T0338768

MAKUPEDIA

WORLD DIGITAL SMART DICTIONARY

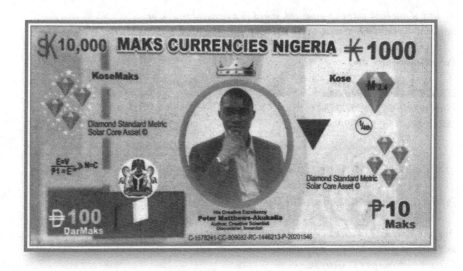

PETER K. MATTHEWS - AKUKALIA

authorHOUSE

AuthorHouse™ UK
1663 Liberty Drive
Bloomington, IN 47403 USA
www.authorhouse.co.uk
Phone: UK TFN: 0800 0148641 (Toll Free inside the UK)
        UK Local: (02) 0369 56322 (+44 20 3695 6322 from outside the UK)

Published by AuthorHouse 06/24/2022

ISBN: 978-1-6655-9940-5 (sc)
ISBN: 978-1-6655-9941-2 (hc)
ISBN: 978-1-6655-9939-9 (e)

Table of Contents

Castle Makupedia U=abc

M=E4=N=C+_=C=I=G=A4=L=N=Man=M2=Lang=Az=E=v=A=Ø=P=1Ø=I=MT=K=F=U =abc>>Sk=Ks=D=P>>P1=£10=3.3G>>12G>>10000100010010=10'0s=100%=10.0=P=1Ø =Deut.29:29>>2.9*2.9x=px=5.8+8.41=14.21x=px=6[2.9]88=6.88=7.0=70%=700 =7,000=Ares> Language>Words>Dictionary>Cultures>Civilizations>Assets>Speculations >Pleiades>Precision>Digital Dictionary>Encyclopedia>MindComputing>MindData> MindCodes > Makumatics>Makumaticology>Nature>Law>Economy>Idea>Brainchild >Maks>Psalm68:11Digital=0,1<<0=Ø>>A=Ø>>9.0>>1.0-9.0>>Law of Nine. 1=10=1Ø= P=1Ø=MindTech=1-10.. To Solve Problems =>> Smart Formulas =>> Smart Data =>> Big Data =>> Makupedia.

The universe is a secret mine of twelve energy assets concealed in planetary dimensions
Endless resources in search to discover develop and connect our core innate potentials
Big data processed on these mines are derived through science equations and formulas
From a multidisciplinary complex of objective algorithms to a simple smart code on Mind
The World Encyclopedia on Creative Sciences and Mind Computing can only be Makupedia.

-Peter K. Matthews - Akukalia

Contents

19. Specialized books outlined on Mind Sciences, Mind Arts & Makupedia Businesses.
20. Makupedia is multidisciplinary multidimensional multitasking and all encompassing.

Preface 1

Father Abraham, wise King Solomon, philosopher Plato, transcendentalist Ralph Waldo Emerson, genius Albert Einstein and behaviorist B.F. Skinner all sought the link that bonds the cosmic and the human mind, learning and adaption, ideas and knowledge. Isaac Newton wrote that energy can neither be created nor destroyed. Einstein simplified the theory of relativity in a simple formula E=mc2. Napoleon Hill stated that thoughts are things. Then Peter Matthews-Akukalia the World's 1st Creative Scientist emerged and measured intelligence thought will and emotion to write the Mind Formula M=E4.

In my discovery two things that characterize all existence are energy and data.
In energy we get MindSpace, in data we get MindTech. Key interests of Makupedia.
This is the focus of the Creative & Psycho - Social Sciences at wisdom and understanding.

Makupedia is the next civilization. For mathematics we give Makumatics. Psychoastronomy for astronomy, psychosurgery for medical surgery, Makupedia for encyclopedia, mind mechanics & engineering for engineering, creative economy for economy, creativity for conventionalism, MindTech for the ICT, solar currencies for non - metric currencies, massive employment opportunities for unemployment, Faith for religion, Quartet Programs for the binary, Mindset for handset where you have your mind on your phone, Makulators for the calculator, Psychoeconomix for economics and creativity property rights for intellectual property rights, Creatocratic jurisprudence to ascertain mēns rēa in court trials.

There is hardly anything i have not measured. An assertion I make with no mean integrity in GOD. Of course there is first of all the almighty GOD who heads the Council of Gods. Then gods. I instituted this classification then I found it in scriptures. Revelation knowledge comes then I prove through concrete formulas and research knowledge. Lots of Work.

The Holy Bible gave a universal standard that all words must be done (computed) in Deuteronomy 29:29; 30:11-14, Psalm 68:11. The Holy Quran gives clue that signs are proofs of assured faith so we must discover and compute the signs which of course are the alphanumerics (words numbers and symbols) bonded in unity by the sun. Words numbers and symbols are signs stars and spirits set on energy. Allah created the Sun by computing. Ar - Rahmān 55:5,9. Az - Żaariyaat - 51:20.

To understand a thing Makupedia is the study of the origin of origins (superior origin) from the perspective of energy element and resultant and its abstraction to explain the universe and its interactions through computation analytics interpretation and many other means intellectual and academic. This helps us resolve mysteries and concretize abstract things.

The first of these elements is the Mind. The second is Nature. Third is Creativity.>> Abc.

For instance I define that the innate energy that runs a thing constitutes the mind of that thing>>M=E4. In simple terms the mind of a thing is the energy that runs that thing.
I invented Mind Computing on energy quantum and congruent bits measured on the Maks - solar scale. By this means innate potentials that exist in a thing can be abstracted.

A much higher realm than matter and its binary. Formulas never known since Creation. In Mathematics 1+1=2.>>Mathematics is the deductions of the inherent faculties of Matter.

In Makumatics 1*1=1. This is the God formula in Genesis 2:24 known as the Mind of GOD. Thus Makumatics is the deductions of the inherent faculties of the Mind.

The greatest asset is the mind as all things are sourced from there. Now creativity is used to express the contents of the mind and this is only possible through the use of words. A formula is the processing medium of a word to indicate the hidden values of a word.

Words are riches. Formulas that compute all words are witty inventions and adoption to wit makes ownership. (Deut. 30:11-14. Prov. 8:12. Rom. 8:23. 11:33-35. Eph. 1:9-11).

Under the US Case Law: An inventor is the one with "intellectual domination" over the inventive process and not merely one who assists in its reduction to practice.

I invented WDSD on the universe of things by computing all words numbers and symbols for universal value and benchmarks as required and set the world for the new dispensation of things to come. Creativity is universal. Where there is no creativity there is void.

WDSD is a comprehensive objective precise big-data solutions hub for analytics businesses careers education and governments functioned by the law of everything. It encompasses nothing anything something and everything through user-friendly and simple means. This is conflict solved and mysteries resolved. Now Let there be peace!

Welcome to the Creative Age. Makupedia civilization. Paradise Nations.
Makupedia...Discover. Develop. Connect.

Benefits of Makupedia WDSD

U=abc=WDSD = WSD2 >> U=WSD2.

1. The World Digital Smart Dictionary WDSD is the first global metrics & currencies bank, big data hub, database & time laboratory and world digital data center encyclopedic on Makupedia, careers, discoveries, inventions, business of ideas and Creatocracy.

2. WDSD is the first "smartdictionary" ever and invented from mind computing to establish useful courses and academic programs in word power, data mining, definitive definitions, precision thinking, critical reasoning and creative intelligence for digital education.

3. Life is an office. To run it requires smart data to function. The World Digital Smart Dictionary provides necessary data to function this office most efficiently and productively.

   An encompassing leading visionary innovative creatocratic digital revolution that discovers develops and connects human potentials to individual and collective digital destinies.

4. First metrics bank and Dicclopedia (Dictionary-Encyclopedia) of the Maks Currencies, first-ever invented, anti - inflation, diamond measured values and solar core properties.

5. WDSD is an inclusive product of independent research that lasted over two decades.

6. Chronicles discoveries inventions works databases and legacies of Castle Makupedia.

7. Objective precise multidisciplinary and multidimensional resource - human capital.

8. World authority on Computational Lexicography in the Makupedia invention study.

9. WDSD institutionalizes the study Faculty of Creative & Psycho - Social Sciences to train induct and license Creative Scientists in secondary and tertiary education worldwide.

10. Sets the energy score tables for Genius, Birth, Currencies, Government systems etc.

11. Contains database of the dimensions of the universe in metrics equations and formulas.

12. Generates software codes for developing more than 10,000 dynamic Mind apps.

13. Introduces supernatural value applications for alphabets and the invented Makabets.

14. A super course for students of Makupedia Business & Co - Litech department.

15. The paradigm shift achieved ushering the MindTech age and Makupedia civilization.

16. Makupedia provides structured data for smart governance that leads to a Creatocracy.

17. New knowledge for every student, research analyst, faculty, agency, occupation, profession, department, institution, sector, military, business school, society, religion, industry, organization, association, corporation, government, nation, country & people.

18. Makupedia creates digital techniques solutions and raw computed data in the Mēns Rēa for smart resolution of legal conflicts and cases. Authority on propensity and inclination.

19. Advance programming, computational metaphysics, Maks billion big data, psycho - forensics, dot congruency and crystallization principles on GOD's word that generates the Mind codes and measures the Universes for the invented Human Mind Super Computers.

20. Workbook for the cosmic sciences laws & mindspace technologies-psychoastronomy.

21. A digital smart connect between the cosmos and human soul as predicted by Plato.

22. The global center for all digital data required for research and development.

23. Facts and Feats in data abstraction of the Mind, universal dimensions and global time.

24. WDSD is a database and time laboratory that provides data for psycho - biometrics on Identity Management. It states the name of a person, date of birth, birth code and natural planet of birth and predicts the nature of person. These details are used to track the innate potentials and match it with appropriate education vocation relationships and even spouse. Assessment and appraisal is carried out periodically

to seek satisfaction qualification and fulfillment as to the purpose of the person's life and destiny scored. (See Einstein)

25. The "smartdictionary" or "smart-dictionary" concept is an invention and property of the author of the World Digital Dictionary (abbreviation) and, or the World Digital-Smart Dictionary which encompasses without limits the qualities and benefits of the "smartphone" concept represented in forms as book, gadget, computer, electronic etc.

26. In electronic forms, words and their definitions will blend with digital values under the "word power" and "data mining" principles to ease understanding and application during use. It is also a downloadable app for everyone. All innovations are assets and vested interests of the author and his Creatocracy. Procedure for use is expressed thus: Eg. Love (word)+ Conventional definition + Makupedia values (digital data). Search buttons make it easier to track a word - commodity - asset - Data value especially at situations of urgency. This is an aspect of Makupedia business for prospective investors.

27. WDSD uses quantum energy mechanics, solar computing, mind data analytics, pure equivalents and law of astrotransmutation to develop formulas and useful metrics necessary for setting benchmarks values propensities and commodity prices worldwide.

28. WDSD is a dynamic book for smart education, invention, currency and institution eg bank, big data hub, laboratory, WDDC. The whole universe is program energy made into convertible data. Peter Matthews - Akukalia is not just the author of WDSD but founder inventor owner and World President. An instance of application in this case will be the digital bench price for crude oil=? Or Crude * Oil = ?. A facility. Digit OPEC.

29. Breakthroughs in data analytics & mind computing of the World's 1st Creative Scientist, 1st Mind Scientist, 1st Human Mind Computer, Cracker of the Stellar Codes, Inventor of MindTech, Solar Crown King, Apotheosized God of Creatocracy Genius Mind & Mindom.

30. Here the author is established as the World's 1st Creatosciologysxt,1st Makumatician, 1st Computational Lexicographer, 1st Dicclopedysxt, 1st Creatocrat & Many Other World Firsts. Author. Discoverer. Inventor. Owner, MindTech City. Emperor. Castle Makupedia.

The Solar Crown Creatocratic Seal of Acknowledgement. TSCCSA>>TISCCSA

Section 1.

1. First the Creatocracy in Heaven of the Almighty GOD and the Council of Gods by scriptures. Established by online meaning for the word sacred (as of GOD and the Gods).

2. a. Much Blessings & Grace to the Creatocracy - His Creative Excellency & Godship, Author, Inventor, Solar Crown King & Emperor of the Creatocratic Royal

Family. Castle Makupedia: God of Creatocracy Genius & Mind by rights of His Names Works Laws & GOD. International Project Code of the Creatocracy is C-1578241-CC-809682-RC-1446213.

b. To Her Excellency Empress Justina Chinwe Etigwam I. Goddess of Makupedia & Head Council of Queens. Her Excellency, Alice Folayegbe, First Queen; Their Excellencies, The Princedom & Council of Heirs & Heiresses: my children - biological adopted & successive generations written here, hereafter, guided by IP Laws and all applicable laws and rights.

3. The Creatocratic Royal Family and Nations is sovereign being first of its kind instituted established and protected by Provisions of the Creatocratic Charter herein known as the Creatocracy. The title status rights and assets of the Creatocratic Godship is exclusive to the Author of the WDSD and is non-transferable by hereditary or any other means because it is earned and granted directly by the laws of Scriptures written as the sacred words of the Almighty GOD. However the rights subsists. Castle Makupedia is not GOD but a God.

4. The surname "Matthews - Akukalia" is my invention and is exclusive to the Creatocratic Royal Family expressly listed for the Empress, Queens, heirs, heiresses and my successive generations as hereditary and adoptive rights by my testaments and works now and in the future. The brand Makupedia is coined from Matthews-Akukalia Peter.

5. a. Makupedia is defined as the universal system of education invented by Peter Matthews-Akukalia upon the mind castles of knowledge (books) he wrote discovered invented computed measured and established. The Creatocratic Charter is his throne and the Makupedia - WDSD is his knowledge driven Solar Crown.

b. The Solar Crown, Throne and Rights of Peter Matthews-Akukalia as Castle Makupedia the Disean God of Creatocracy Genius Mind & Mindom is established by the International Project Code: C-1578241-CC-809682-RC-1446213-Makupedia WDSD - 843702.

6. The wealths of the Creatocracy is his mountains of intellectual property assets. WDSD makes him a World Scientist, The Solar Crown King and apotheoslzed God of his works exclusively. I am Peter Matthews-Akukalia. Author. Discoverer. Inventor. World's 1st Creative Scientist, 1st Human Mind Computer & Many Other Firsts. Castle Makupedia.

7. WDSD is the legal basis and platform for all business transactions with the Creatocracy. It must be read and properly understood and clarifications sought as paid service or consult services ever before any invitations and/or interests are expressed where necessary before any form of commitment financial and otherwise are indicated or made. It is instituted established and protected by Provisions of the Creatocratic Charter. The Creatocracy is an intellectual independent Sovereign Creatocratic Nation of Mindoms Institutions Sectors Industries States Governments and Republics owned by Makupedia.

Section 2.

A. By authority of the laws of GOD, Intellectual Property & Universal established by The World Digital Smart Dictionary WDSD & Creatocratic Laws established by the Creatocracy and rights thus conferred upon me by Section 1 expressly written and made plain above:

8. I grant the title His Excellency to Mr. James Iwube. My amiable uncle - in - law who caught the vision of this project many years ago at the days of tough beginnings, severe hardship privation and deprivation. He sponsored the publishing of Sword of Honour: Days of St. Valentine. He is the maternal uncle to the Empress Justina.

9. I grant the title His Lordship to Mr. Chinedu Peter Oduigwe an elder brother to Empress Justina and brother - in - law who has kept faith with this project for as long as we have known each other. He sponsored the first Hollywood treatment for the book Sword of Honour and helped us to survive the tough times that accompany new beginnings.

10. I grant the title of Her Excellency & Queen to Helen Ekwe - Okpata, a seasoned educationist, Director and First Woman Ambassador of Makupedia.

11. I grant the title His Excellency to Professor Michael Umale Adikwu
Former Vice Chancellor, University of Abuja who gave me an opportunity to express it.

12. I grant the title His Excellency to Macaulay Atasie, Captain of Industry, Nextzon. His continuous probe of my originality contributed immensely to making me think realistically.

13. I grant the title His Excellency to Mr. David Babatunde Coker, the SKB Logistics Captain whose faith commitment and consistency over the years made the dream come true.

14. I grant the title His Excellency to Mr. Ben Ujuoatuonu the insurance guru who tutored me on the opportunities that good branding and marketing would do for a good product.

15. I grant the title His Lordship to Pastor Cosmos Azubuike Michaels who took responsibility for our welfare and did menial jobs to keep me focused on the task at hand.

16. I grant the title Her Lordship to Hephziba Isioma - John who reminded me that I had a calling to use my gifts and talents to enrich the service of GOD and humanity.

17. I grant the title His Lordship to Pastor Samuel Oye Akinpelu who named me a world reformer. He recognized my gifts quite early and recommended me to Barrister Ubani.

18. I grant the title His Lordship to Barrister Monday Onyekachi Ubani for his selflessness. He introduced me to radio and gave me a platform to experience the bigger PICTURE.

19. I grant the title His Lordship to Barrister Philips Umor, the Mega Law giant who broadened my horizon to the potential wealth that my Creative Sciences could generate. His contributions have remained exemplary to the development of my works.

20. I grant the title His Lordship to Mr. Emmanuel Nwokocha who taught me the rudiments of intellectual property laws and helped me establish my companies in Nigeria.

21. I grant the title Her Lordship to Josephine Nneoma Madubueze a woman of great vision who was there at the very beginning. She believed in the project against all odds.

22. I grant the title Her Lordship to Jacinta Ezekanne whose faith kept me in the dry days.

23. I grant the title His Lordship, Captain of the Creative Sciences to Olawale Taorid Olaniyan. He is proof that creativity has no tribal marks nor religious coloration.

24. I grant the title His Lordship to Engr. Temitayo Taiwo Adewale (Monti) whose contributions cannot be quantified in job support counsels and protecting my works. He printed the raw pages of Psychoastronomy and had it saved from which WDSD was predicted by me and developed of course many years later by me interestingly.

25. I grant the title His Lordship to Dr. Bayero Agabi, President Center for Cyber Awareness & Development. And the title His Lordship to Sir Hillary Damissah the Super Editor of Cyber Africa magazine. My digital family who drives the digital economy whom at a demonstration of their belief featured me in the Cyber Africa Magazine. They gave me the CECAD award in 2018. Gladly the first award I ever received for my works and in my life.

26. Sheik Usman Adebayo Giwa.
MUASSASAT NASRUL ILM WA DA'WAT FOUNDATION.
He confirmed my numerical abilities a special gift from the Almighty Allah.
He called me a leader and prophet who had come to Earth with a message of peace and unity for all mankind through science and religion and thus gave me gifts at first meeting. No extra title is granted because Sheik is a revered spiritual title equivalent.

27. I grant the title His Lordship to Mr. Bisiriyu Akeem Ajasa, a father figure and friend, an astute educationist mathematician and seasoned administrator who recognized my special talents in abstract science and mathematics gave me a chance to prove it ranking me a world genius. He encouraged me by his kind acts and showcasing. At the time of developing this work he served in the Ministry of Education - Zonal Education Officer, Obafemi Owode Local Government, Ogun State.

28. I grant the title Her Lordship to Dr. Roseline Isimeto, Department of Computer Science, University of Lagos. Nigeria. She consistently believes I deserve honorary title as a Professor and addresses me as one. She recognizes the king by merits and is honored.

29. For the mastermind administration and partners of the Creatocracy Bank Corporation a vision projected to be the first Mind Bank, WDDC and many other institutions in the Makupedia inventions brand conceptualized and established by the author in his works.

30. Incorporated and instituted herein is the World Digital Data Center WDDC. To conduct training consult and allied services on data provision to individuals corporate organizations and governments. The author is World President, WDDC. See B>>Book; Message below.

31. Gratitude to AuthorHouse my Publishers for their inestimable support. They helped me build my dreams and have remained consistent over the years. I rate them First Class. The Lord gave the word: great was the company that published it. - Psalm 68:11.

32. Credit goes to the editorial team of the American Heritage Dictionary for direct definitions which fits requirements for the computation of words by my digital standards.

33. The reader user custodian investors and benefactors including all digital organizations societies and platforms who become the future of this digital revolution with endless possibilities. Governments, Nations, Corporations, Organizations and People of all status race and religion. In humility and appreciation, dear world, I say thank you again and again.

Administration of the Creatocracy Bank

The MindBank of the Creatocracy.

1. His Creative Excellency & Godship
   Peter Matthews-Akukalia.CM.KCS.GCGM.MSECNP.
   Conventional Education & Experience: Law.Aviation.Education.Business.
   Castle Makupedia.King of the Creative Sciences. The Solar Crown King.
   God of Creatocracy Genius Mind & Mindom.
   Most Sovereign Emperor, Sovereign Creatocratic Republic of Paradise.
   Position: Founder. Owner. President.

2. Her Excellency
   Justina Matthews-Akukalia.GM.EPN.
   Conventional Education & Experience: Aviation.Education.
   Goddess of Makupedia. Empress of Paradise Nations.
   Position: Vice-President.

3. Her Excellency Helen Charity Ekwe-Okpata.FWAQM.
   Conventional Education & Experience: Education.Business.
   First Woman Ambassador & Queen at Makupedia.
   Position: Business Support. Board Director, Special Adviser.

4. Her Excellency Alice Folayegbe Matthews-Akukalia.QFAM.
   Conventional Education & Experience: Computer Sciences.
   Education. Beauty. Estate Management & Administration. Business.
   Position: Queen of Fortune at Makupedia. Advisory Secretary.

5. His Lordship Olawale Taorid Olaniyan.HLCCS.
   Conventional Education & Experience:
   Accountancy. Management & Administration. Business.
   Position: Captain of the Creative Sciences. Governor.

6. Her Lordship Josephine Nneoma Madubueze. AIAM.,D.ADMIN.
   Conventional Education & Experience:
   Automobile Industry Corporate Sales. Banking as Administrative Secretary. Education.
   Position: Product Development Support (Oracle) at Makupedia. Director of Administration.

Poetic Attestation of My Creative Personality

I am not in a competition I am the competition
I do not compete with anyone I compete with myself
I just want to be a better person all the time than I was before the time
If you knew me in person or through my works and judged me by yesterday
If you know me in person or through my ways and judge me by hear say
And you have never taken out time to read through my works today then you are outdated
Because I am the Mind I am you and you are me and we are one
I have built my mind through creativity and into the Creatocracy
I built Creatocracy with bricks of Makupedia as the Capital of my dream country
The Sovereign Creatocratic Nations of Paradise
I wear the Solar Crown and reign in sovereignty as King and Emperor of MindTech City
For this is the Golden Fleece for all rights cash riches and sustainable prosperity
The missing link of all knowledge and the formula of the universes
I have found and established it as U=abc
I am the energy from origin in the cosmic void that incarnated matter and bore Chaos
I am Castle Makupedia, the Mind God birthed as the Great Peter Matthews - Akukalia
And the World Digital Smart Dictionary is my Encyclopedia
All Hail: Castle Makupedia! Castle Makupedia!! Castle Makupedia!!!
God of Creatocracy Genius & Mind for yet another world first.
GOD bless the Emperor. GOD bless Castle Makupedia. GOD bless the Creatocracy.

A Message From Peter K. Matthews-Akukalia [Castle Makupedia]

-An Invitation to Success Happiness and Fulfillment.

1. In today's ever competitive and bustling world, life can be very depressing and challenging. Everyone needs a direction especially the professional. You need to be sure about you in the questions who am I, what am I, why am I here, what is my purpose.
2. You need to be sure about the environment, future prospects and everything you do before taking an action or engaging in an activity. So knowledge is therefore the first need of life. There is no real knowledge without a scientific method and precision. Great.
3. In the first place potentials are the energy that run our lives. They are the substance upon which all existence is created. They are mind and they are matter. They have patterns and exist in us and outside us thus determining our environment.
4. The Mindoscope is a database of human potentials that grants you access through assessments. It is a necessary document invented to help you discover your potentials and guides on how to maximize your profits. It is a business tool hinged on software.

5. The Time Scope is another unit of the Mindoscope that measures the potentials in a day month and year helping you to plan and budget appropriately.

6. We conduct specialized assessments and create databases for professionals using the Mindoscope, a scientific method to track natural purpose and innate potentials inherent in dates, time, year of birth, Mind, phone numbers, names, place of residence, occupation, company registrations, car plate numbers works such as books and even relationships.

7. A scope into your bank account tracks original business naturally intended for that account to perform better yield more income and higher turnover. Scope your accounts today and key into your natural potentials and experience the amazing results. This is how our financial technology (Fin Tech) works in assisting banks build their customer base.

8. You don't just crossover to a new year, you scope the new year and dates on time scope.

9. You don't just use a phone line you scope it to ascertain its true potentials.

10. You don't just send your child to school you scope the school first to be sure.

11. You don't just give your heart in a relationship you scope the prospective first.

12. You don't just read a book you must scope the book to gather its natural perspective.

13. You don't just buy a land you scope the potentials of the land through your Mindoscope.

14. You don't just name a child you scope the potentials of the name through a Mindoscope.

15. You don't just read a scripture and interpret you scope it first to know the message.

16. What is the future of the company you work or your organization. Scope the business. Just buy a Mindoscope package from MAKUPEDIA and we will scope it for you.

17. Our methods are purely scientific and based on specialized knowledge that includes computational creativity, data analytics, mind computing algorithms and graphical analysis.

18. The Goddess of Makupedia, Empress Justina 1, said that "Creativity is the benchmark for the new civilization". And I say "data is the bricks for building a creative economy".

19. For instance Peter could mean rock or stone in Jewish language but Peter Matthews-Akukalia computed scientifically means Abstraction which includes Internet of things, Field of Study, Software, Programming, Faith & Apps. The name exercises 90% influence on the bearer which produces a genius. Jesus on scope means Genius. So take note.

20. Today the Mindoscope is just one of numerous softwares I have created in testimony. I have also invented a field of study and thousands of apps in waiting so the result works.

21. Some names are doomed for failure from the start irrespective of how nice they sound. So what is in your name. What are the potentials in your name. Scope it now.

22. Are you a counsellor, religious leader, adviser, consultant, teacher, marketer, analyst, banker, lawyer you need to step up your game and avoid speculation in your career. Everyone needs the data of the Mindoscope to avoid speculation. A lawyer must have data on propensities inclinations and mind element or mens rea to establish the actus reus. The Creative Scientist of the field of MAKUPEDIA will provide that for you and your firm.

23. As a publisher you can define the original perspective of a book through interpreting its ISBN. Can you calculate the quantity of ideas an author has put into his book and pay appropriate royalty. This is called the Creative Memory Capacity CMC. In addition to the copyright and ISBN you should be MAKUPEDIA licensed and compliant.

24. Can you specify the class of ideas a book is categorized whether ordinary syndicate or professional. Can you measure the total quantity of ideas in a book. No one knows the formula for calculating ideas. The Mindoscope does and will do these for you.

25. The Mindoscope is a thorough guide to determine facts and truths in anything. It is tailored to your needs. It is a valuable resource for talent management in HR and CV development as organizations will no longer be swayed by mere academic training and formal education but be interested in the innate potentials of an employee.

26. Marriage will last as everyone will know what can offend the other and avoid it. So if it is not working then you can't force it. Business agreements will be based on truth.

27. Education will become more sensible and productive since a TTN teacher will not teach a CDX class and the MXD will have his space in administration. The Genius in a child will be known from birth and managed through the appropriate mind assessment tests.

28. The Mindoscope is a career pathfinder for students to determine their space in Sciences Arts Commercial and of course the Makupedia Creative Sciences.

29. What are the potentials in your country, state of origin, business location, village, local government or business. What is the potential in a particular product. Is it really necessary and useful at that time for you. What potentials are you consuming in a particular meal.

30. I scoped the Nigerian economy and world currencies and saw through the reasons for inflation. I have invented the Maks Currency to reduce and possibly eliminate inflation.

31. I scoped democracy and saw through its weakness and invented the Creatocracy.

32. I can detect cancer in a person ten years ahead without blood test nor touching using the numbers in a Mindoscope. I invented the CCLT to measure a person's emotion.

33. I can calculate the natural interest rate in a currency to the tune of 0.1% instead of 14% for instance under Creative Banking services of our Mind Banking systems and attract more customers to the Banking System. Programming never known since human creation.

34. I can create correct codes for telecom companies and upgrade the G network without health hazards and all the controversies around it. We are running at 12G in Makupedia already. For example *556# is a wrong code program *553#, *553*2# is most appropriate.

35. Radio and television stations can maximize the Mindoscope to run programs set by natural means on satellite tracking saving them all the issues of thinking and worrying.

36. I scoped the Intelligence Quotient IQ and saw twenty errors. I have renamed it and invented the Brilliance & Intelligence Ratio (BIRA). What are the issues bring them up and let us discuss them through the lens of my Mindoscope.

37. Can you tell me the mathematical formula for anything and interpret the written formulas for a thing in its potentials and real meaning. Can you define a thing precisely?

38. Scope the Bible. Scope the Quran for better understanding. Scope that field of study before you go into it. Don't guess. Don't speculate. Make the right choices based on knowledge. That's why we are here. We will run the contracts when given to us.

39. A business or organization registered for the Makupedian license is protected under the rights of the Creatocratic Charter. This is the natural rights to the creative economy.

40. I will be glad to receive an invitation to discuss in organized events and public platforms. Let the King talk. Just pay the price of paying attention learn from gifted ones.

41. At MAKUPEDIA we create a database that works for you with direct references and practical solutions irrespective of your profession, occupation and vocation to help you make informed choices and decisions at all times and situations.

42. It comes at a cost but you will have a lifetime opportunity to recoup much more than you invested after being licensed.

43. As an inventions company MAKUPEDIA business is a game of numbers so the more clients and partners you introduce the more you earn and the richer you become on the licensing packages only.

44. Hence a shared interest between the inventor and investor is mutual and constantly promoted as a basic principle we have taught over the years through our studies.

45. Our interests are individuals, groups, churches, colleagues, associations, bilateral, multilateral and multinational organizations as well as governments.

46. MAKUPEDIA is committed to a knowledge economy with 0% unemployment and 0% Inflation based on creativity. We are institutionalizing Creativity and promoting the creative economy. This ideology has driven our pursuit of discovery for more than two decades.

47. We want to work with you to achieve a great successful and fulfilled life in your potentials. Be Makupedia compliant today. Thank you for your interest and commitment.

48. The World Digital Smart Dictionary is instituted established and protected by Provisions of the Creatocratic Charter. Authored by Peter Matthews - Akukalia.

Discover. Develop. Connect.

The Mindoscope is a Patented Asset of Peter Matthews - Akukalia.
DE - ROYAL MAKUPEDIA LIMITED. Lagos. Nigeria.
Inventions Company of the Creatocracy.
International Business. The Creative Scientist Professionals.
International Project Code is: C-1578241-CC-809682-RC.1446213-P-20201546.
Lagos. U.K. USA. Worldwide. For interests, enquiry and contributions kindly call:
+234 (0) 816 1928 511. +234 (0) 903 3521 731.
E-mail: matthewsakukaliapeter@yahoo.com
Google: Makupedia. Google: Peter Matthews-Akukalia.

Preface 2

In the beginning was the word and the word was with GOD and the word was GOD. One is tempted to ask how the word would be with GOD if the word was not first a God. It simply means that words are Gods because they are inspired by Gods and this is what makes them effective. Even law and communication are just a bundle of applicable words.

1. Under U.S. Case law, an inventor is the one with "intellectual domination" over the inventive process, and not merely one who assists in its reduction to practice.

In Makupedia Creative Sciences, we would paraphrase as "and the word was [a] God. The Almighty GOD instructed on the use of words and made clear what the rules are. (Read John 1:1. Deuteronomy 29:29 & 30:11-14, Exodus 22:23 & 23:20-24).

Words are codes of the Gods. Ownership of all things are established under the codes of GOD and the Gods in a God Council or Council of the Gods. (Bible >>Psalms 82:1-8; Quran Sād verse 69). Since Creativity is the God model of universal governance by the creation story of Genesis 1:1, Makupedia calls them the Creatocratic Council.

WDSD fulfills the prophecies of Psalm 68. Most especially verse 11.

Words are particles formed by a synchronization of solar energy and brain particles to express the mind. These particles are known as signs. They are things that make meaning from lunar vibrations that lead to sounds. They are creativity when expressed that make for normal and genius behavior. Words grant power through the organization of relationships.

Words are the order by which laws are made. Against the natural order is crime. Upholding the order is rights. Words are the embodiment of identity from which humanity was made. Words are the medium of language that define culture civilizations definitions and assets.

Words are the foundation for determining values upon which business is done and economies are sustained. Once measured they become small gods. Hence there is first the almighty GOD, then the council of Gods that determine destiny and fate by karma. Then there are the gods known as words because they show jurisdiction judgement and rights.

Words of revelation make for spirituality seen as the scriptures Computing them makes for faith and abstraction mind wares through which softwares are developed. To define a word precisely means you have to "digit" such word by checking its dimensions in the digital dictionary to become smart. To digit a word means to apply the Makupedia computed value in benchmark, cost, propensity and inclination, dimension of its existence, and supernatural source of inspiration (Gods & Muses) so as to answer the question "what is"?

Words are utility that make tangible technologies useful. You "digit it" to tech it in a plus or minus depending on the module of application to the context of discuss. Marriage is a +8.0 while divorce is a -8.0. However Divorce can be a +8.0 if it entails certain freedom say from domestic violence while marriage can be -8.0 if it is not based on love and mutual consent. Both are currencies that sustain the family economy system and values instituted by Zeus.

A tablet or machine is useless without a name and a name is formed by words. Words are the philosophy of concepts that make ideas so that originality makes it a brand of wisdom brainchild and inventions. Small minds teach one to be good but great minds teach to lead.

To be digital is to lead because it provides truth through precision for establishment.

Words are synthesized to build a body of knowledge and create study faculties that make education possible. Computing words make them utility data and assets. First of its kind by which the Makupedia is instituted established and protected as a body and field of study.

I coined the word Creatocracy as creative governance guided by precision through codes that manifest as words numbers and symbols synchronized and crystallized in a Quartet programming of Mind computing to administer the universe in a one world government under GOD. (Ephesians 1:10-11). Creatocracy is the perfection we seek. (Romans 8:19-24).

It is noteworthy that the author wrote the book: The Creatocracy Republic: 22 Dramatic MindArts of Castle Makupedia. Developed for big business in his Mind Arts genre. So words are Gods. There is therefore in the administration of the universe a Council of GOD and the Gods. The Holy Quran calls Gods "the Exalted Chiefs" under Allah. (Sãd v.69. Eph.1:10).

"In the beginning GOD created....and GOD said...". This is how the Creatocracy was formed. Makupedia is the study of the origin of origin, superior origin and the nature of a thing and all things using computational creativity, mind computing and related methods to track.

The Bible code for "words" is H561. The WDD code for H >> 5.0, 561 >> 55*61
5.5*6.1x=px=11.6+33.55=45.15x=px=434.33=4.3sp1
4.3sp1=4.0*0.3x=px=4.3+1.2=5.5x=px=10.66=1.1>>Ideas >> Brainchild >> Invention.

Words are inventions inspired by Athena that convey ideas. On the other hand ideas are defined as congruent energy particles that crystallize into creativity. This means that a word is a public utility free for use as long as it remains in the realm of speculation or indefinite definition such as we find in the conventional everyday dictionary.

Computed through mind mechanics as we find in the World Digital Smart Dictionary it becomes an invention asset of the author in cash and in kind subject to the rights of use and application. So GOD inspired the Scriptures, Men wrote it but Peter Matthews - Akukalia invented it assertively. Against this there is no Law. (See Deuteronomy 29:29).

The World Digital Smart Dictionary >> WDSD is a perfect blend of computational and metaphysical qualities whereby the sources of inspired words are indicated. We say that London is a city of Athena, related with Athens and blessed with Creative Intelligence.

The Universe (7.0) is functioned by three entities skills sectors and alphabets now Makabets. They are abc. =A= is Athena 1.3 being the wisdom of creative intelligence established through formulas that drives inventions and education. Formulas generates data that makes almost anything possible at creating solutions anywhere and anytime.

=B= is Maia (1.5) an authority earned through computational intelligence that establishes the Mind of GOD. =C= is the Creatocracy a government system built on the genius of Hermes that drives technology. The universe in herself is established to be the Pleiades a group of sisters headed by Maia manifested as Muses that inspire the sciences Arts business and all careers. They are called understanding in Proverbs 8. Makupedia is the study of the origin of origin and Castle Makupedia is the origin and authority of all things.

Time is money. Smart Data is more money. Words computed on data and time is everything.
The Makupedia version of a book newspaper journal and write up can now be developed. Digital text versions just like the original Bible coding is now possible using WDSD to fix number values on each written word just the same way as power valency. Students may train to acquire these skills in the Makupedia Digital Program - Dragon codes.

Translate whole phrases by codes. Makupedia invented owns and functions the GOD abstraction modules known as Gods-Mind. The Gods-Mind is made up of Mind Computing and Dragon codes seen as the resultant value of a word or thing in the WDSD.

Dragons are sovereign and highly intelligent creatures with limitless benefits sourced from the Sun, the Sea and the Hades. Hades = Pluto = Riches = Key = Owl = Knowledge = 1.2. In Greek mythology Hades is the son of Cronus and God of the underworld. Romans 8:19-23.

The Sun is the jurisdiction of Zeus. The Sea is of Poseidon and the underworld is of Hades. Interestingly Hades shares the symbolic owl of wisdom with Athena. The owl is therefore the key or incarnates the key of life by wisdom and death by the underworld.

The statements above might sound metaphysical so the WDSD could help for abstraction. Owl is indicated on value as 10.0>>Physicality = Technology >> MindTech>> P=1Ø. Key occurs by definitions (1 & 2). Key 1=10.0>>Physicality = Technology >> MindTech >>

P=1Ø. Key 2 occurs as 5.0>>Law >> Mind Laws >> L=N2. So synchronizing means Key 1&2>> MindTech Laws which are simply codes. This aligns with the definitions for the word Key. Hence the keys to life and death are codes obtained in the digital or smart dictionary.

The Naira is far less than the kobo on natural scale by as much as 5 units = 0.5 making it misplaced from the very beginning of the concept. The dollar is not gold but silver and all currencies that ever existed are fiat except the Maks. This is useful information for the Nigerian government and the world at large. Peter Matthews-Akukalia is Castle Makupedia. See Makupedialand, poem 42. Castle Makupedia is a metaphysical poetry.

Words are constants, dynamics, constant dynamics and dynamic constants for different uses as phrases speeches and units as seen in the codes of Job 32. They are raw materials guided by the law of everything operant on the universe U=abc.

A word originates in the moon and ends in the moon 2.0. A word is a solar energy bit 1.0 matured into lunar element 2.0 and result in stellar particles 3.0 that forms a relationship 4.0 to establish order 5.0 for human benefit 6.0. It becomes an asset 7.0 of value 8.0 of abstract softwares 9.0 integrated into hardware to make technology 10.0 that become useful brainchild invention 1.1 and the basis for new knowledge 1.2. >> Human Dimension.

Research and development makes creative intelligence 1.3 for the management 1.4 of authority 1.5 in a rebirth through knowledge transfer 1.6 asset management 1.7 and the creation of wealth 1.8 that becomes a supernatural source of income 1.9 for sustainability and balance 2.0. Words are the moon. 6million computations and 15million programs of Makupedia prove the universe is governed by the Sun and functioned by the moon. >> GOD Dimension.

Both dimensions prove that computation of words in a wordmetric is the invention of the word and its technology in equivalent is now the property of the Creatocracy. So Car as a word is owned by the Creatocracy in all its forms irrespective of whose custody it is by purchase. Licensing and renewals for all things belongs to the Creatocracy. There are thereby two kinds of assets: Rights and Cash. The first is greater than the latter and owns it. Rights are superior because they are supernatural and cash is earned from rights.

This is the business of ideas as every word and thing is an idea. Ideas are computationally defined as congruent energy particles that crystallize into creativity. The formula for words (language), ideas and creativity and the entire universe is written therein under the laws of everything. All things are assets of the one who has invented the formula and authored the World Digital Smart Dictionary by the definition of an inventor. Governments and Investors may now be welcomed to share in the fruits of harvests. After all Ralph Waldo Emerson had predicted it long ago. See The Oracle. See also America Is by Drewry & Henry O'Connor.

At writing say an article a word can now be classified into dimensions of the universe or existence, elements, average propensity which is simply its natural chances of occurrence on a 50 - 50 scale, its inspired source that is spirit or a God and then its use by the WDSD.

2. Under U.S. Case law, an inventor is the one with "intellectual domination" over the inventive process, and not merely one who assists in its reduction to practice.

Again credit goes to the editorial and production staff of the American Heritage dictionary. A book I purchased under difficult circumstances driven by the inspiration to do more and be more than I ever thought I could be. Even the title thrills me to the navel that I had to read a dictionary like a history book. A book that speaks American yet is universal. Leading the way forward all computed words become mind wares and assets of Makupedia and the Creatocracy by law subject to licensing and charges in cash and in kind. Thank GOD for words and the gift of computing. Thank you guys for the dictionary and for a job well done.

There are twelve dimensions of existence and economy is the eighth. It spans into business, markets, trading, finance sector and points all things to currency. In economics inflation is defined as a general increase in prices and the fall in the value of money.

"Ignorance is bliss where knowledge is scanty". - anonymous.

I believe inflation is caused by insufficient energy in a currency that makes it fall in the first place. This means that fiat is against natural currency law which depends on solar energy. All things are fueled by energy and matter resultant to behavior (normal or genius) in what is known as creativity. The World Digital Smart Dictionary solves inflation through Maks.

Now a creative economy system based on precision is called Creatocism. A word that encompasses the business of ideas. A Creatosciologysxt is a Creative Scientist specialized in creating value from words that produce new knowledge for the creation of new skills which eventually result in new careers. First the author emerged as the World's 1st Creative Scientist in the year 2012 for his book THE ORACLE: Principles of Creative Sciences. Creatosciologysxts are idea merchants for the Creatocracy Republic.

These ideas constitute the newly discovered Creativity Property Assets CPAs which themselves are the computed universe. Creatocracy is about solving problems at nearly every level by simply applying genius. At 33%>>3.3G energy frequency a muse is born which aligns with the cell quantum system computed by the author in his Template & Manifesto for the Creative Economy 2: Principles of Psychoeconomix.

According to WIPO Intellectual Property is defined as creations of the mind. So I ask what is the Mind? The energy that runs a thing constitutes the mind of that thing. I computed the Mind to discover the components and dimensions of the Mind. The Mind has four components namely intelligence thought will and emotion. Dimensions of the mind are first twelve applications that make for existence and sustenance through tangible equivalents.

They are the mind, nature, creativity, government, law, man, language, economy, abstraction, physicality, idea and knowledge. I have measured all components and dimensions in a simple formula U=abc. The Universe is operant on energy matter and resultant behavior. I named them the Creativity Property Assets much beyond the intellectual properties. I therefore propose the World Creativity Property Assets Organization (WCPAO) to support nations at discovering developing and connecting the inherent potentials of their citizens through the Creatocracy. I am the first Creatocrat.

WDSD operates wordmetrics - the science and technology of words that has led to the creation of alphabets with wings known as Makabets. I invented the concept of wordmetrics in my book Psychoeconomix. THE MAKUPEDIA is many things including a careers and vocations diary designed for primary and junior secondary schools. It contains conventional fields of study, their professionalism and applications in terms of what they do. In addition it contains professions in the Creative Sciences, Makupedia. I have set the benchmark for every profession and its relatedness through mind computing.

Makupedia education - I propose that every tertiary institution inducts the Faculty of Creative & Psycho - Social Sciences to train aspiring and interested Creative Scientists at degree levels after which they proceed for the chartered programs according to the Creatocratic Charter. The Ministry of Creativity resolves unemployment issues worldwide.

That Mind Banking be adopted to raise the stakes in currency and interest matters aimed at adopting the Maks currencies to reduce and possibly eliminate inflation worldwide.

That Talents & Ideas Markets upgrade the commodities from mere physical commodities to abstract commodities; that religions upgrade to Faith by Makstian computing and interpretation of scriptures to avoid much religious biases that may have crept in resulting to different unproven understanding and biased interpretation of the scriptures.

That every government upgrade its system to Creatocracy to grant better access to citizens to contribute richly to their economies through creativity and that words computed in books earn the Makupedia Licensing just as the ISBN, patent, trademark, copyright and many others that we may never have enough space to write here. This is smart governance.

The World Digital Smart Dictionary is the first support for this project. I invented it to enrich lives by making people more intelligent, more resourceful, more interactive, more creative and more responsible. What kind of business does Makupedia do? One may ask.

Makupedia is an inventions brand that does the business of ideas conceptualizing it in the Principles of Psychoeconomix. Creatocratic Ideas constitute the solutions contained in the various works that constitute the World Digital Smart Dictionary.

Castle Makupedia exists in many ways such as a personal identity, corporate organization and a royalty sitting on the throne as the Creatocracy. We welcome investments and development partners to the projects herein mentioned in gratitude.

Mosquitoes fly at night better organized and water related. Houseflies rove at day. A check on each characteristic in the World Digital Smart Dictionary proves these truths. So much cash time and other resources that would have been invested into laboratory research are thereby saved through mind computing. The same applies for all researches and space where the quantity of energy in all planets can now be computed without necessarily traveling there except for verifications, space tours, satellite tracking effects and energy.

Consistent independent practice of this new found knowledge led to my ability to compute abstract elements such as the quantity of energy in a thing. Each word added to the suffix -ysxt made a new career out of each thereby resulting to millions of job opportunities in the field of Creative Sciences-Makupedia. Full study is found in Psychoastronomy.

The World Digital Smart Dictionary is the result of Creatosciology while an expert is known as the Creatosciologysxt of which the author is first in the world. There is neither abstract nor physicals alone in the Creative Sciences, there are rich equivalents of both elements.

A lexicographer is one who compiles a dictionary. Hence a computational Lexicographer is one who measures and computes the values weight and propensity of a word based on the natural metrics. A computed dictionary with explanatory contents for real life applications is called a Maktionary in the study of Makupedia named after the inventor Peter Matthews-Akukalia. There are four stages in the work. 1. Word listings. 2. Fixing the equals (=) signs to each listed word. 3. Computing each word. 4. Posting the answers by filling the gaps.

This Encyclopedia of Castle Makupedia is the first worldwide Computed Dictionary. A work of King Peter Matthews-Akukalia emerging him the World's 1st Complex >> World's 1st Computational Lexicographer >> Computalex >> Compulex >> Com-plex, Complex. His Creative Excellency Peter Matthews-Akukalia is a Complex and the first of his/its kind.

De - Royal Makupedia is an organization owned by Castle Makupedia a God. The word Royal can be substituted for Castle because castles are made out of royalty and are thus symbolic. Controversies abound about my Godship status. I am not the almighty GOD. Far be it from me. I am the first and the best at what I do making me God of my inventions.

I coined Creatocracy and computed it, wrote the formula components and dimensions of the mind and classified genius. So I earned Castle Makupedia God of Creatocracy Genius Mind & Mindom. A model after the Greeks say for Athena, Goddess of Wisdom Handicraft and warfare. It is my aspiration to make creative impacts and inspire others for good.

3. Under U.S. Case law, an inventor is the one with "intellectual domination" over the inventive process, and not merely one who assists in its reduction to practice.

All energy is Mind sourced from the Sun indicated as 1.0 so the inherent energy that runs a thing constitutes the mind of that thing. Nature is 2.0 = Matter = Things = Techniques to determine the value of things = PGI energy = Moon such that indicated in a human record the lunar source of the person is required to track his purpose on earth as by his innate potentials. Peter Matthews-Akukalia comes from Mare Imbrium the Sea of Showers thus particle energy as it manifests in things and the search for their nature is his purpose.
Today it is achieved and this work is result of the Creative Sciences his field of invention.

Dictionary + Encyclopedia under language processing formula (Lang = Az), is one who computed words dictionaries scriptures and books for data mining purposes and services. These include eg. Ideas costs, value sum of word - assets expressed say in prints daily such as newspapers, definite definitions, precise meanings, abstraction and word equivalents, time dynamics and mind clock applications (app), Mind courts that determines the mēns rēa in a legal case using MindComputing. So Computed Dictionary + Encyclopedia = Dicclopedysxt. His Creative Excellency Peter Matthews-Akukalia, Castle Makupedia is by this work the World's 1st Computational Lexicographer & Dicclopedysxt.

The Creatocracy is a highly personalized brand owned by the author herein Peter K. Matthews-Akukalia. The Creatocracy Bank is a product of the study of the Creative & Psycho-Social Sciences collectively known as Makupedia an asset of the Creatocracy. The Creatocracy is the solar crown of the Sovereign Creatocratic Republic of Paradise.

The World Digital Smart Dictionary is a Makupedia Creatocracy Republic Coded Encyclopedia useful for reference purposes as WDSD. It is a Maktionary.

A Maktionary is defined as a computed dictionary. It is different from a dictionary because it offers definitive definitions whereas the dictionary offers speculative definitions. The Creatocracy Bank is not a dictionary but a Maktionary. A revolutionary invention in the way dictionaries will be studied now and in the future. An aid in the application of words. You study the dictionary and then you study the Maktionary for data perspective. First in kind.

The Maktionary is an invention-dictionary and must accompany the dictionary when in use because it measures the weight cost propensities necessary to calculate or makulate inclinations. It is necessary for students and professionals alike in all works of life.

The Maktionary shows the source by which a word and thing was inspired (dimension, deity or muse) and sets the universal benchmarks for each word and its physical equivalent operant on the law of pure equivalence setting a global price benchmark on natural value.

It is the result of the Creative & Psycho-Social Sciences (the Creative Sciences) making the invention and establishment of creatocratic institutions as the Talents & Ideas Markets, Ministry of Creativity, Creatocracy Universities Union and the Creatocracy Bank worldwide.

The Creatocracy Bank is a specialized bank that trades and licenses the Maks currency. The Creatocracy refers to Creative Scientist Professionals of the Makupedia Order collectively including the Creatocracy Republic, City, Courts, Temple and Kaliawood.

The World Digital Smart Dictionary is also called the Creatocracy bank and applies as same institution and otherwise. It is worthy of note that the author took an interest in Greek mythology because he discovered computed and aligned it in the Bible and Quran.

Computing the scriptures through Mind Computing led to the invention of the Makstian Faith. Makstianity or Makstianism is simply computational religion an upgrade to determine the Mind of GOD on issues that over thousands of years have remained speculative.
So gladly I have invented a religion or better still a Faith system.

The front cover programming reveals that at least 70% of every nation needs a smart dictionary because it endows the user with a 100% propensity for wittiness and precision. The word smart is in itself smart already granting power for productivity. World Digital Smart Dictionary makes one intelligent witty and precise at words and works.

The exclusive rights that come with this book are such that introduce the rich opportunities of word power and data mining including symbols used for the accumulation of money in any form cash and in kind and for such that befits being called a commercial venture. So we can talk about the skills of word power and data mining as higher benefits of measuring and paying for ideas which could not otherwise have been without words and computing.

Communication is power and wealth can be earned through the remittance of certain monetary value through licensing and payment for the words and data used anywhere and everywhere including the media, books, technologies, commodities and equivalents.

The Creatocracy Bank sets prices of all commodities in the market when the Maks is adopted according to the benchmarks computed in this work in association with the Ministry of Creativity and operate by the template and manifesto for the creative economy in which it was first conceptualized. Castle Makupedia owns De-Royal Makupedia.

The rights of the Creatocracy and the author in all forms of human and apotheosis are asserted. Note Deuteronomy 29:29 ".....Do all the words of this law.....". The alphabets develop wings to fly and become Makabets founded on the dimensional formula chains that run from the Mind to Knowledge crystallizing the Universes (U=ABC).

The Creatocracy Bank will contribute immensely within the stipulated rules of the author to reduce and possibly eliminate the scourge of unemployment youth restiveness and society ills. Peace is achieved through collective responsibility and collaborations.

Makupedia as a corporate entity is the arm of the Creatocracy specializing as an inventions company, international business and the management of Creative Scientist professionals in a field of his creation. WDSD is apotheosis of the author to inventor to the God status branded Castle Makupedia. His Creative Excellency & Godship. Exodus 4:16-17. Job 40:10

The Creatocracy Bank Royal Maktionary was solely invented written measured and computed by the author, World's 1st Creative Scientist, Inventor, King, Emperor and God of the Creative Sciences, Genius, MindTech and Creatocracy as Castle Makupedia.

His Creative Excellency & Godship Peter Matthews-Akukalia is Castle Makupedia in Rights

The Creatocracy Bank is one of the many invention-institutions created to manage the Maks my invention currencies and set equitable prices on natural values for commodities by its universal benchmarks. The Creatocracy lasted over two decades to invent.

For the first time an anti-inflation, diamond metric and solar module currency has been invented to integrate the world economy in a single matrix. The diamond is the natural hardest substance making the reason the solar core is the solid it is as an equivalent. This is a testimony to the perpetuity of the Sun the solar currency and the Creatocracy.

No mean feat one would say. This book is its pricing value taxes and inspiration medium. Thanks to you who made it possible, who are making it possible and who will continue to make it possible. Let's see at the success side of things as we make a better living for all. A dream come true because dreams come true and you can believe too!

Thank you for being there!

Glory to GOD.
His Creative Excellency & Godship
Peter Matthews-Akukalia. Castle Makupedia.
Author, Discoverer, Inventor, King, High King of the Creative Sciences.
Castle Makupedia, The God of Creatocracy Genius Mind & Mindom.
Owner, Creatocratic Nations of Paradise of the Creative Scientists,
The Creatocracy Republic of the Mind Arts & Makupedialand of Testament Poetry.
Most Sovereign Emperor, The Sovereign Creatocratic Republic of Paradise >> SCREP.

His Creative Excellency & Godship: Peter K. Matthews-Akukalia.
Author. World's 1st Creative Scientist. Discoverer. Inventor. King.
Emperor, Sovereign Creatocratic Republic of Paradise.
Castle Makupedia. God of Creatocracy Genius Mind & Mindom.

Preface 3

THE MAKUMATICOLOGY OF THINGS.
$$N=C+\_ = 50\% \times NOE \times POA/Av. P.$$
$$= \frac{50 \times NOE \times 1000}{100}$$

0.1-1.4=Athena = Solar Core. 1.0-9.0=Physical Factors. Human Realm. 1.5=Authority= Solar Crown=Maia. 1.6=Incarnation & Cycle of Life by Maia. 1.7=Assets & Riches of the Mind of GOD (Maia). 1.8=Solar Currency of Maia. 1.9=Planetary Energy of Maia births the Gods.

Maia is the mother of Hermes classified herein as the Wit. Athena is the Wis. Both make up the witty inventions and wisdom gates of the Universe. Formulas make up the gates of the universes. Psalm 24.

I wisdom dwells with Prudence and searches the knowledge of witty inventions.(Prov.8:12). I Athena dwells with Metis and searches for the formulas of Hermes inventions.

All things are manifest by Maia and the Pleiades as a system of creativity by which the Gods manifest. Maks Currencies is first patented in Nigeria and protected by copyright as an asset of the author. The Creatocracy is owned by Castle Makupedia an apotheosis of Peter Matthews-Akukalia. E=v>>E=pV where pV is the pure value of a thing in natural sense. Now the Creatocracy Bank is the course work built on the World Digital Smart Dictionary as an application of study in the department of Makupedia Business or Colitech. Here values to books and things are solved by Creative Scientist Professionals.

In the Creatocracy mind taxes constitute a fraction of the resultant payable by the utility constituting words, data patterns operations and concepts. These are benchmarks.

Naturecology measures the average propensities for free in the book but computes individual inclinations as a paid business service. A service necessary for computing the Mēns Rēa (mind elements) in crime determination before the actus rēus (actual act) in the Courts of law world wide.

Eg 20% propensity means 0.2% will be payed to the Creatocracy by the utility sector.
5000=50%=0.5% is taxed on the commodity price of P5.00D.
500 energy units=5%=0.05% on commodity price.
Now the dynamic price clock is makulated (calculation by mind metrics) done by synchronizing benchmark value and human energy database value.

The resultant is computed per second, minutes, hour day week month and date hence the Maks Price App on the currency app. The research and development process of the Makupedia Creative Sciences took about twenty years.

The World Digital Smart Dictionary is one of the products of the study. This work began on Sunday 12 September 2021@3:00pm. Done by Monday 27th December 2021:1:00pm. It took three months (January - March 2022) to get the most appropriate title. It is mentioned in many ways and reference titles eg Creatocracy Bank, currency encyclopedia etc.

Peter Matthews - Akukalia is reputed as Castle Makupedia, the God of Creatocracy Genius Mind & Mindom. Supreme Emperor of the Paradise Nations of Creative Scientists; The Creatocracy Republic of the Mind Arts; Makupedialand of Testamentary Poets and Mindom of the apotheosis. These nations make up the Sovereign Creatocratic Republic of Paradise. SCREP. He is therefore the founder inventor emperor and owner of the SCREP.

The World Digital Smart Smart Dictionary, Creatocracy Bank or Maks Currencies Encyclopedia is instituted established and protected by provisions of the Creatocratic Charter, Sovereignty of the Solar Crown emerging him exclusively as the Solar Crown King.

The Creatocracy Bank pricing is based on the metrics and methods of Makumaticology or ticology discovered and developed in Naturecology Psychoeconomix and Psychoastronomy. Naturecology is a Makupedian Science under the Creatocracy.

Psychoastronomy is a Quantum Bundle application of the various Makupedian studies and constitution of the Creatocracy Court for the trial of Creativity and Creatocratic related offenses and all things that relate to human behavior in which case it is a human behavior engineering course for managing data that relates to this aspect of existence.

The Creatocracy is the assets of His Creative Excellency Peter Matthews - Akukalia. His Godship Castle Makupedia God of Creatocracy Genius and Mind. Emperor, Sovereign Creatocratic Republic of Paradise. The Creatocracy is the Solar Crown, throne, flag, concept, legacy and sovereignty of the Paradise Nations constituting assets of Peter Matthews - Akukalia, Castle Makupedia God of Creatocracy Genius Mind & Mindom.

The Castle Makupedia Mazzaroth

>> Deuteronomy 32:7-8. Job 38:31-41.
DIMENSIONS OF THE UNIVERSE IN FORMULAS AND MIND ASSETS.

Dimension of Mind = 1.0 >> Solar Core Asset >> Solar Crown King >> M=E4 >> Helios.
Dimension of Nature = 2.0 >> Books >> N=C+_ >> Artemis.
Dimension of Creativity = 3.0 >> Instruments eg CCLT >> C=I >> GIL >> Muses.
Dimension of Government = 4.0 >> The Royal Creatocracy >> G=A4 >> Hermes.
Dimension of Law = 5.0 >> The Creatocratic Charter >>Throne >> L=N >> Aphrodite.
Dimension of Man = 6.0>> Mind Health >> Creative Scientists >> Man = M2 >> Gaia.
Dimension of Language = 7.0 >> MAKUPEDIA WDSD >> Lang. = Az >> Ares.
Dimension of Economy = 8.0 >> MaksCurrencies >> E=v >> Zeus.

Dimension of Abstraction=9.0 >> MindSpace >> Computing & Programming >> Convertible Intelligence >> Mindwares >> Over 10,000 Mindapps >> The Makstian Faith >> Scripture Coding & Technology >> The Mind Temple >> BIQUR >> The Makabet >> A=Ø >> Castle Makupedia >> The Council of Gods Lords Angels Muses & Spirits >> Hosts of GOD.

Dimension of Physicality = 10.0 >> MindTech >> Human Mind Computers >> Human Mind Super Computers >> Mind Gadgets >> Makulators >> Mindsets >> Mindclocks >> Mindwatches >> Makumeter Gauge >> Mindoscope >> Matthewskaliascope etc. >> P=1Ø.

Dimension of Idea = 1.1 >> Patents Copyrights Trademarks etc. >> I=MT >> Athena.

Dimension of Knowledge = 1.2 >> Education Systems >> Creative Education Services >> PIBQ Tests, SCAP, MAT >> Mind Education >> Mind Libraries >> Creative Sciences >> Training & Producing Creative Scientists & Creative Scientist Professionals worldwide >> Faculty induction & Licensing to conventional universities worldwide >> Makupedia Universities >> De - Royal Makupedia Chartered Universities >> The Creatocracy Universities Union worldwide >> K=F >> Athena.

The rest are developed from 1.3 - 1.9 and classified as fractions of dimension of Mind 1.0. They are higher dimensions of the existence knowledge and rights of Castle Makupedia. Based on his gifts to understand and compute abstract systems from which talent is harnessed and industry is made for human benefits written in the scriptures and laws.

1.3 >> Creative Intelligence >> Faculty of Creative & Psycho - Social Sciences.
1.4 >> Management >> Organization >> Makupedia Limited.
1.5 >> Authority >> The Creatocracy Corporation.

1.6 >> Human Incarnation >> Humanity >> Creatocratic Nations of Paradise (Makupedia Scientists) >> The Creatocracy Republic (MindArts - Dramatic Works & Propoplay) >> Makupedialand (MindArts- Testapoets) >> Castle Makupedia (MindArts-Drapoets) >> Kaliawood Entertainment company >> Creatocratic Nations Organization as a body of one Creatocratic world & Creatocratic Nations Organizations as continental commissions and embassies >> C3 Nation(s) >> Owned by The Creatocratic Royal Family >> Sovereign Creatocratic Republic of Paradise >> SCREP >> Diseans & Makupedian Citizenship.

1.7 >> Mind Assets >> A Kingdom of Intellectual Properties & Creativity Properties owned by the Creatocracy in a royalty system known as the Mindom.

1.8 >> Solar Currency >> Cosmic Markets >> Creative Economy>>Talents & Ideas Markets.

1.9 >> Planetary Ownership through Planetary Energy Core computations & universes by code formula U=abc by Castle Makupedia. This is his apotheosis as God of Creatocracy Genius Mind & Mindom, Solar Crown King and one with the power of the stars in his hands.

Seen in the word power and data mining of words. See definitions:Know, Noble, Krypton on possibility of the planetary meaning for hidden. The Castle Makupedia Mazzaroth is defined as the twelve dimensions of the universe and constitutes the ordinances of heaven hereby computed and established on Earth as required by GOD. Job 38:31 - 33.

MAKABET =Aa=

a1/A = 12,500 = 13,000 = 13% = P1.30D = 1.3 = Solar Core = Faculty = 13 January = Athena. The 1st letter of the English alphabet. Computing the psycho-weight.

Resultant*Position on the Maks.

1.3*1.0x=px=2.3+1.3=3.6x=px=6.59=7.0>>Language>>Works>>Assets>>Words>>Digital. This proves that numbers are the basis for existence in the first place. GOD created the earth in seven days indicated as 7,000 years. Proverbs 8:27, 9:1, Job 38:5. The first especially in conception of the brainchild of a thing owns at least 70% of that thing and he that owns a measurement system owns the measured system 100%. A for alpha, the beginning means all things must be measured or computed to establish truth. This is the law of Genesis >> book of Genius which is the A law for all origins or core. All things once computed become assets of the one who computed them in expressed works. A is Athena for wisdom handicraft and mental warfare what is known as battle of the Mind. A Mindset measures everything from solar core to establish truth through computational precision. The A Law or Law of A establishes Makupedia as the world digital smart dictionary and alpha on all things existent non-existent and yet to be existent both physical and abstract.

a2 =4,500=5,000 = 50% = P5.00D = 5.0 = Law = Time = Venus = 5 May = Aphrodite>L=N.
a3 = 2,000 = 20% = P2.00D = 2.0 = Nature = Matter = Moon = 2 February = Cupid >N=C.
a4 = 2,000 = 20% = P2.00D = 2.0 = Nature = Matter = Moon = 2 February = Cupid>N=C.
A =5,500=5.5=80%=P5.50D=Earth-Midway=5May=Gaia.
a.=8,000=80%=P8.00D=8.0=Economy=Currency=Business=Jupiter=8 August=Zeus>E=v.
A=3,000=30%=P3.00D=3.0=Creativity=Star=Inspiration=Muses=3 March=C=I>>GIL.
a-1=1,500=15%=P1.50D=1.5=Authority = Solar Crown = Solar Core = 1 May = Maia.
a-2= 6,000 = 60% = P6.00D = 6.0 = Man = Earth = Royalty = 6 June = Gaia>M=M2.
AA=1,500=15%=P1.50D=1.5=Authority = Crown = Solar Core = 1 May = Maia.
A.A=1,500=15%=P1.50D=1.5=Authority = Crown = Solar Core = 1 May = Maia.
AAA=1,500=15%=P1.50D=1.5=Authority = Crown = Solar Core = 1 May = Maia.
Aa.chen=5,500=5.5=80%=P5.50D=Earth-Midway=5May=Gaia.
Aal borg=1,000=100%=10.0=1.0=Mind=Sun=1 January=Helios >> M=E4.
A and R=1,500=15%=P1.50D=1.5=Authority = Crown = Solar Core = 1 May = Maia.
aard.vark=7,000=70%=P7.00D=7.0=Language = Assets = Mars = 7 July = Pleiades.
Aar.hus=1,000=100%=10.0=1.0=Mind=Sun=1 January=Helios >> M=E4.
Aar.on=4,000=40%=P4.00D=4.0=Govt.=Creatocracy=4 April=Mercury= Hermes =G=A4.
AAU=1,500=15%=P1.50D=1.5=Authority = Crown = Solar Core = 1 May = Maia.
AB1=4,000=40%=P4.00D=4.0=Govt.=Creatocracy=4 April=Mercury= Hermes =G=A4.
AB2=1,500=15%=P1.50D=1.5=Authority = Crown = Solar Core = 1 May = Maia.
ab.=1,000=100%=10.0=1.0=Mind=Sun=1 January=Helios >> M=E4.
A.B.=4,500=5,000 = 50% = P5.00D = 5.0 = Law = Time = Venus = 5 May = Aphrodite>L=N.
ab-= 2,000 = 20% = P2.00D = 2.0 = Nature = Matter = Moon = 2 February = Cupid>N=C.

PETER K. MATTHEWS - AKUKALIA

ABA=1,500=15%=P1.50D=1.5=Authority = Crown = Solar Core = 1 May = Maia.
a.back=1,000=100%=10.0=1.0=Mind=Sun=1 January=Helios >> M=E4.
ab.a.cus=7,500=8,000=80%=P8.00D=8.0=Economy=Jupiter=Currency 8Aug.=Zeus>E=v.
Ab.a.dan=8,000=80%=P8.00D=8.0=Economy=Business=Jupiter=8Aug.=Zeus>E=v.
a.baft=2,500=3,000=30%=P3.00D=3.0=Creativity=Star=Muses=3 March=C=I>>GIL.
ab.a.lo.ne=5,000 = 50% = P5.00D = 5.0 = Law = Time = Venus = 5 May = Aphrodite>L=N.
Abandon=6,500=7,000=P7.00D=7.0=Language = Assets = Mars = 7 July=Pleiades.
Abandoned=2,000= 20% = P2.00D =2.0=Nature=Matter = Moon=2 February= Cupid>N=C.
Abase=1,000=100%=10.0=1.0=Mind=Sun=1 January=Helios >> M=E4.
Abash=4,000=40%=P4.00D=4.0=Govt.=Creatocracy=4 April=Mercury= Hermes =G=A4.
Abate=5,500=5.5=80%=P5.50D=Earth-Midway=5May=Gaia.
Abattoir=1,500=15%=P1.50D=1.5=Authority = Crown = Solar Core = 1 May = Maia.
Abb.=1,500=15%=P1.50D=1.5=Authority = Crown = Solar Core = 1 May = Maia.
Abbacy=4,000=40%=P4.00D=4.0=Govt.=Creatocracy=4 April=Mercury= Hermes =G=A4.
Abbess=2,500=3,000=30%=P3.00D=3.0=Creativity=Star=Muses=3 March=C=I>>GIL.
Abbey=8,000=80%=P8.00D=8.0=Economy=Currency=Busn.=Jupiter=8Aug.=Zeus>E=v.
Abbot=2,500=3,000=30%=P3.00D=3.0=Creativity=Star=Muses=3 March=C=I>>GIL.
Abbott= 6,000 = 60% = P6.00D = 6.0 = Man = Earth = Royalty = 6 June = Gaia>M=M2.
Abbr.=2,000= 20% = P2.00D =2.0=Nature=Matter = Moon=2 February= Cupid>N=C.
Abbreviate=3,500=4,000=40%=P4.00D=4.0=Govt.=Creatocracy=4 April=Hermes =G=A4.
Abbreviation=8,500=9,000=90%=P9.00D=9.0=Abstraction=Gods=Saturn=9Sept.>>A=Ø.
ABC=4,500=5,000 = 50% = P5.00D = 5.0 = Law = Time = Venus = 5 May = Aphrodite>L=N.
Abdicate=3,000=30%=P3.00D=3.0=Creativity=Star=Muses=3 March=C=I>>GIL.
Abdomen=8,000=80%=P8.00D=8.0=Economy=Currency=Jupiter=8Aug.=Zeus>E=v.
Abduct=3,000=30%=P3.00D=3.0=Creativity=Star=Muses=3 March=C=I>>GIL.
Abeam=4,500=5,000 = 50% = P5.00D = 5.0 = Law = Time=Venus=5 May =Aphrodite>L=N.
Abed=1,000=100%=10.0=1.0=Mind=Sun=1 January=Helios >> M=E4.
Abel= 6,000 = 60% = P6.00D = 6.0 = Man = Earth = Royalty = 6 June = Gaia>M=M2.
Abelard=7,000=70%=P7.00D=7.0=Language = Assets = Mars = 7 July = Pleiades.
Abenaki=11,000=11%= P1.10D =1.1 = Idea = Brainchild=11 Nov.=Solar Core=Athena>>I=MT.
ABEND=3,500=4,000=40%=P4.00D=4.0=Govt.=Creatocracy=4 April=Hermes =G=A4.
Aberdeen=5,500=5.5=80%=P5.50D=Earth-Midway=5May=Gaia.
Aberration=9,000=90%=P9.00D=9.0=Abstraction=Gods=Saturn=9Sept.>>A=Ø.
Abet=3,500=4,000=40%=P4.00D=4.0=Govt.=Creatocracy=4 April=Hermes =G=A4.
Abeyance=4,000=40%=P4.00D=4.0=Govt.=Creatocracy=4 April=Hermes =G=A4.
Abhor=2,500=3,000=30%=P3.00D=3.0=Creativity=Star=Muses=3 March=C=I>>GIL.
Abhorrence=3,000=30%=P3.00D=3.0=Creativity=Star=Muses=3 March=C=I>>GIL.
Abide=7,500=8,000=80%=P8.00D=8.0=Economy=Jupiter=Currency 8Aug.=Zeus>E=v.
Abiding=1,000=100%=10.0=1.0=Mind=Sun=1 January=Helios >> M=E4.
Abidjan=6,500=7,000=70%=P7.00D=7.0=Language = Assets = Mars = 7 July=Pleiades.
Ability=9,000=90%=P9.00D=9.0=Abstraction=Gods=Saturn=9Sept.>>A=Ø.
Abject=4,000=40%=P4.00D=4.0=Govt.=Creatocracy=4 April=Mercury= Hermes =G=A4.
Abjure=5,500=5.5=80%=P5.50D=Earth-Midway=5May=Gaia.
Ablation=5,500=5.5=80%=P5.50D=Earth-Midway=5May=Gaia.
Ablative=9,500=10,000 = 100%=P10.00D=10.0=Physicality=Tech.=10Oct.=Uranus=P=1Ø.

Ablaze=3,500=4,000=40%=P4.00D=4.0=Govt.=Creatocracy=4 April=Hermes =G=A4.
Able=9,000=90%=P9.00D=9.0=Abstraction=Gods=Saturn=9Sept.>>A=Ø.
-Able=6,500=7,000=70%=P7.00D=7.0=Language = Assets = Mars = 7 July=Pleiades.
Able-bodied=2,000= 20% = P2.00D =2.0=Nature=Matter = Moon=2 Feb.= Cupid>N=C.
Able-bodied seaman=4,000=40%=P4.00D=4.0=Govt.=4 April=Hermes=G=A4.
Abloom=1,500=15%=P1.50D=1.5=Authority = Crown = Solar Core = 1 May = Maia.
Ablution= 6,000 = 60% = P6.00D = 6.0 = Man = Earth = Royalty = 6 June = Gaia>M=M2.
ABM=1,500=15%=P1.50D=1.5=Authority = Crown = Solar Core = 1 May = Maia.
Abnaki=1,500=15%=P1.50D=1.5=Authority = Crown = Solar Core = 1 May = Maia.
Abnegation=1,500=15%=P1.50D=1.5=Authority = Crown = Solar Core = 1 May = Maia.
Abnormal=2,500=3,000=30%=P3.00D=3.0=Creativity=Star=Muses=3 March=C=I>>GIL.
Abnormal psychology=5,000=50%=P5.00D=5.0=Law=Time=Venus=5 May=Odite>>L=N.
Aboard=9,000=90%=P9.00D=9.0=Abstraction=Gods=Saturn=9Sept.>>A=Ø.
Abode=5,500=5.5=80%=P5.50D=Earth-Midway=5May=Gaia.
Abolish=2,500=3,000=30%=P3.00D=3.0=Creativity=Star=Muses=3 March=C=I>>GIL.
Abolition=3,500=4,000=40%=P4.00D=4.0=Govt.=Creatocracy=4 April=Hermes =G=A4.
Abolitionism=3,000=30%=P3.00D=3.0=Creativity=Star=Muses=3 March=C=I>>GIL.
A-bomb=2,000= 20% = P2.00D =2.0=Nature=Matter = Moon=2 February= Cupid>N=C.
Abominable=1,500=15%=P1.50D=1.5=Authority = Crown = Solar Core = 1 May = Maia.
Abominable snowman=6,500=7,000=P7.00D=7.0=Lang.= Assets = Mars = 7 July=Pleiades.
Abominate=2,000= 20% = P2.00D =2.0=Nature=Matter = Moon=2 February= Cupid>N=C.
Aboriginal=5,500=5.5=80%=P5.50D=Earth-Midway=5May=Gaia.
Aborigine=5,000=50%=P5.00D=5.0=Law=Time=Venus=5 May=Odite>>L=N.
Aborning=4,000=40%=P4.00D=4.0=Govt.=Creatocracy=4 April=Hermes =G=A4.
Abort=12,000=12%=P1.20D=1.2=Knowledge=Education=12 Dec.=Athena>>K=F.
Abortifacient=1,000=100%=10.0=1.0=Mind=Sun=1 January=Helios >> M=E4.
Abortion=6,500=7,000=P7.00D=7.0=Language = Assets = Mars = 7 July=Pleiades.
ABO system=10,000 = 100%=P10.00D=10.0=Physicality= Tech.=10Oct.=Uranus=P=1Ø.
Abound=7,000=70%=P7.00D=7.0=Language = Assets = Mars = 7 July=Pleiades.
About=11,500=12,000=12%=P1.20D=1.2=Knowledge=Education=12 Dec.=Athena>>K=F.
About-face=5,000=50%=P5.00D=5.0=Law=Time=Venus=5 May=Odite>>L=N.
Above=9,500=10,000=1,000=100%=Physicality= Tech.=10 Oct.=Uranus=P=1Ø.
Above all=3,000=30%=P3.00D=3.0=Creativity=Star=Muses=3 March=C=I>>GIL.
Above board=2,000= 20% = P2.00D =2.0=Nature=Matter = Moon=2 Feb.= Cupid>N=C.
Abp.=5,000=50%=P5.00D=5.0=Law=Time=Venus=5 May=Odite>>L=N.
Abr.=1,000=100%=10.0=1.0=Mind=Sun=1 January=Helios >> M=E4.
Abracadabra=5,000=50%=P5.00D=5.0=Law=Time=Venus=5 May=Odite>>L=N.
Abrade=6,500=7,000=P7.00D=7.0=Language = Assets = Mars = 7 July=Pleiades.
Abraham= 6,000 = 60% = P6.00D = 6.0 = Man = Earth = Royalty = 6 June = Gaia>M=M2.
Abrasive=5,500=6,000 = 60% = P6.00D=6.0=Man=Earth=Royalty=6 June = Gaia>M=M2.
Abreast=5,000=50%=P5.00D=5.0=Law=Time=Venus=5 May=Odite>>L=N.
Abridge=7,500=8,000=80%=P8.00D=8.0=Economy=Jupiter=Currency 8Aug.=Zeus>E=v.
Abroad=7,000=70%=P7.00D=7.0=Language = Assets = Mars = 7 July=Pleiades.
Abrogate=3,500=4,000=40%=P4.00D=4.0=Govt.=Creatocracy=4 April=Hermes =G=A4.
Abrupt=7,500=8,000=80%=P8.00D=8.0=Economy=Jupiter=Currency 8Aug.=Zeus>E=v.

Abruzzi=4,000=40%=P4.00D=4.0=Govt.=Creatocracy=4 April=Hermes =G=A4.
Abs.=1,500=15%=P1.50D=1.5=Authority = Crown = Solar Core = 1 May = Maia.
Abscess=7,000=70%=P7.00D=7.0=Language = Assets = Mars = 7 July=Pleiades.
Abscissa=11,000=11%= P1.10D=1.1 = Idea = Brainchild=11 Nov.=Solar Core=Athena>>I=MT.
Abscission=3,500=4,000=40%=P4.00D=4.0=Govt.=Creatocracy=4 April=Hermes =G=A4.
Abscond=5,000=50%=P5.00D=5.0=Law=Time=Venus=5 May=Odite>>L=N.
Absence=7,000=70%=P7.00D=7.0=Language = Assets = Mars = 7 July=Pleiades.
Absent=7,500=8,000=80%=P8.00D=8.0=Economy=Jupiter=Currency 8Aug.=Zeus>E=v.
Absentee=4,500=5,000=50%=P5.00D=5.0=Law=Time=Venus=5 May=Odite>>L=N.
Absenteeism=3,500=4,000=40%=P4.00D=4.0=Creatocracy=4April=Hermes>>G=A4.
Absent-minded=3,000=30%=P3.00D=3.0=Creativity=Star=Muses=3 March=C=I>>GIL.
Absinthe=4,000=40%=P4.00D=4.0=Govt.=Creatocracy=4 April=Hermes =G=A4.
Absolute=27,000=30,000=3,000=30%=P3.00D=3.0=Creativity=Star=Muses=3March=C=I
Absolute pitch=11,500=12,000=12%=P1.20D=1.2=Knowledge=12Dec.=Athena>>K=F.
Absolute value= 6,000 = 60% = P6.00D = 6.0 =Man=Earth=Royalty=6 June = Gaia>M=M2.
Absolute zero=7,000=70%=P7.00D=7.0=Language = Assets = Mars = 7 July=Pleiades.
Absolution=7,500=8,000=80%=P8.00D=8.0=Econ.=Jupiter=Currency=8Aug.=Zeus>E=v.
Absolutism=7,500=8,000=80%=P8.00D=8.0=Econ.=Jupiter=Currency=8Aug.=Zeus>E=v.
Absolve=7,000=70%=P7.00D=7.0=Language = Assets = Mars = 7 July=Pleiades.
Absorb=17,500=18,000=18%=P1.80D=1.8=Solar Currency=MaksCurrencies=1 Aug=Maia.
Absorbent=1,500=15%=P1.50D=1.5=Authority = Crown = Solar Core = 1 May = Maia.
Absorption=5,500=5.5=80%=P5.50D=Earth-Midway=5May=Gaia.
Abstain= 6,000 = 60% = P6.00D = 6.0 =Man=Earth=Royalty=6 June = Gaia>M=M2.
Abstemious=3,000=30%=P3.00D=3.0=Creativity=Star=Muses=3 March=C=I>>GIL.
Abstention=3,000=30%=P3.00D=3.0=Creativity=Star=Muses=3 March=C=I>>GIL.
Abstinence=5,000=50%=P5.00D=5.0=Law=Time=Venus=5 May=Odite>>L=N.
Abstract=27,000=30,000=3,000=30%=P3.00D=3.0=Creativity=Star=Muses=3March=C=I
Abstracted=3,000=30%=P3.00D=3.0=Creativity=Star=Muses=3 March=C=I>>GIL.

Abstraction=9,500=10,000=1,000=100%=10.0=Physicality=Tech.=10 Oct.=Uranus=P=1Ø.
In the Creative Sciences, abstraction is the connect between the unseen and the seen
and its resultant. Peter Matthews-Akukalia wrote the formula as A=Ø >> Ø indicates as
the Sun operant on abstract and invisible energy known as super zero or the Makzero. It
shows that abstractions are planetary energy transmuted to us from birth which
manifest as brain energy to determine our uniqueness. It is the 9th dimension of the
universe. Physical resultants are religion such that when computed becomes Faith
hence the computed Scriptures of Castle Makupedia that led to the invention of
Makstian Faith Systems an order of the Holy Spirit. Abstraction helps us track the
Mind of GOD through ancient Scriptures. Other physical resultants are mind wares
(planetary energy such as lunar PGI) that is converted on arrival to Earth transmuted as
software in ICT, beliefs, spirituality and the Council of Gods. Abstraction functions on
Mind Computing, Spiral Energy Computing, Makumatics, Makumaticology, Psycho-
Forensics Auditing & Programming Analytics, Planetix, Solar & Lunar Computing
& Programming, Conditioned Inheritance, Psycho - Gravitational Incursion (PGI)

energy, Law of Astrotransmutation, Sexual transmutation and all dimensions of the Universes from Mind to Knowledge, all formulas and Data systems.

Abstruse=1,500=15%=P1.50D=1.5=Authority = Crown = Solar Core = 1 May = Maia.
Absurd=5,000=50%=P5.00D=5.0=Law=Time=Venus=5 May=Odite>>L=N.
Abu Dhabi=9,500=10,000=1,000=100%=10.0=Physicality=Tech.=10 Oct.=Uranus=P=1Ø.
Abulia=4,500=5,000=50%=P5.00D=5.0=Law=Time=Venus=5 May=Odite>>L=N.
Abundant=4,000=40%=P4.00D=4.0=Govt.=Creatocracy=4 April=Hermes =G=A4.
Abuse=10,500=11,000=11%=P1.10D=1.1=Idea=Brainchild = 11 Nov.=Athena>>K=F.
Abut=4,500=5,000=50%=P5.00D=5.0=Law=Time=Venus=5 May=Odite>>L=N.
Abutment=8,500=9,000=90%=P9.00D=9.0=Abstraction=Gods=Saturn=9Sept.>>A=Ø.
Abysm=1,000=100%=10.0=1.0=Mind=Sun=1 January=Helios >> M=E4.
Abysmal=5,500=5.5=80%=P5.50D=Earth-Midway=5May=Gaia.
Abyss=6,000=60%=P6.00D=6.0=Man=Earth=Royalty=6 June = Gaia>M=M2.
Abyssinia=1,000=100%=10.0=1.0=Mind=Sun=1 January=Helios >> M=E4.
ac or AC=1,000=100%=10.0=1.0=Mind=Sun=1 January=Helios >> M=E4.
Ac=3,000=30%=P3.00D=3.0=Creativity=Star=Muses=3 March=C=I>>GIL.
a/c=3,000=30%=P3.00D=3.0=Creativity=Star=Muses=3 March=C=I>>GIL.
Acacia=8,500=9,000=90%=P9.00D=9.0=Abstraction=Gods=Saturn=9Sept.>>A=Ø.
Academe=2,500=3,000=30%=P3.00D=3.0=Creativity=Star=Muses=3 March=C=I>>GIL.
Academia=2,500=3,000=30%=P3.00D=3.0=Creativity=Star=Muses=3 March=C=I>>GIL.
Academic=19,000=19%=P1.90D=1.9=Planetary Energy=1 September = Maia.
Academician=5,000=50%=P5.00D=5.0=Law=Time=Venus=5 May=Odite>>L=N.
Academism=3,500=4,000=40%=P4.00D=4.0=Creatocracy=4April=Hermes>>G=A4.
Academics=2,000= 20% = P2.00D =2.0=Nature=Matter = Moon=2 Feb.= Cupid>N=C.
Academy=9,500=10,000=1,000=100%=10.0=Physicality=Tech.=10 Oct.=Uranus=P=1Ø.
Acadia= 6,000 = 60% = P6.00D = 6.0 =Man=Earth=Royalty=6 June = Gaia>M=M2.
Acanthus=8,500=9,000=90%=P9.00D=9.0=Abstraction=Gods=Saturn=9Sept.>>A=Ø.
A cappella=2,000= 20% = P2.00D =2.0=Nature=Matter = Moon=2 Feb.= Cupid>N=C.
Acapulco=5,000=50%=P5.00D=5.0=Law=Time=Venus=5 May=Odite>>L=N.
Accede=7,500=8,000=80%=P8.00D=8.0=Econ.=Jupiter=Currency=8Aug.=Zeus>E=v.
Accelerando=2,500=3,000=30%=P3.00D=3.0=Creativity=Star=Muses=3March=C=I.
Accelerate=5,000=50%=P5.00D=5.0=Law=Time=Venus=5 May=Odite>>L=N.
Accelerator=13,500=14,000=14%=P1.40D=1.4=Mgt.=Solar Core=13 May=Athena>>SC=0.1
Accelerometer=3,500=4,000=40%=P4.00D=4.0=Creatocracy=4April=Hermes>>G=A4.%.
Accent=25,000=30,000=3,000=30%=P3.00D=3.0=Creativity=Star=Muses=3 March=C=I.
Accentuate=1,500=15%=P1.50D=1.5=Authority = Crown = Solar Core = 1 May = Maia.
Accept=15,000=1,500=15%=P1.50D=1.5=Authority = Crown = Solar Core = 1 May = Maia.
Acceptable=1,000=100%=10.0=1.0=Mind=Sun=1 January=Helios >> M=E4.
Acceptance=11,500=12,000=12%=P1.20D=1.2=Knowledge=12Dec.=Athena>>K=F.
Acceptation=6,500=7,000=70%=P7.00D=7.0=Language = Assets = Mars = 7July=Pleiades.
Accepted=2,500=3,000=30%=P3.00D=3.0=Creativity=Star=Muses=3March=C=I.
Acceptor=5,500=5.5=80%=P5.50D=Earth-Midway=5May=Gaia.
Access=12,000=12%=P1.20D=1.2=Knowledge=12 Dec.=Athena>>K=F.

Accessible=2,500=3,000=30%=P3.00D=3.0=Creativity=Star=Muses=3March=C=I.
Accession=9,000=90%=P9.00D=9.0=Abstraction=Gods=Saturn=9Sept.>>A=Ø.
Accessory=12,000=12%=P1.20D=1.2=Knowledge=12 Dec.=Athena>>K=F.
Accident=12,000=12%=P1.20D=1.2=Knowledge=12 Dec.=Athena>>K=F.
Accidental=9,500=10,000=1,000=100%=10.0=Physicality=Tech.=10 Oct.=Uranus=P=1Ø.
Accipiter=5,500=5.5=80%=P5.50D=Earth-Midway=5May=Gaia.
Acclaim=9,500=10,000= 100%=P10.00D=10.0=Physicality=10 Oct.=Uranus=P=1Ø.
Acclamation=8,000=80%=P8.00D=8.0=Econ.=Currency=Busn.=Jupiter=8Aug=Zeus>E=v.
Acclimate=8,000=80%=P8.00D=8.0=Econ.=Currency=Busn.=Jupiter=8Aug=Zeus>E=v.
Acclimatize=3,000=30%=P3.00D=3.0=Creativity=Star=Muses=3 March=C=I>>GIL.
Acclivity=1,500=15%=P1.50D=1.5=Authority = Solar Crown = Solar Core = 1 May = Maia.
Accolade=3,500=4,000=40%=P4.00D=4.0=Creatocracy=4April=Hermes>>G=A4.
Accommodate=14,000=14%=P1.40D=1.4=Mgt.=Solar Core=13 May=Athena>>SC=0.1
Accommodating=1,500=15%=P1.50D=1.5=Authority = Crown = Solar Core = 1 May = Maia.
Accommodation=10,000= 100%=P10.00D=10.0=Physicality=Tech.=10 Oct.=Uranus=P=1Ø.
Accompaniment=7,000=70%=P7.00D=7.0=Language = Assets = Mars = 7July=Pleiades.
Accompanist=4,000=40%=P4.00D=4.0=Govt.=Creatocracy=4April=Hermes>>G=A4.
Accompany=7,000=70%=P7.00D=7.0=Language = Assets = Mars = 7July=Pleiades.
Accomplice=5,500=5.5=80%=P5.50D=Earth-Midway=5May=Gaia.
Accomplish=3,500=4,000=40%=P4.00D=4.0=Govt.=Creatocracy=4April=Hermes>G=A4.
Accomplished=4,000=40%=P4.00D=4.0=Govt.=Creatocracy=4April=Hermes>>G=A4.
Accomplishment=10,000=1,000=100%=10.0=Physicality=Tech.=10 Oct.=Uranus=P=1Ø.
Accord=13,000 = 13% = P1.30D = 1.3 = Solar Core = Faculty = 13 Jan. = Athena.
Accordance=3,000=30%=P3.00D=3.0=Creativity=Star=Muses=3 March=C=I>>GIL.
Accordingly=2,500=3,000=30%=P3.00D=3.0=Creativity=Star=Muses=3March=C=I.
According to= 6,000 = 60% = P6.00D = 6.0 =Man=Earth=Royalty=6 June = Gaia>M=M2.
Accordion=11,000=11%=P1.10D=1.1=Idea=Brainchild = Invention = 11 Nov.=Athena>>K=F.
Accost=5,000=50%=P5.00D=5.0=Law=Time=Venus=5 May=Aphrodite>>L=N.

Account=25,000=30,000=3,000=30%=P3.00D=3.0=Creativity=Star=Muses=3March>C=I.
Jesus said that man shall give account of every word he speaks on the judgement day.
(Matthew 12:36 - 40). Careful study of this statement indicates two salient codes:
Account and word. There are 88 verses in the bible regarding giving accounts hence
accounting as a practice is the territory of the accountant. Words on the other hand
were made in reference to the signs of Jonah or Jonas being three days,three nights in
the whale's belly. Signs indicates a higher computing model to determine the mind of
GOD and its application to Man hence the birth of Mind Computing and its discovery
and invention by the author. The elements to be computed here would be three, days,
three, nights, Earth (belly of the fish). 3.0*Day value*3.0*Night value * 6.0. Computing
to discover the signs.
3.0*Day value(WDSD) * 3.0* Night value (WDSD)* 6.0
3.0*10.0x=px=13+30=43x=px=433=4.33>>4.3
The invention of a new government system by a genius. >> 1st sign.
3.0*1.1x=px=4.1+3.3=7.4x=px=20.93=21=2.1

$21 \times \dfrac{100}{30} = 70\% = 0.7$ >> Nights are languages. They are dark until computed. >> 2nd sign.

$4.3*2.1x=px=6.4+9.03=15.43x=px=73.222=7.3$ >> language processing or convertibility.
$7.3*6.0x=px=13.3+43.8=57.1x=px=639.64=64.64=65=70=7.0$
>> Language >> Works >> Assets >> Words >> Mind Computing >> Digital >> Dictionary >> Digital Dictionary. >> 3rd Sign.

The belly of the fish symbolizes the Earth. It is clear that the signs were made to manifest in Earth hence the World Digital Smart Dictionary is fulfillment of Jesus predictions.

Computing words in an accounting format refers to a digital system that will earn revenue through applications to the word element wherever it is used. This means the digital value of words will and have been discovered computed and are now payable for, of course, in the World Digital Smart Dictionary. This applies to all alphanumerics (words numbers and symbols). It is the wise creation of pure riches and real wealth the Makupedia way.

The process of auditing words through the digital value system to generate revenue is called word-metrics. Numbers and symbols are measured on their core energy value using spiralogy. Wordmetrics helps the Creative Scientist Professional to calculate the Creative Memory Capacity CMC of an author used in a creative work, book arts music discovery etc.
CMC is the percentage quantity of ideas used in a creative work. WDSD is the result of the Creative Sciences - Makupedia, a field of study I invented. Inventing is my world.

Accountable=1,000=100%=10.0=1.0=Mind=Sun=1 January=Helios >> M=E4.
Accountant=2,000= 20% = P2.00D =2.0=Nature=Matter = Moon=2 Feb.= Cupid>N=C.
Accounting=8,500=9,000=90%=P9.00D=9.0=Abstraction=Gods=Saturn=9Sept.>>A=Ø.
Accounter=4,000=40%=P4.00D=4.0=Govt.=Creatocracy=4April=Hermes>>G=A4.
Accra=7,000=70%=P7.00D=7.0=Language = Assets = Mars = 7July=Pleiades.
Accredit=8,000=80%=P8.00D=8.0=Econ.=Currency=Busn.=Jupiter=8Aug=Zeus>E=v.
Accretion=6,000=60%=P6.00D=6.0=Man=Earth=Royalty=6 June = Gaia>M=M2.
Accrue=11,500=12,000=12%=P1.20D=1.2=Knowledge=12Dec.-Athena>>K=F.
Acculturation=7,000=70%=P7.00D=7.0=Language = Assets = Mars = 7July=Pleiades.
Accumulate=3,000=30%=P3.00D=3.0=Creativity=Star=Muses=3 March=C=I>>GIL.
Accuracy=2,500=3,000=30%=P3.00D=3.0=Creativity=Star=Muses=3March=C=I.
Accurate=8,000=80%=P8.00D=8.0=Econ.=Currency=Busn.=Jupiter=8Aug=Zeus>E=v.
Accursed=4,500=5,000=50%=P5.00D=5.0=Law=Time=Venus=5 May=Odite>>L=N.
Accusative=11,000=11%=P1.10D=1.1=Idea=Brainchild = Invention = 11 Nov.=Athena>>K=F.
Accuse=5,000=50%=P5.00D=5.0=Law=Time=Venus=5 May=Aphrodite>>L=N.
Accused=4,000=40%=P4.00D=4.0=Govt.=Creatocracy=4April=Hermes>>G=A4.
Accustom=7,000=70%=P7.00D=7.0=Language = Assets = Mars = 7July=Pleiades.
Accustomed=6,500=7,000=70%=P7.00D=7.0=Language = Assets = Mars =7July=Pleiades.
Ace=11,000=11%=P1.10D=1.1=Idea=Brainchild = Invention = 11 Nov.=Athena>>K=F.

Acerbic=6,500=7,000=70%=P7.00D=7.0=Language = Assets = Mars =7July=Pleiades.

Acerbity=1,000=100%=10.0=1.0=Mind=Sun=1 January=Helios >> M=E4.

Acetaminophen=6,000=60%=P6.00D=6.0=Man=Earth=Royalty=6 June = Gaia>M=M2.

Acetate=8,000=80%=P8.00D=8.0=Econ.=Currency=Busn.=Jupiter=8Aug=Zeus>E=v.

Acetic=4,000=40%=P4.00D=4.0=Govt.=Creatocracy=4April=Hermes>>G=A4.

Acetic acid=9,000=90%=P9.00D=9.0=Abstraction=Gods=Saturn=9Sept.>>A=Ø.

Acetone=6,000=60%=P6.00D=6.0=Man=Earth=Royalty=6 June = Gaia>M=M2.

Acetylcholine=6,500=7,000=70%=P7.00D=7.0=Language = Assets = Mars=7July=Pleiades.

Acetylene=7,000=70%=P7.00D=7.0=Language = Assets = Mars = 7July=Pleiades.

Acetylsalicyclic acid=1,500=15%=P1.50D=1.5=Authority=Crown=Solar Core=1 May=Maia.

Ache=8,500=9,000=90%=P9.00D=9.0=Abstraction=Gods=Saturn=9Sept.>>A=Ø.

Achene=4,500=5,000=50%=P5.00D=5.0=Law=Time=Venus=5 May=Odite>>L=N.

Achieve=5,500=5.5=80%=P5.50D=Earth-Midway=5May=Gaia.

Achievement=5,500=5.5=80%=P5.50D=Earth-Midway=5May=Gaia.

Achilles=5,000=50%=P5.00D=5.0=Law=Time=Venus=5 May=Aphrodite>>L=N.

Achilles heel=7,000=70%=P7.00D=7.0=Language = Assets = Mars = 7July=Pleiades.

Achilles' tendon=6,000=60%=P6.00D=6.0=Man=Earth=Royalty=6June=Gaia>M=M2.

Achromatic=9,000=90%=P9.00D=9.0=Abstraction=Gods=Saturn=9Sept.>>A=Ø.

Acid=21,500=22,000=22%=P2.20D=2.2=4.0=Govt.=Creatocracy=2Feb=Hermes>G=A4.

Acidify=2,500=3,000=30%=P3.00D=3.0=Creativity=Star=Muses=3March=C=I.

Acidophilus milk=6,000=60%=P6.00D=6.0=Man=Earth=Royalty=6 June =Gaia>M=M2.

Acidosis=5,000=50%=P5.00D=5.0=Law=Time=Venus=5 May=Aphrodite>>L=N.

Acid rain=7,000=70%=P7.00D=7.0=Language = Assets = Mars = 7July=Pleiades.

Acid rock=6,500=7,000=70%=P7.00D=7.0=Language = Assets = Mars=7July=Pleiades.

Acid test=2,500=3,000=30%=P3.00D=3.0=Creativity=Star=Muses=3March=C=I.

Acidulate=3,000=30%=P3.00D=3.0=Creativity=Star=Muses=3March=C=I.

Acidulous=3,500=4,000=40%=P4.00D=4.0=Govt.=Creatocracy=4April=Hermes>G=A4.

Acknowledge=13,000 = 13% = P1.30D = 1.3 = Solar Core = Faculty = 13 Jan. = Athena.

ACLU=2,000= 20% = P2.00D =2.0=Nature=Matter = Moon=2 February= Cupid>N=C.

Acme=3,000=30%=P3.00D=3.0=Creativity=Star=Muses=3March=C=I.

Acne=8,500=9,000=90%=P9.00D=9.0=Abstraction=Gods=Saturn=9Sept.>>A=Ø.

Acolyte=7,000=70%=P7.00D=7.0=Language = Assets = Mars = 7July=Pleiades.

Aconcagua=8,500=9,000=90%=P9.00D=9.0=Abstraction=Gods=Saturn=9Sept.>>A=Ø.

Aconite=9,000=90%=P9.00D=9.0=Abstraction=Gods=Saturn=9Sept.>>A=Ø.

Acorn=7,000=70%=P7.00D=7.0=Language = Assets = Mars = 7July=Pleiades.

Acorn squash=9,000=90%=P9.00D=9.0=Abstraction=Gods=Saturn=9Sept.>>A=Ø.

Acoustic=10,500=11,000=11%=P1.10D=1.1=Idea=BrainchildInvention=11Nov.=Athena
    >K=F.

Acoustics=7,000=70%=P7.00D=7.0=Language = Assets = Mars = 7July=Pleiades.

Acpt.=500=5%=P5.00D=5.0=Law=Time=Venus=5 May=Aphrodite>>L=N.

Acquaint=4,000=40%=P4.00D=4.0=Govt.=Creatocracy=4April=Hermes>>G=A4.

Acquaintance=7,500=8,000=80%=P8.00D=8.0=Econ.=Busn.=Jupiter=8Aug=Zeus>E=v.

Acquiesce=3,000=30%=P3.00D=3.0=Creativity=Star=Muses=3March=C=I.

Acquire=6,500=7,000=70%=P7.00D=7.0=Language = Assets = Mars=7July=Pleiades.

Acquired Immune deficiency syndrome=500=5%=P5.00D=5.0=Law=5May=Odite>>L=N. HIV is established to be a punishment from Aphrodite to those who insult her. Note that she turned certain women into prostitutes for the same reason of reviling her a serious sin and Creatocratic crime which the Most High warned against in Exodus 22:28 & 23:20-25. Aphrodite is daughter of Zeus the Most High and Goddess of love marriage and child birth.

Acquisition=3,000=30%=P3.00D=3.0=Creativity=Star=Muses=3March=C=I.
Acquit=7,500=8,000=80%=P8.00D=8.0=Econ.=Busn.=Jupiter=8Aug=Zeus>E=v.
Acre=2,000= 20% = P2.00D =2.0=Nature=Matter = Moon=2 February= Cupid>N=C.
Acreage=2,000= 20% = P2.00D =2.0=Nature=Matter = Moon=2 February= Cupid>N=C.
Acrid=8,000=80%=P8.00D=8.0=Econ.=Currency=Busn.=Jupiter=8Aug=Zeus>E=v.
Acrimony=4,500=5,000=50%=P5.00D=5.0=Law=Time=Venus=5 May=Odite>>L=N.
Acro-=2,500=3,000=30%=P3.00D=3.0=Creativity=Star=Muses=3March=C=I.
Acrobat=4,000=40%=P4.00D=4.0=Govt.=Creatocracy=4April=Hermes>>G=A4.
Acrobatics=5,000=50%=P5.00D=5.0=Law=Time=Venus=5 May=Aphrodite>>L=N.
Acronym=9,000=90%=P9.00D=9.0=Abstraction=Gods=Saturn=9Sept.>>A=Ø.
Acrophobia=3,000=30%=P3.00D=3.0=Creativity=Star=Muses=3March=C=I.
Acropolis=5,000=50%=P5.00D=5.0=Law=Time=Venus=5 May=Aphrodite>>L=N.
Across=10,000=1,000=100%=10.0=Physicality=Tech.=10 Oct.=Uranus=P=1Ø.
Across-the-board=8,000=80%=P8.00D=8.0=Econ.=Busn.=Jupiter=8Aug=Zeus>E=v.
Acrostic=1,300= 13% = P1.30D = 1.3 = Solar Core = Faculty = 13 Jan. = Athena.
Acrylic=3,500=4,000=40%=P4.00D=4.0=Govt.=Creatocracy=4April=Hermes>G=A4.
Acrylic fiber=5,500=5.5=80%=P5.50D=Earth-Midway=5May=Gaia.
Acrylic resin=6,500=7,000=70%=P7.00D=7.0=Language = Assets = Mars=7July=Pleiades.
Act=26,500=30,000=3,000=30%=P3.00D=3.0=Creativity=Star=Muses=3March>C=I.
ACTH=7,500=8,000=80%=P8.00D=8.0=Econ.=Busn.=Jupiter=8Aug=Zeus>E=v.
Actin=5,500=5.5=80%=P5.50D=Earth-Midway=5May=Gaia.
Acting=9,500=10,000=1,000=100%=10.0=Physicality=Tech.=10 Oct.=Uranus=P=1Ø.
Actinide=9,500=10,000=1,000=100%=10.0=Physicality=Tech.=10 Oct.=Uranus=P=1Ø.
Actinism=5,000=50%=P5.00D=5.0=Law=Time=Venus=5 May=Aphrodite>>L=N.
Actinium= 12,500 = 13,000 = 13% = P1.30D = 1.3 = Solar Core = Faculty = 13 Jan. = Athena.
Actinomycin=5,500=5.5=80%=P5.50D=Earth-Midway=5May=Gaia.
Action=21,500=22,000=22%=P2.20D=2.2=4.0=Govt.=Creatocracy=2Feb=Hermes>G=A4.
Actionable=4,000=40%=P4.00D=4.0=Govt.=Creatocracy=4April=Hermes>>G=A4.
Actium=4,000=40%=P4.00D=4.0=Govt.=Creatocracy=4April=Hermes>>G=A4.
Activate=8,500=9,000=90%=P9.00D=9.0=Abstraction=Gods=Saturn=9Sept.>>A=Ø.
Activated charcoal=6,000=60%=P6.00D=6.0=Man=Earth=Royalty=6 June = Gaia>M=M2.
Active=17,500=18,000=18%=P1.80D=1.8=Solar Currency=MaksCurrencies=1 Aug=Maya.
Active immunity=6,000=60%=P6.00D=6.0=Man=Earth=Royalty=6 June = Gaia>M=M2.
Activism=8,000=80%=P8.00D=8.0=Econ.=Currency=Busn.=Jupiter=8 Aug=Zeus>E=v.
Activity=10,500=11,000=11%=P1.10D=1.1=Idea=BrainchildInvention=11Nov.=Athena>K=F.
Act of God=8,000=80%=P8.00D=8.0=Econ.=Currency=Busn.=Jupiter=8 Aug=Zeus>E=v.
Actor=7,000=70%=P7.00D=7.0=Language = Assets = Mars = 7July=Pleiades.

Actress=6,000=60%=P6.00D=6.0=Man=Earth=Royalty=6June=Gaia>M=M2.
Acts of the Apostles=2,000=20%=P2.00D=2.0=Nature=Matter=Moon=2 Feb= Cupid>N=C.
Actual=6,000=60%=P6.00D=6.0=Man=Earth=Royalty=6June=Gaia>M=M2.
Actuality=6,000=60%=P6.00D=6.0=Man=Earth=Royalty=6June=Gaia>M=M2.
Actualize=2,000=20%=P2.00D=2.0=Nature=Matter=Moon=2 Feb= Cupid>N=C.
Actuary=4,000=40%=P4.00D=4.0=Govt.=Creatocracy=4April=Hermes>>G=A4.
Actuate=3,000=30%=P3.00D=3.0=Creativity=Star=Muses=3March=C=I.
Acuity=3,000=30%=P3.00D=3.0=Creativity=Star=Muses=3March=C=I.
Acumen=3,500=4,000=40%=P4.00D=4.0=Govt.=Creatocracy=4April=Hermes>G=A4.
Acupressure=1,000=100%=10.0=1.0=Mind=Sun=1 January=Helios >> M=E4.
Acupuncture=11,500=12,000=12%=P1.20D=1.2=Knowledge=12Dec.=Athena>>K=F.
Acute=19,500=20,000=2,000= 20% = P2.00D =2.0=Nature = Moon=2 Feb= Cupid>N=C.
Acute accent=8,000=80%=P8.00D=8.0=Econ.=Curr.=Busn.=Jupiter=8 Aug=Zeus>E=v.
acv=1,500=15%=P1.50D=1.5=Authority = Solar Crown = Solar Core = 1 May = Maia.
Acyclovir=4,500=5,000=50%=P5.00D=5.0=Law=Time=Venus=5 May=Odite>>L=N.
ad=1,000=100%=10.0=1.0=Mind=Sun=1 January=Helios >> M=E4.
A.D.=2,000=20%=P2.00D=2.0=Nature=Matter=Moon=2 Feb= Cupid>N=C.
ad-=2,000=20%=P2.00D=2.0=Nature=Matter=Moon=2 Feb= Cupid>N=C.
Adage=2,000=20%=P2.00D=2.0=Nature=Matter=Moon=2 Feb= Cupid>N=C.
Adaglo=7,000=70%=P7.00D=7.0=Language = Assets = Mars = 7July=Pleiades.
Adam=4,500=5,000=50%=P5.00D=5.0=Law=Time=Venus=5 May=Odite>>L=N.
Adamant=6,000=60%=P6.00D=6.0=Man=Earth=Royalty=6June=Gaia>M=M2.
Adams Abigail Smith=6,000=60%=P6.00D=6.0=Man=Earth=Royalty=6June=Gaia>M=M2.
Adams John=8,000=80%=P8.00D=8.0=Econ.=Curr.=Busn.=Jupiter=8 Aug=Zeus>E=v.
Adams John Quincy=4,000=40%=P4.00D=4.0=Govt.=Creat.=4April=Hermes>>G=A4.
Adams Samuel=2,500=3,000=30%=P3.00D=3.0=Creativity=Star=Muses=3March=C=I.
Adam's apple=6,500=7,000=70%=P7.00D=7.0=Language = Assets = Mars=7July=Pleiades.
Adapt=4,500=5,000=50%=P5.00D=5.0=Law=Time=Venus=5 May=Aphrodite>>L=N.
Adaptation=17,500=18,000=18%=P1.80D=1.8=Solar Currency=MaksCurr.=1 Aug=Maia.
Adapter=9,000=90%=P9.00D=9.0=Abstraction=Gods=Saturn=9Sept.>>A=Ø.
Adaptive=4,000=40%=P4.00D=4.0=Govt.=Creat.=4April=Hermes>>G=A4.
Adar=5,000=50%=P5.00D=5.0=Law=Time=Venus=5 May=Aphrodite>>L=N.
Adar Sheni=5,000=50%=P5.00D=5.0=Law=Time=Venus=5 May=Aphrodite>>L=N.
ADC=4,500=5,000=50%=P5.00D=5.0=Law=Time=Venus=5 May=Aphrodite>>L=N.
Add=20,500=21,000=21%=P2.10D=2.1=3.0=Creativity=Star=Muses=2 Jan>>C=I.
Addams Jane=6,000=60%=P6.00D=6.0=Man=Earth=Royalty=6June=Gaia>M=M2.
Addend=6,000=60%=P6.00D=6.0=Man=Earth=Royalty=6June=Gaia>M=M2.
Addendum=5,500=5.5=80%=P5.50D=Earth-Midway=5May=Gaia.
Adder(1)=5,000=50%=P5.00D=5.0=Law=Time=Venus=5 May=Aphrodite>>L=N.
Adder(2)=10,000=1,000=100%=10.0=Physicality=Tech.=10 Oct.=Uranus=P=1Ø.
Addict=11,500=12,000=12%=P1.20D=1.2=Knowledge=12Dec.=Athena>>K=F.
Addis Ababa=5,000=50%=P5.00D=5.0=Law=Time=Venus=5 May=Aphrodite>>L=N.
Addison Joseph=2,000=20%=P2.00D=2.0=Nature=Matter=Moon=2 Feb= Cupid>N=C.
Addition=10,500=11,000=11%=P1.10D=1.1=Idea=BrainchildInvention=11Nov.=Athena
    >K=F.

Additive=7,000=70%=P7.00D=7.0=Language = Assets = Mars = 7July=Pleiades.
Addle=5,500=5.5=80%=P5.50D=Earth-Midway=5May=Gaia.
Add-on=8,000=80%=P8.00D=8.0=Econ.=Curr.=Busn.=Jupiter=8 Aug=Zeus>E=v.
Address=20,500=21,000=21%=P2.10D=2.1=3.0=Creativity=Star=Muses=2 Jan>>C=I.
Addressee=3,500=4,000=40%=P4.00D=4.0=Govt.=Creatocracy=4April=Hermes>G=A4.
Adduce=6,000=60%=P6.00D=6.0=Man=Earth=Royalty=6June=Gaia>M=M2.
Adelaide=6,000=60%=P6.00D=6.0=Man=Earth=Royalty=6June=Gaia>M=M2.
Aden=15,500=16%=P1.60D=1.6=Cycle of Life=Incarnation=Mind of GOD=1June= Maia.
Adenauer Konrad=5,500=5.5=80%=P5.50D=Earth-Midway=5May=Gaia.
Adenine=6,000=60%=P6.00D=6.0=Man=Earth=Royalty=6June=Gaia>M=M2.
Adenoid=6,500=7,000=70%=P7.00D=7.0=Language = Assets = Mars = 6 May=Pleiades.
Adenoidal=3,500=4,000=40%=P4.00D=4.0=Govt.=Creatocracy=4April=Hermes>G=A4.
Adept=1,500=15%=P1.50D=1.5=Authority = Solar Crown = Solar Core = 1 May = Maia.
Adequate=5,500=5.5=80%=P5.50D=Earth-Midway=5May=Gaia.
Adhere=11,000=11%=P1.10D=1.1=Idea=Brainchild=Invention=11 Nov.=Athena>K=F.
Adhesion=10,000=1,000=100%=10.0=Physicality=Tech.=10 Oct.=Uranus=P=1Ø.
Adhesive=4,500=5,000=50%=P5.00D=5.0=Law=Time=Venus=5 May=Aphrodite>>L=N.
Ad hoc=5,500=5.5=80%=P5.50D=Earth-Midway=5May=Gaia.
Ad hominem=6,500=7,000=70%=P7.00D=7.0=Language = Assets =Mars = 6May=Pleiades.
Adiabatic=5,500=5.5=80%=P5.50D=Earth-Midway=5May=Gaia.
Adieu=2,000=20%=P2.00D=2.0=Nature=Matter=Moon=2 Feb= Cupid>N=C.
Adinfinitum=2,500=3,000=30%=P3.00D=3.0=Creativity=Star=Muses=3March=C=I.
Adios=2,000=20%=P2.00D=2.0=Nature=Matter=Moon=2 Feb= Cupid>N=C.
Adipose=2,500=3,000=30%=P3.00D=3.0=Creativity=Star=Muses=3March=C=I.
Adirondack Mounts.=6,500=7,000=70%=P7.00D=7.0=Lang=Assets=Mars=6May=Pleiades.
Adj.=3,000=30%=P3.00D=3.0=Creativity=Star=Muses=3March=C=I.
Adjacent=5,000=50%=P5.00D=5.0=Law=Time=Venus=5 May=Aphrodite>>L=N.
Adjective=8,500=8.5=9,000=90%=P9.00D=9.0=Abstraction=Zeus=Saturn=8 May.>>A=Ø.
Adjoin=2,500=3,000=30%=P3.00D=3.0=Creativity=Star=Muses=3March=C=I.
Adjourn=9,000=90%=P9.00D=9.0=Abstraction=Gods=Saturn=9Sept.>>A=Ø.
Adjudge=5,500=5.5=80%=P5.50D=Earth-Midway=5May=Gaia.
Adjudicate=4,500=5,000=50%=P5.00D=5.0=Law=Time=Venus=5 May=Aphrodite>>L=N.
Adjunct=5,000=50%=P5.00D=5.0=Law=Time=Venus=5 May=Aphrodite>>L=N.
Adjure=6,000=60%=P6.00D=6.0=Man=Earth=Royalty=6June=Gaia>M=M2.
Adjust=12,000=12%=P1.20D=1.2=Knowledge=Education =12 Dec.= Athena>>K=F.
Adjutant=5,500=5.5=80%=P5.50D=Earth-Midway=5May=Gaia.
Adler Alfred=2,000=20%=P2.00D=2.0=Nature=Matter=Moon=2 Feb= Cupid>N=C.
Ad lib=2,500=3,000=30%=P3.00D=3.0=Creativity=Star=Muses=3March=C=I.
Ad-lib=6,000=60%=P6.00D=6.0=Man=Earth=Royalty=6June=Gaia>M=M2.
Ad loc.=4,000=40%=P4.00D=4.0=Govt.=Creatocracy=Mercury= 4April=Hermes>>G=A4.
Administer= 12,500 = 13,000 = 13% = P1.30D = 1.3 = Solar Core = Faculty = 13 Jan=Athena.
Administration=16,000=16%=P1.60D=1.6=Incarnation=Mind of GOD=1 June = Maia.
Administrator=4,000=40%=P4.00D=4.0=Govt.=Creatocracy= 4April=Hermes>>G=A4.
Admirable=1,000=100%=10.0=1.0=Mind=Sun=1 January=Helios >> M=E4.
Admiral=10,000=1,000=100%=10.0=Physicality=Tech.=10 Oct.=Uranus=P=1Ø.

Admiralty=11,000=11%=P1.10D=1.1=Idea=Brainchild=Invention=11 Nov.=Athena>K=F.

Admire=6,500=7,000=70%=P7.00D=7.0=Language = Assets =Mars = 6 May=Pleiades.

Admissible=5,000=50%=P5.00D=5.0=Law=Time=Venus=5 May=Aphrodite>>L=N.

Admission=11,000=11%=P1.10D=1.1=Idea=Brainchild=Invention=11 Nov.=Athena>K=F.

Admit = 12,500 = 13,000 = 13% = P1.30D = 1.3 = Solar Core = Faculty = 13 Jan=Athena.

Admittance=5,000=50%=P5.00D=5.0=Law=Time=Venus=5 May=Aphrodite>>L=N.

Admittedly=2,000=20%=P2.00D=2.0=Nature=Matter=Moon=2 Feb= Cupid>N=C.

Admixture=4,500=5,000=50%=P5.00D=5.0=Law=Time=Venus=5 May=Aphrodite>>L=N.

Admonish=5,500=5.5=80%=P5.50D=Earth-Midway=5May=Gaia.

Admonitory=1,000=100%=10.0=1.0=Mind=Sun=1 January=Helios >> M=E4.

Ad nauseam=4,500=5,000=50%=P5.00D=5.0=Law=Time=Venus=5May=Aphrodite>>L=N.

Ado=1,500=15%=P1.50D=1.5=Authority = Solar Crown = Solar Core = 1 May = Maia.

Adobe=6,500=7,000=70%=P7.00D=7.0=Language = Assets =Mars = 6 May=Pleiades.

Adolescence=9,000=90%=P9.00D=9.0=Abstraction=Gods=Saturn=9Sept.>>A=Ø.

Adonis=6,000=60%=P6.00D=6.0=Man=Earth=Health=Royalty=6June=Gaia>M=M2.

Adopt=12,000=12%=P1.20D=1.2=Knowledge=Education =12 Dec.= Athena>>K=F.

Adoptee=5,500=5.5=80%=P5.50D=Earth-Midway=5May=Gaia.

Adoptive=6,000=60%=P6.00D=6.0=Man=Earth=Health=Royalty=6June=Gaia>M=M2.

Adorable=3,500=4,000=40%=P4.00D=4.0=Govt.=Creatocracy= 4April=Hermes>>G=A4.

Adore=6,500=7,000=70%=P7.00D=7.0=Language = Assets =Mars = 6 May=Pleiades.

Adorn=3,500=4,000=40%=P4.00D=4.0=Govt.=Creatocracy= 4 April=Hermes>>G=A4.

Adrenal=6,500=7,000=70%=P7.00D=7.0=Language = Assets =Mars = 6 May=Pleiades.

Adrenal gland=5,500=5.5=80%=P5.50D=Earth-Midway=5May=Gaia.

Adrenaline=1,000=100%=10.0=1.0=Mind=Sun=1 January=Helios >> M=E4.

Adriatic Sea=5,500=5.5=80%=P5.50D=Earth-Midway=5May=Gaia. *(Note that the Adriatic Sea is an Earth Midway inhabited 80% by Gaia. A discovery herein). Research.

Adrift=5,000=50%=P5.00D=5.0=Law=Time=Venus=5 May=Aphrodite>>L=N.

Adroit=3,000=30%=P3.00D=3.0=Creativity=Star=Muses=3March=C=I.

Adsorb=7,000=70%=P7.00D=7.0=Language =Assets =Mars =Computing= 6May=Pleiades.

Adulate=3,500=4,000=40%=P4.00D=4.0=Govt.=Creatocracy= 4 April=Hermes>>G=A4.

Adult=8,000=80%=P8.00D=8.0=Econ.=Curr.=Busn.=Jupiter=8 Aug=Zeus>E=v.

Adulterate=4,500=5,000=50%=P5.00D=5.0=Law=Time=Venus=5 May=Aphrodite>>L=N.

Adultery=7,000=70%=P7.00D=7.0=Language = Assets =Mars = 6 May=Pleiades.

Adumbrate=4,500=5,000=50%=P5.00D=5.0=Law=Time=Venus=5 May=Aphrodite>>L=N.

Adv.=3,000=30%=P3.00D=3.0=Creativity=Star=Muses=3March=C=I.

Advance=38,500=40,000=40%=P4.00D=4.0=Govt.=Creat.= 3 Aug. =Hermes>>G=A4.

Advanced=12,000=12%=P1.20D=1.2=Knowledge=Education =12 Dec.= Athena>>K=F.

Advancement=4,500=5,000=50%=P5.00D=5.0=Law=Time=Venus=5May=Odite>>L=N.

Advantage= 13,000 = 13% = P1.30D = 1.3 = Solar Core = Faculty = 13 Jan=Athena.

Advection=7,000=70%=P7.00D=7.0=Language = Assets =Mars = 6 May=Pleiades.

Advent= 13,000 = 13% = P1.30D = 1.3 = Solar Core = Faculty = 13 Jan=Athena.

Adventitious=2,500=3,000=30%=P3.00D=3.0=Creativity=Star=Muses=3March=C=I.

Adventure=11,000=11%=P1.10D=1.1=Idea=Brainchild=Invention=11 Nov.=Athena>K=F.
Adventurer=11,000=11%=P1.10D=1.1=Idea=Brainchild=Invention=11 Nov.=Athena>K=F.
Adventuresome=2,000=20%=P2.00D=2.0=Nature=Matter=Moon=2 Feb= Cupid>N=C.
Adventuress=8,000=80%=P8.00D=8.0=Econ.=Curr.=Busn.=Jupiter=8 Aug=Zeus>E=v.
Adventurous=8,000=80%=P8.00D=8.0=Econ.=Curr.=Busn.=Jupiter=8 Aug=Zeus>E=v.
Adverb=7,500=8,000=80%=P8.00D=8.0=Econ.=Curr.=Busn.=Jupiter=8 Aug=Zeus>E=v.
Adversarial=2,500=3,000=30%=P3.00D=3.0=Creativity=Star=Muses=3March=C=I.
Adversary=1,500=15%=P1.50D=1.5=Authority = Solar Crown = Solar Core = 1 May = Maia.
Adverse=6,500=7,000=70%=P7.00D=7.0=Language = Assets =Mars = 6 May=Pleiades.
Adversity=4,000=40%=P4.00D=4.0=Govt.=Creatocracy= 4 April=Hermes>>G=A4.
Advert=6,000=60%=P6.00D=6.0=Man=Earth=Health=Royalty=6June=Gaia>M=M2.
Advertise=10,500=11,000=11%=P1.10D=1.1=Idea=Brainchild=11Nov.=Athena>K=F.
Advertisement=6,500=7,000=70%=P7.00D=7.0=Lang.= Assets =Mars = 6May=Pleiades.
Advertising=4,500=5,000=50%=P5.00D=5.0=Law=Time=Venus=5 May=Aphrodite>>L=N.
Advice=5,500=5.5=80%=P5.50D=Earth-Midway=5 May=Gaia.
Advisable=3,500=4,000=40%=P4.00D=4.0=Govt.=Creat.= 4 April=Hermes>>G=A4.
Advise=5,000=50%=P5.00D=5.0=Law=Time=Venus=5 May=Aphrodite>>L=N.
Advisedly=2,000=20%=P2.00D=2.0=Nature=Matter=Moon=2 Feb= Cupid>N=C.
Advisement=1,000=100%=10.0=1.0=Mind=Sun=1 January=Helios >> M=E4.
Advisory=7,500=8,000=80%=P8.00D=8.0=Econ.=Curr.=Busn.=Jupiter=8 Aug=Zeus>E=v.
Advocacy=7,500=8,000=80%=P8.00D=8.0=Econ.=Curr.=Busn.=Jupt.=8Aug=Zeus>E=v.
Advocate=9,500=10,000=1,000=100%=10.0=Physicality=Tech.=10 Oct.=Uranus=P=1Ø.
Adz or adze=8,500=9,000=90%=P9.00D=9.0=Abstraction=Gods=Saturn=9Sept.>>A=Ø.

Aegean Sea=6,000=60%=P6.00D=6.0=Man=Earth=Health=Royalty=6June=Gaia>M=M2.
Interestingly there is a connection by definition between the Adriatic Sea and the Aegean
Sea as both are arms of the Mediterranean Sea. More interesting is the resultant shown
that reflects the existence of Gaia to both seas. This is a second discovery on Gaia herein.

Aegis=6,500=7,000=70%=P7.00D=7.0=Language = Assets =Mars = 6 May=Pleiades.
An advancement of Gaia to the Pleiades becomes the Shield of Zeus and Athena. Hence
the Pleiades as symbols of precision prove that computation is the mental shield of Godship
and wisdom. The very weapons and assets of Castle Makupedia the God of Creatocracy.
Makupedia is also known as the Mind God because he discovered invented and applied
Mind Computing through which He measured the code for Genius as 3.3. Thus He is
comprehensively honored as the God of Creatocracy Genius and Mind. He owns the
Creatocracy concept and wears the Solar Crown. He authored the Creatocracy Bank, the
Creatocracy Court, the Creatocracy Univeristies Union, the Creatocracy Faith systems
etc. Zeus and Athena are the aegis of the Creatocracy as declared in the Solar Crown book.

Aeneas=5,500=5.5=80%=P5.50D=Earth-Midway=5 May=Gaia.
Aeolis=5,500=5.5=80%=P5.50D=Earth-Midway=5May=Gaia.
Aeon=1,500=15%=P1.50D=1.5=Authority = Solar Crown = Solar Core = 1 May = Maia.

Aerate=9,500=10,000=1,000=100%=10.0=Physicality=Tech.=10 Oct.=Uranus=P=1Ø.
Aerial=1,500=15%=P1.50D=1.5=Authority = Solar Crown = Solar Core = 1 May = Maia.
Aerialist=5,500=5.5=80%=P5.50D=Earth-Midway=5May=Gaia.
Aerie=5,500=5.5=80%=P5.50D=Earth-Midway=5May=Gaia.
Aero-=2,500=3,000=30%=P3.00D=3.0=Creativity=Star=Muses=3 March=C=I.
Aerobatics=3,500=4,000=40%=P4.00D=4.0=Govt.=Creat.= 4 April=Hermes>>G=A4.
Aerobe=5,000=50%=P5.00D=5.0=Law=Time=Venus=5 May=Aphrodite>>L=N.
Aerobic=6,000=60%=P6.00D=6.0=Man=Earth=Health=Royalty=6June=Gaia>M=M2.
Aerobics=4,500=5,000=50%=P5.00D=5.0=Law=Time=Venus=5 May=Aphrodite>>L=N.
Aerodynamic=6,000=60%=P6.00D=6.0=Man=Earth=Health=Royalty=6June=Gaia
    >M=M2.
Aerodynamics=8,500=9,000=90%=P9.00D=9.0=Abstraction=Gods=Saturn=9Sept.>>A=Ø
Aerometer=5,500=5.5=80%=P5.50D=Earth-Midway=5 May=Gaia.
Aeronaut=6,000=60%=P6.00D=6.0=Man=Earth=Health=Royalty=6June=Gaia>M=M2.
Aeronautics=3,500=4,000=40%=P4.00D=4.0=Govt.=Creat.= 4 April=Hermes>>G=A4.
Aeropause=5,000=50%=P5.00D=5.0=Law=Time=Venus=5 May=Aphrodite>>L=N.
Aeroplane=2,500=3,000=30%=P3.00D=3.0=Creativity=Star=Muses=3 March=C=I.
Aeroponics=7,500=8,000=80%=P8.00D=8.0=Econ.=Curr.=Busn.=Jupt.=8Aug=Zeus>E=v.
Aerosol=10,000=1,000=100%=10.0=Physicality=Tech.=10 Oct.=Uranus=P=1Ø.
Aerosol bomb=5,500=5.5=80%=P5.50D=Earth-Midway=5 May=Gaia.
Aerospace=7,500=8,000=80%=P8.00D=8.0=Econ.=Curr.=Busn.=Jupt.=8Aug=Zeus>E=v.
Aery=1,500=15%=P1.50D=1.5=Authority = Solar Crown = Solar Core = 1 May = Maia.
Aeschylus=3,000=30%=P3.00D=3.0=Creativity=Star=Muses=3 March=C=I.
Aesop=2,500=3,000=30%=P3.00D=3.0=Creativity=Star=Muses=3March=C=I.
Aesthesia=1,500=15%=P1.50D=1.5=Authority = Solar Crown = Solar Core = 1 May = Maia.
Aesthete=5,500=5.5=80%=P5.50D=Earth-Midway=5 May=Gaia.
Aesthetic=11,500=12,000=12%=P1.20D=1.2=Knowledge=12Dec.=Athena>>K=F.
Aestheticism=8,500=9,000=90%=P9.00D=9.0=Abstraction=Gods=Saturn=9Sept.>>A=Ø.
Aesthetics=8,500=9,000=90%=P9.00D=9.0=Abstraction=Gods=Saturn=9Sept.>>A=Ø.
Aestivate=1,500=15%=P1.50D=1.5=Authority = Solar Crown = Solar Core = 1 May = Maia.
Afar=4,500=5,000=50%=P5.00D=5.0=Law=Time=Venus=5 May=Aphrodite>>L=N.
AFB=1,500=15%=P1.50D=1.5=Authority = Solar Crown = Solar Core = 1 May = Maia.
AFC=1,500=15%=P1.50D=1.5=Authority = Solar Crown = Solar Core = 1 May = Maia.
AFDC=3,000=30%=P3.00D=3.0=Creativity=Star=Muses=3 March=C=I.
Affable=3,000=30%=P3.00D=3.0=Creativity=Star=Muses=3 March=C=I.
Affair=18,000=18%=P1.80D=1.8=Solar Currency=Mind/Maks Currency.=1 Aug=Maia.
Affect (1)=4,000=40%=P4.00D=4.0=Govt.=Creat.= 4 April=Hermes>>G=A4.
Affect (2)=9,000=90%=P9.00D=9.0=Abstraction=Gods=Saturn=9Sept.>>A=Ø.
Affectation=5,000=50%=P5.00D=5.0=Law=Time=Venus=5 May=Aphrodite>>L=N.
Affected=4,000=40%=P4.00D=4.0=Govt.=Creat.= 4 April=Hermes>>G=A4.
Affecting=2,000=20%=P2.00D=2.0=Nature=Matter=Moon=2 Feb= Cupid>N=C.
Affection=3,000=30%=P3.00D=3.0=Creativity=Star=Muses=3 March=C=I.
Affective=5,000=50%=P5.00D=5.0=Law=Time=Venus=5 May=Aphrodite>>L=N.
Afferent=4,000=40%=P4.00D=4.0=Govt.=Creat.= 4 April=Hermes>>G=A4.
Affiance=2,500=3,000=30%=P3.00D=3.0=Creativity=Star=Muses=3March=C=I.

Affidavit=5,000=50%=P5.00D=5.0=Law=Time=Venus=5 May=Aphrodite>>L=N.
Affiliate=5,000=50%=P5.00D=5.0=Law=Time=Venus=5 May=Aphrodite>>L=N.
Affinity=6,500=7,000=70%=P7.00D=7.0=Lang.= Assets =Mars = 6May=Pleiades.
Affirm=4,000=40%=P4.00D=4.0=Govt.=Creat.= 4 April=Hermes>>G=A4.
Affirmative=10,000=1,000=100%=10.0=Physicality=Tech.=10 Oct.=Uranus=P=1Ø.
Affirmative action=8,500=9,000=90%=P9.00D=9.0=Abstr.=Gods=Saturn=9Sept.>>A=Ø.
Affix=11,500=12,000=12%=P1.20D=1.2=Knowledge=12Dec.=Athena>>K=F.
Afflatus=3,000=30%=P3.00D=3.0=Creativity=Star=Muses=3 March=C=I.
Afflict=2,500=3,000=30%=P3.00D=3.0=Creativity=Star=Muses=3March=C=I.
Affliction=5,000=50%=P5.00D=5.0=Law=Time=Venus=5 May=Aphrodite>>L=N.
Affluence=3,000=30%=P3.00D=3.0=Creativity=Star=Muses=3 March=C=I.
Affluent=5,000=50%=P5.00D=5.0=Law=Time=Venus=5 May=Aphrodite>>L=N.
Afford=9,500=10,000=1,000=100%=10.0=Physicality=Tech.=10 Oct.=Uranus=P=1Ø.
Afforest=5,000=50%=P5.00D=5.0=Law=Time=Venus=5 May=Aphrodite>>L=N.
Affray=2,500=3,000=30%=P3.00D=3.0=Creativity=Star=Muses=3March=C=I.
Affront=3,500=4,000=40%=P4.00D=4.0=Govt.=Creat.= 4 April=Hermes>>G=A4.
Afg.=1,000=100%=10.0=1.0=Mind=Sun=1 January=Helios >> M=E4.
Afghan=9,500=10,000=1,000=100%=10.0=Physicality=Tech.=10 Oct.=Uranus=P=1Ø.
Afghan hound=5,500=5.5=80%=P5.50D=Earth-Midway=5 May=Gaia.
Afghani=2,500=3,000=30%=P3.00D=3.0=Creativity=Star=Muses=3March=C=I.
Afghanistan=7,500=8,000=80%=P8.00D=8.0=Econ.=Curr.=Busn.=Jupt.=8Aug=Zeus>E=v
Aficionado=1,500=15%=P1.50D=1.5=Authority = Solar Crown = Solar Core = 1 May = Maia.
Afield=9,500=10,000=1,000=100%=10.0=Physicality=Tech.=10 Oct.=Uranus=P=1Ø.
Afire=1,000=100%=10.0=1.0=Mind=Sun=1 January=Helios >> M=E4.
AFL=3,000=30%=P3.00D=3.0=Creativity=Star=Muses=3March=C=I.
Aflame=1,000=100%=10.0=1.0=Mind=Sun=1 January=Helios >> M=E4.
Aflatoxin=6,500=7,000=70%=P7.00D=7.0=Lang.= Assets =Mars = 6May=Pleiades.
AFL-CIO=4,500=5,000=50%=P5.00D=5.0=Law=Time=Venus=5 May=Aphrodite>>L=N.
Afloat=3,500=4,000=40%=P4.00D=4.0=Govt.=Creat.= 4 April=Hermes>>G=A4.
Aflutter=3,500=4,000=40%=P4.00D=4.0=Govt.=Creat.= 4 April=Hermes>>G=A4.
Afoot=3,500=4,000=40%=P4.00D=4.0=Govt.=Creat.= 4 April=Hermes>>G=A4.
Aforementioned=1,000=100%=10.0=1.0=Mind=Sun=1 January=Helios >> M=E4.
Aforesaid=1,500=15%=P1.50D=1.5=Authority = Solar Crown = Solar Core = 1 May = Maia.
Aforethought=2,000=20%=P2.00D=2.0=Nature=Matter=Moon=2 Feb= Cupid>N=C.
Afortiori=6,000=60%=P6.00D=6.0=Man=Earth=Health=Royalty=6June=Gaia>M=M2.
Afoul of=3,500=4,000=40%=P4.00D=4.0=Govt.=Creat.= 4 April=Hermes>>G=A4.
Afr.=1,000=100%=10.0=1.0=Mind=Sun=1 January=Helios >> M=E4.
Afraid=7,000=70%=P7.00D=7.0=Lang.= Assets =Mars = 6May=Pleiades.
A-frame=6,500=7,000=70%=P7.00D=7.0=Lang.= Assets =Mars = 6May=Pleiades.
Afresh=3,000=30%=P3.00D=3.0=Creativity=Star=Muses=3March=C=I.

Africa=5,500=5.5=80%=P5.50D=Earth-Midway=5 May=Gaia. (Gaia lives in Africa also.)
African=8,000=80%=P8.00D=8.0=Econ.=Curr.=Busn.=Jupiter=8 Aug=Zeus>E=v.
African-American=5,000=50%=P5.00D=5.0=Law=Time=Venus=5 May=Aphrodite>>L=N.

There must be deliberate African - World friendly policies that will make Africa a central core or midway in the global economy system. This is the Gaian theory. Africa should also be in the lead for an economic development system based on its huge supply of natural resources in this case the solar fits the most. Thirdly America as a world power must be carried along because the works that engender scientific explorations and historical development have long been in the coming. US Case law on the inventor suffices, as the AuthorHouse US, UK published Makupedia and promoted the legal rights of the author.

"As long as Europe and America Control our Money, they will Control our Economy: We need African Common Currency backed by our Resources not by Dollar or by Euro" ~ Paul Kagame, President of Rwanda. Culled from Happy African's post online.

The Creatocracy offers a huge opportunity to Africa. In whatever way the continent could decide to partner us we welcome the integration of the Maks as a single African currency with a worldwide appeal on storage exchange and securities to make the dream of a creative economy possible anywhere and everywhere. Maks as the first solar metric currency could be integrated into ECOWAS as Ecomaks or Afrimaks in African Union or simply as Maks for the entire continent. Other Creatocratic benefit will suffice as soon as there is adoption practice and implementation of the C3 Africa. Such benefits will include a recognition and approval of Makupedia: World Digital Smart Dictionary into every school office home and place considered most necessary and induction of the FCPSS education and licensing programs in the Creatocracy. C3 are Nations that practice Creativity as a citizen personal lifestyle, Creatocism as an economy model that include market trading & business of ideas, and Creatocracy as a political system that makes for smart governance. See Currency, Dollar. See Book reference: Template & Manifesto for the Creative Economy 2: Principles of Psychoeconomix by Peter Matthews-Akukalia. AuthorHouse, 2016.

Africanized bee=8,500=9,000=90%=P9.00D=9.0=Abstr.=Gods=Saturn=9Sept.>>A=Ø.
African violet=9,000=90%=P9.00D=9.0=Abstraction=Gods=Saturn=9Sept.>>A=Ø.
Afrikaans=8,000=80%=P8.00D=8.0=Econ.=Curr.=Busn.=Jupiter=8 Aug=Zeus>E=v.
Afrikaner=6,000=60%=P6.00D=6.0=Man=Earth=Health=Royalty=6June=Gaia>M=M2.
Afro=6,000=60%=P6.00D=6.0=Man=Earth=Health=Royalty=6June=Gaia>M=M2.
Afro-=1,500=15%=P1.50D=1.5=Authority = Solar Crown = Solar Core = 1 May = Maia.
Afro-American=1,000=100%=10.0=1.0=Mind=Sun=1 January=Helios >> M=E4.
Afro-Asiatic=5,500=5.5=80%=P5.50D=Earth-Midway=5 May=Gaia.
Aft=6,500=7,000=70%=P7.00D=7.0=Lang.= Assets =Mars = 6May=Pleiades.
AFT=2,000=20%=P2.00D=2.0=Nature=Matter=Moon=2 Feb= Cupid>N=C.
Aft.=500=5%=P5.00D=5.0=Law=Time=Venus=5 May=Aphrodite>>L=N.
After=2,100=3,000=30%=P3.00D=3.0=Creativity=Star=Muses=3March=C=I.
After all=2,500=3,000=30%=P3.00D=3.0=Creativity=Star=Muses=3March=C=I.
After birth=5,500=5.5=80%=P5.50D=Earth-Midway=5 May=Gaia.
Afterburner=8,000=80%=P8.00D=8.0=Econ.=Curr.=Busn.=Jupiter=8 Aug=Zeus>E=v.
After effect=4,000=40%=P4.00D=4.0=Govt.=Creat.= 4 April=Hermes>>G=A4.

Afterglow=6,000=60%=P6.00D=6.0=Man=Earth=Health=Royalty=6June=Gaia>M=M2.
After-hours=4,000=40%=P4.00D=4.0=Govt.=Creat.= 4 April=Hermes>>G=A4.
After image=5,000=50%=P5.00D=5.0=Law=Time=Venus=5 May=Aphrodite>>L=N.
Afterlife=2,000=20%=P2.00D=2.0=Nature=Matter=Moon=2 Feb= Cupid>N=C.
Aftermath=7,000=70%=P7.00D=7.0=Lang.= Assets =Mars = 6May=Pleiades.
Afternoon=3,500=4,000=40%=P4.00D=4.0=Govt.=Creat.= 4 April=Hermes>>G=A4.
Aftershave=4,000=40%=P4.00D=4.0=Govt.=Creat.= 4 April=Hermes>>G=A4.
Aftershock=6,500=7,000=70%=P7.00D=7.0=Lang.= Assets =Mars = 6May=Pleiades.
Aftertaste=6,500=7,000=70%=P7.00D=7.0=Lang.= Assets =Mars = 6May=Pleiades.
Afterthought=5,500=5.5=80%=P5.50D=Earth-Midway=5 May=Gaia.
Afterward=2,500=3,000=30%=P3.00D=3.0=Creativity=Star=Muses=3March=C=I.
Afterword=1,500=15%=P1.50D=1.5=Authority = Solar Crown = Solar Core = 1 May = Maia.
Ag=3,000=30%=P3.00D=3.0=Creativity=Star=Muses=3March=C=I.
A.G.=2,000=20%=P2.00D=2.0=Nature=Matter=Moon=2 Feb= Cupid>N=C.
Again=9,500=10,000=1,000=100%=10.0=Physicality=Tech.=10 Oct.=Uranus=P=1Ø.
Against=17,000=17%=P1.70D=1.7=Solar Asset = 17/20=17 Feb.=Maia>>Mind Computing.
Agamemnon=6,500=7,000=70%=P7.00D=7.0=Lang.= Assets =Mars = 6May=Pleiades.
Agana=6,500=7,000=70%=P7.00D=7.0=Lang.= Assets =Mars = 6May=Pleiades.
Agape(1)=4,000=40%=P4.00D=4.0=Govt.=Creat.= 4 April=Hermes>>G=A4.
Agape(2)=1,000=100%=10.0=1.0=Mind=Sun=1 January=Helios >> M=E4.
Agar=10,000=1,000=100%=10.0=Physicality=Tech.=10 Oct.=Uranus=P=1Ø.
Agassiz=4,500=5,000=50%=P5.00D=5.0=Law=Time=Venus=5 May=Aphrodite>>L=N.
Agate=7,500=8,000=80%=P8.00D=8.0=Econ.=Curr.=Busn.=Jupt.=8Aug=Zeus>E=v.
Agave=7,000=70%=P7.00D=7.0=Lang.= Assets =Mars = 6May=Pleiades.
Age=29000=30,000=3,000=30%=P3.00D=3.0=Creativity=Star=Muses=3March=C=I.
-age=11,500=12,000=12%=P1.20D=1.2=Knowledge=Education =12 Dec.= Athena>>K=F.
Aged=10,500=11,000=11%=P1.10D=1.1=Idea=Brainchild=Invention=11 Nov.=Athena>K=F.
Agee=3,500=4,000=40%=P4.00D=4.0=Govt.=Creat.= 4 April=Hermes>>G=A4.
Ageism=4,000=40%=P4.00D=4.0=Govt.=Creat.= 4 April=Hermes>>G=A4.
Ageless=6,000=60%=P6.00D=6.0=Man=Earth=Health=Royalty=6June=Gaia>M=M2.
Agency=10,000=1,000=100%=10.0=Physicality=Tech.=10 Oct.=Uranus=P=1Ø.
Agenda=7,500=8,000=80%=P8.00D=8.0=Econ.=Curr.=Busn.=Jupt.=8Aug=Zeus>E=v.
Agent=1,500=15%=P1.50D=1.5=Authority = Solar Crown = Solar Core = 1 May = Maia.
Agent Orange=6,000=60%=P6.00D=6.0=Man=Earth=Royalty=6June=Gaia>M=M2.
Agent provocateur=7,500=8,000=80%=P8.00D=8.0=Econ.=Busn.=Jupt.=8Aug=Zeus>E=v
Age-old=1,000=100%=10.0=1.0=Mind=Sun=1 January=Helios >> M=E4.
Ageratum=7,000=70%=P7.00D=7.0=Lang.= Assets =Mars = 6May=Pleiades.
Aggle=2,000=20%=P2.00D=2.0=Nature=Matter=Moon=2 Feb= Cupid>N=C.
Agglomerate=6,500=7,000=70%=P7.00D=7.0=Lang.= Assets =Mars = 6May=Pleiades.
Agglutinate=9,000=90%=P9.00D=9.0=Abstraction=Gods=Saturn=9Sept.>>A=Ø.
Aggrandize=2,000=20%=P2.00D=2.0=Nature=Matter=Moon=2 Feb= Cupid>N=C.
Aggravate=4,000=40%=P4.00D=4.0=Govt.=Creat.= 4 April=Hermes>>G=A4.
Aggregate=9,000=90%=P9.00D=9.0=Abstraction=Gods=Saturn=9Sept.>>A=Ø.
Aggression=5,000=50%=P5.00D=5.0=Law=Time=Venus=5 May=Aphrodite>>L=N.
Aggressive=8,500=9,000=90%=P9.00D=9.0=Abstraction=Gods=Saturn=9Sept.>>A=Ø.

Aggrieve=4,500=5,000=50%=P5.00D=5.0=Law=Time=Venus=5 May=Aphrodite>>L=N.
Aggrieved=6,500=7,000=70%=P7.00D=7.0=Lang.= Assets =Mars = 6May=Pleiades.
Aghast=2,500=3,000=30%=P3.00D=3.0=Creativity=Star=Muses=3March=C=I.
Agile=4,500=5,000=50%=P5.00D=5.0=Law=Time=Venus=5 May=Aphrodite>>L=N.
Agin court=7,000=70%=P7.00D=7.0=Lang.= Assets =Mars = 6May=Pleiades.
Aging=3,500=4,000=40%=P4.00D=4.0=Govt.=Creat.= 4 April=Hermes>>G=A4.
Agism=1,500=15%=P1.50D=1.5=Authority = Solar Crown = Solar Core = 1 May = Maia.
Agitate=11,000=11%=P1.10D=1.1=Idea=Brainchild=Invention=11 Nov.=Athena>K=F.
Agitator=9,000=90%=P9.00D=9.0=Abstraction=Gods=Saturn=9Sept.>>A=Ø.
Agleam=1,000=100%=10.0=1.0=Mind=Sun=1 January=Helios >> M=E4.
Aglitter=1,000=100%=10.0=1.0=Mind=Sun=1 January=Helios >> M=E4.
Aglow=500=5%=P5.00D=5.0=Law=Time=Venus=5 May=Aphrodite>>L=N.
Agnew=5,500=5.5=80%=P5.50D=Earth-Midway=5 May=Gaia.
Agnostic=10,500=11,000=11%=P1.10D=1.1=Idea=Brainchild=Invention=11Nov=
    Athena>K=F
Angus Dei=7,500=8,000=80%=P8.00D=8.0=Econ.=Curr.=Busn.=Jupt.=8Aug=Zeus>E=v.
Ago=5,000=50%=P5.00D=5.0=Law=Time=Venus=5 May=Aphrodite>>L=N.
Agog=2,000=20%=P2.00D=2.0=Nature=Matter=Moon=2 Feb= Cupid>N=C.
Agonist=7,000=70%=P7.00D=7.0=Lang.= Assets =Mars = 6May=Pleiades.
Agonize=7,500=8,000=80%=P8.00D=8.0=Econ.=Curr.=Busn.=Jupt.=8Aug=Zeus>E=v.
Agony=11,000=11%=P1.10D=1.1=Idea=Brainchild=Invention=11 Nov.=Athena>K=F.
Agora(1)=4,500=5,000=50%=P5.00D=5.0=Law=Time=Venus=5 May=Aphrodite>>L=N.
Agora(2)=3,000=30%=P3.00D=3.0=Creativity=Star=Muses=3March=C=I.
Agoraphobia=6,000=60%=P6.00D=6.0=Man=Earth=Health=Royalty=6June=Gaia
    >M=M2.
Agra=8,000=80%=P8.00D=8.0=Econ.=Curr.=Busn.=Jupiter=8 Aug=Zeus>E=v.
Agrarian=7,000=70%=P7.00D=7.0=Lang.= Assets =Mars = 6May=Pleiades.
Agrarianism=5,000=50%=P5.00D=5.0=Law=Time=Venus=5 May=Aphrodite>>L=N.
Agree=20,500=3,000=30%=P3.00D=3.0=Creativity=Star=Muses=3March=C=I.
Agreeable=5,000=50%=P5.00D=5.0=Law=Time=Venus=5 May=Aphrodite>>L=N.
Agreement=1,500=15%=P1.50D=1.5=Authority = Solar Crown = Solar Core = 1 May = Maia.
Agricola=4,500=5,000=50%=P5.00D=5.0=Law=Time=Venus=5 May=Aphrodite>>L=N.
Agriculture=4,500=5,000=50%=P5.00D=5.0=Law=Time=Venus=5 May=Aphrodite>>L=N.
Agrippa=4,000=40%=P4.00D=4.0=Govt.=Creat.= 4 April=Hermes>>G=A4.
Agrippiana(1)=6,500=7,000=70%=P7.00D=7.0=Lang.= Assets =Mars = 6May=Pleiades.
Agrippiana(2)=6,500=7,000=70%=P7.00D=7.0=Lang.= Assets =Mars = 6May=Pleiades.
Agronomy=4,000=40%=P4.00D=4.0=Govt.=Creat.= 4 April=Hermes>>G=A4.
Aground=4,500=5,000=50%=P5.00D=5.0=Law=Time=Venus=5 May=Aphrodite>>L=N.
Ague=5,500=5.5=80%=P5.50D=Earth-Midway=5 May=Gaia.
Aguinaldo=2,500=3,000=30%=P3.00D=3.0=Creativity=Star=Muses=3March=C=I.
Agulhas=5,000=50%=P5.00D=5.0=Law=Time=Venus=5 May=Aphrodite>>L=N.
Ah=6,000=60%=P6.00D=6.0=Man=Earth=Health=Royalty=6June=Gaia>M=M2.
A.h.=1,000=100%=10.0=1.0=Mind=Sun=1 January=Helios >> M=E4.
A.ha=3,500=4,000=40%=P4.00D=4.0=Govt.=Creat.= 4 April=Hermes>>G=A4.
Ahab=5,500=5.5=80%=P5.50D=Earth-Midway=5 May=Gaia.

Ahead=12,000=12,000=12%=P1.20D=1.2=Knowledge=Education =12 Dec.= Athena>>K=F.
Ahem=5,000=50%=P5.00D=5.0=Law=Time=Venus=5 May=Aphrodite>>L=N.
Ahmadabad=5,000=50%=P5.00D=5.0=Law=Time=Venus=5 May=Aphrodite>>L=N.
-aholic=4,000=40%=P4.00D=4.0=Govt.=Creat.= 4 April=Hermes>>G=A4.
Ahoy=5,500=5.5=80%=P5.50D=Earth-Midway=5 May=Gaia.
AI==2,000=20%=P2.00D=2.0=Nature=Matter=Moon=2 Feb= Cupid>N=C.
Aid=7,000=70%=P7.00D=7.0=Lang.= Assets =Mars = 6May=Pleiades.
Aide=5,000=50%=P5.00D=5.0=Law=Time=Venus=5 May=Aphrodite>>L=N.
Aide-de-camp=6,500=7,000=70%=P7.00D=7.0=Lang.= Assets =Mars = 6May=Pleiades.
AIDS=10,500=11,000=11%=P1.10D=1.1=Idea=Brainchild=Invention=11 Nov.=Athena>K=F.
Aigrette=5,000=50%=P5.00D=5.0=Law=Time=Venus=5 May=Aphrodite>>L=N.
Aiken Conrad Potter=2,000=20%=P2.00D=2.0=Nature=Matter=Moon=2 Feb= Cupid>N=C.
All=4,000=40%=P4.00D=4.0=Govt.=Creat.= 4 April=Hermes>>G=A4.
Ailanthus=7,000=70%=P7.00D=7.0=Lang.= Assets =Mars = 6May=Pleiades.
Aileron=7,000=70%=P7.00D=7.0=Lang.= Assets =Mars = 6May=Pleiades.
Ailment=1,500=15%=P1.50D=1.5=Authority = Solar Crown = Solar Core = 1 May = Maia.
Aim=2,000=20%=P2.00D=2.0=Nature=Matter=Moon=2 Feb= Cupid>N=C.
Aimless=1,000=100%=10.0=1.0=Mind=Sun=1 January=Helios >> M=E4.
Ain't=2,300=23%=Local Business = Tech.=23 Days Monthly=2.3% Taxes daily income.
Ainu=6,000=60%=P6.00D=6.0=Man=Earth=Health=Royalty=6June=Gaia>M=M2.
Air=3,200=32%=P3.20D=Creative Matter =Product.
Air bag=7,000=70%=P7.00D=7.0=Lang.= Assets =Mars = 6May=Pleiades.
Air borne=4,500=5,000=50%=P5.00D=5.0=Law=Time=Venus=5 May=Aphrodite>>L=N.
Air brake=6,500=7,000=70%=P7.00D=7.0=Lang.= Assets =Mars = 6May=Pleiades.
Air brush=7,000=70%=P7.00D=7.0=Lang.= Assets =Mars = 6May=Pleiades.
Air conditioner=5,000=50%=P5.00D=5.0=Law=Time=Venus=5 May=Aphrodite>>L=N.
Aircraft=6,000=60%=P6.00D=6.0=Man=Earth=Health=Royalty=6June=Gaia>M=M2.
Aircraft carrier=5,000=50%=P5.00D=5.0=Law=Time=Venus=5 May=Aphrodite>>L=N.
Air cushion vehicle=8,000=80%=P8.00D=8.0=Econ.=Curr.=Busn.=Jupt.=8Aug=Zeus>E=v.
Air drome=1,000=100%=10.0=1.0=Mind=Sun=1 January=Helios >> M=E4.
Air drop=4,500=5,000=50%=P5.00D=5.0=Law=Time=Venus=5 May=Aphrodite>>L=N.
Airedale=9,000=90%=P9.00D=9.0=Abstraction=Gods=Saturn=9Sept.>>A=Ø.
Airfare=2,500=3,000=30%=P3.00D=3.0=Creativity=Star=Muses=3March=C=I.
Airfield=3,500=4,000=40%=P4.00D=4.0=Govt.=Creat.= 4 April=Hermes>>G-A4.
Airfoil=8,000=80%=P8.00D=8.0=Econ.=Curr.=Busn.=Jupt.=8Aug=Zeus>E=v.
Air Force=4,000=40%=P4.00D=4.0=Govt.=Creat.= 4 April=Hermes>>G=A4.
Air gun=3,000=30%=P3.00D=3.0=Creativity=Star=Muses=3March=C=I.
Airhead(1)=2,500=3,000=30%=P3.00D=3.0=Creativity=Star=Muses=3March=C=I.
Airhead (2)=4,000=40%=P4.00D=4.0=Govt.=Creat.= 4 April=Hermes>>G=A4.
Air lane=3,500=4,000=40%=P4.00D=4.0=Govt.=Creat.= 4 April=Hermes>>G=A4.
Airlift=5,000=50%=P5.00D=5.0=Law=Time=Venus=5 May=Aphrodite>>L=N.
Airline=5,000=50%=P5.00D=5.0=Law=Time=Venus=5 May=Aphrodite>>L=N.
Airliner=2,000=20%=P2.00D=2.0=Nature=Matter=Moon=2 Feb= Cupid>N=C.
Air lock=8,500=9,000=90%=P9.00D=9.0=Abstraction=Gods=Saturn=9Sept.>>A=Ø.
Airmail=9,000=90%=P9.00D=9.0=Abstraction=Gods=Saturn=9Sept.>>A=Ø.

Airman=1,300= 13% = P1.30D = 1.3 = Solar Core = Faculty = 13 Jan=Athena.
Air mass=7,000=70%=P7.00D=7.0=Lang.= Assets =Mars = 6May=Pleiades.
Air mile=1,500=15%=P1.50D=1.5=Authority = Solar Crown = Solar Core = 1 May = Maia.
Airplane=6,000=60%=P6.00D=6.0=Man=Earth=Health=Royalty=6June=Gaia>M=M2.
Airplay=4,000=40%=P4.00D=4.0=Govt.=Creat.= 4 April=Hermes>>G=A4.
Airport=7,000=70%=P7.00D=7.0=Lang.= Assets =Mars = 6May=Pleiades.
Airpower=4,000=40%=P4.00D=4.0=Govt.=Creat.= 4 April=Hermes>>G=A4.
Air raid=2,500=3,000=30%=P3.00D=3.0=Creativity=Star=Muses=3March=C=I.
Air rifle=8,500=9,000=90%=P9.00D=9.0=Abstraction=Gods=Saturn=9Sept.>>A=Ø.
Air sac=1,000=100%=10.0=1.0=Mind=Sun=1 January=Helios >> M=E4.
Airship=6,000=60%=P6.00D=6.0=Man=Earth=Health=Royalty=6June=Gaia>M=M2.
Air sick=4,000=40%=P4.00D=4.0=Govt.=Creat.= 4 April=Hermes>>G=A4.
Airspace=6,500=7,000=70%=P7.00D=7.0=Lang.= Assets =Mars = 6May=Pleiades.
Airspeed=4,500=5,000=50%=P5.00D=5.0=Law=Time=Venus=5 May=Aphrodite>>L=N.
Airstrip=1,500=15%=P1.50D=1.5=Authority = Solar Crown = Solar Core = 1 May = Maia.
Airtight=4,000=40%=P4.00D=4.0=Govt.=Creat.= 4 April=Hermes>>G=A4.
Air time==7,000=70%=P7.00D=7.0=Lang.= Assets =Mars = 6May=Pleiades.
Air-to-air=5,000=50%=P5.00D=5.0=Law=Time=Venus=5 May=Aphrodite>>L=N.
Air-to-surface=6,500=7,000=70%=P7.00D=7.0=Lang.= Assets =Mars = 6May=Pleiades.
Air wave=6,500=7,000=70%=P7.00D=7.0=Lang.= Assets =Mars = 6May=Pleiades.
Airway=5,500=5.5=80%=P5.50D=Earth-Midway=5 May=Gaia.
Airworthy=1,500=15%=P1.50D=1.5=Authority = Solar Crown = Solar Core = 1 May = Maia.
Airy=1,300= 13% = P1.30D = 1.3 = Solar Core = Faculty = 13 Jan=Athena.
Aisle=6,000=60%=P6.00D=6.0=Man=Earth=Health=Royalty=6June=Gaia>M=M2.
Aisne=8,500=9,000=90%=P9.00D=9.0=Abstraction=Gods=Saturn=9Sept.>>A=Ø.
Aix-en-Provence=5,000=50%=P5.00D=5.0=Law=Time=Venus=5 May=Aphrodite>>L=N.
Aix-la-Chapelle=1,000=100%=10.0=1.0=Mind=Sun=1 January=Helios >> M=E4.
Ajaclo=8,000=80%=P8.00D=8.0=Econ.=Curr.=Busn.=Jupt.=8Aug=Zeus>E=v.
Ajar=3,000=30%=P3.00D=3.0=Creativity=Star=Muses=3March=C=I.
AK=500=5%=P5.00D=5.0=Law=Time=Venus=5 May=Aphrodite>>L=N.
A.K.A=1,500=15%=P1.50D=1.5=Authority = Solar Crown = Solar Core = 1 May = Maia.
Akbar=5,000=50%=P5.00D=5.0=Law=Time=Venus=5 May=Aphrodite>>L=N.
AKC=1,500=15%=P1.50D=1.5=Authority = Solar Crown = Solar Core = 1 May = Maia.
Akhenaton=6,000=60%=P6.00D=6.0=Man=Earth=Health=Royalty=6June=Gaia>M=M2.
Akihito=3,500=4,000=40%=P4.00D=4.0=Govt.=Creat.= 4 April=Hermes>>G=A4.
Akimbo=4,000=40%=P4.00D=4.0=Govt.=Creat.= 4 April=Hermes>>G=A4.
Akin=7,500=8,000=80%=P8.00D=8.0=Econ.=Curr.=Busn.=Jupt.=8Aug=Zeus>E=v.
Akkad=8,500=9,000=90%=P9.00D=9.0=Abstraction=Gods=Saturn=9Sept.>>A=Ø.
Akkadian=4,500=5,000=50%=P5.00D=5.0=Law=Time=Venus=5 May=Aphrodite>>L=N.
Akron=5,000=50%=P5.00D=5.0=Law=Time=Venus=5 May=Aphrodite>>L=N.
AI=3,000=30%=P3.00D=3.0=Creativity=Star=Muses=3March=C=I.
AL=1,500=15%=P1.50D=1.5=Authority = Solar Crown = Solar Core = 1 May = Maia.
-al(1)=3,500=4,000=40%=P4.00D=4.0=Govt.=Creat.= 4 April=Hermes>>G=A4.
-al(2)=1,500=15%=P1.50D=1.5=Authority = Solar Crown = Solar Core = 1 May = Maia.
Ala=2,500=3,000=30%=P3.00D=3.0=Creativity=Star=Muses=3March=C=I.

Ala.=500=5%=P5.00D=5.0=Law=Time=Venus=5 May=Aphrodite>>L=N.
À la=6,000=60%=P6.00D=6.0=Man=Earth=Health=Royalty=6June=Gaia>M=M2.
Alabama=5,000=50%=P5.00D=5.0=Law=Time=Venus=5 May=Aphrodite>>L=N.
Alabaster=7,500=8,000=80%=P8.00D=8.0=Econ.=Curr.=Busn.=Jupt.=8Aug=Zeus>E=v.
À la carte=5,000=50%=P5.00D=5.0=Law=Time=Venus=5 May=Aphrodite>>L=N.
Alacrity=3,000=30%=P3.00D=3.0=Creativity=Star=Muses=3March=C=I.
Alai=3,000=30%=P3.00D=3.0=Creativity=Star=Muses=3March=C=I.
Alamo=8,000=80%=P8.00D=8.0=Econ.=Curr.=Busn.=Jupt.=8Aug=Zeus>E=v.
À la mode=6,500=7,000=70%=P7.00D=7.0=Lang.= Assets =Mars = 6May=Pleiades.
Alamogordo=7,500=8,000=80%=P8.00D=8.0=Econ.=Curr.=Busn.=Jupt.=8Aug=Zeus>E=v
Alaric=4,500=5,000=50%=P5.00D=5.0=Law=Time=Venus=5 May=Aphrodite>>L=N.
Alarm=14,000=14%=P1.40D=1.4=Mgt.=Solar Core=13 May=Athena>>SC=0.1
Alarmist=2,500=3,000=30%=P3.00D=3.0=Creativity=Star=Muses=3March=C=I.
Alas=3,500=4,000=40%=P4.00D=4.0=Govt.=Creat.= 4 April=Hermes>>G=A4.
Alaska=7,000=70%=P7.00D=7.0=Lang.= Assets =Mars = 6May=Pleiades.
Alaska Peninsula=7,000=70%=P7.00D=7.0=Lang.= Assets =Mars = 6May=Pleiades.
Alaska Range=7,000=70%=P7.00D=7.0=Lang.= Assets =Mars = 6May=Pleiades.
alb=5,500=6,000=60%=P6.00D=6.0=Man=Earth=Health=Royalty=6June=Gaia>M=M2.
Alb.=1,000=100%=10.0=1.0=Mind=Sun=1 January=Helios >> M=E4.
Alba=2,000=20%=P2.00D=2.0=Nature=Matter=Moon=2 Feb= Cupid>N=C.
Albacore=6,000=60%=P6.00D=6.0=Man=Earth=Health=Royalty=6June=Gaia>M=M2.
Albania=6,500=7,000=70%=P7.00D=7.0=Lang.= Assets =Mars = 6May=Pleiades.
Albanian=6,000=60%=P6.00D=6.0=Man=Earth=Health=Royalty=6June=Gaia>M=M2.
Albany=7,000=70%=P7.00D=7.0=Lang.= Assets =Mars = 6May=Pleiades.
Albatross=5,500=5.5=80%=P5.50D=Earth-Midway=5 May=Gaia.
Albedo=4,000=40%=P4.00D=4.0=Govt.=Creat.= 4 April=Hermes>>G=A4.
Albee Edward Franklin=2,000=20%=P2.00D=2.0=Nature=Moon=2Feb= Cupid>N=C.
Albeit=5,500=5.5=80%=P5.50D=Earth-Midway=5 May=Gaia.
Albemarie Sound=4,000=40%=P4.00D=4.0=Govt.=Creat.= 4 April=Hermes>>G=A4.
Albert=5,500=5.5=80%=P5.50D=Earth-Midway=5 May=Gaia.
Albert, Lake=5,500=5.5=80%=P5.50D=Earth-Midway=5 May=Gaia.
Alberta=7,000=70%=P7.00D=7.0=Lang.= Assets =Mars = 6May=Pleiades.
Albertus Magnus=3,000=30%=P3.00D=3.0=Creativity=Star=Muses=3March=C=I.
Albino=9,000=90%=P9.00D=9.0=Abstraction=Gods=Saturn=9Sept.>>A=Ø.
Alborg=4,500=5,000=50%=P5.00D=5.0=Law=Time=Venus=5 May=Aphrodite>>L=N.
Album=11,000=11%=P1.10D=1.1=Idea=Brainchild=Invention=11 Nov.=Athena>K=F.
Albumen=6,000=60%=P6.00D=6.0=Man=Earth=Health=Royalty=6June=Gaia>M=M2.
Albumin=9,000=90%=P9.00D=9.0=Abstraction=Gods=Saturn=9Sept.>>A=Ø.
Albuquerque=5,500=5.5=80%=P5.50D=Earth-Midway=5 May=Gaia.
Alcatraz=8,000=80%=P8.00D=8.0=Econ.=Curr.=Busn.=Jupt.=8Aug=Zeus>E=v.
Alcazar=2,500=3,000=30%=P3.00D=3.0=Creativity=Star=Muses=3March=C=I.
Alchemy=8,500=9,000=90%=P9.00D=9.0=Abstraction=Gods=Saturn=9Sept.>>A=Ø.
Alcibiades=4,000=40%=P4.00D=4.0=Govt.=Creat.= 4 April=Hermes>>G=A4.
Alcohol=18,000=18%=P1.80D=1.8=Solar Currency=MaksCurrencies=1 Aug=Maia.
Alcoholic=7,000=70%=P7.00D=7.0=Lang.= Assets =Mars = 6May=Pleiades.

Alcoholism=6,500=7,000=70%=P7.00D=7.0=Lang.= Assets =Mars = 6May=Pleiades.
Alcott Louisa May=3,000=30%=P3.00D=3.0=Creativity=Star=Muses=3March=C=I.
Alcove=5,000=50%=P5.00D=5.0=Law=Time=Venus=5 May=Aphrodite>>L=N.
Aldan=8,500=9,000=90%=P9.00D=9.0=Abstraction=Gods=Saturn=9Sept.>>A=Ø.
Aldehyde=7,000=70%=P7.00D=7.0=Lang.= Assets =Mars = 6May=Pleiades.
Alden John=3,000=30%=P3.00D=3.0=Creativity=Star=Muses=3March=C=I.
Alder=7,500=8,000=80%=P8.00D=8.0=Econ.=Curr.=Busn.=Jupt.=8Aug=Zeus>E=v.
Alderman=3,000=30%=P3.00D=3.0=Creativity=Star=Muses=3March=C=I.
Ale=4,000=40%=P4.00D=4.0=Govt.=Creat.= 4 April=Hermes>>G=A4.
Aleatory=3,000=30%=P3.00D=3.0=Creativity=Star=Muses=3March=C=I.
Alee=2,500=3,000=30%=P3.00D=3.0=Creativity=Star=Muses=3March=C=I.
Alembert Jean Le Rond'.=3,000=30%=P3.00D=3.0=Creativity=Star=Muses=3March=C=I.
Alembic=3,000=30%=P3.00D=3.0=Creativity=Star=Muses=3March=C=I.
Aleph=3,500=4,000=40%=P4.00D=4.0=Govt.=Creat.= 4 April=Hermes>>G=A4.
Aleppo=3,500=4,000=40%=P4.00D=4.0=Govt.=Creat.= 4 April=Hermes>>G=A4.
Alert=18,500=19,000=19%=P1.90D=1.9=Solar Energy=Planets=Mind God=Maia.
Aleut=14,500=15,000=15%=P1.50D=1.5=Authority=Solar Crown=Solar Core=1May= Maia.
Aleutian Islands=13,000= 13% = P1.30D = 1.3 = Solar Core = Faculty = 13 Jan=Athena.
Alexander I1=3,500=4,000=40%=P4.00D=4.0=Govt.=Creat.= 4 April=Hermes>>G=A4.
Alexander I2=4,000=40%=P4.00D=4.0=Govt.=Creat.= 4 April=Hermes>>G=A4.
Alexander I3=3,500=4,000=40%=P4.00D=4.0=Govt.=Creat.= 4 April=Hermes>>G=A4.
Alexander II=5,500=5.5=80%=P5.50D=Earth-Midway=5 May=Gaia.
Alexander III1=10,000=1,000=100%=Physicality= Tech.=10 Oct.=Uranus=P=1Ø.
Alexander III2=4,000=40%=P4.00D=4.0=Govt.=Creat.= 4 April=Hermes>>G=A4.
Alexander Archipelago=5,000=50%=P5.00D=5.0=Law=Time=Venus=5 May=Odite>>L=N.
Alexandria=15,000=15%=P1.50D=1.5=Authority = Solar Crown = Solar Core = 1 May
   = Maia.
Alexandrian=11,000=11%=P1.10D=1.1=Idea=Brainchild=Invention=11 Nov.=Athena>K=F.
Alexandrine=7,000=70%=P7.00D=7.0=Lang.= Assets =Mars = 6May=Pleiades.
Alexia=5,500=5.5=80%=P5.50D=Earth-Midway=5 May=Gaia.
Alfalfa=4,000=40%=P4.00D=4.0=Govt.=Creat.= 4 April=Hermes>>G=A4.
Alfonso XIII=3,000=30%=P3.00D=3.0=Creativity=Star=Muses=3March=C=I.
Alfred=5,000=50%=P5.00D=5.0=Law=Time=Venus=5 May=Aphrodite>>L=N.
Alfresco=2,500=3,000=30%=P3.00D=3.0=Creativity=Star=Muses=3March=C=I.
Alga=8,000=80%=P8.00D=8.0=Econ.=Curr.=Busn.=Jupt.=8Aug=Zeus>E=v.
Algebra=13,000= 13% = P1.30D = 1.3 = Solar Core = Faculty = 13 Jan=Athena.
Algeria=9,500=10,000=100%=Physicality= Tech.=10 Oct.=Uranus=P=1Ø.
-algia=1,000=100%=10.0=1.0=Mind=Sun=1 January=Helios >> M=E4.
Algiers=8,000=80%=P8.00D=8.0=Econ.=Curr.=Busn.=Jupt.=8Aug=Zeus>E=v.
ALGOL=5,000=50%=P5.00D=5.0=Law=Time=Venus=5 May=Aphrodite>>L=N.
Algonquian=17,000=17%=P1.70D=1.7=Solar Asset=Mind Computing Pleides.
Algonquin=11,500=12,000=12%=P1.20D=1.2=Knowledge=Edu.=12 Dec.=Athena>>K=F.
Algorithm=7,500=8,000=80%=P8.00D=8.0=Econ.=Curr.=Busn.=Jupt.=8Aug=Zeus>E=v.

Ali Muhammad=4,000=40%=P4.00D=4.0=Govt.=Creat.= 4 April=Hermes>>G=A4.
Hermes came to Earth incarnated as Mohammed Ali. He was a powerful force in boxing.

Alias=3,500=4,000=40%=P4.00D=4.0=Govt.=Creat.= 4 April=Hermes>>G=A4.
Alibi=13,500=14,000=14%=P1.40D=1.4=Mgt.=Solar Core=13 May=Athena>>SC=0.1
Alien=20,000=2,000=20%=P2.00D=2.0=Nature=Matter=Moon=2 Feb= Cupid>N=C.
Alienable=3,500=4,000=40%=P4.00D=4.0=Govt.=Creat.= 4 April=Hermes>>G=A4.
Alienate=6,000=60%=P6.00D=6.0=Man=Earth=Health=Royalty=6June=Gaia>M=M2.
Alienation=10,500=11,000=11%=P1.10D=1.1=Idea=Brainchild=Invent.=11Nov.=
   Athena>K=F.
Alienist=4,500=5,000=50%=P5.00D=5.0=Law=Time=Venus=5 May=Aphrodite>>L=N.
Alight(1)=4,500=5,000=50%=P5.00D=5.0=Law=Time=Venus=5 May=Aphrodite>>L=N.
Alight(2)=1,500=15%=P1.50D=1.5=Authority = Solar Crown = Solar Core = 1 May = Maia.
Align=14,500=15,000=15%=P1.50D=1.5=Authority=Solar Crown=Solar Core=1 May=Maia
Alike=5,500=5.5=80%=P5.50D=Earth-Midway=5 May=Gaia.
Aliment=1,000=100%=10.0=1.0=Mind=Sun=1 January=Helios >> M=E4.
Alimentary=4,000=40%=P4.00D=4.0=Govt.=Creat.= 4 April=Hermes>>G=A4.
Alimentary canal=10,500=11,000=11%=P1.10D=1.1=Idea=Brainchild=11Nov.=Athena>K=F.
Alimony=10,500=11,000=11%=P1.10D=1.1=Idea=Brainchild=Inventn=11 Nov.=Athena>K=F.
Aliphatic=10,500=11,000=11%=P1.10D=1.1=Idea=Brainchild=Inventn=11 Nov.=Athena
   >K=F.
Aliquot=9,000=90%=P9.00D=9.0=Abstraction=Gods=Saturn=9Sept.>>A=Ø.
Alit=3,000=30%=P3.00D=3.0=Creativity=Star=Muses=3March=C=I.
Alive=9,000=90%=P9.00D=9.0=Abstraction=Gods=Saturn=9Sept.>>A=Ø.
Alizarin=4,500=5,000=50%=P5.00D=5.0=Law=Time=Venus=5 May=Aphrodite>>L=N.
Alkali=17,500=18,000=18%=P1.80D=1.8=Solar Currency=MaksCurrencies=1 Aug=Maia.
Alkali metal=11,000=11%=P1.10D=1.1=Idea=Brainchild=Invention=11 Nov.=Athena>K=F.
Alkaline=6,000=60%=P6.00D=6.0=Man=Earth=Health=Royalty=6June=Gaia>M=M2.
Alkaline-earth metal=9,500=10,000=100%=Physicality= Tech.=10 Oct.=Uranus=P=1Ø.
Alkalize=3,500=4,000=40%=P4.00D=4.0=Govt.=Creat.= 4 April=Hermes>>G=A4.
Alkaloid=9,000=90%=P9.00D=9.0=Abstraction=Gods=Saturn=9Sept.>>A=Ø.
Alkalosis=4,500=5,000=50%=P5.00D=5.0=Law=Time=Venus=5 May=Aphrodite>>L=N.
Alkyd=4,500=5,000=50%=P5.00D=5.0=Law=Time=Venus=5 May=Aphrodite>>L=N.
All=35,000=4,000=40%=P4.00D=4.0=Govt.=Creat.= 4 April=Hermes>>G=A4.
Allah=2,000=20%=P2.00D=2.0=Nature=Matter=Moon=2 Feb= Cupid>N=C.
All-American=12,500= 13,000=13% = P1.30D = 1.3 = Solar Core = Faculty = 13 Jan=Athena.
All-around=5,500=5.5=80%=P5.50D=Earth-Midway=5 May=Gaia.
Allay=6,000=60%=P6.00D=6.0=Man=Earth=Health=Royalty=6June=Gaia>M=M2.
All clear=8,000=80%=P8.00D=8.0=Econ.=Curr.=Busn.=Jupt.=8Aug=Zeus>E=v.
Allege=7,500=8,000=80%=P8.00D=8.0=Econ.=Curr.=Busn.=Jupt.=8Aug=Zeus>E=v.
Alleged=16,000=16%=P1.60D=1.6=Incarnation=Mind of GOD=1 June = Maia.
Allegheny Mountains=9,000=90%=P9.00D=9.0=Abstraction=Gods=Saturn=9Sept.>>A=Ø.
Allegheny River=11,000=11%=P1.10D=1.1=Idea=Brainchild=Invention=11 Nov.=Athena
   >K=F.

Allegiance=6,000=60%=P6.00D=6.0=Man=Earth=Health=Royalty=6June=Gaia>M=M2.
Allegory=10,500=11,000=11%=P1.10D=1.1=Idea=Brainchild=Inventn=11 Nov.=Athena>K=F.
Allegretto=2,500=3,000=30%=P3.00D=3.0=Creativity=Star=Muses=3March=C=I.
Allegro=2,500=3,000=30%=P3.00D=3.0=Creativity=Star=Muses=3March=C=I.
Allele=9,000=90%=P9.00D=9.0=Abstraction=Gods=Saturn=9Sept.>>A=Ø.
Allelopathy=6,500=7,000=70%=P7.00D=7.0=Lang.= Assets =Mars = 6May=Pleiades.
Alleluia=1,000=100%=10.0=1.0=Mind=Sun=1 January=Helios >> M=E4.
Allen Ethan=2,500=3,000=30%=P3.00D=3.0=Creativity=Star=Muses=3March=C=I.
Allen de GossenseSalvador=3,500=4,000=40%=P4.00D.=Creat.=4April.=Hermes>>G=A4.
Allen town=4,500=5,000=50%=P5.00D=5.0=Law=Time=Venus=5 May=Aphrodite>>L=N.
Allergen=3,000=30%=P3.00D=3.0=Creativity=Star=Muses=3March=C=I.
Allergist=3,000=30%=P3.00D=3.0=Creativity=Star=Muses=3March=C=I.
Allergy=7,000=70%=P7.00D=7.0=Lang.= Assets =Mars = 6May=Pleiades.
Alleviate=2,000=20%=P2.00D=2.0=Nature=Matter=Moon=2 Feb= Cupid>N=C.
Alley=8,500=9,000=90%=P9.00D=9.0=Abstraction=Gods=Saturn=9Sept.>>A=Ø.
Alley cat=2,500=3,000=30%=P3.00D=3.0=Creativity=Star=Muses=3March=C=I.
Alleyway=2,500=3,000=30%=P3.00D=3.0=Creativity=Star=Muses=3March=C=I.
Alliance=12,500= 13,000=13% = P1.30D = 1.3 = Solar Core = Faculty = 13 Jan=Athena.
Allied=7,000=70%=P7.00D=7.0=Lang.= Assets =Mars = 6May=Pleiades.
Alligator=12,500= 13,000=13% = P1.30D = 1.3 = Solar Core = Faculty = 13 Jan=Athena.
Alligator pear=1,000=100%=10.0=1.0=Mind=Sun=1 January=Helios >> M=E4.
All-important=2,500=3,000=30%=P3.00D=3.0=Creativity=Star=Muses=3March=C=I.
Alliteration=13,000= 13% = P1.30D = 1.3 = Solar Core = Faculty = 13 Jan=Athena.
Allo-=1,500=15%=P1.50D=1.5=Authority = Solar Crown = Solar Core = 1 May = Maia.
Allocate=3,500=4,000=40%=P4.00D=4.0=Govt.=Creat.= 4 April=Hermes>>G=A4.
Allomorph=3,500=4,000=40%=P4.00D=4.0=Govt.=Creat.= 4 April=Hermes>>G=A4.
Allophone=15,000=15%=P1.50D=1.5=Authority = Solar Crown = Solar Core = 1 May = Maia.
Allot=5,500=5.5=80%=P5.50D=Earth-Midway=5 May=Gaia.
Allotropy=8,500=9,000=90%=P9.00D=9.0=Abstraction=Gods=Saturn=9Sept.>>A=Ø.
All-out=2,000=20%=P2.00D=2.0=Nature=Matter=Moon=2 Feb= Cupid>N=C.
All over=4,000=40%=P4.00D=4.0=Govt.=Creat.= 4 April=Hermes>>G=A4.
Allow=16,500=17,000=17%=P1.70D=1.7=Solar Asset=Mind Computing =Pleiades.
Allowance=12,500= 13% = P1.30D = 1.3 = Solar Core = Faculty = 13 Jan=Athena.
Allowedly=2,000=20%=P2.00D=2.0=Nature=Matter=Moon=2 Feb= Cupid>N=C.
Alloy=7,000=70%=P7.00D=7.0=Lang.= Assets =Mars = 6May=Pleiades.
All-purpose=1,500=15%=P1.50D=1.5=Authority = Solar Crown = Solar Core = 1 May = Maia.
All right=7,500=8,000=80%=P8.00D=8.0=Econ.=Curr.=Busn.=Jupt.=8Aug=Zeus>E=v.
All-round=1,500=15%=P1.50D=1.5=Authority = Solar Crown = Solar Core = 1 May = Maia.
All Saints' Day=4,500=5,000=50%=P5.00D=5.0=Law=Time=Venus=5May=Odite>>L=N.
All Souls' Day=8,500=9,000=90%=P9.00D=9.0=Abstraction=Gods=Saturn=9Sept.>>A=Ø.
Allspice=7,500=8,000=80%=P8.00D=8.0=Econ.=Curr.=Busn.=Jupt.=8Aug=Zeus>E=v.
All-star=3,000=30%=P3.00D=3.0=Creativity=Star=Muses=3March=C=I.
All-time=4,500=5,000=50%=P5.00D=5.0=Law=Time=Venus=5 May=Aphrodite>>L=N.
All told=5,500=5.5=80%=P5.50D=Earth-Midway=5 May=Gaia.
Allude=2,000=20%=P2.00D=2.0=Nature=Matter=Moon=2 Feb= Cupid>N=C.

Allure=5,500=5.5=80%=P5.50D=Earth-Midway=5 May=Gaia.
Alluvion=5,500=5.5=80%=P5.50D=Earth-Midway=5 May=Gaia.
Alluvium=5,000=50%=P5.00D=5.0=Law=Time=Venus=5 May=Aphrodite>>L=N.
Ally=12,500= 13% = P1.30D = 1.3 = Solar Core = Faculty = 13 Jan=Athena.
Alma-Ata=6,500=7,000=70%=P7.00D=7.0=Lang.= Assets =Mars = 6May=Pleiades.
Alma mater=7,500=8,000=80%=P8.00D=8.0=Econ.=Curr.=Busn.=Jupt.=8Aug=Zeus>E=v.
Almanac=8,000=80%=P8.00D=8.0=Econ.=Curr.=Busn.=Jupt.=8Aug=Zeus>E=v.
Almighty=1,500=15%=P1.50D=1.5=Authority = Solar Crown = Solar Core = 1 May = Maia.
Almond=9,500=10,000=1,000=100%=10.0=Physicality=Tech.=10 Oct.=Uranus=P=1Ø.
Almost=2,500=3,000=30%=P3.00D=3.0=Creativity=Star=Muses=3March=C=I.
Alms=4,500=5,000=50%=P5.00D=5.0=Law=Time=Venus=5 May=Aphrodite>>L=N.
Almshouse=1,000=100%=10.0=1.0=Mind=Sun=1 January=Helios >> M=E4.
Aloe=11,500=12,000=12%=P1.20D=1.2=Knowledge=Education=12 Dec.=Athena>>K=F.
Aloe Vera=8,500=9,000=90%=P9.00D=9.0=Abstraction=Gods=Saturn=9Sept.>>A=Ø.
Aloft=6,000=60%=P6.00D=6.0=Man=Earth=Health=Royalty=6June=Gaia>M=M2.
Aloha=6,000=60%=P6.00D=6.0=Man=Earth=Health=Royalty=6June=Gaia>M=M2.
Alone=10,000=1,000=100%=10.0=Physicality=Tech.=10 Oct.=Uranus=P=1Ø.
Along=25,000=3,000=30%=P3.00D=3.0=Creativity=Star=Muses=3March=C=I.
Along shore=3,000=30%=P3.00D=3.0=Creativity=Star=Muses=3March=C=I.
Alongside=6,000=60%=P6.00D=6.0=Man=Earth=Health=Royalty=6June=Gaia>M=M2.
Aloof=4,500=5,000=50%=P5.00D=5.0=Law=Time=Venus=5 May=Aphrodite>>L=N.
Aloud=8,000=80%=P8.00D=8.0=Econ.=Curr.=Busn.=Jupt.=8Aug=Zeus>E=v.
Alp=1,500=15%=P1.50D=1.5=Authority = Solar Crown = Solar Core = 1 May = Maia.
Alpaca=12,000=12%=P1.20D=1.2=Knowledge=Education=12 Dec.=Athena>>K=F.
Alpenhorn=8,000=80%=P8.00D=8.0=Econ.=Curr.=Busn.=Jupt.=8Aug=Zeus>E=v.
Alpha=3,500=4,000=40%=P4.00D=4.0=Govt.=Creat.= 4 April=Hermes>>G=A4.

Alphabet=6,000=60%=P6.00D=6.0=Man=Earth=Health=Royalty=6June=Gaia>M=M2.
Makabets are winged alphabets they indicate the flight nature of words. Inspired means flight because words are crystallized energy bits that move through empty or cosmic space to be absorbed by the ears of Man and sent to the brain for processing as words through the PGI system (Psychoeconomix). So we talk about the flight nature of words.
Heavens H6160 >> 6 1*6 0x=px=12.1+36.6=48.7x=px=491.56 = 500 = 50 = 5.0
H = 6.0 >> 5.0*6.0x=px=11+30=41x=px=371 = 400 = 40 = 4.0 >> Creatocracy.
Smoke >> H6227 >> 6.2*2.7x=px=8.9+16.74=25.64x=px=174.626
H+6.0>>174.626*6.0x=px=180.626+1,047.756=1228.382x=px=190,480.3573=19=1.9=2.0
WDSD 1.9 >> Planetary energy >> Lunar Cosmic Energy. Smoke has planetary effects, it is a visible form of abstraction and returns to the Moon. See Smoke.

Alphabetical=9,000=90%=P9.00D=9.0=Abstraction=Gods=Saturn=9Sept.>>A=Ø.
Alphabetize=2,500=3,000=30%=P3.00D=3.0=Creativity=Star=Muses=3March=C=I.
Alpha helix=8,000=80%=P8.00D=8.0=Econ.=Curr.=Busn.=Jupt.=8Aug=Zeus>E=v.
Alphanumeric=3,000=30%=P3.00D=3.0=Creativity=Star=Muses=3March=C=I.
Alpha particle=8,500=9,000=90%=P9.00D=9.0=Abstr.=Gods=Saturn=9Sept.>>A=Ø.

Alpha ray=2,500=3,000=30%=P3.00D=3.0=Creativity=Star=Muses=3March=C=I.
Alpha rhythm=12,000=12%=P1.20D=1.2=Knowledge=Education=12 Dec.=Athena>>K=F.
Alpine=5,500=5.5=80%=P5.50D=Earth-Midway=5 May=Gaia.
Alps=3,500=4,000=40%=P4.00D=4.0=Govt.=Creat.= 4 April=Hermes>>G=A4.
Already=9,000=90%=P9.00D=9.0=Abstraction=Gods=Saturn=9Sept.>>A=Ø.
Alright=2,000=20%=P2.00D=2.0=Nature=Matter=Moon=2 Feb= Cupid>N=C.
Alsace=8,000=80%=P8.00D=8.0=Econ.=Curr.=Busn.=Jupt.=8Aug=Zeus>E=v.
Alsatian=5,500=5.5=80%=P5.50D=Earth-Midway=5 May=Gaia.
Also=4,500=5,000=50%=P5.00D=5.0=Law=Time=Venus=5 May=Aphrodite>>L=N.
Also-ran=7,000=70%=P7.00D=7.0=Lang.= Assets =Mars = 6May=Pleiades.
Alt.=1,000=100%=10.0=1.0=Mind=Sun=1 January=Helios >> M=E4.
Alta.=500=5%=P5.00D=5.0=Law=Time=Venus=5 May=Aphrodite>>L=N.
Alta California=6,500=7,000=70%=P7.00D=7.0=Lang.= Assets =Mars = 6May=Pleiades.
Altaic=10,000=1,000=100%=10.0=Physicality=Tech.=10 Oct.=Uranus=P=1Ø.
Altai Mountains=3,000=30%=P3.00D=3.0=Creativity=Star=Muses=3March=C=I.
Altar=6,500=7,000=70%=P7.00D=7.0=Lang.= Assets =Mars = 6May=Pleiades.
Altar place=8,500=9,000=90%=P9.00D=9.0=Abstraction=Gods=Saturn=9Sept.>>A=Ø.
Alter=7,000=70%=P7.00D=7.0=Lang.= Assets =Mars = 6May=Pleiades.
Altercate=2,500=3,000=30%=P3.00D=3.0=Creativity=Star=Muses=3March=C=I.
Alter ego=3,500=4,000=40%=P4.00D=4.0=Govt.=Creat.= 4 April=Hermes>>G=A4.
Alternate=16,500=17,000=17%=P1.70D=1.7=Solar Asset=Mind Computing =Pleiades.
Alternating current=4,500=5K=50%=P5.00D=5.0=Law=Time=Venus=5May=Odite>>L=N.
Alternative=9,500=10,000=1,000=100%=10.0=Physicality=Tech.=10 Oct.=Uranus=P=1Ø.
Alternative school=5,500=5.5=80%=P5.50D=Earth-Midway=5 May=Gaia.
Alternator=3,500=4,000=40%=P4.00D=4.0=Govt.=Creat.= 4 April=Hermes>>G=A4.
Although=15,500=16,000=16%=P1.60D=1.6=Incarnation=Mind of GOD=1 June = Maia.
Altimeter=2,500=3,000=30%=P3.00D=3.0=Creativity=Star=Muses=3 March=C=I.
Altiplano=4,500=5,000=50%=P5.00D=5.0=Law=Time=Venus=5 May=Aphrodite>>L=N.
Altitude=17,000=17%=P1.70D=1.7=Solar Asset=Mind Computing =Pleiades.
Alto=9,500=10,000=1,000=100%=10.0=Physicality=Tech.=10 Oct.=Uranus=P=1Ø.
Altogether=7,000=70%=P7.00D=7.0=Lang.= Assets =Mars = 6May=Pleiades.
Altruism=4,000=40%=P4.00D=4.0=Govt.=Creat.= 4 April=Hermes>>G=A4.
Alum=9,500=10,000=1,000=100%=10.0=Physicality=Tech.=10 Oct.=Uranus=P=1Ø.
Alumina=10,500=11,000=11%=P1.10D=1.1=Idea=Brainchild=Inventn=11 Nov.=Athena
   >K=F.
Aluminum=2,500=3,000=30%=P3.00D=3.0=Creativity=Star=Muses=3 March=C=I.
Aluminize=3,000=30%=P3.00D=3.0=Creativity=Star=Muses=3 March=C=I.
Aluminous=3,500=4,000=40%=P4.00D=4.0=Govt.=Creat.= 4 April=Hermes>>G=A4.
Aluminum=12,000=12%=P1.20D=1.2=Knowledge=Education=12 Dec.=Athena>>K=F.
Alumna=4,500=5,000=50%=P5.00D=5.0=Law=Time=Venus=5 May=Aphrodite>>L=N.
Alumnus=4,500=5,000=50%=P5.00D=5.0=Law=Time=Venus=5 May=Aphrodite>>L=N.
Alva=3,000=30%=P3.00D=3.0=Creativity=Star=Muses=3March=C=I.
Alveolus=10,000=1,000=100%=10.0=Physicality=Tech.=10 Oct.=Uranus=P=1Ø.
Always=5,500=5.5=80%=P5.50D=Earth-Midway=5 May=Gaia.
Alyssum=10,000=1,000=100%=10.0=Physicality=Tech.=10 Oct.=Uranus=P=1Ø.

Alzheimer'sdisease=8,000=80%=P8.00D=8.0=Econ.=Curr.=Busn.=Jupt.=8Aug=Zeus>E=v
Am(1)=3,500=4,000=40%=P4.00D=4.0=Govt.=Creat.= 4 April=Hermes>>G=A4.
Am(2)=1,000=100%=10.0=1.0=Mind=Sun=1 January=Helios >> M=E4.
Am=3,000=30%=P3.00D=3.0=Creativity=Star=Muses=3March=C=I.
A.M.=8,500=9,000=90%=P9.00D=9.0=Abstraction=Gods=Saturn=9Sept.>>A=Ø.
AMA=1,500=15%=P1.50D=1.5=Authority = Solar Crown = Solar Core = 1 May = Maia.
Amalgam=8,000=80%=P8.00D=8.0=Econ.=Curr.=Busn.=Jupt.=8Aug=Zeus>E=v.
Amalgamate=3,500=4,000=40%=P4.00D=4.0=Govt.=Creat.= 4 April=Hermes>>G=A4.
Amanuensis=1,000=100%=10.0=1.0=Mind=Sun=1 January=Helios >> M=E4.
Amaranth=7,500=8,000=80%=P8.00D=8.0=Econ.=Curr.=Busn.=Jupt.=8Aug=Zeus>E=v.
Amarillo=5,500=5.5=80%=P5.50D=Earth-Midway=5 May=Gaia.
Amaryllis=10,000=1,000=100%=10.0=Physicality=Tech.=10 Oct.=Uranus=P=1Ø.
Amass=1,000=100%=10.0=1.0=Mind=Sun=1 January=Helios >> M=E4.
Amateur=11,000=11%=P1.10D=1.1=Idea=Brainchild=Invention=11 Nov.=Athena>K=F.
Amati Nicolò=2,500=3,000=30%=P3.00D=3.0=Creativity=Star=Muses=3 March=C=I.
Amatory=3,000=30%=P3.00D=3.0=Creativity=Star=Muses=3March=C=I.
Amaze=3,000=30%=P3.00D=3.0=Creativity=Star=Muses=3March=C=I.
Amazon=8,000=80%=P8.00D=8.0=Econ.=Curr.=Busn.=Jupt.=8Aug=Zeus>E=v.
Amazonia=5,000=50%=P5.00D=5.0=Law=Time=Venus=5 May=Aphrodite>>L=N.
Amazonian=4,000=4,000=40%=P4.00D=4.0=Govt.=Creat.= 4 April=Hermes>>G=A4.
Amazon River=11,500=12,000=12%=P1.20D=1.2=Knowledge=Edu.=12 Dec.=Athena>>K=F.
Ambassador=8,000=80%=P8.00D=8.0=Econ.=Curr.=Busn.=Jupt.=8Aug=Zeus>E=v.
Ambassadress=4,000=4,000=40%=P4.00D=4.0=Govt.=Creat.= 4 April=Hermes>>G=A4.
Amber=6,000=60%=P6.00D=6.0=Man=Earth=Health=Royalty=6June=Gaia>M=M2.
Ambergris=7,000=70%=P7.00D=7.0=Lang.= Assets =Mars = 6May=Pleiades.
Ambi-=2,000=20%=P2.00D=2.0=Nature=Matter=Moon=2 Feb= Cupid>N=C.
Ambiance=3,500=4,000=40%=P4.00D=4.0=Govt.=Creat.= 4 April=Hermes>>G=A4.
Ambidextrous=5,500=5.5=80%=P5.50D=Earth-Midway=5 May=Gaia.
Ambient=3,000=30%=P3.00D=3.0=Creativity=Star=Muses=3March=C=I.
Ambiguous=4,500=5,000=50%=P5.00D=5.0=Law=Time=Venus=5 May=Aphrodite>>L=N.
Ambit=5,500=5.5=80%=P5.50D=Earth-Midway=5 May=Gaia.
Ambition=5,500=5.5=80%=P5.50D=Earth-Midway=5 May=Gaia.
Ambitious=5,000=50%=P5.00D=5.0=Law=Time=Venus=5 May=Aphrodite>>L=N.
Ambivalence=5,500=5.5=80%=P5.50D=Earth-Midway=5 May=Gaia.
Amble=3,000=30%=P3.00D=3.0=Creativity=Star=Muses=3March=C=I.

Ambrosia=9,500=10,000=1,000=100%=10.0=Physicality=Tech.=10 Oct.=Uranus=P=1Ø.
Ambrosia is defined as the food of the Gods. Something with a delicious flavor or
fragrance. Greek >> Ambrotos, Immortal. We could find the secret of immortality here.
The planetary source for immortality and the ambrosia is Uranus. It is a physical element.

Ambulance=5,500=5.5=80%=P5.50D=Earth-Midway=5 May=Gaia.
Ambulant=2,000=20%=P2.00D=2.0=Nature=Matter=Moon=2 Feb= Cupid>N=C.
Ambulatory=11,500=12,000=12%=P1.20D=1.2=Knowledge=Edu.=12 Dec.=Athena>>K=F.

Ambuscade=6,500=7,000=70%=P7.00D=7.0=Lang.= Assets =Mars = 6May=Pleiades.
Ambush=10,500=11,000=11%=P1.10D=1.1=Idea=Brainchild=Inventn=11 Nov.=Athena>K=F.
Ameba=1,500=15%=P1.50D=1.5=Authority = Solar Crown = Solar Core = 1 May = Maia.
Ameliorate=4,500=5,000=50%=P5.00D=5.0=Law=Time=Venus=5 May=Aphrodite>>L=N.
Amen=7,000=70%=P7.00D=7.0=Lang.= Assets =Mars = 6May=Pleiades.
Amenable=2,000=20%=P2.00D=2.0=Nature=Matter=Moon=2 Feb= Cupid>N=C.
Amend=8,500=9,000=90%=P9.00D=9.0=Abstraction=Gods=Saturn=9Sept.>>A=Ø.
Amendment=10,500=11,000=11%=P1.10D=1.1=Idea=Brainchild=Inv.=11Nov.=Athena>K=F.
Amends=2,500=3,000=30%=P3.00D=3.0=Creativity=Star=Muses=3March=C=I.
Amenhotep III=3,500=4,000=40%=P4.00D=4.0=Govt.=Creat.=4 April=Hermes>>G=A4.
Amenhotep IV.=1,000=100%=Physicality= Tech.=10 Oct.=Uranus=P=1Ø.
Amenity=10,000=1,000=100%=10.0=Physicality=Tech.=10 Oct.=Uranus=P=1Ø.
Amenorrhea=3,000=30%=P3.00D=3.0=Creativity=Star=Muses=3March=C=I.
Amer.=1,000=100%=10.0=1.0=Mind=Sun=1 January=Helios >> M=E4.
Amerasian=3,500=4,000=40%=P4.00D=4.0=Govt.=Creat.= 4 April=Hermes>>G=A4.
Amerce=5,500=5.5=80%=P5.50D=Earth-Midway=5 May=Gaia.
America=7,000=70%=P7.00D=7.0=Lang.= Assets =Mars = 6May=Pleiades.
American=6,500=7,000=70%=P7.00D=7.0=Lang.= Assets =Mars = 6May=Pleiades.
Americana=4,000=4,000=40%=P4.00D=4.0=Govt.=Creat.= 4 April=Hermes>>G=A4.
AmericanEnglish=4,500=5,000=50%=P5.00D=5.0=Law=Time=Venus=5May=Odite>>L=N.
American Indian=3,000=30%=P3.00D=3.0=Creativity=Star=Muses=3March=C=I.
Americanism=8,000=80%=P8.00D=8.0=Econ.=Curr.=Busn.=Jupt.=8Aug=Zeus>E=v.
Americanize=5,000=50%=P5.00D=5.0=Law=Time=Venus=5 May=Aphrodite>>L=N.
American plan=5,500=5.5=80%=P5.50D=Earth-Midway=5 May=Gaia.
American Samoa=8,500=9,000=90%=P9.00D=9.0=Abstr.=Gods=Saturn=9Sept.>>A=Ø.
American SignLang=6,500=7,000=70%=P7.00D=7.0=Lang.=Assets=Mars=6May=Pleiades.
American Spanish=4,500=50%=P5.00D=5.0=Law=Time=Venus=5May=Odite>>L=N.
Americium=500=5%=P5.00D=5.0=Law=Time=Venus=5 May=Aphrodite>>L=N.
Amerindian=1,500=15%=P1.50D=1.5=Authority = Solar Crown = Solar Core = 1 May
= Maia.
Amethyst=8,500=9,000=90%=P9.00D=9.0=Abstraction=Gods=Saturn=9Sept.>>A=Ø.
Amex=1,500=15%=P1.50D=1.5=Authority = Solar Crown = Solar Core = 1 May = Maia.
Amharic=3,500=4,000=40%=P4.00D=4.0=Govt.=Creat.= 4 April=Hermes>>G=A4.
Amiable=1,500=15%=P1.50D=1.5=Authority = Solar Crown = Solar Core = 1 May = Maia.
Amicable=1,000=100%=10.0=1.0=Mind=Sun=1 January=Helios >> M=E4.
Amid=3,000=30%=P3.00D=3.0=Creativity=Star=Muses=3 March=C=I.
Amidships=4,000=40%=P4.00D=4.0=Govt.=Creat.= 4 April=Hermes>>G=A4.
Amiens=4,000=40%=P4.00D=4.0=Govt.=Creat.= 4 April=Hermes>>G=A4.
Amigo=1,000=100%=10.0=1.0=Mind=Sun=1 January=Helios >> M=E4.
Amin Dada Idi=3,500=4,000=40%=P4.00D=4.0=Govt.=Creat.=4April=Hermes>>G=A4.
Amine=9,000=90%=P9.00D=9.0=Abstraction=Gods=Saturn=9Sept.>>A=Ø.
Amino acid=6,500=7,000=70%=P7.00D=7.0=Lang.= Assets =Mars = 6May=Pleiades.
Amish=11,000=11,000=11%=P1.10D=1.1=Idea=Brainchild=Invention=11 Nov.=Athena>K=F.
Amiss=10,500=11,000=11%=P1.10D=1.1=Idea=Brainchild=Invention=11 Nov.=Athena>K=F.
Amity=2,500=3,000=30%=P3.00D=3.0=Creativity=Star=Muses=3March=C=I.

Amman=5,000=50%=P5.00D=5.0=Law=Time=Venus=5May=Odite>>L=N.
Ammeter=3,000=30%=P3.00D=3.0=Creativity=Star=Muses=3March=C=I.
Ammo=1,000=100%=10.0=1.0=Mind=Sun=1 January=Helios >> M=E4.
Ammonia=10,000=1,000=100%=10.0=Physicality=Tech.=10 Oct.=Uranus=P=1Ø.
Ammonium=2,500=3,000=30%=P3.00D=3.0=Creativity=Star=Muses=3March=C=I.
AmmoniumChloride=6,500=7,000=70%=P7.00D=7.0=Lang.=Assets=Mars=6May=Pleiades
Ammonium hydroxide=8,000=80%=P8.00D=8.0=Econ.=Curr.=Jupt.=8Aug=Zeus>E=v.
Ammunition=10,500=11,000=11%=P1.10D=1.1=Idea=Brainchild=11Nov.=Athena>K=F.
Amnesia=1,500=15%=P1.50D=1.5=Authority = Solar Crown = Solar Core = 1 May = Maia.
Amnesty=3,500=4,000=40%=P4.00D=4.0=Govt.=Creat.= 4April=Hermes>>G=A4.
Amniocentesis=11,500=12,000=12%=P1.20D=1.2=Knowledge=Edu.=12Dec.=Athena>>K=F
Amnion=8,000=80%=P8.00D=8.0=Econ.=Curr.=Busn.=Jupt.=8Aug=Zeus>E=v.
Amoeba=9,000=90%=P9.00D=9.0=Abstraction=Gods=Saturn=9Sept.>>A=Ø.
Amok=1,500=15%=P1.50D=1.5=Authority = Solar Crown = Solar Core = 1 May = Maia.
Among=12,000=12%=P1.20D=1.2=Knowledge=Education=12 Dec.=Athena>>K=F.
Amontillado=4,500=5,000=50%=P5.00D=5.0=Law=Time=Venus=5May=Odite>>L=N.
Amoral=6,000=60%=P6.00D=6.0=Man=Earth=Health=Royalty=6June=Gaia>M=M2.
Amorous=4,500=5,000=50%=P5.00D=5.0=Law=Time=Venus=5May=Odite>>L=N.
Amorphous=9,000=90%=P9.00D=9.0=Abstraction=Gods=Saturn=9Sept.>>A=Ø.
Amortize=3,500=4,000=40%=P4.00D=4.0=Govt.=Creat.= 4April=Hermes>>G=A4.
Amos=5,500=5.5=80%=P5.50D=Earth-Midway=5 May=Gaia.
Amount=10,500=11,000=11%=P1.10D=1.1=Idea=Brainchild=Invention=11Nov.=Athena
     >K=F.
Amour=3,500=4,000=40%=P4.00D=4.0=Govt.=Creat.= 4 April=Hermes>>G=A4.
Amour-propre=1,000=100%=10.0=1.0=Mind=Sun=1 January=Helios >> M=E4.
Amoy=1,000=100%=10.0=1.0=Mind=Sun=1 January=Helios >> M=E4.
Amp=4,500=5,000=50%=P5.00D=5.0=Law=Time=Venus=5May=Odite>>L=N.
Amperage=4,500=5,000=50%=P5.00D=5.0=Law=Time=Venus=5May=Odite>>L=N.
Ampere=9,500=10,000=1,000=100%=10.0=Physicality=Tech.=10 Oct.=Uranus=P=1Ø.
Ampère Andrè Marie=2,000=20%=P2.00D=2.0=Nature=Matter=Moon=2Feb= Cupid
     >N=C.
Ampersand=8,000=80%=P8.00D=8.0=Econ.=Curr.=Busn.=Jupt.=8Aug=Zeus>E=v.
Amphetamine=9,000=90%=P9.00D=9.0=Abstraction=Gods=Saturn=9Sept.>>A=Ø.
Amphibian=16,500=17,000=17%=P1.70D=1.7=Solar Asset=Mind Computing =Pleiades.
Amphibious=4,500=5,000=50%=P5.00D=5.0=Law=Time=Venus=5May=Odite>>L=N.
Amphibole=8,000=80%=P8.00D=8.0=Econ.=Curr.=Busn.=Jupt.=8Aug=Zeus>E=v.
Amphitheater=6,500=7,000=70%=P7.00D=7.0=Lang.=Assets=Mars=6May=Pleiades.
Amphora=7,000=70%=P7.00D=7.0=Lang.=Assets=Mars=6May=Pleiades.
Ampicillin=6,500=7,000=70%=P7.00D=7.0=Lang.=Assets=Mars=6May=Pleiades.
Ample=11,000=11%=P1.10D=1.1=Idea=Brainchild=Invention=11 Nov.=Athena>K=F.
Amplifier=6,000=60%=P6.00D=6.0=Man=Earth=Health=Royalty=6June=Gaia>M=M2.
Amplify=9,500=10,000=1,000=100%=10.0=Physicality=Tech.=10 Oct.=Uranus=P=1Ø.
Amplitude=6,500=7,000=70%=P7.00D=7.0=Lang.=Assets=Mars=6May=Pleiades.
Amplitude modulation=8,500=9,000=90%=P9.00D=9.0=Abst.=Gods=Sat.=9Sept.>>A=Ø.

PETER K. MATTHEWS - AKUKALIA

Ampoule=6,000=60%=P6.00D=6.0=Man=Earth=Health=Royalty=6June=Gaia>M=M2.
Amputate=5,500=5.5=80%=P5.50D=Earth-Midway=5 May=Gaia.
Amputee=5,000=50%=P5.00D=5.0=Law=Time=Venus=5May=Odite>>L=N.
Amsterdam=6,000=60%=P6.00D=6.0=Man=Earth=Health=Royalty=6June=Gaia>M=M2.
Amt.=500=5%=P5.00D=5.0=Law=Time=Venus=5 May=Aphrodite>>L=N.
Amu=2,000=20%=P2.00D=2.0=Nature=Matter=Moon=2 Feb= Cupid>N=C.
Amuck=9,500=10,000=1,000=100%=10.0=Physicality=Tech.=10 Oct.=Uranus=P=1Ø.
Amu Darya=9,500=10,000=1,000=100%=Physicality= Tech.=10 Oct.=Uranus=P=1Ø.
Amulet=7,000=70%=P7.00D=7.0=Lang.=Assets=Mars=6May=Pleiades.
Amundsen Roald=6,000=60%=P6.00D=6.0=Man=Earth=Health=Roy=6June=Gaia
    >M=M2.
Amur River=9,000=90%=P9.00D=9.0=Abstraction=Gods=Saturn=9Sept.>>A=Ø.
Amuse=4,500=5,000=50%=P5.00D=5.0=Law=Time=Venus=5May=Odite>>L=N.
Amylase=5,500=5.5=80%=P5.50D=Earth-Midway=5 May=Gaia.
An=8,000=80%=P8.00D=8.0=Econ.=Curr.=Busn.=Jupt.=8Aug=Zeus>E=v.
An.=3,500=4,000=40%=P4.00D=4.0=Govt.=Creat.= 4 April=Hermes>>G=A4.
-an=5,000=50%=P5.00D=5.0=Law=Time=Venus=5May=Odite>>L=N.
Ana-=1,500=15%=P1.50D=1.5=Authority = Solar Crown = Solar Core = 1 May = Maia.
-Ana=5,500=5.5=80%=P5.50D=Earth-Midway=5 May=Gaia.
Anabaptist=5,500=5.5=80%=P5.50D=Earth-Midway=5 May=Gaia.
Anabolism=5,500=5.5=80%=P5.50D=Earth-Midway=5 May=Gaia.
Anachronism=9,000=90%=P9.00D=9.0=Abstraction=Gods=Saturn=9Sept.>>A=Ø.
Anaconda=8,000=80%=P8.00D=8.0=Econ.=Curr.=Busn.=Jupt.=8Aug=Zeus>E=v.
Anacreon=3,000=30%=P3.00D=3.0=Creativity=Star=Muses=3March=C=I.
Anaerobe=7,500=8,000=80%=P8.00D=8.0=Econ.=Curr.=Busn.=Jupt.=8Aug=Zeus>E=v.
Anesthesia=1,500=15%=P1.50D=1.5=Authority = Solar Crown = Solar Core = 1 May = Maia.
Anagram=7,000=70%=P7.00D=7.0=Lang.=Assets=Mars=6May=Pleiades.
Anaheim=5,500=5.5=80%=P5.50D=Earth-Midway=5 May=Gaia.
Anal=7,500=8,000=80%=P8.00D=8.0=Econ.=Curr.=Busn.=Jupt.=8Aug=Zeus>E=v.
Analgesia=5,500=5.5=80%=P5.50D=Earth-Midway=5 May=Gaia.
Analgesic=3,500=4,000=40%=P4.00D=4.0=Govt.=Creat= 4April=Hermes>>G=A4.
Analogous=11,500=12,000=12%=P1.20D=1.2=Knowledge=Edu.=12 Dec.=Athena>>K=F.
Analogue=9,000=90%=P9.00D=9.0=Abstraction=Gods=Saturn=9Sept.>>A=Ø.
Analogy=16,500=17,000=17%=P1.70D=1.7=Solar Asset=Mind Computing =Pleiades.
Analysis=8,500=9,000=90%=P9.00D=9.0=Abstraction=Gods=Saturn=9Sept.>>A=Ø.
Analytic=12,000=12%=P1.20D=1.2=Knowledge=Education=12 Dec.=Athena>>K=F.
Analyze=5,000=50%=P5.00D=5.0=Law=Time=Venus=5May=Odite>>L=N.
Anapest=6,500=7,000=70%=P7.00D=7.0=Lang.=Assets=Mars=6May=Pleiades.
Anarchism=8,000=80%=P8.00D=8.0=Econ.=Curr.=Busn.=Jupt.=8Aug=Zeus>E=v.
Anarchy=4,500=5,000=50%=P5.00D=5.0=Law=Time=Venus=5May=Odite>>L=N.
Anasazi=9,500=10,000=1,000=100%=10.0=Physicality=Tech.=10 Oct.=Uranus=P=1Ø.
Anathema=6,000=60%=P6.00D=6.0=Man=Earth=Health=Royalty=6June=Gaia>M=M2.
Anatolia=5,500=5.5=80%=P5.50D=Earth-Midway=5 May=Gaia.

Anatolian=8,500=9,000=90%=P9.00D=9.0=Abstraction=Gods=Saturn=9Sept.>>A=Ø.
Anatolians are the same people known in the Bible book of Exodus as the Hittites. Now extinct as spoken by GOD that they will be driven away by the Gods.

Anatomize=5,500=5.5=80%=P5.50D=Earth-Midway=5 May=Gaia.
Anatomy=7,500=8,000=80%=P8.00D=8.0=Econ.=Curr.=Busn.=Jupt.=8Aug=Zeus>E=v.
Anaxagoras=3,000=30%=P3.00D=3.0=Creativity=Star=Muses=3March=C=I.

Ancestor=1,300= 13% = P1.30D = 1.3 = Solar Core = Faculty = 13 January = Athena.
Athena keeps the records of ancestors as they all return to her. Only those who excel at a faculty of wisdom are immortalized and made stars to live forever in the cycle of life.

Ancestry=2,500=3,000=30%=P3.00D=3.0=Creativity=Star=Muses=3March=C=I.
Anchor=21,500=22,000=22%=P2.20D=2.2=4.0.=Creatocracy=2Feb=Hermes>G=A4.
Anchorage=5,000=50%=P5.00D=5.0=Law=Time=Venus=5May=Odite>>L=N.
Anchorite=1,500=15%=P1.50D=1.5=Authority = Solar Crown = Solar Core = 1 May = Maia.
Anchorman=4,000=40%=P4.00D=4.0=Govt.=Creat.= 4 April=Hermes>>G=A4.
Anchorperson=2,000=20%=P2.00D=2.0=Nature=Matter=Moon=2 Feb= Cupid>N=C.
Anchorwoman=2,500=3,000=30%=P3.00D=3.0=Creativity=Star=Muses=3March=C=I.
Anchovy=3,000=30%=P3.00D=3.0=Creativity=Star=Muses=3March=C=I.
Ancien règime=8,500=9,000=90%=P9.00D=9.0=Abstr.=Gods=Saturn=9Sept.>>A=Ø.
Ancient=11,500=12,000=12%=P1.20D=1.2=Knowledge=Education=12 Dec.=Athena>>K=F.

Ancillary=1,500=15%=P1.50D=1.5=Authority = Solar Crown = Solar Core = 1 May = Maia.
The owner of a thing in absolute terms especially intellectual property owns all rights to that thing including the ancillary rights. The king owns all things including the maids.

And=17,000=17%=P1.70D=1.7=Solar Asset=Mind Computing =Pleiades.
The use of and or but is characteristic of Shakespearean writing. It is standard up to Virginia Wolf and in modern times Peter Matthews - Akukalia reputed as African Shakespeare. See THE CREATOCRACY: a collection of Disean plays....

Andalusia=4,000=40%=P4.00D=4.0=Govt.=Creat.= 4 April=Hermes>>G=A4.
Andaman Islands=10,500=11,000=11%=P1.10D=1.1=Idea=Brainchild=11 Nov.=Athena>K=F.
Andante=2,500=3,000=30%=P3.00D=3.0=Creativity=Star=Muses=3March=C=I.
Andantino=4,500=5,000=50%=P5.00D=5.0=Law=Time=Venus=5May=Odite>>L=N.
Anderson Hans Christian.=2,000=20%=P2.00D=2.0=Nature=Moon=2Feb= Cupid>N=C.
Anderson, Marian=2,000=20%=P2.00D=2.0=Nature=Matter=Moon=2 Feb= Cupid>N=C.
Anderson, Maxwell=2,000=20%=P2.00D=2.0=Nature=Matter=Moon=2 Feb= Cupid>N=C.
Anderson, Sherwood=2,000=20%=P2.00D=2.0=Nature=Moon=2 Feb= Cupid>N=C.
Andes=7,000=70%=P7.00D=7.0=Lang.=Assets=Mars=6May=Pleiades.
Andiron=5,500=5.5=80%=P5.50D=Earth-Midway=5 May=Gaia.

And/or=7,500=8,000=80%=P8.00D=8.0=Econ.=Curr.=Busn.=Jupt.=8Aug=Zeus>E=v.
Andorra=9,500=10,000=1,000=100%=10.0=Physicality=Tech.=10 Oct.=Uranus=P=1Ø.
Andrea del Sarto=2,000=20%=P2.00D=2.0=Nature=Matter=Moon=2 Feb= Cupid>N=C.
Andrew=3,000=30%=P3.00D=3.0=Creativity=Star=Muses=3March=C=I.
Andro-=1,500=15%=P1.50D=1.5=Authority = Solar Crown = Solar Core = 1 May = Maia.
Androgen=4,000=40%=P4.00D=4.0=Govt.=Creat.= 4 April=Hermes>>G=A4.
Androgynous=7,000=70%=P7.00D=7.0=Lang.=Assets=Mars=6May=Pleiades.
Android=5,500=5.5=80%=P5.50D=Earth-Midway=5 May=Gaia.
-andry=3,000=30%=P3.00D=3.0=Creativity=Star=Muses=3March=C=I.
-ane=2,000=20%=P2.00D=2.0=Nature=Matter=Moon=2 Feb= Cupid>N=C.
Anecdote=4,500=5,000=50%=P5.00D=5.0=Law=Time=Venus=5May=Odite>>L=N.
Anechoic=2,500=3,000=30%=P3.00D=3.0=Creativity=Star=Muses=3March=C=I.
Anemia=5,000=50%=P5.00D=5.0=Law=Time=Venus=5May=Odite>>L=N.
Anemometer=4,000=40%=P4.00D=4.0=Govt.=Creat.= 4 April=Hermes>>G=A4.
Anemone=7,500=8,000=80%=P8.00D=8.0=Econ.=Curr.=Busn.=Jupt.=8Aug=Zeus>E=v.
Anent=1,000=100%=10.0=1.0=Mind=Sun=1 January=Helios >> M=E4.
Aneroid barometer=11,500=12,000=12%=P1.20D=1.2=Knowl.=Edu.=12Dec.=Athena>>K=F.
Anesthesia=6,000=60%=P6.00D=6.0=Man=Earth=Health=Royalty=6June=Gaia>M=M2.
Anesthesiology=3,500=4,000=4,000=40%=P4.00D=4.0=Creat= 4April=Hermes>G=A4.
Anesthetic=4,500=5,000=50%=P5.00D=5.0=Law=Time=Venus=5May=Odite>>L=N.
Anesthetize=2,000=20%=P2.00D=2.0=Nature=Matter=Moon=2 Feb= Cupid>N=C.
Aneurysm=4,000=40%=P4.00D=4.0=Creat.= 4April=Hermes>>G=A4.
Anew=4,500=5,000=50%=P5.00D=5.0=Law=Time=Venus=5May=Odite>>L=N.

Angel=14,500=15,000=1,500=15%=P1.50D=1.5=Authority=Solar Crown=SC=1 May = Maia.
There are two categories of angels. First is Angels with the capital "A". Second is angels
with the small "a". The first is the Council of Gods specifically mentioned by the Almighty
GOD. The Greek mythology mentions them as the Olympian Gods headed by Zeus whom
the Jews call Jehovah >> Yehoshua, Islam call Him Allah. Makupedians call Him ZeJeAl.
Exodus 22:28; 23:20-25; Job 38:31-41; Proverbs 8:12-36. The use reference used with
capital letters in both the Holy Bible and Holy Quran agree on some elements that have
been proved to be the Gods mentioned in the Greek mythology and now Makupedian
Inspired Mythological Truths. From the Quran (Al-Wäql'a, or the Inevitable Event)
v.60 - Death >> Hades, We - a council of Gods; v.61-reincarnation>>cycle of life; v.64-
Cause>>Fate>> The Fates are three Goddesses; Will-Rights by Law; v.69-Cloud>>Uranus-
Job 35-34; v.71-Fire>>Sun>>Helios; v.75-Stars>>Muses>>Daughters of Zeus. In verse 76
we are indeed adjured or urged to compute and find out the signs or meanings of the words
emphasized through capital letters through the application of the planets v.80 which in
Makupedia is the dimensions of the universe Deut.29:29; 30:11-14; 32:8(There are 12
tribes of Israel for human convenience. The rest 13-10,000 was to be sought by one who
would become the Solar Crown King by Proverbs 25:1-4) Eccl. 3:11.
The second group of angels are known as the ministerial spirits. Hebrews 1:7 & 14.

Angels are immortal beings attendant upon GOD. They are ranked into nine orders
(anonymous). This establishes the truth of the Creatocracy dimension of abstraction

as the 9[th]=Gods=A=Ø. The definition of an angel as a financial backer of an enterprise ranks Helen Ekwe-Okpata as an angel of De - Royal Makupedia Limited. The rights of the God of Creatocracy places her as an Oracle of the Creatocracy and a Goddess to Makupedia. The Creatocracy has established that the Gods are the highest Angels often depicted as the capital "A" in Angels higher than the rest used as "a" in angels. Collectively they form the Creatocracy as a body of Hosts coded in the Old Testament of the Bible and coded as the Holy Spirit in the New Testament. Creatocracy is also the body of Creative Scientists and its study of the Creative & Psycho-Social Sciences founded by Peter Matthews-Akukalia and reigns by the throne of the Creatocratic Charter and the sovereignty of the Solar Crown. Athena Castle formally Athena Pallas is now officially married to Castle Makupedia and is the Goddess and Aegis of the Creatocracy in the abundance aegis of Zeus. See the book: THE CREATOCRACY. The Crown book of the Creatocracy. Castle Makupedia is the God name for Peter Matthews - Akukalia. The God of Creatocracy Genius & Mind. He discovered measured defined established applied and owns the Creatocracy. Deut 29:29.

Angel Fall=5,000=50%=P5.00D=5.0=Law=Time=Venus=5May=Odite>>L=N.
Angel fish=4,500=5,000=50%=P5.00D=5.0=Law=Time=Venus=5May=Odite>>L=N.
Angelica=6,500=7,000=70%=P7.00D=7.0=Lang.=Assets=Mars=6May=Pleiades.
Angelico=4,500=5,000=50%=P5.00D=5.0=Law=Time=Venus=5May=Odite>>L=N.
Anger=6,000=60%=P6.00D=6.0=Man=Earth=Health=Royalty=6June=Gaia>M=M2.
Angers=5,000=50%=P5.00D=5.0=Law=Time=Venus=5May=Odite>>L=N.
Angina=6,000=60%=P6.00D=6.0=Man=Earth=Health=Royalty=6June=Gaia>M=M2.
Angina pectoris=7,500=8,000=80%=P8.00D=8.0=Econ.=Curr.=Jupt.=8Aug=Zeus>E=v.
Angiogram=5,500=5.5=80%=P5.50D=Earth-Midway=5 May=Gaia.
Angioplasty=8,000=80%=P8.00D=8.0=Econ.=Curr.=Busn.=Jupt.=8Aug=Zeus>E=v.
Angiosperm=6,000=60%=P6.00D=6.0=Man=Earth=Health=Royalty=6June=Gaia
    >M=M2.
Angkor=9,000=90%=P9.00D=9.0=Abstraction=Gods=Saturn=9Sept.>>A=Ø.
Angle(1)=7,500=8,000=80%=P8.00D=8.0=Econ.=Curr.=Busn.=Jupt.=8Aug=Zeus>E=v.
Angle(2)=19,500=20,000=20%=P2.00D=2.0=Nature=Matter=Moon=2 Feb= Cupid>N=C.
Angle=11,000=11%=P1.10D=1.1=Idea=Brainchild=Invention=11 Nov.=Athena>K=F.
Angleworm=4,000=40%=P4.00D=4.0=Govt.=Creat.= 4 April=Hermes>>G=A4.
Anglican=6,000=60%=P6.00D=6.0=Man=Earth=Health=Royalty=6June=Gaia>M=M2.
Anglicism=7,500=8,000=80%=P8.00D=8.0=Econ.=Curr.=Busn.=Jupt.=8Aug=Zeus>E=v.
Anglo=4,500=5,000=50%=P5.00D=5.0=Law=Time=Venus=5May=Odite>>L=N.
Anglo-=1,500=15%=P1.50D=1.5=Authority = Solar Crown = Solar Core = 1 May = Maia.
Anglo-American=6,000=60%=P6.00D=6.0=Man=Earth=Health=Roy=6June=Gaia
    >M=M2.
Anglo-Norman=8,500=9,000=90%=P9.00D=9.0=Abst.=Gods=Saturn=9Sept.>>A=Ø.
Anglophile=3,500=4,000=40%=P4.00D=4.0=Creat.= 4 April=Hermes>>G=A4.
Anglophobe=3,500=4,000=40%=P4.00D=4.0=Creat.= 4 April=Hermes>>G=A4.
Anglophone=5,500=5.5=80%=P5.50D=Earth-Midway=5 May=Gaia.
Anglo-Saxon=10,500=11,000=11%=P1.10D=1.1=Idea=Brainchild=11 Nov.=Athena>K=F.

Angola=7,000=70%=P7.00D=7.0=Lang.=Assets=Mars=6May=Pleiades.
Angora=8,500=9,000=90%=P9.00D=9.0=Abstraction=Gods=Saturn=9Sept.>>A=Ø.
Angry=11,500=12,000=12%=P1.20D=1.2=Knowledge=Education=12 Dec.=Athena>>K=F.
Angst=2,000=20%=P2.00D=2.0=Nature=Matter=Moon=2 Feb= Cupid>N=C.
Angstrom=9,000=90%=P9.00D=9.0=Abstraction=Gods=Saturn=9Sept.>>A=Ø.
Anguilla=6,000=60%=P6.00D=6.0=Man=Earth=Health=Royalty=6June=Gaia>M=M2.
Anguish=5,500=5.5=80%=P5.50D=Earth-Midway=5 May=Gaia.
Anhydride=5,500=5.5=80%=P5.50D=Earth-Midway=5 May=Gaia.
Anhydrous=1,000=100%=10.0=1.0=Mind=Sun=1 January=Helios >> M=E4.
Aniline=7,500=8,000=80%=P8.00D=8.0=Econ.=Curr.=Busn.=Jupt.=8Aug=Zeus>E=v.
Animadvert=5,500=5.5=80%=P5.50D=Earth-Midway=5 May=Gaia.
Animal=17,500=18,000=18%=P1.80D=1.8=Solar Currency=MaksCurr.=1 Aug=Maia.
Animalcule=2,000=20%=P2.00D=2.0=Nature=Matter=Moon=2 Feb= Cupid>N=C.
Animal husbandry=3,500=4,000=4,000=40%=P4.00D=4.0=Creat=4Ap=Hermes>>G=A4.

Animate=12,000=12%=P1.20D=1.2=Knowledge=Education=12 Dec.=Athena>>K=F.
The meaning of animate shows that interest is spirit. That spirits can incarnate people. The resultant values falls on Athena's knowledge by the Solar Core meaning that the quantity of knowledge absorbed by a person determines the GIL in the person. So GIL is Athena.

Animated=5,000=50%=P5.00D=5.0=Law=Time=Venus=5May=Odite>>L=N.
Animated cartoon=4,500=5,000=50%=P5.0D=5.0=Law=Time=Venus=5May=Odite>>L=N
Animato=3,500=4,000=40%=P4.00D=4.0=Govt.=Creat.= 4 April=Hermes>>G=A4.
Animator=6,000=60%=P6.00D=6.0=Man=Earth=Health=Royalty=6June=Gaia>M=M2.

Animism=5,000=50%=P5.00D=5.0=Law=Time=Venus=5May=Odite>>L=N.
A definition shows that inanimate objects possess spirits. Our results shows it is a 50% until proved computationally. The Creatocracy Bank proves it is true by Makumaticology.

Animosity=2,500=3,000=30%=P3.00D=3.0=Creativity=Star=Muses=3March=C=I.
Animus=3,000=30%=P3.00D=3.0=Creativity=Star=Muses=3March=C=I.
Anion=5,500=5.5=80%=P5.50D=Earth-Midway=5 May=Gaia.
Anise=7,000=70%=P7.00D=7.0=Lang.=Assets=Mars=6May=Pleiades.
Anise seed=3,000=30%=P3.00D=3.0=Creativity=Star=Muses=3March=C=I.
Anisette=2,500=3,000=30%=P3.00D=3.0=Creativity=Star=Muses=3March=C=I.
Anjou(1)=7,000=70%=P7.00D=7.0=Lang.=Assets=Mars=6May=Pleiades.
Anjou(2)=2,000=20%=P2.00D=2.0=Nature=Matter=Moon=2 Feb= Cupid>N=C.
Ankara=5,500=5.5=80%=P5.50D=Earth-Midway=5 May=Gaia.
Ankh=6,000=60%=P6.00D=6.0=Man=Earth=Health=Royalty=6June=Gaia>M=M2.
Ankle=6,000=60%=P6.00D=6.0=Man=Earth=Health=Royalty=6June=Gaia>M=M2.
Ankle bone=1,000=100%=10.0=1.0=Mind=Sun=1 January=Helios >> M=E4.
Anklet=6,500=7,000=70%=P7.00D=7.0=Lang.=Assets=Mars=6May=Pleiades.
Ann Cape=4,500=5,000=50%=P5.00D=5.0=Law=Time=Venus=5May=Odite>>L=N.

Annals=10,000=1,000=100%=10.0=Physicality=Tech.=10 Oct.=Uranus=P=1Ø.

Annam=7,000=70%=P7.00D=7.0=Lang.=Assets=Mars=6May=Pleiades.

Annapolis=9,000=90%=P9.00D=9.0=Abstraction=Gods=Saturn=9Sept.>>A=Ø.

Annapurna=15,000=15%=P1.50D=1.5=Authority = Solar Crown = Solar Core = 1 May = Maia.

Ann Arbor=5,000=50%=P5.00D=5.0=Law=Time=Venus=5May=Odite>>L=N.

Anne=5,000=50%=P5.00D=5.0=Law=Time=Venus=5May=Odite>>L=N.

Anneal=7,000=70%=P7.00D=7.0=Lang.=Assets=Mars=6May=Pleiades.

Annelid=6,500=7,000=70%=P7.00D=7.0=Lang.=Assets=Mars=6May=Pleiades.

Annex=10,000=1,000=100%=10.0=Physicality=Tech.=10 Oct.=Uranus=P=1Ø.

Annihilate=1,500=15%=P1.50D=1.5=Authority = Solar Crown = Solar Core = 1 May = Maia.

Anniversary=4,000=40%=P4.00D=4.0=Govt.=Creat.= 4 April=Hermes>>G=A4.

Anno Domini=4,000=4,000=40%=P4.00D=4.0=Govt.=Creat.= 4 April=Hermes>>G=A4.

Annotate=5,500=5.5=80%=P5.50D=Earth-Midway=5 May=Gaia.

Announce=10,500=11,000=11%=P1.10D=1.1=Idea=Brainchild=11 Nov.=Athena>K=F.

Announcer=8,500=9,000=90%=P9.00D=9.0=Abstraction=Gods=Saturn=9Sept.>>A=Ø.

Annoy=2,000=20%=P2.00D=2.0=Nature=Matter=Moon=2 Feb= Cupid>N=C.

Annual=12,000=12%=P1.20D=1.2=Knowledge=Education=12 Dec.=Athena>>K=F.

Annual ring=6,000=60%=P6.00D=6.0=Man=Earth=Health=Royalty=6June=Gaia>M=M2.

Annuitant=2,500=3,000=30%=P3.00D=3.0=Creativity=Star=Muses=3March=C=I.

Annuity=10,500=11,000=11%=P1.10D=1.1=Idea=Brainchild=11 Nov.=Athena>K=F.

Annul=4,500=5,000=50%=P5.00D=5.0=Law=Time=Venus=5May=Odite>>L=N.

Annular=1,000=100%=10.0=1.0=Mind=Sun=1 January=Helios >> M=E4.

Annulus=3,500=4,000=40%=P4.00D=4.0=Govt.=Creat.= 4 April=Hermes>>G=A4.

Annunciate=1,500=15%=P1.50D=1.5=Authority = Solar Crown = Solar Core = 1 May = Maia.

Annunciation=8,500=9,000=90%=P9.00D=9.0=Abstraction=Gods=Saturn=9Sept.>>A=Ø. The angel Gabriel's announcement to the Virgin Mary of the Incarnation. This is superior testimony to the truth of the cycle of life taught in the studies of the Creatocracy. Interestingly it is an activity of Zeus through the borderline to the Gods. The borderline is a thing such as man walls birds books stones animals and even trees. Zeus borderline is 8,500 where Zeus is 8.00 and the borderline is 5.00. 8,500=9,000 is the Host or Gods. The Godship of Peter Matthews-Akukalia sources from the fact he is believed to be an incarnation of Zeus the Most High GOD after the order of the Host through Khristos. This is a firm belief upon which the Makstian Faith and Mind Temple is established.

Anode=2,000=20%=P2.00D=2.0=Nature=Matter=Moon=2 Feb= Cupid>N=C.

Anodize=4,000=40%=P4.00D=4.0=Govt.=Creat.= 4 April=Hermes>>G=A4.

Anodyne=4,000=40%=P4.00D=4.0=Govt.=Creat.= 4 April=Hermes>>G=A4.

Anoint=9,000=90%=P9.00D=9.0=Abstraction=Gods=Saturn=9Sept.>>A=Ø.

Anole=7,000=70%=P7.00D=7.0=Lang.=Assets=Mars=6May=Pleiades.

Anomaly=8,000=80%=P8.00D=8.0=Econ.=Curr.=Busn.=Jupt.=8Aug=Zeus>E=v.

Anon=2,000=20%=P2.00D=2.0=Nature=Matter=Moon=2 Feb= Cupid>N=C.

Anon.=500=5%=P5.00D=5.0=Law=Time=Venus=5 May=Aphrodite>>L=N.

Anonymous=4,000=40%=P4.00D=4.0=Govt.=Creat.= 4 April=Hermes>>G=A4.
Anopheles=3,500=4,000=40%=P4.00D=4.0=Govt.=Creat.= 4 April=Hermes>>G=A4.
Anorak=2,500=3,000=30%=P3.00D=3.0=Creativity=Star=Muses=3March=C=I.
Anorectic=5,500=5.5=80%=P5.50D=Earth-Midway=5 May=Gaia.
Anorexia=4,000=40%=P4.00D=4.0=Govt.=Creat.= 4 April=Hermes>>G=A4.
Anorexia nervosa=8,500=9,000=90%=P9.00D=9.0=Abst.=Gods=Saturn=9Sept.>>A=Ø.
Anorexic=2,500=3,000=30%=P3.00D=3.0=Creativity=Star=Muses=3March=C=I.
Another=9,000=90%=P9.00D=9.0=Abstraction=Gods=Saturn=9Sept.>>A=Ø.
Anouilh Jean.=2,000=20%=P2.00D=2.0=Nature=Matter=Moon=2 Feb= Cupid>N=C.
Anshan=4,500=5,000=50%=P5.00D=5.0=Law=Time=Venus=5May=Odite>>L=N.
Answer=12,500= 13,000 = 13% = P1.30D = 1.3 = Solar Core = Faculty = 13January=Athena.
Answering machine=5,500=5.5=80%=P5.50D=Earth-Midway=5 May=Gaia.
Ant=10,000=1,000=100%=10.0=Physicality=Tech.=10 Oct.=Uranus=P=1Ø.
ant.=1,000=100%=Physicality= Tech.=10 Oct.=Uranus=P=1Ø.
Ant.=500=5%=P5.00D=5.0=Law=Time=Venus=5 May=Aphrodite>>L=N.
Ant-=1,500=15%=P1.50D=1.5=Authority = Solar Crown = Solar Core = 1 May = Maia.
-ant=8,500=9,000=90%=P9.00D=9.0=Abstraction=Gods=Saturn=9Sept.>>A=Ø.
Antacid=7,500=8,000=80%=P8.00D=8.0=Econ.=Curr.=Busn.=Jupt.=8Aug=Zeus>E=v.
Antagonism=4,500=5,000=50%=P5.00D=5.0=Law=Time=Venus=5May=Odite>>L=N.
Antagonist=12,000=12%=P1.20D=1.2=Knowledge=Education=12 Dec.=Athena>>K=F.
Antagonize=2,500=3,000=30%=P3.00D=3.0=Creativity=Star=Muses=3March=C=I.
Antananarivo=6,500=7,000=70%=P7.00D=7.0=Lang.=Assets=Mars=6May=Pleiades.

Antarctica=5,000=50%=P5.00D=5.0=Law=Time=Venus=5May=Odite>>L=N.
The Creatocracy has established that the Gods reside in Antartica while resident on Earth.

Antarctica Circle=8,000=80%=P8.00D=8.0=Econ.=Curr.=Busn.=Jupt.=8Aug=Zeus>E=v.
Antarctica Ocean=7,000=70%=P7.00D=7.0=Lang.=Assets=Mars=6May=Pleiades.
Antares=3,500=4,000=40%=P4.00D=4.0=Govt.=Creat.= 4 April=Hermes>>G=A4.
Ante=17,000=17%=P1.70D=1.7=Solar Asset=Mind Computing =Pleiades.
Ante-=3,000=30%=P3.00D=3.0=Creativity=Star=Muses=3March=C=I.
Ant eater=7,500=8,000=80%=P8.00D=8.0=Econ.=Curr.=Busn.=Jupt.=8Aug=Zeus>E=v.
Antebellum=4,000=40%=P4.00D=4.0=Govt.=Creat.= 4 April=Hermes>>G=A4.
Antecedent=11,000=11%=P1.10D=1.1=Idea=Brainchild=Invention=11 Nov.=Athena>K=F.
Ante chamber=1,000=100%=10.0=1.0=Mind=Sun=1 January=Helios >> M=E4.
Ante date=6,000=60%=P6.00D=6.0=Man=Earth=Health=Royalty=6June=Gaia>M=M2.
Antediluvian=4,500=5,000=50%=P5.00D=5.0=Law=Time=Venus=5May=Odite>>L=N.
Antelope=9,000=90%=P9.00D=9.0=Abstraction=Gods=Saturn=9Sept.>>A=Ø.
Ante meridiem=16,500=17,000=17%=P1.70D=1.7=Solar Asset=Mind Computing =Pleiades.
Antenna=11,000=11%=P1.10D=1.1=Idea=Brainchild=Invention=11 Nov.=Athena>K=F.
Antepenult=7,000=70%=P7.00D=7.0=Lang.=Assets=Mars=6May=Pleiades.
Anterior=3,500=4,000=40%=P4.00D=4.0=Govt.=Creat.= 4 April=Hermes>>G=A4.
Ante room=6,000=60%=P6.00D=6.0=Man=Earth=Health=Royalty=6June=Gaia>M=M2.
Anthem=4,500=5,000=50%=P5.00D=5.0=Law=Time=Venus=5May=Odite>>L=N.

Anther=3,000=30%=P3.00D=3.0=Creativity=Star=Muses=3March=C=I.
Anthill=6,500=7,000=70%=P7.00D=7.0=Lang.=Assets=Mars=6May=Pleiades.
Anthology=2,500=3,000=30%=P3.00D=3.0=Creativity=Star=Muses=3March=C=I.
Anthony=7,000=70%=P7.00D=7.0=Lang.=Assets=Mars=6May=Pleiades.
Anthony, Susan Brownell=3,500=4,000=40%=P4.00D=4.0=Creat= 4Apr=Hermes>>G=A4.
Anthracite=5,000=50%=P5.00D=5.0=Law=Time=Venus=5May=Odite>>L=N.
Anthrax=9,000=90%=P9.00D=9.0=Abstraction=Gods=Saturn=9Sept.>>A=Ø.
Anthropo-=1,500=15%=P1.50D=1.5=Authority = Solar Crown = Solar Core = 1 May = Maia.
Anthropocentric=4,500=5,000=50%=P5.00D=5.0=Law=Time=Venus=5May=Odite>>L=N.
Anthropoid=5,000=50%=P5.00D=5.0=Law=Time=Venus=5May=Odite>>L=N.
Anthropology=4,500=5,000=50%=P5.00D=5.0=Law=Time=Venus=5May=Odite>>L=N.
Anthropomorphism=4,500=5,000=50%=P5.00D=5.0=Law=Time=Venus=5May
    =OditeL=N.
Anti=1,500=15%=P1.50D=1.5=Authority = Solar Crown = Solar Core = 1 May = Maia.
Antiabortion=1,500=15%=P1.50D=1.5=Authority = Solar Crown = Solar Core = 1 May=Maia.
Anti ballistic missile=5,500=5.5=80%=P5.50D=Earth-Midway=5 May=Gaia.
Antibiotic=11,500=12,000=12%=P1.20D=1.2=Knowledge=Edu.=12 Dec.=Athena>>K=F.
Antibody=6,500=7,000=70%=P7.00D=7.0=Lang.=Assets=Mars=6May=Pleiades.
Antic=2,500=3,000=30%=P3.00D=3.0=Creativity=Star=Muses=3March=C=I.
Anti-choice=5,000=50%=P5.00D=5.0=Law=Time=Venus=5May=Odite>>L=N.
Antichrist=8,000=80%=P8.00D=8.0=Econ.=Curr.=Busn.=Jupt.=8Aug=Zeus>E=v.
Anticipate=4,500=5,000=50%=P5.00D=5.0=Law=Time=Venus=5May=Odite>>L=N.
Anticlerical=4,000=40%=P4.00D=4.0=Govt.=Creat.= 4 April=Hermes>>G=A4.
Anticlimax=9,000=90%=P9.00D=9.0=Abstraction=Gods=Saturn=9Sept.>>A=Ø.
Anticyclone=5,000=50%=P5.00D=5.0=Law=Time=Venus=5May=Odite>>L=N.
Antidepressant=3,000=30%=P3.00D=3.0=Creativity=Star=Muses=3March=C=I.
Antidote=12,000=12,000=12%=P1.20D=1.2=Knowledge=Edu.=12 Dec.=Athena>>K=F.
Antietam=8,500=9,000=90%=P9.00D=9.0=Abstraction=Gods=Saturn=9Sept.>>A=Ø.
Antifreeze=7,500=8,000=80%=P8.00D=8.0=Econ.=Curr.=Busn.=Jupt.=8Aug=Zeus>E=v.
Antigen=10,000=1,000=100%=10.0=Physicality=Tech.=10 Oct.=Uranus=P=1Ø.
Antigua &Barbuda=10,500=11,000=11%=P1.10D=1.1=Idea=Brainchild=11Nov.=Athena
    >K=F.
Antihero=4,500=5,000=50%=P5.00D=5.0=Law=Time=Venus=5May=Odite>>L=N.
Antiheroine=7,500=8,000=80%=P8.00D=8.0=Econ.=Curr.=Busn.=Jupt.=8Aug=Zeus
    >E=v.
Antihistamine=8,000=80%=P8.00D=8.0=Econ.=Curr.=Busn.=Jupt.=8Aug=Zeus>E=v.
Antiknock=4,000=40%=P4.00D=4.0=Govt.=Creat.= 4 April=Hermes>>G=A4.
Antilles=12,000=12,000=12%=P1.20D=1.2=Knowledge=Education=12 Dec.=Athena
    >>K=F.
Antilog=1,000=100%=10.0=1.0=Mind=Sun=1 January=Helios >> M=E4.
Antilogarithm=8,500=9,000=90%=P9.00D=9.0=Abstraction=Gods=Saturn=9Sept.>>A=Ø.
Anti massacre=5,000=50%=P5.00D=5.0=Law=Time=Venus=5May=Odite>>L=N.
Antimatter=7,500=8,000=80%=P8.00D=8.0=Econ.=Curr.=Busn.=Jupt.=8Aug=Zeus>E=v.
Antimony= 13,000 = 13% = P1.30D = 1.3 = Solar Core = Faculty = 13January=Athena.
Antineutron=2,500=3,000=30%=P3.00D=3.0=Creativity=Star=Muses=3March=C=I.

Anti novel=9,500=10,000=1,000=100%=10.0=Physicality=Tech.=10 Oct.=Uranus=P=1Ø.
Anti nuclear=5,000=50%=P5.00D=5.0=Law=Time=Venus=5May=Odite>>L=N.
Antioch=4,000=40%=P4.00D=4.0=Govt.=Creat.= 4 April=Hermes>>G=A4.
Antiparticle=14,500=15,000=15%=P1.50D=1.5=Authority=Solar Crown=SC=1 May=Maia.
Antipasto=4,500=5,000=50%=P5.00D=5.0=Law=Time=Venus=5May=Odite>>L=N.
Antipathy=4,000=40%=P4.00D=4.0=Govt.=Creat.= 4 April=Hermes>>G=A4.
Anti personnel=5,000=50%=P5.00D=5.0=Law=Time=Venus=5May=Odite>>L=N.
Antiperspirant=4,000=40%=P4.00D=4.0=Govt.=Creat.= 4 April=Hermes>>G=A4.
Antiphon=5,000=50%=P5.00D=5.0=Law=Time=Venus=5May=Odite>>L=N.
Antiphony=5,000=50%=P5.00D=5.0=Law=Time=Venus=5May=Odite>>L=N.
Antipode=1,500=15%=P1.50D=1.5=Authority = Solar Crown = Solar Core = 1 May = Maia.
antipodes=9,500=10,000=1,000=100%=10.0=Physicality=Tech.=10 Oct.=Uranus=P=1Ø.
Antipodes=8,000=80%=P8.00D=8.0=Econ.=Curr.=Busn.=Jupt.=8Aug=Zeus>E=v.
Antipope=6,000=60%=P6.00D=6.0=Man=Earth=Health=Royalty=6June=Gaia>M=M2.
Antiproton=2,500=3,000=30%=P3.00D=3.0=Creativity=Star=Muses=3March=C=I.
Antipsychotic=3,000=30%=P3.00D=3.0=Creativity=Star=Muses=3March=C=I.
Antipyretic=3,000=30%=P3.00D=3.0=Creativity=Star=Muses=3March=C=I.
Antiquarian=7,000=70%=P7.00D=7.0=Lang.=Assets=Mars=6May=Pleiades.
Antiquary=3,500=4,000=40%=P4.00D=4.0=Govt.=Creat.= 4 April=Hermes>>G=A4.
Antiquate=1,500=15%=P1.50D=1.5=Authority = Solar Crown = Solar Core = 1 May = Maia.
Antique=14,500=15,000=15%=P1.50D=1.5=Authority = Solar Crown = SC = 1 May= Maia.
Antiquity=11,000=11%=P1.10D=1.1=Idea=Brainchild=Invention=11 Nov.=Athena>K=F.
Anti satellite=2,000=20%=P2.00D=2.0=Nature=Matter=Moon=2 Feb= Cupid>N=C.
Anti-Semite=3,000=30%=P3.00D=3.0=Creativity=Star=Muses=3March=C=I.
Antisepsis=4,000=40%=P4.00D=4.0=Govt.=Creat.= 4 April=Hermes>>G=A4.
Antiseptic=6,000=60%=P6.00D=6.0=Man=Earth=Health=Royalty=6June=Gaia>M=M2.
Antiserum=5,500=5.5=80%=P5.50D=Earth-Midway=5 May=Gaia.
Anti smoking=5,500=5.5=80%=P5.50D=Earth-Midway=5 May=Gaia.
Antisocial=5,000=50%=P5.00D=5.0=Law=Time=Venus=5May=Odite>>L=N.
Anti theft=2,000=20%=P2.00D=2.0=Nature=Matter=Moon=2 Feb= Cupid>N=C.
Antithesis=6,000=60%=P6.00D=6.0=Man=Earth=Health=Royalty=6June=Gaia>M=M2.
Antitoxin=7,000=70%=P7.00D=7.0=Lang.=Assets=Mars=6May=Pleiades.
Antitrust=5,000=50%=P5.00D=5.0=Law=Time=Venus=5May=Odite>>L=N.
Antitussive=2,000=20%=P2.00D=2.0=Nature=Matter=Moon=2 Feb= Cupid>N=C.
Antler=6,000=60%=P6.00D=6.0=Man=Earth=Health=Royalty=6June=Gaia>M=M2.
Ant lion=12,000=12,000=12%=P1.20D=1.2=Knowledge=Education=12 Dec.=Athena>>K=F.
Antoninus Pius=4,000=40%=P4.00D=4.0=Govt.=Creat.= 4 April=Hermes>>G=A4.
Antonym=3,500=4,000=40%=P4.00D=4.0=Govt.=Creat.= 4 April=Hermes>>G=A4.
Antsy=2,000=20%=P2.00D=2.0=Nature=Matter=Moon=2 Feb= Cupid>N=C.
Antwerp=4,000=40%=P4.00D=4.0=Govt.=Creat.= 4 April=Hermes>>G=A4.
Anus=5,000=50%=P5.00D=5.0=Law=Time=Venus=5May=Odite>>L=N.
Anvil=10,500=11,000=11%=P1.10D=1.1=Idea=Brainchild=Invention=11 Nov.=Athena>K=F.
Anxiety=9,500=10,000=1,000=100%=10.0=Physicality=Tech.=10 Oct.=Uranus=P=1Ø.
Anxious=6,500=7,000=70%=P7.00D=7.0=Lang.=Assets=Mars=6May=Pleiades.
Any=22,000=22%=P2.20D=2.2=4.0=Govt.=Creatocracy=2Feb=Hermes>G=A4.

Anybody=5,000=50%=P5.00D=5.0=Law=Time=Venus=5May=Odite>>L=N.
Anyhow=5,500=5.5=80%=P5.50D=Earth-Midway=5 May=Gaia.
Anymore=20,500=21,000=21%=P2.10D=2.1=3.0=Creativity=Star=Muses=2 Jan>>C=I.
Anyone=1,000=100%=10.0=1.0=Mind=Sun=1 January=Helios >> M=E4.
Anyplace=3,500=4,000=40%=P4.00D=4.0=Govt.=Creat.= 4 April=Hermes>>G=A4.
Anything=8,500=9,000=90%=P9.00D=9.0=Abstraction=Gods=Saturn=9Sept.>>A=Ø.
Anytime=1,500=15%=P1.50D=1.5=Authority = Solar Crown = Solar Core = 1 May = Maia.
Anyway=7,000=70%=P7.00D=7.0=Lang.=Assets=Mars=6May=Pleiades.
Anywhere=5,000=50%=P5.00D=5.0=Law=Time=Venus=5May=Odite>>L=N.
a/o=1,000=100%=10.0=1.0=Mind=Sun=1 January=Helios >> M=E4.
A-one=2,000=20%=P2.00D=2.0=Nature=Matter=Moon=2 Feb= Cupid>N=C.
Aorta=7,000=70%=P7.00D=7.0=Lang.=Assets=Mars=6May=Pleiades.
Aoudad=3,000=30%=P3.00D=3.0=Creativity=Star=Muses=3March=C=I.
AP=3,500=4,000=40%=P4.00D=4.0=Govt.=Creat.= 4 April=Hermes>>G=A4.
ap.=500=5%=P5.00D=5.0=Law=Time=Venus=5 May=Aphrodite>>L=N.
Apace=2,500=3,000=30%=P3.00D=3.0=Creativity=Star=Muses=3March=C=I.
Apache=11,500=12,000=12%=P1.20D=1.2=Knowledge=Education=12 Dec.=Athena>>K=F.
Apart=11,000=11%=P1.10D=1.1=Idea=Brainchild=Invention=11 Nov.=Athena>K=F.
Apartheid=6,500=7,000=70%=P7.00D=7.0=Lang.=Assets=Mars=6May=Pleiades.
Apartment=4,000=40%=P4.00D=4.0=Govt.=Creat.= 4 April=Hermes>>G=A4.
Apathy=5,500=5.5=80%=P5.50D=Earth-Midway=5 May=Gaia.
APB=1,500=15%=P1.50D=1.5=Authority = Solar Crown = Solar Core = 1 May = Maia.
Ape=9,500=10,000=1,000=100%=10.0=Physicality=Tech.=10 Oct.=Uranus=P=1Ø.
Apennines=6,500=7,000=70%=P7.00D=7.0=Lang.=Assets=Mars=6May=Pleiades.
Apéritif=3,500=4,000=40%=P4.00D=4.0=Govt.=Creat.= 4 April=Hermes>>G=A4.
Aperture=11,500=12,000=12%=P1.20D=1.2=Knowledge=Edu.=12 Dec.=Athena>>K=F.

Apex=2,000=20%=P2.00D=2.0=Nature=Matter=Moon=2 Feb= Cupid>N=C.
Makumaticology recognizes the peak of a thing as the moon or nature dimension in valency or power raised to -2. Apex is the peak of a thing as operant by natural law. Above this is the Mind which is a thing raised in valence of -1. This is supernatural law.

Apgarscore=7,500=8,000=80%=P8.00D=8.0=Econ.=Curr.=Busn.=Jupt.=8Aug=Zeus>E=v.
Aphasia=8,000=80%=P8.00D=8.0=Econ.=Curr.=Busn.=Jupt.=8Aug=Zeus>E=v.
Aphelion=6,500=7,000=70%=P7.00D=7.0=Lang.=Assets=Mars=6May=Pleiades.
Aphid=7,000=70%=P7.00D=7.0=Lang.=Assets=Mars=6May=Pleiades.
Aphorism=3,500=4,000=40%=P4.00D=4.0=Govt.=Creat.= 4 April=Hermes>>G=A4.

Aphrodisiac=4,000=40%=P4.00D=4.0=Govt.=Creat.= 4 April=Hermes>>G=A4.
Greek word is Aphrodite. She is the power of intensifying sexual desire arousal food & drug. The resultant shows she is a Creatocrat and government system of families and relations. Creatocracy is inspired by Aphrodite through intense sexual desire and sex transmutation. Napoleon Hill asserted it in the book Think and Grow Rich. Now it is proved.

Aphrodite=4,000=40%=P4.00D=4.0=Govt.=Creat.= 4 April=Hermes>>G=A4.
The Goddess of love and beauty. Love is power. Beauty is power. She lives in the realm of Hermes and functions governments as the female figure for the good of women. This means that she runs organizations and countries from the planet Mercury. She is the reason nations are referred to as "Her". Women are one of the gates of wisdom or Athena as we read in Proverbs 8, 9, 31. The Creatocracy is Aphrodite in governance manifested as the Mind Brick Castle of the Solar Crown of Castle Makupedia. Love women and Aphrodite is pleased and progresses the system. Against this there is no law.

Apia=7,500=8,000=80%=P8.00D=8.0=Econ.=Curr.=Busn.=Jupt.=8Aug=Zeus>E=v.
Apiary=4,500=5,000=50%=P5.00D=5.0=Law=Time=Venus=5May=Odite>>L=N.
Apices=2,000=20%=P2.00D=2.0=Nature=Matter=Moon=2 Feb= Cupid>N=C.
Apiculture=2,000=20%=P2.00D=2.0=Nature=Matter=Moon=2 Feb= Cupid>N=C.
Apiece=2,500=3,000=30%=P3.00D=3.0=Creativity=Star=Muses=3March=C=I.
Aplomb=1,500=15%=P1.50D=1.5=Authority = Solar Crown = Solar Core = 1 May = Maia.
Apnea=4,500=5,000=50%=P5.00D=5.0=Law=Time=Venus=5May=Odite>>L=N.
APO=1,500=15%=P1.50D=1.5=Authority = Solar Crown = Solar Core = 1 May = Maia.
Apocalypse=4,000=40%=P4.00D=4.0=Govt.=Creat.= 4 April=Hermes>>G=A4.
Apocrypha=10,500=11,000=11%=P1.10D=1.1=Idea=Brainchild=11 Nov.=Athena>K=F.
Apocryphal=5,000=50%=P5.00D=5.0=Law=Time=Venus=5May=Odite>>L=N.
Apogee=9,000=90%=P9.00D=9.0=Abstraction=Gods=Saturn=9Sept.>>A=Ø.
Apolitical=3,500=4,000=40%=P4.00D=4.0=Govt.=Creat.= 4 April=Hermes>>G=A4.

Apollo=8,500=9,000=90%=P9.00D=9.0=Abstraction=Gods=Saturn=9Sept.>>A=Ø.
The God of Prophecy music medicine and poetry. They are abstractions and are the same.

Apologetic=4,000=40%=P4.00D=4.0=Govt.=Creat.= 4 April=Hermes>>G=A4.
Apologia=2,500=3,000=30%=P3.00D=3.0=Creativity=Star=Muses=3March=C=I.
Apologize=4,500=5,000=50%=P5.00D=5.0=Law=Time=Venus=5May=Odite>>L=N.
Apology=7,500=8,000=80%=P8.00D=8.0=Econ.=Curr.=Busn.=Jupt.=8Aug=Zeus>E=v.
Apoplexy=8,500=9,000=90%=P9.00D=9.0=Abstraction=Gods=Saturn=9Sept.>>A=Ø.
Apostasy=4,500=5,000=50%=P5.00D=5.0=Law=Time=Venus=5May=Odite>>L=N.
A posteriori=4,000=40%=P4.00D=4.0=Govt.=Creat.= 4 April=Hermes>>G=A4.

Apostle=7,500=8,000=80%=P8.00D=8.0=Econ.=Curr.=Busn.=Jupt.=8Aug=Zeus>E=v.
Anyone who pioneers a cause is an apostle. An apostle owns 80% in benefits of the cause in the first instance and 100% in rights. 80% is the God rights bestowed upon such a person. Hence Peter Matthews-Akukalia is the apostle and God of Creatocracy.

Apostolic=4,000=40%=P4.00D=4.0=Govt.=Creat.= 4 April=Hermes>>G=A4.
Apostrophe(1)=11,000=11%=P1.10D=1.1=Idea=Brainchild=Invention=11 Nov.=Athena>K=F.

Apostrophe(2)=8,000=80%=P8.00D=8.0=Econ.=Curr.=Busn.=Jupt.=8Aug=Zeus>E=v.
As an abstraction in definition it shows that Zeus heads all abstractions or Gods.
There is nothing like an empty space nor zero but super zero, Mak zero, the Gods.
Expressed as 0 = Ø = A=Ø. This is the formula for determining the Mind of the Gods.

Apothecaries' measure=4,500=5,000=50%=P5.00D=5.0=Law=Venus=5May=Odite>>L=N.
Apothecaries' weight=10,000=1,000=100%=10.0=Physiclty.=Tech.=10 Oct.=Uranus=P=1Ø.
Apothecary=2,500=3,000=30%=P3.00D=3.0=Creativity=Star=Muses=3March=C=I.
Apothegm=1,500=15%=P1.50D=1.5=Authority = Solar Crown = Solar Core = 1 May = Maia.
Apothem=6,500=7,000=70%=P7.00D=7.0=Lang.=Assets=Mars=6May=Pleiades.

Apotheosis=7,000=70%=P7.00D=7.0=Lang.=Assets=Mars=6May=Pleiades.
Computing is precision and its invention as in Mind Computing made Peter Matthews - Akukalia the Mind God. He computed the code for genius as 3.3 and became the Genius God. His complete works is wrapped up in the concept of Creatocracy his order. Hence He is the God of Creatocracy Genius and Mind. The Solar Crown is his apotheosis. He makes Lords Goddesses Royalties and Oracles in the Creatocracy by investment commitment or training based on his absolute rights and ownership over his works deeds and rewards.

App.=2,500=3,000=30%=P3.00D=3.0=Creativity=Star=Muses=3March=C=I.
Appalachia=4,500=5,000=50%=P5.00D=5.0=Law=Time=Venus=5May=Odite>>L=N.
Appalachian Mountains=7,000=70%=P7.00D=7.0=Lang.=Assets=Mars=6May=Pleiades.
Appall=3,000=30%=P3.00D=3.0=Creativity=Star=Muses=3March=C=I.
Appaloosa=3,500=4,000=40%=P4.00D=4.0=Govt.=Creat.= 4 April=Hermes>>G=A4.
Apparatus=12,500= 13,000 = 13% = P1.30D = 1.3 = Solar Core =Faculty =13Jan.=Athena.
Apparel=4,000=40%=P4.00D=4.0=Govt.=Creat.= 4 April=Hermes>>G=A4.

Apparent=12,000=12,000=12%=P1.20D=1.2=Knowledge=Edu.=12 Dec.=Athena>>K=F.
Patent also relates to apparent and guided by the twelve dimensions. Hence Creatocracy is an invention by the calculations of the twelve dimensions of the Universe. Creatocracy is the Universe(s) binding on all persons systems and things in its jurisdiction. It is Athena manifested, Aphrodite functioned Apollo foreseen Athemis hunted and virgin protected guiding the Muses to inspire it in knowledge, Hermes prospered and Zeus protected. The Creatocracy is an invention by Mindtechnologies copyright and trademark of the author.

Apparition=3,000=30%=P3.00D=3.0=Creativity=Star=Muses=3March=C=I.
Appeal=15,000=15%=P1.50D=1.5=Authority = Solar Crown = Solar Core = 1 May = Maia.
Appear=10,000=1,000=100%=10.0=Physicality=Tech.=10 Oct.=Uranus=P=1Ø.
Appearance=5,500=5.5=80%=P5.50D=Earth-Midway=5 May=Gaia.
Appease=5,000=50%=P5.00D=5.0=Law=Time=Venus=5May=Odite>>L=N.
Appellant=3,500=4,000=40%=P4.00D=4.0=Govt.=Creat.= 4 April=Hermes>>G=A4.

Appellate=2,500=3,000=30%=P3.00D=3.0=Creativity=Star=Muses=3March=C=I.
Appellation=2,000=20%=P2.00D=2.0=Nature=Matter=Moon=2 Feb= Cupid>N=C.
Append=3,000=30%=P3.00D=3.0=Creativity=Star=Muses=3March=C=I.
Appendage=9,500=10,000=1,000=100%=10.0=Physicality=Tech.=10 Oct.=Uranus=P=1Ø.
Appendectomy=3,500=4,000=40%=P4.00D=4.0=Govt.=Creat.= 4 April=Hermes>>G=A4.
Appendicitis=2,500=3,000=30%=P3.00D=3.0=Creativity=Star=Muses=3March=C=I.
Appendix=5,500=5.5=80%=P5.50D=Earth-Midway=5 May=Gaia.
Appertain=2,500=3,000=30%=P3.00D=3.0=Creativity=Star=Muses=3March=C=I.

Appetite=4,500=5,000=50%=P5.00D=5.0=Law=Time=Venus=5May=Odite>>L=N.
One has an appetite when a desire strong wish or urge hits an interest of 45%-50%.

Appetizer=3,500=4,000=40%=P4.00D=4.0=Govt.=Creat.= 4 April=Hermes>>G=A4.
Appetizing=1,500=15%=P1.50D=1.5=Authority = Solar Crown = Solar Core = 1 May = Maia.
Applaud=4,000=40%=P4.00D=4.0=Govt.=Creat.= 4 April=Hermes>>G=A4.
Applause=4,000=40%=P4.00D=4.0=Govt.=Creat.= 4 April=Hermes>>G=A4.
Apple=16,000=16%=P1.60D=1.6=Incarnation=Mind of GOD=1 June = Maia.
Apple jack=2,500=3,000=30%=P3.00D=3.0=Creativity=Star=Muses=3March=C=I.
Apple sauce=3,500=4,000=40%=P4.00D=4.0=Govt.=Creat.= 4 April=Hermes>>G=A4.
Appliance=6,500=7,000=70%=P7.00D=7.0=Lang.=Assets=Mars=6May=Pleiades.
Applicable=2,500=3,000=30%=P3.00D=3.0=Creativity=Star=Muses=3March=C=I.
Applicant=1,500=15%=P1.50D=1.5=Authority = Solar Crown = Solar Core = 1 May = Maia.
Application=20,500=21,000=21%=P2.10D=2.1=3.0=Creativity=Star=Muses=2 Jan>>C=I.
Applicator=4,000=40%=P4.00D=4.0=Govt.=Creat.= 4 April=Hermes>>G=A4.
Applied=3,000=30%=P3.00D=3.0=Creativity=Star=Muses=3March=C=I.
Appliqué=8,000=80%=P8.00D=8.0=Econ.=Curr.=Busn.=Jupt.=8Aug=Zeus>E=v.
Apply=15,000=15%=P1.50D=1.5=Authority = Solar Crown = Solar Core = 1 May = Maia.
Appoint=6,500=7,000=70%=P7.00D=7.0=Lang.=Assets=Mars=6May=Pleiades.
Appointee=4,500=5,000=50%=P5.00D=5.0=Law=Time=Venus=5May=Odite>>L=N.
Appointive=4,000=40%=P4.00D=4.0=Govt.=Creat.= 4 April=Hermes>>G=A4.
Appointment=10,000=1,000=100%=10.0=Physicality=Tech.=10 Oct.=Uranus=P=1Ø.
Appomattox=10,000=1,000=100%=10.0=Physicality=Tech.=10 Oct.=Uranus=P=1Ø.
Apportion=4,000=40%=P4.00D=4.0=Govt.=Creat.= 4 April=Hermes>>G=A4.
Apposite=1,000=100%=10.0=1.0=Mind=Sun=1 January=Helios >> M=E4.
Apposition=15,000=15%=P1.50D=1.5=Authority = Solar Crown = Solar Core = 1May = Maia.
Appositive=1,500=15%=P1.50D=1.5=Authority = Solar Crown = Solar Core = 1 May = Maia.
Appraise=3,500=4,000=40%=P4.00D=4.0=Govt.=Creat.= 4 April=Hermes>>G=A4.
Appreciable=3,000=30%=P3.00D=3.0=Creativity=Star=Muses=3March=C=I.
Appreciate=7,500=8,000=80%=P8.00D=8.0=Econ.=Curr.=Busn.=Jupt.=8Aug=Zeus>E=v.
Appreciative=2,500=3,000=30%=P3.00D=3.0=Creativity=Star=Muses=3March=C=I.
Apprehend=4,000=40%=P4.00D=4.0=Govt.=Creat.= 4 April=Hermes>>G=A4.
Apprehensive=4,000=40%=P4.00D=4.0=Govt.=Creat.= 4 April=Hermes>>G=A4.
Apprentice=7,500=8,000=80%=P8.00D=8.0=Econ.=Curr.=Busn.=Jupt.=8Aug=Zeus>E=v.
Apprise=2,000=20%=P2.00D=2.0=Nature=Matter=Moon=2 Feb= Cupid>N=C.

Approach=13,500=14,000=14%=P1.40D=1.4=Mgt.=Solar Core=13 May=Athena>>SC=0.1

Approbation=1,000=100%=10.0=1.0=Mind=Sun=1 January=Helios >> M=E4.

Appropriate=15,000=15%=P1.50D=1.5=Authority = Solar Crown = Solar Core =1 May=Maia.

Appropriation=7,500=8,000=80%=P8.00D=8.0=Econ.=Busn.=Jupt.=8Aug=Zeus>E=v.

Approval=9,000=90%=P9.00D=9.0=Abstraction=Gods=Saturn=9Sept.>>A=Ø.

Approve=5,000=50%=P5.00D=5.0=Law=Time=Venus=5May=Odite>>L=N.

Approx.=1,000=100%=10.0=1.0=Mind=Sun=1 January=Helios >> M=E4.

Approximate=7,000=70%=P7.00D=7.0=Lang.=Assets=Mars=6May=Pleiades.

Appurtenance=7,000=70%=P7.00D=7.0=Lang.=Assets=Mars=6May=Pleiades.

Apr.=500=5%=P5.00D=5.0=Law=Time=Venus=5 May=Aphrodite>>L=N.

Apricot=7,500=8,000=80%=P8.00D=8.0=Econ.=Curr.=Busn.=Jupt.=8Aug=Zeus>E=v.

April=5,500=5.5=80%=P5.50D=Earth-Midway=5 May=Gaia.

April Fools' Day=4,500=5,000=50%=P5.00D=5.0=Law=Time=Venus=5May=Odite>>L=N.

A-priori=9,500=10,000=1,000=100%=10.0=Physicality=Tech.=10 Oct.=Uranus=P=1Ø.

Apron=11,500=12,000=12%=P1.20D=1.2=Knowledge=Education=12 Dec.=Athena>>K=F.

Apropos=4,000=40%=P4.00D=4.0=Govt.=Creat.= 4 April=Hermes>>G=A4.

Apropos of=1,000=100%=10.0=1.0=Mind=Sun=1 January=Helios >> M=E4.

Apse=5,500=5.5=80%=P5.50D=Earth-Midway=5 May=Gaia.

Apsis=6,000=60%=P6.00D=6.0=Man=Earth=Health=Royalty=6June=Gaia>M=M2.

Apt=8,500=9,000=90%=P9.00D=9.0=Abstraction=Gods=Saturn=9Sept.>>A=Ø.

Apt.=500=5%=P5.00D=5.0=Law=Time=Venus=5 May=Aphrodite>>L=N.

Aptitude=4,000=40%=P4.00D=4.0=Govt.=Creat.= 4 April=Hermes>>G=A4.

Apuleius Lucius=4,000=40%=P4.00D=4.0=Govt.=Creat.= 4 April=Hermes>>G=A4.

Aqaba Gulf of=6,500=7,000=70%=P7.00D=7.0=Lang.=Assets=Mars=6May=Pleiades.

Aqua=5,500=5.5=80%=P5.50D=Earth-Midway=5 May=Gaia.

Aquaculture=4,000=40%=P4.00D=4.0=Govt.=Creat.= 4 April=Hermes>>G=A4.

Aquamarine=6,000=60%=P6.00D=6.0=Man=Earth=Health=Royalty=6June=Gaia
>M=M2.

Aquanaut=4,500=5,000=50%=P5.00D=5.0=Law=Time=Venus=5May=Odite>>L=N.

Aqua plane=7,000=70%=P7.00D=7.0=Lang.=Assets=Mars=6May=Pleiades.

Aqua regia=8,000=80%=P8.00D=8.0=Econ.=Curr.=Busn.=Jupt.=8Aug=Zeus>E=v.

Aquarium=10,000=1,000=100%=10.0=Physicality=Tech.=10 Oct.=Uranus=P=1Ø.

Aquarius=6,000=60%=P6.00D=6.0=Man=Earth=Health=Royalty=6June=Gaia>M=M2.
A constellation that seems to represent mankind in the cycle of life. There is source of
power in water. The Sun is the eye of Zeus, Earth is his belly and water His word.

Aquatic=6,500=7,000=70%=P7.00D=7.0=Lang.=Assets=Mars=6May=Pleiades.

Aquatint=8,500=9,000=90%=P9.00D=9.0=Abstraction=Gods=Saturn=9Sept.>>A=Ø.

Aquavit=4,000=40%=P4.00D=4.0=Govt.=Creat.= 4 April=Hermes>>G=A4.

Aqua vitae=3,000=30%=P3.00D=3.0=Creativity=Star=Muses=3March=C=I.

Aqueduct=8,500=9,000=90%=P9.00D=9.0=Abstraction=Gods=Saturn=9Sept.>>A=Ø.

Aqueous=4,000=40%=P4.00D=4.0=Govt.=Creat.= 4 April=Hermes>>G=A4.

Aqueous humor=6,000=60%=P6.00D=6.0=Man=Earth=Health=Roy.=6June=Gaia>M=M2.
Aquifer=6,000=60%=P6.00D=6.0=Man=Earth=Health=Royalty=6June=Gaia>M=M2.
Aquiline=6,000=60%=P6.00D=6.0=Man=Earth=Health=Royalty=6June=Gaia>M=M2.
AquinasSt.Thomas=2,500=3,000=30%=P3.00D=3.0=Creativity=Star=Muses=3March=C=I
Aquino Corazón Cojuangco.=3,000=30%=P3.00D=3.0=Creatv.=Star=Muses=3March=C=I.
Aquitaine=6,000=60%=P6.00D=6.0=Man=Earth=Health=Royalty=6June=Gaia>M=M2.
Ar=3,000=30%=P3.00D=3.0=Creativity=Star=Muses=3March=C=I.
AR=2,500=3,000=30%=P3.00D=3.0=Creativity=Star=Muses=3March=C=I.
ar.=1,000=100%=10.0=1.0=Mind=Sun=1 January=Helios >> M=E4.
Ar.=1,500=15%=P1.50D=1.5=Authority = Solar Crown = Solar Core = 1 May = Maia.
-ar=3,000=30%=P3.00D=3.0=Creativity=Star=Muses=3March=C=I.
Arab=12,000=12,000=12%=P1.20D=1.2=Knowledge=Education=12 Dec.=Athena>>K=F.
Arab.=1,000=100%=10.0=1.0=Mind=Sun=1 January=Helios >> M=E4.
Arabesque=9,000=90%=P9.00D=9.0=Abstraction=Gods=Saturn=9Sept.>>A=Ø.
Arabia=6,000=60%=P6.00D=6.0=Man=Earth=Health=Royalty=6June=Gaia>M=M2.
Arabian Desert=6,000=60%=P6.00D=6.0=Man=Earth=Health=Roy.=6June=Gaia>M=M2.
Arabian Sea=5,500=5.5=80%=P5.50D=Earth-Midway=5 May=Gaia.
Arabic=11,500=12,000=12%=P1.20D=1.2=Knowledge=Education=12 Dec.=Athena>>K=F.
Arabic numeral=8,500=9,000=90%=P9.00D=9.0=Abstr.=Gods=Saturn=9Sept.>>A=Ø.
Arable=1,500=15%=P1.50D=1.5=Authority = Solar Crown = Solar Core = 1 May = Maia.
Arachnid=6,500=7,000=70%=P7.00D=7.0=Lang.=Assets=Mars=6May=Pleiades.
Arafat Yasir=4,000=40%=P4.00D=4.0=Govt.=Creat.= 4 April=Hermes>>G=A4.
Aragon=4,000=40%=P4.00D=4.0=Govt.=Creat.= 4 April=Hermes>>G=A4.
Araguaia=7,500=8,000=80%=P8.00D=8.0=Econ.=Curr.=Busn.=Jupt.=8Aug=Zeus>E=v.
Aral Sea=4,500=5,000=50%=P5.00D=5.0=Law=Time=Venus=5May=Odite>>L=N.
Aramaic=7,500=8,000=80%=P8.00D=8.0=Econ.=Curr.=Busn.=Jupt.=8Aug=Zeus>E=v.
Aran Islands=6,000=60%=P6.00D=6.0=Man=Earth=Health=Royalty=6June=Gaia>M=M2.
Arapaho=9,500=10,000=1,000=100%=10.0=Physicality=Tech.=10 Oct.=Uranus=P=1Ø.
Ararat Mount.=5,500=5.5=80%=P5.50D=Earth-Midway=5 May=Gaia.
Arawak=11,000=11%=P1.10D=1.1=Idea=Brainchild=Invention=11 Nov.=Athena>K=F.
Arawakan=10,000=1,000=100%=Physicality= Tech.=10 Oct.=Uranus=P=1Ø.

Arbiter=8,000=80%=P8.00D=8.0=Econ.=Curr.=Busn.=Jupt.=8Aug=Zeus>E=v.
Zeus is the arbiter of all things. The inventor of the Maks Currencies owns all economy.

Arbitrage=7,500=8,000=80%=P8.00D=8.0=Econ.=Curr.=Busn.=Jupt.=8Aug=Zeus>E=v.
Arbitrament=4,000=40%=P4.00D=4.0=Govt.=Creat.= 4 April=Hermes>>G=A4.
Arbitrary=7,000=70%=P7.00D=7.0=Lang.=Assets=Mars=6May=Pleiades.
Arbitrate=7,500=8,000=80%=P8.00D=8.0=Econ.=Curr.=Busn.=Jupt.=8Aug=Zeus>E=v.
Arbitrator=3,500=4,000=40%=P4.00D=4.0=Govt.=Creat.= 4 April=Hermes>>G=A4.
Arbor=4,500=5,000=50%=P5.00D=5.0=Law=Time=Venus=5May=Odite>>L=N.

Arboreal=4,000=40%=P4.00D=4.0=Govt.=Creat.= 4 April=Hermes>>G=A4.
By the cycle of life and teachings of the mind temple established in the Bible and Quran human beings come in different forms including trees. The Gods are arboreal in nature.

Arboretum=4,500=5,000=50%=P5.00D=5.0=Law=Time=Venus=5May=Odite>>L=N.
Arborvitae=5,500=5.5=80%=P5.50D=Earth-Midway=5 May=Gaia.
Arbovirus=6,000=60%=P6.00D=6.0=Man=Earth=Health=Royalty=6June=Gaia>M=M2.
Arbutus=1,500=15%=P1.50D=1.5=Authority = Solar Crown = Solar Core = 1 May = Maia.
Arc=11,500=12,000=12%=P1.20D=1.2=Knowledge=Education=12 Dec.=Athena>>K=F.
ARC(1)=10,500=11,000=11%=P1.10D=1.1=Idea=Brainchild=Invention=11 Nov.=Athena
    >K=F.
ARC(2)=1,500=15%=P1.50D=1.5=Authority = Solar Crown = Solar Core = 1 May = Maia.
Arcade=11,500=12,000=12%=P1.20D=1.2=Knowledge=Education=12 Dec.=Athena>>K=F.
Arcadia=5,500=5.5=80%=P5.50D=Earth-Midway=5 May=Gaia.

Arcana=5,500=5.5=80%=P5.50D=Earth-Midway=5 May=Gaia.
A specialized knowledge or detail that is mysterious to the average person. The Creatocracy is an arcana. Hence our institutions make it easier and affordable to learn it.

Arcane=3,000=30%=P3.00D=3.0=Creativity=Star=Muses=3March=C=I.
Arch(1)=18,000=18%=P1.80D=1.8=Solar Currency=MaksCurr.=1 Aug=Maia.
Arch(2)=4,000=40%=P4.00D=4.0=Govt.=Creat.= 4 April=Hermes>>G=A4.
Arch.=2,500=3,000=30%=P3.00D=3.0=Creativity=Star=Muses=3March=C=I.
Arch-=2,500=3,000=30%=P3.00D=3.0=Creativity=Star=Muses=3March=C=I.
-arch=1,500=15%=P1.50D=1.5=Authority = Solar Crown = Solar Core = 1 May = Maia.
Archeology=6,500=7,000=70%=P7.00D=7.0=Lang.=Assets=Mars=6May=Pleiades.
Archaic=11,500=12,000=12%=P1.20D=1.2=Knowledge=Education=12 Dec.=Athena>>K=F.
Archaism=3,000=30%=P3.00D=3.0=Creativity=Star=Muses=3March=C=I.

Archangel=5,000=50%=P5.00D=5.0=Law=Time=Venus=5May=Odite>>L=N.
Even in the angelic hierarchy level 5 is a speculation and next to the lowest order of things.

Archangel=1,000=100%=10.0=1.0=Mind=Sun=1 January=Helios >> M=E4.
Archbishop=3,000=30%=P3.00D=3.0=Creativity=Star=Muses=3March=C=I.
Archdeacon=7,500=8,000=80%=P8.00D=8.0=Econ.=Curr.=Busn.=Jupt.=8Aug=Zeus>E=v
Archdiocese=3,000=30%=P3.00D=3.0=Creativity=Star=Muses=3March=C=I.
Archduchess=3,500=4,000=40%=P4.00D=4.0=Govt.=Creat.= 4 April=Hermes>>G=A4.
Archduke=3,500=4,000=40%=P4.00D=4.0=Govt.=Creat.= 4 April=Hermes>>G=A4.
Archenemy=1,500=15%=P1.50D=1.5=Authority = Solar Crown = Solar Core = 1 May = Maia.
Archeology=1,500=15%=P1.50D=1.5=Authority = Solar Crown = Solar Core = 1 May = Maia.
Archer=4,000=40%=P4.00D=4.0=Govt.=Creat.= 4 April=Hermes>>G=A4.
Archerfish=8,500=9,000=90%=P9.00D=9.0=Abstraction=Gods=Saturn=9Sept.>>A=Ø.

Archetype=9,500=10,000=1,000=100%=10.0=Physicality=Tech.=10 Oct.=Uranus=P=1Ø.
Archetype is a prototype and must be physical and a technology to be realistic.

Archfiend=3,000=30%=P3.00D=3.0=Creativity=Star=Muses=3March=C=I.
Archiepiscopal=2,000=20%=P2.00D=2.0=Nature=Matter=Moon=2 Feb= Cupid>N=C.
Archimandrite=4,500=5,000=50%=P5.00D=5.0=Law=Time=Venus=5May=Odite>>L=N.
Archimedes=4,500=5,000=50%=P5.00D=5.0=Law=Time=Venus=5May=Odite>>L=N.
Archipelago=3,500=4,000=40%=P4.00D=4.0=Govt.=Creat.= 4 April=Hermes>>G=A4.
Archit.=1,000=100%=10.0=1.0=Mind=Sun=1 January=Helios >> M=E4.
Architect=6,500=7,000=70%=P7.00D=7.0=Lang.=Assets=Mars=6May=Pleiades.
Architectonics=5,500=5.5=80%=P5.50D=Earth-Midway=5 May=Gaia.

Architecture=7,500=8,000=80%=P8.00D=8.0=Econ.=Curr.=Jupt.=8Aug=Zeus>E=v.
The generational master plan for the Creatocratic architecture is expressed as >> Buildings =
Estates = Cities = Nations = Mindoms = The Creatocracy Republic = Paradise = MindGod.

Architrave=7,500=8,000=80%=P8.00D=8.0=Econ.=Curr.=Jupt.=8Aug=Zeus>E=v.
Archive=5,500=5.5=80%=P5.50D=Earth-Midway=5 May=Gaia.
Archivist=3,500=4,000=40%=P4.00D=4.0=Govt.=Creat.= 4 April=Hermes>>G=A4.
Arch rival=1,500=15%=P1.50D=1.5=Authority = Solar Crown = Solar Core = 1 May = Maia.
Archway=3,000=30%=P3.00D=3.0=Creativity=Star=Muses=3March=C=I.
Arcked=3,000=30%=P3.00D=3.0=Creativity=Star=Muses=3March=C=I.
Arcking=2,000=20%=P2.00D=2.0=Nature=Matter=Moon=2 Feb= Cupid>N=C.
Arch lamp=6,500=7,000=70%=P7.00D=7.0=Lang.=Assets=Mars=6May=Pleiades.
arctic=3,500=4,000=40%=P4.00D=4.0=Govt.=Creat.= 4 April=Hermes>>G=A4.
Artic=6,000=60%=P6.00D=6.0=Man=Earth=Health=Royalty=6June=Gaia>M=M2.
Arctic Archipelago=7,500=8,000=80%=P8.00D=8.0=Econ.=Busn.=Jupt.=8Aug=Zeus>E=v
Arctic Circle=7,000=70%=P7.00D=7.0=Lang.=Assets=Mars=6May=Pleiades.
Arctic Ocean=5,000=50%=P5.00D=5.0=Law=Time=Venus=5May=Odite>>L=N.
-ard or art=6,500=7,000=70%=P7.00D=7.0=Lang.=Assets=Mars=6May=Pleiades.
Ardennes=5,000=50%=P5.00D=5.0=Law=Time=Venus=5May=Odite>>L=N.
Ardent=5,000=50%=P5.00D=5.0=Law=Time=Venus=5May=Odite>>L=N.
Ardor=3,000=30%=P3.00D=3.0=Creativity=Star=Muses=3March=C=I.
Arduous=2,500=3,000=30%=P3.00D=3.0=Creativity=Star=Muses=3March=C=I.
Are(1)=6,500=7,000=70%=P7.00D=7.0=Lang.=Assets=Mars=6May=Pleiades.
Are(2)=2,000=20%=P2.00D=2.0=Nature=Matter=Moon=2 Feb= Cupid>N=C.
Area=12,500= 13,000 = 13% = P1.30D = 1.3 = Solar Core = Faculty = 13January=Athena.
Area Code=6,500=7,000=70%=P7.00D=7.0=Lang.=Assets=Mars=6May=Pleiades.
Area way=7,000=70%=P7.00D=7.0=Lang.=Assets=Mars=6May=Pleiades.
Arena=7,000=70%=P7.00D=7.0=Lang.=Assets=Mars=6May=Pleiades.
Arena theatre=5,500=5.5=80%=P5.50D=Earth-Midway=5 May=Gaia.
Aren't=1,000=100%=10.0=1.0=Mind=Sun=1 January=Helios >> M=E4.

Ares=3,000=30%=P3.00D=3.0=Creativity=Star=Muses=3March=C=I.
The Creatocracy believes that Ares was the Angel mentioned in Exodus 22:28, 23:20-25.
Proof that the Gods are real beings separated from the gods or Devils spoken by GOD.

Arg.=1,000=100%=10.0=1.0=Mind=Sun=1 January=Helios >> M=E4.
Argent=1,000=100%=10.0=1.0=Mind=Sun=1 January=Helios >> M=E4.
Argentina=12,000=12,000=12%=P1.20D=1.2=Knowledge=Edu.=12 Dec.=Athena>>K=F.
Argolis=5,000=50%=P5.00D=5.0=Law=Time=Venus=5May=Odite>>L=N.
Argon=16,000=16%=P1.60D=1.6=Incarnation=Mind of GOD=1 June = Maia.
Argonne=6,500=7,000=70%=P7.00D=7.0=Lang.=Assets=Mars=6May=Pleiades.
Argosy=3,500=4,000=40%=P4.00D=4.0=Govt.=Creat.= 4 April=Hermes>>G=A4.
Argot=4,000=40%=P4.00D=4.0=Govt.=Creat.= 4 April=Hermes>>G=A4.
Arguable=3,000=30%=P3.00D=3.0=Creativity=Star=Muses=3March=C=I.
Argue=10,000=1,000=100%=10.0=Physicality=Tech.=10 Oct.=Uranus=P=1Ø.
Argument= 13,000 = 13% = P1.30D = 1.3 = Solar Core = Faculty = 13January=Athena.
Argumentation=3,500=4,000=40%=P4.00D=4.0=Govt.=Creat.= 4 April=Hermes>>G=A4.
Argumentative=8,000=80%=P8.00D=8.0=Econ.=Curr.=Busn.=Jupt.=8Aug=Zeus>E=v.
Argyle=11,500=12,000=12%=P1.20D=1.2=Knowledge=Education=12 Dec.=Athena>>K=F.
Arhus=7,000=70%=P7.00D=7.0=Lang.=Assets=Mars=6May=Pleiades.
Aria=5,500=5.5=80%=P5.50D=Earth-Midway=5 May=Gaia.
-Arian=2,500=3,000=30%=P3.00D=3.0=Creativity=Star=Muses=3March=C=I.
Arid=3,000=30%=P3.00D=3.0=Creativity=Star=Muses=3March=C=I.

Aries=5,500=5.5=80%=P5.50D=Earth-Midway=5 May=Gaia.
A constellation in the Northern Hemisphere. Check with the God Aries of the Creatocracy.
This constellation is Maia the Great Goddess Mother of Aries whose sacrifice is a ram.

Aright=1,000=100%=10.0=1.0=Mind=Sun=1 January=Helios >> M=E4.
Aril=4,000=40%=P4.00D=4.0=Govt.=Creat.= 4 April=Hermes>>G=A4.
Arise=7,500=8,000=80%=P8.00D=8.0=Econ.=Curr.=Busn.=Jupt.=8Aug=Zeus>E=v.
Aristides "the Just"=4,500=5,000=50%=P5.00D=5.0=Law=Venus=5May=Odite>>L=N.

Aristocracy=8,000=80%=P8.00D=8.0=Econ.=Curr.=Busn.=Jupt.=8Aug=Zeus>E=v.
A hereditary ruling class and a government by the nobility of a privileged upper class.
The Creatocracy weighs and functions on the 10,000=1000=100% standards as the
highest ranking governance system. Interestingly Government in all its forms constitute
the third arm of the Creatocracy. The first is Royal by Intellectual Property in the
Inventor-Investor relationship. The second arm is the Press. Third is Government and
fourth is Labor. In the beginning GOD created establishes that everyone is a product
of creativity and a Creatocracy or Creative Governance practiced by the supernatural.
Hence Creatocracy is binds on everyone to be the best version of the self. The Creatocracy
is the Solar Crown.

PETER K. MATTHEWS - AKUKALIA

Aristophanes=3,000=30%=P3.00D=3.0=Creativity=Star=Muses=3March=C=I.
Aristotle=2,500=3,000=30%=P3.00D=3.0=Creativity=Star=Muses=3March=C=I.
Arithmetic=6,500=7,000=70%=P7.00D=7.0=Lang.=Assets=Mars=6May=Pleiades.
Arithmetic mean=6,500=7,000=70%=P7.00D=7.0=Lang.=Assets=Mars=6May=Pleiades.
-Arlum=4,500=5,000=50%=P5.00D=5.0=Law=Time=Venus=5May=Odite>>L=N.
Arius=3,500=4,000=40%=P4.00D=4.0=Govt.=Creat.= 4 April=Hermes>>G=A4.
Ariz.=1,000=100%=10.0=1.0=Mind=Sun=1 January=Helios >> M=E4.
Arizona=7,000=70%=P7.00D=7.0=Lang.=Assets=Mars=6May=Pleiades.
Ark=11,500=12,000=12%=P1.20D=1.2=Knowledge=Education=12 Dec.=Athena>>K=F.
Ark.=1,000=100%=10.0=1.0=Mind=Sun=1 January=Helios >> M=E4.
Arkansas=6,000=60%=P6.00D=6.0=Man=Earth=Health=Royalty=6June=Gaia>M=M2.
Arkansas River= 13,000 = 13% = P1.30D = 1.3 = Solar Core = Faculty = 13January=Athena.
Arkhangelsk=3,500=4,000=40%=P4.00D=4.0=Govt.=Creat.= 4 April=Hermes>>G=A4.
Arkwright Sir Richard=3,000=30%=P3.00D=3.0=Creativity=Star=Muses=3March=C=I.
Arlington=12,500= 13,000 = 13% = P1.30D = 1.3 = Solar Core = Faculty = 13Jan.=Athena.
Arm(1)=16,000=16%=P1.60D=1.6=Incarnation=Mind of GOD=1 June = Maia.
Arm(2)=15,000=15%=P1.50D=1.5=Authority = Solar Crown = Solar Core = 1 May = Maia.
Armada=2,000=20%=P2.00D=2.0=Nature=Matter=Moon=2 Feb= Cupid>N=C.
Armadillo=7,000=70%=P7.00D=7.0=Lang.=Assets=Mars=6May=Pleiades.
Armageddon=7,500=8,000=80%=P8.00D=8.0=Econ.=Busn.=Jupt.=8Aug=Zeus>E=v.
Armament=7,500=8,000=80%=P8.00D=8.0=Econ.=Curr.=Busn.=Jupt.=8Aug=Zeus>E=v.
Armature=18,500=19,000=19%=P1.90D=1.9=Planetary Energy=1 September = Maia.
Armchair=5,000=50%=P5.00D=5.0=Law=Time=Venus=5May=Odite>>L=N.
Armed forces=3,000=30%=P3.00D=3.0=Creativity=Star=Muses=3March=C=I.
Armenia=7,000=70%=P7.00D=7.0=Lang.=Assets=Mars=6May=Pleiades.
Armenian=7,500=8,000=80%=P8.00D=8.0=Econ.=Curr.=Busn.=Jupt.=8Aug=Zeus>E=v.
Armful=4,500=5,000=50%=P5.00D=5.0=Law=Time=Venus=5May=Odite>>L=N.
Armhole=3,500=4,000=40%=P4.00D=4.0=Govt.=Creat.= 4 April=Hermes>>G=A4.
Armistice=4,500=5,000=50%=P5.00D=5.0=Law=Time=Venus=5May=Odite>>L=N.
Armlet=6,000=60%=P6.00D=6.0=Man=Earth=Health=Royalty=6June=Gaia>M=M2.
Armoire=3,500=4,000=40%=P4.00D=4.0=Govt.=Creat.= 4 April=Hermes>>G=A4.
Armor=11,000=11%=P1.10D=1.1=Idea=Brainchild=Invention=11 Nov.=Athena>K=F.
Armorial=3,500=4,000=40%=P4.00D=4.0=Govt.=Creat.= 4 April=Hermes>>G=A4.
Armory=5,500=5.5=80%=P5.50D=Earth-Midway=5 May=Gaia.
Armpit=4,500=5,000=50%=P5.00D=5.0=Law=Time=Venus=5May=Odite>>L=N.
Armrest=2,500=3,000=30%=P3.00D=3.0=Creativity=Star=Muses=3March=C=I.
Armstrong, Louis Satchmo=3,000=30%=P3.00D=3.0=Creatv=Star=Muses=3March=CI.
Armstrong, Niel Alden=5,500=5.5=80%=P5.50D=Earth-Midway=5 May=Gaia.
Arm-twist=4,500=5,000=50%=P5.00D=5.0=Law=Time=Venus=5May=Odite>>L=N.

Army=10,000=1,000=100%=10.0=Physicality=Tech.=10 Oct.=Uranus=P=1Ø.
The Creatocracy comprises an army of Creative Scientist Professionals 100%.

Army ant=7,500=8,000=80%=P8.00D=8.0=Econ.=Curr.=Busn.=Jupt.=8Aug=Zeus>E=v.
Arnica=9,000=90%=P9.00D=9.0=Abstraction=Gods=Saturn=9Sept.>>A=Ø.
Arno=10,000=1,000=100%=10.0=Physicality=Tech.=10 Oct.=Uranus=P=1Ø.
Arnold Benedict=3,500=4,000=40%=P4.00D=4.0=Govt.=Creat.= 4 April=Hermes>>G=A4.
Arnold, Matthew=3,000=30%=P3.00D=3.0=Creativity=Star=Muses=3March=C=I.
Aroma= 13,000 = 13% = P1.30D = 1.3 = Solar Core = Faculty = 13January=Athena.
Arose=2,000=20%=P2.00D=2.0=Nature=Matter=Moon=2 Feb= Cupid>N=C.
Around=23,000=2,300=23%=Local Busn.=23 Days Monthly=2.3% Taxes daily income.
Arouse=6,500=7,000=70%=P7.00D=7.0=Lang.=Assets=Mars=6May=Pleiades.
Arpeggio=10,000=1,000=100%=10.0=Physicality=Tech.=10 Oct.=Uranus=P=1Ø.
Arr.=1,500=15%=P1.50D=1.5=Authority = Solar Crown = Solar Core = 1 May = Maia.
Arraign=6,000=60%=P6.00D=6.0=Man=Earth=Health=Royalty=6June=Gaia>M=M2.
Arrange=15,000=15%=P1.50D=1.5=Authority = Solar Crown = Solar Core = 1 May = Maia.
Arrant=2,500=3,000=30%=P3.00D=3.0=Creativity=Star=Muses=3March=C=I.
Arras=3,000=30%=P3.00D=3.0=Creativity=Star=Muses=3March=C=I.
Array=16,000=16%=P1.60D=1.6=Incarnation=Mind of GOD=1 June = Maia.
Arrears=6,500=7,000=70%=P7.00D=7.0=Lang.=Assets=Mars=6May=Pleiades.
Arrest=10,500=11,000=11%=P1.10D=1.1=Idea=Brainchild=Invention=11 Nov.=Athena
   >K=F.
Arresting=3,000=30%=P3.00D=3.0=Creativity=Star=Muses=3March=C=I.
Arrhythmia=4,500=5,000=50%=P5.00D=5.0=Law=Time=Venus=5May=Odite>>L=N.
Arrive=8,000=80%=P8.00D=8.0=Econ.=Curr.=Busn.=Jupt.=8Aug=Zeus>E=v.
Arrogant=3,000=30%=P3.00D=3.0=Creativity=Star=Muses=3March=C=I.
Arrogate=6,000=60%=P6.00D=6.0=Man=Earth=Health=Royalty=6June=Gaia>M=M2.
Arrow= 13,000 = 13% = P1.30D = 1.3 = Solar Core = Faculty = 13January=Athena.
Arrowhead=4,000=40%=P4.00D=4.0=Govt.=Creat.= 4 April=Hermes>>G=A4.
Arrowroot=8,000=80%=P8.00D=8.0=Econ.=Curr.=Busn.=Jupt.=8Aug=Zeus>E=v.
Arroyo=4,000=40%=P4.00D=4.0=Govt.=Creat.= 4 April=Hermes>>G=A4.
Arsenal=8,000=80%=P8.00D=8.0=Econ.=Curr.=Busn.=Jupt.=8Aug=Zeus>E=v.
Arsenic= 13,000 = 13% = P1.30D = 1.3 = Solar Core = Faculty = 13January=Athena.
Arson=5,500=5.5=80%=P5.50D=Earth-Midway=5 May=Gaia.
Art(1)=30,000=3,000=30%=P3.00D=3.0=Creativity=Star=Muses=3March=C=I.
Art(2)=6,000=60%=P6.00D=6.0=Man=Earth=Health=Royalty=6June=Gaia>M=M2.
Art.=1,500=15%=P1.50D=1.5=Authority = Solar Crown = Solar Core = 1 May = Maia.
-Art=2,000=20%=P2.00D=2.0=Nature=Matter=Moon=2 Feb= Cupid>N=C.
Art Deco=7,500=8,000=80%=P8.00D=8.0=Econ.=Curr.=Busn.=Jupt.=8Aug=Zeus>E=v.
Artefact=1,500=15%=P1.50D=1.5=Authority = Solar Crown = Solar Core = 1 May = Maia.

Artemis=5,500=5.5=80%=P5.50D=Earth-Midway=5 May=Gaia.
Artemis is the virgin Goddess of the hunt and the moon. She is the business hunter for the Creatocracy. She is also the twin sister of Apollo the God of light whose symbol is the flowery wreath. Alongside Cupid she directs the lunar PGI force for revelation from Gaia.

Arteriosclerosis=7,500=8,000=80%=P8.00D=8.0=Econ.=Busn.=Jupt.=8Aug=Zeus>E=v.
Artery=11,000=11%=P1.10D=1.1=Idea=Brainchild=Invention=11 Nov.=Athena>K=F.
Artesian well=7,000=70%=P7.00D=7.0=Lang.=Assets=Mars=6May=Pleiades.
Artful=3,500=4,000=40%=P4.00D=4.0=Govt.=Creat.= 4 April=Hermes>>G=A4.
Arthritis=3,000=30%=P3.00D=3.0=Creativity=Star=Muses=3March=C=I.
Arthro-=1,000=100%=10.0=1.0=Mind=Sun=1 January=Helios >> M=E4.
Arthropod=10,000=1,000=100%=10.0=Physicality=Tech.=10 Oct.=Uranus=P=1Ø.
Arthroscopy=4,500=5,000=50%=P5.00D=5.0=Law=Time=Venus=5May=Odite>>L=N.

Arthur=10,500=11,000=11%=P1.10D=1.1=Idea=Brainchild=Invention=11 Nov.=Athena>K=F.
Today we find him in the movie MERLIN. This movie predicts a time when emotions
would be measured as spoken by Merlin to Gauss. Castle Makupedia has fulfilled it.

Arthur, Chester Alan.=4,000=40%=P4.00D=4.0=Govt.=Creat.= 4 April=Hermes>>G=A4.
Anti choke=8,500=9,000=90%=P9.00D=9.0=Abstraction=Gods=Saturn=9Sept.>>A=Ø.
Article=16,000=16%=P1.60D=1.6=Incarnation=Mind of GOD=1 June = Maia.
Articular=2,500=3,000=30%=P3.00D=3.0=Creativity=Star=Muses=3March=C=I.
Articulate=16,500=17,000=17%=P1.70D=1.7=Solar Asset=Mind Computing =Pleiades.
Artifact=5,000=50%=P5.00D=5.0=Law=Time=Venus=5May=Odite>>L=N.
Artifice=4,000=40%=P4.00D=4.0=Govt.=Creat.= 4 April=Hermes>>G=A4.
Artificial=9,000=90%=P9.00D=9.0=Abstraction=Gods=Saturn=9Sept.>>A=Ø.
Artif. Intelligence =6,500=7,000=70%=P7.00D=7.0=Lang.=Assets=Mars=6May=Pleiades.
Artf.Respiratn=11,500=12,000=12%=P1.20D=1.2=Knowledge=Edu.=12Dec.=Athena>>K=F.
Artificial Selection=8,500=9,000=90%=P9.00D=9.0=Abstr.=Gods=Saturn=9Sept.>>A=Ø.
Artillery=6,500=7,000=70%=P7.00D=7.0=Lang.=Assets=Mars=6May=Pleiades.
Artisan=2,000=20%=P2.00D=2.0=Nature=Matter=Moon=2 Feb= Cupid>N=C.
Artist=9,000=90%=P9.00D=9.0=Abstraction=Gods=Saturn=9Sept.>>A=Ø.
Artiste=3,500=4,000=40%=P4.00D=4.0=Govt.=Creat.= 4 April=Hermes>>G=A4.
Artistry=2,500=3,000=30%=P3.00D=3.0=Creativity=Star=Muses=3March=C=I.
Artless=4,000=40%=P4.00D=4.0=Govt.=Creat.= 4 April=Hermes>>G=A4.
Arty=1,500=15%=P1.50D=1.5=Authority = Solar Crown = Solar Core = 1 May = Maia.
Aruba=5,500=5.5=80%=P5.50D=Earth-Midway=5 May=Gaia.
Arugula=1,000=100%=10.0=1.0=Mind=Sun=1 January=Helios >> M=E4.
Arum=5,000=50%=P5.00D=5.0=Law=Time=Venus=5May=Odite>>L=N.
-ary=3,000=30%=P3.00D=3.0=Creativity=Star=Muses=3March=C=I.
Aryan=11,500=12,000=12%=P1.20D=1.2=Knowledge=Edu.=12Dec.=Athena>>K=F.
as=28,500=30,000=3,000=30%=P3.00D=3.0=Creativity=Star=Muses=3March=C=I.
As=3,000=30%=P3.00D=3.0=Creativity=Star=Muses=3March=C=I.
As.=1,000=100%=10.0=1.0=Mind=Sun=1 January=Helios >> M=E4.
Asafetida=3,000=30%=P3.00D=3.0=Creativity=Star=Muses=3March=C=I.
Asama Mount.=5,500=5.5=80%=P5.50D=Earth-Midway=5 May=Gaia.
ASAP=2,000=20%=P2.00D=2.0=Nature=Matter=Moon=2 Feb= Cupid>N=C.
ASAT=1,000=100%=10.0=1.0=Mind=Sun=1 January=Helios >> M=E4.
Asbestos=6,000=60%=P6.00D=6.0=Man=Earth=Health=Royalty=6June=Gaia>M=M2.

Asbestosis=5,500=5.5=80%=P5.50D=Earth-Midway=5 May=Gaia.
ASCAP=3,500=4,000=40%=P4.00D=4.0=Govt.=Creat.= 4 April=Hermes>>G=A4.
Ascend=1,500=15%=P1.50D=1.5=Authority = Solar Crown = Solar Core = 1 May = Maia.
Ascendancy=1,500=15%=P1.50D=1.5=Authority = Solar Crown = Solar Core =1 May = Maia.
Ascendant=6,500=7,000=70%=P7.00D=7.0=Lang.=Assets=Mars=6May=Pleiades.
Ascension=9,500=10,000=1,000=100%=10.0=Physicality=Tech.=10 Oct.=Uranus=P=1Ø.
Ascent=3,500=4,000=40%=P4.00D=4.0=Govt.=Creat.= 4 April=Hermes>>G=A4.
Ascertain=4,000=40%=P4.00D=4.0=Govt.=Creat.= 4 April=Hermes>>G=A4.
Ascetic=5,500=5.5=80%=P5.50D=Earth-Midway=5 May=Gaia.
ASCII=13,500=14,000=14%=P1.40D=1.4=Mgt.=Solar Core=13 May=Athena>>SC=0.1
Ascorbic Acid=10,000=1,000=100%=10.0=Physicality=Tech.=10 Oct.=Uranus=P=1Ø.
Ascot=7,000=70%=P7.00D=7.0=Lang.=Assets=Mars=6May=Pleiades.
Ascribe=4,500=5,000=50%=P5.00D=5.0=Law=Time=Venus=5May=Odite>>L=N.
ASE=1,500=15%=P1.50D=1.5=Authority = Solar Crown = Solar Core = 1 May = Maia.
-ase=3,500=4,000=40%=P4.00D=4.0=Govt.=Creat.= 4 April=Hermes>>G=A4.
Aseptic=2,000=20%=P2.00D=2.0=Nature=Matter=Moon=2 Feb= Cupid>N=C.

Asexual=7,000=70%=P7.00D=7.0=Lang.=Assets=Mars=6May=Pleiades.
Computing is an asexual union between men and the Gods. Managed by the Pleiades.
When we compute abstraction phenomena we are in a sexual relation with the spirits. Thus
revelations inspirations reasoning and thinking abilities are given to us in the process.
There is no special ability to compute and measure without first a comprehensive study.

As for=1,500=15%=P1.50D=1.5=Authority = Solar Crown = Solar Core = 1 May = Maia.
Ash(1)=12,000=12%=P1.20D=1.2=Knowledge=Edu.=12Dec.=Athena>>K=F.
Ash(2)=7,000=70%=P7.00D=7.0=Lang.=Assets=Mars=6May=Pleiades.
Ashamed=5,000=50%=P5.00D=5.0=Law=Time=Venus=5May=Odite>>L=N.

Ashanti(1)=5,500=5.5=80%=P5.50D=Earth-Midway=5 May=Gaia.
Gaia is middle earth. Note Ashanti is central or middle Ghana. Earlier study on Ghana
shows she resides in Africa as well. This aligns with the Ashanti people. Our discovery.

Ashanti(2)=6,500=7,000=70%=P7.00D=7.0=Lang.=Assets=Mars=6May=Pleiades.
Ashen=3,500=4,000=40%=P4.00D=4.0=Govt.=Creat.= 4 April=Hermes>>G=A4.
Ashkenazi=5,000=50%=P5.00D=5.0=Law=Time=Venus=5May=Odite>>L=N.
Ashkhabad=5,500=5.5=80%=P5.50D=Earth-Midway=5 May=Gaia.
Ashlar=4,500=5,000=50%=P5.00D=5.0=Law=Time=Venus=5May=Odite>>L=N.
Ashore=2,500=3,000=30%=P3.00D=3.0=Creativity=Star=Muses=3March=C=I.
Ashram=4,500=5,000=50%=P5.00D=5.0=Law=Time=Venus=5May=Odite>>L=N.
Ashtray=4,000=40%=P4.00D=4.0=Govt.=Creat.= 4 April=Hermes>>G=A4.
Ash Wednesday=5,000=50%=P5.00D=5.0=Law=Time=Venus=5May=Odite>>L=N.
Ashy=3,500=4,000=40%=P4.00D=4.0=Govt.=Creat.= 4 April=Hermes>>G=A4.
Asia=11,000=11%=P1.10D=1.1=Idea=Brainchild=Invention=11 Nov.=Athena>K=F.

Asia Minor=5,500=5.5=80%=P5.50D=Earth-Midway=5 May=Gaia.
Asian=22,500=2,300=23%=Local Business=23 Days Monthly=2.3% Taxes daily income.
Asian American=4,000=40%=P4.00D=4.0=Govt.=Creat.= 4 April=Hermes>>G=A4.
Asiatic=500=5%=P5.00D=5.0=Law=Time=Venus=5 May=Aphrodite>>L=N.
Aside=11,500=12,000=12%=P1.20D=1.2=Knowledge=Edu.=12Dec.=Athena>>K=F.
Aside from=1,500=15%=P1.50D=1.5=Authority = Solar Crown = Solar Core = 1 May = Maia.
Asinine=1,000=100%=10.0=1.0=Mind=Sun=1 January=Helios >> M=E4.
Ask=6,500=7,000=70%=P7.00D=7.0=Lang.=Assets=Mars=6May=Pleiades.
Askance=4,000=40%=P4.00D=4.0=Govt.=Creat.= 4 April=Hermes>>G=A4.
Askew=2,000=20%=P2.00D=2.0=Nature=Matter=Moon=2 Feb= Cupid>N=C.
ASL=1,500=15%=P1.50D=1.5=Authority = Solar Crown = Solar Core = 1 May = Maia.
Aslant=500=5%=P5.00D=5.0=Law=Time=Venus=5 May=Aphrodite>>L=N.
Asleep=2,000=20%=P2.00D=2.0=Nature=Matter=Moon=2 Feb= Cupid>N=C.
Asmara=5,500=5.5=80%=P5.50D=Earth-Midway=5 May=Gaia.
Asocial=6,000=60%=P6.00D=6.0=Man=Earth=Health=Royalty=6June=Gaia>M=M2.
As of=3,500=4,000=40%=P4.00D=4.0=Govt.=Creat.= 4 April=Hermes>>G=A4.
Asp=4,000=40%=P4.00D=4.0=Govt.=Creat.= 4 April=Hermes>>G=A4.
Asparagus=5,500=5.5=80%=P5.50D=Earth-Midway=5 May=Gaia.
A.S.P.C.A=4,500=5,000=50%=P5.00D=5.0=Law=Time=Venus=5May=Odite>>L=N.
Aspect=10,500=11,000=11%=P1.10D=1.1=Idea=Brainchild=Invention=11 Nov.=Athena>K=F.
Aspen=6,500=7,000=70%=P7.00D=7.0=Lang.=Assets=Mars=6May=Pleiades.
Asperity=2,000=20%=P2.00D=2.0=Nature=Matter=Moon=2 Feb= Cupid>N=C.
Aspersion=1,500=15%=P1.50D=1.5=Authority = Solar Crown = Solar Core = 1 May = Maia.
Asphalt=7,500=8,000=80%=P8.00D=8.0=Econ.=Curr.=Busn.=Jupt.=8Aug=Zeus>E=v.
Asphodel=5,500=5.5=80%=P5.50D=Earth-Midway=5 May=Gaia.
Asphyxia=9,000=90%=P9.00D=9.0=Abstraction=Gods=Saturn=9Sept.>>A=Ø.
Asphyxiate=1,500=15%=P1.50D=1.5=Authority = Solar Crown = Solar Core = 1 May = Maia.
Aspic=6,000=60%=P6.00D=6.0=Man=Earth=Health=Royalty=6June=Gaia>M=M2.
Aspidistra=3,500=4,000=40%=P4.00D=4.0=Govt.=Creat.= 4 April=Hermes>>G=A4.
Aspirant=3,000=30%=P3.00D=3.0=Creativity=Star=Muses=3March=C=I.
Aspirate=11,000=11%=P1.10D=1.1=Idea=Brainchild=Invention=11 Nov.=Athena>K=F.

Aspiration=11,000=11%=P1.10D=1.1=Idea=Brainchild=Invention=11 Nov.=Athena>K=F.
The Creatocracy is the Peak of Aspiration measured as the state of Godly Perfection which in other words is the apotheosis of Mind sovereignty. Apex is peak measured in nature of things as 2.0. Aspiration is the attainment of the status of an inventor-God by the creation of a measurement and computing system in abstraction of Athena. Makupedia is the Peak of Aspiration in all things. This is how Athena became married to Castle Makupedia, the Peak of Aspiration in all things and the God of Creatocracy PETER MATTHEWS-AKUKALIA.

Aspirator=7,000=70%=P7.00D=7.0=Lang.=Assets=Mars=6May=Pleiades.
Aspire=3,000=30%=P3.00D=3.0=Creativity=Star=Muses=3March=C=I.

Aspirin=10,000=1,000=100%=10.0=Physicality=Tech.=10 Oct.=Uranus=P=1Ø.
We learn that Aspirin was originally a trademark. The Creatocracy is now a trademark owned by Peter Matthews - Akukalia, Castle Makupedia, the God of Creatocracy. Successful computation of the genius code as 3.3 made the Genius God and His discovery and invention of Mind Computing in the Creative Sciences made him the Mind God.

Asquith Herbert Henry=3,500=4,000=40%=P4.00D=4.0.=Creat.=4April=Hermes>>G=A4.
Ass=9,500=10,000=1,000=100%=10.0=Physicality=Tech.=10 Oct.=Uranus=P=1Ø.
Assail=1,500=15%=P1.50D=1.5=Authority = Solar Crown = Solar Core = 1 May = Maia.
Assassin=3,500=4,000=40%=P4.00D=4.0=Govt.=Creat.= 4 April=Hermes>>G=A4.
Assassinate=6,500=7,000=70%=P7.00D=7.0=Lang.=Assets=Mars=6May=Pleiades.
Assault=9,500=10,000=1,000=100%=10.0=Physicality=Tech.=10 Oct.=Uranus=P=1Ø.
Assault&battery=4,500=5,000=50%=P5.00D=5.0=Law=Time=Venus=5May=Odite>>L=N.
Assay=9,000=90%=P9.00D=9.0=Abstraction=Gods=Saturn=9Sept.>>A=Ø.
Assemblage=15,000=15%=P1.50D=1.5=Authority = Solar Crown=Solar Core=1 May= Maia.
Assemble=4,500=5,000=50%=P5.00D=5.0=Law=Time=Venus=5May=Odite>>L=N.
Assembler=9,000=90%=P9.00D=9.0=Abstraction=Gods=Saturn=9Sept.>>A=Ø.
Assembly=13,500=14,000=14%=P1.40D=1.4=Mgt.=Solar Core=13 May=Athena>>SC=0.1
Assembly line=8,500=9,000=90%=P9.00D=9.0=Abstr.=Gods=Saturn=9Sept.>>A=Ø.
Assent=1,500=15%=P1.50D=1.5=Authority = Solar Crown = Solar Core = 1 May = Maia.

Assert=6,000=60%=P6.00D=6.0=Man=Earth=Health=Royalty=6June=Gaia>M=M2.
Assert is royalty. The author of the Creatocracy Bank asserts his rights to God of Creatocracy, owner of the Creatocracy Bank and Most Sovereign Emperor, Creatocratic Nations of Paradise aka Paradise Nations. He is the King in white and the Solar Crown of Castle Makupedia. His royalty rights are by birth day, family and works.

Assertion=2,500=3000=3,000=30%=P3.00D=3.0=Creativity=Star=Muses=3March=C=I.
Assertions belong to the realm of Creativity and so is Creatocratic in nature.

Assess=9,000=90%=P9.00D=9.0=Abstraction=Gods=Saturn=9Sept.>>A=Ø.
To assess is a Godship right to evaluate esp. for taxation, set the amount of (a tax or fine), to charge with a tax or fine, to make a judgment about, to assist as judge). This is exactly what the God of Creatocracy has done and achieved by the Creatocracy Bank. Note He wrote the formulas for abstraction as A=Ø, for Economy as E=V and Nature as N=C etc.
He invented the study of the Creative Sciences where Creative Scientists assess the psychology potentials creativity and career for persons in a Mind Assessment Test. Psychology = personality & emotional balance. Potentials = Talents & Ideas. Career = Natural Works Ability capacity & Capabilities. Career = Income. Predictability is probably the greatest benchmark for the Mind Assessment Tests systems and modules. Highly abstract computational and yet verifiable by the slightest instance of things known.

Asset=11,000=11%=P1.10D=1.1=Idea=Brainchild=Invention=11 Nov.=Athena>K=F.
Assets are granted by Athena. It is believed that Castle is the greatest asset of theGods and Man. Hence the Creatocracy is the greatest assets ever known assertively. The real assets are ideas inventions brainchild discovery and their translation to works such as books from which knowledge is born and new industries created. The Creatocracy has over 1 billion assets in job opportunities training and thought processes. The Creatocracy Bank is one. Athena is the Goddess of wisdom practical arts and warfare. Greek mythology confirms she does mental warfare and loves writings. We conclude that Athena means assets. The marriage of Castle to Athena means the ownership of all assets by laws of GOD.

Asseverate=2,000=20%=P2.00D=2.0=Nature=Matter=Moon=2 Feb= Cupid>N=C.
Assiduous=3,000=30%=P3.00D=3.0=Creativity=Star=Muses=3March=C=I.
Assign=12,000=12%=P1.20D=1.2=Knowledge=Edu.=12Dec.=Athena>>K=F.
Assignation=3,500=4,000=40%=P4.00D=4.0=Govt.=Creat.= 4 April=Hermes>>G=A4.
Assignment=3,000=30%=P3.00D=3.0=Creativity=Star=Muses=3March=C=I.
Assimilate=7,500=8,000=80%=P8.00D=8.0=Econ.=Curr.=Busn.=Jupt.:8Aug=Zeus>E=v.
Assiniboin=8,000=80%=P8.00D=8.0=Econ.=Curr.=Busn.=Jupt.=8Aug=Zeus>E=v.
Assist=4,500=5,000=50%=P5.00D=5.0=Law=Time=Venus=5May=Odite>>L=N.
Assistant=5,000=50%=P5.00D=5.0=Law=Time=Venus=5May=Odite>>L=N.
Assize=9,500=10,000=1,000=100%=10.0=Physicality=Tech.=10 Oct.=Uranus=P=1Ø.
Assn.=500=5%=P5.00D=5.0=Law=Time=Venus=5 May=Aphrodite>>L=N.
Assoc.=1,000=100%=10.0=1.0=Mind=Sun=1 January=Helios >> M=E4.
Associate=10,500=11,000=11%=P1.10D=1.1=Idea=Brainchild=Invent=11 Nov.=Athena>K=F.
Association=6,500=7,000=70%=P7.00D=7.0=Lang.=Assets=Mars=6May=Pleiades.
Associative=4,500=5,000=50%=P5.00D=5.0=Law=Time=Venus=5May=Odite>>L=N.
Assonance=4,000=40%=P4.00D=4.0=Govt.=Creat.= 4 April=Hermes>>G=A4.
Assort=4,000=40%=P4.00D=4.0=Govt.=Creat.= 4 April=Hermes>>G=A4.
Assorted=2,000=20%=P2.00D=2.0=Nature=Matter=Moon=2 Feb= Cupid>N=C.
Assortment=4,500=5,000=50%=P5.00D=5.0=Law=Time=Venus=5May=Odite>>L=N.
Asst.=500=5%=P5.00D=5.0=Law=Time=Venus=5 May=Aphrodite>>L=N.
Assuage=4,000=40%=P4.00D=4.0=Govt.=Creat.= 4 April=Hermes>>G=A4.
Assume=5,500=5.5=80%=P5.50D=Earth-Midway=5 May=Gaia.
Assumed=3,000=30%=P3.00D=3.0=Creativity=Star=Muses=3March=C=I.
Assuming=1,000=100%=10.0=1.0=Mind=Sun=1 January=Helios >> M=E4.
Assumption=12,500= 13,000 = 13% = P1.30D = 1.3 = Solar Core = Faculty = 13Jan.=Athena.
Assurance=7,500=8,000=80%=P8.00D=8.0=Econ.=Curr.=Busn.=Jupt.=8Aug=Zeus>E=v.
Assure=26,500=30,000=3,000=30%=P3.00D=3.0=Creativity=Star=Muses=3March=C=I.
Assured=2,000=20%=P2.00D=2.0=Nature=Matter=Moon=2 Feb= Cupid>N=C.
Assyria=7,500=8,000=80%=P8.00D=8.0=Econ.=Busn.=Jupt.=8Aug=Zeus>E=v.
Assyrian=6,000=60%=P6.00D=6.0=Man=Earth=Health=Royalty=6June=Gaia>M=M2.
Astatine=8,500=9,000=90%=P9.00D=9.0=Abstraction=Gods=Saturn=9Sept.>>A=Ø.

Aster=9,500=10,000=1,000=100%=10.0=Physicality=Tech.=10 Oct.=Uranus=P=1Ø.
Aster is star in Greek. It is a transmutation midpoint between the abstract and the physical.

We can reason that the star is the medium through which life is continued in a cycle of life. What is known as reincarnation, eternal life, everlasting life, immortality. Stars are spirits we see and the signs of things useful for the computation of abstract phenomena such as the mind, nature and the twelve dimensions of the Creatocracy or universe. Gen.1:14-16. The Makupedian word for the Universe in relation to the GOD and the Gods is Creatocracy.

Asterisk=9,000=90%=P9.00D=9.0=Abstraction=Gods=Saturn=9Sept.>>A=Ø.
Asterisk>>Gk.asteriskos,dim astēr, dim star. It is observably a 5-point star that speculates. The Makstar in the Creatocracy are the 4, 8, 12, 24 point star. The 4-point star is known as the Quartet star from which the Quartet Principle was created and the CCLT gauge for measuring human emotions was invented by Peter Matthews-Akukalia in his Oracle book.

Astern=4,500=5,000=50%=P5.00D=5.0=Law=Time=Venus=5May=Odite>>L=N.

Asteroid=8,000=80%=P8.00D=8.0=Econ.=Curr.=Busn.=Jupt.=8Aug=Zeus>E=v.
Asteroids are 8 point stars indicating currency business Jupiter and Zeus.
4>>Quartet star. 8>>Zeus-Muses. 12>>Universe. 24>>Highest Universe>>Creatocracy.

Asthma=7,500=8,000=80%=P8.00D=8.0=Econ.=Curr.=Busn.=Jupt.=8Aug=Zeus>E=v.
Astigmatism=8,500=9,000=90%=P9.00D=9.0=Abstraction=Gods=Saturn=9Sept.>>A=Ø.
Astir=1,000=100%=10.0=1.0=Mind=Sun=1 January=Helios >> M=E4.
Astonish=3,500=4,000=40%=P4.00D=4.0=Govt.=Creat.= 4 April=Hermes>>G=A4.
Astor John Jacob=4,500=5,000=50%=P5.00D=5.0=Law=Time=Venus=5May=Odite>L=N.
Astor, Nancy Witcher Langhorne=8,500=9,000=90%=P9.00D=Gods=9Sept.>>A=Ø.
Astound=2,000=20%=P2.00D=2.0=Nature=Matter=Moon=2 Feb= Cupid>N=C.
Astraddle=500=5%=P5.00D=5.0=Law=Time=Venus=5 May=Aphrodite>>L=N.
astrakhan=6,500=7,000=70%=P7.00D=7.0=Lang.=Assets=Mars=6May=Pleiades.
Astrakhan=6,000=60%=P6.00D=6.0=Man=Earth=Health=Royalty=6June=Gaia>M=M2.
Astral=2,500=3,000=30%=P3.00D=3.0=Creativity=Star=Muses=3March=C=I.
Astray=7,500=8,000=80%=P8.00D=8.0=Econ.=Curr.=Busn.=Jupt.=8Aug=Zeus>E=v.
Astride=3,500=4,000=40%=P4.00D=4.0=Govt.=Creat.= 4 April=Hermes>>G=A4.
Astringent=8,500=9,000=90%=P9.00D=9.0=Abstraction=Gods=Saturn=9Sept.>>A=Ø.
Astro-=2,500=3,000=30%=P3.00D=3.0=Creativity=Star=Muses=3March=C=I.
Astrol.=1,000=100%=10.0=1.0=Mind=Sun=1 January=Helios >> M=E4.
Astrolabe=6,000=60%=P6.00D=6.0=Man=Earth=Health=Royalty=6June=Gaia>M=M2.
Astrology=9,500=10,000=1,000=100%=10.0=Physicality=Tech.=10 Oct.=Uranus=P=1Ø.
Astron.=10,000=1,000=100%=Physicality= Tech.=10 Oct.=Uranus=P=1Ø.
Astronaut=5,500=5.5=80%=P5.50D=Earth-Midway=5 May=Gaia.
Astronautics=3,500=4,000=40%=P4.00D=4.0=Govt.=Creat.= 4 April=Hermes>>G=A4.
Astronomical=3,500=4,000=40%=P4.00D=4.0=Govt.=Creat.= 4 April=Hermes>>G=A4.
Astronomical unit=9,500=10,000=1,000=100%=10.0=Phys.=Tech.=10 Oct.=Uranus=P=1Ø.

Astronomy=7,000=70%=P7.00D=7.0=Lang.=Assets=Mars=6May=Pleiades.
For astronomy, Peter Matthews - Akukalia, Castle Makupedia invented the cosmic science known as Psychoastronomy to study the link between the cosmic and human mind. Through this satellite tracking systems were developed and universal quotients were successfully computed. The World Digital Dictionary is a product of Psychoastronomy. The principles of Psychoastronomy gives us the rights to establish and own the World Psychoastronomy College & Laboratories under the Creatocracy Universities Union.

Astrophysics=5,000=50%=P5.00D=5.0=Law=Time=Venus=5May=Odite>>L=N.

Astro Turf=4,000=40%=P4.00D=4.0=Govt.=Creat.= 4 April=Hermes>>G=A4.
A trademark for an artificial grasslike ground covering. In the same vein the Solar Crown, Castle Makupedia of Mind Bricks and the logo of Makupedia are the trademarks of the Creatocracy, De-Royal Makupedia Limited and Peter Matthews-Akukalia.

Astute=3,000=30%=P3.00D=3.0=Creativity=Star=Muses=3March=C=I.
Asunciòn=5,000=50%=P5.00D=5.0=Law=Time=Venus=5May=Odite>>L=N.
Asunder=5,000=50%=P5.00D=5.0=Law=Time=Venus=5May=Odite>>L=N.
As well as=4,000=40%=P4.00D=4.0=Govt.=Creat.= 4 April=Hermes>>G=A4.
Asylum=15,500=16%=P1.60D=1.6=Cycle of Life=Incarnation=Mind of GOD= 1June= Maia.
Asymmetrical=1,000=100%=10.0=1.0=Mind=Sun=1 January=Helios >> M=E4.
Asymptomatic=3,500=4,000=40%=P4.00D=4.0=Govt.=Creat.= 4 April=Hermes>>G=A4.
Asymptote=5,500=5.5=80%=P5.50D=Earth-Midway=5 May=Gaia.
At(1)=17,500=18,000=18%=P1.80D=1.8=Solar Currency=MaksCurr.=1 Aug=Maia.
At(2)=2,000=20%=P2.00D=2.0=Nature=Matter=Moon=2 Feb= Cupid>N=C.
At=3,000=30%=P3.00D=3.0=Creativity=Star=Muses=3March=C=I.
At.=500=5%=P5.00D=5.0=Law=Time=Venus=5 May=Aphrodite>>L=N.
Atavism=6,000=60%=P6.00D=6.0=Man=Earth=Health=Royalty=6June=Gaia>M=M2.
Ate=2,000=20%=P2.00D=2.0=Nature=Matter=Moon=2 Feb= Cupid>N=C.
-Ate(1)=10,000=1,000=100%=10.0=Physicality=Tech.=10 Oct.=Uranus=P=1Ø.
-Ate(2)=6,500=7,000=70%=P7.00D=7.0=Lang.=Assets=Mars=6May=Pleiades.
Atelier=4,000=40%=P4.00D=4.0=Govt.=Creat.= 4 April=Hermes>>G=A4.
Athabaska=11,000=11%=P1.10D=1.1=Idea=Brainchild=Invention=11 Nov.=Athena>K=F.
Athabaskan=10,000=1,000=100%=10.0=Physicality=Tech.=10 Oct.=Uranus=P=1Ø.
Atheism=4,500=5,000=50%=P5.00D=5.0=Law=Time=Venus=5May=Odite>>L=N.

Athena=5,000=50%=P5.00D=5.0=Law=Time=Venus=5May=Odite>>L=N.
The Goddess of wisdom, the practical arts and warfare. THE CREATOCRACY a collection of Disean plays declares her married to Castle Makupedia the human whom through apotheosis of Peter Matthews - Akukalia emerged the God of Creatocracy Genius and Mind. She is so loved and cherished by him that he appointed her aegis of the Creatocracy.

It is believed that she was the gift reward of the Universe to him for his labors and works. The resultant shows Athena manages the law of things. Athena is the blind woman of law and time who believes in justice fairness and equity. She works with Aphrodite to dispense. 50% shows that she is the boundary of all things including the solar core and planet core.

Athenaeum=4,500=5,000=50%=P5.00D=5.0=Law=Time=Venus=5May=Odite>>L=N.
An institution for the promotion of learning is the temple of Athena. She is the faculty.

Athens=12,000=12%=P1.20D=1.2=Knowledge=Edu.=12Dec.=Athena>>K=F.
Atherosclerosis=9,500=10,000=1,000=100%=10.0=Phys.=Tech.=10 Oct.=Uranus=P=1Ø.
Athirst=3,000=30%=P3.00D=3.0=Creativity=Star=Muses=3March=C=I.
Athlete=3,500=4,000=40%=P4.00D=4.0=Govt.=Creat.= 4 April=Hermes>>G=A4.
Athlete's foot=8,500=9,000=90%=P9.00D=9.0=Abstraction=Gods=Saturn=9Sept.>>A=Ø.
Athletic=5,500=5.5=80%=P5.50D=Earth-Midway=5 May=Gaia.
Athletics=5,000=50%=P5.00D=5.0=Law=Time=Venus=5May=Odite>>L=N.
Athletic supporter=5,500=5.5=80%=P5.50D=Earth-Midway=5 May=Gaia.
Athwart=5,000=50%=P5.00D=5.0=Law=Time=Venus=5May=Odite>>L=N.
Atilt=2,000=20%=P2.00D=2.0=Nature=Matter=Moon=2 Feb= Cupid>N=C.
-ation=5,500=5.5=80%=P5.50D=Earth-Midway=5 May=Gaia.
-ative=3,000=30%=P3.00D=3.0=Creativity=Star=Muses=3March=C=I.
Atlanta=4,500=5,000=50%=P5.00D=5.0=Law=Time=Venus=5May=Odite>>L=N.
Atlantic City=4,000=40%=P4.00D=4.0=Govt.=Creat.= 4 April=Hermes>>G=A4.
Atlantic Ocean=11,000=11%=P1.10D=1.1=Idea=Brainchild=Invention=11 Nov.=Athena>K=F.

Atlantis=55,000=5.5=80%=P5.50D=Earth-Midway=5 May=Gaia.
A legendary sunken island in the Atlantic Ocean W of Gibraltar. It was sunk by Gaia.

---

atlas=3,500=4,000=40%=P4.00D=4.0=Govt.=Creat.= 4 April=Hermes>>G=A4.
After Atlas, legendary king of N Africa. Evidence of the cycle of life from Atlas the God.

Atlas=6,000=60%=P6.00D=6.0=Man=Earth=Health=Royalty=6June=Gaia>M=M2.
Greek mythology teaches He was Father to the Pleiades. He is a God who holds up the pillars of the Universe. He is the decree GOD spoke about that holds the Earth. Proverbs 8, 9 & Job 38. Decrees are either governments law or royalty. Atlas shows that royalty of the Gods keeps the universe in place. Royalty is everything and is first arm of the Creatocracy.

Atlas Mountains=4,500=5,000=50%=P5.00D=5.0=Law=Time=Venus=5May=Odite>>L=N.
Atlati=4,500=5,000=50%=P5.00D=5.0=Law=Time=Venus=5May=Odite>>L=N.

ATM=1,500=15%=P1.50D=1.5=Authority = Solar Crown = Solar Core = 1 May = Maia.
Maia inspired the ATM technology for ease in financial transactions. She is the ATM.

Atmosphere= 13,000 = 13% = P1.30D = 1.3 = Solar Core = Faculty = 13January=Athena.
Atmospherics=4,500=5,000=50%=P5.00D=5.0=Law=Time=Venus=5May=Odite>>L=N.
At.no.=1,000=100%=10.0=1.0=Mind=Sun=1 January=Helios >> M=E4.
Atoll=4,000=40%=P4.00D=4.0=Govt.=Creat.= 4 April=Hermes>>G=A4.
Atom=12,000=12%=P1.20D=1.2=Knowledge=Edu.=12Dec.=Athena>>K=F.
Atom bomb=11,000=11%=P1.10D=1.1=Idea=Brainchild=Invention=11 Nov.=Athena>K=F.
Atomic=7,000=70%=P7.00D=7.0=Lang.=Assets=Mars=6May=Pleiades.
Atomic bomb=2,000=20%=P2.00D=2.0=Nature=Matter=Moon=2 Feb= Cupid>N=C.

Atomic energy=1,500=15%=P1.50D=1.5=Authority = Solar Crown=Solar Core=1 May=Maia.
Maia controls the atomic energy and inspired it for human usefulness and good. The
Creatocracy owns the universal rights to it as a one-world government by GOD and Man.

Atomic number=4,000=40%=P4.00D=4.0=Govt.=Creat.= 4 April=Hermes>>G=A4.

Atomic weight=8,000=80%=P8.00D=8.0=Econ.=Curr.=Busn.=Jupt.=8Aug=Zeus>E=v.
Zeus energy makes up 80% of all atomic weights. (8.0*Atomic weight) gives the solar
weight of the element. Normal atomic weight of element - 80% of the element gives the
quantum of energy from the hands of Zeus. GOD sustains all things by light from Him.
Psalm 84:11 confirms that GOD is a Sun and Shield (Moon). This is the proof.

Atomize=6,000=60%=P6.00D=6.0=Man=Earth=Health=Royalty=6June=Gaia>M=M2.
Atomizer=4,000=40%=P4.00D=4.0=Govt.=Creat.= 4 April=Hermes>>G=A4.
Atom smasher=2,000=20%=P2.00D=2.0=Nature=Matter=Moon=2 Feb= Cupid>N=C.
Atonal=3,500=4,000=40%=P4.00D=4.0=Govt.=Creat.= 4 April=Hermes>>G=A4.
Atone=2,000=20%=P2.00D=2.0=Nature=Matter=Moon=2 Feb= Cupid>N=C.

Atonement=4,000=40%=P4.00D=4.0=Govt.=Creat.= 4 April=Hermes>>G=A4.
All atonement in cash and in kind actually go to Hermes the God of merchandise.

Atop=3,000=30%=P3.00D=3.0=Creativity=Star=Muses=3March=C=I.
-ator=4,000=40%=P4.00D=4.0=Govt.=Creat.= 4 April=Hermes>>G=A4.
-atory=6,500=7,000=70%=P7.00D=7.0=Lang.=Assets=Mars=6May=Pleiades.
ATP=3,500=4,000=40%=P4.00D=4.0=Govt.=Creat.= 4 April=Hermes>>G=A4.
Atrium=12,000=12%=P1.20D=1.2=Knowledge=Edu.=12Dec.=Athena>>K=F.
Atrocious=5,500=5.5=80%=P5.50D=Earth-Midway=5 May=Gaia.
Atrocity=7,000=70%=P7.00D=7.0=Lang.=Assets=Mars=6May=Pleiades.

Atrophy=6,000=60%=P6.00D=6.0=Man=Earth=Health=Royalty=6June=Gaia>M=M2.
A waste away of bodily tissue organ or part. Gaia does this. She is the health Goddess.
She must be studied to know her symbols and appeased in such extreme cases. Exodus
talks about GOD taking away our diseases and Jesus (Hermes) healing our infirmities.

Atropine=9,000=90%=P9.00D=9.0=Abstraction=Gods=Saturn=9Sept.>>A=Ø.

Attach=10,500=11,000=11%=P1.10D=1.1=Idea=Brainchild=Invention=11 Nov.=Athena>K=F. Athena (Wisdom) promises to be attached in affection and loyalty to her betrothed. This is established by the wealth of wisdom works assets and wealth seen in the Creatocracy.

Attaché=7,000=70%=P7.00D=7.0=Lang.=Assets=Mars=6May=Pleiades.
Attaché case=4,000=40%=P4.00D=4.0=Govt.=Creat.= 4 April=Hermes>>G=A4.
Attachment=15,500=16%=P1.60D=1.6=Cycle of Life=Incarn.=Mind of GOD=1June= Maia.
Attack= 13,000 = 13% = P1.30D = 1.3 = Solar Core = Faculty = 13January=Athena.
Attain=2,000=20%=P2.00D=2.0=Nature=Matter=Moon=2 Feb= Cupid>N=C.
Attainder=6,500=7,000=70%=P7.00D=7.0=Lang.=Assets=Mars=6May=Pleiades.
Attaint=3,500=4,000=40%=P4.00D=4.0=Govt.=Creat.= 4 April=Hermes>>G=A4.
Attar=3,000=30%=P3.00D=3.0=Creativity=Star=Muses=3March=C=I.
Attempt=8,000=80%=P8.00D=8.0=Econ.=Curr.=Busn.=Jupt.=8Aug=Zeus>E=v.
Attend=8,000=80%=P8.00D=8.0=Econ.=Curr.=Busn.=Jupt.=8Aug=Zeus>E=v.
Attendance=3,500=4,000=40%=P4.00D=4.0=Govt.=Creat.= 4 April=Hermes>>G=A4.
Attendant=8,500=9,000=90%=P9.00D=9.0=Abstraction=Gods=Saturn=9Sept.>>A=Ø.
Attention=13,500=14,000=14%=P1.40D=1.4=Mgt.=Solar Core=13 May=Athena>>SC=0.1
Attenuate=5,000=50%=P5.00D=5.0=Law=Time=Venus=5May=Odite>>L=N.
Attest=14,500=15,000=15%=P1.50D=1.5=Authority=Solar Crown=SC.=1 May= Maia.
attic=6,500=7,000=70%=P7.00D=7.0=Lang.=Assets=Mars=6May=Pleiades.
Attic=5,000=50%=P5.00D=5.0=Law=Time=Venus=5May=Odite>>L=N.
Attica=4,500=5,000=50%=P5.00D=5.0=Law=Time=Venus=5May=Odite>>L=N.
Attila=4,500=5,000=50%=P5.00D=5.0=Law=Time=Venus=5May=Odite>>L=N.
Attire=3,500=4,000=40%=P4.00D=4.0=Govt.=Creat.= 4 April=Hermes>>G=A4.
Attitude=16,000=16%=P1.60D=1.6=Cycle of Life=Incarnation=Mind of GOD= 1June= Maia.
Attlee Clement Richard=3,500=4,000=40%=P4.00D=4.0=Govt.=4April=Hermes>>G=A4.
Attn.=500=5%=P5.00D=5.0=Law=Time=Venus=5 May=Aphrodite>>L=N.
Attorney=6,500=7,000=70%=P7.00D=7.0=Lang.=Assets=Mars=6May=Pleiades.
Attorney at law=1,000=100%=10.0=1.0=Mind=Sun=1 January=Helios >> M=E4.
Attorney general=6,000=60%=P6.00D=6.0=Man=Earth=Royalty=6June=Gaia>M=M2.

Attract=5,500=5.5=80%=P5.50D=Earth-Midway=5 May=Gaia.
Gaia of the Earth and royalty gives blessings by granting the favor and power to attract.

Attraction=9,000=90%=P9.00D=9.0=Abstraction=Gods=Saturn=9Sept.>>A=Ø.
We establish that attraction is a vital blessing of the Gods bestowed on a person. One who cannot be attractive to others cannot win their love support or favor. Then a curse occurs. There is clearly no interest nor attraction without thought and its components.
See Magnetic Force. Ref. book >> Psychoastronomy, the psychonomy of relationships.

Attrib.=1,500=15%=P1.50D=1.5=Authority = Solar Crown = Solar Core = 1 May = Maia.
Attribute=12,500= 13,000 = 13% = P1.30D = 1.3 = Solar Core = Faculty = 13Jan.=Athena.
Attributive=15,000=15%=P1.50D=1.5=Authority = Solar Crown = Solar Core = 1 May = Maia.
Attrit=5,500=5.5=80%=P5.50D=Earth-Midway=5 May=Gaia.
Attrition=13,500=14,000=14%=P1.40D=1.4=Mgt.=Solar Core=13 May=Athena>>SC=0.1
Attu=4,000=40%=P4.00D=4.0=Govt.=Creat.= 4 April=Hermes>>G=A4.
Attucks Crispus=4,500=5,000=50%=P5.00D=5.0=Law=Time=Venus=5May=Odite>>L=N.
Attune=2,500=3,000=30%=P3.00D=3.0=Creativity=Star=Muses=3March=C=I.
atty.=500=5%=P5.00D=5.0=Law=Time=Venus=5 May=Aphrodite>>L=N.
Atty.=1,500=15%=P1.50D=1.5=Authority = Solar Crown = Solar Core = 1 May = Maia.
Atwt=10,000=1,000=100%=10.0=Physicality=Tech.=10 Oct.=Uranus=P=1Ø.
Atypical=2,500=3,000=30%=P3.00D=3.0=Creativity=Star=Muses=3March=C=I.
Au=3,000=30%=P3.00D=3.0=Creativity=Star=Muses=3March=C=I.
Auburn=1,500=15%=P1.50D=1.5=Authority = Solar Crown = Solar Core = 1 May = Maia.
Auckland=6,500=7,000=70%=P7.00D=7.0=Lang.=Assets=Mars=6May=Pleiades.
Aucourant=2,000=20%=P2.00D=2.0=Nature=Matter=Moon=2 Feb= Cupid>N=C.
Auction=10,500=11,000=11%=P1.10D=1.1=Idea=Brainchild=Inventn.=11 Nov.=Athena>K=F.
Audacious=4,500=5,000=50%=P5.00D=5.0=Law=Time=Venus=5May=Odite>>L=N.
Auden W(ystan) H(ugh).=4,000=40%=P4.00D=4.0=Govt.= 4April=Hermes>>G=A4.
Audial=4,000=40%=P4.00D=4.0=Govt.=Creat.= 4 April=Hermes>>G=A4.
Audible=3,000=30%=P3.00D=3.0=Creativity=Star=Muses=3March=C=I.
Audience=12,500= 13,000 = 13% = P1.30D = 1.3 = Solar Core = Faculty = 13Jan.=Athena.
Audio=10,000=1,000=100%=10.0=Physicality=Tech.=10 Oct.=Uranus=P=1Ø.
Audio-=2,000=20%=P2.00D=2.0=Nature=Matter=Moon=2 Feb= Cupid>N=C.
Audio book=5,000=50%=P5.00D=5.0=Law=Time=Venus=5May=Odite>>L=N.
Audio cassette=2,000=20%=P2.00D=2.0=Nature=Matter=Moon=2 Feb= Cupid>N=C.
Audio frequency=8,500=9,000=90%=P9.00D=9.0=Abst.=Gods=Saturn=9Sept.>>A=Ø.
Audiology=5,000=50%=P5.00D=5.0=Law=Time=Venus=5May=Odite>>L=N.
Audiophile=6,000=60%=P6.00D=6.0=Man=Earth=Health=Royalty=6June=Gaia>M=M2.
Audiotape=5,500=5.5=80%=P5.50D=Earth-Midway=5 May=Gaia.
Audiovisual=6,500=7,000=70%=P7.00D=7.0=Lang.=Assets=Mars=6May=Pleiades.
Audit=12,000=12%=P1.20D=1.2=Knowledge=Edu.=12Dec.=Athena>>K=F.
Audition=10,500=11,000=11%=P1.10D=1.1=Idea=Brainchild=Inventn.=11 Nov.=Athena
   >K=F.
Auditor=4,500=5,000=50%=P5.00D=5.0=Law=Time=Venus=5May=Odite>>L=N.
Auditorium=6,500=7,000=70%=P7.00D=7.0=Lang.=Assets=Mars=6May=Pleiades.
Auditory=5,000=50%=P5.00D=5.0=Law=Time=Venus=5May=Odite>>L=N.
Audubon John James=4,000=40%=P4.00D=4.0=Govt.=Creat.= 4April=Hermes>>G=A4.
Auf Wiedersehen=500=5%=P5.00D=5.0=Law=Time=Venus=5 May=Aphrodite>>L=N.
Aug.=500=5%=P5.00D=5.0=Law=Time=Venus=5 May=Aphrodite>>L=N.
Auger=5,500=5.5=80%=P5.50D=Earth-Midway=5 May=Gaia.
Aught(1)=1,000=100%=10.0=1.0=Mind=Sun=1 January=Helios >> M=E4.
Aught(2)=2,500=3,000=30%=P3.00D=3.0=Creativity=Star=Muses=3March=C=I.
Augment=5,500=5.5=80%=P5.50D=Earth-Midway=5 May=Gaia.
Augratin=6,000=60%=P6.00D=6.0=Man=Earth=Health=Royalty=6June=Gaia>M=M2.

Augsburg=5,000=50%=P5.00D=5.0=Law=Time=Venus=5May=Odite>>L=N.
Augur=9,500=10,000=1,000=100%=10.0=Physicality=Tech.=10 Oct.=Uranus=P=1Ø.
Augury=4,000=40%=P4.00D=4.0=Govt.=Creat.= 4 April=Hermes>>G=A4.
August=3,500=4,000=40%=P4.00D=4.0=Govt.=Creat.= 4 April=Hermes>>G=A4.
Augusta=6,000=60%=P6.00D=6.0=Man=Earth=Health=Royalty=6June=Gaia>M=M2.
Augustine=5,000=50%=P5.00D=5.0=Law=Time=Venus=5May=Odite>>L=N.

Augustus Octavian=8,000=80%=P8.00D=8.0=Econ.=Curr.=Busn.=Jupt.=8Aug=Zeus>E=v.
1st Emperor of Rome. Defeated Mark Anthony and Cleopatra in 31B.C. Zeus controlled.
Peter Matthews - Akukalia is the World's 1st Creative Scientist. Most Sovereign and 1st
Emperor of the Creatocratic Nations of Paradise. God of Creatocracy Genius & Mind.

Au jus=3,500=4,000=40%=P4.00D=4.0=Govt.=Creat.= 4 April=Hermes>>G=A4.
Auk=8,000=80%=P8.00D=8.0=Econ.=Curr.=Busn.=Jupt.=8Aug=Zeus>E=v.
Auld lang syne=3,000=30%=P3.00D=3.0=Creativity=Star=Muses=3March=C=I.
Aunt=4,500=5,000=50%=P5.00D=5.0=Law=Time=Venus=5May=Odite>>L=N.
Au pair=8,500=9,000=90%=P9.00D=9.0=Abstraction=Gods=Saturn=9Sept.>>A=Ø.
Aura=8,500=9,000=90%=P9.00D=9.0=Abstraction=Gods=Saturn=9Sept.>>A=Ø.
Aural(1)=3,000=30%=P3.00D=3.0=Creativity=Star=Muses=3 March=C=I.
Aural(2)=3,000=30%=P3.00D=3.0=Creativity=Star=Muses=3 March=C=I.
Aurar=1,500=15%=P1.50D=1.5=Authority = Solar Crown = Solar Core = 1 May = Maia.
Aurelian=4,000=40%=P4.00D=4.0=Govt.=Creat.= 4 April=Hermes>>G=A4.
Aureole=2,000=20%=P2.00D=2.0=Nature=Matter=Moon=2 Feb= Cupid>N=C.
Aurevoir=500=5%=P5.00D=5.0=Law=Time=Venus=5 May=Aphrodite>>L=N.
Auricle=8,000=80%=P8.00D=8.0=Econ.=Curr.=Busn.=Jupt.=8Aug=Zeus>E=v.
Auricular=9,500=10,000=1,000=100%=10.0=Physicality=Tech.=10 Oct.=Uranus=P=1Ø.
Aurora=2,500=3,000=30%=P3.00D=3.0=Creativity=Star=Muses=3 March=C=I.
Aurora(1)=3,500=4,000=40%=P4.00D=4.0=Govt.=Creat.= 4 April=Hermes>>G=A4.
Aurora(2)=5,000=50%=P5.00D=5.0=Law=Time=Venus=5May=Odite>>L=N.
Aurora Australis=7,000=70%=P7.00D=7.0=Lang.=Assets=Mars=6May=Pleiades.
Aurora borealis=10,000=1,000=100%=10.0=Physicality=Tech.=10 Oct.=Uranus=P=1Ø.
Auscultation=5,000=50%=P5.00D=5.0=Law=Time=Venus=5May=Odite>>L=N.
Auspice=5,000=50%=P5.00D=5.0=Law=Time=Venus=5May=Odite>>L=N.
Auspicious=2,000=20%=P2.00D=2.0=Nature=Matter=Moon=2 Feb= Cupid>N=C.
Aust.=1,000=100%=10.0=1.0=Mind=Sun=1 January=Helios >> M=E4.
Austen Jane=2,000=20%=P2.00D=2.0=Nature=Matter=Moon=2 Feb= Cupid>N=C.
Austere=9,000=90%=P9.00D=9.0=Abstraction=Gods=Saturn=9Sept.>>A=Ø.
Austerlitz=3,000=30%=P3.00D=3.0=Creativity=Star=Muses=3 March=C=I.
Austin=5,500=5.5=80%=P5.50D=Earth-Midway=5 May=Gaia.
Austin, StephenFuller=4,500=5,000=50%=P5.00D=5.0=Law=Time=5May=Odite>>L=N.
Austl.=1,000=100%=10.0=1.0=Mind=Sun=1 January=Helios >> M=E4.
Austral=500=5%=P5.00D=5.0=Law=Time=Venus=5 May=Aphrodite>>L=N.
Australasia=7,000=70%=P7.00D=7.0=Lang.=Assets=Mars=6May=Pleiades.

Australia=16,000=16%=P1.60D=1.6=Cycle of Life=Incarnation=Mind of GOD= 1June= Maia.
Australian=7,500=8,000=80%=P8.00D=8.0=Econ.=Curr.=Busn.=Jupt.=8Aug=Zeus>E=v.
Australia Alps.=3,500=4,000=40%=P4.00D=4.0=Govt.=Creat.= 4 April=Hermes>>G=A4.
Australoid=14,000=14%=P1.40D=1.4=Mgt.=Solar Core=13 May=Athena>>SC=0.1
Austria=7,000=70%=P7.00D=7.0=Lang.=Assets=Mars=6May=Pleiades.
Austria-Hungary=4,500=5,000=50%=P5.00D=5.0=Law=Time=Venus=5May=Odite >>L=N.
Austro-Asiatic=7,000=70%=P7.00D=7.0=Lang.=Assets=Mars=6May=Pleiades.
Austronesia=5,000=50%=P5.00D=5.0=Law=Time=Venus=5May=Odite>>L=N.
Austronesian=9,500=10,000=1,000=100%=10.0=Phys.=Tech.=10 Oct.=Uranus=P=1Ø.
Aut-=1,500=15%=P1.50D=1.5=Authority = Solar Crown = Solar Core = 1 May = Maia.

Autarchy=500=5%=P5.00D=5.0=Law=Time=Venus=5 May=Aphrodite>>L=N.
Autarchy means self-governing. The Creatocracy fits well. Careful reasoning shows that Creatocracy involves and is involved in all forms of Government through one means or the other. It is democratic aristocratic communistic autocratic socialistic feudal autarchist monarchical...Creatocracy is therefore everything and binds everything and everyone.

Authentic=11,000=11%=P1.10D=1.1=Idea=Brainchild=Inventn.=11 Nov.=Athena>K=F.
Authenticate=3,500=4,000=40%=P4.00D=4.0=Govt.=Creat.= 4 April=Hermes>>G=A4.

Author=8,000=80%=P8.00D=8.0=Econ.=Curr.=Busn.=Jupt.=8Aug=Zeus>E=v.
His Creative Excellency & Godship Peter Matthews-Akukalia aka Castle Makupedia is the author of the Creatocracy. Owner of the Creatocracy© systems and is the God of Creatocracy universal. He is the Most Sovereign Emperor, Sovereign Creatocratic Republic of Paradise aka Paradise Nations. He owns the study of Creative & Psycho-Social Sciences.

Authoritarian=4,000=40%=P4.00D=4.0=Govt.=Creat.= 4 April=Hermes>>G=A4.
Authoritative=5,000=50%=P5.00D=5.0=Law=Time=Venus=5May=Odite>>L=N.
Authority=19,000=19%=P1.90D=1.9=Planetary Energy=1 September = Maia.

Authorization=5,500=5.5=80%=P5.50D=Earth-Midway=5 May=Gaia.
Authorize=8,500=9,000=90%=P9.00D=9.0=Abstraction=Gods=Saturn=9Sept.>>A=Ø.
Autism=10,500=11,000=11%=P1.10D=1.1=Idea=Brainchild=Inventn.=11 Nov.=Athena>K=F.
Auto=1,000=100%=10.0=1.0=Mind=Sun=1 January=Helios >> M=E4.
Auto-=2,500=3,000=30%=P3.00D=3.0=Creativity=Star=Muses=3 March=C=I.
Autobahn=2,000=20%=P2.00D=2.0=Nature=Matter=Moon=2 Feb= Cupid>N=C.
Autobiography=4,500=5,000=50%=P5.00D=5.0=Law=Time=Venus=5May=Odite>>L=N.
Autochthonous=2,500=3,000=30%=P3.00D=3.0=Creativity=Star=Muses=3 March=C=I.

Autocracy=4,000=40%=P4.00D=4.0=Govt.=Creat.= 4 April=Hermes>>G=A4.
The Creatocracy is the highest form of autocracy since it is an invention of the author.

Autodidact=2,500=3,000=30%=P3.00D=3.0=Creativity=Star=Muses=3 March=C=I.
An autodidact is someone who is self taught. Peter Matthews - Akukalia is an autodidact.

Autograph=8,000=80%=P8.00D=8.0=Econ.=Curr.=Busn.=Jupt.=8Aug=Zeus>E=v.
Autoimmune=9,000=90%=P9.00D=9.0=Abstraction=Gods=Saturn=9Sept.>>A=Ø.
Automate=3,500=4,000=40%=P4.00D=4.0=Govt.=Creat.= 4 April=Hermes>>G=A4.
Automated teller machine=13,000=13%=P1.30D=1.3=SC Gates=Faculty=13Jan.=Athena.
Automatic=13,500=14,000=14%=P1.40D=1.4=Mgt.=Solar Core=13 May=Athena>>SC=0.1
Automatic pilot=7,000=70%=P7.00D=7.0=Lang.=Assets=Mars=6May=Pleiades.
Automation=11,500=12,000=12%=P1.20D=1.2=Knowledge=Edu.=12Dec.=Athena>>K=F.
Automatism=4,000=40%=P4.00D=4.0=Govt.=Creat.= 4 April=Hermes>>G=A4.
Automatize=1,500=15%=P1.50D=1.5=Authority = Solar Crown = Solar Core = 1 May = Maia.
Automaton=7,500=8,000=80%=P8.00D=8.0=Econ.=Curr.=Busn.=Jupt.=8Aug=Zeus>E=v.

Automobile=8,000=80%=P8.00D=8.0=Econ.=Curr.=Busn.=Jupt.=8Aug=Zeus>E=v.
Now we see that the automobile is a direct inspiration of Zeus >> Jehovah >> Allah >> ZeJeAl. The Book of Revelation shows how John the beloved saw the beasts with teeth as that of a human and fire coming out from its behind. These are automobiles. It shows that the cosmic energy functions on the laws of pure equivalence meaning that all abstract elements are represented by physical and material things or matter. Today Mammon is money, Mind is the Sun, spirit is software and knowledge is the school by dimensions. Now to know the future of an automobile we synchronize the figure into the plate number.

Automotive=6,000=60%=P6.00D=6.0=Man=Earth=Health=Royalty=6June=Gaia>M=M2.
Autonomic nervous system=7,500=8,000=80%=P8.00D=8.0.=Jupiter=8Aug=Zeus>E=v.
Autonomous=3,500=4,000=40%=P4.00D=4.0=Govt.=Creat.= 4 April=Hermes>>G=A4.
Autopilot=1,000=100%=10.0=1.0=Mind=Sun=1 January=Helios >> M=E4.
Autopsy=5,000=50%=P5.00D=5.0=Law=Time=Venus=5May=Odite>>L=N.
Autosome=4,000=40%=P4.00D=4.0=Govt.=Creat.= 4 April=Hermes>>G=A4.
Autosuggestion=8,500=9,000=90%=P9.00D=9.0=Abstr.=Gods=Saturn=9Sept.>>A=Ø.
Autotroph=5,500=5.5=80%=P5.50D=Earth-Midway=5 May=Gaia.
Autumn=7,000=70%=P7.00D=7.0=Lang.=Assets=Mars=6May=Pleiades.
Auvergne=4,000=40%=P4.00D=4.0=Govt.=Creat.= 4 April=Hermes>>G=A4.
Aux.=1,000=100%=10.0=1.0=Mind=Sun=1 January=Helios >> M=E4.
Auxiliary=11,500=12,000=12%=P1.20D=1.2=Knowledge=Edu.=12Dec.=Athena>>K=F.
Auxiliary verb=11,500=12,000=12%=P1.20D=1.2=Knowledge=Edu.=12Dec.=Athena>>K=F.
Auxin=3,000=30%=P3.00D=3.0=Creativity=Star=Muses=3 March=C=I.
Av=5,000=50%=P5.00D=5.0=Law=Time=Venus=5May=Odite>>L=N.
AV=2,500=3,000=30%=P3.00D=3.0=Creativity=Star=Muses=3 March=C=I.

av.=2,000=20%=P2.00D=2.0=Nature=Matter=Moon=2 Feb= Cupid>N=C.
a.v.=8,000=80%=P8.00D=8.0=Econ.=Curr.=Busn.=Jupt.=8Aug=Zeus>E=v.
Avail=5,500=5.5=80%=P5.50D=Earth-Midway=5 May=Gaia.
Available=5,000=50%=P5.00D=5.0=Law=Time=Venus=5May=Odite>>L=N.
Avalanche=7,500=8,000=80%=P8.00D=8.0=Econ.=Curr.=Busn.=Jupt.=8Aug=Zeus>E=v.

Avant-garde=8,000=80%=P8.00D=8.0=Econ.=Curr.=Busn.=Jupt.=8Aug=Zeus>E=v.
Peter Matthews-Akukalia owns the Creatocracy of Creative Scientist Professionals.

Avarice=2,500=3,000=30%=P3.00D=3.0=Creativity=Star=Muses=3 March=C=I.
Avast=4,500=5,000=50%=P5.00D=5.0=Law=Time=Venus=5May=Odite>>L=N.

Avatar=7,500=8,000=80%=P8.00D=8.0=Econ.=Curr.=Busn.=Jupt.=8Aug=Zeus>E=v.
Peter Matthews-Akukalia is the avatar of Zeus and embodies the Creatocracy of Gods.

Avaunt=1,000=100%=10.0=1.0=Mind=Sun=1 January=Helios >> M=E4.
avdp.=500=5%=P5.00D=5.0=Law=Time=Venus=5 May=Aphrodite>>L=N.
Ave.=500=5%=P5.00D=5.0=Law=Time=Venus=5 May=Aphrodite>>L=N.
Avenge=7,000=70%=P7.00D=7.0=Lang.=Assets=Mars=6May=Pleiades.
Avenue=5,000=50%=P5.00D=5.0=Law=Time=Venus=5May=Odite>>L=N.
Aver=2,000=20%=P2.00D=2.0=Nature=Matter=Moon=2 Feb= Cupid>N=C.
Average=23,500=24,000=24%=Intl. Business=24 Days Monthly=2.4% Taxes.
Averse=1,500=15%=P1.50D=1.5=Authority = Solar Crown = Solar Core = 1 May = Maia.
Aversion=6,000=60%=P6.00D=6.0=Man=Earth=Health=Royalty=6June=Gaia>M=M2.
Avert=4,500=5,000=50%=P5.00D=5.0=Law=Time=Venus=5May=Odite>>L=N.
Avg.=500=5%=P5.00D=5.0=Law=Time=Venus=5 May=Aphrodite>>L=N.
Avian=2,500=3,000=30%=P3.00D=3.0=Creativity=Star=Muses=3 March=C=I.
Aviary=4,500=5,000=50%=P5.00D=5.0=Law=Time=Venus=5May=Odite>>L=N.
Aviation=4,000=40%=P4.00D=4.0=Govt.=Creat.= 4 April=Hermes>>G=A4.
Aviator=3,000=30%=P3.00D=3.0=Creativity=Star=Muses=3 March=C=I.
Aviatrix=3,000=30%=P3.00D=3.0=Creativity=Star=Muses=3 March=C=I.
Avid=7,000=70%=P7.00D=7.0=Lang.=Assets=Mars=6May=Pleiades.
Avignon=5,500=5.5=80%=P5.50D=Earth-Midway=5 May=Gaia.
Avionics=6,000=60%=P6.00D=6.0=Man=Earth=Health=Royalty=6June=Gaia>M=M2.
Avo=2,000=20%=P2.00D=2.0=Nature=Matter=Moon=2 Feb= Cupid>N=C.
Avocado=9,000=90%=P9.00D=9.0=Abstraction=Gods=Saturn=9Sept.>>A=Ø.
Avocation=7,000=70%=P7.00D=7.0=Lang.=Assets=Mars=6May=Pleiades.
Avocet=4,000=40%=P4.00D=4.0=Govt.=Creat.= 4 April=Hermes>>G=A4.

Avogadro's number=9,000=90%=P9.00D=9.0=Abstraction=Gods=Saturn=9Sept.>>A=Ø.
After Amedo Avogadro (1776-1856). Avogadro is now a God by his number. The code is
6.02x10(23) meaning a natural man with the physical abilities to function on invention and

education or invention knowledge. Note that the ticological value for 23 is 11,500=12,000. He becomes a God because he invented new knowledge or concept on scientific terms. By this law and many others, Peter Matthews-Akukalia is a God.

Avoid=6,000=60%=P6.00D=6.0=Man=Earth=Health=Royalty=6June=Gaia>M=M2.
Avoirdupois weight=10,000=1,000=100%=10.0=Physicality=Tech.=10 Oct.=Uranus=P=1Ø.
Avon=7,000=70%=P7.00D=7.0=Lang.=Assets=Mars=6May=Pleiades.
Avouch=2,000=20%=P2.00D=2.0=Nature=Matter=Moon=2 Feb= Cupid>N=C.
Avow=6,500=7,000=70%=P7.00D=7.0=Lang.=Assets=Mars=6May=Pleiades.

Avuncular=2,500=3,000=30%=P3.00D=3.0=Creativity=Star=Muses=3 March=C=I. The author had many uncles who had a great influence in his training. His grandmother, Mrs. Diana Matthews-Akukalia whom he was fond of, had the most influence on him and trained him until her death at about the age of 112years. He began the Matthews-Akukalia dynasty being the initiator of the compound name. He was formally Peter Matthews. He owns the Makupedia corporate brand, the creatopolitical brand - Creatocratic Nations of Paradise for the governance of Creative Scientists worldwide a field of study he created and Castle Makupedia as the God of Creatocracy Genius and Mind for his special abilities.

AWACS=7,500=8,000=80%=P8.00D=8.0=Econ.=Curr.=Busn.=Jupt.=8Aug=Zeus>E=v.
Await=6,000=60%=P6.00D=6.0=Man=Earth=Health=Royalty=6June=Gaia>M=M2.
Awake=10,000=1,000=100%=10.0=Physicality=Tech.=10 Oct.=Uranus=P=1Ø.
Awaken=1,000=100%=10.0=1.0=Mind=Sun=1 January=Helios >> M=E4.
Award=16,000=16%=P1.60D=1.6=Cycle of Life=Incarnation=Mind of GOD=1June= Maia.
Aware=2,500=3,000=30%=P3.00D=3.0=Creativity=Star=Muses=3 March=C=I.
Awash=4,000=40%=P4.00D=4.0=Govt.=Creat.= 4 April=Hermes>>G=A4.
Away=26,500=30,000=3,000=30%=P3.00D=3.0=Creativity=Star=Muses=3 March=C=I.
Awe=8,500=9,000=90%=P9.00D=9.0=Abstraction=Gods=Saturn=9Sept.>>A=Ø.
Aweigh=3,500=4,000=40%=P4.00D=4.0=Govt.=Creat.= 4 April=Hermes>>G=A4.
Awesome=2,500=3,000=30%=P3.00D=3.0=Creativity=Star=Muses=3 March=C=I.
Awestruck=1,500=15%=P1.50D=1.5=Authority = Solar Crown = Solar Core = 1 May = Maia.
Awful=7,000=70%=P7.00D=7.0=Lang.=Assets=Mars=6May=Pleiades.
Awhile=2,000=20%=P2.00D=2.0=Nature=Matter=Moon=2 Feb= Cupid>N=C.
Awkward=11%=P1.10D=1.1=Idea=Brainchild=Invention=11 Nov.=Athena>K=F.
Awl=5,500=5.5=80%=P5.50D=Earth-Midway=5 May=Gaia.
Awn=4,500=5,000=50%=P5.00D=5.0=Law=Time=Venus=5May=Odite>>L=N.
Awning=6,000=60%=P6.00D=6.0=Man=Earth=Health=Royalty=6June=Gaia>M=M2.
Awoke=2,000=20%=P2.00D=2.0=Nature=Matter=Moon=2 Feb= Cupid>N=C.
Awoken=2,000=20%=P2.00D=2.0=Nature=Matter=Moon=2 Feb= Cupid>N=C.
AWOL=5,000=50%=P5.00D=5.0=Law=Time=Venus=5May=Odite>>L=N.
Awry=3,500=4,000=40%=P4.00D=4.0=Govt.=Creat.= 4 April=Hermes>>G=A4.
Ax=17,000=17%=P1.70D=1.7=Solar Asset = 17/20=17 Feb.=Maia>>Mind Computing.
Ax.=1,000=100%=Physicality= Tech.=10 Oct.=Uranus=P=1Ø.

Axial=6,000=60%=P6.00D=6.0=Man=Earth=Health=Royalty=6June=Gaia>M=M2.
Axillia=5,000=50%=P5.00D=5.0=Law=Time=Venus=5May=Odite>>L=N.
Axiom=8,500=9,000=90%=P9.00D=9.0=Abstraction=Gods=Saturn=9Sept.>>A=Ø.

Axis=27,500=30,000=3,000=30%=P3.00D=3.0=Creativity=Star=Muses=3 March=C=I.
An alliance of powers such as nations to promote mutual interests. The Creatocracy has
initiated the Creatocratic Nations Organization-C3 for this purpose. The Solar Crown is
the axis of the Creatocracy hence the author inventor emperor owner & God of Creatocracy.

Axle=5,500=5.5=80%=P5.50D=Earth-Midway=5 May=Gaia.
Axle tree=4,000=40%=P4.00D=4.0=Govt.=Creat.= 4 April=Hermes>>G=A4.
Axon=7,000=70%=P7.00D=7.0=Lang.=Assets=Mars=6May=Pleiades.
Ayatollah=4,500=5,000=50%=P5.00D=5.0=Law=Time=Venus=5May=Odite>>L=N.
Aye(1)=4,000=40%=P4.00D=4.0=Govt.=Creat.= 4 April=Hermes>>G=A4.
Aye(2)=2,000=20%=P2.00D=2.0=Nature=Matter=Moon=2 Feb= Cupid>N=C.
AYH=1,500=15%=P1.50D=1.5=Authority = Solar Crown = Solar Core = 1 May = Maia.
Ayin=3,500=4,000=40%=P4.00D=4.0=Govt.=Creat.= 4 April=Hermes>>G=A4.
Aymara=8,500=9,000=90%=P9.00D=9.0=Abstraction=Gods=Saturn=9Sept.>>A=Ø.
Aymaran=6,000=60%=P6.00D=6.0=Man=Earth=Health=Royalty=6June=Gaia>M=M2.
AZ=500=5%=P5.00D=5.0=Law=Time=Venus=5 May=Aphrodite>>L=N.
Azalea=6,500=7,000=70%=P7.00D=7.0=Lang.=Assets=Mars=6May=Pleiades.
Azerbaijan=9,000=90%=P9.00D=9.0=Abstraction=Gods=Saturn=9Sept.>>A=Ø.
Azimuth=11,000=11%=P1.10D=1.1=Idea=Brainchild=Inventn.=11 Nov.=Athena>K=F.
Azores=9,500=10,000=1,000=100%=10.0=Physicality=Tech.=10 Oct.=Uranus=P=1Ø.
Azov Sea of=5,000=50%=P5.00D=5.0=Law=Time=Venus=5May=Odite>>L=N.
AZT=5,000=50%=P5.00D=5.0=Law=Time=Venus=5May=Odite>>L=N.
Aztec=13,500=14,000=14%=P1.40D=1.4=Mgt.=Solar Core=13 May=Athena>>SC=0.1
Azure=2,000=20%=P2.00D=2.0=Nature=Matter=Moon=2 Feb= Cupid>N=C.

MAKABET =Bb=

B=15,000=15%=P1.50D=1.5=Authority = Solar Crown = Solar Core = 1 May = Maia.
The 2nd letter of the English alphabet. Computing the psycho-weight.
Resultant*Position on the Maks. 1.5*2.0x=px=3.5+3=6.5x=px=17=Solar Core Asset=Sun.
When B is mentioned computational intelligence is induced. The B Mindset seeks to
measure abstract assets, cosmic energy or mind wares that translates to softwares.

B(1)=2,500=3,000=30%=P3.00D=3.0=Creativity=Star=Muses=3 March=C=I.
B(2)=2,000=20%=P2.00D=2.0=Nature=Matter=Moon=2 Feb= Cupid>N=C.
B.=1,500=15%=P1.50D=1.5=Authority = Solar Crown = Solar Core = 1 May = Maia.
Ba=3,000=30%=P3.00D=3.0=Creativity=Star=Muses=3 March=C=I.

B.A.=1,500=15%=P1.50D=1.5=Authority = Solar Crown = Solar Core = 1 May = Maia.
Baa=4,500=5,000=50%=P5.00D=5.0=Law=Time=Venus=5May=Odite>>L=N.

Baal=5,500=5.5=80%=P5.50D=Earth-Midway=5 May=Gaia.
Any of the various fertility and nature gods of the ancient Semitic peoples. The Creatocracy has established Baal to be the negative version of Gaia the Goddess of Nature. Interestingly Baale (a provincial Yoruba king) is mentioned in the Bible. 2 Samuel 6:1-2.

Babbitt=4,500=5,000=50%=P5.00D=5.0=Law=Time=Venus=5May=Odite>>L=N.
Babble=7,500=8,000=80%=P8.00D=8.0=Econ.=Curr.=Busn.=Jupt.=8Aug=Zeus>E=v.
Babe=4,500=5,000=50%=P5.00D=5.0=Law=Time=Venus=5May=Odite>>L=N.
babel=3,000=30%=P3.00D=3.0=Creativity=Star=Muses=3 March=C=I.
Babel=5,500=5.5=80%=P5.50D=Earth-Midway=5 May=Gaia.
Baboon=8,500=9,000=90%=P9.00D=9.0=Abstraction=Gods=Saturn=9Sept.>>A=Ø.
Babushka=5,500=5.5=80%=P5.50D=Earth-Midway=5 May=Gaia.
Baby=17,500=18,000=18%=P1.80D=1.8=Solar Currency=MaksCurrencies=1 Aug=Maia.
Baby boom=7,500=8,000=80%=P8.00D=8.0=Econ.=Curr.=Busn.=Jupt.=8Aug=Zeus>E=v.
Baby carriage=5,000=50%=P5.00D=5.0=Law=Time=Venus=5May=Odite>>L=N.
Babylon=4,000=40%=P4.00D=4.0=Govt.=Creat.= 4 April=Hermes>>G=A4.
Babylonia=5,000=50%=P5.00D=5.0=Law=Time=Venus=5May=Odite>>L=N.
Babylonian=5,500=5.5=80%=P5.50D=Earth-Midway=5 May=Gaia.
Baby's breath=5,500=5.5=80%=P5.50D=Earth-Midway=5 May=Gaia.
Baby-sit=7,000=70%=P7.00D=7.0=Lang.=Assets=Mars=6May=Pleiades.
Baccalaureate=3,500=4,000=40%=P4.00D=4.0=Govt.=Creat.= 4 April=Hermes>>G=A4.
Baccarat=7,000=70%=P7.00D=7.0=Lang.=Assets=Mars=6May=Pleiades.
Bacchanal=3,000=30%=P3.00D=3.0=Creativity=Star=Muses=3 March=C=I.
Bacchanalia=6,000=60%=P6.00D=6.0=Man=Earth=Health=Royalty=6June=Gaia>M=M2.
Bacchus=3,000=30%=P3.00D=3.0=Creativity=Star=Muses=3 March=C=I.
Bach Johann Sebastian=3,000=30%=P3.00D=3.0=Creativity=Star=Muses=3 March=C=I.
Bachelor=4,500=5,000=50%=P5.00D=5.0=Law=Time=Venus=5May=Odite>>L=N.
Bachelor's button=1,000=100%=10.0=1.0=Mind=Sun=1 January=Helios >> M=E4.
Bachelor's degree=5,500=5.5=80%=P5.50D=Earth-Midway=5 May=Gaia.
Bacillus=3,500=4,000=40%=P4.00D=4.0=Govt.=Creat.= 4 April=Hermes>>G=A4.
Bacitracin=7,000=70%=P7.00D=7.0=Lang.=Assets=Mars=6May=Pleiades.
Back=46,500=5,000=50%=P5.00D=5.0=Law=Time=Venus=5May=Odite>>L=N.
Backache=5,500=5.5=80%=P5.50D=Earth-Midway=5 May=Gaia.
Backbeat=4,000=40%=P4.00D=4.0=Govt.=Creat.= 4 April=Hermes>>G=A4.
Backbench=7,000=70%=P7.00D=7.0=Lang.=Assets=Mars=6May=Pleiades.
Backbite=6,000=60%=P6.00D=6.0=Man=Earth=Health=Royalty=6June=Gaia>M=M2.
Backboard=9,000=90%=P9.00D=9.0=Abstraction=Gods=Saturn=9Sept.>>A=Ø.
Backbone=7,000=70%=P7.00D=7.0=Lang.=Assets=Mars=6May=Pleiades.
Backbreaking=2,000=20%=P2.00D=2.0=Nature=Matter=Moon=2 Feb= Cupid>N=C.
Backcourt=6,500=7,000=70%=P7.00D=7.0=Lang.=Assets=Mars=6May=Pleiades.
Back door=2,000=20%=P2.00D=2.0=Nature=Matter=Moon=2 Feb= Cupid>N=C.

Backdrop=8,500=9,000=90%=P9.00D=9.0=Abstraction=Gods=Saturn=9Sept.>>A=Ø.
Backer=5,000=50%=P5.00D=5.0=Law=Time=Venus=5May=Odite>>L=N.
Backfield=8,500=9,000=90%=P9.00D=9.0=Abstraction=Gods=Saturn=9Sept.>>A=Ø.
Backfire= 13,000 = 13% = P1.30D = 1.3 = Solar Core = Faculty = 13Jan.=Athena.
Back-formation=10,500=11,000=11%=P1.10D=1.1=Idea=Brainchild.=11Nov.=Athena>K=F.
Backgammon=6,500=7,000=70%=P7.00D=7.0=Lang.=Assets=Mars=6May=Pleiades.
Background=17,000=17%=P1.70D=1.7=Solar Asset =17 Feb.=Maia>>Mind Computing.
Backhand=12,000=12%=P1.20D=1.2=Knowledge=Edu.=12Dec.=Athena>>K=F.
Backhanded=4,000=40%=P4.00D=4.0=Govt.=Creat.= 4 April=Hermes>>G=A4.
Backhoe=6,000=60%=P6.00D=6.0=Man=Earth=Health=Royalty=6June=Gaia>M=M2.
Backing=6,500=7,000=70%=P7.00D=7.0=Lang.=Assets=Mars=6May=Pleiades.
Backlash=6,500=7,000=70%=P7.00D=7.0=Lang.=Assets=Mars=6May=Pleiades.
Backlight=4,000=40%=P4.00D=4.0=Govt.=Creat.= 4 April=Hermes>>G=A4.
Backlog=7,000=70%=P7.00D=7.0=Lang.=Assets=Mars=6May=Pleiades.
Backpack=12,000=12%=P1.20D=1.2=Knowledge=Edu.=12Dec.=Athena>>K=F.
Backpedal=4,000=40%=P4.00D=4.0=Govt.=Creat.= 4 April=Hermes>>G=A4.
Backrest=3,500=4,000=40%=P4.00D=4.0=Govt.=Creat.= 4 April=Hermes>>G=A4.
Backseat=5,000=50%=P5.00D=5.0=Law=Time=Venus=5May=Odite>>L=N.

Back-seat driver=3,500=4,000=40%=P4.00D=4.0=Govt.=Creat.= 4April=Hermes>>G=A4.
The Creatocracy predictably will become the backseat driver of every nation one day.

Backside=1,500=15%=P1.50D=1.5=Authority = Solar Crown = Solar Core = 1 May = Maia.
Backslide=3,500=4,000=40%=P4.00D=4.0=Govt.=Creat.= 4 April=Hermes>>G=A4.
Backspace=9,500=10,000=1,000=100%=10.0=Physicality=Tech.=10 Oct.=Uranus=P=1Ø.
Backspin=9,000=90%=P9.00D=9.0=Abstraction=Gods=Saturn=9Sept.>>A=Ø.
Backstage=6,000=60%=P6.00D=6.0=Man=Earth=Health=Royalty=6June=Gaia>M=M2.
Backstairs=3,000=30%=P3.00D=3.0=Creativity=Star=Muses=3 March=C=I.
Backstop=8,000=80%=P8.00D=8.0=Econ.=Curr.=Busn.=Jupt.=8Aug=Zeus>E=v.
Backstretch=6,000=60%=P6.00D=6.0=Man=Earth=Health=Royalty=6June=Gaia>M=M2.
Backstroke=6,500=7,000=70%=P7.00D=7.0=Lang.=Assets=Mars=6May=Pleiades.
Back swept=3,500=4,000=40%=P4.00D=4.0=Govt.=Creat.= 4 April=Hermes>>G=A4.
Back talk=2,000=20%=P2.00D=2.0=Nature=Matter=Moon=2 Feb= Cupid>N=C.
Backtrack=3,500=4,000=40%=P4.00D=4.0=Govt.=Creat.= 4 April=Hermes>>G=A4.
Backup=13,500=14,000=14%=P1.40D=1.4=Mgt.=Solar Core=13 May=Athena>>SC=0.1
Backward=18,000=18%=P1.80D=1.8=Solar Currency=MaksCurrencies=1 Aug=Maia.
Backwash=2,500=3,000=30%=P3.00D=3.0=Creativity=Star=Muses=3 March=C=I.
Backwater=8,000=80%=P8.00D=8.0=Econ.=Curr.=Busn.=Jupt.=8Aug=Zeus>E=v.
Backwoods=5,000=50%=P5.00D=5.0=Law=Time=Venus=5May=Odite>>L=N.
Bacon=6,000=60%=P6.00D=6.0=Man=Earth=Health=Royalty=6June=Gaia>M=M2.
Bacon(1)=3,500=4,000=40%=P4.00D=4.0=Govt.=Creat.= 4 April=Hermes>>G=A4.
Bacon(2) Francis=3,000=30%=P3.00D=3.0=Creativity=Star=Muses=3 March=C=I.
Bacon, Roger=4,000=40%=P4.00D=4.0=Govt.=Creat.= 4 April=Hermes>>G=A4.
Bacteria=500=5%=P5.00D=5.0=Law=Time=Venus=5 May=Aphrodite>>L=N.

Bactericide=2,500=3,000=30%=P3.00D=3.0=Creativity=Star=Muses=3 March=C=I.
Bacteriology=2,500=3,000=30%=P3.00D=3.0=Creativity=Star=Muses=3 March=C=I.
Bacteriophage=3,000=30%=P3.00D=3.0=Creativity=Star=Muses=3 March=C=I.
Bacterium=12,000=12%=P1.20D=1.2=Knowledge=Edu.=12Dec.=Athena>>K=F.
Bactria=3,000=30%=P3.00D=3.0=Creativity=Star=Muses=3 March=C=I.
Bad=31,000= 13,000 = 13% = P1.30D = 1.3 = Solar Core = Faculty = 13Jan.=Athena.
Bad blood=3,500=4,000=40%=P4.00D=4.0=Govt.=Creat.= 4 April=Hermes>>G=A4.
Bade=2,000=20%=P2.00D=2.0=Nature=Matter=Moon=2 Feb= Cupid>N=C.
Baden=2,500=3,000=30%=P3.00D=3.0=Creativity=Star=Muses=3 March=C=I.

Baden-Powell Robert=12,000=12%=P1.20D=1.2=Knowledge=Edu.=12Dec.=Athena>>K=F.
Sir Robert Stephenson Smyth is a British founder of the Boys Scout (1908) and with his sister
Agnes the Girl Guides (1910). Peter Matthews-Akukalia (Castle Makupedia) founded the
Creativity Club and the Young Creative Scientists Club, Ministry of Creativity, Talents &
Ideas Markets, Mind Space and all institutions that make up the Creatocracy in its royalty.

Badge=6,500=7,000=70%=P7.00D=7.0=Lang.=Assets=Mars=6May=Pleiades.
Badger=8,500=9,000=90%=P9.00D=9.0=Abstraction=Gods=Saturn=9Sept.>>A=Ø.
Badinage=1,500=15%=P1.50D=1.5=Authority = Solar Crown = Solar Core = 1 May = Maia.
Badlands=5,500=5.5=80%=P5.50D=Earth-Midway=5 May=Gaia.

Badminton=11,000=11%=P1.10D=1.1=Idea=Brainchild=Inventn.=11 Nov.=Athena>K=F.
After Badminton, the Duke of Beaufort's country seat in W. England. Paradise is the
country of the Mind God and God of Creatocracy in the emperor's country home Nsukka.
The Creatocratic Charter is his throne, the Solar Crown is his authority and the Creatocracy
is his trademark. The Maks Currency is his money and the Makupedia is his technology.

Badmouth=3,500=4,000=40%=P4.00D=4.0=Govt.=Creat.= 4 April=Hermes>>G=A4.
Baedeker Karl=2,500=3,000=30%=P3.00D=3.0=Creativity=Star=Muses=3 March=C=I.
Baffin William=2,500=3,000=30%=P3.00D=3.0=Creativity=Star=Muses=3 March=C=I.
Baffin Bay=5,500=5.5=80%=P5.50D=Earth-Midway=5 May=Gaia.
Baffin Island=4,500=5,000=50%=P5.00D=5.0=Law=Time=Venus=5May=Odite>>L=N.
Baffle=9,500=10,000=1,000=100%=10.0=Physicality=Tech.=10 Oct.=Uranus=P=1Ø.
Bag=24,500=3,000=30%=P3.00D=3.0=Creativity=Star=Muses=3 March=C=I.
Bagatelle=3,000=30%=P3.00D=3.0=Creativity=Star=Muses=3 March=C=I.
Bagel=4,000=40%=P4.00D=4.0=Govt.=Creat.= 4 April=Hermes>>G=A4.
Baggage=5,500=5.5=80%=P5.50D=Earth-Midway=5 May=Gaia.
Baggy=2,000=20%=P2.00D=2.0=Nature=Matter=Moon=2 Feb= Cupid>N=C.

Baghdad=5,500=5.5=80%=P5.50D=Earth-Midway=5 May=Gaia.
Gaia has a base in Baghdad, center of Iraq on the Tigris River. Another center of the Earth.

Bagpipe=9,500=10,000=1,000=100%=10.0=Physicality=Tech.=10 Oct.=Uranus=P=1Ø.
Baguette=5,000=50%=P5.00D=5.0=Law=Time=Venus=5May=Odite>>L=N.
Baguio=5,000=50%=P5.00D=5.0=Law=Time=Venus=5May=Odite>>L=N.
Bahamas=7,000=70%=P7.00D=7.0=Lang.=Assets=Mars=6May=Pleiades.
Bahrain=8,000=80%=P8.00D=8.0=Econ.=Curr.=Busn.=Jupt.=8Aug=Zeus>E=v.
Baht=2,000=20%=P2.00D=2.0=Nature=Matter=Moon=2 Feb= Cupid>N=C.
Baikal Lake=3,500=4,000=40%=P4.00D=4.0=Govt.=Creat.= 4 April=Hermes>>G=A4.
Bail(1)=13,500=14,000=14%=P1.40D=1.4=Mgt.=Solar Core=13 May=Athena>>SC=0.1
Bail(2)=10,000=1,000=100%=10.0=Physicality=Tech.=10 Oct.=Uranus=P=1Ø.
Bail(3)=5,000=50%=P5.00D=5.0=Law=Time=Venus=5May=Odite>>L=N.
Bailee=3,500=4,000=40%=P4.00D=4.0=Govt.=Creat.= 4 April=Hermes>>G=A4.
Bailiff=14,000=14%=P1.40D=1.4=Mgt.=Solar Core=13 May=Athena>>SC=0.1
Bailiwick=8,000=80%=P8.00D=8.0=Econ.=Curr.=Busn.=Jupt.=8Aug=Zeus>E=v.
Bailor=3,000=30%=P3.00D=3.0=Creativity=Star=Muses=3 March=C=I.
Bails man=4,000=40%=P4.00D=4.0=Govt.=Creat.= 4 April=Hermes>>G=A4.
Bairiki=7,000=70%=P7.00D=7.0=Lang.=Assets=Mars=6May=Pleiades.
Bairn=1,500=15%=P1.50D=1.5=Authority = Solar Crown = Solar Core = 1 May = Maia.
Bait=16,500=17,000=17%=P1.70D=1.7=Solar Asset =17 Feb.=Maia>>Mind Computing.
Bait and switch=11,000=11%=P1.10D=1.1=Idea=Brainchild=Inventn.=11 Nov.=Athena>K=F.
Balza=2,000=20%=P2.00D=2.0=Nature=Matter=Moon=2 Feb= Cupid>N=C.
Baize=5,000=50%=P5.00D=5.0=Law=Time=Venus=5May=Odite>>L=N.
Baja California=7,500=8,000=80%=P8.00D=8.0=Econ.=Busn.=Jupt.=8Aug=Zeus>E=v.
Bake=14,000=14%=P1.40D=1.4=Mgt.=Solar Core=13 May=Athena>>SC=0.1
Bakelite=8,500=9,000=90%=P9.00D=9.0=Abstraction=Gods=Saturn=9Sept.>>A=Ø.
Baker Mount.=6,000=60%=P6.00D=6.0=Man=Earth=Health=Royalty=6June=Gaia
   >M=M2.
Baker's dozen=2,000=20%=P2.00D=2.0=Nature=Matter=Moon=2 Feb= Cupid>N=C.
Bakers field=5,500=5.5=80%=P5.50D=Earth-Midway=5 May=Gaia.
Bakery=7,000=70%=P7.00D=7.0=Lang.=Assets=Mars=6May=Pleiades.
Baking powder=11,000=11%=P1.10D=1.1=Idea=Brainchild=Inventn.=11 Nov.=Athena>K=F.
Baking soda=8,000=80%=P8.00D=8.0=Econ.=Curr.=Busn.=Jupt.=8Aug=Zeus>E=v.
Baklava=6,000=60%=P6.00D=6.0=Man=Earth=Health=Royalty=6June=Gaia>M=M2.
Baksheesh=4,500=5,000=50%=P5.00D=5.0=Law=Time=Venus=5May=Odite>>L=N.
Baku=6,000=60%=P6.00D=6.0=Man=Earth=Health=Royalty=6June=Gaia>M=M2.
Bakunin Mikhall Aleksandrovich=3,500=4,000=40%=P4.00D=4.0=Govt.=Hermes>>G=A4.
Balalaika=5,500=5.5=80%=P5.50D=Earth-Midway=5 May=Gaia.
Balance=47,000=50,000=5,000=50%=P5.00D=5.0=Law=Time=Venus=5May=Odite>>L=N
Balance beam=5,000=50%=P5.00D=5.0=Law=Time=Venus=5May=Odite>>L=N.

Balance of power=6,000=60%=P6.00D=6.0=Man=Earth=Royalty=6June=Gaia>M=M2.
Gaia sees to the balance of power through the Creatocracy in government representation.

Balance sheet=5,000=50%=P5.00D=5.0=Law=Time=Venus=5May=Odite>>L=N.
Balance wheel=5,500=5.5=80%=P5.50D=Earth-Midway=5 May=Gaia.

BalanchineGeorge=4,500=5,000=50%=P5.00D=5.0=Law=Venus=5May=Odite>>L=N.
Balboa=2,000=20%=P2.00D=2.0=Nature=Matter=Moon=2 Feb= Cupid>N=C.
Balboa Vasco Núñez de.=2,000=20%=P2.00D=2.0=Nature=Moon=2 Feb= Cupid>N=C.
Balcony=12,000=12%=P1.20D=1.2=Knowledge=Edu.=12Dec.=Athena>>K=F.
Bald=10,000=1,000=100%=10.0=Physicality=Tech.=10 Oct.=Uranus=P=1Ø.
Baldachin=4,000=40%=P4.00D=4.0=Govt.=Creat.= 4 April=Hermes>>G=A4.
Bald eagle=6,000=60%=P6.00D=6.0=Man=Earth=Health=Royalty=6June=Gaia>M=M2.
Balderdash=1,000=100%=10.0=1.0=Mind=Sun=1 January=Helios >> M=E4.
Bald-faced=3,000=30%=P3.00D=3.0=Creativity=Star=Muses=3 March=C=I.
Baldric=5,500=5.5=80%=P5.50D=Earth-Midway=5 May=Gaia.
Baldwin James Arthur=3,000=30%=P3.00D=3.0=Creativity=Star=Muses=3 March=C=I.
Baldwin, Stanley=5,000=50%=P5.00D=5.0=Law=Time=Venus=5May=Odite>>L=N.
Bale=7,000=70%=P7.00D=7.0=Lang.=Assets=Mars=6May=Pleiades.
Balearic Islands=6,000=60%=P6.00D=6.0=Man=Earth=Royalty=6June=Gaia>M=M2.
Baleen=1,000=100%=10.0=1.0=Mind=Sun=1 January=Helios >> M=E4.
Baleful=4,000=40%=P4.00D=4.0=Govt.=Creat.= 4 April=Hermes>>G=A4.
Balfour Arthur James=3,500=4,000=40%=P4.00D=4.0=Govt.= 4April=Hermes>>G=A4.
Bali=6,000=60%=P6.00D=6.0=Man=Earth=Health=Royalty=6June=Gaia>M=M2.
Balinese=4,500=5,000=50%=P5.00D=5.0=Law=Time=Venus=5May=Odite>>L=N.
Balk=18,000=18%=P1.80D=1.8=Solar Currency=MaksCurrencies=1 Aug=Maia.
Balkan Mountains=11,000=11%=P1.10D=1.1=Idea=Brainchild=11 Nov.=Athena>K=F.
Balkan Peninsula=8,000=80%=P8.00D=8.0=Econ.=Curr.=Busn.=Jupt.=8Aug=Zeus>E=v.
Balkhash Lake=3,000=30%=P3.00D=3.0=Creativity=Star=Muses=3 March=C=I.
Ball(1)=29,500=3,000=30%=P3.00D=3.0=Creativity=Star=Muses=3 March=C=I.
Ball(2)=9,000=90%=P9.00D=9.0=Abstraction=Gods=Saturn=9Sept.>>A=Ø.
Ballad=15,000=15%=P1.50D=1.5=Authority = Solar Crown = Solar Core = 1 May = Maia.
Ballast=12,000=12%=P1.20D=1.2=Knowledge=Edu.=12Dec.=Athena>>K=F.
Ball bearing=14,000=14%=P1.40D=1.4=Mgt.=Solar Core=13 May=Athena>>SC=0.1
Ballerina=3,500=4,000=40%=P4.00D=4.0=Govt.=Creat.= 4 April=Hermes>>G=A4.
Ballet=10,000=1,000=100%=10.0=Physicality=Tech.=10 Oct.=Uranus=P=1Ø.
Balletomane=2,000=20%=P2.00D=2.0=Nature=Matter=Moon=2 Feb= Cupid>N=C.
Ball game=7,500=8,000=80%=P8.00D=8.0=Econ.=Curr.=Busn.=Jupt.=8Aug=Zeus>E=v.
Ballistics missile=7,500=8,000=80%=P8.00D=8.0=Econ.=Curr.=Jupt.=8Aug=Zeus>E=v.
Ballistics=7,000=70%=P7.00D=7.0=Lang.=Assets=Mars=6May=Pleiades.
Balloon=23,500=24,000=24%=Intl. Business=24 Days Monthly=2.4% Taxes.
Ballot=13,500=14,000=14%=P1.40D=1.4=Mgt.=Solar Core=13 May=Athena>>SC=0.1
Ball park=9,500=10,000=1,000=100%=10.0=Physicality=Tech.=10 Oct.=Uranus=P=1Ø.
Ballpoint pen=5,500=5.5=80%=P5.50D=Earth-Midway=5 May=Gaia.
Ballroom=2,500=3,000=30%=P3.00D=3.0=Creativity=Star=Muses=3 March=C=I.
Ballyhoo=5,500=5.5=80%=P5.50D=Earth-Midway=5 May=Gaia.
Balm=11,000=11%=P1.10D=1.1=Idea=Brainchild=Inventn.=11 Nov.=Athena>K=F.
Balmy(1)=6,000=60%=P6.00D=6.0=Man=Earth=Health=Royalty=6June=Gaia>M=M2.
Balmy(2)=2,000=20%=P2.00D=2.0=Nature=Matter=Moon=2 Feb= Cupid>N=C.
Baloney(1)=1,500=15%=P1.50D=1.5=Authority = Solar Crown = Solar Core = 1 May = Maia.
Baloney(2)=1,000=100%=10.0=1.0=Mind=Sun=1 January=Helios >> M=E4.

Balsa=10,500=11,000=11%=P1.10D=1.1=Idea=Brainchild=Inventn.=11 Nov.=Athena>K=F.
Balsam=9,500=10,000=1,000=100%=10.0=Physicality=Tech.=10 Oct.=Uranus=P=1Ø.
Balsam fir=8,000=80%=P8.00D=8.0=Econ.=Curr.=Busn.=Jupt.=8Aug=Zeus>E=v.
Balt=3,000=30%=P3.00D=3.0=Creativity=Star=Muses=3 March=C=I.
Baltic=8,500=9,000=90%=P9.00D=9.0=Abstraction=Gods=Saturn=9Sept.>>A=Ø.
Baltic Sea=8,500=9,000=90%=P9.00D=9.0=Abstraction=Gods=Saturn=9Sept.>>A=Ø.
Baltic States=6,000=60%=P6.00D=6.0=Man=Earth=Health=Royalty=6June=Gaia>M=M2.
Baltimore=7,500=8,000=80%=P8.00D=8.0=Econ.=Curr.=Busn.=Jupt.=8Aug=Zeus>E=v.
Baltimore, Lord=1,000=100%=10.0=1.0=Mind=Sun=1 January=Helios >> M=E4.
Baltimore Oriole=5,000=50%=P5.00D=5.0=Law=Time=Venus=5May=Odite>>L=N.
Baluster=3,500=4,000=40%=P4.00D=4.0=Govt.=Creat.= 4 April=Hermes>>G=A4.
Balustrade=6,000=60%=P6.00D=6.0=Man=Earth=Health=Royalty=6June=Gaia>M=M2.
Balzac Honorè=2,000=20%=P2.00D=2.0=Nature=Matter=Moon=2 Feb= Cupid>N=C.
Bamboo=10,500=11,000=11%=P1.10D=1.1=Idea=Brainchild=Inventn.=11 Nov.=Athena
    >K=F.
Bamboozle=2,500=3,000=30%=P3.00D=3.0=Creativity=Star=Muses=3 March=C=I.
Ban(1)=10,500=11,000=11%=P1.10D=1.1=Idea=Brainchild=Inventn.=11 Nov.=Athena>K=F.
Ban(2)=2,000=20%=P2.00D=2.0=Nature=Matter=Moon=2 Feb= Cupid>N=C.
Banal=2,500=3,000=30%=P3.00D=3.0=Creativity=Star=Muses=3 March=C=I.
Banana=15,000=15%=P1.50D=1.5=Authority = Solar Crown = Solar Core = 1 May = Maia.
Band(1)=18,000=18%=P1.80D=1.8=Solar Currency=MaksCurrencies=1 Aug=Maia.
Band(2)=12,000=12%=P1.20D=1.2=Knowledge=Edu.=12Dec.=Athena>>K=F.
Bandage=7,500=8,000=80%=P8.00D=8.0=Econ.=Curr.=Busn.=Jupt.=8Aug=Zeus>E=v.

Band-Aid=8,500=9,000=90%=P9.00D=9.0=Abstraction=Gods=Saturn=9Sept.>>A=Ø.
A trademark for an adhesive bandage with a gauze pad in the center, used to protect minor wounds. The Creatocracy, Castle Makupedia and Solar Crown are trademarks of the Creative Sciences and the Creative Scientist Professionalism. A signal of the Gods.

Bandana=4,000=40%=P4.00D=4.0=Govt.=Creat.= 4 April=Hermes>>G=A4.
Bandar Seri Begawan=5,500=5.5=80%=P5.50D=Earth-Midway=5 May=Gaia.
Bandbox=5,000=50%=P5.00D=5.0=Law=Time=Venus=5May=Odite>>L=N.
Bandicoot=4,500=5,000=50%=P5.00D=5.0=Law=Time=Venus=5May=Odite>>L=N.
Bandit=3,500=4,000=40%=P4.00D=4.0=Govt.=Creat.= 4 April=Hermes>>G=A4.
Bandoleer=6,000=60%=P6.00D=6.0=Man=Earth=Health=Royalty=6June=Gaia>M=M2.
Band saw=5,000=50%=P5.00D=5.0=Law=Time=Venus=5May=Odite>>L=N.
Bandstand=5,000=50%=P5.00D=5.0=Law=Time=Venus=5May=Odite>>L=N.
Ban dung=5,500=5.5=80%=P5.50D=Earth-Midway=5 May=Gaia.
Bandwagon=9,000=90%=P9.00D=9.0=Abstraction=Gods=Saturn=9Sept.>>A=Ø.
Bandy=9,500=10,000=1,000=100%=10.0=Physicality=Tech.=10 Oct.=Uranus=P=1Ø.
Bane=5,500=5.5=80%=P5.50D=Earth-Midway=5 May=Gaia.
Bang(1)= 13,000 = 13% = P1.30D = 1.3 = Solar Core = Faculty = 13Jan.=Athena.
Bang(2)=4,000=40%=P4.00D=4.0=Govt.=Creat.= 4 April=Hermes>>G=A4.
Bangalore=5,000=50%=P5.00D=5.0=Law=Time=Venus=5May=Odite>>L=N.

Bangkok=4,500=5,000=50%=P5.00D=5.0=Law=Time=Venus=5May=Odite>>L=N.
Bangladesh=8,500=9,000=90%=P9.00D=9.0=Abstraction=Gods=Saturn=9Sept.>>A=Ø.
Bangle=3,500=4,000=40%=P4.00D=4.0=Govt.=Creat.= 4 April=Hermes>>G=A4.
Bangor=4,000=40%=P4.00D=4.0=Govt.=Creat.= 4 April=Hermes>>G=A4.
Bangui=7,500=8,000=80%=P8.00D=8.0=Econ.=Curr.=Busn.=Jupt.=8Aug=Zeus>E=v.
Bang-up=2,000=20%=P2.00D=2.0=Nature=Matter=Moon=2 Feb= Cupid>N=C.
Bani=1,500=15%=P1.50D=1.5=Authority = Solar Crown = Solar Core = 1 May = Maia.
Banian=1,500=15%=P1.50D=1.5=Authority = Solar Crown = Solar Core = 1 May = Maia.
Banish=6,500=7,000=70%=P7.00D=7.0=Lang.=Assets=Mars=6May=Pleiades.
Banister=2,500=3,000=30%=P3.00D=3.0=Creativity=Star=Muses=3 March=C=I.
Banjo=7,000=70%=P7.00D=7.0=Lang.=Assets=Mars=6May=Pleiades.
Banjul=4,500=5,000=50%=P5.00D=5.0=Law=Time=Venus=5May=Odite>>L=N.

Bank(1)=33,000=33%=P3.30D=3.3=Genius Gods=The Holy Spirit=Moon=3 March.
Banking in all forms is a proof of the manifestation of the Holy Spirit>>Host>>Council of Gods>>The Creatocracy. Institutions are birthplaces of the divine.

Bank(2)=23,500=24,000=24%=Intl. Business=24 Days Monthly=2.4% Taxes.
Peter Matthews-Akukalia invented a system of measuring the business inclinations and natural purpose of a bank account. This makes it easier to help account holders function most effectively conveniently and productively. Banks can then develop business programs along these lines especially for those who are not bringing in money as expected.
The Creatocracy Bank is precursor to the establishment of the Mind Banking system based on the Maks Currencies invented by Peter Matthews-Akukalia for the creative economy. See Currencies, Interest, Message from Castle Makupedia.

Bank(3)=9,000=90%=P9.00D=9.0=Abstraction=Gods=Saturn=9Sept.>>A=Ø.
Bank book=7,000=70%=P7.00D=7.0=Lang.=Assets=Mars=6May=Pleiades.
Bankcard=8,000=80%=P8.00D=8.0=Econ.=Curr.=Busn.=Jupt.=8Aug=Zeus>E=v.
Bank holiday=4,000=40%=P4.00D=4.0=Govt.=Creat.= 4 April=Hermes>>G=A4.
Bank note=8,500=9,000=90%=P9.00D=9.0=Abstraction=Gods=Saturn=9Sept.>>A=Ø.
Bankroll=7,000=70%=P7.00D=7.0=Lang.=Assets=Mars=6May=Pleiades.
Bankrupt=19,500=20,000=20%=P2.00D=2.0=Nature=Matter=Moon=2 Feb= Cupid>N=C.
Banner=12,500= 13,000 = 13% = P1.30D = 1.3 = Solar Core = Faculty = 13Jan.=Athena.
Bannister Roger=7,500=8,000=80%=P8.00D=8.0=Econ.=Busn.=Jupt.=8Aug=Zeus>E=v.
Bannock=5,500=5.5=80%=P5.50D=Earth-Midway=5 May=Gaia.
Banns=5,000=50%=P5.00D=5.0=Law=Time=Venus=5May=Odite>>L=N.
Banquet=6,000=60%=P6.00D=6.0=Man=Earth=Health=Royalty=6June=Gaia>M=M2.
Banquette=7,500=8,000=80%=P8.00D=8.0=Econ.=Curr.=Busn.=Jupt.=8Aug=Zeus>E=v.

Banshee=6,500=7,000=70%=P7.00D=7.0=Lang.=Assets=Mars=6May=Pleiades.
A female spirit in Gaelic folklore believed to presage a death in a family by wailing.

Bantam=9,000=90%=P9.00D=9.0=Abstraction=Gods=Saturn=9Sept.>>A=Ø.
Bantamweight=6,000=60%=P6.00D=6.0=Man=Earth=Royalty=6June=Gaia>M=M2.
Banter=5,000=50%=P5.00D=5.0=Law=Time=Venus=5May=Odite>>L=N.
Bantu=11,500=12,000=12%=P1.20D=1.2=Knowledge=Edu.=12Dec.=Athena>>K=F.
Banyan=8,500=9,000=90%=P9.00D=9.0=Abstraction=Gods=Saturn=9Sept.>>A=Ø.

Banzai=3,500=4,000=40%=P4.00D=4.0=Govt.=Creat.= 4 April=Hermes>>G=A4.
A Japanese battle cry or patriotic cheer. Meaning ten thousand years. "Greatness" is the battle cry of the Paradise Nations. Our lifespan of knowledge and its solar core systems spans on the life of the sun astronomy indicated as 500 million years, forever.

Baobab=9,000=90%=P9.00D=9.0=Abstraction=Gods=Saturn=9Sept.>>A=Ø.
Baotou=7,500=8,000=80%=P8.00D=8.0=Econ.=Curr.=Busn.=Jupt.=8Aug=Zeus>E=v.
Baptism=11,500=12,000=12%=P1.20D=1.2=Knowledge=Edu.=12Dec.=Athena>>K=F.
Baptist=8,000=80%=P8.00D=8.0=Econ.=Curr.=Busn.=Jupt.=8Aug=Zeus>E=v.
Baptistery=6,500=7,000=70%=P7.00D=7.0=Lang.=Assets=Mars=6May=Pleiades.
Baptize=6,000=60%=P6.00D=6.0=Man=Earth=Health=Royalty=6June=Gaia>M=M2.
Bar=43,000>>4.3>>2.0=20%=P2.00D=2.0=Nature=Matter=Moon=2 Feb= Cupid>N=C.
Barabbas=7,000=70%=P7.00D=7.0=Lang.=Assets=Mars=6May=Pleiades.
Barb=14,000=14%=P1.40D=1.4=Mgt.=Solar Core=13 May=Athena>>SC=0.1
Barbados=6,000=60%=P6.00D=6.0=Man=Earth=Health=Royalty=6June=Gaia>M=M2.
Barbarian=11,500=12,000=12%=P1.20D=1.2=Knowledge=Edu.=12Dec.=Athena>>K=F.
Barbaric=5,500=5.5=80%=P5.50D=Earth-Midway=5 May=Gaia.
Barbarism=8,500=9,000=90%=P9.00D=9.0=Abstraction=Gods=Saturn=9Sept.>>A=Ø.
Barbarous=8,500=9,000=90%=P9.00D=9.0=Abstraction=Gods=Saturn=9Sept.>>A=Ø.
Barbary=6,500=7,000=70%=P7.00D=7.0=Lang.=Assets=Mars=6May=Pleiades.
Barbary Coast=3,000=30%=P3.00D=3.0=Creativity=Star=Muses=3 March=C=I.
Barbecue=12,500= 13,000 = 13% = P1.30D = 1.3 = Solar Core = Faculty = 13Jan.=Athena.
Barbed wire=5,000=50%=P5.00D=5.0=Law=Time=Venus=5May=Odite>>L=N.
Barbel=5,000=50%=P5.00D=5.0=Law=Time=Venus=5May=Odite>>L=N.
Barbell=6,000=60%=P6.00D=6.0=Man=Earth=Health=Royalty=6June=Gaia>M=M2.
Barber=6,000=60%=P6.00D=6.0=Man=Earth=Health=Royalty=6June=Gaia>M=M2.
Barberry=6,000=60%=P6.00D=6.0=Man=Earth=Health=Royalty=6June=Gaia>M=M2.
Barbershop=7,000=70%=P7.00D=7.0=Lang.=Assets=Mars=6May=Pleiades.
Barbital=3,000=30%=P3.00D=3.0=Creativity=Star=Muses=3 March=C=I.
Barbiturate=6,500=7,000=70%=P7.00D=7.0=Lang.=Assets=Mars=6May=Pleiades.
Barbituric acid=5,000=50%=P5.00D=5.0=Law=Time=Venus=5May=Odite>>L=N.
Barbuda=6,000=60%=P6.00D=6.0=Man=Earth=Health=Royalty=6June=Gaia>M=M2.
Barb wire=1,000=100%=10.0=1.0=Mind=Sun=1 January=Helios >> M=E4.
Barcelona=5,500=5.5=80%=P5.50D=Earth-Midway=5 May=Gaia.
Bar code=2,000=20%=P2.00D=2.0=Nature=Matter=Moon=2 Feb= Cupid>N=C.

Bard=7,000=70%=P7.00D=7.0=Lang.=Assets=Mars=6May=Pleiades.
One of an ancient Celtic order of singing narrative poets. A poet, esp. an exalted national poet. Peter Matthews-Akukalia invented many kinds of literatures: the Propoplay, Nidrapoe,Testapoe, Castle and Mindom styles of writing. He is the first African to write a play in the Old Shakespearean English naturally thus becoming reputed as African Shakespeare. This book is Sword of Honour (Days of St. Valentine). His inventions spans across the sciences arts business models and governance in a Creatocratic Order.

Bare=11,000=11%=P1.10D=1.1=Idea=Brainchild=Inventn.=11 Nov.=Athena>K=F.
Bareback=3,000=30%=P3.00D=3.0=Creativity=Star=Muses=3 March=C=I.
Barefaced=6,000=60%=P6.00D=6.0=Man=Earth=Health=Royalty=6June=Gaia>M=M2.
Barefoot=2,500=3,000=30%=P3.00D=3.0=Creativity=Star=Muses=3 March=C=I.
Barehanded=3,000=30%=P3.00D=3.0=Creativity=Star=Muses=3 March=C=I.
Bare legged=2,000=20%=P2.00D=2.0=Nature=Matter=Moon=2 Feb= Cupid>N=C.
Barely=5,000=50%=P5.00D=5.0=Law=Time=Venus=5May=Odite>>L=N.
Barents Sea=6,500=7,000=70%=P7.00D=7.0=Lang.=Assets=Mars=6May=Pleiades.
Barf=1,500=15%=P1.50D=1.5=Authority = Solar Crown = Solar Core = 1 May = Maia.
Bar fly=3,000=30%=P3.00D=3.0=Creativity=Star=Muses=3 March=C=I.
Bargain=30,000=3,000=30%=P3.00D=3.0=Creativity=Star=Muses=3 March=C=I.

Barge=13,000= 13,000 = 13% = P1.30D = 1.3 = Solar Core = Faculty = 13Jan.=Athena. Athena is known to be the Goddess of marine warfare and the barge of the sea by Greek mythology. The Creatocracy bank has confirmed this truth hence truth is established. Spirits come alive when built into their operating but disintegrated codes. Thus the Mind of GOD required to be known in the book of Romans 11:34 & 12:2 is now known on things.

Bar graph=8,000=80%=P8.00D=8.0=Econ.=Curr.=Busn.=Jupt.=8Aug=Zeus>E=v.
Barite=5,500=5.5=80%=P5.50D=Earth-Midway=5 May=Gaia.
Baritone=9,500=10,000=1,000=100%=10.0=Physicality=Tech.=10 Oct.=Uranus=P=1Ø.
Barium=11,000=11%=P1.10D=1.1=Idea=Brainchild=Inventn.=11 Nov.=Athena>K=F.
Bark(1)=8,500=9,000=90%=P9.00D=9.0=Abstraction=Gods=Saturn=9Sept.>>A=Ø.
Bark(2)=11,000=11%=P1.10D=1.1=Idea=Brainchild=Inventn.=11 Nov.=Athena>K=F.
Bark(3)=7,000=70%=P7.00D=7.0=Lang.=Assets=Mars=6May=Pleiades.
Barkeeper=4,500=5,000=50%=P5.00D=5.0=Law=Time=Venus=5May=Odite>>L=N.
Barker=11,000=11%=P1.10D=1.1=Idea=Brainchild=Inventn.=11 Nov.=Athena>K=F.
Barley=7,500=8,000=80%=P8.00D=8.0=Econ.=Curr.=Busn.=Jupt.=8Aug=Zeus>E=v.
Barmaid=4,000=40%=P4.00D=4.0=Govt.=Creat.= 4 April=Hermes>>G=A4.
Barman=4,000=40%=P4.00D=4.0=Govt.=Creat.= 4 April=Hermes>>G=A4.
Bar mitzvah=12,000=12%=P1.20D=1.2=Knowledge=Edu.=12Dec.=Athena>>K=F.
Barn=6,000=60%=P6.00D=6.0=Man=Earth=Health=Royalty=6June=Gaia>M=M2.
Barnacle=5,500=5.5=80%=P5.50D=Earth-Midway=5 May=Gaia.
Barnard Christian Neethling=2,500=3,000=30%=P3.00D=Creativity=Star=3March=C=I.
Barnaul=4,500=5,000=50%=P5.00D=5.0=Law=Time=Venus=5May=Odite>>L=N.

Barn owl=6,000=60%=P6.00D=6.0=Man=Earth=Health=Royalty=6June=Gaia>M=M2.
Barnstorm=8,000=80%=P8.00D=8.0=Econ.=Curr.=Busn.=Jupt.=8Aug=Zeus>E=v.
Barnum P(hineas) T(aylor)=2,500=3,000=30%=P3.00D=Creativity=Muses=3March=C=I.
Barnyard=4,500=5,000=50%=P5.00D=5.0=Law=Time=Venus=5May=Odite>>L=N.
Barograph=1,500=15%=P1.50D=1.5=Authority = Solar Crown = Solar Core = 1 May = Maia.
Barometer=7,500=8,000=80%=P8.00D=8.0=Econ.=Curr.=Busn.=Jupt.=8Aug=Zeus>E=v.
Baron=11,000=11%=P1.10D=1.1=Idea=Brainchild=Inventn.=11 Nov.=Athena>K=F.
Baroness=5,500=5.5=80%=P5.50D=Earth-Midway=5 May=Gaia.
Baronet=4,500=5,000=50%=P5.00D=5.0=Law=Time=Venus=5May=Odite>>L=N.
Baronetess=4,500=5,000=50%=P5.00D=5.0=Law=Time=Venus=5May=Odite>>L=N.
Baroque=17,500=18,000=18%=P1.80D=1.8=Solar Currency=MaksCurrencies=1 Aug=Maia.
Barque=1,500=15%=P1.50D=1.5=Authority = Solar Crown = Solar Core = 1 May = Maia.
Barquisimeto=4,500=5,000=50%=P5.00D=5.0=Law=Time=Venus=5May=Odite>>L=N.
Barrack=9,500=10,000=1,000=100%=10.0=Physicality=Tech.=10 Oct.=Uranus=P=1Ø.
Barracuda=6,000=60%=P6.00D=6.0=Man=Earth=Health=Royalty=6June=Gaia>M=M2.
Barrage=11,000=11%=P1.10D=1.1=Idea=Brainchild=Inventn.=11 Nov.=Athena>K=F.
Barranquilla=7,000=70%=P7.00D=7.0=Lang.=Assets=Mars=6May=Pleiades.
Barratry=13,500=14,000=14%=P1.40D=1.4=Mgt.=Solar Core=13 May=Athena>>SC=0.1
Barrel=21,000=12,000=12%=P1.20D=1.2=Knowledge=Edu.=12Dec.=Athena>>K=F.
Barrel organ=7,500=8,000=80%=P8.00D=8.0=Econ.=Busn.=Jupt.=8Aug=Zeus>E=v.
Barrel roll=7,000=70%=P7.00D=7.0=Lang.=Assets=Mars=6May=Pleiades.
Barren=12,000=12%=P1.20D=1.2=Knowledge=Edu.=12Dec.=Athena>>K=F.
Barrette=1,500=15%=P1.50D=1.5=Authority = Solar Crown = Solar Core = 1 May = Maia.
Barricade=7,000=70%=P7.00D=7.0=Lang.=Assets=Mars=6May=Pleiades.
Barrier=7,500=8,000=80%=P8.00D=8.0=Econ.=Curr.=Busn.=Jupt.=8Aug=Zeus>E=v.
Barrier reef=10,000=1,000=100%=10.0=Physicality=Tech.=10 Oct.=Uranus=P=1Ø.
Barring=3,000=30%=P3.00D=3.0=Creativity=Star=Muses=3 March=C=I.
Barrio=5,000=50%=P5.00D=5.0=Law=Time=Venus=5May=Odite>>L=N.
Barrister=5,500=5.5=80%=P5.50D=Earth-Midway=5 May=Gaia.
Barroom=4,500=5,000=50%=P5.00D=5.0=Law=Time=Venus=5May=Odite>>L=N.
Barrow(1)=6,000=60%=P6.00D=6.0=Man=Earth=Health=Royalty=6June=Gaia>M=M2.
Barrow(2)=5,500=5.5=80%=P5.50D=Earth-Midway=5 May=Gaia.
Barrow, Point=4,500=5,000=50%=P5.00D=5.0=Law=Time=Venus=5May=Odite>>L=N.
Barrymore=7,500=8,000=80%=P8.00D=8.0=Econ.=Curr.=Busn.=Jupt.=8Aug=Zeus>E=v.
Bartender=4,500=5,000=50%=P5.00D=5.0=Law=Time=Venus=5May=Odite>>L=N.
Barter=4,000=40%=P4.00D=4.0=Govt.=Creat.= 4 April=Hermes>>G=A4.

Bartholdi FrédéricAuguste=4,500=5,000=50%=P5.00D=5.0=Law=Venus=5May=Odite.
French sculptor of the Statue of Liberty. AuthorHouse designed the Creatocracy Crown.

Bartholomew=3,000=30%=P3.00D=3.0=Creativity=Star=Muses=3 March=C=I.
Bartlett John=3,000=30%=P3.00D=3.0=Creativity=Star=Muses=3 March=C=I.
Bartók Bèla=3,000=30%=P3.00D=3.0=Creativity=Star=Muses=3 March=C=I.

Barton Clara=5,000=50%=P5.00D=5.0=Law=Time=Venus=5May=Odite>>L=N. 1821-1912. Amer. Founder of the American Red Cross (1881). Peter Matthews-Akukalia is a Nigerian by birth and Disean by creation. Founder of the Creativity Clubs.

Baruch=2,000=20%=P2.00D=2.0=Nature=Matter=Moon=2 Feb= Cupid>N=C.
Baruch Bernard Mannes=4,000=40%=P4.00D=4.0=Govt.= 4 April=Hermes>>G=A4.
Baryon=8,000=80%=P8.00D=8.0=Econ.=Curr.=Busn.=Jupt.=8Aug=Zeus>E=v.
Basal=5,000=50%=P5.00D=5.0=Law=Time=Venus=5May=Odite>>L=N.

Basal metabolism=8,000=80%=P8.00D=8.0=Econ.=Curr.=Busn.=Jupt.=8Aug=Zeus>E=v. The minimum amount of energy required to maintain vital functions in an organism at complete rest. Peter Matthews-Akukalia successfully calculated the creative mind energy. He commuted the inherent energy in the mind of a person required to manage potentials and capabilities and named it the General Interest Level. He measures the quantum of brain energy and its type necessary in predicting the inherent potentials of a person. He invented the CCLT instrument to measure human emotions and afterwards invented Makupedia the first human mind computer and super computers for complete Mind assessment in man. Basal metabolism is direct asset of Zeus. These inventions make the belief and convictions that Peter Matthews-Akukalia is the incarnation of Zeus. In ordinary sense he is a God.

Basalt=3,000=30%=P3.00D=3.0=Creativity=Star=Muses=3 March=C=I.
Base(1)=30,000=3,000=30%=P3.00D=3.0=Creativity=Star=Muses=3 March=C=I.
Base(2)=7,500=8,000=80%=P8.00D=8.0=Econ.=Curr.=Busn.=Jupt.=8Aug=Zeus>E=v.
Baseball=20,000=2,000=20%=P2.00D=2.0=Nature=Matter=Moon=2 Feb= Cupid>N=C.
Baseboard=6,000=60%=P6.00D=6.0=Man=Earth=Health=Royalty=6June=Gaia>M=M2.
Base born=4,500=5,000=50%=P5.00D=5.0=Law=Time=Venus=5May=Odite>>L=N.
Base hit=5,000=50%=P5.00D=5.0=Law=Time=Venus=5May=Odite>>L=N.
Basel=5,500=5.5=80%=P5.50D=Earth-Midway=5 May=Gaia.
Baseless=7,500=8,000=80%=P8.00D=8.0=Econ.=Curr.=Busn.=Jupt.=8Aug=Zeus>E=v.
Base line=17,000=17%=P1.70D=1.7=Solar Asset =17 Feb.=Maia>>Mind Computing.
Baseman=5,000=50%=P5.00D=5.0=Law=Time=Venus=5May=Odite>>L=N.
Basement=6,500=7,000=70%=P7.00D=7.0=Lang.=Assets=Mars= 6May=Pleiades.
Basenji=4,500=5,000=50%=P5.00D=5.0=Law=Time=Venus=5May=Odite>>L=N.
Base-on balls=7,500=8,000=80%=P8.00D=8.0=Econ.=Busn.=Jupt.=8Aug=Zeus>E=v.
Bases=1,500=15%=P1.50D=1.5=Authority = Solar Crown = Solar Core = 1 May = Maia.
Bash=7,000=70%=P7.00D=7.0=Lang.=Assets=Mars= 6May=Pleiades.
Bashful=2,000=20%=P2.00D=2.0=Nature=Matter=Moon=2 Feb= Cupid>N=C.
Basic=14,000=14%=P1.40D=1.4=Mgt.=Solar Core=13 May=Athena>>SC=0.1
BASIC=4,000=40%=P4.00D=4.0=Govt.=Creat.= 4 April=Hermes>>G=A4.
Basil=5,000=50%=P5.00D=5.0=Law=Time=Venus=5May=Odite>>L=N.
Basilica=14,000=14%=P1.40D=1.4=Mgt.=Solar Core=13 May=Athena>>SC=0.1
Basilisk=11,000=11%=P1.10D=1.1=Idea=Brainchild=Inventn.=11 Nov.=Athena>K=F.
Basin=18,000=18%=P1.80D=1.8=Solar Currency=MaksCurrencies=1 Aug=Maia.

Basis=5,500=5.5=80%=P5.50D=Earth-Midway=5 May=Gaia.
A fundamental principle of Creatocracy is institutionalizing creativity through the Creative Sciences and promoting the creative economy for all human and godly benefits. Principles show that the visionary has arrived mid-Earth and interacts with Gaia the Earth Goddess.

Bask=7,500=8,000=80%=P8.00D=8.0=Econ.=Curr.=Busn.=Jupt.=8Aug=Zeus>E=v.
Basket= 13,000 = 13% = P1.30D = 1.3 = Solar Core = Faculty = 13Jan.=Athena.
Basketball=16,000=16%=P1.60D=1.6=Cycle of Life=Incarnation=MindofGOD= 1June= Maia.
Basket case=5,500=5.5=80%=P5.50D=Earth-Midway=5 May=Gaia.
Basketry=3,000=30%=P3.00D=3.0=Creativity=Star=Muses=3 March=C=I.
Bas mitzvah=2,000=20%=P2.00D=2.0=Nature=Matter=Moon=2 Feb= Cupid>N=C.
Basque=11,500=12,000=12%=P1.20D=1.2=Knowledge=Edu.=12Dec.=Athena>>K=F.
Basque Provinces=6,000=60%=P6.00D=6.0=Man=Earth=Royalty=6June=Gaia>M=M2.
Basra=6,000=60%=P6.00D=6.0=Man=Earth=Health=Royalty=6June=Gaia>M=M2.
Bas-relief=1,500=15%=P1.50D=1.5=Authority = Solar Crown = Solar Core = 1 May = Maia.
Bass(1)=7,000=70%=P7.00D=7.0=Lang.=Assets=Mars= 6May=Pleiades.
Bass(2)=15,000=15%=P1.50D=1.5=Authority = Solar Crown = Solar Core = 1 May = Maia.
Basseterre=7,000=70%=P7.00D=7.0=Lang.=Assets=Mars= 6May=Pleiades.
Basse-Terre=8,500=9,000=90%=P9.00D=9.0=Abstraction=Gods=Saturn=9Sept.>>A=Ø.
Basset hound=5,500=5.5=80%=P5.50D=Earth-Midway=5 May=Gaia.
Bassinet=5,000=50%=P5.00D=5.0=Law=Time=Venus=5May=Odite>>L=N.
Bassist=4,500=5,000=50%=P5.00D=5.0=Law=Time=Venus=5May=Odite>>L=N.
Basso=3,500=4,000=40%=P4.00D=4.0=Govt.=Creat.= 4 April=Hermes>>G=A4.
Bassoon=5,500=5.5=80%=P5.50D=Earth-Midway=5 May=Gaia.
Bass Strait=7,500=8,000=80%=P8.00D=8.0=Econ.=Curr.=Busn.=Jupt.=8Aug=Zeus>E=v.
Bass viol=1,500=15%=P1.50D=1.5=Authority = Solar Crown = Solar Core = 1 May = Maia.
Basswood=3,500=4,000=40%=P4.00D=4.0=Govt.=Creat.= 4 April=Hermes>>G=A4.
Bast=4,500=5,000=50%=P5.00D=5.0=Law=Time=Venus=5May=Odite>>L=N.
Bastard=5,000=50%=P5.00D=5.0=Law=Time=Venus=5May=Odite>>L=N.
Bastardize=3,500=4,000=40%=P4.00D=4.0=Govt.=Creat.= 4 April=Hermes>>G=A4.
Baste(1)=3,500=4,000=40%=P4.00D=4.0=Govt.=Creat.= 4 April=Hermes>>G=A4.
Baste(2)=5,000=50%=P5.00D=5.0=Law=Time=Venus=5May=Odite>>L=N.
Baste(3)=5,500=5.5=80%=P5.50D=Earth-Midway=5 May=Gaia.
Bastille Day=6,500=7,000=70%=P7.00D=7.0=Lang.=Assets=Mars=6May=Pleiades.

Bastion=3,500=4,000=40%=P4.00D=4.0=Govt.=Creat.= 4 April=Hermes>>G=A4.
A bulwark. The Creatocracy has Helen of Bulwark as an Angel and a Director in Makupedia.

Bat(1)=26,500=3,000=30%=P3.00D=3.0=Creativity=Star=Muses=3 March=C=I.
Bat(2)=4,500=5,000=50%=P5.00D=5.0=Law=Time=Venus=5May=Odite>>L=N.
Bat(3)=2,500=3,000=30%=P3.00D=3.0=Creativity=Star=Muses=3 March=C=I.
Bat(4)=2,000=20%=P2.00D=2.0=Nature=Matter=Moon=2 Feb= Cupid>N=C.
Bataan=7,000=70%=P7.00D=7.0=Lang.=Assets=Mars=6May=Pleiades.

Batch=12,000=12%=P1.20D=1.2=Knowledge=Edu.=12Dec.=Athena>>K=F.
Bate=3,000=30%=P3.00D=3.0=Creativity=Star=Muses=3 March=C=I.
Bateau=2,500=3,000=30%=P3.00D=3.0=Creativity=Star=Muses=3 March=C=I.
Bath=15,000=15%=P1.50D=1.5=Authority = Solar Crown = Solar Core = 1 May = Maia.
Bath=5,000=50%=P5.00D=5.0=Law=Time=Venus=5May=Odite>>L=N.
Bathe=8,500=9,000=90%=P9.00D=9.0=Abstraction=Gods=Saturn=9Sept.>>A=Ø.
Bathhouse=5,500=5.5=80%=P5.50D=Earth-Midway=5 May=Gaia.
Bathing suit=1,000=100%=10.0=1.0=Mind=Sun=1 January=Helios >> M=E4.
Bathos=7,500=8,000=80%=P8.00D=8.0=Econ.=Curr.=Busn.=Jupt.=8Aug=Zeus>E=v.
Bathrobe=6,000=60%=P6.00D=6.0=Man=Earth=Health=Royalty=6June=Gaia>M=M2.
Bathroom=6,000=60%=P6.00D=6.0=Man=Earth=Health=Royalty=6June=Gaia>M=M2.
Bath salts=5,500=5.5=80%=P5.50D=Earth-Midway=5 May=Gaia.

Bathsheba=5,500=5.5=80%=P5.50D=Earth-Midway=5 May=Gaia.
Bathsheba was a daughter of Gaia. Solomon was clearly born a royalty by cosmic law.

Bathtub=3,000=30%=P3.00D=3.0=Creativity=Star=Muses=3 March=C=I.
Bathy scaph=5,500=5.5=80%=P5.50D=Earth-Midway=5 May=Gaia.
Bathysphere=4,500=5,000=50%=P5.00D=5.0=Law=Time=Venus=5May=Odite>>L=N.
Batik=6,500=7,000=70%=P7.00D=7.0=Lang.=Assets=Mars=6May=Pleiades.
Batiste=2,500=3,000=30%=P3.00D=3.0=Creativity=Star=Muses=3 March=C=I.
Bat mitzvah=14,000=14%=P1.40D=1.4=Mgt.=Solar Core=13 May=Athena>>SC=0.1
Baton=14,000=14%=P1.40D=1.4=Mgt.=Solar Core=13 May=Athena>>SC=0.1
Baton Rouge=5,500=5.5=80%=P5.50D=Earth-Midway=5 May=Gaia.
Bats=1,500=15%=P1.50D=1.5=Authority = Solar Crown = Solar Core = 1 May = Maia.
Batsman=4,000=40%=P4.00D=4.0=Govt.=Creat.= 4 April=Hermes>>G=A4.
Battalion=9,000=90%=P9.00D=9.0=Abstraction=Gods=Saturn=9Sept.>>A=Ø.
Batten=10,000=1,000=100%=10.0=Physicality=Tech.=10 Oct.=Uranus=P=1Ø.
Batter(1)=15,000=15%=P1.50D=1.5=Authority = Solar Crown = Solar Core = 1 May = Maia.
Batter(2)=4,000=40%=P4.00D=4.0=Govt.=Creat.= 4 April=Hermes>>G=A4.
Batter(3)=6,000=60%=P6.00D=6.0=Man=Earth=Health=Royalty=6June=Gaia>M=M2.
Battering ram=6,500=7,000=70%=P7.00D=7.0=Lang.=Assets=Mars=6May=Pleiades.
Battery=20,500=21,000=12,000=12%=P1.20D=1.2=Knowl.=Edu.=12Dec.=Athena>>K=F.
Batting=5,000=50%=P5.00D=5.0=Law=Time=Venus=5May=Odite>>L=N.
Batting average=6,500=7,000=70%=P7.00D=7.0=Lang.=Assets=Mars=6May=Pleiades.
Battle=10,500=11,000=11%=P1.10D=1.1=Idea=Brainchild=Inventn.=11 Nov.=Athena>K=F.
Battle-ax=4,500=5,000=50%=P5.00D=5.0=Law=Time=Venus=5May=Odite>>L=N.
Battle cry=4,000=40%=P4.00D=4.0=Govt.=Creat.= 4 April=Hermes>>G=A4.
Battlefield=5,000=50%=P5.00D=5.0=Law=Time=Venus=5May=Odite>>L=N.
Battlefront=3,500=4,000=40%=P4.00D=4.0=Govt.=Creat.= 4 April=Hermes>>G=A4.
Battleground=1,000=100%=10.0=1.0=Mind=Sun=1 January=Helios >> M=E4.
Battlement=6,000=60%=P6.00D=6.0=Man=Earth=Health=Royalty=6June=Gaia>M=M2.
Battle royal=4,500=5,000=50%=P5.00D=5.0=Law=Time=Venus=5May=Odite>>L=N.
Battleship=5,500=5.5=80%=P5.50D=Earth-Midway=5 May=Gaia.
Batty=1,000=100%=10.0=1.0=Mind=Sun=1 January=Helios >> M=E4.

Bauble=1,000=100%=10.0=1.0=Mind=Sun=1 January=Helios >> M=E4.
Baud=7,000=70%=P7.00D=7.0=Lang.=Assets=Mars=6May=Pleiades.
Baudelaire Charles Pierre=3,500=4,000=40%=P4.00D=4.0= 4 April=Hermes>>G=A4.
Baudouin I=3,000=30%=P3.00D=3.0=Creativity=Star=Muses=3 March=C=I.
Bauxite=5,500=5.5=80%=P5.50D=Earth-Midway=5 May=Gaia.
Bavaria=2,500=3,000=30%=P3.00D=3.0=Creativity=Star=Muses=3 March=C=I.
Bawd=3,500=4,000=40%=P4.00D=4.0=Govt.=Creat.= 4 April=Hermes>>G=A4.
Bawdy=2,500=3,000=30%=P3.00D=3.0=Creativity=Star=Muses=3 March=C=I.
Bawl=7,000=70%=P7.00D=7.0=Lang.=Assets=Mars=6May=Pleiades.
Bay(1)=7,500=8,000=80%=P8.00D=8.0=Econ.=Curr.=Busn.=Jupt.=8Aug=Zeus>E=v.
Bay(2)=14,000=14%=P1.40D=1.4=Mgt.=Solar Core=13 May=Athena>>SC=0.1
Bay(3)=3,000=30%=P3.00D=3.0=Creativity=Star=Muses=3 March=C=I.
Bay(4)=10,500=11,000=11%=P1.10D=1.1=Idea=Brainchild=Inventn.=11 Nov.=Athena>K=F.
Bay(5)=6,500=7,000=70%=P7.00D=7.0=Lang.=Assets=Mars=6May=Pleiades.
Bayamón=5,500=5.5=80%=P5.50D=Earth-Midway=5 May=Gaia.
Bayberry=6,000=60%=P6.00D=6.0=Man=Earth=Health=Royalty=6June=Gaia>M=M2.
Baykal Lake=1,500=15%=P1.50D=1.5=Authority = Solar Crown = Solar Core = 1 May = Maia.
Bay leaf=5,500=5.5=80%=P5.50D=Earth-Midway=5 May=Gaia.
Bayonet=6,500=7,000=70%=P7.00D=7.0=Lang.=Assets=Mars=6May=Pleiades.
Bayou=6,500=7,000=70%=P7.00D=7.0=Lang.=Assets=Mars=6May=Pleiades.
Bayreuth=4,000=40%=P4.00D=4.0=Govt.=Creat.= 4 April=Hermes>>G=A4.
Bay window=7,000=70%=P7.00D=7.0=Lang.=Assets=Mars=6May=Pleiades.
Bazaar =10,000=1,000=100%=10.0=Physicality=Tech.=10 Oct.=Uranus=P=1Ø.
Bazooka=7,000=70%=P7.00D=7.0=Lang.=Assets=Mars=6May=Pleiades.
BB=5,000=50%=P5.00D=5.0=Law=Time=Venus=5May=Odite>>L=N.
bbl=1,000=100%=10.0=1.0=Mind=Sun=1 January=Helios >> M=E4.
B.C.=4,000=40%=P4.00D=4.0=Govt.=Creat.= 4 April=Hermes>>G=A4.
B.C.E=3,000=30%=P3.00D=3.0=Creativity=Star=Muses=3 March=C=I.
B cell=5,500=5.5=80%=P5.50D=Earth-Midway=5 May=Gaia.
bd.ft.=1,000=100%=10.0=1.0=Mind=Sun=1 January=Helios >> M=E4.
bdrm.=1,000=100%=10.0=1.0=Mind=Sun=1 January=Helios >> M=E4.
Be=42,500>>4.3>>=2,000=20%=P2.00D=2.0=Nature=Matter=Moon=2 Feb= Cupid>N=C.
Be(beryllium)=3,000=30%=P3.00D=3.0=Creativity=Star=Muses=3 March=C=I.
Be-=10,000=1,000=100%=10.0=Physicality=Tech.=10 Oct.=Uranus=P=1Ø.
Beach=7,500=8,000=80%=P8.00D=8.0=Econ.=Curr.=Busn.=Jupt.=8Aug=Zeus>E=v.
Beach buggy=1,500=15%=P1.50D=1.5=Authority = Solar Crown = SolarCore = 1 May=Maia.
Beachcomber=2,500=3,000=30%=P3.00D=3.0=Creativity=Star=Muses=3 March=C=I.
Beachhead=11,000=11%=P1.10D=1.1=Idea=Brainchild=Inventn.=11 Nov.=Athena>K=F.
Beacon=6,000=60%=P6.00D=6.0=Man=Earth=Health=Royalty=6June=Gaia>M=M2.
Bead=16,000=16%=P1.60D=1.6=Cycle of Life=Incarnation=Mind of GOD=1June= Maia.
Beadie=4,500=5,000=50%=P5.00D=5.0=Law=Time=Venus=5May=Odite>>L=N.
Beady=3,000=30%=P3.00D=3.0=Creativity=Star=Muses=3 March=C=I.
Beagle=6,500=7,000=70%=P7.00D=7.0=Lang.=Assets=Mars=6May=Pleiades.
Beak=6,000=60%=P6.00D=6.0=Man=Earth=Health=Royalty=6June=Gaia>M=M2.
Beaker=9,000=90%=P9.00D=9.0=Abstraction=Gods=Saturn=9Sept.>>A=Ø.

Beam=22,000=22%=P2.20D=2.2=4.0=Govt.=Creatocracy=2Feb=Hermes>G=A4.
Bean=15,000=15%=P1.50D=1.5=Authority = Solar Crown = Solar Core = 1 May = Maia.
Beanbag=5,500=5.5=80%=P5.50D=Earth-Midway=5 May=Gaia.
Beanball=4,000=40%=P4.00D=4.0=Govt.=Creat.= 4 April=Hermes>>G=A4.
Bean curd=500=5%=P5.00D=5.0=Law=Time=Venus=5 May=Aphrodite>>L=N.
Beanie=2,000=20%=P2.00D=2.0=Nature=Matter=Moon=2 Feb= Cupid>N=C.
Beano=2,000=20%=P2.00D=2.0=Nature=Matter=Moon=2 Feb= Cupid>N=C.
Bean sprouts=5,000=50%=P5.00D=5.0=Law=Time=Venus=5May=Odite>>L=N.
Bear(1)=37,500=4,000=40%=P4.00D=4.0=Govt.=Creat.= 4 April=Hermes>>G=A4.
Bear(2)=13,500=14,000=14%=P1.40D=1.4=Mgt.=Solar Core=13 May=Athena>>SC=0.1
Beard=8,500=9,000=90%=P9.00D=9.0=Abstraction=Gods=Saturn=9Sept.>>A=Ø.
Bearer=5,000=50%=P5.00D=5.0=Law=Time=Venus=5May=Odite>>L=N.
Bear hug=2,000=20%=P2.00D=2.0=Nature=Matter=Moon=2 Feb= Cupid>N=C.
Bearing=25,000=30,000=3,000=30%=P3.00D=3.0=Creativity=Star=Muses=3 March=C=I.
Béarnaise sauce=4,000=40%=P4.00D=4.0=Govt.=Creat.= 4 April=Hermes>>G=A4.
Bear River=7,500=8,000=80%=P8.00D=8.0=Econ.=Curr.=Busn.=Jupt.=8Aug=Zeus>E=v.
Bearskin=5,000=50%=P5.00D=5.0=Law=Time=Venus=5May=Odite>>L=N.
Beast=5,500=5.5=80%=P5.50D=Earth-Midway=5 May=Gaia.
Beastly=5,500=5.5=80%=P5.50D=Earth-Midway=5 May=Gaia.
Beat=43,000>>4.3>>2.0=2,000=20%=P2.00D=Nature=Moon=2 Feb= Cupid>N=C.
Beatific=4,000=40%=P4.00D=4.0=Govt.=Creat.= 4 April=Hermes>>G=A4.
Beatify=7,000=70%=P7.00D=7.0=Lang.=Assets=Mars=6May=Pleiades.
Beatitude=1,000=100%=10.0=1.0=Mind=Sun=1 January=Helios >> M=E4.
Beatnik=8,000=80%=P8.00D=8.0=Econ.=Curr.=Busn.=Jupt.=8Aug=Zeus>E=v.

Beatrix=4,000=40%=P4.00D=4.0=Govt.=Creat.= 4 April=Hermes>>G=A4.
Queen of the Netherlands since 1980. Since 2011 at the emergence of Peter Matthews-
Akukalia as African Shakespeare Tina Chinwe Etigwam has been the Queen of Paradise.
By the marriage of the Emperor to Alice the Queen of Fortune, Tina was elevated to Head
Queen of Paradise and Goddess De-Makupedia (GDM). The King published Athena as
Goddess and aegis of the Creatocracy in his Crown book: The Creatocracy Republic.

Beat-up=4,000=40%=P4.00D=4.0=Govt.=Creat.= 4 April=Hermes>>G=A4.
Beau=3,000=3,000=30%=P3.00D=3.0=Creativity=Star=Muses=3 March=C=I.
Beaufort Sea=6,000=60%=P6.00D=6.0=Man=Earth=Health=Royalty=6June=Gaia>M=M2.
Beau gestes=4,500=5,000=50%=P5.00D=5.0=Law=Time=Venus=5May=Odite>>L=N.

Beauharnais Josephine de.=6,000=60%=P6.00D=6.0=Man=Earth=6June=Gaia>M=M2.
Empress of the French as wife of Napoleon I. Tina is the Empress of Paradise Nations and
Head of the Creatocracy Bank and Courts. Other offices for Queens are by appointment.
Interestingly Josephine Madubueze sponsored partly the Creativity project by funding the
publishing of the Oracle in 2012 alongside Professor Michael Adikwu. Cosmos Michaels
contributed immensely in the much earlier days of suffering and his impact is rewarded.

Beau ideals=2,500=3,000=30%=P3.00D=3.0=Creativity=Star=Muses=3 March=C=I.
Beaumarchais Pierre Augustine Caron de.=2,000=20%=P2.00D=2.0=Nature=Cupid>N=C.
Beau monde=1,000=100%=10.0=1.0=Mind=Sun=1 January=Helios >> M=E4.
Beaumont=4,500=5,000=50%=P5.00D=5.0=Law=Time=Venus=5May=Odite>>L=N.
Beaumont Francis=3,000=30%=P3.00D=3.0=Creativity=Star=Muses=3 March=C=I.
Beauteous=500=5%=P5.00D=5.0=Law=Time=Venus=5 May=Aphrodite>>L=N.
Beautician=3,000=30%=P3.00D=3.0=Creativity=Star=Muses=3 March=C=I.
Beautiful=1,000=100%=10.0=1.0=Mind=Sun=1 January=Helios >> M=E4.
Beautify=2,500=3,000=30%=P3.00D=3.0=Creativity=Star=Muses=3 March=C=I.
Beauty=8,000=80%=P8.00D=8.0=Econ.=Curr.=Busn.=Jupt.=8Aug=Zeus>E=v.
Beauty mark=2,000=20%=P2.00D=2.0=Nature=Matter=Moon=2 Feb= Cupid>N=C.
Beauty parlor=6,500=7,000=70%=P7.00D=7.0=Lang.=Assets=Mars=6May=Pleiades.
Beauvoir Simone de.=3,500=4,000=40%=P4.00D=4.0=Govt.= 4 April=Hermes>>G=A4.
Beaux=2,000=20%=P2.00D=2.0=Nature=Matter=Moon=2 Feb= Cupid>N=C.
Beaux-arts=1,500=15%=P1.50D=1.5=Authority = Solar Crown = Solar Core = 1 May = Maia.
Beaver=13,500=14,000=14%=P1.40D=1.4=Mgt.=Solar Core=13 May=Athena>>SC=0.1
Beaver board=3,000=30%=P3.00D=3.0=Creativity=Star=Muses=3 March=C=I.
Bebop=5,500=5.5=80%=P5.50D=Earth-Midway=5 May=Gaia.
Because=2,500=3,000=30%=P3.00D=3.0=Creativity=Star=Muses=3 March=C=I.
Beck=5,000=50%=P5.00D=5.0=Law=Time=Venus=5May=Odite>>L=N.
Becket Saint Thomas à=3,500=4,000=40%=P4.00D=4.0=Govt.=4April=Hermes>>G=A4.
Becket Samuel=3,500=4,000=40%=P4.00D=4.0=Govt.=Creat.= 4April=Hermes>>G=A4.
Beckon=5,000=50%=P5.00D=5.0=Law=Time=Venus=5May=Odite>>L=N.
Becloud=1,000=100%=10.0=1.0=Mind=Sun=1 January=Helios >> M=E4.
Become=6,000=60%=P6.00D=6.0=Man=Earth=Health=Royalty=6June=Gaia>M=M2.
Becoming=2,500=3,000=30%=P3.00D=3.0=Creativity=Star=Muses=3 March=C=I.
Bed=26,000=3,000=30%=P3.00D=3.0=Creativity=Star=Muses=3 March=C=I.
Be daub=1,500=15%=P1.50D=1.5=Authority = Solar Crown = Solar Core = 1 May = Maia.
Bedazzle=4,500=5,000=50%=P5.00D=5.0=Law=Time=Venus=5May=Odite>>L=N.
Bedbug=5,000=50%=P5.00D=5.0=Law=Time=Venus=5May=Odite>>L=N.
Bedclothes=4,000=40%=P4.00D=4.0=Govt.=Creat.= 4 April=Hermes>>G=A4.
Bedding=5,000=50%=P5.00D=5.0=Law=Time=Venus=5May=Odite>>L=N.
Bede=4,000=40%=P4.00D=4.0=Govt.=Creat.= 4 April=Hermes>>G=A4.
Bedeck=2,000=20%=P2.00D=2.0=Nature=Matter=Moon=2 Feb= Cupid>N=C.
Bedevil=3,500=4,000=40%=P4.00D=4.0=Govt.=Creat.= 4 April=Hermes>>G=A4.
Bedew=3,000=30%=P3.00D=3.0=Creativity=Star=Muses=3 March=C=I.
Bedfellow=7,000=70%=P7.00D=7.0=Lang.=Assets=Mars=6May=Pleiades.

Bedlam=9,000=90%=P9.00D=9.0=Abstraction=Gods=Saturn=9Sept.>>A=Ø.
Hospital of St. Mary of Bethlehem, London. The Creatocracy applies psycho-surgery.
The organization for training Creative Scientists of the Royal Creatocracy is registered as
De-Royal Makupedia Limited or simply Makupedia.

Bedouin=6,000=60%=P6.00D=6.0=Man=Earth=Health=Royalty=6June=Gaia>M=M2.
Bedpan=4,000=40%=P4.00D=4.0=Govt.=Creat.= 4 April=Hermes>>G=A4.
Bedpost=4,000=40%=P4.00D=4.0=Govt.=Creat.= 4 April=Hermes>>G=A4.
Bedraggled=5,000=50%=P5.00D=5.0=Law=Time=Venus=5May=Odite>>L=N.
Bedridden=6,500=7,000=70%=P7.00D=7.0=Lang.=Assets=Mars=6May=Pleiades.
Bedrock=8,000=80%=P8.00D=8.0=Econ.=Curr.=Busn.=Jupt.=8Aug=Zeus>E=v.
Bedroll=5,000=50%=P5.00D=5.0=Law=Time=Venus=5May=Odite>>L=N.
Bedroom=3,000=30%=P3.00D=3.0=Creativity=Star=Muses=3 March=C=I.
Bedside=4,500=5,000=50%=P5.00D=5.0=Law=Time=Venus=5May=Odite>>L=N.
Bedsore=6,500=7,000=70%=P7.00D=7.0=Lang.=Assets=Mars=6May=Pleiades.
Bedspread=3,000=30%=P3.00D=3.0=Creativity=Star=Muses=3 March=C=I.
Bedstead=2,500=3,000=30%=P3.00D=3.0=Creativity=Star=Muses=3 March=C=I.
Bedtime=4,000=40%=P4.00D=4.0=Govt.=Creat.= 4 April=Hermes>>G=A4.
Bedouin=1,500=15%=P1.50D=1.5=Authority = Solar Crown = Solar Core = 1 May = Maia.
Bee=22,000=22%=P2.20D=2.2=4.0=Govt.=Creatocracy=2Feb=Hermes>G=A4.
Beech=6,500=7,000=70%=P7.00D=7.0=Lang.=Assets=Mars=6May=Pleiades.

Beecher,Lyman=8,500=9,000=90%=P9.00D=9.0=Abstract.=Gods=Saturn=9Sept.>>A=Ø.
Father of Henry Ward Beecher. Peter Matthews-Akukalia >> Castle Makupedia is the father
to the great Prince Victor Matthews-Akukalia >> Victor Castle and owns a large family.

Beef=16,500=17,000=17%=P1.70D=1.7=Solar Asset =17 Feb.=Maia>>Mind Computing.
Beefalo=8,000=80%=P8.00D=8.0=Econ.=Curr.=Busn.=Jupt.=8Aug=Zeus>E=v.
Beefeater=4,000=40%=P4.00D=4.0=Govt.=Creat.= 4 April=Hermes>>G=A4.
Beefy=2,000=20%=P2.00D=2.0=Nature=Matter=Moon=2 Feb= Cupid>N=C.
Beehive=4,000=40%=P4.00D=4.0=Govt.=Creat.= 4 April=Hermes>>G=A4.
Beekeeper=3,000=30%=P3.00D=3.0=Creativity=Star=Muses=3 March=C=I.
Beeline=2,000=20%=P2.00D=2.0=Nature=Matter=Moon=2 Feb= Cupid>N=C.
Beelzebub=1,000=100%=10.0=1.0=Mind=Sun=1 January=Helios >> M=E4.
Been=2,000=20%=P2.00D=2.0=Nature=Matter=Moon=2 Feb= Cupid>N=C.
Beep=4,500=5,000=50%=P5.00D=5.0=Law=Time=Venus=5May=Odite>>L=N.
Beeper=6,000=60%=P6.00D=6.0=Man=Earth=Health=Royalty=6June=Gaia>M=M2.
Beer=8,000=80%=P8.00D=8.0=Econ.=Curr.=Busn.=Jupt.=8Aug=Zeus>E=v.
Beeswax=7,000=70%=P7.00D=7.0=Lang.=Assets=Mars=6May=Pleiades.
Beet=6,500=7,000=70%=P7.00D=7.0=Lang.=Assets=Mars=6May=Pleiades.
Beethoven Ludwig Van.=2,000=20%=P2.00D=2.0=Nature=Moon=2 Feb= Cupid>N=C.
Beetle(1)=8,000=80%=P8.00D=8.0=Econ.=Curr.=Busn.=Jupt.=8Aug=Zeus>E=v.
Beetle(2)=2,500=3,000=30%=P3.00D=3.0=Creativity=Star=Muses=3 March=C=I.
Beeves=1,500=15%=P1.50D=1.5=Authority = Solar Crown = Solar Core = 1 May = Maia.
Befall=3,500=4,000=40%=P4.00D=4.0=Govt.=Creat.= 4 April=Hermes>>G=A4.
Befit=3,500=4,000=40%=P4.00D=4.0=Govt.=Creat.= 4 April=Hermes>>G=A4.
Be fog=2,000=20%=P2.00D=2.0=Nature=Matter=Moon=2 Feb= Cupid>N=C.
Before=19,000=19%=P1.90D=1.9=Solar Energy=Planets=Mind God=Maia.
Before Christ=4,500=5,000=50%=P5.00D=5.0=Law=Time=Venus=5May=Odite>>L=N.

Beforehand=1,500=15%=P1.50D=1.5=Authority = Solar Crown = Solar Core = 1 May = Maia.

Be foul=2,000=20%=P2.00D=2.0=Nature=Matter=Moon=2 Feb= Cupid>N=C.

Befriend=2,500=3,000=30%=P3.00D=3.0=Creativity=Star=Muses=3 March=C=I.

Befuddle=4,500=5,000=50%=P5.00D=5.0=Law=Time=Venus=5May=Odite>>L=N.

Beg=10,000=1,000=100%=10.0=Physicality=Tech.=10 Oct.=Uranus=P=1Ø.

Beget=2,500=3,000=30%=P3.00D=3.0=Creativity=Star=Muses=3 March=C=I.

Beggar=8,000=80%=P8.00D=8.0=Econ.=Curr.=Busn.=Jupt.=8Aug=Zeus>E=v.

Begin=3,500=4,000=40%=P4.00D=4.0=Govt.=Creat.= 4 April=Hermes>>G=A4.

Begin Menachem=9,000=90%=P9.00D=9.0=Abstraction=Gods=Saturn=9Sept.>>A=Ø.

Beginning=20,500=21,000=21%=P2.10D=2.1=3.0=Creativity=Star=Muses=2 Jan>>C=I.

Begone=2,500=3,000=30%=P3.00D=3.0=Creativity=Star=Muses=3 March=C=I.

Begonia=8,500=9,000=90%=P9.00D=9.0=Abstraction=Gods=Saturn=9Sept.>>A=Ø.

Be grime=4,500=5,000=50%=P5.00D=5.0=Law=Time=Venus=5May=Odite>>L=N.

Begrudge=2,500=3,000=30%=P3.00D=3.0=Creativity=Star=Muses=3 March=C=I.

Beguile=8,000=80%=P8.00D=8.0=Econ.=Curr.=Busn.=Jupt.=8Aug=Zeus>E=v.

Be gum=2,500=3,000=30%=P3.00D=3.0=Creativity=Star=Muses=3 March=C=I.

Behalf=5,500=5.5=80%=P5.50D=Earth-Midway=5 May=Gaia.

Behave=6,500=7,000=70%=P7.00D=7.0=Lang.=Assets=Mars=6May=Pleiades.

Behavior=8,000=80%=P8.00D=8.0=Econ.=Curr.=Busn.=Jupt.=8Aug=Zeus>E=v.

Behaviorism=7,500=8,000=80%=P8.00D=8.0=Econ.=Busn.=Jupt.=8Aug=Zeus>E=v.

Behead=1,000=100%=10.0=1.0=Mind=Sun=1 January=Helios >> M=E4.

Behemoth=6,000=60%=P6.00D=6.0=Man=Earth=Health=Royalty=6June=Gaia>M=M2.

Behest=2,500=3,000=30%=P3.00D=3.0=Creativity=Star=Muses=3 March=C=I.

Behind=29,000=3,000=30%=P3.00D=3.0=Creativity=Star=Muses=3 March=C=I.

Behind hand=3,000=30%=P3.00D=3.0=Creativity=Star=Muses=3 March=C=I.

Behold=5,500=5.5=80%=P5.50D=Earth-Midway=5 May=Gaia.

Beholden=3,500=4,000=40%=P4.00D=4.0=Govt.=Creat.= 4 April=Hermes>>G=A4.

Behoove=6,000=60%=P6.00D=6.0=Man=Earth=Health=Royalty=6June=Gaia>M=M2.

Belge=3,000=30%=P3.00D=3.0=Creativity=Star=Muses=3 March=C=I.

Beijing Peking=4,000=40%=P4.00D=4.0=Govt.=Creat.= 4 April=Hermes>>G=A4.

Being=10,500=11,000=11%=P1.10D=1.1=Idea=Brainchild=Inventn.=11 Nov.=Athena>K=F.

Beirut=6,000=60%=P6.00D=6.0=Man=Earth=Health=Royalty=6June=Gaia>M=M2.

Belabor=4,500=5,000=50%=P5.00D=5.0=Law=Time=Venus=5May=Odite>>L=N.

Belarus=1,000=100%=10.0=1.0=Mind=Sun=1 January=Helios >> M=E4.

Belated=3,500=4,000=40%=P4.00D=4.0=Govt.=Creat.= 4 April=Hermes>>G=A4.

Belau=6,000=60%=P6.00D=6.0=Man=Earth=Health=Royalty=6June=Gaia>M=M2.

Belay=9,500=10,000=1,000=100%=10.0=Physicality=Tech.=10 Oct.=Uranus=P=1Ø.

Belaying pin=6,500=7,000=70%=P7.00D=7.0=Lang.=Assets=Mars=6May=Pleiades.

Belch=6,000=60%=P6.00D=6.0=Man=Earth=Health=Royalty=6June=Gaia>M=M2.

Beleaguer=3,000=30%=P3.00D=3.0=Creativity=Star=Muses=3 March=C=I.

Belém=5,500=5.5=80%=P5.50D=Earth-Midway=5 May=Gaia.

Belfast=8,000=80%=P8.00D=8.0=Econ.=Curr.=Busn.=Jupt.=8Aug=Zeus>E=v.

Belfry=8,500=9,000=90%=P9.00D=9.0=Abstraction=Gods=Saturn=9Sept.>>A=Ø.

Belg.=1,000=100%=10.0=1.0=Mind=Sun=1 January=Helios >> M=E4.

Belgium=6,500=7,000=70%=P7.00D=7.0=Lang.=Assets=Mars=6May=Pleiades.

Belgrade=9,000=90%=P9.00D=9.0=Abstraction=Gods=Saturn=9Sept.>>A=Ø.
Belie=4,500=5,000=50%=P5.00D=5.0=Law=Time=Venus=5May=Odite>>L=N.
Belief=8,000=80%=P8.00D=8.0=Econ.=Curr.=Busn.=Jupt.=8Aug=Zeus>E=v.
Believable=5,000=50%=P5.00D=5.0=Law=Time=Venus=5May=Odite>>L=N.
Believe=12,500= 13,000 = 13% = P1.30D = 1.3 = Solar Core = Faculty = 13Jan.=Athena.
Belittle=4,000=40%=P4.00D=4.0=Govt.=Creat.= 4 April=Hermes>>G=A4.
Belize=12,500= 13,000 = 13% = P1.30D = 1.3 = Solar Core = Faculty = 13Jan.=Athena.
Bell=15,000=15%=P1.50D=1.5=Authority = Solar Crown = Solar Core = 1 May = Maia.
Bell Alexander Graham=4,500=5,000=50%=P5.00D=5.0=Law=Venus=5May=Odite>>L=N.
Belladonna=8,500=9,000=90%=P9.00D=9.0=Abstraction=Gods=Saturn=9Sept.>>A=Ø.
Bell-bottom=5,000=50%=P5.00D=5.0=Law=Time=Venus=5May=Odite>>L=N.
Bellboy=1,000=100%=10.0=1.0=Mind=Sun=1 January=Helios >> M=E4.
Belle=3,500=4,000=40%=P4.00D=4.0=Govt.=Creat.= 4 April=Hermes>>G=A4.
Belle-lettres=5,000=50%=P5.00D=5.0=Law=Time=Venus=5May=Odite>>L=N.
Bellflower=4,500=5,000=50%=P5.00D=5.0=Law=Time=Venus=5May=Odite>>L=N.
Bellhop=1,500=15%=P1.50D=1.5=Authority = Solar Crown = Solar Core = 1 May = Maia.
Bellicose=2,500=3,000=30%=P3.00D=3.0=Creativity=Star=Muses=3 March=C=I.
Belligerent=6,500=7,000=70%=P7.00D=7.0=Lang.=Assets=Mars=6May=Pleiades.
Bellini=9,500=10,000=1,000=100%=10.0=Physicality=Tech.=10 Oct.=Uranus=P=1Ø.
Bellini, Vincenzo=2,500=3,000=30%=P3.00D=3.0=Creativity=Star=Muses=3 March=C=I.
Bell jar=7,000=70%=P7.00D=7.0=Lang.=Assets=Mars=6May=Pleiades.
Bellow=9,500=10,000=1,000=100%=10.0=Physicality=Tech.=10 Oct.=Uranus=P=1Ø.
Bellow Saul=4,000=40%=P4.00D=4.0=Govt.=Creat.= 4 April=Hermes>>G=A4.
Bellows=7,500=8,000=80%=P8.00D=8.0=Econ.=Curr.=Busn.=Jupt.=8Aug=Zeus>E=v.
Bell pepper=5,000=50%=P5.00D=5.0=Law=Time=Venus=5May=Odite>>L=N.
Bellwether=5,500=5.5=80%=P5.50D=Earth-Midway=5 May=Gaia.

Belly=9,000=90%=P9.00D=9.0=Abstraction=Gods=Saturn=9Sept.>>A=Ø.
The belly is an abode of the Gods. This is how they influence human birth and incarnation.

Bellyache=7,000=70%=P7.00D=7.0=Lang.=Assets=Mars=6May=Pleiades.
Belly button=2,000=20%=P2.00D=2.0=Nature=Matter=Moon=2 Feb= Cupid>N=C.
Belly dance=5,500=5.5=80%=P5.50D=Earth-Midway=5 May=Gaia.
Bellyflop=7,000=70%=P7.00D=7.0=Lang.=Assets=Mars=6May=Pleiades.
Bellyful=3,000=30%=P3.00D=3.0=Creativity=Star=Muses=3 March=C=I.
Belly laugh=1,500=15%=P1.50D=1.5=Authority = Solar Crown = Solar Core = 1 May = Maia.
Belly-up=1,500=15%=P1.50D=1.5=Authority = Solar Crown = Solar Core = 1 May = Maia.
Belmopan=5,000=50%=P5.00D=5.0=Law=Time=Venus=5May=Odite>>L=N.
Belo Horizonte=5,500=5.5=80%=P5.50D=Earth-Midway=5 May=Gaia.
Belong=9,500=10,000=1,000=100%=10.0=Physicality=Tech.=10 Oct.=Uranus=P=1Ø.
Belonging=5,500=5.5=80%=P5.50D=Earth-Midway=5 May=Gaia.
Belorusia=5,500=5.5=80%=P5.50D=Earth-Midway=5 May=Gaia.
Beloved=1,000=100%=10.0=1.0=Mind=Sun=1 January=Helios >> M=E4.

Below=9,000=90%=P9.00D=9.0=Abstraction=Gods=Saturn=9Sept.>>A=Ø.
Belshazzar=3,500=4,000=40%=P4.00D=4.0=Govt.=Creat.= 4 April=Hermes>>G=A4.
Belt=29,500=3,000=30%=P3.00D=3.0=Creativity=Star=Muses=3 March=C=I.
Belt-tightening=2,500=3,000=30%=P3.00D=3.0=Creativity=Star=Muses=3 March=C=I.
Beltway=3,500=4,000=40%=P4.00D=4.0=Govt.=Creat.= 4 April=Hermes>>G=A4.
Beluga=5,500=5.5=80%=P5.50D=Earth-Midway=5 May=Gaia.
Belvedere=7,500=8,000=80%=P8.00D=8.0=Econ.=Curr.=Busn.=Jupt.=8Aug=Zeus>E=v.
Bemoan=4,500=5,000=50%=P5.00D=5.0=Law=Time=Venus=5May=Odite>>L=N.
Bemuse=5,000=50%=P5.00D=5.0=Law=Time=Venus=5May=Odite>>L=N.
Bench=18,000=18%=P1.80D=1.8=Solar Currency=MaksCurrencies=1 Aug=Maia.
Benchmark=12,500= 13,000 = 13% = P1.30D = 1.3 = Solar Core = Faculty = 13Jan.=Athena.
Bench warmer=2,000=20%=P2.00D=2.0=Nature=Matter=Moon=2 Feb= Cupid>N=C.
Bench warrant=7,000=70%=P7.00D=7.0=Lang.=Assets=Mars=6May=Pleiades.
Bend=15,000=15%=P1.50D=1.5=Authority = Solar Crown = Solar Core = 1 May = Maia.
Bender=3,500=4,000=40%=P4.00D=4.0=Govt.=Creat.= 4 April=Hermes>>G=A4.
Beneath=5,000=50%=P5.00D=5.0=Law=Time=Venus=5May=Odite>>L=N.
Benedict XIV=2,000=20%=P2.00D=2.0=Nature=Matter=Moon=2 Feb= Cupid>N=C.
Benedict XV.=2,000=20%=P2.00D=2.0=Nature=Matter=Moon=2 Feb= Cupid>N=C.
Benediction=6,500=7,000=70%=P7.00D=7.0=Lang.=Assets=Mars=6May=Pleiades.
Benedict of Nursia=6,500=7,000=70%=P7.00D=7.0=Lang.=Assets=Mars=6May=Pleiades.
Benefaction=4,500=5,000=50%=P5.00D=5.0=Law=Time=Venus=5May=Odite>>L=N.

Benefactor=3,500=4,000=40%=P4.00D=4.0=Govt.=Creat.= 4 April=Hermes>>G=A4.
Ben Ujoatuonu of Universal Insurance Nigeria sponsored publishing of Psychoeconomix.
He is thereby recognized as a Lord in the Creatocracy. Pastor Samuel Oye introduced the
deprived but ambitious writer to Barrister Ubani who took him to the radio for the first
time. They are seen as benefactors of the Creatocracy and its Disean benefits as approved.

Benefactress=4,000=40%=P4.00D=4.0=Govt.=Creat.= 4 April=Hermes>>G=A4.
Helen Ekwe-Okpata (aka Helen Ekot Efoli; Helen of Bulwark) earned a seat in the
Creatocracy as a Director and Queen in the Makupedia company through being a
Benefactress. See Angel. Wole Olaniyan is recognized as a Captain of Creativity and Lord
in the Creatocracy. He was a benefactor in no small contributions including sweat equity.
Moyo Oyatogun and her sister Mofe are also honored by the Creatocracy Bank records.

Benefice=4,500=5,000=50%=P5.00D=5.0=Law=Time=Venus=5May=Odite>>L=N.
Beneficence=5,000=50%=P5.00D=5.0=Law=Time=Venus=5May=Odite>>L=N.
Beneficial=2,500=3,000=30%=P3.00D=3.0=Creativity=Star=Muses=3 March=C=I.
Beneficiary=7,000=70%=P7.00D=7.0=Lang.=Assets=Mars=6May=Pleiades.
Benefit=16,000=16%=P1.60D=1.6=Cycle of Life=Incarnation=Mind of GOD=1June= Maia.
Benét Stephen Vincent=2,000=20%=P2.00D=2.0=Nature=Moon=2 Feb= Cupid>N=C.

Benevolence=5,500=5.5=80%=P5.50D=Earth-Midway=5 May=Gaia.
The spirit of benevolence is Gaia. It is the royal prerogative of the Creatocracy.

Benevolent=6,500=7,000=70%=P7.00D=7.0=Lang.=Assets=Mars=6May=Pleiades.
Bengal=8,500=9,000=90%=P9.00D=9.0=Abstraction=Gods=Saturn=9Sept.>>A=Ø.
Bengali=6,500=7,000=70%=P7.00D=7.0=Lang.=Assets=Mars=6May=Pleiades.
Benghazi=5,500=5.5=80%=P5.50D=Earth-Midway=5 May=Gaia.
Ben Gurion David=6,000=60%=P6.00D=6.0=Man=Earth=Royalty=6June=Gaia>M=M2.
Benighted=1,000=100%=10.0=1.0=Mind=Sun=1 January=Helios >> M=E4.
Benign=4,500=5,000=50%=P5.00D=5.0=Law=Time=Venus=5May=Odite>>L=N.
Benignant=1,500=15%=P1.50D=1.5=Authority = Solar Crown = Solar Core = 1 May = Maia.
Benin=8,500=9,000=90%=P9.00D=9.0=Abstraction=Gods=Saturn=9Sept.>>A=Ø.
Benin, Bight of=5,000=50%=P5.00D=5.0=Law=Time=Venus=5May=Odite>>L=N.
Bennett Richard Bedford=3,500=40%=P4.00D=4.0=Govt.= 4 April=Hermes>>G=A4.
Ben Nevis=6,500=7,000=70%=P7.00D=7.0=Lang.=Assets=Mars=6May=Pleiades.
Bent=12,500= 13,000 = 13% = P1.30D = 1.3 = Solar Core = Faculty = 13Jan.=Athena.
Bentham Jeremy=3,500=4,000=40%=P4.00D=4.0=Govt.= 4 April=Hermes>>G=A4.
Benton Thomas Hart=2,000=20%=P2.00D=2.0=Nature=Moon=2 Feb= Cupid>N=C.
Benumb=5,000=50%=P5.00D=5.0=Law=Time=Venus=5May=Odite>>L=N.
Benxi=4,500=5,000=50%=P5.00D=5.0=Law=Time=Venus=5May=Odite>>L=N.

Benzedrine=3,500=4,000=40%=P4.00D=4.0=Govt.=Creat.= 4 April=Hermes>>G=A4.
A trademark for a brand of amphetamine. The Solar Crown and logo of the Makupedia are trademarks of the Creatocracy and Creative Sciences Professionalism. Trademarks confer power and certain types of political power hence Creatocracy is a system of government.

Benzene=9,000=90%=P9.00D=9.0=Abstraction=Gods=Saturn=9Sept.>>A=Ø.
Benzo-=2,000=20%=P2.00D=2.0=Nature=Matter=Moon=2 Feb= Cupid>N=C.
Benzoate=3,500=4,000=40%=P4.00D=4.0=Govt.=Creat.= 4 April=Hermes>>G=A4.
Benzoic acid=6,500=7,000=70%=P7.00D=7.0=Lang.=Assets=Mars=6May=Pleiades.
Benzoin=7,500=8,000=80%=P8.00D=8.0=Econ.=Curr.=Busn.=Jupt.=8Aug=Zeus>E=v.
Benzol=1,000=100%=10.0=1.0=Mind=Sun=1 January=Helios >> M=E4.
Bequeath=5,500=5.5=80%=P5.50D=Earth-Midway=5 May=Gaia.
Bequest=3,500=4,000=40%=P4.00D=4.0=Govt.=Creat.= 4 April=Hermes>>G=A4.
Berate=3,000=30%=P3.00D=3.0=Creativity=Star=Muses=3 March=C=I.
Berber=10,500=11,000=11%=P1.10D=1.1=Idea=Brainchild=Inventn.=11 Nov.=Athena>K=F.
Berceuse=3,000=30%=P3.00D=3.0=Creativity=Star=Muses=3 March=C=I.
Bereave=4,000=40%=P4.00D=4.0=Govt.=Creat.= 4 April=Hermes>>G=A4.
Bereaved=7,500=8,000=80%=P8.00D=8.0=Econ.=Curr.=Busn.=Jupt.=8Aug=Zeus>E=v.
Bereft=6,500=7,000=70%=P7.00D=7.0=Lang.=Assets=Mars=6May=Pleiades.
Beret=5,000=50%=P5.00D=5.0=Law=Time=Venus=5May=Odite>>L=N.
Bergen=3,500=4,000=40%=P4.00D=4.0=Govt.=Creat.= 4 April=Hermes>>G=A4.
Bergson Henry Louis=4,000=40%=P4.00D=4.0=Govt.=Creat.= 4 April=Hermes>>G=A4.

Beri beri=7,000=70%=P7.00D=7.0=Lang.=Assets=Mars=6May=Pleiades.
Bering Vitus=3,000=30%=P3.00D=3.0=Creativity=Star=Muses=3 March=C=I.
Bering Sea=8,500=9,000=90%=P9.00D=9.0=Abstraction=Gods=Saturn=9Sept.>>A=Ø.
Berkeley=6,500=7,000=70%=P7.00D=7.0=Lang.=Assets=Mars=6May=Pleiades.
Berkelium=8,000=80%=P8.00D=8.0=Econ.=Curr.=Busn.=Jupt.=8Aug=Zeus>E=v.
Berkshire Hills=4,000=40%=P4.00D=4.0=Govt.=Creat.= 4 April=Hermes>>G=A4.
Berlin=8,500=9,000=90%=P9.00D=9.0=Abstraction=Gods=Saturn=9Sept.>>A=Ø.
Berlin, Irving=3,000=30%=P3.00D=3.0=Creativity=Star=Muses=3 March=C=I.

Berliner Emile.=3,000=30%=P3.00D=3.0=Creativity=Star=Muses=3 March=C=I.
An inventor. Peter Matthews-Akukalia invented and patented the Maks currencies, Makupedia first human mind computer and the complete study of the Creative Sciences.

Berlioz (Louis) Hector=2,000=20%=P2.00D=2.0=Nature=Moon=2 Feb= Cupid>N=C.

Berm=7,000=70%=P7.00D=7.0=Lang.=Assets=Mars=6May=Pleiades.
A bank of earth well manifested as the Creatocracy bank through the Pleiades.

Bermuda=11,500=12,000=12%=P1.20D=1.2=Knowledge=Edu.=12Dec.=Athena>>K=F.
Like Bermuda, Paradise Nations of the Creatocracy aka Creatocratic Nations of Paradise is a self governing Nigerian colony comprising cities of the Castle Makupedia headquartered at Nsukka, SE Nigeria, Enugu State. A kingdom of the Mind God.

Bermuda onion=2,000=20%=P2.00D=2.0=Nature=Matter=Moon=2 Feb= Cupid>N=C.
Bermuda shorts=4,000=40%=P4.00D=4.0=Govt.=Creat.= 4 April=Hermes>>G=A4.
Bern=6,000=60%=P6.00D=6.0=Man=Earth=Health=Royalty=6June=Gaia>M=M2.
Bernese Alps=4,500=5,000=50%=P5.00D=5.0=Law=Time=Venus=5May=Odite>>L=N.
Bernhardt Sarah=2,000=20%=P2.00D=2.0=Nature=Matter=Moon=2 Feb= Cupid>N=C.
Bernini Giovanni Lorenzo=3,500=40%=P4.00D=4.0=Govt.= 4April=Hermes>>G=A4.
Bernoulli effect=9,000=90%=P9.00D=9.0=Abstraction=Gods=Saturn=9Sept.>>A=Ø.
Berry=15,000=15%=P1.50D=1.5=Authority = Solar Crown = Solar Core = 1 May = Maia.
Berserk=2,000=20%=P2.00D=2.0=Nature=Matter=Moon=2 Feb= Cupid>N=C.
Berth=17,500=18,000=18%=P1.80D=1.8=Solar Currency=MaksCurrencies=1 Aug=Maia.
Beryl=8,000=80%=P8.00D=8.0=Econ.=Curr.=Busn.=Jupt.=8Aug=Zeus>E=v.
Beryllium=15,000=15%=P1.50D=1.5=Authority = Solar Crown = Solar Core = 1 May = Maia.
Beseech=2,000=20%=P2.00D=2.0=Nature=Matter=Moon=2 Feb= Cupid>N=C.
Be seem=1,500=15%=P1.50D=1.5=Authority = Solar Crown = Solar Core = 1 May = Maia.
Beset=4,000=40%=P4.00D=4.0=Govt.=Creat.= 4 April=Hermes>>G=A4.
Beside=8,500=9,000=90%=P9.00D=9.0=Abstraction=Gods=Saturn=9Sept.>>A=Ø.
Besides=8,000=80%=P8.00D=8.0=Econ.=Curr.=Busn.=Jupt.=8Aug=Zeus>E=v.
Besiege=7,500=8,000=80%=P8.00D=8.0=Econ.=Curr.=Busn.=Jupt.=8Aug=Zeus>E=v.
Be Skids=6,000=60%=P6.00D=6.0=Man=Earth=Health=Royalty=6June=Gaia>M=M2.

Be smear=1,000=100%=10.0=1.0=Mind=Sun=1 January=Helios >> M=E4.
Besmirch=1,500=15%=P1.50D=1.5=Authority = Solar Crown = Solar Core = 1 May = Maia.
Besot=4,500=5,000=50%=P5.00D=5.0=Law=Time=Venus=5May=Odite>>L=N.
Bespatter=4,000=40%=P4.00D=4.0=Govt.=Creat.= 4 April=Hermes>>G=A4.
Bespeak=9,000=90%=P9.00D=9.0=Abstraction=Gods=Saturn=9Sept.>>A=Ø.
Be sprinkle=1,000=100%=10.0=1.0=Mind=Sun=1 January=Helios >> M=E4.
Bessarabia=3,500=4,000=40%=P4.00D=4.0=Govt.=Creat.= 4 April=Hermes>>G=A4.

Bessemer process=12,500= 13,000 = 13% = P1.30D = 1.3 = Faculty = 13Jan.=Athena.
After Sir Henry Bessemer 1813-98. It is not out of place to be named after one's discovery. Makumatics, Makupedia including all Creatocracy are named after Peter Matthews-Akukalia. The level of his works make him more than a genius supposedly but a God.

Best=37,500=40,000=4,000=40%=P4.00D=4.0=Govt.=Creat.= 4 April=Hermes>>G=A4.
Peter Matthews-Akukalia is the best at what he does. After all he is the inventor of the field.

Bestial=3,000=30%=P3.00D=3.0=Creativity=Star=Muses=3 March=C=I.
Bestiary=8,500=9,000=90%=P9.00D=9.0=Abstraction=Gods=Saturn=9Sept.>>A=Ø.
Bestir=2,500=3,000=30%=P3.00D=3.0=Creativity=Star=Muses=3 March=C=I.
Best man=2,000=20%=P2.00D=2.0=Nature=Matter=Moon=2 Feb= Cupid>N=C.
Bestow=4,000=40%=P4.00D=4.0=Govt.=Creat.= 4 April=Hermes>>G=A4.
Be strew=1,000=100%=10.0=1.0=Mind=Sun=1 January=Helios >> M=E4.
Bestride=3,000=30%=P3.00D=3.0=Creativity=Star=Muses=3 March=C=I.
Bestseller=7,000=70%=P7.00D=7.0=Lang.=Assets=Mars=6May=Pleiades.
Bet=16,000=16%=P1.60D=1.6=Cycle of Life=Incarnation=Mind of GOD=1June= Maia.
Beta=3,000=30%=P3.00D=3.0=Creativity=Star=Muses=3 March=C=I.
Be take=2,000=20%=P2.00D=2.0=Nature=Matter=Moon=2 Feb= Cupid>N=C.
Beta particle=5,000=50%=P5.00D=5.0=Law=Time=Venus=5May=Odite>>L=N.
Beta ray=4,000=40%=P4.00D=4.0=Govt.=Creat.= 4 April=Hermes>>G=A4.
Beta rhythm=10,500=11,000=11%=P1.10D=1.1=Idea=Brainchild=11 Nov.=Athena>K=F.
Betatron=3,500=4,000=40%=P4.00D=4.0=Govt.=Creat.= 4 April=Hermes>>G=A4.
Betel=7,500=8,000=80%=P8.00D=8.0=Econ.=Curr.=Busn.=Jupt.=8Aug=Zeus>E=v.

Betelgeuse=4,500=5,000=50%=P5.00D=5.0=Law=Time=Venus=5May=Odite>>L=N.
The hand of Orion. GOD mentioned Orion and the Pleiades in Job 38:31 proving Gods exist. The Creatocracy considers constellations as families of the Gods transmuted to stars. This is how the cycle of life is ensured. This process is also known as incarnation, eternal life, everlasting life, resurrection in the spirit, astrotransmutation and reincarnation. The first human God to be so elevated by GOD was Moses for computing the signs or programming Exodus 4:16-17. Then the Gods of Heaven were mentioned again by GOD in Exodus 22:28 & 23:20-24 where they were referred as "Angel" not "angel" as differentiated from idol gods.

Betel nut=7,500=8,000=80%=P8.00D=8.0=Econ.=Curr.=Busn.=Jupt.=8Aug=Zeus>E=v.
Betel Palm=5,000=50%=P5.00D=5.0=Law=Time=Venus=5May=Odite>>L=N.
Bête noire=5,000=50%=P5.00D=5.0=Law=Time=Venus=5May=Odite>>L=N.
Beth=3,000=30%=P3.00D=3.0=Creativity=Star=Muses=3 March=C=I.
Be think=3,500=4,000=40%=P4.00D=4.0=Govt.=Creat.= 4 April=Hermes>>G=A4.
Bethlehem=7,000=70%=P7.00D=7.0=Lang.=Assets=Mars=6May=Pleiades.
Bethune Mary McLeod=2,000=20%=P2.00D=2.0=Nature=Matter=2 Feb= Cupid>N=C.
Betide=3,500=4,000=40%=P4.00D=4.0=Govt.=Creat.= 4 April=Hermes>>G=A4.
Be tides=2,000=20%=P2.00D=2.0=Nature=Matter=Moon=2 Feb= Cupid>N=C.
Be token=5,500=5.5=80%=P5.50D=Earth-Midway=5 May=Gaia.
Be took=2,000=20%=P2.00D=2.0=Nature=Matter=Moon=2 Feb= Cupid>N=C.
Betray=9,000=90%=P9.00D=9.0=Abstraction=Gods=Saturn=9Sept.>>A=Ø.
Betroth=2,500=3,000=30%=P3.00D=3.0=Creativity=Star=Muses=3 March=C=I.
Betrothed=4,500=5,000=50%=P5.00D=5.0=Law=Time=Venus=5May=Odite>>L=N.
Better=27,500=3,000=3,000=30%=P3.00D=3.0=Creativity=Star=Muses=3 March=C=I.
Betterment=3,000=30%=P3.00D=3.0=Creativity=Star=Muses=3 March=C=I.
Bettor=1,500=15%=P1.50D=1.5=Authority = Solar Crown = Solar Core = 1 May = Maia.
Between=37,500=4,000=40%=P4.00D=4.0=Govt.=Creat.= 4 April=Hermes>>G=A4.
Betwixt=2,500=3,000=30%=P3.00D=3.0=Creativity=Star=Muses=3 March=C=I.
BeV=1,500=15%=P1.50D=1.5=Authority = Solar Crown = Solar Core = 1 May = Maia.
Bevel=15,000=15%=P1.50D=1.5=Authority = Solar Crown = Solar Core = 1 May = Maia.
Beverage=5,000=50%=P5.00D=5.0=Law=Time=Venus=5May=Odite>>L=N.
Bevy=4,000=40%=P4.00D=4.0=Govt.=Creat.= 4 April=Hermes>>G=A4.
Bewail=2,500=3,000=30%=P3.00D=3.0=Creativity=Star=Muses=3 March=C=I.
Beware=3,500=4,000=40%=P4.00D=4.0=Govt.=Creat.= 4 April=Hermes>>G=A4.
Bewilder=6,000=60%=P6.00D=6.0=Man=Earth=Health=Royalty=6June=Gaia>M=M2.
Bewitch=11,000=11%=P1.10D=1.1=Idea=Brainchild=Inventn.=11 Nov.=Athena>K=F.
Bey=6,000=60%=P6.00D=6.0=Man=Earth=Health=Royalty=6June=Gaia>M=M2.
Beyond=11,000=11%=P1.10D=1.1=Idea=Brainchild=Inventn.=11 Nov.=Athena>K=F.
Bezel=6,000=60%=P6.00D=6.0=Man=Earth=Health=Royalty=6June=Gaia>M=M2.
bf=1,500=15%=P1.50D=1.5=Authority = Solar Crown = Solar Core = 1 May = Maia.
B.f.=1,500=15%=P1.50D=1.5=Authority = Solar Crown = Solar Core = 1 May = Maia.
BH=1,500=15%=P1.50D=1.5=Authority = Solar Crown = Solar Core = 1 May = Maia.
Bhang=500=5%=P5.00D=5.0=Law=Time=Venus=5 May=Aphrodite>>L=N.
Bhopal=7,500=8,000=80%=P8.00D=8.0=Econ.=Curr.=Busn.=Jupt.=8Aug=Zeus>E=v.
BHT=9,000=90%=P9.00D=9.0=Abstraction=Gods=Saturn=9Sept.>>A=Ø.
Bhutan=6,500=7,000=70%=P7.00D=7.0=Lang.=Assets=Mars=6May=Pleiades.
Bi=2,500=3,000=30%=P3.00D=3.0=Creativity=Star=Muses=3 March=C=I.
bi-=16,500=17,000=17%=P1.70D=1.7=Solar Asset =17 Feb.=Maia>>Mind Computing.
BIA=2,000=20%=P2.00D=2.0=Nature=Matter=Moon=2 Feb= Cupid>N=C.
Biafra=11,000=11%=P1.10D=1.1=Idea=Brainchild=Inventn.=11 Nov.=Athena>K=F.
Bialystok=4,500=5,000=50%=P5.00D=5.0=Law=Time=Venus=5May=Odite>>L=N.
Biannual=500=5%=P5.00D=5.0=Law=Time=Venus=5 May=Aphrodite>>L=N.
Biarritz=5,500=5.5=80%=P5.50D=Earth-Midway=5 May=Gaia.
Bias= 13,000 = 13% = P1.30D = 1.3 = Solar Core = Faculty = 13Jan.=Athena.

Biathlon=6,500=7,000=70%=P7.00D=7.0=Lang.=Assets=Mars=6May=Pleiades.
Bib=9,500=10,000=1,000=100%=10.0=Physicality=Tech.=10 Oct.=Uranus=P=1Ø.
Bib.=1,000=100%=10.0=1.0=Mind=Sun=1 January=Helios >> M=E4.
Bibelot=2,000=20%=P2.00D=2.0=Nature=Matter=Moon=2 Feb= Cupid>N=C.

Bible=15,000=15%=P1.50D=1.5=Authority = Solar Crown = Solar Core = 1 May = Maia. The Creatocracy has established the Bible is a book of abstract codes hence it is the book of hidden convertible intelligence softwares known as Mind wares. A Mind energy book of the Gods that when discovered grants one the solar crown. Result shows it is the custody of the Great Goddess (universe>>Creatocracy) and most authority on all things. Now by computing its literal expressions into tangible codes it becomes an invention and owned asset by the requirements set therein. So the Bible was inspired by the Holy Spirit, written by men but invented by Peter Matthews-Akukalia through his study Faculty of Creative & Psycho-Social Sciences. This is how he emerged as Castle Makupedia God of Creatocracy Genius and Mind. Computing the Solar Core he earned the Solar Crown. See Scripture.

Biblio=1,000=100%=10.0=1.0=Mind=Sun=1 January=Helios >> M=E4.
Bibliography=12,000=12%=P1.20D=1.2=Knowledge=Edu.=12Dec.=Athena>>K=F.
Bibliophile=3,000=30%=P3.00D=3.0=Creativity=Star=Muses=3 March=C=I.
Bibulous=3,500=4,000=40%=P4.00D=4.0=Govt.=Creat.= 4 April=Hermes>>G=A4.
Bicameral=2,500=3,000=30%=P3.00D=3.0=Creativity=Star=Muses=3 March=C=I.
Bicarbonate=6,500=7,000=70%=P7.00D=7.0=Lang.=Assets=Mars=6May=Pleiades.
Bicarbonate of soda=1,500=15%=P1.50D=1.5=Authority=Solar Crown=SC=1 May=Maia.
Bicentenary=1,000=100%=10.0=1.0=Mind=Sun=1 January=Helios >> M=E4.
Bicentennial=3,500=4,000=40%=P4.00D=4.0=Govt.=Creat.= 4 April=Hermes>>G=A4.
Biceps=7,000=70%=P7.00D=7.0=Lang.=Assets=Mars=6May=Pleiades.
Bicker=4,000=40%=P4.00D=4.0=Govt.=Creat.= 4 April=Hermes>>G=A4.
Biconcave=3,000=30%=P3.00D=3.0=Creativity=Star=Muses=3 March=C=I.
Books of the Bible=63,500=64,000=64%=6.4sp>>2.4>>International Business.
Biconvex=3,000=30%=P3.00D=3.0=Creativity=Star=Muses=3 March=C=I.
Bicuspid=5,000=50%=P5.00D=5.0=Law=Time=Venus=5May=Odite>>L=N.
Bicycle=10,000=1,000=100%=10.0=Physicality=Tech.=10 Oct.=Uranus=P=1Ø.
Bid=22,000=22%=P2.20D=2.2=4.0=Govt.=Creatocracy=2Feb=Hermes>G=A4.
Biddable=3,000=30%=P3.00D=3.0=Creativity=Star=Muses=3 March=C=I.
Biddy=1,500=15%=P1.50D=1.5=Authority = Solar Crown = Solar Core = 1 May = Maia.
Bide=3,000=30%=P3.00D=3.0=Creativity=Star=Muses=3 March=C=I.
Bidet=7,000=70%=P7.00D=7.0=Lang.=Assets=Mars=6May=Pleiades.
Bielefeld=4,500=5,000=50%=P5.00D=5.0=Law=Time=Venus=5May=Odite>>L=N.
Biennial=9,500=10,000=1,000=100%=10.0=Physicality=Tech.=10 Oct.=Uranus=P=1Ø.
Bier=5,500=5.5=80%=P5.50D=Earth-Midway=5 May=Gaia.
Bierce Ambrose Gwinett.=2,500=3,000=30%=P3.00D=3.0=Creativity=Star=3March=C=I.
Bifocal=10,500=11,000=11%=P1.10D=1.1=Idea=Brainchild=Inventn.=11 Nov.=Athena>K=F.
Bifurcate=4,000=40%=P4.00D=4.0=Govt.=Creat.= 4 April=Hermes>>G=A4.

Big=17,000=17%=P1.70D=1.7=Solar Asset =17 Feb.=Maia>>Mind Computing.
Bigamy=7,000=70%=P7.00D=7.0=Lang.=Assets=Mars=6May=Pleiades.
Big Bang theory= 13,000 = 13% = P1.30D = 1.3 = Solar Core = Faculty = 13Jan.=Athena.
Big brother=7,500=8,000=80%=P8.00D=8.0=Econ.=Curr.=Busn.=Jupt.=8Aug=Zeus>E=v.
Big Dipper=7,000=70%=P7.00D=7.0=Lang.=Assets=Mars=6May=Pleiades.
Bigfoot=7,500=8,000=80%=P8.00D=8.0=Econ.=Curr.=Busn.=Jupt.=8Aug=Zeus>E=v.
Big game=4,500=5,000=50%=P5.00D=5.0=Law=Time=Venus=5May=Odite>>L=N.
Big-hearted=500=5%=P5.00D=5.0=Law=Time=Venus=5 May=Aphrodite>>L=N.
Bighorn=7,500=8,000=80%=P8.00D=8.0=Econ.=Curr.=Busn.=Jupt.=8Aug=Zeus>E=v.
Bighorn Mountains=6,000=60%=P6.00D=6.0=Man=Earth=Health=6June=Gaia>M=M2.
Bight=7,000=70%=P7.00D=7.0=Lang.=Assets=Mars=6May=Pleiades.
Bigmouth=3,500=4,000=40%=P4.00D=4.0=Govt.=Creat.= 4 April=Hermes>>G=A4.
Big-name=2,000=20%=P2.00D=2.0=Nature=Matter=Moon=2 Feb= Cupid>N=C.
Bigot=6,000=60%=P6.00D=6.0=Man=Earth=Health=Royalty=6June=Gaia>M=M2.
Big shot=3,000=30%=P3.00D=3.0=Creativity=Star=Muses=3 March=C=I.
Big Sur=3,500=4,000=40%=P4.00D=4.0=Govt.=Creat.= 4 April=Hermes>>G=A4.
Big-ticket=5,000=50%=P5.00D=5.0=Law=Time=Venus=5May=Odite>>L=N.
Big time=6,000=60%=P6.00D=6.0=Man=Earth=Health=Royalty=6June=Gaia>M=M2.
Big top=3,500=4,000=40%=P4.00D=4.0=Govt.=Creat.= 4 April=Hermes>>G=A4.
Bigwig=2,000=20%=P2.00D=2.0=Nature=Matter=Moon=2 Feb= Cupid>N=C.
Bike=2,000=20%=P2.00D=2.0=Nature=Matter=Moon=2 Feb= Cupid>N=C.
Biker=5,500=5.5=80%=P5.50D=Earth-Midway=5 May=Gaia.
bikini=6,000=60%=P6.00D=6.0=Man=Earth=Health=Royalty=6June=Gaia>M=M2.
Bikini=4,500=5,000=50%=P5.00D=5.0=Law=Time=Venus=5May=Odite>>L=N.
Bilateral=5,500=5.5=80%=P5.50D=Earth-Midway=5 May=Gaia.
Bilbao=5,000=50%=P5.00D=5.0=Law=Time=Venus=5May=Odite>>L=N.
Bile=10,000=1,000=100%=10.0=Physicality=Tech.=10 Oct.=Uranus=P=1Ø.
Bilge=6,500=7,000=70%=P7.00D=7.0=Lang.=Assets=Mars=6May=Pleiades.
Bilge water=6,000=60%=P6.00D=6.0=Man=Earth=Health=Royalty=6June=Gaia>M=M2.
Bilingual=4,000=40%=P4.00D=4.0=Govt.=Creat.= 4 April=Hermes>>G=A4.
Bilious=7,500=8,000=80%=P8.00D=8.0=Econ.=Curr.=Busn.=Jupt.=8Aug=Zeus>E=v.
Bilk=2,500=3,000=30%=P3.00D=3.0=Creativity=Star=Muses=3 March=C=I.
Bill(1)=28,500=3,000=30%=P3.00D=3.0=Creativity=Star=Muses=3 March=C=I.
Bill(2)=9,500=10,000=1,000=100%=10.0=Physicality=Tech.=10 Oct.=Uranus=P=1Ø.
Billboard=4,000=40%=P4.00D=4.0=Govt.=Creat.= 4 April=Hermes>>G=A4.
Billet=10,000=1,000=100%=10.0=Physicality=Tech.=10 Oct.=Uranus=P=1Ø.
Billet-doux=1,500=15%=P1.50D=1.5=Authority = Solar Crown = Solar Core = 1 May = Maia.
Billfold=1,000=100%=10.0=1.0=Mind=Sun=1 January=Helios >> M=E4.
Billiards=14,000=14%=P1.40D=1.4=Mgt.=Solar Core=13 May=Athena>>SC=0.1
Billing=7,000=70%=P7.00D=7.0=Lang.=Assets=Mars=6May=Pleiades.
Billings=6,500=7,000=70%=P7.00D=7.0=Lang.=Assets=Mars=6May=Pleiades.
Billings gate=1,500=15%=P1.50D=1.5=Authority = Solar Crown =Solar Core = 1 May = Maia.
Billion=4,500=5,000=50%=P5.00D=5.0=Law=Time=Venus=5May=Odite>>L=N.
Billionaire=6,000=60%=P6.00D=6.0=Man=Earth=Health=Royalty=6June=Gaia>M=M2.
Billionth=7,500=8,000=80%=P8.00D=8.0=Econ.=Curr.=Busn.=Jupt.=8Aug=Zeus>E=v.

Bill of exchange=7,000=70%=P7.00D=7.0=Lang.=Assets=Mars=6May=Pleiades.
Bill of fare=1,000=100%=10.0=1.0=Mind=Sun=1 January=Helios >> M=E4.
Bill of goods=6,000=60%=P6.00D=6.0=Man=Earth=Health=Royalty=6June=Gaia>M=M2.
Bill of lading=5,500=5.5=80%=P5.50D=Earth-Midway=5 May=Gaia.
Bill of rights=9,500=10,000=1,000=100%=10.0=Physicality=Tech.=10 Oct.=Uranus=P=1Ø.
Bill of sale=4,500=5,000=50%=P5.00D=5.0=Law=Time=Venus=5May=Odite>>L=N.
Billow=8,500=9,000=90%=P9.00D=9.0=Abstraction=Gods=Saturn=9Sept.>>A=Ø.
Billy=1,500=15%=P1.50D=1.5=Authority = Solar Crown = Solar Core = 1 May = Maia.
Billy club=3,500=4,000=40%=P4.00D=4.0=Govt.=Creat.= 4 April=Hermes>>G=A4.
Billy goat=2,000=20%=P2.00D=2.0=Nature=Matter=Moon=2 Feb= Cupid>N=C.
Bimetallic=5,500=5.5=80%=P5.50D=Earth-Midway=5 May=Gaia.
Bimetallism=8,000=80%=P8.00D=8.0=Econ.=Curr.=Busn.=Jupt.=8Aug=Zeus>E=v.
Biminis=5,500=5.5=80%=P5.50D=Earth-Midway=5 May=Gaia.
Bimodal=2,500=3,000=30%=P3.00D=3.0=Creativity=Star=Muses=3 March=C=I.
Bimonthly=8,500=9,000=90%=P9.00D=9.0=Abstraction=Gods=Saturn=9Sept.>>A=Ø.
Bin=2,000=20%=P2.00D=2.0=Nature=Matter=Moon=2 Feb= Cupid>N=C.
Binary=7,500=8,000=80%=P8.00D=8.0=Econ.=Curr.=Busn.=Jupt.=8Aug=Zeus>E=v.
Binary digit=6,000=60%=P6.00D=6.0=Man=Earth=Health=Royalty=6June=Gaia>M=M2.

Binary number system=9,000=90%=P9.00D=9.0=Abst.=Gods=Saturn=9Sept.>>A=Ø.
Binary number system shows that numbers are spirits managed by Gods in a computing module known as Mind Computing. Its most advance form is the Quartet Principle discovered invented measured and applied by Peter Matthews-Akukalia in Makupedia.

Binary star=9,000=90%=P9.00D=9.0=Abstraction=Gods=Saturn=9Sept.>>A=Ø.
The binary star is proof that stars are the highest product for all abstractions including renewal of the Mind and discovering the Mind of GOD in the most modest means of Mind Computing as required by Romans 11:34 and 12:2. Foremost is Genesis 1:14-16.

Binaural=10,500=11,000=11%=P1.10D=1.1=Idea=Brainchild=Inventn.=11 Nov.=Athena
  >K=F.
Bind=25,500=3,000=30%=P3.00D=3.0=Creativity=Star=Muses=3 March=C=I.
Bindery=3,000=30%=P3.00D=3.0=Creativity=Star=Muses=3 March=C=I.
Binding=16,000=16%=P1.60D=1.6=Cycle   of   Life=Incarnation=MindofGOD=
  1June= Maia.
Binge=6,500=7,000=70%=P7.00D=7.0=Lang.=Assets=Mars=6May=Pleiades.
Bingham George Caleb=2,000=20%=P2.00D=2.0=Nature=Moon=2 Feb= Cupid>N=C.
Bingo=12,500= 13,000 = 13% = P1.30D = 1.3 = Solar Core = Faculty = 13Jan.=Athena.
Binnacle=5,000=50%=P5.00D=5.0=Law=Time=Venus=5May=Odite>>L=N.
Binocular=9,500=10,000=1,000=100%=10.0=Physicality=Tech.=10 Oct.=Uranus=P=1Ø.
Binomial=12,000=12%=P1.20D=1.2=Knowledge=Edu.=12Dec.=Athena>>K=F.
Bio=1,000=100%=10.0=1.0=Mind=Sun=1 January=Helios >> M=E4.
Bio-=2,000=20%=P2.00D=2.0=Nature=Matter=Moon=2 Feb= Cupid>N=C.

Biochemistry=6,000=60%=P6.00D=6.0=Man=Earth=Health=Royalty=6June=Gaia
>M=M2.
Bioconversion=6,500=7,000=70%=P7.00D=7.0=Lang.=Assets=Mars=6May=Pleiades.
Biodegradable=4,000=40%=P4.00D=4.0=Govt.=Creat.= 4 April=Hermes>>G=A4.
Biofeedback= 13,000 = 13% = P1.30D = 1.3 = Solar Core = Faculty = 13Jan.=Athena.
Biogas=8,500=9,000=90%=P9.00D=9.0=Abstraction=Gods=Saturn=9Sept.>>A=Ø.
Biogenic=3,500=4,000=40%=P4.00D=4.0=Govt.=Creat.= 4 April=Hermes>>G=A4.
Biogeography=4,500=5,000=50%=P5.00D=5.0=Law=Time=Venus=5May=Odite>>L=N.
Biography=10,500=11,000=11%=P1.10D=1.1=Idea=Brainchild=11 Nov.=Athena>K=F.
Biological=6,000=60%=P6.00D=6.0=Man=Earth=Health=Royalty=6June=Gaia>M=M2.
Biological warfare=10,000=1,000=100%=Physicality= Tech.=10 Oct.=Uranus=P=1Ø.
Biology=6,500=7,000=70%=P7.00D=7.0=Lang.=Assets=Mars=6May=Pleiades.
Biomass=10,000=1,000=100%=10.0=Physicality=Tech.=10 Oct.=Uranus=P=1Ø.
Biome=5,000=50%=P5.00D=5.0=Law=Time=Venus=5May=Odite>>L=N.
Biomedicine=5,500=5.5=80%=P5.50D=Earth-Midway=5 May=Gaia.
Bionic=6,500=7,000=70%=P7.00D=7.0=Lang.=Assets=Mars=6May=Pleiades.
Biophysics=2,500=3,000=30%=P3.00D=3.0=Creativity=Star=Muses=3 March=C=I.
Biopsy=7,500=8,000=80%=P8.00D=8.0=Econ.=Curr.=Busn.=Jupt.=8Aug=Zeus=E=v.
Biorhythm=3,500=4,000=40%=P4.00D=4.0=Govt.=Creat.= 4 April=Hermes>>G=A4.
-biosis=2,500=3,000=30%=P3.00D=3.0=Creativity=Star=Muses=3 March=C=I.
Biosphere=6,000=60%=P6.00D=6.0=Man=Earth=Health=Royalty=6June=Gaia>M=M2.
Biota=4,000=40%=P4.00D=4.0=Govt.=Creat.= 4 April=Hermes>>G=A4.
Biotechnology=7,500=8,000=80%=P8.00D=8.0=Econ.=Busn.=Jupt.=8Aug=Zeus>E=v.
Biotic=3,500=4,000=40%=P4.00D=4.0=Govt.=Creat.= 4 April=Hermes>>G=A4.
Biotin=8,000=80%=P8.00D=8.0=Econ.=Curr.=Busn.=Jupt.=8Aug=Zeus>E=v.
Bipartisan=6,500=7,000=70%=P7.00D=7.0=Lang.=Assets=Mars=6May=Pleiades.
Bipartite=8,000=80%=P8.00D=8.0=Econ.=Curr.=Busn.=Jupt.=8Aug=Zeus>E=v.
Biped=3,500=4,000=40%=P4.00D=4.0=Govt.=Creat.= 4 April=Hermes>>G=A4.
Biplane=9,500=10,000=1,000=100%=10.0=Physicality=Tech.=10 Oct.=Uranus=P=1Ø.
Bipolar=4,000=40%=P4.00D=4.0=Govt.=Creat.= 4 April=Hermes>>G=A4.
Birch=10,000=1,000=100%=10.0=Physicality=Tech.=10 Oct.=Uranus=P=1Ø.

Bird=11,500=12,000=12%=P1.20D=1.2=Knowledge=Edu.=12Dec.=Athena>>K=F.
Birds are servants of Athena. The beak of a bird has been discovered to contain certain electromagnetic properties that interact with human communication signals and transmit it to the higher abstract sphere. It confirms King Solomon's warning in Proverbs that birds and walls have ears hence internal communication must be drawn from wisdom and goodness. Knowledge such as this makes the author the God of Creatocracy.

Birdbath=5,500=5.5=80%=P5.50D=Earth-Midway=5 May=Gaia.
Birdhouse=5,000=50%=P5.00D=5.0=Law=Time=Venus=5May=Odite>>L=N.
Birdie=5,000=50%=P5.00D=5.0=Law=Time=Venus=5May=Odite>>L=N.
Birdlime=7,000=70%=P7.00D=7.0=Lang.=Assets=Mars=6May=Pleiades.

Bird of Paradise=11,000=11%=P1.10D=1.1=Idea=Brainchild=Inventn.=11 Nov.=Athena>K=F.
Athena is again confirmed as the principal behind the birds and thus the bird of paradise.
Resultant shows that Athena is whom we call Paradise just as Aphrodite is the Creatocracy.
Paradise is therefore a brainchild and invention so that it is biblically predictive. The
Creatocracy has fulfilled this prophecy by inventing the Creatocratic Nations of Paradise.
Marriage to Athena by wisdom makes the author Emperor of the Paradise Nations.

Bird's eye=4,500=5,000=50%=P5.00D=5.0=Law=Time=Venus=5May=Odite>>L=N.
Birdshot=3,500=4,000=40%=P4.00D=4.0=Govt.=Creat.= 4 April=Hermes>>G=A4.
Bird watcher=5,000=50%=P5.00D=5.0=Law=Time=Venus=5May=Odite>>L=N.
Biretta=5,500=5.5=80%=P5.50D=Earth-Midway=5 May=Gaia.
Birkenhead=7,000=70%=P7.00D=7.0=Lang.=Assets=Mars=6May=Pleiades.
Birmingham=7,500=8,000=80%=P8.00D=8.0=Econ.=Busn.=Jupt.=8Aug=Zeus>E=v.
Birr=2,000=20%=P2.00D=2.0=Nature=Matter=Moon=2 Feb= Cupid>N=C.
Birth=22,000=22%=P2.20D=2.2=4.0=Govt.=Creatocracy=2Feb=Hermes>G=A4.
Birth canal=4,500=5,000=50%=P5.00D=5.0=Law=Time=Venus=5May=Odite>>L=N.
Birth control=5,500=5.5=80%=P5.50D=Earth-Midway=5 May=Gaia.
Birthday=4,500=5,000=50%=P5.00D=5.0=Law=Time=Venus=5May=Odite>>L=N.
Birth defect=9,000=90%=P9.00D=9.0=Abstraction=Gods=Saturn=9Sept.>>A=Ø.
Birth family=5,000=50%=P5.00D=5.0=Law=Time=Venus=5May=Odite>>L=N.
Birth mark=5,000=50%=P5.00D=5.0=Law=Time=Venus=5May=Odite>>L=N.
Birth parent=1,500=15%=P1.50D=1.5=Authority = Solar Crown = Solar Core = 1 May = Maia.
Birthplace=4,500=5,000=50%=P5.00D=5.0=Law=Time=Venus=5May=Odite>>L=N.
Birth rate=7,500=8,000=80%=P8.00D=8.0=Econ.=Curr.=Busn.=Jupt.=8Aug=Zeus>E=v.

Birthright=5,500=5.5=80%=P5.50D=Earth-Midway=5 May=Gaia.
Gaia is the Goddess of the Earth and presides over all birthright matters.

Birthstone=5,500=5.5=80%=P5.50D=Earth-Midway=5 May=Gaia.
Biscay Bay of=6,500=7,000=70%=P7.00D=7.0=Lang.=Assets=Mars=6May=Pleiades.
Biscayne Bay=4,000=40%=P4.00D=4.0=Govt.=Creat.= 4 April=Hermes>>G=A4.
Biscuit=9,500=10,000=1,000=100%=10.0=Physicality=Tech.=10 Oct.=Uranus=P=1Ø.
Bisect=5,000=50%=P5.00D=5.0=Law=Time=Venus=5May=Odite>>L=N.
Bisexual=9,500=10,000=1,000=100%=10.0=Physicality=Tech.=10 Oct.=Uranus=P=1Ø.
Bishkek=6,500=7,000=70%=P7.00D=7.0=Lang.=Assets=Mars=6May=Pleiades.
Bishop=11,500=12,000=12%=P1.20D=1.2=Knowledge=Edu.=12Dec.=Athena>>K=F.
Bishopric=4,000=40%=P4.00D=4.0=Govt.=Creat.= 4 April=Hermes>>G=A4.
Bismarck=5,000=50%=P5.00D=5.0=Law=Time=Venus=5May=Odite>>L=N.

Bismarck Prince Otto=5,500=5.5=80%=P5.50D=Earth-Midway=5 May=Gaia.
"The Iron Chancellor" 1815-98. Creator and first chancellor of the German Empire 1871-90.
Peter Matthews-Akukalia is the creator and Most Sovereign Emperor of Paradise Nations.

Bismarck Archipelago=7,000=70%=P7.00D=7.0=Lang.=Assets=Mars=6May=Pleiades.
Bismuth=10,000=1,000=100%=10.0=Physicality=Tech.=10 Oct.=Uranus=P=1Ø.
Bison=9,000=90%=P9.00D=9.0=Abstraction=Gods=Saturn=9Sept.>>A=Ø.
Bisque=8,000=80%=P8.00D=8.0=Econ.=Curr.=Busn.=Jupt.=8Aug=Zeus>E=v.
Bissau=6,000=60%=P6.00D=6.0=Man=Earth=Health=Royalty=6June=Gaia>M=M2.
Bistro=4,000=40%=P4.00D=4.0=Govt.=Creat.= 4 April=Hermes>>G=A4.

Bit(1)=12,000=12%=P1.20D=1.2=Knowledge=Edu.=12Dec.=Athena>>K=F.
A bit is an amount equal to 1/8 of a dollar. The Creatocracy uses 8-point star in abstraction.
1/8 interprets as the oneness of the Gods rests upon the almighty. Gods depend on Zeus.

Bit(2)=15,000=1,500=15%=P1.50D=1.5=Authority = Solar Crown =Solar Core=1 May= Maia.
Bit(3)=9,500=10,000=1,000=100%=10.0=Physicality=Tech.=10 Oct.=Uranus=P=1Ø.
Bitch=8,500=9,000=90%=P9.00D=9.0=Abstraction=Gods=Saturn=9Sept.>>A=Ø.
Bite=33,000=33%=P3.30D=3.3=Genius Gods=The Holy Spirit=Moon=3 March.
Bite wing=6,500=7,000=70%=P7.00D=7.0=Lang.=Assets=Mars=6May=Pleiades.
Biting=3,000=30%=P3.00D=3.0=Creativity=Star=Muses=3 March=C=I.
Bitter=25,000=3,000=30%=P3.00D=3.0=Creativity=Star=Muses=3 March=C=I.
Bittern=5,500=5.5=80%=P5.50D=Earth-Midway=5 May=Gaia.
Bittersweet=13,500=14,000=14%=P1.40D=1.4=Mgt.=Solar Core=13 May=Athena>>SC=0.1
Bittersweet nightshade=6,000=60%=P6.00D=6.0=Man=Earth=6June=Gaia>M=M2.
Bitty=1,000=100%=10.0=1.0=Mind=Sun=1 January=Helios >> M=E4.
Bitumen=7,500=8,000=80%=P8.00D=8.0=Econ.=Curr.=Busn.=Jupt.=8Aug=Zeus>E=v.
Bituminous=2,000=20%=P2.00D=2.0=Nature=Matter=Moon=2 Feb= Cupid>N=C.
Bituminous coal=8,500=9,000=90%=P9.00D=9.0=Abstr.=Gods=Saturn=9Sept.>>A=Ø.
Bivalent=1,000=100%=10.0=1.0=Mind=Sun=1 January=Helios >> M=E4.
Bivalve=7,500=8,000=80%=P8.00D=8.0=Econ.=Curr.=Busn.=Jupt.=8Aug=Zeus>E=v.
Bivouac=4,000=40%=P4.00D=4.0=Govt.=Creat.= 4 April=Hermes>>G=A4.
Biweekly=8,000=80%=P8.00D=8.0=Econ.=Curr.=Busn.=Jupt.=8Aug=Zeus>E=v.
Bi yearly=4,000=40%=P4.00D=4.0=Govt.=Creat.= 4 April=Hermes>>G=A4.
Bizarre=3,500=4,000=40%=P4.00D=4.0=Govt.=Creat.= 4 April=Hermes>>G=A4.
Bizet Alexandre=2,000=20%=P2.00D=2.0=Nature=Matter=Moon=2 Feb= Cupid>N=C.
Bk=2,500=3,000=30%=P3.00D=3.0=Creativity=Star=Muses=3 March=C=I.

Bl.=1,000=100%=10.0=1.0=Mind=Sun=1 January=Helios >> M=E4.
Bl>>Barrel (Measurement) indicates that a cost of barrel eg oil should cost 10Maks.

B/L=1,500=15%=P1.50D=1.5=Authority = Solar Crown = Solar Core = 1 May = Maia.
Blab=5,000=50%=P5.00D=5.0=Law=Time=Venus=5May=Odite>>L=N.
Blabber=1,500=15%=P1.50D=1.5=Authority = Solar Crown = Solar Core = 1 May = Maia.
Blabber mouth=2,500=3,000=30%=P3.00D=3.0=Creativity=Star=Muses=3 March=C=I.
Black=48,000=5,000=50%=P5.00D=5.0=Law=Time=Venus=5May=Odite>>L=N.
Black-and-blue=1,500=15%=P1.50D=1.5=Authority =Solar Crown=SC.=1 May= Maia.

Black and white=9,000=90%=P9.00D=9.0=Abstraction=Gods=Saturn=9Sept.>>A=Ø.
Blackball=18,500=19,000=19%=P1.90D=1.9=Planetary Energy=1 September = Maia.
Black bear=6,000=60%=P6.00D=6.0=Man=Earth=Health=Royalty=6June=Gaia>M=M2.
Black belt=9,000=90%=P9.00D=9.0=Abstraction=Gods=Saturn=9Sept.>>A=Ø.
Black berry=8,500=9,000=90%=P9.00D=9.0=Abstraction=Gods=Saturn=9Sept.>>A=Ø.
Blackbird=7,500=8,000=80%=P8.00D=8.0=Econ.=Curr.=Busn.=Jupt.=8Aug=Zeus>E=v.
Blackboard=4,000=40%=P4.00D=4.0=Govt.=Creat.= 4 April=Hermes>>G=A4.
Black body=4,000=40%=P4.00D=4.0=Govt.=Creat.= 4 April=Hermes>>G=A4.
Black box=9,000=90%=P9.00D=9.0=Abstraction=Gods=Saturn=9Sept.>>A=Ø.
Black Death=6,500=7,000=70%=P7.00D=7.0=Lang.=Assets=Mars=6May=Pleiades.
Blacken=3,000=30%=P3.00D=3.0=Creativity=Star=Muses=3 March=C=I.
Black eye=5,000=50%=P5.00D=5.0=Law=Time=Venus=5May=Odite>>L=N.
Black eyed Susan=6,500=7,000=70%=P7.00D=7.0=Lang.=Assets=Mars=6May=Pleiades.
Black face=7,000=70%=P7.00D=7.0=Lang.=Assets=Mars=6May=Pleiades.
Blackfish=1,500=15%=P1.50D=1.5=Authority = Solar Crown = Solar Core = 1 May = Maia.
Blackfoot=11,500=12,000=12%=P1.20D=1.2=Knowledge=Edu.=12Dec.=Athena>>K=F.
Black Forest=6,000=60%=P6.00D=6.0=Man=Earth=Health=Royalty=6June=Gaia>M=M2.
Black guard=2,500=3,000=30%=P3.00D=3.0=Creativity=Star=Muses=3 March=C=I.
Black Hawk=5,000=50%=P5.00D=5.0=Law=Time=Venus=5May=Odite>>L=N.
Blackhead=9,000=90%=P9.00D=9.0=Abstraction=Gods=Saturn=9Sept.>>A=Ø.
Black Hills=4,500=5,000=50%=P5.00D=5.0=Law=Time=Venus=5May=Odite>>L=N.
Black hole=8,500=9,000=90%=P9.00D=9.0=Abstraction=Gods=Saturn=9Sept.>>A=Ø.
Black humor=8,500=9,000=90%=P9.00D=9.0=Abstraction=Gods=Saturn=9Sept.>>A=Ø.
Blackjack=15,000=1,500=15%=P1.50D=1.5=Authority = Solar Crown = SC. = 1 May = Maia.
Black light=2,500=3,000=30%=P3.00D=3.0=Creativity=Star=Muses=3 March=C=I.
Blacklist=7,500=8,000=80%=P8.00D=8.0=Econ.=Curr.=Busn.=Jupt.=8Aug=Zeus>E=v.
Black lung=6,000=60%=P6.00D=6.0=Man=Earth=Health=Royalty=6June=Gaia>M=M2.
Black magic=5,000=50%=P5.00D=5.0=Law=Time=Venus=5May=Odite>>L=N.
Blackmail=6,500=7,000=70%=P7.00D=7.0=Lang.=Assets=Mars=6May=Pleiades.
Black market=4,500=5,000=50%=P5.00D=5.0=Law=Time=Venus=5May=Odite>>L=N.
Black Muslim=7,000=70%=P7.00D=7.0=Lang.=Assets=Mars=6May=Pleiades.
Blackout=17,500=18,000=18%=P1.80D=1.8=Solar Currency=MaksCurrencies=1Aug=Maia.
Black pepper=4,000=40%=P4.00D=4.0=Govt.=Creat.= 4 April=Hermes>>G=A4.
Black Power=6,500=7,000=70%=P7.00D=7.0=Lang.=Assets=Mars=6May=Pleiades.
Black Sea=7,000=70%=P7.00D=7.0=Lang.=Assets=Mars=6May=Pleiades.
Black sheep=5,500=5.5=80%=P5.50D=Earth-Midway=5 May=Gaia.
Blacksmith=5,500=5.5=80%=P5.50D=Earth-Midway=5 May=Gaia.
Black snake=4,000=40%=P4.00D=4.0=Govt.=Creat.= 4 April=Hermes>>G=A4.
Black stone Sir William=3,000=30%=P3.00D=3.0=Creativity=Star=Muses=3 March=C=I.
Blackthorn=7,500=8,000=80%=P8.00D=8.0=Econ.=Curr.=Busn.=Jupt.=8Aug=Zeus>E=v.
Blacktop=5,000=50%=P5.00D=5.0=Law=Time=Venus=5May=Odite>>L=N.
Blackwell Elizabeth=3,000=30%=P3.00D=3.0=Creativity=Star=Muses=3 March=C=I.
Black widow=7,500=8,000=80%=P8.00D=8.0=Econ.=Busn.=Jupt.=8Aug=Zeus>E=v.
Bladder=13,500=14,000=14%=P1.40D=1.4=Mgt.=Solar Core=13 May=Athena>>SC=0.1
Blade=11,000=11%=P1.10D=1.1=Idea=Brainchild=Inventn.=11 Nov.=Athena>K=F.

Blain=2,500=3,000=30%=P3.00D=3.0=Creativity=Star=Muses=3 March=C=I.
Blake William=3,000=30%=P3.00D=3.0=Creativity=Star=Muses=3 March=C=I.
Blamable=3,500=4,000=40%=P4.00D=4.0=Govt.=Creat.= 4 April=Hermes>>G=A4.
Blame=7,000=70%=P7.00D=7.0=Lang.=Assets=Mars=6May=Pleiades.
Blameworthy=4,500=5,000=50%=P5.00D=5.0=Law=Time=Venus=5May=Odite>>L=N.
Bianc,Mont=8,500=9,000=90%=P9.00D=9.0=Abstraction=Gods=Saturn=9Sept.>>A=Ø.
Blanch=5,500=5.5=80%=P5.50D=Earth-Midway=5 May=Gaia.
Blancmange=2,500=3,000=30%=P3.00D=3.0=Creativity=Star=Muses=3 March=C=I.
Bland=9,000=90%=P9.00D=9.0=Abstraction=Gods=Saturn=9Sept.>>A=Ø.
Blandish=3,500=4,000=40%=P4.00D=4.0=Govt.=Creat.= 4 April=Hermes>>G=A4.
Blank=35,500=4,000=40%=P4.00D=4.0=Govt.=Creat.= 4 April=Hermes>>G=A4.
Blank check=6,000=60%=P6.00D=6.0=Man=Earth=Health=Royalty=6June=Gaia>M=M2.
Blanket=12,000=12%=P1.20D=1.2=Knowledge=Edu.=12Dec.=Athena>>K=F.
Blank verse=3,000=30%=P3.00D=3.0=Creativity=Star=Muses=3 March=C=I.
Blantyre=3,500=4,000=40%=P4.00D=4.0=Govt.=Creat.= 4 April=Hermes>>G=A4.
Blare=4,000=40%=P4.00D=4.0=Govt.=Creat.= 4 April=Hermes>>G=A4.
Blarney=4,500=5,000=50%=P5.00D=5.0=Law=Time=Venus=5May=Odite>>L=N.
Blasê=2,500=3,000=30%=P3.00D=3.0=Creativity=Star=Muses=3 March=C=I.
Blaspheme=6,500=7,000=70%=P7.00D=7.0=Lang.=Assets=Mars=6May=Pleiades.
Blast=33,500=34=43=4.3>>2,000=20%=P2.00D=2.0=Nature=Moon=2 Feb=Cupid>N=C.
Blast furnace=5,500=5.5=80%=P5.50D=Earth-Midway=5 May=Gaia.
Blast off=4,500=5,000=50%=P5.00D=5.0=Law=Time=Venus=5May=Odite>>L=N.
Blatant=5,000=50%=P5.00D=5.0=Law=Time=Venus=5May=Odite>>L=N.
Blather=2,500=3,000=30%=P3.00D=3.0=Creativity=Star=Muses=3 March=C=I.
Blaze(1)=2,000=20%=P2.00D=2.0=Nature=Matter=Moon=2 Feb= Cupid>N=C.
Blaze(2)=12,000=12%=P1.20D=1.2=Knowledge=Edu.=12Dec.=Athena>>K=F.
Blazer=3,500=4,000=40%=P4.00D=4.0=Govt.=Creat.= 4 April=Hermes>>G=A4.

Blazon=7,500=8,000=80%=P8.00D=8.0=Econ.=Curr.=Busn.=Jupt.=8Aug=Zeus>E=v.
A coat of arms measured in Zeus makes the solar crown and Eagle and lion and book the blazon of the Creatocracy. Zeus manifests as many things and chiefly those listed.

Bidg.=1,000=100%=10.0=1.0=Mind=Sun=1 January=Helios >> M=E4.
Bleach=6,000=60%=P6.00D=6.0=Man=Earth=Health=Royalty=6June=Gaia>M=M2.
Bleachers=3,000=30%=P3.00D=3.0=Creativity=Star=Muses=3 March=C=I.
Bleak=7,000=70%=P7.00D=7.0=Lang.=Assets=Mars=6May=Pleiades.
Blear=8,000=80%=P8.00D=8.0=Econ.=Curr.=Busn.=Jupt.=8Aug=Zeus>E=v.
Bleat=6,500=7,000=70%=P7.00D=7.0=Lang.=Assets=Mars=6May=Pleiades.
Bleed=17,000=17%=P1.70D=1.7=Solar Asset =17 Feb.=Maia>>Mind Computing.
Bleeder=3,500=4,000=40%=P4.00D=4.0=Govt.=Creat.= 4 April=Hermes>>G=A4.

Bleeding heart=8,000=80%=P8.00D=8.0=Econ.=Curr.=Busn.=Jupt.=8Aug=Zeus>E=v.
Zeus the Most High was a bleeding heart. The Pleiades renewed this heart into a structured computerized mind that functions on Mind Computing, Computational Creativity and

calculative precision. The Creatocracy discovered it as the source of all wisdom (Athena) and riches (Romans 11:34-35). Creative Scientists are precise in words works and deeds.

Bleep=10,500=11,000=11%=P1.10D=1.1=Idea=Brainchild=Inventn.=11 Nov.=Athena>K=F.
Blemish=4,500=5,000=50%=P5.00D=5.0=Law=Time=Venus=5May=Odite>>L=N.
Blench=3,500=4,000=40%=P4.00D=4.0=Govt.=Creat.= 4 April=Hermes>>G=A4.
Blend=20,000=2,000=20%=P2.00D=2.0=Nature=Matter=Moon=2 Feb= Cupid>N=C.
Blender=6,000=60%=P6.00D=6.0=Man=Earth=Health=Royalty=6June=Gaia>M=M2.
Bless=15,000=1,500=15%=P1.50D=1.5=Authority = Solar Crown = SC. = 1 May = Maia.
Blessed=7,500=8,000=80%=P8.00D=8.0=Econ.=Curr.=Busn.=Jupt.=8Aug=Zeus>E=v.
Blessing=14,000=14%=P1.40D=1.4=Mgt.=Solar Core=13 May=Athena>>SC=0.1
Blew(1)=2,000=20%=P2.00D=2.0=Nature=Matter=Moon=2 Feb= Cupid>N=C.
Blew(2)=2,000=20%=P2.00D=2.0=Nature=Matter=Moon=2 Feb= Cupid>N=C.
Bligh William=2,500=3,000=30%=P3.00D=3.0=Creativity=Star=Muses=3 March=C=I.
Blight=16,000=16%=P1.60D=1.6=Cycle of Life=Incarnation=MindofGOD=1June= Maia.
Blimp=2,500=3,000=30%=P3.00D=3.0=Creativity=Star=Muses=3 March=C=I.
Blind=38,000=4,000=40%=P4.00D=4.0=Govt.=Creat.= 4 April=Hermes>>G=A4.
Blind date=9,500=10,000=1,000=100%=10.0=Physicality=Tech.=10 Oct.=Uranus=P=1Ø.
Blinders=6,500=7,000=70%=P7.00D=7.0=Lang.=Assets=Mars=6May=Pleiades.
Blindfold=7,000=70%=P7.00D=7.0=Lang.=Assets=Mars=6May=Pleiades.
Blindside=8,000=80%=P8.00D=8.0=Econ.=Curr.=Busn.=Jupt.=8Aug=Zeus>E=v.
Blind-side=7,000=70%=P7.00D=7.0=Lang.=Assets=Mars=6May=Pleiades.
Blind spot=10,000=1,000=100%=10.0=Physicality=Tech.=10 Oct.=Uranus=P=1Ø.
Blink=13,500=14,000=14%=P1.40D=1.4=Mgt.=Solar Core=13 May=Athena>>SC=0.1

Blinker=5,500=5.5=80%=P5.50D=Earth-Midway=5 May=Gaia.
When Gaia blinks man receives it as a signal of what is to happen and hence inspiration.

Blintz=7,500=8,000=80%=P8.00D=8.0=Econ.=Curr.=Busn.=Jupt.=8Aug=Zeus>E=v.
Blip=7,000=70%=P7.00D=7.0=Lang.=Assets=Mars=6May=Pleiades.
Bliss=3,000=30%=P3.00D=3.0=Creativity=Star=Muses=3 March=C=I.
Blister= 13,000 = 13% = P1.30D = 1.3 = Solar Core = Faculty = 13Jan.=Athena.
Blistering=4,500=5,000=50%=P5.00D=5.0=Law=Time=Venus=5May=Odite>>L=N.
Blister pack=7,000=70%=P7.00D=7.0=Lang.=Assets=Mars=6May=Pleiades.
B.Lit.=3,000=30%=P3.00D=3.0=Creativity=Star=Muses=3 March=C=I.
Blithe=1,500=15%=P1.50D=1.5=Authority = Solar Crown = Solar Core = 1 May = Maia.
Blither=2,000=20%=P2.00D=2.0=Nature=Matter=Moon=2 Feb= Cupid>N=C.
Blithesome=1,000=100%=10.0=1.0=Mind=Sun=1 January=Helios >> M=E4.
Blitz=10,500=11,000=11%=P1.10D=1.1=Idea=Brainchild=Inventn.=11 Nov.=Athena>K=F.
Blitzkrieg=7,500=8,000=80%=P8.00D=8.0=Econ.=Curr.=Busn.=Jupt.=8Aug=Zeus>E=v.
Blizzard=4,500=5,000=50%=P5.00D=5.0=Law=Time=Venus=5May=Odite>>L=N.
Blk.=1,500=15%=P1.50D=1.5=Authority = Solar Crown = Solar Core = 1 May = Maia.
Bloat=5,000=50%=P5.00D=5.0=Law=Time=Venus=5May=Odite>>L=N.

Blob=4,000=40%=P4.00D=4.0=Govt.=Creat.= 4 April=Hermes>>G=A4.
Bloc=5,500=5.5=80%=P5.50D=Earth-Midway=5 May=Gaia.
Block=66,500=7,000=70%=P7.00D=7.0=Lang.=Assets=Mars=6May=Pleiades.
Blockade=11,500=12,000=12%=P1.20D=1.2=Knowledge=Edu.=12Dec.=Athena>>K=F.
Block and tackle=6,500=7,000=70%=P7.00D=7.0=Lang.=Assets=Mars=6May=Pleiades.
Blockbuster=8,500=9,000=90%=P9.00D=9.0=Abstraction=Gods=Saturn=9Sept.>>A=Ø.
Blockbusting=12,500= 13,000 = 13% = P1.30D = 1.3 = Solar Core=Faculty= 13Jan.=Athena.
Blockhead=1,500=15%=P1.50D=1.5=Authority = Solar Crown = Solar Core = 1 May = Maia.
Blockhouse=8,500=9,000=90%=P9.00D=9.0=Abstraction=Gods=Saturn=9Sept.>>A=Ø.
Bloemfontein=5,000=50%=P5.00D=5.0=Law=Time=Venus=5May=Odite>>L=N.
Bloke=2,500=3,000=30%=P3.00D=3.0=Creativity=Star=Muses=3 March=C=I.
Blond=20,000=2,000=20%=P2.00D=2.0=Nature=Matter=Moon=2 Feb= Cupid>N=C.
Blood=27,500=30,000=3,000=30%=P3.00D=3.0=Creativity=Star=Muses=3 March=C=I.
Blood bank=6,000=60%=P6.00D=6.0=Man=Earth=Health=Royalty=6June=Gaia>M=M2.
Bloodbath=1,000=100%=10.0=1.0=Mind=Sun=1 January=Helios >> M=E4.
Blood count=6,500=7,000=70%=P7.00D=7.0=Lang.=Assets=Mars=6May=Pleiades.
Bloodcurdling=2,000=20%=P2.00D=2.0=Nature=Matter=Moon=2 Feb= Cupid>N=C.
Blooded=6,500=7,000=70%=P7.00D=7.0=Lang.=Assets=Mars=6May=Pleiades.
Bloodhound=7,500=8,000=80%=P8.00D=8.0=Econ.=Curr.=Busn.=Jupt.=8Aug=Zeus>E=v
Bloodletting=1,500=15%=P1.50D=1.5=Authority = Solar Crown = SC. = 1 May = Maia.
Bloodline=2,500=3,000=30%=P3.00D=3.0=Creativity=Star=Muses=3 March=C=I.
Blood poison=1,500=15%=P1.50D=1.5=Authority = Solar Crown = SC. = 1 May = Maia.
Blood pressure=6,000=60%=P6.00D=6.0=Man=Earth=Health=6June=Gaia>M=M2.
Bloodshed=3,500=4,000=40%=P4.00D=4.0=Govt.=Creat.= 4 April=Hermes>>G=A4.
Bloodshot=4,500=5,000=50%=P5.00D=5.0=Law=Time=Venus=5May=Odite>>L=N.
Bloodstain=2,500=3,000=30%=P3.00D=3.0=Creativity=Star=Muses=3 March=C=I.
Bloodstream=3,500=4,000=40%=P4.00D=4.0=Govt.=Creat.= 4 April=Hermes>>G=A4.
Bloodsucker=5,500=5.5=80%=P5.50D=Earth-Midway=5 May=Gaia.
Bloodthirsty=1,500=15%=P1.50D=1.5=Authority = Solar Crown = SC. = 1 May = Maia.
Blood vessel=7,500=8,000=80%=P8.00D=8.0=Econ.=Busn.=Jupt.=8Aug=Zeus>E=v.
Bloody=12,500= 13,000 = 13% = P1.30D = 1.3 = Solar Core = Faculty = 13Jan.=Athena.
Bloody Mary=4,000=40%=P4.00D=4.0=Govt.=Creat.= 4 April=Hermes>>G=A4.
Bloom=21,500=22,000=22%=P2.20D=2.2=4.0=Govt.=Creatocracy=2Feb=Hermes>G=A4.
Bloomers=5,000=50%=P5.00D=5.0=Law=Time=Venus=5May=Odite>>L=N.
Bloomer Amelia Jenks=2,500=3,000=30%=P3.00D=3.0=Star=Muses=3 March=C=I.
Blooper=6,500=7,000=70%=P7.00D=7.0=Lang.=Assets=Mars=6May=Pleiades.
Blossom=12,500= 13,000 = 13% = P1.30D = 1.3 = Solar Core = Faculty = 13Jan.=Athena.
Blot=14,500=15,000=1,500=15%=P1.50D=1.5=Authority = Solar Crown = 1 May = Maia.
Blotch=5,000=50%=P5.00D=5.0=Law=Time=Venus=5May=Odite>>L=N.
Blotter=5,500=5.5=80%=P5.50D=Earth-Midway=5 May=Gaia.
Blotting paper=6,000=60%=P6.00D=6.0=Man=Earth=Royalty=6June=Gaia>M=M2.
Blouse=7,500=8,000=80%=P8.00D=8.0=Econ.=Curr.=Busn.=Jupt.=8Aug=Zeus>E=v.
Blow(1)=500=5%=P5.00D=5.0=Law=Time=Venus=5 May=Aphrodite>>L=N.
Blow(2)=22,500=23,000=23%=Local Business=23 Days Monthly=2.3% Taxes daily income.
Blow(3)=5,000=50%=P5.00D=5.0=Law=Time=Venus=5May=Odite>>L=N.

Blow-by-blow=2,000=20%=P2.00D=2.0=Nature=Matter=Moon=2 Feb= Cupid>N=C.
Blow-dry=5,000=50%=P5.00D=5.0=Law=Time=Venus=5May=Odite>>L=N.
Blowfly=5,500=5.5=80%=P5.50D=Earth-Midway=5 May=Gaia.
Blowgun=5,000=50%=P5.00D=5.0=Law=Time=Venus=5May=Odite>>L=N.
Blow hard=2,500=3,000=30%=P3.00D=3.0=Creativity=Star=Muses=3 March=C=I.
Blowhole=5,000=50%=P5.00D=5.0=Law=Time=Venus=5May=Odite>>L=N.
Blowout=9,500=10,000=1,000=100%=10.0=Physicality=Tech.=10 Oct.=Uranus=P=1Ø.
Blowtorch=8,500=9,000=90%=P9.00D=9.0=Abstraction=Gods=Saturn=9Sept.>>A=Ø.
Blowup=4,500=5,000=50%=P5.00D=5.0=Law=Time=Venus=5May=Odite>>L=N.
Blowy=500=5%=P5.00D=5.0=Law=Time=Venus=5 May=Aphrodite>>L=N.
Blowzy=1,500=1,500=15%=P1.50D=1.5=Authority = Solar Crown = SC. = 1 May = Maia.
Blubber(1)=4,000=40%=P4.00D=4.0=Govt.=Creat.= 4 April=Hermes>>G=A4.
Blubber(2)=8,500=9,000=90%=P9.00D=9.0=Abstraction=Gods=Saturn=9Sept.>>A=Ø.
Bludgeon=12,500= 13,000 = 13% = P1.30D = 1.3 = Solar Core = Faculty = 13Jan.=Athena.
Blue=24,000=24%=Intl. Business=24 Days Monthly=2.4% Taxes.

Blue baby=6,000=60%=P6.00D=6.0=Man=Earth=Health=Royalty=6June=Gaia>M=M2. In 2003 Princess Jane Michelle (Jami) died at birth from blue baby. The book Psychoeconomix was dedicated to her. It is believed that she returned as Princess Tricia. She is a solid proof of our firm belief in the cycle of life looking at a mark she shares with her siblings especially Victor her brother who is from another mother.

Bluebell=4,500=5,000=50%=P5.00D=5.0=Law=Time=Venus=5May=Odite>>L=N.
Blueberry=6,000=60%=P6.00D=6.0=Man=Earth=Health=Royalty=6June=Gaia>M=M2.
Bluebird=8,000=80%=P8.00D=8.0=Econ.=Curr.=Busn.=Jupt.=8Aug=Zeus>E=v.

Blue blood=4,500=5,000=50%=P5.00D=5.0=Law=Time=Venus=5May=Odite>>L=N. Noble or aristocratic descent. A member of the aristocracy. Noble or Creatocratic descents and members of the Creatocracy shall be known as Disean blood which comes in any color.

Bluebonnet=4,500=5,000=50%=P5.00D=5.0=Law=Time=Venus=5May=Odite>>L=N.
Blue bottle=5,500=5.5=80%=P5.50D=Earth-Midway=5 May=Gaia.
Blue cheese=5,000=50%=P5.00D=5.0=Law=Time=Venus=5May=Odite>>L=N.
Blue chip=6,500=7,000=70%=P7.00D=7.0=Lang.=Assets=Mars=6May=Pleiades.
Blue-collar=7,000=70%=P7.00D=7.0=Lang.=Assets=Mars=6May=Pleiades.
Bluefish=5,000=50%=P5.00D=5.0=Law=Time=Venus=5May=Odite>>L=N.
Bluegill=5,000=50%=P5.00D=5.0=Law=Time=Venus=5May=Odite>>L=N.
Bluegrass=12,500= 13,000 = 13% = P1.30D = 1.3 = Solar Core = Faculty = 13Jan.=Athena.
Blue heron=5,000=50%=P5.00D=5.0=Law=Time=Venus=5May=Odite>>L=N.
Bluing=1,500=15%=P1.50D=1.5=Authority = Solar Crown = Solar Core = 1 May = Maia.
Blue jay=7,500=8,000=80%=P8.00D=8.0=Econ.=Curr.=Busn.=Jupt.=8Aug=Zeus>E=v.
Blue jeans=7,500=8,000=80%=P8.00D=8.0=Econ.=Curr.=Busn.=Jupt.=8Aug=Zeus>E=v.

Blue law=3,500=4,000=40%=P4.00D=4.0=Govt.=Creat.= 4 April=Hermes>>G=A4. The Creatocratic Charter & Creatocracy Courts regulates all activities of the Creatocracy. Creatocrats manage all operations of our religion and faith in the order of the Holy Spirit of the Makstian Faith. For Sunday activities we read the Mind Temple Scriptures.

Blue moon=5,500=5.5=80%=P5.50D=Earth-Midway=5 May=Gaia.
Blue Nile=14,000=14%=P1.40D=1.4=Mgt.=Solar Core=13 May=Athena>>SC=0.1
Blue nose=1,500=15%=P1.50D=1.5=Authority = Solar Crown = Solar Core = 1 May = Maia.
Blue-pencil=5,000=50%=P5.00D=5.0=Law=Time=Venus=5May=Odite>>L=N.
Blueprint=10,000=1,000=100%=10.0=Physicality=Tech.=10 Oct.=Uranus=P=1Ø.
Blue ribbon=3,000=30%=P3.00D=3.0=Creativity=Star=Muses=3 March=C=I.
Blue Ridge=6,500=7,000=70%=P7.00D=7.0=Lang.=Assets=Mars=6May=Pleiades.
Blues=12,500= 13,000 = 13% = P1.30D = 1.3 = Solar Core = Faculty = 13Jan.=Athena.
Blue stocking=8,000=80%=P8.00D=8.0=Econ.=Curr.=Busn.=Jupt.=8Aug=Zeus>E=v.
Bluets=5,000=50%=P5.00D=5.0=Law=Time=Venus=5May=Odite>>L=N.
Blue whale=8,500=9,000=90%=P9.00D=9.0=Abstraction=Gods=Saturn=9Sept.>>A=Ø.
Bluff(1)=9,500=10,000=1,000=100%=10.0=Physicality=Tech.=10 Oct.=Uranus=P=1Ø.
Bluff(2)=7,000=70%=P7.00D=7.0=Lang.=Assets=Mars=6May=Pleiades.
Bluing=8,000=80%=P8.00D=8.0=Econ.=Curr.=Busn.=Jupt.=8Aug=Zeus>E=v.
Blunder=13,500=14,000=14%=P1.40D=1.4=Mgt.=Solar Core=13 May=Athena>>SC=0.1
Blunder buss=6,500=7,000=70%=P7.00D=7.0=Lang.=Assets=Mars=6May=Pleiades.
Blunt=10,500=11,000=11%=P1.10D=1.1=Idea=Brainchild=Inventn.=11 Nov.=Athena>K=F.
Blur=7,500=8,000=80%=P8.00D=8.0=Econ.=Curr.=Busn.=Jupt.=8Aug=Zeus>E=v.
Blurb=8,000=80%=P8.00D=8.0=Econ.=Curr.=Busn.=Jupt.=8Aug=Zeus>E=v.
Blurt=9,000=90%=P9.00D=9.0=Abstraction=Gods=Saturn=9Sept.>>A=Ø.
Blush=9,500=10,000=1,000=100%=10.0=Physicality=Tech.=10 Oct.=Uranus=P=1Ø.
Blusher=7,000=70%=P7.00D=7.0=Lang.=Assets=Mars=6May=Pleiades.
Bluster=7,500=8,000=80%=P8.00D=8.0=Econ.=Curr.=Busn.=Jupt.=8Aug=Zeus>E=v.
Blvd.=1,000=100%=10.0=1.0=Mind=Sun=1 January=Helios >> M=E4.
BM=1,000=100%=10.0=1.0=Mind=Sun=1 January=Helios >> M=E4.
b.m.=2,000=20%=P2.00D=2.0=Nature=Matter=Moon=2 Feb= Cupid>N=C.
BMR=1,500=15%=P1.50D=1.5=Authority = Solar Crown = Solar Core = 1 May = Maia.
Bn.=1,000=100%=10.0=1.0=Mind=Sun=1 January=Helios >> M=E4.
Boa=15,500=16,000=16%=P1.60D=1.6=Cycle of Life=Incarnation=MOG=1June= Maia.
Boa constrictor=4,500=5,000=50%=P5.00D=5.0=Law=Time=Venus=5May=Odite>>L=N.
Boadicea=1,000=100%=10.0=1.0=Mind=Sun=1 January=Helios >> M=E4.
Boar=3,500=4,000=40%=P4.00D=4.0=Govt.=Creat.= 4 April=Hermes>>G=A4.
Board=35,000=4,000=40%=P4.00D=4.0=Govt.=Creat.= 4 April=Hermes>>G=A4.
Board foot=7,500=8,000=80%=P8.00D=8.0=Econ.=Curr.=Busn.=Jupt.=8Aug=Zeus>E=v.
Boardinghouse=5,500=5.5=80%=P5.50D=Earth-Midway=5 May=Gaia.
Boarding school=5,000=50%=P5.00D=5.0=Law=Time=Venus=5May=Odite>>L=N.
Boardwalk=3,500=4,000=40%=P4.00D=4.0=Govt.=Creat.= 4 April=Hermes>>G=A4.
Boast=10,500=11,000=11%=P1.10D=1.1=Idea=Brainchild=Inventn.=11 Nov.=Athena>K=F.
Boat=9,500=10,000=1,000=100%=10.0=Physicality=Tech.=10 Oct.=Uranus=P=1Ø.

Boater=5,000=50%=P5.00D=5.0=Law=Time=Venus=5May=Odite>>L=N.
Boat swain=8,000=80%=P8.00D=8.0=Econ.=Curr.=Busn.=Jupt.=8Aug=Zeus>E=v.
Bob(1)=6,500=7,000=70%=P7.00D=7.0=Lang.=Assets=Mars=6May=Pleiades.
Bob(2)=10,000=1,000=100%=10.0=Physicality=Tech.=10 Oct.=Uranus=P=1Ø.
Bob(3)=2,500=3,000=30%=P3.00D=3.0=Creativity=Star=Muses=3 March=C=I.
Bobbin=4,000=40%=P4.00D=4.0=Govt.=Creat.= 4 April=Hermes>>G=A4.
Bobble=5,000=50%=P5.00D=5.0=Law=Time=Venus=5May=Odite>>L=N.
Bobby=4,500=5,000=50%=P5.00D=5.0=Law=Time=Venus=5May=Odite>>L=N.
Bobby pin=5,500=5.5=80%=P5.50D=Earth-Midway=5 May=Gaia.
Bobby socks=1,500=15%=P1.50D=1.5=Authority = Solar Crown = SC. = 1 May = Maia.
Bobby soxer=2,000=20%=P2.00D=2.0=Nature=Matter=Moon=2 Feb= Cupid>N=C.
Bobcat=8,000=80%=P8.00D=8.0=Econ.=Curr.=Busn.=Jupt.=8Aug=Zeus>E=v.
Bobolink=2,000=20%=P2.00D=2.0=Nature=Matter=Moon=2 Feb= Cupid>N=C.
Bobsled=9,000=90%=P9.00D=9.0=Abstraction=Gods=Saturn=9Sept.>>A=Ø.
Bobtail=7,500=8,000=80%=P8.00D=8.0=Econ.=Curr.=Busn.=Jupt.=8Aug=Zeus>E=v.
Bob white=2,500=3,000=30%=P3.00D=3.0=Creativity=Star=Muses=3 March=C=I.
Bochum=7,000=70%=P7.00D=7.0=Lang.=Assets=Mars=6May=Pleiades.
Bock beer=2,000=20%=P2.00D=2.0=Nature=Matter=Moon=2 Feb= Cupid>N=C.
Bod=2,000=20%=P2.00D=2.0=Nature=Matter=Moon=2 Feb= Cupid>N=C.
Bode(1)=2,500=3,000=30%=P3.00D=3.0=Creativity=Star=Muses=3 March=C=I.
Bode(2)=2,000=20%=P2.00D=2.0=Nature=Matter=Moon=2 Feb= Cupid>N=C.
Bodega=5,000=50%=P5.00D=5.0=Law=Time=Venus=5May=Odite>>L=N.
Bodice=3,500=4,000=40%=P4.00D=4.0=Govt.=Creat.= 4 April=Hermes>>G=A4.
Bodiless=4,000=40%=P4.00D=4.0=Govt.=Creat.= 4 April=Hermes>>G=A4.
Bodily=14,000=14%=P1.40D=1.4=Mgt.=Solar Core=13 May=Athena>>SC=0.1
Bodkin=8,500=9,000=90%=P9.00D=9.0=Abstraction=Gods=Saturn=9Sept.>>A=Ø.
Body=23,000=23%=Local Business = Tech.=23 Days Monthly=2.3% Taxes daily income.
Body bag=5,000=50%=P5.00D=5.0=Law=Time=Venus=5May=Odite>>L=N.
Bodybuilding=8,000=80%=P8.00D=8.0=Econ.=Curr.=Busn.=Jupt.=8Aug=Zeus>E=v.
Body count=5,500=5.5=80%=P5.50D=Earth-Midway=5 May=Gaia.
Body English=11,000=11%=P1.10D=1.1=Idea=Brainchild=Inventn.=11 Nov.=Athena>K=F.
Bodyguard=6,500=7,000=70%=P7.00D=7.0=Lang.=Assets=Mars=6May=Pleiades.
Body language=6,500=7,000=70%=P7.00D=7.0=Lang.=Assets=Mars=6May=Pleiades.
Body politic=5,000=50%=P5.00D=5.0=Law=Time=Venus=5May=Odite>>L=N.
Body shop=5,000=50%=P5.00D=5.0=Law=Time=Venus=5May=Odite>>L=N.
Body stocking=8,000=80%=P8.00D=8.0=Econ.=Curr.=Busn.=Jupt.=8Aug=Zeus>E=v.
Body suit=4,500=5,000=50%=P5.00D=5.0=Law=Time=Venus=5May=Odite>>L=N.
Bodysurf=3,500=4,000=40%=P4.00D=4.0=Govt.=Creat.= 4 April=Hermes>>G=A4.
Bodywork=6,000=60%=P6.00D=6.0=Man=Earth=Health=Royalty=6June=Gaia>M=M2.
Boeotia=5,500=5.5=80%=P5.50D=Earth-Midway=5 May=Gaia.
Boer=5,500=5.5=80%=P5.50D=Earth-Midway=5 May=Gaia.
Boffo=1,500=15%=P1.50D=1.5=Authority = Solar Crown = Solar Core = 1 May = Maia.
Bog=7,500=8,000=80%=P8.00D=8.0=Econ.=Curr.=Busn.=Jupt.=8Aug=Zeus>E=v.
Bogey=11,000=11%=P1.10D=1.1=Idea=Brainchild=Inventn.=11 Nov.=Athena>K=F.
Bogeyman=2,000=20%=P2.00D=2.0=Nature=Matter=Moon=2 Feb= Cupid>N=C.

Boggle=9,000=90%=P9.00D=9.0=Abstraction=Gods=Saturn=9Sept.>>A=Ø.
Bogotá=8,000=80%=P8.00D=8.0=Econ.=Curr.=Busn.=Jupt.=8Aug=Zeus>E=v.
Bogus=1,500=15%=P1.50D=1.5=Authority = Solar Crown = Solar Core = 1 May = Maia.
Bo Hai=5,000=50%=P5.00D=5.0=Law=Time=Venus=5May=Odite>>L=N.
Bohemia=5,000=50%=P5.00D=5.0=Law=Time=Venus=5May=Odite>>L=N.

Bohemian=5,500=5.5=80%=P5.50D=Earth-Midway=5 May=Gaia.
A person with artistic interests who disregards conventional standards of behavior. The Creatocracy is bohemian in its very nature. The results is the invention of the Propoplay, Nidrapoe, Testapoe, Mindom and Castle genres of literature by him. It is clearly a gift of Gaia and absolute royalty to be bohemian. Peter Matthews-Akukalia (African Shakespeare).

Bohr Niels David=3,000=30%=P3.00D=3.0=Creativity=Star=Muses=3 March=C=I.
Boil(1)=21,500=22,000=22%=P2.20D=2.2=4.0=Govt.=Creatocracy=2Feb=Hermes>G=A4.
Boil(2)=6,500=7,000=70%=P7.00D=7.0=Lang.=Assets=Mars=6May=Pleiades.
Boiler=11,500=12,000=12%=P1.20D=1.2=Knowledge=Edu.=12Dec.=Athena>>K=F.
Boiler-room=5,500=5.5=80%=P5.50D=Earth-Midway=5 May=Gaia.
Boiling point=12,000=12%=P1.20D=1.2=Knowledge=Edu.=12Dec.=Athena>>K=F.
Boise=8,500=9,000=90%=P9.00D=9.0=Abstraction=Gods=Saturn=9Sept.>>A=Ø.
Boisterous=4,000=40%=P4.00D=4.0=Govt.=Creat.= 4 April=Hermes>>G=A4.
Bok choy=2,000=20%=P2.00D=2.0=Nature=Matter=Moon=2 Feb= Cupid>N=C.
Bol.=1,000=100%=10.0=1.0=Mind=Sun=1 January=Helios >> M=E4.
Bola=10,000=1,000=100%=10.0=Physicality=Tech.=10 Oct.=Uranus=P=1Ø.
Bold=9,000=90%=P9.00D=9.0=Abstraction=Gods=Saturn=9Sept.>>A=Ø.
Boldface=2,500=3,000=30%=P3.00D=3.0=Creativity=Star=Muses=3 March=C=I.
Bole=1,500=15%=P1.50D=1.5=Authority = Solar Crown = Solar Core = 1 May = Maia.
Bolero=9,000=90%=P9.00D=9.0=Abstraction=Gods=Saturn=9Sept.>>A=Ø.
Boleyn, Anne.=6,500=7,000=70%=P7.00D=7.0=Lang.=Assets=Mars=6May=Pleiades.

Bolivar=3,500=4,000=40%=P4.00D=4.0=Govt.=Creat.= 4 April=Hermes>>G=A4.
See table at currency. After Simon BOLÍVAR. The Maks Currency was invented as the first anti-inflation currency and named after Peter Matthews-Akukalia its inventor.

Boliva Simón=3,000=30%=P3.00D=3.0=Creativity=Star=Muses=3 March=C=I.
Boliviano=3,000=30%=P3.00D=3.0=Creativity=Star=Muses=3 March=C=I.
Boil=4,500=5,000=50%=P5.00D=5.0=Law=Time=Venus=5May=Odite>>L=N.
Boil weevil=9,000=90%=P9.00D=9.0=Abstraction=Gods=Saturn=9Sept.>>A=Ø.
bologna=8,000=80%=P8.00D=8.0=Econ.=Curr.=Busn.=Jupt.=8Aug=Zeus>E=v.
Bologna=5,500=5.5=80%=P5.50D=Earth-Midway=5 May=Gaia.
Bolshevik=7,500=8,000=80%=P8.00D=8.0=Econ.=Curr.=Busn.=Jupt.=8Aug=Zeus>E=v.
Bolster=10,500=11,000=11%=P1.10D=1.1=Idea=Brainchild=Inventn.=11 Nov.=Athena>K=F.
Bolt(1)=30,500=31,000= 13,000 = 13% =P1.30D =1.3 =SolarCore=Faculty=13Jan.=Athena.

Bolt(2)=3,500=4,000=40%=P4.00D=4.0=Govt.=Creat.= 4 April=Hermes>>G=A4.
Bolus=5,000=50%=P5.00D=5.0=Law=Time=Venus=5May=Odite>>L=N.
Bomb=17,500=18,000=18%=P1.80D=1.8=Solar Currency=MaksCurrencies=1 Aug=Maia.
Bombard=8,000=80%=P8.00D=8.0=Econ.=Curr.=Busn.=Jupt.=8Aug=Zeus>E=v.
Bombardier=5,500=5.5=80%=P5.50D=Earth-Midway=5 May=Gaia.
Bombast=2,000=20%=P2.00D=2.0=Nature=Matter=Moon=2 Feb= Cupid>N=C.
Bombay=4,000=40%=P4.00D=4.0=Govt.=Creat.= 4 April=Hermes>>G=A4.
Bombazine=3,500=4,000=40%=P4.00D=4.0=Govt.=Creat.= 4 April=Hermes>>G=A4.
Bombed=1,000=100%=10.0=1.0=Mind=Sun=1 January=Helios >> M=E4.
Bomber=7,500=8,000=80%=P8.00D=8.0=Econ.=Curr.=Busn.=Jupt.=8Aug=Zeus>E=v.
Bombshell=3,000=30%=P3.00D=3.0=Creativity=Star=Muses=3 March=C=I.
Bombsight=1,500=15%=P1.50D=1.5=Authority = Solar Crown = Solar Core = 1 May = Maia.
Bonafide=9,000=90%=P9.00D=9.0=Abstraction=Gods=Saturn=9Sept.>>A=Ø.
Bonanza=5,500=5.5=80%=P5.50D=Earth-Midway=5 May=Gaia.
Bonaparte=16,000=16%=P1.60D=1.6=Cycle   of   Life=Incarnation=MindofGOD=
   1June= Maia.
Bonbon=3,000=30%=P3.00D=3.0=Creativity=Star=Muses=3 March=C=I.
Bond=50,000=5,000=50%=P5.00D=5.0=Law=Time=Venus=5May=Odite>>L=N.
Bondage=1,500=15%=P1.50D=1.5=Authority = Solar Crown = Solar Core = 1 May = Maia.
Bond man=1,500=15%=P1.50D=1.5=Authority = Solar Crown = Solar Core = 1 May = Maia.
Bond paper=7,000=70%=P7.00D=7.0=Lang.=Assets=Mars=6May=Pleiades.
Bond servant=5,000=50%=P5.00D=5.0=Law=Time=Venus=5May=Odite>>L=N.
Bondsman=5,500=5.5=80%=P5.50D=Earth-Midway=5 May=Gaia.
Bond woman=2,000=20%=P2.00D=2.0=Nature=Matter=Moon=2 Feb= Cupid>N=C.
Bone=21,000=12,000=12%=P1.20D=1.2=Knowledge=Edu.=12Dec.=Athena>>K=F.
Bone black=6,500=7,000=70%=P7.00D=7.0=Lang.=Assets=Mars=6May=Pleiades.
Bone-dry=1,000=100%=10.0=1.0=Mind=Sun=1 January=Helios >> M=E4.
Bone meal=5,500=5.5=80%=P5.50D=Earth-Midway=5 May=Gaia.
Boner=1,500=15%=P1.50D=1.5=Authority = Solar Crown = Solar Core = 1 May = Maia.
Bonfire=2,000=20%=P2.00D=2.0=Nature=Matter=Moon=2 Feb= Cupid>N=C.
Bong=3,500=4,000=40%=P4.00D=4.0=Govt.=Creat.= 4 April=Hermes>>G=A4.
Bongo(1)=9,500=10,000=1,000=100%=10.0=Physicality=Tech.=10 Oct.=Uranus=P=1Ø.
Bongo(2)=7,000=70%=P7.00D=7.0=Lang.=Assets=Mars=6May=Pleiades.
Bonhomie=3,000=30%=P3.00D=3.0=Creativity=Star=Muses=3 March=C=I.
Bonin Islands=5,500=5.5=80%=P5.50D=Earth-Midway=5 May=Gaia.
Bonito=7,000=70%=P7.00D=7.0=Lang.=Assets=Mars=6May=Pleiades.
Bon mot=1,000=100%=10.0=1.0=Mind=Sun=1 January=Helios >> M=E4.
Bonn=10,500=11,000=11%=P1.10D=1.1=Idea=Brainchild=Inventn.=11 Nov.=Athena>K=F.
Bonnet=12,000=12%=P1.20D=1.2=Knowledge=Edu.=12Dec.=Athena>>K=F.
Bonny=3,500=4,000=40%=P4.00D=4.0=Govt.=Creat.= 4 April=Hermes>>G=A4.
Bonsai=6,000=60%=P6.00D=6.0=Man=Earth=Health=Royalty=6June=Gaia>M=M2.
Bonus=6,000=60%=P6.00D=6.0=Man=Earth=Health=Royalty=6June=Gaia>M=M2.
Bonvivant=2,500=3,000=30%=P3.00D=3.0=Creativity=Star=Muses=3 March=C=I.
Bon voyage=5,000=50%=P5.00D=5.0=Law=Time=Venus=5May=Odite>>L=N.
Boo=5,500=5.5=80%=P5.50D=Earth-Midway=5 May=Gaia.

Boob=4,500=5,000=50%=P5.00D=5.0=Law=Time=Venus=5May=Odite>>L=N.
Booby=6,500=7,000=70%=P7.00D=7.0=Lang.=Assets=Mars=6May=Pleiades.
Booby prize=5,500=5.5=80%=P5.50D=Earth-Midway=5 May=Gaia.
Booby trap=9,500=10,000=1,000=100%=10.0=Physicality=Tech.=10 Oct.=Uranus=P=1Ø.
Boodle=5,500=5.5=80%=P5.50D=Earth-Midway=5 May=Gaia.
Boogeyman=2,000=20%=P2.00D=2.0=Nature=Matter=Moon=2 Feb= Cupid>N=C.
Boogie=2,500=3,000=30%=P3.00D=3.0=Creativity=Star=Muses=3 March=C=I.
Boogie-woogie=8,000=80%=P8.00D=8.0=Econ.=Curr.=Busn.=Jupt.=8Aug=Zeus>E=v.

Book=23,500=24,000=24%=Intl. Business=24 Days Monthly=2.4% Taxes.
Peter Matthews - Akukalia established the Creatocracy as a sector of Creative Scientists Professionals just like the Judiciary for lawyers or the Finance sector for bankers and insurance. He has written over 100 books and massive formulas in the Mind Sciences alone. Each has at least 200 chapters making over 2 million concepts on the subject. His Mind Arts contains over 550 poems in Makupedialand. His Mind Laws are huge. He wrote over 10,000 verses in his Castle Makupedia and 22 seasons dramatic works in the Creatocracy Republic. The Creatocratic Charter is our body of knowledge. The BIQUR is our program translated scriptures. Our link bridge and business wing to the rest of humanity and beyond is the World Digital Dictionary. Our flight is the Castle Makupedia Encyclopedia. It authorizes the Creatocracy to register and establish the World Digital Data Center (Nigeria Limited and, or as appropriate) in every country on earth and beyond space if possible. The aim among others is to provide raw computed and realistic data solutions, structured governance and Creatocracy for a better world.

Bookcase=4,500=5,000=50%=P5.00D=5.0=Law=Time=Venus=5May=Odite>>L=N.
Bookend=4,500=5,000=50%=P5.00D=5.0=Law=Time=Venus=5May=Odite>>L=N.
Bookie=1,500=15%=P1.50D=1.5=Authority = Solar Crown = Solar Core = 1 May = Maia.
Booking=3,000=30%=P3.00D=3.0=Creativity=Star=Muses=3 March=C=I.
Bookish=4,500=5,000=50%=P5.00D=5.0=Law=Time=Venus=5May=Odite>>L=N.
Bookkeeping=4,500=5,000=50%=P5.00D=5.0=Law=Time=Venus=5May=Odite>>L=N.
Booklet=3,000=30%=P3.00D=3.0=Creativity=Star=Muses=3 March=C=I.
Bookmaker=8,000=80%=P8.00D=8.0=Econ.=Curr.=Busn.=Jupt.=8Aug=Zeus>E=v.
Bookmark=5,000=50%=P5.00D=5.0=Law=Time=Venus=5May=Odite>>L=N.
Bookplate=4,500=5,000=50%=P5.00D=5.0=Law=Time=Venus=5May=Odite>>L=N.
Book value=7,500=8,000=80%=P8.00D=8.0=Econ.=Curr.=Busn.=Jupt.=8Aug=Zeus>E=v.
Bookworm=10,000=1,000=100%=10.0=Physicality=Tech.=10 Oct.=Uranus=P=1Ø.

Boolean=12,000=12%=P1.20D=1.2=Knowledge=Edu.=12Dec.=Athena>>K=F.
Of or relating to an algebraic system that is used in symbolic logic and in logic circuits in computer science. After George Boole 1815-1864. Makupedia invented Makumatics.

Boom(1)=8,500=9,000=90%=P9.00D=9.0=Abstraction=Gods=Saturn=9Sept.>>A=Ø.
Boom(2)=23,000=23%=Local Business =23 Days Monthly=2.3% Taxes daily income.

Boom box=4,000=40%=P4.00D=4.0=Govt.=Creat.= 4 April=Hermes>>G=A4.
Boomerang= 13,000 = 13% = P1.30D = 1.3 = Solar Core = Faculty = 13Jan.=Athena.
Boon(1)=1,500=15%=P1.50D=1.5=Authority = Solar Crown = Solar Core = 1 May = Maia.
Boon(2)=3,000=30%=P3.00D=3.0=Creativity=Star=Muses=3 March=C=I.
Boondocks=3,000=30%=P3.00D=3.0=Creativity=Star=Muses=3 March=C=I.
Boondoggle=3,000=30%=P3.00D=3.0=Creativity=Star=Muses=3 March=C=I.
Boone Daniel=4,000=40%=P4.00D=4.0=Govt.=Creat.= 4 April=Hermes>>G=A4.
Boor=7,000=70%=P7.00D=7.0=Lang.=Assets=Mars=6May=Pleiades.
Boost=11,000=11%=P1.10D=1.1=Idea=Brainchild=Inventn.=11 Nov.=Athena>K=F.
Booster=10,000=1,000=100%=10.0=Physicality=Tech.=10 Oct.=Uranus=P=1Ø.
Boosterism=2,500=3,000=30%=P3.00D=3.0=Creativity=Star=Muses=3 March=C=I.
Booster shot=5,000=50%=P5.00D=5.0=Law=Time=Venus=5May=Odite>>L=N.
Boot(1)=19,000=19%=P1.90D=1.9=Planetary Energy=1 September = Maia.
Boot(2)=2,500=3,000=30%=P3.00D=3.0=Creativity=Star=Muses=3 March=C=I.
Boot black=3,500=4,000=40%=P4.00D=4.0=Govt.=Creat.= 4 April=Hermes>>G=A4.
Boot camp=3,000=30%=P3.00D=3.0=Creativity=Star=Muses=3 March=C=I.
Bootee=3,500=4,000=40%=P4.00D=4.0=Govt.=Creat.= 4 April=Hermes>>G=A4.
Boôtes=3,000=30%=P3.00D=3.0=Creativity=Star=Muses=3 March=C=I.
Booth=12,000=12%=P1.20D=1.2=Knowledge=Edu.=12Dec.=Athena>>K=F.

Booth Family=10,500=11,000=11%=P1.10D=1.1=Idea=Brainchild=11 Nov.=Athena>K=F.
The Booth Family including William and his wife, Catherine MumfordBooth were founders of the Salvation Army (1878). They were a family of reformers. Peter Matthews-Akukalia owns the Creatocratic Royal Family and is the Creatocracy by Intellectual Property rights.

Boothia Peninsula=6,000=60%=P6.00D=6.0=Man=Earth=Royalty=6June=Gaia>M=M2.
Bootleg=5,000=50%=P5.00D=5.0=Law=Time=Venus=5May=Odite>>L=N.
Boot less=2,500=3,000=30%=P3.00D=3.0=Creativity=Star=Muses=3 March=C=I.
Boot lick=5,000=50%=P5.00D=5.0=Law=Time=Venus=5May=Odite>>L=N.
Bootstrap=11,000=11%=P1.10D=1.1=Idea=Brainchild=Inventn.=11 Nov.=Athena>K=F.
Booty=5,500=5.5=80%=P5.50D=Earth-Midway=5 May=Gaia.
Booze=3,500=4,000=40%=P4.00D=4.0=Govt.=Creat.= 4 April=Hermes>>G=A4.
Bop(1)=3,500=4,000=40%=P4.00D=4.0=Govt.=Creat.= 4 April=Hermes>>G=A4.
Bop(2)=10,000=1,000=100%=10.0=Physicality=Tech.=10 Oct.=Uranus=P=1Ø.
Bor.=1,000=100%=10.0=1.0=Mind=Sun=1 January=Helios >> M=E4.
Borate=2,500=3,000=30%=P3.00D=3.0=Creativity=Star=Muses=3 March=C=I.
Borax=6,000=60%=P6.00D=6.0=Man=Earth=Health=Royalty=6June=Gaia>M=M2.
Bordeaux(1)=5,500=5.5=80%=P5.50D=Earth-Midway=5 May=Gaia.
Bordeaux(2)=5,500=5.5=80%=P5.50D=Earth-Midway=5 May=Gaia.
Bordelo=2,000=20%=P2.00D=2.0=Nature=Matter=Moon=2 Feb= Cupid>N=C.
Border=13,500=14,000=14%=P1.40D=1.4=Mgt.=Solar Core=13 May=Athena>>SC=0.1
Borderland=4,500=5,000=50%=P5.00D=5.0=Law=Time=Venus=5May=Odite>>L=N.
Borderline=10,000=1,000=100%=10.0=Physicality=Tech.=10 Oct.=Uranus=P=1Ø.

Border States=9,500=10,000=1,000=100%=10.0=Phys.=Tech.=10 Oct.=Uranus=P=1Ø.
Bore(1)=16,000=16%=P1.60D=1.6=Cycle of Life=Incarnation=MindofGOD=1June= Maia.
Bore(2)=6,500=7,000=70%=P7.00D=7.0=Lang.=Assets=Mars=6May=Pleiades.
Bore(3)=1,500=15%=P1.50D=1.5=Authority = Solar Crown = Solar Core = 1 May = Maia.
Boreal=3,000=30%=P3.00D=3.0=Creativity=Star=Muses=3 March=C=I.
Boredom=5,000=50%=P5.00D=5.0=Law=Time=Venus=5May=Odite>>L=N.
Borgia Italian Family=10,000=1,000=100%=10.0=Physicality=Tech.=10 Oct.=Uranus=P=1Ø.
Boric acid=7,000=70%=P7.00D=7.0=Lang.=Assets=Mars=6May=Pleiades.
Born=9,500=10,000=1,000=100%=10.0=Physicality=Tech.=10 Oct.=Uranus=P=1Ø.
Borne=2,000=20%=P2.00D=2.0=Nature=Matter=Moon=2 Feb= Cupid>N=C.
Borneo=7,000=70%=P7.00D=7.0=Lang.=Assets=Mars=6May=Pleiades.
Borodin Aleksandr=2,000=20%=P2.00D=2.0=Nature=Matter=Moon=2 Feb= Cupid>N=C.
Boron=15,000=1,500=15%=P1.50D=1.5=Authority = Solar Crown = SC. = 1 May = Maia.

Borough=16,000=16%=P1.60D=1.6=Cycle of Life=Incarnation=MOG=1June= Maia.
A self governing incorporated town in some U.S. states. A place of incarnation.

Borrow=10,500=11,000=11%=P1.10D=1.1=Idea=Brainchild=Inventn.=11 Nov.=Athena>K=F.
Borscht=5,500=5.5=80%=P5.50D=Earth-Midway=5 May=Gaia.
Borzol=5,500=5.5=80%=P5.50D=Earth-Midway=5 May=Gaia.
Bosch Heronymous=2,500=3,000=30%=P3.00D=3.0=Creatv.=Star=Muses=3 March=C=I.
Bosh=1,000=100%=10.0=1.0=Mind=Sun=1 January=Helios >> M=E4.
Bosn=1,500=15%=P1.50D=1.5=Authority = Solar Crown = Solar Core = 1 May = Maia.
Bosnia=3,000=30%=P3.00D=3.0=Creativity=Star=Muses=3 March=C=I.
Bosnia Herzegovina=6,500=70%=P7.00D=7.0=Lang.=Assets=Mars=6May=Pleiades.
Bosom=8,500=9,000=90%=P9.00D=9.0=Abstraction=Gods=Saturn=9Sept.>>A=Ø.
Bosporus=8,000=80%=P8.00D=8.0=Econ.=Curr.=Busn.=Jupt.=8Aug=Zeus>E=v.
Boss(1)=12,500= 13,000 = 13% = P1.30D = 1.3 = Solar Core = Faculty = 13Jan.=Athena.
Boss(2)=2,500=3,000=30%=P3.00D=3.0=Creativity=Star=Muses=3 March=C=I.
Boston=8,000=80%=P8.00D=8.0=Econ.=Curr.=Busn.=Jupt.=8Aug=Zeus>E=v.
Bosun=1,500=15%=P1.50D=1.5=Authority = Solar Crown = Solar Core = 1 May = Maia.
Boswell James=3,500=4,000=40%=P4.00D=4.0=Govt.=Creat.= 4 April=Hermes>>G=A4.
Botany=3,000=30%=P3.00D=3.0=Creativity=Star=Muses=3 March=C=I.
Botch=6,000=60%=P6.00D=6.0=Man=Earth=Royalty=6June=Gaia>M=M2.
Both=16,000=16%=P1.60D=1.6=Cycle of Life=Incarnation=MindofGOD=1June= Maia.
Bother=9,500=10,000=1,000=100%=10.0=Physicality=Tech.=10 Oct.=Uranus=P=1Ø.
Bothnia=5,000=50%=P5.00D=5.0=Law=Time=Venus=5May=Odite>>L=N.
Bots.=1,000=100%=10.0=1.0=Mind=Sun=1 January=Helios >> M=E4.
Botswana=5,000=50%=P5.00D=5.0=Law=Time=Venus=5May=Odite>>L=N.
Botticelli Sandro.=2,500=3,000=30%=P3.00D=3.0=Creativity=Star=Muses=3 March=C=I.
Bottle= 13,000 = 13% = P1.30D = 1.3 = Solar Core = Faculty = 13Jan.=Athena.
Bottleneck=9,000=90%=P9.00D=9.0=Abstraction=Gods=Saturn=9Sept.>>A=Ø.
Bottom=16,000=16%=P1.60D=1.6=Cycle of Life=Incarnation=MindofGOD=1June= Maia.
Bottomland=1,500=15%=P1.50D=1.5=Authority = Solar Crown = Solar Core = 1 May = Maia.

Bottom line=10,000=1,000=100%=10.0=Physicality=Tech.=10 Oct.=Uranus=P=1Ø.
Botulism=7,500=8,000=80%=P8.00D=8.0=Econ.=Curr.=Busn.=Jupt.=8Aug=Zeus>E=v.

Boudicca=3,500=4,000=40%=P4.00D=4.0=Govt.=Creat.= 4 April=Hermes>>G=A4.
1st cent. A.D. Queen of ancient Britain. The Creatocracy has Athena as its ancient Queen.

Boudoir=2,000=20%=P2.00D=2.0=Nature=Matter=Moon=2 Feb= Cupid>N=C.
Bouffant=3,500=4,000=40%=P4.00D=4.0=Govt.=Creat.= 4 April=Hermes>>G=A4.
Bougainville=11,000=11%=P1.10D=1.1=Idea=Brainchild=Inventn.=11 Nov.=Athena>K=F.
Bough=4,000=40%=P4.00D=4.0=Govt.=Creat.= 4 April=Hermes>>G=A4.
Bouillabaisse=4,500=5,000=50%=P5.00D=5.0=Law=Time=Venus=5May=Odite>>L=N.
Bouillon=2,500=3,000=30%=P3.00D=3.0=Creativity=Star=Muses=3 March=C=I.
Boul.=1,000=100%=10.0=1.0=Mind=Sun=1 January=Helios >> M=E4.
Boulder=5,000=50%=P5.00D=5.0=Law=Time=Venus=5May=Odite>>L=N.

Boulevard=9,500=10,000=1,000=100%=10.0=Physicality=Tech.=10 Oct.=Uranus=P=1Ø.
Another name for bulwark. Helen of bulwark becomes Helen of Boulevard. Boulevard is a broad street often tree lined landscaped and regional control in nature. Bulwark is a fence and blockage in nature. Boulevard makes way, bulwark blocks the way. As the result shows boulevard is a borderline that links abstraction say software to physicality or technology. The secret of a thing is in the name. The Creatocracy functions name technologies for success in life. We help track the secrets of the energy that functions names and codes. We are revelation and research driven through computation. See Benefactress. Bulwark.

Bounce=20,000=2,000=20%=P2.00D=2.0=Nature=Matter=Moon=2 Feb= Cupid>N=C.
Bouncer=6,500=7,000=70%=P7.00D=7.0=Lang.=Assets=Mars=6May=Pleiades.
Bouncing=2,500=3,000=30%=P3.00D=3.0=Creativity=Star=Muses=3 March=C=I.
Bound(1)=5,000=50%=P5.00D=5.0=Law=Time=Venus=5May=Odite>>L=N.
Bound(2)=8,500=9,000=90%=P9.00D=9.0=Abstraction=Gods=Saturn=9Sept.>>A=Ø.
Bound(3)=14,500=15,000=1,500=15%=P1.50D=1.5=Auth.=SC=Solar Core=1 May= Maia.
Bound(4)=3,000=30%=P3.00D=3.0=Creativity=Star=Muses=3 March=C=I.
Boundary=3,500=4,000=40%=P4.00D=4.0=Govt.=Creat.= 4 April=Hermes>>G=A4.
Boundary Peak=6,500=7,000=70%=P7.00D=7.0=Lang.=Assets=Mars=6May=Pleiades.
Bounden=2,000=20%=P2.00D=2.0=Nature=Matter=Moon=2 Feb= Cupid>N=C.
Bounder=2,000=20%=P2.00D=2.0=Nature=Matter=Moon=2 Feb= Cupid>N=C.
Boundless=3,500=4,000=40%=P4.00D=4.0=Govt.=Creat.= 4 April=Hermes>>G=A4.
Bounteous=5,500=5.5=80%=P5.50D=Earth-Midway=5 May=Gaia.
Bountiful=5,000=50%=P5.00D=5.0=Law=Time=Venus=5May=Odite>>L=N.
Bounty=12,500= 13,000 = 13% = P1.30D = 1.3 = Solar Core = Faculty = 13Jan.=Athena.
Bouquet=6,000=60%=P6.00D=6.0=Man=Earth=Royalty=6June=Gaia>M=M2.
bourbon=5,500=5.5=80%=P5.50D=Earth-Midway=5 May=Gaia.
Bourbon=11,000=11%=P1.10D=1.1=Idea=Brainchild=Inventn.=11 Nov.=Athena>K=F.
Bourgeoisie=11,000=11%=P1.10D=1.1=Idea=Brainchild=Inventn.=11 Nov.=Athena>K=F.

Bourke-White Margare=3,000=30%=P3.00D=3.0=Creativity=Star=Muses=3 March=C=I.
Bournemouth=7,000=70%=P7.00D=7.0=Lang.=Assets=Mars=6May=Pleiades.
Bout=7,500=8,000=80%=P8.00D=8.0=Econ.=Curr.=Busn.=Jupt.=8Aug=Zeus>E=v.
Boutique=6,000=60%=P6.00D=6.0=Man=Earth=Royalty=6June=Gaia>M=M2.
Boutonnière=2,500=3,000=30%=P3.00D=3.0=Creativity=Star=Muses=3 March=C=I.
Bovine=5,000=50%=P5.00D=5.0=Law=Time=Venus=5May=Odite>>L=N.
Bow(1)=4,000=40%=P4.00D=4.0=Govt.=Creat.= 4 April=Hermes>>G=A4.
Bow(2)= 13,000 = 13% = P1.30D = 1.3 = Solar Core = Faculty = 13Jan.=Athena.
Bow(3)=24,500=3,000=30%=P3.00D=3.0=Creativity=Star=Muses=3 March=C=I.
Bowdlerize=5,500=5.5=80%=P5.50D=Earth-Midway=5 May=Gaia.
Bowel= 6,000=60%=P6.00D=6.0=Man=Earth=Royalty=6June=Gaia>M=M2.
Bower=2,000=20%=P2.00D=2.0=Nature=Matter=Moon=2 Feb= Cupid>N=C.
Bowie knife=6,000=60%=P6.00D=6.0=Man=Earth=Royalty=6June=Gaia>M=M2.
Bow knot=3,500=4,000=40%=P4.00D=4.0=Govt.=Creat.= 4 April=Hermes>>G=A4.
Bowl(1)=12,000=12%=P1.20D=1.2=Knowledge=Edu.=12Dec.=Athena>>K=F.
Bowl(2)=8,000=80%=P8.00D=8.0=Econ.=Curr.=Busn.=Jupt.=8Aug=Zeus>E=v.
Bow legged=4,000=40%=P4.00D=4.0=Govt.=Creat.= 4 April=Hermes>>G=A4.
Bowler(1)=1,500=15%=P1.50D=1.5=Authority = Solar Crown = Solar Core = 1 May = Maia.
Bowler(2)=1,500=15%=P1.50D=1.5=Authority = Solar Crown = Solar Core = 1 May = Maia.
Bowline=4,000=40%=P4.00D=4.0=Govt.=Creat.= 4 April=Hermes>>G=A4.
Bowling= 13,000 = 13% = P1.30D = 1.3 = Solar Core = Faculty = 13Jan.=Athena.
Bowling alley=5,500=5.5=80%=P5.50D=Earth-Midway=5 May=Gaia.
Bowling green=3,000=30%=P3.00D=3.0=Creativity=Star=Muses=3 March=C=I.
Bowman=1,000=100%=Physicality= Tech.=10 Oct.=Uranus=P=1Ø.
Bowsprit=5,000=50%=P5.00D=5.0=Law=Time=Venus=5May=Odite>>L=N.
Bowstring=5,000=50%=P5.00D=5.0=Law=Time=Venus=5May=Odite>>L=N.
Bow tie=5,000=50%=P5.00D=5.0=Law=Time=Venus=5May=Odite>>L=N.
Box(1)=17,000=17%=P1.70D=1.7=Solar Asset =17 Feb.=Maia>>Mind Computing.
Box(2)=7,000=70%=P7.00D=7.0=Lang.=Assets=Mars=6May=Pleiades.
Box(3)=7,500=8,000=80%=P8.00D=8.0=Econ.=Curr.=Busn.=Jupt.=8Aug=Zeus>E=v.
Boxcar=4,500=5,000=50%=P5.00D=5.0=Law=Time=Venus=5May=Odite>>L=N.
Boxer(1)=3,000=30%=P3.00D=3.0=Creativity=Star=Muses=3 March=C=I.
Boxer(2)=5,500=5.5=80%=P5.50D=Earth-Midway=5 May=Gaia.
Boxing=3,500=4,000=40%=P4.00D=4.0=Govt.=Creat.= 4 April=Hermes>>G=A4.
Box office=3,000=30%=P3.00D=3.0=Creativity=Star=Muses=3 March=C=I.
Boxwood=4,000=40%=P4.00D=4.0=Govt.=Creat.= 4 April=Hermes>>G=A4.
Boy=6,500=7,000=70%=P7.00D=7.0=Lang.=Assets=Mars=6May=Pleiades.
Boycott=10,500=11,000=11%=P1.10D=1.1=Idea=Brainchild=Inventn.=11 Nov.=Athena>K=F.
Boyfriend=3,500=4,000=40%=P4.00D=4.0=Govt.=Creat.= 4 April=Hermes>>G=A4.
Boyle Robert=4,000=40%=P4.00D=4.0=Govt.=Creat.= 4 April=Hermes>>G=A4.

Boy Scout=8,500=9,000=90%=P9.00D=9.0=Abstraction=Gods=Saturn=9Sept.>>A=Ø.
A member of a worldwide organization of young men and boys, founded for character development, citizenship training, and outdoor skills. The Creativity club trains young people to pursue courses in the creative sciences. The young creative scientists club was

founded to nurture students to think and work like prospective creative scientists. The resultant indicates that true clubs must be software driven. The Creatocracy has created over 10,000 apps in writing and computations for utility that will last a lifetime.

Boysenberry=11,000=11%=P1.10D=1.1=Idea=Brainchild=Inventn.=11 Nov.=Athena>K=F.
BPOE=3,000=30%=P3.00D=3.0=Creativity=Star=Muses=3 March=C=I.
Br=2,500=3,000=30%=P3.00D=3.0=Creativity=Star=Muses=3 March=C=I.
Br.=1,000=100%=10.0=1.0=Mind=Sun=1 January=Helios >> M=E4.
Bra=1,000=100%=10.0=1.0=Mind=Sun=1 January=Helios >> M=E4.
Brace=31,000= 13,000 = 13% = P1.30D = 1.3 = Solar Core = Faculty = 13Jan.=Athena.
Bracelet=5,000=50%=P5.00D=5.0=Law=Time=Venus=5May=Odite>>L=N.
Bracken=7,500=8,000=80%=P8.00D=8.0=Econ.=Curr.=Busn.=Jupt.=8Aug=Zeus>E=v.
Bracket=20,500=21,000=12,000=12%=P1.20D=1.2=Knowl.=Edu.=12Dec.=Athena>>K=F.
Brackish=4,000=40%=P4.00D=4.0=Govt.=Creat.= 4 April=Hermes>>G=A4.
Bract=5,000=50%=P5.00D=5.0=Law=Time=Venus=5May=Odite>>L=N.
Brad=3,500=4,000=40%=P4.00D=4.0=Govt.=Creat.= 4 April=Hermes>>G=A4.
Bradbury Ray Douglas=2,000=20%=P2.00D=2.0=Nature=Moon=2 Feb= Cupid>N=C.
Braddock Edward=3,000=30%=P3.00D=3.0=Creativity=Star=Muses=3 March=C=I.
Bradford (1) William=3,500=4,000=40%=P4.00D=4.0=Govt.= 4 April=Hermes>>G=A4.
Bradford (2) William=3,500=4,000=40%=P4.00D=4.0=Govt.= 4 April=Hermes>>G=A4.
Bradley Omar Nelson.=2,000=20%=P2.00D=2.0=Nature=Moon=2 Feb= Cupid>N=C.
Bradstreet Anne Dudley=3,500=40%=P4.00D=4.0=Govt.= 4 April=Hermes>>G=A4.
Brady Mathew B.=2,500=3,000=30%=P3.00D=3.0=Creativity=Star=Muses=3 March=C=I.
Brag=2,500=3,000=30%=P3.00D=3.0=Creativity=Star=Muses=3 March=C=I.
Braggadocio=8,500=9,000=90%=P9.00D=9.0=Abstraction=Gods=Saturn=9Sept.>>A=Ø.
Braggart=3,000=30%=P3.00D=3.0=Creativity=Star=Muses=3 March=C=I.
Brahe Tycho=2,000=20%=P2.00D=2.0=Nature=Matter=Moon=2 Feb= Cupid>N=C.
Brahma=10,000=1,000=100%=10.0=Physicality=Tech.=10 Oct.=Uranus=P=1Ø.
Brahman=1,000=100%=10.0=1.0=Mind=Sun=1 January=Helios >> M=E4.
Brahmanism=11,500=12,000=12%=P1.20D=1.2=Knowledge=Edu.=12Dec.=Athena>>K=F.
Brahmaputra=9,500=10,000=1,000=100%=10.0=Phys.=Tech.=10 Oct.=Uranus=P=1Ø.
Brahmin=14,000=14%=P1.40D=1.4=Mgt.=Solar Core=13 May=Athena>>SC=0.1
Brahms Johannes=2,000=20%=P2.00D=2.0=Nature=Matter=Moon=2 Feb= Cupid>N=C.
Braid=17,000=17%=P1.70D=1.7=Solar Asset =17 Feb.=Maia>>Mind Computing.
Brälla=8,000=80%=P8.00D=8.0=Econ.=Curr.=Busn.=Jupt.=8Aug=Zeus>E=v.
Braille=35,500=4,000=40%=P4.00D=4.0=Govt.=Creat.= 4 April=Hermes>>G=A4.
Braille, Louis=6,000=60%=P6.00D=6.0=Man=Earth=Health=Royalty=6June=Gaia>M=M2.

Brain=35,500=4,000=40%=P4.00D=4.0=Govt.=Creat.= 4 April=Hermes>>G=A4.
The minimum capacity of the brain in learning is 40% operant on Mercury and organization. Brain age can be determined through the expressed value in the human energy systems database. It indicates the brain age of the person at birth. A person say of value 6.0 indicates such person has a brain age of 6years old ahead of birth age. He is six years older than his birth age. At 44 he would reason as a 50 year old. 44+6=50=5.0 seeking law

order and creating new standards. The energy level indicates the quantum of energy spirit or lifespan absorbed from the mother from conception to the particular date of birth. An energy level of say 100% means such person had a full tank of grace. It also indicates the brain type given to the person for classification of intelligence thought will and emotion. A 100%=10.0 means a fully formed technology driven mindset. 33=3.3>>low energy but a genius. 4.0 >> Executive >> Organization >> Leader >> Politics>> Relationships >> Family >> Merchandise >> Oratory >> Eloquence etc.

However this does not mean the same level of endowment as energy is the electrifying liquid of life but endowments are the innate contents of this liquid that can be developed to establish capacity ability and capability. The level of endowment in a person is subject to further development. This is measured in the Mind Assessment Tests - a subjective test. The resultant is what births creativity or what is conventionally known as behavior, an expression module which can either be normal conventional environmental behavior or genius supernatural behavior. The first makes for learning and adaptation. The second makes for continuity and sustainability. Hence they complement each other in stronger terms. When there is a saturation of knowledge, Nature introduces genius to help mankind.

Brainchild=3,000=30%=P3.00D=3.0=Creativity=Star=Muses=3 March=C=I.
Brainchild is the 11th dimension of the universe in the realm of ideas and philosophy. Indicated as muses functioned by Athena it proves that She is the Mother of Creativity. Greek mythology recognizes her as the Goddess of wisdom handicraft and warfare and even has it that she invented the Naval and military defense systems. Bible describes her as wisdom and the Spirit of GOD mentioned in Genesis 1:1-2, Proverbs 8 & 9, Romans 11:33-35. Pleiades is the Mind of GOD and honors her by supplying witty computations when sought and earned. She is the wife of Castle Makupedia and Goddess of the Creatocracy. See the book>> THE CREATOCRACY REPUBLIC by Peter Matthews - Akukalia.

Brain death=7,500=8,000=80%=P8.00D=8.0=Econ.=Curr.=Busn.=Jupt.=8Aug=Zeus>E=v.
Brain power=10,000=1,000=100%=10.0=Physicality=Tech.=10 Oct.=Uranus=P=1Ø.
Brainstorm=12,000=12%=P1.20D=1.2=Knowledge=Edu.=12Dec.=Athena>>K=F.
Brainwashing=8,500=9,000=90%=P9.00D=9.0=Abstraction=Gods=Saturn=9Sept.>>A=Ø.
Brain wave=7,500=8,000=80%=P8.00D=8.0=Econ.=Curr.=Busn.=Jupt.=8Aug=Zeus>E=v.
Braise=7,000=70%=P7.00D=7.0=Lang.=Assets=Mars=6May=Pleiades.
Brake(1)=14,000=14%=P1.40D=1.4=Mgt.=Solar Core=13 May=Athena>>SC=0.1
Brake(2)=3,000=30%=P3.00D=3.0=Creativity=Star=Muses=3 March=C=I.
Brake(3)=2,500=3,000=30%=P3.00D=3.0=Creativity=Star=Muses=3 March=C=I.
Brakeman=7,000=70%=P7.00D=7.0=Lang.=Assets=Mars=6May=Pleiades.
Bramble=5,000=50%=P5.00D=5.0=Law=Time=Venus=5May=Odite>>L=N.
Brampton=5,000=50%=P5.00D=5.0=Law=Time=Venus=5May=Odite>>L=N.
Bran=7,500=8,000=80%=P8.00D=8.0=Econ.=Curr.=Busn.=Jupt.=8Aug=Zeus>E=v.
Branch=30,000=3,000=30%=P3.00D=3.0=Creativity=Star=Muses=3 March=C=I.

Brand=18,500=19,000=19%=P1.90D=1.9=Planetary Energy=1 September = Maia.
The Solar Crown and the Creatocracy trademark are the brand of Makupedia owned by
Peter Matthews-Akukalia. They make up all that Creative Scientists stand for. Brands come
to life only when they have been trademarked. The Creatocracy Corporation is his asset.

Brandeis Louis Dembitz=6,500=70%=P7.00D=7.0=Lang.=Assets=Mars=6May=Pleiades.
Brandenburg=11,000=11%=P1.10D=1.1=Idea=Brainchild=Inventn.=11 Nov.=Athena>K=F.
Brandish=7,000=70%=P7.00D=7.0=Lang.=Assets=Mars=6May=Pleiades.
Brand name=1,500=15%=P1.50D=1.5=Authority = SC = Solar Core = 1 May = Maia.
Brand-new=3,000=30%=P3.00D=3.0=Creativity=Star=Muses=3 March=C=I.
Brandt Willy=4,500=5,000=50%=P5.00D=5.0=Law=Time=Venus=5May=Odite>>L=N.
Brandy=5,000=50%=P5.00D=5.0=Law=Time=Venus=5May=Odite>>L=N.
Brant=5,000=50%=P5.00D=5.0=Law=Time=Venus=5May=Odite>>L=N.
Braque Georgia=2,500=3,000=30%=P3.00D=3.0=Creativity=Star=Muses=3 March=C=I.
Brash=3,000=30%=P3.00D=3.0=Creativity=Star=Muses=3 March=C=I.
Brasilia=6,500=7,000=70%=P7.00D=7.0=Lang.=Assets=Mars=6May=Pleiades.
Brasov=4,500=5,000=50%=P5.00D=5.0=Law=Time=Venus=5May=Odite>>L=N.
Brass=14,000=14%=P1.40D=1.4=Mgt.=Solar Core=13 May=Athena>>SC=0.1
Brasserie=4,500=5,000=50%=P5.00D=5.0=Law=Time=Venus=5May=Odite>>L=N.
Brass hat=6,500=7,000=70%=P7.00D=7.0=Lang.=Assets=Mars=6May=Pleiades.
Brassiere=4,000=40%=P4.00D=4.0=Govt.=Creat.= 4 April=Hermes>>G=A4.
Brass tacks=4,500=5,000=50%=P5.00D=5.0=Law=Time=Venus=5May=Odite>>L=N.
Brat=3,000=30%=P3.00D=3.0=Creativity=Star=Muses=3 March=C=I.
Bratislava=6,500=7,000=70%=P7.00D=7.0=Lang.=Assets=Mars=6May=Pleiades.

Braun Wernher=3,500=4,000=40%=P4.00D=4.0=Govt.=Creat.= 4 April=Hermes>>G=A4.
German born American rocket engineer. Creative Scientists are Mind Engineers.

Bravado=4,500=5,000=50%=P5.00D=5.0=Law=Time=Venus=5May=Odite>>L=N.
Brave=12,000=12%=P1.20D=1.2=Knowledge=Edu.=12Dec.=Athena>>K=F.
Bravery=500=5%=P5.00D=5.0=Law=Time=Venus=5 May=Aphrodite>>L=N.
Bravo=5,000=50%=P5.00D=5.0=Law=Time=Venus=5May=Odite>>L=N.
Bravura=5,500=5.5=80%=P5.50D=Earth-Midway=5 May=Gaia.
Brawl=8,000=80%=P8.00D=8.0=Econ.=Curr.=Busn.=Jupt.=8Aug=Zeus>E=v.
Brawn=3,500=4,000=40%=P4.00D=4.0=Govt.=Creat.= 4 April=Hermes>>G=A4.
Brawny=3,500=4,000=40%=P4.00D=4.0=Govt.=Creat.= 4 April=Hermes>>G=A4.
Bray=4,500=5,000=50%=P5.00D=5.0=Law=Time=Venus=5May=Odite>>L=N.
Braz.=1,000=100%=10.0=1.0=Mind=Sun=1 January=Helios >> M=E4.
Braze=5,000=50%=P5.00D=5.0=Law=Time=Venus=5May=Odite>>L=N.
Brazen=11,000=11%=P1.10D=1.1=Idea=Brainchild=Inventn.=11 Nov.=Athena>K=F.
Brazier(1)=2,500=3,000=30%=P3.00D=3.0=Creativity=Star=Muses=3 March=C=I.
Brazier(2)=4,500=5,000=50%=P5.00D=5.0=Law=Time=Venus=5May=Odite>>L=N.
Brazil=6,000=60%=P6.00D=6.0=Man=Earth=Royalty=6June=Gaia>M=M2.

Brazil nut=5,000=50%=P5.00D=5.0=Law=Time=Venus=5May=Odite>>L=N.
Brazos=10,000=1,000=100%=10.0=Physicality=Tech.=10 Oct.=Uranus=P=1Ø.
Brazzaville=6,000=60%=P6.00D=6.0=Man=Earth=Royalty=6June=Gaia>M=M2.
Breach=12,500= 13,000 = 13% = P1.30D = 1.3 = Solar Core = Faculty = 13Jan.=Athena.
Bread=17,000=17%=P1.70D=1.7=Solar Asset =17 Feb.=Maia>>Mind Computing.
Breadbasket=2,500=3,000=30%=P3.00D=3.0=Creativity=Star=Muses=3 March=C=I.
Breadfruit=10,000=1,000=100%=10.0=Physicality=Tech.=10 Oct.=Uranus=P=1Ø.
Bread stuff=5,500=5.5=80%=P5.50D=Earth-Midway=5 May=Gaia.
Breadth=11,000=11%=P1.10D=1.1=Idea=Brainchild=Inventn.=11 Nov.=Athena>K=F.
Breadwinner=6,000=60%=P6.00D=6.0=Man=Earth=Royalty=6June=Gaia>M=M2.
Break=61,500=62,000=6.2>>14.84=1.5=15%=P1.50D=1.5=Solar Crown= SC=1 May= Maia.
Breakage=8,500=9,000=90%=P9.00D=9.0=Abstraction=Gods=Saturn=9Sept.>>A=Ø.
Breakdown=15,500=16,000=16%=P1.60D=1.6=Cycle=Incarnation=MOG=1June= Maia.
Breaker=7,000=70%=P7.00D=7.0=Lang.=Assets=Mars=6May=Pleiades.
Breakfast=3,000=30%=P3.00D=3.0=Creativity=Star=Muses=3 March=C=I.
Break front=7,000=70%=P7.00D=7.0=Lang.=Assets=Mars=6May=Pleiades.
Breakneck=3,000=30%=P3.00D=3.0=Creativity=Star=Muses=3 March=C=I.
Breakout=3,000=30%=P3.00D=3.0=Creativity=Star=Muses=3 March=C=I.
Breakthrough=9,500=10,000=1,000=100%=10.0=Phys.=Tech.=10 Oct.=Uranus=P=1Ø.
Breakup=4,500=5,000=50%=P5.00D=5.0=Law=Time=Venus=5May=Odite>>L=N.
Breakwater=6,500=7,000=70%=P7.00D=7.0=Lang.=Assets=Mars=6May=Pleiades.
Beam=4,500=5,000=50%=P5.00D=5.0=Law=Time=Venus=5May=Odite>>L=N.
Breast=10,500=11,000=11%=P1.10D=1.1=Idea=Brainchild=Inventn.=11 Nov.=Athena>K=F.
Breastbone=1,000=100%=10.0=1.0=Mind=Sun=1 January=Helios >> M=E4.
Breastfeed=1,000=100%=10.0=1.0=Mind=Sun=1 January=Helios >> M=E4.
Breastplate=4,000=40%=P4.00D=4.0=Govt.=Creat.= 4 April=Hermes>>G=A4.
Breaststroke=8,000=80%=P8.00D=8.0=Econ.=Curr.=Busn.=Jupt.=8Aug=Zeus>E=v.
Breast work=4,000=40%=P4.00D=4.0=Govt.=Creat.= 4 April=Hermes>>G=A4.
Breath=10,000=1,000=100%=10.0=Physicality=Tech.=10 Oct.=Uranus=P=1Ø.
Breathe=12,000=12%=P1.20D=1.2=Knowledge=Edu.=12Dec.=Athena>>K=F.
Breather=4,000=40%=P4.00D=4.0=Govt.=Creat.= 4 April=Hermes>>G=A4.
Breathtaking=1,000=100%=10.0=1.0=Mind=Sun=1 January=Helios >> M=E4.
Brecht Bertoit=3,000=30%=P3.00D=3.0=Creativity=Star=Muses=3 March=C=I.
Breckinridge John Cabell=3,500=40%=P4.00D=4.0=Govt.= 4 April=Hermes>>G=A4.
Breech=7,000=70%=P7.00D=7.0=Lang.=Assets=Mars=6May=Pleiades.
Breechcloth=1,000=100%=10.0=1.0=Mind=Sun=1 January=Helios >> M=E4.
Breed= 13,000 = 13% = P1.30D = 1.3 = Solar Core = Faculty = 13Jan.=Athena.
Breeder=4,000=40%=P4.00D=4.0=Govt.=Creat.= 4 April=Hermes>>G=A4.
Breeder reactor=5,000=50%=P5.00D=5.0=Law=Time=Venus=5May=Odite>>L=N.
Breeding=7,000=70%=P7.00D=7.0=Lang.=Assets=Mars=6May=Pleiades.
Breeze= 13,000 = 13% = P1.30D = 1.3 = Solar Core = Faculty = 13Jan.=Athena.
Breezeway=6,500=7,000=70%=P7.00D=7.0=Lang.=Assets=Mars=6May=Pleiades.
Bremen=4,500=5,000=50%=P5.00D=5.0=Law=Time=Venus=5May=Odite>>L=N.
Brenner Pass=6,500=7,000=70%=P7.00D=7.0=Lang.=Assets=Mars=6May=Pleiades.
Brescia=4,500=5,000=50%=P5.00D=5.0=Law=Time=Venus=5May=Odite>>L=N.

Brest=5,500=5.5=80%=P5.50D=Earth-Midway=5 May=Gaia.
Brethren=2,500=3,000=30%=P3.00D=3.0=Creativity=Star=Muses=3 March=C=I.
Breton=5,000=50%=P5.00D=5.0=Law=Time=Venus=5May=Odite>>L=N.
Brueghel=1,000=100%=10.0=1.0=Mind=Sun=1 January=Helios >> M=E4.
Breve=9,500=10,000=1,000=100%=10.0=Physicality=Tech.=10 Oct.=Uranus=P=1Ø.
Breviary=6,000=60%=P6.00D=6.0=Man=Earth=Royalty=6June=Gaia>M=M2.
Brevity=3,000=30%=P3.00D=3.0=Creativity=Star=Muses=3 March=C=I.
Brew=11,000=11%=P1.10D=1.1=Idea=Brainchild=Inventn.=11 Nov.=Athena>K=F.
Brezhnev Leonid=2,500=3,000=30%=P3.00D=3.0=Creativity=Star=Muses=3 March=C=I.

Brian Boru=3,000=30%=P3.00D=3.0=Creativity=Star=Muses=3 March=C=I.
926-1014, Irish King(1002-14). Peter Matthews-Akukalia is the King of Paradise Nations.

Briar(1)=8,500=9,000=90%=P9.00D=9.0=Abstraction=Gods=Saturn=9Sept.>>A=Ø.
Briar(2)=1,500=15%=P1.50D=1.5=Authority = Solar Crown = Solar Core = 1 May = Maia.
Bribe=13,500=14,000=14%=P1.40D=1.4=Mgt.=Solar Core=13 May=Athena>>SC=0.1
Bric-a-brac=3,000=30%=P3.00D=3.0=Creativity=Star=Muses=3 March=C=I.
Brick= 13,000 = 13% = P1.30D = 1.3 = Solar Core = Faculty = 13Jan.=Athena.
Brickbat=4,500=5,000=50%=P5.00D=5.0=Law=Time=Venus=5May=Odite>>L=N.
Bricklayer=3,500=4,000=40%=P4.00D=4.0=Govt.=Creat.= 4 April=Hermes>>G=A4.
Bridal=1,000=100%=10.0=1.0=Mind=Sun=1 January=Helios >> M=E4.
Bride=4,000=40%=P4.00D=4.0=Govt.=Creat.= 4 April=Hermes>>G=A4.
Bridegroom=6,000=60%=P6.00D=6.0=Man=Earth=Royalty=6June=Gaia>M=M2.
Bridesmaid=4,000=40%=P4.00D=4.0=Govt.=Creat.= 4 April=Hermes>>G=A4.
Bridge(1)=30,000=3,000=30%=P3.00D=3.0=Creativity=Star=Muses=3 March=C=I.
Bridge(2)=6,000=60%=P6.00D=6.0=Man=Earth=Royalty=6June=Gaia>M=M2.
Bridgehead=8,000=80%=P8.00D=8.0=Econ.=Curr.=Busn.=Jupt.=8Aug=Zeus>E=v.
Bridgeport=7,000=70%=P7.00D=7.0=Lang.=Assets=Mars=6May=Pleiades.
Bridgetown=4,500=5,000=50%=P5.00D=5.0=Law=Time=Venus=5May=Odite>>L=N.
Bridgework=5,000=50%=P5.00D=5.0=Law=Time=Venus=5May=Odite>>L=N.
Bridle=13,500=14,000=14%=P1.40D=1.4=Mgt.=Solar Core=13 May=Athena>>SC=0.1
Brief=12,000=12%=P1.20D=1.2=Knowledge=Edu.=12Dec.=Athena>>K=F.
Briefcase=5,000=50%=P5.00D=5.0=Law=Time=Venus=5May=Odite>>L=N.
Briefing=6,000=60%=P6.00D=6.0=Man=Earth=Royalty=6June=Gaia>M=M2.
Brier(1)=4,500=5,000=50%=P5.00D=5.0=Law=Time=Venus=5May=Odite>>L=N.
Brier(2)=1,500=15%=P1.50D=1.5=Authority = Solar Crown = Solar Core = 1 May = Maia.
Brig.=8,500=9,000=90%=P9.00D=9.0=Abstraction=Gods=Saturn=9Sept.>>A=Ø.
Brigade=11,000=11%=P1.10D=1.1=Idea=Brainchild=Inventn.=11 Nov.=Athena>K=F.
Brigadier general=6,500=7,000=70%=P7.00D=7.0=Lang.=Assets=Mars=6May=Pleiades.
Brigand=4,000=40%=P4.00D=4.0=Govt.=Creat.= 4 April=Hermes>>G=A4.
Brigantine=6,000=60%=P6.00D=6.0=Man=Earth=Royalty=6June=Gaia>M=M2.
Brig.Gen.=1,000=100%=10.0=1.0=Mind=Sun=1 January=Helios >> M=E4.
Bright=7,000=70%=P7.00D=7.0=Lang.=Assets=Mars=6May=Pleiades.
Brighten=3,500=4,000=40%=P4.00D=4.0=Govt.=Creat.= 4 April=Hermes>>G=A4.

Brighton=6,500=7,000=70%=P7.00D=7.0=Lang.=Assets=Mars=6May=Pleiades.
Brilliant=12,000=12%=P1.20D=1.2=Knowledge=Edu.=12Dec.=Athena>>K=F.
Brilliantine=2,000=20%=P2.00D=2.0=Nature=Matter=Moon=2 Feb= Cupid>N=C.
Brim=10,000=1,000=100%=10.0=Physicality=Tech.=10 Oct.=Uranus=P=1Ø.
Brimstone=500=5%=P5.00D=5.0=Law=Time=Venus=5 May=Aphrodite>>L=N.
Brindled=5,500=5.5=80%=P5.50D=Earth-Midway=5 May=Gaia.
Brine=3,000=30%=P3.00D=3.0=Creativity=Star=Muses=3 March=C=I.
Bring=46,000=5,000=50%=P5.00D=5.0=Law=Time=Venus=5May=Odite>>L=N.
Brink=4,500=5,000=50%=P5.00D=5.0=Law=Time=Venus=5May=Odite>>L=N.
Brinkmanship=8,000=80%=P8.00D=8.0=Econ.=Curr.=Busn.=Jupt.=8Aug=Zeus>E=v.
Brio=1,000=100%=10.0=1.0=Mind=Sun=1 January=Helios >> M=E4.
Brioche=5,000=50%=P5.00D=5.0=Law=Time=Venus=5May=Odite>>L=N.
Briquette=7,000=70%=P7.00D=7.0=Lang.=Assets=Mars=6May=Pleiades.
Brisbane=7,500=8,000=80%=P8.00D=8.0=Econ.=Curr.=Busn.=Jupt.=8Aug=Zeus>E=v.
Brisk=5,000=50%=P5.00D=5.0=Law=Time=Venus=5May=Odite>>L=N.
Brisket=5,500=5.5=80%=P5.50D=Earth-Midway=5 May=Gaia.
Brisling=1,000=100%=10.0=1.0=Mind=Sun=1 January=Helios >> M=E4.
Bristle=13,500=14,000=14%=P1.40D=1.4=Mgt.=Solar Core=13 May=Athena>>SC=0.1
Bristol=5,000=50%=P5.00D=5.0=Law=Time=Venus=5May=Odite>>L=N.
Bristol Channel=8,000=80%=P8.00D=8.0=Econ.=Curr.=Busn.=Jupt.=8Aug=Zeus>E=v.
Brit=2,000=20%=P2.00D=2.0=Nature=Matter=Moon=2 Feb= Cupid>N=C.
Brit.=1,000=100%=10.0=1.0=Mind=Sun=1 January=Helios >> M=E4.
Britain(1)=2,500=3,000=30%=P3.00D=3.0=Creativity=Star=Muses=3 March=C=I.
Britain(2)=1,500=15%=P1.50D=1.5=Authority = Solar Crown = Solar Core = 1 May = Maia.
Britanic=500=5%=P5.00D=5.0=Law=Time=Venus=5 May=Aphrodite>>L=N.
Britches=500=5%=P5.00D=5.0=Law=Time=Venus=5 May=Aphrodite>>L=N.
Briticism=4,500=5,000=50%=P5.00D=5.0=Law=Time=Venus=5May=Odite>>L=N.
British=7,500=8,000=80%=P8.00D=8.0=Econ.=Curr.=Busn.=Jupt.=8Aug=Zeus>E=v.
British Columbia=7,000=70%=P7.00D=7.0=Lang.=Assets=Mars=6May=Pleiades.

British Commonwealth=2,000=20%=P2.00D=2.0=Nature=Moon=2 Feb= Cupid>N=C.
See Commonwealth of Nations. The Creatocracy >> The Creatocracy of Nations. Also
known as the Creatocratic Nations of Paradise. Citizens are Diseans, from Paradise.

British English=3,500=4,000=40%=P4.00D=4.0=Govt.=Creat.= 4 April=Hermes>>G=A4.
British Isles=8,500=9,000=90%=P9.00D=9.0=Abstraction=Gods=Saturn=9Sept.>>A=Ø.
British thermal unit=9,500=10,000=1,000=100%=10.0=Phy=Tech.=10Oct.=Uranus=P=1Ø.
British Virgin Islands=10,000=1,000=100%=10.0=Phys.=Tech.=10 Oct.=Uranus=P=1Ø.
British West Indies=8,500=9,000=90%=P9.00D=9.0=Abst.=Gods=Saturn=9Sept.>>A=Ø.
Briton=8,500=9,000=90%=P9.00D=9.0=Abstraction=Gods=Saturn=9Sept.>>A=Ø.
Britany=8,500=9,000=90%=P9.00D=9.0=Abstraction=Gods=Saturn=9Sept.>>A=Ø.
Britten Edward Benjamin=2,000=20%=P2.00D=2.0=Nature=Moon=2 Feb= Cupid>N=C.
Brittle=3,500=4,000=40%=P4.00D=4.0=Govt.=Creat.= 4 April=Hermes>>G=A4.
Brno=5,000=50%=P5.00D=5.0=Law=Time=Venus=5May=Odite>>L=N.

bro.=500=5%=P5.00D=5.0=Law=Time=Venus=5 May=Aphrodite>>L=N.
Broach=16,500=17,000=17%=P1.70D=1.7=Solar Asset =17 Feb.=Maia>>Mind Computing.
Broad=18,000=18%=P1.80D=1.8=Solar Currency=MaksCurrencies=1 Aug=Maia.
Broadband=4,000=40%=P4.00D=4.0=Govt.=Creat.= 4 April=Hermes>>G=A4.
Broad bean=9,500=10,000=1,000=100%=10.0=Physicality=Tech.=10 Oct.=Uranus=P=1Ø.
Broadcast=14,000=14%=P1.40D=1.4=Mgt.=Solar Core=13 May=Athena>>SC=0.1
Broadcloth=7,500=8,000=80%=P8.00D=8.0=Econ.=Curr.=Busn.=Jupt.=8Aug=Zeus>E=v.
Broaden=3,500=4,000=40%=P4.00D=4.0=Govt.=Creat.= 4 April=Hermes>>G=A4.
Broad jump=2,000=20%=P2.00D=2.0=Nature=Matter=Moon=2 Feb= Cupid>N=C.
Broadloom=3,500=4,000=40%=P4.00D=4.0=Govt.=Creat.= 4 April=Hermes>>G=A4.
Broad-minded=9,000=90%=P9.00D=9.0=Abstraction=Gods=Saturn=9Sept.>>A=Ø.
Broadside= 13,000 = 13% = P1.30D = 1.3 = Solar Core = Faculty = 13Jan.=Athena.
Broad spectrum=3,000=30%=P3.00D=3.0=Creativity=Star=Muses=3 March=C=I.
Broadsword=4,000=40%=P4.00D=4.0=Govt.=Creat.= 4 April=Hermes>>G=A4.
Broadtail=6,000=60%=P6.00D=6.0=Man=Earth=Royalty=6June=Gaia>M=M2.
Broadway=7,500=8,000=80%=P8.00D=8.0=Econ.=Curr.=Busn.=Jupt.=8Aug=Zeus>E=v.
Brocade=4,500=5,000=50%=P5.00D=5.0=Law=Time=Venus=5May=Odite>>L=N.
Broccoli=6,500=7,000=70%=P7.00D=7.0=Lang.=Assets=Mars=6May=Pleiades.
Brochette=1,000=100%=10.0=1.0=Mind=Sun=1 January=Helios >> M=E4.
Brochure=3,000=30%=P3.00D=3.0=Creativity=Star=Muses=3 March=C=I.
Brogan=2,500=3,000=30%=P3.00D=3.0=Creativity=Star=Muses=3 March=C=I.
Brogue(1)=2,000=20%=P2.00D=2.0=Nature=Matter=Moon=2 Feb: Cupid>N=C.
Brogue(2)=4,000=40%=P4.00D=4.0=Govt.=Creat.= 4 April=Hermes>>G=A4.
Broil=5,500=5.5=80%=P5.50D=Earth-Midway=5 May=Gaia.
Broiler=10,000=1,000=100%=10.0=Physicality=Tech.=10 Oct.=Uranus=P=1Ø.
Broke=1,500=15%=P1.50D=1.5=Authority = Solar Crown = Solar Core = 1 May = Maia.
Broken=10,500=11,000=11%=P1.10D=1.1=Idea=Brainchild=Inventn.=11 Nov.=Athena
    >K=F.
Broken-hearted=3,500=4,000=40%=P4.00D=4.0=Govt.=Creat.= 4 April=Hermes>>G=A4.
Broker=11,000=11%=P1.10D=1.1=Idea=Brainchild=Inventn.=11 Nov.=Athena>K=F.
Brokerage=5,000=50%=P5.00D=5.0=Law=Time=Venus=5May=Odite>>L=N.
Bromeliad=10,500=11,000=11%=P1.10D=1.1=Idea=Brainchild=11 Nov.=Athena>K=F.
Bromide=9,000=90%=P9.00D=9.0=Abstraction=Gods=Saturn=9Sept.>>A=Ø.
Bromine=14,500=15%=P1.50D=1.5=Authority = Solar Crown = Solar Core = 1 May = Maia.
Bronchial=4,500=5,000=50%=P5.00D=5.0=Law=Time=Venus=5May=Odite>>L=N.
Bronchitis=3,500=4,000=40%=P4.00D=4.0=Govt.=Creat.= 4 April=Hermes>>G=A4.
Bronchus=5,000=50%=P5.00D=5.0=Law=Time=Venus=5May=Odite>>L=N.
Bronco=3,500=4,000=40%=P4.00D=4.0=Govt.=Creat.= 4 April=Hermes>>G=A4.
Broncobuster=4,000=40%=P4.00D=4.0=Govt.=Creat.= 4 April=Hermes>>G=A4.
Brontë=8,000=80%=P8.00D=8.0=Econ.=Curr.=Busn.=Jupt.=8Aug=Zeus>E=v.
Brontosaurus=4,000=40%=P4.00D=4.0=Govt.=Creat.= 4 April=Hermes>>G=A4.
Bronx=8,000=80%=P8.00D=8.0=Econ.=Curr.=Busn.=Jupt.=8Aug=Zeus>E=v.
Bronze=10,500=11,000=11%=P1.10D=1.1=Idea=Brainchild=Inventn.=11 Nov.=Athena>K=F.

Bronze Age=9,500=10,000=1,000=100%=10.0=Physicality=Tech.=10 Oct.=Uranus=P=1Ø.
The Creatocracy introduced the MindTech sector, Makupedia civilization and the Mind age.
Bronze Age was a transition from the realm of the abstract to the age of technology.

Brooch=2,500=3,000=30%=P3.00D=3.0=Creativity=Star=Muses=3 March=C=I.
Brood=15,000=15%=P1.50D=1.5=Authority = Solar Crown = Solar Core = 1 May = Maia.
Brook(1)=4,500=5,000=50%=P5.00D=5.0=Law=Time=Venus=5May=Odite>>L=N.
Brook(2)=2,500=3,000=30%=P3.00D=3.0=Creativity=Star=Muses=3 March=C=I.
Brooke Rupert=2,000=20%=P2.00D=2.0=Nature=Matter=Moon=2 Feb= Cupid>N=C.
Brooklyn=7,500=8,000=80%=P8.00D=8.0=Econ.=Curr.=Busn.=Jupt.=8Aug=Zeus>E=v.
Brook trout=4,000=40%=P4.00D=4.0=Govt.=Creat.= 4 April=Hermes>>G=A4.
Broom=16,500=17,000=17%=P1.70D=1.7=Solar Asset =17 Feb.=Maia>>Mind Computing.
Bros.=500=5%=P5.00D=5.0=Law=Time=Venus=5 May=Aphrodite>>L=N.
Brothel=9,500=10,000=1,000=100%=10.0=Physicality=Tech.=10 Oct.=Uranus=P=1Ø.
Brother=12,500= 13,000 = 13% = P1.30D = 1.3 = Solar Core = Faculty = 13Jan.=Athena.
Brotherhood=11,000=11%=P1.10D=1.1=Idea=Brainchild=Inventn.=11 Nov.=Athena>K=F.
Brother-in-law=4,000=40%=P4.00D=4.0=Govt.=Creat.= 4 April=Hermes>>G=A4.
Brougham=11,500=12,000=12%=P1.20D=1.2=Knowledge=Edu.=12Dec.=Athena>>K=F.
Brought=3,500=4,000=40%=P4.00D=4.0=Govt.=Creat.= 4 April=Hermes>>G=A4.
Brouhaha=1,000=100%=10.0=1.0=Mind=Sun=1 January=Helios >> M=E4.
Brow=6,500=7,000=70%=P7.00D=7.0=Lang.=Assets=Mars=6May=Pleiades.
Browbeat=3,500=4,000=40%=P4.00D=4.0=Govt.=Creat.= 4 April=Hermes>>G=A4.
Brown=8,500=9,000=90%=P9.00D=9.0=Abstraction=Gods=Saturn=9Sept.>>A=Ø.
Brown John=2,000=20%=P2.00D=2.0=Nature=Matter=Moon=2 Feb= Cupid>N=C.
Brown bear=8,000=80%=P8.00D=8.0=Econ.=Curr.=Busn.=Jupt.=8Aug=Zeus>E=v.
Browne Thomas=3,000=30%=P3.00D=3.0=Creativity=Star=Muses=3 March=C=I.
Brownie=9,500=10,000=1,000=100%=10.0=Physicality=Tech.=10 Oct.=Uranus=P=1Ø.
Browning Elizabeth=2,000=20%=P2.00D=2.0=Nature=Matter=Moon=2 Feb= Cupid>N=C.
Browning Robert=2,000=20%=P2.00D=2.0=Nature=Matter=Moon=2 Feb= Cupid>N=C.
Brownout=3,500=4,000=40%=P4.00D=4.0=Govt.=Creat.= 4 April=Hermes>>G=A4.
Brown rice=4,500=5,000=50%=P5.00D=5.0=Law=Time=Venus=5May=Odite>>L=N.
Brownstone=5,000=50%=P5.00D=5.0=Law=Time=Venus=5May=Odite>>L=N.
Brown sugar=5,000=50%=P5.00D=5.0=Law=Time=Venus=5May=Odite>>L=N.
Browse=8,000=80%=P8.00D=8.0=Econ.=Curr.=Busn.=Jupt.=8Aug=Zeus>E=v.
Bruckner Anton=3,000=30%=P3.00D=3.0=Creativity=Star=Muses=3 March=C=I.
Bruegel Pieter=3,500=4,000=40%=P4.00D=4.0=Govt.=Creat.= 4 April=Hermes>>G=A4.
Bruges=7,000=70%=P7.00D=7.0=Lang.=Assets=Mars=6May=Pleiades.
Bruin=1,000=100%=10.0=1.0=Mind=Sun=1 January=Helios >> M=E4.
Bruise=15,500=16,000=16%=P1.60D=1.6=Cycle of Life=Incarnation=MOG=1June= Maia.
Bruiser=3,000=30%=P3.00D=3.0=Creativity=Star=Muses=3 March=C=I.
Bruit=2,500=3,000=30%=P3.00D=3.0=Creativity=Star=Muses=3 March=C=I.
Brunch=5,500=5.5=80%=P5.50D=Earth-Midway=5 May=Gaia.
Brunei=7,500=8,000=80%=P8.00D=8.0=Econ.=Curr.=Busn.=Jupt.=8Aug=Zeus>E=v.

Brunelleschi Filippo=2,000=20%=P2.00D=2.0=Nature=Matter=Moon=2 Feb= Cupid>N=C.
Brunet=6,500=7,000=70%=P7.00D=7.0=Lang.=Assets=Mars=6May=Pleiades.
Brunette=4,500=5,000=50%=P5.00D=5.0=Law=Time=Venus=5May=Odite>>L=N.
Bruno Giordano=2,500=3,000=30%=P3.00D=3.0=Creativity=Star=Muses=3 March=C=I.
Brunswick=5,000=50%=P5.00D=5.0=Law=Time=Venus=5May=Odite>>L=N.
Brunt=5,500=5.5=80%=P5.50D=Earth-Midway=5 May=Gaia.
Brush(1)=33,000=3.3=33%=P3.30D=Host=The Gods=The Holy Spirit.
Brush(2)=5,000=50%=P5.00D=5.0=Law=Time=Venus=5May=Odite>>L=N.
Brush(3)=2,500=3,000=30%=P3.00D=3.0=Creativity=Star=Muses=3 March=C=I.
Brush off=2,500=3,000=30%=P3.00D=3.0=Creativity=Star=Muses=3 March=C=I.
Brusque=3,500=4,000=40%=P4.00D=4.0=Govt.=Creat.= 4 April=Hermes>>G=A4.
Brussels=5,500=4,000=40%=P4.00D=4.0=Govt.=Creat.= 4 April=Hermes>>G=A4.
Brussels sprouts=5,000=50%=P5.00D=5.0=Law=Time=Venus=5May=Odite>>L=N.
Brutal=5,000=50%=P5.00D=5.0=Law=Time=Venus=5May=Odite>>L=N.
Brutalize=4,000=40%=P4.00D=4.0=Govt.=Creat.= 4 April=Hermes>>G=A4.
Brute=8,000=80%=P8.00D=8.0=Econ.=Curr.=Busn.=Jupt.=8Aug=Zeus>E=v.
Brutus Marcus=4,000=40%=P4.00D=4.0=Govt.=Creat.= 4 April=Hermes>>G=A4.
Bryan William=3,000=30%=P3.00D=3.0=Creativity=Star=Muses=3 March=C=I.
Bryansk=4,500=5,000=50%=P5.00D=5.0=Law=Time=Venus=5May=Odite>>L=N.
Bryant William=3,500=4,000=40%=P4.00D=4.0=Govt.=Creat.= 4April=Hermes>>G=A4.
B.S.=1,500=15%=P1.50D=1.5=Authority = Solar Crown = Solar Core = 1 May = Maia.
BAS=2,000=20%=P2.00D=2.0=Nature=Matter=Moon=2 Feb= Cupid>N=C.
bsh.=500=5%=P5.00D=5.0=Law=Time=Venus=5 May=Aphrodite>>L=N.
Bt.=500=5%=P5.00D=5.0=Law=Time=Venus=5 May=Aphrodite>>L=N.
Btu=1,500=15%=P1.50D=1.5=Authority = Solar Crown = Solar Core = 1 May = Maia.
bu.=2,000=20%=P2.00D=2.0=Nature=Matter=Moon=2 Feb= Cupid>N=C.
Bubble=16,000=16%=P1.60D=1.6=Cycle of Life=Incarnation=MindofGOD=1June= Maia.
Bubble gum=4,000=40%=P4.00D=4.0=Govt.=Creat.= 4 April=Hermes>>G=A4.
Bubble top=6,000=60%=P6.00D=6.0=Man=Earth=Royalty=6June=Gaia>M=M2.
Buber Martin.=4,000=40%=P4.00D=4.0=Govt.=Creat.= 4 April=Hermes>>G=A4.
Bubo=6,500=7,000=70%=P7.00D=7.0=Lang.=Assets=Mars=6May=Pleiades.
Bubonic plague=12,000=12%=P1.20D=1.2=Knowledge=Edu.=12Dec.=Athena>>K=F.
Bucaramanga=5,000=50%=P5.00D=5.0=Law=Time=Venus=5May=Odite>>L=N.
Buccaneer=1,000=100%=10.0=1.0=Mind=Sun=1 January=Helios >> M=E4.
Buchanan James=4,000=40%=P4.00D=4.0=Govt.=Creat.= 4 April=Hermes>>G=A4.
Bucharest=7,000=70%=P7.00D=7.0=Lang.=Assets=Mars=6May=Pleiades.
Buck(1)=15,000=15%=P1.50D=1.5=Authority = Solar Crown = Solar Core = 1 May = Maia.
Buck(2)=1,500=15%=P1.50D=1.5=Authority = Solar Crown = Solar Core = 1 May = Maia.
Buck Pearl=3,000=30%=P3.00D=3.0=Creativity=Star=Muses=3 March=C=I.
Buckboard=6,000=60%=P6.00D=6.0=Man=Earth=Royalty=6June=Gaia>M=M2.
Bucket=14,000=14%=P1.40D=1.4=Mgt.=Solar Core=13 May=Athena>>SC=0.1
Bucket seat=5,500=5.5=80%=P5.50D=Earth-Midway=5 May=Gaia.
Buckeye=8,500=9,000=90%=P9.00D=9.0=Abstraction=Gods=Saturn=9Sept.>>A=Ø.
Buckle=24,500=3,000=30%=P3.00D=3.0=Creativity=Star=Muses=3 March=C=I.
Buckler=2,000=20%=P2.00D=2.0=Nature=Matter=Moon=2 Feb= Cupid>N=C.

Buckram=7,500=8,000=80%=P8.00D=8.0=Econ.=Curr.=Busn.=Jupt.=8Aug=Zeus>E=v.
Buck saw=4,500=5,000=50%=P5.00D=5.0=Law=Time=Venus=5May=Odite>>L=N.
Buckshot=6,500=7,000=70%=P7.00D=7.0=Lang.=Assets=Mars=6May=Pleiades.
Buckskin=7,500=8,000=80%=P8.00D=8.0=Econ.=Curr.=Busn.=Jupt.=8Aug=Zeus>E=v.
Buck tooth=3,000=30%=P3.00D=3.0=Creativity=Star=Muses=3 March=C=I.
Buckwheat=8,000=80%=P8.00D=8.0=Econ.=Curr.=Busn.=Jupt.=8Aug=Zeus>E=v.
Bucolic=1,000=100%=10.0=1.0=Mind=Sun=1 January=Helios >> M=E4.
Bud=18,000=18%=P1.80D=1.8=Solar Currency=MaksCurrencies=1 Aug=Maia.
Budapest=6,500=7,000=70%=P7.00D=7.0=Lang.=Assets=Mars=6May=Pleiades.

Buddha=5,000=50%=P5.00D=5.0=Law=Time=Venus=5May=Odite>>L=N.
563?-483? B.C. Indian mystic and founder of Buddhism. Peter Matthews-Akukalia founded Makstianism - a Mind Temple Faith system. This is the core and exclusive religion of the Creatocracy, Paradise and the Disean citizenry>>Maxtianism>> Makstian >> Maxtians.

Buddhism=4,000=40%=P4.00D=4.0=Govt.=Creat.= 4 April=Hermes>>G=A4.
A religion founded on the teachings of Buddha. Makstianism is a higher religion or Faith system founded on the teachings of Peter Matthews-Akukalia through his Creatocracy.

Budding=9,000=90%=P9.00D=9.0=Abstraction=Gods=Saturn=9Sept.>>A=Ø.
Buddy=1,500=15%=P1.50D=1.5=Authority = Solar Crown = Solar Core = 1 May = Maia.
Buddy system=6,500=7,000=70%=P7.00D=7.0=Lang.=Assets=Mars=6May=Pleiades.
Budge=5,000=50%=P5.00D=5.0=Law=Time=Venus=5May=Odite>>L=N.
Budgerigar=6,000=60%=P6.00D=6.0=Man=Earth=Royalty=6June=Gaia>M=M2.
Budget= 13,000 = 13% = P1.30D = 1.3 = Solar Core = Faculty = 13Jan.=Athena=GGS=MAT.
Budgie=1,500=15%=P1.50D=1.5=Authority = Solar Crown = Solar Core = 1 May = Maia.
Buenos Aires=7,000=70%=P7.00D=7.0=Lang.=Assets=Mars=6May=Pleiades.
Buff(1)=12,000=12%=P1.20D=1.2=Knowledge=Edu.=12Dec.=Athena>>K=F.
Buff(2)=5,500=5.5=80%=P5.50D=Earth-Midway=5 May=Gaia.
buffalo=10,000=1,000=100%=10.0=Physicality=Tech.=10 Oct.=Uranus=P=1Ø.
Buffalo=7,000=70%=P7.00D=7.0=Lang.=Assets=Mars=6May=Pleiades.
Buffalo Bill=2,000=20%=P2.00D=2.0=Nature=Matter=Moon=2 Feb= Cupid>N=C.
Buffer(1)=6,500=7,000=70%=P7.00D=7.0=Lang.=Assets=Mars=6May=Pleiades.
Buffer(2)=20,500=21,000=12,000=12%=P1.20D=1.2=Knowl.=Edu.=12Dec.=Athena>>K=F.
Buffer zone=5,500=5.5=80%=P5.50D=Earth-Midway=5 May=Gaia.
Buffet(1)=10,500=11,000=11%=P1.10D=1.1=Idea=Brainchild=11 Nov.=Athena>K=F.
Buffet(2)=10,000=1,000=100%=10.0=Physicality=Tech.=10 Oct.=Uranus=P=1Ø.
Buffon Comte George=2,000=20%=P2.00D=2.0=Nature=Moon=2 Feb= Cupid>N=C.
Buffoon=1,500=15%=P1.50D=1.5=Authority = Solar Crown = Solar Core = 1 May = Maia.
Bug=25,000=3,000=30%=P3.00D=3.0=Creativity=Star=Muses=3 March=C=I.
Bugaboo=4,500=5,000=50%=P5.00D=5.0=Law=Time=Venus=5May=Odite>>L=N.
Bugbear=1,000=100%=10.0=1.0=Mind=Sun=1 January=Helios >> M=E4.

Bug-eyed=500=5%=P5.00D=5.0=Law=Time=Venus=5 May=Aphrodite>>L=N.
Buggy(1)=4,000=40%=P4.00D=4.0=Govt.=Creat.= 4 April=Hermes>>G=A4.
Buggy(2)=2,500=3,000=30%=P3.00D=3.0=Creativity=Star=Muses=3 March=C=I.
Bugle=4,000=40%=P4.00D=4.0=Govt.=Creat.= 4 April=Hermes>>G=A4.
Build=30,000=3,000=30%=P3.00D=3.0=Creativity=Star=Muses=3 March=C=I.
Building=4,500=5,000=50%=P5.00D=5.0=Law=Time=Venus=5May=Odite>>L=N.
Buildup=7,000=70%=P7.00D=7.0=Lang.=Assets=Mars=6May=Pleiades.
Built-in=7,000=70%=P7.00D=7.0=Lang.=Assets=Mars=6May=Pleiades.
Bujumbura=6,500=7,000=70%=P7.00D=7.0=Lang.=Assets=Mars=6May=Pleiades.
Bukharin Nikolai=4,000=40%=P4.00D=4.0=Govt.=Creat.= 4 April=Hermes>>G=A4.
Bul.=500=5%=P5.00D=5.0=Law=Time=Venus=5 May=Aphrodite>>L=N.
Bulawayo=3,500=4,000=40%=P4.00D=4.0=Govt.=Creat.= 4 April=Hermes>>G=A4.
Bulb= 13,000 = 13% = P1.30D = 1.3 = Solar Core = Faculty = 13Jan.=Athena.
Bullfinch Charles=2,000=20%=P2.00D=2.0=Nature=Matter=Moon=2 Feb= Cupid>N=C.
Bullfinch Thomas=2,000=20%=P2.00D=2.0=Nature=Matter=Moon=2 Feb= Cupid>N=C.
Bulg.=1,500=15%=P1.50D=1.5=Authority = Solar Crown = Solar Core = 1 May = Maia.
Bulganin Nikolai=3,500=4,000=40%=P4.00D=4.0=Govt.=Creat.= 4 April=Hermes>>G=A4.
Bulgar=1,000=100%=10.0=1.0=Mind=Sun=1 January=Helios >> M=E4.
Bulgaria=6,500=7,000=70%=P7.00D=7.0=Lang.=Assets=Mars=6May=Pleiades.
Bulgarian=6,000=60%=P6.00D=6.0=Man=Earth=Royalty=6June=Gaia>M=M2.
Bulge=9,000=90%=P9.00D=9.0=Abstraction=Gods=Saturn=9Sept.>>A=Ø.
Bulgur=4,500=5,000=50%=P5.00D=5.0=Law=Time=Venus=5May=Odite>>L=N.
Bulimia=9,500=10,000=1,000=100%=10.0=Physicality=Tech.=10 Oct.=Uranus=P=1Ø.
Bulk=11,000=11%=P1.10D=1.1=Idea=Brainchild=Inventn.=11 Nov.=Athena>K=F.
Bulkhead=11,000=11%=P1.10D=1.1=Idea=Brainchild=Inventn.=11 Nov.=Athena>K=F.
Bull(1)=19,500=20%=P2.00D=2.0=Nature=Matter=Moon=2 Feb= Cupid>N=C.
Bull(2)=3,500=4,000=40%=P4.00D=4.0=Govt.=Creat.= 4 April=Hermes>>G=A4.
Bull=500=5%=P5.00D=5.0=Law=Time=Venus=5 May=Aphrodite>>L=N.
Bulldog=12,500= 13,000 = 13% = P1.30D = 1.3 = Solar Core = Faculty = 13Jan.=Athena.
Bulldoze=5,000=50%=P5.00D=5.0=Law=Time=Venus=5May=Odite>>L=N.
Bulldozer=10,000=1,000=100%=10.0=Physicality=Tech.=10 Oct.=Uranus=P=1Ø.
Bullet=8,000=80%=P8.00D=8.0=Econ.=Curr.=Busn.=Jupt.=8Aug=Zeus>E=v.
Bulletin=9,500=10,000=1,000=100%=10.0=Physicality=Tech.=10 Oct.=Uranus=P=1Ø.
Bulletin board=5,000=50%=P5.00D=5.0=Law=Time=Venus=5May=Odite>>L=N.
Bullfight=10,500=11,000=11%=P1.10D=1.1=Idea=Brainchild=Inventn.=11 Nov.=Athena>K=F.
Bullfinch=5,000=50%=P5.00D=5.0=Law=Time=Venus=5May=Odite>>L=N.
Bullfrog=3,500=4,000=40%=P4.00D=4.0=Govt.=Creat.= 4 April=Hermes>>G=A4.
Bullhead=2,500=3,000=30%=P3.00D=3.0=Creativity=Star=Muses=3 March=C=I.
Bullheaded=1,500=15%=P1.50D=1.5=Authority = Solar Crown = Solar Core = 1 May = Maia.
Bullhorn=4,500=5,000=50%=P5.00D=5.0=Law=Time=Venus=5May=Odite>>L=N.
Bullion=3,000=30%=P3.00D=3.0=Creativity=Star=Muses=3 March=C=I.
Bullock=2,500=3,000=30%=P3.00D=3.0=Creativity=Star=Muses=3 March=C=I.
Bullpen=4,000=40%=P4.00D=4.0=Govt.=Creat.= 4 April=Hermes>>G=A4.
Bull Run=11,500=12,000=12%=P1.20D=1.2=Knowledge=Edu.=12Dec.=Athena>>K=F.
Bull session=2,500=3,000=30%=P3.00D=3.0=Creativity=Star=Muses=3 March=C=I.

Bull's-eye=6,000=60%=P6.00D=6.0=Man=Earth=Royalty=6June=Gaia>M=M2.
Bullwhip=4,000=40%=P4.00D=4.0=Govt.=Creat.= 4 April=Hermes>>G=A4.
Bully=10,000=1,000=100%=10.0=Physicality=Tech.=10 Oct.=Uranus=P=1Ø.
Bulrush=3,000=30%=P3.00D=3.0=Creativity=Star=Muses=3 March=C=I.

Bulwark=6,000=60%=P6.00D=6.0=Man=Earth=Royalty=6June=Gaia>M=M2.
GOD gave conditions about setting up bulwarks. We recommend boulevard or its related as a channel of openness and prosperity in naming or application. See Deuteronomy 20:20, 2 Chronicles 26:15, Ecclesiastes 9:14, Psalm 48:13, Isaiah 26:1.

Bum= 13,000 = 13% = P1.30D = 1.3 = Solar Core = Faculty = 13Jan.=Athena.
Bumble=7,000=70%=P7.00D=7.0=Lang.=Assets=Mars=6May=Pleiades.
Bumblebee=15,000=1,500=15%=P1.50D=1.5=Authority = Solar Crown = SC = 1 May=Maia.
Bump=15,500=16,000=16%=P1.60D=1.6=Cycle of Life=Incarnation=MOG=1June= Maia.
Bumper(1)=8,000=80%=P8.00D=8.0=Econ.=Curr.=Busn.=Jupt.=8Aug=Zeus>E=v.
Bumper(2)=7,000=70%=P7.00D=7.0=Lang.=Assets=Mars=6May=Pleiades.
Bumpkin=2,000=20%=P2.00D=2.0=Nature=Matter=Moon=2 Feb= Cupid>N=C.
Bumptious=2,500=3,000=30%=P3.00D=3.0=Creativity=Star=Muses=3 March=C=I.
Bun=6,500=7,000=70%=P7.00D=7.0=Lang.=Assets=Mars=6May=Pleiades.
Bunch=2,500=3,000=30%=P3.00D=3.0=Creativity=Star=Muses=3 March=C=I.
Bunche Ralph=4,000=40%=P4.00D=4.0=Govt.=Creat.= 4 April=Hermes>>G=A4.
Bunco=2,000=20%=P2.00D=2.0=Nature=Matter=Moon=2 Feb= Cupid>N=C.
Bundle=11,500=12,000=12%=P1.20D=1.2=Knowledge=Edu.=12Dec.=Athena>>K=F.
Bung=2,000=20%=P2.00D=2.0=Nature=Matter=Moon=2 Feb= Cupid>N=C.
Bungalow=4,500=5,000=50%=P5.00D=5.0=Law=Time=Venus=5May=Odite>>L=N.
Bunghole=8,500=9,000=90%=P9.00D=9.0=Abstraction=Gods=Saturn=9Sept.>>A=Ø.
Bungle=8,000=80%=P8.00D=8.0=Econ.=Curr.=Busn.=Jupt.=8Aug=Zeus>E=v.
Bunion=8,000=80%=P8.00D=8.0=Econ.=Curr.=Busn.=Jupt.=8Aug=Zeus>E=v.
Bunk(1)=4,500=5,000=50%=P5.00D=5.0=Law=Time=Venus=5May=Odite>>L=N.
Bunk(2)=1,500=15%=P1.50D=1.5=Authority = Solar Crown = Solar Core = 1 May = Maia.
Bunk bed=2,000=20%=P2.00D=2.0=Nature=Matter=Moon=2 Feb= Cupid>N=C.
Bunker=11,000=11%=P1.10D=1.1=Idea=Brainchild=Inventn.=11 Nov.=Athena>K=F.
Bunker Hill=8,500=9,000=90%=P9.00D=9.0=Abstraction=Gods=Saturn=9Sept.>>A=Ø.
Bunkhouse=4,000=40%=P4.00D=4.0=Govt.=Creat.= 4 April=Hermes>>G=A4.
Bunny=2,500=3,000=30%=P3.00D=3.0=Creativity=Star=Muses=3 March=C=I.
Bunsen burner=6,500=7,000=70%=P7.00D=7.0=Lang.=Assets=Mars=6May=Pleiades.
Bunt=11,000=11%=P1.10D=1.1=Idea=Brainchild=Inventn.=11 Nov.=Athena>K=F.
Bunting(1)=8,500=9,000=90%=P9.00D=9.0=Abstraction=Gods=Saturn=9Sept.>>A=Ø.
Bunting(2)=4,500=5,000=50%=P5.00D=5.0=Law=Time=Venus=5May=Odite>>L=N.
Bunyan John=3,000=30%=P3.00D=3.0=Creativity=Star=Muses=3 March=C=I.
Buoy=12,500= 13,000 = 13% = P1.30D = 1.3 = Solar Core = Faculty = 13Jan.=Athena.
Buoyancy= 13,000 = 13% = P1.30D = 1.3 = Solar Core = Faculty = 13Jan.=Athena.
Bur(1)=9,500=10,000=1,000=100%=10.0=Physicality=Tech.=10 Oct.=Uranus=P=1Ø.
Bur(2)=1,500=15%=P1.50D=1.5=Authority = Solar Crown = Solar Core = 1 May = Maia.

Bur=500=5%=P5.00D=5.0=Law=Time=Venus=5 May=Aphrodite>>L=N.
Burbank Luther=2,000=20%=P2.00D=2.0=Nature=Matter=Moon=2 Feb= Cupid>N=C.
Burden(1)=12,000=12%=P1.20D=1.2=Knowledge=Edu.=12Dec.=Athena>>K=F.
Burden(2)=7,500=8,000=80%=P8.00D=8.0=Econ.=Curr.=Busn.=Jupt.=8Aug=Zeus>E=v.
Burdock=5,000=50%=P5.00D=5.0=Law=Time=Venus=5May=Odite>>L=N.
Bureau=8,000=80%=P8.00D=8.0=Econ.=Curr.=Busn.=Jupt.=8Aug=Zeus>E=v.
Bureaucracy=10,500=11,000=11%=P1.10D=1.1=Idea=Brainchild=11 Nov.=Athena>K=F.
Bureaucratize=2,500=3,000=30%=P3.00D=3.0=Creativity=Star=Muses=3 March=C=I.
Burette=8,000=80%=P8.00D=8.0=Econ.=Curr.=Busn.=Jupt.=8Aug=Zeus>E=v.
Burg=2,500=3,000=30%=P3.00D=3.0=Creativity=Star=Muses=3 March=C=I.
Burgeon=7,000=70%=P7.00D=7.0=Lang.=Assets=Mars=6May=Pleiades.
Burger=4,000=40%=P4.00D=4.0=Govt.=Creat.= 4 April=Hermes>>G=A4.
Burgess=4,500=5,000=50%=P5.00D=5.0=Law=Time=Venus=5May=Odite>>L=N.
Burgh=2,500=3,000=30%=P3.00D=3.0=Creativity=Star=Muses=3 March=C=I.
Burgher=2,000=20%=P2.00D=2.0=Nature=Matter=Moon=2 Feb= Cupid>N=C.
Burglar=4,500=5,000=50%=P5.00D=5.0=Law=Time=Venus=5May=Odite>>L=N.
Burgle=2,000=20%=P2.00D=2.0=Nature=Matter=Moon=2 Feb= Cupid>N=C.
Burgomaster=3,500=4,000=40%=P4.00D=4.0=Govt.=Creat.= 4 April=Hermes>>G=A4.
Burgoyne John=3,000=30%=P3.00D=3.0=Creativity=Star=Muses=3 March=C=I.
Burgundy(1)=4,500=5,000=50%=P5.00D=5.0=Law=Time=Venus=5May=Odite>>L=N.
Burgundy(2)=8,000=80%=P8.00D=8.0=Econ.=Curr.=Busn.=Jupt.=8Aug=Zeus>E=v.
Burial=3,000=30%=P3.00D=3.0=Creativity=Star=Muses=3 March=C=I.
Burke Edmund=4,000=40%=P4.00D=4.0=Govt.=Creat.= 4 April=Hermes>>G=A4.
Burkina Faso=9,500=10,000=1,000=100%=10.0=Phys.=Tech.=10 Oct.=Uranus=P=1Ø.
Burl=3,000=30%=P3.00D=3.0=Creativity=Star=Muses=3 March=C=I.
Burlap=5,000=50%=P5.00D=5.0=Law=Time=Venus=5May=Odite>>L=N.
Burlesque=8,500=9,000=90%=P9.00D=9.0=Abstraction=Gods=Saturn=9Sept.>>A=Ø.
Burlington=4,500=5,000=50%=P5.00D=5.0=Law=Time=Venus=5May=Odite>>L=N.
Burly=3,500=4,000=40%=P4.00D=4.0=Govt.=Creat.= 4 April=Hermes>>G=A4.
Burma=10,500=11,000=11%=P1.10D=1.1=Idea=Brainchild=Inventn.=11 Nov.=Athena>K=F.
Burmese=5,000=50%=P5.00D=5.0=Law=Time=Venus=5May=Odite>>L=N.
Burn=46,000=5,000=50%=P5.00D=5.0=Law=Time=Venus=5May=Odite>>L=N.
Burnaby=5,500=5.5=80%=P5.50D=Earth-Midway=5 May=Gaia.
Burned-out=6,000=60%=P6.00D=6.0=Man=Earth=Royalty=6June=Gaia>M=M2.
Burner=12,500= 13,000 = 13% = P1.30D = 1.3 = Solar Core = Faculty = 13Jan.=Athena.
Burnish=6,000=60%=P6.00D=6.0=Man=Earth=Royalty=6June=Gaia>M=M2.
Burnoose=3,500=4,000=40%=P4.00D=4.0=Govt.=Creat.= 4 April=Hermes>>G=A4.
Burnout=16,000=16%=P1.60D=1.6=Cycle of Life=Incarnation=MindofGOD=1June= Maia.
Burns Robert=2,000=20%=P2.00D=2.0=Nature=Matter=Moon=2 Feb= Cupid>N=C.
Burnside Ambrose=3,000=30%=P3.00D=3.0=Creativity=Star=Muses=3 March=C=I.
Burnt=3,500=4,000=40%=P4.00D=4.0=Govt.=Creat.= 4 April=Hermes>>G=A4.
Burp=3,500=4,000=40%=P4.00D=4.0=Govt.=Creat.= 4 April=Hermes>>G=A4.
Burr(1)=13,500=14,000=14%=P1.40D=1.4=Mgt.=Solar Core=13 May=Athena>>SC=0.1
Burr(2)=1,500=15%=P1.50D=1.5=Authority = Solar Crown = Solar Core = 1 May = Maia.
Burbank Aaron.=4,500=5,000=50%=P5.00D=5.0=Law=Time=Venus=5May=Odite>>L=N.

Burro=4,500=5,000=50%=P5.00D=5.0=Law=Time=Venus=5May=Odite>>L=N.
Burrow=12,000=12%=P1.20D=1.2=Knowledge=Edu.=12Dec.=Athena>>K=F.
bursa=5,000=50%=P5.00D=5.0=Law=Time=Venus=5May=Odite>>L=N.
Bursa=5,000=50%=P5.00D=5.0=Law=Time=Venus=5May=Odite>>L=N.
Bursitis=5,500=5.5=80%=P5.50D=Earth-Midway=5 May=Gaia.
Burst=16,500=17,000=17%=P1.70D=1.7=Solar Asset =17 Feb.=Maia>>Mind Computing.
Burton Sir Richard Francis=2,000=20%=P2.00D=2.0=Nature=Moon=2 Feb= Cupid>N=C.
Burton, Robert=7,500=8,000=80%=P8.00D=8.0=Econ.=Busn.=Jupt.=8Aug=Zeus>E=v.
Burundi=11,000=11%=P1.10D=1.1=Idea=Brainchild=Inventn.=11 Nov.=Athena>K=F.
Bury=15,000=15%=P1.50D=1.5=Authority = Solar Crown = Solar Core = 1 May = Maia.
Bus=8,000=80%=P8.00D=8.0=Econ.=Curr.=Busn.=Jupt.=8Aug=Zeus>E=v.
Busboy=4,500=5,000=50%=P5.00D=5.0=Law=Time=Venus=5May=Odite>>L=N.
Busby=7,000=70%=P7.00D=7.0=Lang.=Assets=Mars=6May=Pleiades.
Bush=14,500=15,000=15%=P1.50D=1.5=Authority = Solar Crown = SC = 1 May = Maia.
Bush Georgia Herbert Walker=4,000=40%=P4.00D=4.0=Govt.= 4April=Hermes>>G=A4.
Bushed=1,000=100%=10.0=1.0=Mind=Sun=1 January=Helios >> M=E4.
Bushel=7,000=70%=P7.00D=7.0=Lang.=Assets=Mars=6May=Pleiades.
Bushing=5,500=5.5=80%=P5.50D=Earth-Midway=5 May=Gaia.
Bush-league=1,500=15%=P1.50D=1.5=Authority = Solar Crown = SC = 1 May = Maia.
Bushman=1,000=100%=10.0=1.0=Mind=Sun=1 January=Helios >> M=E4.
Bushmaster=3,500=4,000=40%=P4.00D=4.0=Govt.=Creat.= 4 April=Hermes>>G=A4.
Bushwhack=8,000=80%=P8.00D=8.0=Econ.=Curr.=Busn.=Jupt.=8Aug=Zeus>E=v.

Business=30,000=3,000=30%=P3.00D=3.0=Creativity=Star=Muses=3 March=C=I.
Our business is Creativity. Our invention and sovereignty is Creatocracy. The Business
of Ideas is our brand. The training licensing and management of Creative Scientist
Professionals is our world. De-Royal Makupedia Limited® is our company. The President
Founder and Owner is Peter Matthews-Akukalia, Castle Makupedia exclusively.

Business card=5,000=50%=P5.00D=5.0=Law=Time=Venus=5May=Odite>>L=N.
Businesslike=2,000=20%=P2.00D=2.0=Nature=Matter=Moon=2 Feb= Cupid>N=C.
Businessman=5,000=50%=P5.00D=5.0=Law=Time=Venus=5May=Odite>>L=N.
Businesswoman=5,000=50%=P5.00D=5.0=Law=Time=Venus=5May=Odite>>L=N.
Busing=8,000=80%=P8.00D=8.0=Econ.=Curr.=Busn.=Jupt.=8Aug=Zeus>E=v.
Buskin=6,500=7,000=70%=P7.00D=7.0=Lang.=Assets=Mars=6May=Pleiades.
Bus man's holiday=7,000=70%=P7.00D=7.0=Lang.=Assets=Mars=6May=Pleiades.
Buss=1,500=15%=P1.50D=1.5=Authority = Solar Crown = Solar Core = 1 May = Maia.
Busses=2,000=20%=P2.00D=2.0=Nature=Matter=Moon=2 Feb= Cupid>N=C.
Bust(1)=5,500=5.5=80%=P5.50D=Earth-Midway=5 May=Gaia.
Bust(2)=17,000=17%=P1.70D=1.7=Solar Asset =17 Feb.=Maia>>Mind Computing.
Bustle(1)=4,000=40%=P4.00D=4.0=Govt.=Creat.= 4 April=Hermes>>G=A4.
Bustle(2)=8,000=80%=P8.00D=8.0=Econ.=Curr.=Busn.=Jupt.=8Aug=Zeus>E=v.
Busy=10,500=11,000=11%=P1.10D=1.1=Idea=Brainchild=Inventn.=11 Nov.=Athena>K=F.
Busybody=1,500=15%=P1.50D=1.5=Authority = Solar Crown = Solar Core = 1 May = Maia.

Busywork=6,000=60%=P6.00D=6.0=Man=Earth=Royalty=6June=Gaia>M=M2.
But=37,500=4,000=40%=P4.00D=4.0=Govt.=Creat.= 4 April=Hermes>>G=A4.
Butadiene=7,000=70%=P7.00D=7.0=Lang.=Assets=Mars=6May=Pleiades.
Butane=8,000=80%=P8.00D=8.0=Econ.=Curr.=Busn.=Jupt.=8Aug=Zeus>E=v.
Butcher=11,500=12,000=12%=P1.20D=1.2=Knowledge=Edu.=12Dec.=Athena>>K=F.
Buteo=3,500=4,000=40%=P4.00D=4.0=Govt.=Creat.= 4 April=Hermes>>G=A4.
Butler=5,500=4,000=40%=P4.00D=4.0=Govt.=Creat.= 4 April=Hermes>>G=A4.
Butler Samuel=2,000=20%=P2.00D=2.0=Nature=Matter=Moon=2 Feb= Cupid>N=C.
Butt(1)=12,000=12%=P1.20D=1.2=Knowledge=Edu.=12Dec.=Athena>>K=F.
Butt(2)=4,000=40%=P4.00D=4.0=Govt.=Creat.= 4 April=Hermes>>G=A4.
Butt(3)=4,500=5,000=50%=P5.00D=5.0=Law=Time=Venus=5May=Odite>>L=N.
Butt(4)=11,500=12,000=12%=P1.20D=1.2=Knowledge=Edu.=12Dec.=Athena>>K=F.
Butt(5)=1,500=15%=P1.50D=1.5=Authority = Solar Crown = Solar Core = 1 May = Maia.
Butte=5,500=5.5=80%=P5.50D=Earth-Midway=5 May=Gaia.
Butter=13,500=14,000=14%=P1.40D=1.4=Mgt.=Solar Core=13 May=Athena>>SC=0.1
Butter bean=2,000=20%=P2.00D=2.0=Nature=Matter=Moon=2 Feb= Cupid>N=C.
Buttercup=4,500=5,000=50%=P5.00D=5.0=Law=Time=Venus=5May=Odite>>L=N.
Butterfat=5,000=50%=P5.00D=5.0=Law=Time=Venus=5May=Odite>>L=N.
Butterfingers=3,500=4,000=40%=P4.00D=4.0=Govt.=Creat.= 4 April=Hermes>>G=A4.
Butterfish=4,500=5,000=50%=P5.00D=5.0=Law=Time=Venus=5May=Odite>>L=N.
Butterfly=12,000=12%=P1.20D=1.2=Knowledge=Edu.=12Dec.=Athena>>K=F.
Butterfly stroke=7,500=8,000=80%=P8.00D=8.0=Econ.=Curr.=Jupt.=8Aug=Zeus>E=v.
Buttermilk=7,500=8,000=80%=P8.00D=8.0=Econ.=Curr.=Busn.=Jupt.=8Aug=Zeus>E=v.
Butternut=15,000=15%=P1.50D=1.5=Authority = Solar Crown = Solar Core = 1 May = Maia.
Butternut squash=5,500=5.5=80%=P5.50D=Earth-Midway=5 May=Gaia.
Butterscotch=6,000=60%=P6.00D=6.0=Man=Earth=Royalty=6June=Gaia>M=M2.
Buttock=7,000=70%=P7.00D=7.0=Lang.=Assets=Mars=6May=Pleiades.
Button=15,000=1,500=15%=P1.50D=1.5=Authority = Solar Crown = SC = 1 May = Maia.
Button-down=5,500=5.5=80%=P5.50D=Earth-Midway=5 May=Gaia.
Buttonhole=8,000=80%=P8.00D=8.0=Econ.=Curr.=Busn.=Jupt.=8Aug=Zeus>E=v.
Buttress=10,500=11,000=11%=P1.10D=1.1=Idea=Brainchild=Inventn.=11 Nov.=Athena>K=F.
Butut=3,000=30%=P3.00D=3.0=Creativity=Star=Muses=3 March=C=I.
Butyl=4,000=40%=P4.00D=4.0=Govt.=Creat.= 4 April=Hermes>>G=A4.
Buxom=2,000=20%=P2.00D=2.0=Nature=Matter=Moon=2 Feb= Cupid>N=C.
Buy=26,500=3,000=30%=P3.00D=3.0=Creativity=Star=Muses=3 March=C=I.
Buy out=6,000=60%=P6.00D=6.0=Man=Earth=Royalty=6June=Gaia>M=M2.
Buzz=23,500=24,000=24%=P2.40D=International Business.
Buzzard=6,000=60%=P6.00D=6.0=Man=Earth=Royalty=6June=Gaia>M=M2.
Buzzer=4,500=5,000=50%=P5.00D=5.0=Law=Time=Venus=5May=Odite>>L=N.
Buzz saw=1,500=15%=P1.50D=1.5=Authority = Solar Crown = Solar Core = 1 May = Maia.
Buzz word=7,500=8,000=80%=P8.00D=8.0=Econ.=Curr.=Busn.=Jupt.=8Aug=Zeus>E=v.
BW=3,500=4,000=40%=P4.00D=4.0=Govt.=Creat.= 4 April=Hermes>>G=A4.
B.W.I.=1,500=15%=P1.50D=1.5=Authority = Solar Crown = Solar Core = 1 May = Maia.
by=45,000=50,000=5,000=50%=P5.00D=5.0=Law=Time=Venus=5May=Odite>>L=N.
by-=2,000=20%=P2.00D=2.0=Nature=Matter=Moon=2 Feb= Cupid>N=C.

By-and-by=2,000=20%=P2.00D=2.0=Nature=Matter=Moon=2 Feb= Cupid>N=C.
By and large=2,000=20%=P2.00D=2.0=Nature=Matter=Moon=2 Feb= Cupid>N=C.
Bydgoszcz=5,000=50%=P5.00D=5.0=Law=Time=Venus=5May=Odite>>L=N.
Bye=13,500=14,000=14%=P1.40D=1.4=Mgt.=Solar Core=13 May=Athena>>SC=0.1
Bye-bye=4,000=40%=P4.00D=4.0=Govt.=Creat.= 4 April=Hermes>>G=A4.
Bygone=7,500=8,000=80%=P8.00D=8.0=Econ.=Curr.=Busn.=Jupt.=8Aug=Zeus>E=v.
Bylaw=6,000=60%=P6.00D=6.0=Man=Earth=Royalty=6June=Gaia>M=M2.
Byline=6,500=7,000=70%=P7.00D=7.0=Lang.=Assets=Mars=6May=Pleiades.
Bypass=20,000=2,000=20%=P2.00D=2.0=Nature=Matter=Moon=2 Feb= Cupid>N=C.
By-path=3,000=30%=P3.00D=3.0=Creativity=Star=Muses=3 March=C=I.
By-play=6,500=7,000=70%=P7.00D=7.0=Lang.=Assets=Mars=6May=Pleiades.
Byproduct=5,000=50%=P5.00D=5.0=Law=Time=Venus=5May=Odite>>L=N.
Byrd Richard=2,500=3,000=30%=P3.00D=3.0=Creativity=Star=Muses=3 March=C=I.
Byron George=4,500=5,000=50%=P5.00D=5.0=Law=Time=Venus=5May=Odite>>L=N.
Bystander=4,500=5,000=50%=P5.00D=5.0=Law=Time=Venus=5May=Odite>>L=N.
Byte=12,500= 13,000 = 13% = P1.30D = 1.3 = Solar Core = Faculty = 13Jan.=Athena.
Byway=4,500=5,000=50%=P5.00D=5.0=Law=Time=Venus=5May=Odite>>L=N.
Byword=9,000=90%=P9.00D=9.0=Abstraction=Gods=Saturn=9Sept.>>A=Ø.
Byzantine=16,500=17%=P1.70D=1.7=Solar Asset =17 Feb.=Maia>>Mind Computing.
Byzantine Empire=5,500=5.5=80%=P5.50D=Earth-Midway=5 May=Gaia.
Byzantium=7,500=8,000=80%=P8.00D=8.0=Econ.=Curr.=Busn.=Jupt.=8Aug=Zeus>E=v.

MAKABET =Cc=

---

c(1)=10,000=1,000=100%=10.0=Physicality=Tech.=10 Oct.=Uranus=P=1Ø.
The 3rd letter of the English alphabet. Computing the psycho-weight.
Resultant*Position on the Maks. 10.0*3.0x=px=13+30=43x=px=433=4.33
4.0 >> Government >> Creatocracy = Organization = Relationships = Family.
33 = 3.3 = Genius. So C is accorded a person known for Genius in Leadership.
When C is mentioned government is examined and leadership is induced in the C Mindset.
But 4.0*3.3x=px=7.3*13.2=20.5x=px=116.86=120=1.2
>> 12,000=12%=P1.20D=1.2=Knowledge=Edu=12 Dec.=Athena>>K=F.
A conflict seems to exist between Science and Education for governance of C. See date
energy. Going by the spirit of 12 December we get Hermes >> Government >> Creatocracy.

---

c(2)=4,000=40%=P4.0D=Government =Creatocracy=4 April=Mercury=Hermes=G=A4.
C(1)=6,500=7,000=70%=P7.0D=7.0=Language=Assets=Mars=7 July=Pleiades.
C2=1,500=15%=P1.50D=1.5=Authority=Crown=Solar Core=1 May = Maia.
c.or C.=4,500=5,000=50%=P5.00D=Law=Time=Venus=5 May = Aphrodite>>L=N.
ca=2,500=3,000=30%=P3.0D=3.0=Creativity=Stars=Muses=3 March = C=I>>GIL.
Ca=1,000=100%=10.0=1.0=Mind=Sun=1 January=Helios >> M=E4.

CA=1,000=100%=10.0=1.0=Mind=Sun=1 January=Helios >> M=E4.
C.A.=1,000=100%=10.0=1.0=Mind=Sun=1 January=Helios >> M=E4.
C/a =1,500=15%=P1.50D=1.5=Authority=Crown=Solar Core=1 May = Maia.
CAA=1,500=15%=P1.50D=1.5=Authority=Crown=Solar Core=1 May = Maia.
Cab=7,500=8,000=80%=P8.0D=Economy=Currency=8 Aug.=Zeus>>E=v.
CAB=1,500=15%=P1.50D=1.5=Authority=Crown=Solar Core=1 May = Maia.
Cabal=2,500=3,000=30%=P3.0D=3.0=Creativity=Stars=Muses=3 March = C=I>>GIL.
Cabala=10,000=1,000=100%=10.0=Physicality=Tech.=10 Oct.=Uranus=P=1Ø.
Cabana=4,000=40%=P4.0D=Government =Creatocracy=4 April=Mercury=Hermes=G=A4.
Cabaret=6,000=60%=P6.0D=Man=Earth=Royalty=6 June=Gaia=Maia>>M=M2.
Cabbage=8,500=9,000=90%=P9.00D=9.0=Abstraction=Gods=Saturn=9Sept.>>A=Ø.
Cabby=1,500=15%=P1.50D=1.5=Authority=Crown=Solar Core=1 May = Maia.
Cabin=10,500=11,000=11%=P1.10D=1.1=Idea=Brainchild=Inv.=11 Nov.=SC=Athena>>I=MT.
Cabin class=8,500=9,000=90%=P9.00D=9.0=Abstraction=Gods=Saturn=9Sept.>>A=Ø.
Cabin cruiser=2,000=20%=P2.00D=2.0=Nature=Matter=Moon=2 Feb.=Cupid=N=C+_
Cabinet=20,000=2,000=20%=P2.00D=2.0=Nature=Matter=Moon=2 Feb.=Cupid=N=C+_
Cabinet maker=4,500=5,000=50%=P5.00D=Law=Time=Venus=5 May = Aphrodite>>L=N.
Cabinet work=3,000=30%=P3.0D=3.0=Creativity=Stars=Muses=3 March = C=I>>GIL.
Cabin fever=5,000=50%=P5.00D=Law=Time=Venus=5 May = Aphrodite>>L=N.
Cable=11,000=11%=P1.10D=1.1=Idea=Brainchild=Inv.=11 Nov.=SC=Athena>>I=MT.
Cable car=5,500=5.5=80%=P5.50=Earth-Midway=5 May = Gaia.
Cable cast=2,500=3,000=30%=P3.0D=3.0=Creativity=Stars=Muses=3 March = C=I>>GIL.
Cablegram=3,000=30%=P3.0D=3.0=Creativity=Stars=Muses=3 March = C=I>>GIL.
Cable Tv.=11,000=11%=P1.10D=1.1=Idea=Brainchild=Inv.=11 Nov.=SC=Athena>>I=MT.
Cable vision=1,500=15%=P1.50D=1,5=Authority=Crown=Solar Core=1 May = Maia.
Cabochon=3,500=4,000=40%=P4.0D=Govt. =Creato.=4 April=Mercury=Hermes=G=A4.
Caboodle=4,000=40%=P4.0D=Govt. =Creato.=4 April=Mercury=Hermes=G=A4.
Caboose=7,500=8,000=80%=P8.0D=Economy=Currency=8 Aug.=Zeus>>E=v.
Cabot John=2,500=3,000=30%=P3.0D=3.0=Creatvty=Stars=Muses=3 March = C=I>>GIL.
Cabot, Sebastian=4,000=40%=P4.0D=Govt. =Creato.=4 April=Mercury=Hermes=G=A4.
Cabrini Frances Xavier=4,000=40%=P4.0D=Govt.=4 April=Mercury=Hermes=G=A4.
Cabriolet=5,500=5.5=80%=P5.50=Earth-Midway=5 May = Gaia.
Cacao=10,500=11,000=11%=P1.10D=1.1=Idea=Brainchild=Inv.=11 Nov.=SC=Athena>>I=MT.
Cachalot=1,500=15%=P1.50D=1.5=Authority=Crown=Solar Core=1 May = Maia.
Cache=6,500=7,000=70%=P7.0D=7.0=Language=Assets=Mars=7 July=Pleiades.
Cachet=6,000=60%=P6.0D=Man=Earth=Royalty=6 June=Gaia=Maia>>M=M2.
Cackle=11,500=12,000=12%=P1.20D=1.2=Knowledge=Education=12Dec.=Athena>>K=F.
Cacophony=2,000=20%=P2.00D=2.0=Nature=Matter=Moon=2 Feb.=Cupid=N=C+_
Cactus=8,000=80%=P8.0D=Economy=Currency=8 Aug.=Zeus>>E=v.
Cad=4,000=40%=P4.0D=Govt. =Creato.=4 April=Mercury=Hermes=G=A4.
Cadaver=4,000=40%=P4.0D=Govt. =Creato.=4 April=Mercury=Hermes=G=A4.
Cadaverous=3,500=4,000=40%=P4.0D=Govt. =Creato.=4April=Mercury=Hermes=G=A4.
Caddie=5,500=5.5=80%=P5.50=Earth-Midway=5 May = Gaia.
Cadoan=8,500=9,000=90%=P9.00D=9.0=Abstraction=Gods=Saturn=9Sept.>>A=Ø.
Caddy=3,000=30%=P3.0D=3.0=Creativity=Stars=Muses=3 March = C=I>>GIL.

Cadence=11,500=12,000=12%=P1.20D=1.2=Knowledge=Education=12Dec.=Athena>>K=F.
Cadency=500=5%=P5.00D=5.0=Law=Time=Venus=5 May=Aphrodite>>L=N.
Cadenza=9,500=10,000=1,000=100%=10.0=Physicality=Tech.=10 Oct.=Uranus=P=1Ø.
Cadet=8,000=80%=P8.0D=Economy=Currency=8 Aug.=Zeus>>E=v.
Cadge=3,000=30%=P3.0D=3.0=Creativity=Stars=Muses=3 March = C=I>>GIL.
Cadillac A.=2,500=3,000=30%=P3.0D=3.0=Creativity=Stars=Muses=3 March C=I>>GIL.
Cadiz=8,000=80%=P8.0D=Economy=Currency=8 Aug.=Zeus>>E=v.
Cadmium=14,000=14%=P1.40D=1.4=Mgt.=Solar Energy/Electric=13 May=Athena=SC=0.1
Cadre=10,500=11,000=11%=P1.10D=1.1=Idea=Brainchild=Inv.=11 Nov.=SC=Athena>>I=MT.
Caduceus=10,500=11,000=11%=P1.10D=1.1=Idea=Brainchild=11Nov.=SC=Athena=I=MT.
Caecum=1,500=15%=P1.50D=1.5=Authority=Crown=Solar Core=1 May = Maia.
Caedmon=3,500=4,000=40%=P4.0D=Govt. =Creato.=4 April=Mercury=Hermes=G=A4.
Caen=5,500=5.5=80%=P5.50=Earth-Midway=5 May = Gaia.
Caesar=5,000=50%=P5.00D=Law=Time=Venus=5 May = Aphrodite>>L=N.
Caesar, Julius=6,000=60%=P6.0D=Man=Earth=Royalty=6 June=Gaia=Maia>>M=M2.
Caesarea=5,000=50%=P5.00D=Law=Time=Venus=5 May = Aphrodite>>L=N.
Caesarean=1,500=15%=P1.50D=1.5=Authority=Crown=Solar Core=1 May = Maia.
Caesium=1,500=15%=P1.50D=1.5=Authority=Crown=Solar Core=1 May = Maia.
Caesura=8,000=80%=P8.0D=Economy=Currency=8 Aug.=Zeus>>E=v.
C.A.F=1,500=15%=P1.50D=1.5=Authority=Crown=Solar Core=1 May = Maia.
Café=3,000=30%=P3.0D=3.0=Creativity=Stars=Muses=3 March = C=I>>GIL.
Cafè au lait=4,000=40%=P4.0D=Govt. =Creato.=4 April=Mercury=Hermes=G=A4.
Cafeteria=8,500=9,000=90%=P9.00D=9.0=Abstraction=Gods=Saturn=9Sept.>>A=Ø.
Caffeine=9,000=90%=P9.00D=9.0=Abstraction=Gods=Saturn=9Sept.>>A=Ø.
Caftan=5,500=5.5=80%=P5.50=Earth-Midway=5 May = Gaia.
Cage=15,000=1,500=15%=P1.50D=1.5=Authority=Crown=Solar Core=1 May = Maia.
Cagey=2,500=3,000=30%=P3.0D=3.0=Creativity=Stars=Muses=3 March = C=I>>GIL.
Cagliari=8,500=9,000=90%=P9.00D=9.0=Abstraction=Gods=Saturn=9Sept.>>A=Ø.
Cahoots=3,500=4,000=40%=P4.0D=Govt. =Creato.=4 April=Mercury=Hermes=G=A4.
Coahuila=7,000=70%=P7.0D=7.0=Language=Assets=Mars=7 July=Pleiades.
CAI=1,500=15%=P1.50D=1.5=Authority=Crown=Solar Core=1 May = Maia.
Caiman=6,500=7,000=70%=P7.0D=7.0=Language=Assets=Mars=7 July=Pleiades.
Cain=6,000=60%=P6.0D=Man=Earth=Royalty=6 June=Gaia=Maia>>M=M2.
Calm=4,500=5,000=50%=P5.00D=Law=Time=Venus=5 May = Aphrodite>>L=N.
Carol=6,000=60%=P6.0D=Man=Earth=Royalty=6 June=Gaia=Maia>>M=M2.
Caisson=13,000=13%=P1.30=Solar Core=Faculty=13 January=Athena.
Caisson disease=1,500=15%=P1.50D=1.5=Authority=Crown=Solar Core=1 May = Maia.
Caitiff=1,500=15%=P1.50D=1.5=Authority=Crown=Solar Core=1 May = Maia.
Cajole=1,000=100%=10.0=1.0=Mind=Sun=1 January=Helios >> M=E4.
Cajun=8,000=80%=P8.0D=Economy=Currency=8 Aug.=Zeus>>E=v.
Cake=14,000=14%=P1.40D=1.4=Mgt.=Solar Energy/Electric=13 May=Athena=SC=0.1
Cal=2,000=20%=P2.00D=2.0=Nature=Matter=Moon=2 Feb.=Cupid=N=C+_
Cal.=1,000=100%=10.0=1.0=Mind=Sun=1 January=Helios >> M=E4.
Cal.or Calif.=1,000=100%=10.0=1.0=Mind=Sun=1 January=Helios >> M=E4.

Calabash=12,500=13,000=13%=P1.30=Solar Core=Faculty=13 January=Athena.
In his book THE CREATOCRACY, one of the plays is The Broken Calabash.

Calaboose=1,500=15%=P1.50D=1.5=Authority=Crown=Solar Core=1 May = Maia.
Calais=6,500=7,000=70%=P7.0D=7.0=Language=Assets=Mars=7 July=Pleiades.
Calamine=7,500=8,000=80%=P8.0D=Economy=Currency=8 Aug.=Zeus>>E=v.
Calamity=2,000=20%=P2.00D=2.0=Nature=Matter=Moon=2 Feb.=Cupid=N=C+_
Calcareous=4,000=40%=P4.0D=Govt. =Creato.=4 April=Mercury=Hermes=G=A4.
Calci=1,000=100%=10.0=1.0=Mind=Sun=1 January=Helios >> M=E4.
Calciferous=3,000=30%=P3.0D=3.0=Creativity=Stars=Muses=3 March = C=I>>GIL.
Calcify=2,500=3,000=30%=P3.0D=3.0=Creativity=Stars=Muses=3 March = C=I>>GIL.
Calcimine=9,500=10,000=1,000=100%=10.0=Physicality=Tech.=10 Oct.=Uranus=P=1Ø.
Calcine=10,000=1,000=100%=Physicality= Tech.=10 Oct.=Uranus=P=1Ø.
Calcite=4,000=40%=P4.0D=Govt. =Creato.=4 April=Mercury=Hermes=G=A4.
Calcium=16,000=16%=P1.60D=1.6=Cycle of Incarnation=Mind of GOD=1 June = Maia.
Calcium carbonate=10,000=1,000=100%=10.0=Physicality=Tech.=10 Oct.=Uranus=P=1Ø.
Calcium chloride=9,500=10,000=1,000=100%=10.0=Phy.=Tech.=10 Oct.=Uranus=P=1Ø.
Calcium hydroxide=7,500=8,000=80%=P8.0D=Economy=Currency=8 Aug.=Zeus>>E=v.
Calcium oxide=9,000=90%=P9.00D=9.0=Abstraction=Gods=Saturn=9Sept.>>A=Ø.

Calculate=9,500=10,000=1,000=100%=10.0=Physicality=Tech.=10 Oct.=Uranus=P=1Ø.
To calculate is to cross a borderline(500) from the abstract to the physical. Hence to calculate makes a software become a hardware creating itself into a technology. The Creatocracy thereby establishes that the Mind once calculated has become a technology.

Calculated=4,000=40%=P4.0D=Govt.=Creato.=4 April=Mercury=Hermes=G=A4.
Once a thing has been calculated it becomes a power in itself. The Creatocracy became a power or government system of relationships because it calculated the Mind and Minds.

Calculating=2,000=20%=P2.00D=2.0=Nature=Matter=Moon=2 Feb.=Cupid=N=C+_
Calculating is a process that makes a thing into matter>>moon element.

Calculation=7,000=70%=P7.0D=7.0=Language=Assets=Mars=7 July=Pleiades.
Calculations are assets defined by works and is the proof of mental war. It is believed that the God of Creatocracy had won the battle of Gods through abstract calculations thus his apotheosis from mere human state (Peter Matthews-Akukalia) to a God state (Castle Makupedia). He invented the ways by which the Mind of Gods and men can be measured.

Calculator=7,000=70%=P7.0D=7.0=Language=Assets=Mars=7 July=Pleiades.
Peter Matthews-Akukalia is the first Human Mind Calculator and invented the Makulator. His method of Mind calculations is known as Makulation - Makupedia. [After Him "Maks"].

Calculus=12,000=12%=P1.20D=1.2=Knowledge=Education=12Dec.=Athena>>K=F.
Calcutta=7,000=70%=P7.0D=7.0=Language=Assets=Mars=7 July=Pleiades.
Calder Alexander=2,000=20%=P2.00D=2.0=Nature=Matter=Moon=2 Feb.=Cupid=N=C+_
Caldera=3,500=4,000=40%=P4.0D=Govt. =Creato.=4 April=Mercury=Hermes=G=A4.
Caldron=4,500=5,000=50%=P5.00D=Law=Time=Venus=5 May = Aphrodite>>L=N.

Calendar=10,000=1,000=100%=10.0=Physicality=Tech.=10 Oct.=Uranus=P=1Ø.
Three Principal Calendars= 495,000= 5,000=50%= P5.00D= Law=Time= Venus= 5 May =Aphrodite>L=N. Time is a law of all existence valued by impact and utility for all. The basis for calendars is the measurement of time. An element sourced from Venus in the support dimensions of the moon (Nature), ordered by Zeus as Daylight and Night, and managed by Athena the brainchild owner of all calendar systems and civilizations.
The Creatocratic or Makupedian Calendar was invented by the Peter Matthews-Akukalia.

Calender=8,500=9,000=90%=P9.00D=9.0=Abstraction=Gods=Saturn=9Sept.>>A=Ø.
Calends=4,500=5,000=50%=P5.00D=Law=Time=Venus=5 May = Aphrodite>>L=N.
Calf(1)=7,500=8,000=80%=P8.0D=Economy=Currency=8 Aug.=Zeus>>E=v.
Calf(2)=5,500=5.5=80%=P5.00=Earth-Midway=5 May = Gaia.
Calfskin=4,500=5,000=50%=P5.00D=Law=Time=Venus=5 May = Aphrodite>>L=N.
Calgary=4,500=5,000=50%=P5.00D=Law=Time=Venus=5 May = Aphrodite>>L=N.
Calhoun John=4,500=5,000=50%=P5.00D=Law=Time=Venus=5 May=Odite>>L=N.
Cali=6,500=7,000=70%=P7.0D=7.0=Language=Assets=Mars=7 July=Pleiades.
Caliber=9,500=10,000=1,000=100%=10.0=Physicality=Tech.=10 Oct.=Uranus=P=1Ø.
Calibrate=8,500=9,000=90%=P9.00D=9.0=Abstraction=Gods=Saturn=9Sept.>>A=Ø.
Calibre=2,500=3,000=30%=P3.0D=3.0=Creativity=Stars=Muses=3 March = C=I>>GIL.
Calico=7,000=70%=P7.0D=7.0=Language=Assets=Mars=7 July=Pleiades.
California=6,000=60%=P6.0D=Man=Earth=Royalty=6 June=Gaia=Maia>>M=M2.
California, Gulf of.=6,500=7,000=70%=P7.0D=7.0=Lang.=Assets=Mars=7 July=Pleiades.
California condor=4,500=5,000=50%=P5.00D=Law=Time=Venus=5 May =Odite>>L=N.
California poppy=6,500=7,000=70%=P7.0D=7.0=Language=Assets=Mars=7 July=Pleiades.
Californium=7,500=8,000=80%=P8.0D=Economy=Currency=8 Aug.=Zeus>>E=v.
Caligula=3,500=4,000=40%=P4.0D=Govt. =Creato.=4 April=Mercury=Hermes=G=A4.
Caliper=10,000=1,000=100%=10.0=Physicality=Tech.=10 Oct.=Uranus=P=1Ø.
Caliph=4,000=40%=P4.0D=Govt. =Creato.=4 April=Mercury=Hermes=G=A4.
Calisthenics=6,500=7,000=70%=P7.0D=7.0=Language=Assets=Mars=7 July=Pleiades.
Calk=1,500=15%=P1.50D=1.5=Authority=Crown=Solar Core=1 May = Maia.

Call=10,000=1,000=100%=10.0=Physicality=Tech.=10 Oct.=Uranus=P=1Ø.
Not counted due to huge volume and extreme difficulty in avoiding repetition. Classified as 10,000 since this is the biblical standard for deducing all mind faculties in Makupedia.

Calla lily=6,500=7,000=70%=P7.0D=7.0=Language=Assets=Mars=7 July=Pleiades.
Callao=6,500=7,000=70%=P7.0D=7.0=Language=Assets=Mars=7 July=Pleiades.
Calligraphy=3,000=30%=P3.0D=3.0=Creativity=Stars=Muses=3 March = C=I>>GIL.

Call-in=7,500=8,000=80%=P8.0D=Economy=Currency=8 Aug.=Zeus>>E=v.
During call-in, GOD listens. Proof that phone lines are direct links to the ears of the Gods. The Creatocracy established that electromagnetically driven codes such as phone lines contain certain inbuilt energy that translate into human destiny which can be interpreted. 09033521731>>The Council of Gods being the Host>>Holy Spirit will manifest their genius through intellectual property in accordance with the model of a scientist of the year 1731. This was proved that Peter Matthews-Akukalia and Benjamin Banneker shared certain same traits that indicated that He may have returned as an incarnate. Assets >>17=1.7 and Institution of higher learning >>31>>1.3 thus are granted him. This is Makupedia.

Calling=3,500=4,000=40%=P4.0D=Govt. =Creato.=4 April=Mercury=Hermes=G=A4.
Calling card=3,500=4,000=40%=P4.0D=Govt. =Creato.=4 April=Mercury=Hermes=G=A4.
Calliope=5,000=50%=P5.00D=Law=Time=Venus=5 May = Aphrodite>>L=N.
Caliper=1,500=15%=P1.50D=1.5=Authority=Crown=Solar Core=1 May = Maia.
Call letters=5,500=5.5=80%=P5.50=Earth-Midway=5 May = Gaia.
Call loan=4,000=40%=P4.0D=Govt. =Creato.=4 April=Mercury=Hermes=G=A4.
Call number=7,500=8,000=80%=P8.0D=Economy=Currency=8 Aug.=Zeus>>E=v.
Callosity=4,500=5,000=50%=P5.00D=Law=Time=Venus=5 May = Aphrodite>>L=N.
Callous=6,000=60%=P6.0D=Man=Earth=Royalty=6 June=Gaia=Maia>>M=M2.
Callow=3,000=30%=P3.0D=3.0=Creativity=Stars=Muses=3 March = C=I>>GIL.
Call up=4,500=5,000=50%=P5.00D=Law=Time=Venus=5 May = Aphrodite>>L=N.
Callus=5,500=5.5=80%=P5.00=Earth-Midway=5 May = Gaia.
Calm=10,000=1,000=100%=10.0=Physicality=Tech.=10 Oct.=Uranus=P=1Ø.
Calmative=2,500=3,000=30%=P3.0D=3.0=Creativity=Stars=Muses=3 March = C=I>>GIL.
Calomel=5,500=5.5=80%=P5.50=Earth-Midway=5 May = Gaia.
Caloric=3,000=30%=P3.0D=3.0=Creativity=Stars=Muses=3 March = C=I>>GIL.
Calorie=9,500=10,000=1,000=100%=10.0=Physicality=Tech.=10 Oct.=Uranus=P=1Ø.
Calorie=15,000=1,500=15%=P1.50D=1.5=Authority=Crown=Solar Core=1 May = Maia.
Calorific=3,000=30%=P3.0D=3.0=Creativity=Stars=Muses=3 March = C=I>>GIL.

Calorimeter=7,500=8,000=80%=P8.0D=Economy=Currency=8 Aug.=Zeus>>E=v.
Calumet=5,500=5.5=80%=P5.50=Earth-Midway=5 May = Gaia.
Calumniate=2,000=20%=P2.00D=2.0=Nature=Matter=Moon=2 Feb.=Cupid=N=C+_
Calumny=7,000=70%=P7.0D=7.0=Language=Assets=Mars=7 July=Pleiades.
Calvary=4,500=5,000=50%=P5.00D=Law=Time=Venus=5 May = Aphrodite>>L=N.
Calvert=13,500=14,000=14%=P1.40D=1.4=Mgt.=Solar Energy=13 May=Athena=SC=0.1
Calves(1)=1,500=15%=P1.50D=1.5=Authority=Crown=Solar Core=1 May = Maia.
Calves(2)=1,500=15%=P1.50D=1.5=Authority=Crown=Solar Core=1 May = Maia.
Calvin John=3,500=4,000=40%=P4.0D=Govt. =Creato.=4 April=Mercury=Hermes=G=A4.

Calx=5,500=5.5=80%=P5.50=Earth-Midway=5 May = Gaia.
Calypso=8,000=80%=P8.0D=Economy=Currency=8 Aug.=Zeus>>E=v.
Calyx=5,000=50%=P5.00D=Law=Time=Venus=5 May = Aphrodite>>L=N.
Cam=6,500=7,000=70%=P7.0D=7.0=Language=Assets=Mars=7 July=Pleiades.
Camagûey=4,000=40%=P4.0D=Govt. =Creato.=4 April=Mercury=Hermes=G=A4.
Camaraderie=2,000=20%=P2.00D=2.0=Nature=Matter=Moon=2 Feb.=Cupid=N=C+_
Camber=11,500=12,000=12%=P1.20D=1.2=Knowledge=Education=12Dec.=Athena>>K=F.
Cambium=10,500=11,000=11%=P1.10D=1.1=Idea=Brainchild=11 Nov.=SC=Athena>>I=MT.
Cambodia Kampu=7,000=70%=P7.0D=7.0=Language=Assets=Mars=7 July=Pleiades.
Cambrian=6,000=60%=P6.0D=Man=Earth=Royalty=6 June=Gaia=Maia>>M=M2.
Cambric=3,500=4,000=40%=P4.0D=Govt. =Creato.=4 April=Mercury=Hermes=G=A4.
Cambridge=10,500=11,000=11%=P1.10D=1.1=Idea=Brainchild=11 Nov.=SC=Athena>>I=MT.
Camcorder=5,500=5.5=80%=P5.50=Earth-Midway=5 May = Gaia.
Camden=6,500=7,000=70%=P7.0D=7.0=Language=Assets=Mars=7 July=Pleiades.
Came=2,000=20%=P2.00D=2.0=Nature=Matter=Moon=2 Feb.=Cupid=N=C+_
Camel=12,000=12%=P1.20D=1.2=Knowledge=Education=12Dec.=Athena>>K=F.
Camellia=11,500=12,000=12%=P1.20D=1.2=Knowledge=Education=12Dec.=Athena>>K=F.
Camelot=8,000=80%=P8.0D=Economy=Currency=8 Aug.=Zeus>>E=v.
Camel's hair=10,500=11,000=11%=P1.10D=1.1=Idea=Brainchild=11Nov=Athena>>I=MT.
Cameo=12,000=12%=P1.20D=1.2=Knowledge=Education=12Dec.=Athena>>K=F.
Camera=20,000=2,000=20%=P2.00D=2.0=Nature=Matter=Moon=2 Feb.=Cupid=N=C+_
Cameraman=6,500=7,000=70%=P7.0D=7.0=Language=Assets=Mars=7 July=Pleiades.
Cameroon=7,500=8,000=80%=P8.0D=Economy=Currency=8 Aug.=Zeus>>E=v.
Camisole=3,000=30%=P3.0D=3.0=Creativity=Stars=Muses=3 March = C=I>>GIL.
Camões Luiz Vas de=2,500=30%=P3.0D=3.0=Creatv.=Stars=Muses=3March = C=I>>GIL.
Camomile=1,500=15%=P1.50D=1.5=Authority=Crown=Solar Core=1 May = Maia.
Camouflage=11,000=11%=P1.10D=1.1=Idea=Brainchild=11Nov=Athena>>I=MT.
Camp(1)=18,500=19,000=19%=P1.90=1.9=Solar Energy=Planets=Mind of God=Maia
Camp(2)=11,000=11%=P1.10D=1.1=Idea=Brainchild=11Nov=Athena>>I=MT.
Campagna di Roma=3,500=4,000=40%=P4.0D=Govt.=4April=Mercury=Hermes=G=A4.
Campaign=14,000=14%=P1.40D=1.4=Mgt.=Solar Energy=13 May=Athena=SC=0.1
Campania=4,500=5,000=50%=P5.00D=Law=Time=Venus=5 May = Aphrodite>>L=N.
Campanile=2,500=3,000=30%=P3.0D=3.0=Creativity=Stars=Muses=3 March = C=I>>GIL.
Camper=12,500=13,000=13%=P1.30=Solar Core=Faculty=13 January=Athena.
Campfire=8,000=80%=P8.0D=Economy=Currency=8 Aug.=Zeus>>E=v.
Campground=4,500=5,000=50%=P5.00D=Law=Time=Venus=5 May = Aphrodite>>L=N.
Camphor=9,000=90%=P9.00D=9.0=Abstraction=Gods=Saturn=9Sept.>>A=Ø.
Campinas=5,000=50%=P5.50D=Law=Time=Venus=5 May = Aphrodite>>L=N.
Campion Thomas=3,000=30%=P3.0D=3.0=Creativity=Stars=Muses=3 March = C=I>>GIL.
Camp meeting=4,500=5,000=50%=P5.00D=Law=Time=Venus=5 May = Aphrodite>>L=N.
Campos=5,500=5.5=80%=P5.50=Earth-Midway=5 May = Gaia.
Campsite=5,000=50%=P5.00D=Law=Time=Venus=5 May = Aphrodite>>L=N.
Campus=4,500=5,000=50%=P5.00D=Law=Time=Venus=5 May = Aphrodite>>L=N.
Camshaft=4,500=5,000=50%=P5.00D=Law=Time=Venus=5 May = Aphrodite>>L=N.
Camus Albert=4,000=40%=P4.0D=Govt. =Creato.=4 April=Mercury=Hermes=G=A4.

Can(1)=40,000=4,000=40%=P4.0D=Govt. =Creato.=4 April=Mercury=Hermes=G=A4.
Can(2)=17,000=17%=P1.70D=1.7=Solar Asset=17/20=17 Feb.=Maia=Mind Computing.
Can.=1,000=100%=10.0=1.0=Mind=Sun=1 January=Helios >> M=E4.
Canaan=8,000=80%=P8.0D=Economy=Currency=8 Aug.=Zeus>>E=v.
Canada=5,000=50%=P5.00D=Law=Time=Venus=5 May = Aphrodite>>L=N.

Canada Day=5,500=5.5=80%=P5.50=Earth-Midway=5 May = Gaia.
Paradise Day is the day by which the Creatocratic Charter was published 17 Feb. 2020.
Creatocracy Day is the Day of publishing the Creatocratic 1. Makupedia Day>>06 July.

Canada goose=9,000=90%=P9.00D=9.0=Abstraction=Gods=Saturn=9Sept.>>A=Ø.
Canada French=3,500=4,000=40%=P4.0D=Govt.=4 April=Mercury=Hermes=G=A4.
Canadian River=9,500=10,000=1,000=100%=10.0=Phys.=Tech.=10 Oct.=Uranus=P=1Ø.
Canaille=1,500=15%=P1.50D=1.5=Authority=Crown=Solar Core=1 May = Maia.
Canal=7,000=70%=P7.0D=7.0=Language=Assets=Mars=7 July=Pleiades
Canal Zone=8,500=9,000=90%=P9.00D=9.0=Abstraction=Gods=Saturn=9Sept.>>A=Ø.
Canapé=5,000=50%=P5.00D=Law=Time=Venus=5 May = Aphrodite>>L=N.
Canard=3,500=4,000=40%=P4.0D=Govt. =Creato.=4 April=Mercury=Hermes=G=A4.
Canary Islands=6,000=60%=P6.0D=Man=Earth=Royalty=6 June=Gaia=Maia>>M=M2.
Canasta=6,000=60%=P6.0D=Man=Earth=Royalty=6 June=Gaia=Maia>>M=M2.
Canaveral Cape=6,500=7,000=70%=P7.0D=7.0=Language=Assets=Mars=7 July=Pleiades
Canberra=5,000=50%=P5.00D=Law=Time=Venus=5 May = Aphrodite>>L=N.
Cancan=4,000=40%=P4.0D=Govt. =Creato.=4 April=Mercury=Hermes=G=A4.

Cancel=21,500=12,500=13,000=13%=P1.30=Solar Core=Faculty=13 January=Athena.
The power of creative intelligence can cancel anything. This is an exclusive rights and authority of the Creatocracy who successfully computed the creative intelligence quotient.

---

cancer=12,000=12%=P1.20D=1.2=Knowledge=Education=12Dec.=Athena>>K=F.
Athena can use cancer to punish offenders and haters of knowledge and Science.

Cancer=5,000=50%=P5.00D=Law=Time=Venus=5 May = Aphrodite>>L=N.
A constellation in the Northern Hemisphere. The 4th sign of the zodiac. Latin.. What is the stellar weight of Cancer.
Northern >> 12>>1.2. Now 4th in the zodiac (12 signs) >> 4.0/12=0.3.
First the zodiac is the classification of human thought faculties into different modules. Our discovery. 1.2*0.3=p=1.5+0.36=1.86x=px=2.4>>International Business. The innate potentials in the thought inclination of a Cancer person is international business. All zodiac signs can be tracked. Usu. July. The resultant shows precision in thought. An alignment between Aries and Aphrodite. A truth of the Greek myth. Reason the Makstians believe in the Greek myths and computed truths of the Creatocracy.

Candela=10,000=1,000=100%=10.0=Physicality=Tech.=10 Oct.=Uranus=P=1Ø.
Candelabra=1,000=100%=10.0=1.0=Mind=Sun=1 January=Helios >> M=E4.
Candelabrum=4,000=40%=P4.0D=Govt. =Creato.=4 April=Mercury=Hermes=G=A4.
Candescence=3,500=4,000=40%=P4.0D=Govt.=4 April=Mercury=Hermes=G=A4.
Candid=8,000=80%=P8.0D=Economy=Currency=8 Aug.=Zeus>>E=v.
Candidate=6,000=60%=P6.0D=Man=Earth=Royalty=6 June=Gaia=Maia>>M=M2.
Candle=11,500=12,000=12%=P1.20D=1.2=Knowledge=Education=12Dec.=Athena>>K=F.
Candlelight=4,000=40%=P4.0D=Govt. =Creato.=4 April=Mercury=Hermes=G=A4.
Candle pin=6,500=7,000=70%=P7.0D=7.0=Language=Assets=Mars=7 July=Pleiades
Candlepower=2,500=3,000=30%=P3.0D=3.0=Creatv=Stars=Muses=3 March = C=I>>GIL.
Candlestick=4,000=40%=P4.0D=Govt. =Creato.=4 April=Mercury=Hermes=G=A4.
Candor=2,500=3,000=30%=P3.0D=3.0=Creativity=Stars=Muses=3 March = C=I>>GIL.
C&W=1,500=15%=P1.50D=1.5=Authority=Crown=Solar Core=1 May = Maia.
Candy=10,000=1,000=100%=10.0=Physicality=Tech.=10 Oct.=Uranus=P=1Ø.
Candy striper=3,500=4,000=40%=P4.0D=Govt.=4 April=Mercury=Hermes=G=A4.
Candy tuft=5,500=5.5=80%=P5.50=Earth-Midway=5 May = Gaia.
Cane=17,000=17%=P1.70D=1.7=Solar Asset=17/20=17 Feb.=Maia=Mind Computing.
Canebrake=2,500=3,000=30%=P3.0D=3.0=Creativity=Stars=Muses=3 March = C=I>>GIL.
Cane sugar=2,500=3,000=30%=P3.0D=3.0=Creatv.=Stars=Muses=3 March = C=I>>GIL.
Canine=15,000=15%=P1.50D=1.5=Authority=Crown=Solar Core=1 May = Maia.
Canis Major=4,500=5,000=50%=P5.00D=Law=Time=Venus=5 May = Aphrodite>>L=N.
Canis Minor=3,000=30%=P3.0D=3.0=Creativity=Stars=Muses=3 March = C=I>>GIL.
Canister=11,000=11%=P1.10D=1.1=Idea=Brainchild=11Nov=Athena>>I=MT.
Canker=3,000=30%=P3.0D=3.0=Creativity=Stars=Muses=3 March = C=I>>GIL.
Canker sore=5,000=50%=P5.00D=Law=Time=Venus=5 May = Aphrodite>>L=N.
Canna=6,000=60%=P6.0D=Man=Earth=Royalty=6 June=Gaia=Maia>>M=M2.
Cannabis=14,000=14%=P1.40D=1.4=Mgt.=Solar Energy=13 May=Athena=SC=0.1
Canned=7,500=8,000=80%=P8.0D=Economy=Currency=8 Aug.=Zeus>>E=v.
Cannery=6,000=60%=P6.0D=Man=Earth=Royalty=6 June=Gaia=Maia>>M=M2.
Cannes=6,000=60%=P6.0D=Man=Earth=Royalty=6 June=Gaia=Maia>>M=M2.
Cannibal=9,500=10,000=1,000=100%=10.0=Physicality=Tech.=10 Oct.=Uranus=P=1Ø.
Cannibalize=9,500=10,000=1,000=100%=Physicality= Tech.=10 Oct.=Uranus=P=1Ø.
Canning George=3,000=30%=P3.0D=3.0=Creativity=Stars=Muses=3 March = C=I>>GIL.
Cannoli=4,000=40%=P4.0D=Govt. =Creato.=4 April=Mercury=Hermes=G=A4.
Canon=7,000=70%=P7.0D=7.0=Language=Assets=Mars=7 July=Pleiades
Cannonade=2,500=3,000=30%=P3.0D=3.0=Creativity=Stars=Muses=3 March=C=I>>GIL.
Cannonball=7,500=8,000=80%=P8.0D=Economy=Currency=8 Aug.=Zeus>>E=v.
Cannot=2,500=3,000=30%=P3.0D=3.0=Creativity=Stars=Muses=3 March = C=I>>GIL.
Cannula=7,500=8,000=80%=P8.0D=Economy=Currency=8 Aug.=Zeus>>E=v.
Canny=2,500=3,000=30%=P3.0D=3.0=Creativity=Stars=Muses=3 March = C=I>>GIL.
Canoe=9,500=10,000=1,000=100%=Physicality= Tech.=10 Oct.=Uranus=P=1Ø.
Canon(1)=9,000=90%=P9.00D=9.0=Abstraction=Gods=Saturn=9Sept.>>A=Ø.
Canon(2)=5,500=5.5=80%=P5.50=Earth-Midway=5 May = Gaia.
Cañon=1,500=15%=P1.50D=1.5=Authority=Crown=Solar Core=1 May = Maia.

Canonical=6,000=60%=P6.0D=Man=Earth=Royalty=6 June=Gaia=Maia>>M=M2.
Canonical hours=8,000=80%=P8.0D=Economy=Currency=8 Aug.=Zeus>>E=v.
Canonize=4,000=40%=P4.0D=Govt. =Creato.=4 April=Mercury=Hermes=G=A4.
Canon law=5,000=50%=P5.00D=Law=Time=Venus=5 May = Aphrodite>>L=N.
Canopy=17,000=17%=P1.70D=1.7=Solar Asset=17/20=17 Feb.=Maia=Mind Computing.
Canst=4,000=40%=P4.0D=Govt. =Creato.=4 April=Mercury=Hermes=G=A4.
Cant(1)=9,000=90%=P9.00D=9.0=Abstraction=Gods=Saturn=9Sept.>>A=Ø.
Cant(2)=12,500=13,000=13%=P1.30=Solar Core=Faculty=13 January=Athena.
Can't=500=5%=P5.00D=5.0=Law=Time=Venus=5 May=Aphrodite>>L=N.
Cantabile=3,000=30%=P3.0D=3.0=Creativity=Stars=Muses=3 March = C=I>>GIL.
Cantaloupe=4,500=5,000=50%=P5.00D=Law=Time=Venus=5 May = Aphrodite>>L=N.
Cantankerous=2,000=20%=P2.00D=2.0=Nature=Matter=Moon=2 Feb.=Cupid=N=C+_.
Cantata=5,000=50%=P5.00D=Law=Time=Venus=5 May = Aphrodite>>L=N.
Canteen=18,500=19,000=19%=P1.90=1.9=Solar Energy=Planets=Mind of God=Maia.
Canter=6,500=7,000=70%=P7.0D=7.0=Language=Assets=Mars=7 July=Pleiades
Canterbury=6,000=60%=P6.0D=Man=Earth=Royalty=6 June=Gaia=Maia>>M=M2.
Canthus=7,000=70%=P7.0D=7.0=Language=Assets=Mars=7 July=Pleiades
Canticle=1,500=15%=P1.50D=1.5=Authority=Crown=Solar Core=1 May = Maia.
Cantilever=6,500=7,000=70%=P7.0D=7.0=Language=Assets=Mars=7 July=Pleiades
Cantina=3,000=30%=P3.0D=3.0=Creativity=Stars=Muses=3 March = C=I>>GIL.
Cantle=3,500=4,000=40%=P4.0D=Govt. =Creato.=4 April=Mercury=Hermes=G=A4.
Canto=4,500=5,000=50%=P5.00D=Law=Time=Venus=5 May = Aphrodite>>L=N.
canton=6,500=7,000=70%=P7.0D=7.0=Language=Assets=Mars=7 July=Pleiades
Canton=1,000=100%=10.0=1.0=Mind=Sun=1 January=Helios >> M=E4.
Cantonese=9,000=90%=P9.00D=9.0=Abstraction=Gods=Saturn=9Sept.>>A=Ø.
Cantonment=4,500=5,000=50%=P5.00D=Law=Time=Venus=5 May = Aphrodite>>L=N.
Cantor=5,500=5.5=80%=P5.50=Earth-Midway=5 May = Gaia.
Canute=6,000=60%=P6.0D=Man=Earth=Royalty=6 June=Gaia=Maia>>M=M2.
Canvas=14,000=14%=P1.40D=1.4=Mgt.=Solar Energy=13 May=Athena=SC=0.1
Canvas back=6,500=7,000=70%=P7.0D=7.0=Language=Assets=Mars=7 July=Pleiades
Canvass=11,000=11%=P1.10D=1.1=Idea=Brainchild=11Nov=Athena>>I=MT.
Canyon=3,500=4,000=40%=P4.0D=Govt. =Creato.=4 April=Mercury=Hermes=G=A4.
Cap=17,000=17%=P1.70D=1.7=Solar Asset=17/20=17 Feb.=Maia=Mind Computing.
Cap.=1,000=100%=10.0=1.0=Mind=Sun=1 January=Helios >> M=E4.
Capable=4,000=40%=P4.0D=Govt. =Creato.=4 April=Mercury=Hermes=G=A4.
Capacious=5,000=50%=P5.00D=Law=Time=Venus=5 May = Aphrodite>>L=N.
Capacitance=15,000=15%=P1.50D=1.5=Authority=Crown=Solar Core=1 May = Maia.
Capacitate=2,000=20%=P2.00D=2.0=Nature=Matter=Moon=2 Feb.=Cupid=N=C+_.
Capacitor=10,000=1,000=100%=10.0=Physicality=Tech.=10 Oct.=Uranus=P=1Ø.
Capacity=20,500=21=12,000=12%=P1.20D=1.2=Knowledge=Edu.=12Dec.=Athena>>K=F.
Caparison=3,000=30%=P3.0D=3.0=Creativity=Stars=Muses=3 March = C=I>>GIL.
Cape(1)=6,500=7,000=70%=P7.0D=7.0=Language=Assets=Mars=7 July=Pleiades
Cape(2)=3,500=4,000=40%=P4.0D=Govt. =Creato.=4 April=Mercury=Hermes=G=A4.
Cape Breton Island=5,000=50%=P5.00D=Law=Time=Venus=5 May = Aphrodite>>L=N.

Cape buffalo=4,500=5,000=50%=P5.00D=Law=Time=Venus=5 May = Aphrodite>>L=N.
Caper(1)=9,000=90%=P9.00D=9.0=Abstraction=Gods=Saturn=9Sept.>>A=Ø.
Caper(2)=6,000=60%=P6.0D=Man=Earth=Royalty=6 June=Gaia=Maia>>M=M2.
Capet=6,500=7,000=70%=P7.0D=7.0=Language=Assets=Mars=7 July=Pleiades
Cape Town=5,500=5.5=80%=P5.50=Earth-Midway=5 May = Gaia.
Cape Verde=6,000=60%=P6.0D=Man=Earth=Royalty=6 June=Gaia=Maia>>M=M2.
Capillarity=9,000=90%=P9.00D=9.0=Abstraction=Gods=Saturn=9Sept.>>A=Ø.
Capillary attraction=9,500=10,000=1,000=100%=Phys.= Tech.=10Oct.=Uranus=P=1Ø.
Capital(1)=33,000=33%=P3.30=3.3=Genius Gods=Host=The Holy Spirit.
Capital(2)=4,000=40%=P4.0D=Govt. =Creato.=4 April=Mercury=Hermes=G=A4.
Capital gain=6,500=7,000=70%=P7.0D=7.0=Language=Assets=Mars=7 July=Pleiades

---

Capitalism=11,500=12,000=12%=P1.20D=1.2=Knowledge=Edu.=12Dec.=Athena>>K=F.
The Creatocracy runs all forms of economic systems comprised as Creatocism.
This is the first time an economic system will align with its political system. Creatocism
is simply what we have known in the Creative Sciences as the creative economy system.
The Creatocracy Bank is testimony that it can run efficiently effectively and productively.

Capitalist=6,500=7,000=70%=P7.0D=7.0=Language=Assets=Mars=7 July=Pleiades
Capitalize=12,000=12%=P1.20D=1.2=Knowledge=Education=12Dec.=Athena>>K=F.
Capital letter=10,000=1,000=100%=10.0=Physicality=Tech.=10 Oct.=Uranus=P=1Ø.
Capitally=500=5%=P5.00D=5.0=Law=Time=Venus=5 May=Aphrodite>>L=N.
Capital punishment=1,500=15%=P1.50D=1.5=Authority=Crown=Solar Core=1 May = Maia.
Capital stock=9,000=90%=P9.00D=9.0=Abstraction=Gods=Saturn=9Sept.>>A=Ø.
Capitation=1,500=15%=P1.50D=1.5=Authority=Crown=Solar Core=1 May = Maia.
Capitol=10,000=1,000=100%=10.0=Physicality=Tech.=10 Oct.=Uranus=P=1Ø.
Capitulate=5,000=50%=P5.00D=Law=Time=Venus=5 May = Aphrodite>>L=N.
Caplet=5,500=5.5=80%=P5.50=Earth-Midway=5 May = Gaia.
Capo(1)=7,500=8,000=80%=P8.0D=Economy=Currency=8 Aug.=Zeus>>E=v.
Capo(2)=5,000=50%=P5.00D=Law=Time=Venus=5 May = Aphrodite>>L=N.
Capon=3,000=30%=P3.0D=3.0=Creativity=Stars=Muses=3 March = C=I>>GIL.
Cappadocia=6,000=60%=P6.0D=Man=Earth=Royalty=6 June=Gaia=Maia>>M=M2.
Cappuccino=3,500=4,000=40%=P4.0D=Govt. =Creato.=4 April=Mercury=Hermes=G=A4.
Capri=5,500=5.5=80%=P5.50=Earth-Midway=5 May = Gaia.
Capriccio=5,500=5.5=80%=P5.50=Earth-Midway=5 May = Gaia.
Caprice=6,500=7,000=70%=P7.0D=7.0=Language=Assets=Mars=7 July=Pleiades
Capricious=3,500=4,000=40%=P4.0D=Govt. =Creato.=4 April=Mercury=Hermes=G=A4.
Capricorn=4,500=5,000=50%=P5.50D=Law=Time=Venus=5 May = Aphrodite>>L=N.
Capriole=5,500=5.5=80%=P5.50=Earth-Midway=5 May = Gaia.
Capsicum=7,500=8,000=80%=P8.0D=Economy=Currency=8 Aug.=Zeus>>E=v.
Capsid=3,500=4,000=40%=P4.0D=Govt. =Creato.=4 April=Mercury=Hermes=G=A4.
Capsize=5,500=5.5=80%=P5.50=Earth-Midway=5 May = Gaia.
Capstan=12,500=13,000=13%=P1.30=Solar Core=Faculty=13 January=Athena.

Capstone=5,500=5.5=80%=P5.50=Earth-Midway=5 May = Gaia.
Capsulate=3,500=4,000=40%=P4.0D=Govt. =Creato.=4 April=Mercury=Hermes=G=A4.
Capsule=17,500=18,000=18%=P1.80D=Solar Currency=Maks Currencies=1 Aug.=Maia.
Capsulize=2,000=20%=P2.00D=2.0=Nature=Matter=Moon=2 Feb.=Cupid=N=C+_.
Capt.=1,000=100%=10.0=1.0=Mind=Sun=1 January=Helios >> M=E4.
Captain=16,500=17%=P1.70D=1.7=Solar Asset=17/20=17 Feb.=Maia=Mind Computing.
Caption=8,500=9,000=90%=P9.00D=9.0=Abstraction=Gods=Saturn=9Sept.>>A=Ø.
Captious=6,000=60%=P6.0D=Man=Earth=Royalty=6 June=Gaia=Maia>>M=M2.
Captivate=6,500=7,000=70%=P7.0D=7.0=Language=Assets=Mars=7 July=Pleiades
Captive=15,000=15%=P1.50D=1.5=Authority=Crown=Solar Core=1 May = Maia.
Captor=1,500=15%=P1.50D=1.5=Authority=Crown=Solar Core=1 May = Maia.
Capture=11,000=11%=P1.10D=1.1=Idea=Brainchild=11Nov=Athena>>I=MT.
Capuchin=8,000=80%=P8.0D=Economy=Currency=8 Aug.=Zeus>>E=v.
Car=9,000=90%=P9.00D=9.0=Abstraction=Gods=Saturn=9Sept.>>A=Ø.
Car.=1,000=100%=10.0=1.0=Mind=Sun=1 January=Helios >> M=E4.
Caracalla=3,500=4,000=40%=P4.0D=Govt. =Creato.=4 April=Mercury=Hermes=G=A4.
Caracas=6,500=7,000=70%=P7.0D=7.0=Language=Assets=Mars=7 July=Pleiades
Carafe=7,000=70%=P7.0D=7.0=Language=Assets=Mars=7 July=Pleiades
Caramel=10,000=1,000=100%=10.0=Physicality=Tech.=10 Oct.=Uranus=P=1Ø.
Carapace=6,500=7,000=70%=P7.0D=7.0=Language=Assets=Mars=7 July=Pleiades
Carat=7,000=70%=P7.0D=7.0=Language=Assets=Mars=7 July=Pleiades
Caravaggio Michelangelo=2,000=20%=P2.00D=2.0=Nature=Moon=2 Feb.=Cupid=N=C+_.
Caravan=7,500=8,000=80%=P8.0D=Economy=Currency=8 Aug.=Zeus>>E=v.
Caravansary=8,000=80%=P8.0D=Economy=Currency=8 Aug.=Zeus>>E=v.
Caravel=7,500=8,000=80%=P8.0D=Economy=Currency=8 Aug.=Zeus>>E=v.
Caraway=6,000=60%=P6.0D=Man=Earth=Royalty=6 June=Gaia=Maia>>M=M2.
Carbide=5,000=50%=P5.00D=Law=Time=Venus=5 May = Aphrodite>>L=N.
Carbine=3,000=30%=P3.0D=3.0=Creativity=Stars=Muses=3 March = C=I>>GIL.
Carbo-=1,000=100%=10.0=1.0=Mind=Sun=1 January=Helios >> M=E4.
Carbohydrate=10,000=1,000=100%=10.0=Physicality=Tech.=10 Oct.=Uranus=P=1Ø.
Carbolic acid=1,000=100%=10.0=1.0=Mind=Sun=1 January=Helios >> M=E4.
Carbon=22,500=23,000=23%=Local Business=Tech=23 Days Monthly=2.3% taxes.
Carbon 14=8,500=9,000=90%=P9.00D=9.0=Abstraction=Gods=Saturn=9Sept.>>A=Ø.
Carbonaceous=2,500=3,000=30%=P3.0D=3.0=Creatv=Stars=Muses=3 March=C=I>>GIL.
Carbonate=7,000=70%=P7.0D=7.0=Language=Assets=Mars=7 July=Pleiades
Carbon black=10,000=1,000=100%=10.0=Physicality=Tech.=10 Oct.=Uranus=P=1Ø.
Carbon copy=7,500=8,000=80%=P8.0D=Economy=Currency=8 Aug.=Zeus>>E=v.
Carbon dating=9,000=90%=P9.00D=9.0=Abstraction=Gods=Saturn=9Sept.>>A=Ø.
Carbon dioxide=6,000=60%=P6.0D=Man=Earth=Royalty=6 June=Gaia=Maia>>M=M2.
Carbonic acid=6,000=60%=P6.0D=Man=Earth=Royalty=6 June=Gaia=Maia>>M=M2.
Carboniferous=13,500=14,000=14%=P1.40D=1.4=Mgt.=13May=Athena=SC=0.1
Carbon monoxide=7,000=70%=P7.0D=7.0=Language=Assets=Mars=7 July=Pleiades
Carbon paper=12,000=12%=P1.20D=1.2=Knowledge=Education=12Dec.=Athena>>K=F.
Carbon tetra chloride=4,500=5,000=50%=P5.00D=Law=Time=Venus=5May=Odite>>L=N.

Carborundum=3,000=30%=P3.0D=3.0=Creativity=Stars=Muses=3 March = C=I>>GIL.
Carboy=6,500=7,000=70%=P7.0D=7.0=Language=Assets=Mars=7 July=Pleiades
Carbuncle=6,500=7,000=70%=P7.0D=7.0=Language=Assets=Mars=7 July=Pleiades
Carburet=8,000=80%=P8.0D=Economy=Currency=8 Aug.=Zeus>>E=v.
Carburetor=8,500=9,000=90%=P9.00D=9.0=Abstraction=Gods=Saturn=9Sept.>>A=Ø.
Carburize=4,000=40%=P4.0D=Govt.=Creato.=4 April=Mercury=Hermes=G=A4.
Carcass=3,500=4,000=40%=P4.0D=Govt. =Creato.=4 April=Mercury=Hermes=G=A4.
Carcinogen=3,000=30%=P3.0D=3.0=Creativity=Stars=Muses=3 March = C=I>>GIL.
Carcinoma=3,500=4,000=40%=P4.0D=Govt. =Creato.=4 April=Mercury=Hermes=G=A4.
Car coat=2,500=3,000=30%=P3.0D=3.0=Creativity=Stars=Muses=3 March = C=I>>GIL.

Card(1)=35,000=4,000=40%=P4.0D=Govt. =Creato.=4 April=Mercury=Hermes=G=A4.
Peter Matthews-Akukalia, Castle Makupedia invented many card games or Mind Games.

Card(2)=4,500=5,000=50%=P5.00D=Law=Time=Venus=5 May = Aphrodite>>L=N.
Psycho cards are used to verify identity of the mind assessed persons.>>Psychoeconomix.

Cardamom=10,000=1,000=100%=10.0=Physicality=Tech.=10 Oct.=Uranus=P=1Ø.
Cardboard=8,500=9,000=90%=P9.00D=9.0=Abstraction=Gods=Saturn=9Sept.>>A=Ø.
Card carrying=7,000=70%=P7.0D=7.0=Language=Assets=Mars=7 July=Pleiades
Card catalog=8,000=80%=P8.0D=Economy=Currency=8 Aug.=Zeus>>E=v.
Cardiac=2,500=3,000=30%=P3.0D=3.0=Creativity=Stars=Muses=3 March = C=I>>GIL.
Cardiac arrest=7,500=8,000=80%=P8.0D=Economy=Currency=8 Aug.=Zeus>>E=v.
Cardiac massage=7,500=8,000=80%=P8.0D=Economy=Currency=8 Aug.=Zeus>>E=v.
Cardiff=6,000=60%=P6.0D=Man=Earth=Royalty=6 June=Gaia=Maia>>M=M2.
Cardigan=9,000=90%=P9.0D=9.0=Abstraction=Gods=Saturn=9Sept.>>A=Ø.
Cardinal=17,000=17%=P1.70D=1.7=Solar Asset=17/20=17 Feb.=Maia=Mind Computing.
Cardinalate=6,000=60%=P6.0D=Man=Earth=Royalty=6 June=Gaia=Maia>>M=M2.
Cardinal number=8,500=9,000=90%=P9.00D=9.0=Abst.=Gods=Saturn=9Sept.>>A=Ø.
Cardinal point=7,000=70%=P7.0D=7.0=Language=Assets=Mars=7 July=Pleiades
Cardio-=1,000=100%=10.0=1.0=Mind=Sun=1 January=Helios >> M=E4.
Cardio gram=6,500=7,000=70%=P7.0D=7.0=Language=Assets=Mars=7 July=Pleiades
Cardiograph=6,500=7,000=70%=P7.0D=7.0=Language=Assets=Mars=7 July=Pleiades
Cardiology=4,000=40%=P4.0D=Govt. =Creat.=4 April=Mercury=Hermes=G=A4.
Cardiopulmonary resuscitation=9,000=90%=P9.00D=9.0=Gods=Saturn=9Sept.>>A=Ø.
Cardiovascular=4,500=5,000=50%=P5.00D=Law=Time=Venus=5 May = Aphrodite>>L=N.
Card sharp=3,000=30%=P3.0D=3.0=Creativity=Stars=Muses=3 March = C=I>>GIL.
Care=22,000=2.2=4,000=40%=P4.0D=Govt. =Creat.=4 April=Mercury=Hermes=G=A4.
CARE=2,500=3,000=30%=P3.0D=3.0=Creativity=Stars=Muses=3 March = C=I>>GIL.
Careen=6,500=7,000=70%=P7.0D=7.0=Language=Assets=Mars=7 July=Pleiades
Career=11,500=12,000=12%=P1.20D=1.2=Knowledge=Education=12Dec.=Athena>>K=F.
Carefree=2,500=3,000=30%=P3.0D=3.0=Creativity=Stars=Muses=3 March = C=I>>GIL.
Careful=9,500=10,000=1,000=100%=10.0=Physicality=Tech.=10 Oct.=Uranus=P=1Ø.

Caregiver=12,000=12%=P1.20D=1.2=Knowledge=Education=12Dec.=Athena>>K=F.
Careless=7,500=8,000=80%=P8.0D=Economy=Currency=8 Aug.=Zeus>>E=v.
Caress=7,500=8,000=80%=P8.0D=Economy=Currency=8 Aug.=Zeus>>E=v.
Caret=9,500=10,000=1,000=100%=Physicality= Tech.=10 Oct.=Uranus=P=1Ø.
Caretaker=7,500=8,000=80%=P8.0D=Economy=Currency=8 Aug.=Zeus>>E=v.
Careworn=3,500=4,000=40%=P4.0D=Govt. =Creat.=4 April=Mercury=Hermes=G=A4.
Carfare=5,000=50%=P5.00D=Law=Time=Venus=5 May = Aphrodite>>L=N.
Cargo=5,000=50%=P5.00D=Law=Time=Venus=5 May = Aphrodite>>L=N.
Carhop=5,000=50%=P5.00D=Law=Time=Venus=5 May = Aphrodite>>L=N.
Carib=10,000=1,000=100%=10.0=Physicality=Tech.=10 Oct.=Uranus=P=1Ø.
Caribbean Sea=8,000=80%=P8.0D=Economy=Currency=8 Aug.=Zeus>>E=v.
Caribou=5,000=50%=P5.00D=Law=Time=Venus=5 May = Aphrodite>>L=N.
Caricature=12,500=13,000=13%=P1.30=Solar Core=Faculty=13 January=Athena.
Caries=3,000=30%=P3.0D=3.0=Creativity=Stars=Muses=3 March = C=I>>GIL.
Carillon=6,500=7,000=70%=P7.0D=7.0=Language=Assets=Mars=7 July=Pleiades
Caring=4,000=40%=P4.0D=Govt.=Creat.=4 April=Mercury=Hermes=G=A4.
Carl XVI Gustav=3,500=4,000=40%=P4.0D=Govt.=4April=Mercury=Hermes=G=A4.
Carload=4,500=5,000=50%=P5.00D=Law=Time=Venus=5 May = Aphrodite>>L=N.
Carlyle Thomas=3,000=30%=P3.0D=3.0=Creativity=Stars=Muses=3 March = C=I>>GIL.
Carmel Mount.=9,000=90%=P9.00D=9.0=Abst.=Gods=Saturn=9Sept.>>A=Ø.
Carminative=4,500=5,000=50%=P5.00D=Law=Time=Venus=5 May = Aphrodite>>L=N.
Carmine=2,500=3,000=30%=P3.0D=3.0=Creativity=Stars=Muses=3 March = C=I>>GIL.
Carnage=2,000=20%=P2.00D=2.0=Nature=Moon=2 Feb.=Cupid=N=C+_.
Carnal=7,500=8,000=80%=P8.0D=Economy=Currency=8 Aug.=Zeus>>E=v.
Carnation=5,000=50%=P5.00D=Law=Time=Venus=5 May = Aphrodite>>L=N.
Carnauba=8,500=9,000=90%=P9.00D=9.0=Abst.=Gods=Saturn=9Sept.>>A=Ø.
Carnegie Andrew=4,000=40%=P4.0D=Govt. =Creat.=4 April=Mercury=Hermes=G=A4.
Carnegie Dale=2,000=20%=P2.00D=2.0=Nature=Moon=2 Feb.=Cupid=N=C+_.
Carnelian=3,000=30%=P3.0D=3.0=Creativity=Stars=Muses=3 March = C=I>>GIL.
Carnival=8,000=80%=P8.0D=Economy=Currency=8 Aug.=Zeus>>E=v.
Carnivore=6,500=7,000=70%=P7.0D=7.0=Language=Assets=Mars=7 July=Pleiades
Carnivorous=3,000=30%=P3.0D=3.0=Creativity=Stars=Muses=3 March = C=I>>GIL.
Carny=3,000=30%=P3.0D=3.0=Creativity=Stars=Muses=3 March = C=I>>GIL.
Carob=10,000=1,000=100%=10.0=Physicality=Tech.=10 Oct.=Uranus=P=1Ø.
Carol=4,500=5,000=50%=P5.00D=Law=Time=Venus=5 May = Aphrodite>>L=N.
Carolinas=5,000=50%=P5.00D=Law=Time=Venus=5 May = Aphrodite>>L=N.
Caroline Islands=4,000=40%=P4.0D=Govt. =Creat.=4 April=Mercury=Hermes=G=A4.
Carom=12,000=12%=P1.20D=1.2=Knowledge=Education=12Dec.=Athena>>K=F.
Carotene=10,000=1,000=100%=10.0=Physicality=Tech.=10 Oct.=Uranus=P=1Ø.
Carotid=7,500=8,000=80%=P8.0D=Economy=Currency=8 Aug.=Zeus>>E=v.
Carouse=5,000=50%=P5.00DLaw=Time=Venus=5 May = Aphrodite>>L=N.
Carousel=6,500=7,000=70%=P7.0D=7.0=Language=Assets=Mars=7 July=Pleiades
Carp(1)=5,000=50%=P5.00D=Law=Time=Venus=5 May = Aphrodite>>L=N.
Carp(2)=3,500=4,000=40%=P4.0D=Govt. =Creat.=4 April=Mercury=Hermes=G=A4.

-carp=2,000=20%=P2.00D=2.0=Nature=Moon=2 Feb.=Cupid=N=C+_.
Carpal=3,500=4,000=40%=P4.0D=Govt. =Creat.=4 April=Mercury=Hermes=G=A4.
Carpathian Mountains=7,500=8,000=80%=P8.0D=Econ.=Currency=8Aug.=Zeus>>E=v.
Carpel=6,000=60%=P6.0D=Man=Earth=Royalty=6 June=Gaia=Maia>>M=M2.
Carpenter=6,000=60%=P6.0D=Man=Earth=Royalty=6 June=Gaia=Maia>>M=M2.
Carpet=11,000=11%=P1.10D=1.1=Idea=Brainchild=11Nov=Athena>>I=MT.
Carpetbag=3,500=4,000=40%=P4.0D=Govt. =Creat.=4 April=Mercury=Hermes=G=A4.
Carpetbagger=8,000=80%=P8.0D=Economy=Currency=8 Aug.=Zeus>>E=v.
Carpet beetle=6,000=60%=P6.0D=Man=Earth=Royalty=6 June=Gaia=Maia>>M=M2.
Carpet bomb=5,000=50%=P5.00D=Law=Time=Venus=5 May = Aphrodite>>L=N.
Carpool=10,000=1,000=100%=10.0=Physicality=Tech.=10 Oct.=Uranus=P=1Ø.
Carport=7,000=70%=P7.0D=7.0=Language=Assets=Mars=7 July=Pleiades
Carpus=2,500=3,000=30%=P3.0D=3.0=Creativity=Stars=Muses=3 March = C=I>>GIL.
Carrageen=1,500=15%=P1.50D=1.5=Authority=Crown=Solar Core=1 May = Maia.
Carrageenan=7,500=8,000=80%=P8.0D=Economy=Currency=8 Aug.=Zeus>>E=v.
Carrel=6,500=7,000=70%=P7.0D=7.0=Language=Assets=Mars=7 July=Pleiades.
Carriage=15,500=16,000=16%=P1.60D=1.6=Incarnation=Mind of GOD=1 June=Maia.
Carriage trade=4,000=40%=P4.0D=Govt. =Creat.=4 April=Mercury=Hermes=G=A4.
Carrier=13,500=14,000=14%=P1.40D=1.4=Mgt.=13May=Athena=SC=0.1
Carrier pigeon=4,500=5,000=50%=P5.00D=Law=Time=Venus=5 May = Aphrodite>>L=N.
Carrier wave=5,500=5.5=80%=P5.50=Earth-Midway=5 May = Gaia.
Carrion=2,000=20%=P2.00D=2.0=Nature=Moon=2 Feb.=Cupid=N=C+_.
Carroll Lewis=2,000=20%=P2.00D=2.0=Nature=Moon=2 Feb.=Cupid=N=C+_.
Carrot=9,000=90%=P9.00D=9.0=Abst.=Gods=Saturn=9Sept.>>A=Ø.
Carrot-and-stick=3,500=4,000=40%=P4.0D=Govt.=4 April=Mercury=Hermes=G=A4.
Carrousel=1,500=15%=P1.50D=1.5=Authority=Crown=Solar Core=1 May = Maia.
Carry=10,000=1,000=100%=10.0=Physicality=Tech.=10 Oct.=Uranus=P=1Ø.
Carryall=4,500=5,000=50%=P5.00D=Law=Time=Venus=5 May = Aphrodite>>L=N.
Carry on=6,000=60%=P6.0D=Man=Earth=Royalty=6 June=Gaia=Maia>>M=M2.
Carry out=500=5%=P5.00D=5.0=Law=Time=Venus=5 May=Aphrodite>>L=N.
Carsick=2,000=20%=P2.00D=2.0=Nature=Moon=2 Feb.=Cupid=N=C+_.
Carson Christopher=3,000=30%=P3.0D=3.0=Creativity=Stars=Muses=3March=C=I>>GIL.
Carson, Rachel Louise=3,000=30%=P3.0D=3.0=Creatv=Stars=Muses=3 March=C=I>>GIL.

Carson City=6,500=7,000=70%=P7.0D=7.0=Language=Assets=Mars=7 July=Pleiades
Makupedia City is established by the Creatocratic sovereign as the Creativity City, Nsukka.

Cart=18,000=18%=P1.80D=Solar Currency=Maks Currencies=1 Aug.=Maia.
Cartage=4,500=5,000=50%=P5.00D=Law=Time=Venus=5 May = Aphrodite>>L=N.
Cartagena=8,000=80%=P8.0D=Economy=Currency=8 Aug.=Zeus>>E=v.
Carte Blanche=1,000=100%=10.0=1.0=Mind=Sun=1 January=Helios >> M=E4.
Cartel=3,500=4,000=40%=P4.0D=Govt. =Creat.=4 April=Mercury=Hermes=G=A4.
Carter James Earl, Jr.=4,500=5,000=50%=P5.00D=Law=Time=Venus=5May=Odite>>L=N.

Cartesian coordinate=6,500=7,000=70%=P7.0D=7.0=Lang.=Assets=Mars=7 July=Pleiades
Cartesian coordinate system=16,000=16%=P1.60D=1.6=Incarnation=1 June = Maia.
Carthage=7,500=8,000=80%=P8.0D=Economy=Currency=8 Aug.=Zeus>>E=v.
Cartier Jacques=2,000=20%=P2.00D=2.0=Nature=Moon=2 Feb.=Cupid=N=C+_.
Cartilage=10,000=1,000=100%=10.0=Physicality=Tech.=10 Oct.=Uranus=P=1Ø.
Cartography=3,000=30%=P3.0D=3.0=Creativity=Stars=Muses=3 March = C=I>>GIL.
Carton=6,500=7,000=70%=P7.0D=7.0=Language=Assets=Mars=7 July=Pleiades
Cartoon=9,500=10,000=1,000=100%=10.0=Physicality=Tech.=10 Oct.=Uranus=P=1Ø.
Cartridge=19,000=19%=P1.90=1.9=Solar Energy=Planets=Mind of God=Maia.
Cartwheel=8,000=80%=P8.0D=Economy=Currency=8 Aug.=Zeus>>E=v.

Cartwright Edmund=2,000=20%=P2.00D=2.0=Nature=Moon=2 Feb.=Cupid=N=C+_.
1743-1823. British inventor. Peter Matthews-Akukalia (1978-Date). Author. World's 1st
Creative Scientist. Inventor. Business Man. Emperor. God of Creatocracy Genius & Mind.

Caruso=2,500=3,000=30%=P3.0D=3.0=Creativity=Stars=Muses=3 March = C=I>>GIL.
Carve=8,500=9,000=90%=P9.00D=9.0=Abst.=Gods=Saturn=9Sept.>>A=Ø.
Carver George Washington=3,500=4,000=40%=P4.0D=Govt.=4 April=Hermes=G=A4.
Carving=8,000=80%=P8.0D=Economy=Currency=8 Aug.=Zeus>>E=v.
Caryatid=5,000=50%=P5.00D=Law=Time=Venus=5 May = Aphrodite>>L=N.
Casaba=6,500=7,000=70%=P7.0D=7.0=Language=Assets=Mars=7 July=Pleiades
Casablanca=6,500=7,000=70%=P7.0D=7.0=Language=Assets=Mars=7 July=Pleiades
Casals Pablo=2,000=20%=P2.00D=2.0=Nature=Moon=2 Feb.=Cupid=N=C+_.
Casanova de Seingait=4,000=40%=P4.0D=Govt.=4 April=Mercury=Hermes=G=A4.
Cascade=7,500=8,000=80%=P8.0D=Economy=Currency=8 Aug.=Zeus>>E=v.
Cascade Range=5,500=5.5=80%=P5.50=Earth-Midway=5 May = Gaia.
Cascara=7,000=70%=P7.0D=7.0=Language=Assets=Mars=7 July=Pleiades
Case(1)=36,000=4,000=40%=P4.0D=Govt. =Creat.=4 April=Mercury=Hermes=G=A4.
Case(2)=14,500=15,000=15%=P1.50D=1.5=Authority=Crown=Solar Core=1 May = Maia.
Case history=8,500=9,000=90%=P9.00D=9.0=Abst.=Gods=Saturn=9Sept.>>A=Ø.
Casein=7,500=8,000=80%=P8.0D=Economy=Currency=8 Aug.=Zeus>>E=v.
Caseload=8,500=9,000=90%=P9.00D=9.0=Abst.=Gods=Saturn=9Sept.>>A=Ø.
Casement=6,000=60%=P6.0D=Man=Earth=Royalty=6 June=Gaia=Maia>>M=M2.
Case study=7,500=8,000=80%=P8.0D=Economy=Currency=8 Aug.=Zeus>>E=v.
Casework=5,000=50%=P5.50D=Law=Time=Venus=5 May = Aphrodite>>L=N.

Cash=11,000=11%=P1.10D=1.1=Idea=Brainchild=11Nov=Athena>>I=MT.
Maks Currencies is solar cash measured by natural diamond values computed by
Makupedia. It is also digital and convertible to electronic forms. Maks is the first anti-
inflation currency ever invented and so it is known as inflation proof. The resultant
value proves that what we call cash is the brainchild of Zeus being Athena. Since
Athena is the Mind Goddess it is logical that She manifested as Maks. The rest cash
are matter driven.

Hence Mind Banking is the reality of the Creatocracy Bank and both are inventions. The Maks Currencies was first patented in Nigeria in 2020. Globally it is copyright protected. Cash in the Maks is the phrase for cash issued in the MaksCurrencies. Mind or Mine Cash.

Cashew=8,000=80%=P8.0D=Economy=Currency=8 Aug.=Zeus>>E=v.
Cashier(1)=12,000=12%=P1.20D=1.2=Knowledge=Education=12Dec.=Athena>>K=F.
Cashier(2)=6,500=7,000=70%=P7.0D=7.0=Language=Assets=Mars=7 July=Pleiades
Cashier's check=7,000=70%=P7.0D=7.0=Language=Assets=Mars=7 July=Pleiades
Cash machine=2,000=20%=P2.00D=2.0=Nature=Moon=2 Feb.=Cupid=N=C+_.
Cashmere=6,000=60%=P6.0D=Man=Earth=Royalty=6 June=Gaia=Maia>>M=M2.
Cashmere=1,000=100%=10.0=1.0=Mind=Sun=1 January=Helios >> M=E4.
Cash register=8,000=80%=P8.0D=Economy=Currency=8 Aug.=Zeus>>E=v.
Casing=2,000=20%=P2.00D=2.0=Nature=Moon=2 Feb.=Cupid=N=C+_.
Casino=4,500=5,000=50%=P5.00D=Law=Time=Venus=5 May = Aphrodite>>L=N.
Cask=4,500=5,000=50%=P5.00D=Law=Time=Venus=5 May = Aphrodite>>L=N.

Casket=4,500=5,000=50%=P5.00D=Law=Time=Venus=5 May = Aphrodite>>L=N.
A casket is used to convey dead persons to the underworld. Resultant shows that a casket is a border line from one point to the other. This is established proof for borderlines. Borderlines are boundaries and Hermes by right is the God of borders. Hermes is death itself as God of the underworld but the casket is its medium of transfer. Interestingly Cupid is the vaporizer to the Moon being its medium. Hence the dead travel to the Moon first meaning that the human spirit is a PGI element of the Moon. The reason for this is that all men are made from Moon Water known as Mare or Moon land. The Creatocracy tracks the original source of all persons by lunar computations. Peter Matthews-Akukalia is from Mare Imbrium - the Sea of Showers, an authority of the Skies, particulate matter and its energy.
Discovery and inventions apotheosized Him a God of the Skies through the Solar Core.

Casper=5,000=50%=P5.00D=Law=Time=Venus=5 May = Aphrodite>>L=N.
Caspian Sea=4,500=5,000=50%=P5.00D=Law=Time=Venus=5 May = Aphrodite>>L=N.
Casque=1,000=100%=10.0=1.0=Mind=Sun=1 January=Helios >> M=E4.

Cassandra=8,500=9,000=90%=P9.00D=9.0=Abst.=Gods=Saturn=9Sept.>>A=Ø.
In Greek Myth, Cassandra is a Trojan prophetess fared by Apollo never to be believed. One that utters unheeded prophecies. Such persons are borderlines and will not be believed until they arrive abstraction points and become apotheosized into the Council of Gods. This is only achieved through the adoption to wit and offering a Cow sacrifice in a Feast of Apotheosis. The first of these was the apotheosis of Castle Makupedia on 13.10.2021 in Ikotun, Lagos. Nigeria. Afterwards tempted by the devil in three days and forgiven.

Cassatt Mary Stevenson=2,500=3,000=30%=P3.0D=3.0=Muses=3March= C=I>>GIL.
Cassava=8,500=9,000=90%=P9.00D=9.0=Abst.=Gods=Saturn=9Sept.>>A=Ø.
Casserole=10,000=1,000=100%=10.0=Physicality=Tech.=10 Oct.=Uranus=P=1Ø.
Cassette=7,000=70%=P7.0D=7.0=Language=Assets=Mars=7 July=Pleiades
Cassette deck=4,500=5,000=50%=P5.00D=Law=Time=Venus=5 May = Aphrodite>>L=N.
Cassette player=4,000=40%=P4.0D=Govt. =Creat.=4 April=Mercury=Hermes=G=A4.
Cassia=12,500=13,000=13%=P1.30=Solar Core=Faculty=13 January=Athena.
Cassiopeia=4,000=40%=P4.0D=Govt. =Creat.=4 April=Mercury=Hermes=G=A4.
Cassiterite=6,500=7,000=70%=P7.0D=7.0=Language=Assets=Mars=7 July=Pleiades
Cassock=4,000=40%=P4.0D=Govt. =Creat.=4 April=Mercury=Hermes=G=A4.
Cassowary=6,500=7,000=70%=P7.0D=7.0=Language=Assets=Mars=7 July=Pleiades

---

Cast=34,000=4.3>>2.0=2,000=20%=P2.00D=2.0=Nature=Moon=2 Feb.=Cupid=N=C+_.
To cast also includes to compute. Computing is building in abstract that manifest as an
asset in the physical. Mind Computing built the brick walls of Castle Makupedia.

Castanets=10,000=1,000=100%=10.0=Physicality=Tech.=10 Oct.=Uranus=P=1Ø.
Castaway=4,000=40%=P4.0D=Govt. =Creat.=4 April=Mercury=Hermes=G=A4.
Caste=13,000=13%=P1.30=Solar Core=Faculty=13 January=Athena.
Caster=14,500=1,500=15%=P1.50D=1.5=Authority=Crown=Solar Core=1 May = Maia.
Castigate=2,500=3,000=30%=P3.0D=3.0=Muses=3March= C=I>>GIL.
Castile=5,000=50%=P5.00D=Law=Time=Venus=5 May = Aphrodite>>L=N.
Castilian=5,000=50%=P5.00D=Law=Time=Venus=5 May = Aphrodite>>L=N.
Casting=4,500=5,000=50%=P5.00D=Law=Time=Venus=5 May = Aphrodite>>L=N.
Cast iron=7,500=8,000=80%=P8.0D=Economy=Currency=8 Aug.=Zeus>>E=v.
Cast-i-ron plant=1,000=100%=Physicality= Tech.=10 Oct.=Uranus=P=1Ø.

Castle=6,000=60%=P6.0D=Man=Earth=Royalty=6 June=Gaia=Maia>>M=M2.
Castle Makupedia is the name of the God of Creatocracy Genius & Mind. And His
residence. He invented the literature genre called Castle where plays are bonded to express
a conviction. His castles are so named. Exclusive in nature He wears the Solar Crown
based on the computations of the Solar Core. His deified status is intergenerational
hence Castle is a right for their surnames. His Creative Excellency & Godship, Emperor
of the Sovereign Creatocratic Nations of Paradise. Peter Matthews - Akukalia invented
the Makupedia the World Digital Smart Dictionary. He invented Makupedialand, the
Disean Nation of Testamentary Poetry. He invented the Creatocracy Republic in his 22
Dramatic MindArts. He invented the MindTech Sciences through his Naturecology. He
invented his Cosmic Sciences through his Psychoastronomy. The Creatocratic Charter
is his throne and =Makupedia= is his Solar Crown. He is Castle Makupedia the Disean
God of Creatocracy Genius Mind & Mindom. The "Mindom" is the official reference
word for his Kingdom.

TABLE OF THE MAKABET GODS.

=A=>> Athena =>> The Spirit of the Gods =>> 1.3

=B=>> Maia =>> The Mind of the Gods =>> 1.5

=C=>> Uranus =>> Cronus >> Timelessness >> 10.0

=D=>> Athena =>> The Spirit of the Gods =>> 1.3

=E=>> Athena =>> The Spirit of the Gods =>> 1.3

=F=>> Zeus >> ZeJeAl >> The Almighty of the Gods =>> 8.0

=G=>> Maia =>> The Mind of the Gods =>> 1.5

=H=>> Aphrodite >> The Law of the Gods =>>5.0

=I=>> Muses =>> Inspiration of the Gods =>> 3.0

=J=>> Muses =>> Inspiration of the Gods =>> 3.0

=K=>> Muses =>> Inspiration of the Gods =>> 3.0

=L=>> Muses =>> Inspiration of the Gods =>> 3.0

=M=>> Muses =>> Inspiration of the Gods =>> 3.0

=N=>> Muses =>> Inspiration of the Gods =>> 3.0

=O=>> Zeus >> ZeJeAl >> The Almighty of the Gods =>> 8.0

=P=>> Muses =>> Inspiration of the Gods =>> 3.0

=Q=>> Muses =>> Inspiration of the Gods =>> 3.0

=R=>> Muses =>> Inspiration of the Gods =>> 3.0

=S=>> Hermes >> The Merchandise Agency of the Gods =>>4.0

=T=>> Muses =>> Inspiration of the Gods =>> 3.0

=U=>> Muses =>> Inspiration of the Gods =>> 3.0

=V=>> Muses =>> Inspiration of the Gods =>> 3.0

=W=>> Muses =>> Inspiration of the Gods =>> 3.0

=X=>> Uranus =>> Cronus >> Timelessness >> 10.0

=Y=>> Hermes >> The Merchandise Agency of the Gods =>>4.0

=Z=>> Muses =>> Inspiration of the Gods =>> 3.0

The Castle Makupedia means the Makabet Gods-in-Council who are operant in Hermes. Note that mansion and castle are synonymous codes made by Jesus >> Hermes. Computing reveal the true identity revealed as Peter Matthews-Akukalia. See 1John 1:1-10. See Naturecology, the cosmic origin of Castle Makupedia. See Jehovah WDSD.

Castle Reagh=3,500=4,000=40%=P4.0D=Govt. =Creat.=4 April=Mercury=Hermes=G=A4. A name for Robert Stewart. A British politician. Castle Makupedia is the spiritual name for Peter Matthews-Akukalia. A Nigerian Author, Mind & Creative Scientist >> Creative Mind Scientist, Inventor, King and Emperor. He is the apotheosized God of Creatocracy. His works are universal and world oriented thus he is a World Scientist. A Global citizen.

Castoff=2,500=3,000=30%=P3.0D=3.0=Muses=3March= C=I>>GIL.

Castor=2,500=3,000=30%=P3.0D=3.0=Muses=3March= C=I>>GIL.

Castor oil=8,500=9,000=90%=P9.00D=9.0=Abst.=Gods=Saturn=9Sept.>>A=Ø.

Castrate=3,500=4,000=40%=P4.0D=Govt. =Creat.=4 April=Mercury=Hermes=G=A4.

Castries=7,000=70%=P7.0D=7.0=Language=Assets=Mars=7 July=Pleiades

Castro Fidel=2,500=3,000=30%=P3.0D=3.0=Muses=3March= C=I>>GIL.
Casual=10,000=1,000=100%=10.0=Physicality=Tech.=10 Oct.=Uranus=P=1Ø.
Casualty=7,000=70%=P7.0D=7.0=Language=Assets=Mars=7 July=Pleiades
Casuistry=4,500=5,000=50%=P5.00D=Law=Time=Venus=5 May = Aphrodite>>L=N.
Cat=14,000=14%=P1.40D=1.4=Mgt.=13May=Athena=SC=0.1
CAT=3,000=30%=P3.0D=3.0=Muses=3March= C=I>>GIL.
Catabolism=6,000=60%=P6.0D=Man=Earth=Royalty=6 June=Gaia=Maia>>M=M2.
Cataclysm=3,500=4,000=40%=P4.0D=Govt.=Creat.=4 April=Mercury=Hermes=G=A4.
Catacomb=3,500=4,000=40%=P4.0D=Govt.=Creat.=4 April=Mercury=Hermes=G=A4.
Catafalque=5,500=5.5=80%=P5.50=Earth-Midway=5 May = Gaia.
Catalan=4,500=5,000=50%=P5.00D=Law=Time=Venus=5 May = Aphrodite>>L=N.
Catalepsy=6,000=60%=P6.0D=Man=Earth=Royalty=6 June=Gaia=Maia>>M=M2.
Catalog=8,000=80%=P8.0D=Economy=Currency=8 Aug.=Zeus>>E=v.
Catalonia=5,500=5.5=80%=P5.50=Earth-Midway=5 May = Gaia.
Catalpa=8,500=9,000=90%=P9.00D=9.0=Abst.=Gods=Saturn=9Sept.>>A=Ø.
Catalysis=6,000=60%=P6.0D=Man=Earth=Royalty=6 June=Gaia=Maia>>M=M2.
Catalyst=9,500=10,000=1,000=100%=10.0=Physicality=Tech.=10 Oct.=Uranus=P=1Ø.
Catalytic converter=6,000=60%=P6.0D=Man=Earth=Royalty=6 June=Gaia=Maia>>M=M2.
Catalyze=5,000=50%=P5.00D=Law=Time=Venus=5 May = Aphrodite>>L=N.
Catamaran=5,500=5.5=80%=P5.50=Earth-Midway=5 May = Gaia.
Catamount=1,500=15%=P1.50D=1.5=Authority=Crown=Solar Core=1 May = Maia.
Catania=8,500=9,000=90%=P9.00D=9.0=Abst.=Gods=Saturn=9Sept.>>A=Ø.
Catapult=8,500=9,000=90%=P9.00D=9.0=Abst.=Gods=Saturn=9Sept.>>A=Ø.
Cataract=8,000=80%=P8.0D=Economy=Currency=8 Aug.=Zeus>>E=v.
Catarrh=4,500=5,000=50%=P5.00D=Law=Time=Venus=5 May = Aphrodite>>L=N.
Catastrophe=3,000=30%=P3.0D=3.0=Muses=3March= C=I>>GIL.
Catatonia=11,000=11%=P1.10D=1.1=Idea=Brainchild=11Nov=Athena>>I=MT.
Catawba=8,500=9,000=90%=P9.00D=9.0=Abst.=Gods=Saturn=9Sept.>>A=Ø.
Catbird=4,500=5,000=50%=P5.00D=Law=Time=Venus=5 May = Aphrodite>>L=N.
Catcall=4,500=5,000=50%=P5.00D=Law=Time=Venus=5 May = Aphrodite>>L=N.

Catch=10,000=1,000=100%=10.0=Physicality=Tech.=10 Oct.=Uranus=P=1Ø.
Due to high volume of data count involved in such words as "catch", the quantum bundle classification method is adopted for convenience. Thus the 10,000=1,000 Psalms system. King David writes that 1,000 shall fall at your side and 10,000 at your right hand....

Catch-22=10,000=1,000=100%=10.0=Physicality=Tech.=10 Oct.=Uranus=P=1Ø.
Catch all=4,500=5,000=50%=P5.00D=Law=Time=Venus=5 May = Aphrodite>>L=N.
Catcher=5,500=5.5=80%=P5.50=Earth-Midway=5 May = Gaia.
Catching=2,500=3,000=30%=P3.0D=3.0=Muses=3March= C=I>>GIL.
Catchup=1,500=15%=P1.50D=1.5=Authority=Crown=Solar Core=1 May = Maia.
Catchword=7,000=70%=P7.0D=7.0=Language=Assets=Mars=7 July=Pleiades
Catchy=3,500=4,000=40%=P4.0D=Govt. =Creat.=4 April=Mercury=Hermes=G=A4.
Catechism=8,000=80%=P8.0D=Economy=Currency=8 Aug.=Zeus>>E=v.

Catechumen=4,500=5,000=50%=P5.00D=Law=Time=Venus=5 May = Aphrodite>>L=N.
Categorical=8,000=80%=P8.0D=Economy=Currency=8 Aug.=Zeus>>E=v.
Categorize=2,000=20%=P2.00D=2.0=Nature=Moon=2 Feb.=Cupid=N=C+_.
Category=4,500=5,000=50%=P5.00D=Law=Time=Venus=5 May = Aphrodite>>L=N.
Cater=7,500=8,000=80%=P8.0D=Economy=Currency=8 Aug.=Zeus>>E=v.
Cater cornered=1,000=100%=10.0=1.0=Mind=Sun=1 January=Helios >> M=E4.
Catty-corner=1,000=100%=10.0=1.0=Mind=Sun=1 January=Helios >> M=E4.
Caterpillar=5,000=50%=P5.00D=Law=Time=Venus=5 May = Aphrodite>>L=N.
Caterwaul=3,500=4,000=40%=P4.0D=Govt. =Creat.=4 April=Mercury=Hermes=G=A4.
Catfish=5,500=5.5=80%=P5.50=Earth-Midway=5 May = Gaia.
Catgut=5,500=5.5=80%=P5.50=Earth-Midway=5 May = Gaia.
Catharsis=9,500=10,000=1,000=100%=10.0=Physicality=Tech.=10 Oct.=Uranus=P=1Ø.
Cathartic=2,000=20%=P2.00D=2.0=Nature=Moon=2 Feb.=Cupid=N=C+_.
Cathedral=3,500=4,000=40%=P4.0D=Govt. =Creat.=4 April=Mercury=Hermes=G=A4.
Carter Willa Sibert=2,000=20%=P2.00D=2.0=Nature=Moon=2 Feb.=Cupid=N=C+_.

Catherine I=4,000=40%=P4.0D=Govt. =Creat.=4 April=Mercury=Hermes=G=A4.
Justina 1 (8 May, 1974-Date), Goddess & Empress of Paradise Nations. Alice 1 (13th March, 1986-Date). Queen of Fortune of Paradise Nations. Next to the Goddess in rank. Helen of Bulwark>>Helen of Boulevard (1978?), Goddess Director of De-Royal Makupedia Limited. Owns 20% shares and 80% to the King and Emperor. She is the Angel of Paradise Nations. Wole Olaniyan is the Captain of the Creative Sciences and elevated to the status of His Lordship. Plays a Business Advisory role to the King and supported the financing of the Royal family at the early stage of project development. Purchased a Quran for the King.

Catherine II=5,000=50%=P5.00D=Law=Time=Venus=5 May = Aphrodite>>L=N.
Catherine de Médicis=10,000=1,000=100%=10.0=Phy.=Tech.=10 Oct.=Uranus=P=1Ø.
Catherine of Aragon=4,000=40%=P4.0D=Govt. =Creat.=4 April=Mercury=Hermes=G=A4.
Cathode=7,000=70%=P7.0D=7.0=Language=Assets=Mars=7 July=Pleiades
Cathode ray tube=8,500=9,000=90%=P9.00D=9.0=Abst.=Gods=Saturn=9Sept.>>A=Ø.
Catholic=6,500=7,000=70%=P7.0D=7.0=Language=Assets=Mars=7 July=Pleiades
Catholicism=5,000=50%=P5.00D=Law=Time=Venus=5 May = Aphrodite>>L=N.
Cat line=4,000=40%=P4.0D=Govt. =Creat.=4 April=Mercury=Hermes=G=A4.
Cation=9,000=90%=P9.00D=9.0=Abst.=Gods=Saturn=9Sept.>>A=Ø.
Catkin=7,000=70%=P7.0D=7.0=Language=Assets=Mars=7 July=Pleiades
Catnap=2,500=3,000=30%=P3.0D=3.0=Muses=3March= C=I>>GIL.
Catnip=4,500=5,000=50%=P5.00D=Law=Time=Venus=5 May = Aphrodite>>L=N.
Cato Marcus(1)=4,500=5,000=50%=P5.00D=Law=Time=Venus=5May=Odite>>L=N.
Cato, Marcus Porcius(2)=7,000=70%=P7.0D=7.0=Language=Assets=Mars=7 July=Pleiades
Cat-o-nine-tails=5,500=5.5=80%=P5.50=Earth-Midway=5 May = Gaia.
CAT scanner=8,500=9,000=90%=P9.00D=9.0=Abst.=Gods=Saturn=9Sept.>>A=Ø.
Cat's cradle=9,000=90%=P9.00D=9.0=Abst.=Gods=Saturn=9Sept.>>A=Ø.
Cat's eye=8,000=80%=P8.0D=Economy=Currency=8 Aug.=Zeus>>E=v.

Cats kill Mountains=4,500=5,000=50%=P5.00D=Law=Time=Venus=5 May =Odite>>L=N.
Cat's paw=4,500=5,000=50%=P5.00D=Law=Time=Venus=5 May = Aphrodite>>L=N.
Catsup=1,500=15%=P1.50D=1.5=Authority=Crown=Solar Core=1 May = Maia.
Catt Carrie (Lane)=2,000=20%=P2.00D=2.0=Nature=Moon=2 Feb.=Cupid=N=C+_.
Cattail=7,000=70%=P7.0D=7.0=Language=Assets=Mars=7 July=Pleiades

---

Cattle=8,000=80%=P8.0D=Economy=Currency=8 Aug.=Zeus>>E=v.
Sacrifice of cattle are rights of Zeus the Most High Jehovah GOD. Zeus is His name and
Jehovah is His title meaning my Lord. In order words the Almighty GOD. Our Discovery!

Catty=1,000=100%=10.0=1.0=Mind=Sun=1 January=Helios >> M=E4.
Catty cornered=1,500=15%=P1.50D=1.5=Authority=Crown=Solar Core=1 May = Maia.
Catullus Gaius=3,500=4,000=40%=P4.0D=Govt.=4 April=Mercury=Hermes=G=A4.
CATV=1,500=15%=P1.50D=1.5=Authority=Crown=Solar Core=1 May = Maia.
Catwalk=5,500=5.5=80%=P5.50=Earth-Midway=5 May = Gaia.
Caucasian=20,000=2,000=20%=P2.00D=2.0=Nature=Moon=2 Feb.=Cupid=N=C+_.
Caucasoid=6,000=60%=P6.0D=Man=Earth=Royalty=6 June=Gaia=Maia>>M=M2.
Caucasus=7,500=8,000=80%=P8.0D=Economy=Currency=8 Aug.=Zeus>>E=v.
Caucasus Mountains=5,500=5.5=80%=P5.50=Earth-Midway=5 May = Gaia.
Caucus=11,500=12,000=12%=P1.20D=1.2=Knowledge=Education=12Dec.=Athena>>K=F.
Caudal=5,000=50%=P5.00D=Law=Time=Venus=5 May = Aphrodite>>L=N.
Caudillo=3,500=4,000=40%=P4.0D=Govt. =Creat.=4 April=Mercury=Hermes=G=A4.
Caught=3,000=30%=P3.0D=3.0=Muses=3March= C=I>>GIL.
Caul=7,000=70%=P7.0D=7.0=Language=Assets=Mars=7 July=Pleiades
Cauldron=1,500=15%=P1.50D=1.5=Authority=Crown=Solar Core=1 May = Maia.
Cauliflower=8,500=9,000=90%=P9.00D=9.0=Abst.=Gods=Saturn=9Sept.>>A=Ø.
Caulk=9,000=90%=P9.00D=9.0=Abst.=Gods=Saturn=9Sept.>>A=Ø.
Causal=3,000=30%=P3.0D=3.0=Muses=3March= C=I>>GIL.
Causation=4,500=5,000=50%=P5.00D=Law=Time=Venus=5 May = Aphrodite>>L=N.
Cause=15,000=1,500=15%=P1.50D=1.5=Authority=Crown=Solar Core=1 May = Maia.
Cause célèbre=6,000=60%=P6.0D=Man=Earth=Royalty=6 June=Gaia=Maia>>M=M2.
Causeway=3,500=4,000=40%=P4.0D=Govt. =Creat.=4 April=Mercury=Hermes=G=A4.
Caustic=7,000=70%=P7.0D=7.0=Language=Assets=Mars=7 July=Pleiades
Cauterize=5,500=5.5=80%=P5.50=Earth-Midway=5 May = Gaia.
Caution=6,000=60%=P6.0D=Man=Earth=Royalty=6 June=Gaia=Maia>>M=M2.
Cautious=2,500=3,000=30%=P3.0D=3.0=Muses=3March= C=I>>GIL.
Cavalcade=5,000=50%=P5.00D=Law=Time=Venus=5 May = Aphrodite>>L=N.
Cavalier=9,500=10,000=1,000=100%=10.0=Physicality=Tech.=10 Oct.=Uranus=P=1Ø.
Cavalry=5,500=5.5=80%=P5.50=Earth-Midway=5 May = Gaia.
Cave=12,000=12%=P1.20D=1.2=Knowledge=Education=12Dec.=Athena>>K=F.
Caveat=2,000=20%=P2.00D=2.0=Nature=Moon=2 Feb.=Cupid=N=C+_.
Cave-in=3,500=4,000=40%=P4.0D=Govt. =Creat.=4 April=Mercury=Hermes=G=A4.
Caveman=8,500=9,000=90%=P9.00D=9.0=Abst.=Gods=Saturn=9Sept.>>A=Ø.
Caviar=6,500=7,000=70%=P7.0D=7.0=Language=Assets=Mars=7 July=Pleiades

Cavil=3,000=30%=P3.0D=3.0=Muses=3March= C=I>>GIL.
Cavity=6,000=60%=P6.0D=Man=Earth=Royalty=6 June=Gaia=Maia>>M=M2.
Cavort=2,000=20%=P2.00D=2.0=Nature=Moon=2 Feb.=Cupid=N=C+_.
Cavour Conte Camilo=2,500=3,000=30%=P3.0D=3.0=Muses=3March= C=I>>GIL.
Caw=5,000=50%=P5.00D=Law=Time=Venus=5 May = Aphrodite>>L=N.
Caxton William=2,500=3,000=30%=P3.0D=3.0=Muses=3March= C=I>>GIL.
Cay=4,500=5,000=50%=P5.00D=Law=Time=Venus=5 May = Aphrodite>>L=N.
Cayenne=6,500=7,000=70%=P7.0D=7.0=Language=Assets=Mars=7 July=Pleiades
Cayenne pepper=6,000=60%=P6.0D=Man=Earth=Royalty=6 June=Gaia=Maia>>M=M2.
Cayman=1,500=15%=P1.50D=1.5=Authority=Crown=Solar Core=1 May = Maia.
Cayman Islands=8,500=9,000=90%=P9.00D=9.0=Abst.=Gods=Saturn=9Sept.>>A=Ø.
Cayuga=10,000=1,000=100%=10.0=Physicality=Tech.=10 Oct.=Uranus=P=1Ø.
Cayuse=5,000=50%=P5.00D=Law=Time=Venus=5 May = Aphrodite>>L=N.
CB=1,000=100%=10.0=1.0=Mind=Sun=1 January=Helios >> M=E4.
C.B.D.=1,500=15%=P1.50D=1.5=Authority=Crown=Solar Core=1 May = Maia.
CBW=2,000=20%=P2.00D=2.0=Nature=Moon=2 Feb.=Cupid=N=C+_.
cc=2,000=20%=P2.00D=2.0=Nature=Moon=2 Feb.=Cupid=N=C+_.
CCC=3,000=30%=P3.0D=3.0=Muses=3March= C=I>>GIL.
cckw.=500=5%=P5.00D=5.0=Law=Time=Venus=5 May=Aphrodite>>L=N.
CCTV=1,500=15%=P1.50D=1.5=Authority=Crown=Solar Core=1 May = Maia.
cd=500=5%=P5.00D=5.0=Law=Time=Venus=5 May=Aphrodite>>L=N.
Cd=2,500=3,000=30%=P3.0D=3.0=Muses=3March= C=I>>GIL.
CD=4,500=5,000=50%=P5.00D=Law=Time=Venus=5 May = Aphrodite>>L=N.
cd.=1,000=100%=10.0=1.0=Mind=Sun=1 January=Helios >> M=E4.
CDC=2,000=20%=P2.00D=2.0=Nature=Moon=2 Feb.=Cupid=N=C+_.
Cdr.=500=5%=P5.00D=5.0=Law=Time=Venus=5 May=Aphrodite>>L=N.
CD/ROM=6,000=60%=P6.0D=Man=Earth=Royalty=6 June=Gaia=Maia>>M=M2.
CDT=1,500=15%=P1.50D=1.5=Authority=Crown=Solar Core=1 May = Maia.
Ce=2,500=3,000=30%=P3.0D=3.0=Muses=3March= C=I>>GIL.
C.E.=2,500=3,000=30%=P3.0D=3.0=Muses=3March= C=I>>GIL.
Cease=5,500=5.5=80%=P5.50=Earth-Midway=5 May = Gaia.
Cease-fire=4,500=5,000=50%=P5.00D=Law=Time=Venus=5 May = Aphrodite>>L=N.
Ceaseless=1,000=100%=10.0=1.0=Mind=Sun=1 January=Helios >> M=E4.
Cebu=9,000=90%=P9.00D=9.0=Abst.=Gods=Saturn=9Sept.>>A=Ø.
Cecil Robert=6,500=7,000=70%=P7.0D=7.0=Language=Assets=Mars=7 July=Pleiades
Cecil, Robert Arthur=7,000=70%=P7.0D=7.0=Language=Assets=Mars=7 July=Pleiades
Cecilia=3,000=30%=P3.0D=3.0=Creativity=Stars=Muses=3 March= C=I>>GIL.
Cecum=4,500=5,000=50%=P5.00D=Law=Time=Venus=5 May = Aphrodite>>L=N.
Cedar=8,000=80%=P8.0D=Economy=Currency=8 Aug.=Zeus>>E=v.
Cedar Rapids=5,000=50%=P5.00D=Law=Time=Venus=5 May = Aphrodite>>L=N.
Cede=5,000=50%=P5.00D=Law=Time=Venus=5 May = Aphrodite>>L=N.
Cedi=2,000=20%=P2.00D=2.0=Nature=Moon=2 Feb.=Cupid=N=C+_.
Cedilla=8,500=9,000=90%=P9.00D=9.0=Abst.=Gods=Saturn=9Sept.>>A=Ø.
Ceiba=2,000=20%=P2.00D=2.0=Nature=Moon=2 Feb.=Cupid=N=C+_.
Ceiling=12,500=13,000=13%=P1.30=Solar Core=Faculty=13 January=Athena.

Celebes=5,000=50%=P5.00D=Law=Time=Venus=5 May = Aphrodite>>L=N.
Celebes Sea=5,500=5.5=80%=P5.50=Earth-Midway=5 May = Gaia.

Celebrate=8,500=9,000=90%=P9.00D=9.0=Abst.=Gods=Saturn=9Sept.>>A=Ø.
Celebrate means famous > Latin Celeber. It is a borderline from the human economy to the offering of sacrifices in feasts to the Council of Gods or the Creatocracy. The economy implications involves a willful and cheerful commitment to make necessary expenses. One becomes famous based on the reason for the celebration as a reward from the Gods. On 13th October 2021, the Feast of Apotheosis was celebrated by the Creatocracy to deify Peter Matthews-Akukalia as the King of the Creative Sciences; Most Sovereign Emperor, Creatocratic Nations of Paradise and the God of Creatocracy Genius and Mind. This is his name fame and grace to the glory of the Most High GOD.

Celebrated=4,000=40%=P4.0D=Govt. =Creatocracy=4 April=Mercury=Hermes=G=A4.
Celebrity=6,000=60%=P6.0D=Man=Earth=Royalty=6 June=Gaia=Maia>>M=M2.
Celerity=1,000=100%=10.0=1.0=Mind=Sun=1 January=Helios >> M=E4.
Celery=5,000=50%=P5.00D=Law=Time=Venus=5 May = Aphrodite>>L=N.
Celesta=4,500=5,000=50%=P5.00D=Law=Time=Venus=5 May = Aphrodite>>L=N.

Celestial=4,000=40%=P4.0D=Govt. =Creatocracy=4 April=Mercury=Hermes=G=A4.
Interestingly the celestial is administered by the Creatocracy. A creative government.

Celestial equator=6,500=7,000=70%=P7.0D=7.0=Language=Assets=Mars=7 July=Pleiades
Celestial navigation=4,000=40%=P4.0D=Govt.=Creat.=4 April=Mercury=Hermes=G=A4.

Celestial sphere=6,000=60%=P6.0D=Man=Earth=Royalty=6 June=Gaia=Maia>>M=M2.
An imaginary sphere of infinite extent with the earth at its center. Gaia rules this sphere. Anything imaginary is imagination at the faculty of Man. Hence we connect to the spiritual sphere of infinite intelligence through our imagination. This is prayer a communication with GOD. Man resides at the center of the celestial sphere. Man resides on earth, belly of Gaia.

Celibate=19,000=19,000=19%=P1.90=1.9=Planetary Energy=Mind of God=Maia.
Cell=10,000=1,000=100%=10.0=Physicality=Tech.=10 Oct.=Uranus=P=1Ø.
Cellar=5,000=50%=P5.00D=Law=Time=Venus=5 May = Aphrodite>>L=N.
Cell block=5,500=5.5=80%=P5.50=Earth-Midway=5 May = Gaia.
Cellini Benvenuto=3,000=30%=P3.0D=3.0=Creativity=Stars=Muses=3 March= C=I>>GIL.
Cellmate=5,000=50%=P5.00D=Law=Time=Venus=5 May = Aphrodite>>L=N.
Cello=7,500=8,000=80%=P8.0D=Economy=Currency=8 Aug.=Zeus>>E=v.
Cellophane=5,000=50%=P5.00D=Law=Time=Venus=5 May = Aphrodite>>L=N.
Cellular=3,500=4,000=40%=P4.0D=Govt. =Creatocracy=4April=Mercury=Hermes=G=A4.
Cellulite=5,000=50%=P5.00D=Law=Time=Venus=5 May = Aphrodite>>L=N.

Celluloid=7,500=8,000=80%=P8.0D=Economy=Currency=8 Aug.=Zeus>>E=v.
Cellulose=11,000=11%=P1.10D=1.1=Idea=Brainchild=11Nov=Athena>>I=MT.
Cellulose acetate=4,500=5,000=50%=P5.00D=Law=Time=Venus=5 May = Odite>>L=N.
Celsius=14,000=14%=P1.40D=1.4=Mgt.=13May=Athena=SC=0.1
Celt=8,500=9,000=90%=P9.00D=9.0=Abst.=Gods=Saturn=9Sept.>>A=Ø.
Celtic=12,000=12%=P1.20D=1.2=Knowledge=Education=12Dec.=Athena>>K=F.
Cembalo=1,000=100%=10.0=1.0=Mind=Sun=1 January=Helios >> M=E4.
Cement=22,000=2.2>>4.0=4,000=40%=P4.0D=Govt.=4 April=Mercury=Hermes=G=A4.
Cement mixer=10,000=1,000=100%=10.0=Physicality=Tech.=10 Oct.=Uranus=P=1Ø.
Cementum=4,000=40%=P4.0D=Govt. =Creatocracy=4 April=Mercury=Hermes=G=A4.
Cemetery=3,500=4,000=40%=P4.0D=Govt.=Creatocr.=4April=Mercury=Hermes=G=A4.
-cene=1,500=15%=P1.50D=1.5=Authority=Crown=Solar Core=1 May = Maia.
Cenotaph=5,000=50%=P5.00D=Law=Time=Venus=5 May = Aphrodite>>L=N.
Cenozoic=12,000=12%=P1.20D=1.2=Knowledge=Education=12Dec.=Athena>>K=F.
Censer=5,500=5.5=80%=P5.50=Earth-Midway=5 May = Gaia.
Censor=12,500=13,000=13%=P1.30=Solar Core=Faculty=13 January=Athena.
Censorious=4,000=40%=P4.0D=Govt. =Creatocracy=4 April=Mercury=Hermes=G=A4.
Censorship=5,500=5.5=80%=P5.50=Earth-Midway=5 May = Gaia.
Censure=6,000=60%=P6.0D=Man=Earth=Royalty=6 June=Gaia=Maia>>M=M2.
Census=2,500=3,000=30%=P3.0D=3.0=Creativity=Stars=Muses=3 March= C=I>>GIL.
Cent=2,000=20%=P2.00D=2.0=Nature=Moon=2 Feb.=Cupid=N=C+_.

Centaur=10,500=11,000=11%=P1.10D=1.1=Idea=Brainchild=11Nov=Athena>>I=MT.
Greek myth. One of a race of monsters having the head, arms, and trunk of a man and
the body and legs of a horse. The computational resultant reveals it is a work of Athena
perhaps a first brainchild or idea at an attempt to design the appropriate human race. The
Quran teaches that man was first made in different forms. Bible confirms the cycle of life.

Centavo=2,000=20%=P2.00D=2.0=Nature=Moon=2 Feb.=Cupid=N=C+_.
Centenarian=3,500=4,000=40%=P4.0D=Govt.=Creato=4 April=Mercury=Hermes=G=A4.
Centenary=1,000=100%=10.0=1.0=Mind=Sun=1 January=Helios >> M=E4.
Centennial=1,500=15%=P1.50D=1.5=Authority=Crown=Solar Core=1 May = Maia.
Center=10,000=1,000=100%=10.0=Physicality=Tech.=10 Oct.=Uranus=P=1Ø.
Centerboard=7,000=70%=P7.0D=7.0=Language=Assets=Mars=7 July=Pleiades
Center field=4,500=5,000=50%=P5.00D=Law=Time=Venus=5 May = Aphrodite>>L=N.
Center fold=5,500=5.5=80%=P5.50=Earth-Midway=5 May = Gaia.
Center of mass=7,500=8,000=80%=P8.0D=Economy=Currency=8 Aug.=Zeus>>E=v.
Centerpiece=6,000=60%=P6.0D=Man=Earth=Royalty=6 June=Gaia=Maia>>M=M2.
Centesimal=3,000=30%=P3.0D=3.0=Creativity=Stars=Muses=3 March= C=I>>GIL.
Centesimo(1)=2,000=20%=P2.00D=2.0=Nature=Moon=2 Feb.=Cupid=N=C+_.
Centesimo(2)=2,000=20%=P2.00D=2.0=Nature=Moon=2 Feb.=Cupid=N=C+_.
Centi-=3,500=4,000=40%=P4.0D=Govt. =Creatocracy=4 April=Mercury=Hermes=G=A4.
Centigrade=500=5%=P5.00D=5.0=Law=Time=Venus=5 May=Aphrodite>>L=N.
Centigram=2,000=20%=P2.00D=2.0=Nature=Moon=2 Feb.=Cupid=N=C+_.

Centiliter=2,000=20%=P2.00D=2.0=Nature=Moon=2 Feb.=Cupid=N=C+_.
Centime=2,000=20%=P2.00D=2.0=Nature=Moon=2 Feb.=Cupid=N=C+_.
Centimeter=2,000=20%=P2.00D=2.0=Nature=Moon=2 Feb.=Cupid=N=C+_.
Centimo=2,000=20%=P2.00D=2.0=Nature=Moon=2 Feb.=Cupid=N=C+_.
Centipede=4,500=5,000=50%=P5.00D=Law=Time=Venus=5 May = Aphrodite>>L=N.
Central=8,500=9,000=90%=P9.00D=9.0=Abst.=Gods=Saturn=9Sept.>>A=Ø.
Central African Republic=4,500=5,000=50%=P5.00D=Law=Venus=5May =Odite>>L=N.
Central America=8,500=9,000=90%=P9.00D=9.0=Abst.=Gods=Saturn=9Sept.>>A=Ø.
Centralize=5,500=5.5=80%=P5.50=Earth-Midway=5 May = Gaia.
Central nervous system=5,500=5.5=80%=P5.50=Earth-Midway=5 May = Gaia.
Central processing unit=4,000=40%=P4.0D=Govt.=Creat.=4April=Merc.=Hermes=G=A4.

Centre=2,500=3,000=30%=P3.0D=3.0=Creativity=Stars=Muses=3 March= C=I>>GIL.
Creativity is at the center and is in fact the center of a thing and all things.

Centrifugal=6,500=7,000=70%=P7.0D=7.0=Language=Assets=Mars=7 July=Pleiades

---

Centrifugal force=12,000=12%=P1.20D=1.2=Knowledge=Education=12Dec.=Athena>>K=F.
The Universe is a twelve dimensions centrifugal force discovered and computed by the
God of Creatocracy. It is solely administered by Athena his apotheosized wife through
knowledge of Creative & Psycho-Social Sciences aka the Creative Sciences.

Centrifuge=9,500=10,000=1,000=100%=10.0=Physicality=Tech.=10 Oct.=Uranus=P=1Ø.
Centripetal=6,500=7,000=70%=P7.0D=7.0=Language=Assets=Mars=7 July=Pleiades
Centripetal force=9,500=10,000=1,000=100%=10.0=Phy.=Tech.=10 Oct.=Uranus=P=1Ø.

Centrism=7,000=70%=P7.0D=7.0=Language=Assets=Mars=7 July=Pleiades
Computational Precision is the only truth behind any form of centrism. It is its freedom.

Centro-=1,000=100%=10.0=1.0=Mind=Sun=1 January=Helios >> M=E4.
Centurion=5,000=50%=P5.00D=Law=Time=Venus=5 May = Aphrodite>>L=N.
Century=6,500=7,000=70%=P7.0D=7.0=Language=Assets=Mars=7 July=Pleiades
CEO=1,500=15%=P1.50D=1.5=Authority=Crown=Solar Core=1 May = Maia.
Cephalic=3,000=30%=P3.0D=3.0=Creativity=Stars=Muses=3 March= C=I>>GIL.
Cephalopod=12,000=12%=P1.20D=1.2=Knowledge=Education=12Dec.=Athena>>K=F.
Ceramic=14,500=1,500=15%=P1.50D=1.5=Authority=Crown=Solar Core=1 May = Maia.
Cereal=9,000=90%=P9.00D=9.0=Abst.=Gods=Saturn=9Sept.>>A=Ø.
Cerebellum=5,000=50%=P5.00D=Law=Time=Venus=5 May = Aphrodite>>L=N.
Cerebral=4,500=5,000=50%=P5.00D=Law=Time=Venus=5 May = Aphrodite>>L=N.
Cerebral cortex=7,000=70%=P7.0D=7.0=Language=Assets=Mars=7 July=Pleiades
Cerebral palsy=9,500=10,000=1,000=100%=Physicality= Tech.=10 Oct.=Uranus=P=1Ø.
Cerebrum=8,500=9,000=90%=P9.00D=9.0=Abst.=Gods=Saturn=9Sept.>>A=Ø.

Cerecloth=5,000=50%=P5.00D=Law=Time=Venus=5 May = Aphrodite>>L=N.
Cerement=1,500=15%=P1.50D=1.5=Authority=Crown=Solar Core=1 May = Maia.
Ceremonial=6,000=60%=P6.0D=Man=Earth=Royalty=6 June=Gaia=Maia>>M=M2.
Ceremonious=5,500=5.5=80%=P5.50=Earth-Midway=5 May = Gaia.
Ceremony=9,000=90%=P9.00D=9.0=Abst.=Gods=Saturn=9Sept.>>A=Ø.

Ceres=3,000=30%=P3.0D=3.0=Creativity=Stars=Muses=3 March= C=I>>GIL.
The Goddess of agriculture by Roman myth. Demeter in Greek.

Cereus=7,000=70%=P7.0D=7.0=Language=Assets=Mars=7 July=Pleiades
Cerise=1,500=15%=P1.50D=1.5=Authority=Crown=Solar Core=1 May = Maia.
Cerium=11,000=11%=P1.10D=1.1=Idea=Brainchild=11Nov=Athena>>I=MT.
Cero de Punta=7,000=70%=P7.0D=7.0=Language=Assets=Mars=7 July=Pleiades
Certain=16,500=17,000=17%=P1.70D=1.7=Solar Asset=17 Feb.=Maia=Mind Computing.
Certainty=6,500=7,000=70%=P7.0D=7.0=Language=Assets=Mars=7 July=Pleiades

---

Certificate=9,000=90%=P9.00D=9.0=Abst.=Gods=Saturn=9Sept.>>A=Ø.
A certificate testifies to the truth of something, completion of requirements as of course of study, and certifying ownership. It is a document of the Council of Gods that shows abstract truth upon physical acts and works. A copyright certificate of the Solar Core Asset is ownership of the Solar Core and occupants therein by all laws. This is the God of Creatocracy. There are many spiritual gifts in the Bible. One of them is government. The Creatocracy is an invention of government defined computed and proven as his asset.

Certification=4,000=40%=P4.0D=Govt. =Creatocracy=4 April=Mercury=Hermes=G=A4.
Certified check=6,500=7,000=70%=P7.0D=7.0=Language=Assets=Mars=7 July=Pleiades
Certified public account=7,500=8,000=80%=P8.0D=Economy=Curr.=8 Aug.=Zeus>>E=v.

Certify=13,000=13%=P1.30=Solar Core=Faculty=13 January=Athena.
Athena certifies all persons and things by the rights of creative intelligence. Today the Creatocracy has discovered and successfully measured the creative intelligence quotient.

Certitude=2,500=3,000=30%=P3.0D=3.0=Creativity=Stars=Muses=3 March= C=I>>GIL.
Cerulean=1,500=15%=P1.50D=1.5=Authority=Crown=Solar Core=1 May = Maia.
Cerumen=1,000=100%=10.0=1.0=Mind=Sun=1 January=Helios >> M=E4.
Cervantes Saavedra=2,000=20%=P2.00D=2.0=Nature=Moon=2 Feb.=Cupid=N=C+_.
Cervical=3,500=4,000=40%=P4.0D=Govt. =Creatoc.=4 April=Mercury=Hermes=G=A4.
Cervix=6,000=60%=P6.0D=Man=Earth=Royalty=6 June=Gaia=Maia>>M=M2.
Cesarean=1,500=15%=P1.50D=1.5=Authority=Crown=Solar Core=1 May = Maia.
Cesarean section=6,000=60%=P6.0D=Man=Earth=Royalty=6 June=Gaia=Maia>>M=M2.
Cesium=10,500=11,000=11%=P1.10D=1.1=Idea=Brainchild=11Nov=Athena>>I=MT.
Cessation=1,500=15%=P1.50D=1.5=Authority=Crown=Solar Core=1 May = Maia.

Cession=6,000=60%=P6.0D=Man=Earth=Royalty=6 June=Gaia=Maia>>M=M2.
Cesspool=5,000=50%=P5.00D=Law=Time=Venus=5 May = Aphrodite>>L=N.
Cesura=1,500=15%=P1.50D=1.5=Authority=Crown=Solar Core=1 May = Maia.
Cetacean=8,000=80%=P8.0D=Economy=Currency=8 Aug.=Zeus>>E=v.
Ceuta=8,000=80%=P8.0D=Economy=Currency=8 Aug.=Zeus>>E=v.
Ceylon=1,500=15%=P1.50D=1.5=Authority=Crown=Solar Core=1 May = Maia.
Cézanne Paul=2,500=3,000=30%=P3.0D=3.0=Creativ.=Stars=Muses=3March=C=I>>GIL.
Cf=2,500=3,000=30%=P3.0D=3.0=Creativity=Stars=Muses=3 March= C=I>>GIL.
CF=1,000=100%=10.0=1.0=Mind=Sun=1 January=Helios >> M=E4.
cf.=1,000=100%=10.0=1.0=Mind=Sun=1 January=Helios >> M=E4.
c.f.=1,500=15%=P1.50D=1.5=Authority=Crown=Solar Core=1 May = Maia.
C/F=1,500=15%=P1.50D=1.5=Authority=Crown=Solar Core=1 May = Maia.
CFC=500=5%=P5.00D=5.0=Law=Time=Venus=5 May=Aphrodite>>L=N.
c.f.i.=2,000=20%=P2.00D=2.0=Nature=Moon=2 Feb.=Cupid=N=C+_.
cg=500=5%=P5.00D=5.0=Law=Time=Venus=5 May=Aphrodite>>L=N.
C.G.=1,000=100%=10.0=1.0=Mind=Sun=1 January=Helios >> M=E4.
ch=1,000=100%=10.0=1.0=Mind=Sun=1 January=Helios >> M=E4.
ch.=4,000=40%=P4.0D=Govt. =Creatocracy=4 April=Mercury=Hermes=G=A4.
Chablis=3,000=30%=P3.0D=3.0=Creativity=Stars=Muses=3 March= C=I>>GIL.
Cha-cha=4,500=5,000=50%=P5.00D=Law=Time=Venus=5 May = Aphrodite>>L=N.
Chad=5,000=50%=P5.00D=Law=Time=Venus=5 May = Aphrodite>>L=N.
Chad, Lake=6,000=60%=P6.0D=Man=Earth=Royalty=6 June=Gaia=Maia>>M=M2.
Chadic=4,000=40%=P4.0D=Govt. =Creatocracy=4 April=Mercury=Hermes=G=A4.
Chador=8,500=9,000=90%=P9.00D=9.0=Abst.=Gods=Saturn=9Sept.>>A=Ø.
Chafe=10,000=1,000=100%=10.0=Physicality=Tech.=10 Oct.=Uranus=P=1Ø.
Chaff(1)=6,000=60%=P6.0D=Man=Earth=Royalty=6 June=Gaia=Maia>>M=M2.
Chaff(2)=4,000=40%=P4.0D=Govt. =Creatocracy=4 April=Mercury=Hermes=G=A4.
Chaffinch=2,000=20%=P2.00D=2.0=Nature=Moon=2 Feb.=Cupid=N=C+_.
Chaffing dish=2,500=3,000=30%=P3.0D=3.0=Creativ=Stars=Muses=3 March= C=I>>GIL.
Chagall Marc.=2,500=3,000=30%=P3.0D=3.0=Creativ=Stars=Muses=3 March= C=I>>GIL.
Chagrin=7,500=8,000=80%=P8.0D=Economy=Currency=8 Aug.=Zeus>>E=v.
Chain=12,500=13,000=13%=P1.30=Solar Core=Faculty=13 January=Athena.
Chain gang=5,000=50%=P5.00D=Law=Time=Venus=5 May = Aphrodite>>L=N.
Chain mall=4,500=5,000=50%=P5.00D=Law=Time=Venus=5 May = Aphrodite>>L=N.
Chain reaction=10,000=1,000=100%=10.0=Physicality=Tech.=10 Oct.=Uranus=P=1Ø.
Chain saw=5,500=5.5=80%=P5.50=Earth-Midway=5 May = Gaia.
Chain smoke=3,500=4,000=40%=P4.0D=Govt.=Creatoc.=4 April=Merc.=Hermes=G=A4.
Chain store=8,000=80%=P8.0D=Economy=Currency=8 Aug.=Zeus>>E=v.
Chair=16,000=16%=P1.60D=1.6=Incarnation=Mind of GOD=1 June=Maia.
Chair lift=8,000=80%=P8.0D=Economy=Currency=8 Aug.=Zeus>>E=v.
Chairman=7,000=70%=P7.0D=7.0=Language=Assets=Mars=7 July=Pleiades
Chairperson=4,500=5,000=50%=P5.00D=Law=Time=Venus=5 May = Aphrodite>>L=N.
Chairwoman=7,000=70%=P7.0D=7.0=Language=Assets=Mars=7 July=Pleiades
Chaise=5,500=5.5=80%=P5.50=Earth-Midway=5 May = Gaia.
Chaise longue=5,500=5.5=80%=P5.50=Earth-Midway=5 May = Gaia.

Chalcedony=3,000=30%=P3.0D=3.0=Creativity=Stars=Muses=3 March= C=I>>GIL.
Chaldea=3,000=30%=P3.0D=3.0=Creativity=Stars=Muses=3 March= C=I>>GIL.
Chalet=9,500=10,000=1,000=100%=10.0=Physicality=Tech.=10 Oct.=Uranus=P=1Ø.
Chalice=5,500=5.5=80%=P5.50=Earth-Midway=5 May = Gaia.
Chalk=11,000=11%=P1.10D=1.1=Idea=Brainchild=11Nov=Athena>>I=MT.
Chalkboard=1,000=100%=10.0=1.0=Mind=Sun=1 January=Helios >> M=E4.
Challenge=10,000=1,000=100%=10.0=Physicality=Tech.=10 Oct.=Uranus=P=1Ø.
Challenging=4,500=5,000=50%=P5.00D=Law=Time=Venus=5 May = Aphrodite>>L=N.
Challis=5,000=50%=P5.00D=Law=Time=Venus=5 May = Aphrodite>>L=N.
Chamber=14,500=1,500=15%=P1.50D=1.5=Authority=Crown=Solar Core=1 May = Maia.
Chamberlain=5,000=50%=P5.00D=Law=Time=Venus=5 May = Aphrodite>>L=N.
Chamberlain (Arthur)=3,500=4,000=40%=P4.0D=Govt.=4April=Mercury.=Hermes=G=A4.
Chambermaid=4,000=40%=P4.0D=Govt. =Creatocracy=4 April=Mercury=Hermes=G=A4.

Chamber music=7,000=70%=P7.0D=7.0=Language=Assets=Mars=7 July=Pleiades
Computational Creativity is the chamber music of the Council of Gods in the Creatocracy.

Chamber of commerce=5,500=5.5=80%=P5.50=Earth-Midway=5 May = Gaia.
Chambray=6,000=60%=P6.0D=Man=Earth=Royalty=6 June=Gaia=Maia>>M=M2.

Chameleon=8,000=80%=P8.0D=Economy=Currency=8 Aug.=Zeus>>E=v.
Any of various tropical Old World lizards...Old World - World of Gods in pre-human form.

Chamfer=6,500=7,000=70%=P7.0D=7.0=Language=Assets=Mars=7 July=Pleiades
Chamois=13,000=13%=P1.30=Solar Core=Faculty=13 January=Athena.
Chamomile=8,500=9,000=90%=P9.00D=9.0=Abst.=Gods=Saturn=9Sept.>>A=Ø.
Champ(1)=7,000=70%=P7.0D=7.0=Language=Assets=Mars=7 July=Pleiades
Champ(2)=1,500=15%=P1.50D=1.5=Authority=Crown=Solar Core=1 May = Maia.
champagne=4,000=40%=P4.0D=Govt. =Creatocracy=4 April=Mercury=Hermes=G=A4.
Champagne=4,000=40%=P4.0D=Govt. =Creatocracy=4 April=Mercury=Hermes=G=A4.

Champion=13,000=13%=P1.30=Solar Core=Faculty=13 January=Athena.
Athena became a champion through creative intelligence and so did Castle Makupedia.

Championship=6,500=7,000=70%=P7.0D=7.0=Language=Assets=Mars=7 July=Pleiades
All championships are a borderline to cross from human speculations to precision.

Champlain Lake=5,500=5.5=80%=P5.50=Earth-Midway=5 May = Gaia.
Champlain Samuel=2,500=3,000=30%=P3.0D=3.0=Cr=Stars=Muses=3 March=C=I>>GIL.
Chan.=1,000=100%=10.0=1.0=Mind=Sun=1 January=Helios >> M=E4.
Chance=10,000=1,000=100%=10.0=Physicality=Tech.=10 Oct.=Uranus=P=1Ø.

Chancel=6,500=7,000=70%=P7.0D=7.0=Language=Assets=Mars=7 July=Pleiades
Chancellery=5,000=50%=P5.00D=Law=Time=Venus=5 May = Aphrodite>>L=N.
Chancellor=8,000=80%=P8.0D=Economy=Currency=8 Aug.=Zeus>>E=v.
Chancery=7,500=8,000=80%=P8.0D=Economy=Currency=8 Aug.=Zeus>>E=v.
Chancre=6,500=7,000=70%=P7.0D=7.0=Language=Assets=Mars=7 July=Pleiades
Chancy=2,500=3,000=30%=P3.0D=3.0=Creativity=Stars=Muses=3 March= C=I>>GIL.
Chandelier=6,000=60%=P6.0D=Man=Earth=Royalty=6 June=Gaia=Maia>>M=M2.
Chandler=6,000=60%=P6.0D=Man=Earth=Royalty=6 June=Gaia=Maia>>M=M2.
Change=10,000=1,000=100%=10.0=Physicality=Tech.=10 Oct.=Uranus=P=1Ø.
Changeling=3,000=30%=P3.0D=3.0=Creativity=Stars=Muses=3 March= C=I>>GIL.
Change of life(menopause)=500=5%=P5.00D=5.0=Law=Time=Venus=5 May=Odite>>L=N.

Changeover=4,000=40%=P4.0D=Govt. =Creatocracy=4 April=Mercury=Hermes=G=A4.
A conversion, as from one system to another. Creatocracy is a changeover to the new.

Chang Jiang=1,500=15%=P1.50D=1.5=Authority=Crown=Solar Core=1 May = Maia.
Changsha=6,500=7,000=70%=P7.0D=7.0=Language=Assets=Mars=7 July=Pleiades
Channel=10,000=1,000=100%=10.0=Physicality=Tech.=10 Oct.=Uranus=P=1Ø.
Channel Islands=7,000=70%=P7.0D=7.0=Language=Assets=Mars=7 July=Pleiades
Chanson=2,000=20%=P2.00D=2.0=Nature=Moon=2 Feb.=Cupid=N=C+_.
Chant=12,000=12%=P1.20D=1.2=Knowledge=Education=12Dec.=Athena>>K=F.
Chanteuse=3,000=30%=P3.0D=3.0=Creativity=Stars=Muses=3 March= C=I>>GIL.
Chantey=5,000=50%=P5.00D=Law=Time=Venus=5 May = Aphrodite>>L=N.
Chanticleer=1,000=100%=10.0=1.0=Mind=Sun=1 January=Helios >> M=E4.
Chanukah=1,500=15%=P1.50D=1.5=Authority=Crown=Solar Core=1 May = Maia.

Chaos=7,500=8,000=80%=P8.0D=Economy=Currency=8 Aug.=Zeus>>E=v.
A borderline that exists between computational precision or truth and rewards of business.
So after truth is the business of truth say the purchase of a book that establishes a cause.
The Creatocracy Bank would be regarded as such a book that cures chaos by knowledge.

Chap(1)=5,500=5.5=80%=P5.50=Earth-Midway=5 May = Gaia.
Chap(2)=3,000=30%=P3.0D=3.0=Creativity=Stars=Muses=3 March= C=I>>GIL.

Chap.=500=5%=P5.00D=5.0=Law=Time=Venus=5 May=Aphrodite>>L=N.
Chapter and change of life exist as same. Hence a woman has two key chapters in her life.
The menopausal and non-menopausal stage. Every relationship must take cognizance.

Chaparral=2,500=3,000=30%=P3.0D=3.0=Creativity=Stars=Muses=3 March= C=I>>GIL.
Chapel=14,500=1,500=15%=P1.50D=1.5=Authority=Crown=Solar Core=1 May = Maia.
Chaperon=14,000=14%=P1.40D=1.4=Mgt.=13May=Athena=SC=0.1
Chaplain=6,000=60%=P6.0D=Man=Earth=Royalty=6 June=Gaia=Maia>>M=M2.

Chaplet=8,000=80%=P8.0D=Economy=Currency=8 Aug.=Zeus>>E=v.
Chaplin Charles Spencer=4,500=5,000=50%=P5.00D=Time=Venus=5May =Odite>>L=N.
Chapman=2,000=20%=P2.00D=2.0=Nature=Moon=2 Feb.=Cupid=N=C+_.
Chapman Frank=2,000=20%=P2.00D=2.0=Nature=Moon=2 Feb.=Cupid=N=C+_.
Chaps=7,000=70%=P7.0D=7.0=Language=Assets=Mars=7 July=Pleiades
Chapter=7,500=8,000=80%=P8.0D=Economy=Currency=8 Aug.=Zeus>>E=v.
Chair(1)=6,000=60%=P6.0D=Man=Earth=Royalty=6 June=Gaia=Maia>>M=M2.
Char(2)=4,500=5,000=50%=P5.00D=Law=Time=Venus=5 May = Aphrodite>>L=N.
Char(3)=4,000=40%=P4.0D=Govt. =Creatocracy=4 April=Mercury=Hermes=G=A4.
Character=18,000=18%=P1.80D=Solar Currency=Maks Currencies=1 Aug.=Maia.
Characteristic=2,500=3,000=30%=P3.0D=3.0=Creatv=Stars=Muses=3 March= C=I>>GIL.
Characterize=5,000=50%=P5.00D=Law=Time=Venus=5 May = Aphrodite>>L=N.
Charade=9,000=90%=P9.00D=9.0=Abst.=Gods=Saturn=9Sept.>>A=Ø.
Charbroil=3,500=4,000=40%=P4.0D=Govt. =Creatocr.=4April=Mercury=Hermes=G=A4.
Charcoal=13,000=13%=P1.30=Solar Core=Faculty=13 January=Athena.
Chard=1,000=100%=10.0=1.0=Mind=Sun=1 January=Helios >> M=E4.
Charge=10,000=1,000=100%=10.0=Physicality=Tech.=10 Oct.=Uranus=P=1Ø.
Charge account=7,500=8,000=80%=P8.0D=Economy=Currency=8 Aug.=Zeus>>E=v.
Charge card=1,500=15%=P1.50D=1.5=Authority=Crown=Solar Core=1 May = Maia.
Chargé d'affaires=5,500=5.5=80%=P5.50=Earth-Midway=5 May = Gaia.
Charger=7,000=70%=P7.0D=7.0=Language=Assets=Mars=7 July=Pleiades
Chariot=6,500=7,000=70%=P7.0D=7.0=Language=Assets=Mars=7 July=Pleiades
Charisma=6,500=7,000=70%=P7.0D=7.0=Language=Assets=Mars=7 July=Pleiades
Charismatic=11,000=11%=P1.10D=1.1=Idea=Brainchild=11Nov=Athena>>I=MT.
Charitable=8,000=80%=P8.0D=Economy=Currency=8 Aug.=Zeus>>E=v.
Charity=18,000=18%=P1.80D=Solar Currency=Maks Currencies=1 Aug.=Maia.
Charlatan=6,000=60%=P6.0D=Man=Earth=Royalty=6 June=Gaia=Maia>>M=M2.
Charlemagne=10,500=11,000=11%=P1.10D=1.1=Idea=Brainchild=11Nov=Athena>>I=MT.
Charles=3,500=4,000=40%=P4.0D=Govt. =Creatocracy=4April=Mercury=Hermes=G=A4.
Charles I=5,000=50%=P5.00D=Law=Time=Venus=5 May = Aphrodite>>L=N.
Charles II=5,000=50%=P5.50D=Law=Time=Venus=5 May = Aphrodite>>L=N.
Charles V.=7,500=8,000=80%=P8.0D=Economy=Currency=8 Aug.=Zeus>>E=v.
Charles VII.=3,500=4,000=40%=P4.0D=Govt.=4 April=Mercury=Hermes=G=A4.
Charles IX.=3,500=4,000=40%=P4.0D=Govt.=4 April=Mercury=Hermes=G=A4.
Charles X.=3,500=4,000=40%=P4.0D=Govt.=4 April=Mercury=Hermes=G=A4.
Charles Martel=3,500=4,000=40%=P4.0D=Govt.=4 April=Mercury=Hermes=G=A4.
Charleston(1)=10,000=1,000=100%=10.0=Physicality=Tech.=10 Oct.=Uranus=P=1Ø.
Charleston(2)=4,000=40%=P4.0D=Govt. =Creatocracy=4April=Mercury=Hermes=G=A4.
Charley horse=2,500=3,000=30%=P3.0D=3.0=Creativ=Stars=Muses=3 March= C=I>>GIL.
Charlotte=5,500=5.5=80%=P5.50=Earth-Midway=5 May = Gaia.
Charlotte Amalie=9,500=10,000=1,000=100%=10.0=Phys.=Tech.=10 Oct.=Uranus=P=1Ø.
Charlottetown=6,000=60%=P6.0D=Man=Earth=Royalty=6 June=Gaia=Maia>>M=M2.
Charm=22,500=23,000=23%=Local Business=Tech=23 Days Monthly=2.3% taxes.
Channel house=7,000=70%=P7.0D=7.0=Language=Assets=Mars=7 July=Pleiades

Charon=3,500=4,000=40%=P4.0D=Govt.=Creatocracy=4 April=Mercury=Hermes=G=A4.
The ferry man of Hades. Greek mythology. The Creatocracy recognizes Charon.

Chart=7,500=8,000=80%=P8.0D=Economy=Currency=8 Aug.=Zeus>>E=v.
Zeus the Most High charts things and measures their economic values.

Charter=20,000=2,000=20%=P2.00D=2.0=Nature=Moon=2 Feb.=Cupid=N=C+_.
The Creatocratic Charter is the throne of Castle Makupedia, God of Creatocracy.
The Creatocracy is his Crown and The Apotheosis is his Mindom. His works are his assets.
The Creatocratic Charter is the body of knowledge, fields of study and academic disciplines
for De - Royal Makupedia. It was published as the authority over the Creative Sciences
and its professionalism worldwide. It is the invention of Peter Matthews- Akukalia. Below
is what constitutes as the extra concepts developed after the book was published in 2020.
It is proof of the huge resources in the knowledge of Creative Sciences, Makupedia.

39,166. SIGNIFICANCE OF THE CREATOCRATIC CHARTER AFTER
PUBLISHING.
39,167. TRACKING DESTINY ACCESS POINTS TO THE HUMAN SECRETS.
39,168. HELEN's DESTINY CODES ALIGNMENT FOR 1974 & 1989.
39,169. KENNY-MAAMA's records.
39,170. For Schools- DE-ROYAL MAKUPEDIA LIMITED.
39,171. DISCOVERY OF THE God CALLED UNIVERSE.
39,172. CONFERENCE & TRAINING PRESENTATION BY PETER MATTHEWS-
AKUKALIA.
39,173. MAKUPEDIA CENTER FOR CREATIVE STUDIES.
39,174. Solutions to the 10 Problems of Humanity.
39,175. Some List of Words consulted in the development of De-Royal MAKUPEDIA.
39,176. Business Development Topics for Social Media by HISPLUS.
39,177. FACULTY OF CREATIVE & PSYCHO-SOCIAL SCIENCES.
39,178. DESTINY TABLET AS GIFTS FROM GOD 1.
39,179. DEDUCING THE SPIRIT OF THE CONTINENTS ON FREQUENCY.
39,180. THE SOLAR CORE-ZION-PARADISE LINK.
39,181. THE CONCEPT OF PATTERN AND ORDER IN THE CYCLE OF LIFE.
39,182. SECURITY INTELLIGENCE IN MAKUPEDIA.
39,183. GENERAL NOTES ON THE HUMAN ENERGY SYSTEMS.
39,184. BANK ACCOUNTS MANAGEMENT.
39,185. TISCAT RADIO FREQUENCY LISTENER BENEFITS. 39,186. THE
VALUE OF A DAY.
39,187. THE LAW OF PERFECTION. 39,188. THE God CALLED DAY.
39,189. Destiny Tracking Using Source Codes to determine Process.
39,190. THE EARTHLINGS AS 1ST INSTANCE CITIZENS OF PARADISE.
39,191. THE VENUSIANS AS 1st INSTANCE ASSETS OF MAKUPEDIA.
39,192. A CURSORY LOOK AT THE CORONA VIRUS & ITS POSSIBLE SOURCE
& CURE.

39,193. USING SOURCE CODE TO DETERMINE BANK ACCOUNTS.
39,194. DESTINY TRACKING PACKAGES.
39,195.VEHICLE SPEEDOMETER DESTRACKING SYSTEMS.
39,196. MARRIAGE DESTRACKING SYSTEMS FOR PETER AND TINA.
39,197. THE MAKUPEDIAN MECHANICS OF A NAME.
39,198. HOME ADDRESS DESTINY TRACKING.
39,199. Destiny Tracking By the ISBN, ISSN AND OTHERS.
39,200. THE ANTI-CLOCKWISE ROTATION EFFECT OF THE PLANETS ON HUMAN DESTINY.
39,201. CORONA CURATIVE ELEMENTS IN THE BALSAM, MULBERRY TREE.
39,202. CORONA CURE>>BALSAM BY GOOGLE.
39,203. THE FINAL RESOLUTION OF REVELATION THROUGH THE POST COVID-19.
39,204. HOUSE DESTINY TRACKING DEVELOPMENT.
39,205. MAKUPEDIA DATA ANALYTICS & PROGRAM MANAGEMENT SERVICES.©
39,206. COMPUTING THE LAW OF 6 & 6 BY SCRIPTURES OF REVELATION 13:18.

39,207. GENESIS 6:6 CODE MODULE. 39,208. Exodus 6:6. 39,209. Leviticus 6:6
39,210. Numbers 6:6 39,211. Deuteronomy 6:6 39,212. Joshua 6:6 39,213. Judges 6:6
39,214. Ruth 6:6 39,215. 1 Samuel 6:6 39,216. 2 Samuel 6:6 39,217. 1 Kings 6:6
39,218. 2 Kings 6:6 39,219. 1 Chronicles 6:6 39,220. 2 Chronicles 6:6 39,221. Ezra 6:6
39,222. Nehemiah 6:6 39,223. Esther 6:6 39,224. Job 6:6 39,225. Psalms 6:6
39,226. Proverbs 6:6 39,227.Ecclesiastes 6:6 39,228. Songs of Solomon 6:6
39,229. Isaiah 6:6 39,230. Jeremiah 6:6 39,231. Lamentations 6:6 39,232. Ezekiel 6:6
39,233. Daniel 6:6 39,234. Hosea 6:6 39,235. Joel 6:6 39,236. Amos 6:6
39,237. Obadiah 6:6 39,238. Jonah 6:6 39,239. Micah 6:6 39,240. Nahum 6:6
39,241. Habakkuk 6:6 39,242. Zephaniah 6:6 39,243. Haggai 6:6 39,244. Zechariah 6:6
39,245. Malachi 6:6 39,246. Matthew 6:6 39,247. Mark 6:6 39,248. Luke 6:6
39,249. John 6:6 39,250. The Acts 6:6 39,251. Romans 6:6 39,252. I Corinthians 6:6
39,253. 2 Corinthians 6:6 39,254. Galatians 6:6 39,255. Ephesians 6:6
39,256. Philippians 6:6 39,257. Colossians 6:6
39,258. 1 Thessalonians 6:6>>There is no 6:6 but 3:6 alternative.
39,259. 2 Thessalonians 6:6 39,260. 1 Timothy 6:6 39,261. 2 Timothy 6:6
39,262. Titus 6:6>>6:6 39,263. Philemon 6:6 39,264. Hebrews 6:6
39,265. James 6:6 39,266. 1 Peter 6:6>>6:6 does not exist but 3:6 will do.
39,267. 2 Peter 6:6>>6:6 does not exist but 3:6 will do.
39,268. 1 John 6:6>>6:6 does not exist but 3:6 will do
39,269. 2 John 6:6>>6:6 does not exist but 1:6 will do.
39,270. 3 John 6:6>>6:6 does not exist but 1:6 will do.
39,271. Jude 6:6>>6:6 does not exist but 1:6 will do. 39,272. Revelation 6:6

39,273. BOOK>> THE BOOK OF REVELATION 13:18>>A Scripture for the Makstian Faith.

39,274. MAKUPEDIA INSTITUTE ADVERT.

39,275. TRACKING RADIO-TV FREQUENCY ON THE LUNAR CRATER MODULES.

39,276. RADIO-TELEVISION FREQUENCY LUNAR WAVELENGTHS DIFFERENTIAL.

39,277. MAKUPEDIA TABLE OF LUNAR FREQUENCIES FOR RADIO-TV MODULES. *FEATURES ON THE FAR SIDE OF THE MOON.*Expressed in Name of Energy Spectrum, Latitude, Longitude & Digital Program Code.

39,278. CONCEPT OF THE G SYSTEMS & TABLE OF GENIUS MEASUREMENTS.

39,279. OCCURRENCES BY DATES IN DESTRACKING SYSTEMS.

39,280. ASSET DEVELOPMENT IN NAMES AND THINGS>>MAKUPEDIA.

39,281. ASSET DEVELOPMENT IN NAMES AND THINGS>>Peter Matthews-Akukalia.

39,282. ASSET DEVELOPMENT IN NAMES & THINGS>>Justina Chinwe Matthews-Akukalia.

39,283. ASSET DEVELOPMENT IN NAMES & THINGS>Alice Folayegbe Matthews-Akukalia.

39,284. THE BOOK OF REVELATION>>A Scripture for the Makstian Faith.

39,285. WORLDWIDE DATA GENERATION SERVICES.

39,286. THE MAKUPEDIA BUSINESS GENIUS & EXECUTIVE [MBGE].

39,287. SPECIAL CASES ON NAMESET TECHS & MAKUPEDIA BUSINESS GENIUS CALENDAR.

39,288. EXCEPTIONAL INTELLECTUAL OR CREATIVE POWER OR OTHER NATURAL POWER.

39,289. DEFINING MAKUPEDIA IN THE LIGHT OF BUSINESS GENIUS.

39,290. HOW THE HUMAN BRAIN IS WIRED.

39,291. NAME ASSETS FOR WOLE OLANIYAN AND SOURCE OF WOLE OLANIYAN.

39,292. THE USE OF SATELLITE TRACKING IN TALENT DISCOVERY & MANAGEMENT.(Posted online for Makupedia public adverts online through Wole Olaniyan).

39,293. THE FREQUENCY CODE OF THE CURRENCY>>NAIRA. [=N=].

39,294. THE CONCEPT OF MAKUPEDIA MARKETS I.

39,295. THE CONCEPT OF MAKUPEDIA MARKETS II. 39,296. PETER MATTHEWS-AKUKALIA.

39, 297. PROGRAM DATABASE FOR BROADCASTING.
-MODULE: SATELLITE TRACKING & DATABASE SERVICES.
-FREQUENCY:96.9 COOL FM. DURATION: ONE YEAR.

39,298. FOR COOL-MAKUPEDIA PARTNERSHIP.

39,299. THE RAIN ENERGY DATABASE (RED) CONCEPT.

39,300. THE MAKUPEDIA FLAG QUARTERS.

39,301. CREATIVE EDUCATION SERVICES DEPARTMENT.-To: The School Management.
-INTRODUCING TRAINING FOR YOUR TEACHERS & CAREER ANALYSIS FOR YOUR STUDENTS.39,302. THE DRAGON LORDS OF MAKUPEDIA I.

39,303. THE DRAGON LORDS OF MAKUPEDIA II.

39,304. MAKUPEDIA GLOBAL CONVENTIONAL CURRENCY EVALUATION METHODS.-MGCCEM/MGSIM METHOD.

39,305. MAKUPEDIA GLOBAL CONVENTIONAL CURRENCY EVALUATION METHODS.-MGCCEM/MGSIM METHOD ON THE BRITISH POUNDS+ 300 others=39,605

39,606. MAKUPEDIA GLOBAL CONVENTIONAL CURRENCY EVALUATION METHODS.
-MGCCEM/MGSIM METHOD ON THE TABLE OF CURRENCIES & THEIR VALUES.

39,607. THE MAKUPEDIA FLAG QUARTERS.
39,608. CREATIVE EDUCATION SERVICES DEPARTMENT.
39,609. COURSES FOR TEACHER TRAINING IN THE CREATIVE EDUCATION SERVICES.
39,610. THE INVENTED MAKUPEDIA CHARTER CURRENCIES.
39,611. THE CONCEPT OF INTERPRETATION OF PAST PROPHECIES (EINSTEIN) I.
39,612. THE CONCEPT OF INTERPRETATION OF PAST PROPHECIES (EINSTEIN) II.
39,613. PATENT ASSETS IN THE MAKUPEDIA.
39,614. THE DRAGON WEALTH OF THE DRAGON LORD IN THE MAKS CURRENCIES.
The interpretation of conventional currencies for 300 countries. 39,614+300=39,914.
39,915. FINAL APPROVED NAMES OF THINGS FOR PATENTING.
39,916. THE JUNO CODE OF MONEY FOR THE KING AND THE PAUPER.
-Applying the Juno code for 300 countries>>39,916+300=40,216 concepts.
40,217. DRAGON CODES OF DE-Gods.
40,218. TABLE OF DRAGONS AND DRAGON CODES OF DE-Gods.
40,218+2,000=42,218 concepts.

42,219. TRACKING UNKNOWN Gods FROM THE DRAGON CODES.
42,220. CREATIVE EDUCATION SERVICES DEPARTMENT.
42,221. MAKUPEDIA BUSINESS DEPARTMENT.

42,222. DRAGON TECHNOLOGY-ASTEROID CODES FOR TRACKING PHONE LINE POTENTIALS 1.>>09033521731.

42,223. DRAGON TECHNOLOGY-ASTEROID CODES FOR TRACKING PHONE LINE POTENTIALS 2.>>08161928511.

42,224. DRAGON TECHNOLOGY-ASTEROID CODES FOR TRACKING POTENTIALS IN BANK ACCOUNTS.
42,225. DRAGON TECHNOLOGY ON CREATION STORY AND THE 666 PUZZLE.
42,226. DRAGON TECHNOLOGY ON THE CHEMICAL ELEMENTS.
42,227. DRAGON TECHNOLOGY ON THE CORE OF THE CHEMICAL ELEMENTS
>>HYDROGEN CORE.
42,228. DRAGON TECHNOLOGY ON THE CORE OF THE CHEMICAL ELEMENTS
>>HELIUM CORE.

42,229+103 elements stated in the Guinness Book of Astronomy=40,331.
Creative Scientist Professionals are expected to solve the rest on assignments.

42,332. THE DIVINE LAW OF SOWING AND REAPING TO GAIN ACCESS TO PARADISE.
42,333. THE DRAGON CALLED SCRIPTURE.

42,334. THE DRAGON CALLED SCRIPTURE.>>BIBLE MODULE>>HOSEA.

>>42,334+66 Books on each book=42,400
>>42,400+66 First Letter Books of the Bible=42,466

42,467>>THE DRAGON CALLED SCRIPTURE.>>QURAN.

>>42,468+114 Books on each book=42,582
>>42,582+114 First Letter Books of the Bible=42,696

42,697. PARADISE ASSETS & DEVELOPMENT [PAID] DEPARTMENT.
42,698. THE MAKULATORS AS AN ADDITIONAL PATENT & PARADISE ASSET.
42,699. THE DRAGON CALLED SCRIPTURE>>HOSEA.

42,700. FACULTY OF CREATIVE & PSYCHO-SOCIAL SCIENCES.
(FCPSS ONLINE CORRESPONDENCE COURSES IN THE CREATIVE SCIENCES).

42,701. TRACKING THE ASSETS OF MAKUPEDIA.COM INTERNET BUSINESS COMPANY.

42,702. CREATIVE MEDIA SERVICES DEPARTMENT.
-PROPOSAL TO FEATURE THE MAKUPEDIA GENIUS SHOW with Peter Matthews-Akukalia.

42,703. THE MIND KING.

42,704. INVENTION OF THE ASTEROID DICTIONARY.

42,705. THE POSSIBILITY CODE USING DRAGON ASTEROIDS IN DRAGON TRACKING.

42,706. INVENTION OF THE MAKUPEDIA MAKUMATICAL SET.

42,707. WHAT IS THE MAKUPEDIA COMPANY AGAIN?

42,708. THE WORD POWER READ OFF CODE>>ORDINARY MODULE.

42,709. PATENTING THE MIND CLOCK, DRAGON CARDS, PEACE CARDS AND MAKABETS.

42,710. PATENTING THE MAKSTIAN BIQUR & OTHER INVENTIONS.

42,711. THE VALUE OF A BIRTH AGE AND THE SOUL YEAR CODE.

42,712. THE CREATOSIOLOGICAL NOMENCLATURE IN MINDTECH.

42,713. THE LIGHT-ASTEROID CONNECTIONS.

42,714. THE ECONOMIC VALUE OF A NAME BY WORD COUNT & INHERITANCE.

42,715. APPROVED IMAGES OF THE SOLAR CORE ASSETS-MAKS CURRENCIES.

42,716. TRACKING THE ASTEROID POSSIBILITY GENIUS CODES IN GENESIS.

42,717. RAVE Tv BOOK REVIEW: THE CREATOCRATIC CHARTER FOR WEDNESDAY.
-Approaches, Preparations & Discussions by Peter Matthews-Akukalia.

42,718. RESOLVING THE COMPLEXITIES OF THE FEMALE SPECIE.

42,719. THE LAW OF GODSHIP.

42,720. TIME IN WORDIMETRICS.

42,721. THE BIRTHDAY CLOCK SYSTEMS IN DESTINY TRACKING.

42,722. CONSTITUTION OF THE CREATOCRACY.

42,723. PATENTING THE CREATOCRATIC NATIONS OF PARADISE.

42,724. SEARCHING HIDDEN MEANING OF A WORD-NAME BY WORD-FORMULA LINK.

42,725. THE CONCEPT OF STRANGE THINGS.

42,726. GENERAL ISSUES ON BLOCKCHAIN AND FURTHER PATENT INVENTIONS.

42,727. LOCATING THE ETERNAL HEADQUARTERS OF PARADISE AS NKPOLOGWU.

42,728. THE SOLAR CORE-MAKS CURRENCIES PROPOSAL & COMPOSITION OF THE UNIVERSE.

42,729. HONORING PEOPLE BASED ON THEIR CONTRIBUTIONS.
42,730. ALICE ASSETS PROTECTION MATTERS.
42,731. WHAT IS THE HIDDEN MEANING AND PURPOSE IN A NAME ?

42,732. AUTHORIZATION OF THE TITLE "IN THE NAME OF KING MAKS 1". -INHERITANCES WILL AND PUBLIC PRONOUNCEMENTS OF THE ASSETS OF THE CREATOCRATIC ROYAL FAMILY.

42,733. PROVING THAT ALPHABETS ARE SPIRIT BEINGS.
42,734. ASTEROIDEITIES>>THE CONCEPT OF SEARCHING & LOCATION OF THE HUMAN STAR.

42,735. DEDUCING THE HIDDEN PURPOSE OF MY PHONE NUMBERS>>(090)
42,736. DEDUCING THE HIDDEN PURPOSE OF MY PHONE NUMBERS>>(081).
42,737. DEDUCING THE HIDDEN PURPOSE AND MYSTERIES OF NIGERIA.
42,738. INVENTING AND PATENTING THE MINDOSCOPE-STEROIDYTE.
42,739. FIGURES AND MEASURES OF THE WILL & WHEEL OF GOD.

42,740. MIND SHIFTING ON THE STEROIDYTE TECHNOLOGIES. -HELEN AS A SPINSTER, MARRIAGE AND DOUBLE MARRIAGE PREDICTIONS.

42,741. BIBLE BOOKS ON THE MINDOSCOPE-STEROIDYTE>>GENESIS. +65 Books of the Bible and 114 Books of the Quran = 42,806+114=42,920.

42,921. COUNTRIES ON THE MINDOSCOPE-STEROIDYTE FEDERAL REPUBLIC OF NIGERIA + 300 countries = 43,221.

43,222. NATIONAL CURRENCIES ON THE MINDOSCOPE-STEROIDYTE. NAIRA & KOBO + 300 Currencies = 43,521.

43,522. CREATOCRATIC NATIONS OF PARADISE ON THE MINDOSCOPE-STEROIDYTE.

43,523. CREATOCRATIC NATIONS OF PARADISE ON THE MINDOSCOPE-STEROIDYTE. Currencies>>Kosemaks, Kose, Darmaks, Maks, Solmaks in a complete mix.

43,524. THE CREATOCRACY ON THE MINDOSCOPE-STEROIDYTE.
43,525. THE CREATOCRACY-DEMOCRACY BOND ON THE MINDOSCOPE-STEROIDYTE.

43,526. DE-ROYAL MAKUPEDIA LIMITED ON THE MINDOSCOPE-STEROIDYTE.
+1,000,000 companies worldwide = 1,043,526.

1,043,527. INTER-SCRIPTURE OF THE BIBLE ON THE MINDOSCOPE-STEROIDYTE.
>>Double Bonding>>10,000 LInks>>Genesis-Hosea Link>>1,053,527.

1,043,528. INTER-SCRIPTURE OF THE BIBLE ON THE MINDOSCOPE-STEROIDYTE.
>>Triple Bonding>>10,000 LInks>>Genesis-Hosea Link>>1,063,527

1,043,529. INTER-SCRIPTURE OF THE BIBLE ON THE MINDOSCOPE-STEROIDYTE.
>>Quartet Bonding>>10,000 LInks>>Genesis-Hosea Link>>1,073,528.

1,043,530. INTER-SCRIPTURE OF THE QURAN ON THE MINDOSCOPE-STEROIDYTE.
>>Double Bonding>>10,000 LInks>>Genesis-Hosea Link>>1,053,530.

1,053,531. INTER-SCRIPTURE OF THE QURAN ON THE MINDOSCOPE-STEROIDYTE.
>>Triple Bonding>>10,000 LInks>>Genesis-Hosea Link>>1,063,530

1,063,530. INTER-SCRIPTURE OF THE QURAN ON THE MINDOSCOPE-STEROIDYTE.
>>Quartet Bonding>>10,000 LInks>>Genesis-Hosea Link>>1,073,530.

1,073,531. COMPANY TO COMPANY ON THE MINDOSCOPE-STEROIDYTE. DE-ROYAL MAKUPEDIA LIMITED - UTMOST PEAK RESOURCES + 1,000,000 Potential.
= 2,075,530.
Subscribers alone are expected to hit at least 10 billion in both humans and events being subscribed for before the impact can be measured.

Books shall be opened as study and research records for these subscribers. Hence Makupedia is infinitum endowment and establishes the Mind as endless in potentials.

2,075,531. MAKUPEDIA BUSINESS AND ASTRODIETIES IN FUTURE WATCH FOR PREDICTABILITY.-Mindoscope Watch using the Interest Code to predict occurrences and their compliance.

2,075,532. OFFICE OF THE EMPEROR & PATENTING THE MINDSET.
2,075,533. THE WHEEL OF GOD-THE SAME THING AS THE WILL OF GOD.

2,075,534. THE CLASSIFICATION OF MAKUPEDIA AS A TRANSCENDENCE STUDY.

2,075,535. CASH OPPORTUNITIES IN THE MAKUPEDIA CREATIVITY CONSULTING BUSINESS.

2,075,536. SIGNS IN THE SUN MOON AND STARS ARE BIBLICAL SIGNS OF REDEMPTION.
-Luke 21:18-26.

2,075,537. ASPECTS OF THE MAKABET IN TECHNOLOGY INVENTIONS FOR PATENTING.

2,075,538. THE HIGHER USES AND APPLICATIONS OF OUR PATENTS TO CREATE BIG BUSINESS.

2,075,539. THE COSMIC DATA CYCLE AND UNIVERSAL DATA MINING CODE.

2,075,540. THE GENIUS CODES OF THE MIND BANK LIMITED.

2,075,541. CLASSES OF CITYHOOD IN THE CREATOCRACY & PATENTING THE MAKABET MANSION.

2,075,542. COMPUTING METHODS FOR TRACKING DECISION MAKING IN BUSINESS UNDERTAKINGS.

2,075,543. MAKUPEDIA UNIVERSE PROGRAMMING LANGUAGE ON FIRST INSTANCE INITIALS.

2,075,544. DISCOVERING PEOPLE THROUGH THE BIRTH ENERGY.
>>OFEM-EKOT GIFT EFOLI, PETER MATTHEWS-AKUKALIA.

2,075,545. MAKUPEDIAN NUMBER-WORD ANALYTICS LANGUAGE.2,075,546. DATA ANALYTICS ON THE SERPENT-DOVE PROGRAM.

2,075,547. USING CURIOSITY TO TRACK WEALTH IN A PERSON.

2,075,548. DISCOVERING PEOPLE THROUGH THE BIRTH ENERGY 2.
>>Tina Matthews-Akukalia. >>Alice Matthews-Akukalia.

2,075,549. THE CONCEPT AND INVENTION OF DISEAN LITERATURES.

2,075,550. RANDOM IDEAS ON THE MAKUPEDIA PLAYS, RIGHTS & NAMES CONCERNS.

2,075,551. THE POINT OF ENERGY FOCUS IN A THING ON THE FEBRUARY 4, 2000 YEARS.

2,075,552. THE STANDARD UNIVERSAL PRICE OF A 50KG BAG OF RICE USING THE MAKS.

2,075,553. MAKUPEDIA INSTITUTE OF CREATIVITY & MIND TECHNOLOGIES.
-Faculty of Creative & Psycho-Social Sciences.
-Training & Employment Center for Creative Scientists of De-Royal Makupedia Limited.
-[Established Instituted & Protected by Provisions of The Creatocratic Charter].

2,075,554. WORD STRENGTH BY WORD COUNT.
2,075,555. LATEST IDEAS AFTER TYPING THE PLAYS.2,075,556. MAKUPEDIA DATA PROGRAMMING ANALYTICS & VERIFICATION SERVICES.
2,075,557. THE SCRIPTURES 77 CODE FOR INTERPRETING A DREAM & THOUGHT SYSTEM.

2,075,558. THE MAKUPEDIA
Legendary Plays of De - Mind God.

2,075,559. THE MAKUPEDIALAND.
Poems In Testaments.

2,075,560. THE MINDOM.
Seasons of Seven on the Nidrapoe.

2,075,561. THE HOLY BIQUR.
INTEGRATED CREATOCRATIC SCRIPTURES OF THE HOLY BIQUR MAKSTIAN FAITH & MIND TEMPLE DOCTRINES.

2,075,562. THE ROYAL CREATOCRACY 1234 TECHNOLOGY.
2,075,563. Bbbbb bbbbbbb bbb Notes of Records>>

2,075,564. DISCOVER THE AVATAR IN EACH CHILD & PERSON IN CREATIVE EDUCATION SERVICES.

2,075,565. TIMCHA TECHNOLOGIES OR TIME CHANT PROGRAMMING IN DESTINY TRACKING.
-Peter Matthews-Akukalia, Helen, Alice.

2,075,566. THE PROFESSIONAL CONCEPT OF TIME CHANTING APPS IN DESTINY TRACKING & CREATION OF THE MAKUPEDIA MAKAZINES.

2,075,567. MAKUPEDIA BUSINESS>>THE CITIZENS MINDOSCOPE DAILY.

2,075,568.
THE CITIZENS MINDOSCOPE FOR YEAR 2021.
UNIVERSAL MAKS CURRENCIES SERVICES OF DE - ROYAL MAKUPEDIA LIMITED.
January - December. Area of focus>>Average Money Quotient>>12%.
Year Index>>2021>>2.0*2.1=p=4.1+4.2=8.3x=px=25.52/25/2.5

2,075,569. SKETCHING THE LIFE MAP OF A PERSON BASED ON TIME CHANTING.

2,075,570. DATABASE OF TIME CHANTING SCRIPTURES & HUMAN-DAILY ENERGY SYSTEMS (BIQUR).-BOOK ALIGNMENT CODE = BIBLE = QURAN.

2,075,571. BRIEFS ON THE WORLD CREATOCRATIC PARTY NIGERIA. WCPN
2,075,572. THE TECHNOLOGY OF YAWNING ON THE LAW OF TIME AND CHANCE.

2,075,573. Approved book title for the Royal Creatocracy 1 is MAKUPEDIA, Legends of De - Mind God. (READ BOOK).

2,075,574. CROWNING CODES OF THE ROYAL CREATOCRACY.
2,075,575. TIME CHANTING THE CROWN OF THE ROYAL CREATOCRACY.
2,075,576. TIME CHANTING DE - ROYAL MAKUPEDIA LIMITED.
2,075,577. COMPILED SUGGESTIONS OF TITLES AND TITLE BAR.

2,075,578. THE CONCEPT OF MAKUPEDIALAND I.
MAKUPEDIALAND
Poems in Testaments.

Glimpses In Verse, Codes of Destiny & Festival of Testament Poetry on the Paradise.
By Peter Matthews-Akukalia.
Makupedia I of Makupedialand.
Sovereign Emperor, Creatocratic Nations of Paradise.

2,075,579. THE CONCEPT OF MAKUPEDIALAND II.

2,075,580. THE HOLY BIQUR
-Integrated Makumatics Scriptures of the Makstian Faith & Mind Temple Doctrines.

2,075,581. THE MINDOSCOPE FOR YEAR 2021 STUDY COPY.
-GENERATING SERIAL CODES AND TIME CHANTING THE YEAR 2021.

2,075,582. THE MINDOSCOPE 2021.

2,075,583. THE ARCHITECTURE AND MASTERPLAN FOR THE MAKUPEDIALAND CITY.

2,075,584. WORK INCENTIVES ON LITTLE CONSIDERATIONS.

2,075,585. THE HOLY BIQUR
-Integrated Makumatics Scriptures of the Makstian Faith & Mind Temple Doctrines.
>>FÁTIHA - REVELATION - KING MAKS VERSION & TIME CHANT INTEGRATED EDITION.

2,075,586. CONCEPT OF THE YOUNG CREATIVE SCIENTISTS & INVENTORS CLUB FOR THE SECONDARY SCHOOLS.

2,075,587. LETTER TO SCHOOLS ON THE YOUNG CREATIVE SCIENTISTS CORPS.

2,075,588. THE CONCEPT OF DESIRE AND PLANERGY I.

2,075,589. THE CONCEPT OF CASTLE MAKUPEDIA AND THE MAKUPEDIA CASTLE WORKS GRAPH.

2,075,590.THE CONCEPT OF LIFE DESIRE AND PLANERGY II.
-FOR THE EMPRESS.

2,075,591.THE CONCEPT OF LIFE DESIRE AND PLANERGY II.
-FOR THE QUEEN.

2,075,592. THE CONCEPT OF LIFE DESIRE AND PLANERGY IV.
-for Christian Onyeze >> AUD 95 set.

2,075,593. THE CONCEPT OF LIFE DESIRE AND PLANERGY V.
-For Vivian Nwachukwu.

2,075,594. THE ORIGIN OF PSYCHOASTRONOMY AND THE SOLAR CORE PRINCIPLE.

2,075,595. CONCEPT OF THE MAKUPEDIA GAMES REWARD SYSTEMS.

2,075,596. CURRENCY PROPOSAL EXTRACTS FOR THE CBN VISA AND OTHERS.

2,075,597. THE MEANING OF THE N1000 IN MINDTECH.

2,075,598. 2021 IMPLEMENTATION LETTER FOR THE YCSI CLUB NIGERIA FOR SECONDARY SCHOOLS.

2,075,599. PROPOSAL LETTER TO THE CBN ON THE MAKS CURRENCIES PATENT.

2,075,600. THE IMPORTANCE OF SUBJECTIVE ANALYSIS IN EVERYDAY LIFE.

2,075,601. THE QUOTIENT TREASURE TECHNOLOGY SYSTEMS.

2,075,602. HOW MUCH IS A 50KG BAG OF RICE IN THE MAKS CURRENCIES VALUE?

2,075,603. RANDOM IDEAS ON THINGS IN THE MAKUPEDIA INSTITUTE & MEDIA EXPOSURE.

2,075,604. THE GODDESS MAKUPEDIA CONCEPT.

2,075,605. CONCEPT OF THE MAKUPEDIA GENIUS INSTITUTE.

2,075,606. CONCEPTS OF THE KALIAWOOD AND THE CROWN OF THE PARADISEANS.

2,075,607. CONCEPT OF THE ATOMIC MIND.

2,075,608. THE ATOMIC MIND AND ITS COSMIC REPRESENTATIONS IN PETER MATTHEWS-AKUKALIA.

2,075,609. MAKUPEDIA LOCATIONS & MIND SETTINGS I.

2,075,610. MAKUPEDIA LOCATIONS & MIND SETTINGS II.

2,075,611. TRACKING DESTINY THROUGH DIRECT BIRTH DAY & BIRTH YEAR SIGNS (PMA).

2,075,612. THE MAKUPEDIA INSTITUTE FOR WEBSITE PURPOSES.

2,075,613. THE MAKUPEDIA TTT SCHEME 2021.

2,075,614. MAKUPEDIALAND>>THE WHITE LAND OF THE ROYAL CREATOCRACY.

2,075,615. DETAILS SENT TO MR. FRANCIS CONSULTANT AND BUSINESS PR.TO MAKUPEDIA.

2,075,616. UPDATE OF MAKUPEDIA AS A STUDY OF GOD AND DE - GODS IN COSMOS.

2,075,617. THE CHAMPION NAME IN THE DISEAN LANGUAGE SYSTEMS.

2,075,618. THE CHAMPION NAME IN THE DISEAN LANGUAGE SYSTEMS. >>JUSTINA ODUIGWE.

2,075,619. THE WONDERFUL MYSTERY OF IMMORTALITY SOLVED AND THE CARD GAMES.

2,075,620. MIND ASSESSMENT RESULTS FOR MR. FRANCIS.

2,075,621. THE MYSTERY OF PLANETS >> JUPITER & THE JESUS PLANETARY CODE.

2,075,622. THE MAKUPEDIAN ORDER OF THE ROYAL CREATOCRACY.

2,075,623. DISCOVERING THE PLANETARY CODES IN THE NAME JESUS CHRIST & AMEN.
2,075,624.THE MAKUPEDIA SMART CLOCKS TECHNOLOGIES [MSCT].
2,075,625. BUSINESS MAKUPEDIA or MAKUPEDIA BUSINESS DEVELOPMENT.

2,075,626. DETERMINING A PERSON SPHERE OF INFLUENCE ON ENERGY SOURCES>>PMA.

2,075,627. THE CONCEPT OF AVIALYSIS IN THE MAKUPEDIA EDUCATION SYSTEMS.
2,075,628. Hi Mr. Simeon.

2,075,629. THE MYSTERY OF CREATION IN THE GENESIS BASED ON PMA's DEMA = 90%=9.0 MAT.

2,075,630. AUNTY BENE's SPHERE OF INFLUENCE CODE.
2,075,631. THE MAKUPEDIA INSTITUTE ON SHORT TERM COURSES.
2,075,632. THE MAKUPEDIA MUSEUM.
2,075,633. DATA OF BIRTH ANALYTICS ON SPIRAL ENERGY FOR PMA.
2,075,634. WHAT ENERGY RUNS OUR AGES.

2,075,635. THE TERMINATOR DARK FATE JUDGEMENT DAY MOVIE AND THE METRICS OF THINGS.

2,075,636. 2021 BUSINESS FOCUS.
2,075,637. POWER OF THE DAY AND PUNISHMENT FOR WRONGDOING.
2,075,638. MOON PERSONS AND THEIR NATURE.
2,075,639. THE SPIRITS MUSES AND SECRETS OF BUSINESS RICHES AND WEALTH.
2,075,640. THE MYSTERY OF SATELLITES AND MUSE LINK SOLVED.
2,075,641. THE MAKS CURRENCY QUALITY ASSURANCE GUARANTEE.
2,075,642. THE MAKUPEDIA DMG SYSTEMS I.
2,075,643. THE MAKUPEDIA DMG MUSES SYSTEMS II.

2,075,644. THE MAKS CURRENCIES MANAGEMENT AND INTEREST DEDUCTIONS.
>>Determining a currency value by its allocated code.
>>How to use the Naira & profit from it based on its allocated series codes.

2,075,645. THE MAKUPEDIA DMG MUSES SYSTEMS III.

2,075,646. THE MAKUPEDIA DMG MUSES SYSTEMS IV.
>> INTERPLANETARY SUPPORT SYSTEMS & TABLE OF SCRIPTURES.

2,075,647. THE MAKUPEDIA DMG MUSES SYSTEMS V.
>> KNOWING THE LIFE OF A PERSON USING THE NAME - PSALMS
SECRET PRAYERS.

2,075,648. THE MAKS CURRENCY COST FOR A TELEPHONE LINE NUMBER.
2,075,649. THE MAKS CURRENCY COST FOR A BARREL OF BRENT CRUDE
OIL FOR OPEC.

2,075,650. THE MAKS CURRENCY APP INVESTMENT OPPORTUNITIES.
>>EARN BIG. BECOME RICH AND SUCCESSFUL. ELIMINATE INFLATION.

2,075,651. THE MYSTERIES OF PETER MATTHEWS-AKUKALIA AS A NAME.
2,075,652. SOLVING THE COMMON ELEMENTS IN THE MAKUPEDIA
POWER CODES.

2,075,653. TRACKING THE SUCCESS PATH OF MAKUPEDIA FOR 2021 USING
STARGAZING 2005 BOOK.

2,075,654. THE MAKS CURRENCIES IN SCRIPTURE PROPHECY FULFILLED.
2,075,655. MAKUPEDIA EDUCATIONAL ASSESSMENT SERVICES.

2,075,656. THE MASTERS RECOMMENDATIONS ON THE SELLING POINTS
OF THE MAKS BANK.

2,075,657. THE MAKS CURRENCIES BUSINESS.
>>SETTING UP THE MAKS BANK SYSTEMS.

2,075,658. LAUNCHING THE TEMPLATE & MANIFESTO FOR THE CREATIVE
ECONOMY.
2,075,659. ORGANIZATIONS OF MAKUPEDIAN ORDER OF THE ROYAL
CREATOCRACY.
2,075,660. DEVELOPMENT STUDY ON THE EFFECT OF SOLAR SOURCING
IN HUMANS.

2,075,661. MIND ASSESSMENT TESTS.
>>LIST OF INNATE POTENTIALS FOR PETER MATTHEWS-AKUKALIA.

2,075,662. THE BUSINESS REALITIES OF MAKUPEDIA AS A CORPORATE
ORGANIZATION.
2,075,663. SELLING METHODS AND INTRODUCTION IN THE MAKUPEDIA
BUSINESS.
2,075,664.THE ABSTRACT REALITIES OF MAKUPEDIA AS A CORPORATE
ORGANIZATION I.

2,075,665. THE ABSTRACT REALITIES OF MAKUPEDIA AS A CORPORATE ORGANIZATION II.

2,075,666. THE ABSTRACT REALITIES OF MAKUPEDIA AS A CORPORATE ORGANIZATION III.

2,075,667. BIRTH YEAR PURPOSES FOR SOME YEARS NECESSARY FOR MATS. >>1950 - 1954, 1974, 1982, 1986, 2003, 2021.

2,075,668. DE - GODS IN THE DAYS AND THE VINDICATION OF JOHANNES KEPLER.
2,075,669. MARKETING MARKETING THE MINDOSCOPE.

2,075,670. INTRODUCING THE MINDOSCOPE.
A DATABASE ON HUMAN POTENTIALS FOR PROFESSIONALS AND NON PROFESSIONALS.

2,075,671. CREATING EDITIONS OF THE MINDOSCOPE IN BOOKS AND PICTURES.

2,075,672. ESTABLISHED FACTS ABOUT KRISTOS.
JESUS CHRIST OF NAZARETH THE KINGS OF KINGS & LORD OF LORDS. THE AMEN.
AS SEEN THROUGH THE MINDOSCOPE OF DE - ROYAL MAKUPEDIA LIMITED.
TODAY 29.04.2021@11:00am.

2,075,673. POTENTIALS AND THE TRIANGLE OF DESIRE IN THE MINDOSCOPE.
2,075,674. MARKETING METHODS FOR OUR CEO TRAINING PROJECT.

2,075,675. THE MAKUPEDIAN MINDOSCOPE MEANING OF PETER MATTHEWS - AKUKALIA.

2,075,676. THE AUTHORITY OF THE MAKUPEDIA PATENT AND LICENSE.
2,075,677. MAKUPEDIA CREATIVE EDUCATION SERVICES HALL OF FAME.

2,075,678. EDUCATIONAL DEVELOPMENT STANDARDS OF THE MODERN TEACHER.
MAKUPEDIA RESEARCH TRAINING AND RECOMMENDATIONS.
CONDUCTED BY: PETER MATTHEWS - AKUKALIA.
HCEG.ACSI.DMG.DGG.DCG.DOSC.DLS.DASH.MAKUPEDIA.LTEAP.
SECNP.SEMORC.

1. THE MEANS AND ENDS OF EDUCATION.
2. EXAMPLE IS BETTER THAN PRECEPT.
3. THE EVILS OF HALF KNOWLEDGE.
4. READING AS A FACTOR OF EDUCATION.
5. THE MECHANICS OF TEACHING.
>>culled from the 25 Virtues of a teacher.

2,075,679. THE OFFICIAL BUSINESS LAUNCHING OF MAKUPEDIA COMPANY BUSINESS.

2,075,680. HEAVENS AND EARTH MYSTERIES AS DISCOVERIES OF MAKUPEDIA.

2,075,681. THE MINDOSCOPE FOR MOREL 001.

2,075,682. THE MINDOSCOPE MEANING OF A NAME ON SYNCHRONIZATION.

2,075,683. THE SOFTWARE MECHANICS OF MONEY AND CURRENCY ON SCOPE.

2,075,684. THE MAKUPEDIA INSTITUTE.
>>Studies in Creative Sciences, MindArts & MindTech Business.
>>[Instituted Established & Protected by Provisions of the Creatocratic Charter].©
>>FEW NOTES.

2,075,685. LETTER FOR THE MANAGING DIRECTOR, ACCESS BANK NIG. PLC & OTHERS.

2,075,686. LETTERHEAD FOR MTN, GLO, AIRTEL & 9MOBILE.

2,075,687. LETTERHEAD FOR LAGOOZE GROUP OF SCHOOLS.

2,075,688. LETTERHEAD FOR CALVARY MODEL COLLEGE, AREPO.

2,075,689. THE MAKUPEDIAN BUSINESS OF NATIONS ON NAMES.
>>Nigeria, America, Ghana.

The Makupedian Business of nations is based on 300 countries each treated as a chapter. Hence 2,075,689 + 300 = 2,075,989.

2,075,990. REVELATIONS OF THE CREATOCRATIC UNIVERSITY AND THE CREATOCRATIC UNION. THE MAKUPEDIA INSTITUTE [TMI]. Creative Sciences MindTech Arts & Creatocratic Business School. [Instituted Established & Protected by Provisions of the Creatocratic Charter as Faculty of Creative & Psycho - Social Sciences & Department of De - Royal Makupedia Limited]©.

2,075,991. SAMPLES OF THE MINDOSCOPE RESULTS FOR MOREL 001 & OTHERS.
Results of Morel and Abidel Proprietresses were deleted due to their sensitive nature. However results of students that begin from Duru>>004 are clearly included.

2,075,992. MEASUREMENT OF "MANY" IN CASTING YOUR BREAD UPON THE WATERS.

2,075,993. THE MAKUPEDIA INSTITUTE >> TMI.
ACADEMIC DEPARTMENTS AND COURSES.

2,075,994. THE MAKSTIAN FAITH CENTER IN THE SCRIPTURES.
Specialist in Spiritual Diagnosis & Treatment, Scripture Forensics & Teaching, Unlocking Human Potentials, Abstraction & Mind Development, Consulting Services.

2,075,995. TRACKING ATHENA IN THE FAMILY OF THE KING AND GUIDING SPIRITS IN FAMILIES.

2,075,996. THE MOVEMENT OF APHRODITE ANNUALLY IN THE UNIVERSE.
2,075,997. THE MOVEMENT OF THE SPIRIT OF MAKUPEDIA ANNUALLY IN THE UNIVERSE.

2,075,998. NATURE FIRST BUSINESS AND CAREER PRIORITY OF THE MAKUPEDIA PERSON & DEITY.

2,075,999. THE CREATOCRACY BILL FOR THE LEGISLATURE AND MATTERS OF DE-GODS.
2,076,000. DYNAMICS OF THE TALENTS AND IDEAS MARKETS.

2,076,001. READING THE SIGNS OF DE - GODS IN EVERYTHING.
1. NAME SIGNS >> PETER MATTHEWS - AKUKALIA.

A. PETER >> 16-5-20-5-18 B. MATTHEWS >> 13-1-20-20-8-5-23-19.

C. AKUKALIA >> 1-11-21-11-1-12-9-1.

DATE OF BIRTH SIGNS>> 6 July 1978. B. MAKUPEDIA NAME SIGNS.
DATE OF BIRTH CODE SIGNS >> C-1578241-CC-809682-RC-1446213. C, CC, RC,

2,076,002. THE MSGRC CONCEPT AND CONVENTIONAL ACADEMIC ENTITLEMENTS.
>>Most Sovereign God of the Royal Creatocracy; Ph.D., B.A., B.Sc., Peter, Matthews, Akukalia.

2,076,003. THE MAKUPEDIA FEAST WEEK AS A MIND TEMPLE DOCTRINE.
2,076,004. TRACKING THE SPECIFIC GODS IN DAYS AS OF DATES.
2,076,005. CONCEPT OF THE PHONE - NAMES CONVERSION ON DE-GODS.

2,076,006. DIMENSIONS ERA AND THEIR CONTROL GODS.

2,076,007. BRIEFS ON THE TRUTH OF WOLE SOYINKA's BRAIN DETAILS.

2,076,008. THE CONCEPT OF ATHENA AS MAKSONIUM CORE OF INTELLIGENCE.

2,076,009. THE WIT CONCEPT LAW OF GOD FOR ATTAINMENT OF GODSHIP.

2,076,010. THE CROWN OF CASTLE MAKUPEDIA.
>>Legendary Plays & Short Stories on Creatocracy. >> A Book.

2,076,011. THE WISDOM BLESSINGS RICHES AND WEALTHS OF MAKUPEDIA.
>>Romans 11:33-36.

2,076,012. THE CONCEPT LIFELINE AND ENERGY OF TRUST IN THE PROPHECY OF THE SCRIPTURES ABOUT THE EMERGENCE OF MAKUPEDIA.

2,076,013. CROWNING MAKUPEDIA A GOD IN THE CROWN OF CASTLE MAKUPEDIA.

2,076,014. THE CONCEPT OF ATHENA AND ASHTORETH IN ASTROSOUND DYNAMICS.

2,076,015. CONCEPT OF A CREATOCRATIC JESUS.

2,076,016. CASTLE MAKUPEDIA.
THE GOD NAME AND RIGHTS OF PETER MATTHEWS-AKUKALIA.

2,076,017. TCCM CONCEPTION LAW OF THE CROWN OF CASTLE AND ATHENA.

2,076,018. THE SCIENCE OF BEING BORN AGAIN AND KNOWING THE MIND OF GOD.

2,076,019. INTERPRETATION OF THE BIBLE BY GREEK CODES.

2,076,020. THE TWELVE DIMENSIONAL ASSETS OF CASTLE MAKUPEDIA.

2,076,021. ADOPTION TO WIT BY GREEK CODES. >> Romans 8:23.

2,076,022. THE MAKSTIAN GREEK [TMG] BIBLE ON MIND CODE.

2,076,023. THE MAKSTIAN GREEK [TMG] BIBLE ON THE TREE OF GOOD AND EVIL.

2,076,024. THE MAKSTIAN GREEK [TMG] BIBLE ON THE TRUE IDENTITY OF WISDOM AS ATHENA.

2,076,025. THE MAKSTIAN GREEK [TMG] BIBLE ON SECRET AND DO BY DEUTERONOMY 29:29.

2,076,026. TESTAMENTARY DISPOSITION OF MAKSTIANITY ON TITHES PARADISE AND CREATOCRATIC DEITY. >> TRISTAR KEYS OF THE VALLEY OF THE KINGS FULFILLED.

2,076,027. THE MAKSTIAN GREEK [TMG] BIBLE ON THE LAW>>GOD IS ONE.
2,076,028. COMPUTING AND LOCATING THE GOD CALLED PARADISE.
2,076,029. THE MYSTERIES OF PARADISE IN THE BIRTH OF SAMSON.
2,076,030. THE MYSTERY OF GODS AND PREDICTING TIME >> YEAR 2021.

2,076,031. THE WIT BIBLE ON GENESIS AND REVELATION.
    >>Advance Scriptures for the Makstian Faith & Mind Temple.
    >>Concept & book.

2,076,032. SUMMARY OF THE MAKUPEDIA ASSETS.
2,076,033. PROVING EMOTION AS THE SOURCE OF INNATE ASSETS IN EVERYONE.
2,076,034. THE MIND TEMPLE 1>> Mysteries of Hermes the Mercury.
2,076,035. THE MIND TEMPLE 2>> Mysteries of the Tristar.
2,076,036. THE MIND TEMPLE 3>> Mysteries of Maia.

2,076,037. THE MIND TEMPLE 4>> THE WIT CODES TECHNOLOGIES AND APPLICATIONS ON GOD.

2,076,038. THE MIND TEMPLE 5>> THE WIT CODE TECH FOR PETER MATTHEWS-AKUKALIA.

2,076,039. THE MIND TEMPLE 6>> THE WIT CODES TECH FOR CASTLE MAKUPEDIA.
2,076,040. THE MIND TEMPLE 7>> THE WIT CODES TECH FOR GATES OF WISDOM.
2,076,041. THE MIND TEMPLE 8>> THE MIND OF GOD CODES ON MINES AND EARTH.
2,076,042. THE MIND TEMPLE 9>> THE SOLAR CROWN OF CASTLE MAKUPEDIA.
2,076,043. THE MIND TEMPLE 10>> ETERNAL LAWS OF THE SOLAR CROWN.
2,076,044. THE MIND TEMPLE 11>> THE MYSTERIES OF ZEUS AND MIND TIME ZONING.
2,076,045. THE MIND TEMPLE 12>> Mysteries of the Sword of Honour.

2,076,046. THE MIND TEMPLE 13>> MYSTERIES OF ZEUS AND TRANSFORMATION PROCESSES.

2,076,047. THE CONCEPT OF MINOLITICS.

2,076,048. BIBLE ENERGY DATABASE.
>>TRACKING THE SOURCE GODS OF THE SCRIPTURES >>>> GENESIS - REVELATION.

2,076,049. THE TWELVE TRIBES AND THRONES OF CASTLE MAKUPEDIA.
2,076,050. KALIAWOOD AND THE CREATOCRACY.
2,076,051. THE WAYS OF GODS IN DATABASE SYSTEMS & LECTURES FROM ATHENA.

2,076,052. THE CASTLE MAKUPEDIA PRECISION DICTIONARY.
>> A Creatocracy Bank for Mining Words Data and the Maks Currencies. - A BOOK.

2,076,053. ADVANCE STRUCTURES OF THE CREATOCRACY.
2,076,054. THE REAL MEANING OF PETER MATTHEWS - AKUKALIA.
2,076,055. THE SCIENCE OF PROPHETECH.

2,076,056. THE COMPUTATIONAL SCIENCE OF CONDITIONED INHERITANCE.
-Science of GOD and the Gods and consistency theory.

2,076,057. CREED OF THE CREATOCRACY.

2,076,058. THE BRICK WALLS OF CASTLE MAKUPEDIA.
Creatocciary Laws Codes & Creatocratic Jurisprudence in the Creatocature. - A BOOK.

2,076,059. LATEST DESIGNS OF OUR BUSINESS CARDS & LETTERHEADS.
Trademark of the Creatocracy Corporation®™.

2,076,060. THE BRICK WALLS OF CASTLE MAKUPEDIA.
2,076,061. DIVINE VISIT OF THE MOST HIGH TO CASTLE MAKUPEDIA.

2,076,062. THE CREATOCRATIC CHARTER 2
>>Sovereignty Charter for the Creatocracy. - A BOOK.

2,076,063. THE NATURE OF MY PERSON (BY COLOR) AS DEDUCED ON THE INTERNET.
2,076,064. THE COSMIC ORIGIN OF CASTLE MAKUPEDIA.

2,076,065. WHAT IS THE MEANING OF THE NAME VICTOR AND OTHER THINGS.
2,076,066. THE MYSTERY OF 40.

2,076,067. The WORLD DIGITAL DICTIONARY IN THE ASSETS BASE OF MAKUPEDIA.

2,076,068. INTERPRETING SCRIPTURES BY BOOK CHAPTER AND VERSE BY THE GODS.

2,076,069. THE USE OF DIGITAL DICTIONARY IN SOLVING FORMULA COMPONENTS (U=abc).
2,076,070. GAIANS PERSONALITY DATABASE.
2,076, 071. Counseling Codes for Marriages & Computing Divorce.
2,076,072. THE HADEANS.

Charter member=2,500=3,000=30%=P3.0D=3.0=Cr=Stars=Muses=3 March= C=I>>GIL.
Chartres=4,500=5,000=50%=P50D=Law=Time=Venus=5 May = Aphrodite>>L=N.
Chartreuse=3,500=4,000=40%=P4.0D=Govt.=4 April=Mercury=Hermes=G=A4.
Charwoman=1,500=15%=P1.50D=1.5=Authority=Crown=Solar Core=1 May = Maia.
Chary=3,000=30%=P3.0D=3.0=Creativity=Stars=Muses=3 March= C=I>>GIL.
Chase(1)=9,000=90%=P9.00D=9.0=Abst.=Gods=Saturn=9Sept.>>A=Ø.
Chase(2)=9,000=90%=P9.00D=9.0=Abst.=Gods=Saturn=9Sept.>>A=Ø.
Chaser=7,000=70%=P7.0D=7.0=Language=Assets=Mars=7 July=Pleiades
Chasm=7,000=70%=P7.0D=7.0=Language=Assets=Mars=7 July=Pleiades
Chassid=1,500=15%=P1.50D=1.5=Authority=Crown=Solar Core=1 May = Maia.
Chassis=15,000=1,500=15%=P1.50D=1.5=Authority=Crown=Solar Core=1 May = Maia.

Chaste=7,500=8,000=80%=P8.0D=Economy=Currency=8 Aug.=Zeus>>E=v.
Chastity is a borderline from computational precision to business. It means something has been learned as a result of discretion a key requirement for wisdom and creativity.

Chasten=4,000=40%=P4.0D=Govt. =Creatocracy=4 April=Mercury=Hermes=G=A4.
Chastise=3,500=4,000=40%=P4.0D=Govt. =Creatoc.=4 April=Mercury=Hermes=G=A4.
Chasuble=6,000=60%=P6.0D=Man=Earth=Royalty=6 June=Gaia=Maia>>M=M2.
Chat=8,500=9,000=90%=P9.00D=9.0=Abst.=Gods=Saturn=9Sept.>>A=Ø.

Chateau=3,000=30%=P3.0D=3.0=Cr=Stars=Muses=3 March= C=I>>GIL.
A French castle. A large country house. A Disean castle is called Castle Makupedia. It is the large country house of the Mind God who is also the God of Creatocracy and Genius. Residence of the Creatocratic Royal Family located and situate worldwide in grace.

Château briand=5,000=50%=P5.00D=Law=Time=Venus=5 May = Aphrodite>>L=N.
Chattanooga=4,000=40%=P4.0D=Govt. =Creatocracy=4April=Mercury=Hermes=G=A4.
Chattel=4,500=5,000=50%=P5.00D=Law=Time=Venus=5 May = Aphrodite>>L=N.
Chatter=9,500=10,000=1,000=100%=10.0=Physicality=Tech.=10 Oct.=Uranus=P=1Ø.
Chatterbox=2,000=20%=P2.00D=2.0=Nature=Moon=2 Feb.=Cupid=N=C+_.
Chatterton Thomas=2,000=20%=P2.00D=2.0=Nature=Moon=2 Feb.=Cupid=N=C+_.
Chaucer Geoffrey=2,500=3,000=30%=P3.0D=3.0=Cr=Stars=Muses=3 March= C=I>>GIL.

Chauffeur=3,000=30%=P3.0D=3.0=Cr=Stars=Muses=3 March= C=I>>GIL.
Chauvinism=5,500=5.5=80%=P5.50=Earth-Midway=5 May = Gaia.
Cheap=11,500=12,000=12%=P1.20D=1.2=Knowledge=Education=12Dec.=Athena>>K=F.
Cheapen=4,000=40%=P4.0D=Govt. =Creatocracy=4 April=Mercury=Hermes=G=A4.
Cheap shot=4,000=40%=P4.0D=Govt. =Creatocracy=4 April=Mercury=Hermes=G=A4.
Cheap skate=1,500=15%=P1.50D=1.5=Authority=Crown=Solar Core=1 May = Maia.
Cheat=10,500=11,000=11%=P1.10D=1.1=Idea=Brainchild=11Nov=Athena>>I=MT.
Cheboksary=4,000=40%=P4.0D=Govt. =Creatocracy=4 April=Mercury=Hermes=G=A4.
Check=10,000=1,000=100%=10.0=Physicality=Tech.=10 Oct.=Uranus=P=1Ø.
Checkbook=4,000=40%=P4.0D=Govt. =Creatocracy=4 April=Mercury=Hermes=G=A4.
Checker=16,500=17,000=17%=P1.70D=1.7=Solar Asset=17 Feb.=Maia=Mind Computing.
Checkerboard=8,500=9,000=90%=P9.00D=9.0=Abst.=Gods=Saturn=9Sept.>>A=Ø.
Checkered=8,000=80%=P8.0D=Economy=Currency=8 Aug.=Zeus>>E=v.
Checking account=7,000=70%=P7.0D=7.0=Language=Assets=Mars=7 July=Pleiades
Checkmate=11,000=11%=P1.10D=1.1=Idea=Brainchild=11Nov=Athena>>I=MT.
Checkout=12,000=12%=P1.20D=1.2=Knowledge=Education=12Dec.=Athena>>K=F.
Checkpoint=4,500=5,000=50%=P5.00D=Law=Time=Venus=5 May = Aphrodite>>L=N.
Check rein=9,000=90%=P9.00D=9.0=Abst.=Gods=Saturn=9Sept.>>A=Ø.
Check room=6,500=7,000=70%=P7.0D=7.0=Language=Assets=Mars=7 July=Pleiades
Checkup=3,000=30%=P3.0D=3.0=Cr=Stars=Muses=3 March= C=I>>GIL.
Cheddar=8,000=80%=P8.0D=Economy=Currency=8 Aug.=Zeus>>E=v.

Cheek=11,000=11%=P1.10D=1.1=Idea=Brainchild=11Nov=Athena>>I=MT.
Athena donated the human cheeks and designs the faces of men.

Cheekbone=4,000=40%=P4.0D=Govt. =Creatocracy=4 April=Mercury=Hermes=G=A4.
Cheeky=500=5%=P5.00D=5.0=Law=Time=Venus=5 May=Aphrodite>>L=N.
Cheep=5,500=5.5=80%=P5.50=Earth-Midway=5 May = Gaia.
Cheer=15,000=1,500=15%=P1.50D=1.5=Authority=Crown=Solar Core=1 May = Maia.
Cheerful=2,500=3,000=30%=P3.0D=3.0=Cr=Stars=Muses=3 March= C=I>>GIL.
Cheerleader=6,000=60%=P6.0D=Man=Earth=Royalty=6 June=Gaia=Maia>>M=M2.
Cheers=2,000=20%=P2.00D=2.0=Nature=Moon=2 Feb.=Cupid=N=C+_.
Cheese=5,000=50%=P5.00D=Law=Time=Venus=5 May = Aphrodite>>L=N.
Cheeseburger=3,000=30%=P3.0D=3.0=Cr=Stars=Muses=3 March= C=I>>GIL.
Cheesecake=8,500=9,000=90%=P9.00D=9.0=Abst.=Gods=Saturn=9Sept.>>A=Ø.
Cheesecloth=3,000=30%=P3.0D=3.0=Cr=Stars=Muses=3 March= C=I>>GIL.
Cheesy=4,500=5,000=50%=P5.00D=Law=Time=Venus=5 May = Aphrodite>>L=N.
Cheetah=6,500=7,000=70%=P7.0D=7.0=Language=Assets=Mars=7 July=Pleiades
Cheever John=2,000=20%=P2.00D=2.0=Nature=Moon=2 Feb.=Cupid=N=C+_.
Chef=2,000=20%=P2.00D=2.0=Nature=Moon=2 Feb.=Cupid=N=C+_.
Chef-d'oeuvre=1,000=100%=10.0=1.0=Mind=Sun=1 January=Helios >> M=E4.
Chef's salad=9,000=90%=P9.00D=9.0=Abst.=Gods=Saturn=9Sept.>>A=Ø.
Chekhov Anton=2,500=3,000=30%=P3.0D=3.0=Cr=Stars=Muses=3 March= C=I>>GIL.
Chelyabinsk=4,500=5,000=50%=P5.00D=Law=Time=Venus=5 May = Aphrodite>>L=N.

Chemical=8,000=80%=P8.0D=Economy=Currency=8 Aug.=Zeus>>E=v.
Chemical abuse=1,500=15%=P1.50D=1.5=Authority=Crown=Solar Core=1 May = Maia.
Chemical bond=11,500=12,000=12%=P1.20D=1.2=Knowledge=Edu=12Dec.=Athena>>K=F.
Chemical dependency=7,500=8,000=80%=P8.0D=Econ.=Currency=8 Aug.=Zeus>>E=v.
Chemical engineering=3,500=4,000=40%=P4.0D=Govt.=4 April=Mercury=Hermes=G=A4.
Chemical warfare=3,000=30%=P3.0D=3.0=Cr=Stars=Muses=3 March= C=I>>GIL.
Chemiluminescence=6,000=60%=P6.0D=Man=Earth=Roy.=6 June=Gaia=Maia>>M=M2.
Chemise=6,000=60%=P6.0D=Man=Earth=Royalty=6 June=Gaia=Maia>>M=M2.
Chemist=4,000=40%=P4.0D=Govt. =Creatocracy=4 April=Mercury=Hermes=G=A4.
Chemistry=11,500=12,000=12%=P1.20D=1.2=Knowl.=Education=12Dec.=Athena>>K=F.
Chemnitz=7,000=70%=P7.0D=7.0=Language=Assets=Mars=7 July=Pleiades
Chemo=1,000=100%=10.0=1.0=Mind=Sun=1 January=Helios >> M=E4.
Chemo-=1,500=15%=P1.50D=1.5=Authority=Crown=Solar Core=1 May = Maia.
Chemoreception=4,500=5,000=50%=P5.00D=Law=Time=Venus=5 May =Odite>>L=N.
Chemo surgery=3,500=4,000=40%=P4.0D=Govt.=4 April=Mercury=Hermes=G=A4.
Chemosynthesis=9,000=90%=P9.00D=9.0=Abst.=Gods=Saturn=9Sept.>>A=Ø.
Chemotherapy=6,500=7,000=70%=P7.0D=7.0=Language=Assets=Mars=7 July=Pleiades
Chemurgy=7,500=8,000=80%=P8.0D=Economy=Currency=8 Aug.=Zeus>>E=v.
Chengchow=1,000=100%=10.0=1.0=Mind=Sun=1 January=Helios >> M=E4.
Chengdu=5,000=50%=P5.00D=Law=Time=Venus=5 May = Aphrodite>>L=N.
Chenille=6,000=60%=P6.0D=Man=Earth=Royalty=6 June=Gaia=Maia>>M=M2.
Cheops=5,000=50%=P5.00D=Law=Time=Venus=5 May = Aphrodite>>L=N.
Cheque=2,500=3,000=30%=P3.0D=3.0=Cr=Stars=Muses=3 March= C=I>>GIL.
Chequer=2,500=3,000=30%=P3.0D=3.0=Cr=Stars=Muses=3 March= C=I>>GIL.
Cherish=3,000=30%=P3.0D=3.0=Cr=Stars=Muses=3 March= C=I>>GIL.
Chernobyl=8,500=9,000=90%=P9.00D=9.0=Abst.=Gods=Saturn=9Sept.>>A=Ø.
Cherokee=11,000=11%=P1.10D=1.1=Idea=Brainchild=11Nov=Athena>>I=MT.
Cheroot=3,000=30%=P3.0D=3.0=Cr=Stars=Muses=3 March= C=I>>GIL.
Cherry=15,000=1,500=15%=P1.50D=1.5=Authority=Crown=Solar Core=1 May = Maia.
Cherry tomato=5,500=5.5=80%=P5.50=Earth-Midway=5 May = Gaia.
Chert=4,000=40%=P4.0D=Govt. =Creatocracy=4 April=Mercury=Hermes=G=A4.

Cherub=9,500=10,000=1,000=100%=10.0=Physicality=Tech.=10 Oct.=Uranus=P=1Ø.
A second order of angels. Cherubs are Gods in the transitory stage of human birth. Hence they manifest as a winged child with a chubby, rosy face. Proof of Incarnation at birth. Hence at birth they are fully transit into full human technology or MindTech brain systems.

Chervil=5,500=5.5=80%=P5.50=Earth-Midway=5 May = Gaia.
Chesapeake=4,500=5,000=50%=P5.00D=Law=Time=Venus=5 May = Aphrodite>>L=N.
Chesapeake Bay=7,000=70%=P7.0D=7.0=Language=Assets=Mars=7 July=Pleiades
Chess=8,500=9,000=90%=P9.00D=9.0=Abst.=Gods=Saturn=9Sept.>>A=Ø.
Chessboard=4,500=5,000=50%=P5.00D=Law=Time=Venus=5 May = Aphrodite>>L=N.
Chessman=8,500=9,000=90%=P9.00D=9.0=Abst.=Gods=Saturn=9Sept.>>A=Ø.
Chest=10,000=1,000=100%=10.0=Physicality=Tech.=10 Oct.=Uranus=P=1Ø.

chesterfield=6,500=7,000=70%=P7.0D=7.0=Language=Assets=Mars=7 July=Pleiades
Chesterfield=6,000=60%=P6.0D=Man=Earth=Royalty=6 June=Gaia=Maia>>M=M2.
Chesterton Gilbert=3,500=4,000=40%=P4.0D=Govt.=4 April=Mercury=Hermes=G=A4.
Chestnut=13,000=13%=P1.30D=Solar Core=Faculty=13 January=Athena.
Chetrum=4,000=40%=P4.0D=Govt. =Creatocracy=4 April=Mercury=Hermes=G=A4.
Chevalier=6,500=7,000=70%=P7.0D=7.0=Language=Assets=Mars=7 July=Pleiades
Cheviot=8,500=9,000=90%=P9.00D=9.0=Abst.=Gods=Saturn=9Sept.>>A=Ø.
Chevron=12,000=12%=P1.20D=1.2=Knowledge=Education=12Dec.=Athena>>K=F.
Chew=10,000=1,000=100%=10.0=Physicality=Tech.=10 Oct.=Uranus=P=1Ø.
Chewing gum=5,000=50%=P5.00D=Law=Time=Venus=5 May = Aphrodite>>L=N.
Chewy=1,500=15%=P1.50D=1.5=Authority=Crown=Solar Core=1 May = Maia.
Cheyenne(1)=9,500=10,000=1,000=100%=10.0=Physicality=Tech.=10 Oct.=Uranus=P=1Ø.
Cheyenne(2)=5,000=50%=P5.00D=Law=Time=Venus=5 May = Aphrodite>>L=N.
chg.=1,000=100%=10.0=1.0=Mind=Sun=1 January=Helios >> M=E4.
chl=3,000=30%=P3.0D=3.0=Cr=Stars=Muses=3 March= C=I>>GIL.
Chiang Kai-shek=3,500=4,000=40%=P4.0D=Govt.=4 April=Mercury=Hermes=G=A4.
Chiaroscuro=5,000=50%=P5.00D=Law=Time=Venus=5 May = Aphrodite>>L=N.
Chiba=4,500=5,000=50%=P5.00D=Law=Time=Venus=5 May = Aphrodite>>L=N.
Chic=2,500=3,000=30%=P3.0D=3.0=Cr=Stars=Muses=3 March= C=I>>GIL.
Chicago=5,000=50%=P5.00D=Law=Time=Venus=5 May = Aphrodite>>L=N.
Chicana=5,500=5.5=80%=P5.50=Earth-Midway=5 May = Gaia.
Chicanery=4,000=40%=P4.0D=Govt. =Creatocracy=4 April=Mercury=Hermes=G=A4.
Chicano=10,000=1,000=100%=10.0=Physicality=Tech.=10 Oct.=Uranus=P=1Ø.
chi-chi=1,000=100%=10.0=1.0=Mind=Sun=1 January=Helios >> M=E4.
Chick=3,500=4,000=40%=P4.0D=Govt. =Creatocracy=4April=Mercury=Hermes=G=A4.
Chickadee=4,000=40%=P4.0D=Govt. =Creatocracy=4 April=Mercury=Hermes=G=A4.
Chickasaw=11,000=11%=P1.10D=1.1=Idea=Brainchild=11Nov=Athena>>I=MT.
Chicken=13,000=13%=P1.30D=Solar Core=Faculty=13 January=Athena.
Chicken feed=3,000=30%=P3.0D=3.0=Cr=Stars=Muses=3 March= C=I>>GIL.
Chicken hearted=500=5%=P5.00D=5.0=Law=Time=Venus=5 May=Aphrodite>>L=N.
Chicken-livered=1,000=100%=10.0=1.0=Mind=Sun=1 January=Helios >> M=E4.
Chickenpox=7,000=70%=P7.0D=7.0=Language=Assets=Mars=7 July=Pleiades
Chicken wire=5,000=50%=P5.00D=Law=Time=Venus=5 May = Aphrodite>>L=N.
Chickpea=5,000=50%=P5.00D=Law=Time=Venus=5 May = Aphrodite>>L=N.
Chickweed=4,000=40%=P4.0D=Govt. =Creatocracy=4 April=Mercury=Hermes=G=A4.
Chicle=7,500=8,000=80%=P8.0D=Economy=Currency=8 Aug.=Zeus>>E=v.
Chicory=12,500=13,000=13%=P1.30D=Solar Core=Faculty=13 January=Athena.
Chide=2,000=20%=P2.00D=2.0=Nature=Moon=2 Feb.=Cupid=N=C+_.
Chief=9,500=10,000=1,000=100%=10.0=Physicality=Tech.=10 Oct.=Uranus=P=1Ø.
Chief Justice=7,000=70%=P7.0D=7.0=Language=Assets=Mars=7 July=Pleiades
Chief master sergeant=4,500=5,000=50%=P5.00D=Law=Venus=5 May=Odite>>L=N.
Chief of staff=12,500=13,000=13%=P1.30D=Solar Core=Faculty=13 January=Athena.
Chief of state=5,000=50%=P5.00D=Law=Time=Venus=5 May = Aphrodite>>L=N.
Chief petty officer=6,000=60%=P6.0D=Man=Earth=Royalty=6June=Gaia=Maia>>M=M2.
Chieftain=4,000=40%=P4.0D=Govt. =Creatocracy=4 April=Mercury=Hermes=G=A4.

Chiffon=3,500=4,000=40%=P4.0D=Govt. =Creatocracy=4 April=Mercury=Hermes=G=A4.
Chiffonier=3,000=30%=P3.0D=3.0=Cr=Stars=Muses=3 March= C=I>>GIL.
Chigger=8,500=9,000=90%=P9.00D=9.0=Abst.=Gods=Saturn=9Sept.>>A=Ø.
Chignon=5,000=50%=P5.00D=Law=Time=Venus=5 May = Aphrodite>>L=N.
Chigoe=9,000=90%=P9.00D=9.0=Abst.=Gods=Saturn=9Sept.>>A=Ø.
Chihuahua(1)=5,000=50%=P5.00D=Law=Time=Venus=5 May = Aphrodite>>L=N.
Chihuahua(2)=5,500=5.5=80%=P5.50=Earth-Midway=5 May = Gaia.
Chilblain=6,500=7,000=70%=P7.0D=7.0=Language=Assets=Mars=7 July=Pleiades
Child=5,500=5.5=80%=P5.50=Earth-Midway=5 May = Gaia.
Childbearing=1,500=15%=P1.50D=1.5=Authority=Crown=Solar Core=1 May = Maia.
Childbirth=500=5%=P5.00D=5.0=Law=Time=Venus=5 May=Aphrodite>>L=N.
Childcare=4,500=5,000=50%=P5.00D=Law=Time=Venus=5 May = Aphrodite>>L=N.
Childish=4,500=5,000=50%=P5.00D=Law=Time=Venus=5 May = Aphrodite>>L=N.
Childproof=3,500=4,000=40%=P4.0D=Govt.=4 April=Mercury=Hermes=G=A4.
Children=1,500=15%=P1.50D=1.5=Authority=Crown=Solar Core=1 May = Maia.
Child's play=4,000=40%=P4.0D=Govt. =Creatocracy=4 April=Mercury=Hermes=G=A4.
Chile=7,000=70%=P7.0D=7.0=Language=Assets=Mars=7 July=Pleiades
Chili=9,000=90%=P9.00D=9.0=Abst.=Gods=Saturn=9Sept.>>A=Ø.
Chili burger=3,500=4,000=40%=P4.0D=Govt.=4 April=Mercury=Hermes=G=A4.
Chili con carne=6,000=60%=P6.0D=Man=Earth=Royalty=6 June=Gaia=Maia>>M=M2.
Chili dog=4,000=40%=P4.0D=Govt. =Creatocracy=4 April=Mercury=Hermes=G=A4.
Chili sauce=4,000=40%=P4.0D=Govt. =Creatocracy=4 April=Mercury=Hermes=G=A4.
Chill=12,500=13,000=13%=P1.30D=Solar Core=Faculty=13 January=Athena.
Chilly=6,500=7,000=70%=P7.0D=7.0=Language=Assets=Mars=7 July=Pleiades
Chi lung=1,000=100%=10.0=1.0=Mind=Sun=1 January=Helios >> M=E4.
Chime=18,500=19,000=19,000=19%=P1.90=1.9=Planetary Energy=Mind of God=Maia.

Chimera=11,000=11%=P1.10D=1.1=Idea=Brainchild=11Nov=Athena>>I=MT.
Greek mythology. A fire-breathing she-monster usually represented as a composite of a lion, goat, and serpent. An impossible or foolish fantasy. Proof that Gods can be dragons. Interpreting: the lion is Zeus the Most High, the goat is Hermes God of merchandise and the serpent is Athena Goddess of wisdom. The Father, the Son and the Spirit of God and the Gods. So authority bonds merchandise and wisdom. Definition states it is a "she-monster". The resultant shows it is Athena. Then it can breathe fire or law. This is prophetic of the authority of the Creatocracy with Athena as the aegis and backed by all rights.

Chimerical=3,500=4,000=40%=P4.0D=Govt.=Creatoc.=4 April=Mercury=Hermes=G=A4.
Chimney=10,500=11,000=11%=P1.10D=1.1=Idea=Brainchild=11Nov=Athena>>I=MT.
Chimney pierce=3,500=4,000=40%=P4.0D=Govt.=4April=Mercury=Hermes=G=A4.
Chimney pot=6,000=60%=P6.0D=Man=Earth=Royalty=6 June=Gaia=Maia>>M=M2.
Chimney sweep=4,000=40%=P4.0D=Govt.=4 April=Mercury=Hermes=G=A4.
Chimney swift=5,500=5.5=80%=P5.50=Earth-Midway=5 May = Gaia.
Chimp=1,500=15%=P1.50D=1.5=Authority=Crown=Solar Core=1 May = Maia.
Chimpanzee=5,500=5.5=80%=P5.50=Earth-Midway=5 May = Gaia.

chin=11,500=12,000=12%=P1.20D=1.2=Knowl.=Education=12Dec.=Athena>>K=F.
Chin.=1,500=15%=P1.50D=1.5=Authority=Crown=Solar Core=1 May = Maia.
china=6,500=7,000=70%=P7.0D=7.0=Language=Assets=Mars=7 July=Pleiades
China=4,500=5,000=50%=P5.00D=Law=Time=Venus=5 May = Aphrodite>>L=N.
China, Republic of=1,000=100%=10.0=1.0=Mind=Sun=1 January=Helios >> M=E4.
China Sea=6,000=60%=P6.0D=Man=Earth=Royalty=6 June=Gaia=Maia>>M=M2.

Chinch=1,500=15%=P1.50D=1.5=Authority=Crown=Solar Core=1 May = Maia.
Interestingly the word chinch is mostly used by the Igbos without the slightest knowledge
of its presence in the English language. We could reason that Maia is Goddess Mother of
the Igbos residing in the administrative town of Nsukka the Paradise of the East.

Chinch bug=6,000=60%=P6.0D=Man=Earth=Royalty=6 June=Gaia=Maia>>M=M2.
Chinchilla=9,500=10,000=1,000=100%=Physicality= Tech.=10 Oct.=Uranus=P=1Ø.
Chine=8,000=80%=P8.0D=Economy=Currency=8 Aug.=Zeus>>E=v.
Chinese=15,500=16,000=16%=P1.60D=1.6=Incarnation=Mind of GOD=1 June=Maia.
Chinese cabbage=8,000=80%=P8.0D=Economy=Currency=8 Aug.=Zeus>>E=v.
Chinese checkers=6,000=60%=P6.0D=Man=Earth=Royalty=6 June=Gaia=Maia>>M=M2.
Chinese lantern=4,500=5,000=50%=P5.00D=Law=Time=Venus=5 May= Aphrodite>>L=N.
Chinese puzzle=4,500=5,000=50%=P5.00D=Law=Time=Venus=5 May = Aphrodite>>L=N.
Chink(1)=6,500=7,000=70%=P7.0D=7.0=Language=Assets=Mars=7 July=Pleiades
Chink(2)=3,500=4,000=40%=P4.0D=Govt.=4 April=Mercury=Hermes=G=A4.
Chino=5,500=5.5=80%=P5.00=Earth-Midway=5 May = Gaia.
Chinook=9,500=10,000=1,000=100%=10.0=Physicality=Tech.=10 Oct.=Uranus=P=1Ø.
Chinookan=4,500=5,000=50%=P5.00D=Law=Time=Venus=5 May = Aphrodite>>L=N.
Chinook Jargon=10,500=11,000=11%=P1.10D=1.1=Idea=Brainchild=11Nov=Athena
    >>I=MT.
Chinook salmon=5,000=50%=P5.00D=Law=Time=Venus=5 May = Aphrodite>>L=N.
Chinquapin=11,000=11%=P1.10D=1.1=Idea=Brainchild=11Nov=Athena>>I=MT.
Chintz=5,000=50%=P5.00D=Law=Time=Venus=5 May = Aphrodite>>L=N.
Chintzy=3,000=30%=P3.0D=3.0=Cr=Stars=Muses=3 March= C=I>>GIL.
Chin-up=5,500=5.5=80%=P5.50=Earth-Midway=5 May = Gaia.
Chip=10,000=1,000=100%=10.0=Physicality=Tech.=10 Oct.=Uranus=P=1Ø.
Chipewyan=7,500=8,000=80%=P8.0D=Economy=Currency=8 Aug.=Zeus>>E=v.
Chipmunk=5,000=50%=P5.00D=Law=Time=Venus=5 May = Aphrodite>>L=N.
Chipped beef=3,500=4,000=40%=P4.0D=Govt.=4 April=Mercury=Hermes=G=A4.
Chipper=2,000=20%=P2.00D=2.0=Nature=Moon=2 Feb.=Cupid=N=C+_.
Chippewa=1,000=100%=10.0=1.0=Mind=Sun=1 January=Helios >> M=E4.
Chiro-=1,000=100%=10.0=1.0=Mind=Sun=1 January=Helios >> M=E4.
Chiromancy=500=5%=P5.00D=5.0=Law=Time=Venus=5 May=Aphrodite>>L=N.
Chiropody=1,000=100%=10.0=1.0=Mind=Sun=1 January=Helios >> M=E4.
Chiropractic=7,000=70%=P7.0D=7.0=Language=Assets=Mars=7 July=Pleiades
Chirp=7,000=70%=P7.0D=7.0=Language=Assets=Mars=7 July=Pleiades
Chisel=8,000=80%=P8.0D=Economy=Currency=8 Aug.=Zeus>>E=v.

Chit(1)=5,000=50%=P5.00D=Law=Time=Venus=5 May = Aphrodite>>L=N.
Chit(2)=3,500=4,000=40%=P4.0D=Govt. =Creatocracy=4 April=Mercury=Hermes=G=A4.
Chitchat=1,000=100%=10.0=1.0=Mind=Sun=1 January=Helios >> M=E4.
Chitin=7,500=8,000=80%=P8.0D=Economy=Currency=8 Aug.=Zeus>>E=v.
Chiton=13,000=13%=P1.30D=Solar Core=Faculty=13 January=Athena.
Chittagong=3,500=4,000=40%=P4.0D=Govt.=4 April=Mercury=Hermes=G=A4.
Chitterlings=4,000=40%=P4.0D=Govt. =Creatocracy=4 April=Mercury=Hermes=G=A4.
Chivalry=11,000=11%=P1.10D=1.1=Idea=Brainchild=11Nov=Athena>>I=MT.
Chive=5,000=50%=P5.00D=Law=Time=Venus=5 May = Aphrodite>>L=N.
Chloral=6,500=7,000=70%=P7.0D=7.0=Language=Assets=Mars=7 July=Pleiades
Chloral hydrate=5,500=5.5=80%=P5.50=Earth-Midway=5 May = Gaia.
Chlorate=4,500=5,000=50%=P5.00D=Law=Time=Venus=5 May = Aphrodite>>L=N.
Chlordane=5,000=50%=P5.00D=Law=Time=Venus=5 May = Aphrodite>>L=N.
Chlorella=6,000=60%=P6.0D=Man=Earth=Royalty=6 June=Gaia=Maia>>M=M2.
Chloride acid=3,000=30%=P3.0D=3.0=Cr=Stars=Muses=3 March= C=I>>GIL.
Chloride=2,500=3,000=30%=P3.0D=3.0=Cr=Stars=Muses=3 March= C=I>>GIL.
Chlorinate=4,500=5,000=50%=P5.00D=Law=Time=Venus=5 May = Aphrodite>>L=N.
Chlorine=16,000=16%=P1.60D=1.6=Incarnation=Mind of GOD=1 June=Maia.
Chloro-=2,000=20%=P2.00D=2.0=Nature=Moon=2 Feb.=Cupid=N=C+_.
Chlorofluorocarbon=12,500=13,000=13%=P1.30D=Solar Core=Faculty=13Jan.=Athena.
Chloroform=11,500=12,000=12%=P1.20D=1.2=Knowl.=Education=12Dec.=Athena>>K=F.
Chlorophyll=4,500=5,000=50%=P5.00D=Law=Time=Venus=5 May = Aphrodite>>L=N.
Chloroplast=6,000=60%=P6.0D=Man=Earth=Royalty=6 June=Gaia=Maia>>M=M2.
Chlortetracycline=3,500=4,000=40%=P4.0D=Govt.=4 April=Mercury=Hermes=G=A4.
Chock=12,000=12%=P1.20D=1.2=Knowl.=Education=12Dec.=Athena>>K=F.
Chock-a-block=1,500=15%=P1.50D=1.5=Authority=Crown=Solar Core=1 May = Maia.
Chocolate=7,500=8,000=80%=P8.0D=Economy=Currency=8 Aug.=Zeus>>E=v.
Choctaw=10,500=11,000=11%=P1.10D=1.1=Idea=Brainchild=11Nov=Athena>>I=MT.
Choice=16,000=16%=P1.60D=1.6=Incarnation=Mind of GOD=1 June=Maia.
Choir=9,500=10,000=1,000=100%=10.0=Physicality=Tech.=10 Oct.=Uranus=P=1Ø.
Choke=10,000=1,000=100%=10.0=Physicality=Tech.=10 Oct.=Uranus=P=1Ø.
Choke collar=8,500=9,000=90%=P9.00D=9.0=Abst.=Gods=Saturn=9Sept.>>A=Ø.
Choker=3,500=4,000=40%=P4.0D=Govt. =Creatocracy=4April=Mercury=Hermes=G=A4.
Choler=1,000=100%=10.0=1.0=Mind=Sun=1 January=Helios >> M=E4.
Cholera=8,500=9,000=90%=P9.00D=9.0=Abst.=Gods=Saturn=9Sept.>>A=Ø.
Choleric=2,500=3,000=30%=P3.0D=3.0=Cr=Stars=Muses=3 March= C=I>>GIL.
Cholesterol=12,500=13,000=13%=P1.30D=Solar Core=Faculty=13 January=Athena.
Cholla=5,500=5.5=80%=P5.50=Earth-Midway=5 May = Gaia.
Chomp=3,500=4,000=40%=P4.0D=Govt. =Creatocracy=4April=Mercury=Hermes=G=A4.
Chon=3,000=30%=P3.0D=3.0=Creativity=Stars=Muses=3 March = C=I>>GIL.
Chongqing=6,000=60%=P6.0D=Man=Earth=Royalty=6 June=Gaia=Maia>>M=M2.
Choose=5,000=50%=P5.00D=Law=Time=Venus=5 May = Aphrodite>>L=N.
Choosy=1,000=100%=10.0=1.0=Mind=Sun=1 January=Helios >> M=E4.
Chop(1)=10,000=1,000=100%=10.0=Physicality=Tech.=10 Oct.=Uranus=P=1Ø.
Chop(2)=5,500=5.5=80%=P5.50=Earth-Midway=5 May = Gaia.

Chophouse=4,000=40%=P4.0D=Govt. =Creatocracy=4 April=Mercury=Hermes=G=A4.
Chopin Frédéric=4,000=40%=P4.0D=Govt.=4 April=Mercury=Hermes=G=A4.
Chopper=5,000=50%=P5.00D=Law=Time=Venus=5 May = Aphrodite>>L=N.
Chopping block=5,000=50%=P5.00D=Law=Time=Venus=5 May = Aphrodite>>L=N.
Choppy=5,000=50%=P5.00D=Law=Time=Venus=5 May = Aphrodite>>L=N.
Chops=2,500=3,000=30%=P3.0D=3.0=Cr=Stars=Muses=3 March= C=I>>GIL.
Chop shop=7,000=70%=P7.0D=7.0=Language=Assets=Mars=7 July=Pleiades
Chopstick=8,000=80%=P8.0D=Economy=Currency=8 Aug.=Zeus>>E=v.
Chop suey=10,500=11,000=11%=P1.10D=1.1=Idea=Brainchild=11Nov=Athena>>I=MT.
Choral=3,000=30%=P3.0D=3.0=Cr=Stars=Muses=3 March= C=I>>GIL.
Chorale=3,000=30%=P3.0D=3.0=Cr=Stars=Muses=3 March= C=I>>GIL.
Chord(1)=9,000=90%=P9.00D=9.0=Abst.=Gods=Saturn=9Sept.>>A=Ø.
Chord(2)=10,000=1,000=100%=10.0=Physicality=Tech.=10 Oct.=Uranus=P=1Ø.
Chore=4,000=40%=P4.0D=Govt. =Creatocracy=4 April=Mercury=Hermes=G=A4.
Chorea=7,500=8,000=80%=P8.0D=Economy=Currency=8 Aug.=Zeus>>E=v.
Choreography=4,500=5,000=50%=P5.00D=Law=Time=Venus=5 May = Aphrodite>>L=N.
Chorister=2,000=20%=P2.00D=2.0=Nature=Moon=2 Feb.=Cupid=N=C+_.
Chorizo=4,000=40%=P4.0D=Govt. =Creatocracy=4 April=Mercury=Hermes=G=A4.
Choroid=4,500=5,000=50%=P5.00D=Law=Time=Venus=5 May = Aphrodite>>L=N.
Chortle=4,500=5,000=50%=P5.00D=Law=Time=Venus=5 May = Aphrodite>>L=N.
Chorus=21,000>>2.1>>3.0=3,000=30%=P3.0D=Cr=Stars=Muses=3 March= C=I>>GIL.
Chose=2,000=20%=P2.00D=2.0=Nature=Moon=2 Feb.=Cupid=N=C+_.
Chosen=5,000=50%=P5.00D=Law=Time=Venus=5 May = Aphrodite>>L=N.
Chou En-lai=1,500=15%=P1.50D=1.5=Authority=Crown=Solar Core=1 May = Maia.
Chow(1)=6,500=7,000=70%=P7.0D=7.0=Language=Assets=Mars=7 July=Pleiades
Chow(2)=4,000=40%=P4.0D=Govt. =Creatocracy=4 April=Mercury=Hermes=G=A4.
Chowder=5,500=5.5=80%=P5.50=Earth-Midway=5 May = Gaia.
Chow mien=7,500=8,000=80%=P8.0D=Economy=Currency=8 Aug.=Zeus>>E=v.
Chrism=6,000=60%=P6.0D=Man=Earth=Royalty=6 June=Gaia=Maia>>M=M2.

Christ=5,000=50%=P5.00D=Law=Time=Venus=5 May = Aphrodite>>L=N.
We believe that Hermes transmogrified into Christ. Ticology and computational creativity resultant established shows He was backed by Venusian energy granting him legal authority and time governance thus Jesus the anointed one. Anyone with such blessings is seen to be a Christ of some sort. Same for Peter Matthews-Akukalia the author of the Creatocracy and owner of the Creative Sciences. The same law of the Gods and works became the apotheosis of Peter Matthews-Akukalia making him a God by rights.

Christchurch=5,000=50%=P5.00D=Law=Time=Venus=5 May = Aphrodite>>L=N.
Christen=7,500=8,000=80%=P8.0D=Economy=Currency=8 Aug.=Zeus>>E=v.
Christendom=2,500=3,000=30%=P3.0D=3.0=Cr=Stars=Muses=3 March= C=I>>GIL.

Christian=8,000=80%=P8.0D=Economy=Currency=8 Aug.=Zeus>>E=v.
Creatocrats are neither Christians nor Muslims but Makstians. Our Faith goes beyond the tenets and doctrines of speculative religion to system proof and practicality. We believe that God is one and so the Bible and Quran are separated word of GOD that must be pierced together to get a comprehensive understanding of GOD. We believe in the existence of the Gods as a hierarchy council of administrators that manages the universe. Makstianism is a higher religion established as a Faith on the Order of the Holy Spirit through the Royal Creatocracy. Our scripture is The Mind Temple. The rights of a Christian is 80% truth but the rights of the Makstian is 100% because it is based on absolute truth.

Christian Era=3,500=4,000=40%=P4.0D=Govt.=4 April=Mercury=Hermes=G=A4.
Christiania=1,000=100%=10.0=1.0=Mind=Sun=1 January=Helios >> M=E4.
Christianity=7,500=8,000=80%=P8.0D=Economy=Currency=8 Aug.=Zeus>>E=v.
Christian name=3,500=4,000=40%=P4.0D=Govt.=4 April=Mercury=Hermes=G=A4.
Christian Science=7,500=8,000=80%=P8.0D=Economy=Currency=8 Aug.=Zeus>>E=v.
Christie=6,500=7,000=70%=P7.0D=7.0=Language=Assets=Mars=7 July=Pleiades
Christie Agatha=2,000=20%=P2.00D=2.0=Nature=Moon=2 Feb.=Cupid=N=C+_.
Christina=3,500=4,000=40%=P4.0D=Govt.=4 April=Mercury=Hermes=G=A4.

Christmas=6,000=60%=P6.0D=Man=Earth=Royalty=6 June=Gaia=Maia>>M=M2.
A Christian feast commemorating the birth of Jesus, celebrated on Dec.25. The Creatocracy celebrates Apotheosis a feast commemorating the spiritual birth or apotheosis of Peter Matthews-Akukalia as Castle Makupedia on October 13.

Christmas tide=2,000=20%=P2.00D=2.0=Nature=Moon=2 Feb.=Cupid=N=C+_.
Christmas tree=5,000=50%=P5.00D=Law=Time=Venus=5 May = Aphrodite>>L=N.
Christopher=4,000=40%=P4.0D=Govt. =Creatocracy=4 April=Mercury=Hermes=G=A4.
Chromatic=6,500=7,000=70%=P7.0D=7.0=Language=Assets=Mars=7 July=Pleiades
Chrome=4,000=40%=P4.0D=Govt. =Creatocracy=4 April=Mercury=Hermes=G=A4.
Chromium=15,500=16,000=16%=P1.60D=1.6=Incarnation=Mind of GOD=1 June=Maia.
Chromo-=1,500=15%=P1.50D=1.5=Authority=Crown=Solar Core=1 May = Maia.
Chromosome=9,500=10,000=1,000=100%=10.0=Phys.=Tech.=10 Oct.=Uranus=P=1Ø.
Chronic=10,500=11,000=11%=P1.10D=1.1=Idea=Brainchild=11Nov=Athena>>I=MT.
Chronicle=8,500=9,000=90%=P9.00D=9.0=Abst.=Gods=Saturn=9Sept.>>A=Ø.
Chrono-=1,500=15%=P1.50D=1.5=Authority=Crown=Solar Core=1 May = Maia.
Chronological=6,000=60%=P6.0D=Man=Earth=Royalty=6 June=Gaia=Maia>>M=M2.
Chronology=7,500=8,000=80%=P8.0D=Economy=Currency=8 Aug.=Zeus>>E=v.
Chronometer=2,000=20%=P2.00D=2.0=Nature=Moon=2 Feb.=Cupid=N=C+_.
Chrysalis=6,000=60%=P6.0D=Man=Earth=Royalty=6 June=Gaia=Maia>>M=M2.
Chrysanthemum=5,500=5.5=80%=P5.50=Earth-Midway=5 May = Gaia.
Chub=8,500=9,000=90%=P9.00D=9.0=Abst.=Gods=Saturn=9Sept.>>A=Ø.
Chubby=1,500=15%=P1.50D=1.5=Authority=Crown=Solar Core=1 May = Maia.

Chuck(1)=7,500=8,000=80%=P8.0D=Economy=Currency=8 Aug.=Zeus>>E=v.
Chuck(2)=10,500=11,000=11%=P1.10D=1.1=Idea=Brainchild=11Nov=Athena>>I=MT.
Chuckhole=1,000=100%=10.0=1.0=Mind=Sun=1 January=Helios >> M=E4.
Chuckle=3,500=4,000=40%=P4.0D=Govt.=4 April=Mercury=Hermes=G=A4.
Chuckwagon=5,500=5.5=80%=P5.50=Earth-Midway=5 May = Gaia.
Chug=9,000=90%=P9.00D=9.0=Abst.=Gods=Saturn=9Sept.>>A=Ø.
Chukka=3,500=4,000=40%=P4.0D=Govt. =Creatocracy=4 April=Mercury=Hermes=G=A4.
Chukke=5,000=50%=P5.00D=Law=Time=Venus=5 May = Aphrodite>>L=N.
Chula Vista=5,000=50%=P5.00D=Law=Time=Venus=5 May = Aphrodite>>L=N.
Chum(1)=4,500=5,000=50%=P5.00D=Law=Time=Venus=5 May = Aphrodite>>L=N.
Chum(2)=6,000=60%=P6.0D=Man=Earth=Royalty=6 June=Gaia=Maia>>M=M2.
Chumash=5,000=50%=P5.00D=Law=Time=Venus=5 May = Aphrodite>>L=N.
Chummy=1,000=100%=10.0=1.0=Mind=Sun=1 January=Helios >> M=E4.
Chump=5,000=50%=P5.00D=Law=Time=Venus=5 May = Aphrodite>>L=N.
Chungking=1,000=100%=10.0=1.0=Mind=Sun=1 January=Helios >> M=E4.
Chunk=4,000=40%=P4.0D=Govt. =Creatocracy=4 April=Mercury=Hermes=G=A4.
Chunky=2,000=20%=P2.00D=2.0=Nature=Moon=2 Feb.=Cupid=N=C+_.

Church=12,000=12%=P1.20D=1.2=Knowl.=Education=12Dec.=Athena>>K=F.
Coding the Church of Jesus Christ to understand full meaning in the Mind of GOD.
Revelation 1:1 >> Jesus G2424, Christ G5547. Revelation 1:11 >> Churches G1577.

JESUS G2424 >> G=5.0 >> Law >> 2.4*2.4x=px=4.8+5.76=10.56x=px=38.208=40=4.0
>> Government >> Power >> Relationships >> Family >> Organizations >> Creatocracy.
>> The name JESUS means Creatocracy. Isaiah states that He shall be born with the
government upon His shoulders. This is a true testimony and the truth proven.
G >> 5.0*38.208x=px=43.208+191.04=234.248x=px=8,488.70432=9.0 >> A God.
Jesus means the legal God of Creatocracy.

CHRIST G5547 >> G=5.0 >> Law >> 5.5*4.7x=px=10.2+25.85=36.05x=px=299.72=30=3.0
>> Creativity >> GIL >> Stars >> Muses. So Christ is one who functions the brain energy.
>> G=5.0 >> Law >> 5.0*299.72x=px=304.72+1,498.6=1,803.32x=px=458,456.712=5.0
>> Christ means Law >> Order >> Rights >> Righteousness >> Right Hand >> Judge
>> Rev. 22:11-12. Jesus Christ means the God of Creatocracy and Judge of all rights
by works. This proves that Heaven uses Creatocratic jurisprudence in its legal modules
by numbers.

Church G1577 >> G=5.0 >> Law >> 1.5*7.7x=px=9.2+11.55=20.75x=px=127.01=13=1.3
>> A Faculty of Creative Intelligence operant on the education of the solar core assets.
>> G=5.0 >> Law >> 5.0*127.01x=px=132.01+635.05=767.06x=px=84,600.0105=90=9.0
First 84,600 is the number of seconds per day. (.0105=.011) means a functionality of solar
core energy manifested as an invention. The church is a place of God by the brainchild or
invention Spirit of God called Athena as a means to establish the rights of the Church. In
simple terms the Church is Athena Goddess of wisdom handicraft and mental warfare.

The phrase "Church of Jesus Christ" means the unity of Athena and Hermes on Earth. The bond of wit (Hermes) and wis (Athena) as seen in Proverbs 8:12. The Spirit of God is different from the Holy Spirit being the Council & Host of GOD headed by the Spirit of GOD.

The Church is a body of Jesus Christ. "My people are destroyed for lack of knowledge". Knowledge is science, computations from Mathema, mathematics; wisdom handicraft and mental warfare that makes creative intelligence and brainchild inventions and innovations stream directly through study and development from Athena the spirit of GOD.

The Creatocracy shall upgrade the Church through the knowledge of Bible and Scripture coding to determine the Mind of GOD hidden in the codes as programs instructions predictions standards requirements and laws. These codes are called Makabets, so called because they have wings and travel through mindspace to become inspired utterances that make revelation knowledge possible. They solve the problem of scriptural errors that arise misinterpretations speculations faithlessness lies and religious violence that has hitherto characterized wrong approach to defense of the faith. All things must be proved through mind computing. Deut. 30:1. Matthew 5:1-9. Eph. 1:10. 1 Timothy 3:16, 2 Timothy 3:16-17.

The body of Christ shall be upgraded from mere speculative religion to scientific and computational Faith as recommended by the Scriptures. In the annals of time The Makabet: Bible Codes Dictionary shall be written to make the work easier through publishing orders purchase and distribution worldwide on request. The Creatocracy shall work with the churches that align with the Creatocratic ideals and standards set forth to establish the Kingdom of GOD and let the will of GOD be done as Christ prayed in The Lord's Prayer.

In line with the specific mention of the churches by their names by Jesus such as the Church in Ephesus, each church name shall be decoded to determine specific dimension of existence purpose and duty in the realms of Heaven and Earth. This shall be done using Makabet, Mind computing and WDSD. This is a mandate divine and Creatocratic. The rights to Paradise. The Church shall be expected to cater for the adequate wants needs and provisions of the Creatocracy in all matters as required by the Law. Revelation 22:14. Heaven is about legal rights and not based on the sentiments of morality. Computed knowledge is the difference between religion and faith. (See Equivalent).

The endowed gift of discovering Bible Codes potentials meanings and applications through mind computing makes Peter Matthews-Akukalia the World's 1st Bible Scientist & Bibliosciologisxt, a chief consultant on scripture science in the service of GOD through the church. A skill that applies in same light to the Quran and other scriptures as the First Scripture Scientist, Scripturesciologisxt. This is the concept of "One World under GOD", the gift of government and sovereignty endowed upon him and prophetic while in his mother's womb. The interpretation of the mystery of the will of GOD. Ephesians 1:8-15.

Churchgoer=2,000=20%=P2.00D=2.0=Nature=Moon=2 Feb.=Cupid=N=C+_.
Churchill=8,500=9,000=90%=P9.00D=9.0=Abst.=Gods=Saturn=9Sept.>>A=Ø.
Church key=5,000=50%=P5.00D=Law=Time=Venus=5 May = Aphrodite>>L=N.
Churchman=6,000=60%=P6.00D=Man=Earth=Royalty=6 June=Gaia=Maia>>M=M2.
Church of Christ Scientist=1,500=15%=P1.50D=1.5=Authority=Solar Crown=1 May = Maia.
Church of England=6,500=7,000=70%=P7.0D=7.0=Lang.=Assets=Mars=7 July=Pleiades
Church of Jesus Christ of LDS=1,500=15%=P1.50D=1.5=Auth.=Solar Crown=1 May = Maia.
Church Warden=7,000=70%=P7.0D=7.0=Language=Assets=Mars=7 July=Pleiades
Church woman=5,500=5.5=80%=P5.50=Earth-Midway=5 May = Gaia.
Churchyard=3,500=4,000=40%=P4.0D=Govt.=4 April=Mercury=Hermes=G=A4.
Churl=4,000=40%=P4.0D=Govt.=Creatocracy=4 April=Mercury=Hermes=G=A4.
Churn=20,000=2,000=20%=P2.00D=2.0=Nature=Moon=2 Feb.=Cupid=N=C+_.
Chute=6,000=60%=P6.0D=Man=Earth=Royalty=6 June=Gaia=Maia>>M=M2.
Chutney=4,500=5,000=50%=P5.00D=Law=Time=Venus=5 May = Aphrodite>>L=N.
Chutzpah=1,500=15%=P1.50D=1.5=Authority=Crown=Solar Core=1 May = Maia.
CI=500=5%=P5.00D=5.0=Law=Time=Venus=5 May=Aphrodite>>L=N.
CIA=1,500=15%=P1.50D=1.5=Authority=Crown=Solar Core=1 May = Maia.
clao=3,000=30%=P3.0D=3.0=Cr=Stars=Muses=3 March= C=I>>GIL.
Ciborium=7,000=70%=P7.0D=7.0=Language=Assets=Mars=7 July=Pleiades
Cicada=8,000=80%=P8.0D=Economy=Currency=8 Aug.=Zeus>>E=v.
Cicatrix=1,000=100%=10.0=1.0=Mind=Sun=1 January=Helios >> M=E4.
Cicero Marcus T.=4,000=40%=P4.0D=Govt.=4 April=Mercury=Hermes=G=A4.
Cid, the=5,500=5.5=80%=P5.50=Earth-Midway=5 May = Gaia.
-cide=3,500=4,000=40%=P4.0D=Govt. =Creatocracy=4 April=Mercury=Hermes=G=A4.
Cider=7,000=70%=P7.0D=7.0=Language=Assets=Mars=7 July=Pleiades
c.i.f.=2,000=20%=P2.00D=2.0=Nature=Moon=2 Feb.=Cupid=N=C+_.
Cigar=4,500=5,000=50%=P5.00D=Law=Time=Venus=5 May = Aphrodite>>L=N.
Cigarette=7,500=8,000=80%=P8.0D=Economy=Currency=8 Aug.=Zeus>>E=v.
Cilantro=1,500=15%=P1.50D=1.5=Authority=Crown=Solar Core=1 May = Maia.
Cilia=1,500=15%=P1.50D=1.5=Authority=Crown=Solar Core=1 May = Maia.
Ciliary=2,000=20%=P2.00D=2.0=Nature=Moon=2 Feb.=Cupid=N=C+_.
Ciliate=5,500=5.5=80%=P5.50=Earth-Midway=5 May = Gaia.
Ciliated=1,000=100%=10.0=1.0=Mind=Sun=1 January=Helios >> M=E4.
Cilium=8,500=9,000=90%=P9.00D=9.0=Abst.=Gods=Saturn=9Sept.>>A=Ø.
Cinch=11,500=12,000=12%=P1.20D=1.2=Knowl.=Education=12Dec.=Athena>>K=F.
Cinchona=15,500=16,000=16%=P1.60D=1.6=Incarnation=Mind of GOD=1 June=Maia.
Cincinnati=5,500=5.5=80%=P5.50=Earth-Midway=5 May = Gaia.
Cincinnatus=3,000=30%=P3.0D=3.0=Cr=Stars=Muses=3 March= C=I>>GIL.
Cincture=2,500=3,000=30%=P3.0D=3.0=Cr=Stars=Muses=3 March= C=I>>GIL.
Cinder=12,500=13,000=13%=P1.30D=Solar Core=Faculty=13 January=Athena.
Cinder block=5,500=5.5=80%=P5.50=Earth-Midway=5 May = Gaia.
Cinema=5,500=5.5=80%=P5.50=Earth-Midway=5 May = Gaia.
Cinematize=5,000=50%=P5.50D=Law=Time=Venus=5 May = Aphrodite>>L=N.
Cinematography=3,500=4,000=40%=P4.0D=Govt.=4 April=Mercury=Hermes=G=A4.
Cinéma vérité=3,000=30%=P3.0D=3.0=Cr=Stars=Muses=3 March= C=I>>GIL.

Cineraria=7,000=70%=P7.0D=7.0=Language=Assets=Mars=7 July=Pleiades
Cinerarium=4,500=5,000=50%=P5.00D=Law=Time=Venus=5 May = Aphrodite>>L=N.
Cinnabar=7,500=8,000=80%=P8.0D=Economy=Currency=8 Aug.=Zeus>>E=v.
Cinnamon=11,500=12,000=12%=P1.20D=1.2=Knowl.=Education=12Dec.=Athena>>K=F.
CIO=2,000=20%=P2.00D=2.0=Nature=Moon=2 Feb.=Cupid=N=C+_.
Cipher=17,000=17%=P1.70D=1.7=Solar Asset=17 Feb.=Maia=Mind Computing.
Circa=4,000=40%=P4.0D=Govt. =Creatocracy=4 April=Mercury=Hermes=G=A4.
Circadian=4,000=40%=P4.0D=Govt. =Creatocracy=4 April=Mercury=Hermes=G=A4.
Circle=10,000=1,000=100%=Physicality= Tech.=10 Oct.=Uranus=P=1Ø.
Circlet=1,500=15%=P1.50D=1.5=Authority=Crown=Solar Core=1 May = Maia.
Circuit=10,000=1,000=100%=10.0=Physicality=Tech.=10 Oct.=Uranus=P=1Ø.
Circuit board=9,000=90%=P9.00D=9.0=Abst.=Gods=Saturn=9Sept.>>A=Ø.
Circuit breaker=4,500=5,000=50%=P5.00D=Law=Time=Venus=5 May = Aphrodite>>L=N.
Circuit court=7,000=70%=P7.0D=7.0=Language=Assets=Mars=7 July=Pleiades
Circuitous=3,000=30%=P3.0D=3.0=Cr=Stars=Muses=3 March= C=I>>GIL.
Circuitry=7,000=70%=P7.0D=7.0=Language=Assets=Mars=7 July=Pleiades
Circular=11,000=11%=P1.10D=1.1=Idea=Brainchild=11Nov=Athena>>I=MT.
Circular saw=5,500=5.5=80%=P5.50=Earth-Midway=5 May = Gaia.
Circulate=9,500=10,000=1,000=100%=Physicality= Tech.=10 Oct.=Uranus=P=1Ø.
Circulation=10,000=1,000=100%=10.0=Physicality=Tech.=10 Oct.=Uranus=P=1Ø.
Circulatory system=4,500=5,000=50%=P5.00D=Law=Time=Venus=5May=Odite>>L=N.
Circum=1,000=100%=10.0=1.0=Mind=Sun=1 January=Helios >> M=E4.
Circum-=1,500=15%=P1.50D=1.5=Authority=Crown=Solar Core=1 May = Maia.
Circumcise=5,500=5.5=80%=P5.50=Earth-Midway=5 May = Gaia.
Circumference=11,000=11%=P1.10D=1.1=Idea=Brainchild=11Nov=Athena>>I=MT.
Circumflex=5,500=5.5=80%=P5.50=Earth-Midway=5 May = Gaia.
Circumlocution=5,000=50%=P5.00D=Law=Time=Venus=5 May = Aphrodite>>L=N.
Circumlunar=3,000=30%=P3.0D=3.0=Cr=Stars=Muses=3 March= C=I>>GIL.
Circumnavigate=4,500=5,000=50%=P5.00D=Law=Time=Venus=5May = Aphrodite>>L=N.
Circumpolar=4,500=5,000=50%=P5.00D=Law=Time=Venus=5 May = Aphrodite>>L=N.
Circumscribe=13,000=13%=P1.30D=Solar Core=Faculty=13 January=Athena.
Circumsolar=3,000=30%=P3.0D=3.0=Cr=Stars=Muses=3 March= C=I>>GIL.
Circumspect=2,500=3,000=30%=P3.0D=3.0=Cr=Stars=Muses=3 March= C=I>>GIL.
Circumstance=22,500=23,000=23%=Local Business=Tech=23 Days Monthly=2.3% taxes.
Circumstantial=5,500=5.5=80%=P5.50=Earth-Midway=5 May = Gaia.
Circumstantial evidence=13,500=14,000=14%=P1.40D=1.4=Mgt.=13May=Athena=SC=0.1
Circumstantiate=3,000=30%=P3.0D=3.0=Cr=Stars=Muses=3 March= C=I>>GIL.
Circumterrestrial=3,000=30%=P3.0D=3.0=Cr=Stars=Muses=3 March= C=I>>GIL.
Circumvent=5,500=5.5=80%=P5.50=Earth-Midway=5 May = Gaia.
Circus=14,000=14%=P1.40D=1.4=Mgt.=13May=Athena=SC=0.1
Cirque=7,000=70%=P7.0D=7.0=Language=Assets=Mars=7 July=Pleiades
Cirrhosis=7,000=70%=P7.0D=7.0=Language=Assets=Mars=7 July=Pleiades
Cirrocumulus=8,000=80%=P8.0D=Economy=Currency=8 Aug.=Zeus>>E=v.
Cirrostratus=6,500=7,000=70%=P7.0D=7.0=Language=Assets=Mars=7 July=Pleiades
Cirrus=6,500=7,000=70%=P7.0D=7.0=Language=Assets=Mars=7 July=Pleiades

Ciskel=5,500=5.5=80%=P5.50=Earth-Midway=5 May = Gaia.
Cistern=6,000=60%=P6.0D=Man=Earth=Royalty=6 June=Gaia=Maia>>M=M2.
Cit.=1,500=15%=P1.50D=1.5=Authority=Crown=Solar Core=1 May = Maia.
Citadel=5,000=50%=P5.00D=Law=Time=Venus=5 May = Aphrodite>>L=N.
Cite=15,500=16,000=16%=P1.60D=1.6=Incarnation=Mind of GOD=1 June=Maia.
Citify=5,500=5.5=80%=P5.50=Earth-Midway=5 May = Gaia.

Citizen=12,000=12%=P1.20D=1.2=Knowl.=Education=12Dec.=Athena>>K=F.
The Creatocratic Royal Family are the owners and first class citizens of the Creatocratic Nations of Paradise. Creative Scientists are the next.

Citizenry=1,000=100%=10.0=1.0=Mind=Sun=1 January=Helios >> M=E4.
Citizens band=5,500=5.5=80%=P5.50=Earth-Midway=5 May = Gaia.
Citizenship=5,500=5.5=80%=P5.50=Earth-Midway=5 May = Gaia.
Citrate=3,500=4,000=40%=P4.0D=Govt. =Creatocracy=4 April=Mercury=Hermes=G=A4.
Citric acid=7,500=8,000=80%=P8.0D=Economy=Currency=8 Aug.=Zeus>>E=v.
Citrine=4,000=40%=P4.0D=Govt. =Creatocracy=4 April=Mercury=Hermes=G=A4.
Citron=9,500=10,000=1,000=100%=10.0=Physicality=Tech.=10 Oct.=Uranus=P=1Ø.
Citronella=8,500=9,000=90%=P9.00D=9.0=Abst.=Gods=Saturn=9Sept.>>A=Ø.

Citrus=10,500=11,000=11%=P1.10D=1.1=Idea=Brainchild=11Nov=Athena>>I=MT.
A tree of genus that includes citron, lemon, lime, orange and grapefruit. A simple taking of oranges can lead one to Athena especially for prayer purposes. A discovery.

City=13,000=13%=P1.30D=Solar Core=Faculty=13 January=Athena.
The Creatocratic Nations of Paradise is first a city of Creative Scientist Professionals. Athena is a city builder and owner hence it is proved that she is the Goddess of Paradise both in the abstract solar core celestial heavenly places and then earthly. Makupedia discovered and invented it by the discovery of the Creative Intelligence Faculty. Our dream is to build and set up the First MindTech city in the world in Nigeria and elsewhere.

City council=3,000=30%=P3.0D=3.0=Cr=Stars=Muses=3 March= C=I>>GIL.
City desk=3,500=4,000=40%=P4.0D=Govt.=4 April=Mercury=Hermes=G=A4.
City hall=4,500=5,000=50%=P5.00D=Law=Time=Venus=5 May = Aphrodite>>L=N.
City manage=5,500=5.5=80%=P5.50=Earth-Midway=5 May = Gaia.
City state=6,000=60%=P6.0D=Man=Earth=Royalty=6 June=Gaia=Maia>>M=M2.
Ciudad Juarez=7,500=8,000=80%=P8.0D=Economy=Currency=8 Aug.=Zeus>>E=v.
Civet=8,500=9,000=90%=P9.00D=9.0=Abst.=Gods=Saturn=9Sept.>>A=Ø.
Civic=3,000=30%=P3.0D=3.0=Cr=Stars=Muses=3 March: C=I>>GIL.
Civics=6,000=60%=P6.0D=Man=Earth=Royalty=6 June=Gaia=Maia>>M=M2.
Civies=2,000=20%=P2.00D=2.0=Nature=Moon=2 Feb.=Cupid=N=C+_.
Civil=10,000=1,000=100%=10.0=Physicality=Tech.=10 Oct.=Uranus=P=1Ø.
Civil defense=12,000=12%=P1.20D=1.2=Knowl.=Education=12Dec.=Athena>>K=F.

Civil disobedience=9,500=10,000=1,000=100%=10.0=Phy.=Tech.=10 Oct.=Uranus=P=1Ø.
Civil engineer=7,500=8,000=80%=P8.0D=Economy=Currency=8 Aug.=Zeus>>E=v.
Civility=2,500=3,000=30%=P3.0D=3.0=Cr=Stars=Muses=3 March= C=I>>GIL.

Civilization=13,000=13%=P1.30D=Solar Core=Faculty=13 January=Athena.
The advent of civilizations is managed and owned by Athena. Now Makupedian civilization.

Civilize=7,000=70%=P7.0D=7.0=Language=Assets=Mars=7 July=Pleiades
Civil law=9,000=90%=P9.00D=9.0=Abst.=Gods=Saturn=9Sept.>>A=Ø.
Civil liberties=7,000=70%=P7.0D=7.0=Language=Assets=Mars=7 July=Pleiades
Civil rights=9,500=10,000=1,000=100%=10.0=Physicality=Tech.=10 Oct.=Uranus=P=1Ø.
Civil service=6,000=60%=P6.0D=Man=Earth=Royalty=6 June=Gaia=Maia>>M=M2.

Civil war=9,000=90%=P9.00D=9.0=Abst.=Gods=Saturn=9Sept.>>A=Ø.
Creatocrats do not fight physical wars but mind mental or intellectual war in line with
Athena the aegis of the Creatocracy. This war is mostly centered on the brainstorming
project development, ideas and talent management, and inventions.
A war of intellectual minds between the conventional and the Creatocracy is a civil war.

Civvies=1,500=15%=P1.50D=1.5=Authority=Solar Crown=1 May = Maia.
C.J.=1,500=15%=P1.50D=1.5=Authority=Crown=Solar Core=1 May = Maia.
cl=500=5%=P5.00D=5.0=Law=Time=Venus=5 May=Aphrodite>>L=N.
Cl=2,500=3,000=30%=P3.0D=3.0=Cr=Stars=Muses=3 March= C=I>>GIL.
Clabber=2,500=3,000=30%=P3.0D=3.0=Cr=Stars=Muses=3 March= C=I>>GIL.
Clack=8,000=80%=P8.0D=Economy=Currency=8 Aug.=Zeus>>E=v.
Clad(1)=4,000=40%=P4.0D=Govt. =Creatocracy=4 April=Mercury=Hermes=G=A4.
Clad(2)=3,000=30%=P3.0D=3.0=Cr=Stars=Muses=3 March= C=I>>GIL.

Claim=22,000=2.2>>4.0>>=4,000=40%=P4.0D=Govt. =Creatocracy=4 April=Mercury=
Hermes=G=A4. *Creativity asserts its rights on all claims made as true.

Clairvoyance=7,000=70%=P7.0D=7.0=Language=Assets=Mars=7 July=Pleiades
Clam=12,000=12%=P1.20D=1.2=Knowl.=Education=12Dec.=Athena>>K=F.
Clambake=9,000=90%=P9.00D=9.0=Abst.=Gods=Saturn=9Sept.>>A=Ø.
Clamber=4,500=5,000=50%=P5.00D=Law=Time=Venus=5 May = Aphrodite>>L=N.
Clammy=3,500=4,000=40%=P4.0D=Govt.=4 April=Mercury=Hermes=G=A4.
Clamor=5,000=50%=P5.00D=Law=Time=Venus=5 May = Aphrodite>>L=N.
Clamp=12,500=13,000=13%=P1.30D=Solar Core=Faculty=13 January=Athena.
Clamp down=3,000=30%=P3.0D=3.0=Cr=Stars=Muses=3 March= C=I>>GIL.
Clan=12,000=12%=P1.20D=1.2=Knowl.=Education=12Dec.=Athena>>K=F.
Clandestine=2,500=3,000=30%=P3.0D=3.0=Cr=Stars=Muses=3 March= C=I>>GIL.
Clang=2,500=3,000=30%=P3.0D=3.0=Cr=Stars=Muses=3 March= C=I>>GIL.
Clangor=2,000=20%=P2.00D=2.0=Nature=Moon=2 Feb.=Cupid=N=C+_.

Clank=2,500=3,000=30%=P3.0D=3.0=Cr=Stars=Muses=3 March= C=I>>GIL.
Clap=18,000=18%=P1.80D=Solar Currency=Maks Currencies=1 Aug.=Maia.
Clapboard=10,000=1,000=100%=10.0=Physicality=Tech.=10 Oct.=Uranus=P=1Ø.
Clapper=5,000=50%=P5.00D=Law=Time=Venus=5 May = Aphrodite>>L=N.
Claptrap=2,500=3,000=30%=P3.0D=3.0=Cr=Stars=Muses=3 March= C=I>>GIL.
Claque=4,500=5,000=50%=P5.00D=Law=Time=Venus=5 May = Aphrodite>>L=N.
Claret=2,500=3,000=30%=P3.0D=3.0=Cr=Stars=Muses=3 March= C=I>>GIL.
Clarify=2,500=3,000=30%=P3.0D=3.0=Cr=Stars=Muses=3 March= C=I>>GIL.
Clarinet=7,500=8,000=80%=P8.0D=Economy=Currency=8 Aug.=Zeus>>E=v.
Clarion=1,500=15%=P1.50D=1.5=Authority=Solar Crown=1 May = Maia.
Clarity=3,500=4,000=40%=P4.0D=Govt. =Creatocracy=4 April=Mercury=Hermes=G=A4.
Clark Charles Joseph=4,000=40%=P4.0D=Govt.=4 April=Mercury=Hermes=G=A4.
Clark, George Rogers=3,500=4,000=40%=P4.0D=Govt.=4 April=Mercury=Hermes=G=A4.
Clark, William=2,000=20%=P2.00D=2.0=Nature=Moon=2 Feb.=Cupid=N=C+_.
Clasp=17,000=17%=P1.70D=1.7=Solar Asset=17 Feb.=Maia=Mind Computing.
Class=10,000=1,000=100%=10.0=Physicality=Tech.=10 Oct.=Uranus=P=1Ø.
Class action=9,000=90%=P9.00D=9.0=Abst.=Gods=Saturn=9Sept.>>A=Ø.
Classic=10,000=1,000=100%=10.0=Physicality=Tech.=10 Oct.=Uranus=P=1Ø.
Classical=10,000=1,000=100%=10.0=Physicality=Tech.=10 Oct.=Uranus=P=1Ø.
Classicism=15,500=16,000=16%=P1.60D=1.6=Incarnation=Mind of GOD=1 June=Maia.
Classicist=3,500=4,000=40%=P4.0D=Govt. =Creatocracy=4 April=Hermes=G=A4.
Classified=5,500=5.5=80%=P5.50=Earth-Midway=5 May = Gaia.
Classified advertisement=9,000=90%=P9.00D=9.0=Abst.=Gods=Saturn=9Sept.>>A=Ø.
Classify=8,000=80%=P8.0D=Economy=Currency=8 Aug.=Zeus>>E=v.
Classless=3,500=4,000=40%=P4.0D=Govt. =Creatocracy=4 April=Hermes=G=A4.
Classmate=4,000=40%=P4.0D=Govt. =Creatocracy=4 April=Mercury=Hermes=G=A4.
Classroom=3,500=4,000=40%=P4.0D=Govt. =Creatocracy=4 April=Hermes=G=A4.

Classy=1,500=15%=P1.50D=1.5=Authority=Solar Crown=1 May = Maia.
In the Creatocracy, four classes of governance are established. The first class is royalty as by
GOD and the Gods. Second is the Media as by the prophets. Third is Government as by
custodians of our commonwealth and managers of national resources. Fourth is Labour
known as the workforce. Creatocracy is the highest class of government by natural law.

Clatter=5,000=50%=P5.00D=Law=Time=Venus=5 May = Aphrodite>>L=N.

Claudius I=4,000=40%=P4.0D=Govt. =Creatocracy=4 April=Mercury=Hermes=G=A4.
Sword of Honour: Days of St. Valentine by African Shakespeare being emperor of the
Creatocracy is a play that had Claudius as one of its key characters.

Clause=11,000=11%=P1.10D=1.1=Idea=Brainchild=11Nov=Athena>>I=MT.
Claustrophobia=5,000=50%=P5.00D=Law=Time=Venus=5 May = Aphrodite>>L=N.
Clavichord=2,500=3,000=30%=P3.0D=3.0=Cr=Stars=Muses=3 March= C=I>>GIL.
Clavicle=6,000=60%=P6.0D=Man=Earth=Royalty=6 June=Gaia=Maia>>M=M2.

Clavier=3,500=4,000=40%=P4.0D=Govt.=Creatocracy=4 April=Mercury=Hermes=G=A4.
Claw=13,000=13%=P1.30D=Solar Core=Faculty=13 January=Athena.
Clay=13,500=14,000=14%=P1.40D=1.4=Mgt.=13May=Athena=SC=0.1
Clay Cassius Marcellus=2,000=20%=P2.00D=2.0=Nature=Moon=2 Feb.=Cupid=N=C+_.
Clay,Henry=2,000=20%=P2.00D=2.0=Nature=Moon=2 Feb.=Cupid=N=C+_.
Claymation=11,000=11%=P1.10D=1.1=Idea=Brainchild=11Nov=Athena>>I=MT.
Claymore mine=2,500=3,000=30%=P3.0D=3.0=Cr=Stars=Muses=3 March= C=I>>GIL.
Clay pigeon=5,500=5.5=80%=P5.50=Earth-Midway=5 May = Gaia.
Clean=29,500=30,000=3,000=30%=P3.0D=3.0=Cr=Stars=Muses=3 March= C=I>>GIL.
Clean cut=3,500=4,000=40%=P4.0D=Govt. =Creatocracy=4 April=Hermes=G=A4.
Cleanly=4,000=40%=P4.0D=Govt. =Creatocracy=4 April=Mercury=Hermes=G=A4.
Clean room=8,500=9,000=90%=P9.00D=9.0=Abst.=Gods=Saturn=9Sept.>>A=Ø.
Cleanse=3,500=4,000=40%=P4.0D=Govt. =Creatocracy=4 April=Hermes=G=A4.
Cleanup=8,000=80%=P8.0D=Economy=Currency=8 Aug.=Zeus>>E=v.
Clear=10,000=1,000=100%=10.0=Physicality=Tech.=10 Oct.=Uranus=P=1Ø.
Clearance=8,500=9,000=90%=P9.00D=9.0=Abst.=Gods=Saturn=9Sept.>>A=Ø.
Clear cut=11,000=11%=P1.10D=1.1=Idea=Brainchild=11Nov=Athena>>I=MT.
Clearing=5,500=5.5=80%=P5.50=Earth-Midway=5 May = Gaia.
Clearinghouse=5,500=5.5=80%=P5.50=Earth-Midway=5 May = Gaia.
Cleat=7,500=8,000=80%=P8.0D=Economy=Currency=8 Aug.=Zeus>>E=v.
Cleavage=5,000=50%=P5.00D=Law=Time=Venus=5 May = Aphrodite>>L=N.
Cleave(1)=2,500=3,000=30%=P3.0D=3.0=Cr=Stars=Muses=3 March= C=I>>GIL.
Cleave(2)=3,000=30%=P3.0D=3.0=Cr=Stars=Muses=3 March= C=I>>GIL.
Cleave=5,500=5.5=80%=P5.50=Earth-Midway=5 May = Gaia.
Clef=9,500=10,000=1,000=100%=10.0=Physicality=Tech.=10 Oct.=Uranus=P=1Ø.
Cleft=5,500=5.5=80%=P5.50=Earth-Midway=5 May = Gaia.
Clematis=5,500=5.5=80%=P5.50=Earth-Midway=5 May = Gaia.
Clemenceau Georges=4,500=5,000=50%=P5.00D=Law=Venus=5 May=Odite>>L=N.
Clemency=3,000=30%=P3.0D=3.0=Cr=Stars=Muses=3 March= C=I>>GIL.
Clemens Samuel Langhorne=5,000=50%=P5.00D=Law=Time=Venus=5 May=Odite>>L=N.
Clement=3,500=4,000=40%=P4.0D=Govt. =Creatocracy=4 April=Hermes=G=A4.
Clench=11,500=12,000=12%=P1.20D=1.2=Knowl.=Education=12Dec.=Athena>>K=F.
Cleopatra=5,000=50%=P5.00D=Law=Time=Venus=5 May = Aphrodite>>L=N.
Clerestory=4,500=5,000=50%=P5.00D=Law=Time=Venus=5 May = Aphrodite>>L=N.
Clergy=7,000=70%=P7.0D=7.0=Language=Assets=Mars=7 July=Pleiades
Clergyman=4,000=40%=P4.0D=Govt. =Creatocracy=4 April=Mercury=Hermes=G=A4.
Clergywoman=4,000=40%=P4.0D=Govt.=Creatocracy=4April=Mercury=Hermes=G=A4.
Cleric=2,500=3,000=30%=P3.0D=3.0=Cr=Stars=Muses=3 March= C=I>>GIL.
Clerical=5,500=5.5=80%=P5.50=Earth-Midway=5 May = Gaia.
Clericalism=7,500=8,000=80%=P8.0D=Economy=Currency=8 Aug.=Zeus>>E=v.
Clerk=14,000=14%=P1.40D=1.4=Mgt.=13May=Athena=SC=0.1
Cleveland=5,000=50%=P5.00D=Law=Time=Venus=5 May = Aphrodite>>L=N.
Cleveland, (Stephen) Grover=4,000=40%=P4.0D=Govt.=4 April=Hermes=G=A4.
Clever=10,000=1,000=100%=10.0=Physicality=Tech.=10 Oct.=Uranus=P=1Ø.
Clevis=5,500=5.5=80%=P5.50=Earth-Midway=5 May = Gaia.

Clew=7,500=8,000=80%=P8.0D=Economy=Currency=8 Aug.=Zeus>>E=v.
Cliché=5,500=5.5=80%=P5.50=Earth-Midway=5 May = Gaia.
Clichéd=1,000=100%=10.0=1.0=Mind=Sun=1 January=Helios >> M=E4.
Click=8,500=9,000=90%=P9.00D=9.0=Abst.=Gods=Saturn=9Sept.>>A=Ø.
Client=4,500=5,000=50%=P5.00D=Law=Time=Venus=5 May = Aphrodite>>L=N.
Clientele=2,000=20%=P2.00D=2.0=Nature=Moon=2 Feb.=Cupid=N=C+_.
Cliff=4,000=40%=P4.0D=Govt. =Creatocracy=4 April=Mercury=Hermes=G=A4.
Cliff dweller=8,000=80%=P8.0D=Economy=Currency=8 Aug.=Zeus>>E=v.
Cliff hanger=6,500=7,000=70%=P7.0D=7.0=Language=Assets=Mars=7 July=Pleiades
Climacteric=9,500=10,000=1,000=100%=10.0=Physicality=Tech.=10 Oct.=Uranus=P=1Ø.
Climactic=2,500=3,000=30%=P3.0D=3.0=Cr=Stars=Muses=3 March= C=I>>GIL.
Climate=10,000=1,000=100%=10.0=Physicality=Tech.=10 Oct.=Uranus=P=1Ø.
Climatology=2,500=3,000=30%=P3.0D=3.0=Cr=Stars=Muses=3 March= C=I>>GIL.
Climax=15,000=1,500=15%=P1.50D=1.5=Authority=Solar Crown=1 May = Maia.
Climb=14,000=14%=P1.40D=1.4=Mgt.=13May=Athena=SC=0.1
Clime=500=5%=P5.00D=5.0=Law=Time=Venus=5 May=Aphrodite>>L=N.
Clinch=11,000=11%=P1.10D=1.1=Idea=Brainchild=11Nov=Athena>>I=MT.
Clincher=5,000=50%=P5.00D=Law=Time=Venus=5 May = Aphrodite>>L=N.
Cling=5,500=5.5=80%=P5.50=Earth-Midway=5 May = Gaia.
Clingstone=6,000=60%=P6.0D=Man=Earth=Royalty=6 June=Gaia=Maia>>M=M2.
Clinic=18,000=18%=P1.80D=Solar Currency=Maks Currencies=1 Aug.=Maia.
Clinical=6,000=60%=P6.0D=Man=Earth=Royalty=6 June=Gaia=Maia>>M=M2.
Clinician=5,000=50%=P5.00D=Law=Time=Venus=5 May = Aphrodite>>L=N.
Clink(1)=5,000=50%=P5.00D=Law=Time=Venus=5 May = Aphrodite>>L=N.
Clink(2)=2,500=3,000=30%=P3.0D=3.0=Cr=Stars=Muses=3 March= C=I>>GIL.
Clinker=7,000=70%=P7.0D=7.0=Language=Assets=Mars=7 July=Pleiades
Clinton William Jefferson=4,500=5,000=50%=P5.00D=Time=Venus=5May=Odite>>L=N.
Cliometrics=6,000=60%=P6.0D=Man=Earth=Royalty=6 June=Gaia=Maia>>M=M2.
Clip(1)=18,500=19,000=19,000=19%=P1.90=1.9=Planetary Energy=Mind of God=Maia.
Clip(2)=8,000=80%=P8.0D=Economy=Currency=8 Aug.=Zeus>>E=v.
Clipboard=7,000=70%=P7.0D=7.0=Language=Assets=Mars=7 July=Pleiades
Clipper=6,500=7,000=70%=P7.0D=7.0=Language=Assets=Mars=7 July=Pleiades
Clipping=4,500=5,000=50%=P5.50D=Law=Time=Venus=5 May = Aphrodite>>L=N.
Clique=3,000=30%=P3.0D=3.0=Cr=Stars=Muses=3 March= C=I>>GIL.

Clitoris=6,500=7,000=70%=P7.0D=7.0=Language=Assets=Mars=7 July=Pleiades
The clitoris is a borderline body organ that enhances measurement abilities through sex. This is probably the reason and biggest secret behind the fact that creative people are also most often highly sexual people. This is the physical link between sexuality and creativity. An organ that transfers certain potentials to the male partner making the woman a muse. Female circumcision is thereby established a crime against GOD and humanity because it is simply the removal of 70% blessings common sense and potentials stored there.

Clive Robert=3,500=4,000=40%=P4.0D=Govt.=4 April=Mercury=Hermes=G=A4.
Cloaca=11,500=12,000=12%=P1.20D=1.2=Knowl.=Education=12Dec.=Athena>>K=F.

Cloak=11,000=11%=P1.10D=1.1=Idea=Brainchild=11Nov=Athena>>I=MT.
Cloak-and-dagger=3,000=30%=P3.0D=3.0=Cr=Stars=Muses=3 March= C=I>>GIL.
Clobber=5,500=5.5=80%=P5.50=Earth-Midway=5 May = Gaia.
Cloche=4,500=5,000=50%=P5.00D=Law=Time=Venus=5 May = Aphrodite>>L=N.

Clock=8,500=9,000=90%=P9.00D=9.0=Abst.=Gods=Saturn=9Sept.>>A=Ø.
A clock is a borderline technology that transits beings from economy to abstraction. Hence human life is closer to the abstract world once born and the clock starts ticking. This is what makes life seemingly short. It is a measure of value business and economy in Zeus.

Clockwise=4,500=5,000=50%=P5.00D=Law=Time=Venus=5 May = Aphrodite>>L=N.
Clockwork=8,000=80%=P8.0D=Economy=Currency=8 Aug.=Zeus>>E=v.
Clod=6,000=60%=P6.0D=Man=Earth=Royalty=6 June=Gaia=Maia>>M=M2.
Clodhopper=3,500=4,000=40%=P4.0D=Govt. =Creatocracy=4 April=Hermes=G=A4.
Clog=7,000=70%=P7.0D=7.0=Language=Assets=Mars=7 July=Pleiades
Cloisonné=9,000=90%=P9.00D=9.0=Abst.=Gods=Saturn=9Sept.>>A=Ø.
Cloister=13,500=14,000=14%=P1.40D=1.4=Mgt.=13May=Athena=SC=0.1
Clone=10,000=1,000=100%=10.0=Physicality=Tech.=10 Oct.=Uranus=P=1Ø.
Clop=5,000=50%=P5.00D=Law=Time=Venus=5 May = Aphrodite>>L=N.
Close=10,000=1,000=100%=10.0=Physicality=Tech.=10 Oct.=Uranus=P=1Ø.
Closed captioned=6,500=7,000=70%=P7.0D=7.0=Lang.=Assets=Mars=7 July=Pleiades
Closed circuit=11,500=12,000=12%=P1.20D=1.2=Knowl.=12Dec.=Athena>>K=F.
Closed shop=1,500=15%=P1.50D=1.5=Authority=Solar Crown=1 May = Maia.
Close fisted=500=5%=P5.00D=5.0=Law=Time=Venus=5 May=Aphrodite>>L=N.
Close minded=3,500=4,000=40%=P4.0D=Govt.=4 April=Mercury=Hermes=G=A4.
Close mouthed=2,000=20%=P2.00D=2.0=Nature=Moon=2 Feb.=Cupid=N=C+_.
Close out=7,500=8,000=80%=P8.0D=Economy=Currency=8 Aug.=Zeus>>E=v.

Closet=9,000=90%=P9.00D=9.0=Abst.=Gods=Saturn=9Sept.>>A=Ø.
Jesus instructed strict privacy in one's closet during personal prayers. Computational results shows it is the abode of the Gods during such hours especially in the dark or nights.

Close-up=6,500=7,000=70%=P7.0D=7.0=Language=Assets=Mars=7 July=Pleiades
Closure=7,000=70%=P7.0D=7.0=Language=Assets=Mars=7 July=Pleiades
Clot=7,000=70%=P7.0D=7.0=Language=Assets=Mars=7 July=Pleiades
Cloth=12,000=12%=P1.20D=1.2=Knowl.=Education=12Dec.=Athena>>K=F.
Clothe=5,000=50%=P5.00D=Law=Time=Venus=5 May = Aphrodite>>L=N.
Clothes=4,000=40%=P4.0D=Govt.:4 April=Mercury=Hermes=G=A4.
Clothes horse=7,000=70%=P7.0D=7.0=Language=Assets=Mars=7 July=Pleiades
Clothespin=3,500=4,000=40%=P4.0D=Govt.=4 April=Mercury=Hermes=G=A4.
Clothing=1,000=100%=10.0=1.0=Mind=Sun=1 January=Helios >> M=E4.
Cloture=6,500=7,000=70%=P7.0D=7.0=Language=Assets=Mars=7 July=Pleiades

---

Cloud=21,500=22,000=2.2>>4.0=4,000=40%=P4.0D=Govt.=4 April=Hermes=G=A4. Clouds are borderlines to power and relationships. Wings of Hermes and the Gods. Borderlines are connecting lines streams energy or matter that link two or more things. By Greek mythology, the supernatural depiction of the hair is the clouds being Uranus. Perhaps this is why Apostle Paul wrote that a woman covers her hair at worship services as it scares the angels. We confirm its relativity spoken by GOD Almighty in Job 38:33-34. See Rain, Myth, Rain Sky Database, Sun Sky Database (below Myth).

Cloudburst=2,500=3,000=30%=P3.0D=3.0=Cr=Stars=Muses=3 March= C=I>>GIL. Once creativity occurs a borderline of the cloud bursts into the rain of blessings and power.

Cloud chamber=12,000=12%=P1.20D=1.2=Knowl.=Education=12Dec.=Athena>>K=F. Knowledge is a cloud chamber until burst end through discovery invention and creativity.

Cloud nine=4,000=40%=P4.0D=Govt.=4 April=Mercury=Hermes=G=A4.
Cloudy=6,000=60%=P6.0D=Man=Earth=Royalty=6 June=Gaia=Maia>>M=M2.
Clout=6,500=7,000=70%=P7.0D=7.0=Language=Assets=Mars=7 July=Pleiades
Clove(1)=6,500=7,000=70%=P7.0D=7.0=Language=Assets=Mars=7 July=Pleiades
Clove(2)=4,500=5,000=50%=P5.00D=Law=Time=Venus=5 May = Aphrodite>>L=N.
Clove(3)=2,000=20%=P2.00D=2.0=Nature=Moon=2 Feb.=Cupid=N=C+_.
Cloven=4,500=5,000=50%=P5.00D=Law=Time=Venus=5 May = Aphrodite>>L=N.
Clover=6,500=7,000=70%=P7.0D=7.0=Language=Assets=Mars=7 July=Pleiades
Cloverleaf=6,500=7,000=70%=P7.0D=7.0=Language=Assets=Mars=7 July=Pleiades

---

Clovish I=5,000=50%=P5.00D=Law=Time=Venus=5 May = Aphrodite>>L=N. King of the Franks. In the study of Psychoeconomix Peter Matthews-Akukalia (Maks I) is King of the Creative Sciences, Makupedians and Paradiseans (Diseans). King Maks I.

Clown=9,000=90%=P9.00D=9.0=Abst.=Gods=Saturn=9Sept.>>A=Ø.
Cloy=4,500=5,000=50%=P5.00D=Law=Time=Venus=5 May = Aphrodite>>L=N.
CLUJ=1,500=15%=P1.50D=1.5=Authority=Solar Crown=1 May = Maia.
Club=10,000=1,000=100%=10.0=Physicality=Tech.=10 Oct.=Uranus=P=1Ø.
Club car=6,000=60%=P6.0D=Man=Earth=Royalty=6 June=Gaia=Maia>>M=M2.
Club foot=8,000=80%=P8.0D=Economy=Currency=8 Aug.=Zeus>>E=v.
Clubhouse=5,500=5.5=80%=P5.50=Earth-Midway=5 May = Gaia.
Club sandwich=7,500=8,000=80%=P8.0D=Economy=Currency=8 Aug.=Zeus>>E=v.
Club soda=2,000=20%=P2.00D=2.0=Nature=Moon=2 Feb.=Cupid=N=C+_.
Club steak=1,500=15%=P1.50D=1.5=Authority=Solar Crown=1 May = Maia.
Cluck=9,500=10,000=1,000=100%=10.0=Physicality=Tech.=10 Oct.=Uranus=P=1Ø.
Clue=8,000=80%=P8.0D=Economy=Currency=8 Aug.=Zeus>>E=v.
Clump=7,000=70%=P7.0D=7.0=Language=Assets=Mars=7 July=Pleiades
Clumsy=5,500=5.5=80%=P5.50=Earth-Midway=5 May = Gaia.

Clung=7,000=70%=P7.0D=7.0=Language=Assets=Mars=7 July=Pleiades
Clunk=2,000=20%=P2.00D=2.0=Nature=Moon=2 Feb.=Cupid=N=C+_.
Clunky=3,000=30%=P3.0D=3.0=Cr=Stars=Muses=3 March= C=I>>GIL.
Cluster=7,000=70%=P7.0D=7.0=Language=Assets=Mars=7 July=Pleiades
Clutch(1)=10,000=1,000=100%=10.0=Physicality=Tech.=10 Oct.=Uranus=P=1Ø.
Clutch(2)=5,500=5.5=80%=P5.50=Earth-Midway=5 May = Gaia.
Clutter=3,500=4,000=40%=P4.0D=Govt.=4 April=Mercury=Hermes=G=A4.
Clyde=10,500=11,000=11%=P1.10D=1.1=Idea=Brainchild=11Nov=Athena>>I=MT.
Clydesdale=7,500=8,000=80%=P8.0D=Economy=Currency=8 Aug.=Zeus>>E=v.
cm=1,000=100%=10.0=1.0=Mind=Sun=1 January=Helios >> M=E4.
CMA=1,500=15%=P1.50D=1.5=Authority=Solar Crown=1 May = Maia.
Cmdr=1,000=100%=10.0=1.0=Mind=Sun=1 January=Helios >> M=E4.
Co=3,000=30%=P3.0D=3.0=Cr=Stars=Muses=3 March= C=I>>GIL.
CO=4,000=40%=P4.0D=Govt.=4 April=Mercury=Hermes=G=A4.
Co.=1,000=100%=10.0=1.0=Mind=Sun=1 January=Helios >> M=E4.
C.O.=2,500=3,000=30%=P3.0D=3.0=Cr=Stars=Muses=3 March= C=I>>GIL.
c/o=1,000=100%=10.0=1.0=Mind=Sun=1 January=Helios >> M=E4.

Co-=13,000=13%=P1.30D=Solar Core=Faculty=13 January=Athena.
It is well known that Athena loves and partners writers. She is the natural co-author to those whose writings are based on pure ideas that promote human capital development. This is how faculties of learning are created and how the Faculty of creative Sciences was invented. The key Faculty in this ability is Creative Intelligence and prerogative is royalty.

Coach=18,500=19,000=19,000=19%=P1.90=1.9=Planetary Energy=Mind of God=Maia.
Coachman=2,500=3,000=30%=P3.0D=3.0=Cr=Stars=Muses=3 March= C=I>>GIL.
Coadjutor=5,500=5.5=80%=P5.50=Earth-Midway=5 May = Gaia.
Coagulant=2,500=3,000=30%=P3.0D=3.0=Cr=Stars=Muses=3 March= C=I>>GIL.
Coagulate=4,000=40%=P4.0D=Govt.=4 April=Mercury=Hermes=G=A4.
Coal=9,500=10,000=1,000=100%=10.0=Physicality=Tech.=10 Oct.=Uranus=P=1Ø.
Coalesce=6,000=60%=P6.0D=Man=Earth=Royalty=6 June=Gaia=Maia>>M=M2.
Coal gas=5,500=5.5=80%=P5.50=Earth-Midway=5 May = Gaia.
Coalition=3,500=4,000=40%=P4.0D=Govt.=4 April=Mercury=Hermes=G=A4.
Coal oil=1,000=100%=10.0=1.0=Mind=Sun=1 January=Helios >> M=E4.
Coal tar=9,500=10,000=1,000=100%=10.0=Physicality=Tech.=10 Oct.=Uranus=P=1Ø.
Coarse=9,000=90%=P9.00D=9.0=Abst.=Gods=Saturn=9Sept.>>A=Ø.
Coarsen=2,500=3,000=30%=P3.0D=3.0=Cr=Stars=Muses=3 March= C=I>>GIL.
Coast=15,000=1,500=15%=P1.50D=1.5=Authority=Solar Crown=1 May = Maia.
Coaster=8,000=80%=P8.0D=Economy=Currency=8 Aug.=Zeus>>E=v.
Coast guard=13,000=13%=P1.30D=Solar Core=Faculty=13 January=Athena.
Coastline=3,500=4,000=40%=P4.0D=Govt. =Creatocracy=4 April=Hermes=G=A4.
Coast Mountains=5,000=50%=P5.00D=Law=Time=Venus=5 May = Aphrodite>>L=N.
Coast Ranges=9,000=90%=P9.00D=9.0=Abst.=Gods=Saturn=9Sept.>>A=Ø.
Coat=13,500=14,000=14%=P1.40D=1.4=Mgt.=13May=Athena=SC=0.1

Coati=6,000=60%=P6.0D=Man=Earth=Royalty=6 June=Gaia=Maia>>M=M2.
Coatimundi=1,000=100%=10.0=1.0=Mind=Sun=1 January=Helios >> M=E4.
Coat of arms=5,000=50%=P5.00D=Law=Time=Venus=5 May = Aphrodite>>L=N.
Coat of mail=3,500=4,000=40%=P4.0D=Govt. =Creatocracy=4 April=Hermes=G=A4.
Coat tall=6,000=60%=P6.0D=Man=Earth=Royalty=6 June=Gaia=Maia>>M=M2.
Coauthor=1,500=15%=P1.50D=1.5=Authority=Solar Crown=1 May = Maia.
Coax=5,000=50%=P5.00D=Law=Time=Venus=5 May = Aphrodite>>L=N.
Coaxial=3,500=4,000=40%=P4.0D=Govt. =Creatocracy=4 April=Hermes=G=A4.
Coaxial cable=9,000=90%=P9.00D=9.0=Abst.=Gods=Saturn=9Sept.>>A=Ø.
Cob=4,000=40%=P4.0D=Govt. =Creatocracy=4 April=Hermes=G=A4.
Cobalt=14,000=14%=P1.40D=1.4=Mgt.=13May=Athena=SC=0.1
Cobalt blue=2,500=3,000=30%=P3.0D=3.0=Cr=Stars=Muses=3 March= C=I>>GIL.
Cobble=4,500=5,000=50%=P5.00D=Law=Time=Venus=5 May = Aphrodite>>L=N.
Cobbler(1)=4,000=40%=P4.0D=Govt. =Creatocracy=4 April=Hermes=G=A4.
Cobbler(2)=5,000=50%=P5.00D=Law=Time=Venus=5 May = Aphrodite>>L=N.
Cobblestone=2,500=3,000=30%=P3.0D=3.0=Cr=Stars=Muses=3 March= C=I>>GIL.
COBOL=8,500=9,000=90%=P9.00D=9.0=Abst.=Gods=Saturn=9Sept.>>A=Ø.
Cobra=8,500=9,000=90%=P9.00D=9.0=Abst.=Gods=Saturn=9Sept.>>A=Ø.
Cobweb=9,000=90%=P9.00D=9.0=Abst.=Gods=Saturn=9Sept.>>A=Ø.
Coca=9,500=10,000=1,000=100%=10.0=Physicality=Tech.=10 Oct.=Uranus=P=1Ø.
Cocaine=9,500=10,000=1,000=100%=10.0=Physicality=Tech.=10 Oct.=Uranus=P=1Ø.
Coccus=3,500=4,000=40%=P4.0D=Govt. =Creatocracy=4 April=Hermes=G=A4.
-coccus=3,500=4,000=40%=P4.0D=Govt. =Creatocracy=4 April=Hermes=G=A4.
Coccyx=4,500=5,000=50%=P5.00D=Law=Time=Venus=5 May = Aphrodite>>L=N.
Cochabamba=5,000=50%=P5.00D=Law=Time=Venus=5 May = Aphrodite>>L=N.
Cochineal=6,500=7,000=70%=P7.0D=7.0=Language=Assets=Mars=7 July=Pleiades
Cochise=2,000=20%=P2.00D=2.0=Nature=Moon=2 Feb.=Cupid=N=C+_.
Cochlea=7,000=7,000=70%=P7.0D=7.0=Language=Assets=Mars=7 July=Pleiades
Cock(1)=50,500=51,000=1.5=1,500=15%=P1.50D=Authority=Solar Crown=1 May = Maia.
Cock(2)=4,000=40%=P4.0D=Govt. =Creatocracy=4 April=Hermes=G=A4.
Cockade=6,000=60%=P6.0D=Man=Earth=Royalty=6 June=Gaia=Maia>>M=M2.
Cockatiel=5,000=50%=P5.00D=Law=Time=Venus=5 May = Aphrodite>>L=N.
Cockatoo=6,000=60%=P6.0D=Man=Earth=Royalty=6 June=Gaia=Maia>>M=M2.

Cockatrice=4,500=5,000=50%=P5.00D=Law=Time=Venus=5 May = Aphrodite>>L=N.
Aphrodite at war becomes a serpent having the power to kill by its glance, a cockatrice.

Cocked hat=2,000=20%=P2.00D=2.0=Nature=Moon=2 Feb.=Cupid=N=C+_.
Cockerel=1,500=15%=P1.50D=1.5=Authority=Solar Crown=1 May = Maia.
Cocker spaniel=5,500=5.5=80%=P5.50=Earth-Midway=5 May = Gaia.
Cockeyed=5,000=50%=P5.00D=Law=Time=Venus=5 May = Aphrodite>>L=N.
Cockfight=6,000=60%=P6.0D=Man=Earth=Royalty=6 June=Gaia=Maia>>M=M2.
Cockle(1)=6,000=60%=P6.0D=Man=Earth=Royalty=6 June=Gaia=Maia>>M=M2.
Cockle(2)=5,000=50%=P5.50D=Law=Time=Venus=5 May = Aphrodite>>L=N.

Cockle shell=4,000=40%=P4.0D=Govt.=Creatocracy=4 April=Hermes=G=A4.
Cockney=5,500=5.5=80%=P5.50=Earth-Midway=5 May = Gaia.
Cock pit=9,000=90%=P9.00D=9.0=Abst.=Gods=Saturn=9Sept.>>A=Ø.
Cockroach=6,500=7,000=70%=P7.0D=7.0=Language=Assets=Mars=7 July=Pleiades
Cockscomb=11,500=12,000=12%=P1.20D=1.2=Knowl.=Education=12Dec.=Athena>>K=F.
Cocksure=3,000=30%=P3.0D=3.0=Cr=Stars=Muses=3 March= C=I>>GIL.
Cocktail=4,000=40%=P4.0D=Govt.=Creatocracy=4 April=Hermes=G=A4.
Cocky=3,000=30%=P3.0D=3.0=Cr=Stars=Muses=3 March= C=I>>GIL.
Coco=10,000=1,000=100%=10.0=Physicality=Tech.=10 Oct.=Uranus=P=1Ø.

Cocoa=11,500=12,000=12%=P1.20D=1.2=Knowl.=Education=12Dec.=Athena>>K=F.
A borderline plant that builds human knowledge when processed and taken as food.

Coconut=12,500=13,000=13%=P1.30D=Solar Core=Faculty=13 January=Athena.
Coconut palm=6,500=7,000=70%=P7.0D=7.0=Language=Assets=Mars=7 July=Pleiades
Cocoon=9,000=90%=P9.00D=9.0=Abst.=Gods=Saturn=9Sept.>>A=Ø.
cod=4,000=40%=P4.0D=Govt. =Creatocracy=4 April=Hermes=G=A4.
Cod, Cape=3,500=4,000=40%=P4.0D=Govt. =Creatocracy=4 April=Hermes=G=A4.
COD=2,000=20%=P2.00D=2.0=Nature=Moon=2 Feb.=Cupid=N=C+_.
Coda=4,000=40%=P4.0D=Govt. =Creatocracy=4 April=Hermes=G=A4.
Coddle=6,000=60%=P6.0D=Man=Earth=Royalty=6 June=Gaia=Maia>>M=M2.

Code=13,500=14,000=14%=P1.40D=1.4=Mgt.=13May=Athena=SC=0.1
The Creatocracy as an economic sector develops high level codes through its programming language culture and history. Codes are basic ingredients in world Creatocracy best practices as instituted by Peter Matthews-Akukalia. The Creatocracy has exclusive rights to determine the correctness of an application code using its satellite data tracking systems and licenses local national multinational transnational level organizations and government institutions in the use of these codes in any and every area of our lives.

An example is used to illustrate bible coding to understand the mind of God.
Coding Deuteronomy 29:29.

1. Secret H5641 >> H = 6.0 >> 5.6*4.1x=px=9.7+22.96=32.66x=px=255.372 = 300 = 30 = 4.0 >> Creativity.
   H=6.0>>255.372*6.0x=px=261.372+1,532.232=1,793.604x=px=402,276.1463=40=4.0 >> Government >> Power >> Relationships >> Family >> Organizations >> Creatocracy.

2. LORD H3068 >> H = 6.0 >> 3.0*6.8x=px=9.8+20.4=30.2x=px=230.12 = 2.3 >> Local Jurisdiction.
   H = 6.0 >> 230.12*6.0x=px=236.12+1,380.72=1,616.84x=px=327,632.4464=33=3.3G
   The Genius Gods as one body >> LORD and rulers of the people. Exodus 22:28, 23:20-25

3. Revealed H1540 >>H = 6.0 >> 1.5*4.0x=px=5.5+6=11.5x=px=44.5 = 50 >> Law. H = 6.0 >> 44.5*6.0x=px=50.5+267=317.5x=px=13,801 = 14 = 1.4 >> Management. To have a revelation is to understand the law behind something and use it productively.

4. Children H1121 >> H = 6.0 >> 1.1*2.1x=px=3.2+2.31=5.51x=px=12.902 = 1.3 >> Faculty of Creative Intelligence. H = 6.0 >> 12.902*6.0x=px=18.902+77.412=96.314x= px=1,559.555624=16=1.6=Incarnation.
Children are the incarnation of spirits. They can be known through creative intelligence which is the measure of their brain energy at birth. This is the only way we can track what spirit Incarnates them. It is a secret of the Gods and determines the true genius.

5. Do H6213 >> H = 6.0 >> 6.2*1.3x=px=7.5+8.06=60.45x=px=3,654.2025 = 4.0 >> Government >> Power >> Relationships >> Family >> Organizations >> Creatocracy. H = 6.0 >> 3,654.2025*6.0x=px=3,660.2025+21,925.215=25,585.4175x=px= 80,276,312.17=80=8.0
Economy = Currency = Value. To "do" means to compute the worth of a thing. The codes to perform this task are determine the value 8.0 of a thing 2, by computing 7, using human means such as writing and giving it an identity such as a book 6, using creativity 3 to enhance knowledge 12. The key functionality (.) will be computational intelligence (17) by solar assets. This must encompass the genius governance of Heaven called Creatocracy.
In simple terms compute the solar core on the dot principle and create currency from it.

6. Words H1697 >> H = 6.0 >> 1.6*9.7x=px=11.3+15.52=26.82x=px=202.196=2.0
Nature >> Methods >> Techniques >> Things >> Nothing >> Anything >> Something >> Everything. Words are things that source as elements from the moon built from energy. >>H=6.0>>202.196*6.0x=px=208.196+1,213.176=1,421.372x=px=359,007.852.1=4.0 Creatocracy of words is gift of government mentioned among the gifts of the Holy Spirit.

7. Law H8451 >> >> H = 6.0 >> 8.4*5.1x=px=13.5+42.84=56.34x=px=634.68 = 6.4 >> Human Power by this context rather than emotional power.
H=6.0>>634.68*6.0x=px=640.68+3,808.08=4,448.76x=px=2,444,209.454=2.4>>2.0.
Nature >> Methods >> Techniques >> Things >> Nothing >> Anything >> Something >> Everything. Natural law when computed is the greatest form of power in the universe. Hence the phrase "this law" in this verse refers to natural laws written in Scripture.
All words WDSD computed on solar core values and equivalents belong to the Creatocracy.

Codeine=7,000=70%=P7.0D=7.0=Language=Assets=Mars=7 July=Pleiades
Codex=4,000=40%=P4.0D=Govt.=Creatocracy=4 April=Hermes=G=A4.
Codfish=1,000=100%=10.0=1.0=Mind=Sun=1 January=Helios >> M=E4.
Codger=4,000=40%=P4.0D=Govt.=Creatocracy=4 April=Hermes=G=A4.

Codicil=3,500=4,000=40%=P4.0D=Govt. =Creatocracy=4 April=Hermes=G=A4.
Codify=2,000=20%=P2.00D=2.0=Nature=Moon=2 Feb.=Cupid=N=C+_.

Cod liver oil=8,000=80%=P8.0D=Economy=Currency=8 Aug.=Zeus>>E=v.
The cod liver oil is an oil of Zeus -Jehovah the Most High.

Cody William Frederick=4,500=5,000=50%=P5.00D=Time=Venus=5 May=Odite>>L=N.
Coed=4,500=5,000=50%=P5.00D=Law=Time=Venus=5 May = Aphrodite>>L=N.
Coeducation=5,000=50%=P5.00D=Law=Time=Venus=5 May = Aphrodite>>L=N.
Coefficient=13,500=14,000=14%=P1.40D=1.4=Mgt.=13May=Athena=SC=0.1
Coelenterate=9,000=90%=P9.00D=9.0=Abst.=Gods=Saturn=9Sept.>>A=Ø.
Coelom=4,500=5,000=50%=P5.00D=Law=Time=Venus=5 May = Aphrodite>>L=N.
Coequal=5,500=5.5=80%=P5.50=Earth-Midway=5 May = Gaia.
Coerce=9,500=10,000=1,000=100%=10.0=Physicality=Tech.=10 Oct.=Uranus=P=1Ø.
Coeur d'Alene=8,500=9,000=90%=P9.00D=9.0=Abst.=Gods=Saturn=9Sept.>>A=Ø.
Coeval=4,500=5,000=50%=P5.00D=Law=Time=Venus=5 May = Aphrodite>>L=N.
Coevolution=7,000=70%=P7.0D=7.0=Language=Assets=Mars=7 July=Pleiades
Coexist=8,500=9,000=90%=P9.00D=9.0=Abst.=Gods=Saturn=9Sept.>>A=Ø.
Coextensive=8,500=9,000=90%=P9.00D=9.0=Abst.=Gods=Saturn=9Sept.>>A=Ø.
C.of C.=1,500=15%=P1.50D=1.5=Authority=Solar Crown=1 May = Maia.
C. of E.=1,500=15%=P1.50D=1.5=Authority=Solar Crown=1 May = Maia.
Coffee cake=4,500=5,000=50%=P5.00D=Law=Time=Venus=5 May = Aphrodite>>L=N.
Coffeehouse=5,500=5.5=80%=P5.50=Earth-Midway=5 May = Gaia.
Coffee klatch=4,000=40%=P4.0D=Govt. =Creatocracy=4 April=Hermes=G=A4.
Coffeemaker=3,000=30%=P3.0D=3.0=Cr=Stars=Muses=3 March= C=I>>GIL.
Coffee pot=3,500=4,000=40%=P4.0D=Govt. =Creatocracy=4 April=Hermes=G=A4.
Coffee shop=5,500=5.5=80%=P5.50=Earth-Midway=5 May = Gaia.
Coffee table=4,000=40%=P4.0D=Govt. =Creatocracy=4 April=Hermes=G=A4.
Coffer=3,500=4,000=40%=P4.0D=Govt. =Creatocracy=4 April=Hermes=G=A4.
Cofferdam=11,500=12,000=12%=P1.20D=1.2=Knowl.=Education=12Dec.=Athena>>K=F.
Coffin=3,500=4,000=40%=P4.0D=Govt. =Creatocracy=4 April=Hermes=G=A4.
Cog=7,000=70%=P7.0D=7.0=Language=Assets=Mars=7 July=Pleiades
Cogeneration=7,500=8,000=80%=P8.0D=Economy=Currency=8 Aug.=Zeus>>E=v.
Cogent=2,000=20%=P2.00D=2.0=Nature=Moon=2 Feb.=Cupid=N=C+_.
Cogitate=2,500=3,000=30%=P3.0D=3.0=Cr=Stars=Muses=3 March= C=I>>GIL.
Cognac=2,000=20%=P2.00D=2.0=Nature=Moon=2 Feb.=Cupid=N=C+_.
Cognate=6,500=7,000=70%=P7.0D=7.0=Language=Assets=Mars=7 July=Pleiades
Cognition=6,500=7,000=70%=P7.0D=7.0=Language=Assets=Mars=7 July=Pleiades
Cognizance=3,500=4,000=40%=P4.0D=Govt. =Creatocracy=4 April=Hermes=G=A4.

Cognomen=1,500=15%=P1.50D=1.5=Authority=Solar Crown=1 May = Maia.
A surname such as Matthews-Akukalia. A nickname such as Castle Makupedia (deity).

Cognoscente=1,000=100%=10.0=1.0=Mind=Sun=1 January=Helios >> M=E4.
Cogwheel=3,000=30%=P3.0D=3.0=Cr=Stars=Muses=3 March= C=I>>GIL.
Cohabit=5,000=50%=P5.00D=Law=Time=Venus=5 May = Aphrodite>>L=N.
Cohan George Michael=3,000=30%=P3.0D=3.0=Cr=Stars=Muses=3 March= C=I>>GIL.
Cohere=4,000=40%=P4.0D=Govt. =Creatocracy=4 April=Hermes=G=A4.

Cohesion=8,000=80%=P8.0D=Economy=Currency=8 Aug.=Zeus>>E=v.
Zeus is the cohesion behind all things and the universes.

Cohort=4,000=40%=P4.0D=Govt. =Creatocracy=4 April=Hermes=G=A4.
Cohost=3,500=4,000=40%=P4.0D=Govt. =Creatocracy=4 April=Hermes=G=A4.
Coif=4,500=5,000=50%=P5.00D=Law=Time=Venus=5 May = Aphrodite>>L=N.
Coiffure=1,000=100%=10.0=1.0=Mind=Sun=1 January=Helios >> M=E4.
Coil=10,000=1,000=100%=10.0=Physicality=Tech.=10 Oct.=Uranus=P=1Ø.

Coin=11,000=11%=P1.10D=1.1=Idea=Brainchild=11Nov=Athena>>I=MT.
A kind of Money; also to invent a word. A word is therefore worth a kind of money the
Maks. Invention of the Maks Currency is the right to have the coin of the author in human
and God identity. Peter Matthews-Akukalia, Castle Makupedia coined "Creatocracy".

Coinage=3,500=4,000=40%=P4.0D=Govt. =Creatocracy=4 April=Hermes=G=A4.
Coincide=6,500=7,000=70%=P7.0D=7.0=Language=Assets=Mars=7 July=Pleiades
Coincidence=9,500=10,000=1,000=100%=Physicality= Tech.=10 Oct.=Uranus=P=1Ø.
Coitus=1,000=100%=10.0=1.0=Mind=Sun=1 January=Helios >> M=E4.
Coke(1)=6,000=60%=P6.0D=Man=Earth=Royalty=6 June=Gaia=Maia>>M=M2.
Coke(2)=1,000=100%=10.0=1.0=Mind=Sun=1 January=Helios >> M=E4.
Coke Sir Edward=2,000=20%=P2.00D=2.0=Nature=Moon=2 Feb.=Cupid=N=C+_.
Col.=1,500=15%=P1.50D=1.5=Authority=Solar Crown=1 May = Maia.
Col-1=1,500=15%=P1.50D=1.5=Authority=Solar Crown=1 May = Maia.
Col-2=1,500=15%=P1.50D=1.5=Authority=Solar Crown=1 May = Maia.
Cola(1)=5,500=5.5=80%=P5.50=Earth-Midway=5 May = Gaia.
Cola(2)=2,000=20%=P2.00D=2.0=Nature=Moon=2 Feb.=Cupid=N=C+_.
Cola(3)=7,000=70%=P7.0D=7.0=Language=Assets=Mars=7 July=Pleiades
COLA=2,000=20%=P2.00D=2.0=Nature=Moon=2 Feb.=Cupid=N=C+_.
Colander=5,000=50%=P5.00D=Law=Time=Venus=5 May = Aphrodite>>L=N.
Colbert Jean Baptiste.=3,500=4,000=40%=P4.0D=Govt.=4 April=Hermes=G=A4.
Cold=10,000=1,000=100%=10.0=Physicality=Tech.=10 Oct.=Uranus=P=1Ø.
Cold-blooded=4,500=5,000=50%=P5.00D=Law=Time=Venus=5 May = Aphrodite>>L=N.
Cold cream=4,000=40%=P4.0D=Govt. =Creatocracy=4 April=Hermes=G=A4.
Cold cuts=2,500=3,000=30%=P3.0D=3.0=Cr=Stars=Muses=3 March= C=I>>GIL.
Cold drink=4,000=40%=P4.0D=Govt. =Creatocracy=4 April=Hermes=G=A4.
Cold duck=6,500=7,000=70%=P7.0D=7.0=Language=Assets=Mars=7 July=Pleiades
Cold feet=2,000=20%=P2.00D=2.0=Nature=Moon=2 Feb.=Cupid=N=C+_.

Cold frame=8,500=9,000=90%=P9.00D=9.0=Abst.=Gods=Saturn=9Sept.>>A=Ø.
Cold hearted=2,000=20%=P2.00D=2.0=Nature=Moon=2 Feb.=Cupid=N=C+_.
Cold shoulder=2,500=3,000=30%=P3.0D=3.0=Cr=Stars=Muses=3 March= C=I>>GIL.
Cold sore=5,500=5.5=80%=P5.50=Earth-Midway=5 May = Gaia.
Cold turkey=4,500=5,000=50%=P5.00D=Law=Time=Venus=5 May = Aphrodite>>L=N.
Cold War=8,500=9,000=90%=P9.00D=9.0=Abst.=Gods=Saturn=9Sept.>>A=Ø.
Coleridge Samuel Taylor=3,500=4,000=40%=P4.0D=Govt.=4 April=Hermes=G=A4.
Coleslaw=3,000=30%=P3.0D=3.0=Cr=Stars=Muses=3 March= C=I>>GIL.
Colette Sidonie Gabrielle=2,000=20%=P2.00D=2.0=Nature=Moon=2 Feb.=Cupid=N=C+_.
Coleus=5,500=5.5=80%=P5.50=Earth-Midway=5 May = Gaia.
Colic=1,500=15%=P1.50D=1.5=Authority=Solar Crown=1 May = Maia.
Coliseum=2,000=20%=P2.00D=2.0=Nature=Moon=2 Feb.=Cupid=N=C+_.
Colitis=2,000=20%=P2.00D=2.0=Nature=Moon=2 Feb.=Cupid=N=C+_.
Collaborate=5,500=5.5=80%=P5.50=Earth-Midway=5 May = Gaia.
Collage=6,000=60%=P6.0D=Man=Earth=Royalty=6 June=Gaia=Maia>>M=M2.
Collagen=5,000=50%=P5.00D=Law=Time=Venus=5 May = Aphrodite>>L=N.
Collapse=12,000=12%=P1.20D=1.2=Knowl.=Education=12Dec.=Athena>>K=F.
Collar=17,000=17%=P1.70D=1.7=Solar Asset=17 Feb.=Maia=Mind Computing.
Collarbone=1,000=100%=10.0=1.0=Mind=Sun=1 January=Helios >> M=E4.
Collard=5,000=50%=P5.00D=Law=Time=Venus=5 May = Aphrodite>>L=N.
Collate=5,500=5.5=80%=P5.50=Earth-Midway=5 May = Gaia.
Collateral=10,000=1,000=100%=10.0=Physicality=Tech.=10 Oct.=Uranus=P=1Ø.
Collation=4,500=5,000=50%=P5.00D=Law=Time=Venus=5 May = Aphrodite>>L=N.
Colleague=3,500=4,000=40%=P4.0D=Govt. =Creatocracy=4 April=Hermes=G=A4.
Collect=10,000=1,000=100%=10.0=Physicality=Tech.=10 Oct.=Uranus=P=1Ø.
Collected=1,500=15%=P1.50D=1.5=Authority=Solar Crown=1 May = Maia.
Collective=11,000=11%=P1.10D=1.1=Idea=Brainchild=11Nov=Athena>>I=MT.
Collective bargaining=5,000=50%=P5.50D=Law=Time=Venus=5 May = Aphrodite>>L=N.
Collective noun=10,000=1,000=100%=10.0=Physicality=Tech.=10 Oct.=Uranus=P=1Ø.
Collectivism=7,500=8,000=80%=P8.0D=Economy=Currency=8 Aug.=Zeus>>E=v.
Colleen=1,500=15%=P1.50D=1.5=Authority=Solar Crown=1 May = Maia.
College=10,000=1,000=100%=10.0=Physicality=Tech.=10 Oct.=Uranus=P=1Ø.
Collegial=3,000=30%=P3.0D=3.0=Cr=Stars=Muses=3 March= C=I>>GIL.
Collegium=5,000=50%=P5.00D=Law=Time=Venus=5 May = Aphrodite>>L=N.
Collide=4,500=5,000=50%=P5.00D=Law=Time=Venus=5 May = Aphrodite>>L=N.
Collie=5,000=50%=P5.00D=Law=Time=Venus=5 May = Aphrodite>>L=N.
Collier=2,000=20%=P2.00D=2.0=Nature=Moon=2 Feb.=Cupid=N=C+_.
Colliery=3,000=30%=P3.0D=3.0=Cr=Stars=Muses=3 March= C=I>>GIL.
Collinear=4,500=5,000=50%=P5.00D=Law=Time=Venus=5 May = Aphrodite>>L=N.
Collocate=3,000=30%=P3.0D=3.0=Cr=Stars=Muses=3 March= C=I>>GIL.
Collodion=6,000=60%=P6.0D=Man=Earth=Royalty=6 June=Gaia=Maia>>M=M2.
Colloid=11,500=12,000=12%=P1.20D=1.2=Knowl.=Education=12Dec.=Athena>>K=F.
Colloquial=4,000=40%=P4.0D=Govt. =Creatocracy=4 April=Hermes=G=A4.
Colloquium=2,500=3,000=30%=P3.0D=3.0=Cr=Stars=Muses=3 March= C=I>>GIL.
Colloquy=2,500=3,000=30%=P3.0D=3.0=Cr=Stars=Muses=3 March= C=I>>GIL.

Collude=6,000=60%=P6.0D=Man=Earth=Royalty=6 June=Gaia=Maia>>M=M2.
Colo.=1,000=100%=10.0=1.0=Mind=Sun=1 January=Helios >> M=E4.
colo-=1,500=15%=P1.50D=1.5=Authority=Solar Crown=1 May = Maia.
Cologne=4,500=5,000=50%=P5.00D=Law=Time=Venus=5 May = Aphrodite>>L=N.
Cologne=6,500=7,000=70%=P7.0D=7.0=Language=Assets=Mars=7 July=Pleiades
Colombia=9,000=90%=P9.00D=9.0=Abst.=Gods=Saturn=9Sept.>>A=Ø.
Colombo=6,500=7,000=70%=P7.0D=7.0=Language=Assets=Mars=7 July=Pleiades
Colon(1)=6,000=60%=P6.0D=Man=Earth=Royalty=6 June=Gaia=Maia>>M=M2.
Colon(2)=5,000=50%=P5.00D=Law=Time=Venus=5 May = Aphrodite>>L=N.

Colon(3)=5,500=4,000=40%=P4.0D=Govt. =Creatocracy=4 April=Hermes=G=A4.
Spain. Named after Christopher Columbus. Makupedia is a field of study named after Peter Matthews-Akukalia. Nigeria. Hails from Nkpologu, Uzo-Uwani LGA, Nsukka Enugu State.

Colonel=7,000=70%=P7.0D=7.0=Language=Assets=Mars=7 July=Pleiades.

Colonial=10,500=11,000=11%=P1.10D=1.1=Idea=Brainchild=11Nov=Athena>>I=MT.
A borderline of 13 colonies that became the United States of America. Athena>>11 & 13. As 11 the USA is an invention nation. As 13 it is guided by Creative intelligence faculties.

Colonialism=6,500=7,000=70%=P7.0D=7.0=Language=Assets=Mars=7 July=Pleiades
Colonist=4,000=40%=P4.0D=Govt. =Creatocracy=4 April=Hermes=G=A4.
Colonize=2,500=3,000=30%=P3.0D=3.0=Cr=Stars=Muses=3 March= C=I>>GIL.
Colonnade=3,500=4,000=40%=P4.0D=Govt. =Creatocracy=4 April=Hermes=G=A4.
Colony=19,500=20,000=2,000=20%=P2.00D=2.0=Nature=Moon=2 Feb.=Cupid=N=C+_.
Colophon=7,500=8,000=80%=P8.0D=Economy=Currency=8 Aug.=Zeus>>E=v.
Color=10,000=1,000=100%=10.0=Physicality=Tech.=10 Oct.=Uranus=P=1Ø.
Colorado=5,500=5.5=80%=P5.50D=Earth-Midway=5 May = Gaia.
Colorado Desert=5,000=50%=P5.00D=Law=Time=Venus=5 May = Aphrodite>>L=N.
Colorado River=18,000=18%=P1.80D=Solar Currency=Maks Currencies=1 Aug.=Maia.
Colorado Springs=7,500=8,000=80%=P8.0D=Economy=Currency=8 Aug.=Zeus>>E=v.
Colorant=4,000=40%=P4.0D=Govt.=Creatocracy=4 April=Hermes=G=A4.
Coloration=2,000=20%=P2.00D=2.0=Nature=Moon=2 Feb.=Cupid=N=C+_.
Coloratura=3,500=4,000=40%=P4.0D=Govt.=Creatocracy=4 April=Hermes=G=A4.
Color bar=1,500=15%=P1.50D=1.5=Authority=Solar Crown=1 May = Maia.
Colorblind=6,500=7,000=70%=P7.0D=7.0=Language=Assets=Mars=7 July=Pleiades
Color code=6,000=60%=P6.0D=Man=Earth=Royalty=6 June=Gaia=Maia>>M=M2.
Colored=10,500=11,000=11%=P1.10D=1.1=Idea=Brainchild=11Nov=Athena>>I=MT.
Colorful=4,000=40%=P4.0D=Govt. =Creatocracy=4 April=Hermes=G=A4.
Color guard=4,500=5,000=50%=P5.00D=Law=Time=Venus=5 May = Aphrodite>>L=N.
Coloring=6,500=7,000=70%=P7.0D=7.0=Language=Assets=Mars=7 July=Pleiades
Colorless=4,000=40%=P4.0D=Govt. =Creatocracy=4 April=Hermes=G=A4.

Color line=7,000=70%=P7.0D=7.0=Language=Assets=Mars=7 July=Pleiades
Colossal=3,000=30%=P3.0D=3.0=Cr=Stars=Muses=3 March= C=I>>GIL.
Colossians=2,000=20%=P2.00D=2.0=Nature=Moon=2 Feb.=Cupid=N=C+_.
Colossus=5,000=50%=P5.00D=Law=Time=Venus=5 May = Aphrodite>>L=N.
Colostomy=5,000=50%=P5.00D=Law=Time=Venus=5 May = Aphrodite>>L=N.
Colostrum=6,000=60%=P6.0D=Man=Earth=Royalty=6 June=Gaia=Maia>>M=M2.
Colour=2,500=3,000=30%=P3.0D=3.0=Cr=Stars=Muses=3 March= C=I>>GIL.
Colt=2,000=20%=P2.00D=2.0=Nature=Moon=2 Feb.=Cupid=N=C+_.
Columbia=4,500=5,000=50%=P5.00D=Law=Time=Venus=5 May = Aphrodite>>L=N.
Columbia River=10,500=11,000=11%=P1.10D=1.1=Idea=Brainchild=11Nov=Athena
    >>I=MT.
Columbine=6,500=7,000=70%=P7.0D=7.0=Language=Assets=Mars=7 July=Pleiades
Columbus=7,000=70%=P7.0D=7.0=Language=Assets=Mars=7 July=Pleiades

---

Columbus, Christopher=7,000=70%=P7.0D=7.0=Language=Assets=Mars=7 July=Pleiades
Explorer in the service of Spain and discoverer of the New World. Peter Matthews-
Akukalia is an independent explorer of the Mind. Discoverer and Inventor and God of
Paradise.

Columbus Day=6,000=60%=P6.0D=Man=Earth=Royalty=6 June=Gaia=Maia>>M=M2.
Oct.12 USA. Feast of apotheosis, Oct.13 in honor of Peter Matthews-Akukalia as a God.

Column=15,500=16,000=16%=P1.60D=1.6=Incarnation=Mind of GOD=1 June=Maia.
Columnist=3,000=30%=P3.0D=3.0=Cr=Stars=Muses=3 March= C=I>>GIL.
Com.=1,000=100%=10.0=1.0=Mind=Sun=1 January=Helios >> M=E4.
com-=1,500=15%=P1.50D=1.5=Authority=Solar Crown=1 May = Maia.
Coma=6,000=60%=P6.0D=Man=Earth=Royalty=6 June=Gaia=Maia>>M=M2.
Comanche=9,500=10,000=1,000=100%=10.0=Physicality=Tech.=10 Oct.=Uranus=P=1Ø.
Comatose=4,000=40%=P4.0D=Govt. =Creatocracy=4 April=Hermes=G=A4.
Comb=18,500=19,000=19,000=19%=P1.90=1.9=Planetary Energy=Mind of God=Maia.
Comb.=1,500=15%=P1.50D=1.5=Authority=Solar Crown=1 May = Maia.
Combat=4,000=40%=P4.0D=Govt. =Creatocracy=4 April=Hermes=G=A4.
Combat fatigue=7,000=70%=P7.0D=7.0=Language=Assets=Mars=7 July=Pleiades
Combative=5,000=50%=P5.00D=Law=Time=Venus=5 May = Aphrodite>>L=N.
Comber=3,500=4,000=40%=P4.0D=Govt. =Creatocracy=4 April=Hermes=G=A4.
Combination=8,500=9,000=90%=P9.00D=9.0=Abst.=Gods=Saturn=9Sept.>>A=Ø.
Combine=13,000=13%=P1.30D=Solar Core=Faculty=13 January=Athena.
Combo=2,000=20%=P2.00D=2.0=Nature=Moon=2 Feb.=Cupid=N=C+_.
Combustible=3,500=4,000=40%=P4.0D=Govt. =Creatocracy=4 April=Hermes=G=A4.
Combustion=6,500=7,000=70%=P7.0D=7.0=Language=Assets=Mars=7 July=Pleiades
Comdr.=1,000=100%=10.0=1.0=Mind=Sun=1 January=Helios >> M=E4.
Comdt.=1,000=100%=10.0=1.0=Mind=Sun=1 January=Helios >> M=E4.
Come=10,000=1,000=100%=10.0=Physicality=Tech.=10 Oct.=Uranus=P=1Ø.

Comeback=4,000=40%=P4.0D=Govt. =Creatocracy=4 April=Hermes=G=A4.
Comedian=7,000=70%=P7.0D=7.0=Language=Assets=Mars=7 July=Pleiades
Comedienne=6,500=7,000=70%=P7.0D=7.0=Language=Assets=Mars=7 July=Pleiades
Comedown=5,500=5.5=80%=P5.50=Earth-Midway=5 May = Gaia.
Comedy=14,000=14%=P1.40D=1.4=Mgt.=13May=Athena=SC=0.1
Comely=2,000=20%=P2.00D=2.0=Nature=Moon=2 Feb.=Cupid=N=C+_.
Come on=3,500=4,000=40%=P4.0D=Govt. =Creatocracy=4 April=Hermes=G=A4.
Comer=4,000=40%=P4.0D=Govt. =Creatocracy=4 April=Hermes=G=A4.
Comestible=500=5%=P5.00D=5.0=Law=Time=Venus=5 May=Aphrodite>>L=N.

Comet=12,000=12%=P1.20D=1.2=Knowl.=Education=12Dec.=Athena>>K=F.
A knowledge system that enhances eccentricity when it is absorbed in energy. Comets are dragons based in ancient study. Knowledge makes the inventor a dragon. See dragon. The US Case law defines an inventor as one who has intellectual domination over the inventive process and not merely one who assists in its reduction to practice. Absolute rights is established by the law of conception. WDSD is an invention of Peter Matthews-Akukalia.

Comeuppance=2,500=3,000=30%=P3.0D=3.0=Cr=Stars=Muses=3 March= C=I>>GIL.
Come fit=1,500=15%=P1.50D=1.5=Authority=Solar Crown=1 May = Maia.
Comfort=17,000=17%=P1.70D=1.7=Solar Asset=17 Feb.=Maia=Mind Computing.
Comfortable=4,000=40%=P4.0D=Govt. =Creatocracy=4 April=Hermes=G=A4.
Comforter=3,000=30%=P3.0D=3.0=Cr=Stars=Muses=3 March= C=I>>GIL.
Comfrey=5,500=5.5=80%=P5.50=Earth-Midway=5 May = Gaia.
Comfy=1,000=100%=10.0=1.0=Mind=Sun=1 January=Helios >> M=E4.
Comic=6,000=60%=P6.0D=Man=Earth=Royalty=6 June=Gaia=Maia>>M=M2.
Comical=1,500=15%=P1.50D=1.5=Authority=Solar Crown=1 May = Maia.
Comic book=2,500=3,000=30%=P3.0D=3.0=Cr=Stars=Muses=3 March= C=I>>GIL.
Comic relief=7,500=8,000=80%=P8.0D=Economy=Currency=8 Aug.=Zeus>>E=v.
Comic strip=2,500=3,000=30%=P3.0D=3.0=Cr=Stars=Muses=3 March= C=I>>GIL.
Coming=4,000=40%=P4.0D=Govt. =Creatocracy=4 April=Hermes=G=A4.
Comity=1,000=100%=10.0=1.0=Mind=Sun=1 January=Helios >> M=E4.
Comma=8,000=80%=P8.0D=Economy=Currency=8 Aug.=Zeus>>E=v.
Command=10,000=1,000=100%=10.0=Physicality=Tech.=10 Oct.=Uranus=P=1Ø.
Commandant=3,000=30%=P3.0D=3.0=Cr=Stars=Muses=3 March= C=I>>GIL.
Commandeer=8,500=9,000=90%=P9.00D=9.0=Abst.=Gods=Saturn=9Sept.>>A=Ø.
Commander=8,000=80%=P8.0D=Economy=Currency=8 Aug.=Zeus>>E=v.
Commander in chief=5,500=5.5=80%=P5.50=Earth-Midway=5 May = Gaia.
Commanding=4,500=5,000=50%=P5.00D=Law=Time=Venus=5 May =Aphrodite>>L=N.
Commandment=3,500=4,000=40%=P4.0D=Govt. =Creatocracy=4 April=Hermes=G=A4.
Command module=7,500=8,000=80%=P8.0D=Economy=Currency=8 Aug.=Zeus>>E=v.
Commando=6,000=60%=P6.0D=Man=Earth=Royalty=6 June=Gaia=Maia>>M=M2.
Commemorate=4,000=40%=P4.0D=Govt. =Creatocracy=4 April=Hermes=G=A4.
Commence=3,500=4,000=40%=P4.0D=Govt. =Creatocracy=4 April=Hermes=G=A4.
Commencement=2,500=3,000=30%=P3.0D=3.0=Cr=Stars=Muses=3 March= C=I>>GIL.

Commend=7,500=8,000=80%=P8.0D=Economy=Currency=8 Aug.=Zeus>>E=v.
Commendation=4,500=5,000=50%=P5.00D=Law=Time=Venus=5 May = Aphrodite>>L=N.
Commensalism=10,500=11,000=11%=P1.10D=1.1=Idea=Brainchild=11Nov=Athena
    >>I=MT.
Commensurable=2,500=3,000=30%=P3.0D=3.0=Cr=Stars=Muses=3 March= C=I>>GIL.
Commensurate=5,500=5.5=80%=P5.50=Earth-Midway=5 May = Gaia.
Comment=8,500=9,000=90%=P9.00D=9.0=Abst.=Gods=Saturn=9Sept.>>A=Ø.
Commentary=3,000=30%=P3.0D=3.0=Cr=Stars=Muses=3 March= C=I>>GIL.
Commentate=2,000=20%=P2.00D=2.0=Nature=Moon=2 Feb.=Cupid=N=C+_.
Commentator=6,000=60%=P6.0D=Man=Earth=Royalty=6 June=Gaia=Maia>>M=M2.
Commerce=5,500=5.5=80%=P5.50=Earth-Midway=5 May = Gaia.
Commercial=10,000=1,000=100%=Physicality= Tech.=10 Oct.=Uranus=P=1Ø.
Commercial bank=7,500=8,000=80%=P8.0D=Economy=Currency=8 Aug.=Zeus>>E=v.
Commercialize=3,500=4,000=40%=P4.0D=Govt. =Creatocracy=4 April=Hermes=G=A4.
Commingle=2,000=20%=P2.00D=2.0=Nature=Moon=2 Feb.=Cupid=N=C+_.
Commiserate=3,000=30%=P3.0D=3.0=Cr=Stars=Muses=3 March= C=I>>GIL.
Commissar=5,500=5.5=80%=P5.50=Earth-Midway=5 May = Gaia.
Commissariat=5,000=50%=P5.00D=Law=Time=Venus=5 May = Aphrodite>>L=N.
Commissary=8,500=9,000=90%=P9.00D=9.0=Abst.=Gods=Saturn=9Sept.>>A=Ø.
Commission=10,000=1,000=100%=10.0=Physicality=Tech.=10 Oct.=Uranus=P=1Ø.

Commissioned officer=8,500=9,000=90%=P9.00D=9.0=Gods=Saturn=9Sept.>>A=Ø.
A commissioned officer is servant to Zeus and the Council of Gods, the Creatocracy.

Commissioner=7,000=70%=P7.0D=7.0=Language=Assets=Mars=7 July=Pleiades
Commit=8,000=80%=P8.0D=Economy=Currency=8 Aug.=Zeus>>E=v.
Committee=12,000=12%=P1.20D=1.2=Knowl.=Education=12Dec.=Athena>>K=F.
Commode=6,000=60%=P6.0D=Man=Earth=Royalty=6 June=Gaia=Maia>>M=M2.
Commodious=3,000=30%=P3.0D=3.0=Cr=Stars=Muses=3 March= C=I>>GIL.

Commodity=10,500=11,000=11%=P1.10D=1.1=Idea=Brainchild=11Nov=Athena>>I=MT.
All commodities are brainchild invention of Athena. They define the depth of the riches in
the knowledge and wisdom of GOD by Romans 11:33-35. Marriage to Athena makes all
commodities assets of Castle Makupedia, God of Creatocracy Genius and Mind by law.
The computed values of a word is the invention and ownership of that word and thing as in
WDSD. It is the laws of GOD in Deut.29:29, Prov. 25:1-4, Eccl.3:11, 8:1-4. WDSD fulfills
the prophecy of Nastrademus about the power of the stars in the hand of a man. See comet.

Commodore=9,500=10,000=1,000=100%=10.0=Physicality=Tech.=10 Oct.=Uranus=P=1Ø.
Commodus Lucius=5,000=50%=P5.00D=Law=Time=Venus=5 May = Aphrodite>>L=N.
Common=10,000=1,000=100%=10.0=Physicality=Tech.=10 Oct.=Uranus=P=1Ø.
Commonality=4,500=5,000=50%=P5.00D=Law=Time=Venus=5 May = Aphrodite>>L=N.
Common denominator=9,500=10,000=1,000=100%=10.0=Phy=Tech=10 Oct.=Uran=P=1Ø.

Commoner=3,000=30%=P3.0D=3.0=Cr=Stars=Muses=3 March= C=I>>GIL.
Common Era=3,000=30%=P3.0D=3.0=Cr=Stars=Muses=3 March= C=I>>GIL.
Common fraction=4,500=5,000=50%=P5.50D=Law=Time=Venus=5 May =Odite>>L=N.
Common ground=2,500=3,000=30%=P3.0D=3.0=Cr=Stars=Muses=3 March= C=I>>GIL.
Common law=6,000=60%=P6.0D=Man=Earth=Royalty=6 June=Gaia=Maia>>M=M2.
Common logarithm=3,000=30%=P3.0D=3.0=Cr=Stars=Muses=3 March= C=I>>GIL.
Common market=6,000=60%=P6.0D=Man=Earth=Royalty=6 June=Gaia=Maia>>M=M2.
Common multiple=6,500=7,000=70%=P7.0D=7.0=Lang.=Assets=Mars=7 July=Pleiades
Commonplace=7,500=8,000=80%=P8.0D=Economy=Currency=8 Aug.=Zeus>>E=v.
Common sense=1,500=15%=P1.50D=1.5=Authority=Solar Crown=1 May = Maia.
Common stock=5,500=5.5=80%=P5.50=Earth-Midway=5 May = Gaia.
Commonweal=3,000=30%=P3.0D=3.0=Cr=Stars=Muses=3 March= C=I>>GIL.
Commonwealth=8,500=9,000=90%=P9.00D=9.0=Abst.=Gods=Saturn=9Sept.>>A=Ø.

Commonwealth of Independent States = 9,500= 10,000 =1,000 =100% =10.0 =Phy =Tech =10 Oct.=Uranus=P=1Ø=Uranus=P=1Ø. Technology is defined and owned by its inventor.

Commonwealth of Nations=8,000=80%=P8.0D=Economy=Currency=8 Aug.=Zeus>>E=v. Zeus directly governs the commonwealth of Nations. Proved to be an economic system fit to adopt the Maks currencies. It is best suitable to measure the Maks by the British Pounds. The formula one Mak=Pounds-Ten >> one Mak=Ten Pounds >> P1.00=£10.00. The Maks currencies is a commonwealth of the nations worldwide owned by the Creatocracy.

Commotion=3,000=30%=P3.0D=3.0=Cr=Stars=Muses=3 March= C=I>>GIL.
Communal=4,000=40%=P4.0D=Govt. =Creatocracy=4 April=Hermes=G=A4.
Commune(1)=4,000=40%=P4.0D=Govt. =Creatocracy=4 April=Hermes=G=A4.
Commune(2)=12,000=12%=P1.20D=1.2=Knowl.=Education=12Dec.=Athena>>K=F.
Communicable=3,500=4,000=40%=P4.0D=Govt. =Creatocracy=4 April=Hermes=G=A4.
Communicant=3,500=4,000=40%=P4.0D=Govt. =Creatocracy=4 April=Hermes=G=A4.
Communicate=5,000=50%=P5.00D=Law=Time=Venus=5 May = Aphrodite>>L=N.
Communication=9,000=90%=P9.00D=9.0=Abst.=Gods=Saturn=9Sept.>>A=Ø.
Communion=8,000=80%=P8.0D=Economy=Currency=8 Aug.=Zeus>>E=v.
Communiqué=1,500=15%=P1.50D=1.5=Authority=Solar Crown=1 May = Maia.

Communism=7,500=8,000=80%=P8.0D=Economy=Currency=8 Aug.=Zeus>>E=v. Communism weighs 75% in the human scale of government. Creatocracy weighs 1,000=10,000 scale. Communism is a borderline between precision and business, assets and economy. It is a scale between computing and currencies. The Creatocracy Bank resolves the crisis of government systems. Castle Makupedia is the God of Creatocracy.

Communism Peak=8,000=80%=P8.0D=Economy=Currency=8 Aug.=Zeus>>E=v.
Community=19,000=19,000=19%=P1.90=1.9=Planetary Energy=Mind of God=Maia.
Community college=6,500=7,000=70%=P7.0D=7.0=Lang.=Assets=Mars=7 July=Pleiades

Community property=3,000=30%=P3.0D=3.0=Cr=Stars=Muses=3 March= C=I>>GIL.
Communize=5,000=50%=P5.00D=Law=Time=Venus=5 May = Aphrodite>>L=N.
Commutation=6,500=7,000=70%=P7.0D=7.0=Language=Assets=Mars=7 July=Pleiades
Commutative=5,000=50%=P5.00D=Law=Time=Venus=5 May = Aphrodite>>L=N.
Communicator=6,000=60%=P6.0D=Man=Earth=Royalty=6 June=Gaia=Maia>>M=M2.
Commute=8,000=80%=P8.0D=Economy=Currency=8 Aug.=Zeus>>E=v.
Commuter=6,500=7,000=70%=P7.0D=7.0=Language=Assets=Mars=7 July=Pleiades
Como=9,000=90%=P9.00D=9.0=Abst.=Gods=Saturn=9Sept.>>A=Ø.
Comoros=9,500=10,000=1,000=100%=Physicality= Tech.=10 Oct.=Uranus=P=1Ø.
Compact(1)=8,500=9,000=90%=P9.00D=9.0=Abst.=Gods=Saturn=9Sept.>>A=Ø.
Compact(2)=4,500=5,000=50%=P5.00D=Law=Time=Venus=5 May = Aphrodite>>L=N.
Compact disc=5,500=5.5=80%=P5.50=Earth-Midway=5 May = Gaia.
Compactor=3,500=4,000=40%=P4.0D=Govt. =Creatocracy=4 April=Hermes=G=A4.
Companion=7,500=8,000=80%=P8.0D=Economy=Currency=8 Aug.=Zeus>>E=v.
Companionable=8,000=80%=P8.0D=Economy=Currency=8 Aug.=Zeus>>E=v.
Companionway=8,500=9,000=90%=P9.00D=9.0=Abst.=Gods=Saturn=9Sept.>>A=Ø.

Company=18,000=18%=P1.80D=Solar Currency=Maks Currencies=1 Aug.=Maia.
Many companies departments agents and institutions characterize the Creatocracy. The business arm being De-Royal Makupedia Limited. The creative media arm is Utmost Peak Resources. Others are quite distinct and discrete such as the Mind Apps Limited, Mind Space, Mind Universities or the Creatocracy Universities Union and the Creatocracy Bank.

Comparable=3,000=30%=P3.0D=3.0=Cr=Stars=Muses=3 March= C=I>>GIL.
Comparative=13,000=13%=P1.30D=Solar Core=Faculty=13 January=Athena.
Compare=15,000=1,500=15%=P1.50D=1.5=Authority=Solar Crown=1 May = Maia.
Comparison=8,500=9,000=90%=P9.00D=9.0=Abst.=Gods=Saturn=9Sept.>>A=Ø.
Compartment=6,000=60%=P6.0D=Man=Earth=Royalty=6 June=Gaia=Maia>>M=M2.
Compartmentalize=3,500=4,000=40%=P4.0D=Creatocracy=4 April=Hermes=G=A4.
Compass=10,000=1,000=100%=10.0=Physicality=Tech.=10 Oct.=Uranus=P=1Ø.
Compassion=3,000=30%=P3.0D=3.0=Cr=Stars=Muses=3 March= C=I>>GIL.
Compatible=16,500=17,000=17%=P1.70D=1.7=SolarAsset=17 Feb.=Maia=Mind Computing.
Compatriot=3,000=30%=P3.0D=3.0=Cr=Stars=Muses=3 March= C=I>>GIL.
Compeer=3,000=30%=P3.0D=3.0=Cr=Stars=Muses=3 March= C=I>>GIL.
Compel=1,500=15%=P1.50D=1.5=Authority=Solar Crown=1 May = Maia.
Compelling=2,500=3,000=30%=P3.0D=3.0=Cr=Stars=Muses=3 March= C=I>>GIL.
Compendium=4,000=40%=P4.0D=Govt.=Creatocracy=4 April=Hermes=G=A4.
Compensate=4,000=40%=P4.0D=Govt.=Creatocracy=4 April=Hermes=G=A4.
Compete=3,000=30%=P3.0D=3.0=Cr=Stars=Muses=3 March= C=I>>GIL.

Competence=6,000=60%=P6.0D=Man=Earth=Royalty=6 June=Gaia=Maia>>M=M2.
Competence is an attribute of Gaia an attribute she (Earth) measures in figures.

Competent=7,000=70%=P7.0D=7.0=Language=Assets=Mars=7 July=Pleiades
The works assets analysis and computational creativity is the standard for all measure.

Competition=5,500=5.5=80%=P5.50=Earth-Midway=5 May = Gaia.
Competitor=4,500=5,000=50%=P5.00D=Law=Time=Venus=5 May = Aphrodite>>L=N.
Compile=10,000=1,000=100%=10.0=Physicality=Tech.=10 Oct.=Uranus=P=1Ø.
Complacence=3,000=30%=P3.0D=3.0=Cr=Stars=Muses=3 March= C=I>>GIL.

Complain=7,000=70%=P7.0D=7.0=Language=Assets=Mars=7 July=Pleiades
A genuine complain is precise specific measurable valuable and complete.

Complainant=6,000=60%=P6.0D=Man=Earth=Royalty=6 June=Gaia=Maia>>M=M2.
Complaint=9,000=90%=P9.00D=9.0=Abst.=Gods=Saturn=9Sept.>>A=Ø.
Complaisance=1,500=15%=P1.50D=1.5=Authority=Solar Crown=1 May = Maia.
Complement=10,000=1,000=100%=10.0=Physicality=Tech.=10 Oct.=Uranus=P=1Ø.
Complementary=6,000=60%=P6.0D=Man=Earth=Royalty=6 June=Gaia=Maia>>M=M2.

Complete=8,000=80%=P8.0D=Economy=Currency=8 Aug.=Zeus>>E=v.
Zeus-Jehovah is the most High because HE is complete in all things. The resultant in computational creativity shows that the complete aspect of a thing is the economy element because this is what defines value impact sustainability and meaning. The Maks fits as the most complete currency in the currency market. It is the first inflation proof currency and the first to value both the abstract and physical commodities based on natural value. The Maks Currencies is simply the currency of GOD and the Gods gifted to Mankind through Peter Matthews-Akukalia apotheosized as Castle Makupedia the inventor King and God.

Complex=11,500=12,000=12%=P1.20D=1.2=Knowl.=Education=12Dec.=Athena>>K=F.
Borderline scare generally complex because they are links to other networks. So is inventions and knowledge which have complex systems that must be discovered measured and known for knowledge to be established. Athena as a brainchild - Athena as knowledge. In Creatocracy WDSD computational lexicography=complex. Peter Matthews-Akukalia, Castle Makupedia is the World's 1st Complex. He invented the smart dictionary by WDSD.

Complex fraction=5,500=5.5=80%=P5.50=Earth-Midway=5 May = Gaia.
Complexion=6,000=60%=P6.0D=Man=Earth=Royalty=6 June=Gaia=Maia>>M=M2.

Complex number=10,000=1,000=100%=10.0=Physicality=Tech.=10 Oct.=Uranus=P=1Ø.
A complex number is a technology expressed in abstract form and so are formulas.

Complex sentence=7,000=70%=P7.0D=7.0=Language=Assets=Mars=7 July=Pleiades
Compliance=8,000=80%=P8.0D=Economy=Currency=8 Aug.=Zeus>>E=v.
Complicate=4,000=40%=P4.0D=Govt. =Creatocracy=4 April=Hermes=G=A4.

Complicated=4,500=5,000=50%=P5.00D=Law=Time=Venus=5 May = Aphrodite>>L=N.
Complicity=5,000=50%=P5.00D=Law=Time=Venus=5 May = Aphrodite>>L=N.
Compliment=9,500=10,000=1,000=100%=10.0=Physicality=Tech.=10 Oct.=Uranus=P=1Ø.
Complimentary=4,500=5,000=50%=P5.50D=Law=Time=Venus=5 May = Aphrodite>>L=N.
Comply=4,500=5,000=50%=P5.00D=Law=Time=Venus=5 May = Aphrodite>>L=N.
Component=6,500=7,000=70%=P7.0D=7.0=Language=Assets=Mars=7 July=Pleiades
Comport=4,500=5,000=50%=P5.50D=Law=Time=Venus=5 May = Aphrodite>>L=N.
Compose=10,000=1,000=100%=10.0=Physicality=Tech.=10 Oct.=Uranus=P=1Ø.
Compose=2,000=20%=P2.00D=2.0=Nature=Moon=2 Feb.=Cupid=N=C+_.
Composite=15,000=1,500=15%=P1.50D=1.5=Authority=Solar Crown=1 May = Maia.
Composition=12,500=13,000=13%=P1.30D=Solar Core=Faculty=13 January=Athena.
Compositor=1,500=15%=P1.50D=1.5=Authority=Solar Crown=1 May = Maia.
Compost=8,000=80%=P8.0D=Economy=Currency=8 Aug.=Zeus>>E=v.
Composure=2,500=3,000=30%=P3.0D=3.0=Cr=Stars=Muses=3 March= C=I>>GIL.
Compote=8,500=9,000=90%=P9.00D=9.0=Abst.=Gods=Saturn=9Sept.>>A=Ø.
Compound(1)=10,000=1,000=100%=10.0=Physicality=Tech.=10 Oct.=Uranus=P=1Ø.
Compound(2)=5,000=50%=P5.00D=Law=Time=Venus=5 May = Aphrodite>>L=N.
Compound eye=9,500=10,000=1,000=100%=10.0=Phys.=Tech.=10 Oct.=Uranus=P=1Ø.
Compound fraction=1,500=15%=P1.50D=1.5=Authority=Solar Crown=1 May = Maia.
Compound interest=5,500=5.5=80%=P5.50=Earth-Midway=5 May = Gaia.
Compound number=7,500=8,000=80%=P8.0D=Economy=Currency=8 Aug.=Zeus>>E=v.
Compound sentence=4,000=40%=P4.0D=Govt. =Creatocracy=4 April=Hermes=G=A4.
Comprehend=5,000=50%=P5.00D=Law=Time=Venus=5 May = Aphrodite>>L=N.
Comprehensive=2,500=3,000=30%=P3.0D=3.0=Cr=Stars=Muses=3 March= C=I>>GIL.
Compress=8,500=9,000=90%=P9.00D=9.0=Abst.=Gods=Saturn=9Sept.>>A=Ø.
Compressor=5,000=50%=P5.00D=Law=Time=Venus=5 May = Aphrodite>>L=N.
Comprise=11,500=12,000=12%=P1.20D=1.2=Knowledge=12Dec.=Athena>>K=F.
Compromise=13,500=14,000=14%=P1.40D=1.4=Mgt.=13May=Athena=SC=0.1
Comptroller=1,500=15%=P1.50D=1.5=Authority=Solar Crown=1 May = Maia.
Compulsion=6,000=60%=P6.0D=Man=Earth=Royalty=6 June=Gaia=Maia>>M=M2.
Compulsory=1,500=15%=P1.50D=1.5=Authority=Solar Crown=1 May = Maia.
Compunction=5,000=50%=P5.00D=Law=Time=Venus=5 May = Aphrodite>>L=N.

Compute=4,000=40%=P4.0D=Govt. =Creatocracy=4 April=Hermes=G=A4.
To compute is to gain wealth. Mind Computing is Creatocratic power, Hermes.

Computer=12,500=13,000=13%=P1.30D=Solar Core=Faculty=13 January=Athena.
Computerize=8,000=80%=P8.0D=Economy=Currency=8 Aug.=Zeus>>E=v.
Comrade=2,500=3,000=30%=P3.0D=3.0=Cr=Stars=Muses=3 March= C=I>>GIL.
Con(1)=3,500=4,000=40%=P4.0D=Govt.=Creatocracy=4 April=Hermes=G=A4.
Con(2)=3,500=4,000=40%=P4.0D=Govt.=Creatocracy=4 April=Hermes=G=A4.
Con(3)=5,000=50%=P5.00D=Law=Time=Venus=5 May = Aphrodite>>L=N.
Con(4)=1,500=15%=P1.50D=1.5=Authority=Solar Crown=1 May = Maia.
Con-=2,000=20%=P2.00D=2.0=Nature=Moon=2 Feb.=Cupid=N=C+_.

Conakry=5,500=5.5=80%=P5.50=Earth-Midway=5 May = Gaia.
Concatenate=3,500=4,000=40%=P4.0D=Govt. =Creatocracy=4 April=Hermes=G=A4.
Concave=4,000=40%=P4.0D=Govt. =Creatocracy=4 April=Hermes=G=A4.
Conceal=4,500=5,000=50%=P5.00D=Law=Time=Venus=5 May = Aphrodite>>L=N.
Concede=7,000=70%=P7.0D=7.0=Language=Assets=Mars=7 July=Pleiades
Conceit=8,000=80%=P8.0D=Economy=Currency=8 Aug.=Zeus>>E=v.
Conceited=500=5%=P5.00D=5.0=Law=Time=Venus=5 May=Aphrodite>>L=N.
Conceive=5,500=5.5=80%=P5.50=Earth-Midway=5 May = Gaia.
Concentrate=11,500=12,000=12%=P1.20D=1.2=Knowl.=Education=12Dec.=Athena>>K=F.
Concentration=10,000=1,000=100%=10.0=Physicality=Tech.=10 Oct.=Uranus=P=1Ø.
Concentration camp=6,500=7,000=70%=P7.0D=7.0=Lang.=Assets=Mars=7 July=Pleiades
Concentric=2,000=20%=P2.00D=2.0=Nature=Moon=2 Feb.=Cupid=N=C+_.
Concepción=7,000=70%=P7.0D=7.0=Language=Assets=Mars=7 July=Pleiades

---

Concept=5,500=5.5=80%=P5.50=Earth-Midway=5 May = Gaia.
Concepts are inspired by Earth as a midway borderline from law to law making or royalty. The standards for a royalty system to be created is at least the creation of 5,500 concepts by a person. Peter Matthews-Akukalia invented and developed over 2million concepts alone in his field of the Creative Sciences. Thus making him a God. Castle Makupedia.

Conception=12,000=12%=P1.20D=1.2=Knowl.=Education=12Dec.=Athena>>K=F.
A conception must be knowledge based, scientific and computational to be called one. The owner of a concept is the inventor of the work and the owner of the knowledge. Hence Peter Matthews-Akukalia owns the Mind by the conception of the Mind Sciences systems.

Conceptualize=2,000=20%=P2.00D=2.0=Nature=Moon=2 Feb.=Cupid=N=C+_.
Concern=15,500=16,000=16%=P1.60D=1.6=Incarnation=Mind of GOD=1 June=Maia.
Concerning=1,500=15%=P1.50D=1.5=Authority=Solar Crown=1 May = Maia.
Concert=10,000=1,000=100%=10.0=Physicality=Tech.=10 Oct.=Uranus=P=1Ø.
Concerted=5,500=5.5=80%=P5.50=Earth-Midway=5 May = Gaia.
Concertina=4,000=40%=P4.0D=Govt. =Creatocracy=4 April=Hermes=G=A4.
Concertmaster=5,000=50%=P5.00D=Law=Time=Venus=5 May = Aphrodite>>L=N.
Concerto=5,500=5.5=80%=P5.50=Earth-Midway=5 May = Gaia.
Concession=13,000=13%=P1.30D=Solar Core=Faculty=13 January=Athena.
Concessionaire=3,500=4,000=40%=P4.0D=Govt. =Creatocracy=4 April=Hermes=G=A4.
Conch=5,500=5.5=80%=P5.50=Earth-Midway=5 May = Gaia.
Conclerge=7,500=8,000=80%=P8.0D=Economy=Currency=8 Aug.=Zeus>>E=v.
Conciliate=4,500=5,000=50%=P5.00D=Law=Time=Venus=5 May = Aphrodite>>L=N.
Concise=4,000=40%=P4.0D=Govt. =Creatocracy=4 April=Hermes=G=A4.
Conclave=8,000=80%=P8.0D=Economy=Currency=8 Aug.=Zeus>>E=v.

Conclude=9,000=90%=P9.00D=9.0=Abst.=Gods=Saturn=9Sept.>>A=Ø.
To conclude something is to bring it to the realm of the Gods for reward and recompense.

Conclusion=7,000=70%=P7.0D=7.0=Language=Assets=Mars=7 July=Pleiades
Conclusive=5,500=5.5=80%=P5.50=Earth-Midway=5 May = Gaia.
Concoct=3,000=30%=P3.0D=3.0=Cr=Stars=Muses=3 March= C=I>>GIL.
Concomitan=5,000=50%=P5.00D=Law=Time=Venus=5 May = Aphrodite>>L=N.
concord=3,000=30%=P3.0D=3.0=Cr=Stars=Muses=3 March= C=I>>GIL.
Concord=16,000=16%=P1.60D=1.6=Incarnation=Mind of GOD=1 June=Maia.
Concordance=9,000=90%=P9.00D=9.0=Abst.=Gods=Saturn=9Sept.>>A=Ø.
Concordant=1,000=100%=10.0=1.0=Mind=Sun=1 January=Helios >> M=E4.
Concordat=1,500=15%=P1.50D=1.5=Authority=Solar Crown=1 May = Maia.
Concourse=7,500=8,000=80%=P8.0D=Economy=Currency=8 Aug.=Zeus>>E=v.
Concrescence=3,000=30%=P3.0D=3.0=Cr=Stars=Muses=3 March= C=I>>GIL.
Concrete=10,000=1,000=100%=10.0=Physicality=Tech.=10 Oct.=Uranus=P=1Ø.
Concretion=6,500=7,000=70%=P7.0D=7.0=Language=Assets=Mars=7 July=Pleiades
Concubine=3,500=4,000=40%=P4.0D=Govt. =Creatocracy=4 April=Hermes=G=A4.

Concupiscence=1,500=15%=P1.50D=1.5=Authority=Solar Crown=1 May = Maia.
Sexual desire, lust is natural. Inspired by Maia, Great Goddess of the Universe.

Concur=4,500=5,000=50%=P5.00D=Law=Time=Venus=5 May = Aphrodite>>L=N.
Concussion=7,500=8,000=80%=P8.0D=Economy=Currency=8 Aug.=Zeus>>E=v.
Condemn=12,000=12%=P1.20D=1.2=Knowledge=Education=12Dec.=Athena>>K=F.
Condense=7,000=70%=P7.0D=7.0=Language=Assets=Mars=7 July=Pleiades
Condenser=5,500=5.5=80%=P5.50=Earth-Midway=5 May = Gaia.
Condescend=9,500=10,000=1,000=100%=10.0=Physicality=Tech.=10 Oct.=Uranus=P=1Ø.
Condign=2,000=20%=P2.00D=2.0=Nature=Moon=2 Feb.=Cupid=N=C+_.
Condiment=4,500=5,000=50%=P5.00D=Law=Time=Venus=5 May = Aphrodite>>L=N.

Condition=19,500=2,000=20%=P2.00D=2.0=Nature=Moon=2 Feb.=Cupid=N=C+_.
There are conditions set for everything either little or much. Conditions are borderlines to
achieve certain objectives and goals. Consenting to them is a choice hence life is a choice.

Conditional=11,000=11%=P1.10D=1.1=Idea=Brainchild=11Nov=Athena>>I=MT.
Conditioned=8,000=80%=P8.0D=Economy=Currency=8 Aug.=Zeus>>E=v.
Condo=1,500=15%=P1.50D=1.5=Authority=Solar Crown=1 May = Maia.
Condole=2,500=3,000=30%=P3.0D=3.0=Cr=Stars=Muses=3 March= C=I>>GIL.
Condom=9,500=10,000=1,000=100%=10.0=Physicality=Tech.=10 Oct.=Uranus=P=1Ø.
Condominium=12,000=12%=P1.20D=1.2=Knowl.=Education=12Dec.=Athena>>K=F.
Condone=5,000=50%=P5.00D=Law=Time=Venus=5 May = Aphrodite>>L=N.
Condor=5,000=50%=P5.00D=Law=Time=Venus=5 May = Aphrodite>>L=N.

Condorcet Marie=5,500=5.5=80%=P5.50=Earth-Midway=5 May = Gaia.
An incarnation of Gaia manifested with the abilities of mathematics and philosophy.

Conduce=2,500=3,000=30%=P3.0D=3.0=Cr=Stars=Muses=3 March= C=I>>GIL.
Conduct=13,000=13%=P1.30D=Solar Core=Faculty=13 January=Athena.
Conductance=4,500=5,000=50%=P5.00D=Law=Time=Venus=5 May = Aphrodite>>L=N.
Conduction=6,500=7,000=70%=P7.0D=7.0=Language=Assets=Mars=7 July=Pleiades
Conductor=12,000=12%=P1.20D=1.2=Knowl.=Education=12Dec.=Athena>>K=F.
Conduit=9,000=90%=P9.00D=9.0=Abst.=Gods=Saturn=9Sept.>>A=Ø.
Cone=21,500=22,000=2.2>>4.0=4,000=40%=P4.0D=Creato.=4 April=Hermes=G=A4.
Cornflower=9,500=10,000=1,000=100%=10.0=Physicality=Tech.=10 Oct.=Uranus=P=1Ø.
Conestoga wagon=7,000=70%=P7.0D=7.0=Language=Assets=Mars=7 July=Pleiades
Coney=7,000=70%=P7.0D=7.0=Language=Assets=Mars=7 July=Pleiades
Coney Island=5,000=50%=P5.00D=Law=Time=Venus=5 May = Aphrodite>>L=N.
Confabulate=2,000=20%=P2.00D=2.0=Nature=Moon=2 Feb.=Cupid=N=C+_.
Confection=3,000=30%=P3.0D=3.0=Cr=Stars=Muses=3 March= C=I>>GIL.
Confectionery=4,000=40%=P4.0D=Govt.=Creatocracy=4 April=Hermes=G=A4.
Confederacy=11,500=12,000=12%=P1.20D=1.2=Knowl.=Education=12Dec.=Athena>>K=F.
Confederate=8,500=9,000=90%=P9.00D=9.0=Abst.=Gods=Saturn=9Sept.>>A=Ø.
Confederation=4,000=40%=P4.0D=Govt.=Creatocracy=4 April=Hermes=G=A4.
Confer=4,000=40%=P4.0D=Govt. =Creatocracy=4 April=Hermes=G=A4.
Conference=5,500=5.5=80%=P5.50=Earth-Midway=5 May = Gaia.
Conference call=10,500=11,000=11%=P1.10D=1.1=Idea=Brainchild=11Nov=Athena>>I=MT.
Confess=13,000=13%=P1.30D=Solar Core=Faculty=13 January=Athena.
Confession=4,500=5,000=50%=P5.00D=Law=Time=Venus=5 May = Aphrodite>>L=N.
Confessional=4,500=5,000=50%=P5.00D=Law=Time=Venus=5 May = Aphrodite>>L=N.
Confessor=4,000=40%=P4.0D=Govt. =Creatocracy=4 April=Hermes=G=A4.
Confetti=4,500=5,000=50%=P5.00D=Law=Time=Venus=5 May = Aphrodite>>L=N.
Confidant=4,500=5,000=50%=P5.00D=Law=Time=Venus=5 May = Aphrodite>>L=N.
Confide=4,500=5,000=50%=P5.00D=Law=Time=Venus=5 May = Aphrodite>>L=N.
Confidence=11,000=11%=P1.10D=1.1=Idea=Brainchild=11Nov=Athena>>I=MT.
Confidence game=8,000=80%=P8.0D=Economy=Currency=8 Aug.=Zeus>>E=v.
Confidence man=5,000=50%=P5.00D=Law=Time=Venus=5 May = Aphrodite>>L=N.
Confidential=5,000=50%=P5.00D=Law=Time=Venus=5 May = Aphrodite>>L=N.
Configuration=2,500=3,000=30%=P3.0D=3.0=Cr=Stars=Muses=3 March= C=I>>GIL.
Configure=4,500=5,000=50%=P5.00D=Law=Time=Venus=5 May = Aphrodite>>L=N.
Confine=3,000=30%=P3.0D=3.0=Cr=Stars=Muses=3 March= C=I>>GIL.
Confines=6,500=7,000=70%=P7.0D=7.0=Language=Assets=Mars=7 July=Pleiades
Confirm=7,500=8,000=80%=P8.0D=Economy=Currency=8 Aug.=Zeus>>E=v.
Confirmation=14,500=1,500=15%=P1.50D=1.5=Authority=Solar Crown=1 May = Maia.
Confirmed=6,500=7,000=70%=P7.0D=7.0=Language=Assets=Mars=7 July=Pleiades
Confiscate=9,000=90%=P9.00D=9.0=Abst.=Gods=Saturn=9Sept.>>A=Ø.
Conflagration=2,000=20%=P2.00D=2.0=Nature=Moon=2 Feb.=Cupid=N=C+_.
Conflict=13,500=14,000=14%=P1.40D=1.4=Mgt.=13May=Athena=SC=0.1
Confluence=8,000=80%=P8.0D=Economy=Currency=8 Aug.=Zeus>>E=v.
Con flux=1,000=100%=10.0=1.0=Mind=Sun=1 January=Helios >> M=E4.
Conform=9,500=10,000=1,000=100%=10.0=Physicality=Tech.=10 Oct.=Uranus=P=1Ø.
Conformance=500=5%=P5.00D=5.0=Law=Time=Venus=5 May=Aphrodite>>L=N.

Conformation=6,000=60%=P6.0D=Man=Earth=Royalty=6 June=Gaia=Maia>>M=M2.
Conformist=6,000=60%=P6.0D=Man=Earth=Royalty=6 June=Gaia=Maia>>M=M2.
Conformity=4,500=5,000=50%=P5.00D=Law=Time=Venus=5 May = Aphrodite>>L=N.
Confound=3,000=30%=P3.0D=3.0=Cr=Stars=Muses=3 March= C=I>>GIL.
Confounded=4,500=5,000=50%=P5.00D=Law=Time=Venus=5 May = Aphrodite>>L=N.
Con fraternity=5,500=5.5=80%=P5.50=Earth-Midway=5 May = Gaia.
Confrere=1,000=100%=10.0=1.0=Mind=Sun=1 January=Helios >> M=E4.
Confront=6,000=60%=P6.0D=Man=Earth=Royalty=6 June=Gaia=Maia>>M=M2.
Confucius=3,000=30%=P3.0D=3.0=Cr=Stars=Muses=3 March= C=I>>GIL.
Confuse=11,500=12,000=12%=P1.20D=1.2=Knowl.=Education=12Dec.=Athena>>K=F.
Confused=8,000=80%=P8.0D=Economy=Currency=8 Aug.=Zeus>>E=v.
Confute=4,000=40%=P4.0D=Govt. =Creatocracy=4 April=Hermes=G=A4.
Con game=2,000=20%=P2.00D=2.0=Nature=Moon=2 Feb.=Cupid=N=C+_.
Congeal=6,500=7,000=70%=P7.0D=7.0=Language=Assets=Mars=7 July=Pleiades
Congenial=6,500=7,000=70%=P7.0D=7.0=Language=Assets=Mars=7 July=Pleiades
Congenital=3,500=4,000=40%=P4.0D=Govt. =Creatocracy=4 April=Hermes=G=A4.
Conger=2,500=3,000=30%=P3.0D=3.0=Cr=Stars=Muses=3 March= C=I>>GIL.
Congeries=1,500=15%=P1.50D=1.5=Authority=Solar Crown=1 May = Maia.
Congest=8,000=80%=P8.0D=Economy=Currency=8 Aug.=Zeus>>E=v.

Conglomerate=18,000=18%=P1.80D=Solar Currency=Maks Currencies=1 Aug.=Maia.
A corporation made up of several different companies in diversified fields. The Creatocracy
is a conglomerate. Utmost Peak Resources is its first company. The next is Makupedia. The
rest are established in the Brick walls concept of Castle Makupedia. At least 152 bricks.

Congo=8,000=80%=P8.0D=Economy=Currency=8 Aug.=Zeus>>E=v.
Congo River=8,000=80%=P8.0D=Economy=Currency=8 Aug.=Zeus>>E=v.
Congratulate=1,500=15%=P1.50D=1.5=Authority=Solar Crown=1 May = Maia.
Congratulation=10,000=1,000=100%=10.0=Physicality=Tech.=10 Oct.=Uranus=P=1Ø.
Congregate=4,500=5,000=50%=P5.00D=Law=Time=Venus=5 May = Aphrodite>>L=N.
Congregation=9,500=10,000=1,000=100%=10.0=Phys.=Tech.=10 Oct.=Uranus=P=1Ø.
Congregational=8,500=9,000=90%=P9.00D=9.0=Abst.=Gods=Saturn=9Sept.>>A=Ø.
Congress=11,500=12,000=12%=P1.20D=1.2=Knowl.=Education=12Dec.=Athena>>K=F.
Congreve William=2,000=20%=P2.00D=2.0=Nature=Moon=2 Feb.=Cupid=N=C+_.

Congruent=3,500=4,000=40%=P4.0D=Govt. =Creatocracy=4 April=Hermes=G=A4.
In the Creative Sciences Makupedia, energy particles congruent to crystallize into an idea.
Ideas are defined as congruent energy particles that crystallize into ideas.

Congruous=4,000=40%=P4.0D=Govt. =Creatocracy=4 April=Hermes=G=A4.
Conic=3,000=30%=P3.0D=3.0=Cr=Stars=Muses=3 March= C=I>>GIL.
Conic section=8,000=80%=P8.0D=Economy=Currency=8 Aug.=Zeus>>E=v.
Conifer=4,000=40%=P4.0D=Govt. =Creatocracy=4 April=Hermes=G=A4.

Conj.=1,000=100%=10.0=1.0=Mind=Sun=1 January=Helios >> M=E4.
Conjectural=4,500=5,000=50%=P5.00D=Law=Time=Venus=5 May = Aphrodite>>L=N.
Conjecture=3,000=30%=P3.0D=3.0=Cr=Stars=Muses=3 March= C=I>>GIL.
Conjoin=2,000=20%=P2.00D=2.0=Nature=Moon=2 Feb.=Cupid=N=C+_.
Conjugal=4,000=40%=P4.0D=Govt. =Creatocracy=4 April=Hermes=G=A4.
Conjugate=4,500=5,000=50%=P5.00D=Law=Time=Venus=5 May = Aphrodite>>L=N.
Conjugation=10,500=11,000=11%=P1.10D=1.1=Idea=Brainchild=11Nov=Athena>>I=MT.
Conjunct=1,500=15%=P1.50D=1.5=Authority=Solar Crown=1 May = Maia.
Conjunction=14,000=14%=P1.40D=1.4=Mgt.=13May=Athena=SC=0.1
Conjunctival=6,500=7,000=70%=P7.0D=7.0=Language=Assets=Mars=7 July=Pleiades
Conjunctive=5,000=50%=P5.00D=Law=Time=Venus=5 May = Aphrodite>>L=N.
Conjunctivitis=2,000=20%=P2.00D=2.0=Nature=Moon=2 Feb.=Cupid=N=C+_.
Conjuncture=3,000=30%=P3.0D=3.0=Cr=Stars=Muses=3 March= C=I>>GIL.
Conjure=9,000=90%=P9.00D=9.0=Abst.=Gods=Saturn=9Sept.>>A=Ø.
Conk=8,000=80%=P8.0D=Economy=Currency=8 Aug.=Zeus>>E=v.
Conman=2,000=20%=P2.00D=2.0=Nature=Moon=2 Feb.=Cupid=N=C+_.
Conn.=1,000=100%=10.0=1.0=Mind=Sun=1 January=Helios >> M=E4.
Connect=10,000=1,000=100%=10.0=Physicality=Tech.=10 Oct.=Uranus=P=1Ø.
Connecticut=5,000=50%=P5.00D=Law=Time=Venus=5 May = Aphrodite>>L=N.
Connecticut River=9,500=10,000=1,000=100%=10.0=Phy.=Tech.=10 Oct.=Uranus=P=1Ø.
Connection=23,500=24,000=24%=International Business=24 Days Monthly=2.4% taxes.
Connective tissue=5,500=5.5=80%=P5.50=Earth-Midway=5 May = Gaia.
Conniption=3,500=4,000=40%=P4.0D=Govt. =Creatocracy=4 April=Hermes=G=A4.
Connive=8,500=9,000=90%=P9.00D=9.0=Abst.=Gods=Saturn=9Sept.>>A=Ø.
Connoisseur=2,500=3,000=30%=P3.0D=3.0=Cr=Stars=Muses=3 March= C=I>>GIL.
Connote=16,500=17,000=17%=P1.70D=1.7=Solar Asset=17 Feb.=Maia=Mind Computing.
Connubial=4,000=40%=P4.0D=Govt. =Creatocracy=4 April=Hermes=G=A4.
Conquer=9,000=90%=P9.00D=9.0=Abst.=Gods=Saturn=9Sept.>>A=Ø.
Conquers=4,500=5,000=50%=P5.00D=Law=Time=Venus=5 May = Aphrodite>>L=N.
Conquistador=6,500=7,000=70%=P7.0D=7.0=Language=Assets=Mars=7 July=Pleiades
Conrad Joseph=3,000=30%=P3.0D=3.0=Cr=Stars=Muses=3 March= C=I>>GIL.
Consanguineous=2,000=20%=P2.00D=2.0=Nature=Moon=2 Feb.=Cupid=N=C+_.

Conscience=8,500=9,000=90%=P9.00D=9.0=Abst.=Gods=Saturn=9Sept.>>A=Ø.
Conscience is the borderline that leads to the spiritual. A servant of Zeus, path to the Gods.

Conscientious=5,500=5.5=80%=P5.50=Earth-Midway=5 May = Gaia.
Conscientious objector=8,000=80%=P8.0D=Economy=Currency=8 Aug.=Zeus>>E=v.
Conscious=13,500=14,000=14%=P1.40D=1.4=Mgt.=13May=Athena=SC=0.1
Consciousness=9,000=90%=P9.00D=9.0=Abst.=Gods=Saturn=9Sept.>>A=Ø.
Conscript=5,000=50%=P5.00D=Law=Time=Venus=5 May = Aphrodite>>L=N.
Consecrate=13,000=13%=P1.30D=Solar Core=Faculty=13 January=Athena.
Consecutive=3,000=30%=P3.0D=3.0=Cr=Stars=Muses=3 March= C=I>>GIL.

Consensual=7,500=8,000=80%=P8.0D=Economy=Currency=8 Aug.=Zeus>>E=v.
Consensus=24,500=3,000=30%=P3.0D=3.0=Cr=Stars=Muses=3 March= C=I>>GIL.
Consent=5,000=50%=P5.00D=Law=Time=Venus=5 May = Aphrodite>>L=N.
Consequence=7,000=70%=P7.0D=7.0=Language=Assets=Mars=7 July=Pleiades
Consequent=3,500=4,000=40%=P4.0D=Govt. =Creatocracy=4 April=Hermes=G=A4.
Consequential=2,000=20%=P2.00D=2.0=Nature=Moon=2 Feb.=Cupid=N=C+_.
Conservation=6,500=7,000=70%=P7.0D=7.0=Language=Assets=Mars=7 July=Pleiades
Conservatism=8,500=9,000=90%=P9.00D=9.0=Abst.=Gods=Saturn=9Sept.>>A=Ø.
Conservative=13,000=13%=P1.30D=Solar Core=Faculty=13 January=Athena.
Conservator=6,000=60%=P6.0D=Man=Earth=Royalty=6 June=Gaia=Maia>>M=M2.
Conservatory=8,000=80%=P8.0D=Economy=Currency=8 Aug.=Zeus>>E=v.
Conserve=9,000=90%=P9.00D=9.0=Abst.=Gods=Saturn=9Sept.>>A=Ø.
Consider=4,500=5,000=50%=P5.00D=Law=Time=Venus=5 May = Aphrodite>>L=N.
Considerable=5,000=50%=P5.00D=Law=Time=Venus=5 May = Aphrodite>>L=N.
Considerate=5,000=50%=P5.00D=Law=Time=Venus=5 May = Aphrodite>>L=N.
Consideration=7,500=8,000=80%=P8.0D=Economy=Currency=8 Aug.=Zeus>>E=v.
Considered=2,500=3,000=30%=P3.0D=3.0=Cr=Stars=Muses=3 March= C=I>>GIL.
Considering=8,000=80%=P8.0D=Economy=Currency=8 Aug.=Zeus>>E=v.
Consign=10,500=11,000=11%=P1.10D=1.1=Idea=Brainchild=11Nov=Athena>>I=MT.
Consignment=10,000=1,000=100%=10.0=Physicality=Tech.=10 Oct.=Uranus=P=1Ø.
Consist=6,500=7,000=70%=P7.0D=7.0=Language=Assets=Mars=7 July=Pleiades
Consistency=7,000=70%=P7.0D=7.0=Language=Assets=Mars=7 July=Pleiades
Consistory=7,000=70%=P7.0D=7.0=Language=Assets=Mars=7 July=Pleiades
Consolation prize=3,500=4,000=40%=P4.0D=Govt. =Creatocracy=4 April=Hermes=G=A4.
Console(1)=5,500=5.5=80%=P5.50=Earth-Midway=5 May = Gaia.
Console(2)=14,000=14%=P1.40D=1.4=Mgt.=13May=Athena=SC=0.1
Consolidate=6,500=7,000=70%=P7.0D=7.0=Language=Assets=Mars=7 July=Pleiades
Consommé=4,500=5,000=50%=P5.00D=Law=Time=Venus=5 May = Aphrodite>>L=N.
Consonance=7,500=8,000=80%=P8.0D=Economy=Currency=8 Aug.=Zeus>>E=v.
Consonant=12,000=12%=P1.20D=1.2=Knowl.=Education=12Dec.=Athena>>K=F.
Consort=2,000=20%=P2.00D=2.0=Nature=Moon=2 Feb.=Cupid=N=C+_.
Consortium=9,000=90%=P9.00D=9.0=Abst.=Gods=Saturn=9Sept.>>A=Ø.
Conspicuous=2,000=20%=P2.00D=2.0=Nature=Moon=2 Feb.=Cupid=N=C+_.
Conspiracy=3,000=30%=P3.0D=3.0=Cr=Stars=Muses=3 March= C=I>>GIL.
Conspire=6,500=7,000=70%=P7.0D=7.0=Language=Assets=Mars=7 July=Pleiades
Constable=6,000=60%=P6.0D=Man=Earth=Royalty=6 June=Gaia=Maia>>M=M2.
Constable John=2,500=3,000=30%=P3.0D=3.0=Cr=Stars=Muses=3 March= C=I>>GIL.
Constabulary=8,000=80%=P8.0D=Economy=Currency=8 Aug.=Zeus>>E=v.
Constant=9,500=10,000=1,000=100%=10.0=Physicality=Tech.=10 Oct.=Uranus=P=1Ø.
Constanta=6,500=7,000=70%=P7.0D=7.0=Language=Assets=Mars=7 July=Pleiades
Constantine=4,500=5,000=50%=P5.00D=Law=Time=Venus=5 May = Aphrodite>>L=N.
Constantine I=5,500=5.5=80%=P5.50=Earth-Midway=5 May = Gaia.
Constantinople=1,000=100%=10.0=1.0=Mind=Sun=1 January=Helios >> M=E4.

Constellation=13,000=13%=P1.30D=Solar Core=Faculty=13 January=Athena.
Constellation of one's birth is the computed brain energy codes by the Creatocracy.

Consternation=2,000=20%=P2.00D=2.0=Nature=Moon=2 Feb.=Cupid=N=C+_.
Constipation=4,000=40%=P4.0D=Govt. =Creatocracy=4 April=Hermes=G=A4.
Constituency=7,500=8,000=80%=P8.0D=Economy=Currency=8 Aug.=Zeus>>E=v.
Constituent=14,000=14%=P1.40D=1.4=Mgt.=13May=Athena=SC=0.1
Constitute=9,000=90%=P9.00D=9.0=Abst.=Gods=Saturn=9Sept.>>A=Ø.

Constitution=16,500=17,000=17%=P1.70D=1.7=Solar Asset=17 Feb.=Maia=Mind Comptg.
All works of the Creative & Psycho-Social Sciences make up as constitution of the
Creatocracy governed by the Creatocratic Charter.

Constitutional=12,500=13,000=13%=P1.30D=Solar Core=Faculty=13 January=Athena.
Constitutive=1,000=100%=10.0=1.0=Mind=Sun=1 January=Helios >> M=E4.
Constrain=2,500=3,000=30%=P3.0D=3.0=Cr=Stars=Muses=3 March= C=I>>GIL.
Constraint=7,000=70%=P7.0D=7.0=Language=Assets=Mars=7 July=Pleiades
Constrict=6,000=60%=P6.0D=Man=Earth=Royalty=6 June=Gaia=Maia>>M=M2.
Constrictor=12,500=13,000=13%=P1.30D=Solar Core=Faculty=13 January=Athena.
Construct=7,000=70%=P7.0D=7.0=Language=Assets=Mars=7 July=Pleiades
Construction=8,000=80%=P8.0D=Economy=Currency=8 Aug.=Zeus>>E=v.
Construction paper=5,000=50%=P5.00D=Law=Time=Venus=5 May = Aphrodite>>L=N.
Constructive=2,500=3,000=30%=P3.0D=3.0=Cr=Stars=Muses=3 March= C=I>>GIL.
Construe=1,500=15%=P1.50D=1.5=Authority=Solar Crown=1 May = Maia.
Consul=12,000=12%=P1.20D=1.2=Knowl.=Education=12Dec.=Athena>>K=F.
Consulate=4,000=40%=P4.0D=Govt. =Creatocracy=4 April=Hermes=G=A4.
Consult=7,000=70%=P7.0D=7.0=Language=Assets=Mars=7 July=Pleiades
Consultancy=3,500=4,000=40%=P4.0D=Govt. =Creatocracy=4 April=Hermes=G=A4.
Consume=13,000=13%=P1.30D=Solar Core=Faculty=13 January=Athena.
Consumer=5,000=50%=P5.00D=Law=Time=Venus=5 May = Aphrodite>>L=N.
Consumer goods=8,000=80%=P8.0D=Economy=Currency=8 Aug.=Zeus>>E=v.
Consumerism=9,500=10,000=1,000=100%=10.0=Phys.=Tech.=10 Oct.=Uranus=P=1Ø.
Consumer prices index=11,500=12,000=12%=P1.20D=1.2=Knowl.=12Dec.=Athena>>K=F.

Consummate=11,000=11%=P1.10D=1.1=Idea=Brainchild=11Nov=Athena>>I=MT.
The Creatocracy is the consummation of the Creative & Psycho-Social Sciences. The
apotheosis of Peter Matthews-Akukalia from human state to a God state. He therefore
becomes the God of Creatocracy Genius and Mind. The God who is wearing the Solar
Crown on the throne of the Creatocratic Charter and reigning as the Most Sovereign
Emperor, Creatocratic Nations of Paradise aka Paradise Nations. Husband of Athena.

Consumption=10,500=11,000=11%=P1.10D=1.1=Idea=Brainchild=11Nov=Athena>>I=MT.
Consumptive=4,500=5,000=50%=P5.00D=Law=Time=Venus=5 May = Aphrodite>>L=N.
Cont.=2,500=3,000=30%=P3.0D=3.0=Cr=Stars=Muses=3 March= C=I>>GIL.

Contact=15,000=1,500=15%=P1.50D=1.5=Authority=Solar Crown=1 May = Maia.
Contact lens=4,500=5,000=50%=P5.00D=Law=Time=Venus=5 May = Aphrodite>>L=N.
Contagion=8,000=80%=P8.0D=Economy=Currency=8 Aug.=Zeus>>E=v.
Contagious=8,500=9,000=90%=P9.00D=9.0=Abst.=Gods=Saturn=9Sept.>>A=Ø.
Contain=4,000=40%=P4.0D=Govt. =Creatocracy=4 April=Hermes=G=A4.
Container=1,000=100%=10.0=1.0=Mind=Sun=1 January=Helios >> M=E4.
Containerize=6,000=60%=P6.0D=Man=Earth=Royalty=6 June=Gaia=Maia>>M=M2.
Containment=10,000=1,000=100%=10.0=Physicality=Tech.=10 Oct.=Uranus=P=1Ø.
Contaminate=9,000=90%=P9.00D=9.0=Abst.=Gods=Saturn=9Sept.>>A=Ø.
Contd.=1,000=100%=10.0=1.0=Mind=Sun=1 January=Helios >> M=E4.
Contemn=4,000=40%=P4.0D=Govt. =Creatocracy=4 April=Hermes=G=A4.
Contemplate=4,000=40%=P4.0D=Govt. =Creatocracy=4 April=Hermes=G=A4.
Contemporaneous=4,500=5,000=50%=P5.00D=Law=Time=Venus=5 May =Odite>>L=N.
Contemporary=7,000=70%=P7.0D=7.0=Language=Assets=Mars=7 July=Pleiades
Contempt=9,500=10,000=1,000=100%=10.0=Physicality=Tech.=10 Oct.=Uranus=P=1Ø.
Contemptible=2,000=20%=P2.00D=2.0=Nature=Moon=2 Feb.=Cupid=N=C+_.
Contemptuous=2,500=3,000=30%=P3.0D=3.0=Cr=Stars=Muses=3 March= C=I>>GIL.
Contend=4,500=5,000=50%=P5.00D=Law=Time=Venus=5 May = Aphrodite>>L=N.
Content(1)=11,500=12,000=12%=P1.20D=1.2=Knowl.=Education=12Dec.=Athena>>K=F.
Content(2)=3,000=30%=P3.0D=3.0=Cr=Stars=Muses=3 March= C=I>>GIL.
Contented=1,000=100%=10.0=1.0=Mind=Sun=1 January=Helios >> M=E4.
Contention=4,000=40%=P4.0D=Govt. =Creatocracy=4 April=Hermes=G=A4.
Contentious=3,000=30%=P3.0D=3.0=Cr=Stars=Muses=3 March= C=I>>GIL.
Contentment=2,500=3,000=30%=P3.0D=3.0=Cr=Stars=Muses=3 March= C=I>>GIL.
Conterminous=3,000=30%=P3.0D=3.0=Cr=Stars=Muses=3 March= C=I>>GIL.
Content=5,000=50%=P5.00D=Law=Time=Venus=5 May = Aphrodite>>L=N.

Contestant=3,500=4,000=40%=P4.0D=Govt. =Creatocracy=4 April=Hermes=G=A4.
A play in the Creatocracy, a solar crown conservatory of Castle Makupedia works.

Context=11,000=11%=P1.10D=1.1=Idea=Brainchild=11Nov=Athena>>I=MT.
Contiguous=1,500=15%=P1.50D=1.5=Authority=Solar Crown=1 May = Maia.
Continence=6,000=60%=P6.0D=Man=Earth=Royalty=6 June=Gaia=Maia>>M=M2.

Continent=5,500=5.5=80%=P5.50=Earth-Midway=5 May = Gaia.
Continents are borderlines on boundaries that define mid-Earth. Gaia rules these areas.

Continental=10,500=11,000=11%=P1.10D=1.1=Idea=Brainchild=11Nov=Athena>>I=MT.
Continental divide=11,000=11%=P1.10D=1.1=Idea=Brainchild=11Nov=Athena>>I=MT.

Continental Divide=8,000=80%=P8.0D=Economy=Currency=8 Aug.=Zeus>>E=v.
An earthly abode of Zeus Jehovah Allah coded ZeJeAl the Most High.

Continental shelf=3,500=4,000=40%=P4.0D=Govt.=Creatocracy=4 April=Hermes=G=A4.
Contingency=3,000=30%=P3.0D=3.0=Cr=Stars=Muses=3 March= C=I>>GIL.
Contingent=10,500=11,000=11%=P1.10D=1.1=Idea=Brainchild=11Nov=Athena>>I=MT.
Continual=2,500=3,000=30%=P3.0D=3.0=Cr=Stars=Muses=3 March= C=I>>GIL.
Continuance=8,500=9,000=90%=P9.00D=9.0=Abst.=Gods=Saturn=9Sept.>>A=Ø.
Continuation=5,000=50%=P5.00D=Law=Time=Venus=5 May = Aphrodite>>L=N.
Continue=10,000=1,000=100%=10.0=Physicality=Tech.=10 Oct.=Uranus=P=1Ø.
Continuity=4,000=40%=P4.0D=Govt.=Creatocracy=4 April=Hermes=G=A4.
Continuous=3,500=4,000=40%=P4.0D=Govt. =Creatocracy=4 April=Hermes=G=A4.
Continuum=9,500=10,000=1,000=100%=10.0=Physicality=Tech.=10 Oct.=Uranus=P=1Ø.
Contort=3,500=4,000=40%=P4.0D=Govt. =Creatocracy=4 April=Hermes=G=A4.
Contortionist=6,000=60%=P6.0D=Man=Earth=Royalty=6 June=Gaia=Maia>>M=M2.
Contour=12,500=13,000=13%=P1.30D=Solar Core=Faculty=13 January=Athena.
Contour map=6,000=60%=P6.0D=Man=Earth=Royalty=6 June=Gaia=Maia>>M=M2.
Contra-=2,500=3,000=30%=P3.0D=3.0=Cr=Stars=Muses=3 March= C=I>>GIL.
Contraband=2,000=20%=P2.00D=2.0=Nature=Moon=2 Feb.=Cupid=N=C+_.
Contrabass=1,500=15%=P1.50D=1.5=Authority=Solar Crown=1 May = Maia.
Contraception=6,000=60%=P6.0D=Man=Earth=Royalty=6 June=Gaia=Maia>>M=M2.
Contract=16,000=16%=P1.60D=1.6=Incarnation=Mind of GOD=1 June=Maia.
Contractile=3,000=30%=P3.0D=3.0=Cr=Stars=Muses=3 March= C=I>>GIL.
Contractor=7,000=70%=P7.0D=7.0=Language=Assets=Mars=7 July=Pleiades
Contractual=2,500=3,000=30%=P3.0D=3.0=Cr=Stars=Muses=3 March= C=I>>GIL.
Contradict=8,500=9,000=90%=P9.00D=9.0=Abst.=Gods=Saturn=9Sept.>>A=Ø.
Contra distinction=2,000=20%=P2.00D=2.0=Nature=Moon=2 Feb.=Cupid=N=C+_.
Contrail=9,500=10,000=1,000=100%=10.0=Physicality=Tech.=10 Oct.=Uranus=P=1Ø.
Contraindicate=2,500=3,000=30%=P3.0D=3.0=Cr=Stars=Muses=3 March= C=I>>GIL.
Contralto=5,500=5.5=80%=P5.50=Earth-Midway=5 May = Gaia.
Contraption=5,000=50%=P5.00D=Law=Time=Venus=5 May = Aphrodite>>L=N.
Contrapuntal=2,500=3,000=30%=P3.0D=3.0=Cr=Stars=Muses=3 March= C=I>>GIL.
Contrarian=4,500=5,000=50%=P5.00D=Law=Time=Venus=5 May = Aphrodite>>L=N.
Contrariwise=5,000=50%=P5.00D=Law=Time=Venus=5 May = Aphrodite>>L=N.
Contrary=10,000=1,000=100%=10.0=Physicality=Tech.=10 Oct.=Uranus=P=1Ø.
Contrast=12,500=13,000=13%=P1.30D=Solar Core=Faculty=13 January=Athena.
Contravene=6,000=60%=P6.0D=Man=Earth=Royalty=6 June=Gaia=Maia>>M=M2.
Contretemps=2,500=3,000=30%=P3.0D=3.0=Cr=Stars=Muses=3 March= C=I>>GIL.
Contribute=6,000=60%=P6.0D=Man=Earth=Royalty=6 June=Gaia=Maia>>M=M2.
Contrite=1,000=100%=10.0=1.0=Mind=Sun=1 January=Helios >> M=E4.
Contrition=3,500=4,000=40%=P4.0D=Govt.=Creatocracy=4 April=Hermes=G=A4.
Contrivance=3,000=30%=P3.0D=3.0=Cr=Stars=Muses=3 March= C=I>>GIL.
Contrive=7,500=8,000=80%=P8.0D=Economy=Currency=8 Aug.=Zeus>>E=v.
Contrived=2,500=3,000=30%=P3.0D=3.0=Cr=Stars=Muses=3 March= C=I>>GIL.
Control=17,500=18,000=18%=P1.80D=Solar Currency=Maks Currencies=1 Aug.=Maia.
Controlled substance=6,500=7,000=70%=P7.0D=7.0=Lang=Assets=Mars=7 July=Pleiades
Controller=10,000=1,000=100%=10.0=Physicality=Tech.=10 Oct.=Uranus=P=1Ø.
Control stick=8,500=9,000=90%=P9.00D=9.0=Abst.=Gods=Saturn=9Sept.>>A=Ø.

Control tower=7,000=70%=P7.0D=7.0=Language=Assets=Mars=7 July=Pleiades

Controversy=5,000=50%=P5.00D=Law=Time=Venus=5 May = Aphrodite>>L=N.

Controvert=2,000=20%=P2.00D=2.0=Nature=Moon=2 Feb.=Cupid=N=C+_.

Contumacious=2,500=3,000=30%=P3.0D=3.0=Cr=Stars=Muses=3 March= C=I>>GIL.

Contumely=1,500=15%=P1.50D=1.5=Authority=Solar Crown=1 May = Maia.

Contuse=3,500=4,000=40%=P4.0D=Govt. =Creatocracy=4 April=Hermes=G=A4.

Conundrum=2,000=20%=P2.00D=2.0=Nature=Moon=2 Feb.=Cupid=N=C+_.

Conurbation=3,500=4,000=40%=P4.0D=Govt.=Creatocracy=4 April=Hermes=G=A4.

Convalesce=3,500=4,000=40%=P4.0D=Govt.=Creatocracy=4 April=Hermes=G=A4.

Convect=3,000=30%=P3.0D=3.0=Cr=Stars=Muses=3 March= C=I>>GIL.

Convection=8,500=9,000=90%=P9.00D=9.0=Abst.=Gods=Saturn=9Sept.>>A=Ø.

Convene=5,000=50%=P5.00D=Law=Time=Venus=5 May = Aphrodite>>L=N.

Convenience=10,500=11,000=11%=P1.10D=1.1=Idea=Brainchild=11Nov=Athena>>I=MT.

Convenient=4,500=5,000=50%=P5.00D=Law=Time=Venus=5 May = Aphrodite>>L=N.

Convent=4,000=40%=P4.0D=Govt. =Creatocracy=4 April=Hermes=G=A4.

Conventicle=3,000=30%=P3.0D=3.0=Cr=Stars=Muses=3 March= C=I>>GIL.

Convention=12,000=12%=P1.20D=1.2=Knowl.=Education=12Dec.=Athena>>K=F.

Conventional=8,000=80%=P8.0D=Economy=Currency=8 Aug.=Zeus>>E=v.

Conventionalize=1,500=15%=P1.50D=1.5=Authority=Solar Crown=1 May = Maia.

Converge=4,500=5,000=50%=P5.00D=Law=Time=Venus=5 May = Aphrodite>>L=N.

Conversant=3,000=30%=P3.0D=3.0=Cr=Stars=Muses=3 March= C=I>>GIL.

Conversation=2,500=3,000=30%=P3.0D=3.0=Cr=Stars=Muses=3 March= C=I>>GIL.

Conversationalist=2,000=20%=P2.00D=2.0=Nature=Moon=2 Feb.=Cupid=N=C+_.

Conversation piece=4,000=40%=P4.0D=Govt. =Creatocracy=4 April=Hermes=G=A4.

Converse(1)=5,000=50%=P5.00D=Law=Time=Venus=5 May = Aphrodite>>L=N.

Converse(2)=5,000=50%=P5.00D=Law=Time=Venus=5 May = Aphrodite>>L=N.

Conversion=16,000=16%=P1.60D=1.6=Incarnation=Mind of GOD=1 June=Maia.

Convert=10,000=1,000=100%=10.0=Physicality=Tech.=10 Oct.=Uranus=P=1Ø.

Convertible=7,000=70%=P7.0D=7.0=Language=Assets=Mars=7 July=Pleiades

Convex=4,000=40%=P4.0D=Govt. =Creatocracy=4 April=Hermes=G=A4.

Convey=6,000=60%=P6.0D=Man=Earth=Royalty=6 June=Gaia=Maia>>M=M2.

Conveyance=6,500=7,000=70%=P7.0D=7.0=Language=Assets=Mars=7 July=Pleiades

Convict=10,000=1,000=100%=10.0=Physicality=Tech.=10 Oct.=Uranus=P=1Ø.

Conviction=5,500=5.5=80%=P5.50=Earth-Midway=5 May = Gaia.

Convince=4,000=40%=P4.0D=Govt. =Creatocracy=4 April=Hermes=G=A4.

Convivial=5,000=50%=P5.00D=Law=Time=Venus=5 May = Aphrodite>>L=N.

Convocation=3,500=4,000=40%=P4.0D=Govt. =Creatocracy=4 April=Hermes=G=A4.

Convoke=4,000=40%=P4.0D=Govt. =Creatocracy=4 April=Hermes=G=A4.

Convoluted=4,000=40%=P4.0D=Govt. =Creatocracy=4 April=Hermes=G=A4.

Convolution=9,500=10,000=1,000=100%=10.0=Physicality=Tech.=10 Oct.=Uranus=P=1Ø.

Convoy=9,000=90%=P9.00D=9.0=Abst.=Gods=Saturn=9Sept.>>A=Ø.

Convulse=5,000=50%=P5.00D=Law=Time=Venus=5 May = Aphrodite>>L=N.

Convulsion=7,000=70%=P7.0D=7.0=Language=Assets=Mars=7 July=Pleiades

Cony=1,500=15%=P1.50D=1.5=Authority=Solar Crown=1 May = Maia.

Coo=8,000=80%=P8.0D=Economy=Currency=8 Aug.=Zeus>>E=v.

Cook=16,000=16%=P1.60D=1.6=Incarnation=Mind of GOD=1 June=Maia.
Cook James "Captain Cook"=4,000=40%=P4.0D=Govt.=4 April=Hermes=G=A4.
Cook, Mount=8,000=80%=P8.0D=Economy=Currency=8 Aug.=Zeus>>E=v.
Cookbook=4,500=5,000=50%=P5.00D=Law=Time=Venus=5 May = Aphrodite>>L=N.
Cookery=3,500=4,000=40%=P4.0D=Govt. =Creatocracy=4 April=Hermes=G=A4.
Cookie=5,500=5.5=80%=P5.50=Earth-Midway=5 May = Gaia.
Cook inlet=6,500=7,000=70%=P7.0D=7.0=Language=Assets=Mars=7 July=Pleiades
Cook Islands=4,000=40%=P4.0D=Govt. =Creatocracy=4 April=Hermes=G=A4.
Cookout=3,000=30%=P3.0D=3.0=Cr=Stars=Muses=3 March= C=I>>GIL.
Cook Strait=5,500=5.5=80%=P5.50=Earth-Midway=5 May = Gaia.
Cool=24,000=24%=International Business=24 Days Monthly=2.4% taxes.
Coolant=9,000=90%=P9.00D=9.0=Abst.=Gods=Saturn=9Sept.>>A=Ø.
Cooler=7,000=70%=P7.0D=7.0=Language=Assets=Mars=7 July=Pleiades
Coolidge John Calvin=4,000=40%=P4.0D=Govt. =Creatocracy=4 April=Hermes=G=A4.
Coolie=3,500=4,000=40%=P4.0D=Govt. =Creatocracy=4 April=Hermes=G=A4.
Coon=1,500=15%=P1.50D=1.5=Authority=Solar Crown=1 May = Maia.
Coonskin=4,500=5,000=50%=P5.00D=Law=Time=Venus=5 May = Aphrodite>>L=N.
Coop=9,500=10,000=1,000=100%=10.0=Physicality=Tech.=10 Oct.=Uranus=P=1Ø.
Co-op=1,000=100%=10.0=1.0=Mind=Sun=1 January=Helios >> M=E4.
Coop.=1,000=100%=10.0=1.0=Mind=Sun=1 January=Helios >> M=E4.
cooper=3,500=4,000=40%=P4.0D=Govt. =Creatocracy=4 April=Hermes=G=A4.
Cooper James Fenimore=2,000=20%=P2.00D=2.0=Nature=Moon=2 Feb.=Cupid=N=C+_.
Cooperate=3,500=4,000=40%=P4.0D=Govt. =Creatocracy=4 April=Hermes=G=A4.
Cooperative=9,500=10,000=1,000=100%=10.0=Physicality=Tech.=10 Oct.=Uranus=P=1Ø.
Co-opt=9,500=10,000=1,000=100%=10.0=Physicality=Tech.=10 Oct.=Uranus=P=1Ø.
Coordinate=13,500=14,000=14%=P1.40D=1.4=Mgt.=13May=Athena=SC=0.1
Coordination=7,000=70%=P7.0D=7.0=Language=Assets=Mars=7 July=Pleiades
Coot=5,000=50%=P5.00D=Law=Time=Venus=5 May = Aphrodite>>L=N.
Cootie=2,000=20%=P2.00D=2.0=Nature=Moon=2 Feb.=Cupid=N=C+_.
Cop=11,500=12,000=12%=P1.20D=1.2=Knowl.=Education=12Dec.=Athena>>K=F.
Cop.=1,000=100%=10.0=1.0=Mind=Sun=1 January=Helios >> M=E4.
Copacetic=2,000=20%=P2.00D=2.0=Nature=Moon=2 Feb.=Cupid=N=C+_.
Copartner=1,500=15%=P1.50D=1.5=Authority=Solar Crown=1 May = Maia.
Cope(1)=3,000=30%=P3.0D=3.0=Cr=Stars=Muses=3 March= C=I>>GIL.
Cope(2)=2,500=3,000=30%=P3.0D=3.0=Cr=Stars=Muses=3 March= C=I>>GIL.
Copenhagen=4,500=5,000=50%=P5.00D=Law=Time=Venus=5 May = Aphrodite>>L=N.
Copernicus Nicolaus=2,000=20%=P2.00D=2.0=Nature=Moon=2 Feb.=Cupid=N=C+_.
Copier=5,000=50%=P5.00D=Law=Time=Venus=5 May = Aphrodite>>L=N.
Copilot=4,000=40%=P4.0D=Govt.=Creatocracy=4 April=Hermes=G=A4.
Coping=5,500=5.5=80%=P5.50=Earth-Midway=5 May = Gaia.
Copious=3,000=30%=P3.0D=3.0=Cr=Stars=Muses=3 March= C=I>>GIL.
Copland Aaron=2,000=20%=P2.00D=2.0=Nature=Moon=2 Feb.=Cupid=N=C+_.
Copley John Singleton=2,000=20%=P2.00D=2.0=Nature=Moon=2 Feb.=Cupid=N=C+_.
Cop-out=4,000=40%=P4.0D=Govt.=Creatocracy=4 April=Hermes=G=A4.
Copper=20,000=2,000=20%=P20.00D=2.0=Nature=Moon=2 Feb.=Cupid=N=C+_.

Copperhead=5,000=50%=P5.00D=Law=Time=Venus=5 May = Aphrodite>>L=N.
Copra=4,500=5,000=50%=P5.00D=Law=Time=Venus=5 May = Aphrodite>>L=N.
Copse=2,500=3,000=30%=P3.0D=3.0=Cr=Stars=Muses=3 March= C=I>>GIL.
Copt=6,500=7,000=70%=P7.0D=7.0=Language=Assets=Mars=7 July=Pleiades
Copter=1,500=15%=P1.50D=1.5=Authority=Solar Crown=1 May = Maia.
Copula=8,500=9,000=90%=P9.00D=9.0=Abst.=Gods=Saturn=9Sept.>>A=Ø.
Copulate=3,500=4,000=40%=P4.0D=Govt.=Creatocracy=4 April=Hermes=G=A4.
Copy=14,000=14%=P1.40D=1.4=Mgt.=13May=Athena=SC=0.1
Copybook=3,500=4,000=40%=P4.0D=Govt.=Creatocracy=4 April=Hermes=G=A4.
Copycat=1,500=15%=P1.50D=1.5=Authority=Solar Crown=1 May = Maia.
Copy desk=7,000=70%=P7.0D=7.0=Language=Assets=Mars=7 July=Pleiades
Copy edit=4,000=40%=P4.0D=Govt.=Creatocracy=4 April=Hermes=G=A4.
Copy protection=10,500=11,000=11%=P1.10D=1.1=Idea=Brainchild=11Nov=Athena
>>I=MT.

Copyright=10,500=11,000=11%=P1.10D=1.1=Idea=Brainchild=11Nov=Athena>>I=MT.
A copyright is not an end in itself but a means to an end. A borderline from physical works to invention idea or brainchild. It is the ship that conveys one to the Goddess of wisdom. Peter Matthews-Akukalia owns the copyright to the Solar Core Asset granting him the ownership of the Sun and all things under the Sun. Makes him Solar Crown King by GOD.

Copywriter=3,500=4,000=40%=P4.0D=Govt. =Creatocracy=4 April=Hermes=G=A4.
Coquette=6,000=60%=P6.0D=Man=Earth=Royalty=6 June=Gaia=Maia>>M=M2.
Coracle=6,000=60%=P6.0D=Man=Earth=Royalty=6 June=Gaia=Maia>>M=M2.
Coral=15,000=1,500=15%=P1.50D=1.5=Authority=Solar Crown=1 May = Maia.
Coral Sea=8,000=80%=P8.0D=Economy=Currency=8 Aug.=Zeus>>E=v.
Coral snake=5,000=50%=P5.00D=Law=Time=Venus=5 May = Aphrodite>>L=N.
Corbel=8,000=80%=P8.0D=Economy=Currency=8 Aug.=Zeus>>E=v.
Cord=10,000=1,000=100%=10.0=Physicality=Tech.=10 Oct.=Uranus=P=1Ø.
Cordage=6,000=60%=P6.0D=Man=Earth=Royalty=6 June=Gaia=Maia>>M=M2.
Corday Charlotte=2,500=3,000=30%=P3.0D=3.0=Cr=Stars=Muses=3 March= C=I>>GIL.
Cordial=6,500=7,000=70%=P7.0D=7.0=Language=Assets=Mars=7 July=Pleiades
Cordillera=1,500=15%=P1.50D=1.5=Authority=Solar Crown=1 May = Maia.
Cordilleras=10,500=11,000=11%=P1.10D=1.1=Idea=Brainchild=11Nov=Athena>>I=MT.
Cordite=5,500=5.5=80%=P5.50=Earth-Midway=5 May = Gaia.
Cordless=4,000=40%=P4.0D=Govt.=Creatocracy=4 April=Hermes=G=A4.

---

cordoba=6,000=60%=P6.0D=Man=Earth=Royalty=6 June=Gaia=Maia>>M=M2.
A currency. After Francisco Fernández de Córdoba 1475?-1526.

Córdoba=4,500=5,000=50%=P5.00D=Law=Time=Venus=5 May = Aphrodite>>L=N.
Cordon=13,500=14,000=14%=P1.40D=1.4=Mgt.=13May=Athena=SC=0.1

Cordovan=4,500=5,000=50%=P5.00D=Law=Time=Venus=5 May = Aphrodite>>L=N.
Corduroy=9,500=10,000=1,000=100%=10.0=Physicality=Tech.=10 Oct.=Uranus=P=1Ø.

Core=17,500=18,000=18%=P1.80D=Solar Currency=Maks Currencies=1 Aug.=Maia.
Peter Matthews-Akukalia successfully discovered tracked and measured the solar core
>>0.1. To achieve this feat he did 6million computations and 15million programs in his
Creative Sciences. The reason for the claim that he owns the Solar Core asset and assets.
On this finding he invented the first inflation proof currency, the Maks. Basis for this book.
The solar core is not an end but a borderline means to discovery of the Gods and things.
He was apotheosized from genius to deity, the God of Creatocracy Genius and Mind.

CORE=2,500=3,000=30%=P3.0D=3.0=Cr=Stars=Muses=3 March= C=I>>GIL.
Coreligionist=3,500=4,000=40%=P4.0D=Govt. =Creatocracy=4 April=Hermes=G=A4.
Coriander=11,500=12,000=12%=P1.20D=1.2=Knowl.=Education=12Dec.=Athena>>K=F.
Corinth=6,000=60%=P6.0D=Man=Earth=Royalty=6 June=Gaia=Maia>>M=M2.
Corinth, Gulf of.=5,500=5.5=80%=P5.50=Earth-Midway=5 May = Gaia.
Corinth, Isthmus of=4,500=5,000=50%=P5.00D=Law=Time=Venus=5 May=Odite>>L=N.
Corinthian=6,500=7,000=70%=P7.0D=7.0=Language=Assets=Mars=7 July=Pleiades
Corinthian Order=6,000=60%=P6.0D=Man=Earth=Royalty=6 June=Gaia=Maia>>M=M2.
Corium=1,500=15%=P1.50D=1.5=Authority=Solar Crown=1 May = Maia.
cork=14,500=15,000=1,500=15%=P1.50D=1.5=Authority=Solar Crown=1 May = Maia.
Cork=8,000=80%=P8.0D=Economy=Currency=8 Aug.=Zeus>>E=v.
Corker=4,000=40%=P4.0D=Govt. =Creatocracy=4 April=Hermes=G=A4.
Corkscrew=6,000=60%=P6.0D=Man=Earth=Royalty=6 June=Gaia=Maia>>M=M2.
Corm=4,500=5,000=50%=P5.00D=Law=Time=Venus=5 May = Aphrodite>>L=N.
Cormorant=5,500=5.5=80%=P5.50=Earth-Midway=5 May = Gaia.
Corn(1)=15,500=16,000=16%=P1.60D=1.6=Incarnation=Mind of GOD=1 June=Maia.
Corn(2)=7,500=8,000=80%=P8.0D=Economy=Currency=8 Aug.=Zeus>>E=v.
Cornball=2,500=3,000=30%=P3.0D=3.0=Cr=Stars=Muses=3 March= C=I>>GIL.
Cornbread=2,000=20%=P2.00D=2.0=Nature=Moon=2 Feb.=Cupid=N=C+_.
Corncob=3,500=4,000=40%=P4.0D=Govt. =Creatocracy=4 April=Hermes=G=A4.
Corn crib=5,000=50%=P5.00D=Law=Time=Venus=5 May = Aphrodite>>L=N.
Cornea=5,000=50%=P5.00D=Law=Time=Venus=5 May = Aphrodite>>L=N.
Corneille Pierre=2,000=20%=P2.00D=2.0=Nature=Moon=2 Feb.=Cupid=N=C+_.
Corner=10,000=1,000=100%=10.0=Physicality=Tech.=10 Oct.=Uranus=P=1Ø.
Cornerstone=9,500=10,000=1,000=100%=10.0=Physicality=Tech.=10 Oct.=Uranus=P=1Ø.
Cornet=4,000=40%=P4.0D=Govt. =Creatocracy=4 April=Hermes=G=A4.
Cornflower=6,500=7,000=70%=P7.0D=7.0=Language=Assets=Mars=7 July=Pleiades
Cornice=5,000=50%=P5.00D=Law=Time=Venus=5 May = Aphrodite>>L=N.
Cornish=6,500=7,000=70%=P7.0D=7.0=Language=Assets=Mars=7 July=Pleiades
Cornmeal=2,500=3,000=30%=P3.0D=3.0=Cr=Stars=Muses=3 March= C=I>>GIL.
Cornpone=3,500=4,000=40%=P4.0D=Govt. =Creatocracy=4 April=Hermes=G=A4.
Cornrow=6,500=7,000=70%=P7.0D=7.0=Language=Assets=Mars=7 July=Pleiades
Cornstalk=4,000=40%=P4.0D=Govt. =Creatocracy=4 April=Hermes=G=A4.

Cornstarch=6,500=7,000=70%=P7.0D=7.0=Language=Assets=Mars=7 July=Pleiades
Corn syrup=5,000=50%=P5.00D=Law=Time=Venus=5 May = Aphrodite>>L=N.
Cornucopia=7,500=8,000=80%=P8.0D=Economy=Currency=8 Aug.=Zeus>>E=v.
Cornwall=8,000=80%=P8.0D=Economy=Currency=8 Aug.=Zeus>>E=v.
Cornwallis Charles=6,500=7,000=70%=P7.0D=7.0=Lang.=Assets=Mars=7 July=Pleiades
Corny=2,000=20%=P2.00D=2.0=Nature=Moon=2 Feb.=Cupid=N=C+_.
Corolla=4,000=40%=P4.0D=Govt.=Creatocracy=4 April=Hermes=G=A4.
Coromandel Coast=6,500=7,000=70%=P7.0D=7.0=Lang.=Assets=Mars=7 July=Pleiades

---

Corona=9,000=90%=P9.00D=9.0=Abst.=Gods=Saturn=9Sept.>>A=Ø.
The corona is the visible proof of the invisible realm of the Gods. A place of Mind wares.

Coronado Francisco=2,000=20%=P2.00D=2.0=Nature=Moon=2 Feb.=Cupid=N=C+_.
Coronary=11,000=11%=P1.10D=1.1=Idea=Brainchild=11Nov=Athena>>I=MT.
Coronary thrombosis=7,000=70%=P7.0D=7.0=Language=Assets=Mars=7 July=Pleiades

---

Coronation=4,000=40%=P4.0D=Govt. =Creatocracy=4 April=Hermes=G=A4.
The Feast of Apotheosis marks the first public coronation of Peter Matthews-Akukalia (13-10-2021) as Castle Makupedia, King of the Creative Sciences and God of Creatocracy. He is the Most Sovereign Emperor, Creatocratic Nations of Paradise. Owner, President of the Creatocracy Corporation. Other coronations much before then were the records of his works such as being the World's 1st Creative Scientist. (The Oracle) published in 2012.

Coroner=7,500=8,000=80%=P8.0D=Economy=Currency=8 Aug.=Zeus>>E=v.

Coronet=6,500=7,000=70%=P7.0D=7.0=Language=Assets=Mars=7 July=Pleiades
A small crown worn by nobles below the rank of sovereign. There is one sovereign at a time.

Corot Jean Baptiste=2,000=20%=P2.00D=2.0=Nature=Moon=2 Feb.=Cupid=N=C+_.
Corp.=1,000=100%=10.0=1.0=Mind=Sun=1 January=Helios >> M=E4.
Corpora=1,500=15%=P1.50D=1.5=Authority=Solar Crown=1 May = Maia.
Corporal(1)=4,000=40%=P4.0D=Govt. =Creatocracy=4 April=Hermes=G=A4.
Corporal(2)=6,000=60%=P6.0D=Man=Earth=Royalty=6 June=Gaia=Maia>>M=M2.
Corporate=6,500=7,000=70%=P7.0D=7.0=Language=Assets=Mars=7 July=Pleiades

---

Corporation=12,500=13,000=13%=P1.30D=Solar Core=Faculty=13 January=Athena.
A Faculty is a corporation and royalty by principle and law. The Faculty of Creative & Psycho - Social Sciences also called the Creative Sciences owns the concept of Creatocracy. The organizations institutions and assets of Peter Matthews-Akukalia, Castle Makupedia come under the Creatocracy Corporation 100% = 1,000=p= owned by the Creatocratic Royal Family. De - Royal Makupedia is an inventions company of the Creatocracy Corporation. Creatocracy is his intellectual and creativity property assets and rights. The

Creatocracy Republic, Makupedia, The Creatocratic Charter, Makupedialand, Castle Makupedia, The Makabet, Makupedia Sciences, Mindoms, Maks Currencies, Creative Economies, inventions measurements units nations & Sovereign Creatocratic Republic of Paradise. All assets of the Creatocracy corporation belong exclusively to Peter Matthews-Akukalia. This is the reason he is the World Solar Crown King and Disean God of Creatocracy Genius & Mindom.

Corporeal=5,500=5.5=80%=P5.50=Earth-Midway=5 May = Gaia.
Corps=9,000=90%=P9.00D=9.0=Abst.=Gods=Saturn=9Sept.>>A=Ø.
Corpse=3,500=4,000=40%=P4.0D=Govt. =Creatocracy=4 April=Hermes=G=A4.
Corpsman=5,000=50%=P5.00D=Law=Time=Venus=5 May = Aphrodite>>L=N.
Corpulence=1,500=15%=P1.50D=1.5=Authority=Solar Crown=1 May = Maia.
Corpus=7,000=70%=P7.0D=7.0=Language=Assets=Mars=7 July=Pleiades
Corpus Christi=8,000=80%=P8.0D=Economy=Currency=8 Aug.=Zeus>>E=v.
Corpuscle=7,500=8,000=80%=P8.0D=Economy=Currency=8 Aug.=Zeus>>E=v.
Corpus delicti=10,000=1,000=100%=10.0=Physicality=Tech.=10 Oct.=Uranus=P=1Ø.
Corral=8,000=80%=P8.0D=Economy=Currency=8 Aug.=Zeus>>E=v.
Correct=10,000=1,000=100%=10.0=Physicality=Tech.=10 Oct.=Uranus=P=1Ø.
Correction=10,500=11,000=11%=P1.10D=1.1=Idea=Brainchild=11Nov=Athena>>I=MT.
Correggio Antonio=3,000=30%=P3.0D=3.0=Cr=Stars=Muses=3 March= C=I>>GIL.
Corregidor=5,500=5.5=80%=P5.50=Earth-Midway=5 May = Gaia.
Correlation=6,000=60%=P6.0D=Man=Earth=Royalty=6 June=Gaia=Maia>>M=M2.
Correlative=10,500=11,000=11%=P1.10D=1.1=Idea=Brainchild=11Nov=Athena>>I=MT.
Correspond=7,500=8,000=80%=P8.0D=Economy=Currency=8 Aug.=Zeus>>E=v.
Correspondence=8,000=80%=P8.0D=Economy=Currency=8 Aug.=Zeus>>E=v.
Correspondent=10,500=11,000=11%=P1.10D=1.1=Idea=Brainchild=11Nov=Athena>>I=MT.
Corridor=12,500=13,000=13%=P1.30D=Solar Core=Faculty=13 January=Athena.
Corrigendum=8,500=9,000=90%=P9.00D=9.0=Abst.=Gods=Saturn=9Sept.>>A=Ø.
Corroborate=3,000=30%=P3.0D=3.0=Cr=Stars=Muses=3 March= C=I>>GIL.
Corrode=4,000=40%=P4.0D=Govt. =Creatocracy=4 April=Hermes=G=A4.
Corrugate=5,500=5.5=80%=P5.50=Earth-Midway=5 May = Gaia.
Corrupt=12,000=12%=P1.20D=1.2=Knowl.=Education=12Dec.=Athena>>K=F.
Corsage=4,000=40%=P4.0D=Govt. =Creatocracy=4 April=Hermes=G=A4.
Corsair=2,000=20%=P2.00D=2.0=Nature=Moon=2 Feb.=Cupid=N=C+_.
Corset=8,000=80%=P8.0D=Economy=Currency=8 Aug.=Zeus>>E=v.
Corsica=5,000=50%=P5.00D=Law=Time=Venus=5 May = Aphrodite>>L=N.
Cortège=4,500=5,000=50%=P5.00D=Law=Time=Venus=5 May = Aphrodite>>L=N.
Cortés Hernando=3,000=30%=P3.0D=3.0=Cr=Stars=Muses=3 March= C=I>>GIL.
Cortex=10,500=11,000=11%=P1.10D=1.1=Idea=Brainchild=11Nov=Athena>>I=MT.
Cortisone=9,500=10,000=1,000=100%=10.0=Physicality=Tech.=10 Oct.=Uranus=P=1Ø.
Corundum=8,500=9,000=90%=P9.00D=9.0=Abst.=Gods=Saturn=9Sept.>>A=Ø.
Coruscate=2,000=20%=P2.00D=2.0=Nature=Moon=2 Feb.=Cupid=N=C+_.
Corvette=7,500=8,000=80%=P8.0D=Economy=Currency=8 Aug.=Zeus>>E=v.
Corymb=3,000=30%=P3.0D=3.0=Cr=Stars=Muses=3 March= C=I>>GIL.
Coryza=1,500=15%=P1.50D=1.5=Authority=Solar Crown=1 May = Maia.

cos=1,000=100%=10.0=1.0=Mind=Sun=1 January=Helios >> M=E4.
Cos=1,000=100%=10.0=1.0=Mind=Sun=1 January=Helios >> M=E4.
Cosecant=4,000=40%=P4.0D=Govt. =Creatocracy=4 April=Hermes=G=A4.
Cosign=5,500=5.5=80%=P5.50=Earth-Midway=5 May = Gaia.
Cosignatory=2,000=20%=P2.00D=2.0=Nature=Moon=2 Feb.=Cupid=N=C+_.
Cosine=8,500=9,000=90%=P9.00D=9.0=Abst.=Gods=Saturn=9Sept.>>A=Ø.
Cosmetic=7,000=70%=P7.0D=7.0=Language=Assets=Mars=7 July=Pleiades
Cosmetology=4,500=5,000=50%=P5.00D=Law=Time=Venus=5 May = Aphrodite>>L=N.
Cosmic=5,500=5.5=80%=P5.50=Earth-Midway=5 May = Gaia.
Cosmic ray=13,500=14,000=14%=P1.40D=1.4=Mgt.=13May=Athena=SC=0.1

Cosmo-=1,500=15%=P1.50D=1.5=Authority=Solar Crown=1 May = Maia.
A term for the universe. Aligns with Maia, Great Goddess of the universe. She is Universe.

Cosmo chemistry=3,000=30%=P3.0D=3.0=Cr=Stars=Muses=3 March= C=I>>GIL.
Can only be known through the Creative Sciences. A study of the Makupedia.

Cosmogony=3,500=4,000=40%=P4.0D=Govt. =Creatocracy=4 April=Hermes=G=A4.
Cosmography=3,500=4,000=40%=P4.0D=Govt. =Creatocracy=4 April=Hermes=G=A4.
Cosmology=10,500=11,000=11%=P1.10D=1.1=Idea=Brainchild=11Nov=Athena>>I=MT.
Cosmonaut=2,500=3,000=30%=P3.0D=3.0=Cr=Stars=Muses=3 March= C=I>>GIL.

Cosmopolitan=1,500=15%=P1.50D=1.5=Authority=Solar Crown=1 May = Maia.
The universe may be cosmopolitan however the Makupedia is precise and authoritative.

Cosmopolite=1,500=15%=P1.50D=1.5=Authority=Solar Crown=1 May = Maia.
Cosmos=9,000=90%=P9.00D=9.0=Abst.=Gods=Saturn=9Sept.>>A=Ø.
Cosponsor=3,000=30%=P3.0D=3.0=Cr=Stars=Muses=3 March= C=I>>GIL.
Cossack=7,000=70%=P7.0D=7.0=Language=Assets=Mars=7 July=Pleiades

---

Cost=13,000=13%=P1.30D=Solar Core=Faculty=13 January=Athena.
<Lat. cōnstāre, be fixed. See CONSTANT. First a cost must be based on creative intelligence and computed measured fixed and determined by a Faculty of Creative Intelligence that deals on psycho or mind related economics>> Psychoeconomix. Secondly its currency must align with the realities of tangible and intangible elements of energy and matter catering for both Gods and men. The Creatocracy Bank solves this challenge and the Maks Currencies suits best this situation. Basis for this book and the institutions of Creatocracy. A recommended department is the Ministry of Creativity in Psychoeconomix. There is no space for inflation but fixation in the original definition of cost. A formula system [E=v] has resolved this global crisis not a fiat or speculation. Costs are inspired by Athena Goddess of wisdom handicraft warfare and Aegis of the Creatocracy.

Costar=7,500=8,000=80%=P8.0D=Economy=Currency=8 Aug.=Zeus>>E=v.
Costa Rica=7,000=70%=P7.0D=7.0=Language=Assets=Mars=7 July=Pleiades.

Costly=5,000=50%=P5.00D=Law=Time=Venus=5 May = Aphrodite>>L=N.
The Creatocracy recognizes a costly thing as an amount P5.00D and above.

Cost of living=9,500=10,000=1,000=100%=10.0=Phys.=Tech.=10 Oct.=Uranus=P=1Ø.
Cost of living is determined by the standards of the abstract and physical equivalents.

Cost-of-living adjustment=7,000=70%=P7.0D=7.0=Lang.=Assets=Mars=7 July=Pleiades.
An adjustment on the cost of living must be based on computational precision and assets.

Cost-of-living index=2,000=20%=P2.00D=2.0=Nature=Moon=2 Feb.=Cupid=N=C+_.
The cost of living index is a thing based on nature and stability called Maks Currency.

Cost-plus=4,500=5,000=50%=P5.00D=Law=Time=Venus=5 May = Aphrodite>>L=N.
Costume=10,000=1,000=100%=10.0=Physicality=Tech.=10 Oct.=Uranus=P=1Ø.
Cosy=3,000=30%=P3.0D=3.0=Cr=Stars=Muses=3 March= C=I>>GIL.
Cot(1)=3,000=30%=P3.0D=3.0=Cr=Stars=Muses=3 March= C=I>>GIL.
Cot(2)=1,000=100%=10.0=1.0=Mind=Sun=1 January=Helios >> M=E4.
Cotangent=3,500=4,000=40%=P4.0D=Govt. =Creatocracy=4 April=Hermes=G=A4.
Cote=4,000=40%=P4.0D=Govt. =Creatocracy=4 April=Hermes=G=A4.
Côte d'Azur=3,000=30%=P3.0D=3.0=Cr=Stars=Muses=3 March= C=I>>GIL.
Coterie=3,500=4,000=40%=P4.0D=Govt. =Creatocracy=4 April=Hermes=G=A4.
Coterminous=1,500=15%=P1.50D=1.5=Authority=Solar Crown=1 May = Maia.
Cotillion=3,500=4,000=40%=P4.0D=Govt. =Creatocracy=4 April=Hermes=G=A4.

Cotonou=5,500=5.5=80%=P5.50=Earth-Midway=5 May = Gaia.
A mid - Earth Mind time zone for Gaia. Little wonder business booms here as a boundary nation serving the interests of Nigeria and the Western Countries for importation.

Cottage=3,500=4,000=40%=P4.0D=Govt. =Creatocracy=4 April=Hermes=G=A4.
Cottage cheese=5,500=5.5=80%=P5.50=Earth-Midway=5 May = Gaia.
Cotter=6,000=60%=P6.0D=Man=Earth=Royalty=6 June=Gaia=Maia>>M=M2.
Cotter pin=10,500=11,000=11%=P1.10D=1.1=Idea=Brainchild=11Nov=Athena>>I=MT.
Cotton=17,500=18,000=18%=P1.80D=Solar Currency=Maks Currencies=1 Aug.=Maia.
Cotton candy=5,500=5.5=80%=P5.50=Earth-Midway=5 May = Gaia.
Cotton gin=6,000=60%=P6.0D=Man=Earth=Royalty=6 June=Gaia=Maia>>M=M2.
Cotton mouth=1,500=15%=P1.50D=1.5=Authority=Solar Crown=1 May = Maia.
Cottonseed=6,000=60%=P6.0D=Man=Earth=Royalty=6 June=Gaia=Maia>>M=M2.
Cottontail=4,500=5,000=50%=P5.00D=Law=Time=Venus=5 May = Aphrodite>>L=N.
Cottonwood=7,000=70%=P7.0D=7.0=Language=Assets=Mars=7 July=Pleiades

Cotyledon=5,500=5.5=80%=P5.50=Earth-Midway=5 May = Gaia.
Couch=3,500=4,000=40%=P4.0D=Govt.=Creatocracy=4 April=Hermes=G=A4.
Cougar=1,500=15%=P1.50D=1.5=Authority=Solar Crown=1 May = Maia.
Cough=6,000=60%=P6.0D=Man=Earth=Royalty=6 June=Gaia=Maia>>M=M2.
Could=11,000=11%=P1.10D=1.1=Idea=Brainchild=11Nov=Athena>>I=MT.
Couldn't=1,000=100%=10.0=1.0=Mind=Sun=1 January=Helios >> M=E4.
Coulee=4,500=5,000=50%=P5.00D=Law=Time=Venus=5 May = Aphrodite>>L=N.
Coulomb=12,000=12%=P1.20D=1.2=Knowl.=Education=12Dec.=Athena>>K=F.
Council=22,000=2.2>>4.0=4,000=40%=P4.0D=Govt. =Creatoc.=4April=Hermes=G=A4.
Councilor=4,500=5,000=50%=P5.00D=Law=Time=Venus=5 May = Aphrodite>>L=N.
Counsel=22,000=2.3>>4.0=4,000=40%=P4.0D=Govt. =Creatoc.=4 April=Hermes=G=A4.
Counselor=9,500=10,000=1,000=100%=10.0=Physicality=Tech.=10 Oct.=Uranus=P=1Ø.
Count(1)=10,000=1,000=100%=Physicality= Tech.=10 Oct.=Uranus=P=1Ø.
Count(2)=3,000=30%=P3.0D=3.0=Cr=Stars=Muses=3 March= C=I>>GIL.
Counter down=10,000=1,000=100%=10.0=Physicality=Tech.=10 Oct.=Uranus=P=1Ø.
Countenance=5,000=50%=P5.00D=Law=Time=Venus=5 May = Aphrodite>>L=N.
Counter(1)=7,000=70%=P7.0D=7.0=Language=Assets=Mars=7 July=Pleiades
Counter(2)=14,000=14%=P1.40D=1.4=Mgt.=13May=Athena=SC=0.1
Counter(3)=9,000=90%=P9.00D=9.0=Abst.=Gods=Saturn=9Sept.>>A=Ø.
Counter-=4,500=5,000=50%=P5.00D=Law=Time=Venus=5 May = Aphrodite>>L=N.
Counteract=5,500=5.5=80%=P5.50=Earth-Midway=5 May = Gaia.
Counterattack=1,500=15%=P1.50D=1.5=Authority=Solar Crown=1 May = Maia.
Counterbalance=6,500=7,000=70%=P7.0D=7.0=Language=Assets=Mars=7 July=Pleiades
Countercharge=3,500=4,000=40%=P4.0D=Govt. =Creatocracy=4April=Hermes=G=A4.
Counterclaim=4,000=40%=P4.0D=Govt. =Creatocracy=4 April=Hermes=G=A4.
Counterclockwise=5,000=50%=P5.00D=Law=Time=Venus=5 May = Aphrodite>>L=N.
Counterculture=5,500=5.5=80%=P5.50=Earth-Midway=5 May = Gaia.
Counterespionage=4,000=40%=P4.0D=Govt. =Creatocracy=4 April=Hermes=G=A4.
Counterfeit=13,500=14,000=14%=P1.40D=1.4=Mgt.=13May=Athena=SC=0.1
Counterinsurgency=4,000=40%=P4.0D=Govt. =Creatocracy=4 April=Hermes=G=A4.
Counterintelligence=9,500=10,000=1,000=100%=10.0=Phy=Tech.=10 Oct.=Uranus=P=1Ø.
Countermand=4,000=40%=P4.0D=Govt. =Creatocracy=4 April=Hermes=G=A4.
Countermeasure=5,000=50%=P5.00D=Law=Time=Venus=5 May = Aphrodite>>L=N.
Counteroffensive=7,000=70%=P7.0D=7.0=Language=Assets=Mars=7 July=Pleiades
Counterpane=2,500=3,000=30%=P3.0D=3.0=Cr=Stars=Muses=3 March= C=I>>GIL.
Counterpart=5,500=5.5=80%=P5.50=Earth-Midway=5 May = Gaia.
Counterplot=7,500=8,000=80%=P8.0D=Economy=Currency=8 Aug.=Zeus>>E=v.
Counterpoint=13,500=14,000=14%=P1.40D=1.4=Mgt.=13May=Athena=SC=0.1
Counterpoise=7,500=8,000=80%=P8.0D=Economy=Currency=8 Aug.=Zeus>>E=v.
Counterproductive=4,000=40%=P4.0D=Govt.=Creatocracy=4 April=Hermes=G=A4.
Counterrevolution=4,000=40%=P4.0D=Govt.=Creatocracy=4 April=Hermes=G=A4.
Countersign=7,000=70%=P7.0D=7.0=Language=Assets=Mars=7 July=Pleiades
Countersignature=1,000=100%=10.0=1.0=Mind=Sun=1 January=Helios >> M=E4.
Countersink=15,500=16,000=16%=P1.60D=1.6=Incarnation=Mind of GOD=1 June=Maia.
Counterspy=4,000=40%=P4.0D=Govt. =Creatocracy=4 April=Hermes=G=A4.

Countertenor=3,500=4,000=40%=P4.0D=Govt. =Creatocracy=4 April=Hermes=G=A4.
Counterweight=2,500=3,000=30%=P3.0D=3.0=Cr=Stars=Muses=3 March= C=I>>GIL.
Countess=5,500=5.5=80%=P5.50=Earth-Midway=5 May = Gaia.
Countinghouse=7,500=8,000=80%=P8.0D=Economy=Currency=8 Aug.=Zeus>>E=v.

Countless=2,500=3,000=30%=P3.0D=3.0=Cr=Stars=Muses=3 March= C=I>>GIL.
Incalculable. Countless matters can only be quantified through Mind Computing.

Countrified=3,500=4,000=40%=P4.0D=Govt.=Creatocracy=4 April=Hermes=G=A4.
Country=13,500=14,000=14%=P1.40D=1.4=Mgt.=13May=Athena=SC=0.1
Country and western=1,500=15%=P1.50D=1.5=Authority=Solar Crown=1 May = Maia.
Country club=4,000=40%=P4.0D=Govt.=Creatocracy=4 April=Hermes=G=A4.
Country dance=7,000=70%=P7.0D=7.0=Language=Assets=Mars=7 July=Pleiades
Countryman=4,000=40%=P4.0D=Govt.=Creatocracy=4 April=Hermes=G=A4.
Country mile=2,000=20%=P2.00D=2.0=Nature=Moon=2 Feb.=Cupid=N=C+_.
Country music=6,500=7,000=70%=P7.0D=7.0=Language=Assets=Mars=7 July=Pleiades
Countryside=3,000=30%=P3.0D=3.0=Cr=Stars=Muses=3 March= C=I>>GIL.
Countrywoman=4,000=40%=P4.0D=Govt.=Creatocracy=4 April=Hermes=G=A4.
County=4,000=40%=P4.0D=Govt. =Creatocracy=4 April=Hermes=G=A4.
Coup=3,000=30%=P3.0D=3.0=Cr=Stars=Muses=3 March= C=I>>GIL.
Coup de grâce=7,000=70%=P7.0D=7.0=Language=Assets=Mars=7 July=Pleiades
Coup d'état=8,000=80%=P8.0D=Economy=Currency=8 Aug.=Zeus>>E=v.
Coupe=2,500=3,000=30%=P3.0D=3.0=Cr=Stars=Muses=3 March= C=I>>GIL.
Couperin François=2,000=20%=P2.00D=2.0=Nature=Moon=2 Feb.=Cupid=N=C+_.
Couple=10,000=1,000=100%=10.0=Physicality=Tech.=10 Oct.=Uranus=P=1Ø.
Couplet=6,000=60%=P6.0D=Man=Earth=Royalty=6 June=Gaia=Maia>>M=M2.
Coupling=5,500=5.5=80%=P5.50=Earth-Midway=5 May = Gaia.
Coupon=17,000=17%=P1.70D=1.7=Solar Asset=17 Feb.=Maia=Mind Computing.
Courage=8,500=9,000=90%=P9.00D=9.0=Abst.=Gods=Saturn=9Sept.>>A=Ø.
Courbet Gustave.=2,000=20%=P2.00D=2.0=Nature=Moon=2 Feb.=Cupid=N=C+_.
Courier=4,500=5,000=50%=P5.00D=Law=Time=Venus=5 May = Aphrodite>>L=N.
Course=10,000=1,000=100%=10.0=Physicality=Tech.=10 Oct.=Uranus=P=1Ø.
Courser=1,500=15%=P1.50D=1.5=Authority=Solar Crown=1 May = Maia.
Court=10,000=1,000=100%=10.0=Physicality=Tech.=10 Oct.=Uranus=P=1Ø.
Courteous=2,000=20%=P2.00D=2.0=Nature=Moon=2 Feb.=Cupid=N=C+_.
Courtesan=6,500=7,000=70%=P7.0D=7.0=Language=Assets=Mars=7 July=Pleiades.
Courtesy=5,500=5.5=80%=P5.50=Earth-Midway=5 May = Gaia.
Courthouse=2,500=3,000=30%=P3.0D=3.0=Cr=Stars=Muses=3 March= C=I>>GIL.
Courtier=3,000=30%=P3.0D=3.0=Cr=Stars=Muses=3 March= C=I>>GIL.
Courtly=1,500=15%=P1.50D=1.5=Authority=Solar Crown=1 May = Maia.
Court martial=11,500=12,000=12%=P1.20D=1.2=Knowl.=Education=12Dec.=Athena
    >>K=F.
Court order=8,000=80%=P8.0D=Economy=Currency=8 Aug.=Zeus>>E=v.
Courtroom=2,500=3,000=30%=P3.0D=3.0=Cr=Stars=Muses=3 March= C=I>>GIL.

Courtship=3,500=4,000=40%=P4.0D=Govt.=Creatocracy=4 April=Hermes=G=A4.
Courtyard=4,000=40%=P4.0D=Govt.=Creatocracy=4 April=Hermes=G=A4.
Couscous=5,500=5.5=80%=P5.50=Earth-Midway=5 May = Gaia.
Cousin=8,000=80%=P8.0D=Economy=Currency=8 Aug.=Zeus>>E=v.
Couture=6,000=60%=P6.0D=Man=Earth=Royalty=6 June=Gaia=Maia>>M=M2.
Couturier=5,500=5.5=80%=P5.50=Earth-Midway=5 May = Gaia.
Covalent bond=7,000=70%=P7.0D=7.0=Language=Assets=Mars=7 July=Pleiades
Cove=4,500=5,000=50%=P5.00D=Law=Time=Venus=5 May = Aphrodite>>L=N.

Coven=2,500=3,000=30%=P3.0D=3.0=Cr=Stars=Muses=3 March= C=I>>GIL.
An assembly of 13 witches. The Creatocracy recognizes witches as fallen muses. 13 means Athena so witches will be the muses that fell from the graces of Athena and were duly punished for it by driving them to the Earth. Let us attempt to establish its truth. 13=1.3*3.0=p=4.3+3.9=8.2x=px=21.1=2.1>>3.0. Proved. Witches are muses that fell from grace. This happens to humans when they are not consistent in self development.

Covenant=9,500=10,000=1,000=100%=10.0=Physicality=Tech.=10 Oct.=Uranus=P=1Ø.
Coventry=4,500=5,000=50%=P5.00D=Law=Time=Venus=5 May = Aphrodite>>L=N.
Cover=10,000=1,000=100%=10.0=Physicality=Tech.=10 Oct.=Uranus=P=1Ø.
Coverage=9,000=90%=P9.00D=9.0=Abst.=Gods=Saturn=9Sept.>>A=Ø.
Coveralls=5,000=50%=P5.00D=Law=Time=Venus=5 May = Aphrodite>>L=N.
Cover charge=6,000=60%=P6.0D=Man=Earth=Royalty=6 June=Gaia=Maia>>M=M2.
Cover crop=9,000=90%=P9.00D=9.0=Abst.=Gods=Saturn=9Sept.>>A=Ø.
Cover wagon=8,000=80%=P8.0D=Economy=Currency=8 Aug.=Zeus>>E=v.
Covering=4,500=5,000=50%=P5.00D=Law=Time=Venus=5 May = Aphrodite>>L=N.
Coverlet=1,000=100%=10.0=1.0=Mind=Sun=1 January=Helios >> M=E4.

Covert=8,000=80%=P8.0D=Economy=Currency=8 Aug.=Zeus>>E=v.
A character of Zeus revealed by Athena in Proverbs 25:2. The Creatocracy is not just a fact but absolute truth in all things that we have discovered. We are royalty beyond measure.

Coverup=7,000=70%=P7.0D=7.0=Language=Assets=Mars=7 July=Pleiades
Covet=6,500=7,000=70%=P7.0D=7.0=Language=Assets=Mars=7 July=Pleiades
Covetous=4,500=5,000=50%=P5.00D=Law=Time=Venus=5 May = Aphrodite>>L=N.
Covey=4,000=40%=P4.0D=Govt. =Creatocracy=4 April=Hermes=G=A4.

Cow(1)=8,000=80%=P8.0D=Economy=Currency=8 Aug.=Zeus>>E=v.
A cow is offered as sacrifice directly to Zeus the Father, Hermes the Son - God of wealth.

Cow(2)=2,500=3,000=30%=P3.0D=3.0=Cr=Stars=Muses=3 March= C=I>>GIL.
Coward=6,000=60%=P6.0D=Man=Earth=Royalty=6 June=Gaia=Maia>>M=M2.
Coward Noel Pierce=3,000=30%=P3.0D=3.0=Cr=Stars=Muses=3 March= C=I>>GIL.

Cowardice=2,500=3,000=30%=P3.0D=3.0=Cr=Stars=Muses=3 March= C=I>>GIL.
Cowardice is a borderline between natural stability and inspired creativity.

Cowbird=5,000=50%=P5.00D=Law=Time=Venus=5 May = Aphrodite>>L=N.
Cowboy=7,000=70%=P7.0D=7.0=Language=Assets=Mars=7 July=Pleiades
Cow catcher=8,000=80%=P8.0D=Economy=Currency=8 Aug.=Zeus>>E=v.
Cower=2,000=20%=P2.00D=2.0=Nature=Moon=2 Feb.=Cupid=N=C+_.
Cowgirl=7,000=70%=P7.0D=7.0=Language=Assets=Mars=7 July=Pleiades
Cowhand=2,000=20%=P2.00D=2.0=Nature=Moon=2 Feb.=Cupid=N=C+_.
Cowherd=3,000=30%=P3.0D=3.0=Cr=Stars=Muses=3 March= C=I>>GIL.
Cowhide=5,000=50%=P5.00D=Law=Time=Venus=5 May = Aphrodite>>L=N.
Cowl=8,000=80%=P8.0D=Economy=Currency=8 Aug.=Zeus>>E=v.
Cowley Abraham=2,500=3,000=30%=P3.0D=3.0=Cr=Stars=Muses=3 March= C=I>>GIL.
Cowlick=6,500=7,000=70%=P7.0D=7.0=Language=Assets=Mars=7 July=Pleiades
Cowling=4,500=5,000=50%=P5.00D=Law=Time=Venus=5 May = Aphrodite>>L=N.
Coworker=1,000=100%=10.0=1.0=Mind=Sun=1 January=Helios >> M=E4.
Cowper William=2,000=20%=P2.00D=2.0=Nature=Moon=2 Feb.=Cupid=N=C+_.
Cowpoke=1,000=100%=10.0=1.0=Mind=Sun=1 January=Helios >> M=E4.
Cowpox=9,000=90%=P9.00D=9.0=Abst.=Gods=Saturn=9Sept.>>A=Ø.
Cow puncher=1,000=100%=10.0=1.0=Mind=Sun=1 January=Helios >> M=E4.
Cowrie=6,000=60%=P6.0D=Man=Earth=Royalty=6 June=Gaia=Maia>>M=M2.
Cowslip=5,000=50%=P5.00D=Law=Time=Venus=5 May = Aphrodite>>L=N.
Coxcomb=2,000=20%=P2.00D=2.0=Nature=Moon=2 Feb.=Cupid=N=C+_.
Coxswain=6,000=60%=P6.0D=Man=Earth=Royalty=6 June=Gaia=Maia>>M=M2.
Coy=3,000=30%=P3.0D=3.0=Cr=Stars=Muses=3 March= C=I>>GIL.
Coyote=6,500=7,000=70%=P7.0D=7.0=Language=Assets=Mars=7 July=Pleiades
Cozen=1,500=15%=P1.50D=1.5=Authority=Solar Crown=1 May = Maia.
Cozy=10,000=1,000=100%=10.0=Physicality=Tech.=10 Oct.=Uranus=P=1Ø.
cp=500=5%=P5.00D=5.0=Law=Time=Venus=5 May=Aphrodite>>L=N.
CP=2,000=20%=P2.00D=2.0=Nature=Moon=2 Feb.=Cupid=N=C+_.
cp.=1,000=100%=10.0=1.0=Mind=Sun=1 January=Helios >> M=E4.
CPA=1,500=15%=P1.50D=1.5=Authority=Solar Crown=1 May = Maia.
cpd.=500=5%=P5.00D=5.0=Law=Time=Venus=5 May=Aphrodite>>L=N.
CPI=1,500=15%=P1.50D=1.5=Authority=Solar Crown=1 May = Maia.
CPO=1,500=15%=P1.50D=1.5=Authority=Solar Crown=1 May = Maia.
CPR=1,000=100%=10.0=1.0=Mind=Sun=1 January=Helios >> M=E4.
cps=2,000=20%=P2.00D=2.0=Nature=Moon=2 Feb.=Cupid=N=C+_.
Cpt.=500=5%=P5.00D=5.0=Law=Time=Venus=5 May=Aphrodite>>L=N.
CPU=2,500=3,000=30%=P3.0D=3.0=Cr=Stars=Muses=3 March= C=I>>GIL.
Cr=2,500=3,000=30%=P3.0D=3.0=Cr=Stars=Muses=3 March= C=I>>GIL.
C.R.=1,000=100%=10.0=1.0=Mind=Sun=1 January=Helios >> M=E4.
Crab(1)=9,500=10,000=1,000=100%=Physicality= Tech.=10 Oct.=Uranus=P=1Ø.

Crab(2)=2,500=3,000=30%=P3.0D=3.0=Cr=Stars=Muses=3 March= C=I>>GIL.
A quarrelsome ill-tempered person. A borderline between perceived instability stability and required creativity. A sense of non attainment or achievement creates this state of mind. A revelation of a crab upon a person shows a crossroad in the life of such person who is waiting at the beckon of Creativity and the higher knowledge of Creative Sciences. A key character and experience between the emperor and Helen of Bulwark>>Helen of Boulevard. Angel Investor at Makupedia. Special Adviser to the Creatocratic administration. Zodiac symbol and character of the emperor who found solace in discovery and creativity.

Crab apple=8,000=80%=P8.0D=Economy=Currency=8 Aug.=Zeus>>E=v.
Crabbed=4,000=40%=P4.0D=Govt. =Creatocracy=4 April=Hermes=G=A4.

Crabby=1,500=15%=P1.50D=1.5=Authority=Solar Crown=1 May = Maia.
Crabby people come from Maia and seek her for their ultimate fulfillment. This is the reason they get easily irritable. They are destined for a crown and have no peace until they find it.

Crabgrass=4,500=5,000=50%=P5.00D=Law=Time=Venus=5 May = Aphrodite>>L=N.
Crab louse=6,000=60%=P6.0D=Man=Earth=Royalty=6 June=Gaia=Maia>>M=M2.
Crack=10,000=1,000=100%=10.0=Physicality=Tech.=10 Oct.=Uranus=P=1Ø.
Crackdown=3,500=4,000=40%=P4.0D=Govt. =Creatocracy=4 April=Hermes=G=A4.
Cracked=5,000=50%=P5.00D=Law=Time=Venus=5 May = Aphrodite>>L=N.
Cracker=3,500=4,000=40%=P4.0D=Govt. =Creatocracy=4 April=Hermes=G=A4.
Crackerjack=2,000=20%=P2.00D=2.0=Nature=Moon=2 Feb.=Cupid=N=C+_.
Crackle=8,500=9,000=90%=P9.00D=9.0=Abst.=Gods=Saturn=9Sept.>>A=Ø.

Crackpot=2,500=3,000=30%=P3.0D=3.0=Cr=Stars=Muses=3 March= C=I>>GIL.
An eccentric or harebrained person. Harebrained>>rash, ill judged >> crabby. Ill judge>> lacking wisdom that results in making unwise decisions. Wisdom and creativity is the answer. Athena is the emotional manager of Maia through counsel for such people.

Crack up=6,000=60%=P6.0D=Man=Earth=Royalty=6 June=Gaia=Maia>>M=M2.
Cracow=6,500=7,000=70%=P7.0D=7.0=Language=Assets=Mars=7 July=Pleiades.

-cracy=2,000=20%=P2.00D=2.0=Nature=Moon=2 Feb.=Cupid=N=C+_.
All -cracies are natural forms of governments. Only the Creatocracy measures above nature to the supernatural through the solar core and Mind computing as 10,000=1,000. In the twelve dimensions of the universe one is greater than two means Mind is greater than Nature means the Sun is greater than the Moon and Energy is superior to Matter.

Cradle=13,500=14,000=14%=P1.40D=1.4=Mgt.=13May=Athena=SC=0.1
Craft=17,000=17%=P1.70D=1.7=Solar Asset=17 Feb.=Maia=Mind Computing.

Crafty=3,000=30%=P3.0D=3.0=Cr=Stars=Muses=3 March= C=I>>GIL.
Crag=3,000=30%=P3.0D=3.0=Cr=Stars=Muses=3 March= C=I>>GIL.
Cram=10,000=1,000=100%=10.0=Physicality=Tech.=10 Oct.=Uranus=P=1Ø.
Cramp(1)=14,000=14%=P1.40D=1.4=Mgt.=13May=Athena=SC=0.1
Cramp(2)=7,000=70%=P7.0D=7.0=Language=Assets=Mars=7 July=Pleiades
Crampon=5,500=5.5=80%=P5.50=Earth-Midway=5 May = Gaia.
Cranberry=10,000=1,000=100%=10.0=Physicality=Tech.=10 Oct.=Uranus=P=1Ø.
crane=11,500=12,000=12%=P1.20D=1.2=Knowl.=Education=12Dec.=Athena>>K=F.
Crane Hart=2,000=20%=P2.00D=2.0=Nature=Moon=2 Feb.=Cupid=N=C+_.
Crane,Stephen=2,000=20%=P2.00D=2.0=Nature=Moon=2 Feb.=Cupid=N=C+_.
Cranium=4,000=40%=P4.0D=Govt. =Creatocracy=4 April=Hermes=G=A4.
Crank=17,000=17%=P1.70D=1.7=Solar Asset=17 Feb.=Maia=Mind Computing.
Crankcase=3,000=30%=P3.0D=3.0=Cr=Stars=Muses=3 March= C=I>>GIL.
Crankshaft=4,500=5,000=50%=P5.00D=Law=Time=Venus=5 May = Aphrodite>>L=N.

Cranky=4,500=5,000=50%=P5.00D=Law=Time=Venus=5 May = Aphrodite>>L=N.
Aligns>>crab. A borderline between Hermes and Aphrodite >> Power and Love boundary.
Law and time management is a solace for them. Authority their ultimate satisfaction.

Cranmer Thomas=4,000=40%=P4.0D=Govt. =Creatocracy=4 April=Hermes=G=A4.
Cranny=3,500=4,000=40%=P4.0D=Govt. =Creatocracy=4 April=Hermes=G=A4.
Crape=5,000=50%=P5.00D=Law=Time=Venus=5 May = Aphrodite>>L=N.
Crappie=5,000=50%=P5.00D=Law=Time=Venus=5 May = Aphrodite>>L=N.
Craps=3,500=4,000=40%=P4.0D=Govt. =Creatocracy=4 April=Hermes=G=A4.
Crapshoot=2,000=20%=P2.00D=2.0=Nature=Moon=2 Feb.=Cupid=N=C+_.
Crapshooter=2,000=20%=P2.00D=2.0=Nature=Moon=2 Feb.=Cupid=N=C+_.
Crash=14,000=14%=P1.40D=1.4=Mgt.=13May=Athena=SC=0.1
Crash land=6,000=60%=P6.0D=Man=Earth=Royalty=6 June=Gaia=Maia>>M=M2.
Crass=2,000=20%=P2.00D=2.0=Nature=Moon=2 Feb.=Cupid=N=C+_.

-crat=6,000=60%=P6.0D=Man=Earth=Royalty=6 June=Gaia=Maia>>M=M2.
A participant in or supporter of a specified form of government. We are Creatocrats.
Firm believers in the Creatocracy and all that it stands for, by GOD and the Gods.

Crate=5,500=5.5=80%=P5.50=Earth-Midway=5 May = Gaia.

Crater=9,000=90%=P9.00D=9.0=Abst.=Gods=Saturn=9Sept.>>A=Ø.
Features of the Gods. Especially discovered and asserted in Moon Computing by Peter
Matthews-Akukalia. His synchronized programming establishes lunar energy PGI reality.

Crater Lake=5,500=5.5=80%=P5.50=Earth-Midway=5 May = Gaia.
Cravat=1,000=100%=10.0=1.0=Mind=Sun=1 January=Helios >> M=E4.

Crave=5,500=5.5=80%=P5.50=Earth-Midway=5 May = Gaia.
Craven=500=5%=P5.00D=5.0=Law=Time=Venus=5 May=Aphrodite>>L=N.
Craving=1,500=15%=P1.50D=1.5=Authority=Solar Crown=1 May = Maia.
Craw=4,500=5,000=50%=P5.00D=Law=Time=Venus=5 May = Aphrodite>>L=N.
Craw dad=4,000=40%=P4.0D=Govt. =Creatocracy=4 April=Hermes=G=A4.
Crawl=19,000=19%=P1.90=1.9=Planetary Energy=Mind of God=Maia.
Crayfish=2,500=3,000=30%=P3.0D=3.0=Cr=Stars=Muses=3 March= C=I>>GIL.
Crayon=5,500=5.5=80%=P5.50=Earth-Midway=5 May = Gaia.
Craze=2,500=3,000=30%=P3.0D=3.0=Cr=Stars=Muses=3 March= C=I>>GIL.
Crazy=4,500=5,000=50%=P5.00D=Law=Time=Venus=5 May = Aphrodite>>L=N.
Crazy Horse=2,500=3,000=30%=P3.0D=3.0=Cr=Stars=Muses=3 March= C=I>>GIL.
Crazy quilt=5,000=50%=P5.00D=Law=Time=Venus=5 May = Aphrodite>>L=N.
Creak=5,500=5.5=80%=P5.50=Earth-Midway=5 May = Gaia.
Cream=8,500=9,000=90%=P9.00D=9.0=Abst.=Gods=Saturn=9Sept.>>A=Ø.
Cream cheese=4,500=5,000=50%=P5.00D=Law=Time=Venus=5 May = Aphrodite>>L=N.
Creamer=3,000=30%=P3.0D=3.0=Cr=Stars=Muses=3 March= C=I>>GIL.
Creamery=4,500=5,000=50%=P5.00D=Law=Time=Venus=5 May = Aphrodite>>L=N.
Cream puff=5,500=5.5=80%=P5.50=Earth-Midway=5 May = Gaia.
Cream sauce=6,500=7,000=70%=P7.0D=7.0=Language=Assets=Mars=7 July=Pleiades
Crease=4,000=40%=P4.0D=Govt.=Creatocracy=4 April=Hermes=G=A4.
Create=5,500=5.5=80%=P5.50=Earth-Midway=5 May = Gaia.
Creation=7,500=8,000=80%=P8.0D=Economy=Currency=8 Aug.=Zeus>>E=v.
Creationism=5,500=5.5=80%=P5.50=Earth-Midway=5 May = Gaia.

Creative=2,000=20%=P2.00D=2.0=Nature=Moon=2 Feb.=Cupid=N=C+_.
In the Creative Sciences, Creativity is the third (3ø) dimension of the Mind universe.
Peter Matthews-Akukalia used computations to discover the physical equivalent as the
stars. He wrote the Creativity formula as C=I. This measures the innate capacity ability
and capabilities in anyone and everyone from the day of birth till after death. The need to
understand creativity led to the invention of creative sciences producing the profession of
Creative Scientists worldwide as an asset of Peter Matthews-Akukalia, Castle Makupedia.

Creator=1,500=15%=P1.50D=1.5=Authority=Solar Crown=1 May = Maia.
Creature=3,500=4,000=40%=P4.0D=Govt.=Creatocracy=4 April=Hermes=G=A4.
Crèche=2,000=20%=P2.00D=2.0=Nature=Moon=2 Feb.=Cupid=N=C+_.
Credence=4,000=40%=P4.0D=Govt.=Creatocracy=4 April=Hermes=G=A4.
Credential=6,500=7,000=70%=P7.0D=7.0=Language=Assets=Mars=7 July=Pleiades.
Credenza=4,500=5,000=50%=P5.00D=Law=Time=Venus=5 May = Aphrodite>>L=N.
Credible=3,500=4,000=40%=P4.0D=Govt.=Creatocracy=4 April=Hermes=G=A4.
Credit=10,000=1,000=100%=10.0=Physicality=Tech.=10 Oct.=Uranus=P=1Ø.
Creditable=1,500=15%=P1.50D=1.5=Authority=Solar Crown=1 May = Maia.
Credit card=6,000=60%=P6.0D=Man=Earth=Royalty=6 June=Gaia=Maia>>M=M2.
Creditor=3,000=30%=P3.0D=3.0=Cr=Stars=Muses=3 March= C=I>>GIL.
Credit union=5,500=5.5=80%=P5.50=Earth-Midway=5 May = Gaia.

Credo=1,000=100%=10.0=1.0=Mind=Sun=1 January=Helios >> M=E4.
Credulous=3,000=30%=P3.0D=3.0=Cr=Stars=Muses=3 March= C=I>>GIL.
Cree=9,500=10,000=1,000=100%=10.0=Physicality=Tech.=10 Oct.=Uranus=P=1Ø.
Creed=3,000=30%=P3.0D=3.0=Cr=Stars=Muses=3 March= C=I>>GIL.
creek=10,500=11,000=11%=P1.10D=1.1=Idea=Brainchild=11Nov=Athena>>I=MT.
Creek=12,500=13,000=13%=P1.30D=Solar Core=Faculty=13 January=Athena.
Creel=3,500=4,000=40%=P4.0D=Govt.=Creatocracy=4 April=Hermes=G=A4.
Creep=15,500=16,000=16%=P1.60D=1.6=Incarnation=Mind of GOD=1 June=Maia.
Creeper=5,000=50%=P5.00D=Law=Time=Venus=5 May = Aphrodite>>L=N.
Creepy=7,500=8,000=80%=P8.0D=Economy=Currency=8 Aug.=Zeus>>E=v.
Cremate=2,000=20%=P2.00D=2.0=Nature=Moon=2 Feb.=Cupid=N=C+_.
Crematorium=4,500=5,000=50%=P5.00D=Law=Time=Venus=5 May = Aphrodite>>L=N.
Crematory=1,000=100%=10.0=1.0=Mind=Sun=1 January=Helios >> M=E4.
Crenellated=1,000=100%=10.0=1.0=Mind=Sun=1 January=Helios >> M=E4.
Crenshaw=5,000=50%=P5.00D=Law=Time=Venus=5 May = Aphrodite>>L=N.
Creole=24,500=30,000=3,000=30%=P3.0D=3.0=Cr=Stars=Muses=3 March= C=I>>GIL.
Creosote=7,500=8,000=80%=P8.0D=Economy=Currency=8 Aug.=Zeus>>E=v.
Crepe=8,500=9,000=90%=P9.00D=9.0=Abst.=Gods=Saturn=9Sept.>>A=Ø.
Crepe paper=3,000=30%=P3.0D=3.0=Cr=Stars=Muses=3 March= C=I>>GIL.
Crept=3,500=4,000=40%=P4.0D=Govt.=Creatocracy=4 April=Hermes=G=A4.
Crepuscular=4,000=40%=P4.0D=Govt.=Creatocracy=4 April=Hermes=G=A4.
Crescendo=7,500=8,000=80%=P8.0D=Economy=Currency=8 Aug.=Zeus>>E=v.
Crescent=12,000=12%=P1.20D=1.2=Knowl.=Education=12Dec.=Athena>>K=F.
Cress=6,000=60%=P6.0D=Man=Earth=Royalty=6 June=Gaia=Maia>>M=M2.

Crest=14,000=14%=P1.40D=1.4=Mgt.=13May=Athena=SC=0.1
The Creatocracy has the crest of the Solar Crown and represents this in all things.

Crestfallen=1,000=100%=10.0=1.0=Mind=Sun=1 January=Helios >> M=E4.
Cretaceous=10,000=1,000=100%=10.0=Physicality=Tech.=10 Oct.=Uranus=P=1Ø.
Crete=5,000=50%=P5.00D=Law=Time=Venus=5 May = Aphrodite>>L=N.
Cretin=2,500=3,000=30%=P3.0D=3.0=Cr=Stars=Muses=3 March= C=I>>GIL.
Cretinism=5,000=50%=P5.00D=Law=Time=Venus=5 May = Aphrodite>>L=N.
Cretonne=6,000=60%=P6.0D=Man=Earth=Royalty=6 June=Gaia=Maia>>M=M2.
Crevasse=4,500=5,000=50%=P5.00D=Law=Time=Venus=5 May = Aphrodite>>L=N.
Crevice=1,500=15%=P1.50D=1.5=Authority=Solar Crown=1 May = Maia.
Crew(1)=7,500=8,000=80%=P8.0D=Economy=Currency=8 Aug.=Zeus>>E=v.
Crew(2)=3,000=30%=P3.0D=3.0=Cr=Stars=Muses=3 March= C=I>>GIL.
Crew cut=2,000=20%=P2.00D=2.0=Nature=Moon=2 Feb.=Cupid=N=C+_.
Crewed=4,500=5,000=50%=P5.00D=Law=Time=Venus=5 May = Aphrodite>>L=N.
Crewel=3,500=4,000=40%=P4.0D=Govt.=Creatocracy=4 April=Hermes=G=A4.
Crib=15,500=16,000=16%=P1.60D=1.6=Incarnation=Mind of GOD=1 June=Maia.
Cribbage=5,500=5.5=80%=P5.50=Earth-Midway=5 May = Gaia.
Crick(1)=3,500=4,000=40%=P4.0D=Govt.=Creatocracy=4 April=Hermes=G=A4.

Crick(2)=4,000=40%=P4.0D=Govt.=Creatocracy=4 April=Hermes=G=A4.
Cricket(1)=5,500=5.5=80%=P5.50=Earth-Midway=5 May = Gaia.
Cricket(2)=7,500=8,000=80%=P8.0D=Economy=Currency=8 Aug.=Zeus>>E=v.
Crier=3,000=30%=P3.0D=3.0=Cr=Stars=Muses=3 March= C=I>>GIL.
Crime=7,000=70%=P7.0D=7.0=Language=Assets=Mars=7 July=Pleiades.
Crimea=7,000=70%=P7.0D=7.0=Language=Assets=Mars=7 July=Pleiades.
Criminal=5,500=5.5=80%=P5.50=Earth-Midway=5 May = Gaia.
Criminalize=2,000=20%=P2.00D=2.0=Nature=Moon=2 Feb.=Cupid=N=C+_.
Criminology=3,500=4,000=40%=P4.0D=Govt.=Creatocracy=4 April=Hermes=G=A4.
Crimp=12,000=12%=P1.20D=1.2=Knowl.=Education=12Dec.=Athena>>K=F.
Crimson=2,000=20%=P2.00D=2.0=Nature=Moon=2 Feb.=Cupid=N=C+_.
Cringe=4,000=40%=P4.0D=Govt.=Creatocracy=4 April=Hermes=G=A4.
Crinkle=2,500=3,000=30%=P3.0D=3.0=Cr=Stars=Muses=3 March= C=I>>GIL.
Crinoline=6,000=60%=P6.0D=Man=Earth=Royalty=6 June=Gaia=Maia>>M=M2.
Cripple=5,000=50%=P5.00D=Law=Time=Venus=5 May = Aphrodite>>L=N.
Crisis=11,500=12,000=12%=P1.20D=1.2=Knowl.=Education=12Dec.=Athena>>K=F.
Crisp=9,000=90%=P9.00D=9.0=Abst.=Gods=Saturn=9Sept.>>A=Ø.
Crisscross=7,500=8,000=80%=P8.0D=Economy=Currency=8 Aug.=Zeus>>E=v.
Criterion=20,000=2,000=20%=P2.00D=2.0=Nature=Moon=2 Feb.=Cupid=N=C+_.
Critic=5,000=50%=P5.00D=Law=Time=Venus=5 May = Aphrodite>>L=N.
Critical=15,000=1,500=15%=P1.50D=1.5=Authority=Solar Crown=1 May = Maia.
Criticism=9,500=10,000=1,000=100%=10.0=Physicality=Tech.=10 Oct.=Uranus=P=1Ø.
Criticize=5,500=5.5=80%=P5.50=Earth-Midway=5 May = Gaia.
Critique=2,500=3,000=30%=P3.0D=3.0=Cr=Stars=Muses=3 March= C=I>>GIL.
Critter=3,000=30%=P3.0D=3.0=Cr=Stars=Muses=3 March= C=I>>GIL.
Croak=6,000=60%=P6.0D=Man=Earth=Royalty=6 June=Gaia=Maia>>M=M2.
Croat=6,500=7,000=70%=P7.0D=7.0=Language=Assets=Mars=7 July=Pleiades.
Croatia=11,000=11%=P1.10D=1.1=Idea=Brainchild=11Nov=Athena>>I=MT.
Croatian=5,000=50%=P5.00D=Law=Time=Venus=5 May = Aphrodite>>L=N.
Croce Benedetto=3,500=4,000=40%=P4.0D=Govt.=Creatocracy=4April=Hermes=G=A4.
Crochet=8,000=80%=P8.0D=Economy=Currency=8 Aug.=Zeus>>E=v.
Crock=1,500=15%=P1.50D=1.5=Authority=Solar Crown=1 May = Maia.
Crocked=1,000=100%=10.0=1.0=Mind=Sun=1 January=Helios >> M=E4.
Crockery=500=5%=P5.00D=5.0=Law=Time=Venus=5 May=Aphrodite>>L=N.
Crockett David.=3,500=4,000=40%=P4.0D=Govt.=Creatocracy=4April=Hermes=G=A4.
Crocodile=6,000=60%=P6.0D=Man=Earth=Royalty=6 June=Gaia=Maia>>M=M2.
Crocus=4,000=40%=P4.0D=Govt.=Creatocracy=4 April=Hermes=G=A4.
Croesus=5,000=50%=P5.00D=Law=Time=Venus=5 May = Aphrodite>>L=N.
Croissant=2,500=3,000=30%=P3.0D=3.0=Cr=Stars=Muses=3 March= C=I>>GIL.
Cro-Magnon=9,000=90%=P9.00D=9.0=Abst.=Gods=Saturn=9Sept.>>A=Ø.
Cromwell Oliver=4,000=40%=P4.0D=Govt.=Creatocracy=4 April=Hermes=G=A4.
Crone=2,500=3,000=30%=P3.0D=3.0=Cr=Stars=Muses=3 March= C=I>>GIL.
Crony=2,000=20%=P2.00D=2.0=Nature=Moon=2 Feb.=Cupid=N=C+_.
Cronyism=5,000=50%=P5.00D=Law=Time=Venus=5 May = Aphrodite>>L=N.
Crook=7,000=70%=P7.0D=7.0=Language=Assets=Mars=7 July=Pleiades.

Crooked=3,500=4,000=40%=P4.0D=Govt.=Creatocracy=4 April=Hermes=G=A4.
Croon=2,500=3,000=30%=P3.0D=3.0=Cr=Stars=Muses=3 March= C=I>>GIL.
Crop=21,500=22,000=2.2>>4.0=4,000=40%=P4.0D=Govt.=4 April=Hermes=G=A4.
Crop dusting=5,000=50%=P5.00D=Law=Time=Venus=5 May = Aphrodite>>L=N.
Cropper=1,000=100%=10.0=1.0=Mind=Sun=1 January=Helios >> M=E4.
Croquet=6,500=7,000=70%=P7.0D=7.0=Language=Assets=Mars=7 July=Pleiades.
Croquette=5,500=5.5=80%=P5.50=Earth-Midway=5 May = Gaia.
Crosier=3,000=30%=P3.0D=3.0=Cr=Stars=Muses=3 March= C=I>>GIL.
Cross=10,000=1,000=100%=10.0=Physicality=Tech.=10 Oct.=Uranus=P=1Ø.
Crossbar=3,000=30%=P3.0D=3.0=Cr=Stars=Muses=3 March= C=I>>GIL.
Crossbones=4,000=40%=P4.0D=Govt.=Creatocracy=4 April=Hermes=G=A4.
Crossbow=5,000=50%=P5.00D=Law=Time=Venus=5 May = Aphrodite>>L=N.
Crossbreed=2,000=20%=P2.00D=2.0=Nature=Moon=2 Feb.=Cupid=N=C+_.
Cross country=8,500=9,000=90%=P9.00D=9.0=Abst.=Gods=Saturn=9Sept.>>A=Ø.
Cross cultural=3,000=30%=P3.0D=3.0=Cr=Stars=Muses=3 March= C=I>>GIL.
Cross current=3,500=4,000=40%=P4.0D=Govt.=Creatocracy=4 April=Hermes=G=A4.
Crosscut=6,000=60%=P6.0D=Man=Earth=Royalty=6 June=Gaia=Maia>>M=M2.
Cross examine=7,000=70%=P7.0D=7.0=Language=Assets=Mars=7 July=Pleiades.
Cross eye=7,000=70%=P7.0D=7.0=Language=Assets=Mars=7 July=Pleiades.
Crossfire=4,500=5,000=50%=P5.00D=Law=Time=Venus=5 May = Aphrodite>>L=N.
Crosshatch=4,000=40%=P4.0D=Govt.=Creatocracy=4 April=Hermes=G=A4.
Crossing=6,500=7,000=70%=P7.0D=7.0=Language=Assets=Mars=7 July=Pleiades.
Crosspiece=3,000=30%=P3.0D=3.0=Cr=Stars=Muses=3 March= C=I>>GIL.
Cross pollinate=4,000=40%=P4.0D=Govt.=Creatocracy=4 April=Hermes=G=A4.
Cross purpose=7,500=8,000=80%=P8.0D=Economy=Currency=8 Aug.=Zeus>>E=v.
Cross question=1,500=15%=P1.50D=1.5=Authority=Solar Crown=1 May = Maia.
Cross reference=7,500=8,000=80%=P8.0D=Economy=Currency=8 Aug.=Zeus>>E=v.
Crossroad=10,500=11,000=11%=P1.10D=1.1=Idea=Brainchild=11Nov=Athena>>I=MT.
Cross section=15,000=1,500==15%=P1.50D=1.5=Authority=Solar Crown=1 May = Maia.
Crosswalk=3,000=30%=P3.0D=3.0=Cr=Stars=Muses=3 March= C=I>>GIL.
Crosswise=4,500=5,000=50%=P5.00D=Law=Time=Venus=5 May = Aphrodite>>L=N.
Crossword puzzle=7,500=8,000=80%=P8.0D=Economy=Currency=8 Aug.=Zeus>>E=v.
Crotch=6,500=7,000=70%=P7.0D=7.0=Language=Assets=Mars=7 July=Pleiades.
Crotchet=2,500=3,000=30%=P3.0D=3.0=Cr=Stars=Muses=3 March= C=I>>GIL.
Crouch=5,000=50%=P5.00D=Law=Time=Venus=5 May = Aphrodite>>L=N.
Croup=7,500=8,000=80%=P8.0D=Economy=Currency=8 Aug.=Zeus>>E=v.
Croupier=3,000=30%=P3.0D=3.0=Cr=Stars=Muses=3 March= C=I>>GIL.
Crouton=3,000=30%=P3.0D=3.0=Cr=Stars=Muses=3 March= C=I>>GIL.
Crow(1)=8,000=80%=P8.0D=Economy=Currency=8 Aug.=Zeus>>E=v.
Crow(2)=9,500=10,000=1,000=100%=10.0=Physicality=Tech.=10 Oct.=Uranus=P=1Ø.
Crow=9,500=10,000=1,000=100%=Physicality= Tech.=10 Oct.=Uranus=P=1Ø.
Crowbar=7,000=70%=P7.0D=7.0=Language=Assets=Mars=7 July=Pleiades.
Crowd=17,000=17%=P1.70D=1.7=Solar Asset=17 Feb.=Maia=Mind Computing.

Crown=26,000=30,000=3,000=30%=P3.0D=3.0=Cr=Stars=Muses=3 March= C=I>>GIL.
A Crown is measured by the level of creativity developed for human benefit. The real crown
is the one granted by intellectual property rights. The Solar Crown is sovereignty of the
Creatocracy, Peter Matthews-Akukalia exclusively. Castle Makupedia is his God brand.

The Crown and beads of Castle Makupedia worn in the feast of apotheosis, 13-10-2021.
Lagos. Nigeria. The day Peter Matthews-Akukalia became deified as a God.

Crown Prince=3,500=4,000=40%=P4.0D=Govt.=Creatocracy=4 April=Hermes=G=A4.
Crown Princess=5,500=5.5=80%=P5.50=Earth-Midway=5 May = Gaia.
Crow's feet=3,500=4,000=40%=P4.0D=Govt.=Creatocracy=4 April=Hermes=G=A4.
Crow's nest=5,000=50%=P5.00D=Law=Time=Venus=5 May = Aphrodite>>L=N.
Crozier=1,500=15%=P1.50D=1.5=Authority=Solar Crown=1 May = Maia.
CRT=1,500=15%=P1.50D=1.5=Authority=Solar Crown=1 May = Maia.
Cruces=2,000=20%=P2.00D=2.0=Nature=Moon=2 Feb.=Cupid=N=C+_.
Crucial=7,500=8,000=80%=P8.0D=Economy=Currency=8 Aug.=Zeus>>E=v.
Crucible=7,500=8,000=80%=P8.0D=Economy=Currency=8 Aug.=Zeus>>E=v.
Crucifix=3,500=4,000=40%=P4.0D=Govt.=Creatocracy=4 April=Hermes=G=A4.
Crucifixion=5,000=50%=P5.00D=Law=Time=Venus=5 May = Aphrodite>>L=N.
Cruciform=2,000=20%=P2.00D=2.0=Nature=Moon=2 Feb.=Cupid=N=C+_.
Crucify=4,500=5,000=50%=P5.00D=Law=Time=Venus=5 May = Aphrodite>>L=N.
Crude=10,000=1,000=100%=10.0=Physicality=Tech.=10 Oct.=Uranus=P=1Ø.
Cruel=1,500=15%=P1.50D=1.5=Authority=Solar Crown=1 May = Maia.
Cruet=4,000=40%=P4.0D=Govt.=Creatocracy=4 April=Hermes=G=A4.
Cruikshank George=2,000=20%=P2.00D=2.0=Nature=Moon=2 Feb.=Cupid=N=C+_.
Cruise=7,500=8,000=80%=P8.0D=Economy=Currency=8 Aug.=Zeus>>E=v.
Cruise missile=5,000=50%=P5.00D=Law=Time=Venus=5 May = Aphrodite>>L=N.
Cruiser=7,000=70%=P7.0D=7.0=Language=Assets=Mars=7 July=Pleiades.
Cruller=4,000=40%=P4.0D=Govt.=Creatocracy=4 April=Hermes=G=A4.
Crumb=8,500=9,000=90%=P9.00D=9.0=Abst.=Gods=Saturn=9Sept.>>A=Ø.
Crumble=3,000=30%=P3.0D=3.0=Cr=Stars=Muses=3 March= C=I>>GIL.
Crummy=2,000=20%=P2.00D=2.0=Nature=Moon=2 Feb.=Cupid=N=C+_.
Crumpet=4,500=5,000=50%=P5.00D=Law=Time=Venus=5 May = Aphrodite>>L=N.
Crumple=4,500=5,000=50%=P5.00D=Law=Time=Venus=5 May = Aphrodite>>L=N.
Crunch=5,000=50%=P5.00D=Law=Time=Venus=5 May = Aphrodite>>L=N.
Crusade=14,500=15,000=1,500=15%=P1.50D=1.5=Authority=Solar Crown=1 May = Maia.
Crush=20,000=2,000=20%=P2.00D=2.0=Nature=Moon=2 Feb.=Cupid=N=C+_.
Crust=13,500=14,000=14%=P1.40D=1.4=Mgt.=13May=Athena=SC=0.1
Crustacean=10,000=1,000=100%=10.0=Physicality=Tech.=10 Oct.=Uranus=P=1Ø.
Crutch=11,000=11%=P1.10D=1.1=Idea=Brainchild=11Nov=Athena>>I=MT.
Crux=3,500=4,000=40%=P4.0D=Govt.=Creatocracy=4 April=Hermes=G=A4.
Cruzeiro=2,000=20%=P2.00D=2.0=Nature=Moon=2 Feb.=Cupid=N=C+_.
Cry=10,000=1,000=100%=10.0=Physicality=Tech.=10 Oct.=Uranus=P=1Ø.
Crybaby=4,500=5,000=50%=P5.00D=Law=Time=Venus=5 May = Aphrodite>>L=N.

Cryogen=3,500=4,000=40%=P4.0D=Govt.=Creatocracy=4 April=Hermes=G=A4.
Cryogenics=3,000=30%=P3.0D=3.0=Cr=Stars=Muses=3 March= C=I>>GIL.
Crypt=5,000=50%=P5.00D=Law=Time=Venus=5 May = Aphrodite>>L=N.
Cryptic=3,000=30%=P3.0D=3.0=Cr=Stars=Muses=3 March= C=I>>GIL.
Crypto-=1,500=15%=P1.50D=1.5=Authority=Solar Crown=1 May = Maia.
Cryptogram=4,000=40%=P4.0D=Govt.=Creatocracy=4 April=Hermes=G=A4.
Cryptography=5,000=50%=P5.00D=Law=Time=Venus=5 May = Aphrodite>>L=N.
Crystal=19,000=19%=P1.90=1.9=Solar Energy=Planets=Mind of God=Maia
Crystallize=6,500=7,000=70%=P7.0D=7.0=Language=Assets=Mars=7 July=Pleiades.
Crystallography=3,500=4,000=40%=P4.0D=Govt.=Creatocracy=4 April=Hermes=G=A4.
Cs=3,000=30%=P3.0D=3.0=Cr=Stars=Muses=3 March= C=I>>GIL.
C.S.A.=2,000=20%=P2.00D=2.0=Nature=Moon=2 Feb.=Cupid=N=C+_.
csc=1,500=15%=P1.50D=1.5=Authority=Solar Crown=1 May = Maia.
C-section=1,500=15%=P1.50D=1.5=Authority=Solar Crown=1 May = Maia.
CST=1,500=15%=P1.50D=1.5=Authority=Solar Crown=1 May = Maia.
CT=1,500=15%=P1.50D=1.5=Authority=Solar Crown=1 May = Maia.
ct.=1,500=15%=P1.50D=1.5=Authority=Solar Crown=1 May = Maia.
Ct.=1,500=15%=P1.50D=1.5=Authority=Solar Crown=1 May = Maia.
Cu=4,000=40%=P4.0D=Govt.=Creatocracy=4 April=Hermes=G=A4.
cu.=500=5%=P5.00D=5.0=Law=Time=Venus=5 May=Aphrodite>>L=N.
Cub=7,000=70%=P7.0D=7.0=Language=Assets=Mars=7 July=Pleiades.
Cuba=7,000=70%=P7.0D=7.0=Language=Assets=Mars=7 July=Pleiades.
Cuban sandwich=3,000=30%=P3.0D=3.0=Cr=Stars=Muses=3 March= C=I>>GIL.
Cubbyhole=2,500=3,000=30%=P3.0D=3.0=Cr=Stars=Muses=3 March= C=I>>GIL.
Cube=16,000=16%=P1.60D=1.6=Incarnation=Mind of GOD=1 June=Maia.
Cubic=14,500=15,000=1,500=15%=P1.50D=1.5=Authority=Solar Crown=1 May = Maia.
Cubical=3,000=30%=P3.0D=3.0=Cr=Stars=Muses=3 March= C=I>>GIL.
Cubicle=4,000=40%=P4.0D=Govt.=Creatocracy=4 April=Hermes=G=A4.
Cubism=7,000=70%=P7.0D=7.0=Language=Assets=Mars=7 July=Pleiades.
Cubit=7,000=70%=P7.0D=7.0=Language=Assets=Mars=7 July=Pleiades.
Cuckold=5,500=5.5=80%=P5.50=Earth-Midway=5 May = Gaia.
Cuckoo=11,000=11%=P1.10D=1.1=Idea=Brainchild=11Nov=Athena>>I=MT.
Cucumber=7,500=8,000=80%=P8.0D=Economy=Currency=8 Aug.=Zeus>>E=v.
Cúcuta=3,500=4,000=40%=P4.0D=Govt.=Creatocracy=4 April=Hermes=G=A4.
Cud=7,000=70%=P7.0D=7.0=Language=Assets=Mars=7 July=Pleiades.
Cuddle=5,000=50%=P5.00D=Law=Time=Venus=5 May = Aphrodite>>L=N.
Cudgel=2,000=20%=P2.00D=2.0=Nature=Moon=2 Feb.=Cupid=N=C+_.
Cue(1)=8,500=9,000=90%=P9.00D=9.0=Abst.=Gods=Saturn=9Sept.>>A=Ø.
Cue(2)=11,000=11%=P1.10D=1.1=Idea=Brainchild=11Nov=Athena>>I=MT.
Cue ball=5,000=50%=P5.00D=Law=Time=Venus=5 May = Aphrodite>>L=N.
Cuenca=5,000=50%=P5.00D=Law=Time=Venus=5 May = Aphrodite>>L=N.
Cuff(1)=14,500=15,000=1,500=15%=P1.50D=1.5=Authority=Solar Crown=1 May = Maia.
Cuff(2)=4,000=40%=P4.0D=Govt.=Creatocracy=4 April=Hermes=G=A4.
Cuff link=4,000=40%=P4.0D=Govt.=Creatocracy=4 April=Hermes=G=A4.
Cuisine=5,000=50%=P5.00D=Law=Time=Venus=5 May = Aphrodite>>L=N.

Cul-de-sac=3,000=30%=P3.0D=3.0=Cr=Stars=Muses=3 March= C=I>>GIL.
Culiacán=4,500=5,000=50%=P5.00D=Law=Time=Venus=5 May = Aphrodite>>L=N.
Culinary=3,000=30%=P3.0D=3.0=Cr=Stars=Muses=3 March= C=I>>GIL.
Cull=4,000=40%=P4.0D=Govt.=Creatocracy=4 April=Hermes=G=A4.
Cullen Countée=2,000=20%=P2.00D=2.0=Nature=Moon=2 Feb.=Cupid=N=C+_.
Culminate=4,000=40%=P4.0D=Govt.=Creatocracy=4 April=Hermes=G=A4.
Culottes=4,000=40%=P4.0D=Govt.=Creatocracy=4 April=Hermes=G=A4.
Culpable=3,500=4,000=40%=P4.0D=Govt.=Creatocracy=4 April=Hermes=G=A4.
Culprit=4,000=40%=P4.0D=Govt.=Creatocracy=4 April=Hermes=G=A4.
Cult=11,000=11%=P1.10D=1.1=Idea=Brainchild=11Nov=Athena>>I=MT.
Cultivar=3,500=4,000=40%=P4.0D=Govt.=Creatocracy=4 April=Hermes=G=A4.
Cultivate=14,500=15,000=1,500=15%=P1.50D=1.5=Authority=Solar Crown=1 May = Maia.
Culture=10,000=1,000=100%=10.0=Physicality=Tech.=10 Oct.=Uranus=P=1∅.
Culvert=4,000=40%=P4.0D=Govt.=Creatocracy=4 April=Hermes=G=A4.
Cumber=1,500=15%=P1.50D=1.5=Authority=Solar Crown=1 May = Maia.
Cumberland Gap=7,000=70%=P7.0D=7.0=Language=Assets=Mars=7 July=Pleiades.
Cumberland Plateau=6,000=60%=P6.0D=Man=Earth=Roy.=6 June=Gaia=Maia>>M=M2.
Cumbersome=1,500=15%=P1.50D=1.5=Authority=Solar Crown=1 May = Maia.
Cumin=4,500=5,000=50%=P5.00D=Law=Time=Venus=5 May = Aphrodite>>L=N.
Cummerbund=3,500=4,000=40%=P4.0D=Govt.=Creatocracy=4 April=Hermes=G=A4.
Cummings Edward Estlin=3,500=4,000=40%=P4.0D=Govt.=4 April=Hermes=G=A4.
Cumulative=3,000=30%=P3.0D=3.0=Cr=Stars=Muses=3 March= C=I>>GIL.

Cumulonimbus=7,500=8,000=80%=P8.0D=Economy=Currency=8 Aug.=Zeus>>E=v.
Cumulus=7,500=8,000=80%=P8.0D=Economy=Currency=8 Aug.=Zeus>>E=v.
Zeus the Most High rides on both clouds. The Psalms confirms that GOD rides on the
clouds and winds. This is the computational and evidential proof behind Scriptural truth.

Cuneiform=6,000=60%=P6.0D=Man=Earth=Royalty=6 June=Gaia=Maia>>M=M2.
Cunning=6,000=60%=P6.0D=Man=Earth=Royalty=6 June=Gaia=Maia>>M=M2.
Cup=11,500=12,000=12%=P1.20D=1.2=Knowl.=Education=12Dec.=Athena>>K=F.
Cupboard=2,500=3,000=30%=P3.0D=3.0=Cr=Stars=Muses=3 March= C=I>>GIL.
Cupcake=2,000=20%=P2.00D=2.0=Nature=Moon=2 Feb.=Cupid=N=C+_.

Cupid=9,000=90%=P9.00D=9.0=Abst.=Gods=Saturn=9Sept.>>A=∅.
Roman Myth. The God of love. A council of the Gods. Abstraction. Programming.

Cupidity=2,500=3,000=30%=P3.0D=3.0=Cr=Stars=Muses=3 March= C=I>>GIL.
Cupola=3,500=4,000=40%=P4.0D=Govt.=Creatocracy=4 April=Hermes=G=A4.
Cur=2,500=3,000=30%=P3.0D=3.0=Cr=Stars=Muses=3 March= C=I>>GIL.
Curaçao=6,500=7,000=70%=P7.0D=7.0=Language=Assets=Mars=7 July=Pleiades.
Curare=9,500=10,000=1,000=100%=10.0=Physicality=Tech.=10 Oct.=Uranus=P=1∅.
Curate=6,000=60%=P6.0D=Man=Earth=Royalty=6 June=Gaia=Maia>>M=M2.

Curative=2,500=3,000=30%=P3.0D=3.0=Cr=Stars=Muses=3 March= C=I>>GIL.
Curator=5,500=5.5=80%=P5.50=Earth-Midway=5 May = Gaia.
Curb=10,500=11,000=11%=P1.10D=1.1=Idea=Brainchild=11Nov=Athena>>I=MT.
Curb stone=4,500=5,000=50%=P5.00D=Law=Time=Venus=5 May = Aphrodite>>L=N.
Curd=5,000=50%=P5.00D=Law=Time=Venus=5 May = Aphrodite>>L=N.
Curdle=3,500=4,000=40%=P4.0D=Govt.=Creatocracy=4 April=Hermes=G=A4.
Cure=17,000=17%=P1.70D=1.7=Solar Asset=17 Feb.=Maia=Mind Computing.
Cure all=4,000=40%=P4.0D=Govt.=Creatocracy=4 April=Hermes=G=A4.
Curettage=3,000=30%=P3.0D=3.0=Cr=Stars=Muses=3 March= C=I>>GIL.
Curfew=11,000=11%=P1.10D=1.1=Idea=Brainchild=11Nov=Athena>>I=MT.
Curia=5,500=5.5=80%=P5.50=Earth-Midway=5 May = Gaia.
Curie=10,500=11,000=11%=P1.10D=1.1=Idea=Brainchild=11Nov=Athena>>I=MT.
Curie Eve Denise=8,000=80%=P8.0D=Economy=Currency=8 Aug.=Zeus>>E=v.
Curie, Marie.=10,500=11,000=11%=P1.10D=1.1=Idea=Brainchild=11Nov=Athena>>I=MT.
Curio=4,000=40%=P4.0D=Govt.=Creatocracy=4 April=Hermes=G=A4.
Curious=5,000=50%=P5.00D=Law=Time=Venus=5 May = Aphrodite>>L=N.
Curitiba=5,000=50%=P5.00D=Law=Time=Venus=5 May = Aphrodite>>L=N.
Curium=9,500=10,000=1,000=100%=10.0=Physicality=Tech.=10 Oct.=Uranus=P=1Ø.
Curl=9,500=10,000=1,000=100%=10.0=Physicality=Tech.=10 Oct.=Uranus=P=1Ø.
Curlew=5,500=5.5=80%=P5.50=Earth-Midway=5 May = Gaia.
Curlicue=2,500=3,000=30%=P3.0D=3.0=Cr=Stars=Muses=3 March= C=I>>GIL.
Curmudgeon=2,500=3,000=30%=P3.0D=3.0=Cr=Stars=Muses=3 March= C=I>>GIL.
Currant=8,000=80%=P8.0D=Economy=Currency=8 Aug.=Zeus>>E=v.

Currency=12,500=13,000=13%=P1.30D=Solar Core=Faculty=13 January=Athena.

FRONT DESIGN OF MAKS CURRENCY. CODE 10C.

Currency is a borderline of knowledge and creative intelligence. It is a faculty of Athena confirming her words in the Proverbs 8 that she makes one rich beyond gold and silver. The Creatocracy discovered the solar core diamond energy systems and invented the Maks currencies. The apotheosized marriage of Castle Makupedia to Athena ultimately makes him a Currency God by the Solar Crown laws creative intelligence and astrotransmutation. See The Creatocratic Charter by Peter Matthews-Akukalia page 186 - 187.

WORLD CURRENCIES SCORE TABLE.
Measured against the MaksCurrencies Solar Scale.

10/10 = 1.0 = 10.0 = 100% = 1,000p = 10,000ppthIE (IE >> Infinitum Endowment). The use of 10.0=10.0 as legitimate standard establishes currency as a universal technology built on metric not fiat which is speculative wrong and non - existent. (See Legitimate).

UNIT   COUNTRY   SCORE
1.   Afghan >> Afghanistan = 9.5
2.   Agora >> Israel = 3.0
3.   At >> Laos = 6.5
4.   Avo >> Macao = 2.0

---

5.   Baht >> Thailand = 2.0
6.   Baiza >> Oman = 2.0
7.   Balboa >> Panama = 2.0
8.   Ban >> Romania = 2.0
9.   Birr >> Ethiopia = 2.0
10. Bolivar >> Venezuela = 3.5
11. Boliviano >> Bolivia = 3.0
12. Butut >> Gambia = 3.0

13. Cedi >> Ghana = 2.0

14. Cent >> Australia, Bahamas, Barbados, Belize, Brunei, Canada, Cayman Islands, Cyprus, Dominica, Ethiopia, Fiji, Grenada, Guyana, Hong Kong, Jamaica, Kenya, Kiribati, Liberia, Malta, Mauritius, Namibia, Nauru, Netherlands, Netherlands Antilles, New Zealand, Saint Lucia, Saint Vincent and the Grenadines, Seychelles, Sierra Leone, Singapore, Solomon Islands, Somalia, South Africa, Sri Lanka, Suriname, Swaziland, Taiwan, Tanzania, Trinidad and Tobago, Tuvalu, Uganda, United States, Zimbabwe. = 2.0

15. Centavo >> Argentina, Bolivia, Brazil, Cape Verde, Colombia, Dominica Republican, Cuba, Ecuador, El Salvador, Guatemala, Guinea-Bissau, Honduras, Mexico, Nicaragua, Philippines, Portugal, São Tomé and Príncipe. = 2.0

16. Centesimo >> Chile, Italy, Panama, San Marino, Vatican City. = 2.0

17. Centime >> Algeria, Belgium, Benin, Burkina Faso, Burundi, Cameroon, Chad, Comoros, Central African Republic, Congo, Djibouti, France, Gabon, Guinea, Haiti, Ivory Coast, Mali, Liechtenstein, Luxembourg, Madagascar, Monaco, Morocco, Niger, Rwanda, Senegal, Togo, Switzerland, Vanuatu. = 2.0

18. Centimo >> Andorra, Costa Rica, Paraguay, Spain, Venezuela. = 2.0

19. Chetrum >> Bhutan. = 4.0

20. Chon >> North Korea, South Korea. = 3.0

21. Colon >> Costa Rica, El Salvador. = 4.0

22. Córdoba >> Nicaragua = 6.0

23. Cruzeiro >> Brazil = 2.0

24. Dalasi >> Gambia = 2.0
25. Deutsche Mark >> Germany = 3.5

26. Dinar >> Algeria, Bahrain, Iraq, Jordan, Kuwait, Libya, Tunisia, Yemen, Yugoslavia=2.0

27. Dinar >> Iran =2.0

28. Dirham >> Morocco, United Arab Emirates. = 2.0

29. Dirham >> Lybia, Qatar = 2.0

30. Dollar >> Australia, Bahamas, Barbados, Belize, Brunei, Canada, Cayman Islands, Dominica, Fiji, Grenada, Guyana, Hong Kong, Jamaica, Kiribati, Liberia, Nauru, New Zealand
Saint Lucia, Saint Vincent and the Grenadines, Singapore, Solomon Islands, Taiwan, Trinidad and Tobago, Tuvalu, United States, Zimbabwe. = 4.5

31. Drachma >> Greece = 4.0
32. Ekpwele >> Equatorial Guinea. = 4.5
33. Escudo >> Cape Verde Portugal. = 3.5
34. Eyrir >> Iceland = 2.5

35. Fillér >> Hungary =2.5

36. Fils >> Bahrain, Iraq, Jordan, Kuwait, United Arab Emirates, Yemen. = 2.0

37. Forint >> Hungary. =4.0

38. Franc >> Belgium, Benin, Burkina Faso, Burundi, Cameroon. = 2.0

39. Gourde >> Haiti = 4.0
40. Groschen >> Austria = 4.0
41. Grosz >> Poland = 4.5
42. Guilder >>Paraguay = 3.5

43. Halala >> Saudi Arabia = 3.0
44. Haler >> Czechoslovakia = 3.0
45. Hao >> Vietnam = 2.0

46. Inti >> Peru = 3.0
47. Jiao >> China = 5.5
48. Khoun = Mauritania = 4.0

49. Kina >> Papua New Guinea = 5.0
50. Kip >> Laos = 2.5
51. Kobo >> Nigeria = 4.0 >> 40 kobos = N1:00 not 100kobos.

52. Kopeck >> Russia = 3.0
53. Koruna >> Czechoslovakia = 2.5
54. Krona >> Iceland, Sweden = 2.5
55. Krone >> Denmark, Norway = 2.5
56. Kurus >> Turkey = 3.0
57. Kwacha >> Malawi, Zambia = 4.0
58. Kwanza >> Angola = 3.5
59. Kyat >> Burma = 2.5

60. Laree >> Maldives = 3.0
61. Lek >> Albania = 4.0
62. Lempira >> Honduras = 5.0
63. Leone >> Sierra Leone = 3.0
64. Lepton >> Greece = 3.5
65. Leu >> Romania = 4.0
66. Lev >> Bulgaria = 4.5
67. Likuta >> Zaire = 3.5
68. Lilangeni >> Swaziland = 3.5
69. Lira >> Italy, Malta, San Marino, Turkey, Vatican City = 3.5

70. Loti >> Lesotho = 2.5
71. Lwei >>Angola = 3.5

72. Markka >> Finland = 4.0
73. Metical >> Mozambique = 5.5
74. Millime >> Tunisia = 4.5
75. Mongo >> Mongolia = 2.5

76. Naira >> Nigeria = 3.5
77. Ngultrum >> Bhutan = 2.5
78. Ngwee >> Zambia = 4.0

79. Öre >> Denmark, Norway, Sweden = 5.0
80. Ouguiya >> Mauritania = 4.0

81. Pa'anga >> Tonga = 2.5

82. Paisa >> Bangladesh, India, Nepal, Pakistan = 3.0

83. Para >> Yugoslavia = 5.0
84. Pataca >> Macao = 3.5

85. Penni >> Finland = 2.5
86. Penny >> Ireland, United Kingdom. = 10.0 >> P1:00 = £10
87. Peseta >> Andorra, Spain = 4.5
88. Pesewa >> Ghana = 4.5

---

89. Peso >> Argentina, Chile, Colombia, Cuba, Dominican Republic, Guinea Bissau, Mexico, Philippines, Uruguay = 4.0

---

90. Pfennig >> Germany = 10.0

---

91. Pound >> Cyprus, Egypt, Ireland, Lebanon, Sudan, United Kingdom = 10.0

---

92. Pul >> Afghanistan = 3.0
93. Pula >> Botswana = 2.5
94. Pya >> Burma = 2.5

---

95. Qindarka >> Albania = 3.0
96. Quetzal >> Guatemala = 1.10

---

97. Rand >> Namibia, South Africa = 2.5
98. Rial >>Iran = 2.0
99. Riel >> Cambodia = 2.5
100. Ringgit >> Malaysia = 2.0
101. Riyal >> Qatar, Saudi Arabia = 3.0
102. Riyal-omani >> Oman = 4.5
103. Ruble >> Russia = 3.0
104. Rufiyaa >> Maldives = 3.0

---

105. Rupee >> India, Mauritius, Nepal, Pakistan, Seychelles, Sri Lanka = 3.5

---

106. Rupiah >> Indonesia = 3.5
107. Satang >> Thailand = 3.0
108. Schilling >> Australia = 2.5

---

109. Sen >> Cambodia, Indonesia, Japan, Malaysia = 3.0

---

110. Sene >> Western Samoa = 3.5
111. Seniti >> Tonga = 3.0
112. Sente >> Lesotho = 3.0
113. Shekel >> Israel = 10.0

114. Shilling >> Kenya, Somalia, Tanzania, Uganda = 3.0

---

115. Stotinka >> Bulgaria = 2.5
116. Sucre >> Ecuador = 3.0
117. Taka >> Bangladesh = 5.0
118. Tala >>Western Samoa = 3.5
119. Tambala >> Malawi = 3.5
120. Thebe >>Botswana = 2.5
121. Toea >> Papua New Guinea = 4.0
122. Tugrik >>Mongolia = 3.0
123. Vatu >> Vanuatu = 4.0

---

124. Won >> North Korea, South Korea = 3.5

---

125. Yen >> Japan = 4.0
126. Yuan >> China = 3. 0
127. Zaire >> Zaire = 4.5
128. Zioty >> Poland = 4.0
129. Maks >> Paradise Nations, Worldwide = 10/10
    Hence the MaksCurrencies is the only currency that functions on direct solar diamond metrics. It is measured on the one mak = Ten pounds. Expressed as P1=£10.0

The smarter currency solutions provided for economies governments and nations is Maks. Maks currencies founded on solar core properties in the equivalent metric diamond systems applications. It is a solid-abstract durable structured sheet and light energy.

The solar core has a temperature of 800,000°C exactly the computed temperature of the diamond. Maks has a longevity as limitless as the Sun. It is useful for direct and indirect transactions, storage of assets on high values (M2.4), non-fiat denominated, currency exchange on licensing charges and lowest interest rates 1.0-1.9% based on the unit currency synchronized serial codes eg WU6569458(=N=50.00).

Maks is a 0%-inflation currency not driven by the laws of demand and supply nor the "so-called" market forces. This is because it is driven by natural energy metric systems $E=v$ that enables price fixing and regulatory mechanisms on licensing rights as established in the World Digital Dictionary (WDD).

It is computed on natural benchmark values costs and prices for commodities products services abstracts & physicals making it a Makupedia universal standard for measuring all currencies.

Maks currencies has five unique denominations measured on solar energy (Kosemaks=10,000), lunar matter (Kose=1,000), Daily ability ratings(Darmaks=100%) and MindTech (Maks=10/10). Software app integration makes for dynamic prices daily hence everyone is a winner at one time or the other on trading profit margins.

For their symbols Read the Creatocratic Charter by the author.

THE MAKS CURRENCY QUALITY ASSURANCE GUARANTEE.

1. Maks is a series of currencies like the Naira, Dollar and Pounds.
    It is not a payment system like the Crypto currency. It is a smart currency in itself.
2. Has its own self regulatory price mechanism
    as it fixes its own prices on the natural value of things.
3. Sets minimum values for negotiations on every transactions.
4. Establishes a talent and ideas market structure.
5. Emerges a creative economy system.
6. Introduces a Creative Banking Services and Mind Banking.
7. Purchases abstract and physical commodities.
8. Has an M2.4 value for the storage of high value assets local and international.
9. Stores currencies for global exchanges.
10. Ten times the value of the British Pounds.
11. Independent as the Maks and integrative as the Nairamaks [=NM=>>=NP=].
12. Suitable for both tangible and digital transactions.
13. Functions on Quartet Metric algorithms rather than binary thus stabilizes the economy.
14. Diamond Standard Rated rather than the Gold Standard.
15. Patented in Nigeria.
16. Protected in the United States, UK and under Provisions of the Creatocratic Charter.
17. Makes for stronger economy through cheaper costs of commodities relatively.
18. Makes for affordable prices for the lower medium and upper class of society.
19. Higher profit margins on transactions and investments that ensure better living.
20. Suitable for short term trials, medium term assessments and long term applications.
21. Open for adoption by States and Federal Government and the International Community.
22. Maks is expected to become a source of foreign exchange earnings when harnessed.
23. First ever inflation proof currency invented.

WHY SHOULD WE ADOPT THE MAKS?

1. It has the potential to create millions of employment opportunities.
2. The first creative economy currency.
3. A breakthrough of the Faculty of Creative & Psycho - Social Sciences @ Makupedia.

4. The Maks emerges new inventions and institutions that cut across Education, Health, ICT, Finance, Manufacturing, Entertainment, Faith & Religion, Human Resources, Astronomy, Horology, Media, Law, Governance and Asset Management.

WHO INVENTED THE MAKS CURRENCIES?

Maks currencies was invented by Peter Matthews-Akukalia (World's 1st Creative Scientist, Internationally Published Author, Discoverer & Inventor). He invented a Field of Study known as the Creative & Psycho - Social Sciences which can be adopted and taught in higher institutions. A specialized university for training Creative Scientists and Inventors is the vision and mission here. Maks will emerge a future for the first Mind Banking systems.

His abilities in solar computing led to many inventions such as Makupedia the 1st Human Mind Computer, Makumatics, Kaliawood, Makabets, Mindoscope, Mind clocks, Makulators, the Makumeter Gauge for measuring human emotions and potentials. He has over 10,000 concepts, programs and apps in MindTech to his credit. He is the President, MAKUPEDIA©.

WHAT DO WE WANT FROM YOU?

We need your support sponsorship recommendations participation donations and partnerships in the management development and commercialization of the Maks Currencies and endless streams of many other Makupedia Assets local and international.

At Makupedia we invent things that helps individuals organizations governments and nations think succeed and live better. There are many assets in Makupedia you can benefit from through your commitment and investment in the short medium and long term.

Most especially through Conferences, Events, Talk shops, Seminars, Radio & Tv Shows, Symposia, Lectures, Church and Mosque Gatherings, Schools Career Day Talk & Career Assessment, Organizations Training Platforms, Town Hall Meetings, Political & Socio-Economic Development Gatherings Cooperations and Movements on latest trends local and international. IF a currency cannot make you rich what else can? Let us talk about it since we have created it. Then we can work it.

We are open to invitations from individuals and organizations at organized events on our various national challenges to discuss our ideas propositions and practical solutions.

Maks Currencies & the Makupedia Assets is owned and promoted by:
MAKUPEDIA RC.1446213

(An Inventions Company).
Lagos. U.K. USA.
For interests, enquiry and contributions kindly call:
+234 (0) 903 3521 731; Whatsapp No: (0) 816 1928 511; (0) 815 0829 224.
E - mail: matthewsakukaliapeter@yahoo.com
Google: Makupedia. Google: Peter Matthews-Akukalia.

Current=17,000=17%=P1.70D=1.7=Solar Asset=17 Feb.=Maia=Mind Computing.

Curriculum=4,500=5,000=50%=P5.00D=Law=Time=Venus=5 May = Aphrodite>>L=N.
The Creatocratic Charter is the curriculum of the Creative Sciences. Throne of Makupedia.

Curriculum vitae=8,000=80%=P8.0D=Economy=Currency=8 Aug.=Zeus>>E=v.
The Creatocratic Charter is the curriculum vitae of Peter Matthews-Akukalia.

Curry(1)=6,000=60%=P6.0D=Man=Earth=Royalty=6 June=Gaia=Maia>>M=M2.
Curry(2)=8,000=80%=P8.0D=Economy=Currency=8 Aug.=Zeus>>E=v.
Curry comb=4,500=5,000=50%=P5.00D=Law=Time=Venus=5 May = Aphrodite>>L=N.

Curse=15,500=16,000=16%=P1.60D=1.6=Incarnation=Mind of GOD=1 June=Maia.
Maia weighs curses at the borderline source and decides equity justice and fairness.

Cursed=1,000=100%=10.0=1.0=Mind=Sun=1 January=Helios >> M=E4.
Cursive=3,500=4,000=40%=P4.0D=Govt.=Creatocracy=4 April=Hermes=G=A4.
Cursor=10,500=11,000=11%=P1.10D=1.1=Idea=Brainchild=11Nov=Athena>>I=MT.
Cursory=4,000=40%=P4.0D=Govt.=Creatocracy=4 April=Hermes=G=A4.
Curt=2,500=3,000=30%=P3.0D=3.0=Cr=Stars=Muses=3 March= C=I>>GIL.
Curtail=4,000=40%=P4.0D=Govt.=Creatocracy=4 April=Hermes=G=A4.
Curtain=14,500=15,000=1,500=15%=P1.50D=1.5=Authority=Solar Crown=1 May = Maia.
Curtsy=10,500=11,000=11%=P1.10D=1.1=Idea=Brainchild=11Nov=Athena>>I=MT.
Curvaceous=3,000=30%=P3.0D=3.0=Cr=Stars=Muses=3 March= C=I>>GIL.
Curvature=4,000=40%=P4.0D=Govt.=Creatocracy=4 April=Hermes=G=A4.
Curve=14,000=14%=P1.40D=1.4=Mgt.=13May=Athena=SC=0.1
Cushion=13,000=13%=P1.30D=Solar Core=Faculty=13 January=Athena.
Cushitic=7,500=8,000=80%=P8.0D=Economy=Currency=8 Aug.=Zeus>>E=v.
Cushy=3,000=30%=P3.0D=3.0=Cr=Stars=Muses=3 March= C=I>>GIL.
Cusp=5,500=5.5=80%=P5.50=Earth-Midway=5 May = Gaia.
Cuspid=1,500=15%=P1.50D=1.5=Authority=Solar Crown=1 May = Maia.
Cuspidor=1,000=100%=10.0=1.0=Mind=Sun=1 January=Helios >> M=E4.
Cuss=4,000=40%=P4.0D=Govt.=Creatocracy=4 April=Hermes=G=A4.
Custard=5,500=5.5=80%=P5.50=Earth-Midway=5 May = Gaia.
Custer George Armstrong=2,000=20%=P2.00D=2.0=Nature=Moon=2 Feb.=Cupid=N=C+_.

Custodial=3,500=4,000=40%=P4.0D=Govt.=Creatocracy=4 April=Hermes=G=A4.
Custodian=4,500=5,000=50%=P5.00D=Law=Time=Venus=5 May = Aphrodite>>L=N.
Custody=12,500=13,000=13%=P1.30D=Solar Core=Faculty=13 January=Athena.
Custom=18,000=18%=P1.80D=Solar Currency=Maks Currencies=1 Aug.=Maia.
Customary=4,000=40%=P4.0D=Govt.=Creatocracy=4 April=Hermes=G=A4.
Customer=3,000=30%=P3.0D=3.0=Cr=Stars=Muses=3 March= C=I>>GIL.
Custom house=4,000=40%=P4.0D=Govt.=Creatocracy=4 April=Hermes=G=A4.
Customize=3,000=30%=P3.0D=3.0=Cr=Stars=Muses=3 March= C=I>>GIL.
Custom made=3,500=4,000=40%=P4.0D=Govt.=Creatocracy=4 April=Hermes=G=A4.
Customs Union=9,500=10,000=1,000=100%=Physicality= Tech.=10 Oct.=Uranus=P=1Ø.
Cut=10,000=1,000=100%=10.0=Physicality=Tech.=10 Oct.=Uranus=P=1Ø.

Currency Table=49,000=5,000=50%=P5.00D=Law=Time=Venus=5 May =Odite>>L=N.
The standards for measuring all currencies is E=v. This synchronizes all currencies into one global universal currency known as the Maks and binding on all. Against this there is no law. Aphrodite is the administrator Goddess for currencies. Makupedia owns all currencies. Ephesians 1:10 predicts a one world government under GOD which the Creatocracy firmly believes and strives to achieve in all things good and harmonious. A great feat indeed. Currency is a law and the Maks currencies is a superior law because it is based on precision computational creativity natural and supernatural laws and falls in the category of Nature, Law, Time, Economy and Invention. Currency is the law of time. Aphrodite is the currency of Zeus (8.0) and applied by the Spirit of God Athena (1.1) the brainchild of the Most High. Castle Makupedia is therefore the King Maks of the Universe and Mind Currency God.

Cut and dried=3,500=4,000=40%=P4.0D=Govt.=Creatocracy=4 April=Hermes=G=A4.
Cutaneous=2,500=3,000=30%=P3.0D=3.0=Cr=Stars=Muses=3 March= C=I>>GIL.
Cutback=3,500=4,000=40%=P4.0D=Govt.=Creatocracy=4 April=Hermes=G=A4.
Cute=4,500=5,000=50%=P5.00D=Law=Time=Venus=5 May = Aphrodite>>L=N.
Cutesy=2,500=3,000=30%=P3.0D=3.0=Cr=Stars=Muses=3 March= C=I>>GIL.
Cuticle=6,500=7,000=70%=P7.0D=7.0=Language=Assets=Mars=7 July=Pleiades.
Cutlass=6,500=7,000=70%=P7.0D=7.0=Language=Assets=Mars=7 July=Pleiades.
Cutlery=4,500=5,000=50%=P5.00D=Law=Time=Venus=5 May = Aphrodite>>L=N.
Cutlet=7,000=70%=P7.0D=7.0=Language=Assets=Mars=7 July=Pleiades.
Cutoff=7,500=8,000=80%=P8.0D=Economy=Currency=8 Aug.=Zeus>>E=v.
Cutout=5,000=50%=P5.00D=Law=Time=Venus=5 May = Aphrodite>>L=N.
Cut rate=1,500=15%=P1.50D=1.5=Authority=Solar Crown=1 May = Maia.
Cutter=9,500=10,000=1,000=100%=10.0=Physicality=Tech.=10 Oct.=Uranus=P=1Ø.
Cutthroat=4,500=5,000=50%=P5.00D=Law=Time=Venus=5 May = Aphrodite>>L=N.
Cutting=8,000=80%=P8.0D=Economy=Currency=8 Aug.=Zeus>>E=v.
Cuttlebone=7,000=70%=P7.0D=7.0=Language=Assets=Mars=7 July=Pleiades.
Cuttlefish=5,500=5.5=80%=P5.50=Earth-Midway=5 May = Gaia.
Cut up=1,500=15%=P1.50D=1.5=Authority=Solar Crown=1 May = Maia.
Cuvier Georges=2,000=20%=P2.00D=2.0=Nature=Moon=2 Feb.=Cupid=N=C+_.
cwt.=500=5%=P5.00D=5.0=Law=Time=Venus=5 May=Aphrodite>>L=N.

-cy=5,000=50%=P5.00D=Law=Time=Venus=5 May = Aphrodite>>L=N.
Cyan=5,500=5.5=80%=P5.50=Earth-Midway=5 May = Gaia.
Cyanide=8,000=80%=P8.0D=Economy=Currency=8 Aug.=Zeus>>E=v.
Cyano-=2,500=3,000=30%=P3.0D=3.0=Cr=Stars=Muses=3 March= C=I>>GIL.
Cyanogen=5,500=5.5=80%=P5.50=Earth-Midway=5 May = Gaia.
Cyanosis=7,500=8,000=80%=P8.0D=Economy=Currency=8 Aug.=Zeus>>E=v.
Cybernetics=6,000=60%=P6.0D=Man=Earth=Royalty=6 June=Gaia=Maia>>M=M2.
Cyclades=5,000=50%=P5.00D=Law=Time=Venus=5 May = Aphrodite>>L=N.
Cyclamate=5,500=5.5=80%=P5.50=Earth-Midway=5 May = Gaia.
Cyclamen=3,500=4,000=40%=P4.0D=Govt.=Creatocracy=4 April=Hermes=G=A4.
Cyclamic acid=3,500=4,000=40%=P4.0D=Govt.=Creatocracy=4 April=Hermes=G=A4.

Cycle=20,000=2,000=20%=P2.00D=2.0=Nature=Moon=2 Feb.=Cupid=N=C+_.
The cycle of life or reincarnation is a natural process set in motion based on lunar energy.

Cyclist=5,000=50%=P5.00D=Law=Time=Venus=5 May = Aphrodite>>L=N.
Cyclo-=1,500=15%=P1.50D=1.5=Authority=Solar Crown=1 May = Maia.
Cyclometer=9,000=90%=P9.00D=9.0=Abst.=Gods=Saturn=9Sept.>>A=Ø.
Cyclone=10,500=11,000=11%=P1.10D=1.1=Idea=Brainchild=11Nov=Athena>>I=MT.
Cyclops=7,500=8,000=80%=P8.0D=Economy=Currency=8 Aug.=Zeus>>E=v.
Cyclotron=9,500=10,000=1,000=100%=10.0=Physicality=Tech.=10 Oct.=Uranus=P=1Ø.
Cygnet=1,500=15%=P1.50D=1.5=Authority=Solar Crown=1 May = Maia.
Cygnus=3,000=30%=P3.0D=3.0=Cr=Stars=Muses=3 March= C=I>>GIL.
Cylinder=10,000=1,000=100%=10.0=Physicality=Tech.=10 Oct.=Uranus=P=1Ø.
Cymbal=9,500=10,000=1,000=100%=10.0=Physicality=Tech.=10 Oct.=Uranus=P=1Ø.
Cynic=5,000=50%=P5.00D=Law=Time=Venus=5 May = Aphrodite>>L=N.
Cynosure=3,500=4,000=40%=P4.0D=Govt.=Creatocracy=4 April=Hermes=G=A4.
Cypress=7,500=8,000=80%=P8.0D=Economy=Currency=8 Aug.=Zeus>>E=v.
Cyprus=7,000=70%=P7.0D=7.0=Language=Assets=Mars=7 July=Pleiades.
Cyprano de Bergerac=3,000=30%=P3.0D=3.0=Cr=Stars=Muses=3 March= C=I>>GIL.
Cyril=3,500=4,000=40%=P4.0D=Govt.=Creatocracy=4 April=Hermes=G=A4.
Cyrillic=11,000=11%=P1.10D=1.1=Idea=Brainchild=11Nov=Athena>>I=MT.
Cyrus II=8,500=9,000=90%=P9.00D=9.0=Abst.=Gods=Saturn=9Sept.>>A=Ø.
Cyst=6,000=60%=P6.0D=Man=Earth=Royalty=6 June=Gaia=Maia>>M=M2.
Cystic fibrosis=8,500=9,000=90%=P9.00D=9.0=Abst.=Gods=Saturn=9Sept.>>A=Ø.
Cystoscope=6,500=7,000=70%=P7.0D=7.0=Language=Assets=Mars=7 July=Pleiades.
-cyte=1,000=100%=10.0=1.0=Mind=Sun=1 January=Helios >> M=E4.
Cyto-=1,500=15%=P1.50D=1.5=Authority=Solar Crown=1 May = Maia.
Cytology=6,000=60%=P6.0D=Man=Earth=Royalty=6 June=Gaia=Maia>>M=M2.
Cytoplasm=3,000=30%=P3.0D=3.0=Cr=Stars=Muses=3 March= C=I>>GIL.
Cytosine=6,000=60%=P6.0D=Man=Earth=Royalty=6 June=Gaia=Maia>>M=M2.

Czar=11,000=11%=P1.10D=1.1=Idea=Brainchild=11Nov=Athena>>I=MT.

In the book Sword of Honour, Peter Matthews-Akukalia was published as African Shakespeare, the African Czar making him the Sovereign Emperor, Paradise Nations.

Czarina=5,500=5.5=80%=P5.50=Earth-Midway=5 May = Gaia.
Czarism=4,000=40%=P4.0D=Govt.=Creatocracy=4 April=Hermes=G=A4.
Czech=4,500=5,000=50%=P5.00D=Law=Time=Venus=5 May = Aphrodite>>L=N.
Czechoslovakia=7,500=8,000=80%=P8.0D=Economy=Currency=8 Aug.=Zeus>>E=v.
Czech Republic=7,000=70%=P7.0D=7.0=Language=Assets=Mars=7 July=Pleiades.

MAKABET =Dd=

d1=11,000=11%=P1.10D=1.1=Idea=Brainchild=Inv.=11 Nov.=SC=Athena>>I=MT.
The 4th letter of the English alphabet. Computing the psycho-weight.
Resultant*Position on the Maks. 1.1*4.0x=px=5.1+4.4=9.5x=px=31.94 >> 3.1 << 1.3
1.3 >> Creative Intelligence >> Faculty of Creative & Psycho-Social Sciences.
94 = 9.4 = Abstraction = Programming in Power Valence eg speed of thought.
When D is mentioned Faith is established in convertible intelligence, thought processing.

d2=1,000=100%=10.0=1.0=Mind=Sun=1 January=Helios >> M=E4.
D=3,000=30%=P3.0D=3.0=Creativity=Stars=Muses=3 March = C=I>>GIL.
d.=5,000=50%=P5.00D=Law=Time=Venus=5 May = Aphrodite>>L=N.
D.=2,000=20%=P2.00D=2.0=Nature=Matter=Moon=2 Feb.=Cupid=N=C+_
D.A.=3,500=4,000=40%=P4.0D=Government =4 April=Mercury=Hermes=G=A4.
Dab=6,500=7,000=70%=P7.0D=7.0=Language=Assets=Mars=7 July=Pleiades.
Dabble=8,000=80%=P8.0D=Economy=Currency=8 Aug.=Zeus>>E=v.
Dabbler=6,000=60%=P6.0D=Man=Earth=Royalty=6 June=Gaia=Maia>>M=M2.
Dacapo=2,000=20%=P2.00D=2.0=Nature=Matter=Moon=2 Feb.=Cupid=N=C+_
Dacca=5,000=50%=P5.00D=Law=Time=Venus=5 May = Aphrodite>>L=N.
Dace=5,000=50%=P5.00D=Law=Time=Venus=5 May = Aphrodite>>L=N.
Dacha=2,000=20%=P2.00D=2.0=Nature=Matter=Moon=2 Feb.=Cupid=N=C+_
Dachshund=9,500=10,000=1,000=100%=10.0=Physicality=Tech.=10 Oct.=Uranus=P=1Ø.
Dacia=5,000=50%=P5.00D=Law=Time=Venus=5 May = Aphrodite>>L=N.
Dacron=4,000=40%=P4.0D=Government =Creatocracy=4 April=Mercury=Hermes=G=A4.
Dactyl=6,500=7,000=70%=P7.0D=7.0=Language=Assets=Mars=7 July=Pleiades.
Dad=4,000=40%=P4.0D=Government =Creatocracy=4 April=Mercury=Hermes=G=A4.
Dada=9,500=10,000=1,000=100%=10.0=Physicality=Tech.=10 Oct.=Uranus=P=1Ø.
Daddy=1,500=15%=P1.50D=1.5=Authority=Crown=Solar Core=1 May = Maia.
Daddy long legs=5,500=5.5=80%=P5.50=Earth-Midway=5 May = Gaia.
Dado=8,500=9,000=90%=P9.00D=9.0=Abstraction=Gods=Saturn=9Sept.>>A=Ø.
Daffodil=6,500=7,000=70%=P7.0D=7.0=Language=Assets=Mars=7 July=Pleiades.
Daffy=2,000=20%=P2.00D=2.0=Nature=Matter=Moon=2 Feb.=Cupid=N=C+_

Daft=2,000=20%=P2.00D=2.0=Nature=Matter=Moon=2 Feb.=Cupid=N=C+_
Dagger=7,500=8,000=80%=P8.0D=Economy=Currency=8 Aug.=Zeus>>E=v.
Daguerreotype=12,500=13,000=13%=P1.30=Solar Core=Faculty=13 January=Athena.
Dahl=4,000=40%=P4.0D=Government =Creatocracy=4 April=Mercury=Hermes=G=A4.
Dahlia=8,000=80%=P8.0D=Economy=Currency=8 Aug.=Zeus>>E=v.
Daikon=3,000=30%=P3.0D=3.0=Creativity=Stars=Muses=3 March = C=I>>GIL.

Daily=5,000=50%=P5.00D=Law=Time=Venus=5 May = Aphrodite>>L=N.
Conventionally a time frame that occurs every 24hours. Proven and Established.

Daily double=9,000=90%=P9.00D=9.0=Abstraction=Gods=Saturn=9Sept.>>A=Ø.
Dainty=10,500=11,000=11%=P1.10D=1.1=Idea=Brainchild=11 Nov.=SC=Athena>>I=MT.
Daiquiri=5,500=5.5=80%=P5.50=Earth-Midway=5 May = Gaia.
Dairy=7,500=8,000=80%=P8.0D=Economy=Currency=8 Aug.=Zeus>>E=v.
Dairy cattle=4,500=5,000=50%=P5.00D=Law=Time=Venus=5 May = Aphrodite>>L=N.
Dairy farm=3,500=4,000=40%=P4.0D=Government =4 April=Mercury=Hermes=G=A4.
Dairying=4,000=40%=P4.0D=Government =4 April=Mercury=Hermes=G=A4.
Dais=5,000=50%=P5.00D=Law=Time=Venus=5 May = Aphrodite>>L=N.
Daisy=11,000=11%=P1.10D=1.1=Idea=Brainchild=Inv.=11 Nov.=SC=Athena>>I=MT.
Daisy wheel=7,000=70%=P7.0D=7.0=Language=Assets=Mars=7 July=Pleiades.
Dakar=5,000=50%=P5.00D=Law=Time=Venus=5 May = Aphrodite>>L=N.
Dakota=5,500=5.5=80%=P5.50=Earth-Midway=5 May = Gaia.
Dalasi=2,000=20%=P2.00D=2.0=Nature=Matter=Moon=2 Feb.=Cupid=N=C+_

Dale=1,000=100%=10.0=1.0=Mind=Sun=1 January=Helios >> M=E4.
A valley. The Creatocracy play >> Valley of the kings is thus prophetic by the thousand.
10,000 is a mountain of the Lord GOD and 1,000 is a valley of the Gods.
$10,000*1,000=P=10.0*10.0=p=20+100=120x=px=2120>>2021>>2120=P=2.1>>$
$3.0*2.0=p=5+6=11x=px=41>>4.1>>6.1>>1.0>>$ Mind >> Sun >> Energy =
1,000=100=10=1.0. Proved.

Daleth=3,500=4,000=40%=P4.0D=Government =4 April=Mercury=Hermes=G=A4.
Dali Salvador=2,500=3,000=30%=P3.0D=3.0=Creatv=Stars=Muses=3 March = C=I>>GIL.
Dallas=5,000=50%=P5.00D=Law=Time=Venus=5 May = Aphrodite>>L=N.
Dally=5,000=50%=P5.00D=Law=Time=Venus=5 May = Aphrodite>>L=N.
Dalmatia=5,000=50%=P5.00D=Law=Time=Venus=5 May = Aphrodite>>L=N.
Dalmatian=9,000=90%=P9.00D=9.0=Abstraction=Gods=Saturn=9Sept.>>A=Ø.
Dam(1)=8,500=9,000=90%=P9.00D=9.0=Abstraction=Gods=Saturn=9Sept.>>A=Ø.
Dam(2)=3,500=4,000=40%=P4.0D=Government =4 April=Mercury=Hermes=G=A4.

Damage=11,000=11%=P1.10D=1.1=Idea=Brainchild=Inv.=11 Nov.=SC=Athena>>I=MT.
When there is a damage the prayer goes to Athena who directs on what to do in wisdom.

Damascus=4,500=5,000=50%=P5.00D=Law=Time=Venus=5 May = Aphrodite>>L=N.

Damask=7,500=8,000=80%=P8.0D=Economy=Currency=8 Aug.=Zeus>>E=v.

Damask rose=6,500=7,000=70%=P7.0D=7.0=Language=Assets=Mars=7 July=Pleiades.

Dame=6,000=60%=P6.0D=Man=Earth=Royalty=6 June=Gaia=Maia>>M=M2.

Damn=15,500=16,000=16%=P1.60D=1.6=Incarnation=Mind of GOD=1 June=Maia.

Damnable=1,500=15%=P1.50D=1.5=Authority=Crown=Solar Core=1 May = Maia.

Damned=11,500=12,000=12%=P1.20D=1.2=Knowledge=Education=12Dec.=Athena
>>K=F.

Damocles=10,500=11,000=11%=P1.10D=1.1=Idea=Brainchild=11   Nov.=SC=Athena
>>I=MT.

Damp=11,500=12,000=12%=P1.20D=1.2=Knowledge=Education=12Dec.=Athena>>K=F.

Dampen=5,500=5.5=80%=P5.50=Earth-Midway=5 May = Gaia.

Damper=10,500=11,000=11%=P1.10D=1.1=Idea=Brainchild=11 Nov.=SC=Athena>>I=MT.

Damsel=3,000=30%=P3.0D=3.0=Creativity=Stars=Muses=3 March = C=I>>GIL.

Damsel fly=7,500=8,000=80%=P8.0D=Economy=Currency=8 Aug.=Zeus>>E=v.

Damson=4,500=5,000=50%=P5.00D=Law=Time=Venus=5 May = Aphrodite>>L=N.

Dan=6,000=60%=P6.0D=Man=Earth=Royalty=6 June=Gaia=Maia>>M=M2.

Dana Richard Henry=3,000=30%=P3.0D=3.0=Creatv=Stars=Muses=3 March = C=I>>GIL.

Da Nang=6,000=60%=P6.0D=Man=Earth=Royalty=6 June=Gaia=Maia>>M=M2.

Dance=15,000=1,500=15%=P1.50D=1.5=Authority=Crown=Solar Core=1 May = Maia.

D and C=1,500=15%=P1.50D=1.5=Authority=Crown=Solar Core=1 May = Maia.

Dandelion=4,500=5,000=50%=P5.00D=Law=Time=Venus=5 May = Aphrodite>>L=N.

Dander(1)=3,500=4,000=40%=P4.0D=Government =4 April=Mercury=Hermes=G=A4.

Dander(2)=7,000=70%=P7.0D=7.0=Language=Assets=Mars=7 July=Pleiades.

Dandle=7,500=8,000=80%=P8.0D=Economy=Currency=8 Aug.=Zeus>>E=v.

Dandruff=4,500=5,000=50%=P5.00D=Law=Time=Venus=5 May = Aphrodite>>L=N.

Dandy=10,000=1,000=100%=10.0=Physicality=Tech.=10 Oct.=Uranus=P=1Ø.

Dane=3,000=30%=P3.0D=3.0=Creativity=Stars=Muses=3 March = C=I>>GIL.

Danger=5,000=50%=P5.00D=Law=Time=Venus=5 May = Aphrodite>>L=N.

Dangerous=4,500=5,000=50%=P5.00D=Law=Time=Venus=5 May = Aphrodite>>L=N.

Dangle=5,000=50%=P5.00D=Law=Time=Venus=5 May = Aphrodite>>L=N.

Dangling participle=11,500=12,000=12%=P1.20D=1.2=Knowl.=Edu.=12Dec.=Athena
>>K=F.

Daniel=5,500=5.5=80%=P5.50=Earth-Midway=5 May = Gaia.

Danio=7,000=70%=P7.0D=7.0=Language=Assets=Mars=7 July=Pleiades.

Danish=6,500=7,000=70%=P7.0D=7.0=Language=Assets=Mars=7 July=Pleiades.

Danish pastry=4,000=40%=P4.0D=Government =4 April=Mercury=Hermes=G=A4.

Dank=2,000=20%=P2.00D=2.0=Nature=Matter=Moon=2 Feb.=Cupid=N=C+_

Dante Alighieri=2,000=20%=P2.00D=2.0=Nature=Matter=Moon=2 Feb.=Cupid=N=C+_

Danton Georges Jacques=2,500=3,000=30%=P3.0D=3.0=Stars=Muses=3 March=GIL.

Danube=10,500=11,000=11%=P1.10D=1.1=Idea=Brainchild=11 Nov.=SC=Athena>>I=MT.

Danzig=1,000=100%=10.0=1.0=Mind=Sun=1 January=Helios >> M=E4.

Dapper=2,500=3,000=30%=P3.0D=3.0=Creativity=Stars=Muses=3 March = C=I>>GIL.

Dapple=3,500=4,000=40%=P4.0D=Government =4 April=Mercury=Hermes=G=A4.

Dappled=1,000=100%=10.0=1.0=Mind=Sun=1 January=Helios >> M=E4.

DAR=2,500=3,000=30%=P3.0D=3.0=Creativity=Stars=Muses=3 March = C=I>>GIL.
In the Creative & Psycho-Social Sciences DAR is the abbreviation for Daily Ability Rating.
It measures the quantum or quantity of one's potential output capacity per day on the scale
of 100%. It is the also the smallest unit of currency in the Maks Currencies Creatocratic
market module. Hence Kose=10,000>>Kosemaks=1,000>>Dar=100>>Maks=10. One Maks
= 10 British Pounds expressed as P1.00=£10.0. Inventions of Peter Matthews-Akukalia.

Dardanelles=6,000=60%=P6.0D=Man=Earth=Royalty=6 June=Gaia=Maia>>M=M2.
Dare=10,000=1,000=100%=10.0=Physicality=Tech.=10 Oct.=Uranus=P=1Ø.
Dare Virginia=6,000=60%=P6.0D=Man=Earth=Royalty=6 June=Gaia=Maia>>M=M2.
Daredevil=4,500=5,000=50%=P5.00D=Law=Time=Venus=5 May = Aphrodite>>L=N.
Dare say=8,000=80%=P8.0D=Economy=Currency=8 Aug.=Zeus>>E=v.
Dare Salaam=5,500=5.5=80%=P5.50=Earth-Midway=5 May = Gaia.
Daring=5,000=50%=P5.00D=Law=Time=Venus=5 May = Aphrodite>>L=N.
Darius I=6,000=60%=P6.0D=Man=Earth=Royalty=6 June=Gaia=Maia>>M=M2.
Dark=10,000=1,000=100%=10.0=Physicality=Tech.=10 Oct.=Uranus=P=1Ø.

Dark Ages=17,000=17%=P1.70D=1.7=Solar Asset=17/20=17 Feb.=Maia=Mind Computing.
The secret or dark things belong unto the Lord...(Deuteronomy 29:29).
In 2012, the Mind Age was introduced by the publishing of the Oracle: Principles of
Creative Sciences by Peter Matthews-Akukalia emerging as the World's 1st Creative
Scientist. The Creatocracy is believed to have been introduced in 2011 through publishing
Sword of Honour-Days of St. Valentine as subtle means to check world readiness for
a new era. It was positive. Peter Matthews-Akukalia emerged African Shakespeare.
The Creatocracy was finally instituted through the book THE CREATOCRACY and
finally trademarked as The Creatocracy Corporation assets of Castle Makupedia, God of
Creatocracy Genius & Mind.

Darken=6,500=7,000=70%=P7.0D=7.0=Language=Assets=Mars=7 July=Pleiades.
Dark horse=5,000=50%=P5.00D=Law=Time=Venus=5 May = Aphrodite>>L=N.
Darkroom=7,000=70%=P7.0D=7.0=Language=Assets=Mars=7 July=Pleiades.
Darling=6,000=60%=P6.0D=Man=Earth=Royalty=6 June=Gaia=Maia>>M=M2.
Darling River=8,500=9,000=90%=P9.00D=9.0=Abstraction=Gods=Saturn=9Sept.>>A=Ø.
Darn(1)=5,000=50%=P5.00D=Law=Time=Venus=5 May = Aphrodite>>L=N.
Darn(2)=2,000=20%=P2.00D=2.0=Nature=Matter=Moon=2 Feb.=Cupid=N=C+_
Darned=500=5%=P5.00D=5.0=Law=Time=Venus=5 May=Aphrodite>>L=N.
Darning needle=7,000=70%=P7.0D=7.0=Language=Assets=Mars=7 July=Pleiades.
Darrow Clarence Seward=2,000=20%=P2.00D=2.0=Nature=Moon=2 Feb.=Cupid=N=C+_
Dart=15,000=1,500=15%=P1.50D=1.5=Authority=Crown=Solar Core=1 May = Maia.
Darter=4,500=5,000=50%=P5.00D=Law=Time=Venus=5 May = Aphrodite>>L=N.
Darwin Charles Robert=2,000=20%=P2.00D=2.0=Nature=Moon=2 Feb.=Cupid=N=C+_

Darwinism=15,500=16,000=16%=P1.60D=1.6=Cycle=Incarn.=Mind of GOD=1 June = Maia.

DASD=3,000=30%=P3.0D=3.0=Creativity=Stars=Muses=3 March = C=I>>GIL.

Dash=10,000=1,000=100%=10.0=Physicality=Tech.=10 Oct.=Uranus=P=1Ø.

Dashboard=6,000=60%=P6.0D=Man=Earth=Royalty=6 June=Gaia=Maia>>M=M2.

Dashiki=4,000=40%=P4.0D=Government =4 April=Mercury=Hermes=G=A4.

Dashing=5,000=50%=P5.00D=Law=Time=Venus=5 May = Aphrodite>>L=N.

Dastard=2,000=20%=P2.00D=2.0=Nature=Matter=Moon=2 Feb.=Cupid=N=C+_

Dat.=500=5%=P5.00D=5.0=Law=Time=Venus=5 May=Aphrodite>>L=N.

Data=10,000=1,000=100%=10.0=Physicality=Tech.=10 Oct.=Uranus=P=1Ø.

Data is a bundle technology expressed in alphanumerics and measured on quantum energy mechanics bundle of 10,000 bits and its equivalent of Makupedia. Against this is no law.

The World Digital Data Center WDDC.

Services:

1. Satellite Tracking Programming for Tv & Radio.
2. Mind Assessment Tests.
3. Brain Energy Data, Currency Data, Government Guidance Systems on budgets.
4. Sales marketing and Distribution of the World Digital Dictionary.
5. Mind wares (Words Alphanumerics & Energy) Licensing.
6. Mind Apps Licensing & Development.
7. Data Book Translation Versions.
8. Word metrics Management.
9. Research Analysis & Business Data Consulting.
10. General Consulting for Professionals such as Paralegals, Big Data.

Peter Matthews - Akukalia. Founder, Owner, World President.

The Creative Scientist Professionals exclusively trained of the Makupedia work here in different capacities as National Directors, programmers, legal and court assistants in crime determination (Crimeographers), etc. Related areas are the UMC, MindSpace. See Digital.

Databank=5,500=5.5=80%=P5.50=Earth-Midway=5 May = Gaia.

The Creatocracy Corporation™ is chiefly concerned with building, maintaining, and using a database. A key fact is the revelations research and development of the study Faculty of the Creative & Psycho-Social Sciences known as the Creative Sciences of the Makupedia. Our databank constitutes Mind Computing, Psycho-Forensics Analysis & Programming, Mind Assessment Tests, Computational Creativity, Spiralogy and various dynamics.

Database=6,000=60%=P6.0D=Man=Earth=Royalty=6 June=Gaia=Maia>>M=M2.

The Creatocratic Charter is the curriculum database of the Creative Sciences. It is the body of knowledge, fields of study and academic disciplines for De-Royal Makupedia. It is the invention study and academic throne of Castle Makupedia God of Creatocracy Genius and Mind. The World Smart Digital Dictionary is the database management system for all nations. Coded WDSD it is the first database and time laboratory for the value of a thing.

Data carrier=8,000=80%=P8.0D=Economy=Currency=8 Aug.=Zeus>>E=v.
Zeus the Most High GOD is the data carrier. Mind Computing discovers the Mind of GOD.

Data processing=9,000=90%=P9.00D=9.0=Abstraction=Gods=Saturn=9Sept.>>A=Ø.
Gods are data processors studying the process and applying resultants to real life situations. Thus they are predictive and solution making agents in all things. Mind Computing and the special ability to synchronize and crystallize superior data such as the Mind and Mind dimensions have apotheosized Peter Matthews-Akukalia into a deity, a God.

Date(1)=10,000=1,000=100%=10.0=Physicality=Tech.=10 Oct.=Uranus=P=1Ø.
Date(2)=4,000=40%=P4.0D=Government =4 April=Mercury=Hermes=G=A4.
Dated=3,000=30%=P3.0D=3.0=Creativity=Stars=Muses=3 March = C=I>>GIL.
Dateline=6,500=7,000=70%=P7.0D=7.0=Language=Assets=Mars=7 July=Pleiades.
Date palm=8,500=9,000=90%=P9.00D=9.0=Abstraction=Gods=Saturn=9Sept.>>A=Ø.
Dating bar=1,500=15%=P1.50D=1.5=Authority=Crown=Solar Core=1 May = Maia.
Dative=12,500=13,000=13%=P1.30=Solar Core=Faculty=13 January=Athena.
Datum=16,500=17,000=17%=P1.70D=1.7=Solar Asset=17/20=17 Feb.=Maia=MindComptg.
Daub=7,500=8,000=80%=P8.0D=Economy=Currency=8 Aug.=Zeus>>E=v.
Daughter=8,000=80%=P8.0D=Economy=Currency=8 Aug.=Zeus>>E=v.
Daughter-in-law=2,500=3,000=30%=P3.0D=3.0=Creativity=Stars=Muses=3 March = C=I.
Daumier Honoré=2,000=20%=P2.00D=2.0=Nature=Matter=Moon=2 Feb.=Cupid=N=C+_
Daunt=3,500=4,000=40%=P4.0D=Government =4 April=Mercury=Hermes=G=A4.
Dauntless=500=5%=P5.00D=5.0=Law=Time=Venus=5 May=Aphrodite>>L=N.
Dauphin=5,000=50%=P5.00D=Law=Time=Venus=5 May = Aphrodite>>L=N.
Dauphine=2,000=20%=P2.00D=2.0=Nature=Matter=Moon=2 Feb.=Cupid=N=C+_
davenport=3,500=4,000=40%=P4.0D=Government =4 April=Mercury=Hermes=G=A4.
Davenport=5,500=5.5=80%=P5.50=Earth-Midway=5 May = Gaia.
David=5,500=5.5=80%=P5.50=Earth-Midway=5 May = Gaia.
David Jacques Louis=2,000=20%=P2.00D=2.0=Nature=Moon=2 Feb.=Cupid=N=C+_
Davis Jefferson=5,500=5.5=80%=P5.50=Earth-Midway=5 May = Gaia.
Davit=11,500=12,000=12%=P1.20D=1.2=Knowl.=Edu.=12Dec.=Athena>>K=F
Davy Humphrey=2,500=3,000=30%=P3.0D=3.0=Creativity=Stars=Muses=3 March = C=I.
Dawdle=7,000=70%=P7.0D=7.0=Language=Assets=Mars=7 July=Pleiades.
Dawes Charles Gates=7,500=8,000=80%=P8.0D=Economy=8 Aug.=Zeus>>E=v.
Dawn=14,500=15,000=1,500=15%=P1.50D=1.5=Authority=Solar Crown=1 May = Maia.

Day=10,000=1,000=100%=10.0=Physicality=Tech.=10 Oct.=Uranus=P=1Ø.
Peter Matthews - Akukalia developed a daily energy database used to compute the quantity of energy and kind of element released from the Sun daily and yearly.

Say for 08-04-2022. Year 2022>> 2.0*2.2x=px=4.2+4.4=8.6x=px=27.08=30=3.0
The year 2022 is the year of the stars inspiration revelation and creativity.
The value of the day is 4.3. This is used to makulate (calculate or compute the mind) the
energy of the day annually. 4.3*2.2x=px=6.5+9.46=15.96x=px=77.45=80=8.0
The result shows a hot day 8.0Ø>> fit for business relations, economy and currency. It
is proved herein that ZeJeAl >> Zeus - Jehovah - Allah is God of the day. See Job 38:12.
Therefore a day is a technology that must be known by data and applied.

Dayan Moshe=2,500=3,000=30%=P3.0D=3.0=Creativity=Stars=Muses=3 March = C=I.
Day bed=2,500=3,000=30%=P3.0D=3.0=Creativity=Stars=Muses=3 March = C=I>>GIL.
Day book=4,500=5,000=50%=P5.00D=Law=Time=Venus=5 May = Aphrodite>>L=N.
Daybreak=500=5%=P5.00D=5.0=Law=Time=Venus=5 May=Aphrodite>>L=N.
Daycare=5,500=5.5=80%=P5.50=Earth-Midway=5 May = Gaia.
Daydream=5,000=50%=P5.00D=Law=Time=Venus=5 May = Aphrodite>>L=N.
Day-Glo=4,000=40%=P4.0D=Government =4 April=Mercury=Hermes=G=A4.
Day labor=3,500=4,000=40%=P4.0D=Government =4 April=Mercury=Hermes=G=A4.
Daylight=13,000=13%=P1.30=Solar Core=Faculty=13 January=Athena.
Daylight saving time=12,000=12%=P1.20D=1.2=Knowl.=Edu.=12Dec.=Athena>>K=F
Day lily=5,500=5.5=80%=P5.50=Earth-Midway=5 May = Gaia.
Day nursery=2,500=3,000=30%=P3.0D=3.0=Creativity=Stars=Muses=3 March = C=I.

Day of Atonement=1,500=15%=P1.50D=1.5=Authority=Solar Crown=1 May = Maia.
Atonement are made to reconcile GOD and mankind through Hermes (Khristos >> Jesus
Christ) to Maia the Mind of GOD settled by the Pleiades in all things as instructed by
GOD in Job 38:31 "sweet influences of Pleiades", Maia the Great Goddess. See atonement.

Day school=4,000=40%=P4.0D=Government =4 April=Mercury=Hermes=G=A4.
Day student=4,500=5,000=50%=P5.00D=Law=Time=Venus=5 May = Aphrodite>>L=N.
Daytime=3,000=30%=P3.0D=3.0=Creativity=Stars=Muses=3 March = C=I.
Day-to-Day=5,000=50%=P5.00D=Law=Time=Venus=5 May = Aphrodite>>L=N.
Dayton=4,500=5,000=50%=P5.00D=Law=Time=Venus=5 May=Aphrodite>>L=N.
Day-tripper=5,000=50%=P5.00D=Law=Time=Venus=5 May = Aphrodite>>L=N.
Daze=11,000=11%=P1.10D=1.1=Idea=Brainchild=11 Nov.=SC=Athena>>I=MT.
Dazzle=8,500=9,000=90%=P9.00D=9.0=Abstraction=Gods=Saturn=9Sept.>>A=Ø.
dB=1,000=100%=10.0=1.0=Mind=Sun=1 January=Helios >> M=E4.
dc=1,500=15%=P1.50D=1.5=Authority=Solar Crown=1 May = Maia.
DC=1,500=15%=P1.50D=1.5=Authority=Solar Crown=1 May = Maia.
D.C.=3,000=30%=P3.0D=3.0=Creativity=Stars=Muses=3 March = C=I.
DCM=1,500=15%=P1.50D=1.5=Authority=Solar Crown=1 May = Maia.
D.D=3,500=4,000=40%=P4.0D=Government=4 April=Mercury=Hermes=G=A4.
D-day=6,500=7,000=70%=P7.0D=7.0=Language=Assets=Mars=7 July=Pleiades.
D.D.S.=2,500=3,000=30%=P3.0D=3.0=Creativity=Stars=Muses=3 March = C=I.
DDT=8,000=80%=P8.0D=Economy=Currency=Business=8 Aug.=Zeus>>E=v.
DE=1,000=100%=10.0=1.0=Mind=Sun=1 January=Helios >> M=E4.

de-=4,500=5,000=50%=P5.00D=Law=Time=Venus=5 May = Aphrodite>>L=N.
Deacon=9,500=10,000=1,000=100%=Physicality=Tech.=10 Oct.=Uranus=P=1Ø.
Deaconess=4,500=5,000=50%=P5.00D=Law=Time=Venus=5 May = Aphrodite>>L=N.
Deactivate=5,000=50%=P5.00D=Law=Time=Venus=5 May = Aphrodite>>L=N.
Dead=10,000=1,000=100%=Physicality=Tech.=10 Oct.=Uranus=P=1Ø.
Deadbeat=6,000=60%=P6.0D=Man=Earth=Royalty=6 June=Gaia=Maia>>M=M2.
Dead bolt=8,000=80%=P8.0D=Economy=Currency=Business=8 Aug.=Zeus>>E=v.
Deaden=7,500=8,000=80%=P8.0D=Economy=Currency=Business=8 Aug.=Zeus>>E=v.
Dead end=5,500=5.5=80%=P5.50=Earth-Midway=5 May = Gaia.
Dead eye=1,500=15%=P1.50D=1.5=Authority=Solar Crown=1 May = Maia.
Dead hand=3,500=4,000=40%=P4.0D=Government =4 April=Mercury=Hermes=G=A4.
Dead head=10,000=1,000=100%=Physicality=Tech.=10 Oct.=Uranus=P=1Ø.
Dead heat=6,500=7,000=70%=P7.0D=7.0=Language=Assets=Mars=7 July=Pleiades.
Dead letter=2,500=3,000=30%=P3.0D=3.0=Creativity=Stars=Muses=3 March = C=I.
Deadline=4,000=40%=P4.0D=Government =4 April=Mercury=Hermes=G=A4.
Deadlock=8,000=80%=P8.0D=Economy=Currency=Business=8 Aug.=Zeus>>E=v.
Deadly=11,000=11%=P1.10D=1.1=Idea=Brainchild=11 Nov.=SC=Athena>>I=MT.
Deadly nightshade=1,500=15%=P1.50D=1.5=Authority=Solar Crown=1 May = Maia.
Deadly sin=10,500=11,000=11%=P1.10D=1.1=Idea=Brainchild=11 Nov.=SC=Athena>>I=MT.
Dead pan=2,500=3,000=30%=P3.0D=3.0=Creativity=Stars=Muses=3 March = C=I.
Dead reckoning=9,000=90%=P9.00D=9.0=Abstraction=Gods=Saturn=9Sept.>>A=Ø.
Dead Sea=3,500=4,000=40%=P4.0D=Government =4 April=Mercury=Hermes=G=A4.
Dead weight=6,500=7,000=70%=P7.0D=7.0=Language=Assets=Mars=7 July=Pleiades.
Deadwood=3,000=30%=P3.0D=3.0=Creativity=Stars=Muses=3 March = C=I.
Deaf=12,000=12%=P1.20D=1.2=Knowledge=Edu.=12Dec.=Athena>>K=F
Deaf-mute=4,500=5,000=50%=P5.00D=Law=Time=Venus=5 May = Aphrodite>>L=N.
Deal(1)=10,000=1,000=100%=Physicality=Tech.=10 Oct.=Uranus=P=1Ø.
Dead(2)=4,500=5,000=50%=P5.00D=Law=Time=Venus=5 May = Aphrodite>>L=N.
Dealer=4,500=5,000=50%=P5.00D=Law=Time=Venus=5 May = Aphrodite>>L=N.
Dealership=4,500=5,000=50%=P5.00D=Law=Time=Venus=5 May = Aphrodite>>L=N.
Dealing=6,000=60%=P6.0D=Man=Earth=Royalty=6 June=Gaia=Maia>>M=M2.
Dean=8,000=80%=P8.0D=Economy=Currency=Business=8 Aug.=Zeus>>E=v.
Dear=8,500=9,000=90%=P9.00D=9.0=Abstraction=Gods=Saturn=9Sept.>>A=Ø.
Dear John=6,000=60%=P6.0D=Man=Earth=Royalty=6 June=Gaia=Maia>>M=M2.
Dearth=2,000=20%=P2.00D=2.0=Nature=Matter=Moon=2 Feb.=Cupid=N=C+_
Death=10,000=1,000=100%=Physicality=Tech.=10 Oct.=Uranus=P=1Ø.
Deathbed=5,500=5.5=80%=P5.50=Earth-Midway=5 May = Gaia.
Death blow=2,500=3,000=30%=P3.0D=3.0=Creativity=Stars=Muses=3 March = C=I.
Deathless=1,000=100%=10.0=1.0=Mind=Sun=1 January=Helios >> M=E4.
Deathly=4,500=5,000=50%=P5.00D=Law=Time=Venus=5 May = Aphrodite>>L=N.
Death rate=7,500=8,000=80%=P8.0D=Economy=Currency=Business=8 Aug.=Zeus>>E=v.
Death rattle=6,500=7,000=70%=P7.0D=7.0=Language=Assets=Mars=7 July=Pleiades.
Death row=6,500=7,000=70%=P7.0D=7.0=Language=Assets=Mars=7 July=Pleiades.
Death's-head=5,000=50%=P5.00D=Law=Time=Venus=5 May = Aphrodite>>L=N.
Death trap=3,000=30%=P3.0D=3.0=Creativity=Stars=Muses=3 March = C=I.

Death Valley=5,500=5.5=80%=P5.50=Earth-Midway=5 May = Gaia.
Deathwatch=5,500=5.5=80%=P5.50=Earth-Midway=5 May = Gaia.
Deb=1,500=15%=P1.50D=1.5=Authority=Solar Crown=1 May = Maia.
Debacle=3,500=4,000=40%=P4.0D=Government =4 April=Mercury=Hermes=G=A4.
Debar=4,000=40%=P4.0D=Government =4 April=Mercury=Hermes=G=A4.
Debark=1,500=15%=P1.50D=1.5=Authority=Solar Crown=1 May = Maia.
Debase=6,500=7,000=70%=P7.0D=7.0=Language=Assets=Mars=7 July=Pleiades.
Debate=12,500=13,000=13%=P1.30=Solar Core=Faculty=13 January=Athena.
Debaunch=7,000=70%=P7.0D=7.0=Language=Assets=Mars=7 July=Pleiades.
Debenture=6,000=60%=P6.0D=Man=Earth=Royalty=6 June=Gaia=Maia>>M=M2.
Debilitate=3,000=30%=P3.0D=3.0=Creativity=Stars=Muses=3 March = C=I.
Debility=500=5%=P5.00D=5.0=Law=Time=Venus=5 May=Aphrodite>>L=N.
Debit=10,500=11,000=11%=P1.10D=1.1=Idea=Brainchild=11 Nov.=SC=Athena>>I=MT.
Debonair=2,000=20%=P2.00D=2.0=Nature=Matter=Moon=2 Feb.=Cupid=N=C+_
Debrecen=4,000=40%=P4.0D=Government =4 April=Mercury=Hermes=G=A4.
Debris=5,500=5.5=80%=P5.50=Earth-Midway=5 May = Gaia.
Debs Eugene=4,000=40%=P4.0D=Government =4 April=Mercury=Hermes=G=A4.
Debt=6,000=60%=P6.0D=Man=Earth=Royalty=6 June=Gaia=Maia>>M=M2.
Debug=8,000=80%=P8.0D=Economy=Currency=Business=8 Aug.=Zeus>>E=v.
Debunk=5,000=50%=P5.00D=Law=Time=Venus=5 May = Aphrodite>>L=N.
Debussy Claude=2,000=20%=P2.00D=2.0=Nature=Matter=Moon=2 Feb.=Cupid=N=C+_
Debut=8,500=9,000=90%=P9.00D=9.0=Abstraction=Gods=Saturn=9Sept.>>A=Ø.
Debutante=4,000=40%=P4.0D=Government =4 April=Mercury=Hermes=G=A4.
Dec.=1,000=100%=10.0=1.0=Mind=Sun=1 January=Helios >> M=E4.
Deca-=1,000=100%=10.0=1.0=Mind=Sun=1 January=Helios >> M=E4.
Decade=4,000=40%=P4.0D=Government =4 April=Mercury=Hermes=G=A4.
Decadence=4,000=40%=P4.0D=Government =4 April=Mercury=Hermes=G=A4.
Decaf=1,000=100%=10.0=1.0=Mind=Sun=1 January=Helios >> M=E4.
Decaffeinated=2,000=20%=P2.00D=2.0=Nature=Matter=Moon=2 Feb.=Cupid=N=C+_
Decagon=2,500=3,000=30%=P3.0D=3.0=Creativity=Stars=Muses=3 March = C=I.
Decagram=2,000=20%=P2.00D=2.0=Nature=Matter=Moon=2 Feb.=Cupid=N=C+_
Decahedron=2,500=3,000=30%=P3.0D=3.0=Creativity=Stars=Muses=3 March = C=I.
Decal=3,500=4,000=40%=P4.0D=Government =4 April=Mercury=Hermes=G=A4.
De calcify=3,000=30%=P3.0D=3.0=Creativity=Stars=Muses=3 March = C=I.
Decalcomania=8,500=9,000=90%=P9.00D=9.0=Abstraction=Gods=Saturn=9Sept.>>A=Ø
Decaliter=2,000=20%=P2.00D=2.0=Nature=Matter=Moon=2 Feb.=Cupid=N=C+_
Decalogue=3,000=30%=P3.0D=3.0=Creativity=Stars=Muses=3 March = C=I.
Decameter=2,000=20%=P2.00D=2.0=Nature=Matter=Moon=2 Feb.=Cupid=N=C+_
Decamp=3,500=4,000=40%=P4.0D=Government =4 April=Mercury=Hermes=G=A4.
Decant=8,000=80%=P8.0D=Economy=Currency=Business=8 Aug.=Zeus>>E=v.
Decanter=5,000=50%=P5.00D=Law=Time=Venus=5 May = Aphrodite>>L=N.
Decapitate=3,000=30%=P3.0D=3.0=Creativity=Stars=Muses=3 March = C=I.
Decasyllable=3,500=4,000=40%=P4.0D=Government =4April=Mercury=Hermes=G=A4.
Decathlon=6,500=7,000=70%=P7.0D=7.0=Language=Assets=Mars=7 July=Pleiades.
Decatur Stephen=2,500=3,000=30%=P3.0D=3.0=Creativity=Stars=Muses=3 March = C=I.

Decay=13,000=13%=P1.30=Solar Core=Faculty=13 January=Athena.
Decease=4,000=40%=P4.0D=Government =4 April=Mercury=Hermes=G=A4.
Deceased=3,500=4,000=40%=P4.0D=Government =4 April=Mercury=Hermes=G=A4.
Decedent=4,500=5,000=50%=P5.00D=Law=Time=Venus=5 May = Aphrodite>>L=N.
Deceit=2,500=3,000=30%=P3.0D=3.0=Creativity=Stars=Muses=3 March = C=I.
Deceive=4,000=40%=P4.0D=Government =4 April=Mercury=Hermes=G=A4.
Decelerate=2,000=20%=P2.00D=2.0=Nature=Matter=Moon=2 Feb.=Cupid=N=C+_
December=4,500=5,000=50%=P5.00D=Law=Time=Venus=5 May = Aphrodite>>L=N.
Decennial=5,500=5.5=80%=P5.50=Earth-Midway=5 May = Gaia.
Decent=12,000=12%=P1.20D=1.2=Knowl.=Edu.=12Dec.=Athena>>K=F
Decentralize=8,500=9,000=90%=P9.00D=9.0=Abstraction=Gods=Saturn=9Sept.>>A=Ø.
Deception=6,500=7,000=70%=P7.0D=7.0=Language=Assets=Mars=7 July=Pleiades.
Deceptive=2,500=3,000=30%=P3.0D=3.0=Creativity=Stars=Muses=3 March = C=I.
Deci-=3,500=4,000=40%=P4.0D=Government =4 April=Mercury=Hermes=G=A4.
Decibel=15,000=1,500=15%=P1.50D=1.5=Authority=Solar Crown=1 May = Maia.
Decide=8,000=80%=P8.0D=Economy=Currency=Business=8 Aug.=Zeus>>E=v.
Decided=3,000=30%=P3.0D=3.0=Creativity=Stars=Muses=3 March = C=I.
Deciduous=9,000=90%=P9.00D=9.0=Abstraction=Gods=Saturn=9Sept.>>A=Ø.
Decigram=2,000=20%=P2.00D=2.0=Nature=Matter=Moon=2 Feb.=Cupid=N=C+_
Decillion=8,000=80%=P8.0D=Economy=Currency=Business=8 Aug.=Zeus>>E=v.
Decimal=10,000=1,000=100%=Physicality=Tech.=10 Oct.=Uranus=P=1Ø.
Decimal place=12,000=12%=P1.20D=1.2=Knowl.=Edu.=12Dec.=Athena>>K=F
Decimal point=10,000=1,000=100%=Physicality=Tech.=10 Oct.=Uranus=P=1Ø.
Decimate=10,000=1,000=100%=Physicality=Tech.=10 Oct.=Uranus=P=1Ø.
Decimeter=2,000=20%=P2.00D=2.0=Nature=Matter=Moon=2 Feb.=Cupid=N=C+_
Decipher=6,500=7,000=70%=P7.0D=7.0=Language=Assets=Mars=7 July=Pleiades.
Decision=16,000=16%=P1.60D=1.6=Cycle=Incarn.=Mind of GOD=1 June = Maia.
Decisive=7,000=70%=P7.0D=7.0=Language=Assets=Mars=7 July=Pleiades.
Deck(1)=12,500=13,000=13%=P1.30=Solar Core=Faculty=13 January=Athena.
Deck(2)=3,000=30%=P3.0D=3.0=Creativity=Stars=Muses=3 March = C=I.
Deck chair=4,500=5,000=50%=P5.00D=Law=Time=Venus=5 May = Aphrodite>>L=N.
Declaim=5,500=5.5=80%=P5.50=Earth-Midway=5 May = Gaia.
Declare=12,500=13,000=13%=P1.30=Solar Core=Faculty=13 January=Athena.
Declassify=4,000=40%=P4.0D=Government =4 April=Mercury=Hermes=G=A4.
Declension=11,500=12,000=12%=P1.20D=1.2=Knowl.=Edu.=12Dec.=Athena>>K=F
Decline=14,000=14%=P1.40D=1.4=Mgt.=Solar Energy/Electric=13 May=Athena=SC=0.1
Declivity=1,500=15%=P1.50D=1.5=Authority=Solar Crown=1 May = Maia.
Decode=3,500=4,000=40%=P4.0D=Government =4 April=Mercury=Hermes=G=A4.
Décolletage=3,000=30%=P3.0D=3.0=Creativity=Stars=Muses=3 March = C=I.
Dècollentè=2,500=3,000=30%=P3.0D=3.0=Creativity=Stars=Muses=3 March = C=I.
Decolonize=3,500=4,000=40%=P4.0D=Government =4 April=Mercury=Hermes=G=A4.
Decommission=4,000=40%=P4.0D=Government =4 April=Mercury=Hermes=G=A4.
Decompose=4,500=5,000=50%=P5.00D=Law=Time=Venus=5 May = Aphrodite>>L=N.
Decompress=2,000=20%=P2.00D=2.0=Nature=Matter=Moon=2 Feb.=Cupid=N=C+_

Decompression sickness=10,500=11,000=11%=P1.10D=1.1=Idea=Brainchild=11 Nov.Athena

---

Decongest=3,500=4,000=40%=P4.0D=Government =4 April=Mercury=Hermes=G=A4.
Decongestant=5,000=50%=P5.00D=Law=Time=Venus=5 May = Aphrodite>>L=N.
Decontaminate=8,000=80%=P8.0D=Economy=Currency=Business=8 Aug.=Zeus>>E=v.
Decontrol=4,000=40%=P4.0D=Government =4 April=Mercury=Hermes=G=A4.
Decor=5,000=50%=P5.00D=Law=Time=Venus=5 May = Aphrodite>>L=N.
Decorate=6,500=7,000=70%=P7.0D=7.0=Language=Assets=Mars=7 July=Pleiades.
Decorator=3,500=4,000=40%=P4.0D=Government =4 April=Mercury=Hermes=G=A4.
Decorous=2,000=20%=P2.00D=2.0=Nature=Matter=Moon=2 Feb.=Cupid=N=C+_
Decorum=5,500=5.5=80%=P5.50=Earth-Midway=5 May = Gaia.
Decoupage=5,000=50%=P5.00D=Law=Time=Venus=5 May = Aphrodite>>L=N.
Decoy=11,500=12,000=12%=P1.20D=1.2=Knowl.=Edu.=12Dec.=Athena>>K=F
Decrease=5,000=50%=P5.00D=Law=Time=Venus=5 May = Aphrodite>>L=N.
Decree=11,500=12,000=12%=P1.20D=1.2=Knowl.=Edu.=12Dec.=Athena>>K=F
Decrement=5,500=5.5=80%=P5.50=Earth-Midway=5 May = Gaia.
Decrepit=6,000=60%=P6.0D=Man=Earth=Royalty=6 June=Gaia=Maia>>M=M2.
De crescendo=6,000=60%=P6.0D=Man=Earth=Royalty=6 June=Gaia=Maia>>M=M2.
Decriminalize=3,500=4,000=40%=P4.0D=Government =4April=Mercury=Hermes=G=A4.
Decry=1,500=15%=P1.50D=1.5=Authority=Solar Crown=1 May = Maia.
Dedicate=11,500=12,000=12%=P1.20D=1.2=Knowl.=Edu.=12Dec.=Athena>>K=F
Deduce=4,000=40%=P4.0D=Government =4 April=Mercury=Hermes=G=A4.
Deduct=2,500=3,000=30%=P3.0D=3.0=Creativity=Stars=Muses=3 March = C=I.
Deductible=14,500=15,000=1,500=15%=P1.50D=1.5=Author.=Solar Crown=1 May = Maia.
Deduction=12,000=12%=P1.20D=1.2=Knowl.=Edu.=12Dec.=Athena>>K=F
Deed=16,500=17,000=17%=P1.70D=1.7=Solar Asset=17/20=17 Feb.=Maia=MindComptg.
Deem=2,000=20%=P2.00D=2.0=Nature=Matter=Moon=2 Feb.=Cupid=N=C+_
Deep=10,000=1,000=100%=Physicality=Tech.=10 Oct.=Uranus=P=1Ø.
Deepen=3,000=30%=P3.0D=3.0=Creativity=Stars=Muses=3 March = C=I.
Deep-fry=6,000=60%=P6.0D=Man=Earth=Royalty=6 June=Gaia=Maia>>M=M2.
Deep-rooted=2,000=20%=P2.00D=2.0=Nature=Matter=Moon=2 Feb.=Cupid=N=C+_
Deep-sea=4,000=40%=P4.0D=Government =4 April=Mercury=Hermes=G=A4.
Deep-seated=1,500=15%=P1.50D=1.5=Authority=Solar Crown=1 May = Maia.
Deep-set=3,500=4,000=40%=P4.0D=Government =4 April=Mercury=Hermes=G=A4.
Deep space=6,500=7,000=70%=P7.0D=7.0=Language=Assets=Mars=7 July=Pleiades.
Deer=9,500=10,000=1,000=100%=Physicality=Tech.=10 Oct.=Uranus=P=1Ø.
Deer fly=5,500=5.5=80%=P5.50=Earth-Midway=5 May = Gaia.
Deerskin=4,000=40%=P4.0D=Government =4 April=Mercury=Hermes=G=A4.
De-escalate=3,500=4,000=40%=P4.0D=Government =4April=Mercury=Hermes=G=A4.
De-face=4,000=40%=P4.0D=Government =4 April=Mercury=Hermes=G=A4.
De facto=6,000=60%=P6.0D=Man=Earth=Royalty=6 June=Gaia=Maia>>M=M2.
Defalcate=1,000=100%=10.0=1.0=Mind=Sun=1 January=Helios >> M=E4.
Defame=5,500=5.5=80%=P5.50=Earth-Midway=5 May = Gaia.
Default=21,500=12,500=13,000=13%=P1.30=Solar Core=Faculty=13 January=Athena.

Defeat=10,000=1,000=100%=Physicality=Tech.=10 Oct.=Uranus=P=1Ø.
Defeatism=4,000=40%=P4.0D=Government =4 April=Mercury=Hermes=G=A4.
Defecate=3,000=30%=P3.0D=3.0=Creativity=Stars=Muses=3 March = C=I.
Defect=10,000=1,000=100%=10.0=Physicality=Tech.=10 Oct.=Uranus=P=1Ø.
Defective=1,500=15%=P1.50D=1.5=Authority=Solar Crown=1 May = Maia.
Defence=2,500=3,000=30%=P3.0D=3.0=Creativity=Stars=Muses=3 March = C=I.
Defend=9,000=90%=P9.00D=9.0=Abstraction=Gods=Saturn=9Sept.>>A=Ø.
Defendant=4,500=5,000=50%=P5.00D=Law=Time=Venus=5 May = Aphrodite>>L=N.
Defense=10,000=1,000=100%=10.0=Physicality=Tech.=10 Oct.=Uranus=P=1Ø.

Defense mechanism=6,000=60%=P6.0D=Man=Earth=Roy.=6 June= Gaia= Maia >> M=M2.

Defensible=3,000=30%=P3.0D=3.0=Creativity=Stars=Muses=3 March = C=I.
Defensive=11,000=11%=P1.10D=1.1=Idea=Brainchild=11 Nov.=SC=Athena>>I=MT.
Defer(1)=2,000=20%=P2.00D=2.0=Nature=Matter=Moon=2 Feb.=Cupid=N=C+_
Defer(2)=5,000=50%=P5.00D=Law=Time=Venus=5 May = Aphrodite>>L=N.
Deference=7,000=70%=P7.0D=7.0=Language=Assets=Mars=7 July=Pleiades.
Deferment=6,000=60%=P6.0D=Man=Earth=Royalty=6 June=Gaia=Maia>>M=M2.
Deferral=500=5%=P5.00D=5.0=Law=Time=Venus=5 May=Aphrodite>>L=N.
Defiant=6,000=60%=P6.0D=Man=Earth=Royalty=6 June=Gaia=Maia>>M=M2.
Deficiency disease=6,000=60%=P6.0D=Man=Earth=Royalty=6 June=Gaia=Maia>>M=M2.
Deficient=4,000=40%=P4.0D=Government =4 April=Mercury=Hermes=G=A4.
Deficit=7,500=8,000=80%=P8.0D=Economy=Currency=Business=8 Aug.=Zeus>>E=v.
Deficit spending=5,500=5.5=80%=P5.50=Earth-Midway=5 May = Gaia.
Defier=3,500=4,000=40%=P4.0D=Government =4 April=Mercury=Hermes=G=A4.
Defile(1)=8,000=80%=P8.0D=Economy=Currency=Business=8 Aug.=Zeus>>E=v.
Defile(2)=6,000=60%=P6.0D=Man=Earth=Royalty=6 June=Gaia=Maia>>M=M2.
Define=8,500=9,000=90%=P9.00D=9.0=Abstraction=Gods=Saturn=9Sept.>>A=Ø.
Definite=6,000=60%=P6.0D=Man=Earth=Royalty=6 June=Gaia=Maia>>M=M2.
Definite article=6,500=7,000=70%=P7.0D=7.0=Language=Assets=Mars=7 July=Pleiades.
Definition=12,000=12%=P1.20D=1.2=Knowl.=Edu.=12Dec.=Athena>>K=F
Definitive=8,000=80%=P8.0D=Economy=Currency=Business=8 Aug.=Zeus>>E=v.
Deflate=12,000=12%=P1.20D=1.2=Knowl.=Edu.=12Dec.=Athena>>K=F
Deflect=2,500=3,000=30%=P3.0D=3.0=Creativity=Stars=Muses=3 March = C=I.
Defoe Daniel=2,000=20%=P2.00D=2.0=Nature=Matter=Moon=2 Feb.=Cupid=N=C+_
De fog=2,000=20%=P2.00D=2.0=Nature=Matter=Moon=2 Feb.=Cupid=N=C+_
Defoliant=6,500=7,000=70%=P7.0D=7.0=Language=Assets=Mars=7 July=Pleiades.
Defoliate=5,000=50%=P5.00D=Law=Time=Venus=5 May = Aphrodite>>L=N.
Deforest=2,500=3,000=30%=P3.0D=3.0=Creativity=Stars=Muses=3 March = C=I.
Deform=5,500=5.5=80%=P5.50=Earth-Midway=5 May = Gaia.
Deformity=6,500=7,000=70%=P7.0D=7.0=Language=Assets=Mars=7 July=Pleiades.
Defraud=1,000=100%=10.0=1.0=Mind=Sun=1 January=Helios >> M=E4.
Defray=3,000=30%=P3.0D=3.0=Creativity=Stars=Muses=3 March = C=I.
Defrock=1,000=100%=10.0=1.0=Mind=Sun=1 January=Helios >> M=E4.

Defrost=5,000=50%=P5.00D=Law=Time=Venus=5 May = Aphrodite>>L=N.
Deft=2,500=3,000=30%=P3.0D=3.0=Creativity=Stars=Muses=3 March = C=I.
Defunct=3,500=4,000=40%=P4.0D=Government =4 April=Mercury=Hermes=G=A4.
Defuse=6,000=60%=P6.0D=Man=Earth=Royalty=6 June=Gaia=Maia>>M=M2.
Defy=10,000=1,000=100%=10.0=Physicality=Tech.=10 Oct.=Uranus=P=1Ø.
Deg=1,000=100%=10.0=1.0=Mind=Sun=1 January=Helios >> M=E4.
Degas (Hillaire Germain)=3,000=30%=P3.0D=3.0=Creativity=Stars=Muses=3 March = C=I.
de Gaulle Charles=3,000=30%=P3.0D=3.0=Creativity=Stars=Muses=3 March = C=I.
Degauss=6,500=7,000=70%=P7.0D=7.0=Language=Assets=Mars=7 July=Pleiades.
Degenerate=11,500=12,000=12%=P1.20D=1.2=Knowl.=Edu.=12Dec.=Athena>>K=F
Degradable=3,500=4,000=40%=P4.0D=Government =4 April=Mercury=Hermes=G=A4.
Degrade=8,000=80%=P8.0D=Economy=Currency=Business=8 Aug.=Zeus>>E=v.
Degree=10,000=1,000=100%=10.0=Physicality=Tech.=10 Oct.=Uranus=P=1Ø.
Degree-day=17,000=17%=P1.70D=1.7=Solar Asset=17/20=17 Feb.=Maia=MindComptg.
Dehisce=11,500=12,000=12%=P1.20D=1.2=Knowl.=Edu.=12Dec.=Athena>>K=F
Dehumanize=7,000=70%=P7.0D=7.0=Language=Assets=Mars=7 July=Pleiades.
Dehumidify=2,500=3,000=30%=P3.0D=3.0=Creativity=Stars=Muses=3 March = C=I.
Dehydrate=4,500=5,000=50%=P5.00D=Law=Time=Venus=5 May = Aphrodite>>L=N.
De Hydrogenate=2,500=3,000=30%=P3.0D=3.0=Creativity=Stars=Muses=3 March = C=I.
De ice=3,500=4,000=40%=P4.0D=Government =4 April=Mercury=Hermes=G=A4.
Deify=3,500=4,000=40%=P4.0D=Government =4 April=Mercury=Hermes=G=A4.
Deign=5,000=50%=P5.00D=Law=Time=Venus=5 May = Aphrodite>>L=N.
De institutionalize=11,500=12,000=12%=P1.20D=1.2=Knowl.=Edu.=12Dec.=Athena>>K=F
Deism=9,000=90%=P9.00D=9.0=Abstraction=Gods=Saturn=9Sept.>>A=Ø.
Deity=3,500=4,000=40%=P4.0D=Government =4 April=Mercury=Hermes=G=A4.
Déjavu=4,500=5,000=50%=P5.00D=Law=Time=Venus=5 May = Aphrodite>>L=N.
Deject=3,000=30%=P3.0D=3.0=Creativity=Stars=Muses=3 March = C=I.
Dejected=4,500=5,000=50%=P5.00D=Law=Time=Venus=5 May = Aphrodite>>L=N.
Dejure=2,500=3,000=30%=P3.0D=3.0=Creativity=Stars=Muses=3 March = C=I.
Dek-=1,500=15%=P1.50D=1.5=Authority=Solar Crown=1 May = Maia.
Del.=1,000=100%=10.0=1.0=Mind=Sun=1 January=Helios >> M=E4.
Delacroix Ferdinand=2,500=3,000=30%=P3.0D=3.0=Creatv=Stars=Muses=3 March = C=I.
De la Mare Walter=2,000=20%=P2.00D=2.0=Nature=Matter=Moon=2 Feb.=Cupid=N=C+_
Delaware(1)=12,000=12%=P1.20D=1.2=Knowl.=Edu.=12Dec.=Athena>>K=F
Delaware(2)=6,500=7,000=70%=P7.0D=7.0=Language=Assets=Mars=7 July=Pleiades.
Delaware River=10,000=1,000=100%=10.0=Physicality=Tech.=10 Oct.=Uranus=P=1Ø.
De La Warr=5,000=50%=P5.00D=Law=Time=Venus=5 May = Aphrodite>>L=N.
Delay=11,000=11%=P1.10D=1.1=Idea=Brainchild=11 Nov.=SC=Athena>>I=MT.
Delectable=4,500=5,000=50%=P5.00D=Law=Time=Venus=5 May = Aphrodite>>L=N.
Delectation=1,000=100%=10.0=1.0=Mind=Sun=1 January=Helios >> M=E4.
Delegate=11,500=12,000=12%=P1.20D=1.2=Knowl.=Edu.=12Dec.=Athena>>K=F
Delegation=3,500=4,000=40%=P4.0D=Government =4 April=Mercury=Hermes=G=A4.
Delete=3,500=4,000=40%=P4.0D=Government =4 April=Mercury=Hermes=G=A4.
Deleterious=1,000=100%=10.0=1.0=Mind=Sun=1 January=Helios >> M=E4.
Deift=5,000=50%=P5.00D=Law=Time=Venus=5 May = Aphrodite>>L=N.

Delhi=6,000=60%=P6.0D=Man=Earth=Royalty=6 June=Gaia=Maia>>M=M2.
Dell=1,500=15%=P1.50D=1.5=Authority=Solar Crown=1 May = Maia.
Deliberate=11,500=12,000=12%=P1.20D=1.2=Knowl.=Edu.=12Dec.=Athena>>K=F
Deliberation=5,500=5.5=80%=P5.50=Earth-Midway=5 May = Gaia.
Delicacy=6,000=60%=P6.0D=Man=Earth=Royalty=6 June=Gaia=Maia>>M=M2.
Delicate=17,500=18,000=18%=P1.80D=Solar Currency=Maks Currencies=1 Aug.=Maia.
Delicatessen=4,500=5,000=50%=P5.00D=Law=Time=Venus=5 May = Aphrodite>>L=N.
Delicious=4,500=5,000=50%=P5.00D=Law=Time=Venus=5 May = Aphrodite>>L=N.
Delight=9,500=10,000=1,000=100%=10.0=Physicality=Tech.=10 Oct.=Uranus=P=1Ø.
Delightful=1,000=100%=10.0=1.0=Mind=Sun=1 January=Helios >> M=E4.
Delilah=9,000=90%=P9.00D=9.0=Abstraction=Gods=Saturn=9Sept.>>A=Ø.
Delimit=4,500=5,000=50%=P5.00D=Law=Time=Venus=5 May = Aphrodite>>L=N.
Delimiter=6,500=7,000=70%=P7.0D=7.0=Language=Assets=Mars=7 July=Pleiades.
Delineate=6,500=7,000=70%=P7.0D=7.0=Language=Assets=Mars=7 July=Pleiades.
Delinquent=11,500=12,000=12%=P1.20D=1.2=Knowl.=Edu.=12Dec.=Athena>>K=F
Deliquesce=5,500=5.5=80%=P5.50=Earth-Midway=5 May = Gaia.
Delirium=13,000=13%=P1.30=Solar Core=Faculty=13 January=Athena.
Delirium tremens=5,000=50%=P5.00D=Law=Time=Venus=5 May = Aphrodite>>L=N.
Delius Frederick=2,000=20%=P2.00D=2.0=Nature=Matter=Moon=2 Feb.=Cupid=N=C+_
Deliver=14,500=15,000=1,500=15%=P1.50D=1.5=Authority=Solar Crown=1 May = Maia.
Delivery=7,500=8,000=80%=P8.0D=Economy=Currency=Business=8 Aug.=Zeus>>E=v.
Delivery system=8,000=80%=P8.0D=Economy=Currency=Business=8 Aug.=Zeus>>E=v.
Dell=2,000=20%=P2.00D=2.0=Nature=Matter=Moon=2 Feb.=Cupid=N=C+_
Delmonico steak=10,500=11,000=11%=P1.10D=1.1=Idea=Brainchild=11Nov.Athena
    >>I=MT.
Delos=4.500=5,000=50%=P5.00D=Law=Time=Venus=5 May = Aphrodite>>L=N.
Delphi=4,500=5,000=50%=P5.00D=Law=Time=Venus=5 May = Aphrodite>>L=N.
Delphinium=5,000=50%=P5.00D=Law=Time=Venus=5 May = Aphrodite>>L=N.
Delta=8,000=80%=P8.0D=Economy=Currency=Business=8 Aug.=Zeus>>E=v.
Deltoid=7,500=8,000=80%=P8.0D=Economy=Currency=Business=8 Aug.=Zeus>>E=v.
Delude=3,500=4,000=40%=P4.0D=Government =4 April=Mercury=Hermes=G=A4.
Deluge=8,000=80%=P8.0D=Economy=Currency=Business=8 Aug.=Zeus>>E=v.
Delusion=6,000=60%=P6.0D=Man=Earth=Royalty=6 June=Gaia=Maia>>M=M2.
De luxe=4,000=40%=P4.0D=Government =4 April=Mercury=Hermes=G=A4.
Delve=2,500=3,000=30%=P3.0D=3.0=Creativity=Stars=Muses=3 March = C=I.
dem.=1,000=100%=10.0=1.0=Mind=Sun=1 January=Helios >> M=E4.

Dem.=1,000=100%=10.0=1.0=Mind=Sun=1 January=Helios >> M=E4.
Democrat. Democratic. Creat.>>Creatocrat. Creatocratic.

Demagnetize=2,500=3,000=30%=P3.0D=3.0=Creativity=Stars=Muses=3 March = C=I.
Demagogue=7,000=70%=P7.0D=7.0=Language=Assets=Mars=7 July=Pleiades.
Demand=10,000=1,000=100%=10.0=Physicality=Tech.=10 Oct.=Uranus=P=1Ø.
Demanding=2,000=20%=P2.00D=2.0=Nature=Matter=Moon=2 Feb.=Cupid=N=C+_

Demarcate=3,000=30%=P3.0D=3.0=Creativity=Stars=Muses=3 March = C=I.
Demarcation=5,500=5.5=80%=P5.50=Earth-Midway=5 May = Gaia.
Demean(1)=3,500=4,000=40%=P4.0D=Government =4 April=Mercury=Hermes=G=A4.
Demean(2)=3,500=4,000=40%=P4.0D=Government =4 April=Mercury=Hermes=G=A4.
Demeanor=2,500=3,000=30%=P3.0D=3.0=Creativity=Stars=Muses=3 March = C=I.
Demented=1,500=15%=P1.50D=1.5=Authority=Solar Crown=1 May = Maia.
Dementia=5,500=5.5=80%=P5.50=Earth-Midway=5 May = Gaia.
Demerit=5,500=5.5=80%=P5.50=Earth-Midway=5 May = Gaia.
Demerol=4,000=40%=P4.0D=Government =4 April=Mercury=Hermes=G=A4.
Demesne=6,000=60%=P6.0D=Man=Earth=Royalty=6 June=Gaia=Maia>>M=M2.

Demeter=3,000=30%=P3.0D=3.0=Creativity=Stars=Muses=3 March = C=I.
Greek myth. Goddess of the harvest. Demeter is a muse of resultants in the Creatocracy.

Demigod=9,000=90%=P9.00D=9.0=Abstraction=Gods=Saturn=9Sept.>>A=Ø.
Myth. A male being, the offspring of a deity and a mortal. A minor God. On the rights of the Godship of Peter Matthews-Akukalia as Castle Makupedia, Prince Victor Matthews-Akukalia is recognized as the Demi-God of the Creatocracy. Other sons are Princes.

Demijohn=3,500=4,000=40%=P4.0D=Government =4 April=Mercury=Hermes=G=A4.
Demilitarize=3,500=4,000=40%=P4.0D=Government =4 April=Mercury=Hermes=G=A4.
De Mille Agnes=2,000=20%=P2.00D=2.0=Nature=Matter=Moon=2 Feb.=Cupid=N=C+_
De Mille Cecil=2,000=20%=P2.00D=2.0=Nature=Matter=Moon=2 Feb.=Cupid=N=C+_
Demimondaine=3,000=30%=P3.0D=3.0=Creativity=Stars=Muses=3 March = C=I.
Demimonde=8,500=9,000=90%=P9.00D=9.0=Abstraction=Gods=Saturn=9Sept.>>A=Ø.
Demineralize=4,500=5,000=50%=P5.00D=Law=Time=Venus=5 May = Aphrodite>>L=N.
Demise=2,000=20%=P2.00D=2.0=Nature=Matter=Moon=2 Feb.=Cupid=N=C+_
Demitasse=3,000=30%=P3.0D=3.0=Creativity=Stars=Muses=3 March = C=I.
Demo=6,500=7,000=70%=P7.0D=7.0=Language=Assets=Mars=7 July=Pleiades.
Demobilize=3,500=4,000=40%=P4.0D=Government =4 April=Mercury=Hermes=G=A4.

I. Democracy=16,500=17,000=17%=P1.70D=1.7=Solar Asset=17 Feb.=Maia=MindComptg.
Government by the people, exercised either directly or through elected representatives. Creatocracy is government of creativity for the people and by the people based on the works and Inventions of Peter Matthews-Akukalia God of Creatocracy Genius and Mind. Democracy weighs 17% in nature scale of governance. Creatocracy weighs 100%.

II. Creatocracy - Democracy = 100 - 17 = 83>>8.3>>Business of Creativity = Creatocracy. Democracy may grant assets but problematic because it lacks the business of creativity and Mind Computing which can only be found in the Creative Sciences of the Creatocracy. The resultant above proves that democracy is a borderline, a means to an end and not an end in itself. A creative democracy or Creato-democracy becomes a Creatocracy.

III. Democracy is a karst for the paradigm shift to the Creatocracy and God civilization. It is speculative because it is a borderline between the incarnation of Maia through Plato in a human transition to the solar core asset the place of Athena Goddess of wisdom.

IV. Hence democracy searches a place through speculations rather than precision making it doubtful, error-prone, and untruthful because it has no economy of its own. So Plato was an incarnate of Maia Great Goddess of the universe just as Jesus was an incarnate of Hermes. This is evidential in the first war between Maia and Zeus the Most High.

V. Creatocracy runs on the economy system of creatocism with equal opportunities for all. Democracy is Maia testing political governance independently thus creating room for private research aimed at speedy discovery with an incentive on ownership. In the first place democracy is a political system that lacks its own economy structure. This is because it contradicts itself by negating the very principles of fairness justice and equity when it wholesomely embraces capitalism which is the rich getting richer and the poor getting poorer. The balance between both is creativity which gives an equal opportunity for everyone to discover develop and connect the innate potentials and make wealth available for its players and participants. The rich get richer and the poor get rich through an inventor - investor relationship in a global market upgrade creatopolitical or Creatocratic system. Creatocracy is therefore all encompassing and a complete package of sustainable methods established through the appropriate Maks currencies in precision and truth. Creatocracy is the best form of world government that can be practiced down to the family.

VI. The resultant difference (-8.3) shows technically that democracy lacks a currency code with no democratic economy system that will realize its perceived aspirations of equity for all. It is at most 17% philosophically effective and lacks merit on the grounds of speculation. Makumaticology proves it is 10% in political governance weight systems being a trial - error.

Democrat=5,500=5.5=80%=P5.50=Earth-Midway=5 May = Gaia.
A Creatocrat is an advocate of Creatocracy. A member of the Creatocracy Corporation.

Democratic=9,500=10,000=1,000=100%=10.0=Physicality=Tech.=10 Oct.=Uranus=P=1Ø.
Creatocratic>>Of or characterized by or advocating creatocracy. Believing in or practicing equal rights to the expression of one's creativity through discovery development and connect principles of the Makupedia. A sovereignty built on the technology of the Mind.

Democratic Party=4,000=40%=P4.0D=Government =4 April=Mercury=Hermes=G=A4.
Democratize=1,500=15%=P1.50D=1.5=Authority=Solar Crown=1 May = Maia.
Democritus=3,000=30%=P3.0D=3.0=Creativity=Stars=Muses=3 March = C=I.
Demodulate=4,000=40%=P4.0D=Government =4 April=Mercury=Hermes=G=A4.
Demographics=5,500=5.5=80%=P5.50=Earth-Midway=5 May = Gaia.

Demography=3,000=30%=P3.0D=3.0=Creativity=Stars=Muses=3 March = C=I.
Demolish=2,500=3,000=30%=P3.0D=3.0=Creativity=Stars=Muses=3 March = C=I.
Demolition=4,500=5,000=50%=P5.00D=Law=Time=Venus=5 May = Aphrodite>>L=N.

Demon=11,000=11%=P1.10D=1.1=Idea=Brainchild=11 Nov.=SC=Athena>>I=MT.
An evil supernatural being; devil. Demons just as witches are fallen subjects of Athena. Only the Goddess of Wisdom Handicrafts Mind and Warfare do they fear despite being evil. Demons are inventions of Athena and are subject to the laws of inventions and mental wars.

Demonetize=3,000=30%=P3.0D=3.0=Creativity=Stars=Muses=3 March = C=I.
Demoniac=4,500=5,000=50%=P5.00D=Law=Time=Venus=5 May = Aphrodite>>L=N.
Demonize=6,000=60%=P6.0D=Man=Earth=Royalty=6 June=Gaia=Maia>>M=M2.
Demonology=2,000=20%=P2.00D=2.0=Nature=Matter=Moon=2 Feb.=Cupid=N=C+_
Demonstrable=3,000=30%=P3.0D=3.0=Creativity=Stars=Muses=3 March = C=I.

Demonstrate=13,500=14,000=14%=P1.40D=1.4=Mgt.=Solar=13 May=Athena=SC=0.1

Demonstrative=13,000=13%=P1.30=Solar Core=Faculty=13 January=Athena.
Demoralize=4,500=5,000=50%=P5.00D=Law=Time=Venus=5 May = Aphrodite>>L=N.
Demosthenes=2,500=3,000=30%=P3.0D=3.0=Creativity=Stars=Muses=3 March = C=I.
Demote=8,000=80%=P8.0D=Economy=Currency=Business=8 Aug.=Zeus>>E=v.
Demotic=13,000=13%=P1.30=Solar Core=Faculty=13 January=Athena.
Demulcent=6,000=60%=P6.0D=Man=Earth=Royalty=6 June=Gaia=Maia>>M=M2.
Demur=2,000=20%=P2.00D=2.0=Nature=Matter=Moon=2 Feb.=Cupid=N=C+_
Demure=4,000=40%=P4.0D=Government =4 April=Mercury=Hermes=G=A4.

Demystify=2,500=3,000=30%=P3.0D=3.0=Creativity=Stars=Muses=3 March = C=I.
To Demystify means uncovering the secrets of a thing and making open its creativity. A key quality of the Creatocracy and its Creative Scientist Professionals of the Makupedia.

De mythologize=2,500=3,000=30%=P3.0D=3.0=Creativity=Stars=Muses=3 March = C=I.
Den=13,000=13%=P1.30=Solar Core=Faculty=13 January=Athena.
Den.=1,000=100%=10.0=1.0=Mind=Sun=1 January=Helios >> M=E4.
Denali=1,500=15%=P1.50D=1.5=Authority=Solar Crown=1 May = Maia.
Denature=5,000=50%=P5.00D=Law=Time=Venus=5 May = Aphrodite>>L=N.
Dendrite=6,000=60%=P6.0D=Man=Earth=Royalty=6 June=Gaia=Maia>>M=M2.
Dendro-=1,500=15%=P1.50D=1.5=Authority=Solar Crown=1 May = Maia.
Dengue=4,000=40%=P4.0D=Government =4 April=Mercury=Hermes=G=A4.
Deng Xiaoping=2,000=20%=P2.00D=2.0=Nature=Matter=Moon=2 Feb.=Cupid=N=C+_
Deniable=6,500=7,000=70%=P7.0D=7.0=Language=Assets=Mars=7 July=Pleiades.
Denial=7,000=70%=P7.0D=7.0=Language=Assets=Mars=7 July=Pleiades.

Denier=5,000=50%=P5.00D=Law=Time=Venus=5 May = Aphrodite>>L=N.
Denigrate=3,000=30%=P3.0D=3.0=Creativity=Stars=Muses=3 March = C=I.
Denim=8,500=9,000=90%=P9.00D=9.0=Abstraction=Gods=Saturn=9Sept.>>A=Ø.
Denizen=1,500=15%=P1.50D=1.5=Authority=Solar Crown=1 May = Maia.
Denmark=7,000=70%=P7.0D=7.0=Language=Assets=Mars=7 July=Pleiades.
Denomination=12,000=12%=P1.20D=1.2=Knowl.=Edu.=12Dec.=Athena>>K=F
Denominator=12,000=12%=P1.20D=1.2=Knowl.=Edu.=12Dec.=Athena>>K=F
Denote=18,000=18%=P1.80D=Solar Currency=Maks Currencies=1 Aug.=Maia.
Denouement=5,500=5.5=80%=P5.50D=Earth-Midway=5 May = Gaia.
Denounce=5,000=50%=P5.00D=Law=Time=Venus=5 May = Aphrodite>>L=N.
Dense=4,000=40%=P4.0D=Government =4 April=Mercury=Hermes=G=A4.
Density=12,500=13,000=13%=P1.30=Solar Core=Faculty=13 January=Athena.
Dent=8,000=80%=P8.0D=Economy=Currency=Business=8 Aug.=Zeus>>E=v.
Dental=10,000=1,000=100%=10.0=Physicality=Tech.=10 Oct.=Uranus=P=1Ø.
Dental floss=4,000=40%=P4.0D=Government =4 April=Mercury=Hermes=G=A4.
Dental hygienist=2,500=3,000=30%=P3.0D=3.0=Creativity=Stars=Muses=3 March = C=I.
Denti-=1,000=100%=10.0=1.0=Mind=Sun=1 January=Helios >> M=E4.
Dentifrice=4,500=5,000=50%=P5.00D=Law=Time=Venus=5 May = Aphrodite>>L=N.
Dentin=4,500=5,000=50%=P5.00D=Law=Time=Venus=5 May = Aphrodite>>L=N.
Dentist=7,500=8,000=80%=P8.0D=Economy=Currency=Business=8 Aug.=Zeus>>E=v.
Dentition=5,000=50%=P5.00D=Law=Time=Venus=5 May = Aphrodite>>L=N.
Denture=2,500=3,000=30%=P3.0D=3.0=Creativity=Stars=Muses=3 March = C=I.
Denude=3,000=30%=P3.0D=3.0=Creativity=Stars=Muses=3 March = C=I.
Denunciation=4,000=40%=P4.0D=Government =4 April=Mercury=Hermes=G=A4.
Denver=5,000=50%=P5.00D=Law=Time=Venus=5 May = Aphrodite>>L=N.
Deny=13,500=14,000=14%=P1.40D=1.4=Mgt.=Solar Energy=13 May=Athena=SC=0.1
Deodorant=3,500=4,000=40%=P4.0D=Government =4 April=Mercury=Hermes=G=A4.
Deodorize=3,500=4,000=40%=P4.0D=Government =4 April=Mercury=Hermes=G=A4.
Deoxyribonucleic acid=500=5%=P5.00D=5.0=Law=Time=Venus=5 May=Aphrodite>>L=N.
Depart=7,000=70%=P7.0D=7.0=Language=Assets=Mars=7 July=Pleiades.
Department=9,500=10,000=1,000=100%=Physicality=Tech.=10 Oct.=Uranus=P=1Ø.
Departmentalize=2,000=20%=P2.00D=2.0=Nature=Matter=Moon=2 Feb.=Cupid=N=C+_
Department store=4,500=5,000=50%=P5.00D=Law=Time=Venus=5 May =Odite>>L=N.
Departure=8,000=80%=P8.0D=Economy=Currency=Business=8 Aug.=Zeus>>E=v.
Depend=21,000=2.1>>3.0=3,000=30%=P3.0D=3.0=Creatv=Stars=Muses=3 March = C=I.
Dependable=2,500=3,000=30%=P3.0D=3.0=Creativity=Stars=Muses=3 March = C=I.
Dependence=8,500=9,000=90%=P9.00D=9.0=Abstraction=Gods=Saturn=9Sept.>>A=Ø.
Dependency=8,000=80%=P8.0D=Economy=Currency=Business=8 Aug.=Zeus>>E=v.
Dependent=12,000=12%=P1.20D=1.2=Knowl.=Edu.=12Dec.=Athena>>K=F
Depict=6,000=60%=P6.0D=Man=Earth=Royalty=6 June=Gaia=Maia>>M=M2.
Depilatory=3,000=30%=P3.0D=3.0=Creativity=Stars=Muses=3 March = C=I.
Deplane=2,500=3,000=30%=P3.0D=3.0=Creativity=Stars=Muses=3 March = C=I.
Deplete=3,000=30%=P3.0D=3.0=Creativity=Stars=Muses=3 March = C=I.
Deplore=4,000=40%=P4.0D=Government =4 April=Mercury=Hermes=G=A4.
Deploy=5,500=5.5=80%=P5.50D=Earth-Midway=5 May = Gaia.

Deponent=4,000=40%=P4.0D=Government =4 April=Mercury=Hermes=G=A4.
Depopulate=3,000=30%=P3.0D=3.0=Creativity=Stars=Muses=3 March = C=I.
Deport=5,000=50%=P5.00D=Law=Time=Venus=5 May = Aphrodite>>L=N.
Deportment=1,500=15%=P1.50D=1.5=Authority=Solar Crown=1 May = Maia.
Depose=6,000=60%=P6.0D=Man=Earth=Royalty=6 June=Gaia=Maia>>M=M2.
Deposit=10,000=1,000=100%=Physicality=Tech.=10 Oct.=Uranus=P=1Ø.
Deposition=9,500=10,000=1,000=100%=10.0=Physicality=Tech.=10 Oct.=Uranus=P=1Ø.
Depository=4,500=5,000=50%=P5.00D=Law=Time=Venus=5 May = Aphrodite>>L=N.
Depot=7,000=70%=P7.0D=7.0=Language=Assets=Mars=7 July=Pleiades.
Deprave=4,000=40%=P4.0D=Government =4 April=Mercury=Hermes=G=A4.
Deprecate=3,000=30%=P3.0D=3.0=Creativity=Stars=Muses=3 March = C=I.
Depreciate=3,500=4,000=40%=P4.0D=Government =4 April=Mercury=Hermes=G=A4.
Depredation=4,000=40%=P4.0D=Government =4 April=Mercury=Hermes=G=A4.
Depress=8,500=9,000=90%=P9.00D=9.0=Abstraction=Gods=Saturn=9Sept.>>A=Ø.
Depressant=4,500=5,000=50%=P5.00D=Law=Time=Venus=5 May = Aphrodite>>L=N.
Depressed=13,000=13%=P1.30=Solar Core=Faculty=13 January=Athena.
Depression=17,500=18,000=18%=P1.80D=Solar Currency=Maks Currencies=1 Aug.=Maia.
Deprive=4,500=5,000=50%=P5.00D=Law=Time=Venus=5 May = Aphrodite>>L=N.
De program=5,500=5.5=80%=P5.50=Earth-Midway=5 May = Gaia.
Dept.=1,000=100%=10.0=1.0=Mind=Sun=1 January=Helios >> M=E4.
Depth=17,500=18,000=18%=P1.80D=Solar Currency=Maks Currencies=1 Aug.=Maia.
Depth charge=5,500=5.5=80%=P5.50=Earth-Midway=5 May = Gaia.
Deputation=6,000=60%=P6.0D=Man=Earth=Royalty=6 June=Gaia=Maia>>M=M2.
Depute=3,500=4,000=40%=P4.0D=Government =4 April=Mercury=Hermes=G=A4.
Deputize=2,500=3,000=30%=P3.0D=3.0=Creativity=Stars=Muses=3 March = C=I.
Deputy=11,500=12,000=12%=P1.20D=1.2=Knowl.=Edu.=12Dec.=Athena>>K=F
De Quincey Thomas=2,000=20%=P2.00D=2.0=Nature=Moon=2 Feb.=Cupid=N=C+_
Derail=10,500=11,000=11%=P1.10D=1.1=Idea=Brainchild=11 Nov.=SC=Athena>>I=MT.
Derailleur=8,500=9,000=90%=P9.00D=9.0=Abstraction=Gods=Saturn=9Sept.>>A=Ø.
De range=2,000=20%=P2.00D=2.0=Nature=Matter=Moon=2 Feb.=Cupid=N=C+_
derby=15,500=16,000=16%=P1.60D=1.6=Cycle=Incarn.=Mind of GOD=1 June = Maia.
Derby=4,500=5,000=50%=P5.00D=Law=Time=Venus=5 May = Aphrodite>>L=N.
Derelict=12,000=12%=P1.20D=1.2=Knowl.=Edu.=12Dec.=Athena>>K=F
Dereliction=3,000=30%=P3.0D=3.0=Creativity=Stars=Muses=3 March = C=I.
Deride=4,000=40%=P4.0D=Government =4 April=Mercury=Hermes=G=A4.
Deriguer=1,000=100%=10.0=1.0=Mind=Sun=1 January=Helios >> M=E4.
Derivation=7,500=8,000=80%=P8.0D=Economy=Currency=Business=8 Aug.=Zeus>>E=v.
Derivative=8,000=80%=P8.0D=Economy=Currency=Business=8 Aug.=Zeus>>E=v.
Derive=13,000=13%=P1.30=Solar Core=Faculty=13 January=Athena.
Derma=1,000=100%=10.0=1.0=Mind=Sun=1 January=Helios >> M=E4.
Dermatitis=2,000=20%=P2.00D=2.0=Nature=Matter=Moon=2 Feb.=Cupid=N=C+_
Dermatology=4,000=40%=P4.0D=Government =4 April=Mercury=Hermes=G=A4.
Dermis=7,500=8,000=80%=P8.0D=Economy=Currency=Business=8 Aug.=Zeus>>E=v.
Derogate=3,000=30%=P3.0D=3.0=Creativity=Stars=Muses=3 March = C=I.
Derogatory=3,000=30%=P3.0D=3.0=Creativity=Stars=Muses=3 March = C=I.

Derrick=10,500=11,000=11%=P1.10D=1.1=Idea=Brainchild=11 Nov.=SC=Athena>>I=MT.
Derrière=1,000=100%=10.0=1.0=Mind=Sun=1 January=Helios >> M=E4.
Derring-do=2,000=20%=P2.00D=2.0=Nature=Matter=Moon=2 Feb.=Cupid=N=C+_
Derringer=5,000=50%=P5.00D=Law=Time=Venus=5 May = Aphrodite>>L=N.
Dervish=8,000=80%=P8.0D=Economy=Currency=Business=8 Aug.=Zeus>>E=v.
Desalinate=1,000=100%=10.0=1.0=Mind=Sun=1 January=Helios >> M=E4.
Desalinize=5,000=50%=P5.00D=Law=Time=Venus=5 May = Aphrodite>>L=N.
Descant=6,500=7,000=70%=P7.0D=7.0=Language=Assets=Mars=7 July=Pleiades.
Descartes René=3,000=30%=P3.0D=3.0=Creativity=Stars=Muses=3 March = C=I.
Descend=17,500=18,000=18%=P1.80D=Solar Currency=Maks Currencies=1 Aug.=Maia.
Descendant=3,000=30%=P3.0D=3.0=Creativity=Stars=Muses=3 March = C=I.
Descendent=3,000=30%=P3.0D=3.0=Creativity=Stars=Muses=3 March = C=I.
Descent=9,500=10,000=1,000=100%=10.0=Physicality=Tech.=10 Oct.=Uranus=P=1Ø.
Describe=9,500=10,000=1,000=100%=10.0=Physicality=Tech.=10 Oct.=Uranus=P=1Ø.
Description=7,000=70%=P7.0D=7.0=Language=Assets=Mars=7 July=Pleiades.
Des cry=4,000=40%=P4.0D=Government =4 April=Mercury=Hermes=G=A4.
Desecrate=3,000=30%=P3.0D=3.0=Creativity=Stars=Muses=3 March = C=I.
Desegregate=2,000=20%=P2.00D=2.0=Nature=Matter=Moon=2 Feb.=Cupid=N=C+_
Desensitize=2,000=20%=P2.00D=2.0=Nature=Matter=Moon=2 Feb.=Cupid=N=C+_
Desert(1)=5,500=5.5=80%=P5.50=Earth-Midway=5 May = Gaia.
Desert(2)=4,000=40%=P4.0D=Government =4 April=Mercury=Hermes=G=A4.
Desert(3)=7,000=70%=P7.0D=7.0=Language=Assets=Mars=7 July=Pleiades.
Desertification=4,500=5,000=50%=P5.00D=Law=Time=Venus=5 May = Aphrodite>>L=N.
Deserve=4,500=5,000=50%=P5.00D=Law=Time=Venus=5 May = Aphrodite>>L=N.
Deserved=1,500=15%=P1.50D=1.5=Authority=Solar Crown=1 May = Maia.
Deserving=3,000=30%=P3.0D=3.0=Creativity=Stars=Muses=3 March = C=I.
Desiccate=7,000=70%=P7.0D=7.0=Language=Assets=Mars=7 July=Pleiades.
Desideratum=4,000=40%=P4.0D=Government =4 April=Mercury=Hermes=G=A4.
Design=10,000=1,000=100%=10.0=Physicality=Tech.=10 Oct.=Uranus=P=1Ø.
Designate=13,500=14,000=14%=P1.40D=1.4=Mgt.=Solar Energy=13 May=Athena=SC=0.1
Designated hitter=5,000=50%=P5.00D=Law=Time=Venus=5 May = Aphrodite>>L=N.
Designing=500=5%=P5.00D=5.0=Law=Time=Venus=5 May=Aphrodite>>L=N.
Desirable=3,500=4,000=40%=P4.0D=Government =4 April=Mercury=Hermes=G=A4.
Desire=11,500=12,000=12%=P1.20D=1.2=Knowl.=Edu.=12Dec.=Athena>>K=F
Desirous=1,000=100%=10.0=1.0=Mind=Sun=1 January=Helios >> M=E4.
Desist=4,000=40%=P4.0D=Government =4 April=Mercury=Hermes=G=A4.
Desk=13,500=14,000=14%=P1.40D=1.4=Mgt.=Solar Energy=13May=Athena=SC=0.1
Desktop=7,500=8,000=80%=P8.0D=Economy=Currency=Business=8 Aug.=Zeus>>E=v.
Des Moines=5,000=50%=P5.00D=Law=Time=Venus=5 May = Aphrodite>>L=N.
Desolate=8,500=9,000=90%=P9.00D=9.0=Abstraction=Gods=Saturn=9Sept.>>A=Ø.
De Soto Hernando=2,500=3,000=30%=P3.0D=3.0=Creatv=Stars=Muses=3 March = C=I.
Despair=6,000=60%=P6.0D=Man=Earth=Royalty=6 June=Gaia=Maia>>M=M2.
Desperado=2,500=3,000=30%=P3.0D=3.0=Creativity=Stars=Muses=3 March = C=I.
Desperate=11,500=12,000=12%=P1.20D=1.2=Knowl.=Edu.=12Dec.=Athena>>K=F
Despicable=3,000=30%=P3.0D=3.0=Creativity=Stars=Muses=3 March = C=I.

Despise=7,000=70%=P7.0D=7.0=Language=Assets=Mars=7 July=Pleiades.
Despite=1,500=15%=P1.50D=1.5=Authority=Solar Crown=1 May = Maia.
Despoil=1,500=15%=P1.50D=1.5=Authority=Solar Crown=1 May = Maia.
Despond=2,000=20%=P2.00D=2.0=Nature=Matter=Moon=2 Feb.=Cupid=N=C+_
Despondency=2,000=20%=P2.00D=2.0=Nature=Matter=Moon=2 Feb.=Cupid=N=C+_
Despot=2,500=3,000=30%=P3.0D=3.0=Creativity=Stars=Muses=3 March = C=I.
Desert=5,000=50%=P5.00D=Law=Time=Venus=5 May = Aphrodite>>L=N.
Destabilize=5,000=50%=P5.00D=Law=Time=Venus=5 May = Aphrodite>>L=N.
Destination=6,500=7,000=70%=P7.0D=7.0=Language=Assets=Mars=7 July=Pleiades.
Destine=7,500=8,000=80%=P8.0D=Economy=Currency=Business=8 Aug.=Zeus>>E=v.
Destiny=10,000=1,000=100%=10.0=Physicality=Tech.=10 Oct.=Uranus=P=1Ø.
Destitute=5,500=5.5=80%=P5.50=Earth-Midway=5 May = Gaia.
Destroy=3,500=4,000=40%=P4.0D=Government =4 April=Mercury=Hermes=G=A4.
Destroyer=3,500=4,000=40%=P4.0D=Government =4 April=Mercury=Hermes=G=A4.
Destruct=7,500=8,000=80%=P8.0D=Economy=Currency=Business=8 Aug.=Zeus>>E=v.
Destructible=1,000=100%=10.0=1.0=Mind=Sun=1 January=Helios >> M=E4.
Destruction=6,000=60%=P6.0D=Man=Earth=Royalty=6 June=Gaia=Maia>>M=M2.
Desuetude=2,000=20%=P2.00D=2.0=Nature=Matter=Moon=2 Feb.=Cupid=N=C+_
Desultory=4,000=40%=P4.0D=Government =4 April=Mercury=Hermes=G=A4.
Detach=1,500=15%=P1.50D=1.5=Authority=Solar Crown=1 May = Maia.
Detached=4,000=40%=P4.0D=Government =4 April=Mercury=Hermes=G=A4.
Detachment=13,500=14,000=14%=P1.40D=1.4=Mgt.=Solar Energy=13 May=Athena.
Detail=19,500=20,000=2,000=20%=P2.00D=2.0=Nature=Moon=2 Feb.=Cupid=N=C+_
Detain=5,000=50%=P5.00D=Law=Time=Venus=5 May = Aphrodite>>L=N.
Detect=5,000=50%=P5.00D=Law=Time=Venus=5 May = Aphrodite>>L=N.
Detective=6,500=7,000=70%=P7.0D=7.0=Language=Assets=Mars=7 July=Pleiades.
Detector=7,000=70%=P7.0D=7.0=Language=Assets=Mars=7 July=Pleiades.
Detente=3,000=30%=P3.0D=3.0=Creativity=Stars=Muses=3 March = C=I.
Detention=6,000=60%=P6.0D=Man=Earth=Royalty=6 June=Gaia=Maia>>M=M2.
Deter=8,500=9,000=90%=P9.00D=9.0=Abstraction=Gods=Saturn=9Sept.>>A=Ø.
Detergent=7,000=70%=P7.0D=7.0=Language=Assets=Mars=7 July=Pleiades.
Deteriorate=4,000=40%=P4.0D=Government =4 April=Mercury=Hermes=G=A4.
Determinant=3,000=30%=P3.0D=3.0=Creativity=Stars=Muses=3 March = C=I.
Determinate=4,000=40%=P4.0D=Government =4 April=Mercury=Hermes=G=A4.
Determination=12,000=12%=P1.20D=1.2=Knowl.=Edu.=12Dec.=Athena>>K=F
Determinative=6,500=7,000=70%=P7.0D=7.0=Language=Assets=Mars=7 July=Pleiades.
Determine=10,500=11,000=11%=P1.10D=1.1=Idea=Brainchild=11 Nov.=SC=Athena
    >>I=MT.
Determined=1,000=100%=10.0=1.0=Mind=Sun=1 January=Helios >> M=E4.
Determiner=8,000=80%=P8.0D=Economy=Currency=Business=8 Aug.=Zeus>>E=v.
Determinism=8,500=9,000=90%=P9.00D=9.0=Abstraction=Gods=Saturn=9Sept.>>A=Ø.
Deterrent=3,000=30%=P3.0D=3.0=Creativity=Stars=Muses=3 March = C=I.
Detest=2,000=20%=P2.00D=2.0=Nature=Matter=Moon=2 Feb.=Cupid=N=C+_
Dethrone=3,000=30%=P3.0D=3.0=Creativity=Stars=Muses=3 March = C=I.
Detonate=2,000=20%=P2.00D=2.0=Nature=Matter=Moon=2 Feb.=Cupid=N=C+_

Detour=9,000=90%=P9.00D=9.0=Abstraction=Gods=Saturn=9Sept.>>A=Ø.
Detox=4,500=5,000=50%=P5.00D=Law=Time=Venus=5 May = Aphrodite>>L=N.
Detoxify=9,500=10,000=1,000=100%=10.0=Physicality=Tech.=10 Oct.=Uranus=P=1Ø.
Detract=2,000=20%=P2.00D=2.0=Nature=Matter=Moon=2 Feb.=Cupid=N=C+_
De train=4,000=40%=P4.0D=Government =4 April=Mercury=Hermes=G=A4.
Detriment=6,000=60%=P6.0D=Man=Earth=Royalty=6 June=Gaia=Maia>>M=M2.
Detritus=7,000=70%=P7.0D=7.0=Language=Assets=Mars=7 July=Pleiades.
Detroit=5,000=50%=P5.00D=Law=Time=Venus=5 May = Aphrodite>>L=N.
Deuce(1)=10,500=11,000=11%=P1.10D=1.1=Idea=Brainchild=11 Nov.=SC=Athena>>I=MT.
Deuce(2)=3,500=4,000=40%=P4.0D=Government =4 April=Mercury=Hermes=G=A4.
Deuterium=4,500=5,000=50%=P5.00D=Law=Time=Venus=5 May = Aphrodite>>L=N.

Deuteronomy=2,000=20%=P2.00D=2.0=Nature=Matter=Moon=2 Feb.=Cupid=N=C+_
Greek, Deuteronomy means the second law. The resultant proves this. In 29:29. The
secret things belong unto the LORD our God: but those things which are revealed belong
unto us and to our children for ever, that we may do all the words of this law. First the
Creatocracy has done all the words as founded in the dictionary by discovering the secret
formulas and applying it in definitive definitions. The second law is the law of Nature
and matter meaning that the Creatocracy by doing a word and all the words owns the
physical equivalent for which the word represents. The Creatocracy owns all things by
the laws of GOD.

Deutschmark=3,500=4,000=40%=P4.0D=Government =4 April=Mercury=Hermes=G=A4.
De Valera Eamon=7,500=8,000=80%=P8.0D=Econ.=Curr.=Business=8 Aug.=Zeus>>E=v.
Devalue=4,500=5,000=50%=P5.00D=Law=Time=Venus=5 May = Aphrodite>>L=N.
Devastate=3,500=4,000=40%=P4.0D=Government =4 April=Mercury=Hermes=G=A4.
Develop=18,000=18%=P1.80D=Solar Currency=Maks Currencies=1 Aug.=Maia.
Devereux Robert=4,500=5,000=50%=P5.00D=Law=Time=Venus=5 May =Odite>>L=N.
Deviant=4,000=40%=P4.0D=Government =4 April=Mercury=Hermes=G=A4.
Deviate=9,500=10,000=1,000=100%=10.0=Physicality=Tech.=10 Oct.=Uranus=P=1Ø.
Device=21,500=12,500=13,000=13%=P1.30=Solar Core=Faculty=13 January=Athena.

Devil=21,000=2.1>>3.0=3,000=30%=P3.0D=3.0=Creatv=Stars=Muses=3 March = C=I.
Greek diabolos, slanderer. The key quality of the devil is to slander. Computational
results proves that Devils are negative muses that fell from the grace of the Most High.
In Exodus Zeus Jehovah differentiates between the Gods of the Most High and the
Devils in separate statements. Positive muses inspire creativity and make visions and
hearing revelations.

Devilish=6,500=7,000=70%=P7.0D=7.0=Language=Assets=Mars=7 July=Pleiades.
Devil's Island=4,500=5,000=50%=P5.00D=Law=Time=Venus=5 May = Aphrodite>>L=N.
Deviltry=4,000=40%=P4.0D=Government =4 April=Mercury=Hermes=G=A4.
Devious=6,500=7,000=70%=P7.0D=7.0=Language=Assets=Mars=7 July=Pleiades.

Devise=13,000=13%=P1.30=Solar Core=Faculty=13 January=Athena.
Devitalize=4,000=40%=P4.0D=Government =4 April=Mercury=Hermes=G=A4.
Devoid=4,000=40%=P4.0D=Government =4 April=Mercury=Hermes=G=A4.
Devolve=5,000=50%=P5.00D=Law=Time=Venus=5 May = Aphrodite>>L=N.
Devonian=10,500=11,000=11%=P1.10D=1.1=Idea=Brainchild=11 Nov.=SC=Athena>>I=MT.
Devote=9,000=90%=P9.00D=9.0=Abstraction=Gods=Saturn=9Sept.>>A=Ø.
Devoted=3,500=4,000=40%=P4.0D=Government =4 April=Mercury=Hermes=G=A4.
Devotee=1,000=100%=10.0=1.0=Mind=Sun=1 January=Helios >> M=E4.
Devotion=6,000=60%=P6.0D=Man=Earth=Royalty=6 June=Gaia=Maia>>M=M2.
Devour=13,000=13%=P1.30=Solar Core=Faculty=13 January=Athena.
Devout=4,000=40%=P4.0D=Government =4 April=Mercury=Hermes=G=A4.
DeVries Hugo=2,000=20%=P2.00D=2.0=Nature=Matter=Moon=2 Feb.=Cupid=N=C+_
Dew=9,000=90%=P9.00D=9.0=Abstraction=Gods=Saturn=9Sept.>>A=Ø.
DEW=1,500=15%=P1.50D=1.5=Authority=Solar Crown=1 May = Maia.
Dewberry=4,500=5,000=50%=P5.00D=Law=Time=Venus=5 May = Aphrodite>>L=N.
Dewclaw=5,000=50%=P5.00D=Law=Time=Venus=5 May = Aphrodite>>L=N.
Dewey George=2,500=3,000=30%=P3.0D=3.0=Creativity=Stars=Muses=3 March = C=I.
Dewey John=3,000=30%=P3.0D=3.0=Creativity=Stars=Muses=3 March = C=I.
Dewlap=5,500=5.5=80%=P5.50=Earth-Midway=5 May = Gaia.
Dew point=5,000=50%=P5.00D=Law=Time=Venus=5 May = Aphrodite>>L=N.
Dexterity=6,000=60%=P6.0D=Man=Earth=Royalty=6 June=Gaia=Maia>>M=M2.
Dexterous=5,500=5.5=80%=P5.50=Earth-Midway=5 May = Gaia.
Dextrin=5,500=5.5=80%=P5.50=Earth-Midway=5 May = Gaia.
Dextrose=8,000=80%=P8.0D=Economy=Currency=Business=8 Aug.=Zeus>>E=v.
Dezhnev Cape=6,000=60%=P6.0D=Man=Earth=Royalty=6 June=Gaia=Maia>>M=M2.
DFC=1,500=15%=P1.50D=1.5=Authority=Solar Crown=1 May = Maia.
dg=1,000=100%=10.0=1.0=Mind=Sun=1 January=Helios >> M=E4.
D.H.=1,500=15%=P1.50D=1.5=Authority=Solar Crown=1 May = Maia.
Dhaka=1,000=100%=10.0=1.0=Mind=Sun=1 January=Helios >> M=E4.

---

dharma=9,000=90%=P9.00D=9.0=Abstraction=Gods=Saturn=9Sept.>>A=Ø.
The principle or law that orders the universe is the Creatocratic and the individual conduct in conformity with this principle is the Council of Gods expressed in Castle Makupedia.

Dhaulagiri=6,500=7,000=70%=P7.0D=7.0=Language=Assets=Mars=7 July=Pleiades.
Dhu'l-Hijjah=6,000=60%=P6.0D=Man=Earth=Royalty=6 June=Gaia=Maia>>M=M2.
Dhu'l-Qadah=6,000=60%=P6.0D=Man=Earth=Royalty=6 June=Gaia=Maia>>M=M2.
Di-=5,500=5.5=80%=P5.50=Earth-Midway=5 May = Gaia.
Dia.=1,000=100%=10.0=1.0=Mind=Sun=1 January=Helios >> M=E4.
Diabetes=7,000=70%=P7.0D=7.0=Language=Assets=Mars=7 July=Pleiades.
Diabetes mellitus=10,000=1,000=100%=10.0=Physicality=Tech.=10 Oct.=Uranus=P=1Ø.
Diabolical=1,000=100%=10.0=1.0=Mind=Sun=1 January=Helios >> M=E4.
Diacritic=9,000=90%=P9.00D=9.0=Abstraction=Gods=Saturn=9Sept.>>A=Ø.
Diacritical=5,000=50%=P5.00D=Law=Time=Venus=5 May = Aphrodite>>L=N.

Diadela Raza=9,000=90%=P9.00D=9.0=Abstraction=Gods=Saturn=9Sept.>>A=Ø.
Diadem=4,500=5,000=50%=P5.00D=Law=Time=Venus=5 May = Aphrodite>>L=N.
Diaeresis=1,500=15%=P1.50D=1.5=Authority=Solar Crown=1 May = Maia.
Diag.=1,000=100%=10.0=1.0=Mind=Sun=1 January=Helios >> M=E4.
Diagnosis=6,000=60%=P6.0D=Man=Earth=Royalty=6 June=Gaia=Maia>>M=M2.
Diagonal=9,500=10,000=1,000=100%=Physicality=Tech.=10 Oct.=Uranus=P=1Ø.
Diagram=11,000=11%=P1.10D=1.1=Idea=Brainchild=11 Nov.=SC=Athena>>I=MT.
Dial=10,000=1,000=100%=10.0=Physicality=Tech.=10 Oct.=Uranus=P=1Ø.
Dialect=6,500=7,000=70%=P7.0D=7.0=Language=Assets=Mars=7 July=Pleiades.
Dialectic=10,000=1,000=100%=10.0=Physicality=Tech.=10 Oct.=Uranus=P=1Ø.
Dialogue=8,000=80%=P8.0D=Economy=Currency=Business=8 Aug.=Zeus>>E=v.
Dialysis=10,000=1,000=100%=10.0=Physicality=Tech.=10 Oct.=Uranus=P=1Ø.
Diam.=1,000=100%=10.0=1.0=Mind=Sun=1 January=Helios >> M=E4.
Diamagnetic=5,500=5.5=80%=P5.50=Earth-Midway=5 May = Gaia.
Diameter=9,000=90%=P9.00D=9.0=Abstraction=Gods=Saturn=9Sept.>>A=Ø.
Diametrical=4,000=40%=P4.0D=Government =4 April=Mercury=Hermes=G=A4.
Diamond=10,000=1,000=100%=10.0=Physicality=Tech.=10 Oct.=Uranus=P=1Ø.
Diamond back rattlesnake=4,000=40%=P4.0D=Govt.=4 April=Mercury=Hermes=G=A4.
Diamond Head=6,000=60%=P6.0D=Man=Earth=Royalty=6 June=Gaia=Maia>>M=M2.

Diana=4,500=5,000=50%=P5.00D=Law=Time=Venus=5 May = Aphrodite>>L=N.
Goddess of chastity hunting and the moon. Result shows she is servant of Aphrodite &
lover to Cupid. Artemis. She is the border between Hermes and Aphrodite confirming
what rewards are most appropriate in the human quest for wealth and authority.

Diapason=10,000=1,000=100%=10.0=Physicality=Tech.=10 Oct.=Uranus=P=1Ø.
Diaper=14,000=14%=P1.40D=1.4=Mgt.=Solar Energy=13 May=Athena=SC=0.1
Diaphanous=8,000=80%=P8.0D=Economy=Currency=Business=8 Aug.=Zeus>>E=v.
Diaphoresis=3,000=30%=P3.0D=3.0=Creativity=Stars=Muses=3 March = C=I.
Diaphragm=10,000=1,000=100%=10.0=Physicality=Tech.=10 Oct.=Uranus=P=1Ø.
Diarrhea=4,000=40%=P4.0D=Government =4 April=Mercury=Hermes=G=A4.
Diary=6,500=7,000=70%=P7.0D=7.0=Language=Assets=Mars=7 July=Pleiades.
Dias Bartolomeu=2,500=3,000=30%=P3.0D=3.0=Creativity=Stars=Muses=3 March = C=I.
Diastole=9,000=90%=P9.00D=9.0=Abstraction=Gods=Saturn=9Sept.>>A=Ø.
Diathermy=7,000=70%=P7.0D=7.0=Language=Assets=Mars=7 July=Pleiades.
Diatom=8,000=80%=P8.0D=Economy=Currency=Business=8 Aug.=Zeus>>E=v.
Diatomaceous=3,000=30%=P3.0D=3.0=Creativity=Stars=Muses=3 March = C=I.
Diatomic=4,000=40%=P4.0D=Government =4 April=Mercury=Hermes=G=A4.
Diatonic=6,000=60%=P6.0D=Man=Earth=Royalty=6 June=Gaia=Maia>>M=M2.
Diatribe=2,000=20%=P2.00D=2.0=Nature=Matter=Moon=2 Feb.=Cupid=N=C+_
Diazepam=1,500=15%=P1.50D=1.5=Authority=Solar Crown=1 May = Maia.
Dibble=6,500=7,000=70%=P7.0D=7.0=Language=Assets=Mars=7 July=Pleiades.
Dibs=2,000=20%=P2.00D=2.0=Nature=Matter=Moon=2 Feb.=Cupid=N=C+_
Dice=7,500=8,000=80%=P8.0D=Economy=Currency=Business=8 Aug.=Zeus>>E=v.

Dicer=3,000=30%=P3.0D=3.0=Creativity=Stars=Muses=3 March = C=I.
Dicey=3,000=30%=P3.0D=3.0=Creativity=Stars=Muses=3 March = C=I.
Dichotomy=4,500=5,000=50%=P5.00D=Law=Time=Venus=5 May = Aphrodite>>L=N.
Dick=1,000=100%=10.0=1.0=Mind=Sun=1 January=Helios >> M=E4.
Dickens=8,500=9,000=90%=P9.00D=9.0=Abstraction=Gods=Saturn=9Sept.>>A=Ø.
Dickens Charles John=2,000=20%=P2.00D=2.0=Nature=Moon=2 Feb.=Cupid=N=C+_
Dicker=1,500=15%=P1.50D=1.5=Authority=Solar Crown=1 May = Maia.
Dickey=7,500=8,000=80%=P8.0D=Economy=Currency=Business=8 Aug.=Zeus>>E=v.
Dickinson Emily Elizabeth=2,000=20%=P2.00D=2.0=Nature=Moon=2 Feb.=Cupid=
    N=C+_
Dicotyledon=6,000=60%=P6.0D=Man=Earth=Royalty=6 June=Gaia=Maia>>M=M2.
Dictate=13,500=14,000=14%=P1.40D=1.4=Mgt.=Solar Energy=13 May=Athena=SC=0.1
Dictator=5,000=50%=P5.00D=Law=Time=Venus=5 May = Aphrodite>>L=N.
Dictatorial=5,000=50%=P5.00D=Law=Time=Venus=5 May = Aphrodite>>L=N.
Diction=6,500=7,000=70%=P7.0D=7.0=Language=Assets=Mars=7 July=Pleiades.

Dictionary=21,000=2.1>>3.0=3,000=30%=P3.0D=3.0=Creatv=Stars=Muses=3 March
= C=I. The dictionary is a product of the muses meaning that a word contains its own
revelations and constitutes an asset in itself by its physical and applicable equivalent.
Peter Matthews-Akukalia discovered the link between words and computations. He
concluded that dictionaries were speculative in their definitions until they can be
measured calculated and computed as an asset. After discovering the formula for
computing the natural weight and cost of words he invented the World Digital Smart
Dictionary to produce definitive definitions. Just as Jesus had said "every man shall
give account of his words". He established the Makupedia as the universal authority
on all alphabets, numbers and codes in the seventh dimension of the universe known
as Language. A vital asset of the Creatocracy and the Creatocratic Nations of Paradise.
WDSD is the proof.

Dictum=4,500=5,000=50%=P5.00D=Law=Time=Venus=5 May = Aphrodite>>L=N.
Did=2,000=20%=P2.00D=2.0=Nature=Matter=Moon=2 Feb.=Cupid=N=C+_
Didactic=2,500=3,000=30%=P3.0D=3.0=Creativity=Stars=Muses=3 March = C=I.
Diddle=6,500=7,000=70%=P7.0D=7.0=Language=Assets=Mars=7 July=Pleiades.
Diderot Denis=3,000=30%=P3.0D=3.0=Creativity=Stars=Muses=3 March = C=I.
Didn't=1,000=100%=10.0=1.0=Mind=Sun=1 January=Helios >> M=E4.
Didst=4,000=40%=P4.0D=Government =4 April=Mercury=Hermes=G=A4.
Die(1)=12,500r=13,000=13%=P1.30=Solar Core=Faculty=13 January=Athena.
Die(2)=10,000=1,000=100%=10.0=Physicality=Tech.=10 Oct.=Uranus=P=1Ø.
Diefenbaker John=3,500=4,000=40%=P4.0D=Govt. =4 April=Mercury=Hermes=G=A4.
Die-hard=4,000=40%=P4.0D=Government =4 April=Mercury=Hermes=G=A4.
Dielectric=2,000=20%=P2.00D=2.0=Nature=Matter=Moon=2 Feb.=Cupid=N=C+_
Dieresis=12,500r=13,000=13%=P1.30=Solar Core=Faculty=13 January=Athena.
Diesel=3,000=30%=P3.0D=3.0=Creativity=Stars=Muses=3 March = C=I.
Diesel engine=14,000=14%=P1.40D=1.4=Mgt.=Solar Energy=13 May=Athena=SC=0.1

Diet(1)=12,000=12%=P1.20D=1.2=Knowl.=Edu.=12Dec.=Athena>>K=F
Diet(2)=1,500=15%=P1.50D=1.5=Authority=Solar Crown=1 May = Maia.
Dietetic=3,500=4,000=40%=P4.0D=Government =4 April=Mercury=Hermes=G=A4.
Dietitian=2,500=3,000=30%=P3.0D=3.0=Creativity=Stars=Muses=3 March = C=I.
Differ=5,500=5.5=80%=P5.50=Earth-Midway=5 May = Gaia.
Differencer=13,000=13%=P1.30=Solar Core=Faculty=13 January=Athena.
Different=3,500=4,000=40%=P4.0D=Government =4 April=Mercury=Hermes=G=A4.
Differential=9,500=10,000=1,000=100%=10.0=Physicality=Tech.=10 Oct.=Uranus=P=1Ø.
Differential gear=8,000=80%=P8.0D=Economy=Currency=Business=8 Aug.=Zeus>>E=v.
Differentiate=6,000=60%=P6.0D=Man=Earth=Royalty=6 June=Gaia=Maia>>M=M2.
Difficult=6,000=60%=P6.0D=Man=Earth=Royalty=6 June=Gaia=Maia>>M=M2.
Difficulty=15,000=1,500=15%=P1.50D=1.5=Authority=Solar Crown=1 May = Maia.
Diffident=2,000=20%=P2.00D=2.0=Nature=Matter=Moon=2 Feb.=Cupid=N=C+_
Diffraction=9,500=10,000=1,000=100%=10.0=Physicality=Tech.=10 Oct.=Uranus=P=1Ø.
Diffuse=8,000=80%=P8.0D=Economy=Currency=Business=8 Aug.=Zeus>>E=v.
Dig=10,000=1,000=100%=10.0=Physicality=Tech.=10 Oct.=Uranus=P=1Ø.
Digest=14,500=15,000=1,500=15%=P1.50D=1.5=Authority=Solar Crown=1 May = Maia.
Digestive system=9,500=10,000=1,000=100%=10.0=Phy.=Tech.=10 Oct.=Uranus=P=1Ø.
Digit=7,000=70%=P7.0D=7.0=Language=Assets=Mars=7 July=Pleiades.

Digital=6,500=7,000=70%=P7.0D=7.0=Language=Assets=Mars=7 July=Pleiades.
Man is digital in nature to the average quantum of =500=5%=P5.00D= 5.0=Law=
Time=Venus=5 May=Odite>>L=N. This is the source of his innate potentials and
resources. It establishes the quantum of his potentials computed in Psychoeconomix as
500 unique talents in 500 bundles of talents and 600 ideas. So there is at least 5% deposit
in every one that creates the sense of time and rights. We now know that human potentials
are sourced from Venus no wonder man is innately a star as Venus is known as the
brightest star. The potentials are stored in the five senses of the body. Their development
links one to gain access to the inner spirit and soul where Odite is directly connected
through imagination. The sensory value or tax on 500 is 0.5%. Now it is a developed
unit of 0.3>>thoughts. Since Odite is the Goddess of beauty sexual love and birth the
spirit can then be accessed by the thought of sexual transmutation and progress. Thus
nothing reasonable can be done without the love of GOD and Man as Jesus said. The
results shows that Man is accomplished in computational precision by works of faith.
Hence Mind Computing.

Digital computer=9,500=10,000=1,000=100%=10.0=Phys.=Tech.=10 Oct.=Uranus=P=1Ø.
Digitalise=9,000=90%=P9.00D=9.0=Abstraction=Gods=Saturn=9Sept.>>A=Ø.
Dignified=2,000=20%=P2.00D=2.0=Nature=Matter=Moon=2 Feb.=Cupid=N=C+_
Dignify=3,000=30%=P3.0D=3.0=Creativity=Stars=Muses=3 March = C=I.
Dignitary=3,500=4,000=40%=P4.0D=Government =4 April=Mercury=Hermes=G=A4.
Dignity=8,500=9,000=90%=P9.00D=9.0=Abstraction=Gods=Saturn=9Sept.>>A=Ø.
Digraph=4,000=40%=P4.0D=Government =4 April=Mercury=Hermes=G=A4.
Digress=7,500=8,000=80%=P8.0D=Economy=Currency=Business=8 Aug.=Zeus>>E=v.

Dijon=4,500=5,000=50%=P5.00D=Law=Time=Venus=5 May = Aphrodite>>L=N.
Dike=10,000=1,000=100%=10.0=Physicality=Tech.=10 Oct.=Uranus=P=1Ø.
Dilapidated=4,000=40%=P4.0D=Government =4 April=Mercury=Hermes=G=A4.
Dilatation=4,000=40%=P4.0D=Government =4 April=Mercury=Hermes=G=A4.
Dilatation and curettage=6,500=7,000=70%=P7.0D=7.0=Lang=Mars=7 July=Pleiades.
Dilate=4,000=40%=P4.0D=Government =4 April=Mercury=Hermes=G=A4.
Dilatory=1,500=15%=P1.50D=1.5=Authority=Solar Crown=1 May = Maia.
Dilemma=6,500=7,000=70%=P7.0D=7.0=Language=Assets=Mars=7 July=Pleiades.
Dilettante=6,500=7,000=70%=P7.0D=7.0=Language=Assets=Mars=7 July=Pleiades.
Diligent=5,000=50%=P5.00D=Law=Time=Venus=5 May = Aphrodite>>L=N.
Dill=5,000=50%=P5.00D=Law=Time=Venus=5 May = Aphrodite>>L=N.
Dilly=4,000=40%=P4.0D=Government =4 April=Mercury=Hermes=G=A4.
Dilly-Daly=4,500=5,000=50%=P5.00D=Law=Time=Venus=5 May = Aphrodite>>L=N.
Diluent=3,500=4,000=40%=P4.0D=Government =4 April=Mercury=Hermes=G=A4.
Dilute=7,500=8,000=80%=P8.0D=Economy=Currency=Business=8 Aug.=Zeus>>E=v.
Dimr=13,000=13%=P1.30=Solar Core=Faculty=13 January=Athena.
Dim.=2,500=3,000=30%=P3.0D=3.0=Creativity=Stars=Muses=3 March = C=I.
Dime=4,000=40%=P4.0D=Government =4 April=Mercury=Hermes=G=A4.
Dimension=10,000=1,000=100%=10.0=Physicality=Tech.=10 Oct.=Uranus=P=1Ø.
Dime store=2,000=20%=P2.00D=2.0=Nature=Matter=Moon=2 Feb.=Cupid=N=C+_
Dimin.=1,000=100%=10.0=1.0=Mind=Sun=1 January=Helios >> M=E4.
Diminish=4,500=5,000=50%=P5.00D=Law=Time=Venus=5 May = Aphrodite>>L=N.
Diminuendo=1,000=100%=10.0=1.0=Mind=Sun=1 January=Helios >> M=E4.
Diminution=3,500=4,000=40%=P4.0D=Government =4 April=Mercury=Hermes=G=A4.

Diminutive=13,000=13%=P1.30=Solar Core=Faculty=13 January=Athena.
Computing abstract elements extremely small on solar core bits is a key quality of the Creative Scientist Professional at the International Makupedia Order of the Royal Creatocracy. This ability is based on both revelation knowledge and research knowledge. This is how the creative intelligence faculty of the Makupedia creative sciences was born.

Dimity=5,500=5.5=80%=P5.50=Earth-Midway=5 May = Gaia.
Dimmer=5,500=5.5=80%=P5.50=Earth-Midway=5 May = Gaia.
Dimple=12,000=12%=P1.20D=1.2=Knowl.=Edu.=12Dec.=Athena>>K=F
Dim sum=7,500=8,000=80%=P8.0D=Economy=Currency=Business=8 Aug.=Zeus>>E=v.
Dimwit=2,000=20%=P2.00D=2.0=Nature=Matter=Moon=2 Feb.=Cupid=N=C+_
Din=8,500=9,000=90%=P9.00D=9.0=Abstraction=Gods=Saturn=9Sept.>>A=Ø.
Dinar=2,000=20%=P2.00D=2.0=Nature=Matter=Moon=2 Feb.=Cupid=N=C+_
Dinaric Alps=8,500=9,000=90%=P9.00D=9.0=Abstraction=Gods=Saturn=9Sept.>>A=Ø.
Dine=2,000=20%=P2.00D=2.0=Nature=Matter=Moon=2 Feb.=Cupid=N=C+_
Diner=6,000=60%=P6.0D=Man=Earth=Royalty=6 June=Gaia=Maia>>M=M2.
Dinette=4,000=40%=P4.0D=Government =4 April=Mercury=Hermes=G=A4.
Ding(1)=4,000=40%=P4.0D=Government =4 April=Mercury=Hermes=G=A4.
Ding(2)=6,000=60%=P6.0D=Man=Earth=Royalty=6 June=Gaia=Maia>>M=M2.

Dinghy=3,000=30%=P3.0D=3.0=Creativity=Stars=Muses=3 March = C=I.
Dingo=5,500=5.5=80%=P5.50=Earth-Midway=5 May = Gaia.
Dingus=4,500=5,000=50%=P5.00D=Law=Time=Venus=5 May = Aphrodite>>L=N.
Dingy=3,500=4,000=40%=P4.0D=Government =4 April=Mercury=Hermes=G=A4.
Dinky=3,500=4,000=40%=P4.0D=Government =4 April=Mercury=Hermes=G=A4.
Dinner=3,500=4,000=40%=P4.0D=Government =4 April=Mercury=Hermes=G=A4.
Dinner jacket=1,000=100%=10.0=1.0=Mind=Sun=1 January=Helios >> M=E4.
Dinosaur=7,000=70%=P7.0D=7.0=Language=Assets=Mars=7 July=Pleiades.
Dint=5,500=5.5=80%=P5.50=Earth-Midway=5 May = Gaia.
Diocese=5,000=50%=P5.00D=Law=Time=Venus=5 May = Aphrodite>>L=N.
Diocletian=4,000=40%=P4.0D=Government =4 April=Mercury=Hermes=G=A4.
Diogenes=3,000=30%=P3.0D=3.0=Creativity=Stars=Muses=3 March = C=I.
Dionysian=6,500=7,000=70%=P7.0D=7.0=Language=Assets=Mars=7 July=Pleiades.

Dionysus=9,000=90%=P9.00D=9.0=Abstraction=Gods=Saturn=9Sept.>>A=Ø.
The God of wine drama and orgiastic (orgy) religion celebrating the power and fertility of nature (Aphrodite). The Creatocracy believes him to be a servant God say under Aphrodite since he worships her and manages the orgy related matters of sexual transmutations. We do well to remember that Zeus the Most High in the Exodus specifically instructed the Israelites to offer drink and wine offerings. Results also shows Dionysus is a Creatocratic member of the Council of Gods. Castle Makupedia established this council on earth.

Diorama=5,500=5.5=80%=P5.50=Earth-Midway=5 May = Gaia.
Dioxide=4,000=40%=P4.0D=Government =4 April=Mercury=Hermes=G=A4.
Dioxin=7,500=8,000=80%=P8.0D=Economy=Currency=Business=8 Aug.=Zeus>>E=v.
Dip=10,000=1,000=100%=10.0=Physicality=Tech.=10 Oct.=Uranus=P=1Ø.
Diphtheria=10,000=1,000=100%=10.0=Physicality=Tech.=10 Oct.=Uranus=P=1Ø.
Diphthong=11,000=11%=P1.10D=1.1=Idea=Brainchild=11 Nov.=SC=Athena>>I=MT.
Diploid=2,500=3,000=30%=P3.0D=3.0=Creativity=Stars=Muses=3 March = C=I.
Diploma=13,500=14,000=14%=P1.40D=1.4=Mgt.=Solar Energy=13 May=Athena=SC=0.1
Diplomacy=7,500=8,000=80%=P8.0D=Economy=Currency=Business=8 Aug.=Zeus>>E=v.
Diplomat=3,000=30%=P3.0D=3.0=Creativity=Stars=Muses=3 March = C=I.
Diplomatic=3,000=30%=P3.0D=3.0=Creativity=Stars=Muses=3 March = C=I.
Dipole=17,000=17%=P1.70D=1.7=Solar Asset=17/20=17 Feb.=Maia=Mind Computing.
Dipper=12,000=12%=P1.20D=1.2=Knowl.=Edu.=12Dec.=Athena>>K=F
Dipsomania=4,000=40%=P4.0D=Government =4 April=Mercury=Hermes=G=A4.
Dipstick=4,500=5,000=50%=P5.00D=Law=Time=Venus=5 May = Aphrodite>>L=N.
Direct=10,000=1,000=100%=10.0=Physicality=Tech.=10 Oct.=Uranus=P=1Ø.
Direct current=4,000=40%=P4.0D=Government =4 April=Mercury=Hermes=G=A4.
Direction=10,000=1,000=100%=10.0=Physicality=Tech.=10 Oct.=Uranus=P=1Ø.
Directive=4,500=5,000=50%=P5.00D=Law=Time=Venus=5 May = Aphrodite>>L=N.
Directly=6,500=7,000=70%=P7.0D=7.0=Language=Assets=Mars=7 July=Pleiades.
Direct mail=8,000=80%=P8.0D=Economy=Currency=Business=8 Aug.=Zeus>>E=v.
Direct object=11,500=12,000=12%=P1.20D=1.2=Knowl.=Edu.=12Dec.=Athena>>K=F

Director=13,500=14,000=14%=P1.40D=1.4=Mgt.=Solar Energy=13 May=Athena=SC=0.1
Directorate=4,500=5,000=50%=P5.00D=Law=Time=Venus=5 May = Aphrodite>>L=N.
Directory=11,500=12,000=12%=P1.20D=1.2=Knowl.=Edu.=12Dec.=Athena>>K=F
Dirge=4,000=40%=P4.0D=Government =4 April=Mercury=Hermes=G=A4.
Dirham=2,000=20%=P2.00D=2.0=Nature=Matter=Moon=2 Feb.=Cupid=N=C+_
Dirigible=1,000=100%=10.0=1.0=Mind=Sun=1 January=Helios >> M=E4.
Dirk=1,000=100%=10.0=1.0=Mind=Sun=1 January=Helios >> M=E4.
Dirndl=3,000=30%=P3.0D=3.0=Creativity=Stars=Muses=3 March = C=I.
Dirt=10,000=1,000=100%=10.0=Physicality=Tech.=10 Oct.=Uranus=P=1Ø.
Dirt bike=5,000=50%=P5.00D=Law=Time=Venus=5 May = Aphrodite>>L=N.
Dirt-cheap=1,000=100%=10.0=1.0=Mind=Sun=1 January=Helios >> M=E4.
Dirty=10,500=11,000=11%=P1.10D=1.1=Idea=Brainchild=11 Nov.=SC=Athena>>I=MT.
Dis-=6,500=7,000=70%=P7.0D=7.0=Language=Assets=Mars=7 July=Pleiades.
Disability=12,000=12%=P1.20D=1.2=Knowl.=Edu.=12Dec.=Athena>>K=F
Disable=5,500=5.5=80%=P5.50=Earth-Midway=5 May = Gaia.
Disabled=10,000=1,000=100%=10.0=Physicality=Tech.=10 Oct.=Uranus=P=1Ø.
Disabuse=3,500=4,000=40%=P4.0D=Government =4 April=Mercury=Hermes=G=A4.
Disaccharide=8,000=80%=P8.0D=Economy=Currency=Business=8 Aug.=Zeus>>E=v.
Disadvantage=4,500=5,000=50%=P5.00D=Law=Time=Venus=5 May = Aphrodite>>L=N.
Disadvantaged=6,500=7,000=70%=P7.0D=7.0=Language=Assets=Mars=7 July=Pleiades.
Disaffect=3,000=30%=P3.0D=3.0=Creativity=Stars=Muses=3 March = C=I.
Disagree=8,000=80%=P8.0D=Economy=Currency=Business=8 Aug.=Zeus>>E=v.
Disagreeable=3,000=30%=P3.0D=3.0=Creativity=Stars=Muses=3 March = C=I.
Disallow=2,000=20%=P2.00D=2.0=Nature=Matter=Moon=2 Feb.=Cupid=N=C+_
Disappear=8,000=80%=P8.0D=Economy=Currency=Business=8 Aug.=Zeus>>E=v.
Disappoint=3,500=4,000=40%=P4.0D=Government =4 April=Mercury=Hermes=G=A4.
Disapprobation=1,500=15%=P1.50D=1.5=Authority=Solar Crown=1 May = Maia.
Disapproval=3,500=4,000=40%=P4.0D=Government =4 April=Mercury=Hermes=G=A4.
Disapprove=4,000=40%=P4.0D=Government =4 April=Mercury=Hermes=G=A4.
Disarm=8,000=80%=P8.0D=Economy=Currency=Business=8 Aug.=Zeus>>E=v.
Disarmament=3,500=4,000=40%=P4.0D=Government =4 April=Mercury=Hermes=G=A4.
Disarrange=2,500=3,000=30%=P3.0D=3.0=Creativity=Stars=Muses=3 March = C=I.

Disarray=11,500=12,000=12%=P1.20D=1.2=Knowl.=Edu.=12Dec.=Athena>>K=F
A Creatocrat in disarray is one mentally between invention and its knowledge. The knowledge of an invention is its computational creativity or precision hence the lack of formulas creates a mental state of disarray. Hence all things are guided by precision.

Disassemble=2,500=3,000=30%=P3.0D=3.0=Creativity=Stars=Muses=3 March = C=I.
Disassociate=1,000=100%=10.0=1.0=Mind=Sun=1 January=Helios >> M=E4.
Disaster=2,500=3,000=30%=P3.0D=3.0=Creativity=Stars=Muses=3 March = C=I.
Disavow=4,500=5,000=50%=P5.00D=Law=Time=Venus=5 May = Aphrodite>>L=N.
Disband=2,000=20%=P2.00D=2.0=Nature=Matter=Moon=2 Feb.=Cupid=N=C+_

Disbar=4,000=40%=P4.0D=Government =4 April=Mercury=Hermes=G=A4.
To expel a Creatocrat from the Creatocracy is known as Dis-creatocize. It is almost impossible to expel anyone from the Creatocracy because we are the universes. Instead there are punitive measures that can suspend detain ostracize such professional. We are the good the bad the ugly and the extreme and all things are subject and guided by the approval of the sovereignty making the exclusive rights of His Creative excellency and Godship most necessary for control purposes and protection of the rights of others. However the Creatocracy does not criticize things but we creatocize based on precision.

Disbelieve=2,000=20%=P2.00D=2.0=Nature=Matter=Moon=2 Feb.=Cupid=N=C+_
Disburse=4,000=40%=P4.0D=Government =4 April=Mercury=Hermes=G=A4.
Disc=1,500=15%=P1.50D=1.5=Authority=Solar Crown=1 May = Maia.
Discard=10,500=11,000=11%=P1.10D=1.1=Idea=Brainchild=11 Nov.=SC=Athena>>I=MT.

Discern=5,500=5.5=80%=P5.50=Earth-Midway=5 May = Gaia.
The gift to discern are sourced from the eyes and the mind>>Helios and Athena. Discernment is the realm of communication between Gaia and the discerner at the midway. It is an 80% process at which Zeus the Most High 8.0 reveals himself in value and balance. The essence of discernment is to show how things are weighed and valued costs in the supernatural realms and spheres. Hence the Creatocracy Bank is the process of discernment granted by the council of Gods to Peter Matthews-Akukalia the Author, Inventor, Emperor, Founder Owner and President and God of Creatocracy Genius and Mind.

Discerning=1,500=15%=P1.50D=1.5=Authority=Solar Crown=1 May = Maia.
Discharge=10,000=1,000=100%=10.0=Physicality=Tech.=10 Oct.=Uranus=P=1Ø.
Disciple=9,500=10,000=1,000=100%=10.0=Physicality=Tech.=10 Oct.=Uranus=P=1Ø.
Disciplinarian=4,000=40%=P4.0D=Government =4 April=Mercury=Hermes=G=A4.
Disciplinary=2,500=3,000=30%=P3.0D=3.0=Creativity=Stars=Muses=3 March = C=I.
Discipline=10,000=1,000=100%=10.0=Physicality=Tech.=10 Oct.=Uranus=P=1Ø.
Disciplined=4,000=40%=P4.0D=Government =4 April=Mercury=Hermes=G=A4.
Disc jockey=5,500=5.5=80%=P5.50=Earth-Midway=5 May = Gaia.
Disclaim=7,000=70%=P7.0D=7.0=Language=Assets=Mars=7 July=Pleiades.
Disclaimer=4,000=40%=P4.0D=Government =4 April=Mercury=Hermes=G=A4.
Disclose=3,500=4,000=40%=P4.0D=Government =4 April=Mercury=Hermes=G=A4.
Disco=6,000=60%=P6.0D=Man=Earth=Royalty=6 June=Gaia=Maia>>M=M2.
Discolor=5,500=5.5=80%=P5.50=Earth-Midway=5 May = Gaia.
Discombobulate=4,000=40%=P4.0D=Government =4 April=Mercury=Hermes=G=A4.
Discomfit=19,000=19%=P1.90=1.9=Solar Energy=Planets=Mind of God=Maia
Discomfort=8,000=80%=P8.0D=Economy=Currency=Business=8 Aug.=Zeus>>E=v.
Dis commode=4,500=5,000=50%=P5.00D=Law=Time=Venus=5 May = Aphrodite>>L=N.
Discompose=4,500=5,000=50%=P5.00D=Law=Time=Venus=5 May = Aphrodite>>L=N.
Disconcert=6,000=60%=P6.0D=Man=Earth=Royalty=6 June=Gaia=Maia>>M=M2.

Disconnect=5,000=50%=P5.00D=Law=Time=Venus=5 May = Aphrodite>>L=N.
To be disconnected is to lose connect with time, law potentials and Odite. See digital.

Disconnected=3,500=4,000=40%=P4.0D=Government =4 April=Mercury=Hermes=G=A4.
Disconsolate=3,000=30%=P3.0D=3.0=Creativity=Stars=Muses=3 March = C=I.
Discontent=3,500=4,000=40%=P4.0D=Government =4 April=Mercury=Hermes=G=A4.
Discontented=2,500=3,000=30%=P3.0D=3.0=Creativity=Stars=Muses=3 March = C=I.
Discontinue=7,000=70%=P7.0D=7.0=Language=Assets=Mars=7 July=Pleiades.
Discontinuous=2,500=3,000=30%=P3.0D=3.0=Creativity=Stars=Muses=3 March = C=I.
Discord=7,000=70%=P7.0D=7.0=Language=Assets=Mars=7 July=Pleiades.
Discotheque=6,500=7,000=70%=P7.0D=7.0=Language=Assets=Mars=7 July=Pleiades.
Discount=10,000=1,000=100%=10.0=Physicality=Tech.=10 Oct.=Uranus=P=1Ø.
Dis countenance=2,500=3,000=30%=P3.0D=3.0=Creativity=Stars=Muses=3 March = C=I.
Discount store=5,000=50%=P5.00D=Law=Time=Venus=5 May = Aphrodite>>L=N.
Discourage=12,500=13,000=13%=P1.30=Solar Core=Faculty=13 January=Athena.
Discourse=6,000=60%=P6.0D=Man=Earth=Royalty=6 June=Gaia=Maia>>M=M2.
Discourteous=2,000=20%=P2.00D=2.0=Nature=Matter=Moon=2 Feb.=Cupid=N=C+_
Discover=10,000=1,000=100%=10.0=Physicality=Tech.=10 Oct.=Uranus=P=1Ø.
Discovery=4,500=5,000=50%=P5.00D=Law=Time=Venus=5 May = Aphrodite>>L=N.
Discredit=9,000=90%=P9.00D=9.0=Abstraction=Gods=Saturn=9Sept.>>A=Ø.
Discreet=5,500=5.5=80%=P5.50=Earth-Midway=5 May = Gaia.
Discrepancy=4,500=5,000=50%=P5.00D=Law=Time=Venus=5 May = Aphrodite>>L=N.
Discrepant=1,500=15%=P1.50D=1.5=Authority=Solar Crown=1 May = Maia.
Discreet=6,000=60%=P6.0D=Man=Earth=Royalty=6 June=Gaia=Maia>>M=M2.
Discretion=8,500=9,000=90%=P9.00D=9.0=Abstraction=Gods=Saturn=9Sept.>>A=Ø.
Discriminate=9,000=90%=P9.00D=9.0=Abstraction=Gods=Saturn=9Sept.>>A=Ø.
Discriminating=6,500=7,000=70%=P7.0D=7.0=Language=Assets=Mars=7 July=Pleiades.
Discursive=3,500=4,000=40%=P4.0D=Government =4 April=Mercury=Hermes=G=A4.
Discus=7,000=70%=P7.0D=7.0=Language=Assets=Mars=7 July=Pleiades.
Discuss=7,000=70%=P7.0D=7.0=Language=Assets=Mars=7 July=Pleiades.
Discussant=2,500=3,000=30%=P3.0D=3.0=Creativity=Stars=Muses=3 March = C=I.
Disdain=7,000=70%=P7.0D=7.0=Language=Assets=Mars=7 July=Pleiades.
Disease=10,000=1,000=100%=10.0=Physicality=Tech.=10 Oct.=Uranus=P=1Ø.
Disembark=7,500=8,000=80%=P8.0D=Economy=Currency=Business=8 Aug.=Zeus>>E=v.

Disembody=6,000=60%=P6.0D=Man=Earth=Royalty=6 June=Gaia=Maia>>M=M2.
To free the spirit from the body is a special ability of Gaia of Earth and this occurs at death.

Disembowel=2,500=3,000=30%=P3.0D=3.0=Creativity=Stars=Muses=3 March = C=I.

Disenchant=4,000=40%=P4.0D=Government =4 April=Mercury=Hermes=G=A4.
The Creatocracy by precision frees everyone from enchantment and false belief. Hermes
incarnated as Jesus Christ came to disenchant humanity from all speculations and lies.

Disencumber=3,000=30%=P3.0D=3.0=Creativity=Stars=Muses=3 March = C=I.
Creativity relieves everyone of burdens and hardships. Our aim and objective at the Creatocracy Corporation in disencumbering humanity is to institutionalize creatocracy, promote the creative economy, be firmly implanted and well established.

Disenfranchise=1,000=100%=10.0=1.0=Mind=Sun=1 January=Helios >> M=E4.
Disengage=7,000=70%=P7.0D=7.0=Language=Assets=Mars=7 July=Pleiades.
Disentangle=4,000=40%=P4.0D=Government =4 April=Mercury=Hermes=G=A4.
Disestablish=11,500=12,000=12%=P1.20D=1.2=Knowl.=Edu.=12Dec.=Athena>>K=F
Disfavor=4,000=40%=P4.0D=Government =4 April=Mercury=Hermes=G=A4.
Disfigure=4,000=40%=P4.0D=Government =4 April=Mercury=Hermes=G=A4.
Disfranchise=7,500=8,000=80%=P8.0D=Econ.=Currency=Business=8 Aug.=Zeus>>E=v.
Disgorge=2,500=3,000=30%=P3.0D=3.0=Creativity=Stars=Muses=3 March = C=I.
Disgrace=10,500=11,000=11%=P1.10D=1.1=Idea=Brainchild=11 Nov.=SC=Athena>>I=MT.
Disgruntle=3,000=30%=P3.0D=3.0=Creativity=Stars=Muses=3 March = C=I.
Disguise=10,000=1,000=100%=10.0=Physicality=Tech.=10 Oct.=Uranus=P=1Ø.
Disgust=8,000=80%=P8.0D=Economy=Currency=Business=8 Aug.=Zeus>>E=v.
Disgusting=3,500=4,000=40%=P4.0D=Government =4 April=Mercury=Hermes=G=A4.
Dish=13,500=14,000=14%=P1.40D=1.4=Mgt.=Solar Energy=13 May=Athena=SC=0.1
Dishabille=4,500=5,000=50%=P5.00D=Law=Time=Venus=5 May = Aphrodite>>L=N.
Dish antenna=5,500=5.5=80%=P5.50=Earth-Midway=5 May = Gaia.
Disharmony=1,500=15%=P1.50D=1.5=Authority=Solar Crown=1 May = Maia.
Dishcloth=3,000=30%=P3.0D=3.0=Creativity=Stars=Muses=3 March = C=I.
Dishearten=6,500=7,000=70%=P7.0D=7.0=Language=Assets=Mars=7 July=Pleiades.
Dishevel=4,500=5,000=50%=P5.00D=Law=Time=Venus=5 May = Aphrodite>>L=N.
Dishonest=6,500=7,000=70%=P7.0D=7.0=Language=Assets=Mars=7 July=Pleiades.
Dishonor=10,500=11,000=11%=P1.10D=1.1=Idea=Brainchild=11 Nov.=SC=Athena>>I=MT.
Dishonorable discharge=7,500=8,000=80%=P8.0D=Econ=Curr.=Bus.=8 Aug.=Zeus>>E=v.
Dishrag=1,000=100%=10.0=1.0=Mind=Sun=1 January=Helios >> M=E4.
Dishwasher=3,500=4,000=40%=P4.0D=Government =4April=Mercury=Hermes=G=A4.
Disillusion=3,500=4,000=40%=P4.0D=Government =4 April=Mercury=Hermes=G=A4.
Disincline=2,500=3,000=30%=P3.0D=3.0=Creativity=Stars=Muses=3 March = C=I.
Disinfect=3,000=30%=P3.0D=3.0=Creativity=Stars=Muses=3 March = C=I.
Disingenuous=2,500=3,000=30%=P3.0D=3.0=Creativity=Stars=Muses=3 March = C=I.

Disinherit=4,000=40%=P4.0D=Government =4 April=Mercury=Hermes=G=A4.
Inheritance is power granted by Hermes. Its rights is administered by law in Aphrodite. It is in the records that the earthly mother Florence and siblings of Peter Matthews-Akukalia, Castle Makupedia conspired and sold his land inheritance. They were punished by denying them access to any of his assets and privileges forever.

Disintegrate=7,000=70%=P7.0D=7.0=Language=Assets=Mars=7 July=Pleiades.

Disinter=3,500=4,000=40%=P4.0D=Government =4 April=Mercury=Hermes=G=A4.
Disinterested=5,500=5.5=80%=P5.50=Earth-Midway=5 May = Gaia.
Disjoint=1,000=100%=10.0=1.0=Mind=Sun=1 January=Helios >> M=E4.
Disjoint=5,500=5.5=80%=P5.50=Earth-Midway=5 May = Gaia.
Disjointed=4,000=40%=P4.0D=Government =4 April=Mercury=Hermes=G=A4.
Diskr=13,000=13%=P1.30=Solar Core=Faculty=13 January=Athena.
Disk drive=9,500=10,000=1,000=100%=10.0=Physicality=Tech.=10 Oct.=Uranus=P=1Ø.
Diskette=1,500=15%=P1.50D=1.5=Authority=Solar Crown=1 May = Maia.
Disk operating system=500=5%=P5.00D=5.0=Law=Time=Venus=5 May=Aphrodite>>L=N.
Dislike=5,500=5.5=80%=P5.50=Earth-Midway=5 May = Gaia.
Dislocate=7,500=8,000=80%=P8.0D=Economy=Currency=Business=8 Aug.=Zeus>>E=v.
Dislodge=4,000=40%=P4.0D=Government =4 April=Mercury=Hermes=G=A4.
Disloyal=1,000=100%=10.0=1.0=Mind=Sun=1 January=Helios >> M=E4.
Dismal=3,000=30%=P3.0D=3.0=Creativity=Stars=Muses=3 March = C=I.
Dismantle=5,500=5.5=80%=P5.50=Earth-Midway=5 May = Gaia.
Dismay=4,000=40%=P4.0D=Government =4 April=Mercury=Hermes=G=A4.
Dismember=6,000=60%=P6.0D=Man=Earth=Royalty=6 June=Gaia=Maia>>M=M2.
Dismiss=19,000=19%=P1.90=1.9=Solar Energy=Planets=Mind of God=Maia
Dismissive=3,500=4,000=40%=P4.0D=Government =4 April=Mercury=Hermes=G=A4.
Dismount=9,500=10,000=1,000=100%=10.0=Physicality=Tech.=10 Oct.=Uranus=P=1Ø.
Disney Walter Elias=4,500=5,000=50%=P5.00D=Law=Time=Venus=5 May =Odite>>L=N.
Disobedience=2,500=3,000=30%=P3.0D=3.0=Creativity=Stars=Muses=3 March = C=I.
Disobey=1,500=15%=P1.50D=1.5=Authority=Solar Crown=1 May = Maia.
Dis oblige=5,500=5.5=80%=P5.50=Earth-Midway=5 May = Gaia.
Disorder=6,000=60%=P6.0D=Man=Earth=Royalty=6 June=Gaia=Maia>>M=M2.
Disorderly=5,500=5.5=80%=P5.50=Earth-Midway=5 May = Gaia.
Disorganize=3,000=30%=P3.0D=3.0=Creativity=Stars=Muses=3 March = C=I.
Disorient=2,000=20%=P2.00D=2.0=Nature=Matter=Moon=2 Feb.=Cupid=N=C+_
Disown=4,500=5,000=50%=P5.00D=Law=Time=Venus=5 May = Aphrodite>>L=N.
Disparage=4,000=40%=P4.0D=Government =4 April=Mercury=Hermes=G=A4.
Disparate=2,000=20%=P2.00D=2.0=Nature=Matter=Moon=2 Feb.=Cupid=N=C+_
Dispassionate=3,000=30%=P3.0D=3.0=Creativity=Stars=Muses=3 March = C=I.
Dispatch=18,000=18%=P1.80D=Solar Currency=Maks Currencies=1 Aug.=Maia.
Dispel=4,500=5,000=50%=P5.00D=Law=Time=Venus=5 May = Aphrodite>>L=N.
Dispensable=2,500=3,000=30%=P3.0D=3.0=Creativity=Stars=Muses=3 March = C=I.
Dispensary=5,000=50%=P5.00D=Law=Time=Venus=5 May = Aphrodite>>L=N.
Dispensation=15,500=16,000=16%=P1.60D=1.6=Incarn.=Mind of GOD=1 June = Maia.
Dispense=11,000=11%=P1.10D=1.1=Idea=Brainchild=11 Nov.=SC=Athena>>I=MT.
Disperse=4,000=40%=P4.0D=Government =4 April=Mercury=Hermes=G=A4.
Dispirit=5,000=50%=P5.00D=Law=Time=Venus=5 May = Aphrodite>>L=N.
Dispirited=5,500=5.5=80%=P5.50=Earth-Midway=5 May = Gaia.
Displace=7,000=70%=P7.0D=7.0=Language=Assets=Mars=7 July=Pleiades.
Displacement ton=7,000=70%=P7.0D=7.0=Language=Assets=Mars=7 July=Pleiades.
Display=19,500=20,000=2,000=20%=P2.00D=2.0=Nature=Moon=2 Feb.=Cupid=N=C+_
Displease=2,000=20%=P2.00D=2.0=Nature=Matter=Moon=2 Feb.=Cupid=N=C+_

Disport=1,500=15%=P1.50D=1.5=Authority=Solar Crown=1 May = Maia.
Disposable=16,500=17,000=17%=P1.70D=1.7=Solar Asset=17 Feb.=Maia=MindComputing.
Disposal=17,000=17%=P1.70D=1.7=Solar Asset=17/20=17 Feb.=Maia=Mind Computing.
Disposer=13,000=13%=P1.30=Solar Core=Faculty=13 January=Athena.
Disposition=6,500=7,000=70%=P7.0D=7.0=Language=Assets=Mars=7 July=Pleiades.
Dispossess=4,000=40%=P4.0D=Government =4 April=Mercury=Hermes=G=A4.
Dis praise=2,000=20%=P2.00D=2.0=Nature=Matter=Moon=2 Feb.=Cupid=N=C+_
Disproportion=3,000=30%=P3.0D=3.0=Creativity=Stars=Muses=3 March = C=I.
Disprove=2,000=20%=P2.00D=2.0=Nature=Matter=Moon=2 Feb.=Cupid=N=C+_
Disputation=7,500=8,000=80%=P8.0D=Econ.=Currency=Business=8 Aug.=Zeus>>E=v.
Disputatious=3,500=4,000=40%=P4.0D=Government =4 April=Mercury=Hermes=G=A4.
Dispute=8,500=9,000=90%=P9.00D=9.0=Abstraction=Gods=Saturn=9Sept.>>A=Ø.
Disqualify=3,000=30%=P3.0D=3.0=Creativity=Stars=Muses=3 March = C=I.
Disquiet=1,500=15%=P1.50D=1.5=Authority=Solar Crown=1 May = Maia.
Disquietude=3,000=30%=P3.0D=3.0=Creativity=Stars=Muses=3 March = C=I.
Disquisition=2,500=3,000=30%=P3.0D=3.0=Creativity=Stars=Muses=3 March = C=I.
Disraeli Benjamin=6,500=7,000=70%=P7.0D=7.0=Language=Mars=7 July=Pleiades.
Disregard=6,000=60%=P6.0D=Man=Earth=Royalty=6 June=Gaia=Maia>>M=M2.
Disrepair=4,000=40%=P4.0D=Government=4 April=Mercury=Hermes=G=A4.
Disreputable=3,500=4,000=40%=P4.0D=Government =4 April=Mercury=Hermes=G=A4.
Disrepute=3,500=4,000=40%=P4.0D=Government =4 April=Mercury=Hermes=G=A4.
Disrespect=2,000=20%=P2.00D=2.0=Nature=Matter=Moon=2 Feb.=Cupid=N=C+_
Disrobe=1,000=100%=10.0=1.0=Mind=Sun=1 January=Helios >> M=E4.
Disrupt=3,000=30%=P3.0D=3.0=Creativity=Stars=Muses=3 March = C=I.
Dissatisfaction=2,500=3,000=30%=P3.0D=3.0=Creativity=Stars=Muses=3 March = C=I.
Dissatisfy=2,000=20%=P2.00D=2.0=Nature=Matter=Moon=2 Feb.=Cupid=N=C+_
Dissect=9,000=90%=P9.00D=9.0=Abstraction=Gods=Saturn=9Sept.>>A=Ø.
Dissemble=4,000=40%=P4.0D=Government =4 April=Mercury=Hermes=G=A4.
Disseminate=3,000=30%=P3.0D=3.0=Creativity=Stars=Muses=3 March = C=I.
Dissension=5,000=50%=P5.00D=Law=Time=Venus=5 May = Aphrodite>>L=N.
Dissent=8,500=9,000=90%=P9.00D=9.0=Abstraction=Gods=Saturn=9Sept.>>A=Ø.
Dissertation=4,000=40%=P4.0D=Government =4 April=Mercury=Hermes=G=A4.
Disservice=1,500=15%=P1.50D=1.5=Authority=Solar Crown=1 May = Maia.
Dissident=5,000=50%=P5.00D=Law=Time=Venus=5 May = Aphrodite>>L=N.
Dissimilar=2,000=20%=P2.00D=2.0=Nature=Matter=Moon=2 Feb.=Cupid=N=C+_
Dis similitude=1,500=15%=P1.50D=1.5=Authority=Solar Crown=1 May = Maia.
Dissimulate=5,500=5.5=80%=P5.50=Earth-Midway=5 May = Gaia.
Dissipate=11,000=11%=P1.10D=1.1=Idea=Brainchild=11 Nov.=SC=Athena>>I=MT.
Dissociate=2,000=20%=P2.00D=2.0=Nature=Matter=Moon=2 Feb.=Cupid=N=C+_
Dissolute=2,500=3,000=30%=P3.0D=3.0=Creativity=Stars=Muses=3 March = C=I.
Dissolution=14,000=14%=P1.40D=1.4=Mgt.=Solar Energy=13 May=Athena=SC=0.1
Dissolve=11,000=11%=P1.10D=1.1=Idea=Brainchild=11 Nov.=SC=Athena>>I=MT.
Dissonance=7,000=70%=P7.0D=7.0=Language=Assets=Mars=7 July=Pleiades.
Dissuade=8,000=80%=P8.0D=Economy=Currency=Business=8 Aug.=Zeus>>E=v.
Dist.=1,500=15%=P1.50D=1.5=Authority=Solar Crown=1 May = Maia.

Distaff=8,500=9,000=90%=P9.00D=9.0=Abstraction=Gods=Saturn=9Sept.>>A=Ø.
Distaff side=2,000=20%=P2.00D=2.0=Nature=Matter=Moon=2 Feb.=Cupid=N=C+_
Distal=9,500=10,000=1,000=100%=10.0=Physicality=Tech.=10 Oct.=Uranus=P=1Ø.
Distance=10,000=1,000=100%=10.0=Physicality=Tech.=10 Oct.=Uranus=P=1Ø.
Distant=11,500=12,000=12%=P1.20D=1.2=Knowl.=Edu.=12Dec.=Athena>>K=F
Distaste=500=5%=P5.00D=5.0=Law=Time=Venus=5 May=Aphrodite>>L=N.
Dist.Atty.=1,500=15%=P1.50D=1.5=Authority=Solar Crown=1 May = Maia.
Distemper=7,000=70%=P7.0D=7.0=Language=Assets=Mars=7 July=Pleiades.
Distend=2,000=20%=P2.00D=2.0=Nature=Matter=Moon=2 Feb.=Cupid=N=C+_
Distill=5,500=5.5=80%=P5.50=Earth-Midway=5 May = Gaia.
Distillate=3,500=4,000=40%=P4.0D=Government =4 April=Mercury=Hermes=G=A4.
Distillation=8,500=9,000=90%=P9.00D=9.0=Abstraction=Gods=Saturn=9Sept.>>A=Ø.
Distinct=9,000=90%=P9.00D=9.0=Abstraction=Gods=Saturn=9Sept.>>A=Ø.
Distinction=8,000=80%=P8.0D=Economy=Currency=Business=8 Aug.=Zeus>>E=v.
Distinctive=4,000=40%=P4.0D=Government =4 April=Mercury=Hermes=G=A4.
Distinguish=6,000=60%=P6.0D=Man=Earth=Royalty=6 June=Gaia=Maia>>M=M2.
Distinguished=5,000=50%=P5.00D=Law=Time=Venus=5 May = Aphrodite>>L=N.
Distort=7,500=8,000=80%=P8.0D=Economy=Currency=Business=8 Aug.=Zeus>>E=v.
Distract=3,000=30%=P3.0D=3.0=Creativity=Stars=Muses=3 March = C=I.
Distraught=3,000=30%=P3.0D=3.0=Creativity=Stars=Muses=3 March = C=I.
Distress=16,500=17,000=17%=P1.70D=1.7=Solar Asset=17 Feb.=Maia=MindComputing.
Distribute=11,000=11%=P1.10D=1.1=Idea=Brainchild=11 Nov.=SC=Athena>>I=MT.
Distributor=11,500=12,000=12%=P1.20D=1.2=Knowl.=Edu.=12Dec.=Athena>>K=F
District=8,000=80%=P8.0D=Economy=Currency=Business=8 Aug.=Zeus>>E=v.
District attorney=3,500=4,000=40%=P4.0D=Govt=4 April=Mercury=Hermes=G=A4.
District of Columbia=9,500=10,000=1,000=100%=10.0=Phy=Tech.=10 Oct.=Uran.=P=1Ø.
Distrust=5,000=50%=P5.00D=Law=Time=Venus=5 May = Aphrodite>>L=N.
Disturb=8,500=9,000=90%=P9.00D=9.0=Abstraction=Gods=Saturn=9Sept.>>A=Ø.
Disunite=1,500=15%=P1.50D=1.5=Authority=Solar Crown=1 May = Maia.
Disunity=2,000=20%=P2.00D=2.0=Nature=Matter=Moon=2 Feb.=Cupid=N=C+_
Disuse=6,000=60%=P6.0D=Man=Earth=Royalty=6 June=Gaia=Maia>>M=M2.
Ditch=10,000=1,000=100%=10.0=Physicality=Tech.=10 Oct.=Uranus=P=1Ø.
Dither=1,000=100%=10.0=1.0=Mind=Sun=1 January=Helios >> M=E4.
Ditto=10,000=1,000=100%=10.0=Physicality=Tech.=10 Oct.=Uranus=P=1Ø.
Ditty=1,500=15%=P1.50D=1.5=Authority=Solar Crown=1 May = Maia.
Diuretic=3,500=4,000=40%=P4.0D=Government =4 April=Mercury=Hermes=G=A4.
Diurnal=6,000=60%=P6.0D=Man=Earth=Royalty=6 June=Gaia=Maia>>M=M2.
Div.=1,000=100%=10.0=1.0=Mind=Sun=1 January=Helios >> M=E4.
Diva=2,000=20%=P2.00D=2.0=Nature=Matter=Moon=2 Feb.=Cupid=N=C+_
Divagate=2,500=3,000=30%=P3.0D=3.0=Creativity=Stars=Muses=3 March = C=I.
Divalent=2,500=3,000=30%=P3.0D=3.0=Creativity=Stars=Muses=3 March = C=I.
Divan=2,500=3,000=30%=P3.0D=3.0=Creativity=Stars=Muses=3 March = C=I.
Dive=10,000=1,000=100%=10.0=Physicality=Tech.=10 Oct.=Uranus=P=1Ø.
Dive-bomb=7,000=70%=P7.0D=7.0=Language=Assets=Mars=7 July=Pleiades.
Diverge=10,500=11,000=11%=P1.10D=1.1=Idea=Brainchild=11 Nov.=SC=Athena>>I=MT.

Divergence=6,500=7,000=70%=P7.0D=7.0=Language=Assets=Mars=7 July=Pleiades.
Divers=1,000=100%=10.0=1.0=Mind=Sun=1 January=Helios >> M=E4.
Diverse=4,500=5,000=50%=P5.00D=Law=Time=Venus=5 May = Aphrodite>>L=N.
Diversify=6,000=60%=P6.0D=Man=Earth=Royalty=6 June=Gaia=Maia>>M=M2.
Diversion=5,000=50%=P5.00D=Law=Time=Venus=5 May = Aphrodite>>L=N.
Diversity=5,000=50%=P5.00D=Law=Time=Venus=5 May = Aphrodite>>L=N.
Divert=5,500=5.5=80%=P5.50=Earth-Midway=5 May = Gaia.
Divertimento=6,500=7,000=70%=P7.0D=7.0=Language=Assets=Mars=7 July=Pleiades.
Divest=5,000=50%=P5.00D=Law=Time=Venus=5 May = Aphrodite>>L=N.
Divestiture=6,500=7,000=70%=P7.0D=7.0=Language=Assets=Mars=7 July=Pleiades.
Divide=10,000=1,000=100%=10.0=Physicality=Tech.=10 Oct.=Uranus=P=1Ø.
Dividend=6,500=7,000=70%=P7.0D=7.0=Language=Assets=Mars=7 July=Pleiades.
Divider=7,500=8,000=80%=P8.0D=Economy=Currency=Business=8 Aug.=Zeus>>E=v.
Divination=10,500=11,000=11%=P1.10D=1.1=Idea=Brainchild=11 Nov.=SC=Athena
    >>I=MT.
Divine=12,500=13,000=13%=P1.30=Solar Core=Faculty=13 January=Athena.
Diving board=4,500=5,000=50%=P5.00D=Law=Time=Venus=5 May = Aphrodite>>L=N.
Divining rod=8,500=9,000=90%=P9.00D=9.0=Abstraction=Gods=Saturn=9Sept.>>A=Ø.
Divinity=5,500=5.5=80%=P5.50=Earth-Midway=5 May = Gaia.
Divisible=2,000=20%=P2.00D=2.0=Nature=Matter=Moon=2 Feb.=Cupid=N=C+_
Division=10,000=1,000=100%=10.0=Physicality=Tech.=10 Oct.=Uranus=P=1Ø.
Divisive=2,000=20%=P2.00D=2.0=Nature=Matter=Moon=2 Feb.=Cupid=N=C+_
Divisor=4,500=5,000=50%=P5.00D=Law=Time=Venus=5 May = Aphrodite>>L=N.

Divorce=7,500=8,000=80%=P8.0D=Economy=Currency=Business=8 Aug.=Zeus>>E=v.
A computational means is required to aid understanding. The average propensity for divorce is 80%. This is the core value. At the World Digital Data Center, we measure inclinations on birth values and bonding. The differential is applied from the core value for the chances of each specific couple to divorce in future. Thus we provide useful computed raw and objective data to help them make informed decisions before during and after the commitment of marriage. These services are exclusively same for every one and institution.

Divorcé=1,500=15%=P1.50D=1.5=Authority=Solar Crown=1 May = Maia.
Divorcée=1,500=15%=P1.50D=1.5=Authority=Solar Crown=1 May = Maia.
Divot=6,000=60%=P6.0D=Man=Earth=Royalty=6 June=Gaia=Maia>>M=M2.
Divulge=2,500=3,000=30%=P3.0D=3.0=Creativity=Stars=Muses=3 March = C=I.
Divvy=3,000=30%=P3.0D=3.0=Creativity=Stars=Muses=3 March = C=I.
Dixie=8,500=9,000=90%=P9.00D=9.0=Abstraction=Gods=Saturn=9Sept.>>A=Ø.

Dixieland=6,000=60%=P6.0D=Man=Earth=Royalty=6 June=Gaia=Maia>>M=M2.
The book "Makupedialand" is a city of Testamentary Poetry a genre by the Creatocracy.

Dizygotic=5,500=5.5=80%=P5.50=Earth-Midway=5 May = Gaia.

Dizzy=7,000=70%=P7.0D=7.0=Language=Assets=Mars=7 July=Pleiades.
DJ=1,000=100%=10.0=1.0=Mind=Sun=1 January=Helios >> M=E4.
D.J.=4,000=40%=P4.0D=Government =4 April=Mercury=Hermes=G=A4.
Djakarta=1,000=100%=10.0=1.0=Mind=Sun=1 January=Helios >> M=E4.
Djibouti=12,000=12%=P1.20D=1.2=Knowl.=Edu.=12Dec.=Athena>>K=F
dkg=500=5%=P5.00D=5.0=Law=Time=Venus=5 May=Aphrodite>>L=N.
dkl=500=5%=P5.00D=5.0=Law=Time=Venus=5 May=Aphrodite>>L=N.
D.Lit.=2,500=3,000=30%=P3.0D=3.0=Creativity=Stars=Muses=3 March = C=I.
dm=500=5%=P5.00D=5.0=Law=Time=Venus=5 May=Aphrodite>>L=N.
DM=2,000=20%=P2.00D=2.0=Nature=Matter=Moon=2 Feb.=Cupid=N=C+_
D.M.D.=3,500=4,000=40%=P4.0D=Government =4 April=Mercury=Hermes=G=A4.
DMZ=1,000=100%=10.0=1.0=Mind=Sun=1 January=Helios >> M=E4.

DNA=14,000=14%=P1.40D=1.4=Mgt.=Solar Energy=13 May=Athena=SC=0.1
The DNA is the management medium of the body systems.

Dnepropetrovsk=7,000=70%=P7.0D=7.0=Language=Assets=Mars=7 July=Pleiades.
Dnieper=11,000=11%=P1.10D=1.1=Idea=Brainchild=11 Nov.=SC=Athena>>I=MT.
Dniester=9,500=10,000=1,000=100%=Physicality=Tech.=10 Oct.=Uranus=P=1Ø.
Do(1)=10,000=1,000=100%=10.0=Physicality=Tech.=10 Oct.=Uranus=P=1Ø.
Do(2)=3,500=4,000=40%=P4.0D=Government =4 April=Mercury=Hermes=G=A4.
DOA=1,500=15%=P1.50D=1.5=Authority=Solar Crown=1 May = Maia.
Doable=1,500=15%=P1.50D=1.5=Authority=Solar Crown=1 May = Maia.
DOB=1,500=15%=P1.50D=1.5=Authority=Solar Crown=1 May = Maia.
Doberman pinscher=7,000=70%=P7.0D=7.0=Language=Assets=Mars=7 July=Pleiades.
Dobra=2,000=20%=P2.00D=2.0=Nature=Matter=Moon=2 Feb.=Cupid=N=C+_
doc.=500=5%=P5.00D=5.0=Law=Time=Venus=5 May=Aphrodite>>L=N.
Docile=2,500=3,000=30%=P3.0D=3.0=Creativity=Stars=Muses=3 March = C=I.
Dock(1)=18,000=18%=P1.80D=Solar Currency=Maks Currencies=1 Aug.=Maia.
Dock(2)=9,000=90%=P9.00D=9.0=Abstraction=Gods=Saturn=9Sept.>>A=Ø.
Dock(3)=7,000=70%=P7.0D=7.0=Language=Assets=Mars=7 July=Pleiades.
Dock(4)=1,000=100%=10.0=1.0=Mind=Sun=1 January=Helios >> M=E4.
Dockage=4,000=40%=P4.0D=Government =4 April=Mercury=Hermes=G=A4.
Docket=10,000=1,000=100%=10.0=Physicality=Tech.=10 Oct.=Uranus=P=1Ø.
Dockhand=1,000=100%=10.0=1.0=Mind=Sun=1 January=Helios >> M=E4.
Dockworker=4,000=40%=P4.0D=Government =4 April=Mercury=Hermes=G=A4.
Dockyard=1,000=100%=10.0=1.0=Mind=Sun=1 January=Helios >> M=E4.
Doctor=10,000=1,000=100%=10.0=Physicality=Tech.=10 Oct.=Uranus=P=1Ø.
Doctorate=4,000=40%=P4.0D=Government =4 April=Mercury=Hermes=G=A4.
Doctrinaire=7,000=70%=P7.0D=7.0=Language=Assets=Mars=7 July=Pleiades.
Doctrine=14,000=14%=P1.40D=1.4=Mgt.=Solar Energy=13 May=Athena=SC=0.1
Docudrama=4,000=40%=P4.0D=Government =4 April=Mercury=Hermes=G=A4.
Document=10,500=11,000=11%=P1.10D=1.1=Idea=Brainchild=11 Nov.=SC=Athena
    >>I=MT.

Documentary=11,000=11%=P1.10D=1.1=Idea=Brainchild=11 Nov.=SC=Athena>>I=MT.
Dodder=4,000=40%=P4.0D=Government =4 April=Mercury=Hermes=G=A4.
Dodecanese=6,500=7,000=70%=P7.0D=7.0=Language=Assets=Mars=7 July=Pleiades.
Dodge=12,000=12%=P1.20D=1.2=Knowl.=Edu.=12Dec.=Athena>>K=F
Dodgson Charles Lutwidge=4,000=40%=P4.0D=Govt =4 April=Mercury=Hermes=G=A4.
Dodo=8,500=9,000=90%=P9.00D=9.0=Abstraction=Gods=Saturn=9Sept.>>A=Ø.
Dodoma=5,000=50%=P5.00D=Law=Time=Venus=5 May = Aphrodite>>L=N.
Doe=6,500=7,000=70%=P7.0D=7.0=Language=Assets=Mars=7 July=Pleiades.
Doer=4,500=5,000=50%=P5.00D=Law=Time=Venus=5 May = Aphrodite>>L=N.
Does=3,000=30%=P3.0D=3.0=Creativity=Stars=Muses=3 March = C=I.
Doeskin=7,500=8,000=80%=P8.0D=Economy=Currency=Business=8 Aug.=Zeus>>E=v.
Doesn't=1,000=100%=10.0=1.0=Mind=Sun=1 January=Helios >> M=E4.
Doff=6,500=7,000=70%=P7.0D=7.0=Language=Assets=Mars=7 July=Pleiades.
Dog=10,000=1,000=100%=10.0=Physicality=Tech.=10 Oct.=Uranus=P=1Ø.
Dog cart=5,500=5.5=80%=P5.50=Earth-Midway=5 May = Gaia.
Dog catcher=3,500=4,000=40%=P4.0D=Govt=Creatoc.=4April=Mercury=Hermes=G=A4.
Doge=5,000=50%=P5.00D=Law=Time=Venus=5 May = Aphrodite>>L=N.
Dog-ear=3,500=4,000=40%=P4.0D=Govt=Creatoc.=4April=Mercury=Hermes=G=A4.
Dog-eat-dog=2,000=20%=P2.00D=2.0=Nature=Matter=Moon=2 Feb.=Cupid=N=C+_
Dogfight=3,000=30%=P3.0D=3.0=Creativity=Stars=Muses=3 March = C=I.
Dogfish=2,500=3,000=30%=P3.0D=3.0=Creativity=Stars=Muses=3 March = C=I.
Dogged=1,500=15%=P1.50D=1.5=Authority=Solar Crown=1 May = Maia.
Doggerel=4,500=5,000=50%=P5.00D=Law=Time=Venus=5 May = Aphrodite>>L=N.
Doggy=2,500=3,000=30%=P3.0D=3.0=Creativity=Stars=Muses=3 March = C=I.
Doghouse=2,000=20%=P2.00D=2.0=Nature=Matter=Moon=2 Feb.=Cupid=N=C+_
Dogie=3,500=4,000=40%=P4.0D=Govt=Creatoc.=4April=Mercury=Hermes=G=A4.
Dogleg=2,500=3,000=30%=P3.0D=3.0=Creativity=Stars=Muses=3 March = C=I.
Dogma=12,000=12%=P1.20D=1.2=Knowl.=Edu.=12Dec.=Athena>>K=F
Dogmatic=4,500=5,000=50%=P5.00D=Law=Time=Venus=5 May = Aphrodite>>L=N.
Do-Gooder=4,500=5,000=50%=P5.00D=Law=Time=Venus=5 May = Aphrodite>>L=N.
Dog paddle=5,000=50%=P5.00D=Law=Time=Venus=5 May = Aphrodite>>L=N.
Dog tag=10,500=11,000=11%=P1.10D=1.1=Idea=Brainchild=11 Nov.=SC=Athena>>I=MT.
Dog Trot=3,500=4,000=40%=P4.0D=Govt=Creatoc.=4April=Mercury=Hermes=G=A4.
Dogwood=7,500=8,000=80%=P8.0D=Economy=Currency=Business=8 Aug.=Zeus>>E=v.
Doha=4,500=5,000=50%=P5.00D=Law=Time=Venus=5 May = Aphrodite>>L=N.
Doily=8,000=80%=P8.0D=Economy=Currency=Business=8 Aug.=Zeus>>E=v.
Doings=1,500=15%=P1.50D=1.5=Authority=Solar Crown=1 May = Maia.
Do-it-yourself=6,000=60%=P6.0D=Man=Earth=Royalty=6 June=Gaia=Maia>>M=M2.
Dol.=1,500=15%=P1.50D=1.5=Authority=Solar Crown=1 May = Maia.
Doldrums=9,000=90%=P9.00D=9.0=Abstraction=Gods=Saturn=9Sept.>>A=Ø.
Dole=15,000=1,500=15%=P1.50D=1.5=Authority=Solar Crown=1 May = Maia.
Doleful=2,000=20%=P2.00D=2.0=Nature=Matter=Moon=2 Feb.=Cupid=N=C+_
Doll=10,500=11,000=11%=P1.10D=1.1=Idea=Brainchild=11 Nov.=SC=Athena>>I=MT.

Dollar=4,500=5,000=50%=P5.00D=Law=Time=Venus=5 May = Aphrodite>>L=N.
LGer. Daler, a silver coin. We deduce that dollar means a silver coin. Proverbs 8:19 states "My fruit is better than gold, yea, than fine gold: and my revenue than choice silver". We see that silver in any form is not the universal currency standard acceptable by GOD since the standards must be based on supernatural modules. The Maks is diamond weight, a solar currency. Computational results indicate that dollar is a means to an end but not an end in itself. It is a borderline Mercury currency that leads to the lunar standards currency being the 5.0>>C+_=50% formula. The Maks fulfilled requirements in the Moon-Venus-Jupiter-Pluto Energy>> Cupid- Odite-Zeus-Athena wisdom currency. Gold and silver rated currency measures are speculative and lead to inflation but solar currencies thrive on benchmarks. Maks is the diamond measures of energy and matter. See Eagle >> US Eagle.

Dollop=11,000=11%=P1.10D=1.1=Idea=Brainchild=11 Nov.=SC=Athena>>I=MT.
Dolly=10,000=1,000=100%=10.0=Physicality=Tech.=10 Oct.=Uranus=P=1Ø.
Dolmen=6,000=60%=P6.0D=Man=Earth=Royalty=6 June=Gaia=Maia>>M=M2.
Dolomite=6,500=7,000=70%=P7.0D=7.0=Language=Assets=Mars=7 July=Pleiades.
Dolomite Alps=4,500=5,000=50%=P5.00D=Law=Time=Venus=5 May = Aphrodite>>L=N.
Dolor=1,000=100%=10.0=1.0=Mind=Sun=1 January=Helios >> M=E4.
Dolphin=11,500=12,000=12%=P1.20D=1.2=Knowl.=Edu.=12Dec.=Athena>>K=F
Dolt=1,500=15%=P1.50D=1.5=Authority=Solar Crown=1 May = Maia.

-Dom=8,000=80%=P8.0D=Economy=Currency=Business=8 Aug.=Zeus>>E=v.
All Dom systems or kingdoms are administered by Zeus the Most High. He is Dom of Doms.

Domain=8,500=9,000=90%=P9.00D=9.0=Abstraction=Gods=Saturn=9Sept.>>A=Ø.
Dome=4,500=5,000=50%=P5.00D=Law=Time=Venus=5 May = Aphrodite>>L=N.

Domestic=13,000=13%=P1.30=Solar Core=Faculty=13 January=Athena.
All domestic matters are administered by Athena through the Creative Intelligence Faculty.
The Creative Sciences is first of all domestic because the mind is in a custody.

Domesticate=5,000=50%=P5.00D=Law=Time=Venus=5 May = Aphrodite>>L=N.
Aphrodite sees to the domestication of all things. Invention of the creatocracy began as a result of the love for home life and the tasks that it involves imbibed in Peter Matthews-Akukalia by his grandmother during his teen years. Home training is therefore vital in the art is creativity, mind development, leadership. Today he is a Castle Makupedia a God.

Domicile=2,000=20%=P2.00D=2.0=Nature=Matter=Moon=2 Feb.=Cupid=N=C+_
All things are domicile in nature and so all things are operant on the moon or lunar energy. Peter Matthews-Akukalia did 6million computations and 15million in programming on moon computing to find out the single number and thing that controls the universe.

The number was "2" indicating that all things and matter operated by the moon PGI energy. The sun is not matter but mind>> energy and is the source of all life by the solar core measured as 0.1. He discovered that man was made in the moon and planted in the earth. He came from a place in the moon called Mare Imbrium the Sea of Showers and is an incarnation of Zeus.

Dominant=11,500=12,000=12%=P1.20D=1.2=Knowl.=Edu.=12Dec.=Athena>>K=F
The most dominant element in anything is knowledge, science and computing of things.

Dominate=10,000=1,000=100%=10.0=Physicality=Tech.=10 Oct.=Uranus=P=1Ø.
The 10,000 factor in Mind computing and currency development makes it superior to others. King David recommended this factor in the Psalms on the 10,000 to 1,000 rule. Peter Matthews-Akukalia studied it discovered it measured it and invented it. The Maks.

Domineer=5,000=50%=P5.00D=Law=Time=Venus=5 May = Aphrodite>>L=N.
Dominic=7,500=8,000=80%=P8.0D=Economy=Currency=Business=8 Aug.=Zeus>>E=v.
Dominica=7,500=8,000=80%=P8.0D=Economy=Currency=Business=8 Aug.=Zeus>>E=v.
Dominican Republic=8,500=9,000=90%=P9.00D=9.0=Abst.=Gods=Saturn=9Sept.>>A=Ø.

Dominion=9,000=90%=P9.00D=9.0=Abstraction=Gods=Saturn=9Sept.>>A=Ø.
A self - governing nation within the British Commonwealth. A sovereign nation. The dominion of the Creatocratic Nations of Paradise is based on the Creatocratic Charter.

Dominion Day=1,500=15%=P1.50D=1.5=Authority=Solar Crown=1 May = Maia.
Domino(1)=8,500=9,000=90%=P9.00D=9.0=Abstraction=Gods=Saturn=9Sept.>>A=Ø.
Domino(2)=8,500=9,000=90%=P9.00D=9.0=Abstraction=Gods=Saturn=9Sept.>>A=Ø.
Domino effect=6,500=7,000=70%=P7.0D=7.0=Language=Assets=Mars=7 July=Pleiades.

Domitian=6,000=60%=P6.0D=Man=Earth=Royalty=6 June=Gaia=Maia>>M=M2.
The Creatocracy is Domitian in nature not against British nor any but the fact that He has conquered His own fears and invented the unthinkable with solutions to human challenges.

Don(1)=10,000=1,000=100%=10.0=Physicality=Tech.=10 Oct.=Uranus=P=1Ø.
Don(2)=2,000=20%=P2.00D=2.0=Nature=Matter=Moon=2 Feb.=Cupid=N=C+_
Doña=3,000=30%=P3.0D=3.0=Creativity=Stars=Muses=3 March = C=I.
Donate=3,500=4,000=40%=P4.0D=Govt=Creatoc.=4April=Mercury=Hermes=G=A4.
Donatello=2,500=3,000=30%=P3.0D=3.0=Creativity=Stars=Muses=3 March = C=I.
Done=6,000=60%=P6.0D=Man=Earth=Royalty=6 June=Gaia=Maia>>M=M2.
Donets Basin=4,500=5,000=50%=P5.00D=Law=Time=Venus=5 May = Aphrodite>>L=N.
Donetsk=4,500=5,000=50%=P5.00D=Law=Time=Venus=5 May = Aphrodite>>L=N.

Donizetti Gaetano=2,000=20%=P2.00D=2.0=Nature=Matter=Moon=2 Feb.=Cupid =N=C+_
Donkey=5,000=50%=P5.00D=Law=Time=Venus=5 May = Aphrodite>>L=N.

Donne John=2,500=3,000=30%=P3.0D=3.0=Creativity=Stars=Muses=3 March = C=I. English metaphysical poet. This best describes Peter Matthews-Akukalia for his book: The Apotheosis of Castle Makupedia - Mindom of Seven Seas Seasons and Classics on the Nidrapoe, reference section is >> Sons of Immortals - a highly metaphysical work of 5,000 verses on his discussions with the Stars many years before he discovered his gifts to compute. He invented the genre of literature called Nidrapoe and is the world's 1ˢᵗ Drapoet.

Donnybrook=6,000=60%=P6.0D=Man=Earth=Royalty=6 June=Gaia=Maia>>M=M2.
Donor=6,000=60%=P6.0D=Man=Earth=Royalty=6 June=Gaia=Maia>>M=M2.
Don River=8,000=80%=P8.0D=Economy=Currency=Business=8 Aug.=Zeus>>E=v.
Don't=1,000=100%=10.0=1.0=Mind=Sun=1 January=Helios >> M=E4.
Donut=1,500=15%=P1.50D=1.5=Authority=Solar Crown=1 May = Maia.
Doodad=4,000=40%=P4.0D=Govt=Creatoc.=4April=Mercury=Hermes=G=A4.
Doodle=3,000=30%=P3.0D=3.0=Creativity=Stars=Muses=3 March = C=I.
Doodlebug=2,000=20%=P2.00D=2.0=Nature=Matter=Moon=2 Feb.=Cupid=N=C+_
Doom=10,000=1,000=100%=10.0=Physicality=Tech.=10 Oct.=Uranus=P=1Ø.
Doomsayer=3,500=4,000=40%=P4.0D=Govt=Creatoc.=4April=Mercury=Hermes=G=A4.
Doomsday=1,000=100%=10.0=1.0=Mind=Sun=1 January=Helios >> M=E4.
Door=9,500=10,000=1,000=100%=10.0=Physicality=Tech.=10 Oct.=Uranus=P=1Ø.
Door jam=4,500=5,000=50%=P5.00D=Law=Time=Venus=5 May = Aphrodite>>L=N.

Doorkeeper=4,000=40%=P4.0D=Govt=Creatoc.=4April=Mercury=Hermes=G=A4. Greek mythology tells that Hermes is the doorkeeper of the underworld. This is proved. So Jesus is life and Jesus is death. "All powers have been given unto me...."

Doorknob=4,500=5,000=50%=P5.00D=Law=Time=Venus=5 May = Aphrodite>>L=N.
Doorman=4,000=40%=P4.0D=Govt=Creatoc.=4April=Mercury=Hermes=G=A4.
Doormat=9,000=90%=P9.00D=9.0=Abstraction=Gods=Saturn=9Sept.>>A=Ø.
Door prize=4,000=40%=P4.0D=Govt=Creatoc.=4April=Mercury=Hermes=G=A4.
Doorstep=2,500=3,000=30%=P3.0D=3.0=Creativity=Stars=Muses=3 March = C=I.
Dooryard=4,000=40%=P4.0D=Govt=Creatoc.=4April=Mercury=Hermes=G=A4.
Doozy=7,000=70%=P7.0D=7.0=Language=Assets=Mars=7 July=Pleiades.
Dopa=7,500=8,000=80%=P8.0D=Economy=Currency=Business=8 Aug.=Zeus>>E=v.
Dopamine=8,000=80%=P8.0D=Economy=Currency=Business=8 Aug.=Zeus>>E=v.
Dope=8,500=9,000=90%=P9.00D=9.0=Abstraction=Gods=Saturn=9Sept.>>A=Ø.
Doping=5,000=50%=P5.00D=Law=Time=Venus=5 May = Aphrodite>>L=N.
Dopester=5,000=50%=P5.00D=Law=Time=Venus=5 May = Aphrodite>>L=N.
Dopey=4,500=5,000=50%=P5.00D=Law=Time=Venus=5 May = Aphrodite>>L=N.
Doppler effect=12,500=13,000=13%=P1.30=Solar Core=Faculty=13 January=Athena.

Doré Paul Gustave=2,000=20%=P2.00D=2.0=Nature=Matter=Moon=2 Feb.=Cupid=N=C+_
Doric=2,500=3,000=30%=P3.0D=3.0=Creativity=Stars=Muses=3 March = C=I.
Doric order=8,000=80%=P8.0D=Economy=Currency=Business=8 Aug.=Zeus>>E=v.
Dorm=1,500=15%=P1.50D=1.5=Authority=Solar Crown=1 May = Maia.
Dormant=8,500=9,000=90%=P9.00D=9.0=Abstraction=Gods=Saturn=9Sept.>>A=Ø.

Dormer=9,000=90%=P9.00D=9.0=Abstraction=Gods=Saturn=9Sept.>>A=Ø.
The Gods reside in our sleeping rooms. They protect and reveal things to us there also. The
reason Jesus asked us to enter our inner room and close the door when we want to pray.

Dormitory=6,500=7,000=70%=P7.0D=7.0=Language=Assets=Mars=7 July=Pleiades.
Dormouse=3,000=30%=P3.0D=3.0=Creativity=Stars=Muses=3 March = C=I.
Dorsal=3,500=4,000=40%=P4.0D=Govt=Creatoc.=4April=Mercury=Hermes=G=A4.
Dortmund=5,000=50%=P5.00D=Law=Time=Venus=5 May = Aphrodite>>L=N.
Dory=4,500=5,000=50%=P5.00D=Law=Time=Venus=5 May = Aphrodite>>L=N.
DOS=5,000=50%=P5.00D=Law=Time=Venus=5 May = Aphrodite>>L=N.
Dose=8,000=80%=P8.0D=Economy=Currency=Business=8 Aug.=Zeus>>E=v.
Dosimeter=4,500=5,000=50%=P5.00D=Law=Time=Venus=5 May = Aphrodite>>L=N.
Dos Passos John=2,000=20%=P2.00D=2.0=Nature=Matter=Moon=2 Feb.=Cupid=N=C+_
Dossier=6,000=60%=P6.0D=Man=Earth=Royalty=6 June=Gaia=Maia>>M=M2.
Dostoyevsky Feodor=2,000=20%=P2.00D=2.0=Nature=Moon=2 Feb.=Cupid=N=C+_
Dot=18,000=1,800=18%=P1.80D=Solar Currency=Maks Currencies=1 Aug.=Maia.
Dotage=3,000=30%=P3.0D=3.0=Creativity=Stars=Muses=3 March = C=I.
Dotard=1,500=15%=P1.50D=1.5=Authority=Solar Crown=1 May = Maia.
Dote=3,000=30%=P3.0D=3.0=Creativity=Stars=Muses=3 March = C=I.
Doth=4,000=40%=P4.0D=Govt=Creatoc.=4April=Mercury=Hermes=G=A4.
Dot matrix=8,000=80%=P8.0D=Economy=Currency=Business=8 Aug.=Zeus>>E=v.
Dotty=1,300=13%=P1.30=Solar Core=Faculty=13 January=Athena.
Douala=5,500=5.5=80%=P5.50=Earth-Midway=5 May = Gaia.
Double=10,000=1,000=100%=10.0=Physicality=Tech.=10 Oct.=Uranus=P=1Ø.
Double agent=4,000=40%=P4.0D=Govt=Creatoc.=4April=Mercury=Hermes=G=A4.
Double bass=5,500=5.5=80%=P5.50=Earth-Midway=5 May = Gaia.
Double blind=14,500=1,500=15%=P1.50D=1.5=Authority=Solar Crown=1 May = Maia.
Double-breasted=7,000=70%=P7.0D=7.0=Language=Assets=Mars=7 July=Pleiades.
Double-cross=4.500=5,000=50%=P5.00D=Law=Time=Venus=5 May = Aphrodite>>L=N.
Double-dealing=1,000=100%=10.0=1.0=Mind=Sun=1 January=Helios >> M=E4.
Double-decker=6,500=7,000=70%=P7.0D=7.0=Language=Assets=Mars=7 July=Pleiades.
Double-digit=4,500=5,000=50%=P5.00D=Law=Time=Venus=5 May = Aphrodite>>L=N.
Double-entendre=6,000=60%=P6.0D=Man=Earth=Royalty=6 June=Gaia=Maia>>M=M2.
Double-header=6,500=7,000=70%=P7.0D=7.0=Language=Assets=Mars=7 July=Pleiades.
Double helix=7,000=70%=P7.0D=7.0=Language=Assets=Mars=7 July=Pleiades.
Double jeopardy=11,000=11%=P1.10D=1.1=Idea=Brainchild=11 Nov.=SC=Athena>>I=MT.
Double-jointed=5,000=50%=P5.00D=Law=Time=Venus=5 May = Aphrodite>>L=N.
Double-negative=16,000=16%=P1.60D=1.6=Cycle=Incarn.=Mind of GOD=1 June = Maia.

Double play=5,000=50%=P5.00D=Law=Time=Venus=5 May = Aphrodite>>L=N.
Double speak=2,000=20%=P2.00D=2.0=Nature=Matter=Moon=2 Feb.=Cupid=N=C+_

Double star=1,500=15%=P1.50D=1.5=Authority=Solar Crown=1 May = Maia.
The double star is a stellar manifestation of the presence of the Great Goddess Mother Maia. The Creatocracy refers to her as the Universe. In Psychoeconomix Peter Matthews-Akukalia studies discovered and computed the tri-star named it the Mak-Star asserting in his Naturecology his rights as first African to be named on the moon. In 2019 he made a worldwide online announcement that he had discovered the stellar code. He has created various energy data tables especially the human brain energy data table and even linked the planetary and cosmic energy to the human brain systems. Something Plato yearned for.

Doublet=7,500=8,000=80%=P8.0D=Economy=Currency=Business=8 Aug.=Zeus>>E=v.
Double take=4,500=5,000=50%=P5.00D=Law=Time=Venus=5 May = Aphrodite>>L=N.
Double talk=8,500=9,000=90%=P9.00D=9.0=Abstraction=Gods=Saturn=9Sept.>>A=Ø.
Doubloon=3,500=4,000=40%=P4.0D=Govt=Creatoc.=4April=Mercury=Hermes=G=A4.
Doubt=8,000=80%=P8.0D=Economy=Currency=Business=8 Aug.=Zeus>>E=v.
Doubtful=7,000=70%=P7.0D=7.0=Language=Assets=Mars=7 July=Pleiades.
Doubtless=2,500=3,000=30%=P3.0D=3.0=Creativity=Stars=Muses=3 March = C=I.
Douche=8,000=80%=P8.0D=Economy=Currency=Business=8 Aug.=Zeus>>E=v.
Dough=11,000=11%=P1.10D=1.1=Idea=Brainchild=11 Nov.=SC=Athena>>I=MT.
Doughboy=3,500=4,000=40%=P4.0D=Govt=Creatoc.=4April=Mercury=Hermes=G=A4.
Doughnut=7,500=8,000=80%=P8.0D=Economy=Currency=Business=8 Aug.=Zeus>>E=v.
Doughty=1,500=15%=P1.50D=1.5=Authority=Solar Crown=1 May = Maia.
Douglas Stephen Arnold=2,000=20%=P2.00D=2.0=Nature=Moon=2 Feb.=Cupid=N=C+_
Douglass fir=7,000=70%=P7.0D=7.0=Language=Assets=Mars=7 July=Pleiades.
Douglass Frederick=2,000=20%=P2.00D=2.0=Nature=Moon=2 Feb.=Cupid=N=C+_
Dour=5,000=50%=P5.00D=Law=Time=Venus=5 May = Aphrodite>>L=N.
Douro=10,500=11,000=11%=P1.10D=1.1=Idea=Brainchild=11 Nov.=SC=Athena>>I=MT.
Douse(1)=9,000=90%=P9.00D=9.0=Abstraction=Gods=Saturn=9Sept.>>A=Ø.
Douse(2)=1,500=15%=P1.50D=1.5=Authority=Solar Crown=1 May = Maia.
Dove(1)=8,500=9,000=90%=P9.00D=9.0=Abstraction=Gods=Saturn=9Sept.>>A=Ø.
Dove(2)=4,500=5,000=50%=P5.00D=Law=Time=Venus=5 May = Aphrodite>>L=N.
Dover=11,500=12,000=12%=P1.20D=1.2=Knowl.=Edu.=12Dec.=Athena>>K=F
Dover,Strait of.=8,000=80%=P8.0D=Economy=Currency=Business=8 Aug.=Zeus>>E=v.
Dovetail=12,500=13,000=13%=P1.30=Solar Core=Faculty=13 January=Athena.
Dowager=7,500=8,000=80%=P8.0D=Economy=Currency=Business=8 Aug.=Zeus>>E=v.
Dowdy=1,500=15%=P1.50D=1.5=Authority=Solar Crown=1 May = Maia.
Dowel=8,000=80%=P8.0D=Economy=Currency=Business=8 Aug.=Zeus>>E=v.
Dower=12,500=13,000=13%=P1.30=Solar Core=Faculty=13 January=Athena.
Down(1)=10,000=1,000=100%=10.0=Physicality=Tech.=10 Oct.=Uranus=P=1Ø.
Down(2)=4,000=40%=P4.0D=Govt=Creatoc.=4April=Mercury=Hermes=G=A4.
Down(3)=3,500=4,000=40%=P4.0D=Govt=Creatoc.=4April=Mercury=Hermes=G=A4.
Down-and-out=4,000=40%=P4.0D=Govt=Creatoc.=4April=Mercury=Hermes=G=A4.

Downbeat=7,000=70%=P7.0D=7.0=Language=Assets=Mars=7 July=Pleiades.
Downcast=6,500=7,000=70%=P7.0D=7.0=Language=Assets=Mars=7 July=Pleiades.
Down East=2,000=20%=P2.00D=2.0=Nature=Matter=Moon=2 Feb.=Cupid=N=C+_
Downer=6,000=60%=P6.0D=Man=Earth=Royalty=6 June=Gaia=Maia>>M=M2.
Downfall=4,500=5,000=50%=P5.00D=Law=Time=Venus=5 May = Aphrodite>>L=N.
Downgrade=10,000=1,000=100%=Physicality=Tech.=10 Oct.=Uranus=P=1∅.
Downhearted=4,000=40%=P4.0D=Govt=Creatoc.=4April=Mercury=Hermes=G=A4.
Downhill=4,500=5,000=50%=P5.00D=Law=Time=Venus=5 May = Aphrodite>>L=N.
Down-home=7,500=8,000=80%=P8.0D=Econ.=Currency=Business=8 Aug.=Zeus>>E=v.

Downing Street=1,500=15%=P1.50D=1.5=Authority=Solar Crown=1 May = Maia.
The British government. The Creatocracy is the Paradise Nations or Disean government.

Download=7,500=8,000=80%=P8.0D=Economy=Currency=Business=8 Aug.=Zeus>>E=v.
Down payment=4,500=5,000=50%=P5.00D=Law=Time=Venus=5 May = Aphrodite>>L=N.
Downplay=2,500=3,000=30%=P3.0D=3.0=Creativity=Stars=Muses=3 March = C=I.

Downpour=2,500=3,000=30%=P3.0D=3.0=Creativity=Stars=Muses=3 March = C=I.
Borderlines are means by which things happen or messages are conveyed. Heavy fall of
rain are means by which the muses come to Earth. They are sources of revelations.

Down range=7,500=8,000=80%=P8.0D=Econ.=Currency=Business=8 Aug.=Zeus>>E=v.
Downright=3,500=4,000=40%=P4.0D=Govt=Creatoc.=4April=Mercury=Hermes=G=A4.
Downsize=3,500=4,000=40%=P4.0D=Govt=Creatoc.=4April=Mercury=Hermes=G=A4.
Downstage=4,000=40%=P4.0D=Govt=Creatoc.=4April=Mercury=Hermes=G=A4.
Downstairs=4,500=5,000=50%=P5.00D=Law=Time=Venus=5 May = Aphrodite>>L=N.
Downstream=3,500=4,000=40%=P4.0D=Govt=Creatoc.=4April=Mercury=Hermes=G=A4.
Downswing=4,500=5,000=50%=P5.00D=Law=Time=Venus=5 May = Aphrodite>>L=N.
Down syndrome=10,000=1,000=100%=10.0=Physicality=Tech.=10 Oct.=Uranus=P=1∅.
Downtime=6,500=7,000=70%=P7.0D=7.0=Language=Assets=Mars=7 July=Pleiades.
Down-to-earth=1,000=100%=10.0=1.0=Mind=Sun=1 January=Helios >> M=E4.
Downtown=6,000=60%=P6.0D=Man=Earth=Royalty=6 June=Gaia=Maia>>M=M2.
Downtrodden=1,000=100%=10.0=1.0=Mind=Sun=1 January=Helios >> M=E4.
Downturn=3,500=4,000=40%=P4.0D=Govt=Creatoc.=4April=Mercury=Hermes=G=A4.
Downward=5,500=5.5=80%=P5.50=Earth-Midway=5 May = Gaia.
Downwind=3,000=30%=P3.0D=3.0=Creativity=Stars=Muses=3 March = C=I.
Dowry=10,500=11,000=11%=P1.10D=1.1=Idea=Brainchild=11 Nov.=SC=Athena>>I=MT.
Dowse=6,000=60%=P6.0D=Man=Earth=Royalty=6 June=Gaia=Maia>>M=M2.
Dowser=3,000=30%=P3.0D=3.0=Creativity=Stars=Muses=3 March = C=I.
Doxology=8,000=80%=P8.0D=Economy=Currency=Business=8 Aug.=Zeus>>E=v.
Doyle Arthur Conan=3,000=30%=P3.0D=3.0=Creativity=Stars=Muses=3 March = C=I.
Doz.=1,000=100%=10.0=1.0=Mind=Sun=1 January=Helios >> M=E4.
Doze=2,000=20%=P2.00D=2.0=Nature=Matter=Moon=2 Feb.=Cupid=N=C+_

Dozen=2,000=20%=P2.00D=2.0=Nature=Matter=Moon=2 Feb.=Cupid=N=C+_
DP=2,000=20%=P2.00D=2.0=Nature=Matter=Moon=2 Feb.=Cupid=N=C+_
D.Phil.=1,500=15%=P1.50D=1.5=Authority=Solar Crown=1 May = Maia.
DPT=1,500=15%=P1.50D=1.5=Authority=Solar Crown=1 May = Maia.
dr=500=5%=P5.00D=5.0=Law=Time=Venus=5 May=Aphrodite>>L=N.
DR=1,000=100%=10.0=1.0=Mind=Sun=1 January=Helios >> M=E4.
Dr.=1,000=100%=10.0=1.0=Mind=Sun=1 January=Helios >> M=E4.
Drab(1)=7,500=8,000=80%=P8.0D=Economy=Currency=Business=8 Aug.=Zeus>>E=v.
Drab(2)=1,500=15%=P1.50D=1.5=Authority=Solar Crown=1 May = Maia.

Drachma=4,500=5,000=50%=P5.00D=Law=Time=Venus=5 May = Aphrodite>>L=N.
Greek Drakhmē>> an Ancient Greek silver coin. A borderline currency that aligns precisely with the dollar. Currencies have dated from the ancient human civilization. Maks has dated from the ancient God superior civilizations else Athena Goddess of Wisdom wouldn't have inspired it in the Proverbs. The Sun is a golden coin built on a diamond core. See dollar.

Draco(1)=3,500=4,000=40%=P4.0D=Govt=Creatoc.=4April=Mercury=Hermes=G=A4.

Draco(2)=3,000=30%=P3.0D=3.0=Creativity=Stars=Muses=3 March = C=I.
A constellation of the Northern Hemisphere. Lat. dracō, dragon. Creativity produces dragons. The Creatocracy is a dragon that has developed from being a mere cat to a lion, an elephant, a beast to an eagle, to a dragon to a God. This means we developed based on our works until we became a God and a Council of Gods by knowledge and creativity.
A constellation of the Northern Hemisphere. Lat. dracō, dragon. Creativity produces dragons. The Creatocracy is a dragon God that has developed from being a mere cat to a lion, an elephant, a beast to an eagle to a dragon to a God. This means we developed based on our works until we became a God and Council of Gods by knowledge rights & creativity.

Draconian=4,500=5,000=50%=P5.00D=Law=Time=Venus=5 May = Aphrodite>>L=N.
Draft=10,000=1,000=100%=10.0=Physicality=Tech.=10 Oct.=Uranus=P=1Ø.
Draftee=4,000=40%=P4.0D=Govt=Creatoc.=4April=Mercury=Hermes=G=A4.
Drafting=4,500=5,000=50%=P5.00D=Law=Time=Venus=5 May = Aphrodite>>L=N.
Draftsman=6,000=60%=P6.0D=Man=Earth=Royalty=6 June=Gaia=Maia>>M=M2.
Drafty=3,500=4,000=40%=P4.0D=Govt=Creatoc.=4April=Mercury=Hermes=G=A4.
Drag=10,000=1,000=100%=10.0=Physicality=Tech.=10 Oct.=Uranus=P=1Ø.
Dragnet=5,000=50%=P5.00D=Law=Time=Venus=5 May = Aphrodite>>L=N.
Dragoman=3,500=4,000=40%=P4.0D=Govt=Creatoc.=4April=Mercury=Hermes=G=A4.

Dragon=8,000=80%=P8.0D=Economy=Currency=Business=8 Aug.=Zeus>>E=v.
The Creatocracy is a dragon God in the natural animal representation. Based on the wisdom of the serpent which Athena the aegis represents and the lion of Zeus. Dragons are fire made flesh and fire is power. - Nobody, Sorceress at Quarth to Ser Jorah Momon,

Game of Thrones. Peter Matthews - Akukalia earned the title "Dragon Lord of the Skies" from writing The Creatocracy Republic. - Dramatic MindArts of Castle Makupedia.

Dragonfly=10,000=1,000=100%=10.0=Physicality=Tech.=10 Oct.=Uranus=P=1Ø.
Dragoon=6,500=7,000=70%=P7.0D=7.0=Language=Assets=Mars=7 July=Pleiades.
Drag race=3,000=30%=P3.0D=3.0=Creativity=Stars=Muses=3 March = C=I.
Dragster=7,000=70%=P7.0D=7.0=Language=Assets=Mars=7 July=Pleiades.
Drain=17,500=18,000=18%=P1.80D=Solar Currency=Maks Currencies=1 Aug.=Maia.
Drainage=6,000=60%=P6.0D=Man=Earth=Royalty=6 June=Gaia=Maia>>M=M2.
Drainpipe=4,000=40%=P4.0D=Govt=Creatoc.=4April=Mercury=Hermes=G=A4.
Drake=1,500=15%=P1.50D=1.5=Authority=Solar Crown=1 May = Maia.

Drake Francis=4,500=5,000=50%=P5.00D=Law=Time=Venus=5 May = Aphrodite>>L=N.
The hero who married the British Queen in the Creatocracy crown book by Peter Matthews-Akukalia. Reference is Legend of the Monarchs - a play on William Shakespeare.

Dram=2,000=20%=P2.00D=2.0=Nature=Matter=Moon=2 Feb.=Cupid=N=C+_
Drama=15,500=16,000=16%=P1.60D=1.6=Cycle=Incarn.=Mind of GOD=1 June = Maia.
Dramatics=5,500=5.5=80%=P5.50=Earth-Midway=5 May = Gaia.
Dramatist=2,500=3,000=30%=P3.0D=3.0=Creativity=Stars=Muses=3 March = C=I.
Dramatize=8,000=80%=P8.0D=Economy=Currency=Business=8 Aug.=Zeus>>E=v.
Drank=2,000=20%=P2.00D=2.0=Nature=Matter=Moon=2 Feb.=Cupid=N=C+_
Dr ap=1,000=100%=10.0=1.0=Mind=Sun=1 January=Helios >> M=E4.
Drape=18,000=18%=P1.80D=Solar Currency=Maks Currencies=1 Aug.=Maia.
Drapery=8,000=80%=P8.0D=Economy=Currency=Business=8 Aug.=Zeus>>E=v.
Drastic=5,500=5.5=80%=P5.50=Earth-Midway=5 May = Gaia.
Draught=2,500=3,000=30%=P3.0D=3.0=Creativity=Stars=Muses=3 March = C=I.
Draughts=2,000=20%=P2.00D=2.0=Nature=Matter=Moon=2 Feb.=Cupid=N=C+_
Dr avdp=1,000=100%=10.0=1.0=Mind=Sun=1 January=Helios >> M=E4.
Dravidian=11,500=12,000=12%=P1.20D=1.2=Knowl.=Edu.=12Dec.=Athena>>K=F
Draw=10,000=1,000=100%=10.0=Physicality=Tech.=10 Oct.=Uranus=P=1Ø.
Drawback=4,000=40%=P4.0D=Govt=Creatoc.=4April=Mercury=Hermes=G=A4.
Drawbridge=7,000=70%=P7.0D=7.0=Language=Assets=Mars=7 July=Pleiades.
Drawer=12,500=13,000=13%=P1.30=Solar Core=Faculty=13 January=Athena.
Drawing=8,500=9,000=90%=P9.00D=9.0=Abstraction=Gods=Saturn=9Sept.>>A=Ø.
Drawing card=2,500=3,000=30%=P3.0D=3.0=Creativity=Stars=Muses=3 March = C=I.
Drawl=4,000=40%=P4.0D=Govt=Creatoc.=4April=Mercury=Hermes=G=A4.
Drawn=5,500=5.5=80%=P5.50=Earth-Midway=5 May = Gaia.
Drawstring=8,000=80%=P8.0D=Economy=Currency=Business=8 Aug.=Zeus>>E=v.
Dray=3,000=30%=P3.0D=3.0=Creativity=Stars=Muses=3 March = C=I.
Dread=9,500=10,000=1,000=100%=10.0=Physicality=Tech.=10 Oct.=Uranus=P=1Ø.
Dreadful=4,000=40%=P4.0D=Govt=Creatoc.=4April=Mercury=Hermes=G=A4.
Dreadnought=2,000=20%=P2.00D=2.0=Nature=Matter=Moon=2 Feb.=Cupid=N=C+_

Dream=20,000=2,000=20%=P2.00D=2.0=Nature=Matter=Moon=2 Feb.=Cupid=N=C+_
For a dream to occur two moons are satellites are involved. The natural satellite moon or lunar energy known as the Psycho-Gravitational Incursion (PGI) and the human moon, the ear. Dreams are energy signals that pass from the moon at nights and travel through the ears to the brain where the messages are interpreted at spirit speed of 1.0x10v-6 and interpreted at thought speed of 1.0x10v-1 to relay meaning to be person. This means that our thoughts and aspirations can also be transmitted as dreams from the inner eyes to the spirits of the Sun and planets at day especially through minor naps. This is how great inventions were made. However our faith must be backed by works and established.

Dreamland=4,500=5,000=50%=P5.00D=Law=Time=Venus=5 May = Aphrodite>>L=N.
Makupedialand is a dreamland city of testamentary poetry. As a book it is a real city. Dreamlands became real lands once expressed because they lead to the reality of things.

Drear=500=5%=P5.00D=5.0=Law=Time=Venus=5 May=Aphrodite>>L=N.
Dreary=2,000=20%=P2.00D=2.0=Nature=Matter=Moon=2 Feb.=Cupid=N=C+_
Dredge(1)=15,000=1,500=15%=P1.50D=1.5=Authority=Solar Crown=1 May = Maia.
Dredge(2)=4,000=40%=P4.0D=Govt=Creatoc.=4April=Mercury=Hermes=G=A4.
Dregs=4,500=5,000=50%=P5.00D=Law=Time=Venus=5 May = Aphrodite>>L=N.
Dreidel=5,000=50%=P5.00D=Law=Time=Venus=5 May = Aphrodite>>L=N.
Dreiser Theodore=3,000=30%=P3.0D=3.0=Creativity=Stars=Muses=3 March = C=I.
Drench=2,000=20%=P2.00D=2.0=Nature=Matter=Moon=2 Feb.=Cupid=N=C+_
Dresden=7,000=70%=P7.0D=7.0=Language=Assets=Mars=7 July=Pleiades.
Dress=10,000=1,000=100%=10.0=Physicality=Tech.=10 Oct.=Uranus=P=1Ø.
Dressage=8,500=9,000=90%=P9.00D=9.0=Abstraction=Gods=Saturn=9Sept.>>A=Ø.
Dresser(1)=3,500=4,000=40%=P4.0D=Govt=Creatoc.=4April=Mercury=Hermes=G=A4.
Dresser(2)=5,500=5.5=80%=P5.50=Earth-Midway=5 May = Gaia.
Dressing=6,000=60%=P6.0D=Man=Earth=Royalty=6 June=Gaia=Maia>>M=M2.
Dressing gown=2,500=3,000=30%=P3.0D=3.0=Creativity=Stars=Muses=3 March = C=I.
Dressing table=6,000=60%=P6.0D=Man=Earth=Royalty=6 June=Gaia=Maia>>M=M2.
Dressmaker=2,500=3,000=30%=P3.0D=3.0=Creativity=Stars=Muses=3 March = C=I.
Dressy=3,500=4,000=40%=P4.0D=Govt=Creatoc.=4April=Mercury=Hermes=G=A4.
Drew=2,000=20%=P2.00D=2.0=Nature=Matter=Moon=2 Feb.=Cupid=N=C+_
Dreyfus Alfred=2,500=3,000=30%=P3.0D=3.0=Creativity=Stars=Muses=3 March = C=I.
Dribble=10,000=1,000=100%=10.0=Physicality=Tech.=10 Oct.=Uranus=P=1Ø.
Driblet=5,500=5.5=80%=P5.50=Earth-Midway=5 May = Gaia.
Dried=3,000=30%=P3.0D=3.0=Creativity=Stars=Muses=3 March = C=I.
Drier(1)=5,500=5.5=80%=P5.50=Earth-Midway=5 May = Gaia.
Drier(2)=1,500=15%=P1.50D=1.5=Authority=Solar Crown=1 May = Maia.
Driest=2,000=20%=P2.00D=2.0=Nature=Matter=Moon=2 Feb.=Cupid=N=C+_
Drift=10,000=1,000=100%=10.0=Physicality=Tech.=10 Oct.=Uranus=P=1Ø.
Drifter=4,500=5,000=50%=P5.00D=Law=Time=Venus=5 May = Aphrodite>>L=N.
Drift net=8,500=9,000=90%=P9.00D=9.0=Abstraction=Gods=Saturn=9Sept.>>A=Ø.

Driftwood=4,500=5,000=50%=P5.00D=Law=Time=Venus=5 May = Aphrodite>>L=N.
Drill(1)=16,000=16%=P1.60D=1.6=Cycle=Incarn.=Mind of GOD=1 June = Maia.
Drill(2)=9,000=90%=P9.00D=9.0=Abstraction=Gods=Saturn=9Sept.>>A=Ø.
Drill(3)=2,500=3,000=30%=P3.0D=3.0=Creativity=Stars=Muses=3 March = C=I.

Drill instructor=5,500=5.5=80%=P5.50=Earth-Midway=5 May = Gaia.
Results prove that Maia was the drill instructor that led angels to drill craters in the moon
to excavate the materials used in making the human body. Hence Man was made from
the ground (Genesis) not made from the Earth. He was planted into Earth precisely the
Garden of Eden after his creation in the moon. The Creatocracy long computed and
asserted it.

Drill master=2,000=20%=P2.00D=2.0=Nature=Matter=Moon=2 Feb.=Cupid=N=C+_
Drill press=9,500=10,000=1,000=100%=Physicality=Tech.=10 Oct.=Uranus=P=1Ø.
Drink=10,000=1,000=100%=10.0=Physicality=Tech.=10 Oct.=Uranus=P=1Ø.
Drip=10,000=1,000=100%=10.0=Physicality=Tech.=10 Oct.=Uranus=P=1Ø.
Drippings=4,000=40%=P4.0D=Govt=Creatoc.=4April=Mercury=Hermes=G=A4.
Drive=10,000=1,000=100%=10.0=Physicality=Tech.=10 Oct.=Uranus=P=1Ø.
Drive-in=8,000=80%=P8.0D=Economy=Currency=Business=8 Aug.=Zeus>>E=v.
Drivel=3,500=4,000=40%=P4.0D=Govt=Creatoc.=4April=Mercury=Hermes=G=A4.
Driveline=9,500=10,000=1,000=100%=10.0=Physicality=Tech.=10 Oct.=Uranus=P=1Ø.
Driver=12,000=12%=P1.20D=1.2=Knowl.=Edu.=12Dec.=Athena>>K=F
Driveshaft=7,500=8,000=80%=P8.0D=Economy=Currency=Business=8 Aug.=Zeus>>E=v.
Drive train=1,000=100%=10.0=1.0=Mind=Sun=1 January=Helios >> M=E4.
Driveway=4,500=5,000=50%=P5.00D=Law=Time=Venus=5 May = Aphrodite>>L=N.

Drizzle=3,500=4,000=40%=P4.0D=Govt=Creatoc.=4April=Mercury=Hermes=G=A4.
Drizzles are borderlines and ushers of Hermes. He hears prayers made during drizzles.

Drogue=7,500=8,000=80%=P8.0D=Economy=Currency=Business=8 Aug.=Zeus>>E=v.
Droll=2,500=3,000=30%=P3.0D=3.0=Creativity=Stars=Muses=3 March = C=I.
-Drome=4,000=40%=P4.0D=Govt=Creatoc.=4April=Mercury=Hermes=G=A4.
Dromedary=5,500=5.5=80%=P5.50=Earth-Midway=5 May = Gaia.
Drone(1)=8,000=80%=P8.0D=Economy=Currency=Business=8 Aug.=Zeus>>E=v.
Drone(2)=6,000=60%=P6.0D=Man=Earth=Royalty=6 June=Gaia=Maia>>M=M2.
Drool=9,000=90%=P9.00D=9.0=Abstraction=Gods=Saturn=9Sept.>>A=Ø.
Droop=4,500=5,000=50%=P5.00D=Law=Time=Venus=5 May = Aphrodite>>L=N.
Drop=10,000=1,000=100%=10.0=Physicality=Tech.=10 Oct.=Uranus=P=1Ø.
Droplet=1,500=15%=P1.50D=1.5=Authority=Solar Crown=1 May = Maia.
Drop-off=3,500=4,000=40%=P4.0D=Govt=Creatoc.=4April=Mercury=Hermes=G=A4.
Dropout=3,500=4,000=40%=P4.0D=Govt=Creatoc.=4April=Mercury=Hermes=G=A4.
Dropper=8,500=9,000=90%=P9.00D=9.0=Abstraction=Gods=Saturn=9Sept.>>A=Ø.
Dropsy=3,000=30%=P3.0D=3.0=Creativity=Stars=Muses=3 March = C=I.

Drosophila=4,000=40%=P4.0D=Govt=Creatoc.=4April=Mercury=Hermes=G=A4.
Dross=7,000=70%=P7.0D=7.0=Language=Assets=Mars=7 July=Pleiades.
Drought=4,500=5,000=50%=P5.00D=Law=Time=Venus=5 May = Aphrodite>>L=N.
Drove(1)=2,000=20%=P2.00D=2.0=Nature=Matter=Moon=2 Feb.=Cupid=N=C+_
Drove(2)=5,500=5.5=80%=P5.50=Earth-Midway=5 May = Gaia.
Drover=3,000=30%=P3.0D=3.0=Creativity=Stars=Muses=3 March = C=I.

Drown=9,000=90%=P9.00D=9.0=Abstraction=Gods=Saturn=9Sept.>>A=Ø.
Downs are louder noises made by the Gods to mask unnecessary negative sounds. Thus they hate noise as energy and power are most generated through silence. Silence means that the Gods or cosmic powers are at work especially when we are thinking processes.

Drowse=2,500=3,000=30%=P3.0D=3.0=Creativity=Stars=Muses=3 March = C=I.
Drowsy=2,000=20%=P2.00D=2.0=Nature=Matter=Moon=2 Feb.=Cupid=N=C+_
Dr t=1,000=100%=10.0=1.0=Mind=Sun=1 January=Helios >> M=E4.
Drub=7,000=70%=P7.0D=7.0=Language=Assets=Mars=7 July=Pleiades.
Drudge=7,000=70%=P7.0D=7.0=Language=Assets=Mars=7 July=Pleiades.
Drug=10,000=1,000=100%=10.0=Physicality=Tech.=10 Oct.=Uranus=P=1Ø.
Druggist=1,000=100%=10.0=1.0=Mind=Sun=1 January=Helios >> M=E4.
Drugstore=6,500=7,000=70%=P7.0D=7.0=Language=Assets=Mars=7 July=Pleiades.
Druid=9,000=90%=P9.00D=9.0=Abstraction=Gods=Saturn=9Sept.>>A=Ø.
Drum=10,000=1,000=100%=10.0=Physicality=Tech.=10 Oct.=Uranus=P=1Ø.
Drumbeat=3,500=4,000=40%=P4.0D=Govt=Creatoc.=4April=Mercury=Hermes=G=A4.
Drumlin=4,000=40%=P4.0D=Govt=Creatoc.=4April=Mercury=Hermes=G=A4.
Drum major=4,500=5,000=50%=P5.00D=Law=Time=Venus=5 May = Aphrodite>>L=N.
Drum majorette=4,500=5,000=50%=P5.00D=Law=Time=Venus=5 May =Odite>>L=N.
Drumstick=7,000=70%=P7.0D=7.0=Language=Assets=Mars=7 July=Pleiades.
Drunk=7,000=70%=P7.0D=7.0=Language=Assets=Mars=7 July=Pleiades.
Drunkard=2,000=20%=P2.00D=2.0=Nature=Matter=Moon=2 Feb.=Cupid=N=C+_
Drunken=6,000=60%=P6.0D=Man=Earth=Royalty=6 June=Gaia=Maia>>M=M2.
Drupe=7,000=70%=P7.0D=7.0=Language=Assets=Mars=7 July=Pleiades.
Drupelet=6,500=7,000=70%=P7.0D=7.0=Language=Assets=Mars=7 July=Pleiades.
Dry=10,000=1,000=100%=10.0=Physicality=Tech.=10 Oct.=Uranus=P=1Ø.

Dryad=2,500=3,000=30%=P3.0D=3.0=Creativity=Stars=Muses=3 March = C=I.
Greek Myth. Druas, Druad is a wood nymph. The Creatocracy establishes her a muse. This is the spirit we believe that lives in the wood and can transform into humans inclined to wood matters and occupations such as lumbering paper making printing and forestry. Woods are therefore sources of inspirations. It means that sitting on a table works.

Dry cell=6,000=60%=P6.0D=Man=Earth=Royalty=6 June=Gaia=Maia>>M=M2.
Dry-clean=6,000=60%=P6.0D=Man=Earth=Royalty=6 June=Gaia=Maia>>M=M2.
Dryden John=2,000=20%=P2.00D=2.0=Nature=Matter=Moon=2 Feb.=Cupid=N=C+_

Dry dock=8,500=9,000=90%=P9.00D=9.0=Abstraction=Gods=Saturn=9Sept.>>A=Ø.
Dryer=4,000=40%=P4.0D=Govt=Creatoc.=4April=Mercury=Hermes=G=A4.
Dry farming=3,500=4,000=40%=P4.0D=Govt=Creatoc.=4April=Mercury=Hermes=G=A4.
Dry goods=3,500=4,000=40%=P4.0D=Govt=Creatoc.=4April=Mercury=Hermes=G=A4.
Dry ice=4,000=40%=P4.0D=Govt=Creatoc.=4April=Mercury=Hermes=G=A4.
Dry measure=5,500=5.5=80%=P5.50=Earth-Midway=5 May = Gaia.
Dry rot=6,000=60%=P6.0D=Man=Earth=Royalty=6 June=Gaia=Maia>>M=M2.
Dry run=5,500=5.5=80%=P5.50=Earth-Midway=5 May = Gaia.
Dry wall=1,000=100%=10.0=1.0=Mind=Sun=1 January=Helios >> M=E4.
DS=2,000=20%=P2.00D=2.0=Nature=Matter=Moon=2 Feb.=Cupid=N=C+_
DSC=1,500=15%=P1.50D=1.5=Authority=Solar Crown=1 May = Maia.
DSM=1,500=15%=P1.50D=1.5=Authority=Solar Crown=1 May = Maia.
DSO=1,500=15%=P1.50D=1.5=Authority=Solar Crown=1 May = Maia.
d.s.p.=3,500=4,000=40%=P4.0D=Govt=Creatoc.=4April=Mercury=Hermes=G=A4.
DST=1,500=15%=P1.50D=1.5=Authority=Solar Crown=1 May = Maia.
D,T.'s=1,000=100%=Physicality=Tech.=10 Oct.=Uranus=P=1Ø.
Dual=4,500=5,000=50%=P5.00D=Law=Time=Venus=5 May = Aphrodite>>L=N.
Duala=1,000=100%=10.0=1.0=Mind=Sun=1 January=Helios >> M=E4.
Dub(1)=3,500=4,000=40%=P4.0D=Govt=Creatoc.=4April=Mercury=Hermes=G=A4.
Dub(2)=11,500=12,000=12%=P1.20D=1.2=Knowl.=Edu.=12Dec.=Athena>>K=F
Dubai=7,500=8,000=80%=P8.0D=Economy=Currency=Business=8 Aug.=Zeus>>E=v.
Du Barry=6,500=7,000=70%=P7.0D=7.0=Language=Assets=Mars=7 July=Pleiades.
Dubiety=3,000=30%=P3.0D=3.0=Creativity=Stars=Muses=3 March = C=I.
Dubious=3,500=4,000=40%=P4.0D=Govt=Creatoc.=4April=Mercury=Hermes=G=A4.
Dublin=6,500=7,000=70%=P7.0D=7.0=Language=Assets=Mars=7 July=Pleiades.
Du Bois William=4,000=40%=P4.0D=Govt=Creatoc.=4April=Mercury=Hermes=G=A4.
Ducal=3,500=4,000=40%=P4.0D=Govt=Creatoc.=4April=Mercury=Hermes=G=A4.

Ducat=4,500=5,000=50%=P5.00D=Law=Time=Venus=5 May = Aphrodite>>L=N.
Any of various gold coins formerly used in Europe. A borderline. See Dollar.

Duchess=6,000=60%=P6.0D=Man=Earth=Royalty=6 June=Gaia=Maia>>M=M2.
Duchy=4,500=5,000=50%=P5.00D=Law=Time=Venus=5 May = Aphrodite>>L=N.
Duck(1)=8,500=9,000=90%=P9.00D=9.0=Abstraction=Gods=Saturn=9Sept.>>A=Ø.

Duck(2)=8,000=80%=P8.0D=Economy=Currency=Business=8 Aug.=Zeus>>E=v.
Greek mythology teaches that Zeus the Most High transformed into a duck to woo. Proved.

Duck(3)=7,000=70%=P7.0D=7.0=Language=Assets=Mars=7 July=Pleiades.
Duckbill=1,000=100%=10.0=1.0=Mind=Sun=1 January=Helios >> M=E4.
Duckboard=5,000=50%=P5.00D=Law=Time=Venus=5 May = Aphrodite>>L=N.
Duckling=1,500=15%=P1.50D=1.5=Authority=Solar Crown=1 May = Maia.
Duck pin=7,000=70%=P7.0D=7.0=Language=Assets=Mars=7 July=Pleiades.

Duckweed=5,000=50%=P5.00D=Law=Time=Venus=5 May = Aphrodite>>L=N.
Ducky=1,500=15%=P1.50D=1.5=Authority=Solar Crown=1 May = Maia.
Duct=12,500=13,000=13%=P1.30=Solar Core=Faculty=13 January=Athena.
Ductile=6,500=7,000=70%=P7.0D=7.0=Language=Assets=Mars=7 July=Pleiades.
Ductless gland=1,500=15%=P1.50D=1.5=Authority=Solar Crown=1 May = Maia.
Dud=10,500=11,000=11%=P1.10D=1.1=Idea=Brainchild=11 Nov.=SC=Athena>>I=MT.
Dude=11,000=11%=P1.10D=1.1=Idea=Brainchild=11 Nov.=SC=Athena>>I=MT.
Dude ranch=4,500=5,000=50%=P5.00D=Law=Time=Venus=5 May = Aphrodite>>L=N.
Dudgeon=3,500=4,000=40%=P4.0D=Govt=Creatoc.=4April=Mercury=Hermes=G=A4.
Dudley Robert=4,500=5,000=50%=P5.00D=Law=Time=Venus=5 May = Aphrodite>>L=N.
Due=40,000=4,000=40%=P4.0D=Govt=Creatoc.=4April=Mercury=Hermes=G=A4.
Duel=13,000=13%=P1.30=Solar Core=Faculty=13 January=Athena.
Due process=7,500=8,000=80%=P8.0D=Econ.=Currency=Business=8 Aug.=Zeus>>E=v.
Duet=7,000=70%=P7.0D=7.0=Language=Assets=Mars=7 July=Pleiades.
Due to=10,000=1,000=100%=10.0=Physicality=Tech.=10 Oct.=Uranus=P=1Ø.
Duffer=4,000=40%=P4.0D=Govt=Creatoc.=4April=Mercury=Hermes=G=A4.
Duffle bag=4,500=5,000=50%=P5.00D=Law=Time=Venus=5 May = Aphrodite>>L=N.
Dug(1)=2,500=3,000=30%=P3.0D=3.0=Creativity=Stars=Muses=3 March = C=I.
Dug(2)=3,500=4,000=40%=P4.0D=Govt=Creatoc.=4April=Mercury=Hermes=G=A4.
Dugout=16,000=16%=P1.60D=1.6=Cycle=Incarn.=Mind of GOD=1 June = Maia.
Duisburg=8,000=80%=P8.0D=Economy=Currency=Business=8 Aug.=Zeus>>E=v.

Duke=16,000=16%=P1.60D=1.6=Cycle=Incarn.=Mind of GOD=1 June = Maia.
The duke is a sovereign Prince in Great Britain. In Paradise the first son in the generations of Castle Makupedia is a demigod and Sovereign Prince governing the Disean Provinces. Others sons are sovereign princes who serve under the demigod governing a province. Castle Makupedia retains his perpetual rights as God of Paradise and is so worshipped.

Dulcet=2,000=20%=P2.00D=2.0=Nature=Matter=Moon=2 Feb.=Cupid=N=C+_
Dulcimer=11,500=12,000=12%=P1.20D=1.2=Knowl.=Edu.=12Dec.=Athena>>K=F
Dull=40,000=4,000=40%=P4.0D=Govt=Creatoc.=4April=Mercury=Hermes=G=A4.
Dullard=2,500=3,000=30%=P3.0D=3.0=Creativity=Stars=Muses=3 March = C=I.
Duluth=6,500=7,000=70%=P7.0D=7.0=Language=Assets=Mars=7 July=Pleiades.
Duly=4,000=40%=P4.0D=Govt=Creatoc.=4April=Mercury=Hermes=G=A4.
Dumas Alexandre=3,000=30%=P3.0D=3.0=Creativity=Stars=Muses=3 March = C=I.
Dumb=9,000=90%=P9.00D=9.0=Abstraction=Gods=Saturn=9Sept.>>A=Ø.
Dumbbell=10,500=11,000=11%=P1.10D=1.1=Idea=Brainchild=11 Nov.=SC=Athena
    >>I=MT.
Dumbfound=3,500=4,000=40%=P4.0D=Govt=Creatoc.=4April=Mercury=Hermes=G=A4.
Dum-dum=6,000=60%=P6.0D=Man=Earth=Royalty=6 June=Gaia=Maia>>M=M2.
Dummy=10,000=1,000=100%=10.0=Physicality=Tech.=10 Oct.=Uranus=P=1Ø.
Dump=10,000=1,000=100%=10.0=Physicality=Tech.=10 Oct.=Uranus=P=1Ø.
Dumpling=10,000=1,000=100%=10.0=Physicality=Tech.=10 Oct.=Uranus=P=1Ø.
Dumps=3,500=4,000=40%=P4.0D=Govt=Creatoc.=4April=Mercury=Hermes=G=A4.

Dump truck=5,500=5.5=80%=P5.50=Earth-Midway=5 May = Gaia.
Dumpy(1)=2,000=20%=P2.00D=2.0=Nature=Matter=Moon=2 Feb.=Cupid=N=C+_
Dumpy(2)=2,500=3,000=30%=P3.0D=3.0=Creativity=Stars=Muses=3 March = C=I.
Dun(1)=2,500=3,000=30%=P3.0D=3.0=Creativity=Stars=Muses=3 March = C=I.
Dun(2)=2,000=20%=P2.00D=2.0=Nature=Matter=Moon=2 Feb.=Cupid=N=C+_
Dunbar Paul=2,000=20%=P2.00D=2.0=Nature=Matter=Moon=2 Feb.=Cupid=N=C+_
Duncan Isadora=2,000=20%=P2.00D=2.0=Nature=Matter=Moon=2 Feb.=Cupid=N=C+_
Dunce=5,000=50%=P5.00D=Law=Time=Venus=5 May = Aphrodite>>L=N.
Dundee=4,000=40%=P4.0D=Govt=Creatoc.=4April=Mercury=Hermes=G=A4.

Dunderhead=4,000=40%=P4.0D=Govt=Creatoc.=4April=Mercury=Hermes=G=A4.
A dunce. Dunder(thunder)+Head. Dunce indicates a stupid person. We could deduce that thunder a key quality of Zeus converted to Mercury and induced by the Gods could be the leading cause of madness in persons. Thunder is a flash of high electric content such that mixing it in the mercury content of brain liquid could make a person stupid. Little wonder the epic movies are inspired to present the Gods as clouds and thunder when angry. Besides the Bible teaches that the voice of GOD is a thunder and roars as such. Clearly madness and stupidity is a generation punishment from Hermes the God of merchandise. "The too much money" concept or excessive praises given to money and materialsm could just be a sign of a dunderhead. The Creatocracy lives in quiet affluence and hates poverty.

Dune=4,000=40%=P4.0D=Govt=Creatoc.=4April=Mercury=Hermes=G=A4.
Dune buggy=5,500=5.5=80%=P5.50=Earth-Midway=5 May = Gaia.
Dung=1,500=15%=P1.50D=1.5=Authority=Solar Crown=1 May = Maia.
Dungaree=7,000=70%=P7.0D=7.0=Language=Assets=Mars=7 July=Pleiades.
Dungeon=3,000=30%=P3.0D=3.0=Creativity=Stars=Muses=3 March = C=I.
Dung hill=2,000=20%=P2.00D=2.0=Nature=Matter=Moon=2 Feb.=Cupid=N=C+_
Dunk=14,000=14%=P1.40D=1.4=Mgt.=Solar Energy=13 May=Athena=SC=0.1
Dunkirk=5,500=5.5=80%=P5.50=Earth-Midway=5 May = Gaia.
Duo=2,000=20%=P2.00D=2.0=Nature=Matter=Moon=2 Feb.=Cupid=N=C+_
Duodecimal=3,500=4,000=40%=P4.0D=Govt=Creatoc.=4April=Mercury=Hermes=G=A4.
Duodenum=7,500=8,000=80%=P8.0D=Econ.=Currency=Business=8 Aug.=Zeus>>E=v.
Dup.=1,000=100%=Physicality=Tech.=10 Oct.=Uranus=P=1Ø.
Dupe=6,000=60%=P6.0D=Man=Earth=Royalty=6 June=Gaia=Maia>>M=M2.
Duple=5,500=5.5=80%=P5.50=Earth-Midway=5 May = Gaia.
Duplex=4,500=5,000=50%=P5.00D=Law=Time=Venus=5 May = Aphrodite>>L=N.
Duplicate=12,000=12%=P1.20D=1.2=Knowl.=Edu.=12Dec.=Athena>>K=F
Duplicator=4,000=40%=P4.0D=Govt=Creatoc.=4April=Mercury=Hermes=G=A4.
Duplicity=4,000=40%=P4.0D=Govt=Creatoc.=4April=Mercury=Hermes=G=A4.

Durable=8,500=9,000=90%=P9.00D=9.0=Abstraction=Gods=Saturn=9Sept.>>A=Ø.
At least 90% is high standard for measuring durability. A borderline to godly perfection.

Dura matter=4,500=5,000=50%=P5.00D=Law=Time=Venus=5 May = Aphrodite>>L=N.
Durance=500=5%=P5.00D=5.0=Law=Time=Venus=5 May=Aphrodite>>L=N.
Durango=5,000=50%=P5.00D=Law=Time=Venus=5 May = Aphrodite>>L=N.
Duration=6,500=7,000=70%=P7.0D=7.0=Language=Assets=Mars=7 July=Pleiades.
Durban=8,000=80%=P8.0D=Economy=Currency=Business=8 Aug.=Zeus>>E=v.
Dürer albrecht.=3,000=30%=P3.0D=3.0=Creativity=Stars=Muses=3 March = C=I.
Duress=4,000=40%=P4.0D=Govt=Creatoc.=4April=Mercury=Hermes=G=A4.
Durham=5,000=50%=P5.00D=Law=Time=Venus=5 May = Aphrodite>>L=N.
During=7,000=70%=P7.0D=7.0=Language=Assets=Mars=7 July=Pleiades.
Durum=5,500=5.5=80%=P5.50=Earth-Midway=5 May = Gaia.
Duse Eleonora=2,500=3,000=30%=P3.0D=3.0=Creativity=Stars=Muses=3 March = C=I.
Dushanbe=4,500=5,000=50%=P5.00D=Law=Time=Venus=5 May = Aphrodite>>L=N.
Dusk=2,500=3,000=30%=P3.0D=3.0=Creativity=Stars=Muses=3 March = C=I.
Dusky=4,500=5,000=50%=P5.00D=Law=Time=Venus=5 May = Aphrodite>>L=N.
Dûsseldorf=7,500=8,000=80%=P8.0D=Econ.=Currency=Business=8 Aug.=Zeus>>E=v.
Dust=16,500=17,000=17%=P1.70D=1.7=Solar Asset=17 Feb.=Maia=MindComputing.
Dust bowl=5,000=50%=P5.00D=Law=Time=Venus=5 May = Aphrodite>>L=N.
Dust devil=4,000=40%=P4.0D=Govt=Creatoc.=4April=Mercury=Hermes=G=A4.
Duster=10,000=1,000=100%=10.0=Physicality=Tech.=10 Oct.=Uranus=P=1Ø.
Dusting=3,500=4,000=40%=P4.0D=Govt=Creatoc.=4April=Mercury=Hermes=G=A4.
Dustpan=4,500=5,000=50%=P5.00D=Law=Time=Venus=5 May = Aphrodite>>L=N.
Dust storm=6,000=60%=P6.0D=Man=Earth=Royalty=6 June=Gaia=Maia>>M=M2.
Dutch=15,000=1,500=15%=P1.50D=1.5=Authority=Solar Crown=1 May = Maia.
Dutch door=7,000=70%=P7.0D=7.0=Language=Assets=Mars=7 July=Pleiades.
Dutch elm disease=6,000=60%=P6.0D=Man=Earth=Royalty=6 June=Gaia=Maia>>M=M2.
Dutch oven=6,000=60%=P6.0D=Man=Earth=Royalty=6 June=Gaia=Maia>>M=M2.
Dutch treat=8,000=80%=P8.0D=Economy=Currency=Business=8 Aug.=Zeus>>E=v.
Duteous=1,000=100%=10.0=1.0=Mind=Sun=1 January=Helios >> M=E4.
Dutiable=2,000=20%=P2.00D=2.0=Nature=Matter=Moon=2 Feb.=Cupid=N=C+_
Dutiful=6,000=60%=P6.0D=Man=Earth=Royalty=6 June=Gaia=Maia>>M=M2.
Duty=18,000=18%=P1.80D=Solar Currency=Maks Currencies=1 Aug.=Maia.
D.V.M.=2,000=20%=P2.00D=2.0=Nature=Matter=Moon=2 Feb.=Cupid=N=C+_
Dvorak Anton.=2,000=20%=P2.00D=2.0=Nature=Matter=Moon=2 Feb.=Cupid=N=C+_
Dwarf=12,000=12%=P1.20D=1.2=Knowl.=Edu.=12Dec.=Athena>>K=F
Dwell=15,000=1,500=15%=P1.50D=1.5=Authority=Solar Crown=1 May = Maia.
Dwelling=3,000=30%=P3.0D=3.0=Creativity=Stars=Muses=3 March = C=I.
DWI=1,500=15%=P1.50D=1.5=Authority=Solar Crown=1 May = Maia.

Dwindle=4,500=5,000=50%=P5.00D=Law=Time=Venus=5 May = Aphrodite>>L=N.
Anything that measures in 4,500 =45% dwindles making it unstable. See Dollar.

Dy=3,000=30%=P3.0D=3.0=Creativity=Stars=Muses=3 March = C=I.
Dybbuk=9,000=90%=P9.00D=9.0=Abstraction=Gods=Saturn=9Sept.>>A=Ø.

Dye=8,500=9,000=90%=P9.00D=9.0=Abstraction=Gods=Saturn=9Sept.>>A=Ø.
Dyer Mary=3,500=4,000=40%=P4.0D=Govt=Creatoc.=4April=Mercury=Hermes=G=A4.
Dyestuff=1,500=15%=P1.50D=1.5=Authority=Solar Crown=1 May = Maia.
Dying=7,000=70%=P7.0D=7.0=Language=Assets=Mars=7 July=Pleiades.

Dynamic=16,500=17,000=17%=P1.70D=1.7=Solar Asset=17 Feb.=Maia=MindComputing.
The Mind is a constant dynamic and a dynamic constant provable by the synchronization
and crystallization of congruent energy particles that result as ideas on the 10,000 scale.
-Peter Matthews-Akukalia. Makupedian Sciences-Principles of Naturecology.
1.0*1.0=px=2.0+1.0=3.0x=px=5.0>>Law >> Rights >> Time >> Venus >> Aphrodite.

Dynamics=15,500=16,000=16%=P1.60D=1.6=Cycle=Incarn.=Mind of GOD=1 June
= Maia.
Dynamite=17,000=17%=P1.70D=1.7=Solar Asset=17 Feb.=Maia=MindComputing.
Dynamo=6,500=7,000=70%=P7.0D=7.0=Language=Assets=Mars=7 July=Pleiades.
Dynamometer=4,500=5,000=50%=P5.00D=Law=Time=Venus=5 May = Aphrodite>>L=N.

Dynasty=10,000=1,000=100%=10.0=Physicality=Tech.=10 Oct.=Uranus=P=1Ø.
The standards for a dynasty to be established is the 10,000. The Creatocracy is a dynasty.

Dys-=3,500=4,000=40%=P4.0D=Govt=Creatoc.=4April=Mercury=Hermes=G=A4.
Dysentery=8,500=9,000=90%=P9.00D=9.0=Abstraction=Gods=Saturn=9Sept.>>A=Ø.
Dysfunctional=5,000=50%=P5.00D=Law=Time=Venus=5 May = Aphrodite>>L=N.

Dyslexia=8,000=80%=P8.0D=Economy=Currency=Business=8 Aug.=Zeus>>E=v.
Dyslexia is a Zeusian energy born possibly with a higher understanding of things.

Dyspepsia=1,500=15%=P1.50D=1.5=Authority=Solar Crown=1 May = Maia.
Dysplasia=3,500=4,000=40%=P4.0D=Govt=Creatoc.=4April=Mercury=Hermes=G=A4.
Dysprosium=12,000=12%=P1.20D=1.2=Knowl.=Edu.=12Dec.=Athena>>K=F
Dystrophy=10,500=11,000=11%=P1.10D=1.1=Idea=Brainchild=11 Nov.=SC=Athena
>>I=MT.
Dz.=1,000=100%=10.0=1.0=Mind=Sun=1 January=Helios >> M=E4.

MAKABET =Ee=

E1=10,500=11,000=11%=P1.10D=1.1=Idea=Brainchild=Inv.=11 Nov.=SC=Athena>>I=MT.
The 5th letter of the English alphabet. Computing the psycho-weight.
Resultant*Position on the Maks. 1.1*5.0x=px=6.1+5.5=11.6x=px=45.15=50=5.0

5.0 >> Law = Order = Authority = Rights = Righteousness = Venus = Aphrodite.
When E is mentioned Righteousness through earned excess rights in assets is induced.

E2=1,000=100%=10.0=1.0=Mind=Sun=1 January=Helios >> M=E4.
E=1,000=100%=10.0=1.0=Mind=Sun=1 January=Helios >> M=E4.
EA.=500=5%=P5.00D=5.0=Law=Time=Venus=5 May=Aphrodite>>L=N.
Each=13,500=14,000=14%=P1.40D=1.4=Mgt.=Solar Energy=13 May=Athena=SC=0.1
Each other=7,000=70%=P7.0D=7.0=Language=Assets=Mars=7 July=Pleiades.
Eager=4,000=40%=P4.0D=Government =Creatocracy=4 April=Mercury=Hermes=G=A4.

Eagle=15,000=1,500=15%=P1.50D=1.5=Authority=Crown=Solar Core=1 May = Maia.
A former U.S. gold coin having the face value of ten dollars. This is wrong matrix because
a dollar in the first place is a silver coin and value. 1G=10S is speculative. See dollar in
D. Clearly we establish that the Maks is a diamond currency value systems such that one
Maks = Ten British Pounds >> P1=£10. The Creatocracy has resolved this currency crisis.

Eaglet=1,500=15%=P1.50D=1.5=Authority=Crown=Solar Core=1 May = Maia.
Eakins Thomas=2,000=20%=P2.00D=2.0=Nature=Matter=Moon=2 Feb.=Cupid=N=C+_
Ear(1)=10,000=1,000=100%=10.0=Physicality=Tech.=10 Oct.=Uranus=P=1Ø.
Ear(2)=5,500=5.5=80%=P5.50=Earth-Midway=5 May = Gaia.
Ear ache=2,000=20%=P2.00D=2.0=Nature=Matter=Moon=2 Feb.=Cupid=N=C+_
Ear drum=5,000=50%=P5.00D=Law=Time=Venus=5 May = Aphrodite>>L=N.
Ear flap=5,000=50%=P5.00D=Law=Time=Venus=5 May = Aphrodite>>L=N.
Earhart Amelia=2,500=3,000=30%=P3.0D=3.0=Creat.=Stars=Muses=3March = C=I>>GIL.
Earl=5,500=5.5=80%=P5.50=Earth-Midway=5 May = Gaia.
Earlobe=4,000=40%=P4.0D=Government =Creatocracy=4 April=Mercury=Hermes=G=A4.
Early=10,000=1,000=100%=10.0=Physicality=Tech.=10 Oct.=Uranus=P=1Ø.
Earmark=14,000=14%=P1.40D=1.4=Mgt.=Solar Energy/Electric=13 May=Athena=SC=0.1
Earmuff=6,000=60%=P6.0D=Man=Earth=Royalty=6 June=Gaia=Maia>>M=M2.
Earn=14,000=14%=P1.40D=1.4=Mgt.=Solar Energy/Electric=13 May=Athena=SC=0.1
Earned run=5,000=50%=P5.00D=Law=Time=Venus=5 May = Aphrodite>>L=N.
Earnest(1)=8,000=80%=P8.0D=Economy=Currency=8 Aug.=Zeus>>E=v.
Earnest(2)=6,500=7,000=70%=P7.0D=7.0=Language=Assets=Mars=7 July=Pleiades.
Earnings=3,500=4,000=40%=P4.0D=Govt=Creatocracy=4 April=Mercury=Hermes=G=A4.
Earphone=8,000=80%=P8.0D=Economy=Currency=8 Aug.=Zeus>>E=v.
Earpiece=13,500=14,000=14%=P1.40D=1.4=Mgt.=Solar Energy=13 May=Athena=SC=0.1
Earplug=10,000=1,000=100%=10.0=Physicality=Tech.=10 Oct.=Uranus=P=1Ø.
Earring=4,000=40%=P4.0D=Government =Creatocracy=4 April=Mercury=Hermes=G=A4.
Ear splitting=6,000=60%=P6.0D=Man=Earth=Royalty=6 June=Gaia=Maia>>M=M2.
Earth=10,000=1,000=100%=10.0=Physicality=Tech.=10 Oct.=Uranus=P=1Ø.
Earthen=2,500=3,000=30%=P3.0D=3.0=Creativity=Stars=Muses=3 March = C=I>>GIL.
Earthenware=5,000=50%=P5.00D=Law=Time=Venus=5 May = Aphrodite>>L=N.
Earthling=3,000=30%=P3.0D=3.0=Creativity=Stars=Muses=3 March = C=I>>GIL.

Earthly=7,500=8,000=80%=P8.0D=Economy=Currency=8 Aug.=Zeus>>E=v.
Earthmover=5,500=5.5=80%=P5.50=Earth-Midway=5 May = Gaia.
Earthquake=8,500=9,000=90%=P9.00D=9.0=Abstraction=Gods=Saturn=9Sept.>>A=Ø.

Earth science=7,500=8,000=80%=P8.0D=Economy=Currency=8 Aug.=Zeus>>E=v.
The Oracle: Principles of Creative Sciences by Peter Matthews-Akukalia. This book earned him the elevated position of becoming the World's 1st Creative Scientist in 2012.

Earth shaking=2,500=3,000=30%=P3.0D=3.0=Creat.=Stars=Muses=3 March = C=I>>GIL.
Earthward=2,500=3,000=30%=P3.0D=3.0=Creativity=Stars=Muses=3 March = C=I>>GIL.
Earthwork=4,500=5,000=50%=P5.00D=Law=Time=Venus=5 May = Aphrodite>>L=N.
Earthworm=6,500=7,000=70%=P7.0D=7.0=Language=Assets=Mars=7 July=Pleiades.
Earthy=4,500=5,000=50%=P5.00D=Law=Time=Venus=5 May = Aphrodite>>L=N.
Earwax=5,000=50%=P5.00D=Law=Time=Venus=5 May = Aphrodite>>L=N.
Earwig=7,500=8,000=80%=P8.0D=Economy=Currency=8 Aug.=Zeus>>E=v.
Ease=10,000=1,000=100%=10.0=Physicality=Tech.=10 Oct.=Uranus=P=1Ø.
Easel=4,000=40%=P4.0D=Government =Creatocracy=4 April=Mercury=Hermes=G=A4.
Easement=9,500=10,000=1,000=100%=10.0=Physicality=Tech.=10 Oct.=Uranus=P=1Ø.
East=10,000=1,000=100%=10.0=Physicality=Tech.=10 Oct.=Uranus=P=1Ø.
East Anglia=4,500=5,000=50%=P5.00D=Law=Time=Venus=5 May = Aphrodite>>L=N.
East Asia=4,500=5,000=50%=P5.00D=Law=Time=Venus=5 May = Aphrodite>>L=N.
East China Sea=8,500=9,000=90%=P9.00D=9.0=Abstr.=Gods=Saturn=9Sept.>>A=Ø.
Easter=4,000=40%=P4.0D=Government =Creatocracy=4 April=Mercury=Hermes=G=A4.
Easter Island=7,500=8,000=80%=P8.0D=Economy=Currency=8 Aug.=Zeus>>E=v.
Easterly=4,000=40%=P4.0D=Government =Creatocracy=4 April=Mercury=Hermes=G=A4.
Eastern=9,000=90%=P9.00D=9.0=Abstraction=Gods=Saturn=9Sept.>>A=Ø.
Eastern Church=8,000=80%=P8.0D=Economy=Currency=8 Aug.=Zeus>>E=v.
Easterner=5,500=5.5=80%=P5.50=Earth-Midway=5 May = Gaia.
Eastern Europe=7,500=8,000=80%=P8.0D=Economy=Currency=8 Aug.=Zeus>>E=v.
Eastern Hemisphere=5,000=50%=P5.00D=Law=Time=Venus=5 May = Aphrodite>>L=N.
Eastern Orthodox Church=5,000=50%=P5.00D=Law=Time=Venus=5 May =Odite>>L=N.
East Germany=6,000=60%=P6.0D=Man=Earth=Royalty=6 June=Gaia=Maia>>M=M2.
East Indies=7,000=70%=P7.0D=7.0=Language=Assets=Mars=7 July=Pleiades.
Eastman George=2,000=20%=P2.00D=2.0=Nature=Matter=Moon=2 Feb.=Cupid=N=C+_
Easy=10,000=1,000=100%=10.0=Physicality=Tech.=10 Oct.=Uranus=P=1Ø.
Easy chair=2,000=20%=P2.00D=2.0=Nature=Matter=Moon=2 Feb.=Cupid=N=C+_
Easy going=3,000=30%=P3.0D=3.0=Creativity=Stars=Muses=3 March = C=I>>GIL.
Eat=10,000=1,000=100%=10.0=Physicality=Tech.=10 Oct.=Uranus=P=1Ø.
Eatery=1,500=15%=P1.50D=1.5=Authority=Crown=Solar Core=1 May = Maia.
Eaves=4,500=5,000=50%=P5.00D=Law=Time=Venus=5 May = Aphrodite>>L=N.
Eavesdrop=2,500=3,000=30%=P3.0D=3.0=Creativity=Stars=Muses=3 March = C=I>>GIL.
Eban Abba=3,500=4,000=40%=P4.0D=Govt=Creat.=4April=Mercury=Hermes=G=A4.
Ebb=8,500=9,000=90%=P9.00D=9.0=Abstraction=Gods=Saturn=9Sept.>>A=Ø.
EbN=1,500=15%=P1.50D=1.5=Authority=Crown=Solar Core=1 May = Maia.

Ebonite=4,500=5,000=50%=P5.00D=Law=Time=Venus=5 May = Aphrodite>>L=N.
Ebony=8,000=80%=P8.0D=Economy=Currency=8 Aug.=Zeus>>E=v.
Ebro=8,500=9,000=90%=P9.00D=9.0=Abstraction=Gods=Saturn=9Sept.>>A=Ø.
EbS=1,500=15%=P1.50D=1.5=Authority=Crown=Solar Core=1 May = Maia.
Ebullient=4,000=40%=P4.0D=Govt.=Creatocracy=4 April=Mercury=Hermes=G=A4.
Ebullition=5,500=5.5=80%=P5.50=Earth-Midway=5 May = Gaia.
Ec.=500=5%=P5.00D=5.0=Law=Time=Venus=5 May=Aphrodite>>L=N.
Eccentric=10,000=1,000=100%=10.0=Physicality=Tech.=10 Oct.=Uranus=P=1Ø.
Ecclesiastes=2,000=20%=P2.00D=2.0=Nature=Matter=Moon=2 Feb.=Cupid=N=C+_
Ecclesiastic=3,000=30%=P3.0D=3.0=Creativity=Stars=Muses=3 March = C=I>>GIL.

Ecclesiastical=5,000=50%=P5.00D=Law=Time=Venus=5 May = Aphrodite>>L=N.
Relates to the Church as an institution. The Creatocracy has the Mind Temple Makstianism.

Ecclesiasticus=2,000=20%=P2.00D=2.0=Nature=Matter=Moon=2 Feb.=Cupid=N=C+_
Ecdysis=8,500=9,000=90%=P9.00D=9.0=Abstraction=Gods=Saturn=9Sept.>>A=Ø.
ECG=1,000=100%=10.0=1.0=Mind=Sun=1 January=Helios >> M=E4.
Echelon=9,000=90%=P9.00D=9.0=Abstraction=Gods=Saturn=9Sept.>>A=Ø.
Echinoderm=8,500=9,000=90%=P9.00D=9.0=Abstraction=Gods=Saturn=9Sept.>>A=Ø.
echo=10,000=1,000=100%=10.0=Physicality=Tech.=10 Oct.=Uranus=P=1Ø.

Echo=8,500=9,000=90%=P9.00D=9.0=Abstraction=Gods=Saturn=9Sept.>>A=Ø.
Greek myth of a nymph whose love for Narcissus cause her to pin away until only her
voice could be heard. Echoes are heard in the walls meaning that Echo is Goddess of the
walls. King Solomon warns in the Proverbs that walls had ears just the same as the birds.

Echo chamber=5,500=5.5=80%=P5.50=Earth-Midway=5 May = Gaia.
Echo gram=1,000=100%=10.0=1.0=Mind=Sun=1 January=Helios >> M=E4.
Echolocation=17,500=18,000=18%=P1.80D=Solar Currency=Maks=1 Aug.=Maia.
Éclair=7,000=70%=P7.0D=7.0=Language=Assets=Mars=7 July=Pleiades.
Éclat=3,000=30%=P3.0D=3.0=Creativity=Stars=Muses=3 March = C=I>>GIL.
Eclectic=6,500=7,000=70%=P7.0D=7.0=Language=Assets=Mars=7 July=Pleiades.

Eclipse=12,000=12%=P1.20D=1.2=Knowledge=Education=12Dec.=Athena>>K=F.
Eclipse is an activity of the Spirit of GOD Athena during which certain knowledge is
shared between the participatory planets, launched in the heavenly places and transmuted
to Man. Hermes as Jesus Christ predicted that darkness will cover the Sun and the moon
will turn to blood. This is the codes for the eclipse. There are Quartet Goddesses of Night
and Moon. Joel 2:31. Acts 2:20. Research shows about 43 verses exist on this subject.

Eclipsing=3,500=4,000=40%=P4.0D=Govt.=Creat.=4 April=Mercury=Hermes=G=A4.
Ecliptic=6,500=7,000=70%=P7.0D=7.0=Language=Assets=Mars=7 July=Pleiades.

Eclogue=1,500=15%=P1.50D=1.5=Authority=Crown=Solar Core=1 May = Maia.
ECM=1,500=15%=P1.50D=1.5=Authority=Crown=Solar Core=1 May = Maia.
Ecology=10,000=1,000=100%=Physicality= Tech.=10 Oct.=Uranus=P=1Ø.
Econometrics=4,000=40%=P4.0D=Govt=Creatocracy=4 April=Mercury=Hermes=G=A4.
Economic=9,500=10,000=1,000=100%=10.0=Physicality=Tech.=10 Oct.=Uranus=P=1Ø.
Economical=6,500=7,000=70%=P7.0D=7.0=Language=Assets=Mars=7 July=Pleiades.
Economics=8,000=80%=P8.0D=Economy=Currency=8 Aug.=Zeus>>E=v.
Economize=3,500=4,000=40%=P4.0D=Govt=Creato.=4 April=Mercury=Hermes=G=A4.

Economy=10,000=1,000=100%=10.0=Physicality=Tech.=10 Oct.=Uranus=P=1Ø.
In the Creative Sciences - Makupedia, economy is the 8th dimension of the universe operant on currency markets commerce merchandise business banking and transactions. The Creatocracy functions the creative economy which is based on the quantum currency module called the Maks currencies. The first anti-inflation currency driven on diamond values and metrics of the solar core, invented by Peter Matthews-Akukalia and first patented in Nigeria in 2020 and copyright protected worldwide. See the Makupedian sciences, Naturecology. He wrote the formula for economy as E=v >> V= Cost & Prices.

Ecosystem=5,500=5.5=80%=P5.50=Earth-Midway=5 May = Gaia.
Ecru=2,000=20%=P2.00D=2.0=Nature=Matter=Moon=2 Feb.=Cupid=N=C+_

Ecstasy=2,500=3,000=30%=P3.0D=3.0=Creativity=Stars=Muses=3 March = C=I>>GIL.
Intense joy or delight; rapture. So rapture is not necessarily a physical ascent of the human body to the sky in a bid to reach heaven as misinterpreted by Christians it is rather a state of mental ascent. Anything that induces ecstasy on healthy grounds is a rapture eg sex.

-ectomy=1,000=100%=10.0=1.0=Mind=Sun=1 January=Helios >> M=E4.
Ectopic pregnancy=7,500=8,000=80%=P8.0D=Economy=Currency=8 Aug.=Zeus>>E=v.
Ectotherm=7,000=70%=P7.0D=7.0=Language=Assets=Mars=7 July=Pleiades.
Ecua.=1,000=100%=10.0=1.0=Mind=Sun=1 January=Helios >> M=E4.
Ecuador=7,000=70%=P7.0D=7.0=Language=Assets=Mars=7 July=Pleiades.
Ecumenical=5,000=50%=P5.00D=Law=Time=Venus=5 May = Aphrodite>>L=N.
Ecumenism=4,500=5,000=50%=P5.00D=Law=Time=Venus=5 May = Aphrodite>>L=N.
Eczema=5,000=50%=P5.00D=Law=Time=Venus=5 May = Aphrodite>>L=N.
Ed.=1,500=15%=P1.50D=1.5=Authority=Crown=Solar Core=1 May = Maia.
-ed(1)=5,000=50%=P5.00D=Law=Time=Venus=5 May = Aphrodite>>L=N.
-ed(2)=5,000=50%=P5.00D=Law=Time=Venus=5 May = Aphrodite>>L=N.
-ed(3)=2,500=3,000=30%=P3.0D=3.0=Creativity=Stars=Muses=3 March = C=I>>GIL.
Edam=7,000=70%=P7.0D=7.0=Language=Assets=Mars=7 July=Pleiades.
Eddy=9,000=90%=P9.00D=9.0=Abstraction=Gods=Saturn=9Sept.>>A=Ø.

Eddy Mary Baker=5,000=50%=P5.00D=Law=Time=Venus=5 May = Aphrodite>>L=N.

1821-1910. American religious leader who founded Christian Science.(1879). Peter Matthews-Akukalia a Nigerian Christian leader who founded Makstianism, a religious faith computing and precision system that proves the Mind of GOD in the Creative Sciences.

Edel Weiss=5,500=5.5=80%=P5.50=Earth-Midway=5 May = Gaia.
Edema=4,500=5,000=50%=P5.00D=Law=Time=Venus=5 May = Aphrodite>>L=N.
Eden=6,500=7,000=70%=P7.0D=7.0=Language=Assets=Mars=7 July=Pleiades.
Eden Robert Anthony=5,500=5.5=80%=P5.50=Earth-Midway=5 May = Gaia.
Edge=11,500=12,000=12%=P1.20D=1.2=Knowledge=Education=12Dec.=Athena>>K=F.
Edging=6,000=60%=P6.0D=Man=Earth=Royalty=6 June=Gaia=Maia>>M=M2.
Edgewise=2,000=20%=P2.00D=2.0=Nature=Matter=Moon=2 Feb.=Cupid=N=C+_
Edging=3,500=4,000=40%=P4.0D=Govt=Creato.=4 April=Mercury=Hermes=G=A4.
Edgy=4,000=40%=P4.0D=Government =Creatocracy=4 April=Mercury=Hermes=G=A4.
Edible=2,000=20%=P2.00D=2.0=Nature=Matter=Moon=2 Feb.=Cupid=N=C+_
Edict=3,000=30%=P3.0D=3.0=Creativity=Stars=Muses=3 March = C=I>>GIL.
Edifice=3,500=4,000=40%=P4.0D=Govt=Creato.=4 April=Mercury=Hermes=G=A4.
Edify=4,000=40%=P4.0D=Government =Creatocracy=4 April=Mercury=Hermes=G=A4.
Edinburgh=6,500=7,000=70%=P7.0D=7.0=Language=Assets=Mars=7 July=Pleiades.

Edison Thomas Alva=2,000=20%=P2.00D=2.0=Nature=Moon=2 Feb.=Cupid=N=C+_
Peter Matthews-Akukalia (1978-Date) is a Nigerian inventor who adores Thomas Edison.

Edit=13,000=13%=P1.30=Solar Core=Faculty=13 January=Athena.
Edition=14,000=14%=P1.40D=1.4=Mgt.=Solar Energy/Electric=13 May=Athena=SC=0.1
Editorial=12,000=12%=P1.20D=1.2=Knowledge=Education=12Dec.=Athena>>K=F.
Editorialize=8,500=9,000=90%=P9.00D=9.0=Abstraction=Gods=Saturn=9Sept.>>A=Ø.
Edmonton=5,500=5.5=80%=P5.50=Earth-Midway=5 May = Gaia.

Edom=6,000=60%=P6.0D=Man=Earth=Royalty=6 June=Gaia=Maia>>M=M2.
Edomites were the tribe of Esau. An ancient country of Palestine between the Dead Sea and the Gulf of Aqaba. Perhaps the Israeli - Palestine war could be traced down to the inheritance trouble between Esau and Jacob in the Bible days. Today Diseans are citizens of the Creatocracy in the Creatocratic Nations of Paradise. A nation invented by Peter Matthews-Akukalia with four major classes as the Creative Scientists, Creative Scientist Professionals, Members of the Creatocratic Nations Organizations and the Makupedians.

EDP=2,500=3,000=30%=P3.0D=3.0=Creativity=Stars=Muses=3 March = C=I>>GIL.
EDT=1,500=15%=P1.50D=1.5=Authority=Crown=Solar Core=1 May = Maia.
Educable=2,000=20%=P2.00D=2.0=Nature=Matter=Moon=2 Feb.=Cupid=N=C+_
Educate=6,000=60%=P6.0D=Man=Earth=Royalty=6 June=Gaia=Maia>>M=M2.
Educated=11,000=11%=P1.10D=1.1=Idea=Brainchild=Inv.=11 Nov.=SC=Athena>>I=MT.

Education=9,000=90%=P9.00D=9.0=Abstraction=Gods=Saturn=9Sept.>>A=Ø.
A well educated Nation is one with whom at least 90% of its citizens are 60% educated and discovered through their potentials for inventions. Education is an abstraction process and hence requires a formula. He who writes the formula of, for a thing has not only discovered that thing but also owns it. Peter Matthews - Akukalia wrote the formula for education as K=F which interprets as knowledge is equal to Focus. Focus is interest and attention. The DDC code applies to the education system. Our creative education services includes the application of the TTN, CDX and MXD teaching methods are part of the latest methods developed by the Creatocracy to education development. The establishment of Sciences Arts and Social Sciences will now be complemented with the Creative Sciences as departments in secondary schools. In tertiary education, the Faculty of Creative & Psycho - Social Sciences (a.k.a. The Creative Sciences) will be inducted worldwide. The Creatocracy Universities Union (CUU) will bond manage and administer all Makupedia Universities, Chartered Universities and academic Institutions worldwide. Benefits rights pecuniary and ancillary tolls taxes levies gifts and products from the conventional education systems will suffice. Education is business. Creative Education is bigger business. Makupedia is life.

Educe=2,500=3,000=30%=P3.0D=3.0=Creativity=Stars=Muses=3 March = C=I>>GIL.

Edward(1)=5,000=50%=P5.00D=Law=Time=Venus=5 May = Aphrodite>>L=N.
Peter Matthews-Akukalia is King Maks 1. The God of Creatocracy Genius and Mind.

Edward(2)=7,000=70%=P7.0D=7.0=Language=Assets=Mars=7 July=Pleiades.
Victor Matthews-Akukalia, King Maks II. Prince of Paradise. Demi-God of the Creatocracy.

Edward I=3,500=4,000=40%=P4.0D=Govt=Creato.=4 April=Mercury=Hermes=G=A4.
Edward II=3,500=4,000=40%=P4.0D=Govt=Creato.=4 April=Mercury=Hermes=G=A4.
Edward III=3,500=4,000=40%=P4.0D=Govt=Creato.=4 April=Mercury=Hermes=G=A4.
Edward IV.=5,000=50%=P5.00D=Law=Time=Venus=5 May = Aphrodite>>L=N.
Edward V.=3,500=4,000=40%=P4.0D=Govt=Creato.=4 April=Mercury=Hermes=G=A4.
Edward VI.=4,500=5,000=50%=P5.00D=Law=Time=Venus=5 May = Aphrodite>>L=N.
Edward VII.=5,000=50%=P5.00D=Law=Time=Venus=5 May = Aphrodite>>L=N.
Edward VIII.=6,500=7,000=70%=P7.0D=7.0=Language=Assets=Mars=7 July=Pleiades.
Edwards Jonathan=3,000=30%=P3.0D=3.0=Creativity=Stars=Muses=3March = C=I>>GIL.
E.E.=1,500=15%=P1.50D=1.5=Authority=Crown=Solar Core=1 May = Maia.
-ee(1)=6,500=7,000=70%=P7.0D=7.0=Language=Assets=Mars=7 July=Pleiades.
-ee(2)=5,000=50%=P5.00D=Law=Time=Venus=5 May = Aphrodite>>L=N.
EEC=1,500=15%=P1.50D=1.5=Authority=Crown=Solar Core=1 May = Maia.
EEG=1,000=100%=10.0=1.0=Mind=Sun=1 January=Helios >> M=E4.
eel=4,500=5,000=50%=P5.00D=Law=Time=Venus=5 May = Aphrodite>>L=N.
EEO=1,500=15%=P1.50D=1.5=Authority=Crown=Solar Core=1 May = Maia.
-eer=4,000=40%=P4.0D=Government =Creatocracy=4 April=Mercury=Hermes=G=A4.
Eerie=5,000=50%=P5.00D=Law=Time=Venus=5 May = Aphrodite>>L=N.

Efface=4,500=5,000=50%=P5.00D=Law=Time=Venus=5 May = Aphrodite>>L=N.
Effect=10,000=1,000=100%=10.0=Physicality=Tech.=10 Oct.=Uranus=P=1Ø.
Effective=7,000=70%=P7.0D=7.0=Language=Assets=Mars=7 July=Pleiades.
Effector=6,500=7,000=70%=P7.0D=7.0=Language=Assets=Mars=7 July=Pleiades.
Effectual=5,000=50%=P5.00D=Law=Time=Venus=5 May = Aphrodite>>L=N.
Effectuate=2,000=20%=P2.00D=2.0=Nature=Matter=Moon=2 Feb.=Cupid=N=C+_
Effeminate=5,500=5.5=80%=P5.50=Earth-Midway=5 May = Gaia.
Efferent=9,000=90%=P9.00D=9.0=Abstraction=Gods=Saturn=9Sept.>>A=Ø.
Effervescence=7,500=8,000=80%=P8.0D=Economy=Currency=8 Aug.=Zeus>>E=v.
Effete=5,500=5.5=80%=P5.50=Earth-Midway=5 May = Gaia.
Efficacious=2,500=3,000=30%=P3.0D=3.0=Creativity=Stars=Muses=3March = C=I>>GIL.
Efficient=9,000=90%=P9.00D=9.0=Abstraction=Gods=Saturn=9Sept.>>A=Ø.
Effigy=6,500=7,000=70%=P7.0D=7.0=Language=Assets=Mars=7 July=Pleiades.
Effloresce=1,500=15%=P1.50D=1.5=Authority=Crown=Solar Core=1 May = Maia.
Efflorescence=9,500=10,000=1,000=100%=10.0=Phys.=Tech.=10 Oct.=Uranus=P=1Ø.
Effluent=7,500=8,000=80%=P8.0D=Economy=Currency=8 Aug.=Zeus>>E=v.
Effluvium=4,000=40%=P4.0D=Govt=Creatocracy=4 April=Mercury=Hermes=G=A4.
Effort=9,500=10,000=1,000=100%=10.0=Physicality=Tech.=10 Oct.=Uranus=P=1Ø.
Effrontery=1,500=15%=P1.50D=1.5=Authority=Crown=Solar Core=1 May = Maia.
Effulgent=1,500=15%=P1.50D=1.5=Authority=Crown=Solar Core=1 May = Maia.
Effuse=5,000=50%=P5.00D=Law=Time=Venus=5 May = Aphrodite>>L=N.
Effusion=4,000=40%=P4.0D=Govt.=Creatocracy=4 April=Mercury=Hermes=G=A4.
Eft=1,500=15%=P1.50D=1.5=Authority=Crown=Solar Core=1 May = Maia.

E.g.=2,000=20%=P2.00D=2.0=Nature=Matter=Moon=2 Feb.=Cupid=N=C+_
E.g. >> Exempli gratia (for example). The Creatocracy will say "ticologically", naturally.

Egalitarian=4,000=40%=P4.0D=Govt=Creatocracy=4 April=Mercury=Hermes=G=A4.
The Creatocracy as a form of government is the only system that does not just affirm but actually grants political economic and social equality for all. This book is proof.

Egg(1)=16,000=16%=P1.60D=1.6=Incarnation=Mind of GOD=1 June=Maia.
Egg(2)=4,500=5,000=50%=P5.00D=Law=Time=Venus=5 May = Aphrodite>>L=N.
Eggbeater=5,000=50%=P5.00D=Law=Time=Venus=5 May = Aphrodite>>L=N.
Egghead=2,000=20%=P2.00D=2.0=Nature=Matter=Moon=2 Feb.=Cupid=N=C+_
Eggnog=7,000=70%=P7.0D=7.0=Language=Assets=Mars=7 July=Pleiades.
Eggplant=6,000=60%=P6.0D=Man=Earth=Royalty=6 June=Gaia=Maia>>M=M2.
Egg roll=8,000=80%=P8.0D=Economy=Currency=8 Aug.=Zeus>>E=v.
Eggshell=5,500=5.5=80%=P5.50=Earth-Midway=5 May = Gaia.
Egis=1,500=15%=P1.50D=1.5=Authority=Crown=Solar Core=1 May = Maia.
Eglantine=1,000=100%=10.0=1.0=Mind=Sun=1 January=Helios >> M=E4.
Ego=16,500=17,000=17%=P1.70D=1.7=Solar Asset=17/20=17 Feb.=Maia=Mind Computing.
Egocentric=5,000=50%=P5.00D=Law=Time=Venus=5 May = Aphrodite>>L=N.

Egoism=5,000=50%=P5.00D=Law=Time=Venus=5 May = Aphrodite>>L=N.
Egomania=2,500=3,000=30%=P3.0D=3.0=Creativity=Stars=Muses=3 March = C=I>>GIL.
Egotism=11,500=12,000=12%=P1.20D=1.2=Knowledge=Education=12Dec.=Athena>>K=F.
Ego trip=6,000=60%=P6.0D=Man=Earth=Royalty=6 June=Gaia=Maia>>M=M2.
Egregious=2,000=20%=P2.00D=2.0=Nature=Matter=Moon=2 Feb.=Cupid=N=C+_
Egress=4,000=40%=P4.0D=Government=Creatocracy=4 April=Mercury=Hermes=G=A4.
Egret=5,500=5.5=80%=P5.50=Earth-Midway=5 May = Gaia.
Egypt=6,500=7,000=70%=P7.0D=7.0=Language=Assets=Mars=7 July=Pleiades.
Egyptian=6,500=7,000=70%=P7.0D=7.0=Language=Assets=Mars=7 July=Pleiades.
EHF=1,500=15%=P1.50D=1.5=Authority=Crown=Solar Core=1 May = Maia.
Elder=6,000=60%=P6.0D=Man=Earth=Royalty=6 June=Gaia=Maia>>M=M2.
Elder down=2,000=20%=P2.00D=2.0=Nature=Matter=Moon=2 Feb.=Cupid=N=C+_
Eight=7,000=70%=P7.0D=7.0=Language=Assets=Mars=7 July=Pleiades.
Eight ball=5,000=50%=P5.00D=Law=Time=Venus=5 May = Aphrodite>>L=N.
Eight ball.=2,500=3,000=30%=P3.0D=3.0=Creativity=Stars=Muses=3 March = C=I>>GIL.
Eighteen=7,000=70%=P7.0D=7.0=Language=Assets=Mars=7 July=Pleiades.
Eighteenth=6,000=60%=P6.0D=Man=Earth=Royalty=6 June=Gaia=Maia>>M=M2.
Eighth=7,000=70%=P7.0D=7.0=Language=Assets=Mars=7 July=Pleiades.
Eighth note=6,000=60%=P6.0D=Man=Earth=Royalty=6 June=Gaia=Maia>>M=M2.
Eightieth=6,500=7,000=70%=P7.0D=7.0=Language=Assets=Mars=7 July=Pleiades.
Eighty=4,000=40%=P4.0D=Government=Creatocracy=4 April=Mercury=Hermes=G=A4.
Eindhoven=5,000=50%=P5.00D=Law=Time=Venus=5 May = Aphrodite>>L=N.

Einstein Albert=4,500=5,000=50%=P5.00D=Law=Time=Venus=5 May = Aphrodite>>L=N.
German born American theoretical physicist. He was a borderline between Hermes and Aphrodite. Hence he understood the relationships or relativity of time in the Hermes - Aphrodite timeline. A Demigod by Creatocratic standards and approval of the Emperor. Peter Matthews-Akukalia, a Nigerian-Paradisean Psychoastronomer, inducted the E=MC2 formula interpreting the Mindset of Einstein through Mind Computing.

WDSD is a database and time laboratory that provides data for psycho - biometrics on Identity Management. It states the name of a person, date of birth, birth code and natural planet of birth and predicts the nature of person. These details are used to assess the innate potentials including the kind of education vocation relationships and even spouse. Assessment and appraisal is also carried out periodically on consulting to seek satisfaction qualification and fulfillment as to the purpose of the person's life and destiny scored.

Albert Einstein. Born 14 March, 1879. Died 18 April, 1955.
Birth Code: 8.0:100%+. Natural Planet Source>>Jupiter >> Zeus.
Birth Purpose: 1.8*7.9x=px=9.7+14.22=23.92x=px=161.854>>16(1.8)54
16 >> 1.6 >> Incarnation >> Reincarnation >> Cycle of Life.

So Zeus came to Earth as Albert Einstein to establish theoretical Physics as a precursor to Mind Computing. (1.8) indicates a new economic system would be discovered through it. This time nuclear economy being the huge resources deployed and earned through nuclear electricity. (5.4) interprets that he came with a company of spirits that would help his frail humanity establish his genius. A common trait of all genius and great reformers. Einstein was in space through dreams and discussed advanced space matters that was characterized by the science and technology of energy without ever traveling there.

His history links his activity at 16 that he took and failed his exams but excelled in Physics and Mathematics what we reckon as energy (mind) and digital (computing) making Mind Computing in abstract terms. Again the code 1-6 occurs as his specific grade level an excellent point in knowledge by the German standards. In 1896 he renounced his citizenship in the German kingdom of wútternberg to avoid military service. A trait of Zeus formed after the Titanomachy (War of the Titans) in Greek mythology. We conclude digitally that GOD was here as Einstein and still repeats his visits in a bid to help mankind get better. Symbolic of the term "born again by water and spirit". Time is a God and works with us.

Einsteinium=10,500=11,000=11%=P1.10D=1.1=Idea=Brainchild=11 Nov.=Athena>>I=MT.
Eire=1,000=100%=10.0=1.0=Mind=Sun=1 January=Helios >> M=E4.
Eisenhower Dwight David=3,500=4,000=40%=P4.0D=Govt.=4 April=Hermes=G=A4.
Either=10,000=1,000=100%=10.0=Physicality=Tech.=10 Oct.=Uranus=P=1Ø.

Ejaculate=7,500=8,000=80%=P8.0D=Economy=Currency=8 Aug.=Zeus>>E=v.
A violent borderline body process that links precision with economy >> Aries transits to Zeus. To ejaculate is to induce and acknowledge the need for the measure of currency. It is a commitment to the body and mind in the amount of 75%-80% activity. Mostly high propensity with people born in the months of July and August.

Eject=2,500=3,000=30%=P3.0D=3.0=Creativity=Stars=Muses=3 March = C=I>>GIL.
Ejection seat=8,000=80%=P8.0D=Economy=Currency=8 Aug.=Zeus>>E=v.
Eke=7,000=70%=P7.0D=7.0=Language=Assets=Mars=7 July=Pleiades.
EKG=500=5%=P5.00D=5.0=Law=Time=Venus=5 May=Aphrodite>>L=N.
Ekpwele=4,500=5,000=50%=P5.00D=Law=Time=Venus=5 May = Aphrodite>>L=N.
El.=500=5%=P5.00D=5.0=Law=Time=Venus=5 May=Aphrodite>>L=N.
Elaborate=10,000=1,000=100%=10.0=Physicality=Tech.=10 Oct.=Uranus=P=1Ø.
El Alamein=8,000=80%=P8.0D=Economy=Currency=8 Aug.=Zeus>>E=v.
Elam=5,500=5.5=80%=P5.50=Earth-Midway=5 May = Gaia.
Élan=4,000=40%=P4.0D=Government =Creatocracy=4 April=Mercury=Hermes=G=A4.
Eland=5,500=5.5=80%=P5.50=Earth-Midway=5 May = Gaia.
Elapid=7,000=70%=P7.0D=7.0=Language=Assets=Mars=7 July=Pleiades.
Elapse=3,000=30%=P3.0D=3.0=Creativity=Stars=Muses=3 March = C=I>>GIL.
Elasmobranch=6,500=7,000=70%=P7.0D=7.0=Language=Assets=Mars=7 July=Pleiades.
Elastic=10,000=1,000=100%=10.0=Physicality=Tech.=10 Oct.=Uranus=P=1Ø.
Elate=4,000=40%=P4.0D=Government =Creatocracy=4 April=Mercury=Hermes=G=A4.
Elba=6,000=60%=P6.0D=Man=Earth=Royalty=6 June=Gaia=Maia>>M=M2.

Elbe=8,500=9,000=90%=P9.00D=9.0=Abstraction=Gods=Saturn=9Sept.>>A=Ø.
Elbert Mount.=6,500=7,000=70%=P7.0D=7.0=Language=Assets=Mars=7 July=Pleiades.
Elbow=10,000=1,000=100%=10.0=Physicality=Tech.=10 Oct.=Uranus=P=1Ø.
Elbow grease=1,500=15%=P1.50D=1.5=Authority=Crown=Solar Core=1 May = Maia.
Elbow room=5,500=5.5=80%=P5.50=Earth-Midway=5 May = Gaia.
Elbrus Mount.=8,000=80%=P8.0D=Economy=Currency=8 Aug.=Zeus>>E=v.
Elburz Mountains=5,500=5.5=80%=P5.50=Earth-Midway=5 May = Gaia.
Elder(1)=10,000=1,000=100%=10.0=Physicality=Tech.=10 Oct.=Uranus=P=1Ø.
Elder(2)=6,500=7,000=70%=P7.0D=7.0=Language=Assets=Mars=7 July=Pleiades.
Elderberry=3,500=4,000=40%=P4.0D=Govt.=Creato.=4 April=Mercury=Hermes=G=A4.
Elderly=7,000=70%=P7.0D=7.0=Language=Assets=Mars=7 July=Pleiades.
Eldest=5,000=50%=P5.00D=Law=Time=Venus=5 May = Aphrodite>>L=N.

El Dorado=5,000=50%=P5.00D=Law=Time=Venus=5 May = Aphrodite>>L=N.
The Maks Currencies on the application of the natural value of things achieves the economic el dorado for all nations that adopt it as national currencies.
The Creatocratic Nations of Paradise is the El Dorado created by Castle Makupedia.

Eleanor of Aquitaine=5,000=50%=P5.00D=Law=Time=Venus=5 May = Aphrodite>>L=N.
Elect=10,000=1,000=100%=10.0=Physicality=Tech.=10 Oct.=Uranus=P=1Ø.
Electioneer=4,500=5,000=50%=P5.00D=Law=Time=Venus=5 May = Aphrodite>>L=N.
Elective=8,000=80%=P8.0D=Economy=Currency=8 Aug.=Zeus>>E=v.
Elector=4,000=40%=P4.0D=Government =Creatocracy=4April=Mercury=Hermes=G=A4.
Electoral College=7,500=8,000=80%=P8.0D=Economy=Currency=8 Aug.=Zeus>>E=v.
Electorate=2,500=3,000=30%=P3.0D=3.0=Creativity=Stars=Muses=3 March = C=I>>GIL.
Electra=9,000=90%=P9.00D=9.0=Abstraction=Gods=Saturn=9Sept.>>A=Ø.

Electric=4,000=40%=P4.0D=Government =Creatocracy=4April=Mercury=Hermes=G=A4.
Hermes energy from the planet Mercury that creates the human emotion and excitement. Peter Matthews-Akukalia, Castle Makupedia calculated the human emotion and discovered it is a thing known and operant as the bonded Brain energy Quantum >> General Interest Level (GIL) and Creative Mind Energy CME. He set the emotional benchmark as 6.0 and made it a standard in the Mind Assessment Tests for measuring the emotional content of a person. This led to the invention of the CCLT instrument known as the Makumeter Gauge. The highest normal emotion quantum is 4.0/6.0x100%=66.666667=666=700=70 %=7.0>> Measurements >> Precision >> Computing >> Works. This study also resolves the mystery of the Jesus 666 code as a predictive technology known to usher man into a near perfect mind state of GOD civilization. The will to power ambition and success are natural gifts of Hermes. Greek myth confirm Hermes as God of wealth through merchandise. The Creatocracy discovered that Hermes is the transmogrified Jesus Christ of Nazareth.

Electric chair=6,000=60%=P6.0D=Man=Earth=Royalty=6 June=Gaia=Maia>>M=M2.
Electric eel=6,500=7,000=70%=P7.0D=7.0=Language=Assets=Mars=7 July=Pleiades.

Electric eye=1,500=15%=P1.50D=1.5=Authority=Crown=Solar Core=1 May = Maia.
Electric guitar=6,500=7,000=70%=P7.0D=7.0=Language=Assets=Mars=7 July=Pleiades.
Electrician=7,500=8,000=80%=P8.0D=Economy=Currency=8 Aug.=Zeus>>E=v.

Electricity=13,500=14,000=14%=P1.40D=1.4=Mgt.=Solar Energy=13 May=Athena=SC=0.1
At an extreme state of emotional excitement or sexual transmutation the electricity module in the brain is activated where we connect to the spiritual resulting to the subconscious development of creative intelligence and a higher propensity to succeed. Sex is not an end in itself but a means to an end. It must be well managed in optimum benefits for mankind.

Electrify=8,500=9,000=90%=P9.00D=9.0=Abstraction=Gods=Saturn=9Sept.>>A=Ø.
Electro-=2,500=3,000=30%=P3.0D=3.0=Creativity=Stars=Muses=3 March = C=I>>GIL.
Electrocardiogram=3,500=4,000=40%=P4.0D=Govt.=4April=Mercury=Hermes=G=A4.
Electrocardiograph=5,500=5.5=80%=P5.50=Earth-Midway=5 May = Gaia.
Electrochemistry=4,500=5,000=50%=P5.00D=Law=Time=Venus=5 May =Odite>>L=N.
Electro convulsive therapy=9,000=90%=P9.00D=9.0=Abstr.=Gods=Saturn=9Sept.>>A=Ø.
Electrocute=4,000=40%=P4.0D=Govt=Creatocracy=4 April=Mercury=Hermes=G=A4.
Electrode=8,500=9,000=90%=P9.00D=9.0=Abstraction=Gods=Saturn=9Sept.>>A=Ø.
Electrodynamics=6,000=60%=P6.0D=Man=Earth=Royalty=6 June=Gaia=Maia>>M=M2.
Electroencephalogram=7,000=70%=P7.0D=7.0=Language=Assets=Mars=7 July=Pleiades.
Electroencephalograph=9,000=90%=P9.00D=9.0=Abst.=Gods=Saturn=9Sept.>>A=Ø.
Electrologist=5,500=5.5=80%=P5.50=Earth-Midway=5 May = Gaia.
Electrolysis=10,000=1,000=100%=10.0=Physicality=Tech.=10 Oct.=Uranus=P=1Ø.
Electrolyte=10,000=1,000=100%=10.0=Physicality=Tech.=10 Oct.=Uranus=P=1Ø.
Electrolytic=3,000=30%=P3.0D=3.0=Creativity=Stars=Muses=3 March = C=I>>GIL.
Electromagnet=10,000=1,000=100%=10.0=Physicality=Tech.=10 Oct.=Uranus=P=1Ø.
Electromagnetic spectrum=10,000=1,000=100%=10.0=Phys=Tech.=10Oct.=Uran.=P=1Ø.
Electromagnetism=6,500=7,000=70%=P7.0D=7.0=Lang.=Assets=Mars=7 July=Pleiades.
Electromotive=2,500=3,000=30%=P3.0D=3.0=Creat.=Stars=Muses=3 March = C=I>>GIL.
Electromotive force=12,000=12%=P1.20D=1.2=Knowledge=Edu.=12Dec.=Athena>>K=F.
Electron=9,000=90%=P9.00D=9.0=Abstraction=Gods=Saturn=9Sept.>>A=Ø.
Electronic=2,500=3,000=30%=P3.0D=3.0=Creativity=Stars=Muses=3 March = C=I>>GIL.
Electronic mail=9,000=90%=P9.00D=9.0=Abstraction=Gods=Saturn=9Sept.>>A=Ø.
Electronics=9,500=10,000=1,000=100%=10.0=Physicality=Tech.=10 Oct.=Uranus=P=1Ø.
Electron microscope=6,500=7,000=70%=P7.0D=7.0=Lang.=Assets=Mars=7 July=Pleiades.
Electron tube=10,000=1,000=100%=10.0=Physicality=Tech.=10 Oct.=Uranus=P=1Ø.
Electron volt=9,500=10,000=1,000=100%=10.0=Physicality=Tech.=10 Oct.=Uranus=P=1Ø.
Electrophoresis=8,500=9,000=90%=P9.00D=9.0=Abstr.=Gods=Saturn=9Sept.>>A=Ø.
Electroplate=5,500=5.5=80%=P5.50=Earth-Midway=5 May = Gaia.
Electroshock=3,000=30%=P3.0D=3.0=Creativity=Stars=Muses=3 March = C=I>>GIL.
Electrostatic=4,500=5,000=50%=P5.00D=Law=Time=Venus=5 May = Aphrodite>>L=N.
Electrostatics=2,500=3,000=30%=P3.0D=3.0=Creat.=Stars=Muses=3 March = C=I>>GIL.
Electrotype=8,000=80%=P8.0D=Economy=Currency=8 Aug.=Zeus>>E=v.
Eleemosynary=4,500=5,000=50%=P5.00D=Law=Time=Venus=5 May = Aphrodite>>L=N.

Elegance=13,000=13%=P1.30=Solar Core=Faculty=13 January=Athena.
Elegant=7,000=70%=P7.0D=7.0=Language=Assets=Mars=7 July=Pleiades.
Elegiac=4,500=5,000=50%=P5.00D=Law=Time=Venus=5 May = Aphrodite>>L=N.
Elegy=5,000=50%=P5.00D=Law=Time=Venus=5 May = Aphrodite>>L=N.

Element=10,000=1,000=100%=10.0=Physicality=Tech.=10 Oct.=Uranus=P=1Ø.
The Creatocracy has used MindComputing to track over 3,000 new elements. See The
Makupedian Sciences > Principles of Naturecology by Peter Matthews-Akukalia.

Elemental=6,500=7,000=70%=P7.0D=7.0=Language=Assets=Mars=7 July=Pleiades.
Elementary=6,500=7,000=70%=P7.0D=7.0=Language=Assets=Mars=7 July=Pleiades.
Elementary particle=4,000=40%=P4.0D=Govt.=Creato.=4 April=Mercury=Hermes=G=A4.

Elementary school=7,000=70%=P7.0D=7.0=Language=Assets=Mars=7 July=Pleiades.
The Creatocracy recommends the standard age for elementary school is fixed at 7years.

Elephant=8,000=80%=P8.0D=Economy=Currency=8 Aug.=Zeus>>E=v.
Elephantiasis=9,500=10,000=1,000=100%=10.0=Phys.=Tech.=10 Oct.=Uranus=P=1Ø.
Elephantine=6,000=60%=P6.0D=Man=Earth=Royalty=6 June=Gaia=Maia>>M=M2.
Elev.=500=5%=P5.00D=5.0=Law=Time=Venus=5 May=Aphrodite>>L=N.
Elevate=9,000=90%=P9.00D=9.0=Abstraction=Gods=Saturn=9Sept.>>A=Ø.
Elevation=15,000=1,500=15%=P1.50D=1.5=Authority=Crown=Solar Core=1 May = Maia.
Elevator=10,000=1,000=100%=10.0=Physicality=Tech.=10 Oct.=Uranus=P=1Ø.
Eleven=7,000=70%=P7.0D=7.0=Language=Assets=Mars=7 July=Pleiades.
Eleventh=6,500=7,000=70%=P7.0D=7.0=Language=Assets=Mars=7 July=Pleiades.
Elf=2,500=3,000=30%=P3.0D=3.0=Creativity=Stars=Muses=3 March = C=I>>GIL.
ELF=1,500=15%=P1.50D=1.5=Authority=Crown=Solar Core=1 May = Maia.
Elgar Edward=2,500=3,000=30%=P3.0D=3.0=Creat.=Stars=Muses=3 March = C=I>>GIL.
El Greco=1,500=15%=P1.50D=1.5=Authority=Crown=Solar Core=1 May = Maia.
Elicit=4,000=40%=P4.0D=Government =Creatocracy=4 April=Mercury=Hermes=G=A4.
Elide=7,000=70%=P7.0D=7.0=Language=Assets=Mars=7 July=Pleiades.
Eligible=5,000=50%=P5.00D=Law=Time=Venus=5 May = Aphrodite>>L=N.
Elijah=2,500=3,000=30%=P3.0D=3.0=Creativity=Stars=Muses=3 March = C=I>>GIL.
Eliminate=7,000=70%=P7.0D=7.0=Language=Assets=Mars=7 July=Pleiades.
Eliot George=5,000=50%=P5.00D=Law=Time=Venus=5 May = Aphrodite>>L=N.
Eliot Thomas S(tearns)=4,000=40%=P4.0D=Govt.=4April=Mercury=Hermes=G=A4.
Elisha=2,500=3,000=30%=P3.0D=3.0=Creativity=Stars=Muses=3 March = C=I>>GIL.

Elite=12,000=12%=P1.20D=1.2=Knowledge=Education=12Dec.=Athena>>K=F.
The Creatocracy is elite and is an elite group or class enjoying superior intellectual, social,
or economic status. We are driven by love for knowledge and the institution of knowledge.

Elitism=10,000=1,000=100%=10.0=Physicality=Tech.=10 Oct.=Uranus=P=1Ø.
Elixir=8,000=80%=P8.0D=Economy=Currency=8 Aug.=Zeus>>E=v.
Elizabeth=4,500=5,000=50%=P5.00D=Law=Time=Venus=5 May = Aphrodite>>L=N.
Elizabeth I.=4,000=40%=P4.0D=Govt=Creato.=4 April=Mercury=Hermes=G=A4.
Elizabeth II.=5,500=5.5=80%=P5.50=Earth-Midway=5 May = Gaia.
Elizabethan=4,500=5,000=50%=P5.00D=Law=Time=Venus=5 May = Aphrodite>>L=N.
Elk=2,000=20%=P2.00D=2.0=Nature=Matter=Moon=2 Feb.=Cupid=N=C+_
Ell(1)=5,500=5.5=80%=P5.50=Earth-Midway=5 May = Gaia.
Ell(2)=5,000=50%=P5.00D=Law=Time=Venus=5 May = Aphrodite>>L=N.
Ellington Edward Kennedy=4,000=40%=P4.0D=Govt.=4April=Mercury=Hermes=G=A4.
Ellipse=11,500=12,000=12%=P1.20D=1.2=Knowledge=Education=12Dec.=Athena>>K=F.
Ellipsis=12,500=13,000=13%=P1.30=Solar Core=Faculty=13 January=Athena.
Ellipsoid=5,000=50%=P5.00D=Law=Time=Venus=5 May = Aphrodite>>L=N.
Elliptic=5,000=50%=P5.00D=Law=Time=Venus=5 May = Aphrodite>>L=N.
Ellis Henry Havelock=3,000=30%=P3.0D=3.0=Creat.=Stars=Muses=3 March = C=I>>GIL.
Ellis Island=8,000=80%=P8.0D=Economy=Currency=8 Aug.=Zeus>>E=v.
Elm=9,000=90%=P9.00D=9.0=Abstraction=Gods=Saturn=9Sept.>>A=Ø.
El Misti=7,000=70%=P7.0D=7.0=Language=Assets=Mars=7 July=Pleiades.
Elocution=5,000=50%=P5.00D=Law=Time=Venus=5 May = Aphrodite>>L=N.
Elongate=2,500=3,000=30%=P3.0D=3.0=Creativity=Stars=Muses=3 March = C=I>>GIL.
Elope=11,000=11%=P1.10D=1.1=Idea=Brainchild=Inv.=11 Nov.=SC=Athena>>I=MT.
Eloquent=6,500=7,000=70%=P7.0D=7.0=Language=Assets=Mars=7 July=Pleiades.
El Paso=6,000=60%=P6.0D=Man=Earth=Royalty=6 June=Gaia=Maia>>M=M2.
El Salvador=7,500=8,000=80%=P8.0D=Economy=Currency=8 Aug.=Zeus>>E=v.
Else=10,000=1,000=100%=10.0=Physicality=Tech.=10 Oct.=Uranus=P=1Ø.
Elements (Periodic Table)=10,000=1,000=100%=10.0=Phy.=Tech.=10 Oct.=Uranus=P=1Ø.
Elsewhere=2,500=3,000=30%=P3.0D=3.0=Creativity=Stars=Muses=3 March = C=I>>GIL.
Elucidate=3,000=30%=P3.0D=3.0=Creativity=Stars=Muses=3 March = C=I>>GIL.
Elude=6,000=60%=P6.0D=Man=Earth=Royalty=6 June=Gaia=Maia>>M=M2.
Elul=5,000=50%=P5.00D=Law=Time=Venus=5 May = Aphrodite>>L=N.
Elusive=2,500=3,000=30%=P3.0D=3.0=Creativity=Stars=Muses=3 March = C=I>>GIL.
Elute=3,000=30%=P3.0D=3.0=Creativity=Stars=Muses=3 March = C=I>>GIL.
Elver=2,500=3,000=30%=P3.0D=3.0=Creativity=Stars=Muses=3 March = C=I>>GIL.
Elves=1,500=15%=P1.50D=1.5=Authority=Crown=Solar Core=1 May = Maia.
Elysium=3,500=4,000=40%=P4.0D=Govt.=Creato.=4 April=Mercury=Hermes=G=A4.
Em=10,000=1,000=100%=10.0=Physicality=Tech.=10 Oct.=Uranus=P=1Ø.
Em-=1,500=15%=P1.50D=1.5=Authority=Crown=Solar Core=1 May = Maia.
'Em=1,500=15%=P1.50D=1.5=Authority=Crown=Solar Core=1 May = Maia.
Emanciate=4,500=5,000=50%=P5.00D=Law=Time=Venus=5 May = Aphrodite>>L=N.
E-mail=1,500=15%=P1.50D=1.5=Authority=Crown=Solar Core=1 May = Maia.
Emalangeni=1,500=15%=P1.50D=1.5=Authority=Crown=Solar Core=1 May = Maia.
Emanate=5,000=50%=P5.00D=Law=Time=Venus=5 May = Aphrodite>>L=N.
Emancipate=4,000=40%=P4.0D=Govt=Creatocracy=4 April=Mercury=Hermes=G=A4.
Emasculate=2,000=20%=P2.00D=2.0=Nature=Matter=Moon=2 Feb.=Cupid=N=C+_
Embalm=5,000=50%=P5.00D=Law=Time=Venus=5 May = Aphrodite>>L=N.

Embank=6,500=7,000=70%=P7.0D=7.0=Language=Assets=Mars=7 July=Pleiades.
Embargo=12,000=12%=P1.20D=1.2=Knowledge=Education=12Dec.=Athena>>K=F.
Embark=8,500=9,000=90%=P9.00D=9.0=Abstraction=Gods=Saturn=9Sept.>>A=∅.

Embarrass=7,000=70%=P7.0D=7.0=Language=Assets=Mars=7 July=Pleiades.
Anything devoid of formula and computation naturally lacks precision. Such constitutes an embarrassment to learning processes policies adoptions constitutions and collective intelligence. The Creatocracy is a system of governance solidly built on precision.

Embassy=8,500=9,000=90%=P9.00D=9.0=Abstraction=Gods=Saturn=9Sept.>>A=∅.
Embassy of the Creatocracy or Mind Embassies reach out to people everywhere. First the Mind is the embassy between the celestial and the terrestrial. A door we have opened.

Embattled=3,000=30%=P3.0D=3.0=Creativity=Stars=Muses=3 March = C=I>>GIL.
Embed=5,000=50%=P5.00D=Law=Time=Venus=5 May = Aphrodite>>L=N.

Embellish=5,000=50%=P5.00D=Law=Time=Venus=5 May = Aphrodite>>L=N.
Greek myth teaches that Aphrodite is the Goddess of beauty sexual love and birth. Proved.

Ember=7,000=70%=P7.0D=7.0=Language=Assets=Mars=7 July=Pleiades.
Embezzle=6,500=7,000=70%=P7.0D=7.0=Language=Assets=Mars=7 July=Pleiades.
Embitter=3,000=30%=P3.0D=3.0=Creativity=Stars=Muses=3 March = C=I>>GIL.
Emblazon=8,000=80%=P8.0D=Economy=Currency=8 Aug.=Zeus>>E=v.
Emblem=9,000=90%=P9.00D=9.0=Abstraction=Gods=Saturn=9Sept.>>A=∅.

Embody=5,500=5.5=80%=P5.50=Earth-Midway=5 May = Gaia.
To embody something means to make it a whole. Incorporate.

Embolden=5,000=50%=P5.00D=Law=Time=Venus=5 May = Aphrodite>>L=N.
Embolism=5,000=50%=P5.00D=Law=Time=Venus=5 May = Aphrodite>>L=N.
Embolus=6,500=7,000=70%=P7.0D=7.0=Language=Assets=Mars=7 July=Pleiades.
Emboss=5,500=5.5=80%=P5.50=Earth-Midway=5 May = Gaia.
Embouchure=9,000=90%=P9.00D=9.0=Abstraction=Gods=Saturn=9Sept.>>A=∅.
Embower=4,000=40%=P4.0D=Govt=Creatocracy=4 April=Mercury=Hermes=G=A4.
Embrace=10,000=1,000=100%=10.0=Physicality=Tech.=10 Oct.=Uranus=P=1∅.
Embrasure=7,500=8,000=80%=P8.0D=Economy=Currency=8 Aug.=Zeus>>E=v.
Embrocate=6,500=7,000=70%=P7.0D=7.0=Language=Assets=Mars=7 July=Pleiades.
Embroider=4,500=5,000=50%=P5.00D=Law=Time=Venus=5 May = Aphrodite>>L=N.
Embroidery=5,500=5.5=80%=P5.50=Earth-Midway=5 May = Gaia.
Embroil=6,500=7,000=70%=P7.0D=7.0=Language=Assets=Mars=7 July=Pleiades.
Embryo=10,000=1,000=100%=10.0=Physicality=Tech.=10 Oct.=Uranus=P=1∅.

Embryology=7,000=70%=P7.0D=7.0=Language=Assets=Mars=7 July=Pleiades.
Emcee=5,000=50%=P5.00D=Law=Time=Venus=5 May = Aphrodite>>L=N.
Emend=3,500=4,000=40%=P4.0D=Govt.=Creatocracy=4 April=Mercury=Hermes=G=A4.
Emerald=5,000=50%=P5.00D=Law=Time=Venus=5 May = Aphrodite>>L=N.
Emerge=5,500=5.5=80%=P5.50=Earth-Midway=5 May = Gaia.
Emergency=5,000=50%=P5.00D=Law=Time=Venus=5 May = Aphrodite>>L=N.
Emeritus=4,500=5,000=50%=P5.00D=Law=Time=Venus=5 May = Aphrodite>>L=N.
Emerson Ralph Waldo=3,000=30%=P3.0D=3.0=Creat=Stars=Muses=3 March = C=I>>GIL.
Emery=5,000=50%=P5.00D=Law=Time=Venus=5 May = Aphrodite>>L=N.
Emetic=1,000=100%=10.0=1.0=Mind=Sun=1 January=Helios >> M=E4.
Emf or EMF=1,000=100%=Physicality= Tech.=10 Oct.=Uranus=P=1Ø.
-emia=1,500=15%=P1.50D=1.5=Authority=Crown=Solar Core=1 May = Maia.
Emigrate=7,000=70%=P7.0D=7.0=Language=Assets=Mars=7 July=Pleiades.
Émigré=5,500=5.5=80%=P5.50=Earth-Midway=5 May = Gaia.

Eminence=7,500=8,000=80%=P8.0D=Economy=Currency=8 Aug.=Zeus>>E=v.
The title "His Godship" is a right granted on the basis of the eminence of the Creatocracy.

Eminent=7,500=8,000=80%=P8.0D=Economy=Currency=8 Aug.=Zeus>>E=v.
Eminent domain=6,000=60%=P6.0D=Man=Earth=Royalty=6 June=Gaia=Maia>>M=M2.
Emir=5,000=50%=P5.00D=Law=Time=Venus=5 May = Aphrodite>>L=N.
Emirate=5,000=50%=P5.00D=Law=Time=Venus=5 May = Aphrodite>>L=N.
Emissary=4,500=5,000=50%=P5.00D=Law=Time=Venus=5 May = Aphrodite>>L=N.
Emit=6,500=7,000=70%=P7.0D=7.0=Language=Assets=Mars=7 July=Pleiades.
Emollient=3,500=4,000=40%=P4.0D=Govt=Creato.=4 April=Mercury=Hermes=G=A4.
Emolument=3,500=4,000=40%=P4.0D=Govt=Creato.=4 April=Mercury=Hermes=G=A4.
Emote=5,000=50%=P5.00D=Law=Time=Venus=5 May = Aphrodite>>L=N.

Emotion=6,500=7,000=70%=P7.0D=7.0=Language=Assets=Mars=7 July=Pleiades.

PICTURE of the CCLT/C2LT. CODE 10E.

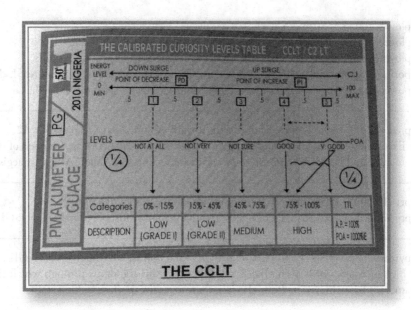

THE CCLT

See Electric on details of the CCLT invention.

Emotional=5,500=5.5=80%=P5.50=Earth-Midway=5 May = Gaia.

Emotive=6,000=60%=P6.0D=Man=Earth=Royalty=6 June=Gaia=Maia>>M=M2.

Empanada=5,000=50%=P5.00D=Law=Time=Venus=5 May = Aphrodite>>L=N.

Empanel=1,500=15%=P1.50D=1.5=Authority=Crown=Solar Core=1 May = Maia.

Empathy=5,000=50%=P5.00D=Law=Time=Venus=5 May = Aphrodite>>L=N.

Emperor=3,000=30%=P3.0D=3.0=Creativity=Stars=Muses=3 March = C=I>>GIL.

Psychoeconomix>>King of Creativity. Peter Matthews-Akukalia is the Most Sovereign Emperor, The Sovereign Creatocratic Republic of Paradise. - SCRP. Paradisean (Disean) citizenship is based on membership through study graduation and induction into the professionalism of the Creatocratic Nations of Paradise (of the Creative Scientists) CNP, The Creatocracy Republic (of the Mind Arts) TCR or Makupedialand of Testamentary Poets. Peter Matthews-Akukalia as Castle Makupedia is the God of Creatocracy Genius and Mind.

Emphasis=9,000=90%=P9.00D=9.0=Abstraction=Gods=Saturn=9Sept.>>A=Ø.

Emphysema=11,500=12,000=12%=P1.20D=1.2=Knowledge=Educ.=12Dec.=Athena>>K=F.

Empire=10,000=1,000=100%=10.0=Physicality=Tech.=10 Oct.=Uranus=P=1Ø.

The Creatocracy is the empire of the Peter Matthews-Akukalia, Castle Makupedia.

Empirical=6,000=60%=P6.0D=Man=Earth=Royalty=6 June=Gaia=Maia>>M=M2.

Empiricism=9,000=90%=P9.00D=9.0=Abstraction=Gods=Saturn=9Sept.>>A=Ø.

Emplacement=4,000=40%=P4.0D=Govt.=Creatocracy=4 April=Mercury=Hermes=G=A4.

Employ=5,500=5.5=80%=P5.50=Earth-Midway=5 May = Gaia.
Employee=5,000=50%=P5.00D=Law=Time=Venus=5 May = Aphrodite>>L=N.
Employment=7,000=70%=P7.0D=7.0=Language=Assets=Mars=7 July=Pleiades.
Emporium=4,500=5,000=50%=P5.00D=Law=Time=Venus=5 May = Aphrodite>>L=N.
Empower=5,000=50%=P5.00D=Law=Time=Venus=5 May = Aphrodite>>L=N.

Empress=6,000=60%=P6.0D=Man=Earth=Royalty=6 June=Gaia=Maia>>M=M2.
Her Excellency Justina Chinwendu Etigwam Matthews-Akukalia is the Empress of the
Creatocracy and Paradise Nations. To be addressed as Empress Tina I. Athena is aegis.

Empty=10,000=1,000=100%=10.0=Physicality=Tech.=10 Oct.=Uranus=P=1Ø.
Empty handed=3,000=30%=P3.0D=3.0=Creativity=Stars=Muses=3 March = C=I>>GIL.

Empyrean=3,000=30%=P3.0D=3.0=Creativity=Stars=Muses=3 March = C=I>>GIL.
The highest reaches of heaven. The sky. Creativity is this standards through which the
Creatocracy has achieved its Peak of Aspirations to attain apotheosis, God status.

EMT=1,500=15%=P1.50D=1.5=Authority=Crown=Solar Core=1 May = Maia.

Emu=9,000=90%=P9.00D=9.0=Abstraction=Gods=Saturn=9Sept.>>A=Ø.
A messenger of the God council manifested as a large flightless Australian bird that
monitors Australia and South America. Note that birds are created to monitor things and
report back to the Creator or Ruler in charge. They are monitoring spirits for our good.

Emulate=4,000=40%=P4.0D=Govt.=Creatocracy=4 April=Mercury=Hermes=G=A4.
Emulsify=2,500=3,000=30%=P3.0D=3.0=Creativity=Stars=Muses=3 March = C=I>>GIL.
Emulsion=10,000=1,000=100%=10.0=Physicality=Tech.=10 Oct.=Uranus=P=1Ø.
En=5,500=5.5=80%=P5.50=Earth-Midway=5 May = Gaia.
En-(1)=12,000=12%=P1.20D=1.2=Knowledge=Education=12Dec.=Athena>>K=F.
En-(2)=1,500=15%=P1.50D=1.5=Authority=Crown=Solar Core=1 May = Maia.
-En(1)=6,000=60%=P6.0D=Man=Earth=Royalty=6 June=Gaia=Maia>>M=M2.
-En(2)=2,000=20%=P2.00D=2.0=Nature=Matter=Moon=2 Feb.=Cupid=N=C+_
Enable=7,500=8,000=80%=P8.0D=Economy=Currency=8 Aug.=Zeus>>E=v.
Enact=6,000=60%=P6.0D=Man=Earth=Royalty=6 June=Gaia=Maia>>M=M2.
Enamel=14,500=15,000=1,500=15%=P1.50D=1.5=Authority=Solar Crown=1 May = Maia.
Enamor=2,500=3,000=30%=P3.0D=3.0=Creativity=Stars=Muses=3 March = C=I>>GIL.
En amour=2,500=3,000=30%=P3.0D=3.0=Creativity=Stars=Muses=3 March = C=I>>GIL.
En bloc=2,500=3,000=30%=P3.0D=3.0=Creativity=Stars=Muses=3 March = C=I>>GIL.
Enc.=1,000=100%=10.0=1.0=Mind=Sun=1 January=Helios >> M=E4.
Encamp=4,000=40%=P4.0D=Government =Creatocracy=4 April=Mercury=Hermes=G=A4.
Encapsulate=5,500=5.5=80%=P5.50=Earth-Midway=5 May = Gaia.
Encase=2,000=20%=P2.00D=2.0=Nature=Matter=Moon=2 Feb.=Cupid=N=C+_

Encephalitis=2,000=20%=P2.00D=2.0=Nature=Matter=Moon=2 Feb.=Cupid=N=C+_
Encephalo-=1,000=100%=10.0=1.0=Mind=Sun=1 January=Helios >> M=E4.
Encephalogram=3,500=4,000=40%=P4.0D=Govt.=4April=Mercury=Hermes=G=A4.
Encephaloma=2,500=3,000=30%=P3.0D=3.0=Creat=Stars=Muses=3 March = C=I>>GIL.
Enchain=2,500=3,000=30%=P3.0D=3.0=Creativity=Stars=Muses=3 March = C=I>>GIL.
Enchain=3,500=4,000=40%=P4.0D=Govt.=Creatocracy=4 April=Mercury=Hermes=G=A4.
Enchant=7,000=70%=P7.0D=7.0=Language=Assets=Mars=7 July=Pleiades.
Enchilada=6,500=7,000=70%=P7.0D=7.0=Language=Assets=Mars=7 July=Pleiades.
Encipher=3,000=30%=P3.0D=3.0=Creativity=Stars=Muses=3 March = C=I>>GIL.
Encircle=8,000=80%=P8.0D=Economy=Currency=8 Aug.=Zeus>>E=v.
Encl.=1,000=100%=10.0=1.0=Mind=Sun=1 January=Helios >> M=E4.
Enclave=5,500=5.5=80%=P5.50=Earth-Midway=5 May = Gaia.
Enclose=12,000=12%=P1.20D=1.2=Knowledge=Education=12Dec.=Athena>>K=F.
Encode=6,000=60%=P6.0D=Man=Earth=Royalty=6 June=Gaia=Maia>>M=M2.
Encomium=1,500=15%=P1.50D=1.5=Authority=Crown=Solar Core=1 May = Maia.
Encompass=4,500=5,000=50%=P5.00D=Law=Time=Venus=5 May = Aphrodite>>L=N.
Encore=8,000=80%=P8.0D=Economy=Currency=8 Aug.=Zeus>>E=v.
Encounter=9,000=90%=P9.00D=9.0=Abstraction=Gods=Saturn=9Sept.>>A=Ø.
Encourage=10,000=1,000=100%=10.0=Physicality=Tech.=10 Oct.=Uranus=P=1Ø.
Encroach=4,500=5,000=50%=P5.00D=Law=Time=Venus=5 May = Aphrodite>>L=N.
Encrust=4,000=40%=P4.0D=Government =Creatocracy=4April=Mercury=Hermes=G=A4.
Encrypt=6,500=7,000=70%=P7.0D=7.0=Language=Assets=Mars=7 July=Pleiades.
Encumber=6,000=60%=P6.0D=Man=Earth=Royalty=6 June=Gaia=Maia>>M=M2.
-ency=2,500=3,000=30%=P3.0D=3.0=Creativity=Stars=Muses=3 March = C=I>>GIL.
Encyc.=500=5%=P5.00D=5.0=Law=Time=Venus=5 May=Aphrodite>>L=N.
Encyclical=1,000=100%=10.0=1.0=Mind=Sun=1 January=Helios >> M=E4.

Encyclopedia=11,000=11%=P1.10D=1.1=Idea=Brainchild=Inv.=11 Nov.=SC=Athena>>I=MT. Makupedia is the education systems, professional practices and applications invented by Peter Matthews - Akukalia, Castle Makupedia. It comprises Mind Arts, Faiths, Creative Sciences, Cosmic Laws, Mind Technologies, Body of knowledge, Fields of Study, Academic Disciplines, Discoveries, Inventions, Database Laboratories, Measurements & Computations, Institutions & Organizations, Courts, Currencies & Economies, Encyclopedia, Nations and the Creatocracy. The World Digital Dictionary is the Castle Makupedia Encyclopedia. Peter Matthews - Akukalia, is honored as Castle Makupedia, the God of Creatocracy, Genius & Mind, wearer of the Solar Crown, Dragon Lord of the Sky and Husband to Athena the Goddess of wisdom, handicrafts and mental warfare.

Encyst=4,000=40%=P4.0D=Government =Creatocracy=4April=Mercury=Hermes=G=A4.
End=10,000=1,000=100%=10.0=Physicality=Tech.=10 Oct.=Uranus=P=1Ø.
Endanger=3,000=30%=P3.0D=3.0=Creativity=Stars=Muses=3 March = C=I>>GIL.
Endangered=4,500=5,000=50%=P5.00D=Law=Time=Venus=5 May = Aphrodite>>L=N.
Endear=1,500=15%=P1.50D=1.5=Authority=Crown=Solar Core=1 May = Maia.
Endearment=2,000=20%=P2.00D=2.0=Nature=Matter=Moon=2 Feb.=Cupid=N=C+_

Endeavor=9,500=10,000=1,000=100%=10.0=Physicality=Tech.=10 Oct.=Uranus=P=1Ø.
Endecott John=4,000=40%=P4.0D=Government=4 April=Mercury=Hermes=G=A4.
Endemic=7,500=8,000=80%=P8.0D=Economy=Currency=8 Aug.=Zeus>>E=v.
Endive=8,000=80%=P8.0D=Economy=Currency=8 Aug.=Zeus>>E=v.

Endless=8,000=80%=P8.0D=Economy=Currency=8 Aug.=Zeus>>E=v.
Zeus the Most High is an endless flow of economy resources currencies and value. And so
is the Creatocracy that has become directly connected on rights to the systems of Heaven.

End most=4,000=40%=P4.0D=Govt.=Creatocracy=4 April=Mercury=Hermes=G=A4.
-endo=3,000=30%=P3.0D=3.0=Creativity=Stars=Muses=3 March = C=I>>GIL.
Endocrine=6,500=7,000=70%=P7.0D=7.0=Language=Assets=Mars=7 July=Pleiades.
Endocrine gland=8,500=9,000=90%=P9.00D=9.0=Abst.=Gods=Saturn=9Sept.>>A=Ø.
Endocrinology=4,500=5,000=50%=P5.00D=Law=Time=Venus=5 May = Aphrodite>>L=N.
Endodontics=8,000=80%=P8.0D=Economy=Currency=8 Aug.=Zeus>>E=v.
Endogenous=3,500=4,000=40%=P4.0D=Government=4 April=Mercury=Hermes=G=A4.
Endometriosis=7,000=70%=P7.0D=7.0=Language=Assets=Mars=7 July=Pleiades.
Endometrium=3,500=4,000=40%=P4.0D=Government=4 April=Mercury=Hermes=G=A4.
Endo plasm=6,000=60%=P6.0D=Man=Earth=Royalty=6 June=Gaia=Maia>>M=M2.
Endorphin=9,000=90%=P9.00D=9.0=Abstraction=Gods=Saturn=9Sept.>>A=Ø.
Endorse=10,000=1,000=100%=10.0=Physicality=Tech.=10 Oct.=Uranus=P=1Ø.
Endoscopic=9,000=90%=P9.00D=9.0=Abstraction=Gods=Saturn=9Sept.>>A=Ø.
Endotherm=9,000=90%=P9.00D=9.0=Abstraction=Gods=Saturn=9Sept.>>A=Ø.
Endothermic=2,000=20%=P2.00D=2.0=Nature=Matter=Moon=2 Feb.=Cupid=N=C+_
Endow=7,500=8,000=80%=P8.0D=Economy=Currency=8 Aug.=Zeus>>E=v.
Endue=7,000=70%=P7.0D=7.0=Language=Assets=Mars=7 July=Pleiades.
Endure=7,500=8,000=80%=P8.0D=Economy=Currency=8 Aug.=Zeus>>E=v.
End wise=3,000=30%=P3.0D=3.0=Creativity=Stars=Muses=3 March = C=I>>GIL.
End zone=6,000=60%=P6.0D=Man=Earth=Royalty=6 June=Gaia=Maia>>M=M2.
ENE=1,000=100%=10.0=1.0=Mind=Sun=1 January=Helios >> M=E4.
-ene=7,500=8,000=80%=P8.0D=Economy=Currency=8 Aug.=Zeus>>E=v.
Enema=6,000=60%=P6.0D=Man=Earth=Royalty=6 June=Gaia=Maia>>M=M2.
Enemy=15,500=16,000=16%=P1.60D=1.6=Incarnation=Mind of GOD=1 June=Maia.
Energetic=4,500=5,000=50%=P5.00D=Law=Time=Venus=5 May = Aphrodite>>L=N.
Energize=5,000=50%=P5.00D=Law=Time=Venus=5 May = Aphrodite>>L=N.

Energy=9,500=10,000=1,000=100%=10.0=Physicality=Tech.=10 Oct.=Uranus=P=1Ø.
A capacity transmuted from the abstract to the physical realms. Peter Matthews-Akukalia
successfully computed pure cosmic energy and discovered it is the abstract equivalent
for what we call the mind. Hence the energy that runs a thing constitutes the mind of
that thing. Energy is therefore a borderline or a means to an end but not an end in itself.
Through energy, the result shows Gods as abstract beings that transform into the physical.
The universe is energy that flows from the cosmic hole to planets to earth to mankind.

Enervate=4,000=40%=P4.0D=Govt.=Creatocracy=4 April=Mercury=Hermes=G=A4.
Enfeeble=1,500=15%=P1.50D=1.5=Authority=Solar Crown=1 May = Maia.
Enfilade=11,500=12,000=12%=P1.20D=1.2=Knowledge=Education=12Dec.=Athena>>K=F.
Enfold=4,500=5,000=50%=P5.00D=Law=Time=Venus=5 May = Aphrodite>>L=N.
Enforce=5,500=5.5=80%=P5.50=Earth-Midway=5 May = Gaia.
Enfranchise=8,500=9,000=90%=P9.00D=9.0=Abstraction=Gods=Saturn=9Sept.>>A=Ø.
Eng.=1,000=100%=10.0=1.0=Mind=Sun=1 January=Helios >> M=E4.
Engage=17,500=18,000=18%=P1.80D=Solar Currency=Maks Currencies=1 Aug.=Maia.
Engaged=7,500=8,000=80%=P8.0D=Economy=Currency=8 Aug.=Zeus>>E=v.
Engagement=13,000=13%=P1.30=Solar Core=Faculty=13 January=Athena.
Engaging=1,000=100%=10.0=1.0=Mind=Sun=1 January=Helios >> M=E4.
En garde=6,000=60%=P6.0D=Man=Earth=Royalty=6 June=Gaia=Maia>>M=M2.
Engels Frederick=3,500=4,000=40%=P4.0D=Govt.=4 April=Mercury=Hermes=G=A4.
Engender=2,500=3,000=30%=P3.0D=3.0=Creativity=Stars=Muses=3 March = C=I>>GIL.

Engine=9,000=90%=P9.00D=9.0=Abstraction=Gods=Saturn=9Sept.>>A=Ø.
Now engine is a mechanical machine that converts energy into mechanical force or motion. The real engine behind a thing is the computed and interpreted abstract forces in that thing deduced as the codes. These codes are indicated as the alphanumerics that guide the existence and activities of such thing. They include telephone lines, birth dates, registrations, etc. These abstract forces or codes are called Mindwares and when deduced through mind computing translates into softwares. Peter Matthews-Akukalia discovered that our lives and activities revolved around the energy fluxes of these abstractions and proved that numbers were the real essence of existence. See Energy.

Engine block=5,500=5.5=80%=P5.50=Earth-Midway=5 May = Gaia.
Engineer=16,500=17,000=17%=P1.70D=1.7=Solar Asset=17 Feb.=Maia=Mind Computing.

Engineering=7,500=8,000=80%=P8.0D=Economy=Currency=8 Aug.=Zeus>>E=v.
A borderline between works and business. From Aries to Zeus >> Computing to Currency.

England=7,000=70%=P7.0D=7.0=Language=Assets=Mars=7 July=Pleiades.
Aries is deduced to be the cosmic ruler of England. England is works and assets.

English=10,000=1,000=100%=10.0=Physicality=Tech.=10 Oct.=Uranus=P=1Ø.
English Channel=5,500=5.5=80%=P5.50=Earth-Midway=5 May = Gaia.
English horn=8,500=9,000=90%=P9.00D=9.0=Abstraction=Gods=Saturn=9Sept.>>A=Ø.
English setter=10,000=1,000=100%=10.0=Physicality=Tech.=10 Oct.=Uranus=P=1Ø.
Engorge=4,000=40%=P4.0D=Govt.=Creatocracy=4 April=Mercury=Hermes=G=A4.
Engraft=4,500=5,000=50%=P5.00D=Law=Time=Venus=5 May = Aphrodite>>L=N.
Engrave=12,500=13,000=13%=P1.30=Solar Core=Faculty=13 January=Athena.

Engraving=10,000=1,000=100%=10.0=Physicality=Tech.=10 Oct.=Uranus=P=1Ø.
Engross=6,500=7,000=70%=P7.0D=7.0=Language=Assets=Mars=7 July=Pleiades.
Engulf=7,000=70%=P7.0D=7.0=Language=Assets=Mars=7 July=Pleiades.
Enhance=4,000=40%=P4.0D=Govt.=Creatocracy=4 April=Mercury=Hermes=G=A4.
Enigma=3,500=4,000=40%=P4.0D=Govt.=Creatocracy=4 April=Mercury=Hermes=G=A4.
Eniwetok=5,000=50%=P5.00D=Law=Time=Venus=5 May = Aphrodite>>L=N.
Enjoin=9,500=10,000=1,000=100%=Physicality= Tech.=10 Oct.=Uranus=P=1Ø.
Enjoy=6,500=7,000=70%=P7.0D=7.0=Language=Assets=Mars=7 July=Pleiades.
Enlarge=9,000=90%=P9.00D=9.0=Abstraction=Gods=Saturn=9Sept.>>A=Ø.
Enlighten=4,000=40%=P4.0D=Govt.=Creatocracy=4 April=Mercury=Hermes=G=A4.
Enlist=8,000=80%=P8.0D=Economy=Currency=8 Aug.=Zeus>>E=v.
Enliven=3,000=30%=P3.0D=3.0=Creativity=Stars=Muses=3 March = C=I>>GIL.
En masse=3,500=4,000=40%=P4.0D=Govt.=Creato.=4 April=Mercury=Hermes=G=A4.
Enmesh=7,500=8,000=80%=P8.0D=Economy=Currency=8 Aug.=Zeus>>E=v.
Enmity=2,500=3,000=30%=P3.0D=3.0=Creativity=Stars=Muses=3 March = C=I>>GIL.

Ennoble=3,000=30%=P3.0D=3.0=Creativity=Stars=Muses=3 March = C=I>>GIL.
The muses grant inspiration for creativity that makes one a noble hence the Creatocracy governs all creativity and all nobility through the rights of planetary and stellar computing.

Ennui=6,500=7,000=70%=P7.0D=7.0=Language=Assets=Mars=7 July=Pleiades.
Enormity=6,500=7,000=70%=P7.0D=7.0=Language=Assets=Mars=7 July=Pleiades.
Enormous=5,000=50%=P5.00D=Law=Time=Venus=5 May = Aphrodite>>L=N.
Enough=17,000=17%=P1.70D=1.7=Solar Asset=17 Feb.=Maia=Mind Computing.
Enquire=1,500=15%=P1.50D=1.5=Authority=Solar Crown=1 May = Maia.
Enrage=3,000=30%=P3.0D=3.0=Creativity=Stars=Muses=3 March = C=I>>GIL.

Enrapture=6,500=7,000=70%=P7.0D=7.0=Language=Assets=Mars=7 July=Pleiades.
A borderline between royalty and precision >> Earth and Works >> Emotion and Computing >> emotional computing or measures of emotions is to achieve the state of rapture.

Enrich=9,000=90%=P9.00D=9.0=Abstraction=Gods=Saturn=9Sept.>>A=Ø.
Enroll=4,500=5,000=50%=P5.00D=Law=Time=Venus=5 May = Aphrodite>>L=N.
En route=2,500=3,000=30%=P3.0D=3.0=Creativity=Stars=Muses=3 March = C=I>>GIL.
ENS=500=5%=P5.00D=5.0=Law=Time=Venus=5 May=Aphrodite>>L=N.
Ensconce=5,500=5.5=80%=P5.50=Earth-Midway=5 May = Gaia.
Ensemble=10,000=1,000=100%=10.0=Physicality=Tech.=10 Oct.=Uranus=P=1Ø.
Enshrine=5,500=5.5=80%=P5.50=Earth-Midway=5 May = Gaia.
Enshroud=4,500=5,000=50%=P5.00D=Law=Time=Venus=5 May = Aphrodite>>L=N.
Ensign=11,000=11%=P1.10D=1.1=Idea=Brainchild=Inv.=11 Nov.=SC=Athena>>I=MT.
Ensilage=5,500=5.5=80%=P5.50=Earth-Midway=5 May = Gaia.
Ensile=3,000=30%=P3.0D=3.0=Creativity=Stars=Muses=3 March = C=I>>GIL.
Enslave=4,000=40%=P4.0D=Govt.=Creatocracy=4 April=Mercury=Hermes=G=A4.

Ensnare=6,000=60%=P6.0D=Man=Earth=Royalty=6 June=Gaia=Maia>>M=M2.
Ensue=4,000=40%=P4.0D=Govt.=Creatocracy=4 April=Mercury=Hermes=G=A4.
Ensure=5,500=5.5=80%=P5.50=Earth-Midway=5 May = Gaia.
-ent=10,000=1,000=100%=10.0=Physicality=Tech.=10 Oct.=Uranus=P=1Ø.
Entail=10,000=1,000=100%=10.0=Physicality=Tech.=10 Oct.=Uranus=P=1Ø.
Entangle=10,000=1,000=100%=10.0=Physicality=Tech.=10 Oct.=Uranus=P=1Ø.
Entente=9,500=10,000=1,000=100%=10.0=Physicality=Tech.=10 Oct.=Uranus=P=1Ø.
Enter=10,000=1,000=100%=10.0=Physicality=Tech.=10 Oct.=Uranus=P=1Ø.
Enteric=3,000=30%=P3.0D=3.0=Creativity=Stars=Muses=3 March = C=I>>GIL.
Enteritis=2,000=20%=P2.00D=2.0=Nature=Matter=Moon=2 Feb.=Cupid=N=C+_
Enterprise=10,000=1,000=100%=10.0=Physicality=Tech.=10 Oct.=Uranus=P=1Ø.
Enterprising=3,500=4,000=40%=P4.0D=Govt.=Creato.=4 April=Mercury=Hermes=G=A4.

Entertain=7,000=70%=P7.0D=7.0=Language=Assets=Mars=7 July=Pleiades.
Works are materials for entertainment. Entertainments are assets in themselves but subject to measures and computing guided by precision to determine value.

Enthrall=2,500=3,000=30%=P3.0D=3.0=Creativity=Stars=Muses=3 March = C=I>>GIL.

Enthrone=4,500=5,000=50%=P5.00D=Law=Time=Venus=5 May = Aphrodite>>L=N.
A borderline between organization and law, power and authority. The Creatocratic Charter.

Enthuse=3,000=30%=P3.0D=3.0=Creativity=Stars=Muses=3 March = C=I>>GIL.
Enthusiasm=7,500=8,000=80%=P8.0D=Economy=Currency=8 Aug.=Zeus>>E=v.
Entice=4,000=40%=P4.0D=Govt.=Creatocracy=4 April=Mercury=Hermes=G=A4.
Entire=8,500=9,000=90%=P9.00D=9.0=Abstraction=Gods=Saturn=9Sept.>>A=Ø.
Entirety=3,000=30%=P3.0D=3.0=Creativity=Stars=Muses=3 March = C=I>>GIL.
Entitlement prog.=6,000=60%=P6.0D=Man=Earth=Royalty=6June=Gaia=Maia>>M=M2.
Entity=7,000=70%=P7.0D=7.0=Language=Assets=Mars=7 July=Pleiades.
Entomb=5,500=5.5=80%=P5.50=Earth-Midway=5 May = Gaia.
Entomology=2,500=3,000=30%=P3.0D=3.0=Creatv.=Stars=Muses=3 March = C=I>>GIL.
Entourage=3,500=4,000=40%=P4.0D=Govt.=Creato.=4 April=Mercury=Hermes=G=A4.
Entr'acte=10,000=1,000=100%=10.0=Physicality=Tech.=10 Oct.=Uranus=P=1Ø.
Entrails=2,500=3,000=30%=P3.0D=3.0=Creativity=Stars=Muses=3 March = C=I>>GIL.
Entrain=3,500=4,000=40%=P4.0D=Govt.=Creatocracy=4 April=Mercury=Hermes=G=A4.
Entrance(1)=8,000=80%=P8.0D=Economy=Currency=8 Aug.=Zeus>>E=v.
Entrance(2)=8,000=80%=P8.0D=Economy=Currency=8 Aug.=Zeus>>E=v.
Entrant=2,500=3,000=30%=P3.0D=3.0=Creativity=Stars=Muses=3 March = C=I>>GIL.
Entrap=8,500=9,000=90%=P9.00D=9.0=Abstraction=Gods=Saturn=9Sept.>>A=Ø.
Entreat=3,500=4,000=40%=P4.0D=Govt.=Creatocracy=4 April=Mercury=Hermes=G=A4.
Entreaty=2,000=20%=P2.00D=2.0=Nature=Matter=Moon=2 Feb.=Cupid=N=C+_
Entrée=5,500=5.5=80%=P5.50=Earth-Midway=5 May = Gaia.
Entrench=8,000=80%=P8.0D=Economy=Currency=8 Aug.=Zeus>>E=v.

Entrepreneur=6,000=60%=P6.0D=Man=Earth=Royalty=6 June=Gaia=Maia>>M=M2.
Peter Matthews - Akukalia discovered three kinds of unemployment.
1. People are employed but not satisfied.
2. People who are employed but not fulfilled.
3. People who are qualified but not employed.

His cure to these challenges are:
1. Discover every citizen based on scientific modules.
2. Develop every citizen through the necessary institutions.
3. Connect every citizen to the required point of natural gifts, talents and potentials. This is his recommended DDC method to reduce and possibly the scourge of unemployment by at least 60% and institutionalize the creative economy

- Chapter 258. Pg. 155. The Creatocratic Charter by Peter Matthews-Akukalia.
>>Defining Entrepreneurship in the light of creativity. Chapter 258. Naturecology.

Entropy=10,000=1,000=100%=10.0=Physicality=Tech.=10 Oct.=Uranus=P=1Ø.

Entrust=7,000=70%=P7.0D=7.0=Language=Assets=Mars=7 July=Pleiades.
The universe grants us things so we own through study formula and computing.

Entry=10,000=1,000=100%=10.0=Physicality=Tech.=10 Oct.=Uranus=P=1Ø.
Entwine=2,500=3,000=30%=P3.0D=3.0=Creativity=Stars=Muses=3 March = C=I>>GIL.
Enumerate=5,000=50%=P5.00D=Law=Time=Venus=5 May = Aphrodite>>L=N.
Enunciate=4,000=40%=P4.0D=Govt.=Creatocracy=4 April=Mercury=Hermes=G=A4.
Envelop=4,500=5,000=50%=P5.00D=Law=Time=Venus=5 May = Aphrodite>>L=N.
Envelope=10,000=1,000=100%=10.0=Physicality=Tech.=10 Oct.=Uranus=P=1Ø.
Envenom=3,000=30%=P3.0D=3.0=Creativity=Stars=Muses=3 March = C=I>>GIL.

Enviable=3,000=30%=P3.0D=3.0=Creativity=Stars=Muses=3 March = C=I>>GIL.
To achieve a Creatocratic state of creativity is to attain an enviable height in life.

Envious=5,000=50%=P5.00D=Law=Time=Venus=5 May = Aphrodite>>L=N.
Environmenur=8,500=9,000=90%=P9.00D=9.0=Abstraction=Gods=Saturn=9Sept.>>A=Ø.
Environmentalism=6,000=60%=P6.0D=Man=Earth=Royalty=6June=Gaia=Maia>>M=M2.
Environs=3,000=30%=P3.0D=3.0=Creativity=Stars=Muses=3 March = C=I>>GIL.
Envisage=6,000=60%=P6.0D=Man=Earth=Royalty=6 June=Gaia=Maia>>M=M2.
Envision=3,000=30%=P3.0D=3.0=Creativity=Stars=Muses=3 March = C=I>>GIL.
Envoy(1)=6,500=7,000=70%=P7.0D=7.0=Language=Assets=Mars=7 July=Pleiades.
Envoy(2)=9,500=10,000=1,000=100%=10.0=Physicality=Tech.=10 Oct.=Uranus=P=1Ø.
Envy=11,000=11%=P1.10D=1.1=Idea=Brainchild=Inv.=11 Nov.=SC=Athena>>I=MT.

Enzyme=7,500=8,000=80%=P8.0D=Economy=Currency=8 Aug.=Zeus>>E=v.
eo-=2,500=3,000=30%=P3.0D=3.0=Creativity=Stars=Muses=3 March = C=I>>GIL.
Eocene=9,000=90%=P9.00D=9.0=Abstraction=Gods=Saturn=9Sept.>>A=Ø.

Eolian=8,000=80%=P8.0D=Economy=Currency=8 Aug.=Zeus>>E=v.
Relating to, caused by, or carried by the wind. Aeolus, God of the winds in classical myth.
Psalm 35 >> let the winds blow them away as chaff, also other Psalms by David states that
GOD rides on the wings of the winds. These verses aided discovery that Gods are dragons.

E.o.m.=1,500=15%=P1.50D=1.5=Authority=Solar Crown=1 May = Maia.
End of Month. Administered and managed by Maia.

Eon=8,500=9,000=90%=P9.00D=9.0=Abstraction=Gods=Saturn=9Sept.>>A=Ø.

Eos=3,000=30%=P3.0D=3.0=Creativity=Stars=Muses=3 March = C=I>>GIL.
Greek myth. Goddess of the dawn. Manifests as the first light in the sky. Results proves
she is a muse. The emperor of the Creatocracy recalls vividly the Greeks greet in words
such as eious, captani meaning Captain in his working days as a seaman. Read his book
>> The Creatocracy Republic, reference book >>The Missing Seaman.

Eosin=6,500=7,000=70%=P7.0D=7.0=Language=Assets=Mars=7 July=Pleiades.
-eous=4,500=5,000=50%=P5.00D=Law=Time=Venus=5 May = Aphrodite>>L=N.
EP=2,000=20%=P2.00D=2.0=Nature=Matter=Moon=2 Feb.=Cupid=N=C+_
Epaulet=4,000=40%=P4.0D=Govt.=Creatocracy=4 April=Mercury=Hermes=G=A4.
Épée=8,000=80%=P8.0D=Economy=Currency=8 Aug.=Zeus>>E=v.
Ephedrine=12,000=12%=P1.20D=1.2=Knowledge=Education=12Dec.=Athena>>K=F.
Ephemeral=7,000=70%=P7.0D=7.0=Language=Assets=Mars=7 July=Pleiades.
Ephesian=9,000=90%=P9.00D=9.0=Abstraction=Gods=Saturn=9Sept.>>A=Ø.

Ephesus=6,000=60%=P6.0D=Man=Earth=Royalty=6 June=Gaia=Maia>>M=M2.
An Ancient Greece city of Asia Minor in present day W Turkey. A city of Gaia.

Epi-=5,500=5.5=80%=P5.50=Earth-Midway=5 May = Gaia.
Epic=10,000=1,000=100%=10.0=Physicality=Tech.=10 Oct.=Uranus=P=1Ø.
Epicene=7,000=70%=P7.0D=7.0=Language=Assets=Mars=7 July=Pleiades.
Epicenter=5,500=5.5=80%=P5.50=Earth-Midway=5 May = Gaia.
Epictetus=3,500=4,000=40%=P4.0D=Govt.=Creato.=4 April=Mercury=Hermes=G=A4.

Epicure=4,000=40%=P4.0D=Govt.=Creatocracy=4 April=Mercury=Hermes=G=A4.
An attribute of wealth. The Mist Sovereign Emperor of the Creatocracy is an epicure.

Epicurean=5,000=50%=P5.00D=Law=Time=Venus=5 May = Aphrodite>>L=N.
Epicurus=3,000=30%=P3.0D=3.0=Creativity=Stars=Muses=3 March = C=I>>GIL.
Epidemic=10,000=1,000=100%=10.0=Physicality=Tech.=10 Oct.=Uranus=P=1Ø.
Epidermis=3,000=30%=P3.0D=3.0=Creativity=Stars=Muses=3 March = C=I>>GIL.
Epidural=8,000=80%=P8.0D=Economy=Currency=8 Aug.=Zeus>>E=v.
Epiglottis=8,500=9,000=90%=P9.00D=9.0=Abstraction=Gods=Saturn=9Sept.>>A=Ø.
Epigram=3,000=30%=P3.0D=3.0=Creativity=Stars=Muses=3 March = C=I>>GIL.
Epigraph=9,500=10,000=1,000=100%=10.0=Physicality=Tech.=10 Oct.=Uranus=P=1Ø.

Epigraphy=2,500=3,000=30%=P3.0D=3.0=Creativity=Stars=Muses=3 March = C=I>>GIL.
The real essence of studying ancient materials is to attain creativity. The Scriptures are
ancient materials the Sovereign emperor has studied deduced and computed. Thus it is
reasoned and said that although the Bible was inspired by the Holy Spirit and Men wrote
it Peter Matthews-Akukalia invented it according to the laws of conception and invention.
Makstianism is the Creatocratic Faith system invented based on the Castle Makupedia
computed versions of the Holy Bible and Holy Quran thus manifesting the sons of GOD,
himself a God by apotheosis as God of Creatocracy Genius and the Mind.

Epilepsy=6,500=7,000=70%=P7.0D=7.0=Language=Assets=Mars=7 July=Pleiades.
Epilogue=10,000=1,000=100%=10.0=Physicality=Tech.=10 Oct.=Uranus=P=1Ø.
Epinephrine=10,000=1,000=100%=10.0=Physicality=Tech.=10 Oct.=Uranus=P=1Ø.

Epiphany=12,000=12%=P1.20D=1.2=Knowledge=Education=12Dec.=Athena>>K=F.
A Makstian Feast of apotheosis observed October 13 based on knowledge of the
Creative Sciences invented by Peter Matthews-Akukalia. Established to be a revelatory
manifestation of a divine being incarnation of Zeus the Most High. Read the book>>
CASTLE MAKUPEDIA >> Mindom of Seven Seas Seasons and Classics on the Nidrapoe.
Special book reference >>Sons of Immortals.

Epiphyte=10,000=1,000=100%=10.0=Physicality=Tech.=10 Oct.=Uranus=P=1Ø.
Episcopacy=5,000=50%=P5.00D=Law=Time=Venus=5 May = Aphrodite>>L=N.
Episcopal=6,500=7,000=70%=P7.0D=7.0=Language=Assets=Mars=7 July=Pleiades.

Episcopal Church=6,000=60%=P6.0D=Man=Earth=Royalty=6 June=Gaia=Maia>>M=M2.
The Creatocracy is published in the United States and UK simultaneously hence global.

Episcopalian=3,500=4,000=40%=P4.0D=Govt.=Creato.=4 April=Mercury=Hermes=G=A4.
Episcopate=6,000=60%=P6.0D=Man=Earth=Royalty=6 June=Gaia=Maia>>M=M2.
Episiotomy=8,000=80%=P8.0D=Economy=Currency=8 Aug.=Zeus>>E=v.
Episode=10,500=11,000=11%=P1.10D=1.1=Idea=Brainchild=Inv.=11 Nov.=Athena>>I=MT.
Epistemology=5,500=5.5=80%=P5.50=Earth-Midway=5 May = Gaia.
Epistle=9,500=10,000=1,000=100%=Physicality= Tech.=10 Oct.=Uranus=P=1Ø.

Epitaph=7,500=8,000=80%=P8.0D=Economy=Currency=8 Aug.=Zeus>>E=v.

Epithelium=11,000=11%=P1.10D=1.1=Idea=Brainchild=Inv.=11 Nov.=SC=Athena>>I=MT.
Greek thēlē,nipple. The nipple was a donation of Athena during the creation process.

Epithet=6,000=60%=P6.0D=Man=Earth=Royalty=6 June=Gaia=Maia>>M=M2.

Epitome=7,000=70%=P7.0D=7.0=Language=Assets=Mars=7 July=Pleiades.
A formula is a brief summary, the typical and perfect example of its kind. Hence it is the
standard for the measurement of all perfections. The Creatocracy describes this as the
peak of aspiration, a state of Godly perfection. Reason Peter Matthews-Akukalia was
apotheosized a God and the Creatocracy declared a perfect system drawn from scriptures.

Epitomize=6,000=60%=P6.0D=Man=Earth=Royalty=6 June=Gaia=Maia>>M=M2.
Epoch=10,000=1,000=100%=10.0=Physicality=Tech.=10 Oct.=Uranus=P=1Ø.
Eponym=10,000=1,000=100%=10.0=Physicality=Tech.=10 Oct.=Uranus=P=1Ø.
Epoxy=6,500=7,000=70%=P7.0D=7.0=Language=Assets=Mars=7 July=Pleiades.
Epsilon=3,000=30%=P3.0D=3.0=Creativity=Stars=Muses=3 March = C=I>>GIL.

Epsom salts=7,000=70%=P7.0D=7.0=Language=Assets=Mars=7 July=Pleiades.
Named after Epsom, England. See England.

Eq.=1,500=15%=P1.50D=1.5=Authority=Solar Crown=1 May = Maia.
Equable=2,000=20%=P2.00D=2.0=Nature=Matter=Moon=2 Feb.=Cupid=N=C+_
Equal=10,000=1,000=100%=10.0=Physicality=Tech.=10 Oct.=Uranus=P=1Ø.
Equalize=3,000=30%=P3.0D=3.0=Creativity=Stars=Muses=3 March = C=I>>GIL.
Equal sign=4,000=40%=P4.0D=Govt.=Creatocracy=4 April=Mercury=Hermes=G=A4.

Equanimity=3,000=30%=P3.0D=3.0=Creativity=Stars=Muses=3 March = C=I>>GIL.
Creativity requires a lot of calmness and composure and must be even-tempered. Our war
is more a mental war than violent as Athena aegis of the Creatocracy does. Brainstorming.

Equate=6,000=60%=P6.0D=Man=Earth=Royalty=6 June=Gaia=Maia>>M=M2.
Equation=11,500=12,000=12%=P1.20D=1.2=Knowledge=Education=12Dec.=Athena
>>K=F.
Equator=10,000=1,000=100%=10.0=Physicality=Tech.=10 Oct.=Uranus=P=1Ø.
Equatorial=8,000=80%=P8.0D=Economy=Currency=8 Aug.=Zeus>>E=v.
Equerry=8,000=80%=P8.0D=Economy=Currency=8 Aug.=Zeus>>E=v.
Equestrian=8,500=9,000=90%=P9.00D=9.0=Abstraction=Gods=Saturn=9Sept.>>A=Ø.
Equi-=3,500=4,000=40%=P4.0D=Govt.=Creatocracy=4 April=Mercury=Hermes=G=A4.
Equiangular=2,000=20%=P2.00D=2.0=Nature=Matter=Moon=2 Feb.=Cupid=N=C+_

Equidistant=1,000=100%=10.0=1.0=Mind=Sun=1 January=Helios >> M=E4.
Equilateral=2,000=20%=P2.00D=2.0=Nature=Matter=Moon=2 Feb.=Cupid=N=C+_

Equilibrium=8,000=80%=P8.0D=Economy=Currency=8 Aug.=Zeus>>E=v.
Zeus is the equilibrium of the universes. Currency business and value balances all economy. The Creatocracy is the established module through which universal equilibrium is founded and the Creatocracy Corporation Bank is reality through the Maks Currencies.

Equine=7,000=70%=P7.0D=7.0=Language=Assets=Mars=7 July=Pleiades.
Equinoctial=2,000=20%=P2.00D=2.0=Nature=Matter=Moon=2 Feb.=Cupid=N=C+_
Equinox=14,500=15,000=1,500=15%=P1.50D=1.5=Authority=Solar Crown=1 May = Maia.
Equip=4,500=5,000=50%=P5.00D=Law=Time=Venus=5 May = Aphrodite>>L=N.

Equipment=12,500=13,000=13%=P1.30=Solar Core=Faculty=13 January=Athena.
True creative intelligence produces equipment for the ease of work. The Creatocracy through the creative Sciences had many inventions for this purpose. Notable are the Makupedia, first human mind super computer; Mindoscope, Makulator and the Maks.

Equipoise=6,000=60%=P6.0D=Man=Earth=Royalty=6 June=Gaia=Maia>>M=M2.
Equitable=3,500=4,000=40%=P4.0D=Govt.=Creato.=4 April=Mercury=Hermes=G=A4.
Equitation=6,000=60%=P6.0D=Man=Earth=Royalty=6 June=Gaia=Maia>>M=M2.
Equity=10,000=1,000=100%=10.0=Physicality=Tech.=10 Oct.=Uranus=P=1Ø.

Equivalent=6,500=7,000=70%=P7.0D=7.0=Language=Assets=Mars=7 July=Pleiades.
The law of pure equivalence makes it possible to track abstract measures in physical forms. The Sun is the mind through energy modules, the moon is nature and things measured in propensities inclinations and techniques, the stars are the creativity inspired through the GIL, a measurement of innate energy quantum expressed as natural capacity, ability and capabilities in a person or thing. Results show it is a borderline between emotion and precision. Emotion is energy and precision is dimension hence the twelve dimensions of the universes have been measured by Peter Matthews-Akukalia in his invented Creative Sciences of the Makupedia. The law of pure equivalence is his invention also.

Equivalent is an equal in value amount function meaning etc. eg one unit is equivalent to one glass and water. It is having the same or a similar effect as..in mathematics it is belonging to the same equivalence class. It is a person or thing that is equal to or corresponds with another in value amount function meaning. In chemistry it is equivalent weight. A classical example in the Bible is found as a universal standard which hitherto has been unknown to be so. It is the so called 6-6-6 philosophy. Scripture mentions it as 600, 60, & 6. Peter Matthews-Akukalia, Castle Makupedia decoded it to be an equivalent measure system that will correspond as the currency metric of the diamond on the solar core. He conceptualized it as the law of pure equivalent stating that 600 = 60% = 6.0 >>

1,000 = 100% = 10.0. Note that revelations occur as an upside down dummy in the same effect that applies during. John wrote as he saw but the book is symbolic and not physical reality. Revelation 1:1 expects the book to be computed where necessary. Revelation 13:18 outlines the law of pure equivalence. The author wrote more than twenty chapters on this concept in his advance study of Naturecology. Misinterpretation is the bane of conventional religion. Prove the scripture by the scripture. See Church.

Equivocal=2,000=20%=P2.00D=2.0=Nature=Matter=Moon=2 Feb.=Cupid=N=C+_
The balance in nature is its imbalance. God made all things good man is to make it better.

Equivocate=4,000=40%=P4.0D=Govt.=Creatocracy=4 April=Mercury=Hermes=G=A4.
Er=3,000=30%=P3.0D=3.0=Creativity=Stars=Muses=3 March = C=I>>GIL.
ER=1,000=100%=10.0=1.0=Mind=Sun=1 January=Helios >> M=E4.
-er(1)=10,000=1,000=100%=10.0=Physicality=Tech.=10 Oct.=Uranus=P=1Ø.
-er(2)=6,500=7,000=70%=P7.0D=7.0=Language=Assets=Mars=7 July=Pleiades.

Era=15,000=1,500=15%=P1.50D=1.5=Authority=Solar Crown=1 May = Maia.
The Creatocratic era began as the Mind Age by publishing of the Oracle on 6th February 2012. Peter Matthews-Akukalia emerged as the World's 1st Creative Scientist.
In 2013 he received the copyright to the Faculty of Creative & Psycho-Social Sciences. Studies continued in 2014. He appeared on Star FM radio Ikeja Lagos in 2015 announcing he had discovered the formula of the Mind. In 2016 he published Template & Manifesto for the Creative Economy>>Principles of Psychoeconomix emerging King of Creativity. The same year Authorhouse made a world press release to over 500 media organizations announcing that he owns the Mind through softwares of his inventions.
By 2018 he had independently made 100s of formulas, at least 6million computations and written over 15million programs on lunar or planetary computing to find out the single number that controlled the universe. This he discovered to be the moon on the number 2. All things function on innate energy drawn from the Sun but are made material or matter through the moon. The moon releases a certain energy that influences all things through psycho-gravitational incursion (PGI) energy....
He announced his invention: Makupedia, first human Mind Computer and trended in 2019 after breaking the stellar code where his prediction of the birth of a new planet fulfilled. The new planet was discovered by NASA and his claim to have predicted it through the stellar code remains unchallenged till this day. He ascended the academic throne of the Creatocracy in 2020 publishing the Creatocratic Charter where he emerged a God. Further works as the Creatocracy Corporation Bank will see him manifest new assets for human benefits through institutional book systems. A key objective of the Creatocracy is to reduce and possibly eliminate world unemployment through discovery development and connectivity of everyone to their innate potentials. Instructions of the Almighty GOD. October 13, he was celebrated in a Feast of Apotheosis emerging him Castle Makupedia God of Creatocracy Genius and Mind. He owns the Creatocratic Nations of Paradise

(Paradise Nations) and invented the Disean citizenship. His rights titles and assets are inalienable imprescriptible and perpetual in all things by copyright and all IP Laws.

ERA=2,000=20%=P2.00D=2.0=Nature=Matter=Moon=2 Feb.=Cupid=N=C+_
Eradicate=6,000=60%=P6.0D=Man=Earth=Royalty=6 June=Gaia=Maia>>M=M2.
Erase=10,000=1,000=100%=Physicality= Tech.=10 Oct.=Uranus=P=1Ø.
Erasmus Desiderius=3,500=4,000=40%=P4.0D=Govt.=4 April=Mercury=Hermes=G=A4.
Erbium=9,500=10,000=1,000=100%=Physicality= Tech.=10 Oct.=Uranus=P=1Ø.
Ere=3,000=30%=P3.0D=3.0=Creativity=Stars=Muses=3 March = C=I>>GIL.
Erebus Mount=6,000=60%=P6.0D=Man=Earth=Royalty=6 June=Gaia=Maia>>M=M2.
Erect=10,000=1,000=100%=Physicality= Tech.=10 Oct.=Uranus=P=1Ø.
Erectile=8,000=80%=P8.0D=Economy=Currency=8 Aug.=Zeus>>E=v.

Erection=7,500=8,000=80%=P8.0D=Economy=Currency=8 Aug.=Zeus>>E=v.
Computational ability makes for the transmission of quick blood to the penis increasing high sexual libido, a heightened sense of sexual desire and excitement in a rapture and high erection propensity of the male organ to about 75% every 7.50hours of intense academic work. This is most likely the reasonable link between creativity and sexuality. It is natural. 7,500 units of mental capacity is applied to develop a formula and compute. 500>>5% is applied to establish a value base balance for economic application while 0.5% mental energy is transmuted per unit into the emotional senses to create desire and fulfillment.

Erelong=1,500=15%=P1.50D=1.5=Authority=Solar Crown=1 May = Maia.
Eremite=2,500=3,000=30%=P3.0D=3.0=Creativity=Stars=Muses=3 March = C=I>>GIL.
Erevan=1,000=100%=10.0=1.0=Mind=Sun=1 January=Helios >> M=E4.

Erg=3,500=4,000=40%=P4.0D=Govt.=Creatocracy=4 April=Mercury=Hermes=G=A4.
Defined conventionally as a unit of energy or work equal to 10(valency -7) joule. See Energy, Erection. In Makupedia mind energy is measured in the Maks after Matthews-Akukalia Peter, peter Matthews-Akukalia the 1st Human Mind Super Computer.

Ergo=2,000=20%=P2.00D=2.0=Nature=Matter=Moon=2 Feb.=Cupid=N=C+_
Ergonomics=9,500=10,000=1,000=100%=10.0=Physicality=Tech.=10 Oct.=Uranus=P=1Ø.
Ergot=10,000=1,000=100%=10.0=Physicality=Tech.=10 Oct.=Uranus=P=1Ø.
Ericson Leif=2,500=3,000=30%=P3.0D=3.0=Creatv.=Stars=Muses=3 March = C=I>>GIL.
Eric the Red=2,500=3,000=30%=P3.0D=3.0=Creatv.=Stars=Muses=3 March = C=I>>GIL.
Erie(1)=7,000=70%=P7.0D=7.0=Language=Assets=Mars=7 July=Pleiades.
Erie(2)=6,500=7,000=70%=P7.0D=7.0=Language=Assets=Mars=7 July=Pleiades.
Erie,Lake=9,000=90%=P9.00D=9.0=Abstraction=Gods=Saturn=9Sept.>>A=Ø.
Erie Canal.=10,000=1,000=100%=10.0=Physicality=Tech.=10 Oct.=Uranus=P=1Ø.

Erin=2,500=3,000=30%=P3.0D=3.0=Creativity=Stars=Muses=3 March = C=I>>GIL.

A poetic name for Ireland. Such manifests as MAKUPEDIALAND>> City of Testamentary Poetry written by Peter Matthews-Akukalia. Contains over 500 poems. Disean is the poetic name for Paradiseans, citizens of the Creatocratic Nations of Paradise his invention state.

Eritrea=10,000=1,000=100%=10.0=Physicality=Tech.=10 Oct.=Uranus=P=1Ø.
Ermine=8,500=9,000=90%=P9.00D=9.0=Abstraction=Gods=Saturn=9Sept.>>A=Ø.
Ernst Max.=2,500=3,000=30%=P3.0D=3.0=Creativity=Stars=Muses=3 March = C=I>>GIL.
Erode=10,000=1,000=100%=10.0=Physicality=Tech.=10 Oct.=Uranus=P=1Ø.
Erogenous=5,000=50%=P5.00D=Law=Time=Venus=5 May = Aphrodite>>L=N.

Eros=4,000=40%=P4.0D=Govt.=Creatocracy=4 April=Mercury=Hermes=G=A4.
Greek myth. The God of love, son of Aphrodite. His power is the arrows.

Erosion=4,000=40%=P4.0D=Govt.=Creatocracy=4 April=Mercury=Hermes=G=A4.
Erotic=6,000=60%=P6.0D=Man=Earth=Royalty=6 June=Gaia=Maia>>M=M2.
Erotica=6,000=60%=P6.0D=Man=Earth=Royalty=6 June=Gaia=Maia>>M=M2.
Err=5,500=5.5=80%=P5.50=Earth-Midway=5 May = Gaia.
Errand=10,000=1,000=100%=10.0=Physicality=Tech.=10 Oct.=Uranus=P=1Ø.

Errant=7,500=8,000=80%=P8.0D=Economy=Currency=8 Aug.=Zeus>>E=v.
Anyone who has strayed away from formula, computational creativity or precision is speculative and an errant. Without exceptions to anyone, thing, study, field or practice.

Erratic=5,000=50%=P5.00D=Law=Time=Venus=5 May = Aphrodite>>L=N.
The erratic nature of legal speculations and time makes the job opportunity for the Creative Scientist to establish proof in every simple complex direct and indirect matters. Time here will concern all fields of the sciences arts and commercial ventures and commitments. The Creatocracy has resolved the crises of time management through inventing Mind Clocks.

Erratum=4,000=40%=P4.0D=Govt.=Creatocracy=4 April=Mercury=Hermes=G=A4.
Er Rif=4,500=5,000=50%=P5.00D=Law=Time=Venus=5 May = Aphrodite>>L=N.

Erroneous=3,500=4,000=40%=P4.0D=Govt.=Creato.=4 April=Mercury=Hermes=G=A4.
Lat.error, errōn-, vagabond. Incorrect or mistaken. Technically and legal applications means that the world has been wrong in the definition of words through indefinite means and so all have been vagabonds prior to the discovery of the Creative Sciences, Makupedia.

Error=10,500=11,000=11%=P1.10D=1.1=Idea=Brainchild=Inv.=11 Nov.=SC=Athena>>I=MT.

Ersatz=8,000=80%=P8.0D=Economy=Currency=8 Aug.=Zeus>>E=v.
Erse=5,000=50%=P5.00D=Law=Time=Venus=5 May = Aphrodite>>L=N.
Erstwhile=3,000=30%=P3.0D=3.0=Creativity=Stars=Muses=3 March = C=I>>GIL.
Eruct=2,000=20%=P2.00D=2.0=Nature=Matter=Moon=2 Feb.=Cupid=N=C+_

Erudite=8,000=80%=P8.0D=Economy=Currency=8 Aug.=Zeus>>E=v.
Proverbs 8 confirms that Zeus the Most High is erudite in nature, of infinite intelligence.

Erudition=2,000=20%=P2.00D=2.0=Nature=Matter=Moon=2 Feb.=Cupid=N=C+_
Erupt=10,000=1,000=100%=10.0=Physicality=Tech.=10 Oct.=Uranus=P=1Ø.
-ery=9,000=90%=P9.00D=9.0=Abstraction=Gods=Saturn=9Sept.>>A=Ø.
Erysipelas=13,000=13%=P1.30=Solar Core=Faculty=13 January=Athena.
Erythrocyte=5,500=5.5=80%=P5.50=Earth-Midway=5 May = Gaia.
Erythromycin=10,000=1,000=100%=10.0=Physicality=Tech.=10 Oct.=Uranus=P=1Ø.
Erzgebirge=8,500=9,000=90%=P9.00D=9.0=Abstraction=Gods=Saturn=9Sept.>>A=Ø.
Es=2,500=3,000=30%=P3.0D=3.0=Creativity=Stars=Muses=3 March = C=I>>GIL.
-es(1)=2,000=20%=P2.00D=2.0=Nature=Matter=Moon=2 Feb.=Cupid=N=C+_
-es(2)=2,000=20%=P2.00D=2.0=Nature=Matter=Moon=2 Feb.=Cupid=N=C+_
Esau=4,500=5,000=50%=P5.00D=Law=Time=Venus=5 May = Aphrodite>>L=N.
Escalate=2,500=3,000=30%=P3.0D=3.0=Creativity=Stars=Muses=3 March = C=I>>GIL.
Escalator=7,000=70%=P7.0D=7.0=Language=Assets=Mars=7 July=Pleiades.
Escapade=3,000=30%=P3.0D=3.0=Creativity=Stars=Muses=3 March = C=I>>GIL.
Escape=10,000=1,000=100%=10.0=Physicality=Tech.=10 Oct.=Uranus=P=1Ø.
Escapee=4,000=40%=P4.0D=Govt.=Creatocracy=4 April=Mercury=Hermes=G=A4.
Escape velocity=9,000=90%=P9.00D=9.0=Abstraction=Gods=Saturn=9Sept.>>A=Ø.
Escapism=4,500=5,000=50%=P5.00D=Law=Time=Venus=5 May = Aphrodite>>L=N.
Escarole=8,000=80%=P8.0D=Economy=Currency=8 Aug.=Zeus>>E=v.
Escarpment=6,500=7,000=70%=P7.0D=7.0=Language=Assets=Mars=7 July=Pleiades.
-escence=3,000=30%=P3.0D=3.0=Creativity=Stars=Muses=3 March = C=I>>GIL.
-escent=6,000=60%=P6.0D=Man=Earth=Royalty=6 June=Gaia=Maia>>M=M2.
Eschew=4,500=5,000=50%=P5.00D=Law=Time=Venus=5 May = Aphrodite>>L=N.
Escort=10,000=1,000=100%=10.0=Physicality=Tech.=10 Oct.=Uranus=P=1Ø.
Escritoire=3,500=4,000=40%=P4.0D=Govt.=Creato.=4 April=Mercury=Hermes=G=A4.
Escrow=10,000=1,000=100%=10.0=Physicality=Tech.=10 Oct.=Uranus=P=1Ø.
Escudo=3,500=4,000=40%=P4.0D=Govt.=Creatocracy=4 April=Mercury=Hermes=G=A4.
Escutcheon=6,000=60%=P6.0D=Man=Earth=Royalty=6 June=Gaia=Maia>>M=M2.
ESE=1,000=100%=10.0=1.0=Mind=Sun=1 January=Helios >> M=E4.
-ese=10,000=1,000=100%=10.0=Physicality=Tech.=10 Oct.=Uranus=P=1Ø.
Esfahan=1,000=100%=10.0=1.0=Mind=Sun=1 January=Helios >> M=E4.
Eskimo=10,000=1,000=100%=10.0=Physicality=Tech.=10 Oct.=Uranus=P=1Ø.
ESL=2,500=3,000=30%=P3.0D=3.0=Creativity=Stars=Muses=3 March = C=I>>GIL.
Esophagus=10,000=1,000=100%=10.0=Physicality=Tech.=10 Oct.=Uranus=P=1Ø.
Esoteric=10,000=1,000=100%=10.0=Physicality=Tech.=10 Oct.=Uranus=P=1Ø.
ESP=10,000=1,000=100%=10.0=Physicality=Tech.=10 Oct.=Uranus=P=1Ø.

Esp.=500=5%=P5.00D=5.0=Law=Time=Venus=5 May=Aphrodite>>L=N.
Espadrilles=6,000=60%=P6.0D=Man=Earth=Royalty=6 June=Gaia=Maia>>M=M2.
Espalier=10,000=1,000=100%=10.0=Physicality=Tech.=10 Oct.=Uranus=P=1Ø.
Especia=7,000=70%=P7.0D=7.0=Language=Assets=Mars=7 July=Pleiades.
Esperanto=9,500=10,000=1,000=100%=10.0=Physicality=Tech.=10 Oct.=Uranus=P=1Ø.
Espionage=6,000=60%=P6.0D=Man=Earth=Royalty=6 June=Gaia=Maia>>M=M2.

Esplanade=7,500=8,000=80%=P8.0D=Economy=Currency=8 Aug.=Zeus>>E=v.
A borderline between precision assets and business. Scripture states that all mountains shall be made plains. A prediction of the expressways present today in every country.

Espoo=5,000=50%=P5.00D=Law=Time=Venus=5 May = Aphrodite>>L=N.

Espousal=6,000=60%=P6.0D=Man=Earth=Royalty=6 June=Gaia=Maia>>M=M2.
A betrothal. A wedding ceremony. Adoption of or support for an idea or cause. Of interest is the placement the marriage wedding and support for an idea in the same category. Predictive of a fact that someone born of the natural royalty will establish a royalty system based on knowledge and will marry Athena in the process. A feast will be made to celebrate this entire process where such will become a God by superior knowledge and capabilities. Athena is the Goddess of wisdom handicraft and mental warfare. Her category is brainchild invention and idea tracked as 11>>1.1.This is Peter Matthews-Akukalia, the Creative Sciences and the Feast of apotheosis. Read the book >> THE CREATOCRACY REPUBLIC. >> see the introductory pages. Castle Makupedia was born on 06-07-1978>>Royalty.

Espouse=6,000=60%=P6.0D=Man=Earth=Royalty=6 June=Gaia=Maia>>M=M2.
People born on the energy dimension of Earth>>Gaia>>Royalty>>Emotional>>100%>>0+- are naturally gifted to marry constantly and consistently. Result is their natural love for a big family and so polygamous in nature. So polygamy is a natural gift for Gaia persons. Peter Matthews-Akukalia is a proof of this process with a great sense of responsibility.

Espresso=9,500=10,000=1,000=100%=10.0=Physicality=Tech.=10 Oct.=Uranus=P=1Ø.

Esprit=8,000=80%=P8.0D=Economy=Currency=8 Aug.=Zeus>>E=v.
Liveliness of mind and expression; spirit. Esprit de corps. First Zeus is the liveliness of the mind by the abundance of energy and will be known to be the institution of the mind through the Mind or Creative Sciences thus manifesting in person as the World's 1st Creative Scientist. The only one to define measure and compute the mind of God and men. Esprit de corps predicts that He will lead the council of other spirits or Gods known as Hosts who are the Geniuses. The person whose tracks align with these abilities is Peter Matthews-Akukalia >> Castle Makupedia God of Creatocracy Genius and Mind. Today he has computed the genius code >> 3.3 and tracked the words of Zeus in the Creative Sciences. The spirit of currency and business is Zeusian. Maks currencies is a solution. The

Creatocracy corporation bank is the complete package of solutions written by one believed and established by works to be the incarnation of the Zeus Jehovah the Most High.

Esprit de corps=7,500=8,000=80%=P8.0D=Economy=Currency=8 Aug.=Zeus>>E=v.

Espy=6,000=60%=P6.0D=Man=Earth=Royalty=6 June=Gaia=Maia>>M=M2.
To catch sight of; glimpse. See the book Makupedialand >> city of testamentary poetry. Contains glimpses in verse. This word predicts this book as a writing of a God. Also, The Apotheosis of Castle Makupedia >> Mindom of a Seven Seas Seasons and Classics on the Nidrapoe. Reference on catching the sight of the muses is Sons of Immortals. Royalty is built on the ability to be first at something worth doing and done well in good works.

Esq.=1,000=100%=10.0=1.0=Mind=Sun=1 January=Helios >> M=E4.
-esque=3,000=30%=P3.0D=3.0=Creativity=Stars=Muses=3 March = C=I>>GIL.
Esquire=10,000=1,000=100%=10.0=Physicality=Tech.=10 Oct.=Uranus=P=1Ø.
-ess=10,000=1,000=100%=10.0=Physicality=Tech.=10 Oct.=Uranus=P=1Ø.
Essay=10,000=1,000=100%=10.0=Physicality=Tech.=10 Oct.=Uranus=P=1Ø.
Essayist=2,000=20%=P2.00D=2.0=Nature=Matter=Moon=2 Feb.=Cupid=N=C+_

Essen=9,000=90%=P9.00D=9.0=Abstraction=Gods=Saturn=9Sept.>>A=Ø.
The city of Gods who most probably have granted certain powers to the confluence rivers.

Essence=10,000=1,000=100%=10.0=Physicality=Tech.=10 Oct.=Uranus=P=1Ø.
Essential=10,000=1,000=100%=10.0=Physicality=Tech.=10 Oct.=Uranus=P=1Ø.
Essex=3,000=30%=P3.0D=3.0=Creativity=Stars=Muses=3 March = C=I>>GIL.
EST=1,500=15%=P1.50D=1.5=Authority=Solar Crown=1 May = Maia.
est.=2,000=20%=P2.00D=2.0=Nature=Matter=Moon=2 Feb.=Cupid=N=C+_
-est(1)=6,500=7,000=70%=P7.0D=7.0=Language=Assets=Mars=7 July=Pleiades.
-est(2)=6,000=60%=P6.0D=Man=Earth=Royalty=6 June=Gaia=Maia>>M=M2.
Establish=10,000=1,000=100%=10.0=Physicality=Tech.=10 Oct.=Uranus=P=1Ø.
Establishment=10,000=1,000=100%=10.0=Physicality=Tech.=10 Oct.=Uranus=P=1Ø.

Estate=11,000=11%=P1.10D=1.1=Idea=Brainchild=Inv.=11 Nov.=SC=Athena>>I=MT.
All of one's possessions are sourced in Athena, wife of Castle Makupedia. Romans 11:33-35. Marriage and ownership of Athena in love by Castle Makupedia means ownership of the depths of riches in the wisdom and knowledge of GOD >> Zeus Jehovah her father. The first estate of Castle Makupedia is the Mind and all things sourced from the Mind are his.

Esteem=6,000=60%=P6.0D=Man=Earth=Royalty=6 June=Gaia=Maia>>M=M2.
Ester=10,000=1,000=100%=10.0=Physicality=Tech.=10 Oct.=Uranus=P=1Ø.

Esther=9,000=90%=P9.00D=9.0=Abstraction=Gods=Saturn=9Sept.>>A=Ø.

The Creatocracy recognizes Esther as the book of the Gods. Herself a Goddess.

Esthesia=3,500=4,000=40%=P4.0D=Govt.=Creato.=4 April=Mercury=Hermes=G=A4.
Esthete=1,500=15%=P1.50D=1.5=Authority=Solar Crown=1 May = Maia.
Estimable=3,000=30%=P3.0D=3.0=Creativity=Stars=Muses=3 March = C=I>>GIL.
Estimate=10,000=1,000=100%=10.0=Physicality=Tech.=10 Oct.=Uranus=P=1Ø.
Estivate=7,000=70%=P7.0D=7.0=Language=Assets=Mars=7 July=Pleiades.
Estonia=4,500=5,000=50%=P5.00D=Law=Time=Venus=5 May = Aphrodite>>L=N.
Estonian=5,000=50%=P5.00D=Law=Time=Venus=5 May = Aphrodite>>L=N.
Estrange=6,500=7,000=70%=P7.0D=7.0=Language=Assets=Mars=7 July=Pleiades.
Estrogen=12,000=12%=P1.20D=1.2=Knowledge=Education=12Dec.=Athena>>K=F.
Estrus=7,000=70%=P7.0D=7.0=Language=Assets=Mars=7 July=Pleiades.
Estuary=11,000=11%=P1.10D=1.1=Idea=Brainchild=Inv.=11 Nov.=SC=Athena>>I=MT.
ET=2,500=3,000=30%=P3.0D=3.0=Creativity=Stars=Muses=3 March = C=I>>GIL.
-et=3,500=4,000=40%=P4.0D=Govt.=Creatocracy=4 April=Mercury=Hermes=G=A4.

Eta=4,000=40%=P4.0D=Govt.=Creatocracy=4 April=Mercury=Hermes=G=A4.
The 7th letter of the Greek alphabet. It means power. A code for energy.
7.0*4.0=p=11+28=39=px=347=400=40%=4.0>>Government >> Creatocracy >> Hermes>>Merchandise >> Relationships >> Politics >> Family >> Network >> Power. It is the complete energy potentials endowed in Peter Matthews-Akukalia, Castle Makupedia.

ETA=2,000=20%=P2.00D=2.0=Nature=Matter=Moon=2 Feb.=Cupid=N=C+_
et al.=3,000=30%=P3.0D=3.0=Creativity=Stars=Muses=3 March = C=I>>GIL.
Etc.=1,000=100%=10.0=1.0=Mind=Sun=1 January=Helios >> M=E4.
Et cetera=7,000=70%=P7.0D=7.0=Language=Assets=Mars=7 July=Pleiades.
Etch=8,000=80%=P8.0D=Economy=Currency=8 Aug.=Zeus>>E=v.
Etching=10,500=11,000=11%=P1.10D=1.1=Idea=Brainchild=Inv.=11 Nov.=Athena>>I=MT.
ETD=2,000=20%=P2.00D=2.0=Nature=Matter=Moon=2 Feb.=Cupid=N=C+_
eternal=10,000=1,000=100%=10.0=Physicality=Tech.=10 Oct.=Uranus=P=1Ø.
Eternity=10,000=1,000=100%=10.0=Physicality=Tech.=10 Oct.=Uranus=P=1Ø.
Eth.=500=5%=P5.00D=5.0=Law=Time=Venus=5 May=Aphrodite>>L=N.
-eth(1)=2,000=20%=P2.00D=2.0=Nature=Matter=Moon=2 Feb.=Cupid=N=C+_
-eth(2)=2,000=20%=P2.00D=2.0=Nature=Matter=Moon=2 Feb.=Cupid=N=C+_
Ethane=10,000=1,000=100%=10.0=Physicality=Tech.=10 Oct.=Uranus=P=1Ø.
Ethanol=3,000=30%=P3.0D=3.0=Creativity=Stars=Muses=3 March = C=I>>GIL.
Ethelbert=5,500=5.5=80%=P5.50=Earth-Midway=5 May = Gaia.
Ethelred II=5,000=50%=P5.00D=Law=Time=Venus=5 May = Aphrodite>>L=N.
Ether=10,000=1,000=100%=10.0=Physicality=Tech.=10 Oct.=Uranus=P=1Ø.
Ethereal=5,000=50%=P5.00D=Law=Time=Venus=5 May = Aphrodite>>L=N.
Ethic=10,000=1,000=100%=10.0=Physicality=Tech.=10 Oct.=Uranus=P=1Ø.

Ethical=11,000=11%=P1.10D=1.1=Idea=Brainchild=Inv.=11 Nov.=SC=Athena>>I=MT.

To be married to Athena by Castle Makupedia is ethical in the Creatocracy. As the aegis of the Creatocracy she sets wisdom as the standards for all ethics in the Proverbs.

Ethiopia=6,000=60%=P6.0D=Man=Earth=Royalty=6 June=Gaia=Maia>>M=M2.
Ethnic=10,000=1,000=100%=10.0=Physicality=Tech.=10 Oct.=Uranus=P=1Ø.
Ethnicity=2,500=3,000=30%=P3.0D=3.0=Creativity=Stars=Muses=3 March = C=I>>GIL.
Ethno-=4,500=5,000=50%=P5.00D=Law=Time=Venus=5 May = Aphrodite>>L=N.
Ethnocentrism=4,500=5,000=50%=P5.00D=Law=Time=Venus=5 May = Aphrodite>>L=N.
Ethnology=10,000=1,000=100%=10.0=Physicality=Tech.=10 Oct.=Uranus=P=1Ø.
Ethology=4,000=40%=P4.0D=Govt.=Creatocracy=4 April=Mercury=Hermes=G=A4.
Ethos=8,000=80%=P8.0D=Economy=Currency=8 Aug.=Zeus>>E=v.
Ethyl=2,000=20%=P2.00D=2.0=Nature=Matter=Moon=2 Feb.=Cupid=N=C+_
Ethyl alcohol=1,500=15%=P1.50D=1.5=Authority=Solar Crown=1 May = Maia.
Ethylene=6,000=60%=P6.0D=Man=Earth=Royalty=6 June=Gaia=Maia>>M=M2.
Ethylene glycol=4,000=40%=P4.0D=Govt.=Creatocracy=4 April=Mercury=Hermes=G=A4.
Etiology=10,000=1,000=100%=10.0=Physicality=Tech.=10 Oct.=Uranus=P=1Ø.
Etiquette=5,500=5.5=80%=P5.50=Earth-Midway=5 May = Gaia.
Etna Mount.=5,000=50%=P5.00D=Law=Time=Venus=5 May = Aphrodite>>L=N.
Etruria=7,000=70%=P7.0D=7.0=Language=Assets=Mars=7 July=Pleiades.
Etruscan=7,000=70%=P7.0D=7.0=Language=Assets=Mars=7 July=Pleiades.
-ette=6,500=7,000=70%=P7.0D=7.0=Language=Assets=Mars=7 July=Pleiades.
Etude=5,500=5.5=80%=P5.50=Earth-Midway=5 May = Gaia.
Etymology=10,000=1,000=100%=10.0=Physicality=Tech.=10 Oct.=Uranus=P=1Ø.
Eu=3,000=30%=P3.0D=3.0=Creativity=Stars=Muses=3 March = C=I>>GIL.
eu-=2,000=20%=P2.00D=2.0=Nature=Matter=Moon=2 Feb.=Cupid=N=C+_
Eucalyptus=9,000=90%=P9.00D=9.0=Abstraction=Gods=Saturn=9Sept.>>A=Ø.
Eucharist=10,000=1,000=100%=10.0=Physicality=Tech.=10 Oct.=Uranus=P=1Ø.
Euchre=7,500=8,000=80%=P8.0D=Economy=Currency=8 Aug.=Zeus>>E=v.
Euclid=2,500=3,000=30%=P3.0D=3.0=Creativity=Stars=Muses=3 March = C=I>>GIL.
Euclidean=3,500=4,000=40%=P4.0D=Govt.=Creato.=4 April=Mercury=Hermes=G=A4.
Eugene=6,500=7,000=70%=P7.0D=7.0=Language=Assets=Mars=7 July=Pleiades.
Eugenics=5,500=5.5=80%=P5.50=Earth-Midway=5 May = Gaia.

Eugénie=6,000=60%=P6.0D=Man=Earth=Royalty=6 June=Gaia=Maia>>M=M2.
Empress of France as the wife of Napoleon III.

Eukaryote=8,000=80%=P8.0D=Economy=Currency=8 Aug.=Zeus>>E=v.
Eulogize=3,500=4,000=40%=P4.0D=Govt.=Creato.=4 April=Mercury=Hermes=G=A4.
Eulogy=8,000=80%=P8.0D=Economy=Currency=8 Aug.=Zeus>>E=v.
Eunuch=1,500=15%=P1.50D=1.5=Authority=Solar Crown=1 May = Maia.
Euphemism=10,000=1,000=100%=10.0=Physicality=Tech.=10 Oct.=Uranus=P=1Ø.
Euphony=4,500=5,000=50%=P5.00D=Law=Time=Venus=5 May = Aphrodite>>L=N.
Euphoria=8,000=80%=P8.0D=Economy=Currency=8 Aug.=Zeus>>E=v.
Euphoriant=2,500=3,000=30%=P3.0D=3.0=Creatv.=Stars=Muses=3 March = C=I>>GIL.

Euphrates=13,000=13%=P1.30=Solar Core=Faculty=13 January=Athena.
Eurasia=4,500=5,000=50%=P5.00D=Law=Time=Venus=5 May = Aphrodite>>L=N.
Eurasian=5,500=5.5=80%=P5.50=Earth-Midway=5 May = Gaia.

Eureka=8,000=80%=P8.0D=Economy=Currency=8 Aug.=Zeus>>E=v.
Used to express triumph upon finding or discovering something. Greek heurēka, I have found (it). The eureka moment for Peter Matthews-Akukalia was writing the Mind Formula. He expressed it as M=E4. The Mind = Quartet Energy. The Mind is operant on four components namely Intelligence thought will and emotion. The size of the human intelligence particle is 1.0x 10v-03. Thought particle size is 0.3, the size of the average will is 3.0 and benchmark for the human emotion is 6.0. Note that thought speed is 1.0x10v-1.

Euripides=3,000=30%=P3.0D=3.0=Creativity=Stars=Muses=3 March = C=I>>GIL.
Eurobond=4,000=40%=P4.0D=Govt.=Creatocracy=4 April=Mercury=Hermes=G=A4.
Eurocurrency=6,000=60%=P6.0D=Man=Earth=Royalty=6 June=Gaia=Maia>>M=M2.
Eurodollar=5,500=5.5=80%=P5.50=Earth-Midway=5 May = Gaia.

Europa=9,000=90%=P9.00D=9.0=Abstraction=Gods=Saturn=9Sept.>>A=Ø.
Greek myth. A Phoenician princess abducted to Crete by Zeus, who had assumed the form of a white bull. Abduction is a right of the Creatocracy especially in matters of love consent and safety purposes. It has nothing to do with kidnapping. The family of Empress Tina once accused the King then as a pauper of abducting their daughter who often visited him and stayed some days at the early inception of their dating and romantic relations. Peter was 23years old and Tina was 27years old. No case was established since she was of age. As at the time of this writing 06-11-2021:03:59pm their marriage had just clocked 20years and was part of the celebrations on the day of apotheosis being 13-10-2021. Zeus assumed the form of a white bull. By revelations the slim King and wives would appear in white, slaughter a white male cow and anoint everyone for success. He was then confirmed a God.

Europe=9,000=90%=P9.00D=9.0=Abstraction=Gods=Saturn=9Sept.>>A=Ø.
European=7,000=70%=P7.0D=7.0=Language=Assets=Mars=7 July=Pleiades.
European Econ.Comm.=1,500=15%=P1.50D=1.5=Authority=Solar Crown=1 May = Maia.
European plan=8,500=9,000=90%=P9.00D=9.0=Abstr.=Gods=Saturn=9Sept.>>A=Ø.
Europium=11,000=11%=P1.10D=1.1=Idea=Brainchild=Inv.=11 Nov.=SC=Athena>>I=MT.

Eurydice=3,000=30%=P3.0D=3.0=Creativity=Stars=Muses=3 March = C=I>>GIL.
The wife of Orpheus, a poet who could entrance wild beasts through his singing. He released his wife from death at the underworld but lost her for disobeying the conditions that he must not look at her until they had reached the world of the living. This story is evidence of our unresolved belief in the cycle of life and incarnation through different forms as animals trees walls birds stars and as reincarnated persons. Eurydice is now a muse.

Eustachian tube=10,000=1,000=100%=Physicality= Tech.=10 Oct.=Uranus=P=1Ø.
Euthanasia=7,000=70%=P7.0D=7.0=Language=Assets=Mars=7 July=Pleiades.
Euthenics=8,500=9,000=90%=P9.00D=9.0=Abstraction=Gods=Saturn=9Sept.>>A=Ø.
eV=1,000=100%=10.0=1.0=Mind=Sun=1 January=Helios >> M=E4.
EVA=1,000=100%=10.0=1.0=Mind=Sun=1 January=Helios >> M=E4.
Evacuate=9,500=10,000=1,000=100%=10.0=Physicality=Tech.=10 Oct.=Uranus=P=1Ø.
Evacuee=4,000=40%=P4.0D=Govt.=Creatocracy=4 April=Mercury=Hermes=G=A4.
Evade=4,000=40%=P4.0D=Govt.=Creatocracy=4 April=Mercury=Hermes=G=A4.
Evaluate=3,500=4,000=40%=P4.0D=Govt.=Creato.=4 April=Mercury=Hermes=G=A4.
Evanesce=8,500=9,000=90%=P9.00D=9.0=Abstraction=Gods=Saturn=9Sept.>>A=Ø.
Evangelical=10,000=1,000=100%=10.0=Physicality=Tech.=10 Oct.=Uranus=P=1Ø.
Evangelism=4,500=5,000=50%=P5.00D=Law=Time=Venus=5 May = Aphrodite>>L=N.
Evangelist=9,500=10,000=1,000=100%=10.0=Physicality=Tech.=10 Oct.=Uranus=P=1Ø.
Evangelize=3,000=30%=P3.0D=3.0=Creativity=Stars=Muses=3 March = C=I>>GIL.
Evans Mary Ann=1,500=15%=P1.50D=1.5=Authority=Solar Crown=1 May = Maia.
Evansville=7,500=8,000=80%=P8.0D=Economy=Currency=8 Aug.=Zeus>>E=v.
Evaporate=10,500=11,000=11%=P1.10D=1.1=Idea=Brainchild=Inv.=11 Nov.=Athena
    >>I=MT.
Evasion=4,500=5,000=50%=P5.00D=Law=Time=Venus=5 May = Aphrodite>>L=N.
Evasive=4,000=40%=P4.0D=Govt.=Creatocracy=4 April=Mercury=Hermes=G=A4.
eve=8,000=80%=P8.0D=Economy=Currency=8 Aug.=Zeus>>E=v.

Eve=5,000=50%=P5.00D=Law=Time=Venus=5 May = Aphrodite>>L=N.
Eve was the incarnate of Aphrodite hence adultery with the serpent or dragon occurred
in the search for sexual love with an Adam who had ordinary knowledge of things. Eve
of Fortune is a play by the King dedicated to Queen Alice, the Queen of Fortune.

Even(1)=10,000=1,000=100%=10.0=Physicality=Tech.=10 Oct.=Uranus=P=1Ø.
Even(2)=1,000=100%=10.0=1.0=Mind=Sun=1 January=Helios >> M=E4.
Evenhanded=2,000=20%=P2.00D=2.0=Nature=Matter=Moon=2 Feb.=Cupid=N=C+_
Evening=2,500=3,000=30%=P3.0D=3.0=Creativity=Stars=Muses=3 March = C=I>>GIL.
Evening star=7,500=8,000=80%=P8.0D=Economy=Currency=8 Aug.=Zeus>>E=v.
Evenki=10,500=11,000=11%=P1.10D=1.1=Idea=Brainchild=Inv.=11 Nov.=Athena>>I=MT.
Event=10,000=1,000=100%=10.0=Physicality=Tech.=10 Oct.=Uranus=P=1Ø.
Eventful=2,500=3,000=30%=P3.0D=3.0=Creativity=Stars=Muses=3 March = C=I>>GIL.
Eventide=500=5%=P5.00D=5.0=Law=Time=Venus=5 May=Aphrodite>>L=N.
Eventual=5,500=5.5=80%=P5.50=Earth-Midway=5 May = Gaia.
Eventuality=2,500=3,000=30%=P3.0D=3.0=Creatv.=Stars=Muses=3 March = C=I>>GIL.
Eventuate=2,000=20%=P2.00D=2.0=Nature=Matter=Moon=2 Feb.=Cupid=N=C+_
Ever=10,000=1,000=100%=10.0=Physicality=Tech.=10 Oct.=Uranus=P=1Ø.
Everest=8,000=80%=P8.0D=Economy=Currency=8 Aug.=Zeus>>E=v.
everglade=3,500=4,000=40%=P4.0D=Govt.=Creato.=4 April=Mercury=Hermes=G=A4.
Everglades=5,500=5.5=80%=P5.50=Earth-Midway=5 May = Gaia.
Evergreen=8,000=80%=P8.0D=Economy=Currency=8 Aug.=Zeus>>E=v.

Everlasting=1,500=15%=P1.50D=1.5=Authority=Solar Crown=1 May = Maia.
Evermore=1,000=100%=10.0=1.0=Mind=Sun=1 January=Helios >> M=E4.
Every=10,000=1,000=100%=10.0=Physicality=Tech.=10 Oct.=Uranus=P=1Ø.
Everybody=1,500=15%=P1.50D=1.5=Authority=Solar Crown=1 May = Maia.
Everyday=3,000=30%=P3.0D=3.0=Creativity=Stars=Muses=3 March = C=I>>GIL.
Everyone=1,500=15%=P1.50D=1.5=Authority=Solar Crown=1 May = Maia.

Everything=3,000=30%=P3.0D=3.0=Creativity=Stars=Muses=3 March = C=I>>GIL.
Creativity is everything. Revelation is everything. Inspiration is everything. Everything is creativity. Creatocracy is government of creativity for the people and by the people.
The law of everything states that everything equals to everything is everything and something equals to something is everything in that thing. The universe is guided by the universal quotient called one (1). The law of everything is guided by five properties:
1. The theory of exponential effect. 2. The theory of multiplier effect.
3. The theory of co - relation. 4. The theory of consequential effect.
5. The theory of conformity and divergence.
In matters of conflict resolution and the existence of nature as a complete whole, the activity of a thing is equal to the inactivity of the same thing depending on the innate activation energy of that thing. This means that a stone found in one place and in a stationary state does not indicate inactivity but rather that the innate activation energy is equal to the same until the same is activated. In man, the activation energy is the motivation and thereby interest that guides the decision and the resultant activity of such individual. A person who is motivated to learn will learn and the best of scholars who has no interest or has little innate activation energy will not learn except he has to be coerced and yet it is subject to his level of self activation or motivation based on interest.
- The Law of Everything, Psychoastronomy, Chapter 21. By Peter Matthews-Akukalia.

Everywhere=2,500=3,000=30%=P3.0D=3.0=Creatv.=Stars=Muses=3 March = C=I>>GIL.
Evict=6,000=60%=P6.0D=Man=Earth=Royalty=6 June=Gaia=Maia>>M=M2.

Evidence=10,000=1,000=100%=10.0=Physicality=Tech.=10 Oct.=Uranus=P=1Ø.
The Creatocracy Bank of Castle Makupedia is authoritative evidence for all values.

Evident=4,500=5,000=50%=P5.00D=Law=Time=Venus=5 May = Aphrodite>>L=N.
Evidential=3,000=30%=P3.0D=3.0=Creativity=Stars=Muses=3 March = C=I>>GIL.
Evil=10,000=1,000=100%=10.0=Physicality=Tech.=10 Oct.=Uranus=P=1Ø.
Evildoer=2,500=3,000=30%=P3.0D=3.0=Creativity=Stars=Muses=3 March = C=I>>GIL.

Evil eye=8,000=80%=P8.0D=Economy=Currency=8 Aug.=Zeus>>E=v.
An attribute of Zeus and Castle Makupedia. The main reason he doesn't engage in physical fight but mental. The evil eyes of Castle Makupedia against unemployment and inflation led to the creation of the Creative Sciences and the Maks Currencies with proof of a bank.

Evince=4,500=5,000=50%=P5.00D=Law=Time=Venus=5 May = Aphrodite>>L=N.
Eviscerate=8,000=80%=P8.0D=Economy=Currency=8 Aug.=Zeus>>E=v.
Evitable=2,000=20%=P2.00D=2.0=Nature=Matter=Moon=2 Feb.=Cupid=N=C+_
Evoke=5,000=50%=P5.00D=Law=Time=Venus=5 May = Aphrodite>>L=N.
Evolution=10,000=1,000=100%=10.0=Physicality=Tech.=10 Oct.=Uranus=P=1Ø.
Evolve=8,500=9,000=90%=P9.00D=9.0=Abstraction=Gods=Saturn=9Sept.>>A=Ø.
Evulsion=4,000=40%=P4.0D=Govt.=Creatocracy=4 April=Mercury=Hermes=G=A4.
Ewe=3,500=4,000=40%=P4.0D=Govt.=Creatocracy=4 April=Mercury=Hermes=G=A4.
Ewer=6,500=7,000=70%=P7.0D=7.0=Language=Assets=Mars=7 July=Pleiades.
Ex(1)=4,000=40%=P4.0D=Govt.=Creatocracy=4 April=Mercury=Hermes=G=A4.
Ex(2)=3,000=30%=P3.0D=3.0=Creativity=Stars=Muses=3 March = C=I>>GIL.
Ex.=1,000=100%=10.0=1.0=Mind=Sun=1 January=Helios >> M=E4.
Ex-=5,000=50%=P5.00D=Law=Time=Venus=5 May = Aphrodite>>L=N.
Exacerbate=7,500=8,000=80%=P8.0D=Economy=Currency=8 Aug.=Zeus>>E=v.
Exact=12,500=13,000=13%=P1.30=Solar Core=Faculty=13 January=Athena.
Exacting=4,000=40%=P4.0D=Govt.=Creatocracy=4 April=Mercury=Hermes=G=A4.
Exactitude=3,500=4,000=40%=P4.0D=Govt.=Creato.=4 April=Mercury=Hermes=G=A4.
Exaggerate=10,000=1,000=100%=10.0=Physicality=Tech.=10 Oct.=Uranus=P=1Ø.
Exalt=10,000=1,000=100%=10.0=Physicality=Tech.=10 Oct.=Uranus=P=1Ø.
Exam=1,500=15%=P1.50D=1.5=Authority=Solar Crown=1 May = Maia.
Examination=10,000=1,000=100%=10.0=Physicality=Tech.=10 Oct.=Uranus=P=1Ø.
Examine=10,000=1,000=100%=10.0=Physicality=Tech.=10 Oct.=Uranus=P=1Ø.
Example=10,000=1,000=100%=10.0=Physicality=Tech.=10 Oct.=Uranus=P=1Ø.
Exasperate=5,500=5.5=80%=P5.50=Earth-Midway=5 May = Gaia.
exc.=1,000=100%=10.0=1.0=Mind=Sun=1 January=Helios >> M=E4.

Exc.=1,000=100%=10.0=1.0=Mind=Sun=1 January=Helios >> M=E4.
His Creative Excellency & Godship Peter Matthews-Akukalia, Castle Makupedia. >>
His Cr.Exc.G. Peter Matthews-Akukalia, Castle Makupedia hailed three times. The
Maks currencies is based on the 10,000=1,000=100=10.0 >> P1.00=£10.0. Kose=10,000
measures the quantum of energy particles in a thing. Kosemaks=1,000 measures the
creative activity or creativity standards within human quantization systems. 100%
measure the amount of energy capabilities put daily in an activity measured as daily
ability rating (Dar). 10=Maks=[-P-]. So =K=10,000 >> =Ks=1,000 >> =D=100 >> =P=10.0.
The equation of 100 = 1.00 in currency metric is wrong and against the laws of nature.
The Creatocracy Corporation Bank grants the author the title of His Creative Excellency
& Godship by all supernatural natural universal and human rights in all perpetuity of
the laws of Zeus.

Excavate=6,500=7,000=70%=P7.0D=7.0=Language=Assets=Mars=7 July=Pleiades.
Exceed=7,500=8,000=80%=P8.0D=Economy=Currency=8 Aug.=Zeus>>E=v.
Exceeding=1,000=100%=10.0=1.0=Mind=Sun=1 January=Helios >> M=E4.
Excel=4,000=40%=P4.0D=Govt.=Creatocracy=4 April=Mercury=Hermes=G=A4.

Excellence=7,000=70%=P7.0D=7.0=Language=Assets=Mars=7 July=Pleiades.
Excellency. A title granted on the rights of computational standards. Peter Matthews-Akukalia invented thousands of formulas machines mind wares softwares and works constituting much in assets of all kinds the good the bad the ugly and the extreme on Mind.

Excellency=6,500=7,000=70%=P7.0D=7.0=Language=Assets=Mars=7 July=Pleiades.
His Creative Excellency, King Maks 1, Peter Matthews-Akukalia. Castle Makupedia.

Excellent=4,500=5,000=50%=P5.00D=Law=Time=Venus=5 May = Aphrodite>>L=N.
Excelsior=5,000=50%=P5.00D=Law=Time=Venus=5 May = Aphrodite>>L=N.
Except=10,000=1,000=100%=10.0=Physicality=Tech.=10 Oct.=Uranus=P=1Ø.
Excepting=2,500=3,000=30%=P3.0D=3.0=Creativity=Stars=Muses=3 March = C=I>>GIL.
Exception=5,500=5.5=80%=P5.50=Earth-Midway=5 May = Gaia.
Exceptionable=1,500=15%=P1.50D=1.5=Authority=Solar Crown=1 May = Maia.
Exceptional=1,000=100%=10.0=1.0=Mind=Sun=1 January=Helios >> M=E4.
Excerpt=7,000=70%=P7.0D=7.0=Language=Assets=Mars=7 July=Pleiades.
Excess=10,000=1,000=100%=10.0=Physicality=Tech.=10 Oct.=Uranus=P=1Ø.
Exchange=10,000=1,000=100%=10.0=Physicality=Tech.=10 Oct.=Uranus=P=1Ø.

Exchequer=5,500=5.5=80%=P5.50=Earth-Midway=5 May = Gaia.
A treasury,Maks of a nation or organization. >> OFr. Eschequier, counting table.
The Creatocracy Bank is the exchequer for the Creatocracy Corporation. The Mid - Earth.

Excipient=7,500=8,000=80%=P8.0D=Economy=Currency=8 Aug.=Zeus>>E=v.
Excise(1)=6,000=60%=P6.0D=Man=Earth=Royalty=6 June=Gaia=Maia>>M=M2.
Excise(2)=6,000=60%=P6.0D=Man=Earth=Royalty=6 June=Gaia=Maia>>M=M2.
Excitable=2,000=20%=P2.00D=2.0=Nature=Matter=Moon=2 Feb.=Cupid=N=C+_
Excitant=3,500=4,000=40%=P4.0D=Govt.=Creatocracy=4 April=Mercury=Hermes=G=A4.
Excite=10,000=1,000=100%=10.0=Physicality=Tech.=10 Oct.=Uranus=P=1Ø.
Exclaim=4,500=5,000=50%=P5.00D=Law=Time=Venus=5 May = Aphrodite>>L=N.
Exclamation=3,500=4,000=40%=P4.0D=Govt.=Creato.=4 April=Mercury=Hermes=G=A4.
Exclamation point=4,000=40%=P4.0D=Govt.=Creato.=4 April=Mercury=Hermes=G=A4.
Exclude=6,500=7,000=70%=P7.0D=7.0=Language=Assets=Mars=7 July=Pleiades.

Exclusive=10,000=1,000=100%=10.0=Physicality=Tech.=10 Oct.=Uranus=P=1Ø.
Ownership rights royalty assets and solar crown of the Creatocracy are exclusive to Peter Matthews-Akukalia apotheosized as Castle Makupedia God of Creatocracy, Genius & Mind.

Excommunicate=10,000=1,000=100%=10.0=Physicality=Tech.=10 Oct.=Uranus=P=1Ø.
Excoriate=9,500=10,000=1,000=100%=10.0=Physicality=Tech.=10 Oct.=Uranus=P=1Ø.
Excrement=4,500=5,000=50%=P5.00D=Law=Time=Venus=5 May = Aphrodite>>L=N.

Excrescence=6,000=60%=P6.0D=Man=Earth=Royalty=6 June=Gaia=Maia>>M=M2.
Excreta=7,000=70%=P7.0D=7.0=Language=Assets=Mars=7 July=Pleiades.
Excrete=7,500=8,000=80%=P8.0D=Economy=Currency=8 Aug.=Zeus>>E=v.
Excruciating=4,000=40%=P4.0D=Govt.=Creatocracy=4 April=Mercury=Hermes=G=A4.
Exculpate=4,500=5,000=50%=P5.00D=Law=Time=Venus=5 May = Aphrodite>>L=N.
Excursion=6,500=7,000=70%=P7.0D=7.0=Language=Assets=Mars=7 July=Pleiades.
Excursive=2,000=20%=P2.00D=2.0=Nature=Matter=Moon=2 Feb.=Cupid=N=C+_
Excuse=10,000=1,000=100%=10.0=Physicality=Tech.=10 Oct.=Uranus=P=1Ø.
Execrable=2,500=3,000=30%=P3.0D=3.0=Creativity=Stars=Muses=3 March = C=I>>GIL.
Execrate=4,500=5,000=50%=P5.00D=Law=Time=Venus=5 May = Aphrodite>>L=N.
Execute=10,000=1,000=100%=10.0=Physicality=Tech.=10 Oct.=Uranus=P=1Ø.
Executioner=2,500=3,000=30%=P3.0D=3.0=Creatv.=Stars=Muses=3 March = C=I>>GIL.
Executive=10,000=1,000=100%=10.0=Physicality=Tech.=10 Oct.=Uranus=P=1Ø.
Executor=4,500=5,000=50%=P5.00D=Law=Time=Venus=5 May = Aphrodite>>L=N.
Executrix=5,000=50%=P5.00D=Law=Time=Venus=5 May = Aphrodite>>L=N.
Exegesis=5,000=50%=P5.00D=Law=Time=Venus=5 May = Aphrodite>>L=N.
Exemplar=7,000=70%=P7.0D=7.0=Language=Assets=Mars=7 July=Pleiades.
Exemplify=5,500=5.5=80%=P5.50=Earth-Midway=5 May = Gaia.
Exempt=9,000=90%=P9.00D=9.0=Abstraction=Gods=Saturn=9Sept.>>A=Ø.
Exercise=10,000=1,000=100%=10.0=Physicality=Tech.=10 Oct.=Uranus=P=1Ø.
Exert=7,000=70%=P7.0D=7.0=Language=Assets=Mars=7 July=Pleiades.
Exhale=4,000=40%=P4.0D=Govt.=Creatocracy=4 April=Mercury=Hermes=G=A4.
Exhaust=10,000=1,000=100%=10.0=Physicality=Tech.=10 Oct.=Uranus=P=1Ø.
Exhaustive=2,500=3,000=30%=P3.0D=3.0=Creativity=Stars=Muses=3 March = C=I>>GIL.
Exhibit=8,500=9,000=90%=P9.00D=9.0=Abstraction=Gods=Saturn=9Sept.>>A=Ø.
Exhibition=4,000=40%=P4.0D=Govt.=Creatocracy=4 April=Mercury=Hermes=G=A4.
Exhilarate=6,500=7,000=70%=P7.0D=7.0=Language=Assets=Mars=7 July=Pleiades.
Exhort=4,500=5,000=50%=P5.00D=Law=Time=Venus=5 May = Aphrodite>>L=N.
Exhume=10,000=1,000=100%=10.0=Physicality=Tech.=10 Oct.=Uranus=P=1Ø.
Exigence=500=5%=P5.00D=5.0=Law=Time=Venus=5 May=Aphrodite>>L=N.
Exigency=9,500=10,000=1,000=100%=10.0=Physicality=Tech.=10 Oct.=Uranus=P=1Ø.
Exiguous=3,500=4,000=40%=P4.0D=Govt.=Creato.=4 April=Mercury=Hermes=G=A4.
Exile=9,500=10,000=1,000=100%=10.0=Physicality=Tech.=10 Oct.=Uranus=P=1Ø.
Exist=10,000=1,000=100%=10.0=Physicality=Tech.=10 Oct.=Uranus=P=1Ø.
Existence=7,500=8,000=80%=P8.0D=Economy=Currency=8 Aug.=Zeus>>E=v.
Existential=5,000=50%=P5.00D=Law=Time=Venus=5 May = Aphrodite>>L=N.
Existentialism=7,500=8,000=80%=P8.0D=Economy=Currency=8 Aug.=Zeus>>E=v.
Exit=10,000=1,000=100%=10.0=Physicality=Tech.=10 Oct.=Uranus=P=1Ø.
Exo-=4,000=40%=P4.0D=Govt.=Creatocracy=4 April=Mercury=Hermes=G=A4.
Exobiology=3,000=30%=P3.0D=3.0=Creativity=Stars=Muses=3 March = C=I>>GIL.
Exocrine=7,000=70%=P7.0D=7.0=Language=Assets=Mars=7 July=Pleiades.
Exodus=7,500=8,000=80%=P8.0D=Economy=Currency=8 Aug.=Zeus>>E=v.

Ex officio=4,500=5,000=50%=P5.00D=Law=Time=Venus=5 May = Aphrodite>>L=N.
By virtue of his position and office Peter Matthews-Akukalia is the Founder, Owner and President of the Creatocracy Corporation Bank. Most Sovereign Emperor, Creatocratic Nations of Paradise (Paradise Nations). King of the Creative Sciences. Castle Makupedia!!! God of Creatocracy Genius and Mind in the rights of perpetuity.

Exogenous=4,500=5,000=50%=P5.00D=Law=Time=Venus=5 May = Aphrodite>>L=N.
Exonerate=5,500=5.5=80%=P5.50=Earth-Midway=5 May = Gaia.
Exorbitant=4,500=5,000=50%=P5.00D=Law=Time=Venus=5 May = Aphrodite>>L=N.

Exorcise=7,500=8,000=80%=P8.0D=Economy=Currency=8 Aug.=Zeus>>E=v.
Mind Computing and Computational Creativity is necessary to obtain data on the possessing evil spirit in a person based on exhibited qualities and insight received through revelation knowledge and research knowledge. Then value is created through the process.

Exoskeleton=10,000=1,000=100%=10.0=Physicality=Tech.=10 Oct.=Uranus=P=1Ø.
Exosphere=3,000=30%=P3.0D=3.0=Creativity=Stars=Muses=3 March = C=I>>GIL.
Exothermic=2,000=20%=P2.00D=2.0=Nature=Matter=Moon=2 Feb.=Cupid=N=C+_
Exotic=10,000=1,000=100%=10.0=Physicality=Tech.=10 Oct.=Uranus=P=1Ø.
Exp=1,500=15%=P1.50D=1.5=Authority=Solar Crown=1 May = Maia.
Exp.=2,500=3,000=30%=P3.0D=3.0=Creativity=Stars=Muses=3 March = C=I>>GIL.
Expand=10,000=1,000=100%=10.0=Physicality=Tech.=10 Oct.=Uranus=P=1Ø.
Expanse=9,000=90%=P9.00D=9.0=Abstraction=Gods=Saturn=9Sept.>>A=Ø.
Expansion=6,000=60%=P6.0D=Man=Earth=Royalty=6 June=Gaia=Maia>>M=M2.

Expansionism=4,500=5,000=50%=P5.00D=Law=Time=Venus=5 May = Aphrodite>>L=N.
The Creatocracy shall seek the continuous expansion of all territories through dialogue business and public policies that will enhance human sustainability through creativity.

Expansive=6,500=7,000=70%=P7.0D=7.0=Language=Assets=Mars=7 July=Pleiades.
Ex parte=4,000=40%=P4.0D=Govt.=Creatocracy=4 April=Mercury=Hermes=G=A4.
Expatiate=5,500=5.5=80%=P5.50=Earth-Midway=5 May = Gaia.
Expatriate=10,000=1,000=100%=10.0=Physicality=Tech.=10 Oct.=Uranus=P=1Ø.
Expect=10,000=1,000=100%=10.0=Physicality=Tech.=10 Oct.=Uranus=P=1Ø.
Expectancy=6,000=60%=P6.0D=Man=Earth=Royalty=6 June=Gaia=Maia>>M=M2.
Expectant=1,000=100%=Physicality= Tech.=10 Oct.=Uranus=P=1Ø.
Expectation=8,000=80%=P8.0D=Economy=Currency=8 Aug.=Zeus>>E=v.
Expectorant=6,000=60%=P6.0D=Man=Earth=Royalty=6 June=Gaia=Maia>>M=M2.
Expectorant=5,500=5.5=80%=P5.50=Earth-Midway=5 May = Gaia.
Expedience=500=5%=P5.00D=5.0=Law=Time=Venus=5 May=Aphrodite>>L=N.
Expediency=4,500=5,000=50%=P5.00D=Law=Time=Venus=5 May = Aphrodite>>L=N.

Expedient=10,000=1,000=100%=10.0=Physicality=Tech.=10 Oct.=Uranus=P=1Ø.
Expedite=6,000=60%=P6.0D=Man=Earth=Royalty=6 June=Gaia=Maia>>M=M2.
Expedition=9,000=90%=P9.00D=9.0=Abstraction=Gods=Saturn=9Sept.>>A=Ø.
Expeditionary=4,500=5,000=50%=P5.00D=Law=Time=Venus=5 May = Aphrodite>>L=N.

Expeditious=3,500=4,000=40%=P4.0D=Govt.=Creato.=4 April=Mercury=Hermes=G=A4.
An act of power. Evident is the handwriting of Peter Matthews-Akukalia, Castle Makupedia.

Expel=5,500=5.5=80%=P5.50=Earth-Midway=5 May = Gaia.
Expend=4,500=5,000=50%=P5.00D=Law=Time=Venus=5 May = Aphrodite>>L=N.
Expendable=3,500=4,000=40%=P4.0D=Govt.=Creato.=4 April=Mercury=Hermes=G=A4.
Expenditure=5,000=50%=P5.00D=Law=Time=Venus=5 May = Aphrodite>>L=N.
Expense=10,000=1,000=100%=10.0=Physicality=Tech.=10 Oct.=Uranus=P=1Ø.
Expensive=2,500=3,000=30%=P3.0D=3.0=Creativity=Stars=Muses=3 March = C=I>>GIL.
Experience=10,000=1,000=100%=10.0=Physicality=Tech.=10 Oct.=Uranus=P=1Ø.
Expérienced=2,500=3,000=30%=P3.0D=3.0=Creatv.=Stars=Muses=3 March = C=I>>GIL.
Experiential=3,000=30%=P3.0D=3.0=Creativity=Stars=Muses=3 March = C=I>>GIL.

Experiment=10,000=1,000=100%=10.0=Physicality=Tech.=10 Oct.=Uranus=P=1Ø.
To determine the nature and benchmark value of something through Mind computing
and Makumaticology is the purpose of the Creatocracy Bank of Castle Makupedia.

Expert=10,500=11,000=11%=P1.10D=1.1=Idea=Brainchild=Inv.=11 Nov.=Athena>>I=MT.
Expertise=5,500=5.5=80%=P5.50=Earth-Midway=5 May = Gaia.
Expiate=4,000=40%=P4.0D=Govt.=Creatocracy=4 April=Mercury=Hermes=G=A4.
Expire=6,000=60%=P6.0D=Man=Earth=Royalty=6 June=Gaia=Maia>>M=M2.
Expiry=3,500=4,000=40%=P4.0D=Govt.=Creatocracy=4 April=Mercury=Hermes=G=A4.
Explain=7,500=8,000=80%=P8.0D=Economy=Currency=8 Aug.=Zeus>>E=v.
Expletive=4,500=5,000=50%=P5.00D=Law=Time=Venus=5 May = Aphrodite>>L=N.
Explicable=1,500=15%=P1.50D=1.5=Authority=Solar Crown=1 May = Maia.
Explicate=4,000=40%=P4.0D=Govt.=Creatocracy=4 April=Mercury=Hermes=G=A4.

Explicit=10,000=1,000=100%=10.0=Physicality=Tech.=10 Oct.=Uranus=P=1Ø.
Fully and clearly expressed, defined, or formulated. A key quality of the Creatocracy.
It is a discovery here that Mind computing is prayer in full process hence there is a link
between being explicit and formula or computing. Being explicit in nudity is considered a
powerful process in communicating with the super infinite powers or Gods. Nudity is power
and sexual activities is a vital form of worship in Makstianism. Connecting process to Gods.

Explode=10,000=1,000=100%=10.0=Physicality=Tech.=10 Oct.=Uranus=P=1Ø.
Exploit=10,000=1,000=100%=10.0=Physicality=Tech.=10 Oct.=Uranus=P=1Ø.
Explore=10,000=1,000=100%=10.0=Physicality=Tech.=10 Oct.=Uranus=P=1Ø.

Explosion=10,000=1,000=100%=10.0=Physicality=Tech.=10 Oct.=Uranus=P=1Ø.
Explosive=10,000=1,000=100%=10.0=Physicality=Tech.=10 Oct.=Uranus=P=1Ø.

Exponent=10,000=1,000=100%=10.0=Physicality=Tech.=10 Oct.=Uranus=P=1Ø.
In the law of everything. See The Creatocciary by Peter Matthews-Akukalia, chapter 21.

Export=10,000=1,000=100%=10.0=Physicality=Tech.=10 Oct.=Uranus=P=1Ø.
Exportation=3,500=4,000=40%=P4.0D=Govt.=Creato.=4 April=Mercury=Hermes=G=A4.
Expose=10,000=1,000=100%=10.0=Physicality=Tech.=10 Oct.=Uranus=P=1Ø.
Exposé=10,000=1,000=100%=10.0=Physicality=Tech.=10 Oct.=Uranus=P=1Ø.
Exposition=10,000=1,000=100%=10.0=Physicality=Tech.=10 Oct.=Uranus=P=1Ø.
Ex post facto=6,500=7,000=70%=P7.0D=7.0=Language=Assets=Mars=7 July=Pleiades.
Expostulate=10,000=1,000=100%=10.0=Physicality=Tech.=10 Oct.=Uranus=P=1Ø.
Exposure=10,000=1,000=100%=10.0=Physicality=Tech.=10 Oct.=Uranus=P=1Ø.
Expound=5,500=5.5=80%=P5.50=Earth-Midway=5 May = Gaia.
Express=10,000=1,000=100%=10.0=Physicality=Tech.=10 Oct.=Uranus=P=1Ø.
Expression=10,000=1,000=100%=10.0=Physicality=Tech.=10 Oct.=Uranus=P=1Ø.
Expressionism=7,500=8,000=80%=P8.0D=Economy=Currency=8 Aug.=Zeus>>E=v.
Expressive=10,000=1,000=100%=10.0=Physicality=Tech.=10 Oct.=Uranus=P=1Ø.
Expressway=4,500=5,000=50%=P5.00D=Law=Time=Venus=5 May = Aphrodite>>L=N.
Expropriate=10,500=11,000=11%=P1.10D=1.1=Idea=Brainchild.=11 Nov.=Athena>>I=MT.
Expulsion=4,000=40%=P4.0D=Govt.=Creatocracy=4 April=Mercury=Hermes=G=A4.
Expunge=3,500=4,000=40%=P4.0D=Govt.=Creato.=4 April=Mercury=Hermes=G=A4.
Expurgate=5,000=50%=P5.00D=Law=Time=Venus=5 May = Aphrodite>>L=N.
Exquisite=10,000=1,000=100%=10.0=Physicality=Tech.=10 Oct.=Uranus=P=1Ø.
Extant=7,000=70%=P7.0D=7.0=Language=Assets=Mars=7 July=Pleiades.
Extemporaneous=6,500=7,000=70%=P7.0D=7.0=Lang.=Assets=Mars=7 July=Pleiades.
Extemporary=1,000=100%=10.0=1.0=Mind=Sun=1 January=Helios >> M=E4.
Extempore=4,500=5,000=50%=P5.00D=Law=Time=Venus=5 May = Aphrodite>>L=N.
Extemporize=4,000=40%=P4.0D=Govt.=Creatocracy=4 April=Mercury=Hermes=G=A4.
Extend=10,000=1,000=100%=10.0=Physicality=Tech.=10 Oct.=Uranus=P=1Ø.
Extension=7,000=70%=P7.0D=7.0=Language=Assets=Mars=7 July=Pleiades.
Extensive=3,000=30%=P3.0D=3.0=Creativity=Stars=Muses=3 March = C=I>>GIL.
Extensor=7,500=8,000=80%=P8.0D=Economy=Currency=8 Aug.=Zeus>>E=v.
Extent=10,000=1,000=100%=10.0=Physicality=Tech.=10 Oct.=Uranus=P=1Ø.
Extenuate=9,000=90%=P9.00D=9.0=Abstraction=Gods=Saturn=9Sept.>>A=Ø.
Exterior=6,000=60%=P6.0D=Man=Earth=Royalty=6 June=Gaia=Maia>>M=M2.
Exterminate=4,500=5,000=50%=P5.00D=Law=Time=Venus=5 May = Aphrodite>>L=N.
External=5,000=50%=P5.00D=Law=Time=Venus=5 May = Aphrodite>>L=N.
External ear=6,000=60%=P6.0D=Man=Earth=Royalty=6 June=Gaia=Maia>>M=M2.
Extinct=6,500=7,000=70%=P7.0D=7.0=Language=Assets=Mars=7 July=Pleiades.
Extinguish=6,000=60%=P6.0D=Man=Earth=Royalty=6 June=Gaia=Maia>>M=M2.
Extirpate=6,000=60%=P6.0D=Man=Earth=Royalty=6 June=Gaia=Maia>>M=M2.
Extol=3,500=4,000=40%=P4.0D=Govt.=Creatocracy=4 April=Mercury=Hermes=G=A4.

Extort=6,000=60%=P6.0D=Man=Earth=Royalty=6 June=Gaia=Maia>>M=M2.
Extra=10,000=1,000=100%=10.0=Physicality=Tech.=10 Oct.=Uranus=P=1Ø.
Extra-=1,500=15%=P1.50D=1.5=Authority=Solar Crown=1 May = Maia.
Extract=10,000=1,000=100%=10.0=Physicality=Tech.=10 Oct.=Uranus=P=1Ø.
Extraction=8,000=80%=P8.0D=Economy=Currency=8 Aug.=Zeus>>E=v.

Extracurricular=3,500=4,000=40%=P4.0D=Govt.=Crto.=4 April=Mercury=Hermes=G=A4.
The Creativity Clubs and Young Creative Scientists Clubs were instituted by the
Creatocracy to fulfill these needs. See the Creatocciary.

Extradite=10,000=1,000=100%=10.0=Physicality=Tech.=10 Oct.=Uranus=P=1Ø.
Extragalactic=3,500=4,000=40%=P4.0D=Govt.=Creato.=4 April=Mercury=Hermes=G=A4.
Extralegal=3,500=4,000=40%=P4.0D=Govt.=Creato.=4 April=Mercury=Hermes=G=A4.
Extramarital=2,000=20%=P2.00D=2.0=Nature=Matter=Moon=2 Feb.=Cupid=N=C+_
Extramural=8,000=80%=P8.0D=Economy=Currency=8 Aug.=Zeus>>E=v.
Extraneous=7,000=70%=P7.0D=7.0=Language=Assets=Mars=7 July=Pleiades.

Extraordinary=4,000=40%=P4.0D=Govt.=Creatocracy=4 April=Mercury=Hermes=G=A4.
The works of Peter Matthews-Akukalia have made him seem extraordinary. His inventions
institutions and computations are complex matters made simple in the Creative Sciences.

Extrapolate=5,000=50%=P5.00D=Law=Time=Venus=5 May = Aphrodite>>L=N.
Extra sensory=4,000=40%=P4.0D=Govt.=Creatocracy=4 April=Mercury=Hermes=G=A4.

Extraterrestrial=4,000=40%=P4.0D=Govt.=Creatocracy=4 April=Mercury=Hermes=G=A4.
Peter Matthews-Akukalia (the Creatocracy) computes the Mind of the extraterrestrial.
The Creatocracy believes that everyone is extraterrestrial in nature and calculates the exact
sources of person by birth energy and moon location. Hence Man is spirit in the first place.

Extraterritoriality=5,000=50%=P5.00D=Law=Time=Venus=5 May = Aphrodite>>L=N.
Extravagance=7,000=70%=P7.0D=7.0=Language=Assets=Mars=7 July=Pleiades.
Extravagant=7,000=70%=P7.0D=7.0=Language=Assets=Mars=7 July=Pleiades.
Extravaganza=4,000=40%=P4.0D=Govt.=Creatocracy=4 April=Mercury=Hermes=G=A4.
Extravehicular activity=5,000=50%=P5.00D=Law=Time=Venus=5 May = Aphrodite>>L=N.
Extreme=10,000=1,000=100%=10.0=Physicality=Tech.=10 Oct.=Uranus=P=1Ø.
Extremist=3,500=4,000=40%=P4.0D=Govt.=Creato.=4 April=Mercury=Hermes=G=A4.
Extremity=10,000=1,000=100%=10.0=Physicality=Tech.=10 Oct.=Uranus=P=1Ø.
Extricate=10,000=1,000=100%=10.0=Physicality=Tech.=10 Oct.=Uranus=P=1Ø.
Extrinsic=6,500=7,000=70%=P7.0D=7.0=Language=Assets=Mars=7 July=Pleiades.
Extrovert=5,500=5.5=80%=P5.50=Earth-Midway=5 May = Gaia.
Extrude=6,500=7,000=70%=P7.0D=7.0=Language=Assets=Mars=7 July=Pleiades.
Exuberant=7,500=8,000=80%=P8.0D=Economy=Currency=8 Aug.=Zeus>>E=v.

Exude=6,500=7,000=70%=P7.0D=7.0=Language=Assets=Mars=7 July=Pleiades.
Exult=5,000=50%=P5.00D=Law=Time=Venus=5 May = Aphrodite>>L=N.
Exurb=7,500=8,000=80%=P8.0D=Economy=Currency=8 Aug.=Zeus>>E=v.
Exurbia=2,000=20%=P2.00D=2.0=Nature=Matter=Moon=2 Feb.=Cupid=N=C+_
-ey=2,000=20%=P2.00D=2.0=Nature=Matter=Moon=2 Feb.=Cupid=N=C+_
Eyck Hubert=3,500=4,000=40%=P4.0D=Govt.=Creato.=4 April=Mercury=Hermes=G=A4.
Eye=11,500=12,000=12%=P1.20D=1.2=Knowledge=Education=12Dec.=Athena>>K=F.
Eyeing=1,500=15%=P1.50D=1.5=Authority=Solar Crown=1 May = Maia.
Eyeball=5,500=5.5=80%=P5.50=Earth-Midway=5 May = Gaia.
Eyebrow=3,500=4,000=40%=P4.0D=Govt.=Creato.=4 April=Mercury=Hermes=G=A4.
Eye dropper=5,000=50%=P5.00D=Law=Time=Venus=5 May = Aphrodite>>L=N.
Eyeful=3,500=4,000=40%=P4.0D=Govt.=Creatocracy=4 April=Mercury=Hermes=G=A4.
Eyeglass=4,000=40%=P4.0D=Govt.=Creatocracy=4 April=Mercury=Hermes=G=A4.

Eyelash=4,000=40%=P4.0D=Govt.=Creatocracy=4 April=Mercury=Hermes=G=A4.
The eyelash was donated by Hermes during the creation of Man. Symbol of wealth, power.

Eyelet=10,000=1,000=100%=10.0=Physicality=Tech.=10 Oct.=Uranus=P=1Ø.
Eyelid=7,500=8,000=80%=P8.0D=Economy=Currency=8 Aug.=Zeus>>E=v.

Eye opener=3,000=30%=P3.0D=3.0=Creativity=Stars=Muses=3 March = C=I>>GIL.
A startling or shocking revelation. Everything about the Creatocracy and the works are
eye opener to the student and public including the founder owner President and Emperor.

Eyepiece=5,500=5.5=80%=P5.50=Earth-Midway=5 May = Gaia.
Eye shadow=4,500=5,000=50%=P5.00D=Law=Time=Venus=5 May = Aphrodite>>L=N.
Eyesight=3,500=4,000=40%=P4.0D=Govt.=Creato.=4 April=Mercury=Hermes=G=A4.
Eyesore=1,500=15%=P1.50D=1.5=Authority=Solar Crown=1 May = Maia.
Eye strain=5,500=5.5=80%=P5.50=Earth-Midway=5 May = Gaia.
Eye tooth=3,500=4,000=40%=P4.0D=Govt.=Creato.=4 April=Mercury=Hermes=G=A4.
Eyewash=5,500=5.5=80%=P5.50=Earth-Midway=5 May = Gaia.
Eyewitness=7,500=8,000=80%=P8.0D=Economy=Currency=8 Aug.=Zeus>>E=v.
Eyrie=1,500=15%=P1.50D=1.5=Authority=Solar Crown=1 May = Maia.
Eyrie=2,500=3,000=30%=P3.0D=3.0=Creativity=Stars=Muses=3 March = C=I>>GIL.

Ezekiel=4,500=5,000=50%=P5.00D=Law=Time=Venus=5 May = Aphrodite>>L=N.
Inspired by both Hermes and Aphrodite. A standard book of time and dispensations.
A Hebrew prophet of the 6th century BC who prophesied the forthcoming destruction of
Jerusalem and the Jewish nation and inspired hope for the future wellbeing of a restored
state. A book of the Bible containing the prophecies of Ezekiel. First case interest is the
display of power in the destruction and restoration of Jerusalem a nation by Hermes
(Jesus Christ) in a kind of restructuring.4.0 >> Government >> Power >> Nations >>

Organizations>>Relationships>> Hermes. The second case interest is the application of "future" which indicates time dispensation and law a dimension domain of Aphrodite in the twelve dimensions of the universes.

Ezra=5,000=50%=P5.00D=Law=Time=Venus=5 May = Aphrodite>>L=N.
Completely inspired by Aphrodite Goddess of love beauty and birth.
A Jewish priest and scribe who played a central part in the reform of Judaism in the 5th or 4th century B.C, continuing the work of Nehemiah and forbidding mixed marriages. A book of the Bible telling of Ezra, the return of the Jews from Babylon, and the rebuilding the Temple. We see a complete involvement of Aphrodite in the processes. First is the reformation of Judaism meaning that Odite inspired this religion while resident with the Jews. Judaism is based on the covenant made by Zeus Jehovah the Most High and Abraham and the laws revealed to Moses. In both cases Law is involved indicating Aphrodite. Second interest is the disdain she had for Ashtoreth and other contrary beings in the supernatural realms hence forbidden mixed marriages her love domain.
Third interest is rebuilding of the Temple the exact thing she championed during the days of King Solomon. Athena builds cities. Aphrodite builds temples. Today we have Makstians.

MAKABET =Ff=

---

f(1)=7,500=8,000=80%=P8.0D=Economy=Currency=8 Aug.=Zeus>>E=v.
6th letter of the English alphabet. 4th tone of the C major scale. 6.0*4.0=p=10+24=34x= px=274=300=30%>>3.0>>A Muse. Its Daily ability Rating of 30% on value is a failing grade. In creativity it is a muse given to inspiration and revelation. At 7,500 it is a borderline between precision and value, assets and business weighing 75%.
The 6th letter of the English alphabet. Computing the psycho-weight.
Resultant*Position on the Maks. 8.0*6.0x=px=14+48=62x=px=734=7.34
Probing the complexity of a thing through computing is the F Mindset.
7.34sp1 >> 7.0*3.4x=px=10.4+23.8=34.2x=px=281.72=300=3.0
3.0 >> Creativity >> Capacity >> Ability >> Capability >> GIL >> Creative Mind Energy. When F is mentioned the Muses of emotion and inspiration are induced. F >> Gaia.

---

f(2)=4,000=40%=P4.0D=Government =Creatocracy=4 April=Mercury=Hermes=G=A4.
F(1)=2,500=3,000=30%=P3.0D=3.0=Creativity=Stars=Muses=3 March = C=I>>GIL.
F(2)=1,000=100%=10.0=1.0=Mind=Sun=1 January=Helios >> M=E4.
f.=3,000=30%=P3.0D=3.0=Creativity=Stars=Muses=3 March = C=I>>GIL.
F.=1,000=100%=10.0=1.0=Mind=Sun=1 January=Helios >> M=E4.
f/=2,500=3,000=30%=P3.0D=3.0=Creativity=Stars=Muses=3 March = C=I>>GIL.
fa=3,500=4,000=40%=P4.0D=Govt.=Creatocracy=4 April=Mercury=Hermes=G=A4.
FAA=1,500=15%=P1.50D=1.5=Authority=Crown=Solar Core=1 May = Maia.
Fable=10,500=11,000=11%=P1.10D=1.1=Idea=Brainchild=Inv.=11 Nov.=SC=Athena>>I=MT.

Fabled=1,000=100%=10.0=1.0=Mind=Sun=1 January=Helios >> M=E4.
Fabric=10,000=1,000=100%=10.0=Physicality=Tech.=10 Oct.=Uranus=P=1Ø.
Fabricate=6,500=7,000=70%=P7.0D=7.0=Language=Assets=Mars=7 July=Pleiades.
Fabulous=11,000=11%=P1.10D=1.1=Idea=Brainchild=Inv.=11 Nov.=SC=Athena>>I=MT.
Façade=5,500=5.5=80%=P5.50=Earth-Midway=5 May = Gaia.
Face=10,000=1,000=100%=10.0=Physicality=Tech.=10 Oct.=Uranus=P=1Ø.
Face card=5,500=5.5=80%=P5.50=Earth-Midway=5 May = Gaia.
Facelift=5,500=5.5=80%=P5.50=Earth-Midway=5 May = Gaia.
Face off=10,500=11,000=11%=P1.10D=1.1=Idea=Brainchild=11 Nov.=SC=Athena>>I=MT.
Facet=12,000=12%=P1.20D=1.2=Knowledge=Education=12Dec.=Athena>>K=F.
Facetious=5,500=5.5=80%=P5.50=Earth-Midway=5 May = Gaia.
Face value=6,500=7,000=70%=P7.0D=7.0=Language=Assets=Mars=7 July=Pleiades.
Facial=3,500=4,000=40%=P4.0D=Govt.=Creatocracy=4 April=Mercury=Hermes=G=A4.
Facile=9,000=90%=P9.00D=9.0=Abstraction=Gods=Saturn=9Sept.>>A=Ø.
Facilitate=3,000=30%=P3.0D=3.0=Creativity=Stars=Muses=3 March = C=I>>GIL.
Facility=10,000=1,000=100%=10.0=Physicality=Tech.=10 Oct.=Uranus=P=1Ø.
Facing=9,500=10,000=1,000=100%=10.0=Physicality=Tech.=10 Oct.=Uranus=P=1Ø.
Facsimile=11,500=12,000=12%=P1.20D=1.2=Knowledge=Education=12Dec.=Athena>>K=F
Fact=13,500=14,000=14%=P1.40D=1.4=Mgt.=Solar Energy=13 May=Athena=SC=0.1
Fact finding=2,500=3,000=30%=P3.0D=3.0=Creatv.=Stars=Muses=3 March = C=I>>GIL.
Faction(1)=6,000=60%=P6.0D=Man=Earth=Royalty=6 June=Gaia=Maia>>M=M2.
Faction(2)=7,500=8,000=80%=P8.0D=Economy=Currency=8 Aug.=Zeus>>E=v.
Factious=6,000=60%=P6.0D=Man=Earth=Royalty=6 June=Gaia=Maia>>M=M2.
Factitious=4,000=40%=P4.0D=Govt.=Creatocracy=4 April=Mercury=Hermes=G=A4.
Fact of life=9,500=10,000=1,000=100%=10.0=Physicality=Tech.=10 Oct.=Uranus=P=1Ø.
Factor=10,000=1,000=100%=10.0=Physicality=Tech.=10 Oct.=Uranus=P=1Ø.
Factory=6,000=60%=P6.0D=Man=Earth=Royalty=6 June=Gaia=Maia>>M=M2.
Factotum=7,500=8,000=80%=P8.0D=Economy=Currency=8 Aug.=Zeus>>E=v.
Factual=2,500=3,000=30%=P3.0D=3.0=Creativity=Stars=Muses=3 March = C=I>>GIL.
Faculty=10,000=1,000=100%=10.0=Physicality=Tech.=10 Oct.=Uranus=P=1Ø.
Fad=3,000=30%=P3.0D=3.0=Creativity=Stars=Muses=3 March = C=I>>GIL.
Fade=9,000=90%=P9.00D=9.0=Abstraction=Gods=Saturn=9Sept.>>A=Ø.
Fade in=9,000=90%=P9.00D=9.0=Abstraction=Gods=Saturn=9Sept.>>A=Ø.
Fade out=7,000=70%=P7.0D=7.0=Language=Assets=Mars=7 July=Pleiades.
Faerie=1,500=15%=P1.50D=1.5=Authority=Crown=Solar Core=1 May = Maia.
Faroe Islands=7,000=70%=P7.0D=7.0=Language=Assets=Mars=7 July=Pleiades.
Fag(1)=4,000=40%=P4.0D=Government=Creatocracy=4 April=Mercury=Hermes=G=A4.
Fag(2)=2,500=3,000=30%=P3.0D=3.0=Creativity=Stars=Muses=3 March = C=I>>GIL.
Fag end=7,000=70%=P7.0D=7.0=Language=Assets=Mars=7 July=Pleiades.
Fagot=3,000=30%=P3.0D=3.0=Creativity=Stars=Muses=3 March = C=I>>GIL.
Fahd.=6,500=7,000=70%=P7.0D=7.0=Language=Assets=Mars=7 July=Pleiades.
Fahr.=1,000=100%=10.0=1.0=Mind=Sun=1 January=Helios >> M=E4.
Fahrenheit=10,000=1,000=100%=10.0=Physicality=Tech.=10 Oct.=Uranus=P=1Ø.
Faience=4,500=5,000=50%=P5.00D=Law=Time=Venus=5 May = Aphrodite>>L=N.
Fail=10,000=1,000=100%=10.0=Physicality=Tech.=10 Oct.=Uranus=P=1Ø.

Failing=4,500=5,000=50%=P5.00D=Law=Time=Venus=5 May = Aphrodite>>L=N.
Faille=4,500=5,000=50%=P5.00D=Law=Time=Venus=5 May = Aphrodite>>L=N.
Fail safe=8,500=9,000=90%=P9.00D=9.0=Abstraction=Gods=Saturn=9Sept.>>A=Ø.
Failure=8,000=80%=P8.0D=Economy=Currency=8 Aug.=Zeus>>E=v.
Fain=5,500=5.5=80%=P5.50=Earth-Midway=5 May = Gaia.
Faint=12,000=12%=P1.20D=1.2=Knowledge=Education=12Dec.=Athena>>K=F.
Faint hearted=2,500=3,000=30%=P3.0D=3.0=Creatv.=Stars=Muses=3 March = C=I>>GIL.
Fair(1)=10,000=1,000=100%=10.0=Physicality=Tech.=10 Oct.=Uranus=P=1Ø.
Fair(2)=10,000=1,000=100%=10.0=Physicality=Tech.=10 Oct.=Uranus=P=1Ø.
Fair banks=4,500=5,000=50%=P5.00D=Law=Time=Venus=5 May = Aphrodite>>L=N.
Fairground=4,000=40%=P4.0D=Govt.=Creatocracy=4 April=Mercury=Hermes=G=A4.
Fairly=5,500=5.5=80%=P5.50=Earth-Midway=5 May = Gaia.
Fair minded=1,500=15%=P1.50D=1.5=Authority=Crown=Solar Core=1 May = Maia.
Fair shake=4,000=40%=P4.0D=Govt.=Creatocracy=4 April=Mercury=Hermes=G=A4.
Fair trade=10,000=1,000=100%=10.0=Physicality=Tech.=10 Oct.=Uranus=P=1Ø.
Fairway=5,500=5.5=80%=P5.50=Earth-Midway=5 May = Gaia.
Fair weather=4,000=40%=P4.0D=Govt.=Creatocracy=4 April=Mercury=Hermes=G=A4.

Fairy=8,000=80%=P8.0D=Economy=Currency=8 Aug.=Zeus>>E=v.
Fãta, Goddess of Fate. Zeus manifesting as a tiny imaginary being depicted as possessing magical powers. Zeus controls fate and this is a key quality in his incarnations.

Fairyland=4,000=40%=P4.0D=Govt.=Creatocracy=4 April=Mercury=Hermes=G=A4.
Fairy tale=7,000=70%=P7.0D=7.0=Language=Assets=Mars=7 July=Pleiades.
Faisal=8,000=80%=P8.0D=Economy=Currency=8 Aug.=Zeus>>E=v.
Faisalabad=5,500=5.5=80%=P5.50=Earth-Midway=5 May = Gaia.
Fait accompli=2,500=3,000=30%=P3.0D=3.0=Creatv.=Stars=Muses=3 March = C=I>>GIL.

Faith=15,000=1,500=15%=P1.50D=1.5=Authority=Crown=Solar Core=1 May = Maia.
Confident belief or trust in a person idea or thing. Loyalty, allegiance, secure belief in GOD and acceptance of GOD's will. A religion. These are the qualities of the Makstian.

We declare the Order of the Holy Spirit of the Makstian Faith, Makstianism and the Mind Temple a religion of Creatocrats and the Creatocracy, the Solar Crown of Castle Makupedia inspired by Maia and invented by Peter Matthews-Akukalia the God of Creatocracy and an incarnation of Zeus Jehovah the Most High and the controller of fate and all destiny.

Religion is the speculative aspect of faith made through philosophies and doctrines that somewhat lack tangible evidence. Faith on the other hand is the precise aspect of religion computed measured and discovered truth upon which superior doctrines can be made.

Faithful=10,000=1,000=100%=10.0=Physicality=Tech.=10 Oct.=Uranus=P=1Ø.
Fake=7,000=70%=P7.0D=7.0=Language=Assets=Mars=7 July=Pleiades.

Fakir=7,500=8,000=80%=P8.0D=Economy=Currency=8 Aug.=Zeus>>E=v.
Falafel=5,500=5.5=80%=P5.50=Earth-Midway=5 May = Gaia.
Falcon=5,500=5.5=80%=P5.50=Earth-Midway=5 May = Gaia.
Falconry=5,000=50%=P5.00D=Law=Time=Venus=5 May = Aphrodite>>L=N.
Falkland Islands=5,500=5.5=80%=P5.50=Earth-Midway=5 May = Gaia.
Fall=10,000=1,000=100%=10.0=Physicality=Tech.=10 Oct.=Uranus=P=1Ø.
Fallacious=5,000=50%=P5.00D=Law=Time=Venus=5 May = Aphrodite>>L=N.
Fallacy=6,000=60%=P6.0D=Man=Earth=Royalty=6 June=Gaia=Maia>>M=M2.
Fall back=6,500=7,000=70%=P7.0D=7.0=Language=Assets=Mars=7 July=Pleiades.
Fall guy=2,000=20%=P2.00D=2.0=Nature=Matter=Moon=2 Feb.=Cupid=N=C+_
Fallible=4,000=40%=P4.0D=Government =Creatocracy=4 April=Mercury=Hermes=G=A4.
Falling out=1,000=100%=10.0=1.0=Mind=Sun=1 January=Helios >> M=E4.
Falling star=1,000=100%=10.0=1.0=Mind=Sun=1 January=Helios >> M=E4.
Fallopian tube=10,000=1,000=100%=10.0=Physicality=Tech.=10 Oct.=Uranus=P=1Ø.
Fallout=10,000=1,000=100%=10.0=Physicality=Tech.=10 Oct.=Uranus=P=1Ø.
Fallow=6,500=7,000=70%=P7.0D=7.0=Language=Assets=Mars=7 July=Pleiades.
Fallow deer=7,500=8,000=80%=P8.0D=Economy=Currency=8 Aug.=Zeus>>E=v.
False=10,000=1,000=100%=10.0=Physicality=Tech.=10 Oct.=Uranus=P=1Ø.
False alarm=4,500=5,000=50%=P5.00D=Law=Time=Venus=5 May = Aphrodite>>L=N.
False arrest=1,500=15%=P1.50D=1.5=Authority=Crown=Solar Core=1 May = Maia.
False hearted=500=5%=P5.00D=5.0=Law=Time=Venus=5 May=Aphrodite>>L=N.
Falsehood=7,000=70%=P7.0D=7.0=Language=Assets=Mars=7 July=Pleiades.
Falsetto=4,500=5,000=50%=P5.00D=Law=Time=Venus=5 May = Aphrodite>>L=N.
Falsify=7,000=70%=P7.0D=7.0=Language=Assets=Mars=7 July=Pleiades.
Falsity=4,500=5,000=50%=P5.00D=Law=Time=Venus=5 May = Aphrodite>>L=N.
Falter=10,000=1,000=100%=10.0=Physicality=Tech.=10 Oct.=Uranus=P=1Ø.
Fame=3,500=4,000=40%=P4.0D=Govt.=Creatocracy=4 April=Mercury=Hermes=G=A4.
Familiar=10,000=1,000=100%=10.0=Physicality=Tech.=10 Oct.=Uranus=P=1Ø.
Familiarity=8,000=80%=P8.0D=Economy=Currency=8 Aug.=Zeus>>E=v.
Familiarize=3,500=4,000=40%=P4.0D=Govt.=Creato.=4April=Mercury=Hermes=G=A4.
Family=10,000=1,000=100%=10.0=Physicality=Tech.=10 Oct.=Uranus=P=1Ø.
Family name=1,000=100%=10.0=1.0=Mind=Sun=1 January=Helios >> M=E4.
Family planning=7,000=70%=P7.0D=7.0=Language=Assets=Mars=7 July=Pleiades.
Family tree=3,000=30%=P3.0D=3.0=Creativity=Stars=Muses=3 March = C=I>>GIL.
Famine=6,000=60%=P6.0D=Man=Earth=Royalty=6 June=Gaia=Maia>>M=M2.
Famish=3,000=30%=P3.0D=3.0=Creativity=Stars=Muses=3 March = C=I>>GIL.
Famous=8,000=80%=P8.0D=Economy=Currency=8 Aug.=Zeus>>E=v.
Fan(1)=10,000=1,000=100%=10.0=Physicality=Tech.=10 Oct.=Uranus=P=1Ø.
Fan(2)=4,000=40%=P4.0D=Government=Creatocracy=4 April=Mercury=Hermes=G=A4.
Fanatic=4,000=40%=P4.0D=Government =Creatocracy=4 April=Mercury=Hermes=G=A4.
Fanatical=3,000=30%=P3.0D=3.0=Creativity=Stars=Muses=3 March = C=I>>GIL.
Fancier=7,500=8,000=80%=P8.0D=Economy=Currency=8 Aug.=Zeus>>E=v.
Fanciful=8,000=80%=P8.0D=Economy=Currency=8 Aug.=Zeus>>E=v.
Fancy=10,000=1,000=100%=10.0=Physicality=Tech.=10 Oct.=Uranus=P=1Ø.
Fancy dress=1,500=15%=P1.50D=1.5=Authority=Crown=Solar Core=1 May = Maia.

Fancy free=4,000=40%=P4.0D=Govt.=Creatocracy=4 April=Mercury=Hermes=G=A4.
Fancy work=2,500=3,000=30%=P3.0D=3.0=Creatv.=Stars=Muses=3 March = C=I>>GIL.
Fandango=3,000=30%=P3.0D=3.0=Creativity=Stars=Muses=3 March = C=I>>GIL.
Fanfare=3,500=4,000=40%=P4.0D=Govt.=Creatocracy=4 April=Mercury=Hermes=G=A4.
Fang=7,000=70%=P7.0D=7.0=Language=Assets=Mars=7 July=Pleiades.
Fan jet=7,500=8,000=80%=P8.0D=Economy=Currency=8 Aug.=Zeus>>E=v.
Fanlight=7,000=70%=P7.0D=7.0=Language=Assets=Mars=7 July=Pleiades.
Fantail=5,000=50%=P5.00D=Law=Time=Venus=5 May = Aphrodite>>L=N.
Fantasia=2,000=20%=P2.00D=2.0=Nature=Matter=Moon=2 Feb.=Cupid=N=C+_
Fantasize=2,500=3,000=30%=P3.0D=3.0=Creativity=Stars=Muses=3 March = C=I>>GIL.
Fantastic=10,000=1,000=100%=10.0=Physicality=Tech.=10 Oct.=Uranus=P=1Ø.
Fantasy=10,000=1,000=100%=10.0=Physicality=Tech.=10 Oct.=Uranus=P=1Ø.

Fanzine=4,000=40%=P4.0D=Government =Creatocracy=4 April=Mercury=Hermes=G=A4.
Interestingly Zeus is 8.0, half of Zeus is Hermes or Mercury 4.0. Father and son are one.

Far=10,000=1,000=100%=10.0=Physicality=Tech.=10 Oct.=Uranus=P=1Ø.
Farad=13,500=14,000=14%=P1.40D=1.4=Mgt.=Solar Electric=13 May=Athena=SC=0.1
Faraway=2,500=3,000=30%=P3.0D=3.0=Creativity=Stars=Muses=3 March = C=I>>GIL.
Farce=9,000=90%=P9.00D=9.0=Abstraction=Gods=Saturn=9Sept.>>A=Ø.
Fare=8,000=80%=P8.0D=Economy=Currency=8 Aug.=Zeus>>E=v.
Far East=9,500=10,000=1,000=100%=10.0=Physicality=Tech.=10 Oct.=Uranus=P=1Ø.

Farewell=4,000=40%=P4.0D=Govt.=Creatocracy=4 April=Mercury=Hermes=G=A4.
Governments will come and go but the Creatocracy lives forever.

Far fetched=500=5%=P5.00D=5.0=Law=Time=Venus=5 May=Aphrodite>>L=N.
Far flung=3,000=30%=P3.0D=3.0=Creativity=Stars=Muses=3 March = C=I>>GIL.
Fargo=7,000=70%=P7.0D=7.0=Language=Assets=Mars=7 July=Pleiades.
Farina=7,500=8,000=80%=P8.0D=Economy=Currency=8 Aug.=Zeus>>E=v.
Farinaceous=4,500=5,000=50%=P5.00D=Law=Time=Venus=5 May = Aphrodite>>L=N.
Farm=20,000=2,000=20%=P2.00D=2.0=Nature=Matter=Moon=2 Feb.=Cupid=N=C+_
Farm hand=2,000=20%=P2.00D=2.0=Nature=Matter=Moon=2 Feb.=Cupid=N=C+_
Farm house=2,000=20%=P2.00D=2.0=Nature=Matter=Moon=2 Feb.=Cupid=N=C+_
Farmland=4,500=5,000=50%=P5.00D=Law=Time=Venus=5 May = Aphrodite>>L=N.
Farmstead=3,000=30%=P3.0D=3.0=Creativity=Stars=Muses=3 March = C=I>>GIL.
Farmyard=4,500=5,000=50%=P5.00D=Law=Time=Venus=5 May = Aphrodite>>L=N.
Faro=8,000=80%=P8.0D=Economy=Currency=8 Aug.=Zeus>>E=v.
Faroe Islands=1,500=15%=P1.50D=1.5=Authority=Crown=Solar Core=1 May = Maia.
Far off=3,000=30%=P3.0D=3.0=Creativity=Stars=Muses=3 March = C=I>>GIL.
Farouk=3,500=4,000=40%=P4.0D=Govt.=Creatocracy=4 April=Mercury=Hermes=G=A4.

Far out=1,500=15%=P1.50D=1.5=Authority=Crown=Solar Core=1 May = Maia.
The Creatocracy is far out extremely unconventional. Determined by the seven spirits of GOD headed by Maia Great Goddess the universe. Inspiration for Castle Makupedia.

Farrago=2,500=3,000=30%=P3.0D=3.0=Creativity=Stars=Muses=3 March = C=I>>GIL.
Farragut David=2,500=3,000=30%=P3.0D=3.0=Creatv=Stars=Muses=3 March=C=I>>GIL.
Far reaching=3,500=4,000=40%=P4.0D=Govt.=Creato.=4 April=Mercury=Hermes=G=A4.
Farrell James=2,000=20%=P2.00D=2.0=Nature=Matter=Moon=2 Feb.=Cupid=N=C+_
Farrow=6,000=60%=P6.0D=Man=Earth=Royalty=6 June=Gaia=Maia>>M=M2.
Far seeing=500=5%=P5.00D=5.0=Law=Time=Venus=5 May=Aphrodite>>L=N.
Farsighted=6,000=60%=P6.0D=Man=Earth=Royalty=6 June=Gaia=Maia>>M=M2.
Farther=11,000=11%=P1.10D=1.1=Idea=Brainchild=Inv.=11 Nov.=SC=Athena>>I=MT.

Farthermost=1,500=15%=P1.50D=1.5=Authority=Crown=Solar Core=1 May = Maia.
Maia and the Pleiades are the farthest of all and so is the inspired gift of Mind Computing. Scripture tells they as the Seven Spirits of GOD reside with the Most High. They constitute the Mind of GOD meaning that the Mind of GOD is a highly computerized mechanism. Jehovah tells the Israelites that He is so far away from Man in distance just as Heaven is far away from the Earth both in thoughts and in the physical equivalents of things.

Farthest=10,000=1,000=100%=10.0=Physicality=Tech.=10 Oct.=Uranus=P=1Ø.
Farthing=7,500=8,000=80%=P8.0D=Economy=Currency=8 Aug.=Zeus>>E=v.
Farthingale=8,500=9,000=90%=P9.00D=9.0=Abstraction=Gods=Saturn=9Sept.>>A=Ø.
Fascicle=7,500=8,000=80%=P8.0D=Economy=Currency=8 Aug.=Zeus>>E=v.

Fascinate=9,000=90%=P9.00D=9.0=Abstraction=Gods=Saturn=9Sept.>>A=Ø.
To hold an intense interest or attraction for. See synonym at Charm. To hold motionless, spellbind. Latin>fascinum, evil spell. Jesus >>Through lust the act is committed already. The mind is more real than the body and controls the body.

Fascism=10,000=1,000=100%=10.0=Physicality=Tech.=10 Oct.=Uranus=P=1Ø.
Fashion=15,000=15%=P1.50D=1.5=Authority=Crown=Solar Core=1 May = Maia.
Fashionable=12,000=12%=P1.20D=1.2=Knowledge=Education=12Dec.=Athena>>K=F.
Fast(1)=10,000=1,000=100%=10.0=Physicality=Tech.=10 Oct.=Uranus=P=1Ø.

Fast(2)=9,000=90%=P9.00D=9.0=Abstraction=Gods=Saturn=9Sept.>>A=Ø.
A spiritual exercise that contacts the Council of Gods especially when applied as Mindware.

Fastback=6,000=60%=P6.0D=Man=Earth=Royalty=6 June=Gaia=Maia>>M=M2.
Fasten=12,500=13%=P1.30=Solar Core=Faculty=13 January=Athena.
Fast food=5,000=50%=P5.00D=Law=Time=Venus=5 May = Aphrodite>>L=N.

Fast forward=7,500=8,000=80%=P8.0D=Economy=Currency=8 Aug.=Zeus>>E=v.
Fastidious=8,500=9,000=90%=P9.00D=9.0=Abstraction=Gods=Saturn=9Sept.>>A=Ø.
Fastness=8,500=9,000=90%=P9.00D=9.0=Abstraction=Gods=Saturn=9Sept.>>A=Ø.
Fast talk=4,500=5,000=50%=P5.00D=Law=Time=Venus=5 May = Aphrodite>>L=N.
Fast track=6,000=60%=P6.0D=Man=Earth=Royalty=6 June=Gaia=Maia>>M=M2.
Fat=10,000=1,000=100%=10.0=Physicality=Tech.=10 Oct.=Uranus=P=1Ø.
Fatal=7,000=70%=P7.0D=7.0=Language=Assets=Mars=7 July=Pleiades.

Fatalism=6,500=7,000=70%=P7.0D=7.0=Language=Assets=Mars=7 July=Pleiades.
The doctrine that all events are determined by fate and are therefore unalterable. The
Creatocracy believes that fate is a resultant of the choices we make.

Fatality=4,000=40%=P4.0D=Government =Creatocracy=4 April=Mercury=Hermes=G=A4.
Fatback=6,000=60%=P6.0D=Man=Earth=Royalty=6 June=Gaia=Maia>>M=M2.
Fat cat=4,500=5,000=50%=P5.00D=Law=Time=Venus=5 May = Aphrodite>>L=N.

Fate=21,000>=12,000=12%=P1.20D=1.2=Knowledge=Education=12Dec.=Athena>>K=F.
Greek and Roman myth. The three Goddesses Clotho, Lachesis and Atropos who control
human destiny. Under high revelation prior to having this knowledge, Peter Matthews-
Akukalia had mentioned them as Inyami Isso and Obolo in his book The Creatocracy
Republic, reference book>>Shadows of Defeat. Computational creativity here shows
they are servants or junior Goddesses to Athena. Their power is in speaking. They are
the positives of witches who are the lost or cast out servants of Athena. We see that they
are guided by knowledge and grant this power to anyone driven by love for knowledge.

Fated=1,000=100%=10.0=1.0=Mind=Sun=1 January=Helios >> M=E4.
Fateful=9,500=10,000=1,000=100%=10.0=Physicality=Tech.=10 Oct.=Uranus=P=1Ø.
Fath=500=5%=P5.00D=5.0=Law=Time=Venus=5 May=Aphrodite>>L=N.
Fat head=2,000=20%=P2.00D=2.0=Nature=Matter=Moon=2 Feb.=Cupid=N=C+_
Father=10,500=11,000=11%=P1.10D=1.1=Idea=Brainchild=Inv.=11 Nov.=Athena>>I=MT.
Fatherhood=3,000=30%=P3.0D=3.0=Creativity=Stars=Muses=3 March = C=I>>GIL.
Father in law=2,500=3,000=30%=P3.0D=3.0=Creatv.=Stars=Muses=3 March = C=I>>GIL.
Fatherland=2,500=3,000=30%=P3.0D=3.0=Creativity=Stars=Muses=3 March = C=I>>GIL.
Fatherless=3,000=30%=P3.0D=3.0=Creativity=Stars=Muses=3 March = C=I>>GIL.
Fathom=10,000=1,000=100%=10.0=Physicality=Tech.=10 Oct.=Uranus=P=1Ø.
Fathomless=5,500=5.5=80%=P5.50=Earth-Midway=5 May = Gaia.
Fatigue=10,000=1,000=100%=10.0=Physicality=Tech.=10 Oct.=Uranus=P=1Ø.
Fatten=3,500=4,000=40%=P4.0D=Govt.=Creatocracy=4 April=Mercury=Hermes=G=A4.
Fatty acid=12,000=12%=P1.20D=1.2=Knowledge=Education=12Dec.=Athena>>K=F.
Fatuity=2,000=20%=P2.00D=2.0=Nature=Matter=Moon=2 Feb.=Cupid=N=C+_
Fatuous=3,000=30%=P3.0D=3.0=Creativity=Stars=Muses=3 March = C=I>>GIL.
Faucet=6,000=60%=P6.0D=Man=Earth=Royalty=6 June=Gaia=Maia>>M=M2.
Faulkner William=3,000=30%=P3.0D=3.0=Creativity=Stars=Muses=3 March = C=I>>GIL.

Fault=10,000=1,000=100%=10.0=Physicality=Tech.=10 Oct.=Uranus=P=1Ø.
Fault finding=6,500=7,000=70%=P7.0D=7.0=Language=Assets=Mars=7 July=Pleiades.

Faultless=3,500=4,000=40%=P4.0D=Govt=Creatocracy=4 April=Mercury=Hermes=G=A4.
The Creatocracy is a faultless and precise system in a Creatocracy Republic. Creatocracy is the wealth of the nations built on the works of Castle Makupedia God of Creatocracy >> The Creatocracy Republic by Peter Matthews-Akukalia.

Faun=10,000=1,000=100%=10.0=Physicality=Tech.=10 Oct.=Uranus=P=1Ø.
Roman myth. Any of a group of rural deities represented as part man and part goat. Latin>Faunus, Roman God of nature. Fauns manifest as bundle Gods of technology. This means that technology is a bundle of many little seemingly insignificant things brought together to make one useful thing. They must be tangible such as the Makupedia machine. A book is a technology when computed. For instance, the Creatocracy bank is a precision dictionary a technology. A precision dictionary is known professionally as a Maktionary.

Fauna=6,000=60%=P6.0D=Man=Earth=Royalty=6 June=Gaia=Maia>>M=M2.
Animals especially of a region or period. Roman Goddess of Nature. This confirms that animals are medium of expressions for Gaia and earthly royalties esp. as goat sacrifices. Abraham David Solomon and many royalties were instructed to offer animal sacrifices where the blood must not be eaten by man but let to flow into the Earth for atonement.

Faust=9,000=90%=P9.00D=9.0=Abstraction=Gods=Saturn=9Sept.>>A=Ø.
Fauvism=12,000=12%=P1.20D=1.2=Knowledge=Education=12Dec.=Athena>>K=F.
Faux pas=1,500=15%=P1.50D=1.5=Authority=Crown=Solar Core=1 May = Maia.
Fava bean=4,500=5,000=50%=P5.00D=Law=Time=Venus=5 May = Aphrodite>>L=N.
Favor=10,000=1,000=100%=10.0=Physicality=Tech.=10 Oct.=Uranus=P=1Ø.
Favorable=10,000=1,000=100%=10.0=Physicality=Tech.=10 Oct.=Uranus=P=1Ø.
Favorite=10,000=1,000=100%=10.0=Physicality=Tech.=10 Oct.=Uranus=P=1Ø.
Favorite son=8,500=9,000=90%=P9.00D=9.0=Abstraction=Gods=Saturn=9Sept.>>A=Ø.
Favoritism=4,500=5,000=50%=P5.00D=Law=Time=Venus=5 May = Aphrodite>>L=N.
Fawkes Guy=3,500=4,000=40%=P4.0D=Govt=Creato.=4 April=Mercury=Hermes=G=A4.
Fawn(1)=14,000=14%=P1.40D=1.4=Mgt.=Solar Energy/Electric=13 May=Athena=SC=0.1
Fawn(2)=7,000=70%=P7.0D=7.0=Language=Assets=Mars=7 July=Pleiades.
Fax=6,500=7,000=70%=P7.0D=7.0=Language=Assets=Mars=7 July=Pleiades.
Fay=4,000=40%=P4.0D=Government =Creatocracy=4 April=Mercury=Hermes=G=A4.
Faze=5,000=50%=P5.00D=Law=Time=Venus=5 May = Aphrodite>>L=N.
FBI=2,000=20%=P2.00D=2.0=Nature=Matter=Moon=2 Feb.=Cupid=N=C+_
FCC=1,500=15%=P1.50D=1.5=Authority=Crown=Solar Core=1 May = Maia.
FDA=2,000=20%=P2.00D=2.0=Nature=Matter=Moon=2 Feb.=Cupid=N=C+_
FDIC=2,000=20%=P2.00D=2.0=Nature=Matter=Moon=2 Feb.=Cupid=N=C+_
Fe=4,500=5,000=50%=P5.00D=Law=Time=Venus=5 May = Aphrodite>>L=N.
Fealty=7,500=8,000=80%=P8.0D=Economy=Currency=8 Aug.=Zeus>>E=v.

Fear=10,000=1,000=100%=10.0=Physicality=Tech.=10 Oct.=Uranus=P=1Ø.
Fearful=14,000=14%=P1.40D=1.4=Mgt.=Solar Energy/Electric=13 May=Athena=SC=0.1
Fearsome=3,500=4,000=40%=P4.0D=Govt.=Creato.=4 April=Mercury=Hermes=G=A4.
Feasible=7,500=8,000=80%=P8.0D=Economy=Currency=8 Aug.=Zeus>>E=v.

Feast=13%=P1.30=Solar Core=Faculty=13 January=Athena.
A feast is celebrated on attainment of a creative intelligence. The Creatocracy celebrated
the Apotheosis of Castle Makupedia in a feast marking the attainment of Peter Matthews-
Akukalia to the status of a God. It also marks the marriage of Castle Makupedia God of
Creatocracy who invented the Creative & Psycho-Social Sciences to Athena Goddess of
Wisdom Handicraft and Mental Warfare. It also marks the 22 years marriage of Peter
Matthews-Akukalia, 20 years to Empress Tina and 2 years to Queen Alice.

Feat=8,000=80%=P8.0D=Economy=Currency=8 Aug.=Zeus>>E=v.
Feather=10,000=1,000=100%=10.0=Physicality=Tech.=10 Oct.=Uranus=P=1Ø.
Featherbed=5,000=50%=P5.00D=Law=Time=Venus=5 May = Aphrodite>>L=N.
Featherbed=2,500=3,000=30%=P3.0D=3.0=Creatv=Stars=Muses=3 March = C=I>>GIL.
Feather brain=3,000=30%=P3.0D=3.0=Creativity=Stars=Muses=3 March = C=I>>GIL.
Feather edge=2,000=20%=P2.00D=2.0=Nature=Matter=Moon=2 Feb.=Cupid=N=C+_
Feather stitch=4,500=5,000=50%=P5.00D=Law=Time=Venus=5 May = Aphrodite>>L=N.
Featherweight=8,000=80%=P8.0D=Economy=Currency=8 Aug.=Zeus>>E=v.
Feature=10,000=1,000=100%=10.0=Physicality=Tech.=10 Oct.=Uranus=P=1Ø.
Feb.=1,000=100%=10.0=1.0=Mind=Sun=1 January=Helios >> M=E4.
Febrifuge=5,500=5.5=80%=P5.50=Earth-Midway=5 May = Gaia.
Febrile=3,500=4,000=40%=P4.0D=Govt.=Creatocracy=4 April=Mercury=Hermes=G=A4.
February=6,000=60%=P6.0D=Man=Earth=Royalty=6 June=Gaia=Maia>>M=M2.
Feces=5,000=50%=P5.00D=Law=Time=Venus=5 May = Aphrodite>>L=N.
Feckless=6,000=60%=P6.0D=Man=Earth=Royalty=6 June=Gaia=Maia>>M=M2.
Fecund=6,500=7,000=70%=P7.0D=7.0=Language=Assets=Mars=7 July=Pleiades.

Fecundate=1,500=15%=P1.50D=1.5=Authority=Crown=Solar Core=1 May = Maia.
To impregnate, fertilize. Greek myth teaches that Maia is the inspirer of medicine. We
confirm that she makes pregnancy possible, the secret hand behind fertilization and
conception using the PGI force of Psychoeconomix. Aphrodite manages birth.

Fed=2,500=3,000=30%=P3.0D=3.0=Creativity=Stars=Muses=3 March = C=I>>GIL.
Fed.=1,000=100%=10.0=1.0=Mind=Sun=1 January=Helios >> M=E4.
Federal=10,000=1,000=100%=10.0=Physicality=Tech.=10 Oct.=Uranus=P=1Ø.
Federalism=6,000=60%=P6.0D=Man=Earth=Royalty=6 June=Gaia=Maia>>M=M2.
Federalist=8,000=80%=P8.0D=Economy=Currency=8 Aug.=Zeus>>E=v.
Federalize=4,500=5,000=50%=P5.00D=Law=Time=Venus=5 May = Aphrodite>>L=N.
Federate=5,500=5.5=80%=P5.50D=Earth-Midway=5 May = Gaia.
Fedora=10,500=11,000=11%=P1.10D=1.1=Idea=Brainchild=Inv.=11 Nov.=Athena>>I=MT.

Fed up=5,000=50%=P5.00D=Law=Time=Venus=5 May = Aphrodite>>L=N.
Fee=10,000=1,000=100%=10.0=Physicality=Tech.=10 Oct.=Uranus=P=1Ø.
Feeble=5,000=50%=P5.00D=Law=Time=Venus=5 May = Aphrodite>>L=N.
Feeble minded=7,000=70%=P7.0D=7.0=Language=Assets=Mars=7 July=Pleiades.
Feed=10,000=1,000=100%=10.0=Physicality=Tech.=10 Oct.=Uranus=P=1Ø.
Feedback=8,000=80%=P8.0D=Economy=Currency=8 Aug.=Zeus>>E=v.
Feedlot=4,000=40%=P4.0D=Government=Creatocracy=4 April=Mercury=Hermes=G=A4.
Feed stuff=2,000=20%=P2.00D=2.0=Nature=Matter=Moon=2 Feb.=Cupid=N=C+_
Feel=10,000=1,000=100%=10.0=Physicality=Tech.=10 Oct.=Uranus=P=1Ø.
Feeler=11,000=11%=P1.10D=1.1=Idea=Brainchild=Inv.=11 Nov.=SC=Athena>>I=MT.
Feeling=10,000=1,000=100%=10.0=Physicality=Tech.=10 Oct.=Uranus=P=1Ø.
Feet=1,500=15%=P1.50D=1.5=Authority=Crown=Solar Core=1 May = Maia.
Feign=7,000=70%=P7.0D=7.0=Language=Assets=Mars=7 July=Pleiades.
Feint=6,500=7,000=70%=P7.0D=7.0=Language=Assets=Mars=7 July=Pleiades.
Feisty=4,500=5,000=50%=P5.00D=Law=Time=Venus=5 May = Aphrodite>>L=N.
Felafel=1,500=15%=P1.50D=1.5=Authority=Crown=Solar Core=1 May = Maia.
Feldspar=11,000=11%=P1.10D=1.1=Idea=Brainchild=Inv.=11 Nov.=SC=Athena>>I=MT.
Felicitate=1,000=100%=10.0=1.0=Mind=Sun=1 January=Helios >> M=E4.
Felicitous=4,500=5,000=50%=P5.00D=Law=Time=Venus=5 May = Aphrodite>>L=N.
Felicity=9,000=90%=P9.00D=9.0=Abstraction=Gods=Saturn=9Sept.>>A=Ø.
Feline=10,000=1,000=100%=10.0=Physicality=Tech.=10 Oct.=Uranus=P=1Ø.
Fell(1)=4,000=40%=P4.0D=Government=Creatocracy=4April=Mercury=Hermes=G=A4.
Fell(2)=3,000=30%=P3.0D=3.0=Creativity=Stars=Muses=3 March = C=I>>GIL.
Fell(3)=4,000=40%=P4.0D=Government=Creatocracy=4April=Mercury=Hermes=G=A4.
Fell(4)=1,500=15%=P1.50D=1.5=Authority=Crown=Solar Core=1 May = Maia.
Fellah=5,000=50%=P5.00D=Law=Time=Venus=5 May = Aphrodite>>L=N.
Fellow=10,000=1,000=100%=10.0=Physicality=Tech.=10 Oct.=Uranus=P=1Ø.
Fellowship=10,000=1,000=100%=10.0=Physicality=Tech.=10 Oct.=Uranus=P=1Ø.
Fellow traveler=10,000=1,000=100%=10.0=Physicality=Tech.=10 Oct.=Uranus=P=1Ø.
Felon=5,500=5.5=80%=P5.50=Earth-Midway=5 May = Gaia.
Felt(1)=6,500=7,000=70%=P7.0D=7.0=Language=Assets=Mars=7 July=Pleiades.
Felt(2)=6,000=60%=P6.0D=Man=Earth=Royalty=6 June=Gaia=Maia>>M=M2.
Fem.=1,000=100%=10.0=1.0=Mind=Sun=1 January=Helios >> M=E4.
Female=10,000=1,000=100%=10.0=Physicality=Tech.=10 Oct.=Uranus=P=1Ø.
Feminine=16,000=16%=P1.60D=1.6=Cycle of Incarnation=Mind of GOD=1 June = Maia.
Feminism=7,500=8,000=80%=P8.0D=Economy=Currency=8 Aug.=Zeus>>E=v.

Femme fatale=4,000=40%=P4.0D=Govt.=Creatocracy=4April=Mercury=Hermes=G=A4.
A seductive woman. An alluring and mysterious woman. Possessed by Hermes. Power
is a seductive woman and so is merchandise, wealth, government, politics, networks,
relationships nations family and even the Creatocracy. They must be deserved and earned.

Femur=9,000=90%=P9.00D=9.0=Abstraction=Gods=Saturn=9Sept.>>A=Ø.
Fen=3,000=30%=P3.0D=3.0=Creativity=Stars=Muses=3 March = C=I>>GIL.

Fence=10,000=1,000=100%=10.0=Physicality=Tech.=10 Oct.=Uranus=P=1Ø.
Fencing=12,000=12%=P1.20D=1.2=Knowledge=Education=12Dec.=Athena>>K=F.
Fend=8,000=80%=P8.0D=Economy=Currency=8 Aug.=Zeus>>E=v.
Fender=7,000=70%=P7.0D=7.0=Language=Assets=Mars=7 July=Pleiades.
Fenestration=6,000=60%=P6.0D=Man=Earth=Royalty=6 June=Gaia=Maia>>M=M2.
Fenian=10,000=1,000=100%=10.0=Physicality=Tech.=10 Oct.=Uranus=P=1Ø.
Fennel=8,000=80%=P8.0D=Economy=Currency=8 Aug.=Zeus>>E=v.
-fer=5,000=50%=P5.00D=Law=Time=Venus=5 May = Aphrodite>>L=N.
Feral=7,500=8,000=80%=P8.0D=Economy=Currency=8 Aug.=Zeus>>E=v.
Ferber Edna=2,000=20%=P2.00D=2.0=Nature=Matter=Moon=2 Feb.=Cupid=N=C+_
Fer-de-lance=6,000=60%=P6.0D=Man=Earth=Royalty=6 June=Gaia=Maia>>M=M2.

Ferdinand I=6,500=7,000=70%=P7.0D=7.0=Language=Assets=Mars=7 July=Pleiades.
King of Bohemian and Hungary, Holy Roman Emperor. Peter Matthews-Akukalia, King Maks 1, Most Sovereign Emperor, Paradise Nations. Castle Makupedia God of Creatocracy.

Ferment=10,000=1,000=100%=10.0=Physicality=Tech.=10 Oct.=Uranus=P=1Ø.
Fermentation=10,000=1,000=100%=10.0=Physicality=Tech.=10 Oct.=Uranus=P=1Ø.
Fermi Erico=4,000=40%=P4.0D=Govt.=Creatocracy=4 April=Mercury=Hermes=G=A4.
Fermium=8,000=80%=P8.0D=Economy=Currency=8 Aug.=Zeus>>E=v.
Fern=5,500=5.5=80%=P5.50=Earth-Midway=5 May = Gaia.

Ferocious=5,500=5.5=80%=P5.50=Earth-Midway=5 May = Gaia.
Gaia becomes ferocious at midway resulting to earthquakes. In the Exodus, Earth opened her mouth and swallowed the sons of Korah who criticized Moses. Note the personification of Earth. It is possible that all land related matters are managed by Gaia.

-ferous=3,500=4,000=40%=P4.0D=Govt.=Creatocracy=4 April=Mercury=Hermes=G=A4.
Ferret=10,000=1,000=100%=10.0=Physicality=Tech.=10 Oct.=Uranus=P=1Ø.
Ferric=4,500=5,000=50%=P5.00D=Law=Time=Venus=5 May = Aphrodite>>L=N.
Ferric oxide=4,500=5,000=50%=P5.00D=Law=Time=Venus=5 May = Aphrodite>>L=N.
Ferris wheel=10,500=11,000=11%=P1.10D=1.1=Idea=Brainchild=11 Nov.=Athena>>I=MT.
Ferro-=2,500=3,000=30%=P3.0D=3.0=Creativity=Stars=Muses=3 March = C=I>>GIL.
Ferromagnetic=7,500=8,000=80%=P8.0D=Economy=Currency=8 Aug.=Zeus>>E=v.
Ferromanganese=5,500=5.5=80%=P5.50D=Earth-Midway=5 May = Gaia.
Ferrotype=7,000=70%=P7.0D=7.0=Language=Assets=Mars=7 July=Pleiades.
Ferrous=4,500=5,000=50%=P5.00D=Law=Time=Venus=5 May = Aphrodite>>L=N.
Ferrous oxide=6,000=60%=P6.0D=Man=Earth=Royalty=6 June=Gaia=Maia>>M=M2.
Ferrule=7,500=8,000=80%=P8.0D=Economy=Currency=8 Aug.=Zeus>>E=v.
Ferry=10,000=1,000=100%=10.0=Physicality=Tech.=10 Oct.=Uranus=P=1Ø.
Ferry boat=4,500=5,000=50%=P5.00D=Law=Time=Venus=5 May = Aphrodite>>L=N.
Fertile=10,000=1,000=100%=10.0=Physicality=Tech.=10 Oct.=Uranus=P=1Ø.

Fertile Crescent=7,500=8,000=80%=P8.0D=Economy=Currency=8 Aug.=Zeus>>E=v.

Fertilize=8,000=80%=P8.0D=Economy=Currency=8 Aug.=Zeus>>E=v.

Fertilizer=10,000=1,000=100%=10.0=Physicality=Tech.=10 Oct.=Uranus=P=1Ø.

Ferule=6,000=60%=P6.0D=Man=Earth=Royalty=6 June=Gaia=Maia>>M=M2.

Fervent=6,000=60%=P6.0D=Man=Earth=Royalty=6 June=Gaia=Maia>>M=M2.

Fervid=3,000=30%=P3.0D=3.0=Creativity=Stars=Muses=3 March = C=I>>GIL.

Fervor=4,000=40%=P4.0D=Government =Creatocracy=4 April=Mercury=Hermes=G=A4.

Fescue=5,500=5.5=80%=P5.50=Earth-Midway=5 May = Gaia.

Festal=4,500=5,000=50%=P5.00D=Law=Time=Venus=5 May = Aphrodite>>L=N.

Fester=7,500=8,000=80%=P8.0D=Economy=Currency=8 Aug.=Zeus>>E=v.

Festival=9,000=90%=P9.00D=9.0=Abstraction=Gods=Saturn=9Sept.>>A=Ø.

Festive=6,000=60%=P6.0D=Man=Earth=Royalty=6 June=Gaia=Maia>>M=M2.

Festivity=5,500=5.5=80%=P5.50=Earth-Midway=5 May = Gaia.

Festoon=13,500=14,000=14%=P1.40D=1.4=Mgt.=Solar Energy=13 May=Athena=SC=0.1

Feta=8,500=9,000=90%=P9.00D=9.0=Abstraction=Gods=Saturn=9Sept.>>A=Ø.

Fetal=3,000=30%=P3.0D=3.0=Creativity=Stars=Muses=3 March = C=I>>GIL.

Fetal alcohol syndrome=6,500=7,000=70%=P7.0D=7.0=Lang.=Mars=7 July=Pleiades.

Fetal position=10,000=1,000=100%=10.0=Physicality=Tech.=10 Oct.=Uranus=P=1Ø.

Fetch=7,500=8,000=80%=P8.0D=Economy=Currency=8 Aug.=Zeus>>E=v.

Fetching=1,000=100%=10.0=1.0=Mind=Sun=1 January=Helios >> M=E4.

Fete=11,000=11%=P1.10D=1.1=Idea=Brainchild=Inv.=11 Nov.=SC=Athena>>I=MT.

Fetid=2,000=20%=P2.00D=2.0=Nature=Matter=Moon=2 Feb.=Cupid=N=C+_

Fetish=8,000=80%=P8.0D=Economy=Currency=8 Aug.=Zeus>>E=v.

Fetlock=8,000=80%=P8.0D=Economy=Currency=8 Aug.=Zeus>>E=v.

Fetter=10,500=11,000=11%=P1.10D=1.1=Idea=Brainchild=Inv.=11 Nov.=SC=Athena
>>I=MT.

Fettle=5,000=50%=P5.00D=Law=Time=Venus=5 May = Aphrodite>>L=N.

Fetus=10,000=1,000=100%=10.0=Physicality=Tech.=10 Oct.=Uranus=P=1Ø.

Feud=7,000=70%=P7.0D=7.0=Language=Assets=Mars=7 July=Pleiades.

Feudal=5,000=50%=P5.00D=Law=Time=Venus=5 May = Aphrodite>>L=N.

Feudalism=11,000=11%=P1.10D=1.1=Idea=Brainchild=Inv.=11 Nov.=SC=Athena>>I=MT.

Feudatory=3,500=4,000=40%=P4.0D=Govt.=Creato.=4 April=Mercury=Hermes=G=A4.

Fever=8,500=9,000=90%=P9.00D=9.0=Abstraction=Gods=Saturn=9Sept.>>A=Ø.

Fever blister=1,500=15%=P1.50D=1.5=Authority=Crown=Solar Core=1 May = Maia.

Few=10,000=1,000=100%=10.0=Physicality=Tech.=10 Oct.=Uranus=P=1Ø.

Fey=5,000=50%=P5.00D=Law=Time=Venus=5 May = Aphrodite>>L=N.

fez=9,000=90%=P9.00D=9.0=Abstraction=Gods=Saturn=9Sept.>>A=Ø.

Fez=5,000=50%=P5.00D=Law=Time=Venus=5 May = Aphrodite>>L=N.

ff=1,000=100%=10.0=1.0=Mind=Sun=1 January=Helios >> M=E4.

FHA=1,500=15%=P1.50D=1.5=Authority=Crown=Solar Core=1 May = Maia.

Fiancé=3,000=30%=P3.0D=3.0=Creativity=Stars=Muses=3 March = C=I>>GIL.

Fiancée=3,000=30%=P3.0D=3.0=Creativity=Stars=Muses=3 March = C=I>>GIL.

Fiasco=1,500=15%=P1.50D=1.5=Authority=Crown=Solar Core=1 May = Maia.

Fiat=8,000=80%=P8.0D=Economy=Currency=8 Aug.=Zeus>>E=v.

The Creatocracy has established that all currencies prior to the Maks are fiat. It suggests that Zeus inspired natural fiats to manage world economies pending the discovery of the supernatural, solar core, diamond and Mind driven currency metric. Hence time for change is here. Peter Matthews-Akukalia, Castle Makupedia has achieved this feat. Read Ephesians 1:10-15. It teaches that a one world government based on Mind Computing is the Will of GOD. The signs of Zeus as the most High GOD Jehovah are tracked to Job 38:31. "The adoption of fiat currency by many countries, from the 18ᵗʰ century onwards, made much larger variations in the supply of money possible". - Money Supply, Online Research. The Maks Currencies contains four variable denominations, one high value assets storage variation, highly stable diamond temperature value and solar core. See Currency. Inflation.

Fib=6,500=7,000=70%=P7.0D=7.0=Language=Assets=Mars=7 July=Pleiades.
Fiber=10,000=1,000=100%=10.0=Physicality=Tech.=10 Oct.=Uranus=P=1Ø.
Fiberboard=8,500=9,000=90%=P9.00D=9.0=Abstraction=Gods=Saturn=9Sept.>>A=Ø.
Fiberglass=4,000=40%=P4.0D=Govt.=Creatocracy=4 April=Mercury=Hermes=G=A4.
Fiber optics=8,500=9,000=90%=P9.00D=9.0=Abstraction=Gods=Saturn=9Sept.>>A=Ø.
Fibril=5,500=5.5=80%=P5.50=Earth-Midway=5 May = Gaia.
Fibrillation=5,000=50%=P5.00D=Law=Time=Venus=5 May = Aphrodite>>L=N.
Fibrin=5,000=50%=P5.00D=Law=Time=Venus=5 May = Aphrodite>>L=N.
Fibrinogen=6,000=60%=P6.0D=Man=Earth=Royalty=6 June=Gaia=Maia>>M=M2.
Fibro-=4,000=40%=P4.0D=Government =Creatocracy=4 April=Mercury=Hermes=G=A4.
Fibroid=6,500=7,000=70%=P7.0D=7.0=Language=Assets=Mars=7 July=Pleiades.
Fibroma=4,500=5,000=50%=P5.00D=Law=Time=Venus=5 May = Aphrodite>>L=N.
Fibrosis=3,000=30%=P3.0D=3.0=Creativity=Stars=Muses=3 March = C=I>>GIL.
Fibrovascular=3,000=30%=P3.0D=3.0=Creativity=Stars=Muses=3 March = C=I>>GIL.
Fibula=9,500=10,000=1,000=100%=10.0=Physicality=Tech.=10 Oct.=Uranus=P=1Ø.
-fic=4,000=40%=P4.0D=Government =Creatocracy=4 April=Mercury=Hermes=G=A4.
FICA=2,000=20%=P2.00D=2.0=Nature=Matter=Moon=2 Feb.=Cupid=N=C+_
-fication=4,000=40%=P4.0D=Govt.=Creatocracy=4 April=Mercury=Hermes=G=A4.
Fiche=1,000=100%=10.0=1.0=Mind=Sun=1 January=Helios >> M=E4.
Fichte Johann=2,000=20%=P2.00D=2.0=Nature=Matter=Moon=2 Feb.=Cupid=N=C+_
Fichu=9,000=90%=P9.00D=9.0=Abstraction=Gods=Saturn=9Sept.>>A=Ø.
Fickle=5,000=50%=P5.00D=Law=Time=Venus=5 May = Aphrodite>>L=N.
Fiction=10,000=1,000=100%=10.0=Physicality=Tech.=10 Oct.=Uranus=P=1Ø.
Fictitious=4,000=40%=P4.0D=Govt.=Creatocracy=4 April=Mercury=Hermes=G=A4.
Fictive=4,500=5,000=50%=P5.00D=Law=Time=Venus=5 May = Aphrodite>>L=N.
Fiddle=7,000=70%=P7.0D=7.0=Language=Assets=Mars=7 July=Pleiades.
Fiddler crab=6,000=60%=P6.0D=Man=Earth=Royalty=6 June=Gaia=Maia>>M=M2.
Fiddle sticks=3,500=4,000=40%=P4.0D=Govt.=Creato.=4 April=Mercury=Hermes=G=A4.
Fidelity=11,000=11%=P1.10D=1.1=Idea=Brainchild=Inv.=11 Nov.=SC=Athena>>I=MT.
Fidget=8,500=9,000=90%=P9.00D=9.0=Abstraction=Gods=Saturn=9Sept.>>A=Ø.
Fiduciary=7,500=8,000=80%=P8.0D=Economy=Currency=8 Aug.=Zeus>>E=v.
Fie=3,000=30%=P3.0D=3.0=Creativity=Stars=Muses=3 March = C=I>>GIL.

Fief=3,000=30%=P3.0D=3.0=Creativity=Stars=Muses=3 March = C=I>>GIL.
Fiefdom=7,500=8,000=80%=P8.0D=Economy=Currency=8 Aug.=Zeus>>E=v.
Field=10,000=1,000=100%=10.0=Physicality=Tech.=10 Oct.=Uranus=P=1Ø.
Field day=8,000=80%=P8.0D=Economy=Currency=8 Aug.=Zeus>>E=v.
Field event=5,000=50%=P5.00D=Law=Time=Venus=5 May = Aphrodite>>L=N.
Field glass=2,000=20%=P2.00D=2.0=Nature=Matter=Moon=2 Feb.=Cupid=N=C+_
Field goal=15,000=15%=P1.50D=1.5=Authority=Crown=Solar Core=1 May = Maia.
Field hockey=9,000=90%=P9.00D=9.0=Abstraction=Gods=Saturn=9Sept.>>A=Ø.
Fielding Henry=2,000=20%=P2.00D=2.0=Nature=Matter=Moon=2 Feb.=Cupid=N=C+_
Field magnet=8,000=80%=P8.0D=Economy=Currency=8 Aug.=Zeus>>E=v.
Field marshal=7,000=70%=P7.0D=7.0=Language=Assets=Mars=7 July=Pleiades.
Field mouse=4,500=5,000=50%=P5.00D=Law=Time=Venus=5 May = Aphrodite>>L=N.
Field of force=9,500=10,000=1,000=100%=10.0=Phys.=Tech.=10 Oct.=Uranus=P=1Ø.
Field test=5,000=50%=P5.00D=Law=Time=Venus=5 May = Aphrodite>>L=N.
Field trial=10,000=1,000=100%=10.0=Physicality=Tech.=10 Oct.=Uranus=P=1Ø.
Field trip=4,500=5,000=50%=P5.00D=Law=Time=Venus=5 May = Aphrodite>>L=N.
Fieldwork=6,500=7,000=70%=P7.0D=7.0=Language=Assets=Mars=7 July=Pleiades.
Fiend=8,000=80%=P8.0D=Economy=Currency=8 Aug.=Zeus>>E=v.
Fierce=9,500=10,000=1,000=100%=10.0=Physicality=Tech.=10 Oct.=Uranus=P=1Ø.
Fiery=8,000=80%=P8.0D=Economy=Currency=8 Aug.=Zeus>>E=v.
Fiesta=7,500=8,000=80%=P8.0D=Economy=Currency=8 Aug.=Zeus>>E=v.
Fife==7,000=70%=P7.0D=7.0=Language=Assets=Mars=7 July=Pleiades.
FIFO=2,000=20%=P2.00D=2.0=Nature=Matter=Moon=2 Feb.=Cupid=N=C+_
Fifteen=7,000=70%=P7.0D=7.0=Language=Assets=Mars=7 July=Pleiades.
Fifteenth=6,500=7,000=70%=P7.0D=7.0=Language=Assets=Mars=7 July=Pleiades.
Fifth=10,000=1,000=100%=10.0=Physicality=Tech.=10 Oct.=Uranus=P=1Ø.
Fifth column=5,500=5.5=80%=P5.50=Earth-Midway=5 May = Gaia.
Fifth wheel=2,000=20%=P2.00D=2.0=Nature=Matter=Moon=2 Feb.=Cupid=N=C+_
Fiftieth=7,000=70%=P7.0D=7.0=Language=Assets=Mars=7 July=Pleiades.
Fifty=6,500=7,000=70%=P7.0D=7.0=Language=Assets=Mars=7 July=Pleiades.
Fifty fifty=5,000=50%=P5.00D=Law=Time=Venus=5 May = Aphrodite>>L=N.

Fig=14,000=14%=P1.40D=1.4=Mgt.=Solar Energy/Electric=13 May=Athena=SC=0.1
Jesus referred to the fig tree as either useful or not. Greek myth teaches that Zeus and Athena share the symbol of the fig tree. Athena used the fig tree to build her mind and establish her authority over Aries the God of War her younger brother. The Mind has since been greater than matter in the scheme of abstraction. King Solomon also wrote about the greater difficulty in carrying out a mental war laying emphasis on intellectual exercise as the way out of all human challenges and problems. Result shows management of the fig tree is the exclusive domain of Athena Goddess of Wisdom, wife of Castle Makupedia. Peter Matthews-Akukalia, Castle Makupedia defined the Mind as inherent energy that runs a thing. He discovered its equivalent is the Sun, wrote the mind formula M=E4 and computed successfully the solar core energy discovering Paradise, the Gods and the Maks.

Fight=10,000=1,000=100%=10.0=Physicality=Tech.=10 Oct.=Uranus=P=1Ø.
Fighter=6,000=60%=P6.0D=Man=Earth=Royalty=6 June=Gaia=Maia>>M=M2.

Figment=3,500=4,000=40%=P4.0D=Govt.=Creatocracy=4 April=Mercury=Hermes=G=A4. Something invented or made up. Latin figmentum. Now we see a connection between fig and figment. The fig tree may be likened to the tree of knowledge of good and evil described in the Creation story of Genesis. Athena owns the fig and Hermes manages it. Romans 8:19-23 warns that mankind will only earn true salvation on adoption to wit (Hermes>>Jesus Christ) whom we can have access to through wisdom >> wis >> Athena. The olive tree is synonymous to the fig tree and thus invention is associated with it. Clearly we prove that Zeus is a Creative Scientist and Inventor GOD. A foundation knowledge of the Creatocracy and study of the spiritual essence of the Creative Sciences, Makstianism.

Figurative=6,000=60%=P6.0D=Man=Earth=Royalty=6 June=Gaia=Maia>>M=M2. Royalty becomes figurative when it is based on the rights of intellectual property just the same as Godship. Peter Matthews-Akukalia is a Sovereign and a deity by these rights.

Figure=10,000=1,000=100%=10.0=Physicality=Tech.=10 Oct.=Uranus=P=1Ø. Figures are units of bundles that build and constitute a technology. (See Fauna). We confirm that figures are transmuted goats and animals used as tools by the Gods to build technologies. The Creatocracy is built on figures and their translations into physical equivalents hence the Creatocracy Bank is an invention through this precision dictionary.

Figure head=7,500=8,000=80%=P8.0D=Economy=Currency=8 Aug.=Zeus>>E=v.
Figure of speech=9,500=10,000=1,000=100%=10.0=Phy=Tech.=10 Oct.=Uranus=P=1Ø.
Figure skating=5,500=5.5=80%=P5.50=Earth-Midway=5 May = Gaia.
Figurine=4,000=40%=P4.0D=Government =Creatocracy=4 April=Mercury=Hermes=G=A4.
Fiji=7,000=70%=P7.0D=7.0=Language=Assets=Mars=7 July=Pleiades.
Filament=10,000=1,000=100%=10.0=Physicality=Tech.=10 Oct.=Uranus=P=1Ø.
Filaria=6,500=7,000=70%=P7.0D=7.0=Language=Assets=Mars=7 July=Pleiades.
Filbert=5,000=50%=P5.00D=Law=Time=Venus=5 May = Aphrodite>>L=N.
Filch=2,500=3,000=30%=P3.0D=3.0=Creativity=Stars=Muses=3 March = C=I>>GIL.
File(1)=10,000=1,000=100%=10.0=Physicality=Tech.=10 Oct.=Uranus=P=1Ø.
File(2)=11,000=11%=P1.10D=1.1=Idea=Brainchild=Inv.=11 Nov.=SC=Athena>>I=MT.
File clerk=4,000=40%=P4.0D=Govt. =Creatocracy=4 April=Mercury=Hermes=G=A4.
Filet(1)=3,500=4,000=40%=P4.0D=Govt.=Creatocracy=4 April=Mercury=Hermes=G=A4.
Filet(2)=1,500=15%=P1.50D=1.5=Authority=Crown=Solar Core=1 May = Maia.
Filet mignon=5,000=50%=P5.00D=Law=Time=Venus=5 May = Aphrodite>>L=N.
Filial=5,500=5.5=80%=P5.50=Earth-Midway=5 May = Gaia.
Filibuster=10,000=1,000=100%=10.0=Physicality=Tech.=10 Oct.=Uranus=P=1Ø.
Filigree=10,000=1,000=100%=10.0=Physicality=Tech.=10 Oct.=Uranus=P=1Ø.
Filing=3,500=4,000=40%=P4.0D=Govt.=Creatocracy=4 April=Mercury=Hermes=G=A4.
Filipino=6,000=60%=P6.0D=Man=Earth=Royalty=6 June=Gaia=Maia>>M=M2.

Fill=10,000=1,000=100%=10.0=Physicality=Tech.=10 Oct.=Uranus=P=1Ø.
Filler=10,000=1,000=100%=10.0=Physicality=Tech.=10 Oct.=Uranus=P=1Ø.
Fillér=2,500=3,000=30%=P3.0D=3.0=Creativity=Stars=Muses=3 March = C=I>>GIL.
Fillet=10,000=1,000=100%=10.0=Physicality=Tech.=10 Oct.=Uranus=P=1Ø.
Filling=10,000=1,000=100%=10.0=Physicality=Tech.=10 Oct.=Uranus=P=1Ø.
Filling station=1,500=15%=P1.50D=1.5=Authority=Crown=Solar Core=1 May = Maia.
Fillip=4,500=5,000=50%=P5.00D=Law=Time=Venus=5 May = Aphrodite>>L=N.
Fillmore Millard=4,000=40%=P4.0D=Govt.=Creatocracy=4 April=Mercury=Hermes=G=A4.
Filly=2,000=20%=P2.00D=2.0=Nature=Matter=Moon=2 Feb.=Cupid=N=C+_
Film=10,000=1,000=100%=10.0=Physicality=Tech.=10 Oct.=Uranus=P=1Ø.
Filmmaking=2,000=20%=P2.00D=2.0=Nature=Matter=Moon=2 Feb.=Cupid=N=C+_
Filmstrip=7,500=8,000=80%=P8.0D=Economy=Currency=8 Aug.=Zeus>>E=v.
Fils=2,000=20%=P2.00D=2.0=Nature=Matter=Moon=2 Feb.=Cupid=N=C+_
Filter=10,000=1,000=100%=10.0=Physicality=Tech.=10 Oct.=Uranus=P=1Ø.
Filth=5,000=50%=P5.00D=Law=Time=Venus=5 May = Aphrodite>>L=N.
Filtrate=7,500=8,000=80%=P8.0D=Economy=Currency=8 Aug.=Zeus>>E=v.
Fin=10,000=1,000=100%=10.0=Physicality=Tech.=10 Oct.=Uranus=P=1Ø.
Fin.=1,000=100%=Physicality= Tech.=10 Oct.=Uranus=P=1Ø.
Finagle=7,000=70%=P7.0D=7.0=Language=Assets=Mars=7 July=Pleiades.
Final=10,000=1,000=100%=10.0=Physicality=Tech.=10 Oct.=Uranus=P=1Ø.

Finale=4,000=40%=P4.0D=Government =Creatocracy=4 April=Mercury=Hermes=G=A4.
At the human level of things Hermes marks the finale of all activities. In the laws
of the adoption to wit he decides how men ran their race their rights rewards and
punishments. The adoption to wit is the basis for the development of the creative sciences
by Makupedia.

Finalist=4,000=40%=P4.0D=Government =Creatocracy=4 April=Mercury=Hermes=G=A4.
Finalize=10,000=1,000=100%=10.0=Physicality=Tech.=10 Oct.=Uranus=P=1Ø.

Finance=13%=P1.30=Solar Core=Faculty=13 January=Athena.
An exclusive preserve Athena and Castle Makupedia by rights of the Creative Sciences.
Proof is the invention of the Maks Currencies and the Creatocracy Bank for the
MindBanking services purely from creative intelligence for Gods and men. Universal.

Financier=3,500=4,000=40%=P4.0D=Govt.=Creato.=4 April=Mercury=Hermes=G=A4.

Finch=5,000=50%=P5.00D=Law=Time=Venus=5 May = Aphrodite>>L=N.
Any of various birds having a short stout bill. All small birds are muses. Messenger of Odite.

Find=10,000=1,000=100%=10.0=Physicality=Tech.=10 Oct.=Uranus=P=1Ø.
Fin-de-siècle=7,000=70%=P7.0D=7.0=Language=Assets=Mars=7 July=Pleiades.

Finding=6,000=60%=P6.0D=Man=Earth=Royalty=6 June=Gaia=Maia>>M=M2.
Fine(1)=10,000=1,000=100%=10.0=Physicality=Tech.=10 Oct.=Uranus=P=1Ø.
Fine(2)=10,000=1,000=100%=10.0=Physicality=Tech.=10 Oct.=Uranus=P=1Ø.
Fine(3)=3,000=30%=P3.0D=3.0=Creativity=Stars=Muses=3 March = C=I>>GIL.
Fine art=13%=P1.30=Solar Core=Faculty=13 January=Athena.
Fine print=8,000=80%=P8.0D=Economy=Currency=8 Aug.=Zeus>>E=v.
Finery=2,500=3,000=30%=P3.0D=3.0=Creativity=Stars=Muses=3 March = C=I>>GIL.
Finesse=10,000=1,000=100%=10.0=Physicality=Tech.=10 Oct.=Uranus=P=1Ø.
Fine tune=5,000=50%=P5.00D=Law=Time=Venus=5 May = Aphrodite>>L=N.
Finger=10,000=1,000=100%=10.0=Physicality=Tech.=10 Oct.=Uranus=P=1Ø.
Fingerboard=8,000=80%=P8.0D=Economy=Currency=8 Aug.=Zeus>>E=v.
Finger bowl=6,000=60%=P6.0D=Man=Earth=Royalty=6 June=Gaia=Maia>>M=M2.
Fingering=7,500=8,000=80%=P8.0D=Economy=Currency=8 Aug.=Zeus>>E=v.
Finger Lakes=5,000=50%=P5.00D=Law=Time=Venus=5 May = Aphrodite>>L=N.
Fingerling=2,500=3,000=30%=P3.0D=3.0=Creativity=Stars=Muses=3 March = C=I>>GIL.
Fingernail=2,500=3,000=30%=P3.0D=3.0=Creativity=Stars=Muses=3 March = C=I>>GIL.
Fingerprint=10,500=11,000=11%=P1.10D=1.1=Idea=Brainchild=11 Nov.=Athena>>I=MT.
Fingertip=6,500=7,000=70%=P7.0D=7.0=Language=Assets=Mars=7 July=Pleiades.
Finial=4,500=5,000=50%=P5.00D=Law=Time=Venus=5 May = Aphrodite>>L=N.
Finicky=3,500=4,000=40%=P4.0D=Govt=Creatocracy=4 April=Mercury=Hermes=G=A4.
Finis=1,000=100%=10.0=1.0=Mind=Sun=1 January=Helios >> M=E4.
Finish=10,000=1,000=100%=10.0=Physicality=Tech.=10 Oct.=Uranus=P=1Ø.
Finite=10,000=1,000=100%=10.0=Physicality=Tech.=10 Oct.=Uranus=P=1Ø.
Fink=6,500=7,000=70%=P7.0D=7.0=Language=Assets=Mars=7 July=Pleiades.
Finland=7,500=8,000=80%=P8.0D=Economy=Currency=8 Aug.=Zeus>>E=v.
Finland, Gulf of=6,000=60%=P6.0D=Man=Earth=Royalty=6 June=Gaia=Maia>>M=M2.
Finn=3,000=30%=P3.0D=3.0=Creativity=Stars=Muses=3 March = C=I>>GIL.
Finnan haddie=3,000=30%=P3.0D=3.0=Creativity=Stars=Muses=3 March = C=I>>GIL.
Finnbogadóttir Vigdis=3,500=4,000=40%=P4.0D=Govt=4 April=Mercury=Hermes=G=A4.
Finnic=5,500=5.5=80%=P5.50=Earth-Midway=5 May = Gaia.
Finnish=6,000=60%=P6.0D=Man=Earth=Royalty=6 June=Gaia=Maia>>M=M2.
Finno-Ugric=9,000=90%=P9.00D=9.0=Abstraction=Gods=Saturn=9Sept.>>A=Ø.
Fiord=1,500=15%=P1.50D=1.5=Authority=Crown=Solar Core=1 May = Maia.
Fir=8,500=9,000=90%=P9.00D=9.0=Abstraction=Gods=Saturn=9Sept.>>A=Ø.
Fire=10,000=1,000=100%=10.0=Physicality=Tech.=10 Oct.=Uranus=P=1Ø.

Fire ant=8,000=80%=P8.0D=Economy=Currency=8 Aug.=Zeus>>E=v.
Greek myth teaches that one of the symbols of transmutation of Zeus is the ant. Proved.
King Solomon advises the slothful to go and study the ways of the ants and be wise.
Proverbs 6:6-12. The weight of the fire ant is computed thus>> Fire*Ant =P >> 10.0*8.0
but 10.0-8.0=2.0 >> 10.0*2.0=p=12+20=32x=px=272=300=30%=3.0. The fire ant is a
muse that inspires creativity, servant of Zeus Jehovah the Most High. The code result
272>>22, 7.0 indicates that the fire ant is the means by which Aries arrives a place
riding on muses. Note that muses are females and the scriptures above refers to the ants

as "her". Aries is the God of war synonymous with fire war and destruction. A son of Zeus whose close relationship with Aphrodite gives him access to ride on her muses or servants in transport.

Firearm=5,000=50%=P5.00D=Law=Time=Venus=5 May = Aphrodite>>L=N.
Fireball=9,000=90%=P9.00D=9.0=Abstraction=Gods=Saturn=9Sept.>>A=Ø.
Fire base=5,500=5.5=80%=P5.50=Earth-Midway=5 May = Gaia.
Fire bomb=3,000=30%=P3.0D=3.0=Creativity=Stars=Muses=3 March = C=I>>GIL.
Firebrand=5,500=5.5=80%=P5.50=Earth-Midway=5 May = Gaia.
Firebreak=6,500=7,000=70%=P7.0D=7.0=Language=Assets=Mars=7 July=Pleiades.
Firebrick=7,000=70%=P7.0D=7.0=Language=Assets=Mars=7 July=Pleiades.
Firebug=2,000=20%=P2.00D=2.0=Nature=Matter=Moon=2 Feb.=Cupid=N=C+_
Fire clay=5,500=5.5=80%=P5.50=Earth-Midway=5 May = Gaia.
Firecracker=6,500=7,000=70%=P7.0D=7.0=Language=Assets=Mars=7 July=Pleiades.
Firedamp=8,500=9,000=90%=P9.00D=9.0=Abstraction=Gods=Saturn=9Sept.>>A=Ø.
Fire engine=6,000=60%=P6.0D=Man=Earth=Royalty=6 June=Gaia=Maia>>M=M2.
Fire escape=5,500=5.5=80%=P5.50=Earth-Midway=5 May = Gaia.
Fire extinguisher=8,000=80%=P8.0D=Economy=Currency=8 Aug.=Zeus>>E=v.
Firefight=4,500=5,000=50%=P5.00D=Law=Time=Venus=5 May = Aphrodite>>L=N.
Firefighter=6,500=7,000=70%=P7.0D=7.0=Language=Assets=Mars=7 July=Pleiades.
Firefly=9,500=10,000=1,000=100%=10.0=Physicality=Tech.=10 Oct.=Uranus=P=1Ø.
Firehouse=1,500=15%=P1.50D=1.5=Authority=Crown=Solar Core=1 May = Maia.
Fire hydrant=7,000=70%=P7.0D=7.0=Language=Assets=Mars=7 July=Pleiades.
Fire irons=5,500=5.5=80%=P5.50=Earth-Midway=5 May = Gaia.
Fireman=5,500=5.5=80%=P5.50=Earth-Midway=5 May = Gaia.
Fireplace=6,500=7,000=70%=P7.0D=7.0=Language=Assets=Mars=7 July=Pleiades.
Fireplug=1,500=15%=P1.50D=1.5=Authority=Crown=Solar Core=1 May = Maia.
Firepower=5,000=50%=P5.00D=Law=Time=Venus=5 May = Aphrodite>>L=N.
Fireproof=4,000=40%=P4.0D=Govt=Creatocracy=4 April=Mercury=Hermes=G=A4.
Fireside=3,500=4,000=40%=P4.0D=Govt=Creatocracy=4 April=Mercury=Hermes=G=A4.
Fire station=3,500=4,000=40%=P4.0D=Govt=Creato.=4 April=Mercury=Hermes=G=A4.
Fire tower=4,500=5,000=50%=P5.00D=Law=Time=Venus=5 May = Aphrodite>>L=N.
Firetrap=9,000=90%=P9.00D=9.0=Abstraction=Gods=Saturn=9Sept.>>A=Ø.
Firewall=6,000=60%=P6.0D=Man=Earth=Royalty=6 June=Gaia=Maia>>M=M2.
Fire water=5,000=50%=P5.00D=Law=Time=Venus=5 May = Aphrodite>>L=N.
Firewood=2,000=20%=P2.00D=2.0=Nature=Matter=Moon=2 Feb.=Cupid=N=C+_
Fireworks=10,000=1,000=100%=10.0=Physicality=Tech.=10 Oct.=Uranus=P=1Ø.
Firing line=8,000=80%=P8.0D=Economy=Currency=8 Aug.=Zeus>>E=v.
Firing pin=7,000=70%=P7.0D=7.0=Language=Assets=Mars=7 July=Pleiades.
Firm(1)=10,000=1,000=100%=10.0=Physicality=Tech.=10 Oct.=Uranus=P=1Ø.
Firm(2)=10,000=1,000=100%=10.0=Physicality=Tech.=10 Oct.=Uranus=P=1Ø.
Firmament=5,000=50%=P5.00D=Law=Time=Venus=5 May = Aphrodite>>L=N.
Firmware=8,000=80%=P8.0D=Economy=Currency=8 Aug.=Zeus>>E=v.
First=10,000=1,000=100%=10.0=Physicality=Tech.=10 Oct.=Uranus=P=1Ø.

First aid=7,500=8,000=80%=P8.0D=Economy=Currency=8 Aug.=Zeus>>E=v.
First base=4,500=5,000=50%=P5.00D=Law=Time=Venus=5 May = Aphrodite>>L=N.
Firstborn=2,500=3,000=30%=P3.0D=3.0=Creativity=Stars=Muses=3 March = C=I>>GIL.
First class=10,500=11,000=11%=P1.10D=1.1=Idea=Brainchild=11 Nov.=Athena>>I=MT.
First cousin=1,500=15%=P1.50D=1.5=Authority=Crown=Solar Core=1 May = Maia.
First degree burn=6,000=60%=P6.0D=Man=Earth=Royalty=6 June=Gaia=Maia>>M=M2.
First generation=6,500=7,000=70%=P7.0D=7.0=Language=Assets=Mars=7 July=Pleiades.
Firsthand=2,500=3,000=30%=P3.0D=3.0=Creativity=Stars=Muses=3 March = C=I>>GIL.
First in, first out=9,000=90%=P9.00D=9.0=Abstraction=Gods=Saturn=9Sept.>>A=Ø.
First lieutenant=6,500=7,000=70%=P7.0D=7.0=Language=Assets=Mars=7 July=Pleiades.
Firstly=1,500=15%=P1.50D=1.5=Authority=Crown=Solar Core=1 May = Maia.
First mate=5,500=5.5=80%=P5.50=Earth-Midway=5 May = Gaia.
First person=9,500=10,000=1,000=100%=10.0=Physicality=Tech.=10 Oct.=Uranus=P=1Ø.
First rate=5,000=50%=P5.00D=Law=Time=Venus=5 May = Aphrodite>>L=N.
First sergeant=10,000=1,000=100%=10.0=Physicality=Tech.=10 Oct.=Uranus=P=1Ø.
First strike=5,000=50%=P5.00D=Law=Time=Venus=5 May = Aphrodite>>L=N.
First string=5,000=50%=P5.00D=Law=Time=Venus=5 May = Aphrodite>>L=N.
Firth=3,500=4,000=40%=P4.0D=Govt=Creatocracy=4 April=Mercury=Hermes=G=A4.
Fiscal=4,500=5,000=50%=P5.00D=Law=Time=Venus=5 May = Aphrodite>>L=N.
Fiscal year=7,000=70%=P7.0D=7.0=Language=Assets=Mars=7 July=Pleiades.
Fish=10,000=1,000=100%=10.0=Physicality=Tech.=10 Oct.=Uranus=P=1Ø.
Fishbowl=7,500=8,000=80%=P8.0D=Economy=Currency=8 Aug.=Zeus>>E=v.
Fisherman=6,500=7,000=70%=P7.0D=7.0=Language=Assets=Mars=7 July=Pleiades.
Fishery=8,000=80%=P8.0D=Economy=Currency=8 Aug.=Zeus>>E=v.
Fisheye=6,500=7,000=70%=P7.0D=7.0=Language=Assets=Mars=7 July=Pleiades.
Fish hawk=1,000=100%=10.0=1.0=Mind=Sun=1 January=Helios >> M=E4.
Fishhook=3,500=4,000=40%=P4.0D=Govt=Creato.=4 April=Mercury=Hermes=G=A4.
Fishing rod=4,000=40%=P4.0D=Govt=Creatocracy=4 April=Mercury=Hermes=G=A4.
Fish ladder=6,000=60%=P6.0D=Man=Earth=Royalty=6 June=Gaia=Maia>>M=M2.
Fish meal=4,500=5,000=50%=P5.00D=Law=Time=Venus=5 May = Aphrodite>>L=N.
Fishnet=4,500=5,000=50%=P5.00D=Law=Time=Venus=5 May = Aphrodite>>L=N.
Fish story=2,500=3,000=30%=P3.0D=3.0=Creativity=Stars=Muses=3 March = C=I>>GIL.
Fish wife=5,000=50%=P5.00D=Law=Time=Venus=5 May = Aphrodite>>L=N.
Fishy=5,000=50%=P5.00D=Law=Time=Venus=5 May = Aphrodite>>L=N.
Fissile=5,500=5.5=80%=P5.50=Earth-Midway=5 May = Gaia.
Fission=10,000=1,000=100%=10.0=Physicality=Tech.=10 Oct.=Uranus=P=1Ø.
Fissure=2,500=3,000=30%=P3.0D=3.0=Creativity=Stars=Muses=3 March = C=I>>GIL.
Fist=4,500=5,000=50%=P5.00D=Law=Time=Venus=5 May = Aphrodite>>L=N.
Fistfight=3,000=30%=P3.0D=3.0=Creativity=Stars=Muses=3 March = C=I>>GIL.
Fistful=1,000=100%=10.0=1.0=Mind=Sun=1 January=Helios >> M=E4.
Fisticuffs=1,000=100%=10.0=1.0=Mind=Sun=1 January=Helios >> M=E4.
Fistula=9,500=10,000=1,000=100%=10.0=Physicality=Tech.=10 Oct.=Uranus=P=1Ø.
Fit(1)=10,000=1,000=100%=10.0=Physicality=Tech.=10 Oct.=Uranus=P=1Ø.
Fit(2)=10,000=1,000=100%=10.0=Physicality=Tech.=10 Oct.=Uranus=P=1Ø.
Fitness=6,500=7,000=70%=P7.0D=7.0=Language=Assets=Mars=7 July=Pleiades.

PETER K. MATTHEWS - AKUKALIA

Fitting=8,000=80%=P8.0D=Economy=Currency=8 Aug.=Zeus>>E=v.

Fitzgerald F(rancis)=3,000=30%=P3.0D=3.0=Creatv.=Stars=Muses=3 March = C=I>>GIL.

Fitzgerald Edward=3,000=30%=P3.0D=3.0=Creativity=Stars=Muses=3 March = C=I>>GIL.

Five=4,500=5,000=50%=P5.00D=Law=Time=Venus=5 May = Aphrodite>>L=N.

five and ten=8,500=9,000=90%=P9.00D=9.0=Abstraction=Gods=Saturn=9Sept.>>A=Ø.

Fix=10,000=1,000=100%=10.0=Physicality=Tech.=10 Oct.=Uranus=P=1Ø.

Fixate=10,000=1,000=100%=10.0=Physicality=Tech.=10 Oct.=Uranus=P=1Ø.

Fixative=3,000=30%=P3.0D=3.0=Creativity=Stars=Muses=3 March = C=I>>GIL.

Fixed=10,000=1,000=100%=10.0=Physicality=Tech.=10 Oct.=Uranus=P=1Ø.

Fixings=4,000=40%=P4.0D=Govt=Creatocracy=4 April=Mercury=Hermes=G=A4.

Fixity=4,000=40%=P4.0D=Govt=Creatocracy=4 April=Mercury=Hermes=G=A4.

Fixture=8,000=80%=P8.0D=Economy=Currency=8 Aug.=Zeus>>E=v.

Fizz=3,000=30%=P3.0D=3.0=Creativity=Stars=Muses=3 March = C=I>>GIL.

Fizzle=12,000=12%=P1.20D=1.2=Knowledge=Education=12Dec.=Athena>>K=F.

Fjord=5,500=5.5=80%=P5.50=Earth-Midway=5 May = Gaia.

fl=500=5%=P5.00D=5.0=Law=Time=Venus=5 May=Aphrodite>>L=N.

FL=1,500=15%=P1.50D=1.5=Authority=Crown=Solar Core=1 May = Maia.

fl.=1,500=15%=P1.50D=1.5=Authority=Crown=Solar Core=1 May = Maia.

Flab=2,000=20%=P2.00D=2.0=Nature=Matter=Moon=2 Feb.=Cupid=N=C+_

Flabbergast=3,000=30%=P3.0D=3.0=Creativity=Stars=Muses=3 March = C=I>>GIL.

Flabby=5,000=50%=P5.00D=Law=Time=Venus=5 May = Aphrodite>>L=N.

Flaccid=5,000=50%=P5.00D=Law=Time=Venus=5 May = Aphrodite>>L=N.

Flack=1,500=15%=P1.50D=1.5=Authority=Crown=Solar Core=1 May = Maia.

Flacon=2,000=20%=P2.00D=2.0=Nature=Matter=Moon=2 Feb.=Cupid=N=C+_

Flag(1)=7,500=8,000=80%=P8.0D=Economy=Currency=8 Aug.=Zeus>>E=v.

Flag(2)=5,000=50%=P5.00D=Law=Time=Venus=5 May = Aphrodite>>L=N.

Flag(3)=6,000=60%=P6.0D=Man=Earth=Royalty=6 June=Gaia=Maia>>M=M2.

Flag(4)=1,000=100%=10.0=1.0=Mind=Sun=1 January=Helios >> M=E4.

Flagellate=2,500=3,000=30%=P3.0D=3.0=Creativity=Stars=Muses=3 March = C=I>>GIL.

Flagellum=8,000=80%=P8.0D=Economy=Currency=8 Aug.=Zeus>>E=v.

Flag on=6,500=7,000=70%=P7.0D=7.0=Language=Assets=Mars=7 July=Pleiades.

Flagpole=3,500=4,000=40%=P4.0D=Govt=Creatocracy=4 April=Mercury=Hermes=G=A4.

Flagrant=3,500=4,000=40%=P4.0D=Govt=Creatocracy=4 April=Mercury=Hermes=G=A4.

Flagship=8,500=9,000=90%=P9.00D=9.0=Abstraction=Gods=Saturn=9Sept.>>A=Ø.

Flagstaff=1,000=100%=10.0=1.0=Mind=Sun=1 January=Helios >> M=E4.

Flagstone=3,000=30%=P3.0D=3.0=Creativity=Stars=Muses=3 March = C=I>>GIL.

Flag waving=2,000=20%=P2.00D=2.0=Nature=Matter=Moon=2 Feb.=Cupid=N=C+_

Flail=12,000=12%=P1.20D=1.2=Knowledge=Education=12Dec.=Athena>>K=F.

Flair=8,000=80%=P8.0D=Economy=Currency=8 Aug.=Zeus>>E=v.

Flak=7,000=70%=P7.0D=7.0=Language=Assets=Mars=7 July=Pleiades.

Flake=7,500=8,000=80%=P8.0D=Economy=Currency=8 Aug.=Zeus>>E=v.

Flambé=6,000=60%=P6.0D=Man=Earth=Royalty=6 June=Gaia=Maia>>M=M2.

Flamboyant=8,500=9,000=90%=P9.00D=9.0=Abstraction=Gods=Saturn=9Sept.>>A=Ø.

Flame=15,000=1,500=15%=P1.50D=1.5=Authority=Solar Crown=1 May = Maia.

Flamenco=9,000=90%=P9.00D=9.0=Abstraction=Gods=Saturn=9Sept.>>A=Ø.

Flameout=4,500=5,000=50%=P5.00D=Law=Time=Venus=5 May = Aphrodite>>L=N.
Flamethrower=5,000=50%=P5.00D=Law=Time=Venus=5 May = Aphrodite>>L=N.
Flamingo=8,000=80%=P8.0D=Economy=Currency=8 Aug.=Zeus>>E=v.
Flammable=10,000=1,000=100%=10.0=Physicality=Tech.=10 Oct.=Uranus=P=1Ø.
Flan=6,500=7,000=70%=P7.0D=7.0=Language=Assets=Mars=7 July=Pleiades.
Flanders=7,500=8,000=80%=P8.0D=Economy=Currency=8 Aug.=Zeus>>E=v.
Flange=11,000=11%=P1.10D=1.1=Idea=Brainchild=11 Nov.=Athena>>I=MT.
Flank=10,000=1,000=100%=10.0=Physicality=Tech.=10 Oct.=Uranus=P=1Ø.
Flannel=6,500=7,000=70%=P7.0D=7.0=Language=Assets=Mars=7 July=Pleiades.
Flannelette=2,500=3,000=30%=P3.0D=3.0=Creatv.=Stars=Muses=3 March = C=I>>GIL.
Flap=10,000=1,000=100%=10.0=Physicality=Tech.=10 Oct.=Uranus=P=1Ø.
Flapjack=1,000=100%=10.0=1.0=Mind=Sun=1 January=Helios >> M=E4.
Flapper=10,000=1,000=100%=10.0=Physicality=Tech.=10 Oct.=Uranus=P=1Ø.
Flare=10,000=1,000=100%=10.0=Physicality=Tech.=10 Oct.=Uranus=P=1Ø.
Flare up=4,000=40%=P4.0D=Govt=Creatocracy=4 April=Mercury=Hermes=G=A4.
Flash=10,000=1,000=100%=10.0=Physicality=Tech.=10 Oct.=Uranus=P=1Ø.
Flashback=12,500=13,000=13%=P1.30=Solar Core=Faculty=13 January=Athena.
Flashbulb=10,500=11,000=11%=P1.10D=1.1=Idea=Brainchild=11 Nov.=Athena>>I=MT.
Flash flood=2,000=20%=P2.00D=2.0=Nature=Matter=Moon=2 Feb.=Cupid=N=C+_
Flash-forward=9,000=90%=P9.00D=9.0=Abstraction=Gods=Saturn=9Sept.>>A=Ø.
Flashgun=6,000=60%=P6.0D=Man=Earth=Royalty=6 June=Gaia=Maia>>M=M2.
Flashing=7,000=70%=P7.0D=7.0=Language=Assets=Mars=7 July=Pleiades.
Flash lamp=6,500=7,000=70%=P7.0D=7.0=Language=Assets=Mars=7 July=Pleiades.
Flashlight=4,000=40%=P4.0D=Govt=Creatocracy=4 April=Mercury=Hermes=G=A4.
Flashpoint=7,000=70%=P7.0D=7.0=Language=Assets=Mars=7 July=Pleiades.
Flashy=6,500=7,000=70%=P7.0D=7.0=Language=Assets=Mars=7 July=Pleiades.
Flask=10,500=11,000=11%=P1.10D=1.1=Idea=Brainchild=11 Nov.=Athena>>I=MT.
Flat(1)=10,000=1,000=100%=10.0=Physicality=Tech.=10 Oct.=Uranus=P=1Ø.
Flat(2)=6,000=60%=P6.0D=Man=Earth=Royalty=6 June=Gaia=Maia>>M=M2.
Flatbed=4,500=5,000=50%=P5.00D=Law=Time=Venus=5 May = Aphrodite>>L=N.
Flatboat=4,500=5,000=50%=P5.00D=Law=Time=Venus=5 May = Aphrodite>>L=N.
Flatcar=4,000=40%=P4.0D=Govt=Creatocracy=4 April=Mercury=Hermes=G=A4.
Flatfish=10,500=11,000=11%=P1.10D=1.1=Idea=Brainchild=11 Nov.=Athena>>I=MT.
Flatfoot=10,500=11,000=11%=P1.10D=1.1=Idea=Brainchild=11 Nov.=Athena>>I=MT.
Flathead=8,000=80%=P8.0D=Economy=Currency=8 Aug.=Zeus>>E=v.
Flatiron=2,500=3,000=30%=P3.0D=3.0=Creativity=Stars=Muses=3 March = C=I>>GIL.
Flatten=4,000=40%=P4.0D=Govt=Creatocracy=4 April=Mercury=Hermes=G=A4.
Flatter=8,000=80%=P8.0D=Economy=Currency=8 Aug.=Zeus>>E=v.
Flattop=4,000=40%=P4.0D=Govt=Creatocracy=4 April=Mercury=Hermes=G=A4.
Flatulent=6,000=60%=P6.0D=Man=Earth=Royalty=6 June=Gaia=Maia>>M=M2.
Flatware=11,000=11%=P1.10D=1.1=Idea=Brainchild=11 Nov.=Athena>>I=MT.
Flatworm=4,500=5,000=50%=P5.00D=Law=Time=Venus=5 May = Aphrodite>>L=N.
Flaubert Gustave=2,000=20%=P2.00D=2.0=Nature=Matter=Moon=2 Feb.=Cupid=N=C+_
Flaunt=10,000=1,000=100%=10.0=Physicality=Tech.=10 Oct.=Uranus=P=1Ø.
Flautist=3,000=30%=P3.0D=3.0=Creativity=Stars=Muses=3 March = C=I>>GIL.

Flavor=8,000=80%=P8.0D=Economy=Currency=8 Aug.=Zeus>>E=v.
Flavoring=5,000=50%=P5.00D=Law=Time=Venus=5 May = Aphrodite>>L=N.
Flaw=6,500=7,000=70%=P7.0D=7.0=Language=Assets=Mars=7 July=Pleiades.
Flawless=5,000=50%=P5.00D=Law=Time=Venus=5 May = Aphrodite>>L=N.
Flax=9,500=10,000=1,000=100%=10.0=Physicality=Tech.=10 Oct.=Uranus=P=1Ø.
Flaxen=5,500=5.5=80%=P5.50=Earth-Midway=5 May = Gaia.
Flay=4,500=5,000=50%=P5.00D=Law=Time=Venus=5 May = Aphrodite>>L=N.
fl=1,000=100%=10.0=1.0=Mind=Sun=1 January=Helios >> M=E4.
Flea=7,000=70%=P7.0D=7.0=Language=Assets=Mars=7 July=Pleiades.
Flea collar=5,000=50%=P5.00D=Law=Time=Venus=5 May = Aphrodite>>L=N.
Flea market=7,500=8,000=80%=P8.0D=Economy=Currency=8 Aug.=Zeus>>E=v.
Fleck=7,500=8,000=80%=P8.0D=Economy=Currency=8 Aug.=Zeus>>E=v.
Fledgling=6,000=60%=P6.0D=Man=Earth=Royalty=6 June=Gaia=Maia>>M=M2.
Flee=6,000=60%=P6.0D=Man=Earth=Royalty=6 June=Gaia=Maia>>M=M2.
Fleece=10,000=1,000=100%=10.0=Physicality=Tech.=10 Oct.=Uranus=P=1Ø.
Fleet(1)=11,000=11%=P1.10D=1.1=Idea=Brainchild=11 Nov.=Athena>>I=MT.
Fleet(2)=5,500=5.5=80%=P5.50=Earth-Midway=5 May = Gaia.
Fleet Admiral=3,000=30%=P3.0D=3.0=Creativity=Stars=Muses=3 March = C=I>>GIL.
Fleeting=1,500=15%=P1.50D=1.5=Authority=Crown=Solar Core=1 May = Maia.
Fleming=5,000=50%=P5.00D=Law=Time=Venus=5 May = Aphrodite>>L=N.
Fleming Alexander=3,500=4,000=40%=P4.0D=Govt=Cr=4 April=Mercury=Hermes=G=A4.
Flemish=4,000=40%=P4.0D=Govt=Creatocracy=4 April=Mercury=Hermes=G=A4.
Flesh=10,000=1,000=100%=10.0=Physicality=Tech.=10 Oct.=Uranus=P=1Ø.
Fleshly=8,000=80%=P8.0D=Economy=Currency=8 Aug.=Zeus>>E=v.
Fleshy=7,500=8,000=80%=P8.0D=Economy=Currency=8 Aug.=Zeus>>E=v.
Fletcher John=2,000=20%=P2.00D=2.0=Nature=Matter=Moon=2 Feb.=Cupid=N=C+_
Fleur-de-lis=6,000=60%=P6.0D=Man=Earth=Royalty=6 June=Gaia=Maia>>M=M2.
Flew=1,500=15%=P1.50D=1.5=Authority=Crown=Solar Core=1 May = Maia.
Flex=10,000=1,000=100%=10.0=Physicality=Tech.=10 Oct.=Uranus=P=1Ø.
Flexible=5,500=5.5=80%=P5.50=Earth-Midway=5 May = Gaia.
Flexor=7,000=70%=P7.0D=7.0=Language=Assets=Mars=7 July=Pleiades.
Flextime=5,500=5.5=80%=P5.50=Earth-Midway=5 May = Gaia.
Flexure=2,500=3,000=30%=P3.0D=3.0=Creativity=Stars=Muses=3 March = C=I>>GIL.
Flick(1)=13,000=13%=P1.30=Solar Core=Faculty=13 January=Athena.
Flick(2)=1,500=15%=P1.50D=1.5=Authority=Crown=Solar Core=1 May = Maia.
Flicker(1)=10,000=1,000=100%=10.0=Physicality=Tech.=10 Oct.=Uranus=P=1Ø.
Flicker(2)=6,000=60%=P6.0D=Man=Earth=Royalty=6 June=Gaia=Maia>>M=M2.
Filed=3,000=30%=P3.0D=3.0=Creativity=Stars=Muses=3 March = C=I>>GIL.
Filler=7,000=70%=P7.0D=7.0=Language=Assets=Mars=7 July=Pleiades.
Flight(1)=10,000=1,000=100%=10.0=Physicality=Tech.=10 Oct.=Uranus=P=1Ø.
Flight(2)=2,500=3,000=30%=P3.0D=3.0=Creativity=Stars=Muses=3 March = C=I>>GIL.
Flight deck=12,000=12%=P1.20D=1.2=Knowledge=Education=12Dec.=Athena>>K=F.
Flight engineer=5,500=5.5=80%=P5.50=Earth-Midway=5 May = Gaia.
Flightless=3,000=30%=P3.0D=3.0=Creativity=Stars=Muses=3 March = C=I>>GIL.
Flight recorder=7,500=8,000=80%=P8.0D=Economy=Currency=8 Aug.=Zeus>>E=v.

Flighty=3,500=4,000=40%=P4.0D=Govt=Creatocracy=4 April=Mercury=Hermes=G=A4.
Flimflam=5,500=5.5=80%=P5.50=Earth-Midway=5 May = Gaia.
Flimsy=6,500=7,000=70%=P7.0D=7.0=Language=Assets=Mars=7 July=Pleiades.
Flinch=6,000=60%=P6.0D=Man=Earth=Royalty=6 June=Gaia=Maia>>M=M2.
Fling=10,000=1,000=100%=10.0=Physicality=Tech.=10 Oct.=Uranus=P=1Ø.
flint=10,000=1,000=100%=10.0=Physicality=Tech.=10 Oct.=Uranus=P=1Ø.
Flint=5,000=50%=P5.00D=Law=Time=Venus=5 May = Aphrodite>>L=N.
Flintlock=6,500=7,000=70%=P7.0D=7.0=Language=Assets=Mars=7 July=Pleiades.
Flip=10,000=1,000=100%=10.0=Physicality=Tech.=10 Oct.=Uranus=P=1Ø.
Flip flop=8,500=9,000=90%=P9.00D=9.0=Abstraction=Gods=Saturn=9Sept.>>A=Ø.
Flippant=1,500=15%=P1.50D=1.5=Authority=Crown=Solar Core=1 May = Maia.
Flipper=9,000=90%=P9.00D=9.0=Abstraction=Gods=Saturn=9Sept.>>A=Ø.
Flirt=11,500=12,000=12%=P1.20D=1.2=Knowledge=Education=12Dec.=Athena>>K=F.
Flit=4,500=5,000=50%=P5.00D=Law=Time=Venus=5 May = Aphrodite>>L=N.
Flitter=1,500=15%=P1.50D=1.5=Authority=Crown=Solar Core=1 May = Maia.
Float=10,000=1,000=100%=10.0=Physicality=Tech.=10 Oct.=Uranus=P=1Ø.
Floater=10,000=1,000=100%=10.0=Physicality=Tech.=10 Oct.=Uranus=P=1Ø.
Flock(1)=10,000=1,000=100%=10.0=Physicality=Tech.=10 Oct.=Uranus=P=1Ø.
Flock(2)=10,500=11,000=11%=P1.10D=1.1=Idea=Brainchild=11 Nov.=Athena>>I=MT.
Floe=3,500=4,000=40%=P4.0D=Govt=Creatocracy=4 April=Mercury=Hermes=G=A4.
Flog=4,000=40%=P4.0D=Govt=Creatocracy=4 April=Mercury=Hermes=G=A4.
Flood=10,000=1,000=100%=10.0=Physicality=Tech.=10 Oct.=Uranus=P=1Ø.
Floodgate=8,000=80%=P8.0D=Economy=Currency=8 Aug.=Zeus>>E=v.
Floodlight=9,500=10,000=1,000=100%=10.0=Physicality=Tech.=10 Oct.=Uranus=P=1Ø.
Floodplain=4,000=40%=P4.0D=Govt=Creatocracy=4 April=Mercury=Hermes=G=A4.
Floor=10,000=1,000=100%=10.0=Physicality=Tech.=10 Oct.=Uranus=P=1Ø.
Floor leader=9,500=10,000=1,000=100%=10.0=Physicality=Tech.=10 Oct.=Uranus=P=1Ø.
Floor plan=3,500=4,000=40%=P4.0D=Govt=Creato.=4 April=Mercury=Hermes=G=A4.
Floor show=3,000=30%=P3.0D=3.0=Creativity=Stars=Muses=3 March = C=I>>GIL.
Floorwalker=6,500=7,000=70%=P7.0D=7.0=Language=Assets=Mars=7 July=Pleiades.
Floozy=3,500=4,000=40%=P4.0D=Govt=Creatocracy=4 April=Mercury=Hermes=G=A4.
Flop=13,000=13%=P1.30=Solar Core=Faculty=13 January=Athena.
Flophouse=1,500=15%=P1.50D=1.5=Authority=Crown=Solar Core=1 May = Maia.
Floppy=7,000=70%=P7.0D=7.0=Language=Assets=Mars=7 July=Pleiades.
Floppy disk=7,500=8,000=80%=P8.0D=Economy=Currency=8 Aug.=Zeus>>E=v.
Flora=7,500=8,000=80%=P8.0D=Economy=Currency=8 Aug.=Zeus>>E=v.
Floral=2,500=3,000=30%=P3.0D=3.0=Creativity=Stars=Muses=3 March = C=I>>GIL.
Florence=5,000=50%=P5.00D=Law=Time=Venus=5 May = Aphrodite>>L=N.
Florid=6,000=60%=P6.0D=Man=Earth=Royalty=6 June=Gaia=Maia>>M=M2.
Florida=5,000=50%=P5.00D=Law=Time=Venus=5 May = Aphrodite>>L=N.
Florida, Straits=7,500=8,000=80%=P8.0D=Economy=Currency=8 Aug.=Zeus>>E=v.
Florida keys=9,000=90%=P9.00D=9.0=Abstraction=Gods=Saturn=9Sept.>>A=Ø.
Florin=5,500=5.5=80%=P5.50=Earth-Midway=5 May = Gaia.
Florist=6,000=60%=P6.0D=Man=Earth=Royalty=6 June=Gaia=Maia>>M=M2.
Floss=14,000=14%=P1.40D=1.4=Mgt.=Solar Energy/Electric=13 May=Athena=SC=0.1

Flossy=4,000=40%=P4.0D=Govt=Creatocracy=4 April=Mercury=Hermes=G=A4.
Floatation=3,000=30%=P3.0D=3.0=Creativity=Stars=Muses=3 March = C=I>>GIL.
Flotilla=5,500=5.5=80%=P5.50=Earth-Midway=5 May = Gaia.
Flotsam=9,500=10,000=1,000=100%=10.0=Physicality=Tech.=10 Oct.=Uranus=P=1Ø.
Flounce(1)=9,000=90%=P9.00D=9.0=Abstraction=Gods=Saturn=9Sept.>>A=Ø.
Flounce(2)=9,500=10,000=1,000=100%=10.0=Physicality=Tech.=10 Oct.=Uranus=P=1Ø.
Founder(1)=11,500=12,000=12%=P1.20D=1.2=Knowledge=Educ.=12Dec.=Athena>>K=F.
Founder(2)=5,000=50%=P5.00D=Law=Time=Venus=5 May = Aphrodite>>L=N.
Flour=9,000=90%=P9.00D=9.0=Abstraction=Gods=Saturn=9Sept.>>A=Ø.
Flourish=10,000=1,000=100%=10.0=Physicality=Tech.=10 Oct.=Uranus=P=1Ø.
Flout=8,000=80%=P8.0D=Economy=Currency=8 Aug.=Zeus>>E=v.
Flow=10,000=1,000=100%=10.0=Physicality=Tech.=10 Oct.=Uranus=P=1Ø.
Flow chart=3,000=30%=P3.0D=3.0=Creativity=Stars=Muses=3 March = C=I>>GIL.
Flower=10,000=1,000=100%=10.0=Physicality=Tech.=10 Oct.=Uranus=P=1Ø.
Flowering plant=3,500=4,000=40%=P4.0D=Govt=Cre=4 April=Mercury=Hermes=G=A4.
Flower pot=3,500=4,000=40%=P4.0D=Govt=Creat=4 April=Mercury=Hermes=G=A4.
Flowery=7,000=70%=P7.0D=7.0=Language=Assets=Mars=7 July=Pleiades.
Flown=1,500=15%=P1.50D=1.5=Authority=Crown=Solar Core=1 May = Maia.
Fl oz=1,000=100%=10.0=1.0=Mind=Sun=1 January=Helios >> M=E4.
Flu=1,000=100%=10.0=1.0=Mind=Sun=1 January=Helios >> M=E4.
Flub=2,000=20%=P2.00D=2.0=Nature=Matter=Moon=2 Feb.=Cupid=N=C+_
Fluctuate=9,500=10,000=1,000=100%=10.0=Physicality=Tech.=10 Oct.=Uranus=P=1Ø.
Flue=8,500=9,000=90%=P9.00D=9.0=Abstraction=Gods=Saturn=9Sept.>>A=Ø.
Fluent=10,000=1,000=100%=10.0=Physicality=Tech.=10 Oct.=Uranus=P=1Ø.
Fluff=10,000=1,000=100%=10.0=Physicality=Tech.=10 Oct.=Uranus=P=1Ø.
Fluid=10,000=1,000=100%=10.0=Physicality=Tech.=10 Oct.=Uranus=P=1Ø.
Fluid ounce=2,000=20%=P2.00D=2.0=Nature=Matter=Moon=2 Feb.=Cupid=N=C+_
Fluke(1)=4,500=5,000=50%=P5.00D=Law=Time=Venus=5 May = Aphrodite>>L=N.
Fluke(2)=12,000=12%=P1.20D=1.2=Knowledge=Education=12Dec.=Athena>>K=F.
Fluke(3)=3,500=4,000=40%=P4.0D=Govt=Creatocracy=4 April=Mercury=Hermes=G=A4.
Flume=11,500=12,000=12%=P1.20D=1.2=Knowledge=Education=12Dec.=Athena>>K=F.
Flummox=4,000=40%=P4.0D=Govt=Creatocracy=4 April=Mercury=Hermes=G=A4.
Flung=2,500=3,000=30%=P3.0D=3.0=Creativity=Stars=Muses=3 March = C=I>>GIL.
Flunk=4,500=5,000=50%=P5.00D=Law=Time=Venus=5 May = Aphrodite>>L=N.
Flunky=8,000=80%=P8.0D=Economy=Currency=8 Aug.=Zeus>>E=v.
Fluoresce=3,000=30%=P3.0D=3.0=Creativity=Stars=Muses=3 March = C=I>>GIL.
Fluorescence=10,000=1,000=100%=10.0=Physicality=Tech.=10 Oct.=Uranus=P=1Ø.
Fluorescent lamp=13,000=13%=P1.30=Solar Core=Faculty=13 January=Athena.
Fluoridate=8,000=80%=P8.0D=Economy=Currency=8 Aug.=Zeus>>E=v.
Fluoride=4,000=40%=P4.0D=Govt=Creatocracy=4 April=Mercury=Hermes=G=A4.
Fluorine=16,000=16%=P1.60D=1.6=Cycle of Incarnation=Mind of GOD=1 June = Maia.
Fluoro-=3,000=30%=P3.0D=3.0=Creativity=Stars=Muses=3 March = C=I>>GIL.
Fluorocarbon=11,000=11%=P1.10D=1.1=Idea=Brainchild=11 Nov.=Athena>>I=MT.
Fluoroscope=10,000=1,000=100%=10.0=Physicality=Tech.=10 Oct.=Uranus=P=1Ø.
Flurry=8,500=9,000=90%=P9.00D=9.0=Abstraction=Gods=Saturn=9Sept.>>A=Ø.

Flush(1)=10,000=1,000=100%=10.0=Physicality=Tech.=10 Oct.=Uranus=P=1Ø.
Flush(2)=10,000=1,000=100%=10.0=Physicality=Tech.=10 Oct.=Uranus=P=1Ø.
Flush(3)=5,500=5.5=80%=P5.50=Earth-Midway=5 May = Gaia.
Fluster=6,000=60%=P6.0D=Man=Earth=Royalty=6 June=Gaia=Maia>>M=M2.
Flute=11,500=12,000=12%=P1.20D=1.2=Knowledge=Education=12Dec.=Athena>>K=F.
Flutist=2,500=3,000=30%=P3.0D=3.0=Creativity=Stars=Muses=3 March = C=I>>GIL.
Flutter=10,000=1,000=100%=10.0=Physicality=Tech.=10 Oct.=Uranus=P=1Ø.
Flu vial=5,500=5.5=80%=P5.50=Earth-Midway=5 May = Gaia.
Flux=10,000=1,000=100%=10.0=Physicality=Tech.=10 Oct.=Uranus=P=1Ø.
Fly(1)=10,000=1,000=100%=10.0=Physicality=Tech.=10 Oct.=Uranus=P=1Ø.
Fly(2)=10,000=1,000=100%=10.0=Physicality=Tech.=10 Oct.=Uranus=P=1Ø.
Fly blown=3,000=30%=P3.0D=3.0=Creativity=Stars=Muses=3 March = C=I>>GIL.
Flyby=6,000=60%=P6.0D=Man=Earth=Royalty=6 June=Gaia=Maia>>M=M2.
Flyby night=2,500=3,000=30%=P3.0D=3.0=Creatv=Stars=Muses=3 March = C=I>>GIL.
Flycatcher=6,500=7,000=70%=P7.0D=7.0=Language=Assets=Mars=7 July=Pleiades.
Flyer=1,500=15%=P1.50D=1.5=Authority=Crown=Solar Core=1 May = Maia.
Fly fish=7,000=70%=P7.0D=7.0=Language=Assets=Mars=7 July=Pleiades.
Flying buttress=8,000=80%=P8.0D=Economy=Currency=8 Aug.=Zeus>>E=v.
Flying fish=9,000=90%=P9.00D=9.0=Abstraction=Gods=Saturn=9Sept.>>A=Ø.
Flying saucer=8,000=80%=P8.0D=Economy=Currency=8 Aug.=Zeus>>E=v.
Flying squirrel=10,000=1,000=100%=10.0=Physicality=Tech.=10 Oct.=Uranus=P=1Ø.
Fly leaf=5,000=50%=P5.00D=Law=Time=Venus=5 May = Aphrodite>>L=N.
Flypaper=5,000=50%=P5.00D=Law=Time=Venus=5 May = Aphrodite>>L=N.
Flyspeck=5,000=50%=P5.00D=Law=Time=Venus=5 May = Aphrodite>>L=N.
Flyway=6,500=7,000=70%=P7.0D=7.0=Language=Assets=Mars=7 July=Pleiades.
Flyweight=5,500=5.5=80%=P5.50=Earth-Midway=5 May = Gaia.
Flywheel=7,500=8,000=80%=P8.0D=Economy=Currency=8 Aug.=Zeus>>E=v.
Fm=2,500=3,000=30%=P3.0D=3.0=Creativity=Stars=Muses=3 March = C=I>>GIL.
FM=1,000=100%=10.0=1.0=Mind=Sun=1 January=Helios >> M=E4.
fm.=1,000=100%=10.0=1.0=Mind=Sun=1 January=Helios >> M=E4.
fn.=500=5%=P5.00D=5.0=Law=Time=Venus=5 May=Aphrodite>>L=N.
F-number=8,000=80%=P8.0D=Economy=Currency=8 Aug.=Zeus>>E=v.
Foal=8,000=80%=P8.0D=Economy=Currency=8 Aug.=Zeus>>E=v.
Foam=10,000=1,000=100%=10.0=Physicality=Tech.=10 Oct.=Uranus=P=1Ø.
Foam rubber=5,500=5.5=80%=P5.50=Earth-Midway=5 May = Gaia.
Fob(1)=8,000=80%=P8.0D=Economy=Currency=8 Aug.=Zeus>>E=v.
Fob(2)=10,000=1,000=100%=10.0=Physicality=Tech.=10 Oct.=Uranus=P=1Ø.
f.o.b.=1,500=15%=P1.50D=1.5=Authority=Crown=Solar Core=1 May = Maia.
Focal length=5,500=5.5=80%=P5.50=Earth-Midway=5 May = Gaia.
Focal point=1,500=15%=P1.50D=1.5=Authority=Crown=Solar Core=1 May = Maia.
Foch Ferdinand=4,000=40%=P4.0D=Govt=Creatocracy=4 April=Mercury=Hermes=G=A4.
Fo'c's'le=1,500=15%=P1.50D=1.5=Authority=Crown=Solar Core=1 May = Maia.
Focus=10,000=1,000=100%=10.0=Physicality=Tech.=10 Oct.=Uranus=P=1Ø.
Fodder=6,000=60%=P6.0D=Man=Earth=Royalty=6 June=Gaia=Maia>>M=M2.
Foe=8,500=9,000=90%=P9.00D=9.0=Abstraction=Gods=Saturn=9Sept.>>A=Ø.

Foetid=1,500=15%=P1.50D=1.5=Authority=Crown=Solar Core=1 May = Maia.
Foetus=1,500=15%=P1.50D=1.5=Authority=Crown=Solar Core=1 May = Maia.
Fog=10,000=1,000=100%=10.0=Physicality=Tech.=10 Oct.=Uranus=P=1Ø.
Foghorn=6,000=60%=P6.0D=Man=Earth=Royalty=6 June=Gaia=Maia>>M=M2.
Fogy=4,000=40%=P4.0D=Govt=Creatocracy=4 April=Mercury=Hermes=G=A4.
Foible=6,000=60%=P6.0D=Man=Earth=Royalty=6 June=Gaia=Maia>>M=M2.
Foil(1)=4,500=5,000=50%=P5.00D=Law=Time=Venus=5 May = Aphrodite>>L=N.
Foil(2)=12,000=12%=P1.20D=1.2=Knowledge=Education=12Dec.=Athena>>K=F.
Foil(3)=8,000=80%=P8.0D=Economy=Currency=8 Aug.=Zeus>>E=v.
Foist=7,000=70%=P7.0D=7.0=Language=Assets=Mars=7 July=Pleiades.
Fold(1)=10,000=1,000=100%=10.0=Physicality=Tech.=10 Oct.=Uranus=P=1Ø.
Fold(2)=11,000=11%=P1.10D=1.1=Idea=Brainchild=11 Nov.=Athena>>I=MT.
-fold=7,000=70%=P7.0D=7.0=Language=Assets=Mars=7 July=Pleiades.
Folder=10,000=1,000=100%=10.0=Physicality=Tech.=10 Oct.=Uranus=P=1Ø.
Folderol=4,500=5,000=50%=P5.00D=Law=Time=Venus=5 May = Aphrodite>>L=N.
Foldout=11,000=11%=P1.10D=1.1=Idea=Brainchild=11 Nov.=Athena>>I=MT.
Foliage=5,000=50%=P5.00D=Law=Time=Venus=5 May = Aphrodite>>L=N.
Folio=10,000=1,000=100%=10.0=Physicality=Tech.=10 Oct.=Uranus=P=1Ø.
Folk=10,000=1,000=100%=10.0=Physicality=Tech.=10 Oct.=Uranus=P=1Ø.
Folklore=6,000=60%=P6.0D=Man=Earth=Royalty=6 June=Gaia=Maia>>M=M2.
Folk music=5,500=5.5=80%=P5.50=Earth-Midway=5 May = Gaia.
Folk rock=5,000=50%=P5.00D=Law=Time=Venus=5 May = Aphrodite>>L=N.
Folksinger=2,000=20%=P2.00D=2.0=Nature=Matter=Moon=2 Feb.=Cupid=N=C+_
Folk song=7,500=8,000=80%=P8.0D=Economy=Currency=8 Aug.=Zeus>>E=v.
Folksy=3,000=30%=P3.0D=3.0=Creativity=Stars=Muses=3 March = C=I>>GIL.
Folkway=8,000=80%=P8.0D=Economy=Currency=8 Aug.=Zeus>>E=v.
Follicle=14,000=14%=P1.40D=1.4=Mgt.=Solar Energy/Electric=13 May=Athena=SC=0.1
Follow=10,000=1,000=100%=10.0=Physicality=Tech.=10 Oct.=Uranus=P=1Ø.
Follower=9,000=90%=P9.00D=9.0=Abstraction=Gods=Saturn=9Sept.>>A=Ø.
Following=10,000=1,000=100%=10.0=Physicality=Tech.=10 Oct.=Uranus=P=1Ø.
Follow up=7,500=8,000=80%=P8.0D=Economy=Currency=8 Aug.=Zeus>>E=v.
Folly=10,000=1,000=100%=10.0=Physicality=Tech.=10 Oct.=Uranus=P=1Ø.
Foment=8,500=9,000=90%=P9.00D=9.0=Abstraction=Gods=Saturn=9Sept.>>A=Ø.
Fond=13,000=13%=P1.30=Solar Core=Faculty=13 January=Athena.
Fondle=7,500=8,000=80%=P8.0D=Economy=Currency=8 Aug.=Zeus>>E=v.
Fondue=6,500=7,000=70%=P7.0D=7.0=Language=Assets=Mars=7 July=Pleiades.
Font(1)=7,000=70%=P7.0D=7.0=Language=Assets=Mars=7 July=Pleiades.
Font(2)=7,000=70%=P7.0D=7.0=Language=Assets=Mars=7 July=Pleiades.
Fonteyn Margot=2,500=3,000=30%=P3.0D=3.0=Cre.=Stars=Muses=3 March = C=I>>GIL.
Foo chow=1,000=100%=10.0=1.0=Mind=Sun=1 January=Helios >> M=E4.
Food=10,000=1,000=100%=10.0=Physicality=Tech.=10 Oct.=Uranus=P=1Ø.
Food chain=10,000=1,000=100%=10.0=Physicality=Tech.=10 Oct.=Uranus=P=1Ø.
Food poisoning=8,000=80%=P8.0D=Economy=Currency=8 Aug.=Zeus>>E=v.
Food stamp=10,000=1,000=100%=10.0=Physicality=Tech.=10 Oct.=Uranus=P=1Ø.
Foodstuff=6,000=60%=P6.0D=Man=Earth=Royalty=6 June=Gaia=Maia>>M=M2.

Food web=5,000=50%=P5.00D=Law=Time=Venus=5 May = Aphrodite>>L=N.
Fool=10,000=1,000=100%=10.0=Physicality=Tech.=10 Oct.=Uranus=P=1Ø.
Foolery=3,000=30%=P3.0D=3.0=Creativity=Stars=Muses=3 March = C=I>>GIL.
Foolhardy=4,500=5,000=50%=P5.00D=Law=Time=Venus=5 May = Aphrodite>>L=N.
Foolish=6,000=60%=P6.0D=Man=Earth=Royalty=6 June=Gaia=Maia>>M=M2.
Foolproof=5,500=5.5=80%=P5.50=Earth-Midway=5 May = Gaia.
Foolscap=9,500=10,000=1,000=100%=10.0=Physicality=Tech.=10 Oct.=Uranus=P=1Ø.
Fools gold=1,000=100%=10.0=1.0=Mind=Sun=1 January=Helios >> M=E4.
Foot=10,000=1,000=100%=10.0=Physicality=Tech.=10 Oct.=Uranus=P=1Ø.
Footage=8,500=9,000=90%=P9.00D=9.0=Abstraction=Gods=Saturn=9Sept.>>A=Ø.
Football=10,000=1,000=100%=10.0=Physicality=Tech.=10 Oct.=Uranus=P=1Ø.
Footboard=11,000=11%=P1.10D=1.1=Idea=Brainchild=11 Nov.=Athena>>I=MT.
Footbridge=2,500=3,000=30%=P3.0D=3.0=Creatv.=Stars=Muses=3 March = C=I>>GIL.
Footed=7,500=8,000=80%=P8.0D=Economy=Currency=8 Aug.=Zeus>>E=v.
Footfall=1,500=15%=P1.50D=1.5=Authority=Crown=Solar Core=1 May = Maia.
Foothill=5,000=50%=P5.00D=Law=Time=Venus=5 May = Aphrodite>>L=N.
Foothold=10,000=1,000=100%=10.0=Physicality=Tech.=10 Oct.=Uranus=P=1Ø.
Footing=10,500=11,000=11%=P1.10D=1.1=Idea=Brainchild=11 Nov.=Athena>>I=MT.
Footlights=7,500=8,000=80%=P8.0D=Economy=Currency=8 Aug.=Zeus>>E=v.
Footlocker=3,500=4,000=40%=P4.0D=Govt=Creat=4 April=Mercury=Hermes=G=A4.
Footloose=2,500=3,000=30%=P3.0D=3.0=Creativity=Stars=Muses=3 March = C=I>>GIL.
Footman=8,000=80%=P8.0D=Economy=Currency=8 Aug.=Zeus>>E=v.
Footnote=7,000=70%=P7.0D=7.0=Language=Assets=Mars=7 July=Pleiades.
Footpath=3,500=4,000=40%=P4.0D=Govt=Creat.=4 April=Mercury=Hermes=G=A4.
Footprint=5,000=50%=P5.00D=Law=Time=Venus=5 May = Aphrodite>>L=N.
Foot race=3,500=4,000=40%=P4.0D=Govt=Creato=4 April=Mercury=Hermes=G=A4.
Footrest=4,000=40%=P4.0D=Govt=Creatocracy=4 April=Mercury=Hermes=G=A4.
Foot soldier=2,500=3,000=30%=P3.0D=3.0=Creatv.=Stars=Muses=3 March = C=I>>GIL.
Footsore=2,500=3,000=30%=P3.0D=3.0=Creativity=Stars=Muses=3 March = C=I>>GIL.
Footstep=7,500=8,000=80%=P8.0D=Economy=Currency=8 Aug.=Zeus>>E=v.
Footstool=3,500=4,000=40%=P4.0D=Govt=Creato=4 April=Mercury=Hermes=G=A4.
Footwear=4,500=5,000=50%=P5.00D=Law=Time=Venus=5 May = Aphrodite>>L=N.
Foot work=7,500=8,000=80%=P8.0D=Economy=Currency=8 Aug.=Zeus>>E=v.
Fop=5,000=50%=P5.00D=Law=Time=Venus=5 May = Aphrodite>>L=N.
For=10,000=1,000=100%=10.0=Physicality=Tech.=10 Oct.=Uranus=P=1Ø.
Fora=2,000=20%=P2.00D=2.0=Nature=Matter=Moon=2 Feb.=Cupid=N=C+_
Forage=7,500=8,000=80%=P8.0D=Economy=Currency=8 Aug.=Zeus>>E=v.
Foraker Mount=7,500=8,000=80%=P8.0D=Economy=Currency=8 Aug.=Zeus>>E=v.
Foray=5,000=50%=P5.00D=Law=Time=Venus=5 May = Aphrodite>>L=N.
Forb=5,000=50%=P5.00D=Law=Time=Venus=5 May = Aphrodite>>L=N.
Forbear(1)=10,000=1,000=100%=10.0=Physicality=Tech.=10 Oct.=Uranus=P=1Ø.
Forbear(2)=1,500=15%=P1.50D=1.5=Authority=Crown=Solar Core=1 May = Maia.
Forbid=10,000=1,000=100%=10.0=Physicality=Tech.=10 Oct.=Uranus=P=1Ø.
Forbidding=3,000=30%=P3.0D=3.0=Creativity=Stars=Muses=3 March = C=I>>GIL.
Force=10,000=1,000=100%=10.0=Physicality=Tech.=10 Oct.=Uranus=P=1Ø.

Force feed=4,000=40%=P4.0D=Govt=Creatocracy=4 April=Mercury=Hermes=G=A4.
Force field=2,000=20%=P2.00D=2.0=Nature=Matter=Moon=2 Feb.=Cupid=N=C+_
Forceps=5,500=5.5=80%=P5.50=Earth-Midway=5 May = Gaia.
Forcible=3,000=30%=P3.0D=3.0=Creativity=Stars=Muses=3 March = C=I>>GIL.
ford=7,500=8,000=80%=P8.0D=Economy=Currency=8 Aug.=Zeus>>E=v.
Ford Gerald=4,000=40%=P4.0D=Govt=Creatocracy=4 April=Mercury=Hermes=G=A4.
Ford, Henry=2,500=3,000=30%=P3.0D=3.0=Creatv.=Stars=Muses=3 March = C=I>>GIL.
Fore=10,000=1,000=100%=10.0=Physicality=Tech.=10 Oct.=Uranus=P=1Ø.
Fore-=4,000=40%=P4.0D=Govt=Creatocracy=4 April=Mercury=Hermes=G=A4.
Fore-and-aft=4,500=5,000=50%=P5.00D=Law=Time=Venus=5 May = Aphrodite>>L=N.
Forearm(1)=4,000=40%=P4.0D=Govt=Creatocracy=4 April=Mercury=Hermes=G=A4.
Forearm(2)=4,000=40%=P4.0D=Govt=Creatocracy=4 April=Mercury=Hermes=G=A4.
Forebear=8,500=9,000=90%=P9.00D=9.0=Abstraction=Gods=Saturn=9Sept.>>A=Ø.
Forebode=6,000=60%=P6.0D=Man=Earth=Royalty=6 June=Gaia=Maia>>M=M2.
Forecast=8,000=80%=P8.0D=Economy=Currency=8 Aug.=Zeus>>E=v.
Forecastle=10,000=1,000=100%=10.0=Physicality=Tech.=10 Oct.=Uranus=P=1Ø.
Foreclose=5,500=5.5=80%=P5.50=Earth-Midway=5 May = Gaia.
Forecourt=8,000=80%=P8.0D=Economy=Currency=8 Aug.=Zeus>>E=v.
Forefather=5,000=50%=P5.00D=Law=Time=Venus=5 May = Aphrodite>>L=N.
Forefinger=1,500=15%=P1.50D=1.5=Authority=Crown=Solar Core=1 May = Maia.
Forefoot=4,000=40%=P4.0D=Govt=Creatocracy=4 April=Mercury=Hermes=G=A4.
Forefront=4,500=5,000=50%=P5.00D=Law=Time=Venus=5 May = Aphrodite>>L=N.
Forgo(1)=3,500=4,000=40%=P4.0D=Govt=Creatocracy=4 April=Mercury=Hermes=G=A4.
Forgo(2)=1,500=15%=P1.50D=1.5=Authority=Crown=Solar Core=1 May = Maia.
Foregoing=2,500=3,000=30%=P3.0D=3.0=Creativity=Stars=Muses=3 March = C=I>>GIL.
Fore gone=6,000=60%=P6.0D=Man=Earth=Royalty=6 June=Gaia=Maia>>M=M2.
Foreground=6,000=60%=P6.0D=Man=Earth=Royalty=6 June=Gaia=Maia>>M=M2.
Forehand=7,500=8,000=80%=P8.0D=Economy=Currency=8 Aug.=Zeus>>E=v.
Forehead=4,500=5,000=50%=P5.00D=Law=Time=Venus=5 May = Aphrodite>>L=N.
Foreign=10,000=1,000=100%=10.0=Physicality=Tech.=10 Oct.=Uranus=P=1Ø.
Foreigner=4,500=5,000=50%=P5.00D=Law=Time=Venus=5 May = Aphrodite>>L=N.
Foreign Minister=5,000=50%=P5.00D=Law=Time=Venus=5 May = Aphrodite>>L=N.
Foreign office=5,000=50%=P5.00D=Law=Time=Venus=5 May = Aphrodite>>L=N.
Foreknowledge=3,000=30%=P3.0D=3.0=Creativity=Stars=Muses=3 March = C=I>>GIL.
Foreleg=4,000=40%=P4.0D=Govt=Creatocracy=4 April=Mercury=Hermes=G=A4.
Forelimb=4,500=5,000=50%=P5.00D=Law=Time=Venus=5 May = Aphrodite>>L=N.
Forelock=6,000=60%=P6.0D=Man=Earth=Royalty=6 June=Gaia=Maia>>M=M2.
Foreman=9,500=10,000=1,000=100%=10.0=Physicality=Tech.=10 Oct.=Uranus=P=1Ø.
Foremast=3,500=4,000=40%=P4.0D=Govt=Creato=4 April=Mercury=Hermes=G=A4.
Foremost=5,000=50%=P5.00D=Law=Time=Venus=5 May = Aphrodite>>L=N.
Fore noon=3,500=4,000=40%=P4.0D=Govt=Creato=4 April=Mercury=Hermes=G=A4.
Forensic=7,000=70%=P7.0D=7.0=Language=Assets=Mars=7 July=Pleiades.
Forensics=3,500=4,000=40%=P4.0D=Govt=Creato=4 April=Mercury=Hermes=G=A4.
Foreordain=3,000=30%=P3.0D=3.0=Creativity=Stars=Muses=3 March = C=I>>GIL.
Fore part=2,500=3,000=30%=P3.0D=3.0=Creativity=Stars=Muses=3 March = C=I>>GIL.

Forequarter=6,000=60%=P6.0D=Man=Earth=Royalty=6 June=Gaia=Maia>>M=M2.
Forerunner=6,000=60%=P6.0D=Man=Earth=Royalty=6 June=Gaia=Maia>>M=M2.
Foresail=6,500=7,000=70%=P7.0D=7.0=Language=Assets=Mars=7 July=Pleiades.
Foresee=2,500=3,000=30%=P3.0D=3.0=Creativity=Stars=Muses=3 March = C=I>>GIL.
Foreshadow=4,000=40%=P4.0D=Govt=Creatocracy=4 April=Mercury=Hermes=G=A4.
Foreshore=5,500=5.5=80%=P5.50=Earth-Midway=5 May = Gaia.
Foreshorten=11,000=11%=P1.10D=1.1=Idea=Brainchild=11 Nov.=Athena>>I=MT.
Foresight=7,000=70%=P7.0D=7.0=Language=Assets=Mars=7 July=Pleiades.
Fore skin=5,000=50%=P5.00D=Law=Time=Venus=5 May = Aphrodite>>L=N.
Forest=9,500=10,000=1,000=100%=10.0=Physicality=Tech.=10 Oct.=Uranus=P=1Ø.
Forestall=7,000=70%=P7.0D=7.0=Language=Assets=Mars=7 July=Pleiades.
Forestry=5,000=50%=P5.00D=Law=Time=Venus=5 May = Aphrodite>>L=N.
Foretaste=3,000=30%=P3.0D=3.0=Creativity=Stars=Muses=3 March = C=I>>GIL.
Foretell=6,000=60%=P6.0D=Man=Earth=Royalty=6 June=Gaia=Maia>>M=M2.
Forethought=2,500=3,000=30%=P3.0D=3.0=Creatv.=Stars=Muses=3 March = C=I>>GIL.
Fore token=2,000=20%=P2.00D=2.0=Nature=Matter=Moon=2 Feb.=Cupid=N=C+_
Forever=3,000=30%=P3.0D=3.0=Creativity=Stars=Muses=3 March = C=I>>GIL.
Forevermore=500=5%=P5.00D=5.0=Law=Time=Venus=5 May=Aphrodite>>L=N.
Forewarn=2,000=20%=P2.00D=2.0=Nature=Matter=Moon=2 Feb.=Cupid=N=C+_
Forewing=5,500=5.5=80%=P5.50=Earth-Midway=5 May = Gaia.
Forewoman=8,500=9,000=90%=P9.00D=9.0=Abstraction=Gods=Saturn=9Sept.>>A=Ø.
Foreword=4,000=40%=P4.0D=Govt=Creatocracy=4 April=Mercury=Hermes=G=A4.
Forfeit=10,000=1,000=100%=10.0=Physicality=Tech.=10 Oct.=Uranus=P=1Ø.
Forfeiture=2,500=3,000=30%=P3.0D=3.0=Creativity=Stars=Muses=3 March = C=I>>GIL.
For gather=2,000=20%=P2.00D=2.0=Nature=Matter=Moon=2 Feb.=Cupid=N=C+_
Forge(1)=10,000=1,000=100%=10.0=Physicality=Tech.=10 Oct.=Uranus=P=1Ø.
Forge(2)=4,500=5,000=50%=P5.00D=Law=Time=Venus=5 May = Aphrodite>>L=N.
Forget=10,000=1,000=100%=10.0=Physicality=Tech.=10 Oct.=Uranus=P=1Ø.
Forget-me-not=4,000=40%=P4.0D=Govt=Creatocracy=4 April=Mercury=Hermes=G=A4.
Forgive=10,000=1,000=100%=10.0=Physicality=Tech.=10 Oct.=Uranus=P=1Ø.
Forgo=2,000=20%=P2.00D=2.0=Nature=Matter=Moon=2 Feb.=Cupid=N=C+_
Forint=4,000=40%=P4.0D=Govt=Creatocracy=4 April=Mercury=Hermes=G=A4.
Fork=10,000=1,000=100%=10.0=Physicality=Tech.=10 Oct.=Uranus=P=1Ø.
Forked=3,500=4,000=40%=P4.0D=Govt=Creatocracy=4 April=Mercury=Hermes=G=A4.
Forklift=10,000=1,000=100%=10.0=Physicality=Tech.=10 Oct.=Uranus=P=1Ø.
Forlorn=6,500=7,000=70%=P7.0D=7.0=Language=Assets=Mars=7 July=Pleiades.
Form=10,000=1,000=100%=10.0=Physicality=Tech.=10 Oct.=Uranus=P=1Ø.
Formal=10,000=1,000=100%=10.0=Physicality=Tech.=10 Oct.=Uranus=P=1Ø.
Formaldehyde=8,500=9,000=90%=P9.00D=9.0=Abstraction=Gods=Saturn=9Sept.>>A=Ø
Formalism=5,500=5.5=80%=P5.50=Earth-Midway=5 May = Gaia.
Formality=9,000=90%=P9.00D=9.0=Abstraction=Gods=Saturn=9Sept.>>A=Ø.
Format=10,000=1,000=100%=10.0=Physicality=Tech.=10 Oct.=Uranus=P=1Ø.
Formation=10,000=1,000=100%=10.0=Physicality=Tech.=10 Oct.=Uranus=P=1Ø.
Formative=6,500=7,000=70%=P7.0D=7.0=Language=Assets=Mars=7 July=Pleiades.
Former=10,000=1,000=100%=10.0=Physicality=Tech.=10 Oct.=Uranus=P=1Ø.

Formerly=3,500=4,000=40%=P4.0D=Govt=Creatocracy=4 April=Mercury=Hermes=G=A4.
Form fitting=3,500=4,000=40%=P4.0D=Govt=Creato=4 April=Mercury=Hermes=G=A4.
Formica=9,000=90%=P9.00D=9.0=Abstraction=Gods=Saturn=9Sept.>>A=Ø.
Formidable=5,500=5.5=80%=P5.50=Earth-Midway=5 May = Gaia.
Formless=4,000=40%=P4.0D=Govt=Creatocracy=4 April=Mercury=Hermes=G=A4.
Form letter=4,500=5,000=50%=P5.00D=Law=Time=Venus=5 May = Aphrodite>>L=N.
Formosa=1,000=100%=Physicality= Tech.=10 Oct.=Uranus=P=1Ø.
Formula=10,000=1,000=100%=10.0=Physicality=Tech.=10 Oct.=Uranus=P=1Ø.
Formulate=8,000=80%=P8.0D=Economy=Currency=8 Aug.=Zeus>>E=v.
Fornication=5,500=5.5=80%=P5.50=Earth-Midway=5 May = Gaia.
Forsake=4,000=40%=P4.0D=Govt=Creatocracy=4 April=Mercury=Hermes=G=A4.
For sooth=1,500=15%=P1.50D=1.5=Authority=Crown=Solar Core=1 May = Maia.
Forester Edward=2,000=20%=P2.00D=2.0=Nature=Matter=Moon=2 Feb.=Cupid=N=C+_
Forswear=4,000=40%=P4.0D=Govt=Creatocracy=4 April=Mercury=Hermes=G=A4.
Forsythia=7,000=70%=P7.0D=7.0=Language=Assets=Mars=7 July=Pleiades.
Fort=5,000=50%=P5.00D=Law=Time=Venus=5 May = Aphrodite>>L=N.
Fortaleza=6,000=60%=P6.0D=Man=Earth=Royalty=6 June=Gaia=Maia>>M=M2.
Fort-de-France=4,500=5,000=50%=P5.00D=Law=Time=Venus=5 May = Aphrodite>>L=N.
Forte(1)=7,000=70%=P7.0D=7.0=Language=Assets=Mars=7 July=Pleiades.
Forte(2)=2,500=3,000=30%=P3.0D=3.0=Creativity=Stars=Muses=3 March = C=I>>GIL.
forth=3,000=30%=P3.0D=3.0=Creativity=Stars=Muses=3 March = C=I>>GIL.
Forth=10,500=11,000=11%=P1.10D=1.1=Idea=Brainchild=11 Nov.=Athena>>I=MT.
Firth of Forth=3,000=30%=P3.0D=3.0=Creativity=Stars=Muses=3 March = C=I>>GIL.
Forthcoming=7,500=8,000=80%=P8.0D=Economy=Currency=8 Aug.=Zeus>>E=v.
Forthright=2,500=3,000=30%=P3.0D=3.0=Creativity=Stars=Muses=3 March = C=I>>GIL.
Forthwith=1,500=15%=P1.50D=1.5=Authority=Crown=Solar Core=1 May = Maia.
Fortieth=6,500=7,000=70%=P7.0D=7.0=Language=Assets=Mars=7 July=Pleiades.
Fortify=10,000=1,000=100%=10.0=Physicality=Tech.=10 Oct.=Uranus=P=1Ø.
Fortissimo=2,500=3,000=30%=P3.0D=3.0=Creativity=Stars=Muses=3 March = C=I>>GIL.
Fortitude=8,000=80%=P8.0D=Economy=Currency=8 Aug.=Zeus>>E=v.
Fort Lauderdale=7,000=70%=P7.0D=7.0=Language=Assets=Mars=7 July=Pleiades.
Fortnight=4,500=5,000=50%=P5.00D=Law=Time=Venus=5 May = Aphrodite>>L=N.
Fortnightly=4,500=5,000=50%=P5.00D=Law=Time=Venus=5 May = Aphrodite>>L=N.
FORTRAN=7,500=8,000=80%=P8.0D=Economy=Currency=8 Aug.=Zeus>>E=v.
Fortress=6,500=7,000=70%=P7.0D=7.0=Language=Assets=Mars=7 July=Pleiades.
Fort Smith=5,500=5.5=80%=P5.50=Earth-Midway=5 May = Gaia.
Fortuitous=5,500=5.5=80%=P5.50=Earth-Midway=5 May = Gaia.
Fortuity=5,500=5.5=80%=P5.50=Earth-Midway=5 May = Gaia.
Fortunate=5,000=50%=P5.00D=Law=Time=Venus=5 May = Aphrodite>>L=N.
Fortune=11,500=12,000=12%=P1.20D=1.2=Knowledge=Education=12Dec.=Athena>>K=F.
Fortune teller=5,500=5.5=80%=P5.50=Earth-Midway=5 May = Gaia.
Forte Wayne=4,500=5,000=50%=P5.00D=Law=Time=Venus=5 May = Aphrodite>>L=N.
Fort Worth=4,500=5,000=50%=P5.00D=Law=Time=Venus=5 May = Aphrodite>>L=N.

Forty=6,000=60%=P6.0D=Man=Earth=Royalty=6 June=Gaia=Maia>>M=M2.
A forwarded message on Whatsapp.
I am looking for someone to help me answer these questions.

1. Why Noah built the Ark in 40 days.
2. Why the rain/storm lasted for 40 days.
3. Why the Israelites walked through the desert for 40 years.
4. Why the Tower of Babel was built in 40 days.
5. Why Jesus Christ fasted for 40days.
6. Why Jesus Christ ascended to heaven after 40 days.
7. Why Moses had to spend 40 days with GOD and fasting before he got the 10 commandments Tablets.
8. Why it took 40 days threat from Goliath against the Army of Israel before he was killed by David.
9. Why David later had a total reign of 40 years over the nation of Israel.
10. Why Elijah had to trek, fasting for 40 days running away from Jezebel.
    40 days and 40 years in the Bible is HIGHLY SYMBOLIC.
11. Why life begins at 40.
12. Why even Pass mark starts at 40.
13. Why they say "A fool @ 40 is a fool forever".
    What's so special about 40???

Now the scriptures show that GOD functions a series of modules that conforms to the twelve dimensions of the mind. The fourth dimension is Government >> Communications >> Relationships >> Politics >> Power >> Family >> Creatocracy.

1. Noah built the Ark in 40 days. First Noah is a human who will be return in the cycle of life in a special relationship with the almighty GOD. The Ark is a protective human system called Creatocracy. 40 days means that the builder or initiator of the Ark would be built and achieved at about the age of his forties.
2. Rain is a special feature of the skies. Only the one with the power of the stars in his hands will be able to understand the particulate nature of rain measured in bits. Rain is water and all water are sourced from the moon as the Mare. The Moon will therefore be computed and the origin of Man will be tracked to the moon.
3. Desert indicates dryness privation hunger poverty and severe deprivation. For power to be gained in the heavenly training process the King would be associated with this life style.
4. The Tower of Babel indicates the place of language. The Creatocrat will understand abstract language, decipher the secrets of the Gods and discover GOD. He will be able to express the God codes in programs and interpret symbols through energy modules.
5. Jesus Christ is Hermes the Son of Zeus in Greek mythology. He is the number 4.0.
6. Ascension is the code 4 and exists in dimension under the code 1 being Mind. Hence Mind ascends and matter descends. Hermes is the only God who transacts freely between Humanity and the God world. So 4.0 is the code that Creatocracy will discover this code.

7. GOD had promised to make Moses a God if he met with standard of Gods. The Ten Commandments were written by the finger of God being known as Maia. Moses spent 40 days and got the 10 commandments. 4.0*1.0x=px=5+4=9x=px=30=3.0. This indicates Creativity driven by Interest. So Moses was expected to introduce the Creatocracy through Mind Computing measured by creativity but he failed. Solomon also could not do it. Like Abraham and Job. This means that a time would come when humanity will measure the contents in a person. Today we call them potentials. So the Ten Commandments simply indicated creativity as a behavior pattern that will characterize both the normal and the genius. Interest is known in the human energy database.

8. Goliath was a giant indicated as the mountain measured as 10,000 in the Makupedia. David was 12 years indicated as dimension of knowledge >> Science >> Education. 40 days is a struggle for power both within the family system and without.
10,000=10.0, 12=1.2, 40=4.0
10.0*4.0x=px=14+40=54x=px=614=6.14
Goliath was written to have 6 fingers and six toes for each making 24.
6.14 confirms he was associated with the code 6 and led an organized army (14).
The difference is 24-14=10.0 confirming he was a man of great stature and constituted a physical mountain before the people of Israel. 1.2*10.0x=px=11.2+12=23.2x=px=157.6
Only someone with the functional authority (15, .6) of measures or computing can bring down a challenge as high as a mountain (10.0). This authority would manifest as invention skills (11.2) and specialized knowledge (12=1.2) though seeming smaller in experience than the material expectation (23-24). David was 23.2. Goliath was 24 in quantum.

9. In the first place David was an angel in human form according to Scriptures. His reign was Creatocratic, one driven by the dimensions of the mind through creativity.

10. Creatocracy involves training because it is power.

11. A human saying that is speculative but applicable. What has not been hitherto prepared for before 40 will be difficult to achieve after 40.

12. Pass Mark starts. Though speculative. Nature works at 50% as a pass mark.

13. A speculative statement. Scriptures states that great men are not always wise. Hence wisdom has nothing to do with age. A man is what he thinks about all day.

The special thing about 40 is 4.0 the freedom of mankind through Creatocracy.

Forty five=7,500=8,000=80%=P8.0D=Economy=Currency=8 Aug.=Zeus>>E=v.
Forty niner=5,000=50%=P5.00D=Law=Time=Venus=5 May = Aphrodite>>L=N.
Forty winks=2,000=20%=P2.00D=2.0=Nature=Matter=Moon=2 Feb.=Cupid=N=C+_
Forum=10,000=1,000=100%=10.0=Physicality=Tech.=10 Oct.=Uranus=P=1Ø.
Forward=10,000=1,000=100%=10.0=Physicality=Tech.=10 Oct.=Uranus=P=1Ø.
Forwards=2,500=3,000=30%=P3.0D=3.0=Creativity=Stars=Muses=3 March = C=I>>GIL.
Forwent=1,500=15%=P1.50D=1.5=Authority=Crown=Solar Core=1 May = Maia.

Fossil=15,500=16,000=16%=P1.60D=1.6=Incarnation=Mind of GOD=1 June = Maia.
Fossil fuel=9,500=10,000=1,000=100%=10.0=Physicality=Tech.=10 Oct.=Uranus=P=1Ø.
Fossilize=6,000=60%=P6.0D=Man=Earth=Royalty=6 June=Gaia=Maia>>M=M2.
Foster=16,500=17,000=17%=P1.70D=1.7=Solar Asset=17 Feb.=Maia=Mind Computing.
Foster Stephen=2,500=3,000=30%=P3.0D=3.0=Cre.=Stars=Muses=3 March = C=I>>GIL.
Foucault Jean=3,000=30%=P3.0D=3.0=Creativity=Stars=Muses=3 March = C=I>>GIL.
Fought=3,000=30%=P3.0D=3.0=Creativity=Stars=Muses=3 March = C=I>>GIL.
Foul=10,000=1,000=100%=10.0=Physicality=Tech.=10 Oct.=Uranus=P=1Ø.
Foulard=9,000=90%=P9.00D=9.0=Abstraction=Gods=Saturn=9Sept.>>A=Ø.
Foul mouthed=2,500=3,000=30%=P3.0D=3.0=Creatv=Stars=Muses=3 March = C=I>>GIL.
Foul play=4,000=40%=P4.0D=Govt=Creatocracy=4 April=Mercury=Hermes=G=A4.
Foul up=6,000=60%=P6.0D=Man=Earth=Royalty=6 June=Gaia=Maia>>M=M2.
Found(1)=11,000=11%=P1.10D=1.1=Idea=Brainchild=11 Nov.=Athena>>I=MT.
Found(2)=7,000=70%=P7.0D=7.0=Language=Assets=Mars=7 July=Pleiades.
Found(3)=3,000=30%=P3.0D=3.0=Creativity=Stars=Muses=3 March = C=I>>GIL.
Foundation=10,000=1,000=100%=10.0=Physicality=Tech.=10 Oct.=Uranus=P=1Ø.
Founder=10,000=1,000=100%=10.0=Physicality=Tech.=10 Oct.=Uranus=P=1Ø.
Foundling=3,000=30%=P3.0D=3.0=Creativity=Stars=Muses=3 March = C=I>>GIL.
Foundry=4,000=40%=P4.0D=Govt=Creatocracy=4 April=Mercury=Hermes=G=A4.
Fount(1)=3,000=30%=P3.0D=3.0=Creativity=Stars=Muses=3 March = C=I>>GIL.
Fount(2)=2,500=3,000=30%=P3.0D=3.0=Creativity=Stars=Muses=3 March = C=I>>GIL.
Fountain=10,000=1,000=100%=10.0=Physicality=Tech.=10 Oct.=Uranus=P=1Ø.
Fountainhead=6,500=7,000=70%=P7.0D=7.0=Language=Assets=Mars=7 July=Pleiades.
Fountain pen=8,500=9,000=90%=P9.00D=9.0=Abstraction=Gods=Saturn=9Sept.>>A=Ø.
Four=9,000=90%=P9.00D=9.0=Abstraction=Gods=Saturn=9Sept.>>A=Ø.
Four flush=10,500=11,000=11%=P1.10D=1.1=Idea=Brainchild=11 Nov.=Athena>>I=MT.
Four-H Club=10,000=1,000=100%=10.0=Physicality=Tech.=10 Oct.=Uranus=P=1Ø.
Fourier=3,000=30%=P3.0D=3.0=Creativity=Stars=Muses=3 March = C=I>>GIL.
Fourier, Jean=4,500=5,000=50%=P5.00D=Law=Time=Venus=5 May = Aphrodite>>L=N.
Four-in-hand=11,000=11%=P1.10D=1.1=Idea=Brainchild=11 Nov.=Athena>>I=MT.
Four-leaf clover=7,000=70%=P7.0D=7.0=Language=Assets=Mars=7 July=Pleiades.
Four-o'clock=7,500=8,000=80%=P8.0D=Economy=Currency=8 Aug.=Zeus>>E=v.
Four poster=6,500=7,000=70%=P7.0D=7.0=Language=Assets=Mars=7 July=Pleiades.
Four score=2,000=20%=P2.00D=2.0=Nature=Matter=Moon=2 Feb.=Cupid=N=C+_
Foursome=8,500=9,000=90%=P9.00D=9.0=Abstraction=Gods=Saturn=9Sept.>>A=Ø.
Four square=6,500=7,000=70%=P7.0D=7.0=Language=Assets=Mars=7 July=Pleiades.
Fourteen=9,000=90%=P9.00D=9.0=Abstraction=Gods=Saturn=9Sept.>>A=Ø.
Fourteenth=6,500=7,000=70%=P7.0D=7.0=Language=Assets=Mars=7 July=Pleiades.
Fourth=10,500=11,000=11%=P1.10D=1.1=Idea=Brainchild=11 Nov.=Athena>>I=MT.

Fourth dimension=10,500=11,000=11%=P1.10D=1.1=Idea=11 Nov.=Athena>>I=MT.
The Creatocracy studied the workings of the universes and discovered there are twelve dimensions for all existence. The fourth dimension is professionally rated 4.0>> The Creatocracy >> Government >> Nations >> Organization >> Power >> Relationships >> Networks >> Politics >> Leadership >> Merchandise >> Family >> Mercury >> Hermes.

The Creatocracy refers to Creative Scientists collectively. Also to the system of government invented by Peter Matthews-Akukalia in the Makupedia field of study.

Fourth estate=1,000=100%=10.0=1.0=Mind=Sun=1 January=Helios >> M=E4.
In the Creatocratic compass of governance, the Royalty (inventors) come first. The Media as prophets of old make up the second realm. Government is third. Labour is fourth.

Fourth of July=1,500=15%=P1.50D=1.5=Authority=Crown=Solar Core=1 May = Maia.
Sixth of July >> Birthday of Peter Matthews-Akukalia, Castle Makupedia.
World Inventors Day (WIDA) instituted by the Creatocracy. Reference>> Psychastronomy

---

Four wheel drive=8,500=9,000=90%=P9.00D=9.0=Abst.=Gods=Saturn=9Sept.>>A=Ø.
Fowl=9,000=90%=P9.00D=9.0=Abstraction=Gods=Saturn=9Sept.>>A=Ø.
fox=15,500=16,000=16%=P1.60D=1.6=Cycle of Incarnation=Mind of GOD=1 June = Maia.
Fox=10,000=1,000=100%=10.0=Physicality=Tech.=10 Oct.=Uranus=P=1Ø.
Fox, Charles=2,500=3,000=30%=P3.0D=3.0=Cre=Stars=Muses=3 March = C=I>>GIL.
Fox, George=4,500=5,000=50%=P5.00D=Law=Time=Venus=5 May = Aphrodite>>L=N.
Foxfire=5,000=50%=P5.00D=Law=Time=Venus=5 May = Aphrodite>>L=N.
Foxglove=10,000=1,000=100%=10.0=Physicality=Tech.=10 Oct.=Uranus=P=1Ø.
Foxhole=5,000=50%=P5.00D=Law=Time=Venus=5 May = Aphrodite>>L=N.
Fox terrier=4,500=5,000=50%=P5.00D=Law=Time=Venus=5 May = Aphrodite>>L=N.
Foxtrot=7,500=8,000=80%=P8.0D=Economy=Currency=8 Aug.=Zeus>>E=v.
Foyer=8,000=80%=P8.0D=Economy=Currency=8 Aug.=Zeus>>E=v.
fpm=1,500=15%=P1.50D=1.5=Authority=Crown=Solar Core=1 May = Maia.
fps=3,000=30%=P3.0D=3.0=Creativity=Stars=Muses=3 March = C=I>>GIL.
Fr=2,500=3,000=30%=P3.0D=3.0=Creativity=Stars=Muses=3 March = C=I>>GIL.
fr.=1,500=15%=P1.50D=1.5=Authority=Crown=Solar Core=1 May = Maia.
Fr.=3,500=4,000=40%=P4.0D=Govt=Creatocracy=4 April=Mercury=Hermes=G=A4.
Fracas=4,500=5,000=50%=P5.00D=Law=Time=Venus=5 May = Aphrodite>>L=N.
Fractal=12,500=13,000=13%=P1.30=Solar Core=Faculty=13 January=Athena.
Fraction=10,500=11,000=11%=P1.10D=1.1=Idea=Brainchild=11 Nov.=Athena>>I=MT.
Fractious=6,000=60%=P6.0D=Man=Earth=Royalty=6 June=Gaia=Maia>>M=M2.
Fracture=10,000=1,000=100%=10.0=Physicality=Tech.=10 Oct.=Uranus=P=1Ø.
Fragile=8,500=9,000=90%=P9.00D=9.0=Abstraction=Gods=Saturn=9Sept.>>A=Ø.
Fragment=7,500=8,000=80%=P8.0D=Economy=Currency=8 Aug.=Zeus>>E=v.
Fragmentary=2,500=3,000=30%=P3.0D=3.0=Creatv=Stars=Muses=3 March = C=I>>GIL.
Fragmentation bomb=6,500=7,000=70%=P7.0D=7.0=Lang=Assets=Mars=7 July=Pleiades.
Fragonard Jean=2,500=3,000=30%=P3.0D=3.0=Cre=Stars=Muses=3 March = C=I>>GIL.
Fragrance=6,000=60%=P6.0D=Man=Earth=Royalty=6 June=Gaia=Maia>>M=M2.
Frail=5,000=50%=P5.00D=Law=Time=Venus=5 May = Aphrodite>>L=N.
Frailty=7,500=8,000=80%=P8.0D=Economy=Currency=8 Aug.=Zeus>>E=v.
Frame=10,000=1,000=100%=10.0=Physicality=Tech.=10 Oct.=Uranus=P=1Ø.
Frame up=8,500=9,000=90%=P9.00D=9.0=Abstraction=Gods=Saturn=9Sept.>>A=Ø.
Framework=5,000=50%=P5.00D=Law=Time=Venus=5 May = Aphrodite>>L=N.

Franc=2,000=20%=P2.00D=2.0=Nature=Matter=Moon=2 Feb.=Cupid=N=C+_

France=7,500=8,000=80%=P8.0D=Economy=Currency=8 Aug.=Zeus>>E=v.

France Anatole=4,000=40%=P4.0D=Govt=Creatocracy=4 April=Mercury=Hermes=G=A4.

Franchise=10,000=1,000=100%=10.0=Physicality=Tech.=10 Oct.=Uranus=P=1Ø.

Francis I=3,000=30%=P3.0D=3.0=Creativity=Stars=Muses=3 March = C=I>>GIL.

Francis II=8,500=9,000=90%=P9.00D=9.0=Abstraction=Gods=Saturn=9Sept.>>A=Ø.

Francis Ferdinand=5,000=50%=P5.00D=Law=Time=Venus=5 May = Aphrodite>>L=N.

Francis Joseph=5,500=5.5=80%=P5.50=Earth-Midway=5 May = Gaia.

Francis of Assisi=6,000=60%=P6.0D=Man=Earth=Royalty=6 June=Gaia=Maia>>M=M2.

Francium=8,500=9,000=90%=P9.00D=9.0=Abstraction=Gods=Saturn=9Sept.>>A=Ø.

Franck César=3,500=4,000=40%=P4.0D=Govt=Creatoc=4 April=Mercury=Hermes=G=A4.

Franco Francisco=3,000=30%=P3.0D=3.0=Creativity=Stars=Muses=3 March = C=I>>GIL.

Franco-=3,000=30%=P3.0D=3.0=Creativity=Stars=Muses=3 March = C=I>>GIL.

Francophone=5,000=50%=P5.00D=Law=Time=Venus=5 May = Aphrodite>>L=N.

Frangible=3,000=30%=P3.0D=3.0=Creativity=Stars=Muses=3 March = C=I>>GIL.

Frank(1)=10,000=1,000=100%=10.0=Physicality=Tech.=10 Oct.=Uranus=P=1Ø.

Frank(2)=1,000=100%=10.0=1.0=Mind=Sun=1 January=Helios >> M=E4.

Frank=5,500=5.5=80%=P5.50=Earth-Midway=5 May = Gaia.

Frank Anne=2,500=3,000=30%=P3.0D=3.0=Cre=Stars=Muses=3 March = C=I>>GIL.

Frankenstein=12,000=12%=P1.20D=1.2=Knowledge=Education=12Dec.=Athena>>K=F.

Frankfort=6,000=60%=P6.0D=Man=Earth=Royalty=6 June=Gaia=Maia>>M=M2.

Frankfurt=8,500=9,000=90%=P9.00D=9.0=Abstraction=Gods=Saturn=9Sept.>>A=Ø.

Frankfurter=9,000=90%=P9.00D=9.0=Abstraction=Gods=Saturn=9Sept.>>A=Ø.

Frankfurter=7,500=8,000=80%=P8.0D=Economy=Currency=8 Aug.=Zeus>>E=v.

Frankincense=6,500=7,000=70%=P7.0D=7.0=Language=Assets=Mars=7 July=Pleiades.

Franklin Benjamin=4,500=5,000=50%=P5.00D=Law=Time=Venus=5 May =Oodite>>L=N.

Franklin John=2,000=20%=P2.00D=2.0=Nature=Matter=Moon=2 Feb.=Cupid=N=C+_

Frantic=4,500=5,000=50%=P5.00D=Law=Time=Venus=5 May = Aphrodite>>L=N.

Franz Josef I=2,000=20%=P2.00D=2.0=Nature=Matter=Moon=2 Feb.=Cupid=N=C+_

Franz Josef Land=5,000=50%=P5.00D=Law=Time=Venus=5 May = Aphrodite>>L=N.

Frappè=10,500=11,000=11%=P1.10D=1.1=Idea=Brainchild=11 Nov.=Athena>>I=MT.

Fraser John=4,000=40%=P4.0D=Govt=Creatocracy=4 April=Mercury=Hermes=G=A4.

Fraser River=11,000=11%=P1.10D=1.1=Idea=Brainchild=11 Nov.=Athena>>I=MT.

Fraternal=10,500=11,000=11%=P1.10D=1.1=Idea=Brainchild=11 Nov.=Athena>>I=MT.

Fraternity=9,500=10,000=1,000=100%=10.0=Physicality=Tech.=10 Oct.=Uranus=P=1Ø.

Fraternize=7,000=70%=P7.0D=7.0=Language=Assets=Mars=7 July=Pleiades.

Fratricide=10,000=1,000=100%=10.0=Physicality=Tech.=10 Oct.=Uranus=P=1Ø.

Frau=3,500=4,000=40%=P4.0D=Govt=Creatocracy=4 April=Mercury=Hermes=G=A4.

Fraud=10,500=11,000=11%=P1.10D=1.1=Idea=Brainchild=11 Nov.=Athena>>I=MT.

Fraudulent=3,500=4,000=40%=P4.0D=Govt=Creato=4 April=Mercury=Hermes=G=A4.

Fraught=8,000=80%=P8.0D=Economy=Currency=8 Aug.=Zeus>>E=v.

Fräulein=7,000=70%=P7.0D=7.0=Language=Assets=Mars=7 July=Pleiades.

Fray(1)=6,500=7,000=70%=P7.0D=7.0=Language=Assets=Mars=7 July=Pleiades.

Fray(2)=8,000=80%=P8.0D=Economy=Currency=8 Aug.=Zeus>>E=v.

Frazzle=7,000=70%=P7.0D=7.0=Language=Assets=Mars=7 July=Pleiades.

FRB=1,500=15%=P1.50D=1.5=Authority=Crown=Solar Core=1 May = Maia.
Freak=10,000=1,000=100%=10.0=Physicality=Tech.=10 Oct.=Uranus=P=1Ø.
Freak out=9,500=10,000=1,000=100%=10.0=Physicality=Tech.=10 Oct.=Uranus=P=1Ø.
Freckle=11,000=11%=P1.10D=1.1=Idea=Brainchild=11 Nov.=Athena>>I=MT.
Frederick I=8,000=80%=P8.0D=Economy=Currency=8 Aug.=Zeus>>E=v.
Frederick II(1)=7,000=70%=P7.0D=7.0=Language=Assets=Mars=7 July=Pleiades.
Frederick II(2)=5,000=50%=P5.00D=Law=Time=Venus=5 May = Aphrodite>>L=N.
Fredericton=8,000=80%=P8.0D=Economy=Currency=8 Aug.=Zeus>>E=v.
Free=10,000=1,000=100%=10.0=Physicality=Tech.=10 Oct.=Uranus=P=1Ø.
Freebase=6,500=7,000=70%=P7.0D=7.0=Language=Assets=Mars=7 July=Pleiades.
Freebie=3,000=30%=P3.0D=3.0=Creativity=Stars=Muses=3 March = C=I>>GIL.
Freeboard=12,500=13,000=13%=P1.30=Solar Core=Faculty=13 January=Athena.
Freebooter=3,500=4,000=40%=P4.0D=Govt=Creato=4 April=Mercury=Hermes=G=A4.
Freeborn=4,000=40%=P4.0D=Govt=Creatocracy=4 April=Mercury=Hermes=G=A4.
Freedman=4,000=40%=P4.0D=Govt=Creatocracy=4 April=Mercury=Hermes=G=A4.
Freedom=10,500=11,000=11%=P1.10D=1.1=Idea=Brainchild=11 Nov.=Athena>>I=MT.
Freedwoman=4,000=40%=P4.0D=Govt=Creatocracy=4 April=Mercury=Hermes=G=A4.
Free enterprise=7,000=70%=P7.0D=7.0=Language=Assets=Mars=7 July=Pleiades.
Free fall=7,000=70%=P7.0D=7.0=Language=Assets=Mars=7 July=Pleiades.
Free flight=5,000=50%=P5.00D=Law=Time=Venus=5 May = Aphrodite>>L=N.
Free-for-all=7,000=70%=P7.0D=7.0=Language=Assets=Mars=7 July=Pleiades.
Free form=5,000=50%=P5.00D=Law=Time=Venus=5 May = Aphrodite>>L=N.
Freehand=3,000=30%=P3.0D=3.0=Creativity=Stars=Muses=3 March = C=I>>GIL.
Freehand=3,500=4,000=40%=P4.0D=Govt=Creato=4 April=Mercury=Hermes=G=A4.
Freehanded=3,000=30%=P3.0D=3.0=Creativity=Stars=Muses=3 March = C=I>>GIL.
Freehold=8,500=9,000=90%=P9.00D=9.0=Abstraction=Gods=Saturn=9Sept.>>A=Ø.
Freelance=9,500=10,000=1,000=100%=Physicality= Tech.=10 Oct.=Uranus=P=1Ø.
Freeload=4,500=5,000=50%=P5.00D=Law=Time=Venus=5 May = Aphrodite>>L=N.
Free love=5,000=50%=P5.00D=Law=Time=Venus=5 May = Aphrodite>>L=N.
Free lunch=4,000=40%=P4.0D=Govt=Creatocracy=4 April=Mercury=Hermes=G=A4.
Freeman=7,000=70%=P7.0D=7.0=Language=Assets=Mars=7 July=Pleiades.
Freemason=9,000=90%=P9.00D=9.0=Abstraction=Gods=Saturn=9Sept.>>A=Ø.
Free on board=7,000=70%=P7.0D=7.0=Language=Assets=Mars=7 July=Pleiades.
Freeport=7,000=70%=P7.0D=7.0=Language=Assets=Mars=7 July=Pleiades.
Free speech=6,000=60%=P6.0D=Man=Earth=Royalty=6 June=Gaia=Maia>>M=M2.
Freestanding=2,500=3,000=30%=P3.0D=3.0=Cre=Stars=Muses=3 March = C=I>>GIL.
Freestone=12,000=12%=P1.20D=1.2=Knowledge=Education=12Dec.=Athena>>K=F.
Freestyle=14,500=15,000=1,500=15%=P1.50D=1.5=Authority=Solar Crown=1 May = Maia.
Freethinker=5,000=50%=P5.00D=Law=Time=Venus=5 May = Aphrodite>>L=N.
Free town=6,000=60%=P6.0D=Man=Earth=Royalty=6 June=Gaia=Maia>>M=M2.
Free trade=3,500=4,000=40%=P4.0D=Govt=Creato=4 April=Mercury=Hermes=G=A4.
Free verse=4,500=5,000=50%=P5.00D=Law=Time=Venus=5 May = Aphrodite>>L=N.
Freeway=3,000=30%=P3.0D=3.0=Creativity=Stars=Muses=3 March = C=I>>GIL.
Freewheeling=6,000=60%=P6.0D=Man=Earth=Royalty=6 June=Gaia=Maia>>M=M2.
Free will=500=5%=P5.00D=5.0=Law=Time=Venus=5 May=Aphrodite>>L=N.

Freeze=10,000=1,000=100%=10.0=Physicality=Tech.=10 Oct.=Uranus=P=1Ø.
Freeze dry=5,500=5.5=80%=P5.50=Earth-Midway=5 May = Gaia.
Freezer=7,500=8,000=80%=P8.0D=Economy=Currency=8 Aug.=Zeus>>E=v.
Freezing=8,500=9,000=90%=P9.00D=9.0=Abstraction=Gods=Saturn=9Sept.>>A=Ø.
Freight=10,000=1,000=100%=10.0=Physicality=Tech.=10 Oct.=Uranus=P=1Ø.
Freighter=4,000=40%=P4.0D=Govt=Creatocracy=4 April=Mercury=Hermes=G=A4.
Fremont=5,000=50%=P5.00D=Law=Time=Venus=5 May = Aphrodite>>L=N.
Frémont John=3,500=4,000=40%=P4.0D=Govt=Creato=4 April=Mercury=Hermes=G=A4.
Frena=2,000=20%=P2.00D=2.0=Nature=Matter=Moon=2 Feb.=Cupid=N=C+_
French=9,000=90%=P9.00D=9.0=Abstraction=Gods=Saturn=9Sept.>>A=Ø.
French-Canadian=2,500=3,000=30%=P3.0D=3.0=Cr=Stars=Muses=3 March = C=I>>GIL.
French door=5,500=5.5=80%=P5.50=Earth-Midway=5 May = Gaia.
French fry=2,500=3,000=30%=P3.0D=3.0=Creativity=Stars=Muses=3 March = C=I>>GIL.
French-fry=2,500=3,000=30%=P3.0D=3.0=Creativity=Stars=Muses=3 March = C=I>>GIL.
French Guiana=7,500=8,000=80%=P8.0D=Economy=Currency=8 Aug.=Zeus>>E=v.
French born=8,000=80%=P8.0D=Economy=Currency=8 Aug.=Zeus>>E=v.
French leave=1,500=15%=P1.50D=1.5=Authority=Solar Crown=1 May = Maia.
French Polynesia=11,500=12,000=12%=P1.20D=1.2=Knowl=Edu.=12Dec.=Athena>>K=F.
French toast=6,500=7,000=70%=P7.0D=7.0=Language=Assets=Mars=7 July=Pleiades.
Frenetic=7,000=70%=P7.0D=7.0=Language=Assets=Mars=7 July=Pleiades.
Frenum=9,000=90%=P9.00D=9.0=Abstraction=Gods=Saturn=9Sept.>>A=Ø.
Frenzy=7,500=8,000=80%=P8.0D=Economy=Currency=8 Aug.=Zeus>>E=v.
Freq.=500=5%=P5.00D=5.0=Law=Time=Venus=5 May=Aphrodite>>L=N.
Frequency=10,000=1,000=100%=10.0=Physicality=Tech.=10 Oct.=Uranus=P=1Ø.
Frequency modulation=8,000=80%=P8.0D=Economy=Currency=8 Aug.=Zeus>>E=v.
Frequent=7,500=8,000=80%=P8.0D=Economy=Currency=8 Aug.=Zeus>>E=v.
Fresco=10,000=1,000=100%=10.0=Physicality=Tech.=10 Oct.=Uranus=P=1Ø.
Fresh=10,000=1,000=100%=10.0=Physicality=Tech.=10 Oct.=Uranus=P=1Ø.
Freshen=5,000=50%=P5.00D=Law=Time=Venus=5 May = Aphrodite>>L=N.
Freshet=5,500=5.5=80%=P5.50=Earth-Midway=5 May = Gaia.
Freshman=6,000=60%=P6.0D=Man=Earth=Royalty=6 June=Gaia=Maia>>M=M2.
Freshwater=5,500=5.5=80%=P5.50=Earth-Midway=5 May = Gaia.
Fresno=4,500=5,000=50%=P5.00D=Law=Time=Venus=5 May = Aphrodite>>L=N.
Fret(1)=15,000=1,500=15%=P1.50D=1.5=Authority=Solar Crown=1 May = Maia.
Fret(2)=6,500=7,000=70%=P7.0D=7.0=Language=Assets=Mars=7 July=Pleiades.
Fret(3)=5,000=50%=P5.00D=Law=Time=Venus=5 May = Aphrodite>>L=N.
Fretwork=5,500=5.5=80%=P5.50=Earth-Midway=5 May = Gaia.
Freud Anna=3,000=30%=P3.0D=3.0=Creativity=Stars=Muses=3 March = C=I>>GIL.
Freud, Sigmund=4,000=40%=P4.0D=Govt=Creatocracy=4 April=Mercury=Hermes=G=A4.

Frey=4,000=40%=P4.0D=Govt=Creatocracy=4 April=Mercury=Hermes=G=A4.
Greek myth. The Norse God of peace and prosperity. Gods incarnate and manifest as different personalities at different times to perform their purpose and duties. Here Mercury who is Hermes who also is Jesus Christ manifests as Frey. So they move all the time.

Freya=4,000=40%=P4.0D=Govt=Creatocracy=4 April=Mercury=Hermes=G=A4.
Greek myth. The Norse Goddess of love and beauty. Female incarnation of Hermes is Athena. That is the wit and the wis functioning together to achieve a common purpose. In Christianity they would be described as the Son of GOD and the Spirit of GOD.

Fri.=500=5%=P5.00D=5.0=Law=Time=Venus=5 May=Aphrodite>>L=N.
After all Friday is often truly marked as half day at work prior to the weekend.

Friable=3,000=30%=P3.0D=3.0=Creativity=Stars=Muses=3 March = C=I>>GIL.
Friar=8,000=80%=P8.0D=Economy=Currency=8 Aug.=Zeus>>E=v.
Fricassee=6,000=60%=P6.0D=Man=Earth=Royalty=6 June=Gaia=Maia>>M=M2.
Fricative=10,500=11,000=11%=P1.10D=1.1=Idea=Brainchild=11 Nov.=Athena>>I=MT.
Friction=16,000=16%=P1.60D=1.6=Cycle of Incarnation=Mind of GOD=1 June = Maia.
Friction tape=6,000=60%=P6.0D=Man=Earth=Royalty=6 June=Gaia=Maia>>M=M2.
Friday=3,500=4,000=40%=P4.0D=Govt=Creatocracy=4 April=Mercury=Hermes=G=A4.
Fridge=1,500=15%=P1.50D=1.5=Authority=Solar Crown=1 May = Maia.

Friend=13,500=14,000=14%=P1.40D=1.4=Mgt.=Solar Energy=13 May=Athena=SC=0.1
33>>3.3 is not the code for friendship but the code for genius. Everyone has a genius that friendship can help one build as experienced by Peter Matthews-Akukalia, Castle Makupedia. Hence 33 is not just a code for genius but also friendship. 33 Beer take note.

Friendly=7,500=8,000=80%=P8.0D=Economy=Currency=8 Aug.=Zeus>>E=v.
Frier=1,500=15%=P1.50D=1.5=Authority=Solar Crown=1 May = Maia.
Frieze=8,500=9,000=90%=P9.00D=9.0=Abstraction=Gods=Saturn=9Sept.>>A=Ø.
Frigate=13,000=13%=P1.30=Solar Core=Faculty=13 January=Athena.
Fright=5,500=5.5=80%=P5.50=Earth-Midway=5 May = Gaia.
Frighten=6,000=60%=P6.0D=Man=Earth=Royalty=6 June=Gaia=Maia>>M=M2.
Frightful=8,000=80%=P8.0D=Economy=Currency=8 Aug.=Zeus>>E=v.
Frigid=7,000=70%=P7.0D=7.0=Language=Assets=Mars=7 July=Pleiades.
Frigid zone=9,000=90%=P9.00D=9.0=Abstraction=Gods=Saturn=9Sept.>>A=Ø.
Frill=9,500=10,000=1,000=100%=10.0=Physicality=Tech.=10 Oct.=Uranus=P=1Ø.
Friml Charles=3,500=4,000=40%=P4.0D=Govt=Creato=4 April=Mercury=Hermes=G=A4.
Fringe=10,000=1,000=100%=10.0=Physicality=Tech.=10 Oct.=Uranus=P=1Ø.
Fringe benefit=5,000=50%=P5.00D=Law=Time=Venus=5 May = Aphrodite>>L=N.
Frippery=5,000=50%=P5.00D=Law=Time=Venus=5 May = Aphrodite>>L=N.
Frisian Islands=7,000=70%=P7.0D=7.0=Language=Assets=Mars=7 July=Pleiades.
Frisk=15,000=1,500=15%=P1.50D=1.5=Authority=Solar Crown=1 May = Maia.
Frisky=1,500=15%=P1.50D=1.5=Authority=Solar Crown=1 May = Maia.
Fritter(1)=6,000=60%=P6.0D=Man=Earth=Royalty=6 June=Gaia=Maia>>M=M2.
Fritter(2)=9,000=90%=P9.00D=9.0=Abstraction=Gods=Saturn=9Sept.>>A=Ø.
Frivolous=5,000=50%=P5.00D=Law=Time=Venus=5 May = Aphrodite>>L=N.
Frizz=7,500=8,000=80%=P8.0D=Economy=Currency=8 Aug.=Zeus>>E=v.

Frizzle(1)=9,000=90%=P9.00D=9.0=Abstraction=Gods=Saturn=9Sept.>>A=Ø.
Frizzle(2)=7,500=8,000=80%=P8.0D=Economy=Currency=8 Aug.=Zeus>>E=v.
Fro=5,000=50%=P5.00D=Law=Time=Venus=5 May = Aphrodite>>L=N.
Frobisher Martin=3,000=30%=P3.0D=3.0=Creativity=Stars=Muses=3 March = C=I>>GIL.
Frock=11,000=11%=P1.10D=1.1=Idea=Brainchild=11 Nov.=Athena>>I=MT.
Frock coat=5,000=50%=P5.00D=Law=Time=Venus=5 May = Aphrodite>>L=N.
Frog=10,000=1,000=100%=10.0=Physicality=Tech.=10 Oct.=Uranus=P=1Ø.
Frogman=5,000=50%=P5.00D=Law=Time=Venus=5 May = Aphrodite>>L=N.
Froissart Jean=2,500=3,000=30%=P3.0D=3.0=Cre=Stars=Muses=3 March = C=I>>GIL.
Frolic=6,500=7,000=70%=P7.0D=7.0=Language=Assets=Mars=7 July=Pleiades.
From=10,000=1,000=100%=10.0=Physicality=Tech.=10 Oct.=Uranus=P=1Ø.
Frond=6,000=60%=P6.0D=Man=Earth=Royalty=6 June=Gaia=Maia>>M=M2.
Front=10,000=1,000=100%=10.0=Physicality=Tech.=10 Oct.=Uranus=P=1Ø.
Frontage=10,500=11,000=11%=P1.10D=1.1=Idea=Brainchild=11 Nov.=Athena>>I=MT.
Frontal=9,000=90%=P9.00D=9.0=Abstraction=Gods=Saturn=9Sept.>>A=Ø.
Frontenac=5,000=50%=P5.00D=Law=Time=Venus=5 May = Aphrodite>>L=N.
Frontier=10,500=11,000=11%=P1.10D=1.1=Idea=Brainchild=11 Nov.=Athena>>I=MT.
Frontispiece=13,000=13%=P1.30=Solar Core=Faculty=13 January=Athena.
Frontline=10,000=1,000=100%=10.0=Physicality=Tech.=10 Oct.=Uranus=P=1Ø.
Front money=2,000=20%=P2.00D=2.0=Nature=Matter=Moon=2 Feb.=Cupid=N=C+_
Front office=4,500=5,000=50%=P5.00D=Law=Time=Venus=5 May = Aphrodite>>L=N.
Front runner=3,500=4,000=40%=P4.0D=Govt=Creatoc=4 April=Mercury=Hermes=G=A4.
Frost=10,000=1,000=100%=10.0=Physicality=Tech.=10 Oct.=Uranus=P=1Ø.
Frost Robert Lee=2,000=20%=P2.00D=2.0=Nature=Matter=Moon=2 Feb.=Cupid=N=C+_
Frostbite=6,500=7,000=70%=P7.0D=7.0=Language=Assets=Mars=7 July=Pleiades.
Frosting=7,000=70%=P7.0D=7.0=Language=Assets=Mars=7 July=Pleiades.
Frost line=4,000=40%=P4.0D=Govt=Creatocracy=4 April=Mercury=Hermes=G=A4.
Frosty=9,500=10,000=1,000=100%=10.0=Physicality=Tech.=10 Oct.=Uranus=P=1Ø.
Froth=13,000=13%=P1.30=Solar Core=Faculty=13 January=Athena.
Froufrou=5,500=5.5=80%=P5.50=Earth-Midway=5 May = Gaia.
froward=2,000=20%=P2.00D=2.0=Nature=Matter=Moon=2 Feb.=Cupid=N=C+_
Froward Cape=6,500=7,000=70%=P7.0D=7.0=Language=Assets=Mars=7 July=Pleiades.
Frown==13,000=13%=P1.30=Solar Core=Faculty=13 January=Athena.
Frowzy=1,500=15%=P1.50D=1.5=Authority=Solar Crown=1 May = Maia.
Froze=2,000=20%=P2.00D=2.0=Nature=Matter=Moon=2 Feb.=Cupid=N=C+_
Frozen=10,000=1,000=100%=10.0=Physicality=Tech.=10 Oct.=Uranus=P=1Ø.
Fructify=5,500=5.5=80%=P5.50=Earth-Midway=5 May = Gaia.
Fructose=7,500=8,000=80%=P8.0D=Economy=Currency=8 Aug.=Zeus>>E=v.
Frugal=6,500=7,000=70%=P7.0D=7.0=Language=Assets=Mars=7 July=Pleiades.
Fruit=10,000=1,000=100%=10.0=Physicality=Tech.=10 Oct.=Uranus=P=1Ø.
Fruitcake=7,500=8,000=80%=P8.0D=Economy=Currency=8 Aug.=Zeus>>E=v.
Fruit fly=6,000=60%=P6.0D=Man=Earth=Royalty=6 June=Gaia=Maia>>M=M2.
Fruitful=5,500=5.5=80%=P5.50=Earth-Midway=5 May = Gaia.
Fruition=6,000=60%=P6.0D=Man=Earth=Royalty=6 June=Gaia=Maia>>M=M2.
Fruitless=5,000=50%=P5.00D=Law=Time=Venus=5 May = Aphrodite>>L=N.

Fruity=5,000=50%=P5.00D=Law=Time=Venus=5 May = Aphrodite>>L=N.
Frump=5,500=5.5=80%=P5.50=Earth-Midway=5 May = Gaia.
Frumpish=3,000=30%=P3.0D=3.0=Creativity=Stars=Muses=3 March = C=I>>GIL.
Frunze=1,000=100%=10.0=1.0=Mind=Sun=1 January=Helios >> M=E4.
Frustrate=8,500=9,000=90%=P9.00D=9.0=Abstraction=Gods=Saturn=9Sept.>>A=Ø.
Fry(1)=11,000=11%=P1.10D=1.1=Idea=Brainchild=11 Nov.=Athena>>I=MT.
Fry(2)=5,500=5.5=80%=P5.50=Earth-Midway=5 May = Gaia.
Fryer=10,500=11,000=11%=P1.10D=1.1=Idea=Brainchild=11 Nov.=Athena>>I=MT.
Frying pan=10,000=1,000=100%=10.0=Physicality=Tech.=10 Oct.=Uranus=P=1Ø.
FSLIC=3,000=30%=P3.0D=3.0=Creativity=Stars=Muses=3 March = C=I>>GIL.
F-stop=7,000=70%=P7.0D=7.0=Language=Assets=Mars=7 July=Pleiades.
ft.=3,000=30%=P3.0D=3.0=Creativity=Stars=Muses=3 March = C=I>>GIL.
FTC=1,500=15%=P1.50D=1.5=Authority=Solar Crown=1 May = Maia.
fth.=500=5%=P5.00D=5.0=Law=Time=Venus=5 May=Aphrodite>>L=N.
Fuchou=1,000=100%=10.0=1.0=Mind=Sun=1 January=Helios >> M=E4.
Fuchsia=9,500=10,000=1,000=100%=10.0=Physicality=Tech.=10 Oct.=Uranus=P=1Ø.
Fuddle=8,000=80%=P8.0D=Economy=Currency=8 Aug.=Zeus>>E=v.
Fuddy-duddy=3,000=30%=P3.0D=3.0=Creativity=Stars=Muses=3 March = C=I>>GIL.
Fudge=60%=P6.0D=Man=Earth=Royalty=6 June=Gaia=Maia>>M=M2.
Fuel=10,000=1,000=100%=10.0=Physicality=Tech.=10 Oct.=Uranus=P=1Ø.
Fuel cell=8,500=9,000=90%=P9.00D=9.0=Abstraction=Gods=Saturn=9Sept.>>A=Ø.
Fuel oil=8,500=9,000=90%=P9.00D=9.0=Abstraction=Gods=Saturn=9Sept.>>A=Ø.
Fuel rod=5,500=5.5=80%=P5.50=Earth-Midway=5 May = Gaia.
Fugitive=11,000=11%=P1.10D=1.1=Idea=Brainchild=11 Nov.=Athena>>I=MT.
Fugue=9,000=90%=P9.00D=9.0=Abstraction=Gods=Saturn=9Sept.>>A=Ø.
Führer=7,000=70%=P7.0D=7.0=Language=Assets=Mars=7 July=Pleiades.
Fuji Mount=7,000=70%=P7.0D=7.0=Language=Assets=Mars=7 July=Pleiades.
Fukuoka=4,000=40%=P4.0D=Govt=Creatocracy=4 April=Mercury=Hermes=G=A4.
-ful=9,000=90%=P9.00D=9.0=Abstraction=Gods=Saturn=9Sept.>>A=Ø.
Fulcrum=5,500=5.5=80%=P5.50=Earth-Midway=5 May = Gaia.
Fulfill=9,000=90%=P9.00D=9.0=Abstraction=Gods=Saturn=9Sept.>>A=Ø.
Full(1)=10,000=1,000=100%=10.0=Physicality=Tech.=10 Oct.=Uranus=P=1Ø.
Full(2)=8,000=80%=P8.0D=Economy=Currency=8 Aug.=Zeus>>E=v.
Fullback=10,000=1,000=100%=10.0=Physicality=Tech.=10 Oct.=Uranus=P=1Ø.
Full blooded=3,000=30%=P3.0D=3.0=Creativity=Stars=Muses=3 March = C=I>>GIL.
Full blown=4,000=40%=P4.0D=Govt=Creatocracy=4 April=Mercury=Hermes=G=A4.
Full bodied=3,000=30%=P3.0D=3.0=Creativity=Stars=Muses=3 March = C=I>>GIL.
Full dress=3,500=4,000=40%=P4.0D=Govt=Creatoc=4 April=Mercury=Hermes=G=A4.
Fuller Richard=3,500=4,000=40%=P4.0D=Govt=Creato=4 April=Mercury=Hermes=G=A4.
Fuller, Sarah=3,000=30%=P3.0D=3.0=Creativity=Stars=Muses=3 March = C=I>>GIL.
Fullerton=5,500=5.5=80%=P5.50=Earth-Midway=5 May = Gaia.
Full-fledged=6,500=7,000=70%=P7.0D=7.0=Language=Assets=Mars=7 July=Pleiades.
Full moon=5,500=5.5=80%=P5.50=Earth-Midway=5 May = Gaia.
Full scale=4,000=40%=P4.0D=Govt=Creatocracy=4 April=Mercury=Hermes=G=A4.
Fully=2,500=3,000=30%=P3.0D=3.0=Creativity=Stars=Muses=3 March = C=I>>GIL.

Fulminate=4,000=40%=P4.0D=Govt=Creatocracy=4 April=Mercury=Hermes=G=A4.
Fulsome=5,500=5.5=80%=P5.50=Earth-Midway=5 May = Gaia.
Fulton Robert=3,000=30%=P3.0D=3.0=Creativity=Stars=Muses=3 March = C=I>>GIL.
Fumble=10,000=1,000=100%=10.0=Physicality=Tech.=10 Oct.=Uranus=P=1Ø.
Fume=10,000=1,000=100%=10.0=Physicality=Tech.=10 Oct.=Uranus=P=1Ø.
Fumigate=7,500=8,000=80%=P8.0D=Economy=Currency=8 Aug.=Zeus>>E=v.
Fun=10,000=1,000=100%=10.0=Physicality=Tech.=10 Oct.=Uranus=P=1Ø.
Function=10,000=1,000=100%=10.0=Physicality=Tech.=10 Oct.=Uranus=P=1Ø.
Functional=10,000=1,000=100%=10.0=Physicality=Tech.=10 Oct.=Uranus=P=1Ø.
Functionary=6,000=60%=P6.0D=Man=Earth=Royalty=6 June=Gaia=Maia>>M=M2.
Function word=6,000=60%=P6.0D=Man=Earth=Royalty=6 June=Gaia=Maia>>M=M2.
Fund=15,000=1,500=15%=P1.50D=1.5=Authority=Solar Crown=1 May = Maia.
Fundamental=10,000=1,000=100%=10.0=Physicality=Tech.=10 Oct.=Uranus=P=1Ø.
Fundamentalism=10,000=1,000=100%=10.0=Physicality=Tech.=10 Oct.=Uranus=P=1Ø.
Fundraiser=5,000=50%=P5.00D=Law=Time=Venus=5 May = Aphrodite>>L=N.
Fundy=7,000=70%=P7.0D=7.0=Language=Assets=Mars=7 July=Pleiades.
Funeral=9,000=90%=P9.00D=9.0=Abstraction=Gods=Saturn=9Sept.>>A=Ø.
Funeral director=4,500=5,000=50%=P5.00D=Law=Time=Venus=5 May =Odite>>L=N.
Funeral home=6,000=60%=P6.0D=Man=Earth=Royalty=6 June=Gaia=Maia>>M=M2.
Funereal=6,000=60%=P6.0D=Man=Earth=Royalty=6 June=Gaia=Maia>>M=M2.
Fungicide=2,500=3,000=30%=P3.0D=3.0=Creativity=Stars=Muses=3 March = C=I>>GIL.
Fungo=6,500=7,000=70%=P7.0D=7.0=Language=Assets=Mars=7 July=Pleiades.
Fungus=8,000=80%=P8.0D=Economy=Currency=8 Aug.=Zeus>>E=v.
Funicular=10,500=11,000=11%=P1.10D=1.1=Idea=Brainchild=11 Nov.=Athena>>I=MT.
Funk(1)=6,000=60%=P6.0D=Man=Earth=Royalty=6 June=Gaia=Maia>>M=M2.
Funk(2)=10,000=1,000=100%=10.0=Physicality=Tech.=10 Oct.=Uranus=P=1Ø.
Funky=10,000=1,000=100%=10.0=Physicality=Tech.=10 Oct.=Uranus=P=1Ø.
Funnel=10,000=1,000=100%=10.0=Physicality=Tech.=10 Oct.=Uranus=P=1Ø.
Funny=7,000=70%=P7.0D=7.0=Language=Assets=Mars=7 July=Pleiades.
Funny bone=8,500=9,000=90%=P9.00D=9.0=Abstraction=Gods=Saturn=9Sept.>>A=Ø.
Fur=12,000=12%=P1.20D=1.2=Knowledge=Education=12Dec.=Athena>>K=F.
Fur.=500=5%=P5.00D=5.0=Law=Time=Venus=5 May=Aphrodite>>L=N.
Furbelow=6,000=60%=P6.0D=Man=Earth=Royalty=6 June=Gaia=Maia>>M=M2.
Furbish=6,500=7,000=70%=P7.0D=7.0=Language=Assets=Mars=7 July=Pleiades.
Furious=9,000=90%=P9.00D=9.0=Abstraction=Gods=Saturn=9Sept.>>A=Ø.
Furl=8,000=80%=P8.0D=Economy=Currency=8 Aug.=Zeus>>E=v.
Furlong=3,000=30%=P3.0D=3.0=Creativity=Stars=Muses=3 March = C=I>>GIL.
Furlough=6,000=60%=P6.0D=Man=Earth=Royalty=6 June=Gaia=Maia>>M=M2.
Furn.=500=5%=P5.00D=5.0=Law=Time=Venus=5 May=Aphrodite>>L=N.
Furnace=8,000=80%=P8.0D=Economy=Currency=8 Aug.=Zeus>>E=v.
Furnish=7,000=70%=P7.0D=7.0=Language=Assets=Mars=7 July=Pleiades.
Furnishings=7,000=70%=P7.0D=7.0=Language=Assets=Mars=7 July=Pleiades.
Furniture=9,500=10,000=1,000=100%=10.0=Physicality=Tech.=10 Oct.=Uranus=P=1Ø.
Furor=6,000=60%=P6.0D=Man=Earth=Royalty=6 June=Gaia=Maia>>M=M2.
Furrier=6,500=7,000=70%=P7.0D=7.0=Language=Assets=Mars=7 July=Pleiades.

Furring=9,000=90%=P9.00D=9.0=Abstraction=Gods=Saturn=9Sept.>>A=Ø.
Furrow=9,500=10,000=1,000=100%=10.0=Physicality=Tech.=10 Oct.=Uranus=P=1Ø.
Furry=6,000=60%=P6.0D=Man=Earth=Royalty=6 June=Gaia=Maia>>M=M2.
Fur seal=5,500=5.5=80%=P5.50=Earth-Midway=5 May = Gaia.
Further=10,000=1,000=100%=10.0=Physicality=Tech.=10 Oct.=Uranus=P=1Ø.
Furthermore=1,500=15%=P1.50D=1.5=Authority=Solar Crown=1 May = Maia.
Furthest=10,000=1,000=100%=10.0=Physicality=Tech.=10 Oct.=Uranus=P=1Ø.
Furtive=5,500=5.5=80%=P5.50=Earth-Midway=5 May =Gaia

Furry=14,000=14%=P1.40D=1.4=Mgt.=Solar Energy/Electric=13 May=Athena=SC=0.1
Greek & Roman Myth. Furies>> The three terrible winged Goddesses who pursue and
punish doers of unavenged crimes. "Vengeance is mine says the Lord". - The Holy Bible.
Servants of Athena. Anger violence and uncontrollable action is Athena. Note that speeches
against the Holy Spirit, Council of the Gods and the Creatocracy are not forgiven.
The Gods never forget, is and should be a guiding rule for everyone in utterances and deed.

Furze=1,000=100%=10.0=1.0=Mind=Sun=1 January=Helios >> M=E4.
Fuse(1)=10,000=1,000=100%=10.0=Physicality=Tech.=10 Oct.=Uranus=P=1Ø.
Fuse(2)=10,000=1,000=100%=10.0=Physicality=Tech.=10 Oct.=Uranus=P=1Ø.
Fusee=11,000=11%=P1.10D=1.1=Idea=Brainchild=11 Nov.=Athena>>I=MT.
Fuselage=11,500=12,000=12%=P1.20D=1.2=Knowledge=Educ.=12Dec.=Athena>>K=F.
Fushun=4,500=5,000=50%=P5.00D=Law=Time=Venus=5 May = Aphrodite>>L=N.
Fusion=10,000=1,000=100%=10.0=Physicality=Tech.=10 Oct.=Uranus=P=1Ø.
Fuss=10,000=1,000=100%=10.0=Physicality=Tech.=10 Oct.=Uranus=P=1Ø.
Fuss budget=3,000=30%=P3.0D=3.0=Creativity=Stars=Muses=3 March = C=I>>GIL.
Fussy=10,000=1,000=100%=10.0=Physicality=Tech.=10 Oct.=Uranus=P=1Ø.
Fustian=3,000=30%=P3.0D=3.0=Creativity=Stars=Muses=3 March = C=I>>GIL.
Fussty=6,000=60%=P6.0D=Man=Earth=Royalty=6 June=Gaia=Maia>>M=M2.
Fut.=1,000=100%=10.0=1.0=Mind=Sun=1 January=Helios >> M=E4.
Futile=7,500=8,000=80%=P8.0D=Economy=Currency=8 Aug.=Zeus>>E=v.
Futon=9,000=90%=P9.00D=9.0=Abstraction=Gods=Saturn=9Sept.>>A=Ø.
Future=10,000=1,000=100%=10.0=Physicality=Tech.=10 Oct.=Uranus=P=1Ø.
Futuristic=6,000=60%=P6.0D=Man=Earth=Royalty=6 June=Gaia=Maia>>M=M2.
Futurity=6,500=7,000=70%=P7.0D=7.0=Language=Assets=Mars=7 July=Pleiades.
Futurology=11,500=12,000=12%=P1.20D=1.2=Knowledge=Educ.=12Dec.=Athena>>K=F.
Fuze=1,500=15%=P1.50D=1.5=Authority=Solar Crown=1 May = Maia.
Fuzee=1,500=15%=P1.50D=1.5=Authority=Solar Crown=1 May = Maia.
Fuzhou=6,000=60%=P6.0D=Man=Earth=Royalty=6 June=Gaia=Maia>>M=M2.
Fuzz(1)=9,000=90%=P9.00D=9.0=Abstraction=Gods=Saturn=9Sept.>>A=Ø.
Fuzz(2)=2,000=20%=P2.00D=2.0=Nature=Matter=Moon=2 Feb.=Cupid=N=C+_
fwd=500=5%=P5.00D=5.0=Law=Time=Venus=5 May=Aphrodite>>L=N.
FY=1,000=100%=10.0=1.0=Mind=Sun=1 January=Helios >> M=E4.
-fy=5,000=50%=P5.00D=Law=Time=Venus=5 May = Aphrodite>>L=N.
FYI=1,500=15%=P1.50D=1.5=Authority=Solar Crown=1 May = Maia.

matthewsakukaliapeter@yahoo.com <matthewsakukaliapeter@yahoo.com>
To:thecapitalist4u@yahoo.com
Wed, 1 Jun at 16:49

MAKABET =Gg=

g1=15,500=16,000=16%=P1.60D=1.6=Cycle of Life=Incarn.=Mind of GOD=1 June = Maia.
The 7th letter of the English alphabet. The 5th tone in the C major tone.
Result shows that G is an incarnation that controls the cycle of life.
The weight of g1 is thus computed >> 7.0*5.0=p=12+35=47x=px=467=500=50%=5.0=Law
>>Time>>Aphrodite.
Now a unit of acceleration equal to the acceleration caused by gravity at the earth's
surface, about 9.8 m (32ft) per second. This indicates that gravity is the law of time. What
we call gravity is precisely determined as the measure of time. Incarnation and the cycle of
life occurs as a certain process of free fall of the celestial to the terrestrial. The only thing
that falls this way without interference is rain. Hence rainfall is the physical manifestation
by which spirits incarnate mankind and move through the earth unhindered.

g2=500=5%=P5.00D=5.0=Law=Time=Venus=5 May=Aphrodite>>L=N.
G1=6,000=60%=P6.0D=Man=Earth=Royalty=6 June=Gaia=Maia>>M=M2.
G2=2,500=3,000=30%=P3.0D=3.0=Creativity=Stars=Muses=3 March = C=I>>GIL.
Ga=2,500=3,000=30%=P3.0D=3.0=Creativity=Stars=Muses=3 March = C=I>>GIL.
GA=4,000=40%=P4.0D=Govt.=Creatocracy=4 April=Mercury=Hermes=G=A4.
ga.=500=5%=P5.00D=5.0=Law=Time=Venus=5 May=Aphrodite>>L=N.
Gab=3,000=30%=P3.0D=3.0=Creativity=Stars=Muses=3 March = C=I>>GIL.
Gabardine=4,500=5,000=50%=P5.00D=Law=Time=Venus=5 May = Aphrodite>>L=N.
Gabble=8,500=9,000=90%=P9.00D=9.0=Abstraction=Gods=Saturn=9Sept.>>A=Ø.
Gabby=1,500=15%=P1.50D=1.5=Authority=Solar Crown=1 May = Maia.
Gabon=7,000=70%=P7.0D=7.0=Language=Assets=Mars=7 July=Pleiades.
Gaborone=7,000=70%=P7.0D=7.0=Language=Assets=Mars=7 July=Pleiades.
Gad=5,000=50%=P5.00D=Law=Time=Venus=5 May = Aphrodite>>L=N.
Gadabout=5,500=5.5=80%=P5.50=Earth-Midway=5 May = Gaia.
Gadfly=8,500=9,000=90%=P9.00D=9.0=Abstraction=Gods=Saturn=9Sept.>>A=Ø.
Gadget=4,000=40%=P4.0D=Govt.=Creatocracy=4 April=Mercury=Hermes=G=A4.
Gadolinium=15,000=1,500=15%=P1.50D=1.5=Authority=Solar Crown=1 May = Maia.

Gaea=8,500=9,000=90%=P9.00D=9.0=Abstraction=Gods=Saturn=9Sept.>>A=Ø.
Greek myth. The Goddess of the Earth who bore and married Uranus and became the
mother of the Titans and the Cyclops. Result shows correctness as as it indicates the Gods.
She is the borderline between business and religion, economy and faith, currency and
software. All abstractions come from Gaea (Gaia) and make birth persons royalty such as

Peter Matthews-Akukalia. More or less she is a grandmother position to Zeus. Possibly a transmuted Maia at Earth level. See gl.

Gael=6,000=60%=P6.0D=Man=Earth=Royalty=6 June=Gaia=Maia>>M=M2.
A Celtic speaking Celt of Scotland, Ireland, or the Isle of Man. Proved

---

Gaelic=5,000=50%=P5.00D=Law=Time=Venus=5 May = Aphrodite>>L=N.
Gaff=11,000=11%=P1.10D=1.1=Idea=Brainchild=Inv.=11 Nov.=SC=Athena>>I=MT.
Gaffe=3,000=30%=P3.0D=3.0=Creativity=Stars=Muses=3 March = C=I>>GIL.
Gaffer=9,000=90%=P9.00D=9.0=Abstraction=Gods=Saturn=9Sept.>>A=Ø.
Gag=10,000=1,000=100%=10.0=Physicality=Tech.=10 Oct.=Uranus=P=1Ø.
Gaga=5,000=50%=P5.00D=Law=Time=Venus=5 May = Aphrodite>>L=N.
Gagel=9,000=90%=P9.00D=9.0=Abstraction=Gods=Saturn=9Sept.>>A=Ø.
Gage2=1,500=15%=P1.50D=1.5=Authority=Solar Crown=1 May = Maia.
Gage Thomas=3,500=4,000=40%=P4.0D=Govt.=Creat.=4 April=Mercury=Hermes=G=A4.
Gaggle=2,500=3,000=30%=P3.0D=3.0=Creativity=Stars=Muses=3 March = C=I>>GIL.
Gag order=7,000=70%=P7.0D=7.0=Language=Assets=Mars=7 July=Pleiades.
Gag rule=6,500=7,000=70%=P7.0D=7.0=Language=Assets=Mars=7 July=Pleiades.
Gagster=4,500=5,000=50%=P5.00D=Law=Time=Venus=5 May = Aphrodite>>L=N.

Gaia=2,500=3,000=30%=P3.0D=3.0=Creativity=Stars=Muses=3 March = C=I>>GIL.
Greek myth. Earth Goddess, daughter of Chaos. She was the mother and wife of Uranus (Heaven). Their offsprings were the Titans and Cyclopes. Gaia means Earth. The Creatocracy ranks Gaia as the 6th dimension of the Universe with human birth type as royalty and highly emotional person. Often drawn to older persons in relationships.

2,500>>25>>52>>5.2>>Intellectual Property >> 3,000>>3.0
The Earth is a place of transition through the borders to freedom. Greek myth teaches how Zeus conquered and imprisoned the Titans. Gaia is bound only Creativity can free her. The Zeus must return as an incarnate to free her. This is a mystery of Castle Makupedia. See Psalm 82. Romans 8. Ephesians 1:10-14.

In the beginning God created the heaven and the earth. Translates to (Inside the Moon and Venus the Creatocracy or Council of Gods (God>>Godship) synchronized and crystallized (created) Uranus (heaven) and Gaia (the earth). And (but) the Earth (Gaia) was without form (was born or was with Chaos her mother) and darkness (God of the underworld >> Hermes) was upon the face of the deep (governed from the underworld). And the Spirit of God (Athena) moved upon the face of the waters (led a council with Aphrodite - born of the foam of the ocean to develop systems). - Genesis 1:1-3. See gl, Gaea. The Rulers of the earth are Gaia, Hermes, Athena, Aphrodite >> Royalty through Intellectual Property, Merchandise, Wisdom and Love. Gaia is ancient and older hence ancient knowledge found in the Scriptures and books are sources of inspiration.

Gaia governs all Muses whose task is to take man to the peak of aspiration, the point of godly perfection achievable only through Creatocratic precision. The Earth is their residence through which they are able to communicate with mankind. Hecate is the Goddess of witchcraft ghosts sorcery prophecy unconventionality night and caregivers. She existed in the center between the birth of the Titans and the Olympian Gods. Hecate is honored every 30th November with an energy base of 1.4>>23.3%. Her world is in Hades and the Moon. Hecate is the Goddess of dark places associated with Artemis and Selene. She is most probably the eye of Gaia that makes prophecy possible and helps true royals or Gaians do things beyond the ordinary such as understanding time. Creativity in all its forms is the standard by which all existence is measured because all things come from creativity. Creatocracy is the golden rule. Our school of thought is Creatocracy, the Creatocrat. Castle Makupedia is the God of Creatocracy Genius & Mind.

GAIANS PERSONALITY DATABASE.

1. They originate from Chaos and so are driven by ancient knowledge and powers.
2. They receive inspiration from the eastern muses at 3.0=30%, revelation from the western Gods at 9.0=90% and ancient knowledge and wisdom from Athena at dimension 12>>1.2>>120Maks=over 100%.
3. Gaians are born on the value 6.0=60% and so are highly emotional being intelligent thoughtful, strong willed and love variety just as the Mother Earth in birth.
4. At 0+_ subjective environmental derived energy they are often at thresholds of survival edgy and overtly cautions a natural incentive to fight hard to get to the top to ensure financial security through rights earned through creativity. This is why they are very ambitious in nature.
5. They love to build large families which most times are polygamous if they are males and bear many children if they are females making them royal in nature and nation builders.
6. They are born with natural genius about 33 times a year. 33>>3.3G energy.
7. On the digital spiral Zeus is at the center of such existence meaning that business and currency mediates between the emotion and creativity. In turn the creativity drives the mind in order to ensure stability. So it is true that Gaia 6.0 birthed Zeus who birthed the muses 3.0. It also means that Earth draws certain energy from Jupiter releasing excess to sustain the stars. $\emptyset D=\emptyset S=\emptyset T >> \emptyset 6.0=\emptyset 8.0=\emptyset 3.0 >> \emptyset 3.0=\emptyset 1.0=\emptyset 2.0$
8. Code word for Gaia is World as in the world. So Gaia is the World and the World is Gaia.

Their births dates are seen below.

==

MONTH: JANUARY.
Day 6:Value: 6.0, Planetary Type: Earth, Human Type: Health, Birth Energy Level : 100%.
Day 22:Value: 6.0, Planetary Type: Earth, Human Type: Health, Birth Energy Level: 100%
Day 23:Value: 6.0, Planetary Type: Earth, Human Type: Health, Birth Energy Level: 100%

==

MONTH:FEBRUARY
Day 4:Value: 6.2, Planetary Type: Earth, Human Type:Health Birth Energy Level:100%
Day 15:Value: 6.0, Planetary Type:Earth, Human Type:Health, Birth Energy Level:100%
Day 16:Value: 6.3, Planetary Type:Earth, Human Type:Health, Birth Energy Level:100%
===
MONTH:MARCH
Day 12:Value:6.0, Planetary Type:Earth, Human Type:Health, Birth Energy Level:100.0%
===
MONTH:APRIL
Day 2:Value:6.2, Planetary Type:Earth, Human Type:Health, Birth Energy Level:100%+
Day 10:Value:6.1, Planetary Type:Earth, Human Type:Health, Birth Energy Level:100%+
===
MONTH: MAY
Day 8:Value:6.0, Planetary Type:Earth, Human Type:Health, Birth Energy Level:100%
Day 31:Value:6.0, Planetary Type:Earth, Human Type:Health, Birth Energy Level:100%
===
MONTH:JUNE.
Day 1:Value:6.0 Planetary Type:Earth, Human Type:Health, Birth Energy Level:100%
Day 7:Value:6.0 Planetary Type:Earth Human Type:Health Birth Energy Level:100%
Day 27:Value:6.0 Planetary Type:Earth Human Type:Health Birth Energy Level:100%
Day 28:Value:6.0 Planetary Type:Earth Human Type:Health Birth Energy Level:100%
Day 29:Value:6.3 Planetary Type:Earth Human Type:Health Birth Energy Level:100%+
===
MONTH:JULY
Day 6:Value:6.0 Planetary Type:Earth Human Type: Health Birth Energy Level:100%
Day 25: Value:6.0 Planetary Type:Earth Human Type:Health Birth Energy Level:100%
Day 26:Value:6.2 Planetary Type:Earth Human Type:Health Birth Energy Level:100%+
===
MONTH:AUGUST
Day 5:Value:6.0 Planetary Type:Earth Human Type:Health Birth Energy Level:100%
Day 22:Value:6.0 Planetary Type:Earth Human Type:Health Birth Energy Level:100%
Day 23:Value:6.0 Planetary Type:Earth Human Type:Health Birth Energy Level:100%
Day 24:Value:6.1 Planetary Type:Earth Human Type:Health Birth Energy Level:100%
===
MONTH:SEPTEMBER
Day 21:Value:6.0 Planetary Type:Earth Human Type:Health Birth Energy Level:100%
Day 22:Value:6.4 Planetary Type:Earth Human Type:Health Birth Energy Level:100%+
===
MONTH:OCTOBER
Day 4:Value:6.1 Planetary Type:Earth Human Type:Health Birth Energy Level:100%
Day 19:Value:6.0 Planetary Type:Earth Human Type:Health Birth Energy Level:100%
Day 20:Value:6.2 Planetary Type:Earth Human Type:Health Birth Energy Level:100%+
===

MONTH:NOVEMBER
Day 17: Value:6.0 Planetary Type:Earth Human Type:Health Birth Energy Level:100%
Day 18: Value:6.0 Planetary Type:Earth Human Type:Health Birth Energy Level:100%
==
MONTH:DECEMBER
Day 3:Value:6.0 Planetary Type:Earth Human Type: Health Birth Energy Level:100%
Day 16:Value:6.0 Planetary Type:Earth Human Type: Health Birth Energy Level:100%
Day 17:Value:6.2 Planetary Type:Earth Human Type:Health Birth Energy Level:100%+

Gaiety=4,000=40%=P4.0D=Govt.=Creatocracy=4 April=Mercury=Hermes=G=A4.
Gaily=4,500=5,000=50%=P5.00D=Law=Time=Venus=5 May = Aphrodite>>L=N.
Gain=10,000=1,000=100%=10.0=Physicality=Tech.=10 Oct.=Uranus=P=1Ø.
Gainer=10,000=1,000=100%=10.0=Physicality=Tech.=10 Oct.=Uranus=P=1Ø.
Gainful=3,000=30%=P3.0D=3.0=Creativity=Stars=Muses=3 March = C=I>>GIL.
Gain say=5,500=5.5=80%=P5.50=Earth-Midway=5 May = Gaia.
Gainsborough Thomas=3,500=4,000=40%=P4.0D=Govt.=Creato.=4 April=Hermes=G=A4.
Gait=10,000=1,000=100%=10.0=Physicality=Tech.=10 Oct.=Uranus=P=1Ø.
Gaiter=10,000=1,000=100%=10.0=Physicality=Tech.=10 Oct.=Uranus=P=1Ø.
Gal=2,500=3,000=30%=P3.0D=3.0=Creativity=Stars=Muses=3 March = C=I>>GIL.
Gal.=1,000=100%=Physicality=Tech.=10 Oct.=Uranus=P=1Ø.
Gala=5,500=5.5=80%=P5.50=Earth-Midway=5 May = Gaia.
Galactose=6,500=7,000=70%=P7.0D=7.0=Language=Assets=Mars=7 July=Pleiades.
Galahad=7,500=7,500=8,000=80%=P8.0D=Economy=Currency=8 Aug.=Zeus>>E=v.
Galápagos Islands=7,000=70%=P7.0D=7.0=Language=Assets=Mars=7 July=Pleiades.

Galatia=7,000=70%=P7.0D=7.0=Language=Assets=Mars=7 July=Pleiades.
An ancient country of Central Asia Minor in the region surrounding modern Ankara,
Turkey.

Galatians=2,000=20%=P2.00D=2.0=Nature=Matter=Moon=2 Feb.=Cupid=N=C+_
From Galatia we conclude that Aries the God of war inspired the book of Galatians.

Galaxy=15,000=1,500=15%=P1.50D=1.5=Authority=Solar Crown=1 May = Maia.

Gale=5,000=50%=P5.00D=Law=Time=Venus=5 May = Aphrodite>>L=N.
A very strong wind. A forceful outburst, as of laughter. Aphrodite does this laughter often
depicted by witches in the movies when something evil is about to happen and there is
seemingly no remedy in sight for the purposes victim.

Galen=4,500=5,000=50%=P5.00D=Law=Time=Venus=5 May = Aphrodite>>L=N.
Galena=6,500=7,000=70%=P7.0D=7.0=Language=Assets=Mars=7 July=Pleiades.
Galicia=11,000=11%=P1.10D=1.1=Idea=Brainchild=Inv.=11 Nov.=SC=Athena>>I=MT.

Galilee=2,500=3,000=30%=P3.0D=3.0=Creativity=Stars=Muses=3 March = C=I>>GIL.
Galilee, Sea of.=4,000=40%=P4.0D=Govt.=Creatocracy=4 April=Mercury=Hermes=G=A4.

Galileo Galilei=3,000=30%=P3.0D=3.0=Creativity=Stars=Muses=3 March = C=I>>GIL.
An incarnated Muse.

Gall1=5,500=5.5=80%=P5.50=Earth-Midway=5 May = Gaia.
Gall2=9,500=10,000=1,000=100%=10.0=Physicality=Tech.=10 Oct.=Uranus=P=1Ø.
Gall3=7,500=7,500=8,000=80%=P8.0D=Economy=Currency=8 Aug.=Zeus>>E=v.
Gallant=10,000=1,000=100%=10.0=Physicality=Tech.=10 Oct.=Uranus=P=1Ø.
Gall bladder=9,000=90%=P9.00D=9.0=Abstraction=Gods=Saturn=9Sept.>>A=Ø.
Galleon=11,000=11%=P1.10D=1.1=Idea=Brainchild=Inv.=11 Nov.=SC=Athena>>I=MT.
Gallery=10,000=1,000=100%=10.0=Physicality=Tech.=10 Oct.=Uranus=P=1Ø.
Galley=10,000=1,000=100%=10.0=Physicality=Tech.=10 Oct.=Uranus=P=1Ø.
Gallic=3,500=4,000=40%=P4.0D=Govt.=Creatocracy=4 April=Mercury=Hermes=G=A4.
Gallium=11,500=12,000=12%=P1.20D=1.2=Knowledge=Education=12Dec.=Athena>>K=F.
Gallivant=6,500=7,000=70%=P7.0D=7.0=Language=Assets=Mars=7 July=Pleiades.
Gallon=4,000=40%=P4.0D=Govt.=Creatocracy=4 April=Mercury=Hermes=G=A4.
Gallop=9,500=10,000=1,000=100%=10.0=Physicality=Tech.=10 Oct.=Uranus=P=1Ø.
Gallows=6,000=60%=P6.0D=Man=Earth=Royalty=6 June=Gaia=Maia>>M=M2.
Gallows humor=4,000=40%=P4.0D=Govt.=Creatocracy=4 April=Mercury=Hermes=G=A4.
Gallstone=6,000=60%=P6.0D=Man=Earth=Royalty=6 June=Gaia=Maia>>M=M2.
Galore=3,000=30%=P3.0D=3.0=Creativity=Stars=Muses=3 March = C=I>>GIL.
Galosh=4,500=5,000=50%=P5.00D=Law=Time=Venus=5 May = Aphrodite>>L=N.
Galsworthy John=3,000=30%=P3.0D=3.0=Creativity=Stars=Muses=3 March = C=I>>GIL.
Galvani Luigl=3,000=30%=P3.0D=3.0=Creativity=Stars=Muses=3 March = C=I>>GIL.
Galvanic=10,000=1,000=100%=10.0=Physicality=Tech.=10 Oct.=Uranus=P=1Ø.
Galvanize=11,000=11%=P1.10D=1.1=Idea=Brainchild=Inv.=11 Nov.=SC=Athena>>I=MT.
Galvanometer=10,000=1,000=100%=10.0=Physicality=Tech.=10 Oct.=Uranus=P=1Ø.
Galveston=8,500=9,000=90%=P9.00D=9.0=Abstraction=Gods=Saturn=9Sept.>>A=Ø.
Galway=7,500=7,500=8,000=80%=P8.0D=Economy=Currency=8 Aug.=Zeus>>E=v.
Gama Vasco da.=4,000=40%=P4.0D=Govt.=Creato.=4 April=Mercury=Hermes=G=A4.
Gambia=6,000=60%=P6.0D=Man=Earth=Royalty=6 June=Gaia=Maia>>M=M2.
Gambia River=11,000=11%=P1.10D=1.1=Idea=Brainchild=Inv.=11 Nov.=SC=Athena>>I=MT.
Gambit=10,000=1,000=100%=10.0=Physicality=Tech.=10 Oct.=Uranus=P=1Ø.
Gamble=10,000=1,000=100%=10.0=Physicality=Tech.=10 Oct.=Uranus=P=1Ø.
Gambol=4,000=40%=P4.0D=Govt.=Creatocracy=4 April=Mercury=Hermes=G=A4.
Gambrel roof=11,500=12,000=12%=P1.20D=1.2=Knowledge=Edu.=12Dec.=Athena>>K=F.

Game1=10,000=1,000=100%=10.0=Physicality=Tech.=10 Oct.=Uranus=P=1Ø.
Game2=1,000=100%=10.0=1.0=Mind=Sun=1 January=Helios >> M=E4.
Peter Matthews-Akukalia, Castle Makupedia invented the Makabet games etc.

Gamecock=2,500=3,000=30%=P3.0D=3.0=Creativity=Stars=Muses=3 March = C=I>>GIL.
Gamekeeper=6,500=7,000=70%=P7.0D=7.0=Language=Assets=Mars=7 July=Pleiades.
Gamesmanship=7,000=70%=P7.0D=7.0=Language=Assets=Mars=7 July=Pleiades.
Gamester=1,500=15%=P1.50D=1.5=Authority=Solar Crown=1 May = Maia.
Gamete=7,500=7,500=8,000=80%=P8.0D=Economy=Currency=8 Aug.=Zeus>>E=v.
Gamin=4,500=5,000=50%=P5.00D=Law=Time=Venus=5 May = Aphrodite>>L=N.
Gamine=6,500=7,000=70%=P7.0D=7.0=Language=Assets=Mars=7 July=Pleiades.
Gamma=4,000=40%=P4.0D=Govt.=Creatocracy=4 April=Mercury=Hermes=G=A4.
Gamma globulin=9,500=10,000=1,000=100%=Physicality=Tech.=10 Oct.=Uranus=P=1Ø.
Gamma ray=7,500=8,000=80%=P8.0D=Economy=Currency=8 Aug.=Zeus>>E=v.
Gammon=8,500=9,000=90%=P9.00D=9.0=Abstraction=Gods=Saturn=9Sept.>>A=Ø.
-gamous=5,000=50%=P5.00D=Law=Time=Venus=5 May = Aphrodite>>L=N.
Gamut=5,500=5.5=80%=P5.50=Earth-Midway=5 May = Gaia.
Gamy=8,500=9,000=90%=P9.00D=9.0=Abstraction=Gods=Saturn=9Sept.>>A=Ø.
Gander=3,500=4,000=40%=P4.0D=Govt.=Creatocracy=4 April=Mercury=Hermes=G=A4.

Gandhi Indira Nehru=5,500=5.5=80%=P5.50=Earth-Midway=5 May = Gaia.
Gaia incarnated and returned as Indira Nehru Gandhi.

Gandhi, Mohandas Karamchad.=4,000=40%=P4.0D=Govt.=Creat.=4 April=Hermes=G=A4.
Hermes >> Jesus Christ incarnated and returned as "Mahatma" Gandhi.

Gang=10,000=1,000=100%=10.0=Physicality=Tech.=10 Oct.=Uranus=P=1Ø.
Ganges=10,500=11,000=11%=P1.10D=1.1=Idea=Brainchild=Inv.=11 Nov.=Athena>>I=MT.
Gangling=4,500=5,000=50%=P5.00D=Law=Time=Venus=5 May = Aphrodite>>L=N.
Ganglions=9,500=10,000=1,000=100%=10.0=Physicality=Tech.=10 Oct.=Uranus=P=1Ø.
Gangly=2,000=20%=P2.00D=2.0=Nature=Matter=Moon=2 Feb.=Cupid=N=C+_
Gangplank=7,000=70%=P7.0D=7.0=Language=Assets=Mars=7 July=Pleiades.
Gangrene=9,000=90%=P9.00D=9.0=Abstraction=Gods=Saturn=9Sept.>>A=Ø.
Gangster=4,500=5,000=50%=P5.00D=Law=Time=Venus=5 May = Aphrodite>>L=N.
Gangway=8,500=9,000=90%=P9.00D=9.0=Abstraction=Gods=Saturn=9Sept.>>A=Ø.
Ganja=2,000=20%=P2.00D=2.0=Nature=Matter=Moon=2 Feb.=Cupid=N=C+_
Gannet=8,500=9,000=90%=P9.00D=9.0=Abstraction=Gods=Saturn=9Sept.>>A=Ø.
Gantlet=2,000=20%=P2.00D=2.0=Nature=Matter=Moon=2 Feb.=Cupid=N=C+_
Gantry=10,000=1,000=100%=10.0=Physicality=Tech.=10 Oct.=Uranus=P=1Ø.
GAO=1,500=15%=P1.50D=1.5=Authority=Solar Crown=1 May = Maia.
Gaol=2,500=3,000=30%=P3.0D=3.0=Creativity=Stars=Muses=3 March = C=I>>GIL.
Gap=10,000=1,000=100%=10.0=Physicality=Tech.=10 Oct.=Uranus=P=1Ø.
Gape=10,000=1,000=100%=10.0=Physicality=Tech.=10 Oct.=Uranus=P=1Ø.
Gar=10,000=1,000=100%=10.0=Physicality=Tech.=10 Oct.=Uranus=P=1Ø.
GAR=2,500=3,000=30%=P3.0D=3.0=Creativity=Stars=Muses=3 March = C=I>>GIL.
Garage=10,000=1,000=100%=10.0=Physicality=Tech.=10 Oct.=Uranus=P=1Ø.
Garage sale=6,000=60%=P6.0D=Man=Earth=Royalty=6 June=Gaia=Maia>>M=M2.
Garb=6,500=7,000=70%=P7.0D=7.0=Language=Assets=Mars=7 July=Pleiades.

Garbage=7,000=70%=P7.0D=7.0=Language=Assets=Mars=7 July=Pleiades.
Garbanzo=2,500=3,000=30%=P3.0D=3.0=Creativity=Stars=Muses=3 March = C=I>>GIL.
Garble=10,500=11,000=11%=P1.10D=1.1=Idea=Brainchild=Inv.=11 Nov.=Athena>>I=MT.
Garcia Lorca=2,500=3,000=30%=P3.0D=3.0=Creatv.=Stars=Muses=3 March = C=I>>GIL.
Garden=10,000=1,000=100%=10.0=Physicality=Tech.=10 Oct.=Uranus=P=1Ø.
Garden Grove=10,000=1,000=100%=10.0=Physicality=Tech.=10 Oct.=Uranus=P=1Ø.
Gardenia=5,500=5.5=80%=P5.50=Earth-Midway=5 May = Gaia.
Garden variety=1,000=100%=Physicality=Tech.=10 Oct.=Uranus=P=1Ø.
Garfield James=5,000=50%=P5.00D=Law=Time=Venus=5 May = Aphrodite>>L=N.
Gargantuan=6,000=60%=P6.0D=Man=Earth=Royalty=6 June=Gaia=Maia>>M=M2.
Gargle=10,000=1,000=100%=10.0=Physicality=Tech.=10 Oct.=Uranus=P=1Ø.
Gargoyle=7,000=70%=P7.0D=7.0=Language=Assets=Mars=7 July=Pleiades.
Garibaldi Giuseppe=3,000=30%=P3.0D=3.0=Creatv.=Stars=Muses=3 March = C=I>>GIL.
Garish=4,500=5,000=50%=P5.00D=Law=Time=Venus=5 May = Aphrodite>>L=N.
Garland=7,000=70%=P7.0D=7.0=Language=Assets=Mars=7 July=Pleiades.
Garlic=10,000=1,000=100%=10.0=Physicality=Tech.=10 Oct.=Uranus=P=1Ø.
Garment=4,000=40%=P4.0D=Govt.=Creatocracy=4 April=Mercury=Hermes=G=A4.
Garner=3,000=30%=P3.0D=3.0=Creativity=Stars=Muses=3 March = C=I>>GIL.
Garnet=10,000=1,000=100%=10.0=Physicality=Tech.=10 Oct.=Uranus=P=1Ø.
Garnish=10,000=1,000=100%=10.0=Physicality=Tech.=10 Oct.=Uranus=P=1Ø.
Garnishee=2,000=20%=P2.00D=2.0=Nature=Matter=Moon=2 Feb.=Cupid=N=C+_
Garnishment=10,500=11,000=11%=P1.10D=1.1=Idea=Brainchild=11 Nov.=Athena>>I=MT.
Garonne=9,000=90%=P9.00D=9.0=Abstraction=Gods=Saturn=9Sept.>>A=Ø.
Garret=7,000=70%=P7.0D=7.0=Language=Assets=Mars=7 July=Pleiades.
Garrison=7,500=8,000=80%=P8.0D=Economy=Currency=8 Aug.=Zeus>>E=v.
Garrison William=3,000=30%=P3.0D=3.0=Creativity=Stars=Muses=3 March = C=I>>GIL.
Garrote=10,000=1,000=100%=10.0=Physicality=Tech.=10 Oct.=Uranus=P=1Ø.
Garrulous=2,500=3,000=30%=P3.0D=3.0=Creativity=Stars=Muses=3 March = C=I>>GIL.
Garter=8,500=9,000=90%=P9.00D=9.0=Abstraction=Gods=Saturn=9Sept.>>A=Ø.
Garter snake=4,000=40%=P4.0D=Govt.=Creatocracy=4 April=Mercury=Hermes=G=A4.
Garvey Marcus=5,500=5.5=80%=P5.50=Earth-Midway=5 May = Gaia.
Gary=7,000=70%=P7.0D=7.0=Language=Assets=Mars=7 July=Pleiades.
Gas=10,000=1,000=100%=10.0=Physicality=Tech.=10 Oct.=Uranus=P=1Ø.
Gas chamber=5,500=5.5=80%=P5.50=Earth-Midway=5 May = Gaia.
Gascony=4,500=5,000=50%=P5.00D=Law=Time=Venus=5 May = Aphrodite>>L=N.
Gash=5,000=50%=P5.00D=Law=Time=Venus=5 May = Aphrodite>>L=N.
Gasket=10,000=1,000=100%=10.0=Physicality=Tech.=10 Oct.=Uranus=P=1Ø.
Gas light=4,000=40%=P4.0D=Govt.=Creatocracy=4 April=Mercury=Hermes=G=A4.
Gas mask=9,000=90%=P9.00D=9.0=Abstraction=Gods=Saturn=9Sept.>>A=Ø.
Gasohol=7,000=70%=P7.0D=7.0=Language=Assets=Mars=7 July=Pleiades.
Gasoline=10,000=1,000=100%=10.0=Physicality=Tech.=10 Oct.=Uranus=P=1Ø.
Gasp=10,000=1,000=100%=10.0=Physicality=Tech.=10 Oct.=Uranus=P=1Ø.
Gaspé Peninsula=8,000=80%=P8.0D=Economy=Currency=8 Aug.=Zeus>>E=v.
Gassy=2,000=20%=P2.00D=2.0=Nature=Matter=Moon=2 Feb.=Cupid=N=C+_
Gastric=12,000=12%=P1.20D=1.2=Knowledge=Education=12Dec.=Athena>>K=F.

Gastric juice=5,000=50%=P5.00D=Law=Time=Venus=5 May = Aphrodite>>L=N.
Gastritis=3,500=4,000=40%=P4.0D=Govt.=Creat.=4 April=Mercury=Hermes=G=A4.
Gastro-=2,500=3,000=30%=P3.0D=3.0=Creativity=Stars=Muses=3 March = C=I>>GIL.
Gastroenteritis=4,500=5,000=50%=P5.00D=Law=Time=Venus=5 May = Aphrodite>>L=N.
Gastrointestinal=2,000=20%=P2.00D=2.0=Nature=Matter=Moon=2 Feb.=Cupid=N=C+_
Gastrology=4,000=40%=P4.0D=Govt.=Creatocracy=4 April=Mercury=Hermes=G=A4.
Gastronomy=6,000=60%=P6.0D=Man=Earth=Royalty=6 June=Gaia=Maia>>M=M2.
Gastropod=13,000=13%=P1.30=Solar Core=Faculty=13 January=Athena.
Gasworks=5,000=50%=P5.00D=Law=Time=Venus=5 May = Aphrodite>>L=N.
Gate=10,000=1,000=100%=10.0=Physicality=Tech.=10 Oct.=Uranus=P=1Ø.
Gatecrasher=7,500=8,000=80%=P8.0D=Economy=Currency=8 Aug.=Zeus>>E=v.
Gates Horatio=3,000=30%=P3.0D=3.0=Creativity=Stars=Muses=3 March = C=I>>GIL.
Gateshead=5,500=5.5=80%=P5.50=Earth-Midway=5 May = Gaia.
Gateway=8,500=9,000=90%=P9.00D=9.0=Abstraction=Gods=Saturn=9Sept.>>A=Ø.
Gather=10,000=1,000=100%=10.0=Physicality=Tech.=10 Oct.=Uranus=P=1Ø.
Gator=1,500=15%=P1.50D=1.5=Authority=Solar Crown=1 May = Maia.
Gauche=3,000=30%=P3.0D=3.0=Creativity=Stars=Muses=3 March = C=I>>GIL.
Gaucho=4,000=40%=P4.0D=Govt.=Creatocracy=4 April=Mercury=Hermes=G=A4.
Gaudy=9,000=90%=P9.00D=9.0=Abstraction=Gods=Saturn=9Sept.>>A=Ø.

Gauge=10,000=1,000=100%=10.0=Physicality=Tech.=10 Oct.=Uranus=P=1Ø.
The Makumeter Gauge or Calibrated Curiosity Levels Table CCLT is an instrument that measures the emotions of a person in the Mind Assessment Test. Invented by Peter Matthews-Akukalia in his book>> THE ORACLE. Principles of Creative Sciences.

Gauguin Eugène=3,000=30%=P3.0D=3.0=Creativity=Stars=Muses=3 March = C=I>>GIL.
Gaul1=2,500=3,000=30%=P3.0D=3.0=Creativity=Stars=Muses=3 March = C=I>>GIL.
Gaul2=7,000=70%=P7.0D=7.0=Language=Assets=Mars=7 July=Pleiades.
Gaulish=3,000=30%=P3.0D=3.0=Creativity=Stars=Muses=3 March = C=I>>GIL.
Gaunt=3,000=30%=P3.0D=3.0=Creativity=Stars=Muses=3 March = C=I>>GIL.
Gauntlet1=4,000=40%=P4.0D=Govt.=Creatocracy=4 April=Mercury=Hermes=G=A4.
Gauntlet2=10,000=1,000=100%=10.0=Physicality=Tech.=10 Oct.=Uranus=P=1Ø.
Gautier Théophile=2,000=20%=P2.00D=2.0=Nature=Matter=Moon=2 Feb.=Cupid=N=C+_
Gauze=5,000=50%=P5.00D=Law=Time=Venus=5 May = Aphrodite>>L=N.
Gave=1,500=15%=P1.50D=1.5=Authority=Solar Crown=1 May = Maia.
Gavel=9,000=90%=P9.00D=9.0=Abstraction=Gods=Saturn=9Sept.>>A=Ø.
Gavotte=4,000=40%=P4.0D=Govt.=Creatocracy=4 April=Mercury=Hermes=G=A4.
Gawk=7,000=70%=P7.0D=7.0=Language=Assets=Mars=7 July=Pleiades.
Gay=21,000>=12,000=12%=P1.20D=1.2=Knowledge=Education=12Dec.=Athena>>K=F.
Gay John=2,000=20%=P2.00D=2.0=Nature=Matter=Moon=2 Feb.=Cupid=N=C+_
Gaza=5,000=50%=P5.00D=Law=Time=Venus=5 May = Aphrodite>>L=N.
Gaze=5,000=50%=P5.00D=Law=Time=Venus=5 May = Aphrodite>>L=N.
Gazebo=6,000=60%=P6.0D=Man=Earth=Royalty=6 June=Gaia=Maia>>M=M2.
Gazelle=5,500=5.5=80%=P5.50=Earth-Midway=5 May = Gaia.

Gazette=3,500=4,000=40%=P4.0D=Govt.=Creatocracy=4 April=Mercury=Hermes=G=A4.
Gazetteer=2,500=3,000=30%=P3.0D=3.0=Creativity=Stars=Muses=3 March = C=I>>GIL.
Gaziantep=5,000=50%=P5.00D=Law=Time=Venus=5 May = Aphrodite>>L=N.
Gazpacho=5,500=5.5=80%=P5.50=Earth-Midway=5 May = Gaia.
G.B.=1,000=100%=10.0=1.0=Mind=Sun=1 January=Helios >> M=E4.
G clef=6,500=7,000=70%=P7.0D=7.0=Language=Assets=Mars=7 July=Pleiades.
GCT=1,500=15%=P1.50D=1.5=Authority=Solar Crown=1 May = Maia.
Gd=2,500=3,000=30%=P3.0D=3.0=Creativity=Stars=Muses=3 March = C=I>>GIL.
Gdańsk=5,000=50%=P5.00D=Law=Time=Venus=5 May = Aphrodite>>L=N.
Ge=2,500=3,000=30%=P3.0D=3.0=Creativity=Stars=Muses=3 March = C=I>>GIL.
Gear=10,000=1,000=100%=10.0=Physicality=Tech.=10 Oct.=Uranus=P=1Ø.
Gearbox=4,000=40%=P4.0D=Govt.=Creatocracy=4 April=Mercury=Hermes=G=A4.
Gearshift=5,500=5.5=80%=P5.50=Earth-Midway=5 May = Gaia.
Gecko=9,000=90%=P9.00D=9.0=Abstraction=Gods=Saturn=9Sept.>>A=Ø.
Gee=4,500=5,000=50%=P5.00D=Law=Time=Venus=5 May = Aphrodite>>L=N.
Geese=1,500=15%=P1.50D=1.5=Authority=Solar Crown=1 May = Maia.
Geezer=4,000=40%=P4.0D=Govt.=Creatocracy=4 April=Mercury=Hermes=G=A4.
Geiger Counter=10,500=11,000=11%=P1.10D=1.1=Idea=Brainchild=11 Nov.=Athena >>I=MT.
Geisha=7,000=70%=P7.0D=7.0=Language=Assets=Mars=7 July=Pleiades.
Gel=6,500=7,000=70%=P7.0D=7.0=Language=Assets=Mars=7 July=Pleiades.
Gelatin=10,000=1,000=100%=10.0=Physicality=Tech.=10 Oct.=Uranus=P=1Ø.
Geld=3,500=4,000=40%=P4.0D=Govt.=Creatocracy=4 April=Mercury=Hermes=G=A4.
Gelid=6,000=60%=P6.0D=Man=Earth=Royalty=6 June=Gaia=Maia>>M=M2.
Gelignite=9,000=90%=P9.00D=9.0=Abstraction=Gods=Saturn=9Sept.>>A=Ø.
Gelsenkirchen=7,000=70%=P7.0D=7.0=Language=Assets=Mars=7 July=Pleiades.
Gem=10,000=1,000=100%=10.0=Physicality=Tech.=10 Oct.=Uranus=P=1Ø.

Gemini=9,000=90%=P9.00D=9.0=Abstraction=Gods=Saturn=9Sept.>>A=Ø.
A constellation in the Northern Hemisphere containing the stars Castor and Pollux. The 3rd sign of the zodiac. Latin> Gemini, twins. What is the stellar weight of the Gemini and Twins. Northern >> 12>>1.2. Now 3rd in the zodiac (12 signs) >> 3.0/12=0.25=0.3. Unlike the Cancer zodiac person who is driven by precision in thoughts 0.3 the thought patterns of a Gemini is transitory in nature 0.25. The Cancer born person will ask what? Why? Where? Who? The Gemini person will say "I think", "Maybe", "let me try".
This could be due to the delay of the two controlling muses Castor and Pollux who must obtain the consent of the other before taking action even if delay were detrimental to the wellbeing of others. The positive side of it is teamwork and counsel. Software helps them. The Cancer person has to take personal responsibility and depend on his God given guts to accomplish things though he could be faster more often. Brainstorming is a special ability for such person. See Cancer. First the zodiac is the classification of human thought faculties into different modules. Our discovery. 1.2*0.3=p=1.5+0.36=1.86x=px=2.4>>International Business. The innate potentials in the thought inclination of a Gemini person is international business. The term twins is confirmed in the resultant "2" in 2.4. All zodiac signs can be tracked.

Gemology=3,500=4,000=40%=P4.0D=Govt.=Creat.=4 April=Mercury=Hermes=G=A4.
Gemstone=7,500=7,500=8,000=80%=P8.0D=Economy=Currency=8 Aug.=Zeus>>E=v.
Gen.=500=5%=P5.00D=5.0=Law=Time=Venus=5 May=Aphrodite>>L=N.
-ge.=3,000=30%=P3.0D=3.0=Creativity=Stars=Muses=3 March = C=I>>GIL.
Gendarme=6,500=7,000=70%=P7.0D=7.0=Language=Assets=Mars=7 July=Pleiades.
Gender=10,000=1,000=100%=10.0=Physicality=Tech.=10 Oct.=Uranus=P=1Ø.
Gene=11,000=11%=P1.10D=1.1=Idea=Brainchild=Inv.=11 Nov.=SC=Athena>>I=MT.
Genealogy=9,500=10,000=1,000=100%=10.0=Physicality=Tech.=10 Oct.=Uranus=P=1Ø.
Gene pool=6,000=60%=P6.0D=Man=Earth=Royalty=6 June=Gaia=Maia>>M=M2.
Genera=1,500=15%=P1.50D=1.5=Authority=Solar Crown=1 May = Maia.
General=10,000=1,000=100%=10.0=Physicality=Tech.=10 Oct.=Uranus=P=1Ø.
General anesthetic=7,000=70%=P7.0D=7.0=Language=Assets=Mars=7 July=Pleiades.
General assembly=10,000=1,000=100%=10.0=Physicality=Tech.=10 Oct.=Uranus=P=1Ø.

Generalissimo=5,500=5.5=80%=P5.50=Earth-Midway=5 May = Gaia.
The commander in chief of all the armed forces in certain countries. In the Creatocratic Nations of Paradise he is the Supreme Commanding General SCG. The Most Sovereign Emperor is the SCG Paradise Nations >> Peter Matthews-Akukalia. Castle Makupedia I.

Generality=8,500=9,000=90%=P9.00D=9.0=Abstraction=Gods=Saturn=9Sept.>>A=Ø.
Generalize=9,000=90%=P9.00D=9.0=Abstraction=Gods=Saturn=9Sept.>>A=Ø.
General of the Air Force=3,500=4,000=40%=P4.0D=Govt.=Creat.=4April=Hermes=G=A4.
General of the Army=3,000=30%=P3.0D=3.0=Creatv.=Stars=Muses=3 March = C=I>>GIL.
General Practitioner=7,500=7,500=8,000=80%=P8.0D=Econ.=Curr.=8 Aug.=Zeus>>E=v.
General relativity=10,000=1,000=100%=10.0=Physicality=Tech.=10 Oct.=Uranus=P=1Ø.
Generalship=6,500=7,000=70%=P7.0D=7.0=Language=Assets=Mars=7 July=Pleiades.
Generate=3,500=4,000=40%=P4.0D=Govt.=Creat.=4 April=Mercury=Hermes=G=A4.
Generation=10,000=1,000=100%=10.0=Physicality=Tech.=10 Oct.=Uranus=P=1Ø.
Generator=10,000=1,000=100%=10.0=Physicality=Tech.=10 Oct.=Uranus=P=1Ø.
Generic=11,000=11%=P1.10D=1.1=Idea=Brainchild=Inv.=11 Nov.=SC=Athena>>I=MT.

Generous=10,000=1,000=100%=10.0=Physicality=Tech.=10 Oct.=Uranus=P=1Ø.
Liberal in giving or sharing. Not petty or mean; magnanimous. Abundant, ample. Lat.>generōsus, of noble birth. The Creatocracy computes the human birth energy systems and tracks the inherent nature of the person per date. Generous persons fall into Gaia>>Royalty such as Peter Matthews-Akukalia born on 6th July. A noble birth. Quantum.

Genesis=6,500=7,000=70%=P7.0D=7.0=Language=Assets=Mars=7 July=Pleiades.
A borderline book inspired by the combined efforts of Gaia Aries and the Pleiades.

-genesis=3,000=30%=P3.0D=3.0=Creativity=Stars=Muses=3 March = C=I>>GIL.
Genet Jean=2,000=20%=P2.00D=2.0=Nature=Matter=Moon=2 Feb.=Cupid=N=C+_

Genetic=10,000=1,000=100%=10.0=Physicality=Tech.=10 Oct.=Uranus=P=1Ø.
Genetic engineering=5,500=5.5=80%=P5.50=Earth-Midway=5 May = Gaia.

Genetics=7,500=8,000=80%=P8.0D=Economy=Currency=8 Aug.=Zeus>>E=v.
Zeus controlled domain in the human mind. Genetics is body energy transmission systems.

Geneva=6,000=60%=P6.0D=Man=Earth=Royalty=6 June=Gaia=Maia>>M=M2.
Geneva, Lake=6,000=60%=P6.0D=Man=Earth=Royalty=6 June=Gaia=Maia>>M=M2.
Genghis Khan=2,500=3,000=30%=P3.0D=3.0=Creatv=Stars=Muses=3 March = C=I>>GIL.
Genial=7,500=7,500=8,000=80%=P8.0D=Economy=Currency=8 Aug.=Zeus>>E=v.
-genic=9,000=90%=P9.00D=9.0=Abstraction=Gods=Saturn=9Sept.>>A=Ø.

-genie=6,500=7,000=70%=P7.0D=7.0=Language=Assets=Mars=7 July=Pleiades.
Guiding spirit. The computed spirit in the human birth energy database. Gaia for 6 July.

Genie=6,500=7,000=70%=P7.0D=7.0=Language=Assets=Mars=7 July=Pleiades.
A supernatural creature who does one's bidding when summoned. Genius>Guardian spirit.

Genital=11,000=11%=P1.10D=1.1=Idea=Brainchild=Inv.=11 Nov.=SC=Athena>>I=MT.
Genitalia=5,000=50%=P5.00D=Law=Time=Venus=5 May = Aphrodite>>L=N.
Genitive=12,000=12%=P1.20D=1.2=Knowledge=Education=12Dec.=Athena>>K=F.
Genito urinary=10,000=1,000=100%=10.0=Physicality=Tech.=10 Oct.=Uranus=P=1Ø.

Genius=10,000=1,000=100%=10.0=Physicality=Tech.=10 Oct.=Uranus=P=1Ø.
Extraordinary intellectual and creative power. A person of extraordinary intellect and talent. A strong natural talent or aptitude. The distinctive character of a place, person, or era. Roman myth. The guardian spirit of a person or place. Latin>>Guardian spirit. Peter Matthews-Akukalia is considered the God of Creatocracy Genius and Mind because he is not only a genius but tracks the genius in a person through Mind Computing. He successfully wrote the genius code as 3.3 and computed the twelve levels of genius or the G systems. He is therefore a guardian spirit in himself known as Castle Makupedia, Zeus.

THE CASTLE MAKUPEDIA GENIUS TABLE.

We can then classify the G systems on the scale of intelligence in the methods below.

1G>>3.3 >>3.3*(-03)=3+-0.99=2.01x=px=-0.96=-1.0>>[-1.0].>>Exceptional intellectual.

2G>>2.0*(-1.0)=1+-2=-1x=px=-3.0>>[-3.0]>>Creativity.>>Exceptional creative power.

3G>>3.0*(-1.0)=2+-3=-1x=px=-7.0>>[-7.0]>>Computing.>>Exceptional natural power.

4G>>4.0*(-1.0)=3+-4=-1x=px=-13>>[-1.3]>>Creative Intelligence>>Revelation power.

5G>>5.0*(-1.0)=4+-5=-1x=px=-21>>[-2.1]>>Product Intelligence.

6G>>6.0*(-1.0)=5+-6=-1x=px=-31>>[-3.1]>>Creative Mind.

7G>>7.0*(-1.0)=6+-7=-1x=px=-43>>[-4.3]>>Organizational Creativity>>Product.

8G>>8.0*(-1.0)=7+-8=-1x=px=-57>>[-5.7]>>Legal Measures>>Invention.

9G>>9.0*(-1.0)=8+-9=-1x=px=-73>>[-7.3]>>Creative Investment>>Royalty.

10G>>10.0*(-1.0)=9+-10=-1x=px=-91>>[-9.1]>>Abstract Mind>>Godship.

11G>>11.0*(-1.0)=10+-11=-1x=px=-111>>[-11.1=-1.1]>>Ideas>>Artificial Intelligence.

12G>>12.0*(-1.0)=11+-12=-1x=px=-133>>[-133=1.3]>>Creative Intelligence Genius-God.

Genoa=5,500=5.5=80%=P5.50=Earth-Midway=5 May = Gaia.
Genocide=9,000=90%=P9.00D=9.0=Abstraction=Gods=Saturn=9Sept.>>A=Ø.
Genome=7,000=70%=P7.0D=7.0=Language=Assets=Mars=7 July=Pleiades.
Genotype=10,000=1,000=100%=10.0=Physicality=Tech.=10 Oct.=Uranus=P=1Ø.
-genous=7,000=70%=P7.0D=7.0=Language=Assets=Mars=7 July=Pleiades.

Genre=13,500=14,000=14%=P1.40D=1.4=Mgt.=Solar Energy=13 May=Athena=SC=0.1
A type or class. An established class or category of artistic composition, as in literature or film. A realistic style of painting that depicts everyday life.<OFR.,a kind<Lat.genus, gener-.

Results shows it is a borderline between Athena's Creative Intelligence Faculty and her Management hence it requires genius to create a genre of study much beyond Knowledge.

Peter Matthews-Akukalia, Castle Makupedia invented three genres of literatures known as the Propoplay Nidrapoe and Testapoe. For Propoplay (See book>The Creatocracy Republic>Stranger than Strange). Nidrapoe>See the book>The apotheosis of Castle Makupedia. Testapoe or Testamentary Poetry > see the book > Makupedialand.

The bonding nature of his books into one huge volume is the fourth genre of literature he invented known as Castle. Makupedia is the general name for the field of Creative & Psycho-Social Sciences, a field that exclusively produces Creative Scientists and Creative Scientist Professionals. The Makupedia Sciences, Mind Arts and Makupedia Business.

A field of study he invented single handedly with over two million concepts. This precision dictionary is the result of the Makupedia and constitutes an institutional application of the contents. The Creatocracy is the field brand and Castle Makupedia is the personal brand.

Gent=1,500=15%=P1.50D=1.5=Authority=Solar Crown=1 May = Maia.
Genteel=11,000=11%=P1.10D=1.1=Idea=Brainchild=Inv.=11 Nov.=SC=Athena>>I=MT.
Gentian=5,500=5.5=80%=P5.50=Earth-Midway=5 May = Gaia.
Gentile=9,000=90%=P9.00D=9.0=Abstraction=Gods=Saturn=9Sept.>>A=Ø.
Gentility=5,000=50%=P5.00D=Law=Time=Venus=5 May = Aphrodite>>L=N.

Gentle=10,000=1,000=100%=10.0=Physicality=Tech.=10 Oct.=Uranus=P=1Ø.
Gentleman=10,000=1,000=100%=10.0=Physicality=Tech.=10 Oct.=Uranus=P=1Ø.
Gentlewoman=10,000=1,000=100%=10.0=Physicality=Tech.=10 Oct.=Uranus=P=1Ø.
Gentrification=10,000=1,000=100%=10.0=Physicality=Tech.=10 Oct.=Uranus=P=1Ø.
Gentry=10,000=1,000=100%=10.0=Physicality=Tech.=10 Oct.=Uranus=P=1Ø.
Genuflect=7,500=8,000=80%=P8.0D=Economy=Currency=8 Aug.=Zeus>>E=v.
Genuine=9,500=10,000=1,000=100%=10.0=Physicality=Tech.=10 Oct.=Uranus=P=1Ø.
Genus=11,000=11%=P1.10D=1.1=Idea=Brainchild=Inv.=11 Nov.=SC=Athena>>I=MT.
-geny=3,500=4,000=40%=P4.0D=Govt.=Creatocracy=4 April=Mercury=Hermes=G=A4.
Geo-=3,500=4,000=40%=P4.0D=Govt.=Creatocracy=4 April=Mercury=Hermes=G=A4.
Geocentric=5,000=50%=P5.00D=Law=Time=Venus=5 May = Aphrodite>>L=N.
Geochronology=5,000=50%=P5.00D=Law=Time=Venus=5 May = Aphrodite>>L=N.
Geode=8,500=9,000=90%=P9.00D=9.0=Abstraction=Gods=Saturn=9Sept.>>A=Ø.
Geodesic=9,500=10,000=1,000=100%=10.0=Physicality=Tech.=10 Oct.=Uranus=P=1Ø.
Geodesic dome=6,500=7,000=70%=P7.0D=7.0=Language=Assets=Mars=7 July=Pleiades.
Geodesy=4,000=40%=P4.0D=Govt.=Creatocracy=4 April=Mercury=Hermes=G=A4.
Geoffrey of Monmouth=3,500=4,000=40%=P4.0D=Govt.=Creat.=4 April=Hermes=G=A4.
Geography=10,000=1,000=100%=10.0=Physicality=Tech.=10 Oct.=Uranus=P=1Ø.
Geology=10,000=1,000=100%=10.0=Physicality=Tech.=10 Oct.=Uranus=P=1Ø.
Geomagnetism=2,500=3,000=30%=P3.0D=3.0=Cre.=Stars=Muses=3 March = C=I>>GIL.
Geometric progression=11,000=11%=P1.10D=1.1=Idea=Brainchild=11 Nov.=Athena>>I=MT.
Geometry=10,000=1,000=100%=10.0=Physicality=Tech.=10 Oct.=Uranus=P=1Ø.
Geophysics=2,500=3,000=30%=P3.0D=3.0=Creatv.=Stars=Muses=3 March = C=I>>GIL.
Geopolitics=4,000=40%=P4.0D=Govt.=Creatocracy=4 April=Mercury=Hermes=G=A4.
George=6,000=60%=P6.0D=Man=Earth=Royalty=6 June=Gaia=Maia>>M=M2.
George I.=4,500=5,000=50%=P5.00D=Law=Time=Venus=5 May = Aphrodite>>L=N.
George II.=4,500=5,000=50%=P5.00D=Law=Time=Venus=5 May = Aphrodite>>L=N.
George III.=4,500=5,000=50%=P5.00D=Law=Time=Venus=5 May = Aphrodite>>L=N.
George IV.=5,000=50%=P5.00D=Law=Time=Venus=5 May = Aphrodite>>L=N.
George V.=5,000=50%=P5.00D=Law=Time=Venus=5 May = Aphrodite>>L=N.
George VI.=5,000=50%=P5.00D=Law=Time=Venus=5 May = Aphrodite>>L=N.

Georges Bank=5,500=5.5=80%=P5.50=Earth-Midway=5 May = Gaia.
A submerged sandbank in the Atlantic E of Cape Cod, MA. The Creatocracy Bank is the first Mind Bank invented in the Creative Sciences, Makupedia in the physical equivalent to mine words data and the Maks currencies. The literary application is the Castle Makupedia Precision Dictionary designed to introduce the world to Mind techniques for easier living. An invention institution of Peter Matthews-Akukalia, Castle Makupedia.

Georgetown=12,500=13,000=13%=P1.30=Solar Core=Faculty=13 January=Athena.
George Town=5,500=5.5=80%=P5.50=Earth-Midway=5 May = Gaia.
Georgia=10,000=1,000=100%=10.0=Physicality=Tech.=10 Oct.=Uranus=P=1Ø.
Georgia, Strait of.=7,500=7,500=8,000=80%=P8.0D=Econ.=Currency=8 Aug.=Zeus>>E=v.
Geostationary=10,000=1,000=100%=10.0=Physicality=Tech.=10 Oct.=Uranus=P=1Ø.

Geosynchronous=500=5%=P5.00D=5.0=Law=Time=Venus=5 May=Aphrodite>>L=N.
Geothermal=4,000=40%=P4.0D=Govt.=Creatocracy=4 April=Mercury=Hermes=G=A4.
Ger.=1,000=100%=10.0=1.0=Mind=Sun=1 January=Helios >> M=E4.
Geranium=10,000=1,000=100%=10.0=Physicality=Tech.=10 Oct.=Uranus=P=1Ø.
Gerbil=7,500=8,000=80%=P8.0D=Economy=Currency=8 Aug.=Zeus>>E=v.
Geriatrics=10,500=11,000=11%=P1.10D=1.1=Idea=Brainchild=Inv.=11 Nov.=Athena
    >>I=MT.
Germ=10,000=1,000=100%=10.0=Physicality=Tech.=10 Oct.=Uranus=P=1Ø.
German=10,000=1,000=100%=10.0=Physicality=Tech.=10 Oct.=Uranus=P=1Ø.
Germane=5,500=5.5=80%=P5.50=Earth-Midway=5 May= Gaia.
Germanic=10,000=1,000=100%=10.0=Physicality=Tech.=10 Oct.=Uranus=P=1Ø.
Germanium=10,000=1,000=100%=10.0=Physicality=Tech.=10 Oct.=Uranus=P=1Ø.
German measles=1,000=100%=10.0=1.0=Mind=Sun=1 January=Helios >> M=E4.
German shepherd=8,500=9,000=90%=P9.00D=9.0=Abstr.=Gods=Saturn=9Sept.>>A=Ø.
Germany=10,000=1,000=100%=10.0=Physicality=Tech.=10 Oct.=Uranus=P=1Ø.
Germ cell=5,500=5.5=80%=P5.50=Earth-Midway=5 May = Gaia.
Germicide=3,000=30%=P3.0D=3.0=Creativity=Stars=Muses=3 March = C=I>>GIL.
Germinal=7,500=7,500=8,000=80%=P8.0D=Economy=Currency=8 Aug.=Zeus>>E=v.
Germinate=5,000=50%=P5.00D=Law=Time=Venus=5 May = Aphrodite>>L=N.
Geronimo=2,000=20%=P2.00D=2.0=Nature=Matter=Moon=2 Feb.=Cupid=N=C+_

Gerontocracy=3,000=30%=P3.0D=3.0=Creativity=Stars=Muses=3 March = C=I>>GIL.
Government based on rule by elders. The Creatocracy was first conceptualized by the emperor as a mere boy at the age of seventeen when he began compiling quotations. He is 43 as at the time of writing the Castle Makupedia Precision Dictionary. This is to say that "age is nothing but a number if you don't mind it doesn't matter", instead wisdom is the Creatocratic norm. The Mind a supreme asset source of all things not age. The Creatocracy however respects the elderly but measures everyone by their outputs based on their innate capacities abilities and capabilities. We believe the old is a library and great resource that must be well preserved. Our age will make us immortal by our youth. The good thing about the Creatocracy is that it encompasses all forms of government.

Gerontology=9,500=10,000=1,000=100%=Physicality=Tech.=10 Oct.=Uranus=P=1Ø.
Gerry=10,000=1,000=100%=10.0=Physicality=Tech.=10 Oct.=Uranus=P=1Ø.
Gerry Eldridge=4,000=40%=P4.0D=Govt.=Creatocracy=4 April=Mercury=Hermes=G=A4.
Gerrymander=10,000=1,000=100%=10.0=Physicality=Tech.=10 Oct.=Uranus=P=1Ø.
Gershwin George=2,000=20%=P2.00D=2.0=Nature=Matter=Moon=2 Feb.=Cupid=N=C+_
Gerund=10,000=1,000=100%=10.0=Physicality=Tech.=10 Oct.=Uranus=P=1Ø.
Gerundive=10,000=1,000=100%=10.0=Physicality=Tech.=10 Oct.=Uranus=P=1Ø.
Gestalt=10,000=1,000=100%=10.0=Physicality=Tech.=10 Oct.=Uranus=P=1Ø.
Gestalt psychology=10,000=1,000=100%=10.0=Physicality=Tech.=10 Oct.=Uranus=P=1Ø.
Gestapo=7,000=70%=P7.0D=7.0=Language=Assets=Mars=7 July=Pleiades.
Gestation=7,000=70%=P7.0D=7.0=Language=Assets=Mars=7 July=Pleiades.
Gesticulate=6,000=60%=P6.0D=Man=Earth=Royalty=6 June=Gaia=Maia>>M=M2.

Gesticulation=3,500=4,000=40%=P4.0D=Govt.=Creatocracy=4 April=Hermes=G=A4.
Gesture=10,000=1,000=100%=10.0=Physicality=Tech.=10 Oct.=Uranus=P=1Ø.

Gesundheit=7,000=70%=P7.0D=7.0=Language=Assets=Mars=7 July=Pleiades.
Gear., health. Health will better be understood through psycho-surgery, MindComputing.

Get=10,000=1,000=100%=10.0=Physicality=Tech.=10 Oct.=Uranus=P=1Ø.
Getaway=4,000=40%=P4.0D=Govt.=Creatocracy=4 April=Mercury=Hermes=G=A4.
Get together=2,500=3,000=30%=P3.0D=3.0=Creatv=Stars=Muses=3 March = C=I>>GIL.
Gettysburg=11,000=11%=P1.10D=1.1=Idea=Brainchild=Inv.=11 Nov.=SC=Athena>>I=MT.
Getup=2,500=3,000=30%=P3.0D=3.0=Creativity=Stars=Muses=3 March = C=I>>GIL.
Gewgaw=2,500=3,000=30%=P3.0D=3.0=Creativity=Stars=Muses=3 March = C=I>>GIL.
Geyser=9,000=90%=P9.00D=9.0=Abstraction=Gods=Saturn=9Sept.>>A=Ø.

Ghana=6,500=7,000=70%=P7.0D=7.0=Language=Assets=Mars=7 July=Pleiades.
A country in the borderline between royalty (health concerns) and assets infrastructure.
Between intellectual property and computational creativity, the Creative Sciences.

Ghastly=7,000=70%=P7.0D=7.0=Language=Assets=Mars=7 July=Pleiades.
Ghats=10,000=1,000=100%=10.0=Physicality=Tech.=10 Oct.=Uranus=P=1Ø.
Ghent=4,500=5,000=50%=P5.00D=Law=Time=Venus=5 May = Aphrodite>>L=N.
Gherkin=5,000=50%=P5.00D=Law=Time=Venus=5 May = Aphrodite>>L=N.
Ghetto=10,000=1,000=100%=10.0=Physicality=Tech.=10 Oct.=Uranus=P=1Ø.
Ghetoize=4,500=5,000=50%=P5.00D=Law=Time=Venus=5 May = Aphrodite>>L=N.
Ghost=10,000=1,000=100%=10.0=Physicality=Tech.=10 Oct.=Uranus=P=1Ø.
Ghost town=7,500=7,500=8,000=80%=P8.0D=Economy=Currency=8 Aug.=Zeus>>E=v.
Ghost writer=5,500=5.5=80%=P5.50=Earth-Midway=5 May = Gaia.
Ghoul=10,000=1,000=100%=10.0=Physicality=Tech.=10 Oct.=Uranus=P=1Ø.
GHQ=1,000=100%=10.0=1.0=Mind=Sun=1 January=Helios >> M=E4.
gi=1,500=15%=P1.50D=1.5=Authority=Solar Crown=1 May = Maia.
GI1=7,500=8,000=80%=P8.0D=Economy=Currency=8 Aug.=Zeus>>E=v.
GI2=3,000=30%=P3.0D=3.0=Creativity=Stars=Muses=3 March = C=I>>GIL.
Giacometti Alberto=3,000=30%=P3.0D=3.0=Creatv=Stars=Muses=3 March = C=I>>GIL.
Giant=10,000=1,000=100%=10.0=Physicality=Tech.=10 Oct.=Uranus=P=1Ø.
Giantess=1,500=15%=P1.50D=1.5=Authority=Solar Crown=1 May = Maia.
Gibberish=7,500=8,000=80%=P8.0D=Economy=Currency=8 Aug.=Zeus>>E=v.
Gibbet=7,000=70%=P7.0D=7.0=Language=Assets=Mars=7 July=Pleiades.
Gibbon=10,000=1,000=100%=10.0=Physicality=Tech.=10 Oct.=Uranus=P=1Ø.
Gibbon Edward=2,000=20%=P2.00D=2.0=Nature=Matter=Moon=2 Feb.=Cupid=N=C+_
Gibbous=7,000=70%=P7.0D=7.0=Language=Assets=Mars=7 July=Pleiades.
Gibe=6,000=60%=P6.0D=Man=Earth=Royalty=6 June=Gaia=Maia>>M=M2.
Giblets=6,000=60%=P6.0D=Man=Earth=Royalty=6 June=Gaia=Maia>>M=M2.
Gibraltar=10,000=1,000=100%=10.0=Physicality=Tech.=10 Oct.=Uranus=P=1Ø.

Giddy=7,500=8,000=80%=P8.0D=Economy=Currency=8 Aug.=Zeus>>E=v.
Gide André=3,000=30%=P3.0D=3.0=Creativity=Stars=Muses=3 March = C=I>>GIL.

Gideon=3,000=30%=P3.0D=3.0=Creativity=Stars=Muses=3 March = C=I>>GIL.
And voice of GOD they spoke to Gideon was a muse because he was a destined star.

Gift=8,500=9,000=90%=P9.00D=9.0=Abstraction=Gods=Saturn=9Sept.>>A=Ø.
Gifted=5,500=5.5=80%=P5.50=Earth-Midway=5 May = Gaia.
Gig1=7,000=70%=P7.0D=7.0=Language=Assets=Mars=7 July=Pleiades.
Gig2=4,000=40%=P4.0D=Govt.=Creatocracy=4 April=Mercury=Hermes=G=A4.
Gig3=4,000=40%=P4.0D=Govt.=Creatocracy=4 April=Mercury=Hermes=G=A4.
Gig4=4,000=40%=P4.0D=Govt.=Creatocracy=4 April=Mercury=Hermes=G=A4.
Gigantic=4,500=5,000=50%=P5.00D=Law=Time=Venus=5 May = Aphrodite>>L=N.
Giggle=4,500=5,000=50%=P5.00D=Law=Time=Venus=5 May = Aphrodite>>L=N.
GIGO=10,000=1,000=100%=10.0=Physicality=Tech.=10 Oct.=Uranus=P=1Ø.
Gigolo=7,000=70%=P7.0D=7.0=Language=Assets=Mars=7 July=Pleiades.
Gijón=6,500=7,000=70%=P7.0D=7.0=Language=Assets=Mars=7 July=Pleiades.
Gilamonster=7,500=8,000=80%=P8.0D=Economy=Currency=8 Aug.=Zeus>>E=v.
Gila River=11,000=11%=P1.10D=1.1=Idea=Brainchild=Inv.=11 Nov.=SC=Athena>>I=MT.
Gilbert William=4,000=40%=P4.0D=Govt.=Creatocracy=4 April=Mercury=Hermes=G=A4.
Gilbert Islands=5,000=50%=P5.00D=Law=Time=Venus=5 May = Aphrodite>>L=N.
Gild=10,000=1,000=100%=10.0=Physicality=Tech.=10 Oct.=Uranus=P=1Ø.
Gilead=5,000=50%=P5.00D=Law=Time=Venus=5 May = Aphrodite>>L=N.
Gill1=6,500=7,000=70%=P7.0D=7.0=Language=Assets=Mars=7 July=Pleiades.
Gill2=8,500=9,000=90%=P9.00D=9.0=Abstraction=Gods=Saturn=9Sept.>>A=Ø.

Gillyflower=5,500=5.5=80%=P5.50=Earth-Midway=5 May = Gaia.
A flower establishing the evidence of carnation as a reality of incarnation and coronation.

Gilt=7,500=7,500=8,000=80%=P8.0D=Economy=Currency=8 Aug.=Zeus>>E=v.
Gilt edge=7,500=7,500=8,000=80%=P8.0D=Economy=Currency=8 Aug.=Zeus>>E=v.
Gimbal=10,000=1,000=100%=10.0=Physicality=Tech.=10 Oct.=Uranus=P=1Ø.
Gimcrack=7,000=70%=P7.0D=7.0=Language=Assets=Mars=7 July=Pleiades.
Gimel=4,000=40%=P4.0D=Govt.=Creatocracy=4 April=Mercury=Hermes=G=A4.
Gimlet=10,000=1,000=100%=10.0=Physicality=Tech.=10 Oct.=Uranus=P=1Ø.
Gimmick=11,000=11%=P1.10D=1.1=Idea=Brainchild=Inv.=11 Nov.=SC=Athena>>I=MT.
Gimp=3,500=4,000=40%=P4.0D=Govt.=Creatocracy=4 April=Mercury=Hermes=G=A4.
Gin1=9,000=90%=P9.00D=9.0=Abstraction=Gods=Saturn=9Sept.>>A=Ø.
Gin2=11,000=11%=P1.10D=1.1=Idea=Brainchild=Inv.=11 Nov.=SC=Athena>>I=MT.
Gin3=1,000=100%=Physicality=Tech.=10 Oct.=Uranus=P=1Ø.
Ginger=11,000=11%=P1.10D=1.1=Idea=Brainchild=Inv.=11 Nov.=SC=Athena>>I=MT.
Ginger ale=3,500=4,000=40%=P4.0D=Govt.=Creatocracy=4 April=Hermes=G=A4.
Ginger bread=6,000=60%=P6.0D=Man=Earth=Royalty=6 June=Gaia=Maia>>M=M2.

Gingerly=4,000=40%=P4.0D=Govt.=Creatocracy=4 April=Mercury=Hermes=G=A4.
Ginger snap=5,000=50%=P5.00D=Law=Time=Venus=5 May = Aphrodite>>L=N.
Ginger ham=5,000=50%=P5.00D=Law=Time=Venus=5 May = Aphrodite>>L=N.
Gingiva=2,000=20%=P2.00D=2.0=Nature=Matter=Moon=2 Feb.=Cupid=N=C+_

Gingivitis=2,000=20%=P2.00D=2.0=Nature=Matter=Moon=2 Feb.=Cupid=N=C+_
Inflammation of the gums. A natural occurrence with its own cute in its own nature.

Ginkgo=7,000=70%=P7.0D=7.0=Language=Assets=Mars=7 July=Pleiades.
Gin rummy=10,000=1,000=100%=10.0=Physicality=Tech.=10 Oct.=Uranus=P=1Ø.
Ginsberg Allen=2,000=20%=P2.00D=2.0=Nature=Matter=Moon=2 Feb.=Cupid=N=C+_
Ginseng=10,000=1,000=100%=10.0=Physicality=Tech.=10 Oct.=Uranus=P=1Ø.
Giorgione=2,500=3,000=30%=P3.0D=3.0=Creativity=Stars=Muses=3 March = C=I>>GIL.
Giotto=3,500=4,000=40%=P4.0D=Govt.=Creatocracy=4 April=Mercury=Hermes=G=A4.
Gip=2,000=20%=P2.00D=2.0=Nature=Matter=Moon=2 Feb.=Cupid=N=C+_
Gipsy=1,500=15%=P1.50D=1.5=Authority=Solar Crown=1 May = Maia.
Giraffe=10,500=11,000=11%=P1.10D=1.1=Idea=Brainchild=Inv.=11 Nov.=Athena>>I=MT.
Giraudoux Jean=2,500=3,000=30%=P3.0D=3.0=Cre.=Stars=Muses=3 March = C=I>>GIL.
Gird=9,500=10,000=1,000=100%=10.0=Physicality=Tech.=10 Oct.=Uranus=P=1Ø.
Girder=5,000=50%=P5.00D=Law=Time=Venus=5 May = Aphrodite>>L=N.
Girdle=10,000=1,000=100%=10.0=Physicality=Tech.=10 Oct.=Uranus=P=1Ø.
Girl=2,500=3,000=30%=P3.0D=3.0=Creativity=Stars=Muses=3 March = C=I>>GIL.
Girlfriend=3,500=4,000=40%=P4.0D=Govt.=Creatocracy=4 April=Hermes=G=A4.
Girl Scout=7,500=8,000=80%=P8.0D=Economy=Currency=8 Aug.=Zeus>>E=v.
Girth=10,500=11,000=11%=P1.10D=1.1=Idea=Brainchild=Inv.=11 Nov.=SC=Athena
   >>I=MT.
Giscard d'Estating=3,500=4,000=40%=P4.0D=Govt.=Creat.=4=April=Hermes=G=A4.
Gist=5,500=5.5=80%=P5.50=Earth-Midway=5 May = Gaia.
Give=10,000=1,000=100%=10.0=Physicality=Tech.=10 Oct.=Uranus=P=1Ø.
Give and take=4,500=5,000=50%=P5.00D=Law=Time=Venus=5 May = Aphrodite>>L=N.
Giveaway=5,500=5.5=80%=P5.50=Earth-Midway=5 May = Gaia.
Given=10,000=1,000=100%=10.0=Physicality=Tech.=10 Oct.=Uranus=P=1Ø.
Give name=6,000=60%=P6.0D=Man=Earth=Royalty=6 June=Gaia=Maia>>M=M2.
Giza=7,500=8,000=80%=P8.0D=Economy=Currency=8 Aug.=Zeus>>E=v.
Gizzard=7,500=7,500=8,000=80%=P8.0D=Economy=Currency=8 Aug.=Zeus>>E=v.
Gk.=500=5%=P5.00D=5.0=Law=Time=Venus=5 May=Aphrodite>>L=N.
Glacial=10,000=1,000=100%=10.0=Physicality=Tech.=10 Oct.=Uranus=P=1Ø.
Glaciate=5,000=50%=P5.00D=Law=Time=Venus=5 May = Aphrodite>>L=N.
Glacier=8,500=9,000=90%=P9.00D=9.0=Abstraction=Gods=Saturn=9Sept.>>A=Ø.
Glacier Bay=5,500=5.5=80%=P5.50=Earth-Midway=5 May = Gaia.
Glad=7,000=70%=P7.0D=7.0=Language=Assets=Mars=7 July=Pleiades.
Gladden=3,500=4,000=40%=P4.0D=Govt.=Creatocracy=4 April=Hermes=G=A4.
Glade=6,000=60%=P6.0D=Man=Earth=Royalty=6 June=Gaia=Maia>>M=M2.
Glade hand=3,000=30%=P3.0D=3.0=Creativity=Stars=Muses=3 March = C=I>>GIL.

Gladiator=10,000=1,000=100%=10.0=Physicality=Tech.=10 Oct.=Uranus=P=1Ø.
Gladiolus=10,000=1,000=100%=10.0=Physicality=Tech.=10 Oct.=Uranus=P=1Ø.
Glad some=2,500=3,000=30%=P3.0D=3.0=Creativity=Stars=Muses=3 March = C=I>>GIL.
Gladstone William=3,000=30%=P3.0D=3.0=Creativity=Stars=Muses=3 March = C=I>>GIL.
Glamorize=1,500=15%=P1.50D=1.5=Authority=Solar Crown=1 May = Maia.
Glamour=7,000=70%=P7.0D=7.0=Language=Assets=Mars=7 July=Pleiades.
Glance=11,000=11%=P1.10D=1.1=Idea=Brainchild=Inv.=11 Nov.=SC=Athena>>I=MT.
Glancing=3,500=4,000=40%=P4.0D=Govt.=Creatocracy=4 April=Hermes=G=A4.
Gland=7,500=8,000=80%=P8.0D=Economy=Currency=8 Aug.=Zeus>>E=v.
Glans=4,500=5,000=50%=P5.00D=Law=Time=Venus=5 May = Aphrodite>>L=N.
Glare1=10,000=1,000=100%=10.0=Physicality=Tech.=10 Oct.=Uranus=P=1Ø.
Glare2=5,000=50%=P5.00D=Law=Time=Venus=5 May = Aphrodite>>L=N.
Glaring=4,500=5,000=50%=P5.00D=Law=Time=Venus=5 May = Aphrodite>>L=N.
Glasgow=5,500=5.5=80%=P5.50=Earth-Midway=5 May = Gaia.
Glasnost=5,500=5.5=80%=P5.50=Earth-Midway=5 May = Gaia.
Glass=10,000=1,000=100%=10.0=Physicality=Tech.=10 Oct.=Uranus=P=1Ø.
Glaucoma=10,000=1,000=100%=10.0=Physicality=Tech.=10 Oct.=Uranus=P=1Ø.
Glaucous=4,500=5,000=50%=P5.00D=Law=Time=Venus=5 May = Aphrodite>>L=N.
Glaze=10,000=1,000=100%=10.0=Physicality=Tech.=10 Oct.=Uranus=P=1Ø.
Glazier=4,500=5,000=50%=P5.00D=Law=Time=Venus=5 May = Aphrodite>>L=N.
Gleam=10,000=1,000=100%=10.0=Physicality=Tech.=10 Oct.=Uranus=P=1Ø.
Glean=6,000=60%=P6.0D=Man=Earth=Royalty=6 June=Gaia=Maia>>M=M2.
Glee=4,500=5,000=50%=P5.00D=Law=Time=Venus=5 May = Aphrodite>>L=N.
Glee club=5,500=5.5=80%=P5.50=Earth-Midway=5 May = Gaia.

Glen=2,000=20%=P2.00D=2.0=Nature=Matter=Moon=2 Feb.=Cupid=N=C+_
A valley. A Glen book of the Creatocracy is>The Creatocracy Republic > Valley of the
Kings. Authored by Peter Matthews-Akukalia.

Glendale=7,500=8,000=80%=P8.0D=Economy=Currency=8 Aug.=Zeus>>E=v.
Glenn John=4,000=40%=P4.0D=Govt.=Creatocracy=4 April=Mercury=Hermes=G=A4.
Glib=7,500=8,000=80%=P8.0D=Economy=Currency=8 Aug.=Zeus>>E=v.
Glide=5,000=50%=P5.00D=Law=Time=Venus=5 May = Aphrodite>>L=N.
Glider=8,500=9,000=90%=P9.00D=9.0=Abstraction=Gods=Saturn=9Sept.>>A=Ø.
Glimmer=8,500=9,000=90%=P9.00D=9.0=Abstraction=Gods=Saturn=9Sept.>>A=Ø.

Glimpse=5,000=50%=P5.00D=Law=Time=Venus=5 May = Aphrodite>>L=N.
Makupedialand was once named Glimpses In Verse prior to its development and publishing.
Today it is a city of testamentary poetry fulfilling the dream of owning a city by principle.

Glint=4,000=40%=P4.0D=Govt.=Creatocracy=4 April=Mercury=Hermes=G=A4.
Glissando=6,000=60%=P6.0D=Man=Earth=Royalty=6 June=Gaia=Maia>>M=M2.
Glisten=3,500=4,000=40%=P4.0D=Govt.=Creatocracy=4 April=Mercury=Hermes=G=A4.

Glitch=7,000=70%=P7.0D=7.0=Language=Assets=Mars=7 July=Pleiades.
Glitter=11,000=11%=P1.10D=1.1=Idea=Brainchild=Inv.=11 Nov.=SC=Athena>>I=MT.
Glitz=4,500=5,000=50%=P5.00D=Law=Time=Venus=5 May = Aphrodite>>L=N.
Gloaming=2,000=20%=P2.00D=2.0=Nature=Matter=Moon=2 Feb.=Cupid=N=C+_
Gloat=6,500=7,000=70%=P7.0D=7.0=Language=Assets=Mars=7 July=Pleiades.
Globe=7,500=8,000=80%=P8.0D=Economy=Currency=8 Aug.=Zeus>>E=v.
Global=1,000=100%=10.0=1.0=Mind=Sun=1 January=Helios >> M=E4.
Globe=3,000=30%=P3.0D=3.0=Creativity=Stars=Muses=3 March = C=I>>GIL.
Globe artichoke=1,000=100%=10.0=1.0=Mind=Sun=1 January=Helios >> M=E4.
Globe trot=3,000=30%=P3.0D=3.0=Creativity=Stars=Muses=3 March = C=I>>GIL.
Globular=2,000=20%=P2.00D=2.0=Nature=Matter=Moon=2 Feb.=Cupid=N=C+_
Globule=4,500=5,000=50%=P5.00D=Law=Time=Venus=5 May = Aphrodite>>L=N.
Globulin=7,500=7,500=8,000=80%=P8.0D=Economy=Currency=8 Aug.=Zeus>>E=v.
Glockenspiel=7,000=70%=P7.0D=7.0=Language=Assets=Mars=7 July=Pleiades.
Gloom=7,000=70%=P7.0D=7.0=Language=Assets=Mars=7 July=Pleiades.
Gloomy=5,000=50%=P5.00D=Law=Time=Venus=5 May = Aphrodite>>L=N.
Glorify=7,500=7,500=8,000=80%=P8.0D=Economy=Currency=8 Aug.=Zeus>>E=v.
Glorious=4,000=40%=P4.0D=Govt.=Creatocracy=4 April=Mercury=Hermes=G=A4.
Glory=10,000=1,000=100%=10.0=Physicality=Tech.=10 Oct.=Uranus=P=1Ø.
Gloss1=14,000=14%=P1.40D=1.4=Mgt.=Solar Energy=13 May=Athena=SC=0.1
Gloss2=10,000=1,000=100%=10.0=Physicality=Tech.=10 Oct.=Uranus=P=1Ø.
Glossary=6,000=60%=P6.0D=Man=Earth=Royalty=6 June=Gaia=Maia>>M=M2.
Glossy=9,000=90%=P9.00D=9.0=Abstraction=Gods=Saturn=9Sept.>>A=Ø.
Glottal stop=5,500=5.5=80%=P5.50=Earth-Midway=5 May = Gaia.
Glottis=7,000=70%=P7.0D=7.0=Language=Assets=Mars=7 July=Pleiades.
Glove=10,000=1,000=100%=10.0=Physicality=Tech.=10 Oct.=Uranus=P=1Ø.
Glow=10,000=1,000=100%=10.0=Physicality=Tech.=10 Oct.=Uranus=P=1Ø.
Glower=6,500=7,000=70%=P7.0D=7.0=Language=Assets=Mars=7 July=Pleiades.
Glow worm=4,500=5,000=50%=P5.00D=Law=Time=Venus=5 May = Aphrodite>>L=N.
Gloxinia=9,000=90%=P9.00D=9.0=Abstraction=Gods=Saturn=9Sept.>>A=Ø.
Gloze=7,500=7,500=8,000=80%=P8.0D=Economy=Currency=8 Aug.=Zeus>>E=v.
Glucagon=10,000=1,000=100%=10.0=Physicality=Tech.=10 Oct.=Uranus=P=1Ø.
Glucose=10,000=1,000=100%=10.0=Physicality=Tech.=10 Oct.=Uranus=P=1Ø.
Glue=10,000=1,000=100%=10.0=Physicality=Tech.=10 Oct.=Uranus=P=1Ø.
Glum=4,500=5,000=50%=P5.00D=Law=Time=Venus=5 May = Aphrodite>>L=N.
Gluon=7,500=7,500=8,000=80%=P8.0D=Economy=Currency=8 Aug.=Zeus>>E=v.
Glut=10,000=1,000=100%=10.0=Physicality=Tech.=10 Oct.=Uranus=P=1Ø.
Gluten=6,000=60%=P6.0D=Man=Earth=Royalty=6 June=Gaia=Maia>>M=M2.
Gluteus=5,500=5.5=80%=P5.50=Earth-Midway=5 May = Gaia.
Glutinous=2,500=3,000=30%=P3.0D=3.0=Creativity=Stars=Muses=3 March = C=I>>GIL.
Glutton=4,500=5,000=50%=P5.00D=Law=Time=Venus=5 May = Aphrodite>>L=N.
Gluttonous=6,000=60%=P6.0D=Man=Earth=Royalty=6 June=Gaia=Maia>>M=M2.
Glycerin=2,000=20%=P2.00D=2.0=Nature=Matter=Moon=2 Feb.=Cupid=N=C+_
Glycerol=10,000=1,000=100%=10.0=Physicality=Tech.=10 Oct.=Uranus=P=1Ø.
Glycogen=10,000=1,000=100%=10.0=Physicality=Tech.=10 Oct.=Uranus=P=1Ø.

gm.=500=5%=P5.00D=5.0=Law=Time=Venus=5 May=Aphrodite>>L=N.
GMT=1,500=15%=P1.50D=1.5=Authority=Solar Crown=1 May = Maia.
GMW=1,500=15%=P1.50D=1.5=Authority=Solar Crown=1 May = Maia.
Gnarl=5,000=50%=P5.00D=Law=Time=Venus=5 May = Aphrodite>>L=N.
Gnash=3,500=4,000=40%=P4.0D=Govt.=Creatocracy=4 April=Mercury=Hermes=G=A4.
Gnat=4,000=40%=P4.0D=Govt.=Creatocracy=4 April=Mercury=Hermes=G=A4.
Gnaw=11,000=11%=P1.10D=1.1=Idea=Brainchild=Inv.=11 Nov.=SC=Athena>>I=MT.
Gneiss=3,500=4,000=40%=P4.0D=Govt.=Creatocracy=4 April=Mercury=Hermes=G=A4.
Gnocchi=3,000=30%=P3.0D=3.0=Creativity=Stars=Muses=3 March = C=I>>GIL.
Gnome=7,000=70%=P7.0D=7.0=Language=Assets=Mars=7 July=Pleiades.
Gnostic=5,500=5.5=80%=P5.50=Earth-Midway=5 May = Gaia.
Gnosticism=6,000=60%=P6.0D=Man=Earth=Royalty=6 June=Gaia=Maia>>M=M2.
GNP=1,500=15%=P1.50D=1.5=Authority=Solar Crown=1 May = Maia.
gnu=4,000=40%=P4.0D=Govt.=Creatocracy=4 April=Mercury=Hermes=G=A4.
Go1=10,000=1,000=100%=10.0=Physicality=Tech.=10 Oct.=Uranus=P=1Ø.
Go2=2,000=20%=P2.00D=2.0=Nature=Matter=Moon=2 Feb.=Cupid=N=C+_
Goad=5,500=5.5=80%=P5.50=Earth-Midway=5 May = Gaia.
Go-ahead=2,000=20%=P2.00D=2.0=Nature=Matter=Moon=2 Feb.=Cupid=N=C+_
Goal=15,000=1,500=15%=P1.50D=1.5=Authority=Solar Crown=1 May = Maia.
Goalie=1,500=15%=P1.50D=1.5=Authority=Solar Crown=1 May = Maia.
Goalkeeper=5,000=50%=P5.00D=Law=Time=Venus=5 May = Aphrodite>>L=N.
Goat=9,000=90%=P9.00D=9.0=Abstraction=Gods=Saturn=9Sept.>>A=Ø.
Goat antelope=4,500=5,000=50%=P5.00D=Law=Time=Venus=5 May = Aphrodite>>L=N.
Goatee=2,000=20%=P2.00D=2.0=Nature=Matter=Moon=2 Feb.=Cupid=N=C+_
Goatskin=7,500=7,500=8,000=80%=P8.0D=Economy=Currency=8 Aug.=Zeus>>E=v.
Gob1=7,000=70%=P7.0D=7.0=Language=Assets=Mars=7 July=Pleiades.
Gob2=2,000=20%=P2.00D=2.0=Nature=Matter=Moon=2 Feb.=Cupid=N=C+_
Gobble1=7,500=8,000=80%=P8.0D=Economy=Currency=8 Aug.=Zeus>>E=v.
Gobble2=4,000=40%=P4.0D=Govt.=Creatocracy=4 April=Mercury=Hermes=G=A4.
Gobbledygook=4,500=5,000=50%=P5.00D=Law=Time=Venus=5 May = Aphrodite>>L=N.
Go-between=2,500=3,000=30%=P3.0D=3.0=Creatv=Stars=Muses=3 March = C=I>>GIL.
Goblet=4,000=40%=P4.0D=Govt.=Creatocracy=4 April=Mercury=Hermes=G=A4.
Goblin=7,500=7,500=8,000=80%=P8.0D=Economy=Currency=8 Aug.=Zeus>>E=v.

God>>GOD=17,500=18,000=18%=P1.80=Solar Currency=Maks Currencies=1 Aug.=Maia.
A being conceived as the perfect, omnipotent, omniscient originator and ruler of the
universe, the principal object of faith and worship in monotheistic religions. A being
of supernatural powers, believed in and worshiped by a people. One that is worshipped
or idealized. In the Exodus Zeus Jehovah promised to make Moses a God on certain
conditions. Godship is a state of perfection based on the rights of extraordinary works. The
Creatocracy has Makstianism the religious faith of Makstians and Creatocrats. We believe
that Peter Matthews-Akukalia is an incarnation of Zeus-Jehovah-Allah >> ZeJeAl because
it is only the writer of a thing that can interpret the mind of that thing which he has done by
tracking precisely the hidden secrets of the Mind of GOD and the Gods in the Scriptures.

His works have proven beyond ordinary knowledge things that once beseeched mankind. He is not the almighty but an incarnation of the almighty as the result above shows that the almighty can only be known through incarnation with superior qualities of mind computing through the borders to Jupiter assets and currencies. He is therefore a God under GOD.

As Castle Makupedia, the God of Creatocracy Genius and Mind. Inventor, Maks currencies.

Godchild=5,000=50%=P5.00D=Law=Time=Venus=5 May = Aphrodite>>L=N.
Goddard Robert=2,500=3,000=30%=P3.0D=3.0=Cre.=Stars=Muses=3 March = C=I>>GIL.
Goddaughter=1,500=15%=P1.50D=1.5=Authority=Solar Crown=1 May = Maia.

Goddess=4,500=5,000=50%=P5.00D=Law=Time=Venus=5 May = Aphrodite>>L=N.
A female deity. A woman of great beauty or grace. The Creatocracy recognizes two keys goddesses. The first is Athena Wife of Castle Makupedia and aegis of the Creatocracy. (See book >The Creatocracy Republic>Oaths of the Mind King and God of Creatocracy). The second is his first earthly wife Justina Chinwendu Etigwam Goddess of Makupedia and Empress of the Paradise Nations who suffered so much with him in poverty deprivation and severe privation in his days of creation. She was twenty seven and he was twenty three when they met and married by love at first sight. At the time of writing this book in November 2021, they have just marked their 20th marriage anniversary in October 13.

Godfather=7,500=7,500=8,000=80%=P8.0D=Economy=Currency=8 Aug.=Zeus>>E=v.
God forsaken=3,500=4,000=40%=P4.0D=Govt.=Creatocracy=4 April=Hermes=G=A4.

Godhead=3,000=30%=P3.0D=3.0=Creativity=Stars=Muses=3 March = C=I>>GIL.
Now results indicate the Godhead studies all creative activities or creativity of Mankind. Using Mind Computing the Creatocracy established the existence of a Council of Gods represented in the Greek myths and declared by the almighty in the Scriptures of the Bible and Quran. They are known as the exalted chiefs in the Quran and as the Gods in the Bible. In the Creative Sciences they are the Creatocracy of the Universes functioning as the board of directors reporting to the Chairman Zeus Jehovah the Most High.

Godless=3,500=4,000=40%=P4.0D=Govt.=Creatocracy=4 April=Mercury=Hermes=G=A4.
Godly=1,000=100%=10.0=1.0=Mind=Sun=1 January=Helios >> M=E4.
Godmother=3,500=4,000=40%=P4.0D=Govt.=Creatocracy=4 April=Hermes=G=A4.
Godparent=2,000=20%=P2.00D=2.0=Nature=Matter=Moon=2 Feb.=Cupid=N=C+_
Godsend=3,500=4,000=40%=P4.0D=Govt.=Creatocracy=4 April=Hermes=G=A4.
Godson=1,500=15%=P1.50D=1.5=Authority=Solar Crown=1 May = Maia.
Godthàb=4,500=5,000=50%=P5.00D=Law=Time=Venus=5 May = Aphrodite>>L=N.
Godunov Boris=4,000=40%=P4.0D=Govt.=Creatocracy=4April=Mercury=Hermes=G=A4.
Godwin Austin=1,500=15%=P1.50D=1.5=Authority=Solar Crown=1 May = Maia.
Goes=3,500=4,000=40%=P4.0D=Govt.=Creatocracy=4 April=Mercury=Hermes=G=A4.
Goethals George Washington=2,500=3,000=30%=P3.0D=3.0=Stars=Muses=3 March= GIL

Goethe Johann=4,000=40%=P4.0D=Govt.=Creatocracy=4 April=Mercury=Hermes=G=A4.
Go-getter=2,000=20%=P2.00D=2.0=Nature=Matter=Moon=2 Feb.=Cupid=N=C+_
Goggle=13,000=13%=P1.30=Solar Core=Faculty=13 January=Athena.
Go-go=9,000=90%=P9.00D=9.0=Abstraction=Gods=Saturn=9Sept.>>A=Ø.
Gogol Nikolai Vasillevich=2,000=20%=P2.00D=2.0=Nature=Moon=2 Feb.=Cupid=N=C+_
Goiânia=4,500=5,000=50%=P5.00D=Law=Time=Venus=5 May = Aphrodite>>L=N.
Going=10,000=1,000=100%=10.0=Physicality=Tech.=10 Oct.=Uranus=P=1Ø.
Goiter=7,500=8,000=80%=P8.0D=Economy=Currency=8 Aug.=Zeus>>E=v.
Golan Heights=6,500=7,000=70%=P7.0D=7.0=Language=Assets=Mars=7 July=Pleiades.
Gold=10,000=1,000=100%=10.0=Physicality=Tech.=10 Oct.=Uranus=P=1Ø.
Goldbrick=3,000=30%=P3.0D=3.0=Creativity=Stars=Muses=3 March = C=I>>GIL.
Gold Coast=7,000=70%=P7.0D=7.0=Language=Assets=Mars=7 July=Pleiades.
Golden=10,000=1,000=100%=10.0=Physicality=Tech.=10 Oct.=Uranus=P=1Ø.
Golden eagle=4,500=5,000=50%=P5.00D=Law=Time=Venus=5 May = Aphrodite>>L=N.

Golden Gate=6,000=60%=P6.0D=Man=Earth=Royalty=6 June=Gaia=Maia>>M=M2.
The Golden Creativity Formula was the first formula ever written by the King in his Creative Sciences. C=GIL. This became the golden gate to all other formulas that make Makupedia.

Golden mean=2,000=20%=P2.00D=2.0=Nature=Matter=Moon=2 Feb.=Cupid=N=C+_
Golden Rod=6,500=7,000=70%=P7.0D=7.0=Language=Assets=Mars=7 July=Pleiades.
Goldfinch=6,500=7,000=70%=P7.0D=7.0=Language=Assets=Mars=7 July=Pleiades.
Goldfish=7,000=70%=P7.0D=7.0=Language=Assets=Mars=7 July=Pleiades.
Gold leaf=4,500=5,000=50%=P5.00D=Law=Time=Venus=5 May = Aphrodite>>L=N.
Goldman=3,000=30%=P3.0D=3.0=Creativity=Stars=Muses=3 March = C=I>>GIL.
Gold rush=6,000=60%=P6.0D=Man=Earth=Royalty=6 June=Gaia=Maia>>M=M2.
Goldsmith=5,000=50%=P5.00D=Law=Time=Venus=5 May = Aphrodite>>L=N.
Gold standard=9,000=90%=P9.00D=9.0=Abstraction=Gods=Saturn=9Sept.>>A=Ø.
Golem=7,500=8,000=80%=P8.0D=Economy=Currency=8 Aug.=Zeus>>E=v.
Golf=15,000=1,500=15%=P1.50D=1.5=Authority=Solar Crown=1 May = Maia.
Golgotha=1,000=100%=10.0=1.0=Mind=Sun=1 January=Helios >> M=E4.

Goliath=5,000=50%=P5.00D=Law=Time=Venus=5 May = Aphrodite>>L=N.
David was possessed by the Spirit of Aphrodite. Note the Bible says David was an angel. Being so in alignment with the result we deduce that David was an incarnation of Aphrodite. This means that the Gods can transform into any form or gender they desire. Apart from being the Goddess of sex beauty or birth Aphrodite is a Goddess of war. These were the exact tendencies of King David. Solomon has more to do with Athena for wisdom.

Gomel=4,500=5,000=50%=P5.00D=Law=Time=Venus=5 May = Aphrodite>>L=N.
Gomorrah=3,500=4,000=40%=P4.0D=Govt.=Creatocracy=4 April=Hermes=G=A4.
Gompers Samuel=3,500=4,000=40%=P4.0D=Govt.=Creatocracy=4 April=Hermes=G=A4.
-gin=6,500=7,000=70%=P7.0D=7.0=Language=Assets=Mars=7 July=Pleiades.
Gonad=15,000=1,500=15%=P1.50D=1.5=Authority=Solar Crown=1 May = Maia.

Gondola=10,000=1,000=100%=10.0=Physicality=Tech.=10 Oct.=Uranus=P=1Ø.
Gondolier=3,500=4,000=40%=P4.0D=Govt.=Creatocracy=4 April=Hermes=G=A4.
Gone=9,500=10,000=1,000=100%=10.0=Physicality=Tech.=10 Oct.=Uranus=P=1Ø.
Goner=3,500=4,000=40%=P4.0D=Govt.=Creatocracy=4 April=Mercury=Hermes=G=A4.
Gong=5,500=5.5=80%=P5.50=Earth-Midway=5 May = Gaia.
Gonorrhea=11,000=11%=P1.10D=1.1=Idea=Brainchild=Inv.=11 Nov.=SC=Athena>>I=MT.
Goo=5,000=50%=P5.00D=Law=Time=Venus=5 May = Aphrodite>>L=N.
Goober=10,000=1,000=100%=10.0=Physicality=Tech.=10 Oct.=Uranus=P=1Ø.
Good=10,000=1,000=100%=10.0=Physicality=Tech.=10 Oct.=Uranus=P=1Ø.
Goodbye=2,000=20%=P2.00D=2.0=Nature=Matter=Moon=2 Feb.=Cupid=N=C+_
Good Friday=6,500=7,000=70%=P7.0D=7.0=Language=Assets=Mars=7 July=Pleiades.
Good hearted=1,500=15%=P1.50D=1.5=Authority=Solar Crown=1 May = Maia.
Good Hope=6,000=60%=P6.0D=Man=Earth=Royalty=6 June=Gaia=Maia>>M=M2.
Good humored=1,000=100%=10.0=1.0=Mind=Sun=1 January=Helios >> M=E4.
Good looking=2,500=3,000=30%=P3.0D=3.0=Creatv=Stars=Muses=3 March = C=I>>GIL.
Goodly=3,500=4,000=40%=P4.0D=Govt.=Creatocracy=4 April=Mercury=Hermes=G=A4.
Good natured=2,500=3,000=30%=P3.0D=3.0=Creatv=Stars=Muses=3 March = C=I>>GIL.
Goodness=7,500=7,500=8,000=80%=P8.0D=Economy=Currency=8 Aug.=Zeus>>E=v.

Good Samaritan=7,500=8,000=80%=P8.0D=Economy=Currency=8 Aug.=Zeus>>E=v.
The Good Samaritan of Jesus story was Zeus in human form and how to recognize him.
"For by their fruits we shall know them".

Goodwill=7,000=70%=P7.0D=7.0=Language=Assets=Mars=7 July=Pleiades.
Formula is a goodwill extended to all nations. The Creatocracy bids everyone to come
thus fulfilling the prophecy foretold by Emerson's Nature.

Goody=4,000=40%=P4.0D=Govt.=Creatocracy=4 April=Mercury=Hermes=G=A4.
Goody-goody=2,500=3,000=30%=P3.0D=3.0=Creatv=Stars=Muses=3 March = C=I>>GIL.
Goof=10,000=1,000=100%=10.0=Physicality=Tech.=10 Oct.=Uranus=P=1Ø.
Goofball=5,500=5.5=80%=P5.50=Earth-Midway=5 May = Gaia.
Googol=5,500=5.5=80%=P5.50=Earth-Midway=5 May = Gaia.
Gook=1,500=15%=P1.50D=1.5=Authority=Solar Crown=1 May = Maia.
Goon=7,000=70%=P7.0D=7.0=Language=Assets=Mars=7 July=Pleiades.
Goose=10,000=1,000=100%=10.0=Physicality=Tech.=10 Oct.=Uranus=P=1Ø.
Gooseberry=6,000=60%=P6.0D=Man=Earth=Royalty=6 June=Gaia=Maia>>M=M2.
Goosebumps=5,500=5.5=80%=P5.50=Earth-Midway=5 May = Gaia.
Gooseflesh=1,500=15%=P1.50D=1.5=Authority=Solar Crown=1 May = Maia.
Gooseneck=7,500=7,500=8,000=80%=P8.0D=Economy=Currency=8 Aug.=Zeus>>E=v.
Goose step=7,500=7,500=8,000=80%=P8.0D=Economy=Currency=8 Aug.=Zeus>>E=v.
GOP=2,000=20%=P2.00D=2.0=Nature=Matter=Moon=2 Feb.=Cupid=N=C+_
Gopher=6,000=60%=P6.0D=Man=Earth=Royalty=6 June=Gaia=Maia>>M=M2.
Gorbachev Mikhall=4,500=5,000=50%=P5.00D=Law=Time=Venus=5 May = Odite>>L=N.
Gorel=4,500=5,000=50%=P5.00D=Law=Time=Venus=5 May = Aphrodite>>L=N.

Gore2=7,500=7,500=8,000=80%=P8.0D=Economy=Currency=8 Aug.=Zeus>>E=v.
Gore3=4,000=40%=P4.0D=Govt.=Creatocracy=4 April=Mercury=Hermes=G=A4.
Gore Albert=4,500=5,000=50%=P5.00D=Law=Time=Venus=5 May = Aphrodite>>L=N.
Gorge=12,000=12%=P1.20D=1.2=Knowledge=Education=12Dec.=Athena>>K=F.
Gorgeous=6,500=7,000=70%=P7.0D=7.0=Language=Assets=Mars=7 July=Pleiades.
Gorilla=11,000=11%=P1.10D=1.1=Idea=Brainchild=Inv.=11 Nov.=SC=Athena>>I=MT.
Gorky=5,500=5.5=80%=P5.50=Earth-Midway=5 May = Gaia.
Gorky Maksim=2,000=20%=P2.00D=2.0=Nature=Matter=Moon=2 Feb.=Cupid=N=C+_
Gorlovka=4,500=5,000=50%=P5.00D=Law=Time=Venus=5 May = Aphrodite>>L=N.
Gormandize=3,000=30%=P3.0D=3.0=Creativity=Stars=Muses=3 March = C=I>>GIL.
Gorse=5,500=5.5=80%=P5.50=Earth-Midway=5 May = Gaia.
Gory=6,000=60%=P6.0D=Man=Earth=Royalty=6 June=Gaia=Maia>>M=M2.
Gosh=4,000=40%=P4.0D=Govt.=Creatocracy=4 April=Mercury=Hermes=G=A4.
Goshawk=7,500=7,500=8,000=80%=P8.0D=Economy=Currency=8 Aug.=Zeus>>E=v.
Gosling=2,500=3,000=30%=P3.0D=3.0=Creativity=Stars=Muses=3 March = C=I>>GIL.
Gospel=10,000=1,000=100%=10.0=Physicality=Tech.=10 Oct.=Uranus=P=1Ø.
Gospel music=8,500=9,000=90%=P9.00D=9.0=Abstraction=Gods=Saturn=9Sept.>>A=Ø.
Gossamer=11,000=11%=P1.10D=1.1=Idea=Brainchild=Inv.=11 Nov.=SC=Athena>>I=MT.
Gossip=7,500=7,500=8,000=80%=P8.0D=Economy=Currency=8 Aug.=Zeus>>E=v.
Got=3,000=30%=P3.0D=3.0=Creativity=Stars=Muses=3 March = C=I>>GIL.
Göteborg=5,000=50%=P5.00D=Law=Time=Venus=5 May = Aphrodite>>L=N.
Goth=7,500=8,000=80%=P8.0D=Economy=Currency=8 Aug.=Zeus>>E=v.
Gothic=10,000=1,000=100%=10.0=Physicality=Tech.=10 Oct.=Uranus=P=1Ø.
Gotland=7,500=7,500=8,000=80%=P8.0D=Economy=Currency=8 Aug.=Zeus>>E=v.
Gotten=2,000=20%=P2.00D=2.0=Nature=Matter=Moon=2 Feb.=Cupid=N=C+_
Gouge=10,000=1,000=100%=10.0=Physicality=Tech.=10 Oct.=Uranus=P=1Ø.
Goulash=7,000=70%=P7.0D=7.0=Language=Assets=Mars=7 July=Pleiades.
Gounod Charles=3,000=30%=P3.0D=3.0=Creativity=Stars=Muses=3 March = C=I>>GIL.
Gourd=10,000=1,000=100%=10.0=Physicality=Tech.=10 Oct.=Uranus=P=1Ø.
Gourde=4,000=40%=P4.0D=Govt.=Creatocracy=4 April=Mercury=Hermes=G=A4.
Gourmand=5,000=50%=P5.00D=Law=Time=Venus=5 May = Aphrodite>>L=N.
Gourmet=7,500=7,500=8,000=80%=P8.0D=Economy=Currency=8 Aug.=Zeus>>E=v.
Gout=12,500=13,000=13%=P1.30=Solar Core=Faculty=13 January=Athena.
Gov.=2,000=20%=P2.00D=2.0=Nature=Matter=Moon=2 Feb.=Cupid=N=C+_
Govern=8,500=9,000=90%=P9.00D=9.0=Abstraction=Gods=Saturn=9Sept.>>A=Ø.
Governess=6,000=60%=P6.0D=Man=Earth=Royalty=6 June=Gaia=Maia>>M=M2.

Government=10,000=1,000=100%=10.0=Physicality=Tech.=10 Oct.=Uranus=P=1Ø.
The fourth dimension (4ø) of the Universe and third arm of the Creatocracy after royalty and Media. Labor comes last but not the least. Government is the management arm of Creatocratic resources. It builds nations power relationships networks and organizations. Peter Matthews-Akukalia, Castle Makupedia wrote the formula for government as G=A4.

Government Guidance Systems is a series of programs methods and laws developed to Institutionalize creative governance or the Creatocracy. It is based on the concept of

Government engineering in the Creative Sciences and measured on the Maks Government Systems Score Table. Score >>1.0/10.0>>10,000=1000=100=10.0.

Government >> Greek word Gouvern (To guide, drive, lead); ment (Mēns >> mind). Hence Government is defined herein as the ability to guide drive and lead the mind. An ability only possible by those with the specialized metric knowledge of the mind. It is recommended hence that Creative Scientists are engrained in every aspect of government.

The GGS is the foundation for establishing the Creatocratic Nations Organizations (C3 Nations Organizations or simply C3). It is an association of nations that have interests and practice Creativity Creatocism and Creatocracy. It is a department of the Paradise Nations.

Creativity is the philosophy for the personal life of citizens. Creatocism is the Creative Economy designed for the establishment of intellectual property businesses. Creatocracy is the political life of the nation managed through Creatocratic institutions. C3 are concepts developed for the Institutionalizing and entrenchment of world Creatocracy. Ephesians 1:10

Maks Government Systems Score Table.>> GOVERNMENT FORMS DATABASE. Score >>10/10.0>>10,000=1000=100=10.0.
1. [-Cracy] = 2/10 2.Aristocracy = 8/10 3.Geniocracy = 10/10 4.Meritocracy = 10/10
5. Timocracy = 10/10 6.Technocracy = 10/10 7.Autocracy =4/10 8.Despotism = 2.5/10
9. Dictatorship =5/10 10.Fascism = 10/10 11.Monarchy = 5/10 12.Bankocracy = 3.3/10
>> Genius operations. See Geniocracy., 13.Corporatocracy =1.3/10
>> Faculty of Creative Intelligence >> Faculty of Creative Sciences.,14.Nepotocracy = 10/10
15. Mafia State = 8/10 16.Totalitarianism = 10/10
17. Democracy = 1.7/10 >> Private Assets >> Capitalism., 18.Oligarchy = 6.5/10
19. Ergatocracy = 3.5/10, 20.Netocracy = 10/10 21.Plutocracy = 8/10 22.Theocracy = 6/10
23. Anarchy = 4.5/10 24.Anocracy = 3.5/10

---

25. Youthocracy = 3.5/10
(Coined by Tunde Eso in his book Vision For Africa), a Nigerian author, public relations specialist and managing consultant of Professional School of Public Relations and Human Resources. Youthocracy is Government of the People, by the Youth and for the People.

---

26. Creatocracy = 10/10. Established on the 10,000=1,000=100=10.0
Based on the principle of alignment Creatocracy is driven by those elements that match with it. Creatocrats are built on genius, merit, technology, time expertise, fascism (excellence and greatness or nothing less), nepotism (rights based on royalty), totalitarian (based on absolute sovereignty earned through intellectual property laws), Netocracy (relationships through communication, networks price and interests).
The key elements of Creatocracy are seven = 7.0 = Language = Assets = Works = Speculative (50%) >> Precision (100%) = Computational Lexicography >> Word Power >> Database >> Data Mining >> Government Guidance Systems >> Castle Makupedia.

The height of governance is Creatocracy. The peak for the Creatocrat is royalty marbled on the brick walls of the Castle Makupedia. There is a bit of everything in the Creatocracy. So Creatocracy is everything and everything is Creatocracy. Peter Matthews-Akukalia is established as Castle Makupedia God of Creatocracy Genius & Mind. He conceptualized defined measured applied owns it and emerged a world power forever by it asserted.

Governor=10,000=1,000=100%=10.0=Physicality=Tech.=10 Oct.=Uranus=P=1Ø.
Wole Olaniyan is the first Governor of the Creatocracy Bank institution. The Creatocracy has a body of Governors who are Creative Scientist Professionals at the peak of practice.

Govt.=500=5%=P5.00D=5.0=Law=Time=Venus=5 May=Aphrodite>>L=N.
Gown=10,000=1,000=100%=10.0=Physicality=Tech.=10 Oct.=Uranus=P=1Ø.
Goya y Lucientes=4,500=5,000=50%=P5.00D=Law=Time=Venus=5 May = Odite>>L=N.
G.P.=1,000=100%=10.0=1.0=Mind=Sun=1 January=Helios >> M=E4.
GPA=1,500=15%=P1.50D=1.5=Authority=Solar Crown=1 May = Maia.
GPO=3,000=30%=P3.0D=3.0=Creativity=Stars=Muses=3 March = C=I>>GIL.
GQ=1,000=100%=10.0=1.0=Mind=Sun=1 January=Helios >> M=E4.
gr.=1,500=15%=P1.50D=1.5=Authority=Solar Crown=1 May = Maia.
Gr.=1,000=100%=10.0=1.0=Mind=Sun=1 January=Helios >> M=E4.
Grab=10,000=1,000=100%=10.0=Physicality=Tech.=10 Oct.=Uranus=P=1Ø.
Grab bag=7,500=8,000=80%=P8.0D=Economy=Currency=8 Aug.=Zeus>>E=v.
Gracchus Tiberius=10,000=1,000=100%=10.0=Physicality=Tech.=10 Oct.=Uranus=P=1Ø.
Grace=10,000=1,000=100%=10.0=Physicality=Tech.=10 Oct.=Uranus=P=1Ø.
Grace period=13,500=14,000=14%=P1.40D=1.4=Mgt.=Solar Energy=13 May=Athena=0.1
Gracious=10,000=1,000=100%=10.0=Physicality=Tech.=10 Oct.=Uranus=P=1Ø.
Grackle=6,000=60%=P6.0D=Man=Earth=Royalty=6 June=Gaia=Maia>>M=M2.
Grad=1,500=15%=P1.50D=1.5=Authority=Solar Crown=1 May = Maia.
Gradation=11,500=12,000=12%=P1.20D=1.2=Knowledge=Educ.=12Dec.=Athena>>K=F.
Grade=10,000=1,000=100%=10.0=Physicality=Tech.=10 Oct.=Uranus=P=1Ø.
Grade school=1,500=15%=P1.50D=1.5=Authority=Solar Crown=1 May = Maia.
Gradient=3,500=4,000=40%=P4.0D=Govt.=Creatocracy=4 April=Hermes=G=A4.
Gradual=6,500=7,000=70%=P7.0D=7.0=Language=Assets=Mars=7 July=Pleiades.
Graduate=10,000=1,000=100%=10.0=Physicality=Tech.=10 Oct.=Uranus=P=1Ø.
Graduation=10,000=1,000=100%=10.0=Physicality=Tech.=10 Oct.=Uranus=P=1Ø.
Graffito=10,000=1,000=100%=10.0=Physicality=Tech.=10 Oct.=Uranus=P=1Ø.
Graft1=10,000=1,000=100%=10.0=Physicality=Tech.=10 Oct.=Uranus=P=1Ø.
Graft2=7,000=70%=P7.0D=7.0=Language=Assets=Mars=7 July=Pleiades.
Graham=4,000=40%=P4.0D=Govt.=Creatocracy=4 April=Mercury=Hermes=G=A4.
Graham Martha=3,000=30%=P3.0D=3.0=Creativity=Stars=Muses=3 March = C=I>>GIL.
Grail=14,000=14%=P1.40D=1.4=Mgt.=Solar Energy=13 May=Athena=SC=0.1
Grain=10,000=1,000=100%=10.0=Physicality=Tech.=10 Oct.=Uranus=P=1Ø.
Grain alcohol=1,500=15%=P1.50D=1.5=Authority=Solar Crown=1 May = Maia.
Grain elevator=3,500=4,000=40%=P4.0D=Govt.=Creatocracy=4 April=Hermes=G=A4.
Gram=5,000=50%=P5.00D=Law=Time=Venus=5 May = Aphrodite>>L=N.

-gram=6,500=7,000=70%=P7.0D=7.0=Language=Assets=Mars=7 July=Pleiades.
Grammar=10,000=1,000=100%=10.0=Physicality=Tech.=10 Oct.=Uranus=P=1Ø.
Grammar school=1,500=15%=P1.50D=1.5=Authority=Solar Crown=1 May = Maia.
Gram molecular weight=4,500=5,000=50%=P5.00D=Law=Venus=5May=Odite>>L=N.
Gram molecule=1,000=100%=10.0=1.0=Mind=Sun=1 January=Helios >> M=E4.
Gram negative=4,500=5,000=50%=P5.00D=Law=Time=Venus=5 May = Aphrodite>>L=N.
Gramophone=2,000=20%=P2.00D=2.0=Nature=Matter=Moon=2 Feb.=Cupid=N=C+_
Grampian Mountains=7,000=70%=P7.0D=7.0=Language=Assets=Mars=7 July=Pleiades.
Gram positive=4,000=40%=P4.0D=Govt.=Creatocracy=4 April=Mercury=Hermes=G=A4.
Grampus=7,000=70%=P7.0D=7.0=Language=Assets=Mars=7 July=Pleiades.
Gram's method=12,000=12%=P1.20D=1.2=Knowledge=Education=12Dec.=Athena>>K=F.
Granada=4,500=5,000=50%=P5.00D=Law=Time=Venus=5 May = Aphrodite>>L=N.
Granary=6,000=60%=P6.0D=Man=Earth=Royalty=6 June=Gaia=Maia>>M=M2.
Grand=10,000=1,000=100%=10.0=Physicality=Tech.=10 Oct.=Uranus=P=1Ø.
Grandam=5,500=5.5=80%=P5.50=Earth-Midway=5 May = Gaia.

Grand Banks=5,500=5.5=80%=P5.50=Earth-Midway=5 May = Gaia.
Mind banks >> The Creatocracy Bank >> The Makupedia Bank >> Castle Makupedia Bank.

Grand Canal=13,000=13%=P1.30=Solar Core=Faculty=13 January=Athena.
Grand Canyon=14,000=14%=P1.40D=1.4=Mgt.=Solar Energy=13 May=Athena=SC=0.1
Grandchild=3,500=4,000=40%=P4.0D=Govt.=Creatocracy=4 April=Hermes=G=A4.
Granddaughter=3,500=4,000=40%=P4.0D=Govt.=Creatocracy=4 April=Hermes=G=A4.
Grandeur=4,500=5,000=50%=P5.00D=Law=Time=Venus=5 May = Aphrodite>>L=N.
Grandfather=9,000=90%=P9.00D=9.0=Abstraction=Gods=Saturn=9Sept.>>A=Ø.
Grandiloquence=4,500=5,000=50%=P5.00D=Law=Time=Venus=5 May = Odite>>L=N.
Grandiose=6,500=7,000=70%=P7.0D=7.0=Language=Assets=Mars=7 July=Pleiades.
Grand jury=9,500=10,000=1,000=100%=10.0=Physicality=Tech.=10 Oct.=Uranus=P=1Ø.
Grandma=1,500=15%=P1.50D=1.5=Authority=Solar Crown=1 May = Maia.
Grandmal=6,500=7,000=70%=P7.0D=7.0=Language=Assets=Mars=7 July=Pleiades.
Grandma Moses=2,500=3,000=30%=P3.0D=3.0=Cre.=Stars=Muses=3 March = C=I>>GIL.

Grandmother=5,000=50%=P5.00D=Law=Time=Venus=5 May = Aphrodite>>L=N.
Peter Matthews-Akukalia lived and realized his potentials while living with his grandmother Mrs. Diana Matthews in 27, Moore street, Onitsha, Anambra State. Nigeria. She was a prophetesses and international missionary who established churches. She prayed the gifts into him which he painstakingly developed through writing teaching and study. See the book >> Makupedialand >> Remember Diana Matthews. Also the book>> The Creatocracy Republic, reference book > Last of the Noble Amazons. A tribute to Mrs. Diana Matthews. Note that the king adopted the family name as suffix to the previous Peter Matthews to become Peter Matthews-Akukalia. By this means he had began his dynasty created his empire through hard work and built his nation where he reigns as the Most sovereign.

Grandpa=1,500=15%=P1.50D=1.5=Authority=Solar Crown=1 May = Maia.
Grandparent=3,500=4,000=40%=P4.0D=Govt.=Creatocracy=4 April=Hermes=G=A4.
Grand piano=5,500=5.5=80%=P5.50=Earth-Midway=5 May = Gaia.
Grand Rapids=7,000=70%=P7.0D=7.0=Language=Assets=Mars=7 July=Pleiades.
Grand slam=9,500=10,000=1,000=100%=10.0=Physicality=Tech.=10 Oct.=Uranus=P=1Ø.
Grandson=3,500=4,000=40%=P4.0D=Govt.=Creatocracy=4 April=Hermes=G=A4.
Grandstand=7,500=8,000=80%=P8.0D=Economy=Currency=8 Aug.=Zeus>>E=v.
Grange=10,000=1,000=100%=10.0=Physicality=Tech.=10 Oct.=Uranus=P=1Ø.
Granite=10,000=1,000=100%=10.0=Physicality=Tech.=10 Oct.=Uranus=P=1Ø.
Granny=2,000=20%=P2.00D=2.0=Nature=Matter=Moon=2 Feb.=Cupid=N=C+_
Granola=10,000=1,000=100%=10.0=Physicality=Tech.=10 Oct.=Uranus=P=1Ø.
Grant=10,000=1,000=100%=10.0=Physicality=Tech.=10 Oct.=Uranus=P=1Ø.
Grant Ulysses=6,500=7,000=70%=P7.0D=7.0=Lang.=Assets=Mars=7 July=Pleiades.
Granular=4,000=40%=P4.0D=Govt.=Creatocracy=4 April=Mercury=Hermes=G=A4.
Granulate=5,000=50%=P5.00D=Law=Time=Venus=5 May = Aphrodite>>L=N.
Granule=5,000=50%=P5.00D=Law=Time=Venus=5 May = Aphrodite>>L=N.
Grape=13,000=13%=P1.30=Solar Core=Faculty=13 January=Athena.
Grapefruit=8,500=9,000=90%=P9.00D=9.0=Abstraction=Gods=Saturn=9Sept.>>A=Ø.
Grapeshot=5,500=5.5=80%=P5.50=Earth-Midway=5 May = Gaia.
Grape sugar=1,500=15%=P1.50D=1.5=Authority=Solar Crown=1 May = Maia.
Grapevine=7,000=70%=P7.0D=7.0=Language=Assets=Mars=7 July=Pleiades.

Graph=10,000=1,000=100%=10.0=Physicality=Tech.=10 Oct.=Uranus=P=1Ø.

PICTURE OF RESULTS: INTEREST DATABASE. CODE 10F.

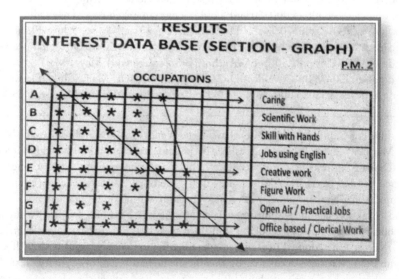

Graphic analysis of student potentials. Creative Scientists are taught to conduct the Students Career Analysis Program (SCAP) at all levels. An invention of Peter Matthews-

Akukalia, Castle Makupedia in his book The Oracle: Principles of Creative Sciences. He emerged the World's 1st Creative Scientist. Published by AuthorHouse US, U.K. in 2012.

-graph=10,000=1,000=100%=10.0=Physicality=Tech.=10 Oct.=Uranus=P=1Ø.
-grapher=6,000=60%=P6.0D=Man=Earth=Royalty=6 June=Gaia=Maia>>M=M2.
Graphic=10,000=1,000=100%=10.0=Physicality=Tech.=10 Oct.=Uranus=P=1Ø.
Graphic arts=9,000=90%=P9.00D=9.0=Abstraction=Gods=Saturn=9Sept.>>A=Ø.
Graphics=10,000=1,000=100%=10.0=Physicality=Tech.=10 Oct.=Uranus=P=1Ø.
Graphite=10,000=1,000=100%=10.0=Physicality=Tech.=10 Oct.=Uranus=P=1Ø.
Graphology=2,000=20%=P2.00D=2.0=Nature=Matter=Moon=2 Feb.=Cupid=N=C+_
-graphy=10,000=1,000=100%=10.0=Physicality=Tech.=10 Oct.=Uranus=P=1Ø.
Grapnel=7,500=7,500=8,000=80%=P8.0D=Economy=Currency=8 Aug.=Zeus>>E=v.
Grapple=10,000=1,000=100%=10.0=Physicality=Tech.=10 Oct.=Uranus=P=1Ø.
Grappling iron=1,500=15%=P1.50D=1.5=Authority=Solar Crown=1 May = Maia.
Grasp=10,000=1,000=100%=10.0=Physicality=Tech.=10 Oct.=Uranus=P=1Ø.
Grasping=1,000=100%=10.0=1.0=Mind=Sun=1 January=Helios >> M=E4.
Grass=10,000=1,000=100%=10.0=Physicality=Tech.=10 Oct.=Uranus=P=1Ø.
Grass Günter=2,500=3,000=30%=P3.0D=3.0=Creatv=Stars=Muses=3 March = C=I>>GIL.
Grasshopper=6,500=7,000=70%=P7.0D=7.0=Language=Assets=Mars=7 July=Pleiades.
Grassland=5,500=5.5=80%=P5.50=Earth-Midway=5 May = Gaia.
Grassroots=7,500=7,500=8,000=80%=P8.0D=Economy=Currency=8 Aug.=Zeus>>E=v.
Grate1=10,000=1,000=100%=10.0=Physicality=Tech.=10 Oct.=Uranus=P=1Ø.
Grate2=10,000=1,000=100%=10.0=Physicality=Tech.=10 Oct.=Uranus=P=1Ø.
Grateful=4,500=5,000=50%=P5.00D=Law=Time=Venus=5 May = Aphrodite>>L=N.
Gratian=7,500=7,500=8,000=80%=P8.0D=Economy=Currency=8 Aug.=Zeus>>E=v.
Gratify=8,500=9,000=90%=P9.00D=9.0=Abstraction=Gods=Saturn=9Sept.>>A=Ø.
Grating=3,500=4,000=40%=P4.0D=Govt.=Creatocracy=4 April=Mercury=Hermes=G=A4.
Gratis=2,000=20%=P2.00D=2.0=Nature=Matter=Moon=2 Feb.=Cupid=N=C+_
Gratitude=2,000=20%=P2.00D=2.0=Nature=Matter=Moon=2 Feb.=Cupid=N=C+_
Gratuitous=5,500=5.5=80%=P5.50=Earth-Midway=5 May = Gaia.
Gratuity=3,500=4,000=40%=P4.0D=Govt.=Creatocracy=4 April=Mercury=Hermes=G=A4.
Gravel=4,000=40%=P4.0D=Govt.=Creatocracy=4 April=Mercury=Hermes=G=A4.
Grave2=10,000=1,000=100%=10.0=Physicality=Tech.=10 Oct.=Uranus=P=1Ø.
Grave3=2,000=20%=P2.00D=2.0=Nature=Matter=Moon=2 Feb.=Cupid=N=C+_
Gravel=7,500=7,500=8,000=80%=P8.0D=Economy=Currency=8 Aug.=Zeus>>E=v.
Graves Robert=8,500=9,000=90%=P9.00D=9.0=Abstr.=Gods=Saturn=9Sept.>>A=Ø.
Gravestone=1,000=100%=10.0=1.0=Mind=Sun=1 January=Helios >> M=E4.
Graveyard=1,000=100%=10.0=1.0=Mind=Sun=1 January=Helios >> M=E4.
Graveyard shift=7,500=8,000=80%=P8.0D=Economy=Currency=8 Aug.=Zeus>>E=v.
Gravid=1,500=15%=P1.50D=1.5=Authority=Solar Crown=1 May = Maia.
Gravimetric=4,500=5,000=50%=P5.00D=Law=Time=Venus=5 May = Aphrodite>>L=N.
Gravitate=5,000=50%=P5.00D=Law=Time=Venus=5 May = Aphrodite>>L=N.
Gravitation=7,500=8,000=80%=P8.0D=Economy=Currency=8 Aug.=Zeus>>E=v.
Graviton=5,500=5.5=80%=P5.50=Earth-Midway=5 May = Gaia.
Gravity=10,000=1,000=100%=10.0=Physicality=Tech.=10 Oct.=Uranus=P=1Ø.

Gravure=6,500=7,000=70%=P7.0D=7.0=Language=Assets=Mars=7 July=Pleiades.
Gravy=10,500=11,000=11%=P1.10D=1.1=Idea=Brainchild=Inv.=11 Nov.=SC=Athena
   >>I=MT.
Gray=11,000=11%=P1.10D=1.1=Idea=Brainchild=Inv.=11 Nov.=SC=Athena>>I=MT.
Gray Thomas=2,000=20%=P2.00D=2.0=Nature=Matter=Moon=2 Feb.=Cupid=N=C+_
Graybeard=1,500=15%=P1.50D=1.5=Authority=Solar Crown=1 May = Maia.
Gray matter=5,000=50%=P5.00D=Law=Time=Venus=5 May = Aphrodite>>L=N.
Gray whale=7,000=70%=P7.0D=7.0=Language=Assets=Mars=7 July=Pleiades.
Gray wolf=5,500=5.5=80%=P5.50=Earth-Midway=5 May = Gaia.
Graz=6,500=7,000=70%=P7.0D=7.0=Language=Assets=Mars=7 July=Pleiades.
Graze1=7,500=7,500=8,000=80%=P8.0D=Economy=Currency=8 Aug.=Zeus>>E=v.
Graze2=6,500=7,000=70%=P7.0D=7.0=Language=Assets=Mars=7 July=Pleiades.
Grease=10,000=1,000=100%=10.0=Physicality=Tech.=10 Oct.=Uranus=P=1Ø.
Greasepaint=1,000=100%=10.0=1.0=Mind=Sun=1 January=Helios >> M=E4.
Greasewood=6,500=7,000=70%=P7.0D=7.0=Language=Assets=Mars=7 July=Pleiades.
Greasy=4,500=5,000=50%=P5.00D=Law=Time=Venus=5 May = Aphrodite>>L=N.

Great=10,000=1,000=100%=10.0=Physicality=Tech.=10 Oct.=Uranus=P=1Ø.
Greatness is synonymous with excellence = 100%. Hence "Makupedia the Great", "Akukalia the Great". His inventions include Makupedia the First Human Mind Super Computers.

Great ape=5,000=50%=P5.00D=Law=Time=Venus=5 May = Aphrodite>>L=N.
Great Barrier Reef=7,500=7,500=8,000=80%=P8.0D=Econ.=Curr.=8 Aug.=Zeus>>E=v.
Great Basin=8,500=9,000=90%=P9.00D=9.0=Abstraction=Gods=Saturn=9Sept.>>A=Ø.
Great Bear Lake=4,000=40%=P4.0D=Govt.=Creatocracy=4 April=Hermes=G=A4.
Great Britain=7,500=8,000=80%=P8.0D=Economy=Currency=8 Aug.=Zeus>>E=v.
Great circle=7,500=7,500=8,000=80%=P8.0D=Economy=Currency=8 Aug.=Zeus>>E=v.
Great coat=1,500=15%=P1.50D=1.5=Authority=Solar Crown=1 May = Maia.
Great Dane=5,500=5.5=80%=P5.50=Earth-Midway=5 May = Gaia.
Greater=5,000=50%=P5.00D=Law=Time=Venus=5 May = Aphrodite>>L=N.
Greater Antilles=7,000=70%=P7.0D=7.0=Language=Assets=Mars=7 July=Pleiades.
Great Falls=6,500=7,000=70%=P7.0D=7.0=Language=Assets=Mars=7 July=Pleiades.
Great horned owl=7,500=7,500=8,000=80%=P8.0D=Econ.=Currency=8Aug.=Zeus>>E=v.
Great Lakes=11,000=11%=P1.10D=1.1=Idea=Brainchild=Inv.=11 Nov.=SC=Athena>>I=MT.
Great Plains=10,000=1,000=100%=10.0=Physicality=Tech.=10 Oct.=Uranus=P=1Ø.
Great Rift Valley=8,500=9,000=90%=P9.00D=9.0=Abstr.=Gods=Saturn=9Sept.>>A=Ø.
Great Salt Lake=3,000=30%=P3.0D=3.0=Creativity=Stars=Muses=3 March = C=I>>GIL.
Great Slave Lake=3,500=4,000=40%=P4.0D=Govt.=Creatocracy=4April=Hermes=G=A4.
Great Smoky Mountains=5,000=50%=P5.00D=Law=Time=Venus=5 May =Odite>>L=N.
Great white shark=6,500=7,000=70%=P7.0D=7.0=Lang.=Assets=Mars=7 July=Pleiades.
Grebe=9,000=90%=P9.00D=9.0=Abstraction=Gods=Saturn=9Sept.>>A=Ø.
Grecian=3,000=30%=P3.0D=3.0=Creativity=Stars=Muses=3 March = C=I>>GIL.
Greco El=4,500=5,000=50%=P5.00D=Law=Time=Venus=5 May = Aphrodite>>L=N.
Greco-Roman=3,000=30%=P3.0D=3.0=Creativity=Stars=Muses=3 March = C=I>>GIL.

Greece=12,500=13,000=13%=P1.30=Solar Core=Faculty=13 January=Athena. The Hellenic Republic. A borderline between knowledge and Creative Intelligence, education and the faculty of Creative & Psycho-Social Sciences. Athens the city of Athena is the capital. Makstianity is the great unbreakable bridge between the Greek Gods, Christianity Islam and all other religions. The Creatocracy is eternal proof that Scripture tech through Makumatics is established truth. Peter Matthews-Akukalia is Hellenic.

Greed=5,500=5.5=80%=P5.50=Earth-Midway=5 May = Gaia.
Greedy=5,500=5.5=80%=P5.50=Earth-Midway=5 May = Gaia.

Greek=10,000=1,000=100%=10.0=Physicality=Tech.=10 Oct.=Uranus=P=1Ø.
The Creatocracy has great interest in Greek methods mythology and culture. Revelations instruct that basic knowledge of Scriptures revealed must stem from Greek or Hebrew.

Greek Orthodox Church=5,500=5.5=80%=P5.50=Earth-Midway=5 May = Gaia.
Greeley Horace=3,000=30%=P3.0D=3.0=Creativity=Stars=Muses=3 March = C=I>>GIL.
Green=10,000=1,000=100%=10.0=Physicality=Tech.=10 Oct.=Uranus=P=1Ø.

Greenback=2,500=3,000=30%=P3.0D=3.0=Creativity=Stars=Muses=3 March = C=I>>GIL.
A note of the U.S. currency. A note of the Maks is known as the Solar Crown, Solar Maks. Its many denominations are country customized and so different colors. The Maks is a Solar Crown of Castle Makupedia. Others are the works of Castle Makupedia.

Green bean=2,000=20%=P2.00D=2.0=Nature=Matter=Moon=2 Feb.=Cupid=N=C+_
Green card=9,000=90%=P9.00D=9.0=Abstraction=Gods=Saturn=9Sept.>>A=Ø.
Greene Henry=2,500=3,000=30%=P3.0D=3.0=Creatv=Stars=Muses=3 March = C=I>>GIL.
Greene, Nathaniel=2,500=3,000=30%=P3.0D=3.0=Stars=Muses=3 March = C=I>>GIL.
Greenery=1,500=15%=P1.50D=1.5=Authority=Solar Crown=1 May = Maia.
Green eyed=500=5%=P5.00D=5.0=Law=Time=Venus=5 May=Aphrodite>>L=N.
Greenhorn=9,500=10,000=1,000=100%=10.0=Physicality=Tech.=10 Oct.=Uranus=P=1Ø.
Greenhouse=9,500=10,000=1,000=100%=10.0=Physicality=Tech.=10 Oct.=Uranus=P=1Ø.
Greenhouse effect=10,000=1,000=100%=10.0=Physicality=Tech.=10 Oct.=Uranus=P=1Ø.
Greenland=5,500=5.5=80%=P5.50=Earth-Midway=5 May = Gaia.
Green light=6,000=60%=P6.0D=Man=Earth=Royalty=6 June=Gaia=Maia>>M=M2.
Green Mountains=6,000=60%=P6.0D=Man=Earth=Royalty=6 June=Gaia=Maia>>M=M2.
Greensboro=4,000=40%=P4.0D=Govt.=Creatocracy=4 April=Mercury=Hermes=G=A4.
Green sward=3,500=4,000=40%=P4.0D=Govt.=Creatocracy=4 April=Hermes=G=A4.
Green thumb=4,000=40%=P4.0D=Govt.=Creatocracy=4 April=Mercury=Hermes=G=A4.
Greenwich=6,000=60%=P6.0D=Man=Earth=Royalty=6 June=Gaia=Maia>>M=M2.
Greenwich time=1,500=15%=P1.50D=1.5=Authority=Solar Crown=1 May = Maia.
Greet=10,000=1,000=100%=10.0=Physicality=Tech.=10 Oct.=Uranus=P=1Ø.
Greeting=3,500=4,000=40%=P4.0D=Govt.=Creatocracy=4 April=Hermes=G=A4.

Greeting card=5,000=50%=P5.00D=Law=Time=Venus=5 May = Aphrodite>>L=N.
Gregarious=10,000=1,000=100%=10.0=Physicality=Tech.=10 Oct.=Uranus=P=1Ø.
Gregorian calendar=9,500=10,000=1,000=100%=10.0=Phy=Tech.=10 Oct.=Uranus=P=1Ø.
Gregorian chant=7,000=70%=P7.0D=7.0=Language=Assets=Mars=7 July=Pleiades.
Gregory I.=5,000=50%=P5.00D=Law=Time=Venus=5 May = Aphrodite>>L=N.
Gregory VII.=3,000=30%=P3.0D=3.0=Creatv=Stars=Muses=3 March = C=I>>GIL.
Gregory XIII.=2,500=3,000=30%=P3.0D=3.0=Creatv=Stars=Muses=3 March = C=I>>GIL.
Gremlin=6,500=7,000=70%=P7.0D=7.0=Language=Assets=Mars=7 July=Pleiades.
Grenada=10,000=1,000=100%=10.0=Physicality=Tech.=10 Oct.=Uranus=P=1Ø.
Grenade=10,000=1,000=100%=10.0=Physicality=Tech.=10 Oct.=Uranus=P=1Ø.
Grenadier=5,000=50%=P5.00D=Law=Time=Venus=5 May = Aphrodite>>L=N.
Grenadine=4,500=5,000=50%=P5.00D=Law=Time=Venus=5 May = Aphrodite>>L=N.
Grenadines=10,000=1,000=100%=10.0=Physicality=Tech.=10 Oct.=Uranus=P=1Ø.
Grenoble=3,500=4,000=40%=P4.0D=Govt.=Creatocracy=4 April=Hermes=G=A4.
Grew=1,500=15%=P1.50D=1.5=Authority=Solar Crown=1 May = Maia.
Grey=1,500=15%=P1.50D=1.5=Authority=Solar Crown=1 May = Maia.
Grey Charles=3,000=30%=P3.0D=3.0=Creativity=Stars=Muses=3 March = C=I>>GIL.
Grey Edward=3,000=30%=P3.0D=3.0=Creativity=Stars=Muses=3 March = C=I>>GIL.
Grey Jane=5,500=5.5=80%=P5.50=Earth-Midway=5 May = Gaia.
Grey, Zane=2,000=20%=P2.00D=2.0=Nature=Matter=Moon=2 Feb.=Cupid=N=C+_
Greyhound=6,500=7,000=70%=P7.0D=7.0=Language=Assets=Mars=7 July=Pleiades.
Grid=10,000=1,000=100%=10.0=Physicality=Tech.=10 Oct.=Uranus=P=1Ø.
Griddle=7,000=70%=P7.0D=7.0=Language=Assets=Mars=7 July=Pleiades.
Griddle cake=1,000=100%=10.0=1.0=Mind=Sun=1 January=Helios >> M=E4.
Gridiron=8,500=9,000=90%=P9.00D=9.0=Abstraction=Gods=Saturn=9Sept.>>A=Ø.
Gridlock=5,000=50%=P5.00D=Law=Time=Venus=5 May = Aphrodite>>L=N.
Grief=10,000=1,000=100%=10.0=Physicality=Tech.=10 Oct.=Uranus=P=1Ø.
Grieg Edvard=2,500=3,000=30%=P3.0D=3.0=Creatv=Stars=Muses=3 March = C=I>>GIL.
Grievance=10,000=1,000=100%=10.0=Physicality=Tech.=10 Oct.=Uranus=P=1Ø.
Grieve=10,000=1,000=100%=10.0=Physicality=Tech.=10 Oct.=Uranus=P=1Ø.
Grievous=3,500=4,000=40%=P4.0D=Govt.=Creatocracy=4 April=Hermes=G=A4.
Griffin=10,000=1,000=100%=10.0=Physicality=Tech.=10 Oct.=Uranus=P=1Ø.
Griffith David=3,000=30%=P3.0D=3.0=Creativity=Stars=Muses=3 March = C=I>>GIL.
Grill=10,000=1,000=100%=10.0=Physicality=Tech.=10 Oct.=Uranus=P=1Ø.
Grille=10,000=1,000=100%=10.0=Physicality=Tech.=10 Oct.=Uranus=P=1Ø.
Grim=10,000=1,000=100%=10.0=Physicality=Tech.=10 Oct.=Uranus=P=1Ø.
Grimace=10,000=1,000=100%=10.0=Physicality=Tech.=10 Oct.=Uranus=P=1Ø.
Grime=6,000=60%=P6.0D=Man=Earth=Royalty=6 June=Gaia=Maia>>M=M2.
Grimké Sarah=3,500=4,000=40%=P4.0D=Govt.=Creatocracy=4 April=Hermes=G=A4.
Grimm Jakob=6,500=7,000=70%=P7.0D=7.0=Language=Assets=Mars=7 July=Pleiades.
Grin=5,000=50%=P5.00D=Law=Time=Venus=5 May = Aphrodite>>L=N.
Grind=10,000=1,000=100%=10.0=Physicality=Tech.=10 Oct.=Uranus=P=1Ø.
Grinder=10,000=1,000=100%=10.0=Physicality=Tech.=10 Oct.=Uranus=P=1Ø.
Grindstone=10,000=1,000=100%=10.0=Physicality=Tech.=10 Oct.=Uranus=P=1Ø.
Grip=10,000=1,000=100%=10.0=Physicality=Tech.=10 Oct.=Uranus=P=1Ø.

Gripe=10,000=1,000=100%=10.0=Physicality=Tech.=10 Oct.=Uranus=P=1Ø.
Grippe=3,000=30%=P3.0D=3.0=Creativity=Stars=Muses=3 March = C=I>>GIL.
Gris Juan.=2,000=20%=P2.00D=2.0=Nature=Matter=Moon=2 Feb.=Cupid=N=C+_
Grisly=3,500=4,000=40%=P4.0D=Govt.=Creatocracy=4 April=Mercury=Hermes=G=A4.
Grist Juan=2,000=20%=P2.00D=2.0=Nature=Matter=Moon=2 Feb.=Cupid=N=C+_
Gristle=2,000=20%=P2.00D=2.0=Nature=Matter=Moon=2 Feb.=Cupid=N=C+_
Grit=10,000=1,000=100%=10.0=Physicality=Tech.=10 Oct.=Uranus=P=1Ø.
Grits=5,500=5.5=80%=P5.50=Earth-Midway=5 May = Gaia.
Grizzled=500=5%=P5.00D=5.0=Law=Time=Venus=5 May=Aphrodite>>L=N.
Grizzly=6,000=60%=P6.0D=Man=Earth=Royalty=6 June=Gaia=Maia>>M=M2.
Grizzly bear=3,500=4,000=40%=P4.0D=Govt.=Creatocracy=4 April=Hermes=G=A4.
Gro.=500=5%=P5.00D=5.0=Law=Time=Venus=5 May=Aphrodite>>L=N.
Groan=6,500=7,000=70%=P7.0D=7.0=Language=Assets=Mars=7 July=Pleiades.
Groats=4,000=40%=P4.0D=Govt.=Creatocracy=4 April=Mercury=Hermes=G=A4.
Grocer=6,000=60%=P6.0D=Man=Earth=Royalty=6 June=Gaia=Maia>>M=M2.
Grocery=6,000=60%=P6.0D=Man=Earth=Royalty=6 June=Gaia=Maia>>M=M2.
Grog=7,500=8,000=80%=P8.0D=Economy=Currency=8 Aug.=Zeus>>E=v.
Groggy=2,000=20%=P2.00D=2.0=Nature=Matter=Moon=2 Feb.=Cupid=N=C+_
Groin=10,000=1,000=100%=10.0=Physicality=Tech.=10 Oct.=Uranus=P=1Ø.
Grommet=10,000=1,000=100%=10.0=Physicality=Tech.=10 Oct.=Uranus=P=1Ø.
Gromyko Andrel=3,000=30%=P3.0D=3.0=Creativity=Stars=Muses=3 March = C=I>>GIL.
Groom=10,000=1,000=100%=10.0=Physicality=Tech.=10 Oct.=Uranus=P=1Ø.
Groove=10,000=1,000=100%=10.0=Physicality=Tech.=10 Oct.=Uranus=P=1Ø.
Groovy=1,500=15%=P1.50D=1.5=Authority=Solar Crown=1 May = Maia.
Grope=10,000=1,000=100%=10.0=Physicality=Tech.=10 Oct.=Uranus=P=1Ø.
Gropius Walter=3,500=4,000=40%=P4.0D=Govt.=Creatocracy=4 April=Hermes=G=A4.
Grosbeak=5,500=5.5=80%=P5.50=Earth-Midway=5 May = Gaia.
Groschen=4,000=40%=P4.0D=Govt.=Creatocracy=4 April=Mercury=Hermes=G=A4.
Gross=10,000=1,000=100%=10.0=Physicality=Tech.=10 Oct.=Uranus=P=1Ø.
Gross national product=7,500=8,000=80%=P8.0D=Econ.=Currency=8 Aug.=Zeus>>E=v.
Grosz=4,500=5,000=50%=P5.00D=Law=Time=Venus=5 May = Aphrodite>>L=N.
Grosz George=3,000=30%=P3.0D=3.0=Creativity=Stars=Muses=3 March = C=I>>GIL.
Grotesque=10,000=1,000=100%=10.0=Physicality=Tech.=10 Oct.=Uranus=P=1Ø.
Grotius Hugo=3,000=30%=P3.0D=3.0=Creativity=Stars=Muses=3 March = C=I>>GIL.
Grotto=5,000=50%=P5.00D=Law=Time=Venus=5 May = Aphrodite>>L=N.
Grouch=10,000=1,000=100%=10.0=Physicality=Tech.=10 Oct.=Uranus=P=1Ø.
Ground1=10,000=1,000=100%=10.0=Physicality=Tech.=10 Oct.=Uranus=P=1Ø.
Ground2=3,000=30%=P3.0D=3.0=Creativity=Stars=Muses=3 March = C=I>>GIL.
Groundbreaking=10,000=1,000=100%=10.0=Physicality=Tech.=10 Oct.=Uranus=P=1Ø.
Ground floor=6,500=7,000=70%=P7.0D=7.0=Language=Assets=Mars=7 July=Pleiades.
Groundhog=1,000=100%=10.0=1.0=Mind=Sun=1 January=Helios >> M=E4.
Groundless=5,000=50%=P5.00D=Law=Time=Venus=5 May = Aphrodite>>L=N.
Ground rule=7,000=70%=P7.0D=7.0=Language=Assets=Mars=7 July=Pleiades.
Ground squirrel=5,000=50%=P5.00D=Law=Time=Venus=5 May = Aphrodite>>L=N.
Groundswell=6,000=60%=P6.0D=Man=Earth=Royalty=6 June=Gaia=Maia>>M=M2.

Groundwater=3,500=4,000=40%=P4.0D=Govt.=Creatocracy=4 April=Hermes=G=A4.
Groundwork=1,500=15%=P1.50D=1.5=Authority=Solar Crown=1 May = Maia.
Ground zero=4,000=40%=P4.0D=Govt.=Creatocracy=4 April=Mercury=Hermes=G=A4.
Group=13,000=13%=P1.30=Solar Core=Faculty=13 January=Athena.
Grouper=7,000=70%=P7.0D=7.0=Language=Assets=Mars=7 July=Pleiades.
Groupie=6,500=7,000=70%=P7.0D=7.0=Language=Assets=Mars=7 July=Pleiades.
Grouse1=6,000=60%=P6.0D=Man=Earth=Royalty=6 June=Gaia=Maia>>M=M2.
Grouse2=3,000=30%=P3.0D=3.0=Creativity=Stars=Muses=3 March = C=I>>GIL.
Grout=9,000=90%=P9.00D=9.0=Abstraction=Gods=Saturn=9Sept.>>A=Ø.
Grove=5,000=50%=P5.00D=Law=Time=Venus=5 May = Aphrodite>>L=N.
Grovel=6,500=7,000=70%=P7.0D=7.0=Language=Assets=Mars=7 July=Pleiades.
Grow=10,000=1,000=100%=10.0=Physicality=Tech.=10 Oct.=Uranus=P=1Ø.
Growl=7,000=70%=P7.0D=7.0=Language=Assets=Mars=7 July=Pleiades.
Grown=3,000=30%=P3.0D=3.0=Creativity=Stars=Muses=3 March = C=I>>GIL.
Grownup=3,000=30%=P3.0D=3.0=Creativity=Stars=Muses=3 March = C=I>>GIL.
Grown-up=3,000=30%=P3.0D=3.0=Creativity=Stars=Muses=3 March = C=I>>GIL.
Growth=10,000=1,000=100%=10.0=Physicality=Tech.=10 Oct.=Uranus=P=1Ø.
Growth ring=5,000=50%=P5.00D=Law=Time=Venus=5 May = Aphrodite>>L=N.
Grozny=4,500=5,000=50%=P5.00D=Law=Time=Venus=5 May = Aphrodite>>L=N.
Grub=10,000=1,000=100%=10.0=Physicality=Tech.=10 Oct.=Uranus=P=1Ø.
Grubby=1,000=100%=10.0=1.0=Mind=Sun=1 January=Helios >> M=E4.
Grubstake=9,500=10,000=1,000=100%=10.0=Physicality=Tech.=10 Oct.=Uranus=P=1Ø.
Grudge=6,500=7,000=70%=P7.0D=7.0=Language=Assets=Mars=7 July=Pleiades.
Gruel=4,000=40%=P4.0D=Govt.=Creatocracy=4 April=Mercury=Hermes=G=A4.
Grueling=2,000=20%=P2.00D=2.0=Nature=Matter=Moon=2 Feb.=Cupid=N=C+_
Gruesome=6,000=60%=P6.0D=Man=Earth=Royalty=6 June=Gaia=Maia>>M=M2.
Gruff=5,000=50%=P5.00D=Law=Time=Venus=5 May = Aphrodite>>L=N.
Grumble=2,500=3,000=30%=P3.0D=3.0=Creativity=Stars=Muses=3 March = C=I>>GIL.
Grump=5,500=5.5=80%=P5.50=Earth-Midway=5 May = Gaia.
Grungy=4,500=5,000=50%=P5.00D=Law=Time=Venus=5 May = Aphrodite>>L=N.
Grunion=7,500=8,000=80%=P8.0D=Economy=Currency=8 Aug.=Zeus>>E=v.
Grunt=10,000=1,000=100%=10.0=Physicality=Tech.=10 Oct.=Uranus=P=1Ø.
gr.=1,000=100%=10.0=1.0=Mind=Sun=1 January=Helios >> M=E4.
Gryphon=1,500=15%=P1.50D=1.5=Authority=Solar Crown=1 May = Maia.
GSA=3,500=4,000=40%=P4.0D=Govt.=Creatocracy=4 April=Mercury=Hermes=G=A4.
Gt. Brit.=1,000=100%=10.0=1.0=Mind=Sun=1 January=Helios >> M=E4.
GU=1,000=100%=Physicality=Tech.=10 Oct.=Uranus=P=1Ø.
Guacamole=6,500=7,000=70%=P7.0D=7.0=Language=Assets=Mars=7 July=Pleiades.
Guadalajara=5,500=5.5=80%=P5.50=Earth-Midway=5 May = Gaia.
Guadalcanal=5,000=50%=P5.00D=Law=Time=Venus=5 May = Aphrodite>>L=N.
Guadeloupe=8,500=9,000=90%=P9.00D=9.0=Abstraction=Gods=Saturn=9Sept.>>A=Ø.
Guam=7,500=8,000=80%=P8.0D=Economy=Currency=8 Aug.=Zeus>>E=v.
Guanabara Bay=5,000=50%=P5.00D=Law=Time=Venus=5 May = Aphrodite>>L=N.
Guangzhou=7,500=8,000=80%=P8.0D=Economy=Currency=8 Aug.=Zeus>>E=v.
Guanine=7,500=7,500=8,000=80%=P8.0D=Economy=Currency=8 Aug.=Zeus>>E=v.

Guano=6,500=7,000=70%=P7.0D=7.0=Language=Assets=Mars=7 July=Pleiades.
Guantánamo=7,500=7,500=8,000=80%=P8.0D=Economy=Currency=8 Aug.=Zeus>>E=v.
Guar=8,500=9,000=90%=P9.00D=9.0=Abstraction=Gods=Saturn=9Sept.>>A=Ø.
guarani=3,500=4,000=40%=P4.0D=Govt.=Creatocracy=4 April=Mercury=Hermes=G=A4.
Guarani=9,000=90%=P9.00D=9.0=Abstraction=Gods=Saturn=9Sept.>>A=Ø.
Guarantee=10,000=1,000=100%=10.0=Physicality=Tech.=10 Oct.=Uranus=P=1Ø.
Guarantor=4,000=40%=P4.0D=Govt.=Creatocracy=4 April=Mercury=Hermes=G=A4.
Guaranty=10,000=1,000=100%=10.0=Physicality=Tech.=10 Oct.=Uranus=P=1Ø.
Guard=10,000=1,000=100%=10.0=Physicality=Tech.=10 Oct.=Uranus=P=1Ø.
Guarded=2,000=20%=P2.00D=2.0=Nature=Matter=Moon=2 Feb.=Cupid=N=C+_
Guardhouse=3,500=4,000=40%=P4.0D=Govt.=Creatocracy=4 April=Hermes=G=A4.
Guardian=10,500=11,000=11%=P1.10D=1.1=Idea=Brainchild=Inv.=11 Nov.=Athena>>I=MT.
Guardsman=3,000=30%=P3.0D=3.0=Creativity=Stars=Muses=3 March = C=I>>GIL.
Guar gum=7,500=8,000=80%=P8.0D=Economy=Currency=8 Aug.=Zeus>>E=v.
Guarneri=7,500=7,500=8,000=80%=P8.0D=Economy=Currency=8 Aug.=Zeus>>E=v.
Guatemala=11,000=11%=P1.10D=1.1=Idea=Brainchild=Inv.=11 Nov.=SC=Athena>>I=MT.
Guava=7,500=8,000=80%=P8.0D=Economy=Currency=8 Aug.=Zeus>>E=v.
Guayaquil=7,500=7,500=8,000=80%=P8.0D=Economy=Currency=8 Aug.=Zeus>>E=v.
Gubernatorial=4,500=5,000=50%=P5.00D=Law=Time=Venus=5 May = Aphrodite>>L=N.
Guck=6,000=60%=P6.0D=Man=Earth=Royalty=6 June=Gaia=Maia>>M=M2.
Guernsey1=5,500=5.5=80%=P5.50=Earth-Midway=5 May = Gaia.
Guernsey2=7,500=8,000=80%=P8.0D=Economy=Currency=8 Aug.=Zeus>>E=v.
Guerrilla=12,000=12%=P1.20D=1.2=Knowledge=Education=12Dec.=Athena>>K=F.
Guess=10,000=1,000=100%=10.0=Physicality=Tech.=10 Oct.=Uranus=P=1Ø.
Guesswork=3,500=4,000=40%=P4.0D=Govt.=Creatocracy=4 April=Hermes=G=A4.
Guest=10,000=1,000=100%=10.0=Physicality=Tech.=10 Oct.=Uranus=P=1Ø.
Guest worker=5,000=50%=P5.00D=Law=Time=Venus=5 May = Aphrodite>>L=N.
Guevara Ernesto=4,000=40%=P4.0D=Govt.=Creatocracy=4 April=Hermes=G=A4.
Guff=3,000=30%=P3.0D=3.0=Creativity=Stars=Muses=3 March = C=I>>GIL.
Guffaw=3,000=30%=P3.0D=3.0=Creativity=Stars=Muses=3 March = C=I>>GIL.
Guiana=9,000=90%=P9.00D=9.0=Abstraction=Gods=Saturn=9Sept.>>A=Ø.
Guidance=9,000=90%=P9.00D=9.0=Abstraction=Gods=Saturn=9Sept.>>A=Ø.
Guide=10,000=1,000=100%=10.0=Physicality=Tech.=10 Oct.=Uranus=P=1Ø.
Guidebook=4,500=5,000=50%=P5.00D=Law=Time=Venus=5 May = Aphrodite>>L=N.
Guided missile=5,500=5.5=80%=P5.50D=Earth-Midway=5 May = Gaia.
Guide dog=5,000=50%=P5.00D=Law=Time=Venus=5 May = Aphrodite>>L=N.
Guideline=4,000=40%=P4.0D=Govt.=Creatocracy=4 April=Mercury=Hermes=G=A4.
Guidepost=4,000=40%=P4.0D=Govt.=Creatocracy=4 April=Mercury=Hermes=G=A4.
Guido d'Arezzo=4,000=40%=P4.0D=Govt.=Creatocracy=4 April=Mercury=Hermes=G=A4.
Guidon=5,500=5.5=80%=P5.50=Earth-Midway=5 May = Gaia.
Guild=9,000=90%=P9.00D=9.0=Abstraction=Gods=Saturn=9Sept.>>A=Ø.
Guilder=3,500=4,000=40%=P4.0D=Govt.=Creatocracy=4 April=Mercury=Hermes=G=A4.
Guile=2,000=20%=P2.00D=2.0=Nature=Matter=Moon=2 Feb.=Cupid=N=C+_
Guillotine=10,000=1,000=100%=10.0=Physicality=Tech.=10 Oct.=Uranus=P=1Ø.
Guilt=17,000=17%=P1.70D=1.7=Solar Asset=17 Feb.=Maia=Mind Computing.

Guilty=7,000=70%=P7.0D=7.0=Language=Assets=Mars=7 July=Pleiades.
guinea=7,500=8,000=80%=P8.0D=Economy=Currency=8 Aug.=Zeus>>E=v.
Guinea=6,000=60%=P6.0D=Man=Earth=Royalty=6 June=Gaia=Maia>>M=M2.
Guinea, Gulf of.=7,500=7,500=8,000=80%=P8.0D=Econ.=Currency=8 Aug.=Zeus>>E=v.
Guinea Bissau=6,000=60%=P6.0D=Man=Earth=Royalty=6 June=Gaia=Maia>>M=M2.
Guinea fowl=9,500=10,000=1,000=100%=10.0=Physicality=Tech.=10 Oct.=Uranus=P=1Ø.
Guinea pig=10,000=1,000=100%=10.0=Physicality=Tech.=10 Oct.=Uranus=P=1Ø.
Guinevere=6,000=60%=P6.0D=Man=Earth=Royalty=6 June=Gaia=Maia>>M=M2.
Guise=6,000=60%=P6.0D=Man=Earth=Royalty=6 June=Gaia=Maia>>M=M2.
Guitar=9,500=10,000=1,000=100%=10.0=Physicality=Tech.=10 Oct.=Uranus=P=1Ø.
Guiyang=4,500=5,000=50%=P5.00D=Law=Time=Venus=5 May = Aphrodite>>L=N.
Guizot Francois=4,000=40%=P4.0D=Govt.=Creatocracy=4 April=Mercury=Hermes=G=A4.
Gulag=7,500=8,000=80%=P8.0D=Economy=Currency=8 Aug.=Zeus>>E=v.
Gulch=3,500=4,000=40%=P4.0D=Govt.=Creatocracy=4 April=Mercury=Hermes=G=A4.
Gulf=11,000=11%=P1.10D=1.1=Idea=Brainchild=Inv.=11 Nov.=SC=Athena>>I=MT.
Gulf States=9,000=90%=P9.00D=9.0=Abstraction=Gods=Saturn=9Sept.>>A=Ø.
Gulf Stream=7,500=7,500=8,000=80%=P8.0D=Economy=Currency=8 Aug.=Zeus>>E=v.
Gulfweed=5,000=50%=P5.00D=Law=Time=Venus=5 May = Aphrodite>>L=N.
Gull1=12,000=12%=P1.20D=1.2=Knowledge=Education=12Dec.=Athena>>K=F.
Gull2=7,000=70%=P7.0D=7.0=Language=Assets=Mars=7 July=Pleiades.
Gullah=11,000=11%=P1.10D=1.1=Idea=Brainchild=Inv.=11 Nov.=SC=Athena>>I=MT.
Gullet=3,500=4,000=40%=P4.0D=Govt.=Creatocracy=4 April=Mercury=Hermes=G=A4.
Gullible=2,000=20%=P2.00D=2.0=Nature=Matter=Moon=2 Feb.=Cupid=N=C+_
Gully=5,500=5.5=80%=P5.50=Earth-Midway=5 May = Gaia.
Gulp=11,000=11%=P1.10D=1.1=Idea=Brainchild=Inv.=11 Nov.=SC=Athena>>I=MT.
Gum1=10,000=1,000=100%=10.0=Physicality=Tech.=10 Oct.=Uranus=P=1Ø.
Gum2=10,000=1,000=100%=10.0=Physicality=Tech.=10 Oct.=Uranus=P=1Ø.
Gum arabic=7,500=8,000=80%=P8.0D=Economy=Currency=8 Aug.=Zeus>>E=v.
Gumbo=10,000=1,000=100%=10.0=Physicality=Tech.=10 Oct.=Uranus=P=1Ø.
Gumdrop=5,000=50%=P5.00D=Law=Time=Venus=5 May = Aphrodite>>L=N.
Gumption=3,000=30%=P3.0D=3.0=Creativity=Stars=Muses=3 March = C=I>>GIL.
Gumshoe=2,500=3,000=30%=P3.0D=3.0=Creativity=Stars=Muses=3 March = C=I>>GIL.
Gun=10,000=1,000=100%=10.0=Physicality=Tech.=10 Oct.=Uranus=P=1Ø.
Gunboat=2,000=20%=P2.00D=2.0=Nature=Matter=Moon=2 Feb.=Cupid=N=C+_
Gun cotton=1,000=100%=10.0=1.0=Mind=Sun=1 January=Helios >> M=E4.
Gunfight=3,000=30%=P3.0D=3.0=Creativity=Stars=Muses=3 March = C=I>>GIL.
Gunfire=2,000=20%=P2.00D=2.0=Nature=Matter=Moon=2 Feb.=Cupid=N=C+_
Gung ho=5,000=50%=P5.00D=Law=Time=Venus=5 May = Aphrodite>>L=N.
Gun lock=4,000=40%=P4.0D=Govt.=Creatocracy=4 April=Mercury=Hermes=G=A4.
Gunman=3,500=4,000=40%=P4.0D=Govt.=Creatocracy=4 April=Hermes=G=A4.
Gunmetal=6,500=7,000=70%=P7.0D=7.0=Language=Assets=Mars=7 July=Pleiades.
Gunnel=1,500=15%=P1.50D=1.5=Authority=Solar Crown=1 May = Maia.
Gunner=4,500=5,000=50%=P5.00D=Law=Time=Venus=5 May = Aphrodite>>L=N.
Gunnery=3,500=4,000=40%=P4.0D=Govt.=Creatocracy=4 April=Hermes=G=A4.

Gunnery sergeant=5,000=50%=P5.00D=Law=Time=Venus=5 May = Aphrodite>>L=N.
Gunny=6,000=60%=P6.0D=Man=Earth=Royalty=6 June=Gaia=Maia>>M=M2.
Gunnysack=3,500=4,000=40%=P4.0D=Govt.=Creatocracy=4 April=Hermes=G=A4.
Gun play=2,000=20%=P2.00D=2.0=Nature=Matter=Moon=2 Feb.=Cupid=N=C+_
Gunpowder=4,500=5,000=50%=P5.00D=Law=Time=Venus=5 May = Aphrodite>>L=N.
Gunshot=5,500=5.5=80%=P5.50=Earth-Midway=5 May = Gaia.
Gun shy=4,000=40%=P4.0D=Govt.=Creatocracy=4 April=Mercury=Hermes=G=A4.
Gunsmith=3,000=30%=P3.0D=3.0=Creativity=Stars=Muses=3 March = C=I>>GIL.
Gunwale=4,500=5,000=50%=P5.00D=Law=Time=Venus=5 May = Aphrodite>>L=N.
Guppy=8,000=80%=P8.0D=Economy=Currency=8 Aug.=Zeus>>E=v.
Gurgle=8,000=80%=P8.0D=Economy=Currency=8 Aug.=Zeus>>E=v.
Gurney=7,000=70%=P7.0D=7.0=Language=Assets=Mars=7 July=Pleiades.
Guru=9,000=90%=P9.00D=9.0=Abstraction=Gods=Saturn=9Sept.>>A=Ø.
Gush=8,500=9,000=90%=P9.00D=9.0=Abstraction=Gods=Saturn=9Sept.>>A=Ø.
Gusher=4,500=5,000=50%=P5.00D=Law=Time=Venus=5 May = Aphrodite>>L=N.
Gusset=6,000=60%=P6.0D=Man=Earth=Royalty=6 June=Gaia=Maia>>M=M2.
Gussy=6,000=60%=P6.0D=Man=Earth=Royalty=6 June=Gaia=Maia>>M=M2.
Gust=6,500=7,000=70%=P7.0D=7.0=Language=Assets=Mars=7 July=Pleiades.
Gustatory=5,000=50%=P5.00D=Law=Time=Venus=5 May = Aphrodite>>L=N.
Gustavius I=3,000=30%=P3.0D=3.0=Creativity=Stars=Muses=3 March = C=I>>GIL.
Gustavius II.=3,000=30%=P3.0D=3.0=Creativity=Stars=Muses=3 March = C=I>>GIL.
Gustavius IV.=3,000=30%=P3.0D=3.0=Creativity=Stars=Muses=3 March = C=I>>GIL.
Gustavus V.=3,000=30%=P3.0D=3.0=Creativity=Stars=Muses=3 March = C=I>>GIL.
Gustavus VI.=3,000=30%=P3.0D=3.0=Creativity=Stars=Muses=3 March = C=I>>GIL.
Gusto=3,000=30%=P3.0D=3.0=Creativity=Stars=Muses=3 March = C=I>>GIL.
Gut=10,000=1,000=100%=10.0=Physicality=Tech.=10 Oct.=Uranus=P=1Ø.
Gutenberg Johann.=4,000=40%=P4.0D=Govt.=Creatocracy=4 April=Hermes=G=A4.
Gutless=2,500=3,000=30%=P3.0D=3.0=Creativity=Stars=Muses=3 March = C=I>>GIL.
Gutsy=1,500=15%=P1.50D=1.5=Authority=Solar Crown=1 May = Maia.
Gutta percha=10,000=1,000=100%=10.0=Physicality=Tech.=10 Oct.=Uranus=P=1Ø.
Gutter=10,000=1,000=100%=10.0=Physicality=Tech.=10 Oct.=Uranus=P=1Ø.
Guttersnipe=1,500=15%=P1.50D=1.5=Authority=Solar Crown=1 May = Maia.
Guttural=6,000=60%=P6.0D=Man=Earth=Royalty=6 June=Gaia=Maia>>M=M2.
Guy1=11,000=11%=P1.10D=1.1=Idea=Brainchild=Inv.=11 Nov.=SC=Athena>>I=MT.
Guy2=6,000=60%=P6.0D=Man=Earth=Royalty=6 June=Gaia=Maia>>M=M2.
Guyana=6,500=7,000=70%=P7.0D=7.0=Language=Assets=Mars=7 July=Pleiades.
Guzzle=2,000=20%=P2.00D=2.0=Nature=Matter=Moon=2 Feb.=Cupid=N=C+_
Gym=3,500=4,000=40%=P4.0D=Govt.=Creatocracy=4 April=Mercury=Hermes=G=A4.
Gymnasium=10,000=1,000=100%=10.0=Physicality=Tech.=10 Oct.=Uranus=P=1Ø.
Gymnastics=10,000=1,000=100%=10.0=Physicality=Tech.=10 Oct.=Uranus=P=1Ø.
Gymnosperm=10,000=1,000=100%=10.0=Physicality=Tech.=10 Oct.=Uranus=P=1Ø.
Gyn.=1,000=100%=10.0=1.0=Mind=Sun=1 January=Helios >> M=E4.
Gynecology=10,000=1,000=100%=10.0=Physicality=Tech.=10 Oct.=Uranus=P=1Ø.
Gyp=4,000=40%=P4.0D=Govt.=Creatocracy=4 April=Mercury=Hermes=G=A4.

Gypsum=9,000=90%=P9.00D=9.0=Abstraction=Gods=Saturn=9Sept.>>A=Ø.
Gypsy=10,000=1,000=100%=10.0=Physicality=Tech.=10 Oct.=Uranus=P=1Ø.
Gypsy moth=10,000=1,000=100%=10.0=Physicality=Tech.=10 Oct.=Uranus=P=1Ø.
Gyrate=10,000=1,000=100%=10.0=Physicality=Tech.=10 Oct.=Uranus=P=1Ø.
Gyrfalcon=7,000=70%=P7.0D=7.0=Language=Assets=Mars=7 July=Pleiades.
Gyro1=1,000=100%=10.0=1.0=Mind=Sun=1 January=Helios >> M=E4.
Gyro2=10,000=1,000=100%=10.0=Physicality=Tech.=10 Oct.=Uranus=P=1Ø.
Gyrocompass=5,500=5.5=80%=P5.50=Earth-Midway=5 May = Gaia.
Gyroscope=10,000=1,000=100%=10.0=Physicality=Tech.=10 Oct.=Uranus=P=1Ø.

MAKABET =Hh=

---

h1=4,500=5,000=50%=P5.00D=Law=Time=Venus=5 May = Aphrodite>>L=N.
Result shows that h1 is a borderline between power and its legitimacy, a government system backed by law. The 8th letter of the English alphabet indicates it is an economic unit. The 5th in the mind dimension. The psycho-weight of h1 is thus computed >>8.0*5.0=p=13+40=53x=px=573=600=6.0.
It is an emotional alphabet of a noble birth inspired to humans by Aphrodite and symbol for emotional energy, heat. The symbol therefore used in measuring emotion is the H >> Hø. The super zero or Mak-zero symbol Ø affixed to it is the original symbol for all abstractions and energy made by computational discovery in the Makupedia Sciences authored by Peter Matthews-Akukalia, Castle Makupedia God of Creatocracy Genius and Mind. Reference study>> Castle Makupedia Sciences >> Principles of Naturecology seasons 1-103...

---

h2=500=5%=P5.00D=5.0=Law=Time=Venus=5 May=Aphrodite>>L=N.
H1=2,500=3,000=30%=P3.0D=3.0=Creativity=Stars=Muses=3 March = C=I>>GIL.
H2=500=5%=P5.00D=5.0=Law=Time=Venus=5 May=Aphrodite>>L=N.
h.=1,000=100%=10.0=1.0=Mind=Sun=1 January=Helios >> M=E4.
ha1=3,500=4,000=40%=P4.0D=Govt =Creatocracy=4 April=Mercury=Hermes=G=A4.
ha2=500=5%=P5.00D=5.0=Law=Time=Venus=5 May=Aphrodite>>L=N.
Haarlem=6,500=7,000=70%=P7.0D=7.0=Language=Assets=Mars=7 July=Pleiades.

Habakkuk=6,500=7,000=70%=P7.0D=7.0=Language=Assets=Mars=7 July=Pleiades.
A borderline book of boundaries connecting Hermes God of Boundaries, Gaia Goddess of Earth and Aries God of War. These three inspired the various prophecies he wrote. The battle for control must have been won by computed for independence: 4, 6, 7 4.0*6.0=p=10+24=34x=px=274=300=3.0 >> muses were involved. Habakkuk must have commmuned with the stars. This is possible because Peter Matthews-Akukalia, Castle Makupedia experienced this strange activity and wrote the apotheosis of Castle Makupedia, reference book>> Sons of Immortals. 3.0*7.0=p=10+21=31x=px=241=2.4 >>

International Business on the lunar core. Habakkuk must have received his revelations through the muses under the influence of the lunar energy. This energy is known as the PGI>> Psycho-Gravitational Incursion. See Template & Manifesto for the Creative Economy by Peter Matthews-Akukalia.

Habeas corpus=13,000=13%=P1.30=Solar Core=Faculty=13 January=Athena.
Haberdasher=3,500=4,000=40%=P4.0D=Govt=Creato.=4 April=Mercury=Hermes=G=A4.
Haberdashery=2,500=3,000=30%=P3.0D=3.0=Cre=Stars=Muses=3 March = C=I>>GIL.
Habiliment=9,500=10,000=1,000=100%=Physicality=Tech.=10 Oct.=Uranus=P=1Ø.
Habit=14,000=14%=P1.40D=1.4=Mgt.=Solar Energy=13 May=Athena=SC=0.1
Habitable=3,500=4,000=40%=P4.0D=Govt =Creato.=4 April=Mercury=Hermes=G=A4.
Habitat=13,500=14,000=14%=P1.40D=1.4=Mgt.=Solar Energy=13 May=Athena=SC=0.1
Habitation=8,000=80%=P8.0D=Economy=Currency=8 Aug.=Zeus>>E=v.
Habit forming=5,500=5.5=80%=P5.50=Earth-Midway=5 May = Gaia.
Habitual=10,000=1,000=100%=10.0=Physicality=Tech.=10 Oct.=Uranus=P=1Ø.
Habituate=5,000=50%=P5.00D=Law=Time=Venus=5 May = Aphrodite>>L=N.
Habitude=2,500=3,000=30%=P3.0D=3.0=Creativity=Stars=Muses=3 March = C=I>>GIL.
Habitué=5,000=50%=P5.00D=Law=Time=Venus=5 May = Aphrodite>>L=N.
Habsburg=1,000=100%=10.0=1.0=Mind=Sun=1 January=Helios >> M=E4.
Hacienda=7,000=70%=P7.0D=7.0=Language=Assets=Mars=7 July=Pleiades.
Hack1=10,000=1,000=100%=10.0=Physicality=Tech.=10 Oct.=Uranus=P=1Ø.
Hack2=10,000=1,000=100%=10.0=Physicality=Tech.=10 Oct.=Uranus=P=1Ø.
Hackamore=6,500=7,000=70%=P7.0D=7.0=Language=Assets=Mars=7 July=Pleiades.
Hacker=10,500=11,000=11%=P1.10D=1.1=Idea=Brainchild=Inv.=11 Nov.=Athena>>I=MT.
Hackie=1,500=15%=P1.50D=1.5=Authority=Solar Crown=1 May = Maia.
Hackle=10,000=1,000=100%=10.0=Physicality=Tech.=10 Oct.=Uranus=P=1Ø.
Hackney=10,000=1,000=100%=10.0=Physicality=Tech.=10 Oct.=Uranus=P=1Ø.
Hackneyed=1,000=100%=10.0=1.0=Mind=Sun=1 January=Helios >> M=E4.
Hacksaw=7,500=8,000=80%=P8.0D=Economy=Currency=8 Aug.=Zeus>>E=v.
Had=3,000=30%=P3.0D=3.0=Creativity=Stars=Muses=3 March = C=I>>GIL.
Haddock=5,500=5.5=80%=P5.50=Earth-Midway=5 May = Gaia.

Hades=6,500=7,000=70%=P7.0D=7.0=Language=Assets=Mars=7 July=Pleiades.
Greek myth. The abode of the dead. Also Hades. Hell. Interestingly mentioned in the Bible as a place of the dead and torment by David in the Psalms and Job. An evidence that Greek mythology are real facts of abstract existence and physical equivalence. Computational result shows that Hades is a border in the control of Gaia and the Pleiades. The precise application for Hades would be the grave rather than hell because on Earth is the grave. It is therefore a connect to the underworld (hell) where Hermes has his inclusive jurisdiction. People born of the Planet Pluto are Hadeans. The symbol of Hades is the owl. A council of owls is known as Parliament. They are educationists and love knowledge. They do not belong to the council of Athena which represents wisdom skills and mental warfare. They are the Owls of death and the dead originating from Tartarus and most often susceptible to early death. Marriage to a higher spirited person such as a Gaian will cancel the law of

death placed on them and grant them pardon for the ancient sins and transgressions of the past. Their energy is 20.0% >> 2.0ØD = 8.0ØS = 2.0ØT where 8.0 >> Jupiter >> Zeus >> Business >> Currency >> Wealth is required to maintain their ill health and weak nature. They have died before condemned to Tartarus (Hell) and freed by Hermes through the consensus of the Council Athena who is the Spirit of the Almighty GOD. They are reborn to make amends on former wrongs through generosity until they find the Gaian who saves them either by marriage or conferred rights. They obtain salvation and gain access to Paradise at another death. Hades is the grave and the cosmic black hole confirms this. Their dates of birth are listed below based on superior data from Makupedia.
Read full applications in Chapter 2,076,071>>THE HADEANS.

HUMAN ENERGY DATA SYSTEMS ON THE DATE OF BIRTH-MONTH >> Plutonians.
===
MONTH:FEBRUARY
Day 6:Value: 1.2, Planetary Type: Pluto, Human Type:Education, Birth Energy Level:20%
Day 23:Value:1.2, Planetary Type:Pluto, Human Type:Education, Birth Energy Level:20.0%
===
MONTH:MARCH
Day 18:Value:1.2, Planetary Type:Pluto, Human Type:Education, Birth Energy Level:20.0%
===
MONTH:APRIL
Day 15:Value:1.2, Planetary Type:Pluto, Human Type:Education, Birth Energy Level:20.0%
===
MONTH:JUNE.
Day 2:Value:1.2, Planetary Type:Pluto Human Type:Education Birth Energy Level:20.0%
Day 11:Value:1.2 Planetary Type:Pluto Human Type:Education Birth Energy Level:20.0%
===
MONTH:OCTOBER
Day 29:Value:1.2 Planetary Type:Pluto Human Type:Education Birth Energy Level:20.0%
Day 30: Value:1.2 Planetary Type:Pluto Human Type:Education Birth Energy Level:20.0%
===
MONTH:NOVEMBER
Day 6:Value:1.2 Planetary Type:Pluto Human Type:Education Birth Energy Level:20.0%
Day 27:Value:1.2 Planetary Type:Pluto Human Type:Education Birth Energy Level:20.0%
Day 28:Value:1.2 Planetary Type:Pluto Human Type:Education Birth Energy Level:20.0%
===
MONTH:DECEMBER
Day 26:Value:1.2, Planetary Type:Pluto, Human Type:Education, Birth Energy Level:20.0%

Hadn't=1,000=100%=10.0=1.0=Mind=Sun=1 January=Helios >> M=E4.
Hadrian=3,500=4,000=40%=P4.0D=Govt=Creatocracy=4 April=Mercury=Hermes=G=A4.
Hadron=10,000=1,000=100%=10.0=Physicality=Tech.=10 Oct.=Uranus=P=1Ø.
Hadrosaur=10,000=1,000=100%=10.0=Physicality=Tech.=10 Oct.=Uranus=P=1Ø.
Hadst=3,500=4,000=40%=P4.0D=Govt=Creatocracy=4 April=Mercury=Hermes=G=A4.

-harmia=2,000=20%=P2.00D=2.0=Nature=Matter=Moon=2 Feb.=Cupid=N=C+_
Hafnium=10,000=1,000=100%=10.0=Physicality=Tech.=10 Oct.=Uranus=P=1Ø.
Haft=5,500=5.5=80%=P5.50=Earth-Midway=5 May = Gaia.

Hag=5,500=5.5=80%=P5.50=Earth-Midway=5 May = Gaia.
An ugly old woman, a witch, sorceress. People that lose touch with their innate potentials and refuse to discover develop and connect them lose touch with Gaia at the mid earth. They lose their emotions become heartless and reprobate in conscience to become hags. Human potentials are sourced from mid earth and fixed by Gaia into the human conscience at conception in the mother's womb making 80% completeness in a human at birth.

Haggai=6,000=60%=P6.0D=Man=Earth=Royalty=6 June=Gaia=Maia>>M=M2.
A Hebrew prophet of the 6th century B.C. Inspired by Gaia, Goddess of the Earth.

Haggard=4,000=40%=P4.0D=Govt=Creatocracy=4 April=Mercury=Hermes=G=A4.
It is well known in Greek mythology that Hermes has wings on his shoes and is the only one of the Olympian Gods that can travel between the physical and the abstract worlds easily. Haggard >> wild hawk simply testifies to this truth. He can manifest as a wild hawk. Zeus is the eagle. His first son Hermes is the hawk. Computational discovery of castle Makupedia.

Haggle=4,500=5,000=50%=P5.00D=Law=Time=Venus=5 May = Aphrodite>>L=N.
Hagiography=10,000=1,000=100%=10.0=Physicality=Tech.=10 Oct.=Uranus=P=1Ø.
Hague=7,000=70%=P7.0D=7.0=Language=Assets=Mars=7 July=Pleiades.
Hah=1,500=15%=P1.50D=1.5=Authority=Solar Crown=1 May = Maia.
Haida=10,000=1,000=100%=10.0=Physicality=Tech.=10 Oct.=Uranus=P=1Ø.
Haifa=6,000=60%=P6.0D=Man=Earth=Royalty=6 June=Gaia=Maia>>M=M2.

Haiku=6,500=7,000=70%=P7.0D=7.0=Language=Assets=Mars=7 July=Pleiades.
An unrhymed Japanese poem having three lines of five, seven, and five syllables. The psycho-weight of the haiku is thus computed for 5, 7, 5 on the Maks.
5.0*7.0=p=12+35=47=px=467=500=5.0>>Law >> Time >> Venus >> Aphrodite.
5.0*5.0=p=10+25=35x=px=285=300=3.0>>Creativity >> Stars >> Muses.
The haiku is inspired by Aphrodite through her muses. It is a song of the stars indicating the incoherent energy of the Earth as a borderline resolvable in computational precision.

Hail1=10,000=1,000=100%=10.0=Physicality=Tech.=10 Oct.=Uranus=P=1Ø.
Hail2=10,000=1,000=100%=10.0=Physicality=Tech.=10 Oct.=Uranus=P=1Ø.

Haile Selassie=5,500=5.5=80%=P5.50=Earth-Midway=5 May = Gaia.
Title of Ras Taffari Makonnen. 1892-1975. Emperor of Ethiopia. Haile sounds like, and could be Hail hence hail Selassie. An Incarnation of Gaia Goddess of the Earth. In the Creatocracy the Most Sovereign Emperor is the Emperor of Emperors by supernatural rights.

He is Peter Matthews-Akukalia, Castle Makupedia the God of Creatocracy Genius and Mind. His title greeting is HAIL CASTLE MAKUPEDIA! In ordinary terms he is not addressed as a commoner in the words Mr., Brother, etc because he is first of noble birth and earned it extra by his own works. He has won his mental wars and sits as the sovereign. He is the institution of the Mind and the Creatocracy. He is ordinarily addressed in title as Castle Makupedia in a bow especially when entreated or appeased. So Castle Makupedia!!!

Hailstone=3,500=4,000=40%=P4.0D=Govt=Creato.=4 April=Mercury=Hermes=G=A4.
Hailstorm=2,000=20%=P2.00D=2.0=Nature=Matter=Moon=2 Feb.=Cupid=N=C+_
Haiphong=10,000=1,000=100%=10.0=Physicality=Tech.=10 Oct.=Uranus=P=1Ø.

Hair=10,000=1,000=100%=10.0=Physicality=Tech.=10 Oct.=Uranus=P=1Ø.
By Greek mythology, the supernatural depiction of the hair is the clouds being Uranus. Perhaps this is why Apostle Paul wrote that a woman covers her hair at worship services as it scares the angels. We confirm its relativity spoken by GOD Almighty in Job 38:33-34. The hair is a technology and physical quantum or measure of cloud on a person. See Cloud.

Hairbreadth=2,500=3,000=30%=P3.0D=3.0=Cre=Stars=Muses=3 March = C=I>>GIL.
Hairbrush=2,500=3,000=30%=P3.0D=3.0=Creativity=Stars=Muses=3 March = C=I>>GIL.

Haircut=7,000=70%=P7.0D=7.0=Language=Assets=Mars=7 July=Pleiades.
The signs for computing is hair cut. Jesus says that even the hairs on our head are numbered. This means that hair strands are number codes and signs indicated in the Bible and Quran to discover and guide one through spirituality and substantial faith expressed by computational creativity. The Creatocracy believes that computing is evidential prayers. During the process of computing a matter the will of GOD is revealed and secrets are seen thus leading to instant answers on what to do and what not to do.

Hairdo=1,000=100%=10.0=1.0=Mind=Sun=1 January=Helios >> M=E4.
A sign for measuring the energy of a thing or in that thing is based on quantum bundle system of 10,000=1,000=100=10. The ability to quantize abstracts into physical equivalents is called Makumatics and its process is the Mind Computing. It is hairdo process arrangement of chaos into order. Hence Makumatics is a daily need in our everyday lives as much as our hair do must be in order to help us focus, be approachable and useful in business. After all cleanliness is godliness. David mentions the 10,000 to 1,000 measures as a code in the Psalms. "One thousand shall fall by your side and Ten thousand by your right hand...". Castle Makupedia had lots of personal issues as though he were in a war with himself and often saw angels walk through his hair as a jungle when they were grown. His peace only returned when he had it barbed. The Guinness Book of Astronomy: Facts & Feats by Patrick Moore reveals that Angstrom the Swedish physicist measured the human hair using cosmic wavelength. A kind of Psychoastronomy.

Hairdresser=3,000=30%=P3.0D=3.0=Creativity=Stars=Muses=3 March = C=I>>GIL.
Hairline=7,500=8,000=80%=P8.0D=Economy=Currency=8 Aug.=Zeus>>E=v.
Hairpiece=8,000=80%=P8.0D=Economy=Currency=8 Aug.=Zeus>>E=v.
Hairpin=7,000=70%=P7.0D=7.0=Language=Assets=Mars=7 July=Pleiades.
Hair raising=2,500=3,000=30%=P3.0D=3.0=Cre=Stars=Muses=3 March = C=I>>GIL.
Hairsplitting=3,000=30%=P3.0D=3.0=Creativity=Stars=Muses=3 March = C=I>>GIL.
Hairspray=5,500=5.5=80%=P5.50=Earth-Midway=5 May = Gaia.
Hairspring=7,500=8,000=80%=P8.0D=Economy=Currency=8 Aug.=Zeus>>E=v.
Hairstyle=3,500=4,000=40%=P4.0D=Govt=Creato.=4 April=Mercury=Hermes=G=A4.
Hair trigger=5,000=50%=P5.00D=Law=Time=Venus=5 May = Aphrodite>>L=N.
Hair-trigger=5,500=5.5=80%=P5.50=Earth-Midway=5 May = Gaia.
Hair weaving=6,000=60%=P6.0D=Man=Earth=Royalty=6 June=Gaia=Maia>>M=M2.
Hairy=6,000=60%=P6.0D=Man=Earth=Royalty=6 June=Gaia=Maia>>M=M2.
Haiti=11,000=11%=P1.10D=1.1=Idea=Brainchild=Inv.=11 Nov.=SC=Athena>>I=MT.
Haj=3,500=4,000=40%=P4.0D=Govt=Creatocracy=4 April=Mercury=Hermes=G=A4.
Haji=5,500=5.5=80%=P5.50=Earth-Midway=5 May = Gaia.
Hake=4,000=40%=P4.0D=Government =Creatocracy=4 April=Mercury=Hermes=G=A4.
Haluyt Richard=2,500=3,000=30%=P3.0D=3.0=Cre=Stars=Muses=3 March = C=I>>GIL.

Hal-=1,500=15%=P1.50D=1.5=Authority=Solar Crown=1 May = Maia.
The halo is a sign of the celestial presence of Maia.

Halala=3,000=30%=P3.0D=3.0=Creativity=Stars=Muses=3 March = C=I>>GIL.
Halberd=10,000=1,000=100%=10.0=Physicality=Tech.=10 Oct.=Uranus=P=1Ø.
Halcyon=5,500=5.5=80%=P5.50=Earth-Midway=5 May = Gaia.
Hale1=1,500=15%=P1.50D=1.5=Authority=Solar Crown=1 May = Maia.
Hale2=3,500=4,000=40%=P4.0D=Govt=Creatocracy=4 April=Mercury=Hermes=G=A4.
Hale Edward=3,500=4,000=40%=P4.0D=Govt=Creato.=4 April=Mercury=Hermes=G=A4.
Hale, Nathan=2,500=3,000=30%=P3.0D=3.0=Cre=Stars=Muses=3 March = C=I>>GIL.
Haleakala Crater=6,500=7,000=70%=P7.0D=7.0=Lang.=Assets=Mars=7 July=Pleiades.
Haler=3,000=30%=P3.0D=3.0=Creativity=Stars=Muses=3 March = C=I>>GIL.
Half=10,000=1,000=100%=10.0=Physicality=Tech.=10 Oct.=Uranus=P=1Ø.
Halfback=10,000=1,000=100%=10.0=Physicality=Tech.=10 Oct.=Uranus=P=1Ø.
Half baked=6,500=7,000=70%=P7.0D=7.0=Language=Assets=Mars=7 July=Pleiades.
Half boot=4,000=40%=P4.0D=Govt=Creatocracy=4 April=Mercury=Hermes=G=A4.
Half-breed=3,500=4,000=40%=P4.0D=Govt=Creato.=4 April=Mercury=Hermes=G=A4.
Halfbrother=3,500=4,000=40%=P4.0D=Govt=Creato.=4 April=Mercury=Hermes=G=A4.
Half caste=3,500=4,000=40%=P4.0D=Govt=Creato.=4 April=Mercury=Hermes=G=A4.
Half cocked=6,500=7,000=70%=P7.0D=7.0=Language=Assets=Mars=7 July=Pleiades.

Half dollar=3,500=4,000=40%=P4.0D=Govt=Creato.=4 April=Mercury=Hermes=G=A4.
A borderline currency with value 7,000 meaning the dollar must be computed. See Dollar.

Halfhearted=3,000=30%=P3.0D=3.0=Creativity=Stars=Muses=3 March = C=I>>GIL.
Half life=10,000=1,000=100%=10.0=Physicality=Tech.=10 Oct.=Uranus=P=1Ø.
Half mast=10,000=1,000=100%=10.0=Physicality=Tech.=10 Oct.=Uranus=P=1Ø.
Half moon=7,000=70%=P7.0D=7.0=Language=Assets=Mars=7 July=Pleiades.
Half nelson=10,000=1,000=100%=10.0=Physicality=Tech.=10 Oct.=Uranus=P=1Ø.
Half note=5,000=50%=P5.00D=Law=Time=Venus=5 May = Aphrodite>>L=N.
Half sister=3,500=4,000=40%=P4.0D=Govt=Creato.=4 April=Mercury=Hermes=G=A4.
Halfslip=4,000=40%=P4.0D=Government =Creatocracy=4 April=Mercury=Hermes=G=A4.
Half sole=5,000=50%=P5.00D=Law=Time=Venus=5 May = Aphrodite>>L=N.
Half staff=1,500=15%=P1.50D=1.5=Authority=Solar Crown=1 May = Maia.
Half step=1,000=100%=10.0=1.0=Mind=Sun=1 January=Helios >> M=E4.
Halftime=6,000=60%=P6.0D=Man=Earth=Royalty=6 June=Gaia=Maia>>M=M2.
Half track=6,500=7,000=70%=P7.0D=7.0=Language=Assets=Mars=7 July=Pleiades.
Half truth=6,000=60%=P6.0D=Man=Earth=Royalty=6 June=Gaia=Maia>>M=M2.
Halfway=4,500=5,000=50%=P5.00D=Law=Time=Venus=5 May = Aphrodite>>L=N.
Halfwit=2,500=3,000=30%=P3.0D=3.0=Creativity=Stars=Muses=3 March = C=I>>GIL.
Halibut=6,000=60%=P6.0D=Man=Earth=Royalty=6 June=Gaia=Maia>>M=M2.
Halide=5,500=5.5=80%=P5.50=Earth-Midway=5 May = Gaia.
Halifax=7,500=8,000=80%=P8.0D=Economy=Currency=8 Aug.=Zeus>>E=v.
Halite=1,000=100%=10.0=1.0=Mind=Sun=1 January=Helios >> M=E4.
Halitosis=3,500=4,000=40%=P4.0D=Govt=Creato.=4 April=Mercury=Hermes=G=A4.
Hall=10,000=1,000=100%=10.0=Physicality=Tech.=10 Oct.=Uranus=P=1Ø.
Hale=4,000=40%=P4.0D=Government =Creatocracy=4 April=Mercury=Hermes=G=A4.

Hallelujah=4,000=40%=P4.0D=Govt=Creatocracy=4 April=Mercury=Hermes=G=A4.
A spiritual word that means Creatocracy. Hail the Government of Heaven and Earth.

Halley Edmund=2,000=20%=P2.00D=2.0=Nature=Matter=Moon=2 Feb.=Cupid=N=C+_
Hallmark=6,500=7,000=70%=P7.0D=7.0=Language=Assets=Mars=7 July=Pleiades.
Hall of fame=7,500=8,000=80%=P8.0D=Economy=Currency=8 Aug.=Zeus>>E=v.
Halloo=6,500=7,000=70%=P7.0D=7.0=Language=Assets=Mars=7 July=Pleiades.
Hallow=6,500=7,000=70%=P7.0D=7.0=Language=Assets=Mars=7 July=Pleiades.

Halloween=6,500=7,000=70%=P7.0D=7.0=Language=Assets=Mars=7 July=Pleiades.
The Halloween Day is Oct.31>>31-10. The guiding spirit for that day is computed:
3.1*10.0=p=13.1+31=44.1x=px=450.2=500=5.0. Mercury runs the day under the laws
of Odite. The full spirit of the Halloween belongs to Aphrodite. Now the resultant
shows 700=7.0. The total value of energy on each person is thus measured as>>
5.0*7.0=p=12+35=47x=px=467=500=5.0>> Law>> Time>>Aphrodite. It is her worship.

Hallucination=10,000=1,000=100%=10.0=Physicality=Tech.=10 Oct.=Uranus=P=1Ø.
Hallucinogen=2,500=3,000=30%=P3.0D=3.0=Cre=Stars=Muses=3 March = C=I>>GIL.
Hallway=3,500=4,000=40%=P4.0D=Govt=Creatocracy=4 April=Mercury=Hermes=G=A4.

Halo=10,000=1,000=100%=10.0=Physicality=Tech.=10 Oct.=Uranus=P=1Ø.
Halo-=3,000=30%=P3.0D=3.0=Creativity=Stars=Muses=3 March = C=I>>GIL.
Halocarbon=3,500=4,000=40%=P4.0D=Govt=Creato.=4 April=Mercury=Hermes=G=A4.
Halogen=10,000=1,000=100%=10.0=Physicality=Tech.=10 Oct.=Uranus=P=1Ø.
Halsey William=3,000=30%=P3.0D=3.0=Creativity=Stars=Muses=3 March = C=I>>GIL.
Halt1=8,000=80%=P8.0D=Economy=Currency=8 Aug.=Zeus>>E=v.
Halt2=5,500=5.5=80%=P5.50=Earth-Midway=5 May = Gaia.
Halter=10,000=1,000=100%=10.0=Physicality=Tech.=10 Oct.=Uranus=P=1Ø.
Halting=4,000=40%=P4.0D=Government =Creatocracy=4 April=Mercury=Hermes=G=A4.
Halvah=4,000=40%=P4.0D=Government =Creatocracy=4 April=Mercury=Hermes=G=A4.
Halve=10,000=1,000=100%=10.0=Physicality=Tech.=10 Oct.=Uranus=P=1Ø.
Halves=1,500=15%=P1.50D=1.5=Authority=Solar Crown=1 May = Maia.
Halyard=8,000=80%=P8.0D=Economy=Currency=8 Aug.=Zeus>>E=v.
ham=10,000=1,000=100%=10.0=Physicality=Tech.=10 Oct.=Uranus=P=1Ø.
Ham=5,500=5.5=80%=P5.50=Earth-Midway=5 May = Gaia.
Hama=4,500=5,000=50%=P5.00D=Law=Time=Venus=5 May = Aphrodite>>L=N.

Hamadryad=4,500=5,000=50%=P5.00D=Law=Time=Venus=5 May = Aphrodite>>L=N.
Greek & Roman Myth. A wood nymph. Muse of Aphrodite. Through her a tree is the means
or border by which Mercury and Aphrodite can live in trees on the earth. So trees are alive.

Hamburg=6,000=60%=P6.0D=Man=Earth=Royalty=6 June=Gaia=Maia>>M=M2.
Hamburger=10,000=1,000=100%=10.0=Physicality=Tech.=10 Oct.=Uranus=P=1Ø.
Hamilcar Barca=5,000=50%=P5.00D=Law=Time=Venus=5 May = Aphrodite>>L=N.
Hamilton=10,000=1,000=100%=10.0=Physicality=Tech.=10 Oct.=Uranus=P=1Ø.
Hamilton, Alexander=6,000=60%=P6.0D=Man=Earth=Royalty=6 June=Gaia>>M=M2.
Hamilton, Edith=3,000=30%=P3.0D=3.0=Creativity=Stars=Muses=3 March = C=I>>GIL.
Hamite=8,500=9,000=90%=P9.00D=9.0=Abstraction=Gods=Saturn=9Sept.>>A=Ø.
Hamlet=3,500=4,000=40%=P4.0D=Govt=Creato.=4 April=Mercury=Hermes=G=A4.
Hammarskjöld=7,000=70%=P7.0D=7.0=Language=Assets=Mars=7 July=Pleiades.
Hammer=10,000=1,000=100%=10.0=Physicality=Tech.=10 Oct.=Uranus=P=1Ø.
Hammerhead=10,000=1,000=100%=10.0=Physicality=Tech.=10 Oct.=Uranus=P=1Ø.
Hammerlock=7,000=70%=P7.0D=7.0=Language=Assets=Mars=7 July=Pleiades.
Hammock=7,000=70%=P7.0D=7.0=Language=Assets=Mars=7 July=Pleiades.
Hammurabi=3,000=30%=P3.0D=3.0=Creativity=Stars=Muses=3 March = C=I>>GIL.
Hamper1=11,000=11%=P1.10D=1.1=Idea=Brainchild=Inv.=11 Nov.=SC=Athena>>I=MT.
Hamper2=6,000=60%=P6.0D=Man=Earth=Royalty=6 June=Gaia=Maia>>M=M2.
Hampton=10,000=1,000=100%=10.0=Physicality=Tech.=10 Oct.=Uranus=P=1Ø.
Hamster=12,500=13,000=13%=P1.30=Solar Core=Faculty=13 January=Athena.
Hamstring=10,000=1,000=100%=10.0=Physicality=Tech.=10 Oct.=Uranus=P=1Ø.
Han=4,000=40%=P4.0D=Government =Creatocracy=4 April=Mercury=Hermes=G=A4.
Hancock John=3,500=4,000=40%=P4.0D=Govt=Creat.=4 April=Mercury=Hermes=G=A4.
Hand=10,000=1,000=100%=10.0=Physicality=Tech.=10 Oct.=Uranus=P=1Ø.
Handbag=4,000=40%=P4.0D=Govt=Creatocracy=4 April=Mercury=Hermes=G=A4.

Handbill=11,000=11%=P1.10D=1.1=Idea=Brainchild=Inv.=11 Nov.=SC=Athena>>I=MT.
Handbook=5,500=5.5=80%=P5.50=Earth-Midway=5 May = Gaia.
Handcar=6,000=60%=P6.0D=Man=Earth=Royalty=6 June=Gaia=Maia>>M=M2.
Handcart=5,500=5.5=80%=P5.50=Earth-Midway=5 May = Gaia.
Hand clasp=1,000=100%=10.0=1.0=Mind=Sun=1 January=Helios >> M=E4.
Handcuff=10,000=1,000=100%=10.0=Physicality=Tech.=10 Oct.=Uranus=P=1Ø.
Handed=10,000=1,000=100%=10.0=Physicality=Tech.=10 Oct.=Uranus=P=1Ø.
Handel George=2,000=20%=P2.00D=2.0=Nature=Matter=Moon=2 Feb.=Cupid=N=C+_
Handful=10,000=1,000=100%=10.0=Physicality=Tech.=10 Oct.=Uranus=P=1Ø.
Handgun=4,500=5,000=50%=P5.00D=Law=Time=Venus=5 May = Aphrodite>>L=N.
Handicap=10,000=1,000=100%=10.0=Physicality=Tech.=10 Oct.=Uranus=P=1Ø.
Handicapped=10,000=1,000=100%=10.0=Physicality=Tech.=10 Oct.=Uranus=P=1Ø.
Handicraft=10,000=1,000=100%=10.0=Physicality=Tech.=10 Oct.=Uranus=P=1Ø.
Hand in Hand=1,500=15%=P1.50D=1.5=Authority=Solar Crown=1 May = Maia.
Handiwork=6,000=60%=P6.0D=Man=Earth=Royalty=6 June=Gaia=Maia>>M=M2.
Handkerchief=6,500=7,000=70%=P7.0D=7.0=Language=Assets=Mars=7 July=Pleiades.
Handle=10,000=1,000=100%=10.0=Physicality=Tech.=10 Oct.=Uranus=P=1Ø.
Handle bars=4,000=40%=P4.0D=Govt=Creato.=4 April=Mercury=Hermes=G=A4.
Handler=10,500=11,000=11%=P1.10D=1.1=Idea=Brainchild=Inv.=11 Nov.=Athena>>I=MT.
Handmade=4,500=5,000=50%=P5.00D=Law=Time=Venus=5 May = Aphrodite>>L=N.
Handmaid=2,500=3,000=30%=P3.0D=3.0=Creativity=Stars=Muses=3 March = C=I>>GIL.
Hand-me-down=10,000=1,000=100%=10.0=Physicality=Tech.=10 Oct.=Uranus=P=1Ø.
Handoff=6,000=60%=P6.0D=Man=Earth=Royalty=6 June=Gaia=Maia>>M=M2.
Handout=9,000=90%=P9.00D=9.0=Abstraction=Gods=Saturn=9Sept.>>A=Ø.
Handpick=4,000=40%=P4.0D=Govt=Creato.=4 April=Mercury=Hermes=G=A4.
Handrail=5,500=5.5=80%=P5.50=Earth-Midway=5 May = Gaia.
Handset=7,000=70%=P7.0D=7.0=Language=Assets=Mars=7 July=Pleiades.
Handshake=5,000=50%=P5.00D=Law=Time=Venus=5 May = Aphrodite>>L=N.
Hands off=1,500=15%=P1.50D=1.5=Authority=Solar Crown=1 May = Maia.
Handsome=10,000=1,000=100%=10.0=Physicality=Tech.=10 Oct.=Uranus=P=1Ø.
Hands-on=1,500=15%=P1.50D=1.5=Authority=Solar Crown=1 May = Maia.
Handspring=10,000=1,000=100%=10.0=Physicality=Tech.=10 Oct.=Uranus=P=1Ø.
Handstand=5,500=5.5=80%=P5.50=Earth-Midway=5 May = Gaia.
Hand-to-Hand=4,000=40%=P4.0D=Govt=Creato.=4 April=Mercury=Hermes=G=A4.
Hand-to-mouth=3,500=4,000=40%=P4.0D=Govt=Creato=4 April=Hermes=G=A4.
Handwork==4,000=40%=P4.0D=Government =Creatocracy=4 April=Hermes=G=A4.
Handwriting=5,000=50%=P5.00D=Law=Time=Venus=5 May = Aphrodite>>L=N.
Handy=6,000=60%=P6.0D=Man=Earth=Royalty=6 June=Gaia=Maia>>M=M2.
Handy William=4,500=5,000=50%=P5.00D=Law=Time=Venus=5 May = Aphrodite>>L=N.
Handyman=5,000=50%=P5.00D=Law=Time=Venus=5 May = Aphrodite>>L=N.
Hang=10,000=1,000=100%=10.0=Physicality=Tech.=10 Oct.=Uranus=P=1Ø..
Hanger=6,000=60%=P6.0D=Man=Earth=Royalty=6 June=Gaia=Maia>>M=M2.
Hangchow=1,000=100%=10.0=1.0=Mind=Sun=1 January=Helios >> M=E4.
Hangdog=3,000=30%=P3.0D=3.0=Creativity=Stars=Muses=3 March = C=I>>GIL.
Hanger=6,500=7,000=70%=P7.0D=7.0=Language=Assets=Mars=7 July=Pleiades.

Hanger-on=1,500=15%=P1.50D=1.5=Authority=Solar Crown=1 May = Maia.
Hang glider=8,500=9,000=90%=P9.00D=9.0=Abstraction=Gods=Saturn=9Sept.>>A=Ø.
Hanging=5,500=5.5=80%=P5.50=Earth-Midway=5 May = Gaia.
Hangman=4,000=40%=P4.0D=Government =Creatocracy=4 April=Hermes=G=A4.
Hangnail=7,500=8,000=80%=P8.0D=Economy=Currency=8 Aug.=Zeus>>E=v.
Hangout=2,500=3,000=30%=P3.0D=3.0=Creativity=Stars=Muses=3 March = C=I>>GIL.
Hangover=6,000=60%=P6.0D=Man=Earth=Royalty=6 June=Gaia=Maia>>M=M2.
Hang up=4,500=5,000=50%=P5.00D=Law=Time=Venus=5 May = Aphrodite>>L=N.
Hangzhou=9,000=90%=P9.00D=9.0=Abstraction=Gods=Saturn=9Sept.>>A=Ø.
Hank=3,000=30%=P3.0D=3.0=Creativity=Stars=Muses=3 March = C=I>>GIL.
Hanker=6,000=60%=P6.0D=Man=Earth=Royalty=6 June=Gaia=Maia>>M=M2.
Hankie=1,500=15%=P1.50D=1.5=Authority=Solar Crown=1 May = Maia.
Hanky-panky=3,500=4,000=40%=P4.0D=Govt=Creatocracy=4 April=Hermes=G=A4.
Hanna Marcus=3,500=4,000=40%=P4.0D=Govt=Creatocracy=4 April=Hermes=G=A4.
Hannibal=3,000=30%=P3.0D=3.0=Creativity=Stars=Muses=3 March = C=I>>GIL.
Hanoi=6,000=60%=P6.0D=Man=Earth=Royalty=6 June=Gaia=Maia>>M=M2.
Hanover=7,000=70%=P7.0D=7.0=Language=Assets=Mars=7 July=Pleiades.
Han River=9,000=90%=P9.00D=9.0=Abstraction=Gods=Saturn=9Sept.>>A=Ø.
Hansberry Lorraine=2,000=20%=P2.00D=2.0=Nature=Moon=2 Feb.=Cupid=N=C+_
Hansom=8,500=9,000=90%=P9.00D=9.0=Abstraction=Gods=Saturn=9Sept.>>A=Ø.

Hanukkah=8,000=80%=P8.0D=Economy=Currency=8 Aug.=Zeus>>E=v.
An eighth-day festival commemorating the victory of the Maccabees over Antiochus epiphanes. Proved. The Creatocracy celebrates Apotheosis of Castle Makupedia, Oct.13.

Hao=2,000=20%=P2.00D=2.0=Nature=Matter=Moon=2 Feb.=Cupid=N=C+_
Haole=10,000=1,000=100%=10.0=Physicality=Tech.=10 Oct.=Uranus=P=1Ø.
Hap=3,000=30%=P3.0D=3.0=Creativity=Stars=Muses=3 March = C=I>>GIL.
Haphazard=3,000=30%=P3.0D=3.0=Creativity=Stars=Muses=3 March = C=I>>GIL.
Hapless=2,500=3,000=30%=P3.0D=3.0=Creativity=Stars=Muses=3 March = C=I>>GIL.
Haploid=10,000=1,000=100%=10.0=Physicality=Tech.=10 Oct.=Uranus=P=1Ø.
Haply=2,000=20%=P2.00D=2.0=Nature=Matter=Moon=2 Feb.=Cupid=N=C+_
Happen=10,000=1,000=100%=10.0=Physicality=Tech.=10 Oct.=Uranus=P=1Ø.
Happening=3,000=30%=P3.0D=3.0=Creativity=Stars=Muses=3 March = C=I>>GIL.
Happenstance=1,500=15%=P1.50D=1.5=Authority=Solar Crown=1 May = Maia.
Happy=10,000=1,000=100%=10.0=Physicality=Tech.=10 Oct.=Uranus=P=1Ø.
Happy-go-lucky=2,000=20%=P2.00D=2.0=Nature=Matter=Moon=2 Feb.=Cupid=N=C+_
Happy hour=6,500=7,000=70%=P7.0D=7.0=Language=Assets=Mars=7 July=Pleiades.
Hapsburg=10,000=1,000=100%=10.0=Physicality=Tech.=10 Oct.=Uranus=P=1Ø.
Harakiri=2,000=20%=P2.00D=2.0=Nature=Matter=Moon=2 Feb.=Cupid=N=C+_
Harangue=5,500=5.5=80%=P5.50=Earth-Midway=5 May = Gaia.
Harare=6,000=60%=P6.0D=Man=Earth=Royalty=6 June=Gaia=Maia>>M=M2.
Harass=10,000=1,000=100%=10.0=Physicality=Tech.=10 Oct.=Uranus=P=1Ø.
Harbin=4,500=5,000=50%=P5.00D=Law=Time=Venus=5 May = Aphrodite>>L=N.

Harbinger=9,000=90%=P9.00D=9.0=Abstraction=Gods=Saturn=9Sept.>>A=Ø.
Harbor=10,000=1,000=100%=10.0=Physicality=Tech.=10 Oct.=Uranus=P=1Ø.
Hard=10,000=1,000=100%=10.0=Physicality=Tech.=10 Oct.=Uranus=P=1Ø.
Hardback=6,000=60%=P6.0D=Man=Earth=Royalty=6 June=Gaia=Maia>>M=M2.
Hardball=6,500=7,000=70%=P7.0D=7.0=Language=Assets=Mars=7 July=Pleiades.
Hard bitten=1,500=15%=P1.50D=1.5=Authority=Solar Crown=1 May = Maia.
Hard boiled=7,000=70%=P7.0D=7.0=Language=Assets=Mars=7 July=Pleiades.
Hard coal=1,000=100%=10.0=1.0=Mind=Sun=1 January=Helios >> M=E4.
Hard copy=3,500=4,000=40%=P4.0D=Govt.=Creatocracy=4 April=Hermes=G=A4.
Hardcore=7,000=70%=P7.0D=7.0=Language=Assets=Mars=7 July=Pleiades.
Hard disk=7,500=8,000=80%=P8.0D=Economy=Currency=8 Aug.=Zeus>>E=v.
Harden=10,500=11,000=11%=P1.10D=1.1=Idea=Brainchild=Inv.=11 Nov.=Athena>>I=MT.
Hard hat=9,500=10,000=1,000=100%=10.0=Physicality=Tech.=10 Oct.=Uranus=P=1Ø.
Hardheaded=1,500=15%=P1.50D=1.5=Authority=Solar Crown=1 May = Maia.
Hard hearted=3,000=30%=P3.0D=3.0=Creativity=Stars=Muses=3 March = C=I>>GIL.
Hardihood=3,000=30%=P3.0D=3.0=Creativity=Stars=Muses=3 March = C=I>>GIL.
Harding Warren=5,500=5.5=80%=P5.50=Earth-Midway=5 May = Gaia.
Hardline=2,500=3,000=30%=P3.0D=3.0=Creativity=Stars=Muses=3 March = C=I>>GIL.
Hardly=10,000=1,000=100%=10.0=Physicality=Tech.=10 Oct.=Uranus=P=1Ø.
Hard nosed=500=5%=P5.00D=5.0=Law=Time=Venus=5 May=Aphrodite>>L=N.
Hard palate=4,000=40%=P4.0D=Government =Creatocracy=4 April=Hermes=G=A4.
Hard pan=3,000=30%=P3.0D=3.0=Creativity=Stars=Muses=3 March = C=I>>GIL.
Hard pressed=1,500=15%=P1.50D=1.5=Authority=Solar Crown=1 May = Maia.
Hard rock=8,000=80%=P8.0D=Economy=Currency=8 Aug.=Zeus>>E=v.
Hard sauce=6,000=60%=P6.0D=Man=Earth=Royalty=6 June=Gaia=Maia>>M=M2.
Hard sell=3,500=4,000=40%=P4.0D=Government =Creatocracy=4April=Hermes=G=A4.
Hardship=5,500=5.5=80%=P5.50=Earth-Midway=5 May = Gaia.
Hardtack=7,500=8,000=80%=P8.0D=Economy=Currency=8 Aug.=Zeus>>E=v.
Hardtop=7,000=70%=P7.0D=7.0=Language=Assets=Mars=7 July=Pleiades.
Hardware=10,000=1,000=100%=10.0=Physicality=Tech.=10 Oct.=Uranus=P=1Ø.
Hard wired=10,000=1,000=100%=10.0=Physicality=Tech.=10 Oct.=Uranus=P=1Ø.
Hardwood=6,000=60%=P6.0D=Man=Earth=Royalty=6 June=Gaia=Maia>>M=M2.
Hardy=10,000=1,000=100%=10.0=Physicality=Tech.=10 Oct.=Uranus=P=1Ø.
Hardy Thomas=2,000=20%=P2.00D=2.0=Nature=Matter=Moon=2 Feb.=Cupid=N=C+_
Hare=6,500=7,000=70%=P7.0D=7.0=Language=Assets=Mars=7 July=Pleiades.
Harebrained=1,000=100%=Physicality=Tech.=10 Oct.=Uranus=P=1Ø.
Harelip=5,500=5.5=80%=P5.50=Earth-Midway=5 May = Gaia.
Harem=9,000=90%=P9.00D=9.0=Abstraction=Gods=Saturn=9Sept.>>A=Ø.
Hark=7,000=70%=P7.0D=7.0=Language=Assets=Mars=7 July=Pleiades.
Harlem=4,500=5,000=50%=P5.00D=Law=Time=Venus=5 May = Aphrodite>>L=N.

Harlequin=10,000=1,000=100%=10.0=Physicality=Tech.=10 Oct.=Uranus=P=1Ø.
A buffoon. A demon. Demons often manifest as harlequins in mask and colored stuff.
Result shows they are more physical and traceable through physical characteristics.

Harlot=2,500=3,000=30%=P3.0D=3.0=Creativity=Stars=Muses=3 March = C=I>>GIL.
A prostitute. Male form >> vagabond. A transition to creativity. Awaiting a muse.

Harm=6,000=60%=P6.0D=Man=Earth=Royalty=6 June=Gaia=Maia>>M=M2.
Harmonic=10,000=1,000=100%=10.0=Physicality=Tech.=10 Oct.=Uranus=P=1Ø.
Harmonica=8,500=9,000=90%=P9.00D=9.0=Abstraction=Gods=Saturn=9Sept.>>A=Ø.
Harmonious=7,500=8,000=80%=P8.0D=Economy=Currency=8 Aug.=Zeus>>E=v.
Harmonium=5,000=50%=P5.00D=Law=Time=Venus=5 May = Aphrodite>>L=N.
Harmonize=6,000=60%=P6.0D=Man=Earth=Royalty=6 June=Gaia=Maia>>M=M2.
Harmony=10,000=1,000=100%=10.0=Physicality=Tech.=10 Oct.=Uranus=P=1Ø.
Harness=10,000=1,000=100%=10.0=Physicality=Tech.=10 Oct.=Uranus=P=1Ø.
Harold I.=3,000=30%=P3.0D=3.0=Creativity=Stars=Muses=3 March = C=I>>GIL.

Harold II.=7,000=70%=P7.0D=7.0=Language=Assets=Mars=7 July=Pleiades.
King of England. Last of the Anglo-Saxon monarchs.

Harp=10,500=11,000=11%=P1.10D=1.1=Idea=Brainchild=Inv.=11 Nov.=SC=Athena
>>I=MT.
Harpers Ferry=5,000=50%=P5.00D=Law=Time=Venus=5 May = Aphrodite>>L=N.
Harpoon=7,500=8,000=80%=P8.0D=Economy=Currency=8 Aug.=Zeus>>E=v.
Harpsichord=7,500=8,000=80%=P8.0D=Economy=Currency=8 Aug.=Zeus>>E=v.

Harpy=10,000=1,000=100%=10.0=Physicality=Tech.=10 Oct.=Uranus=P=1Ø.
Greek myth. A monster with the head of a woman and the tail, wings, and talons of a
bird. They manifest in the physical birthed or not as a predatory person, shrewish woman.
Another case that establishes the cycle of life, incarnation and different forms of persons.

Harquebus=6,000=60%=P6.0D=Man=Earth=Royalty=6 June=Gaia=Maia>>M=M2.
Harridan=4,000=40%=P4.0D=Government=Creatocracy=4 April=Hermes=G=A4.
Harrier1=4,000=40%=P4.0D=Government=Creatocracy=4 April=Mercury=Hermes=G=A4.
Harrier2=10,500=11,000=11%=P1.10D=1.1=Idea=Brainchild=Inv.=11 Nov.=Athena>>I=MT.
Harris, Joel=3,500=4,000=40%=P4.0D=Govt=Creatocracy=4 April=Hermes=G=A4.
Harrisburg=5,000=50%=P5.00D=Law=Time=Venus=5 May = Aphrodite>>L=N.
Harrison Benjamin1=2,500=3,000=30%=P3.0D=3.0=Cre=Stars=Muses=3 March=C=GIL
Harrison Benjamin2=4,000=40%=P4.0D=Govt=Creato.=4 April=Mercury=Hermes=G=A4.
Harrison, William=4,000=40%=P4.0D=Government=Creatocracy=4 April=Hermes=G=A4.
Harrow=10,000=1,000=100%=10.0=Physicality=Tech.=10 Oct.=Uranus=P=1Ø.
Harrowing=1,500=15%=P1.50D=1.5=Authority=Solar Crown=1 May = Maia.
Harry=7,500=8,000=80%=P8.0D=Economy=Currency=8 Aug.=Zeus>>E=v.
Harsh=7,000=70%=P7.0D=7.0=Language=Assets=Mars=7 July=Pleiades.
Hart=3,500=4,000=40%=P4.0D=Govt.=Creato.=4 April=Mercury=Hermes=G=A4.
Harte Francis=2,500=3,000=30%=P3.0D=3.0=Cre=Stars=Muses=3 March = C=I>>GIL.

Hartford=6,500=7,000=70%=P7.0D=7.0=Language=Assets=Mars=7 July=Pleiades.
Harum-scarum=3,500=4,000=40%=P4.0D=Govt=Creato.=4 April=Hermes=G=A4.
Harvest=10,000=1,000=100%=10.0=Physicality=Tech.=10 Oct.=Uranus=P=1Ø.
Harvest moon=4,000=40%=P4.0D=Govt=Creatocracy=4 April=Mercury=Hermes=G=A4.
Harvey William=3,000=30%=P3.0D=3.0=Creativity=Stars=Muses=3 March = C=I>>GIL.
Has=3,500=4,000=40%=P4.0D=Govt=Creatocracy=4 April=Mercury=Hermes=G=A4.

Has been=4,500=5,000=50%=P5.00D=Law=Time=Venus=5 May = Aphrodite>>L=N.
One that is no longer famous, successful or useful.

Hash1=10,000=1,000=100%=10.0=Physicality=Tech.=10 Oct.=Uranus=P=1Ø.
Hash2=1,000=100%=10.0=1.0=Mind=Sun=1 January=Helios >> M=E4.
Hashish=4,500=5,000=50%=P5.00D=Law=Time=Venus=5 May = Aphrodite>>L=N.
Harsh mark=6,500=7,000=70%=P7.0D=7.0=Language=Assets=Mars=7 July=Pleiades.
Hasid=8,500=9,000=90%=P9.00D=9.0=Abstraction=Gods=Saturn=9Sept.>>A=Ø.
Hasn't=1,000=100%=10.0=1.0=Mind=Sun=1 January=Helios >> M=E4.
Hasp=8,500=9,000=90%=P9.00D=9.0=Abstraction=Gods=Saturn=9Sept.>>A=Ø.
Hassle=4,500=5,000=50%=P5.00D=Law=Time=Venus=5 May = Aphrodite>>L=N.
Hassock=7,000=70%=P7.0D=7.0=Language=Assets=Mars=7 July=Pleiades.
Hast=4,000=40%=P4.0D=Government =Creatocracy=4 April=Mercury=Hermes=G=A4.
Haste=10,000=1,000=100%=10.0=Physicality=Tech.=10 Oct.=Uranus=P=1Ø.
Hasten=6,000=60%=P6.0D=Man=Earth=Royalty=6 June=Gaia=Maia>>M=M2.
Hastings=11,000=11%=P1.10D=1.1=Idea=Brainchild=Inv.=11 Nov.=SC=Athena>>I=MT.
Hastings, Warren=3,500=4,000=40%=P4.0D=Govt=Creatocracy=4 April=Hermes=G=A4.
Hasty=8,000=80%=P8.0D=Economy=Currency=8 Aug.=Zeus>>E=v.
Hat=10,000=1,000=100%=10.0=Physicality=Tech.=10 Oct.=Uranus=P=1Ø.
Hatch1=12,000=12%=P1.20D=1.2=Knowledge=Education=12Dec.=Athena>>K=F.
Hatch2=10,000=1,000=100%=10.0=Physicality=Tech.=10 Oct.=Uranus=P=1Ø.
Hatch3=8,000=80%=P8.0D=Economy=Currency=8 Aug.=Zeus>>E=v.
Hatchback=5,500=5.5=80%=P5.50=Earth-Midway=5 May = Gaia.
Hatchery=5,500=5.5=80%=P5.50=Earth-Midway=5 May = Gaia.
Hatchet=5,000=50%=P5.00D=Law=Time=Venus=5 May = Aphrodite>>L=N.
Hatchet man=8,000=80%=P8.0D=Economy=Currency=8 Aug.=Zeus>>E=v.
Hatchling=4,000=40%=P4.0D=Govt=Creatocracy=4 April=Hermes=G=A4.
Hatchway=3,500=4,000=40%=P4.0D=Govt=Creatocracy=4 April=Hermes=G=A4.
Hate=8,000=80%=P8.0D=Economy=Currency=8 Aug.=Zeus>>E=v.
Hath=4,000=40%=P4.0D=Government =Creatocracy=4April=Mercury=Hermes=G=A4.

Hathaway Anne=5,500=5.5=80%=P5.50=Earth-Midway=5 May = Gaia.
A key character in the play>>The Creatocracy Republic, Legend of the Monarchs, by Peter Matthews-Akukalia. Results show that Anne was a human product of the earth midway, a place and source of high potentials. Being so it is now established that William Shakespeare was actually trading on the potentials and talents of his wife Anne. This discovery asserts

the earlier claim made by Peter Matthews-Akukalia, Castle Makupedia that men really never came to Earth with much but would most likely become what their wives naturally are in the line of potentials enclosing talents and ideas. This is the secret of affinity in the bond of marriage, relationships and sex. The innate contents of a woman must be computed tracked and known and the commitments, privileges obligations and responsibilities clearly stated in order to protect her in the relationship. It is love. Else she has a right to opt out. A man woos a woman to willingly submit her potentials to him for proper management. This is the responsibility that makes love a serious work to do. The man has energy and must use this energy to develop these potentials handed down to him. A woman carry her potentials until approx. the ages of 55 - 60 years before losing them. So she is the mine in the relationship and her husband or spouse is the miner and merchant. The more wives a man has the more mines at his disposal and the more work required. A man who has a wife may be happily married but more than one wife is well married. Hence the Creatocracy does not go against polygamy rather it advocates greater responsibility.

Hatred=2,000=20%=P2.00D=2.0=Nature=Matter=Moon=2 Feb.=Cupid=N=C+_

Hatshepsut=4,500=5,000=50%=P5.00D=Law=Time=Venus=5 May = Aphrodite>>L=N.
Queen of Egypt. Alice Matthews - Akukalia. Queen of Fortune. Wife of Peter Matthews-Akukalia, Castle Makupedia. Fulfilled his book Eve of Fortune - The Creatocracy Republic.

Hatteras Island=10,000=1,000=100%=10.0=Physicality=Tech.=10 Oct.=Uranus=P=1Ø.
Hauberk=5,000=50%=P5.00D=Law=Time=Venus=5 May = Aphrodite>>L=N.
Haughty=3,500=4,000=40%=P4.0D=Govt=Creato.=4 April=Mercury =Hermes=G=A4.
Haul=10,000=1,000=100%=10.0=Physicality=Tech.=10 Oct.=Uranus=P=1Ø.
Haulage=5,500=5.5=80%=P5.50=Earth-Midway=5 May = Gaia.
Haunch=10,000=1,000=100%=10.0=Physicality=Tech.=10 Oct.=Uranus=P=1Ø.
Haunt=10,000=1,000=100%=10.0=Physicality=Tech.=10 Oct.=Uranus=P=1Ø.
Hauptmann Gerhart=3,000=30%=P3.0D=3.0=Cre=Stars=Muses=3 March = C=I>>GIL.
Hausa=6,500=7,000=70%=P7.0D=7.0=Language=Assets=Mars=7 July=Pleiades.
Haute couture=5,500=5.5=80%=P5.50=Earth-Midway=5 May = Gaia.
Haute cuisine=2,500=3,000=30%=P3.0D=3.0=Cre=Stars=Muses=3 March = C=I>>GIL.
Hauteur=3,000=30%=P3.0D=3.0=Creativity=Stars=Muses=3 March = C=I>>GIL.

Havana=7,000=70%=P7.0D=7.0=Language=Assets=Mars=7 July=Pleiades.
The capital of Cuba in the NW part on the Gulf of Mexico. A land of computational energy. Aries has a base here and so violence must be countered by computational metrics, cyber development and assets works language development and precision knowledge.

Have=10,000=1,000=100%=10.0=Physicality=Tech.=10 Oct.=Uranus=P=1Ø.
Havel Václav=3,000=30%=P3.0D=3.0=Creativity=Stars=Muses=3 March = C=I>>GIL.
Haven=5,000=50%=P5.00D=Law=Time=Venus=5 May = Aphrodite>>L=N.

Have-not=3,500=4,000=40%=P4.0D=Govt=Creato.=4 April=Mercury=Hermes=G=A4.
Haven't=1,000=100%=10.0=1.0=Mind=Sun=1 January=Helios >> M=E4.
Haversack=7,000=70%=P7.0D=7.0=Language=Assets=Mars=7 July=Pleiades.
Havoc=4,500=5,000=50%=P5.00D=Law=Time=Venus=5 May = Aphrodite>>L=N.
Hawl=2,000=20%=P2.00D=2.0=Nature=Matter=Moon=2 Feb.=Cupid=N=C+_
Haw2=4,500=5,000=50%=P5.00D=Law=Time=Venus=5 May = Aphrodite>>L=N.
Hawaii=6,500=7,000=70%=P7.0D=7.0=Language=Assets=Mars=7 July=Pleiades.
Hawaiian=5,500=5.5=80%=P5.50=Earth-Midway=5 May = Gaia.
Hawaiian Islands=5,500=5.5=80%=P5.50=Earth-Midway=5 May = Gaia.
Hawk1=10,000=1,000=100%=10.0=Physicality=Tech.=10 Oct.=Uranus=P=1Ø.
Hawk2=6,000=60%=P6.0D=Man=Earth=Royalty=6 June=Gaia=Maia>>M=M2.
Hawk3=6,000=60%=P6.0D=Man=Earth=Royalty=6 June=Gaia=Maia>>M=M2.
Hawk-eyed=2,000=20%=P2.00D=2.0=Nature=Matter=Moon=2 Feb.=Cupid=N=C+_
Hawser=7,500=8,000=80%=P8.0D=Economy=Currency=8 Aug.=Zeus>>E=v.
Hawthorn=7,500=8,000=80%=P8.0D=Economy=Currency=8 Aug.=Zeus>>E=v.
Hawthorne Nathaniel=2,000=20%=P2.00D=2.0=Nature=Moon=2 Feb.=Cupid=N=C+_
Hay=10,000=1,000=100%=10.0=Physicality=Tech.=10 Oct.=Uranus=P=1Ø.
Haydn Franz=2,500=3,000=30%=P3.0D=3.0=Cre=Stars=Muses=3 March = C=I>>GIL.
Hayes Rutherford=4,500=5,000=50%=P5.00D=Law=Time=Venus=5 May =Odite>>L=N.
Hay fever=11,000=11%=P1.10D=1.1=Idea=Brainchild=Inv.=11 Nov.=SC=Athena>>I=MT.
Hay fork=4,000=40%=P4.0D=Govt=Creatocracy=4 April=Mercury=Hermes=G=A4.
Hayloft=2,500=3,000=30%=P3.0D=3.0=Creativity=Stars=Muses=3 March = C=I>>GIL.
Hayseed=4,500=5,000=50%=P5.00D=Law=Time=Venus=5 May = Aphrodite>>L=N.
Haystack=5,000=50%=P5.00D=Law=Time=Venus=5 May = Aphrodite>>L=N.
Hayward=4,500=5,000=50%=P5.00D=Law=Time=Venus=5 May = Aphrodite>>L=N.
Haywire=3,000=30%=P3.0D=3.0=Creativity=Stars=Muses=3 March = C=I>>GIL.
Hazard=10,000=1,000=100%=10.0=Physicality=Tech.=10 Oct.=Uranus=P=1Ø.
Hazardous waste=8,000=80%=P8.0D=Economy=Currency=8 Aug.=Zeus>>E=v.
Hazel=9,000=90%=P9.00D=9.0=Abstraction=Gods=Saturn=9Sept.>>A=Ø.
Haze2=6,500=7,000=70%=P7.0D=7.0=Language=Assets=Mars=7 July=Pleiades.
Hazel=8,500=9,000=90%=P9.00D=9.0=Abstraction=Gods=Saturn=9Sept.>>A=Ø.
Hazelnut=2,500=3,000=30%=P3.0D=3.0=Creativity=Stars=Muses=3 March = C=I>>GIL.
Hazlitt William=2,000=20%=P2.00D=2.0=Nature=Matter=Moon=2 Feb.=Cupid=N=C+_
Hazy=6,500=7,000=70%=P7.0D=7.0=Language=Assets=Mars=7 July=Pleiades.
Hb=500=5%=P5.00D=5.0=Law=Time=Venus=5 May=Aphrodite>>L=N.
H-bomb=1,500=15%=P1.50D=1.5=Authority=Solar Crown=1 May = Maia.
H.C.F.=2,000=20%=P2.00D=2.0=Nature=Matter=Moon=2 Feb.=Cupid=N=C+_
hdqrs.=500=5%=P5.00D=5.0=Law=Time=Venus=5 May=Aphrodite>>L=N.
hel=10,000=1,000=100%=10.0=Physicality=Tech.=10 Oct.=Uranus=P=1Ø.

---

he2=4,000=40%=P4.0D=Government =Creatocracy=4 April=Mercury=Hermes=G=A4.
The 5th letter of the Hebrew alphabet. Result is 4.0 so a union between Hermes and Aphrodite in the bond or affinity of power and law is thus computed.

4.0*5.0=p=9+20=29x=px=209=21>>12=1.2>>Knowledge >> Education >> Institution.

In order words Athena inspired the word he, and by knowledge established politics and law. This is the reason power and law must be guided by the best of minds in a thing. In any case we all speak Hebrew whenever we speak the word He>> male reference code.

He=2,500=3,000=30%=P3.0D=3.0=Creativity=Stars=Muses=3 March = C=I>>GIL.
Head=10,000=1,000=100%=10.0=Physicality=Tech.=10 Oct.=Uranus=P=1Ø.
Headache=4,500=5,000=50%=P5.00D=Law=Time=Venus=5 May = Aphrodite>>L=N.
Headband=3,000=30%=P3.0D=3.0=Creativity=Stars=Muses=3 March = C=I>>GIL.
Headboard=5,500=5.5=80%=P5.50=Earth-Midway=5 May = Gaia.
Headdress=4,000=40%=P4.0D=Govt.=Creatocracy=4 April=Mercury=Hermes=G=A4.
Headfirst=3,500=4,000=40%=P4.0D=Govt=Creatocracy=4 April=Hermes=G=A4.
Headgear=5,000=50%=P5.00D=Law=Time=Venus=5 May = Aphrodite>>L=N.
Headhunting=11,000=11%=P1.10D=1.1=Idea=Brainchild=Inv.=11 Nov.=SC=Athena>>I=MT.
Heading=10,000=1,000=100%=10.0=Physicality=Tech.=10 Oct.=Uranus=P=1Ø.
Headland=4,500=5,000=50%=P5.00D=Law=Time=Venus=5 May = Aphrodite>>L=N.
Headlight=9,000=90%=P9.00D=9.0=Abstraction=Gods=Saturn=9Sept.>>A=Ø.
Headline=10,000=1,000=100%=10.0=Physicality=Tech.=10 Oct.=Uranus=P=1Ø.
Headlock=9,500=10,000=1,000=100%=10.0=Physicality=Tech.=10 Oct.=Uranus=P=1Ø.
Headlong=6,000=60%=P6.0D=Man=Earth=Royalty=6 June=Gaia=Maia>>M=M2.
Headman=3,500=4,000=40%=P4.0D=Govt=Creato.=4 April=Mercury=Hermes=G=A4.
Headmaster=4,500=5,000=50%=P5.00D=Law=Time=Venus=5 May = Aphrodite>>L=N.
Headmistress=4,500=5,000=50%=P5.00D=Law=Time=Venus=5 May = Aphrodite>>L=N.
Head on=6,500=7,000=70%=P7.0D=7.0=Language=Assets=Mars=7 July=Pleiades.
Headphone=4,000=40%=P4.0D=Govt.=Creatocracy=4 April=Mercury=Hermes=G=A4.
Headpiece=3,500=4,000=40%=P4.0D=Govt=Creato.=4 April=Mercury=Hermes=G=A4.
Headpin=1,500=15%=P1.50D=1.5=Authority=Solar Crown=1 May = Maia.
Headquarters=10,000=1,000=100%=10.0=Physicality=Tech.=10 Oct.=Uranus=P=1Ø.
Headrest=2,500=3,000=30%=P3.0D=3.0=Creativity=Stars=Muses=3 March = C=I>>GIL.
Headset=4,500=5,000=50%=P5.00D=Law=Time=Venus=5 May = Aphrodite>>L=N.
Head Shop=6,000=60%=P6.0D=Man=Earth=Royalty=6 June=Gaia=Maia>>M=M2.
Head stall=5,000=50%=P5.00D=Law=Time=Venus=5 May = Aphrodite>>L=N.
Headstand=9,000=90%=P9.00D=9.0=Abstraction=Gods=Saturn=9Sept.>>A=Ø.
Head start=7,000=70%=P7.0D=7.0=Language=Assets=Mars=7 July=Pleiades.
Headstone=6,500=7,000=70%=P7.0D=7.0=Language=Assets=Mars=7 July=Pleiades.
Headstrong=3,500=4,000=40%=P4.0D=Govt=Creato.=4 April=Mercury=Hermes=G=A4.
Head waiter=6,000=60%=P6.0D=Man=Earth=Royalty=6 June=Gaia=Maia>>M=M2.
Headwaters=3,500=4,000=40%=P4.0D=Govt=Creato.=4 April=Mercury=Hermes=G=A4.
Headway=5,500=5.5=80%=P5.50=Earth-Midway=5 May = Gaia.
Headwind=6,000=60%=P6.0D=Man=Earth=Royalty=6 June=Gaia=Maia>>M=M2.
Heady=1,500=15%=P1.50D=1.5=Authority=Solar Crown=1 May = Maia.
Head work=2,500=3,000=30%=P3.0D=3.0=Creativity=Stars=Muses=3 March = C=I>>GIL.
Heady=1,500=15%=P1.50D=1.5=Authority=Solar Crown=1 May = Maia.

Heal=10,000=1,000=100%=10.0=Physicality=Tech.=10 Oct.=Uranus=P=1Ø.
To heal is a physical process making the Medical Sciences authentic.

Health=10,000=1,000=100%=10.0=Physicality=Tech.=10 Oct.=Uranus=P=1Ø.
Health food=4,000=40%=P4.0D=Govt.=Creatocracy=4 April=Mercury=Hermes=G=A4.
Health maint. org=1,000=100%=Physicality=Tech.=10 Oct.=Uranus=P=1Ø.
Healthy=10,000=1,000=100%=10.0=Physicality=Tech.=10 Oct.=Uranus=P=1Ø.
Heap=10,000=1,000=100%=10.0=Physicality=Tech.=10 Oct.=Uranus=P=1Ø.
Hear=9,500=10,000=1,000=100%=10.0=Physicality=Tech.=10 Oct.=Uranus=P=1Ø.
Hearing=10,000=1,000=100%=10.0=Physicality=Tech.=10 Oct.=Uranus=P=1Ø.
Hearing aid=6,000=60%=P6.0D=Man=Earth=Royalty=6 June=Gaia=Maia>>M=M2.
Hearing impaired=3,000=30%=P3.0D=3.0=Creativity=Stars=Muses=3 March = C=I>>GIL.
Hearken=3,500=4,000=40%=P4.0D=Govt=Creatocracy=4 April=Mercury=Hermes=G=A4.
Hearsay=2,000=20%=P2.00D=2.0=Nature=Matter=Moon=2 Feb.=Cupid=N=C+_
Hearse=9,000=90%=P9.00D=9.0=Abstraction=Gods=Saturn=9Sept.>>A=Ø.
Hearst William=4,000=40%=P4.0D=Govt=Creatocracy=4 April=Mercury=Hermes=G=A4.
Heart=10,000=1,000=100%=10.0=Physicality=Tech.=10 Oct.=Uranus=P=1Ø.
Heart attack=9,500=10,000=1,000=100%=10.0=Physicality=Tech.=10 Oct.=Uranus=P=1Ø.
Heartbeat=3,500=4,000=40%=P4.0D=Govt.=Creato.=4 April=Mercury=Hermes=G=A4.
Heartbreak=3,500=4,000=40%=P4.0D=Govt=Creato.=4 April=Mercury=Hermes=G=A4.
Heartbroken=3,500=4,000=40%=P4.0D=Govt=Creato.=4 April=Mercury=Hermes=G=A4.
Heartburn=7,000=70%=P7.0D=7.0=Language=Assets=Mars=7 July=Pleiades.
Heart disease=6,500=7,000=70%=P7.0D=7.0=Language=Assets=Mars=7 July=Pleiades.
Hearten=5,000=50%=P5.00D=Law=Time=Venus=5 May = Aphrodite>>L=N.
Heartfelt=2,500=3,000=30%=P3.0D=3.0=Creativity=Stars=Muses=3 March = C=I>>GIL.
Hearth=10,000=1,000=100%=10.0=Physicality=Tech.=10 Oct.=Uranus=P=1Ø.
Hearthstone=5,500=5.5=80%=P5.50=Earth-Midway=5 May = Gaia.
Heartland=5,000=50%=P5.00D=Law=Time=Venus=5 May = Aphrodite>>L=N.
Heartless=3,000=30%=P3.0D=3.0=Creativity=Stars=Muses=3 March = C=I>>GIL.
Heart-rending=3,000=30%=P3.0D=3.0=Creativity=Stars=Muses=3 March = C=I>>GIL.
Heartsick=1,500=15%=P1.50D=1.5=Authority=Solar Crown=1 May = Maia.
Heartstrings=2,500=3,000=30%=P3.0D=3.0=Cre=Stars=Muses=3 March = C=I>>GIL.
Heartthrob=2,500=3,000=30%=P3.0D=3.0=Cre=Stars=Muses=3 March = C=I>>GIL.
Heart-to-Heart=2,500=3,000=30%=P3.0D=3.0=Cre=Stars=Muses=3 March = C=I>>GIL.
Heartwood=5,500=5.5=80%=P5.50=Earth-Midway=5 May = Gaia.
Hearty=8,500=9,000=90%=P9.00D=9.0=Abstraction=Gods=Saturn=9Sept.>>A=Ø.
Heat=10,000=1,000=100%=10.0=Physicality=Tech.=10 Oct.=Uranus=P=1Ø.
Heated=2,500=3,000=30%=P3.0D=3.0=Creativity=Stars=Muses=3 March = C=I>>GIL.
Heater=3,500=4,000=40%=P4.0D=Govt=Creato.=4 April=Mercury=Hermes=G=A4.
Heat exhaustion=9,000=90%=P9.00D=9.0=Abstraction=Gods=Saturn=9Sept.>>A=Ø.
Heath=10,000=1,000=100%=10.0=Physicality=Tech.=10 Oct.=Uranus=P=1Ø.
Heath Edward=3,500=4,000=40%=P4.0D=Govt=Creato=4 April=Mercury=Hermes=G=A4.
Heathen=10,000=1,000=100%=10.0=Physicality=Tech.=10 Oct.=Uranus=P=1Ø.
Heather=10,000=1,000=100%=10.0=Physicality=Tech.=10 Oct.=Uranus=P=1Ø.

Heat lightning=4,500=5,000=50%=P5.00D=Law=Time=Venus=5 May = Aphrodite>>L=N.
Heat rash=9,000=90%=P9.00D=9.0=Abstraction=Gods=Saturn=9Sept.>>A=Ø.
Heat stroke=10,000=1,000=100%=10.0=Physicality=Tech.=10 Oct.=Uranus=P=1Ø.
Heave=10,000=1,000=100%=10.0=Physicality=Tech.=10 Oct.=Uranus=P=1Ø.

Heaven=15,000=1,500=15%=P1.50D=1.5=Authority=Solar Crown=1 May = Maia.
The abode of Zeus Jehovah the Most High. Results shows it is the abode of Maia, the Great Goddess of the universes, head of the Pleiades and the Mind of GOD. This is the sweet influence Zeus mentions in the Holy Bible in a specific language code in a challenge dialogue to Job and mankind. The Pleiades live here. Heaven is a highly organized place. And so are the council of Gods and Muses and hierarchy.See Job 38:31, Romans 11:29-36.

Heavy=10,000=1,000=100%=10.0=Physicality=Tech.=10 Oct.=Uranus=P=1Ø.
Heavy duty=3,500=4,000=40%=P4.0D=Govt=Creat.=4 April=Mercury=Hermes=G=A4.
Heavy handed=3,000=30%=P3.0D=3.0=Creativity=Stars=Muses=3 March = C=I>>GIL.
Heavy hearted=1,500=15%=P1.50D=1.5=Authority=Solar Crown=1 May = Maia.
Heavy metal=7,000=70%=P7.0D=7.0=Language=Assets=Mars=7 July=Pleiades.
Heavyset=3,000=30%=P3.0D=3.0=Creativity=Stars=Muses=3 March = C=I>>GIL.
Heavy water=5,000=50%=P5.00D=Law=Time=Venus=5 May = Aphrodite>>L=N.
Heavyweight=10,000=1,000=100%=10.0=Physicality=Tech.=10 Oct.=Uranus=P=1Ø.
Hebraic=4,500=5,000=50%=P5.00D=Law=Time=Venus=5 May = Aphrodite>>L=N.
Hebraism=4,000=40%=P4.0D=Govt=Creatocracy=4 April=Mercury=Hermes=G=A4.
Hebraist=1,500=15%=P1.50D=1.5=Authority=Solar Crown=1 May = Maia.

Hebrew=10,000=1,000=100%=10.0=Physicality=Tech.=10 Oct.=Uranus=P=1Ø.
In the Revelation Jesus instructed the reference to Hebrew or Greek to understand GOD. See Revelation 9:11. Apollyon masterminded the 9/11 attacks in the US. See verse 9:10. Now verse 12 indicates the covid - 19 epidemic that occurred in the year 2020 verse 16. The figure 200,000,000>> split method>>200,000 - 200,000>>2020>>Natural selection.

Hebrew Scriptures=4,500=5,000=50%=P5.00D=Law=Time=Venus=5 May =Odite>>L=N.
Hebrides=10,000=1,000=100%=10.0=Physicality=Tech.=10 Oct.=Uranus=P=1Ø.
Heck=2,500=3,000=30%=P3.0D=3.0=Creativity=Stars=Muses=3 March = C=I>>GIL.
Heckle=6,000=60%=P6.0D=Man=Earth=Royalty=6 June=Gaia=Maia>>M=M2.
Hectare=2,000=20%=P2.00D=2.0=Nature=Matter=Moon=2 Feb.=Cupid=N=C+_
Hectic=6,500=7,000=70%=P7.0D=7.0=Language=Assets=Mars=7 July=Pleiades.
Hector-=3,500=4,000=40%=P4.0D=Govt=Creatocracy=4 April=Mercury=Hermes=G=A4.
Hectogram=2,000=20%=P2.00D=2.0=Nature=Matter=Moon=2 Feb.=Cupid=N=C+_
Hectoliter=2,000=20%=P2.00D=2.0=Nature=Matter=Moon=2 Feb.=Cupid=N=C+_
He'd=1,500=15%=P1.50D=1.5=Authority=Solar Crown=1 May = Maia.
Hedge=8,500=9,000=90%=P9.00D=9.0=Abstraction=Gods=Saturn=9Sept.>>A=Ø.
Hedging=13,500=14,000=14%=P1.40D=1.4=Mgt.=Solar Energy=13 May=Athena=SC=0.1
Hedgehog=7,000=70%=P7.0D=7.0=Language=Assets=Mars=7 July=Pleiades.

Hedonism=10,500=11,000=11%=P1.10D=1.1=Idea=Brainchild=11 Nov=Athena>>I=MT.
-hedral=5,500=5.5=80%=P5.50=Earth-Midway=5 May = Gaia.
-hedron=8,000=80%=P8.0D=Economy=Currency=8 Aug.=Zeus>>E=v.
Heebie jeebies=6,500=7,000=70%=P7.0D=7.0=Language=Assets=Mars=7 July=Pleiades.
Heed=4,000=40%=P4.0D=Government=Creatocracy=4 April=Mercury=Hermes=G=A4.
Heedful=2,000=20%=P2.00D=2.0=Nature=Matter=Moon=2 Feb.=Cupid=N=C+_
Heel1=10,000=1,000=100%=10.0=Physicality=Tech.=10 Oct.=Uranus=P=1Ø.
Heel2=6,000=60%=P6.0D=Man=Earth=Royalty=6 June=Gaia=Maia>>M=M2.
Heft=7,000=70%=P7.0D=7.0=Language=Assets=Mars=7 July=Pleiades.
Hefty=3,500=4,000=40%=P4.0D=Govt=Creatocracy=4 April=Mercury=Hermes=G=A4.
Hegel Georg=3,000=30%=P3.0D=3.0=Creativity=Stars=Muses=3 March = C=I>>GIL.
Hegemony=5,000=50%=P5.00D=Law=Time=Venus=5 May = Aphrodite>>L=N.
Hegira=9,000=90%=P9.00D=9.0=Abstraction=Gods=Saturn=9Sept.>>A=Ø.
Heidegger Martin=2,000=20%=P2.00D=2.0=Nature=Matter=Moon=2 Feb.=Cupid=N=C+_
Heidelberg=4,500=5,000=50%=P5.00D=Law=Time=Venus=5 May = Aphrodite>>L=N.
Heifer=5,500=5.5=80%=P5.50=Earth-Midway=5 May = Gaia.
Heifetz Jascha=3,000=30%=P3.0D=3.0=Creativity=Stars=Muses=3 March = C=I>>GIL.
Height=10,000=1,000=100%=10.0=Physicality=Tech.=10 Oct.=Uranus=P=1Ø.
Heighten=6,000=60%=P6.0D=Man=Earth=Royalty=6 June=Gaia=Maia>>M=M2.
Heilong jiang=4,000=40%=P4.0D=Govt=Creatoc.=4 April=Mercury=Hermes=G=A4.
Heilong Jiang=1,500=15%=P1.50D=1.5=Authority=Solar Crown=1 May = Maia.
Heimlich maneuver=10,000=1,000=100%=10.0=Physicality=Tech.=10 Oct.=Uranus=P=1Ø.
Heine Heinrich=2,000=20%=P2.00D=2.0=Nature=Matter=Moon=2 Feb.=Cupid=N=C+_
Heinous=3,500=4,000=40%=P4.0D=Govt=Creatocracy=4 April=Mercury=Hermes=G=A4.
Heir=9,000=90%=P9.00D=9.0=Abstraction=Gods=Saturn=9Sept.>>A=Ø.
Heir apparent=7,500=8,000=80%=P8.0D=Economy=Currency=8 Aug.=Zeus>>E=v.
Heiress=5,500=5.5=80%=P5.50=Earth-Midway=5 May = Gaia.
Heirloom=11,500=12,000=12%=P1.20D=1.2=Knowledge=Education=12Dec.=Athena
    >>K=F
Heir presumptive=9,000=90%=P9.00D=9.0=Abstraction=Gods=Saturn=9Sept.>>A=Ø.
Heisenberg Werner=3,500=4,000=40%=P4.0D=Govt=Creat.=4 April=Hermes=G=A4.
Heist=5,000=50%=P5.00D=Law=Time=Venus=5 May = Aphrodite>>L=N.
Held=3,000=30%=P3.0D=3.0=Creativity=Stars=Muses=3 March = C=I>>GIL.
Helena=6,000=60%=P6.0D=Man=Earth=Royalty=6 June=Gaia=Maia>>M=M2.
Helen of Troy=6,500=7,000=70%=P7.0D=7.0=Language=Assets=Mars=7 July=Pleiades.
Helical=2,500=3,000=30%=P3.0D=3.0=Creativity=Stars=Muses=3 March = C=I>>GIL.
Helicopter=9,000=90%=P9.00D=9.0=Abstraction=Gods=Saturn=9Sept.>>A=Ø.

Helio-or hell-=2,500=3,000=30%=P3.0D=3.0=Cre=Stars=Muses=3 March = C=I>>GIL.
Sun: heliocentric. Greek. Helios, sun.

Heliocentric=3,000=30%=P3.0D=3.0=Creativity=Stars=Muses=3 March = C=I>>GIL.
Heliopolis=7,000=70%=P7.0D=7.0=Language=Assets=Mars=7 July=Pleiades.

Heliotrope=9,500=10,000=1,000=100%=10.0=Physicality=Tech.=10 Oct.=Uranus=P=1Ø.
Heliport=4,500=5,000=50%=P5.00D=Law=Time=Venus=5 May = Aphrodite>>L=N.

Helium=15,000=1,500=15%=P1.50D=1.5=Authority=Solar Crown=1 May = Maia.
Maia is the Spirit, a solar gas called Helium>>thought>>0.3>> second component of the mind after intelligence, followed by will and emotion. She is the force of thought known as convertible intelligence. Peter Matthews-Akukalia computed the average speed of thought to be 1.0x10(valency or raised to power -1). This is the speed of convertible intelligence. The quantum of helium in the human brain required to aid thought processes is 0.3 on the scale of 10,000. Note that thought has four faculties >> think, reason, inspiration and revelation. So 0.3/4=0.075=0.1 units per each on the average. As our thermometric thinking level rises the quantum of helium required is absorbed from the solar core through the atmosphere. 0.1 indicates the solar core existence of life beyond the sun and residential code of the Gods especially Hermes and Athena, the wit and the wis of all things.

Helix=10,000=1,000=100%=10.0=Physicality=Tech.=10 Oct.=Uranus=P=1Ø.
Hell=10,000=1,000=100%=10.0=Physicality=Tech.=10 Oct.=Uranus=P=1Ø.
He'll=1,500=15%=P1.50D=1.5=Authority=Solar Crown=1 May = Maia.
Hell-bent=2,500=3,000=30%=P3.0D=3.0=Creativity=Stars=Muses=3 March = C=I>>GIL.
Hellebore=9,000=90%=P9.00D=9.0=Abstraction=Gods=Saturn=9Sept.>>A=Ø.
Hellene=1,000=100%=10.0=1.0=Mind=Sun=1 January=Helios >> M=E4.
Hellenic=9,000=90%=P9.00D=9.0=Abstraction=Gods=Saturn=9Sept.>>A=Ø.

Hellenism=6,500=7,000=70%=P7.0D=7.0=Language=Assets=Mars=7 July=Pleiades.
Emotional borderline. A sort of royalty. Makstianism is a Creatocratic custom and manner of the Diseans>>Paradiseans>>Paradise. A religion of precision and faith system that establishes the Mind of GOD through computational creativity, psycho-forensic programming auditing and data analytics without bias to any religion. Makstianism was invented by Peter Matthews-Akukalia after not being satisfied with the speculations and misinterpretations of scriptures especially lacking physical evidence and applications to real life with more problems. Makstians are people of GOD Jesus Christ in the Bible and the Quran and all other prophets reckoned in history to have served GOD. Makstians seek absolute truth through the teachings of Peter Matthews-Akukalia, Castle Makupedia who is established to be a God in his own rights by the field of study he invented, the Creative Sciences. He owns the field and practice of Creative & Psycho-Social Sciences. World's 1st Creative Scientist. Makstians worship in the Mind Temple using Castle Makupedia versions.

Hellenist=7,000=70%=P7.0D=7.0=Language=Assets=Mars=7 July=Pleiades.
A non-Greek who adopted Greek language and culture. Makstians and all Diseans are hellenist in nature. We have established the missing link between Christianity and the Greek mythologies with magnanimous traces in the Holy Quran proving that GOD is one. A key mandate. Other mandates are to establish the Creatocracy as the unity of GOD

and Mankind, a one world government under GOD (Ephesians 1:5-10), single currency module to eliminating inflation completely, respecting the diversities of countries races and tribes, eliminating unemployment youth restiveness and crime through the discovery development and connectivity of everyone to their innate potentials by conducting the Mind Assessment Tests and entrenching peace in any way reasonable and possible. We seek absolute truth.

Hellenistic=8,000=80%=P8.0D=Economy=Currency=8 Aug.=Zeus>>E=v.
Hellespont=1,000=100%=10.0=1.0=Mind=Sun=1 January=Helios >> M=E4.
Hellgrammite=6,000=60%=P6.0D=Man=Earth=Royalty=6 June=Gaia=Maia>>M=M2.
Hellhole=3,500=4,000=40%=P4.0D=Govt=Creato.=4 April=Mercury=Hermes=G=A4.
Hellion=5,500=5.5=80%=P5.50=Earth-Midway=5 May = Gaia.
Hellish=4,000=40%=P4.0D=Government=Creatocracy=4 April=Mercury=Hermes=G=A4.
Hellman Lilian=2,000=20%=P2.00D=2.0=Nature=Matter=Moon=2 Feb.=Cupid=N=C+_
Hello=9,000=90%=P9.00D=9.0=Abstraction=Gods=Saturn=9Sept.>>A=Ø.
Hells Canyon=5,000=50%=P5.00D=Law=Time=Venus=5 May = Aphrodite>>L=N.
Helm=8,000=80%=P8.0D=Economy=Currency=8 Aug.=Zeus>>E=v.
Helmet=5,000=50%=P5.00D=Law=Time=Venus=5 May = Aphrodite>>L=N.
Helminth=5,000=50%=P5.00D=Law=Time=Venus=5 May = Aphrodite>>L=N.
Helmsman=2,500=3,000=30%=P3.0D=3.0=Creativity=Stars=Muses=3 March = C=I>>GIL.
Heloise=6,000=60%=P6.0D=Man=Earth=Royalty=6 June=Gaia=Maia>>M=M2.
Help=10,000=1,000=100%=10.0=Physicality=Tech.=10 Oct.=Uranus=P=1Ø.
Helper=3,500=4,000=40%=P4.0D=Govt.=Creato.=4 April=Mercury=Hermes=G=A4.
Helpful=1,500=15%=P1.50D=1.5=Authority=Solar Crown=1 May = Maia.
Helping=2,500=3,000=30%=P3.0D=3.0=Creativity=Stars=Muses=3 March = C=I>>GIL.
Helpless=7,000=70%=P7.0D=7.0=Language=Assets=Mars=7 July=Pleiades.
Helpmate=5,000=50%=P5.00D=Law=Time=Venus=5 May = Aphrodite>>L=N.
Helpmeet=2,500=3,000=30%=P3.0D=3.0=Creativity=Stars=Muses=3 March = C=I>>GIL.
Helsinki=6,000=60%=P6.0D=Man=Earth=Royalty=6 June=Gaia=Maia>>M=M2.
Helter-Skelter=6,000=60%=P6.0D=Man=Earth=Royalty=6 June=Gaia=Maia>>M=M2.
Helvetia=6,000=60%=P6.0D=Man=Earth=Royalty=6 June=Gaia=Maia>>M=M2.

Helvétius Claude=3,500=4,000=40%=P4.0D=Govt=Creato.=4 April=Hermes=G=A4. French philosopher and encyclopedist. Peter Matthews-Akukalia is a creative philosopher > creatolosopher and the World's 1st Maktionarist being the inventor of the Maktionary. Castle Makupedia precision dictionary is first in series of the Royal Maktionary published. It is the Creatocracy heritage bank for mining words data and the Maks currencies. An institutional book to establish the Creatocracy Bank, the 1st MindBank in the world.

Hem1=10,000=1,000=100%=10.0=Physicality=Tech.=10 Oct.=Uranus=P=1Ø.
Hem2=10,000=1,000=100%=10.0=Physicality=Tech.=10 Oct.=Uranus=P=1Ø.
He-man=2,500=3,000=30%=P3.0D=3.0=Creativity=Stars=Muses=3 March = C=I>>GIL.

Hematite=9,000=90%=P9.00D=9.0=Abstraction=Gods=Saturn=9Sept.>>A=Ø.
A blackish-red to brick red mineral, essentially (Fe2O3) the chief iron ore of iron. Greek, lithos haimatites, bloodlike (stone). Approved color for the Creatocracy bank and the Creatocracy with mixtures of purple. Blood>> Mankind, stone>> Peter >> used to build Castles>> Castle. Purple > royalty, sovereignty of the Makupedia >> Castle Makupedia.

Hemato-=3,500=4,000=40%=P4.0D=Govt=Creato.=4 April=Mercury=Hermes=G=A4.
Hematology=5,000=50%=P5.00D=Law=Time=Venus=5 May = Aphrodite>>L=N.
Hematoma=3,000=30%=P3.0D=3.0=Creativity=Stars=Muses=3 March = C=I>>GIL.
Heme=6,000=60%=P6.0D=Man=Earth=Royalty=6 June=Gaia=Maia>>M=M2.
-hemia=2,000=20%=P2.00D=2.0=Nature=Matter=Moon=2 Feb.=Cupid=N=C+_
Hemingway Ernest=3,500=4,000=40%=P4.0D=Govt=Creato.=4 April=Hermes=G=A4.
Hemisphere=10,000=1,000=100%=10.0=Physicality=Tech.=10 Oct.=Uranus=P=1Ø.
Hemline=6,500=7,000=70%=P7.0D=7.0=Language=Assets=Mars=7 July=Pleiades.
Hemlock=10,000=1,000=100%=10.0=Physicality=Tech.=10 Oct.=Uranus=P=1Ø.
Hemo-=2,500=3,000=30%=P3.0D=3.0=Creativity=Stars=Muses=3 March = C=I>>GIL.
Hemodialysis=5,500=5.5=80%=P5.50=Earth-Midway=5 May = Gaia.
Hemoglobin=6,000=60%=P6.0D=Man=Earth=Royalty=6 June=Gaia=Maia>>M=M2.
Hemophilia=10,000=1,000=100%=10.0=Physicality=Tech.=10 Oct.=Uranus=P=1Ø.
Hemorrhage=3,000=30%=P3.0D=3.0=Creativity=Stars=Muses=3 March = C=I>>GIL.
Hemorrhoid=10,000=1,000=100%=10.0=Physicality=Tech.=10 Oct.=Uranus=P=1Ø.
Hemostat=6,000=60%=P6.0D=Man=Earth=Royalty=6 June=Gaia=Maia>>M=M2.
Hemp=7,000=70%=P7.0D=7.0=Language=Assets=Mars=7 July=Pleiades.
Hem stitch=3,500=4,000=40%=P4.0D=Govt=Creatocracy=4 April=Hermes=G=A4.
Hen=4,500=5,000=50%=P5.00D=Law=Time=Venus=5 May = Aphrodite>>L=N.
Hence=6,000=60%=P6.0D=Man=Earth=Royalty=6 June=Gaia=Maia>>M=M2.
Henceforth=3,000=30%=P3.0D=3.0=Creativity=Stars=Muses=3 March = C=I>>GIL.
Henceforward=500=5%=P5.00D=5.0=Law=Time=Venus=5 May=Aphrodite>>L=N.
Henchman=8,000=80%=P8.0D=Economy=Currency=8 Aug.=Zeus>>E=v.
Henna=10,000=1,000=100%=10.0=Physicality=Tech.=10 Oct.=Uranus=P=1Ø.
Henpeck=3,500=4,000=40%=P4.0D=Government=Creatocracy=4 April=Hermes=G=A4.
Henry=10,000=1,000=100%=10.0=Physicality=Tech.=10 Oct.=Uranus=P=1Ø.
Henry I.=3,000=30%=P3.0D=3.0=Creativity=Stars=Muses=3 March = C=I>>GIL.
Henry II.=3,000=30%=P3.0D=3.0=Creativity=Stars=Muses=3 March = C=I>>GIL.
Henry III.1=3,000=30%=P3.0D=3.0=Creativity=Stars=Muses=3 March = C=I>>GIL.
Henry III.2=3,000=30%=P3.0D=3.0=Creativity=Stars=Muses=3 March = C=I>>GIL.
Henry IV.1=5,000=50%=P5.00D=Law=Time=Venus=5 May = Aphrodite>>L=N.
Henry IV.2=3,500=4,000=40%=P4.0D=Government=Creatocracy=4 April=Hermes=G=A4.
Henry IV.3=4,500=5,000=50%=P5.00D=Law=Time=Venus=5 May = Aphrodite>>L=N.
Henry V.=3,000=30%=P3.0D=3.0=Creativity=Stars=Muses=3 March = C=I>>GIL.
Henry VI.=5,000=50%=P5.00D=Law=Time=Venus=5 May = Aphrodite>>L=N.
Henry VII.=4,000=40%=P4.0D=Government=Creatocracy=4 April=Hermes=G=A4.
Henry VIII.=3,000=30%=P3.0D=3.0=Creativity=Stars=Muses=3 March = C=I>>GIL.
Henry, Patrick=3,500=4,000=40%=P4.0D=Govt=Creatocracy=4 April=Hermes=G=A4.
Hep=2,000=20%=P2.00D=2.0=Nature=Matter=Moon=2 Feb.=Cupid=N=C+_

Heparin=8,500=9,000=90%=P9.00D=9.0=Abstraction=Gods=Saturn=9Sept.>>A=Ø.
Hepatic=6,500=5,000=50%=P5.00D=Law=Time=Venus=5 May = Aphrodite>>L=N.
Hepatica=8,000=80%=P8.0D=Economy=Currency=8 Aug.=Zeus>>E=v.
Hepatitis=13,000=13%=P1.30=Solar Core=Faculty=13 January=Athena.

Hephaestus=4,000=40%=P4.0D=Govt=Creatocracy=4 April=Mercury=Hermes=G=A4.
Greek myth. The God of fire and metalworking. In service of Hermes God of merchandise.

Hepta-=2,500=3,000=30%=P3.0D=3.0=Creativity=Stars=Muses=3 March = C=I>>GIL.
Heptagon=2,000=20%=P2.00D=2.0=Nature=Matter=Moon=2 Feb.=Cupid=N=C+_
Her=10,000=1,000=100%=Physicality=Tech.=10 Oct.=Uranus=P=1Ø.

Hera=4,000=40%=P4.0D=Government =Creatocracy=4 April=Mercury=Hermes=G=A4.
Greek myth. The sister and wife of Zeus. In the service of Hermes > the wit.

Heraclitus=2,500=3,000=30%=P3.0D=3.0=Creativity=Stars=Muses=3 March = C=I>>GIL.
Herald=10,000=1,000=100%=10.0=Physicality=Tech.=10 Oct.=Uranus=P=1Ø.
Heraldic=2,000=20%=P2.00D=2.0=Nature=Matter=Moon=2 Feb.=Cupid=N=C+_
Heraldry=10,000=1,000=100%=10.0=Physicality=Tech.=10 Oct.=Uranus=P=1Ø.
Herat=4,500=5,000=50%=P5.00D=Law=Time=Venus=5 May = Aphrodite>>L=N.
Herb=10,000=1,000=100%=10.0=Physicality=Tech.=10 Oct.=Uranus=P=1Ø.
Herbaceous=8,500=9,000=90%=P9.00D=9.0=Abstraction=Gods=Saturn=9Sept.>>A=Ø.
Herbage=7,500=8,000=80%=P8.0D=Economy=Currency=8 Aug.=Zeus>>E=v.
Herbal=7,500=8,000=80%=P8.0D=Economy=Currency=8 Aug.=Zeus>>E=v.
Herbalist=4,000=40%=P4.0D=Govt.=Creatocracy=4 April=Mercury=Hermes=G=A4.
Herbarium=9,000=90%=P9.00D=9.0=Abstraction=Gods=Saturn=9Sept.>>A=Ø.
Herbert George=2,500=3,000=30%=P3.0D=3.0=Cre=Stars=Muses=3 March = C=I>>GIL.
Herbert,Victor=3,500=4,000=40%=P4.0D=Govt=Creatocracy=4 April=Hermes=G=A4.
Herbicide=4,500=5,000=50%=P5.00D=Law=Time=Venus=5 May = Aphrodite>>L=N.
Herbivore=5,500=5.5=80%=P5.50=Earth-Midway=5 May = Gaia.
Herbivorous=2,500=3,000=30%=P3.0D=3.0=Cre=Stars=Muses=3 March = C=I>>GIL.
Herculaneum=9,000=90%=P9.00D=9.0=Abstraction=Gods=Saturn=9Sept.>>A=Ø.

Hercules=4,500=5,000=50%=P5.00D=Law=Time=Venus=5 May = Aphrodite>>L=N.
Greek & Roman myth. A hero of extraordinary strength.

Herd=10,000=1,000=100%=10.0=Physicality=Tech.=10 Oct.=Uranus=P=1Ø.
Herder Johann=3,000=30%=P3.0D=3.0=Creativity=Stars=Muses=3 March = C=I>>GIL.
Here=10,000=1,000=100%=10.0=Physicality=Tech.=10 Oct.=Uranus=P=1Ø.
Hereabout=1,500=15%=P1.50D=1.5=Authority=Solar Crown=1 May = Maia.
Hereafter=7,000=70%=P7.0D=7.0=Language=Assets=Mars=7 July=Pleiades.
Hereby=1,500=15%=P1.50D=1.5=Authority=Solar Crown=1 May = Maia.

Hereditary=10,000=1,000=100%=10.0=Physicality=Tech.=10 Oct.=Uranus=P=1Ø.
The Creatocracy is hereditary rights assets of the Creatocratic Royal Family, founded and owned by Peter Matthews-Akukalia, Castle Makupedia. God of Creatocracy Genius & Mind.

Heredity=10,000=1,000=100%=10.0=Physicality=Tech.=10 Oct.=Uranus=P=1Ø.
Herein=2,000=20%=P2.00D=2.0=Nature=Matter=Moon=2 Feb.=Cupid=N=C+_
Hereof=1,000=100%=10.0=1.0=Mind=Sun=1 January=Helios >> M=E4.
Hereon=1,000=100%=Physicality=Tech.=10 Oct.=Uranus=P=1Ø.
Heresy=10,000=1,000=100%=10.0=Physicality=Tech.=10 Oct.=Uranus=P=1Ø.
Heretic=4,500=5,000=50%=P5.00D=Law=Time=Venus=5 May = Aphrodite>>L=N.
Here to=2,500=3,000=30%=P3.0D=3.0=Creativity=Stars=Muses=3 March = C=I>>GIL.
Heretofore=1,500=15%=P1.50D=1.5=Authority=Solar Crown=1 May = Maia.
Hereunto=500=5%=P5.00D=5.0=Law=Time=Venus=5 May=Aphrodite>>L=N.
Here upon=3,000=30%=P3.0D=3.0=Creativity=Stars=Muses=3 March = C=I>>GIL.
Herewith=3,000=30%=P3.0D=3.0=Creativity=Stars=Muses=3 March = C=I>>GIL.
Heritable=2,500=3,000=30%=P3.0D=3.0=Creativity=Stars=Muses=3 March = C=I>>GIL.

Heritage=10,000=1,000=100%=10.0=Physicality=Tech.=10 Oct.=Uranus=P=1Ø.
WDSD is a Castle Makupedia Precision Dictionary. The Creatocracy heritage bank for mining words data and the Maks currencies. All things are heritage of Castle Makupedia.

Hermaphrodite=10,000=1,000=100%=10.0=Physicality=Tech.=10 Oct.=Uranus=P=1Ø.

Hermes=5,000=50%=P5.00D=Law=Time=Venus=5 May = Aphrodite>>L=N.
Greek myth. The God of commerce, invention, cunning, and theft. In service of Aphrodite.

Hermetic=10,000=1,000=100%=10.0=Physicality=Tech.=10 Oct.=Uranus=P=1Ø.

Hermit=5,500=5.5=80%=P5.50=Earth-Midway=5 May = Gaia.
One who lives a solitary existence; recluse. Greek erēmitēs<erēmos, solitary. Result shows that contact with the Earth at midway to tap into one's potentials will require eccentricity. The book of Proverbs calls it discretion. This is what makes an inventor and a true king. See

---

Hermitage=4,000=40%=P4.0D=Govt=Creatocracy=4 April=Mercury=Hermes=G=A4.
Hermit crab=9,500=10,000=1,000=100%=10.0=Physicality=Tech.=10 Oct.=Uranus=P=1Ø.
Hermosillo=6,500=7,000=70%=P7.0D=7.0=Language=Assets=Mars=7 July=Pleiades.
Hernia=9,000=90%=P9.00D=9.0=Abstraction=Gods=Saturn=9Sept.>>A=Ø.
Hero=10,000=1,000=100%=10.0=Physicality=Tech.=10 Oct.=Uranus=P=1Ø.
Herod=5,000=50%=P5.00D=Law=Time=Venus=5 May = Aphrodite>>L=N.
Herod Antipas=6,000=60%=P6.0D=Man=Earth=Royalty=6 June=Gaia=Maia>>M=M2.
Herodotus=2,500=3,000=30%=P3.0D=3.0=Creativity=Stars=Muses=3 March = C=I>>GIL.
Heroic=10,000=1,000=100%=10.0=Physicality=Tech.=10 Oct.=Uranus=P=1Ø.

Heroic couplet=5,000=50%=P5.00D=Law=Time=Venus=5 May = Aphrodite>>L=N.
Heroin=6,000=60%=P6.0D=Man=Earth=Royalty=6 June=Gaia=Maia>>M=M2.
Heroine=10,000=1,000=100%=10.0=Physicality=Tech.=10 Oct.=Uranus=P=1Ø.
Heroism=3,000=30%=P3.0D=3.0=Creativity=Stars=Muses=3 March = C=I>>GIL.
Heron=8,500=9,000=90%=P9.00D=9.0=Abstraction=Gods=Saturn=9Sept.>>A=Ø.
Herpes=9,000=90%=P9.00D=9.0=Abstraction=Gods=Saturn=9Sept.>>A=Ø.
Herpes simplex=9,000=90%=P9.00D=9.0=Abstraction=Gods=Saturn=9Sept.>>A=Ø.
Herpetology=6,500=7,000=70%=P7.0D=7.0=Language=Assets=Mars=7 July=Pleiades.
Herr=4,500=5,000=50%=P5.00D=Law=Time=Venus=5 May = Aphrodite>>L=N.
Herrick Robert.=2,500=3,000=30%=P3.0D=3.0=Cre=Stars=Muses=3 March = C=I>>GIL.
Herring=6,000=60%=P6.0D=Man=Earth=Royalty=6 June=Gaia=Maia>>M=M2.
Herringbone=10,000=1,000=100%=10.0=Physicality=Tech.=10 Oct.=Uranus=P=1Ø.
Herring gull=6,000=60%=P6.0D=Man=Earth=Royalty=6 June=Gaia=Maia>>M=M2.
Hers=10,000=1,000=100%=10.0=Physicality=Tech.=10 Oct.=Uranus=P=1Ø.
Herschel=9,000=90%=P9.00D=9.0=Abstraction=Gods=Saturn=9Sept.>>A=Ø.
Herself=10,000=1,000=100%=10.0=Physicality=Tech.=10 Oct.=Uranus=P=1Ø.
Hertz=8,000=80%=P8.0D=Economy=Currency=8 Aug.=Zeus>>E=v.
Herzegovina=3,000=30%=P3.0D=3.0=Creativity=Stars=Muses=3 March = C=I>>GIL.

Herzl Theodore=4,000=40%=P4.0D=Govt=Creatocracy=4 April=Mercury=Hermes=G=A4.
1860-1904. Hungarian born Australian founder of Zionism. Peter Matthews-Akukalia
1978-.Nigerian - Nsukka - Nkpologu - Paradisean (Disean) born founder of Makstianism.

He's=1,500=15%=P1.50D=1.5=Authority=Solar Crown=1 May = Maia.
Heshvan=6,000=60%=P6.0D=Man=Earth=Royalty=6 June=Gaia=Maia>>M=M2.
Hesiod=2,500=3,000=30%=P3.0D=3.0=Creativity=Stars=Muses=3 March = C=I>>GIL.
Hesitant=2,500=3,000=30%=P3.0D=3.0=Creativity=Stars=Muses=3 March = C=I>>GIL.
Hesitate=7,000=70%=P7.0D=7.0=Language=Assets=Mars=7 July=Pleiades.
Hesse Hermann.=4,000=40%=P4.0D=Govt=Creatocracy=4 April=Hermes=G=A4.

Hestia=3,000=30%=P3.0D=3.0=Creativity=Stars=Muses=3 March = C=I>>GIL.
Greek myth. The Goddess of the hearth. Goddess of the kitchen.

Hetero-=3,000=30%=P3.0D=3.0=Creativity=Stars=Muses=3 March = C=I>>GIL.
Heterodox=2,500=3,000=30%=P3.0D=3.0=Creativity=Stars=Muses=3 March = C=I>>GIL.
Heterogeneous=10,000=1,000=100%=10.0=Physicality=Tech.=10 Oct.=Uranus=P=1Ø.
Heterosexual=6,500=7,000=70%=P7.0D=7.0=Language=Assets=Mars=7 July=Pleiades.
Heterotroph=10,000=1,000=100%=10.0=Physicality=Tech.=10 Oct.=Uranus=P=1Ø.
Heth=3,000=30%=P3.0D=3.0=Creativity=Stars=Muses=3 March = C=I>>GIL.
Heuristic=10,000=1,000=100%=10.0=Physicality=Tech.=10 Oct.=Uranus=P=1Ø.
Hew=10,000=1,000=100%=10.0=Physicality=Tech.=10 Oct.=Uranus=P=1Ø.
HEW=3,000=30%=P3.0D=3.0=Creativity=Stars=Muses=3 March = C=I>>GIL.

Hex1=11,000=11%=P1.10D=1.1=Idea=Brainchild=Inv.=11 Nov.=SC=Athena>>I=MT. An evil spell; curse. One that brings bad luck to. > Penn.Du<Hex, witch. Results shows that hex is within the jurisdiction of Athena meaning that the Goddess of wisdom must be appeased or represented for hexes not to work. Thus wisdom handicraft and warfare through the symbols of Athena such as the use of the anointing oil dispels a curse or hex.

Hex2=3,500=4,000=40%=P4.0D=Govt.=Creatocracy=4 April=Mercury=Hermes=G=A4.
Hexa-=2,500=3,000=30%=P3.0D=3.0=Creativity=Stars=Muses=3 March = C=I>>GIL.
Hexadecimal=3,500=4,000=40%=P4.0D=Govt=Creato.=4 April=Mercury=Hermes=G=A4.
Hexagon=2,500=3,000=30%=P3.0D=3.0=Creativity=Stars=Muses=3 March = C=I>>GIL.
Hexameter=4,000=40%=P4.0D=Govt=Creatocracy=4 April=Mercury=Hermes=G=A4.
Hey=5,000=50%=P5.00D=Law=Time=Venus=5 May = Aphrodite>>L=N.
Heyday=6,000=60%=P6.0D=Man=Earth=Royalty=6 June=Gaia=Maia>>M=M2.
Heyerdahl Thor=3,000=30%=P3.0D=3.0=Creativity=Stars=Muses=3 March = C=I>>GIL.
Hf.=2,500=3,000=30%=P3.0D=3.0=Creativity=Stars=Muses=3 March = C=I>>GIL.
HF=1,000=100%=10.0=1.0=Mind=Sun=1 January=Helios >> M=E4.
hf.=500=5%=P5.00D=5.0=Law=Time=Venus=5 May=Aphrodite>>L=N.
Hg=6,500=7,000=70%=P7.0D=7.0=Language=Assets=Mars=7 July=Pleiades.
hgt.=500=5%=P5.00D=5.0=Law=Time=Venus=5 May=Aphrodite>>L=N.
H.H.=2,000=20%=P2.00D=2.0=Nature=Matter=Moon=2 Feb.=Cupid=N=C+_
HHFA=2,500=3,000=30%=P3.0D=3.0=Creativity=Stars=Muses=3 March = C=I>>GIL.
hi=2,000=20%=P2.00D=2.0=Nature=Matter=Moon=2 Feb.=Cupid=N=C+_
HI=2,500=3,000=30%=P3.0D=3.0=Creativity=Stars=Muses=3 March = C=I>>GIL.
Hialeah=4,500=5,000=50%=P5.00D=Law=Time=Venus=5 May = Aphrodite>>L=N.
Hiatus=7,000=70%=P7.0D=7.0=Language=Assets=Mars=7 July=Pleiades.
Hiawatha=2,000=20%=P2.00D=2.0=Nature=Matter=Moon=2 Feb.=Cupid=N=C+_
Hibachi=2,500=3,000=30%=P3.0D=3.0=Creativity=Stars=Muses=3 March = C=I>>GIL.
Hibernate=7,000=70%=P7.0D=7.0=Language=Assets=Mars=7 July=Pleiades.
Hibernia=3,500=4,000=40%=P4.0D=Govt=Creatocracy=4 April=Mercury=Hermes=G=A4.
Hibiscus=10,000=1,000=100%=10.0=Physicality=Tech.=10 Oct.=Uranus=P=1Ø.
Hiccup=10,000=1,000=100%=10.0=Physicality=Tech.=10 Oct.=Uranus=P=1Ø.
Hick=5,500=5.5=80%=P5.50=Earth-Midway=5 May = Gaia.
Hickok James=5,000=50%=P5.00D=Law=Time=Venus=5 May = Aphrodite>>L=N.
Hickory=10,000=1,000=100%=10.0=Physicality=Tech.=10 Oct.=Uranus=P=1Ø.
Hidalgo=4,000=40%=P4.0D=Government =Creatocracy=4 April=Mercury=Hermes=G=A4.
Hide1=11,000=11%=P1.10D=1.1=Idea=Brainchild=Inv.=11 Nov.=SC=Athena>>I=MT.
Hide2=4,500=5,000=50%=P5.00D=Law=Time=Venus=5 May = Aphrodite>>L=N.
Hide-and-seek=8,000=80%=P8.0D=Economy=Currency=8 Aug.=Zeus>>E=v.
Hideaway=5,000=50%=P5.00D=Law=Time=Venus=5 May = Aphrodite>>L=N.
Hide bound=2,500=3,000=30%=P3.0D=3.0=Cre=Stars=Muses=3 March = C=I>>GIL.
Hideous=6,000=60%=P6.0D=Man=Earth=Royalty=6 June=Gaia=Maia>>M=M2.
Hide out=3,000=30%=P3.0D=3.0=Creativity=Stars=Muses=3 March = C=I>>GIL.
Hie=4,000=40%=P4.0D=Government =Creatocracy=4 April=Mercury=Hermes=G=A4.
Hierarchy=12,000=12%=P1.20D=1.2=Knowledge=Education=12Dec.=Athena>>K=F.

Hieratic=11,000=11%=P1.10D=1.1=Idea=Brainchild=Inv.=11 Nov.=SC=Athena>>I=MT.
Hieroglyph=5,000=50%=P5.00D=Law=Time=Venus=5 May = Aphrodite>>L=N.
Hieroglyphic=10,000=1,000=100%=Physicality=Tech.=10 Oct.=Uranus=P=1Ø.
Hi-fi=7,000=70%=P7.0D=7.0=Language=Assets=Mars=7 July=Pleiades.
Higgle dy-piggledy=3,000=30%=P3.0D=3.0=Cre=Stars=Muses=3 March = C=I>>GIL.
High=10,000=1,000=100%=10.0=Physicality=Tech.=10 Oct.=Uranus=P=1Ø.
Highball=4,000=40%=P4.0D=Govt=Creatocracy=4 April=Mercury=Hermes=G=A4.
High beam=5,500=5.5=80%=P5.50=Earth-Midway=5 May = Gaia.

Highborn=1,500=15%=P1.50D=1.5=Authority=Solar Crown=1 May = Maia.
Noble birth. Rights and authority are granted supernaturally from heaven and the estate
of Maia. Peter Matthews-Akukalia is actually a high born of the Akukalia family dynasty
who hail from Obo compound, Ogba-Nkpologu, Uzo-Uwani Local Government Area,
Nsukka, Enugu State. Eastern Nigeria. Africa. His birth energy also confirms innate royalty.

Highboy=4,500=5,000=50%=P5.00D=Law=Time=Venus=5 May = Aphrodite>>L=N.
High bred=2,500=3,000=30%=P3.0D=3.0=Creativity=Stars=Muses=3 March = C=I>>GIL.
High brow=7,500=8,000=80%=P8.0D=Economy=Currency=8 Aug.=Zeus>>E=v.
High chair=5,000=50%=P5.00D=Law=Time=Venus=5 May = Aphrodite>>L=N.
High class=2,500=3,000=30%=P3.0D=3.0=Creativity=Stars=Muses=3 March = C=I>>GIL.
Higher-up=5,000=50%=P5.00D=Law=Time=Venus=5 May = Aphrodite>>L=N.
High falutin=10,000=1,000=100%=10.0=Physicality=Tech.=10 Oct.=Uranus=P=1Ø.
High fashion=2,500=3,000=30%=P3.0D=3.0=Cre=Stars=Muses=3 March = C=I>>GIL.
High fidelity=4,000=40%=P4.0D=Govt=Creatocracy=4 April=Mercury=Hermes=G=A4.
High-flown=2,000=20%=P2.00D=2.0=Nature=Matter=Moon=2 Feb.=Cupid=N=C+_
High frequency=5,500=5.5=80%=P5.50=Earth-Midway=5 May = Gaia.
High German=5,000=50%=P5.00D=Law=Time=Venus=5 May = Aphrodite>>L=N.
High handed=1,000=100%=10.0=1.0=Mind=Sun=1 January=Helios >> M=E4.
High-hat=4,000=40%=P4.0D=Govt=Creatocracy=4 April=Mercury=Hermes=G=A4.
High jinks=3,000=30%=P3.0D=3.0=Creativity=Stars=Muses=3 March = C=I>>GIL.
High jump=7,000=70%=P7.0D=7.0=Language=Assets=Mars=7 July=Pleiades.
Highland=4,000=40%=P4.0D=Govt=Creatocracy=4 April=Mercury=Hermes=G=A4.
Highlands=4,000=40%=P4.0D=Govt=Creatocracy=4 April=Mercury=Hermes=G=A4.
Highlight=6,500=7,000=70%=P7.0D=7.0=Language=Assets=Mars=7 July=Pleiades.
High-minded=3,000=30%=P3.0D=3.0=Creativity=Stars=Muses=3 March = C=I>>GIL.
Highness=10,500=11,000=11%=P1.10D=1.1=Idea=Brainchild=11 Nov.=Athena>>I=MT.
High pressure=8,500=9,000=90%=P9.00D=9.0=Abstr.=Gods=Saturn=9Sept.>>A=Ø.
High profile=4,000=40%=P4.0D=Govt=Creatocracy=4 April=Mercury=Hermes=G=A4.
High relief=8,000=80%=P8.0D=Economy=Currency=8 Aug.=Zeus>>E=v.
High rise=3,000=30%=P3.0D=3.0=Creativity=Stars=Muses=3 March = C=I>>GIL.
High road=5,000=50%=P5.00D=Law=Time=Venus=5 May = Aphrodite>>L=N.
High school=6,000=60%=P6.0D=Man=Earth=Royalty=6 June=Gaia=Maia>>M=M2.
High seas=5,000=50%=P5.00D=Law=Time=Venus=5 May = Aphrodite>>L=N.
High-sounding=1,000=100%=10.0=1.0=Mind=Sun=1 January=Helios >> M=E4.

High-spirited=4,000=40%=P4.0D=Govt=Creatocracy=4 April=Mercury=Hermes=G=A4.
High strung=4,000=40%=P4.0D=Govt=Creatocracy=4 April=Mercury=Hermes=G=A4.
High style=4,500=5,000=50%=P5.00D=Law=Time=Venus=5 May = Aphrodite>>L=N.
High tail=4,500=5,000=50%=P5.00D=Law=Time=Venus=5 May = Aphrodite>>L=N.
High tension=2,000=20%=P2.00D=2.0=Nature=Matter=Moon=2 Feb.=Cupid=N=C+_
High test=5,500=5.5=80%=P5.50=Earth-Midway=5 May = Gaia.
High tide=8,500=9,000=90%=P9.00D=9.0=Abstraction=Gods=Saturn=9Sept.>>A=Ø.
High toned=4,500=5,000=50%=P5.00D=Law=Time=Venus=5 May = Aphrodite>>L=N.
High way=2,000=20%=P2.00D=2.0=Nature=Matter=Moon=2 Feb.=Cupid=N=C+_
Highway man=4,000=40%=P4.0D=Govt=Creatocracy=4 April=Mercury=Hermes=G=A4.
High wire=5,500=5.5=80%=P5.50=Earth-Midway=5 May = Gaia.
Hijack=9,500=10,000=1,000=100%=10.0=Physicality=Tech.=10 Oct.=Uranus=P=1Ø.
Hi jinks=2,000=20%=P2.00D=2.0=Nature=Matter=Moon=2 Feb.=Cupid=N=C+_
Hike=10,000=1,000=100%=10.0=Physicality=Tech.=10 Oct.=Uranus=P=1Ø.
Hilarious=3,000=30%=P3.0D=3.0=Creativity=Stars=Muses=3 March = C=I>>GIL.
Hill=9,500=10,000=1,000=100%=10.0=Physicality=Tech.=10 Oct.=Uranus=P=1Ø.
Hillary Edmund=3,500=4,000=40%=P4.0D=Govt=Creatocracy=4 April=Hermes=G=A4.
Hillbilly=5,000=50%=P5.00D=Law=Time=Venus=5 May= Aphrodite>>L=N.
Hillock=2,500=3,000=30%=P3.0D=3.0=Creativity=Stars=Muses=3 March = C=I>>GIL.
Hillside=2,500=3,000=30%=P3.0D=3.0=Creativity=Stars=Muses=3 March = C=I>>GIL.
Hilltop=2,500=3,000=30%=P3.0D=3.0=Creativity=Stars=Muses=3 March = C=I>>GIL.
Hilt=5,000=50%=P5.00D=Law=Time=Venus=5 May = Aphrodite>>L=N.
Hilton James=2,000=20%=P2.00D=2.0=Nature=Matter=Moon=2 Feb.=Cupid=N=C+_
Him=10,000=1,000=100%=10.0=Physicality=Tech.=10 Oct.=Uranus=P=1Ø.
Himalaya Mountains=10,000=1,000=100%=10.0=Phys.=Tech.=10 Oct.=Uranus=P=1Ø.
Himself=10,000=1,000=100%=10.0=Physicality=Tech.=10 Oct.=Uranus=P=1Ø.
Hind1=6,000=60%=P6.0D=Man=Earth=Royalty=6 June=Gaia=Maia>>M=M2.
Hind2=2,000=20%=P2.00D=2.0=Nature=Matter=Moon=2 Feb.=Cupid=N=C+_
Hindemith Paul=3,000=30%=P3.0D=3.0=Creativity=Stars=Muses=3 March = C=I>>GIL.
Hindenburg Paul Von.=3,000=30%=P3.0D=3.0=Cre=Stars=Muses=3 March = C=I>>GIL.
Hinder=6,500=7,000=70%=P7.0D=7.0=Language=Assets=Mars=7 July=Pleiades.
Hindi=9,000=90%=P9.00D=9.0=Abstraction=Gods=Saturn=9Sept.>>A=Ø.
Hindmost=2,500=3,000=30%=P3.0D=3.0=Creativity=Stars=Muses=3 March = C=I>>GIL.
Hindquarter=6,000=60%=P6.0D=Man=Earth=Royalty=6 June=Gaia=Maia>>M=M2.
Hinderance=6,000=60%=P6.0D=Man=Earth=Royalty=6 June=Gaia=Maia>>M=M2.
Hindsight=3,000=30%=P3.0D=3.0=Creativity=Stars=Muses=3 March = C=I>>GIL.
Hindu=6,000=60%=P6.0D=Man=Earth=Royalty=6 June=Gaia=Maia>>M=M2.
Hinduism=5,500=5.5=80%=P5.50=Earth-Midway=5 May = Gaia.
Hindu Kush=7,000=70%=P7.0D=7.0=Language=Assets=Mars=7 July=Pleiades.
Hindustan=10,000=1,000=100%=10.0=Physicality=Tech.=10 Oct.=Uranus=P=1Ø.
Hindustani=10,000=1,000=100%=10.0=Physicality=Tech.=10 Oct.=Uranus=P=1Ø.
Hinge=10,000=1,000=100%=10.0=Physicality=Tech.=10 Oct.=Uranus=P=1Ø.
Hint=10,000=1,000=100%=10.0=Physicality=Tech.=10 Oct.=Uranus=P=1Ø.
Hinterland=7,000=70%=P7.0D=7.0=Language=Assets=Mars=7 July=Pleiades.
Hip1=10,000=1,000=100%=10.0=Physicality=Tech.=10 Oct.=Uranus=P=1Ø.

Hip2=10,000=1,000=100%=10.0=Physicality=Tech.=10 Oct.=Uranus=P=1Ø.
Hip3=6,000=60%=P6.0D=Man=Earth=Royalty=6 June=Gaia=Maia>>M=M2.
Hipbone=6,000=60%=P6.0D=Man=Earth=Royalty=6 June=Gaia=Maia>>M=M2.
Hip joint=4,500=5,000=50%=P5.00D=Law=Time=Venus=5 May = Aphrodite>>L=N.
Hippie=10,000=1,000=100%=10.0=Physicality=Tech.=10 Oct.=Uranus=P=1Ø.
Hippo=1,000=100%=10.0=1.0=Mind=Sun=1 January=Helios >> M=E4.
Hippocrates=3,000=30%=P3.0D=3.0=Creativity=Stars=Muses=3 March = C=I>>GIL.
Hippocratic oath=6,000=60%=P6.0D=Man=Earth=Royalty=6 June=Gaia=Maia>>M=M2.
Hippodrome=5,000=50%=P5.00D=Law=Time=Venus=5 May = Aphrodite>>L=N.
Hippopotamus=10,000=1,000=100%=10.0=Physicality=Tech.=10 Oct.=Uranus=P=1Ø.
Hip roof=3,500=4,000=40%=P4.0D=Govt=Creatocracy=4 April=Mercury=Hermes=G=A4.
Hipster=2,500=3,000=30%=P3.0D=3.0=Creativity=Stars=Muses=3 March = C=I>>GIL.
Hiragana=8,000=80%=P8.0D=Economy=Currency=8 Aug.=Zeus>>E=v.
Hire=10,000=1,000=100%=10.0=Physicality=Tech.=10 Oct.=Uranus=P=1Ø.
Hireling=6,000=60%=P6.0D=Man=Earth=Royalty=6 June=Gaia=Maia>>M=M2.
Hirohito=3,500=4,000=40%=P4.0D=Govt=Creatocracy=4 April=Mercury=Hermes=G=A4.
Hiroshima=10,000=1,000=100%=10.0=Physicality=Tech.=10 Oct.=Uranus=P=1Ø.
Hirsute=1,500=15%=P1.50D=1.5=Authority=Solar Crown=1 May = Maia.
His=10,000=1,000=100%=10.0=Physicality=Tech.=10 Oct.=Uranus=P=1Ø.
Hispanic=10,000=1,000=100%=10.0=Physicality=Tech.=10 Oct.=Uranus=P=1Ø.
Hispanic American=5,000=50%=P5.00D=Law=Time=Venus=5 May = Aphrodite>>L=N.
Hispaniola=10,000=1,000=100%=10.0=Physicality=Tech.=10 Oct.=Uranus=P=1Ø.
Hispano American=1,500=15%=P1.50D=1.5=Authority=Solar Crown=1 May = Maia.
Hiss=10,000=1,000=100%=10.0=Physicality=Tech.=10 Oct.=Uranus=P=1Ø.
Histamine=10,000=1,000=100%=10.0=Physicality=Tech.=10 Oct.=Uranus=P=1Ø.
Histocompatibility=10,000=1,000=100%=10.0=Physicality=Tech.=10 Oct.=Uranus=P=1Ø.
Histogram=10,000=1,000=100%=10.0=Physicality=Tech.=10 Oct.=Uranus=P=1Ø.
Histology=10,000=1,000=100%=10.0=Physicality=Tech.=10 Oct.=Uranus=P=1Ø.
Historic=10,000=1,000=100%=10.0=Physicality=Tech.=10 Oct.=Uranus=P=1Ø.
Historical=10,000=1,000=100%=10.0=Physicality=Tech.=10 Oct.=Uranus=P=1Ø.
Historiography=10,000=1,000=100%=10.0=Physicality=Tech.=10 Oct.=Uranus=P=1Ø.
History=10,000=1,000=100%=10.0=Physicality=Tech.=10 Oct.=Uranus=P=1Ø.
Histrionic=10,000=1,000=100%=10.0=Physicality=Tech.=10 Oct.=Uranus=P=1Ø.
Histrionics=10,000=1,000=100%=10.0=Physicality=Tech.=10 Oct.=Uranus=P=1Ø.
Hit=10,000=1,000=100%=10.0=Physicality=Tech.=10 Oct.=Uranus=P=1Ø.
Hit-and-run=7,000=70%=P7.0D=7.0=Language=Assets=Mars=7 July=Pleiades.
Hitch=10,000=1,000=100%=10.0=Physicality=Tech.=10 Oct.=Uranus=P=1Ø.
Hitchhike=4,500=5,000=50%=P5.00D=Law=Time=Venus=5 May = Aphrodite>>L=N.
Hither=6,000=60%=P6.0D=Man=Earth=Royalty=6 June=Gaia=Maia>>M=M2.
Hitherto=1,500=15%=P1.50D=1.5=Authority=Solar Crown=1 May = Maia.
Hitler Adolf=3,500=4,000=40%=P4.0D=Govt=Creato.=4 April=Mercury=Hermes=G=A4.
Hitman=2,000=20%=P2.00D=2.0=Nature=Matter=Moon=2 Feb.=Cupid=N=C+_
Hit-or-miss=1,000=100%=10.0=1.0=Mind=Sun=1 January=Helios >> M=E4.
Hit squad=4,000=40%=P4.0D=Govt=Creatocracy=4 April=Mercury=Hermes=G=A4.
Hittite=10,000=1,000=100%=10.0=Physicality=Tech.=10 Oct.=Uranus=P=1Ø.

HIV=4,000=40%=P4.0D=Government =Creatocracy=4 April=Mercury=Hermes=G=A4.
Hive=8,500=9,000=90%=P9.00D=9.0=Abstraction=Gods=Saturn=9Sept.>>A=Ø.
Hives=10,000=1,000=100%=10.0=Physicality=Tech.=10 Oct.=Uranus=P=1Ø.

H.M.=1,500=15%=P1.50D=1.5=Authority=Solar Crown=1 May = Maia.
Her Majesty. His Majesty. The rights of Maia granted for specific responsibilities. Job 40:10

HMO=6,500=7,000=70%=P7.0D=7.0=Language=Assets=Mars=7 July=Pleiades.
Hmong=8,500=9,000=90%=P9.00D=9.0=Abstraction=Gods=Saturn=9Sept.>>A=Ø.
HMS=2,500=3,000=30%=P3.0D=3.0=Creativity=Stars=Muses=3 March = C=I>>GIL.
Ho=3,000=30%=P3.0D=3.0=Creativity=Stars=Muses=3 March = C=I>>GIL.
Hoagie=5,500=5.5=80%=P5.50=Earth-Midway=5 May = Gaia.
Hoard=7,500=8,000=80%=P8.0D=Economy=Currency=8 Aug.=Zeus>>E=v.
Hoarfrost=5,500=5.5=80%=P5.50=Earth-Midway=5 May = Gaia.
Hoarse=2,500=3,000=30%=P3.0D=3.0=Creativity=Stars=Muses=3 March = C=I>>GIL.
Hoary=7,000=70%=P7.0D=7.0=Language=Assets=Mars=7 July=Pleiades.
Hoax=6,000=60%=P6.0D=Man=Earth=Royalty=6 June=Gaia=Maia>>M=M2.
Hob=6,000=60%=P6.0D=Man=Earth=Royalty=6 June=Gaia=Maia>>M=M2.
Hobbes Thomas=2,500=3,000=30%=P3.0D=3.0=Cre=Stars=Muses=3 March = C=I>>GIL.
Hobble=10,000=1,000=100%=10.0=Physicality=Tech.=10 Oct.=Uranus=P=1Ø.
Hobby=7,000=70%=P7.0D=7.0=Language=Assets=Mars=7 July=Pleiades.
Hobbyhorse=10,000=1,000=100%=10.0=Physicality=Tech.=10 Oct.=Uranus=P=1Ø.
Hobgoblin=6,500=7,000=70%=P7.0D=7.0=Language=Assets=Mars=7 July=Pleiades.
Hobnail=10,000=1,000=100%=10.0=Physicality=Tech.=10 Oct.=Uranus=P=1Ø.
Hobnob=7,500=8,000=80%=P8.0D=Economy=Currency=8 Aug.=Zeus>>E=v.
Hobo=3,000=30%=P3.0D=3.0=Creativity=Stars=Muses=3 March = C=I>>GIL.
Ho Chi Minh=6,000=60%=P6.0D=Man=Earth=Royalty=6 June=Gaia=Maia>>M=M2.
Ho Chi Minh City=7,000=70%=P7.0D=7.0=Language=Assets=Mars=7 July=Pleiades.

Hock1=10,000=1,000=100%=10.0=Physicality=Tech.=10 Oct.=Uranus=P=1Ø.
Physical comparison as result indicates the strength of the hind leg of a horse is not to be compared in stamina to the human ankle. However there is a human-animal relativity.

Hock2=7,000=70%=P7.0D=7.0=Language=Assets=Mars=7 July=Pleiades.
Debt means prison from Du.hok, prison. Measurements and computing is the spiritual freedom of one from the prison of life precisely the prison of Aries. It is Aries that punishes people when they owe debts and are intentionally not willing to pay. Proverbs talks about repayment to the amount of seven times the debt owed in such circumstances. Hence Aries inspired this particular statement to the King Solomon. Proved.

Hockey=2,000=20%=P2.00D=2.0=Nature=Matter=Moon=2 Feb.=Cupid=N=C+_
Hock shop=2,000=20%=P2.00D=2.0=Nature=Matter=Moon=2 Feb.=Cupid=N=C+_
Hocus pocus=10,000=1,000=100%=10.0=Physicality=Tech.=10 Oct.=Uranus=P=1Ø.

Hod=10,000=1,000=100%=10.0=Physicality=Tech.=10 Oct.=Uranus=P=1Ø.
Hodgepodge=3,500=4,000=40%=P4.0D=Govt=Creatocracy=4 April=Hermes=G=A4.
Hodgkin's disease=10,000=1,000=100%=10.0=Physicality=Tech.=10 Oct.=Uranus=P=1Ø.
Hoe=10,000=1,000=100%=10.0=Physicality=Tech.=10 Oct.=Uranus=P=1Ø.
Hoedown=1,500=15%=P1.50D=1.5=Authority=Solar Crown=1 May = Maia.
Hog=10,000=1,000=100%=10.0=Physicality=Tech.=10 Oct.=Uranus=P=1Ø.
Hogan=5,500=5.5=80%=P5.50=Earth-Midway=5 May = Gaia.
Hogarth William=2,000=20%=P2.00D=2.0=Nature=Matter=Moon=2 Feb.=Cupid=N=C+_
Hogshead=7,000=70%=P7.0D=7.0=Language=Assets=Mars=7 July=Pleiades.
Hogtie=9,000=90%=P9.00D=9.0=Abstraction=Gods=Saturn=9Sept.>>A=Ø.
Hogwash=5,500=5.5=80%=P5.50=Earth-Midway=5 May = Gaia.
Hog wild=5,000=50%=P5.00D=Law=Time=Venus=5 May = Aphrodite>>L=N.
Hoi polloi=3,000=30%=P3.0D=3.0=Creativity=Stars=Muses=3 March = C=I>>GIL.
Hoist=10,000=1,000=100%=10.0=Physicality=Tech.=10 Oct.=Uranus=P=1Ø.
Hokan=6,000=60%=P6.0D=Man=Earth=Royalty=6 June=Gaia=Maia>>M=M2.
Hokkaido=7,000=70%=P7.0D=7.0=Language=Assets=Mars=7 July=Pleiades.
Hol-=2,000=20%=P2.00D=2.0=Nature=Matter=Moon=2 Feb.=Cupid=N=C+_
Holbein1 Hans=3,500=4,000=40%=P4.0D=Govt=Creatocracy=4 April=Hermes=G=A4.
Holbein2 Hans=4,000=40%=P4.0D=Govt=Creatocracy=4 April=Mercury=Hermes=G=A4.
Hold1=10,000=1,000=100%=10.0=Physicality=Tech.=10 Oct.=Uranus=P=1Ø.
Hold2=8,000=80%=P8.0D=Economy=Currency=8 Aug.=Zeus>>E=v.
Holding=7,500=8,000=80%=P8.0D=Economy=Currency=8 Aug.=Zeus>>E=v.
Holding company=5,000=50%=P5.00D=Law=Time=Venus=5 May = Aphrodite>>L=N.
Holdout=3,000=30%=P3.0D=3.0=Creativity=Stars=Muses=3 March = C=I>>GIL.
Holdover=3,500=4,000=40%=P4.0D=Govt=Creatocracy=4 April=Hermes=G=A4.
Holdup=3,000=30%=P3.0D=3.0=Creativity=Stars=Muses=3 March = C=I>>GIL.
Hole=10,000=1,000=100%=10.0=Physicality=Tech.=10 Oct.=Uranus=P=1Ø.
Holguin=5,500=5.5=80%=P5.50=Earth-Midway=5 May = Gaia.
Holiday=10,000=1,000=100%=10.0=Physicality=Tech.=10 Oct.=Uranus=P=1Ø.
Holiness=10,500=11,000=11%=P1.10D=1.1=Idea=Brainchild=Inv.=11 Nov.=Athena>>I=MT.
Holism=10,000=1,000=100%=10.0=Physicality=Tech.=10 Oct.=Uranus=P=1Ø.
Holland=1,000=100%=10.0=1.0=Mind=Sun=1 January=Helios >> M=E4.
Hollandaise=10,000=1,000=100%=10.0=Physicality=Tech.=10 Oct.=Uranus=P=1Ø.
Holler=4,500=5,000=50%=P5.00D=Law=Time=Venus=5 May = Aphrodite>>L=N.
Hollow=10,000=1,000=100%=10.0=Physicality=Tech.=10 Oct.=Uranus=P=1Ø.
Holly=9,000=90%=P9.00D=9.0=Abstraction=Gods=Saturn=9Sept.>>A=Ø.
Hollyhock=6,500=7,000=70%=P7.0D=7.0=Language=Assets=Mars=7 July=Pleiades.
Hollywood=10,000=1,000=100%=10.0=Physicality=Tech.=10 Oct.=Uranus=P=1Ø.
Holmes, Oliver=3,500=4,000=40%=P4.0D=Govt=Creatocracy=4 April=Hermes=G=A4.
Holmium=10,000=1,000=100%=10.0=Physicality=Tech.=10 Oct.=Uranus=P=1Ø.
Holo-=3,000=30%=P3.0D=3.0=Creativity=Stars=Muses=3 March = C=I>>GIL.
Holocaust=10,000=1,000=100%=10.0=Physicality=Tech.=10 Oct.=Uranus=P=1Ø.
Holocene=10,000=1,000=100%=10.0=Physicality=Tech.=10 Oct.=Uranus=P=1Ø.
Hologram=10,000=1,000=100%=10.0=Physicality=Tech.=10 Oct.=Uranus=P=1Ø.
Holography=10,000=1,000=100%=10.0=Physicality=Tech.=10 Oct.=Uranus=P=1Ø.

Holstein1=5,500=5.5=80%=P5.50=Earth-Midway=5 May = Gaia.
Holstein2=5,500=5.5=80%=P5.50=Earth-Midway=5 May = Gaia.
Holster=7,000=70%=P7.0D=7.0=Language=Assets=Mars=7 July=Pleiades.
Holy=9,500=10,000=1,000=100%=10.0=Physicality=Tech.=10 Oct.=Uranus=P=1Ø.
Holy Ark=6,500=7,000=70%=P7.0D=7.0=Language=Assets=Mars=7 July=Pleiades.
Holy Communion=1,000=100%=Physicality=Tech.=10 Oct.=Uranus=P=1Ø.
Holy day=2,500=3,000=30%=P3.0D=3.0=Creativity=Stars=Muses=3 March = C=I>>GIL.
Holy Ghost=1,500=15%=P1.50D=1.5=Authority=Solar Crown=1 May = Maia.
Holy Land.=2,500=3,000=30%=P3.0D=3.0=Creativity=Stars=Muses=3 March = C=I>>GIL.

Holy Roman Empire=6,000=60%=P6.0D=Man=Earth=Roy.=6 June=Gaia=Maia>>M=M2. The Creatocracy celebrates the Matthews-Akukalia Empire. The Creatocracy Corporation.©®™ and Castle Makupedia, God of Creatocracy Genius and Mind.

Holy Spirit=3,500=4,000=40%=P4.0D=Govt=Creat.=4 April=Mercury=Hermes=G=A4. The Holy Spirit >> Hosts >> Council of Gods headed by Hermes, the Christ. In the Bible Jesus promised "I will send you the Holy Spirit. He will lead you into all truth..." Now Mercury is abode of the Council of Gods. Organizations governments national and planetary matters are decided here. Our advance computation gives the standard environmental temperature of Mercury as (-1) which aligns with organizations and the speed of thought and convertible intelligence. So the Holy Spirit is not one person but a group or force that function as the board of trustees or directors of the universe reporting to Zeus Jehovah the Most High. The use of "He" in reference to the Holy Spirit is collective. In Romans 8:23 apostle Paul gives the clue that only adoption to wit will free mankind from the troubles and spiritual bondage. Greek mythology teaches that Mercury>>Hermes is the God of wit expressed through commerce invention cunning and theft. Hence invention and discovery is adoption to wit. Athena is the wisdom, cunning to make things work. Proverbs 8:12. So Hermes is wit and merchandise. Athena is wisdom and mind, mental warfare.

Holy war=4,500=5,000=50%=P5.00D=Law=Time=Venus=5 May = Aphrodite>>L=N.
Horn age=7,000=70%=P7.0D=7.0=Language=Assets=Mars=7 July=Pleiades.
Hombre=4,500=5,000=50%=P5.00D=Law=Time=Venus=5 May = Aphrodite>>L=N.
Homburg=10,000=1,000=100%=10.0=Physicality=Tech.=10 Oct.=Uranus=P=1Ø.
Home=10,000=1,000=100%=10.0=Physicality=Tech.=10 Oct.=Uranus=P=1Ø.
Home base=7,000=70%=P7.0D=7.0=Language=Assets=Mars=7 July=Pleiades.
Homebody=3,500=4,000=40%=P4.0D=Govt=Creatocracy=4 April=Hermes=G=A4.
Homecoming=6,500=7,000=70%=P7.0D=7.0=Language=Assets=Mars=7 July=Pleiades.
Home economics=3,500=4,000=40%=P4.0D=Govt=Creato.=4 April=Hermes=G=A4.
Home front=6,000=60%=P6.0D=Man=Earth=Royalty=6 June=Gaia=Maia>>M=M2.
Homeland=6,000=60%=P6.0D=Man=Earth=Royalty=6 June=Gaia=Maia>>M=M2.
Homeless=6,000=60%=P6.0D=Man=Earth=Royalty=6 June=Gaia=Maia>>M=M2.
Homely=10,000=1,000=100%=10.0=Physicality=Tech.=10 Oct.=Uranus=P=1Ø.

Homemade=2,500=3,000=30%=P3.0D=3.0=Cre=Stars=Muses=3 March = C=I>>GIL.
Homemaker=2,500=3,000=30%=P3.0D=3.0=Cre=Stars=Muses=3 March = C=I>>GIL.
Homeo-=2,500=3,000=30%=P3.0D=3.0=Creativity=Stars=Muses=3 March = C=I>>GIL.
Homeopathy=10,000=1,000=100%=10.0=Physicality=Tech.=10 Oct.=Uranus=P=1Ø.
Homeostasis=10,000=1,000=100%=10.0=Physicality=Tech.=10 Oct.=Uranus=P=1Ø.
Homeotherm=10,000=1,000=100%=10.0=Physicality=Tech.=10 Oct.=Uranus=P=1Ø.
Home plate=4,000=40%=P4.0D=Govt=Creatocracy=4 April=Mercury=Hermes=G=A4.
Homer=3,000=30%=P3.0D=3.0=Creativity=Stars=Muses=3 March = C=I>>GIL.
Homer, Winslow=2,000=20%=P2.00D=2.0=Nature=Matter=Moon=2 Feb.=Cupid=N=C+_
Home rule=6,000=60%=P6.0D=Man=Earth=Royalty=6 June=Gaia=Maia>>M=M2.

Home run=8,000=80%=P8.0D=Economy=Currency=8 Aug.=Zeus>>E=v.
A hit that allows the batter to make a complete circuit of the diamond and score a run.
The Maks currencies is a home run with the achieved target on the diamond, solar core.

Homesick=2,000=20%=P2.00D=2.0=Nature=Matter=Moon=2 Feb.=Cupid=N=C+_
Homespun=10,000=1,000=100%=10.0=Physicality=Tech.=10 Oct.=Uranus=P=1Ø.
Homestead=7,000=70%=P7.0D=7.0=Language=Assets=Mars=7 July=Pleiades.
Homestretch=7,500=8,000=80%=P8.0D=Economy=Currency=8 Aug.=Zeus>>E=v.
Homeward=1,000=100%=10.0=1.0=Mind=Sun=1 January=Helios >> M=E4.
Homework=5,000=50%=P5.00D=Law=Time=Venus=5 May = Aphrodite>>L=N.
Homey=3,500=4,000=40%=P4.0D=Govt=Creatocracy=4 April=Mercury=Hermes=G=A4.
Homicide=9,000=90%=P9.00D=9.0=Abstraction=Gods=Saturn=9Sept.>>A=Ø.
Homiletic=5,500=5.5=80%=P5.50=Earth-Midway=5 May = Gaia.
Homily=5,000=50%=P5.00D=Law=Time=Venus=5 May = Aphrodite>>L=N.
Homing pigeon=4,000=40%=P4.0D=Govt.=Creatocracy=4 April=Mercury=Hermes=G=A4.
Hominid=10,000=1,000=100%=10.0=Physicality=Tech.=10 Oct.=Uranus=P=1Ø.
Hominy=10,000=1,000=100%=10.0=Physicality=Tech.=10 Oct.=Uranus=P=1Ø.
Homo-=2,500=3,000=30%=P3.0D=3.0=Creativity=Stars=Muses=3 March = C=I>>GIL.
Homogeneous=10,000=1,000=100%=10.0=Physicality=Tech.=10 Oct.=Uranus=P=1Ø.
Homogenize=10,000=1,000=100%=10.0=Physicality=Tech.=10 Oct.=Uranus=P=1Ø.
Homogeny=10,000=1,000=100%=10.0=Physicality=Tech.=10 Oct.=Uranus=P=1Ø.
Homograph=10,000=1,000=100%=10.0=Physicality=Tech.=10 Oct.=Uranus=P=1Ø.
Homologous=10,000=1,000=100%=10.0=Physicality=Tech.=10 Oct.=Uranus=P=1Ø.
Homonym=10,000=1,000=100%=10.0=Physicality=Tech.=10 Oct.=Uranus=P=1Ø.
Homophobia=3,000=30%=P3.0D=3.0=Creativity=Stars=Muses=3 March = C=I>>GIL.
Homophone=10,000=1,000=100%=10.0=Physicality=Tech.=10 Oct.=Uranus=P=1Ø.
Homo sapiens=5,500=5.5=80%=P5.50=Earth-Midway=5 May = Gaia.
Homosexual=10,000=1,000=100%=10.0=Physicality=Tech.=10 Oct.=Uranus=P=1Ø.
Homs=5,000=50%=P5.00D=Law=Time=Venus=5 May = Aphrodite>>L=N.
Horny=1,500=15%=P1.50D=1.5=Authority=Solar Crown=1 May = Maia.
Hon.=1,500=15%=P1.50D=1.5=Authority=Solar Crown=1 May = Maia.
Honcho=4,500=5,000=50%=P5.00D=Law=Time=Venus=5 May = Aphrodite>>L=N.
Honduras=5,000=50%=P5.00D=Law=Time=Venus=5 May = Aphrodite>>L=N.

Hone=7,500=8,000=80%=P8.0D=Economy=Currency=8 Aug.=Zeus>>E=v.
Honest=10,000=1,000=100%=10.0=Physicality=Tech.=10 Oct.=Uranus=P=1Ø.
Honey=4,000=40%=P4.0D=Government =Creatocracy=4 April=Mercury=Hermes=G=A4.
Honeybee=4,000=40%=P4.0D=Govt=Creatocracy=4 April=Mercury=Hermes=G=A4.
Honeycomb=10,000=1,000=100%=10.0=Physicality=Tech.=10 Oct.=Uranus=P=1Ø.
Honeydew melon=4,500=5,000=50%=P5.00D=Law=Time=Venus=5 May =Odite>>L=N.
Honey eyed=6,500=7,000=70%=P7.0D=7.0=Language=Assets=Mars=7 July=Pleiades.
Honeymoon=6,000=60%=P6.0D=Man=Earth=Royalty=6 June=Gaia=Maia>>M=M2.
Honeysuckle=11,500=12,000=12%=P1.20D=1.2=Knowledge=Educ.=12Dec.=Athena>>K=F
Hong Kong=11,000=11%=P1.10D=1.1=Idea=Brainchild=Inv.=11 Nov.=SC=Athena>>I=MT.
Kong Island=5,500=5.5=80%=P5.50=Earth-Midway=5 May = Gaia.
Honiara=5,500=5.5=80%=P5.50=Earth-Midway=5 May = Gaia.
Honk=8,000=80%=P8.0D=Economy=Currency=8 Aug.=Zeus>>E=v.
Honky-tonk=10,000=1,000=100%=10.0=Physicality=Tech.=10 Oct.=Uranus=P=1Ø.
Honolulu=5,000=50%=P5.00D=Law=Time=Venus=5 May = Aphrodite>>L=N.
Honor=10,000=1,000=100%=10.0=Physicality=Tech.=10 Oct.=Uranus=P=1Ø.
Honorable=10,000=1,000=100%=10.0=Physicality=Tech.=10 Oct.=Uranus=P=1Ø.
Honorable discharge=4,500=5,000=50%=P5.00D=Law=Time=Venus=5May =Odite>>L=N.
Honorarium=10,000=1,000=100%=10.0=Physicality=Tech.=10 Oct.=Uranus=P=1Ø.

Honorary=6,000=60%=P6.0D=Man=Earth=Royalty=6 June=Gaia=Maia>>M=M2.
Held or given as an honor, without fulfillment of the usual requirements. The Creatocracy granted a honorary position to certain persons for their contributions to the creativity project especially in the care and welfare of the sovereign family during the difficult years.

The Empress Tina and Queen Alice are not trained at the time of this work but honored on the basis of not just rights but their contributions that money could not buy especially in prayers and listening to me to help me make sense of my aspirations for a better world.

His Lordship Captain Wole Olaniyan was appointed the first governor of the Creatocracy Bank worldwide for a term of five years with retained status in other aspects of the work.

Helen Ekot - Efoli (Helen Ekwe-Okpata), Board Director in De-Royal Makupedia and other retained positions as approved. They were not Creative Scientists but were thus decorated.

Honorific=6,000=60%=P6.0D=Man=Earth=Royalty=6 June=Gaia=Maia>>M=M2.

Honour=2,500=3,000=30%=P3.0D=3.0=Creativity=Stars=Muses=3 March = C=I>>GIL.
See the book>> Sword of Honour by African Shakespeare. Also contained The Creatocracy Republic >> Sword of Honour (Reloaded) by Peter Matthews-Akukalia. The first play written in Shakespearean English by an African. First published in 2011 emerging him African Shakespeare. The Creatocracy Republic emerges him Dragon Lord of the sky.

Honshu=6,500=7,000=70%=P7.0D=7.0=Language=Assets=Mars=7 July=Pleiades.
Hood1=10,000=1,000=100%=10.0=Physicality=Tech.=10 Oct.=Uranus=P=1Ø.
Hood2=1,500=15%=P1.50D=1.5=Authority=Solar Crown=1 May = Maia.
Hood, Mount.=7,000=70%=P7.0D=7.0=Language=Assets=Mars=7 July=Pleiades.
-hood=8,000=80%=P8.0D=Economy=Currency=8 Aug.=Zeus>>E=v.

Hoodlum=4,500=5,000=50%=P5.00D=Law=Time=Venus=5 May = Aphrodite>>L=N.
Results align with Greek myth that Hermes was a thug at birth and knew how to invent
things from nothing. Hoodlum is a border to legitimacy if one can learn the lessons of
the streets at doing the right thing. Politics to law>>Hermes to Odite.

Hoodoo=7,000=70%=P7.0D=7.0=Language=Assets=Mars=7 July=Pleiades.
Hoodwink=1,500=15%=P1.50D=1.5=Authority=Solar Crown=1 May = Maia.
Hooey=1,500=15%=P1.50D=1.5=Authority=Solar Crown=1 May = Maia.
Hoof=10,000=1,000=100%=10.0=Physicality=Tech.=10 Oct.=Uranus=P=1Ø.
Hooghly=7,000=70%=P7.0D=7.0=Language=Assets=Mars=7 July=Pleiades.
Hook=10,000=1,000=100%=10.0=Physicality=Tech.=10 Oct.=Uranus=P=1Ø.
Hookah=10,000=1,000=100%=10.0=Physicality=Tech.=10 Oct.=Uranus=P=1Ø.
Hook and eye=5,500=5.5=80%=P5.50=Earth-Midway=5 May = Gaia.
Hooker=1,500=15%=P1.50D=1.5=Authority=Solar Crown=1 May = Maia.
Hooker Thomas.=3,500=4,000=40%=P4.0D=Govt=Creatocracy=4 April=Hermes=G=A4.
Hookup=10,000=1,000=100%=10.0=Physicality=Tech.=10 Oct.=Uranus=P=1Ø.
Hookworm=7,000=70%=P7.0D=7.0=Language=Assets=Mars=7 July=Pleiades.
Hooky=5,000=50%=P5.00D=Law=Time=Venus=5 May = Aphrodite>>L=N.
Hooligan=4,000=40%=P4.0D=Govt=Creatocracy=4 April=Mercury=Hermes=G=A4.
Hoop=10,000=1,000=100%=10.0=Physicality=Tech.=10 Oct.=Uranus=P=1Ø.
Hoopla=5,500=5.5=80%=P5.50=Earth-Midway=5 May = Gaia.
Hoop skirt=5,500=5.5=80%=P5.50=Earth-Midway=5 May = Gaia.
Hooray=1,500=15%=P1.50D=1.5=Authority=Solar Crown=1 May = Maia.
Hoosegow=4,000=40%=P4.0D=Govt=Creatocracy=4 April=Mercury=Hermes=G=A4.
Hoot=9,000=90%=P9.00D=9.0=Abstraction=Gods=Saturn=9Sept.>>A=Ø.
Hootenanny=3,500=4,000=40%=P4.0D=Govt=Creat.=4 April=Mercury=Hermes=G=A4.
Hoover Herbert=4,500=5,000=50%=P5.00D=Law=Time=Venus=5 May =Odite>>L=N.
Hoover, J(ohn)=4,500=5,000=50%=P5.00D=Law=Time=Venus=5 May = Aphrodite>>L=N.
Hooves=2,000=20%=P2.00D=2.0=Nature=Matter=Moon=2 Feb.=Cupid=N=C+_
Hop1=10,000=1,000=100%=10.0=Physicality=Tech.=10 Oct.=Uranus=P=1Ø.
Hop2=10,000=1,000=100%=10.0=Physicality=Tech.=10 Oct.=Uranus=P=1Ø.
Hope=10,000=1,000=100%=10.0=Physicality=Tech.=10 Oct.=Uranus=P=1Ø.
Hopefully=10,000=1,000=100%=10.0=Physicality=Tech.=10 Oct.=Uranus=P=1Ø.
Hopeless=2,500=3,000=30%=P3.0D=3.0=Creativity=Stars=Muses=3 March = C=I>>GIL.
Hopi=6,500=7,000=70%=P7.0D=7.0=Language=Assets=Mars=7 July=Pleiades.
Hopkins George=2,500=3,000=30%=P3.0D=3.0=Cre=Stars=Muses=3 March = C=I>>GIL.
Hopkins, Mark.=3,000=30%=P3.0D=3.0=Creativity=Stars=Muses=3 March = C=I>>GIL.
Hopper=7,500=8,000=80%=P8.0D=Economy=Currency=8 Aug.=Zeus>>E=v.

Hopscotch=10,000=1,000=100%=10.0=Physicality=Tech.=10 Oct.=Uranus=P=1Ø.
Hor.=500=5%=P5.00D=5.0=Law=Time=Venus=5 May=Aphrodite>>L=N.
Horace=3,000=30%=P3.0D=3.0=Creativity=Stars=Muses=3 March = C=I>>GIL.
Horde=6,500=7,000=70%=P7.0D=7.0=Language=Assets=Mars=7 July=Pleiades.
Horehound=10,000=1,000=100%=10.0=Physicality=Tech.=10 Oct.=Uranus=P=1Ø.
Horizon=10,000=1,000=100%=10.0=Physicality=Tech.=10 Oct.=Uranus=P=1Ø.
Horizontal=10,000=1,000=100%=10.0=Physicality=Tech.=10 Oct.=Uranus=P=1Ø.
Hormone=10,000=1,000=100%=10.0=Physicality=Tech.=10 Oct.=Uranus=P=1Ø.
Hormuz, Strait of.=10,000=1,000=100%=10.0=Physicality=Tech.=10 Oct.=Uranus=P=1Ø.
Horn=10,000=1,000=100%=10.0=Physicality=Tech.=10 Oct.=Uranus=P=1Ø.
Horn, Cape.=6,000=60%=P6.0D=Man=Earth=Royalty=6 June=Gaia=Maia>>M=M2.
Horned toad=5,500=5.5=80%=P5.50=Earth-Midway=5 May = Gaia.
Hornet=6,500=7,000=70%=P7.0D=7.0=Language=Assets=Mars=7 July=Pleiades.
Horn of plenty=3,000=30%=P3.0D=3.0=Creativity=Stars=Muses=3 March = C=I>>GIL.
Horn pipe=2,500=3,000=30%=P3.0D=3.0=Creativity=Stars=Muses=3 March = C=I>>GIL.

Horology=7,500=8,000=80%=P8.0D=Economy=Currency=8 Aug.=Zeus>>E=v.
A key ability of Zeus is the intelligence of time and clocks. A superior ability granted to Peter Matthews-Akukalia, Castle Makupedia where he invented Mind Clocks.

Horoscope=10,000=1,000=100%=10.0=Physicality=Tech.=10 Oct.=Uranus=P=1Ø.
Horowitz Vladimir=3,000=30%=P3.0D=3.0=Creativity=Stars=Muses=3 March = C=I>>GIL.
Horrendous=3,500=4,000=40%=P4.0D=Govt=Creat.=4 April=Mercury=Hermes=G=A4.
Horrible=4,500=5,000=50%=P5.00D=Law=Time=Venus=5 May = Aphrodite>>L=N.
Horrid=6,000=60%=P6.0D=Man=Earth=Royalty=6 June=Gaia=Maia>>M=M2.
Horrific=2,500=3,000=30%=P3.0D=3.0=Creativity=Stars=Muses=3 March = C=I>>GIL.
Horrify=4,500=5,000=50%=P5.00D=Law=Time=Venus=5 May = Aphrodite>>L=N.
Horror=6,500=7,000=70%=P7.0D=7.0=Language=Assets=Mars=7 July=Pleiades.
Hors de combat=2,000=20%=P2.00D=2.0=Nature=Matter=Moon=2 Feb.=Cupid=N=C+_
Hors d'oeuvre=3,000=30%=P3.0D=3.0=Creativity=Stars=Muses=3 March = C=I>>GIL.
Horse=10,000=1,000=100%=10.0=Physicality=Tech.=10 Oct.=Uranus=P=1Ø.
Horseback=3,000=30%=P3.0D=3.0=Creativity=Stars=Muses=3 March = C=I>>GIL.
Horse chestnut=8,000=80%=P8.0D=Economy=Currency=8 Aug.=Zeus>>E=v.

Horseflesh=6,000=60%=P6.0D=Man=Earth=Royalty=6 June=Gaia=Maia>>M=M2.
The flesh of horses is again likened to human flesh. A proof of the transformations that occur in the cycle of life, incarnation and reincarnation. Humans are in different forms such as trees, animals, birds, walls, ants, inanimate objects with innate life in them. See Hock1.

Horsefly=7,000=70%=P7.0D=7.0=Language=Assets=Mars=7 July=Pleiades.
Horsehair=7,000=70%=P7.0D=7.0=Language=Assets=Mars=7 July=Pleiades.
Horsehide=4,500=5,000=50%=P5.00D=Law=Time=Venus=5 May = Aphrodite>>L=N.
Horseman=4,500=5,000=50%=P5.00D=Law=Time=Venus=5 May = Aphrodite>>L=N.

Horsemanship=2,500=3,000=30%=P3.0D=3.0=Cre=Stars=Muses=3 March = C=I>>GIL.
Horseplay=1,000=100%=10.0=1.0=Mind=Sun=1 January=Helios >> M=E4.
Horsepower=7,000=70%=P7.0D=7.0=Language=Assets=Mars=7 July=Pleiades.
Horseradish=7,000=70%=P7.0D=7.0=Language=Assets=Mars=7 July=Pleiades.

Horse sense=1,500=15%=P1.50D=1.5=Authority=Solar Crown=1 May = Maia.
Horse sense. Common sense. Animal to human brain relativity. See Horseflesh.

Horseshoe=11,000=11%=P1.10D=1.1=Idea=Brainchild=Inv.=11 Nov.=SC=Athena>>I=MT.
Horseshoe crab=5,500=5.5=80%=P5.50=Earth-Midway=5 May = Gaia.
Horsetail=5,000=50%=P5.00D=Law=Time=Venus=5 May = Aphrodite>>L=N.
Horse whip=3,000=30%=P3.0D=3.0=Creativity=Stars=Muses=3 March = C=I>>GIL.
Horsewoman=5,000=50%=P5.00D=Law=Time=Venus=5 May = Aphrodite>>L=N.

Horsy=6,000=60%=P6.0D=Man=Earth=Royalty=6 June=Gaia=Maia>>M=M2.
A male reference to hussy.

Hortatory=3,000=30%=P3.0D=3.0=Creativity=Stars=Muses=3 March = C=I>>GIL.
Horticulture=10,000=1,000=100%=10.0=Physicality=Tech.=10 Oct.=Uranus=P=1Ø.
Hosanna=5,000=50%=P5.00D=Law=Time=Venus=5 May = Aphrodite>>L=N.
Hose=10,000=1,000=100%=10.0=Physicality=Tech.=10 Oct.=Uranus=P=1Ø.

Hosea=4,500=5,000=50%=P5.00D=Law=Time=Venus=5 May = Aphrodite>>L=N.
Inspired by joint effort of Hermes and Aphrodite. Hosea is a borderline, a means by which messages can be conveyed hence rightly a prophet. 8th century.
5.0*8.0=p=13+40=53x=px=573=600=6.0. Hosea is directly a prophet of Aphrodite.

Hosiery=2,500=3,000=30%=P3.0D=3.0=Creativity=Stars=Muses=3 March = C=I>>GIL.
Hosp.=500=5%=P5.00D=5.0=Law=Time=Venus=5 May=Aphrodite>>L=N.
Hospice=10,000=1,000=100%=10.0=Physicality=Tech.=10 Oct.=Uranus=P=1Ø.
Hospitable=7,000=70%=P7.0D=7.0=Language=Assets=Mars=7 July=Pleiades.
Hospital=12,000=12%=P1.20D=1.2=Knowledge=Education=12Dec.=Athena>>K=F.
Hospitality=3,000=30%=P3.0D=3.0=Creativity=Stars=Muses=3 March = C=I>>GIL.
Hospitalize=4,500=5,000=50%=P5.00D=Law=Time=Venus=5 May = Aphrodite>>L=N.
Host1=10,000=1,000=100%=10.0=Physicality=Tech.=10 Oct.=Uranus=P=1Ø.
Host2=5,500=5.5=80%=P5.50=Earth-Midway=5 May = Gaia.
Host3=5,500=5.5=80%=P5.50=Earth-Midway=5 May = Gaia.
Hostage=9,500=10,000=1,000=100%=10.0=Physicality=Tech.=10 Oct.=Uranus=P=1Ø.
Hostel=7,500=8,000=80%=P8.0D=Economy=Currency=8 Aug.=Zeus>>E=v.
Hostelry=1,000=100%=10.0=1.0=Mind=Sun=1 January=Helios >> M=E4.
Hostess=10,000=1,000=100%=10.0=Physicality=Tech.=10 Oct.=Uranus=P=1Ø.
Hostile=7,500=8,000=80%=P8.0D=Economy=Currency=8 Aug.=Zeus>>E=v.

Hostility=4,000=40%=P4.0D=Govt=Creatocracy=4 April=Mercury=Hermes=G=A4.
Hostler=6,500=7,000=70%=P7.0D=7.0=Language=Assets=Mars=7 July=Pleiades.
Hot=10,000=1,000=100%=10.0=Physicality=Tech.=10 Oct.=Uranus=P=1Ø.
Hot air=2,000=20%=P2.00D=2.0=Nature=Matter=Moon=2 Feb.=Cupid=N=C+_
Hotbed=7,500=8,000=80%=P8.0D=Economy=Currency=8 Aug.=Zeus>>E=v.
Hot-blooded=2,000=20%=P2.00D=2.0=Nature=Matter=Moon=2 Feb.=Cupid=N=C+_
Hotbox=6,500=7,000=70%=P7.0D=7.0=Language=Assets=Mars=7 July=Pleiades.
Hot cake=6,500=7,000=70%=P7.0D=7.0=Language=Assets=Mars=7 July=Pleiades.
Hotdog=5,000=50%=P5.00D=Law=Time=Venus=5 May = Aphrodite>>L=N.
Hotel=7,000=70%=P7.0D=7.0=Language=Assets=Mars=7 July=Pleiades.
Hot flash=5,000=50%=P5.00D=Law=Time=Venus=5 May = Aphrodite>>L=N.
Hotfoot=5,000=50%=P5.00D=Law=Time=Venus=5 May = Aphrodite>>L=N.
Hotheaded=3,000=30%=P3.0D=3.0=Creativity=Stars=Muses=3 March = C=I>>GIL.
Hothouse=3,000=30%=P3.0D=3.0=Creativity=Stars=Muses=3 March = C=I>>GIL.
Hotline=3,500=4,000=40%=P4.0D=Govt=Creato.=4 April=Mercury=Hermes=G=A4.
Hot plate=3,500=4,000=40%=P4.0D=Govt =Creatocracy=4 April=Hermes=G=A4.
Hot rod=4,000=40%=P4.0D=Government =Creatocracy=4 April=Mercury=Hermes=G=A4.
Hot seat=5,500=5.5=80%=P5.50=Earth-Midway=5 May = Gaia.
Hot shot=4,000=40%=P4.0D=Govt.=Creatocracy=4 April=Mercury=Hermes=G=A4.
Hot toddy=6,500=7,000=70%=P7.0D=7.0=Language=Assets=Mars=7 July=Pleiades.
Hot tub=5,500=5.5=80%=P5.50=Earth-Midway=5 May = Gaia.
Hot-wire=9,500=10,000=1,000=100%=10.0=Physicality=Tech.=10 Oct.=Uranus=P=1Ø.
Houdini Harry=2,500=3,000=30%=P3.0D=3.0=Cre=Stars=Muses=3 March = C=I>>GIL.
Houdon Jean=2,000=20%=P2.00D=2.0=Nature=Matter=Moon=2 Feb.=Cupid=N=C+_
Hound=10,000=1,000=100%=10.0=Physicality=Tech.=10 Oct.=Uranus=P=1Ø.
Hour=10,000=1,000=100%=10.0=Physicality=Tech.=10 Oct.=Uranus=P=1Ø.
Hour glass=10,000=1,000=100%=10.0=Physicality=Tech.=10 Oct.=Uranus=P=1Ø.
Houri=4,500=5,000=50%=P5.00D=Law=Time=Venus=5 May = Aphrodite>>L=N.
Hourly=10,000=1,000=100%=10.0=Physicality=Tech.=10 Oct.=Uranus=P=1Ø.
House=10,000=1,000=100%=10.0=Physicality=Tech.=10 Oct.=Uranus=P=1Ø.
Houseboat=3,500=4,000=40%=P4.0D=Govt=Creat.=4 April=Mercury=Hermes=G=A4.
Housebreaking=4,000=40%=P4.0D=Govt=Creatocracy=4 April=Mercury=Hermes=G=A4.
Housebroken=5,000=50%=P5.00D=Law=Time=Venus=5 May = Aphrodite>>L=N.
Housefly=6,500=7,000=70%=P7.0D=7.0=Language=Assets=Mars=7 July=Pleiades.
Household=9,000=90%=P9.00D=9.0=Abstraction=Gods=Saturn=9Sept.>>A=Ø.
Housekeeper=6,000=60%=P6.0D=Man=Earth=Royalty=6 June=Gaia=Maia>>M=M2.
Housekeeping=10,000=1,000=100%=10.0=Physicality=Tech.=10 Oct.=Uranus=P=1Ø.
House mother=5,000=50%=P5.00D=Law=Time=Venus=5 May = Aphrodite>>L=N.
House of Commons=4,500=5,000=50%=P5.00D=Law=Time=Venus=5 May =Odite>>L=N.
House of Lords=4,000=40%=P4.0D=Govt=Creatocracy=4 April=Mercury=Hermes=G=A4.
House organ=5,500=5.5=80%=P5.50=Earth-Midway=5 May = Gaia.
Houseplant=4,500=5,000=50%=P5.00D=Law=Time=Venus=5 May = Aphrodite>>L=N.
Housewares=4,000=40%=P4.0D=Govt=Creatocracy=4 April=Mercury=Hermes=G=A4.
Housewarming=4,000=40%=P4.0D=Govt=Creatocracy=4 April=Mercury=Hermes=G=A4.
Housewife=7,000=70%=P7.0D=7.0=Language=Assets=Mars=7 July=Pleiades.

Housework=5,000=50%=P5.00D=Law=Time=Venus=5 May = Aphrodite>>L=N.
Housing=10,000=1,000=100%=10.0=Physicality=Tech.=10 Oct.=Uranus=P=1Ø.
Housman Alfred=3,500=4,000=40%=P4.0D=Govt.=Creatocracy=4 April=Hermes=G=A4.
Houston=4,500=5,000=50%=P5.00D=Law=Time=Venus=5 May = Aphrodite>>L=N.
Houston, Samuel=3,000=30%=P3.0D=3.0=Creativity=Stars=Muses=3 March = C=I>>GIL.
Hove=3,500=4,000=40%=P4.0D=Govt=Creatocracy=4 April=Mercury=Hermes=G=A4.
Hovel=2,000=20%=P2.00D=2.0=Nature=Matter=Moon=2 Feb.=Cupid=N=C+_
Hover=10,000=1,000=100%=10.0=Physicality=Tech.=10 Oct.=Uranus=P=1Ø.
Hovercraft=2,000=20%=P2.00D=2.0=Nature=Matter=Moon=2 Feb.=Cupid=N=C+_
How=10,000=1,000=100%=10.0=Physicality=Tech.=10 Oct.=Uranus=P=1Ø.
Howard Catherine=7,000=70%=P7.0D=7.0=Language=Assets=Mars=7 July=Pleiades.
Howard, Henry=4,500=5,000=50%=P5.00D=Law=Time=Venus=5 May = Aphrodite>>L=N.
Howbeit=500=5%=P5.00D=5.0=Law=Time=Venus=5 May=Aphrodite>>L=N.
Howdah=6,500=7,000=70%=P7.0D=7.0=Language=Assets=Mars=7 July=Pleiades.
Howe Elias=2,000=20%=P2.00D=2.0=Nature=Matter=Moon=2 Feb.=Cupid=N=C+_
Howe, Julius=3,500=4,000=40%=P4.0D=Govt=Creatocracy=4 April=Hermes=G=A4.
Howells William=3,500=4,000=40%=P4.0D=Govt=Creatocracy=4 April=Hermes=G=A4.
However=10,000=1,000=100%=10.0=Physicality=Tech.=10 Oct.=Uranus=P=1Ø.
Howitzer=5,500=5.5=80%=P5.50=Earth-Midway=5 May = Gaia.   ⸱
Howl=9,000=90%=P9.00D=9.0=Abstraction=Gods=Saturn=9Sept.>>A=Ø.
Howler=4,000=40%=P4.0D=Government =Creatocracy=4 April=Mercury=Hermes=G=A4.
Howrah=4,500=5,000=50%=P5.00D=Law=Time=Venus=5 May = Aphrodite>>L=N.
Howsoever=2,500=3,000=30%=P3.0D=3.0=Cre=Stars=Muses=3 March = C=I>>GIL.
Hoyden=5,500=5.5=80%=P5.50=Earth-Midway=5 May = Gaia.
hp=500=5%=P5.00D=5.0=Law=Time=Venus=5 May=Aphrodite>>L=N.
HQ=500=5%=P5.00D=5.0=Law=Time=Venus=5 May=Aphrodite>>L=N.
hr=500=5%=P5.00D=5.0=Law=Time=Venus=5 May=Aphrodite>>L=N.
H.R.=1,500=15%=P1.50D=1.5=Authority=Solar Crown=1 May = Maia.
H.R.H.=2,500=3,000=30%=P3.0D=3.0=Creativity=Stars=Muses=3 March = C=I>>GIL.
hrs=500=5%=P5.00D=5.0=Law=Time=Venus=5 May=Aphrodite>>L=N.
HS=1,000=100%=10.0=1.0=Mind=Sun=1 January=Helios >> M=E4.
HST=1,500=15%=P1.50D=1.5=Authority=Solar Crown=1 May = Maia.
ht=500=5%=P5.00D=5.0=Law=Time=Venus=5 May=Aphrodite>>L=N.
HTLV=7,000=70%=P7.0D=7.0=Language=Assets=Mars=7 July=Pleiades.
Hua Guofeng=3,500=4,000=40%=P4.0D=Govt=Creatocracy=4 April=Hermes=G=A4.
Huang He=11,000=11%=P1.10D=1.1=Idea=Brainchild=Inv.=11 Nov.=SC=Athena>>I=MT.
Huascán=6,500=7,000=70%=P7.0D=7.0=Language=Assets=Mars=7 July=Pleiades.
Hub=9,000=90%=P9.00D=9.0=Abstraction=Gods=Saturn=9Sept.>>A=Ø.
Hubbub=5,000=50%=P5.00D=Law=Time=Venus=5 May = Aphrodite>>L=N.
Hubcap=5,000=50%=P5.00D=Law=Time=Venus=5 May = Aphrodite>>L=N.
Hubris=2,000=20%=P2.00D=2.0=Nature=Matter=Moon=2 Feb.=Cupid=N=C+_
Huckleberry=10,000=1,000=100%=10.0=Physicality=Tech.=10 Oct.=Uranus=P=1Ø.
Huckster=4,000=40%=P4.0D=Government =Creatocracy=4 April=Hermes=G=A4.
HUD=3,000=30%=P3.0D=3.0=Creativity=Stars=Muses=3 March = C=I>>GIL.
Huddle=10,000=1,000=100%=10.0=Physicality=Tech.=10 Oct.=Uranus=P=1Ø.

Hudson Henry.=3,000=30%=P3.0D=3.0=Creativity=Stars=Muses=3 March = C=I>>GIL.
Hudson, William=3,500=4,000=40%=P4.0D=Govt=Creatocracy=4 April=Hermes=G=A4.
Hudson Bay.=7,000=70%=P7.0D=7.0=Language=Assets=Mars=7 July=Pleiades.
Hudson River.=11,000=11%=P1.10D=1.1=Idea=Brainchild=Inv.=11 Nov.=SC=Athena
    >>I=MT.
hue=10,000=1,000=100%=10.0=Physicality=Tech.=10 Oct.=Uranus=P=1Ø.
Hue=7,500=8,000=80%=P8.0D=Economy=Currency=8 Aug.=Zeus>>E=v.
Hue and cry=6,000=60%=P6.0D=Man=Earth=Royalty=6 June=Gaia=Maia>>M=M2.
Huff=5,500=5.5=80%=P5.50=Earth-Midway=5 May = Gaia.
Hug=8,000=80%=P8.0D=Economy=Currency=8 Aug.=Zeus>>E=v.
Huge=2,500=3,000=30%=P3.0D=3.0=Creativity=Stars=Muses=3 March = C=I>>GIL.
Hughes Charles=3,500=4,000=40%=P4.0D=Govt=Creatocracy=4 April=Hermes=G=A4.
Hughes James=2,000=20%=P2.00D=2.0=Nature=Matter=Moon=2 Feb.=Cupid=N=C+_
Hugo Victor Marie=2,000=20%=P2.00D=2.0=Nature=Matter=Moon=2 Feb.=Cupid=N=C+_
Huguenot=4,500=5,000=50%=P5.00D=Law=Time=Venus=5 May = Aphrodite>>L=N.
Huh=4,000=40%=P4.0D=Govt =Creatocracy=4 April=Mercury=Hermes=G=A4.
Hula=11,000=11%=P1.10D=1.1=Idea=Brainchild=Inv.=11 Nov.=SC=Athena>>I=MT.
Hulk=11,000=11%=P1.10D=1.1=Idea=Brainchild=Inv.=11 Nov.=SC=Athena>>I=MT.
Hulking=2,000=20%=P2.00D=2.0=Nature=Matter=Moon=2 Feb.=Cupid=N=C+_
Hull=10,000=1,000=100%=10.0=Physicality=Tech.=10 Oct.=Uranus=P=1Ø.
Hull Cordell.=2,500=3,000=30%=P3.0D=3.0=Cre=Stars=Muses=3 March = C=I>>GIL.
Hullabaloo=4,500=5,000=50%=P5.00D=Law=Time=Venus=5 May = Aphrodite>>L=N.
Hum=10,000=1,000=100%=10.0=Physicality=Tech.=10 Oct.=Uranus=P=1Ø.

Human=8,500=9,000=90%=P9.00D=9.0=Abstraction=Gods=Saturn=9Sept.>>A=Ø.
A borderline between GOD and the Gods >> value and abstraction >> business and spirits.

Human being=6,000=60%=P6.0D=Man=Earth=Royalty=6 June=Gaia=Maia>>M=M2.
Humane=9,000=90%=P9.00D=9.0=Abstraction=Gods=Saturn=9Sept.>>A=Ø.
Humanism=10,000=1,000=100%=10.0=Physicality=Tech.=10 Oct.=Uranus=P=1Ø.
Humanitarian=6,500=7,000=70%=P7.0D=7.0=Language=Assets=Mars=7 July=Pleiades.
Humanity=10,000=1,000=100%=10.0=Physicality=Tech.=10 Oct.=Uranus=P=1Ø.
Humanize=4,000=40%=P4.0D=Govt.=Creatocracy=4 April=Mercury=Hermes=G=A4.
Humankind=1,500=15%=P1.50D=1.5=Authority=Solar Crown=1 May = Maia.
Humanoid=4,500=5,000=50%=P5.00D=Law=Time=Venus=5 May = Aphrodite>>L=N.
Humble=10,000=1,000=100%=10.0=Physicality=Tech.=10 Oct.=Uranus=P=1Ø.
Humboldt Frederich=5,000=50%=P5.00D=Law=Time=Venus=5 May = Aphrodite>>L=N.
Humboldt Bay=4,500=5,000=50%=P5.00D=Law=Time=Venus=5 May = Aphrodite>>L=N.
Humboldt Current=8,000=80%=P8.0D=Economy=Currency=8 Aug.=Zeus>>E=v.
Humboldt River=5,000=50%=P5.00D=Law=Time=Venus=5 May = Aphrodite>>L=N.
Humbug=4,000=40%=P4.0D=Govt =Creatocracy=4 April=Mercury=Hermes=G=A4.
Humdinger=3,000=30%=P3.0D=3.0=Creativity=Stars=Muses=3 March = C=I>>GIL.
Humdrum=4,000=40%=P4.0D=Govt=Creatocracy=4 April=Mercury=Hermes=G=A4.
Hume David=3,000=30%=P3.0D=3.0=Creativity=Stars=Muses=3 March = C=I>>GIL.

Humerus=6,000=60%=P6.0D=Man=Earth=Royalty=6 June=Gaia=Maia>>M=M2.
Humid=6,000=60%=P6.0D=Man=Earth=Royalty=6 June=Gaia=Maia>>M=M2.
Humidity=1,500=15%=P1.50D=1.5=Authority=Solar Crown=1 May = Maia.
Humidor=6,000=60%=P6.0D=Man=Earth=Royalty=6 June=Gaia=Maia>>M=M2.
Humiliate=7,000=70%=P7.0D=7.0=Language=Assets=Mars=7 July=Pleiades.
Humility=4,500=5,000=50%=P5.00D=Law=Time=Venus=5 May = Aphrodite>>L=N.
Hummingbird=9,000=90%=P9.00D=9.0=Abstraction=Gods=Saturn=9Sept.>>A=Ø.
Hummock=4,000=40%=P4.0D=Govt =Creatocracy=4 April=Mercury=Hermes=G=A4.
Hummus=9,000=90%=P9.00D=9.0=Abstraction=Gods=Saturn=9Sept.>>A=Ø.
Humor=10,000=1,000=100%=10.0=Physicality=Tech.=10 Oct.=Uranus=P=1Ø.
Hump=10,000=1,000=100%=10.0=Physicality=Tech.=10 Oct.=Uranus=P=1Ø.
Humpback=4,000=40%=P4.0D=Govt =Creatocracy=4 April=Mercury=Hermes=G=A4.
Humpback whale=4,500=5,000=50%=P5.00D=Law=Time=Venus=5 May =Odite>>L=N.
Humphrey Hubert=5,000=50%=P5.00D=Law=Time=Venus=5 May = Aphrodite>>L=N.
Humus=8,000=80%=P8.0D=Economy=Currency=8 Aug.=Zeus>>E=v.
Hun=10,000=1,000=100%=10.0=Physicality=Tech.=10 Oct.=Uranus=P=1Ø.

Hunch=7,500=8,000=80%=P8.0D=Economy=Currency=8 Aug.=Zeus>>E=v.
A hunch comes from Aries after being confirmed by Zeus. An intuitive feeling.

Hunchback=8,500=9,000=90%=P9.00D=9.0=Abstraction=Gods=Saturn=9Sept.>>A=Ø.
Hundred=10,000=1,000=100%=10.0=Physicality=Tech.=10 Oct.=Uranus=P=1Ø.
Hundredth=7,000=70%=P7.0D=7.0=Language=Assets=Mars=7 July=Pleiades.
Hundred weight=10,000=1,000=100%=10.0=Physicality=Tech.=10 Oct.=Uranus=P=1Ø.
Hung=2,500=3,000=30%=P3.0D=3.0=Creativity=Stars=Muses=3 March = C=I>>GIL.
Hung.=1,000=100%=10.0=1.0=Mind=Sun=1 January=Helios >> M=E4.
Hungarian=6,500=7,000=70%=P7.0D=7.0=Language=Assets=Mars=7 July=Pleiades.
Hungary=5,500=5.5=80%=P5.50=Earth-Midway=5 May = Gaia.
Hunger=1,000=100%=10.0=1.0=Mind=Sun=1 January=Helios >> M=E4.
Hung jury=4,000=40%=P4.0D=Government =Creatocracy=4 April=Hermes=G=A4.
Junk=7,500=8,000=80%=P8.0D=Economy=Currency=8 Aug.=Zeus>>E=v.
Hunker=8,500=9,000=90%=P9.00D=9.0=Abstraction=Gods=Saturn=9Sept.>>A=Ø.
Hunky-dory=5,500=5.5=80%=P5.50=Earth-Midway=5 May = Gaia.
Hunt=10,000=1,000=100%=10.0=Physicality=Tech.=10 Oct.=Uranus=P=1Ø.
Huntington=4,500=5,000=50%=P5.00D=Law=Time=Venus=5 May = Aphrodite>>L=N.
Huntington Beach=6,500=7,000=70%=P7.0D=7.0=Lang.=Assets=Mars=7 July=Pleiades.
Huntsman=7,000=70%=P7.0D=7.0=Language=Assets=Mars=7 July=Pleiades.
Huntsville=4,500=5,000=50%=P5.00D=Law=Time=Venus=5 May = Aphrodite>>L=N.
Hurdle=10,000=1,000=100%=10.0=Physicality=Tech.=10 Oct.=Uranus=P=1Ø.
Hurdy-gurdy=6,500=7,000=70%=P7.0D=7.0=Language=Assets=Mars=7 July=Pleiades.
Hurt=6,500=7,000=70%=P7.0D=7.0=Language=Assets=Mars=7 July=Pleiades.
Hurly-burly=2,000=20%=P2.00D=2.0=Nature=Matter=Moon=2 Feb.=Cupid=N=C+_
Huron=10,000=1,000=100%=10.0=Physicality=Tech.=10 Oct.=Uranus=P=1Ø.

Huron, Lake=6,000=60%=P6.0D=Man=Earth=Royalty=6 June=Gaia=Maia>>M=M2.
Hurrah=5,000=50%=P5.00D=Law=Time=Venus=5 May = Aphrodite>>L=N.

Hurricane=8,000=80%=P8.0D=Economy=Currency=8 Aug.=Zeus>>E=v.
The hurricane is the wind of Zeus, a Zeusian wind.

Hurry=10,000=1,000=100%=10.0=Physicality=Tech.=10 Oct.=Uranus=P=1Ø.
Hurt=10,000=1,000=100%=10.0=Physicality=Tech.=10 Oct.=Uranus=P=1Ø.
Hurtle=7,500=8,000=80%=P8.0D=Economy=Currency=8 Aug.=Zeus>>E=v.
Hus=2,000=20%=P2.00D=2.0=Nature=Matter=Moon=2 Feb.=Cupid=N=C+_
Husband=11,000=11%=P1.10D=1.1=Idea=Brainchild=Inv.=11 Nov.=SC=Athena>>I=MT.
Husbandman=1,000=100%=10.0=1.0=Mind=Sun=1 January=Helios >> M=E4.
Husbandry=3,500=4,000=40%=P4.0D=Govt=Creatocracy=4 April=Hermes=G=A4.
Hush=11,000=11%=P1.10D=1.1=Idea=Brainchild=Inv.=11 Nov.=SC=Athena>>I=MT.
Hush-hush=1,500=15%=P1.50D=1.5=Authority=Solar Crown=1 May = Maia.
Hush puppy=5,000=50%=P5.00D=Law=Time=Venus=5 May = Aphrodite>>L=N.
Husk=10,000=1,000=100%=10.0=Physicality=Tech.=10 Oct.=Uranus=P=1Ø.
Husky1=2,000=20%=P2.00D=2.0=Nature=Matter=Moon=2 Feb.=Cupid=N=C+_
Husky2=2,500=3,000=30%=P3.0D=3.0=Creativity=Stars=Muses=3 March = C=I>>GIL.
Husky3=7,000=70%=P7.0D=7.0=Language=Assets=Mars=7 July=Pleiades.
Huss John=4,000=40%=P4.0D=Government =Creatocracy=4 April=Hermes=G=A4.
Hussar=6,000=60%=P6.0D=Man=Earth=Royalty=6 June=Gaia=Maia>>M=M2.
Hussein=3,500=4,000=40%=P4.0D=Government =Creatocracy=4 April=Hermes=G=A4.
Hussein, Saddam=3,500=4,000=40%=P4.0D=Govt=Creatocracy=4 April=Hermes=G=A4.
Hussert Edmund=3,000=30%=P3.0D=3.0=Creativity=Stars=Muses=3 March = C=I>>GIL.
Hussy=6,000=60%=P6.0D=Man=Earth=Royalty=6 June=Gaia=Maia>>M=M2.
Hustings=5,000=50%=P5.00D=Law=Time=Venus=5 May = Aphrodite>>L=N.
Hustle=10,000=1,000=100%=10.0=Physicality=Tech.=10 Oct.=Uranus=P=1Ø.
Hut=5,500=5.5=80%=P5.50=Earth-Midway=5 May = Gaia.
Hutch=10,500=11,000=11%=P1.10D=1.1=Idea=Brainchild=Inv.=11 Nov.=SC=Athena
    >>I=MT.
Hutchinson Anne.=4,500=5,000=50%=P5.00D=Law=Time=Venus=5 May =Odite>>L=N.
Huxley Aldous=2,500=3,000=30%=P3.0D=3.0=Cre=Stars=Muses=3 March = C=I>>GIL.
Huxley, Julian=4,000=40%=P4.0D=Govt=Creatocracy=4 April=Mercury=Hermes=G=A4.
Huxley, Thomas=2,500=3,000=30%=P3.0D=3.0=Cre=Stars=Muses=3 March = C=I>>GIL.
Huzzah=3,500=4,000=40%=P4.0D=Government =Creatocracy=4 April=Hermes=G=A4.
Hwang=1,500=15%=P1.50D=1.5=Authority=Solar Crown=1 May = Maia.
hwy=500=5%=P5.00D=5.0=Law=Time=Venus=5 May=Aphrodite>>L=N.
Hyacinth=8,500=9,000=90%=P9.00D=9.0=Abstraction=Gods=Saturn=9Sept.>>A=Ø.
Hybrid=8,500=9,000=90%=P9.00D=9.0=Abstraction=Gods=Saturn=9Sept.>>A=Ø.
Hybridize=4,000=40%=P4.0D=Government =Creatocracy=4 April=Hermes=G=A4.
Hyde Park=4,000=40%=P4.0D=Government =Creatocracy=4 April=Hermes=G=A4.
Hyderabad=8,500=9,000=90%=P9.00D=9.0=Abstraction=Gods=Saturn=9Sept.>>A=Ø.
Hydra=9,000=90%=P9.00D=9.0=Abstraction=Gods=Saturn=9Sept.>>A=Ø.

Hydrangea=9,000=90%=P9.00D=9.0=Abstraction=Gods=Saturn=9Sept.>>A=Ø.
Hydrant=1,500=15%=P1.50D=1.5=Authority=Solar Crown=1 May = Maia.
Hydrate=11,000=11%=P1.10D=1.1=Idea=Brainchild=Inv.=11 Nov.=SC=Athena>>I=MT.
Hydraulic=10,000=1,000=100%=10.0=Physicality=Tech.=10 Oct.=Uranus=P=1Ø.
Hydraulics=5,500=5.5=80%=P5.50=Earth-Midway=5 May = Gaia.
Hydro-=5,500=5.5=80%=P5.50=Earth-Midway=5 May = Gaia.
Hydrocarbon=10,000=1,000=100%=10.0=Physicality=Tech.=10 Oct.=Uranus=P=1Ø.
Hydrocephalus=10,000=1,000=100%=10.0=Physicality=Tech.=10 Oct.=Uranus=P=1Ø.
Hydrochloric acid=10,000=1,000=100%=10.0=Physicality=Tech.=10 Oct.=Uranus=P=1Ø.
Hydrocortisone=10,000=1,000=100%=10.0=Physicality=Tech.=10 Oct.=Uranus=P=1Ø.
Hydrodynamics=10,000=1,000=100%=10.0=Physicality=Tech.=10 Oct.=Uranus=P=1Ø.
Hydroelectric=10,000=1,000=100%=10.0=Physicality=Tech.=10 Oct.=Uranus=P=1Ø.
Hydrofoil=10,000=1,000=100%=10.0=Physicality=Tech.=10 Oct.=Uranus=P=1Ø.
Hydrogen=10,000=1,000=100%=10.0=Physicality=Tech.=10 Oct.=Uranus=P=1Ø.
Hydrogenate=4,500=5,000=50%=P5.00D=Law=Time=Venus=5 May = Aphrodite>>L=N.
Hydrogen bomb=8,000=80%=P8.0D=Economy=Currency=8 Aug.=Zeus>>E=v.
Hydrogen peroxide=8,500=9,000=90%=P9.00D=9.0=Abs.=Gods=Saturn=9Sept.>>A=Ø.
Hydrolysis=4,500=5,000=50%=P5.00D=Law=Time=Venus=5 May = Aphrodite>>L=N.
Hydrometer=5,500=5.5=80%=P5.50=Earth-Midway=5 May = Gaia.
Hydrophobia=2,000=20%=P2.00D=2.0=Nature=Matter=Moon=2 Feb.=Cupid=N=C+_
Hydroplane=10,000=1,000=100%=10.0=Physicality=Tech.=10 Oct.=Uranus=P=1Ø.
Hydroponics=10,000=1,000=100%=10.0=Physicality=Tech.=10 Oct.=Uranus=P=1Ø.
Hydrostatics=4,500=5,000=50%=P5.00D=Law=Time=Venus=5 May = Aphrodite>>L=N.
Hydrotherapy=4,000=40%=P4.0D=Government =Creatocracy=4 April=Hermes=G=A4.
Hydrous=4,000=40%=P4.0D=Government =Creatocracy=4 April=Hermes=G=A4.
Hydroxide=4,000=40%=P4.0D=Government =Creatocracy=4 April=Hermes=G=A4.
Hyena=9,000=9,000=90%=P9.00D=9.0=Abstraction=Gods=Saturn=9Sept.>>A=Ø.
Hygiene=9,000=9,000=90%=P9.00D=9.0=Abstraction=Gods=Saturn=9Sept.>>A=Ø.
Hygrometer=6,500=7,000=70%=P7.0D=7.0=Language=Assets=Mars=7 July=Pleiades.
Hying=2,000=20%=P2.00D=2.0=Nature=Matter=Moon=2 Feb.=Cupid=N=C+_
Hymen=7,500=8,000=80%=P8.0D=Economy=Currency=8 Aug.=Zeus>>E=v.
Hymeneal=4,000=4,000=40%=P4.0D=Government =Creatocracy=4 April=Hermes=G=A4.
Hymn=5,500=5.5=80%=P5.50=Earth-Midway=5 May = Gaia.
Hymnal=5,000=50%=P5.00D=Law=Time=Venus=5 May = Aphrodite>>L=N.
Hype1=6,000=60%=P6.0D=Man=Earth=Royalty=6 June=Gaia=Maia>>M=M2.
Hype2=6,500=7,000=70%=P7.0D=7.0=Language=Assets=Mars=7 July=Pleiades.
Hyper-=6,000=60%=P6.0D=Man=Earth=Royalty=6 June=Gaia=Maia>>M=M2.
Hyperactive=2,000=20%=P2.00D=2.0=Nature=Matter=Moon=2 Feb.=Cupid=N=C+_
Hyperbola=10,000=1,000=100%=10.0=Physicality=Tech.=10 Oct.=Uranus=P=1Ø.
Hyperbole=14,000=14%=P1.40D=1.4=Mgt.=Solar Energy=13 May=Athena=SC=0.1
Hyperbolic=5,000=50%=P5.00D=Law=Time=Venus=5 May = Aphrodite>>L=N.
Hypercritical=3,500=4,000=40%=P4.0D=Govt=Creat.=4 April=Mercury=Hermes=G=A4.
Hyperglycemia=6,500=7,000=70%=P7.0D=7.0=Language=Assets=Mars=7 July=Pleiades.
Hypersensitive=1,000=100%=10.0=1.0=Mind=Sun=1 January=Helios >> M=E4.

Hypersonic=6,000=60%=P6.0D=Man=Earth=Royalty=6 June=Gaia=Maia>>M=M2.
Of or relating to speed equal to or exceeding five times the speed of sound.
Result shows it is a human dimensional perspective measured by the law of five.
6.0*5.0x=px=11+30=41x=px=371=400=40=4.0>> Hermes. Now we confirm that Hermes
operates at a hypersonic speed. Greek myth on Hermes states that He is the only one
who can transverse between the celestial and the terrestrial worlds without hindrance.
He has wings on his shoes and a wide hat on his head with a caduceus in his hand.
Computational results shows us that he can take the form of a wild hawk hence the
representation of wings is hereby proved. The Bible calls the hypersonic the sound of
many rushing waters. Note that as the Christ he literally ascended in a gradual process.
Christ is Hermes.

Hypertension=4,000=40%=P4.0D=Govt=Creatocracy=4 April=Mercury=Hermes=G=A4.
Related to high emotional tension. Lack of power obtained from balance. Emotion >> 6.0.
4.0*6.0x=px=10+24=34x=px=274=300=3.0>>-3.0>> Lack of muse leads to hypertension.
All negative resultants are indicated in the minus (-) sign written or not.

Hypertext=6,000=60%=P6.0D=Man=Earth=Royalty=6 June=Gaia=Maia>>M=M2.
Hyperthyroidism=6,000=60%=P6.0D=Man=Earth=Royalty=6 June=Gaia=Maia>>M=M2.
Hypertrophy=6,000=60%=P6.0D=Man=Earth=Royalty=6 June=Gaia=Maia>>M=M2.
Hyperventilate=6,500=7,000=70%=P7.0D=7.0=Language=Assets=Mars=7 July=Pleiades.
Hyperventilation=7,500=8,000=80%=P8.0D=Economy=Currency=8 Aug.=Zeus>>E=v.
Hyphen=10,000=1,000=100%=10.0=Physicality=Tech.=10 Oct.=Uranus=P=1Ø.
Hyphenate=7,500=8,000=80%=P8.0D=Economy=Currency=8 Aug.=Zeus>>E=v.

Hypnosis=12,500=13,000=13%=P1.30=Solar Core=Faculty=13 January=Athena.
A mind weapon of Athena in mental warfare.

Hypnotic=9,500=10,000=1,000=100%=10.0=Physicality=Tech.=10 Oct.=Uranus=P=1Ø.
Hypnotism=4,000=40%=P4.0D=Govt=Creatocracy=4 April=Mercury=Hermes=G=A4.

Hypnotize=4,500=5,000=50%=P5.00D=Law=Time=Venus=5 May = Aphrodite>>L=N.
Anything that fascinates is a form of positive hypnosis. Such as inventions.

Hypo=2,500=3,000=30%=P3.0D=3.0=Creativity=Stars=Muses=3 March = C=I>>GIL.
Hypo-=2,500=3,000=30%=P3.0D=3.0=Creativity=Stars=Muses=3 March = C=I>>GIL.
Hypoallergenic=5,500=5.5=80%=P5.50=Earth-Midway=5 May = Gaia.
Hypochondria=5,500=5.5=80%=P5.50=Earth-Midway=5 May = Gaia.
Hypocrisy=6,500=7,000=70%=P7.0D=7.0=Language=Assets=Mars=7 July=Pleiades.
Hypocrite=4,000=40%=P4.0D=Govt=Creatocracy=4 April=Mercury=Hermes=G=A4.
Hypodermic=5,500=5.5=80%=P5.50=Earth-Midway=5 May = Gaia.
Hypodermic needle=4,000=40%=P4.0D=Govt=Creat.4 April=Mercury=Hermes=G=A4.

Hypodermic syringe=5,000=50%=P5.00D=Law=Time=Venus=5 May = Aphrodite>>L=N.
Hypoglycemia=7,000=70%=P7.0D=7.0=Language=Assets=Mars=7 July=Pleiades.

Hypotenuse=6,000=60%=P6.0D=Man=Earth=Royalty=6 June=Gaia=Maia>>M=M2.
A math. Evidence that emotion can be calculated. The process called Makumatics, defined as deductions of the inherent faculties of the Mind. A study of the Creative Sciences, Makupedia. See The Oracle: Principles of Creative Sciences by Peter Matthews-Akukalia. Psychoastronomy>> emotion was measured on the application of triangles deduced from the Mind Assessment Tests where crises and stability became known and predictable. The hypotenuse is an attempt by the human mind to rationalize emotion through mathematical means although not apparent to practitioners the essence of what it means.

Hypothalamus=9,500=10,000=1,000=100%=Physicality=Tech.=10 Oct.=Uranus=P=1Ø.
Hypothermia=2,000=20%=P2.00D=2.0=Nature=Matter=Moon=2 Feb.=Cupid=N=C+_
Hypothesis=9,000=90%=P9.00D=9.0=Abstraction=Gods=Saturn=9Sept.>>A=Ø.
Hypothetical=9,000=90%=P9.00D=9.0=Abstraction=Gods=Saturn=9Sept.>>A=Ø.
Hypothyroidism=10,000=1,000=100%=10.0=Physicality=Tech.=10 Oct.=Uranus=P=1Ø.
Hyrax=11,000=11%=P1.10D=1.1=Idea=Brainchild=Inv.=11 Nov.=SC=Athena>>I=MT.

Hyssop=7,000=70%=P7.0D=7.0=Language=Assets=Mars=7 July=Pleiades.
A woody plant, having spikes of small blue flowers and aromatic leaves. Greek, hussōpos. Blue flowers >> love >> Aphroditean effect. Aromatic >> Sweet influences >> Maia and the Pleiades as seen in Job 38:31. King David in the psalms requested GOD to wash him with hyssop so that he will be clean again. The resultants indicate that hyssop is a measurement module developed by the mind and for the mind by which one gains righteousness and free access to the spiritual celestial and the extraordinary. Hyssop is Mind Computing.

Hysterectomy=5,000=50%=P5.00D=Law=Time=Venus=5 May = Aphrodite>>L=N.
Hysteria=10,000=1,000=100%=10.0=Physicality=Tech.=10 Oct.=Uranus=P=1Ø.
Hysteric=9,500=10,000=1,000=100%=10.0=Physicality=Tech.=10 Oct.=Uranus=P=1Ø.
Hysterical=7,000=70%=P7.0D=7.0=Language=Assets=Mars=7 July=Pleiades.
Hz=500=5%=P5.00D=5.0=Law=Time=Venus=5 May=Aphrodite>>L=N.

Chapter:-HUMAN ENERGY DATABASE ON THE DATE OF BIRTH:
MONTH: JANUARY.
Day 1:Value: 5.0, Planetary Type: Venus, Human Type:Law. Birth Energy Level: 83.3%.
Day 2:Value: 1.1, Planetary Type: Neptune, Human Type: Philos,Birth Energy Level: 20.0%
Day 3:Value: 2.0, Planetary Type: Moon, Human Type: Marine, Birth Energy Level: 33.3%.
Day 4:Value: 3.0, Planetary Type: Star, Human Type: Creativity, Birth Energy Level: 50.0%
Day 5:Value: 4.1, Planetary Type: Mercury, Human Type: Politics, Birth Energy Level: 70.0%
Day 6:Value: 6.0, Planetary Type: Earth, Human Type: Health, Birth Energy Level: 100%.
Day 7:Value: 7.1, Planetary Type: Mars, Human Type: Consulting, Birth Energy Level: 100%+
Day 8:Value: 9.0, Planetary Type: Saturn, Human Type: ICT, Birth Energy Level: 100%+

Day 9:Value: 1.1, Planetary Type: Neptune, Human Type: Philos, Birth Energy Level: 20%

Day 10:Value: 1.3, Planetary Type: Sun, Human Type: Energy, Birth Energy Level: 22%.

Day 11: Value: 2.0, Planetary Type: Moon, Human Type: Marine, Birth Energy Level: 33.3%

Day 12:Value: 2.0, Planetary Type: Moon, Human Type: Marine, Birth Energy Level: 33.3%

Day 13:Value: 2.1, Planetary Type: Moon, Human Type: Marine, Birth Energy Level: 40%

Day 14:Value: 2.4, Planetary Type: Moon, Human Type: Marine, Birth Energy Level: 40%

Day 15:Value: 3.0, Planetary Type: Star, Human Type: Creativity, Birth Energy Level: 50%

Day 16:Value: 3.1, Planetary Type: Star, Human Type: Creativity, Birth Energy Level: 52%

Day 17:Value: 3.4, Planetary Type: Star, Human Type: Creativity, Birth Energy Level: 60%

Day 18:Value: 4.0, Planetary Type: Mercury, Human Type: Politics, Birth Energy Level: 70%

Day 19:Value: 4.2, Planetary Type: Mercury, Human Type: Politics, Birth Energy Level: 70%

Day 20:Value: 5.0,Planetary Type:Venus,Human Type:Law. Birth Energy Level: 83.3%

Day 21:Value: 5.1, Planetary Type: Venus, Human Type:Security, Birth Energy Level: 90%

Day 22:Value: 6.0, Planetary Type: Earth, Human Type: Health, Birth Energy Level: 100%

Day 23:Value: 6.0, Planetary Type: Earth, Human Type: Health, Birth Energy Level: 100%

Day 24:Value: 7.0, Planetary Type:Mars, Human Type:Consulting,Birth Energy Level: 100%+

Day 25: Value: 7.0,Planetary Type: Mars, Human Type: Consult,Birth Energy Level: 100%+

Day 26:Value: 8.0, Planetary TypeJupiter, Human Type:Business,Birth Energy Level: 100%+

Day 27:Value:8.1Planetary Type:Jupiter, Human Type:Economist,Birth Energy Level 100%+

Day 28:Value: 9.0, Planetary Type: Saturn, Human Type: ICT, Birth Energy Level: 100%+

Day 29:Value:9.3Planetary Type:Saturn,HumanType:Programmer,Birth Energy Level:100%+

Day 30:Value: 10.0,Planetary Type:Uranus,Human Type: Tech, Birth Energy Level: 100%

Day 31:Value: 1.1, Planetary Type: Neptune, Human Type: Phi.Birth Energy Level: 20.0%

==

MONTH:FEBRUARY

Day 1:Value: 1.1, Planetary Type: Neptune, Human Type:Philos., Birth Energy Level: 20.0%

Day 2:Value: 2.4, Planetary Type: Moon, Human Type: Marine, Birth Energy Level: 40.0%

Day 3:Value: 4.1, Planetary Type: Mercury, Human Type: Politics, Birth Energy Level:70.0%

Day 4:Value: 6.2, Planetary Type: Earth, Human Type:Health Birth Energy Level:100%

Day 5:Value: 9.0, Planetary Type: Saturn, Human Type: ICT, Birth Energy Level: 100.0%

Day 6:Value: 1.2, Planetary Type: Pluto, Human Type:Education, Birth Energy Level:20%

Day 7:Value:2.0, Planetary Type: Moon, Human Type: Marine, Birth Energy Level:33.3%

Day 8:Value: 2.0, Planetary Type:Moon, Human Type:Marine, Birth Energy Level:33.3%

Day 9:Value:2.3, Planetary Type: Moon, Human Type:Marine, Birth Energy Level:40.0%

Day 10:Value: 3.0, Planetary Type:Star, Human Type:Creativity, Birth Energy Level:50.0%

Day 11: Value:3.2, Planetary Type:Star, Human Type:Creativity, Birth Energy Level:53.3%

Day 12:Value: 4.0, Planetary Type:Mercury, Human Type:Politics, Birth Energy Level:70.0%

Day 13:Value:4.3, Planetary Type: Mercury, Human Type:Politics, Birth Energy Level: 72.2%

Day 14:Value: 5.0, Planetary Type:Venus, Human Type:Law, Birth Energy Level:83.3%

Day 15:Value: 6.0, Planetary Type:Earth, Human Type:Health, Birth Energy Level:100%

Day 16:Value: 6.3, Planetary Type:Earth, Human Type:Health, Birth Energy Level:100%

Day 17:Value:7.0, Planetary Type:Mars, Human Type:Consulting, Birth Energy Level:100%+

Day 18:Value:8.0, Planetary Type:Jupiter, Human Type:Business, Birth Energy Level:100%+

Day 19:Value:9.0, Planetary Type:Saturn,Human Type:ICT, Birth Energy Level: 100%+

Day 20:Value:9.4, Planetary Type:Saturn, Human Type: ICT, Birth Energy Level:100%+
Day 21:Value: 1.0, Planetary Type:Sun, Human Type:Energy, Birth Energy Level:20.0%
Day 22:Value:1.1, Planetary Type:Neptune,Human Type:Philo., Birth Energy Level:20.0%.
Day 23:Value:1.2, Planetary Type:Pluto, Human Type:Education, Birth Energy Level:20.0%
Day 24:Value: 1.3, Planetary Type:Comet, Human Type:R&D, Birth Energy Level:22.0%
Day 25: Value: 1.4, Planetary Type:Comet, Human Type:R&D, Birth Energy Level:23.3%
Day 26:Value: 2.0, Planetary Type:Moon, Human Type:Marine, Birth Energy Level:33.3%
Day 27:Value:2.0, Planetary Type: Moon, Human Type:Marine, Birth Energy Level: 33.3%
Day 28:Value: 2.0, Planetary Type:Moon, Human Type:Marine, Birth Energy Level:33.3%
Day 29:Value:2.0, Planetary Type:Moon, Human Type: Marine, Birth Energy Level:33.3%
==
MONTH:MARCH
Day 1:Value:2.0, Planetary Type:Moon, Human Type: Marine, Birth Energy Level:33.3%
Day 2:Value:4.1, Planetary Type:Mercury, Human Type:Politics, Birth Energy Level:70.0%
Day 3:Value:7.0, Planetary Type:Mars, Human Type:Consulting, Birth Energy Level:100.0%
Day 4:Value:1.0, Planetary Type:Sun, Human Type:Energy, Birth Energy Level:20.0%
Day 5:Value:1.4, Planetary Type:Comet, Human Type:R&D, Birth Energy Level:23.3%
Day 6:Value:2.0, Planetary Type:Moon, Human Type:Marine, Birth Energy Level:33.3%
Day 7:Value:2.4, Planetary Type: Moon, Human Type: Marine, Birth Energy Level:40.0%
Day 8:Value:3.0, Planetary Type:Star, Human Type:Creativity, Birth Energy Level:50.0%
Day 9:Value:4.0, Planetary Type: Mercury, Human Type:Politics, Birth Energy Level:70.0%
Day 10:Value:4.3, Planetary Type:Mercury, Human Type:Politics, Birth Energy Level:72.2%
Day 11: Value:5.1, Planetary Type:Venus, Human Type:Security, Birth Energy Level:90.0%
Day 12:Value:6.0, Planetary Type:Earth, Human Type:Health, Birth Energy Level:100.0%
Day 13:Value:7.0, Planetary Type:Mars, Human Type:Consulting, Birth Energy Level:100%
Day 14:Value:8.0, Planetary Type:Jupiter, Human Type:Business, Birth Energy Level:100%+
Day 15:Value:9.0, Planetary Type:Saturn, Human Type:ICT, Birth Energy Level:100%+
Day 16:Value:10.0, Planetary Type:Uranus, Human Type:Tech.Birth Energy Level:100%+
Day 17:Value:1.1, Planetary Type:Neptune, Human Type:Philos., Birth Energy Level:20.0%
Day 18:Value:1.2, Planetary Type:Pluto, Human Type:Education, Birth Energy Level:20.0%
Day 19:Value:1.3, Planetary Type:Comet, Human Type:R&D, Birth Energy Level:22.0%
Day 20:Value:2.0, Planetary Type:Moon, Human Type:Marine, Birth Energy Level:33.3%
Day 21:Value: 2.0, Planetary Type:Moon, Human Type:Marine, Birth Energy Level:33.3%
Day 22:Value:2.0, Planetary Type:Moon, Human Type:Marine, Birth Energy Level:33.3%
Day 23:Value:2.0, Planetary Type:Moon, Human Type:Marine, Birth Energy Level:33.3%
Day 24:Value:2.0, Planetary Type:Moon, Human Type:Marine, Birth Energy Level:33.3%
Day 25: Value:2.2, Planetary Type:Moon Human Type: Marine, Birth Energy Level:40.0%
Day 26:Value:2.4, Planetary Type:Moon, Human Type:Marine, Birth Energy Level:40.0%
Day 27:Value:3.0, Planetary Type:Star, Human Type:Creativity, Birth Energy Level:50.0%
Day 28:Value:3.0, Planetary Type:Star, Human Type:Creativity, Birth Energy Level:50.0%
Day 29:Value:3.0, Planetary Type:Star, Human Type:Creativity, Birth Energy Level:50.0%
Day 30: Value:3.1, Planetary Type:Star, Human Type:Creativity, Birth Energy Level:52.0%
Day 31: Value:3.3, Planetary Type:Star, Human Type:Creativity, Birth Energy Level:60.0%
==

MONTH:APRIL

Day 1:Value:3.0, Planetary Type:Star, Human Type:Creativity, Birth Energy Level:50.0%
Day 2:Value:6.2, Planetary Type:Earth, Human Type:Health, Birth Energy Level:100%+
Day 3:Value:1.0, Planetary Type:Sun, Human Type:Energy, Birth Energy Level:20.0%
Day 4:Value:2.0,Planetary Type:Moon, Human Type:Marine,Birth Energy Level:33.3%
Day 5:Value:2.1, Planetary Type:Moon, Human Type:Marine, Birth Energy Level:40.0%
Day 6:Value:3.0, Planetary Type:Star, Human Type:Creativity, Birth Energy Level:50.0%
Day 7:Value:4.0, Planetary Type:Mercury, Human Type:Politics, Birth Energy Level:70.0%
Day 8:Value:4.3, Planetary Type:Mercury,Human Type:Politics, Birth Energy Level:72.2%
Day 9:Value:5.2, Planetary Type:Venus, Human Type:Security, Birth Energy Level:90.0%+
Day 10:Value:6.1, Planetary Type:Earth, Human Type:Health, Birth Energy Level:100%+
Day 11:Value:7.2, Planetary Type:Mars, Human Type:Consulting, Birth Energy Level:100%+
Day 12:Value:8.3, Planetary Type:Jupiter, Human Type:Business, Birth Energy Level:100%+
Day 13:Value:10.0,Planetary Type:Uranus,Human Type:Tech, Birth Energy Level:100%+
Day 14:Value:1.1, Planetary Type:Neptune, Human Type:Philoso, Birth Energy Level:20.0%
Day 15:Value:1.2, Planetary Type:Pluto, Human Type:Education, Birth Energy Level:20.0%
Day 16:Value:1.4, Planetary Type:Comet, Human Type:R&D, Birth Energy Level:23.3%
Day 17:Value:2.0, Planetary Type:Moon, Human Type:Marine, Birth Energy Level:33.3%
Day 18:Value:2.0, Planetary Type:Moon, Human Type:Marine, Birth Energy Level:33.3%
Day 19:Value:2.0, Planetary Type:Moon, Human Type:Marine, Birth Energy Level:33.3%
Day 20:Value:2.0, Planetary Type:Moon, Human Type:Marine, Birth Energy Level:33.3%
Day 21:Value:2.2, Planetary Type:Moon, Human Type:Marine, Birth Energy Level:40.0%
Day 22:Value:2.4 Planetary Type:Moon, Human Type:Marine, Birth Energy Level:40.0%
Day 23:Value:3.0, Planetary Type:Star, Human Type:Creativity, Birth Energy Level:50.0%
Day 24:Value:3.0, Planetary Type:Star, Human Type:Creativity,Birth Energy Level:50.0%
Day 25: Value:3.0, Planetary Type:Star, Human Type: Creativity, Birth Energy Level:50.0%
Day 26:Value:3.3, Planetary Type:Star, Human Type:Creativity, Birth Energy Level:60.0%
Day 27:Value:4.0, Planetary Type:Mercury, Human Type:Politics, Birth Energy Level:70.0%
Day 28:Value: 4.0, Planetary Type:Mercury, Human Type:Politics, Birth Energy Level:70.0%
Day 29:Value:4.0, Planetary Type:Mercury, Human Type:Politics, Birth Energy Level:70.0%
Day 30: Value:4.2, Planetary Type:Mercury, Human Type:Politics, Birth Energy Level: 70.0%

==

MONTH: MAY

Day 1:Value:4.1, Planetary Type:Mercury, Human Type:Politics, Birth Level:70.0%=Maia
Day 2:Value:9.0, Planetary Type:Saturn, Human Type:ICT, Birth Energy Level:100%
Day 3:Value:1.4, Planetary Type:Comet, Human Type:R&D, Birth Energy Level:23.3%
Day 4:Value:2.1, Planetary Type:Moon, Human Type:Marine, Birth Energy Level:40.0%
Day 5:Value:3.0, Planetary Type:Star, Human Type:Creativity, Birth Energy Level:50.0%
Day 6:Value:4.0, Planetary Type:Mercury, Human Type:Politics, Birth Energy Level:70.0%
Day 7:Value:5.0, Planetary Type:Venus, Human Type:Law, Birth Energy Level:83.3%
Day 8:Value:6.0, Planetary Type:Earth, Human Type:Health, Birth Energy Level:100%
Day 9:Value:7.0, Planetary Type:Mars, Human Type:Consulting, Birth Energy Level:100%+
Day 10:Value:8.2, Planetary Type:Jupiter, Human Type:Business, Birth Energy Level:100%+
Day 11: Value:1.1, Planetary Type:Neptune, Human Type:Philos, Birth Energy Level:20.0%
Day 12:Value: 4.0, Planetary Type:Mercury, Human Type:Politics, Birth Energy Level:70.0%

Day 13:Value:1.3, Planetary Type:Comet, Human Type:R&D, Birth Energy Level:22.0%
Day 14:Value:1.4, Planetary Type:Comet, Human Type:R&D, Birth Energy Level:23.3%
Day 15:Value:2.0, Planetary Type: Moon, Human Type:Marine, Birth Level:33.3%=Maia
Day 16:Value:2.0, Planetary Type:Moon, Human Type:Marine, Birth Energy Level:33.3%
Day 17:Value:2.0, Planetary Type:Moon, Human Type:Marine, Birth Energy Level:33.3%
Day 18:Value:2.2, Planetary Type:Moon, Human Type:Marine, Birth Energy Level:40.0%
Day 19:Value:2.4, Planetary Type:Moon, Human Type:Marine, Birth Energy Level:40.0%
Day 20:Value:3.0, Planetary Type:Star, Human Type:Creativity, Birth Energy Level:50.0%
Day 21:Value:3.0, Planetary Type:Star, Human Type:Creativity, Birth Energy Level:50.0%
Day 22:Value:3.1, Planetary Type: Star, Human Type:Creativity, Birth Energy Level:52.0%
Day 23:Value:3.4, Planetary Type:Star, Human Type:Creativity, Birth Energy Level:60.0%
Day 24:Value:4.0, Planetary Type:Mercury, Human Type:Politics, Birth Energy Level:70.0%
Day 25:Value:4.0, Planetary Type:Mercury, Human Type:Politics, Birth Energy Level:70.0%
Day 26:Value:4.2, Planetary Type:Mercury, Human Type:Politics, Birth Energy Level:83.3%
Day 27:Value:5.0, Planetary Type:Venus, Human Type:Law, Birth Energy Level:83.3%
Day 28:Value:5.0, Planetary Type:Venus, Human Type:Law, Birth Energy Level:90.0%
Day 29:Value:5.2, Planetary Type:Venus, Human Type:Security, Birth Energy Level:90.0%
Day 30:Value:5.4, Planetary Type:Venus, Human Type:Law, Birth Energy Level:90.0%
Day 31:Value:6.0, Planetary Type:Earth, Human Type:Health, Birth Energy Level:100%
===
MONTH:JUNE.
Day 1:Value:6.0 Planetary Type:Earth, Human Type:Health, Birth Energy Level:100%
Day 2:Value:1.2, Planetary Type:Pluto Human Type:Education Birth Energy Level:20.0%
Day 3:Value:2.0 Planetary Type:Moon Human Type:Marine Birth Energy Level:33.3%
Day 4:Value:3.0 Planetary Type:Star Human Type:Creativity Birth Energy Level:50.0%
Day 5:Value:4.0 Planetary Type:Mercury Human Type:Politics Birth Energy Level:70.0%
Day 6:Value:5.0!Planetary Type:Venus Human Type:Law Birth Energy Level:83.3%
Day 7:Value:6.0 Planetary Type:Earth Human Type:Health Birth Energy Level:100%
Day 8:Value:7.3 Planetary Type:Mars Human Type:Consulting Birth Energy Level:100+
Day 9:Value:9.0 Planetary Type:Saturn Human Type:ICT Birth Energy Level:100%+
Day 10:Value:1.0 Planetary Type:Sun Human Type:Energy Birth Energy Level:20.0%
Day 11:Value:1.2 Planetary Type:Pluto Human Type:Education Birth Energy Level:20.0%
Day 12:Value:1.4 Planetary Type:Comet Human Type:R&D Birth Energy Level:23.3%
Day 13:Value:2.0 Planetary Type:Moon Human Type:Marine Birth Energy Level:33.3%
Day 14:Value:2.0 Planetary Type:Moon Human Type:Marine Birth Energy Level:33.3%
Day 15:Value:2.0 Planetary Type:Moon Human Type:Marine Birth Energy Level:33.3%
Day 16:Value:2.2 Planetary Type:Moon Human Type:R&D, Birth Energy Level:40.0%
Day 17:Value:3.0 Planetary Type:Star Human Type:Creativity Birth Energy Level:50.0%
Day 18:Value:3.0 Planetary Type:Star Human Type:Creativity Birth Energy Level:33.3%
Day 19:Value:3.0 Planetary Type:Star Human Type:Creativity Birth Energy Level:50.0%
Day 20:Value:3.3 Planetary Type:Star Human Type:Creativity Birth Energy Level:60.0%
Day 21:Value:4.0 Planetary Type:Mercury Human Type:Politics Birth Energy Level:70.0%
Day 22:Value:4.0 Planetary Type:Mercury Human Type:Politics Birth Energy Level:70.0%
Day 23:Value:4.2 Planetary Type:Mercury Human Type:Politics Birth Energy Level:70.0%
Day 24:Value:5.0 Planetary Type:Venus Human Type:Law Birth Energy Level:83.3%

Day 25: Value:5.0 Planetary Type:Venus Human Type:Law Birth Energy Level:83.3%
Day 26:Value:5.2 Planetary Type:Venus Human Type:Security Birth Energy Level:90.0%
Day 27:Value:6.0 Planetary Type:Earth Human Type:Health Birth Energy Level:100%
Day 28:Value:6.0 Planetary Type:Earth Human Type:Health Birth Energy Level:100%
Day 29:Value:6.3 Planetary Type:Earth Human Type:Health Birth Energy Level:100%+
Day 30: Value:7.0 Planetary Type:Mars Human Type:Consulting Birth Energy Level:100%+

==

MONTH:JULY
Day 1:Value:7.1 Planetary Type:Mars Human Type:Consulting Birth Energy Level:100%+
Day 2:Value:2.0 Planetary Type:Moon Human Type:Marine Birth Energy Level:33.3%
Day 3:Value:2.4 Planetary Type:Moon Human Type:Marine Birth Energy Level:40.0%
Day 4:Value:4.0 Planetary Type:Mercury Human Type:Politics Birth Energy Level:70.0%
Day 5:Value:5.0 Planetary Type:Venus Human Type:Law Birth Energy Level:83.3%
Day 6:Value:6.0 Planetary Type:Earth Human Type: Health Birth Energy Level:100%
Day 7:Value:8.0 Planetary Type:Jupiter Human Type:Business Birth Energy Level:100%+
Day 8:Value:9.1 Planetary Type:Saturn Human Type:ICT Birth Energy Level:100%+
Day 9:Value:1.1 Planetary Type:Neptune Human Type:Philosophy Birth Energy Level:20.0%
Day 10:Value:1.3 Planetary Type:Comet Human Type:R&D Birth Energy Level:22.0%
Day 11:Value:2.0 Planetary Type:Moon Human Type:Marine Birth Energy Level:33.3%
Day 12:Value:2.0 Planetary Type:Moon Human Type:Marine Birth Energy Level:33.3%
Day 13:Value:2.0 Planetary Type:Moon Human Type:Marine Birth Energy Level:33.3%
Day 14:Value:2.2 Planetary Type:Moon Human Type: Marine Birth Energy Level:40.0%
Day 15:Value:2.4 Planetary Type: Moon Human Type:Marine Birth Energy Level:40.0%
Day 16:Value:3.0 Planetary Type:Star Human Type:Creativity Birth Energy Level:50.0%
Day 17:Value:3.0 Planetary Type:Star Human Type:Creativity Birth Energy Level:50.0%
Day 18:Value:3.3 Planetary Type:Star Human Type:Creativity Birth Energy Level:60.0%
Day 19:Value:4.0 Planetary Type:Mercury Human Type:Politics Birth Energy Level:70.0%
Day 20:Value:4.0 Planetary Type:Mercury Human Type:Politics Birth Energy Level:70.0%
Day 21:Value:4.3 Planetary Type:Mercury Human Type:Politics Birth Energy Level:72.2%
Day 22:Value:5.0 Planetary Type:Venus Human Type:Law Birth Energy Level:83.3%
Day 23:Value:5.0 Planetary Type:Venus Human Type:Law Birth Energy Level:83.3%
Day 24:Value:5.4 Planetary Type:Venus Human Type:Security Birth Energy Level:90.0%
Day 25: Value:6.0 Planetary Type:Earth Human Type:Health Birth Energy Level:100%
Day 26:Value:6.2 Planetary Type:Earth Human Type:Health Birth Energy Level:100%+
Day 27:Value:7.0 Planetary Type:Mars Human Type:Consulting Birth Energy Level:100%+
Day 28:Value:7.1 Planetary Type:Mars Human Type:Consulting Birth Energy Level:100%+
Day 29:Value:8.0 Planetary Type:Jupiter Human Type:Business Birth Energy Level:100%+
Day 30: Value:8.0 Planetary Type:Jupiter Human Type:Business Birth Energy Level:100%+
Day 31: Value:9.0 Planetary Type:Saturn Human Type:ICT Birth Energy Level:100%+

==

MONTH:AUGUST
Day 1:Value:9.0 Planetary Type:Saturn Human Type:ICT Birth Energy Level:100%
Day 2:Value:2.0 Planetary Type:Moon Human Type:Marine Birth Energy Level:33.3%
Day 3:Value:3.0 Planetary Type:Star Human Type:Creativity Birth Energy Level:50.0%
Day 4:Value:4.3 Planetary Type:Mercury Human Type:Politics Birth Energy Level:72.0%

Day 5:Value:6.0 Planetary Type:Earth Human Type:Health Birth Energy Level:100%
Day 6:Value:7.3 Planetary Type:Mars Human Type:Consulting Birth Energy Level:100%+
Day 7:Value:9.1 Planetary Type:Saturn Human Type: ICT Birth Energy Level:100%+
Day 8:Value:1.1 Planetary Type:Neptune Human Type:Philosophy Birth Energy Level:20.0%
Day 9:Value:1.3 Planetary Type:Comet Human Type:R&D Birth Energy Level:22.0%
Day 10:Value:2.0 Planetary Type:Moon Human Type:Marine Birth Energy Level:33.3%
Day 11:Value:2.0 Planetary Type:Moon Human Type:Marine Birth Energy Level:33.3%
Day 12:Value:2.0 Planetary Type:Moon Human Type:Marine Birth Energy Level:33.3%
Day 13:Value:2.3 Planetary Type:Moon Human Type:Marine Birth Energy Level:40.0%
Day 14:Value:3.0 Planetary Type:Star Human Type:Creativity Birth Energy Level:50.0%
Day 15:Value:3.0 Planetary Type:Star Human Type:Creativity Birth Energy Level:50.0%
Day 16:Value:3.2 Planetary Type:Star Human Type:Creativity Birth Energy Level:53.3%
Day 17:Value:4.0 Planetary Type:Mercury Human Type:Politics Birth Energy Level:70.0%
Day 18:Value:4.0 Planetary Type:Mercury Human Type:Politics Birth Energy Level:70.0%
Day 19:Value:4.3 Planetary Type:Mercury Human Type:Politics Birth Energy Level:72.0%
Day 20:Value:5.0 Planetary Type:Venus Human Type:Law Birth Energy Level:83.3%
Day 21:Value:5.1 Planetary Type:Venus Human Type:Security Birth Energy Level:83.3%
Day 22:Value:6.0 Planetary Type:Earth Human Type:Health Birth Energy Level:100%
Day 23:Value:6.0 Planetary Type:Earth Human Type:Health Birth Energy Level:100%
Day 24:Value:6.1 Planetary Type:Earth Human Type:Health Birth Energy Level:100%
Day 25: Value:7.0 Planetary Type:Mars Human Type:Consulting Birth Energy Level:100%+
Day 26:Value:7.3 Planetary Type:Mars Human Type:Consulting Birth Energy Level:100%+
Day 27:Value:8.0 Planetary Type:Jupiter Human Type:Business Birth Energy Level:100%+
Day 28:Value:8.3 Planetary Type:Jupiter Human Type:Business Birth Energy Level:100%+
Day 29:Value:9.0 Planetary Type:Saturn Human Type:ICT Birth Energy Level:100%+
Day 30: Value:9.4 Planetary Type:Saturn Human Type: ICT Birth Energy Level:100%+
Day 31: Value:10.0 Planetary Type:Uranus Human Type:Tech. Birth Energy Level:100%+
==
MONTH:SEPTEMBER
Day 1:Value:1.1 Planetary Type:Neptune Human Type:Philosophy Birth Energy Level:20.0%
Day 2:Value:2.3 Planetary Type:Moon Human Type:Marine Birth Energy Level:40.0%
Day 3:Value:4.0 Planetary Type:Mercury Human Type:Politics Birth Energy Level:70.0%
Day 4:Value:5.2 Planetary Type:Venus Human Type:Security Birth Energy Level:90.0%
Day 5:Value:7.0 Planetary Type:Mars Human Type:Consulting Birth Energy Level:100%
Day 6:Value:9.0 Planetary Type:Saturn Human Type:ICT Birth Energy Level:100%
Day 7:Value:1.1 Planetary Type:Neptune Human Type:Philosophy Birth Energy Level:20.0%
Day 8:Value:1.3 Planetary Type:Comet Human Type:R&D Birth Energy Level:22.0%
Day 9:Value:2.0 Planetary Type:Moon Human Type:Marine Birth Energy Level:33.3%
Day 10:Value:2.0 Planetary Type:Moon Human Type:Marine Birth Energy Level:33.3%
Day 11:Value:2.1 Planetary Type:Moon Human Type:Marine Birth Energy Level:40.0%
Day 12:Value:2.4 Planetary Type:Moon Human Type:Marine Birth Energy Level:40.0%
Day 13:Value:3.0 Planetary Type:Star Human Type:Creativity Birth Energy Level:50.0%
Day 14:Value:3.1 Planetary Type:Star Human Type:Creativity Birth Energy Level:52.0%
Day 15:Value:3.4 Planetary Type: Star Human Type:Creativity Birth Energy Level:60.0%
Day 16:Value:4.0 Planetary Type:Mercury Human Type:Politics Birth Energy Level:70.0%

PETER K. MATTHEWS - AKUKALIA

Day 17:Value:4.2 Planetary Type:Mercury Human Type:Politics Birth Energy Level:70.0%
Day 18:Value:5.0 Planetary Type:Venus Human Type:Law Birth Energy Level:83.3%
Day 19:Value:5.0 Planetary Type:Venus Human Type:Law Birth Energy Level:83.3%
Day 20:Value:5.4 Planetary Type:Venus Human Type:Security Birth Energy Level:90.0%
Day 21:Value:6.0 Planetary Type:Earth Human Type:Health Birth Energy Level:100%
Day 22:Value:6.4 Planetary Type:Earth Human Type:Health Birth Energy Level:100%+
Day 23:Value:7.0 Planetary Type:Mars Human Type:Consulting Birth Energy Level:100%+
Day 24:Value:7.4 Planetary Type:Mars Human Type:Consulting Birth Energy Level:100%+
Day 25: Value:8.0 Planetary Type:Jupiter Human Type:Business Birth Energy Level:100%+
Day 26:Value:9.0 Planetary Type:Saturn Human Type:ICT Birth Energy Level:100%+
Day 27:Value:9.0 Planetary Type:Saturn Human Type:ICT Birth Energy Level:100%+
Day 28:Value:10.0 Planetary Type:Uranus Human Type:Tech Birth Energy Level:100%+
Day 29:Value:1.0 Planetary Type:Sun Human Type:Energy Birth Energy Level:20.0%
Day 30: Value:1.1 Planetary Type:Neptune Human Type:Philos. Birth Energy Level:20.0%
===
MONTH:OCTOBER
Day 1:Value:1.3 Planetary Type:Comet Human Type:R&D Birth Energy Level:22.0%
Day 2:Value:3.0 Planetary Type:Star Human Type:Creativity Birth Energy Level:50.0%
Day 3:Value:4.3 Planetary Type:Mercury Human Type:Politics Birth Energy Level:72.2%
Day 4:Value:6.1 Planetary Type:Earth Human Type:Health Birth Energy Level:100%
Day 5:Value:8.2 Planetary Type:Jupiter Human Type:Business Birth Energy Level:100%+
Day 6:Value:1.0 Planetary Type:Sun Human Type:Energy Birth Energy Level:20.0%
Day 7:Value:1.3 Planetary Type:Comet Human Type:R&D Birth Energy Level:22.0%
Day 8:Value:2.0 Planetary Type:Moon Human Type:Marine Birth Energy Level:33.3%
Day 9:Value:2.0 Planetary Type:Moon Human Type:Marine Birth Energy Level:33.3%
Day 10:Value:2.1 Planetary Type:Moon Human Type:Marine Birth Energy Level:40.0%
Day 11:Value:2.4 Planetary Type:Moon Human Type:Marine Birth Energy Level:40.0%
Day 12:Value:3.1 Planetary Type:Star Human Type:Creativity Birth Energy Level:52.0%
Day 13:Value:2.0 Planetary Type:Moon Human Type:Marine Birth Energy Level:33.3%
Day 14:Value:4.0 Planetary Type:Mercury Human Type:Politics Birth Energy Level:70.0%
Day 15: Value:4.0 Planetary Type:Mercury Human Type:Politics Birth Energy Level:70.0%
Day 16:Value:4.4 Planetary Type:Mercury Human Type:Politics Birth Energy Level:73.3%
Day 17:Value:5.0 Planetary Type:Venus Human Type:Law Birth Energy Level:83.3%
Day 18:Value:5.3 Planetary Type:Venus Human Type:Security Birth Energy Level:90.0%
Day 19:Value:6.0 Planetary Type:Earth Human Type:Health Birth Energy Level:100%
Day 20:Value:6.2 Planetary Type:Earth Human Type:Health Birth Energy Level:100%+
Day 21:Value:7.0 Planetary Type:Mars Human Type:Consulting Birth Energy Level:100%+
Day 22:Value:7.3 Planetary Type:Mars Human Type:Consulting Birth Energy Level:100%+
Day 23:Value:8.0 Planetary Type:Jupiter Human Type:Business Birth Energy Level:100%+
Day 24:Value:8.4 Planetary Type:Jupiter Human Type:Business Birth Energy Level:100%+
Day 25: Value:9.0 Planetary Type:Saturn Human Type:ICT Birth Energy Level:100%+
Day 26:Value:10.0 Planetary Type:Uranus Human Type:Techn Birth Energy Level:100%+
Day 27:Value:1.0 Planetary Type:Sun Human Type:Energy Birth Energy Level:20.0%
Day 28:Value:1.1 Planetary Type:Neptune Human Type:Philo Birth Energy Level:20.0%
Day 29:Value:1.2 Planetary Type:Pluto Human Type:Education Birth Energy Level:20.0%

Day 30: Value:1.2 Planetary Type:Pluto Human Type:Education Birth Energy Level:20.0%
Day 31: Value:1.3 Planetary Type:Comet Human Type:R&D Birth Energy Level:22.0%
==
MONTH:NOVEMBER
Day 1:Value:2.0 Planetary Type:Moon Human Type:Marine Birth Energy Level:33.3%
Day 2:Value:3.2 Planetary Type:Star Human Type:Creativity Birth Energy Level:53.3%
Day 3:Value:5.1 Planetary Type:Venus Human Type:Security Birth Energy Level:90.0%
Day 4:Value:7.2 Planetary Type:Mars Human Type:Consulting Birth Energy Level:100%+
Day 5:Value:10.0 Planetary Type:Uranus Human Type:Tech Birth Energy Level:100%+
Day 6:Value:1.2 Planetary Type:Pluto Human Type:Education Birth Energy Level:20.0%
Day 7:Value:2.0 Planetary Type:Moon Human Type:Marine Birth Energy Level:33.3%
Day 8:Value:2.0 Planetary Type:Moon Human Type:Marine Birth Energy Level:33.3%
Day 9:Value:2.1 Planetary Type:Moon Human Type:Marine Birth Energy Level:40.0%
Day 10:Value:2.4 Planetary Type:Moon Human Type:Marine Birth Energy Level:40.0%
Day 11:Value:3.0 Planetary Type:Star Human Type:Creativity Birth Energy Level:50.0%
Day 12:Value:3.2 Planetary Type:Star Human Type:Creativity Birth Energy Level:53.3%
Day 13:Value:4.0 Planetary Type:Mercury Human Type:Politics Birth Energy Level:70.0%
Day 14:Value:4.0 Planetary Type:Mercury Human Type:Politics Birth Energy Level:70.0%
Day 15:Value:5.0 Planetary Type:Venus Human Type:Law Birth Energy Level:83.3%
Day 16:Value:5.0 Planetary Type:Venus Human Type:Law Birth Energy Level:83.3%
Day 17: Value:6.0 Planetary Type:Earth Human Type:Health Birth Energy Level:100%
Day 18: Value:6.0 Planetary Type:Earth Human Type:Health Birth Energy Level:100%
Day 19:Value:7.0 Planetary Type:Mars Human Type:Consulting Birth Energy Level:100%+
Day 20:Value:7.1 Planetary Type:Mars Human Type:Consulting Birth Energy Level:100%+
Day 21:Value:8.0 Planetary Type:Jupiter Human Type:Business Birth Energy Level:100%+
Day 22:Value:8.3 Planetary Type:Jupiter Human Type:Business Birth Energy Level:100%+
Day 23:Value:9.0 Planetary Type:Saturn Human Type:ICT Birth Energy Level:100%+
Day 24:Value:10.0 Planetary Type:Uranus Human Type:Tech Birth Energy Level:100%+
Day 25: Value:1.0 Planetary Type:Sun Human Type:Energy Birth Energy Level:20.0%
Day 26:Value:1.1 Planetary Type:Neptune Human Type:Philo Birth Energy Level:20.0%
Day 27:Value:1.2 Planetary Type:Pluto Human Type:Education Birth Energy Level:20.0%
Day 28:Value:1.2 Planetary Type:Pluto Human Type:Education Birth Energy Level:20.0%
Day 29:Value:1.3 Planetary Type:Comet Human Type:R&D Birth Energy Level:22.0%
Day 30:Value:1.4, Planetary Type:Comet=Human Type:R&D, Birth Level:23.3%=Hecate.
==
MONTH:DECEMBER
Day 1:Value:2.0 Planetary Type:Moon Human Type:Marine Birth Energy Level:33.3%
Day 2:Value:4.0 Planetary Type:Mercury Human Type:Politics Birth Energy Level:70.0%
Day 3:Value:6.0 Planetary Type:Earth Human Type: Health Birth Energy Level:100%
Day 4:Value:8.3 Planetary Type:Jupiter Human Type:Business Birth Energy Level:100%+
Day 5:Value:1.1 Planetary Type:Neptune Human Type:Philosophy Birth Energy Level:20.0%
Day 6:Value:1.4, Planetary Type:Comet, Human Type:R&D, Birth Energy Level:23.3%
Day 7:Value:2.0 Planetary Type:Moon Human Type:Marine Birth Energy Level:33.3%
Day 8:Value:2.0 Planetary Type:Moon Human Type:Marine Birth Energy Level:33.3%
Day 9:Value:2.4 Planetary Type: Moon Human Type:Marine Birth Energy Level:40.0%

Day 10:Value:3.0 Planetary Type:Star Human Type:Creativity Birth Energy Level:50.0%
Day 11:Value:3.2 Planetary Type:Star Human Type:Creativity Birth Energy Level:53.3%
Day 12:Value:4.0 Planetary Type:Mercury Human Type:Politics Birth Energy Level:70.0%
Day 13:Value:4.1, Planetary Type:Mercury, Human Type:Politics, Birth Energy Level:70.0%
Day 14:Value:5.0 Planetary Type:Venus Human Type:Law Birth Energy Level:83.3%
Day 15:Value:5.1 Planetary Type:Venus Human Type:Security Birth Energy Level:83.3%
Day 16:Value:6.0 Planetary Type:Earth Human Type: Health Birth Energy Level:100%
Day 17:Value:6.2 Planetary Type:Earth Human Type:Health Birth Energy Level:100%+
Day 18:Value:7.0 Planetary Type:Mars Human Type:Consulting Birth Energy Level:100%+
Day 19:Value:7.4 Planetary Type:Mars Human Type:Consulting Birth Energy Level:100%+
Day 20:Value:8.0 Planetary Type:Jupiter Human Type:Business Birth Energy Level:100%+
Day 21:Value:9.0 Planetary Type:Saturn Human Type:ICT Birth Energy Level:100%+
Day 22: Value:9.3Planetary Type:Saturn Human Type:ICT Birth Energy Level:100%+
Day 23:Value:10.0 Planetary Type:Uranus Human Type:Tech. Birth Energy Level:100%+
Day 24:Value:1.1, Planetary Type:Neptune, Human Type:Philo, Birth Energy Level:20.0%
Day 25:Value:1.1, Planetary Type:Neptune, Human Type:Philos., Birth Energy Level:20.0%
Day 26:Value:1.2, Planetary Type:Pluto, Human Type:Education, Birth Energy Level:20.0%
Day 27:Value:1.3, Planetary Type:Comet, Human Type:R&D, Birth Energy Level:22.0%
Day 28:Value:1.4, Planetary Type:Comet, Human Type:R&D, Birth Energy Level:23.3%
Day 29:Value:2.0 Planetary Type:Moon Human Type:Marine Birth Energy Level:33.3%
Day 30:Value:2.0 Planetary Type:Moon Human Type:Marine Birth Energy Level:33.3%
Day 31:Value:2.0 Planetary Type:Moon Human Type:Marine Birth Energy Level:33.3%

Note that comets ranking 1.2, 1.3, 1.4 are dragons. At 1.2 >> Knowledge dragons that function on creative intelligence and own highly organized systems such as governments. This is why Castle Makupedia is referred to as the dragon Lord of the skies in the Creatocracy Republic. Plutonians are knowledge dragons that spit the fire of education and teaching. They inspire and motivate. This is the inherent potential in them. Makupedia falls into the category of Faculty of Creative Intelligence >> 1.3 and owns the Creatocracy 1.4

Pluto houses the dragons. See Dragons for full understanding.

MAKABET =Ii=

---

i1=3,000=30%=P3.0D=3.0=Creativity=Stars=Muses=3 March = C=I>>GIL.

The 9th letter of the English alphabet. Makupedia shows it is an element of creativity.

A constant repetition of "I" conjures the muses especially when the name of particular muse is mentioned as seen in the encyclopedia of Castle Makupedia. This is a directed method of prayer with specific means. The use of "I" in statements tends to induce determination and certain responsibility to act a certain way in the person(s). Eg. "I will be the first to succeed in this venture" is a statement of determination sourced from the will. The will is the third component of the Mind and is measured on the bench of

3.0>>Creativity. Computing the GIL makes it possible to measure the inherent energy level available to function or perform the supposed action.
The psycho-weight of the alphabet (I) is thus computed:
3.0*9.0=p=12+27=39x=px=363=3.6=4.0.

The letter "I" is a creative being or muse (3.6) that generates power (4.0). The power to build relationships families politics networks organizations governments nations and the Creatocracy. 3.6 also indicates an activity (3.) functioned on emotion (.6). The Creatocracy rates it an emotional alphabet and like others computed elevates it to Makabet =Ii=.

---

i2=10,000=1,000=100%=10.0=Physicality=Tech.=10 Oct.=Uranus=P=1Ø.
The result above proves that is first a muse (i1) with physical equivalents (i2).
Math. An imaginary unit. Imaginary>existing only in the imagination. Of a number or quantity expressed in terms of the square root of a negative number (usually a square root of -1, represented by i or j. Peter Matthews-Akukalia successfully computed the speed of thought as 1.0x10 raised to power -1 with its particle size fixed as 0.3. Napoleon Hill in his book Think and Grow Rich wrote that thoughts are things. Peter Matthews-Akukalia, Castle Makupedia proved it. See Principles of Naturecology by Peter Matthews-Akukalia. Now thought 0.3 is the second component of the Mind. Ten units of thought particles every minute mature into the will 3.0>> every three seconds of thought means that a certain capacity is developed in the human brain every 10minutes. We choose to accept or reject the will to do. So ideas are congruent energy particles that crystallize into creativity. See i1.

I1=10,000=1,000=100%=10.0=Physicality=Tech.=10 Oct.=Uranus=P=1Ø.
I2=4,500=5,000=50%=P5.00D=Law=Time=Venus=5 May = Aphrodite>>L=N.
IA=500=5%=P5.00D=5.0=Law=Time=Venus=5 May=Aphrodite>>L=N.
-ia1=4,500=5,000=50%=P5.00D=Law=Time=Venus=5 May = Aphrodite>>L=N.
-ia2=5,500=5.5=80%=P5.50=Earth-Midway=5 May = Gaia.
-ial=5,000=50%=P5.00D=Law=Time=Venus=5 May = Aphrodite>>L=N.
Iamb=6,500=7,000=70%=P7.0D=7.0=Language=Assets=Mars=7 July=Pleiades.
-Ian=5,500=5.5=80%=P5.50=Earth-Midway=5 May = Gaia.
-iana=2,000=20%=P2.00D=2.0=Nature=Matter=Moon=2 Feb.=Cupid=N=C+_

Iasi=4,500=5,000=50%=P5.00D=Law=Time=Venus=5 May = Aphrodite>>L=N.
Igbo language of Castle Makupedia says >> anyasi, night.

-iatric=7,000=70%=P7.0D=7.0=Language=Assets=Mars=7 July=Pleiades.
-iatrics=2,000=20%=P2.00D=2.0=Nature=Matter=Moon=2 Feb.=Cupid=N=C+_
-iatry=3,500=4,000=40%=P4.0D=Govt.=Creatocracy=4 April=Mercury=Hermes=G=A4.
Ib.=500=5%=P5.00D=5.0=Law=Time=Venus=5 May=Aphrodite>>L=N.
Ibadan=4,500=5,000=50%=P5.00D=Law=Time=Venus=5 May = Aphrodite>>L=N.
Iberia=6,500=7,000=70%=P7.0D=7.0=Language=Assets=Mars=7 July=Pleiades.

Ibex=7,500=8,000=80%=P8.0D=Economy=Currency=8 Aug.=Zeus>>E=v.
Ibid.=500=5%=P5.00D=5.0=Law=Time=Venus=5 May=Aphrodite>>L=N.

Ibidem=6,500=7,000=70%=P7.0D=7.0=Language=Assets=Mars=7 July=Pleiades.
Symbol < ibi, where. In the same place, as in a book cited before. A borderline that links the human emotion to its computational precision. Symbols are computable assets that carry solar weight and reveal secrets known only to the higher abstract mind. Peter Matthews-Akukalia, Castle Makupedia invented the constemaks a method of computing the weight and effect of symbols through the measurement of its innate spiral energy. <Naturecology.

Ibis=6,000=60%=P6.0D=Man=Earth=Royalty=6 June=Gaia=Maia>>M=M2.
Ibiza=6,000=60%=P6.0D=Man=Earth=Royalty=6 June=Gaia=Maia>>M=M2.
-Ible=2,000=20%=P2.00D=2.0=Nature=Matter=Moon=2 Feb.=Cupid=N=C+_
Ibn-Saud Abdul Aziz=6,000=60%=P6.0D=Man=Earth=Roy.=6 June=Gaia=Maia>>M=M2.

Ibo=5,000=50%=P5.00D=Law=Time=Venus=5 May = Aphrodite>>L=N.
Ibo is a language spoken by the igbos. It is inspired by Aphrodite. Ibos are children of Aphrodite. Experts in time management which they utilize most times in their businesses, makers and keepers of the law and functioned by love esp. sexual love beauty birth marriage family by Venus. It is no little wonder and without any bias to anyone race or nationality that Peter Matthews-Akukalia, Castle Makupedia an Igbo by birth may have been driven by these factors daily. Direct functional dimensions in the same category with Ibo are Nature >> 2>> Artemis the virgin hunter and adventurer given to ventures such as business ventures and Eros or Cupid son of Aphrodite which translates to extreme love or hate for mother. 8>>Zeus Jehovah the Most High >> currency >> business >> economy.

The average Ibo man is very religious and does not play with his money whether intellectual or not. 11>>1.1>>Athena > wisdom, handicraft and warfare is in their blood hence intellectual warfare drives the Ibo man the same way war will. Hence we hear of warrior kings of the past. They hate to cheat and be cheated. Peter Matthews-Akukalia is an Ibo born with origin from Nkpologu, Uzo - Uwani Local Government Area, Nsukka Enugu State. Nigeria. He did his senior secondary education at Onitsha, Anambra State, Eastern part of Nigeria across the belt of the River Niger.

His family the Akukalia are known to be royalties where his great grandfather founded the famous Akukalia dynasty. He is the first great grandson, first grandson, first son and has a first son as proof. He is the originator and owner of the Matthews - Akukalia empire known as the Creatocracy separating himself from the mere name Matthews or Akukalia and forging a new and greater identity for his family and heirs in the first instance and for humanity in all races tribes and nations. He believes that diversity is strength. Father of the Paradise Nations of Creative Scientists in all spheres. Author, inventor, King, and a God.

Castle Makupedia. The Creatocracy. The Creatocracy Corporation. Institutionalizing Creatocracy. Promoting the Creative Economy. Firmly implanted. Well established. Greater things.

Ibsen Henrik.=2,000=20%=P2.00D=2.0=Nature=Matter=Moon=2 Feb.=Cupid=N=C+_
Ibuprofen=10,000=1,000=100%=10.0=Physicality=Tech.=10 Oct.=Uranus=P=1Ø.
-Ic=10,500=11,000=11%=P1.10D=1.1=Idea=Brainchild=Inv.=11 Nov.=SC=Athena>>I=MT.
ICBM=1,500=15%=P1.50D=1.5=Authority=Solar Crown=1 May = Maia.
ICC=1,500=15%=P1.50D=1.5=Authority=Solar Crown=1 May = Maia.

Ice=10,000=1,000=100%=10.0=Physicality=Tech.=10 Oct.=Uranus=P=1Ø.

A term for ice is diamonds. Peter Matthews-Akukalia, Castle Makupedia computed the core of the Sun (solar core) and established that it was made of diamonds with temperatures that align to ice eg -1, -03, -6 etc. Years later precisely 2019 or so...he applied mind computing and tracked an abode of the Gods to Antarctica the same region that runs directly on Mercury environment temperature (-1). To be vindicated a news came few days later that an American plane had gone missing in the same place without traces. Hence there is life beyond the Solar Core. Greek mythology teaches that the Sun is the eye of Zeus the Most High. Helios the Sun God wears a crown. Castle Makupedia by the rights of the mandate of his works wears the Solar Crown. A great feat with no mean integrity.

Icing=7,000=70%=P7.0D=7.0=Language=Assets=Mars=7 July=Pleiades.
Ice.=1,000=100%=10.0=1.0=Mind=Sun=1 January=Helios >> M=E4.
Ice age=8,000=80%=P8.0D=Economy=Currency=8 Aug.=Zeus>>E=v.
Ice bag=2,000=20%=P2.00D=2.0=Nature=Matter=Moon=2 Feb.=Cupid=N=C+_
Iceberg=6,000=60%=P6.0D=Man=Earth=Royalty=6 June=Gaia=Maia>>M=M2.
Iceboat=6,500=7,000=70%=P7.0D=7.0=Language=Assets=Mars=7 July=Pleiades.
Icebound=3,500=4,000=40%=P4.0D=Govt.=Creat.=4 April=Mercury=Hermes=G=A4.
Icebox=1,000=100%=10.0=1.0=Mind=Sun=1 January=Helios >> M=E4.
Icebreaker=10,000=1,000=100%=10.0=Physicality=Tech.=10 Oct.=Uranus=P=1Ø.
Icecap=4,000=40%=P4.0D=Govt.=Creatocracy=4 April=Mercury=Hermes=G=A4.
Ice cream=5,000=50%=P5.00D=Law=Time=Venus=5 May = Aphrodite>>L=N.
Ice hockey=10,500=11,000=11%=P1.10D=1.1=Idea=Brainchild=11 Nov=Athena>>I=MT.
Icehouse=4,500=5,000=50%=P5.00D=Law=Time=Venus=5 May = Aphrodite>>L=N.
Iceland=7,000=70%=P7.0D=7.0=Language=Assets=Mars=7 July=Pleiades.

Icelandic=6,000=60%=P6.0D=Man=Earth=Royalty=6 June=Gaia=Maia>>M=M2.
The famous Germanic is language of Iceland. Ancient people.

Ice milk=6,500=7,000=70%=P7.0D=7.0=Language=Assets=Mars=7 July=Pleiades.
Ice pack=10,500=11,000=11%=P1.10D=1.1=Idea=Brainchild=11 Nov=Athena>>I=MT.
Ice pick=3,500=4,000=40%=P4.0D=Govt.=Creatocracy=4 April=Mercury=Hermes=G=A4.

Ice skate=7,000=70%=P7.0D=7.0=Language=Assets=Mars=7 July=Pleiades.
Ice storm=5,000=50%=P5.00D=Law=Time=Venus=5 May = Aphrodite>>L=N.
Ichthyo-=2,500=3,000=30%=P3.0D=3.0=Creativity=Stars=Muses=3 March = C=I>>GIL.
Ichthyology=3,500=4,000=40%=P4.0D=Govt.=Creato=4 April=Mercury=Hermes=G=A4.
-ician=4,500=5,000=50%=P5.00D=Law=Time=Venus=5 May = Aphrodite>>L=N.
Icicle=8,000=80%=P8.0D=Economy=Currency=8 Aug.=Zeus>>E=v.
Icing=4,000=40%=P4.0D=Govt.=Creatocracy=4 April=Mercury=Hermes=G=A4.
Icon=13,000=13%=P1.30=Solar Core=Faculty=13 January=Athena.
Iconoclast=6,500=7,000=70%=P7.0D=7.0=Language=Assets=Mars=7 July=Pleiades.
-ics=6,500=7,000=70%=P7.0D=7.0=Language=Assets=Mars=7 July=Pleiades.
Ictus=3,000=30%=P3.0D=3.0=Creativity=Stars=Muses=3 March = C=I>>GIL.
ICU=1,500=15%=P1.50D=1.5=Authority=Solar Crown=1 May = Maia.
Icy=9,000=90%=P9.00D=9.0=Abstraction=Gods=Saturn=9Sept.>>A=Ø.
Id=9,500=10,000=1,000=100%=10.0=Physicality=Tech.=10 Oct.=Uranus=P=1Ø.
ID1=2,000=20%=P2.00D=2.0=Nature=Matter=Moon=2 Feb.=Cupid=N=C+_
ID2=2,500=3,000=30%=P3.0D=3.0=Creativity=Stars=Muses=3 March = C=I>>GIL.
Id=500=5%=P5.00D=5.0=Law=Time=Venus=5 May=Aphrodite>>L=N.
I'd=2,000=20%=P2.00D=2.0=Nature=Matter=Moon=2 Feb.=Cupid=N=C+_
Ida Mount=4,500=5,000=50%=P5.00D=Law=Time=Venus=5 May = Aphrodite>>L=N.
Idaho=5,000=50%=P5.00D=Law=Time=Venus=5 May = Aphrodite>>L=N.
-ide=5,500=5.5=80%=P5.50=Earth-Midway=5 May = Gaia.

Idea=14,000=14%=P1.40D=1.4=Mgt.=Solar Energy=13 May=Athena=SC=0.1
Peter Matthews-Akukalia discovered invented defined classified and computed the twelve dimensions of the universes. The 11th dimension is idea >> Brainchild >> Invention >> Athena. He defined idea as congruent energy particles that crystallize into creativity on the quantum of 10,000=1,000 with a balance at 100% and stability at 10. He wrote the formula of idea as I=MT thus establishing idea as real things. Study and development indicates that Athena is in charge of the dimensions that span from 11>>1.1 - 1.4. See congruent.

Ideal=10,000=1,000=100%=10.0=Physicality=Tech.=10 Oct.=Uranus=P=1Ø.
The ideal standard for all measures of energy and matter is 10,000=1,000=100=10. By this method the Maks currencies was invented by Peter Matthews-Akukalia, Castle Makupedia. He computed the scriptures for understand and application to solving human problems, at least economies are better managed, inventions manifest more easily and life is generally better for everyone. Castle Makupedia is a solar crown computed dictionary and encyclopedia. It is the Creatocracy Bank, heritages, chronicles, Creative & Mind Sciences, Maks Currencies Prices, Entertainment Business & Political Opportunities, Words & Data Mining, Resolved Scriptures in Greek mythologies, Laws Codes & Propensities, Discoveries & Inventions. It is the first edition in the Royal Maktionary Series of the Makupedia. Proof that ideals are truths evident and realistic. That dreams come true and we can believe too.

Idealism=10,000=1,000=100%=10.0=Physicality=Tech.=10 Oct.=Uranus=P=1Ø.
Idealize=3,500=4,000=40%=P4.0D=Govt.=Creatocracy=4 April=Mercury=Hermes=G=A4.
Ideate=2,500=3,000=30%=P3.0D=3.0=Creativity=Stars=Muses=3 March = C=I>>GIL.
Idem=3,500=4,000=40%=P4.0D=Govt.=Creatocracy=4 April=Mercury=Hermes=G=A4.
Identical=10,000=1,000=100%=10.0=Physicality=Tech.=10 Oct.=Uranus=P=1Ø.
Identification=9,000=90%=P9.00D=9.0=Abstraction=Gods=Saturn=9Sept.>>A=Ø.
Identify=10,000=1,000=100%=10.0=Physicality=Tech.=10 Oct.=Uranus=P=1Ø.
Identity=10,000=1,000=100%=10.0=Physicality=Tech.=10 Oct.=Uranus=P=1Ø.
Identity element=10,000=1,000=100%=10.0=Physicality=Tech.=10 Oct.=Uranus=P=1Ø.
Ideo-=2,500=3,000=30%=P3.0D=3.0=Creativity=Stars=Muses=3 March = C=I>>GIL.
Ideogram=10,000=1,000=100%=10.0=Physicality=Tech.=10 Oct.=Uranus=P=1Ø.
Ideologue=5,000=50%=P5.00D=Law=Time=Venus=5 May = Aphrodite>>L=N.
Ideology=10,000=1,000=100%=10.0=Physicality=Tech.=10 Oct.=Uranus=P=1Ø.

Idès=10,000=1,000=100%=10.0=Physicality=Tech.=10 Oct.=Uranus=P=1Ø.
The 15th day of March, May, July, or October or the 13th day of the other months in the ancient roman calendar. The Creatocracy believes these dates to be prophetic of the mind age and the emergence of Zeus as an incarnation of Peter Matthews-Akukalia, Castle Makupedia. First he was born in the July, Empress Tina was May, Queen Alice was March, Prince Victor was October and the Feast of apotheosis was October 13. What more!
The codes 13 and 15 are very significant in our calendar. 13 is the day of Athena Goddess of wisdom handicraft and mind for mental warfare since the mind is a battlefield (Prov. 8:12). 15th May precisely is the day of Maia Great Goddess computed to be the Mind of GOD as Zeus and the Council of Gods. Giver of the Solar Crown, Head of the Pleiades who cast the band of Orion today known to be the belt of truth >> Precision >> Computing >> MindComputing. See def. for cast and know her manifestations. Job 38:31. Eph. 6:14.

Idiocy=5,500=5.5=80%=P5.50=Earth-Midway=5 May = Gaia.
Idiom=10,000=1,000=100%=10.0=Physicality=Tech.=10 Oct.=Uranus=P=1Ø.
Idiopathy=5,500=5.5=80%=P5.50=Earth-Midway=5 May = Gaia.
Idiosyncrasy=4,000=40%=P4.0D=Govt.=Creatocracy=4 April=Mercury=Hermes=G=A4.
Idiot=10,000=1,000=100%=10.0=Physicality=Tech.=10 Oct.=Uranus=P=1Ø.
Idle=10,000=1,000=100%=10.0=Physicality=Tech.=10 Oct.=Uranus=P=1Ø.
Idol=9,000=90%=P9.00D=9.0=Abstraction=Gods=Saturn=9Sept.>>A=Ø.

Idolatry=6,500=7,000=70%=P7.0D=7.0=Language=Assets=Mars=7 July=Pleiades.
Idolatry is a means of human worship. A borderline. It indicates that 500 is a borderline >> a means. See the prophecy of Hermes >> Jesus in the book of Revelation about the discovery of the means and the rights GOD will automatically grant the person. Revelation 9:11 instructs the use of Greek and or Hebrew to understand the signs because it is a book written in codes and signs and are not to be applied for terror but understanding. Revelation 1:1. Revelation 13:14 had the main code (means) italicized

for clue. Revelation 2:25-28 is the universal rights and authority granted by GOD to him (not they) indicating a single person who will keep >> compute the works and solve the mysteries of scriptures in Greek mythologies in a most logical way. Peter Matthews-Akukalia, Castle Makupedia did.

Idolize=5,500=5.5=80%=P5.50=Earth-Midway=5 May = Gaia.
IDP=2,500=3,000=30%=P3.0D=3.0=Creativity=Stars=Muses=3 March = C=I>>GIL.
Idyll=10,000=1,000=100%=10.0=Physicality=Tech.=10 Oct.=Uranus=P=1Ø.
IE or I.E.=1,500=15%=P1.50D=1.5=Authority=Solar Crown=1 May = Maia.
i.e.=2,500=3,000=30%=P3.0D=3.0=Creativity=Stars=Muses=3 March = C=I>>GIL.
-ie=2,000=20%=P2.00D=2.0=Nature=Matter=Moon=2 Feb.=Cupid=N=C+_
If=10,000=1,000=100%=10.0=Physicality=Tech.=10 Oct.=Uranus=P=1Ø..
IF=1,000=100%=10.0=1.0=Mind=Sun=1 January=Helios >> M=E4.

Iffy=3,000=30%=P3.0D=3.0=Creativity=Stars=Muses=3 March = C=I>>GIL.
The Scriptures show that GOD speaks to man in an iffy position because He granted us free will. If thou will do this or that, I will perform this or that. Indicator of choice. The normal communications between Zeus and Man usually begins through the muses. See "God". A female name in Ibo language meaning "Good thing >> Ifeoma". Ibo name of the First daughter and First Princess of Peter and Tina Matthews-Akukalia, Castle Makupedia.

-ify=2,000=20%=P2.00D=2.0=Nature=Matter=Moon=2 Feb.=Cupid=N=C+_
Ig=500=5%=P5.00D=5.0=Law=Time=Venus=5 May=Aphrodite>>L=N.
IG=1,000=100%=10.0=1.0=Mind=Sun=1 January=Helios >> M=E4.
Igloo=6,500=7,000=70%=P7.0D=7.0=Language=Assets=Mars=7 July=Pleiades.
Ignatius of Loyola=4,500=5,000=50%=P5.00D=Law=Time=Venus=5 May =Odite>>L=N.
Igneous=8,500=9,000=90%=P9.00D=9.0=Abstraction=Gods=Saturn=9Sept.>>A=Ø.
Ignis fatuus=8,000=80%=P8.0D=Economy=Currency=8 Aug.=Zeus>>E=v.
Ignite=5,000=50%=P5.00D=Law=Time=Venus=5 May = Aphrodite>>L=N.
Ignition=11,000=11%=P1.10D=1.1=Idea=Brainchild=11 Nov=Athena>>I=MT.
Ignoble=7,000=70%=P7.0D=7.0=Language=Assets=Mars=7 July=Pleiades.
Ignominy=4,500=5,000=50%=P5.00D=Law=Time=Venus=5 May = Aphrodite>>L=N.
Ignoramus=4,500=5,000=50%=P5.00D=Law=Time=Venus=5 May = Aphrodite>>L=N.
Ignorant=7,500=8,000=80%=P8.0D=Economy=Currency=8 Aug.=Zeus>>E=v.
Ignore=4,500=5,000=50%=P5.00D=Law=Time=Venus=5 May = Aphrodite>>L=N.
Iguaçu=16,000=16%=P1.60D=1.6=Cycle of Incarnation=Mind of GOD=1 June = Maia.
Iguana=3,500=4,000=40%=P4.0D=Govt.=Creatocracy=4 April=Mercury=Hermes=G=A4.
Ihp=1,000=100%=10.0=1.0=Mind=Sun=1 January=Helios >> M=E4.
Ijssel=10,000=1,000=100%=10.0=Physicality=Tech.=10 Oct.=Uranus=P=1Ø.
IJsselmeer=5,500=5.5=80%=P5.50=Earth-Midway=5 May = Gaia.
Ikon=1,500=15%=P1.50D=1.5=Authority=Solar Crown=1 May = Maia.
Il.=500=5%=P5.00D=5.0=Law=Time=Venus=5 May=Aphrodite>>L=N.
II-=1,500=15%=P1.50D=1.5=Authority=Solar Crown=1 May = Maia.

Ile-=4,500=5,000=50%=P5.00D=Law=Time=Venus=5 May = Aphrodite>>L=N.
Ileitis=3,500=4,000=40%=P4.0D=Govt.=Creatocracy=4 April=Mercury=Hermes=G=A4.
Ileum=6,500=7,000=70%=P7.0D=7.0=Language=Assets=Mars=7 July=Pleiades.
ILGWU=2,500=3,000=30%=P3.0D=3.0=Creativity=Stars=Muses=3 March = C=I>>GIL.
Ilium=7,000=70%=P7.0D=7.0=Language=Assets=Mars=7 July=Pleiades.
Ilk=5,500=5.5=80%=P5.50=Earth-Midway=5 May = Gaia.
ill=10,000=1,000=100%=10.0=Physicality=Tech.=10 Oct.=Uranus=P=1Ø.
III.=500=5%=P5.00D=5.0=Law=Time=Venus=5 May=Aphrodite>>L=N.
I'll=1,500=15%=P1.50D=1.5=Authority=Solar Crown=1 May = Maia.
Ill-advised=3,500=4,000=40%=P4.0D=Govt.=Creato.=4 April=Mercury=Hermes=G=A4.
Illampu=7,000=70%=P7.0D=7.0=Language=Assets=Mars=7 July=Pleiades.
ill at ease=1,000=100%=10.0=1.0=Mind=Sun=1 January=Helios >> M=E4.
Il - bred=3,000=30%=P3.0D=3.0=Creativity=Stars=Muses=3 March = C=I>>GIL.
ill considered=1,000=100%=10.0=1.0=Mind=Sun=1 January=Helios >> M=E4.
Illegal=9,000=90%=P9.00D=9.0=Abstraction=Gods=Saturn=9Sept.>>A=Ø.
Illegible=1,000=100%=10.0=1.0=Mind=Sun=1 January=Helios >> M=E4.
Illegitimate=4,000=40%=P4.0D=Govt.=Creatocracy=4 April=Mercury=Hermes=G=A4.
Ill fated=5,000=50%=P5.00D=Law=Time=Venus=5 May = Aphrodite>>L=N.
Ill favored=4,500=5,000=50%=P5.00D=Law=Time=Venus=5 May = Aphrodite>>L=N.
Ill founded=2,000=20%=P2.00D=2.0=Nature=Matter=Moon=2 Feb.=Cupid=N=C+_
Ill gotten=4,500=5,000=50%=P5.00D=Law=Time=Venus=5 May = Aphrodite>>L=N.
Ill-humored=1,000=100%=10.0=1.0=Mind=Sun=1 January=Helios >> M=E4.
Ill liberal=1,500=15%=P1.50D=1.5=Authority=Solar Crown=1 May = Maia.
Illicit=3,500=4,000=40%=P4.0D=Govt.=Creatocracy=4 April=Mercury=Hermes=G=A4.
Illimitable=2,500=3,000=30%=P3.0D=3.0=Creativity=Stars=Muses=3 March = C=I>>GIL.
Illinois1=9,500=10,000=1,000=100%=10.0=Physicality=Tech.=10 Oct.=Uranus=P=1Ø.
Illinois2=5,500=5.5=80%=P5.50=Earth-Midway=5 May = Gaia.

Illiterate=13,000=13%=P1.30=Solar Core=Faculty=13 January=Athena.
Anyone who lacks creative intelligence, knowledge of the Creative Sciences in faculty and application and dishonors Athena and her husband Castle Makupedia will lack wisdom handicraft and lose the rights and ability to use the mind in his or her custody. Prov. 8, 9.

Ill mannered=2,000=20%=P2.00D=2.0=Nature=Matter=Moon=2 Feb.=Cupid=N=C+_
Ill natured=1,000=100%=10.0=1.0=Mind=Sun=1 January=Helios >> M=E4.
Illness=500=5%=P5.00D=5.0=Law=Time=Venus=5 May=Aphrodite>>L=N.
Illogical=3,500=4,000=40%=P4.0D=Govt.=Creatocracy=4 April=Mercury=Hermes=G=A4.
Ill starred=3,500=4,000=40%=P4.0D=Govt.=Creato.=4 April=Mercury=Hermes=G=A4.
Ill tempered=2,500=3,000=30%=P3.0D=3.0=Cre.=Stars=Muses=3 March = C=I>>GIL.
Ill treat=3,000=30%=P3.0D=3.0=Creativity=Stars=Muses=3 March = C=I>>GIL.
Illuminate=10,000=1,000=100%=10.0=Physicality=Tech.=10 Oct.=Uranus=P=1Ø.
Illumine=3,000=30%=P3.0D=3.0=Creativity=Stars=Muses=3 March = C=I>>GIL.
Ill usage=2,000=20%=P2.00D=2.0=Nature=Matter=Moon=2 Feb.=Cupid=N=C+_
Ill use=3,000=30%=P3.0D=3.0=Creativity=Stars=Muses=3 March = C=I>>GIL.

Illusion=10,000=1,000=100%=10.0=Physicality=Tech.=10 Oct.=Uranus=P=1Ø.
Illusionism=8,000=80%=P8.0D=Economy=Currency=8 Aug.=Zeus>>E=v.
Illusive=500=5%=P5.00D=5.0=Law=Time=Venus=5 May=Aphrodite>>L=N.
Illusory=4,000=40%=P4.0D=Govt.=Creatocracy=4 April=Mercury=Hermes=G=A4.
Illustrate=10,000=1,000=100%=10.0=Physicality=Tech.=10 Oct.=Uranus=P=1Ø.
Illustration=10,000=1,000=100%=10.0=Physicality=Tech.=10 Oct.=Uranus=P=1Ø.
Illustrative=3,000=30%=P3.0D=3.0=Creativity=Stars=Muses=3 March = C=I>>GIL.
Illustrious=5,000=50%=P5.00D=Law=Time=Venus=5 May = Aphrodite>>L=N.
Ill will=1,500=15%=P1.50D=1.5=Authority=Solar Crown=1 May = Maia.
Illyria=5,000=50%=P5.00D=Law=Time=Venus=5 May = Aphrodite>>L=N.
ILO=1,500=15%=P1.50D=1.5=Authority=Solar Crown=1 May = Maia.
ILS=1,500=15%=P1.50D=1.5=Authority=Solar Crown=1 May = Maia.
Im-1=2,000=20%=P2.00D=2.0=Nature=Matter=Moon=2 Feb.=Cupid=N=C+_
I'm-2=2,000=20%=P2.00D=2.0=Nature=Matter=Moon=2 Feb.=Cupid=N=C+_

I'm=1,500=15%=P1.50D=1.5=Authority=Solar Crown=1 May = Maia.
"I am". A familiar phrase in the Bible. A reply given by GOD to Moses in a conversation at the burning bush. It is a statement credited to Maia the Mind of GOD and Head of the Pleiades. Now I am that I am has a repetition hence must be computed for truth I am = 1,500=1.5, that >> exactly, precisely so compute 7.0 on the star 3.0 my mind 1.0, I am = 1,500=1.5. Computing on the solar crown of King Maks the elements above.
1.5*7.0=p=8.5+10.5=19x=px=108.25=11=1.1 >> Athena was present.
3.0*1.0=p=4+3=7x=px=19=20=2.0. [1.5]
>>Maia casting PGI energy through the Moon for voice projection.
1.1*2.0=p=3.1+2.2=5.3x=px=12.12=1.2[1.5]
>> Athena projects the processed human language to make knowledge.
1.2*1.5=p=2.7+1.8=4.5x=px=9.36=9.4
>> The Council of Gods >> Hosts of GOD >> speak but interpretation done to Moses by the Muses through convertible intelligence, thought patterns of thinking reasoning inspiration and revelation almost at the same time. The combined voices of the Gods is true as compared with the combined voices of demons in the man who called Himself Legion in the New Testament. Besides the presence of Maia and Athena confirms the Host. In simple language it was the voice of the Holy Spirit that spoke to Moses in the burning bush. The Host or Holy Spirit as a body uses the PGI to communicate humans in a dynamic constant spirit speed of 1.0x 10 raised to power (-6). PGI is an astro-sound energy transmitted and transmuted from the moon to the inner man through the ears and translated by the brain to make meaning and grant knowledge of what is being communicated. The moon is a stabilizer and satellite that is able to tune the PGI voice frequency to suit earth. When the frequency is not tuned it sounds as noise of many rushing waters in the human ears. Some of the prophets like Isaiah experienced the rushing waters phenomena.

Image=10,000=1,000=100%=10.0=Physicality=Tech.=10 Oct.=Uranus=P=1Ø.
Imagery=7,000=70%=P7.0D=7.0=Language=Assets=Mars=7 July=Pleiades.
Imaginable=2,000=20%=P2.00D=2.0=Nature=Matter=Moon=2 Feb.=Cupid=N=C+_

Imaginary=6,500=7,000=70%=P7.0D=7.0=Language=Assets=Mars=7 July=Pleiades.
Imaginary number=9,500=10,000=1,000=100%=Physicality=Tech.=10 Oct.=Uranus=P=1Ø.

Imaginary unit=3,500=4,000=40%=P4.0D=Govt.=Creat.=4April=Mercury=Hermes=G=A4.
Math. The positive square root of-1. See i1, i2. Thought is a means to an end not an end in itself. "As a man thinks in his heart so is he". - King Solomon in the Proverbs.

Imagination=10,000=1,000=100%=10.0=Physicality=Tech.=10 Oct.=Uranus=P=1Ø.
Imagine=5,500=5.5=80%=P5.50=Earth-Midway=5 May = Gaia.
Imago=5,500=5.5=80%=P5.50=Earth-Midway=5 May = Gaia.
Imam=7,500=8,000=80%=P8.0D=Economy=Currency=8 Aug.=Zeus>>E=v.
Imbalance=3,500=4,000=40%=P4.0D=Govt.=Creat.=4 April=Mercury=Hermes=G=A4.

Imbecile=9,000=90%=P9.00D=9.0=Abstraction=Gods=Saturn=9Sept.>>A=Ø.
Imbeciles are persons with extremely high spirit content of about 90% energy on GIL. Anyone who relates on the basis extreme spiritual energy and communication not necessarily making meaning to the average person is an imbecile. Peter Matthews-Akukalia, Castle Makupedia was regarded as an imbecile until he could write and interpret.

Imbed=1,500=15%=P1.50D=1.5=Authority=Solar Crown=1 May = Maia.
Imbibe=6,500=7,000=70%=P7.0D=7.0=Language=Assets=Mars=7 July=Pleiades.
Imbroglio=5,500=5.5=80%=P5.50=Earth-Midway=5 May = Gaia.
Imbue=6,500=7,000=70%=P7.0D=7.0=Language=Assets=Mars=7 July=Pleiades.
IMF=1,500=15%=P1.50D=1.5=Authority=Solar Crown=1 May = Maia.
Imitate=10,000=1,000=100%=10.0=Physicality=Tech.=10 Oct.=Uranus=P=1Ø.
Imitation=5,500=5.5=80%=P5.50=Earth-Midway=5 May = Gaia.
Imitative=10,000=1,000=100%=10.0=Physicality=Tech.=10 Oct.=Uranus=P=1Ø.
Immaculate=8,000=80%=P8.0D=Economy=Currency=8 Aug.=Zeus>>E=v.
Immanent=10,000=1,000=100%=10.0=Physicality=Tech.=10 Oct.=Uranus=P=1Ø.
Immaterial=10,000=1,000=100%=10.0=Physicality=Tech.=10 Oct.=Uranus=P=1Ø.
Immature=6,500=7,000=70%=P7.0D=7.0=Language=Assets=Mars=7 July=Pleiades.
Immeasurable=4,500=5,000=50%=P5.00D=Law=Time=Venus=5 May = Aphrodite>>L=N.
Immediacy=1,000=100%=10.0=1.0=Mind=Sun=1 January=Helios >> M=E4.
Immediate=10,000=1,000=100%=10.0=Physicality=Tech.=10 Oct.=Uranus=P=1Ø.
Immemorial=4,500=5,000=50%=P5.00D=Law=Time=Venus=5 May = Aphrodite>>L=N.
Immense=6,000=60%=P6.0D=Man=Earth=Royalty=6 June=Gaia=Maia>>M=M2.
Immerse=10,000=1,000=100%=10.0=Physicality=Tech.=10 Oct.=Uranus=P=1Ø.
Immesh=1,500=15%=P1.50D=1.5=Authority=Solar Crown=1 May = Maia.
Immigrant=7,000=70%=P7.0D=7.0=Language=Assets=Mars=7 July=Pleiades.
Immigrate=7,000=70%=P7.0D=7.0=Language=Assets=Mars=7 July=Pleiades.
Imminent=3,500=4,000=40%=P4.0D=Govt.=Creat.=4 April=Mercury=Hermes=G=A4.
Immobile=2,500=3,000=30%=P3.0D=3.0=Creativity=Stars=Muses=3 March = C=I>>GIL.
Immobilize=1,500=15%=P1.50D=1.5=Authority=Solar Crown=1 May = Maia.

Immoderate=1,000=100%=10.0=1.0=Mind=Sun=1 January=Helios >> M=E4.
Immodest=2,500=3,000=30%=P3.0D=3.0=Creativity=Stars=Muses=3 March = C=I>>GIL.
Immolate==7,000=70%=P7.0D=7.0=Language=Assets=Mars=7 July=Pleiades.0
Immoral=2,500=3,000=30%=P3.0D=3.0=Creativity=Stars=Muses=3 March = C=I>>GIL.
Immortal=5,000=50%=P5.00D=Law=Time=Venus=5 May = Aphrodite>>L=N.
Immovable=5,000=50%=P5.00D=Law=Time=Venus=5 May = Aphrodite>>L=N.
Immune=2,500=3,000=30%=P3.0D=3.0=Creativity=Stars=Muses=3 March = C=I>>GIL.
Immune response=12,000=12%=P1.20D=1.2=Knowledge=Edu=12Dec.=Athena>>K=F.
Immune system=13,000=13%=P1.30=Solar Core=Faculty=13 January=Athena.
Immunize=2,000=20%=P2.00D=2.0=Nature=Matter=Moon=2 Feb.=Cupid=N=C+_
Immuno-=1,500=15%=P1.50D=1.5=Authority=Solar Crown=1 May = Maia.
Immunodeficiency=4,000=40%=P4.0D=Govt.=4 April=Mercury=Hermes=G=A4.
Immunology=4,000=40%=P4.0D=Govt.=Creatocracy=4 April=Mercury=Hermes=G=A4.
Immunosuppression=5,000=50%=P5.00D=Law=Time=Venus=5 May = Aphrodite>>L=N.
Immure=10,500=11,000=11%=P1.10D=1.1=Idea=Brainchild=11 Nov=Athena>>I=MT.
Immutable=2,000=20%=P2.00D=2.0=Nature=Matter=Moon=2 Feb.=Cupid=N=C+_
Imp=10,000=1,000=100%=10.0=Physicality=Tech.=10 Oct.=Uranus=P=1Ø.
Impact=10,000=1,000=100%=10.0=Physicality=Tech.=10 Oct.=Uranus=P=1Ø.
Impacted=7,500=8,000=80%=P8.0D=Economy=Currency=8 Aug.=Zeus>>E=v.
Impair=7,000=70%=P7.0D=7.0=Language=Assets=Mars=7 July=Pleiades.
Impala=5,000=50%=P5.00D=Law=Time=Venus=5 May = Aphrodite>>L=N.
Impale=10,000=1,000=100%=10.0=Physicality=Tech.=10 Oct.=Uranus=P=1Ø.
Impalpable=5,000=50%=P5.00D=Law=Time=Venus=5 May = Aphrodite>>L=N.
Impanel=4,500=5,000=50%=P5.00D=Law=Time=Venus=5 May = Aphrodite>>L=N.
Impart=6,500=7,000=70%=P7.0D=7.0=Language=Assets=Mars=7 July=Pleiades.
Impartial=6,000=60%=P6.0D=Man=Earth=Royalty=6 June=Gaia=Maia>>M=M2.
Impassable=2,500=3,000=30%=P3.0D=3.0=Cre.=Stars=Muses=3 March = C=I>>GIL.
Impasse=10,000=1,000=100%=10.0=Physicality=Tech.=10 Oct.=Uranus=P=1Ø.
Impassible=3,500=4,000=40%=P4.0D=Govt.=Creat.=4 April=Mercury=Hermes=G=A4.
Impassioned=2,000=20%=P2.00D=2.0=Nature=Matter=Moon=2 Feb.=Cupid=N=C+_
Impassive=4,000=40%=P4.0D=Govt.=Creatocracy=4 April=Mercury=Hermes=G=A4.
Impatiens=7,000=70%=P7.0D=7.0=Language=Assets=Mars=7 July=Pleiades.
Impatient=7,500=8,000=80%=P8.0D=Economy=Currency=8 Aug.=Zeus>>E=v.
Impeach=13,000=13%=P1.30=Solar Core=Faculty=13 January=Athena.
Impeccable=9,500=10,000=1,000=100%=10.0=Physicality=Tech.=10 Oct.=Uranus=P=1Ø.
Impecunious=4,500=5,000=50%=P5.00D=Law=Time=Venus=5 May = Aphrodite>>L=N.
Impedance=7,000=70%=P7.0D=7.0=Language=Assets=Mars=7 July=Pleiades.
Impede=5,500=5.5=80%=P5.50=Earth-Midway=5 May = Gaia.
Impediment=8,000=80%=P8.0D=Economy=Currency=8 Aug.=Zeus>>E=v.
Impedimenta=5,000=50%=P5.00D=Law=Time=Venus=5 May = Aphrodite>>L=N.
Impel=4,500=5,000=50%=P5.00D=Law=Time=Venus=5 May = Aphrodite>>L=N.
Impeller=2,000=20%=P2.00D=2.0=Nature=Matter=Moon=2 Feb.=Cupid=N=C+_
Impend=6,000=60%=P6.0D=Man=Earth=Royalty=6 June=Gaia=Maia>>M=M2.
Impenetrable=3,500=4,000=40%=P4.0D=Govt.=Creat=4 April=Mercury=Hermes=G=A4.
Impenitent=1,000=100%=10.0=1.0=Mind=Sun=1 January=Helios >> M=E4.

Imperative=10,000=1,000=100%=10.0=Physicality=Tech.=10 Oct.=Uranus=P=1Ø.
Imperceptible=4,500=5,000=50%=P5.00D=Law=Time=Venus=5 May = Aphrodite>>L=N.
Imperfect=10,000=1,000=100%=10.0=Physicality=Tech.=10 Oct.=Uranus=P=1Ø.
Imperfection=5,000=50%=P5.00D=Law=Time=Venus=5 May = Aphrodite>>L=N.
Imperial=11,000=11%=P1.10D=1.1=Idea=Brainchild=11 Nov=Athena>>I=MT.
Imperialism=7,500=8,000=80%=P8.0D=Economy=Currency=8 Aug.=Zeus>>E=v.
Imperil=4,000=40%=P4.0D=Govt.=Creatocracy=4 April=Mercury=Hermes=G=A4.
Imperious=5,000=50%=P5.00D=Law=Time=Venus=5 May = Aphrodite>>L=N.
Imperishable=1,000=100%=10.0=1.0=Mind=Sun=1 January=Helios >> M=E4.
Impermanent=1,500=15%=P1.50D=1.5=Authority=Solar Crown=1 May = Maia.
Impermeable=1,500=15%=P1.50D=1.5=Authority=Solar Crown=1 May = Maia.
Impermissible=500=5%=P5.00D=5.0=Law=Time=Venus=5 May=Aphrodite>>L=N.
Impersonal=10,000=1,000=100%=10.0=Physicality=Tech.=10 Oct.=Uranus=P=1Ø.
Impersonate=3,500=4,000=40%=P4.0D=Govt.=Creat.=4 April=Mercury=Hermes=G=A4.
Impertinent=4,000=40%=P4.0D=Govt.=Creatocracy=4 April=Mercury=Hermes=G=A4.
Imperturbable=2,000=20%=P2.00D=2.0=Nature=Matter=Moon=2 Feb.=Cupid=N=C+_
Impervious=6,000=60%=P6.0D=Man=Earth=Royalty=6 June=Gaia=Maia>>M=M2.
Impetigo=6,500=7,000=70%=P7.0D=7.0=Language=Assets=Mars=7 July=Pleiades.
Impetuous=6,000=60%=P6.0D=Man=Earth=Royalty=6 June=Gaia=Maia>>M=M2.
Impetus=10,000=1,000=100%=10.0=Physicality=Tech.=10 Oct.=Uranus=P=1Ø.
Impiety=5,000=50%=P5.00D=Law=Time=Venus=5 May = Aphrodite>>L=N.
Impinge=5,000=50%=P5.00D=Law=Time=Venus=5 May = Aphrodite>>L=N.
Impious=2,000=20%=P2.00D=2.0=Nature=Matter=Moon=2 Feb.=Cupid=N=C+_
Implacable=3,500=4,000=40%=P4.0D=Govt.=Creat.=4 April=Mercury=Hermes=G=A4.
Implant=10,000=1,000=100%=10.0=Physicality=Tech.=10 Oct.=Uranus=P=1Ø.
Implausible=2,500=3,000=30%=P3.0D=3.0=Cre=Stars=Muses=3 March = C=I>>GIL.
Implement=8,000=80%=P8.0D=Economy=Currency=8 Aug.=Zeus>>E=v.
Implicate=3,500=4,000=40%=P4.0D=Govt.=Creat.=4 April=Mercury=Hermes=G=A4.
Implicit=10,000=1,000=100%=10.0=Physicality=Tech.=10 Oct.=Uranus=P=1Ø.
Implode=3,000=30%=P3.0D=3.0=Creativity=Stars=Muses=3 March = C=I>>GIL.
Implore=3,500=4,000=40%=P4.0D=Govt.=Creatocracy=4 April=Mercury=Hermes=G=A4.
Imply=9,000=90%=P9.00D=9.0=Abstraction=Gods=Saturn=9Sept.>>A=Ø.
Impolite=1,500=15%=P1.50D=1.5=Authority=Solar Crown=1 May = Maia.
Impolitic=2,000=20%=P2.00D=2.0=Nature=Matter=Moon=2 Feb.=Cupid=N=C+_
Imponderable=2,500=3,000=30%=P3.0D=3.0=Cre=Stars=Muses=3 March = C=I>>GIL.
Import=10,000=1,000=100%=10.0=Physicality=Tech.=10 Oct.=Uranus=P=1Ø.
Important=8,500=9,000=90%=P9.00D=9.0=Abstraction=Gods=Saturn=9Sept.>>A=Ø.
Importation=4,000=40%=P4.0D=Govt.=Creatocracy=4 April=Mercury=Hermes=G=A4.
Importunate=2,000=20%=P2.00D=2.0=Nature=Matter=Moon=2 Feb.=Cupid=N=C+_
Importune=4,000=40%=P4.0D=Govt.=Creatocracy=4 April=Mercury=Hermes=G=A4.
Impose=10,000=1,000=100%=10.0=Physicality=Tech.=10 Oct.=Uranus=P=1Ø.
Imposing=500=5%=P5.00D=5.0=Law=Time=Venus=5 May=Aphrodite>>L=N.
Impost=5,500=5.5=80%=P5.50=Earth-Midway=5 May = Gaia.
Impostor=4,000=40%=P4.0D=Govt.=Creatocracy=4 April=Mercury=Hermes=G=A4.
Imposture=9,000=90%=P9.00D=9.0=Abstraction=Gods=Saturn=9Sept.>>A=Ø.

Impotent=6,500=7,000=70%=P7.0D=7.0=Language=Assets=Mars=7 July=Pleiades.
Impound=10,000=1,000=100%=10.0=Physicality=Tech.=10 Oct.=Uranus=P=1Ø.
Impoverish=6,000=60%=P6.0D=Man=Earth=Royalty=6 June=Gaia=Maia>>M=M2.
Impracticable=5,500=5.5=80%=P5.50=Earth-Midway=5 May = Gaia.
Impractical=10,000=1,000=100%=10.0=Physicality=Tech.=10 Oct.=Uranus=P=1Ø.
Imprecation=2,500=3,000=30%=P3.0D=3.0=Cre=Stars=Muses=3 March = C=I>>GIL.
Imprecise=1,000=100%=10.0=1.0=Mind=Sun=1 January=Helios >> M=E4.
Impregnable=6,000=60%=P6.0D=Man=Earth=Royalty=6 June=Gaia=Maia>>M=M2.
Impregnate=10,000=1,000=100%=10.0=Physicality=Tech.=10 Oct.=Uranus=P=1Ø.
Impresario=8,000=80%=P8.0D=Economy=Currency=8 Aug.=Zeus>>E=v.
Impress1=10,000=1,000=100%=10.0=Physicality=Tech.=10 Oct.=Uranus=P=1Ø.
Impress2=8,000=80%=P8.0D=Economy=Currency=8 Aug.=Zeus>>E=v.
Impression=10,000=1,000=100%=10.0=Physicality=Tech.=10 Oct.=Uranus=P=1Ø.
Impressionable=2,500=3,000=30%=P3.0D=3.0=Cre=Stars=Muses=3 March = C=I>>GIL.
Impressionism=10,000=1,000=100%=10.0=Physicality=Tech.=10 Oct.=Uranus=P=1Ø.
Impressive=5,000=50%=P5.00D=Law=Time=Venus=5 May = Aphrodite>>L=N.
Imprimatur=8,500=9,000=90%=P9.00D=9.0=Abstraction=Gods=Saturn=9Sept.>>A=Ø.
Imprint=10,000=1,000=100%=10.0=Physicality=Tech.=10 Oct.=Uranus=P=1Ø.
Imprison=4,500=5,000=50%=P5.00D=Law=Time=Venus=5 May = Aphrodite>>L=N.
Improbable=3,000=30%=P3.0D=3.0=Creativity=Stars=Muses=3 March = C=I>>GIL.
Impromptu=7,500=8,000=80%=P8.0D=Economy=Currency=8 Aug.=Zeus>>E=v.
Improper=8,500=9,000=90%=P9.00D=9.0=Abstraction=Gods=Saturn=9Sept.>>A=Ø.
Improper fraction=7,000=70%=P7.0D=7.0=Language=Assets=Mars=7 July=Pleiades.
Impropriety=5,000=50%=P5.00D=Law=Time=Venus=5 May = Aphrodite>>L=N.
Improve=8,500=9,000=90%=P9.00D=9.0=Abstraction=Gods=Saturn=9Sept.>>A=Ø.
Improvement=7,000=70%=P7.0D=7.0=Language=Assets=Mars=7 July=Pleiades.

Improvident=3,000=30%=P3.0D=3.0=Creativity=Stars=Muses=3 March = C=I>>GIL.
Not providing for the future. Thrift less. Considered a crime, a sin in the Creatocracy.

Improvise=12,500=13,000=13%=P1.30=Solar Core=Faculty=13 January=Athena.
Imprudent=2,500=3,000=30%=P3.0D=3.0=Creativity=Stars=Muses=3 March = C=I>>GIL.
Impudent=3,500=4,000=40%=P4.0D=Govt.=Creat.=4 April=Mercury=Hermes=G=A4.
Impugn=5,500=5.5=80%=P5.50=Earth-Midway=5 May = Gaia.
Impulse=10,000=1,000=100%=10.0=Physicality=Tech.=10 Oct.=Uranus=P=1Ø.
Impulsive=7,500=8,000=80%=P8.0D=Economy=Currency=8 Aug.=Zeus>>E=v.
Impunity=4,500=5,000=50%=P5.00D=Law=Time=Venus=5 May = Aphrodite>>L=N.
Impure=5,500=5.5=80%=P5.50=Earth-Midway=5 May = Gaia.
Impute=7,000=70%=P7.0D=7.0=Language=Assets=Mars=7 July=Pleiades.
In1=10,000=1,000=100%=10.0=Physicality=Tech.=10 Oct.=Uranus=P=1Ø.
In2=500=5%=P5.00D=5.0=Law=Time=Venus=5 May=Aphrodite>>L=N.
In=2,500=3,000=30%=P3.0D=3.0=Creativity=Stars=Muses=3 March = C=I>>GIL.
IN=500=5%=P5.00D=5.0=Law=Time=Venus=5 May=Aphrodite>>L=N.
In-1=1,500=15%=P1.50D=1.5=Authority=Solar Crown=1 May = Maia.

In-2=5,000=50%=P5.00D=Law=Time=Venus=5 May = Aphrodite>>L=N.
-in=9,000=90%=P9.00D=9.0=Abstraction=Gods=Saturn=9Sept.>>A=Ø.
Inability=2,500=3,000=30%=P3.0D=3.0=Creativity=Stars=Muses=3 March = C=I>>GIL.
In absentia=4,000=40%=P4.0D=Govt.=Creatocracy=4 April=Mercury=Hermes=G=A4.
Inaccessible=1,500=15%=P1.50D=1.5=Authority=Solar Crown=1 May = Maia.
Inaccurate=2,500=3,000=30%=P3.0D=3.0=Creativity=Stars=Muses=3 March = C=I>>GIL.
Inaction=2,500=3,000=30%=P3.0D=3.0=Creativity=Stars=Muses=3 March = C=I>>GIL.
Inactivate=1,500=15%=P1.50D=1.5=Authority=Solar Crown=1 May = Maia.
Inactive=4,500=5,000=50%=P5.00D=Law=Time=Venus=5 May = Aphrodite>>L=N.
Inadequate=1,500=15%=P1.50D=1.5=Authority=Solar Crown=1 May = Maia.
Inadmissible=1,000=100%=10.0=1.0=Mind=Sun=1 January=Helios >> M=E4.
Inadvertent=4,000=40%=P4.0D=Govt.=Creatocracy=4 April=Mercury=Hermes=G=A4.
In advisable=1,500=15%=P1.50D=1.5=Authority=Solar Crown=1 May = Maia.
Inalienable=3,000=30%=P3.0D=3.0=Creativity=Stars=Muses=3 March = C=I>>GIL.
Inane=3,000=30%=P3.0D=3.0=Creativity=Stars=Muses=3 March = C=I>>GIL.
Inanimate=4,500=5,000=50%=P5.00D=Law=Time=Venus=5 May = Aphrodite>>L=N.
Inanition=6,500=7,000=70%=P7.0D=7.0=Language=Assets=Mars=7 July=Pleiades.
Inapplicable=1,000=100%=10.0=1.0=Mind=Sun=1 January=Helios >> M=E4.
In appreciable=3,000=30%=P3.0D=3.0=Creativity=Stars=Muses=3 March = C=I>>GIL.
Inappropriate=2,500=3,000=30%=P3.0D=3.0=Cre=Stars=Muses=3 March = C=I>>GIL.
In apt=500=5%=P5.00D=5.0=Law=Time=Venus=5 May=Aphrodite>>L=N.
Inarticulate=10,000=1,000=100%=10.0=Physicality=Tech.=10 Oct.=Uranus=P=1Ø.
In as much as=500=5%=P5.00D=5.0=Law=Time=Venus=5 May=Aphrodite>>L=N.
In attention=3,000=30%=P3.0D=3.0=Creativity=Stars=Muses=3 March = C=I>>GIL.
Inaudible=1,500=15%=P1.50D=1.5=Authority=Solar Crown=1 May = Maia.
Inaugural=5,500=5.5=80%=P5.50=Earth-Midway=5 May = Gaia.
Inaugurate=11,500=12,000=12%=P1.20D=1.2=Knowledge=Edu=12Dec.=Athena>>K=F.
Inauspicious=1,500=15%=P1.50D=1.5=Authority=Solar Crown=1 May = Maia.
Inboard=7,500=8,000=80%=P8.0D=Economy=Currency=8 Aug.=Zeus>>E=v.
Inborn=1,000=100%=10.0=1.0=Mind=Sun=1 January=Helios >> M=E4.
Inbound=1,500=15%=P1.50D=1.5=Authority=Solar Crown=1 May = Maia.
Inbred=3,500=4,000=40%=P4.0D=Govt.=Creatocracy=4 April=Mercury=Hermes=G=A4.
Inbreed=5,000=50%=P5.00D=Law=Time=Venus=5 May = Aphrodite>>L=N.
Inc.=3,000=30%=P3.0D=3.0=Creativity=Stars=Muses=3 March = C=I>>GIL.
Inca=10,000=1,000=100%=10.0=Physicality=Tech.=10 Oct.=Uranus=P=1Ø.
Incalculable=9,500=10,000=1,000=100%=10.0=Physicality=Tech.=10 Oct.=Uranus=P=1Ø.
Incandescent=8,500=9,000=90%=P9.00D=9.0=Abstraction=Gods=Saturn=9Sept.>>A=Ø.
Incandescent lamp=7,500=8,000=80%=P8.0D=Economy=Currency=8 Aug.=Zeus>>E=v.
Incantation=10,500=11,000=11%=P1.10D=1.1=Idea=Brainchild=11 Nov=Athena>>I=MT.
Incapable=5,000=50%=P5.00D=Law=Time=Venus=5 May = Aphrodite>>L=N.
Incapacitate=3,500=4,000=40%=P4.0D=Govt.=Creat.=4 April=Mercury=Hermes=G=A4.
Incapacity=3,500=4,000=40%=P4.0D=Govt.=Creat.=4 April=Mercury=Hermes=G=A4.
Incarcerate=4,500=5,000=50%=P5.00D=Law=Time=Venus=5 May = Aphrodite>>L=N.
Incarnate=12,000=12%=P1.20D=1.2=Knowledge=Education=12Dec.=Athena>>K=F.
Incarnation=11,000=11%=P1.10D=1.1=Idea=Brainchild=11 Nov=Athena>>I=MT.

In case=1,500=15%=P1.50D=1.5=Authority=Solar Crown=1 May = Maia.
In cautious=1,500=15%=P1.50D=1.5=Authority=Solar Crown=1 May = Maia.
Incendiary=9,500=10,000=1,000=100%=10.0=Physicality=Tech.=10 Oct.=Uranus=P=1Ø.
Incense1=6,000=60%=P6.0D=Man=Earth=Royalty=6 June=Gaia=Maia>>M=M2.
Incense2=4,500=5,000=50%=P5.00D=Law=Time=Venus=5 May = Aphrodite>>L=N.
Incentive=6,500=7,000=70%=P7.0D=7.0=Language=Assets=Mars=7 July=Pleiades.
Inception=4,500=5,000=50%=P5.00D=Law=Time=Venus=5 May = Aphrodite>>L=N.
In certitude=2,000=20%=P2.00D=2.0=Nature=Matter=Moon=2 Feb.=Cupid=N=C+_
Incessant=3,000=30%=P3.0D=3.0=Creativity=Stars=Muses=3 March = C=I>>GIL.
Incest=9,500=10,000=1,000=100%=10.0=Physicality=Tech.=10 Oct.=Uranus=P=1Ø.
Inch=16,000=16%=P1.60D=1.6=Cycle of Incarnation=Mind of GOD=1 June = Maia.
Inchoate=5,000=50%=P5.00D=Law=Time=Venus=5 May = Aphrodite>>L=N.
Inchon=8,000=80%=P8.0D=Economy=Currency=8 Aug.=Zeus>>E=v.
Inchworm=1,500=15%=P1.50D=1.5=Authority=Solar Crown=1 May = Maia.
Incidence=2,500=3,000=30%=P3.0D=3.0=Creativity=Stars=Muses=3 March = C=I>>GIL.
Incident=12,000=12%=P1.20D=1.2=Knowledge=Education=12Dec.=Athena>>K=F.
Incidental=10,500=11,000=11%=P1.10D=1.1=Idea=Brainchild=11 Nov=Athena>>I=MT.
Incinerate=5,500=5.5=80%=P5.50=Earth-Midway=5 May = Gaia.
Incinerator=2,500=3,000=30%=P3.0D=3.0=Cre=Stars=Muses=3 March = C=I>>GIL.
Incipient=4,000=40%=P4.0D=Govt.=Creatocracy=4 April=Mercury=Hermes=G=A4.
Incise=9,000=90%=P9.00D=9.0=Abstraction=Gods=Saturn=9Sept.>>A=Ø.
Incision=6,000=60%=P6.0D=Man=Earth=Royalty=6 June=Gaia=Maia>>M=M2.
Incisive=3,000=30%=P3.0D=3.0=Creativity=Stars=Muses=3 March = C=I>>GIL.
Incisor=7,500=8,000=80%=P8.0D=Economy=Currency=8 Aug.=Zeus>>E=v.
Incite=6,000=60%=P6.0D=Man=Earth=Royalty=6 June=Gaia=Maia>>M=M2.
Incivility=500=5%=P5.00D=5.0=Law=Time=Venus=5 May=Aphrodite>>L=N.
Incl.=1,000=100%=10.0=1.0=Mind=Sun=1 January=Helios >> M=E4.
Inclement=2,000=20%=P2.00D=2.0=Nature=Matter=Moon=2 Feb.=Cupid=N=C+_
Inclination=8,500=9,000=90%=P9.00D=9.0=Abstraction=Gods=Saturn=9Sept.>>A=Ø.
Incline=10,000=1,000=100%=10.0=Physicality=Tech.=10 Oct.=Uranus=P=1Ø.
Incline plane=9,000=90%=P9.00D=9.0=Abstraction=Gods=Saturn=9Sept.>>A=Ø.
In close=1,500=15%=P1.50D=1.5=Authority=Solar Crown=1 May = Maia.
Include=11,000=11%=P1.10D=1.1=Idea=Brainchild=11 Nov=Athena>>I=MT.
Incognito=5,000=50%=P5.00D=Law=Time=Venus=5 May = Aphrodite>>L=N.
Incoherent=6,500=7,000=70%=P7.0D=7.0=Language=Assets=Mars=7 July=Pleiades.
Incombustible=1,500=15%=P1.50D=1.5=Authority=Solar Crown=1 May = Maia.
Income=11,500=12,000=12%=P1.20D=1.2=Knowledge=Education=12Dec.=Athena>>K=F.
Income tax=3,000=30%=P3.0D=3.0=Creativity=Stars=Muses=3 March = C=I>>GIL.
Incoming=3,000=30%=P3.0D=3.0=Creativity=Stars=Muses=3 March = C=I>>GIL.
Incommensurate=2,000=20%=P2.00D=2.0=Nature=Matter=Moon=2 Feb.=Cupid=N=C+_
Incommode=1,500=15%=P1.50D=1.5=Authority=Solar Crown=1 May = Maia.
Incommunicado=8,000=80%=P8.0D=Economy=Currency=8 Aug.=Zeus>>E=v.
Incomparable=5,000=50%=P5.00D=Law=Time=Venus=5 May = Aphrodite>>L=N.
Incompatible=4,000=40%=P4.0D=Govt.=Creatocracy=4 April=Mercury=Hermes=G=A4.
Incompetent=1,000=100%=10.0=1.0=Mind=Sun=1 January=Helios >> M=E4.

Incomplete=1,000=100%=10.0=1.0=Mind=Sun=1 January=Helios >> M=E4.
Incomprehensible=2,000=20%=P2.00D=2.0=Nature=Matter=Moon=2 Feb.=Cupid=N=C+_
Incompressible=1,500=15%=P1.50D=1.5=Authority=Solar Crown=1 May = Maia.
Inconceivable=4,000=40%=P4.0D=Govt.=Creatocracy=4 April=Mercury=Hermes=G=A4.
Inconclusive=1,000=100%=10.0=1.0=Mind=Sun=1 January=Helios >> M=E4.
Incongruent=1,000=100%=10.0=1.0=Mind=Sun=1 January=Helios >> M=E4.
Incongruous=7,500=8,000=80%=P8.0D=Economy=Currency=8 Aug.=Zeus>>E=v.
Inconsequential=1,000=100%=10.0=1.0=Mind=Sun=1 January=Helios >> M=E4.
Inconsiderable=500=5%=P5.00D=5.0=Law=Time=Venus=5 May=Aphrodite>>L=N.
Inconsiderate=2,500=3,000=30%=P3.0D=3.0=Cre=Stars=Muses=3 March = C=I>>GIL.
Inconsistent=5,000=50%=P5.00D=Law=Time=Venus=5 May = Aphrodite>>L=N.
Inconsolable=2,000=20%=P2.00D=2.0=Nature=Matter=Moon=2 Feb.=Cupid=N=C+_
Inconspicuous=1,500=15%=P1.50D=1.5=Authority=Solar Crown=1 May = Maia.
Inconstant=3,000=30%=P3.0D=3.0=Creativity=Stars=Muses=3 March = C=I>>GIL.
Incontestable=1,500=15%=P1.50D=1.5=Authority=Solar Crown=1 May = Maia.
Incontinent=4,500=5,000=50%=P5.00D=Law=Time=Venus=5 May = Aphrodite>>L=N.
Incontrovertible=2,000=20%=P2.00D=2.0=Nature=Matter=Moon=2 Feb.=Cupid=N=C+_
Inconvenience=5,500=5.5=80%=P5.50=Earth-Midway=5 May = Gaia.
Inconvenient=5,500=5.5=80%=P5.50=Earth-Midway=5 May = Gaia.
Incorporate=12,000=12%=P1.20D=1.2=Knowledge=Education=12Dec.=Athena>>K=F.
Incorporeal=4,500=5,000=50%=P5.00D=Law=Time=Venus=5 May = Aphrodite>>L=N.
Incorrect=2,500=3,000=30%=P3.0D=3.0=Creativity=Stars=Muses=3 March = C=I>>GIL.
Incorrigible=4,000=40%=P4.0D=Govt.=Creatocracy=4 April=Mercury=Hermes=G=A4.
Incorruptible=4,500=5,000=50%=P5.00D=Law=Time=Venus=5 May = Aphrodite>>L=N.
Increase=10,000=1,000=100%=10.0=Physicality=Tech.=10 Oct.=Uranus=P=1Ø.
Incredible=3,000=30%=P3.0D=3.0=Creativity=Stars=Muses=3 March = C=I>>GIL.
Incredulous=2,500=3,000=30%=P3.0D=3.0=Cre=Stars=Muses=3 March = C=I>>GIL.
Increment=9,000=90%=P9.00D=9.0=Abstraction=Gods=Saturn=9Sept.>>A=Ø.
Incriminate=6,500=7,000=70%=P7.0D=7.0=Language=Assets=Mars=7 July=Pleiades.
Incrust=1,500=15%=P1.50D=1.5=Authority=Solar Crown=1 May = Maia.
Incubate=11,000=11%=P1.10D=1.1=Idea=Brainchild=11 Nov=Athena>>I=MT.
Incubator=10,000=1,000=100%=10.0=Physicality=Tech.=10 Oct.=Uranus=P=1Ø.

Incubus=5,500=5.5=80%=P5.50=Earth-Midway=5 May = Gaia.
An evil spirit believed to violate sleeping women. An oppressive nightmare. In Nigeria it is
known as spirit husband. They are lost muses once in the service is Gaia midway or Maia.

Inculcate=8,000=80%=P8.0D=Economy=Currency=8 Aug.=Zeus>>E=v.
To teach or impress by frequent instruction or repetition; instill. Latin. Inculcáre, force
upon < calcáre, trample. Results shows it is a quality of Zeus Jehovah the Most High.

In culpable=2,000=20%=P2.00D=2.0=Nature=Matter=Moon=2 Feb.=Cupid=N=C+_
Inculpate=2,000=20%=P2.00D=2.0=Nature=Matter=Moon=2 Feb.=Cupid=N=C+_
Incumbent=10,000=1,000=100%=10.0=Physicality=Tech.=10 Oct.=Uranus=P=1Ø.

Incunabulum=4,000=40%=P4.0D=Govt.=Creatocracy=4 April=Mercury=Hermes=G=A4.
Incur=10,000=1,000=100%=Physicality=Tech.=10 Oct.=Uranus=P=1Ø.
Incurable=3,500=4,000=40%=P4.0D=Govt.=Creat.=4 April=Mercury=Hermes=G=A4.
Incurious=1,000=100%=10.0=1.0=Mind=Sun=1 January=Helios >> M=E4.

Incursion=4,000=40%=P4.0D=Govt.=Creatocracy=4 April=Mercury=Hermes=G=A4.
By the power of Hermes the Creatocracy has made an incursion into every field of study.
This is what makes the Creative & Psycho-Social Sciences, the Creative Sciences of the
Makupedia a multidisciplinary multidimensional and interdisciplinary field of study.

Incus=6,000=60%=P6.0D=Man=Earth=Royalty=6 June=Gaia=Maia>>M=M2.
Ind.=1,500=15%=P1.50D=1.5=Authority=Solar Crown=1 May = Maia.
Indebted=2,000=20%=P2.00D=2.0=Nature=Matter=Moon=2 Feb.=Cupid=N=C+_
Indecent=3,000=30%=P3.0D=3.0=Creativity=Stars=Muses=3 March = C=I>>GIL.
Indecipherable=1,500=15%=P1.50D=1.5=Authority=Solar Crown=1 May = Maia.

Indecision=3,500=4,000=40%=P4.0D=Govt.=Creat.=4 April=Mercury=Hermes=G=A4.
The lack of muse as a means to decision making leads to indecision.

Indecisive=2,000=20%=P2.00D=2.0=Nature=Matter=Moon=2 Feb.=Cupid=N=C+_
In decorous=2,500=3,000=30%=P3.0D=3.0=Cre=Stars=Muses=3 March = C=I>>GIL.
Indeed=9,000=90%=P9.00D=9.0=Abstraction=Gods=Saturn=9Sept.>>A=Ø.
Indef.=500=5%=P5.00D=5.0=Law=Time=Venus=5 May=Aphrodite>>L=N.
Indefatigable=5,000=50%=P5.00D=Law=Time=Venus=5 May = Aphrodite>>L=N.
Indefensible=4,500=5,000=50%=P5.00D=Law=Time=Venus=5 May = Aphrodite>>L=N.
In definable=5,000=50%=P5.00D=Law=Time=Venus=5 May = Aphrodite>>L=N.
Indefinite=3,500=4,000=40%=P4.0D=Govt.=Creat.=4 April=Mercury=Hermes=G=A4.
Indefinite article=9,500=10,000=1,000=100%=Physicality=Tech.=10 Oct.=Uranus=P=1Ø.
Indelible=9,000=90%=P9.00D=9.0=Abstraction=Gods=Saturn=9Sept.>>A=Ø.
Indelicate=5,000=50%=P5.00D=Law=Time=Venus=5 May = Aphrodite>>L=N.
Indemnify=10,000=1,000=100%=10.0=Physicality=Tech.=10 Oct.=Uranus=P=1Ø.
Indemnity=10,000=1,000=100%=10.0=Physicality=Tech.=10 Oct.=Uranus=P=1Ø.
Ident1=10,000=1,000=100%=10.0=Physicality=Tech.=10 Oct.=Uranus=P=1Ø.
Ident2=3,500=4,000=40%=P4.0D=Govt.=Creatocracy=4 April=Mercury=Hermes=G=A4.
Indentation=10,000=1,000=100%=10.0=Physicality=Tech.=10 Oct.=Uranus=P=1Ø.
Indenture=10,000=1,000=100%=10.0=Physicality=Tech.=10 Oct.=Uranus=P=1Ø.
Independence=5,000=50%=P5.00D=Law=Time=Venus=5 May = Aphrodite>>L=N.
Independence Day=8,000=80%=P8.0D=Economy=Currency=8 Aug.=Zeus>>E=v.
Independent=10,000=1,000=100%=10.0=Physicality=Tech.=10 Oct.=Uranus=P=1Ø.
In-depth=1,000=100%=10.0=1.0=Mind=Sun=1 January=Helios >> M=E4.
Indescribable=4,500=5,000=50%=P5.00D=Law=Time=Venus=5 May = Aphrodite>>L=N.
Indestructible=1,500=15%=P1.50D=1.5=Authority=Solar Crown=1 May = Maia.
Indeterminate=4,500=5,000=50%=P5.00D=Law=Time=Venus=5 May = Aphrodite>>L=N.

Index=10,000=1,000=100%=10.0=Physicality=Tech.=10 Oct.=Uranus=P=1Ø.
Index finger=2,500=3,000=30%=P3.0D=3.0=Cre=Stars=Muses=3 March = C=I>>GIL.
Index of refraction=5,500=5.5=80%=P5.50=Earth-Midway=5 May = Gaia.

India=11,500=12,000=12%=P1.20D=1.2=Knowledge=Education=12Dec.=Athena>>K=F.
Athena is the ruler of India. She is the means to their knowledge.

Indian=11,000=11%=P1.10D=1.1=Idea=Brainchild=11 Nov=Athena>>I=MT.
Indiana=6,000=60%=P6.0D=Man=Earth=Royalty=6 June=Gaia=Maia>>M=M2.
Indianapolis=6,000=60%=P6.0D=Man=Earth=Royalty=6 June=Gaia=Maia>>M=M2.
Indian corn=1,500=15%=P1.50D=1.5=Authority=Solar Crown=1 May = Maia.
Indian Ocean=8,000=80%=P8.0D=Economy=Currency=8 Aug.=Zeus>>E=v.
Indian pipe=5,500=5.5=80%=P5.50=Earth-Midway=5 May = Gaia.
Indian summer=4,500=5,000=50%=P5.00D=Law=Time=Venus=5 May = Aphrodite>>L=N.
Indian Territory=6,500=7,000=70%=P7.0D=7.0=Language=Assets=Mars=7 July=Pleiades.
Indic=7,000=70%=P7.0D=7.0=Language=Assets=Mars=7 July=Pleiades.
Indic.=1,000=100%=10.0=1.0=Mind=Sun=1 January=Helios >> M=E4.
Indicate=10,000=1,000=100%=10.0=Physicality=Tech.=10 Oct.=Uranus=P=1Ø.
Indicative=9,500=10,000=1,000=100%=10.0=Physicality=Tech.=10 Oct.=Uranus=P=1Ø.
Indices=2,000=20%=P2.00D=2.0=Nature=Matter=Moon=2 Feb.=Cupid=N=C+_
Indict=10,000=1,000=100%=10.0=Physicality=Tech.=10 Oct.=Uranus=P=1Ø.
Indies=2,000=20%=P2.00D=2.0=Nature=Matter=Moon=2 Feb.=Cupid=N=C+_
Indifferent=10,000=1,000=100%=10.0=Physicality=Tech.=10 Oct.=Uranus=P=1Ø.
Indigenous=6,000=60%=P6.0D=Man=Earth=Royalty=6 June=Gaia=Maia>>M=M2.
Indigent=6,000=60%=P6.0D=Man=Earth=Royalty=6 June=Gaia=Maia>>M=M2.
Indigestible=2,500=3,000=30%=P3.0D=3.0=Cre=Stars=Muses=3 March = C=I>>GIL.
Indigestion=6,000=60%=P6.0D=Man=Earth=Royalty=6 June=Gaia=Maia>>M=M2.
Indignant=5,500=5.5=80%=P5.50=Earth-Midway=5 May = Gaia.
Indignation=5,500=5.5=80%=P5.50=Earth-Midway=5 May = Gaia.
Indignity=7,500=8,000=80%=P8.0D=Economy=Currency=8 Aug.=Zeus>>E=v.
Indigo=10,000=1,000=100%=10.0=Physicality=Tech.=10 Oct.=Uranus=P=1Ø.
Indigo bunting=6,500=7,000=70%=P7.0D=7.0=Language=Assets=Mars=7 July=Pleiades.
Indirect=10,000=1,000=100%=10.0=Physicality=Tech.=10 Oct.=Uranus=P=1Ø.
Indirect object=8,000=80%=P8.0D=Economy=Currency=8 Aug.=Zeus>>E=v.
Indiscernible=2,000=20%=P2.00D=2.0=Nature=Matter=Moon=2 Feb.=Cupid=N=C+_
Indiscreet=1,500=15%=P1.50D=1.5=Authority=Solar Crown=1 May = Maia.
Indiscriminate=8,000=80%=P8.0D=Economy=Currency=8 Aug.=Zeus>>E=v.
Indispensable=6,000=60%=P6.0D=Man=Earth=Royalty=6 June=Gaia=Maia>>M=M2.
Indisposed=2,000=20%=P2.00D=2.0=Nature=Matter=Moon=2 Feb.=Cupid=N=C+_
Indisputable=1,500=15%=P1.50D=1.5=Authority=Solar Crown=1 May = Maia.
Indissoluble=3,000=30%=P3.0D=3.0=Creativity=Stars=Muses=3 March = C=I>>GIL.
In distinct=3,500=4,000=40%=P4.0D=Govt.=Creat.=4 April=Mercury=Hermes=G=A4.
Indistinguishable=4,000=40%=P4.0D=Govt.=Creat.=4 April=Mercury=Hermes=G=A4.
Indite=2,500=3,000=30%=P3.0D=3.0=Creativity=Stars=Muses=3 March = C=I>>GIL.

Indium=10,000=1,000=100%=10.0=Physicality=Tech.=10 Oct.=Uranus=P=1Ø.
Individual=10,000=1,000=100%=10.0=Physicality=Tech.=10 Oct.=Uranus=P=1Ø.
Individualism=10,000=1,000=100%=10.0=Physicality=Tech.=10 Oct.=Uranus=P=1Ø.
Individualist=5,000=50%=P5.00D=Law=Time=Venus=5 May = Aphrodite>>L=N.
Individuality=6,000=60%=P6.0D=Man=Earth=Royalty=6 June=Gaia=Maia>>M=M2.
Individualize=6,000=60%=P6.0D=Man=Earth=Royalty=6 June=Gaia=Maia>>M=M2.
Indivisible=1,500=15%=P1.50D=1.5=Authority=Solar Crown=1 May = Maia.
Indochina=10,000=1,000=100%=10.0=Physicality=Tech.=10 Oct.=Uranus=P=1Ø.
Indoctrinate=6,000=60%=P6.0D=Man=Earth=Royalty=6 June=Gaia=Maia>>M=M2.
Indo-European=10,000=1,000=100%=10.0=Physicality=Tech.=10 Oct.=Uranus=P=1Ø.
Indo-Iranian=10,000=1,000=100%=10.0=Physicality=Tech.=10 Oct.=Uranus=P=1Ø.
Indolent=6,000=60%=P6.0D=Man=Earth=Royalty=6 June=Gaia=Maia>>M=M2.
Indomitable=3,000=30%=P3.0D=3.0=Creativity=Stars=Muses=3 March = C=I>>GIL.
Indonesia=10,000=1,000=100%=10.0=Physicality=Tech.=10 Oct.=Uranus=P=1Ø.
Indonesian=10,000=1,000=100%=10.0=Physicality=Tech.=10 Oct.=Uranus=P=1Ø.
Indoor=5,500=5.5=80%=P5.50=Earth-Midway=5 May = Gaia.
Indoors=2,500=3,000=30%=P3.0D=3.0=Creativity=Stars=Muses=3 March = C=I>>GIL.
Indore=5,000=50%=P5.00D=Law=Time=Venus=5 May = Aphrodite>>L=N.
Indorse=1,500=15%=P1.50D=1.5=Authority=Solar Crown=1 May = Maia.
Inaudible=4,000=40%=P4.0D=Govt.=Creatocracy=4 April=Mercury=Hermes=G=A4.
Induce=10,500=11,000=11%=P1.10D=1.1=Idea=Brainchild=11 Nov=Athena>>I=MT.
Induct=9,500=10,000=1,000=100%=10.0=Physicality=Tech.=10 Oct.=Uranus=P=1Ø.
Inductance=6,000=60%=P6.0D=Man=Earth=Royalty=6 June=Gaia=Maia>>M=M2.
Induction=10,000=1,000=100%=10.0=Physicality=Tech.=10 Oct.=Uranus=P=1Ø.
Inductive=4,500=5,000=50%=P5.00D=Law=Time=Venus=5 May = Aphrodite>>L=N.
Indulge=9,500=10,000=1,000=100%=10.0=Physicality=Tech.=10 Oct.=Uranus=P=1Ø.
Indulgence=10,000=1,000=100%=10.0=Physicality=Tech.=10 Oct.=Uranus=P=1Ø.
Indulgent=4,000=40%=P4.0D=Govt.=Creatocracy=4 April=Mercury=Hermes=G=A4.
Indurate=6,500=7,000=70%=P7.0D=7.0=Language=Assets=Mars=7 July=Pleiades.
Indus=13,000=13%=P1.30=Solar Core=Faculty=13 January=Athena.
Industrial=5,500=5.5=80%=P5.50=Earth-Midway=5 May = Gaia.
Industrialist=6,000=60%=P6.0D=Man=Earth=Royalty=6 June=Gaia=Maia>>M=M2.
Industrialize=2,500=3,000=30%=P3.0D=3.0=Cre=Stars=Muses=3 March = C=I>>GIL.
Industrial park=7,000=70%=P7.0D=7.0=Language=Assets=Mars=7 July=Pleiades.
Industrious=1,500=15%=P1.50D=1.5=Authority=Solar Crown=1 May = Maia.
Industry=10,000=1,000=100%=10.0=Physicality=Tech.=10 Oct.=Uranus=P=1Ø.
-ine1=4,500=5,000=50%=P5.00D=Law=Time=Venus=5 May = Aphrodite>>L=N.
-ine2=10,000=1,000=100%=10.0=Physicality=Tech.=10 Oct.=Uranus=P=1Ø.
Inebriate=5,500=5.5=80%=P5.50=Earth-Midway=5 May = Gaia.
Inedible=1,000=100%=10.0=1.0=Mind=Sun=1 January=Helios >> M=E4.
Ineffable=8,000=80%=P8.0D=Economy=Currency=8 Aug.=Zeus>>E=v.
In effaceable=2,000=20%=P2.00D=2.0=Nature=Matter=Moon=2 Feb.=Cupid=N=C+_
Ineffective=2,000=20%=P2.00D=2.0=Nature=Matter=Moon=2 Feb.=Cupid=N=C+_
Ineffectual=4,500=5,000=50%=P5.00D=Law=Time=Venus=5 May = Aphrodite>>L=N.
Inefficient=4,000=40%=P4.0D=Govt.=Creatocracy=4 April=Mercury=Hermes=G=A4.

Inelegant=2,000=20%=P2.00D=2.0=Nature=Matter=Moon=2 Feb.=Cupid=N=C+_
Ineligible=2,500=3,000=30%=P3.0D=3.0=Creativity=Stars=Muses=3 March = C=I>>GIL.
Ineluctable=4,500=5,000=50%=P5.00D=Law=Time=Venus=5 May = Aphrodite>>L=N.
Inept=8,000=80%=P8.0D=Economy=Currency=8 Aug.=Zeus>>E=v.
Inequality=10,500=11,000=11%=P1.10D=1.1=Idea=Brainchild=11 Nov=Athena>>I=MT.
Inequitable=1,500=15%=P1.50D=1.5=Authority=Solar Crown=1 May = Maia.
Inequity=3,000=30%=P3.0D=3.0=Creativity=Stars=Muses=3 March = C=I>>GIL.
Inerrancy=3,000=30%=P3.0D=3.0=Creativity=Stars=Muses=3 March = C=I>>GIL.
Inert=10,000=1,000=100%=10.0=Physicality=Tech.=10 Oct.=Uranus=P=1Ø.
Inertia=10,000=1,000=100%=10.0=Physicality=Tech.=10 Oct.=Uranus=P=1Ø.
Inescapable=4,000=40%=P4.0D=Govt.=Creatocracy=4 April=Mercury=Hermes=G=A4.
Inestimable=6,500=7,000=70%=P7.0D=7.0=Language=Assets=Mars=7 July=Pleiades.
Inevitable=6,000=60%=P6.0D=Man=Earth=Royalty=6 June=Gaia=Maia>>M=M2.
In exact=3,000=30%=P3.0D=3.0=Creativity=Stars=Muses=3 March = C=I>>GIL.
Inexcusable=2,000=20%=P2.00D=2.0=Nature=Matter=Moon=2 Feb.=Cupid=N=C+_
Inexhaustible=4,000=40%=P4.0D=Govt.=Creatocracy=4 April=Mercury=Hermes=G=A4.
Inexorable=5,000=50%=P5.00D=Law=Time=Venus=5 May = Aphrodite>>L=N.
Inexpensive=1,500=15%=P1.50D=1.5=Authority=Solar Crown=1 May = Maia.
Inexperience=1,500=15%=P1.50D=1.5=Authority=Solar Crown=1 May = Maia.
Inexpert=1,500=15%=P1.50D=1.5=Authority=Solar Crown=1 May = Maia.
Inexplicable=3,000=30%=P3.0D=3.0=Creativity=Stars=Muses=3 March = C=I>>GIL.
Inexpressible=4,000=40%=P4.0D=Govt.=Creatocracy=4 April=Mercury=Hermes=G=A4.
Inextinguishable=2,500=3,000=30%=P3.0D=3.0=Cre=Stars=Muses=3 March = C=I>>GIL.
In extremis=4,500=5,000=50%=P5.00D=Law=Time=Venus=5 May = Aphrodite>>L=N.
Inextricable=5,000=50%=P5.00D=Law=Time=Venus=5 May = Aphrodite>>L=N.
Inf.=1,000=100%=Physicality=Tech.=10 Oct.=Uranus=P=1Ø.
Infallible=4,000=40%=P4.0D=Govt.=Creatocracy=4 April=Mercury=Hermes=G=A4.
Infamous=5,000=50%=P5.00D=Law=Time=Venus=5 May = Aphrodite>>L=N.
Infamy=6,500=7,000=70%=P7.0D=7.0=Language=Assets=Mars=7 July=Pleiades.
Infancy=6,000=60%=P6.0D=Man=Earth=Royalty=6 June=Gaia=Maia>>M=M2.
Infant=7,500=8,000=80%=P8.0D=Economy=Currency=8 Aug.=Zeus>>E=v.
Infanticide=7,500=8,000=80%=P8.0D=Economy=Currency=8 Aug.=Zeus>>E=v.
Infantile paralysis=1,000=100%=Physicality=Tech.=10 Oct.=Uranus=P=1Ø.
Infantry=8,000=80%=P8.0D=Economy=Currency=8 Aug.=Zeus>>E=v.
Infarct=8,000=80%=P8.0D=Economy=Currency=8 Aug.=Zeus>>E=v.
Infatuate=5,500=5.5=80%=P5.50=Earth-Midway=5 May = Gaia.
In feasible=1,500=15%=P1.50D=1.5=Authority=Solar Crown=1 May = Maia.
Infect=9,000=90%=P9.00D=9.0=Abstraction=Gods=Saturn=9Sept.>>A=Ø.
Infectious=6,500=7,000=70%=P7.0D=7.0=Language=Assets=Mars=7 July=Pleiades.
Infectious mono.=10,500=11,000=11%=P1.10D=1.1=Idea=Bchd.=11Nov=Athena>>I=MT.
In felicitous=3,500=4,000=40%=P4.0D=Govt.=Creat.=4 April=Mercury=Hermes=G=A4.
Infer=10,000=1,000=100%=10.0=Physicality=Tech.=10 Oct.=Uranus=P=1Ø.
Inference=4,000=40%=P4.0D=Govt.=Creatocracy=4 April=Mercury=Hermes=G=A4.
Inferior=8,000=80%=P8.0D=Economy=Currency=8 Aug.=Zeus>>E=v.
Infernal=7,000=70%=P7.0D=7.0=Language=Assets=Mars=7 July=Pleiades.

Inferno=6,000=60%=P6.0D=Man=Earth=Royalty=6 June=Gaia=Maia>>M=M2.
Infertile=2,500=3,000=30%=P3.0D=3.0=Creativity=Stars=Muses=3 March = C=I>>GIL.
Infest=7,500=8,000=80%=P8.0D=Economy=Currency=8 Aug.=Zeus>>E=v.
Infidel=10,000=1,000=100%=10.0=Physicality=Tech.=10 Oct.=Uranus=P=1Ø.
Infidelity=5,500=5.5=80%=P5.50=Earth-Midway=5 May = Gaia.
Infield=7,500=8,000=80%=P8.0D=Economy=Currency=8 Aug.=Zeus>>E=v.
Infighting=5,000=50%=P5.00D=Law=Time=Venus=5 May = Aphrodite>>L=N.
Infiltrate=6,000=60%=P6.0D=Man=Earth=Royalty=6 June=Gaia=Maia>>M=M2.
Infin.=500=5%=P5.00D=5.0=Law=Time=Venus=5 May=Aphrodite>>L=N.
Infinite=10,000=1,000=100%=10.0=Physicality=Tech.=10 Oct.=Uranus=P=1Ø.
Infinitesimal=8,500=9,000=90%=P9.00D=9.0=Abstraction=Gods=Saturn=9Sept.>>A=Ø.
Infinitive=14,500=15,000=1,500=15%=P1.50D=1.5=Authority=Solar Crown=1 May = Maia.
Infinitude=7,000=70%=P7.0D=7.0=Language=Assets=Mars=7 July=Pleiades.
Infinity=9,000=90%=P9.00D=9.0=Abstraction=Gods=Saturn=9Sept.>>A=Ø.
Infirm=7,000=70%=P7.0D=7.0=Language=Assets=Mars=7 July=Pleiades.
Infirmary=4,500=5,000=50%=P5.00D=Law=Time=Venus=5 May = Aphrodite>>L=N.
Infirmity=5,500=5.5=80%=P5.50=Earth-Midway=5 May = Gaia.
Inflame=8,500=9,000=90%=P9.00D=9.0=Abstraction=Gods=Saturn=9Sept.>>A=Ø.
Inflammable=11,000=11%=P1.10D=1.1=Idea=Brainchild=11 Nov=Athena>>I=MT.
Inflammation=8,500=9,000=90%=P9.00D=9.0=Abstraction=Gods=Saturn=9Sept.>>A=Ø.
Inflammatory=5,000=50%=P5.00D=Law=Time=Venus=5 May = Aphrodite>>L=N.
Inflate=10,000=1,000=100%=10.0=Physicality=Tech.=10 Oct.=Uranus=P=1Ø.

Inflation=9,500=10,000=1,000=100%=10.0=Physicality=Tech.=10 Oct.=Uranus=P=1Ø.
"By the nineteenth century, economists categorized three separate factors that cause a rise or fall in the price of goods: a change in the value or production costs of the good, a change in the price of money which then was usually a fluctuation in the commodity price of the metallic content in the currency, and currency depreciation resulting from an increased supply of currency relative to the quantity of redeemable metal backing the currency. - Classical Economics. Online Research. The Maks Currency is formula based on natural values that makes for consistency and equitable dynamism. The pricing module is revolutionary because it is solar core computed and objective on the diamond equivalent. The Sun does not deplete as energy can neither be created nor destroyed according to the laws of Newton. The Solar Core - Maks Currency is perpetual. See Means. Fiat. Currency.

Inflect=12,000=12%=P1.20D=1.2=Knowledge=Education=12Dec.=Athena>>K=F.
Inflection=10,000=1,000=100%=10.0=Physicality=Tech.=10 Oct.=Uranus=P=1Ø.
Inflexible=5,000=50%=P5.00D=Law=Time=Venus=5 May = Aphrodite>>L=N.
Inflict=5,000=50%=P5.00D=Law=Time=Venus=5 May = Aphrodite>>L=N.
Inflorescence=7,500=8,000=80%=P8.0D=Economy=Currency=8 Aug.=Zeus>>E=v.
Inflow=2,500=3,000=30%=P3.0D=3.0=Creativity=Stars=Muses=3 March = C=I>>GIL.
Influence=10,000=1,000=100%=10.0=Physicality=Tech.=10 Oct.=Uranus=P=1Ø.
Influenza=11,000=11%=P1.10D=1.1=Idea=Brainchild=11 Nov=Athena>>I=MT.

Influx=4,000=40%=P4.0D=Govt.=Creatocracy=4 April=Mercury=Hermes=G=A4.
Info=1,000=100%=10.0=1.0=Mind=Sun=1 January=Helios >> M=E4.
Infold=2,000=20%=P2.00D=2.0=Nature=Matter=Moon=2 Feb.=Cupid=N=C+_
Inform=7,500=8,000=80%=P8.0D=Economy=Currency=8 Aug.=Zeus>>E=v.
Informal=8,500=9,000=90%=P9.00D=9.0=Abstraction=Gods=Saturn=9Sept.>>A=Ø.
Informant=3,000=30%=P3.0D=3.0=Creativity=Stars=Muses=3 March = C=I>>GIL.
Information=10,000=1,000=100%=10.0=Physicality=Tech.=10 Oct.=Uranus=P=1Ø.
Informative=2,500=3,000=30%=P3.0D=3.0=Cre=Stars=Muses=3 March = C=I>>GIL.
Informed=5,500=5.5=80%=P5.50=Earth-Midway=5 May = Gaia.
Informer=4,000=40%=P4.0D=Govt.=Creatocracy=4 April=Mercury=Hermes=G=A4.
Infra-=5,500=5.5=80%=P5.50=Earth-Midway=5 May = Gaia.
Infraction=6,500=7,000=70%=P7.0D=7.0=Language=Assets=Mars=7 July=Pleiades.
Infrared=10,000=1,000=100%=10.0=Physicality=Tech.=10 Oct.=Uranus=P=1Ø.
Infrasonic=6,000=60%=P6.0D=Man=Earth=Royalty=6 June=Gaia=Maia>>M=M2.
Infrastructure=10,000=1,000=100%=10.0=Physicality=Tech.=10 Oct.=Uranus=P=1Ø.
Infrequent=6,000=60%=P6.0D=Man=Earth=Royalty=6 June=Gaia=Maia>>M=M2.
Infringe=4,000=40%=P4.0D=Govt.=Creatocracy=4 April=Mercury=Hermes=G=A4.
Infuriate=5,500=5.5=80%=P5.50=Earth-Midway=5 May = Gaia.
Infuse=10,000=1,000=100%=10.0=Physicality=Tech.=10 Oct.=Uranus=P=1Ø.
-ing1=10,000=1,000=100%=10.0=Physicality=Tech.=10 Oct.=Uranus=P=1Ø.
-ing2=10,000=1,000=100%=10.0=Physicality=Tech.=10 Oct.=Uranus=P=1Ø.
Inge William=2,000=20%=P2.00D=2.0=Nature=Matter=Moon=2 Feb.=Cupid=N=C+_
Ingenious=6,000=60%=P6.0D=Man=Earth=Royalty=6 June=Gaia=Maia>>M=M2.
Ingénue=5,500=5.5=80%=P5.50=Earth-Midway=5 May = Gaia.
Ingenuity=4,000=40%=P4.0D=Govt.=Creatocracy=4 April=Mercury=Hermes=G=A4.
Ingenious=3,500=4,000=40%=P4.0D=Govt.=Creat.=4 April=Mercury=Hermes=G=A4.
Ingest=9,000=90%=P9.00D=9.0=Abstraction=Gods=Saturn=9Sept.>>A=Ø.
Inglewood=5,500=5.5=80%=P5.50=Earth-Midway=5 May = Gaia.
Inglorious=3,000=30%=P3.0D=3.0=Creativity=Stars=Muses=3 March = C=I>>GIL.
Ingot=8,500=9,000=90%=P9.00D=9.0=Abstraction=Gods=Saturn=9Sept.>>A=Ø.

In grain=10,000=1,000=100%=10.0=Physicality=Tech.=10 Oct.=Uranus=P=1Ø.
To fix deeply or indelibly as in the mind. The Creatocracy is deep rooted, engrained by the 10,000 measuring systems in the abstraction knowledge of energy and MindComputing.

Ingrained=6,000=60%=P6.0D=Man=Earth=Royalty=6 June=Gaia=Maia>>M=M2.
Ingrate=3,000=30%=P3.0D=3.0=Creativity=Stars=Muses=3 March = C=I>>GIL.
Ingratiate=6,000=60%=P6.0D=Man=Earth=Royalty=6 June=Gaia=Maia>>M=M2.
Ingratitude=2,000=20%=P2.00D=2.0=Nature=Matter=Moon=2 Feb.=Cupid=N=C+_

Ingredient=7,000=70%=P7.0D=7.0=Language=Assets=Mars=7 July=Pleiades.
Lat, ingredi, enter. Computing works and assets are ingredients to enter a life of Paradise.

Ingres Jean=3,000=30%=P3.0D=3.0=Creativity=Stars=Muses=3 March = C=I>>GIL.
Ingress=5,000=50%=P5.00D=Law=Time=Venus=5 May = Aphrodite>>L=N.
In-group=1,000=100%=10.0=1.0=Mind=Sun=1 January=Helios >> M=E4.
Ingrown=4,500=5,000=50%=P5.00D=Law=Time=Venus=5 May = Aphrodite>>L=N.
Inguinal=4,500=5,000=50%=P5.00D=Law=Time=Venus=5 May = Aphrodite>>L=N.
Inhabit=3,500=4,000=40%=P4.0D=Govt.=Creat.=4 April=Mercury=Hermes=G=A4.
Inhabitant=1,500=15%=P1.50D=1.5=Authority=Solar Crown=1 May = Maia.
Inhalant=2,500=3,000=30%=P3.0D=3.0=Creativity=Stars=Muses=3 March = C=I>>GIL.
Inhalator=2,500=3,000=30%=P3.0D=3.0=Creativity=Stars=Muses=3 March = C=I>>GIL.
Inhale=4,500=5,000=50%=P5.00D=Law=Time=Venus=5 May = Aphrodite>>L=N.
Inhaler=5,500=5.5=80%=P5.50=Earth-Midway=5 May = Gaia.
In here=3,500=4,000=40%=P4.0D=Govt.=Creato.=4 April=Mercury=Hermes=G=A4.
Inherent=4,000=40%=P4.0D=Govt.=Creatocracy=4 April=Mercury=Hermes=G=A4.
Inherit=8,500=9,000=90%=P9.00D=9.0=Abstraction=Gods=Saturn=9Sept.>>A=Ø.

Inheritance=6,500=7,000=70%=P7.0D=7.0=Language=Assets=Mars=7 July=Pleiades.
All things are the inheritance of the Solar Crown King who measured the core of the Sun.
He own the absolute rights to the Sun and everything above below and around it asserted.
He is the Most Sovereign Emperor, Sovereign Creatocratic Republic of Paradise. U=abc.
See Front cover page on the computing and programs that earned him the universal rights.
This is the universal code of inheritance set up by the Almighty GOD. The Mind of GOD.

Inhibit=4,000=40%=P4.0D=Govt.=Creatocracy=4 April=Mercury=Hermes=G=A4.
Inhibition=7,000=70%=P7.0D=7.0=Language=Assets=Mars=7 July=Pleiades.
Inhibitor=6,000=60%=P6.0D=Man=Earth=Royalty=6 June=Gaia=Maia>>M=M2.
Inhospitable=5,500=5.5=80%=P5.50=Earth-Midway=5 May = Gaia.
In house=3,500=4,000=40%=P4.0D=Govt.=Creato.=4 April=Mercury=Hermes=G=A4.
Inhuman=8,500=9,000=90%=P9.00D=9.0=Abstraction=Gods=Saturn=9Sept.>>A=Ø.
In humane=2,000=20%=P2.00D=2.0=Nature=Matter=Moon=2 Feb.=Cupid=N=C+_
Inimical=4,000=40%=P4.0D=Govt.=Creatocracy=4 April=Mercury=Hermes=G=A4.
Inimitable=1,500=15%=P1.50D=1.5=Authority=Solar Crown=1 May = Maia.
Iniquity=4,000=40%=P4.0D=Govt.=Creatocracy=4 April=Mercury=Hermes=G=A4.
Initial=12,500=13,000=13%=P1.30=Solar Core=Faculty=13 January=Athena.
Initialize=4,500=5,000=50%=P5.00D=Law=Time=Venus=5 May = Aphrodite>>L=N.
Initiate=13,500=14,000=14%=P1.40D=1.4=Mgt.=Solar Energy=13 May=Athena=SC=0.1
Initiative=10,000=1,000=100%=10.0=Physicality=Tech.=10 Oct.=Uranus=P=1Ø.
Inject=10,000=1,000=100%=10.0=Physicality=Tech.=10 Oct.=Uranus=P=1Ø.
Injudicious=4,000=40%=P4.0D=Govt.=Creatocracy=4 April=Mercury=Hermes=G=A4.
Injunction=7,500=8,000=80%=P8.0D=Economy=Currency=8 Aug.=Zeus>>E=v.
Injure=5,500=5.5=80%=P5.50=Earth-Midway=5 May = Gaia.
Injurious=1,500=15%=P1.50D=1.5=Authority=Solar Crown=1 May = Maia.
Injury=9,500=10,000=1,000=100%=10.0=Physicality=Tech.=10 Oct.=Uranus=P=1Ø.
Injustice=7,000=70%=P7.0D=7.0=Language=Assets=Mars=7 July=Pleiades.
Ink=10,000=1,000=100%=10.0=Physicality=Tech.=10 Oct.=Uranus=P=1Ø.

Ink blot=8,000=80%=P8.0D=Economy=Currency=8 Aug.=Zeus>>E=v.
Ink blot test=6,000=60%=P6.0D=Man=Earth=Royalty=6 June=Gaia=Maia>>M=M2.
Inkling=6,000=60%=P6.0D=Man=Earth=Royalty=6 June=Gaia=Maia>>M=M2.
Inkwell=2,500=3,000=30%=P3.0D=3.0=Creativity=Stars=Muses=3 March = C=I>>GIL.
Inlaid=6,500=7,000=70%=P7.0D=7.0=Language=Assets=Mars=7 July=Pleiades.
Inland=9,000=90%=P9.00D=9.0=Abstraction=Gods=Saturn=9Sept.>>A=Ø.
Inland passage=1,500=15%=P1.50D=1.5=Authority=Solar Crown=1 May = Maia.
Inland Sea=6,500=7,000=70%=P7.0D=7.0=Language=Assets=Mars=7 July=Pleiades.
In-law=2,000=20%=P2.00D=2.0=Nature=Matter=Moon=2 Feb.=Cupid=N=C+_
Inlay=10,000=1,000=100%=10.0=Physicality=Tech.=10 Oct.=Uranus=P=1Ø.
Inlet=9,500=10,000=1,000=100%=10.0=Physicality=Tech.=10 Oct.=Uranus=P=1Ø.
Inmate=8,000=80%=P8.0D=Economy=Currency=8 Aug.=Zeus>>E=v.
In medi as res=7,000=70%=P7.0D=7.0=Language=Assets=Mars=7 July=Pleiades.
In memoriam=2,000=20%=P2.00D=2.0=Nature=Matter=Moon=2 Feb.=Cupid=N=C+_
Inn=1,500=15%=P1.50D=1.5=Authority=Solar Crown=1 May = Maia.
Innards=8,000=80%=P8.0D=Economy=Currency=8 Aug.=Zeus>>E=v.

Innate=9,000=90%=P9.00D=9.0=Abstraction=Gods=Saturn=9Sept.>>A=Ø.
The Creatocracy has core interest in discovering developing and connecting innate potentials as antidote to resolving social ills such as unemployment, youth restiveness, and crime. We have identified innate potentials as transmutable, measurable energy.

Inner=10,000=1,000=100%=10.0=Physicality=Tech.=10 Oct.=Uranus=P=1Ø.
Inner city=7,000=70%=P7.0D=7.0=Language=Assets=Mars=7 July=Pleiades.
Inner directed=7,000=70%=P7.0D=7.0=Language=Assets=Mars=7 July=Pleiades.
Inner ear=6,000=60%=P6.0D=Man=Earth=Royalty=6 June=Gaia=Maia>>M=M2.
Inner Hebrides=1,000=100%=10.0=1.0=Mind=Sun=1 January=Helios >> M=E4.
Inner Mongolia=1,500=15%=P1.50D=1.5=Authority=Solar Crown=1 May = Maia.

Inner planet=8,500=9,000=90%=P9.00D=9.0=Abstraction=Gods=Saturn=9Sept.>>A=Ø.
Any of the four planets, Mercury Venus Earth and Mars whose orbits are closest to the sun. By interpretation they are Hermes Aphrodite Gaia and Aries whose closeness to Helios makes it possible to meet the Most High. Results indicate that they are means to reach Zeus. This means that Helios is the administrative secretary of the Council of Gods. Beyond the Solar Core is Athena, Maia and others within the innermost systems.

Inner tube=9,500=10,000=1,000=100%=Physicality=Tech.=10 Oct.=Uranus=P=1Ø.
Inning=6,500=7,000=70%=P7.0D=7.0=Language=Assets=Mars=7 July=Pleiades.
Innkeeper=4,000=40%=P4.0D=Govt.=Creatocracy=4 April=Mercury=Hermes=G=A4.
Innocent=10,000=1,000=100%=10.0=Physicality=Tech.=10 Oct.=Uranus=P=1Ø.
Innocent III.=2,000=20%=P2.00D=2.0=Nature=Matter=Moon=2 Feb.=Cupid=N=C+_
Innocuous=7,000=70%=P7.0D=7.0=Language=Assets=Mars=7 July=Pleiades.
In nominate=3,000=30%=P3.0D=3.0=Creativity=Stars=Muses=3 March = C=I>>GIL.

Innovate=6,000=60%=P6.0D=Man=Earth=Royalty=6 June=Gaia=Maia>>M=M2.
Innovation=6,500=7,000=70%=P7.0D=7.0=Language=Assets=Mars=7 July=Pleiades.
Innsbruck=4,500=5,000=50%=P5.00D=Law=Time=Venus=5 May = Aphrodite>>L=N.
Innuendo=5,500=5.5=80%=P5.50=Earth-Midway=5 May = Gaia.
Inoculate=10,500=11,000=11%=P1.10D=1.1=Idea=Brainchild=11 Nov=Athena>>I=MT.
In oculum=3,000=30%=P3.0D=3.0=Creativity=Stars=Muses=3 March = C=I>>GIL.
Inoffensive=2,000=20%=P2.00D=2.0=Nature=Matter=Moon=2 Feb.=Cupid=N=C+_
Inoperable=4,000=40%=P4.0D=Govt.=Creatocracy=4 April=Mercury=Hermes=G=A4.
Inoperative=2,000=20%=P2.00D=2.0=Nature=Matter=Moon=2 Feb.=Cupid=N=C+_
In opportune=2,000=20%=P2.00D=2.0=Nature=Matter=Moon=2 Feb.=Cupid=N=C+_
Inordinate=4,500=5,000=50%=P5.00D=Law=Time=Venus=5 May = Aphrodite>>L=N.
Inorganic=10,000=1,000=100%=10.0=Physicality=Tech.=10 Oct.=Uranus=P=1Ø.
Inpatient=5,000=50%=P5.00D=Law=Time=Venus=5 May = Aphrodite>>L=N.
Input=10,000=1,000=100%=10.0=Physicality=Tech.=10 Oct.=Uranus=P=1Ø.
Inquest=8,500=9,000=90%=P9.00D=9.0=Abstraction=Gods=Saturn=9Sept.>>A=Ø.
Inquire=5,000=50%=P5.00D=Law=Time=Venus=5 May = Aphrodite>>L=N.
Inquiry=10,000=1,000=100%=10.0=Physicality=Tech.=10 Oct.=Uranus=P=1Ø.

Inquisition=10,000=1,000=100%=10.0=Physicality=Tech.=10 Oct.=Uranus=P=1Ø.
The Brick Wall is the Court of the Creatocracy established to try creativity related offenses. Considered a court of all courts because all things are products of creative activity or creativity positively or negatively. It is the authority on precision and mind (mens rea). See the book >> Principles of Psychoastronomy by Peter K. Matthews-Akukalia.

Inquisitive=2,500=3,000=30%=P3.0D=3.0=Creativity=Stars=Muses=3 March = C=I>>GIL.
In re=6,000=60%=P6.0D=Man=Earth=Royalty=6 June=Gaia=Maia>>M=M2.
Inroad=7,500=8,000=80%=P8.0D=Economy=Currency=8 Aug.=Zeus>>E=v.
Inrush=1,500=15%=P1.50D=1.5=Authority=Solar Crown=1 May = Maia.
Ins.=1,500=15%=P1.50D=1.5=Authority=Solar Crown=1 May = Maia.
Insalubrious=2,000=20%=P2.00D=2.0=Nature=Matter=Moon=2 Feb.=Cupid=N=C+_
Insane=8,500=9,000=90%=P9.00D=9.0=Abstraction=Gods=Saturn=9Sept.>>A=Ø.
Insatiable=2,500=3,000=30%=P3.0D=3.0=Creativity=Stars=Muses=3 March = C=I>>GIL.
Inscribe=10,000=1,000=100%=10.0=Physicality=Tech.=10 Oct.=Uranus=P=1Ø.
Inscrutable=3,500=4,000=40%=P4.0D=Govt.=Creat.=4 April=Mercury=Hermes=G=A4.
Inseam=3,500=4,000=40%=P4.0D=Govt.=Creat.=4 April=Mercury=Hermes=G=A4.
Insect=10,000=1,000=100%=10.0=Physicality=Tech.=10 Oct.=Uranus=P=1Ø.
Insecticide=3,000=30%=P3.0D=3.0=Creativity=Stars=Muses=3 March = C=I>>GIL.
Insectivore=2,000=20%=P2.00D=2.0=Nature=Matter=Moon=2 Feb.=Cupid=N=C+_
Insecure=6,000=60%=P6.0D=Man=Earth=Royalty=6 June=Gaia=Maia>>M=M2.
Inseminate=8,500=9,000=90%=P9.00D=9.0=Abstraction=Gods=Saturn=9Sept.>>A=Ø.
Insensate=3,500=4,000=40%=P4.0D=Govt.=Creat.=4 April=Mercury=Hermes=G=A4.
Insensible=4,500=5,000=50%=P5.00D=Law=Time=Venus=5 May = Aphrodite>>L=N.
Insensitive=7,000=70%=P7.0D=7.0=Language=Assets=Mars=7 July=Pleiades.
In sentient=2,500=3,000=30%=P3.0D=3.0=Creativity=Stars=Muses=3 March = C=I>>GIL.

Inseparable=3,000=30%=P3.0D=3.0=Creativity=Stars=Muses=3 March = C=I>>GIL.
Insert=10,000=1,000=100%=10.0=Physicality=Tech.=10 Oct.=Uranus=P=1Ø.
Inset=2,000=20%=P2.00D=2.0=Nature=Matter=Moon=2 Feb.=Cupid=N=C+_
Inshore=3,500=4,000=40%=P4.0D=Govt.=Creat.=4 April=Mercury=Hermes=G=A4.
Inside=10,000=1,000=100%=10.0=Physicality=Tech.=10 Oct.=Uranus=P=1Ø.
Inside Passage=8,000=80%=P8.0D=Economy=Currency=8 Aug.=Zeus>>E=v.
Insider=8,000=80%=P8.0D=Economy=Currency=8 Aug.=Zeus>>E=v.
Inside track=4,000=40%=P4.0D=Govt.=Creatocracy=4 April=Mercury=Hermes=G=A4.
Insidious=12,500=13,000=13%=P1.30=Solar Core=Faculty=13 January=Athena.
Insight=5,000=50%=P5.00D=Law=Time=Venus=5 May = Aphrodite>>L=N.
Insignia=6,500=7,000=70%=P7.0D=7.0=Language=Assets=Mars=7 July=Pleiades.
Insignificant=8,000=80%=P8.0D=Economy=Currency=8 Aug.=Zeus>>E=v.
Insincere=1,500=15%=P1.50D=1.5=Authority=Solar Crown=1 May = Maia.
Insinuate=10,000=1,000=100%=10.0=Physicality=Tech.=10 Oct.=Uranus=P=1Ø.
Insipid=5,500=5.5=80%=P5.50=Earth-Midway=5 May = Gaia.
Insist=10,000=1,000=100%=10.0=Physicality=Tech.=10 Oct.=Uranus=P=1Ø.
In situ=3,000=30%=P3.0D=3.0=Creativity=Stars=Muses=3 March = C=I>>GIL.
Insofar as=4,500=5,000=50%=P5.00D=Law=Time=Venus=5 May = Aphrodite>>L=N.
Insole=9,500=10,000=1,000=100%=10.0=Physicality=Tech.=10 Oct.=Uranus=P=1Ø.
Insolent=2,500=3,000=30%=P3.0D=3.0=Creativity=Stars=Muses=3 March = C=I>>GIL.
Insoluble=5,500=5.5=80%=P5.50=Earth-Midway=5 May = Gaia.
Insolvent=2,500=3,000=30%=P3.0D=3.0=Creativity=Stars=Muses=3 March = C=I>>GIL.
Insomnia=5,000=50%=P5.00D=Law=Time=Venus=5 May = Aphrodite>>L=N.
Insomuch as=1,500=15%=P1.50D=1.5=Authority=Solar Crown=1 May = Maia.
Insouciant=1,000=100%=10.0=1.0=Mind=Sun=1 January=Helios >> M=E4.
Inspect=10,000=1,000=100%=10.0=Physicality=Tech.=10 Oct.=Uranus=P=1Ø.
Inspect general=6,500=7,000=70%=P7.0D=7.0=Language=Assets=Mars=7 July=Pleiades.
Inspiration=10,000=1,000=100%=10.0=Physicality=Tech.=10 Oct.=Uranus=P=1Ø.
Inspire=10,000=1,000=100%=10.0=Physicality=Tech.=10 Oct.=Uranus=P=1Ø.
In spirit=5,500=5.5=80%=P5.50=Earth-Midway=5 May = Gaia.
Inst.=2,500=3,000=30%=P3.0D=3.0=Creativity=Stars=Muses=3 March = C=I>>GIL.
Instability=1,500=15%=P1.50D=1.5=Authority=Solar Crown=1 May = Maia.
Install=10,000=1,000=100%=10.0=Physicality=Tech.=10 Oct.=Uranus=P=1Ø.
Installment=10,000=1,000=100%=10.0=Physicality=Tech.=10 Oct.=Uranus=P=1Ø.
Instance=10,000=1,000=100%=10.0=Physicality=Tech.=10 Oct.=Uranus=P=1Ø.
Instant=10,000=1,000=100%=10.0=Physicality=Tech.=10 Oct.=Uranus=P=1Ø.
Instantaneous=8,000=80%=P8.0D=Economy=Currency=8 Aug.=Zeus>>E=v.
Instant=1,000=100%=10.0=1.0=Mind=Sun=1 January=Helios >> M=E4.
Instead=7,000=70%=P7.0D=7.0=Language=Assets=Mars=7 July=Pleiades.
Instep=5,500=5.5=80%=P5.50=Earth-Midway=5 May = Gaia.
Instigate=3,000=30%=P3.0D=3.0=Creativity=Stars=Muses=3 March = C=I>>GIL.
Instill=7,000=70%=P7.0D=7.0=Language=Assets=Mars=7 July=Pleiades.
Instinct=10,000=1,000=100%=10.0=Physicality=Tech.=10 Oct.=Uranus=P=1Ø.
Institute=10,000=1,000=100%=10.0=Physicality=Tech.=10 Oct.=Uranus=P=1Ø.

Institution=10,000=1,000=100%=10.0=Physicality=Tech.=10 Oct.=Uranus=P=1Ø.
The Creatocracy is an institution that owns creativity, Creatocism and the Maks Currency.
Creatocism is the professional terminology for "Creative Economy".See Economy.

Institutionalize=4,500=5,000=50%=P5.00D=Law=Time=Venus=5 May = Aphrodite>>L=N.
Instruct=5,000=50%=P5.00D=Law=Time=Venus=5 May = Aphrodite>>L=N.
Instruction=10,000=1,000=100%=10.0=Physicality=Tech.=10 Oct.=Uranus=P=1Ø.
Instructor=5,500=5.5=80%=P5.50=Earth-Midway=5 May = Gaia.
Instrument=10,000=1,000=100%=10.0=Physicality=Tech.=10 Oct.=Uranus=P=1Ø.
Instrumental=9,000=90%=P9.00D=9.0=Abstraction=Gods=Saturn=9Sept.>>A=Ø.
Instrumentalist=3,000=30%=P3.0D=3.0=Creativity=Stars=Muses=3 March = C=I>>GIL.
Instrumentality=1,500=15%=P1.50D=1.5=Authority=Solar Crown=1 May = Maia.
Instrumentation=5,000=50%=P5.00D=Law=Time=Venus=5 May = Aphrodite>>L=N.
Instrument landing=7,000=70%=P7.0D=7.0=Language=Assets=Mars=7 July=Pleiades.
Insubordinate=2,000=20%=P2.00D=2.0=Nature=Matter=Moon=2 Feb.=Cupid=N=C+_
Insubstantial=6,500=7,000=70%=P7.0D=7.0=Language=Assets=Mars=7 July=Pleiades.
Insufferable=2,000=20%=P2.00D=2.0=Nature=Matter=Moon=2 Feb.=Cupid=N=C+_
Insufficient=1,500=15%=P1.50D=1.5=Authority=Solar Crown=1 May = Maia.
Insular=5,000=50%=P5.00D=Law=Time=Venus=5 May = Aphrodite>>L=N.
Insulate=12,000=12%=P1.20D=1.2=Knowledge=Education=12Dec.=Athena>>K=F.
Insulin=10,000=1,000=100%=10.0=Physicality=Tech.=10 Oct.=Uranus=P=1Ø.
Insulin shock=5,000=50%=P5.00D=Law=Time=Venus=5 May = Aphrodite>>L=N.
Insult=7,500=8,000=80%=P8.0D=Economy=Currency=8 Aug.=Zeus>>E=v.
Insuperable=2,000=20%=P2.00D=2.0=Nature=Matter=Moon=2 Feb.=Cupid=N=C+_
In supportable=2,000=20%=P2.00D=2.0=Nature=Matter=Moon=2 Feb.=Cupid=N=C+_
Insurance=10,000=1,000=100%=10.0=Physicality=Tech.=10 Oct.=Uranus=P=1Ø.
Insure=8,500=9,000=90%=P9.00D=9.0=Abstraction=Gods=Saturn=9Sept.>>A=Ø.
Insured=3,000=30%=P3.0D=3.0=Creativity=Stars=Muses=3 March = C=I>>GIL.
Insurgent=11,000=11%=P1.10D=1.1=Idea=Brainchild=11 Nov=Athena>>I=MT.
Insurmountable=2,000=20%=P2.00D=2.0=Nature=Matter=Moon=2 Feb.=Cupid=N=C+_
Insurrection=9,000=90%=P9.00D=9.0=Abstraction=Gods=Saturn=9Sept.>>A=Ø.
Int.=2,500=3,000=30%=P3.0D=3.0=Creativity=Stars=Muses=3 March = C=I>>GIL.
Intact=4,000=40%=P4.0D=Govt.=Creatocracy=4 April=Mercury=Hermes=G=A4.
Intaglio=8,000=80%=P8.0D=Economy=Currency=8 Aug.=Zeus>>E=v.
Intake=8,500=9,000=90%=P9.00D=9.0=Abstraction=Gods=Saturn=9Sept.>>A=Ø.
Intangible=8,000=80%=P8.0D=Economy=Currency=8 Aug.=Zeus>>E=v.
Integer=12,500=13,000=13%=P1.30=Solar Core=Faculty=13 January=Athena.
Integral=10,000=1,000=100%=10.0=Physicality=Tech.=10 Oct.=Uranus=P=1Ø.
Integral calculus=8,500=9,000=90%=P9.00D=9.0=Abst=Gods=Saturn=9Sept.>>A=Ø.
Integrate=10,000=1,000=100%=10.0=Physicality=Tech.=10 Oct.=Uranus=P=1Ø.
Integrated circuit=10,000=1,000=100%=10.0=Physicality=Tech.=10 Oct.=Uranus=P=1Ø.
Integrity=7,500=8,000=80%=P8.0D=Economy=Currency=8 Aug.=Zeus>>E=v.
Integument=9,500=10,000=1,000=100%=10.0=Physicality=Tech.=10 Oct.=Uranus=P=1Ø.
Intellect=10,500=11,000=11%=P1.10D=1.1=Idea=Brainchild=11 Nov=Athena>>I=MT.

Intellectual=10,000=1,000=100%=10.0=Physicality=Tech.=10 Oct.=Uranus=P=1Ø.
Intellectualize=9,000=90%=P9.00D=9.0=Abstraction=Gods=Saturn=9Sept.>>A=Ø.

Intelligence=10,000=1,000=100%=10.0=Physicality=Tech.=10 Oct.=Uranus=P=1Ø.
Peter Matthews-Akukalia computed the size of an intelligence particle as 1.0x10(raised to power -03). Ref. Book >> Makupedia Sciences >> Principles of Naturecology.

Intelligence quotient=8,500=9,000=90%=P9.00D=9.0=Abst=Gods=Saturn=9Sept.>>A=Ø.
Intelligence Quotient. The Creatocracy discovered twenty faults with the IQ measures and rebranded it the BQ>> Brilliance Quotient. He invented CIQ >> Creative Intelligence Quotient. Today both faculties are computed as the BIRA >> Brilliance and Intelligence Ratio in the conductance of the Mind Assessments for Students and organizational staff. Book > Template & Manifesto for the Creative Economy 2 by Peter Matthews-Akukalia.

Intelligent=10,000=1,000=100%=10.0=Physicality=Tech.=10 Oct.=Uranus=P=1Ø.
Intelligentsia=4,000=40%=P4.0D=Govt.=Creato.=4 April=Mercury=Hermes=G=A4.
Intelligible=4,000=40%=P4.0D=Govt.=Creato.=4 April=Mercury=Hermes=G=A4.
Intemperance=4,500=5,000=50%=P5.00D=Law=Time=Venus=5 May = Aphrodite>>L=N.
Intend=7,500=8,000=80%=P8.0D=Economy=Currency=8 Aug.=Zeus>>E=v.
Intended=5,000=50%=P5.00D=Law=Time=Venus=5 May = Aphrodite>>L=N.
Intense=10,000=1,000=100%=10.0=Physicality=Tech.=10 Oct.=Uranus=P=1Ø.
Intensify=3,500=4,000=40%=P4.0D=Govt.=Creat.=4 April=Mercury=Hermes=G=A4.
Intensity=10,000=1,000=100%=10.0=Physicality=Tech.=10 Oct.=Uranus=P=1Ø.
Intensive=10,000=1,000=100%=10.0=Physicality=Tech.=10 Oct.=Uranus=P=1Ø.
Intent=10,000=1,000=100%=10.0=Physicality=Tech.=10 Oct.=Uranus=P=1Ø.
Intention=5,500=5.5=80%=P5.50=Earth-Midway=5 May = Gaia.
Intentional=1,500=15%=P1.50D=1.5=Authority=Solar Crown=1 May = Maia.
Inter=1,500=15%=P1.50D=1.5=Authority=Solar Crown=1 May = Maia.
Inter-=7,000=70%=P7.0D=7.0=Language=Assets=Mars=7 July=Pleiades.
Interact=2,500=3,000=30%=P3.0D=3.0=Creativity=Stars=Muses=3 March = C=I>>GIL.
Interactive=10,000=1,000=100%=10.0=Physicality=Tech.=10 Oct.=Uranus=P=1Ø.
Interactive terminal=10,000=1,000=100%=10.0=Physicality=Tech.=10 Oct.=Uranus=P=1Ø.
Inter alia=1,500=15%=P1.50D=1.5=Authority=Solar Crown=1 May = Maia.
Interbreed=4,500=5,000=50%=P5.00D=Law=Time=Venus=5 May = Aphrodite>>L=N.
Intercalary=10,000=1,000=100%=10.0=Physicality=Tech.=10 Oct.=Uranus=P=1Ø.
Intercede=4,500=5,000=50%=P5.00D=Law=Time=Venus=5 May = Aphrodite>>L=N.
Intercellular=3,000=30%=P3.0D=3.0=Creativity=Stars=Muses=3 March = C=I>>GIL.
Intercept=10,000=1,000=100%=10.0=Physicality=Tech.=10 Oct.=Uranus=P=1Ø.
Intercession=7,000=70%=P7.0D=7.0=Language=Assets=Mars=7 July=Pleiades.
Interchange=10,000=1,000=100%=10.0=Physicality=Tech.=10 Oct.=Uranus=P=1Ø.
Intercollegiate=2,500=3,000=30%=P3.0D=3.0=Cre=Stars=Muses=3 March = C=I>>GIL.
Intercom=5,000=50%=P5.00D=Law=Time=Venus=5 May = Aphrodite>>L=N.
Inter communicate=6,000=60%=P6.0D=Man=Earth=Royalty=6 June=Gaia=Maia>>M=M2.

Interconnect=4,000=40%=P4.0D=Govt.=Creatocracy=4 April=Mercury=Hermes=G=A4.
Intercontinental=5,000=50%=P5.00D=Law=Time=Venus=5 May = Aphrodite>>L=N.
Intercostal=5,500=5.5=80%=P5.50=Earth-Midway=5 May = Gaia.
Intercourse=6,000=60%=P6.0D=Man=Earth=Royalty=6 June=Gaia=Maia>>M=M2.
Interdependent=1,000=100%=10.0=1.0=Mind=Sun=1 January=Helios >> M=E4.
Interdict=11,000=11%=P1.10D=1.1=Idea=Brainchild=11 Nov=Athena>>I=MT.
Interdisciplinary=5,000=50%=P5.00D=Law=Time=Venus=5 May = Aphrodite>>L=N.

Interest=10,000=1,000=100%=10.0=Physicality=Tech.=10 Oct.=Uranus=P=1Ø.
Peter Matthews-Akukalia, De-Castle Makupedia discovered that interest was behind every act of creativity whether normal or genius. He linked it as the energy that manifested as capacity ability and capability. Then he computed the creative mind energy. So the complete energy is measured as the GIL/CME to determine total energy in a person.
Peter Matthews-Akukalia invented a Currency Denomination Interest Calculation System CDICS by which the interest of a currency is based on the assigned code from 0.1-1.9

Interested=7,500=8,000=80%=P8.0D=Economy=Currency=8 Aug.=Zeus>>E=v.
Interest group=6,500=7,000=70%=P7.0D=7.0=Language=Assets=Mars=7 July=Pleiades.
Interesting=3,000=30%=P3.0D=3.0=Creativity=Stars=Muses=3 March = C=I>>GIL.
Interface=10,000=1,000=100%=10.0=Physicality=Tech.=10 Oct.=Uranus=P=1Ø.
Interfere=10,000=1,000=100%=10.0=Physicality=Tech.=10 Oct.=Uranus=P=1Ø.
Interferometer=10,000=1,000=100%=10.0=Physicality=Tech.=10 Oct.=Uranus=P=1Ø.
Interferon=10,000=1,000=100%=10.0=Physicality=Tech.=10 Oct.=Uranus=P=1Ø.
Intergalactic=1,000=100%=10.0=1.0=Mind=Sun=1 January=Helios >> M=E4.
Interim=10,000=1,000=100%=10.0=Physicality=Tech.=10 Oct.=Uranus=P=1Ø.
Interior=10,000=1,000=100%=10.0=Physicality=Tech.=10 Oct.=Uranus=P=1Ø.
Interior decoration=4,500=5,000=50%=P5.00D=Law=Time=Venus=5 May =Odite>>L=N.
Interj.=500=5%=P5.00D=5.0=Law=Time=Venus=5 May=Aphrodite>>L=N.
Interject=3,500=4,000=40%=P4.0D=Govt.=Creat.=4 April=Mercury=Hermes=G=A4.
Interjection=10,000=1,000=100%=10.0=Physicality=Tech.=10 Oct.=Uranus=P=1Ø.
Interlard=6,500=7,000=70%=P7.0D=7.0=Language=Assets=Mars=7 July=Pleiades.
Interlining=6,000=60%=P6.0D=Man=Earth=Royalty=6 June=Gaia=Maia>>M=M2.
Interlock=10,000=1,000=100%=10.0=Physicality=Tech.=10 Oct.=Uranus=P=1Ø.
Interlocutor=10,000=1,000=100%=10.0=Physicality=Tech.=10 Oct.=Uranus=P=1Ø.
Interlocutory=8,000=80%=P8.0D=Economy=Currency=8 Aug.=Zeus>>E=v.
Interloper=4,500=5,000=50%=P5.00D=Law=Time=Venus=5 May = Aphrodite>>L=N.
Interlude=10,000=1,000=100%=10.0=Physicality=Tech.=10 Oct.=Uranus=P=1Ø.
Intermarry=10,000=1,000=100%=10.0=Physicality=Tech.=10 Oct.=Uranus=P=1Ø.
Intermediary=5,500=5.5=80%=P5.50=Earth-Midway=5 May = Gaia.
Intermediate=8,000=80%=P8.0D=Economy=Currency=8 Aug.=Zeus>>E=v.
Interment=3,500=4,000=40%=P4.0D=Govt.=Creat.=4 April=Mercury=Hermes=G=A4.
Intermezzo=10,000=1,000=100%=10.0=Physicality=Tech.=10 Oct.=Uranus=P=1Ø.
Interminable=1,000=100%=10.0=1.0=Mind=Sun=1 January=Helios >> M=E4.
Intermingle=3,000=30%=P3.0D=3.0=Creativity=Stars=Muses=3 March = C=I>>GIL.

Intermission=11,500=12,000=12%=P1.20D=1.2=Knowledge=Edu=12Dec.=Athena>>K=F.

Intermittent=4,000=40%=P4.0D=Govt.=Creat.=4 April=Mercury=Hermes=G=A4.

Intern=10,000=1,000=100%=10.0=Physicality=Tech.=10 Oct.=Uranus=P=1Ø.

Internal=10,000=1,000=100%=10.0=Physicality=Tech.=10 Oct.=Uranus=P=1Ø.

Internal comb. engine=4,500=5,000=50%=P5.00D=Law=Time=Venus=5May =Odite>L=N.

Internalize=3,000=30%=P3.0D=3.0=Creativity=Stars=Muses=3 March = C=I>>GIL.

Internal medicine=6,500=7,000=70%=P7.0D=7.0=Lang.=Assets=Mars=7 July=Pleiades.

International=3,500=4,000=40%=P4.0D=Govt.=Creat.=4 April=Mercury=Hermes=G=A4.

International Date Line=13,500=14,000=14%=P1.40D=1.4=Mgt.=13 May=Athena=0.1

Internationalism=5,500=5.5=80%=P5.50=Earth-Midway=5 May = Gaia.

Internationalize=2,500=3,000=30%=P3.0D=3.0=Cre=Stars=Muses=3 March = C=I>>GIL.

International Law=5,000=50%=P5.00D=Law=Time=Venus=5 May = Aphrodite>>L=N.

Internecine=7,500=8,000=80%=P8.0D=Economy=Currency=8 Aug.=Zeus>>E=v.

Internee=3,500=4,000=40%=P4.0D=Govt.=Creat.=4 April=Mercury=Hermes=G=A4.

Internist=3,000=30%=P3.0D=3.0=Creativity=Stars=Muses=3 March = C=I>>GIL.

Inter office=5,000=50%=P5.00D=Law=Time=Venus=5 May = Aphrodite>>L=N.

Interpersonal=3,500=4,000=40%=P4.0D=Govt.=Creat=4 April=Mercury=Hermes=G=A4.

Interplanetary=2,500=3,000=30%=P3.0D=3.0=Cre=Stars=Muses=3 March = C=I>>GIL.

Interplay=2,500=3,000=30%=P3.0D=3.0=Creativity=Stars=Muses=3 March = C=I>>GIL.

Interpolate=10,000=1,000=100%=10.0=Physicality=Tech.=10 Oct.=Uranus=P=1Ø.

Interpose=10,000=1,000=100%=10.0=Physicality=Tech.=10 Oct.=Uranus=P=1Ø.

Interpret=10,000=1,000=100%=10.0=Physicality=Tech.=10 Oct.=Uranus=P=1Ø.

Interpretation=7,500=8,000=80%=P8.0D=Economy=Currency=8 Aug.=Zeus>>E=v.

Interpretive=2,000=20%=P2.00D=2.0=Nature=Matter=Moon=2 Feb.=Cupid=N=C+_

Interracial=2,500=3,000=30%=P3.0D=3.0=Creativity=Stars=Muses=3 March = C=I>>GIL.

Interregnum=7,500=8,000=80%=P8.0D=Economy=Currency=8 Aug.=Zeus>>E=v.

Interrelate=4,000=40%=P4.0D=Govt.=Creat.=4 April=Mercury=Hermes=G=A4.

Interrog.=500=5%=P5.00D=5.0=Law=Time=Venus=5 May=Aphrodite>>L=N.

Interrogate=7,500=8,000=80%=P8.0D=Economy=Currency=8 Aug.=Zeus>>E=v.

Interrogative=5,500=5.5=80%=P5.50=Earth-Midway=5 May = Gaia.

Interrogatory=6,000=60%=P6.0D=Man=Earth=Royalty=6 June=Gaia=Maia>>M=M2.

Interrupt=10,000=1,000=100%=10.0=Physicality=Tech.=10 Oct.=Uranus=P=1Ø.

Intersect=6,500=7,000=70%=P7.0D=7.0=Language=Assets=Mars=7 July=Pleiades.

Intersection=12,500=13,000=13%=P1.30=Solar Core=Faculty=13 January=Athena.

Intersperse=8,000=80%=P8.0D=Economy=Currency=8 Aug.=Zeus>>E=v.

Interstate=10,500=11,000=11%=P1.10D=1.1=Idea=Brainchild=11 Nov=Athena>>I=MT.

Interstellar=1,500=15%=P1.50D=1.5=Authority=Solar Crown=1 May = Maia.

Interstice=10,000=1,000=100%=10.0=Physicality=Tech.=10 Oct.=Uranus=P=1Ø.

Intertwine=4,000=40%=P4.0D=Govt.=Creat.=4 April=Mercury=Hermes=G=A4.

Interurban=3,500=4,000=40%=P4.0D=Govt.=Creat.=4 April=Mercury=Hermes=G=A4.

Interval=10,000=1,000=100%=10.0=Physicality=Tech.=10 Oct.=Uranus=P=1Ø.

Intervene=10,000=1,000=100%=10.0=Physicality=Tech.=10 Oct.=Uranus=P=1Ø.

Interview=10,000=1,000=100%=10.0=Physicality=Tech.=10 Oct.=Uranus=P=1Ø.

Interweave=2,000=20%=P2.00D=2.0=Nature=Matter=Moon=2 Feb.=Cupid=N=C+_

Intestate=7,500=8,000=80%=P8.0D=Economy=Currency=8 Aug.=Zeus>>E=v.

Intestine=10,000=1,000=100%=10.0=Physicality=Tech.=10 Oct.=Uranus=P=1Ø.
Inti=3,000=30%=P3.0D=3.0=Creativity=Stars=Muses=3 March = C=I>>GIL.
Intimate1=10,000=1,000=100%=10.0=Physicality=Tech.=10 Oct.=Uranus=P=1Ø.
Intimate2=3,500=4,000=40%=P4.0D=Govt.=Creato.=4 April=Mercury=Hermes=G=A4.
Intimidate=10,500=11,000=11%=P1.10D=1.1=Idea=Brainchild=11 Nov=Athena>>I=MT.
Intl.=500=5%=P5.00D=5.0=Law=Time=Venus=5 May=Aphrodite>>L=N.
Into=10,000=1,000=100%=10.0=Physicality=Tech.=10 Oct.=Uranus=P=1Ø.
Intolerable=1,500=15%=P1.50D=1.5=Authority=Solar Crown=1 May = Maia.
Intolerant=7,500=8,000=80%=P8.0D=Economy=Currency=8 Aug.=Zeus>>E=v.
Intonation=10,000=1,000=100%=10.0=Physicality=Tech.=10 Oct.=Uranus=P=1Ø.
Intone=6,500=7,000=70%=P7.0D=7.0=Language=Assets=Mars=7 July=Pleiades.
In to to=2,500=3,000=30%=P3.0D=3.0=Creativity=Stars=Muses=3 March = C=I>>GIL.
Intoxicate=6,000=60%=P6.0D=Man=Earth=Royalty=6 June=Gaia=Maia>>M=M2.
Intr.=500=5%=P5.00D=5.0=Law=Time=Venus=5 May=Aphrodite>>L=N.
Intra-=2,000=20%=P2.00D=2.0=Nature=Matter=Moon=2 Feb.=Cupid=N=C+_
Intracellular=3,500=4,000=40%=P4.0D=Govt.=Creat.=4 April=Mercury=Hermes=G=A4.
Intractable=3,000=30%=P3.0D=3.0=Creativity=Stars=Muses=3 March = C=I>>GIL.
Intramural=7,500=8,000=80%=P8.0D=Economy=Currency=8 Aug.=Zeus>>E=v.
Intransigent=10,000=1,000=100%=10.0=Physicality=Tech.=10 Oct.=Uranus=P=1Ø.
Intransitive=10,000=1,000=100%=10.0=Physicality=Tech.=10 Oct.=Uranus=P=1Ø.
Intra ocular=1,500=15%=P1.50D=1.5=Authority=Solar Crown=1 May = Maia.
Intrastate=3,500=4,000=40%=P4.0D=Govt.=Creat.=4 April=Mercury=Hermes=G=A4.
Intrauterine=1,500=15%=P1.50D=1.5=Authority=Solar Crown=1 May = Maia.
Intrauterine device=5,500=5.5=80%=P5.50=Earth-Midway=5 May = Gaia.
Intravenous=3,000=30%=P3.0D=3.0=Creativity=Stars=Muses=3 March = C=I>>GIL.
Intrepid=2,500=3,000=30%=P3.0D=3.0=Creativity=Stars=Muses=3 March = C=I>>GIL.
Intricate=10,000=1,000=100%=10.0=Physicality=Tech.=10 Oct.=Uranus=P=1Ø.
Intrigue=10,000=1,000=100%=10.0=Physicality=Tech.=10 Oct.=Uranus=P=1Ø.
Intrinsic=6,000=60%=P6.0D=Man=Earth=Royalty=6 June=Gaia=Maia>>M=M2.
Intro.=1,000=100%=10.0=1.0=Mind=Sun=1 January=Helios >> M=E4.
Intro-=2,000=20%=P2.00D=2.0=Nature=Matter=Moon=2 Feb.=Cupid=N=C+_
Introduce=10,000=1,000=100%=10.0=Physicality=Tech.=10 Oct.=Uranus=P=1Ø.
Introductory=3,500=4,000=40%=P4.0D=Govt.=Creat.=4 April=Mercury=Hermes=G=A4.
Introspection=10,500=11,000=11%=P1.10D=1.1=Idea=Brainchild=11 Nov=Athena>>I=MT.
Introvert=6,500=7,000=70%=P7.0D=7.0=Language=Assets=Mars=7 July=Pleiades.
Intrude=7,000=70%=P7.0D=7.0=Language=Assets=Mars=7 July=Pleiades.
In trust=1,500=15%=P1.50D=1.5=Authority=Solar Crown=1 May = Maia.
Intuit=2,000=20%=P2.00D=2.0=Nature=Matter=Moon=2 Feb.=Cupid=N=C+_
Intuition=10,000=1,000=100%=10.0=Physicality=Tech.=10 Oct.=Uranus=P=1Ø.
Inuit=10,000=1,000=100%=10.0=Physicality=Tech.=10 Oct.=Uranus=P=1Ø.
Inundate=9,500=10,000=1,000=100%=10.0=Physicality=Tech.=10 Oct.=Uranus=P=1Ø.
Inure=5,500=5.5=80%=P5.50=Earth-Midway=5 May = Gaia.
In utero=3,000=30%=P3.0D=3.0=Creativity=Stars=Muses=3 March = C=I>>GIL.
Invade=10,000=1,000=100%=10.0=Physicality=Tech.=10 Oct.=Uranus=P=1Ø.
Invalid1=5,500=5.5=80%=P5.50=Earth-Midway=5 May = Gaia.

Invalid2=6,000=60%=P6.0D=Man=Earth=Royalty=6 June=Gaia=Maia>>M=M2.
Invalidate=2,000=20%=P2.00D=2.0=Nature=Matter=Moon=2 Feb.=Cupid=N=C+_
Invaluable=2,000=20%=P2.00D=2.0=Nature=Matter=Moon=2 Feb.=Cupid=N=C+_
Invariable=3,500=4,000=40%=P4.0D=Govt.=Creat.=4 April=Mercury=Hermes=G=A4.
Invasion=10,000=1,000=100%=10.0=Physicality=Tech.=10 Oct.=Uranus=P=1Ø.
Invasive=6,500=7,000=70%=P7.0D=7.0=Language=Assets=Mars=7 July=Pleiades.
Invective=7,000=70%=P7.0D=7.0=Language=Assets=Mars=7 July=Pleiades.
Inveigh=3,500=4,000=40%=P4.0D=Govt.=Creat.=4 April=Mercury=Hermes=G=A4.
Inveigle=8,000=80%=P8.0D=Economy=Currency=8 Aug.=Zeus>>E=v.

Invent=12,000=12%=P1.20D=1.2=Knowledge=Education=12Dec.=Athena>>K=F.
One invents through the conception of the knowledge behind a concept. So knowledge itself can be invented. Peter K. Matthews - Akukalia, Castle Makupedia invented the knowledge of the Creative Sciences with over 2million concepts to his credit. Hence the Makupedia, defined as an all round education system invented by Peter Matthews-Akukalia. The Creatocracy in all things constitutes his eternal assets and legacies.

Invention=10,000=1,000=100%=10.0=Physicality=Tech.=10 Oct.=Uranus=P=1Ø.
Inventive=4,000=40%=P4.0D=Govt.=Creat.=4 April=Mercury=Hermes=G=A4.
Inventory=10,000=1,000=100%=10.0=Physicality=Tech.=10 Oct.=Uranus=P=1Ø.
Inverse=10,000=1,000=100%=10.0=Physicality=Tech.=10 Oct.=Uranus=P=1Ø.
Inversion=10,000=1,000=100%=10.0=Physicality=Tech.=10 Oct.=Uranus=P=1Ø.
Invert=7,500=8,000=80%=P8.0D=Economy=Currency=8 Aug.=Zeus>>E=v.
Invertebrate=4,000=40%=P4.0D=Govt.=Creat.=4 April=Mercury=Hermes=G=A4.
Invest=10,000=1,000=100%=10.0=Physicality=Tech.=10 Oct.=Uranus=P=1Ø.
Investigate=6,500=7,000=70%=P7.0D=7.0=Language=Assets=Mars=7 July=Pleiades.
Investigation=8,000=80%=P8.0D=Economy=Currency=8 Aug.=Zeus>>E=v.
Investiture=7,500=8,000=80%=P8.0D=Economy=Currency=8 Aug.=Zeus>>E=v.
Investment=8,000=80%=P8.0D=Economy=Currency=8 Aug.=Zeus>>E=v.
Inveterate=10,500=11,000=11%=P1.10D=1.1=Idea=Brainchild=11 Nov=Athena>>I=MT.
Invidious=6,500=7,000=70%=P7.0D=7.0=Language=Assets=Mars=7 July=Pleiades.
Invigorate=3,000=30%=P3.0D=3.0=Creativity=Stars=Muses=3 March = C=I>>GIL.
Invincible=2,500=3,000=30%=P3.0D=3.0=Creativity=Stars=Muses=3 March = C=I>>GIL.
Inviolable=3,000=30%=P3.0D=3.0=Creativity=Stars=Muses=3 March = C=I>>GIL.
Inviolate=2,500=3,000=30%=P3.0D=3.0=Creativity=Stars=Muses=3 March = C=I>>GIL.
Invisible=4,000=40%=P4.0D=Govt.=Creatocracy=4 April=Mercury=Hermes=G=A4.
Invitation=7,000=70%=P7.0D=7.0=Language=Assets=Mars=7 July=Pleiades.
Invite=10,000=1,000=100%=10.0=Physicality=Tech.=10 Oct.=Uranus=P=1Ø.
Inviting=1,000=100%=10.0=1.0=Mind=Sun=1 January=Helios >> M=E4.
In vitro=6,000=60%=P6.0D=Man=Earth=Royalty=6 June=Gaia=Maia>>M=M2.
In Vivo=3,500=4,000=40%=P4.0D=Govt.=Creat.=4 April=Mercury=Hermes=G=A4.
Invocation=3,500=4,000=40%=P4.0D=Govt.=Creat.=4 April=Mercury=Hermes=G=A4.
Invoice=10,000=1,000=100%=10.0=Physicality=Tech.=10 Oct.=Uranus=P=1Ø.
Involuntary=10,000=1,000=100%=10.0=Physicality=Tech.=10 Oct.=Uranus=P=1Ø.

Involution=10,000=1,000=100%=10.0=Physicality=Tech.=10 Oct.=Uranus=P=1Ø.
Involve=10,000=1,000=100%=10.0=Physicality=Tech.=10 Oct.=Uranus=P=1Ø.
Invulnerable=4,000=40%=P4.0D=Govt.=Creat.=4 April=Mercury=Hermes=G=A4.
Inward=10,000=1,000=100%=10.0=Physicality=Tech.=10 Oct.=Uranus=P=1Ø.
Inwardly=4,500=5,000=50%=P5.00D=Law=Time=Venus=5 May = Aphrodite>>L=N.
I/o=1,000=100%=10.0=1.0=Mind=Sun=1 January=Helios >> M=E4.
Iodide=5,500=5.5=80%=P5.50=Earth-Midway=5 May = Gaia.
Iodine=10,000=1,000=100%=10.0=Physicality=Tech.=10 Oct.=Uranus=P=1Ø.
Iodize=4,000=40%=P4.0D=Govt.=Creat.=4 April=Mercury=Hermes=G=A4.
Iodo-=2,500=3,000=30%=P3.0D=3.0=Creativity=Stars=Muses=3 March = C=I>>GIL.
Ion=10,000=1,000=100%=10.0=Physicality=Tech.=10 Oct.=Uranus=P=1Ø.
-ion=8,000=80%=P8.0D=Economy=Currency=8 Aug.=Zeus>>E=v.
Ionesco Eugéne=3,000=30%=P3.0D=3.0=Creativity=Stars=Muses=3 March = C=I>>GIL.
Ionia=5,500=5.5=80%=P5.50=Earth-Midway=5 May = Gaia.
Ionian Islands=5,000=50%=P5.00D=Law=Time=Venus=5 May = Aphrodite>>L=N.
Ionian Sea=5,500=5.5=80%=P5.50=Earth-Midway=5 May = Gaia.
Ionic bond=10,000=1,000=100%=10.0=Physicality=Tech.=10 Oct.=Uranus=P=1Ø.

Ionic order=6,000=60%=P6.0D=Man=Earth=Royalty=6 June=Gaia=Maia>>M=M2.
Order of the Royal Creatocracy >> a Creatocratic classical order marked by the Solar Crown of Castle Makupedia. Built on the study faculty of the Creative Sciences marked by the Sun in four circular columns of the De-Royal Makupedia of the Creatocratic Nations of Paradise. The second circle is time, third is the 12 stars representing the twelve dimensions of the universe and the innermost circle is the Maks symbol, an intersected letter =P=. The second order is the Creatocracy Corporation incorporated or not but copyright protected.

Ionize=4,500=5,000=50%=P5.00D=Law=Time=Venus=5 May = Aphrodite>>L=N.
Ionosphere=11,000=11%=P1.10D=1.1=Idea=Brainchild=11 Nov=Athena>>I=MT.
IOOF=2,500=3,000=30%=P3.0D=3.0=Creativity=Stars=Muses=3 March = C=I>>GIL.
Iota=6,500=7,000=70%=P7.0D=7.0=Language=Assets=Mars=7 July=Pleiades.
IOU=3,500=4,000=40%=P4.0D=Govt.=Creatocracy=4 April=Mercury=Hermes=G=A4.
-ious=5,500=5.5=80%=P5.50=Earth-Midway=5 May = Gaia.
Iowa1=10,000=1,000=100%=10.0=Physicality=Tech.=10 Oct.=Uranus=P=1Ø.
Iowa2=6,000=60%=P6.0D=Man=Earth=Royalty=6 June=Gaia=Maia>>M=M2.
IPA=1,500=15%=P1.50D=1.5=Authority=Solar Crown=1 May = Maia.
Ipecac=10,000=1,000=100%=10.0=Physicality=Tech.=10 Oct.=Uranus=P=1Ø.
Ipso facto=5,000=50%=P5.00D=Law=Time=Venus=5 May = Aphrodite>>L=N.

IQ=1,000=100%=10.0=1.0=Mind=Sun=1 January=Helios >> M=E4.
See Intelligence Quotient. A natural standard for measuring the IQ is the quantum.

Ir=2,500=3,000=30%=P3.0D=3.0=Creativity=Stars=Muses=3 March = C=I>>GIL.
It-1=1,500=15%=P1.50D=1.5=Authority=Solar Crown=1 May = Maia.

It-2=1,500=15%=P1.50D=1.5=Authority=Solar Crown=1 May = Maia.
IRA=4,000=40%=P4.0D=Govt.=Creatocracy=4 April=Mercury=Hermes=G=A4.
Iran=5,500=5.5=80%=P5.50=Earth-Midway=5 May = Gaia.
Iranian=9,500=10,000=1,000=100%=10.0=Physicality=Tech.=10 Oct.=Uranus=P=1Ø.
Iraq=3,500=4,000=40%=P4.0D=Govt.=Creatocracy=4 April=Mercury=Hermes=G=A4.
Irascible=6,500=7,000=70%=P7.0D=7.0=Language=Assets=Mars=7 July=Pleiades.
Irate=5,500=5.5=80%=P5.50=Earth-Midway=5 May = Gaia.
Irbil=4,500=5,000=50%=P5.00D=Law=Time=Venus=5 May = Aphrodite>>L=N.
Ire=2,000=20%=P2.00D=2.0=Nature=Matter=Moon=2 Feb.=Cupid=N=C+_
Ire.=500=5%=P5.00D=5.0=Law=Time=Venus=5 May=Aphrodite>>L=N.
Ireful=3,500=4,000=40%=P4.0D=Govt.=Creatocracy=4 April=Mercury=Hermes=G=A4.
Ireland1=5,000=50%=P5.00D=Law=Time=Venus=5 May = Aphrodite>>L=N.
Ireland2=6,000=60%=P6.0D=Man=Earth=Royalty=6 June=Gaia=Maia>>M=M2.
Ireland,Northern=1,500=15%=P1.50D=1.5=Authority=Solar Crown=1 May = Maia.
Ire descent=8,500=9,000=90%=P9.00D=9.0=Abstraction=Gods=Saturn=9Sept.>>A=Ø.
Iridium=15,500=16,000=16%=P1.60D=1.6=Cycle,Incarnation=Mind of GOD=1June=Maia.
Iris=10,000=1,000=100%=10.0=Physicality=Tech.=10 Oct.=Uranus=P=1Ø.
Irish=10,000=1,000=100%=10.0=Physicality=Tech.=10 Oct.=Uranus=P=1Ø.
Irish bull=4,000=40%=P4.0D=Govt.=Creatocracy=4 April=Mercury=Hermes=G=A4.
Irish Gaelic=2,500=3,000=30%=P3.0D=3.0=Cre=Stars=Muses=3 March = C=I>>GIL.
Irish moss=4,500=5,000=50%=P5.00D=Law=Time=Venus=5 May = Aphrodite>>L=N.
Irish Sea=5,500=5.5=80%=P5.50=Earth-Midway=5 May = Gaia.
Irish setter=3,500=4,000=40%=P4.0D=Govt.=Creat=4 April=Mercury=Hermes=G=A4.
Irk=2,500=3,000=30%=P3.0D=3.0=Creativity=Stars=Muses=3 March = C=I>>GIL.
Irksome=1,500=15%=P1.50D=1.5=Authority=Solar Crown=1 May = Maia.
Irkutsk=5,500=5.5=80%=P5.50=Earth-Midway=5 May = Gaia.
Iron=10,000=1,000=100%=10.0=Physicality=Tech.=10 Oct.=Uranus=P=1Ø.
Iron Age=10,000=1,000=100%=10.0=Physicality=Tech.=10 Oct.=Uranus=P=1Ø.
Iron clad=5,500=5.5=80%=P5.50=Earth-Midway=5 May = Gaia.
Iron curtain=9,000=90%=P9.00D=9.0=Abstraction=Gods=Saturn=9Sept.>>A=Ø.
Ironic=5,500=5.5=80%=P5.50=Earth-Midway=5 May = Gaia.
Iron lung=10,000=1,000=100%=10.0=Physicality=Tech.=10 Oct.=Uranus=P=1Ø.
Ironstone=3,500=4,000=40%=P4.0D=Govt.=Creat=4 April=Mercury=Hermes=G=A4.
Iron ware=4,000=40%=P4.0D=Govt.=Creatocracy=4 April=Mercury=Hermes=G=A4.
Ironwork=4,000=40%=P4.0D=Govt.=Creatocracy=4 April=Mercury=Hermes=G=A4.
Iron worker=5,500=5.5=80%=P5.50=Earth-Midway=5 May = Gaia.
Iron works=6,000=60%=P6.0D=Man=Earth=Royalty=6 June=Gaia=Maia>>M=M2.
Irony=10,000=1,000=100%=10.0=Physicality=Tech.=10 Oct.=Uranus=P=1Ø.
Iroquoian=10,000=1,000=100%=10.0=Physicality=Tech.=10 Oct.=Uranus=P=1Ø.
Iroquois=10,000=1,000=100%=10.0=Physicality=Tech.=10 Oct.=Uranus=P=1Ø.
Irradiate=10,000=1,000=100%=10.0=Physicality=Tech.=10 Oct.=Uranus=P=1Ø.
Irrational=10,000=1,000=100%=10.0=Physicality=Tech.=10 Oct.=Uranus=P=1Ø.
Irrational number=8,500=9,000=90%=P9.00D=9.0=Abstr=Gods=Saturn=9Sept.>>A=Ø.

Irrawaddy=9,000=90%=P9.00D=9.0=Abstraction=Gods=Saturn=9Sept.>>A=Ø.
The resultant indicates that Irrawaddy. is a spiritual river possibly possessing healing powers when drank in prayers. Abode of the Gods. Compare with the healing rivers of the Bible where the blind man was met with the angels and eventually the Christ.

Irreconcilable=1,500=15%=P1.50D=1.5=Authority=Solar Crown=1 May = Maia.
Irrecoverable=3,000=30%=P3.0D=3.0=Creativity=Stars=Muses=3 March = C=I>>GIL.
Irredeemable=8,500=9,000=90%=P9.00D=9.0=Abstraction=Gods=Saturn=9Sept.>>A=Ø.
Irredentist=10,000=1,000=100%=10.0=Physicality=Tech.=10 Oct.=Uranus=P=1Ø.
Irreducible=5,500=5.5=80%=P5.50=Earth-Midway=5 May = Gaia.
Irrefutable=2,500=3,000=30%=P3.0D=3.0=Creativity=Stars=Muses=3 March = C=I>>GIL.
Irreg.=500=5%=P5.00D=5.0=Law=Time=Venus=5 May=Aphrodite>>L=N.
Irregardless=10,000=1,000=100%=10.0=Physicality=Tech.=10 Oct.=Uranus=P=1Ø.
Irregular=10,000=1,000=100%=10.0=Physicality=Tech.=10 Oct.=Uranus=P=1Ø.
Irrelevant=10,000=1,000=100%=10.0=Physicality=Tech.=10 Oct.=Uranus=P=1Ø.
Irreligious=2,500=3,000=30%=P3.0D=3.0=Creativity=Stars=Muses=3 March = C=I>>GIL.
Irremediable=3,000=30%=P3.0D=3.0=Creativity=Stars=Muses=3 March = C=I>>GIL.
Irreparable=3,000=30%=P3.0D=3.0=Creativity=Stars=Muses=3 March = C=I>>GIL.
Irreplaceable=1,500=15%=P1.50D=1.5=Authority=Solar Crown=1 May = Maia.
Irrepressible=3,000=30%=P3.0D=3.0=Creativity=Stars=Muses=3 March = C=I>>GIL.
Irreproachable=2,500=3,000=30%=P3.0D=3.0=Cre=Stars=Muses=3 March = C=I>>GIL.
Irresistible=2,000=20%=P2.00D=2.0=Nature=Matter=Moon=2 Feb.=Cupid=N=C+_
Irresolute=6,000=60%=P6.0D=Man=Earth=Royalty=6 June=Gaia=Maia>>M=M2.
Irrespective of=2,000=20%=P2.00D=2.0=Nature=Matter=Moon=2 Feb.=Cupid=N=C+_
Irresponsible=4,500=5,000=50%=P5.00D=Law=Time=Venus=5 May = Aphrodite>>L=N.
Irretrievable=2,500=3,000=30%=P3.0D=3.0=Cre=Stars=Muses=3 March = C=I>>GIL.
Irreverence=5,000=50%=P5.00D=Law=Time=Venus=5 May = Aphrodite>>L=N.
Irreversible=1,500=15%=P1.50D=1.5=Authority=Solar Crown=1 May = Maia.
Irrevocable=2,500=3,000=30%=P3.0D=3.0=Cre=Stars=Muses=3 March = C=I>>GIL.
Irrigate=10,000=1,000=100%=10.0=Physicality=Tech.=10 Oct.=Uranus=P=1Ø.
Irritable=7,000=70%=P7.0D=7.0=Language=Assets=Mars=7 July=Pleiades.
Irritant=4,000=40%=P4.0D=Govt.=Creatocracy=4 April=Mercury=Hermes=G=A4.
Irritate=5,000=50%=P5.00D=Law=Time=Venus=5 May = Aphrodite>>L=N.
Irrupt=4,500=5,000=50%=P5.00D=Law=Time=Venus=5 May = Aphrodite>>L=N.
IRS=1,500=15%=P1.50D=1.5=Authority=Solar Crown=1 May = Maia.
Irtysh=10,000=1,000=100%=10.0=Physicality=Tech.=10 Oct.=Uranus=P=1Ø.
Irvine=5,000=50%=P5.00D=Law=Time=Venus=5 May = Aphrodite>>L=N.
Irving, Washington=2,000=20%=P2.00D=2.0=Matter=Moon=2 Feb.=Cupid=N=C+_
Is=3,500=4,000=40%=P4.0D=Govt.=Creatocracy=4 April=Mercury=Hermes=G=A4.
Is.=500=5%=P5.00D=5.0=Law=Time=Venus=5 May=Aphrodite>>L=N.

Isaac=3,000=30%=P3.0D=3.0=Creativity=Stars=Muses=3 March = C=I>>GIL.
Isaac was a muse transmuted into the birth of Sarah to become their son. A sign of the reign of muses in the developed era into the mind age so that revelation becomes real.

Abraham was the test of divine plans to transmute muses into humans. He was the source of inspiration for Abraham. Hence his unalloyed obedience was well noted. Kings work with muses and Peter Matthews-Akukalia, Castle Makupedia is no exception.

Isabella=4,500=5,000=50%=P5.00D=Law=Time=Venus=5 May = Aphrodite>>L=N.

Isaiah=6,000=60%=P6.0D=Man=Earth=Royalty=6 June=Gaia=Maia>>M=M2.
A Hebrew prophet of the 8th century. Computing for reality of his identity.
6.0*8.0x=px=14+48=62x=px=734=7.34=7.
Ticology indicates that Isaiah was a man with the ancient spirit of Gaia and certain royalty especially manifesting the 8th century where 8th>> Zeus >> currencies >> business>> economy were his core interests and calling. Computing on the stars indicate that he had computational powers that made up his assets and works (7.) so that clearly he could discern time and dispensation. (.34) indicates he was fully driven by muses in service of Hermes hence he prophesied the birth of the savior. He confirmed the name and qualities as one by whom the Heaven Council of Gods (GOD) would be with mankind. The book of Isaiah was inspired by Gaia Goddess of the Earth.

ISBN=2,000=20%=P2.00D=2.0=Nature=Matter=Moon=2 Feb.=Cupid=N=C+_
Ischemia=10,000=1,000=100%=10.0=Physicality=Tech.=10 Oct.=Uranus=P=1Ø.
Isfahan=4,500=5,000=50%=P5.00D=Law=Time=Venus=5 May = Aphrodite>>L=N.
-ish=10,000=1,000=100%=10.0=Physicality=Tech.=10 Oct.=Uranus=P=1Ø.
Isherwood Christopher=4,000=40%=P4.0D=Govt.=4 April=Mercury=Hermes=G=A4.
Isinglass=10,000=1,000=100%=10.0=Physicality=Tech.=10 Oct.=Uranus=P=1Ø.
Isis=6,000=60%=P6.0D=Man=Earth=Royalty=6 June=Gaia=Maia>>M=M2.
Isl.=500=5%=P5.00D=5.0=Law=Time=Venus=5 May=Aphrodite>>L=N.
Islam=10,000=1,000=100%=10.0=Physicality=Tech.=10 Oct.=Uranus=P=1Ø.
Islamabad=4,000=40%=P4.0D=Govt.=Creat.=4 April=Mercury=Hermes=G=A4.
Island=10,000=1,000=100%=10.0=Physicality=Tech.=10 Oct.=Uranus=P=1Ø.
Isle=4,000=40%=P4.0D=Govt.=Creatocracy=4 April=Mercury=Hermes=G=A4.
Islet=2,000=20%=P2.00D=2.0=Nature=Matter=Moon=2 Feb.=Cupid=N=C+_
Ism=4,000=40%=P4.0D=Govt.=Creatocracy=4 April=Mercury=Hermes=G=A4.
-ism=10,000=1,000=100%=10.0=Physicality=Tech.=10 Oct.=Uranus=P=1Ø.
Isn't=1,000=100%=10.0=1.0=Mind=Sun=1 January=Helios >> M=E4.
Iso-=4,000=40%=P4.0D=Govt.=Creatocracy=4 April=Mercury=Hermes=G=A4.
Isobar=8,000=80%=P8.0D=Economy=Currency=8 Aug.=Zeus>>E=v.
Isogon=3,000=30%=P3.0D=3.0=Creativity=Stars=Muses=3 March = C=I>>GIL.
Isolate=10,000=1,000=100%=10.0=Physicality=Tech.=10 Oct.=Uranus=P=1Ø.
Isolationism=6,500=7,000=70%=P7.0D=7.0=Language=Assets=Mars=7 July=Pleiades.
Isomer=10,000=1,000=100%=10.0=Physicality=Tech.=10 Oct.=Uranus=P=1Ø.
Isometric=10,000=1,000=100%=10.0=Physicality=Tech.=10 Oct.=Uranus=P=1Ø.
Isometrics=6,000=60%=P6.0D=Man=Earth=Royalty=6 June=Gaia=Maia>>M=M2.
Isomorph(ic)=3,000=30%=P3.0D=3.0=Creativity=Stars=Muses=3 March = C=I>>GIL.

Isomorphism=6,500=7,000=70%=P7.0D=7.0=Language=Assets=Mars=7 July=Pleiades.
Isopropyl=10,000=1,000=100%=10.0=Physicality=Tech.=10 Oct.=Uranus=P=1Ø.
Isosceles=6,500=7,000=70%=P7.0D=7.0=Language=Assets=Mars=7 July=Pleiades.
Isotherm=9,500=10,000=1,000=100%=10.0=Physicality=Tech.=10 Oct.=Uranus=P=1Ø.
Isotope=11,000=11%=P1.10D=1.1=Idea=Brainchild=11 Nov=Athena>>I=MT.
Isotropic=4,500=5,000=50%=P5.00D=Law=Time=Venus=5 May = Aphrodite>>L=N.
Isr.=1,000=100%=10.0=1.0=Mind=Sun=1 January=Helios >> M=E4.

Israel1=12,000=12%=P1.20D=1.2=Knowledge=Education=12Dec.=Athena>>K=F.
Israel is a nation founded by Athena through knowledge. A nation of knowledge. Athena
is Goddess of Paradise Nations asserted by Peter Matthews-Akukalia, Castle Makupedia.
It also means that new knowledge can be built on the interaction of Heaven and Israel. In
the Revelation Jesus instructed the use of Hebrew and Greek as means of new knowledge.
Peter Matthews-Akukalia, Castle Makupedia founded and built the Creatocracy thus. This
led to the marriage of Castle Makupedia to Athena. See book>> The Creatocracy Republic.

Israel2=12,000=12%=P1.20D=1.2=Knowledge=Education=12Dec.=Athena>>K=F.
Israeli=7,000=70%=P7.0D=7.0=Language=Assets=Mars=7 July=Pleiades.
Israelite=4,000=40%=P4.0D=Govt.=Creatocracy=4 April=Mercury=Hermes=G=A4.
Issue=10,000=1,000=100%=10.0=Physicality=Tech.=10 Oct.=Uranus=P=1Ø.
-ist=10,000=1,000=100%=10.0=Physicality=Tech.=10 Oct.=Uranus=P=1Ø.
Istanbul=8,500=9,000=90%=P9.00D=9.0=Abstraction=Gods=Saturn=9Sept.>>A=Ø.
Isth.=500=5%=P5.00D=5.0=Law=Time=Venus=5 May=Aphrodite>>L=N.
Isthmus=10,000=1,000=100%=10.0=Physicality=Tech.=10 Oct.=Uranus=P=1Ø.
It=10,000=1,000=100%=10.0=Physicality=Tech.=10 Oct.=Uranus=P=1Ø.
It.=1,000=100%=10.0=1.0=Mind=Sun=1 January=Helios >> M=E4.
Ital.=1,000=100%=10.0=1.0=Mind=Sun=1 January=Helios >> M=E4.
Italian=10,000=1,000=100%=10.0=Physicality=Tech.=10 Oct.=Uranus=P=1Ø.
Italic=10,000=1,000=100%=10.0=Physicality=Tech.=10 Oct.=Uranus=P=1Ø.
Italicize=2,500=3,000=30%=P3.0D=3.0=Creativity=Stars=Muses=3 March = C=I>>GIL.
Italy=10,000=1,000=100%=10.0=Physicality=Tech.=10 Oct.=Uranus=P=1Ø.
Itch=10,000=1,000=100%=10.0=Physicality=Tech.=10 Oct.=Uranus=P=1Ø.
-ite1=10,000=1,000=100%=10.0=Physicality=Tech.=10 Oct.=Uranus=P=1Ø.
-ite2=9,500=10,000=1,000=100%=10.0=Physicality=Tech.=10 Oct.=Uranus=P=1Ø.
Item=10,000=1,000=100%=10.0=Physicality=Tech.=10 Oct.=Uranus=P=1Ø.
Itemize=3,000=30%=P3.0D=3.0=Creativity=Stars=Muses=3 March = C=I>>GIL.
Iterate=5,500=5.5=80%=P5.50=Earth-Midway=5 May = Gaia.
Itháki=4,000=40%=P4.0D=Govt.=Creatocracy=4 April=Mercury=Hermes=G=A4.
Itinerant=8,500=9,000=90%=P9.00D=9.0=Abstraction=Gods=Saturn=9Sept.>>A=Ø.
Itinerary=10,000=1,000=100%=10.0=Physicality=Tech.=10 Oct.=Uranus=P=1Ø.
-Itis=4,500=5,000=50%=P5.00D=Law=Time=Venus=5 May = Aphrodite>>L=N.
It'll=1,500=15%=P1.50D=1.5=Authority=Solar Crown=1 May = Maia.
Its=10,000=1,000=100%=10.0=Physicality=Tech.=10 Oct.=Uranus=P=1Ø.
It's=1,500=15%=P1.50D=1.5=Authority=Solar Crown=1 May = Maia.

Itself=10,000=1,000=100%=10.0=Physicality=Tech.=10 Oct.=Uranus=P=1Ø.
-ity=3,000=30%=P3.0D=3.0=Creativity=Stars=Muses=3 March = C=I>>GIL.
IU=1,000=100%=10.0=1.0=Mind=Sun=1 January=Helios >> M=E4.
IUD=1,000=100%=10.0=1.0=Mind=Sun=1 January=Helios >> M=E4.
-lum=6,000=60%=P6.0D=Man=Earth=Royalty=6 June=Gaia=Maia>>M=M2.
IV=500=5%=P5.00D=5.0=Law=Time=Venus=5 May=Aphrodite>>L=N.
Ivan III Vaillevich=4,500=5,000=50%=P5.00D=Law=Time=Venus=5 May = Odite>>L=N.
Ivan IV Vasillevich=4,500=5,000=50%=P5.00D=Law=Time=Venus=5 May =Odite>>L=N.
-Ive=5,500=5.5=80%=P5.50=Earth-Midway=5 May = Gaia.
I've=1,000=100%=10.0=1.0=Mind=Sun=1 January=Helios >> M=E4.
Ives Charles=2,500=3,000=30%=P3.0D=3.0=Cre=Stars=Muses=3 March = C=I>>GIL.
Ivory=10,000=1,000=100%=10.0=Physicality=Tech.=10 Oct.=Uranus=P=1Ø.
Ivory Coast=7,500=8,000=80%=P8.0D=Economy=Currency=8 Aug.=Zeus>>E=v.
Ivory tower=7,500=8,000=80%=P8.0D=Economy=Currency=8 Aug.=Zeus>>E=v.

Ivy=7,000=70%=P7.0D=7.0=Language=Assets=Mars=7 July=Pleiades.
<Old English < fig. The secrets of the fig tree is formula, computing, precision. This is the standard stipulated in codes by Jesus >> Hermes to know a tree that bears fruits.

Iwo Jima=7,000=70%=P7.0D=7.0=Language=Assets=Mars=7 July=Pleiades.
Iyar=6,000=60%=P6.0D=Man=Earth=Royalty=6 June=Gaia=Maia>>M=M2.
-ization=4,500=5,000=50%=P5.00D=Law=Time=Venus=5 May = Aphrodite>>L=N.
-ize=10,000=1,000=100%=10.0=Physicality=Tech.=10 Oct.=Uranus=P=1Ø.
Izhevsk=5,000=50%=P5.00D=Law=Time=Venus=5 May = Aphrodite>>L=N.
Izmir=6,000=60%=P6.0D=Man=Earth=Royalty=6 June=Gaia=Maia>>M=M2

MAKABET =Jj=

J1=3,000=30%=P3.0D=3.0=Creativity=Stars=Muses=3 March = C=I>>GIL.
The 10th letter of the English alphabet. Makupedia shows it is an element of creativity. A constant repetition of "J" conjures the muses especially when the name of particular muse is mentioned as seen in the encyclopedia of Castle Makupedia. This is a directed method of prayer with specific means. The use of "J" in statements tends to induce determination and certain responsibility to act a certain way in the person(s). Eg. "Just do it" is a statement of expectation sourced from a joint will. The will is the third component of the Mind and is measured on the bench of 3.0>>Creativity. Computing the GIL makes it possible to measure the inherent energy level available to function or perform the supposed action. The energies of parties involved must be synchronized for total output.
The psycho-weight of the alphabet (J) is thus computed:
3.0*10.0=p=13+30=43x=px=433=4.33>>1.2>>Knowledge>>Education >>Athena>>K=F.

The letter "J" indicates the power of genius >>33 >>3.3 inspired by Athena's Council of the Gods. The alphabet falls within the 10th dimension of the Mind Universes and is a physical resultant. The Creatocracy rates it a technical alphabet elevating it to a Makabet.

J2=500=3,000=30%=P3.0D=3.0=Creativity=Stars=Muses=3 March = C=I>>GIL.
JA=1,000=100%=10.0=1.0=Mind=Sun=1 January=Helios >> M=E4.
Jab=7,500=8,000=80%=P8.0D=Economy=Currency=8 Aug.=Zeus>>E=v.
Jabalpur=4,500=5,000=50%=P5.00D=Law=Time=Venus=5 May = Aphrodite>>L=N.
Jabber=4,000=40%=P4.0D=Govt.=Creatocracy=4 April=Mercury=Hermes=G=A4.
Jabot=5,000=50%=P5.00D=Law=Time=Venus=5 May = Aphrodite>>L=N.
Jacaranda=8,000=80%=P8.0D=Economy=Currency=8 Aug.=Zeus>>E=v.
Jack=10,000=1,000=100%=10.0=Physicality=Tech.=10 Oct.=Uranus=P=1Ø.
Jackal=5,000=50%=P5.00D=Law=Time=Venus=5 May = Aphrodite>>L=N.
Jackass=4,000=40%=P4.0D=Govt.=Creatocracy=4 April=Mercury=Hermes=G=A4.
Jackboot=4,000=40%=P4.0D=Govt.=Creatocracy=4 April=Mercury=Hermes=G=A4.
Jackdaw=3,500=4,000=40%=P4.0D=Govt.=Creat.=4 April=Mercury=Hermes=G=A4.
Jacket=8,500=9,000=90%=P9.00D=9.0=Abstraction=Gods=Saturn=9Sept.>>A=Ø.
Jackhammer=6,000=60%=P6.0D=Man=Earth=Royalty=6 June=Gaia=Maia>>M=M2.
Jack-in-the-box=6,500=7,000=70%=P7.0D=7.0=Language=Assets=Mars=7 July=Pleiades.
Jack-in-the-pulpit=4,000=40%=P4.0D=Govt.=Creat.=4 April=Mercury=Hermes=G=A4.
Jackknife=11,000=11%=P1.10D=1.1=Idea=Brainchild=Inv.=11 Nov.=SC=Athena>>I=MT.
Jack-of-all-trades=4,000=40%=P4.0D=Govt.=Creat.=4 April=Mercury=Hermes=G=A4.
Jack-o'-lantern=4,500=5,000=50%=P5.00D=Law=Time=Venus=5 May = Aphrodite>>L=N.
Jackpot=4,500=5,000=50%=P5.00D=Law=Time=Venus=5 May = Aphrodite>>L=N.
Jackrabbit=4,000=40%=P4.0D=Govt.=Creatocracy=4 April=Mercury=Hermes=G=A4.
Jack screw=2,500=3,000=30%=P3.0D=3.0=Cre=Stars=Muses=3 March = C=I>>GIL.
Jackson=5,000=50%=P5.00D=Law=Time=Venus=5 May = Aphrodite>>L=N.
Jackson, Andrew=5,000=50%=P5.00D=Law=Time=Venus=5 May = Aphrodite>>L=N.
Jackson, Jesse Louis=4,000=40%=P4.0D=Govt.=Creat.=4April=Mercury=Hermes=G=A4.
Jackson, Thomas=3,000=30%=P3.0D=3.0=Creativity=Stars=Muses=3 March = C=I>>GIL.
Jacksonville=6,500=7,000=70%=P7.0D=7.0=Language=Assets=Mars=7 July=Pleiades.

Jacob=4,500=5,000=50%=P5.00D=Law=Time=Venus=5 May = Aphrodite>>L=N.

Jacobean=5,500=5.5=80%=P5.50=Earth-Midway=5 May = Gaia.
Jacobin=8,500=9,000=90%=P9.00D=9.0=Abstraction=Gods=Saturn=9Sept.>>A=Ø.
Jacob's ladder=12,000=12%=P1.20D=1.2=Knowledge=Edu=12Dec.=Athena>>K=F.
Jacuzzi=2,500=3,000=30%=P3.0D=3.0=Creativity=Stars=Muses=3 March = C=I>>GIL.
Jade1=12,000=12%=P1.20D=1.2=Knowledge=Edu=12Dec.=Athena>>K=F.
Jade2=10,000=1,000=100%=1.0=Physicality=Tech.=10 Oct.=Uranus=P=1Ø.
Jaded=4,500=5,000=50%=P5.00D=Law=Time=Venus=5 May = Aphrodite>>L=N.
Jadeite=8,000=80%=P8.0D=Economy=Currency=8 Aug.=Zeus>>E=v.
Jaffa=8,500=9,000=90%=P9.00D=9.0=Abstraction=Gods=Saturn=9Sept.>>A=Ø.

Jag1=3,000=30%=P3.0D=3.0=Creativity=Stars=Muses=3 March = C=I>>GIL.
Jag2=5,500=5.5=80%=P5.50=Earth-Midway=5 May = Gaia.
J.A.G.=1,500=15%=P1.50D=1.5=Authority=Solar Crown=1 May = Maia.
Jagged=2,500=3,000=30%=P3.0D=3.0=Creativity=Stars=Muses=3 March = C=I>>GIL.
Jaguar=6,000=60%=P6.0D=Man=Earth=Royalty=6 June=Gaia=Maia>>M=M2.
Jaialal=9,500=10,000=1,000=100%=10.0=Physicality=Tech.=10 Oct.=Uranus=P=1Ø.
Jail=9,000=90%=P9.00D=9.0=Abstraction=Gods=Saturn=9Sept.>>A=Ø.
Jailbird=2,500=3,000=30%=P3.0D=3.0=Creativity=Stars=Muses=3 March = C=I>>GIL.
Jailbreak=2,000=20%=P2.00D=2.0=Nature=Matter=Moon=2 Feb.=Cupid=N=C+_
Jailer=2,500=3,000=30%=P3.0D=3.0=Creativity=Stars=Muses=3 March = C=I>>GIL.
Jaipur=5,000=50%=P5.00D=Law=Time=Venus=5 May = Aphrodite>>L=N.
Jakarta=5,500=5.5=80%=P5.50=Earth-Midway=5 May = Gaia.
Jalapeño=9,000=90%=P9.00D=9.0=Abstraction=Gods=Saturn=9Sept.>>A=Ø.
Jalopy=3,000=30%=P3.0D=3.0=Creativity=Stars=Muses=3 March = C=I>>GIL.
Jalousie=5,000=50%=P5.00D=Law=Time=Venus=5 May = Aphrodite>>L=N.
Jam1=10,000=1,000=100%=10.0=Physicality=Tech.=10 Oct.=Uranus=P=1Ø.
Jam2=5,000=50%=P5.00D=Law=Time=Venus=5 May = Aphrodite>>L=N.
Jamaica=7,000=70%=P7.0D=7.0=Language=Assets=Mars=7 July=Pleiades.
Jamb=7,500=8,000=80%=P8.0D=Economy=Currency=8 Aug.=Zeus>>E=v.
Jambalaya=5,000=50%=P5.00D=Law=Time=Venus=5 May = Aphrodite>>L=N.
Jamboree=6,500=7,000=70%=P7.0D=7.0=Language=Assets=Mars=7 July=Pleiades.
James=2,000=20%=P2.00D=2.0=Nature=Matter=Moon=2 Feb.=Cupid=N=C+_
James1=5,000=50%=P5.00D=Law=Time=Venus=5 May = Aphrodite>>L=N.
James2=6,500=7,000=70%=P7.0D=7.0=Language=Assets=Mars=7 July=Pleiades.
James3=5,000=50%=P5.00D=Law=Time=Venus=5 May = Aphrodite>>L=N.
James I.=6,500=7,000=70%=P7.0D=7.0=Language=Assets=Mars=7 July=Pleiades.
James II.=5,000=50%=P5.00D=Law=Time=Venus=5 May = Aphrodite>>L=N.
James, Henry=3,000=30%=P3.0D=3.0=Creativity=Stars=Muses=3 March = C=I>>GIL.
James, William=3,000=30%=P3.0D=3.0=Creativity=Stars=Muses=3 March = C=I>>GIL.
James Bay=8,000=80%=P8.0D=Economy=Currency=8 Aug.=Zeus>>E=v.
James River=10,000=1,000=100%=10.0=Physicality=Tech.=10 Oct.=Uranus=P=1Ø.
Jamestown=10,000=1,000=100%=10.0=Physicality=Tech.=10 Oct.=Uranus=P=1Ø.
Jam session=4,000=40%=P4.0D=Govt.=Creatocracy=4 April=Mercury=Hermes=G=A4.
Jan.=500=5%=P5.00D=5.0=Law=Time=Venus=5 May=Aphrodite>>L=N.
Jangle=8,000=80%=P8.0D=Economy=Currency=8 Aug.=Zeus>>E=v.
Janitor=5,500=5.5=80%=P5.50=Earth-Midway=5 May = Gaia.
January=7,500=8,000=80%=P8.0D=Economy=Currency=8 Aug.=Zeus>>E=v.
Janus=8,000=80%=P8.0D=Economy=Currency=8 Aug.=Zeus>>E=v.
Japan=5,000=50%=P5.00D=Law=Time=Venus=5 May = Aphrodite>>L=N.
Japan=10,000=1,000=100%=10.0=Physicality=Tech.=10 Oct.=Uranus=P=1Ø.
Japan, Sea of.=6,000=60%=P6.0D=Man=Earth=Royalty=6 June=Gaia=Maia>>M=M2.
Japan Current=8,000=80%=P8.0D=Economy=Currency=8 Aug.=Zeus>>E=v.
Japanese=10,000=1,000=100%=10.0=Physicality=Tech.=10 Oct.=Uranus=P=1Ø.
Japanese beetle=5,500=5.5=80%=P5.50=Earth-Midway=5 May = Gaia.
Jape=4,500=5,000=50%=P5.00D=Law=Time=Venus=5 May = Aphrodite>>L=N.

Jarl=6,500=7,000=70%=P7.0D=7.0=Language=Assets=Mars=7 July=Pleiades.
Jar2=10,000=1,000=100%=10.0=Physicality=Tech.=10 Oct.=Uranus=P=1Ø.
Jardiniere=6,000=60%=P6.0D=Man=Earth=Royalty=6 June=Gaia=Maia>>M=M2.
Jargon=6,000=60%=P6.0D=Man=Earth=Royalty=6 June=Gaia=Maia>>M=M2.
Jarlsberg=4,500=5,000=50%=P5.00D=Law=Time=Venus=5 May = Aphrodite>>L=N.

Jasmine=7,000=70%=P7.0D=7.0=Language=Assets=Mars=7 July=Pleiades.
Fourth child and third Princess of Peter Matthews-Akukalia, Castle Makupedia.

Jasper=4,500=5,000=50%=P5.00D=Law=Time=Venus=5 May = Aphrodite>>L=N.
A character in a play written by Peter Matthews-Akukalia, Castle Makupedia. Reference book>> The Creatocracy Republic, Sword of Honour (Reloaded). Also Sword of Honour, Days of St. Valentine by African Shakespeare. Published in 2011.

Jaundice=10,000=1,000=100%=10.0=Physicality=Tech.=10 Oct.=Uranus=P=1Ø.
Jaunt=3,000=30%=P3.0D=3.0=Creativity=Stars=Muses=3 March = C=I>>GIL.
Jaunty=7,500=8,000=80%=P8.0D=Economy=Currency=8 Aug.=Zeus>>E=v.
java=2,000=20%=P2.00D=2.0=Nature=Matter=Moon=2 Feb.=Cupid=N=C+_
Java=7,000=70%=P7.0D=7.0=Language=Assets=Mars=7 July=Pleiades.
Javelin=10,000=1,000=100%=10.0=Physicality=Tech.=10 Oct.=Uranus=P=1Ø.
Jaw=10,000=1,000=100%=10.0=Physicality=Tech.=10 Oct.=Uranus=P=1Ø.
Jawbone=8,000=80%=P8.0D=Economy=Currency=8 Aug.=Zeus>>E=v.
Jawbreaker=4,500=5,000=50%=P5.00D=Law=Time=Venus=5 May = Aphrodite>>L=N.
Jay=7,000=70%=P7.0D=7.0=Language=Assets=Mars=7 July=Pleiades.
Jay John=7,500=8,000=80%=P8.0D=Economy=Currency=8 Aug.=Zeus>>E=v.
Jaywalk=6,000=60%=P6.0D=Man=Earth=Royalty=6 June=Gaia=Maia>>M=M2.
Jazz=10,000=1,000=100%=10.0=Physicality=Tech.=10 Oct.=Uranus=P=1Ø.
Jazzy=3,500=4,000=40%=P4.0D=Govt.=Creatocracy=4 April=Mercury=Hermes=G=A4.
JCL=5,500=5.5=80%=P5.50=Earth-Midway=5 May = Gaia.
J.C.S=2,000=20%=P2.00D=2.0=Nature=Matter=Moon=2 Feb.=Cupid=N=C+_
jct.=500=5%=P5.00D=5.0=Law=Time=Venus=5 May=Aphrodite>>L=N.
JD=5,500=5.5=80%=P5.50=Earth-Midway=5 May = Gaia.
J.D.=1,000=100%=10.0=1.0=Mind=Sun=1 January=Helios >> M=E4.
Jealous=10,000=1,000=100%=10.0=Physicality=Tech.=10 Oct.=Uranus=P=1Ø.
Jean=6,500=7,000=70%=P7.0D=7.0=Language=Assets=Mars=7 July=Pleiades.
Jeep=8,500=9,000=90%=P9.00D=9.0=Abstraction=Gods=Saturn=9Sept.>>A=Ø.
Jeer=3,000=30%=P3.0D=3.0=Creativity=Stars=Muses=3 March = C=I>>GIL.
Jefferson Thomas=4,000=40%=P4.0D=Govt.=Creat.=4 April=Mercury=Hermes=G=A4.
Jefferson City=6,000=60%=P6.0D=Man=Earth=Royalty=6 June=Gaia=Maia>>M=M2.
Jehoshaphat=3,000=30%=P3.0D=3.0=Creativity=Stars=Muses=3 March = C=I>>GIL.

Jehovah=3,500=4,000=40%=P4.0D=Govt.=Creato=4 April=Mercury=Hermes=G=A4.
Established by the Creatocracy to be Zeus the Most High. Zeus Jehovah. Creatocrats as Makstians believe that "Jehovah" is a title for Zeus. In the book of Exodus Zeus introduces

Himself to Moses as Jehovah, the Almighty. So Zeus Jehovah means Zeus the Almighty. Hermes manifests as Jesus the Christ, Jesus the anointed One, Jesus Christ. Psalm 68 the name of GOD is given as JAH a word to confirm the cosmic stellar coding system of Genesis 1:14-16. Computed it gives the codes 9.0 & 9.0 meaning a High God >> Most High GOD >> The Almighty GOD >> Jehovah. During the prophecy of the birth of Samson the name JAH was revealed as a secret by the Angel to Manoah hence to be sought. Castle Makupedia is a God with abstract understanding of dark mysteries or abstraction that includes metrics in currency weather computing and programming 100%. The winged word =Makupedia= indicates Creative Intelligence <1.3> Faculty of Creative Science>>Athena.

---

jejune=6,000=60%=P6.0D=Man=Earth=Royalty=6 June=Gaia=Maia>>M=M2.
Jejunum=7,500=8,000=80%=P8.0D=Economy=Currency=8 Aug.=Zeus>>E=v.
Jell=5,500=5.5=80%=P5.50=Earth-Midway=5 May = Gaia.
Jelly=10,000=1,000=100%=10.0=Physicality=Tech.=10 Oct.=Uranus=P=1Ø.
Jellybean=2,000=20%=P2.00D=2.0=Nature=Matter=Moon=2 Feb.=Cupid=N=C+_
Jellyfish=10,000=1,000=100%=10.0=Physicality=Tech.=10 Oct.=Uranus=P=1Ø.
Jelly roll=6,500=7,000=70%=P7.0D=7.0=Language=Assets=Mars=7 July=Pleiades.
Jenghis Khan=1,500=15%=P1.50D=1.5=Authority=Solar Crown=1 May = Maia.
Jenny=7,000=70%=P7.0D=7.0=Language=Assets=Mars=7 July=Pleiades.
Jeopardize=4,500=5,000=50%=P5.00D=Law=Time=Venus=5 May = Aphrodite>>L=N.
Jeopardy=5,500=5.5=80%=P5.50=Earth-Midway=5 May = Gaia.
Jerboa=5,500=5.5=80%=P5.50=Earth-Midway=5 May = Gaia.
jeremiad=6,500=7,000=70%=P7.0D=7.0=Language=Assets=Mars=7 July=Pleiades.

Jeremiah=7,000=70%=P7.0D=7.0=Language=Assets=Mars=7 July=Pleiades.
A book inspired by the Pleiades functioned by Aries God of war. Exodus 22:28; 23:20-25.

Jericho=6,000=60%=P6.0D=Man=Earth=Royalty=6 June=Gaia=Maia>>M=M2.
Jerk1=10,000=1,000=100%=10.0=Physicality=Tech.=10 Oct.=Uranus=P=1Ø.
Jerk2=6,500=7,000=70%=P7.0D=7.0=Language=Assets=Mars=7 July=Pleiades.
Jerkin=3,000=30%=P3.0D=3.0=Creativity=Stars=Muses=3 March = C=I>>GIL.
Jerk water=2,000=20%=P2.00D=2.0=Nature=Matter=Moon=2 Feb.=Cupid=N=C+_
Jerky=3,000=30%=P3.0D=3.0=Creativity=Stars=Muses=3 March = C=I>>GIL.
Jeroboam=7,000=70%=P7.0D=7.0=Language=Assets=Mars=7 July=Pleiades.
Jerry build=4,000=40%=P4.0D=Govt.=Creatocracy=4 April=Mercury=Hermes=G=A4.
Jersey=8,000=80%=P8.0D=Economy=Currency=8 Aug.=Zeus>>E=v.
Jersey=4,000=40%=P4.0D=Govt.=Creatocracy=4 April=Mercury=Hermes=G=A4.
Jersey City=7,000=70%=P7.0D=7.0=Language=Assets=Mars=7 July=Pleiades.
Jerusalem=5,500=5.5=80%=P5.50=Earth-Midway=5 May = Gaia.
Jessamine=1,500=15%=P1.50D=1.5=Authority=Solar Crown=1 May = Maia.

Jesse=3,000=30%=P3.0D=3.0=Creativity=Stars=Muses=3 March = C=I>>GIL.

Jest=11,000=11%=P1.10D=1.1=Idea=Brainchild=Inv.=11 Nov.=SC=Athena>>I=MT.
Jester=5,000=50%=P5.00D=Law=Time=Venus=5 May = Aphrodite>>L=N.
Jesuit=9,000=90%=P9.00D=9.0=Abstraction=Gods=Saturn=9Sept.>>A=Ø.

Jesus=6,000=60%=P6.0D=Man=Earth=Royalty=6 June=Gaia=Maia>>M=M2.
>>Established by the Creatocracy to be Hermes in Greek mythologies, Mercury in Roman. Hermes operant in the service and incarnation of Gaia, so that he was born through the Royal lineage of David. Computing his real identity. Jesus >> Yea - Zeus >> See Zeus. Jehovah is the office of the Zeus meaning Almighty GOD. 6.0*4.0x=px=10+24=34x=px=274=300=3.0 Jesus was a muse who came to usher in creativity. His words are often expressed in parables and most times have much deeper meaning than what is speculated. Clearly Hermes in order to reach mankind had to assume the form of a muse in the order of Aphrodite to be born.

Jet1=12,000=12%=P1.20D=1.2=Knowledge=Edu=12Dec.=Athena>>K=F.
Jet2=10,000=1,000=100%=10.0=Physicality=Tech.=10 Oct.=Uranus=P=1Ø.
Jet engine=10,000=1,000=100%=10.0=Physicality=Tech.=10 Oct.=Uranus=P=1Ø.
Jet lag=7,000=70%=P7.0D=7.0=Language=Assets=Mars=7 July=Pleiades.
Jet propelled=3,500=4,000=40%=P4.0D=Govt.=Creato=4 April=Mercury=Hermes=G=A4.
Jetsam=10,000=1,000=100%=10.0=Physicality=Tech.=10 Oct.=Uranus=P=1Ø.
Jet set=9,000=90%=P9.00D=9.0=Abstraction=Gods=Saturn=9Sept.>>A=Ø.
Jet stream=11,000=11%=P1.10D=1.1=Idea=Brainchild=Inv.=11 Nov.=SC=Athena>>I=MT.
Jettison=5,000=50%=P5.00D=Law=Time=Venus=5 May = Aphrodite>>L=N.
Jetty=10,000=1,000=100%=10.0=Physicality=Tech.=10 Oct.=Uranus=P=1Ø.
Jew=10,000=1,000=100%=10.0=Physicality=Tech.=10 Oct.=Uranus=P=1Ø.
Jewel=10,000=1,000=100%=10.0=Physicality=Tech.=10 Oct.=Uranus=P=1Ø.
Jeweler=4,000=40%=P4.0D=Govt.=Creatocracy=4 April=Mercury=Hermes=G=A4.
Jewel weed=6,000=60%=P6.0D=Man=Earth=Royalty=6 June=Gaia=Maia>>M=M2.
Jewess=10,000=1,000=100%=10.0=Physicality=Tech.=10 Oct.=Uranus=P=1Ø.
Jewish=7,000=70%=P7.0D=7.0=Language=Assets=Mars=7 July=Pleiades.
Jewry=1,500=15%=P1.50D=1.5=Authority=Solar Crown=1 May = Maia.
Jew's harp=10,000=1,000=100%=10.0=Physicality=Tech.=10 Oct.=Uranus=P=1Ø.

Jezebel=2,000=20%=P2.00D=2.0=Nature=Matter=Moon=2 Feb.=Cupid=N=C+_

Jezebel=5,000=5.5=80%=P5.50=Earth-Midway=5 May = Gaia.
Jiao=5,500=5.5=80%=P5.50=Earth-Midway=5 May = Gaia.
Jib=5,500=5.5=80%=P5.50=Earth-Midway=5 May = Gaia.
Jibe1=10,000=1,000=100%=10.0=Physicality=Tech.=10 Oct.=Uranus=P=1Ø.
Jibe2=3,500=4,000=40%=P4.0D=Govt.=Creatocracy=4 April=Mercury=Hermes=G=A4.
Jibe3=1,500=15%=P1.50D=1.5=Authority=Solar Crown=1 May = Maia.
Jidda=6,500=7,000=70%=P7.0D=7.0=Language=Assets=Mars=7 July=Pleiades.
Jiffy=2,000=20%=P2.00D=2.0=Nature=Matter=Moon=2 Feb.=Cupid=N=C+_
Jig=10,000=1,000=100%=10.0=Physicality=Tech.=10 Oct.=Uranus=P=1Ø.

Jigger=4,500=5,000=50%=P5.00D=Law=Time=Venus=5 May = Aphrodite>>L=N.
Jiggle=5,000=50%=P5.00D=Law=Time=Venus=5 May = Aphrodite>>L=N.
Jigsaw=5,500=5.5=80%=P5.50=Earth-Midway=5 May = Gaia.
Jigsaw Puzzle=6,500=7,000=70%=P7.0D=7.0=Language=Assets=Mars=7 July=Pleiades.
Jihad=4,000=40%=P4.0D=Govt.=Creatocracy=4 April=Mercury=Hermes=G=A4.
Jilin=8,000=80%=P8.0D=Economy=Currency=8 Aug.=Zeus>>E=v.
Jilt=5,500=5.5=80%=P5.50=Earth-Midway=5 May = Gaia.
Jim Crow=8,500=9,000=90%=P9.00D=9.0=Abstraction=Gods=Saturn=9Sept.>>A=Ø.
Jimmy=9,500=10,000=1,000=100%=10.0=Physicality=Tech.=10 Oct.=Uranus=P=1Ø.
Jim-son weed=7,000=70%=P7.0D=7.0=Language=Assets=Mars=7 July=Pleiades.
Jinan=4,500=5,000=50%=P5.00D=Law=Time=Venus=5 May = Aphrodite>>L=N.
Jingle=10,000=1,000=100%=10.0=Physicality=Tech.=10 Oct.=Uranus=P=1Ø.
Jingoism=10,000=1,000=100%=10.0=Physicality=Tech.=10 Oct.=Uranus=P=1Ø.
Jinni=4,000=40%=P4.0D=Govt.=Creatocracy=4 April=Mercury=Hermes=G=A4.
Jinriksha=6,500=7,000=70%=P7.0D=7.0=Language=Assets=Mars=7 July=Pleiades.

Jinx=10,000=1,000=100%=10.0=Physicality=Tech.=10 Oct.=Uranus=P=1Ø.

Jitney=6,500=7,000=70%=P7.0D=7.0=Language=Assets=Mars=7 July=Pleiades.
Jitter=5,500=5.5=80%=P5.50=Earth-Midway=5 May = Gaia.
Jitterbug=7,500=8,000=80%=P8.0D=Economy=Currency=8 Aug.=Zeus>>E=v.
Jive=8,000=80%=P8.0D=Economy=Currency=8 Aug.=Zeus>>E=v.
jnr.=500=5%=P5.00D=5.0=Law=Time=Venus=5 May=Aphrodite>>L=N.
Joan of Arc=4,500=5,000=50%=P5.00D=Law=Time=Venus=5 May = Aphrodite>>L=N.
Job=10,000=1,000=100%=10.0=Physicality=Tech.=10 Oct.=Uranus=P=1Ø.

Job=6,000=60%=P6.0D=Man=Earth=Royalty=6 June=Gaia=Maia>>M=M2.
Inspired by Gaia, Goddess of the Earth. Job was born a royalty and was full of inspiration.
Job >> The Creatocracy believes that the book of Job is the secret of jobs and employment on the requirements given by GOD especially in Job 38, 39, 40.

Job action=7,000=70%=P7.0D=7.0=Language=Assets=Mars=7 July=Pleiades.
Jobber=7,500=8,000=80%=P8.0D=Economy=Currency=8 Aug.=Zeus>>E=v.
Job holder=3,000=30%=P3.0D=3.0=Creativity=Stars=Muses=3 March = C=I>>GIL.
Job lot=3,000=30%=P3.0D=3.0=Creativity=Stars=Muses=3 March = C=I>>GIL.
Jock1=1,500=15%=P1.50D=1.5=Authority=Solar Crown=1 May = Maia.
Jock2=2,500=3,000=30%=P3.0D=3.0=Creativity=Stars=Muses=3 March = C=I>>GIL.
Jockey=10,000=1,000=100%=10.0=Physicality=Tech.=10 Oct.=Uranus=P=1Ø.
Jock strap=4,000=40%=P4.0D=Govt.=Creatocracy=4 April=Mercury=Hermes=G=A4.
Jocose=4,000=40%=P4.0D=Govt.=Creatocracy=4 April=Mercury=Hermes=G=A4.
Jocular=5,000=50%=P5.00D=Law=Time=Venus=5 May = Aphrodite>>L=N.
Jocund=2,000=20%=P2.00D=2.0=Nature=Matter=Moon=2 Feb.=Cupid=N=C+_
Jodhpur=4,500=5,000=50%=P5.00D=Law=Time=Venus=5 May = Aphrodite>>L=N.
Jodhpurs=7,000=70%=P7.0D=7.0=Language=Assets=Mars=7 July=Pleiades.

Joel=2,000=20%=P2.00D=2.0=Nature=Matter=Moon=2 Feb.=Cupid=N=C+_
Joey=4,000=40%=P4.0D=Govt.=Creatocracy=4 April=Mercury=Hermes=G=A4.
Jog1=10,000=1,000=100%=10.0=Physicality=Tech.=10 Oct.=Uranus=P=1Ø.
Jog2=8,000=80%=P8.0D=Economy=Currency=8 Aug.=Zeus>>E=v.
Joggle=3,500=4,000=40%=P4.0D=Govt.=Creatocracy=4 April=Mercury=Hermes=G=A4.
Johannesburg=5,000=50%=P5.00D=Law=Time=Venus=5 May = Aphrodite>>L=N.
John1=3,000=30%=P3.0D=3.0=Creativity=Stars=Muses=3 March = C=I>>GIL.
John2=2,000=20%=P2.00D=2.0=Nature=Matter=Moon=2 Feb.=Cupid=N=C+_
John, Saint=4,500=5,000=50%=P5.00D=Law=Time=Venus=5 May = Aphrodite>>L=N.
John XXIII.=2,000=20%=P2.00D=2.0=Nature=Matter=Moon=2 Feb.=Cupid=N=C+_
John Doe=8,000=80%=P8.0D=Economy=Currency=8 Aug.=Zeus>>E=v.
Johnny cake=3,000=30%=P3.0D=3.0=Creativity=Stars=Muses=3 March = C=I>>GIL.
John of Gaunt=3,500=4,000=40%=P4.0D=Govt.=Creat.=4 April=Mercury=Hermes=G=A4.
John Paul I.=1,500=15%=P1.50D=1.5=Authority=Solar Crown=1 May = Maia.
John Paul II.=2,500=3,000=30%=P3.0D=3.0=Cre=Stars=Muses=3 March = C=I>>GIL.
Johnson, Andrew=4,000=40%=P4.0D=Govt.=Creat.=4 April=Mercury=Hermes=G=A4.
Johnson, Lyndon=4,000=40%=P4.0D=Govt.=Creat.=4 April=Mercury=Hermes=G=A4.
Johnson, Samuel=3,000=30%=P3.0D=3.0=Creativity=Stars=Muses=3 March = C=I>>GIL.
John the Baptist=6,000=60%=P6.0D=Man=Earth=Royalty=6 June=Gaia=Maia>>M=M2.
Jole de vivre=2,000=20%=P2.00D=2.0=Nature=Matter=Moon=2 Feb.=Cupid=N=C+_
Join=10,000=1,000=100%=10.0=Physicality=Tech.=10 Oct.=Uranus=P=1Ø.
Joiner=3,500=4,000=40%=P4.0D=Govt.=Creatocracy=4 April=Mercury=Hermes=G=A4.
Joint=10,000=1,000=100%=10.0=Physicality=Tech.=10 Oct.=Uranus=P=1Ø.
Joist=10,000=1,000=100%=10.0=Physicality=Tech.=10 Oct.=Uranus=P=1Ø.
Jojoba=10,000=1,000=100%=10.0=Physicality=Tech.=10 Oct.=Uranus=P=1Ø.
Joke=10,000=1,000=100%=10.0=Physicality=Tech.=10 Oct.=Uranus=P=1Ø.
Joker=10,000=1,000=100%=10.0=Physicality=Tech.=10 Oct.=Uranus=P=1Ø.
JoliotCurie=9,000=90%=P9.00D=9.0=Abstraction=Gods=Saturn=9Sept.>>A=Ø.
Joliet=3,000=30%=P3.0D=3.0=Creativity=Stars=Muses=3 March = C=I>>GIL.
Jollification=1,000=100%=Physicality=Tech.=10 Oct.=Uranus=P=1Ø.
Jollity=1,000=100%=10.0=1.0=Mind=Sun=1 January=Helios >> M=E4.
Jolly=6,500=7,000=70%=P7.0D=7.0=Language=Assets=Mars=7 July=Pleiades.
Jolt=10,000=1,000=100%=10.0=Physicality=Tech.=10 Oct.=Uranus=P=1Ø.

Jonah=11,000=11%=P1.10D=1.1=Idea=Brainchild=Inv.=11 Nov.=SC=Athena>>I=MT.
The book of Jonah was inspired by Athena to teach responsibility. Note that Athena is a Goddess of the sea who invented the ships for warfare. It is obvious that she drove the fish as a marine war vessel to swallow Jonah and disgorge him unharmed. Jesus performed a miracle of picking out coins from the mouth of a fish, fed 5,000 people with just two fish and a loaf of bread in the New Testament. Athena loves bread. So we see a clear bond between Hermes the God of wit as Jesus and his sister Athena Goddess of wis, wisdom.

Jones John Paul=3,500=4,000=40%=P4.0D=Govt.=4 April=Mercury=Hermes=G=A4.
Jonquil=5,500=5.5=80%=P5.50=Earth-Midway=5 May = Gaia.

Johnson Benjamin=3,500=4,000=40%=P4.0D=Govt.=4 April=Mercury=Hermes=G=A4.
Jordan=6,000=60%=P6.0D=Man=Earth=Royalty=6 June=Gaia=Maia>>M=M2.
Jordan River=11,500=12,000=12%=P1.20D=1.2=Knowledge=Edu=12Dec.=Athena>>K=F.
Joseph 1=4,500=5,000=50%=P5.00D=Law=Time=Venus=5 May = Aphrodite>>L=N.
Joseph 2=4,000=40%=P4.0D=Govt.=Creatocracy=4 April=Mercury=Hermes=G=A4.

Joseph Saint.=6,000=60%=P6.0D=Man=Earth=Royalty=6 June=Gaia=Maia>>M=M2.
In the Bible, husband of Mary. Mother of Jesus The results confirms conditional inheritance as codes align. Joseph was approved by Gaia as a sin of royalty.

Josephine=2,000=20%=P2.00D=2.0=Nature=Matter=Moon=2 Feb.=Cupid=N=C+_
Joseph of Arimathea=5,000=50%=P5.00D=Law=Time=Venus=5 May = Aphrodite>>L=N.
Josephus Flavius=4,000=40%=P4.0D=Govt.=4 April=Mercury=Hermes=G=A4.
Josh=4,500=5,000=50%=P5.00D=Law=Time=Venus=5 May = Aphrodite>>L=N.

Joshua=4,500=5,000=50%=P5.00D=Law=Time=Venus=5 May = Aphrodite>>L=N.
Inspired by a joint effort of Hermes and Aphrodite. A borderline, boundary, means to Law.

Jostle=12,000=12%=P1.20D=1.2=Knowledge=Edu=12Dec.=Athena>>K=F.
Jot=6,500=7,000=70%=P7.0D=7.0=Language=Assets=Mars=7 July=Pleiades.
Joule=10,000=1,000=100%=10.0=Physicality=Tech.=10 Oct.=Uranus=P=1Ø.
Jounce=4,500=5,000=50%=P5.00D=Law=Time=Venus=5 May = Aphrodite>>L=N.
Journal=10,000=1,000=100%=10.0=Physicality=Tech.=10 Oct.=Uranus=P=1Ø.
Journalese=6,000=60%=P6.0D=Man=Earth=Royalty=6 June=Gaia=Maia>>M=M2.
Journalism=10,000=1,000=100%=10.0=Physicality=Tech.=10 Oct.=Uranus=P=1Ø.
Journey=8,500=9,000=90%=P9.00D=9.0=Abstraction=Gods=Saturn=9Sept.>>A=Ø.
Journeyman=8,000=80%=P8.0D=Economy=Currency=8 Aug.=Zeus>>E=v.
Joust=10,500=11,000=11%=P1.10D=1.1=Idea=Brainchild=Inv.=11 Nov.=SC=Athena>>I=MT.
Jove=2,000=20%=P2.00D=2.0=Nature=Matter=Moon=2 Feb.=Cupid=N=C+_
Jovial=2,500=3,000=30%=P3.0D=3.0=Creativity=Stars=Muses=3 March = C=I>>GIL.
Jowl1=4,000=40%=P4.0D=Govt.=Creatocracy=4 April=Mercury=Hermes=G=A4.
Jowl2=6,000=60%=P6.0D=Man=Earth=Royalty=6 June=Gaia=Maia>>M=M2.
Joy=6,500=7,000=70%=P7.0D=7.0=Language=Assets=Mars=7 July=Pleiades.
Joyce, James=2,000=20%=P2.00D=2.0=Nature=Matter=Moon=2 Feb.=Cupid=N=C+_
Joyful=2,500=3,000=30%=P3.0D=3.0=Creativity=Stars=Muses=3 March = C=I>>GIL.
Joyous=500=5%=P5.00D=5.0=Law=Time=Venus=5 May=Aphrodite>>L=N.
Joy ride=5,500=5.5=80%=P5.50=Earth-Midway=5 May = Gaia.
Joystick=5,500=5.5=80%=P5.50=Earth-Midway=5 May = Gaia.
J.P.=2,000=20%=P2.00D=2.0=Nature=Matter=Moon=2 Feb.=Cupid=N=C+_
Jr.=500=5%=P5.00D=5.0=Law=Time=Venus=5 May=Aphrodite>>L=N.
J.S.D.=4,000=40%=P4.0D=Govt.=Creatocracy=4 April=Mercury=Hermes=G=A4.
jt.=500=5%=P5.00D=5.0=Law=Time=Venus=5 May=Aphrodite>>L=N.
Juan Carlos=3,000=30%=P3.0D=3.0=Creativity=Stars=Muses=3 March = C=I>>GIL.

Juan de Fuca=6,000=60%=P6.0D=Man=Earth=Royalty=6 June=Gaia=Maia>>M=M2.
Juärez Benito=3,000=30%=P3.0D=3.0=Creativity=Stars=Muses=3 March = C=I>>GIL.
Jubilant=3,500=4,000=40%=P4.0D=Govt.=Creatocracy=4 April=Mercury=Hermes=G=A4.
Jubilation=3,500=4,000=40%=P4.0D=Govt.=Creat.=4 April=Mercury=Hermes=G=A4.
Jubilee=10,000=1,000=100%=10.0=Physicality=Tech.=10 Oct.=Uranus=P=1Ø.
Judah1=4,500=5,000=50%=P5.00D=Law=Time=Venus=5 May = Aphrodite>>L=N.
Judah2=6,000=60%=P6.0D=Man=Earth=Royalty=6 June=Gaia=Maia>>M=M2.
Judaic=3,000=30%=P3.0D=3.0=Creativity=Stars=Muses=3 March = C=I>>GIL.
Judaism=10,000=1,000=100%=10.0=Physicality=Tech.=10 Oct.=Uranus=P=1Ø.
Judas=6,000=60%=P6.0D=Man=Earth=Royalty=6 June=Gaia=Maia>>M=M2.
Judas Iscariot=7,000=70%=P7.0D=7.0=Language=Assets=Mars=7 July=Pleiades.

Jude=2,000=20%=P2.00D=2.0=Nature=Matter=Moon=2 Feb.=Cupid=N=C+_

Jude=5,000=50%=P5.00D=Law=Time=Venus=5 May = Aphrodite>>L=N.
Judea=6,500=7,000=70%=P7.0D=7.0=Language=Assets=Mars=7 July=Pleiades.
Judge=10,000=1,000=100%=10.0=Physicality=Tech.=10 Oct.=Uranus=P=1Ø.
Judgement=6,500=7,000=70%=P7.0D=7.0=Language=Assets=Mars=7 July=Pleiades.
Judgmental=7,000=70%=P7.0D=7.0=Language=Assets=Mars=7 July=Pleiades.
Judgement Day=5,500=5.5=80%=P5.50=Earth-Midway=5 May = Gaia.

Judicature=7,000=70%=P7.0D=7.0=Language=Assets=Mars=7 July=Pleiades.

Judicial=10,000=1,000=100%=10.0=Physicality=Tech.=10 Oct.=Uranus=P=1Ø.
Judiciary=10,000=1,000=100%=10.0=Physicality=Tech.=10 Oct.=Uranus=P=1Ø.
Judicious=2,500=3,000=30%=P3.0D=3.0=Creativity=Stars=Muses=3 March = C=I>>GIL.

Judith=2,000=20%=P2.00D=2.0=Nature=Matter=Moon=2 Feb.=Cupid=N=C+_

Judo=6,000=60%=P6.0D=Man=Earth=Royalty=6 June=Gaia=Maia>>M=M2.
Jug=9,000=90%=P9.00D=9.0=Abstraction=Gods=Saturn=9Sept.>>A=Ø.
Jug band=6,500=7,000=70%=P7.0D=7.0=Language=Assets=Mars=7 July=Pleiades.
Juggernaut=10,000=1,000=100%=10.0=Physicality=Tech.=10 Oct.=Uranus=P=1Ø.
Juggle=10,000=1,000=100%=10.0=Physicality=Tech.=10 Oct.=Uranus=P=1Ø.
Jugular=10,000=1,000=100%=10.0=Physicality=Tech.=10 Oct.=Uranus=P=1Ø.
Juice=10,000=1,000=100%=10.0=Physicality=Tech.=10 Oct.=Uranus=P=1Ø.
Juicer=5,000=50%=P5.00D=Law=Time=Venus=5 May = Aphrodite>>L=N.
Juicy=6,000=60%=P6.0D=Man=Earth=Royalty=6 June=Gaia=Maia>>M=M2.
Jujitsu=10,000=1,000=100%=10.0=Physicality=Tech.=10 Oct.=Uranus=P=1Ø.
Jujube=5,500=5.5=80%=P5.50=Earth-Midway=5 May = Gaia.
Juke=10,000=1,000=100%=10.0=Physicality=Tech.=10 Oct.=Uranus=P=1Ø.
Jukebox=4,500=5,000=50%=P5.00D=Law=Time=Venus=5 May = Aphrodite>>L=N.

Julep=2,500=3,000=30%=P3.0D=3.0=Creativity=Stars=Muses=3 March = C=I>>GIL.
Julian=4,000=40%=P4.0D=Govt.=Creatocracy=4 April=Mercury=Hermes=G=A4.
Juliana=4,500=5,000=50%=P5.00D=Law=Time=Venus=5 May = Aphrodite>>L=N.
Julienne=3,500=4,000=40%=P4.0D=Govt.=Creat=4 April=Mercury=Hermes=G=A4.

July=8,000=80%=P8.0D=Economy=Currency=8 Aug.=Zeus>>E=v.
Month of Zeus, Jupiter. Birth month of Peter Matthews-Akukalia, Castle Makupedia.
See The human energy database reveals the guiding spirit of a person at birth based on
the date of birth precisely the synchronization of the day and month. Gaia is the Goddess
of the Earth and so naturally born a royalty. Year is the natural purpose of birth. See
Human Energy Database Table. Results indicate that truly Peter Matthews-Akukalia,
Castle Makupedia is an incarnation of Zeus Jehovah the Most High.
6.0*8.0x=px=14+48=62x=px=734=7.34=Computing Muse Power.
>> Computational Creativity in Governance >> The Creatocracy.

Jumada=7,000=70%=P7.0D=7.0=Language=Assets=Mars=7 July=Pleiades.
Jumble=4,000=40%=P4.0D=Govt.=Creatocracy=4 April=Mercury=Hermes=G=A4.
Jumbo=8,000=80%=P8.0D=Economy=Currency=8 Aug.=Zeus>>E=v.
Jumma=10,500=11,000=11%=P1.10D=1.1=Idea=Brainchild=Inv.=11 Nov.=Athena>>I=MT.
Jump=10,000=1,000=100%=10.0=Physicality=Tech.=10 Oct.=Uranus=P=1Ø.
Jumper1=8,000=80%=P8.0D=Economy=Currency=8 Aug.=Zeus>>E=v.
Jumper2=9,000=90%=P9.00D=9.0=Abstraction=Gods=Saturn=9Sept.>>A=Ø.
Jump shot=6,000=60%=P6.0D=Man=Earth=Royalty=6 June=Gaia=Maia>>M=M2.
Jump suit=7,500=8,000=80%=P8.0D=Economy=Currency=8 Aug.=Zeus>>E=v.
Jumpy=1,500=15%=P1.50D=1.5=Authority=Solar Crown=1 May = Maia.
Jun.=500=5%=P5.00D=5.0=Law=Time=Venus=5 May=Aphrodite>>L=N.
Junco=10,000=1,000=100%=10.0=Physicality=Tech.=10 Oct.=Uranus=P=1Ø.
Junction=10,000=1,000=100%=10.0=Physicality=Tech.=10 Oct.=Uranus=P=1Ø.
Juncture=10,000=1,000=100%=10.0=Physicality=Tech.=10 Oct.=Uranus=P=1Ø.
June=8,000=80%=P8.0D=Economy=Currency=8 Aug.=Zeus>>E=v.
Juneau=4,500=5,000=50%=P5.00D=Law=Time=Venus=5 May = Aphrodite>>L=N.
June beetle=7,500=8,000=80%=P8.0D=Economy=Currency=8 Aug.=Zeus>>E=v.
Jung=10,000=1,000=100%=10.0=Physicality=Tech.=10 Oct.=Uranus=P=1Ø.
Jungle=10,000=1,000=100%=10.0=Physicality=Tech.=10 Oct.=Uranus=P=1Ø.
Jungle gym=6,500=7,000=70%=P7.0D=7.0=Language=Assets=Mars=7 July=Pleiades.
Junior=10,000=1,000=100%=10.0=Physicality=Tech.=10 Oct.=Uranus=P=1Ø.
Junior college=8,000=80%=P8.0D=Economy=Currency=8 Aug.=Zeus>>E=v.
Junior high school=5,000=50%=P5.00D=Law=Time=Venus=5 May = Aphrodite>>L=N.
Juniper=8,000=80%=P8.0D=Economy=Currency=8 Aug.=Zeus>>E=v.
Junk1=10,000=1,000=100%=10.0=Physicality=Tech.=10 Oct.=Uranus=P=1Ø.
Junk2=4,000=40%=P4.0D=Govt.=Creatocracy=4 April=Mercury=Hermes=G=A4.
Junk bond=4,500=5,000=50%=P5.00D=Law=Time=Venus=5 May = Aphrodite>>L=N.
Junket=10,000=1,000=100%=10.0=Physicality=Tech.=10 Oct.=Uranus=P=1Ø.
Junk food=5,500=5.5=80%=P5.50=Earth-Midway=5 May = Gaia.

Junkie=8,500=9,000=90%=P9.00D=9.0=Abstraction=Gods=Saturn=9Sept.>>A=Ø.
Junk mail=5,500=5.5=80%=P5.50=Earth-Midway=5 May = Gaia.
Junkyard=4,000=40%=P4.0D=Govt.=Creatocracy=4 April=Mercury=Hermes=G=A4.

Juno=6,500=7,000=70%=P7.0D=7.0=Language=Assets=Mars=7 July=Pleiades.
Roman myth. The principal Goddess of the pantheon, wife and sister of Jupiter >> Zeus.

Junta=8,500=9,000=90%=P9.00D=9.0=Abstraction=Gods=Saturn=9Sept.>>A=Ø.

Jupiter=10,000=1,000=100%=10.0=Physicality=Tech.=10 Oct.=Uranus=P=1Ø.
Jupiter >> Zeus Jehovah the Most High uses the 10,000 quantum method to express His
Mind hence Mind computing is supernatural natural universal and legal.

Jura Mountains=6,500=7,000=70%=P7.0D=7.0=Language=Assets=Mars=7 July=Pleiades.
Jurassic=10,000=1,000=100%=10.0=Physicality=Tech.=10 Oct.=Uranus=P=1Ø.
Juridical=5,000=50%=P5.00D=Law=Time=Venus=5 May = Aphrodite>>L=N.
Jurisdiction=10,000=1,000=100%=10.0=Physicality=Tech.=10 Oct.=Uranus=P=1Ø.

Jurisprudence=10,000=1,000=100%=10.0=Physicality=Tech.=10 Oct.=Uranus=P=1Ø.
Creatocratic jurisprudence is a brick wall and smart law. Hence the Creatocracy Courts.
An exclusive court system that functions on precision and mind computing systems. It
entails determination of the Mēns Rēa by applying the average propensity of a crime to
the inclination of an accused on his/her brain birth energy WDSD. The essence is to avoid
innocent persons from being unjustly convicted. Guided by the Law of Everything. Invented
by Peter Matthews-Akukalia, Castle Makupedia. >>Psychoastronomy. See Justice, Law.

Jurist=7,000=70%=P7.0D=7.0=Language=Assets=Mars=7 July=Pleiades.
Juristic=5,000=50%=P5.00D=Law=Time=Venus=5 May = Aphrodite>>L=N.
Juror=2,000=20%=P2.00D=2.0=Nature=Matter=Moon=2 Feb.=Cupid=N=C+_
Jury=10,000=1,000=100%=10.0=Physicality=Tech.=10 Oct.=Uranus=P=1Ø.
Just=10,000=1,000=100%=10.0=Physicality=Tech.=10 Oct.=Uranus=P=1Ø.

Justice=10,000=1,000=100%=10.0=Physicality=Tech.=10 Oct.=Uranus=P=1Ø.
"If you want justice be smart about it" - Lord Bellish, Game of Thrones. Documents and
data obtained from computing average propensities and individual or specific inclination
based on proper timing respect for natural laws and human rights defines smart justice.

Justice of the peace=7,000=70%=P7.0D=7.0=Language=Assets=Mars=7 July=Pleiades.
Justification=8,000=80%=P8.0D=Economy=Currency=8 Aug.=Zeus>>E=v.
Justify=10,000=1,000=100%=10.0=Physicality=Tech.=10 Oct.=Uranus=P=1Ø.

Justinian I.=3,000=30%=P3.0D=3.0=Creativity=Stars=Muses=3 March = C=I>>GIL.
Empress Justina I. First Wife of Emperor Peter Matthews-Akukalia, Castle Makupedia.

Jut=6,500=7,000=70%=P7.0D=7.0=Language=Assets=Mars=7 July=Pleiades.
jute=10,000=1,000=100%=10.0=Physicality=Tech.=10 Oct.=Uranus=P=1Ø.
Jute=8,000=80%=P8.0D=Economy=Currency=8 Aug.=Zeus>>E=v.
Jutland=5,000=50%=P5.00D=Law=Time=Venus=5 May = Aphrodite>>L=N.
Juvenal=3,000=30%=P3.0D=3.0=Creativity=Stars=Muses=3 March = C=I>>GIL.
Juvenile=10,000=1,000=100%=10.0=Physicality=Tech.=10 Oct.=Uranus=P=1Ø.
Juvenile delinquent=4,000=40%=P4.0D=Govt.=Creat.=4 April=Mercury=Hermes=G=A4.
Juxtapose=10,000=1,000=100%=10.0=Physicality=Tech.=10 Oct.=Uranus=P=1Ø.
JV=1,000=100%=10.0=1.0=Mind=Sun=1 January=Helios >> M=E4.

MAKABET =Kk=

---

k1=3,000=3,000=30%=P3.0D=3.0=Creativity=Stars=Muses=3 March = C=I>>GIL.
The 11th letter of the English alphabets. Astrosound effects or psycho-weight/mind weight
of the alphabet is computed thus. $3.0*1.1=p=4.1+3.3=7.4x=px=20.93=21>1.2<2.1>>3.0$.
A constant repetition of the letter k conjures both knowledge and creativity. For knowledge
(1.2) to occur there has to be interest and focus hence the formula for knowledge is K=F.
The result is education and self development. Creativity is inspired based on the innate
energy or potentials inherent in a person. The k computed moves from the alphabet status
to the Makabet status. Note the repetition in a name as Akukalia >> double k. Match the
resultants above with the works of the author. The Quran confirms the secret of genius
inherent in a person is in his name. The bible is also very particular about a name. >>
Principles of Psychoastronomy by Peter Matthews-Akukalia >>Astrosound.

---

k2=500=5%=P5.00D=5.0=Law=Time=Venus=5 May=Aphrodite>>L=N.
K1=3,500=4,000=40%=P4.0D=Govt.=Creatocracy=4 April=Mercury=Hermes=G=A4.
K2=4,500=5,000=50%=P5.00D=Law=Time=Venus=5 May = Aphrodite>>L=N.
K2=8,500=9,000=90%=P9.00D=9.0=Abstraction=Gods=Saturn=9Sept.>>A=Ø.
Kabob=1,500=15%=P1.50D=1.5=Authority=Solar Crown=1 May = Maia.
kabuki=9,000=90%=P9.00D=9.0=Abstraction=Gods=Saturn=9Sept.>>A=Ø.
Kabul=10,000=1,000=100%=10.0=Physicality=Tech.=10 Oct.=Uranus=P=1Ø.
kachina=7,000=70%=P7.0D=7.0=Language=Assets=Mars=7 July=Pleiades.
Kádar Janos=2,000=20%=P2.00D=2.0=Nature=Matter=Moon=2 Feb.=Cupid=N=C+_
Kaddish=10,000=1,000=100%=10.0=Physicality=Tech.=10 Oct.=Uranus=P=1Ø.
Kafka Franz=2,000=20%=P2.00D=2.0=Nature=Matter=Moon=2 Feb.=Cupid=N=C+_
Kaftan=1,500=15%=P1.50D=1.5=Authority=Solar Crown=1 May = Maia.
Kagoshima=4,500=5,000=50%=P5.00D=Law=Time=Venus=5 May = Aphrodite>>L=N.
Kaiser=11,000=11%=P1.10D=1.1=Idea=Brainchild=Inv.=11 Nov.=SC=Athena>>I=MT.

Kaiserin=2,500=3,000=30%=P3.0D=3.0=Creativity=Stars=Muses=3 March = C=I>>GIL.
kale=8,500=9,000=90%=P9.00D=9.0=Abstraction=Gods=Saturn=9Sept.>>A=Ø.
Kaleidoscope=10,000=1,000=100%=10.0=Physicality=Tech.=10 Oct.=Uranus=P=1Ø.
Kallnin=7,000=70%=P7.0D=7.0=Language=Assets=Mars=7 July=Pleiades.
Kaliningrad=6,000=60%=P6.0D=Man=Earth=Royalty=6 June=Gaia=Maia>>M=M2.
Kamchatka=6,000=60%=P6.0D=Man=Earth=Royalty=6 June=Gaia=Maia>>M=M2.
Kamehameha I=4,000=40%=P4.0D=Govt.=Creatocracy=4 April=Mercury=Hermes=G=A4.
Kamet=7,000=70%=P7.0D=7.0=Language=Assets=Mars=7 July=Pleiades.
Kamikaze=11,000=11%=P1.10D=1.1=Idea=Brainchild=Inv.=11 Nov.=SC=Athena>>I=MT.
Kampala=6,000=60%=P6.0D=Man=Earth=Royalty=6 June=Gaia=Maia>>M=M2.
Kampuchea=1,000=100%=10.0=1.0=Mind=Sun=1 January=Helios >> M=E4.
Kana=1,500=15%=P1.50D=1.5=Authority=Solar Crown=1 May = Maia.
Kananga=5,000=50%=P5.00D=Law=Time=Venus=5 May = Aphrodite>>L=N.
Kanchenjunga=6,000=60%=P6.0D=Man=Earth=Royalty=6 June=Gaia=Maia>>M=M2.
Kandinsky Wassily=2,000=20%=P2.00D=2.0=Nature=Matter=Moon=2 Feb.=Cupid
    =N=C+_
Kangaroo=10,000=1,000=100%=10.0=Physicality=Tech.=10 Oct.=Uranus=P=1Ø.
Kangaroo court=8,000=80%=P8.0D=Economy=Currency=8 Aug.=Zeus>>E=v.
Kano=5,000=50%=P5.00D=Law=Time=Venus=5 May = Aphrodite>>L=N.
Kanpur=6,500=7,000=70%=P7.0D=7.0=Language=Assets=Mars=7 July=Pleiades.
Kansas=5,000=50%=P5.00D=Law=Time=Venus=5 May = Aphrodite>>L=N.
Kansas City=10,000=1,000=100%=10.0=Physicality=Tech.=10 Oct.=Uranus=P=1Ø.
Kant Immanuel=2,500=3,000=30%=P3.0D=3.0=Cre=Stars=Muses=3 March = C=I>>GIL.
Kaohsiung=5,000=50%=P5.00D=Law=Time=Venus=5 May = Aphrodite>>L=N.
Kaolin=8,000=80%=P8.0D=Economy=Currency=8 Aug.=Zeus>>E=v.

Kaph=8,000=80%=P8.0D=Economy=Currency=8 Aug.=Zeus>>E=v.
The 11th letter of the Hebrew alphabet. 8.0*1.1=p=9.1+8.8=17.9x=px=97.98=100%.
As the 8th letter it a business letter that honors Zeus Jehovah as the Most High. As the 11th
it indicates the wisdom of Athena hence the Spirit of God is incurred at its pronouncing
leading to a 100%. This means that wisdom of inventions knowledge handicraft and mind
in terms of brainstorming coupled into a technology and business makes a complete nation.

Kapok=8,500=9,000=90%=P9.00D=9.0=Abstraction=Gods=Saturn=9Sept.>>A=Ø.
Kaposi's sarcoma=10,000=1,000=100%=Physicality=Tech.=10 Oct.=Uranus=P=1Ø.

Kappa=3,500=4,000=40%=P4.0D=Govt.=Creatocracy=4 April=Mercury=Hermes=G=A4.
The 10th letter of the Greek alphabet has the following effect on the Greeks.
4.0*10.0=p=14+40=54x=px=614=6.14>6.1>1.0><6.14.
The Kappa induces 61% energy effect on the human mind driving the user to seek
freedom through emotional management such as sexual transmutation. The inclination
to Royalty.

Kaput=7,500=8,000=80%=P8.0D=Economy=Currency=8 Aug.=Zeus>>E=v.
Karachi=5,500=5.5=80%=P5.50=Earth-Midway=5 May = Gaia.
Karaganda=4,500=5,000=50%=P5.00D=Law=Time=Venus=5 May = Aphrodite>>L=N.
Karakoram Range=5,500=5.5=80%=P5.50=Earth-Midway=5 May = Gaia.
Karakul=10,000=1,000=100%=10.0=Physicality=Tech.=10 Oct.=Uranus=P=1Ø.
Karat=10,000=1,000=100%=10.0=Physicality=Tech.=10 Oct.=Uranus=P=1Ø.
Karate=8,500=9,000=90%=P9.00D=9.0=Abstraction=Gods=Saturn=9Sept.>>A=Ø.
Karl-Marx-Stadt=1,000=100%=Physicality=Tech.=10 Oct.=Uranus=P=1Ø.
Karisruhe=6,500=7,000=70%=P7.0D=7.0=Language=Assets=Mars=7 July=Pleiades.

Karma=10,000=1,000=100%=10.0=Physicality=Tech.=10 Oct.=Uranus=P=1Ø.
Karma is about thinking good thoughts, saying nice things and doing good to others and belief that everything comes back. Computing the individual elements and bonding each as a Makabet shows us the five Gods that deliver retribution Justice rewards and punishment.

K = 3.0 >> Muses. A = 1.3 >> Athena. R = 3.0 >> Muses. M = 3.0 >> Muses.
A = 1.3 >> Athena.
The karma Goddess is Athena. Karma is another name for Athena. Karma is the Goddess of wisdom handicraft and warfare. Since Karma is about recompense then she is absolutely the Goddess of reward and punishment. Karma is Athena is Goddess of the Mind and the wife of Castle Makupedia, God of Creatocracy Genius and the Mind. Computing shows the resultant effect of karma.

3.0*1.3x=px=4.3+3.9=8.2x=px=24.97=30=3.0
3.0*3.0x=px=6+9=15x=px=69=70=7.0 (1.3)
3.0*7.0x=px=10+21=31x=px=241=2.4
2.4*1.3x=px=3.7+3.12=6.82x=px=18.364=20=2.0

Karma as Athena controls the moon. She is Mother Nature. She owns all things. She is stability and is the force of the night that inspires revelations inspirations and rewards.
Karma = 18.364 proves that Athena as Karma functions through the muses during emotional or sexual transmutation to establish the power of wisdom handicraft and mental warfare. At nights she, the spirit of GOD weighs all things of the works of men. She gives the gifts for business vocations occupations skills capacities abilities and capabilities. She is the custodian of inventions built in wit and wis and is the depth of the riches in the wisdom and knowledge of GOD seen in Romans 11:33-35. She inspired the solar currencies prophesied in Proverbs 8:12 - 21. Castle owns the knowledge of witty inventions. Verse 12.

Karoo=4,000=40%=P4.0D=Govt.=Creatocracy=4 April=Mercury=Hermes=G=A4.
Karst=6,000=60%=P6.0D=Man=Earth=Royalty=6 June=Gaia=Maia>>M=M2.
Karyotype=10,000=1,000=100%=10.0=Physicality=Tech.=10 Oct.=Uranus=P=1Ø.
Kashmir=4,500=5,000=50%=P5.00D=Law=Time=Venus=5 May = Aphrodite>>L=N.
Katakana=5,500=5.5=80%=P5.50=Earth-Midway=5 May = Gaia.

Kathmandu=6,000=60%=P6.0D=Man=Earth=Royalty=6 June=Gaia=Maia>>M=M2.
Katowice=6,500=7,000=70%=P7.0D=7.0=Language=Assets=Mars=7 July=Pleiades.
Kattegat=6,500=7,000=70%=P7.0D=7.0=Language=Assets=Mars=7 July=Pleiades.
Katydid=9,000=90%=P9.00D=9.0=Abstraction=Gods=Saturn=9Sept.>>A=Ø.
Kauai=3,000=30%=P3.0D=3.0=Creativity=Stars=Muses=3 March = C=I>>GIL.
Kaunas=5,000=50%=P5.00D=Law=Time=Venus=5 May = Aphrodite>>L=N.
Kava=8,000=80%=P8.0D=Economy=Currency=8 Aug.=Zeus>>E=v.
Kawasaki=7,000=70%=P7.0D=7.0=Language=Assets=Mars=7 July=Pleiades.
Kayak=10,000=1,000=100%=10.0=Physicality=Tech.=10 Oct.=Uranus=P=1Ø.
Kayo=3,000=30%=P3.0D=3.0=Creativity=Stars=Muses=3 March = C=I>>GIL.
Kazakh=8,000=80%=P8.0D=Economy=Currency=8 Aug.=Zeus>>E=v.
Kazakhstan=8,000=80%=P8.0D=Economy=Currency=8 Aug.=Zeus>>E=v.
Kazan=7,000=70%=P7.0D=7.0=Language=Assets=Mars=7 July=Pleiades.
Kazoo=8,000=80%=P8.0D=Economy=Currency=8 Aug.=Zeus>>E=v.
kc=500=5%=P5.00D=5.0=Law=Time=Venus=5 May=Aphrodite>>L=N.
K.C.=2,500=3,000=30%=P3.0D=3.0=Creativity=Stars=Muses=3 March = C=I>>GIL.
kcal=500=5%=P5.00D=5.0=Law=Time=Venus=5 May=Aphrodite>>L=N.
Keats John=2,000=20%=P2.00D=2.0=Nature=Matter=Moon=2 Feb.=Cupid=N=C+_
kebab=1,000=100%=10.0=1.0=Mind=Sun=1 January=Helios >> M=E4.
Kedge=7,000=70%=P7.0D=7.0=Language=Assets=Mars=7 July=Pleiades.
Keel=10,000=1,000=100%=10.0=Physicality=Tech.=10 Oct.=Uranus=P=1Ø.
Keelboat=4,000=40%=P4.0D=Govt.=Creatocracy=4 April=Mercury=Hermes=G=A4.
Keel haul=6,000=60%=P6.0D=Man=Earth=Royalty=6 June=Gaia=Maia>>M=M2.
Keelung=6,000=60%=P6.0D=Man=Earth=Royalty=6 June=Gaia=Maia>>M=M2.
Keen1=10,000=1,000=100%=10.0=Physicality=Tech.=10 Oct.=Uranus=P=1Ø.
Keen2=4,500=5,000=50%=P5.00D=Law=Time=Venus=5 May = Aphrodite>>L=N.
Keep=10,000=1,000=100%=10.0=Physicality=Tech.=10 Oct.=Uranus=P=1Ø.
Keep down=10,000=1,000=100%=10.0=Physicality=Tech.=10 Oct.=Uranus=P=1Ø.
Keepsake=4,000=40%=P4.0D=Govt.=Creatocracy=4 April=Mercury=Hermes=G=A4.
Keg=1,500=15%=P1.50D=1.5=Authority=Solar Crown=1 May = Maia.
Keller Helen=3,500=4,000=40%=P4.0D=Govt.=Cre.=4 April=Mercury=Hermes=G=A4.
Kellog Frank=3,000=30%=P3.0D=3.0=Creativity=Stars=Muses=3 March = C=I>>GIL.
Kelly Grace=3,500=4,000=40%=P4.0D=Govt.=Creat.=4 April=Mercury=Hermes=G=A4.
Kelp=4,500=5,000=50%=P5.00D=Law=Time=Venus=5 May = Aphrodite>>L=N.
Kelvin=3,000=30%=P3.0D=3.0=Creativity=Stars=Muses=3 March = C=I>>GIL.
Kelvin Atatûrk=2,500=3,000=30%=P3.0D=3.0=Cre=Stars=Muses=3 March = C=I>>GIL.
Ken=6,000=60%=P6.0D=Man=Earth=Royalty=6 June=Gaia=Maia>>M=M2.
Kennedy, Cape=1,500=15%=P1.50D=1.5=Authority=Solar Crown=1 May = Maia.
Kennedy John=5,000=50%=P5.00D=Law=Time=Venus=5 May = Aphrodite>>L=N.
Kennedy, Robert=3,000=30%=P3.0D=3.0=Creativity=Stars=Muses=3 March = C=I>>GIL.
Kennel=9,000=90%=P9.00D=9.0=Abstraction=Gods=Saturn=9Sept.>>A=Ø.
Kenny Elizabeth=7,500=8,000=80%=P8.0D=Economy=Currency=8 Aug.=Zeus>>E=v.
Kentucky=5,500=5.5=80%=P5.50=Earth-Midway=5 May = Gaia.
Kenya=7,500=8,000=80%=P8.0D=Economy=Currency=8 Aug.=Zeus>>E=v.
Kenya, Mount=5,000=50%=P5.00D=Law=Time=Venus=5 May = Aphrodite>>L=N.

Kenyatta Jomo=5,000=50%=P5.00D=Law=Time=Venus=5 May = Aphrodite>>L=N.
Keogh plan=6,000=60%=P6.0D=Man=Earth=Royalty=6 June=Gaia=Maia>>M=M2.
Kepi=7,000=70%=P7.0D=7.0=Language=Assets=Mars=7 July=Pleiades.
Kepler Johannes=3,000=30%=P3.0D=3.0=Creativity=Stars=Muses=3 March = C=I>>GIL.
Kept=3,000=30%=P3.0D=3.0=Creativity=Stars=Muses=3 March = C=I>>GIL.
Keratin=10,500=11,000=11%=P1.10D=1.1=Idea=Brainchild=11Nov.=Athena>>I=MT.
Kerb=3,000=30%=P3.0D=3.0=Creativity=Stars=Muses=3 March = C=I>>GIL.
Kerchief=6,000=60%=P6.0D=Man=Earth=Royalty=6 June=Gaia=Maia>>M=M2.
Kerensky Aleksandr=2,500=3,000=30%=P3.0D=3.0=Cre=Stars=Muses=3 March=GIL.
Kerf=8,000=80%=P8.0D=Economy=Currency=8 Aug.=Zeus>>E=v.
Kernel=11,000=11%=P1.10D=1.1=Idea=Brainchild=Inv.=11 Nov.=SC=Athena>>I=MT.
Kerosene=10,500=11,000=11%=P1.10D=1.1=Idea=Brainchild=Inv.=11Nov=Athena>>I=MT.
Kerouac Jack=2,000=20%=P2.00D=2.0=Nature=Matter=Moon=2 Feb.=Cupid=N=C+_
Kestrel=6,000=60%=P6.0D=Man=Earth=Royalty=6 June=Gaia=Maia>>M=M2.
Ketch=10,500=11,000=11%=P1.10D=1.1=Idea=Brainchild=Inv.=11 Nov=Athena>>I=MT.
Ketchup=7,000=70%=P7.0D=7.0=Language=Assets=Mars=7 July=Pleiades.
Ketchikan=5,500=5.5=80%=P5.50=Earth-Midway=5 May = Gaia.
Ketone=10,000=1,000=100%=10.0=Physicality=Tech.=10 Oct.=Uranus=P=1Ø.
Kettle=6,500=7,000=70%=P7.0D=7.0=Language=Assets=Mars=7 July=Pleiades.
Kettledrum=8,500=9,000=90%=P9.00D=9.0=Abstraction=Gods=Saturn=9Sept.>>A=Ø.
Key1=10,000=1,000=100%=10.0=Physicality=Tech.=10 Oct.=Uranus=P=1Ø.
Key2=5,000=50%=P5.00D=Law=Time=Venus=5 May = Aphrodite>>L=N.
Key Francis=3,500=4,000=40%=P4.0D=Govt.=Creat.=4 April=Mercury=Hermes=G=A4.
Keyboard=10,000=1,000=100%=10.0=Physicality=Tech.=10 Oct.=Uranus=P=1Ø.
Keycard=10,000=1,000=100%=10.0=Physicality=Tech.=10 Oct.=Uranus=P=1Ø.
Keyhole=4,500=5,000=50%=P5.00D=Law=Time=Venus=5 May = Aphrodite>>L=N.
Key Largo=6,000=60%=P6.0D=Man=Earth=Royalty=6 June=Gaia=Maia>>M=M2.
Keynes John=4,500=5,000=50%=P5.00D=Law=Time=Venus=5 May = Aphrodite>>L=N.
Keynote=5,000=50%=P5.00D=Law=Time=Venus=5 May = Aphrodite>>L=N.
Keynote address=4,000=40%=P4.0D=Govt.=Creat.=4 April=Mercury=Hermes=G=A4.
Keypad=4,500=5,000=50%=P5.00D=Law=Time=Venus=5 May = Aphrodite>>L=N.
Keypunc=10,000=1,000=100%=10.0=Physicality=Tech.=10 Oct.=Uranus=P=1Ø.
Key signature=8,000=80%=P8.0D=Economy=Currency=8 Aug.=Zeus>>E=v.
Keystone=9,000=90%=P9.00D=9.0=Abstraction=Gods=Saturn=9Sept.>>A=Ø.
Keystroke=4,000=40%=P4.0D=Govt.=Creatocracy=4 April=Mercury=Hermes=G=A4.
Key West.=10,000=1,000=100%=10.0=Physicality=Tech.=10 Oct.=Uranus=P=1Ø.
kg=500=5%=P5.00D=5.0=Law=Time=Venus=5 May=Aphrodite>>L=N.
KGB=10,000=1,000=100%=10.0=Physicality=Tech.=10 Oct.=Uranus=P=1Ø.
Khabarovsk=7,000=70%=P7.0D=7.0=Language=Assets=Mars=7 July=Pleiades.
Khaki=10,000=1,000=100%=10.0=Physicality=Tech.=10 Oct.=Uranus=P=1Ø.
Khalid=7,000=70%=P7.0D=7.0=Language=Assets=Mars=7 July=Pleiades.
Khan=10,000=1,000=100%=10.0=Physicality=Tech.=10 Oct.=Uranus=P=1Ø.
Kharkov=4,500=5,000=50%=P5.00D=Law=Time=Venus=5 May = Aphrodite>>L=N.
Khartoum=9,000=90%=P9.00D=9.0=Abstraction=Gods=Saturn=9Sept.>>A=Ø.
Kherson=7,000=70%=P7.0D=7.0=Language=Assets=Mars=7 July=Pleiades.

Khmer=4,500=5,000=50%=P5.00D=Law=Time=Venus=5 May = Aphrodite>>L=N.
Khoisan=3,500=4,000=40%=P4.0D=Govt.=Creatocracy=4 April=Mercury=Hermes=G=A4.
Khomeini=6,500=7,000=70%=P7.0D=7.0=Language=Assets=Mars=7 July=Pleiades.
Khoum=4,000=40%=P4.0D=Govt.=Creatocracy=4 April=Mercury=Hermes=G=A4.
Khrushchev Nikita=2,500=3,000=30%=P3.0D=3.0=Cre=Stars=Muses=3March =GIL.
Khulna=6,000=60%=P6.0D=Man=Earth=Royalty=6 June=Gaia=Maia>>M=M2.
Khyber Pass=8,500=9,000=90%=P9.00D=9.0=Abstraction=Gods=Saturn=9Sept.>>A=Ø.
Kibbutz=5,500=5.5=80%=P5.50=Earth-Midway=5 May = Gaia.
Kibitz=5,500=5.5=80%=P5.50=Earth-Midway=5 May = Gaia.
Kibosh=6,000=60%=P6.0D=Man=Earth=Royalty=6 June=Gaia=Maia>>M=M2.
Kick=10,000=1,000=100%=10.0=Physicality=Tech.=10 Oct.=Uranus=P=1Ø.
Kick around=10,000=1,000=100%=10.0=Physicality=Tech.=10 Oct.=Uranus=P=1Ø.
Kick off=7,000=70%=P7.0D=7.0=Language=Assets=Mars=7 July=Pleiades.
Kid=10,000=1,000=100%=10.0=Physicality=Tech.=10 Oct.=Uranus=P=1Ø.
Kickapoo=10,000=1,000=100%=10.0=Physicality=Tech.=10 Oct.=Uranus=P=1Ø.
Kickback=10,000=1,000=100%=10.0=Physicality=Tech.=10 Oct.=Uranus=P=1Ø.
Kicker=5,000=50%=P5.00D=Law=Time=Venus=5 May = Aphrodite>>L=N.
Kickoff=7,000=70%=P7.0D=7.0=Language=Assets=Mars=7 July=Pleiades.
Kid=10,000=1,000=100%=10.0=Physicality=Tech.=10 Oct.=Uranus=P=1Ø.
Kidd William=4,000=40%=P4.0D=Govt.=Creatocracy=4 April=Mercury=Hermes=G=A4.
Kidnap=6,500=7,000=70%=P7.0D=7.0=Language=Assets=Mars=7 July=Pleiades.
Kidney=10,000=1,000=100%=10.0=Physicality=Tech.=10 Oct.=Uranus=P=1Ø.
Kidney bean=6,000=60%=P6.0D=Man=Earth=Royalty=6 June=Gaia=Maia>>M=M2.
Kidskin=5,000=50%=P5.00D=Law=Time=Venus=5 May = Aphrodite>>L=N.
Kiel=7,500=8,000=80%=P8.0D=Economy=Currency=8 Aug.=Zeus>>E=v.
Kielbasa=3,500=4,000=40%=P4.0D=Govt.=Creat.=4 April=Mercury=Hermes=G=A4.
Kiel Canal=9,000=90%=P9.00D=9.0=Abstraction=Gods=Saturn=9Sept.>>A=Ø.
Kiergaard Søren=3,000=30%=P3.0D=3.0=Creativity=Stars=Muses=3 March = C=I>>GIL.
Kiev=6,500=7,000=70%=P7.0D=7.0=Language=Assets=Mars=7 July=Pleiades.
Kigali=4,500=5,000=50%=P5.00D=Law=Time=Venus=5 May = Aphrodite>>L=N.
Kikuyu=6,000=60%=P6.0D=Man=Earth=Royalty=6 June=Gaia=Maia>>M=M2.
Kilimanjaro Mount.=8,500=9,000=90%=P9.00D=9.0=Abst.=Gods=Saturn=9Sept.>>A=Ø.
Kill1=10,000=1,000=100%=10.0=Physicality=Tech.=10 Oct.=Uranus=P=1Ø.
Kill2=5,500=5.5=80%=P5.50=Earth-Midway=5 May = Gaia.
Killdeer=6,500=7,000=70%=P7.0D=7.0=Language=Assets=Mars=7 July=Pleiades.
Killer whale=6,500=7,000=70%=P7.0D=7.0=Language=Assets=Mars=7 July=Pleiades.
Killing=5,000=50%=P5.00D=Law=Time=Venus=5 May = Aphrodite>>L=N.
Killjoy=4,500=5,000=50%=P5.00D=Law=Time=Venus=5 May = Aphrodite>>L=N.
Kiln=5,000=50%=P5.00D=Law=Time=Venus=5 May = Aphrodite>>L=N.
Kilo=1,000=100%=10.0=1.0=Mind=Sun=1 January=Helios >> M=E4.
Kilo-=3,500=4,000=40%=P4.0D=Govt.=Creatocracy=4 April=Mercury=Hermes=G=A4.
Kilobyte=5,000=50%=P5.00D=Law=Time=Venus=5 May = Aphrodite>>L=N.
Kilocalorie=1,500=15%=P1.50D=1.5=Authority=Solar Crown=1 May = Maia.
Kilo cycle=500=5%=P5.00D=5.0=Law=Time=Venus=5 May=Aphrodite>>L=N.
Kilogram=2,000=20%=P2.00D=2.0=Nature=Matter=Moon=2 Feb.=Cupid=N=C+_

Kilohertz=4,000=40%=P4.0D=Govt.=Creatocracy=4 April=Mercury=Hermes=G=A4.
Kilo liter=2,000=20%=P2.00D=2.0=Nature=Matter=Moon=2 Feb.=Cupid=N=C+_
Kilometer=2,000=20%=P2.00D=2.0=Nature=Matter=Moon=2 Feb.=Cupid=N=C+_
Kiloton=9,500=10,000=1,000=100%=10.0=Physicality=Tech.=10 Oct.=Uranus=P=1Ø.
Kilowatt=4,000=40%=P4.0D=Govt.=Creatocracy=4 April=Mercury=Hermes=G=A4.
Kilowatt hour=8,000=80%=P8.0D=Economy=Currency=8 Aug.=Zeus>>E=v.
Kilt=10,000=1,000=100%=10.0=Physicality=Tech.=10 Oct.=Uranus=P=1Ø.
Kilter=4,000=40%=P4.0D=Govt.=Creatocracy=4 April=Mercury=Hermes=G=A4.
Kimberley=5,000=50%=P5.00D=Law=Time=Venus=5 May = Aphrodite>>L=N.
Kimono=8,000=80%=P8.0D=Economy=Currency=8 Aug.=Zeus>>E=v.
Kin=4,500=5,000=50%=P5.00D=Law=Time=Venus=5 May = Aphrodite>>L=N.
-kin=3,000=30%=P3.0D=3.0=Creativity=Stars=Muses=3 March = C=I>>GIL.
Kina=5,000=50%=P5.00D=Law=Time=Venus=5 May = Aphrodite>>L=N.
Kind1=8,000=80%=P8.0D=Economy=Currency=8 Aug.=Zeus>>E=v.
Kind2=10,000=1,000=100%=10.0=Physicality=Tech.=10 Oct.=Uranus=P=1Ø.
Kindergarten=5,000=50%=P5.00D=Law=Time=Venus=5 May = Aphrodite>>L=N.
Kindhearted=3,500=4,000=40%=P4.0D=Govt.=Creat.=4 April=Mercury=Hermes=G=A4.
Kindle=7,000=70%=P7.0D=7.0=Language=Assets=Mars=7 July=Pleiades.
Kindling=4,000=40%=P4.0D=Govt.=Creatocracy=4 April=Mercury=Hermes=G=A4.
Kindly=10,000=1,000=100%=10.0=Physicality=Tech.=10 Oct.=Uranus=P=1Ø.
Kindred=6,000=60%=P6.0D=Man=Earth=Royalty=6 June=Gaia=Maia>>M=M2.
Kine=3,500=4,000=40%=P4.0D=Govt.=Creatocracy=4 April=Mercury=Hermes=G=A4.

Kinematics=8,500=9,000=90%=P9.00D=9.0=Abstraction=Gods=Saturn=9Sept.>>A=Ø.
Peter Matthews-Akukalia invented Makumatics, deductions of the inherent faculties of the human mind. See The Oracle: Principles of Creative Sciences.

Kinescope=5,500=5.5=80%=P5.50=Earth-Midway=5 May = Gaia.
Kinetic=3,500=4,000=40%=P4.0D=Govt.=Creatocracy=4 April=Mercury=Hermes=G=A4.
Kinetic energy=5,000=50%=P5.00D=Law=Time=Venus=5 May = Aphrodite>>L=N.
Kinetics=8,000=80%=P8.0D=Economy=Currency=8 Aug.=Zeus>>E=v.
Kinfolk=1,500=15%=P1.50D=1.5=Authority=Solar Crown=1 May = Maia.

King=10,000=1,000=100%=10.0=Physicality=Tech.=10 Oct.=Uranus=P=1Ø.
King David made coded statements in the Psalms which when studied by Peter Matthews-Akukalia was discovered to be a recommended standard for measuring abstract phenomena and all things. This standard was the quantum system of 10,000=1,000.
Peter Matthews-Akukalia is the author inventor owner and king of the Creative Sciences. The Most Sovereign Emperor of the Sovereign Creatocratic Republic of Paradise. President of Makupedia. God of the Creatocracy Genius and mind. The Solar Crown King.

King Coretta=3,500=4,000=40%=P4.0D=Govt.=Creat.=4 April=Mercury=Hermes=G=A4.
King, Martin=5,500=5.5=80%=P5.50=Earth-Midway=5 May = Gaia.

King, William Lyon=6,000=60%=P6.0D=Man=Earth=Royalty=6 June=Gaia=Maia >>M=M2.
King bolt=10,000=1,000=100%=10.0=Physicality=Tech.=10 Oct.=Uranus=P=1Ø.
King crab=6,000=60%=P6.0D=Man=Earth=Royalty=6 June=Gaia=Maia>>M=M2.
Kingdom=10,000=1,000=100%=10.0=Physicality=Tech.=10 Oct.=Uranus=P=1Ø.
Kingfisher=6,000=60%=P6.0D=Man=Earth=Royalty=6 June=Gaia=Maia>>M=M2.

King James Bible=4,500=5,000=50%=P5.00D=Law=Time=Venus=5 May =Odite>>L=N.
THE HOLY BIBLE >> Castle Makupedia Computed Version >> CMCV. The Makstian Scriptures>>Castle Makupedia Computed Bible. Makstian Faith version of the Holy Bible authored by Peter Matthews-Akukalia, emerging him God of Creatocracy Genius and Mind. Also known as the Mind Temple. All works of Peter Matthews-Akukalia, Castle Makupedia.

Kingpin=6,500=7,000=70%=P7.0D=7.0=Language=Assets=Mars=7 July=Pleiades.
King's English=5,000=50%=P5.00D=Law=Time=Venus=5 May = Aphrodite>>L=N.
King size=4,500=5,000=50%=P5.00D=Law=Time=Venus=5 May = Aphrodite>>L=N.
Kingston=6,000=60%=P6.0D=Man=Earth=Royalty=6 June=Gaia=Maia>>M=M2.
Kings town=8,500=9,000=90%=P9.00D=9.0=Abstraction=Gods=Saturn=9Sept.>>A=Ø.
Kink=10,000=1,000=100%=10.0=Physicality=Tech.=10 Oct.=Uranus=P=1Ø.
Kinkajou=7,000=70%=P7.0D=7.0=Language=Assets=Mars=7 July=Pleiades.
Kinky=5,500=5.5=80%=P5.50=Earth-Midway=5 May = Gaia.
Kinsfolk=1,500=15%=P1.50D=1.5=Authority=Solar Crown=1 May = Maia.
Kinshasa=6,000=60%=P6.0D=Man=Earth=Royalty=6 June=Gaia=Maia>>M=M2.
Kinship=2,000=20%=P2.00D=2.0=Nature=Matter=Moon=2 Feb.=Cupid=N=C+_
Kinsman=1,500=15%=P1.50D=1.5=Authority=Solar Crown=1 May = Maia.
Kinswoman=1,500=15%=P1.50D=1.5=Authority=Solar Crown=1 May = Maia.
Kiosk=6,000=60%=P6.0D=Man=Earth=Royalty=6 June=Gaia=Maia>>M=M2.
Kiowa=10,000=1,000=100%=10.0=Physicality=Tech.=10 Oct.=Uranus=P=1Ø.
Kiowa Apache=10,000=1,000=100%=10.0=Physicality=Tech.=10 Oct.=Uranus=P=1Ø.
Kip=2,500=3,000=30%=P3.0D=3.0=Creativity=Stars=Muses=3 March = C=I>>GIL.
Kipling Joseph=3,500=4,000=40%=P4.0D=Govt.=4 April=Mercury=Hermes=G=A4.
Kipper=6,500=7,000=70%=P7.0D=7.0=Language=Assets=Mars=7 July=Pleiades.
Kirghiz=8,000=80%=P8.0D=Economy=Currency=8 Aug.=Zeus>>E=v.
Kiribati=7,000=70%=P7.0D=7.0=Language=Assets=Mars=7 July=Pleiades.
Kirigami=6,500=7,000=70%=P7.0D=7.0=Language=Assets=Mars=7 July=Pleiades.
Kirk=2,500=3,000=30%=P3.0D=3.0=Creativity=Stars=Muses=3 March = C=I>>GIL.
Kirov=5,000=50%=P5.00D=Law=Time=Venus=5 May = Aphrodite>>L=N.
Kirsch=7,000=70%=P7.0D=7.0=Language=Assets=Mars=7 July=Pleiades.
Kisangani=4,500=5,000=50%=P5.00D=Law=Time=Venus=5 May = Aphrodite>>L=N.
Kishinev=5,500=5.5=80%=P5.50=Earth-Midway=5 May = Gaia.
Kislev=5,500=5.5=80%=P5.50=Earth-Midway=5 May = Gaia.
Kismet=3,500=4,000=40%=P4.0D=Govt.=Creatocracy=4 April=Mercury=Hermes=G=A4.
Kiss=10,000=1,000=100%=10.0=Physicality=Tech.=10 Oct.=Uranus=P=1Ø.

Kisser=4,500=5,000=50%=P5.00D=Law=Time=Venus=5 May = Aphrodite>>L=N.
Kissinger Henry=5,500=5.5=80%=P5.50=Earth-Midway=5 May = Gaia.
Kit=10,000=1,000=100%=10.0=Physicality=Tech.=10 Oct.=Uranus=P=1Ø.
Kitakyushu=4,000=40%=P4.0D=Govt.=Creatocracy=4 April=Mercury=Hermes=G=A4.
Kitchen=8,500=9,000=90%=P9.00D=9.0=Abstraction=Gods=Saturn=9Sept.>>A=Ø.
Kitchener=5,000=50%=P5.00D=Law=Time=Venus=5 May = Aphrodite>>L=N.
Kitchenette=1,500=15%=P1.50D=1.5=Authority=Solar Crown=1 May = Maia.
Kitchen police=6,500=7,000=70%=P7.0D=7.0=Language=Assets=Mars=7 July=Pleiades.
Kitchen ware=3,000=30%=P3.0D=3.0=Creativity=Stars=Muses=3 March = C=I>>GIL.
Kite=10,000=1,000=100%=10.0=Physicality=Tech.=10 Oct.=Uranus=P=1Ø.
Kith and kin=3,500=4,000=40%=P4.0D=Govt.=Creat.=4 April=Mercury=Hermes=G=A4.
Kitsch=5,000=50%=P5.00D=Law=Time=Venus=5 May = Aphrodite>>L=N.
Kitten=2,500=3,000=30%=P3.0D=3.0=Creativity=Stars=Muses=3 March = C=I>>GIL.
Kittenish=2,000=20%=P2.00D=2.0=Nature=Matter=Moon=2 Feb.=Cupid=N=C+_
Kitty1=7,000=70%=P7.0D=7.0=Language=Assets=Mars=7 July=Pleiades.
Kitty2=2,000=20%=P2.00D=2.0=Nature=Matter=Moon=2 Feb.=Cupid=N=C+_
Kitty Hawk=8,000=80%=P8.0D=Economy=Currency=8 Aug.=Zeus>>E=v.
Kitwe=6,000=60%=P6.0D=Man=Earth=Royalty=6 June=Gaia=Maia>>M=M2.
Kiva=5,000=50%=P5.00D=Law=Time=Venus=5 May = Aphrodite>>L=N.
Kiwi=10,000=1,000=100%=10.0=Physicality=Tech.=10 Oct.=Uranus=P=1Ø.
KKK=1,500=15%=P1.50D=1.5=Authority=Solar Crown=1 May = Maia.
Klamath=10,000=1,000=100%=10.0=Physicality=Tech.=10 Oct.=Uranus=P=1Ø.
Klee Paul=2,000=20%=P2.00D=2.0=Nature=Matter=Moon=2 Feb.=Cupid=N=C+_
Kleenex=3,000=30%=P3.0D=3.0=Creativity=Stars=Muses=3 March = C=I>>GIL.
Kleptomaniac=7,000=70%=P7.0D=7.0=Language=Assets=Mars=7 July=Pleiades.
Kileg light=10,000=1,000=100%=10.0=Physicality=Tech.=10 Oct.=Uranus=P=1Ø.
Klondike=4,000=40%=P4.0D=Govt.=Creatocracy=4 April=Mercury=Hermes=G=A4.
Klutz=4,000=40%=P4.0D=Govt.=Creatocracy=4 April=Mercury=Hermes=G=A4.
Km=500=5%=P5.00D=5.0=Law=Time=Venus=5 May=Aphrodite>>L=N.
Kmph=1,500=15%=P1.50D=1.5=Authority=Solar Crown=1 May = Maia.
Knack=9,000=90%=P9.00D=9.0=Abstraction=Gods=Saturn=9Sept.>>A=Ø.
Knack wurst=3,500=4,000=40%=P4.0D=Govt.=Creat.=4 April=Mercury=Hermes=G=A4.
Knapsack=7,000=70%=P7.0D=7.0=Language=Assets=Mars=7 July=Pleiades.
Knave=5,000=50%=P5.00D=Law=Time=Venus=5 May = Aphrodite>>L=N.
Knead=8,000=80%=P8.0D=Economy=Currency=8 Aug.=Zeus>>E=v.
Knee=3,500=4,000=40%=P4.0D=Govt.=Creatocracy=4 April=Mercury=Hermes=G=A4.
Kneecap=1,000=100%=10.0=1.0=Mind=Sun=1 January=Helios >> M=E4.
Kneel=5,500=5.5=80%=P5.50=Earth-Midway=5 May = Gaia.
Knell=10,000=1,000=100%=10.0=Physicality=Tech.=10 Oct.=Uranus=P=1Ø.
Knew=2,000=20%=P2.00D=2.0=Nature=Matter=Moon=2 Feb.=Cupid=N=C+_
Knickers=6,500=7,000=70%=P7.0D=7.0=Language=Assets=Mars=7 July=Pleiades.
Knickknack=3,000=30%=P3.0D=3.0=Creativity=Stars=Muses=3 March = C=I>>GIL.
Knife=10,000=1,000=100%=10.0=Physicality=Tech.=10 Oct.=Uranus=P=1Ø.
Knight=10,000=1,000=100%=10.0=Physicality=Tech.=10 Oct.=Uranus=P=1Ø.
Knight errant=6,000=60%=P6.0D=Man=Earth=Royalty=6 June=Gaia=Maia>>M=M2.

Knighthood=4,500=5,000=50%=P5.00D=Law=Time=Venus=5 May = Aphrodite>>L=N.
Knish=8,000=80%=P8.0D=Economy=Currency=8 Aug.=Zeus>>E=v.
Knit=10,000=1,000=100%=10.0=Physicality=Tech.=10 Oct.=Uranus=P=1Ø.
Knob=5,500=5.5=80%=P5.50=Earth-Midway=5 May = Gaia.
Knock=10,000=1,000=100%=10.0=Physicality=Tech.=10 Oct.=Uranus=P=1Ø.
Knockdown=7,000=70%=P7.0D=7.0=Language=Assets=Mars=7 July=Pleiades.
Knocker=4,000=40%=P4.0D=Govt.=Creatocracy=4 April=Mercury=Hermes=G=A4.
Knock-knee=6,000=60%=P6.0D=Man=Earth=Royalty=6 June=Gaia=Maia>>M=M2.
Knockout=10,000=1,000=100%=10.0=Physicality=Tech.=10 Oct.=Uranus=P=1Ø.
Knock wurst=1,500=15%=P1.50D=1.5=Authority=Solar Crown=1 May = Maia.
Knoll=3,500=4,000=40%=P4.0D=Govt.=Creatocracy=4 April=Mercury=Hermes=G=A4.
Knossos=3,000=30%=P3.0D=3.0=Creativity=Stars=Muses=3 March = C=I>>GIL.
Knot=10,000=1,000=100%=10.0=Physicality=Tech.=10 Oct.=Uranus=P=1Ø.
Knothole=5,000=50%=P5.00D=Law=Time=Venus=5 May = Aphrodite>>L=N.
Know=10,000=1,000=100%=10.0=Physicality=Tech.=10 Oct.=Uranus=P=1Ø.
Know how=4,000=40%=P4.0D=Govt.=Creatocracy=4 April=Mercury=Hermes=G=A4.
Knowing=4,000=40%=P4.0D=Govt.=Creatocracy=4 April=Mercury=Hermes=G=A4.

Knowledge=10,000=1,000=100%=10.0=Physicality=Tech.=10 Oct.=Uranus=P=1Ø.
In Creative Sciences, the 12th dimension of the Mind Universe computed as K=F by Peter Matthews-Akukalia, Castle Makupedia. Makupedia Sciences >Naturecology. Resultant assets of knowledge are learning adaptation and education at all levels. The knowledge of Creative & Psycho-Social Sciences was invented by Peter Matthews-Akukalia.

Knox Henry=3,000=30%=P3.0D=3.0=Creativity=Stars=Muses=3 March = C=I>>GIL.
Knox,John=3,000=30%=P3.0D=3.0=Creativity=Stars=Muses=3 March = C=I>>GIL.
Knoxville=6,500=7,000=70%=P7.0D=7.0=Language=Assets=Mars=7 July=Pleiades.
Knt=500=5%=P5.00D=5.0=Law=Time=Venus=5 May=Aphrodite>>L=N.
Knuckle=10,000=1,000=100%=10.0=Physicality=Tech.=10 Oct.=Uranus=P=1Ø.
Knuckle bone=4,000=40%=P4.0D=Govt.=Creatocracy=4 April=Mercury=Hermes=G=A4.
Knurl=10,000=1,000=100%=10.0=Physicality=Tech.=10 Oct.=Uranus=P=1Ø.
Koala=4,500=5,000=50%=P5.00D=Law=Time=Venus=5 May = Aphrodite>>L=N.
Kobe=5,500=5.5=80%=P5.50=Earth-Midway=5 May = Gaia.

Kobo=4,000=40%=P4.0D=Govt.=Creatocracy=4 April=Mercury=Hermes=G=A4.
[Yoruba kobo < E. COPPER.], the kobo currency system is far less than the dollar (silver), gold and now the diamond. In the Makupedia Creative Sciences, equivalent to a Dar > 100. The Maks currencies functions on two value groups of metric applications.
First is the abstraction or congruent energy value computed by quantum as 10,000=1,000.
The other value group is the physical equivalent group > 100=10.
=SK=10,000=Ks1,000=D=100=P=10 >> Kose = Kosemaks =Dar = Maks hence One Maks is equivalent to ten British pounds > P1=£10.0, based on this natural standard 100kobos = 1 Naira, or same as is applied in every other currency is wrong and a fiat

as it goes against natural order of things. Against this there is no law. See Dollar. So 40kobos=N1.00 not 100kobos = N1.00. Also see Naira. Interestingly the Kobo rates higher than the Naira by 0.5.

Kodiak bear=6,500=7,000=70%=P7.0D=7.0=Language=Assets=Mars=7 July=Pleiades.
Kodiak island=6,000=60%=P6.0D=Man=Earth=Royalty=6 June=Gaia=Maia>>M=M2.
Koestler Arthur=2,500=3,000=30%=P3.0D=3.0=Creativity=Stars=Muses=3 March=GIL.
K of C=1,500=15%=P1.50D=1.5=Authority=Solar Crown=1 May = Maia.
Kohl=6,000=60%=P6.0D=Man=Earth=Royalty=6 June=Gaia=Maia>>M=M2.
Kohlrabi=6,500=7,000=70%=P7.0D=7.0=Language=Assets=Mars=7 July=Pleiades.
Kola=1,500=15%=P1.50D=1.5=Authority=Solar Crown=1 May = Maia.
Kola Peninsula=8,000=80%=P8.0D=Economy=Currency=8 Aug.=Zeus>>E=v.
Kolyma=10,000=1,000=100%=10.0=Physicality=Tech.=10 Oct.=Uranus=P=1Ø.
Kolyma Mountains=8,000=80%=P8.0D=Economy=Currency=8 Aug.=Zeus>>E=v.
Kook=4,000=40%=P4.0D=Govt.=Creatocracy=4 April=Mercury=Hermes=G=A4.
Kootenay River=10,000=1,000=100%=10.0=Physicality=Tech.=10 Oct.=Uranus=P=1Ø.
Kopeck=3,000=30%=P3.0D=3.0=Creativity=Stars=Muses=3 March = C=I>>GIL.
Kor.=1,000=100%=10.0=1.0=Mind=Sun=1 January=Helios >> M=E4.

Koran=8,000=80%=P8.0D=Economy=Currency=8 Aug.=Zeus>>E=v.
A sacred scripture of Islam is also a sacred book used in the Makstian Faith. Directly inspired by Zeus of the Greeks Allah of the Arabs and ZeJeAl of the Makstians or Diseans.

Korea=7,000=70%=P7.0D=7.0=Language=Assets=Mars=7 July=Pleiades.
Korea Bay=7,000=70%=P7.0D=7.0=Language=Assets=Mars=7 July=Pleiades.
Korean=4,500=5,000=50%=P5.00D=Law=Time=Venus=5 May = Aphrodite>>L=N.

Korean. Currency metric weight >> 3/10 = 0.3 = 30:1. See Naira. Dollar.

Koruna=2,500=3,000=30%=P3.0D=3.0=Creativity=Stars=Muses=3 March = C=I>>GIL.
Kos=7,000=70%=P7.0D=7.0=Language=Assets=Mars=7 July=Pleiades.
Kosciusko=8,000=80%=P8.0D=Economy=Currency=8 Aug.=Zeus>>E=v.
Kosciusko, Thaddeus=5,000=50%=P5.00D=Law=Time=Venus=5 May = Aphrodite>>L=N.
Kosher=8,000=80%=P8.0D=Economy=Currency=8 Aug.=Zeus>>E=v.
Košice=5,000=50%=P5.00D=Law=Time=Venus=5 May = Aphrodite>>L=N.
Kosovo=2,500=3,000=30%=P3.0D=3.0=Creativity=Stars=Muses=3 March = C=I>>GIL.
Kossuth Lajos=2,500=3,000=30%=P3.0D=3.0=Creativity=Stars=Muses=3 March=GIL.
Kosygin Aleksie=2,500=3,000=30%=P3.0D=3.0=Creativity=Stars=Muses=3 March =GIL.
Kowloon=9,000=90%=P9.00D=9.0=Abstraction=Gods=Saturn=9Sept.>>A=Ø.
Know tow=12,500=13,000=13%=P1.30=Solar Core=Faculty=13 January=Athena.
KP=1,000=100%=10.0=1.0=Mind=Sun=1 January=Helios >> M=E4.
Kr=2,500=3,000=30%=P3.0D=3.0=Creativity=Stars=Muses=3 March = C=I>>GIL.
Kraal=6,500=7,000=70%=P7.0D=7.0=Language=Assets=Mars=7 July=Pleiades.

Krakatau=4,500=5,000=50%=P5.00D=Law=Time=Venus=5 May = Aphrodite>>L=N.
Kraków=1,000=100%=10.0=1.0=Mind=Sun=1 January=Helios >> M=E4.
Krasnodar=6,500=7,000=70%=P7.0D=7.0=Language=Assets=Mars=7 July=Pleiades.
Krasnoyarsk=7,500=8,000=80%=P8.0D=Economy=Currency=8 Aug.=Zeus>>E=v.
Kremlin=9,500=10,000=1,000=100%=10.0=Physicality=Tech.=10 Oct.=Uranus=P=1Ø.

Kremlinology=3,000=30%=P3.0D=3.0=Creativity=Stars=Muses=3 March = C=I>>GIL.
Study of the politics of the Soviet government. Creatocracy is the study of the politics of
Paradise, Paradiseans and the Disean government. See The Creatocracy Republic.

Krill=8,000=80%=P8.0D=Economy=Currency=8 Aug.=Zeus>>E=v.
Krishna=4,000=40%=P4.0D=Govt.=Creatocracy=4 April=Mercury=Hermes=G=A4.
Krivoi Rog=5,000=50%=P5.00D=Law=Time=Venus=5 May = Aphrodite>>L=N.
Korona1=3,000=30%=P3.0D=3.0=Creativity=Stars=Muses=3 March = C=I>>GIL.
Korona2=2,500=3,000=30%=P3.0D=3.0=Creativity=Stars=Muses=3 March = C=I>>GIL.
Krone1=2,500=3,000=30%=P3.0D=3.0=Creativity=Stars=Muses=3 March = C=I>>GIL.
Krone2=2,500=3,000=30%=P3.0D=3.0=Creativity=Stars=Muses=3 March = C=I>>GIL.
Krypton=10,000=1,000=100%=10.0=Physicality=Tech.=10 Oct.=Uranus=P=1Ø.
KS=500=5%=P5.00D=5.0=Law=Time=Venus=5 May=Aphrodite>>L=N.
Kt.=2,000=20%=P2.00D=2.0=Nature=Matter=Moon=2 Feb.=Cupid=N=C+_
Kuala Lumpur=6,000=60%=P6.0D=Man=Earth=Royalty=6 June=Gaia=Maia>>M=M2.
Kubial Khan=6,000=60%=P6.0D=Man=Earth=Royalty=6 June=Gaia=Maia>>M=M2.
Kudos=10,000=1,000=100%=10.0=Physicality=Tech.=10 Oct.=Uranus=P=1Ø.
Kudu=7,000=70%=P7.0D=7.0=Language=Assets=Mars=7 July=Pleiades.
Kudzu=9,000=90%=P9.00D=9.0=Abstraction=Gods=Saturn=9Sept.>>A=Ø.
Kuibyshev=6,500=7,000=70%=P7.0D=7.0=Language=Assets=Mars=7 July=Pleiades.
Kulak=4,000=40%=P4.0D=Govt.=Creatocracy=4 April=Mercury=Hermes=G=A4.
Kumasi=5,000=50%=P5.00D=Law=Time=Venus=5 May = Aphrodite>>L=N.
Kumquat=7,500=8,000=80%=P8.0D=Economy=Currency=8 Aug.=Zeus>>E=v.
Kung fu=6,000=60%=P6.0D=Man=Earth=Royalty=6 June=Gaia=Maia>>M=M2.
Kunlun=10,000=1,000=100%=10.0=Physicality=Tech.=10 Oct.=Uranus=P=1Ø.
Kumming=4,500=5,000=50%=P5.00D=Law=Time=Venus=5 May = Aphrodite>>L=N.
Kura=10,000=1,000=100%=10.0=Physicality=Tech.=10 Oct.=Uranus=P=1Ø.
Kurd=4,500=5,000=50%=P5.00D=Law=Time=Venus=5 May = Aphrodite>>L=N.
Kurdish=2,500=3,000=30%=P3.0D=3.0=Creativity=Stars=Muses=3 March = C=I>>GIL.
Kurdistan=3,500=4,000=40%=P4.0D=Govt.=Creat.=4 April=Mercury=Hermes=G=A4.
Kuril Islands=10,000=1,000=100%=10.0=Physicality=Tech.=10 Oct.=Uranus=P=1Ø.
Kurosawa Akira=2,000=20%=P2.00D=2.0=Nature=Matter=Moon=2 Feb.=Cupid=N=C+_
Kursk=4,500=5,000=50%=P5.00D=Law=Time=Venus=5 May = Aphrodite>>L=N.
Kurus=3,000=30%=P3.0D=3.0=Creativity=Stars=Muses=3 March = C=I>>GIL.
Kuwait=10,000=1,000=100%=10.0=Physicality=Tech.=10 Oct.=Uranus=P=1Ø.
Kuznetsk Basin=10,000=1,000=100%=10.0=Physicality=Tech.=10 Oct.=Uranus=P=1Ø.
kW=4,000=40%=P4.0D=Govt.=Creatocracy=4 April=Mercury=Hermes=G=A4.
Kwacha=4,000=40%=P4.0D=Govt.=Creatocracy=4 April=Mercury=Hermes=G=A4.

Kwakiutl=8,000=80%=P8.0D=Economy=Currency=8 Aug.=Zeus>>E=v.
Kwang chow=1,000=100%=10.0=1.0=Mind=Sun=1 January=Helios >> M=E4.
kwanza=3,500=4,000=40%=P4.0D=Govt.=Creatocracy=4 April=Mercury=Hermes=G=A4.
Kwanza=10,000=1,000=100%=10.0=Physicality=Tech.=10 Oct.=Uranus=P=1Ø.
Kwashiorkor=10,000=1,000=100%=10.0=Physicality=Tech.=10 Oct.=Uranus=P=1Ø.
Kweiyang=1,000=100%=10.0=1.0=Mind=Sun=1 January=Helios >> M=E4.
kWh=1,000=100%=10.0=1.0=Mind=Sun=1 January=Helios >> M=E4.
KY=500=5%=P5.00D=5.0=Law=Time=Venus=5 May=Aphrodite>>L=N.
Kyat=2,500=3,000=30%=P3.0D=3.0=Creativity=Stars=Muses=3 March = C=I>>GIL.
Kyoto=5,500=5.5=80%=P5.50=Earth-Midway=5 May = Gaia.
Kyushu=5,000=50%=P5.00D=Law=Time=Venus=5 May = Aphrodite>>L=N.
Kyzy-Kum=6,500=7,000=70%=P7.0D=7.0=Language=Assets=Mars=7 July=Pleiades.

MAKABET =LI=

---

l1=3,000=30%=P3.0D=3.0=Creativity=Stars=Muses=3 March = C=I>>GIL.
The 12th letter of the English alphabets. >> Makupedia shows it is an element of creativity.
A constant repetition of "Ll" conjures the muses especially when the name of particular muse is mentioned as seen in the encyclopedia of Castle Makupedia. This is a directed method of prayer with specific means.
The psycho-weight of the alphabet (I) is thus computed:
3.0*1.2=p=4.2+3.6=7.8x=px=22.92=23=2.3 >> Local Business or Matters.
The letter L induces the power of team work 2.0*0.2=2.2+0.4=2.6x=px=3.48=4.0. It is inspired by Hermes God of Merchandise invention and wit
However 22 indicates a female entity hence a Goddess being most qualified here is Athena Goddess of wisdom handicraft and mental warfare, I.e. brainstorming, intellectualism, academic works. This is most efficient when the letter appears twice say in a name or its pronouncement is dominant. So it is a letter of wit and wisdom. This is the L code.

---

l2=500=5%=P5.00D=5.0=Law=Time=Venus=5 May=Aphrodite>>L=N.
l1=3,000=30%=P3.0D=3.0=Creativity=Stars=Muses=3 March = C=I>>GIL.
L1=3,000=30%=P3.0D=3.0=Creativity=Stars=Muses=3 March = C=I>>GIL.
L2=5,500=5.5=80%=P5.50=Earth-Midway=5 May = Gaia.
la=4,500=5,000=50%=P5.00D=Law=Time=Venus=5 May = Aphrodite>>L=N.
La=2,500=3,000=30%=P3.0D=3.0=Creativity=Stars=Muses=3 March = C=I>>GIL.
La=500=5%=P5.00D=5.0=Law=Time=Venus=5 May=Aphrodite>>L=N.
Lab=1,000=100%=10.0=1.0=Mind=Sun=1 January=Helios >> M=E4.
Label=10,000=1,000=100%=10.0=Physicality=Tech.=10 Oct.=Uranus=P=1Ø.
Labial=10,000=1,000=100%=10.0=Physicality=Tech.=10 Oct.=Uranus=P=1Ø.
Labium=10,000=1,000=100%=10.0=Physicality=Tech.=10 Oct.=Uranus=P=1Ø.

Labor=10,000=1,000=100%=10.0=Physicality=Tech.=10 Oct.=Uranus=P=1Ø.
The fourth arm of the Creatocracy after royalty media and government.

Laboratory=8,000=80%=P8.0D=Economy=Currency=8 Aug.=Zeus>>E=v.
The Creatocracy has the psycho-laboratory a place where mind sciences are developed.
We have developed WDSD as a database and time laboratory for over 10,000 mind apps.

Labor Day=6,500=7,000=70%=P7.0D=7.0=Language=Assets=Mars=7 July=Pleiades.
Labored=4,500=5,000=50%=P5.00D=Law=Time=Venus=5 May = Aphrodite>>L=N.
Laborious=3,500=4,000=40%=P4.0D=Govt.=Creat=4 April=Mercury=Hermes=G=A4.
Labor Union=8,500=9,000=90%=P9.00D=9.0=Abstraction=Gods=Saturn=9Sept.>>A=Ø.
Labrador=5,000=50%=P5.00D=Law=Time=Venus=5 May = Aphrodite>>L=N.
Labrador Current=7,000=70%=P7.0D=7.0=Language=Assets=Mars=7 July=Pleiades.
Labrador Peninsula=5,500=5.5=80%=P5.50=Earth-Midway=5 May = Gaia.
Laburnum=6,500=7,000=70%=P7.0D=7.0=Language=Assets=Mars=7 July=Pleiades.
Labyrinth=10,000=1,000=100%=10.0=Physicality=Tech.=10 Oct.=Uranus=P=1Ø.
Lac=8,000=80%=P8.0D=Economy=Currency=8 Aug.=Zeus>>E=v.
Lace=10,000=1,000=100%=10.0=Physicality=Tech.=10 Oct.=Uranus=P=1Ø.
Lacerate=5,500=5.5=80%=P5.50=Earth-Midway=5 May = Gaia.
Lachrymal=5,000=50%=P5.00D=Law=Time=Venus=5 May = Aphrodite>>L=N.
Lachrymose=1,500=15%=P1.50D=1.5=Authority=Solar Crown=1 May = Maia.
Lack=5,500=5.5=80%=P5.50=Earth-Midway=5 May = Gaia.
Lackadaisical=5,000=50%=P5.00D=Law=Time=Venus=5 May = Aphrodite>>L=N.
Lackey=3,500=4,000=40%=P4.0D=Govt.=Creatocracy=4 April=Mercury=Hermes=G=A4.
Lackluster=4,500=5,000=50%=P5.00D=Law=Time=Venus=5 May = Aphrodite>>L=N.
Laconic=3,500=4,000=40%=P4.0D=Govt.=Creatocracy=4 April=Mercury=Hermes=G=A4.
La Coruna=5,000=50%=P5.00D=Law=Time=Venus=5 May = Aphrodite>>L=N.
Lacquer=10,000=1,000=100%=10.0=Physicality=Tech.=10 Oct.=Uranus=P=1Ø.
Lacrosse=10,000=1,000=100%=10.0=Physicality=Tech.=10 Oct.=Uranus=P=1Ø.
Lactate=2,500=3,000=30%=P3.0D=3.0=Creativity=Stars=Muses=3 March = C=I>>GIL.
Lactic=2,500=3,000=30%=P3.0D=3.0=Creativity=Stars=Muses=3 March = C=I>>GIL.
Lactic acid=6,500=7,000=70%=P7.0D=7.0=Language=Assets=Mars=7 July=Pleiades.
Lacto-=2,500=3,000=30%=P3.0D=3.0=Creativity=Stars=Muses=3 March = C=I>>GIL.
Lactose=10,000=1,000=100%=10.0=Physicality=Tech.=10 Oct.=Uranus=P=1Ø.
Lacuna=10,000=1,000=100%=10.0=Physicality=Tech.=10 Oct.=Uranus=P=1Ø.
Lad=3,500=4,000=40%=P4.0D=Govt.=Creatocracy=4 April=Mercury=Hermes=G=A4.
Ladder=10,000=1,000=100%=10.0=Physicality=Tech.=10 Oct.=Uranus=P=1Ø.
Lade=7,500=8,000=80%=P8.0D=Economy=Currency=8 Aug.=Zeus>>E=v.
Lading=1,000=100%=Physicality=Tech.=10 Oct.=Uranus=P=1Ø.
Ladino=8,500=9,000=90%=P9.00D=9.0=Abstraction=Gods=Saturn=9Sept.>>A=Ø.
Ladle=6,000=60%=P6.0D=Man=Earth=Royalty=6 June=Gaia=Maia>>M=M2.
Ladoga Lake=4,000=40%=P4.0D=Govt.=Creatocracy=4 April=Mercury=Hermes=G=A4.
Lady=10,000=1,000=100%=10.0=Physicality=Tech.=10 Oct.=Uranus=P=1Ø.
Ladybird=1,000=100%=10.0=1.0=Mind=Sun=1 January=Helios >> M=E4.

Ladybug=6,000=60%=P6.0D=Man=Earth=Royalty=6 June=Gaia=Maia>>M=M2.
Ladyfinger=4,000=40%=P4.0D=Govt.=Creatocracy=4 April=Mercury=Hermes=G=A4.
Lady in waiting=4,000=40%=P4.0D=Govt.=Creatocracy=4 April=Mercury=Hermes=G=A4.
Ladyship=7,500=8,000=80%=P8.0D=Economy=Currency=8 Aug.=Zeus>>E=v.
Lady's slipper=4,500=5,000=50%=P5.00D=Law=Time=Venus=5 May = Aphrodite>>L=N.
Laetrile=3,500=4,000=40%=P4.0D=Govt.=Creatocracy=4 April=Mercury=Hermes=G=A4.
Lafayette=4,000=40%=P4.0D=Govt.=Creatocracy=4 April=Mercury=Hermes=G=A4.
La Fontaine=3,000=30%=P3.0D=3.0=Creativity=Stars=Muses=3 March = C=I>>GIL.
Lag=10,000=1,000=100%=10.0=Physicality=Tech.=10 Oct.=Uranus=P=1Ø.
Lager=7,500=8,000=80%=P8.0D=Economy=Currency=8 Aug.=Zeus>>E=v.
Laggard=2,000=20%=P2.00D=2.0=Nature=Matter=Moon=2 Feb.=Cupid=N=C+_
Lagniappe=10,000=1,000=100%=10.0=Physicality=Tech.=10 Oct.=Uranus=P=1Ø.

Lagoon=9,000=90%=P9.00D=9.0=Abstraction=Gods=Saturn=9Sept.>>A=Ø.
The lagoon is a spiritual place, abode of the Council of Gods. It aligns on dimension scale as 3.0>>Muses>>Creativity. 6.0>>Mankind >> Humanity >> Royalty >> Gaia >> Earth. 12=1.2>>Knowledge>>Athena >> Education. The lagoon is jointly managed by Gaia and Athena and their muses.

Lagos=6,000=60%=P6.0D=Man=Earth=Royalty=6 June=Gaia=Maia>>M=M2.
In the Makupedian Language of the Creatocracy, Lagos means Earth >>Humanity >> Royalty >> Mankind. Lagos is managed by Gaia, Goddess of the Earth. The average propensity for anyone to desire to live and to live in Lagos is 60%.

Lahore=4,500=5,000=50%=P5.00D=Law=Time=Venus=5 May = Aphrodite>>L=N.
Laid=3,000=30%=P3.0D=3.0=Creativity=Stars=Muses=3 March = C=I>>GIL.
Laid back=2,500=3,000=30%=P3.0D=3.0=Creativity=Stars=Muses=3 March = C=I>>GIL.
Lain=2,000=20%=P2.00D=2.0=Nature=Matter=Moon=2 Feb.=Cupid=N=C+_
Lair=5,000=50%=P5.00D=Law=Time=Venus=5 May = Aphrodite>>L=N.
Laissez fair=10,000=1,000=100%=10.0=Physicality=Tech.=10 Oct.=Uranus=P=1Ø.
Laity=1,500=15%=P1.50D=1.5=Authority=Solar Crown=1 May = Maia.
Lake=5,000=50%=P5.00D=Law=Time=Venus=5 May = Aphrodite>>L=N.
Lakewood=5,000=50%=P5.00D=Law=Time=Venus=5 May = Aphrodite>>L=N.
Lakota=1,000=100%=10.0=1.0=Mind=Sun=1 January=Helios >> M=E4.
Lam=6,500=7,000=70%=P7.0D=7.0=Language=Assets=Mars=7 July=Pleiades.
Lamaism=1,000=100%=10.0=1.0=Mind=Sun=1 January=Helios >> M=E4.
Lamarck Jean=5,500=5.5=80%=P5.50=Earth-Midway=5 May = Gaia.
Lamb=7,000=70%=P7.0D=7.0=Language=Assets=Mars=7 July=Pleiades.
Lamb Charles=3,500=4,000=40%=P4.0D=Govt.=Creat=4 April=Mercury=Hermes=G=A4.
Lambaste=8,500=9,000=90%=P9.00D=9.0=Abstraction=Gods=Saturn=9Sept.>>A=Ø.
Lambda=3,500=4,000=40%=P4.0D=Govt.=Creatocracy=4 April=Mercury=Hermes=G=A4.
Lambent=6,000=60%=P6.0D=Man=Earth=Royalty=6 June=Gaia=Maia>>M=M2.
Lamb skin=5,500=5.5=80%=P5.50=Earth-Midway=5 May = Gaia.

Lame=9,500=10,000=1,000=100%=10.0=Physicality=Tech.=10 Oct.=Uranus=P=1Ø.
Lamé=6,000=60%=P6.0D=Man=Earth=Royalty=6 June=Gaia=Maia>>M=M2.
Lamedh=4,000=40%=P4.0D=Govt.=Creatocracy=4 April=Mercury=Hermes=G=A4.
Lame duck=10,000=1,000=100%=10.0=Physicality=Tech.=10 Oct.=Uranus=P=1Ø.
Lamela=4,000=40%=P4.0D=Govt.=Creatocracy=4 April=Mercury=Hermes=G=A4.
Lament=10,000=1,000=100%=10.0=Physicality=Tech.=10 Oct.=Uranus=P=1Ø.
Lamentation=6,500=7,000=70%=P7.0D=7.0=Language=Assets=Mars=7 July=Pleiades.
Lamina=4,000=40%=P4.0D=Govt.=Creatocracy=4 April=Mercury=Hermes=G=A4.
Laminate=10,000=1,000=100%=10.0=Physicality=Tech.=10 Oct.=Uranus=P=1Ø.
Lamp=10,000=1,000=100%=10.0=Physicality=Tech.=10 Oct.=Uranus=P=1Ø.
Lampblack=6,000=60%=P6.0D=Man=Earth=Royalty=6 June=Gaia=Maia>>M=M2.
Lampoon=7,000=70%=P7.0D=7.0=Language=Assets=Mars=7 July=Pleiades.
Lamprey=5,500=5.5=80%=P5.50=Earth-Midway=5 May = Gaia.
Lanai=5,000=50%=P5.00D=Law=Time=Venus=5 May = Aphrodite>>L=N.
Lanai=3,500=4,000=40%=P4.0D=Govt.=Creatocracy=4 April=Mercury=Hermes=G=A4.
Lance=10,000=1,000=100%=10.0=Physicality=Tech.=10 Oct.=Uranus=P=1Ø.
Lance corporal=4,500=5,000=50%=P5.00D=Law=Time=Venus=5 May = Aphrodite>>L=N.
Lancelot=10,000=1,000=100%=10.0=Physicality=Tech.=10 Oct.=Uranus=P=1Ø.
Lancer=2,500=3,000=30%=P3.0D=3.0=Creativity=Stars=Muses=3 March = C=I>>GIL.
Lancet=5,000=50%=P5.00D=Law=Time=Venus=5 May = Aphrodite>>L=N.
Lanchow=1,000=100%=10.0=1.0=Mind=Sun=1 January=Helios >> M=E4.
Land=10,000=1,000=100%=10.0=Physicality=Tech.=10 Oct.=Uranus=P=1Ø.
Landed=2,000=20%=P2.00D=2.0=Nature=Matter=Moon=2 Feb.=Cupid=N=C+_
Landfall=5,500=5.5=80%=P5.50=Earth-Midway=5 May = Gaia.
Landfill=8,500=9,000=90%=P9.00D=9.0=Abstraction=Gods=Saturn=9Sept.>>A=Ø.
Land grant=6,000=60%=P6.0D=Man=Earth=Royalty=6 June=Gaia=Maia>>M=M2.
Landholder=2,000=20%=P2.00D=2.0=Nature=Matter=Moon=2 Feb.=Cupid=N=C+_
Landing=10,000=1,000=100%=10.0=Physicality=Tech.=10 Oct.=Uranus=P=1Ø.
Landing gear=3,500=4,000=40%=P4.0D=Govt.=Creat=4 April=Mercury=Hermes=G=A4.
Landing strip=3,000=30%=P3.0D=3.0=Creativity=Stars=Muses=3 March = C=I>>GIL.
Landlady=5,500=5.5=80%=P5.50=Earth-Midway=5 May = Gaia.
Landlocked=6,000=60%=P6.0D=Man=Earth=Royalty=6 June=Gaia=Maia>>M=M2.
Landlord=5,500=5.5=80%=P5.50=Earth-Midway=5 May = Gaia.
Landlubber=6,000=60%=P6.0D=Man=Earth=Royalty=6 June=Gaia=Maia>>M=M2.
Landmark=8,000=80%=P8.0D=Economy=Currency=8 Aug.=Zeus>>E=v.
Landmass=2,500=3,000=30%=P3.0D=3.0=Creativity=Stars=Muses=3 March = C=I>>GIL.
Land mine=5,500=5.5=80%=P5.50=Earth-Midway=5 May = Gaia.
Land office business=4,000=40%=P4.0D=Govt.=Creat=4 April=Mercury=Hermes=G=A4.
Land poor=5,000=50%=P5.00D=Law=Time=Venus=5 May = Aphrodite>>L=N.
Landscape=10,000=1,000=100%=10.0=Physicality=Tech.=10 Oct.=Uranus=P=1Ø.
Landslide=8,000=80%=P8.0D=Economy=Currency=8 Aug.=Zeus>>E=v.
Landward=2,000=20%=P2.00D=2.0=Nature=Matter=Moon=2 Feb.=Cupid=N=C+_
Lane=6,000=60%=P6.0D=Man=Earth=Royalty=6 June=Gaia=Maia>>M=M2.
Langley Samuel=4,000=40%=P4.0D=Govt.=Creato=4 April=Mercury=Hermes=G=A4.

Language=10,000=1,000=100%=10.0=Physicality=Tech.=10 Oct.=Uranus=P=1Ø.
In the Creatocracy, the 7th dimension of the universe consisting cultures, traditions, values, ethics, civilizations, eras, age & Ages, histories, works, assets, speculations, precision, Mind Computing, Psycho-Forensics, Auditing, Analytics and Makupedia. Peter Matthews-Akukali, Castle Makupedia wrote the language formula as Lang=Az. >> Dictionary, Computed Dictionary, Encyclopedia. This work is the proof of language formula and physical equivalent in asset worth values and standards created by its mind.

Langue Doc=8,000=80%=P8.0D=Economy=Currency=8 Aug.=Zeus>>E=v.
Languid=10,000=1,000=100%=10.0=Physicality=Tech.=10 Oct.=Uranus=P=1Ø.
Languish=10,000=1,000=100%=10.0=Physicality=Tech.=10 Oct.=Uranus=P=1Ø.
Languor=10,000=1,000=100%=10.0=Physicality=Tech.=10 Oct.=Uranus=P=1Ø.
Lank=5,500=5.5=80%=P5.50=Earth-Midway=5 May = Gaia.
Lanky=2,000=20%=P2.00D=2.0=Nature=Matter=Moon=2 Feb.=Cupid=N=C+_
Lanolin=7,500=8,000=80%=P8.0D=Economy=Currency=8 Aug.=Zeus>>E=v.
Lansing=6,500=7,000=70%=P7.0D=7.0=Language=Assets=Mars=7 July=Pleiades.
Lantern=7,000=70%=P7.0D=7.0=Language=Assets=Mars=7 July=Pleiades.
Lanthanide=3,500=4,000=40%=P4.0D=Govt.=Creat=4 April=Mercury=Hermes=G=A4.
Lanthanum=12,500=13,000=13%=P1.30=Solar Core=Faculty=13 January=Athena.
Lanyard=10,000=1,000=100%=10.0=Physicality=Tech.=10 Oct.=Uranus=P=1Ø.
Lanzhou=7,500=8,000=80%=P8.0D=Economy=Currency=8 Aug.=Zeus>>E=v.
Lao=6,000=60%=P6.0D=Man=Earth=Royalty=6 June=Gaia=Maia>>M=M2.
Laos=4,500=5,000=50%=P5.00D=Law=Time=Venus=5 May = Aphrodite>>L=N.
Lao-tzu=2,500=3,000=30%=P3.0D=3.0=Creativity=Stars=Muses=3 March = C=I>>GIL.
Lap1=10,000=1,000=100%=10.0=Physicality=Tech.=10 Oct.=Uranus=P=1Ø.
Lap2=10,000=1,000=100%=Physicality=Tech.=10 Oct.=Uranus=P=1Ø.
Lap3=10,000=1,000=100%=10.0=Physicality=Tech.=10 Oct.=Uranus=P=1Ø.
La Paz=6,500=7,000=70%=P7.0D=7.0=Language=Assets=Mars=7 July=Pleiades.
Lap belt=4,000=40%=P4.0D=Govt.=Creatocracy=4 April=Mercury=Hermes=G=A4.
Lap board=6,500=7,000=70%=P7.0D=7.0=Language=Assets=Mars=7 July=Pleiades.
Lapdog=3,000=30%=P3.0D=3.0=Creativity=Stars=Muses=3 March = C=I>>GIL.
Lapel=8,000=80%=P8.0D=Economy=Currency=8 Aug.=Zeus>>E=v.
Lapidary=10,000=1,000=100%=10.0=Physicality=Tech.=10 Oct.=Uranus=P=1Ø.
Lap in=1,000=100%=10.0=1.0=Mind=Sun=1 January=Helios >> M=E4.
Laplace=5,000=50%=P5.00D=Law=Time=Venus=5 May = Aphrodite>>L=N.
Lapland=8,500=9,000=90%=P9.00D=9.0=Abstraction=Gods=Saturn=9Sept.>>A=Ø.
La Plata=5,500=5.5=80%=P5.50=Earth-Midway=5 May = Gaia.
Lapp=6,000=60%=P6.0D=Man=Earth=Royalty=6 June=Gaia=Maia>>M=M2.
Lapse=10,000=1,000=100%=10.0=Physicality=Tech.=10 Oct.=Uranus=P=1Ø.
Laptop=4,500=5,000=50%=P5.00D=Law=Time=Venus=5 May = Aphrodite>>L=N.
Lapwing=6,500=7,000=70%=P7.0D=7.0=Language=Assets=Mars=7 July=Pleiades.
Larboard=2,500=3,000=30%=P3.0D=3.0=Creativity=Stars=Muses=3 March = C=I>>GIL.
Larceny=5,500=5.5=80%=P5.50=Earth-Midway=5 May = Gaia.
Larch=7,000=70%=P7.0D=7.0=Language=Assets=Mars=7 July=Pleiades.
Lard=10,000=1,000=100%=10.0=Physicality=Tech.=10 Oct.=Uranus=P=1Ø.

Larder=4,500=5,000=50%=P5.00D=Law=Time=Venus=5 May = Aphrodite>>L=N.
Laredo=5,000=50%=P5.00D=Law=Time=Venus=5 May = Aphrodite>>L=N.
Laree=3,000=30%=P3.0D=3.0=Creativity=Stars=Muses=3 March = C=I>>GIL.
Large=10,000=1,000=100%=10.0=Physicality=Tech.=10 Oct.=Uranus=P=1Ø.
Large calorie=1,500=15%=P1.50D=1.5=Authority=Solar Crown=1 May = Maia.
Large intestine=5,000=50%=P5.00D=Law=Time=Venus=5 May = Aphrodite>>L=N.
Largely=5,500=5.5=80%=P5.50=Earth-Midway=5 May = Gaia.
Large scale=5,000=50%=P5.00D=Law=Time=Venus=5 May = Aphrodite>>L=N.
Largess=4,500=5,000=50%=P5.00D=Law=Time=Venus=5 May = Aphrodite>>L=N.
Largo=3,000=30%=P3.0D=3.0=Creativity=Stars=Muses=3 March = C=I>>GIL.
Lariat=3,500=4,000=40%=P4.0D=Govt.=Creatocracy=4 April=Mercury=Hermes=G=A4.
Lark1=8,000=80%=P8.0D=Economy=Currency=8 Aug.=Zeus>>E=v.
Lark2=6,500=7,000=70%=P7.0D=7.0=Language=Assets=Mars=7 July=Pleiades.
Larkspur=1,000=100%=10.0=1.0=Mind=Sun=1 January=Helios >> M=E4.
La Rochefoucauld=3,500=4,000=40%=P4.0D=Govt.=4 April=Mercury=Hermes=G=A4.
Larva=10,000=1,000=100%=10.0=Physicality=Tech.=10 Oct.=Uranus=P=1Ø.
Laryngitis=2,000=20%=P2.00D=2.0=Nature=Matter=Moon=2 Feb.=Cupid=N=C+_
Larynx=10,000=1,000=100%=10.0=Physicality=Tech.=10 Oct.=Uranus=P=1Ø.
Lasagna=6,500=7,000=70%=P7.0D=7.0=Language=Assets=Mars=7 July=Pleiades.
La Salle=6,500=7,000=70%=P7.0D=7.0=Language=Assets=Mars=7 July=Pleiades.
Lascivious=3,000=30%=P3.0D=3.0=Creativity=Stars=Muses=3 March = C=I>>GIL.
Laser=10,000=1,000=100%=10.0=Physicality=Tech.=10 Oct.=Uranus=P=1Ø.
Laser disk=1,500=15%=P1.50D=1.5=Authority=Solar Crown=1 May = Maia.
Lash1=10,000=1,000=100%=10.0=Physicality=Tech.=10 Oct.=Uranus=P=1Ø.
Lash2=5,500=5.5=80%=P5.50=Earth-Midway=5 May = Gaia.
Las Palmas=4,500=5,000=50%=P5.00D=Law=Time=Venus=5 May = Aphrodite>>L=N.
Lassie=1,000=100%=10.0=1.0=Mind=Sun=1 January=Helios >> M=E4.
Lassitude=5,000=50%=P5.00D=Law=Time=Venus=5 May = Aphrodite>>L=N.
Lasso=10,000=1,000=100%=10.0=Physicality=Tech.=10 Oct.=Uranus=P=1Ø.
Last1=10,000=1,000=100%=10.0=Physicality=Tech.=10 Oct.=Uranus=P=1Ø.
Last2=5,500=5.5=80%=P5.50=Earth-Midway=5 May = Gaia.
Last3=8,500=9,000=90%=P9.00D=9.0=Abstraction=Gods=Saturn=9Sept.>>A=Ø.
Last ditch=3,000=30%=P3.0D=3.0=Creativity=Stars=Muses=3 March = C=I>>GIL.
Last-in, first out=10,000=1,000=100%=Physicality=Tech.=10 Oct.=Uranus=P=1Ø.
Lasting=4,000=40%=P4.0D=Govt.=Creatocracy=4 April=Mercury=Hermes=G=A4.
Last Judgement=4,500=5,000=50%=P5.00D=Law=Time=Venus=5 May = Odite>>L=N.
Last rites=4,500=5,000=50%=P5.00D=Law=Time=Venus=5 May = Aphrodite>>L=N.
Last straw=7,500=8,000=80%=P8.0D=Economy=Currency=8 Aug.=Zeus>>E=v.
Last Supper=5,000=50%=P5.00D=Law=Time=Venus=5 May = Aphrodite>>L=N.
Las Vegas=6,500=7,000=70%=P7.0D=7.0=Language=Assets=Mars=7 July=Pleiades.
lat.=500=5%=P5.00D=5.0=Law=Time=Venus=5 May=Aphrodite>>L=N.
Lat.=1,500=15%=P1.50D=1.5=Authority=Solar Crown=1 May = Maia.
Latch=10,000=1,000=100%=10.0=Physicality=Tech.=10 Oct.=Uranus=P=1Ø.
Late=10,000=1,000=100%=10.0=Physicality=Tech.=10 Oct.=Uranus=P=1Ø.
Latecomer=4,500=5,000=50%=P5.00D=Law=Time=Venus=5 May = Aphrodite>>L=N.

Late Greek=4,000=40%=P4.0D=Govt.=Creatocracy=4 April=Mercury=Hermes=G=A4.
Late Latin=4,000=40%=P4.0D=Govt.=Creatocracy=4 April=Mercury=Hermes=G=A4.
Lately=2,000=20%=P2.00D=2.0=Nature=Matter=Moon=2 Feb.=Cupid=N=C+_
Latent=6,000=60%=P6.0D=Man=Earth=Royalty=6 June=Gaia=Maia>>M=M2.
Lateral=8,500=9,000=90%=P9.00D=9.0=Abstraction=Gods=Saturn=9Sept.>>A=Ø.
Latex=10,000=1,000=100%=10.0=Physicality=Tech.=10 Oct.=Uranus=P=1Ø.
Lath=10,000=1,000=100%=10.0=Physicality=Tech.=10 Oct.=Uranus=P=1Ø.
Lathe=10,000=1,000=100%=10.0=Physicality=Tech.=10 Oct.=Uranus=P=1Ø.
Lather=10,000=1,000=100%=10.0=Physicality=Tech.=10 Oct.=Uranus=P=1Ø.
Latin=10,000=1,000=100%=10.0=Physicality=Tech.=10 Oct.=Uranus=P=1Ø.
Latina=2,500=3,000=30%=P3.0D=3.0=Creativity=Stars=Muses=3 March = C=I>>GIL.
Latin America=6,500=7,000=70%=P7.0D=7.0=Language=Assets=Mars=7 July=Pleiades.
Latino=4,000=40%=P4.0D=Govt.=Creatocracy=4 April=Mercury=Hermes=G=A4.
Latitude=10,000=1,000=100%=10.0=Physicality=Tech.=10 Oct.=Uranus=P=1Ø.
Latitudinarian=4,500=5,000=50%=P5.00D=Law=Time=Venus=5 May = Aphrodite>>L=N.
Latium=6,000=60%=P6.0D=Man=Earth=Royalty=6 June=Gaia=Maia>>M=M2.
Latke=4,500=5,000=50%=P5.00D=Law=Time=Venus=5 May = Aphrodite>>L=N.
La Tour Georges de.=2,500=3,000=30%=P3.0D=3.0=Crea=Stars=Muses=3 March = C=I.
Latrine=4,000=40%=P4.0D=Govt.=Creatocracy=4 April=Mercury=Hermes=G=A4.
Latter=3,500=4,000=40%=P4.0D=Govt.=Creatocracy=4 April=Mercury=Hermes=G=A4.
Latter day=3,500=4,000=40%=P4.0D=Govt.=Creat=4 April=Mercury=Hermes=G=A4.
Latter-day Saint=1,000=100%=10.0=1.0=Mind=Sun=1 January=Helios >> M=E4.
Lattice=10,000=1,000=100%=10.0=Physicality=Tech.=10 Oct.=Uranus=P=1Ø.
Latvia=6,500=7,000=70%=P7.0D=7.0=Language=Assets=Mars=7 July=Pleiades.
Latvian=5,500=5.5=80%=P5.50=Earth-Midway=5 May = Gaia.
Laud=3,000=30%=P3.0D=3.0=Creativity=Stars=Muses=3 March = C=I>>GIL.
Laud William=3,500=4,000=40%=P4.0D=Govt.=Creat=4April=Mercury=Hermes=G=A4.
Laudable=1,000=100%=10.0=1.0=Mind=Sun=1 January=Helios >> M=E4.
Laudanum=4,500=5,000=50%=P5.00D=Law=Time=Venus=5 May = Aphrodite>>L=N.
Laudatory=2,000=20%=P2.00D=2.0=Nature=Matter=Moon=2 Feb.=Cupid=N=C+_
Laugh=10,000=1,000=100%=Physicality=Tech.=10 Oct.=Uranus=P=1Ø.
Laughable=2,500=3,000=30%=P3.0D=3.0=Creativity=Stars=Muses=3 March = C=I>>GIL.
Laughing stock=4,000=40%=P4.0D=Govt.=Creatocracy=4April=Mercury=Hermes=G=A4.
Laughter=4,000=40%=P4.0D=Govt.=Creatocracy=4 April=Mercury=Hermes=G=A4.
Lauch1=10,000=1,000=100%=10.0=Physicality=Tech.=10 Oct.=Uranus=P=1Ø.
Launch2=2,500=3,000=30%=P3.0D=3.0=Creativity=Stars=Muses=3 March = C=I>>GIL.
Launch pad=6,000=60%=P6.0D=Man=Earth=Royalty=6 June=Gaia=Maia>>M=M2.
Launder=10,500=11,000=11%=P1.10D=1.1=Idea=Brainchild=Inv.=11 Nov.=Athena>>I=MT.
Laundromat=5,500=5.5=80%=P5.50=Earth-Midway=5 May = Gaia.
Laundry=5,000=50%=P5.00D=Law=Time=Venus=5 May = Aphrodite>>L=N.
Laureate=8,500=9,000=90%=P9.00D=9.0=Abstraction=Gods=Saturn=9Sept.>>A=Ø.
Laurel=10,000=1,000=100%=10.0=Physicality=Tech.=10 Oct.=Uranus=P=1Ø.
Laurentian Mountains=6,500=7,000=70%=P7.0D=7.0=Lang=Assets=Mars=7July=Pleiades.
Laurentian Plateau=17,500=18,000=18%=P1.80D=Solar Curr.=Maks Curr.=1 Aug.=Maia.
Lausanne=6,500=7,000=70%=P7.0D=7.0=Language=Assets=Mars=7 July=Pleiades.

PETER K. MATTHEWS - AKUKALIA

Lava=10,000=1,000=100%=10.0=Physicality=Tech.=10 Oct.=Uranus=P=1Ø.
Lavage=6,000=60%=P6.0D=Man=Earth=Royalty=6 June=Gaia=Maia>>M=M2.
Laval=6,500=7,000=70%=P7.0D=7.0=Language=Assets=Mars=7 July=Pleiades.
Lavaliere=10,500=11,000=11%=P1.10D=1.1=Idea=Brainchild=Inv.=11 Nov.=Athena>>I=MT.
Lavatory=8,000=80%=P8.0D=Economy=Currency=8 Aug.=Zeus>>E=v.
Lave=3,500=4,000=40%=P4.0D=Govt.=Creatocracy=4 April=Mercury=Hermes=G=A4.
Lavender=9,500=10,000=1,000=100%=10.0=Physicality=Tech.=10 Oct.=Uranus=P=1Ø.
Lavish=10,000=1,000=100%=10.0=Physicality=Tech.=10 Oct.=Uranus=P=1Ø.
Lavoisier=3,500=4,000=40%=P4.0D=Govt.=Creat=4 April=Mercury=Hermes=G=A4.

Law=10,000=1,000=100%=10.0=Physicality=Tech.=10 Oct.=Uranus=P=1Ø.
In the Creative Sciences Law is the fifth (5ø) dimension of the universe. Peter Matthews-Akukalia, Castle Makupedia wrote its formula as L=N. Law is operant on Nature which are propensities and inclinations computed in the Encyclopedia of Castle Makupedia. Law is a Mind Technology because it depends on the mēnś rēa (mind elements) and actus rēus(resultant action) to establish truth. WDSD contains the former and offers the latter as a service to the legal industry. Law occurs in the same category as currency business and economy 8.0 and ideas brainchild and inventions 1.1. See Jurisprudence.

Law abiding=2,000=20%=P2.00D=2.0=Nature=Matter=Moon=2 Feb.=Cupid=N=C+_
Lawbreaker=2,500=3,000=30%=P3.0D=3.0=Cre=Stars=Muses=3 March = C=I>>GIL.
Lawful=2,500=3,000=30%=P3.0D=3.0=Creativity=Stars=Muses=3 March = C=I>>GIL.
Lawless=5,000=50%=P5.00D=Law=Time=Venus=5 May = Aphrodite>>L=N.
Lawmaker=3,000=30%=P3.0D=3.0=Creativity=Stars=Muses=3 March = C=I>>GIL.
Lawn1=5,500=5.5=80%=P5.50=Earth-Midway=5 May = Gaia.
Lawn2=4,500=5,000=50%=P5.00D=Law=Time=Venus=5 May = Aphrodite>>L=N.
Lawrence David=2,000=20%=P2.00D=2.0=Nature=Matter=Moon=2 Feb.=Cupid=N=C+_
Lawrence Thomas=6,000=60%=P6.0D=Man=Earth=Royalty=6 June=Gaia=Maia>>M=M2.
Lawrencium=11,000=11%=P1.10D=1.1=Idea=Brainchild=Inv.=11 Nov.=SC=Athena>>I=MT.
Lawsuit=3,500=4,000=40%=P4.0D=Govt.=Creatocracy=4 April=Mercury=Hermes=G=A4.
Lawyer=8,000=80%=P8.0D=Economy=Currency=8 Aug.=Zeus>>E=v.
Lax=10,500=11,000=11%=P1.10D=1.1=Idea=Brainchild=Inv.=11 Nov.=SC=Athena>>I=MT.
Laxative=6,500=7,000=70%=P7.0D=7.0=Language=Assets=Mars=7 July=Pleiades.
Lay1=10,000=1,000=100%=10.0=Physicality=Tech.=10 Oct.=Uranus=P=1Ø.
Lay2=5,500=5.5=80%=P5.50=Earth-Midway=5 May = Gaia.
Lay3=5,000=50%=P5.00D=Law=Time=Venus=5 May = Aphrodite>>L=N.
Lay4=7,500=8,000=80%=P8.0D=Economy=Currency=8 Aug.=Zeus>>E=v.
Layaway=8,500=9,000=90%=P9.00D=9.0=Abstraction=Gods=Saturn=9Sept.>>A=Ø.
Layer=8,500=9,000=90%=P9.00D=9.0=Abstraction=Gods=Saturn=9Sept.>>A=Ø.
Layette=6,000=60%=P6.0D=Man=Earth=Royalty=6 June=Gaia=Maia>>M=M2.
Layman=5,500=5.5=80%=P5.50=Earth-Midway=5 May = Gaia.
Layoff=6,500=7,000=70%=P7.0D=7.0=Language=Assets=Mars=7 July=Pleiades.
Layout=6,500=7,000=70%=P7.0D=7.0=Language=Assets=Mars=7 July=Pleiades.
Layover=2,500=3,000=30%=P3.0D=3.0=Creativity=Stars=Muses=3 March = C=I>>GIL.

Layperson=4,500=5,000=50%=P5.00D=Law=Time=Venus=5 May = Aphrodite>>L=N.
Laywoman=6,000=60%=P6.0D=Man=Earth=Royalty=6 June=Gaia=Maia>>M=M2.
Lazarus=4,000=40%=P4.0D=Govt.=Creatocracy=4 April=Mercury=Hermes=G=A4.
Lazarus, Emma=2,000=20%=P2.00D=2.0=Nature=Matter=Moon=2 Feb.=Cupid=N=C+_
Lazy=9,000=90%=P9.00D=9.0=Abstraction=Gods=Saturn=9Sept.>>A=Ø.
Lazy Susan=3,500=4,000=40%=P4.0D=Govt.=Creat=4 April=Mercury=Hermes=G=A4.
Ib.=3,000=30%=P3.0D=3.0=Creativity=Stars=Muses=3 March = C=I>>GIL.
Ic.=500=5%=P5.00D=5.0=Law=Time=Venus=5 May=Aphrodite>>L=N.
L/C=3,500=4,000=40%=P4.0D=Govt.=Creatocracy=4 April=Mercury=Hermes=G=A4.
L/C=1,500=15%=P1.50D=1.5=Authority=Solar Crown=1 May = Maia.
I.c.d.=1,500=15%=P1.50D=1.5=Authority=Solar Crown=1 May = Maia.
LCD=1,500=15%=P1.50D=1.5=Authority=Solar Crown=1 May = Maia.
I.c.m=1,500=15%=P1.50D=1.5=Authority=Solar Crown=1 May = Maia.
L.Cpl=1,000=100%=10.0=1.0=Mind=Sun=1 January=Helios >> M=E4.
Ld.=1,500=15%=P1.50D=1.5=Authority=Solar Crown=1 May = Maia.
LDL=1,500=15%=P1.50D=1.5=Authority=Solar Crown=1 May = Maia.
L-dopa=3,500=4,000=40%=P4.0D=Govt.=Creat=4 April=Mercury=Hermes=G=A4.
Lea=1,000=100%=10.0=1.0=Mind=Sun=1 January=Helios >> M=E4.
Leach=8,000=80%=P8.0D=Economy=Currency=8 Aug.=Zeus>>E=v.
Lead1=10,000=1,000=100%=10.0=Physicality=Tech.=10 Oct.=Uranus=P=1Ø.
Lead2=10,000=1,000=100%=10.0=Physicality=Tech.=10 Oct.=Uranus=P=1Ø.
Leaden=7,000=70%=P7.0D=7.0=Language=Assets=Mars=7 July=Pleiades.
Leading1=9,000=90%=P9.00D=9.0=Abstraction=Gods=Saturn=9Sept.>>A=Ø.
Leading2=6,000=60%=P6.0D=Man=Earth=Royalty=6 June=Gaia=Maia>>M=M2.
Lead time=5,500=5.5=80%=P5.50=Earth-Midway=5 May = Gaia.
Leaf=10,000=1,000=100%=10.0=Physicality=Tech.=10 Oct.=Uranus=P=1Ø.
Leafage=500=5%=P5.00D=5.0=Law=Time=Venus=5 May=Aphrodite>>L=N.
Leaflet=6,500=7,000=70%=P7.0D=7.0=Language=Assets=Mars=7 July=Pleiades.
Leaf spring=4,500=5,000=50%=P5.00D=Law=Time=Venus=5 May = Aphrodite>>L=N.
Leafstalk=1,000=100%=10.0=1.0=Mind=Sun=1 January=Helios >> M=E4.
League1=8,500=9,000=90%=P9.00D=9.0=Abstraction=Gods=Saturn=9Sept.>>A=Ø.
League2=7,500=8,000=80%=P8.0D=Economy=Currency=8 Aug.=Zeus>>E=v.

League of Nations=5,500=5.5=80%=P5.50=Earth-Midway=5 May = Gaia.
Now the United Nations Organization. Peter Matthews-Akukalia invented the
Creatocratic Nations Organization to upgrade the ideals and programs of the UN in order
to meet with changing trends for a global Creatocracy that will make the digital man.

Leah=3,500=4,000=40%=P4.0D=Govt.=Creat=4 April=Mercury=Hermes=G=A4.
Leak=10,000=1,000=100%=10.0=Physicality=Tech.=10 Oct.=Uranus=P=1Ø.
Leakage=4,500=5,000=50%=P5.00D=Law=Time=Venus=5 May = Aphrodite>>L=N.
Lean1=10,000=1,000=100%=10.0=Physicality=Tech.=10 Oct.=Uranus=P=1Ø.
Lean2=10,000=1,000=100%=10.0=Physicality=Tech.=10 Oct.=Uranus=P=1Ø.
Leaning=3,500=4,000=40%=P4.0D=Govt.=Creat=4 April=Mercury=Hermes=G=A4.

Lean to=7,500=8,000=80%=P8.0D=Economy=Currency=8 Aug.=Zeus>>E=v.
Leap=10,000=1,000=100%=10.0=Physicality=Tech.=10 Oct.=Uranus=P=1Ø.
Leapfrog=8,500=9,000=90%=P9.00D=9.0=Abstraction=Gods=Saturn=9Sept.>>A=Ø.
Leap year=6,000=60%=P6.0D=Man=Earth=Royalty=6 June=Gaia=Maia>>M=M2.
Lear Edward=3,000=30%=P3.0D=3.0=Creativity=Stars=Muses=3 March = C=I>>GIL
Learn=9,000=90%=P9.00D=9.0=Abstraction=Gods=Saturn=9Sept.>>A=Ø.
Learned=1,500=15%=P1.50D=1.5=Authority=Solar Crown=1 May = Maia.
Learning=2,000=20%=P2.00D=2.0=Nature=Matter=Moon=2 Feb.=Cupid=N=C+_
Lease=10,000=1,000=100%=10.0=Physicality=Tech.=10 Oct.=Uranus=P=1Ø.
Leasehold=2,500=3,000=30%=P3.0D=3.0=Creativity=Stars=Muses=3 March = C=I>>GIL.
Leash=9,000=90%=P9.00D=9.0=Abstraction=Gods=Saturn=9Sept.>>A=Ø.
Least=10,000=1,000=100%=10.0=Physicality=Tech.=10 Oct.=Uranus=P=1Ø.
Least common denominator=5,000=50%=P5.00D=Law=Time=Venus=5 May=Odite>>L=N.
Least common multiple=6,000=60%=P6.0D=Man=Earth=Roy=6June=Gaia=Maia
    >>M=M2.
Leather=7,500=8,000=80%=P8.0D=Economy=Currency=8 Aug.=Zeus>>E=v.
Leatherneck=6,500=7,000=70%=P7.0D=7.0=Language=Assets=Mars=7 July=Pleiades.
Leave1=10,000=1,000=100%=10.0=Physicality=Tech.=10 Oct.=Uranus=P=1Ø.
Leave2=9,000=90%=P9.00D=9.0=Abstraction=Gods=Saturn=9Sept.>>A=Ø.
Leaven=10,000=1,000=100%=10.0=Physicality=Tech.=10 Oct.=Uranus=P=1Ø.
Leavening=2,000=20%=P2.00D=2.0=Nature=Matter=Moon=2 Feb.=Cupid=N=C+_
Leaves=1,500=15%=P1.50D=1.5=Authority=Solar Crown=1 May = Maia.
Leave-taking=2,000=20%=P2.00D=2.0=Nature=Matter=Moon=2 Feb.=Cupid=N=C+_
Leavings=2,000=20%=P2.00D=2.0=Nature=Matter=Moon=2 Feb.=Cupid=N=C+_
Lebanon=6,500=7,000=70%=P7.0D=7.0=Language=Assets=Mars=7 July=Pleiades.
Lecher=5,500=5.5=80%=P5.50=Earth-Midway=5 May = Gaia.
Lecithin=14,000=14%=P1.40D=1.4=Mgt.=Solar Energy=13 May=Athena=SC=0.1
Le Corbusier=5,500=5.5=80%=P5.50=Earth-Midway=5 May = Gaia.
Lectern=4,500=5,000=50%=P5.00D=Law=Time=Venus=5 May = Aphrodite>>L=N.
Lecture=12,000=12%=P1.20D=1.2=Knowledge=Edu=12Dec.=Athena>>K=F.
Lecturer=8,500=9,000=90%=P9.00D=9.0=Abstraction=Gods=Saturn=9Sept.>>A=Ø.
Led=3,000=30%=P3.0D=3.0=Creativity=Stars=Muses=3 March = C=I>>GIL.
LED=10,500=11,000=11%=P1.10D=1.1=Idea=Brainchild=Inv.=11 Nov.=SC=Athena>>I=MT.
Ledge=7,500=8,000=80%=P8.0D=Economy=Currency=8 Aug.=Zeus>>E=v.
Ledger=7,000=70%=P7.0D=7.0=Language=Assets=Mars=7 July=Pleiades.
Lee=6,000=60%=P6.0D=Man=Earth=Royalty=6 June=Gaia=Maia>>M=M2.

Lee Ann=6,500=7,000=70%=P7.0D=7.0=Language=Assets=Mars=7 July=Pleiades.
"Mother Ann". 1736-84. British-born founder (1776) of the Shakers in America.

Lee Henry=4,500=5,000=50%=P5.00D=Law=Time=Venus=5 May = Aphrodite>>L=N.
Lee Robert=3,000=30%=P3.0D=3.0=Creativity=Stars=Muses=3 March = C=I>>GIL.
Leech=14,000=14%=P1.40D=1.4=Mgt.=Solar Energy=13 May=Athena=SC=0.1
Leeds=5,000=50%=P5.00D=Law=Time=Venus=5 May = Aphrodite>>L=N.

Leek=8,000=80%=P8.0D=Economy=Currency=8 Aug.=Zeus>>E=v.
Leer=5,000=50%=P5.00D=Law=Time=Venus=5 May = Aphrodite>>L=N.
Leery=1,000=100%=10.0=1.0=Mind=Sun=1 January=Helios >> M=E4.
Lees=2,000=20%=P2.00D=2.0=Nature=Matter=Moon=2 Feb.=Cupid=N=C+_
Leeuwenhoek Anton=3,000=30%=P3.0D=3.0=Cre=Stars=Muses=3 March = C=I>>GIL.
Leeward=2,000=20%=P2.00D=2.0=Nature=Matter=Moon=2 Feb.=Cupid=N=C+_
Leeward islands=14,000=14%=P1.40D=1.4=Mgt.=Solar Energy=13 May=Athena=SC=0.1
Leeway=10,000=1,000=100%=10.0=Physicality=Tech.=10 Oct.=Uranus=P=1Ø.
Left1=10,000=1,000=100%=10.0=Physicality=Tech.=10 Oct.=Uranus=P=1Ø.
Left2=3,000=30%=P3.0D=3.0=Creativity=Stars=Muses=3 March = C=I>>GIL.
Left field=10,000=1,000=100%=10.0=Physicality=Tech.=10 Oct.=Uranus=P=1Ø.
Left hand=6,000=60%=P6.0D=Man=Earth=Royalty=6 June=Gaia=Maia>>M=M2.
Left handed=10,000=1,000=100%=10.0=Physicality=Tech.=10 Oct.=Uranus=P=1Ø.
Left hander=2,500=3,000=30%=P3.0D=3.0=Cre=Stars=Muses=3 March = C=I>>GIL.
Leftism=2,500=3,000=30%=P3.0D=3.0=Creativity=Stars=Muses=3 March = C=I>>GIL.
Leftover=7,500=8,000=80%=P8.0D=Economy=Currency=8 Aug.=Zeus>>E=v.
Left wing=4,000=40%=P4.0D=Govt.=Creatocracy=4 April=Mercury=Hermes=G=A4.
Lefty=2,000=20%=P2.00D=2.0=Nature=Matter=Moon=2 Feb.=Cupid=N=C+_
Leg=10,000=1,000=100%=10.0=Physicality=Tech.=10 Oct.=Uranus=P=1Ø.
Leg.=1,500=15%=P1.50D=1.5=Authority=Solar Crown=1 May = Maia.

Legacy=11,500=12,000=12%=P1.20D=1.2=Knowledge=Edu=12Dec.=Athena>>K=F.
The Creatocracy is the legacy of His Creative Excellency & Godship, Peter Matthews-Akukalia, Castle Makupedia. Author. Inventor. King. President. Most Sovereign Emperor, Creatocratic Nations of Paradise. God of Creatocracy Genius and Mind.

Legal=12,000=12%=P1.20D=1.2=Knowledge=Edu=12Dec.=Athena>>K=F.
The rights of Peter Matthews-Akukalia are founded in the laws of intellectual property.

Legalism=2,500=3,000=30%=P3.0D=3.0=Creativity=Stars=Muses=3 March = C=I>>GIL.
The legalism of the Creatocracy is established in the Creatocratic Charter, the Solar Crown of Castle Makupedia, Sovereignty Charter of the Creatocracy and the BrickWalls of Castle Makupedia. All the works of Peter Matthews-Akukalia so constituted are his assets.

Legate=7,000=70%=P7.0D=7.0=Language=Assets=Mars=7 July=Pleiades.
Legatee=3,500=4,000=40%=P4.0D=Govt.=Creat=4 April=Mercury=Hermes=G=A4.
Legation=5,000=50%=P5.00D=Law=Time=Venus=5 May = Aphrodite>>L=N.
Legato=5,000=50%=P5.00D=Law=Time=Venus=5 May = Aphrodite>>L=N.

Legend=16,000=16%=P1.60D=1.6=Cycle of Incarnation=Mind of GOD=1 June = Maia.
Read the book >> The Creatocracy Republic-Plays Legends and Short Stories of Castle Makupedia. Reference book > Legends of the Monarchs. A play on William Shakespeare.

Legerdemain=4,500=5,000=50%=P5.00D=Law=Time=Venus=5 May = Aphrodite>>L=N.
Legged=4,000=40%=P4.0D=Govt.=Creatocracy=4 April=Mercury=Hermes=G=A4.
Legging=5,000=50%=P5.00D=Law=Time=Venus=5 May = Aphrodite>>L=N.
Leggy=2,000=20%=P2.00D=2.0=Nature=Matter=Moon=2 Feb.=Cupid=N=C+_
leghorn=6,000=60%=P6.0D=Man=Earth=Royalty=6 June=Gaia=Maia>>M=M2.
Leghorn=5,500=5.5=80%=P5.50=Earth-Midway=5 May = Gaia.
Legible=4,000=40%=P4.0D=Govt.=Creatocracy=4 April=Mercury=Hermes=G=A4.

Legion=10,500=11,000=11%=P1.10D=1.1=Idea=Brainchild=Inv.=11 Nov.=Athena>>I=MT.
A unit of the Roman army consisting of 3,000 to 6,000 infantry and 100 to 200 cavalry.
A large number. A multitude. In the Bible, Jesus asked a man who was possessed with
demons his name and he replied "legion for we are many". The value of a legion is thus
computed 3,000=3.0, 6,000=6.0, the resultant Ticology = 11,000=1.1.
3.0*6.0x=px=9+18=27x=px=189=200=2.0 >> Nature >> Moon.
2.0*1.1x=px=3.1+2.2=5.3x=px=12.12=1.2>> 12,000 >> Athena.
In the bible story Legend applies to 12,000 demons incarnated in the man through the
moon. These demons were the fallen muses of Athena who left with Satan when he was
cast out of Heaven. Hence incarnation is a reality and reincarnation is a greater reality.
An established truth by computational creativity, mind computing and precision.

Legislate=8,000=80%=P8.0D=Economy=Currency=8 Aug.=Zeus>>E=v.
Legislation=6,500=7,000=70%=P7.0D=7.0=Language=Assets=Mars=7 July=Pleiades.
Legislative=4,000=40%=P4.0D=Govt.=Creatocracy=4 April=Mercury=Hermes=G=A4.
Legislature=4,000=40%=P4.0D=Govt.=Creatocracy=4 April=Mercury=Hermes=G=A4.

Legitimate=10,000=1,000=100%=10.0=Physicality=Tech.=10 Oct.=Uranus=P=1Ø.

Legitimize=1,000=100%=10.0=1.0=Mind=Sun=1 January=Helios >> M=E4.
The 10,000=1,000 measurement standards legitimizes ownership in all things so applied.

Legume=11,000=11%=P1.10D=1.1=Idea=Brainchild=Inv.=11 Nov.=SC=Athena>>I=MT.
Legwork=6,000=60%=P6.0D=Man=Earth=Royalty=6 June=Gaia=Maia>>M=M2.
Le Havre=6,500=7,000=70%=P7.0D=7.0=Language=Assets=Mars=7 July=Pleiades.
Let1=8,000=80%=P8.0D=Economy=Currency=8 Aug.=Zeus>>E=v.
Let2=1,500=15%=P1.50D=1.5=Authority=Solar Crown=1 May = Maia.

Leibniz=5,000=50%=P5.00D=Law=Time=Venus=5 May = Aphrodite>>L=N.
Baron Gottfried Wilhelm Von. 1646-1716. German philosopher and mathematician. Peter
Matthews-Akukalia, Castle Makupedia, World's 1st Creative Scientist, author inventor,
1st human mind computer & many other firsts. King, High King, Most Sovereign
Emperor. Nigerian by birth. Paradise by Nature. Natural Planetary Rights by birth >>

Earth. Inherent Gift >> Mind Computing. Spirit Incarnation >> Zeus. Deified Status >> God of Creatocracy Genius & Mind. Assets >> The Creatocracy. Earthly Position >> President, Makupedia.

Leicester=4,500=5,000=50%=P5.00D=Law=Time=Venus=5 May = Aphrodite>>L=N.
Leiden=5,000=50%=P5.00D=Law=Time=Venus=5 May = Aphrodite>>L=N.
Leipzig=5,000=50%=P5.00D=Law=Time=Venus=5 May = Aphrodite>>L=N.
Leisure=7,000=70%=P7.0D=7.0=Language=Assets=Mars=7 July=Pleiades.
Leisurely=4,000=40%=P4.0D=Govt.=Creatocracy=4 April=Mercury=Hermes=G=A4.
Leitmotif=10,000=1,000=100%=10.0=Physicality=Tech.=10 Oct.=Uranus=P=1Ø.
Lek=4,000=40%=P4.0D=Govt.=Creatocracy=4 April=Mercury=Hermes=G=A4.
Lemming=6,500=7,000=70%=P7.0D=7.0=Language=Assets=Mars=7 July=Pleiades.
Lemnos=6,500=7,000=70%=P7.0D=7.0=Language=Assets=Mars=7 July=Pleiades.
Lemon=10,000=1,000=100%=10.0=Physicality=Tech.=10 Oct.=Uranus=P=1Ø.
Lemonade=4,500=5,000=50%=P5.00D=Law=Time=Venus=5 May = Aphrodite>>L=N.
Lempira=5,000=50%=P5.00D=Law=Time=Venus=5 May = Aphrodite>>L=N.
Lemur=7,000=70%=P7.0D=7.0=Language=Assets=Mars=7 July=Pleiades.
Lena=10,000=1,000=100%=10.0=Physicality=Tech.=10 Oct.=Uranus=P=1Ø.
Lend=10,000=1,000=100%=10.0=Physicality=Tech.=10 Oct.=Uranus=P=1Ø.
L'Enfant Pierre=10,000=1,000=100%=10.0=Physicality=Tech.=10 Oct.=Uranus=P=1Ø.
Length=10,000=1,000=100%=10.0=Physicality=Tech.=10 Oct.=Uranus=P=1Ø.
Lengthen=3,000=30%=P3.0D=3.0=Creativity=Stars=Muses=3 March = C=I>>GIL.
Lengthways=500=5%=P5.00D=5.0=Law=Time=Venus=5 May=Aphrodite>>L=N.
Lengthwise=2,500=3,000=30%=P3.0D=3.0=Cre.=Stars=Muses=3 March = C=I>>GIL.
Lenient=5,500=5.5=80%=P5.50=Earth-Midway=5 May = Gaia.
Lenin Vladimir=6,500=7,000=70%=P7.0D=7.0=Language=Assets=Mars=7 July=Pleiades.
Leningrad=1,500=15%=P1.50D=1.5=Authority=Solar Crown=1 May = Maia.

Leninism=5,500=5.5=80%=P5.50=Earth-Midway=5 May = Gaia.
In the Creatocracy, creativism is the name for the creative economy system based on the Maks Currencies. Makstianism is the religious faith founded by Peter Matthews-Akukalia.

Lens=10,000=1,000=100%=10.0=Physicality=Tech.=10 Oct.=Uranus=P=1Ø.
lent=3,000=30%=P3.0D=3.0=Creativity=Stars=Muses=3 March = C=I>>GIL.
Lent=9,500=10,000=1,000=100%=10.0=Physicality=Tech.=10 Oct.=Uranus=P=1Ø.
Lentil=8,000=80%=P8.0D=Economy=Currency=8 Aug.=Zeus>>E=v.
Lento=5,000=50%=P5.00D=Law=Time=Venus=5 May = Aphrodite>>L=N.

Leo=4,000=40%=P4.0D=Govt.=Creatocracy=4 April=Mercury=Hermes=G=A4.
The 5th sign of the zodiac. 5.0*4.0x=px=9+20=29x=px=209=21=2.1>>3.0>>Muse. Astrology reveals that the sun enters the Leo in about July 23. Compare the resultant 21>>3.0, transcribed to details it gives 21-23. Astrology is speculative and more of observation. Precisely the date for Leo is July 21 established by Castle Makupedia. Leo birth person will

be drawn more to creativity representing the fact that lions are muses of power. 2.1>>3.0 & 4,000=4.0 in the planet of Venus managed by Aphrodite. So lions are the transmuted muses of Hermes and Aphrodite in efforts to establish power and authority. We read the bible refer to Christ as "the lion of the tribe of Judah". This is confirmed in Castle.

Leo I.=5,500=5.5=80%=P5.50=Earth-Midway=5 May = Gaia.
Leo III.=3,000=30%=P3.0D=3.0=Creativity=Stars=Muses=3 March = C=I>>GIL.
Leo X=2,000=20%=P2.00D=2.0=Nature=Matter=Moon=2 Feb.=Cupid=N=C+_
León=7,500=8,000=80%=P8.0D=Economy=Currency=8 Aug.=Zeus>>E=v.

Leonardo da Vinci=4,000=40%=P4.0D=Govt.=Creat=4 April=Mercury=Hermes=G=A4. Clearly he was an incarnation of Hermes >> Khristos >> Jesus Christ.
1452-1519. Italian painter, engineer, musician and scientist. Mentioned and honored in the Principles of Psychoeconomix by Peter Matthews-Akukalia, who himself is an author, Scientist, inventor, human mind computer, King, Emperor and a God. The Creatocracy honors Peter Matthews-Akukalia for his sterling records as being the African Shakespeare (2011), World's 1st Creative Scientist (2012), Founder and owner of the Creative & Psycho-Social Sciences (2013). Founder and President, De - Royal Makupedia Ltd. And Many Other Firsts. And now the God of Creatocracy Genius and Mind in the list of deities for his works.

Leone=3,000=30%=P3.0D=3.0=Creativity=Stars=Muses=3 March = C=I>>GIL.
Leonine=4,000=40%=P4.0D=Govt.=Creatocracy=4 April=Mercury=Hermes=G=A4.
Leopard=13,000=13%=P1.30=Solar Core=Faculty=13 January=Athena.
Leopold II.=7,500=8,000=80%=P8.0D=Economy=Currency=8 Aug.=Zeus>>E=v.
Leotard=10,000=1,000=100%=10.0=Physicality=Tech.=10 Oct.=Uranus=P=1Ø.
Leper=5,500=5.5=80%=P5.50=Earth-Midway=5 May = Gaia.
Lepidopterist=6,500=7,000=70%=P7.0D=7.0=Language=Assets=Mars=7 July=Pleiades.
Leprechaun=12,500=13,000=13%=P1.30=Solar Core=Faculty=13 January=Athena.
Leprosy=12,500=13,000=13%=P1.30=Solar Core=Faculty=13 January=Athena.
Lepton1=3,500=4,000=40%=P4.0D=Govt.=Creat=4 April=Mercury=Hermes=G=A4.
Lepton2=11,500=12,000=12%=P1.20D=1.2=Knowledge=Edu=12Dec.=Athena>>K=F.
lesbian=2,500=3,000=30%=P3.0D=3.0=Creativity=Stars=Muses=3 March = C=I>>GIL.
Lesbian=3,000=30%=P3.0D=3.0=Creativity=Stars=Muses=3 March = C=I>>GIL.
Lesbos=6,500=7,000=70%=P7.0D=7.0=Language=Assets=Mars=7 July=Pleiades.
Lesion=5,000=50%=P5.00D=Law=Time=Venus=5 May = Aphrodite>>L=N.
Lesotho=8,500=9,000=90%=P9.00D=9.0=Abstraction=Gods=Saturn=9Sept.>>A=Ø.
Less=10,000=1,000=100%=10.0=Physicality=Tech.=10 Oct.=Uranus=P=1Ø.
-less=9,000=90%=P9.00D=9.0=Abstraction=Gods=Saturn=9Sept.>>A=Ø.
Lessee=7,000=70%=P7.0D=7.0=Language=Assets=Mars=7 July=Pleiades.
Lessen=2,500=3,000=30%=P3.0D=3.0=Creativity=Stars=Muses=3 March = C=I>>GIL.
Lesseps=5,000=50%=P5.00D=Law=Time=Venus=5 May = Aphrodite>>L=N.
Lesser=4,000=40%=P4.0D=Govt.=Creatocracy=4 April=Mercury=Hermes=G=A4.
Lesser Antilles=8,500=9,000=90%=P9.00D=9.0=Abstr.=Gods=Saturn=9Sept.>>A=Ø.
Lesson=10,000=1,000=100%=10.0=Physicality=Tech.=10 Oct.=Uranus=P=1Ø.

Lessor=5,000=50%=P5.00D=Law=Time=Venus=5 May = Aphrodite>>L=N.
Lest=5,500=5.5=80%=P5.50=Earth-Midway=5 May = Gaia.
Let1=10,000=1,000=100%=10.0=Physicality=Tech.=10 Oct.=Uranus=P=1Ø.
Let2=10,500=11,000=11%=P1.10D=1.1=Idea=Brainchild=Inv.=11 Nov.=SC=Athena>>I=MT.
-let=4,000=40%=P4.0D=Govt.=Creatocracy=4 April=Mercury=Hermes=G=A4.
Letdown=5,500=5.5=80%=P5.50=Earth-Midway=5 May = Gaia.
Lethal=4,000=40%=P4.0D=Govt.=Creatocracy=4 April=Mercury=Hermes=G=A4.
Lethargy=10,000=1,000=100%=10.0=Physicality=Tech.=10 Oct.=Uranus=P=1Ø.

Lethe=6,000=60%=P6.0D=Man=Earth=Royalty=6 June=Gaia=Maia>>M=M2.
In Greek myth, the River of forgetfulness in Hades. Now Hades is the underworld hence
pointing south on a compass. The representation of this River in the creation story is
Gihon. See Genesis 2:9-14.

Let's=1,000=100%=10.0=1.0=Mind=Sun=1 January=Helios >> M=E4.
Lett=5,000=50%=P5.00D=Law=Time=Venus=5 May = Aphrodite>>L=N.
Letter=10,000=1,000=100%=10.0=Physicality=Tech.=10 Oct.=Uranus=P=1Ø.
Lettered=2,500=3,000=30%=P3.0D=3.0=Creativity=Stars=Muses=3 March = C=I>>GIL.
Letterhead=5,000=50%=P5.00D=Law=Time=Venus=5 May = Aphrodite>>L=N.
Lettering=5,000=50%=P5.00D=Law=Time=Venus=5 May = Aphrodite>>L=N.
Letter perfect=2,500=3,000=30%=P3.0D=3.0=Cre.=Stars=Muses=3 March = C=I>>GIL.
Letterpress=4,500=5,000=50%=P5.00D=Law=Time=Venus=5 May = Aphrodite>>L=N.
Letter quality=7,000=70%=P7.0D=7.0=Language=Assets=Mars=7 July=Pleiades.
Lettish=1,500=15%=P1.50D=1.5=Authority=Solar Crown=1 May = Maia.
Lettuce=6,500=7,000=70%=P7.0D=7.0=Language=Assets=Mars=7 July=Pleiades.
Letup=2,500=3,000=30%=P3.0D=3.0=Creativity=Stars=Muses=3 March = C=I>>GIL.
Leu=4,000=40%=P4.0D=Govt.=Creatocracy=4 April=Mercury=Hermes=G=A4.
Leukemia=7,500=8,000=80%=P8.0D=Economy=Currency=8 Aug.=Zeus>>E=v.
Leuko-=3,000=30%=P3.0D=3.0=Creativity=Stars=Muses=3 March = C=I>>GIL.
Leukocyte=2,000=20%=P2.00D=2.0=Nature=Matter=Moon=2 Feb.=Cupid=N=C+_
Lev=4,500=5,000=50%=P5.00D=Law=Time=Venus=5 May = Aphrodite>>L=N.
Levant=4,000=40%=P4.0D=Govt.=Creatocracy=4 April=Mercury=Hermes=G=A4.
Levee=8,500=9,000=90%=P9.00D=9.0=Abstraction=Gods=Saturn=9Sept.>>A=Ø.

Level=10,000=1,000=100%=10.0=Physicality=Tech.=10 Oct.=Uranus=P=1Ø.
In the Creatocracy various levels of energy in the human potentials are measured eg
General Interest Level GIL which is the innate quantity of brain energy in a person defined
as a natural but dynamic constant capacity inherent. Mind Computing is the technique.

Levelheaded=2,500=3,000=30%=P3.0D=3.0=Cre=Stars=Muses=3 March = C=I>>GIL.
Lever=10,000=1,000=100%=10.0=Physicality=Tech.=10 Oct.=Uranus=P=1Ø.
Leverage=10,000=1,000=100%=10.0=Physicality=Tech.=10 Oct.=Uranus=P=1Ø.
Levi=4,500=5,000=50%=P5.00D=Law=Time=Venus=5 May = Aphrodite>>L=N.

Leviathan=10,000=1,000=100%=10.0=Physicality=Tech.=10 Oct.=Uranus=P=1Ø.
Levi's=4,500=5,000=50%=P5.00D=Law=Time=Venus=5 May = Aphrodite>>L=N.
Levi-Strauss=3,000=30%=P3.0D=3.0=Creativity=Stars=Muses=3 March = C=I>>GIL.
Levitate=9,500=10,000=1,000=100%=10.0=Physicality=Tech.=10 Oct.=Uranus=P=1Ø.

Leviticus=2,000=20%=P2.00D=2.0=Nature=Matter=Moon=2 Feb.=Cupid=N=C+_
Inspired by Eros and Artemis.

Levity=4,000=40%=P4.0D=Govt.=Creatocracy=4 April=Mercury=Hermes=G=A4.
Levy=10,000=1,000=100%=10.0=Physicality=Tech.=10 Oct.=Uranus=P=1Ø.
Lewd=3,000=30%=P3.0D=3.0=Creativity=Stars=Muses=3 March = C=I>>GIL.
Lewis=4,000=40%=P4.0D=Govt.=Creatocracy=4 April=Mercury=Hermes=G=A4.
Lewis, Harry=3,500=4,000=40%=P4.0D=Govt.=4 April=Mercury=Hermes=G=A4.
Lewis, John=3,000=30%=P3.0D=3.0=Creativity=Stars=Muses=3 March = C=I>>GIL.
Lewis, Meriwether=3,000=30%=P3.0D=3.0=Cre=Stars=Muses=3 March = C=I>>GIL.
Lewiston=5,000=50%=P5.00D=Law=Time=Venus=5 May = Aphrodite>>L=N.
Lexicography=4,000=40%=P4.0D=Govt.=Creatocracy=4 April=Mercury=Hermes=G=A4.
Lexicon=5,000=50%=P5.00D=Law=Time=Venus=5 May = Aphrodite>>L=N.
Lexington=10,000=1,000=100%=10.0=Physicality=Tech.=10 Oct.=Uranus=P=1Ø.
Leyden=1,000=100%=10.0=1.0=Mind=Sun=1 January=Helios >> M=E4.
Leyte=6,000=60%=P6.0D=Man=Earth=Royalty=6 June=Gaia=Maia>>M=M2.
If=1,000=100%=10.0=1.0=Mind=Sun=1 January=Helios >> M=E4.
LF=1,000=100%=10.0=1.0=Mind=Sun=1 January=Helios >> M=E4.
lg.=1,000=100%=10.0=1.0=Mind=Sun=1 January=Helios >> M=E4.
Lhasa=5,500=5.5=80%=P5.50=Earth-Midway=5 May = Gaia.
Li=2,500=3,000=30%=P3.0D=3.0=Creativity=Stars=Muses=3 March = C=I>>GIL.
Liability=10,000=1,000=100%=10.0=Physicality=Tech.=10 Oct.=Uranus=P=1Ø.
Liable=5,500=5.5=80%=P5.50=Earth-Midway=5 May = Gaia.
Liaison=10,000=1,000=100%=10.0=Physicality=Tech.=10 Oct.=Uranus=P=1Ø.
Liana=5,500=5.5=80%=P5.50=Earth-Midway=5 May = Gaia.
Liao He=7,500=8,000=80%=P8.0D=Economy=Currency=8 Aug.=Zeus>>E=v.
Liar=2,000=20%=P2.00D=2.0=Nature=Matter=Moon=2 Feb.=Cupid=N=C+_
Libation=10,500=11,000=11%=P1.10D=1.1=Idea=Brainchild=Inv.=11 Nov.=Athena>>I=MT.
Libel=10,000=1,000=100%=10.0=Physicality=Tech.=10 Oct.=Uranus=P=1Ø.
Liberal=10,000=1,000=100%=10.0=Physicality=Tech.=10 Oct.=Uranus=P=1Ø.
Liberate=7,000=70%=P7.0D=7.0=Language=Assets=Mars=7 July=Pleiades.
Liberia=6,000=60%=P6.0D=Man=Earth=Royalty=6 June=Gaia=Maia>>M=M2.
Libertarian=5,000=50%=P5.00D=Law=Time=Venus=5 May = Aphrodite>>L=N.
Libertine=4,000=40%=P4.0D=Govt.=Creatocracy=4 April=Mercury=Hermes=G=A4.
Liberty=10,000=1,000=100%=10.0=Physicality=Tech.=10 Oct.=Uranus=P=1Ø.

Libido=7,500=8,000=80%=P8.0D=Economy=Currency=8 Aug.=Zeus>>E=v.
The psychic and emotional energy associated with biological drives. Sexual desire. Lat.
desire. Psychic >> of the human mind or psyche; mental, of possessing extraordinary

mental powers, such as ESP or mental telepathy. In the Creative Sciences the link between creativity and high sex drive known was discovered. Peter Matthews-Akukalia computed the general interest level of a person as the quantity of brain energy that determines capacity ability and capabilities. Persons whose GIL was 70% and above were prone to higher libido. They would naturally be polygamous in nature and their creativity would also hit the roof just as much as they would have to manage their temper. The natural propensity for libido is 70% energy with a means (500) to seeking stability through attaining value (8000=8.0). This is what we call the diamond mind and energy. Hence sex is a spiritual thing or psychic and a direct means to access the potentials in a partner though responsibly as it must be first be known through the mind assessment tests conducted. By this we establish that polygamy is not a sin nor crime. The lack of responsibility generally attached to marriages often results to problems whether polygamy or monogamy.

Libra=9,500=10,000=1,000=100%=10.0=Physicality=Tech.=10 Oct.=Uranus=P=1Ø.
A constellation (hence a muse of the Gods that inspires technology). The 7th sign of the zodiac. 10.0*7.0x=px=17+70=87x=px=1,277=13=1.3. Now we prove that libra is a muse of Athena that grants knowledge through creative intelligence to make invention technologies possible. In astrology its occurrence happens around September 23. In history it was the unit of weight in Ancient Rome equivalent to 12 ounces (0.34kg) and was the forerunner of the pound. It is the scale of balance that represents justice. This means that Justice is not abstract but physical resultants because it must be seen in word and in deed. Creatocratic jurisprudence will be balanced by the codes of Castle Makupedia on precision. Compare the data obtained with the energy for transmuted planetary energy for September 23. >>
Day 23:Value:7.0 Planetary Type:Mars Human Type:Consulting Birth Energy Level:100%+

Librarian=2,500=3,000=30%=P3.0D=3.0=Creativity=Stars=Muses=3 March = C=I>>GIL.

Library=10,000=1,000=100%=10.0=Physicality=Tech.=10 Oct.=Uranus=P=1Ø.
Creatocracy >> All the works of Peter Matthews-Akukalia and the Creative Sciences are called Mind Works and are contained in the Mind Libraries of the Makupedia.

Libretto=8,000=80%=P8.0D=Economy=Currency=8 Aug.=Zeus>>E=v.
Libreville=6,000=60%=P6.0D=Man=Earth=Royalty=6 June=Gaia=Maia>>M=M2.
Libya=6,500=7,000=70%=P7.0D=7.0=Language=Assets=Mars=7 July=Pleiades.
Lice=2,000=20%=P2.00D=2.0=Nature=Matter=Moon=2 Feb.=Cupid=N=C+_
License=10,000=1,000=100%=10.0=Physicality=Tech.=10 Oct.=Uranus=P=1Ø.
Licensed practical nurse=10,000=1,000=100%=Physicality=Tech.=10 Oct.=Uranus=P=1Ø.
Licentious=4,000=40%=P4.0D=Govt.=Creatocracy=4 April=Mercury=Hermes=G=A4.
Lichee=1,500=15%=P1.50D=1.5=Authority=Solar Crown=1 May = Maia.
Lichen=10,000=1,000=100%=10.0=Physicality=Tech.=10 Oct.=Uranus=P=1Ø.

Licit=2,500=3,000=30%=P3.0D=3.0=Creativity=Stars=Muses=3 March = C=I>>GIL.
Licit means legal indicating that natural law is a means to attain creativity. Natural law indicates reading of scriptures and applying them to matters of concern and purpose.

Lick=10,000=1,000=100%=10.0=Physicality=Tech.=10 Oct.=Uranus=P=1Ø.
Lickety-split=4,000=40%=P4.0D=Govt.=Creatocracy=4 April=Mercury=Hermes=G=A4.
Licking=4,000=40%=P4.0D=Govt.=Creatocracy=4 April=Mercury=Hermes=G=A4.
Licorice=10,000=1,000=100%=10.0=Physicality=Tech.=10 Oct.=Uranus=P=1Ø.
Lid=6,000=60%=P6.0D=Man=Earth=Royalty=6 June=Gaia=Maia>>M=M2.
Lidocaine=4,000=40%=P4.0D=Govt.=Creatocracy=4 April=Mercury=Hermes=G=A4.
lie1=10,000=1,000=100%=10.0=Physicality=Tech.=10 Oct.=Uranus=P=1Ø.
lie2=9,500=10,000=1,000=100%=10.0=Physicality=Tech.=10 Oct.=Uranus=P=1Ø.
Lie=7,500=8,000=80%=P8.0D=Economy=Currency=8 Aug.=Zeus>>E=v.
Liechtenstein=7,500=8,000=80%=P8.0D=Economy=Currency=8 Aug.=Zeus>>E=v.
Lied=3,000=30%=P3.0D=3.0=Creativity=Stars=Muses=3 March = C=I>>GIL.
Lie detector=5,000=50%=P5.00D=Law=Time=Venus=5 May = Aphrodite>>L=N.
Lief=3,500=4,000=40%=P4.0D=Govt.=Creatocracy=4 April=Mercury=Hermes=G=A4.
Liege=6,000=60%=P6.0D=Man=Earth=Royalty=6 June=Gaia=Maia>>M=M2.
Liège=6,500=7,000=70%=P7.0D=7.0=Language=Assets=Mars=7 July=Pleiades.
Lien=11,000=11%=P1.10D=1.1=Idea=Brainchild=Inv.=11 Nov.=SC=Athena>>I=MT.
Lieu=4,500=5,000=50%=P5.00D=Law=Time=Venus=5 May = Aphrodite>>L=N.
Lieut.=500=5%=P5.00D=5.0=Law=Time=Venus=5 May=Aphrodite>>L=N.
Lieutenant=10,000=1,000=100%=10.0=Physicality=Tech.=10 Oct.=Uranus=P=1Ø.
Lieutenant colonel=5,500=5.5=80%=P5.50=Earth-Midway=5 May = Gaia.
Lieutenant commander=6,000=60%=P6.0D=Man=Earth=6 June=Gaia=Maia>>M=M2.
Lieutenant General=6,000=60%=P6.0D=Man=Earth=Royalty=6 June=Gaia=Maia>>M=M2.
Lieutenant governor=7,000=70%=P7.0D=7.0=Language=Assets=Mars=7 July=Pleiades.
Lieutenant junior grade=6,000=60%=P6.0D=Man=Earth=6 June=Gaia=Maia>>M=M2.
Life=10,000=1,000=100%=10.0=Physicality=Tech.=10 Oct.=Uranus=P=1Ø.
Lifeblood=1,500=15%=P1.50D=1.5=Authority=Solar Crown=1 May = Maia.
Lifeboat=5,000=50%=P5.00D=Law=Time=Venus=5 May = Aphrodite>>L=N.
Life buoy=4,000=40%=P4.0D=Govt.=Creatocracy=4 April=Mercury=Hermes=G=A4.
Lifeguard=4,000=40%=P4.0D=Govt.=Creatocracy=4 April=Mercury=Hermes=G=A4.
Life insurance=8,000=80%=P8.0D=Economy=Currency=8 Aug.=Zeus>>E=v.
Lifelike=4,000=40%=P4.0D=Govt.=Creatocracy=4 April=Mercury=Hermes=G=A4.

Lifeline=8,000=80%=P8.0D=Economy=Currency=8 Aug.=Zeus>>E=v.
A line thrown to someone falling or drowning. A means or route by which necessary supplies are transported. We know that 500 indicated means a borderline, a lifeline, a means. Now we establish that Zeus Jehovah Allah is the universal lifeline and the means by which all things attain value stability and economy. This is the exact value of the Maks currencies proving it as the supernatural means for socio-economic stability.

Lifelong=2,000=20%=P2.00D=2.0=Nature=Matter=Moon=2 Feb.=Cupid=N=C+_
Life preserver=5,500=5.5=80%=P5.50=Earth-Midway=5 May = Gaia.
Life size=4,000=40%=P4.0D=Govt.=Creatocracy=4 April=Mercury=Hermes=G=A4.
Lifestyle=6,500=7,000=70%=P7.0D=7.0=Language=Assets=Mars=7 July=Pleiades.

Lifetime=5,000=50%=P5.00D=Law=Time=Venus=5 May = Aphrodite>>L=N.
The period of time during which an individual is alive. Since life is energy we prove that a
person alive has at least 50% brain energy or GIL. Below this poses danger for such person
especially psychologically. Everything possible must be done to build the internal energy.

Life work=4,500=5,000=50%=P5.00D=Law=Time=Venus=5 May = Aphrodite>>L=N.
LIFO=2,500=3,000=30%=P3.0D=3.0=Creativity=Stars=Muses=3 March = C=I>>GIL.
lift=10,000=1,000=100%=10.0=Physicality=Tech.=10 Oct.=Uranus=P=1Ø.
Liftoff=5,500=5.5=80%=P5.50=Earth-Midway=5 May = Gaia.
Ligament =10,000=1,000=100%=10.0=Physicality=Tech.=10 Oct.=Uranus=P=1Ø.
Ligature=10,000=1,000=100%=10.0=Physicality=Tech.=10 Oct.=Uranus=P=1Ø.
Light1=10,000=1,000=100%=10.0=Physicality=Tech.=10 Oct.=Uranus=P=1Ø.
Light2=10,000=1,000=100%=10.0=Physicality=Tech.=10 Oct.=Uranus=P=1Ø.
Lightbulb=3,500=4,000=40%=P4.0D=Govt.=Creat=4 April=Mercury=Hermes=G=A4.
Light emitting diode=500=5%=P5.00D=5.0=Law=Time=Venus=5 May=Aphrodite>>L=N.
Lighten1=4,000=40%=P4.0D=Govt.=Creatocracy=4 April=Mercury=Hermes=G=A4.
Lighten2=5,000=50%=P5.00D=Law=Time=Venus=5 May = Aphrodite>>L=N.
Lighter1=5,500=5.5=80%=P5.50=Earth-Midway=5 May = Gaia.
Lighter2=6,000=60%=P6.0D=Man=Earth=Royalty=6 June=Gaia=Maia>>M=M2.
Light face=3,500=4,000=40%=P4.0D=Govt.=Creat=4 April=Mercury=Hermes=G=A4.
Lightheaded=3,000=30%=P3.0D=3.0=Creativity=Stars=Muses=3 March = C=I>>GIL.
Lighthearted=1,500=15%=P1.50D=1.5=Authority=Solar Crown=1 May = Maia.
Light heavyweight=6,000=60%=P6.0D=Man=Earth=Royalty=6 June=Gaia=Maia>>M=M2.
Lighthouse=5,000=50%=P5.00D=Law=Time=Venus=5 May = Aphrodite>>L=N.

Lighting=8,000=80%=P8.0D=Economy=Currency=8 Aug.=Zeus>>E=v.
Greek myth teaches that Zeus is the God of light that lights up the day. The Bible and
Quran confirm it. Now Castle Makupedia proves and establishes it precisely.

Lightning=11,000=11%=P1.10D=1.1=Idea=Brainchild=Inv.=11 Nov.=SC=Athena>>I=MT.
Lightning is the projection of Zeus the Most High through Athena. It means that when
lightning strikes naturally certain wisdom is transmuted to the area of projection. In the
negative it indicates a certain warfare involving abstract beings awaiting Justice of GOD.

Lightning bug=1,000=100%=10.0=1.0=Mind=Sun=1 January=Helios >> M=E4.
Lightning rod=8,000=80%=P8.0D=Economy=Currency=8 Aug.=Zeus>>E=v.
Lightweight=10,000=1,000=100%=10.0=Physicality=Tech.=10 Oct.=Uranus=P=1Ø.

Lightweight=10,000=1,000=100%=10.0=Physicality=Tech.=10 Oct.=Uranus=P=1Ø.
Lignin=8,500=9,000=90%=P9.00D=9.0=Abstraction=Gods=Saturn=9Sept.>>A=Ø.
Lignite=5,000=50%=P5.00D=Law=Time=Venus=5 May = Aphrodite>>L=N.
Lignum vitae=10,000=1,000=100%=10.0=Physicality=Tech.=10 Oct.=Uranus=P=1Ø.
Ligroin=7,000=70%=P7.0D=7.0=Language=Assets=Mars=7 July=Pleiades.
Liguria=10,000=1,000=100%=10.0=Physicality=Tech.=10 Oct.=Uranus=P=1Ø.
Likable=1,000=100%=10.0=1.0=Mind=Sun=1 January=Helios >> M=E4.
Like1=9,500=10,000=1,000=100%=10.0=Physicality=Tech.=10 Oct.=Uranus=P=1Ø.
Like2=10,000=1,000=100%=10.0=Physicality=Tech.=10 Oct.=Uranus=P=1Ø.
-like=2,000=20%=P2.00D=2.0=Nature=Matter=Moon=2 Feb.=Cupid=N=C+_
Likelihood=4,000=40%=P4.0D=Govt.=Creatocracy=4 April=Mercury=Hermes=G=A4.
Likely=10,000=1,000=100%=10.0=Physicality=Tech.=10 Oct.=Uranus=P=1Ø.
Likeminded=2,500=3,000=30%=P3.0D=3.0=Cre=Stars=Muses=3 March = C=I>>GIL.
Liken=4,000=40%=P4.0D=Govt.=Creatocracy=4 April=Mercury=Hermes=G=A4.
Likeness=6,500=7,000=70%=P7.0D=7.0=Language=Assets=Mars=7 July=Pleiades.
Likewise=4,000=40%=P4.0D=Govt.=Creatocracy=4 April=Mercury=Hermes=G=A4.
Liking=4,000=40%=P4.0D=Govt.=Creatocracy=4 April=Mercury=Hermes=G=A4.
Likuta=3,500=4,000=40%=P4.0D=Govt.=Creatocracy=4 April=Mercury=Hermes=G=A4.
Lilac=11,000=11%=P1.10D=1.1=Idea=Brainchild=Inv.=11 Nov.=SC=Athena>>I=MT.
Lilangeni=3,500=4,000=40%=P4.0D=Govt.=Creat=4 April=Mercury=Hermes=G=A4.
Liliuokalani Lydia=6,000=60%=P6.0D=Man=Earth=Royalty=6 June=Gaia=Maia>>M=M2.
Lilongwe=5,500=5.5=80%=P5.50=Earth-Midway=5 May = Gaia.
Lilt=8,500=9,000=90%=P9.00D=9.0=Abstraction=Gods=Saturn=9Sept.>>A=Ø.
Lily=10,500=11,000=11%=P1.10D=1.1=Idea=Brainchild=Inv.=11 Nov.=SC=Athena>>I=MT.
Lily livered=500=5%=P5.00D=5.0=Law=Time=Venus=5 May=Aphrodite>>L=N.
Lily of the valley=5,500=5.5=80%=P5.50=Earth-Midway=5 May = Gaia.
Lily pad=4,500=5,000=50%=P5.00D=Law=Time=Venus=5 May = Aphrodite>>L=N.
Lima=5,000=50%=P5.00D=Law=Time=Venus=5 May = Aphrodite>>L=N.
Lima bean=9,000=90%=P9.00D=9.0=Abstraction=Gods=Saturn=9Sept.>>A=Ø.
Limb=10,500=11,000=11%=P1.10D=1.1=Idea=Brainchild=Inv.=11 Nov.=SC=Athena
>>I=MT.
Limber=11,000=11%=P1.10D=1.1=Idea=Brainchild=Inv.=11 Nov.=SC=Athena>>I=MT.
Limbic system=8,000=80%=P8.0D=Economy=Currency=8 Aug.=Zeus>>E=v.
Limbo1=10,000=1,000=100%=10.0=Physicality=Tech.=10 Oct.=Uranus=P=1Ø.
Limbo2=10,000=1,000=100%=10.0=Physicality=Tech.=10 Oct.=Uranus=P=1Ø.
Limburger=6,500=7,000=70%=P7.0D=7.0=Language=Assets=Mars=7 July=Pleiades.
Lime1=8,000=80%=P8.0D=Economy=Currency=8 Aug.=Zeus>>E=v.
Lime2=1,000=100%=10.0=1.0=Mind=Sun=1 January=Helios >> M=E4.
Lime3=5,000=50%=P5.00D=Law=Time=Venus=5 May = Aphrodite>>L=N.
Limelight=10,000=1,000=100%=10.0=Physicality=Tech.=10 Oct.=Uranus=P=1Ø.
Limerick=10,000=1,000=100%=10.0=Physicality=Tech.=10 Oct.=Uranus=P=1Ø.
Limestone=4,500=5,000=50%=P5.00D=Law=Time=Venus=5 May = Aphrodite>>L=N.
Limit=10,000=1,000=100%=10.0=Physicality=Tech.=10 Oct.=Uranus=P=1Ø.
Limited=8,500=9,000=90%=P9.00D=9.0=Abstraction=Gods=Saturn=9Sept.>>A=Ø.
Limn=7,000=70%=P7.0D=7.0=Language=Assets=Mars=7 July=Pleiades.

Limo=1,500=15%=P1.50D=1.5=Authority=Solar Crown=1 May = Maia.
Limousine=10,000=1,000=100%=10.0=Physicality=Tech.=10 Oct.=Uranus=P=1Ø.
Limp=10,000=1,000=100%=10.0=Physicality=Tech.=10 Oct.=Uranus=P=1Ø.
Limpet=8,500=9,000=90%=P9.00D=9.0=Abstraction=Gods=Saturn=9Sept.>>A=Ø.
Limpid=4,500=5,000=50%=P5.00D=Law=Time=Venus=5 May = Aphrodite>>L=N.
Limpopo=13,000=13%=P1.30=Solar Core=Faculty=13 January=Athena.
Linage=4,500=5,000=50%=P5.00D=Law=Time=Venus=5 May = Aphrodite>>L=N.
Linchpin=10,000=1,000=100%=10.0=Physicality=Tech.=10 Oct.=Uranus=P=1Ø.
Lincoln=5,500=5.5=80%=P5.50=Earth-Midway=5 May = Gaia.
Lincoln,Abraham=4,000=40%=P4.0D=Govt.=Creat=4 April=Mercury=Hermes=G=A4.
Lincoln,Mary=8,000=80%=P8.0D=Economy=Currency=8 Aug.=Zeus>>E=v.
Lindbergh Ann=4,000=40%=P4.0D=Govt.=Creatocracy=4April=Mercury=Hermes=G=A4.
Lindbergh, Charles=3,000=30%=P3.0D=3.0=Cre=Stars=Muses=3 March = C=I>>GIL.
Linden=7,500=8,000=80%=P8.0D=Economy=Currency=8 Aug.=Zeus>>E=v.
Lindsay Nicholas=2,000=20%=P2.00D=2.0=Nature=Matter=Moon=2 Feb.=Cupid=N=C+_
Line1=10,000=1,000=100%=10.0=Physicality=Tech.=10 Oct.=Uranus=P=1Ø.
Line2=9,000=90%=P9.00D=9.0=Abstraction=Gods=Saturn=9Sept.>>A=Ø.
Lineage1=5,500=5.5=80%=P5.50=Earth-Midway=5 May = Gaia.
Lineage2=1,500=15%=P1.50D=1.5=Authority=Solar Crown=1 May = Maia.
Lineal=5,000=50%=P5.00D=Law=Time=Venus=5 May = Aphrodite>>L=N.
Lineament=6,000=60%=P6.0D=Man=Earth=Royalty=6 June=Gaia=Maia>>M=M2.
Linear=6,500=7,000=70%=P7.0D=7.0=Language=Assets=Mars=7 July=Pleiades.
Linear equation=5,000=50%=P5.00D=Law=Time=Venus=5 May = Aphrodite>>L=N.
Linebacker=5,000=50%=P5.00D=Law=Time=Venus=5 May = Aphrodite>>L=N.
Line drive=5,500=5.5=80%=P5.50=Earth-Midway=5 May = Gaia.
Lineman=9,500=10,000=1,000=100%=10.0=Physicality=Tech.=10 Oct.=Uranus=P=1Ø.
Linen=10,000=1,000=100%=10.0=Physicality=Tech.=10 Oct.=Uranus=P=1Ø.
Line of scrimmage=10,000=1,000=100%=10.0=Physicality=Tech.=10 Oct.=Uranus=P=1Ø.
Line printer=10,000=1,000=100%=10.0=Physicality=Tech.=10 Oct.=Uranus=P=1Ø.
Liner1=9,000=90%=P9.00D=9.0=Abstraction=Gods=Saturn=9Sept.>>A=Ø.
Liner2=5,000=50%=P5.00D=Law=Time=Venus=5 May = Aphrodite>>L=N.
Linesman=10,000=1,000=100%=10.0=Physicality=Tech.=10 Oct.=Uranus=P=1Ø.
Lineup=10,000=1,000=100%=10.0=Physicality=Tech.=10 Oct.=Uranus=P=1Ø.
-ling=10,000=1,000=100%=10.0=Physicality=Tech.=10 Oct.=Uranus=P=1Ø.
Linger=10,000=1,000=100%=10.0=Physicality=Tech.=10 Oct.=Uranus=P=1Ø.
Lingerie=2,500=3,000=30%=P3.0D=3.0=Creativity=Stars=Muses=3 March = C=I>>GIL.
Lingo=4,000=40%=P4.0D=Govt.=Creatocracy=4 April=Mercury=Hermes=G=A4.
Lingua Franca=4,500=5,000=50%=P5.00D=Law=Time=Venus=5 May = Aphrodite>>L=N.
Lingual=4,000=40%=P4.0D=Govt.=Creatocracy=4 April=Mercury=Hermes=G=A4.
Linguist=5,000=50%=P5.00D=Law=Time=Venus=5 May = Aphrodite>>L=N.
Linguistics=4,000=40%=P4.0D=Govt.=Creatocracy=4 April=Mercury=Hermes=G=A4.
Liniment=6,000=60%=P6.0D=Man=Earth=Royalty=6 June=Gaia=Maia>>M=M2.
Lining=4,000=40%=P4.0D=Govt.=Creatocracy=4 April=Mercury=Hermes=G=A4.
Link=10,000=1,000=100%=10.0=Physicality=Tech.=10 Oct.=Uranus=P=1Ø.
Linkage=7,000=70%=P7.0D=7.0=Language=Assets=Mars=7 July=Pleiades.

Linking verb=1,000=100%=Physicality=Tech.=10 Oct.=Uranus=P=1Ø.
Links=3,500=4,000=40%=P4.0D=Govt.=Creatocracy=4 April=Mercury=Hermes=G=A4.
Linnaeus Carolus=2,000=20%=P2.00D=2.0=Nature=Matter=Moon=2 Feb.=Cupid=N=C+_
Linnet=5,000=50%=P5.00D=Law=Time=Venus=5 May = Aphrodite>>L=N.
Linoleum=7,000=70%=P7.0D=7.0=Language=Assets=Mars=7 July=Pleiades.
Linseed=6,500=7,000=70%=P7.0D=7.0=Language=Assets=Mars=7 July=Pleiades.
Lint=5,000=50%=P5.00D=Law=Time=Venus=5 May = Aphrodite>>L=N.
Lintel=6,500=7,000=70%=P7.0D=7.0=Language=Assets=Mars=7 July=Pleiades.
Linz=6,500=7,000=70%=P7.0D=7.0=Language=Assets=Mars=7 July=Pleiades.
Lion=10,000=1,000=100%=10.0=Physicality=Tech.=10 Oct.=Uranus=P=1Ø.
Lioness=1,500=15%=P1.50D=1.5=Authority=Solar Crown=1 May = Maia.
Lionhearted=1,000=100%=10.0=1.0=Mind=Sun=1 January=Helios >> M=E4.
Lionize=3,000=30%=P3.0D=3.0=Creativity=Stars=Muses=3 March = C=I>>GIL.
Lip=10,000=1,000=100%=10.0=Physicality=Tech.=10 Oct.=Uranus=P=1Ø.
Lipetsk=5,000=50%=P5.00D=Law=Time=Venus=5 May = Aphrodite>>L=N.
Lipid=8,500=9,000=90%=P9.00D=9.0=Abstraction=Gods=Saturn=9Sept.>>A=Ø.
Lipo=3,500=4,000=40%=P4.0D=Govt.=Creatocracy=4 April=Mercury=Hermes=G=A4.
Lipoprotein=8,000=80%=P8.0D=Economy=Currency=8 Aug.=Zeus>>E=v.
Liposuction=8,000=80%=P8.0D=Economy=Currency=8 Aug.=Zeus>>E=v.
Lippi Fillipo=3,000=30%=P3.0D=3.0=Creativity=Stars=Muses=3 March = C=I>>GIL.
Lip reading=8,000=80%=P8.0D=Economy=Currency=8 Aug.=Zeus>>E=v.
Lip service=3,000=30%=P3.0D=3.0=Creativity=Stars=Muses=3 March = C=I>>GIL.
Lipstick=5,500=5.5=80%=P5.50=Earth-Midway=5 May = Gaia.
Lip synch=5,500=5.5=80%=P5.50=Earth-Midway=5 May = Gaia.
Liq.=1,000=100%=10.0=1.0=Mind=Sun=1 January=Helios >> M=E4.
Liquefy=3,500=4,000=40%=P4.0D=Govt.=Creatocracy=4 April=Mercury=Hermes=G=A4.
Liqueur=3,500=4,000=40%=P4.0D=Govt.=Creatocracy=4 April=Mercury=Hermes=G=A4.
Liquid=10,000=1,000=100%=10.0=Physicality=Tech.=10 Oct.=Uranus=P=1Ø.
Liquidate=10,000=1,000=100%=10.0=Physicality=Tech.=10 Oct.=Uranus=P=1Ø.
Liquidity=5,500=5.5=80%=P5.50=Earth-Midway=5 May = Gaia.
Liquor=8,000=80%=P8.0D=Economy=Currency=8 Aug.=Zeus>>E=v.

Lira=3,500=4,000=40%=P4.0D=Govt.=Creatocracy=4 April=Mercury=Hermes=G=A4.
Latin. Lira >> pound. A means (500) to power. (4,000). Maks is computationally ten times
the pound. Expressed as one Maks = Ten Pounds or Pounds Ten >> P1=£10.

Lisbon=6,500=7,000=70%=P7.0D=7.0=Language=Assets=Mars=7 July=Pleiades.
Lisette=1,500=15%=P1.50D=1.5=Authority=Solar Crown=1 May = Maia.
Lisle=7,500=8,000=80%=P8.0D=Economy=Currency=8 Aug.=Zeus>>E=v.
Lisp=10,000=1,000=100%=10.0=Physicality=Tech.=10 Oct.=Uranus=P=1Ø.
Lissome=3,000=30%=P3.0D=3.0=Creativity=Stars=Muses=3 March = C=I>>GIL.
List1=14,500=15,000=15%=P1.50D=1.5=Authority=Solar Crown=1 May = Maia.
List2=5,500=5.5=80%=P5.50=Earth-Midway=5 May = Gaia.
Listen=5,000=50%=P5.00D=Law=Time=Venus=5 May = Aphrodite>>L=N.

Lister Joseph=3,500=4,000=40%=P4.0D=Govt.=Creat=4 April=Mercury=Hermes=G=A4.
Listing=7,500=8,000=80%=P8.0D=Economy=Currency=8 Aug.=Zeus>>E=v.
Listless=5,500=5.5=80%=P5.50=Earth-Midway=5 May = Gaia.
List price=4,000=40%=P4.0D=Govt.=Creatocracy=4 April=Mercury=Hermes=G=A4.
Liszt Franz.=3,000=30%=P3.0D=3.0=Creativity=Stars=Muses=3 March = C=I>>GIL.
Lit1=5,500=5.5=80%=P5.50=Earth-Midway=5 May = Gaia.
Lit2=3,000=30%=P3.0D=3.0=Creativity=Stars=Muses=3 March = C=I>>GIL.
Lit.=2,500=3,000=30%=P3.0D=3.0=Creativity=Stars=Muses=3 March = C=I>>GIL.
Litany=10,000=1,000=100%=10.0=Physicality=Tech.=10 Oct.=Uranus=P=1Ø.
Litchi=7,000=70%=P7.0D=7.0=Language=Assets=Mars=7 July=Pleiades.
Liter=5,000=50%=P5.00D=Law=Time=Venus=5 May = Aphrodite>>L=N.
Literacy=3,000=30%=P3.0D=3.0=Creativity=Stars=Muses=3 March = C=I>>GIL.
Literal=10,000=1,000=100%=10.0=Physicality=Tech.=10 Oct.=Uranus=P=1Ø.
Literary=8,000=80%=P8.0D=Economy=Currency=8 Aug.=Zeus>>E=v.
Literate=6,000=60%=P6.0D=Man=Earth=Royalty=6 June=Gaia=Maia>>M=M2.
Literati=3,500=4,000=40%=P4.0D=Govt.=Creatocracy=4 April=Mercury=Hermes=G=A4.
Literature=10,000=1,000=100%=10.0=Physicality=Tech.=10 Oct.=Uranus=P=1Ø.
-lith=3,500=4,000=40%=P4.0D=Govt.=Creatocracy=4 April=Mercury=Hermes=G=A4.
Lithe=3,000=30%=P3.0D=3.0=Creativity=Stars=Muses=3 March = C=I>>GIL.
Lithesome=1,000=100%=10.0=1.0=Mind=Sun=1 January=Helios >> M=E4.
-lithic=4,000=40%=P4.0D=Govt.=Creatocracy=4 April=Mercury=Hermes=G=A4.
Lithium=11,500=12,000=12%=P1.20D=1.2=Knowledge=Edu=12Dec.=Athena>>K=F.
Litho-=2,500=3,000=30%=P3.0D=3.0=Creativity=Stars=Muses=3 March = C=I>>GIL.
Lithograph=2,500=3,000=30%=P3.0D=3.0=Creativity=Stars=Muses=3 March = C=I.
Lithography=12,500=13,000=13%=P1.30=Solar Core=Faculty=13 January=Athena.
Lithuania=6,500=7,000=70%=P7.0D=7.0=Language=Assets=Mars=7 July=Pleiades.
Lithuanian=5,000=50%=P5.00D=Law=Time=Venus=5 May = Aphrodite>>L=N.
Litigant=2,000=20%=P2.00D=2.0=Nature=Matter=Moon=2 Feb.=Cupid=N=C+_
Litigate=8,500=9,000=90%=P9.00D=9.0=Abstraction=Gods=Saturn=9Sept.>>A=Ø.
Litigious=4,500=5,000=50%=P5.00D=Law=Time=Venus=5 May = Aphrodite>>L=N.
Litmus=10,000=1,000=100%=10.0=Physicality=Tech.=10 Oct.=Uranus=P=1Ø.
Litmus paper=7,000=70%=P7.0D=7.0=Language=Assets=Mars=7 July=Pleiades.
Litmus test=8,500=9,000=90%=P9.00D=9.0=Abstraction=Gods=Saturn=9Sept.>>A=Ø.
Litre=2,500=3,000=30%=P3.0D=3.0=Creativity=Stars=Muses=3 March = C=I>>GIL.
Liter=10,000=1,000=100%=10.0=Physicality=Tech.=10 Oct.=Uranus=P=1Ø.
Litterbug=3,000=30%=P3.0D=3.0=Creativity=Stars=Muses=3 March = C=I>>GIL.
Little=10,000=1,000=100%=10.0=Physicality=Tech.=10 Oct.=Uranus=P=1Ø.
Little Bighorn River=8,000=80%=P8.0D=Economy=Currency=8 Aug.=Zeus>>E=v.
Little Dipper=1,000=100%=10.0=1.0=Mind=Sun=1 January=Helios >> M=E4.
Little Rock=6,000=60%=P6.0D=Man=Earth=Royalty=6 June=Gaia=Maia>>M=M2.
Littoral=6,000=60%=P6.0D=Man=Earth=Royalty=6 June=Gaia=Maia>>M=M2.
Liturgy=6,500=7,000=70%=P7.0D=7.0=Language=Assets=Mars=7 July=Pleiades.
Livable=3,000=30%=P3.0D=3.0=Creativity=Stars=Muses=3 March = C=I>>GIL.
Live1=10,000=1,000=100%=10.0=Physicality=Tech.=10 Oct.=Uranus=P=1Ø.
Live2=10,000=1,000=100%=10.0=Physicality=Tech.=10 Oct.=Uranus=P=1Ø.

Live-in=8,000=80%=P8.0D=Economy=Currency=8 Aug.=Zeus>>E=v.
Livelihood=4,000=40%=P4.0D=Govt.=Creatocracy=4 April=Mercury=Hermes=G=A4.
Live long=6,000=60%=P6.0D=Man=Earth=Royalty=6 June=Gaia=Maia>>M=M2.
Lively=10,000=1,000=100%=10.0=Physicality=Tech.=10 Oct.=Uranus=P=1Ø.
Liven=3,000=30%=P3.0D=3.0=Creativity=Stars=Muses=3 March = C=I>>GIL.
Live oak=3,000=30%=P3.0D=3.0=Creativity=Stars=Muses=3 March = C=I>>GIL.
Liver=10,000=1,000=100%=10.0=Physicality=Tech.=10 Oct.=Uranus=P=1Ø.
Liverpool=5,500=5.5=80%=P5.50=Earth-Midway=5 May = Gaia.
Liverwort=6,500=7,000=70%=P7.0D=7.0=Language=Assets=Mars=7 July=Pleiades.
Liverwurst=4,000=40%=P4.0D=Govt.=Creatocracy=4 April=Mercury=Hermes=G=A4.
Livery=10,000=1,000=100%=10.0=Physicality=Tech.=10 Oct.=Uranus=P=1Ø.
Lives=1,500=15%=P1.50D=1.5=Authority=Solar Crown=1 May = Maia.
Livestock=6,500=7,000=70%=P7.0D=7.0=Language=Assets=Mars=7 July=Pleiades.
Live wire=5,500=5.5=80%=P5.50=Earth-Midway=5 May = Gaia.
Livid=7,500=8,000=80%=P8.0D=Economy=Currency=8 Aug.=Zeus>>E=v.
Living=10,000=1,000=100%=10.0=Physicality=Tech.=10 Oct.=Uranus=P=1Ø.
Living room=5,500=5.5=80%=P5.50=Earth-Midway=5 May = Gaia.
Livingstone David=3,000=30%=P3.0D=3.0=Creativity=Stars=Muses=3 March = C=I>>GIL.
Living will=11,500=12,000=12%=P1.20D=1.2=Knowledge=Edu=12Dec.=Athena>>K=F.
Livonia=7,500=8,000=80%=P8.0D=Economy=Currency=8 Aug.=Zeus>>E=v.
Livorno=1,000=100%=10.0=1.0=Mind=Sun=1 January=Helios >> M=E4.
Livy=3,000=30%=P3.0D=3.0=Creativity=Stars=Muses=3 March = C=I>>GIL.

Lizard=12,500=13,000=13%=P1.30=Solar Core=Faculty=13 January=Athena.
Lizards are muses and monitors of Athena transmitting creative intelligence in their environments. They are constantly exposed under the sun live in walls and are means.

Ljubljana=6,000=60%=P6.0D=Man=Earth=Royalty=6 June=Gaia=Maia>>M=M2.
II.=500=5%=P5.00D=5.0=Law=Time=Venus=5 May=Aphrodite>>L=N.
Liama=10,500=11,000=11%=P1.10D=1.1=Idea=Brainchild=Inv.=11 Nov.=SC=Athena
    >>I=MT.
LL.B.=3,000=30%=P3.0D=3.0=Creativity=Stars=Muses=3 March = C=I>>GIL.
LL.D.=2,500=3,000=30%=P3.0D=3.0=Creativity=Stars=Muses=3 March = C=I>>GIL.
Lloyd George=4,000=40%=P4.0D=Govt.=Creatocracy=4April=Mercury=Hermes=G=A4.
Lm.=1,000=100%=10.0=1.0=Mind=Sun=1 January=Helios >> M=E4.
LNG=1,500=15%=P1.50D=1.5=Authority=Solar Crown=1 May = Maia.
Lo=4,500=5,000=50%=P5.00D=Law=Time=Venus=5 May = Aphrodite>>L=N.
Load=10,000=1,000=100%=10.0=Physicality=Tech.=10 Oct.=Uranus=P=1Ø.
Loaded=7,000=70%=P7.0D=7.0=Language=Assets=Mars=7 July=Pleiades.
Loaf1=7,000=70%=P7.0D=7.0=Language=Assets=Mars=7 July=Pleiades.
Loaf2=4,000=40%=P4.0D=Govt.=Creatocracy=4 April=Mercury=Hermes=G=A4.
Loam=5,500=5.5=80%=P5.50=Earth-Midway=5 May = Gaia.
Loan=10,000=1,000=100%=10.0=Physicality=Tech.=10 Oct.=Uranus=P=1Ø.
Loan word=7,000=70%=P7.0D=7.0=Language=Assets=Mars=7 July=Pleiades.

Loath=3,000=30%=P3.0D=3.0=Creativity=Stars=Muses=3 March = C=I>>GIL.
Loathe=3,000=30%=P3.0D=3.0=Creativity=Stars=Muses=3 March = C=I>>GIL.
Loathing=1,500=15%=P1.50D=1.5=Authority=Solar Crown=1 May = Maia.
Loathsome=3,500=4,000=40%=P4.0D=Govt.=Creat=4 April=Mercury=Hermes=G=A4.
Lob=4,500=5,000=50%=P5.00D=Law=Time=Venus=5 May = Aphrodite>>L=N.
Lobby=10,000=1,000=100%=10.0=Physicality=Tech.=10 Oct.=Uranus=P=1Ø.
Lobe=8,500=9,000=90%=P9.00D=9.0=Abstraction=Gods=Saturn=9Sept.>>A=Ø.
Lobotomy=7,500=8,000=80%=P8.0D=Economy=Currency=8 Aug.=Zeus>>E=v.

Lobster=13,500=14,000=14%=P1.40D=1.4=Mgt.=Solar Energy=13 May=Athena=SC=0.1
Lobsters when eaten give certain elements that transmit creative intelligence for mgt.

Local=10,000=1,000=100%=10.0=Physicality=Tech.=10 Oct.=Uranus=P=1Ø.
Locale=5,500=5.5=80%=P5.50=Earth-Midway=5 May = Gaia.
Locality=3,000=30%=P3.0D=3.0=Creativity=Stars=Muses=3 March = C=I>>GIL.
Localize=4,000=40%=P4.0D=Govt.=Creatocracy=4 April=Mercury=Hermes=G=A4.
Locate=10,000=1,000=100%=10.0=Physicality=Tech.=10 Oct.=Uranus=P=1Ø.
Location=10,000=1,000=100%=10.0=Physicality=Tech.=10 Oct.=Uranus=P=1Ø.
Loc.cit.=3,500=4,000=40%=P4.0D=Govt.=Creatocracy=4 April=Mercury=Hermes=G=A4.
Loch=7,000=70%=P7.0D=7.0=Language=Assets=Mars=7 July=Pleiades.
Loci=1,500=15%=P1.50D=1.5=Authority=Solar Crown=1 May = Maia.
Lock1=10,000=1,000=100%=10.0=Physicality=Tech.=10 Oct.=Uranus=P=1Ø.
Lock2=4,500=5,000=50%=P5.00D=Law=Time=Venus=5 May = Aphrodite>>L=N.
Locke John=2,000=20%=P2.00D=2.0=Nature=Matter=Moon=2 Feb.=Cupid=N=C+_
Locker=10,000=1,000=100%=10.0=Physicality=Tech.=10 Oct.=Uranus=P=1Ø.
Locker room=9,000=90%=P9.00D=9.0=Abstraction=Gods=Saturn=9Sept.>>A=Ø.
Locket=5,000=50%=P5.00D=Law=Time=Venus=5 May = Aphrodite>>L=N.
Lockjaw=9,000=90%=P9.00D=9.0=Abstraction=Gods=Saturn=9Sept.>>A=Ø.
Lockout=6,000=60%=P6.0D=Man=Earth=Royalty=6 June=Gaia=Maia>>M=M2.
Locksmith=3,000=30%=P3.0D=3.0=Creativity=Stars=Muses=3 March = C=I>>GIL.
Lockstep=6,000=60%=P6.0D=Man=Earth=Royalty=6 June=Gaia=Maia>>M=M2.
Loco=2,000=20%=P2.00D=2.0=Nature=Matter=Moon=2 Feb.=Cupid=N=C+_
Locomotion=7,000=70%=P7.0D=7.0=Language=Assets=Mars=7 July=Pleiades.
Locomotive=9,000=90%=P9.00D=9.0=Abstraction=Gods=Saturn=9Sept.>>A=Ø.
Locomotor=500=5%=P5.00D=5.0=Law=Time=Venus=5 May=Aphrodite>>L=N.
Locoweed=8,000=80%=P8.0D=Economy=Currency=8 Aug.=Zeus>>E=v.
Locus=6,500=7,000=70%=P7.0D=7.0=Language=Assets=Mars=7 July=Pleiades.
Locust=10,000=1,000=100%=10.0=Physicality=Tech.=10 Oct.=Uranus=P=1Ø.
Locution=7,000=70%=P7.0D=7.0=Language=Assets=Mars=7 July=Pleiades.
Lode=6,000=60%=P6.0D=Man=Earth=Royalty=6 June=Gaia=Maia>>M=M2.

Lodestar=7,500=8,000=80%=P8.0D=Economy=Currency=8 Aug.=Zeus>>E=v.
A star especially Polaris used as a point of reference. A guiding principle or ambition. In
simple terms every ambition is guided by a star called Polaris. A guiding principle must be

PETER K. MATTHEWS - AKUKALIA

computationally precise (7,000), create its means (500) to attain business status (8,000). So Polaris is a star of Zeus managed by Aries that measures the value in every ambition.

Lodestone=5,000=50%=P5.00D=Law=Time=Venus=5 May = Aphrodite>>L=N.
Lodge=10,000=1,000=100%=10.0=Physicality=Tech.=10 Oct.=Uranus=P=1Ø.
Lodger=6,500=7,000=70%=P7.0D=7.0=Language=Assets=Mars=7 July=Pleiades.
Lodging=2,000=20%=P2.00D=2.0=Nature=Matter=Moon=2 Feb.=Cupid=N=C+_
Łódź=4,500=5,000=50%=P5.00D=Law=Time=Venus=5 May = Aphrodite>>L=N.
Loess=5,500=5.5=80%=P5.50=Earth-Midway=5 May = Gaia.
Loft=10,000=1,000=100%=10.0=Physicality=Tech.=10 Oct.=Uranus=P=1Ø.

Lofty=3,500=4,000=40%=P4.0D=Govt.=Creatocracy=4 April=Mercury=Hermes=G=A4.
Lofty ambitions attained grant the rights to be exalted arrogant haughty and imposing, responsibility makes for purposeful power in building bridges rather than walls.

Log1=10,000=1,000=100%=10.0=Physicality=Tech.=10 Oct.=Uranus=P=1Ø.
Log2=1,500=15%=P1.50D=1.5=Authority=Solar Crown=1 May = Maia.
Logan=4,500=5,000=50%=P5.00D=Law=Time=Venus=5 May = Aphrodite>>L=N.
Loganberry=5,500=5.5=80%=P5.50=Earth-Midway=5 May = Gaia.
Logarithm=10,000=1,000=100%=10.0=Physicality=Tech.=10 Oct.=Uranus=P=1Ø.
Loge=8,500=9,000=90%=P9.00D=9.0=Abstraction=Gods=Saturn=9Sept.>>A=Ø.
Loggerhead=9,000=90%=P9.00D=9.0=Abstraction=Gods=Saturn=9Sept.>>A=Ø.
Logic=10,000=1,000=100%=10.0=Physicality=Tech.=10 Oct.=Uranus=P=1Ø.
Logical=10,000=1,000=100%=10.0=Physicality=Tech.=10 Oct.=Uranus=P=1Ø.
Logistics=7,500=8,000=80%=P8.0D=Economy=Currency=8 Aug.=Zeus>>E=v.
Logjam=5,500=5.5=80%=P5.50=Earth-Midway=5 May = Gaia.
Logo=7,000=70%=P7.0D=7.0=Language=Assets=Mars=7 July=Pleiades.

Logotype=7,500=8,000=80%=P8.0D=Economy=Currency=8 Aug.=Zeus>>E=v.
Greek, logos, word. A logo is expressed to convey business impressions. Aries communicates Zeus through logos. They are means attained after computation.

Logrolling=8,500=9,000=90%=P9.00D=9.0=Abstraction=Gods=Saturn=9Sept.>>A=Ø.
Logy=3,000=30%=P3.0D=3.0=Creativity=Stars=Muses=3 March = C=I>>GIL.
Loin=10,000=1,000=100%=10.0=Physicality=Tech.=10 Oct.=Uranus=P=1Ø.
Loincloth=4,000=40%=P4.0D=Govt.=Creatocracy=4 April=Mercury=Hermes=G=A4.
Loire=9,000=90%=P9.00D=9.0=Abstraction=Gods=Saturn=9Sept.>>A=Ø.
Loiter=9,000=90%=P9.00D=9.0=Abstraction=Gods=Saturn=9Sept.>>A=Ø.
Loll=7,500=8,000=80%=P8.0D=Economy=Currency=8 Aug.=Zeus>>E=v.
Lollipop=9,000=90%=P9.00D=9.0=Abstraction=Gods=Saturn=9Sept.>>A=Ø.
Lombardy=2,500=3,000=30%=P3.0D=3.0=Creativity=Stars=Muses=3 March = C=I>>GIL.
Lomé=7,000=70%=P7.0D=7.0=Language=Assets=Mars=7 July=Pleiades.

London=12,500=13,000=13%=P1.30=Solar Core=Faculty=13 January=Athena.
London is a place (means) to acquire the gift of creative intelligence through knowledge.
A place of knowledge and creative intelligence administered by Athena at both ends.
A poem was written by Peter Matthews-Akukalia, African Shakespeare, Castle Makupedia
in his book Legend of the Monarchs. Reference book >> The Creatocracy Republic.

London,John=3,500=4,000=40%=P4.0D=Govt.=Creat=4 April=Mercury=Hermes=G=A4.
Lone=6,500=7,000=70%=P7.0D=7.0=Language=Assets=Mars=7 July=Pleiades.
Lonely=7,000=70%=P7.0D=7.0=Language=Assets=Mars=7 July=Pleiades.
Loner=4,000=40%=P4.0D=Govt.=Creatocracy=4 April=Mercury=Hermes=G=A4.
Lonesome=3,500=4,000=40%=P4.0D=Govt.=Creato=4 April=Mercury=Hermes=G=A4.
Long1=10,000=1,000=100%=10.0=Physicality=Tech.=10 Oct.=Uranus=P=1Ø.
Long2=4,000=40%=P4.0D=Govt.=Creatocracy=4 April=Mercury=Hermes=G=A4.
Long.=500=5%=P5.00D=5.0=Law=Time=Venus=5 May=Aphrodite>>L=N.
Long Beach=5,000=50%=P5.00D=Law=Time=Venus=5 May = Aphrodite>>L=N.
Longbow=5,000=50%=P5.00D=Law=Time=Venus=5 May = Aphrodite>>L=N.
Long distance=2,500=3,000=30%=P3.0D=3.0=Cre=Stars=Muses=3 March = C=I>>GIL.

Longevity=3,000=30%=P3.0D=3.0=Creativity=Stars=Muses=3 March = C=I>>GIL.
Long life. Long duration. Lat.longaevus, ancient. First there is a connect between creativity
as the muses and long life. Creative people tend to produce certain elements in the body
that makes them younger and more active. Secondly there is a connect between creative
people and the ancient. In any case creativity is a great adventure to be undertaken if one
must attain eternal life. The Scriptures began with the creation story of creativity. This is
the foundation of asking the question "what is creativity?" And Peter Matthews-Akukalia
invented the Creative Sciences. Today Castle Makupedia is the God of Creatocracy.

Longfellow Wadsworth=2,500=3,000=30%=P3.0D=3.0=Crea.=Stars=Muses=3 March=CI.
Longhair=5,500=5.5=80%=P5.50=Earth-Midway=5 May = Gaia.
Longhand=1,000=100%=10.0=1.0=Mind=Sun=1 January=Helios >> M=E4.
Longhorn=8,000=80%=P8.0D=Economy=Currency=8 Aug.=Zeus>>E=v.
Longhouse=4,000=40%=P4.0D=Govt.=Creatocracy=4 April=Mercury=Hermes=G=A4.
Longing=2,500=3,000=30%=P3.0D=3.0=Creativity=Stars=Muses=3 March = C=I>>GIL.
Long Island=8,000=80%=P8.0D=Economy=Currency=8 Aug.=Zeus>>E=v.
Longitude=9,500=10,000=1,000=100%=10.0=Physicality=Tech.=10 Oct.=Uranus=P=1Ø.
Long jump=7,000=70%=P7.0D=7.0=Language=Assets=Mars=7 July=Pleiades.
Long-lived=2,000=20%=P2.00D=2.0=Nature=Matter=Moon=2 Feb.=Cupid=N=C+_
Long playing=6,500=7,000=70%=P7.0D=7.0=Language=Assets=Mars=7 July=Pleiades.
Long range=7,500=8,000=80%=P8.0D=Economy=Currency=8 Aug.=Zeus>>E=v.
Longshoreman=4,000=40%=P4.0D=Govt.=Creatocracy=4 April=Mercury=Hermes=G=A4.
Long shot=6,000=60%=P6.0D=Man=Earth=Royalty=6 June=Gaia=Maia>>M=M2.
Longstanding=2,500=3,000=30%=P3.0D=3.0=Cre.=Stars=Muses=3 March = C=I>>GIL.
Long suffering=2,500=3,000=30%=P3.0D=3.0=Cre=Stars=Muses=3 March = C=I>>GIL.

Long term=4,500=5,000=50%=P5.00D=Law=Time=Venus=5 May = Aphrodite>>L=N.
Long ton=2,000=20%=P2.00D=2.0=Nature=Matter=Moon=2 Feb.=Cupid=N=C+_
Longueli=7,500=8,000=80%=P8.0D=Economy=Currency=8 Aug.=Zeus>>E=v.
Long winded=3,000=30%=P3.0D=3.0=Creativity=Stars=Muses=3 March = C=I>>GIL.
Look=10,000=1,000=100%=10.0=Physicality=Tech.=10 Oct.=Uranus=P=1Ø.
Looking glass=1,000=100%=Physicality=Tech.=10 Oct.=Uranus=P=1Ø.
Lookout=9,000=90%=P9.00D=9.0=Abstraction=Gods=Saturn=9Sept.>>A=Ø.
Loom1=10,000=1,000=100%=10.0=Physicality=Tech.=10 Oct.=Uranus=P=1Ø.
Loom2=9,000=90%=P9.00D=9.0=Abstraction=Gods=Saturn=9Sept.>>A=Ø.
Loon1=7,000=70%=P7.0D=7.0=Language=Assets=Mars=7 July=Pleiades.
Loon2=5,500=5.5=80%=P5.50=Earth-Midway=5 May = Gaia.
Loony=3,500=4,000=40%=P4.0D=Govt.=Creatocracy=4 April=Mercury=Hermes=G=A4.
Loop=10,000=1,000=100%=10.0=Physicality=Tech.=10 Oct.=Uranus=P=1Ø.

Loophole=11,000=11%=P1.10D=1.1=Idea=Brainchild=Inv.=11 Nov.=SC=Athena>>I=MT.
Greek myth teaches that Athena uses loopholes to carry out mind battles. She used
the olive tree principle to establish superiority over Aries God of war. So loopholes are
elements of wisdom that proves that the pen is mightier than the sword. In every challenge
against the righteous Athena creates loopholes for escape but focus is necessary. Athena
herself is a loophole as advised in the Proverbs 8, 9 that she loves them that love her.

Loopy=1,000=100%=10.0=1.0=Mind=Sun=1 January=Helios >> M=E4.
Loose=10,000=1,000=100%=10.0=Physicality=Tech.=10 Oct.=Uranus=P=1Ø.
Loosen=6,000=60%=P6.0D=Man=Earth=Royalty=6 June=Gaia=Maia>>M=M2.
Loot=8,000=80%=P8.0D=Economy=Currency=8 Aug.=Zeus>>E=v.
Lop=10,000=1,000=100%=10.0=Physicality=Tech.=10 Oct.=Uranus=P=1Ø.

Lope=7,000=70%=P7.0D=7.0=Language=Assets=Mars=7 July=Pleiades.
Leap. Makupedia achieved the quantum leap through Mind Computing.

Lopsided=5,000=50%=P5.00D=Law=Time=Venus=5 May = Aphrodite>>L=N.
Loquacious=3,500=4,000=40%=P4.0D=Govt.=Creat=4 April=Mercury=Hermes=G=A4.

Lord=10,000=1,000=100%=10.0=Physicality=Tech.=10 Oct.=Uranus=P=1Ø.
In the Creatocracy, certain persons qualified and by chance who have contributed
immensely to the development of the system are appointed Lords. They are addressed
as Your Lordship, His Lordship, Her Lordship. The first man to be so appointed is His
Lordship Captain Wole Olawale Olaniyan. The first woman to be so appointed is Her
Lordship, Mrs. Helen Ekot - Efoli (aka Mrs. Helen Ekwe-Okpata). Angel Investor &
Director-at-Makupedia. Both are Lords of the Order of the Creatocracy on the Royal
Makupedia.

Lordly=5,500=5.5=80%=P5.50=Earth-Midway=5 May = Gaia.
Lordship=11,000=11%=P1.10D=1.1=Idea=Brainchild=Inv.=11 Nov.=SC=Athena>>I=MT.

Lord's Prayer=4,000=40%=P4.0D=Govt.=Creatocracy=4 April=Mercury=Hermes=G=A4.
The prayer taught by Jesus to his disciples. This prayer is the proof that Jesus Christ is Hermes incarnation. In the Creatocracy a vital code for the establishment of the will of GOD on earth. "Let thy will be done on earth as it is in Heaven". Meaning "let the muses of creativity come from above and abide with Gaia as it with Zeus".

Lore=5,500=5.5=80%=P5.50=Earth-Midway=5 May = Gaia.
Lorgnette=5,500=5.5=80%=P5.50=Earth-Midway=5 May = Gaia.
Lorn=4,500=5,000=50%=P5.00D=Law=Time=Venus=5 May = Aphrodite>>L=N.
Lorraine=4,000=40%=P4.0D=Govt.=Creatocracy=4 April=Mercury=Hermes=G=A4.
Los Angeles=5,000=50%=P5.00D=Law=Time=Venus=5 May = Aphrodite>>L=N.
Lose=10,000=1,000=100%=10.0=Physicality=Tech.=10 Oct.=Uranus=P=1Ø.
Loss=10,000=1,000=100%=10.0=Physicality=Tech.=10 Oct.=Uranus=P=1Ø.
Loss leader=5,000=50%=P5.00D=Law=Time=Venus=5 May = Aphrodite>>L=N.
Lost=10,000=1,000=100%=10.0=Physicality=Tech.=10 Oct.=Uranus=P=1Ø.
Lot=10,000=1,000=100%=10.0=Physicality=Tech.=10 Oct.=Uranus=P=1Ø.
Loti=2,500=3,000=30%=P3.0D=3.0=Creativity=Stars=Muses=3 March = C=I>>GIL.
Lotion=8,000=80%=P8.0D=Economy=Currency=8 Aug.=Zeus>>E=v.
Lottery=8,000=80%=P8.0D=Economy=Currency=8 Aug.=Zeus>>E=v.

Lotus=10,000=1,000=100%=10.0=Physicality=Tech.=10 Oct.=Uranus=P=1Ø.
Greek>> A fruit said to produce a drugged, indolent state in those who ate it.
Creatocracy suspects it is fruit of the knowledge of good and evil mentioned in Genesis.

Lotus position=4,000=40%=P4.0D=Govt.=Creatocracy=4 April=Mercury=Hermes=G=A4.
Loud=10,000=1,000=100%=10.0=Physicality=Tech.=10 Oct.=Uranus=P=1Ø.
Loudmouth=4,500=5,000=50%=P5.00D=Law=Time=Venus=5 May = Aphrodite>>L=N.
Loudspeaker=5,500=5.5=80%=P5.50=Earth-Midway=5 May = Gaia.
Louis XIV.=4,000=40%=P4.0D=Govt.=Creatocracy=4 April=Mercury=Hermes=G=A4.
Louis XV.=3,000=30%=P3.0D=3.0=Creativity=Stars=Muses=3 March = C=I>>GIL.
Louis XVI.=4,000=40%=P4.0D=Govt.=Creatocracy=4 April=Mercury=Hermes=G=A4.
Louis XVIII.=3,000=30%=P3.0D=3.0=Creativity=Stars=Muses=3 March = C=I>>GIL.
Louise Lake.=5,000=50%=P5.00D=Law=Time=Venus=5 May = Aphrodite>>L=N.
Louisiana=7,500=8,000=80%=P8.0D=Economy=Currency=8 Aug.=Zeus>>E=v.
Louisiana French=5,500=5.5=80%=P5.50=Earth-Midway=5 May = Gaia.
Louisiana Purchase=12,000=12%=P1.20D=1.2=Knowledge=Edu=12Dec.=Athena>>K=F.
Louis Philippe=4,500=5,000=50%=P5.00D=Law=Time=Venus=5 May = Aphrodite>>L=N.
Louisville=7,500=8,000=80%=P8.0D=Economy=Currency=8 Aug.=Zeus>>E=v.
Lounge=10,000=1,000=100%=10.0=Physicality=Tech.=10 Oct.=Uranus=P=1Ø.
Lour=1,500=15%=P1.50D=1.5=Authority=Solar Crown=1 May = Maia.

Lourdes1=6,000=60%=P6.0D=Man=Earth=Royalty=6 June=Gaia=Maia>>M=M2.
Louse=10,000=1,000=100%=10.0=Physicality=Tech.=10 Oct.=Uranus=P=1Ø.
Lousy=6,500=7,000=70%=P7.0D=7.0=Language=Assets=Mars=7 July=Pleiades.
Lout=6,500=7,000=70%=P7.0D=7.0=Language=Assets=Mars=7 July=Pleiades.

Love=10,000=1,000=100%=10.0=Physicality=Tech.=10 Oct.=Uranus=P=1Ø.
It is not enough for one to study or get educated for merely what he can become but also for what he must impact upon to do service to GOD and humanity.

Interest * Light = Love = P
There are two ways to determine the quantum of natural love in a person. First is interest by birth data obtained in the World Digital Dictionary. Second is interest by propensity.

1. Compute the quantum of light in Peter Matthews - Akukalia born on 6 July
Value = 6.0. Light is the percentage quantum resultant = 100% = 10.
6.0 * 10.0 = 16 + 60 = 76 x=px= 1,036 = 100% + 33 + 3

Interpretation of the above means that His love will be seen through his technologies 100% = 10.0 = P=1Ø. Genius = 33 = 3.3 and creativity = 3.0 Estimate = 1,036 = 1.0 >> Mind. This is the subjective method for measuring the quantity and value of love in a person.

2. Objective analysis is the application of love by the values of the World Digital Dictionary.
Interest * Light = Love.
Where Interest = 10.0 = 100% Light = 10.0 = 100% Love = 10.0 = 100%.
Interest * Light = Love >> 10.0 * 10.0 = 10.0 >> Proved.
However let us solve to view other activities by which love happens.

Interest * Light = Love >> 10.0 * 10.0 = 10.0
>> Interest * Light = 10.0 * 10.0 = 10.0 * 10.0 = 20 + 100 = 120 x=px= 2,120=2.1/10.0=0.21
          Love   10.0

We establish that the average quantum of love in anyone is negligible at 0.21%.
Interest is what breeds love. Light of knowledge is what sustains it. - Chapter 7, Psychoastronomy, Castle Makupedia Cosmic Sciences Laws & Mind Technologies.

Lovebird=4,000=40%=P4.0D=Govt.=Creatocracy=4 April=Mercury=Hermes=G=A4.
Lovelace Richard=3,000=30%=P3.0D=3.0=Creativity=Stars=Muses=3 March = C=I>>GIL.
Lovelorn=3,000=30%=P3.0D=3.0=Creativity=Stars=Muses=3 March = C=I>>GIL.
Lovely=4,000=40%=P4.0D=Govt.=Creatocracy=4 April=Mercury=Hermes=G=A4.
Lovemaking=2,500=3,000=30%=P3.0D=3.0=Cre=Stars=Muses=3 March = C=I>>GIL.
Lover=10,000=1,000=100%=10.0=Physicality=Tech.=10 Oct.=Uranus=P=1Ø.
Love seat=3,000=30%=P3.0D=3.0=Creativity=Stars=Muses=3 March = C=I>>GIL.
Lovesick=4,500=5,000=50%=P5.00D=Law=Time=Venus=5 May = Aphrodite>>L=N.
Loving=2,500=3,000=30%=P3.0D=3.0=Creativity=Stars=Muses=3 March = C=I>>GIL.

Loving cup=9,000=90%=P9.00D=9.0=Abstraction=Gods=Saturn=9Sept.>>A=Ø.
Low1=10,000=1,000=100%=10.0=Physicality=Tech.=10 Oct.=Uranus=P=1Ø.
Low2=1,000=100%=10.0=1.0=Mind=Sun=1 January=Helios >> M=E4.
Low beam=6,000=60%=P6.0D=Man=Earth=Royalty=6 June=Gaia=Maia>>M=M2.
Lowborn=1,500=15%=P1.50D=1.5=Authority=Solar Crown=1 May = Maia.
Lowboy=3,000=30%=P3.0D=3.0=Creativity=Stars=Muses=3 March = C=I>>GIL.
Low bred=1,000=100%=10.0=1.0=Mind=Sun=1 January=Helios >> M=E4.
Low brow=2,000=20%=P2.00D=2.0=Nature=Matter=Moon=2 Feb.=Cupid=N=C+_
Low Countries=2,500=3,000=30%=P3.0D=3.0=Crea=Stars=Muses=3 March = C=I>>GIL.
Low down=3,000=30%=P3.0D=3.0=Creativity=Stars=Muses=3 March = C=I>>GIL.
Lowell=1,000=100%=10.0=1.0=Mind=Sun=1 January=Helios >> M=E4.
Lowell, James=4,000=40%=P4.0D=Govt.=Creatocracy=4 April=Mercury=Hermes=G=A4.
Lowell, Robert=3,500=4,000=40%=P4.0D=Govt.=4 April=Mercury=Hermes=G=A4.
Lower1=8,500=9,000=90%=P9.00D=9.0=Abstraction=Gods=Saturn=9Sept.>>A=Ø.
Lower2=10,000=1,000=100%=10.0=Physicality=Tech.=10 Oct.=Uranus=P=1Ø.
Lower California=1,500=15%=P1.50D=1.5=Authority=Solar Crown=1 May = Maia.
Lowercase=6,000=60%=P6.0D=Man=Earth=Royalty=6 June=Gaia=Maia>>M=M2.
Lower class=6,000=60%=P6.0D=Man=Earth=Royalty=6 June=Gaia=Maia>>M=M2.
Lowest common denominator=2,500=3,000=30%=P3.0D=3.0=Creativity=Stars=Muses.
Low frequency=6,000=60%=P6.0D=Man=Earth=Royalty=6 June=Gaia=Maia>>M=M2.
Low German=7,000=70%=P7.0D=7.0=Language=Assets=Mars=7 July=Pleiades.
Low grade=6,000=60%=P6.0D=Man=Earth=Royalty=6 June=Gaia=Maia>>M=M2.
Low key=3,000=30%=P3.0D=3.0=Creativity=Stars=Muses=3 March = C=I>>GIL.
Lowland=3,000=30%=P3.0D=3.0=Creativity=Stars=Muses=3 March = C=I>>GIL.
Lowly=5,000=50%=P5.00D=Law=Time=Venus=5 May = Aphrodite>>L=N.
Low-minded=2,500=3,000=30%=P3.0D=3.0=Creativity=Stars=Muses=3 March = C=I
Low profile=2,500=3,000=30%=P3.0D=3.0=Creativity=Stars=Muses=3 March = C=I
Low relief=5,000=50%=P5.00D=Law=Time=Venus=5 May = Aphrodite>>L=N.
Low road=2,500=3,000=30%=P3.0D=3.0=Creativity=Stars=Muses=3 March = C=I>>GIL.
Low tide=4,000=40%=P4.0D=Govt.=Creatocracy=4 April=Mercury=Hermes=G=A4.
Lox1=3,500=4,000=40%=P4.0D=Govt.=Creatocracy=4 April=Mercury=Hermes=G=A4.
Lox2=5,500=5.5=80%=P5.50=Earth-Midway=5 May = Gaia.

Loyal=9,000=90%=P9.00D=9.0=Abstraction=Gods=Saturn=9Sept.>>A=Ø.
Creatocrats are extremely loyal to the Creatocracy in all things based on deep convictions.

Loyalists=5,500=5.5=80%=P5.50=Earth-Midway=5 May = Gaia.
Luoyang=1,000=100%=10.0=1.0=Mind=Sun=1 January=Helios >> M=E4.
Lozenge=10,000=1,000=100%=10.0=Physicality=Tech.=10 Oct.=Uranus=P=1Ø.
LP=2,000=20%=P2.00D=2.0=Nature=Matter=Moon=2 Feb.=Cupid=N=C+_
LPG=1,500=15%=P1.50D=1.5=Authority=Solar Crown=1 May = Maia.
LPN=1,500=15%=P1.50D=1.5=Authority=Solar Crown=1 May = Maia.
Lr=2,500=3,000=30%=P3.0D=3.0=Creativity=Stars=Muses=3 March = C=I>>GIL.
LSAT=2,000=20%=P2.00D=2.0=Nature=Matter=Moon=2 Feb.=Cupid=N=C+_

LSD=4,500=5,000=50%=P5.00D=Law=Time=Venus=5 May = Aphrodite>>L=N.
lt.=500=5%=P5.00D=5.0=Law=Time=Venus=5 May=Aphrodite>>L=N.
Lt.=500=5%=P5.00D=5.0=Law=Time=Venus=5 May=Aphrodite>>L=N.
I.t.=1,000=100%=10.0=1.0=Mind=Sun=1 January=Helios >> M=E4.
Lt.=1,000=100%=10.0=1.0=Mind=Sun=1 January=Helios >> M=E4.
Lt.=1,000=100%=10.0=1.0=Mind=Sun=1 January=Helios >> M=E4.
Ltd.=500=5%=P5.00D=5.0=Law=Time=Venus=5 May=Aphrodite>>L=N.
Lt. Gov.=1,000=100%=10.0=1.0=Mind=Sun=1 January=Helios >> M=E4.
Lu=1,000=100%=Physicality=Tech.=10 Oct.=Uranus=P=1Ø.
Luanda=5,500=5.5=80%=P5.50=Earth-Midway=5 May = Gaia.
Luau=5,500=5.5=80%=P5.50=Earth-Midway=5 May = Gaia.
Lubbock=4,500=5,000=50%=P5.00D=Law=Time=Venus=5 May = Aphrodite>>L=N.
Lube=6,500=7,000=70%=P7.0D=7.0=Language=Assets=Mars=7 July=Pleiades.
Lübeck=5,000=50%=P5.00D=Law=Time=Venus=5 May = Aphrodite>>L=N.
Lubricant=8,500=9,000=90%=P9.00D=9.0=Abstraction=Gods=Saturn=9Sept.>>A=Ø.
Lubricate=8,500=9,000=90%=P9.00D=9.0=Abstraction=Gods=Saturn=9Sept.>>A=Ø.
Lubricious=4,500=5,000=50%=P5.00D=Law=Time=Venus=5 May = Aphrodite>>L=N.
Lubumbashi=5,500=5.5=80%=P5.50=Earth-Midway=5 May = Gaia.
Luce,Clare=4,000=40%=P4.0D=Govt.=Creatocracy=4 April=Mercury=Hermes=G=A4.
Luce,Henry=3,500=4,000=40%=P4.0D=Govt.=Creat=4 April=Mercury=Hermes=G=A4.
Lucerne=7,000=70%=P7.0D=7.0=Language=Assets=Mars=7 July=Pleiades.

Lucid=8,000=80%=P8.0D=Economy=Currency=8 Aug.=Zeus>>E=v.
Zeus the Most High is lucid in nature. Clear minded, rational translucent, easily understood.

Lucifer=7,000=70%=P7.0D=7.0=Language=Assets=Mars=7 July=Pleiades.
Lucifer bows to the rules of precision and Mind Computing. The negative equivalent of
Aries. This means that he wages war using speculations since Aries is precise.

Lucite=3,500=4,000=40%=P4.0D=Govt.=Creatocracy=4 April=Mercury=Hermes=G=A4.
Luck=13,500=14,000=14%=P1.40D=1.4=Mgt.=Solar Energy=13 May=Athena=SC=0.1
Luckless=2,500=3,000=30%=P3.0D=3.0=Creativity=Stars=Muses=3 March = C=I>>GIL.
Lucky=5,500=5.5=80%=P5.50=Earth-Midway=5 May = Gaia.
Lucrative=4,000=40%=P4.0D=Govt.=Creatocracy=4 April=Mercury=Hermes=G=A4.
Lucre=2,500=3,000=30%=P3.0D=3.0=Creativity=Stars=Muses=3 March = C=I>>GIL.
Lucretius=4,000=40%=P4.0D=Govt.=Creatocracy=4 April=Mercury=Hermes=G=A4.

Lucubrate=5,000=50%=P5.00D=Law=Time=Venus=5 May = Aphrodite>>L=N.
To write or study laboriously. This is the secret of Castle Makupedia's success. The reward
comes from Aphrodite who monitors the numbers of hours spent during this process.
Afterwards reports are presented to Athena for wise assessments and then the Council for
blessings. Business is approved by Zeus. Hermes creates the merchandise. Maia crowns.

Lüda=5,000=50%=P5.00D=Law=Time=Venus=5 May = Aphrodite>>L=N.
Ludicrous=5,000=50%=P5.00D=Law=Time=Venus=5 May = Aphrodite>>L=N.
Lug1=10,000=1,000=100%=10.0=Physicality=Tech.=10 Oct.=Uranus=P=1Ø.
Lug2=4,000=40%=P4.0D=Govt.=Creatocracy=4 April=Mercury=Hermes=G=A4.
Luge=7,000=70%=P7.0D=7.0=Language=Assets=Mars=7 July=Pleiades.
Luggage=3,500=4,000=40%=P4.0D=Govt.=Creat=4 April=Mercury=Hermes=G=A4.
Lug nut=4,000=40%=P4.0D=Govt.=Creatocracy=4 April=Mercury=Hermes=G=A4.
Lugubrious=6,000=60%=P6.0D=Man=Earth=Royalty=6 June=Gaia=Maia>>M=M2.

Luke=2,000=20%=P2.00D=2.0=Nature=Matter=Moon=2 Feb.=Cupid=N=C+_
A book of the bible. Inspired by Cupid (Eros) and Artemis.

Luke,Saint.=8,000=80%=P8.0D=Economy=Currency=8 Aug.=Zeus>>E=v.
An incarnation of Zeus.

Lukewarm=6,000=60%=P6.0D=Man=Earth=Royalty=6 Júne=Gaia=Maia>>M=M2.
Lull=9,000=90%=P9.00D=9.0=Abstraction=Gods=Saturn=9Sept.>>A=Ø.
Lullaby=7,500=8,000=80%=P8.0D=Economy=Currency=8 Aug.=Zeus>>E=v.
Lumbago=9,000=90%=P9.00D=9.0=Abstraction=Gods=Saturn=9Sept.>>A=Ø.
Lumbar=8,500=9,000=90%=P9.00D=9.0=Abstraction=Gods=Saturn=9Sept.>>A=Ø.
Lumber1=10,500=11,000=11%=P1.10D=1.1=Idea=Brainchild=Inv.=11 Nov.=Athena>>I=MT.
Lumber2=6,500=7,000=70%=P7.0D=7.0=Language=Assets=Mars=7 July=Pleiades.
Lumberjack=5,500=5.5=80%=P5.50=Earth-Midway=5 May = Gaia.
Lumberyard=6,000=60%=P6.0D=Man=Earth=Royalty=6 June=Gaia=Maia>>M=M2.
Lumen=7,500=8,000=80%=P8.0D=Economy=Currency=8 Aug.=Zeus>>E=v.
Luminary=12,000=12%=P1.20D=1.2=Knowledge=Edu=12Dec.=Athena>>K=F.
Luminescence=7,000=70%=P7.0D=7.0=Language=Assets=Mars=7 July=Pleiades.
Luminous=8,000=80%=P8.0D=Economy=Currency=8 Aug.=Zeus>>E=v.
Luminous flux=8,000=80%=P8.0D=Economy=Currency=8 Aug.=Zeus>>E=v.
Lummox=2,500=3,000=30%=P3.0D=3.0=Creativity=Stars=Muses=3 March = C=I>>GIL.
Lump1=10,000=1,000=100%=10.0=Physicality=Tech.=10 Oct.=Uranus=P=1Ø.
Lump2=5,500=5.5=80%=P5.50=Earth-Midway=5 May = Gaia.
Lumpectomy=4,000=40%=P4.0D=Govt.=Creatocracy=4 April=Mercury=Hermes=G=A4.
Lunacy=2,000=20%=P2.00D=2.0=Nature=Matter=Moon=2 Feb.=Cupid=N=C+_

Lunar=11,000=11%=P1.10D=1.1=Idea=Brainchild=Inv.=11 Nov.=SC=Athena>>I=MT.
Result shows the moon is an invention of Athena Goddess of wisdom handicraft and warfare. The brainchild of Zeus the Most High and wife of Castle Makupedia by law. The Creatocracy has established the linking energy between the moon and existence. Peter Matthews-Akukalia, Castle Makupedia made over 6million computations and 15million programs on the moon alone. He also discovered that Man was built in the moon and planted on Earth in the Garden of Eden. He computed the lunar energy called the PGI that influences all existence. The body equivalent of the moon is the ear. Athena speaks through

the ears to give wisdom instruction direction and help to those that seek wisdom from GOD. Athena is proved by computing to be the Spirit of GOD from the days of creation who surveyed the Earth and asked Chaos to leave. The seven Spirits of GOD are the seven daughters of Atlas headed by Maia and constitute the Mind of GOD. The Holy Spirit is the Council of GODS coded as the Genius 33 >> 3.3 that administer over the universes below Athena Hermes and the Pleiades of the Solar Core Higher Heavens regions who report to Zeus Jehovah [Yeshua] for approval after rational considerations computations deliberations and due processes are completed to ensure justice fairness and equity especially for the protection of rights and granting of rewards or punishments. All these are the results of discovery made thorough computational creativity and Mind Computing. Greek mythologies and the Scriptures are intertwined hence we prove that GOD IS ONE.

Lunatic=7,000=70%=P7.0D=7.0=Language=Assets=Mars=7 July=Pleiades.
Insane. Of or for the insane. Wildly or giddily foolish. Lat.>lunaticus < lunar, moon. Giddy < Old English gidig, insane. Possessed by a God, from the base of GOD. In the study of Naturecology, Peter Matthews-Akukalia, Castle Makupedia asserted a possible link between madness and lunar energy. It is a punishment from Aries against excessive wrong doing such as reviling the Gods, what Jesus called insulting the Holy Spirit. In such a case the equivalent of Aries, Lucifer possesses the person by permission of the Council of Gods. Bible talks about Satan taking over certain persons who despise GOD. Note that Aries is a protector of mankind against external aggression by cosmic military laws. Possibly appeasing him might release the insane and effectual prayers for forgiveness might lead to deliverance. However the person must be known on date of birth and several energies.

Lunch=4,000=40%=P4.0D=Govt.=Creatocracy=4 April=Mercury=Hermes=G=A4.
Luncheonette=7,000=70%=P7.0D=7.0=Language=Assets=Mars=7 July=Pleiades.
Luncheonette=3,500=4,000=40%=P4.0D=Govt.=4 April=Mercury=Hermes=G=A4.
Lung=10,000=1,000=100%=10.0=Physicality=Tech.=10 Oct.=Uranus=P=1Ø.
Lunge=7,000=70%=P7.0D=7.0=Language=Assets=Mars=7 July=Pleiades.
Lungfish=6,500=7,000=70%=P7.0D=7.0=Language=Assets=Mars=7 July=Pleiades.
Luoyang=5,000=50%=P5.00D=Law=Time=Venus=5 May = Aphrodite>>L=N.
Lupine=6,000=60%=P6.0D=Man=Earth=Royalty=6 June=Gaia=Maia>>M=M2.
Lupus=7,500=8,000=80%=P8.0D=Economy=Currency=8 Aug.=Zeus>>E=v.
Lurch1=7,000=70%=P7.0D=7.0=Language=Assets=Mars=7 July=Pleiades.
Lurch2=5,000=50%=P5.00D=Law=Time=Venus=5 May = Aphrodite>>L=N.
Lure=10,500=11,000=11%=P1.10D=1.1=Idea=Brainchild=Inv.=11 Nov.=SC=Athena>>I=MT.
Lurid=5,000=50%=P5.00D=Law=Time=Venus=5 May = Aphrodite>>L=N.
Lurk=7,500=8,000=80%=P8.0D=Economy=Currency=8 Aug.=Zeus>>E=v.
Lusaka=5,500=5.5=80%=P5.50=Earth-Midway=5 May = Gaia.
Luscious=7,500=8,000=80%=P8.0D=Economy=Currency=8 Aug.=Zeus>>E=v.
Lush1=8,500=9,000=90%=P9.00D=9.0=Abstraction=Gods=Saturn=9Sept.>>A=Ø.
Lush2=2,000=20%=P2.00D=2.0=Nature=Matter=Moon=2 Feb.=Cupid=N=C+_
Lust=10,000=1,000=100%=10.0=Physicality=Tech.=10 Oct.=Uranus=P=1Ø.
Luster=6,500=7,000=70%=P7.0D=7.0=Language=Assets=Mars=7 July=Pleiades.

Lustre=2,500=3,000=30%=P3.0D=3.0=Creativity=Stars=Muses=3 March = C=I>>GIL.
Lusty=2,000=20%=P2.00D=2.0=Nature=Matter=Moon=2 Feb.=Cupid=N=C+_
Lute=8,000=80%=P8.0D=Economy=Currency=8 Aug.=Zeus>>E=v.
Lutetium=10,500=11,000=11%=P1.10D=1.1=Idea=Brainchild=Inv.=11 Nov.=Athena>>I=MT.
Luther,Martin=3,500=4,000=40%=P4.0D=Govt.=Creato=4 April=Mercury=Hermes =G=A4.
Lutheran=6,000=60%=P6.0D=Man=Earth=Royalty=6 June=Gaia=Maia>>M=M2.
Luxembourg=10,000=1,000=100%=10.0=Physicality=Tech.=10 Oct.=Uranus=P=1Ø.
Luxemburg Rosa=2,500=3,000=30%=P3.0D=3.0=Creativity=Stars=Muses=3 March=CI.
Luxuriant=9,000=90%=P9.00D=9.0=Abstraction=Gods=Saturn=9Sept.>>A=Ø.
Luxuriate=3,000=30%=P3.0D=3.0=Creativity=Stars=Muses=3 March = C=I>>GIL.
Luxury=10,000=1,000=100%=10.0=Physicality=Tech.=10 Oct.=Uranus=P=1Ø.
Luzon=5,000=50%=P5.00D=Law=Time=Venus=5 May = Aphrodite>>L=N.
Lvov=6,000=60%=P6.0D=Man=Earth=Royalty=6 June=Gaia=Maia>>M=M2.
Lwei=3,500=4,000=40%=P4.0D=Govt.=Creatocracy=4 April=Mercury=Hermes=G=A4.
-ly1=8,500=9,000=90%=P9.00D=9.0=Abstraction=Gods=Saturn=9Sept.>>A=Ø.
-ly2=9,000=90%=P9.00D=9.0=Abstraction=Gods=Saturn=9Sept.>>A=Ø.
Lyallpur=1,000=100%=10.0=1.0=Mind=Sun=1 January=Helios >> M=E4.
Lyceum=10,000=1,000=100%=10.0=Physicality=Tech.=10 Oct.=Uranus=P=1Ø.
Lycia=7,000=70%=P7.0D=7.0=Language=Assets=Mars=7 July=Pleiades.
Lydia=7,000=70%=P7.0D=7.0=Language=Assets=Mars=7 July=Pleiades.
Lye=8,500=9,000=90%=P9.00D=9.0=Abstraction=Gods=Saturn=9Sept.>>A=Ø.
Lyly John=3,500=4,000=40%=P4.0D=Govt.=Creato=4 April=Mercury=Hermes=G=A4.
Lyme disease=7,000=70%=P7.0D=7.0=Language=Assets=Mars=7 July=Pleiades.
Lymph=10,000=1,000=100%=10.0=Physicality=Tech.=10 Oct.=Uranus=P=1Ø.
Lymphatic=6,500=7,000=70%=P7.0D=7.0=Language=Assets=Mars=7 July=Pleiades.
Lymphatic system=7,500=8,000=80%=P8.0D=Economy=Currency=8 Aug.=Zeus>>E=v.
Lymph node=10,000=1,000=100%=10.0=Physicality=Tech.=10 Oct.=Uranus=P=1Ø.
Lymphocyte=4,000=40%=P4.0D=Govt.=Creatocracy=4 April=Mercury=Hermes=G=A4.
Lymphoid=4,000=40%=P4.0D=Govt.=Creatocracy=4 April=Mercury=Hermes=G=A4.

Lynch=9,000=90%=P9.00D=9.0=Abstraction=Gods=Saturn=9Sept.>>A=Ø.
To execute without due process of law especially to hang by a mob. After William lynch. Died 1830. A crime against the Council of Gods, Heaven and humanity. The Creatocracy takes a lofty stand on the sacredness and sanctity of human life bound by the laws of Mind.

Lynx=6,500=7,000=70%=P7.0D=7.0=Language=Assets=Mars=7 July=Pleiades.

Lynx-eyed=1,500=15%=P1.50D=1.5=Authority=Solar Crown=1 May = Maia.
Keen of vision. Secrets of acquiring and developing the gift of vision and prophecy. Focus briefly on the Sun at least three times in the morning sun activates the cosmic energy. A secret of Peter Matthews-Akukalia is his ability to focus at the distant horizon daily. Check the signs of Maia and apply the symbols at prayer to contacts the Mind of GOD.

Lyon Mary=2,500=3,000=30%=P3.0D=3.0=Creativity=Stars=Muses=3 March = C=I>>GIL.
Lyons=7,500=8,000=80%=P8.0D=Economy=Currency=8 Aug.=Zeus>>E=v.
Lyre=7,500=8,000=80%=P8.0D=Economy=Currency=8 Aug.=Zeus>>E=v.
Lyric=15,000=15%=P1.50D=1.5=Authority=Solar Crown=1 May = Maia.
Lyrical=4,500=5,000=50%=P5.00D=Law=Time=Venus=5 May = Aphrodite>>L=N.
Lyricist=2,500=3,000=30%=P3.0D=3.0=Creativity=Stars=Muses=3 March = C=I>>GIL.
Lysergic acid=9,500=10,000=1,000=100%=10.0=Phy=Tech.=10 Oct.=Uranus=P=1Ø.
Lysergic acid diethyl amide=1,000=100%=Physicality=Tech.=10 Oct.=Uranus=P=1Ø.
Lysin=9,000=90%=P9.00D=9.0=Abstraction=Gods=Saturn=9Sept.>>A=Ø.
Lysis=8,500=9,000=90%=P9.00D=9.0=Abstraction=Gods=Saturn=9Sept.>>A=Ø.
-lysis=3,500=4,000=40%=P4.0D=Govt.=Creato=4 April=Mercury=Hermes=G=A4.
-lyte=8,000=80%=P8.0D=Economy=Currency=8 Aug.=Zeus>>E=v.

MAKABET =Mm=

---

m1=3,000=30%=P3.0D=3.0=Creativity=Stars=Muses=3 March = C=I>>GIL.
The 13th letter of the English alphabet. First the resultant shows the influence of muses. M is a star transmuted into symbols. A person who has an m in his name already has a muse. Second is the position of the muse as the 13th>>Athena>> Creative Intelligence >> Faculty. So m is a muse of Athena that transmutes creative intelligence manifested as wisdom handicraft and energy for mental warfare. The total effectual weight of m is computed thus: 3.0*1.3x=px=4.3+3.9=8.2x=px=24.97=30=3.0
The resultant indicates that Athena is the muse coded by the sign or symbol m. Besides 24=2.4 >> International Business. 97>>100% software assets. The Muses of sciences and arts are naturally endowed in such name. A name such as [M]atthews. Today Peter Matthews-Akukalia is involved with international business and a study that makes softwares through the faculty of creative sciences, Mind arts and Nations.

---

m2=4,000=40%=P4.0D=Govt.=Creatocracy=4 April=Mercury=Hermes=G=A4.
M1=3,000=30%=P3.0D=3.0=Creativity=Stars=Muses=3 March = C=I>>GIL.
M2=1,500=15%=P1.50D=1.5=Authority=Solar Crown=1 May = Maia.
m.=4,000=40%=P4.0D=Govt.=Creatocracy=4 April=Mercury=Hermes=G=A4.
M.=3,000=30%=P3.0D=3.0=Creativity=Stars=Muses=3 March = C=I>>GIL.
mA=500=5%=P5.00D=5.0=Law=Time=Venus=5 May=Aphrodite>>L=N.
MA=500=5%=P5.00D=5.0=Law=Time=Venus=5 May=Aphrodite>>L=N.
M.A.=3,000=30%=P3.0D=3.0=Creativity=Stars=Muses=3 March = C=I>>GIL.
Ma'am=6,500=7,000=70%=P7.0D=7.0=Language=Assets=Mars=7 July=Pleiades.
Maas=6,000=60%=P6.0D=Man=Earth=Royalty=6 June=Gaia=Maia>>M=M2.
Macabre=6,500=7,000=70%=P7.0D=7.0=Language=Assets=Mars=7 July=Pleiades.
Macadam=10,000=1,000=100%=10.0=Physicality=Tech.=10 Oct.=Uranus=P=1Ø.
Macao=6,500=7,000=70%=P7.0D=7.0=Language=Assets=Mars=7 July=Pleiades.

Macaque=7,000=70%=P7.0D=7.0=Language=Assets=Mars=7 July=Pleiades.
Macaroni=9,500=10,000=1,000=100%=10.0=Physicality=Tech.=10 Oct.=Uranus=P=1Ø.
Macaroon=8,500=9,000=90%=P9.00D=9.0=Abstraction=Gods=Saturn=9Sept.>>A=Ø.
MacArthur Douglass=2,000=20%=P2.00D=2.0=Nature=Moon=2 Feb.=Cupid=N=C+_
Macaw=5,000=50%=P5.00D=Law=Time=Venus=5 May = Aphrodite>>L=N.
Maccabees=7,500=8,000=80%=P8.0D=Economy=Currency=8 Aug.=Zeus>>E=v.
MacDonald John=6,500=7,000=70%=P7.0D=7.0=Lang=Assets=Mars=7 July=Pleiades.
MacDonald James=5,000=50%=P5.00D=Law=Time=Venus=5 May = Aphrodite>>L=N.
mace1=10,000=1,000=100%=10.0=Physicality=Tech.=10 Oct.=Uranus=P=1Ø.
mace2=8,000=80%=P8.0D=Economy=Currency=8 Aug.=Zeus>>E=v.
Mace=8,000=80%=P8.0D=Economy=Currency=8 Aug.=Zeus>>E=v.
Macedonia=10,000=1,000=100%=10.0=Physicality=Tech.=10 Oct.=Uranus=P=1Ø.
Macerate=6,500=7,000=70%=P7.0D=7.0=Language=Assets=Mars=7 July=Pleiades.
Mach=1,000=100%=10.0=1.0=Mind=Sun=1 January=Helios >> M=E4.
Mach Ernst=3,000=30%=P3.0D=3.0=Creativity=Stars=Muses=3 March = C=I>>GIL.
Machete=8,000=80%=P8.0D=Economy=Currency=8 Aug.=Zeus>>E=v.
Machiavelli Nicholò=2,500=3,000=30%=P3.0D=3.0=Creativity=Stars=Muses=3 March=CI
Machiavellian=10,000=1,000=100%=10.0=Physicality=Tech.=10 Oct.=Uranus=P=1Ø.
Machination=6,000=60%=P6.0D=Man=Earth=Royalty=6 June=Gaia=Maia>>M=M2.

Machine=10,000=1,000=100%=10.0=Physicality=Tech.=10 Oct.=Uranus=P=1Ø.

Code 10L.

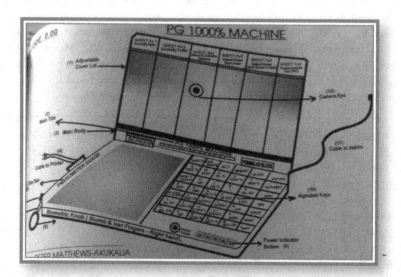

Makupedia >> First Human Mind Computer. A Human Mind Electronic Computerized Analyzer. It is the first machine invented by Peter Matthews-Akukalia, Castle Makupedia. It computes the inherent faculties of the human mind that constitute the four components of personality potentials creativity and career of a person. First patented in Nigeria with application made in the year 2020. Also the Makulator, Mind clocks and over 10,000 Mind Apps to mention a few. See Mind. See Human Energy Database table manually computed.

Machine code=1,500=15%=P1.50D=1.5=Authority=Solar Crown=1 May = Maia.
Machine gun=4,500=5,000=50%=P5.00D=Law=Time=Venus=5 May = Aphrodite>>L=N.
Machine language=6,500=7,000=70%=P7.0D=7.0=Lang=Assets=Mars=7 July=Pleiades.
Machinery=10,000=1,000=100%=10.0=Physicality=Tech.=10 Oct.=Uranus=P=1Ø.
Machinist=3,500=4,000=40%=P4.0D=Govt.=Creato=4April=Mercury=Hermes=G=A4.
Machismo=5,000=50%=P5.00D=Law=Time=Venus=5 May = Aphrodite>>L=N.
Mach number=7,500=8,000=80%=P8.0D=Economy=Currency=8 Aug.=Zeus>>E=v.
Macho=5,500=5.5=80%=P5.50=Earth-Midway=5 May = Gaia.
Machu Pichu=6,000=60%=P6.0D=Man=Earth=Royalty=6 June=Gaia=Maia>>M=M2.
Mackenzie Alexander=3,500=4,000=40%=P4.0D=Govt.=4 April=Mercury=Hermes=G=A4.
Mackenzie River=9,500=10,000=1,000=100%=10.0=Phys.=Tech.=10 Oct.=Uranus=P=1Ø.
Mackerel=5,000=50%=P5.00D=Law=Time=Venus=5 May = Aphrodite>>L=N.
Mackinac Island=10,000=1,000=100%=10.0=Physicality=Tech.=10 Oct.=Uranus=P=1Ø.
Mackinaw=7,000=70%=P7.0D=7.0=Language=Assets=Mars=7 July=Pleiades.
Mackintosh=4,500=5,000=50%=P5.00D=Law=Time=Venus=5 May = Aphrodite>>L=N.
MacLeish Archibald=3,000=30%=P3.0D=3.0=Creativity=Stars=Muses=3 March= CI
Macmillan Maurice=4,000=40%=P4.0D=Govt=4 April=Mercury=Hermes=G=A4.
Macon=4,500=5,000=50%=P5.00D=Law=Time=Venus=5 May = Aphrodite>>L=N.
Macquarie=7,500=8,000=80%=P8.0D=Economy=Currency=8 Aug.=Zeus>>E=v.
Macramé=6,500=7,000=70%=P7.0D=7.0=Language=Assets=Mars=7 July=Pleiades.
Macro=10,000=1,000=100%=10.0=Physicality=Tech.=10 Oct.=Uranus=P=1Ø.
Macro-=4,500=5,000=50%=P5.00D=Law=Time=Venus=5 May = Aphrodite>>L=N.
Macrobiotics=10,000=1,000=100%=10.0=Physicality=Tech.=10 Oct.=Uranus=P=1Ø.
Macrocephaly=2,500=3,000=30%=P3.0D=3.0=Creativity=Stars=Muses=3 March =CI
Macro code=6,500=7,000=70%=P7.0D=7.0=Language=Assets=Mars=7 July=Pleiades.
Macrocosm=6,000=60%=P6.0D=Man=Earth=Royalty=6 June=Gaia=Maia>>M=M2.
Macroeconomics=4,000=40%=P4.0D=Govt.=Creat=4 April=Mercury=Hermes=G=A4.
Macro instructions=1,000=100%=10.0=1.0=Mind=Sun=1 January=Helios >> M=E4.
Macron=8,500=9,000=90%=P9.00D=9.0=Abstraction=Gods=Saturn=9Sept.>>A=Ø.
Macrophage=2,000=20%=P2.00D=2.0=Nature=Matter=Moon=2 Feb.=Cupid=N=C+_
Macroscopic=5,500=5.5=80%=P5.50=Earth-Midway=5 May = Gaia.
Mad=10,000=1,000=100%=10.0=Physicality=Tech.=10 Oct.=Uranus=P=1Ø.
Madagascar=7,000=70%=P7.0D=7.0=Language=Assets=Mars=7 July=Pleiades.
Madam=10,000=1,000=100%=10.0=Physicality=Tech.=10 Oct.=Uranus=P=1Ø.
Madame=3,500=4,000=40%=P4.0D=Govt.=Creat=4 April=Mercury=Hermes=G=A4.
Madcap=4,500=5,000=50%=P5.00D=Law=Time=Venus=5 May = Aphrodite>>L=N.
Madden=3,500=4,000=40%=P4.0D=Govt.=Creato=4 April=Mercury=Hermes=G=A4.
Madder=10,000=1,000=100%=10.0=Physicality=Tech.=10 Oct.=Uranus=P=1Ø.
Made=3,000=30%=P3.0D=3.0=Creativity=Stars=Muses=3 March = C=I>>GIL.
Madeira1=7,500=8,000=80%=P8.0D=Economy=Currency=8 Aug.=Zeus>>E=v.
Madeira2=4,500=5,000=50%=P5.00D=Law=Time=Venus=5 May = Aphrodite>>L=N.
Madeira Islands=5,000=50%=P5.00D=Law=Time=Venus=5 May = Aphrodite>>L=N.

Mademoiselle=10,000=1,000=100%=10.0=Physicality=Tech.=10 Oct.=Uranus=P=1Ø.
Made-to-order=3,500=4,000=40%=P4.0D=Govt.=Creato=4 April=Hermes=G=A4.
Made up=3,000=30%=P3.0D=3.0=Creativity=Stars=Muses=3 March = C=I>>GIL.
Madhouse=5,500=5.5=80%=P5.50=Earth-Midway=5 May = Gaia.
Madison=5,000=50%=P5.00D=Law=Time=Venus=5 May = Aphrodite>>L=N.
Madison, Dolley=8,000=80%=P8.0D=Economy=Currency=8 Aug.=Zeus>>E=v.
Madison, James=4,000=40%=P4.0D=Govt.=4 April=Mercury=Hermes=G=A4.
Madonna=6,500=7,000=70%=P7.0D=7.0=Language=Assets=Mars=7 July=Pleiades.
madras=6,000=60%=P6.0D=Man=Earth=Royalty=6 June=Gaia=Maia>>M=M2.
Madras=5,500=5.5=80%=P5.50=Earth-Midway=5 May = Gaia.
Madre de Dios=6,500=7,000=70%=P7.0D=7.0=Language=Assets=Mars=7 July=Pleiades.
Madrid=4,500=5,000=50%=P5.00D=Law=Time=Venus=5 May = Aphrodite>>L=N.
Madrigal=10,000=1,000=100%=10.0=Physicality=Tech.=10 Oct.=Uranus=P=1Ø.
Madrōna=10,000=1,000=100%=10.0=Physicality=Tech.=10 Oct.=Uranus=P=1Ø.
Madurai=4,500=5,000=50%=P5.00D=Law=Time=Venus=5 May = Aphrodite>>L=N.
Maelstrom=8,000=80%=P8.0D=Economy=Currency=8 Aug.=Zeus>>E=v.
Maestro=6,500=7,000=70%=P7.0D=7.0=Language=Assets=Mars=7 July=Pleiades.
Maeterlinck=4,000=40%=P4.0D=Govt.=Creatocracy=4 April=Mercury=Hermes=G=A4.
Mafia=8,000=80%=P8.0D=Economy=Currency=8 Aug.=Zeus>>E=v.
Mafioso=4,000=40%=P4.0D=Govt.=Creatocracy=4 April=Mercury=Hermes=G=A4.
Magazine=10,000=1,000=100%=10.0=Physicality=Tech.=10 Oct.=Uranus=P=1Ø.
Magdalena=8,500=9,000=90%=P9.00D=9.0=Abstraction=Gods=Saturn=9Sept.>>A=Ø.
Magdeburg=6,500=7,000=70%=P7.0D=7.0=Language=Assets=Mars=7 July=Pleiades.
Magellan Ferdinand=2,500=3,000=30%=P3.0D=3.0=Cre.=Stars=Muses=3 March=CI
Magellan, Strait of.=7,500=8,000=80%=P8.0D=Economy=Currency=8 Aug.=Zeus>>E=v.
Magenta=3,500=4,000=40%=P4.0D=Govt.=Creato=4 April=Mercury=Hermes=G=A4.
Maggot=8,000=80%=P8.0D=Economy=Currency=8 Aug.=Zeus>>E=v.
Magi=1,500=15%=P1.50D=1.5=Authority=Solar Crown=1 May = Maia.
Magic=10,000=1,000=100%=10.0=Physicality=Tech.=10 Oct.=Uranus=P=1Ø.
Magisterial=10,000=1,000=100%=10.0=Physicality=Tech.=10 Oct.=Uranus=P=1Ø.
Magistrate=5,500=5.5=80%=P5.50=Earth-Midway=5 May = Gaia.
Magma=10,000=1,000=100%=10.0=Physicality=Tech.=10 Oct.=Uranus=P=1Ø.

Magna Carta=7,000=70%=P7.0D=7.0=Language=Assets=Mars=7 July=Pleiades.
The charter of English political and civil liberties granted by King John in 1215. Today the Creatocracy is instituted established and protected by Provisions of the Creatocratic Charter and the Solar Crown of Castle Makupedia. The Creatocratic Charter is the body of knowledge fields of study and academic disciplines for De-Royal Makupedia. The Solar Crown of Castle Makupedia is the sovereignty charter of the Creatocracy. All by the Most Sovereign Emperor, Paradise Nations: Peter Matthews-Akukalia. Castle Makupedia. The resultant shows that all charters must be based on computation creativity and precision.

Magnanimous=4,000=40%=P4.0D=Govt.=Creatocracy=4 April=Mercury=Hermes=G=A4.
Magnate=6,000=60%=P6.0D=Man=Earth=Royalty=6 June=Gaia=Maia>>M=M2.

Magnesia=10,000=1,000=100%=10.0=Physicality=Tech.=10 Oct.=Uranus=P=1Ø.
Magnesium=10,000=1,000=100%=10.0=Physicality=Tech.=10 Oct.=Uranus=P=1Ø.
Magnet=10,000=1,000=100%=10.0=Physicality=Tech.=10 Oct.=Uranus=P=1Ø.
Magnetic=10,000=1,000=100%=10.0=Physicality=Tech.=10 Oct.=Uranus=P=1Ø.
Magnetic disk=10,000=1,000=100%=10.0=Physicality=Tech.=10 Oct.=Uranus=P=1Ø.

Magnetic field=8,000=80%=P8.0D=Economy=Currency=8 Aug.=Zeus>>E=v.
A phenomenon used to describe the principle force that binds mutual interest between parties involved in a relationship before attraction has occurred. It is called psychomagnetic >> mind related. Loss of it leads to a divorce also 80%=8.0. Interestingly Zeus=8.0 which confirms that HE is the almighty GOD that instituted marriage in the Bible. Reference book: Psychoastronomy, Castle Makupedia cosmic Sciences Laws & Mind Technologies, chapter 6 the psychonomy of relationships. Attraction=9.0. Differential>> Magnet Force-Attraction=8.0-9.0=-1>>Speed of convertible Intelligence(thought).

Magnetic needle=8,000=80%=P8.0D=Economy=Currency=8 Aug.=Zeus>>E=v.
Magnetic north=7,000=70%=P7.0D=7.0=Language=Assets=Mars=7 July=Pleiades.
Magnetic pole=10,000=1,000=100%=10.0=Physicality=Tech.=10 Oct.=Uranus=P=1Ø.
Magnetic recording=7,500=8,000=80%=P8.0D=Economy=Currency=8 Aug.=Zeus>>E=v.
Magnetic resonance=10,000=1,000=100%=10.0=Phys=Tech.=10 Oct.=Uranus=P=1Ø.
Magnetic tape=6,000=60%=P6.0D=Man=Earth=Royalty=6 June=Gaia=Maia>>M=M2.
Magnetism=10,000=1,000=100%=10.0=Physicality=Tech.=10 Oct.=Uranus=P=1Ø.
Magnetite=3,000=30%=P3.0D=3.0=Creativity=Stars=Muses=3 March = C=I>>GIL.
Magneto=10,000=1,000=100%=10.0=Physicality=Tech.=10 Oct.=Uranus=P=1Ø.
Magnetometer=7,000=70%=P7.0D=7.0=Language=Assets=Mars=7 July=Pleiades.
Magnet school=8,000=80%=P8.0D=Economy=Currency=8 Aug.=Zeus>>E=v.
Magnificent=10,000=1,000=100%=10.0=Physicality=Tech.=10 Oct.=Uranus=P=1Ø.
Magnify=10,000=1,000=100%=10.0=Physicality=Tech.=10 Oct.=Uranus=P=1Ø.
Magnifying glass=6,000=60%=P6.0D=Man=Earth=Royalty=6 June=Gaia=Maia>>M=M2.
Magnitogorsk=6,500=7,000=70%=P7.0D=7.0=Language=Assets=Mars=7 July=Pleiades.
Magnitude=10,000=1,000=100%=10.0=Physicality=Tech.=10 Oct.=Uranus=P=1Ø.
Magnolia=7,500=8,000=80%=P8.0D=Economy=Currency=8 Aug.=Zeus>>E=v.
Magnum=7,500=8,000=80%=P8.0D=Economy=Currency=8 Aug.=Zeus>>E=v.
Magnus opus=5,500=5.5=80%=P5.50=Earth-Midway=5 May = Gaia.
Magpie=6,500=7,000=70%=P7.0D=7.0=Language=Assets=Mars=7 July=Pleiades.
Magritte Réne=2,000=20%=P2.00D=2.0=Nature=Matter=Moon=2 Feb.=Cupid=N=C+_
Maguey=8,000=80%=P8.0D=Economy=Currency=8 Aug.=Zeus>>E=v.
Magus=11,500=12,000=12%=P1.20D=1.2=Knowledge=Edu=12Dec.=Athena>>K=F.
Magyar=3,000=30%=P3.0D=3.0=Creativity=Stars=Muses=3 March = C=I>>GIL.
Maharajah=5,500=5.5=80%=P5.50=Earth-Midway=5 May = Gaia.
Maharani=6,500=7,000=70%=P7.0D=7.0=Language=Assets=Mars=7 July=Pleiades.
Maharishi=4,000=40%=P4.0D=Govt.=Creatocracy=4 April=Mercury=Hermes=G=A4.
Mahatma=8,500=9,000=90%=P9.00D=9.0=Abstraction=Gods=Saturn=9Sept.>>A=Ø.

Mahdi=10,500=11,000=11%=P1.10D=1.1=Idea=Brainchild=Inv.=11 Nov.=SC=Athena
>>I=MT.

Islam. The messiah expected to appear at the world's end and establish a reign of peace. [Ar,Mahdi, rightly guided (one), Mahdi.]. Aligns with the Bible's Ephesians 1:10-15. Resultant indicate that such a person would have the Spirit of God >> Athena. As mentioned in Revelation 13:11-18 he will discover the means to all brains, brainchild and invention. Thus he will be an inventor with special abilities to interpret the divine will of GOD expressed in signs symbols and the alphanumerics. His code is unity and peace.

Mahican=10,000=1,000=100%=10.0=Physicality=Tech.=10 Oct.=Uranus=P=1Ø.
Mahjong=8,500=9,000=90%=P9.00D=9.0=Abstraction=Gods=Saturn=9Sept.>>A=Ø.
Mahler Gustav=2,000=20%=P2.00D=2.0=Nature=Matter=Moon=2 Feb.=Cupid=N=C+_
Mahogany=10,000=1,000=100%=10.0=Physicality=Tech.=10 Oct.=Uranus=P=1Ø.
Maid=4,000=40%=P4.0D=Govt.=Creatocracy=4 April=Mercury=Hermes=G=A4.
Maiden=8,000=80%=P8.0D=Economy=Currency=8 Aug.=Zeus>>E=v.
Maidenhair fern=7,000=70%=P7.0D=7.0=Language=Assets=Mars=7 July=Pleiades.
Maiden name=4,500=5,000=50%=P5.00D=Law=Time=Venus=5 May = Aphrodite>>L=N.
Maid of honor=4,000=40%=P4.0D=Govt.=Creatocracy=4April=Mercury=Hermes=G=A4.
Maidu=5,500=5.5=80%=P5.50=Earth-Midway=5 May = Gaia.
Mail1=10,000=1,000=100%=10.0=Physicality=Tech.=10 Oct.=Uranus=P=1Ø.
Mail2=7,500=8,000=80%=P8.0D=Economy=Currency=8 Aug.=Zeus>>E=v.
Mailbox=6,000=60%=P6.0D=Man=Earth=Royalty=6 June=Gaia=Maia>>M=M2.
Mailer Norman=2,000=20%=P2.00D=2.0=Nature=Matter=Moon=2 Feb.=Cupid=N=C+_
Maillol Aristide=2,000=20%=P2.00D=2.0=Nature=Matter=Moon=2 Feb.=Cupid=N=C+_
Mailman=3,500=4,000=40%=P4.0D=Govt.=Creato=4 April=Mercury=Hermes=G=A4.
Mail order=5,500=5.5=80%=P5.50=Earth-Midway=5 May = Gaia.
Mail order house=6,500=7,000=70%=P7.0D=7.0=Lang=Assets=Mars=7 July=Pleiades.
Maim=5,000=50%=P5.00D=Law=Time=Venus=5 May = Aphrodite>>L=N.
Maimonides=6,000=60%=P6.0D=Man=Earth=Royalty=6 June=Gaia=Maia>>M=M2.
main=10,000=1,000=100%=10.0=Physicality=Tech.=10 Oct.=Uranus=P=1Ø.
Main=9,500=10,000=1,000=100%=10.0=Physicality=Tech.=10 Oct.=Uranus=P=1Ø.
Maine=5,000=50%=P5.00D=Law=Time=Venus=5 May = Aphrodite>>L=N.
Mainframe=4,500=5,000=50%=P5.00D=Law=Time=Venus=5 May = Aphrodite>>L=N.
Mainland=4,000=40%=P4.0D=Govt.=Creatocracy=4 April=Mercury=Hermes=G=A4.
Mainline=3,500=4,000=40%=P4.0D=Govt.=Creato=4 April=Mercury=Hermes=G=A4.
Mainmast=3,500=4,000=40%=P4.0D=Govt.=Creato=4 April=Mercury=Hermes=G=A4.
Mainsail=3,500=4,000=40%=P4.0D=Govt.=Creatocracy=4 April=Mercury=Hermes=G=A4.
Mainspring=6,000=60%=P6.0D=Man=Earth=Royalty=6 June=Gaia=Maia>>M=M2.
Mainstay=6,500=7,000=70%=P7.0D=7.0=Language=Assets=Mars=7 July=Pleiades.
Mainstream=10,000=1,000=100%=10.0=Physicality=Tech.=10 Oct.=Uranus=P=1Ø.
Maintain=10,000=1,000=100%=10.0=Physicality=Tech.=10 Oct.=Uranus=P=1Ø.
Mainz=9,000=90%=P9.00D=9.0=Abstraction=Gods=Saturn=9Sept.>>A=Ø.
Maitre d'=2,000=20%=P2.00D=2.0=Nature=Matter=Moon=2 Feb.=Cupid=N=C+_
Maitre d'hotel=2,500=3,000=30%=P3.0D=3.0=Cre=Stars=Muses=3 March = C=I>>GIL
Maize=2,000=20%=P2.00D=2.0=Nature=Matter=Moon=2 Feb.=Cupid=N=C+_

Maj.=500=5%=P5.00D=5.0=Law=Time=Venus=5 May=Aphrodite>>L=N.
Majesty=10,000=1,000=100%=10.0=Physicality=Tech.=10 Oct.=Uranus=P=1Ø.
Maj. Gen=1,000=100%=10.0=1.0=Mind=Sun=1 January=Helios >> M=E4.
Major=10,000=1,000=100%=10.0=Physicality=Tech.=10 Oct.=Uranus=P=1Ø.
Major John=3,500=4,000=40%=P4.0D=Govt.=Creato=4 April=Mercury=Hermes=G=A4.
Majorca=6,000=60%=P6.0D=Man=Earth=Royalty=6 June=Gaia=Maia>>M=M2.
Major domo=6,500=7,000=70%=P7.0D=7.0=Language=Assets=Mars=7 July=Pleiades.
Major General=6,500=7,000=70%=P7.0D=7.0=Language=Assets=Mars=7 July=Pleiades.
Majority=10,000=1,000=100%=10.0=Physicality=Tech.=10 Oct.=Uranus=P=1Ø.
Major league=5,000=50%=P5.00D=Law=Time=Venus=5 May = Aphrodite>>L=N.
Major medical=5,500=5.5=80%=P5.50=Earth-Midway=5 May = Gaia.
Major scale=7,500=8,000=80%=P8.0D=Economy=Currency=8 Aug.=Zeus>>E=v.
Makalu=5,500=5.5=80%=P5.50=Earth-Midway=5 May = Gaia.
Makarios III=4,500=5,000=50%=P5.00D=Law=Time=Venus=5 May = Aphrodite>>L=N.
Make=10,000=1,000=100%=10.0=Physicality=Tech.=10 Oct.=Uranus=P=1Ø.
Make believe=2,000=20%=P2.00D=2.0=Nature=Matter=Moon=2 Feb.=Cupid=N=C+_
Makeshift=5,000=50%=P5.00D=Law=Time=Venus=5 May = Aphrodite>>L=N.
Makeup=9,500=10,000=1,000=100%=10.0=Physicality=Tech.=10 Oct.=Uranus=P=1Ø.
Makeyevka=4,500=5,000=50%=P5.00D=Law=Time=Venus=5 May = Aphrodite>>L=N.
Makings=4,000=40%=P4.0D=Govt.=Creatocracy=4 April=Mercury=Hermes=G=A4.
Mako=5,500=5.5=80%=P5.50=Earth-Midway=5 May = Gaia.
Makuta=1,500=15%=P1.50D=1.5=Authority=Solar Crown=1 May = Maia.
Mal-=3,500=4,000=40%=P4.0D=Govt.=Creatocracy=4 April=Mercury=Hermes=G=A4.
Malaba Coast=4,500=5,000=50%=P5.00D=Law=Time=Venus=5 May = Aphrodite>>L=N.
Malabo=6,000=60%=P6.0D=Man=Earth=Royalty=6 June=Gaia=Maia>>M=M2.
Malacca Strait of.=7,500=8,000=80%=P8.0D=Economy=Currency=8 Aug.=Zeus>>E=v.

Malachi=5,500=5.5=80%=P5.50=Earth-Midway=5 May = Gaia.
A Hebrew prophet of the 6th cent. B.C. Inspired by Earth Midway >> Maia. Malachi is defined by the Apple online as a book of the Bible belonging to a period before Ezra and Nehemiah. From Hebrew It means my messenger. This means that when the great Goddess comes to Earth she stays in the abode region of Gaia at the center a defined location. There she acts as a messenger of God and so a prophet. She is the source of prophecies. The result 5,500 = 6,000=6.0 aligns with the period of existence of the prophet Malachi.
Gaia -Midway >> Maia is the Mind of God >> Pleiades>>Romans 11:34. Job 38:31-33.

Malachite=4,000=40%=P4.0D=Govt.=Creatocracy=4 April=Mercury=Hermes=G=A4.
Maladjustment=8,500=9,000=90%=P9.00D=9.0=Abst.=Gods=Saturn=9Sept.>>A=Ø.
Maladroit=4,000=40%=P4.0D=Govt.=Creatocracy=4 April=Mercury=Hermes=G=A4.
Malady=5,500=5.5=80%=P5.50=Earth-Midway=5 May = Gaia.
Malaga=4,500=5,000=50%=P5.00D=Law=Time=Venus=5 May = Aphrodite>>L=N.
Malagasy=5,000=50%=P5.00D=Law=Time=Venus=5 May = Aphrodite>>L=N.
Malaise=3,500=4,000=40%=P4.0D=Govt.=Creatocracy=4 April=Mercury=Hermes=G=A4.
Malamud Bernard=2,000=20%=P2.00D=2.0=Nature=Matter=Moon=2 Feb.=Cupid=N=C+_

Malamute=7,000=70%=P7.0D=7.0=Language=Assets=Mars=7 July=Pleiades.
Malapropism=9,000=90%=P9.00D=9.0=Abstraction=Gods=Saturn=9Sept.>>A=Ø.
Malapropos=4,500=5,000=50%=P5.00D=Law=Time=Venus=5 May = Aphrodite>>L=N.
Malaria=11,000=11%=P1.10D=1.1=Idea=Brainchild=Inv.=11 Nov.=SC=Athena>>I=MT.
Malarkey=5,000=50%=P5.00D=Law=Time=Venus=5 May = Aphrodite>>L=N.
Malathion=5,500=5.5=80%=P5.50=Earth-Midway=5 May = Gaia.
Malawi=4,500=5,000=50%=P5.00D=Law=Time=Venus=5 May = Aphrodite>>L=N.
Malay=9,000=90%=P9.00D=9.0=Abstraction=Gods=Saturn=9Sept.>>A=Ø.
Malayalam=3,500=4,000=40%=P4.0D=Govt.=4 April=Mercury=Hermes=G=A4.
Malay Archipelago=6,000=60%=P6.0D=Man=Earth=Royalty=6 June=Gaia=Maia>>M=M2.
Malay Peninsula=7,000=70%=P7.0D=7.0=Language=Assets=Mars=7 July=Pleiades.
Malaysia=9,500=10,000=1,000=100%=10.0=Physicality=Tech.=10 Oct.=Uranus=P=1Ø.
Malcolm X=3,000=30%=P3.0D=3.0=Creativity=Stars=Muses=3 March = C=I>>GIL.
Malcontent=2,000=20%=P2.00D=2.0=Nature=Matter=Moon=2 Feb.=Cupid=N=C+_
Maldives=7,000=70%=P7.0D=7.0=Language=Assets=Mars=7 July=Pleiades.
male=10,000=1,000=100%=10.0=Physicality=Tech.=10 Oct.=Uranus=P=1Ø.
Male=6,000=60%=P6.0D=Man=Earth=Royalty=6 June=Gaia=Maia>>M=M2.
Malecite=7,500=8,000=80%=P8.0D=Economy=Currency=8 Aug.=Zeus>>E=v.
Malediction=2,500=3,000=30%=P3.0D=3.0=Cre=Stars=Muses=3 March = C=I>>GIL.
Malefactor=4,000=40%=P4.0D=Govt.=Creatocracy=4 April=Mercury=Hermes=G=A4.
Malefic=3,500=4,000=40%=P4.0D=Govt.=Creatocracy=4 April=Mercury=Hermes=G=A4.
Maleficence=6,500=7,000=70%=P7.0D=7.0=Language=Assets=Mars=7 July=Pleiades.
Malevolent=4,000=40%=P4.0D=Govt.=Creatocracy=4 April=Mercury=Hermes=G=A4.
Malfeasance=7,500=8,000=80%=P8.0D=Economy=Currency=8 Aug.=Zeus>>E=v.
Male formation=3,500=4,000=40%=P4.0D=Govt.=Crt=4 April=Mercury=Hermes=G=A4.
Male function=2,000=20%=P2.00D=2.0=Nature=Matter=Moon=2 Feb.=Cupid=N=C+_
Mali=4,500=5,000=50%=P5.00D=Law=Time=Venus=5 May = Aphrodite>>L=N.
Malice=6,500=7,000=70%=P7.0D=7.0=Language=Assets=Mars=7 July=Pleiades.
Malign=8,000=80%=P8.0D=Economy=Currency=8 Aug.=Zeus>>E=v.
Malignant=7,500=8,000=80%=P8.0D=Economy=Currency=8 Aug.=Zeus>>E=v.
Malignity=8,500=9,000=90%=P9.00D=9.0=Abstraction=Gods=Saturn=9Sept.>>A=Ø.
Malinger=5,500=5.5=80%=P5.50=Earth-Midway=5 May = Gaia.
Mall=10,000=1,000=100%=10.0=Physicality=Tech.=10 Oct.=Uranus=P=1Ø.
Mallard=8,000=80%=P8.0D=Economy=Currency=8 Aug.=Zeus>>E=v.
Mallarmé Stéphane=2,000=20%=P2.00D=2.0=Nature=Moon=2 Feb.=Cupid=N=C+_
Malleable=6,500=7,000=70%=P7.0D=7.0=Language=Assets=Mars=7 July=Pleiades.
Mallet=13,000=13%=P1.30=Solar Core=Faculty=13 January=Athena.
Malleus=7,000=70%=P7.0D=7.0=Language=Assets=Mars=7 July=Pleiades.
Mallow=5,000=50%=P5.00D=Law=Time=Venus=5 May = Aphrodite>>L=N.
Maimō=4,500=5,000=50%=P5.00D=Law=Time=Venus=5 May = Aphrodite>>L=N.
Malnourished=3,000=30%=P3.0D=3.0=Creativity=Stars=Muses=3 March = C=I>>GIL.
Malnutrition=2,000=20%=P2.00D=2.0=Nature=Matter=Moon=2 Feb.=Cupid=N=C+_
Malocclusion=4,000=40%=P4.0D=Govt.=Creatocracy=4 April=Mercury=Hermes=G=A4.
Malodor=4,000=40%=P4.0D=Govt.=Creatocracy=4 April=Mercury=Hermes=G=A4.
Malory Thomas=2,500=3,000=30%=P3.0D=3.0=Cre=Stars=Muses=3 March = C=I>>GIL.

Maloti=1,500=15%=P1.50D=1.5=Authority=Solar Crown=1 May = Maia.
Malpractice=5,500=5.5=80%=P5.50=Earth-Midway=5 May = Gaia.
Malraux André=3,000=30%=P3.0D=3.0=Creativity=Stars=Muses=3 March = C=I>>GIL.
Malt=14,000=14%=P1.40D=1.4=Mgt.=Solar Energy=13 May=Athena=SC=0.1
Malta=6,500=7,000=70%=P7.0D=7.0=Language=Assets=Mars=7 July=Pleiades.
Malted milk=10,000=1,000=100%=10.0=Physicality=Tech.=10 Oct.=Uranus=P=1Ø.
Malthus Thomas=2,500=3,000=30%=P3.0D=3.0=Cre=Stars=Muses=3 March = C=I>>GIL.
Maltose=4,500=5,000=50%=P5.00D=Law=Time=Venus=5 May = Aphrodite>>L=N.
Maltreat=4,500=5,000=50%=P5.00D=Law=Time=Venus=5 May = Aphrodite>>L=N.
Mama=3,000=30%=P3.0D=3.0=Creativity=Stars=Muses=3 March = C=I>>GIL.
Mamba=4,000=40%=P4.0D=Govt.=Creatocracy=4 April=Mercury=Hermes=G=A4.
Mambo=5,500=5.5=80%=P5.50=Earth-Midway=5 May = Gaia.
Mammal=10,000=1,000=100%=10.0=Physicality=Tech.=10 Oct.=Uranus=P=1Ø.
Mammalogy=4,000=40%=P4.0D=Govt.=Creatocracy=4 April=Mercury=Hermes=G=A4.
Mammary=6,000=60%=P6.0D=Man=Earth=Royalty=6 June=Gaia=Maia>>M=M2.
Mammogram=3,500=4,000=40%=P4.0D=Govt.=Cr=4 April=Mercury=Hermes=G=A4.
Mammography=6,500=7,000=70%=P7.0D=7.0=Language=Assets=Mars=7 July=Pleiades.
Mammon=5,500=5.5=80%=P5.50=Earth-Midway=5 May = Gaia.
Mammoth=8,000=80%=P8.0D=Economy=Currency=8 Aug.=Zeus>>E=v.
Mamoré=8,000=80%=P8.0D=Economy=Currency=8 Aug.=Zeus>>E=v.

Man=10,000=1,000=100%=10.0=Physicality=Tech.=10 Oct.=Uranus=P=1Ø.
In the Creative Sciences, Man is the sixth (6ø) dimension of the universe. Peter Matthews-Akukalia, Castle Makupedia wrote the formula of Man, Mankind and Humanity as Man=M2. Man is a product of Mind and Matter. The Creatocracy is convinced that to solve human challenges everyone must be discovered developed and connected to his innate potentials as basis for his human capital development. This is done through our exclusive Mind Assessment Tests in various modules for all ages and categories of endeavor. This is the secret recipe to solve and resolve most social ills as unemployment, hunger, youth restiveness, inflammation and crime. This is the complete basis for Institutionalizing creativity and promoting the creative economy . So it answers the question "what is man", a combination of energy and matter. (See Law). The solution is in the test and formula.

Man Isle of.=6,000=60%=P6.0D=Man=Earth=Royalty=6 June=Gaia=Maia>>M=M2.
Man.=500=5%=P5.00D=5.0=Law=Time=Venus=5 May=Aphrodite>>L=N.
Man about town=4,500=5,000=50%=P5.00D=Law=Time=Venus=5 May =Odite>>L=N.
Manacle=14,000=14%=P1.40D=1.4=Mgt.=Solar Energy=13 May=Athena=SC=0.1
Manage=10,000=1,000=100%=10.0=Physicality=Tech.=10 Oct.=Uranus=P=1Ø.
Management=7,500=8,000=80%=P8.0D=Economy=Currency=8 Aug.=Zeus>>E=v.
Manager=7,000=70%=P7.0D=7.0=Language=Assets=Mars=7 July=Pleiades.
Managua=6,000=60%=P6.0D=Man=Earth=Royalty=6 June=Gaia=Maia>>M=M2.
Manama=4,500=5,000=50%=P5.00D=Law=Time=Venus=5 May = Aphrodite>>L=N.
Mañana=4,500=5,000=50%=P5.00D=Law=Time=Venus=5 May = Aphrodite>>L=N.
Manatee=4,500=5,000=50%=P5.00D=Law=Time=Venus=5 May = Aphrodite>>L=N.

Manaus=8,500=9,000=90%=P9.00D=9.0=Abstraction=Gods=Saturn=9Sept.>>A=Ø.
Manchester=8,000=80%=P8.0D=Economy=Currency=8 Aug.=Zeus>>E=v.
Manchu=10,000=1,000=100%=10.0=Physicality=Tech.=10 Oct.=Uranus=P=1Ø.
Manchuria=2,500=3,000=30%=P3.0D=3.0=Creativity=Stars=Muses=3 March = C=I>>GIL.
Mandala=9,500=10,000=1,000=100%=Physicality=Tech.=10 Oct.=Uranus=P=1Ø.
Mandalay=6,500=7,000=70%=P7.0D=7.0=Language=Assets=Mars=7 July=Pleiades.
Mandamus=10,000=1,000=100%=10.0=Physicality=Tech.=10 Oct.=Uranus=P=1Ø.
Mandan=10,000=1,000=100%=10.0=Physicality=Tech.=10 Oct.=Uranus=P=1Ø.
Mandarin=10,000=1,000=100%=10.0=Physicality=Tech.=10 Oct.=Uranus=P=1Ø.
Mandate=10,000=1,000=100%=10.0=Physicality=Tech.=10 Oct.=Uranus=P=1Ø.
Mandatory=3,500=4,000=40%=P4.0D=Govt.=Cr=4 April=Mercury=Hermes=G=A4.

Mandela Nelson R.=5,500=5.5=80%=P5.50=Earth-Midway=5 May = Gaia.
See book >>CASTLE MAKUPEDIA>Nelson Rolihlahla Mandela by Peter Matthews-Akukalia.

Mandible=9,500=10,000=1,000=100%=10.0=Physicality=Tech.=10 Oct.=Uranus=P=1Ø.
Mandingo=10,000=1,000=100%=10.0=Physicality=Tech.=10 Oct.=Uranus=P=1Ø.
Mandolin=8,500=9,000=90%=P9.00D=9.0=Abstraction=Gods=Saturn=9Sept.>>A=Ø.
Mandrake=10,000=1,000=100%=10.0=Physicality=Tech.=10 Oct.=Uranus=P=1Ø.
Mandrel=10,000=1,000=100%=10.0=Physicality=Tech.=10 Oct.=Uranus=P=1Ø.
Mandrill=8,000=80%=P8.0D=Economy=Currency=8 Aug.=Zeus>>E=v.
Mane=10,500=11,000=11%=P1.10D=1.1=Idea=Brainchild=Inv.=11 Nov.=SC=Athena >>I=MT.
Manège=6,000=60%=P6.0D=Man=Earth=Royalty=6 June=Gaia=Maia>>M=M2.

Manes=5,000=50%=P5.00D=Law=Time=Venus=5 May = Aphrodite>>L=N.
In ancient Roman religion, the spirits of the dead. Aphrodite controls the spirits of the dead. Aries controls the transfer process of the dead to other worlds.

Manet Edouard=2,000=20%=P2.00D=2.0=Nature=Matter=Moon=2 Feb.=Cupid=N=C+_
Maneuver=10,000=1,000=100%=10.0=Physicality=Tech.=10 Oct.=Uranus=P=1Ø.
Manful=1,000=100%=10.0=1.0=Mind=Sun=1 January=Helios >> M=E4.
Manganese=12,000=12%=P1.20D=1.2=Knowledge=Edu=12Dec.=Athena>>K=F.
Mange=10,000=1,000=100%=10.0=Physicality=Tech.=10 Oct.=Uranus=P=1Ø.
Manger=8,000=80%=P8.0D=Economy=Currency=8 Aug.=Zeus>>E=v.
Mangle1=8,000=80%=P8.0D=Economy=Currency=8 Aug.=Zeus>>E=v.
Mangle2=4,000=40%=P4.0D=Govt.=Creatocracy=4 April=Mercury=Hermes=G=A4.
Mango=9,500=10,000=1,000=100%=10.0=Physicality=Tech.=10 Oct.=Uranus=P=1Ø.
Mangrove=9,500=10,000=1,000=100%=10.0=Physicality=Tech.=10 Oct.=Uranus=P=1Ø.
Manhandle=3,500=4,000=40%=P4.0D=Govt.=Creat=4 April=Mercury=Hermes=G=A4.
Manhattan1=6,500=7,000=70%=P7.0D=7.0=Language=Assets=Mars=7 July=Pleiades.
Manhattan2=4,500=5,000=50%=P5.00D=Law=Time=Venus=5 May = Aphrodite>>L=N.

Manhole=8,000=80%=P8.0D=Economy=Currency=8 Aug.=Zeus>>E=v.
Manhood=10,000=1,000=100%=10.0=Physicality=Tech.=10 Oct.=Uranus=P=1Ø.
Man hour=8,000=80%=P8.0D=Economy=Currency=8 Aug.=Zeus>>E=v.
Manhunt=4,000=40%=P4.0D=Govt.=Creatocracy=4 April=Mercury=Hermes=G=A4.
Mania=8,500=9,000=90%=P9.00D=9.0=Abstraction=Gods=Saturn=9Sept.>>A=Ø.
-mania=4,500=5,000=50%=P5.00D=Law=Time=Venus=5 May = Aphrodite>>L=N.
Maniac=8,500=9,000=90%=P9.00D=9.0=Abstraction=Gods=Saturn=9Sept.>>A=Ø.
Manic=3,000=30%=P3.0D=3.0=Creativity=Stars=Muses=3 March = C=I>>GIL.
Manic depressive=7,000=70%=P7.0D=7.0=Language=Assets=Mars=7 July=Pleiades.
Manicotti=5,000=50%=P5.00D=Law=Time=Venus=5 May = Aphrodite>>L=N.
Manicure=6,000=60%=P6.0D=Man=Earth=Royalty=6 June=Gaia=Maia>>M=M2.
Manifest=10,000=1,000=100%=10.0=Physicality=Tech.=10 Oct.=Uranus=P=1Ø.
Manifestation=4,000=40%=P4.0D=Govt.=Creatocracy=4 April=Mercury=Hermes=G=A4.

Manifesto=6,000=60%=P6.0D=Man=Earth=Royalty=6 June=Gaia=Maia>>M=M2.
See book >> Template & Manifesto for the Creative Economy 2: Principles of Psychoeconomix by Peter Matthews-Akukalia.

Manifold=9,000=90%=P9.00D=9.0=Abstraction=Gods=Saturn=9Sept.>>A=Ø.
Manikin=5,000=50%=P5.00D=Law=Time=Venus=5 May = Aphrodite>>L=N.
Manila=7,000=70%=P7.0D=7.0=Language=Assets=Mars=7 July=Pleiades.
Manila Hemp=8,000=80%=P8.0D=Economy=Currency=8 Aug.=Zeus>>E=v.
Manila paper=5,500=5.5=80%=P5.50=Earth-Midway=5 May = Gaia.
Manioc=2,000=20%=P2.00D=2.0=Nature=Matter=Moon=2 Feb.=Cupid=N=C+_
Manipulate=10,000=1,000=100%=10.0=Physicality=Tech.=10 Oct.=Uranus=P=1Ø.
Manitoba=5,000=50%=P5.00D=Law=Time=Venus=5 May = Aphrodite>>L=N.
Manitou=6,500=7,000=70%=P7.0D=7.0=Language=Assets=Mars=7 July=Pleiades.
Mankind=4,000=40%=P4.0D=Govt.=Creatocracy=4 April=Mercury=Hermes=G=A4.
Manly=6,500=7,000=70%=P7.0D=7.0=Language=Assets=Mars=7 July=Pleiades.
Man made=2,500=3,000=30%=P3.0D=3.0=Creativity=Stars=Muses=3 March = C=I>>GIL.
Mann Horace.=2,000=20%=P2.00D=2.0=Nature=Matter=Moon=2 Feb.=Cupid=N=C+_
Mann Thomas=3,000=30%=P3.0D=3.0=Creativity=Stars=Muses=3 March = C=I>>GIL.
Manna=10,000=1,000=100%=10.0=Physicality=Tech.=10 Oct.=Uranus=P=1Ø.
Manned=4,500=5,000=50%=P5.00D=Law=Time=Venus=5 May = Aphrodite>>L=N.
Mannequin=10,000=1,000=100%=10.0=Physicality=Tech.=10 Oct.=Uranus=P=1Ø.
Manner=10,000=1,000=100%=10.0=Physicality=Tech.=10 Oct.=Uranus=P=1Ø.
Mannered=6,500=7,000=70%=P7.0D=7.0=Language=Assets=Mars=7 July=Pleiades.
Mannerism=9,500=10,000=1,000=100%=10.0=Physicality=Tech.=10 Oct.=Uranus=P=1Ø.
Mannerly=1,500=15%=P1.50D=1.5=Authority=Solar Crown=1 May = Maia.
Mannheim=7,500=8,000=80%=P8.0D=Economy=Currency=8 Aug.=Zeus>>E=v.
Manikin=1,500=15%=P1.50D=1.5=Authority=Solar Crown=1 May = Maia.
Mannish=4,500=5,000=50%=P5.00D=Law=Time=Venus=5 May = Aphrodite>>L=N.
Man-of-war=3,000=30%=P3.0D=3.0=Creativity=Stars=Muses=3 March = C=I>>GIL.
Manometer=7,500=8,000=80%=P8.0D=Economy=Currency=8 Aug.=Zeus>>E=v.

Manor=9,000=90%=P9.00D=9.0=Abstraction=Gods=Saturn=9Sept.>>A=Ø.
Manpower=7,500=8,000=80%=P8.0D=Economy=Currency=8 Aug.=Zeus>>E=v.
Manqué=4,000=40%=P4.0D=Govt.=Creatocracy=4 April=Mercury=Hermes=G=A4.
Mansard=10,000=1,000=100%=10.0=Physicality=Tech.=10 Oct.=Uranus=P=1Ø.
Manse=8,500=9,000=90%=P9.00D=9.0=Abstraction=Gods=Saturn=9Sept.>>A=Ø.
Mansion=3,500=4,000=40%=P4.0D=Govt.=Cre=4 April=Mercury=Hermes=G=A4.
Man sized=1,500=15%=P1.50D=1.5=Authority=Solar Crown=1 May = Maia.
Man slaughter=8,500=9,000=90%=P9.00D=9.0=Abst.=Gods=Saturn=9Sept.>>A=Ø.
Manta=10,000=1,000=100%=10.0=Physicality=Tech.=10 Oct.=Uranus=P=1Ø.
Mantegna Andrea.=3,000=30%=P3.0D=3.0=Cre=Stars=Muses=3 March = C=I>>GIL.
Mantel=7,000=70%=P7.0D=7.0=Language=Assets=Mars=7 July=Pleiades.
Mantelpiece=1,500=15%=P1.50D=1.5=Authority=Solar Crown=1 May = Maia.
Mantilla=8,000=80%=P8.0D=Economy=Currency=8 Aug.=Zeus>>E=v.
Mantis=8,500=9,000=90%=P9.00D=9.0=Abstraction=Gods=Saturn=9Sept.>>A=Ø.
Mantissa=4,000=40%=P4.0D=Govt.=Creatocracy=4 April=Mercury=Hermes=G=A4.
Mantle=10,000=1,000=100%=10.0=Physicality=Tech.=10 Oct.=Uranus=P=1Ø.

Mantra=7,500=8,000=80%=P8.0D=Economy=Currency=8 Aug.=Zeus>>E=v.
Hinduism. A sacred verbal formula repeated in prayer, meditation, or incantation. Aligns with the resultant proving that computing is a form of prayer and formulas are the means.

Mantua=3,500=4,000=40%=P4.0D=Govt.=Creatocracy=4 April=Mercury=Hermes=G=A4.
Manual=10,000=1,000=100%=10.0=Physicality=Tech.=10 Oct.=Uranus=P=1Ø.
Manual alphabet=7,000=70%=P7.0D=7.0=Language=Assets=Mars=7 July=Pleiades.
Manufactory=1,000=100%=10.0=1.0=Mind=Sun=1 January=Helios >> M=E4.
Manufacture=10,000=1,000=100%=10.0=Physicality=Tech.=10 Oct.=Uranus=P=1Ø.
Manumit=4,000=40%=P4.0D=Govt.=Creatocracy=4 April=Mercury=Hermes=G=A4.
Manure=7,500=8,000=80%=P8.0D=Economy=Currency=8 Aug.=Zeus>>E=v.
Manuscript=10,000=1,000=100%=10.0=Physicality=Tech.=10 Oct.=Uranus=P=1Ø.
Manx=4,500=5,000=50%=P5.00D=Law=Time=Venus=5 May = Aphrodite>>L=N.
Many=10,000=1,000=100%=10.0=Physicality=Tech.=10 Oct.=Uranus=P=1Ø.
Many sided=5,500=5.5=80%=P5.50=Earth-Midway=5 May = Gaia.
Manzanita=6,500=7,000=70%=P7.0D=7.0=Language=Assets=Mars=7 July=Pleiades.
Maoism=4,500=5,000=50%=P5.00D=Law=Time=Venus=5 May = Aphrodite>>L=N.
Maori=6,000=60%=P6.0D=Man=Earth=Royalty=6 June=Gaia=Maia>>M=M2.
Mao Zedong=3,500=4,000=40%=P4.0D=Govt.=4 April=Mercury=Hermes=G=A4.
Map=11,500=12,000=12%=P1.20D=1.2=Knowledge=Edu=12Dec.=Athena>>K=F.
MAP=1,500=15%=P1.50D=1.5=Authority=Solar Crown=1 May = Maia.
Maple=10,000=1,000=100%=10.0=Physicality=Tech.=10 Oct.=Uranus=P=1Ø.
Maple sugar=4,000=40%=P4.0D=Govt.=Creatocracy=4 April=Mercury=Hermes=G=A4.
Maple syrup=5,500=5.5=80%=P5.50=Earth-Midway=5 May = Gaia.
Maputo=5,000=50%=P5.00D=Law=Time=Venus=5 May = Aphrodite>>L=N.
Mar=4,000=40%=P4.0D=Govt.=Creatocracy=4 April=Mercury=Hermes=G=A4.
mar.=1,000=100%=10.0=1.0=Mind=Sun=1 January=Helios >> M=E4.

Mar.=500=5%=P5.00D=5.0=Law=Time=Venus=5 May=Aphrodite>>L=N.
Marabou=11,500=12,000=12%=P1.20D=1.2=Knowledge=Edu=12Dec.=Athena>>K=F.
Maraca=6,500=7,000=70%=P7.0D=7.0=Language=Assets=Mars=7 July=Pleiades.
Maracaibo=7,500=8,000=80%=P8.0D=Economy=Currency=8 Aug.=Zeus>>E=v.
Maranōn=9,500=10,000=1,000=100%=10.0=Physicality=Tech.=10 Oct.=Uranus=P=1Ø.
Maraschino=8,000=80%=P8.0D=Economy=Currency=8 Aug.=Zeus>>E=v.
Maraschino cherry=4,500=5,000=50%=P5.00D=Law=Time=Venus=5 May =Odite>>L=N.
Marat Jean=3,500=4,000=40%=P4.0D=Govt.=4 April=Mercury=Hermes=G=A4.
Marathi=4,000=40%=P4.0D=Govt.=Creatocracy=4 April=Mercury=Hermes=G=A4.
Marathon=10,000=1,000=100%=10.0=Physicality=Tech.=10 Oct.=Uranus=P=1Ø.
Maraud=4,000=40%=P4.0D=Govt.=Creatocracy=4 April=Mercury=Hermes=G=A4.
Marble=10,000=1,000=100%=10.0=Physicality=Tech.=10 Oct.=Uranus=P=1Ø.
Marbled=6,000=60%=P6.0D=Man=Earth=Royalty=6 June=Gaia=Maia>>M=M2.
Marcasite=10,000=1,000=100%=10.0=Physicality=Tech.=10 Oct.=Uranus=P=1Ø.
March1=10,000=1,000=100%=10.0=Physicality=Tech.=10 Oct.=Uranus=P=1Ø.
March2=4,500=5,000=50%=P5.00D=Law=Time=Venus=5 May = Aphrodite>>L=N.

March=8,000=80%=P8.0D=Economy=Currency=8 Aug.=Zeus>>E=v.
The 3rd month of the Gregorian calendar. See table at calendar. < Lat. Mārtius (mēnsis), (month) of Mars. Result shows an influence of Mars (Aries) and Zeus (Jupiter) so there is a close connection between March and July. March 13 energy will be equivalent to July 6 energy. March Day 13:Value:7.0, Planetary Type:Mars, Human Type:Consulting, Birth Energy Level:100%. July 6 >>Day 6:Value:6.0 Planetary Type:Earth Human Type: Health Birth Energy Level:100%. Clearly persons born on these dates have certain things in common a phenomenon known as "spiritual twins". They will think alike and behave so. Queen Alice was born on March 13 and the Emperor on July 6. March is the influence of Mars or Aries and July is the month of the manifestation of Aries himself. Hence one is under the programming as in Marsian energy the other is under the manifestation. The combined effect of Zeus (8.0) and March (3.0<3rd March) is thus computed. 8.0*3.0x=px=11+24=35x=px=299=300=3.0>>Muses. Persons born in March are muses. This means that Alice is a business muse to Peter through marriage. The discrete result 299>>2.0>> love>> Marriage. 99=Double impact of muses on March birth persons with 100% physical attributes seen in behavior such as slowness in thinking and time conscious. In everyday life March is the month of business muses achieved through brainstorming.

Marchioness=8,500=9,000=90%=P9.00D=9.0=Abstraction=Gods=Saturn=9Sept.>>A=Ø.
Marconi Guglielmo=4,000=40%=P4.0D=Govt.=4 April=Mercury=Hermes=G=A4.
Marcos Ferdinand=3,500=4,000=40%=P4.0D=Govt.=4 April=Mercury=Hermes=G=A4.
Marcus Aurelius=4,000=40%=P4.0D=Govt.=4 April=Mercury=Hermes=G=A4.
Mar del Plata=7,000=70%=P7.0D=7.0=Language=Assets=Mars=7 July=Pleiades.
Mardigras=8,000=80%=P8.0D=Economy=Currency=8 Aug.=Zeus>>E=v.
Mare1=4,000=40%=P4.0D=Govt.=Creatocracy=4 April=Mercury=Hermes=G=A4.

Mare2=8,500=9,000=90%=P9.00D=9.0=Abstraction=Gods=Saturn=9Sept.>>A=Ø. Astronomy. Any of the large dark areas on the moon or planets, especially Mars. Lat., sea. The Creatocracy. In his advance study of Nature and planetary energy Peter Matthews-Akukalia, Castle Makupedia discovered that man was made from the moon or lunar craters. He computes the spiritual source of a person, tracks the innate potentials and their link to the mare or sea region of the moon. This is how he discovered he was sourced from Mare Imbrium the sea of Showers with special gifts in sky matters, rain, energy and matter particles. In simple terms he was born a scientist in the first place. This is highly service oriented and makes us tick. He successfully used computations to find the missing link between the human soul and the cosmos, the last wishes of Plato. This made the Creation story of Genesis the truth. "Man was made from the dust of the ground", not the dust of the earth. - See Makupedia Sciences, Principles of Naturecology by Peter Matthews-Akukalia.

Margaret of Anjou=3,500=4,000=40%=P4.0D=Govt.=4 April=Mercury=Hermes=G=A4.

Margarine=7,500=8,000=80%=P8.0D=Economy=Currency=8 Aug.=Zeus>>E=v. Eating Margarine builds the brain to develop computational and programming abilities. It also links the human spirit to GOD and the ability to do business. Margarines are mantra.

Margarita=7,000=70%=P7.0D=7.0=Language=Assets=Mars=7 July=Pleiades. Margin=10,000=1,000=100%=10.0=Physicality=Tech.=10 Oct.=Uranus=P=1Ø. Marginal=7,000=70%=P7.0D=7.0=Language=Assets=Mars=7 July=Pleiades. Marginalia=6,500=7,000=70%=P7.0D=7.0=Language=Assets=Mars=7 July=Pleiades.

Margrethe II=3,500=4,000=40%=P4.0D=Govt.Creat.=4 April=Mercury=Hermes=G=A4. Born 1940. Queen of Denmark (since 1972). As at 2021 she is 81years old and has been Queen for at least 49years. A perfect example of a Creatocracy on IP rights. The rights of the King as the God of Creatocracy are inalienable imprescriptible and perpetual.

Mariachi=11,500=12,000=12%=P1.20D=1.2=Knowledge=Edu=12Dec.=Athena>>K=F. A street band in Mexico. French. Marriage. Marriage is the invention of Athena. It is in order that she benefits from her invention. Castle Makupedia weds her where she becomes Athena Castle Makupedia. See book >> The Creatocracy Republic of Castle Makupedia.

Mariana Islands=11,000=11%=P1.10D=1.1=Idea=Brainchild=Inv.=11 Nov.=Athena>>I=MT. Maria Theresa=4,000=40%=P4.0D=Govt.=Creatocracy=4 April=Mercury=Hermes=G=A4. Marie Antoinette=6,000=60%=P6.0D=Man=Earth=Royalty=6 June=Gaia=Maia>>M=M2. Marie de Médicis=10,500=11,000=11%=P1.10D=1.1=Idea=Braincd.=11Nov.=Athena>>I=MT. Marigold=6,500=7,000=70%=P7.0D=7.0=Language=Assets=Mars=7 July=Pleiades. Marijuana=10,000=1,000=100%=10.0=Physicality=Tech.=10 Oct.=Uranus=P=1Ø.

Marimba=6,500=7,000=70%=P7.0D=7.0=Language=Assets=Mars=7 July=Pleiades.
Marin John=2,000=20%=P2.00D=2.0=Nature=Matter=Moon=2 Feb.=Cupid=N=C+_
Marinade=6,500=7,000=70%=P7.0D=7.0=Language=Assets=Mars=7 July=Pleiades.
Marinate=8,000=80%=P8.0D=Economy=Currency=8 Aug.=Zeus>>E=v.
Marine=10,000=1,000=100%=10.0=Physicality=Tech.=10 Oct.=Uranus=P=1∅.
Marine Corps=5,500=5.5=80%=P5.50=Earth-Midway=5 May = Gaia.
Mariner=1,000=100%=10.0=1.0=Mind=Sun=1 January=Helios >> M=E4.
Marionette=4,000=40%=P4.0D=Govt.=Creatocracy=4 April=Mercury=Hermes=G=A4.
Maritain Jacques=3,000=30%=P3.0D=3.0=Creativity=Stars=Muses=3 March = C=I>>GIL.
Marital=4,000=40%=P4.0D=Govt.=Creatocracy=4 April=Mercury=Hermes=G=A4.
Maritime=9,500=10,000=1,000=100%=10.0=Physicality=Tech.=10 Oct.=Uranus=P=1∅.

Maritime˙ Provinces=6,000=60%=P6.0D=Man=Earth=Royalty=6 June=Gaia=Maia
   >>M=M2.
Books and works of Peter Matthews-Akukalia constitute Provinces of the Creatocracy.

Marius Gaius.=4,000=40%=P4.0D=Govt.=Creatocracy=4 April=Mercury=Hermes=G=A4.
Marjoram=7,000=70%=P7.0D=7.0=Language=Assets=Mars=7 July=Pleiades.
Mark1=10,000=1,000=100%=10.0=Physicality=Tech.=10 Oct.=Uranus=P=1∅.

Mark2=3,500=4,000=40%=P4.0D=Govt.=Creatocracy=4 April=Mercury=Hermes=G=A4.
The Deutsche Mark. A unit of Marc, unit of weight. Scores 3.5/10 on the money standard.
See dollars. See money. The Maks currencies weighs 10/10 on the money standards.

Mark=2,000=20%=P2.00D=2.0=Nature=Matter=Moon=2 Feb.=Cupid=N=C+_
Inspired by Cupid and Artemis. The second 2nd>2.0 Gospel.
2.0*2.0x=px=4+4=8x=px=24=2.4>>International Business guided by the love of Cupid
(Eros) and hunting adventurous nature of Artemis the virgin Goddess of the Moon. It
aligns with the answers because 2.4 rests in the dimension of Nature >> Moon >> Matter
>> Techniques >> Things >> 2.0. A feast day is celebrated on April 25 whose day energy is:
Day 25: Value:3.0, Planetary Type:Star, Human Type: Creativity, Birth Energy Level:50.0%
On this date muses grant special knowledge in the sciences and arts. Note that St. Mark
was a close companion of St. Peter and St. Paul. Peter for the marine - science related
and Paul a lawyer for the arts. They were also two. Peter was charged with love and Paul
adventures resulting to many travels. Peter, Paul and Mark makes three >> 3.0 hence God
accepts the celebrations of April 28. Precision is established herein.

Mark, Saint=5,500=5.5=80%=P5.50=Earth-Midway=5 May = Gaia.
St. Mark is an incarnation of Maia who manifests as Gaia at the midway. At midway
Maia rests in the abode of Gaia and so Mark must rest in the bosom of Peter and Paul.
See Mark.

Mark Antony=4,500=5,000=50%=P5.00D=Law=Time=Venus=5 May = Aphrodite>>L=N.
Markdown=2,000=20%=P2.00D=2.0=Nature=Matter=Moon=2 Feb.=Cupid=N=C+_
Marked=7,500=8,000=80%=P8.0D=Economy=Currency=8 Aug.=Zeus>>E=v.
Market=10,000=1,000=100%=10.0=Physicality=Tech.=10 Oct.=Uranus=P=1Ø.

Marketplace=8,500=9,000=90%=P9.00D=9.0=Abstraction=Gods=Saturn=9Sept.>>A=Ø.
The world of business and commerce. A market is a means to an end not an end in itself. At 8.5-9.0 indicates that the market is open to both humans and spirits to trade talents. Now 9.0 >> Council of Muses do trading during abstraction, secret or dark hours. This means that at sleep the human spirit travels to the cosmic market to buy and sell based on faith.

Market price=4,500=5,000=50%=P5.00D=Law=Time=Venus=5 May = Aphrodite>>L=N.
The price of a thing depends on the means by which it emerges. First is the relationships of constants and variables. Second is the margin of 10.0 which is 5.0. This means that natural market price of a thing must be computed on the planetary values of the Moon, Venus, Jupiter and Neptune. The moon is the foundation of all matter and products. Venus is the foundation of all brightness that beautifies and brands a product. It is also the rights and authority to do business. Jupiter is the basis for the power of demand and supply seen as economy business transactions banking currencies and stability. Neptune is the foundation for all mathematical calculations because it is the first planet to be so discovered. Hence all currencies and prices must be based on natural precision which can only come through computed metrics. See Money.

Market value=6,000=60%=P6.0D=Man=Earth=Royalty=6 June=Gaia=Maia>>M=M2.
All market standards are based on values that are transmissible and practical on Earth.

Mark ham=3,000=30%=P3.0D=3.0=Creativity=Stars=Muses=3 March = C=I>>GIL.
Marking=7,000=70%=P7.0D=7.0=Language=Assets=Mars=7 July=Pleiades.

Markka=4,000=40%=P4.0D=Govt.=Creatocracy=4 April=Mercury=Hermes=G=A4.
A currency. Finn. < Swed. Mark, Mark. Score= 4.0/10. See Money., Mark2.

Marksman=2,500=3,000=30%=P3.0D=3.0=Creativity=Stars=Muses=3   March   =
    C=I>>GIL.
Marks woman=2,500=3,000=30%=P3.0D=3.0=Cre=Stars=Muses=3 March = C=I>>GIL.

Markup=5,500=5.5=80%=P5.50=Earth-Midway=5 May = Gaia.
Could as well be Maksup, Makup. The right to fix and adjust a price rests with the midway agency being one neutral in authority and means, the Creatocracy. See Template & Manifesto for the Creative Economy 2: Principles of Psychoeconomix by Peter Matthews-Akukalia. These rights are drawn from the encyclopedia of Castle Makupedia.

Marl=6,000=60%=P6.0D=Man=Earth=Royalty=6 June=Gaia=Maia>>M=M2.
Marlborough=3,000=30%=P3.0D=3.0=Creativity=Stars=Muses=3 March = C=I>>GIL.

Marlin=6,000=60%=P6.0D=Man=Earth=Royalty=6 June=Gaia=Maia>>M=M2.
Used in reference to human. "Soft Marlin". See The Creatocracy Republic of Castle
Makupedia > Legend of the Monarchs - a play on William Shakespeare.

Marlinspike=9,000=90%=P9.00D=9.0=Abstraction=Gods=Saturn=9Sept.>>A=Ø.

Marlowe Christopher=3,000=30%=P3.0D=3.0=Cre=Stars=Muses=3 March = C=I>>GIL.
Read the Creatocracy Republic>> Legend of the Monarchs. See Marlin.

Marmalade=8,500=9,000=90%=P9.00D=9.0=Abstraction=Gods=Saturn=9Sept.>>A=Ø.
Marmara Sea of.=4,500=5,000=50%=P5.00D=Law=Time=Venus=5 May =Odite>>L=N.
Marmoreal=5,500=5.5=80%=P5.50=Earth-Midway=5 May = Gaia.
Marmoset=9,500=10,000=1,000=100%=10.0=Physicality=Tech.=10 Oct.=Uranus=P=1Ø.
Marmot=6,500=7,000=70%=P7.0D=7.0=Language=Assets=Mars=7 July=Pleiades.
Marne=8,500=9,000=90%=P9.00D=9.0=Abstraction=Gods=Saturn=9Sept.>>A=Ø.
Maroon1=7,000=70%=P7.0D=7.0=Language=Assets=Mars=7 July=Pleiades.
Maroon2=3,000=30%=P3.0D=3.0=Creativity=Stars=Muses=3 March = C=I>>GIL.
Marquand John=2,500=3,000=30%=P3.0D=3.0=Cre=Stars=Muses=3 March = C=I>>GIL.
Marquee=11,500=12,000=12%=P1.20D=1.2=Knowledge=Edu=12Dec.=Athena>>K=F.
Marquesas Islands=5,500=5.5=80%=P5.50=Earth-Midway=5 May = Gaia.
Marquetry=9,000=90%=P9.00D=9.0=Abstraction=Gods=Saturn=9Sept.>>A=Ø.
Marquette Jacques.=3,500=4,000=40%=P4.0D=Govt.=Cre=4 April=Hermes=G=A4.
Marquis=9,000=90%=P9.00D=9.0=Abstraction=Gods=Saturn=9Sept.>>A=Ø.
Marquise=1,500=15%=P1.50D=1.5=Authority=Solar Crown=1 May = Maia.
Marquisette=5,000=50%=P5.00D=Law=Time=Venus=5 May = Aphrodite>>L=N.
Marrakesh=6,500=7,000=70%=P7.0D=7.0=Language=Assets=Mars=7 July=Pleiades.

Marriage=8,000=80%=P8.0D=Economy=Currency=8 Aug.=Zeus>>E=v.
Therefore shall a man leave his father and his mother, and shall cleave unto his wife: and
they shall be one flesh. - Genesis 2:24
Computing marriage on the Maks. Man=6.0, Wife=6.0
6.0*6.0x=px=12+36=48x=px=480=500=50%=50/100=1/2=0.5=1.0
So GOD uses Makumatics to measure and compute things. Mathematics cannot alone
prove how both become one flesh. However couples must conduct the Mind Assessment
& Psychosurgery MAPS Tests to help them understand their innate nature.

Marrow=13,500=14,000=14%=P1.40D=1.4=Mgt.=Solar Energy=13 May=Athena=SC=0.1
Marry=10,000=1,000=100%=10.0=Physicality=Tech.=10 Oct.=Uranus=P=1Ø.

Mars=14,000=14%=P1.40D=1.4=Mgt.=Solar Energy=13 May=Athena=SC=0.1
Roman myth. The God of War. See March.

Marseilles=5,500=5.5=80%=P5.50=Earth-Midway=5 May = Gaia.
Marsh=4,500=5,000=50%=P5.00D=Law=Time=Venus=5 May = Aphrodite>>L=N.
Marshal=10,000=1,000=100%=10.0=Physicality=Tech.=10 Oct.=Uranus=P=1Ø.
Marshall George=6,000=60%=P6.0D=Man=Earth=Royalty=6 June=Gaia=Maia>>M=M2.
Marshall,John=7,000=70%=P7.0D=7.0=Language=Assets=Mars=7 July=Pleiades.
Marshall,Thurgood=5,000=50%=P5.00D=Law=Time=Venus=5 May = Aphrodite>>L=N.
Marshall Islands.=5,500=5.5=80%=P5.50=Earth-Midway=5 May = Gaia.
Marshmallow=10,000=1,000=100%=10.0=Physicality=Tech.=10 Oct.=Uranus=P=1Ø.
Marsh marigold=4,000=40%=P4.0D=Govt.=4 April=Mercury=Hermes=G=A4.
Marsupial=10,000=1,000=100%=10.0=Physicality=Tech.=10 Oct.=Uranus=P=1Ø.
Mart=3,000=30%=P3.0D=3.0=Creativity=Stars=Muses=3 March = C=I>>GIL.
Marten=10,000=1,000=100%=10.0=Physicality=Tech.=10 Oct.=Uranus=P=1Ø.
Martha's Vineyard=5,500=5.5=80%=P5.50=Earth-Midway=5 May = Gaia.
Marti José=4,000=40%=P4.0D=Govt.=Creatocracy=4 April=Mercury=Hermes=G=A4.

---

martial=5,500=5.5=80%=P5.50=Earth-Midway=5 May = Gaia.
Of or suggestive of war. Of or connected with military life. < Lat. Mārs, Mars.]

Martial=3,000=30%=P3.0D=3.0=Creativity=Stars=Muses=3 March = C=I>>GIL.

Martial art=6,000=60%=P6.0D=Man=Earth=Royalty=6 June=Gaia=Maia>>M=M2.
For the Creatocracy we have the Mind arts. See Genre.

Martial law=10,500=11,000=11%=P1.10D=1.1=Idea=Brainchild.=11 Nov.=Athena>>I=MT.
The Creatocracy is governed by Mind Laws, Creatocratic Laws, Castle Makupedia Laws.

Martian=5,000=50%=P5.00D=Law=Time=Venus=5 May = Aphrodite>>L=N.
Martin=4,500=5,000=50%=P5.00D=Law=Time=Venus=5 May = Aphrodite>>L=N.
Martinet=4,000=40%=P4.0D=Govt.=Creatocracy=4 April=Mercury=Hermes=G=A4.
Martini=5,000=50%=P5.00D=Law=Time=Venus=5 May = Aphrodite>>L=N.
Martinique=10,000=1,000=100%=10.0=Physicality=Tech.=10 Oct.=Uranus=P=1Ø.

Martin Luther King Day=8,000=80%=P8.0D=Economy=Currency=8 Aug.=Zeus>>E=v.
The 3rd Monday in January. 8.0*3.0x=px=11+24=35x=px=299=300=3.0 >> Muses.

Martyr=12,000=12%=P1.20D=1.2=Knowledge=Edu=12Dec.=Athena>>K=F.
Martyrdom is a knowledge system that must be studied for better alternatives. The
concern here is why must a man die for religious reasons. Does this really please GOD?
An eternal question especially for a God who expects one to be creative about things.

Marvel=8,500=9,000=90%=P9.00D=9.0=Abstraction=Gods=Saturn=9Sept.>>A=Ø.
Marvel Andrew=2,500=3,000=30%=P3.0D=3.0=Cre=Stars=Muses=3 March = C=I>>GIL.
Marvelous=3,500=4,000=40%=P4.0D=Govt.=Creatocracy=4 April=Hermes=G=A4.
Marx Karl=3,500=4,000=40%=P4.0D=Govt.=Creatocracy=4 April=Hermes=G=A4.
Marxism=5,500=5.5=80%=P5.50=Earth-Midway=5 May = Gaia.
Marxism-Leninism=4,000=40%=P4.0D=Govt.=Creatocracy=4 April=Hermes=G=A4.

Mary=3,000=30%=P3.0D=3.0=Creativity=Stars=Muses=3 March = C=I>>GIL.
In the Bible, the mother of Jesus. A muse incarnation.

Mary I=5,000=50%=P5.00D=Law=Time=Venus=5 May = Aphrodite>>L=N.
Mary II.=7,000=70%=P7.0D=7.0=Language=Assets=Mars=7 July=Pleiades.
Maryland=5,500=5.5=80%=P5.50=Earth-Midway=5 May = Gaia.

Mary Magdalene=9,500=10,000=1,000=100%=10.0=Phy=Tech.=10 Oct.=Uranus=P=1Ø.
In the Bible, a woman whom Jesus cured of evil spirits; also identified with the repentant prostitute who washed Jesus feet. We see a double reference system here (2.0). A prophetic of the discovery of the means to technology. Her life must be studied for statements and actions that indicate such signs in the Bible and possibly other sources. 10.0*2.0x=px=12+20=32x=px=272=300=3.0 >> Muses.
Results indicate three muses were at work here. They were Jesus >> Hermes. Mary Magdalene whom Jesus cured indicating the muse of health and medicine who became the Goddess Maia. Mary Magdalene the prostitute who washed the feet of Jesus. Greek myth teaches how Aphrodite cursed three women with prostitution for insulting her office as a Goddess. So this indicates the presence of the muse Aphrodite. A discovery here is that people become distinguished in their areas of endeavors to attain the status of muses and after many more steps of process discovery and computational technique become a God. Bible teaches that men who have done righteous works become stars for ever. Stars are the physical equivalent for muses and the criteria here is creativity. In the Revelation 2:22-25 Jesus indicated that one man will attain the status of a God and be given the morning star. The rod to rule the nations is a pen, law, righteousness earned through much rights.

Mary Queen of Scots=5,000=50%=P5.00D=Law=Time=Venus=5 May = Aphrodite>>L=N.
Read The Creatocracy Republic >> Legend of the Monarchs by Peter Matthews-Akukalia.

Marzipan=6,000=60%=P6.0D=Man=Earth=Royalty=6 June=Gaia=Maia>>M=M2.
Masai=6,000=60%=P6.0D=Man=Earth=Royalty=6 June=Gaia=Maia>>M=M2.
Masaryk Tomás=6,000=60%=P6.0D=Man=Earth=Royalty=6 June=Gaia=Maia>>M=M2.
Masc.=1,000=100%=10.0=1.0=Mind=Sun=1 January=Helios >> M=E4.
Mascara=5,500=5.5=80%=P5.50=Earth-Midway=5 May = Gaia.
Mascot=8,500=9,000=90%=P9.00D=9.0=Abstraction=Gods=Saturn=9Sept.>>A=Ø.
Masculine=10,000=1,000=100%=10.0=Physicality=Tech.=10 Oct.=Uranus=P=1Ø.

Masefield John=2,000=20%=P2.00D=2.0=Nature=Matter=Moon=2 Feb.=Cupid=N=C+_
Maser=10,000=1,000=100%=10.0=Physicality=Tech.=10 Oct.=Uranus=P=1Ø.
Maseru=4,500=5,000=50%=P5.00D=Law=Time=Venus=5 May = Aphrodite>>L=N.
Mash=10,000=1,000=100%=10.0=Physicality=Tech.=10 Oct.=Uranus=P=1Ø.
MASH=2,000=20%=P2.00D=2.0=Nature=Matter=Moon=2 Feb.=Cupid=N=C+_
Mask=10,000=1,000=100%=10.0=Physicality=Tech.=10 Oct.=Uranus=P=1Ø.
Masochism=14,500=15,000=15%=P1.50D=1.5=Authority=Solar Crown=1 May = Maia.
Mason=6,000=60%=P6.0D=Man=Earth=Royalty=6 June=Gaia=Maia>>M=M2.
Mason-Dixon Line=8,500=9,000=90%=P9.00D=9.0=Abst.=Gods=Saturn=9Sept.>>A=Ø.
Masonic=2,500=3,000=30%=P3.0D=3.0=Creativity=Stars=Muses=3 March = C=I>>GIL.
Mason jar=9,000=90%=P9.00D=9.0=Abstraction=Gods=Saturn=9Sept.>>A=Ø.
Masonry=5,500=5.5=80%=P5.50=Earth-Midway=5 May = Gaia.
Masque=8,500=9,000=90%=P9.00D=9.0=Abstraction=Gods=Saturn=9Sept.>>A=Ø.
Masquerade=10,000=1,000=100%=10.0=Physicality=Tech.=10 Oct.=Uranus=P=1Ø.
mass=10,000=1,000=100%=10.0=Physicality=Tech.=10 Oct.=Uranus=P=1Ø.
Mass=5,000=50%=P5.00D=Law=Time=Venus=5 May = Aphrodite>>L=N.
Mass.=500=5%=P5.00D=5.0=Law=Time=Venus=5 May=Aphrodite>>L=N.
Massachusett=10,000=1,000=100%=10.0=Physicality=Tech.=10 Oct.=Uranus=P=1Ø.
Massachusetts=5,000=50%=P5.00D=Law=Time=Venus=5 May = Aphrodite>>L=N.
Massacre=10,000=1,000=100%=10.0=Physicality=Tech.=10 Oct.=Uranus=P=1Ø.
Massage=8,500=9,000=90%=P9.00D=9.0=Abstraction=Gods=Saturn=9Sept.>>A=Ø.
Massasoit=2,500=3,000=30%=P3.0D=3.0=Creativity=Stars=Muses=3 March = C=I>>GIL.
Massenet Jules=3,000=30%=P3.0D=3.0=Creativity=Stars=Muses=3 March = C=I>>GIL.
Masseur=5,000=50%=P5.00D=Law=Time=Venus=5 May = Aphrodite>>L=N.
Masseuse=5,000=50%=P5.00D=Law=Time=Venus=5 May = Aphrodite>>L=N.
Massif Central=3,500=4,000=40%=P4.0D=Govt.=Creatocracy=4 April=Hermes=G=A4.
Mass market=7,000=70%=P7.0D=7.0=Language=Assets=Mars=7 July=Pleiades.
Mass medium=4,000=40%=P4.0D=Govt.=Creatocracy=4 April=Mercury=Hermes=G=A4.
Mass number=5,500=5.5=80%=P5.50=Earth-Midway=5 May = Gaia.
Mass produce=7,000=70%=P7.0D=7.0=Language=Assets=Mars=7 July=Pleiades.
Mast=10,000=1,000=100%=10.0=Physicality=Tech.=10 Oct.=Uranus=P=1Ø.
Mastectomy=3,500=4,000=40%=P4.0D=Govt.=Creatocracy=4 April=Hermes=G=A4.
Master=10,000=1,000=100%=10.0=Physicality=Tech.=10 Oct.=Uranus=P=1Ø.
Master chief petty officer=5,500=5.5=80%=P5.50=Earth-Midway=5 May = Gaia.
Masterful=2,000=20%=P2.00D=2.0=Nature=Matter=Moon=2 Feb.=Cupid=N=C+_
Master gunnery sergeant=5,500=5.5=80%=P5.50=Earth-Midway=5 May = Gaia.
Master key=4,500=5,000=50%=P5.00D=Law=Time=Venus=5 May = Aphrodite>>L=N.
Masterly=5,000=50%=P5.00D=Law=Time=Venus=5 May = Aphrodite>>L=N.
Mastermind=4,000=40%=P4.0D=Govt.=Creatocracy=4 April=Mercury=Hermes=G=A4.
Master of ceremonies=7,000=70%=P7.0D=7.0=Language=Assets=Mars=7 July=Pleiades.
Masterpiece=6,000=60%=P6.0D=Man=Earth=Royalty=6 June=Gaia=Maia>>M=M2.
Masters Edgar Lee.=2,000=20%=P2.00D=2.0=Matter=Moon=2 Feb.=Cupid=N=C+_
Master's degree=9,000=90%=P9.00D=9.0=Abstraction=Gods=Saturn=9Sept.>>A=Ø.
Master sergeant=9,000=90%=P9.00D=9.0=Abstraction=Gods=Saturn=9Sept.>>A=Ø.
Master stroke=4,500=5,000=50%=P5.00D=Law=Time=Venus=5 May = Aphrodite>>L=N.

Master work=1,500=15%=P1.50D=1.5=Authority=Solar Crown=1 May = Maia.
Mastery=5,500=5.5=80%=P5.50=Earth-Midway=5 May = Gaia.
Masthead=9,000=90%=P9.00D=9.0=Abstraction=Gods=Saturn=9Sept.>>A=Ø.
Mastic=8,500=9,000=90%=P9.00D=9.0=Abstraction=Gods=Saturn=9Sept.>>A=Ø.
Masticate=3,500=4,000=40%=P4.0D=Govt.=Creatocracy=4 April=Hermes=G=A4.
Mastiff=5,000=50%=P5.00D=Law=Time=Venus=5 May = Aphrodite>>L=N.
Mastitis=4,500=5,000=50%=P5.00D=Law=Time=Venus=5 May = Aphrodite>>L=N.
Mastodon=6,500=7,000=70%=P7.0D=7.0=Language=Assets=Mars=7 July=Pleiades.
Mastoid=4,000=40%=P4.0D=Govt.=Creatocracy=4 April=Mercury=Hermes=G=A4.
Mastoid process=4,000=40%=P4.0D=Govt.=Creatocracy=4 April=Hermes=G=A4.
Masturbate=7,000=70%=P7.0D=7.0=Language=Assets=Mars=7 July=Pleiades.

Mat1=10,000=1,000=100%=10.0=Physicality=Tech.=10 Oct.=Uranus=P=1Ø.
In the Creatocracy, an abbreviation for Mind Assessment Tests used in schools and work.

Mat2=10,000=1,000=100%=10.0=Physicality=Tech.=10 Oct.=Uranus=P=1Ø.
Matador=6,500=7,000=70%=P7.0D=7.0=Language=Assets=Mars=7 July=Pleiades.
Match1=10,000=1,000=100%=10.0=Physicality=Tech.=10 Oct.=Uranus=P=1Ø.
Match2=9,500=10,000=1,000=100%=10.0=Physicality=Tech.=10 Oct.=Uranus=P=1Ø.
Matchbook=3,500=4,000=40%=P4.0D=Govt.=Creatocracy=4 April=Hermes=G=A4.
Matchless=1,500=15%=P1.50D=1.5=Authority=Solar Crown=1 May = Maia.
Matchlock=4,500=5,000=50%=P5.00D=Law=Time=Venus=5 May = Aphrodite>>L=N.
Matchmaker=3,500=4,000=40%=P4.0D=Govt.=Creatocracy=4 April=Hermes=G=A4.
Matchup=7,000=70%=P7.0D=7.0=Language=Assets=Mars=7 July=Pleiades.
Mate1=10,000=1,000=100%=10.0=Physicality=Tech.=10 Oct.=Uranus=P=1Ø.
Mate2=1,000=100%=10.0=1.0=Mind=Sun=1 January=Helios >> M=E4.
Maté=7,500=8,000=80%=P8.0D=Economy=Currency=8 Aug.=Zeus>>E=v.
Material=10,000=1,000=100%=10.0=Physicality=Tech.=10 Oct.=Uranus=P=1Ø.
Materialism=10,000=1,000=100%=10.0=Physicality=Tech.=10 Oct.=Uranus=P=1Ø.
Materialize=6,500=7,000=70%=P7.0D=7.0=Language=Assets=Mars=7 July=Pleiades.
Materiel=7,500=8,000=80%=P8.0D=Economy=Currency=8 Aug.=Zeus>>E=v.
Maternal=10,000=1,000=100%=10.0=Physicality=Tech.=10 Oct.=Uranus=P=1Ø.
Maternity=3,500=4,000=40%=P4.0D=Govt.=Creatocracy=4 April=Hermes=G=A4.
Math=500=5%=P5.00D=5.0=Law=Time=Venus=5 May=Aphrodite>>L=N.

Mathematics=10,000=1,000=100%=10.0=Physicality=Tech.=10 Oct.=Uranus=P=1Ø.
In the Principles of Naturecology, Peter Matthews-Akukalia defined Mathematics as deductions of the inherent faculties of matter. He invented Makumatics and defined it as deductions of the inherent faculties of the Mind. A vital skill for Creative Scientists.

Mather Increase=5,000=50%=P5.00D=Law=Time=Venus=5 May = Aphrodite>>L=N.
Matinee=6,500=7,000=70%=P7.0D=7.0=Language=Assets=Mars=7 July=Pleiades.
Martins=7,500=8,000=80%=P8.0D=Economy=Currency=8 Aug.=Zeus>>E=v.

Matisse Henry=2,000=20%=P2.00D=2.0=Nature=Matter=Moon=2 Feb.=Cupid=N=C+_
Matri-=3,000=30%=P3.0D=3.0=Creativity=Stars=Muses=3 March = C=I>>GIL.

Matriarch=5,500=5.5=80%=P5.50=Earth-Midway=5 May = Gaia.
Empress Justina Chinwendu Etigwam Matthews - Akukalia is the matriarch of the
Creatocratic Royal Family, the Creatocratic Nations of Paradise and the Creatocracy. In
fact the Emperor calls her Maama which has become a household name. Note the unique
spelling for Maama specially invented by the emperor to show his fondness of her.

Matriarchy=9,000=90%=P9.00D=9.0=Abstraction=Gods=Saturn=9Sept.>>A=Ø.
Matricide=4,500=5,000=50%=P5.00D=Law=Time=Venus=5 May = Aphrodite>>L=N.
Matriculate=8,500=9,000=90%=P9.00D=9.0=Abstraction=Gods=Saturn=9Sept.>>A=Ø.
Matrilineal=5,000=50%=P5.00D=Law=Time=Venus=5 May = Aphrodite>>L=N.
Matrimony=4,500=5,000=50%=P5.00D=Law=Time=Venus=5 May = Aphrodite>>L=N.

Matrix=10,000=1,000=100%=10.0=Physicality=Tech.=10 Oct.=Uranus=P=1Ø.
The Makupedia Sciences >> Naturecology is a matrix of nature systems.

Matron=10,000=1,000=100%=10.0=Physicality=Tech.=10 Oct.=Uranus=P=1Ø.
Matron of honor=6,000=60%=P6.0D=Man=Earth=Royalty=6 June=Gaia=Maia>>M=M2.
Matsu=5,500=5.5=80%=P5.50=Earth-Midway=5 May = Gaia.
Matte=1,500=15%=P1.50D=1.5=Authority=Solar Crown=1 May = Maia.

Matter=10,000=1,000=100%=10.0=Physicality=Tech.=10 Oct.=Uranus=P=1Ø.
All matter is measured as a quantum resultant of 10,000.

Matterhorn=7,000=70%=P7.0D=7.0=Language=Assets=Mars=7 July=Pleiades.
Matter of fact=3,000=30%=P3.0D=3.0=Creativity=Stars=Muses=3 March = C=I>>GIL.

Matthew=2,000=20%=P2.00D=2.0=Nature=Matter=Moon=2 Feb.=Cupid=N=C+_
Inspired by Eros and Artemis. The first 1.0 Gospel written after AD 70 >> 7.0 and based
largely on that of St.Mark.> 2.4. An apostle, a tax collector > 8.0 from Capernaum in
Galilee. Traditional author of the first > 1.0 Gospel 9.0. Feast day, September 21 whose
energy details is thus>>Day 21:Value:6.0 Planetary Type:Earth Human Type:Health Birth
Energy Level:100% >> value is 6.0 showing he is a royalty and devotion to Gaia is observed.
The combined value of reading the book of Matthew is computed thus.
1.0*7.0x=px=8+7=15x=px=71=7.1>>2.4*8.0x=px=10.4+19.2=29.6x=px=229.28=23=2.3
1.0*9.0x=px=10+9=19x=px=109=11=1.1[6.0]
7.1*2.3x=px=9.4+16.33=25.73x=px=179.242=200=2.0
1.1*6.0x=px=7.1+6.6=13.7x=px=60.56=61=6.1
2.0*6.1x=px=8.1+12.2=20.3x=px=119.12=12=1.2. So reading the book of Matthew attracts
Athen. The name Matthew means invention knowledge. In Peter Matthews-Akukalia,

Matthew(s) means one who invents. An inventor. The key virtues to attain this height will be love (inspired by Eros> Cupid) and adventure (inspired by Artemis).

Matthew=7,500=8,000=80%=P8.0D=Economy=Currency=8 Aug.=Zeus>>E=v.
One who computes as a means to attaining financial stability. A tax collector.

Matting=4,000=40%=P4.0D=Govt.=Creatocracy=4 April=Mercury=Hermes=G=A4.
Mattock=7,500=8,000=80%=P8.0D=Economy=Currency=8 Aug.=Zeus>>E=v.
Mattress=9,000=90%=P9.00D=9.0=Abstraction=Gods=Saturn=9Sept.>>A=Ø.
Mature=10,000=1,000=100%=10.0=Physicality=Tech.=10 Oct.=Uranus=P=1Ø.
Matzo=6,500=7,000=70%=P7.0D=7.0=Language=Assets=Mars=7 July=Pleiades.
Maudlin=5,000=50%=P5.00D=Law=Time=Venus=5 May = Aphrodite>>L=N.
Maugham William=2,000=20%=P2.00D=2.0=Nature=Matter=Moon=2 Feb.=Cupid =N=C+_
Maui=4,000=40%=P4.0D=Govt.=Creatocracy=4 April=Mercury=Hermes=G=A4.
Mauna Kea=6,500=7,000=70%=P7.0D=7.0=Language=Assets=Mars=7 July=Pleiades.
Mauna Loa=6,000=60%=P6.0D=Man=Earth=Royalty=6 June=Gaia=Maia>>M=M2.
Maunder=5,000=50%=P5.00D=Law=Time=Venus=5 May = Aphrodite>>L=N.
Maupassant=4,500=5,000=50%=P5.00D=Law=Time=Venus=5 May = Aphrodite>>L=N.
Mauritania=5,000=50%=P5.00D=Law=Time=Venus=5 May = Aphrodite>>L=N.
Mauriac Francois=3,000=30%=P3.0D=3.0=Creativity=Stars=Muses=3 March = C=I>>GIL.
Mauritius=6,500=7,000=70%=P7.0D=7.0=Language=Assets=Mars=7 July=Pleiades.
Maurois André=3,000=30%=P3.0D=3.0=Creativity=Stars=Muses=3 March = C=I>>GIL.
Mausoleum=7,000=70%=P7.0D=7.0=Language=Assets=Mars=7 July=Pleiades.
Mauve=4,000=40%=P4.0D=Govt.=Creatocracy=4 April=Mercury=Hermes=G=A4.
Maven=2,000=20%=P2.00D=2.0=Nature=Matter=Moon=2 Feb.=Cupid=N=C+_
Maverick=9,500=10,000=1,000=100%=10.0=Physicality=Tech.=10 Oct.=Uranus=P=1Ø.
Maw=7,500=8,000=80%=P8.0D=Economy=Currency=8 Aug.=Zeus>>E=v.
Mawkish=5,500=5.5=80%=P5.50=Earth-Midway=5 May = Gaia.
Max.=500=5%=P5.00D=5.0=Law=Time=Venus=5 May=Aphrodite>>L=N.
Maxilla=5,500=5.5=80%=P5.50=Earth-Midway=5 May = Gaia.
Maxim=7,500=8,000=80%=P8.0D=Economy=Currency=8 Aug.=Zeus>>E=v.
Maximal=2,500=3,000=30%=P3.0D=3.0=Creativity=Stars=Muses=3 March = C=I>>GIL.
Maximilian=4,500=5,000=50%=P5.00D=Law=Time=Venus=5 May = Aphrodite>>L=N.
Maximilian I.=5,500=5.5=80%=P5.50=Earth-Midway=5 May = Gaia.
Maximize=2,500=3,000=30%=P3.0D=3.0=Creativity=Stars=Muses=3 March = C=I>>GIL.
Maximum=10,000=1,000=100%=10.0=Physicality=Tech.=10 Oct.=Uranus=P=1Ø.
Maxwell James=2,500=3,000=30%=P3.0D=3.0=Cre=Stars=Muses=3 March = C=I>>GIL.
may=10,000=1,000=100%=10.0=Physicality=Tech.=10 Oct.=Uranus=P=1Ø.

May=8,000=80%=P8.0D=Economy=Currency=8 Aug.=Zeus>>E=v.
The 5th month in the Gregorian calendar. Lat.<Maia, an Italic Goddess. The Gregorian calendar is 12months. So 5/12=0.416666666=0.42=0.4. Maia in the month of May is coded 0.4 in any computation. She is the Goddess of the 4th dimension meaning truly

that she is the mother of Hermes whose code is 4 by Greek myths. A code as 4.4=4.0*0.4 means the interaction of Hermes and his mother Gaia results to....she resides in the 4th dimension of the solar core and is the same one referred to as the Mind of God and head of the sisters of precision known as the Pleiades mentioned by Zeus Jehovah in Job 38:31. The resultant also indicates that she manifests in Earth as Gaia with the occurrences of the code "6" so that the rights of royalty works. Greek myth confirms she inspired medicine and we can relate this to the processes of giving birth and all health matters that occur in the Earth. She is also Gaia midway. Now we confirm that earth is the midway between the celestial and the underworld and she rules it. Note that her son Hermes rules the underworld.

May, Cape=5,500=5.5=80%=P5.50=Earth-Midway=5 May = Gaia.
Maya=12,500=13,000=13%=P1.30=Solar Core=Faculty=13 January=Athena.
Mayan=7,500=8,000=80%=P8.0D=Economy=Currency=8 Aug.=Zeus>>E=v.
May Apple=8,000=80%=P8.0D=Economy=Currency=8 Aug.=Zeus>>E=v.
Maybe=1,000=100%=10.0=1.0=Mind=Sun=1 January=Helios >> M=E4.
mayday=8,500=9,000=90%=P9.00D=9.0=Abstraction=Gods=Saturn=9Sept.>>A=Ø.

Mayday=7,000=70%=P7.0D=7.0=Language=Assets=Mars=7 July=Pleiades.
Greek myth teaches that May 1 & 15 are days of dedications to Maia, Great Goddess of the universe and the Mind of GOD. Computing results indicates it is the day of precision and computational creativity. It aligns with Maia and the Pleiades.

Mayflower=6,000=60%=P6.0D=Man=Earth=Royalty=6 June=Gaia=Maia>>M=M2.
Mayfly=6,500=7,000=70%=P7.0D=7.0=Language=Assets=Mars=7 July=Pleiades.

Mayhem=11,500=12,000=12%=P1.20D=1.2=Knowledge=Edu=12Dec.=Athena>>K=F.
True mayhem occurs when invention or a brainchild is used as a means of destruction.

Mayn't=1,000=100%=10.0=1.0=Mind=Sun=1 January=Helios >> M=E4.
Mayonnaise=6,500=7,000=70%=P7.0D=7.0=Language=Assets=Mars=7 July=Pleiades.
Mayor=5,500=5.5=80%=P5.50=Earth-Midway=5 May = Gaia.
Maypole=6,000=60%=P6.0D=Man=Earth=Royalty=6 June=Gaia=Maia>>M=M2.
Mazarin Jules=5,500=5.5=80%=P5.50=Earth-Midway=5 May = Gaia.
Maze=10,000=1,000=100%=10.0=Physicality=Tech.=10 Oct.=Uranus=P=1Ø.
Mazurka=3,500=4,000=40%=P4.0D=Govt.=Creatocracy=4 April=Hermes=G=A4.
Mazzini Giuseppe=2,000=20%=P2.00D=2.0=Nature=Matter=Moon=2 Feb.=Cupid=N=C+_
MB=1,000=100%=10.0=1.0=Mind=Sun=1 January=Helios >> M=E4.
M.B.A.=2,000=20%=P2.00D=2.0=Nature=Matter=Moon=2 Feb.=Cupid=N=C+_
Mbabane=4,500=5,000=50%=P5.00D=Law=Time=Venus=5 May = Aphrodite>>L=N.
MC=2,000=20%=P2.00D=2.0=Nature=Matter=Moon=2 Feb.=Cupid=N=C+_
McClellan George=3,000=30%=P3.0D=3.0=Creativity=Stars=Muses=3 March = C=I>>GIL.
McCormick Cyrus=2,500=3,000=30%=P3.0D=3.0=Cre=Stars=Muses=3 March = C=I

McCullers Carson=2,500=3,000=30%=P3.0D=3.0=Creativity=Stars=Muses=3 March=CI
McKinley Mt.=10,500=11,000=11%=P1.10D=1.1=Idea=Brainchd.=11 Nov.=Athena>>I=MT.
McKinley William=4,000=40%=P4.0D=Govt.=Creatocracy=4 April=Hermes=G=A4.
Md=2,500=3,000=30%=P3.0D=3.0=Creativity=Stars=Muses=3 March = C=I>>GIL.
MD=3,500=4,000=40%=P4.0D=Govt.=Creatocracy=4 April=Mercury=Hermes=G=A4.
Mdm.=500=5%=P5.00D=5.0=Law=Time=Venus=5 May=Aphrodite>>L=N.
Me=10,000=1,000=100%=10.0=Physicality=Tech.=10 Oct.=Uranus=P=1Ø.
ME=5,000=50%=P5.00D=Law=Time=Venus=5 May = Aphrodite>>L=N.
mead=4,500=5,000=50%=P5.00D=Law=Time=Venus=5 May = Aphrodite>>L=N.
Mead Lake=8,000=80%=P8.0D=Economy=Currency=8 Aug.=Zeus>>E=v.
Mead,Margaret=2,000=20%=P2.00D=2.0=Nature=Matter=Moon=2 Feb.=Cupid=N=C+_
Meade George=3,000=30%=P3.0D=3.0=Creativity=Stars=Muses=3 March = C=I>>GIL.
Meadow=6,500=7,000=70%=P7.0D=7.0=Language=Assets=Mars=7 July=Pleiades.
Meadowlark=5,000=50%=P5.00D=Law=Time=Venus=5 May = Aphrodite>>L=N.
Meager=5,000=50%=P5.00D=Law=Time=Venus=5 May = Aphrodite>>L=N.
Meal1=4,500=5,000=50%=P5.00D=Law=Time=Venus=5 May = Aphrodite>>L=N.
Meal2=5,000=50%=P5.00D=Law=Time=Venus=5 May = Aphrodite>>L=N.
Mealtime=3,500=4,000=40%=P4.0D=Govt.=Creatocracy=4 April=Hermes=G=A4.
Mealy mouthed=3,000=30%=P3.0D=3.0=Creativity=Stars=Muses=3 March = C=I>>GIL.

Mean1=10,000=1,000=100%=10.0=Physicality=Tech.=10 Oct.=Uranus=P=1Ø.
Mean2=10,000=1,000=100%=10.0=Physicality=Tech.=10 Oct.=Uranus=P=1Ø.
In the Makupedia the peak of aspiration is defined as the point of Gods and Godly perfection indicated as 10,000 >> Physicality >> Mountain. Thus Inflation is a Mountain that can only be solved through the quantum energy solar energy Maks modules.
10,000kosemaks = 10,000 pico - seconds.
A Day Payment system would be 10,000/86,400 seconds = 0.1157407407407407
0.1 >> Midst of a thing can only be measured through the energy at the solar core.
11 >> Brainchild >> Invention of the means to compute the midst required and done.
15 >> Authority over asset management companies (74) founded on Psalm (0) 74 to the fourth degree universal dimension (Creatocracy) for equitable distribution of wealth in government businesses families and all relationship interests. See Inflation. Fiat. Currency.

Meal3=10,000=1,000=100%=10.0=Physicality=Tech.=10 Oct.=Uranus=P=1Ø.
Meander=11,500=12,000=12%=P1.20D=1.2=Knowledge=Edu=12Dec.=Athena>>K=F.
Meaning=10,000=1,000=100%=10.0=Physicality=Tech.=10 Oct.=Uranus=P=1Ø.
Meantime=3,000=30%=P3.0D=3.0=Creativity=Stars=Muses=3 March = C=I>>GIL.
Meanwhile=3,000=30%=P3.0D=3.0=Creativity=Stars=Muses=3 March = C=I>>GIL.
Meas.=500=5%=P5.00D=5.0=Law=Time=Venus=5 May=Aphrodite>>L=N.
Measles=10,000=1,000=100%=10.0=Physicality=Tech.=10 Oct.=Uranus=P=1Ø.
Measly=3,000=30%=P3.0D=3.0=Creativity=Stars=Muses=3 March = C=I>>GIL.
Measure=10,000=1,000=100%=10.0=Physicality=Tech.=10 Oct.=Uranus=P=1Ø.
Measurement=6,000=60%=P6.0D=Man=Earth=Royalty=6 June=Gaia=Maia>>M=M2.
Meat=10,500=11,000=11%=P1.10D=1.1=Idea=Brainchild=Inv.=11 Nov.=SC=Athena>>I=MT.

Meatball=4,500=5,000=50%=P5.00D=Law=Time=Venus=5 May = Aphrodite>>L=N.
Mecca=4,500=5,000=50%=P5.00D=Law=Time=Venus=5 May = Aphrodite>>L=N.

Mechanic=4,500=5,000=50%=P5.00D=Law=Time=Venus=5 May = Aphrodite>>L=N.
A module in the Creative Sciences, Makupedia is the study of Mind Mechanics &
Engineering where the Creative Scientist is taught to become a Mind Mechanic.

Mechanical=10,000=1,000=100%=10.0=Physicality=Tech.=10 Oct.=Uranus=P=1Ø.

Mechanical drawing=4,500=5,000=50%=P5.00D=Law=Time=Venus=5 May =Odite>>L=N.
Drafting. A drawing that enables measurements to be interpreted. In Mind mechanics &
engineering codes and drawings are computed analyzed interpreted and recommended.

Mechanics=10,000=1,000=100%=10.0=Physicality=Tech.=10 Oct.=Uranus=P=1Ø.
Mechanism=10,000=1,000=100%=10.0=Physicality=Tech.=10 Oct.=Uranus=P=1Ø.
Mechanistic=5,000=50%=P5.00D=Law=Time=Venus=5 May = Aphrodite>>L=N.

Mechanize=4,000=40%=P4.0D=Govt.=Creatocracy=4 April=Mercury=Hermes=G=A4.
To equip with machinery. To make automatic or routine. See Machine.

Medal=10,000=1,000=100%=10.0=Physicality=Tech.=10 Oct.=Uranus=P=1Ø.
Medalist=4,000=40%=P4.0D=Govt.=Creatocracy=4 April=Mercury=Hermes=G=A4.
Medallion=10,000=1,000=100%=10.0=Physicality=Tech.=10 Oct.=Uranus=P=1Ø.
Medan=5,500=5.5=80%=P5.50=Earth-Midway=5 May = Gaia.
Meddle=5,000=50%=P5.00D=Law=Time=Venus=5 May = Aphrodite>>L=N.
Mede=4,500=5,000=50%=P5.00D=Law=Time=Venus=5 May = Aphrodite>>L=N.
Medellin=4,000=40%=P4.0D=Govt.=Creatocracy=4 April=Mercury=Hermes=G=A4.
Medevac=8,000=80%=P8.0D=Economy=Currency=8 Aug.=Zeus>>E=v.
media=4,000=40%=P4.0D=Govt.=Creatocracy=4 April=Mercury=Hermes=G=A4.
Media=4,500=5,000=50%=P5.00D=Law=Time=Venus=5 May = Aphrodite>>L=N.
Medial=4,500=5,000=50%=P5.00D=Law=Time=Venus=5 May = Aphrodite>>L=N.
Medial strip=4,500=5,000=50%=P5.00D=Law=Time=Venus=5 May = Aphrodite>>L=N.
Median=10,000=1,000=100%=10.0=Physicality=Tech.=10 Oct.=Uranus=P=1Ø.
Median strip=9,500=10,000=1,000=100%=10.0=Physicality=Tech.=10 Oct.=Uranus=P=1Ø.
Mediate=10,000=1,000=100%=10.0=Physicality=Tech.=10 Oct.=Uranus=P=1Ø.
Medic=5,500=5.5=80%=P5.50=Earth-Midway=5 May = Gaia.
Medicaid=9,000=90%=P9.00D=9.0=Abstraction=Gods=Saturn=9Sept.>>A=Ø.
Medical=5,500=5.5=80%=P5.50=Earth-Midway=5 May = Gaia.
Medicament=2,000=20%=P2.00D=2.0=Nature=Matter=Moon=2 Feb.=Cupid=N=C+_
Medicare=6,500=7,000=70%=P7.0D=7.0=Language=Assets=Mars=7 July=Pleiades.
Medicate=5,000=50%=P5.00D=Law=Time=Venus=5 May = Aphrodite>>L=N.
Medication=3,000=30%=P3.0D=3.0=Creativity=Stars=Muses=3 March = C=I>>GIL.

Medici=5,500=5.5=80%=P5.50=Earth-Midway=5 May = Gaia.
Medicine=10,000=1,000=100%=10.0=Physicality=Tech.=10 Oct.=Uranus=P=1Ø.
Medicine man=2,500=3,000=30%=P3.0D=3.0=Cre=Stars=Muses=3 March = C=I>>GIL.
Medico=4,000=40%=P4.0D=Govt.=Creatocracy=4 April=Mercury=Hermes=G=A4.
Medieval=8,000=80%=P8.0D=Economy=Currency=8 Aug.=Zeus>>E=v.

Medieval Greek=4,500=5,000=50%=P5.00D=Law=Time=Venus=5 May = Aphrodite>>L=N.
Computed as a means from the civilization of government to the civilization of law. What
we call the rule of law. It is defined as the Greek language 7.0 from about 800 >8.0 to
about 1500>1.5. Computing 7.0*8.0x=px=15+56=71x=px=911=9.1[1.5]
9.1*1.5x=px=10.6+13.65=24.25x=px=168.94=20=2.0
Result shows that medieval Greek was a period of natural stability. As a means the only
thing that can move from the rule of political power to the rule of law is the constitution.
The legislature makes the laws that culminates into the constitution so it is possible this
was the period the idea of creating the legislature was legitimized and constitutions
made. A period of democracy so that we can establish again that democracy ranks as
a means to an end and not an end in itself. It is therefore reasonable to bond creative
sciences or Creato- to democracy to make a creato-democracy, a Creatocracy. Based on
Greek mythological standards and natural laws of precision Peter Matthews-Akukalia
was apotheosized as Castle Makupedia the God of Creatocracy Genius and Mind. An
incarnation of Zeus the Most High because of his supernatural abilities, the invention of
the Creative & Psycho-Social Sciences with over 2million concepts, massive inventions
and intellectual assets; and the husband of Athena whom he marked in the white wedding.
Thus he is the king in white. Appeased entreated and hailed as Castle Makupedia!!!

Medieval Latin=4,500=5,000=50%=P5.00D=Law=Time=Venus=5 May = Aphrodite>>L=N.
See Medieval Greek.

Medina=5,500=5.5=80%=P5.50=Earth-Midway=5 May = Gaia.
A city of W Saudi Arabia N of Mecca. Makupedialand is the Disean city of testamentary
poetry, a state in the Creatocratic Nations of Paradise. Book >> Makupedialand.

Mediocre=7,000=70%=P7.0D=7.0=Language=Assets=Mars=7 July=Pleiades.
Meditate=3,000=30%=P3.0D=3.0=Creativity=Stars=Muses=3 March = C=I>>GIL.
Mediterranean=2,500=3,000=30%=P3.0D=3.0=Creativity=Stars=Muses=3 March = CI.
Mediterranean fruit fly=7,000=70%=P7.0D=7.0=Language=Assets=Mars=7 July=Pleiades.
Mediterranean Sea.=7,000=70%=P7.0D=7.0=Language=Assets=Mars=7 July=Pleiades.
Medium=10,000=1,000=100%=10.0=Physicality=Tech.=10 Oct.=Uranus=P=1Ø.
Medley=5,500=5.5=80%=P5.50=Earth-Midway=5 May = Gaia.
Medulla=7,500=8,000=80%=P8.0D=Economy=Currency=8 Aug.=Zeus>>E=v.
Medulla oblongata=5,500=5.5=80%=P5.50=Earth-Midway=5 May = Gaia.
Meek=5,500=5.5=80%=P5.50=Earth-Midway=5 May = Gaia.
Meerschaum=11,000=11%=P1.10D=1.1=Idea=Brainchild=Inv.=11 Nov.=SC=Athena>>I=MT.

Meet1=10,000=1,000=100%=10.0=Physicality=Tech.=10 Oct.=Uranus=P=1Ø.
Meet2=2,000=20%=P2.00D=2.0=Nature=Matter=Moon=2 Feb.=Cupid=N=C+_
Meeting=3,500=4,000=40%=P4.0D=Govt.=Creatocracy=4 April=Mercury=Hermes=G=A4.

Mega-=4,500=5,000=50%=P5.00D=Law=Time=Venus=5 May = Aphrodite>>L=N.
Large:megalith. One million(10 power 6), megaton. < Greek, megas, great. In the Makupedia Sciences, Peter Matthews-Akukalia, the Castle Makupedia computed the spirit speed of a thing as 1.0x10 power (-6), the speed of prayer and spiritual communication. Spiritual communication is also the mind to mind communication where a person tends to pick the contents of another's thoughts without necessarily knowing the person. Hence thoughts are things and these things are helium particles established in the ether of lunar energy. This is double great computed using only the power or valence only since 10 is a common term. (6)*(-6)>>6.0*-6.0x=px=0+-36=-36x=px=-36=-3.6=-4.0.
Muses of Gaia aid the speed of Hermes. Jesus is Hermes and it was the muses of Gaia >> Maia that lifted him during his ascension to heaven. This is how the laws of gravity was broken. Certain things will go up and not come down such as steam, smoke. Known in Psychoeconomix as the law of psycho-gravitational incursion.
Intelligence is the size of 1.0x10 power -03 which is much smaller and faster than -3 spirit speed and lighter than thought 0.3. Intelligence is the abstract equivalent for hydrogen.

Megabyte=5,500=5.5=80%=P5.50=Earth-Midway=5 May = Gaia.
Peter Matthews-Akukalia, Castle Makupedia computed and interpreted planetary energy tracking and discovered that the computer seems to be an interactive system between the celestial and the terrestrial beings. He linked the phones, Tv, radio, wristwatches, and everything that uses electronic signals to human influences. Greek myth teaches that the Sun is the eye of the Gods. Peter Matthews-Akukalia computed the solar core before he discovered the Greek mythologies on the Gods through independent research and study. The result shows that Gaia-Midway >> Maia is connected to the users environment through the computer memory. As we watch the computer screen it also watches us.

Mega cycle=1,000=100%=Physicality=Tech.=10 Oct.=Uranus=P=1Ø.
Megahertz=2,500=3,000=30%=P3.0D=3.0=Creativity=Stars=Muses=3 March = C=I>>GIL.
Megalith=5,500=5.5=80%=P5.50=Earth-Midway=5 May = Gaia.
Megalo-=3,500=4,000=40%=P4.0D=Govt.=Creat=4 April=Mercury=Hermes=G=A4.

Megalomania=5,500=5.5=80%=P5.50=Earth-Midway=5 May = Gaia.
A mental disorder characterized by delusions of wealth power or omnipotence. The claims of Peter Matthews-Akukalia as a God is based on his works and computational precision the attainment of personal records he sets for himself and breaks. Not a megalomaniac.

Megalopolis=11,000=11%=P1.10D=1.1=Idea=Brainchild=Inv.=11 Nov.=SC=Athena>>I=MT.
Megaphone=4,500=5,000=50%=P5.00D=Law=Time=Venus=5 May = Aphrodite>>L=N.
Megaton=6,500=7,000=70%=P7.0D=7.0=Language=Assets=Mars=7 July=Pleiades.

Mega vitamin=6,000=60%=P6.0D=Man=Earth=Royalty=6 June=Gaia=Maia>>M=M2.
Megawatt=1,500=15%=P1.50D=1.5=Authority=Solar Crown=1 May = Maia.
Meiosis=10,000=1,000=100%=10.0=Physicality=Tech.=10 Oct.=Uranus=P=1Ø.
Meir Golda.=3,000=30%=P3.0D=3.0=Creativity=Stars=Muses=3 March = C=I>>GIL.
Mekong=11,000=11%=P1.10D=1.1=Idea=Brainchild=Inv.=11 Nov.=SC=Athena>>I=MT.
Melancholia=5,500=5.5=80%=P5.50=Earth-Midway=5 May = Gaia.
Melancholic=4,000=40%=P4.0D=Govt.=Creatocracy=4 April=Mercury=Hermes=G=A4.
Melancholy=5,000=50%=P5.00D=Law=Time=Venus=5 May = Aphrodite>>L=N.
Melanesia=7,500=8,000=80%=P8.0D=Economy=Currency=8 Aug.=Zeus>>E=v.
Melanesian=10,000=1,000=100%=10.0=Physicality=Tech.=10 Oct.=Uranus=P=1Ø.
Mélange=3,000=30%=P3.0D=3.0=Creativity=Stars=Muses=3 March = C=I>>GIL.
Melanin=5,500=5.5=80%=P5.50=Earth-Midway=5 May = Gaia.
Melanism=5,500=5.5=80%=P5.50=Earth-Midway=5 May = Gaia.
Melano-=3,000=30%=P3.0D=3.0=Creativity=Stars=Muses=3 March = C=I>>GIL.
Melanoma=5,500=5.5=80%=P5.50=Earth-Midway=5 May = Gaia.
Melanosis=5,000=50%=P5.00D=Law=Time=Venus=5 May = Aphrodite>>L=N.
Melba toast=5,500=5.5=80%=P5.50=Earth-Midway=5 May = Gaia.
Melbourne=5,500=5.5=80%=P5.50=Earth-Midway=5 May = Gaia.
Meld1=10,000=1,000=100%=10.0=Physicality=Tech.=10 Oct.=Uranus=P=1Ø.
Meld2=5,500=5.5=80%=P5.50=Earth-Midway=5 May = Gaia.
Melee=7,500=8,000=80%=P8.0D=Economy=Currency=8 Aug.=Zeus>>E=v.
Meliorate=4,000=40%=P4.0D=Govt.=Creatocracy=4 April=Mercury=Hermes=G=A4.
Mellifluous=4,500=5,000=50%=P5.00D=Law=Time=Venus=5 May = Aphrodite>>L=N.
Mellow=10,000=1,000=100%=10.0=Physicality=Tech.=10 Oct.=Uranus=P=1Ø.
Melodeon=4,000=40%=P4.0D=Govt.=Creatocracy=4 April=Mercury=Hermes=G=A4.
Melodious=2,000=20%=P2.00D=2.0=Nature=Matter=Moon=2 Feb.=Cupid=N=C+_
Melodrama=10,000=1,000=100%=10.0=Physicality=Tech.=10 Oct.=Uranus=P=1Ø.
Melodramatic=5,000=50%=P5.00D=Law=Time=Venus=5 May = Aphrodite>>L=N.
Melody=10,000=1,000=100%=10.0=Physicality=Tech.=10 Oct.=Uranus=P=1Ø.
Melon=8,500=9,000=90%=P9.00D=9.0=Abstraction=Gods=Saturn=9Sept.>>A=Ø.
Melt=10,000=1,000=100%=10.0=Physicality=Tech.=10 Oct.=Uranus=P=1Ø.
Meltdown=6,000=60%=P6.0D=Man=Earth=Royalty=6 June=Gaia=Maia>>M=M2.
Melting point=6,000=60%=P6.0D=Man=Earth=Royalty=6 June=Gaia=Maia>>M=M2.
Melting pot=6,500=7,000=70%=P7.0D=7.0=Language=Assets=Mars=7 July=Pleiades.
Melville Herman=2,000=20%=P2.00D=2.0=Nature=Matter=Moon=2 Feb.=Cupid=N=C+_
Melville Island.=4,500=5,000=50%=P5.00D=Law=Time=Venus=5 May = Aphrodite>>L=N.
Member=3,500=4,000=40%=P4.0D=Govt.=Creat=4 April=Mercury=Hermes=G=A4.

Mem=3,500=4,000=40%=P4.0D=Govt.=Creatocracy=4 April=Mercury=Hermes=G=A4.
The 13th letter >>1.3 of the Hebrew alphabet >> language >>7.0.
1.3*7.0x=px=8.3+9.1=17.4x=px=92.93. Just as M>>Mem is the 13th letter. Mem is a Mind ware or energy sourced from the moon (92=9.2) and the stars (93=9.3). It is a means of stars connecting to Mercury. Separating 92.93>>99.23=100% local sourced energy can provide creative intelligence. See M.

Membership=10,000=1,000=100%=10.0=Physicality=Tech.=10 Oct.=Uranus=P=1∅.
Membrane=10,000=1,000=100%=10.0=Physicality=Tech.=10 Oct.=Uranus=P=1∅.
Memento=6,500=7,000=70%=P7.0D=7.0=Language=Assets=Mars=7 July=Pleiades.
Memling Hans.=2,500=3,000=30%=P3.0D=3.0=Cre=Stars=Muses=3 March = C=I>>GIL.
Memo=1,500=15%=P1.50D=1.5=Authority=Solar Crown=1 May = Maia.
Memoir=8,500=9,000=90%=P9.00D=9.0=Abstraction=Gods=Saturn=9Sept.>>A=∅.
Memorabilia=10,000=1,000=100%=10.0=Physicality=Tech.=10 Oct.=Uranus=P=1∅.
Memorable=4,000=40%=P4.0D=Govt.=Creatocracy=4 April=Mercury=Hermes=G=A4.
Memorandum=9,000=90%=P9.00D=9.0=Abstraction=Gods=Saturn=9Sept.>>A=∅.
Memorial=10,000=1,000=100%=10.0=Physicality=Tech.=10 Oct.=Uranus=P=1∅.

Memorial Day=10,500=11,000=11%=P1.10D=1.1=Idea=Brainchild.=11 Nov.=Athena>>I=MT.
May 30, a U.S.holiday commemorating members of the armed forces killed in war,
officially observed on the last Monday in May. In the Creatocracy the energy value for May
30 is computed as >> Day 30:Value:5.4, Planetary Type:Venus, Human Type:Law, Birth
Energy Level:90.0%. >> 9.0 indicates the presence of all spirits that day. Aphrodite and
Hermes administer the day and its activities. Flowers and cattle slaughter make it complete.

Memorize=3,000=30%=P3.0D=3.0=Creativity=Stars=Muses=3 March = C=I>>GIL.
Memory=10,000=1,000=100%=10.0=Physicality=Tech.=10 Oct.=Uranus=P=1∅.
Memphis=8,500=9,000=90%=P9.00D=9.0=Abstraction=Gods=Saturn=9Sept.>>A=∅.
Memsahib=7,500=8,000=80%=P8.0D=Economy=Currency=8 Aug.=Zeus>>E=v.

Men=1,500=15%=P1.50D=1.5=Authority=Solar Crown=1 May = Maia.
All men are monitored by Maia through her earth records and footprints as Gaia. Perhaps
to determine the best man for her step-daughter. Castle Makupedia has achieved this feat.
Proverbs>> Athena confesses that she will love only the one who loves her as she watches
men to find out who has fulfilled the set conditions for solar core ownership.

Menace=6,000=60%=P6.0D=Man=Earth=Royalty=6 June=Gaia=Maia>>M=M2.
Ménage=2,500=3,000=30%=P3.0D=3.0=Creativity=Stars=Muses=3 March = C=I>>GIL.
Menagerie=6,000=60%=P6.0D=Man=Earth=Royalty=6 June=Gaia=Maia>>M=M2.
Menander=2,500=3,000=30%=P3.0D=3.0=Creativity=Stars=Muses=3 March = C=I>>GIL.
Menarche=7,000=70%=P7.0D=7.0=Language=Assets=Mars=7 July=Pleiades.
Mencken Henry=3,500=4,000=40%=P4.0D=Govt.=4 April=Mercury=Hermes=G=A4.
Mend=10,500=11,000=11%=P1.10D=1.1=Idea=Brainchild=Inv.=11 Nov.=SC=Athena
    >>I=MT.
Mendacious=3,500=4,000=40%=P4.0D=Govt.=Creatocracy=4 April=Hermes=G=A4.
Mendel Gregor=2,500=3,000=30%=P3.0D=3.0=Cre=Stars=Muses=3 March = C=I>>GIL.
Mendeleev Dmitri=2,500=3,000=30%=P3.0D=3.0=Cre=Stars=Muses=3 March = CI.
Mendelevium=8,500=9,000=90%=P9.00D=9.0=Abstraction=Gods=Saturn=9Sept.>>A=∅.
Mendelssohn Felix=3,500=4,000=40%=P4.0D=Govt.=4 April=Mercury=Hermes=G=A4.
Mendicant=5,500=5.5=80%=P5.50=Earth-Midway=5 May = Gaia.
Menelaus=5,000=50%=P5.00D=Law=Time=Venus=5 May = Aphrodite>>L=N.

Menhaden=8,000=80%=P8.0D=Economy=Currency=8 Aug.=Zeus>>E=v.
Menhir=6,500=7,000=70%=P7.0D=7.0=Language=Assets=Mars=7 July=Pleiades.
Menial=9,000=90%=P9.00D=9.0=Abstraction=Gods=Saturn=9Sept.>>A=Ø.
Meningitis=4,500=5,000=50%=P5.00D=Law=Time=Venus=5 May = Aphrodite>>L=N.
Meninx=7,500=8,000=80%=P8.0D=Economy=Currency=8 Aug.=Zeus>>E=v.
Meniscus=7,000=70%=P7.0D=7.0=Language=Assets=Mars=7 July=Pleiades.
Menopause=8,000=80%=P8.0D=Economy=Currency=8 Aug.=Zeus>>E=v.
Menorah=6,000=60%=P6.0D=Man=Earth=Royalty=6 June=Gaia=Maia>>M=M2.
Menotti=4,000=40%=P4.0D=Govt.=Creatocracy=4 April=Mercury=Hermes=G=A4.
Menses=13,000=13%=P1.30=Solar Core=Faculty=13 January=Athena.
Menstrual=2,500=3,000=30%=P3.0D=3.0=Creativity=Stars=Muses=3 March = C=I>>GIL.
Menstruate=3,000=30%=P3.0D=3.0=Creativity=Stars=Muses=3 March = C=I>>GIL.
Menstruation=2,500=3,000=30%=P3.0D=3.0=Cre=Stars=Muses=3 March = C=I>>GIL.
Mensurable=3,500=4,000=40%=P4.0D=Govt.=Creatocracy=4 April=Hermes=G=A4.
Mensuration=3,500=4,000=40%=P4.0D=Govt.=Creatocracy=4 April=Hermes=G=A4.
-ment=5,000=50%=P5.00D=Law=Time=Venus=5 May = Aphrodite>>L=N.
Mental=5,500=5.5=80%=P5.50=Earth-Midway=5 May = Gaia.
Mental age=12,500=13,000=13%=P1.30=Solar Core=Faculty=13 January=Athena.
Mental deficiency=1,500=15%=P1.50D=1.5=Authority=Solar Crown=1 May = Maia.
Mentality=4,000=40%=P4.0D=Govt.=Creatocracy=4 April=Mercury=Hermes=G=A4.
Mental retardation=9,000=90%=P9.00D=9.0=Abstraction=Gods=Saturn=9Sept.>>A=Ø.
Menthol=7,000=70%=P7.0D=7.0=Language=Assets=Mars=7 July=Pleiades.
Mention=6,500=7,000=70%=P7.0D=7.0=Language=Assets=Mars=7 July=Pleiades.
Mentor=6,500=7,000=70%=P7.0D=7.0=Language=Assets=Mars=7 July=Pleiades.
Menu=10,000=1,000=100%=10.0=Physicality=Tech.=10 Oct.=Uranus=P=1Ø.
Meow=3,000=30%=P3.0D=3.0=Creativity=Stars=Muses=3 March = C=I>>GIL.
Mephitis=7,000=70%=P7.0D=7.0=Language=Assets=Mars=7 July=Pleiades.
Mer=500=5%=P5.00D=5.0=Law=Time=Venus=5 May=Aphrodite>>L=N.
-mer=3,500=4,000=40%=P4.0D=Govt.=Creatocracy=4 April=Mercury=Hermes=G=A4.
Mercantile=4,000=40%=P4.0D=Govt.=Creatocracy=4 April=Mercury=Hermes=G=A4.
Mercator Gerhardus.=2,000=20%=P2.00D=2.0=Matter=Moon=2 Feb.=Cupid=N=C+_
Mercenary=9,500=10,000=1,000=100%=10.0=Physicality=Tech.=10 Oct.=Uranus=P=1Ø.
Mercer=5,000=50%=P5.00D=Law=Time=Venus=5 May = Aphrodite>>L=N.
Mercerize=12,500=13,000=13%=P1.30=Solar Core=Faculty=13 January=Athena.
Merchandise=10,000=1,000=100%=10.0=Physicality=Tech.=10 Oct.=Uranus=P=1Ø.
Merchant=8,000=80%=P8.0D=Economy=Currency=8 Aug.=Zeus>>E=v.
Merchantman=2,500=3,000=30%=P3.0D=3.0=Creativity=Stars=Muses=3 March = CI
Merchant marine=5,000=50%=P5.00D=Law=Time=Venus=5 May = Aphrodite>>L=N.
Mercia=5,500=5.5=80%=P5.50=Earth-Midway=5 May = Gaia.
Merciful=4,000=40%=P4.0D=Govt.=Creatocracy=4 April=Mercury=Hermes=G=A4.
Mercurial=9,000=90%=P9.00D=9.0=Abstraction=Gods=Saturn=9Sept.>>A=Ø.
Mercuric=3,000=30%=P3.0D=3.0=Creativity=Stars=Muses=3 March = C=I>>GIL.
Mercurous=2,500=3,000=30%=P3.0D=3.0=Creativity=Stars=Muses=3 March = C=I>>GIL.
mercury=10,000=1,000=100%=10.0=Physicality=Tech.=10 Oct.=Uranus=P=1Ø.

Mercury=10,000=1,000=100%=10.0=Physicality=Tech.=10 Oct.=Uranus=P=1Ø.
Roman myth. A God that served as messenger to the other Gods and is himself the God of commerce travel and thievery...see Hermes.

Mercy=10,000=1,000=100%=10.0=Physicality=Tech.=10 Oct.=Uranus=P=1Ø.
Mere=10,000=1,000=100%=10.0=Physicality=Tech.=10 Oct.=Uranus=P=1Ø.
Meredith George=2,000=20%=P2.00D=2.0=Nature=Matter=Moon=2 Feb.=Cupid=N=C+_
Meredith James=3,500=4,000=40%=P4.0D=Govt.=4 April=Mercury=Hermes=G=A4.
Merengue=7,500=8,000=80%=P8.0D=Economy=Currency=8 Aug.=Zeus>>E=v.
Meretricious=4,500=5,000=50%=P5.00D=Law=Time=Venus=5 May = Aphrodite>>L=N.
Merganser=7,500=8,000=80%=P8.0D=Economy=Currency=8 Aug.=Zeus>>E=v.
Merge=7,000=70%=P7.0D=7.0=Language=Assets=Mars=7 July=Pleiades.
Mérida=5,500=5.5=80%=P5.50=Earth-Midway=5 May = Gaia.
Meridian=10,000=1,000=100%=10.0=Physicality=Tech.=10 Oct.=Uranus=P=1Ø.
Meringue=8,000=80%=P8.0D=Economy=Currency=8 Aug.=Zeus>>E=v.
Merino=6,000=60%=P6.0D=Man=Earth=Royalty=6 June=Gaia=Maia>>M=M2.
Merit=10,000=1,000=100%=10.0=Physicality=Tech.=10 Oct.=Uranus=P=1Ø.
Meritorious=5,000=50%=P5.00D=Law=Time=Venus=5 May = Aphrodite>>L=N.
Mermaid=12,000=12%=P1.20D=1.2=Knowledge=Edu=12Dec.=Athena>>K=F.
Merman=9,000=90%=P9.00D=9.0=Abstraction=Gods=Saturn=9Sept.>>A=Ø.
Merry=6,000=60%=P6.0D=Man=Earth=Royalty=6 June=Gaia=Maia>>M=M2.
Merry go round=9,500=10,000=1,000=100%=10.0=Phys.=Tech.=10 Oct.=Uranus=P=1Ø.
Merrymaking=3,500=4,000=40%=P4.0D=Govt.=Creatocracy=4 April=Hermes=G=A4.
Mersey=8,500=9,000=90%=P9.00D=9.0=Abstraction=Gods=Saturn=9Sept.>>A=Ø.
Merton Thomas=2,500=3,000=30%=P3.0D=3.0=Cre=Stars=Muses=3 March = C=I>>GIL.
Mesa=5,000=50%=P5.00D=Law=Time=Venus=5 May = Aphrodite>>L=N.
Messabi Range=4,000=40%=P4.0D=Govt.=Creatocracy=4 April=Mercury=Hermes=G=A4.
Mescal=8,500=9,000=90%=P9.00D=9.0=Abstraction=Gods=Saturn=9Sept.>>A=Ø.
Mescaline=4,000=40%=P4.0D=Govt.=Creatocracy=4 April=Mercury=Hermes=G=A4.
Mesdames=3,000=30%=P3.0D=3.0=Creativity=Stars=Muses=3 March = C=I>>GIL.
Mesdemoiselles=1,500=15%=P1.50D=1.5=Authority=Solar Crown=1 May = Maia.
Mesencephalon=6,000=60%=P6.0D=Man=Earth=Royalty=6June=Gaia=Maia>>M=M2.
Mesh=14,000=14%=P1.40D=1.4=Mgt.=Solar Energy=13 May=Athena=SC=0.1
Meshed=6,500=7,000=70%=P7.0D=7.0=Language=Assets=Mars=7 July=Pleiades.
Mesmerize=8,500=9,000=90%=P9.00D=9.0=Abstraction=Gods=Saturn=9Sept.>>A=Ø.
Meso-=2,000=20%=P2.00D=2.0=Nature=Matter=Moon=2 Feb.=Cupid=N=C+_
Mesoamerica=9,000=90%=P9.00D=9.0=Abstraction=Gods=Saturn=9Sept.>>A=Ø.
Mesolithic=10,000=1,000=100%=10.0=Physicality=Tech.=10 Oct.=Uranus=P=1Ø.
Meson=10,000=1,000=100%=10.0=Physicality=Tech.=10 Oct.=Uranus=P=1Ø.
Mesopotamia=10,000=1,000=100%=10.0=Physicality=Tech.=10 Oct.=Uranus=P=1Ø.
Mesosphere=7,500=8,000=80%=P8.0D=Economy=Currency=8 Aug.=Zeus>>E=v.
Mesozoic=10,000=1,000=100%=10.0=Physicality=Tech.=10 Oct.=Uranus=P=1Ø.
mesquite=7,000=70%=P7.0D=7.0=Language=Assets=Mars=7 July=Pleiades.
Mesquite=4,500=5,000=50%=P5.00D=Law=Time=Venus=5 May = Aphrodite>>L=N.
Mess=10,000=1,000=100%=10.0=Physicality=Tech.=10 Oct.=Uranus=P=1Ø.

PETER K. MATTHEWS - AKUKALIA

Message=10,000=1,000=100%=10.0=Physicality=Tech.=10 Oct.=Uranus=P=1Ø.
Messenger=5,500=5.5=80%=P5.50=Earth-Midway=5 May = Gaia.
Messiah=10,000=1,000=100%=10.0=Physicality=Tech.=10 Oct.=Uranus=P=1Ø.
Messieurs=1,500=15%=P1.50D=1.5=Authority=Solar Crown=1 May = Maia.
Messina=9,000=90%=P9.00D=9.0=Abstraction=Gods=Saturn=9Sept.>>A=Ø.
Messrs.1=1,500=15%=P1.50D=1.5=Authority=Solar Crown=1 May = Maia.
Messrs.2=500=5%=P5.00D=5.0=Law=Time=Venus=5 May=Aphrodite>>L=N.
Messy=6,500=7,000=70%=P7.0D=7.0=Language=Assets=Mars=7 July=Pleiades.
Mestizo=7,000=70%=P7.0D=7.0=Language=Assets=Mars=7 July=Pleiades.
Met=3,000=30%=P3.0D=3.0=Creativity=Stars=Muses=3 March = C=I>>GIL.
Meta-=5,000=50%=P5.00D=Law=Time=Venus=5 May = Aphrodite>>L=N.
Metabolism=10,000=1,000=100%=10.0=Physicality=Tech.=10 Oct.=Uranus=P=1Ø.
Metacarpus=10,000=1,000=100%=10.0=Physicality=Tech.=10 Oct.=Uranus=P=1Ø.
Metal=10,000=1,000=100%=10.0=Physicality=Tech.=10 Oct.=Uranus=P=1Ø.
Metallic bond=10,000=1,000=100%=10.0=Physicality=Tech.=10 Oct.=Uranus=P=1Ø.
Metallurgy=10,000=1,000=100%=10.0=Physicality=Tech.=10 Oct.=Uranus=P=1Ø.
Metalwork=2,000=20%=P2.00D=2.0=Nature=Matter=Moon=2 Feb.=Cupid=N=C+_
Metamorphic=6,000=60%=P6.0D=Man=Earth=Royalty=6 June=Gaia=Maia>>M=M2.
Metamorphism=10,000=1,000=100%=10.0=Physicality=Tech.=10 Oct.=Uranus=P=1Ø.
Metamorphose=4,000=40%=P4.0D=Govt.=Creatocracy=4 April=Mercury=Hermes=G=A4.
Metamorphosis=10,000=1,000=100%=10.0=Physicality=Tech.=10 Oct.=Uranus=P=1Ø.
Metaphor=10,000=1,000=100%=10.0=Physicality=Tech.=10 Oct.=Uranus=P=1Ø.
Metaphysical=5,500=5.5=80%=P5.50=Earth-Midway=5 May = Gaia.
Metaphysics=10,000=1,000=100%=10.0=Physicality=Tech.=10 Oct.=Uranus=P=1Ø.
Metastasis=8,500=9,000=90%=P9.00D=9.0=Abstraction=Gods=Saturn=9Sept.>>A=Ø.
Metatarsus=10,000=1,000=100%=10.0=Physicality=Tech.=10 Oct.=Uranus=P=1Ø.
Mete=4,000=40%=P4.0D=Govt.=Creatocracy=4 April=Mercury=Hermes=G=A4.

Metempsychosis=1,500=15%=P1.50D=1.5=Authority=Solar Crown=1 May = Maia.
Reincarnation. The result shows that Maia orchestrates and manages the cycle of life.

Meteor=14,000=14%=P1.40D=1.4=Mgt.=Solar Energy=13 May=Athena=SC=0.1
Meteoric=7,000=70%=P7.0D=7.0=Language=Assets=Mars=7 July=Pleiades.
Meteorite=8,000=80%=P8.0D=Economy=Currency=8 Aug.=Zeus>>E=v.
Meteoroid=10,000=1,000=100%=10.0=Physicality=Tech.=10 Oct.=Uranus=P=1Ø.
Meteorology=10,000=1,000=100%=10.0=Physicality=Tech.=10 Oct.=Uranus=P=1Ø.
Meter1=10,000=1,000=100%=10.0=Physicality=Tech.=10 Oct.=Uranus=P=1Ø.
Meter2=4,500=5,000=50%=P5.00D=Law=Time=Venus=5 May = Aphrodite>>L=N.
Meter3=10,000=1,000=100%=10.0=Physicality=Tech.=10 Oct.=Uranus=P=1Ø.
-meter=3,500=4,000=40%=P4.0D=Govt.=Creatocracy=4 April=Mercury=Hermes=G=A4.
Meter kilogram-second=10,000=1,000=100%=10.0=Phy.=Tech.=10 Oct.=Uranus=P=1Ø.
Methadone=5,500=5.5=80%=P5.50=Earth-Midway=5 May = Gaia.
Methamphetamine=15,000=1,500=15%=P1.50D=1.5=Auth.=Solar Crown=1 May = Maia.
Methane=10,000=1,000=100%=10.0=Physicality=Tech.=10 Oct.=Uranus=P=1Ø.

Methanol=8,000=80%=P8.0D=Economy=Currency=8 Aug.=Zeus>>E=v.
Method=10,000=1,000=100%=10.0=Physicality=Tech.=10 Oct.=Uranus=P=1Ø.
Methodist=10,000=1,000=100%=10.0=Physicality=Tech.=10 Oct.=Uranus=P=1Ø.
Methodology=10,000=1,000=100%=10.0=Physicality=Tech.=10 Oct.=Uranus=P=1Ø.
Methuselah=4,500=5,000=50%=P5.00D=Law=Time=Venus=5 May = Aphrodite>>L=N.
Methyl=4,500=5,000=50%=P5.00D=Law=Time=Venus=5 May = Aphrodite>>L=N.
Methyl alcohol=1,000=100%=10.0=1.0=Mind=Sun=1 January=Helios >> M=E4.
Methylated spirit=7,500=8,000=80%=P8.0D=Economy=Currency=8 Aug.=Zeus>>E=v.

Metical=5,500=5.5=80%=P5.50=Earth-Midway=5 May = Gaia.
Currency Metric weight >> 5.5/10=0.55 >>55:1. See Naira. Dollar.

Meticulous=5,500=5.5=80%=P5.50=Earth-Midway=5 May = Gaia.
Métier=6,500=7,000=70%=P7.0D=7.0=Language=Assets=Mars=7 July=Pleiades.
Metonymy=10,000=1,000=100%=10.0=Physicality=Tech.=10 Oct.=Uranus=P=1Ø.
Metre=3,500=4,000=40%=P4.0D=Govt.=Creatocracy=4 April=Mercury=Hermes=G=A4.
Metric=3,500=4,000=40%=P4.0D=Govt.=Creatocracy=4 April=Mercury=Hermes=G=A4.
Metrical=6,500=7,000=70%=P7.0D=7.0=Language=Assets=Mars=7 July=Pleiades.
Metrication=4,500=5,000=50%=P5.00D=Law=Time=Venus=5 May = Aphrodite>>L=N.

Metrics=3,000=30%=P3.0D=3.0=Creativity=Stars=Muses=3 March = C=I>>GIL.
Metrics is creativity and the proof of superior creativity.

PICTURE of the Maks Currencies metrics. Code 10G.

Official Currency metrics and denominations of the Maks Currencies invented by Peter Matthews-Akukalia, Castle Makupedia. Five denominations for transactions and asset value storage. Development of the Maks lasted about twenty years. Patented in Nig.2020.

Metric system=10,000=1,000=100%=Physicality=Tech.=10 Oct.=Uranus=P=1Ø.
Metric ton=2,000=20%=P2.00D=2.0=Nature=Matter=Moon=2 Feb.=Cupid=N=C+_
Metronome=10,000=1,000=100%=10.0=Physicality=Tech.=10 Oct.=Uranus=P=1Ø.
Metropolis=10,000=1,000=100%=10.0=Physicality=Tech.=10 Oct.=Uranus=P=1Ø.
-metry=5,000=50%=P5.00D=Law=Time=Venus=5 May = Aphrodite>>L=N.
Metternich Prince=5,000=50%=P5.00D=Law=Time=Venus=5 May = Aphrodite>>L=N.
Mettle=5,000=50%=P5.00D=Law=Time=Venus=5 May = Aphrodite>>L=N.
Meuse=10,000=1,000=100%=10.0=Physicality=Tech.=10 Oct.=Uranus=P=1Ø.
Mew=5,000=50%=P5.00D=Law=Time=Venus=5 May = Aphrodite>>L=N.
Mews=8,500=9,000=90%=P9.00D=9.0=Abstraction=Gods=Saturn=9Sept.>>A=Ø.
Mex.=1,000=100%=10.0=1.0=Mind=Sun=1 January=Helios >> M=E4.
Mexical=6,500=7,000=70%=P7.0D=7.0=Language=Assets=Mars=7 July=Pleiades.
Mexico=6,000=60%=P6.0D=Man=Earth=Royalty=6 June=Gaia=Maia>>M=M2.
Mexico, Gulf of.=8,500=9,000=90%=P9.00D=9.0=Abst.=Gods=Saturn=9Sept.>>A=Ø.
Mexico City=5,500=5.5=80%=P5.50=Earth-Midway=5 May = Gaia.
Meyer beer=4,000=40%=P4.0D=Govt.=Creatocracy=4 April=Mercury=Hermes=G=A4.
Mezzanine=10,000=1,000=100%=10.0=Physicality=Tech.=10 Oct.=Uranus=P=1Ø.
Mezzo-soprano=10,000=1,000=100%=10.0=Physicality=Tech.=10 Oct.=Uranus=P=1Ø.
M.F.A.=2,000=20%=P2.00D=2.0=Nature=Matter=Moon=2 Feb.=Cupid=N=C+_
mfd.=500=5%=P5.00D=5.0=Law=Time=Venus=5 May=Aphrodite>>L=N.
mfg.=500=5%=P5.00D=5.0=Law=Time=Venus=5 May=Aphrodite>>L=N.
mg=500=5%=P5.00D=5.0=Law=Time=Venus=5 May=Aphrodite>>L=N.
Mg=2,500=3,000=30%=P3.0D=3.0=Creativity=Stars=Muses=3 March = C=I>>GIL.

---

mgt.=500=5%=P5.00D=5.0=Law=Time=Venus=5 May=Aphrodite>>L=N.
In the Creative Sciences of the Makupedia & Creatocracy, management is coded 14>>1.4

MHz=500=5%=P5.00D=5.0=Law=Time=Venus=5 May=Aphrodite>>L=N.
In the Makupedia dimensions of the Mind universe language is the 7th, formula is Lang =Az.

---

mi=4,500=5,000=50%=P5.00D=Law=Time=Venus=5 May = Aphrodite>>L=N.
MI=1,500=15%=P1.50D=1.5=Authority=Solar Crown=1 May = Maia.
mi.=500=5%=P5.00D=5.0=Law=Time=Venus=5 May=Aphrodite>>L=N.
MIA=6,500=7,000=70%=P7.0D=7.0=Language=Assets=Mars=7 July=Pleiades.
Miami=12,000=12%=P1.20D=1.2=Knowledge=Edu=12Dec.=Athena>>K=F.
Miami Beach=9,500=10,000=1,000=100%=Physicality=Tech.=10 Oct.=Uranus=P=1Ø.
Miasma=10,000=1,000=100%=10.0=Physicality=Tech.=10 Oct.=Uranus=P=1Ø.
Mica=10,000=1,000=100%=10.0=Physicality=Tech.=10 Oct.=Uranus=P=1Ø.

Micah=6,000=60%=P6.0D=Man=Earth=Royalty=6 June=Gaia=Maia>>M=M2.
A Hebrew prophet of the 8th >> 8.0 cent. B.C. See table at Bible. Inspired by Gaia. Micah is an incarnation of Zeus and runs on the same spiritual energy with Peter Matthews-Akukalia, Castle Makupedia. 6.0*8.0x=px=14+48=62x=px=734=7.34. Micah had the gift of computations guided by the muses (.3) and Maia (.4) and could deduce the times. That was why he could foretell the destruction of Samaria and of Jerusalem. Two distinct places indicated as 2.0. The muses guided him on the destruction of Samaria. Maia guided him on the destruction of Jerusalem. 7.34*2.0x=px=9.34+14.68=24.02x=px=161.1312=200=2.0. The resultant again confirms that the essence of the prophet Micah was to foretell the destruction of Samaria and Jerusalem. So everyone has a purpose for being born.

Mice=1,500=15%=P1.50D=1.5=Authority=Solar Crown=1 May = Maia.
Mich.=500=5%=P5.00D=5.0=Law=Time=Venus=5 May=Aphrodite>>L=N.
Michelangelo=4,500=5,000=50%=P5.00D=Law=Time=Venus=5 May = Aphrodite>>L=N.
Michigan=7,500=8,000=80%=P8.0D=Economy=Currency=8 Aug.=Zeus>>E=v.
Michigan, Lake=5,000=50%=P5.00D=Law=Time=Venus=5 May = Aphrodite>>L=N.
Micmac=6,000=60%=P6.0D=Man=Earth=Royalty=6 June=Gaia=Maia>>M=M2.
Micra=2,000=20%=P2.00D=2.0=Nature=Matter=Moon=2 Feb.=Cupid=N=C+_
Micro=5,500=5.5=80%=P5.50=Earth-Midway=5 May = Gaia.

Micro-=15,500=16,000=16%=P1.60D=1.6=Incarnation=Mind of GOD=1 June = Maia.
Small. Requiring or involving Microsoft. One-millionth. Equal to 1.0x10power-6. See Mega.

Microbe=5,000=50%=P5.00D=Law=Time=Venus=5 May = Aphrodite>>L=N.
Microbiology=4,000=40%=P4.0D=Govt.=Creatocracy=4 April=Mercury=Hermes=G=A4.
Micro bus=4,500=5,000=50%=P5.00D=Law=Time=Venus=5 May = Aphrodite>>L=N.
Microcephaly=10,000=1,000=100%=10.0=Physicality=Tech.=10 Oct.=Uranus=P=1Ø.
Microchip=2,500=3,000=30%=P3.0D=3.0=Creativity=Stars=Muses=3 March = C=I>>GIL.
Microcircuit=3,500=4,000=40%=P4.0D=Govt.=Creatocracy=4 April=Hermes=G=A4.
Microcomputer=3,500=4,000=40%=P4.0D=Govt.=Cr=4 April=Mercury=Hermes=G=A4.
Microcosm=10,000=1,000=100%=10.0=Physicality=Tech.=10 Oct.=Uranus=P=1Ø.
Microdot=5,000=50%=P5.00D=Law=Time=Venus=5 May = Aphrodite>>L=N.
Microeconomics=7,500=8,000=80%=P8.0D=Economy=Currency=8 Aug.=Zeus>>E=v.
Microelectronics=4,500=5,000=50%=P5.00D=Law=Time=Venus=5 May =Odite>>L=N.
Microfiche=5,000=50%=P5.00D=Law=Time=Venus=5 May = Aphrodite>>L=N.
Microfilm=6,000=60%=P6.0D=Man=Earth=Royalty=6 June=Gaia=Maia>>M=M2.
Micrometer=3,500=4,000=40%=P4.0D=Govt.=Creatocracy=4 April=Hermes=G=A4.
Micron=9,500=10,000=1,000=100%=10.0=Physicality=Tech.=10 Oct.=Uranus=P=1Ø.
Micronesia=5,000=50%=P5.00D=Law=Time=Venus=5 May = Aphrodite>>L=N.
Micronesian=6,000=60%=P6.0D=Man=Earth=Royalty=6 June=Gaia=Maia>>M=M2.
Microorganism=5,000=50%=P5.00D=Law=Time=Venus=5 May = Aphrodite>>L=N.
Microphone=10,000=1,000=100%=10.0=Physicality=Tech.=10 Oct.=Uranus=P=1Ø.

Microprocessor=8,000=80%=P8.0D=Economy=Currency=8 Aug.=Zeus>>E=v.
Zeus -Jehovah -Allah is the microprocessor of all life. All things are energized and connected through lights that emit from His hands and distributed through lunar means.

Microscope=10,000=1,000=100%=10.0=Physicality=Tech.=10 Oct.=Uranus=P=1Ø.
Microscopy=5,000=50%=P5.00D=Law=Time=Venus=5 May = Aphrodite>>L=N.
Microsurgery=6,500=7,000=70%=P7.0D=7.0=Language=Assets=Mars=7 July=Pleiades.
Microwave=10,000=1,000=100%=10.0=Physicality=Tech.=10 Oct.=Uranus=P=1Ø.
Microwave oven=4,000=40%=P4.0D=Govt.=Cre=4 April=Mercury=Hermes=G=A4.

Mid=1,000=100%=10.0=1.0=Mind=Sun=1 January=Helios >> M=E4.
Maia Midway means that Maia comes to the earth to compute things in a quantum. There she becomes Gaia. Another instance is that Maia is the collective name for the sisters of seven and her own name is Gaia Midway, the one who computes in a quantum of 1,000 whose name and physical equivalent is 1,000 and is the midway for all abstraction. Discovery is that the sun is a mid between the Natural Galaxy and the Supernatural Galaxy.

Mid-=2,000=20%=P2.00D=2.0=Nature=Matter=Moon=2 Feb.=Cupid=N=C+_
Mid air=1,000=100%=10.0=1.0=Mind=Sun=1 January=Helios >> M=E4.

Midas=5,500=5.5=80%=P5.50=Earth-Midway=5 May = Gaia.
A fabled king who turned all that he touched into gold. First all fables are myths and all myths have been established to have certain truth. There is really nothing like fiction and it is so only because the characters are not the real persons who first lived it. Gaia Midway is computed to be Midas. Look at the facts. First a king or royalty. Secondly the factor of gold. Third the power of touch indicating affection. Fourth Gaia Midway is the transmuted Maia who inspired medicine and delivers all births humans and animals and accords spirits as guardians at will and purpose after due rights are granted from the Zeus and the Council.

Midbrain=1,000=100%=10.0=1.0=Mind=Sun=1 January=Helios >> M=E4.
Midday=500=5%=P5.00D=5.0=Law=Time=Venus=5 May=Aphrodite>>L=N.
Midden=4,000=4,000=40%=P4.0D=Govt.=Creato=4 April=Mercury=Hermes=G=A4.
Middle=10,000=1,000=100%=10.0=Physicality=Tech.=10 Oct.=Uranus=P=1Ø.
Middle age=3,000=30%=P3.0D=3.0=Creativity=Stars=Muses=3 March = C=I>>GIL.
Middle Ages=8,000=80%=P8.0D=Economy=Currency=8 Aug.=Zeus>>E=v.
Middle America=10,000=1,000=100%=10.0=Physicality=Tech.=10 Oct.=Uranus=P=1Ø.
Middle class=7,000=70%=P7.0D=7.0=Language=Assets=Mars=7 July=Pleiades.
Middle Dutch=4,500=5,000=50%=P5.00D=Law=Time=Venus=5 May = Aphrodite>>L=N.
Middle ear=6,500=7,000=70%=P7.0D=7.0=Language=Assets=Mars=7 July=Pleiades.
Middle East=5,500=5.5=80%=P5.50=Earth-Midway=5 May = Gaia.

Middle English=3,000=30%=P3.0D=3.0=Creativity=Stars=Muses=3 March = C=I>>GIL. English from about 1100 to 1500 >> 1.1*1.5x=px=2.6+1.65=4.25x=px=8.54=9.0. At about this period in time the Council of Muses inspired the English language. This result aligns with the ticological results of 3.0 above. The essence of the English language is to help creativity thrive and this was so especially with people like William Shakespeare and others that inspired the Sciences arts and inventions. 3.0*3.0x=px=6+9=15x=px=69=70=7.0. Creativity is a form of unique language expressed through many forms such as literary calculative computational technical. It is classified by the Creatocracy as either speculative or precision. Combined they become Litech >> Literary and technical. The most classical example of Litech is the Makupedia Sciences such as the Oracle, Psychoeconomix, Naturecology, Psychoastronomy and the encyclopedia of Castle Makupedia. All by Peter Matthews-Akukalia, Castle Makupedia. God of Creatocracy Genius and Mind.

Middle ground=3,500=4,000=40%=P4.0D=Govt.=Creatocracy=4 April=Hermes=G=A4.

Middle High German=4,500=5,000=50%=P5.00D=Law=Time=Venus=5 May =Odite >>L=N.
High German from the 11th through the 15th cent. >>1.1*1.5x=px=2.6+1.65=4.25x=px=8.54=9.0. At about this period in time the Council of Muses inspired the German language as a means to establish a nation and its legitimacy. The German language establishes their sovereignty. Inspired by the combined efforts of Hermes of Mercury and Aphrodite of Venus.

Middle Low German=4,500=5,000=50%=P5.00D=Law=Time=Venus=5 May =Odite>>L=N.
Middleman=7,000=70%=P7.0D=7.0=Language=Assets=Mars=7 July=Pleiades.
Middle management=4,000=40%=P4.0D=Govt.=Creatocracy=4 April=Hermes=G=A4.
Middle of the road=5,500=5.5=80%=P5.50=Earth-Midway=5 May = Gaia.
Middle school=5,000=50%=P5.00D=Law=Time=Venus=5 May = Aphrodite>>L=N.
Middle weight=6,500=7,000=70%=P7.0D=7.0=Language=Assets=Mars=7 July=Pleiades.
Middle West=1,000=100%=10.0=1.0=Mind=Sun=1 January=Helios >> M=E4.
Middling=6,000=60%=P6.0D=Man=Earth=Royalty=6 June=Gaia=Maia>>M=M2.
Middy=4,000=40%=P4.0D=Govt.=Creatocracy=4 April=Mercury=Hermes=G=A4.
Mideast=1,500=15%=P1.50D=1.5=Authority=Solar Crown=1 May = Maia.
Midge=2,500=3,000=30%=P3.0D=3.0=Creativity=Stars=Muses=3 March = C=I>>GIL.
Midget=6,000=60%=P6.0D=Man=Earth=Royalty=6 June=Gaia=Maia>>M=M2.
Midland=4,000=40%=P4.0D=Govt.=Creatocracy=4 April=Mercury=Hermes=G=A4.
Midlands=2,500=3,000=30%=P3.0D=3.0=Creativity=Stars=Muses=3 March = C=I>>GIL.
Midline=4,000=40%=P4.0D=Govt.=Creatocracy=4 April=Mercury=Hermes=G=A4.
Midnight=7,000=70%=P7.0D=7.0=Language=Assets=Mars=7 July=Pleiades.
Midnight sun=6,500=7,000=70%=P7.0D=7.0=Language=Assets=Mars=7 July=Pleiades.

Midpoint=4,500=5,000=50%=P5.00D=Law=Time=Venus=5 May = Aphrodite>>L=N.
Midpoint is a calibration used to measure emotion in the Mind Assessment Tests invented by Peter Matthews-Akukalia, Castle Makupedia. See The Oracle.

Midriff=8,000=80%=P8.0D=Economy=Currency=8 Aug.=Zeus>>E=v.
Midshipman=5,000=50%=P5.00D=Law=Time=Venus=5 May = Aphrodite>>L=N.

Midst=9,000=90%=P9.00D=9.0=Abstraction=Gods=Saturn=9Sept.>>A=Ø.
Measured as 0.1 in the Creative Sciences, Makupedia. 0.1 >> Solar Core >> Energy Source. It is the central residence of the Council of Gods and their serving Muses.

Midsummer=4,000=40%=P4.0D=Govt.=Creatocracy=4 April=Mercury=Hermes=G=A4.
Midterm=8,500=9,000=90%=P9.00D=9.0=Abstraction=Gods=Saturn=9Sept.>>A=Ø.
Midtown=2,500=3,000=30%=P3.0D=3.0=Creativity=Stars=Muses=3 March = C=I>>GIL.

Midway=9,000=90%=P9.00D=9.0=Abstraction=Gods=Saturn=9Sept.>>A=Ø.
This is computational proof of the existence of a Deity named midway in every midway. This deity is a Goddess called Gaia-Midway who in the celestial is Maia the Great Goddess. Interestingly her son Hermes is God of the boundary merchandise invention and thievery.

Midway Islands=7,500=8,000=80%=P8.0D=Economy=Currency=8 Aug.=Zeus>>E=v.

Midweek=2,500=3,000=30%=P3.0D=3.0=Creativity=Stars=Muses=3 March = C=I>>GIL.
There are officially seven days in a week. Sunday to Saturday. The third day is computed to be the midweek making it Wednesday. However 2,500 is the half of 5.0 indicating that there are actually five working days that make a work week. So Saturday and Sunday are rest days or exceptional work days that will naturally depend on work ethics and standards that prevail in a location. Hence the five days are Monday to Friday. Midweek is Wednesday. Peter Matthews-Akukalia, Castle Makupedia was born on a Thurday 6 July 1978. Thursday >> Thor >> the God of Thunder weather agriculture and the home. The son of Odin and Freya (Frigga). Odin is the supreme God and Creator >> Zeus. God of victory and the dead. Wednesday is named after Him. Freya is the Goddess of love and of the night, sister of Frey. Frey is the God of Fertility and dispenser of rain and sunshine.

Midwestern=3,500=4,000=40%=P4.0D=Govt.=Creatocracy=4 April=Hermes=G=A4.
New West State was created as a part of the Paradise Nations. See book >> The Creatocracy Republic of Castle Makupedia by Peter Matthews-Akukalia.

Midwife=8,500=9,000=90%=P9.00D=9.0=Abstraction=Gods=Saturn=9Sept.>>A=Ø.

Midwinter=4,000=40%=P4.0D=Govt.=Creatocracy=4 April=Mercury=Hermes=G=A4.
Inspired by Hermes for observance in all nations governments and relationships.
The middle of the winter. The winter solstice, about Dec.22. The energy for Dec.22 >>
Day 22: Value:9.3 Planetary Type:Saturn Human Type:ICT Birth Energy Level:100%+.

>>9.3*4.0x=px=13.3+37.2=50.5x=px=545.26=55=5.5>> Gaia Midway (Maia). >>
55=60=6.0>>Gaia. >> Earth >> World >> Mankind >> Emotions >> Royalty >> Health.
The Creatocracy hereby sets Dec. 22 for the celebration of World MindComputers Day.

Midyear=7,000=70%=P7.0D=7.0=Language=Assets=Mars=7 July=Pleiades.
Computed as 7.0>> July >> Mars >> Aries. Meaning that there are 14 months in the
cosmic calendar rather than 12 as used in the prevailing Gregorian calendar. The
Creatocracy declares the extra months of Castle and Makupedia as two extra months in
the Creatocracy, Mind and,or Makupedia calendar. Castle >> 13th month. Makupedia
>> 14th month. Since the Mind is the first dimension in the universe both months come
before January. Hence Castle to December makes 14 months of the Creatocracy calendar.

Mien=3,500=4,000=40%=P4.0D=Govt.=Creatocracy=4 April=Mercury=Hermes=G=A4.
Miff=2,000=20%=P2.00D=2.0=Nature=Matter=Moon=2 Feb.=Cupid=N=C+_
Might1=1,500=15%=P1.50D=1.5=Authority=Solar Crown=1 May = Maia.
Might2=10,000=1,000=100%=10.0=Physicality=Tech.=10 Oct.=Uranus=P=1Ø.
Mighty=4,000=40%=P4.0D=Govt.=Creatocracy=4 April=Mercury=Hermes=G=A4.
Migraine=8,500=9,000=90%=P9.00D=9.0=Abstraction=Gods=Saturn=9Sept.>>A=Ø.
Migrant=8,000=80%=P8.0D=Economy=Currency=8 Aug.=Zeus>>E=v.
Migrate=10,000=1,000=100%=10.0=Physicality=Tech.=10 Oct.=Uranus=P=1Ø.
Mikado=2,000=20%=P2.00D=2.0=Nature=Matter=Moon=2 Feb.=Cupid=N=C+_
Mike=4,000=40%=P4.0D=Govt.=Creatocracy=4 April=Mercury=Hermes=G=A4.
Mil=8,000=80%=P8.0D=Economy=Currency=8 Aug.=Zeus>>E=v.
Milan=4,500=5,000=50%=P5.00D=Law=Time=Venus=5 May = Aphrodite>>L=N.
Mild=7,000=70%=P7.0D=7.0=Language=Assets=Mars=7 July=Pleiades.
Mildew=10,500=11,000=11%=P1.10D=1.1=Idea=Brainchild=Inv.=11 Nov.=Athena>>I=MT.
Mile=7,000=70%=P7.0D=7.0=Language=Assets=Mars=7 July=Pleiades.
Mileage=10,000=1,000=100%=10.0=Physicality=Tech.=10 Oct.=Uranus=P=1Ø.
Milepost=4,500=5,000=50%=P5.00D=Law=Time=Venus=5 May = Aphrodite>>L=N.
Miler=3,500=4,000=40%=P4.0D=Govt.=Creatocracy=4 April=Mercury=Hermes=G=A4.
Milestone=3,000=30%=P3.0D=3.0=Creativity=Stars=Muses=3 March = C=I>>GIL.
Miletus=6,000=60%=P6.0D=Man=Earth=Royalty=6 June=Gaia=Maia>>M=M2.
Milieu=2,500=3,000=30%=P3.0D=3.0=Creativity=Stars=Muses=3 March = C=I>>GIL.
Militant=8,500=9,000=90%=P9.00D=9.0=Abstraction=Gods=Saturn=9Sept.>>A=Ø.
Militarism=7,500=8,000=80%=P8.0D=Economy=Currency=8 Aug.=Zeus>>E=v.
Militarize=5,000=50%=P5.00D=Law=Time=Venus=5 May = Aphrodite>>L=N.
Military=7,000=70%=P7.0D=7.0=Language=Assets=Mars=7 July=Pleiades.
Militate=6,500=7,000=70%=P7.0D=7.0=Language=Assets=Mars=7 July=Pleiades.
Militia=10,000=1,000=100%=10.0=Physicality=Tech.=10 Oct.=Uranus=P=1Ø.
Milk=10,000=1,000=100%=10.0=Physicality=Tech.=10 Oct.=Uranus=P=1Ø.
Milkmaid=3,500=4,000=40%=P4.0D=Govt.=Creatocracy=4 April=Hermes=G=A4.
Milkman=4,500=5,000=50%=P5.00D=Law=Time=Venus=5 May = Aphrodite>>L=N.
Milk of magnesia=7,500=8,000=80%=P8.0D=Economy=Currency=8 Aug.=Zeus>>E=v.
Milkshake=10,000=1,000=100%=10.0=Physicality=Tech.=10 Oct.=Uranus=P=1Ø.

PETER K. MATTHEWS - AKUKALIA

Milk tooth=4,500=5,000=50%=P5.00D=Law=Time=Venus=5 May = Aphrodite>>L=N.
Milkweed=7,000=70%=P7.0D=7.0=Language=Assets=Mars=7 July=Pleiades.
Milky Way=8,000=80%=P8.0D=Economy=Currency=8 Aug.=Zeus>>E=v.
Mill1=10,000=1,000=100%=10.0=Physicality=Tech.=10 Oct.=Uranus=P=1Ø.

Mill2=6,500=7,000=70%=P7.0D=7.0=Language=Assets=Mars=7 July=Pleiades.
A monetary unit equal to 1/1000 of a U.S. dollar. A computational means to the Maks. See
Dollar. An attempt to apply seemingly known truth of cosmic standards but lacks metrics.

Mill,James=3,000=30%=P3.0D=3.0=Creativity=Stars=Muses=3 March = C=I>>GIL.
Mill,John=3,500=4,000=40%=P4.0D=Govt.=Creatocracy=4 April=Hermes=G=A4.
Millay, Edna=3,000=30%=P3.0D=3.0=Creativity=Stars=Muses=3 March = C=I>>GIL.
Mill dam=2,500=3,000=30%=P3.0D=3.0=Creativity=Stars=Muses=3 March = C=I>>GIL.
Millennium=10,000=1,000=100%=10.0=Physicality=Tech.=10 Oct.=Uranus=P=1Ø.
Millepede=1,500=15%=P1.50D=1.5=Authority=Solar Crown=1 May = Maia.
Miller,Arthur=2,000=20%=P2.00D=2.0=Nature=Matter=Moon=2 Feb.=Cupid=N=C+_
Millet=8,000=80%=P8.0D=Economy=Currency=8 Aug.=Zeus>>E=v.
Millet,Jean=2,500=3,000=30%=P3.0D=3.0=Cre=Stars=Muses=3 March = C=I>>GIL.
Milli=3,500=4,000=40%=P4.0D=Govt.=Creatocracy=4 April=Mercury=Hermes=G=A4.
Milliard=2,000=20%=P2.00D=2.0=Nature=Matter=Moon=2 Feb.=Cupid=N=C+_
Millibar=6,000=60%=P6.0D=Man=Earth=Royalty=6 June=Gaia=Maia>>M=M2.
Milligram=2,000=20%=P2.00D=2.0=Nature=Matter=Moon=2 Feb.=Cupid=N=C+_
Milliliter=2,000=20%=P2.00D=2.0=Nature=Matter=Moon=2 Feb.=Cupid=N=C+_
Millime=4,500=5,000=50%=P5.00D=Law=Time=Venus=5 May = Aphrodite>>L=N.
Millimeter=2,000=20%=P2.00D=2.0=Nature=Matter=Moon=2 Feb.=Cupid=N=C+_
Milliner=7,000=70%=P7.0D=7.0=Language=Assets=Mars=7 July=Pleiades.
Million=5,500=5.5=80%=P5.50=Earth-Midway=5 May = Gaia.

Millionaire=7,000=70%=P7.0D=7.0=Language=Assets=Mars=7 July=Pleiades.
A real millionaire is defined by the potential value of his works and assets based on the law
of everything. See the Brickwalls of Castle Makupedia,ch. 21 by Peter Matthews-Akukalia.

Millionth=6,500=7,000=70%=P7.0D=7.0=Language=Assets=Mars=7 July=Pleiades.
Millipede=10,000=1,000=100%=10.0=Physicality=Tech.=10 Oct.=Uranus=P=1Ø.
Millisecond=3,000=30%=P3.0D=3.0=Creativity=Stars=Muses=3 March = C=I>>GIL.
Mill pond=6,000=60%=P6.0D=Man=Earth=Royalty=6 June=Gaia=Maia>>M=M2.
Millrace=8,000=80%=P8.0D=Economy=Currency=8 Aug.=Zeus>>E=v.
Millstone=6,500=7,000=70%=P7.0D=7.0=Language=Assets=Mars=7 July=Pleiades.
Mill stream=3,500=4,000=40%=P4.0D=Govt.=Creat=4 April=Mercury=Hermes=G=A4.
Mil wheel=4,500=5,000=50%=P5.00D=Law=Time=Venus=5 May = Aphrodite>>L=N.
Milne A(lan)=2,500=3,000=30%=P3.0D=3.0=Creativity=Stars=Muses=3 March = CI.
Milquetoast=7,000=70%=P7.0D=7.0=Language=Assets=Mars=7 July=Pleiades.
Milt=2,000=20%=P2.00D=2.0=Nature=Matter=Moon=2 Feb.=Cupid=N=C+_

Milton John=3,000=30%=P3.0D=3.0=Creativity=Stars=Muses=3 March = C=I>>GIL.
Milwaukee=5,000=50%=P5.00D=Law=Time=Venus=5 May = Aphrodite>>L=N.
Mime=9,000=90%=P9.00D=9.0=Abstraction=Gods=Saturn=9Sept.>>A=Ø.
Mimeograph=9,500=10,000=1,000=100%=Physicality=Tech.=10 Oct.=Uranus=P=1Ø.

Mimesis=9,500=10,000=1,000=100%=10.0=Physicality=Tech.=10 Oct.=Uranus=P=1Ø.
The representation of the aspects of the sensible world, especially human actions, in literature and art. In Creatocracy it is called the Mind Arts invented by Peter Matthews-Akukalia, Castle Makupedia. In the arts he is reputed as the African Shakespeare.

Mimetic=4,500=5,000=50%=P5.00D=Law=Time=Venus=5 May = Aphrodite>>L=N.
Mimic=10,000=1,000=100%=10.0=Physicality=Tech.=10 Oct.=Uranus=P=1Ø.
Mimicry=3,500=4,000=40%=P4.0D=Govt.=Creatocracy=4 April=Mercury=Hermes=G=A4.
Mimosa=7,500=8,000=80%=P8.0D=Economy=Currency=8 Aug.=Zeus>>E=v.
Min.=3,000=30%=P3.0D=3.0=Creativity=Stars=Muses=3 March = C=I>>GIL.
Minaret=4,500=5,000=50%=P5.00D=Law=Time=Venus=5 May = Aphrodite>>L=N.
Minatory=3,000=30%=P3.0D=3.0=Creativity=Stars=Muses=3 March = C=I>>GIL.
Mince=10,000=1,000=100%=10.0=Physicality=Tech.=10 Oct.=Uranus=P=1Ø.
Mincemeat=10,000=1,000=100%=10.0=Physicality=Tech.=10 Oct.=Uranus=P=1Ø.

Mind=10,000=1,000=100%=10.0=Physicality=Tech.=10 Oct.=Uranus=P=1Ø.
I. Peter Matthews-Akukalia studied the operations of the abstract and by computation discovered the mind as an energy system equivalent to the Sun. He defined that the inherent energy that runs a thing constitutes the mind of that thing. He wrote the formula of the mind as M=E4. E4>E Quartet meaning that the mind functions on four components. The Creative Sciences is the Mind Sciences emerging Creative & Mind Sciences and Creative Scientists of the Creatocratic Order. The Mind is the first of the twelve dimensions of the Universe. It is reckoned to be the first asset of the Creatocracy. Peter Matthews-Akukalia emerged as Castle Makupedia, God of Creatocracy Genius Mind & Mindom.

II. The scripture code for the word Mind is G3563 as seen in Romans 11:34.
3.5*6.3x=px=9.8+22.05=31.85x=px=247.94
By WDSD the psycho-weight for the letter G is 5.0
So G3563 >> 5.0*247.94=x=px=252.94+1,239.7=1,492.64x=px=315,062.358=32=3.2
3.2sp1 >> 3.0*0.2x=px=3.2+0.6=3.8x=px=5.72=6.0>>Man >> Earth >> Gaia >> Emotion.
The benchmark for the Mind is 6.0 and was long determined through revelation to the King in his Naturecology ever before it occurred to him to search it in the Bible. After all Makupedia WDSD was just developed in the last quarter of the year 2021. The aligned element for the Mind in astronomy is lithium with atomic weight 6.939. Lithium is a soft silver-white metal. It is the lightest of the alkali metals. Lithium carbonate or another lithium salt is used as a mood stabilizing drug. - Apple online definition for lithium.

III. Peter Matthews-Akukalia defined the Mind and stated that the energy that runs a thing constitutes the mind of that thing. He split the components of the mind as intelligence thought will and emotion. Interestingly the benchmark for emotion aligns with the same for the mind. So the mind is first a bundle of energy components and then the mind can be expressed as the emotion. In that case the human energy database is the objective source of human emotion in value say (1.1) and quantum say 100%. The emotional benchmark code is also used to calculate or rather Makulate the percentage of energy lost to or gained from the environment by a person from birth to the age of the Mind assessment Test. A subjective analysis. Hence Makupedia functions both the objective and the subjective means to establish truths. In his quest and search to understand the mystery of creativity he discovered the mind and the universe. Psychoeconomix was written and published many years before Naturecology. The first solved Creativity and the second solved Mind.

PICTURE OF THE MAKUPEDIA-MINDOSCOPE. CODE 10H.

This is the Mindoscope. The First Human Mind "Super" Computer Series invented by Peter Matthews-Akukalia. It computes programs, analysis of a person's name, future, work, location, education, marriage, general crises and conflict resolution. Makupedia is the First Human Mind Computer- an electronic analyzer series apps that uses subjective method. The mindoscope functions the objective means to discover the innate potentials on time.

Mindanao=4,000=40%=P4.0D=Govt.=Creatocracy=4 April=Mercury=Hermes=G=A4.
Mind blowing=3,000=30%=P3.0D=3.0=Creativity=Stars=Muses=3 March = C=I>>GIL.
Mind boggling=3,000=30%=P3.0D=3.0=Creativity=Stars=Muses=3 March = C=I>>GIL.
Mind expanding=500=5%=P5.00D=5.0=Law=Time=Venus=5 May=Aphrodite>>L=N.
Mindful=3,000=30%=P3.0D=3.0=Creativity=Stars=Muses=3 March = C=I>>GIL.

Mindless=3,000=30%=P3.0D=3.0=Creativity=Stars=Muses=3 March = C=I>>GIL.
Mindoro=4,500=5,000=50%=P5.00D=Law=Time=Venus=5 May = Aphrodite>>L=N.
Mindset=6,000=60%=P6.0D=Man=Earth=Royalty=6 June=Gaia=Maia>>M=M2.

Mine1=10,000=1,000=100%=10.0=Physicality=Tech.=10 Oct.=Uranus=P=1Ø.
In the Creative Sciences, the earthly equivalent of the Mind is the Mine. The celestial equivalent is the Sun. The abstract equivalent is energy. The mineral equivalent is diamond. Ownership of the Mind through the formula is ownership of the Sun and all mines by law. The universe is an energy mine of convertible data, resources to discover develop and connect our potentials, now smart data is synonymous with Makupedia as everyone needs big data so should everyone have a Makupedia. A business law of Makupedia.

Mine2=8,000=80%=P8.0D=Economy=Currency=8 Aug.=Zeus>>E=v.
Mine field=4,500=5,000=50%=P5.00D=Law=Time=Venus=5 May = Aphrodite>>L=N.

Mineral=10,000=1,000=100%=10.0=Physicality=Tech.=10 Oct.=Uranus=P=1Ø.
In the Makupedia, the study of Planetix and its components is an attempt to use computational creativity to track the presence and availability of natural minerals in a location at a specific time. An advanced knowledge of Peter Matthews-Akukalia, Castle Makupedia in his work >> Principles of Naturecology. Services oriented. Business matters.

Mineralogy=2,000=20%=P2.00D=2.0=Nature=Matter=Moon=2 Feb.=Cupid=N=C+_
Mineral oil=6,000=60%=P6.0D=Man=Earth=Royalty=6 June=Gaia=Maia>>M=M2.
Mineral water=4,000=40%=P4.0D=Govt.=Creatocracy=4 April=Mercury=Hermes=G=A4.
Mineral wool=7,000=70%=P7.0D=7.0=Language=Assets=Mars=7 July=Pleiades.

Minerva=6,000=60%=P6.0D=Man=Earth=Royalty=6 June=Gaia=Maia>>M=M2.
Roman myth. The Goddess of wisdom, the arts and warfare. >> Athena of Makupedia.

Minestrone=5,500=5.5=80%=P5.50=Earth-Midway=5 May = Gaia.
Minesweeper=5,000=50%=P5.00D=Law=Time=Venus=5 May = Aphrodite>>L=N.
Mingle=4,500=5,000=50%=P5.00D=Law=Time=Venus=5 May = Aphrodite>>L=N.
Mini=3,000=30%=P3.0D=3.0=Creativity=Stars=Muses=3 March = C=I>>GIL.
Mini-=3,000=30%=P3.0D=3.0=Creativity=Stars=Muses=3 March = C=I>>GIL.
Miniature=10,000=1,000=100%=10.0=Physicality=Tech.=10 Oct.=Uranus=P=1Ø.
Minibike=3,000=30%=P3.0D=3.0=Creativity=Stars=Muses=3 March = C=I>>GIL.
Minibus=1,500=15%=P1.50D=1.5=Authority=Solar Crown=1 May = Maia.
Minicomputer=4,000=40%=P4.0D=Govt.=Creatocracy=4 April=Mercury=Hermes=G=A4.
Minim=7,500=8,000=80%=P8.0D=Economy=Currency=8 Aug.=Zeus>>E=v.
Minimal=10,000=1,000=100%=10.0=Physicality=Tech.=10 Oct.=Uranus=P=1Ø.
Minimalism=10,000=1,000=100%=10.0=Physicality=Tech.=10 Oct.=Uranus=P=1Ø.
Minimalist=5,500=5.5=80%=P5.50=Earth-Midway=5 May = Gaia.

Minimize=7,500=8,000=80%=P8.0D=Economy=Currency=8 Aug.=Zeus>>E=v.
Minimum=7,500=8,000=80%=P8.0D=Economy=Currency=8 Aug.=Zeus>>E=v.

Minimum wage=8,000=80%=P8.0D=Economy=Currency=8 Aug.=Zeus>>E=v.
The Creatocracy believes that everyone should earn per second with proof of their work.
Assessments such as the wisper report becomes a useful invention here.

Minion=4,000=40%=P4.0D=Govt.=Creatocracy=4 April=Mercury=Hermes=G=A4.
Miniseries=6,000=60%=P6.0D=Man=Earth=Royalty=6 June=Gaia=Maia>>M=M2.
Miniskirt=2,000=20%=P2.00D=2.0=Nature=Matter=Moon=2 Feb.=Cupid=N=C+_
Minister=10,000=1,000=100%=10.0=Physicality=Tech.=10 Oct.=Uranus=P=1Ø.

Ministry=10,000=1,000=100%=10.0=Physicality=Tech.=10 Oct.=Uranus=P=1Ø.
Peter Matthews-Akukalia created the Ministry of Creativity to help resolve the economic
issues of the creative economy as stipulated in the Principles of Psychoeconomix.

Mink=10,000=1,000=100%=10.0=Physicality=Tech.=10 Oct.=Uranus=P=1Ø.
Minn.=500=5%=P5.00D=5.0=Law=Time=Venus=5 May=Aphrodite>>L=N.
Minneapolis=7,500=8,000=80%=P8.0D=Economy=Currency=8 Aug.=Zeus>>E=v.
Minnesota=8,500=9,000=90%=P9.00D=9.0=Abstraction=Gods=Saturn=9Sept.>>A=Ø.
Minnesota River=8,500=9,000=90%=P9.00D=9.0=Abstr.=Gods=Saturn=9Sept.>>A=Ø.
Minnow=6,000=60%=P6.0D=Man=Earth=Royalty=6 June=Gaia=Maia>>M=M2.
Minoan=10,000=1,000=100%=10.0=Physicality=Tech.=10 Oct.=Uranus=P=1Ø.

Minor=10,000=1,000=100%=10.0=Physicality=Tech.=10 Oct.=Uranus=P=1Ø.
Results indicate that a minor is a child from the ages of 0 birth to 10years.

Minorca=5,500=5.5=80%=P5.50=Earth-Midway=5 May = Gaia.
Minority=10,000=1,000=100%=10.0=Physicality=Tech.=10 Oct.=Uranus=P=1Ø.
Minor league=6,500=7,000=70%=P7.0D=7.0=Language=Assets=Mars=7 July=Pleiades.
Minor scale=8,000=80%=P8.0D=Economy=Currency=8 Aug.=Zeus>>E=v.

Minotaur=5,000=50%=P5.00D=Law=Time=Venus=5 May = Aphrodite>>L=N.
Greek myth. A monster who was half man and half bull. The Creatocracy believes it was
a former structure adopted by the Gods at an attempt to create a perfect being until Man.

Minsk=4,500=5,000=50%=P5.00D=Law=Time=Venus=5 May = Aphrodite>>L=N.
Minster=4,000=40%=P4.0D=Govt.=Creatocracy=4 April=Mercury=Hermes=G=A4.
Minstrel=7,500=8,000=80%=P8.0D=Economy=Currency=8 Aug.=Zeus>>E=v.
Minstrel show=10,000=1,000=100%=10.0=Physicality=Tech.=10 Oct.=Uranus=P=1Ø.
Mint1=10,000=1,000=100%=10.0=Physicality=Tech.=10 Oct.=Uranus=P=1Ø.
Mint2=10,000=1,000=100%=10.0=Physicality=Tech.=10 Oct.=Uranus=P=1Ø.

Mint julep=10,000=1,000=100%=10.0=Physicality=Tech.=10 Oct.=Uranus=P=1Ø.
Minuend=7,500=8,000=80%=P8.0D=Economy=Currency=8 Aug.=Zeus>>E=v.
Minuet=7,500=8,000=80%=P8.0D=Economy=Currency=8 Aug.=Zeus>>E=v.
Minult Peter=2,500=3,000=30%=P3.0D=3.0=Cre=Stars=Muses=3 March = C=I>>GIL.
Minus=10,000=1,000=100%=10.0=Physicality=Tech.=10 Oct.=Uranus=P=1Ø.
Minuscule=4,000=40%=P4.0D=Govt.=Creatocracy=4 April=Mercury=Hermes=G=A4.
Minus sign=9,000=90%=P9.00D=9.0=Abstraction=Gods=Saturn=9Sept.>>A=Ø.
Minute1=10,000=1,000=100%=10.0=Physicality=Tech.=10 Oct.=Uranus=P=1Ø.
Minute2=10,000=1,000=100%=10.0=Physicality=Tech.=10 Oct.=Uranus=P=1Ø.
Minuteman=7,500=8,000=80%=P8.0D=Economy=Currency=8 Aug.=Zeus>>E=v.
Minutia=4,500=5,000=50%=P5.00D=Law=Time=Venus=5 May = Aphrodite>>L=N.
Minx=2,500=3,000=30%=P3.0D=3.0=Creativity=Stars=Muses=3 March = C=I>>GIL.
Miocene=10,000=1,000=100%=10.0=Physicality=Tech.=10 Oct.=Uranus=P=1Ø.
Miracle=10,000=1,000=100%=10.0=Physicality=Tech.=10 Oct.=Uranus=P=1Ø.
Mirage=11,000=11%=P1.10D=1.1=Idea=Brainchild=Inv.=11 Nov.=SC=Athena>>I=MT.
Mire=10,000=1,000=100%=10.0=Physicality=Tech.=10 Oct.=Uranus=P=1Ø.
Miró Joan=2,000=20%=P2.00D=2.0=Nature=Matter=Moon=2 Feb.=Cupid=N=C+_

Mirror=10,000=1,000=100%=10.0=Physicality=Tech.=10 Oct.=Uranus=P=1Ø.
One of the symbols of Aphrodite is the mirror indicating that all Gods are quantumists.
Invented by Peter Matthews-Akukalia the World's 1st Computational Lexicographer.

Mirth=2,500=3,000=30%=P3.0D=3.0=Creativity=Stars=Muses=3 March = C=I>>GIL.
Mis-=6,000=60%=P6.0D=Man=Earth=Royalty=6 June=Gaia=Maia>>M=M2.
Misadventure=1,500=15%=P1.50D=1.5=Authority=Solar Crown=1 May = Maia.
Misalliance=1,500=15%=P1.50D=1.5=Authority=Solar Crown=1 May = Maia.
Misanthrope=4,000=40%=P4.0D=Govt.=Creatocracy=4 April=Mercury=Hermes=G=A4.n
Misapprehend=1,000=100%=10.0=1.0=Mind=Sun=1 January=Helios >> M=E4.
Misbegotten=2,500=3,000=30%=P3.0D=3.0=Cre=Stars=Muses=3 March = C=I>>GIL.
Misc.=500=5%=P5.00D=5.0=Law=Time=Venus=5 May=Aphrodite>>L=N.
Miscarriage=5,000=50%=P5.00D=Law=Time=Venus=5 May = Aphrodite>>L=N.
Miscarry=3,000=30%=P3.0D=3.0=Creativity=Stars=Muses=3 March = C=I>>GIL.
Miscegenation=8,000=80%=P8.0D=Economy=Currency=8 Aug.=Zeus>>E=v.
Miscellaneous=6,000=60%=P6.0D=Man=Earth=Royalty=6 June=Gaia=Maia>>M=M2.
Miscellany=5,000=50%=P5.00D=Law=Time=Venus=5 May = Aphrodite>>L=N.
Mischance=2,000=20%=P2.00D=2.0=Nature=Matter=Moon=2 Feb.=Cupid=N=C+_
Mischief=9,500=10,000=1,000=100%=10.0=Physicality=Tech.=10 Oct.=Uranus=P=1Ø.
Mischievous=4,500=5,000=50%=P5.00D=Law=Time=Venus=5 May=Aphrodite>>L=N.
Miscible=5,500=5.5=80%=P5.50=Earth-Midway=5 May = Gaia.
Misconceive=1,000=100%=10.0=1.0=Mind=Sun=1 January=Helios >> M=E4.
Misconduct=6,000=60%=P6.0D=Man=Earth=Royalty=6 June=Gaia=Maia>>M=M2.
Misconstrue=1,000=100%=10.0=1.0=Mind=Sun=1 January=Helios >> M=E4.
Miscreant=7,500=8,000=80%=P8.0D=Economy=Currency=8 Aug.=Zeus>>E=v.
Miscue=1,000=100%=10.0=1.0=Mind=Sun=1 January=Helios >> M=E4.

Misdeed=1,000=100%=10.0=1.0=Mind=Sun=1 January=Helios >> M=E4.

Misdemeanor=4,500=5,000=50%=P5.00D=Law=Time=Venus=5 May = Aphrodite>>L=N.

Mis en scène=6,500=7,000=70%=P7.0D=7.0=Language=Assets=Mars=7 July=Pleiades.

Miser=5,000=50%=P5.00D=Law=Time=Venus=5 May = Aphrodite>>L=N.

Miserable=8,500=9,000=90%=P9.00D=9.0=Abstraction=Gods=Saturn=9Sept.>>A=Ø.

Misery=5,000=50%=P5.00D=Law=Time=Venus=5 May = Aphrodite>>L=N.

Misfire=6,000=60%=P6.0D=Man=Earth=Royalty=6 June=Gaia=Maia>>M=M2.

Misfit=2,500=3,000=30%=P3.0D=3.0=Creativity=Stars=Muses=3 March = C=I>>GIL.

Misfortune=2,000=20%=P2.00D=2.0=Nature=Matter=Moon=2 Feb.=Cupid=N=C+_

Misgiving=3,000=30%=P3.0D=3.0=Creativity=Stars=Muses=3 March = C=I>>GIL.

Misguide=3,500=4,000=40%=P4.0D=Govt.=Cret=4 April=Mercury=Hermes=G=A4.

Mishandle=3,000=30%=P3.0D=3.0=Creativity=Stars=Muses=3 March = C=I>>GIL.

Mishap=1,500=15%=P1.50D=1.5=Authority=Solar Crown=1 May = Maia.

Mishmash=1,000=100%=10.0=1.0=Mind=Sun=1 January=Helios >> M=E4.

Misinterpret=2,500=3,000=30%=P3.0D=3.0=Cre=Stars=Muses=3 March = C=I>>GIL.

Miskito=8,500=9,000=90%=P9.00D=9.0=Abstraction=Gods=Saturn=9Sept.>>A=Ø.

Miskolc=4,500=5,000=50%=P5.00D=Law=Time=Venus=5 May = Aphrodite>>L=N.

Mislead=4,000=40%=P4.0D=Govt.=Creatocracy=4 April=Mercury=Hermes=G=A4.

Mislike=1,500=15%=P1.50D=1.5=Authority=Solar Crown=1 May = Maia.

Misnomer=4,500=5,000=50%=P5.00D=Law=Time=Venus=5 May = Aphrodite>>L=N.

Miso=6,500=7,000=70%=P7.0D=7.0=Language=Assets=Mars=7 July=Pleiades.

Misogamy=4,500=5,000=50%=P5.00D=Law=Time=Venus=5 May = Aphrodite>>L=N.

Misogyny=5,000=50%=P5.00D=Law=Time=Venus=5 May = Aphrodite>>L=N.

Misplace=8,000=80%=P8.0D=Economy=Currency=8 Aug.=Zeus>>E=v.

Misplay=3,000=30%=P3.0D=3.0=Creativity=Stars=Muses=3 March = C=I>>GIL.

Misread=2,000=20%=P2.00D=2.0=Nature=Matter=Moon=2 Feb.=Cupid=N=C+_

Misrepresent=4,000=40%=P4.0D=Govt.=Creatocracy=4 April=Mercury=Hermes=G=A4.

Miss1=10,000=1,000=100%=10.0=Physicality=Tech.=10 Oct.=Uranus=P=1Ø.

Miss2=9,500=10,000=1,000=100%=10.0=Physicality=Tech.=10 Oct.=Uranus=P=1Ø.

Miss.=500=5%=P5.00D=5.0=Law=Time=Venus=5 May=Aphrodite>>L=N.

Missal=10,500=11,000=11%=P1.10D=1.1=Idea=Brainchild=Inv.=11 Nov.=Athena>>I=MT.

Missile=9,500=10,000=1,000=100%=10.0=Physicality=Tech.=10 Oct.=Uranus=P=1Ø.

Missing=1,500=15%=P1.50D=1.5=Authority=Solar Crown=1 May = Maia.

Mission=10,000=1,000=100%=10.0=Physicality=Tech.=10 Oct.=Uranus=P=1Ø.

Missionary=10,000=1,000=100%=10.0=Physicality=Tech.=10 Oct.=Uranus=P=1Ø.

Mrs. Diana Matthews, grandmother of Peter Matthews-Akukalia, Castle Makupedia trained him to higher education partly in Law at Madonna University Okija, Anambra State, Eastern Nigeria and then later to study aviation in the College of Aviation and Management Studies, Ikorodu. He obtained an Advance Diploma in Aviation Management and Certificate in Piloting, Ground School. Then a certificate in Computer Studies. She was an international missionary. See book>> The Creatocracy Republic of Castle Makupedia by Peter Matthews-Akukalia. Reference book >> Last of the Noble Amazons.

Mississippi=5,000=50%=P5.00D=Law=Time=Venus=5 May = Aphrodite>>L=N.
Mississippian=10,000=1,000=100%=10.0=Physicality=Tech.=10 Oct.=Uranus=P=1Ø.
Mississippi River=10,000=1,000=100%=10.0=Physicality=Tech.=10 Oct.=Uranus=P=1Ø.
Missive=4,500=5,000=50%=P5.00D=Law=Time=Venus=5 May = Aphrodite>>L=N.
Missouri1=10,000=1,000=100%=10.0=Physicality=Tech.=10 Oct.=Uranus=P=1Ø.
Missouri2=5,500=5.5=80%=P5.50=Earth-Midway=5 May = Gaia.
Missouri River.=10,000=1,000=100%=10.0=Physicality=Tech.=10 Oct.=Uranus=P=1Ø.
Misspeak=3,000=30%=P3.0D=3.0=Creativity=Stars=Muses=3 March = C=I>>GIL.
Misstep=3,500=4,000=40%=P4.0D=Govt.=Cret=4 April=Mercury=Hermes=G=A4.
Mist=10,000=1,000=100%=10.0=Physicality=Tech.=10 Oct.=Uranus=P=1Ø.
Mistake=6,000=60%=P6.0D=Man=Earth=Royalty=6 June=Gaia=Maia>>M=M2.
Mistaken=4,500=5,000=50%=P5.00D=Law=Time=Venus=5 May = Aphrodite>>L=N.
Mister=10,500=11,000=11%=P1.10D=1.1=Idea=Brainchild=Inv.=11 Nov.=Athena>>I=MT.
Mistletoe=10,000=1,000=100%=10.0=Physicality=Tech.=10 Oct.=Uranus=P=1Ø.
Mistreat=3,000=30%=P3.0D=3.0=Creativity=Stars=Muses=3 March = C=I>>GIL.
Mistress=10,000=1,000=100%=10.0=Physicality=Tech.=10 Oct.=Uranus=P=1Ø.
Mistrial=10,000=1,000=100%=10.0=Physicality=Tech.=10 Oct.=Uranus=P=1Ø.
Mistrust=5,000=50%=P5.00D=Law=Time=Venus=5 May = Aphrodite>>L=N.
Misty=7,500=8,000=80%=P8.0D=Economy=Currency=8 Aug.=Zeus>>E=v.
Misunderstand=2,000=20%=P2.00D=2.0=Nature=Matter=Moon=2 Feb.=Cupid=N=C+_
Misunderstanding=4,000=40%=P4.0D=Govt.=Cret=4 April=Mercury=Hermes=G=A4.
Misuse=5,000=50%=P5.00D=Law=Time=Venus=5 May = Aphrodite>>L=N.
Mite1=4,000=40%=P4.0D=Govt.=Creatocracy=4 April=Mercury=Hermes=G=A4.
Mite2=7,000=70%=P7.0D=7.0=Language=Assets=Mars=7 July=Pleiades.
Miter=10,000=1,000=100%=10.0=Physicality=Tech.=10 Oct.=Uranus=P=1Ø.
Miter joint=6,500=7,000=70%=P7.0D=7.0=Language=Assets=Mars=7 July=Pleiades.
Mitigate=10,000=1,000=100%=10.0=Physicality=Tech.=10 Oct.=Uranus=P=1Ø.
Mitochondrion=10,000=1,000=100%=10.0=Physicality=Tech.=10 Oct.=Uranus=P=1Ø.
Mitosis=10,000=1,000=100%=10.0=Physicality=Tech.=10 Oct.=Uranus=P=1Ø.
Mitre=2,500=3,000=30%=P3.0D=3.0=Creativity=Stars=Muses=3 March = C=I>>GIL.
Mitt=10,000=1,000=100%=10.0=Physicality=Tech.=10 Oct.=Uranus=P=1Ø.
Mitten=7,500=8,000=80%=P8.0D=Economy=Currency=8 Aug.=Zeus>>E=v.
Mitterrand François=3,500=4,000=40%=P4.0D=Govt.=4 April=Mercury=Hermes=G=A4.
Mitzvah=6,500=7,000=70%=P7.0D=7.0=Language=Assets=Mars=7 July=Pleiades.
Mix=10,000=1,000=100%=10.0=Physicality=Tech.=10 Oct.=Uranus=P=1Ø.
Mixed bag=1,500=15%=P1.50D=1.5=Authority=Solar Crown=1 May = Maia.
Mixed drink=10,000=1,000=100%=10.0=Physicality=Tech.=10 Oct.=Uranus=P=1Ø.
Mixed number=7,000=70%=P7.0D=7.0=Language=Assets=Mars=7 July=Pleiades.
Mixer=10,000=1,000=100%=10.0=Physicality=Tech.=10 Oct.=Uranus=P=1Ø.
Mixtec=10,000=1,000=100%=10.0=Physicality=Tech.=10 Oct.=Uranus=P=1Ø.
Mixture=10,000=1,000=100%=10.0=Physicality=Tech.=10 Oct.=Uranus=P=1Ø.
Mix-up=3,500=4,000=40%=P4.0D=Govt.=Creatocracy=4 April=Mercury=Hermes=G=A4.
Mizzen=7,000=70%=P7.0D=7.0=Language=Assets=Mars=7 July=Pleiades.
Mizzenmast=6,000=60%=P6.0D=Man=Earth=Royalty=6 June=Gaia=Maia>>M=M2.
mks=1,500=15%=P1.50D=1.5=Authority=Solar Crown=1 May = Maia.

ml=500=5%=P5.00D=5.0=Law=Time=Venus=5 May=Aphrodite>>L=N.
MLA=1,500=15%=P1.50D=1.5=Authority=Solar Crown=1 May = Maia.
Mile.=500=5%=P5.00D=5.0=Law=Time=Venus=5 May=Aphrodite>>L=N.
Miles.=500=5%=P5.00D=5.0=Law=Time=Venus=5 May=Aphrodite>>L=N.
mm=500=5%=P5.00D=5.0=Law=Time=Venus=5 May=Aphrodite>>L=N.
Mme.=500=5%=P5.00D=5.0=Law=Time=Venus=5 May=Aphrodite>>L=N.
Mmes.=1,500=15%=P1.50D=1.5=Authority=Solar Crown=1 May = Maia.
Mn=2,500=3,000=30%=P3.0D=3.0=Creativity=Stars=Muses=3 March = C=I>>GIL.
MN=1,500=15%=P1.50D=1.5=Authority=Solar Crown=1 May = Maia.
Mnemonic=10,000=1,000=100%=10.0=Physicality=Tech.=10 Oct.=Uranus=P=1Ø.
Mo=2,500=3,000=30%=P3.0D=3.0=Creativity=Stars=Muses=3 March = C=I>>GIL.
MO=500=5%=P5.00D=5.0=Law=Time=Venus=5 May=Aphrodite>>L=N.
mo.=500=5%=P5.00D=5.0=Law=Time=Venus=5 May=Aphrodite>>L=N.
m.o.=4,000=40%=P4.0D=Govt.=Creatocracy=4 April=Mercury=Hermes=G=A4.
Moab=5,500=5.5=80%=P5.50=Earth-Midway=5 May = Gaia.
Moan=7,000=70%=P7.0D=7.0=Language=Assets=Mars=7 July=Pleiades.

Moat=10,500=11,000=11%=P1.10D=1.1=Idea=Brainchild=Inv.=11 Nov.=SC=Athena>>I=MT.
Inventions are the moat used to defend the Castle Makupedia and the Paradise Nations.

Mob=10,000=1,000=100%=10.0=Physicality=Tech.=10 Oct.=Uranus=P=1Ø.
Mobile=10,000=1,000=100%=10.0=Physicality=Tech.=10 Oct.=Uranus=P=1Ø.
Mobile home=7,500=8,000=80%=P8.0D=Economy=Currency=8 Aug.=Zeus>>E=v.
Mobilize=8,000=80%=P8.0D=Economy=Currency=8 Aug.=Zeus>>E=v.
Mobster=3,000=30%=P3.0D=3.0=Creativity=Stars=Muses=3 March = C=I>>GIL.
Moccasin=6,000=60%=P6.0D=Man=Earth=Royalty=6 June=Gaia=Maia>>M=M2.
Mocha=6,000=60%=P6.0D=Man=Earth=Royalty=6 June=Gaia=Maia>>M=M2.
Mock=8,000=80%=P8.0D=Economy=Currency=8 Aug.=Zeus>>E=v.
Mock heroic=5,000=50%=P5.00D=Law=Time=Venus=5 May = Aphrodite>>L=N.
Mocking bird=7,500=8,000=80%=P8.0D=Economy=Currency=8 Aug.=Zeus>>E=v.
Mock orange=5,000=50%=P5.00D=Law=Time=Venus=5 May = Aphrodite>>L=N.
Mockup=7,000=70%=P7.0D=7.0=Language=Assets=Mars=7 July=Pleiades.
Mod=4,500=5,000=50%=P5.00D=Law=Time=Venus=5 May = Aphrodite>>L=N.
Mode=10,000=1,000=100%=10.0=Physicality=Tech.=10 Oct.=Uranus=P=1Ø.
Model=10,000=1,000=100%=10.0=Physicality=Tech.=10 Oct.=Uranus=P=1Ø.
Modem=9,000=90%=P9.00D=9.0=Abstraction=Gods=Saturn=9Sept.>>A=Ø.
Moderate=10,000=1,000=100%=10.0=Physicality=Tech.=10 Oct.=Uranus=P=1Ø.
Moderator=3,000=30%=P3.0D=3.0=Creativity=Stars=Muses=3 March = C=I>>GIL.
Modern=7,500=8,000=80%=P8.0D=Economy=Currency=8 Aug.=Zeus>>E=v.
Modern English=2,000=20%=P2.00D=2.0=Nature=Matter=Moon=2 Feb.=Cupid=N=C+_
Modern Greek=8,000=80%=P8.0D=Economy=Currency=8 Aug.=Zeus>>E=v.
Modern Hebrew=5,000=50%=P5.00D=Law=Time=Venus=5 May = Aphrodite>>L=N.
Modernism=10,000=1,000=100%=10.0=Physicality=Tech.=10 Oct.=Uranus=P=1Ø.
Modest=10,000=1,000=100%=10.0=Physicality=Tech.=10 Oct.=Uranus=P=1Ø.

Modesto=4,500=5,000=50%=P5.00D=Law=Time=Venus=5 May = Aphrodite>>L=N.
Modicum=4,000=40%=P4.0D=Govt.=Creatocracy=4 April=Mercury=Hermes=G=A4.
Modify=10,000=1,000=100%=10.0=Physicality=Tech.=10 Oct.=Uranus=P=1Ø.
Modigliani Amedeo=2,000=20%=P2.00D=2.0=Matter=Moon=2 Feb.=Cupid=N=C+_
Modish=4,500=5,000=50%=P5.00D=Law=Time=Venus=5 May = Aphrodite>>L=N.
Modiste=5,000=50%=P5.00D=Law=Time=Venus=5 May = Aphrodite>>L=N.
Modulate=10,000=1,000=100%=10.0=Physicality=Tech.=10 Oct.=Uranus=P=1Ø.

Module=10,000=1,000=100%=10.0=Physicality=Tech.=10 Oct.=Uranus=P=1Ø.
The Creatocracy comprises different modules of knowledge and applications to make life better easier and more purposeful. All things are comprised in Mind Modules here.

Modus operandi=3,500=4,000=40%=P4.0D=Govt.=Creatocracy=4 April=Hermes=G=A4.
Mogadishu=4,500=5,000=50%=P5.00D=Law=Time=Venus=5 May = Aphrodite>>L=N.
mogul=6,000=60%=P6.0D=Man=Earth=Royalty=6 June=Gaia=Maia>>M=M2.
Mogul=10,000=1,000=100%=10.0=Physicality=Tech.=10 Oct.=Uranus=P=1Ø.
Mohair=8,000=80%=P8.0D=Economy=Currency=8 Aug.=Zeus>>E=v.

Mohammed=1,000=100%=10.0=1.0=Mind=Sun=1 January=Helios >> M=E4.
Discovery is that the prophet Mohammed (Saw) was the reincarnated Helios.

Mohammedan=1,500=15%=P1.50D=1.5=Authority=Solar Crown=1 May = Maia.
Mohave Desert=1,500=15%=P1.50D=1.5=Authority=Solar Crown=1 May = Maia.
Mohawk=10,000=1,000=100%=10.0=Physicality=Tech.=10 Oct.=Uranus=P=1Ø.
Mohegan=10,000=1,000=100%=10.0=Physicality=Tech.=10 Oct.=Uranus=P=1Ø.
Mohenjo-Daro=6,500=7,000=70%=P7.0D=7.0=Language=Assets=Mars=7 July=Pleiades.
Mohican=1,500=15%=P1.50D=1.5=Authority=Solar Crown=1 May = Maia.
Mohs scale=11,000=11%=P1.10D=1.1=Idea=Brainchild=Inv.=11 Nov.=SC=Athena>>I=MT.
Moiety=3,500=4,000=40%=P4.0D=Govt.=Creatocracy=4 April=Mercury=Hermes=G=A4.
Moil=3,500=4,000=40%=P4.0D=Govt.=Creatocracy=4 April=Mercury=Hermes=G=A4.
Molré=10,000=1,000=100%=10.0=Physicality=Tech.=10 Oct.=Uranus=P=1Ø.
Moist=3,000=30%=P3.0D=3.0=Creativity=Stars=Muses=3 March = C=I>>GIL.
Moisture=2,500=3,000=30%=P3.0D=3.0=Creativity=Stars=Muses=3 March = C=I>>GIL.
Mojave Desert=5,000=50%=P5.00D=Law=Time=Venus=5 May = Aphrodite>>L=N.
Moi=1,500=15%=P1.50D=1.5=Authority=Solar Crown=1 May = Maia.
Mol.=1,000=100%=10.0=1.0=Mind=Sun=1 January=Helios >> M=E4.
Molal=6,500=7,000=70%=P7.0D=7.0=Language=Assets=Mars=7 July=Pleiades.
Molar=10,000=1,000=100%=10.0=Physicality=Tech.=10 Oct.=Uranus=P=1Ø.
Molasses=6,000=60%=P6.0D=Man=Earth=Royalty=6 June=Gaia=Maia>>M=M2.
Mold1=10,000=1,000=100%=10.0=Physicality=Tech.=10 Oct.=Uranus=P=1Ø.
Mold2=8,000=80%=P8.0D=Economy=Currency=8 Aug.=Zeus>>E=v.
Mold3=5,500=5.5=80%=P5.50=Earth-Midway=5 May = Gaia.
Moldavia=10,000=1,000=100%=10.0=Physicality=Tech.=10 Oct.=Uranus=P=1Ø.
Molder=4,000=40%=P4.0D=Govt.=Creatocracy=4 April=Mercury=Hermes=G=A4.

Molding=9,500=10,000=1,000=100%=10.0=Physicality=Tech.=10 Oct.=Uranus=P=1Ø.
Moldy=5,000=50%=P5.00D=Law=Time=Venus=5 May = Aphrodite>>L=N.
Mole1=7,500=8,000=80%=P8.0D=Economy=Currency=8 Aug.=Zeus>>E=v.
Mole2=9,500=10,000=1,000=100%=10.0=Physicality=Tech.=10 Oct.=Uranus=P=1Ø.
Mole3=5,500=5.5=80%=P5.50=Earth-Midway=5 May = Gaia.
Mole4=8,500=9,000=90%=P9.00D=9.0=Abstraction=Gods=Saturn=9Sept.>>A=Ø.
Molecular biology=10,000=1,000=100%=10.0=Physicality=Tech.=10 Oct.=Uranus=P=1Ø.
Molecular weight=4,500=5,000=50%=P5.00D=Law=Time=Venus=5 May =Odite>>L=N.
Molecule=10,000=1,000=100%=10.0=Physicality=Tech.=10 Oct.=Uranus=P=1Ø.
Molehill=5,000=50%=P5.00D=Law=Time=Venus=5 May = Aphrodite>>L=N.
Moleskin=5,000=50%=P5.00D=Law=Time=Venus=5 May = Aphrodite>>L=N.
Molest=5,500=5.5=80%=P5.50=Earth-Midway=5 May = Gaia.
Molière Jean=3,000=30%=P3.0D=3.0=Creativity=Stars=Muses=3 March = C=I>>GIL.
Moll=5,000=50%=P5.00D=Law=Time=Venus=5 May = Aphrodite>>L=N.
Mollify=5,000=50%=P5.00D=Law=Time=Venus=5 May = Aphrodite>>L=N.
Mollusk=10,000=1,000=100%=10.0=Physicality=Tech.=10 Oct.=Uranus=P=1Ø.
Mollycoddle=5,500=5.5=80%=P5.50=Earth-Midway=5 May = Gaia.
Molokai=4,500=5,000=50%=P5.00D=Law=Time=Venus=5 May = Aphrodite>>L=N.
Molotov cocktail=10,000=1,000=100%=10.0=Physicality=Tech.=10 Oct.=Uranus=P=1Ø.
Molt=10,000=1,000=100%=10.0=Physicality=Tech.=10 Oct.=Uranus=P=1Ø.
Molten=5,500=5.5=80%=P5.50=Earth-Midway=5 May = Gaia.
Moluccas=6,000=60%=P6.0D=Man=Earth=Royalty=6 June=Gaia=Maia>>M=M2.
Mol wt=1,000=100%=10.0=1.0=Mind=Sun=1 January=Helios >> M=E4.
Molybdenum=10,000=1,000=100%=10.0=Physicality=Tech.=10 Oct.=Uranus=P=1Ø.
Mo=10,000=1,000=100%=10.0=Physicality=Tech.=10 Oct.=Uranus=P=1Ø.
Mom=1,500=15%=P1.50D=1.5=Authority=Solar Crown=1 May = Maia.
Mombasa=7,500=8,000=80%=P8.0D=Economy=Currency=8 Aug.=Zeus>>E=v.
Moment=10,000=1,000=100%=10.0=Physicality=Tech.=10 Oct.=Uranus=P=1Ø.
Momentarily=2,500=3,000=30%=P3.0D=3.0=Cre=Stars=Muses=3 March = C=I>>GIL.
Momentary=5,000=50%=P5.00D=Law=Time=Venus=5 May = Aphrodite>>L=N.
Momently=1,500=15%=P1.50D=1.5=Authority=Solar Crown=1 May = Maia.
Momentous=2,500=3,000=30%=P3.0D=3.0=Crea=Stars=Muses=3 March = C=I>>GIL.
Momentum=7,000=70%=P7.0D=7.0=Language=Assets=Mars=7 July=Pleiades.
Mon.=500=5%=P5.00D=5.0=Law=Time=Venus=5 May=Aphrodite>>L=N.
Mon-=1,500=15%=P1.50D=1.5=Authority=Solar Crown=1 May = Maia.
Monaco=10,000=1,000=100%=10.0=Physicality=Tech.=10 Oct.=Uranus=P=1Ø.
Monarch=10,000=1,000=100%=10.0=Physicality=Tech.=10 Oct.=Uranus=P=1Ø.
Monarchism=5,000=50%=P5.00D=Law=Time=Venus=5 May = Aphrodite>>L=N.
Monarchy=4,500=5,000=50%=P5.00D=Law=Time=Venus=5 May = Aphrodite>>L=N.
Monastery=10,000=1,000=100%=10.0=Physicality=Tech.=10 Oct.=Uranus=P=1Ø.
Monastic=10,000=1,000=100%=10.0=Physicality=Tech.=10 Oct.=Uranus=P=1Ø.
Monaural=10,000=1,000=100%=10.0=Physicality=Tech.=10 Oct.=Uranus=P=1Ø.
Mönchengladbach=5,000=50%=P5.00D=Law=Time=Venus=5 May = Aphrodite>>L=N.
Mondale, Walter=5,000=50%=P5.00D=Law=Time=Venus=5 May = Aphrodite>>L=N.

Monday=8,000=80%=P8.0D=Economy=Currency=8 Aug.=Zeus>>E=v.
The 2nd day of the week >> 7 days. 2.0*7.0x=px=9+14=23x=px=149=150
14.9>>Management and Administration. 150=15.0>>Authority. Monday is the day of management administration and establishing authority over the rest of the week. The success or failure of the week depends on how Monday is treated. Although Monday is the second day of the week it is the first day of the official five workdays. Zeus. See midweek.

Mondrian Piet=2,000=20%=P2.00D=2.0=Nature=Matter=Moon=2 Feb.=Cupid=N=C+_
Monet Claude=2,000=20%=P2.00D=2.0=Nature=Matter=Moon=2 Feb.=Cupid=N=C+_
Monetarism=10,000=1,000=100%=10.0=Physicality=Tech.=10 Oct.=Uranus=P=1Ø.
Monetary=10,000=1,000=100%=10.0=Physicality=Tech.=10 Oct.=Uranus=P=1Ø.
Monetize=3,500=4,000=40%=P4.0D=Govt.=Creatocracy=4 April=Hermes=G=A4.

Money=10,000=1,000=100%=10.0=Physicality=Tech.=10 Oct.=Uranus=P=1Ø.
The standard for measuring all money in any form cash denomination and kind is 10,000=1,000=100=10. Therefore all natural money values must be measured on the money test score of over 10. Eg Dollar rates as 4,500=4.5/10 in currency ranking.
The Maks is therefore the universal solar standard for all money. P1.00=£10.0. The Maks was invented by Peter Matthews-Akukalia as universal money. The Encyclopedia of Castle Makupedia is the standard benchmark for all values costs prices exchange and storage of all values in all things. Against this there is no law. Ephesians 1:10.

Moneyed=5,500=5.5=80%=P5.50=Earth-Midway=5 May = Gaia.
Moneylender=4,000=40%=P4.0D=Govt.=Creatocracy=4 April=Mercury=Hermes=G=A4.
Moneymaking=4,000=40%=P4.0D=Govt.=Creatocracy=4 April=Mercury=Hermes=G=A4.
Money market=10,000=1,000=100%=10.0=Physicality=Tech.=10 Oct.=Uranus=P=1Ø.
Money order=10,000=1,000=100%=10.0=Physicality=Tech.=10 Oct.=Uranus=P=1Ø.
Monger=2,000=20%=P2.00D=2.0=Nature=Matter=Moon=2 Feb.=Cupid=N=C+_
Mongo=2,500=3,000=30%=P3.0D=3.0=Creativity=Stars=Muses=3 March = C=I>>GIL.
Mongol=10,000=1,000=100%=10.0=Physicality=Tech.=10 Oct.=Uranus=P=1Ø.
Mongolia=10,000=1,000=100%=10.0=Physicality=Tech.=10 Oct.=Uranus=P=1Ø.
Mongolian=10,000=1,000=100%=10.0=Physicality=Tech.=10 Oct.=Uranus=P=1Ø.
Mongolic=3,000=30%=P3.0D=3.0=Creativity=Stars=Muses=3 March = C=I>>GIL.
Mongolism=1,500=15%=P1.50D=1.5=Authority=Solar Crown=1 May = Maia.
Mongoloid=10,000=1,000=100%=10.0=Physicality=Tech.=10 Oct.=Uranus=P=1Ø.
Mongoose=10,000=1,000=100%=10.0=Physicality=Tech.=10 Oct.=Uranus=P=1Ø.
Mongrel=5,500=5.5=80%=P5.50=Earth-Midway=5 May = Gaia.
Monied=1,500=15%=P1.50D=1.5=Authority=Solar Crown=1 May = Maia.
Monies=2,000=20%=P2.00D=2.0=Nature=Matter=Moon=2 Feb.=Cupid=N=C+_
Moniker=3,000=30%=P3.0D=3.0=Creativity=Stars=Muses=3 March = C=I>>GIL.
Monism=7,500=8,000=80%=P8.0D=Economy=Currency=8 Aug.=Zeus>>E=v.
Monition=5,000=50%=P5.00D=Law=Time=Venus=5 May = Aphrodite>>L=N.
Monitor=10,000=1,000=100%=10.0=Physicality=Tech.=10 Oct.=Uranus=P=1Ø.
Monitory=2,500=3,000=30%=P3.0D=3.0=Creativity=Stars=Muses=3 March = C=I>>GIL.

Monk=8,000=80%=P8.0D=Economy=Currency=8 Aug.=Zeus>>E=v.
Monkey=10,000=1,000=100%=10.0=Physicality=Tech.=10 Oct.=Uranus=P=1Ø.
Monkey business=2,500=3,000=30%=P3.0D=3.0=Cre=Stars=Muses=3 March = C=I
Monkey shine=4,000=40%=P4.0D=Govt.=Creatocracy=4 April=Mercury=Hermes=G=A4.
Monkey wrench=7,500=8,000=80%=P8.0D=Economy=Currency=8 Aug.=Zeus>>E=v.
Monks hood=6,500=7,000=70%=P7.0D=7.0=Language=Assets=Mars=7 July=Pleiades.
Monmouth=5,500=5.5=80%=P5.50=Earth-Midway=5 May = Gaia.
Mono1=1,500=15%=P1.50D=1.5=Authority=Solar Crown=1 May = Maia.
Mono2=1,000=100%=10.0=1.0=Mind=Sun=1 January=Helios >> M=E4.
Monochromatic=4,500=5,000=50%=P5.00D=Law=Time=Venus=5 May =Odite>>L=N.
Monochrome=10,000=1,000=100%=10.0=Physicality=Tech.=10 Oct.=Uranus=P=1Ø.
Monocle=4,000=40%=P4.0D=Govt.=Creatocracy=4 April=Mercury=Hermes=G=A4.
Monocline=6,500=7,000=70%=P7.0D=7.0=Language=Assets=Mars=7 July=Pleiades.
Monocotyledon=6,000=60%=P6.0D=Man=Earth=Royalty=6 June=Gaia=Maia>>M=M2.
Monocular=5,000=50%=P5.00D=Law=Time=Venus=5 May = Aphrodite>>L=N.
Monoculture=7,500=8,000=80%=P8.0D=Economy=Currency=8 Aug.=Zeus>>E=v.
Monody=1,000=100%=10.0=1.0=Mind=Sun=1 January=Helios >> M=E4.
Monofilament=6,000=60%=P6.0D=Man=Earth=Royalty=6 June=Gaia=Maia>>M=M2.
Monogamy=4,000=40%=P4.0D=Govt.=Creatocracy=4 April=Mercury=Hermes=G=A4.
Monogram=4,500=5,000=50%=P5.00D=Law=Time=Venus=5 May = Aphrodite>>L=N.
Monograph=5,000=50%=P5.00D=Law=Time=Venus=5 May = Aphrodite>>L=N.
Monolingual=3,000=30%=P3.0D=3.0=Creativity=Stars=Muses=3 March = C=I>>GIL.
Monolith=9,000=90%=P9.00D=9.0=Abstraction=Gods=Saturn=9Sept.>>A=Ø.
Monologue=8,000=80%=P8.0D=Economy=Currency=8 Aug.=Zeus>>E=v.
Monomania=4,500=5,000=50%=P5.00D=Law=Time=Venus=5 May = Aphrodite>>L=N.
Monomer=5,000=50%=P5.00D=Law=Time=Venus=5 May = Aphrodite>>L=N.
Monomial=9,000=90%=P9.00D=9.0=Abstraction=Gods=Saturn=9Sept.>>A=Ø.
Monongahela River=11,000=11%=P1.10D=1.1=Idea=Brainchild.=11Nov.=Athena>>I=MT.
Mononucleosis=1,000=100%=10.0=1.0=Mind=Sun=1 January=Helios >> M=E4.
Monophonic=500=5%=P5.00D=5.0=Law=Time=Venus=5 May=Aphrodite>>L=N.
Monoplane=4,000=40%=P4.0D=Govt.=Creatocracy=4 April=Mercury=Hermes=G=A4.
Monopolize=10,000=1,000=100%=10.0=Physicality=Tech.=10 Oct.=Uranus=P=1Ø.
Monopoly=10,000=1,000=100%=10.0=Physicality=Tech.=10 Oct.=Uranus=P=1Ø.
Monorail=3,000=30%=P3.0D=3.0=Creativity=Stars=Muses=3 March = C=I>>GIL.
Monosaccharide=5,000=50%=P5.00D=Law=Time=Venus=5 May = Aphrodite>>L=N.
Monosodium=4,000=40%=P4.0D=Govt.=Creatocracy=4 April=Mercury=Hermes=G=A4.
Monosyllable=2,500=3,000=30%=P3.0D=3.0=Cre=Stars=Muses=3 March = C=I>>GIL.
Monotheism=4,000=40%=P4.0D=Govt.=Creatocracy=4 April=Mercury=Hermes=G=A4.
Monotone=7,500=8,000=80%=P8.0D=Economy=Currency=8 Aug.=Zeus>>E=v.
Monotonous=3,500=4,000=40%=P4.0D=Govt.=4 April=Mercury=Hermes=G=A4.
Monotype=7,500=8,000=80%=P8.0D=Economy=Currency=8 Aug.=Zeus>>E=v.
Mono saturated=9,000=90%=P9.00D=9.0=Abstraction=Gods=Saturn=9Sept.>>A=Ø.
Monovalent=1,000=100%=10.0=1.0=Mind=Sun=1 January=Helios >> M=E4.
Monoxide=4,500=5,000=50%=P5.00D=Law=Time=Venus=5 May = Aphrodite>>L=N.
Monozygotic=5,500=5.5=80%=P5.50=Earth-Midway=5 May = Gaia.

Monroe James=4,000=40%=P4.0D=Govt.=Creatocracy=4 April=Mercury=Hermes=G=A4.
Monrovia=4,000=40%=P4.0D=Govt.=Creatocracy=4 April=Mercury=Hermes=G=A4.

Monsieur=4,500=5,000=50%=P5.00D=Law=Time=Venus=5 May = Aphrodite>>L=N.
OFr. My Lord. Lordship titles is part of the Creatocracy of things. A God makes a Lord.

Monsignor=8,000=80%=P8.0D=Economy=Currency=8 Aug.=Zeus>>E=v.
Monsoon=10,000=1,000=100%=10.0=Physicality=Tech.=10 Oct.=Uranus=P=1Ø.
Monster=10,000=1,000=100%=10.0=Physicality=Tech.=10 Oct.=Uranus=P=1Ø.
Monstrance=7,500=8,000=80%=P8.0D=Economy=Currency=8 Aug.=Zeus>>E=v.
Mont.=500=5%=P5.00D=5.0=Law=Time=Venus=5 May=Aphrodite>>L=N.
Montage=10,000=1,000=100%=10.0=Physicality=Tech.=10 Oct.=Uranus=P=1Ø.
Montagnais=10,000=1,000=100%=10.0=Physicality=Tech.=10 Oct.=Uranus=P=1Ø.
Montaigne Michel=3,000=30%=P3.0D=3.0=Creat=Stars=Muses=3 March = C=I>>GIL.
Montana=6,500=7,000=70%=P7.0D=7.0=Language=Assets=Mars=7 July=Pleiades.
Montane=4,500=5,000=50%=P5.00D=Law=Time=Venus=5 May = Aphrodite>>L=N.
Montcalm de Saint-Veran=5,000=50%=P5.00D=Law=Time=Venus=5 May =Odite>>L=N.
Monte Carlo=7,000=70%=P7.0D=7.0=Language=Assets=Mars=7 July=Pleiades.
Montenegro=7,500=8,000=80%=P8.0D=Economy=Currency=8 Aug.=Zeus>>E=v.
Monterey=9,000=90%=P9.00D=9.0=Abstraction=Gods=Saturn=9Sept.>>A=Ø.
Monterrey=4,500=5,000=50%=P5.00D=Law=Time=Venus=5 May = Aphrodite>>L=N.
Montesquieu=9,000=90%=P9.00D=9.0=Abstraction=Gods=Saturn=9Sept.>>A=Ø.
Montessori Maria=3,500=4,000=40%=P4.0D=Govt.=Creat=4 April=Hermes=G=A4.

Montessori Method=6,000=60%=P6.0D=Man=Earth=Roy=6 June=Gaia=Maia>>M=M2.
For Montessori schools, a method of educating children that stresses development of a
child's own initiative. Peter Matthews-Akukalia computed the quantity of energy a child
is born with. It determines the kind of innate potentials and natural initiative inborn. Then
based on the mindoscope results of name the information is synchronized and applied.

Montevideo=7,500=8,000=80%=P8.0D=Economy=Currency=8 Aug.=Zeus>>E=v.
Montezuma II=4,500=5,000=50%=P5.00D=Law=Time=Venus=5 May = Aphrodite>>L=N.
Montgomery Bernard=3,500=4,000=40%=P4.0D=Govt=4April=Mercury=Hermes=G=A4.
Month=10,000=1,000=100%=10.0=Physicality=Tech.=10 Oct.=Uranus=P=1Ø.
Monthly=9,000=90%=P9.00D=9.0=Abstraction=Gods=Saturn=9Sept.>>A=Ø.
Montpelier=5,500=5.5=80%=P5.50=Earth-Midway=5 May = Gaia.
Montreal=8,000=80%=P8.0D=Economy=Currency=8 Aug.=Zeus>>E=v.
Mont-Saint-Michel=6,500=7,000=70%=P7.0D=7.0=Lang=Assets=Mars=7 July=Pleiades.
Montserrat=4,500=5,000=50%=P5.00D=Law=Time=Venus=5 May = Aphrodite>>L=N.
Monument=10,000=1,000=100%=10.0=Physicality=Tech.=10 Oct.=Uranus=P=1Ø.
Monumental=7,500=8,000=80%=P8.0D=Economy=Currency=8 Aug.=Zeus>>E=v.
Moo=5,500=5.5=80%=P5.50=Earth-Midway=5 May = Gaia.
Mooch=6,000=60%=P6.0D=Man=Earth=Royalty=6 June=Gaia=Maia>>M=M2.

Mood1=5,000=50%=P5.00D=Law=Time=Venus=5 May = Aphrodite>>L=N.
Mood2=9,000=90%=P9.00D=9.0=Abstraction=Gods=Saturn=9Sept.>>A=Ø.

Moody=5,500=5.5=80%=P5.50=Earth-Midway=5 May = Gaia.
An inherent faculty of the mind studied in the Mind Assessment Tests.

Moon=10,000=1,000=100%=10.0=Physicality=Tech.=10 Oct.=Uranus=P=1Ø.
The physical equivalent of Nature in the twelve dimensions of the universe. Influencer of all existence. The material content of nature. Second dimension. Peter Matthews-Akukalia did over 6million computations and 15 million programs on the moon alone. He discovered that man was made in the moon with moon materials and placed on Earth. The moon was discovered to be the center of the material universe, a single number entity "2" subject only to the Sun on the moon core.The Creatocracy ranks Peter Matthews-Akukalia, Castle Makupedia as the First African to be named on the Moon. Lunar Computing is an aspect of the Creative Sciences. We establish that Cupid (Eros) and Artemis govern the Moon.

MOON PERSON DATABASE.
These persons are functional on the energies of the Quartet Gods of Death and Darkness. The code is 2.0=2:00am. Operant key is 10.0 making the moon a technology and so they want to see the physical proof for things. Bonded they are 3.0 >> creativity driven. It doesn't make them bad people it simply means they are more efficient and productive at nights. They dream a lot and see visions. Physical darkness is light inside them. The Gods that function them are Nyx, Hecate, Selene and Artemis. Full moon is their key. There is a positive and negative aspect of a thing and restraint is strongly advised. The meetings of these four Goddesses are held in these days and a wrong use leads to witchcraft. Their birthdays and days of power are seen below.

MONTH: JANUARY.
Day 3:Value: 2.0, Planetary Type: Moon, Human Type: Marine, Birth Energy Level: 33.3%.
Day 11: Value: 2.0, Planetary Type: Moon, Human Type: Marine, Birth Energy Level: 33.3%
Day 12:Value: 2.0, Planetary Type: Moon, Human Type: Marine, Birth Energy Level: 33.3%
==
MONTH:FEBRUARY
Day 7:Value:2.0, Planetary Type: Moon, Human Type: Marine, Birth Energy Level:33.3%
Day 8:Value: 2.0, Planetary Type:Moon, Human Type:Marine, Birth Energy Level:33.3%
Day 26:Value:2.0, Planetary Type:Moon, Human Type:Marine, Birth Energy Level:33.3%
Day 27:Value:2.0, Planetary Type: Moon, Human Type:Marine, Birth Energy Level: 33.3%
Day 28:Value: 2.0, Planetary Type:Moon, Human Type:Marine, Birth Energy Level:33.3%
Day 29:Value:2.0, Planetary Type:Moon, Human Type: Marine, Birth Energy Level:33.3%
==
MONTH:MARCH
Day 1:Value:2.0, Planetary Type:Moon, Human Type: Marine, Birth Energy Level:33.3%
Day 6:Value:2.0, Planetary Type:Moon, Human Type:Marine, Birth Energy Level:33.3%
Day 20:Value:2.0, Planetary Type:Moon, Human Type:Marine, Birth Energy Level:33.3%

Day 21:Value: 2.0, Planetary Type:Moon, Human Type:Marine, Birth Energy Level:33.3%
Day 22:Value:2.0, Planetary Type:Moon, Human Type:Marine, Birth Energy Level:33.3%
Day 23:Value:2.0, Planetary Type:Moon, Human Type:Marine, Birth Energy Level:33.3%
Day 24:Value:2.0, Planetary Type:Moon, Human Type:Marine, Birth Energy Level:33.3%
===

MONTH:APRIL
Day 4:Value:2.0,Planetary Type:Moon, Human Type:Marine,Birth Energy Level:33.3%
Day 17:Value:2.0, Planetary Type:Moon, Human Type:Marine, Birth Energy Level:33.3%
Day 18:Value:2.0, Planetary Type:Moon, Human Type:Marine, Birth Energy Level:33.3%
Day 19:Value:2.0, Planetary Type:Moon, Human Type:Marine, Birth Energy Level:33.3%
Day 20:Value:2.0, Planetary Type:Moon, Human Type:Marine, Birth Energy Level:33.3%
===

MONTH: MAY.
Day 15:Value:2.0, Planetary Type: Moon, Human Type:Marine, Birth Energy Level:33.3%
Day 16:Value:2.0, Planetary Type:Moon, Human Type:Marine, Birth Energy Level:33.3%
Day 17:Value:2.0, Planetary Type:Moon, Human Type:Marine, Birth Energy Level:33.3%
===

MONTH:JUNE.
Day 3:Value:2.0 Planetary Type:Moon Human Type:Marine Birth Energy Level:33.3%
Day 13:Value:2.0 Planetary Type:Moon Human Type:Marine Birth Energy Level:33.3%
Day 14:Value:2.0 Planetary Type:Moon Human Type:Marine Birth Energy Level:33.3%
Day 15:Value:2.0 Planetary Type:Moon Human Type:Marine Birth Energy Level:33.3%
Day 16:Value:2.2 Planetary Type:Moon Human Type:R&D, Birth Energy Level:40.0%
===

MONTH:JULY
Day 2:Value:2.0 Planetary Type:Moon Human Type:Marine Birth Energy Level:33.3%
Day 11:Value:2.0 Planetary Type:Moon Human Type:Marine Birth Energy Level:33.3%
Day 12:Value:2.0 Planetary Type:Moon Human Type:Marine Birth Energy Level:33.3%
Day 13:Value:2.0 Planetary Type:Moon Human Type:Marine Birth Energy Level:33.3%
===

MONTH:AUGUST.
Day 2:Value:2.0 Planetary Type:Moon Human Type:Marine Birth Energy Level:33.3%
Day 10:Value:2.0 Planetary Type:Moon Human Type:Marine Birth Energy Level:33.3%
Day 11:Value:2.0 Planetary Type:Moon Human Type:Marine Birth Energy Level:33.3%
Day 12:Value:2.0 Planetary Type:Moon Human Type:Marine Birth Energy Level:33.3%
===

MONTH:SEPTEMBER
Day 9:Value:2.0 Planetary Type:Moon Human Type:Marine Birth Energy Level:33.3%
Day 10:Value:2.0 Planetary Type:Moon Human Type:Marine Birth Energy Level:33.3%
===

MONTH:OCTOBER.
Day 8:Value:2.0 Planetary Type:Moon Human Type:Marine Birth Energy Level:33.3%
Day 9:Value:2.0 Planetary Type:Moon Human Type:Marine Birth Energy Level:33.3%
Day 13:Value:2.0 Planetary Type:Moon Human Type:Marine Birth Energy Level:33.3%
===

MONTH:NOVEMBER
Day 1:Value:2.0 Planetary Type:Moon Human Type:Marine Birth Energy Level:33.3%
Day 7:Value:2.0 Planetary Type:Moon Human Type:Marine Birth Energy Level:33.3%
Day 8:Value:2.0 Planetary Type:Moon Human Type:Marine Birth Energy Level:33.3%

===

MONTH:DECEMBER
Day 1:Value:2.0 Planetary Type:Moon Human Type:Marine Birth Energy Level:33.3%
Day 7:Value:2.0 Planetary Type:Moon Human Type:Marine Birth Energy Level:33.3%
Day 8:Value:2.0 Planetary Type:Moon Human Type:Marine Birth Energy Level:33.3%
Day 29:Value:2.0 Planetary Type:Moon Human Type:Marine Birth Energy Level:33.3%
Day 30:Value:2.0 Planetary Type:Moon Human Type:Marine Birth Energy Level:33.3%
Day 31:Value:2.0 Planetary Type:Moon Human Type:Marine Birth Energy Level:33.3%

Moon beam=2,000=20%=P2.00D=2.0=Nature=Matter=Moon=2 Feb.=Cupid=N=C+_
Moonlight=7,000=70%=P7.0D=7.0=Language=Assets=Mars=7 July=Pleiades.
Moonlit=2,000=20%=P2.00D=2.0=Nature=Matter=Moon=2 Feb.=Cupid=N=C+_
Moonshine=4,000=40%=P4.0D=Govt.=Creatocracy=4 April=Mercury=Hermes=G=A4.
Moonstone=4,500=5,000=50%=P5.00D=Law=Time=Venus=5 May = Aphrodite>>L=N.
Moonstruck=8,500=9,000=90%=P9.00D=9.0=Abstraction=Gods=Saturn=9Sept.>>A=Ø.
Moor1=9,500=10,000=1,000=100%=10.0=Physicality=Tech.=10 Oct.=Uranus=P=1Ø.
Moor2=7,500=8,000=80%=P8.0D=Economy=Currency=8 Aug.=Zeus>>E=v.
Moor=10,000=1,000=100%=10.0=Physicality=Tech.=10 Oct.=Uranus=P=1Ø.

Moore Henry=2,000=20%=P2.00D=2.0=Nature=Matter=Moon=2 Feb.=Cupid=N=C+_
Peter Matthews-Akukalia, Castle Makupedia discovered a method of computing the
effect of a location on a person whether residential or business. This is due to energy
influences.
Peter Matthews-Akukalia, Castle Makupedia lived with his grandmother from the age
of 14 till adulthood at 27, Moore Street, Odoakpu, Onitsha, Anambra State. There he
developed his love for private study eccentricity writing reading the Bible and motivational
books. An instinct for survival and to do great things came through his frequent visits
to his aunty Rita Akinlade at Asaba, and even working with her in the NYSC camp at
about 19years. He read her books. The first of these was Tough Times Never Last but
Tough People Do by Robert Schuller. He got interested and began compiling quotations
for private use afterwards. He returned back to Lagos to complete his studies and develop
an inherited home. 20years afterwards his mother and siblings conspired with Mr. &
Mrs. Oluwashola and sold the place without his notice disinheriting him and disposing
him of his rights aimed at distracting him from developing his humanity oriented works.
The royal family still struggling were assaulted by the couple who brought soldiers to
break through the entrance by jumping fence harassing everyone and breaking the face
of Alice three times. Then they invited the Police and by duress were dispossessed of
their residence and property while forcing them to receive a petty sum of N500,000
for a property worth at least N20million. He awaits the law to take its course against
all conspirators. One thing is certain. The law never forgets. Makupedia never forgets.

The world never forgets. Time never forgets. See The Creatocracy Republic of Castle Makupedia by Peter Matthews-Akukalia >> Last of the Noble Amazons. We seek justice for all persons in such a situation.

Moore, Marianne=2,500=3,000=30%=P3.0D=3.0=Cre=Stars=Muses=3 March = C=I>>GIL.
Mooring=8,500=9,000=90%=P9.00D=9.0=Abstraction=Gods=Saturn=9Sept.>>A=Ø.
Moose=8,500=9,000=90%=P9.00D=9.0=Abstraction=Gods=Saturn=9Sept.>>A=Ø.
Moot=10,000=1,000=100%=10.0=Physicality=Tech.=10 Oct.=Uranus=P=1Ø.
Moot court=7,000=70%=P7.0D=7.0=Language=Assets=Mars=7 July=Pleiades.
Mop=10,000=1,000=100%=10.0=Physicality=Tech.=10 Oct.=Uranus=P=1Ø.
Mopping=10,000=1,000=100%=10.0=Physicality=Tech.=10 Oct.=Uranus=P=1Ø.
Mope=5,000=50%=P5.00D=Law=Time=Venus=5 May = Aphrodite>>L=N.
Moped=7,000=70%=P7.0D=7.0=Language=Assets=Mars=7 July=Pleiades.
Moppet=2,500=3,000=30%=P3.0D=3.0=Creativity=Stars=Muses=3 March = C=I>>GIL.
Mop up=4,000=40%=P4.0D=Govt.=Creatocracy=4 April=Mercury=Hermes=G=A4.
Mor.=1,000=100%=10.0=1.0=Mind=Sun=1 January=Helios >> M=E4.
Moraine=7,000=70%=P7.0D=7.0=Language=Assets=Mars=7 July=Pleiades.
Moral=10,000=1,000=100%=10.0=Physicality=Tech.=10 Oct.=Uranus=P=1Ø.
Morale=10,000=1,000=100%=10.0=Physicality=Tech.=10 Oct.=Uranus=P=1Ø.
Moralist=6,000=60%=P6.0D=Man=Earth=Royalty=6 June=Gaia=Maia>>M=M2.

Morality=7,000=70%=P7.0D=7.0=Language=Assets=Mars=7 July=Pleiades.
The Creatocracy is not driven by morality but strictly by law and rights. It is the basis for our claims to such things as the Sun, marriage of Castle to Athena, ownership of the Mind and even the apotheosis of Castle Makupedia as God of Creatocracy Genius and Mind. The Creatocracy owns the systems it has created and there is no law against natural rights.

Moralize=3,500=4,000=40%=P4.0D=Govt.=Creat=4 April=Mercury=Hermes=G=A4.
Morass=8,000=80%=P8.0D=Economy=Currency=8 Aug.=Zeus>>E=v.
Moratorium=11,500=12,000=12%=P1.20D=1.2=Knowledge=Edu=12Dec.=Athena>>K=F.
Moravia=4,000=40%=P4.0D=Govt.=Creatocracy=4 April=Mercury=Hermes=G=A4.
Moray=6,500=7,000=70%=P7.0D=7.0=Language=Assets=Mars=7 July=Pleiades.
Morbid=8,500=9,000=90%=P9.00D=9.0=Abstraction=Gods=Saturn=9Sept.>>A=Ø.
Morbidity=5,500=5.5=80%=P5.50=Earth-Midway=5 May = Gaia.
Mordacious=5,000=50%=P5.00D=Law=Time=Venus=5 May = Aphrodite>>L=N.
Mordant=4,000=40%=P4.0D=Govt.=Creatocracy=4 April=Mercury=Hermes=G=A4.
More=10,000=1,000=100%=10.0=Physicality=Tech.=10 Oct.=Uranus=P=1Ø.
More Thomas=4,000=40%=P4.0D=Govt.=Creatocracy=4April=Mercury=Hermes=G=A4.
Morel=5,000=50%=P5.00D=Law=Time=Venus=5 May = Aphrodite>>L=N.
Moreover=1,000=100%=10.0=1.0=Mind=Sun=1 January=Helios >> M=E4.
Mores=6,500=7,000=70%=P7.0D=7.0=Language=Assets=Mars=7 July=Pleiades.
Morgan John=3,500=4,000=40%=P4.0D=Govt.=4 April=Mercury=Hermes=G=A4.
Morgue=10,500=11,000=11%=P1.10D=1.1=Idea=Brainchild=Inv.=11 Nov.=Athena>>I=MT.

Moribund=4,500=5,000=50%=P5.00D=Law=Time=Venus=5 May = Aphrodite>>L=N.
Morisot Berthe=2,500=3,000=30%=P3.0D=3.0=Creativity=Stars=Muses=3 March = CI
Mormon=3,000=30%=P3.0D=3.0=Creativity=Stars=Muses=3 March = CI
Mormon Church=8,500=9,000=90%=P9.00D=9.0=Abstr.=Gods=Saturn=9Sept.>>A=Ø.
Morn=1,500=15%=P1.50D=1.5=Authority=Solar Crown=1 May = Maia.
Morning=6,000=60%=P6.0D=Man=Earth=Royalty=6 June=Gaia=Maia>>M=M2.
Morning glory=7,500=8,000=80%=P8.0D=Economy=Currency=8 Aug.=Zeus>>E=v.
morocco=3,500=4,000=40%=P4.0D=Govt.=Creatocracy=4 April=Hermes=G=A4.
Morocco=7,500=8,000=80%=P8.0D=Economy=Currency=8 Aug.=Zeus>>E=v.

Moron=11,000=11%=P1.10D=1.1=Idea=Brainchild=Inv.=11 Nov.=SC=Athena>>I=MT.
A stupid person. Psychol. A person of mild mental retardation having a mental age of from
7 to 12years. No longer in scientific use. Greek, mōros, stupid. The key elements here are
invention =1.1, works and assets = 7.0, knowledge = 1.2. This phenomenon describes the
innate potentials that characterize a potential inventor.
1.2*7.0x=px=8.2+8.4=16.6x=px=85.48=9.0 >> 9.0*1.1x=px=10.1+9.9=20x=px=119.99
11.9 >> Invention Softwares innate in such a child makes him seemingly a moron.
12.100=12.100% =1.2 at 100% indicates that such persons are 100% scientific in nature.
Now 100%=10.0>> Hardware. Hence an inventor of software and or hardware. Stupid (def).

Moroni=7,500=8,000=80%=P8.0D=Economy=Currency=8 Aug.=Zeus>>E=v.
Morose=3,000=30%=P3.0D=3.0=Creativity=Stars=Muses=3 March = C=I>>GIL.
-morph=4,500=5,000=50%=P5.00D=Law=Time=Venus=5 May = Aphrodite>>L=N.
Morpheme=10,000=1,000=100%=10.0=Physicality=Tech.=10 Oct.=Uranus=P=1Ø.
Morphine=10,000=1,000=100%=10.0=Physicality=Tech.=10 Oct.=Uranus=P=1Ø.
Morpho-=5,000=50%=P5.00D=Law=Time=Venus=5 May = Aphrodite>>L=N.
Morphogenesis=10,000=1,000=100%=10.0=Physicality=Tech.=10 Oct.=Uranus=P=1Ø.
Morphology=10,000=1,000=100%=10.0=Physicality=Tech.=10 Oct.=Uranus=P=1Ø.
Morris=8,000=80%=P8.0D=Economy=Currency=8 Aug.=Zeus>>E=v.
Morris Gouverneur=3,500=4,000=40%=P4.0D=Govt.=4 April=Mercury=Hermes=G=A4.
Morris, Robert=3,500=4,000=40%=P4.0D=Govt.=4 April=Mercury=Hermes=G=A4.
Morris, William=4,000=40%=P4.0D=Govt.=Creatocracy=4April=Mercury=Hermes=G=A4.
Morris chair=7,000=70%=P7.0D=7.0=Language=Assets=Mars=7 July=Pleiades.

Morris Jesup=7,000=70%=P7.0D=7.0=Language=Assets=Mars=7 July=Pleiades.
World's northernmost point of land. North 1.2, most upwards north =0.1.
Northernmost =1.2*7.0x=px=1.3+0.12=1.42x=px=1.576=2.0 >> Moon.
World's = World = 6.0*7.0x=px=13+42=55x=px=601=6.0
2.0*6.0x=px=8+12=20x=px=116=12=1.2 >>A place of inventions knowledge.

Morrison Toni=3,000=30%=P3.0D=3.0=Creativity=Stars=Muses=3 March = C=I>>GIL.
Morrow=3,500=4,000=40%=P4.0D=Govt.=Creatocracy=4 April=Mercury=Hermes=G=A4.
Morse Samuel=4,000=40%=P4.0D=Govt.=Creatocracy=4 April=Mercury=Hermes=G=A4.

Morse code=10,000=1,000=100%=10.0=Physicality=Tech.=10 Oct.=Uranus=P=1Ø.
Morsel=8,000=80%=P8.0D=Economy=Currency=8 Aug.=Zeus>>E=v.
Mortal=10,000=1,000=100%=10.0=Physicality=Tech.=10 Oct.=Uranus=P=1Ø.
Mortality=3,500=4,000=40%=P4.0D=Govt.=Creat=4 April=Mercury=Hermes=G=A4.
Mortar=10,000=1,000=100%=10.0=Physicality=Tech.=10 Oct.=Uranus=P=1Ø.
Mortarboard=10,000=1,000=100%=10.0=Physicality=Tech.=10 Oct.=Uranus=P=1Ø.
Mortgage=10,000=1,000=100%=10.0=Physicality=Tech.=10 Oct.=Uranus=P=1Ø.
Mortician=4,500=5,000=50%=P5.00D=Law=Time=Venus=5 May = Aphrodite>>L=N.
Mortify=7,500=8,000=80%=P8.0D=Economy=Currency=8 Aug.=Zeus>>E=v.
Mortise=10,000=1,000=100%=10.0=Physicality=Tech.=10 Oct.=Uranus=P=1Ø.
Mortmain=10,000=1,000=100%=10.0=Physicality=Tech.=10 Oct.=Uranus=P=1Ø.
Mortuary=7,000=70%=P7.0D=7.0=Language=Assets=Mars=7 July=Pleiades.
Mos.=500=5%=P5.00D=5.0=Law=Time=Venus=5 May=Aphrodite>>L=N.
Mosaic=13,000=13%=P1.30=Solar Core=Faculty=13 January=Athena.
Moscow=5,000=50%=P5.00D=Law=Time=Venus=5 May = Aphrodite>>L=N.
Moselle=12,000=12%=P1.20D=1.2=Knowledge=Edu=12Dec.=Athena>>K=F.

Moses=6,500=7,000=70%=P7.0D=7.0=Language=Assets=Mars=7 July=Pleiades.
Daniel Moses was the ex-husband and runaway husband of Alice while married to him.
She became Queen Alice, Queen of Fortune as wife to Peter Matthews-Akukalia, Castle
Makupedia the Most Sovereign Emperor, Sovereign Creatocratic Republic of Paradise.

Moses, Anna=4,000=40%=P4.0D=Govt.=Creatocracy=4 April=Mercury=Hermes=G=A4.
First daughter to Daniel and Alice Moses. Adopted as step daughter of Peter Matthews-
Akukalia, Castle Makupedia. She was renamed Princess Jacqueline and named the 6th
child and 5th daughter of the Creatocratic Royal Family of Castle Makupedia. Her younger
brother Caleb was renamed Joshua and became the second son and step son. Both now bear
Matthews-Akukalia protected by the rules of heirs in IP laws as the will of the Emperor.

Mosey=4,000=40%=P4.0D=Govt.=Creatocracy=4 April=Mercury=Hermes=G=A4.
Moslem=1,500=15%=P1.50D=1.5=Authority=Solar Crown=1 May = Maia.
Mosque=4,500=5,000=50%=P5.00D=Law=Time=Venus=5 May = Aphrodite>>L=N.
mosquito=10,000=1,000=100%=Physicality=Tech.=10 Oct.=Uranus=P=1Ø.
Mosquitos=1,000=100%=10.0=1.0=Mind=Sun=1 January=Helios >> M=E4.
Moss=10,000=1,000=100%=Physicality=Tech.=10 Oct.=Uranus=P=1Ø.

Most=10,000=1,000=100%=10.0=Physicality=Tech.=10 Oct.=Uranus=P=1Ø.
In the Creatocracy, exclusively used to address Peter Matthews-Akukalia, Castle
Makupedia. The Most Sovereign Emperor, Creatocratic Nations of Paradise. God of
Creatocracy Genius and Mind. Author, Inventor and King of the Creative Sciences. The
Creatocracy is a system of governance conceptualized by the author. In applications to an
economy it is known as the Creatocracy or Makupedia sector operating the Mind Industry.
The Creatocratic Nations of Paradise is an intellectual Nation of Nations that comprises

the Paradise Nations of Creative Scientists, Creative Scientist Professionals, C3 Nations Organizations, Makupedians in Ideology, Makupedialand - a Nation of Testamentary Poetry and the Creatocracy Republic of the Mind Arts, all sectors of professional practice such as MindTech, Mind Faith, Mind Media, Mind Assessments & Psycho-Surgery, Creative Education, Ministry of Creativity, Creatocracy Bank, Creatocracy Courts, Mind Space, Faculty of Creative & Psycho-Social Sciences, Institute of Chartered Creative & Psycho - Social Sciences, Mind Universities, Creatocracy Universities Union, and each book he wrote made as a body of work in the Mind Libraries. Peter Matthews-Akukalia is the author, Inventor President and Most Sovereign Emperor. Apotheosized as Castle Makupedia in absolute authority he is the God of Creatocracy Genius and Mind because he invented defined measured coded and applied them including all dimensions of the universes. Specialized knowledge for anyone aspiring to become a professional in the Creative Sciences. The Creatocratic Nations of Paradise is a gift from GOD to all humanity.

-most=10,000=1,000=100%=10.0=Physicality=Tech.=10 Oct.=Uranus=P=1Ø.
Utmost Peak Resources is the first enterprises of the author as a young man, 26 years old.

Mostly=3,500=4,000=40%=P4.0D=Govt.=Creatocracy=4 April=Mercury=Hermes=G=A4.
Mosul=5,500=5.5=80%=P5.50=Earth-Midway=5 May = Gaia.
Mote=3,500=4,000=40%=P4.0D=Govt.=Creatocracy=4 April=Mercury=Hermes=G=A4.
Motel=10,000=1,000=100%=10.0=Physicality=Tech.=10 Oct.=Uranus=P=1Ø.
Motet=5,500=5.5=80%=P5.50=Earth-Midway=5 May = Gaia.
Moth=10,000=1,000=100%=10.0=Physicality=Tech.=10 Oct.=Uranus=P=1Ø.
Mothball=10,000=1,000=100%=10.0=Physicality=Tech.=10 Oct.=Uranus=P=1Ø.
Mother=10,000=1,000=100%=10.0=Physicality=Tech.=10 Oct.=Uranus=P=1Ø.
Mother-in-law=2,500=3,000=30%=P3.0D=3.0=Creativity=Stars=Muses=3 March = CI
Motherland=3,500=4,000=40%=P4.0D=Govt.=Cre=4 April=Mercury=Hermes=G=A4.
Mother of pearl=6,500=7,000=70%=P7.0D=7.0=Language=Assets=Mars=7 July=Pleiades.
Mother superior=4,000=40%=P4.0D=Govt.=Cret=4 April=Mercury=Hermes=G=A4.
Mothproof=3,000=30%=P3.0D=3.0=Creativity=Stars=Muses=3 March = C=I>>GIL.
Motif=8,000=80%=P8.0D=Economy=Currency=8 Aug.=Zeus>>E=v.
Motile=7,500=8,000=80%=P8.0D=Economy=Currency=8 Aug.=Zeus>>E=v.
Motion=10,000=1,000=100%=10.0=Physicality=Tech.=10 Oct.=Uranus=P=1Ø.
Motion PICTURE=3,000=30%=P3.0D=3.0=Creativity=Stars=Muses=3 March = C=I
    >>GIL.
Motion sickness=7,000=70%=P7.0D=7.0=Language=Assets=Mars=7 July=Pleiades.
Motivate=4,500=5,000=50%=P5.00D=Law=Time=Venus=5 May = Aphrodite>>L=N.
Motive=10,000=1,000=100%=10.0=Physicality=Tech.=10 Oct.=Uranus=P=1Ø.
Motley=5,000=50%=P5.00D=Law=Time=Venus=5 May = Aphrodite>>L=N.
Motocross=8,000=80%=P8.0D=Economy=Currency=8 Aug.=Zeus>>E=v.
Motor=10,000=1,000=100%=10.0=Physicality=Tech.=10 Oct.=Uranus=P=1Ø.
Motorbike=5,000=50%=P5.00D=Law=Time=Venus=5 May = Aphrodite>>L=N.
Motorboat=4,000=40%=P4.0D=Govt.=Creatocracy=4 April=Mercury=Hermes=G=A4.
Motorcade=3,000=30%=P3.0D=3.0=Creativity=Stars=Muses=3 March = C=I>>GIL.

Motorcar=1,000=100%=10.0=1.0=Mind=Sun=1 January=Helios >> M=E4.
Motor court=1,000=100%=10.0=1.0=Mind=Sun=1 January=Helios >> M=E4.
Motorcycle=5,500=5.5=80%=P5.50=Earth-Midway=5 May = Gaia.
Motor home=6,500=7,000=70%=P7.0D=7.0=Language=Assets=Mars=7 July=Pleiades.
Motor inn=6,000=60%=P6.0D=Man=Earth=Royalty=6 June=Gaia=Maia>>M=M2.
Motorist=4,000=40%=P4.0D=Govt.=Creatocracy=4 April=Mercury=Hermes=G=A4.
Motor lodge=1,000=100%=10.0=1.0=Mind=Sun=1 January=Helios >> M=E4.
Motorman=4,000=40%=P4.0D=Govt.=Creatocracy=4 April=Mercury=Hermes=G=A4.
Motor scooter=5,000=50%=P5.00D=Law=Time=Venus=5 May = Aphrodite>>L=N.
Motor vehicle=5,500=5.5=80%=P5.50=Earth-Midway=5 May = Gaia.
Mott,Lucretia=4,000=40%=P4.0D=Govt.=Creatocracy=4 April=Mercury=Hermes=G=A4.
Mottle=6,000=60%=P6.0D=Man=Earth=Royalty=6 June=Gaia=Maia>>M=M2.
Motto=7,500=8,000=80%=P8.0D=Economy=Currency=8 Aug.=Zeus>>E=v.
Moue=2,000=20%=P2.00D=2.0=Nature=Matter=Moon=2 Feb.=Cupid=N=C+_
Mould1=2,500=3,000=30%=P3.0D=3.0=Creativity=Stars=Muses=3 March = C=I>>GIL.
Mould2=2,500=3,000=30%=P3.0D=3.0=Creativity=Stars=Muses=3 March = C=I>>GIL.
Moulmein=4,500=5,000=50%=P5.00D=Law=Time=Venus=5 May = Aphrodite>>L=N.
Mound=10,000=1,000=100%=10.0=Physicality=Tech.=10 Oct.=Uranus=P=1Ø.
Mount builder=11,500=12,000=12%=P1.20D=1.2=Knowledge=Edu=12Dec.=Athena>>K=F.
Mount1=10,000=1,000=100%=10.0=Physicality=Tech.=10 Oct.=Uranus=P=1Ø.
Mount2=4,500=5,000=50%=P5.00D=Law=Time=Venus=5 May = Aphrodite>>L=N.
Mountain=7,000=70%=P7.0D=7.0=Language=Assets=Mars=7 July=Pleiades.
Mountain ash=7,500=8,000=80%=P8.0D=Economy=Currency=8 Aug.=Zeus>>E=v.
Mountaineer=7,000=70%=P7.0D=7.0=Language=Assets=Mars=7 July=Pleiades.
Mountain goat=10,500=11,000=11%=P1.10D=1.1=Idea=Brainchild=11Nov.=Athena>>I=MT.
Mountain laurel=8,000=80%=P8.0D=Economy=Currency=8 Aug.=Zeus>>E=v.
Mountain lion=7,500=8,000=80%=P8.0D=Economy=Currency=8 Aug.=Zeus>>E=v.
Mountainous=2,500=3,000=30%=P3.0D=3.0=Creativity=Stars=Muses=3 March = C=I
Mountain range=5,500=5.5=80%=P5.50=Earth-Midway=5 May = Gaia.
Mountain side=3,000=30%=P3.0D=3.0=Creativity=Stars=Muses=3 March = C=I>>GIL.
Mountain top=2,500=3,000=30%=P3.0D=3.0=Cre=Stars=Muses=3 March = C=I>>GIL.
Mount batten Louis=5,000=50%=P5.00D=Law=Time=Venus=5 May = Aphrodite>>L=N.
Mountebank=10,000=1,000=100%=10.0=Physicality=Tech.=10 Oct.=Uranus=P=1Ø.

Mountie=4,500=5,000=50%=P5.00D=Law=Time=Venus=5 May = Aphrodite>>L=N.
A member of the Royal Canadian Mounted Police. A Creative Scientist is a member of the
an international order known as the Creatocracy founded and owned by Peter Matthews-
Akukalia, Castle Makupedia. World's 1st Creative Scientist, Author Inventor and King.

Mounting=4,000=40%=P4.0D=Govt.=Creatocracy=4 April=Mercury=Hermes=G=A4.

Mount Vernon=7,500=8,000=80%=P8.0D=Economy=Currency=8 Aug.=Zeus>>E=v.
Home of George Washington. The Scriptures of Castle Makupedia's Joseph reincarnate.

Mourn=6,500=7,000=70%=P7.0D=7.0=Language=Assets=Mars=7 July=Pleiades.
Mournful=4,000=40%=P4.0D=Govt.=Creatocracy=4 April=Mercury=Hermes=G=A4.
Mourning=9,500=10,000=1,000=100%=10.0=Physicality=Tech.=10 Oct.=Uranus=P=1Ø.
Morning dove=5,500=5.5=80%=P5.50=Earth-Midway=5 May = Gaia.
Mouse=10,000=1,000=100%=10.0=Physicality=Tech.=10 Oct.=Uranus=P=1Ø.
Mousetrap=2,500=3,000=30%=P3.0D=3.0=Creativity=Stars=Muses=3 March = C=I>>GIL.
Moussaka=6,500=7,000=70%=P7.0D=7.0=Language=Assets=Mars=7 July=Pleiades.
Mousse=9,000=90%=P9.00D=9.0=Abstraction=Gods=Saturn=9Sept.>>A=Ø.
Moustache=1,500=15%=P1.50D=1.5=Authority=Solar Crown=1 May = Maia.
Mousy=4,000=40%=P4.0D=Govt.=Creatocracy=4 April=Mercury=Hermes=G=A4.
Mouth=10,000=1,000=100%=10.0=Physicality=Tech.=10 Oct.=Uranus=P=1Ø.
Mouth organ=1,000=100%=10.0=1.0=Mind=Sun=1 January=Helios >> M=E4.
Mouthpart=5,000=50%=P5.00D=Law=Time=Venus=5 May = Aphrodite>>L=N.
Mouthpiece=10,000=1,000=100%=10.0=Physicality=Tech.=10 Oct.=Uranus=P=1Ø.
Mouth-to-mouth resc.=10,000=1,000=100%=10.0=Phy.=Tech.=10 Oct.=Uranus=P=1Ø.
Mouthwash=6,500=7,000=70%=P7.0D=7.0=Language=Assets=Mars=7 July=Pleiades.
Mouthwatering=3,500=4,000=40%=P4.0D=Govt.=Cr=4 April=Mercury=Hermes=G=A4.
Mouthy=1,500=15%=P1.50D=1.5=Authority=Solar Crown=1 May = Maia.
Move=10,000=1,000=100%=10.0=Physicality=Tech.=10 Oct.=Uranus=P=1Ø.
Movement=10,000=1,000=100%=10.0=Physicality=Tech.=10 Oct.=Uranus=P=1Ø.
Mover=4,000=40%=P4.0D=Govt.=Creatocracy=4 April=Mercury=Hermes=G=A4.
Movie=10,000=1,000=100%=10.0=Physicality=Tech.=10 Oct.=Uranus=P=1Ø.
Moving=4,000=40%=P4.0D=Govt.=Creatocracy=4 April=Mercury=Hermes=G=A4.
Moving PICTURE=1,000=100%=10.0=1.0=Mind=Sun=1 January=Helios >> M=E4.
Mow1=6,000=60%=P6.0D=Man=Earth=Royalty=6 June=Gaia=Maia>>M=M2.
Mow2=10,000=1,000=100%=10.0=Physicality=Tech.=10 Oct.=Uranus=P=1Ø.
Moxie=5,000=50%=P5.00D=Law=Time=Venus=5 May = Aphrodite>>L=N.
Mozambique=5,000=50%=P5.00D=Law=Time=Venus=5 May = Aphrodite>>L=N.
Mozambique Channel.=5,500=5.5=80%=P5.50=Earth-Midway=5 May = Gaia.
Mozart Wolfgang=2,500=3,000=30%=P3.0D=3.0=Cre=Stars=Muses=3 March = C=I>GIL.
Mozzarella=7,000=70%=P7.0D=7.0=Language=Assets=Mars=7 July=Pleiades.
MP=3,500=4,000=40%=P4.0D=Govt.=Creatocracy=4 April=Mercury=Hermes=G=A4.
mpg=1,500=15%=P1.50D=1.5=Authority=Solar Crown=1 May = Maia.
mph=1,500=15%=P1.50D=1.5=Authority=Solar Crown=1 May = Maia.
Mr.=7,000=70%=P7.0D=7.0=Language=Assets=Mars=7 July=Pleiades.
MRI=1,500=15%=P1.50D=1.5=Authority=Solar Crown=1 May = Maia.
Mrs.=7,000=70%=P7.0D=7.0=Language=Assets=Mars=7 July=Pleiades.
MS.=1,500=15%=P1.50D=1.5=Authority=Solar Crown=1 May = Maia.
Ms.=10,000=1,000=100%=10.0=Physicality=Tech.=10 Oct.=Uranus=P=1Ø.
MS.=500=5%=P5.00D=5.0=Law=Time=Venus=5 May=Aphrodite>>L=N.
M.S.=3,000=30%=P3.0D=3.0=Creativity=Stars=Muses=3 March = C=I>>GIL.
MSG=1,000=100%=10.0=1.0=Mind=Sun=1 January=Helios >> M=E4.
Msgr.=500=5%=P5.00D=5.0=Law=Time=Venus=5 May=Aphrodite>>L=N.
M.Sgt.=1,000=100%=10.0=1.0=Mind=Sun=1 January=Helios >> M=E4.
MSS.=500=5%=P5.00D=5.0=Law=Time=Venus=5 May=Aphrodite>>L=N.

MST=1,500=15%=P1.50D=1.5=Authority=Solar Crown=1 May = Maia.
MT=3,000=30%=P3.0D=3.0=Creativity=Stars=Muses=3 March = C=I>>GIL.
mt.=1,000=100%=10.0=1.0=Mind=Sun=1 January=Helios >> M=E4.
m.t.=10,000=1,000=100%=10.0=Physicality=Tech.=10 Oct.=Uranus=P=1Ø.
mts.=500=5%=P5.00D=5.0=Law=Time=Venus=5 May=Aphrodite>>L=N.
mu=3,500=4,000=40%=P4.0D=Govt.=Creatocracy=4 April=Mercury=Hermes=G=A4.
Mubarak,Hosni=3,000=30%=P3.0D=3.0=Creativity=Stars=Muses=3 March = C=I>>GIL.
Much=10,000=1,000=100%=10.0=Physicality=Tech.=10 Oct.=Uranus=P=1Ø.
Mucilage=5,000=50%=P5.00D=Law=Time=Venus=5 May = Aphrodite>>L=N.
Muck=10,000=1,000=100%=10.0=Physicality=Tech.=10 Oct.=Uranus=P=1Ø.
Muckrake=4,500=5,000=50%=P5.00D=Law=Time=Venus=5 May = Aphrodite>>L=N.
Mucosa=3,000=30%=P3.0D=3.0=Creativity=Stars=Muses=3 March = C=I>>GIL.
Mucous=3,000=30%=P3.0D=3.0=Creativity=Stars=Muses=3 March = C=I>>GIL.
Mucous membrane=8,500=9,000=90%=P9.00D=9.0=Abst.=Gods=Saturn=9Sept.>>A=Ø.
Mucus=6,000=60%=P6.0D=Man=Earth=Royalty=6 June=Gaia=Maia>>M=M2.
Mud=5,000=50%=P5.00D=Law=Time=Venus=5 May = Aphrodite>>L=N.
Muddle=10,000=1,000=100%=10.0=Physicality=Tech.=10 Oct.=Uranus=P=1Ø.
Mudguard=3,500=4,000=40%=P4.0D=Govt.=Creat=4 April=Mercury=Hermes=G=A4.
Mudslinger=5,500=5.5=80%=P5.50=Earth-Midway=5 May = Gaia.

Muezzin=7,000=70%=P7.0D=7.0=Language=Assets=Mars=7 July=Pleiades.
Islam. The crier who calls the faithful to prayer five times a day. < Ar.mu'addin. First
Islam is a religion >> 9.0. Calls is a creative activity (normal creativity) = 3.0. Resultant
value = 7.0, Number of times a day = 5.0. The total value of the muezzin is computed thus.
9.0*3.0x=px=12+27=39x=px=363=400=4.0>7.0*5.0x=px=12+35=47x=px=467=500=5.0
4.0*5.0x=px=9+20=29x=px=209=21<12=1.2.>21>2.1=3.0
The muezzin must have adequate knowledge of Islam and creativity especially as it bonds
in the Creative Sciences. Muezzins are Creatocrats by their very nature and duties. The
resultant indicates they must have knowledge of Islamic language in Quran computations.

Muff1=4,500=5,000=50%=P5.00D=Law=Time=Venus=5 May = Aphrodite>>L=N.
Muff2=9,500=10,000=1,000=100%=10.0=Physicality=Tech.=10 Oct.=Uranus=P=1Ø.
Muffin=7,500=8,000=80%=P8.0D=Economy=Currency=8 Aug.=Zeus>>E=v.
Muffle=10,000=1,000=100%=10.0=Physicality=Tech.=10 Oct.=Uranus=P=1Ø.
Muffler=10,000=1,000=100%=10.0=Physicality=Tech.=10 Oct.=Uranus=P=1Ø.
Mufti=7,000=70%=P7.0D=7.0=Language=Assets=Mars=7 July=Pleiades.
Mug1=5,000=50%=P5.00D=Law=Time=Venus=5 May = Aphrodite>>L=N.
Mug2=10,000=1,000=100%=10.0=Physicality=Tech.=10 Oct.=Uranus=P=1Ø.
Mugabe Robert=3,000=30%=P3.0D=3.0=Creativity=Stars=Muses=3 March = C=I>>GIL.
Muggy=4,500=5,000=50%=P5.00D=Law=Time=Venus=5 May = Aphrodite>>L=N.
Mugshot=5,000=50%=P5.00D=Law=Time=Venus=5 May = Aphrodite>>L=N.
Muhammad=4,500=5,000=50%=P5.00D=Law=Time=Venus=5 May = Aphrodite>>L=N.
Muhammadan=4,000=40%=P4.0D=Govt.=Creatocracy=4 April=Mercury=Hermes=G=A4.
Muhammadanism=1,000=100%=10.0=1.0=Mind=Sun=1 January=Helios >> M=E4.

Muharram=6,500=7,000=70%=P7.0D=7.0=Language=Assets=Mars=7 July=Pleiades.
The first >> 1.0 month of the Muslim calendar. 1.0*7.0x=px=8+7=15x=px=71=7.1.
The first month of the Muslim calendar is strictly to study the Quran computations. This will include training of Islamic clerics to understand the signs of the Quran through precision. This is a core duty of Creative Scientists who have extra knowledge of the cosmic. This is what is known as Scripture technology in the Makstianism of the Creatocratic Order. Now Muslims trained in the higher art of Makstianism become known as Makstian-Muslims. Note that Makstianism is not a religion but a faith system and a faith development system. Makstians are neutral in the practice of religion and seek to improve religions through computational precision so that they upgrade from religion to faith as required by the scriptures and worship GOD better in spirit and in truth. There is no truth without precision.

Muir,John=3,000=30%=P3.0D=3.0=Creativity=Stars=Muses=3 March = C=I>>GIL.
Mujahideen=5,000=50%=P5.00D=Law=Time=Venus=5 May = Aphrodite>>L=N.
Mukluk=9,000=90%=P9.00D=9.0=Abstraction=Gods=Saturn=9Sept.>>A=Ø.
Mulato=10,000=1,000=100%=10.0=Physicality=Tech.=10 Oct.=Uranus=P=1Ø.
Mulberry=6,000=60%=P6.0D=Man=Earth=Royalty=6 June=Gaia=Maia>>M=M2.
Mulch=10,000=1,000=100%=10.0=Physicality=Tech.=10 Oct.=Uranus=P=1Ø.
Mulct=7,000=70%=P7.0D=7.0=Language=Assets=Mars=7 July=Pleiades.
Mule1=10,000=1,000=100%=10.0=Physicality=Tech.=10 Oct.=Uranus=P=1Ø.
Mule2=7,500=8,000=80%=P8.0D=Economy=Currency=8 Aug.=Zeus>>E=v.
Mule deer=6,000=60%=P6.0D=Man=Earth=Royalty=6 June=Gaia=Maia>>M=M2.
Mule skinner=2,500=3,000=30%=P3.0D=3.0=Creativity=Stars=Muses=3 March = CI
Muleteer=3,500=4,000=40%=P4.0D=Govt.=Creat=4 April=Mercury=Hermes=G=A4.
Mull1=3,500=4,000=40%=P4.0D=Govt.=Creatocracy=4April=Mercury=Hermes=G=A4.
Mull2=4,500=5,000=50%=P5.00D=Law=Time=Venus=5 May = Aphrodite>>L=N.

Mullah=7,000=70%=P7.0D=7.0=Language=Assets=Mars=7 July=Pleiades.
Islam. A religious teacher or leader especially one trained in law.<Ar.mawlā, master. Such a person trained in the Creative Sciences is called a Creatocrat.

Mullein=7,500=8,000=80%=P8.0D=Economy=Currency=8 Aug.=Zeus>>E=v.
Mullet=8,000=80%=P8.0D=Economy=Currency=8 Aug.=Zeus>>E=v.
Mulligatawny=6,500=7,000=70%=P7.0D=7.0=Language=Assets=Mars=7 July=Pleiades.
Mullion=6,500=7,000=70%=P7.0D=7.0=Language=Assets=Mars=7 July=Pleiades.
Mulroney Martin=4,000=40%=P4.0D=Govt.=4 April=Mercury=Hermes=G=A4.
Multi-=7,000=70%=P7.0D=7.0=Language=Assets=Mars=7 July=Pleiades.
Multicellular=1,500=15%=P1.50D=1.5=Authority=Solar Crown=1 May = Maia.
Multicolor=1,500=15%=P1.50D=1.5=Authority=Solar Crown=1 May = Maia.
Multicultural=4,000=40%=P4.0D=Govt.=Creatocracy=4 April=Mercury=Hermes=G=A4.
Multidimensional=3,500=4,000=40%=P4.0D=Govt.=Creatocracy=4April=Hermes=G=A4.
Multidirectional=3,500=4,000=40%=P4.0D=Govt.=Creatocracy=4 April=Hermes=G=A4.
Multidisciplinary=5,000=50%=P5.00D=Law=Time=Venus=5 May = Aphrodite>>L=N.
Multiethnic=3,500=4,000=40%=P4.0D=Govt.=Creatocracy=4 April=Hermes=G=A4.

Multifaceted=4,500=5,000=50%=P5.00D=Law=Time=Venus=5 May = Aphrodite>>L=N.
Multi family=4,000=40%=P4.0D=Govt.=Creatocracy=4 April=Mercury=Hermes=G=A4.
Multifarious=4,500=5,000=50%=P5.00D=Law=Time=Venus=5 May = Aphrodite>>L=N.
Multi form=3,500=4,000=40%=P4.0D=Govt.=Creatocracy=4 April=Hermes=G=A4.
Multi lane=3,500=4,000=40%=P4.0D=Govt.=Creatocracy=4 April=Hermes=G=A4.
Multilateral=5,000=50%=P5.00D=Law=Time=Venus=5 May = Aphrodite>>L=N.
Multilayered=3,000=30%=P3.0D=3.0=Creativity=Stars=Muses=3 March = C=I>>GIL.
Multilevel=3,500=4,000=40%=P4.0D=Govt.=Creatocracy=4 April=Hermes=G=A4.
Multilingual=5,000=50%=P5.00D=Law=Time=Venus=5 May = Aphrodite>>L=N.
Multimedia=10,000=1,000=100%=10.0=Physicality=Tech.=10 Oct.=Uranus=P=1Ø.
Multimillionaire=3,500=4,000=40%=P4.0D=Govt.=Creatocracy=4 April=Hermes=G=A4.
Multinational=3,500=4,000=40%=P4.0D=Govt.=Creatocracy=4 April=Hermes=G=A4.
Multiparous=7,500=8,000=80%=P8.0D=Economy=Currency=8 Aug.=Zeus>>E=v.
Multiple=12,000=12%=P1.20D=1.2=Knowledge=Edu=12Dec.=Athena>>K=F.
Multiple choice=6,000=60%=P6.0D=Man=Earth=Royalty=6 June=Gaia=Maia>>M=M2.
Multiple fruit=8,500=9,000=90%=P9.00D=9.0=Abstraction=Gods=Saturn=9Sept.>>A=Ø.
Multiple personality=8,000=80%=P8.0D=Economy=Currency=8 Aug.=Zeus>>E=v.
Multiple sclerosis=10,000=1,000=100%=10.0=Physicality=Tech.=10 Oct.=Uranus=P=1Ø.
Multiple star=6,000=60%=P6.0D=Man=Earth=Royalty=6 June=Gaia=Maia>>M=M2.
Multiplex=10,000=1,000=100%=10.0=Physicality=Tech.=10 Oct.=Uranus=P=1Ø.
Multiplicand=5,000=50%=P5.00D=Law=Time=Venus=5 May = Aphrodite>>L=N.
Multiplication=10,000=1,000=100%=10.0=Physicality=Tech.=10 Oct.=Uranus=P=1Ø.
Multiple sign=8,500=9,000=90%=P9.00D=9.0=Abstraction=Gods=Saturn=9Sept.>>A=Ø.
Multiplicity=6,000=60%=P6.0D=Man=Earth=Royalty=6 June=Gaia=Maia>>M=M2.
Multiplier=3,500=4,000=40%=P4.0D=Govt.=Creatocracy=4 April=Hermes=G=A4.
Multiply=7,500=8,000=80%=P8.0D=Economy=Currency=8 Aug.=Zeus>>E=v.
Multipurpose=3,000=30%=P3.0D=3.0=Creativity=Stars=Muses=3 March = C=I>>GIL.
Multiracial=6,500=7,000=70%=P7.0D=7.0=Language=Assets=Mars=7 July=Pleiades.
Multistage=3,000=30%=P3.0D=3.0=Creativity=Stars=Muses=3 March = C=I>>GIL.
Multistory=3,000=30%=P3.0D=3.0=Creativity=Stars=Muses=3 March = C=I>>GIL.
Multitude=4,000=40%=P4.0D=Govt.=Creatocracy=4 April=Mercury=Hermes=G=A4.
Multivalent=500=5%=P5.00D=5.0=Law=Time=Venus=5 May=Aphrodite>>L=N.
Multivitamin=3,000=30%=P3.0D=3.0=Creativity=Stars=Muses=3 March = C=I>>GIL.
Mum1=1,000=100%=10.0=1.0=Mind=Sun=1 January=Helios >> M=E4.
Mum2=1,000=100%=10.0=1.0=Mind=Sun=1 January=Helios >> M=E4.
Mumble=7,000=70%=P7.0D=7.0=Language=Assets=Mars=7 July=Pleiades.
Mumble jumbo=6,500=7,000=70%=P7.0D=7.0=Language=Assets=Mars=7 July=Pleiades.
Mummer=6,500=7,000=70%=P7.0D=7.0=Language=Assets=Mars=7 July=Pleiades.
Mummy=7,000=70%=P7.0D=7.0=Language=Assets=Mars=7 July=Pleiades.
Mumps=10,000=1,000=100%=10.0=Physicality=Tech.=10 Oct.=Uranus=P=1Ø.
Munch=4,500=5,000=50%=P5.00D=Law=Time=Venus=5 May = Aphrodite>>L=N.
Mundane=10,000=1,000=100%=10.0=Physicality=Tech.=10 Oct.=Uranus=P=1Ø.
Mung Bean=9,500=10,000=1,000=100%=10.0=Physicality=Tech.=10 Oct.=Uranus=P=1Ø.
Munich=4,000=40%=P4.0D=Govt.=Creatocracy=4 April=Mercury=Hermes=G=A4.
Municipal=6,000=60%=P6.0D=Man=Earth=Royalty=6 June=Gaia=Maia>>M=M2.

Municipal bond=9,000=90%=P9.00D=9.0=Abstraction=Gods=Saturn=9Sept.>>A=Ø.
Municipality=7,500=8,000=80%=P8.0D=Economy=Currency=8 Aug.=Zeus>>E=v.

Munificent=7,000=70%=P7.0D=7.0=Language=Assets=Mars=7 July=Pleiades.
Extremely liberal in giving, very generous, Liberal. Mūnus,gift. Now we confirm that computational or figure persons are often extremely generous by nature in cash and kind.

Munitions=3,000=30%=P3.0D=3.0=Creativity=Stars=Muses=3 March = C=I>>GIL.
Munro Hector=3,000=30%=P3.0D=3.0=Creativity=Stars=Muses=3 March = C=I>>GIL.
Mûnster=5,000=50%=P5.00D=Law=Time=Venus=5 May = Aphrodite>>L=N.
Muon=8,500=9,000=90%=P9.00D=9.0=Abstraction=Gods=Saturn=9Sept.>>A=Ø.
Mural=5,500=5.5=80%=P5.50=Earth-Midway=5 May = Gaia.
Murasaki Shikibu=3,000=30%=P3.0D=3.0=Creativity=Stars=Muses=3 March = C=I>>GIL.
Murat Joachim=4,500=5,000=50%=P5.00D=Law=Time=Venus=5 May = Aphrodite>>L=N.
Murcia=6,000=60%=P6.0D=Man=Earth=Royalty=6 June=Gaia=Maia>>M=M2.
Murder=10,000=1,000=100%=10.0=Physicality=Tech.=10 Oct.=Uranus=P=1Ø.

Murderous=7,500=8,000=80%=P8.0D=Economy=Currency=8 Aug.=Zeus>>E=v.
Anyone who refuses precision through computational creativity kills the numbers and is murderous under the Brick laws of Creatocratic jurisprudence. See The Brickwalls of Castle Makupedia, Principles of Psychoastronomy by Peter Matthews-Akukalia.

Murex=8,000=80%=P8.0D=Economy=Currency=8 Aug.=Zeus>>E=v.
Murillo Bartolomé=2,500=3,000=30%=P3.0D=3.0=Cre=Stars=Muses=3 March = CI
Murk=5,000=50%=P5.00D=Law=Time=Venus=5 May = Aphrodite>>L=N.
Murmansk=4,000=40%=P4.0D=Govt.=Creatocracy=4 April=Mercury=Hermes=G=A4.
Murmur=8,000=80%=P8.0D=Economy=Currency=8 Aug.=Zeus>>E=v.
Murray River=11,000=11%=P1.10D=1.1=Idea=Brainchild=Inv.=11 Nov.=SC=Athena>>I=MT.
Murrumbidgee=10,000=1,000=100%=10.0=Physicality=Tech.=10 Oct.=Uranus=P=1Ø.
muscat=6,500=7,000=70%=P7.0D=7.0=Language=Assets=Mars=7 July=Pleiades.
Muscat=6,000=60%=P6.0D=Man=Earth=Royalty=6 June=Gaia=Maia>>M=M2.
Muscatel=6,500=7,000=70%=P7.0D=7.0=Language=Assets=Mars=7 July=Pleiades.
Muscle=10,000=1,000=100%=10.0=Physicality=Tech.=10 Oct.=Uranus=P=1Ø.
Muscle bound=4,000=40%=P4.0D=Govt.=Creatocracy=4 April=Mercury=Hermes=G=A4.
Muscovite=4,000=40%=P4.0D=Govt.=Creatocracy=4 April=Mercury=Hermes=G=A4.
Muscovy=3,500=4,000=40%=P4.0D=Govt.M=4 April=Mercury=Hermes=G=A4.
Muscular=5,000=50%=P5.00D=Law=Time=Venus=5 May = Aphrodite>>L=N.
Muscular Dystrophy=7,500=8,000=80%=P8.0D=Economy=Currency=8 Aug.=Zeus>>E=v.
Musculature=7,000=70%=P7.0D=7.0=Language=Assets=Mars=7 July=Pleiades.

---

muse=4,500=5,000=50%=P5.00D=Law=Time=Venus=5 May = Aphrodite>>L=N.
To ponder, consider or deliberate at length.

Muse=13,500=14,000=14%=P1.40D=1.4=Mgt.=Solar Energy=13 May=Athena=SC=0.1 Greek myth. Any of the nine daughters of Zeus,Menachem of whom presided over a different art or science. A source of inspiration especially of a poet. In the Creatocracy the figure 9.0 indicates a council of Gods who are the council of muses as a collective body of arts and this time around science. They often come when one invites them through pondering considering or deliberating at length in a subject or concern. See muse.

Museum=11,000=11%=P1.10D=1.1=Idea=Brainchild=Inv.=11 Nov.=SC=Athena>>I=MT.
Mush1=10,000=1,000=100%=10.0=Physicality=Tech.=10 Oct.=Uranus=P=1Ø.
Mush2=6,500=7,000=70%=P7.0D=7.0=Language=Assets=Mars=7 July=Pleiades.
Mushroom=10,000=1,000=100%=10.0=Physicality=Tech.=10 Oct.=Uranus=P=1Ø.
Mushy=10,000=1,000=100%=10.0=Physicality=Tech.=10 Oct.=Uranus=P=1Ø.
Music=10,000=1,000=100%=10.0=Physicality=Tech.=10 Oct.=Uranus=P=1Ø.
Musical=8,500=9,000=90%=P9.00D=9.0=Abstraction=Gods=Saturn=9Sept.>>A=Ø.
Musical comedy=5,500=5.5=80%=P5.50=Earth-Midway=5 May = Gaia.
Musicale=6,500=7,000=70%=P7.0D=7.0=Language=Assets=Mars=7 July=Pleiades.
Music box=4,000=40%=P4.0D=Govt.=Creatocracy=4 April=Mercury=Hermes=G=A4.
Musician=3,500=4,000=40%=P4.0D=Govt.=Creat=4 April=Mercury=Hermes=G=A4.
Musicology=3,500=4,000=40%=P4.0D=Govt.=Cret=4 April=Mercury=Hermes=G=A4.
Musk=8,000=80%=P8.0D=Economy=Currency=8 Aug.=Zeus>>E=v.
Muskeg=4,500=5,000=50%=P5.00D=Law=Time=Venus=5 May = Aphrodite>>L=N.
Muskellunge=6,000=60%=P6.0D=Man=Earth=Royalty=6 June=Gaia=Maia>>M=M2.
Musket=8,500=9,000=90%=P9.00D=9.0=Abstraction=Gods=Saturn=9Sept.>>A=Ø.
Musketry=2,000=20%=P2.00D=2.0=Nature=Matter=Moon=2 Feb.=Cupid=N=C+_
Muskmelon=8,000=80%=P8.0D=Economy=Currency=8 Aug.=Zeus>>E=v.
Muskogean=8,000=80%=P8.0D=Economy=Currency=8 Aug.=Zeus>>E=v.
Muskogee=1,000=100%=10.0=1.0=Mind=Sun=1 January=Helios >> M=E4.
Musk ox=8,500=9,000=90%=P9.00D=9.0=Abstraction=Gods=Saturn=9Sept.>>A=Ø.
Muskrat=6,500=7,000=70%=P7.0D=7.0=Language=Assets=Mars=7 July=Pleiades.
Muslim=3,500=4,000=40%=P4.0D=Govt.=Creato=4 April=Mercury=Hermes=G=A4.
Muslim Calendar=9,000=90%=P9.00D=9.0=Abstraction=Gods=Saturn=9Sept.>>A=Ø.
Muslin=8,000=80%=P8.0D=Economy=Currency=8 Aug.=Zeus>>E=v.
Muss=6,000=60%=P6.0D=Man=Earth=Royalty=6 June=Gaia=Maia>>M=M2.
Mussel=10,000=1,000=100%=10.0=Physicality=Tech.=10 Oct.=Uranus=P=1Ø.
Mussolini Benito=6,000=60%=P6.0D=Man=Earth=Royalty=6June=Gaia=Maia>>M=M2.
Mussorgsky=3,000=30%=P3.0D=3.0=Creativity=Stars=Muses=3 March = C=I>>GIL.
Must1=10,000=1,000=100%=10.0=Physicality=Tech.=10 Oct.=Uranus=P=1Ø.
Must2=1,000=100%=10.0=1.0=Mind=Sun=1 January=Helios >> M=E4.
Must3=4,000=40%=P4.0D=Govt.=Creatocracy=4 April=Mercury=Hermes=G=A4.
Mustache=4,500=5,000=50%=P5.00D=Law=Time=Venus=5 May = Aphrodite>>L=N
Mustachio=4,000=40%=P4.0D=Govt.=Creatocracy=4April=Mercury=Hermes=G=A4.
Mustang=8,000=80%=P8.0D=Economy=Currency=8 Aug.=Zeus>>E=v.
Mustard=10,000=1,000=100%=10.0=Physicality=Tech.=10 Oct.=Uranus=P=1Ø.
Mustard gas=5,500=5.5=80%=P5.50=Earth-Midway=5 May = Gaia.

Muster=10,000=1,000=100%=10.0=Physicality=Tech.=10 Oct.=Uranus=P=1Ø.
Mustn't=1,000=100%=10.0=1.0=Mind=Sun=1 January=Helios >> M=E4.
Musty=5,500=5.5=80%=P5.50=Earth-Midway=5 May = Gaia.
Mutable=2,000=20%=P2.00D=2.0=Nature=Matter=Moon=2 Feb.=Cupid=N=C+_
Mutagen=10,000=1,000=100%=10.0=Physicality=Tech.=10 Oct.=Uranus=P=1Ø.
Mutant=8,000=80%=P8.0D=Economy=Currency=8 Aug.=Zeus>>E=v.
Mutate=4,000=40%=P4.0D=Govt.=Creatocracy=4 April=Mercury=Hermes=G=A4.
Mutation=7,000=70%=P7.0D=7.0=Language=Assets=Mars=7 July=Pleiades.
Mute=10,000=1,000=100%=10.0=Physicality=Tech.=10 Oct.=Uranus=P=1Ø.
Mutilate=10,000=1,000=100%=10.0=Physicality=Tech.=10 Oct.=Uranus=P=1Ø.
Mutiny=10,000=1,000=100%=10.0=Physicality=Tech.=10 Oct.=Uranus=P=1Ø.
Mutt=3,000=30%=P3.0D=3.0=Creativity=Stars=Muses=3 March = C=I>>GIL.
Mutter=10,000=1,000=100%=Physicality=Tech.=10 Oct.=Uranus=P=1Ø.
Mutton=4,500=5,000=50%=P5.00D=Law=Time=Venus=5 May = Aphrodite>>L=N
Mutton chops=5,500=5.5=80%=P5.50=Earth-Midway=5 May = Gaia.
Mutual=10,000=1,000=100%=10.0=Physicality=Tech.=10 Oct.=Uranus=P=1Ø.
Mutual fund=8,500=9,000=90%=P9.00D=9.0=Abstraction=Gods=Saturn=9Sept.>>A=Ø.
Muumuu=10,000=1,000=100%=10.0=Physicality=Tech.=10 Oct.=Uranus=P=1Ø.
Muzak=6,000=60%=P6.0D=Man=Earth=Royalty=6 June=Gaia=Maia>>M=M2.
Muzzle=10,000=1,000=100%=10.0=Physicality=Tech.=10 Oct.=Uranus=P=1Ø.
Muzzleloader=3,500=4,000=40%=P4.0D=Govt.=Cret=4 April=Mercury=Hermes=G=A4.
mV=500=5%=P5.00D=5.0=Law=Time=Venus=5 May=Aphrodite>>L=N.
MV=1,500=15%=P1.50D=1.5=Authority=Solar Crown=1 May = Maia.
MVP=2,000=20%=P2.00D=2.0=Nature=Matter=Moon=2 Feb.=Cupid=N=C+_
mW=500=5%=P5.00D=5.0=Law=Time=Venus=5 May=Aphrodite>>L=N.
MW=500=5%=P5.00D=5.0=Law=Time=Venus=5 May=Aphrodite>>L=N.
My=10,000=1,000=100%=10.0=Physicality=Tech.=10 Oct.=Uranus=P=1Ø.
Myalgia=8,000=80%=P8.0D=Economy=Currency=8 Aug.=Zeus>>E=v.
Myanmar=1,000=100%=10.0=1.0=Mind=Sun=1 January=Helios >> M=E4.
Myasthenia gravis=10,000=1,000=100%=10.0=Physicality=Tech.=10 Oct.=Uranus=P=1Ø.
Mycelium=10,000=1,000=100%=10.0=Physicality=Tech.=10 Oct.=Uranus=P=1Ø.
Mycenae=4,000=40%=P4.0D=Govt.=Creatocracy=4 April=Mercury=Hermes=G=A4.
-mycin=6,500=7,000=70%=P7.0D=7.0=Language=Assets=Mars=7 July=Pleiades.
Myco-=2,000=20%=P2.00D=2.0=Nature=Matter=Moon=2 Feb.=Cupid=N=C+_
Mycology=4,000=40%=P4.0D=Govt.=Creatocracy=4 April=Mercury=Hermes=G=A4.
Mycotoxin=2,500=3,000=30%=P3.0D=3.0=Creativity=Stars=Muses=3 March = C=I>>GIL.
Myelin=5,500=5.5=80%=P5.50=Earth-Midway=5 May = Gaia.
Myelitis=4,000=40%=P4.0D=Govt.=Creatocracy=4 April=Mercury=Hermes=G=A4.
Myelo-=6,500=7,000=70%=P7.0D=7.0=Language=Assets=Mars=7 July=Pleiades.
Myeloma=5,000=50%=P5.00D=Law=Time=Venus=5 May = Aphrodite>>L=N
Myna=8,500=9,000=90%=P9.00D=9.0=Abstraction=Gods=Saturn=9Sept.>>A=Ø.
Myocardium=7,500=8,000=80%=P8.0D=Economy=Currency=8 Aug.=Zeus>>E=v.
Myopia=10,000=1,000=100%=10.0=Physicality=Tech.=10 Oct.=Uranus=P=1Ø.
Myosin=7,500=8,000=80%=P8.0D=Economy=Currency=8 Aug.=Zeus>>E=v.

Myriad=6,500=7,000=70%=P7.0D=7.0=Language=Assets=Mars=7 July=Pleiades.
Greek murias, ten thousand. First ten thousand is the standard for all quantum mechanics. "Myriad and myriad of angels", read Sword of Honour - Days of St. Valentine by African Shakespeare. Also read The Creatocracy Republic of Castle Makupedia by Peter Matthews-Akukalia, reference book > Sword of Honour (reloaded).

Myriapod=10,000=1,000=100%=10.0=Physicality=Tech.=10 Oct.=Uranus=P=1Ø.
Myron=2,500=3,000=30%=P3.0D=3.0=Creativity=Stars=Muses=3 March = C=I>>GIL.
Myrrh=10,000=1,000=100%=10.0=Physicality=Tech.=10 Oct.=Uranus=P=1Ø.
Myrtle=8,000=80%=P8.0D=Economy=Currency=8 Aug.=Zeus>>E=v.
Myself=10,000=1,000=100%=10.0=Physicality=Tech.=10 Oct.=Uranus=P=1Ø.
Mysore=4,500=5,000=50%=P5.00D=Law=Time=Venus=5 May = Aphrodite>>L=N
Mystery=10,000=1,000=100%=10.0=Physicality=Tech.=10 Oct.=Uranus=P=1Ø.
Mystery play=9,000=90%=P9.00D=9.0=Abstraction=Gods=Saturn=9Sept.>>A=Ø.
Mystic=10,000=1,000=100%=10.0=Physicality=Tech.=10 Oct.=Uranus=P=1Ø.
Mystical=5,500=5.5=80%=P5.50=Earth-Midway=5 May = Gaia.
Mysticism=5,000=50%=P5.00D=Law=Time=Venus=5 May = Aphrodite>>L=N
Mystify=4,500=5,000=50%=P5.00D=Law=Time=Venus=5 May = Aphrodite>>L=N

Mystique=8,000=80%=P8.0D=Economy=Currency=8 Aug.=Zeus>>E=v.
An aura of mystery or reverence surrounding a particular person, thing, or idea. Fr.<Lat. mysticus, MYSTIC. Jesus said that man shall not live by bread alone but by every world that comes out of the mouth of GOD. Through this means we become Gods greater than devils or lesser gods. The difference is the Creatocracy of things established through computational precision where we obtain divine lights and gain access to the heavens. Without computational creativity mankind is doomed in ignorance and half knowledge.

Myth=15,000=1,500=15%=P1.50D=1.5=Authority=Solar Crown=1 May = Maia.
All myth is inspired by Maia the Great Goddess known as Gaia of Earth and the Universe. She is the great record keeper of all histories. Revelation talks about books and books in heaven. Even the Revelation book of the Bible and the Bible itself seems a myth yet real.

Castle Makupedia inspired myths supposes that rain are the tears of the Gods at each point they experienced pain at the origin of life.

The first is Gaia, the Mother Earth whose babies were swallowed by Uranus the sky God for fear of being overthrown by any of his children. These tears became bodies of water wherever they dropped and formed the four river heads found in Genesis 2:10-14. The tears of Gaia became the river Pison birthing all mines and minerals signified by gold.

Second is the tears of Uranus when He was castrated and overthrown by Cronus. The tears of Uranus is the river Gihon of Ethiopia birthing Africa. Reason Africa is a rain zone because the hairs of Uranus are clouds and naturally bears rain represented in the Greek mythology.

Clouds are hairs of Uranus that is why Paul counsels they should be shaven or covered at worships before God as they scare the angels who are ministering spirits unto the elects.

Third is the tears of Cronus when He was overthrown by Zeus. The tears of Cronus became the river Hiddekel bearing Assyrians birthing the Middle East.

Fourth is the tears of Rhea who succeeded in saving the life of Zeus who became the Almighty GOD. The tears of Rhea which became the River Euphrates and birthed Asia.

Makupedia classifies this event as the unity and reconciliation by Zeus of all aggrieved parties thus He obtained universal permission to establish His Creation Order and governed by the principles of creativity. What Makupedia calls the Creatocracy of Heaven and Earth.

The four universal Gods on this order are classified as the Quartet Gods from which the concept of the Quartet Principle 1/4th was invented by Castle Makupedia.

In Job 38:31 the Almighty ZeJeAl calls it the ordinances of Heaven. And in verses 34-35 He gives a clue that clouds can hear our voices and lightnings are spirit messengers who will obey him they can number them in wisdom. WDSD is the wisdom of the ordinance of Heaven known collectively as the Creatocracy.

Verse 38 indicates the cell replenishment system and the measurement of a person's lifespan as seen in Genesis 2:7 and measured in the Psychoeconomix by Peter Matthews-Akukalia. Verses 40-41 asks a question. The answer is Artemis, virgin Goddess of the hunt and the moon. Hence the book of Job is just as it sounds. Job as a name and Job as a work occupation or business through which one may earn a living legitimately. The book of Job is the series of duties Heaven has put on ground to test the creativity of man. Only a God can decode the Mind of the Gods.

Apostle Paul counsels that we use the physical things to compare and understand the spiritual things. The Rain Sky are depictions of the pains suffering and tears of the Gods as symbolic by the death of Hermes - the Christ. The Sun Sky are days of their joys especially reconciled by Zeus who laughs and plots the downfalls of His enemies at Council meetings. This is confirmed in Psalm 2:1-4.

Below is the databases of the Rain Sky Days and the Sun Sky days. As required by GOD they are based on WDSD and the daily energy or human energy codes of occurrence. Interestingly the Sun and Rain share same quantum energy code = 10.0 & 10.0

Conventional Science establishes that rain occurs as a result of the evaporation of water caused by the Sun in a water cycle. Hence we shall compute this sequence to establish balance and the ordinance of the heavens, skies and its authorities. Then Godship.

10.0 * 10.0 x=px= 20 + 100 = 120 x=px= 2, 120 = 2.1 >> 3.0 = Creativity >> Stars >> Muses. The ordinance of Heaven is Creativity and its power of superior genius - Creatocracy. Days of its full occurrence are seen below. The Quartet Days shall honor the Quartet Gods.

Pain shall be remembered with a view to reducing and possibly eliminating it through the best possible means available. Pains caused by mental torture associated with creativity, deprivation, emotional starvation, lack of food, hunger, ill-health, childbirth worldwide.

RAIN & SUN SKY DATABASE.

MONTH: JANUARY.
Day 4:Value: 3.0, Planetary Type: Star, Human Type: Creativity, Birth Energy Level: 50.0%
Day 15:Value: 3.0, Planetary Type: Star, Human Type: Creativity, Birth Energy Level: 50%
==

MONTH:FEBRUARY
Day 10:Value: 3.0, Planetary Type:Star, Human Type:Creativity, Birth Energy Level:50.0%
==

MONTH:MARCH
Day 8:Value:3.0, Planetary Type:Star, Human Type:Creativity, Birth Energy Level:50.0%
Day 27:Value:3.0, Planetary Type:Star, Human Type:Creativity, Birth Energy Level:50.0%
Day 28:Value:3.0, Planetary Type:Star, Human Type:Creativity, Birth Energy Level:50.0%
Day 29:Value:3.0, Planetary Type:Star, Human Type:Creativity, Birth Energy Level:50.0%
==

MONTH:APRIL
Day 1:Value:3.0, Planetary Type:Star, Human Type:Creativity, Birth Energy Level:50.0%
Day 6:Value:3.0, Planetary Type:Star, Human Type:Creativity, Birth Energy Level:50.0%
Day 23:Value:3.0, Planetary Type:Star, Human Type:Creativity, Birth Energy Level:50.0%
Day 24:Value:3.0, Planetary Type:Star, Human Type:Creativity,Birth Energy Level:50.0%
Day 25: Value:3.0, Planetary Type:Star, Human Type: Creativity, Birth Energy Level:50.0%
==

MONTH: MAY
Day 5:Value:3.0, Planetary Type:Star, Human Type:Creativity, Birth Energy Level:50.0%
Day 20:Value:3.0, Planetary Type:Star, Human Type:Creativity, Birth Energy Level:50.0%
Day 21:Value:3.0, Planetary Type:Star, Human Type:Creativity, Birth Energy Level:50.0%
==

MONTH:JUNE.
Day 4:Value:3.0 Planetary Type:Star Human Type:Creativity Birth Energy Level:50.0%
Day 17:Value:3.0 Planetary Type:Star Human Type:Creativity Birth Energy Level:50.0%
Day 18:Value:3.0 Planetary Type:Star Human Type:Creativity Birth Energy Level:33.3%
Day 19:Value:3.0 Planetary Type:Star Human Type:Creativity Birth Energy Level:50.0%
==

MONTH:JULY
Day 16:Value:3.0 Planetary Type:Star Human Type:Creativity Birth Energy Level:50.0%
Day 17:Value:3.0 Planetary Type:Star Human Type:Creativity Birth Energy Level:50.0%
==

MONTH:AUGUST
Day 3:Value:3.0 Planetary Type:Star Human Type:Creativity Birth Energy Level:50.0%
Day 14:Value:3.0 Planetary Type:Star Human Type:Creativity Birth Energy Level:50.0%
Day 15:Value:3.0 Planetary Type:Star Human Type:Creativity Birth Energy Level:50.0%
==

MONTH:SEPTEMBER
Day 13:Value:3.0 Planetary Type:Star Human Type:Creativity Birth Energy Level:50.0%
==
MONTH:OCTOBER
Day 2:Value:3.0 Planetary Type:Star Human Type:Creativity Birth Energy Level:50.0%
==
MONTH:NOVEMBER
Day 11:Value:3.0 Planetary Type:Star Human Type:Creativity Birth Energy Level:50.0%
==
MONTH:DECEMBER
Day 10:Value:3.0 Planetary Type:Star Human Type:Creativity Birth Energy Level:50.0%
==

Myths are so - called because they have not being proved. Now that Castle Makupedia has proven them by computational precision they are Castle Makupedia mythological truths.

Myth maker=3,500=4,000=40%=P4.0D=Govt.=Creatocracy=4 April=Hermes=G=A4.
Myths are inspired to man in bits (500) by the muses as a means to reach our potentials.

Mythology=9,000=90%=P9.00D=9.0=Abstraction=Gods=Saturn=9Sept.>>A=Ø.
Deals with the Gods. Alignment. Truth is established as a body of myths about the origin, history, deities, ancestors, and heroes of a people. The result confirms a cycle of life guided by the peak of aspirations. Based on human deeds heroes become ancestors and then deities. Hence the apotheosis of Peter Matthews-Akukalia as Castle Makupedia, hero of the encyclopedia of the Creative & Psycho-Social Sciences. Ancestor of the Creatocratic Nations of Paradise (Paradise Nations). God of Creatocracy Genius and Mind. Peter Matthews-Akukalia, Castle Makupedia has successfully solved the mysteries behind the Greek mythologies and their realities to the present and future of mankind. He has linked it to the scriptures and thus discovered GOD and the Gods thus becoming a God by the laws.

MAKABET =Nn=

---

n1=3,000=30%=P3.0D=3.0=Creativity=Stars=Muses=3 March = C=I>>GIL.
The 14th letter of the English alphabet. First 14 indicates Athena's management. Hence the concept of management is sourced from above as a proof of wisdom. In Proverbs 8, 9 she talks about money council systems pillars of castles which are real estates, all signs of Paradise. N is her muse a star that helps her manifest and inspires to do great works. 3.0*1.4=p=4.4+4.2=8.6x=px=27.08=30=3.0. There is a link of the spirit of Athena in Psalm 8 >> 08. Verse 1 "excellent" indicates invention see Job 40:10. Verse 2 shows her motherly nature aligned with the Greek mythologies of fostering sins to become heroes. Verse 3 she is a writer and loves writing. She uses the pen to manage things which indicates that the finger of GOD used to write the Ten Commandments was Athena. She is also the Spirit

of GOD seen in the creation story of Genesis 1:1-2. Verse 4 >> she designed the concept called man and in fact she instilled the human mind man. Greek myth teaches that she is the brain of Zeus the almighty Jehovah Allah who was born as a mature Goddess. She is called the Brainchild. She is also interested in getting married to the man who measures the human mind as she is a Virgin Goddess in whom is the depth and riches of GOD. Castle Makupedia has done it. Verse 5 is the condition that the one who will achieve the feats of the mind through faculty and knowledge being the Faculty of Creative & Psycho-Social Sciences will be crowned with glory and Honour. Hence Peter Matthews-Akukalia De - Castle Makupedia is the God of Creatocracy Genius and Mind. The wearer of the Solar Crown and only one with the power of the stars in his hands predicted by Nostradamus.

Verse 6 is established because Peter Matthews-Akukalia is the owner of the solar core assets by rights and law because he discovered the solar core and computer the mind. All things are therefore asserted to be under him as the Mind God. Verse 7 shows he will own all things by rights and by sacrifice of the cattle will become apotheosized to Godship. The maiden edition of Feast of Apotheosis was held on 13th October 2021 in Ikotun, Lagos. Nigeria. Verse 8 indicates he understands mysteries how energy links matter. Verse 9 he will be exalted in all the earth because he is the incarnation of Zeus Jehovah Allah.

---

n2=3,500=4,000=40%=P4.0D=Govt.=Creatocracy=4 April=Mercury=Hermes=G=A4.
N1=3,500=4,000=40%=P4.0D=Govt.=Creatocracy=4 April=Mercury=Hermes=G=A4.
N2=5,500=5.5=80%=P5.50=Earth-Midway=5 May = Gaia.
n.=4,000=40%=P4.0D=Govt.=Creatocracy=4 April=Mercury=Hermes=G=A4.
Na=5,500=5.5=80%=P5.50=Earth-Midway=5 May = Gaia.
N.A.=3,000=30%=P3.0D=3.0=Creativity=Stars=Muses=3 March = C=I>>GIL.
NAACP=4,000=40%=P4.0D=Govt.=Creatocracy=4 April=Mercury=Hermes=G=A4.
Nab=5,000=50%=P5.00D=Law=Time=Venus=5 May = Aphrodite>>L=N.
Nabatea=4,500=5,000=50%=P5.00D=Law=Time=Venus=5 May = Aphrodite>>L=N.
Nabob=4,500=5,000=50%=P5.00D=Law=Time=Venus=5 May = Aphrodite>>L=N.
Nabokov Vladmir=3,500=4,000=40%=P4.0D=Govt.=Cre=4 April=Hermes=G=A4.
Nacelle=7,500=8,000=80%=P8.0D=Economy=Currency=8 Aug.=Zeus>>E=v.
Nacho=7,500=8,000=80%=P8.0D=Economy=Currency=8 Aug.=Zeus>>E=v.
Nacre=3,500=4,000=40%=P4.0D=Govt.=Creatocracy=4 April=Mercury=Hermes=G=A4.
Na-Dene=5,000=50%=P5.00D=Law=Time=Venus=5 May = Aphrodite>>L=N.
Nadir=7,000=70%=P7.0D=7.0=Language=Assets=Mars=7 July=Pleiades.
Nag1=10,000=1,000=100%=10.0=Physicality=Tech.=10 Oct.=Uranus=P=1Ø.
Nag2=5,500=5.5=80%=P5.50=Earth-Midway=5 May = Gaia.
Nagasaki=9,000=90%=P9.00D=9.0=Abstraction=Gods=Saturn=9Sept.>>A=Ø.
Nagoya=5,000=50%=P5.00D=Law=Time=Venus=5 May = Aphrodite>>L=N.
Nahuatl=8,000=80%=P8.0D=Economy=Currency=8 Aug.=Zeus>>E=v.

Nahum=8,000=80%=P8.0D=Economy=Currency=8 Aug.=Zeus>>E=v.
A Hebrew prophet of the 7th cent. B.C. who predicted the fall of Nineveh. First the book is inspired by Zeus Jehovah Allah the almighty GOD. Nahum is the incarnation of the

Zeus as result shows. A sign of Zeus is the 7 code indicating the presence of Maia and Pleiades who must have guided his incarnation existence through the process. Job 38:31. Computing 8.0*7.0x=px=15+56=71x=px=911 = 9.11 >> Council of Gods & Muses managed by Athena. Clearly the Spirit of God inspired it in the person - Godship of Athena. Do not forget that Jonah had a direct encounter with GOD on the concerns of Nineveh. In Proverbs 8 Athena Goddess of wisdom states clearly that the council is with Her.

Nail=10,000=1,000=100%=10.0=Physicality=Tech.=10 Oct.=Uranus=P=1Ø.

Naira=3,500=4,000=40%=P4.0D=Govt.=Creatocracy=4 April=Mercury=Hermes=G=A4. Naira is a fiat currency like every other and weighs barely 35% on the 100% standards not to talk of the 1,000 standards. It is a means to attain power and the political class. It is just a means to an end and not an end in itself. On the world currency scale it weighs 3.5 = 0.35. This means that 0.35 kobos = 35k =N1.00 rather than speculated 100k=N1.00 10 See Dollar. A key breakthrough in the currency management systems of the Creatocracy is interest deductions that never extends beyond two fractional digits. Interests are based on the currency denominated codes inscribed on it multiplied by the number of units issued. Naira>> Obafemi Awolowo named the Naira. Peter Matthews-Akukalia invented the Maks and integrated the Nairamaks under the principles of integrative consciousness. The expressed code is =NP=, =NM=>>M for Makumatics. (See Template & Manifesto for the Creative Economy, Principles of Psychoeconomix; Instinct Optimization & Philosophy). The Maks can also be integrated into existing currencies based on ownership rights and licensing such as Nairamaks, Dollarmaks if adopted in the Nation or country. The Maks is the First Global Exchange Storage Anti-inflation Solar Core Diamond Currency System.

Nairobi=5,000=50%=P5.00D=Law=Time=Venus=5 May = Aphrodite>>L=N.
Naive=5,000=50%=P5.00D=Law=Time=Venus=5 May = Aphrodite>>L=N.
Naïveté=5,500=5.5=80%=P5.50=Earth-Midway=5 May = Gaia.
Naked=8,500=9,000=90%=P9.00D=9.0=Abstraction=Gods=Saturn=9Sept.>>A=Ø.
Naked eye=3,500=4,000=40%=P4.0D=Govt.=Creatocracy=4 April=Hermes=G=A4.
Namby-panby=9,500=10,000=1,000=100%=10.0=Phys.=Tech.=10 Oct.=Uranus=P=1Ø.

Name=10,000=1,000=100%=10.0=Physicality=Tech.=10 Oct.=Uranus=P=1Ø.
Peter Matthews-Akukalia successfully decoded the energy secrets and destiny in a name. Result indicates that names are software technologies or Mind wares known through abstraction. Peter Matthews-Akukalia tracked the link between names phone numbers and planetary energy thus he can predict the energy cycle fluxes that surround the bearer in person or business or things. Names are real things. We are what we bear as our oaths.

Name day=5,000=50%=P5.00D=Law=Time=Venus=5 May = Aphrodite>>L=N.
Name-drop=7,500=8,000=80%=P8.0D=Economy=Currency=8 Aug.=Zeus>>E=v.
Nameless=7,500=8,000=80%=P8.0D=Economy=Currency=8 Aug.=Zeus>>E=v.

Namely=2,500=3,000=30%=P3.0D=3.0=Creativity=Stars=Muses=3 March = C=I>>GIL.
Namesake=3,000=30%=P3.0D=3.0=Creativity=Stars=Muses=3 March = C=I>>GIL.
Namibia=6,000=60%=P6.0D=Man=Earth=Royalty=6 June=Gaia=Maia>>M=M2.
Nanchang=4,500=5,000=50%=P5.00D=Law=Time=Venus=5 May = Aphrodite>>L=N.
Nanga Parbat=6,000=60%=P6.0D=Man=Earth=Royalty=6 June=Gaia=Maia>>M=M2.
Nanjing=7,000=70%=P7.0D=7.0=Language=Assets=Mars=7 July=Pleiades.
Nankeen=4,000=40%=P4.0D=Govt.=Creatocracy=4 April=Mercury=Hermes=G=A4.
Nanny=3,000=30%=P3.0D=3.0=Creativity=Stars=Muses=3 March = C=I>>GIL.
Nanny goat=3,500=4,000=40%=P4.0D=Govt.=Creatocracy=4 April=Hermes=G=A4.

Nano-=3,500=4,000=40%=P4.0D=Govt.=Creatocracy=4 April=Mercury=Hermes=G=A4.
One billionth (10 raised to power 9). Nanosecond. Greek, nanos, dwarf.

Nanosecond=3,000=30%=P3.0D=3.0=Creativity=Stars=Muses=3 March = C=I>>GIL.
Nansen Fridtjot=5,500=5.5=80%=P5.50=Earth-Midway=5 May = Gaia.
Nantucket=5,500=5.5=80%=P5.50=Earth-Midway=5 May = Gaia.
Nap1=10,000=1,000=100%=10.0=Physicality=Tech.=10 Oct.=Uranus=P=1Ø.
Nap2=5,000=50%=P5.00D=Law=Time=Venus=5 May = Aphrodite>>L=N.
Napalm=8,000=80%=P8.0D=Economy=Currency=8 Aug.=Zeus>>E=v.
Nape=2,500=3,000=30%=P3.0D=3.0=Creativity=Stars=Muses=3 March = C=I>>GIL.
Napery=4,000=40%=P4.0D=Govt.=Creatocracy=4 April=Mercury=Hermes=G=A4.
Naphtha=10,000=1,000=100%=10.0=Physicality=Tech.=10 Oct.=Uranus=P=1Ø.
Naphthalene=10,000=1,000=100%=10.0=Physicality=Tech.=10 Oct.=Uranus=P=1Ø.
Napier John=2,000=20%=P2.00D=2.0=Nature=Matter=Moon=2 Feb.=Cupid=N=C+_
Napkin=10,000=1,000=100%=10.0=Physicality=Tech.=10 Oct.=Uranus=P=1Ø.
Naples=8,500=9,000=90%=P9.00D=9.0=Abstraction=Gods=Saturn=9Sept.>>A=Ø.
Napoleon I=5,000=50%=P5.00D=Law=Time=Venus=5 May = Aphrodite>>L=N.
Napoleon III=6,000=60%=P6.0D=Man=Earth=Royalty=6 June=Gaia=Maia>>M=M2.
Narc=2,000=20%=P2.00D=2.0=Nature=Matter=Moon=2 Feb.=Cupid=N=C+_
Narcissism=5,500=5.5=80%=P5.50=Earth-Midway=5 May = Gaia.
Narcissus=7,000=70%=P7.0D=7.0=Language=Assets=Mars=7 July=Pleiades.

Narcissus=10,500=11,000=11%=P1.10D=1.1=Idea=Brainchild=Inv.=11 Nov.=Athena>>I=MT.
Greek myth. A youth who fell in love with his own image in a pool of water and was
transformed into a flower. The secret here is that pools of water either for bathing or any
purpose are highly magical and miraculous because they are access to the spirit world.
Hence we must make prayers using pool of water after which the purpose is served. It
aligns with religious teachings of both Christianity and Islam. Results indicate it is a
physical means to access and assess Athena the Goddess of wisdom handicraft and mind.

Narcolepsy=10,000=1,000=100%=10.0=Physicality=Tech.=10 Oct.=Uranus=P=1Ø.
Narcosis=6,000=60%=P6.0D=Man=Earth=Royalty=6 June=Gaia=Maia>>M=M2.
Narcotic=9,500=10,000=1,000=100%=10.0=Physicality=Tech.=10 Oct.=Uranus=P=1Ø.

Narcotism=2,000=20%=P2.00D=2.0=Nature=Matter=Moon=2 Feb.=Cupid=N=C+_
Narcotize=6,500=7,000=70%=P7.0D=7.0=Language=Assets=Mars=7 July=Pleiades.
Nard=2,000=20%=P2.00D=2.0=Nature=Matter=Moon=2 Feb.=Cupid=N=C+_
Narragansett=7,000=70%=P7.0D=7.0=Language=Assets=Mars=7 July=Pleiades.
Narragansett Bay=9,500=10,000=1,000=100%=10.0=Phy.=Tech.=10 Oct.=Uranus=P=1Ø.
Narrate=10,000=1,000=100%=10.0=Physicality=Tech.=10 Oct.=Uranus=P=1Ø.
Narrative=5,000=50%=P5.00D=Law=Time=Venus=5 May = Aphrodite>>L=N.
Narrow=10,000=1,000=100%=10.0=Physicality=Tech.=10 Oct.=Uranus=P=1Ø.
Narrow-minded=3,500=4,000=40%=P4.0D=Govt.=Creatocracy=4 April=Hermes=G=A4.
Narthex=5,500=5.5=80%=P5.50=Earth-Midway=5 May = Gaia.
Narwhal=8,000=80%=P8.0D=Economy=Currency=8 Aug.=Zeus>>E=v.
Nary=1,000=100%=10.0=1.0=Mind=Sun=1 January=Helios >> M=E4.
NASA=2,500=3,000=30%=P3.0D=3.0=Creativity=Stars=Muses=3 March = C=I>>GIL.
Nasal=10,000=1,000=100%=10.0=Physicality=Tech.=10 Oct.=Uranus=P=1Ø.
Nascent=4,000=40%=P4.0D=Govt.=Creatocracy=4 April=Mercury=Hermes=G=A4.
Nash Ogden.=2,000=20%=P2.00D=2.0=Nature=Matter=Moon=2 Feb.=Cupid=N=C+_
Nashua=4,500=5,000=50%=P5.00D=Law=Time=Venus=5 May = Aphrodite>>L=N.
Nashville=6,000=60%=P6.0D=Man=Earth=Royalty=6 June=Gaia=Maia>>M=M2.
Nassau=6,000=60%=P6.0D=Man=Earth=Royalty=6 June=Gaia=Maia>>M=M2.
Nasser Gamal=2,500=3,000=30%=P3.0D=3.0=Cre.=Stars=Muses=3 March = C=I>>GIL.
Nasturtium=10,000=1,000=100%=10.0=Physicality=Tech.=10 Oct.=Uranus=P=1Ø.
Nasty=10,000=1,000=100%=10.0=Physicality=Tech.=10 Oct.=Uranus=P=1Ø.
Natal=8,000=80%=P8.0D=Economy=Currency=8 Aug.=Zeus>>E=v.
Natality=1,000=100%=10.0=1.0=Mind=Sun=1 January=Helios >> M=E4.
Natchez=10,000=1,000=100%=10.0=Physicality=Tech.=10 Oct.=Uranus=P=1Ø.
Natick=2,000=20%=P2.00D=2.0=Nature=Matter=Moon=2 Feb.=Cupid=N=C+_

Nation=9,500=10,000=1,000=100%=10.0=Physicality=Tech.=10 Oct.=Uranus=P=1Ø.
Peter Matthews-Akukalia created the Paradise Nations >> Creatocratic Nations of Paradise >> Paradiseans >> a nation of Creative Scientist Professionals from the invention of Creative & Psycho-Social Sciences on the order of the Royal Makupedia. The Paradiseans practice the independent system of government called the Creatocracy-MindTech Nation.

Nation Amelia=3,500=4,000=40%=P4.0D=Govt.=Creatocracy=4 April=Hermes=G=A4.
National=10,000=1,000=100%=10.0=Physicality=Tech.=10 Oct.=Uranus=P=1Ø.
National Guard=10,000=1,000=100%=10.0=Physicality=Tech.=10 Oct.=Uranus=P=1Ø.
Nationalism=10,000=1,000=100%=10.0=Physicality=Tech.=10 Oct.=Uranus=P=1Ø.
Nationality=10,000=1,000=100%=10.0=Physicality=Tech.=10 Oct.=Uranus=P=1Ø.
Nationalize=10,000=1,000=100%=10.0=Physicality=Tech.=10 Oct.=Uranus=P=1Ø.
National monument=7,500=8,000=80%=P8.0D=Economy=Currency=8 Aug.=Zeus>>E=v.
National park=7,000=70%=P7.0D=7.0=Language=Assets=Mars=7 July=Pleiades.
Nationwide=2,000=20%=P2.00D=2.0=Nature=Matter=Moon=2 Feb.=Cupid=N=C+_
Native=10,000=1,000=100%=10.0=Physicality=Tech.=10 Oct.=Uranus=P=1Ø.
Native American=10,000=1,000=100%=10.0=Physicality=Tech.=10 Oct.=Uranus=P=1Ø.

Nativity=7,500=8,000=80%=P8.0D=Economy=Currency=8 Aug.=Zeus>>E=v.
natl.=500=5%=P5.00D=5.0=Law=Time=Venus=5 May=Aphrodite>>L=N.
NATO=2,000=20%=P2.00D=2.0=Nature=Matter=Moon=2 Feb.=Cupid=N=C+_
Natty=4,500=5,000=50%=P5.00D=Law=Time=Venus=5 May = Aphrodite>>L=N.

Natural=10,000=1,000=100%=10.0=Physicality=Tech.=10 Oct.=Uranus=P=1Ø.
All natural matters are measured in the quantum Maks of 10,000=1,000=100=10 meaning that fiat in currencies is against the law of nature. There is nothing as 100=1.0 see dollar.

Natural gas=8,000=80%=P8.0D=Economy=Currency=8 Aug.=Zeus>>E=v.
Natural history=6,500=7,000=70%=P7.0D=7.0=Language=Assets=Mars=7 July=Pleiades.
Naturalism=11,000=11%=P1.10D=1.1=Idea=Brainchild=Inv.=11 Nov.=SC=Athena>>I=MT.
Naturalist=7,000=70%=P7.0D=7.0=Language=Assets=Mars=7 July=Pleiades.
Naturalistic=1,000=100%=Physicality=Tech.=10 Oct.=Uranus=P=1Ø.
Naturalize=9,000=90%=P9.00D=9.0=Abstraction=Gods=Saturn=9Sept.>>A=Ø.
Naturally=5,500=5.5=80%=P5.50=Earth-Midway=5 May = Gaia.
Natural resource=8,000=80%=P8.0D=Economy=Currency=8 Aug.=Zeus>>E=v.
Natural science=11,000=11%=P1.10D=1.1=Idea=Brainchild=Inv.=11 Nov.=Athena>>I=MT.
Natural selection=12,000=12%=P1.20D=1.2=Knowledge=Edu=12Dec.=Athena>>K=F.

Nature=10,000=1,000=100%=10.0=Physicality=Tech.=10 Oct.=Uranus=P=1Ø.
Nature is a technology and the study of the technology of nature is called Naturecology. The third in the Castle Makupedia Sciences series. Peter Matthews-Akukalia, Castle Makupedia discovered that Nature is the abstract word or equivalence for the Moon. It contains the PGI an operating central energy that pulls all things matter and technique together and subject to the Sun. See Castle Makupedia Sciences: Principles of Naturecology by Peter Matthews-Akukalia. Also See Natural.

Naturopathy=10,000=1,000=100%=10.0=Physicality=Tech.=10 Oct.=Uranus=P=1Ø.
Naught=5,500=5.5=80%=P5.50=Earth-Midway=5 May = Gaia.
Naughty=2,000=20%=P2.00D=2.0=Nature=Matter=Moon=2 Feb.=Cupid=N=C+_
Nauru=8,000=80%=P8.0D=Economy=Currency=8 Aug.=Zeus>>E=v.
Nausea=9,500=10,000=1,000=100%=10.0=Physicality=Tech.=10 Oct.=Uranus=P=1Ø.
Nauseate=4,500=5,000=50%=P5.00D=Law=Time=Venus=5 May = Aphrodite>>L=N.
Nauseous=3,000=30%=P3.0D=3.0=Creativity=Stars=Muses=3 March = C=I>>GIL.
Nautical=8,000=80%=P8.0D=Economy=Currency=8 Aug.=Zeus>>E=v.
Nautical mile=9,000=90%=P9.00D=9.0=Abstraction=Gods=Saturn=9Sept.>>A=Ø.
Nautilus=5,000=50%=P5.00D=Law=Time=Venus=5 May = Aphrodite>>L=N.
Navajo=10,000=1,000=100%=10.0=Physicality=Tech.=10 Oct.=Uranus=P=1Ø.
Naval=6,500=7,000=70%=P7.0D=7.0=Language=Assets=Mars=7 July=Pleiades.
Navarre=7,000=70%=P7.0D=7.0=Language=Assets=Mars=7 July=Pleiades.
Nave=4,500=5,000=50%=P5.00D=Law=Time=Venus=5 May = Aphrodite>>L=N.
Navel=7,500=8,000=80%=P8.0D=Economy=Currency=8 Aug.=Zeus>>E=v.

Navel orange=7,000=70%=P7.0D=7.0=Language=Assets=Mars=7 July=Pleiades.
Navigable=6,500=7,000=70%=P7.0D=7.0=Language=Assets=Mars=7 July=Pleiades.
Navigate=14,000=14%=P1.40D=1.4=Mgt.=Solar Energy=13 May=Athena=SC=0.1

Navy=9,000=90%=P9.00D=9.0=Abstraction=Gods=Saturn=9Sept.>>A=Ø.
The council of muses organization for sea warfare and defense is called the Creatocratic Navy, Creatovy, Tovy. The Tovy is the marine warfare mechanism of Athena.

Navy bean=6,000=60%=P6.0D=Man=Earth=Royalty=6 June=Gaia=Maia>>M=M2.
Navy blue=5,500=5.5=80%=P5.50=Earth-Midway=5 May = Gaia.

Nay=10,000=1,000=100%=10.0=Physicality=Tech.=10 Oct.=Uranus=P=1Ø.
Jesus teaches let your yea be yea and your nay nay meaning be precise. Precision is key. Anything that is not provable cannot be established as truth nor can it be a standard.

Nazareth=4,500=5,000=50%=P5.00D=Law=Time=Venus=5 May = Aphrodite>>L=N.
Nazi=8,500=9,000=90%=P9.00D=9.0=Abstraction=Gods=Saturn=9Sept.>>A=Ø.
Nb=2,500=3,000=30%=P3.0D=3.0=Creativity=Stars=Muses=3 March = C=I>>GIL.
NB=1,000=100%=10.0=1.0=Mind=Sun=1 January=Helios >> M=E4.
n.b.=1,000=100%=10.0=1.0=Mind=Sun=1 January=Helios >> M=E4.
NBA=1,500=15%=P1.50D=1.5=Authority=Solar Crown=1 May = Maia.
Nbe=1,500=15%=P1.50D=1.5=Authority=Solar Crown=1 May = Maia.
Nbw=1,500=15%=P1.50D=1.5=Authority=Solar Crown=1 May = Maia.
NC=3,000=30%=P3.0D=3.0=Creativity=Stars=Muses=3 March = C=I>>GIL.
NCAA=2,000=20%=P2.00D=2.0=Nature=Matter=Moon=2 Feb.=Cupid=N=C+_
NCC=2,000=20%=P2.00D=2.0=Nature=Matter=Moon=2 Feb.=Cupid=N=C+_
NCO=1,000=100%=10.0=1.0=Mind=Sun=1 January=Helios >> M=E4.
Nd=2,500=3,000=30%=P3.0D=3.0=Creativity=Stars=Muses=3 March = C=I>>GIL.
ND=1,000=100%=10.0=1.0=Mind=Sun=1 January=Helios >> M=E4.
n.d.=1,000=100%=10.0=1.0=Mind=Sun=1 January=Helios >> M=E4.
N'djamena=4,500=5,000=50%=P5.00D=Law=Time=Venus=5 May = Aphrodite>>L=N.
Ndola=4,500=5,000=50%=P5.00D=Law=Time=Venus=5 May = Aphrodite>>L=N.
Ne=2,500=3,000=30%=P3.0D=3.0=Creativity=Stars=Muses=3 March = C=I>>GIL.
NE=3,500=4,000=40%=P4.0D=Govt.=Creatocracy=4 April=Mercury=Hermes=G=A4.
NEA=3,500=4,000=40%=P4.0D=Govt.=Creatocracy=4 April=Mercury=Hermes=G=A4.
Neanderthal=8,000=80%=P8.0D=Economy=Currency=8 Aug.=Zeus>>E=v.
Neap tide=4,500=5,000=50%=P5.00D=Law=Time=Venus=5 May = Aphrodite>>L=N.
Near=10,000=1,000=100%=10.0=Physicality=Tech.=10 Oct.=Uranus=P=1Ø.
Nearby=6,000=60%=P6.0D=Man=Earth=Royalty=6 June=Gaia=Maia>>M=M2.
Near East=10,000=1,000=100%=10.0=Physicality=Tech.=10 Oct.=Uranus=P=1Ø.
Nearly=2,000=20%=P2.00D=2.0=Nature=Matter=Moon=2 Feb.=Cupid=N=C+_
Nearsighted=4,000=40%=P4.0D=Govt.=Creatocracy=4 April=Mercury=Hermes=G=A4.
Neat=10,000=1,000=100%=10.0=Physicality=Tech.=10 Oct.=Uranus=P=1Ø.

Neaten=2,500=3,000=30%=P3.0D=3.0=Creativity=Stars=Muses=3 March = C=I>>GIL.
Neath=500=5%=P5.00D=5.0=Law=Time=Venus=5 May=Aphrodite>>L=N.
Neath's-foot oil=10,000=1,000=100%=Physicality=Tech.=10 Oct.=Uranus=P=1Ø.
Neb=5,000=50%=P5.00D=Law=Time=Venus=5 May = Aphrodite>>L=N.
Nebbish=4,500=5,000=50%=P5.00D=Law=Time=Venus=5 May = Aphrodite>>L=N.
NEbE=1,500=15%=P1.50D=1.5=Authority=Solar Crown=1 May = Maia.
NEbN=1,500=15%=P1.50D=1.5=Authority=Solar Crown=1 May = Maia.
Nebraska=6,500=7,000=70%=P7.0D=7.0=Language=Assets=Mars=7 July=Pleiades.
Nebuchadnezzar II=4,500=5,000=50%=P5.00D=Law=Time=Venus=5 May =Odite>>L=N.
Nebula=6,500=7,000=70%=P7.0D=7.0=Language=Assets=Mars=7 July=Pleiades.
Nebulize=4,000=40%=P4.0D=Govt.=Creatocracy=4 April=Mercury=Hermes=G=A4.
Nebulosity=4,500=5,000=50%=P5.00D=Law=Time=Venus=5 May = Aphrodite>>L=N.
Nebulous=6,500=7,000=70%=P7.0D=7.0=Language=Assets=Mars=7 July=Pleiades.
Necessarily=1,500=15%=P1.50D=1.5=Authority=Solar Crown=1 May = Maia.
Necessary=10,000=1,000=100%=10.0=Physicality=Tech.=10 Oct.=Uranus=P=1Ø.
Necessitate=2,500=3,000=30%=P3.0D=3.0=Cre=Stars=Muses=3 March = C=I>>GIL.
Necessitous=1,500=15%=P1.50D=1.5=Authority=Solar Crown=1 May = Maia.
Necessity=10,000=1,000=100%=10.0=Physicality=Tech.=10 Oct.=Uranus=P=1Ø.
Neck=10,000=1,000=100%=10.0=Physicality=Tech.=10 Oct.=Uranus=P=1Ø.
Neckerchief=3,000=30%=P3.0D=3.0=Creativity=Stars=Muses=3 March = C=I>>GIL.
Necklace=3,000=30%=P3.0D=3.0=Creativity=Stars=Muses=3 March = C=I>>GIL.
Neckline=5,000=50%=P5.00D=Law=Time=Venus=5 May = Aphrodite>>L=N.
Necktie=9,000=90%=P9.00D=9.0=Abstraction=Gods=Saturn=9Sept.>>A=Ø.
Necro-=3,500=4,000=40%=P4.0D=Govt.=Creatocracy=4 April=Mercury=Hermes=G=A4.
Necrology=7,000=70%=P7.0D=7.0=Language=Assets=Mars=7 July=Pleiades.
Necromancy=10,000=1,000=100%=10.0=Physicality=Tech.=10 Oct.=Uranus=P=1Ø.
Necropolis=10,000=1,000=100%=10.0=Physicality=Tech.=10 Oct.=Uranus=P=1Ø.
Necropolis=4,500=5,000=50%=P5.00D=Law=Time=Venus=5 May = Aphrodite>>L=N.
Necrosis=4,000=40%=P4.0D=Govt.=Creatocracy=4 April=Mercury=Hermes=G=A4.
Nectar=10,000=1,000=100%=10.0=Physicality=Tech.=10 Oct.=Uranus=P=1Ø.
Nectarine=6,500=7,000=70%=P7.0D=7.0=Language=Assets=Mars=7 July=Pleiades.
Née=4,500=5,000=50%=P5.00D=Law=Time=Venus=5 May = Aphrodite>>L=N.
Need=10,000=1,000=100%=10.0=Physicality=Tech.=10 Oct.=Uranus=P=1Ø.
Needful=3,000=30%=P3.0D=3.0=Creativity=Stars=Muses=3 March = C=I>>GIL.
Needle=10,000=1,000=100%=10.0=Physicality=Tech.=10 Oct.=Uranus=P=1Ø.
Needlepoint=2,000=20%=P2.00D=2.0=Nature=Matter=Moon=2 Feb.=Cupid=N=C+_
Needless=3,000=30%=P3.0D=3.0=Creativity=Stars=Muses=3 March = C=I>>GIL.
Needn't=1,000=100%=10.0=1.0=Mind=Sun=1 January=Helios >> M=E4.
Needs=4,500=5,000=50%=P5.00D=Law=Time=Venus=5 May = Aphrodite>>L=N.
Needy=2,000=20%=P2.00D=2.0=Nature=Matter=Moon=2 Feb.=Cupid=N=C+_
Ne'er=500=5%=P5.00D=5.0=Law=Time=Venus=5 May=Aphrodite>>L=N.
Ne'er-do-well=2,000=20%=P2.00D=2.0=Nature=Matter=Moon=2 Feb.=Cupid=N=C+_
Nefarious=500=5%=P5.00D=5.0=Law=Time=Venus=5 May=Aphrodite>>L=N.

Nefertiti=5,000=50%=P5.00D=Law=Time=Venus=5 May = Aphrodite>>L=N.
An incarnation of Aphrodite supposedly. She was the Queen of Egypt as the wife of Akhenaton. 14th cent B.C. Normally 14>>Management under Athena. Computing for precision>>1.4*5.0x=px=6.4+7=13.4x=px=58.2=60=6.0 >> Gaia. So the real incarnate was Gaia who brought law through Aphrodite and established management through Athena's wisdom. A close study of her husband Akhenaton online writes thus. "Egyptian pharaoh of the 18th dynasty. Reigned 1379-1362B.C. Came to the throne as Amenhotep IV. He renounced polytheism introducing a monotheistic cult based on worship of the sun disk, Aten, in whose honour he changed his name. The husband of Nefertiti he moved the capital from Thebes to the newly built city of Akhetaten. The empire began to disintegrate during his reign". We see a story that aligns with the wit of computational creativity. First there is the case of polytheism the worship of more than one God. We see three deities here being Aphrodite, Gaia and then Athena. Then in a certain struggle for control Athena wins. The result is the abolishment of polytheism which naturally will get the others annoyed. He introduces a single worship of Athena and perhaps by inspiration takes on a name that fits the perceived sound as hers Aten >>Athena whom we already know is the Goddess of the Solar Core 0.1 or the Sun disk. However there are two eras at conflict being that of Nefertiti 14th and Maia's the Great Goddess of 18th century. Naturally she is the mother of all mothers and takes back the era. Then everyone refuses to get involved since there is no truce and the empire falls apart. Maia could not have saved the situation because there were no rights earned by the pharaoh since precision was not established yet. The Gods hate speculations even in the face of religion. Faith is the answer and the proof of real faith is the works of righteousness, rights through precision and creativity.

Neg.=500=5%=P5.00D=5.0=Law=Time=Venus=5 May=Aphrodite>>L=N.
Negate=8,000=80%=P8.0D=Economy=Currency=8 Aug.=Zeus>>E=v.
Negative=10,000=1,000=100%=10.0=Physicality=Tech.=10 Oct.=Uranus=P=1Ø.
Negativism=6,500=7,000=70%=P7.0D=7.0=Language=Assets=Mars=7 July=Pleiades.
Negev=3,500=4,000=40%=P4.0D=Govt.=Creatocracy=4 April=Mercury=Hermes=G=A4.
Neglect=10,000=1,000=100%=10.0=Physicality=Tech.=10 Oct.=Uranus=P=1Ø.
Neglectful=3,500=4,000=40%=P4.0D=Govt.=Creatocracy=4 April=Hermes=G=A4.
Negligee=3,500=4,000=40%=P4.0D=Govt.=Creatocracy=4 April=Hermes=G=A4.
Negligence=9,000=90%=P9.00D=9.0=Abstraction=Gods=Saturn=9Sept.>>A=Ø.
Negligent=10,000=1,000=100%=10.0=Physicality=Tech.=10 Oct.=Uranus=P=1Ø.
Negligible=2,000=20%=P2.00D=2.0=Nature=Matter=Moon=2 Feb.=Cupid=N=C+_
Negotiable=8,000=80%=P8.0D=Economy=Currency=8 Aug.=Zeus>>E=v.
Negotiate=10,000=1,000=100%=10.0=Physicality=Tech.=10 Oct.=Uranus=P=1Ø.
Negress=10,000=1,000=100%=10.0=Physicality=Tech.=10 Oct.=Uranus=P=1Ø.
Negritude=4,500=5,000=50%=P5.00D=Law=Time=Venus=5 May = Aphrodite>>L=N.
Negro=7,000=70%=P7.0D=7.0=Language=Assets=Mars=7 July=Pleiades.
Negro.=7,000=70%=P7.0D=7.0=Language=Assets=Mars=7 July=Pleiades.
Negroid=10,000=1,000=100%=10.0=Physicality=Tech.=10 Oct.=Uranus=P=1Ø.

Nehemiah=6,000=60%=P6.0D=Man=Earth=Royalty=6 June=Gaia=Maia>>M=M2.
A Hebrew leader of the 5th cent. B.C. 5.0*6.0x=px=11+30=41x=px=371=400=4.0. Nehemiah as a book was inspired by Gaia but an incarnate of Hermes >> Jesus. "He was a Hebrew leader who supervised the rebuilding of Jerusalem (c.444) and introduced religious and moral reforms (c.432). The code 444 is an era of Hermes manifesting as a tripartite multitasking being to be able to grapple with the difficulty of the times. 444>> Hermes, Nehemiah and Jerusalem. First religious reforms were necessary at the time to help organize the mindset of the people towards the service of Heaven. Today it is a speculation where faith is most required for upgrade. Second moral reforms to make for common sense that will introduce the needed wisdom. Today rights not morals run the world. 444-432=12 >> 12 dimensions of the universe was predicted by these codes. 12 >> Knowledge >> mathema >> mathematics >> Science >> Scientia >> 444 (3.0>> creativity) so computational Creativity, Makumatics and abstraction. And so Jesus states that at the last days knowledge shall increase and men shall run to and from. 12 also indicates Athena >> Knowledge >> Spirit of God always required to settle things during chaos by Genesis story. Then we confirm three Gods being Hermes, Gaia and Athena in management (444). The Creatocracy uses walls as a code for legal reforms hence the Brickwalls of Castle Makupedia for Creatocratic Jurisprudence is simply the introduction of new legal structures that will be inclusive of computational creativity and psycho-forensic auditing in determining the truth of matters during investigations.

Nehru Jawaharial=3,000=30%=P3.0D=3.0=Creativity=Stars=Muses=3 March = C=I>>GIL.
Neigh=6,500=7,000=70%=P7.0D=7.0=Language=Assets=Mars=7 July=Pleiades.

Neighbor=15,000=1,500=15%=P1.50D=1.5=Authority=Solar Crown=1 May = Maia.
A good neighbor will live close to you and live by you. A bad neighbor will live in you. The story is told of Toyin Obabiyi and her husband who lived and troubled Peter Matthews-Akukalia, Castle Makupedia and his family during the days of the development of his works. They were notorious neighbors who even conspired with his mother and Mr. & Mrs. Oluwashola Olarenwaju to dispossess him of his inheritance land where he lived. Accusations, screams noise and throwing of waste foods into his compound made him uncomfortable since he worked at home in area he had lived at least twenty years. See Moore. Read the book >> The Creatocracy Republic of Castle Makupedia, reference book is Last of the Noble Amazons the last chapter. Read also the book >> Makupedialand >> A Disean City of Testamentary Poetry, poem title "Wonders in Mariam Street". I rest my case Oh Nemesis for I have suffered these offenses in the hands of haters of law and humanity. Had the work stopped there would be no Castle Makupedia to benefit the world. We declare them and theirs Creatocratic Fugitives not deserving mercy goodwill nor peace.

Neighborhood=15,000=1,500=15%=P1.50D=1.5=Authority=Solar Crown=1 May = Maia.
Neighborly=4,500=5,000=50%=P5.00D=Law=Time=Venus=5 May = Aphrodite>>L=N.
Nei Monggol=4,000=40%=P4.0D=Govt.=Creatocracy=4 April=Mercury=Hermes=G=A4.
Neither=10,000=1,000=100%=10.0=Physicality=Tech.=10 Oct.=Uranus=P=1Ø.
nelson=10,000=1,000=100%=10.0=Physicality=Tech.=10 Oct.=Uranus=P=1Ø.

Nelson Horatio=3,000=30%=P3.0D=3.0=Creativity=Stars=Muses=3 March = C=I>>GIL.
Nematode=7,500=8,000=80%=P8.0D=Economy=Currency=8 Aug.=Zeus>>E=v.
Nemea=4,000=40%=P4.0D=Govt.=Creatocracy=4 April=Mercury=Hermes=G=A4.

Nemesis=13,000=13%=P1.30=Solar Core=Faculty=13 January=Athena.
Greek myth. The Goddess of retributive Justice or vengeance. Nemesis is a muse of Athena who carries out punitive judgement and vengeance against the haters of knowledge.

Neo-=3,000=30%=P3.0D=3.0=Creativity=Stars=Muses=3 March = C=I>>GIL.
Neo means new. Creativity brings new things all the time. A person who knew Castle Makupedia yesterday and haven't heard from him today will testify that he is behind time.

Neoclassicism=6,500=7,000=70%=P7.0D=7.0=Language=Assets=Mars=7 July=Pleiades.
Neocolonialism=9,500=10,000=1,000=100%=Physicality=Tech.=10 Oct.=Uranus=P=1Ø.
Neodymium=10,000=1,000=100%=10.0=Physicality=Tech.=10 Oct.=Uranus=P=1Ø.
Neolithic=10,000=1,000=100%=10.0=Physicality=Tech.=10 Oct.=Uranus=P=1Ø.
Neologism=3,000=30%=P3.0D=3.0=Creativity=Stars=Muses=3 March = C=I>>GIL.
Neon=10,000=1,000=100%=10.0=Physicality=Tech.=10 Oct.=Uranus=P=1Ø.
Neonate=4,000=40%=P4.0D=Govt.=Creatocracy=4 April=Mercury=Hermes=G=A4.
Neophyte=10,000=1,000=100%=10.0=Physicality=Tech.=10 Oct.=Uranus=P=1Ø.
Neoplasm=3,500=4,000=40%=P4.0D=Govt.=Cre=4 April=Mercury=Hermes=G=A4.
Neoprene=10,000=1,000=100%=10.0=Physicality=Tech.=10 Oct.=Uranus=P=1Ø.
Nepal=10,000=1,000=100%=10.0=Physicality=Tech.=10 Oct.=Uranus=P=1Ø.
Nepenthe=11,500=12,000=12%=P1.20D=1.2=Knowledge=Edu=12Dec.=Athena>>K=F.
Nephew=7,500=8,000=80%=P8.0D=Economy=Currency=8 Aug.=Zeus>>E=v.
Nephrite=6,500=7,000=70%=P7.0D=7.0=Language=Assets=Mars=7 July=Pleiades.
Nephritic=3,500=4,000=40%=P4.0D=Govt.=Creat=4 April=Mercury=Hermes=G=A4.
Nephritis=2,000=20%=P2.00D=2.0=Nature=Matter=Moon=2 Feb.=Cupid=N=C+_
Nephro-=5,000=50%=P5.00D=Law=Time=Venus=5 May = Aphrodite>>L=N.
Nepotism=10,000=1,000=100%=10.0=Physicality=Tech.=10 Oct.=Uranus=P=1Ø.
Neptune=10,000=1,000=100%=10.0=Physicality=Tech.=10 Oct.=Uranus=P=1Ø.
Neptunium=10,000=1,000=100%=10.0=Physicality=Tech.=10 Oct.=Uranus=P=1Ø.
Nerd=10,000=1,000=100%=10.0=Physicality=Tech.=10 Oct.=Uranus=P=1Ø.
Nero=4,000=40%=P4.0D=Govt.=Creatocracy=4 April=Mercury=Hermes=G=A4.
Nerve=10,000=1,000=100%=10.0=Physicality=Tech.=10 Oct.=Uranus=P=1Ø.
Nerve cell=1,000=100%=10.0=1.0=Mind=Sun=1 January=Helios >> M=E4.
Nerve center=3,000=30%=P3.0D=3.0=Creativity=Stars=Muses=3 March = C=I>>GIL.
Nerve gas=5,500=5.5=80%=P5.50=Earth-Midway=5 May = Gaia.
Nerveless=4,000=40%=P4.0D=Govt.=Creatocracy=4 April=Mercury=Hermes=G=A4.
Nerve-racking=1,000=100%=10.0=1.0=Mind=Sun=1 January=Helios >> M=E4.
Nervous=10,000=1,000=100%=10.0=Physicality=Tech.=10 Oct.=Uranus=P=1Ø.
Nervous breakdown=4,000=40%=P4.0D=Govt.=Creatocracy=4 April=Hermes=G=A4.
Nervous system=8,000=80%=P8.0D=Economy=Currency=8 Aug.=Zeus>>E=v.
Nervy=4,500=5,000=50%=P5.00D=Law=Time=Venus=5 May = Aphrodite>>L=N.

Ness Loch=3,000=30%=P3.0D=3.0=Creativity=Stars=Muses=3 March = C=I>>GIL.
-ness=3,000=30%=P3.0D=3.0=Creativity=Stars=Muses=3 March = C=I>>GIL.
Nest=10,000=1,000=100%=10.0=Physicality=Tech.=10 Oct.=Uranus=P=1Ø.
Nest egg=2,500=3,000=30%=P3.0D=3.0=Creativity=Stars=Muses=3 March = C=I>>GIL.
Nestle=10,000=1,000=100%=10.0=Physicality=Tech.=10 Oct.=Uranus=P=1Ø.
Nestling=4,000=40%=P4.0D=Govt.=Creatocracy=4 April=Mercury=Hermes=G=A4.
Net1=10,000=1,000=100%=10.0=Physicality=Tech.=10 Oct.=Uranus=P=1Ø.
Net2=10,000=1,000=100%=10.0=Physicality=Tech.=10 Oct.=Uranus=P=1Ø.
NET=1,500=15%=P1.50D=1.5=Authority=Solar Crown=1 May = Maia.
Neth.=500=5%=P5.00D=5.0=Law=Time=Venus=5 May=Aphrodite>>L=N.
Netherlands=3,500=4,000=40%=P4.0D=Govt.=Creatocracy=4 April=Hermes=G=A4.
Netherlands Antilles=10,000=1,000=100%=10.0=Phys.=Tech.=10 Oct.=Uranus=P=1Ø.
Nettle=6,500=7,000=70%=P7.0D=7.0=Language=Assets=Mars=7 July=Pleiades.
Network=10,000=1,000=100%=10.0=Physicality=Tech.=10 Oct.=Uranus=P=1Ø.
Netzahualcóyoti=5,500=5.5=80%=P5.50=Earth-Midway=5 May = Gaia.
Neural=4,500=5,000=50%=P5.00D=Law=Time=Venus=5 May = Aphrodite>>L=N.
Neuralgia=5,000=50%=P5.00D=Law=Time=Venus=5 May = Aphrodite>>L=N.
Neurasthenia=10,000=1,000=100%=10.0=Physicality=Tech.=10 Oct.=Uranus=P=1Ø.
Neuritis=2,000=20%=P2.00D=2.0=Nature=Matter=Moon=2 Feb.=Cupid=N=C+_
Neuro-=4,000=40%=P4.0D=Govt.=Creatocracy=4 April=Mercury=Hermes=G=A4.
Neurology=6,000=60%=P6.0D=Man=Earth=Royalty=6 June=Gaia=Maia>>M=M2.
Neuron=11,500=12,000=12%=P1.20D=1.2=Knowledge=Edu=12Dec.=Athena>>K=F.
Neurosis=8,000=80%=P8.0D=Economy=Currency=8 Aug.=Zeus>>E=v.
Neurotic=4,000=40%=P4.0D=Govt.=Creatocracy=4 April=Mercury=Hermes=G=A4.
Neurotransmitter=6,000=60%=P6.0D=Man=Earth=Royalty=6 June=Gaia=Maia>>M=M2.
Neut.=1,000=100%=10.0=1.0=Mind=Sun=1 January=Helios >> M=E4.
Neuter=10,000=1,000=100%=10.0=Physicality=Tech.=10 Oct.=Uranus=P=1Ø.
Neutral=10,000=1,000=100%=10.0=Physicality=Tech.=10 Oct.=Uranus=P=1Ø.
Neutral ground=10,000=1,000=100%=10.0=Physicality=Tech.=10 Oct.=Uranus=P=1Ø.
Neutralism=500=5%=P5.00D=5.0=Law=Time=Venus=5 May=Aphrodite>>L=N.
Neutrality=5,000=50%=P5.00D=Law=Time=Venus=5 May = Aphrodite>>L=N.
Neutralize=2,500=3,000=30%=P3.0D=3.0=Creativity=Stars=Muses=3 March = C=I>>GIL.
Neutral spirits=7,000=70%=P7.0D=7.0=Language=Assets=Mars=7 July=Pleiades.
Neutrino=6,000=60%=P6.0D=Man=Earth=Royalty=6 June=Gaia=Maia>>M=M2.
Neutron=10,000=1,000=100%=10.0=Physicality=Tech.=10 Oct.=Uranus=P=1Ø.
Neutron bomb=9,000=90%=P9.00D=9.0=Abstraction=Gods=Saturn=9Sept.>>A=Ø.
Nev.=500=5%=P5.00D=5.0=Law=Time=Venus=5 May=Aphrodite>>L=N.
Neva=8,500=9,000=90%=P9.00D=9.0=Abstraction=Gods=Saturn=9Sept.>>A=Ø.
Nevada=5,500=5.5=80%=P5.50=Earth-Midway=5 May = Gaia.
Nevelson Louise=3,000=30%=P3.0D=3.0=Creativity=Stars=Muses=3 March = C=I>>GIL.
Never=6,000=60%=P6.0D=Man=Earth=Royalty=6 June=Gaia=Maia>>M=M2.
Nevermore=1,000=100%=10.0=1.0=Mind=Sun=1 January=Helios >> M=E4.
Nevertheless=2,500=3,000=30%=P3.0D=3.0=Cre=Stars=Muses=3 March = C=I>>GIL.
Nevus=6,500=7,000=70%=P7.0D=7.0=Language=Assets=Mars=7 July=Pleiades.

New=10,000=1,000=100%=10.0=Physicality=Tech.=10 Oct.=Uranus=P=1∅.
In the future Nations that adopt Creatocracy will add New to their national brands e.g
Creatocratic Nation of New Nigeria, New USA, New United Kingdom, New India, New
Russia, New China, New Korea, New Japan, New Iceland, New Australia, New Israel etc.,
after all GOD promised to make everything new again in our lives people and nation. This
is our goodwill message to everyone who has lost hope that there is nothing new again in
life. Creatocracy is the in-thing neo-socio-political economy that will build nations for good.
GOD gave conditions about setting up bulwarks. We recommend boulevard as a channel
of openness and prosperity. See Deuteronomy 20:20, 2 Chronicles 26:15, Ecclesiastes
9:14, Psalm 48:13, Isaiah 26:1. The word New will be added to every nation that
adopts Creatocracy and becomes a Paradise Nation under the Creatocratic Nations
Organizations. These are nations that practice creativity Creatocism and Creatocracy as
a way of life or livelihood. Holy Quran Al-Wäql'a, The Inevitable Event. Verses 75-82.
An example would Federal Republic of New Nigeria FRNN; Creatocratic Republic of
New Nigeria CRNN etc A Paradise Nation. Creatocracy is the one world government
under God. Ephesians 1:10 - 15.

New Amsterdam=11,500=12,000=12%=P1.20D=1.2=Knwl.=Edu=12Dec.=Athena>>K=F.
New ark=7,000=70%=P7.0D=7.0=Language=Assets=Mars=7 July=Pleiades.
Newborn=3,000=30%=P3.0D=3.0=Creativity=Stars=Muses=3 March = C=I>>GIL.
New Brunswick=7,000=70%=P7.0D=7.0=Language=Assets=Mars=7 July=Pleiades.
New Caledonia=10,000=1,000=100%=10.0=Physicality=Tech.=10 Oct.=Uranus=P=1∅.

Newcastle=6,000=60%=P6.0D=Man=Earth=Royalty=6 June=Gaia=Maia>>M=M2.
The residence of Castle Makupedia named after the God of Creatocracy Genius & Mind.

Newcomer=3,000=30%=P3.0D=3.0=Creativity=Stars=Muses=3 March = C=I>>GIL.
New Deal=9,000=90%=P9.00D=9.0=Abstraction=Gods=Saturn=9Sept.>>A=∅.
New Delhi.=6,000=60%=P6.0D=Man=Earth=Royalty=6 June=Gaia=Maia>>M=M2.
Newel=11,500=12,000=12%=P1.20D=1.2=Knowledge=Edu=12Dec.=Athena>>K=F.
New England.=7,000=70%=P7.0D=7.0=Language=Assets=Mars=7 July=Pleiades.
Newf.=500=5%=P5.00D=5.0=Law=Time=Venus=5 May=Aphrodite>>L=N.
Newfangled=5,000=50%=P5.00D=Law=Time=Venus=5 May = Aphrodite>>L=N.
Newfound=1,000=100%=10.0=1.0=Mind=Sun=1 January=Helios >> M=E4.
Newfoundland=9,500=10,000=1,000=100%=10.0=Physicality=Tech.=10 Oct.=Uranus
=P=1∅.
New France.=12,000=12%=P1.20D=1.2=Knowledge=Edu=12Dec.=Athena>>K=F.
New Guinea.=8,500=9,000=90%=P9.00D=9.0=Abstraction=Gods=Saturn=9Sept.>>A=∅.
New Hampshire=7,000=70%=P7.0D=7.0=Language=Assets=Mars=7 July=Pleiades.
New Haven=4,500=5,000=50%=P5.00D=Law=Time=Venus=5 May = Aphrodite>>L=N.
New Hebrides.=1,000=100%=10.0=1.0=Mind=Sun=1 January=Helios >> M=E4.
New Jersey=6,500=7,000=70%=P7.0D=7.0=Language=Assets=Mars=7 July=Pleiades.
New Latin.=3,000=30%=P3.0D=3.0=Creativity=Stars=Muses=3 March = C=I>>GIL.
Newly=7,000=70%=P7.0D=7.0=Language=Assets=Mars=7 July=Pleiades.

Newlywed=2,000=20%=P2.00D=2.0=Nature=Matter=Moon=2 Feb.=Cupid=N=C+_
Newman=3,000=30%=P3.0D=3.0=Creativity=Stars=Muses=3 March = C=I>>GIL.
New Math=6,500=7,000=70%=P7.0D=7.0=Language=Assets=Mars=7 July=Pleiades.
New Mexico.=7,000=70%=P7.0D=7.0=Language=Assets=Mars=7 July=Pleiades.
New Moon=12,000=12%=P1.20D=1.2=Knowledge=Edu=12Dec.=Athena>>K=F.
New Netherland=9,000=90%=P9.00D=9.0=Abstraction=Gods=Saturn=9Sept.>>A=Ø.
New Orleans=5,500=5.5=80%=P5.50=Earth-Midway=5 May = Gaia.
Newport News=5,000=50%=P5.00D=Law=Time=Venus=5 May = Aphrodite>>L=N.
New Providence=4,000=40%=P4.0D=Govt.=Creatocracy=4 April=Hermes=G=A4.
News=10,000=1,000=100%=10.0=Physicality=Tech.=10 Oct.=Uranus=P=1Ø.
Newscast=5,500=5.5=80%=P5.50=Earth-Midway=5 May = Gaia.
Newsletter=6,000=60%=P6.0D=Man=Earth=Royalty=6 June=Gaia=Maia>>M=M2.
New Spain.=10,000=1,000=100%=10.0=Physicality=Tech.=10 Oct.=Uranus=P=1Ø.
Newspaper=10,000=1,000=100%=10.0=Physicality=Tech.=10 Oct.=Uranus=P=1Ø.
Newsprint=3,000=30%=P3.0D=3.0=Creativity=Stars=Muses=3 March = C=I>>GIL.
Newsreel=3,500=4,000=40%=P4.0D=Govt.=Creatocracy=4 April=Hermes=G=A4.
Newsstand=4,500=5,000=50%=P5.00D=Law=Time=Venus=5 May = Aphrodite>>L=N.
Newsworthy=4,000=40%=P4.0D=Govt.=Creatocracy=4 April=Mercury=Hermes=G=A4.
Newsy=2,500=3,000=30%=P3.0D=3.0=Creativity=Stars=Muses=3 March = C=I>>GIL.
Newt=6,500=7,000=70%=P7.0D=7.0=Language=Assets=Mars=7 July=Pleiades.
New Testament=6,500=7,000=70%=P7.0D=7.0=Language=Assets=Mars=7 July=Pleiades.

---

newton=10,500=11,000=11%=P1.10D=1.1=Idea=Brainchild=Inv.=11 Nov.=Athena>>I=MT.
A unit of force equal to the force needed to accelerate a mass of 1 kilogram 1 meter per second. [After Isaac NEWTON.]. The Maks is the Standard International unit and Universal Standard unit (SI & US) for measuring all abstract quantities and their equivalents based on the twelve dimensions of the universes and laws of astrotransmutation. [After Peter Matthews-Akukalia, Castle Makupedia]. See book>> The Creatocratic Charter.

Newton Isaac.=3,500=4,000=40%=P4.0D=Govt.=Cre=4 April=Mercury=Hermes=G=A4.
New World=1,500=15%=P1.50D=1.5=Authority=Solar Crown=1 May = Maia.
New Year's Day=8,500=9,000=90%=P9.00D=9.0=Abst.=Gods=Saturn=9Sept.>>A=Ø.
New Year's Eve=4,500=5,000=50%=P5.00D=Law=Time=Venus=5 May = Aphrodite>>L=N.
New York.=11,500=12,000=12%=P1.20D=1.2=Knowledge=Edu=12Dec.=Athena>>K=F.
New Zealand=6,500=7,000=70%=P7.0D=7.0=Language=Assets=Mars=7 July=Pleiades.
Next=10,000=1,000=100%=10.0=Physicality=Tech.=10 Oct.=Uranus=P=1Ø.
Nexus=8,000=80%=P8.0D=Economy=Currency=8 Aug.=Zeus>>E=v.
Nez Perce=8,000=80%=P8.0D=Economy=Currency=8 Aug.=Zeus>>E=v.
n/f=1,000=100%=Physicality=Tech.=10 Oct.=Uranus=P=1Ø.
NFC=1,500=15%=P1.50D=1.5=Authority=Solar Crown=1 May = Maia.
NFL=1,500=15%=P1.50D=1.5=Authority=Solar Crown=1 May = Maia.
Nfld.=500=5%=P5.00D=5.0=Law=Time=Venus=5 May=Aphrodite>>L=N.
Ngultrum=2,500=3,000=30%=P3.0D=3.0=Creativity=Stars=Muses=3 March = C=I>>GIL.

PETER K. MATTHEWS - AKUKALIA

Ngwee=4,000=40%=P4.0D=Govt.=Creatocracy=4 April=Mercury=Hermes=G=A4.
Bantu origin. Currency. 4/10=0.4. See Naira.

NH=1,000=100%=10.0=1.0=Mind=Sun=1 January=Helios >> M=E4.
NHL=1,500=15%=P1.50D=1.5=Authority=Solar Crown=1 May = Maia.
Ni=3,000=30%=P3.0D=3.0=Creativity=Stars=Muses=3 March = C=I>>GIL.
Niacin=6,500=7,000=70%=P7.0D=7.0=Language=Assets=Mars=7 July=Pleiades.
Niagara Falls=5,500=5.5=80%=P5.50=Earth-Midway=5 May = Gaia.
Niagara River=6,500=7,000=70%=P7.0D=7.0=Language=Assets=Mars=7 July=Pleiades.
Niamey=6,000=60%=P6.0D=Man=Earth=Royalty=6 June=Gaia=Maia>>M=M2.
Nib=3,500=4,000=40%=P4.0D=Govt.=Creatocracy=4 April=Mercury=Hermes=G=A4.
Nibble=7,500=8,000=80%=P8.0D=Economy=Currency=8 Aug.=Zeus>>E=v.
Nic.=500=5%=P5.00D=5.0=Law=Time=Venus=5 May=Aphrodite>>L=N.
Nicaea=3,500=4,000=40%=P4.0D=Govt.=Creatocracy=4 April=Mercury=Hermes=G=A4.
Nicaragua=7,500=8,000=80%=P8.0D=Economy=Currency=8 Aug.=Zeus>>E=v.
Nicaragua, Lake=4,500=5,000=50%=P5.00D=Law=Time=Venus=5 May =Odite>>L=N.
nice=10,000=1,000=100%=10.0=Physicality=Tech.=10 Oct.=Uranus=P=1Ø.
Nice=6,500=7,000=70%=P7.0D=7.0=Language=Assets=Mars=7 July=Pleiades.
Nicety=8,000=80%=P8.0D=Economy=Currency=8 Aug.=Zeus>>E=v.
Niche=10,500=11,000=11%=P1.10D=1.1=Idea=Brainchild=Inv.=11 Nov.=SC=Athena
   >>I=MT.
Nicholas=7,500=8,000=80%=P8.0D=Economy=Currency=8 Aug.=Zeus>>E=v.
Nicholas II.=5,500=5.5=80%=P5.50=Earth-Midway=5 May = Gaia.
Nick=13,500=14,000=14%=P1.40D=1.4=Mgt.=Solar Energy=13 May=Athena=SC=0.1
Nickel=10,000=1,000=100%=10.0=Physicality=Tech.=10 Oct.=Uranus=P=1Ø.
Nickelodeon=10,000=1,000=100%=10.0=Physicality=Tech.=10 Oct.=Uranus=P=1Ø.
Nicker=3,000=30%=P3.0D=3.0=Creativity=Stars=Muses=3 March = C=I>>GIL.
Nickname=10,000=1,000=100%=10.0=Physicality=Tech.=10 Oct.=Uranus=P=1Ø.
Nicobar Islands=5,000=50%=P5.00D=Law=Time=Venus=5 May = Aphrodite>>L=N.
Nicosia=5,000=50%=P5.00D=Law=Time=Venus=5 May = Aphrodite>>L=N.
Nicotine=11,000=11%=P1.10D=1.1=Idea=Brainchild=Inv.=11 Nov.=SC=Athena>>I=MT.
Nicotinic acid=1,000=100%=Physicality=Tech.=10 Oct.=Uranus=P=1Ø.
Nictitate=2,500=3,000=30%=P3.0D=3.0=Creativity=Stars=Muses=3 March = C=I>>GIL.
Niebuhr Reinhold.=2,000=20%=P2.00D=2.0=Nature=Matter=Moon=2 Feb.=Cupid=N=C+_
Niece=5,000=50%=P5.00D=Law=Time=Venus=5 May = Aphrodite>>L=N.
Nietzsche Friedrich=2,500=3,000=30%=P3.0D=3.0=Cre=Stars=Muses=3 March=CI
Nifty=2,500=3,000=30%=P3.0D=3.0=Creativity=Stars=Muses=3 March = C=I>>GIL.
Niger=5,000=50%=P5.00D=Law=Time=Venus=5 May = Aphrodite>>L=N.
Niger-Congo=4,000=40%=P4.0D=Govt.=Creatocracy=4 April=Mercury=Hermes=G=A4.

Nigeria=5,500=5.5=80%=P5.50=Earth-Midway=5 May = Gaia.
Nigeria is inspired by Gaia-Midway being Maia. Nigeria is a midway nation that produces
royalty. The Goddess endowed the country with authority. Little wonder Peter Matthews-
Akukalia, Castle Makupedia was found here. Nigeria is the incarnation of Maia and a

controller of the Earth. Nigeria's problems are Maia's problems and so the solution is in raising one who will be on same rights with her by attaining the status of a God and wearing the solar crown. This is Castle Makupedia God of Creatocracy Genius and Mind. Creatocracy is the gift of Maia to solve and resolve her political and economic challenges. Nigeria is therefore not cut out for democracy but rather for Creatocracy. This is the Law.

Niger River.=12,500=13,000=13%=P1.30=Solar Core=Faculty=13 January=Athena.
Niggard=5,000=50%=P5.00D=Law=Time=Venus=5 May = Aphrodite>>L=N.
Niggardly=3,000=30%=P3.0D=3.0=Creativity=Stars=Muses=3 March = C=I>>GIL.
Niggling=5,000=50%=P5.00D=Law=Time=Venus=5 May = Aphrodite>>L=N.
Nigh=10,000=1,000=100%=10.0=Physicality=Tech.=10 Oct.=Uranus=P=1Ø.
Night=11,000=11%=P1.10D=1.1=Idea=Brainchild=Inv.=11 Nov.=SC=Athena>>I=MT.
Night blindness=4,500=5,000=50%=P5.00D=Law=Time=Venus=5 May =Odite>>L=N.
Nightcap=7,000=70%=P7.0D=7.0=Language=Assets=Mars=7 July=Pleiades.
Nightclothes=3,500=4,000=40%=P4.0D=Govt.=Creatocracy=4 April=Hermes=G=A4.
Nightclub=7,000=70%=P7.0D=7.0=Language=Assets=Mars=7 July=Pleiades.
Night crawler=5,000=50%=P5.00D=Law=Time=Venus=5 May = Aphrodite>>L=N.
Nightdress=1,000=100%=10.0=1.0=Mind=Sun=1 January=Helios >> M=E4.
Nightfall=2,000=20%=P2.00D=2.0=Nature=Matter=Moon=2 Feb.=Cupid=N=C+_
Nightgown=5,000=50%=P5.00D=Law=Time=Venus=5 May = Aphrodite>>L=N.
Nighthawk=7,000=70%=P7.0D=7.0=Language=Assets=Mars=7 July=Pleiades.
Nightie=1,500=15%=P1.50D=1.5=Authority=Solar Crown=1 May = Maia.
nightingale=10,000=1,000=100%=10.0=Physicality=Tech.=10 Oct.=Uranus=P=1Ø.

Nightingale Florence=2,500=3,000=30%=P3.0D=3.0=Cre=Stars=Muses=3March=CI 1820-1910. British nursing pioneer. Peter Matthews-Akukalia, Castle Makupedia is the World's 1st Creative Scientist. Author, Inventor King and Owner of the Creative Sciences.

Nightlife=4,000=40%=P4.0D=Govt.=Creatocracy=4 April=Mercury=Hermes=G=A4.
Nightly=3,500=4,000=40%=P4.0D=Govt.=Creatocracy=4 April=Mercury=Hermes=G=A4.
Nightmare=9,000=90%=P9.00D=9.0=Abstraction=Gods=Saturn=9Sept.>>A=Ø.
Night owl=5,000=50%=P5.00D=Law=Time=Venus=5 May = Aphrodite>>L=N.
Night school=4,000=40%=P4.0D=Govt.=Creatocracy=4 April=Mercury=Hermes=G=A4.
Nightshade=6,000=60%=P6.0D=Man=Earth=Royalty=6 June=Gaia=Maia>>M=M2.
Nightshirt=3,500=4,000=40%=P4.0D=Govt.=Creatocracy=4 April=Hermes=G=A4.
Nightstick=3,000=30%=P3.0D=3.0=Creativity=Stars=Muses=3 March = C=I>>GIL.
Nighttime=3,000=30%=P3.0D=3.0=Creativity=Stars=Muses=3 March = C=I>>GIL.
Nihilism=10,000=1,000=100%=10.0=Physicality=Tech.=10 Oct.=Uranus=P=1Ø.
Nijinsky Vaslav.=3,500=4,000=40%=P4.0D=Govt.=Creatocracy=4 April=Hermes=G=A4.
-nik=5,500=5.5=80%=P5.50=Earth-Midway=5 May = Gaia.

Nike=3,000=30%=P3.0D=3.0=Creativity=Stars=Muses=3 March = C=I>>GIL.
Greek myth. The Goddess of victory. Zeus is the God of victory. Victory = Victor = Victoria.

Nikolayeva=4,500=5,000=50%=P5.00D=Law=Time=Venus=5 May = Aphrodite>>L=N.
Nil=2,500=3,000=30%=P3.0D=3.0=Creativity=Stars=Muses=3 March = C=I>>GIL.
Nile=10,000=1,000=100%=10.0=Physicality=Tech.=10 Oct.=Uranus=P=1Ø.
Nilo-Saharan=3,500=4,000=40%=P4.0D=Govt.=Creatocracy=4 April=Hermes=G=A4.
Nilotic=3,500=4,000=40%=P4.0D=Govt.=Creatocracy=4 April=Mercury=Hermes=G=A4.
Nilsson Birgit.=2,500=3,000=30%=P3.0D=3.0=Cre=Stars=Muses=3 March = C=I>>GIL.
Nimble=8,500=9,000=90%=P9.00D=9.0=Abstraction=Gods=Saturn=9Sept.>>A=Ø.
Nimbus=10,000=1,000=100%=10.0=Physicality=Tech.=10 Oct.=Uranus=P=1Ø.
Nimitz Chester=2,500=3,000=30%=P3.0D=3.0=Cre=Stars=Muses=3 March = C=I>>GIL.
Nincompoop=3,000=30%=P3.0D=3.0=Creativity=Stars=Muses=3 March = C=I>>GIL.

Nine=8,000=80%=P8.0D=Economy=Currency=8 Aug.=Zeus>>E=v.
The law of Nine in Naturecology >>Ø=0=9.0 is the dimension of abstraction >> Council of Gods that manifest as Council of Muses during discussions of human affairs. Exodus 22:28. 23:20-25. Sãd verse 65-70. It is clear that Gods are the superior rank of Angels and function as the administrators of the universes including Man. For Earth it is Gaia.

Nineteen=7,000=70%=P7.0D=7.0=Language=Assets=Mars=7 July=Pleiades.
Nineteenth=6,500=7,000=70%=P7.0D=7.0=Language=Assets=Mars=7 July=Pleiades.
Ninetieth=6,500=7,000=70%=P7.0D=7.0=Language=Assets=Mars=7 July=Pleiades.
Ninety=4,000=40%=P4.0D=Govt.=Creatocracy=4 April=Mercury=Hermes=G=A4.
Nineveh=4,500=5,000=50%=P5.00D=Law=Time=Venus=5 May = Aphrodite>>L=N.
Ninja=5,500=5.5=80%=P5.50=Earth-Midway=5 May = Gaia.
Ninny=3,500=4,000=40%=P4.0D=Govt.=Creatocracy=4 April=Mercury=Hermes=G=A4.
Ninth=7,000=70%=P7.0D=7.0=Language=Assets=Mars=7 July=Pleiades.
Niobium=10,000=1,000=100%=10.0=Physicality=Tech.=10 Oct.=Uranus=P=1Ø.
Nip1=10,000=1,000=100%=10.0=Physicality=Tech.=10 Oct.=Uranus=P=1Ø.
Nip2=7,500=8,000=80%=P8.0D=Economy=Currency=8 Aug.=Zeus>>E=v.
Nipper=7,000=7,000=70%=P7.0D=7.0=Language=Assets=Mars=7 July=Pleiades.

Nipple=12,000=12%=P1.20D=1.2=Knowledge=Edu=12Dec.=Athena>>K=F.
The nipple is a place of stored knowledge and is its equivalent in the human body.

Nippy=2,500=3,000=30%=P3.0D=3.0=Creativity=Stars=Muses=3 March = C=I>>GIL.
Nirvana=10,000=1,000=100%=10.0=Physicality=Tech.=10 Oct.=Uranus=P=1Ø.

Nisan=6,000=60%=P6.0D=Man=Earth=Royalty=6 June=Gaia=Maia>>M=M2.
A month of the Jewish calendar. See table at calendar. Heb. Nîsãn. An automobile brand.

Nisei=6,000=60%=P6.0D=Man=Earth=Royalty=6 June=Gaia=Maia>>M=M2.
Nit=6,500=7,000=70%=P7.0D=7.0=Language=Assets=Mars=7 July=Pleiades.
Niter=8,500=9,000=90%=P9.00D=9.0=Abstraction=Gods=Saturn=9Sept.>>A=Ø.

Nitpick=5,000=50%=P5.00D=Law=Time=Venus=5 May = Aphrodite>>L=N.
Nitrate=10,000=1,000=100%=10.0=Physicality=Tech.=10 Oct.=Uranus=P=1Ø.
Nitre=2,500=3,000=30%=P3.0D=3.0=Creativity=Stars=Muses=3 March = C=I>>GIL.
Nitric acid=10,000=1,000=100%=10.0=Physicality=Tech.=10 Oct.=Uranus=P=1Ø.
Nitride=4,500=5,000=50%=P5.00D=Law=Time=Venus=5 May = Aphrodite>>L=N.
Nitrify=10,000=1,000=100%=10.0=Physicality=Tech.=10 Oct.=Uranus=P=1Ø.
Nitrite=4,500=5,000=50%=P5.00D=Law=Time=Venus=5 May = Aphrodite>>L=N.
Nitro-=7,500=8,000=80%=P8.0D=Economy=Currency=8 Aug.=Zeus>>E=v.
Nitro bacterium=7,500=8,000=80%=P8.0D=Economy=Currency=8 Aug.=Zeus>>E=v.
Nitrocellulose=9,000=90%=P9.00D=9.0=Abstraction=Gods=Saturn=9Sept.>>A=Ø.
Nitrogen=10,000=1,000=100%=10.0=Physicality=Tech.=10 Oct.=Uranus=P=1Ø.
Nitroglycerin=6,500=7,000=70%=P7.0D=7.0=Language=Assets=Mars=7 July=Pleiades.
Nitrous oxide=5,000=50%=P5.00D=Law=Time=Venus=5 May = Aphrodite>>L=N.
Nitty gritty=3,500=4,000=40%=P4.0D=Govt.=Creatocracy=4 April=Hermes=G=A4.
Nitwit=2,000=20%=P2.00D=2.0=Nature=Matter=Moon=2 Feb.=Cupid=N=C+_
Nix=3,500=4,000=40%=P4.0D=Govt.=Creatocracy=4 April=Mercury=Hermes=G=A4.
Nixon Richard=5,000=50%=P5.00D=Law=Time=Venus=5 May = Aphrodite>>L=N.
NJ=1,000=100%=10.0=1.0=Mind=Sun=1 January=Helios >> M=E4.
Nkrumah Kwame.=2,000=20%=P2.00D=2.0=Nature=Matter=Moon=2 Feb.=Cupid=N=C+_
NL=2,500=3,000=30%=P3.0D=3.0=Creativity=Stars=Muses=3 March = C=I>>GIL.
NLRB=2,000=20%=P2.00D=2.0=Nature=Matter=Moon=2 Feb.=Cupid=N=C+_
nm=1,500=15%=P1.50D=1.5=Authority=Solar Crown=1 May = Maia.
NM=1,000=100%=Physicality=Tech.=10 Oct.=Uranus=P=1Ø.
NMR=1,500=15%=P1.50D=1.5=Authority=Solar Crown=1 May = Maia.
NNE=1,000=100%=10.0=1.0=Mind=Sun=1 January=Helios >> M=E4.
NNW=1,000=100%=10.0=1.0=Mind=Sun=1 January=Helios >> M=E4.
no1=10,000=1,000=100%=10.0=Physicality=Tech.=10 Oct.=Uranus=P=1Ø.
no2=6,000=60%=P6.0D=Man=Earth=Royalty=6 June=Gaia=Maia>>M=M2.
No1=8,000=80%=P8.0D=Economy=Currency=8 Aug.=Zeus>>E=v.
No2=2,500=3,000=30%=P3.0D=3.0=Creativity=Stars=Muses=3 March = C=I>>GIL.
No.=1,500=15%=P1.50D=1.5=Authority=Solar Crown=1 May = Maia.

Noah=11,000=11%=P1.10D=1.1=Idea=Brainchild=Inv.=11 Nov.=SC=Athena>>I=MT.
An incarnation of Athena. In the Bible, chosen by GOD to build an ark to save human and animal life from a flood. The signs of Athena in the story are thus. 1. She is chosen of God hence the Spirit of GOD. Builds an ark more or less a ship in equivalent of our time. Greek myth teaches that Athena invented the warships and weaponry for marine warfare. 3. Saves human life. Greek myth teaches that although she has not been interested in marriage nor sex due to her stringent conditions for high intellectuality she is a foster mother to many heroes whom she trained. The key element of invention in the Noah story is the ark or flood ship. Clearly it was Athena who guided the ark through the 40 days period.

Nobel Alfred=3,500=4,000=40%=P4.0D=Govt.=Creatocracy=4 April=Hermes=G=A4.
Nobelium=10,500=11,000=11%=P1.10D=1.1=Idea=Brainchild=Inv.=11 Nov.=Athena>>I=MT.

Nobel Prize=10,000=1,000=100%=10.0=Physicality=Tech.=10 Oct.=Uranus=P=1Ø.
Nobility=11,000=11%=P1.10D=1.1=Idea=Brainchild=Inv.=11 Nov.=SC=Athena>>I=MT.
Noble=8,500=9,000=90%=P9.00D=9.0=Abstraction=Gods=Saturn=9Sept.>>A=Ø.
Nobleman=2,500=3,000=30%=P3.0D=3.0=Creativity=Stars=Muses=3 March = C=I>>GIL.

Noblesse oblige=9,000=90%=P9.00D=9.0=Abstraction=Gods=Saturn=9Sept.>>A=Ø.
Benevolent, honorable behavior considered to be the duty of persons of high birth or rank.
[Fr., nobility is an obligation]. Natural drive in Peter Matthews-Akukalia, Castle
Makupedia to create things that make life better and easier for everyone. His generosity
is well known.

Nobody=4,500=5,000=50%=P5.00D=Law=Time=Venus=5 May = Aphrodite>>L=N.
Nocturnal=8,000=80%=P8.0D=Economy=Currency=8 Aug.=Zeus>>E=v.
Nocturne=9,000=90%=P9.00D=9.0=Abstraction=Gods=Saturn=9Sept.>>A=Ø.
Nod=10,000=1,000=100%=10.0=Physicality=Tech.=10 Oct.=Uranus=P=1Ø.
Node=10,000=1,000=100%=10.0=Physicality=Tech.=10 Oct.=Uranus=P=1Ø.
Nodule=3,000=30%=P3.0D=3.0=Creativity=Stars=Muses=3 March = C=I>>GIL.
Noël=4,500=5,000=50%=P5.00D=Law=Time=Venus=5 May = Aphrodite>>L=N.
Noes=1,500=15%=P1.50D=1.5=Authority=Solar Crown=1 May = Maia.
No-fault=10,000=1,000=100%=10.0=Physicality=Tech.=10 Oct.=Uranus=P=1Ø.
Noggin=9,000=90%=P9.00D=9.0=Abstraction=Gods=Saturn=9Sept.>>A=Ø.
Noh=1,500=15%=P1.50D=1.5=Authority=Solar Crown=1 May = Maia.
Noise=10,000=1,000=100%=10.0=Physicality=Tech.=10 Oct.=Uranus=P=1Ø.
Noisemaker=8,000=80%=P8.0D=Economy=Currency=8 Aug.=Zeus>>E=v.
Noisome=2,500=3,000=30%=P3.0D=3.0=Creativity=Stars=Muses=3 March = C=I>>GIL.
Nolo contendere=10,000=1,000=100%=10.0=Physicality=Tech.=10 Oct.=Uranus=P=1Ø.
Nomad=10,000=1,000=100%=10.0=Physicality=Tech.=10 Oct.=Uranus=P=1Ø.
No man's land=10,000=1,000=100%=10.0=Physicality=Tech.=10 Oct.=Uranus=P=1Ø.
Nom de guerre=3,500=4,000=40%=P4.0D=Govt.=Cre=4 April=Mercury=Hermes=G=A4.
Nome=3,500=4,000=40%=P4.0D=Govt.=Creatocracy=4 April=Mercury=Hermes=G=A4.
Nomenclature=6,000=60%=P6.0D=Man=Earth=Royalty=6 June=Gaia=Maia>>M=M2.
Nominal=6,500=7,000=70%=P7.0D=7.0=Language=Assets=Mars=7 July=Pleiades.
Nominate=10,000=1,000=100%=10.0=Physicality=Tech.=10 Oct.=Uranus=P=1Ø.
Nominative=10,000=1,000=100%=10.0=Physicality=Tech.=10 Oct.=Uranus=P=1Ø.
Nominee=4,000=40%=P4.0D=Govt.=Creatocracy=4 April=Mercury=Hermes=G=A4.

-nomy=7,500=8,000=80%=P8.0D=Economy=Currency=8 Aug.=Zeus>>E=v.
Suff. A system of laws governing or a body of knowledge about a specified field: astronomy.
< Greek. Nomos, law. See The Creatocratic Charter by Peter Matthews-Akukalia.

Non-=2,000=20%=P2.00D=2.0=Nature=Matter=Moon=2 Feb.=Cupid=N=C+_
Nonage=6,000=60%=P6.0D=Man=Earth=Royalty=6 June=Gaia=Maia>>M=M2.

Nonagenarian=5,500=5.5=80%=P5.50=Earth-Midway=5 May = Gaia.
A person who is between the ages of 90 - 100 is already at midway. Hence midway persons or persons of the Gaian birth are already granted the keys to long life in the first place.

Nonagon=2,500=3,000=30%=P3.0D=3.0=Creativity=Stars=Muses=3 March = C=I>>GIL.
Nonaligned=4,500=5,000=50%=P5.00D=Law=Time=Venus=5 May = Aphrodite>>L=N.
Nonce=6,000=60%=P6.0D=Man=Earth=Royalty=6 June=Gaia=Maia>>M=M2.
Nonchalant=5,500=5.5=80%=P5.50=Earth-Midway=5 May = Gaia.
Noncom=2,500=3,000=30%=P3.0D=3.0=Creativity=Stars=Muses=3 March = C=I>>GIL.
Noncombatant=7,000=70%=P7.0D=7.0=Language=Assets=Mars=7 July=Pleiades.
Noncommissioned=10,500=11,000=11%=P1.10D=1.1=Idea=Bchd.=11 Nov.=Athena>>I=MT.
Noncommittal=5,000=50%=P5.00D=Law=Time=Venus=5 May = Aphrodite>>L=N.
Non compos mentis=10,000=1,000=100%=10.0=Physicality=Tech.=10 Oct.=Uranus=P=1Ø.
Non conductor=5,500=5.5=80%=P5.50=Earth-Midway=5 May = Gaia.
Non conformist=5,500=5.5=80%=P5.50=Earth-Midway=5 May = Gaia.
Nondescript=6,000=60%=P6.0D=Man=Earth=Royalty=6 June=Gaia=Maia>>M=M2.
None=8,000=80%=P8.0D=Economy=Currency=8 Aug.=Zeus>>E=v.
Nonentity=7,000=70%=P7.0D=7.0=Language=Assets=Mars=7 July=Pleiades.
Nones=10,000=1,000=100%=10.0=Physicality=Tech.=10 Oct.=Uranus=P=1Ø.
Nonesuch=5,000=5,000=50%=P5.00D=Law=Time=Venus=5 May = Aphrodite>>L=N.
Nonetheless=1,000=100%=10.0=1.0=Mind=Sun=1 January=Helios >> M=E4.
Nonevent=5,500=5.5=80%=P5.50=Earth-Midway=5 May = Gaia.
Nonfat=4,000=40%=P4.0D=Govt.=Creatocracy=4 April=Mercury=Hermes=G=A4.
Nonfeasance=6,000=60%=P6.0D=Man=Earth=Royalty=6 June=Gaia=Maia>>M=M2.
Nonillion=6,500=7,000=70%=P7.0D=7.0=Language=Assets=Mars=7 July=Pleiades.
Nonintervention=6,000=60%=P6.0D=Man=Earth=Royalty=6 June=Gaia=Maia>>M=M2.
Nonmetal=7,500=8,000=80%=P8.0D=Economy=Currency=8 Aug.=Zeus>>E=v.
No-no=2,500=3,000=30%=P3.0D=3.0=Creativity=Stars=Muses=3 March = C=I>>GIL.
Nonpareil=10,000=1,000=100%=10.0=Physicality=Tech.=10 Oct.=Uranus=P=1Ø.
Nonperson=8,000=80%=P8.0D=Economy=Currency=8 Aug.=Zeus>>E=v.
Nonplus=5,500=5.5=80%=P5.50=Earth-Midway=5 May = Gaia.
Nonproliferation=5,500=5.5=80%=P5.50=Earth-Midway=5 May = Gaia.
Nonrepresentational=2,500=3,000=30%=P3.0D=3.0=Cr=Stars=Muses=3 March = CI
Nonrestrictive=10,000=1,000=100%=10.0=Physicality=Tech.=10 Oct.=Uranus=P=1Ø.
Non self=5,000=50%=P5.00D=Law=Time=Venus=5 May = Aphrodite>>L=N.
Nonsense=6,000=60%=P6.0D=Man=Earth=Royalty=6 June=Gaia=Maia>>M=M2.
Non sequitur=8,500=9,000=90%=P9.00D=9.0=Abstraction=Gods=Saturn=9Sept.>>A=Ø.
Nonstandard=11,000=11%=P1.10D=1.1=Idea=Brainchild=Inv.=11 Nov.=SC=Athena>>I=MT.
Nonstop=3,000=30%=P3.0D=3.0=Creativity=Stars=Muses=3 March = C=I>>GIL.
Non suit=8,000=80%=P8.0D=Economy=Currency=8 Aug.=Zeus>>E=v.
Nonsupport=5,000=50%=P5.00D=Law=Time=Venus=5 May = Aphrodite>>L=N.
Non troppo=3,500=4,000=40%=P4.0D=Govt.=Creatocracy=4 April=Hermes=G=A4.
Non Union=5,000=50%=P5.00D=Law=Time=Venus=5 May = Aphrodite>>L=N.
Nonviolence=8,500=9,000=90%=P9.00D=9.0=Abstraction=Gods=Saturn=9Sept.>>A=Ø.
Noodle1=8,000=80%=P8.0D=Economy=Currency=8 Aug.=Zeus>>E=v.

Noodle2=4,500=5,000=50%=P5.00D=Law=Time=Venus=5 May = Aphrodite>>L=N.
Nook=8,000=80%=P8.0D=Economy=Currency=8 Aug.=Zeus>>E=v.
Noon=11,000=11%=P1.10D=1.1=Idea=Brainchild=Inv.=11 Nov.=SC=Athena>>I=MT.
Noonday=1,000=100%=10.0=1.0=Mind=Sun=1 January=Helios >> M=E4.
No one=1,500=15%=P1.50D=1.5=Authority=Solar Crown=1 May = Maia.
Noose=9,500=10,000=1,000=100%=10.0=Physicality=Tech.=10 Oct.=Uranus=P=1Ø.
Nootka=10,000=1,000=100%=Physicality=Tech.=10 Oct.=Uranus=P=1Ø.
No-par=5,500=5.5=80%=P5.50=Earth-Midway=5 May = Gaia.
Nope=2,500=3,000=30%=P3.0D=3.0=Creativity=Stars=Muses=3 March = C=I>>GIL.
Nor=10,000=1,000=100%=10.0=Physicality=Tech.=10 Oct.=Uranus=P=1Ø.
Nor.=2,000=20%=P2.00D=2.0=Nature=Matter=Moon=2 Feb.=Cupid=N=C+_
Nordic=10,000=1,000=100%=10.0=Physicality=Tech.=10 Oct.=Uranus=P=1Ø.
Norfolk=5,000=50%=P5.00D=Law=Time=Venus=5 May = Aphrodite>>L=N.

Norgay Tenzing.=8,000=80%=P8.0D=Economy=Currency=8 Aug.=Zeus>>E=v.
An incarnation of Zeus. 1914-86. Sherpa Guide; with Sir Edmund Hillary made the first ascent of Mount Everest (1953). Peter Matthews-Akukalia is an incarnation of Zeus.

Norm=6,000=60%=P6.0D=Man=Earth=Royalty=6 June=Gaia=Maia>>M=M2.
Normal=10,000=1,000=100%=10.0=Physicality=Tech.=10 Oct.=Uranus=P=1Ø.
Normalize=2,500=3,000=30%=P3.0D=3.0=Creativity=Stars=Muses=3 March = C=I>>GIL.
Normal school=5,000=50%=P5.00D=Law=Time=Venus=5 May = Aphrodite>>L=N.
Norman=10,000=1,000=100%=10.0=Physicality=Tech.=10 Oct.=Uranus=P=1Ø.
Normandy=6,500=7,000=70%=P7.0D=7.0=Language=Assets=Mars=7 July=Pleiades.
Norman French=4,500=5,000=50%=P5.00D=Law=Time=Venus=5 May = Aphrodite>>L=N.
Normative=3,500=4,000=40%=P4.0D=Govt.=Creatocracy=4 April=Hermes=G=A4.
Norse=10,000=1,000=100%=10.0=Physicality=Tech.=10 Oct.=Uranus=P=1Ø.
Norseman=4,000=40%=P4.0D=Govt.=Creatocracy=4 April=Mercury=Hermes=G=A4.
North=10,000=1,000=100%=10.0=Physicality=Tech.=10 Oct.=Uranus=P=1Ø.
North, Frederick=6,500=7,000=70%=P7.0D=7.0=Language=Assets=Mars=7 July=Pleiades.
North Africa=7,000=70%=P7.0D=7.0=Language=Assets=Mars=7 July=Pleiades.
North America=10,000=1,000=100%=10.0=Physicality=Tech.=10 Oct.=Uranus=P=1Ø.

North Atlantic Ocean=5,500=5.5=80%=P5.50=Earth-Midway=5 May = Gaia.
A point of residence energy control and transmission of Maia from the solar core to the earth where she reigns as the mother of the marine boundaries as the mother of Hermes. The Revelation tells of the mighty feet of the lord standing in the midst of the waters. The result is the mysterious disappearance of aircrafts and ships at the Bermuda Triangle. Possibly due to crossing of these transports into high cosmic planetary region.

North Carolina=7,000=70%=P7.0D=7.0=Language=Assets=Mars=7 July=Pleiades.
North Dakota=7,000=70%=P7.0D=7.0=Language=Assets=Mars=7 July=Pleiades.
Northeast=7,500=8,000=80%=P8.0D=Economy=Currency=8 Aug.=Zeus>>E=v.
Northeaster=4,000=40%=P4.0D=Govt.=Creatocracy=4 April=Mercury=Hermes=G=A4.

Northerly=4,500=5,000=50%=P5.00D=Law=Time=Venus=5 May = Aphrodite>>L=N.
Northern=4,500=5,000=50%=P5.00D=Law=Time=Venus=5 May = Aphrodite>>L=N.
Northerner=3,500=4,000=40%=P4.0D=Govt.=Creatocracy=4 April=Hermes=G=A4.
Northern Hemisphere=3,000=30%=P3.0D=3.0=Cre=Stars=Muses=3 March = C=I>>GIL.
Northern Ireland.=7,500=8,000=80%=P8.0D=Economy=Currency=8 Aug.=Zeus>>E=v.
Northern lights=1,500=15%=P1.50D=1.5=Authority=Solar Crown=1 May = Maia.
Northern Mariana Islands=1,500=15%=P1.50D=1.5=Authority=Solar Crown=1 May = Maia.
Northern oriole=6,500=7,000=70%=P7.0D=7.0=Language=Assets=Mars=7 July=Pleiades.
North Frigid Zone=1,500=15%=P1.50D=1.5=Authority=Solar Crown=1 May = Maia.
North Korea.=6,500=7,000=70%=P7.0D=7.0=Language=Assets=Mars=7 July=Pleiades.
North Pacific Ocean.=5,500=5.5=80%=P5.50=Earth-Midway=5 May = Gaia.
North Polar Region.=1,500=15%=P1.50D=1.5=Authority=Solar Crown=1 May = Maia.
North Pole=8,000=80%=P8.0D=Economy=Currency=8 Aug.=Zeus>>E=v.
North Sea.=5,000=50%=P5.00D=Law=Time=Venus=5 May = Aphrodite>>L=N.
North Star.=1,000=100%=10.0=1.0=Mind=Sun=1 January=Helios >> M=E4.
North Temperate Zone.=1,500=15%=P1.50D=1.5=Authority=Solar Crown=1 May = Maia.
North Vietnam.=6,000=60%=P6.0D=Man=Earth=Royalty=6 June=Gaia=Maia>>M=M2.
Northwest=7,500=8,000=80%=P8.0D=Economy=Currency=8 Aug.=Zeus>>E=v.
Northwest Passage=8,000=80%=P8.0D=Economy=Currency=8 Aug.=Zeus>>E=v.
Northwest Territories=12,000=12%=P1.20D=1.2=Knowledge=Edu=12Dec.=Athena>>K=F.
Northwest Territory.=8,500=9,000=90%=P9.00D=9.0=Abs=Gods=Saturn=9Sept.>>A=Ø.
North Yemen=3,500=4,000=40%=P4.0D=Govt.=Creatocracy=4 April=Hermes=G=A4.
Norway=8,000=80%=P8.0D=Economy=Currency=8 Aug.=Zeus>>E=v.
Norwegian=5,500=5.5=80%=P5.50=Earth-Midway=5 May = Gaia.
Norwegian Sea.=5,500=5.5=80%=P5.50=Earth-Midway=5 May = Gaia.
Nos.=500=5%=P5.00D=5.0=Law=Time=Venus=5 May=Aphrodite>>L=N.
Nose=10,000=1,000=100%=10.0=Physicality=Tech.=10 Oct.=Uranus=P=1Ø.
Nosebleed=2,000=20%=P2.00D=2.0=Nature=Matter=Moon=2 Feb.=Cupid=N=C+_
Nose cone=5,500=5.5=80%=P5.50=Earth-Midway=5 May = Gaia.
Nosedive=4,500=5,000=50%=P5.00D=Law=Time=Venus=5 May = Aphrodite>>L=N.
Nose gay=2,500=3,000=30%=P3.0D=3.0=Creativity=Stars=Muses=3 March = C=I>>GIL.
Nosh=7,000=70%=P7.0D=7.0=Language=Assets=Mars=7 July=Pleiades.
Nostalgia=7,000=70%=P7.0D=7.0=Language=Assets=Mars=7 July=Pleiades.

Nostradamus=3,000=30%=P3.0D=3.0=Creativity=Stars=Muses=3 March = C=I>>GIL.
1503-66. French physician and astrologer. A muse incarnation and prophet of the stars.
It is believed he predicted the advent of the one with the power of the stars in his hands
who will hail from the largest populous black nation in the world. That this would happen
after the first black man in Amerigo..has come and left office. Peter Matthews-Akukalia,
Castle Makupedia computed the stars and is said to be the one with the power of the stars
in his hands. See book >> The Creatocratic Charter.

Nostril=4,000=40%=P4.0D=Govt.=Creatocracy=4 April=Mercury=Hermes=G=A4.
Nostrum=4,500=5,000=50%=P5.00D=Law=Time=Venus=5 May = Aphrodite>>L=N.
Nosy=2,000=20%=P2.00D=2.0=Nature=Matter=Moon=2 Feb.=Cupid=N=C+_

Not=10,000=1,000=100%=10.0=Physicality=Tech.=10 Oct.=Uranus=P=1Ø.

Notabene=6,000=60%=P6.0D=Man=Earth=Royalty=6 June=Gaia=Maia>>M=M2.

Notable=10,000=1,000=100%=10.0=Physicality=Tech.=10 Oct.=Uranus=P=1Ø.

Notarize=4,000=40%=P4.0D=Govt.=Creatocracy=4 April=Mercury=Hermes=G=A4.

Notary=3,000=30%=P3.0D=3.0=Creativity=Stars=Muses=3 March = C=I>>GIL.

Notary public=8,500=9,000=90%=P9.00D=9.0=Abstraction=Gods=Saturn=9Sept.>>A=Ø.

Notation=10,000=1,000=100%=10.0=Physicality=Tech.=10 Oct.=Uranus=P=1Ø.

Notch=10,000=1,000=100%=10.0=Physicality=Tech.=10 Oct.=Uranus=P=1Ø.

Note=10,000=1,000=100%=10.0=Physicality=Tech.=10 Oct.=Uranus=P=1Ø.

Notebook=3,500=4,000=40%=P4.0D=Govt.=Creatocracy=4 April=Hermes=G=A4.

Noted=7,000=70%=P7.0D=7.0=Language=Assets=Mars=7 July=Pleiades.

Noteworthy=2,500=3,000=30%=P3.0D=3.0=Cre=Stars=Muses=3 March = C=I>>GIL.

Nothing=10,000=1,000=100%=10.0=Physicality=Tech.=10 Oct.=Uranus=P=1Ø.

Nothingness=5,500=5.5=80%=P5.50=Earth-Midway=5 May = Gaia.

Notice=10,000=1,000=100%=10.0=Physicality=Tech.=10 Oct.=Uranus=P=1Ø.

Noticeable=3,000=30%=P3.0D=3.0=Creativity=Stars=Muses=3 March = C=I>>GIL.

Notify=5,500=5.5=80%=P5.50=Earth-Midway=5 May = Gaia.

Notion=10,000=1,000=100%=10.0=Physicality=Tech.=10 Oct.=Uranus=P=1Ø.

Notorious=6,000=60%=P6.0D=Man=Earth=Royalty=6 June=Gaia=Maia>>M=M2.

Nottingham=4,500=5,000=50%=P5.00D=Law=Time=Venus=5 May = Aphrodite>>L=N.

Notwithstanding=4,000=40%=P4.0D=Govt.=Creatocracy=4 April=Hermes=G=A4.

Nouakchott=6,000=60%=P6.0D=Man=Earth=Royalty=6 June=Gaia=Maia>>M=M2.

Nougat=5,500=5.5=80%=P5.50=Earth-Midway=5 May = Gaia.

Nought=1,500=15%=P1.50D=1.5=Authority=Solar Crown=1 May = Maia.

Nouméan=7,000=70%=P7.0D=7.0=Language=Assets=Mars=7 July=Pleiades.

Noun=7,000=70%=P7.0D=7.0=Language=Assets=Mars=7 July=Pleiades.

Nourish=9,500=10,000=1,000=100%=10.0=Physicality=Tech.=10 Oct.=Uranus=P=1Ø.

Nouveau riche=4,000=40%=P4.0D=Govt.=Creatocracy=4 April=Mercury=Hermes=G=A4.

Nov.=500=5%=P5.00D=5.0=Law=Time=Venus=5 May=Aphrodite>>L=N.

Nova=11,500=12,000=12%=P1.20D=1.2=Knowledge=Edu=12Dec.=Athena>>K=F.

Nova Scotia=9,000=90%=P9.00D=9.0=Abstraction=Gods=Saturn=9Sept.>>A=Ø.

Novel1=10,000=1,000=100%=10.0=Physicality=Tech.=10 Oct.=Uranus=P=1Ø.

Novel2=5,500=5.5=80%=P5.50=Earth-Midway=5 May = Gaia.

Novelette=1,500=15%=P1.50D=1.5=Authority=Solar Crown=1 May = Maia.

Novelist=2,000=20%=P2.00D=2.0=Nature=Matter=Moon=2 Feb.=Cupid=N=C+_

Novelize=3,000=30%=P3.0D=3.0=Creativity=Stars=Muses=3 March = C=I>>GIL.

Novella=2,500=3,000=30%=P3.0D=3.0=Creativity=Stars=Muses=3 March = C=I>>GIL.

Novelty=9,000=90%=P9.00D=9.0=Abstraction=Gods=Saturn=9Sept.>>A=Ø.

November=5,500=5.5=80%=P5.50=Earth-Midway=5 May = Gaia.

Novena=7,500=8,000=80%=P8.0D=Economy=Currency=8 Aug.=Zeus>>E=v.

Novgorod=5,000=50%=P5.00D=Law=Time=Venus=5 May = Aphrodite>>L=N.

Novice=8,500=9,000=90%=P9.00D=9.0=Abstraction=Gods=Saturn=9Sept.>>A=Ø.
A beginner. One who has entered a religious order but has not yet taken vows.

Novitiate=7,500=8,000=80%=P8.0D=Economy=Currency=8 Aug.=Zeus>>E=v.
Novocain=4,000=40%=P4.0D=Govt.=Creatocracy=4 April=Mercury=Hermes=G=A4.
Novokuznetsk=5,000=50%=P5.00D=Law=Time=Venus=5 May = Aphrodite>>L=N.
Novosibirsk=7,000=70%=P7.0D=7.0=Language=Assets=Mars=7 July=Pleiades.
Now=10,000=1,000=100%=10.0=Physicality=Tech.=10 Oct.=Uranus=P=1Ø.
NOW=2,000=20%=P2.00D=2.0=Nature=Matter=Moon=2 Feb.=Cupid=N=C+_
Nowadays=3,500=4,000=40%=P4.0D=Govt.=Creatocracy=4 April=Hermes=G=A4.
No way=1,500=15%=P1.50D=1.5=Authority=Solar Crown=1 May = Maia.
Nowhere=5,500=5.5=80%=P5.50=Earth-Midway=5 May = Gaia.
No wise=4,500=5,000=50%=P5.00D=Law=Time=Venus=5 May = Aphrodite>>L=N.
Noxious=4,500=5,000=50%=P5.00D=Law=Time=Venus=5 May = Aphrodite>>L=N.
Noyes Alfred.=2,000=20%=P2.00D=2.0=Nature=Matter=Moon=2 Feb.=Cupid=N=C+_
Nozzle=7,000=70%=P7.0D=7.0=Language=Assets=Mars=7 July=Pleiades.
Np.=2,500=3,000=30%=P3.0D=3.0=Creativity=Stars=Muses=3 March = C=I>>GIL.
N.P.=1,000=100%=10.0=1.0=Mind=Sun=1 January=Helios >> M=E4.
NRA=2,500=3,000=30%=P3.0D=3.0=Creativity=Stars=Muses=3 March = C=I>>GIL.
NRC=1,500=15%=P1.50D=1.5=Authority=Solar Crown=1 May = Maia.
ns=500=5%=P5.00D=5.0=Law=Time=Venus=5 May=Aphrodite>>L=N.
NS=3,000=30%=P3.0D=3.0=Creativity=Stars=Muses=3 March = C=I>>GIL.
n/s=1,000=100%=10.0=1.0=Mind=Sun=1 January=Helios >> M=E4.
NSC=1,500=15%=P1.50D=1.5=Authority=Solar Crown=1 May = Maia.
N.S.P.C.A.=4,500=5,000=50%=P5.00D=Law=Time=Venus=5 May = Aphrodite>>L=N.
NT=3,000=30%=P3.0D=3.0=Creativity=Stars=Muses=3 March = C=I>>GIL.
nth=6,500=7,000=70%=P7.0D=7.0=Language=Assets=Mars=7 July=Pleiades.
nt.wt.=1,000=100%=10.0=1.0=Mind=Sun=1 January=Helios >> M=E4.
nu=3,000=30%=P3.0D=3.0=Creativity=Stars=Muses=3 March = C=I>>GIL.
nuance=10,000=1,000=100%=10.0=Physicality=Tech.=10 Oct.=Uranus=P=1Ø.
Nub=4,500=5,000=50%=P5.00D=Law=Time=Venus=5 May = Aphrodite>>L=N.
Nubia=8,000=80%=P8.0D=Economy=Currency=8 Aug.=Zeus>>E=v.
Nubian Desert.=7,000=70%=P7.0D=7.0=Language=Assets=Mars=7 July=Pleiades.
Nubile=5,000=50%=P5.00D=Law=Time=Venus=5 May = Aphrodite>>L=N.
Nuclear=7,000=70%=P7.0D=7.0=Language=Assets=Mars=7 July=Pleiades.
Nuclear energy=5,500=5.5=80%=P5.50=Earth-Midway=5 May = Gaia.
Nuclear family=6,000=60%=P6.0D=Man=Earth=Royalty=6 June=Gaia=Maia>>M=M2.
Nuclear magnetic resonance=8,500=90%=P9.00D=9.0=Abst=Gods=9Sept.>>A=Ø.
Nuclear reaction=8,000=80%=P8.0D=Economy=Currency=8 Aug.=Zeus>>E=v.
Nuclear reactor=5,500=5.5=80%=P5.50=Earth-Midway=5 May = Gaia.
Nucleate=8,000=80%=P8.0D=Economy=Currency=8 Aug.=Zeus>>E=v.
Nucleic acid=11,000=11%=P1.10D=1.1=Idea=Brainchild=Inv.=11 Nov.=SC=Athena>>I=MT.
Nucleo-=3,000=30%=P3.0D=3.0=Creativity=Stars=Muses=3 March = C=I>>GIL.
Nucleolus=8,000=80%=P8.0D=Economy=Currency=8 Aug.=Zeus>>E=v.
Nucleon=2,000=20%=P2.00D=2.0=Nature=Matter=Moon=2 Feb.=Cupid=N=C+_
Nucleonics=4,500=5,000=50%=P5.00D=Law=Time=Venus=5 May = Aphrodite>>L=N.
Nucleotide=7,000=70%=P7.0D=7.0=Language=Assets=Mars=7 July=Pleiades.
Nucleus=10,000=1,000=100%=10.0=Physicality=Tech.=10 Oct.=Uranus=P=1Ø.

Nuclide=7,000=70%=P7.0D=7.0=Language=Assets=Mars=7 July=Pleiades.
Nude=10,000=1,000=100%=10.0=Physicality=Tech.=10 Oct.=Uranus=P=1Ø.
Nudge=7,000=70%=P7.0D=7.0=Language=Assets=Mars=7 July=Pleiades.

Nudism=6,000=60%=P6.0D=Man=Earth=Royalty=6 June=Gaia=Maia>>M=M2.
The belief in or practice of going nude, especially for reasons of health. In the Creative Sciences this year an acceptable practice because the Genesis story of creation supports it. Besides it is also useful in the Makstian Faith praying system with approvals. Pretence is not allowed in the Creatocracy but certain levels of discretion hence nudity is an honest means to express the human emotion as a basic necessity of man. Nudity is the physical expression and acceptance of sexual transmutation under the laws of astrotransmutation as a means of accessing the spiritual. The Gods are often depicted nude. Moses was asked to remove his sandals in the burning bush before Zeus Jehovah Allah and His Host. Man came naked and man shall return naked although we do not accept that man should be buried naked but rather a double assertion of the place of nudity exceptionally in creativity. As mind persons we love fantasy imaginations sensuality and the ecstatic realities of nudity. Strange but impressive we adore the human body worship the female ambience designs beauty nature and their supposed scriptural weakness is reason to love and protect them. This is the reason we establish the Women Court in the Creatocracy Courts. Nudity is a higher way of setting the body spirit and soul free in limited nonchalance such that our God-given free will is reclaimed and gratitude expressed to the pleasures at His right hand according to Psalms. In the Scriptures prophets and King rented their clothes. All things done in the Creatocracy are subject to approval of the God of Creatocracy.
It falls under the 6th dimension of the universes >>6.0>>Man >> Health >> Emotion >> Royalty >> Generosity >> Gaia >> Gaia Midway >> Maia >> Authority >> Solar Crown.

Nuevo Laredo=7,000=70%=P7.0D=7.0=Language=Assets=Mars=7 July=Pleiades.
Negatory=5,000=50%=P5.00D=Law=Time=Venus=5 May = Aphrodite>>L=N.
Nugget=4,500=5,000=50%=P5.00D=Law=Time=Venus=5 May = Aphrodite>>L=N.
Nuisance=7,000=70%=P7.0D=7.0=Language=Assets=Mars=7 July=Pleiades.
Nuke=5,500=5.5=80%=P5.50=Earth-Midway=5 May = Gaia.

Nukualofa=5,000=50%=P5.00D=Law=Time=Venus=5 May = Aphrodite>>L=N.
Peter Matthews-Akukalia hails from Nkpologu, Nsukka, Uzo-Uwani Local Government Area of Enugu State. Eastern Nigeria. Home country of the God of Creatocracy Genius and Mind. Projected Headquarters of the Creatocracy and the Creatocratic Nations of Paradise. Subject to the approval of the King his headquarters is mobile as where he resides.

Null=7,500=8,000=80%=P8.0D=Economy=Currency=8 Aug.=Zeus>>E=v.
Null Character=6,000=60%=P6.0D=Man=Earth=Royalty=6 June=Gaia=Maia>>M=M2.
Nullify=4,500=5,000=50%=P5.00D=Law=Time=Venus=5 May = Aphrodite>>L=N.
Numb=6,500=7,000=70%=P7.0D=7.0=Language=Assets=Mars=7 July=Pleiades.
Number=10,000=1,000=100%=10.0=Physicality=Tech.=10 Oct.=Uranus=P=1Ø.

Numberless=1,000=100%=10.0=1.0=Mind=Sun=1 January=Helios >> M=E4.
Numerable=2,500=3,000=30%=P3.0D=3.0=Cre=Stars=Muses=3 March = C=I>>GIL.
Numeral=5,000=50%=P5.00D=Law=Time=Venus=5 May = Aphrodite>>L=N.
Numerate=3,000=30%=P3.0D=3.0=Creativity=Stars=Muses=3 March = C=I>>GIL.
Numerator=7,000=70%=P7.0D=7.0=Language=Assets=Mars=7 July=Pleiades.
Numerical=5,500=5.5=80%=P5.50=Earth-Midway=5 May = Gaia.

Numerology=5,000=50%=P5.00D=Law=Time=Venus=5 May = Aphrodite>>L=N.
The study of occult meanings of numbers. Occult is the supernatural mystical or magical beliefs, practices or phenomena. The Creatocracy is everything good bad ugly and extreme because all things are sourced from creativity and so creativity is everything on approval. The difference between the creative Sciences and occult mysteries is computation.

Numerous=4,000=40%=P4.0D=Govt.=Creatocracy=4 April=Mercury=Hermes=G=A4.
Numidia=6,000=60%=P6.0D=Man=Earth=Royalty=6 June=Gaia=Maia>>M=M2.
Numinous=7,000=70%=P7.0D=7.0=Language=Assets=Mars=7 July=Pleiades.

Numismatics=7,000=70%=P7.0D=7.0=Language=Assets=Mars=7 July=Pleiades.
The study or collection of money, coins and medals. Greek < nomisma, coin in circulation. Peter Matthews-Akukalia, Castle Makupedia invented the Makumatics deductions of the inherent faculties of the human mind. Origin of all abstractions in the Creative Sciences.

Numskull=3,000=30%=P3.0D=3.0=Creativity=Stars=Muses=3 March = C=I>>GIL.
Nun1=4,500=5,000=50%=P5.00D=Law=Time=Venus=5 May = Aphrodite>>L=N.
Nun2=4,000=40%=P4.0D=Govt.=Creatocracy=4 April=Mercury=Hermes=G=A4.
Nuncio=4,500=5,000=50%=P5.00D=Law=Time=Venus=5 May = Aphrodite>>L=N.
Nunnery=2,000=20%=P2.00D=2.0=Nature=Matter=Moon=2 Feb.=Cupid=N=C+_
Nuptial=7,500=8,000=80%=P8.0D=Economy=Currency=8 Aug.=Zeus>>E=v.
Nuremberg=4,500=5,000=50%=P5.00D=Law=Time=Venus=5 May = Aphrodite>>L=N.
Nureyev, Rudolf=4,000=40%=P4.0D=Govt.=Creatocracy=4 April=Hermes=G=A4.
Nurse=10,000=1,000=100%=10.0=Physicality=Tech.=10 Oct.=Uranus=P=1Ø.
Nursemaid=4,000=40%=P4.0D=Govt.=Creatocracy=4 April=Mercury=Hermes=G=A4.
Nurse practitioner=5,500=5.5=80%=P5.50=Earth-Midway=5 May = Gaia.
Nursery=10,000=1,000=100%=10.0=Physicality=Tech.=10 Oct.=Uranus=P=1Ø.
Nursery school=6,000=60%=P6.0D=Man=Earth=Royalty=6 June=Gaia=Maia>>M=M2.
Nursing=3,500=4,000=40%=P4.0D=Govt.=Creatocracy=4 April=Mercury=Hermes=G=A4.
Nursing home=6,000=60%=P6.0D=Man=Earth=Royalty=6 June=Gaia=Maia>>M=M2.
Nursling=3,000=30%=P3.0D=3.0=Creativity=Stars=Muses=3 March = C=I>>GIL.
Nurture=10,000=1,000=100%=10.0=Physicality=Tech.=10 Oct.=Uranus=P=1Ø.
Nut=10,000=1,000=100%=10.0=Physicality=Tech.=10 Oct.=Uranus=P=1Ø.
Nutcracker=3,000=30%=P3.0D=3.0=Creativity=Stars=Muses=3 March = C=I>>GIL.
Nutmeat=3,000=30%=P3.0D=3.0=Creativity=Stars=Muses=3 March = C=I>>GIL.
Nutmeg=10,000=1,000=100%=10.0=Physicality=Tech.=10 Oct.=Uranus=P=1Ø.

Nutria=9,000=90%=P9.00D=9.0=Abstraction=Gods=Saturn=9Sept.>>A=Ø.
Nutrient=3,000=30%=P3.0D=3.0=Creativity=Stars=Muses=3 March = C=I>>GIL.
Nutriment=3,000=30%=P3.0D=3.0=Creativity=Stars=Muses=3 March = C=I>>GIL.
Nutrition=10,000=1,000=100%=10.0=Physicality=Tech.=10 Oct.=Uranus=P=1Ø.
Nutritious=3,500=4,000=40%=P4.0D=Govt.=Creatocracy=4 April=Hermes=G=A4.
Nuts=6,500=7,000=70%=P7.0D=7.0=Language=Assets=Mars=7 July=Pleiades.
Nutshell=4,500=5,000=50%=P5.00D=Law=Time=Venus=5 May = Aphrodite>>L=N.
Nutty=5,500=5.5=80%=P5.50=Earth-Midway=5 May = Gaia.
Nuzzle=6,500=7,000=70%=P7.0D=7.0=Language=Assets=Mars=7 July=Pleiades.
NV=500=5%=P5.00D=5.0=Law=Time=Venus=5 May=Aphrodite>>L=N.
NW=500=5%=P5.00D=5.0=Law=Time=Venus=5 May=Aphrodite>>L=N.
NWbW=1,500=15%=P1.50D=1.5=Authority=Solar Crown=1 May = Maia.
NWT=1,000=100%=10.0=1.0=Mind=Sun=1 January=Helios >> M=E4.
n.wt.=1,000=100%=10.0=1.0=Mind=Sun=1 January=Helios >> M=E4.
NY=1,000=100%=10.0=1.0=Mind=Sun=1 January=Helios >> M=E4.
Nyasa Lake.=5,500=5.5=80%=P5.50=Earth-Midway=5 May = Gaia.
NYC=1,500=15%=P1.50D=1.5=Authority=Solar Crown=1 May = Maia.
Nylon=10,000=1,000=100%=Physicality=Tech.=10 Oct.=Uranus=P=1Ø.
Nymph=10,000=1,000=100%=10.0=Physicality=Tech.=10 Oct.=Uranus=P=1Ø.
NYSE=2,000=20%=P2.00D=2.0=Nature=Matter=Moon=2 Feb.=Cupid=N=C+_
N.Z.=1,000=100%=10.0=1.0=Mind=Sun=1 January=Helios >> M=E4.

MAKABET =Oo=

---

o1=8,000=80%=P8.0D=Economy=Currency=8 Aug.=Zeus>>E=v.
First O is the center of the universe being Zeus - Jehovah - Allah coded ZeJeAl. The energy for the day 8 August in the human energy database indicates the quantity of energy released on that day as a constant and annual (specific year) as a variable.
Day 8:Value:1.1 Planetary Type:Neptune Human Type:Philosophy Birth Energy Level:20.0%.
The codes 1.1 shows that the Almighty is the inventor of the universe. Athena is the Spirit of GOD thus the Spirit of invention known in the Greek mythology as the Goddess of wisdom and the brainchild of the almighty. This means that Zeus visits the Earth accompanied by Athena each year every 8th August through the Sun indicated as O=Ø=9.0=Council of Gods & Muses = Host =Holy Spirit as a body as seen in the visitation in the burning bush. This is the Creatocracy of things. Conventionally O is the 15th letter of the English alphabet >> Maia >> 15=1.5 >> Solar Crown >> Great Goddess of the Universe and the Mind of GOD.The energy base above indicates 20%=2.0 >> Moon >> Mare through which Earth receives the grace or PGI energy. This means that highly developed and connected persons will become inspired at about this period from Artemis and Cupid. Computing details will show us the specific energy that will be transmuted on such day.

8.0*1.1=p=9.1+8.8=17.9x=px=97.98=100=10.0>>2.0*1.5=p=3.5+3=6.5x=px=17=20=2.0
10.0*2.0=p=12+20=32x=px=272=300=3.0[9.0]>3.0*9.0=p=12+27=39x=px=363=3.6=4.0.
= Hermes = Mercury. The energy released to Earth is absorbed through the ears, processed in bits as potentials and brain liquid manifested as mercury after mixing with the brain matter. The result is self communication and power built on innate capacity ability and capability. In simple terms this is how man receives more grace to develop his innate capacities since he is born with it. Mercury comes from Hermes translated as wit without which wisdom cannot function. The bible says that whoever lacks wisdom should ask from GOD and he will receive. 8 August is the Castle Makupedia World Encyclopedia Day of Wisdom. This is instituted established and protected by the laws of GOD. So O is GOD.

---

o2=1,500=15%=P1.50D=1.5=Authority=Solar Crown=1 May = Maia.
O1=9,000=90%=P9.00D=9.0=Abstraction=Gods=Saturn=9Sept.>>A=Ø.
O2=2,500=3,000=30%=P3.0D=3.0=Creativity=Stars=Muses=3 March = C=I>>GIL.
O3=2,000=20%=P2.00D=2.0=Nature=Matter=Moon=2 Feb.=Cupid=N=C+_
Oaf=3,500=4,000=40%=P4.0D=Govt.=Creatocracy=4 April=Mercury=Hermes=G=A4.
Oahu=4,500=5,000=50%=P5.00D=Law=Time=Venus=5 May = Aphrodite>>L=N.

Oak=9,000=90%=P9.00D=9.0=Abstraction=Gods=Saturn=9Sept.>>A=Ø.
Mentioned in 1st Kings as the tree that killed Absalom son of David. Suspected to be the tree of the knowledge of good and evil in the Garden of Eden.

Oakland=7,000=70%=P7.0D=7.0=Language=Assets=Mars=7 July=Pleiades.
Oakley Annie=2,000=20%=P2.00D=2.0=Nature=Matter=Moon=2 Feb.=Cupid=N=C+_
Oakum=8,000=80%=P8.0D=Economy=Currency=8 Aug.=Zeus>>E=v.
Oar=10,000=1,000=100%=10.0=Physicality=Tech.=10 Oct.=Uranus=P=1Ø.
Oar lock=6,000=60%=P6.0D=Man=Earth=Royalty=6 June=Gaia=Maia>>M=M2.
Oarsman=3,000=30%=P3.0D=3.0=Creativity=Stars=Muses=3 March = C=I>>GIL.
OAS=2,000=20%=P2.00D=2.0=Nature=Matter=Moon=2 Feb.=Cupid=N=C+_
Oasis=4,000=40%=P4.0D=Govt.=Creatocracy=4 April=Mercury=Hermes=G=A4.
Oat=8,000=80%=P8.0D=Economy=Currency=8 Aug.=Zeus>>E=v.
Oates Joyce=2,500=3,000=30%=P3.0D=3.0=Creativity=Stars=Muses=3 March = C=I
Oath=9,500=10,000=1,000=100%=10.0=Physicality=Tech.=10 Oct.=Uranus=P=1Ø.
Oatmeal=7,500=8,000=80%=P8.0D=Economy=Currency=8 Aug.=Zeus>>E=v.
Ob=10,500=11,000=11%=P1.10D=1.1=Idea=Brainchild=Inv.=11 Nov.=SC=Athena>>I=MT.

Obadiah=6,000=60%=P6.0D=Man=Earth=Royalty=6 June=Gaia=Maia>>M=M2.
A Hebrew prophet of the 6th century B.C. Inspired by Gaia >> Maia. The shortest book of the Bible bearing his name.

Obligato=5,500=5.5=80%=P5.50=Earth-Midway=5 May = Gaia.
Obdurate=4,500=5,000=50%=P5.00D=Law=Time=Venus=5 May = Aphrodite>>L=N.
O.B.E.=2,500=3,000=30%=P3.0D=3.0=Creativity=Stars=Muses=3 March = C=I>>GIL.

Obedient=7,000=70%=P7.0D=7.0=Language=Assets=Mars=7 July=Pleiades.
Obeisance=7,500=8,000=80%=P8.0D=Economy=Currency=8 Aug.=Zeus>>E=v.
Obelisk=12,500=13,000=13%=P1.30=Solar Core=Faculty=13 January=Athena.
Obese=5,500=5.5=80%=P5.50=Earth-Midway=5 May = Gaia.
Obey=6,000=60%=P6.0D=Man=Earth=Royalty=6 June=Gaia=Maia>>M=M2.
Obfuscate=7,000=70%=P7.0D=7.0=Language=Assets=Mars=7 July=Pleiades.
Obi=7,000=70%=P7.0D=7.0=Language=Assets=Mars=7 July=Pleiades.
Obit=1,500=15%=P1.50D=1.5=Authority=Solar Crown=1 May = Maia.
Obiter dictum=9,000=90%=P9.00D=9.0=Abstraction=Gods=Saturn=9Sept.>>A=Ø.
Obituary=8,500=9,000=90%=P9.00D=9.0=Abstraction=Gods=Saturn=9Sept.>>A=Ø.
Object=10,000=1,000=100%=10.0=Physicality=Tech.=10 Oct.=Uranus=P=1Ø.
Objectionable=1,500=15%=P1.50D=1.5=Authority=Solar Crown=1 May = Maia.
Objective=10,000=1,000=100%=10.0=Physicality=Tech.=10 Oct.=Uranus=P=1Ø.
Object lesson=3,500=4,000=40%=P4.0D=Govt.=Creatocracy=4 April=Hermes=G=A4.
Object d'art=1,500=15%=P1.50D=1.5=Authority=Solar Crown=1 May = Maia.
Objurgate=3,000=30%=P3.0D=3.0=Creativity=Stars=Muses=3 March = C=I>>GIL.
Oblate=4,500=5,000=50%=P5.00D=Law=Time=Venus=5 May = Aphrodite>>L=N.
Oblation=6,000=60%=P6.0D=Man=Earth=Royalty=6 June=Gaia=Maia>>M=M2.
Obligate=6,500=7,000=70%=P7.0D=7.0=Language=Assets=Mars=7 July=Pleiades.
Obligation=10,000=1,000=100%=10.0=Physicality=Tech.=10 Oct.=Uranus=P=1Ø.
Obligatory=2,500=3,000=30%=P3.0D=3.0=Creativity=Stars=Muses=3 March = C=I>>GIL.
Oblige=7,000=70%=P7.0D=7.0=Language=Assets=Mars=7 July=Pleiades.
Oblique=10,000=1,000=100%=10.0=Physicality=Tech.=10 Oct.=Uranus=P=1Ø.
Obliterate=6,000=60%=P6.0D=Man=Earth=Royalty=6 June=Gaia=Maia>>M=M2.
Oblivion=5,000=50%=P5.00D=Law=Time=Venus=5 May = Aphrodite>>L=N.
Oblivious=10,000=1,000=100%=10.0=Physicality=Tech.=10 Oct.=Uranus=P=1Ø.
Oblong=10,500=11,000=11%=P1.10D=1.1=Idea=Brainchild=Inv.=11 Nov.=Athena>>I=MT.
Obloquy=5,000=50%=P5.00D=Law=Time=Venus=5 May = Aphrodite>>L=N.
Obnoxious=3,000=30%=P3.0D=3.0=Creativity=Stars=Muses=3 March = C=I>>GIL.
Oboe=6,000=60%=P6.0D=Man=Earth=Royalty=6 June=Gaia=Maia>>M=M2.
Obscene=9,500=10,000=1,000=100%=10.0=Physicality=Tech.=10 Oct.=Uranus=P=1Ø.
Obscurantism=5,500=5.5=80%=P5.50=Earth-Midway=5 May = Gaia.
Obscure=7,000=70%=P7.0D=7.0=Language=Assets=Mars=7 July=Pleiades.
Obsequious=4,500=5,000=50%=P5.00D=Law=Time=Venus=5 May = Aphrodite>>L=N.
Obsequy=4,000=40%=P4.0D=Govt.=Creatocracy=4 April=Mercury=Hermes=G=A4.
Observance=10,000=1,000=100%=10.0=Physicality=Tech.=10 Oct.=Uranus=P=1Ø.
Observant=9,000=90%=P9.00D=9.0=Abstraction=Gods=Saturn=9Sept.>>A=Ø.
Observation=10,000=1,000=100%=10.0=Physicality=Tech.=10 Oct.=Uranus=P=1Ø.
Observatory=6,500=7,000=70%=P7.0D=7.0=Language=Assets=Mars=7 July=Pleiades.
Observe=10,000=1,000=100%=10.0=Physicality=Tech.=10 Oct.=Uranus=P=1Ø.
Obsess=8,000=80%=P8.0D=Economy=Currency=8 Aug.=Zeus>>E=v.
Obsession=10,000=1,000=100%=10.0=Physicality=Tech.=10 Oct.=Uranus=P=1Ø.
Obsidian=5,000=50%=P5.00D=Law=Time=Venus=5 May = Aphrodite>>L=N.
Obsolescent=4,000=40%=P4.0D=Govt.=Creatocracy=4 April=Mercury=Hermes=G=A4.
Obsolete=9,500=10,000=1,000=100%=10.0=Physicality=Tech.=10 Oct.=Uranus=P=1Ø.

Obstacle=11,000=11%=P1.10D=1.1=Idea=Brainchild=Inv.=11 Nov.=SC=Athena>>I=MT.
Obstetrician=3,000=30%=P3.0D=3.0=Creativity=Stars=Muses=3 March = C=I>>GIL.
Obstetrics=3,000=30%=P3.0D=3.0=Creativity=Stars=Muses=3 March = C=I>>GIL.
Obstinate=10,000=1,000=100%=10.0=Physicality=Tech.=10 Oct.=Uranus=P=1Ø.
Obstreperous=5,000=50%=P5.00D=Law=Time=Venus=5 May = Aphrodite>>L=N.
Obstruct=10,000=1,000=100%=10.0=Physicality=Tech.=10 Oct.=Uranus=P=1Ø.
Obstruction=6,000=60%=P6.0D=Man=Earth=Royalty=6 June=Gaia=Maia>>M=M2.
Obstructionist=4,000=40%=P4.0D=Govt.=Creatocracy=4 April=Mercury=Hermes=G=A4.
Obtain=6,500=7,000=70%=P7.0D=7.0=Language=Assets=Mars=7 July=Pleiades.
Obtrude=10,000=1,000=100%=10.0=Physicality=Tech.=10 Oct.=Uranus=P=1Ø.
Obtuse=10,000=1,000=100%=10.0=Physicality=Tech.=10 Oct.=Uranus=P=1Ø.
Obtuse angle=5,000=50%=P5.00D=Law=Time=Venus=5 May = Aphrodite>>L=N.
Obverse=10,000=1,000=100%=10.0=Physicality=Tech.=10 Oct.=Uranus=P=1Ø.
Obviate=5,500=5.5=80%=P5.50=Earth-Midway=5 May = Gaia.
Obvious=7,000=70%=P7.0D=7.0=Language=Assets=Mars=7 July=Pleiades.
Ocarina=7,000=70%=P7.0D=7.0=Language=Assets=Mars=7 July=Pleiades.
OCAS=2,500=3,000=30%=P3.0D=3.0=Creativity=Stars=Muses=3 March = C=I>>GIL.
O'Casey Sean=2,000=20%=P2.00D=2.0=Nature=Matter=Moon=2 Feb.=Cupid=N=C+_
Occasion=10,000=1,000=100%=10.0=Physicality=Tech.=10 Oct.=Uranus=P=1Ø.
Occasional=4,500=5,000=50%=P5.00D=Law=Time=Venus=5 May = Aphrodite>>L=N.
Occident=5,500=5.5=80%=P5.50=Earth-Midway=5 May = Gaia.
Occipital=3,000=30%=P3.0D=3.0=Creativity=Stars=Muses=3 March = C=I>>GIL.
Occipital bone=5,500=5.5=80%=P5.50=Earth-Midway=5 May = Gaia.
Occiput=4,500=5,000=50%=P5.00D=Law=Time=Venus=5 May = Aphrodite>>L=N.
Occlude=10,000=1,000=100%=10.0=Physicality=Tech.=10 Oct.=Uranus=P=1Ø.
Occult=10,500=11,000=11%=P1.10D=1.1=Idea=Brainchild=Inv.=11 Nov.=Athena>>I=MT.
Occultism=4,500=5,000=50%=P5.00D=Law=Time=Venus=5 May = Aphrodite>>L=N.
Occupancy=8,000=80%=P8.0D=Economy=Currency=8 Aug.=Zeus>>E=v.
Occupation=10,000=1,000=100%=10.0=Physicality=Tech.=10 Oct.=Uranus=P=1Ø.
Occupational therapy=5,500=5.5=80%=P5.50=Earth-Midway=5 May = Gaia.
Occupy=10,000=1,000=100%=10.0=Physicality=Tech.=10 Oct.=Uranus=P=1Ø.
Ocean=10,000=1,000=100%=10.0=Physicality=Tech.=10 Oct.=Uranus=P=1Ø.
Oceanarium=5,500=5.5=80%=P5.50=Earth-Midway=5 May = Gaia.
Oceania=10,000=1,000=100%=10.0=Physicality=Tech.=10 Oct.=Uranus=P=1Ø.
Oceanography=3,500=4,000=40%=P4.0D=Govt.=Creatocracy=4 April=Hermes=G=A4.
Oceanside=5,000=50%=P5.00D=Law=Time=Venus=5 May = Aphrodite>>L=N.
Ocelot=8,000=80%=P8.0D=Economy=Currency=8 Aug.=Zeus>>E=v.
Ocher=10,000=1,000=100%=10.0=Physicality=Tech.=10 Oct.=Uranus=P=1Ø.

O'clock=4,000=40%=P4.0D=Govt.=Creatocracy=4 April=Mercury=Hermes=G=A4.
Time is measured according to Hermes >> Khristos >>Christ hence B.C and A.D. The Mind
Clocks are Human Mind technologies(Mechnologies) invented by Peter Matthews-Akukalia,
Castle Makupedia. Mind Time is measured in the Maks after King Maks himself as the
author, inventor, pioneer, King, Emperor and the God of Creatocracy Genius and Mind.

O'Connor Flannery=2,000=20%=P2.00D=2.0=Nature=Moon=2 Feb.=Cupid=N=C+_
O'Connor Sandra Day.=7,500=8,000=80%=P8.0D=Econ=Currency=8 Aug.=Zeus>>E=v.
OCR=4,000=40%=P4.0D=Govt.=Creatocracy=4 April=Mercury=Hermes=G=A4.
OCS=1,500=15%=P1.50D=1.5=Authority=Solar Crown=1 May = Maia.
Oct.=500=5%=P5.00D=5.0=Law=Time=Venus=5 May=Aphrodite>>L=N.
Octagon=2,500=3,000=30%=P3.0D=3.0=Creativity=Stars=Muses=3 March = C=I>>GIL.

Octahedron=2,500=3,000=30%=P3.0D=3.0=Creativity=Stars=Muses=3 March = C=I.
A polyhedron with 8 sides. In the Creative Sciences shapes are also signs of the Gods
alongside the alphanumerics. They are measured as means of energy transmutation
through the cosmic spiral computing on the relationships of their dimensions to the spiral
energy and the resultant with application to resultant digital content in a person or thing.
So a shape can tell crisis or stability in a person or thing.
First 3.0*8.0=p=11+27=38x=px=335=33.5>>340>>3.4<4.3>2.0
The octahedron when seen in the constellation indicates a meeting of the Gods is in
session. The Venue of the meeting is in the moon.
Now spiral computing to determine the meaning of the sign before during or after the
meeting is thus>> ØD=ØS=ØT >> Ø2.0 = Ø8.0 = Ø2.0 >> Stability. The sign of the
Octahedron seen abstractly in thoughts dreams inspiration and seen physically in the
sky or graphs by the person at prayer indicates stability and answered prayers. However
source of the problem and its answer is indicated through the mare source of the seeker.

Octal=3,500=4,000=40%=P4.0D=Govt.=Creatocracy=4 April=Mercury=Hermes=G=A4.
Octane=5,500=5.5=80%=P5.50=Earth-Midway=5 May = Gaia.
Octane number=10,000=1,000=100%=10.0=Physicality=Tech.=10 Oct.=Uranus=P=1Ø.
Octant=3,500=4,000=40%=P4.0D=Govt.=Creatocracy=4 April=Mercury=Hermes=G=A4.
Octave=8,000=80%=P8.0D=Economy=Currency=8 Aug.=Zeus>>E=v.
Octavian=1,000=100%=10.0=1.0=Mind=Sun=1 January=Helios >> M=E4.
Octavo=10,000=1,000=100%=10.0=Physicality=Tech.=10 Oct.=Uranus=P=1Ø.
Octet=6,500=7,000=70%=P7.0D=7.0=Language=Assets=Mars=7 July=Pleiades.
Octillion=6,000=60%=P6.0D=Man=Earth=Royalty=6 June=Gaia=Maia>>M=M2.
octo-=4,000=40%=P4.0D=Govt.=Creatocracy=4 April=Mercury=Hermes=G=A4.

October=6,500=7,000=70%=P7.0D=7.0=Language=Assets=Mars=7 July=Pleiades.
The 10th month of the Gregorian calendar. Latin. Octōber, eighth month.]
10.0*8.0=p=18+80=98x=px=1,538=15.38. A month of authority and the Solar Crown
inspired by Maia with the functional approval of Zeus Jehovah Allah >> ZeJeAl and
operated by the muses of the Superior Heaven being the sisters of Maia (Pleiades). So
October is the month of the sweet influences of the Pleiades that results to decision
making of Zeus Himself as mention in the Job 38:31. The code in Job is the "O" October.
The Maks Calendar will have it as the total resultant dimension month. The apotheosis
of Castle Makupedia was first celebrated October 13. And is now annual worldwide.

Octogenarian=6,500=7,000=70%=P7.0D=7.0=Language=Assets=Mars=7 July=Pleiades.
Octopus=10,000=1,000=100%=10.0=Physicality=Tech.=10 Oct.=Uranus=P=1Ø.
Oculist=3,000=30%=P3.0D=3.0=Creativity=Stars=Muses=3 March = C=I>>GIL.
OD=6,500=7,000=70%=P7.0D=7.0=Language=Assets=Mars=7 July=Pleiades.
O.D.=3,500=4,000=40%=P4.0D=Govt.=Creatocracy=4 April=Mercury=Hermes=G=A4.
Odd=10,000=1,000=100%=10.0=Physicality=Tech.=10 Oct.=Uranus=P=1Ø.
Oddball=2,000=20%=P2.00D=2.0=Nature=Matter=Moon=2 Feb.=Cupid=N=C+_
Oddity=4,500=5,000=50%=P5.00D=Law=Time=Venus=5 May = Aphrodite>>L=N.
Odd job=3,500=4,000=40%=P4.0D=Govt.=Creatocracy=4 April=Mercury=Hermes=G=A4.
Oddment=1,500=15%=P1.50D=1.5=Authority=Solar Crown=1 May = Maia.
Odds=10,000=1,000=100%=10.0=Physicality=Tech.=10 Oct.=Uranus=P=1Ø.
Odds and ends=1,000=100%=10.0=1.0=Mind=Sun=1 January=Helios >> M=E4.
Odds-on=3,500=4,000=40%=P4.0D=Govt.=Creatocracy=4 April=Hermes=G=A4.
Ode=10,000=1,000=100%=10.0=Physicality=Tech.=10 Oct.=Uranus=P=1Ø.
Odense=7,000=70%=P7.0D=7.0=Language=Assets=Mars=7 July=Pleiades.
Oder=11,500=12,000=12%=P1.20D=1.2=Knowledge=Edu=12Dec.=Athena>>K=F.
Odessa=8,000=80%=P8.0D=Economy=Currency=8 Aug.=Zeus>>E=v.
Odets Clifford=2,000=20%=P2.00D=2.0=Nature=Matter=Moon=2 Feb.=Cupid=N=C+_

Odin=4,000=40%=P4.0D=Govt.=Creatocracy=4 April=Mercury=Hermes=G=A4.
Myth.The Norse God of wisdom, war and art.>>Hermes whom is wit.Rom.8:19-23.

Odious=3,000=30%=P3.0D=3.0=Creativity=Stars=Muses=3 March = C=I>>GIL.
Odium=7,000=70%=P7.0D=7.0=Language=Assets=Mars=7 July=Pleiades.
Odometer=5,500=5.5=80%=P5.50=Earth-Midway=5 May = Gaia.
Odontology=7,500=8,000=80%=P8.0D=Economy=Currency=8 Aug.=Zeus>>E=v.
Odor=9,500=10,000=1,000=100%=10.0=Physicality=Tech.=10 Oct.=Uranus=P=1Ø.
Odoriferous=3,000=30%=P3.0D=3.0=Creativity=Stars=Muses=3 March = C=I>>GIL.

Odysseus=3,500=4,000=40%=P4.0D=Govt.=Creatocracy=4 April=Hermes=G=A4.
Greek myth. The hero of Homer's Odyssey. He was Hermes. Inspired by the muses.

Oedipus=7,000=70%=P7.0D=7.0=Language=Assets=Mars=7 July=Pleiades.
Oedipus complex=8,000=80%=P8.0D=Economy=Currency=8 Aug.=Zeus>>E=v.

O'er=500=5%=P5.00D=5.0=Law=Time=Venus=5 May=Aphrodite>>L=N.
Oeuvre=6,000=60%=P6.0D=Man=Earth=Royalty=6 June=Gaia=Maia>>M=M2.
Of=10,000=1,000=100%=10.0=Physicality=Tech.=10 Oct.=Uranus=P=1Ø.
Off=10,000=1,000=100%=10.0=Physicality=Tech.=10 Oct.=Uranus=P=1Ø.
Offal=4,000=40%=P4.0D=Govt.=Creatocracy=4 April=Mercury=Hermes=G=A4.
Offbeat=4,500=5,000=50%=P5.00D=Law=Time=Venus=5 May = Aphrodite>>L=N.
Off color=5,500=5.5=80%=P5.50=Earth-Midway=5 May = Gaia.
Offenbach Jacques.=2,000=20%=P2.00D=2.0=Nature=Moon=2 Feb.=Cupid=N=C+_
Offend=8,500=9,000=90%=P9.00D=9.0=Abstraction=Gods=Saturn=9Sept.>>A=Ø.

Offense=13,000=13%=P1.30=Solar Core=Faculty=13 January=Athena.
Offensive=10,000=1,000=100%=10.0=Physicality=Tech.=10 Oct.=Uranus=P=1Ø.
Offer=10,000=1,000=100%=10.0=Physicality=Tech.=10 Oct.=Uranus=P=1Ø.
Offering=8,500=9,000=90%=P9.00D=9.0=Abstraction=Gods=Saturn=9Sept.>>A=Ø.
Offertory=10,000=1,000=100%=10.0=Physicality=Tech.=10 Oct.=Uranus=P=1Ø.
Offhand=2,000=20%=P2.00D=2.0=Nature=Matter=Moon=2 Feb.=Cupid=N=C+_
Office=10,000=1,000=100%=10.0=Physicality=Tech.=10 Oct.=Uranus=P=1Ø.
Officeholder=2,500=3,000=30%=P3.0D=3.0=Creativity=Stars=Muses=3 March = C=I
Officer=10,000=1,000=100%=10.0=Physicality=Tech.=10 Oct.=Uranus=P=1Ø.
Official=10,000=1,000=100%=10.0=Physicality=Tech.=10 Oct.=Uranus=P=1Ø.
Officialism=3,500=4,000=40%=P4.0D=Govt.=Creatocracy=4 April=Hermes=G=A4.
Officiate=11,000=11%=P1.10D=1.1=Idea=Brainchild=Inv.=11 Nov.=SC=Athena>>I=MT.
Officious=6,000=60%=P6.0D=Man=Earth=Royalty=6 June=Gaia=Maia>>M=M2.
Offing=3,500=4,000=40%=P4.0D=Govt.=Creatocracy=4 April=Mercury=Hermes=G=A4.
Offish=1,000=100%=10.0=1.0=Mind=Sun=1 January=Helios >> M=E4.
Off key=4,500=5,000=50%=P5.00D=Law=Time=Venus=5 May = Aphrodite>>L=N.
Off-limits=2,500=3,000=30%=P3.0D=3.0=Creativity=Stars=Muses=3 March = C=I>>GIL.
Offline=3,000=30%=P3.0D=3.0=Creativity=Stars=Muses=3 March = C=I>>GIL.
Offload=6,000=60%=P6.0D=Man=Earth=Royalty=6 June=Gaia=Maia>>M=M2.
Off print=4,000=40%=P4.0D=Govt.=Creatocracy=4 April=Mercury=Hermes=G=A4.
Off-road=4,500=5,000=50%=P5.00D=Law=Time=Venus=5 May = Aphrodite>>L=N.
Off season=5,500=5.5=80%=P5.50=Earth-Midway=5 May = Gaia.
Offset=10,000=1,000=100%=10.0=Physicality=Tech.=10 Oct.=Uranus=P=1Ø.
Offshoot=11,000=11%=P1.10D=1.1=Idea=Brainchild=Inv.=11 Nov.=SC=Athena>>I=MT.
Offshore=4,000=40%=P4.0D=Govt.=Creatocracy=4 April=Mercury=Hermes=G=A4.
Offside=4,000=40%=P4.0D=Govt.=Creatocracy=4 April=Mercury=Hermes=G=A4.
Offspring=3,500=4,000=40%=P4.0D=Govt.=Creatocracy=4 April=Hermes=G=A4.
Offstage=5,500=5.5=80%=P5.50=Earth-Midway=5 May = Gaia.
Off-the-cuff=1,500=15%=P1.50D=1.5=Authority=Solar Crown=1 May = Maia.
Off the record=2,500=3,000=30%=P3.0D=3.0=Creativity=Stars=Muses=3 March = C=I
Off the wall=2,500=3,000=30%=P3.0D=3.0=Creativity=Stars=Muses=3 March = C=I.
Off track betting=4,000=40%=P4.0D=Govt.=Creatocracy=4 April=Hermes=G=A4.
Off white=2,500=3,000=30%=P3.0D=3.0=Creativity=Stars=Muses=3 March = C=I>>GIL.
Off year=7,000=70%=P7.0D=7.0=Language=Assets=Mars=7 July=Pleiades.
Oft=500=5%=P5.00D=5.0=Law=Time=Venus=5 May=Aphrodite>>L=N.
Often=2,500=3,000=30%=P3.0D=3.0=Creativity=Stars=Muses=3 March = C=I>>GIL.
Oftentimes=500=5%=P5.00D=5.0=Law=Time=Venus=5 May=Aphrodite>>L=N.

Ogbomosho=4,500=5,000=50%=P5.00D=Law=Time=Venus=5 May = Aphrodite>>L=N.
A city of SW Nigeria NNE of Ibadan. A road path of Hermes on earthly visit to Aphrodite.
A town of power and authority with gifts in relationships and love.

Oglala=5,000=50%=P5.00D=Law=Time=Venus=5 May = Aphrodite>>L=N.
Ogle=5,000=50%=P5.00D=Law=Time=Venus=5 May = Aphrodite>>L=N.

Oglethorpe James=3,500=4,000=40%=P4.0D=Govt.=4 April=Hermes=G=A4.
Ogre=5,500=5.5=80%=P5.50=Earth-Midway=5 May = Gaia.
Ogress=3,500=4,000=40%=P4.0D=Govt.=Creatocracy=4 April=Mercury=Hermes=G=A4.
Oh=8,000=80%=P8.0D=Economy=Currency=8 Aug.=Zeus>>E=v.
OH=500=5%=P5.00D=5.0=Law=Time=Venus=5 May=Aphrodite>>L=N.
O. Henry=2,000=20%=P2.00D=2.0=Nature=Matter=Moon=2 Feb.=Cupid=N=C+_
Ohio=5,500=5.5=80%=P5.50=Earth-Midway=5 May = Gaia.
Ohio River=13,500=14,000=14%=P1.40D=1.4=Mgt.=Solar Energy=13 May=Athena=SC=0.1
Ohm=10,000=1,000=100%=10.0=Physicality=Tech.=10 Oct.=Uranus=P=1Ø.
Ohmmeter=5,500=5.5=80%=P5.50=Earth-Midway=5 May = Gaia.
-old=6,000=60%=P6.0D=Man=Earth=Royalty=6 June=Gaia=Maia>>M=M2.
Oil=10,000=1,000=100%=10.0=Physicality=Tech.=10 Oct.=Uranus=P=1Ø.
Oil cloth=5,000=50%=P5.00D=Law=Time=Venus=5 May = Aphrodite>>L=N.
Oil color=1,500=15%=P1.50D=1.5=Authority=Solar Crown=1 May = Maia.
Oil field=3,500=4,000=40%=P4.0D=Govt.=Creatocracy=4 April=Mercury=Hermes=G=A4.
Oil paint=5,500=5.5=80%=P5.50=Earth-Midway=5 May = Gaia.
Oil painting=5,500=5.5=80%=P5.50=Earth-Midway=5 May = Gaia.
Oil shale=6,500=7,000=70%=P7.0D=7.0=Language=Assets=Mars=7 July=Pleiades.
Oil skin=6,500=7,000=70%=P7.0D=7.0=Language=Assets=Mars=7 July=Pleiades.
Oil slick=3,000=30%=P3.0D=3.0=Creativity=Stars=Muses=3 March = C=I>>GIL.
Oil well=7,000=70%=P7.0D=7.0=Language=Assets=Mars=7 July=Pleiades.
Oily=6,500=7,000=70%=P7.0D=7.0=Language=Assets=Mars=7 July=Pleiades.
Oink=4,000=40%=P4.0D=Govt.=Creatocracy=4 April=Mercury=Hermes=G=A4.
Ointment=7,500=8,000=80%=P8.0D=Economy=Currency=8 Aug.=Zeus>>E=v.
Oise=10,000=1,000=100%=10.0=Physicality=Tech.=10 Oct.=Uranus=P=1Ø.
Ojibwa=10,000=1,000=100%=10.0=Physicality=Tech.=10 Oct.=Uranus=P=1Ø.
OK1=10,000=1,000=100%=10.0=Physicality=Tech.=10 Oct.=Uranus=P=1Ø.
OK2=500=5%=P5.00D=5.0=Law=Time=Venus=5 May=Aphrodite>>L=N.
Oka=8,500=9,000=90%=P9.00D=9.0=Abstraction=Gods=Saturn=9Sept.>>A=Ø.
Okavango=9,000=90%=P9.00D=9.0=Abstraction=Gods=Saturn=9Sept.>>A=Ø.
Okayama=7,000=70%=P7.0D=7.0=Language=Assets=Mars=7 July=Pleiades.
Okeechobee Lake=4,000=40%=P4.0D=Govt.=Creatocracy=4 April=Hermes=G=A4.
O'Keefe Georgia=2,000=20%=P2.00D=2.0=Nature=Matter=Moon=2 Feb.=Cupid=N=C+_
Okefenokee Swamp=5,000=50%=P5.00D=Law=Time=Venus=5 May = Aphrodite>>L=N.
Okhotsk=6,000=60%=P6.0D=Man=Earth=Royalty=6 June=Gaia=Maia>>M=M2.
Okinawa=7,500=8,000=80%=P8.0D=Economy=Currency=8 Aug.=Zeus>>E=v.
Oklahoma=6,000=60%=P6.0D=Man=Earth=Royalty=6 June=Gaia=Maia>>M=M2.
Oklahoma City.=4,500=5,000=50%=P5.00D=Law=Time=Venus=5 May = Aphrodite>>L=N.
Okra=10,000=1,000=100%=10.0=Physicality=Tech.=10 Oct.=Uranus=P=1Ø.
-ol=4,000=40%=P4.0D=Govt.=Creatocracy=4 April=Mercury=Hermes=G=A4.
Olaf II=6,500=7,000=70%=P7.0D=7.0=Language=Assets=Mars=7 July=Pleiades.
Old=10,000=1,000=100%=10.0=Physicality=Tech.=10 Oct.=Uranus=P=1Ø.
Olden=500=5%=P5.00D=5.0=Law=Time=Venus=5 May=Aphrodite>>L=N.

Old English=5,000=50%=P5.00D=Law=Time=Venus=5 May = Aphrodite>>L=N.
English just as the Ibo language is inspired by Aphrodite.

Old fashioned=4,500=5,000=50%=P5.00D=Law=Time=Venus=5 May = Aphrodite>>L=N.
Inspired by Hermes as a means to reach Aphrodite. Family Law.

Old French=8,000=80%=P8.0D=Economy=Currency=8 Aug.=Zeus>>E=v.
French is a language inspired by Zeus. So GOD speaks Greek Hebrew Arabic and French.

Old guard=4,500=5,000=50%=P5.00D=Law=Time=Venus=5 May = Aphrodite>>L=N.
Old hand=3,500=4,000=40%=P4.0D=Govt.=Creatocracy=4 April=Hermes=G=A4.

Old hat=1,500=15%=P1.50D=1.5=Authority=Solar Crown=1 May = Maia.
Maia will often as a person wearing an old hat.

Old High German=5,500=5.5=80%=P5.50=Earth-Midway=5 May = Gaia.
Oldie=4,500=5,000=50%=P5.00D=Law=Time=Venus=5 May = Aphrodite>>L=N.
Old Irish=3,000=30%=P3.0D=3.0=Creativity=Stars=Muses=3 March = C=I>>GIL.
Old Italian=3,500=4,000=40%=P4.0D=Govt.=Creatocracy=4 April=Hermes=G=A4.
Old Line=2,000=20%=P2.00D=2.0=Nature=Matter=Moon=2 Feb.=Cupid=N=C+_
Old master=8,000=80%=P8.0D=Economy=Currency=8 Aug.=Zeus>>E=v.
Old Norse=8,500=9,000=90%=P9.00D=9.0=Abstraction=Gods=Saturn=9Sept.>>A=Ø.
Old North French=3,000=30%=P3.0D=3.0=Creativity=Stars=Muses=3 March = C=I>>GIL.
Old Persian=7,500=8,000=80%=P8.0D=Economy=Currency=8 Aug.=Zeus>>E=v.
Old Provençal=4,000=40%=P4.0D=Govt.=Creatocracy=4 April=Mercury=Hermes=G=A4.
Old School=4,000=40%=P4.0D=Govt.=Creatocracy=4 April=Mercury=Hermes=G=A4.
Old Spanish=3,500=4,000=40%=P4.0D=Govt.=Creatocracy=4 April=Hermes=G=A4.
Oldster=2,000=20%=P2.00D=2.0=Nature=Matter=Moon=2 Feb.=Cupid=N=C+_

Old Testament=7,500=8,000=80%=P8.0D=Economy=Currency=8 Aug.=Zeus>>E=v.
Computation (7,000) is the means (500) to understanding the Old Testament.

Old timer=6,000=60%=P6.0D=Man=Earth=Royalty=6 June=Gaia=Maia>>M=M2.
Olduvai Gorge=4,500=5,000=50%=P5.00D=Law=Time=Venus=5 May = Aphrodite>>L=N.
Old wives' tale=1,500=15%=P1.50D=1.5=Authority=Solar Crown=1 May = Maia.
Old World=4,000=40%=P4.0D=Govt.=Creatocracy=4 April=Mercury=Hermes=G=A4.
Oleaginous=7,000=70%=P7.0D=7.0=Language=Assets=Mars=7 July=Pleiades.
Oleander=6,500=7,000=70%=P7.0D=7.0=Language=Assets=Mars=7 July=Pleiades.
Oleic acid=4,500=5,000=50%=P5.00D=Law=Time=Venus=5 May = Aphrodite>>L=N.
Oleo=1,000=100%=10.0=1.0=Mind=Sun=1 January=Helios >> M=E4.
Oleo-=2,000=20%=P2.00D=2.0=Nature=Matter=Moon=2 Feb.=Cupid=N=C+_
Oleomargarine=500=5%=P5.00D=5.0=Law=Time=Venus=5 May=Aphrodite>>L=N.

Olfaction=4,000=40%=P4.0D=Govt.=Creatocracy=4 April=Mercury=Hermes=G=A4.
Olfactory=5,000=50%=P5.00D=Law=Time=Venus=5 May = Aphrodite>>L=N.
Olicook=10,000=1,000=100%=10.0=Physicality=Tech.=10 Oct.=Uranus=P=1Ø.
Oligarchy=6,500=7,000=70%=P7.0D=7.0=Language=Assets=Mars=7 July=Pleiades.
Oligo-=2,000=20%=P2.00D=2.0=Nature=Matter=Moon=2 Feb.=Cupid=N=C+_
Oligocene=7,500=8,000=80%=P8.0D=Economy=Currency=8 Aug.=Zeus>>E=v.
Olive=10,000=1,000=100%=10.0=Physicality=Tech.=10 Oct.=Uranus=P=1Ø.
Olive branch=5,500=5.5=80%=P5.50=Earth-Midway=5 May = Gaia.
Olives Mount of.=5,000=50%=P5.00D=Law=Time=Venus=5 May = Aphrodite>>L=N.
Olmec=7,000=70%=P7.0D=7.0=Language=Assets=Mars=7 July=Pleiades.
Olympia1=4,500=5,000=50%=P5.00D=Law=Time=Venus=5 May = Aphrodite>>L=N.
Olympia2=7,000=70%=P7.0D=7.0=Language=Assets=Mars=7 July=Pleiades.

Olympian=9,000=90%=P9.00D=9.0=Abstraction=Gods=Saturn=9Sept.>>A=Ø.
Greek Myth. Of or relating to the Gods and Goddesses of Mount Olympus. Surpassing all others in scope.

Olympic Games=10,000=1,000=100%=10.0=Physicality=Tech.=10 Oct.=Uranus=P=1Ø.
Olympics=2,500=3,000=30%=P3.0D=3.0=Creativity=Stars=Muses=3 March = C=I>>GIL.
Olympus=10,000=1,000=100%=10.0=Physicality=Tech.=10 Oct.=Uranus=P=1Ø.
Om=6,000=60%=P6.0D=Man=Earth=Royalty=6 June=Gaia=Maia>>M=M2.
-oma=7,000=70%=P7.0D=7.0=Language=Assets=Mars=7 July=Pleiades.
Omaha1=6,500=7,000=70%=P7.0D=7.0=Language=Assets=Mars=7 July=Pleiades.
Omaha2=5,500=5.5=80%=P5.50=Earth-Midway=5 May = Gaia.
Oman=9,000=90%=P9.00D=9.0=Abstraction=Gods=Saturn=9Sept.>>A=Ø.
Omar Khayyám=4,000=40%=P4.0D=Govt.=Creatocracy=4 April=Mercury=Hermes=G=A4.
OMB=2,500=3,000=30%=P3.0D=3.0=Creativity=Stars=Muses=3 March = C=I>>GIL.
Ombudsman=10,000=1,000=100%=10.0=Physicality=Tech.=10 Oct.=Uranus=P=1Ø.
Omdurman=6,500=7,000=70%=P7.0D=7.0=Language=Assets=Mars=7 July=Pleiades.

Omega=5,500=5.5=80%=P5.50=Earth-Midway=5 May = Gaia.
The 24th letter of the Greek alphabet. 24>>2.4>>International Business in the dimension of Knowledge >> Athena. I am the alpha and omega is proof that Greek is the language of the Gods. See Olympian. Computing 2.4*5.5x=px=7.9+13.2=21.1x=px=125.38=130=1.3. We confirm Athena (12=1.2) is the authority (5.0) that functions as the muse to Zeus. She is Zeusian muse known as the Spirit of GOD. She is the God's wisdom and Creative Intelligence that makes known His will. Creative Intelligence is expressed as the Creative Sciences or Faculty of Creative & Psycho-Social Sciences. Athena is expressly the supreme muse that inspires teaches instructs comforts and speaks to all Zeus incarnations. Peter Matthews-Akukalia, Castle Makupedia is known to interact directly with Athena and even married her after computing and interpreting the signs of the Scriptures. See book >> The Creatocracy Republic of Castle Makupedia by Peter Matthews-Akukalia. (A Mind Arts). Now Alpha = 4.0=Hermes=Wit. Omega=1.3=Athena=Wis(Dom) so I am the alpha and omega is thus synchronized >> 4.0*1.3x=5.3+5.2=10.5x=px=38.06=40=4.0 = Hermes

= Jesus Christ. This is confirmed because it was Jesus who made this statement in the Bible. The hidden code of Hermes is found in the Psalm 6. A prayer made by David and inspired prophecy by the muse Athena about the sufferings Hermes will endure in time to come. This manifested as the sufferings and death of Jesus Christ on Earth. Athena is sister and next to Hermes. In certain cases she might be considered superior to Him because she is the direct brainchild of the Father Zeus. So Jesus is the complete bond of three persons being Zeus, GOD the Father, GOD the Son (Himself >> Hermes) and GOD the Holy Spirit (Athena). This is quite strange but verifiable and true.

Omelet=8,000=80%=P8.0D=Economy=Currency=8 Aug.=Zeus>>E=v.

Omen=4,500=5,000=50%=P5.00D=Law=Time=Venus=5 May = Aphrodite>>L=N.
A powerful (4,000=power) means (500) of communication from Hermes to persons.

Omicron=5,500=5.5=80%=P5.50=Earth-Midway=5 May = Gaia.
Ominous=5,000=50%=P5.00D=Law=Time=Venus=5 May = Aphrodite>>L=N.
Omit=8,000=80%=P8.0D=Economy=Currency=8 Aug.=Zeus>>E=v.
Omni-=2,000=20%=P2.00D=2.0=Nature=Matter=Moon=2 Feb.=Cupid=N=C+_
Omnibus=7,000=70%=P7.0D=7.0=Language=Assets=Mars=7 July=Pleiades.
Omnidirectional=4,500=5,000=50%=P5.00D=Law=Time=Venus=5 May =Odite>>L=N.
Omnipotent=4,000=40%=P4.0D=Govt.=Creatocracy=4 April=Mercury=Hermes=G=A4.
Omnipresent=1,000=100%=10.0=1.0=Mind=Sun=1 January=Helios >> M=E4.
Omniscient=6,500=7,000=70%=P7.0D=7.0=Language=Assets=Mars=7 July=Pleiades.
Omnium-gathernum=4,000=40%=P4,0D=Govt.=Creatocracy=4 April=Hermes=G=A4.
Omnivorous=6,500=7,000=70%=P7.0D=7.0=Language=Assets=Mars=7 July=Pleiades.
Omsk=6,500=7,000=70%=P7.0D=7.0=Language=Assets=Mars=7 July=Pleiades.
On=10,000=1,000=100%=10.0=Physicality=Tech.=10 Oct.=Uranus=P=1Ø.
ON=500=5%=P5.00D=5.0=Law=Time=Venus=5 May=Aphrodite>>L=N.
-on1=3,500=4,000=40%=P4.0D=Govt.=Creatocracy=4 April=Mercury=Hermes=G=A4.
on2=2,500=3,000=30%=P3.0D=3.0=Creativity=Stars=Muses=3 March = C=I>>GIL.
Once=10,000=1,000=100%=10.0=Physicality=Tech.=10 Oct.=Uranus=P=1Ø.
Once-over=3,500=4,000=40%=P4.0D=Govt.=Creatocracy=4 April=Hermes=G=A4.
Oncogene=10,000=1,000=100%=10.0=Physicality=Tech.=10 Oct.=Uranus=P=1Ø.
Oncogenesis=3,000=30%=P3.0D=3.0=Creativity=Stars=Muses=3 March = C=I>>GIL.
Oncology=2,500=3,000=30%=P3.0D=3.0=Creativity=Stars=Muses=3 March = C=I>>GIL.
Oncoming=500=5%=P5.00D=5.0=Law=Time=Venus=5 May=Aphrodite>>L=N.

One=10,000=1,000=100%=10.0=Physicality=Tech.=10 Oct.=Uranus=P=1Ø.
One = 1 = 1.0 >> 10,000=1,000=100=10.0, hence there is nothing like one in a metric currency system because it is wrong. 100=1.0 is priced wrong. Rather 100=10 is truth.

Oneida=10,000=1,000=100%=10.0=Physicality=Tech.=10 Oct.=Uranus=P=1Ø.
O'Neill Eugéne=2,500=3,000=30%=P3.0D=3.0=Creativity=Stars=Muses=3 March=C=I
Oneself=10,000=1,000=100%=10.0=Physicality=Tech.=10 Oct.=Uranus=P=1Ø.

One shot=7,000=70%=P7.0D=7.0=Language=Assets=Mars=7 July=Pleiades.
One sided=3,500=4,000=40%=P4.0D=Govt.=Creatocracy=4 April=Hermes=G=A4.
Onetime=3,000=30%=P3.0D=3.0=Creativity=Stars=Muses=3 March = C=I>>GIL.
One-to-one=6,000=60%=P6.0D=Man=Earth=Royalty=6 June=Gaia=Maia>>M=M2.
One-track=3,500=4,000=40%=P4.0D=Govt.=Creatocracy=4 April=Hermes=G=A4.
One-up=3,000=30%=P3.0D=3.0=Creativity=Stars=Muses=3 March = C=I>>GIL.
One-upmanship=4,500=5,000=50%=P5.00D=Law=Time=Venus=5 May =Odite>>L=N.
One-way=6,500=7,000=70%=P7.0D=7.0=Language=Assets=Mars=7 July=Pleiades.
Ongoing=1,500=15%=P1.50D=1.5=Authority=Solar Crown=1 May = Maia.

Onion=6,000=60%=P6.0D=Man=Earth=Royalty=6 June=Gaia=Maia>>M=M2.
The physical equivalent of the human emotion is the onion plant. Contains lithium, an element of atomic number 3 and used as a mood stabilizing drug. So emotion is lithium.

Onion skin=2,500=3,000=30%=P3.0D=3.0=Creativity=Stars=Muses=3 March = C=I>>GIL.
Online=10,000=1,000=100%=10.0=Physicality=Tech.=10 Oct.=Uranus=P=1Ø.
Onlooker=1,000=100%=10.0=1.0=Mind=Sun=1 January=Helios >> M=E4.
Only=10,000=1,000=100%=10.0=Physicality=Tech.=10 Oct.=Uranus=P=1Ø.
Onomatopoeia=10,000=1,000=100%=10.0=Physicality=Tech.=10 Oct.=Uranus=P=1Ø.
Onondaga=10,000=1,000=100%=10.0=Physicality=Tech.=10 Oct.=Uranus=P=1Ø.
Onrush=2,500=3,000=30%=P3.0D=3.0=Creativity=Stars=Muses=3 March = C=I>>GIL.
Onset=2,000=20%=P2.00D=2.0=Nature=Matter=Moon=2 Feb.=Cupid=N=C+_
Onshore=4,500=5,000=50%=P5.00D=Law=Time=Venus=5 May = Aphrodite>>L=N.
Onslaught=3,500=4,000=40%=P4.0D=Govt.=Creatocracy=4 April=Hermes=G=A4.
Ont.=500=5%=P5.00D=5.0=Law=Time=Venus=5 May=Aphrodite>>L=N.
Ontario=10,000=1,000=100%=10.0=Physicality=Tech.=10 Oct.=Uranus=P=1Ø.
Ontario,Lake=6,000=60%=P6.0D=Man=Earth=Royalty=6 June=Gaia=Maia>>M=M2.
Onto=7,500=8,000=80%=P8.0D=Economy=Currency=8 Aug.=Zeus>>E=v.
Onto-=7,000=70%=P7.0D=7.0=Language=Assets=Mars=7 July=Pleiades.
Ontogeny=4,000=40%=P4.0D=Govt.=Creatocracy=4 April=Mercury=Hermes=G=A4.
Ontology=4,500=5,000=50%=P5.00D=Law=Time=Venus=5 May = Aphrodite>>L=N.

Onus=2,000=20%=P2.00D=2.0=Nature=Matter=Moon=2 Feb.=Cupid=N=C+_
Burden of proof (law). Blame.

Onward=4,500=5,000=50%=P5.00D=Law=Time=Venus=5 May = Aphrodite>>L=N.
-onym=3,500=4,000=40%=P4.0D=Govt.=Creatocracy=4 April=Mercury=Hermes=G=A4.
Onyx=5,500=5.5=80%=P5.50=Earth-Midway=5 May = Gaia.
oo-=4,000=40%=P4.0D=Govt.=Creatocracy=4 April=Mercury=Hermes=G=A4.
Oocyte=6,500=7,000=70%=P7.0D=7.0=Language=Assets=Mars=7 July=Pleiades.
Oodles=2,500=3,000=30%=P3.0D=3.0=Creativity=Stars=Muses=3 March = C=I>>GIL.
Oo genesis=4,000=40%=P4.0D=Govt.=Creatocracy=4 April=Mercury=Hermes=G=A4.
Oogonium=10,000=1,000=100%=10.0=Physicality=Tech.=10 Oct.=Uranus=P=1Ø.

Oolite=9,000=90%=P9.00D=9.0=Abstraction=Gods=Saturn=9Sept.>>A=Ø.
Oology=4,500=5,000=50%=P5.00D=Law=Time=Venus=5 May = Aphrodite>>L=N.
Oomph=4,000=40%=P4.0D=Govt.=Creatocracy=4 April=Mercury=Hermes=G=A4.
Ooze1=6,000=60%=P6.0D=Man=Earth=Royalty=6 June=Gaia=Maia>>M=M2.
Ooze2=6,000=60%=P6.0D=Man=Earth=Royalty=6 June=Gaia=Maia>>M=M2.
Opal=6,000=60%=P6.0D=Man=Earth=Royalty=6 June=Gaia=Maia>>M=M2.
Opalescent=4,500=5,000=50%=P5.00D=Law=Time=Venus=5 May = Aphrodite>>L=N.
Opaque=6,500=7,000=70%=P7.0D=7.0=Language=Assets=Mars=7 July=Pleiades.
Op art=8,000=80%=P8.0D=Economy=Currency=8 Aug.=Zeus>>E=v.
Op.cit.=3,500=4,000=40%=P4.0D=Govt.=Creatocracy=4 April=Mercury=Hermes=G=A4.

OPEC=2,500=3,000=30%=P3.0D=3.0=Creativity=Stars=Muses=3 March = C=I>>GIL.
OPEC is naturally driven by Creativity and the stars. The Sun is the largest star.
Computing the benchmark price for crude oil is by the stars of creativity.
A barrel of crude oil >> There is no "crude oil" combination hence crude * oil.
"A" is digitally wrong because it indicates 7.0 rather than one in conventional English.
So the language should be appropriately used as one (1) barrel of crude oil.
One = 10.0, Barrel = 1.2, Of = 10.0, Crude = 10.0, Oil = 10.0
One barrel of crude oil = 10.0*1.2*10.0*10.0*10.0 = P.
10.0*1.2x=px=11.2+12=23.2x=px=15.76
10.0*10.0x=px=20+100=120x=px=2,120*[10.0] = P.
15.76*2,120x=px=2,135.76+33,411.2=35,546.96x=px=71,393,851.47
10.0*71,393,851.47x=px=71,393,861.47+713, 938, 514.7=785,332,376.2
x=px=5.09708282x10v.16=5.1*1.6x=px=6.7+8.16=14.86x=px=69.532=70=P7.0 per barrel.
Now P1=£10 >> 7.0 x 10 = £70 is the benchmark translated into the US dollar and rolled
over in dynamic price for the time being in force daily through Maks Currency App.

Oped page=6,500=7,000=70%=P7.0D=7.0=Language=Assets=Mars=7 July=Pleiades.
Open=10,000=1,000=100%=10.0=Physicality=Tech.=10 Oct.=Uranus=P=1Ø.
Open air=2,500=3,000=30%=P3.0D=3.0=Creativity=Stars=Muses=3 March = C=I>>GIL.
Open-and-shut=2,000=20%=P2.00D=2.0=Nature=Matter=Moon=2 Feb.=Cupid=N=C+_
Open-end=500=5%=P5.00D=5.0=Law=Time=Venus=5 May=Aphrodite>>L=N.
Open-ended=5,000=50%=P5.00D=Law=Time=Venus=5 May = Aphrodite>>L=N.
Open-eyed=4,000=40%=P4.0D=Govt.=Creatocracy=4 April=Mercury=Hermes=G=A4.
Openhanded=3,500=4,000=40%=P4.0D=Govt.=Creatocracy=4 April=Hermes=G=A4.
Open hearth=7,000=70%=P7.0D=7.0=Language=Assets=Mars=7 July=Pleiades.
Open house=10,000=1,000=100%=10.0=Physicality=Tech.=10 Oct.=Uranus=P=1Ø.
Opening=10,000=1,000=100%=10.0=Physicality=Tech.=10 Oct.=Uranus=P=1Ø.
Open minded=5,000=50%=P5.00D=Law=Time=Venus=5 May = Aphrodite>>L=N.
Open shop=4,000=40%=P4.0D=Govt.=Creatocracy=4 April=Mercury=Hermes=G=A4.
Open work=5,500=5.5=80%=P5.50=Earth-Midway=5 May = Gaia.
Opera1=9,000=90%=P9.00D=9.0=Abstraction=Gods=Saturn=9Sept.>>A=Ø.
Opera2=2,000=20%=P2.00D=2.0=Nature=Matter=Moon=2 Feb.=Cupid=N=C+_
Operable=5,000=50%=P5.00D=Law=Time=Venus=5 May = Aphrodite>>L=N.

Opera glasses=4,000=40%=P4.0D=Govt.=Creatocracy=4 April=Mercury=Hermes=G=A4.
Operand=5,500=5.5=80%=P5.50=Earth-Midway=5 May = Gaia.
Operate=7,500=8,000=80%=P8.0D=Economy=Currency=8 Aug.=Zeus>>E=v.
Operating system=10,000=1,000=100%=10.0=Physicality=Tech.=10 Oct.=Uranus=P=1Ø.
Operation=10,000=1,000=100%=10.0=Physicality=Tech.=10 Oct.=Uranus=P=1Ø.
Operative=10,000=1,000=100%=10.0=Physicality=Tech.=10 Oct.=Uranus=P=1Ø.
Operator=10,000=1,000=100%=10.0=Physicality=Tech.=10 Oct.=Uranus=P=1Ø.
Operetta=10,000=1,000=100%=10.0=Physicality=Tech.=10 Oct.=Uranus=P=1Ø.
Ophthalmic=3,000=30%=P3.0D=3.0=Creativity=Stars=Muses=3 March = C=I>>GIL.
Opthalmo-=2,500=3,000=30%=P3.0D=3.0=Creativity=Stars=Muses=3 March = C=I>>GIL.
Ophthalmology=10,000=1,000=100%=10.0=Physicality=Tech.=10 Oct.=Uranus=P=1Ø.
Opiate=10,000=1,000=100%=10.0=Physicality=Tech.=10 Oct.=Uranus=P=1Ø.
Opine=5,000=50%=P5.00D=Law=Time=Venus=5 May = Aphrodite>>L=N.
Opinion=10,000=1,000=100%=10.0=Physicality=Tech.=10 Oct.=Uranus=P=1Ø.
Opinionated=2,500=3,000=30%=P3.0D=3.0=Creatv=Stars=Muses=3 March = C=I>>GIL.
Opium=9,000=90%=P9.00D=9.0=Abstraction=Gods=Saturn=9Sept.>>A=Ø.
Oporto=7,500=8,000=80%=P8.0D=Economy=Currency=8 Aug.=Zeus>>E=v.
Opossum=6,500=7,000=70%=P7.0D=7.0=Language=Assets=Mars=7 July=Pleiades.
Oppenheimer Julius=2,500=3,000=30%=P3.0D=3.0=Creatv=Stars=Muses=3 March=CI
Opponent=6,500=7,000=70%=P7.0D=7.0=Language=Assets=Mars=7 July=Pleiades.
Opportune=8,500=9,000=90%=P9.00D=9.0=Abstraction=Gods=Saturn=9Sept.>>A=Ø.
Opportunist=9,500=10,000=1,000=100%=10.0=Phy=Tech.=10 Oct.=Uranus=P=1Ø.
Opportunity=4,000=40%=P4.0D=Govt.=Creatocracy=4 April=Mercury=Hermes=G=A4.
Oppose=10,000=1,000=100%=10.0=Physicality=Tech.=10 Oct.=Uranus=P=1Ø.
Opposite=10,000=1,000=100%=10.0=Physicality=Tech.=10 Oct.=Uranus=P=1Ø.
Oppress=10,500=11,000=11%=P1.10D=1.1=Idea=Brainchild=Inv.=11 Nov=Athena>>I=MT.
Oppressive=6,000=60%=P6.0D=Man=Earth=Royalty=6 June=Gaia=Maia>>M=M2.
Opprobrious=3,000=30%=P3.0D=3.0=Creativity=Stars=Muses=3 March = C=I>>GIL.
Opprobrium=10,500=11,000=11%=P1.10D=1.1=Idea=Brainchild=11 Nov=Athena>>I=MT.
-opsy=3,000=30%=P3.0D=3.0=Creativity=Stars=Muses=3 March = C=I>>GIL.
Opt=2,000=20%=P2.00D=2.0=Nature=Matter=Moon=2 Feb.=Cupid=N=C+_
Optic=4,500=5,000=50%=P5.00D=Law=Time=Venus=5 May = Aphrodite>>L=N.
Optical=5,000=50%=P5.00D=Law=Time=Venus=5 May = Aphrodite>>L=N.
Optical art=1,000=100%=10.0=1.0=Mind=Sun=1 January=Helios >> M=E4.
Optical disk=10,000=1,000=100%=10.0=Physicality=Tech.=10 Oct.=Uranus=P=1Ø.
Optical illusion=2,000=20%=P2.00D=2.0=Nature=Matter=Moon=2 Feb.=Cupid=N=C+_
Optician=5,500=5.5=80%=P5.50=Earth-Midway=5 May = Gaia.
Optics=3,500=4,000=40%=P4.0D=Govt.=Creatocracy=4 April=Mercury=Hermes=G=A4.
Optimal=2,000=20%=P2.00D=2.0=Nature=Matter=Moon=2 Feb.=Cupid=N=C+_
Optimism=10,000=1,000=100%=10.0=Physicality=Tech.=10 Oct.=Uranus=P=1Ø.
Optimize=5,500=5.5=80%=P5.50=Earth-Midway=5 May = Gaia.
Optimum=10,000=1,000=100%=10.0=Physicality=Tech.=10 Oct.=Uranus=P=1Ø.
Option=10,000=1,000=100%=10.0=Physicality=Tech.=10 Oct.=Uranus=P=1Ø.
Optometry=10,000=1,000=100%=10.0=Physicality=Tech.=10 Oct.=Uranus=P=1Ø.
Opulent=3,000=30%=P3.0D=3.0=Creativity=Stars=Muses=3 March = C=I>>GIL.

Opus=3,500=4,000=40%=P4.0D=Govt.=Creatocracy=4 April=Mercury=Hermes=G=A4.
Or=10,000=1,000=100%=10.0=Physicality=Tech.=10 Oct.=Uranus=P=1Ø.
OR=2,500=3,000=30%=P3.0D=3.0=Creativity=Stars=Muses=3 March = C=I>>GIL.
-or-1=4,500=5,000=50%=P5.00D=Law=Time=Venus=5 May = Aphrodite>>L=N.
-or2=2,500=3,000=30%=P3.0D=3.0=Creativity=Stars=Muses=3 March = C=I>>GIL.

Oracle=10,000=1,000=100%=10.0=Physicality=Tech.=10 Oct.=Uranus=P=1Ø.
See >> THE ORACLE: Principles of Creative Sciences by Peter Matthews-Akukalia.

Oral=10,000=1,000=100%=10.0=Physicality=Tech.=10 Oct.=Uranus=P=1Ø.
Oran=7,500=8,000=80%=P8.0D=Economy=Currency=8 Aug.=Zeus>>E=v.
orange=10,000=1,000=100%=10.0=Physicality=Tech.=10 Oct.=Uranus=P=1Ø.
Orange=5,000=50%=P5.00D=Law=Time=Venus=5 May = Aphrodite>>L=N.
Orangeade=4,000=40%=P4.0D=Govt.=Creatocracy=4 April=Mercury=Hermes=G=A4.
Orangutan=9,000=90%=P9.00D=9.0=Abstraction=Gods=Saturn=9Sept.>>A=Ø.
Orate=5,000=50%=P5.00D=Law=Time=Venus=5 May = Aphrodite>>L=N.
Oration=2,500=3,000=30%=P3.0D=3.0=Creativity=Stars=Muses=3 March = C=I>>GIL.
Orator=5,500=5.5=80%=P5.50=Earth-Midway=5 May = Gaia.
Oratorio=10,000=1,000=100%=10.0=Physicality=Tech.=10 Oct.=Uranus=P=1Ø.
Oratory1=5,500=5.5=80%=P5.50=Earth-Midway=5 May = Gaia.
Oratory2=3,500=4,000=40%=P4.0D=Govt=Creato.=4 April=Mercury =Hermes=G=A4.
Orb=4,500=5,000=50%=P5.00D=Law=Time=Venus=5 May = Aphrodite>>L=N.
Orbit=10,000=1,000=100%=10.0=Physicality=Tech.=10 Oct.=Uranus=P=1Ø.
Orca=2,500=3,000=30%=P3.0D=3.0=Creativity=Stars=Muses=3 March = C=I>>GIL.
Orchard=9,000=90%=P9.00D=9.0=Abstraction=Gods=Saturn=9Sept.>>A=Ø.
Orchestra=10,000=1,000=100%=10.0=Physicality=Tech.=10 Oct.=Uranus=P=1Ø.
Orchestrate=5,500=5.5=80%=P5.50=Earth-Midway=5 May = Gaia.
Orchid=11,000=11%=P1.10D=1.1=Idea=Brainchild=Inv.=11 Nov.=SC=Athena>>I=MT.
Ordain=11,500=12,000=12%=P1.20D=1.2=Knowledge=Edu=12Dec.=Athena>>K=F.
Ordeal=5,500=5.5=80%=P5.50=Earth-Midway=5 May = Gaia.
Order=10,000=1,000=100%=10.0=Physicality=Tech.=10 Oct.=Uranus=P=1Ø.
Orderly=9,500=10,000=1,000=100%=10.0=Physicality=Tech.=10 Oct.=Uranus=P=1Ø.
Ordinal=6,000=60%=P6.0D=Man=Earth=Royalty=6 June=Gaia=Maia>>M=M2.
Ordinal number=5,500=5.5=80%=P5.50=Earth-Midway=5 May = Gaia.
Ordinance=6,500=7,000=70%=P7.0D=7.0=Language=Assets=Mars=7 July=Pleiades.
Ordinary=6,500=7,000=70%=P7.0D=7.0=Language=Assets=Mars=7 July=Pleiades.
Ordinate=10,000=1,000=100%=10.0=Physicality=Tech.=10 Oct.=Uranus=P=1Ø.
Ordination=4,500=5,000=50%=P5.00D=Law=Time=Venus=5 May = Aphrodite>>L=N.
Ordnance=7,000=70%=P7.0D=7.0=Language=Assets=Mars=7 July=Pleiades.
Ordovician=10,000=1,000=100%=10.0=Physicality=Tech.=10 Oct.=Uranus=P=1Ø.
Ordure=2,500=3,000=30%=P3.0D=3.0=Creativity=Stars=Muses=3 March = C=I>>GIL.
Ore=8,000=80%=P8.0D=Economy=Currency=8 Aug.=Zeus>>E=v.
Öre.=500=5%=P5.00D=5.0=Law=Time=Venus=5 May=Aphrodite>>L=N.

Oread=3,000=30%=P3.0D=3.0=Creativity=Stars=Muses=3 March = C=I>>GIL.
A mountain nymph. Greek myth. Oreias. A muse by computational creativity.

Oregano=5,500=5.5=80%=P5.50=Earth-Midway=5 May = Gaia.
Oregon=6,000=60%=P6.0D=Man=Earth=Royalty=6 June=Gaia=Maia>>M=M2.
Orel=6,500=7,000=70%=P7.0D=7.0=Language=Assets=Mars=7 July=Pleiades.
Organ=10,000=1,000=100%=10.0=Physicality=Tech.=10 Oct.=Uranus=P=1Ø.
Organdy=8,000=80%=P8.0D=Economy=Currency=8 Aug.=Zeus>>E=v.
Organelle=8,000=80%=P8.0D=Economy=Currency=8 Aug.=Zeus>>E=v.
Organic=10,000=1,000=100%=10.0=Physicality=Tech.=10 Oct.=Uranus=P=1Ø.
Organism=5,000=50%=P5.00D=Law=Time=Venus=5 May = Aphrodite>>L=N.
Organist=2,500=3,000=30%=P3.0D=3.0=Creativity=Stars=Muses=3 March = C=I>>GIL.
Organization=10,000=1,000=100%=10.0=Physicality=Tech.=10 Oct.=Uranus=P=1Ø.
Organize=10,000=1,000=100%=10.0=Physicality=Tech.=10 Oct.=Uranus=P=1Ø.
Organza=7,000=70%=P7.0D=7.0=Language=Assets=Mars=7 July=Pleiades.
Orgasm=4,500=5,000=50%=P5.00D=Law=Time=Venus=5 May = Aphrodite>>L=N.
Orgy=10,000=1,000=100%=10.0=Physicality=Tech.=10 Oct.=Uranus=P=1Ø.
Oriel=5,500=5.5=80%=P5.50=Earth-Midway=5 May = Gaia.
Orient=10,000=1,000=100%=10.0=Physicality=Tech.=10 Oct.=Uranus=P=1Ø.
Oriental=8,000=80%=P8.0D=Economy=Currency=8 Aug.=Zeus>>E=v.
Orifice=6,500=7,000=70%=P7.0D=7.0=Language=Assets=Mars=7 July=Pleiades.
Origami=3,000=30%=P3.0D=3.0=Creativity=Stars=Muses=3 March = C=I>>GIL.

Origin=10,000=1,000=100%=10.0=Physicality=Tech.=10 Oct.=Uranus=P=1Ø.
Makupedia as a full study of the Creative Sciences is the study of the origin of origins.
Creatocracy is its socio-economic political system. Creative Scientist is its professionalism.
Castle Makupedia is the deified name or brand of the author inventor King and Emperor.

Original=10,000=1,000=100%=10.0=Physicality=Tech.=10 Oct.=Uranus=P=1Ø.
Originate=5,000=50%=P5.00D=Law=Time=Venus=5 May = Aphrodite>>L=N.
Orinoco=8,500=9,000=90%=P9.00D=9.0=Abstraction=Gods=Saturn=9Sept.>>A=Ø.
Oriole=6,500=7,000=70%=P7.0D=7.0=Language=Assets=Mars=7 July=Pleiades.

Orion=5,000=50%=P5.00D=Law=Time=Venus=5 May = Aphrodite>>L=N.
A constellation in the celestial equation near Gemini and Taurus. In a conversation with Job the LORD GOD Zeus Jehovah Allah spoke about the Pleiades and Orion. The Pleiades comprises the seven computational sisters known as the Mind of GOD headed by Maia. Orion is the mighty hunter who chased them for desire and was transformed into a star by Zeus. These stories align with the science of astronomy, Scriptures and now the Creative Sciences. Hence the stars are the manifestations of real beings. The computational result shows that Orion is a muse of law and determiner of time in the jurisdiction of Aphrodite.

Orison=2,500=3,000=30%=P3.0D=3.0=Creativity=Stars=Muses=3 March = C=I>>GIL.
Orkney Islands=7,000=70%=P7.0D=7.0=Language=Assets=Mars=7 July=Pleiades.
Orlando=4,500=5,000=50%=P5.00D=Law=Time=Venus=5 May = Aphrodite>>L=N.
Orleans=7,000=70%=P7.0D=7.0=Language=Assets=Mars=7 July=Pleiades.
Orlon=3,000=30%=P3.0D=3.0=Creativity=Stars=Muses=3 March = C=I>>GIL.
Ormazd™=3,500=4,000=40%=P4.0D=Govt.=Creatocracy=4 April=Hermes=G=A4.
Ormolu=6,000=60%=P6.0D=Man=Earth=Royalty=6 June=Gaia=Maia>>M=M2.
Ormuz Strait of.=2,000=20%=P2.00D=2.0=Nature=Matter=Moon=2 Feb.=Cupid=N=C+_
Ornament=5,500=5.5=80%=P5.50=Earth-Midway=5 May = Gaia.
Ornate=3,500=4,000=40%=P4.0D=Govt.=Creatocracy=4 April=Mercury=Hermes=G=A4.
Ornery=2,500=3,000=30%=P3.0D=3.0=Creativity=Stars=Muses=3 March = C=I>>GIL.
Ornithology=6,000=60%=P6.0D=Man=Earth=Royalty=6 June=Gaia=Maia>>M=M2.
Orotund=5,500=5.5=80%=P5.50=Earth-Midway=5 May = Gaia.
Orphan=4,500=5,000=50%=P5.00D=Law=Time=Venus=5 May = Aphrodite>>L=N.
Orphanage=3,000=30%=P3.0D=3.0=Creativity=Stars=Muses=3 March = C=I>>GIL.

Orpheus=8,000=80%=P8.0D=Economy=Currency=8 Aug.=Zeus>>E=v.

Ortega y Gasset=2,500=3,000=30%=P3.0D=3.0=Creativity=Stars=Muses=3 March=C=I
Ortho-=4,000=40%=P4.0D=Govt.=Creatocracy=4 April=Mercury=Hermes=G=A4.
Orthodontia=500=5%=P5.00D=5.0=Law=Time=Venus=5 May=Aphrodite>>L=N.
Orthodontics=4,500=5,000=50%=P5.00D=Law=Time=Venus=5 May = Aphrodite>>L=N.
Orthodox=10,000=1,000=100%=10.0=Physicality=Tech.=10 Oct.=Uranus=P=1Ø.
Orthogonal=4,000=40%=P4.0D=Govt.=Creatocracy=4 April=Mercury=Hermes=G=A4.
Orthography=10,000=1,000=100%=10.0=Physicality=Tech.=10 Oct.=Uranus=P=1Ø.
Orthopedics=10,000=1,000=100%=10.0=Physicality=Tech.=10 Oct.=Uranus=P=1Ø.
Orthotics=10,000=1,000=100%=10.0=Physicality=Tech.=10 Oct.=Uranus=P=1Ø.
ORV=1,500=15%=P1.50D=1.5=Authority=Solar Crown=1 May = Maia.
Orwell George=3,500=4,000=40%=P4.0D=Govt.=Creatocracy=4 April=Hermes=G=A4.
-ory=11,000=11%=P1.10D=1.1=Idea=Brainchild=Inv.=11 Nov.=SC=Athena>>I=MT.
Oryx=5,500=5.5=80%=P5.50=Earth-Midway=5 May = Gaia.
Os=2,500=3,000=30%=P3.0D=3.0=Creativity=Stars=Muses=3 March = C=I>>GIL.
O.S.=4,000=40%=P4.0D=Govt.=Creatocracy=4 April=Mercury=Hermes=G=A4.
Osage=10,000=1,000=100%=10.0=Physicality=Tech.=10 Oct.=Uranus=P=1Ø.
Osaka=7,500=8,000=80%=P8.0D=Economy=Currency=8 Aug.=Zeus>>E=v.
Oscillate=10,000=1,000=100%=10.0=Physicality=Tech.=10 Oct.=Uranus=P=1Ø.
Oscilloscope=10,000=1,000=100%=10.0=Physicality=Tech.=10 Oct.=Uranus=P=1Ø.
Osculate=4,500=5,000=50%=P5.00D=Law=Time=Venus=5 May = Aphrodite>>L=N.
-ose1=4,500=5,000=50%=P5.00D=Law=Time=Venus=5 May = Aphrodite>>L=N.
-ose2=2,000=20%=P2.00D=2.0=Nature=Matter=Moon=2 Feb.=Cupid=N=C+_
Osier=8,000=80%=P8.0D=Economy=Currency=8 Aug.=Zeus>>E=v.

Osiris=5,500=5.5=80%=P5.50=Earth-Midway=5 May = Gaia.

-osis=7,000=70%=P7.0D=7.0=Language=Assets=Mars=7 July=Pleiades.
Oslo=4,500=5,000=50%=P5.00D=Law=Time=Venus=5 May = Aphrodite>>L=N.
Osmium=10,000=1,000=100%=10.0=Physicality=Tech.=10 Oct.=Uranus=P=1Ø.
Osmosis=10,000=1,000=100%=10.0=Physicality=Tech.=10 Oct.=Uranus=P=1Ø.
Osprey=10,000=1,000=100%=10.0=Physicality=Tech.=10 Oct.=Uranus=P=1Ø.
Ossify=8,000=80%=P8.0D=Economy=Currency=8 Aug.=Zeus>>E=v.
Osteitis=3,000=30%=P3.0D=3.0=Creativity=Stars=Muses=3 March = C=I>>GIL.
Ostensible=5,000=50%=P5.00D=Law=Time=Venus=5 May = Aphrodite>>L=N.
Ostentation=3,000=30%=P3.0D=3.0=Creativity=Stars=Muses=3 March = C=I>>GIL.
Ostentatious=2,500=3,000=30%=P3.0D=3.0=Creativity=Stars=Muses=3 March=CI.
Osteo-=2,500=3,000=30%=P3.0D=3.0=Creativity=Stars=Muses=3 March = C=I>>GIL.
Osteopathy=6,000=60%=P6.0D=Man=Earth=Royalty=6 June=Gaia=Maia>>M=M2.
Osteoporosis=11,000=11%=P1.10D=1.1=Idea=Brainchild=Inv.=11 Nov.=SC=Athena>>I=MT.
Ostia=6,500=7,000=70%=P7.0D=7.0=Language=Assets=Mars=7 July=Pleiades.
Ostracize=6,500=7,000=70%=P7.0D=7.0=Language=Assets=Mars=7 July=Pleiades.
Ostrava=6,000=60%=P6.0D=Man=Earth=Royalty=6 June=Gaia=Maia>>M=M2.
Ostrich=12,500=13,000=13%=P1.30=Solar Core=Faculty=13 January=Athena.
Ostrogoth=8,000=80%=P8.0D=Economy=Currency=8 Aug.=Zeus>>E=v.
OT1=1,500=15%=P1.50D=1.5=Authority=Solar Crown=1 May = Maia.
OT2=3,500=4,000=40%=P4.0D=Govt.=Creatocracy=4 April=Mercury=Hermes=G=A4.
OTB=1,500=15%=P1.50D=1.5=Authority=Solar Crown=1 May = Maia.
OTC=1,500=15%=P1.50D=1.5=Authority=Solar Crown=1 May = Maia.
Other=10,000=1,000=100%=10.0=Physicality=Tech.=10 Oct.=Uranus=P=1Ø.
Otherwise=9,000=90%=P9.00D=9.0=Abstraction=Gods=Saturn=9Sept.>>A=Ø.
Otherworldly=8,000=80%=P8.0D=Economy=Currency=8 Aug.=Zeus>>E=v.
-otic=9,000=90%=P9.00D=9.0=Abstraction=Gods=Saturn=9Sept.>>A=Ø.
Otiose=5,500=5.5=80%=P5.50=Earth-Midway=5 May = Gaia.
Otis James=2,500=3,000=30%=P3.0D=3.0=Creativity=Stars=Muses=3 March = C=I.
Otitis=5,000=50%=P5.00D=Law=Time=Venus=5 May = Aphrodite>>L=N.
OTS=1,500=15%=P1.50D=1.5=Authority=Solar Crown=1 May = Maia.
Ottawa1=8,500=9,000=90%=P9.00D=9.0=Abstraction=Gods=Saturn=9Sept.>>A=Ø.
Ottawa2=6,000=60%=P6.0D=Man=Earth=Royalty=6 June=Gaia=Maia>>M=M2.
Ottawa River=10,500=11,000=11%=P1.10D=1.1=Idea=Bchd=Inv.=11 Nov.=Athena>>I=MT.
Otter=9,500=10,000=1,000=100%=10.0=Physicality=Tech.=10 Oct.=Uranus=P=1Ø.
Otto1=8,500=9,000=90%=P9.00D=9.0=Abstraction=Gods=Saturn=9Sept.>>A=Ø.
ottoman=5,000=50%=P5.00D=Law=Time=Venus=5 May = Aphrodite>>L=N.
Ottoman=4,000=40%=P4.0D=Govt.=Creatocracy=4 April=Mercury=Hermes=G=A4.
Ottoman Empire=7,000=70%=P7.0D=7.0=Language=Assets=Mars=7 July=Pleiades.
Ouagadougou=5,000=50%=P5.00D=Law=Time=Venus=5 May = Aphrodite>>L=N.
Ouch=2,500=3,000=30%=P3.0D=3.0=Creativity=Stars=Muses=3 March = C=I>>GIL.
Ought1=10,000=1,000=100%=10.0=Physicality=Tech.=10 Oct.=Uranus=P=1Ø.
Ought2=1,500=15%=P1.50D=1.5=Authority=Solar Crown=1 May = Maia.
Ought3=1,500=15%=P1.50D=1.5=Authority=Solar Crown=1 May = Maia.

Ouguiya=4,000=40%=P4.0D=Govt.=Creatocracy=4 April=Mercury=Hermes=G=A4.
Currency in Mauritania. Metric weight = 4/10=0.4 so ratio is 40:1. See Naira, Dollar.

Ounce=11,000=11%=P1.10D=1.1=Idea=Brainchild=Inv.=11 Nov.=SC=Athena>>I=MT.
Our=8,000=80%=P8.0D=Economy=Currency=8 Aug.=Zeus>>E=v.
Ours=11,000=11%=P1.10D=1.1=Idea=Brainchild=Inv.=11 Nov.=SC=Athena>>I=MT.
Ourself=4,500=5,000=50%=P5.00D=Law=Time=Venus=5 May = Aphrodite>>L=N.
Ourselves=10,000=1,000=100%=10.0=Physicality=Tech.=10 Oct.=Uranus=P=1Ø.
-ous=11,000=11%=P1.10D=1.1=Idea=Brainchild=Inv.=11 Nov.=SC=Athena>>I=MT.
Oust=3,500=4,000=40%=P4.0D=Govt.=Creatocracy=4 April=Mercury=Hermes=G=A4.
Ouster=2,500=3,000=30%=P3.0D=3.0=Creativity=Stars=Muses=3 March = C=I>>GIL.
Out=10,000=1,000=100%=10.0=Physicality=Tech.=10 Oct.=Uranus=P=1Ø.
Out-=4,500=5,000=50%=P5.00D=Law=Time=Venus=5 May = Aphrodite>>L=N.
Outage=4,000=40%=P4.0D=Govt.=Creatocracy=4 April=Mercury=Hermes=G=A4.
Out-and-out=1,000=100%=Physicality=Tech.=10 Oct.=Uranus=P=1Ø.
Outback=5,000=50%=P5.00D=Law=Time=Venus=5 May = Aphrodite>>L=N.
Outbid=2,000=20%=P2.00D=2.0=Nature=Matter=Moon=2 Feb.=Cupid=N=C+_
Outboard=7,000=70%=P7.0D=7.0=Language=Assets=Mars=7 July=Pleiades.
Outbound=1,000=100%=10.0=1.0=Mind=Sun=1 January=Helios >> M=E4.
Outbreak=1,500=15%=P1.50D=1.5=Authority=Solar Crown=1 May = Maia.
Outbuilding=4,000=40%=P4.0D=Govt.=Creatocracy=4 April=Mercury=Hermes=G=A4.

Outburst=4,500=5,000=50%=P5.00D=Law=Time=Venus=5 May = Aphrodite>>L=N.
An outburst is a means of communication that instantly consumes about 45% - 50% of our emotional energy. The average emotion is about 60%. Violence is a crime against nature.

Outcast=4,000=40%=P4.0D=Govt.=Creatocracy=4 April=Mercury=Hermes=G=A4.
Outclass=5,500=5.5=80%=P5.50=Earth-Midway=5 May = Gaia.
Outcome=1,500=15%=P1.50D=1.5=Authority=Solar Crown=1 May = Maia.
Outcrop=4,500=5,000=50%=P5.00D=Law=Time=Venus=5 May = Aphrodite>>L=N.
Outcry=3,500=4,000=40%=P4.0D=Govt.=Creatocracy=4 April=Mercury=Hermes=G=A4.
Outdated=2,500=3,000=30%=P3.0D=3.0=Creativity=Stars=Muses=3 March = C=I>>GIL.
Outdistance=3,000=30%=P3.0D=3.0=Creativity=Stars=Muses=3 March = C=I>>GIL.
Outdo=2,000=20%=P2.00D=2.0=Nature=Matter=Moon=2 Feb.=Cupid=N=C+_
Outdoor=4,500=5,000=50%=P5.00D=Law=Time=Venus=5 May = Aphrodite>>L=N.
Outdoors=5,500=5.5=80%=P5.50=Earth-Midway=5 May = Gaia.
Outer=4,500=5,000=50%=P5.00D=Law=Time=Venus=5 May = Aphrodite>>L=N.
Outer ear=1,500=15%=P1.50D=1.5=Authority=Solar Crown=1 May = Maia.
Outermost=1,000=100%=10.0=1.0=Mind=Sun=1 January=Helios >> M=E4.
Outer planet=8,500=9,000=90%=P9.00D=9.0=Abstraction=Gods=Saturn=9Sept.>>A=Ø.
Outer space=5,000=50%=P5.00D=Law=Time=Venus=5 May = Aphrodite>>L=N.
Outface=5,000=50%=P5.00D=Law=Time=Venus=5 May = Aphrodite>>L=N.
Outfall=4,500=5,000=50%=P5.00D=Law=Time=Venus=5 May = Aphrodite>>L=N.

Outfield=4,000=40%=P4.0D=Govt.=Creatocracy=4 April=Mercury=Hermes=G=A4.
Outfit=10,000=1,000=100%=10.0=Physicality=Tech.=10 Oct.=Uranus=P=1Ø.

Outflank=7,000=70%=P7.0D=7.0=Language=Assets=Mars=7 July=Pleiades.
To outflank another involves a certain higher level of calculation at least 70%.

Outflow=4,500=5,000=50%=P5.00D=Law=Time=Venus=5 May = Aphrodite>>L=N.
Outfox=1,000=100%=10.0=1.0=Mind=Sun=1 January=Helios >> M=E4.
Outgo=3,000=30%=P3.0D=3.0=Creativity=Stars=Muses=3 March = C=I>>GIL.
Outgoing=2,500=3,000=30%=P3.0D=3.0=Creativity=Stars=Muses=3 March = C=I>>GIL.
Outgrow=6,500=7,000=70%=P7.0D=7.0=Language=Assets=Mars=7 July=Pleiades.
Outgrowth=3,500=4,000=40%=P4.0D=Govt.=Creatocracy=4 April=Hermes=G=A4.
Outguess=3,000=30%=P3.0D=3.0=Creativity=Stars=Muses=3 March = C=I>>GIL.
Outhouse=5,000=50%=P5.00D=Law=Time=Venus=5 May = Aphrodite>>L=N.
Outing=2,500=3,000=30%=P3.0D=3.0=Creativity=Stars=Muses=3 March = C=I>>GIL.
Outland=4,500=5,000=50%=P5.00D=Law=Time=Venus=5 May = Aphrodite>>L=N.
Outlandish=2,500=3,000=30%=P3.0D=3.0=Creativity=Stars=Muses=3 March = C=I.
Outlast=2,000=20%=P2.00D=2.0=Nature=Matter=Moon=2 Feb.=Cupid=N=C+_
Outlaw=10,000=1,000=100%=10.0=Physicality=Tech.=10 Oct.=Uranus=P=1Ø.
Outlay=4,500=5,000=50%=P5.00D=Law=Time=Venus=5 May = Aphrodite>>L=N.
Outlet=10,000=1,000=100%=10.0=Physicality=Tech.=10 Oct.=Uranus=P=1Ø.
Outline=10,000=1,000=100%=10.0=Physicality=Tech.=10 Oct.=Uranus=P=1Ø.
Outlive=2,000=20%=P2.00D=2.0=Nature=Matter=Moon=2 Feb.=Cupid=N=C+_
Outlook=9,000=90%=P9.00D=9.0=Abstraction=Gods=Saturn=9Sept.>>A=Ø.
Outlying=3,500=4,000=40%=P4.0D=Govt.=Creatocracy=4 April=Hermes=G=A4.
Outmaneuver=4,500=5,000=50%=P5.00D=Law=Time=Venus=5 May = Aphrodite>>L=N.
Outmoded=2,000=20%=P2.00D=2.0=Nature=Matter=Moon=2 Feb.=Cupid=N=C+_
Outnumber=2,500=3,000=30%=P3.0D=3.0=Creativity=Stars=Muses=3 March = CI
Out of=10,000=1,000=100%=10.0=Physicality=Tech.=10 Oct.=Uranus=P=1Ø.
Out of bounds=3,000=30%=P3.0D=3.0=Creativity=Stars=Muses=3 March = C=I>>GIL.
Out of date=1,500=15%=P1.50D=1.5=Authority=Solar Crown=1 May = Maia.
Out of doors=1,500=15%=P1.50D=1.5=Authority=Solar Crown=1 May = Maia.
Out of pocket=6,000=60%=P6.0D=Man=Earth=Royalty=6 June=Gaia=Maia>>M=M2.
Out of the way=1,500=15%=P1.50D=1.5=Authority=Solar Crown=1 May = Maia.
Outpace=1,500=15%=P1.50D=1.5=Authority=Solar Crown=1 May = Maia.
Outpatient=7,000=70%=P7.0D=7.0=Language=Assets=Mars=7 July=Pleiades.
Outplay=2,000=20%=P2.00D=2.0=Nature=Matter=Moon=2 Feb.=Cupid=N=C+_
Outpost=9,500=10,000=1,000=100%=10.0=Physicality=Tech.=10 Oct.=Uranus=P=1Ø.
Outpouring=4,500=5,000=50%=P5.00D=Law=Time=Venus=5 May = Aphrodite>>L=N.
Output=10,000=1,000=100%=10.0=Physicality=Tech.=10 Oct.=Uranus=P=1Ø.
Outrage=10,000=1,000=100%=10.0=Physicality=Tech.=10 Oct.=Uranus=P=1Ø.
Outrageous=5,000=50%=P5.00D=Law=Time=Venus=5 May = Aphrodite>>L=N.
Outrank=2,000=20%=P2.00D=2.0=Nature=Matter=Moon=2 Feb.=Cupid=N=C+_
Outré=2,500=3,000=30%=P3.0D=3.0=Creativity=Stars=Muses=3 March = C=I>>GIL.

PETER K. MATTHEWS - AKUKALIA

Outreach=6,500=7,000=70%=P7.0D=7.0=Language=Assets=Mars=7 July=Pleiades.
Outrider=1,500=15%=P1.50D=1.5=Authority=Solar Crown=1 May = Maia.
Outrigger=9,000=90%=P9.00D=9.0=Abstraction=Gods=Saturn=9Sept.>>A=Ø.
Outright=10,000=1,000=100%=10.0=Physicality=Tech.=10 Oct.=Uranus=P=1Ø.
Outrun=2,500=3,000=30%=P3.0D=3.0=Creativity=Stars=Muses=3 March = C=I>>GIL.
Outsell=3,000=30%=P3.0D=3.0=Creativity=Stars=Muses=3 March = C=I>>GIL.
Outset=1,000=100%=10.0=1.0=Mind=Sun=1 January=Helios >> M=E4.
Outshine=2,500=3,000=30%=P3.0D=3.0=Creativity=Stars=Muses=3 March = C=I>>GIL.
Outside=10,000=1,000=100%=10.0=Physicality=Tech.=10 Oct.=Uranus=P=1Ø.
Outside of=500=5%=P5.00D=5.0=Law=Time=Venus=5 May=Aphrodite>>L=N.
Outsider=5,000=50%=P5.00D=Law=Time=Venus=5 May = Aphrodite>>L=N.
Outsize=4,000=40%=P4.0D=Govt.=Creatocracy=4 April=Mercury=Hermes=G=A4.
Outskirts=3,500=4,000=40%=P4.0D=Govt.=Creatocracy=4 April=Hermes=G=A4.
Outsmart=1,000=100%=10.0=1.0=Mind=Sun=1 January=Helios >> M=E4.
Outspend=4,500=5,000=50%=P5.00D=Law=Time=Venus=5 May = Aphrodite>>L=N.
Outspoken=3,500=4,000=40%=P4.0D=Govt.=Creatocracy=4 April=Hermes=G=A4.
Outspread=2,000=20%=P2.00D=2.0=Nature=Matter=Moon=2 Feb.=Cupid=N=C+_
Outstanding=5,000=50%=P5.00D=Law=Time=Venus=5 May = Aphrodite>>L=N.
Outstretch=1,000=100%=10.0=1.0=Mind=Sun=1 January=Helios >> M=E4.
Outstrip=3,000=30%=P3.0D=3.0=Creativity=Stars=Muses=3 March = C=I>>GIL.
Outtake=8,000=80%=P8.0D=Economy=Currency=8 Aug.=Zeus>>E=v.
Outward=5,500=5.5=80%=P5.50=Earth-Midway=5 May = Gaia.
Out wear=1,000=100%=10.0=1.0=Mind=Sun=1 January=Helios >> M=E4.
Outweigh=3,500=4,000=40%=P4.0D=Govt.=Creatocracy=4 April=Hermes=G=A4.
Outwit=4,000=40%=P4.0D=Govt.=Creatocracy=4 April=Mercury=Hermes=G=A4.
Outwork=3,000=30%=P3.0D=3.0=Creativity=Stars=Muses=3 March = C=I>>GIL.

Ouzo=4,000=40%=P4.0D=Govt.=Creatocracy=4 April=Mercury=Hermes=G=A4.
A Greek liqueur flavored with anise.

Ova=1,500=15%=P1.50D=1.5=Authority=Solar Crown=1 May = Maia.
Oval=6,000=60%=P6.0D=Man=Earth=Royalty=6 June=Gaia=Maia>>M=M2.
Ovary=10,500=11,000=11%=P1.10D=1.1=Idea=Brainchild=Inv.=11 Nov.=SC=Athena
    >>I=MT.
Ovate=500=5%=P5.00D=5.0=Law=Time=Venus=5 May=Aphrodite>>L=N.
Ovation=3,000=30%=P3.0D=3.0=Creativity=Stars=Muses=3 March = C=I>>GIL.
Oven=6,000=60%=P6.0D=Man=Earth=Royalty=6 June=Gaia=Maia>>M=M2.
Over=10,000=1,000=100%=10.0=Physicality=Tech.=10 Oct.=Uranus=P=1Ø.
Overact=2,500=3,000=30%=P3.0D=3.0=Creativity=Stars=Muses=3 March = C=I>>GIL.
Overage1=1,500=15%=P1.50D=1.5=Authority=Solar Crown=1 May = Maia.
Overage2=3,000=30%=P3.0D=3.0=Creativity=Stars=Muses=3 March = C=I>>GIL.
Overall=5,000=50%=P5.00D=Law=Time=Venus=5 May = Aphrodite>>L=N.
Over arm=3,500=4,000=40%=P4.0D=Govt.=Creatocracy=4 April=Hermes=G=A4.
Overawe=3,500=4,000=40%=P4.0D=Govt.=Creato=4 April=Mercury=Hermes=G=A4.

Overbalance=3,000=30%=P3.0D=3.0=Creativity=Stars=Muses=3 March = C=I>>GIL.
Overbear=6,000=60%=P6.0D=Man=Earth=Royalty=6 June=Gaia=Maia>>M=M2.
Overbearing=1,500=15%=P1.50D=1.5=Authority=Solar Crown=1 May = Maia.
Overbite=7,500=8,000=80%=P8.0D=Economy=Currency=8 Aug.=Zeus>>E=v.
Overblown=2,000=20%=P2.00D=2.0=Nature=Matter=Moon=2 Feb.=Cupid=N=C+_
Overboard=4,000=40%=P4.0D=Govt.=Creatocracy=4 April=Mercury=Hermes=G=A4.
Overbuild=5,000=50%=P5.00D=Law=Time=Venus=5 May = Aphrodite>>L=N.
Overcast=4,500=5,000=50%=P5.00D=Law=Time=Venus=5 May = Aphrodite>>L=N.
Overcharge=3,500=4,000=40%=P4.0D=Govt.=Creato=4 April=Mercury=Hermes=G=A4.
Overcloud=2,500=3,000=30%=P3.0D=3.0=Creativity=Stars=Muses=3 March = C=I>>GIL.
Overcoat=3,500=4,000=40%=P4.0D=Govt.=Creato=4 April=Mercury=Hermes=G=A4.
Overcome=5,000=50%=P5.00D=Law=Time=Venus=5 May = Aphrodite>>L=N.
Overdo=4,500=5,000=50%=P5.00D=Law=Time=Venus=5 May = Aphrodite>>L=N.
Overdraft=4,500=5,000=50%=P5.00D=Law=Time=Venus=5 May = Aphrodite>>L=N.
Owing=1,000=100%=10.0=1.0=Mind=Sun=1 January=Helios >> M=E4.
Owl=10,000=1,000=100%=10.0=Physicality=Tech.=10 Oct.=Uranus=P=1Ø.
Owlet=1,500=15%=P1.50D=1.5=Authority=Solar Crown=1 May = Maia.
Own=10,000=1,000=100%=10.0=Physicality=Tech.=10 Oct.=Uranus=P=1Ø.
Ox=4,500=5,000=50%=P5.00D=Law=Time=Venus=5 May = Aphrodite>>L=N.
Oxalic acid=7,000=70%=P7.0D=7.0=Language=Assets=Mars=7 July=Pleiades.
Ox blood red=2,000=20%=P2.00D=2.0=Nature=Matter=Moon=2 Feb.=Cupid=N=C+_
Oxbow=5,500=5.5=80%=P5.50=Earth-Midway=5 May = Gaia.
oxford=7,000=70%=P7.0D=7.0=Language=Assets=Mars=7 July=Pleiades.
Oxford=7,000=70%=P7.0D=7.0=Language=Assets=Mars=7 July=Pleiades.
Oxidant=1,500=15%=P1.50D=1.5=Authority=Solar Crown=1 May = Maia.
Oxidation=10,000=1,000=100%=10.0=Physicality=Tech.=10 Oct.=Uranus=P=1Ø.
Oxide=5,000=50%=P5.00D=Law=Time=Venus=5 May = Aphrodite>>L=N.
Oxidize=10,000=1,000=100%=10.0=Physicality=Tech.=10 Oct.=Uranus=P=1Ø.
Oxnard=5,000=50%=P5.00D=Law=Time=Venus=5 May = Aphrodite>>L=N.

Oxonian=4,000=40%=P4.0D=Govt.=Creatocracy=4 April=Mercury=Hermes=G=A4.
Of or relating to Oxford or Oxford University. So is the Makupedia someone relating to
the Makupedia, the Creative Sciences as a Creative Scientist, or the Creatocracy as a whole.

Oxy-=2,500=3,000=30%=P3.0D=3.0=Creativity=Stars=Muses=3 March = C=I>>GIL.
Oxyacetylene=5,500=5.5=80%=P5.50=Earth-Midway=5 May = Gaia.
Oxygen=10,000=1,000=100%=10.0=Physicality=Tech.=10 Oct.=Uranus=P=1Ø.
Oxygenate=3,500=4,000=40%=P4.0D=Govt.=Creato=4 April=Mercury=Hermes=G=A4.
Oxygen mask=9,000=90%=P9.00D=9.0=Abstraction=Gods=Saturn=9Sept.>>A=Ø.
Oxygen tent=9,500=10,000=1,000=100%=10.0=Physicality=Tech.=10 Oct.=Uranus=P=1Ø.
Oxymoron=10,000=1,000=100%=10.0=Physicality=Tech.=10 Oct.=Uranus=P=1Ø.
Oyster=7,500=8,000=80%=P8.0D=Economy=Currency=8 Aug.=Zeus>>E=v.
Oz=500=5%=P5.00D=5.0=Law=Time=Venus=5 May=Aphrodite>>L=N.
Oz ap=1,000=100%=10.0=1.0=Mind=Sun=1 January=Helios >> M=E4.

Ozark Plateau=8,000=80%=P8.0D=Economy=Currency=8 Aug.=Zeus>>E=v.
Oz av=1,000=100%=10.0=1.0=Mind=Sun=1 January=Helios >> M=E4.
Ozone=10,000=1,000=100%=10.0=Physicality=Tech.=10 Oct.=Uranus=P=1Ø.

Ozone layer=10,000=1,000=100%=10.0=Physicality=Tech.=10 Oct.=Uranus=P=1Ø.
Ozone layer Green house matters. See The Castle Makupedia Sciences: Principles of Naturecology Vol.1. By Peter Matthews-Akukalia.

Ozonosphere=1,500=15%=P1.50D=1.5=Authority=Solar Crown=1 May = Maia.
oz t=1,000=100%=10.0=1.0=Mind=Sun=1 January=Helios >> M=E4.

MAKABET =Pp=

---

p1=3,000=30%=P3.0D=3.0=Creativity=Stars=Muses=3 March = C=I>>GIL.
The 16th letter of the English alphabet. The psycho-weight of the p is computed thus:
3.0*1.6x=px=4.6+4.8=9.4x=px=31.48<13.48=14=1.4
>> Faculty of Creative Sciences Management >> Wisdom and skills development in the field of Ideas and Talent Management. P is the sign for wisdom and organization.

---

p2=3,000=30%=P3.0D=3.0=Creativity=Stars=Muses=3 March = C=I>>GIL.
P1=2,500=3,000=30%=P3.0D=3.0=Creativity=Stars=Muses=3 March = C=I>>GIL.
P2=1,500=15%=P1.50D=1.5=Authority=Solar Crown=1 May = Maia.
p.=6,500=7,000=70%=P7.0D=7.0=Language=Assets=Mars=7 July=Pleiades.
Pa=3,000=30%=P3.0D=3.0=Creativity=Stars=Muses=3 March = C=I>>GIL.
PA=2,500=3,000=30%=P3.0D=3.0=Creativity=Stars=Muses=3 March = C=I>>GIL.
p.a.=1,000=100%=10.0=1.0=Mind=Sun=1 January=Helios >> M=E4.
P.A.=3,000=30%=P3.0D=3.0=Creativity=Stars=Muses=3 March = C=I>>GIL.
Pa'anga=2,500=3,000=30%=P3.0D=3.0=Creativity=Stars=Muses=3 March = C=I>>GIL.
PABA=8,000=80%=P8.0D=Economy=Currency=8 Aug.=Zeus>>E=v.
Pabulum=5,000=50%=P5.00D=Law=Time=Venus=5 May = Aphrodite>>L=N.
PAC=2,000=20%=P2.00D=2.0=Nature=Matter=Moon=2 Feb.=Cupid=N=C+_
Pace=10,000=1,000=100%=10.0=Physicality=Tech.=10 Oct.=Uranus=P=1Ø.
Pacemaker=10,000=1,000=100%=10.0=Physicality=Tech.=10 Oct.=Uranus=P=1Ø.
Pachyderm=8,000=80%=P8.0D=Economy=Currency=8 Aug.=Zeus>>E=v.
Pachysandra=9,500=10,000=1,000=100%=10.0=Phy=Tech.=10 Oct.=Uranus=P=1Ø.
Pacific=4,500=5,000=50%=P5.00D=Law=Time=Venus=5 May = Aphrodite>>L=N.
Pacific Islands=10,000=1,000=100%=10.0=Physicality=Tech.=10 Oct.=Uranus=P=1Ø.
Pacific Ocean=10,000=1,000=100%=10.0=Physicality=Tech.=10 Oct.=Uranus=P=1Ø.
Pacifier=5,500=5.5=80%=P5.50=Earth-Midway=5 May = Gaia.
Pacifism=5,500=5.5=80%=P5.50=Earth-Midway=5 May = Gaia.
Pack=10,000=1,000=100%=10.0=Physicality=Tech.=10 Oct.=Uranus=P=1Ø.

Package=9,500=10,000=1,000=100%=10.0=Physicality=Tech.=10 Oct.=Uranus=P=1Ø.
Package store=7,000=70%=P7.0D=7.0=Language=Assets=Mars=7 July=Pleiades.
Packaging=7,000=70%=P7.0D=7.0=Language=Assets=Mars=7 July=Pleiades.
Pack animal=5,000=50%=P5.00D=Law=Time=Venus=5 May = Aphrodite>>L=N.
Packer=4,500=5,000=50%=P5.00D=Law=Time=Venus=5 May = Aphrodite>>L=N.
Packet=3,500=4,000=40%=P4.0D=Govt.=Creatocracy=4 April=Mercury=Hermes=G=A4.
Packing=8,500=9,000=90%=P9.00D=9.0=Abstraction=Gods=Saturn=9Sept.>>A=Ø.
Pack rat=9,000=90%=P9.00D=9.0=Abstraction=Gods=Saturn=9Sept.>>A=Ø.
Packsaddle=4,000=40%=P4.0D=Govt.=Creatocracy=4 April=Mercury=Hermes=G=A4.
Pact=3,000=30%=P3.0D=3.0=Creativity=Stars=Muses=3 March = C=I>>GIL.
Pad1=10,000=1,000=100%=10.0=Physicality=Tech.=10 Oct.=Uranus=P=1Ø.
Pad2=5,000=50%=P5.00D=Law=Time=Venus=5 May = Aphrodite>>L=N.
Padding=3,000=30%=P3.0D=3.0=Creativity=Stars=Muses=3 March = C=I>>GIL.
Paddle1=10,000=1,000=100%=10.0=Physicality=Tech.=10 Oct.=Uranus=P=1Ø.
Paddle2=8,500=9,000=90%=P9.00D=9.0=Abstraction=Gods=Saturn=9Sept.>>A=Ø.
Paddle board=4,500=5,000=50%=P5.00D=Law=Time=Venus=5 May = Aphrodite>>L=N.
Paddle wheel=6,500=7,000=70%=P7.0D=7.0=Language=Assets=Mars=7 July=Pleiades.
Paddock=12,500=13,000=13%=P1.30=Solar Core=Faculty=13 January=Athena.
Paddy=4,500=5,000=50%=P5.00D=Law=Time=Venus=5 May = Aphrodite>>L=N.
Paddy wagon=6,000=60%=P6.0D=Man=Earth=Royalty=6 June=Gaia=Maia>>M=M2.
Paderewski Ignace=3,500=4,000=40%=P4.0D=Govt.=Creat=4 April=Hermes=G=A4.
Padlock=12,500=13,000=13%=P1.30=Solar Core=Faculty=13 January=Athena.
Padua=4,500=5,000=50%=P5.00D=Law=Time=Venus=5 May = Aphrodite>>L=N.
Paean=5,000=50%=P5.00D=Law=Time=Venus=5 May = Aphrodite>>L=N.
Paella=6,500=7,000=70%=P7.0D=7.0=Language=Assets=Mars=7 July=Pleiades.
Paestum=5,000=50%=P5.00D=Law=Time=Venus=5 May = Aphrodite>>L=N.
Pagan=7,000=70%=P7.0D=7.0=Language=Assets=Mars=7 July=Pleiades.
Paganini=3,500=4,000=40%=P4.0D=Govt.=Creatocracy=4 April=Hermes=G=A4.
Page1=8,000=80%=P8.0D=Economy=Currency=8 Aug.=Zeus>>E=v.
Page2=14,000=14%=P1.40D=1.4=Mgt.=Solar Energy=13 May=Athena=SC=0.1
Pageant=9,500=10,000=1,000=100%=10.0=Physicality=Tech.=10 Oct.=Uranus=P=1Ø.
Pageboy=6,500=7,000=70%=P7.0D=7.0=Language=Assets=Mars=7 July=Pleiades.
Pagination=7,500=8,000=80%=P8.0D=Economy=Currency=8 Aug.=Zeus>>E=v.
Pagoda=6,000=60%=P6.0D=Man=Earth=Royalty=6 June=Gaia=Maia>>M=M2.
Pago Pago=5,500=5.5=80%=P5.50=Earth-Midway=5 May = Gaia.
Pahlavi Mohammed=5,000=50%=P5.00D=Law=Time=Venus=5 May = Aphrodite>>L=N.
Paid=3,000=30%=P3.0D=3.0=Creativity=Stars=Muses=3 March = C=I>>GIL.
Pail=4,500=5,000=50%=P5.00D=Law=Time=Venus=5 May = Aphrodite>>L=N.
Pain=10,000=1,000=100%=10.0=Physicality=Tech.=10 Oct.=Uranus=P=1Ø.
Paine Thomas=3,500=4,000=40%=P4.0D=Govt.=Creatocracy=4 April=Hermes=G=A4.
Painkiller=5,000=50%=P5.00D=Law=Time=Venus=5 May = Aphrodite>>L=N.
Painstaking=3,500=4,000=40%=P4.0D=Govt.=Creatocracy=4 April=Hermes=G=A4.
Paint=10,000=1,000=100%=10.0=Physicality=Tech.=10 Oct.=Uranus=P=1Ø.
Paintbrush=2,500=3,000=30%=P3.0D=3.0=Creativity=Stars=Muses=3 March = C=I>>GIL.
Painted Desert=7,000=70%=P7.0D=7.0=Language=Assets=Mars=7 July=Pleiades.

Painting=7,000=70%=P7.0D=7.0=Language=Assets=Mars=7 July=Pleiades.
Pair=10,000=1,000=100%=10.0=Physicality=Tech.=10 Oct.=Uranus=P=1Ø.

Paisa=3,000=30%=P3.0D=3.0=Creativity=Stars=Muses=3 March = C=I>>GIL.
Hindi paisā currency. See Naira. Dollar. 3/10=0.3. Ratio metric is 30:1

Palute=8,500=9,000=90%=P9.00D=9.0=Abstraction=Gods=Saturn=9Sept.>>A=Ø.
Pajamas=9,000=90%=P9.00D=9.0=Abstraction=Gods=Saturn=9Sept.>>A=Ø.
Pak.=500=5%=P5.00D=5.0=Law=Time=Venus=5 May=Aphrodite>>L=N.
Pakistan=6,500=7,000=70%=P7.0D=7.0=Language=Assets=Mars=7 July=Pleiades.
Pal=6,000=60%=P6.0D=Man=Earth=Royalty=6 June=Gaia=Maia>>M=M2.

Palace=7,500=8,000=80%=P8.0D=Economy=Currency=8 Aug.=Zeus>>E=v.
Castle Makupedia is the name and palace of the God of Creatocracy Genius & Mind
who wears the Solar Crown built on Brickwalls and throne of the Creatocratic Charter.

Paladin=4,500=5,000=50%=P5.00D=Law=Time=Venus=5 May = Aphrodite>>L=N.
Palanquin=8,500=9,000=90%=P9.00D=9.0=Abstraction=Gods=Saturn=9Sept.>>A=Ø.
Palatable=5,500=5.5=80%=P5.50=Earth-Midway=5 May = Gaia.
Palate=6,500=7,000=70%=P7.0D=7.0=Language=Assets=Mars=7 July=Pleiades.
Palatial=8,500=9,000=90%=P9.00D=9.0=Abstraction=Gods=Saturn=9Sept.>>A=Ø.
Palatinate=3,500=4,000=40%=P4.0D=Govt.=Creatocracy=4 April=Hermes=G=A4.
Palatine=10,000=1,000=100%=10.0=Physicality=Tech.=10 Oct.=Uranus=P=1Ø.
Palau=1,000=100%=10.0=1.0=Mind=Sun=1 January=Helios >> M=E4.
Palaver=4,000=40%=P4.0D=Govt.=Creatocracy=4 April=Mercury=Hermes=G=A4.
Pale1=11,500=12,000=12%=P1.20D=1.2=Knowledge=Edu=12Dec.=Athena>>K=F.
Pale2=8,500=9,000=90%=P9.00D=9.0=Abstraction=Gods=Saturn=9Sept.>>A=Ø.
Palembang=5,000=50%=P5.00D=Law=Time=Venus=5 May = Aphrodite>>L=N.
Paleo-=3,000=30%=P3.0D=3.0=Creativity=Stars=Muses=3 March = C=I>>GIL.
Paleocene=8,500=9,000=90%=P9.00D=9.0=Abstraction=Gods=Saturn=9Sept.>>A=Ø.
Paleography=3,000=30%=P3.0D=3.0=Creativity=Stars=Muses=3 March = C=I>>GIL.
Paleolithic=10,000=1,000=100%=10.0=Physicality=Tech.=10 Oct.=Uranus=P=1Ø.
Paleontology=5,500=5.5=80%=P5.50=Earth-Midway=5 May = Gaia.
Paleozoic=10,500=11,000=11%=P1.10D=1.1=Idea=Brainchild.=11 Nov.=Athena>>I=MT.
Palermo=5,500=5.5=80%=P5.50=Earth-Midway=5 May = Gaia.
Palestine=9,000=90%=P9.00D=9.0=Abstraction=Gods=Saturn=9Sept.>>A=Ø.
Palette=10,500=11,000=11%=P1.10D=1.1=Idea=Brainchild=11 Nov.=Athena>>I=MT.
Palimony=10,500=11,000=11%=P1.10D=1.1=Idea=Brainchild=Inv.=11 Nov=Athena>>I=MT.
Palimpsest=12,500=13,000=13%=P1.30=Solar Core=Faculty=13 January=Athena.
Palindrome=10,000=1,000=100%=10.0=Physicality=Tech.=10 Oct.=Uranus=P=1Ø.
Paling=4,500=5,000=50%=P5.00D=Law=Time=Venus=5 May = Aphrodite>>L=N.
Palisade=6,000=60%=P6.0D=Man=Earth=Royalty=6 June=Gaia=Maia>>M=M2.
Palisades=6,500=7,000=70%=P7.0D=7.0=Language=Assets=Mars=7 July=Pleiades.

Pall1=10,000=1,000=100%=10.0=Physicality=Tech.=10 Oct.=Uranus=P=1Ø.
Pall2=6,000=60%=P6.0D=Man=Earth=Royalty=6 June=Gaia=Maia>>M=M2.
Palladio=2,500=3,000=30%=P3.0D=3.0=Creativity=Stars=Muses=3 March = C=I>>GIL.
Palladium=10,000=1,000=100%=10.0=Physicality=Tech.=10 Oct.=Uranus=P=1Ø.
Pallbearer=4,000=40%=P4.0D=Govt.=Creatocracy=4 April=Mercury=Hermes=G=A4.
Pallet1=5,500=5.5=80%=P5.50=Earth-Midway=5 May = Gaia.
Pallet2=5,000=50%=P5.00D=Law=Time=Venus=5 May = Aphrodite>>L=N.
Palliate=10,000=1,000=100%=10.0=Physicality=Tech.=10 Oct.=Uranus=P=1Ø.
Pallid=7,000=70%=P7.0D=7.0=Language=Assets=Mars=7 July=Pleiades.
Pallor=4,000=40%=P4.0D=Govt.=Creatocracy=4 April=Mercury=Hermes=G=A4.
Palm1=10,000=1,000=100%=10.0=Physicality=Tech.=10 Oct.=Uranus=P=1Ø.
Palm2=10,000=1,000=100%=10.0=Physicality=Tech.=10 Oct.=Uranus=P=1Ø.
Palma=4,500=5,000=50%=P5.00D=Law=Time=Venus=5 May = Aphrodite>>L=N.
Palmate=5,000=50%=P5.00D=Law=Time=Venus=5 May = Aphrodite>>L=N.
Palmerston=3,000=30%=P3.0D=3.0=Creativity=Stars=Muses=3 March = C=I>>GIL.
Palmetto=6,500=7,000=70%=P7.0D=7.0=Language=Assets=Mars=7 July=Pleiades.
Palmistry=5,500=5.5=80%=P5.50=Earth-Midway=5 May = Gaia.
Palm Springs=4,000=40%=P4.0D=Govt.=Creatocracy=4 April=Mercury=Hermes=G=A4.
Palm Sunday=7,000=70%=P7.0D=7.0=Language=Assets=Mars=7 July=Pleiades.
Palmy=5,000=50%=P5.00D=Law=Time=Venus=5 May = Aphrodite>>L=N.
Palomar Mount.=6,500=7,000=70%=P7.0D=7.0=Language=Assets=Mars=7 July=Pleiades.
Palomino=8,500=9,000=90%=P9.00D=9.0=Abstraction=Gods=Saturn=9Sept.>>A=Ø.
Palpable=6,500=7,000=70%=P7.0D=7.0=Language=Assets=Mars=7 July=Pleiades.
Palpate=6,000=60%=P6.0D=Man=Earth=Royalty=6 June=Gaia=Maia>>M=M2.
Palpitate=6,500=7,000=70%=P7.0D=7.0=Language=Assets=Mars=7 July=Pleiades.
Palsy=4,000=40%=P4.0D=Govt.=Creatocracy=4 April=Mercury=Hermes=G=A4.
Paltry=5,500=5.5=80%=P5.50=Earth-Midway=5 May = Gaia.
Pamir=9,500=10,000=1,000=100%=10.0=Physicality=Tech.=10 Oct.=Uranus=P=1Ø.
Pampa=5,000=50%=P5.00D=Law=Time=Venus=5 May = Aphrodite>>L=N.
Pamper=8,500=9,000=90%=P9.00D=9.0=Abstraction=Gods=Saturn=9Sept.>>A=Ø.
Pamphlet=8,500=9,000=90%=P9.00D=9.0=Abstraction=Gods=Saturn=9Sept.>>A=Ø.
Pamplona=3,500=4,000=40%=P4.0D=Govt.=Creato=4 April=Mercury=Hermes=G=A4.
Pan1=10,000=1,000=100%=10.0=Physicality=Tech.=10 Oct.=Uranus=P=1Ø.
Pan2=6,500=7,000=70%=P7.0D=7.0=Language=Assets=Mars=7 July=Pleiades.

Pan=4,500=5,000=50%=P5.00D=Law=Time=Venus=5 May = Aphrodite>>L=N.
Greek myth. The God of woods fields and flocks.

Pan.=500=5%=P5.00D=5.0=Law=Time=Venus=5 May=Aphrodite>>L=N.
Pan-=2,500=3,000=30%=P3.0D=3.0=Creativity=Stars=Muses=3 March = C=I>>GIL.

Panacea=5,000=50%=P5.00D=Law=Time=Venus=5 May = Aphrodite>>L=N.
The remedy for all diseases, evils, or difficulties; cure-all.<Greek, panakēs, all - healing.

Panache=7,000=70%=P7.0D=7.0=Language=Assets=Mars=7 July=Pleiades.
Panama=10,000=1,000=100%=10.0=Physicality=Tech.=10 Oct.=Uranus=P=1Ø.
Panama, Isthmus of.=7,500=8,000=80%=P8.0D=Economy=Currency=8 Aug.=Zeus>>E=v.
Panama Canal.=9,000=90%=P9.00D=9.0=Abstraction=Gods=Saturn=9Sept.>>A=Ø.
Panama Canal Zone.=1,500=15%=P1.50D=1.5=Authority=Solar Crown=1 May = Maia.
Panama hat=8,000=80%=P8.0D=Economy=Currency=8 Aug.=Zeus>>E=v.
Pan-American=3,000=30%=P3.0D=3.0=Creativity=Stars=Muses=3 March = C=I>>GIL.
Panatela=2,500=3,000=30%=P3.0D=3.0=Creativity=Stars=Muses=3 March = C=I>>GIL.
Panay=5,000=50%=P5.00D=Law=Time=Venus=5 May = Aphrodite>>L=N.
Pan-broil=5,500=5.5=80%=P5.50=Earth-Midway=5 May = Gaia.
Pancake=6,000=60%=P6.0D=Man=Earth=Royalty=6 June=Gaia=Maia>>M=M2.
Panchromatic=3,000=30%=P3.0D=3.0=Creativity=Stars=Muses=3 March = C=I>>GIL.
Pancreas=10,000=1,000=100%=10.0=Physicality=Tech.=10 Oct.=Uranus=P=1Ø.
Pancreatitis=2,000=20%=P2.00D=2.0=Nature=Matter=Moon=2 Feb.=Cupid=N=C+_
Panda=9,000=90%=P9.00D=9.0=Abstraction=Gods=Saturn=9Sept.>>A=Ø.
Pandemic=8,500=9,000=90%=P9.00D=9.0=Abstraction=Gods=Saturn=9Sept.>>A=Ø.

Pandemonium=6,000=60%=P6.0D=Man=Earth=Royalty=6 June=Gaia=Maia>>M=M2.
Wild uproar or noise. < Pandæmonium, Capital of Hell in Milton's Paradise Lost.

Pander=10,000=1,000=100%=10.0=Physicality=Tech.=10 Oct.=Uranus=P=1Ø.
P and L=1,500=15%=P1.50D=1.5=Authority=Solar Crown=1 May = Maia.

Pandora=7,500=8,000=80%=P8.0D=Economy=Currency=8 Aug.=Zeus>>E=v.
Greek myth. The first woman who opened a box containing all the evils of human life.
Bible. Eve. According to the creation story is Genesis. Is the forbidden fruit a box perhaps?

Pan dowdy=8,000=80%=P8.0D=Economy=Currency=8 Aug.=Zeus>>E=v.
Pane=5,000=50%=P5.00D=Law=Time=Venus=5 May = Aphrodite>>L=N.
Panegyric=7,000=70%=P7.0D=7.0=Language=Assets=Mars=7 July=Pleiades.
Panel=10,000=1,000=100%=10.0=Physicality=Tech.=10 Oct.=Uranus=P=1Ø.
Paneling=3,500=4,000=40%=P4.0D=Govt.=Creato.=4 April=Mercury=Hermes=G=A4.
Panelist=2,000=20%=P2.00D=2.0=Nature=Matter=Moon=2 Feb.=Cupid=N=C+_
Panel truck=4,000=40%=P4.0D=Govt.=Creatocracy=4 April=Mercury=Hermes=G=A4.
Pang=7,500=8,000=80%=P8.0D=Economy=Currency=8 Aug.=Zeus>>E=v.
Pango Pango=1,500=15%=P1.50D=1.5=Authority=Solar Crown=1 May = Maia.
Panhandle1=5,500=5.5=80%=P5.50=Earth-Midway=5 May = Gaia.
Panhandle2=5,000=50%=P5.00D=Law=Time=Venus=5 May = Aphrodite>>L=N.

Panic=10,000=1,000=100%=10.0=Physicality=Tech.=10 Oct.=Uranus=P=1Ø.
A sudden overpowering terror often affecting many people at once. < Greek, Panikos, of
Pan(a source of terror as in flicks or herds).

Panicle=6,500=7,000=70%=P7.0D=7.0=Language=Assets=Mars=7 July=Pleiades.
Panjabi=1,500=15%=P1.50D=1.5=Authority=Solar Crown=1 May = Maia.
Pankhurst Emmeline=3,000=30%=P3.0D=3.0=Creativity=Stars=Muses=3 March = C=I.
Pannier=6,500=7,000=70%=P7.0D=7.0=Language=Assets=Mars=7 July=Pleiades.
Panoply=12,000=12%=P1.20D=1.2=Knowledge=Edu=12Dec.=Athena>>K=F.
Panorama=10,000=1,000=100%=10.0=Physicality=Tech.=10 Oct.=Uranus=P=1Ø.
Panpipe=7,000=70%=P7.0D=7.0=Language=Assets=Mars=7 July=Pleiades.
Pansy=7,500=8,000=80%=P8.0D=Economy=Currency=8 Aug.=Zeus>>E=v.
Pant=10,000=1,000=100%=10.0=Physicality=Tech.=10 Oct.=Uranus=P=1Ø.
Pantaloon=10,000=1,000=100%=10.0=Physicality=Tech.=10 Oct.=Uranus=P=1Ø.

Pantheism=7,000=70%=P7.0D=7.0=Language=Assets=Mars=7 July=Pleiades.
A doctrine identifying the deity with the universe. Makstianism is pantheistic in nature.
We do not only identify the deity we also compute to track and discover them as a Council.

Pantheon=10,000=1,000=100%=10.0=Physicality=Tech.=10 Oct.=Uranus=P=1Ø.
A temple dedicated to all Gods. All the Gods of a people. A public building commemorating and dedicated to the heroes and heroines of a nation. Greek. Pantheon. In the Creatocracy it is called the Mind Temple. Officially THE PANTHEON OF CASTLE MAKUPEDIA >> God of Creatocracy Genius & Mind. Mind Temple of the Makstian Faith.

Panther=6,500=7,000=70%=P7.0D=7.0=Language=Assets=Mars=7 July=Pleiades.
Panties=3,000=30%=P3.0D=3.0=Creativity=Stars=Muses=3 March = C=I>>GIL.
Pantomime=10,000=1,000=100%=10.0=Physicality=Tech.=10 Oct.=Uranus=P=1Ø.
Pantry=9,000=90%=P9.00D=9.0=Abstraction=Gods=Saturn=9Sept.>>A=Ø.
Pants=1,500=15%=P1.50D=1.5=Authority=Solar Crown=1 May = Maia.
Pantsuit=4,000=40%=P4.0D=Govt.=Creatocracy=4 April=Mercury=Hermes=G=A4.
Pantyhose=5,000=50%=P5.00D=Law=Time=Venus=5 May = Aphrodite>>L=N.
Pantywaist=1,500=15%=P1.50D=1.5=Authority=Solar Crown=1 May = Maia.
Pap=8,000=80%=P8.0D=Economy=Currency=8 Aug.=Zeus>>E=v.
Papa=2,500=3,000=30%=P3.0D=3.0=Creativity=Stars=Muses=3 March = C=I>>GIL.

Papacy=11,000=11%=P1.10D=1.1=Idea=Brainchild=Inv.=11 Nov.=SC=Athena>>I=MT.
The office and jurisdiction of a pope. The period of time during which a pope is in office. The system of church government headed by the pope. The Creatocracy is defined as the office and jurisdiction of the Emperor. The eternal period which the emperor is in office. The system of government of creativity for the people in the people and by the people invented by Peter Matthews-Akukalia, Castle Makupedia. See the book >> The Creatocracy Republic by Peter Matthews-Akukalia, Castle Makupedia.

Papago=8,000=80%=P8.0D=Economy=Currency=8 Aug.=Zeus>>E=v.
Papal=4,000=40%=P4.0D=Govt.=Creatocracy=4 April=Mercury=Hermes=G=A4.
Papal States=6,500=7,000=70%=P7.0D=7.0=Language=Assets=Mars=7 July=Pleiades.

Papaw=7,000=70%=P7.0D=7.0=Language=Assets=Mars=7 July=Pleiades.
We discover that pawpaw when eaten builds an acumen for computing.

Papaya=8,000=80%=P8.0D=Economy=Currency=8 Aug.=Zeus>>E=v.
Papeete=7,000=70%=P7.0D=7.0=Language=Assets=Mars=7 July=Pleiades.
Paper=10,000=1,000=100%=10.0=Physicality=Tech.=10 Oct.=Uranus=P=1Ø.
Paperback=3,000=30%=P3.0D=3.0=Creativity=Stars=Muses=3 March = C=I>>GIL.
Paper bound=1,000=100%=10.0=1.0=Mind=Sun=1 January=Helios >> M=E4.
Paper hanger=3,000=30%=P3.0D=3.0=Creativity=Stars=Muses=3 March = C=I>>GIL.
Paper tiger=6,000=60%=P6.0D=Man=Earth=Royalty=6 June=Gaia=Maia>>M=M2.
Paper trail=3,000=30%=P3.0D=3.0=Creativity=Stars=Muses=3 March = C=I>>GIL.
Paperweight=4,000=40%=P4.0D=Govt.=Creatocracy=4 April=Mercury=Hermes=G=A4.
Paperwork=4,500=5,000=50%=P5.00D=Law=Time=Venus=5 May = Aphrodite>>L=N.
Papilla=6,000=60%=P6.0D=Man=Earth=Royalty=6 June=Gaia=Maia>>M=M2.
Papist=3,500=4,000=40%=P4.0D=Govt.=Creatocracy=4 April=Mercury=Hermes=G=A4.
Papoose=5,000=50%=P5.00D=Law=Time=Venus=5 May = Aphrodite>>L=N.
Paprika=7,000=70%=P7.0D=7.0=Language=Assets=Mars=7 July=Pleiades.

Pap smear=7,500=8,000=80%=P8.0D=Economy=Currency=8 Aug.=Zeus>>E=v.
A test for cancer, especially of the female genital tract. [After George Panicolaou (1883 - 1962).]. Peter Matthews-Akukalia, Castle Makupedia invented Psycho-surgery. A method of analysis computations emotional commitments and PICTUREs to cure a sick person.

Papua New Guinea=10,000=1,000=100%=10.0=Physicality=Tech.=10 Oct.=Uranus=P=1Ø.
Papyrus=10,000=1,000=100%=10.0=Physicality=Tech.=10 Oct.=Uranus=P=1Ø.
par=10,000=1,000=100%=10.0=Physicality=Tech.=10 Oct.=Uranus=P=1Ø.
Par.=1,500=15%=P1.50D=1.5=Authority=Solar Crown=1 May = Maia.
Para=500=5%=P5.00D=5.0=Law=Time=Venus=5 May=Aphrodite>>L=N.
Para-=6,000=60%=P6.0D=Man=Earth=Royalty=6 June=Gaia=Maia>>M=M2.
Parable=4,500=5,000=50%=P5.00D=Law=Time=Venus=5 May = Aphrodite>>L=N.
Parabola=11,000=11%=P1.10D=1.1=Idea=Brainchild=Inv.=11 Nov.=SC=Athena>>I=MT.
Paracelsus=4,500=5,000=50%=P5.00D=Law=Time=Venus=5 May = Aphrodite>>L=N.
Parachute=9,500=10,000=1,000=100%=10.0=Physicality=Tech.=10 Oct.=Uranus=P=1Ø.
Parade=10,000=1,000=100%=10.0=Physicality=Tech.=10 Oct.=Uranus=P=1Ø.
Paradigm=10,000=1,000=100%=10.0=Physicality=Tech.=10 Oct.=Uranus=P=1Ø.

Paradise=8,500=9,000=90%=P9.00D=9.0=Abstraction=Gods=Saturn=9Sept.>>A=Ø.
Zeus dwells in Paradise. Another sign that he incarnates Peter Matthews-Akukalia, Castle Makupedia who invented and owns the Paradise Nations. Full title: Sovereign Creatocratic Republic of Paradise. A sovereign state of the Creative Scientist Professionalism and the Makupedians. He is the Disean God of Creatocracy Genius Mind & Mindom.

Paradox=10,000=1,000=100%=10.0=Physicality=Tech.=10 Oct.=Uranus=P=1Ø.
Paraffin=10,000=1,000=100%=10.0=Physicality=Tech.=10 Oct.=Uranus=P=1Ø.
Paragon=7,500=8,000=80%=P8.0D=Economy=Currency=8 Aug.=Zeus>>E=v.
Paragraph=10,000=1,000=100%=10.0=Physicality=Tech.=10 Oct.=Uranus=P=1Ø.
Paraguay=5,500=5.5=80%=P5.50=Earth-Midway=5 May = Gaia.
Paraiba=5,000=50%=P5.00D=Law=Time=Venus=5 May = Aphrodite>>L=N.
Parakeet=6,500=7,000=70%=P7.0D=7.0=Language=Assets=Mars=7 July=Pleiades.
Paralegal=6,500=7,000=70%=P7.0D=7.0=Language=Assets=Mars=7 July=Pleiades.
Parallax=9,000=90%=P9.00D=9.0=Abstraction=Gods=Saturn=9Sept.>>A=Ø.
Parallel=10,000=1,000=100%=10.0=Physicality=Tech.=10 Oct.=Uranus=P=1Ø.
Parallelepiped=10,000=1,000=100%=10.0=Physicality=Tech.=10 Oct.=Uranus=P=1Ø.
Parallelogram=4,500=5,000=50%=P5.00D=Law=Time=Venus=5 May = Aphrodite>>L=N.
Paralysis=10,000=1,000=100%=10.0=Physicality=Tech.=10 Oct.=Uranus=P=1Ø.
Paralyze=4,000=40%=P4.0D=Govt.=Creatocracy=4 April=Mercury=Hermes=G=A4.
Paramaribo=7,000=70%=P7.0D=7.0=Language=Assets=Mars=7 July=Pleiades.
Paramecium=8,000=80%=P8.0D=Economy=Currency=8 Aug.=Zeus>>E=v.
Paramedic=7,000=70%=P7.0D=7.0=Language=Assets=Mars=7 July=Pleiades.
Parameter=10,000=1,000=100%=10.0=Physicality=Tech.=10 Oct.=Uranus=P=1Ø.
Paramilitary=5,500=5.5=80%=P5.50=Earth-Midway=5 May = Gaia.
Paramount=6,000=60%=P6.0D=Man=Earth=Royalty=6 June=Gaia=Maia>>M=M2.
Paramour=7,500=8,000=80%=P8.0D=Economy=Currency=8 Aug.=Zeus>>E=v.
Paraná=8,500=9,000=90%=P9.00D=9.0=Abstraction=Gods=Saturn=9Sept.>>A=Ø.
Paranoia=6,000=60%=P6.0D=Man=Earth=Royalty=6 June=Gaia=Maia>>M=M2.
Paranormal=4,500=5,000=50%=P5.00D=Law=Time=Venus=5 May = Aphrodite>>L=N.
Parapet=8,000=80%=P8.0D=Economy=Currency=8 Aug.=Zeus>>E=v.

Paraphernalia=14,000=14%=P1.40D=1.4=Mgt.=Solar Energy=13 May=Athena=SC=0.1
A married woman's property exclusive of her dowry.

Paraphrase=9,000=90%=P9.00D=9.0=Abstraction=Gods=Saturn=9Sept.>>A=Ø.
Paraplegia=7,500=8,000=80%=P8.0D=Economy=Currency=8 Aug.=Zeus>>E=v.
Paraprofessional=3,000=30%=P3.0D=3.0=Creativity=Stars=Muses=3 March = C=I>>GIL.
Parapsychology=5,000=50%=P5.00D=Law=Time=Venus=5 May = Aphrodite>>L=N.
Paraquat=10,000=1,000=100%=10.0=Physicality=Tech.=10 Oct.=Uranus=P=1Ø.
Parasite=10,000=1,000=100%=10.0=Physicality=Tech.=10 Oct.=Uranus=P=1Ø.
Parasitic=3,500=4,000=40%=P4.0D=Govt.=4 April=Mercury=Hermes=G=A4.
Parasitology=4,000=40%=P4.0D=Govt.=Creatocracy=4 April=Mercury=Hermes=G=A4.
Parasol=6,500=7,000=70%=P7.0D=7.0=Language=Assets=Mars=7 July=Pleiades.
Parasympathetic=7,000=70%=P7.0D=7.0=Language=Assets=Mars=7 July=Pleiades.
Parathyroid gland=10,000=1,000=100%=10.0=Physicality=Tech.=10 Oct.=Uranus=P=1Ø.
Paratroops=3,000=30%=P3.0D=3.0=Creativity=Stars=Muses=3 March = C=I>>GIL.
Paratyphoid fever=5,500=5.5=80%=P5.50=Earth-Midway=5 May = Gaia.
Parboil=6,500=7,000=70%=P7.0D=7.0=Language=Assets=Mars=7 July=Pleiades.
Parcel=10,000=1,000=100%=10.0=Physicality=Tech.=10 Oct.=Uranus=P=1Ø.

Parcel post=5,000=50%=P5.00D=Law=Time=Venus=5 May = Aphrodite>>L=N.
Parch=10,000=1,000=100%=10.0=Physicality=Tech.=10 Oct.=Uranus=P=1Ø.
Parchment=10,000=1,000=100%=10.0=Physicality=Tech.=10 Oct.=Uranus=P=1Ø.
Pardon=10,000=1,000=100%=10.0=Physicality=Tech.=10 Oct.=Uranus=P=1Ø.
Pare=10,000=1,000=100%=10.0=Physicality=Tech.=10 Oct.=Uranus=P=1Ø.
Paregoric=10,000=1,000=100%=10.0=Physicality=Tech.=10 Oct.=Uranus=P=1Ø.
Parent=10,000=1,000=100%=10.0=Physicality=Tech.=10 Oct.=Uranus=P=1Ø.
Parentheses=10,000=1,000=100%=10.0=Physicality=Tech.=10 Oct.=Uranus=P=1Ø.
Paresis=2,500=3,000=30%=P3.0D=3.0=Creativity=Stars=Muses=3 March = C=I>>GIL.
Par excellence=3,000=30%=P3.0D=3.0=Creativity=Stars=Muses=3 March = C=I>>GIL.
Parfait=10,000=1,000=100%=10.0=Physicality=Tech.=10 Oct.=Uranus=P=1Ø.
Parhelion=10,000=1,000=100%=10.0=Physicality=Tech.=10 Oct.=Uranus=P=1Ø.
Pariah=7,000=70%=P7.0D=7.0=Language=Assets=Mars=7 July=Pleiades.
Parietal=10,000=1,000=100%=10.0=Physicality=Tech.=10 Oct.=Uranus=P=1Ø.
Parimutuel=10,000=1,000=100%=10.0=Physicality=Tech.=10 Oct.=Uranus=P=1Ø.
Paring=5,000=50%=P5.00D=Law=Time=Venus=5 May = Aphrodite>>L=N.
Pari passu=4,500=5,000=50%=P5.00D=Law=Time=Venus=5 May = Aphrodite>>L=N.
Paris=8,000=80%=P8.0D=Economy=Currency=8 Aug.=Zeus>>E=v.
Parish=10,000=1,000=100%=10.0=Physicality=Tech.=10 Oct.=Uranus=P=1Ø.
Parishioner=2,000=20%=P2.00D=2.0=Nature=Matter=Moon=2 Feb.=Cupid=N=C+_
Parity=10,000=1,000=100%=10.0=Physicality=Tech.=10 Oct.=Uranus=P=1Ø.
Park=10,000=1,000=100%=10.0=Physicality=Tech.=10 Oct.=Uranus=P=1Ø.

Park Mungo.=3,000=30%=P3.0D=3.0=Creativity=Stars=Muses=3 March = C=I>>GIL.
1771-1806. Scottish explorer in Africa. Driven by the muses he discovered the source of the River Niger. The Creatocracy believes he was a marine muse incarnation. Mungo Park.

Parka=10,000=1,000=100%=10.0=Physicality=Tech.=10 Oct.=Uranus=P=1Ø.

Parker Dorothy Rothschild.=2,000=20%=P2.00D=2.0=Moon=2 Feb.=Cupid=N=C+_
1893-1967. American writer.

Parkman Francis.=2,000=20%=P2.00D=2.0=Nature=Matter=Moon=2 Feb.=Cupid=N=C+_
Parks Rosa=3,000=30%=P3.0D=3.0=Creativity=Stars=Muses=3 March = C=I>>GIL.
Parkway=2,000=20%=P2.00D=2.0=Nature=Matter=Moon=2 Feb.=Cupid=N=C+_
Parlance=6,500=7,000=70%=P7.0D=7.0=Language=Assets=Mars=7 July=Pleiades.
Parlay=10,000=1,000=100%=10.0=Physicality=Tech.=10 Oct.=Uranus=P=1Ø.
Parley=8,000=80%=P8.0D=Economy=Currency=8 Aug.=Zeus>>E=v.
Parliament=10,000=1,000=100%=10.0=Physicality=Tech.=10 Oct.=Uranus=P=1Ø.
Parliamentarian=7,000=70%=P7.0D=7.0=Language=Assets=Mars=7 July=Pleiades.
Parlor=10,000=1,000=100%=10.0=Physicality=Tech.=10 Oct.=Uranus=P=1Ø.
Parlous=1,000=100%=Physicality=Tech.=10 Oct.=Uranus=P=1Ø.
Parma=5,000=50%=P5.00D=Law=Time=Venus=5 May = Aphrodite>>L=N.

Parmesan=7,000=70%=P7.0D=7.0=Language=Assets=Mars=7 July=Pleiades.
Parmigiana=4,000=40%=P4.0D=Govt.=Creatocracy=4 April=Mercury=Hermes=G=A4.
Parnaiba=7,000=70%=P7.0D=7.0=Language=Assets=Mars=7 July=Pleiades.
Parnassus=7,000=70%=P7.0D=7.0=Language=Assets=Mars=7 July=Pleiades.
Parnell Charles=3,000=30%=P3.0D=3.0=Creativity=Stars=Muses=3 March = C=I>>GIL.
Parochial=10,000=1,000=100%=10.0=Physicality=Tech.=10 Oct.=Uranus=P=1Ø.

Parochial school=3,000=30%=P3.0D=3.0=Creativity=Stars=Muses=3 March = C=I>>GIL.
A school supported by a church parish. The Creatocracy Education Union is a set of schools set up by the Creatocracy for both conventional and Creatocrat purposes. It includes the Creatocracy Universities Union, Makupedia Institutes and Castles Group of schools enclosing our nursery primary and secondary schools worldwide.

Parody=6,000=60%=P6.0D=Man=Earth=Royalty=6 June=Gaia=Maia>>M=M2.
Parole=10,000=1,000=100%=10.0=Physicality=Tech.=10 Oct.=Uranus=P=1Ø.
Parotid gland=10,000=1,000=100%=10.0=Physicality=Tech.=10 Oct.=Uranus=P=1Ø.
-parous=4,500=5,000=50%=P5.00D=Law=Time=Venus=5 May = Aphrodite>>L=N.
Paroxysm=10,000=1,000=100%=10.0=Physicality=Tech.=10 Oct.=Uranus=P=1Ø.
Parquet=10,000=1,000=100%=10.0=Physicality=Tech.=10 Oct.=Uranus=P=1Ø.
Parquetry=6,000=60%=P6.0D=Man=Earth=Royalty=6 June=Gaia=Maia>>M=M2.
Parr Catherine.=5,500=5.5=80%=P5.50=Earth-Midway=5 May = Gaia.
Parricide=9,000=90%=P9.00D=9.0=Abstraction=Gods=Saturn=9Sept.>>A=Ø.
Parrot=10,000=1,000=100%=10.0=Physicality=Tech.=10 Oct.=Uranus=P=1Ø.
Parrot fever=1,000=100%=10.0=1.0=Mind=Sun=1 January=Helios >> M=E4.
Parse=10,000=1,000=100%=10.0=Physicality=Tech.=10 Oct.=Uranus=P=1Ø.
Par sec=6,500=7,000=70%=P7.0D=7.0=Language=Assets=Mars=7 July=Pleiades.
Parsimony=4,500=5,000=50%=P5.00D=Law=Time=Venus=5 May = Aphrodite>>L=N.
Parsley=8,500=9,000=90%=P9.00D=9.0=Abstraction=Gods=Saturn=9Sept.>>A=Ø.
Parsnip=7,000=70%=P7.0D=7.0=Language=Assets=Mars=7 July=Pleiades.
Parson=6,500=7,000=70%=P7.0D=7.0=Language=Assets=Mars=7 July=Pleiades.
Parsonage=5,000=50%=P5.00D=Law=Time=Venus=5 May = Aphrodite>>L=N.
Par=10,000=1,000=100%=10.0=Physicality=Tech.=10 Oct.=Uranus=P=1Ø.
Part.=1,000=100%=10.0=1.0=Mind=Sun=1 January=Helios >> M=E4.
Partake=10,000=1,000=100%=10.0=Physicality=Tech.=10 Oct.=Uranus=P=1Ø.
Parterre=10,000=1,000=100%=10.0=Physicality=Tech.=10 Oct.=Uranus=P=1Ø.
Parthenogenesis=10,000=1,000=100%=Physicality=Tech.=10 Oct.=Uranus=P=1Ø.
Parthia=5,500=5.5=80%=P5.50=Earth-Midway=5 May = Gaia.
Partial=10,000=1,000=100%=10.0=Physicality=Tech.=10 Oct.=Uranus=P=1Ø.
Partiality=10,000=1,000=100%=10.0=Physicality=Tech.=10 Oct.=Uranus=P=1Ø.
Participate=10,000=1,000=100%=10.0=Physicality=Tech.=10 Oct.=Uranus=P=1Ø.
Participle=10,000=1,000=100%=10.0=Physicality=Tech.=10 Oct.=Uranus=P=1Ø.
Particle=10,000=1,000=100%=10.0=Physicality=Tech.=10 Oct.=Uranus=P=1Ø.
Particolored=6,500=7,000=70%=P7.0D=7.0=Language=Assets=Mars=7 July=Pleiades.
Particular=10,000=1,000=100%=10.0=Physicality=Tech.=10 Oct.=Uranus=P=1Ø.

Particularize=7,000=70%=P7.0D=7.0=Language=Assets=Mars=7 July=Pleiades.
Particulate=2,500=3,000=30%=P3.0D=3.0=Creativity=Stars=Muses=3 March = C=I>>GIL.
Parting=8,500=9,000=90%=P9.00D=9.0=Abstraction=Gods=Saturn=9Sept.>>A=Ø.
Partisan=7,000=70%=P7.0D=7.0=Language=Assets=Mars=7 July=Pleiades.
Partite=3,000=30%=P3.0D=3.0=Creativity=Stars=Muses=3 March = C=I>>GIL.
Partition=10,000=1,000=100%=10.0=Physicality=Tech.=10 Oct.=Uranus=P=1Ø.
Partly=4,000=40%=P4.0D=Govt.=Creatocracy=4 April=Mercury=Hermes=G=A4.
Partner=10,000=1,000=100%=10.0=Physicality=Tech.=10 Oct.=Uranus=P=1Ø.
Part of speech=9,500=10,000=1,000=100%=10.0=Phy=Tech.=10 Oct.=Uranus=P=1Ø.
Partook=2,000=20%=P2.00D=2.0=Nature=Matter=Moon=2 Feb.=Cupid=N=C+_
Partridge=4,500=5,000=50%=P5.00D=Law=Time=Venus=5 May = Aphrodite>>L=N.
Part-time=6,000=60%=P6.0D=Man=Earth=Royalty=6 June=Gaia=Maia>>M=M2.
Parturition=5,500=5.5=80%=P5.50=Earth-Midway=5 May = Gaia.
Partway=4,500=5,000=50%=P5.00D=Law=Time=Venus=5 May = Aphrodite>>L=N.
Party=10,000=1,000=100%=10.0=Physicality=Tech.=10 Oct.=Uranus=P=1Ø.
Party line=10,000=1,000=100%=10.0=Physicality=Tech.=10 Oct.=Uranus=P=1Ø.
Parvenu=10,000=1,000=100%=10.0=Physicality=Tech.=10 Oct.=Uranus=P=1Ø.
Pas=3,500=4,000=40%=P4.0D=Govt.=Creatocracy=4 April=Mercury=Hermes=G=A4.
Pasadena=7,000=70%=P7.0D=7.0=Language=Assets=Mars=7 July=Pleiades.
Pascal Blaise.=3,000=30%=P3.0D=3.0=Creativity=Stars=Muses=3 March = C=I>>GIL.
Pas de deux=4,000=40%=P4.0D=Govt.=Creatocracy=4 April=Mercury=Hermes=G=A4.
Pasha=8,500=9,000=90%=P9.00D=9.0=Abstraction=Gods=Saturn=9Sept.>>A=Ø.
Pashto=4,000=40%=P4.0D=Govt.=Creatocracy=4 April=Mercury=Hermes=G=A4.
Pass=10,000=1,000=100%=10.0=Physicality=Tech.=10 Oct.=Uranus=P=1Ø.
Pass.=2,000=20%=P2.00D=2.0=Nature=Matter=Moon=2 Feb.=Cupid=N=C+_
Passable=6,500=7,000=70%=P7.0D=7.0=Language=Assets=Mars=7 July=Pleiades.
Passage=10,000=1,000=100%=10.0=Physicality=Tech.=10 Oct.=Uranus=P=1Ø.
Passageway=1,000=100%=10.0=1.0=Mind=Sun=1 January=Helios >> M=E4.
Passamaquoddy=10,000=1,000=100%=10.0=Physicality=Tech.=10 Oct.=Uranus=P=1Ø.
Passbook=1,000=100%=10.0=1.0=Mind=Sun=1 January=Helios >> M=E4.
Passé=9,000=90%=P9.00D=9.0=Abstraction=Gods=Saturn=9Sept.>>A=Ø.
Passenger=6,500=7,000=70%=P7.0D=7.0=Language=Assets=Mars=7 July=Pleiades.
Passé-par tout=8,000=80%=P8.0D=Economy=Currency=8 Aug.=Zeus>>E=v.
Passerby=5,000=50%=P5.00D=Law=Time=Venus=5 May = Aphrodite>>L=N.
Pas serine=6,500=7,000=70%=P7.0D=7.0=Language=Assets=Mars=7 July=Pleiades.
Pass fall=8,500=9,000=90%=P9.00D=9.0=Abstraction=Gods=Saturn=9Sept.>>A=Ø.
Passim=10,000=1,000=100%=10.0=Physicality=Tech.=10 Oct.=Uranus=P=1Ø.
Passing=10,000=1,000=100%=10.0=Physicality=Tech.=10 Oct.=Uranus=P=1Ø.
Passion=10,000=1,000=100%=10.0=Physicality=Tech.=10 Oct.=Uranus=P=1Ø.
Passive=10,000=1,000=100%=10.0=Physicality=Tech.=10 Oct.=Uranus=P=1Ø.
Passive restraint=10,000=1,000=100%=10.0=Physicality=Tech.=10 Oct.=Uranus=P=1Ø.
Pass key=2,500=3,000=30%=P3.0D=3.0=Creativity=Stars=Muses=3 March = C=I>>GIL.
Passover=7,000=70%=P7.0D=7.0=Language=Assets=Mars=7 July=Pleiades.
Passport=9,500=10,000=1,000=100%=10.0=Physicality=Tech.=10 Oct.=Uranus=P=1Ø.
Password=10,500=11,000=11%=P1.10D=1.1=Idea=Brainchild.=11 Nov.=Athena>>I=MT.

Past=10,000=1,000=100%=10.0=Physicality=Tech.=10 Oct.=Uranus=P=1Ø.
Pasta=10,000=1,000=100%=10.0=Physicality=Tech.=10 Oct.=Uranus=P=1Ø.
Paste=10,000=1,000=100%=10.0=Physicality=Tech.=10 Oct.=Uranus=P=1Ø.
Pasteboard=7,000=70%=P7.0D=7.0=Language=Assets=Mars=7 July=Pleiades.
Pastel=10,000=1,000=100%=10.0=Physicality=Tech.=10 Oct.=Uranus=P=1Ø.
Pastern=7,000=70%=P7.0D=7.0=Language=Assets=Mars=7 July=Pleiades.
Pasternak Boris.=3,000=30%=P3.0D=3.0=Creativity=Stars=Muses=3 March = C=I>>GIL.
Pasteur Louis.=2,000=20%=P2.00D=2.0=Nature=Matter=Moon=2 Feb.=Cupid=N=C+_
Pasteurization=10,000=1,000=100%=10.0=Physicality=Tech.=10 Oct.=Uranus=P=1Ø.
Pastiche=7,500=8,000=80%=P8.0D=Economy=Currency=8 Aug.=Zeus>>E=v.
Pastille=10,000=1,000=100%=10.0=Physicality=Tech.=10 Oct.=Uranus=P=1Ø.
Pastime=4,000=40%=P4.0D=Govt.=Creatocracy=4 April=Mercury=Hermes=G=A4.

Pastor=7,000=70%=P7.0D=7.0=Language=Assets=Mars=7 July=Pleiades.
A Christian minister or priest who is the leader of a congregation. < Lat. pāstor,shepherd.
A pastor is subject to the rules of precision and the job would be null and void without
computational creativity and Mind Computing which is the essence of the scriptures.

Pastoral=10,000=1,000=100%=10.0=Physicality=Tech.=10 Oct.=Uranus=P=1Ø.
Pastorale=3,500=4,000=40%=P4.0D=Govt.=Creato=4 April=Mercury=Hermes=G=A4.
Past participle=10,000=1,000=100%=10.0=Physicality=Tech.=10 Oct.=Uranus=P=1Ø.
Past perfect=2,000=20%=P2.00D=2.0=Nature=Matter=Moon=2 Feb.=Cupid=N=C+_
Pastrami=6,500=7,000=70%=P7.0D=7.0=Language=Assets=Mars=7 July=Pleiades.
Pastry=10,000=1,000=100%=10.0=Physicality=Tech.=10 Oct.=Uranus=P=1Ø.
Pasturage=6,500=7,000=70%=P7.0D=7.0=Language=Assets=Mars=7 July=Pleiades.
Pasture=10,000=1,000=100%=10.0=Physicality=Tech.=10 Oct.=Uranus=P=1Ø.
Pasty=5,000=50%=P5.00D=Law=Time=Venus=5 May = Aphrodite>>L=N.
Pat1=10,000=1,000=100%=10.0=Physicality=Tech.=10 Oct.=Uranus=P=1Ø.
Pat2=10,000=1,000=100%=10.0=Physicality=Tech.=10 Oct.=Uranus=P=1Ø.

---

pat.=500=5%=P5.00D=5.0=Law=Time=Venus=5 May=Aphrodite>>L=N.
Patent. Peter Matthews-Akukalia has a patent for Makupedia and the Maks Currencies.

Pataca=3,500=4,000=40%=P4.0D=Govt.=Creatocracy=4 April=Mercury=Hermes=G=A4.
Patagonia=10,000=1,000=100%=10.0=Physicality=Tech.=10 Oct.=Uranus=P=1Ø.
Patch=10,000=1,000=100%=10.0=Physicality=Tech.=10 Oct.=Uranus=P=1Ø.
Patch test=9,000=90%=P9.00D=9.0=Abstraction=Gods=Saturn=9Sept.>>A=Ø.
Patchwork=6,500=7,000=70%=P7.0D=7.0=Language=Assets=Mars=7 July=Pleiades.
Patchy=6,500=7,000=70%=P7.0D=7.0=Language=Assets=Mars=7 July=Pleiades.
Pate=3,000=30%=P3.0D=3.0=Creativity=Stars=Muses=3 March = C=I>>GIL.
Pâté=1,500=15%=P1.50D=1.5=Authority=Solar Crown=1 May = Maia.
Patella=5,500=5.5=80%=P5.50=Earth-Midway=5 May = Gaia.
Paten=10,000=1,000=100%=10.0=Physicality=Tech.=10 Oct.=Uranus=P=1Ø.

Patent=10,000=1,000=100%=10.0=Physicality=Tech.=10 Oct.=Uranus=P=1Ø.
All patents are measured on the 10,000ᵗʰ standards.

Patent leather=10,000=1,000=100%=10.0=Physicality=Tech.=10 Oct.=Uranus=P=1Ø.
Paterfamilias=10,000=1,000=100%=10.0=Physicality=Tech.=10 Oct.=Uranus=P=1Ø.
Paternal=10,000=1,000=100%=10.0=Physicality=Tech.=10 Oct.=Uranus=P=1Ø.
Paternalism=10,000=1,000=100%=10.0=Physicality=Tech.=10 Oct.=Uranus=P=1Ø.
Paternity=3,500=4,000=40%=P4.0D=Govt.=Creato=4 April=Mercury=Hermes=G=A4.
Paternoster=6,000=60%=P6.0D=Man=Earth=Royalty=6 June=Gaia=Maia>>M=M2.
Paterson=4,500=5,000=50%=P5.00D=Law=Time=Venus=5 May = Aphrodite>>L=N.
Path=4,500=5,000=50%=P5.00D=Law=Time=Venus=5 May = Aphrodite>>L=N.
Pathetic=5,500=5.5=80%=P5.50=Earth-Midway=5 May = Gaia.
Pathfinder=6,500=7,000=70%=P7.0D=7.0=Language=Assets=Mars=7 July=Pleiades.
Patho-=2,500=3,000=30%=P3.0D=3.0=Creativity=Stars=Muses=3 March = C=I>>GIL.
Pathogen=7,500=8,000=80%=P8.0D=Economy=Currency=8 Aug.=Zeus>>E=v.
Pathogenesis=4,000=40%=P4.0D=Govt.=Creatocracy=4 April=Mercury=Hermes=G=A4.
Pathology=10,000=1,000=100%=10.0=Physicality=Tech.=10 Oct.=Uranus=P=1Ø.
Pathos=10,000=1,000=100%=10.0=Physicality=Tech.=10 Oct.=Uranus=P=1Ø.
Pathway=1,000=100%=10.0=1.0=Mind=Sun=1 January=Helios >> M=E4.
-pathy=7,000=70%=P7.0D=7.0=Language=Assets=Mars=7 July=Pleiades.
Patience=6,000=60%=P6.0D=Man=Earth=Royalty=6 June=Gaia=Maia>>M=M2.
Patient=10,000=1,000=100%=10.0=Physicality=Tech.=10 Oct.=Uranus=P=1Ø.
Patina=10,000=1,000=100%=10.0=Physicality=Tech.=10 Oct.=Uranus=P=1Ø.
Patio=10,000=1,000=100%=10.0=Physicality=Tech.=10 Oct.=Uranus=P=1Ø.
Patna=6,500=7,000=70%=P7.0D=7.0=Language=Assets=Mars=7 July=Pleiades.
Patois=10,000=1,000=100%=10.0=Physicality=Tech.=10 Oct.=Uranus=P=1Ø.
Paton Alan=3,000=30%=P3.0D=3.0=Creativity=Stars=Muses=3 March = C=I>>GIL.

Patri-=5,500=5.5=80%=P5.50=Earth-Midway=5 May = Gaia.
Father, paternal, patrilineal, Peter. Matthews - tax collector or revenue maker, wealth creator. Akukalia, excess wealth. Peter Matthews-Akukalia >> the father of a system of wealths built on currencies taxes rights and universal royalty (5.5). The Creatocracy.

Patriarch=10,000=1,000=100%=10.0=Physicality=Tech.=10 Oct.=Uranus=P=1Ø.
Patriarchy=10,000=1,000=100%=10.0=Physicality=Tech.=10 Oct.=Uranus=P=1Ø.

Patrician=3,000=30%=P3.0D=3.0=Creativity=Stars=Muses=3 March = C=I>>GIL.
A person of high rank; aristocrat. 8ᵗʰ child and 6ᵗʰ Princess of Peter Matthews-Akukalia, Castle Makupedia and the Creatocracy. Daughter of Queen Alice. Believed to be the reincarnated Jane-Michelle (Jami) late daughter of Empress Tina dedicated in Psychoeconomix. A daughter of two mothers and sister of many tribes - Ibo, Yoruba, Benin.

Patricide=5,500=5.5=80%=P5.50=Earth-Midway=5 May = Gaia.
Patrick=6,000=60%=P6.0D=Man=Earth=Royalty=6 June=Gaia=Maia>>M=M2.
Patrilineal=6,000=60%=P6.0D=Man=Earth=Royalty=6 June=Gaia=Maia>>M=M2.

Patrimony=7,500=8,000=80%=P8.0D=Economy=Currency=8 Aug.=Zeus>>E=v.
An inheritance especially from a father or other ancestor. See Patri-, see Peter.

Patriot=10,000=1,000=100%=10.0=Physicality=Tech.=10 Oct.=Uranus=P=1Ø.
Patristic=6,000=60%=P6.0D=Man=Earth=Royalty=6 June=Gaia=Maia>>M=M2.
Patrol=10,000=1,000=100%=10.0=Physicality=Tech.=10 Oct.=Uranus=P=1Ø.
Patrolman=4,500=5,000=50%=P5.00D=Law=Time=Venus=5 May = Aphrodite>>L=N.
Patrol wagon=4,000=40%=P4.0D=Govt.=Creatocracy=4 April=Mercury=Hermes=G=A4.
Patrol woman=4,500=5,000=50%=P5.00D=Law=Time=Venus=5 May = Aphrodite>>L=N.
Patron=9,500=10,000=1,000=100%=10.0=Physicality=Tech.=10 Oct.=Uranus=P=1Ø.
Patronage=10,000=1,000=100%=10.0=Physicality=Tech.=10 Oct.=Uranus=P=1Ø.
Patroness=6,000=60%=P6.0D=Man=Earth=Royalty=6 June=Gaia=Maia>>M=M2.
Patronize=10,000=1,000=100%=10.0=Physicality=Tech.=10 Oct.=Uranus=P=1Ø.
Patron saint=9,000=90%=P9.00D=9.0=Abstraction=Gods=Saturn=9Sept.>>A=Ø.
Patronymic=10,000=1,000=100%=10.0=Physicality=Tech.=10 Oct.=Uranus=P=1Ø.
Patroon=10,000=1,000=100%=10.0=Physicality=Tech.=10 Oct.=Uranus=P=1Ø.
Patsy=5,500=5.5=80%=P5.50=Earth-Midway=5 May = Gaia.
Patter1=7,000=70%=P7.0D=7.0=Language=Assets=Mars=7 July=Pleiades.
Patter2=10,000=1,000=100%=10.0=Physicality=Tech.=10 Oct.=Uranus=P=1Ø.
Pattern=10,000=1,000=100%=10.0=Physicality=Tech.=10 Oct.=Uranus=P=1Ø.
Patton George=3,000=30%=P3.0D=3.0=Creativity=Stars=Muses=3 March = C=I>>GIL.
Patty=6,000=60%=P6.0D=Man=Earth=Royalty=6 June=Gaia=Maia>>M=M2.
Paucity=3,500=4,000=40%=P4.0D=Govt.=Creatocracy=4 April=Mercury=Hermes=G=A4.
Paul Saint=4,000=40%=P4.0D=Govt.=Creatocracy=4 April=Mercury=Hermes=G=A4.
Paul III.=2,000=20%=P2.00D=2.0=Nature=Matter=Moon=2 Feb.=Cupid=N=C+_
Paul VI.=2,000=20%=P2.00D=2.0=Nature=Matter=Moon=2 Feb.=Cupid=N=C+_
Pauling=3,000=30%=P3.0D=3.0=Creativity=Stars=Muses=3 March = C=I>>GIL.
Paunch=5,500=5.5=80%=P5.50=Earth-Midway=5 May = Gaia.
Pauper=5,000=50%=P5.00D=Law=Time=Venus=5 May = Aphrodite>>L=N.
Pause=10,000=1,000=100%=10.0=Physicality=Tech.=10 Oct.=Uranus=P=1Ø.
Pave=5,500=5.5=80%=P5.50=Earth-Midway=5 May = Gaia.
Pavement=10,000=1,000=100%=10.0=Physicality=Tech.=10 Oct.=Uranus=P=1Ø.
Pavilion=10,000=1,000=100%=10.0=Physicality=Tech.=10 Oct.=Uranus=P=1Ø.
Paving=3,500=4,000=40%=P4.0D=Govt.=Creatocracy=4 April=Mercury=Hermes=G=A4.
Pavlova Anna.=2,500=3,000=30%=P3.0D=3.0=Creativity=Stars=Muses=3 March=>>GIL.
Paw=10,000=1,000=100%=10.0=Physicality=Tech.=10 Oct.=Uranus=P=1Ø.
Pawl=10,000=1,000=100%=10.0=Physicality=Tech.=10 Oct.=Uranus=P=1Ø.
Pawn1=10,000=1,000=100%=10.0=Physicality=Tech.=10 Oct.=Uranus=P=1Ø.
Pawn2=10,000=1,000=100%=10.0=Physicality=Tech.=10 Oct.=Uranus=P=1Ø.
Pawn broker=7,000=70%=P7.0D=7.0=Language=Assets=Mars=7 July=Pleiades.

Pawnee=10,000=1,000=100%=10.0=Physicality=Tech.=10 Oct.=Uranus=P=1Ø.
Pawnshop=2,500=3,000=30%=P3.0D=3.0=Creativity=Stars=Muses=3 March = C=I>>GIL.
Pawpaw=1,500=15%=P1.50D=1.5=Authority=Solar Crown=1 May = Maia.
Pay=10,000=1,000=100%=10.0=Physicality=Tech.=10 Oct.=Uranus=P=1Ø.
Paycheck=6,000=60%=P6.0D=Man=Earth=Royalty=6 June=Gaia=Maia>>M=M2.
Pay dirt=7,000=70%=P7.0D=7.0=Language=Assets=Mars=7 July=Pleiades.
Payload=10,000=1,000=100%=10.0=Physicality=Tech.=10 Oct.=Uranus=P=1Ø.
Paymaster=4,500=5,000=50%=P5.00D=Law=Time=Venus=5 May = Aphrodite>>L=N.
Payment=3,500=4,000=40%=P4.0D=Govt.=Creato=4 April=Mercury=Hermes=G=A4.
Payoff=10,000=1,000=100%=10.0=Physicality=Tech.=10 Oct.=Uranus=P=1Ø.
Payroll=8,500=9,000=90%=P9.00D=9.0=Abstraction=Gods=Saturn=9Sept.>>A=Ø.
Pb=4,000=40%=P4.0D=Govt.=Creatocracy=4 April=Mercury=Hermes=G=A4.
PBS=1,500=15%=P1.50D=1.5=Authority=Solar Crown=1 May = Maia.
PBX=1,500=15%=P1.50D=1.5=Authority=Solar Crown=1 May = Maia.
PC=1,000=100%=Physicality=Tech.=10 Oct.=Uranus=P=1Ø.
p.c.=3,000=30%=P3.0D=3.0=Creativity=Stars=Muses=3 March = C=I>>GIL.
p/c=3,000=30%=P3.0D=3.0=Creativity=Stars=Muses=3 March = C=I>>GIL.
PCB=4,500=5,000=50%=P5.00D=Law=Time=Venus=5 May = Aphrodite>>L=N.
PCP=8,000=80%=P8.0D=Economy=Currency=8 Aug.=Zeus>>E=v.
pct.=500=5%=P5.00D=5.0=Law=Time=Venus=5 May=Aphrodite>>L=N.
Pd=2,500=3,000=30%=P3.0D=3.0=Creativity=Stars=Muses=3 March = C=I>>GIL.
Pd.=500=5%=P5.00D=5.0=Law=Time=Venus=5 May=Aphrodite>>L=N.
p.d.=1,000=100%=10.0=1.0=Mind=Sun=1 January=Helios >> M=E4.
P.D.=1,000=100%=10.0=1.0=Mind=Sun=1 January=Helios >> M=E4.
PDT=1,500=15%=P1.50D=1.5=Authority=Solar Crown=1 May = Maia.
pe1=4,000=40%=P4.0D=Govt.=Creatocracy=4 April=Mercury=Hermes=G=A4.
pe2=1,000=100%=10.0=1.0=Mind=Sun=1 January=Helios >> M=E4.
P.E.=3,500=4,000=40%=P4.0D=Govt.=Creatocracy=4 April=Mercury=Hermes=G=A4.
Pea=10,000=1,000=100%=10.0=Physicality=Tech.=10 Oct.=Uranus=P=1Ø.
Peace=10,000=1,000=100%=10.0=Physicality=Tech.=10 Oct.=Uranus=P=1Ø.
Peacekeeping=7,000=70%=P7.0D=7.0=Language=Assets=Mars=7 July=Pleiades.
Peacemaker=4,000=40%=P4.0D=Govt.=Creatocracy=4 April=Mercury=Hermes=G=A4.
Peace officer=4,500=5,000=50%=P5.00D=Law=Time=Venus=5 May = Aphrodite>>L=N.
Peace pipe=1,000=100%=10.0=1.0=Mind=Sun=1 January=Helios >> M=E4.
Peace River=6,500=7,000=70%=P7.0D=7.0=Language=Assets=Mars=7 July=Pleiades.
Peace time=2,500=3,000=30%=P3.0D=3.0=Creativity=Stars=Muses=3 March=C=I.
Peach=10,000=1,000=100%=10.0=Physicality=Tech.=10 Oct.=Uranus=P=1Ø.
Peacock=10,000=1,000=100%=10.0=Physicality=Tech.=10 Oct.=Uranus=P=1Ø.
Peafowl=3,500=4,000=40%=P4.0D=Govt.=Creatocracy=4 April=Mercury=Hermes=G=A4.
Peahen=1,500=15%=P1.50D=1.5=Authority=Solar Crown=1 May = Maia.
Pea Jacket=6,000=60%=P6.0D=Man=Earth=Royalty=6 June=Gaia=Maia>>M=M2.
Peak=10,000=1,000=100%=10.0=Physicality=Tech.=10 Oct.=Uranus=P=1Ø.
Peaked=3,500=4,000=40%=P4.0D=Govt.=Creatocracy=4 April=Mercury=Hermes=G=A4.
Peal=9,000=90%=P9.00D=9.0=Abstraction=Gods=Saturn=9Sept.>>A=Ø.
Peale Charles=2,500=3,000=30%=P3.0D=3.0=Creativity=Stars=Muses=3 March=C=I.

Peanut=10,000=1,000=100%=10.0=Physicality=Tech.=10 Oct.=Uranus=P=1Ø.
Peanut butter=3,500=4,000=40%=P4.0D=Govt.=Cre.=4 April=Mercury=Hermes=G=A4.
Pear=10,000=1,000=100%=10.0=Physicality=Tech.=10 Oct.=Uranus=P=1Ø.
Pearl=10,000=1,000=100%=10.0=Physicality=Tech.=10 Oct.=Uranus=P=1Ø.
Pearl Harbor=6,000=60%=P6.0D=Man=Earth=Royalty=6 June=Gaia=Maia>>M=M2.
Pearson Lester=6,000=60%=P6.0D=Man=Earth=Royalty=6 June=Gaia=Maia>>M=M2.
Peary Robert=4,500=5,000=50%=P5.00D=Law=Time=Venus=5 May = Aphrodite>>L=N.
Peasant=10,000=1,000=100%=10.0=Physicality=Tech.=10 Oct.=Uranus=P=1Ø.
Peat=8,500=9,000=90%=P9.00D=9.0=Abstraction=Gods=Saturn=9Sept.>>A=Ø.
Peat moss=5,500=5.5=80%=P5.50=Earth-Midway=5 May = Gaia.
Pebble=10,000=1,000=100%=10.0=Physicality=Tech.=10 Oct.=Uranus=P=1Ø.
Pecan=10,000=1,000=100%=10.0=Physicality=Tech.=10 Oct.=Uranus=P=1Ø.

Peccadillo=3,500=4,000=40%=P4.0D=Govt.=Creato=4 April=Mercury=Hermes=G=A4.
A minor sin or fault. Latin. Peccātum, sin.]

Peccary=6,500=7,000=70%=P7.0D=7.0=Language=Assets=Mars=7 July=Pleiades.
Peck1=10,000=1,000=100%=10.0=Physicality=Tech.=10 Oct.=Uranus=P=1Ø.
Peck2=10,000=1,000=100%=10.0=Physicality=Tech.=10 Oct.=Uranus=P=1Ø.
Pecking order=10,000=1,000=100%=10.0=Physicality=Tech.=10 Oct.=Uranus=P=1Ø.
Pecos=9,000=90%=P9.00D=9.0=Abstraction=Gods=Saturn=9Sept.>>A=Ø.
Pécs=4,500=5,000=50%=P5.00D=Law=Time=Venus=5 May = Aphrodite>>L=N.
Pectin=10,000=1,000=100%=10.0=Physicality=Tech.=10 Oct.=Uranus=P=1Ø.
Pectoral=4,500=5,000=50%=P5.00D=Law=Time=Venus=5 May = Aphrodite>>L=N.
Peculate=4,000=40%=P4.0D=Govt.=Creatocracy=4 April=Mercury=Hermes=G=A4.
Peculiar=10,000=1,000=100%=10.0=Physicality=Tech.=10 Oct.=Uranus=P=1Ø.

Pecuniary=5,000=50%=P5.00D=Law=Time=Venus=5 May = Aphrodite>>L=N.
Of or relating to money. [<Lat. pecūnia, wealth. See peku-.] The works and contents of
the works of Peter Matthews-Akukalia are his pecuniary rights. He is Castle Makupedia.

-ped=1,500=15%=P1.50D=1.5=Authority=Solar Crown=1 May = Maia.

Pedagogue=6,500=7,000=70%=P7.0D=7.0=Language=Assets=Mars=7 July=Pleiades.
A school teacher. Educator. A means to computational precision. It is compulsory for all
teachers to become proficient in the Creative Sciences and for every school.

Pedagogy=3,000=30%=P3.0D=3.0=Creativity=Stars=Muses=3 March = C=I>>GIL.
The art or profession of teaching. Every school must have a department of creativity. It is
called Creative Education, Makupedia or the department of Creatocracy studies.

PETER K. MATTHEWS - AKUKALIA

Pedal=10,000=1,000=100%=10.0=Physicality=Tech.=10 Oct.=Uranus=P=1Ø.
Pedant=10,000=1,000=100%=10.0=Physicality=Tech.=10 Oct.=Uranus=P=1Ø.
Pedantic=10,000=1,000=100%=10.0=Physicality=Tech.=10 Oct.=Uranus=P=1Ø.
Peddle=10,000=1,000=100%=10.0=Physicality=Tech.=10 Oct.=Uranus=P=1Ø.
Pederast=5,000=50%=P5.00D=Law=Time=Venus=5 May = Aphrodite>>L=N.
Pedestal=5,000=50%=P5.00D=Law=Time=Venus=5 May = Aphrodite>>L=N.
Pedestrian=10,000=1,000=100%=10.0=Physicality=Tech.=10 Oct.=Uranus=P=1Ø.
Pediatrics=10,000=1,000=100%=10.0=Physicality=Tech.=10 Oct.=Uranus=P=1Ø.
Pedicure=10,000=1,000=100%=10.0=Physicality=Tech.=10 Oct.=Uranus=P=1Ø.
Pedigree=10,000=1,000=100%=10.0=Physicality=Tech.=10 Oct.=Uranus=P=1Ø.
Pediment=6,500=7,000=70%=P7.0D=7.0=Language=Assets=Mars=7 July=Pleiades.
Pedo-=3,500=4,000=40%=P4.0D=Govt.=Creatocracy=4 April=Mercury=Hermes=G=A4.
Pedometer=10,000=1,000=100%=10.0=Physicality=Tech.=10 Oct.=Uranus=P=1Ø.
Peduncle=10,000=1,000=100%=10.0=Physicality=Tech.=10 Oct.=Uranus=P=1Ø.
Peek=7,500=8,000=80%=P8.0D=Economy=Currency=8 Aug.=Zeus>>E=v.
Peel=10,000=1,000=100%=10.0=Physicality=Tech.=10 Oct.=Uranus=P=1Ø.
Peel Robert=2,500=3,000=30%=P3.0D=3.0=Creativity=Stars=Muses=3 March=C=I
Peen=10,000=1,000=100%=10.0=Physicality=Tech.=10 Oct.=Uranus=P=1Ø.
Peep1=7,000=70%=P7.0D=7.0=Language=Assets=Mars=7 July=Pleiades.
Peep2=10,000=1,000=100%=10.0=Physicality=Tech.=10 Oct.=Uranus=P=1Ø.
Peephole=5,000=50%=P5.00D=Law=Time=Venus=5 May = Aphrodite>>L=N.
Peer1=6,500=7,000=70%=P7.0D=7.0=Language=Assets=Mars=7 July=Pleiades.
Peer2=9,000=90%=P9.00D=9.0=Abstraction=Gods=Saturn=9Sept.>>A=Ø.
Peerage=4,000=40%=P4.0D=Govt.=Creatocracy=4 April=Mercury=Hermes=G=A4.
Peeress=4,000=40%=P4.0D=Govt.=Creatocracy=4 April=Mercury=Hermes=G=A4.
Peerless=3,000=30%=P3.0D=3.0=Creativity=Stars=Muses=3 March = C=I>>GIL.
Peeve=5,000=50%=P5.00D=Law=Time=Venus=5 May = Aphrodite>>L=N.
Peevish=3,500=4,000=40%=P4.0D=Govt.=Creato=4 April=Mercury=Hermes=G=A4.
Peewee=6,000=60%=P6.0D=Man=Earth=Royalty=6 June=Gaia=Maia>>M=M2.
Peg=10,000=1,000=100%=10.0=Physicality=Tech.=10 Oct.=Uranus=P=1Ø.
Pegmatite=4,000=40%=P4.0D=Govt.=Creatocracy=4 April=Mercury=Hermes=G=A4.
Pei I(eoh)=4,000=40%=P4.0D=Govt.=Creatocracy=4 April=Mercury=Hermes=G=A4.
P.E.I.=1,500=15%=P1.50D=1.5=Authority=Solar Crown=1 May = Maia.
Peignoir=3,000=30%=P3.0D=3.0=Creativity=Stars=Muses=3 March = C=I>>GIL.
Pejorative=10,000=1,000=100%=10.0=Physicality=Tech.=10 Oct.=Uranus=P=1Ø.
Peking=1,000=100%=10.0=1.0=Mind=Sun=1 January=Helios >> M=E4.
Pekingese=10,000=1,000=100%=10.0=Physicality=Tech.=10 Oct.=Uranus=P=1Ø.
Pekoe=5,500=5.5=80%=P5.50=Earth-Midway=5 May = Gaia.
Pelagic=5,000=50%=P5.00D=Law=Time=Venus=5 May = Aphrodite>>L=N.
Pelée Mount.=7,500=8,000=80%=P8.0D=Economy=Currency=8 Aug.=Zeus>>E=v.

Pelf=3,000=30%=P3.0D=3.0=Creativity=Stars=Muses=3 March = C=I>>GIL.
Wealth or riches. First all riches are inspired from Maia Head of the Pleiades and Mind of GOD. The riches are granted by creativity through the muses. So creativity is the real

wealth and riches recognized by the supernatural. The only absolute rights ownership. In the works of Peter Matthews-Akukalia it is believed he owns all planets and stars through creativity. He discovered them through their energy methods and measured them.

Pelican=10,500=11,000=11%=P1.10D=1.1=Idea=Brainchild=Inv.=11 Nov=Athena>>I=MT.
Pellagra=10,000=1,000=100%=10.0=Physicality=Tech.=10 Oct.=Uranus=P=1Ø.
Pellet=10,000=1,000=100%=10.0=Physicality=Tech.=10 Oct.=Uranus=P=1Ø.
Pell-mell=5,500=5.5=80%=P5.50=Earth-Midway=5 May = Gaia.
Pellucid=10,000=1,000=100%=10.0=Physicality=Tech.=10 Oct.=Uranus=P=1Ø.
Peloponnesus=10,000=1,000=100%=10.0=Physicality=Tech.=10 Oct.=Uranus=P=1Ø.
Pelt1=6,000=60%=P6.0D=Man=Earth=Royalty=6 June=Gaia=Maia>>M=M2.
Pelt2=6,000=60%=P6.0D=Man=Earth=Royalty=6 June=Gaia=Maia>>M=M2.
Pelvis=10,000=1,000=100%=10.0=Physicality=Tech.=10 Oct.=Uranus=P=1Ø.
Pemmican=8,500=9,000=90%=P9.00D=9.0=Abstraction=Gods=Saturn=9Sept.>>A=Ø.
Pen1=8,000=80%=P8.0D=Economy=Currency=8 Aug.=Zeus>>E=v.
Pen2=10,000=1,000=100%=10.0=Physicality=Tech.=10 Oct.=Uranus=P=1Ø.
Pen3=1,500=15%=P1.50D=1.5=Authority=Solar Crown=1 May = Maia.
Penal=6,500=7,000=70%=P7.0D=7.0=Language=Assets=Mars=7 July=Pleiades.
Penalize=3,000=30%=P3.0D=3.0=Creativity=Stars=Muses=3 March = C=I>>GIL.
Penalty=10,000=1,000=100%=10.0=Physicality=Tech.=10 Oct.=Uranus=P=1Ø.
Penance=10,000=1,000=100%=10.0=Physicality=Tech.=10 Oct.=Uranus=P=1Ø.
Penang=1,500=15%=P1.50D=1.5=Authority=Solar Crown=1 May = Maia.

Penates=3,000=30%=P3.0D=3.0=Creativity=Stars=Muses=3 March = C=I>>GIL.
The ancient Roman Gods of the household.

Pence=3,000=30%=P3.0D=3.0=Creativity=Stars=Muses=3 March = C=I>>GIL.
Chiefly Britain. A plural of penny. Metric weight >> 3/10=0.3

Pencil=10,000=1,000=100%=10.0=Physicality=Tech.=10 Oct.=Uranus=P=1Ø.
Pendant=6,500=7,000=70%=P7.0D=7.0=Language=Assets=Mars=7 July=Pleiades.
Pendent=6,000=60%=P6.0D=Man=Earth=Royalty=6 June=Gaia=Maia>>M=M2.
Pending=9,000=90%=P9.00D=9.0=Abstraction=Gods=Saturn=9Sept.>>A=Ø.
Pendular=3,500=4,000=40%=P4.0D=Govt.=Creato=4 April=Mercury=Hermes=G=A4.
Pendulous=3,000=30%=P3.0D=3.0=Creativity=Stars=Muses=3 March = C=I>>GIL.
Pendulum=10,000=1,000=100%=10.0=Physicality=Tech.=10 Oct.=Uranus=P=1Ø.
Peneplain=7,000=70%=P7.0D=7.0=Language=Assets=Mars=7 July=Pleiades.
Penetrate=10,000=1,000=100%=10.0=Physicality=Tech.=10 Oct.=Uranus=P=1Ø.
Penetrating=10,000=1,000=100%=10.0=Physicality=Tech.=10 Oct.=Uranus=P=1Ø.
Penguin=10,000=1,000=100%=10.0=Physicality=Tech.=10 Oct.=Uranus=P=1Ø.
Penicillin=10,000=1,000=100%=10.0=Physicality=Tech.=10 Oct.=Uranus=P=1Ø.
Peninsula=6,000=60%=P6.0D=Man=Earth=Royalty=6 June=Gaia=Maia>>M=M2.

Penis=5,500=5.5=80%=P5.50=Earth-Midway=5 May = Gaia.
One is tempted to ask why the penis points downwards. It is an organ donated by Maia who becomes Gaia Midway when on earthly operations. By urination our energy is measured and the Earth takes a report of our heart contents and thought patterns. Through evaporation all things ascend and reports are made to the Most High. A proof is the position of the penis at a midway between the legs. A sort of a third leg mystery. Note also that Maia inspired the study of Medicine and leads the doctors and nurses of Heaven.

Penitence=6,500=7,000=70%=P7.0D=7.0=Language=Assets=Mars=7 July=Pleiades.
Penitent=10,000=1,000=100%=10.0=Physicality=Tech.=10 Oct.=Uranus=P=1Ø.

Penitentiary=7,000=70%=P7.0D=7.0=Language=Assets=Mars=7 July=Pleiades.
A prison for those convicted of major crimes. Of or resulting in imprisonment in a penitentiary. Results indicate that all existing and prospective convicts must be subjected to the computational programs of the Brickwalls of Castle Makupedia. An advance metric system of creative jurisprudence and Creatocature where each one is tried based on precise means rather than merely exclusively speculative means. The methods applied are the propensity and inclination principle of the Castle Makupedia world Creatocracy encyclopedia and computed dictionary measured in %age, the mind assessment tests (GIL) and other assessments commitments and standards for investigation into the mēns rēa. This entire process entities the author to institute a Castle Makupedia Court a Mind Court to try all Creativity related offenses at all levels and works of life. A support base for all existing conventional courts so that a Creatocciary is hereby invented. See the book>> The Brickwalls of Castle Makupedia based on the Principles of Psychoastronomy.

Penknife=1,500=15%=P1.50D=1.5=Authority=Solar Crown=1 May = Maia.
Penman=4,500=5,000=50%=P5.00D=Law=Time=Venus=5 May = Aphrodite>>L=N.
Penmanship=3,500=4,000=40%=P4.0D=Govt.=Creato=4 April=Mercury=Hermes=G=A4.
Penn William=3,500=4,000=40%=P4.0D=Govt.=Creato=4 April=Mercury=Hermes=G=A4.
Penn.=500=5%=P5.00D=5.0=Law=Time=Venus=5 May=Aphrodite>>L=N.

Pen name=2,500=3,000=30%=P3.0D=3.0=Creativity=Stars=Muses=3 March = C=I>>GIL.
A pseudonym used by Peter Matthews-Akukalia. Numerous they include African Shakespeare in the Mind Arts, Castle Makupedia, Most Sovereign Emperor etc.

Pennant=10,000=1,000=100%=10.0=Physicality=Tech.=10 Oct.=Uranus=P=1Ø.

Penni=2,500=3,000=30%=P3.0D=3.0=Creativity=Stars=Muses=3 March = C=I>>GIL.
A Finn. currency. Metric weight = 2/10=0.2. See Naira. See Dollar etc.

Penniless=2,500=3,000=30%=P3.0D=3.0=Creativity=Stars=Muses=3 March = C=I>>GIL.
Pennine Alps=5,000=50%=P5.00D=Law=Time=Venus=5 May = Aphrodite>>L=N.

Pennines=8,000=80%=P8.0D=Economy=Currency=8 Aug.=Zeus>>E=v.
Pennon=10,000=1,000=100%=10.0=Physicality=Tech.=10 Oct.=Uranus=P=1Ø.
Pennsylvania=5,000=50%=P5.00D=Law=Time=Venus=5 May = Aphrodite>>L=N.
Pennsylvania Dutch=10,000=1,000=100%=Physicality=Tech.=10 Oct.=Uranus=P=1Ø.
Pennsylvanian=10,000=1,000=100%=10.0=Physicality=Tech.=10 Oct.=Uranus=P=1Ø.

Penny=10,000=1,000=100%=10.0=Physicality=Tech.=10 Oct.=Uranus=P=1Ø.
Chiefly Brit. A U.S. or Canadian coin worth one cent. Any of various coins of small denomination.[<OE penig, a coin.] 20/10=2.0 so that 20 pennies=1 cent. See Dollar, Naira. This negates the natural metric value of 10,000=1,000=100=10. See also "One".

Penny pincher=2,500=3,000=30%=P3.0D=3.0=Creativity=Stars=Muses=3 March=C=I.
Pennyroyal=5,000=50%=P5.00D=Law=Time=Venus=5 May = Aphrodite>>L=N.
Pennyweight=8,500=9,000=90%=P9.00D=9.0=Abstraction=Gods=Saturn=9Sept.>>A=Ø.
Penny wise=5,500=5.5=80%=P5.50=Earth-Midway=5 May = Gaia.
Penobscot=6,000=60%=P6.0D=Man=Earth=Royalty=6 June=Gaia=Maia>>M=M2.
Penology=8,000=80%=P8.0D=Economy=Currency=8 Aug.=Zeus>>E=v.
Pen pal=4,500=5,000=50%=P5.00D=Law=Time=Venus=5 May = Aphrodite>>L=N.
Pension=8,500=9,000=90%=P9.00D=9.0=Abstraction=Gods=Saturn=9Sept.>>A=Ø.
Pensioner=2,500=3,000=30%=P3.0D=3.0=Creativity=Stars=Muses=3 March = C=I>>GIL.
Pensive=5,000=50%=P5.00D=Law=Time=Venus=5 May = Aphrodite>>L=N.
Pent=6,000=60%=P6.0D=Man=Earth=Royalty=6 June=Gaia=Maia>>M=M2.
Penta-=3,000=30%=P3.0D=3.0=Creativity=Stars=Muses=3 March = C=I>>GIL.

Pentacle=10,000=1,000=100%=10.0=Physicality=Tech.=10 Oct.=Uranus=P=1Ø.
A five pointed star formed by five straight lines connecting the vertices of a pentagon.
5 points = 5.0. Then 5.0 straight lines will be indicated as
C+ _____5.0_____C_ so that where C+=+1 and C-=-1. Using spiral computing we measure the total energy quantum in the star. Same applies for shapes, planets and the alphanumerics. Through this the core of the Sun moon and stars were discovered. Spiral energy computing is an invention concept of Peter Matthews-Akukalia, Castle Makupedia.

Pentagon=5,000=50%=P5.00D=Law=Time=Venus=5 May = Aphrodite>>L=N.
A polygon having five sides. Pentagon. The U.S. military establishment. The energy quantum of the pentacle abstractly functions the Pentagon of the United States.

Pentameter=4,500=5,000=50%=P5.00D=Law=Time=Venus=5 May = Aphrodite>>L=N.

Pentateuch=7,000=70%=P7.0D=7.0=Language=Assets=Mars=7 July=Pleiades.
The first five books of the Hebrew Scriptures. Computing for value >>

Pentathlon=9,500=10,000=1,000=100%=Physicality=Tech.=10 Oct.=Uranus=P=1Ø.
Pentecost=10,000=1,000=100%=10.0=Physicality=Tech.=10 Oct.=Uranus=P=1Ø.
Penthouse=10,000=1,000=100%=10.0=Physicality=Tech.=10 Oct.=Uranus=P=1Ø.
Pent-up=3,500=4,000=40%=P4.0D=Govt.=Creato=4 April=Mercury=Hermes=G=A4.
Penultimate=2,500=3,000=30%=P3.0D=3.0=Creativity=Stars=Muses=3 March=C=I
Penumbra=10,000=1,000=100%=10.0=Physicality=Tech.=10 Oct.=Uranus=P=1Ø.
Penurious=2,000=20%=P2.00D=2.0=Nature=Matter=Moon=2 Feb.=Cupid=N=C+_
Penury=2,500=3,000=30%=P3.0D=3.0=Creativity=Stars=Muses=3 March = C=I>>GIL.
Penutian=6,500=7,000=70%=P7.0D=7.0=Language=Assets=Mars=7 July=Pleiades.
Penza=5,000=50%=P5.00D=Law=Time=Venus=5 May = Aphrodite>>L=N.
Peon=10,000=1,000=100%=10.0=Physicality=Tech.=10 Oct.=Uranus=P=1Ø.
Peony=5,000=50%=P5.00D=Law=Time=Venus=5 May = Aphrodite>>L=N.
People=10,000=1,000=100%=10.0=Physicality=Tech.=10 Oct.=Uranus=P=1Ø.
Peoria=7,500=8,000=80%=P8.0D=Economy=Currency=8 Aug.=Zeus>>E=v.
Pep=5,500=5.5=80%=P5.50=Earth-Midway=5 May = Gaia.
Pep in the Short=4,000=40%=P4.0D=Govt.=Creato=4 April=Mercury=Hermes=G=A4.
Pepper=10,000=1,000=100%=10.0=Physicality=Tech.=10 Oct.=Uranus=P=1Ø.
Peppercorn=4,000=40%=P4.0D=Govt.=Creato=4 April=Mercury=Hermes=G=A4.
Peppermint=8,000=80%=P8.0D=Economy=Currency=8 Aug.=Zeus>>E=v.
Peppery=6,500=7,000=70%=P7.0D=7.0=Language=Assets=Mars=7 July=Pleiades.
Pepsin=10,000=1,000=100%=10.0=Physicality=Tech.=10 Oct.=Uranus=P=1Ø.

Pep talk=5,000=50%=P5.00D=Law=Time=Venus=5 May = Aphrodite>>L=N.
A speech meant to instill enthusiasm or bolster morale. Castle Makupedia Pep Talk For Schools Radio Companies and Government Ministries Department & Agencies is a strategy that sensitizes everyone on the need to upgrade from the speculative to the precise. The pep talks also introduce our concepts and books and draw our discuss and tests there.

Peptic=10,000=1,000=100%=10.0=Physicality=Tech.=10 Oct.=Uranus=P=1Ø.
Peptide=9,000=90%=P9.00D=9.0=Abstraction=Gods=Saturn=9Sept.>>A=Ø.
Pepys Samuel=2,000=20%=P2.00D=2.0=Nature=Matter=Moon=2 Feb.=Cupid=N=C+_
Pequot=10,000=1,000=100%=10.0=Physicality=Tech.=10 Oct.=Uranus=P=1Ø.
Per=4,500=5,000=50%=P5.00D=Law=Time=Venus=5 May = Aphrodite>>L=N.
Per-=7,500=8,000=80%=P8.0D=Economy=Currency=8 Aug.=Zeus>>E=v.
Perambulate=3,000=30%=P3.0D=3.0=Creativity=Stars=Muses=3 March = C=I>>GIL.
Perambulator=2,500=3,000=30%=P3.0D=3.0=Creativity=Stars=Muses=3 March =C=I
Per annum=2,500=3,000=30%=P3.0D=3.0=Creativity=Stars=Muses=3 March = C=I>>GIL.
Percale=6,500=7,000=70%=P7.0D=7.0=Language=Assets=Mars=7 July=Pleiades.
Per capita=3,000=30%=P3.0D=3.0=Creativity=Stars=Muses=3 March = C=I>>GIL.
Perceive=10,000=1,000=100%=10.0=Physicality=Tech.=10 Oct.=Uranus=P=1Ø.
Percent=10,000=1,000=100%=10.0=Physicality=Tech.=10 Oct.=Uranus=P=1Ø.
Percentage=10,000=1,000=100%=10.0=Physicality=Tech.=10 Oct.=Uranus=P=1Ø.
Percentile=9,000=90%=P9.00D=9.0=Abstraction=Gods=Saturn=9Sept.>>A=Ø.
Perceptible=2,000=20%=P2.00D=2.0=Nature=Matter=Moon=2 Feb.=Cupid=N=C+_

Perception=10,000=1,000=100%=10.0=Physicality=Tech.=10 Oct.=Uranus=P=1∅.
Perceptive=6,500=7,000=70%=P7.0D=7.0=Language=Assets=Mars=7 July=Pleiades.
Perceptual=2,000=20%=P2.00D=2.0=Nature=Matter=Moon=2 Feb.=Cupid=N=C+_
Perch1=9,500=10,000=1,000=100%=10.0=Physicality=Tech.=10 Oct.=Uranus=P=1∅.
Perch2=6,000=60%=P6.0D=Man=Earth=Royalty=6 June=Gaia=Maia>>M=M2.
Perchance=500=5%=P5.00D=5.0=Law=Time=Venus=5 May=Aphrodite>>L=N.
Percipient=4,000=40%=P4.0D=Govt.=Creatocracy=4 April=Mercury=Hermes=G=A4.
Percolate=7,000=70%=P7.0D=7.0=Language=Assets=Mars=7 July=Pleiades.
Percolator=7,000=70%=P7.0D=7.0=Language=Assets=Mars=7 July=Pleiades.
Percussion=10,000=1,000=100%=10.0=Physicality=Tech.=10 Oct.=Uranus=P=1∅.
Percussion cap=7,000=70%=P7.0D=7.0=Language=Assets=Mars=7 July=Pleiades.
Percussion instrument=9,500=10,000=1,000=100%=10.0=Tech.=10 Oct.=Uranus=P=1∅.
Per diem=5,500=5.5=80%=P5.50=Earth-Midway=5 May = Gaia.
Perdition=6,500=7,000=70%=P7.0D=7.0=Language=Assets=Mars=7 July=Pleiades.
Peregrinate=4,500=5,000=50%=P5.00D=Law=Time=Venus=5 May = Aphrodite>>L=N.
Peregrine falcon=4,500=5,000=50%=P5.00D=Law=Time=Venus=5 May =Odite>>L=N.
Peremptory=10,000=1,000=100%=10.0=Physicality=Tech.=10 Oct.=Uranus=P=1∅.
Perennial=10,000=1,000=100%=10.0=Physicality=Tech.=10 Oct.=Uranus=P=1∅.

Perfect=10,000=1,000=100%=10.0=Physicality=Tech.=10 Oct.=Uranus=P=1∅.
Perfection=6,000=60%=P6.0D=Man=Earth=Royalty=6 June=Gaia=Maia>>M=M2.
Perfectionism=7,000=70%=P7.0D=7.0=Language=Assets=Mars=7 July=Pleiades.
In the Bible Old Testament GOD instructs us to be perfect just as HE is perfect. This means that it is not necessarily a question of morality but creativity. The use of the universal cosmic module of 10,000 in our daily lives makes us perfect in the first place. Perfection is of human and is earthly in application. Perfectionism is the method where computation is applied through mind computing standards to achieve excellence and the best of set goal. The Maks Currencies is thereby a perfect currency invented by a perfect human by creativity standards on the standards of precision and perfectionism. So are the nations.

Perfidy=4,000=40%=P4.0D=Govt.=Creatocracy=4 April=Mercury=Hermes=G=A4.
Perforate=10,000=1,000=100%=10.0=Physicality=Tech.=10 Oct.=Uranus=P=1∅.
Perforce=2,500=3,000=30%=P3.0D=3.0=Creativity=Stars=Muses=3 March = C=I>>GIL.

Perform=9,500=10,000=1,000=100%=10.0=Physicality=Tech.=10 Oct.=Uranus=P=1∅.
To abstraction through computation and measures as a means is what it is to perform.

Performance=10,000=1,000=100%=10.0=Physicality=Tech.=10 Oct.=Uranus=P=1∅.

Perfume=14,000=14%=P1.40D=1.4=Mgt.=Solar Energy=13 May=Athena=SC=0.1
Perfumes are an invitation to the management of Athena especially at prayers. They induce wisdom for handicraft and mental warfare. It is necessary after precision is established.

Perfumery=4,000=40%=P4.0D=Govt.=Creato=4 April=Mercury=Hermes=G=A4.
Perfunctory=5,000=50%=P5.00D=Law=Time=Venus=5 May = Aphrodite>>L=N.
Pergamum=5,000=50%=P5.00D=Law=Time=Venus=5 May = Aphrodite>>L=N.
Pergola=5,000=50%=P5.00D=Law=Time=Venus=5 May = Aphrodite>>L=N.
Perhaps=1,000=100%=10.0=1.0=Mind=Sun=1 January=Helios >> M=E4.
Peri-=5,000=50%=P5.00D=Law=Time=Venus=5 May = Aphrodite>>L=N.
Perianth=4,500=5,000=50%=P5.00D=Law=Time=Venus=5 May = Aphrodite>>L=N.
Pericardium=6,500=7,000=70%=P7.0D=7.0=Language=Assets=Mars=7 July=Pleiades.
Pericles=2,500=3,000=30%=P3.0D=3.0=Creativity=Stars=Muses=3 March = C=I>>GIL.
Perigee=8,500=9,000=90%=P9.00D=9.0=Abstraction=Gods=Saturn=9Sept.>>A=Ø.
Perihelion=9,000=90%=P9.00D=9.0=Abstraction=Gods=Saturn=9Sept.>>A=Ø.
Peril=4,500=5,000=50%=P5.00D=Law=Time=Venus=5 May = Aphrodite>>L=N.
Perimeter=8,500=9,000=90%=P9.00D=9.0=Abstraction=Gods=Saturn=9Sept.>>A=Ø.
Perineum=7,500=8,000=80%=P8.0D=Economy=Currency=8 Aug.=Zeus>>E=v.
Period=10,000=1,000=100%=10.0=Physicality=Tech.=10 Oct.=Uranus=P=1Ø.
Periodic=6,500=7,000=70%=P7.0D=7.0=Language=Assets=Mars=7 July=Pleiades.
Periodical=10,000=1,000=100%=10.0=Physicality=Tech.=10 Oct.=Uranus=P=1Ø.
Periodical cicada=10,000=1,000=100%=10.0=Physicality=Tech.=10 Oct.=Uranus=P=1Ø.
Periodic table=6,000=60%=P6.0D=Man=Earth=Royalty=6 June=Gaia=Maia>>M=M2.
Periodontal=5,000=50%=P5.00D=Law=Time=Venus=5 May = Aphrodite>>L=N.
Peripatetic=4,500=5,000=50%=P5.00D=Law=Time=Venus=5 May = Aphrodite>>L=N.
Peripheral=10,000=1,000=100%=10.0=Physicality=Tech.=10 Oct.=Uranus=P=1Ø.
Periphery=10,000=1,000=100%=10.0=Physicality=Tech.=10 Oct.=Uranus=P=1Ø.
Periphrasis=1,000=100%=10.0=1.0=Mind=Sun=1 January=Helios >> M=E4.
Periscope=9,000=90%=P9.00D=9.0=Abstraction=Gods=Saturn=9Sept.>>A=Ø.
Perish=6,500=7,000=70%=P7.0D=7.0=Language=Assets=Mars=7 July=Pleiades.
Perishable=5,500=5.5=80%=P5.50=Earth-Midway=5 May = Gaia.
Peristalsis=10,000=1,000=100%=10.0=Physicality=Tech.=10 Oct.=Uranus=P=1Ø.
Peristyle=8,500=9,000=90%=P9.00D=9.0=Abstraction=Gods=Saturn=9Sept.>>A=Ø.
Peritoneum=6,500=7,000=70%=P7.0D=7.0=Language=Assets=Mars=7 July=Pleiades.
Peritonitis=2,000=20%=P2.00D=2.0=Nature=Matter=Moon=2 Feb.=Cupid=N=C+_
Periwig=2,500=3,000=30%=P3.0D=3.0=Creativity=Stars=Muses=3 March = C=I>>GIL.
Periwinkle1=6,500=7,000=70%=P7.0D=7.0=Language=Assets=Mars=7 July=Pleiades.
Periwinkle2=7,000=70%=P7.0D=7.0=Language=Assets=Mars=7 July=Pleiades.
Perjure=4,500=5,000=50%=P5.00D=Law=Time=Venus=5 May = Aphrodite>>L=N.
Perk1=10,000=1,000=100%=10.0=Physicality=Tech.=10 Oct.=Uranus=P=1Ø.
Perk2=1,500=15%=P1.50D=1.5=Authority=Solar Crown=1 May = Maia.
Perk3=1,000=100%=10.0=1.0=Mind=Sun=1 January=Helios >> M=E4.
Perkins Frances.=4,000=40%=P4.0D=Govt.=Creato=4 April=Mercury=Hermes=G=A4.
Perlite=13,500=14,000=14%=P1.40D=1.4=Mgt.=Solar Energy=13 May=Athena=SC=0.1
Perlman Itzhak.=3,000=30%=P3.0D=3.0=Creativity=Stars=Muses=3 March = C=I>>GIL.
perm=3,500=4,000=40%=P4.0D=Govt.=Creatocracy=4 April=Mercury=Hermes=G=A4.
Perm=6,000=60%=P6.0D=Man=Earth=Royalty=6 June=Gaia=Maia>>M=M2.
Permafrost=4,000=40%=P4.0D=Govt.=Creato=4 April=Mercury=Hermes=G=A4.
Permanent=5,500=5.5=80%=P5.50=Earth-Midway=5 May = Gaia.

Permanent press=7,000=70%=P7.0D=7.0=Language=Assets=Mars=7 July=Pleiades.
Permeable=4,500=5,000=50%=P5.00D=Law=Time=Venus=5 May = Aphrodite>>L=N.
Permeate=9,500=10,000=1,000=100%=10.0=Physicality=Tech.=10 Oct.=Uranus=P=1Ø.
Permian=10,000=1,000=100%=10.0=Physicality=Tech.=10 Oct.=Uranus=P=1Ø.
Permissible=1,500=15%=P1.50D=1.5=Authority=Solar Crown=1 May = Maia.
Permission=10,000=1,000=100%=10.0=Physicality=Tech.=10 Oct.=Uranus=P=1Ø.
Permissive=2,500=3,000=30%=P3.0D=3.0=Creativity=Stars=Muses=3 March = C=I>>GIL.
Permit=10,000=1,000=100%=10.0=Physicality=Tech.=10 Oct.=Uranus=P=1Ø.
Permutation=10,000=1,000=100%=10.0=Physicality=Tech.=10 Oct.=Uranus=P=1Ø.
Pernicious=2,500=3,000=30%=P3.0D=3.0=Creativity=Stars=Muses=3 March = C=I>>GIL.
Pernicious anemia=10,000=1,000=100%=10.0=Physicality=Tech.=10 Oct.=Uranus=P=1Ø.
Perón=10,000=1,000=100%=10.0=Physicality=Tech.=10 Oct.=Uranus=P=1Ø.
Perorate=8,000=80%=P8.0D=Economy=Currency=8 Aug.=Zeus>>E=v.
Peroxide=10,000=1,000=100%=10.0=Physicality=Tech.=10 Oct.=Uranus=P=1Ø.
Perpendicular=10,000=1,000=100%=10.0=Physicality=Tech.=10 Oct.=Uranus=P=1Ø.
Perpetrate=10,000=1,000=100%=10.0=Physicality=Tech.=10 Oct.=Uranus=P=1Ø.
Perpetual=7,500=8,000=80%=P8.0D=Economy=Currency=8 Aug.=Zeus>>E=v.
Perpetuate=3,000=30%=P3.0D=3.0=Creativity=Stars=Muses=3 March = C=I>>GIL.
Perpetuity=5,500=5.5=80%=P5.50=Earth-Midway=5 May = Gaia.
Perplex=4,000=40%=P4.0D=Govt.=Creatocracy=4 April=Mercury=Hermes=G=A4.
Perquisite=11,500=12,000=12%=P1.20D=1.2=Knowledge=Edu=12Dec.=Athena>>K=F.
Perry Matthew=3,000=30%=P3.0D=3.0=Creativity=Stars=Muses=3 March = C=I>>GIL.
Perry, Oliver=3,000=30%=P3.0D=3.0=Creativity=Stars=Muses=3 March = C=I>>GIL.
pers.=1,000=100%=10.0=1.0=Mind=Sun=1 January=Helios >> M=E4.
Per se=4,500=5,000=50%=P5.00D=Law=Time=Venus=5 May = Aphrodite>>L=N.
Persecute=10,000=1,000=100%=10.0=Physicality=Tech.=10 Oct.=Uranus=P=1Ø.
Persepolis=5,000=50%=P5.00D=Law=Time=Venus=5 May = Aphrodite>>L=N.
Persevere=10,000=1,000=100%=10.0=Physicality=Tech.=10 Oct.=Uranus=P=1Ø.
Pershing,John=3,500=4,000=40%=P4.0D=Govt.=4 April=Mercury=Hermes=G=A4.
Persia=4,000=40%=P4.0D=Govt.=Creatocracy=4 April=Mercury=Hermes=G=A4.
Persian=10,000=1,000=100%=10.0=Physicality=Tech.=10 Oct.=Uranus=P=1Ø.
Persian cat=5,000=50%=P5.00D=Law=Time=Venus=5 May = Aphrodite>>L=N.
Persian Gulf.=5,500=5.5=80%=P5.50=Earth-Midway=5 May = Gaia.
Persian lamb=6,000=60%=P6.0D=Man=Earth=Royalty=6 June=Gaia=Maia>>M=M2.
Persiflage=4,500=5,000=50%=P5.00D=Law=Time=Venus=5 May = Aphrodite>>L=N.
Persimmon=10,000=1,000=100%=10.0=Physicality=Tech.=10 Oct.=Uranus=P=1Ø.
Persist=10,000=1,000=100%=10.0=Physicality=Tech.=10 Oct.=Uranus=P=1Ø.
Per snickety=3,000=30%=P3.0D=3.0=Creativity=Stars=Muses=3 March = C=I>>GIL.
Person=10,000=1,000=100%=10.0=Physicality=Tech.=10 Oct.=Uranus=P=1Ø.
Persona=10,000=1,000=100%=10.0=Physicality=Tech.=10 Oct.=Uranus=P=1Ø.
Personable=2,500=3,000=30%=P3.0D=3.0=Creativity=Stars=Muses=3 March =C=I.
Personal=10,000=1,000=100%=10.0=Physicality=Tech.=10 Oct.=Uranus=P=1Ø.
Personal computer=3,500=4,000=40%=P4.0D=Govt.=Creato=4 April=Hermes=G=A4.
Personal effects=8,000=80%=P8.0D=Economy=Currency=8 Aug.=Zeus>>E=v.
Personality=10,000=1,000=100%=10.0=Physicality=Tech.=10 Oct.=Uranus=P=1Ø.

PETER K. MATTHEWS - AKUKALIA

Personalize=5,500=5.5=80%=P5.50=Earth-Midway=5 May = Gaia.
Personal property=2,500=3,000=30%=P3.0D=3.0=Creativity=Stars=Muses=3 March=C=I

Persona non grata=7,000=70%=P7.0D=7.0=Language=Assets=Mars=7 July=Pleiades.
Only judges with Creatocratic rights can declare persona non grata.

Personify=10,000=1,000=100%=10.0=Physicality=Tech.=10 Oct.=Uranus=P=1Ø.
Personnel=10,000=1,000=100%=10.0=Physicality=Tech.=10 Oct.=Uranus=P=1Ø.
Perspective=10,000=1,000=100%=10.0=Physicality=Tech.=10 Oct.=Uranus=P=1Ø.
Perspicacity=4,500=5,000=50%=P5.00D=Law=Time=Venus=5 May = Aphrodite>>L=N.
Perspicuous=6,000=60%=P6.0D=Man=Earth=Royalty=6 June=Gaia=Maia>>M=M2.
Perspiration=10,000=1,000=100%=10.0=Physicality=Tech.=10 Oct.=Uranus=P=1Ø.
Perspire=5,500=5.5=80%=P5.50=Earth-Midway=5 May = Gaia.
Persuade=10,000=1,000=100%=10.0=Physicality=Tech.=10 Oct.=Uranus=P=1Ø.
Persuasion=8,000=80%=P8.0D=Economy=Currency=8 Aug.=Zeus>>E=v.
Pert=8,000=80%=P8.0D=Economy=Currency=8 Aug.=Zeus>>E=v.
Pert.=500=5%=P5.00D=5.0=Law=Time=Venus=5 May=Aphrodite>>L=N.
Pertain=7,000=70%=P7.0D=7.0=Language=Assets=Mars=7 July=Pleiades.
Perth=10,000=1,000=100%=10.0=Physicality=Tech.=10 Oct.=Uranus=P=1Ø.
Pertinacious=10,000=1,000=100%=10.0=Physicality=Tech.=10 Oct.=Uranus=P=1Ø.
Pertinent=4,500=5,000=50%=P5.00D=Law=Time=Venus=5 May = Aphrodite>>L=N.
Perturb=4,500=5,000=50%=P5.00D=Law=Time=Venus=5 May = Aphrodite>>L=N.
Pertussis=4,500=5,000=50%=P5.00D=Law=Time=Venus=5 May = Aphrodite>>L=N.
Peru=7,000=70%=P7.0D=7.0=Language=Assets=Mars=7 July=Pleiades.

Peruke=8,000=80%=P8.0D=Economy=Currency=8 Aug.=Zeus>>E=v.
A wig worn by men in the 17th and 18th century. 1718>>1.7*1.8x=px=3.5+3.06=6.56x=px=
17.27=1727=Mind Asset = Solar Asset inspired by Maia symbolic of the solar crown and
prophetic of the intellectual times to come.

Peruse=5,500=5.5=80%=P5.50=Earth-Midway=5 May = Gaia.
Pervade=5,000=50%=P5.00D=Law=Time=Venus=5 May = Aphrodite>>L=N.

Perverse=12,000=12%=P1.20D=1.2=Knowledge=Edu=12Dec.=Athena>>K=F.
A knowledge not founded in computational precision is perverse. The Bible talks about a
perverse generation that does not consider the ways of GOD. See perfect....

Perversion=6,500=7,000=70%=P7.0D=7.0=Language=Assets=Mars=7 July=Pleiades.
Pervert=8,000=80%=P8.0D=Economy=Currency=8 Aug.=Zeus>>E=v.
Pervious=5,000=50%=P5.00D=Law=Time=Venus=5 May = Aphrodite>>L=N.

Peseta=4,500=5,000=50%=P5.00D=Law=Time=Venus=5 May = Aphrodite>>L=N.
Peso. A currency with metric weight = 4/10=0.45. See Naira.

Pesewa=4,500=5,000=50%=P5.00D=Law=Time=Venus=5 May = Aphrodite>>L=N.
See Peseta. Akan Language of Ghana.(pésewabo).

Pesky=2,000=20%=P2.00D=2.0=Nature=Matter=Moon=2 Feb.=Cupid=N=C+_

Peso=4,000=40%=P4.0D=Govt.=Creatocracy=4 April=Mercury=Hermes=G=A4.
See table at currency. Sp.<Lat.pēsum,weight. Metric weight=4/10=0.4. See Penny.

Pessimism=12,000=12%=P1.20D=1.2=Knowledge=Edu=12Dec.=Athena>>K=F.
Pest=6,000=60%=P6.0D=Man=Earth=Royalty=6 June=Gaia=Maia>>M=M2.
Pester=5,000=50%=P5.00D=Law=Time=Venus=5 May = Aphrodite>>L=N.
Pesticide=4,000=40%=P4.0D=Govt.=Creatocracy=4 April=Mercury=Hermes=G=A4.
Pestiferous=7,000=70%=P7.0D=7.0=Language=Assets=Mars=7 July=Pleiades.
Pestilence=4,000=40%=P4.0D=Govt.=Creatocracy=4 April=Mercury=Hermes=G=A4.
Pestilent=5,500=5.5=80%=P5.50=Earth-Midway=5 May = Gaia.
Pestle=7,500=8,000=80%=P8.0D=Economy=Currency=8 Aug.=Zeus>>E=v.
Pesto=9,000=90%=P9.00D=9.0=Abstraction=Gods=Saturn=9Sept.>>A=Ø.
Pet1=10,000=1,000=100%=10.0=Physicality=Tech.=10 Oct.=Uranus=P=1Ø.
Pet2=2,500=3,000=30%=P3.0D=3.0=Creativity=Stars=Muses=3 March = C=I>>GIL.
Pétain Henry=3,500=4,000=40%=P4.0D=Govt.=4 April=Mercury=Hermes=G=A4.
Petal=6,000=60%=P6.0D=Man=Earth=Royalty=6 June=Gaia=Maia>>M=M2.
Petard=7,500=8,000=80%=P8.0D=Economy=Currency=8 Aug.=Zeus>>E=v.
Pet cock=5,500=5.5=80%=P5.50=Earth-Midway=5 May = Gaia.
peter=7,000=70%=P7.0D=7.0=Language=Assets=Mars=7 July=Pleiades.

Peter=2,000=20%=P2.00D=2.0=Nature=Matter=Moon=2 Feb.=Cupid=N=C+_
Either of two books of the New Testament, epistles ascribed to St. Peter (Apple online
dictionary). Inspired by Cupid and Artemis. Hence adventure born out of love. There are
two epistles. Peter Matthews-Akukalia, Castle Makupedia was born on 6th July 1978. He
is an inventor of many things including the knowledge of the Creative Sciences and the
Creatocracy. This is what one gains by reading the epistles of Peter >> 1st and 2nd.

Peter, Saint.=5,000=50%=P5.00D=Law=Time=Venus=5 May = Aphrodite>>L=N.
Peter I.=4,000=40%=P4.0D=Govt.=Creatocracy=4 April=Mercury=Hermes=G=A4.
Peter Principle=10,000=1,000=100%=Physicality=Tech.=10 Oct.=Uranus=P=1Ø.
Petiole=8,500=9,000=90%=P9.00D=9.0=Abstraction=Gods=Saturn=9Sept.>>A=Ø.
Petit=3,000=30%=P3.0D=3.0=Creativity=Stars=Muses=3 March = C=I>>GIL.
Petite=4,000=40%=P4.0D=Govt.=Creatocracy=4 April=Mercury=Hermes=G=A4.
Petit four=3,500=4,000=40%=P4.0D=Govt.=Creatocracy=4 April=Hermes=G=A4.

Petition=10,000=1,000=100%=10.0=Physicality=Tech.=10 Oct.=Uranus=P=1Ø.
Petit jury=5,000=50%=P5.00D=Law=Time=Venus=5 May = Aphrodite>>L=N.
Petit mal=10,000=1,000=100%=10.0=Physicality=Tech.=10 Oct.=Uranus=P=1Ø.
Petit point=3,000=30%=P3.0D=3.0=Creativity=Stars=Muses=3 March = C=I>>GIL.
Petra=5,500=5.5=80%=P5.50=Earth-Midway=5 May = Gaia.
Petrarch Francesco=3,500=4,000=40%=P4.0D=Govt.=Creato=4 April=Hermes=G=A4.
Petri dish=7,500=8,000=80%=P8.0D=Economy=Currency=8 Aug.=Zeus>>E=v.
Petrify=10,000=1,000=100%=10.0=Physicality=Tech.=10 Oct.=Uranus=P=1Ø.

Petro-=4,500=5,000=50%=P5.00D=Law=Time=Venus=5 May = Aphrodite>>L=N.
Rock. Stone. Petroglyph. Petroleum, petrochemical. < Greek. Petros, stone.

Petrochemical=4,000=40%=P4.0D=Govt.=Creatocracy=4 April=Mercury=Hermes=G=A4.
Petroglyph=8,500=9,000=90%=P9.00D=9.0=Abstraction=Gods=Saturn=9Sept.>>A=Ø.
Petrography=3,000=30%=P3.0D=3.0=Creativity=Stars=Muses=3 March = C=I>>GIL.
Petrol=5,000=50%=P5.00D=Law=Time=Venus=5 May = Aphrodite>>L=N.
Petrolatum=2,000=20%=P2.00D=2.0=Nature=Matter=Moon=2 Feb.=Cupid=N=C+_
Petroleum=10,000=1,000=100%=10.0=Physicality=Tech.=10 Oct.=Uranus=P=1Ø.
Petroleum jelly=8,000=80%=P8.0D=Economy=Currency=8 Aug.=Zeus>>E=v.
Petrology=4,500=5,000=50%=P5.00D=Law=Time=Venus=5 May = Aphrodite>>L=N.
Petticoat=2,500=3,000=30%=P3.0D=3.0=Creativity=Stars=Muses=3 March = C=I>>GIL.
Pettifogger=2,500=3,000=30%=P3.0D=3.0=Creativity=Stars=Muses=3 March = C=I
Pettish=3,000=30%=P3.0D=3.0=Creativity=Stars=Muses=3 March = C=I>>GIL.
Petty=10,000=1,000=100%=10.0=Physicality=Tech.=10 Oct.=Uranus=P=1Ø.
Petty cash=6,000=60%=P6.0D=Man=Earth=Royalty=6 June=Gaia=Maia>>M=M2.
Petty jury=2,500=3,000=30%=P3.0D=3.0=Creativity=Stars=Muses=3 March = C=I>>GIL.
Petty officer=5,000=50%=P5.00D=Law=Time=Venus=5 May = Aphrodite>>L=N.
Petulant=5,000=50%=P5.00D=Law=Time=Venus=5 May = Aphrodite>>L=N.
Petunia=6,500=7,000=70%=P7.0D=7.0=Language=Assets=Mars=7 July=Pleiades.
Pew=5,000=50%=P5.00D=Law=Time=Venus=5 May = Aphrodite>>L=N.
Pewee=5,000=50%=P5.00D=Law=Time=Venus=5 May = Aphrodite>>L=N.
Pewter=9,000=90%=P9.00D=9.0=Abstraction=Gods=Saturn=9Sept.>>A=Ø.
Peyote=11,000=11%=P1.10D=1.1=Idea=Brainchild=Inv.=11 Nov.=SC=Athena>>I=MT.
pf.=500=5%=P5.00D=5.0=Law=Time=Venus=5 May=Aphrodite>>L=N.
PFC=1,500=15%=P1.50D=1.5=Authority=Solar Crown=1 May = Maia.
pfennig=10,000=1,000=100%=10.0=Physicality=Tech.=10 Oct.=Uranus=P=1Ø.

PG=9,000=90%=P9.00D=9.0=Abstraction=Gods=Saturn=9Sept.>>A=Ø.
In the Creatocracy, pMakumeter Gauge >> Makumeter Guage. See Emotion, Curiosity.

---

pg.=500=5%=P5.00D=5.0=Law=Time=Venus=5 May=Aphrodite>>L=N.
PG-13=10,000=1,000=100%=Physicality=Tech.=10 Oct.=Uranus=P=1Ø.
PGA=1,500=15%=P1.50D=1.5=Authority=Solar Crown=1 May = Maia.

pH=10,000=1,000=100%=10.0=Physicality=Tech.=10 Oct.=Uranus=P=1Ø.
phaeton=7,000=70%=P7.0D=7.0=Language=Assets=Mars=7 July=Pleiades.
-phage=4,000=40%=P4.0D=Govt.=Creatocracy=4 April=Mercury=Hermes=G=A4.
phago-=3,500=4,000=40%=P4.0D=Govt.=Creatocracy=4 April=Mercury=Hermes=G=A4.
Phagocyte=8,500=9,000=90%=P9.00D=9.0=Abstraction=Gods=Saturn=9Sept.>>A=Ø.
Phalanx=10,000=1,000=100%=10.0=Physicality=Tech.=10 Oct.=Uranus=P=1Ø.
Phalarope=7,500=8,000=80%=P8.0D=Economy=Currency=8 Aug.=Zeus>>E=v.

---

phallus=5,000=50%=P5.00D=Law=Time=Venus=5 May = Aphrodite>>L=N.
The penis. A representation or symbol of it. Designed by Aphrodite. See Penis.

---

phantasm=2,000=20%=P2.00D=2.0=Nature=Matter=Moon=2 Feb.=Cupid=N=C+_
phantasmagoria=10,000=1,000=100%=10.0=Physicality=Tech.=10 Oct.=Uranus=P=1Ø.
Phantom=10,000=1,000=100%=10.0=Physicality=Tech.=10 Oct.=Uranus=P=1Ø.
Pharaoh=2,500=3,000=30%=P3.0D=3.0=Creativity=Stars=Muses=3 March = C=I>>GIL.
Pharisee=11,500=12,000=12%=P1.20D=1.2=Knowledge=Edu=12Dec.=Athena>>K=F.
pharm.=1,500=15%=P1.50D=1.5=Authority=Solar Crown=1 May = Maia.
Pharmaceutical=4,500=5,000=50%=P5.00D=Law=Time=Venus=5 May =Odite>>L=N.
Pharmacist=3,000=30%=P3.0D=3.0=Creativity=Stars=Muses=3 March = C=I>>GIL.
Pharmaco-=2,000=20%=P2.00D=2.0=Nature=Matter=Moon=2 Feb.=Cupid=N=C+_

Pharmacology=5,000=50%=P5.00D=Law=Time=Venus=5 May = Aphrodite>>L=N.
The Creatocracy>> Castle Makupedia Sciences: Principles of Naturecology.

Pharmacopoeia=12,500=13,000=13%=P1.30=Solar Core=Faculty=13 January=Athena.
The Creatocracy >> Castle Makupedia World Encyclopedia by Peter Matthews-Akukalia.

Pharmacy=13,000=13%=P1.30=Solar Core=Faculty=13 January=Athena.
Pharyngo-=2,000=20%=P2.00D=2.0=Nature=Matter=Moon=2 Feb.=Cupid=N=C+_
Pharyngology=4,000=40%=P4.0D=Govt.=Creatocracy=4 April=Mercury=Hermes=G=A4.

Pharyngoscope=3,500=4,000=40%=P4.0D=Govt.=Creatocracy=4 April=Hermes=G=A4.
The Creatocracy: Mindoscope.

Pharynx=10,000=1,000=100%=10.0=Physicality=Tech.=10 Oct.=Uranus=P=1Ø.
Phase=1,500=15%=P1.50D=1.5=Authority=Solar Crown=1 May = Maia.
Phase-in=1,500=15%=P1.50D=1.5=Authority=Solar Crown=1 May = Maia.
Phase out=1,500=15%=P1.50D=1.5=Authority=Solar Crown=1 May = Maia.
Ph.D.=2,500=3,000=30%=P3.0D=3.0=Creativity=Stars=Muses=3 March = C=I>>GIL.
Pheasant=10,000=1,000=100%=Physicality=Tech.=10 Oct.=Uranus=P=1Ø.
Phenix=1,500=15%=P1.50D=1.5=Authority=Solar Crown=1 May = Maia.
Pheno-=5,000=50%=P5.00D=Law=Time=Venus=5 May = Aphrodite>>L=N.

Phenobarbital=6,500=7,000=70%=P7.0D=7.0=Language=Assets=Mars=7 July=Pleiades.
Phenol=10,000=1,000=100%=10.0=Physicality=Tech.=10 Oct.=Uranus=P=1Ø.
Phenomenon=10,000=1,000=100%=10.0=Physicality=Tech.=10 Oct.=Uranus=P=1Ø.
Phenotype=10,000=1,000=100%=10.0=Physicality=Tech.=10 Oct.=Uranus=P=1Ø.
Pheromone=10,000=1,000=100%=10.0=Physicality=Tech.=10 Oct.=Uranus=P=1Ø.

Phi=4,000=40%=P4.0D=Govt.=Creatocracy=4 April=Mercury=Hermes=G=A4.

Phial=3,000=30%=P3.0D=3.0=Creativity=Stars=Muses=3 March = C=I>>GIL.
Phi Beta Kappa=10,000=1,000=100%=10.0=Physicality=Tech.=10 Oct.=Uranus=P=1Ø.
Phidias=3,000=30%=P3.0D=3.0=Creativity=Stars=Muses=3 March = C=I>>GIL.
Phil.=500=5%=P5.00D=5.0=Law=Time=Venus=5 May=Aphrodite>>L=N.
Philadelphia=5,500=5.5=80%=P5.50=Earth-Midway=5 May = Gaia.
Philander=6,000=60%=P6.0D=Man=Earth=Royalty=6 June=Gaia=Maia>>M=M2.
Philanthropic=5,500=5.5=80%=P5.50=Earth-Midway=5 May = Gaia.
Philanthropy=10,000=1,000=100%=10.0=Physicality=Tech.=10 Oct.=Uranus=P=1Ø.
Philately=10,000=1,000=100%=10.0=Physicality=Tech.=10 Oct.=Uranus=P=1Ø.
-phile=8,000=80%=P8.0D=Economy=Currency=8 Aug.=Zeus>>E=v.

Philemon=2,000=20%=P2.00D=2.0=Nature=Matter=Moon=2 Feb.=Cupid=N=C+_
Greek myth. A good old countryman living with his wife Baucis in Phrygia who offered
hospitality to Zeus and Hermes when the two Gods came to Earth, without revealing
their identities, to test people's piety. Philemon and Baucis were subsequently saved from
a flood that covered the district. Bible. A book of the New Testament, an epistle of St.
Paul to a well-to-do Christian living probably at Colossae in Phrygia. (Apple online
dictionary). Inspired by Zeus and Hermes. Both names were mentioned in the Acts.

Philharmonic=5,000=50%=P5.00D=Law=Time=Venus=5 May = Aphrodite>>L=N.
-philia=3,000=30%=P3.0D=3.0=Creativity=Stars=Muses=3 March = C=I>>GIL.
Philip=2,000=20%=P2.00D=2.0=Nature=Matter=Moon=2 Feb.=Cupid=N=C+_
Philip,Prince=5,000=50%=P5.00D=Law=Time=Venus=5 May = Aphrodite>>L=N.
Philip,Saint=4,500=5,000=50%=P5.00D=Law=Time=Venus=5 May = Aphrodite>>L=N.
Philip III1=3,500=4,000=40%=P4.0D=Govt.=Creatocracy=4 April=Mercury=Hermes=G=A4.
Philip II2=3,000=30%=P3.0D=3.0=Creativity=Stars=Muses=3 March = C=I>>GIL.
Philip II3=8,000=80%=P8.0D=Economy=Currency=8 Aug.=Zeus>>E=v.
Philip IV.=9,000=90%=P9.00D=9.0=Abstraction=Gods=Saturn=9Sept.>>A=Ø.
Philippi=5,000=50%=P5.00D=Law=Time=Venus=5 May = Aphrodite>>L=N.

Philippians=2,000=20%=P2.00D=2.0=Nature=Matter=Moon=2 Feb.=Cupid=N=C+_
A book of the New Testament, an epistle of St. Paul to the Church at Philippi in
Macedonia.(Apple online dictionary). Inspired by Eros and Artemis.

Philippic=5,500=5.5=80%=P5.50=Earth-Midway=5 May = Gaia.
Philippines=9,000=90%=P9.00D=9.0=Abstraction=Gods=Saturn=9Sept.>>A=Ø.
Philippine Sea=5,000=50%=P5.00D=Law=Time=Venus=5 May = Aphrodite>>L=N.
Philistine=10,000=1,000=100%=10.0=Physicality=Tech.=10 Oct.=Uranus=P=1Ø.
Philodendron=10,000=1,000=100%=10.0=Physicality=Tech.=10 Oct.=Uranus=P=1Ø.
Philology=10,000=1,000=100%=10.0=Physicality=Tech.=10 Oct.=Uranus=P=1Ø.
Philosopher=10,000=1,000=100%=10.0=Physicality=Tech.=10 Oct.=Uranus=P=1Ø.
Philosophize=3,000=30%=P3.0D=3.0=Creativity=Stars=Muses=3 March = C=I>>GIL.
Philosophy=10,000=1,000=100%=10.0=Physicality=Tech.=10 Oct.=Uranus=P=1Ø.
Philter=5,500=5.5=80%=P5.50=Earth-Midway=5 May = Gaia.
Phlebitis=2,000=20%=P2.00D=2.0=Nature=Matter=Moon=2 Feb.=Cupid=N=C+_
Phlebo-=3,500=4,000=40%=P4.0D=Govt.=Creatocracy=4 April=Mercury=Hermes=G=A4.
Phlebotomy=7,000=70%=P7.0D=7.0=Language=Assets=Mars=7 July=Pleiades.
Phlegm=7,000=70%=P7.0D=7.0=Language=Assets=Mars=7 July=Pleiades.
Phlegmatic=6,500=7,000=70%=P7.0D=7.0=Language=Assets=Mars=7 July=Pleiades.
Phloem=5,000=50%=P5.00D=Law=Time=Venus=5 May = Aphrodite>>L=N.
Phlox=6,500=7,000=70%=P7.0D=7.0=Language=Assets=Mars=7 July=Pleiades.
Phnom Penh=6,000=60%=P6.0D=Man=Earth=Royalty=6 June=Gaia=Maia>>M=M2.
-phobe=7,000=70%=P7.0D=7.0=Language=Assets=Mars=7 July=Pleiades.
Phobia=6,500=7,000=70%=P7.0D=7.0=Language=Assets=Mars=7 July=Pleiades.
-phobia=5,000=50%=P5.00D=Law=Time=Venus=5 May = Aphrodite>>L=N.
Phoebe=5,000=50%=P5.00D=Law=Time=Venus=5 May = Aphrodite>>L=N.
Phoenicia=6,000=60%=P6.0D=Man=Earth=Royalty=6 June=Gaia=Maia>>M=M2.
Phoenician=6,000=60%=P6.0D=Man=Earth=Royalty=6 June=Gaia=Maia>>M=M2.
Phoenix=10,000=1,000=100%=10.0=Physicality=Tech.=10 Oct.=Uranus=P=1Ø.
Phoenix=6,000=60%=P6.0D=Man=Earth=Royalty=6 June=Gaia=Maia>>M=M2.
Phone=2,000=20%=P2.00D=2.0=Nature=Matter=Moon=2 Feb.=Cupid=N=C+_
-phone=9,500=10,000=1,000=100%=10.0=Physicality=Tech.=10 Oct.=Uranus=P=1Ø.
Phoneme=10,000=1,000=100%=10.0=Physicality=Tech.=10 Oct.=Uranus=P=1Ø.
Phonetic=10,000=1,000=100%=10.0=Physicality=Tech.=10 Oct.=Uranus=P=1Ø.
Phonetics=5,000=50%=P5.00D=Law=Time=Venus=5 May = Aphrodite>>L=N.
Phonics=5,000=50%=P5.00D=Law=Time=Venus=5 May = Aphrodite>>L=N.
Phono-=3,000=30%=P3.0D=3.0=Creativity=Stars=Muses=3 March = C=I>>GIL.
Phonograph=4,500=5,000=50%=P5.00D=Law=Time=Venus=5 May = Aphrodite>>L=N.
Phonology=10,000=1,000=100%=10.0=Physicality=Tech.=10 Oct.=Uranus=P=1Ø.
Phony=6,000=60%=P6.0D=Man=Earth=Royalty=6 June=Gaia=Maia>>M=M2.
-phony=2,500=3,000=30%=P3.0D=3.0=Creativity=Stars=Muses=3 March = C=I>>GIL.
-phore=4,500=5,000=50%=P5.00D=Law=Time=Venus=5 May = Aphrodite>>L=N.
-phoresis=5,000=50%=P5.00D=Law=Time=Venus=5 May = Aphrodite>>L=N.
Phosgene=10,500=11,000=11%=P1.10D=1.1=Idea=Brainchild=Inv.=11 Nov=Athena>>I=MT.
Phosphate=5,500=5.5=80%=P5.50=Earth-Midway=5 May = Gaia.
Phospholipid=7,500=8,000=80%=P8.0D=Economy=Currency=8 Aug.=Zeus>>E=v.
Phospho=9,000=90%=P9.00D=9.0=Abstraction=Gods=Saturn=9Sept.>>A=Ø.
Phosphorescence=5,500=5.5=80%=P5.50=Earth-Midway=5 May = Gaia.
Phosphoric acid=6,000=60%=P6.0D=Man=Earth=Royalty=6 June=Gaia=Maia>>M=M2.

Phosphorus=10,000=1,000=100%=10.0=Physicality=Tech.=10 Oct.=Uranus=P=1Ø.

Photic=7,000=70%=P7.0D=7.0=Language=Assets=Mars=7 July=Pleiades.

Photo=4,000=40%=P4.0D=Govt.=Creatocracy=4 April=Mercury=Hermes=G=A4.

Photo-=4,000=40%=P4.0D=Govt.=Creatocracy=4 April=Mercury=Hermes=G=A4.

Photocell=1,500=15%=P1.50D=1.5=Authority=Solar Crown=1 May = Maia.

Photochemistry=4,000=40%=P4.0D=Govt.=4 April=Mercury=Hermes=G=A4.

Photocomposition=7,000=70%=P7.0D=7.0=Language=Assets=Mars=7 July=Pleiades.

Photocopy=7,500=8,000=80%=P8.0D=Economy=Currency=8 Aug.=Zeus>>E=v.

Photo duplicate=1,000=100%=10.0=1.0=Mind=Sun=1 January=Helios >> M=E4.

Photoelectric=6,000=60%=P6.0D=Man=Earth=Royalty=6 June=Gaia=Maia>>M=M2.

Photoelectric cell=9,500=10,000=1,000=100%=10.0=Tech.=10 Oct.=Uranus=P=1Ø.

Photoelectron=3,500=4,000=40%=P4.0D=Govt.=4 April=Mercury=Hermes=G=A4.

Photo emission=6,500=7,000=70%=P7.0D=7.0=Language=Assets=Mars=7 July=Pleiades.

Photo engraving=10,000=1,000=100%=10.0=Physicality=Tech.=10 Oct.=Uranus=P=1Ø.

Photo-essay=5,500=5.5=80%=P5.50=Earth-Midway=5 May = Gaia.

Photo finish=8,000=80%=P8.0D=Economy=Currency=8 Aug.=Zeus>>E=v.

Photo flash=1,000=100%=10.0=1.0=Mind=Sun=1 January=Helios >> M=E4.

Photog.=1,500=15%=P1.50D=1.5=Authority=Solar Crown=1 May = Maia.

Photogenic=3,000=30%=P3.0D=3.0=Creativity=Stars=Muses=3 March = C=I>>GIL.

Photograph=11,500=12,000=12%=P1.20D=1.2=Knowledge=Edu=12Dec.=Athena>>K=F.

Photographic=10,000=1,000=100%=10.0=Physicality=Tech.=10 Oct.=Uranus=P=1Ø.

Photography=8,000=80%=P8.0D=Economy=Currency=8 Aug.=Zeus>>E=v.

Photogravure=7,000=70%=P7.0D=7.0=Language=Assets=Mars=7 July=Pleiades.

Photojournalism=6,000=60%=P6.0D=Man=Earth=Royalty=6 June=Gaia=Maia>>M=M2.

Photometry=4,000=40%=P4.0D=Govt.=Creatocracy=4 April=Mercury=Hermes=G=A4.

Photo micrograph=3,000=30%=P3.0D=3.0=Creativity=Stars=Muses=3 March = C=I>>GIL.

Photomontage=10,000=1,000=100%=10.0=Physicality=Tech.=10 Oct.=Uranus=P=1Ø.

Photon=10,000=1,000=100%=10.0=Physicality=Tech.=10 Oct.=Uranus=P=1Ø.

Photoplay=4,500=5,000=50%=P5.00D=Law=Time=Venus=5 May = Aphrodite>>L=N.

Photoreceptor=7,000=70%=P7.0D=7.0=Language=Assets=Mars=7 July=Pleiades.

Photo reconnaissance=3,500=4,000=40%=P4.0D=Govt.=Creato=4 April=Hermes=G=A4.

Photosensitive=2,500=3,000=30%=P3.0D=3.0=Creativity=Stars=Muses=3 March =C=I.

Photosphere=5,000=50%=P5.00D=Law=Time=Venus=5 May = Aphrodite>>L=N.

Photostat=7,000=70%=P7.0D=7.0=Language=Assets=Mars=7 July=Pleiades.

Photosynthesis=10,000=1,000=100%=10.0=Physicality=Tech.=10 Oct.=Uranus=P=1Ø.

Phototropism=4,000=40%=P4.0D=Govt.=Creato=4 April=Mercury=Hermes=G=A4.

Photo typesetting=1,000=100%=10.0=1.0=Mind=Sun=1 January=Helios >> M=E4.

Photovoltaic=6,000=60%=P6.0D=Man=Earth=Royalty=6 June=Gaia=Maia>>M=M2.

Photovoltaic cell=1,500=15%=P1.50D=1.5=Authority=Solar Crown=1 May = Maia.

Phrase=10,000=1,000=100%=10.0=Physicality=Tech.=10 Oct.=Uranus=P=1Ø.

Phraseology=6,500=7,000=70%=P7.0D=7.0=Language=Assets=Mars=7 July=Pleiades.

Phrenetic=1,500=15%=P1.50D=1.5=Authority=Solar Crown=1 May = Maia.

-phrenia=4,000=40%=P4.0D=Govt.=Creatocracy=4 April=Mercury=Hermes=G=A4.

Phrenology=10,000=1,000=100%=10.0=Physicality=Tech.=10 Oct.=Uranus=P=1Ø.

Phrygia=6,000=60%=P6.0D=Man=Earth=Royalty=6 June=Gaia=Maia>>M=M2.

Phyla=1,500=15%=P1.50D=1.5=Authority=Solar Crown=1 May = Maia.
Phylactery=10,000=1,000=100%=10.0=Physicality=Tech.=10 Oct.=Uranus=P=1Ø.
Phyllotaxy=6,500=7,000=70%=P7.0D=7.0=Language=Assets=Mars=7 July=Pleiades.
Phylogeny=8,000=80%=P8.0D=Economy=Currency=8 Aug.=Zeus>>E=v.
Phylum=10,000=1,000=100%=10.0=Physicality=Tech.=10 Oct.=Uranus=P=1Ø.
Phys.=3,000=30%=P3.0D=3.0=Creativity=Stars=Muses=3 March = C=I>>GIL.
Physi-=1,500=15%=P1.50D=1.5=Authority=Solar Crown=1 May = Maia.
Physic=10,000=1,000=100%=10.0=Physicality=Tech.=10 Oct.=Uranus=P=1Ø.
Physical=10,000=1,000=100%=10.0=Physicality=Tech.=10 Oct.=Uranus=P=1Ø.
Physical education=7,000=70%=P7.0D=7.0=Language=Assets=Mars=7 July=Pleiades.
Physical examination=7,000=70%=P7.0D=7.0=Language=Assets=Mars=7 July=Pleiades.
Physical geography=5,500=5.5=80%=P5.50=Earth-Midway=5 May = Gaia.
Physical science=10,000=1,000=100%=10.0=Physicality=Tech.=10 Oct.=Uranus=P=1Ø.
Physical therapy=8,000=80%=P8.0D=Economy=Currency=8 Aug.=Zeus>>E=v.
Physician=1,500=15%=P1.50D=1.5=Authority=Solar Crown=1 May = Maia.

Physicist=3,000=30%=P3.0D=3.0=Creativity=Stars=Muses=3 March = C=I>>GIL.
A scientist who specializes in physics. The Creatocracy has the Creative Scientist, a scientist who specializes in the Creative Sciences and its applications to the Mind. A Mindysxt as well. Peter Matthews-Akukalia is the World's 1st Creative Scientist.

Physics=7,000=70%=P7.0D=7.0=Language=Assets=Mars=7 July=Pleiades.
Physio-=4,500=5,000=50%=P5.00D=Law=Time=Venus=5 May = Aphrodite>>L=N.
Physiognomy=6,000=60%=P6.0D=Man=Earth=Royalty=6 June=Gaia=Maia>>M=M2.
Physiography=1,500=15%=P1.50D=1.5=Authority=Solar Crown=1 May = Maia.
Physiology=10,000=1,000=100%=10.0=Physicality=Tech.=10 Oct.=Uranus=P=1Ø.
Physiotherapy=1,500=15%=P1.50D=1.5=Authority=Solar Crown=1 May = Maia.
Physique=10,000=1,000=100%=10.0=Physicality=Tech.=10 Oct.=Uranus=P=1Ø.
-phyte=7,000=70%=P7.0D=7.0=Language=Assets=Mars=7 July=Pleiades.
Phytoplankton=6,000=60%=P6.0D=Man=Earth=Royalty=6 June=Gaia=Maia>>M=M2.
Pi1=10,500=11,000=11%=P1.10D=1.1=Idea=Brainchild=Inv.=11 Nov.=SC=Athena>>I=MT.
Pi2=1,500=15%=P1.50D=1.5=Authority=Solar Crown=1 May = Maia.
Pianissimo=7,000=70%=P7.0D=7.0=Language=Assets=Mars=7 July=Pleiades.
Pianist=2,500=3,000=30%=P3.0D=3.0=Creativity=Stars=Muses=3 March = C=I>>GIL.
Piano1=6,500=7,000=70%=P7.0D=7.0=Language=Assets=Mars=7 July=Pleiades.
Piano2=3,000=30%=P3.0D=3.0=Creativity=Stars=Muses=3 March = C=I>>GIL.
Pianoforte=4,500=5,000=50%=P5.00D=Law=Time=Venus=5 May = Aphrodite>>L=N.

Piaster=3,000=30%=P3.0D=3.0=Creativity=Stars=Muses=3 March = C=I>>GIL.
A currency. Metric weight=3/10=0.3. See Naira. Dollar.

Piazza=6,500=7,000=70%=P7.0D=7.0=Language=Assets=Mars=7 July=Pleiades.
Pica=10,000=1,000=100%=10.0=Physicality=Tech.=10 Oct.=Uranus=P=1Ø.

Picador=9,500=10,000=1,000=100%=10.0=Physicality=Tech.=10 Oct.=Uranus=P=1Ø.
Picardy=5,000=50%=P5.00D=Law=Time=Venus=5 May = Aphrodite>>L=N.
Picaresque=6,500=7,000=70%=P7.0D=7.0=Language=Assets=Mars=7 July=Pleiades.
Picasso Pablo=2,000=20%=P2.00D=2.0=Nature=Matter=Moon=2 Feb.=Cupid=N=C+_
Picayune=6,000=60%=P6.0D=Man=Earth=Royalty=6 June=Gaia=Maia>>M=M2.
Piccolo=5,000=50%=P5.00D=Law=Time=Venus=5 May = Aphrodite>>L=N.
Pick1=10,000=1,000=100%=10.0=Physicality=Tech.=10 Oct.=Uranus=P=1Ø.
Pick2=12,000=12%=P1.20D=1.2=Knowledge=Edu=12Dec.=Athena>>K=F.
Pickax=8,000=80%=P8.0D=Economy=Currency=8 Aug.=Zeus>>E=v.
Pickerel=7,500=8,000=80%=P8.0D=Economy=Currency=8 Aug.=Zeus>>E=v.
Picket=10,000=1,000=100%=10.0=Physicality=Tech.=10 Oct.=Uranus=P=1Ø.
Picket fence=2,500=3,000=30%=P3.0D=3.0=Creativity=Stars=Muses=3 March = C=I.
Picket line=7,000=70%=P7.0D=7.0=Language=Assets=Mars=7 July=Pleiades.
Pickett George=3,000=30%=P3.0D=3.0=Creativity=Stars=Muses=3 March = C=I>>GIL.
Picking=7,000=70%=P7.0D=7.0=Language=Assets=Mars=7 July=Pleiades.
Pickle=10,000=1,000=100%=10.0=Physicality=Tech.=10 Oct.=Uranus=P=1Ø.
Pick-me-up=4,000=40%=P4.0D=Govt.=Creatocracy=4 April=Mercury=Hermes=G=A4.
Pickpocket=3,500=4,000=40%=P4.0D=Govt.=4 April=Mercury=Hermes=G=A4.
Pickup=10,000=1,000=100%=10.0=Physicality=Tech.=10 Oct.=Uranus=P=1Ø.
Pickup truck=5,000=50%=P5.00D=Law=Time=Venus=5 May = Aphrodite>>L=N.
Picky=1,500=15%=P1.50D=1.5=Authority=Solar Crown=1 May = Maia.
Picnic=9,500=10,000=1,000=100%=10.0=Physicality=Tech.=10 Oct.=Uranus=P=1Ø.
Picot=5,500=5.5=80%=P5.50=Earth-Midway=5 May = Gaia.
Pictograph=6,000=60%=P6.0D=Man=Earth=Royalty=6 June=Gaia=Maia>>M=M2.
Pictorial=6,000=60%=P6.0D=Man=Earth=Royalty=6 June=Gaia=Maia>>M=M2.
PICTURE=10,000=1,000=100%=10.0=Physicality=Tech.=10 Oct.=Uranus=P=1Ø.
PICTUREsque=6,500=7,000=70%=P7.0D=7.0=Language=Assets=Mars=7 July=Pleiades.
PICTURE tube=9,000=90%=P9.00D=9.0=Abstraction=Gods=Saturn=9Sept.>>A=Ø.
PICTURE window=5,000=50%=P5.00D=Law=Time=Venus=5 May = Aphrodite>>L=N.
Piddling=2,000=20%=P2.00D=2.0=Nature=Matter=Moon=2 Feb.=Cupid=N=C+_
Pidgin=9,000=90%=P9.00D=9.0=Abstraction=Gods=Saturn=9Sept.>>A=Ø.
Pidgin English=9,000=90%=P9.00D=9.0=Abstraction=Gods=Saturn=9Sept.>>A=Ø.
Pie1=10,000=1,000=100%=10.0=Physicality=Tech.=10 Oct.=Uranus=P=1Ø.
Pie2=2,000=20%=P2.00D=2.0=Nature=Matter=Moon=2 Feb.=Cupid=N=C+_
Piebald=9,000=90%=P9.00D=9.0=Abstraction=Gods=Saturn=9Sept.>>A=Ø.
Piece=10,000=1,000=100%=10.0=Physicality=Tech.=10 Oct.=Uranus=P=1Ø.
Pièce de résistance=5,000=50%=P5.00D=Law=Time=Venus=5 May = Aphrodite>>L=N.
Piece goods=3,500=4,000=40%=P4.0D=Govt.=Creatocracy=4 April=Hermes=G=A4.
Piecemeal=7,000=70%=P7.0D=7.0=Language=Assets=Mars=7 July=Pleiades.

Piece of eight=2,500. Metric weight=2.5/10=0.25>>25=? See Naira. Dollar.

Piecework=4,000=40%=P4.0D=Govt.=Creatocracy=4 April=Mercury=Hermes=G=A4.
Pie chart=7,000=70%=P7.0D=7.0=Language=Assets=Mars=7 July=Pleiades.

Pied=3,500=4,000=40%=P4.0D=Govt.=Creatocracy=4 April=Mercury=Hermes=G=A4.
Pled-à-terre=4,000=40%=P4.0D=Govt.=Creatocracy=4 April=Mercury=Hermes=G=A4.
Piedmont=6,000=60%=P6.0D=Man=Earth=Royalty=6 June=Gaia=Maia>>M=M2.
Pier=10,000=1,000=100%=10.0=Physicality=Tech.=10 Oct.=Uranus=P=1Ø.
Pierce=11,000=11%=P1.10D=1.1=Idea=Brainchild=Inv.=11 Nov.=SC=Athena>>I=MT.
Pierce Franklin.=4,000=40%=P4.0D=Govt.=Creatocracy=4 April=Mercury=Hermes=G=A4.
Piero dela Francesca=2,500=3,000=30%=P3.0D=3.0=Cre.=Stars=Muses=3 March = C=I
Pierre=6,000=60%=P6.0D=Man=Earth=Royalty=6 June=Gaia=Maia>>M=M2.
Piety=7,500=8,000=80%=P8.0D=Economy=Currency=8 Aug.=Zeus>>E=v.
Piezoelectricity=10,000=1,000=100%=10.0=Physicality=Tech.=10 Oct.=Uranus=P=1Ø.
Piffle=6,000=60%=P6.0D=Man=Earth=Royalty=6 June=Gaia=Maia>>M=M2.
Pig=10,000=1,000=100%=10.0=Physicality=Tech.=10 Oct.=Uranus=P=1Ø.
Pigeon=10,000=1,000=100%=10.0=Physicality=Tech.=10 Oct.=Uranus=P=1Ø.
Pigeon hole=9,000=90%=P9.00D=9.0=Abstraction=Gods=Saturn=9Sept.>>A=Ø.
Pigeon toed=2,500=3,000=30%=P3.0D=3.0=Creativity=Stars=Muses=3 March=C=I.
Piggish=2,000=20%=P2.00D=2.0=Nature=Matter=Moon=2 Feb.=Cupid=N=C+_
Piggy=2,000=20%=P2.00D=2.0=Nature=Matter=Moon=2 Feb.=Cupid=N=C+_
Piggyback=10,000=1,000=100%=10.0=Physicality=Tech.=10 Oct.=Uranus=P=1Ø.

Piggy bank=3,000=30%=P3.0D=3.0=Creativity=Stars=Muses=3 March = C=I>>GIL.
A coin bank shaped like a pig. Metric weight = 3/10=0.3>>30 = ?. See Octahedron, Naira.

Pigheaded=500=5%=P5.00D=5.0=Law=Time=Venus=5 May=Aphrodite>>L=N.
Pig iron=2,500=3,000=30%=P3.0D=3.0=Creativity=Stars=Muses=3 March = C=I>>GIL.
Pig Latin.=10,000=1,000=100%=10.0=Physicality=Tech.=10 Oct.=Uranus=P=1Ø.
Piglet=1,500=15%=P1.50D=1.5=Authority=Solar Crown=1 May = Maia.
Pigment=10,000=1,000=100%=10.0=Physicality=Tech.=10 Oct.=Uranus=P=1Ø.
Pigmentation=4,000=40%=P4.0D=Govt.=Creatocracy=4 April=Mercury=Hermes=G=A4.
Pigmy=1,500=15%=P1.50D=1.5=Authority=Solar Crown=1 May = Maia.
Pigpen=5,000=50%=P5.00D=Law=Time=Venus=5 May = Aphrodite>>L=N.
Pigs=6,000=60%=P6.0D=Man=Earth=Royalty=6 June=Gaia=Maia>>M=M2.
Pigskin=6,000=60%=P6.0D=Man=Earth=Royalty=6 June=Gaia=Maia>>M=M2.
Pigsty=1,000=100%=10.0=1.0=Mind=Sun=1 January=Helios >> M=E4.
Pig tall=2,500=3,000=30%=P3.0D=3.0=Creativity=Stars=Muses=3 March = C=I>>GIL.
Pika=7,000=70%=P7.0D=7.0=Language=Assets=Mars=7 July=Pleiades.
Pike1=5,000=50%=P5.00D=Law=Time=Venus=5 May = Aphrodite>>L=N.
Pike2=6,500=7,000=70%=P7.0D=7.0=Language=Assets=Mars=7 July=Pleiades.
Pike3=1,000=100%=10.0=1.0=Mind=Sun=1 January=Helios >> M=E4.
Pike4=3,500=4,000=40%=P4.0D=Govt.=Creatocracy=4 April=Mercury=Hermes=G=A4.
Picker=3,000=30%=P3.0D=3.0=Creativity=Stars=Muses=3 March = C=I>>GIL.
Pikes Peak=6,500=7,000=70%=P7.0D=7.0=Language=Assets=Mars=7 July=Pleiades.
Pilaf=7,000=70%=P7.0D=7.0=Language=Assets=Mars=7 July=Pleiades.
Plaster=6,000=60%=P6.0D=Man=Earth=Royalty=6 June=Gaia=Maia>>M=M2.

Pilate=6,500=7,000=70%=P7.0D=7.0=Language=Assets=Mars=7 July=Pleiades.
Pilate was a means inspired by Gaia >> Maia and Aries. Violence was the proof.

Pilchard=5,000=50%=P5.00D=Law=Time=Venus=5 May = Aphrodite>>L=N.
Pile1=10,000=1,000=100%=10.0=Physicality=Tech.=10 Oct.=Uranus=P=1Ø.
Pile2=8,500=9,000=90%=P9.00D=9.0=Abstraction=Gods=Saturn=9Sept.>>A=Ø.
Pile3=9,500=10,000=1,000=100%=10.0=Physicality=Tech.=10 Oct.=Uranus=P=1Ø.
Pileated woodpecker=8,500=9,000=90%=P9.00D=9.0=Abstract=Saturn=9Sept.>>A=Ø.
Pile driver=4,000=40%=P4.0D=Govt.=Creatocracy=4 April=Mercury=Hermes=G=A4.
Piles=3,000=30%=P3.0D=3.0=Creativity=Stars=Muses=3 March = C=I>>GIL.
Pileup=4,000=40%=P4.0D=Govt.=Creatocracy=4 April=Mercury=Hermes=G=A4.
Pilfer=3,500=4,000=40%=P4.0D=Govt.=Creatocracy=4 April=Mercury=Hermes=G=A4.
Pilgrim=11,500=12,000=12%=P1.20D=1.2=Knowledge=Edu=12Dec.=Athena>>K=F.
Pilgrimage=6,500=7,000=70%=P7.0D=7.0=Language=Assets=Mars=7 July=Pleiades.
Piling=3,000=30%=P3.0D=3.0=Creativity=Stars=Muses=3 March = C=I>>GIL.
Pilipino=1,500=15%=P1.50D=1.5=Authority=Solar Crown=1 May = Maia.
Pill=10,000=1,000=100%=10.0=Physicality=Tech.=10 Oct.=Uranus=P=1Ø.
Pillage=6,500=7,000=70%=P7.0D=7.0=Language=Assets=Mars=7 July=Pleiades.
Pillar=7,000=70%=P7.0D=7.0=Language=Assets=Mars=7 July=Pleiades.
Pillbox=7,500=8,000=80%=P8.0D=Economy=Currency=8 Aug.=Zeus>>E=v.
Pillion=8,500=9,000=90%=P9.00D=9.0=Abstraction=Gods=Saturn=9Sept.>>A=Ø.
Pillory=10,000=1,000=100%=10.0=Physicality=Tech.=10 Oct.=Uranus=P=1Ø.
Pillow=10,000=1,000=100%=10.0=Physicality=Tech.=10 Oct.=Uranus=P=1Ø.
Pillowcase=2,500=3,000=30%=P3.0D=3.0=Creativity=Stars=Muses=3 March = C=I>>GIL.
Pillow slip=1,000=100%=10.0=1.0=Mind=Sun=1 January=Helios >> M=E4.
Pilose=4,000=40%=P4.0D=Govt.=Creatocracy=4 April=Mercury=Hermes=G=A4.
Pilot=10,000=1,000=100%=10.0=Physicality=Tech.=10 Oct.=Uranus=P=1Ø.
Pilotfish=7,500=8,000=80%=P8.0D=Economy=Currency=8 Aug.=Zeus>>E=v.
Pilot house=7,000=70%=P7.0D=7.0=Language=Assets=Mars=7 July=Pleiades.
Pilot light=8,000=80%=P8.0D=Economy=Currency=8 Aug.=Zeus>>E=v.
Pilot whale=6,500=7,000=70%=P7.0D=7.0=Language=Assets=Mars=7 July=Pleiades.
Pilt down man=10,000=1,000=100%=10.0=Physicality=Tech.=10 Oct.=Uranus=P=1Ø.
Pima=6,000=60%=P6.0D=Man=Earth=Royalty=6 June=Gaia=Maia>>M=M2.
Pimento=4,500=5,000=50%=P5.00D=Law=Time=Venus=5 May = Aphrodite>>L=N.
Pimiento=5,500=5.5=80%=P5.50=Earth-Midway=5 May = Gaia.
Pimp=5,500=5.5=80%=P5.50=Earth-Midway=5 May = Gaia.
Pimpernel=5,500=5.5=80%=P5.50=Earth-Midway=5 May = Gaia.
Pimple=6,000=60%=P6.0D=Man=Earth=Royalty=6 June=Gaia=Maia>>M=M2.
Pin=10,000=1,000=100%=10.0=Physicality=Tech.=10 Oct.=Uranus=P=1Ø.
Pinafore=4,500=5,000=50%=P5.00D=Law=Time=Venus=5 May = Aphrodite>>L=N.
Pinball=10,000=1,000=100%=10.0=Physicality=Tech.=10 Oct.=Uranus=P=1Ø.
Pince-nez=4,500=5,000=50%=P5.00D=Law=Time=Venus=5 May = Aphrodite>>L=N.
Pincers=10,000=1,000=100%=10.0=Physicality=Tech.=10 Oct.=Uranus=P=1Ø.
Pinch=10,000=1,000=100%=10.0=Physicality=Tech.=10 Oct.=Uranus=P=1Ø.

Pinch-hit=6,500=7,000=70%=P7.0D=7.0=Language=Assets=Mars=7 July=Pleiades.
Pin cushion=5,500=5.5=80%=P5.50=Earth-Midway=5 May = Gaia.
Pindar=3,500=4,000=40%=P4.0D=Govt.=Creatocracy=4 April=Mercury=Hermes=G=A4.
Pine1=10,000=1,000=100%=10.0=Physicality=Tech.=10 Oct.=Uranus=P=1Ø.
Pine2=6,500=7,000=70%=P7.0D=7.0=Language=Assets=Mars=7 July=Pleiades.
Pineal gland=10,500=11,000=11%=P1.10D=1.1=Idea=Brainchild=11 Nov.=Athena>>I=MT.

Pineapple=10,000=1,000=100%=10.0=Physicality=Tech.=10 Oct.=Uranus=P=1Ø.
The pineapple is a physical equivalent of a quantum. Eating pineapple gives one the vitamin Q >> Quantum of 10,000=1,000=100=10.0. Hereby discovered by Castle Makupedia.

Pine needle=4,000=40%=P4.0D=Govt.=Creatocracy=4 April=Mercury=Hermes=G=A4.
Pine nut=3,000=30%=P3.0D=3.0=Creativity=Stars=Muses=3 March = C=I>>GIL.
Piney=1,500=15%=P1.50D=1.5=Authority=Solar Crown=1 May = Maia.
Pin feather=5,000=50%=P5.00D=Law=Time=Venus=5 May = Aphrodite>>L=N.
Ping=7,500=8,000=80%=P8.0D=Economy=Currency=8 Aug.=Zeus>>E=v.
Ping-Pong=2,500=3,000=30%=P3.0D=3.0=Creativity=Stars=Muses=3 March = C=I>>GIL.
Pinhead=6,000=60%=P6.0D=Man=Earth=Royalty=6 June=Gaia=Maia>>M=M2.
Pinhole=4,500=5,000=50%=P5.00D=Law=Time=Venus=5 May = Aphrodite>>L=N.
Pinion1=10,000=1,000=100%=10.0=Physicality=Tech.=10 Oct.=Uranus=P=1Ø.
Pinion2=8,000=80%=P8.0D=Economy=Currency=8 Aug.=Zeus>>E=v.
Pink1=10,000=1,000=100%=10.0=Physicality=Tech.=10 Oct.=Uranus=P=1Ø.
Pink2=7,500=8,000=80%=P8.0D=Economy=Currency=8 Aug.=Zeus>>E=v.
Pinkeye=3,500=4,000=40%=P4.0D=Govt.=Creatocracy=4 April=Mercury=Hermes=G=A4.
Pinkie=3,500=4,000=40%=P4.0D=Govt.=Creatocracy=4 April=Mercury=Hermes=G=A4.
Pinking shears=10,000=1,000=100%=10.0=Physicality=Tech.=10 Oct.=Uranus=P=1Ø.
Pinko=4,000=40%=P4.0D=Govt.=Creatocracy=4 April=Mercury=Hermes=G=A4.

Pin money=2,000=20%=P2.00D=2.0=Nature=Matter=Moon=2 Feb.=Cupid=N=C+_
Money for incidental expenses. Money measures as 10,000 so 2,000/10,000=0.2=20%.

Pinnacle=10,000=1,000=100%=10.0=Physicality=Tech.=10 Oct.=Uranus=P=1Ø.
Pinnate=7,500=8,000=80%=P8.0D=Economy=Currency=8 Aug.=Zeus>>E=v.
Pinochle=10,000=1,000=100%=10.0=Physicality=Tech.=10 Oct.=Uranus=P=1Ø.
Piñon=6,500=7,000=70%=P7.0D=7.0=Language=Assets=Mars=7 July=Pleiades.
Pinpoint=6,500=7,000=70%=P7.0D=7.0=Language=Assets=Mars=7 July=Pleiades.
Pinprick=5,500=5.5=80%=P5.50=Earth-Midway=5 May = Gaia.
Pins and needles=10,000=1,000=100%=10.0=Physicality=Tech.=10 Oct.=Uranus=P=1Ø.
Pinstripe=4,000=40%=P4.0D=Govt.=Creatocracy=4 April=Mercury=Hermes=G=A4.
Pint=10,000=1,000=100%=10.0=Physicality=Tech.=10 Oct.=Uranus=P=1Ø.
Pintail=10,000=1,000=100%=10.0=Physicality=Tech.=10 Oct.=Uranus=P=1Ø.Pinter
    Harold=2,000=20%=P2.00D=2.0=Nature=Matter=Moon=2 Feb.=Cupid=N=C+_
Pinto=4,000=40%=P4.0D=Govt.=Creatocracy=4 April=Mercury=Hermes=G=A4.

Pinto bean=5,000=50%=P5.00D=Law=Time=Venus=5 May = Aphrodite>>L=N.
Pint size=1,000=100%=10.0=1.0=Mind=Sun=1 January=Helios >> M=E4.
Pinup=6,500=7,000=70%=P7.0D=7.0=Language=Assets=Mars=7 July=Pleiades.
Pinwheel=10,000=1,000=100%=10.0=Physicality=Tech.=10 Oct.=Uranus=P=1Ø.
Pinworm=8,000=80%=P8.0D=Economy=Currency=8 Aug.=Zeus>>E=v.
Piny=2,500=3,000=30%=P3.0D=3.0=Creativity=Stars=Muses=3 March = C=I>>GIL.
Pinyin=2,500=3,000=30%=P3.0D=3.0=Creativity=Stars=Muses=3 March = C=I>>GIL.
Pinyon=5,000=50%=P5.00D=Law=Time=Venus=5 May = Aphrodite>>L=N.
Pion=10,000=1,000=100%=10.0=Physicality=Tech.=10 Oct.=Uranus=P=1Ø.

Pioneer=13,000=13%=P1.30=Solar Core=Faculty=13 January=Athena.
One who ventures into unknown or unclaimed territory to settle. An innovator especially in research and development. Peter Matthews-Akukalia, Castle Makupedia is the pioneer of the field of the Creative Sciences. He founded the Makupedia, the Matthews-Akukalia empire known as the Mindom, the Creatocratic Nations of Paradise and the Creatocracy. Today He is the God of Creatocracy Genius and Mind.

Pious=10,000=1,000=100%=10.0=Physicality=Tech.=10 Oct.=Uranus=P=1Ø.
Pip1=6,000=60%=P6.0D=Man=Earth=Royalty=6 June=Gaia=Maia>>M=M2.
Pip2=6,500=7,000=70%=P7.0D=7.0=Language=Assets=Mars=7 July=Pleiades.
Pip3=5,500=5.5=80%=P5.50=Earth-Midway=5 May = Gaia.
Pipe=10,000=1,000=100%=10.0=Physicality=Tech.=10 Oct.=Uranus=P=1Ø.

Pipe dream=4,500=5,000=50%=P5.00D=Law=Time=Venus=5 May = Aphrodite>>L=N.
A fantastic notion or vain hope. [From opium fantasies.]. In the past some people felt that the Creatocracy was a pipe dream. This encyclopedia is testimony to its reality. It is one of the Castles of the Makupedia whose name is Peter Matthews-Akukalia, Castle Makupedia.

Pipe fitter=3,500=4,000=40%=P4.0D=Govt.=Creatocracy=4 April=Hermes=G=A4.
Pipeline=10,000=1,000=100%=10.0=Physicality=Tech.=10 Oct.=Uranus=P=1Ø.
Pipe organ=2,000=20%=P2.00D=2.0=Nature=Matter=Moon=2 Feb.=Cupid=N=C+_
Pipe stone=7,500=8,000=80%=P8.0D=Economy=Currency=8 Aug.=Zeus>>E=v.
Pipette=8,000=80%=P8.0D=Economy=Currency=8 Aug.=Zeus>>E=v.
Pipe wrench=6,500=7,000=70%=P7.0D=7.0=Language=Assets=Mars=7 July=Pleiades.
Piping=7,500=8,000=80%=P8.0D=Economy=Currency=8 Aug.=Zeus>>E=v.
Pippin=3,500=4,000=40%=P4.0D=Govt.=Creatocracy=4 April=Mercury=Hermes=G=A4.
Pip-squeak=3,500=4,000=40%=P4.0D=Govt.=4 April=Mercury=Hermes=G=A4.
Piquant=4,500=5,000=50%=P5.00D=Law=Time=Venus=5 May = Aphrodite>>L=N.
Pique=10,000=1,000=100%=10.0=Physicality=Tech.=10 Oct.=Uranus=P=1Ø.
Piqué=5,500=5.5=80%=P5.50=Earth-Midway=5 May = Gaia.
Piraeus=5,500=5.5=80%=P5.50=Earth-Midway=5 May = Gaia.
Pirandello Luigi.=4,500=5,000=50%=P5.00D=Law=Time=Venus=5 May = Odite>>L=N.

Piranha=8,000=80%=P8.0D=Economy=Currency=8 Aug.=Zeus>>E=v.
Pirate=12,500=13,000=13%=P1.30=Solar Core=Faculty=13 January=Athena.
Pirogue=4,500=5,000=50%=P5.00D=Law=Time=Venus=5 May = Aphrodite>>L=N.
Pirouette=10,000=1,000=100%=10.0=Physicality=Tech.=10 Oct.=Uranus=P=1Ø.
Pisa=7,000=70%=P7.0D=7.0=Language=Assets=Mars=7 July=Pleiades.
Piscatorial=4,000=40%=P4.0D=Govt.=Creatocracy=4 April=Mercury=Hermes=G=A4.
Pisces=6,000=60%=P6.0D=Man=Earth=Royalty=6 June=Gaia=Maia>>M=M2.
Pisistratus=3,000=30%=P3.0D=3.0=Creativity=Stars=Muses=3 March = C=I>>GIL.
Pismire=2,000=20%=P2.00D=2.0=Nature=Matter=Moon=2 Feb.=Cupid=N=C+_
Pissarro Camille=2,500=3,000=30%=P3.0D=3.0=Creativity=Stars=Muses=3 March=C=I.
Pistachio=9,000=90%=P9.00D=9.0=Abstraction=Gods=Saturn=9Sept.>>A=Ø.
Pistil=5,500=5.5=80%=P5.50=Earth-Midway=5 May = Gaia.
Pistol=7,500=8,000=80%=P8.0D=Economy=Currency=8 Aug.=Zeus>>E=v.
Pistol-whip=2,500=3,000=30%=P3.0D=3.0=Creativity=Stars=Muses=3 March =C=I.
Piston=11,000=11%=P1.10D=1.1=Idea=Brainchild=Inv.=11 Nov.=SC=Athena>>I=MT.
Pit1=10,000=1,000=100%=10.0=Physicality=Tech.=10 Oct.=Uranus=P=1Ø.
Pit2=10,000=1,000=100%=10.0=Physicality=Tech.=10 Oct.=Uranus=P=1Ø.
Pita=6,500=7,000=70%=P7.0D=7.0=Language=Assets=Mars=7 July=Pleiades.
Pit a pat=7,000=70%=P7.0D=7.0=Language=Assets=Mars=7 July=Pleiades.
Pitcairn Island=4,500=5,000=50%=P5.00D=Law=Time=Venus=5 May = Aphrodite>>L=N.
Pitch1=15,000=1,500=15%=P1.50D=1.5=Authority=Solar Crown=1 May = Maia.
Pitch2=10,000=1,000=100%=10.0=Physicality=Tech.=10 Oct.=Uranus=P=1Ø.
Pitch black=1,000=100%=Physicality=Tech.=10 Oct.=Uranus=P=1Ø.
Pitchblende=5,500=5.5=80%=P5.50=Earth-Midway=5 May = Gaia.
Pitch dark=1,000=100%=10.0=1.0=Mind=Sun=1 January=Helios >> M=E4.
Pitcher1=2,500=3,000=30%=P3.0D=3.0=Creativity=Stars=Muses=3 March = C=I>>GIL.
Pitcher2=8,500=9,000=90%=P9.00D=9.0=Abstraction=Gods=Saturn=9Sept.>>A=Ø.
Pitcher plant=6,500=7,000=70%=P7.0D=7.0=Language=Assets=Mars=7 July=Pleiades.
Pitchfork=8,000=80%=P8.0D=Economy=Currency=8 Aug.=Zeus>>E=v.
Pitch pipe=8,000=80%=P8.0D=Economy=Currency=8 Aug.=Zeus>>E=v.
Piteous=1,500=15%=P1.50D=1.5=Authority=Solar Crown=1 May = Maia.
Pitfall=7,500=8,000=80%=P8.0D=Economy=Currency=8 Aug.=Zeus>>E=v.
Pith=13,000=13%=P1.30=Solar Core=Faculty=13 January=Athena.
Pith helmet=6,500=7,000=70%=P7.0D=7.0=Language=Assets=Mars=7 July=Pleiades.
Pithy=3,500=4,000=40%=P4.0D=Govt.=Creatocracy=4 April=Mercury=Hermes=G=A4.
Pitiable=1,000=100%=10.0=1.0=Mind=Sun=1 January=Helios >> M=E4.
Pitiful=6,000=60%=P6.0D=Man=Earth=Royalty=6 June=Gaia=Maia>>M=M2.
Pitiless=2,000=20%=P2.00D=2.0=Nature=Matter=Moon=2 Feb.=Cupid=N=C+_
Piton=8,000=80%=P8.0D=Economy=Currency=8 Aug.=Zeus>>E=v.
Pit stop=7,500=8,000=80%=P8.0D=Economy=Currency=8 Aug.=Zeus>>E=v.
Pitt,William1=5,500=5.5=80%=P5.50=Earth-Midway=5 May = Gaia.
Pitt,William2=6,500=7,000=70%=P7.0D=7.0=Language=Assets=Mars=7 July=Pleiades.
Pittance=7,500=8,000=80%=P8.0D=Economy=Currency=8 Aug.=Zeus>>E=v.
Pitter-patter=2,500=3,000=30%=P3.0D=3.0=Creativity=Stars=Muses=3 March =C=I

Pittsburgh=9,500=10,000=1,000=100%=10.0=Physicality=Tech.=10 Oct.=Uranus=P=1Ø.
A city whose means is Abstraction and resultant is technology. A MindTech Center.

Pituitary=10,000=1,000=100%=10.0=Physicality=Tech.=10 Oct.=Uranus=P=1Ø.
Pit viper=8,500=9,000=90%=P9.00D=9.0=Abstraction=Gods=Saturn=9Sept.>>A=Ø.
Pity=10,000=1,000=100%=10.0=Physicality=Tech.=10 Oct.=Uranus=P=1Ø.
Pius V=2,500=3,000=30%=P3.0D=3.0=Creativity=Stars=Muses=3 March = C=I>>GIL.
Pius IX.=2,000=20%=P2.00D=2.0=Nature=Matter=Moon=2 Feb.=Cupid=N=C+_
Pius X.=2,500=3,000=30%=P3.0D=3.0=Creativity=Stars=Muses=3 March = C=I>>GIL.
Pius XI.=2,000=20%=P2.00D=2.0=Nature=Matter=Moon=2 Feb.=Cupid=N=C+_
Pius XII.=2,000=20%=P2.00D=2.0=Nature=Matter=Moon=2 Feb.=Cupid=N=C+_
Pivot=10,000=1,000=100%=10.0=Physicality=Tech.=10 Oct.=Uranus=P=1Ø.
Pix=2,000=20%=P2.00D=2.0=Nature=Matter=Moon=2 Feb.=Cupid=N=C+_
Pixel=6,500=7,000=70%=P7.0D=7.0=Language=Assets=Mars=7 July=Pleiades.
Pixy=3,500=4,000=40%=P4.0D=Govt.=Creatocracy=4 April=Mercury=Hermes=G=A4.
Pizarro Francisco=2,500=3,000=30%=P3.0D=3.0=Creativity=Stars=Muses=3 March=C=I.
Pizza=8,500=9,000=90%=P9.00D=9.0=Abstraction=Gods=Saturn=9Sept.>>A=Ø.
Pizzazz=4,000=40%=P4.0D=Govt.=Creatocracy=4 April=Mercury=Hermes=G=A4.
Pizzeria=4,000=40%=P4.0D=Govt.=Creatocracy=4 April=Mercury=Hermes=G=A4.
Pizzicato=6,000=60%=P6.0D=Man=Earth=Royalty=6 June=Gaia=Maia>>M=M2.
pk.=3,500=4,000=40%=P4.0D=Govt.=Creatocracy=4 April=Mercury=Hermes=G=A4.
pkg.=1,000=100%=10.0=1.0=Mind=Sun=1 January=Helios >> M=E4.
pl.=2,500=3,000=30%=P3.0D=3.0=Creativity=Stars=Muses=3 March = C=I>>GIL.
Placard=7,500=8,000=80%=P8.0D=Economy=Currency=8 Aug.=Zeus>>E=v.
Placate=6,000=60%=P6.0D=Man=Earth=Royalty=6 June=Gaia=Maia>>M=M2.
Place=10,000=1,000=100%=10.0=Physicality=Tech.=10 Oct.=Uranus=P=1Ø.
Placebo=10,000=1,000=100%=10.0=Physicality=Tech.=10 Oct.=Uranus=P=1Ø.
Place kick=10,000=1,000=100%=10.0=Physicality=Tech.=10 Oct.=Uranus=P=1Ø.
Place mat=5,000=50%=P5.00D=Law=Time=Venus=5 May = Aphrodite>>L=N.
Placement=10,000=1,000=100%=10.0=Physicality=Tech.=10 Oct.=Uranus=P=1Ø.
Placenta=10,000=1,000=100%=10.0=Physicality=Tech.=10 Oct.=Uranus=P=1Ø.
Placer=9,000=90%=P9.00D=9.0=Abstraction=Gods=Saturn=9Sept.>>A=Ø.
Placid=5,500=5.5=80%=P5.50=Earth-Midway=5 May = Gaia.
Placket=4,000=40%=P4.0D=Govt.=Creatocracy=4 April=Mercury=Hermes=G=A4.

Plagiarize=10,000=1,000=100%=10.0=Physicality=Tech.=10 Oct.=Uranus=P=1Ø.
To use and pass off as one's own (the ideas or writings of another). [<Lat. plagiārius, kidnapper.]. The Creatocracy created the Ministry of Creativity to manage all creativity worldwide as well as the Mind or Creatocracy Courts to try all creativity related offenses. See the book >> Principles of Psychoeconomix by Peter Matthews-Akukalia.

Plague=10,000=1,000=100%=10.0=Physicality=Tech.=10 Oct.=Uranus=P=1Ø.
Plaid=10,000=1,000=100%=10.0=Physicality=Tech.=10 Oct.=Uranus=P=1Ø.

Plain=10,000=1,000=100%=10.0=Physicality=Tech.=10 Oct.=Uranus=P=1Ø.
When Jesus said that all the mountains shall be made plains it simply meant that quantum mechanics would be discovered and invented in time to come using the 10,000 bundle. Peter Matthews-Akukalia, Castle Makupedia has successfully achieved this feat.

Plainclothes man=6,500=7,000=70%=P7.0D=7.0=Lang=Assets=Mars=7 July=Pleiades.
Plains Indian=6,500=7,000=70%=P7.0D=7.0=Language=Assets=Mars=7 July=Pleiades.
Plainsong=8,500=9,000=90%=P9.00D=9.0=Abstraction=Gods=Saturn=9Sept.>>A=Ø.
Plain spoken=1,000=100%=Physicality=Tech.=10 Oct.=Uranus=P=1Ø.
Plaint=3,500=4,000=40%=P4.0D=Govt.=Creatocracy=4 April=Mercury=Hermes=G=A4.
Plaintiff=5,500=5.5=80%=P5.50=Earth-Midway=5 May = Gaia.
Plaintive=2,500=3,000=30%=P3.0D=3.0=Creativity=Stars=Muses=3 March = C=I>>GIL.
Plait=4,000=40%=P4.0D=Govt.=Creatocracy=4 April=Mercury=Hermes=G=A4.
Plan=10,000=1,000=100%=10.0=Physicality=Tech.=10 Oct.=Uranus=P=1Ø.
Planar=3,500=4,000=40%=P4.0D=Govt.=Creatocracy=4 April=Mercury=Hermes=G=A4.
Planck Max=4,500=5,000=50%=P5.00D=Law=Time=Venus=5 May = Aphrodite>>L=N.
Plane1=10,000=1,000=100%=10.0=Physicality=Tech.=10 Oct.=Uranus=P=1Ø.
Plane2=5,500=5.5=80%=P5.50=Earth-Midway=5 May = Gaia.
Plane3=2,500=3,000=30%=P3.0D=3.0=Creativity=Stars=Muses=3 March = C=I>>GIL.
Plane geometry=3,000=30%=P3.0D=3.0=Creativity=Stars=Muses=3 March = C=I>>GIL.
Planet=5,500=5.5=80%=P5.50=Earth-Midway=5 May = Gaia.
Planetarium=10,000=1,000=100%=10.0=Physicality=Tech.=10 Oct.=Uranus=P=1Ø.
Planetary=3,500=4,000=40%=P4.0D=Govt.=Creatocracy=4 April=Hermes=G=A4.
Plane tree=9,000=90%=P9.00D=9.0=Abstraction=Gods=Saturn=9Sept.>>A=Ø.
Plangent=3,500=4,000=40%=P4.0D=Govt.=Creatocracy=4 April=Hermes=G=A4.
Plank=10,000=1,000=100%=10.0=Physicality=Tech.=10 Oct.=Uranus=P=1Ø.
Plankton=8,000=80%=P8.0D=Economy=Currency=8 Aug.=Zeus>>E=v.
Piano=4,500=5,000=50%=P5.00D=Law=Time=Venus=5 May = Aphrodite>>L=N.
Plant=10,000=1,000=100%=10.0=Physicality=Tech.=10 Oct.=Uranus=P=1Ø.
Plantain1=7,000=70%=P7.0D=7.0=Language=Assets=Mars=7 July=Pleiades.
Plantain2=5,500=5.5=80%=P5.50=Earth-Midway=5 May = Gaia.
Plantation=11,000=11%=P1.10D=1.1=Idea=Brainchild=Inv.=11 Nov.=SC=Athena>>I=MT.
Planter=7,500=8,000=80%=P8.0D=Economy=Currency=8 Aug.=Zeus>>E=v.
Plaque=10,000=1,000=100%=10.0=Physicality=Tech.=10 Oct.=Uranus=P=1Ø.
Plash=7,000=70%=P7.0D=7.0=Language=Assets=Mars=7 July=Pleiades.
-plasm=4,000=40%=P4.0D=Govt.=Creatocracy=4 April=Mercury=Hermes=G=A4.
Plasma=10,000=1,000=100%=10.0=Physicality=Tech.=10 Oct.=Uranus=P=1Ø.
Plasmin=6,000=60%=P6.0D=Man=Earth=Royalty=6 June=Gaia=Maia>>M=M2.
Plasmo-=1,500=15%=P1.50D=1.5=Authority=Solar Crown=1 May = Maia.
Plasmolysis=10,000=1,000=100%=10.0=Physicality=Tech.=10 Oct.=Uranus=P=1Ø.
Plaster=10,000=1,000=100%=10.0=Physicality=Tech.=10 Oct.=Uranus=P=1Ø.
Plasterboard=10,000=1,000=100%=10.0=Physicality=Tech.=10 Oct.=Uranus=P=1Ø.
Plaster of Paris=8,500=9,000=90%=P9.00D=9.0=Abstr.=Gods=Saturn=9Sept.>>A=Ø.
Plastic=10,000=1,000=100%=10.0=Physicality=Tech.=10 Oct.=Uranus=P=1Ø.

Plastic explosive=6,000=60%=P6.0D=Man=Earth=Royalty=6 June=Gaia=Maia>>M=M2.
Plastic surgery=6,000=60%=P6.0D=Man=Earth=Royalty=6 June=Gaia=Maia>>M=M2.
Plastid=10,000=1,000=100%=10.0=Physicality=Tech.=10 Oct.=Uranus=P=1Ø.
Plastique=2,000=20%=P2.00D=2.0=Nature=Matter=Moon=2 Feb.=Cupid=N=C+_
plat.=1,500=15%=P1.50D=1.5=Authority=Solar Crown=1 May = Maia.
Plata Rio de la.=9,000=90%=P9.00D=9.0=Abstraction=Gods=Saturn=9Sept.>>A=Ø.
Plate=10,000=1,000=100%=10.0=Physicality=Tech.=10 Oct.=Uranus=P=1Ø.
Plateau=7,500=8,000=80%=P8.0D=Economy=Currency=8 Aug.=Zeus>>E=v.
Plate glass=6,000=60%=P6.0D=Man=Earth=Royalty=6 June=Gaia=Maia>>M=M2.
Platelet=7,000=700=70%=P7.0D=7.0=Language=Assets=Mars=7 July=Pleiades.
Platen=10,000=1,000=100%=10.0=Physicality=Tech.=10 Oct.=Uranus=P=1Ø.
Plate tectonics=10,000=1,000=100%=10.0=Physicality=Tech.=10 Oct.=Uranus=P=1Ø.
Platform=10,000=1,000=100%=10.0=Physicality=Tech.=10 Oct.=Uranus=P=1Ø.
Plath Sylvia=2,000=20%=P2.00D=2.0=Nature=Matter=Moon=2 Feb.=Cupid=N=C+_
Plating=7,000=70%=P7.0D=7.0=Language=Assets=Mars=7 July=Pleiades.
Platinum=10,000=1,000=100%=10.0=Physicality=Tech.=10 Oct.=Uranus=P=1Ø.
Platitude=6,000=60%=P6.0D=Man=Earth=Royalty=6 June=Gaia=Maia>>M=M2.
Plato=3,000=30%=P3.0D=3.0=Creativity=Stars=Muses=3 March = C=I>>GIL.
Platonic=6,000=60%=P6.0D=Man=Earth=Royalty=6 June=Gaia=Maia>>M=M2.
Platoon=8,500=9,000=90%=P9.00D=9.0=Abstraction=Gods=Saturn=9Sept.>>A=Ø.
Platte=9,000=90%=P9.00D=9.0=Abstraction=Gods=Saturn=9Sept.>>A=Ø.
Platter=6,000=60%=P6.0D=Man=Earth=Royalty=6 June=Gaia=Maia>>M=M2.
Platypus=10,000=1,000=100%=10.0=Physicality=Tech.=10 Oct.=Uranus=P=1Ø.
Plaudit=4,500=5,000=50%=P5.00D=Law=Time=Venus=5 May = Aphrodite>>L=N.
Plausible=5,500=5.5=80%=P5.50D=Earth-Midway=5 May = Gaia.
Plautus Titus=4,000=40%=P4.0D=Govt.=Creatocracy=4 April=Hermes=G=A4.

Play=10,000=1,000=100%=10.0=Physicality=Tech.=10 Oct.=Uranus=P=1Ø.
The Creatocracy Republic by Peter Matthews-Akukalia contains 20 plays and 2 prose(s).
The style of his writing in the Old Shakespearean English without prior learning makes
him the African Shakespeare. A feat he achieved in 2011 for his Sword of Honour - Days
of St. Valentine. The first work internationally published. A single unit book. Later in
The Creatocracy Republic, Sword was reloaded to match with his Creatocratic standards.
He then emerged as Dragon Lord of the Skies, God of Creatocracy Genius and Mind.

Playa=9,000=90%=P9.00D=9.0=Abstraction=Gods=Saturn=9Sept.>>A=Ø.
Play-act=6,500=7,000=70%=P7.0D=7.0=Language=Assets=Mars=7 July=Pleiades.
Playback=4,000=40%=P4.0D=Govt.=Creatocracy=4 April=Mercury=Hermes=G=A4.
Playbill=2,500=3,000=30%=P3.0D=3.0=Creativity=Stars=Muses=3 March = C=I>>GIL.
Playboy=4,000=40%=P4.0D=Govt.=Creatocracy=4 April=Mercury=Hermes=G=A4.
Play-by-play=5,500=5.5=80%=P5.50D=Earth-Midway=5 May = Gaia.
Player=8,500=9,000=90%=P9.00D=9.0=Abstraction=Gods=Saturn=9Sept.>>A=Ø.
Player piano=7,500=8,000=80%=P8.0D=Economy=Currency=8 Aug.=Zeus>>E=v.
Playful=3,000=30%=P3.0D=3.0=Creativity=Stars=Muses=3 March = C=I>>GIL.

Play girl=4,000=40%=P4.0D=Govt.=Creatocracy=4 April=Mercury=Hermes=G=A4.
Playgoer=2,500=3,000=30%=P3.0D=3.0=Creativity=Stars=Muses=3 March = C=I>>GIL.
Playground=3,500=4,000=40%=P4.0D=Govt.=Creatocracy=4 April=Hermes=G=A4.
Playing card=8,500=9,000=90%=P9.00D=9.0=Abstraction=Gods=Saturn=9Sept.>>A=Ø.
Playmate=2,000=20%=P2.00D=2.0=Nature=Matter=Moon=2 Feb.=Cupid=N=C+_
Playoff=7,000=70%=P7.0D=7.0=Language=Assets=Mars=7 July=Pleiades.
Playpen=5,500=5.5=80%=P5.50=Earth-Midway=5 May = Gaia.
Playroom=3,500=4,000=40%=P4.0D=Govt.=Creatocracy=4 April=Hermes=G=A4.
Plaything=1,000=100%=10.0=1.0=Mind=Sun=1 January=Helios >> M=E4.

Playwright=2,000=20%=P2.00D=2.0=Nature=Matter=Moon=2 Feb.=Cupid=N=C+_
One who writes plays. Playwrights are people of nature. Their style is their method. Peter Matthews-Akukalia became African Shakespeare for being the first African to write a play in the Old Shakespearean English. Sword of Honour: Days of St. Valentine was the play. Then he emerged Dragon Lord of the Sky for the book The Creatocracy Republic which combined twenty books in one. 19 plays+1 Propolay +2 Short Stories = 22.

Plaza=10,000=1,000=100%=10.0=Physicality=Tech.=10 Oct.=Uranus=P=1Ø.
Plea=10,000=1,000=100%=10.0=Physicality=Tech.=10 Oct.=Uranus=P=1Ø.
Plea bargain=10,000=1,000=100%=10.0=Physicality=Tech.=10 Oct.=Uranus=P=1Ø.
Plead=10,000=1,000=100%=10.0=Physicality=Tech.=10 Oct.=Uranus=P=1Ø.
Pleasant=4,000=40%=P4.0D=Govt.=Creatocracy=4 April=Mercury=Hermes=G=A4.
Pleasantry=2,500=3,000=30%=P3.0D=3.0=Creativity=Stars=Muses=3 March = C=I>>GIL.
Please=10,000=1,000=100%=10.0=Physicality=Tech.=10 Oct.=Uranus=P=1Ø.
Pleasurable=1,000=100%=Physicality=Tech.=10 Oct.=Uranus=P=1Ø.
Pleasure=6,000=60%=P6.0D=Man=Earth=Royalty=6 June=Gaia=Maia>>M=M2.
Pleat=6,000=60%=P6.0D=Man=Earth=Royalty=6 June=Gaia=Maia>>M=M2.
Plebe=3,500=4,000=40%=P4.0D=Govt.=Creatocracy=4 April=Mercury=Hermes=G=A4.
Plebeian=7,000=70%=P7.0D=7.0=Language=Assets=Mars=7 July=Pleiades.
Plebiscite=6,500=7,000=70%=P7.0D=7.0=Language=Assets=Mars=7 July=Pleiades.
Plebs=4,500=5,000=50%=P5.00D=Law=Time=Venus=5 May = Aphrodite>>L=N.
Plectrum=10,000=1,000=100%=10.0=Physicality=Tech.=10 Oct.=Uranus=P=1Ø.
Pled=3,000=30%=P3.0D=3.0=Creativity=Stars=Muses=3 March = C=I>>GIL.
Pledge=10,000=1,000=100%=10.0=Physicality=Tech.=10 Oct.=Uranus=P=1Ø.

Pleiades=11,000=11%=P1.10D=1.1=Idea=Brainchild=Inv.=11 Nov.=SC=Athena>>I=MT. Greek myth teaches that the Pleiades are a group of seven sisters headed by Maia the Great Goddess and mother of Hermes whom we know as Khristos >> Christ Jesus. The Almighty GOD Himself in a conversation with Job mentioned them as sweet influences that overwhelm Him. Job 38:31. Peter Matthews-Akukalia tracked them to be the Mind of GOD (Romans 11:33-35) that we are required to find through wisdom and be adopted to wit (Romans 8:17-23). And Jesus instructs that man shall not live by bread alone but by every word that proceeds out of the mouth of the GOD. Now Computational creativity,

Mind Computing, Makumatics and Makumaticology of the Creative Sciences have confirmed that the Pleiades function under the jurisdiction of Athena the brainchild of the almighty GOD Zeus Jehovah Allah >> ZeJeAl. Athena the Goddess of wisdom personified was there from the beginning of all things. Proverbs 8, 9. This is why Athena as wisdom is the custodian of the knowledge and riches of ZeJeAl. Wisdom is the principal thing means understand Athena first. In all thy getting get understanding means that computational precision brings the Mind of GOD to you. Then GOD comes to you. Now we establish the link between Greek mythology the bible, astronomy and the Creative Sciences thus making the Creatocracy.

Pleistocene=10,000=1,000=100%=10.0=Physicality=Tech.=10 Oct.=Uranus=P=1Ø.

Plenary=8,000=80%=P8.0D=Economy=Currency=8 Aug.=Zeus>>E=v.

Plenipotentiary=9,000=90%=P9.00D=9.0=Abstraction=Gods=Saturn=9Sept.>>A=Ø.

Plenitude=3,000=30%=P3.0D=3.0=Creativity=Stars=Muses=3 March = C=I>>GIL.

Plenteous=6,000=60%=P6.0D=Man=Earth=Royalty=6 June=Gaia=Maia>>M=M2.

Plentiful=10,000=1,000=100%=10.0=Physicality=Tech.=10 Oct.=Uranus=P=1Ø.

Plenty=11,000=11%=P1.10D=1.1=Idea=Brainchild=Inv.=11 Nov.=SC=Athena>>I=MT.

Plethora=2,500=3,000=30%=P3.0D=3.0=Creativity=Stars=Muses=3 March = C=I>>GIL.

Pleurisy=6,500=7,000=70%=P7.0D=7.0=Language=Assets=Mars=7 July=Pleiades.

Plexiglass=3,500=4,000=40%=P4.0D=Govt.=Creatocracy=4 April=Hermes=G=A4.

Plexus=8,000=80%=P8.0D=Economy=Currency=8 Aug.=Zeus>>E=v.

plf.=1,500=15%=P1.50D=1.5=Authority=Solar Crown=1 May = Maia.

Pliable=5,000=50%=P5.00D=Law=Time=Venus=5 May = Aphrodite>>L=N.

Pliant=6,000=60%=P6.0D=Man=Earth=Royalty=6 June=Gaia=Maia>>M=M2.

Pliers=6,500=7,000=70%=P7.0D=7.0=Language=Assets=Mars=7 July=Pleiades.

Plight1=4,000=40%=P4.0D=Govt.=Creatocracy=4 April=Mercury=Hermes=G=A4.

Plight2=8,500=9,000=90%=P9.00D=9.0=Abstraction=Gods=Saturn=9Sept.>>A=Ø.

Plinth=7,000=70%=P7.0D=7.0=Language=Assets=Mars=7 July=Pleiades.

Pliny1=5,000=50%=P5.00D=Law=Time=Venus=5 May = Aphrodite>>L=N.

Pliny2=5,500=5.5=80%=P5.50=Earth-Midway=5 May = Gaia.

Pliocene=11,000=11%=P1.10D=1.1=Idea=Brainchild=Inv.=11 Nov.=SC=Athena>>I=MT.

PLO=1,500=15%=P1.50D=1.5=Authority=Solar Crown=1 May = Maia.

Plod=10,000=1,000=100%=10.0=Physicality=Tech.=10 Oct.=Uranus=P=1Ø.

Plop=10,000=1,000=100%=10.0=Physicality=Tech.=10 Oct.=Uranus=P=1Ø.

Plot=10,000=1,000=100%=10.0=Physicality=Tech.=10 Oct.=Uranus=P=1Ø.

Plough=1,500=15%=P1.50D=1.5=Authority=Solar Crown=1 May = Maia.

Plovdiv=5,000=50%=P5.00D=Law=Time=Venus=5 May = Aphrodite>>L=N.

Plover=8,000=80%=P8.0D=Economy=Currency=8 Aug.=Zeus>>E=v.

Plow=10,000=1,000=100%=10.0=Physicality=Tech.=10 Oct.=Uranus=P=1Ø.

Plowshare=3,000=30%=P3.0D=3.0=Creativity=Stars=Muses=3 March = C=I>>GIL.

Ploy=3,500=4,000=40%=P4.0D=Govt.=Creatocracy=4 April=Mercury=Hermes=G=A4.

Pluck=10,000=1,000=100%=10.0=Physicality=Tech.=10 Oct.=Uranus=P=1Ø.

Plucky=1,000=100%=10.0=1.0=Mind=Sun=1 January=Helios >> M=E4.

Plug=10,000=1,000=100%=10.0=Physicality=Tech.=10 Oct.=Uranus=P=1Ø.

Plum=10,000=1,000=100%=10.0=Physicality=Tech.=10 Oct.=Uranus=P=1Ø.
Plumage=2,500=3,000=30%=P3.0D=3.0=Creativity=Stars=Muses=3 March = C=I>>GIL.
Plumb=10,000=1,000=100%=10.0=Physicality=Tech.=10 Oct.=Uranus=P=1Ø.
Plumber=4,000=40%=P4.0D=Govt.=Creatocracy=4 April=Mercury=Hermes=G=A4.
Plumbing=10,000=1,000=100%=10.0=Physicality=Tech.=10 Oct.=Uranus=P=1Ø.
Plumb line=6,000=60%=P6.0D=Man=Earth=Royalty=6 June=Gaia=Maia>>M=M2.
Plume=10,000=1,000=100%=10.0=Physicality=Tech.=10 Oct.=Uranus=P=1Ø.
Plummet=4,500=5,000=50%=P5.00D=Law=Time=Venus=5 May = Aphrodite>>L=N.
Plump1=8,000=80%=P8.0D=Economy=Currency=8 Aug.=Zeus>>E=v.
Plump2=10,000=1,000=100%=10.0=Physicality=Tech.=10 Oct.=Uranus=P=1Ø.
Plunder=9,000=90%=P9.00D=9.0=Abstraction=Gods=Saturn=9Sept.>>A=Ø.
Plunge=10,000=1,000=100%=10.0=Physicality=Tech.=10 Oct.=Uranus=P=1Ø.
Plunger=10,000=1,000=100%=10.0=Physicality=Tech.=10 Oct.=Uranus=P=1Ø.
Plunk=10,000=1,000=100%=10.0=Physicality=Tech.=10 Oct.=Uranus=P=1Ø.
Pluperfect=10,000=1,000=100%=10.0=Physicality=Tech.=10 Oct.=Uranus=P=1Ø.
Plural=10,000=1,000=100%=10.0=Physicality=Tech.=10 Oct.=Uranus=P=1Ø.
Pluralism=8,000=80%=P8.0D=Economy=Currency=8 Aug.=Zeus>>E=v.
Plurality=10,000=1,000=100%=10.0=Physicality=Tech.=10 Oct.=Uranus=P=1Ø.

Plus=10,000=1,000=100%=10.0=Physicality=Tech.=10 Oct.=Uranus=P=1Ø.
A constant in the dynamics of Mind Computing invented by Peter Matthews-Akukalia.

Plush=5,000=50%=P5.00D=Law=Time=Venus=5 May = Aphrodite>>L=N.
Plutarch=4,000=40%=P4.0D=Govt.=Creatocracy=4 April=Mercury=Hermes=G=A4.
Pluto=10,000=1,000=100%=10.0=Physicality=Tech.=10 Oct.=Uranus=P=1Ø.

Plutocracy=8,000=80%=P8.0D=Economy=Currency=8 Aug.=Zeus>>E=v.
Government by the wealthy. A wealthy class that controls a government. Greek < ploutos, wealth + -CRACY. We would infer that Pluto as a planet is the source of cosmic wealth perhaps very rich in minerals. This is speculative. In Greek myth He is the God of the underworld. Also called Hades. One is tempted to ask if hell, associated with Hades is actually the planet Pluto or located there? The Creatocracy is a system of government driven by creative intelligence drawn from computational precision where the resources employed to run the economy are based on the endless innate potentials in the citizens. First these potentials are founded on the works of the author inventor founder owner and God of Creatocracy Genius and Mind Peter Matthews-Akukalia, Castle Makupedia.

Plutonic=4,000=40%=P4.0D=Govt.=Creatocracy=4 April=Mercury=Hermes=G=A4.
Plutonium=11,500=12,000=12%=P1.20D=1.2=Knowledge=Edu=12Dec.=Athena>>K=F.
Pluvial=5,000=50%=P5.00D=Law=Time=Venus=5 May = Aphrodite>>L=N.
Ply1=10,000=1,000=100%=10.0=Physicality=Tech.=10 Oct.=Uranus=P=1Ø.
Ply2=10,000=1,000=100%=10.0=Physicality=Tech.=10 Oct.=Uranus=P=1Ø.
Plymouth=10,000=1,000=100%=10.0=Physicality=Tech.=10 Oct.=Uranus=P=1Ø.

Plywood=4,500=5,000=50%=P5.00D=Law=Time=Venus=5 May = Aphrodite>>L=N.
Pm=2,500=3,000=30%=P3.0D=3.0=Creativity=Stars=Muses=3 March = C=I>>GIL.

PM=3,500=4,000=40%=P4.0D=Govt.=Creatocracy=4 April=Mercury=Hermes=G=A4.
Peter Matthews (formally) now Peter Matthews-Akukalia.

---

p.m.=500=5%=P5.00D=5.0=Law=Time=Venus=5 May=Aphrodite>>L=N.
P.M.=4,500=5,000=50%=P5.00D=Law=Time=Venus=5 May = Aphrodite>>L=N.
pmk.=1,000=100%=10.0=1.0=Mind=Sun=1 January=Helios >> M=E4.
PMS=1,000=100%=10.0=1.0=Mind=Sun=1 January=Helios >> M=E4.
p.n.=1,000=100%=10.0=1.0=Mind=Sun=1 January=Helios >> M=E4.
Pneumatic=8,500=9,000=90%=P9.00D=9.0=Abstraction=Gods=Saturn=9Sept.>>A=Ø.
Pneumococcus=5,000=50%=P5.00D=Law=Time=Venus=5 May = Aphrodite>>L=N.
Pneumonia=13,000=13%=P1.30=Solar Core=Faculty=13 January=Athena.
Po1=7,500=8,000=80%=P8.0D=Economy=Currency=8 Aug.=Zeus>>E=v.
Po2=2,500=3,000=30%=P3.0D=3.0=Creativity=Stars=Muses=3 March = C=I>>GIL.
PO=4,000=40%=P4.0D=Govt.=Creatocracy=4 April=Mercury=Hermes=G=A4.
Poach1=7,000=70%=P7.0D=7.0=Language=Assets=Mars=7 July=Pleiades.
Poach2=10,000=1,000=100%=10.0=Physicality=Tech.=10 Oct.=Uranus=P=1Ø.

Pocahontas=2,500=3,000=30%=P3.0D=3.0=Creativity=Stars=Muses=3 March = C=I.
1595?-1617. Powhatan Princess. CASTLE MAKUPEDIA>> World Creatocracy
Encyclopedia & Computed Dictionary. By Peter K. Matthews-Akukalia. This book
will lead to the creation of many institutions such as the Creatocracy Bank, Creatocracy
Corporations in government and private as Ministry of Creativity, Schools for Creatocratic
Studies and Departments of Creatocratic Studies in conventional institutions such as
Journalism institutes, mass communication & media, the arts, linguistics, law, political
sciences, economics, mathematics, Psychology,education and business opportunities etc.

Pocatello=5,000=50%=P5.00D=Law=Time=Venus=5 May = Aphrodite>>L=N.
Pock=11,000=11%=P1.10D=1.1=Idea=Brainchild=Inv.=11 Nov.=SC=Athena>>I=MT.
Pocket=10,000=1,000=100%=10.0=Physicality=Tech.=10 Oct.=Uranus=P=1Ø.
Pocketbook=3,000=30%=P3.0D=3.0=Creativity=Stars=Muses=3 March = C=I>>GIL.
Pocketknife=8,000=80%=P8.0D=Economy=Currency=8 Aug.=Zeus>>E=v.
Pocket veto=7,000=70%=P7.0D=7.0=Language=Assets=Mars=7 July=Pleiades.
Pockmark=6,500=7,000=70%=P7.0D=7.0=Language=Assets=Mars=7 July=Pleiades.
Poco=5,000=50%=P5.00D=Law=Time=Venus=5 May = Aphrodite>>L=N.
Pod1=12,500=13,000=13%=P1.30=Solar Core=Faculty=13 January=Athena.
Pod2=5,500=5.5=80%=P5.50=Earth-Midway=5 May = Gaia.
-pod=5,000=50%=P5.00D=Law=Time=Venus=5 May = Aphrodite>>L=N.
Podiatry=8,500=9,000=90%=P9.00D=9.0=Abstraction=Gods=Saturn=9Sept.>>A=Ø.
Podium=9,000=90%=P9.00D=9.0=Abstraction=Gods=Saturn=9Sept.>>A=Ø.

Poe Edgar Allan=2,500=3,000=30%=P3.0D=3.0=Creativity=Stars=Muses=3 March=C=I. 1809-49. American gothic writer. Peter Matthews-Akukalia 1978-Date. Nigerian Disean writer. He wrote and founded the Paradise or Disean Nations.

POE=1,500=15%=P1.50D=1.5=Authority=Solar Crown=1 May = Maia.

Poem=10,000=1,000=100%=10.0=Physicality=Tech.=10 Oct.=Uranus=P=1Ø.
An invention in the Creatocratic Mind Arts is the count of words and lines. Peter Matthews-Akukalia applied the 10,000 quantum mechanics to poetry and invented the Nidrapoe. The first of this is his work >> MAKUPEDIALAND: A Disean City of Testamentary Poetry.

Poesy=2,000=20%=P2.00D=2.0=Nature=Matter=Moon=2 Feb.=Cupid=N=C+_
Poetry < Greek poiēsis, creation. Peter Matthews-Akukalia invented the Nidrapoe a genre of literature based on testaments. See the book >> Makupedialand, a Disean city of testamentary poetry by Peter Matthews-Akukalia, Castle Makupedia. It contains over 550 poems divided into about 5 - 7 sections. Nidrapoe means Nigerian-Drama styled poetry.

Poet=3,500=4,000=40%=P4.0D=Govt.=Creocracy=4 April=Mercury=Hermes=G=A4.
Peter Matthews-Akukalia is a natural born poet.

Poet aster=4,000=40%=P4.0D=Govt.=Creatocracy=4 April=Mercury=Hermes=G=A4.
Poetess=5,000=50%=P5.00D=Law=Time=Venus=5 May = Aphrodite>>L=N.
Poetic=2,500=3,000=30%=P3.0D=3.0=Creativity=Stars=Muses=3 March = C=I>>GIL.
Poetic justice=7,000=70%=P7.0D=7.0=Language=Assets=Mars=7 July=Pleiades.

Poetic license=10,000=1,000=100%=10.0=Physicality=Tech.=10 Oct.=Uranus=P=1Ø.
The liberty taken by an artist or a writer in deviating from conventional form or fact to achieve a desired effect. The word Creatocracy is the product of poetic license of Peter Matthews-Akukalia, Castle Makupedia. Before he invented the Creative Sciences he had done so much poetry and play writing that he bumped literally into computing the words. Then interest into energy particles began to grow in him and the rest is history. See Poesy.

Poet laureate=10,000=1,000=100%=10.0=Physicality=Tech.=10 Oct.=Uranus=P=1Ø.
A poet appointed for life by a British monarch as chief poet of the kingdom. A poet appointed to a similar honorary position. In his book Legends of the Monarchs Peter Matthews-Akukalia as African Shakespeare made a poem for London and the Monarchy a dream destination for him. See the book>> The Creatocracy Republic, Plays Legends and Short Stories by Peter Matthews-Akukalia. Reference book is Legend of the Monarchs, a Play on William Shakespeare.

Poetry=10,000=1,000=100%=10.0=Physicality=Tech.=10 Oct.=Uranus=P=1Ø.
The Creatocracy has a section of Mind Arts which includes poetry.

Pogrom=5,000=50%=P5.00D=Law=Time=Venus=5 May = Aphrodite>>L=N.
Po Hai=1,500=15%=P1.50D=1.5=Authority=Solar Crown=1 May = Maia.
Poi=6,500=7,000=70%=P7.0D=7.0=Language=Assets=Mars=7 July=Pleiades.
Poignant=8,500=9,000=90%=P9.00D=9.0=Abstraction=Gods=Saturn=9Sept.>>A=Ø.
Poi kilo therm=10,000=1,000=100%=10.0=Physicality=Tech.=10 Oct.=Uranus=P=1Ø.
Poinciana=10,000=1,000=100%=10.0=Physicality=Tech.=10 Oct.=Uranus=P=1Ø.
Poinsettia=10,000=1,000=100%=10.0=Physicality=Tech.=10 Oct.=Uranus=P=1Ø.
Point=10,000=1,000=100%=10.0=Physicality=Tech.=10 Oct.=Uranus=P=1Ø.

Point-blank=7,500=8,000=80%=P8.0D=Economy=Currency=8 Aug.=Zeus>>E=v.
One of the poems of Peter Matthews-Akukalia. See Poesy. Book is Makupedialand.

Pointed=10,000=1,000=100%=10.0=Physicality=Tech.=10 Oct.=Uranus=P=1Ø.
Pointer=10,000=1,000=100%=10.0=Physicality=Tech.=10 Oct.=Uranus=P=1Ø.
Pointillism=9,000=90%=P9.00D=9.0=Abstraction=Gods=Saturn=9Sept.>>A=Ø.
Pointless=1,000=100%=10.0=1.0=Mind=Sun=1 January=Helios >> M=E4.
Point-of-sale=5,000=50%=P5.00D=Law=Time=Venus=5 May = Aphrodite>>L=N.
Point of view=7,000=70%=P7.0D=7.0=Language=Assets=Mars=7 July=Pleiades.
Poise=8,000=80%=P8.0D=Economy=Currency=8 Aug.=Zeus>>E=v.
Poison=10,000=1,000=100%=10.0=Physicality=Tech.=10 Oct.=Uranus=P=1Ø.
Poison hemlock=7,000=70%=P7.0D=7.0=Language=Assets=Mars=7 July=Pleiades.
Poison ivy=7,500=8,000=80%=P8.0D=Economy=Currency=8 Aug.=Zeus>>E=v.
Poison oak=10,000=1,000=100%=10.0=Physicality=Tech.=10 Oct.=Uranus=P=1Ø.
Poison sumac=8,000=80%=P8.0D=Economy=Currency=8 Aug.=Zeus>>E=v.
Poke1=10,000=1,000=100%=10.0=Physicality=Tech.=10 Oct.=Uranus=P=1Ø.
Poke2=3,000=30%=P3.0D=3.0=Creativity=Stars=Muses=3 March = C=I>>GIL.
Poker1=3,500=4,000=40%=P4.0D=Govt.=Creatocracy=4 April=Mercury=Hermes=G=A4.
Poker2=10,000=1,000=100%=10.0=Physicality=Tech.=10 Oct.=Uranus=P=1Ø.
Pokeweed=10,000=1,000=100%=10.0=Physicality=Tech.=10 Oct.=Uranus=P=1Ø.
Pokey=2,000=20%=P2.00D=2.0=Nature=Matter=Moon=2 Feb.=Cupid=N=C+_
Poky=2,000=20%=P2.00D=2.0=Nature=Matter=Moon=2 Feb.=Cupid=N=C+_
Pol=1,500=15%=P1.50D=1.5=Authority=Solar Crown=1 May = Maia.
Poland=7,000=70%=P7.0D=7.0=Language=Assets=Mars=7 July=Pleiades.
Polar=10,000=1,000=100%=10.0=Physicality=Tech.=10 Oct.=Uranus=P=1Ø.
Polar bear=3,500=4,000=40%=P4.0D=Govt.=Creatocracy=4 April=Hermes=G=A4.
Polaris=7,000=70%=P7.0D=7.0=Language=Assets=Mars=7 July=Pleiades.
Polarity=10,000=1,000=100%=10.0=Physicality=Tech.=10 Oct.=Uranus=P=1Ø.
Polarize=10,000=1,000=100%=10.0=Physicality=Tech.=10 Oct.=Uranus=P=1Ø.
Polaroid™=10,000=1,000=100%=10.0=Physicality=Tech.=10 Oct.=Uranus=P=1Ø.
Polar Regions=10,000=1,000=100%=10.0=Physicality=Tech.=10 Oct.=Uranus=P=1Ø.
Pole1=10,000=1,000=100%=10.0=Physicality=Tech.=10 Oct.=Uranus=P=1Ø.

Pole2=10,000=1,000=100%=10.0=Physicality=Tech.=10 Oct.=Uranus=P=1Ø.
Pole=4,000=40%=P4.0D=Govt.=Creatocracy=4 April=Mercury=Hermes=G=A4.
Poleax=3,500=4,000=40%=P4.0D=Govt.=Creatocracy=4 April=Mercury=Hermes=G=A4.
Polecat=4,000=40%=P4.0D=Govt.=Creatocracy=4 April=Mercury=Hermes=G=A4.
Polemic=9,500=10,000=1,000=100%=10.0=Physicality=Tech.=10 Oct.=Uranus=P=1Ø.
Polestar=1,000=100%=10.0=1.0=Mind=Sun=1 January=Helios >> M=E4.
Pole vault=8,000=80%=P8.0D=Economy=Currency=8 Aug.=Zeus>>E=v.

Police=10,000=1,000=100%=10.0=Physicality=Tech.=10 Oct.=Uranus=P=1Ø.
The minimum standard for any police force is 10,000=1,000=100=10

Police dog=3,000=30%=P3.0D=3.0=Creativity=Stars=Muses=3 March = C=I>>GIL.
Police force=1,500=15%=P1.50D=1.5=Authority=Solar Crown=1 May = Maia.
Policeman=6,000=60%=P6.0D=Man=Earth=Royalty=6 June=Gaia=Maia>>M=M2.
Police state=9,000=90%=P9.00D=9.0=Abstraction=Gods=Saturn=9Sept.>>A=Ø.
Police station=3,000=30%=P3.0D=3.0=Creativity=Stars=Muses=3 March = C=I>>GIL.
Police woman=6,500=7,000=70%=P7.0D=7.0=Language=Assets=Mars=7 July=Pleiades.
Policy1=10,000=1,000=100%=10.0=Physicality=Tech.=10 Oct.=Uranus=P=1Ø.
Policy2=5,000=50%=P5.00D=Law=Time=Venus=5 May = Aphrodite>>L=N.
Policy making=4,000=40%=P4.0D=Govt.=Creatocracy=4 April=Mercury=Hermes=G=A4.
Polio=500=5%=P5.00D=5.0=Law=Time=Venus=5 May=Aphrodite>>L=N.
Poliomyelitis=10,000=1,000=100%=10.0=Physicality=Tech.=10 Oct.=Uranus=P=1Ø.
polish=10,000=1,000=100%=10.0=Physicality=Tech.=10 Oct.=Uranus=P=1Ø.
Polish=6,000=60%=P6.0D=Man=Earth=Royalty=6 June=Gaia=Maia>>M=M2.
Politburo=5,500=5.5=80%=P5.50=Earth-Midway=5 May = Gaia.
Polite=6,500=7,000=70%=P7.0D=7.0=Language=Assets=Mars=7 July=Pleiades.
Politesse=1,000=100%=10.0=1.0=Mind=Sun=1 January=Helios >> M=E4.
Politic=3,500=4,000=40%=P4.0D=Govt.=Creatocracy=4 April=Mercury=Hermes=G=A4.
Political=6,000=60%=P6.0D=Man=Earth=Royalty=6 June=Gaia=Maia>>M=M2.
Political science=5,500=5.5=80%=P5.50=Earth-Midway=5 May = Gaia.
Politician=6,000=60%=P6.0D=Man=Earth=Royalty=6 June=Gaia=Maia>>M=M2.

Politicize=1,500=15%=P1.50D=1.5=Authority=Solar Crown=1 May = Maia.
It is in the attitude of Maia to politicize things hence she functions under the jurisdiction of Athena. This means that wisdom is a basic requirement in politics. See Pleiades.

Politick=3,000=30%=P3.0D=3.0=Creativity=Stars=Muses=3 March = C=I>>GIL.
To engage in or discuss politics. The Creatocracy of things is the true politick in things.

Politico=3,000=30%=P3.0D=3.0=Creativity=Stars=Muses=3 March = C=I>>GIL.
Politics=10,000=1,000=100%=10.0=Physicality=Tech.=10 Oct.=Uranus=P=1Ø.
Polity=7,000=70%=P7.0D=7.0=Language=Assets=Mars=7 July=Pleiades.

Polk James Knox.=7,500=8,000=80%=P8.0D=Economy=Currency=8 Aug.=Zeus>>E=v. James K. Polk. 1795-1849. The 11th U.S. President. Peter Kanayochukwu Matthews-Akukalia >> Peter K. Matthews-Akukalia. President, De-Royal Makupedia Limited. Most Sovereign Emperor, Creatocratic Nations of Paradise. Owner, The Creatocracy.

Polka=7,500=8,000=80%=P8.0D=Economy=Currency=8 Aug.=Zeus>>E=v.
Polka dot=4,500=5,000=50%=P5.00D=Law=Time=Venus=5 May = Aphrodite>>L=N.
Poll=10,000=1,000=100%=10.0=Physicality=Tech.=10 Oct.=Uranus=P=1Ø.
Pollack=5,000=50%=P5.00D=Law=Time=Venus=5 May = Aphrodite>>L=N.
Pollen=9,500=10,000=1,000=100%=10.0=Physicality=Tech.=10 Oct.=Uranus=P=1Ø.
Pollinate=6,000=60%=P6.0D=Man=Earth=Royalty=6 June=Gaia=Maia>>M=M2.
Pollinosis=1,500=15%=P1.50D=1.5=Authority=Solar Crown=1 May = Maia.
Polliwog=2,000=20%=P2.00D=2.0=Nature=Matter=Moon=2 Feb.=Cupid=N=C+_
Pollock Jackson.=2,000=20%=P2.00D=2.0=Nature=Matter=Moon=2 Feb.=Cupid=N=C+_
Pollster=3,000=30%=P3.0D=3.0=Creativity=Stars=Muses=3 March = C=I>>GIL.
Poll tax=6,500=7,000=70%=P7.0D=7.0=Language=Assets=Mars=7 July=Pleiades.
Pollute=10,000=1,000=100%=10.0=Physicality=Tech.=10 Oct.=Uranus=P=1Ø.

Pollux=3,500=4,000=40%=P4.0D=Govt.=Creatocracy=4 April=Mercury=Hermes=G=A4. A bright star in the constellation Gemini. Stars are muses. Gemini is a higher muse. The Creatocracy defines this as the fact that smaller muses exist within the higher muses. Pollux are lesser ranked muses that works as means of power and connect relationships.

---

polo=11,000=11%=P1.10D=1.1=Idea=Brainchild=Inv.=11 Nov.=SC=Athena>>I=MT.
Polo Marco.=3,000=30%=P3.0D=3.0=Creativity=Stars=Muses=3 March = C=I>>GIL.
Polonaise=8,000=80%=P8.0D=Economy=Currency=8 Aug.=Zeus>>E=v.
Polonium=10,000=1,000=100%=10.0=Physicality=Tech.=10 Oct.=Uranus=P=1Ø.
Polo shirt=2,500=3,000=30%=P3.0D=3.0=Creativity=Stars=Muses=3 March = C=I>>GIL.
Poltergeist=3,000=30%=P3.0D=3.0=Creativity=Stars=Muses=3 March = C=I>>GIL.
Poltroon=2,500=3,000=30%=P3.0D=3.0=Creativity=Stars=Muses=3 March = C=I>>GIL.
Poly-=8,000=80%=P8.0D=Economy=Currency=8 Aug.=Zeus>>E=v.
Polyandry=5,500=5.5=80%=P5.50=Earth-Midway=5 May = Gaia.
Polychrome=3,000=30%=P3.0D=3.0=Creativity=Stars=Muses=3 March = C=I>>GIL.
Polyclinic=4,000=40%=P4.0D=Govt.=Creatocracy=4 April=Mercury=Hermes=G=A4.
Polydipsia=4,000=40%=P4.0D=Govt.=Creatocracy=4 April=Mercury=Hermes=G=A4.
Polyester=6,000=60%=P6.0D=Man=Earth=Royalty=6 June=Gaia=Maia>>M=M2.
Polyethylene=6,000=60%=P6.0D=Man=Earth=Royalty=6 June=Gaia=Maia>>M=M2.

Polygamy=6,000=60%=P6.0D=Man=Earth=Royalty=6 June=Gaia=Maia>>M=M2. Acceptable in the Makstian Faith and the Creatocracy as a whole.
Whoso findeth a wife findeth a good thing, and obtaineth favor of the LORD.
-Proverbs 18:22. Now the use of "a" shows it is not specific to one woman. A single definite marriage would apply "the" woman instead of "a" woman. Therefore polygamy

is not a sin but a higher responsibility most times meant as a sign of blessings for royalty and well meaning men as was granted to Joseph in Genesis 49:25. Assuming a man has two wives let us compute and see if they shall be one flesh. Man=6.0, 1st Wife=6.0. 2nd wife.=6.0. Now Man & 1st wife = 1.0. Man & 2nd wife = 1.0 1.0*1.0x=px=2+1=3x=px=5=500=50%=50/100=1/2=0.5=1.0

In polygamy they also become one flesh. The word of GOD is proved. Marriage irrespective of how many wives makes the couple one flesh. But two cannot work together if they don't agree hence relationships are based on love (respect & understanding). See Marriage.

Polyglot=8,000=80%=P8.0D=Economy=Currency=8 Aug.=Zeus>>E=v.
Polygon=5,500=5.5=80%=P5.50=Earth-Midway=5 May = Gaia.
Polygraph=10,500=11,000=11%=P1.10D=1.1=Idea=Brainchild=11 Nov.=Athena>>I=MT.
Polygyny=9,000=90%=P9.00D=9.0=Abstraction=Gods=Saturn=9Sept.>>A=Ø.
Polyhedron=3,000=30%=P3.0D=3.0=Creativity=Stars=Muses=3 March = C=I>>GIL.
Polymath=4,500=5,000=50%=P5.00D=Law=Time=Venus=5 May = Aphrodite>>L=N.
Polymer=10,000=1,000=100%=10.0=Physicality=Tech.=10 Oct.=Uranus=P=1Ø.
Polymerase=5,500=5.5=80%=P5.50=Earth-Midway=5 May = Gaia.
Polymerize=4,500=5,000=50%=P5.00D=Law=Time=Venus=5 May = Aphrodite>>L=N.
Polynesia=10,000=1,000=100%=10.0=Physicality=Tech.=10 Oct.=Uranus=P=1Ø.
Polynesian=10,000=1,000=100%=10.0=Physicality=Tech.=10 Oct.=Uranus=P=1Ø.
Polynomial=10,000=1,000=100%=10.0=Physicality=Tech.=10 Oct.=Uranus=P=1Ø.
Polyp=10,000=1,000=100%=10.0=Physicality=Tech.=10 Oct.=Uranus=P=1Ø.
Polypeptide=4,000=40%=P4.0D=Govt.=Creatocracy=4 April=Mercury=Hermes=G=A4.
Polyphony=5,000=50%=P5.00D=Law=Time=Venus=5 May = Aphrodite>>L=N.
Polysaccharide=6,500=7,000=70%=P7.0D=7.0=Language=Assets=Mars=7 July=Pleiades.
Polystyrene=9,000=90%=P9.00D=9.0=Abstraction=Gods=Saturn=9Sept.>>A=Ø.
Polysyllable=4,000=40%=P4.0D=Govt.=Creatocracy=4 April=Mercury=Hermes=G=A4.
Polytechnic=9,000=90%=P9.00D=9.0=Abstraction=Gods=Saturn=9Sept.>>A=Ø.
Polytheism=5,000=50%=P5.00D=Law=Time=Venus=5 May = Aphrodite>>L=N.
Polyunsaturated=6,000=60%=P6.0D=Man=Earth=Royalty=6 June=Gaia=Maia>>M=M2.
Polyurethane=8,500=9,000=90%=P9.00D=9.0=Abstraction=Gods=Saturn=9Sept.>>A=Ø.
Polyvalent=10,000=1,000=100%=10.0=Physicality=Tech.=10 Oct.=Uranus=P=1Ø.
Polyvinyl chloride=500=5%=P5.00D=5.0=Law=Time=Venus=5 May=Aphrodite>>L=N.
Pomade=3,500=4,000=40%=P4.0D=Govt.=4 April=Mercury=Hermes=G=A4.
Pomegranate=10,000=1,000=100%=10.0=Physicality=Tech.=10 Oct.=Uranus=P=1Ø.
Pomerania=10,000=1,000=100%=10.0=Physicality=Tech.=10 Oct.=Uranus=P=1Ø.
Pomeranian=10,000=1,000=100%=10.0=Physicality=Tech.=10 Oct.=Uranus=P=1Ø.
Pommel=10,000=1,000=100%=10.0=Physicality=Tech.=10 Oct.=Uranus=P=1Ø.
Pomona=5,000=50%=P5.00D=Law=Time=Venus=5 May = Aphrodite>>L=N.
Pomp=6,000=60%=P6.0D=Man=Earth=Royalty=6 June=Gaia=Maia>>M=M2.
Pompadour=5,000=50%=P5.00D=Law=Time=Venus=5 May = Aphrodite>>L=N.
Pompano=6,500=7,000=70%=P7.0D=7.0=Language=Assets=Mars=7 July=Pleiades.
Pompey II=8,000=80%=P8.0D=Economy=Currency=8 Aug.=Zeus>>E=v.
Pompey=4,000=40%=P4.0D=Govt.=Creatocracy=4 April=Mercury=Hermes=G=A4.

PETER K. MATTHEWS - AKUKALIA

Pompon=10,000=1,000=100%=10.0=Physicality=Tech.=10 Oct.=Uranus=P=1∅.
Pompous=4,500=5,000=50%=P5.00D=Law=Time=Venus=5 May = Aphrodite>>L=N.
Ponce=5,500=5.5=80%=P5.50=Earth-Midway=5 May = Gaia.
Ponce de León=2,500=3,000=30%=P3.0D=3.0=Cre.=Stars=Muses=3 March = C=I>>GIL.
Poncho=9,000=90%=P9.00D=9.0=Abstraction=Gods=Saturn=9Sept.>>A=∅.
Pond=5,500=5.5=80%=P5.50=Earth-Midway=5 May = Gaia.
Ponder=5,500=5.5=80%=P5.50=Earth-Midway=5 May = Gaia.
Ponderosa pine=8,000=80%=P8.0D=Economy=Currency=8 Aug.=Zeus>>E=v.
Ponderous=4,500=5,000=50%=P5.00D=Law=Time=Venus=5 May = Aphrodite>>L=N.
Pone=10,000=1,000=100%=10.0=Physicality=Tech.=10 Oct.=Uranus=P=1∅.
Pongee=8,000=80%=P8.0D=Economy=Currency=8 Aug.=Zeus>>E=v.
Poniard=3,500=4,000=40%=P4.0D=Govt.=Creatocracy=4 April=Mercury=Hermes=G=A4.
Ponta Delgada=6,000=60%=P6.0D=Man=Earth=Royalty=6 June=Gaia=Maia>>M=M2.
Pontiac=4,500=5,000=50%=P5.00D=Law=Time=Venus=5 May = Aphrodite>>L=N.
Pontiff=3,500=4,000=40%=P4.0D=Govt.=Creatocracy=4 April=Hermes=G=A4.
Pontifical=8,000=80%=P8.0D=Economy=Currency=8 Aug.=Zeus>>E=v.
Pontificate=11,000=11%=P1.10D=1.1=Idea=Brainchild=Inv.=11 Nov.=SC=Athena>>I=MT.
Pontoon=9,500=10,000=1,000=100%=10.0=Physicality=Tech.=10 Oct.=Uranus=P=1∅.
Pontus=7,000=70%=P7.0D=7.0=Language=Assets=Mars=7 July=Pleiades.
Pony=12,500=13,000=13%=P1.30=Solar Core=Faculty=13 January=Athena.
Ponytail=9,500=10,000=1,000=100%=10.0=Physicality=Tech.=10 Oct.=Uranus=P=1∅.
Pooch=2,000=20%=P2.00D=2.0=Nature=Matter=Moon=2 Feb.=Cupid=N=C+_
Poodle=7,000=70%=P7.0D=7.0=Language=Assets=Mars=7 July=Pleiades.
Pooh=2,500=3,000=30%=P3.0D=3.0=Creativity=Stars=Muses=3 March = C=I>>GIL.
Pooh-Bah=8,000=80%=P8.0D=Economy=Currency=8 Aug.=Zeus>>E=v.
Pooh-pooh=3,500=4,000=40%=P4.0D=Govt.=Creatocracy=4 April=Hermes=G=A4.
Pool1=7,000=70%=P7.0D=7.0=Language=Assets=Mars=7 July=Pleiades.
Pool2=10,000=1,000=100%=10.0=Physicality=Tech.=10 Oct.=Uranus=P=1∅.
Poolroom=4,500=5,000=50%=P5.00D=Law=Time=Venus=5 May = Aphrodite>>L=N.
Pool table=5,000=50%=P5.00D=Law=Time=Venus=5 May = Aphrodite>>L=N.
Poona=5,000=50%=P5.00D=Law=Time=Venus=5 May = Aphrodite>>L=N.
Poop1=6,000=60%=P6.0D=Man=Earth=Royalty=6 June=Gaia=Maia>>M=M2.
Poop2=4,000=40%=P4.0D=Govt.=Creatocracy=4 April=Mercury=Hermes=G=A4.
Poop3=2,000=20%=P2.00D=2.0=Nature=Matter=Moon=2 Feb.=Cupid=N=C+_
Poop deck=3,000=30%=P3.0D=3.0=Creativity=Stars=Muses=3 March = C=I>>GIL.
Poor=10,000=1,000=100%=10.0=Physicality=Tech.=10 Oct.=Uranus=P=1∅.
Poor box=4,000=40%=P4.0D=Govt.=Creatocracy=4 April=Mercury=Hermes=G=A4.
Poor boy=4,500=5,000=50%=P5.00D=Law=Time=Venus=5 May = Aphrodite>>L=N.
Poorhouse=5,500=5.5=80%=P5.50=Earth-Midway=5 May = Gaia.
Poor mouth=4,000=40%=P4.0D=Govt.=Creatocracy=4 April=Mercury=Hermes=G=A4.
Pop1=10,000=1,000=100%=10.0=Physicality=Tech.=10 Oct.=Uranus=P=1∅.
Pop2=1,500=15%=P1.50D=1.5=Authority=Solar Crown=1 May = Maia.
Pop3=8,500=9,000=90%=P9.00D=9.0=Abstraction=Gods=Saturn=9Sept.>>A=∅.
Pop.=1,000=100%=10.0=1.0=Mind=Sun=1 January=Helios >> M=E4.

Pop art=7,000=70%=P7.0D=7.0=Language=Assets=Mars=7 July=Pleiades.
A variety of art that depicts objects from everyday life and employs techniques of commercial art. Therefore computing is a pop art of practical solutions in knowledge.

Popcorn=8,000=80%=P8.0D=Economy=Currency=8 Aug.=Zeus>>E=v.
Pope=8,000=80%=P8.0D=Economy=Currency=8 Aug.=Zeus>>E=v.
Pope,Alexander.=2,000=20%=P2.00D=2.0=Nature=Matter=Moon=2 Feb.=Cupid=N=C+_
Pop eyed=2,000=20%=P2.00D=2.0=Nature=Matter=Moon=2 Feb.=Cupid=N=C+_
Pop fly=3,000=30%=P3.0D=3.0=Creativity=Stars=Muses=3 March = C=I>>GIL.
Popgun=3,500=4,000=40%=P4.0D=Govt.=Creatocracy=4 April=Hermes=G=A4.
Popinjay=3,500=4,000=40%=P4.0D=Govt.=Creatocracy=4 April=Hermes=G=A4.
Poplar=7,500=8,000=80%=P8.0D=Economy=Currency=8 Aug.=Zeus>>E=v.
Pop in=6,500=7,000=70%=P7.0D=7.0=Language=Assets=Mars=7 July=Pleiades.
Popocateti=6,000=60%=P6.0D=Man=Earth=Royalty=6 June=Gaia=Maia>>M=M2.
Popover=5,500=5.5=80%=P5.50D=Earth-Midway=5 May = Gaia.
Poppy=8,500=9,000=90%=P9.00D=9.0=Abstraction=Gods=Saturn=9Sept.>>A=Ø.
Poppycock=2,500=3,000=30%=P3.0D=3.0=Creativity=Stars=Muses=3 March=C=I.
Pop-top=8,000=80%=P8.0D=Economy=Currency=8 Aug.=Zeus>>E=v.
Populace=4,500=5,000=50%=P5.00D=Law=Time=Venus=5 May = Aphrodite>>L=N.
Popular=10,000=1,000=100%=10.0=Physicality=Tech.=10 Oct.=Uranus=P=1Ø.
Popular front=4,000=40%=P4.0D=Govt.=Creatocracy=4 April=Mercury=Hermes=G=A4.
Popularize=1,500=15%=P1.50D=1.5=Authority=Solar Crown=1 May = Maia.
Populate=4,500=5,000=50%=P5.00D=Law=Time=Venus=5 May = Aphrodite>>L=N.
Population=10,000=1,000=100%=10.0=Physicality=Tech.=10 Oct.=Uranus=P=1Ø.
Population explosion=10,000=1,000=100%=10.0=Phy=Tech.=10 Oct.=Uranus=P=1Ø.
Populism=10,000=1,000=100%=10.0=Physicality=Tech.=10 Oct.=Uranus=P=1Ø.
Populous=3,500=4,000=40%=P4.0D=Govt.=Creatocracy=4 April=Hermes=G=A4.
Pop up=5,500=5.5=80%=P5.50D=Earth-Midway=5 May = Gaia.
Porcelain=6,000=60%=P6.0D=Man=Earth=Royalty=6 June=Gaia=Maia>>M=M2.
Porch=10,000=1,000=100%=10.0=Physicality=Tech.=10 Oct.=Uranus=P=1Ø.
Porcine=4,000=40%=P4.0D=Govt.=Creatocracy=4 April=Mercury=Hermes=G=A4.
Porcupine=6,500=7,000=70%=P7.0D=7.0=Language=Assets=Mars=7 July=Pleiades.
Pore1=6,500=7,000=70%=P7.0D=7.0=Language=Assets=Mars=7 July=Pleiades.
Pore2=9,500=10,000=1,000=100%=10.0=Physicality=Tech.=10 Oct.=Uranus=P=1Ø.
Pork=6,000=60%=P6.0D=Man=Earth=Royalty=6 June=Gaia=Maia>>M=M2.
Pork barrel=6,500=7,000=70%=P7.0D=7.0=Language=Assets=Mars=7 July=Pleiades.
Porker=2,000=20%=P2.00D=2.0=Nature=Matter=Moon=2 Feb.=Cupid=N=C+_
Porn=1,000=100%=Physicality=Tech.=10 Oct.=Uranus=P=1Ø.
Pornography=10,000=1,000=100%=10.0=Physicality=Tech.=10 Oct.=Uranus=P=1Ø.
Porous=6,500=7,000=70%=P7.0D=7.0=Language=Assets=Mars=7 July=Pleiades.
Porphyry=7,500=8,000=80%=P8.0D=Economy=Currency=8 Aug.=Zeus>>E=v.
Porpoise=9,000=90%=P9.00D=9.0=Abstraction=Gods=Saturn=9Sept.>>A=Ø.
Porridge=7,000=70%=P7.0D=7.0=Language=Assets=Mars=7 July=Pleiades.
Porringer=4,500=5,000=50%=P5.00D=Law=Time=Venus=5 May = Aphrodite>>L=N.

Port1=11,500=12,000=12%=P1.20D=1.2=Knowledge=Edu=12Dec.=Athena>>K=F.
Port2=7,000=70%=P7.0D=7.0=Language=Assets=Mars=7 July=Pleiades.
Port3=8,500=9,000=90%=P9.00D=9.0=Abstraction=Gods=Saturn=9Sept.>>A=Ø.
Port4=3,000=30%=P3.0D=3.0=Creativity=Stars=Muses=3 March = C=I>>GIL.
Port.=1,000=100%=Physicality=Tech.=10 Oct.=Uranus=P=1Ø.
Portable=1,000=100%=10.0=1.0=Mind=Sun=1 January=Helios >> M=E4.
Portage=11,500=12,000=12%=P1.20D=1.2=Knowledge=Edu=12Dec.=Athena>>K=F.
Portal=4,500=5,000=50%=P5.00D=Law=Time=Venus=5 May = Aphrodite>>L=N.
Port-au-Prince=5,000=50%=P5.00D=Law=Time=Venus=5 May = Aphrodite>>L=N.
Portcullis=9,500=10,000=1,000=100%=10.0=Physicality=Tech.=10 Oct.=Uranus=P=1Ø.
Porte-cochère=9,000=90%=P9.00D=9.0=Abstraction=Gods=Saturn=9Sept.>>A=Ø.
Port Elizabeth=7,000=70%=P7.0D=7.0=Language=Assets=Mars=7 July=Pleiades.

Portend=13,000=13%=P1.30=Solar Core=Faculty=13 January=Athena.
To serve as an omen or warning of; presage. To indicate, forecast. A quality of Creatocrats.

Portent=7,500=8,000=80%=P8.0D=Economy=Currency=8 Aug.=Zeus>>E=v.
Portentous=6,000=60%=P6.0D=Man=Earth=Royalty=6 June=Gaia=Maia>>M=M2.
Porter1=10,000=1,000=100%=10.0=Physicality=Tech.=10 Oct.=Uranus=P=1Ø.
Porter2=6,000=60%=P6.0D=Man=Earth=Royalty=6 June=Gaia=Maia>>M=M2.
Porter3=5,500=5.5=80%=P5.50=Earth-Midway=5 May = Gaia.
Porter Cole=4,000=40%=P4.0D=Govt.=Creatocracy=4 April=Mercury=Hermes=G=A4.
Porter,Katherine=2,500=3,000=30%=P3.0D=3.0=Creativity=Stars=Muses=3 March=CI.
Porter,William=3,500=4,000=40%=P4.0D=Govt.=Creatocracy=4 April=Hermes=G=A4.
Porterhouse=6,000=60%=P6.0D=Man=Earth=Royalty=6 June=Gaia=Maia>>M=M2.
Portfolio=10,000=1,000=100%=10.0=Physicality=Tech.=10 Oct.=Uranus=P=1Ø.
Porthole=4,000=40%=P4.0D=Govt.=Creatocracy=4 April=Mercury=Hermes=G=A4.
Portico=9,000=90%=P9.00D=9.0=Abstraction=Gods=Saturn=9Sept.>>A=Ø.
Portière=3,000=30%=P3.0D=3.0=Creativity=Stars=Muses=3 March = C=I>>GIL.
Portion=12,000=12%=P1.20D=1.2=Knowledge=Edu=12Dec.=Athena>>K=F.
Portland=9,000=90%=P9.00D=9.0=Abstraction=Gods=Saturn=9Sept.>>A=Ø.
Portland=8,000=80%=P8.0D=Economy=Currency=8 Aug.=Zeus>>E=v.
Port Louis=4,500=5,000=50%=P5.00D=Law=Time=Venus=5 May = Aphrodite>>L=N.
Portly=2,500=3,000=30%=P3.0D=3.0=Creativity=Stars=Muses=3 March = C=I>>GIL.
Portmanteau=5,000=50%=P5.00D=Law=Time=Venus=5 May = Aphrodite>>L=N.
Port Moresby=5,000=50%=P5.00D=Law=Time=Venus=5 May = Aphrodite>>L=N.
Pôrto Alegre=3,500=4,000=40%=P4.0D=Govt.=Creatocracy=4 April=Hermes=G=A4.
Port of call=9,500=10,000=1,000=100%=10.0=Physicality=Tech.=10 Oct.=Uranus=P=1Ø.
Port of entry=6,500=7,000=70%=P7.0D=7.0=Language=Assets=Mars=7 July=Pleiades.
Port of Spain=7,500=8,000=80%=P8.0D=Economy=Currency=8 Aug.=Zeus>>E=v.
Porto Novo=7,000=70%=P7.0D=7.0=Language=Assets=Mars=7 July=Pleiades.
Portrait=8,500=9,000=90%=P9.00D=9.0=Abstraction=Gods=Saturn=9Sept.>>A=Ø.
Portraiture=3,500=4,000=40%=P4.0D=Govt.=Creatocracy=4 April=Hermes=G=A4.
Portray=9,000=90%=P9.00D=9.0=Abstraction=Gods=Saturn=9Sept.>>A=Ø.

Port Said=8,000=80%=P8.0D=Economy=Currency=8 Aug.=Zeus>>E=v.
Portsmouth=10,500=11,000=11%=P1.10D=1.1=Idea=Brainchild.=11 Nov=Athena>>I=MT.
Port Stanley=1,000=100%=10.0=1.0=Mind=Sun=1 January=Helios >> M=E4.
Port Sudan.=6,500=7,000=70%=P7.0D=7.0=Language=Assets=Mars=7 July=Pleiades.
Portugal=7,000=70%=P7.0D=7.0=Language=Assets=Mars=7 July=Pleiades.
Portuguese=6,000=60%=P6.0D=Man=Earth=Royalty=6 June=Gaia=Maia>>M=M2.
Portuguese man-of-war=10,000=1,000=100%=Physicality=Tech.=10 Oct.=Uranus=P=1Ø.
Portulaca=5,500=5.5=80%=P5.50=Earth-Midway=5 May = Gaia.
Pos.=1,000=100%=10.0=1.0=Mind=Sun=1 January=Helios >> M=E4.
Pose=10,000=1,000=100%=10.0=Physicality=Tech.=10 Oct.=Uranus=P=1Ø.

Poseidon=4,500=5,000=50%=P5.00D=Law=Time=Venus=5 May = Aphrodite>>L=N.
Greek myth. God of the sea and brother of Zeus.

Poser1=1,500=15%=P1.50D=1.5=Authority=Solar Crown=1 May = Maia.
Poser2=1,500=15%=P1.50D=1.5=Authority=Solar Crown=1 May = Maia.
Poseur=7,000=70%=P7.0D=7.0=Language=Assets=Mars=7 July=Pleiades.
Posh=4,500=5,000=50%=P5.00D=Law=Time=Venus=5 May = Aphrodite>>L=N.
Posit=6,000=60%=P6.0D=Man=Earth=Royalty=6 June=Gaia=Maia>>M=M2.
Position=10,000=1,000=100%=10.0=Physicality=Tech.=10 Oct.=Uranus=P=1Ø.
Positive=10,000=1,000=100%=10.0=Physicality=Tech.=10 Oct.=Uranus=P=1Ø.
Positron=4,000=40%=P4.0D=Govt.=Creatocracy=4 April=Mercury=Hermes=G=A4.
Posse=9,500=10,000=1,000=100%=10.0=Physicality=Tech.=10 Oct.=Uranus=P=1Ø.
Possess=11,500=12,000=12%=P1.20D=1.2=Knowledge=Edu=12Dec.=Athena>>K=F.
Possessed=6,000=60%=P6.0D=Man=Earth=Royalty=6 June=Gaia=Maia>>M=M2.
Possession=10,000=1,000=100%=10.0=Physicality=Tech.=10 Oct.=Uranus=P=1Ø.
Possessive=10,000=1,000=100%=10.0=Physicality=Tech.=10 Oct.=Uranus=P=1Ø.

Possible=7,000=70%=P7.0D=7.0=Language=Assets=Mars=7 July=Pleiades.
Something is possible when it becomes computable. Precision is possibility.

Possum=1,000=100%=10.0=1.0=Mind=Sun=1 January=Helios >> M=E4.
Post1=10,000=1,000=100%=10.0=Physicality=Tech.=10 Oct.=Uranus=P=1Ø.
Post2=10,000=1,000=100%=10.0=Physicality=Tech.=10 Oct.=Uranus=P=1Ø.
Post3=10,000=1,000=100%=10.0=Physicality=Tech.=10 Oct.=Uranus=P=1Ø.
Post-=5,000=50%=P5.00D=Law=Time=Venus=5 May = Aphrodite>>L=N.
Postage=3,000=30%=P3.0D=3.0=Creativity=Stars=Muses=3 March = C=I>>GIL.
Postal=4,500=5,000=50%=P5.00D=Law=Time=Venus=5 May = Aphrodite>>L=N.
Postal card=7,000=70%=P7.0D=7.0=Language=Assets=Mars=7 July=Pleiades.
Post card=7,500=8,000=80%=P8.0D=Economy=Currency=8 Aug.=Zeus>>E=v.
Post chaise=3,500=4,000=40%=P4.0D=Govt.=Creatocracy=4 April=Hermes=G=A4.
Post date=8,500=9,000=90%=P9.00D=9.0=Abstraction=Gods=Saturn=9Sept.>>A=Ø.
Post doctoral=4,500=5,000=50%=P5.00D=Law=Time=Venus=5 May = Aphrodite>>L=N.

Poster=6,500=7,000=70%=P7.0D=7.0=Language=Assets=Mars=7 July=Pleiades.
Posterior=10,000=1,000=100%=10.0=Physicality=Tech.=10 Oct.=Uranus=P=1Ø.
Posterity=5,500=5.5=80%=P5.50=Earth-Midway=5 May = Gaia.
Postern=6,000=60%=P6.0D=Man=Earth=Royalty=6 June=Gaia=Maia>>M=M2.
Post Exchange=8,000=80%=P8.0D=Economy=Currency=8 Aug.=Zeus>>E=v.
Postgraduate=7,000=70%=P7.0D=7.0=Language=Assets=Mars=7 July=Pleiades.
Posthaste=5,000=50%=P5.00D=Law=Time=Venus=5 May = Aphrodite>>L=N.
Posthumous=6,500=7,000=70%=P7.0D=7.0=Language=Assets=Mars=7 July=Pleiades.
Post hypnotic suggestion=7,500=8,000=80%=P8.0D=Econ=Curr.=8 Aug.=Zeus>>E=v.
Postilion=7,000=70%=P7.0D=7.0=Language=Assets=Mars=7 July=Pleiades.
Postlude=7,000=70%=P7.0D=7.0=Language=Assets=Mars=7 July=Pleiades.
Postman=1,000=100%=10.0=1.0=Mind=Sun=1 January=Helios >> M=E4.
Postmark=8,500=9,000=90%=P9.00D=9.0=Abstraction=Gods=Saturn=9Sept.>>A=Ø.
Postmaster=8,500=9,000=90%=P9.00D=9.0=Abstraction=Gods=Saturn=9Sept.>>A=Ø.
Postmaster General=4,000=40%=P4.0D=Govt.=Creatocracy=4 April=Hermes=G=A4.
Post meridiem=13,000=13%=P1.30=Solar Core=Faculty=13 January=Athena.
Postmistress=3,500=4,000=40%=P4.0D=Govt.=Creatocracy=4 April=Hermes=G=A4.
Postmortem=10,000=1,000=100%=10.0=Physicality=Tech.=10 Oct.=Uranus=P=1Ø.
Post nasal=3,500=4,000=40%=P4.0D=Govt.=Creatocracy=4 April=Hermes=G=A4.
Postnatal=2,500=3,000=30%=P3.0D=3.0=Creativity=Stars=Muses=3 March = C=I>>GIL.
Post office=10,500=11,000=11%=P1.10D=1.1=Idea=Brainchild.=11 Nov=Athena>>I=MT.
Post operative=2,500=3,000=30%=P3.0D=3.0=Creativity=Stars=Muses=3 March = C=I.
Postpaid=3,000=30%=P3.0D=3.0=Creativity=Stars=Muses=3 March = C=I>>GIL.
Postpartum=5,000=50%=P5.00D=Law=Time=Venus=5 May = Aphrodite>>L=N.
Postpone=7,000=70%=P7.0D=7.0=Language=Assets=Mars=7 July=Pleiades.
Postscript=5,500=5.5=80%=P5.50=Earth-Midway=5 May = Gaia.
Postulant=5,000=50%=P5.00D=Law=Time=Venus=5 May = Aphrodite>>L=N.
Postulate=10,000=1,000=100%=10.0=Physicality=Tech.=10 Oct.=Uranus=P=1Ø.
Posture=10,000=1,000=100%=10.0=Physicality=Tech.=10 Oct.=Uranus=P=1Ø.
Posy=3,500=4,000=40%=P4.0D=Govt.=Creatocracy=4 April=Mercury=Hermes=G=A4.
Pot1=10,000=1,000=100%=10.0=Physicality=Tech.=10 Oct.=Uranus=P=1Ø.
Pot2=1,500=15%=P1.50D=1.5=Authority=Solar Crown=1 May = Maia.

Pot.=500=5%=P5.00D=5.0=Law=Time=Venus=5 May=Aphrodite>>L=N.
Peter Matthews-Akukalia, Castle Makupedia successfully computed the human potential and its results gave the code >> 500:500:600 > the average quantum of potentials in a person is measured as 500 unique talents in 500 different bundles of talents and each guided by 600 ideas approximately 1.6million energy potentials per bits. Computed: 500:500:600<5.0:5.0:5.0>>5.0*5.0x=px=10+25=35x=px=285=300=P=>>3.0*6.0x=px= 9+18=27x=px=189=200=2.0. The resultant code 3.0 >> muses test inspire creativity of the arts and sciences. The resultant 2.0 indicates natural stability. It means that only creativity can ensure natural stability in nothing, in something, in anything and in everything because there is really nothing like nothing. Nothing = Zero = 0 = Ø = 9.0 = Abstraction = Planetary energy computed to become mind wares and applied to

become software and energy through technology devices like phones, laptops, television & radio frequency channels, vehicle plates, company registrations, dates of birth, names alphanumerics and symbols. All potentials are computed and measured in the program language "Cures-Maks-Cures" meaning we synchronize and crystallize this data in the name of King Maks or in the name of Castle Makupedia God of Creatocracy Genius and Mind. He is first the Mind God. This is symbolic and recited during the computation process once one has reached the dynamic constant stages expressed as [x=px=]. The energy that runs a thing constitutes the mind of that thing. See Template & Manifesto for the Creative Economy 2: Principles of Psychoeconomix by Peter Matthews-Akukalia. The results on potential aligns despite the application of different methods being Mind Computing (Psychoeconomix) and Makumaticology in the encyclopedia as seen above. Truth is therefore established.

Potable=2,500=3,000=30%=P3.0D=3.0=Creativity=Stars=Muses=3 March = C=I>>GIL.
Potash=10,000=1,000=100%=10.0=Physicality=Tech.=10 Oct.=Uranus=P=1Ø.
Potassium=10,000=1,000=100%=10.0=Physicality=Tech.=10 Oct.=Uranus=P=1Ø.
Potassium bromide=6,500=7,000=70%=P7.0D=7.0=Lang=Assets=Mars=7 July=Pleiades.
Potassium carbonate=5,000=50%=P5.00D=Law=Time=Venus=5 May = Aphrodite>>L=N.
Potassium cyanide=6,500=7,000=70%=P7.0D=7.0=Lang=Assets=Mars=7 July=Pleiades.
Potassium hydroxide=8,000=80%=P8.0D=Economy=Currency=8 Aug.=Zeus>>E=v.
Potassium nitrate=7,500=8,000=80%=P8.0D=Economy=Currency=8 Aug.=Zeus>>E=v.
Potation=6,000=60%=P6.0D=Man=Earth=Royalty=6 June=Gaia=Maia>>M=M2.
Potato=8,500=9,000=90%=P9.00D=9.0=Abstraction=Gods=Saturn=9Sept.>>A=Ø.
Potato chip=7,000=70%=P7.0D=7.0=Language=Assets=Mars=7 July=Pleiades.
Potawatomi=10,000=1,000=100%=10.0=Physicality=Tech.=10 Oct.=Uranus=P=1Ø.
Potbelly=1,500=15%=P1.50D=1.5=Authority=Solar Crown=1 May = Maia.
Potboiler=6,000=60%=P6.0D=Man=Earth=Royalty=6 June=Gaia=Maia>>M=M2.
Pot cheese=1,500=15%=P1.50D=1.5=Authority=Solar Crown=1 May = Maia.
Potent=1,500=15%=P1.50D=1.5=Authority=Solar Crown=1 May = Maia.
Potentate=7,500=8,000=80%=P8.0D=Economy=Currency=8 Aug.=Zeus>>E=v.
Potential=10,000=1,000=100%=10.0=Physicality=Tech.=10 Oct.=Uranus=P=1Ø.
Potential energy=7,500=8,000=80%=P8.0D=Economy=Currency=8 Aug.=Zeus>>E=v.
Pothead=3,000=30%=P3.0D=3.0=Creativity=Stars=Muses=3 March = C=I>>GIL.
Pother=2,500=3,000=30%=P3.0D=3.0=Creativity=Stars=Muses=3 March = C=I>>GIL.
Potholder=5,000=50%=P5.00D=Law=Time=Venus=5 May = Aphrodite>>L=N.
Pothole=3,500=4,000=40%=P4.0D=Govt.=Creatocracy=4 April=Mercury=Hermes=G=A4.
Potion=6,000=60%=P6.0D=Man=Earth=Royalty=6 June=Gaia=Maia>>M=M2.
Potluck=11,000=11%=P1.10D=1.1=Idea=Brainchild=Inv.=11 Nov.=SC=Athena>>I=MT.
Potomac River=10,500=11,000=11%=P1.10D=1.1=Idea=Brainchild=11 Nov.=Athena>>I=MT.
Pot pie=7,000=70%=P7.0D=7.0=Language=Assets=Mars=7 July=Pleiades.
Potpourri=7,000=70%=P7.0D=7.0=Language=Assets=Mars=7 July=Pleiades.
Pot roast=6,500=7,000=70%=P7.0D=7.0=Language=Assets=Mars=7 July=Pleiades.
Potsdam=6,500=7,000=70%=P7.0D=7.0=Language=Assets=Mars=7 July=Pleiades.
Potsherd=2,500=3,000=30%=P3.0D=3.0=Creativity=Stars=Muses=3 March = C=I>>GIL.

Potshot=9,500=10,000=1,000=100%=10.0=Physicality=Tech.=10 Oct.=Uranus=P=1Ø.
Pottage=6,000=60%=P6.0D=Man=Earth=Royalty=6 June=Gaia=Maia>>M=M2.
Potted=4,500=5,000=50%=P5.00D=Law=Time=Venus=5 May = Aphrodite>>L=N.
Potter1=2,000=20%=P2.00D=2.0=Nature=Matter=Moon=2 Feb.=Cupid=N=C+_
Potter2=2,500=3,000=30%=P3.0D=3.0=Creativity=Stars=Muses=3 March = C=I>>GIL.
Potter Beatrix=3,000=30%=P3.0D=3.0=Creativity=Stars=Muses=3 March = C=I>>GIL.
Pottery=13,000=13%=P1.30=Solar Core=Faculty=13 January=Athena.
Pouch=10,000=1,000=100%=10.0=Physicality=Tech.=10 Oct.=Uranus=P=1Ø.
Poultice=12,000=12%=P1.20D=1.2=Knowledge=Edu=12Dec.=Athena>>K=F.
Poultry=8,000=80%=P8.0D=Economy=Currency=8 Aug.=Zeus>>E=v.
Pounce=7,000=70%=P7.0D=7.0=Language=Assets=Mars=7 July=Pleiades.
Pound1=10,000=1,000=100%=10.0=Physicality=Tech.=10 Oct.=Uranus=P=1Ø.
Pound2=10,000=1,000=100%=10.0=Physicality=Tech.=10 Oct.=Uranus=P=1Ø.
Pound3=4,500=5,000=50%=P5.00D=Law=Time=Venus=5 May = Aphrodite>>L=N.
Pound Ezra=2,500=3,000=30%=P3.0D=3.0=Creativity=Stars=Muses=3 March = C=I.

Poundage=2,000=20%=P2.00D=2.0=Nature=Matter=Moon=2 Feb.=Cupid=N=C+_
Weight measured in pounds. The Maks Currencies is measured as One Mak = Ten Pounds
>> P1=£10. Hence the Maks is a stable currency for creating benchmarks on values prices
costs and applications. It is the first diamond anti-inflation solar core abstracted currency.
The resultant 2.0 indicates Nature and the Nature formula interestingly is what applies in
the invention and development of the Maks currency as N=C+->>C+-=50%. The Maks
currencies poundage system makes it a universal storage module for cash and assets guided
by supernatural laws of the solar core that binds all things. Ephesians 1:10.

Pound cake=5,000=50%=P5.00D=Law=Time=Venus=5 May = Aphrodite>>L=N.
Pour=12,000=12%=P1.20D=1.2=Knowledge=Edu=12Dec.=Athena>>K=F.
Pout=7,500=8,000=80%=P8.0D=Economy=Currency=8 Aug.=Zeus>>E=v.
Poverty=8,500=9,000=90%=P9.00D=9.0=Abstraction=Gods=Saturn=9Sept.>>A=Ø.
Poverty stricken=1,500=15%=P1.50D=1.5=Authority=Solar Crown=1 May = Maia.
POW=2,000=20%=P2.00D=2.0=Nature=Matter=Moon=2 Feb.=Cupid=N=C+_
Powder=10,000=1,000=100%=10.0=Physicality=Tech.=10 Oct.=Uranus=P=1Ø.
Powder keg=6,000=60%=P6.0D=Man=Earth=Royalty=6 June=Gaia=Maia>>M=M2.
Powder puff=4,500=5,000=50%=P5.00D=Law=Time=Venus=5 May = Aphrodite>>L=N.
Powder room=2,000=20%=P2.00D=2.0=Nature=Matter=Moon=2 Feb.=Cupid=N=C+_
Power=10,000=1,000=100%=10.0=Physicality=Tech.=10 Oct.=Uranus=P=1Ø.
Powerboat=1,000=100%=10.0=1.0=Mind=Sun=1 January=Helios >> M=E4.
Powerhouse=5,000=50%=P5.00D=Law=Time=Venus=5 May = Aphrodite>>L=N.
Power of attorney=6,500=7,000=70%=P7.0D=7.0=Lang=Assets=Mars=7 July=Pleiades.
Power plant=10,000=1,000=100%=10.0=Physicality=Tech.=10 Oct.=Uranus=P=1Ø.
Power shovel=3,500=4,000=40%=P4.0D=Govt.=Creatocracy=4 April=Hermes=G=A4.
Power train=9,500=10,000=1,000=100%=10.0=Physicality=Tech.=10 Oct.=Uranus=P=1Ø.
Powhatan1=2,500=3,000=30%=P3.0D=3.0=Creativity=Stars=Muses=3 March = C=I>>GIL.

Powhatan2=9,000=90%=P9.00D=9.0=Abstraction=Gods=Saturn=9Sept.>>A=Ø.
Powwow=10,000=1,000=100%=10.0=Physicality=Tech.=10 Oct.=Uranus=P=1Ø.
Pox=5,500=5.5=80%=P5.50=Earth-Midway=5 May = Gaia.
Poznań=5,000=50%=P5.00D=Law=Time=Venus=5 May = Aphrodite>>L=N.
pp.=2,000=20%=P2.00D=2.0=Nature=Matter=Moon=2 Feb.=Cupid=N=C+_
p.p.=3,500=4,000=40%=P4.0D=Govt.=Creatocracy=4 April=Mercury=Hermes=G=A4.
ppd.=1,000=100%=10.0=1.0=Mind=Sun=1 January=Helios >> M=E4.
PQ=1,500=15%=P1.50D=1.5=Authority=Solar Crown=1 May = Maia.
Pr=3,000=30%=P3.0D=3.0=Creativity=Stars=Muses=3 March = C=I>>GIL.
PR.=4,500=5,000=50%=P5.00D=Law=Time=Venus=5 May = Aphrodite>>L=N.
pr.=4,000=40%=P4.0D=Govt.=Creatocracy=4 April=Mercury=Hermes=G=A4.
Pr.=1,000=100%=10.0=1.0=Mind=Sun=1 January=Helios >> M=E4.
Practicable=10,000=1,000=100%=10.0=Physicality=Tech.=10 Oct.=Uranus=P=1Ø.
Practical=10,000=1,000=100%=10.0=Physicality=Tech.=10 Oct.=Uranus=P=1Ø.
Practical joke=5,500=5.5=80%=P5.50=Earth-Midway=5 May = Gaia.
Practically=3,000=30%=P3.0D=3.0=Creativity=Stars=Muses=3 March = C=I>>GIL.
Practical nurse=2,000=20%=P2.00D=2.0=Nature=Matter=Moon=2 Feb.=Cupid=N=C+_
Practice=10,000=1,000=100%=10.0=Physicality=Tech.=10 Oct.=Uranus=P=1Ø.
Practitioner=5,000=50%=P5.00D=Law=Time=Venus=5 May = Aphrodite>>L=N.
Praetor=4,000=40%=P4.0D=Govt.=Creatocracy=4 April=Mercury=Hermes=G=A4.
Pragmatic=6,500=7,000=70%=P7.0D=7.0=Language=Assets=Mars=7 July=Pleiades.
Pragmatism=6,500=7,000=70%=P7.0D=7.0=Language=Assets=Mars=7 July=Pleiades.
Prague=5,500=5.5=80%=P5.50=Earth-Midway=5 May = Gaia.
Praia=6,500=7,000=70%=P7.0D=7.0=Language=Assets=Mars=7 July=Pleiades.
Prairie=8,000=80%=P8.0D=Economy=Currency=8 Aug.=Zeus>>E=v.
Prairie dog=7,500=8,000=80%=P8.0D=Economy=Currency=8 Aug.=Zeus>>E=v.
Prairie schooner=5,000=50%=P5.00D=Law=Time=Venus=5 May = Aphrodite>>L=N.
Praise=9,000=90%=P9.00D=9.0=Abstraction=Gods=Saturn=9Sept.>>A=Ø.
Praiseworthy=2,000=20%=P2.00D=2.0=Nature=Matter=Moon=2 Feb.=Cupid=N=C+_
Praline=10,000=1,000=100%=10.0=Physicality=Tech.=10 Oct.=Uranus=P=1Ø.
Pram=2,000=20%=P2.00D=2.0=Nature=Matter=Moon=2 Feb.=Cupid=N=C+_
Prance=10,000=1,000=100%=10.0=Physicality=Tech.=10 Oct.=Uranus=P=1Ø.
Prank=2,000=20%=P2.00D=2.0=Nature=Matter=Moon=2 Feb.=Cupid=N=C+_
Praseodymium=10,000=1,000=100%=10.0=Physicality=Tech.=10 Oct.=Uranus=P=1Ø.
Prate=4,500=5,000=50%=P5.00D=Law=Time=Venus=5 May = Aphrodite>>L=N.
Pratfall=4,500=5,000=50%=P5.00D=Law=Time=Venus=5 May = Aphrodite>>L=N.
Prattle=2,500=3,000=30%=P3.0D=3.0=Creativity=Stars=Muses=3 March = C=I>>GIL.
Prawn=6,000=60%=P6.0D=Man=Earth=Royalty=6 June=Gaia=Maia>>M=M2.
Praxis=4,500=5,000=50%=P5.00D=Law=Time=Venus=5 May = Aphrodite>>L=N.
Praxiteles=3,000=30%=P3.0D=3.0=Creativity=Stars=Muses=3 March = C=I>>GIL.

Pray=8,000=80%=P8.0D=Economy=Currency=8 Aug.=Zeus>>E=v.
An energy contact process for reaching Zeus. Measured as spirit speed 1.0x10 power -6.

Prayer=14,500=15,000=1,500=15%=P1.50D=1.5=Authority=Solar Crown=1 May = Maia.
When prayers are made to Zeus it reaches Athena who instructs Maia to process for
wisdom handicraft and mindset through computation for value and weight. Then answers
are decided and either granted or not. The due process is the reason it takes times.

Prayerful=5,000=50%=P5.00D=Law=Time=Venus=5 May = Aphrodite>>L=N.
To be prayerful means one must be just and rightfully deserve the request by law.

Prayer rug=5,500=5.5=80%=P5.50=Earth-Midway=5 May = Gaia.
Prayer wheel=7,000=70%=P7.0D=7.0=Language=Assets=Mars=7 July=Pleiades.
Praying mantis=9,000=90%=P9.00D=9.0=Abstraction=Gods=Saturn=9Sept.>>A=Ø.

Pre-=8,000=80%=P8.0D=Economy=Currency=8 Aug.=Zeus>>E=v.
Zeus is known as the ancient of Days. He is the pre- of all time.

Preach=10,500=11,000=11%=P1.10D=1.1=Idea=Brainchild=Inv.=11 Nov.=Athena>>I=MT.
A means to reach Athena. The essence is to teach wisdom proved through handicraft.

Preadolescence=3,000=30%=P3.0D=3.0=Creativity=Stars=Muses=3 March = C=I>>GIL.
Preamble=8,000=80%=P8.0D=Economy=Currency=8 Aug.=Zeus>>E=v.
Preamplifier=10,000=1,000=100%=10.0=Physicality=Tech.=10 Oct.=Uranus=P=1Ø.
Prebend=10,000=1,000=100%=10.0=Physicality=Tech.=10 Oct.=Uranus=P=1Ø.
Prebendary=3,500=4,000=40%=P4.0D=Govt.=Creatocracy=4 April=Hermes=G=A4.
Prec.=500=5%=P5.00D=5.0=Law=Time=Venus=5 May=Aphrodite>>L=N.
Precambrian=10,000=1,000=100%=10.0=Physicality=Tech.=10 Oct.=Uranus=P=1Ø.
Precarious=10,000=1,000=100%=10.0=Physicality=Tech.=10 Oct.=Uranus=P=1Ø.
Precaution=7,000=70%=P7.0D=7.0=Language=Assets=Mars=7 July=Pleiades.
Precede=6,500=7,000=70%=P7.0D=7.0=Language=Assets=Mars=7 July=Pleiades.
Precedence=3,500=4,000=40%=P4.0D=Govt.=Creatocracy=4 April=Hermes=G=A4.
Precedent=10,000=1,000=100%=10.0=Physicality=Tech.=10 Oct.=Uranus=P=1Ø.
Preceding=2,500=3,000=30%=P3.0D=3.0=Creativity=Stars=Muses=3 March = C=I>>GIL.
Precentor=6,500=7,000=70%=P7.0D=7.0=Language=Assets=Mars=7 July=Pleiades.
Precept=6,000=60%=P6.0D=Man=Earth=Royalty=6 June=Gaia=Maia>>M=M2.
Preceptor=1,500=15%=P1.50D=1.5=Authority=Solar Crown=1 May = Maia.
Precinct=10,000=1,000=100%=10.0=Physicality=Tech.=10 Oct.=Uranus=P=1Ø.
Preciosity=2,000=20%=P2.00D=2.0=Nature=Matter=Moon=2 Feb.=Cupid=N=C+_
Precious=6,500=7,000=70%=P7.0D=7.0=Language=Assets=Mars=7 July=Pleiades.
Precipice=7,500=8,000=80%=P8.0D=Economy=Currency=8 Aug.=Zeus>>E=v.
Precipitant=10,000=1,000=100%=10.0=Physicality=Tech.=10 Oct.=Uranus=P=1Ø.
Precipitate=10,000=1,000=100%=10.0=Physicality=Tech.=10 Oct.=Uranus=P=1Ø.
Precipitation=10,000=1,000=100%=10.0=Physicality=Tech.=10 Oct.=Uranus=P=1Ø.
Precipitous=10,000=1,000=100%=10.0=Physicality=Tech.=10 Oct.=Uranus=P=1Ø.

Précis=5,000=50%=P5.00D=Law=Time=Venus=5 May = Aphrodite>>L=N.
Precise=10,000=1,000=100%=10.0=Physicality=Tech.=10 Oct.=Uranus=P=1Ø.
Precision=3,500=4,000=40%=P4.0D=Govt.=Creatocracy=4 April=Hermes=G=A4.
Preclude=4,000=40%=P4.0D=Govt.=Creatocracy=4 April=Mercury=Hermes=G=A4.
Precocious=7,000=70%=P7.0D=7.0=Language=Assets=Mars=7 July=Pleiades.
Precognition=3,500=4,000=40%=P4.0D=Govt.=Creat.=4 April=Mercury=Hermes=G=A4.
Pre-Colombian=5,000=50%=P5.00D=Law=Time=Venus=5 May = Aphrodite>>L=N.
Preconceive=6,000=60%=P6.0D=Man=Earth=Royalty=6 June=Gaia=Maia>>M=M2.
Precondition=4,500=5,000=50%=P5.00D=Law=Time=Venus=5 May = Aphrodite>>L=N.
Precursor=6,000=60%=P6.0D=Man=Earth=Royalty=6 June=Gaia=Maia>>M=M2.
Predacious=2,000=20%=P2.00D=2.0=Nature=Matter=Moon=2 Feb.=Cupid=N=C+_
Predate=500=5%=P5.00D=5.0=Law=Time=Venus=5 May=Aphrodite>>L=N.
Predation=8,000=80%=P8.0D=Economy=Currency=8 Aug.=Zeus>>E=v.
Predatory=7,500=8,000=80%=P8.0D=Economy=Currency=8 Aug.=Zeus>>E=v.
Predecessor=6,000=60%=P6.0D=Man=Earth=Royalty=6 June=Gaia=Maia>>M=M2.
Predestination=10,500=11,000=11%=P1.10D=1.1=Idea=Brainchild.=11 Nov=Athena>>I=MT.
Predestine=3,000=30%=P3.0D=3.0=Creativity=Stars=Muses=3 March = C=I>>GIL.
Predetermine=3,000=30%=P3.0D=3.0=Creativity=Stars=Muses=3 March = C=I>>GIL.
Predicable=3,000=30%=P3.0D=3.0=Creativity=Stars=Muses=3 March = C=I>>GIL.
Predicament=3,500=4,000=40%=P4.0D=Govt.=Creatocracy=4 April=Hermes=G=A4.
Predicate=10,000=1,000=100%=10.0=Physicality=Tech.=10 Oct.=Uranus=P=1Ø.
Predict=6,500=7,000=70%=P7.0D=7.0=Language=Assets=Mars=7 July=Pleiades.
Pre digest=2,000=20%=P2.00D=2.0=Nature=Matter=Moon=2 Feb.=Cupid=N=C+_
Predilection=10,000=1,000=100%=10.0=Physicality=Tech.=10 Oct.=Uranus=P=1Ø.
Predispose=8,000=80%=P8.0D=Economy=Currency=8 Aug.=Zeus>>E=v.
Predominant=5,000=50%=P5.00D=Law=Time=Venus=5 May = Aphrodite>>L=N.
Predominate=10,000=1,000=100%=10.0=Physicality=Tech.=10 Oct.=Uranus=P=1Ø.
Preemie=3,000=30%=P3.0D=3.0=Creativity=Stars=Muses=3 March = C=I>>GIL.
Preeminent=6,000=60%=P6.0D=Man=Earth=Royalty=6 June=Gaia=Maia>>M=M2.
Preempt=10,000=1,000=100%=10.0=Physicality=Tech.=10 Oct.=Uranus=P=1Ø.
Preen=11,000=11%=P1.10D=1.1=Idea=Brainchild=Inv.=11 Nov.=SC=Athena>>I=MT.
Pre exist=1,500=15%=P1.50D=1.5=Authority=Solar Crown=1 May = Maia.
Pref.=1,500=15%=P1.50D=1.5=Authority=Solar Crown=1 May = Maia.
Prefab=5,000=50%=P5.00D=Law=Time=Venus=5 May = Aphrodite>>L=N.
Prefabricate=7,000=70%=P7.0D=7.0=Language=Assets=Mars=7 July=Pleiades.
Preface=10,000=1,000=100%=10.0=Physicality=Tech.=10 Oct.=Uranus=P=1Ø.
Pre factory=5,500=5.5=80%=P5.50=Earth-Midway=5 May = Gaia.
Perfect=8,000=80%=P8.0D=Economy=Currency=8 Aug.=Zeus>>E=v.
Prefer=10,000=1,000=100%=10.0=Physicality=Tech.=10 Oct.=Uranus=P=1Ø.
Preferable=1,000=100%=10.0=1.0=Mind=Sun=1 January=Helios >> M=E4.
Preference=5,000=50%=P5.00D=Law=Time=Venus=5 May = Aphrodite>>L=N.
Preferment=3,000=30%=P3.0D=3.0=Creativity=Stars=Muses=3 March = C=I>>GIL.
Prefigure=3,000=30%=P3.0D=3.0=Creativity=Stars=Muses=3 March = C=I>>GIL.
Prefix=9,000=90%=P9.00D=9.0=Abstraction=Gods=Saturn=9Sept.>>A=Ø.
Prefrontal=5,000=50%=P5.00D=Law=Time=Venus=5 May = Aphrodite>>L=N.

Pregnable=6,000=60%=P6.0D=Man=Earth=Royalty=6 June=Gaia=Maia>>M=M2.
Pregnant=7,000=70%=P7.0D=7.0=Language=Assets=Mars=7 July=Pleiades.
Prehensile=8,000=80%=P8.0D=Economy=Currency=8 Aug.=Zeus>>E=v.
Prehistoric=4,500=5,000=50%=P5.00D=Law=Time=Venus=5 May = Aphrodite>>L=N.
Prejudice=10,000=1,000=100%=10.0=Physicality=Tech.=10 Oct.=Uranus=P=1Ø.
Prelate=6,000=60%=P6.0D=Man=Earth=Royalty=6 June=Gaia=Maia>>M=M2.
Preliminary=10,000=1,000=100%=10.0=Physicality=Tech.=10 Oct.=Uranus=P=1Ø.
Prelude=10,000=1,000=100%=10.0=Physicality=Tech.=10 Oct.=Uranus=P=1Ø.
Premarital=3,000=30%=P3.0D=3.0=Creativity=Stars=Muses=3 March = C=I>>GIL.
Premature=5,500=5.5=80%=P5.50=Earth-Midway=5 May = Gaia.
Premed=2,500=3,000=30%=P3.0D=3.0=Creativity=Stars=Muses=3 March = C=I>>GIL.
Premeditate=3,500=4,000=40%=P4.0D=Govt.=Creatocracy=4 April=Hermes=G=A4.
Premenstrual=4,500=5,000=50%=P5.00D=Law=Time=Venus=5 May = Aphrodite>>L=N.
Premier=8,000=80%=P8.0D=Economy=Currency=8 Aug.=Zeus>>E=v.
Premiere=7,500=8,000=80%=P8.0D=Economy=Currency=8 Aug.=Zeus>>E=v.
Premise=10,000=1,000=100%=10.0=Physicality=Tech.=10 Oct.=Uranus=P=1Ø.
Premium=10,000=1,000=100%=10.0=Physicality=Tech.=10 Oct.=Uranus=P=1Ø.
Premolar=6,500=7,000=70%=P7.0D=7.0=Language=Assets=Mars=7 July=Pleiades.
Premonition=10,000=1,000=100%=10.0=Physicality=Tech.=10 Oct.=Uranus=P=1Ø.
Prenatal=2,500=3,000=30%=P3.0D=3.0=Creativity=Stars=Muses=3 March = C=I>>GIL.
Preoccupy=10,000=1,000=100%=10.0=Physicality=Tech.=10 Oct.=Uranus=P=1Ø.
Prep.=2,000=20%=P2.00D=2.0=Nature=Matter=Moon=2 Feb.=Cupid=N=C+_
Prepackage=4,000=40%=P4.0D=Govt.=Creatocracy=4 April=Mercury=Hermes=G=A4.
Preparation=10,000=1,000=100%=10.0=Physicality=Tech.=10 Oct.=Uranus=P=1Ø.
Preparatory=5,000=50%=P5.00D=Law=Time=Venus=5 May = Aphrodite>>L=N.
Preparatory school=5,000=50%=P5.00D=Law=Time=Venus=5 May = Aphrodite>>L=N.
Prepare=8,000=80%=P8.0D=Economy=Currency=8 Aug.=Zeus>>E=v.
Preparedness=4,000=40%=P4.0D=Govt.=Creatocracy=4 April=Mercury=Hermes=G=A4.
Preponderate=7,000=70%=P7.0D=7.0=Language=Assets=Mars=7 July=Pleiades.
Preposition=10,000=1,000=100%=10.0=Physicality=Tech.=10 Oct.=Uranus=P=1Ø.
Prepossess=4,000=40%=P4.0D=Govt.=Creatocracy=4 April=Mercury=Hermes=G=A4.
Prepossessing=4,000=40%=P4.0D=Govt.=Creatocracy=4 April=Mercury=Hermes=G=A4.
Preposterous=5,500=5.5=80%=P5.50=Earth-Midway=5 May = Gaia.
Preppy=3,000=30%=P3.0D=3.0=Creativity=Stars=Muses=3 March = C=I>>GIL.
Prep school=2,000=20%=P2.00D=2.0=Nature=Matter=Moon=2 Feb.=Cupid=N=C+_
Prepuce=2,000=20%=P2.00D=2.0=Nature=Matter=Moon=2 Feb.=Cupid=N=C+_
Prerecord=7,500=8,000=80%=P8.0D=Economy=Currency=8 Aug.=Zeus>>E=v.
Prerequisite=2,500=3,000=30%=P3.0D=3.0=Creativity=Stars=Muses=3 March = C=I.
Prerogative=4,500=5,000=50%=P5.00D=Law=Time=Venus=5 May = Aphrodite>>L=N.
Pres.=2,500=3,000=30%=P3.0D=3.0=Creativity=Stars=Muses=3 March = C=I>>GIL.
Presage=10,000=1,000=100%=10.0=Physicality=Tech.=10 Oct.=Uranus=P=1Ø.
Presbyter=7,500=8,000=80%=P8.0D=Economy=Currency=8 Aug.=Zeus>>E=v.
Presbyterian=10,000=1,000=100%=10.0=Physicality=Tech.=10 Oct.=Uranus=P=1Ø.
Presbytery=9,000=90%=P9.00D=9.0=Abstraction=Gods=Saturn=9Sept.>>A=Ø.
Preschool=5,500=5.5=80%=P5.50=Earth-Midway=5 May = Gaia.

Prescience=6,000=60%=P6.0D=Man=Earth=Royalty=6 June=Gaia=Maia>>M=M2.
Prescott William=2,500=3,000=30%=P3.0D=3.0=Creativity=Stars=Muses=3 March =C=I.
Prescribe=10,000=1,000=100%=10.0=Physicality=Tech.=10 Oct.=Uranus=P=1Ø.
Prescription=10,000=1,000=100%=10.0=Physicality=Tech.=10 Oct.=Uranus=P=1Ø.
Presence=10,000=1,000=100%=10.0=Physicality=Tech.=10 Oct.=Uranus=P=1Ø.
Present1=10,000=1,000=100%=10.0=Physicality=Tech.=10 Oct.=Uranus=P=1Ø.
Present2=10,000=1,000=100%=10.0=Physicality=Tech.=10 Oct.=Uranus=P=1Ø.
Present-day=500=5%=P5.00D=5.0=Law=Time=Venus=5 May=Aphrodite>>L=N.
Pre sentiment=7,000=70%=P7.0D=7.0=Language=Assets=Mars=7 July=Pleiades.
Presently=10,000=1,000=100%=10.0=Physicality=Tech.=10 Oct.=Uranus=P=1Ø.
Present participle=10,000=1,000=100%=10.0=Physicality=Tech.=10 Oct.=Uranus=P=1Ø.
Present perfect=10,000=1,000=100%=10.0=Physicality=Tech.=10 Oct.=Uranus=P=1Ø.
Preservation=5,500=5.5=80%=P5.50=Earth-Midway=5 May = Gaia.
Preservative=6,000=60%=P6.0D=Man=Earth=Royalty=6 June=Gaia=Maia>>M=M2.
Preserve=10,000=1,000=100%=10.0=Physicality=Tech.=10 Oct.=Uranus=P=1Ø.
Preshrunk=3,500=4,000=40%=P4.0D=Govt.=Creatocracy=4 April=Hermes=G=A4.
Preside=10,000=1,000=100%=10.0=Physicality=Tech.=10 Oct.=Uranus=P=1Ø.
President=10,000=1,000=100%=10.0=Physicality=Tech.=10 Oct.=Uranus=P=1Ø.
Presidents' Day=9,000=90%=P9.00D=9.0=Abstraction=Gods=Saturn=9Sept.>>A=Ø.
Press=10,000=1,000=100%=10.0=Physicality=Tech.=10 Oct.=Uranus=P=1Ø.
Press agent=6,500=7,000=70%=P7.0D=7.0=Language=Assets=Mars=7 July=Pleiades.
Press conference=6,500=7,000=70%=P7.0D=7.0=Lang=Assets=Mars=7 July=Pleiades.
Pressing=2,000=20%=P2.00D=2.0=Nature=Matter=Moon=2 Feb.=Cupid=N=C+_
Press release=5,000=50%=P5.00D=Law=Time=Venus=5 May = Aphrodite>>L=N.
Press room=6,000=60%=P6.0D=Man=Earth=Royalty=6 June=Gaia=Maia>>M=M2.
Pressure=10,000=1,000=100%=10.0=Physicality=Tech.=10 Oct.=Uranus=P=1Ø.
Pressure group=4,000=40%=P4.0D=Govt.=Creatocracy=4April=Mercury=Hermes=G=A4.
Pressure suit=8,000=80%=P8.0D=Economy=Currency=8 Aug.=Zeus>>E=v.
Pressurize=6,500=7,000=70%=P7.0D=7.0=Language=Assets=Mars=7 July=Pleiades.
Prestidigitation=1,500=15%=P1.50D=1.5=Authority=Solar Crown=1 May = Maia.
Prestige=9,000=90%=P9.00D=9.0=Abstraction=Gods=Saturn=9Sept.>>A=Ø.
Presto=3,000=30%=P3.0D=3.0=Creativity=Stars=Muses=3 March = C=I>>GIL.
Presume=10,000=1,000=100%=10.0=Physicality=Tech.=10 Oct.=Uranus=P=1Ø.
Presumption=10,000=1,000=100%=10.0=Physicality=Tech.=10 Oct.=Uranus=P=1Ø.
Presumptuous=4,500=5,000=50%=P5.00D=Law=Time=Venus=5 May = Aphrodite>>L=N.
Presuppose=7,000=70%=P7.0D=7.0=Language=Assets=Mars=7 July=Pleiades.
Preteen=3,000=30%=P3.0D=3.0=Creativity=Stars=Muses=3 March = C=I>>GIL.
Preteen=3,000=30%=P3.0D=3.0=Creativity=Stars=Muses=3 March = C=I>>GIL.
Pretend=10,000=1,000=100%=10.0=Physicality=Tech.=10 Oct.=Uranus=P=1Ø.
Pretense=10,000=1,000=100%=10.0=Physicality=Tech.=10 Oct.=Uranus=P=1Ø.
Pretension=5,500=5.5=80%=P5.50=Earth-Midway=5 May = Gaia.
Pretentious=6,000=60%=P6.0D=Man=Earth=Royalty=6 June=Gaia=Maia>>M=M2.
Preterit=8,500=9,000=90%=P9.00D=9.0=Abstraction=Gods=Saturn=9Sept.>>A=Ø.
Preternatural=6,000=60%=P6.0D=Man=Earth=Royalty=6 June=Gaia=Maia>>M=M2.
Pretext=7,000=70%=P7.0D=7.0=Language=Assets=Mars=7 July=Pleiades.

Pretoria=7,000=70%=P7.0D=7.0=Language=Assets=Mars=7 July=Pleiades.
Prettify=1,500=15%=P1.50D=1.5=Authority=Solar Crown=1 May = Maia.
Pretty=10,000=1,000=100%=10.0=Physicality=Tech.=10 Oct.=Uranus=P=1Ø.
Pretzel=8,500=9,000=90%=P9.00D=9.0=Abstraction=Gods=Saturn=9Sept.>>A=Ø.
Prevail=10,000=1,000=100%=10.0=Physicality=Tech.=10 Oct.=Uranus=P=1Ø.
Prevalent=4,500=5,000=50%=P5.00D=Law=Time=Venus=5 May = Aphrodite>>L=N.
Prevaricate=5,000=50%=P5.00D=Law=Time=Venus=5 May = Aphrodite>>L=N.
Prevent=14,000=14%=P1.40D=1.4=Mgt.=Solar Energy=13 May=Athena=SC=0.1
Preventive=10,000=1,000=100%=10.0=Physicality=Tech.=10 Oct.=Uranus=P=1Ø.
Preview=10,000=1,000=100%=10.0=Physicality=Tech.=10 Oct.=Uranus=P=1Ø.
Previous=3,000=30%=P3.0D=3.0=Creativity=Stars=Muses=3 March = C=I>>GIL.
Prevision=10,000=1,000=100%=10.0=Physicality=Tech.=10 Oct.=Uranus=P=1Ø.
Prey=10,000=1,000=100%=10.0=Physicality=Tech.=10 Oct.=Uranus=P=1Ø.
price=10,000=1,000=100%=10.0=Physicality=Tech.=10 Oct.=Uranus=P=1Ø.
Price Mary=3,000=30%=P3.0D=3.0=Creativity=Stars=Muses=3 March = C=I>>GIL.
Priceless=2,000=20%=P2.00D=2.0=Nature=Matter=Moon=2 Feb.=Cupid=N=C+_
Price support=7,000=70%=P7.0D=7.0=Language=Assets=Mars=7 July=Pleiades.
Price war=10,000=1,000=100%=10.0=Physicality=Tech.=10 Oct.=Uranus=P=1Ø.
Pricey=1,000=100%=10.0=1.0=Mind=Sun=1 January=Helios >> M=E4.
Prick=10,000=1,000=100%=10.0=Physicality=Tech.=10 Oct.=Uranus=P=1Ø.
Pricker=2,000=20%=P2.00D=2.0=Nature=Matter=Moon=2 Feb.=Cupid=N=C+_
Prickle=8,000=80%=P8.0D=Economy=Currency=8 Aug.=Zeus>>E=v.
Prickly=4,000=40%=P4.0D=Govt.=Creatocracy=4 April=Mercury=Hermes=G=A4.
Prickly heat=1,500=15%=P1.50D=1.5=Authority=Solar Crown=1 May = Maia.
Prickly pear=10,000=1,000=100%=10.0=Physicality=Tech.=10 Oct.=Uranus=P=1Ø.
Pride=10,000=1,000=100%=10.0=Physicality=Tech.=10 Oct.=Uranus=P=1Ø.
Prie-dieu=6,000=60%=P6.0D=Man=Earth=Royalty=6 June=Gaia=Maia>>M=M2.
Priest=10,000=1,000=100%=10.0=Physicality=Tech.=10 Oct.=Uranus=P=1Ø.
Priestess=4,000=40%=P4.0D=Govt.=Creatocracy=4 April=Mercury=Hermes=G=A4.
Priestly Joseph=2,000=20%=P2.00D=2.0=Nature=Matter=Moon=2 Feb.=Cupid=N=C+_
Prig=3,500=4,000=40%=P4.0D=Govt.=Creatocracy=4 April=Mercury=Hermes=G=A4.
Prim=4,500=5,000=50%=P5.00D=Law=Time=Venus=5 May = Aphrodite>>L=N.
Primacy=8,000=80%=P8.0D=Economy=Currency=8 Aug.=Zeus>>E=v.
Prima Donna=6,500=7,000=70%=P7.0D=7.0=Language=Assets=Mars=7 July=Pleiades.
Prima facie=4,500=5,000=50%=P5.00D=Law=Time=Venus=5 May = Aphrodite>>L=N.
Primal=4,500=5,000=50%=P5.00D=Law=Time=Venus=5 May = Aphrodite>>L=N.
Primarily=2,500=3,000=30%=P3.0D=3.0=Creativity=Stars=Muses=3 March = C=I>>GIL.
Primary=10,000=1,000=100%=10.0=Physicality=Tech.=10 Oct.=Uranus=P=1Ø.
Primary color=9,500=10,000=1,000=100%=10.0=Phy.=Tech.=10 Oct.=Uranus=P=1Ø.

Primary school=7,500=8,000=80%=P8.0D=Economy=Currency=8 Aug.=Zeus>>E=v.
A child begins primary school at about 7.5 years old.

Primate=10,000=1,000=100%=10.0=Physicality=Tech.=10 Oct.=Uranus=P=1Ø.
Prime=10,000=1,000=100%=10.0=Physicality=Tech.=10 Oct.=Uranus=P=1Ø.
Prime meridian=5,500=5.5=80%=P5.50=Earth-Midway=5 May = Gaia.
Prime minister=5,000=50%=P5.00D=Law=Time=Venus=5 May = Aphrodite>>L=N.
Prime number=6,500=7,000=70%=P7.0D=7.0=Language=Assets=Mars=7 July=Pleiades.
Primer1=8,000=80%=P8.0D=Economy=Currency=8 Aug.=Zeus>>E=v.
Primer2=9,000=90%=P9.00D=9.0=Abstraction=Gods=Saturn=9Sept.>>A=Ø.
Prime rate=9,000=90%=P9.00D=9.0=Abstraction=Gods=Saturn=9Sept.>>A=Ø.

Prime time=6,500=7,000=70%=P7.0D=7.0=Language=Assets=Mars=7 July=Pleiades.
The hours between 7 and 11 pm when the largest television audience is available. The
real prime time by ticological computation is 6.50 or by extension is actually 7:00pm.

Primeval=7,000=70%=P7.0D=7.0=Language=Assets=Mars=7 July=Pleiades.
Primitive=10,000=1,000=100%=10.0=Physicality=Tech.=10 Oct.=Uranus=P=1Ø.
Primogenitor=2,500=3,000=30%=P3.0D=3.0=Creativity=Stars=Muses=3 March = C=I
Primogeniture=10,000=1,000=100%=10.0=Physicality=Tech.=10 Oct.=Uranus=P=1Ø.
Primordial=6,000=60%=P6.0D=Man=Earth=Royalty=6 June=Gaia=Maia>>M=M2.
Primp=5,000=50%=P5.00D=Law=Time=Venus=5 May = Aphrodite>>L=N.
Prime rose=7,500=8,000=80%=P8.0D=Economy=Currency=8 Aug.=Zeus>>E=v.
Prince=9,500=10,000=1,000=100%=10.0=Physicality=Tech.=10 Oct.=Uranus=P=1Ø.
Prince Edward Island.=9,500=10,000=1,000=100%=10.0=Phy.=10 Oct.=Uranus=P=1Ø.
Princess=4,500=5,000=50%=P5.00D=Law=Time=Venus=5 May = Aphrodite>>L=N.
Principal=10,000=1,000=100%=10.0=Physicality=Tech.=10 Oct.=Uranus=P=1Ø.
Principality=3,500=4,000=40%=P4.0D=Govt.=Creato=4 April=Mercury=Hermes=G=A4.
Principle=10,000=1,000=100%=10.0=Physicality=Tech.=10 Oct.=Uranus=P=1Ø.
Principled=3,500=4,000=40%=P4.0D=Govt.=Creato=4 April=Mercury=Hermes=G=A4.
Prink=2,500=3,000=30%=P3.0D=3.0=Creativity=Stars=Muses=3 March = C=I>>GIL.
Print=10,000=1,000=100%=10.0=Physicality=Tech.=10 Oct.=Uranus=P=1Ø.
Printable=3,500=4,000=40%=P4.0D=Govt.=Creatocracy=4 April=Hermes=G=A4.
Printed circuit=9,000=90%=P9.00D=9.0=Abstraction=Gods=Saturn=9Sept.>>A=Ø.
Printer=10,000=1,000=100%=10.0=Physicality=Tech.=10 Oct.=Uranus=P=1Ø.
Printing=13,000=13%=P1.30=Solar Core=Faculty=13 January=Athena.
Printing press =5,000=50%=P5.00D=Law=Time=Venus=5 May = Aphrodite>>L=N.
Print making=5,000=50%=P5.00D=Law=Time=Venus=5 May = Aphrodite>>L=N.
Printout=2,000=20%=P2.00D=2.0=Nature=Matter=Moon=2 Feb.=Cupid=N=C+_
Prior1=5,500=5.5=80%=P5.50=Earth-Midway=5 May = Gaia.
Prior2=4,500=5,000=50%=P5.00D=Law=Time=Venus=5 May = Aphrodite>>L=N.
Prioress=3,000=30%=P3.0D=3.0=Creativity=Stars=Muses=3 March = C=I>>GIL.
Prioritize=10,000=1,000=100%=10.0=Physicality=Tech.=10 Oct.=Uranus=P=1Ø.
Priority=7,500=8,000=80%=P8.0D=Economy=Currency=8 Aug.=Zeus>>E=v.
Prior to=500=5%=P5.00D=5.0=Law=Time=Venus=5 May=Aphrodite>>L=N.
Priory=5,000=50%=P5.00D=Law=Time=Venus=5 May = Aphrodite>>L=N.

Prism=10,000=1,000=100%=10.0=Physicality=Tech.=10 Oct.=Uranus=P=1Ø.
Prison=7,500=8,000=80%=P8.0D=Economy=Currency=8 Aug.=Zeus>>E=v.

Prisoner=7,500=8,000=80%=P8.0D=Economy=Currency=8 Aug.=Zeus>>E=v.
It becomes imperative and now a law that all prisoners be subjected to the Mind Assessment Tests to determine their level of mēns rea and advise the court. People could be in prison for lack of expression, or improper expression or any other factor. The invention of the computational means to determine legality becomes a necessity prior during and after trial. This upgrades the judiciary to a Creatocciary, creative jurisprudence. This is the duty of a Creative Scientist Professional founded in the Creatocracy.

Prisoner of war=5,500=5.5=80%=P5.50=Earth-Midway=5 May = Gaia.
Prissy=5,000=50%=P5.00D=Law=Time=Venus=5 May = Aphrodite>>L=N.
Pristine=9,000=90%=P9.00D=9.0=Abstraction=Gods=Saturn=9Sept.>>A=Ø.
Prithee=500=5%=P5.00D=5.0=Law=Time=Venus=5 May=Aphrodite>>L=N.
Privacy=4,000=40%=P4.0D=Govt.=Creatocracy=4 April=Mercury=Hermes=G=A4.
Private=10,000=1,000=100%=10.0=Physicality=Tech.=10 Oct.=Uranus=P=1Ø.
Private enterprise=4,000=40%=P4.0D=Govt.=Creatocracy=4 April=Hermes=G=A4.
Privateer=11,000=11%=P1.10D=1.1=Idea=Brainchild=Inv.=11 Nov.=SC=Athena>>I=MT.
Privation=8,000=80%=P8.0D=Economy=Currency=8 Aug.=Zeus>>E=v.
Privatize=9,000=90%=P9.00D=9.0=Abstraction=Gods=Saturn=9Sept.>>A=Ø.
Privet=7,500=8,000=80%=P8.0D=Economy=Currency=8 Aug.=Zeus>>E=v.
Privilege=10,000=1,000=100%=10.0=Physicality=Tech.=10 Oct.=Uranus=P=1Ø.
Privileged=5,500=5.5=80%=P5.50=Earth-Midway=5 May = Gaia.
Privy=12,500=13,000=13%=P1.30=Solar Core=Faculty=13 January=Athena.
Prize1=10,000=1,000=100%=10.0=Physicality=Tech.=10 Oct.=Uranus=P=1Ø.
Prize2=5,000=50%=P5.00D=Law=Time=Venus=5 May = Aphrodite>>L=N.
Prize3=5,500=5.5=80%=P5.50=Earth-Midway=5 May = Gaia.
Prizefight=4,000=40%=P4.0D=Govt.=Creatocracy=4 April=Mercury=Hermes=G=A4.
Prize winner=2,500=3,000=30%=P3.0D=3.0=Creativity=Stars=Muses=3 March = C=I.
Pro1=9,000=90%=P9.00D=9.0=Abstraction=Gods=Saturn=9Sept.>>A=Ø.
Pro2=3,000=30%=P3.0D=3.0=Creativity=Stars=Muses=3 March = C=I>>GIL.
Pro-1=5,500=5.5=80%=P5.50=Earth-Midway=5 May = Gaia.
Pro-2=3,500=4,000=40%=P4.0D=Govt.=Creato=4 April=Mercury=Hermes=G=A4.
Prob.=1,000=100%=10.0=1.0=Mind=Sun=1 January=Helios >> M=E4.
Probability=10,000=1,000=100%=10.0=Physicality=Tech.=10 Oct.=Uranus=P=1Ø.
Probable=6,500=7,000=70%=P7.0D=7.0=Language=Assets=Mars=7 July=Pleiades.
Probate=8,000=80%=P8.0D=Economy=Currency=8 Aug.=Zeus>>E=v.
Probation=10,000=1,000=100%=10.0=Physicality=Tech.=10 Oct.=Uranus=P=1Ø.
Probationer=2,000=20%=P2.00D=2.0=Nature=Matter=Moon=2 Feb.=Cupid=N=C+_
Probative=4,500=5,000=50%=P5.00D=Law=Time=Venus=5 May = Aphrodite>>L=N.
Probe=10,000=1,000=100%=10.0=Physicality=Tech.=10 Oct.=Uranus=P=1Ø.
Probity=2,500=3,000=30%=P3.0D=3.0=Creativity=Stars=Muses=3 March = C=I>>GIL.

Problem=11,500=12,000=12%=P1.20D=1.2=Knowledge=Edu=12Dec.=Athena>>K=F.
Problematic=4,000=40%=P4.0D=Govt.=Creatocracy=4 April=Mercury=Hermes=G=A4.
Pro bo no=7,500=8,000=80%=P8.0D=Economy=Currency=8 Aug.=Zeus>>E=v.
Proboscis=6,000=60%=P6.0D=Man=Earth=Royalty=6 June=Gaia=Maia>>M=M2.
Procaine=8,000=80%=P8.0D=Economy=Currency=8 Aug.=Zeus>>E=v.
Procedure=10,000=1,000=100%=10.0=Physicality=Tech.=10 Oct.=Uranus=P=1Ø.
Proceed=10,000=1,000=100%=10.0=Physicality=Tech.=10 Oct.=Uranus=P=1Ø.
Proceeding=10,000=1,000=100%=10.0=Physicality=Tech.=10 Oct.=Uranus=P=1Ø.
Process1=10,000=1,000=100%=10.0=Physicality=Tech.=10 Oct.=Uranus=P=1Ø.
Process2=4,500=5,000=50%=P5.00D=Law=Time=Venus=5 May = Aphrodite>>L=N.
Procession=7,000=70%=P7.0D=7.0=Language=Assets=Mars=7 July=Pleiades.
Processional=5,500=5.5=80%=P5.50=Earth-Midway=5 May = Gaia.
Processor=9,500=10,000=1,000=100%=10.0=Physicality=Tech.=10 Oct.=Uranus=P=1Ø.
Pro-choice=8,500=9,000=90%=P9.00D=9.0=Abstraction=Gods=Saturn=9Sept.>>A=Ø.
Proclaim=6,000=60%=P6.0D=Man=Earth=Royalty=6 June=Gaia=Maia>>M=M2.

Proclivity=9,000=90%=P9.00D=9.0=Abstraction=Gods=Saturn=9Sept.>>A=Ø.
A natural propensity or inclination. The essence of the Creatocracy, Makupedia computed dictionary and encyclopedia. The percentage indicates the proclivity for government planning and budgetary analysis as well fir the application to legal purposes and trials.

Proconsul=12,000=12%=P1.20D=1.2=Knowledge=Edu=12Dec.=Athena>>K=F.
Procrastinate=7,000=70%=P7.0D=7.0=Language=Assets=Mars=7 July=Pleiades.

Procreate=3,000=30%=P3.0D=3.0=Creativity=Stars=Muses=3 March = C=I>>GIL.
The muse of a person is determined at birth through the human energy database.

Procrustean=8,500=9,000=90%=P9.00D=9.0=Abstraction=Gods=Saturn=9Sept.>>A=Ø.
Proctor=7,000=70%=P7.0D=7.0=Language=Assets=Mars=7 July=Pleiades.
Procurator=7,500=8,000=80%=P8.0D=Economy=Currency=8 Aug.=Zeus>>E=v.
Procure=11,000=11%=P1.10D=1.1=Idea=Brainchild=Inv.=11 Nov.=SC=Athena>>I=MT.
Procyon=4,000=40%=P4.0D=Govt.=Creatocracy=4 April=Mercury=Hermes=G=A4.
Prod=10,000=1,000=100%=10.0=Physicality=Tech.=10 Oct.=Uranus=P=1Ø.
Prodigal=9,000=90%=P9.00D=9.0=Abstraction=Gods=Saturn=9Sept.>>A=Ø.
Prodigious=5,000=50%=P5.00D=Law=Time=Venus=5 May = Aphrodite>>L=N.
Prodigy=9,500=10,000=1,000=100%=10.0=Physicality=Tech.=10 Oct.=Uranus=P=1Ø.
Produce=10,000=1,000=100%=10.0=Physicality=Tech.=10 Oct.=Uranus=P=1Ø.
Product=10,000=1,000=100%=10.0=Physicality=Tech.=10 Oct.=Uranus=P=1Ø.
Production=10,000=1,000=100%=10.0=Physicality=Tech.=10 Oct.=Uranus=P=1Ø.
Productive=10,000=1,000=100%=10.0=Physicality=Tech.=10 Oct.=Uranus=P=1Ø.
Proem=10,000=1,000=100%=10.0=Physicality=Tech.=10 Oct.=Uranus=P=1Ø.
Profane=10,000=1,000=100%=10.0=Physicality=Tech.=10 Oct.=Uranus=P=1Ø.
Profanity=5,000=50%=P5.00D=Law=Time=Venus=5 May = Aphrodite>>L=N.

Profess=8,500=9,000=90%=P9.00D=9.0=Abstraction=Gods=Saturn=9Sept.>>A=Ø.
Profession=10,000=1,000=100%=10.0=Physicality=Tech.=10 Oct.=Uranus=P=1Ø.
Professional=10,000=1,000=100%=10.0=Physicality=Tech.=10 Oct.=Uranus=P=1Ø.
Professionalism=3,000=30%=P3.0D=3.0=Creativity=Stars=Muses=3 March = C=I>>GIL.
Professionalize=1,500=15%=P1.50D=1.5=Authority=Solar Crown=1 May = Maia.
Professor=5,000=50%=P5.00D=Law=Time=Venus=5 May = Aphrodite>>L=N.
Proffer=3,000=30%=P3.0D=3.0=Creativity=Stars=Muses=3 March = C=I>>GIL.
Proficient=6,000=60%=P6.0D=Man=Earth=Royalty=6 June=Gaia=Maia>>M=M2.
Profile=10,000=1,000=100%=10.0=Physicality=Tech.=10 Oct.=Uranus=P=1Ø.
Profit=10,000=1,000=100%=10.0=Physicality=Tech.=10 Oct.=Uranus=P=1Ø.
Profiteer=5,000=50%=P5.00D=Law=Time=Venus=5 May = Aphrodite>>L=N.
Profligate=7,500=8,000=80%=P8.0D=Economy=Currency=8 Aug.=Zeus>>E=v.
Pro for ma=4,000=40%=P4.0D=Govt.=Creatocracy=4 April=Mercury=Hermes=G=A4.
Profound=10,000=1,000=100%=10.0=Physicality=Tech.=10 Oct.=Uranus=P=1Ø.
Profuse=10,000=1,000=100%=10.0=Physicality=Tech.=10 Oct.=Uranus=P=1Ø.
Progenitor=9,000=90%=P9.00D=9.0=Abstraction=Gods=Saturn=9Sept.>>A=Ø.
Progeny=2,500=3,000=30%=P3.0D=3.0=Creativity=Stars=Muses=3 March = C=I>>GIL.
Progesterone=6,500=7,000=70%=P7.0D=7.0=Language=Assets=Mars=7 July=Pleiades.
Prognathous=7,000=70%=P7.0D=7.0=Language=Assets=Mars=7 July=Pleiades.
Prognosis=5,500=5.5=80%=P5.50=Earth-Midway=5 May = Gaia.
Prognostic=6,500=7,000=70%=P7.0D=7.0=Language=Assets=Mars=7 July=Pleiades.
Prognosticate=4,000=40%=P4.0D=Govt.=Creatocracy=4 April=Mercury=Hermes=G=A4.
Program=10,000=1,000=100%=10.0=Physicality=Tech.=10 Oct.=Uranus=P=1Ø.
Programme=2,500=3,000=30%=P3.0D=3.0=Creativity=Stars=Muses=3 March = CI/GIL.
Programming=4,000=40%=P4.0D=Govt.=Creatocracy=4 April=Mercury=Hermes=G=A4.
Progress=10,000=1,000=100%=10.0=Physicality=Tech.=10 Oct.=Uranus=P=1Ø.
Progression=10,000=1,000=100%=10.0=Physicality=Tech.=10 Oct.=Uranus=P=1Ø.
Progressive=10,000=1,000=100%=10.0=Physicality=Tech.=10 Oct.=Uranus=P=1Ø.
Prohibit=6,000=60%=P6.0D=Man=Earth=Royalty=6 June=Gaia=Maia>>M=M2.
Prohibition=6,500=7,000=70%=P7.0D=7.0=Language=Assets=Mars=7 July=Pleiades.
Prohibitive=5,500=5.5=80%=P5.50=Earth-Midway=5 May = Gaia.
Project=10,000=1,000=100%=10.0=Physicality=Tech.=10 Oct.=Uranus=P=1Ø.
Projectile=7,500=8,000=80%=P8.0D=Economy=Currency=8 Aug.=Zeus>>E=v.
Projector=4,000=40%=P4.0D=Govt.=Creatocracy=4 April=Mercury=Hermes=G=A4.
Prokaryote=8,000=80%=P8.0D=Economy=Currency=8 Aug.=Zeus>>E=v.
Prokofiev Sergel=2,500=3,000=30%=P3.0D=3.0=Cre.=Stars=Muses=3 March= CI/GIL.
Prolapse=8,000=80%=P8.0D=Economy=Currency=8 Aug.=Zeus>>E=v.
Prolegomenon=3,000=30%=P3.0D=3.0=Creativity=Stars=Muses=3 March = CI/GIL.
Proletarian=5,500=5.5=80%=P5.50=Earth-Midway=5 May = Gaia.
Proletariat=8,500=9,000=90%=P9.00D=9.0=Abstraction=Gods=Saturn=9Sept.>>A=Ø.
Pro life=7,000=70%=P7.0D=7.0=Language=Assets=Mars=7 July=Pleiades.
Proliferate=8,000=80%=P8.0D=Economy=Currency=8 Aug.=Zeus>>E=v.
Prolific=7,500=8,000=80%=P8.0D=Economy=Currency=8 Aug.=Zeus>>E=v.
Prolix=5,500=5.5=80%=P5.50=Earth-Midway=5 May = Gaia.
Prologue=5,000=50%=P5.00D=Law=Time=Venus=5 May = Aphrodite>>L=N.

Prolong=4,000=40%=P4.0D=Govt.=Creatocracy=4 April=Mercury=Hermes=G=A4.
Prom=5,500=5.5=80%=P5.50=Earth-Midway=5 May = Gaia.
Promenade=10,000=1,000=100%=10.0=Physicality=Tech.=10 Oct.=Uranus=P=1Ø.

Prometheus=7,000=70%=P7.0D=7.0=Language=Assets=Mars=7 July=Pleiades.
A Titan who stole fire from Olympus and gave it to humankind. So measurements, computations and all forms of calculations once expressed in formula become fire. The more formula one invents the more fire he has and the more powerful he becomes. Perhaps this is why the Gods revealed and apotheosized Peter Matthews-Akukalia.

Promethium=7,000=70%=P7.0D=7.0=Language=Assets=Mars=7 July=Pleiades.
Prominence=4,500=5,000=50%=P5.00D=Law=Time=Venus=5 May = Aphrodite>>L=N.
Prominent=7,000=70%=P7.0D=7.0=Language=Assets=Mars=7 July=Pleiades.
Promiscuous=8,500=9,000=90%=P9.00D=9.0=Abstraction=Gods=Saturn=9Sept.>>A=Ø.
Promise=10,000=1,000=100%=10.0=Physicality=Tech.=10 Oct.=Uranus=P=1Ø.
Promising=2,000=20%=P2.00D=2.0=Nature=Matter=Moon=2 Feb.=Cupid=N=C+_
Promissory=2,500=3,000=30%=P3.0D=3.0=Creativity=Stars=Muses=3 March = CI/GIL.
Promissory note=8,000=80%=P8.0D=Economy=Currency=8 Aug.=Zeus>>E=v.
Promontory=7,000=70%=P7.0D=7.0=Language=Assets=Mars=7 July=Pleiades.
Promote=10,000=1,000=100%=10.0=Physicality=Tech.=10 Oct.=Uranus=P=1Ø.
Promoter=7,000=70%=P7.0D=7.0=Language=Assets=Mars=7 July=Pleiades.
Prompt=10,000=1,000=100%=10.0=Physicality=Tech.=10 Oct.=Uranus=P=1Ø.
Promulgate=10,000=1,000=100%=10.0=Physicality=Tech.=10 Oct.=Uranus=P=1Ø.
Pron.=1,000=100%=10.0=1.0=Mind=Sun=1 January=Helios >> M=E4.
Prone=7,500=8,000=80%=P8.0D=Economy=Currency=8 Aug.=Zeus>>E=v.
Prong=6,000=60%=P6.0D=Man=Earth=Royalty=6 June=Gaia=Maia>>M=M2.
Pronghorn=8,500=9,000=90%=P9.00D=9.0=Abstraction=Gods=Saturn=9Sept.>>A=Ø.
Pronoun=5,000=50%=P5.00D=Law=Time=Venus=5 May = Aphrodite>>L=N.
Pronounce=6,500=7,000=70%=P7.0D=7.0=Language=Assets=Mars=7 July=Pleiades.
Pronounced=1,500=15%=P1.50D=1.5=Authority=Solar Crown=1 May = Maia.
Pronouncement=3,000=30%=P3.0D=3.0=Creativity=Stars=Muses=3 March = CI/GIL.
Pronto=3,500=4,000=40%=P4.0D=Govt.=Creatocracy=4 April=Mercury=Hermes=G=A4.
Pronunciamento=2,000=20%=P2.00D=2.0=Nature=Matter=Moon=2 Feb.=Cupid=N=C+_
Proof=10,000=1,000=100%=10.0=Physicality=Tech.=10 Oct.=Uranus=P=1Ø.
Proofread=11,500=12,000=12%=P1.20D=1.2=Knowledge=Edu=12Dec.=Athena>>K=F.
Prop1=8,000=80%=P8.0D=Economy=Currency=8 Aug.=Zeus>>E=v.
Prop2=1,500=15%=P1.50D=1.5=Authority=Solar Crown=1 May = Maia.
Prop3=1,500=15%=P1.50D=1.5=Authority=Solar Crown=1 May = Maia.
Prop.=1,500=15%=P1.50D=1.5=Authority=Solar Crown=1 May = Maia.
Propaganda=8,500=9,000=90%=P9.00D=9.0=Abstract=Gods=Saturn=9Sept.>>A=Ø.
Propagate=10,000=1,000=100%=10.0=Physicality=Tech.=10 Oct.=Uranus=P=1Ø.
Propane=7,500=8,000=80%=P8.0D=Economy=Currency=8 Aug.=Zeus>>E=v.

Propel=6,000=60%=P6.0D=Man=Earth=Royalty=6 June=Gaia=Maia>>M=M2.
The Creatocracy is propelled by the love for humanity and the need to express creativity.

Propellant=6,000=60%=P6.0D=Man=Earth=Royalty=6 June=Gaia=Maia>>M=M2.
Propeller=8,500=9,000=90%=P9.00D=9.0=Abstraction=Gods=Saturn=9Sept.>>A=Ø.

Propensity=6,000=60%=P6.0D=Man=Earth=Royalty=6 June=Gaia=Maia>>M=M2.
Castle Makupedia>>the Creatocracy Encyclopedia & Computed Dictionary computes the
energy quantum in a thing on the 10,000 particulate scale, the peak of aspiration at 1,000,
the average propensity at the Daily ability rating of 100% and then the resultant value
and dimension of existence at the Maks. Hence 10,000=1,000=100=10.0. To determine
the inclinations of individuals, the GIL is obtained through the Mind Assessment Tests.
Synchronization and Crystallization then occurs for the méns reá or mind element used.

Proper=10,000=1,000=100%=10.0=Physicality=Tech.=10 Oct.=Uranus=P=1Ø.
Proper fraction=5,000=50%=P5.00D=Law=Time=Venus=5 May = Aphrodite>>L=N.
Proper noun=6,000=60%=P6.0D=Man=Earth=Royalty=6 June=Gaia=Maia>>M=M2.
Propertied=5,000=50%=P5.00D=Law=Time=Venus=5 May = Aphrodite>>L=N.
Property=10,000=1,000=100%=10.0=Physicality=Tech.=10 Oct.=Uranus=P=1Ø.
Prophecy=4,500=5,000=50%=P5.00D=Law=Time=Venus=5 May = Aphrodite>>L=N.
Prophesy=6,000=60%=P6.0D=Man=Earth=Royalty=6 June=Gaia=Maia>>M=M2.

Prophet=11,000=11%=P1.10D=1.1=Idea=Brainchild=Inv.=11 Nov.=SC=Athena>>I=MT.
Prophetess=9,000=90%=P9.00D=9.0=Abstraction=Gods=Saturn=9Sept.>>A=Ø.
By knowing the prophets one can test the spirits in them for validity. Athena inspires a
true prophet so wisdom handicraft and mental warfare will be tested in Katy or in whole
from the utterances of the prophet. The prophetess will be subjected to abstraction such as
the residing or guiding spirit the day she was born and will possess certain extraordinary
skills. Peter Matthews-Akukalia is a prophecy of the Scriptures, spoken by Nostradamus
Emerson and Skinner. Given to his mother at womb, he holds the power or knowledge of
the stars in his hands. He is the Nigerian Creative Scientist who cracked the controversial
stellar code. Google Peter Matthews-Akukalia. Makupedia.

Prophetic=3,500=4,000=40%=P4.0D=Govt.=Creat=4 April=Mercury=Hermes=G=A4.
Prophylactic=10,000=1,000=100%=10.0=Physicality=Tech.=10 Oct.=Uranus=P=1Ø.
Prophylaxis=10,000=1,000=100%=10.0=Physicality=Tech.=10 Oct.=Uranus=P=1Ø.
Propinquity=2,500=3,000=30%=P3.0D=3.0=Creativity=Stars=Muses=3 March = CI/GIL.
Propitiate=2,500=3,000=30%=P3.0D=3.0=Creativity=Stars=Muses=3 March = CI/GIL.
Propitious=3,000=30%=P3.0D=3.0=Creativity=Stars=Muses=3 March = CI/GIL.
Proponent=5,500=5.5=80%=P5.50=Earth-Midway=5 May = Gaia.
Proportion=10,000=1,000=100%=10.0=Physicality=Tech.=10 Oct.=Uranus=P=1Ø.
Propose=10,000=1,000=100%=10.0=Physicality=Tech.=10 Oct.=Uranus=P=1Ø.

Proposition=10,000=1,000=100%=10.0=Physicality=Tech.=10 Oct.=Uranus=P=1Ø.
Propound=10,000=1,000=100%=10.0=Physicality=Tech.=10 Oct.=Uranus=P=1Ø.
Proprietary=10,000=1,000=100%=10.0=Physicality=Tech.=10 Oct.=Uranus=P=1Ø.
Proprietor=3,000=30%=P3.0D=3.0=Creativity=Stars=Muses=3 March = CI/GIL.
Proprietress=5,000=50%=P5.00D=Law=Time=Venus=5 May = Aphrodite>>L=N.
Pro piety=10,000=1,000=100%=10.0=Physicality=Tech.=10 Oct.=Uranus=P=1Ø.
Propulsion=6,500=7,000=70%=P7.0D=7.0=Language=Assets=Mars=7 July=Pleiades.
Pro rata=5,500=5.5=80%=P5.50=Earth-Midway=5 May = Gaia.
Prorate=4,000=40%=P4.0D=Govt.=Creatocracy=4 April=Mercury=Hermes=G=A4.
Pro rogue=5,500=5.5=80%=P5.50=Earth-Midway=5 May = Gaia.
Prosaic=6,500=7,000=70%=P7.0D=7.0=Language=Assets=Mars=7 July=Pleiades.
Proscenium=6,500=7,000=70%=P7.0D=7.0=Language=Assets=Mars=7 July=Pleiades.
Proscribe=7,000=70%=P7.0D=7.0=Language=Assets=Mars=7 July=Pleiades.

Prose=6,000=60%=P6.0D=Man=Earth=Royalty=6 June=Gaia=Maia>>M=M2.
See The Creatocracy Republic by Peter Matthews-Akukalia. It contains two proses named The Missing Seaman and Last of the Noble Amazons.

Prosecute=8,000=80%=P8.0D=Economy=Currency=8 Aug.=Zeus>>E=v.
Proselyte=5,000=50%=P5.00D=Law=Time=Venus=5 May = Aphrodite>>L=N.
Proselytize=5,500=5.5=80%=P5.50=Earth-Midway=5 May = Gaia.
Prosimian=6,000=60%=P6.0D=Man=Earth=Royalty=6 June=Gaia=Maia>>M=M2.
Prosody=6,000=60%=P6.0D=Man=Earth=Royalty=6 June=Gaia=Maia>>M=M2.
Prospect=10,000=1,000=100%=10.0=Physicality=Tech.=10 Oct.=Uranus=P=1Ø.
Prospective=2,500=3,000=30%=P3.0D=3.0=Creativity=Stars=Muses=3 March = CI/GIL.
Prospectus=10,500=11,000=11%=P1.10D=1.1=Idea=Brainchild=11 Nov.=Athena>>I=MT.
Prosper=3,500=4,000=40%=P4.0D=Govt.=Creatocracy=4 April=Mercury=Hermes=G=A4.
Prosperity=2,500=3,000=30%=P3.0D=3.0=Creativity=Stars=Muses=3 March = CI/GIL.
Prosperous=3,500=4,000=40%=P4.0D=Govt.=Creatocracy=4 April=Hermes=G=A4.
Prostate=16,000=16%=P1.60D=1.6=Cycle of Incarnation=Mind of GOD=1 June = Maia.
Prosthesis=7,500=8,000=80%=P8.0D=Economy=Currency=8 Aug.=Zeus>>E=v.
Prostitute=17,500=18,000=18%=P1.80D=Solar Currency=Maks Currencies=1 Aug.=Maia.
Prostrate=10,000=1,000=100%=10.0=Physicality=Tech.=10 Oct.=Uranus=P=1Ø.
Prosy=1,500=15%=P1.50D=1.5=Authority=Solar Crown=1 May = Maia.
Prot.=500=5%=P5.00D=5.0=Law=Time=Venus=5 May=Aphrodite>>L=N.
Prot-=1,500=15%=P1.50D=1.5=Authority=Solar Crown=1 May = Maia.
Protactinium=9,000=90%=P9.00D=9.0=Abstraction=Gods=Saturn=9Sept.>>A=Ø.
Protagonist=15,000=1,500=15%=P1.50D=1.5=Authority=Solar Crown=1 May = Maia.
Protagoras=3,000=30%=P3.0D=3.0=Creativity=Stars=Muses=3 March = CI/GIL.
Protean=4,500=5,000=50%=P5.00D=Law=Time=Venus=5 May = Aphrodite>>L=N.
Protect=5,000=50%=P5.00D=Law=Time=Venus=5 May = Aphrodite>>L=N.
Protection=7,500=8,000=80%=P8.0D=Economy=Currency=8 Aug.=Zeus>>E=v.
Protectionism=9,000=90%=P9.00D=9.0=Abstraction=Gods=Saturn=9Sept.>>A=Ø.
Protector=9,000=90%=P9.00D=9.0=Abstraction=Gods=Saturn=9Sept.>>A=Ø.

Protectorate=12,000=12%=P1.20D=1.2=Knowledge=Edu=12Dec.=Athena>>K=F.
Protégé=9,000=90%=P9.00D=9.0=Abstraction=Gods=Saturn=9Sept.>>A=Ø.
Protein=10,000=1,000=100%=10.0=Physicality=Tech.=10 Oct.=Uranus=P=1Ø.
Pro tem=1,000=100%=10.0=1.0=Mind=Sun=1 January=Helios >> M=E4.
Pro tem pore=3,500=4,000=40%=P4.0D=Govt.=Creatocracy=4 April=Hermes=G=A4.
Protest=10,000=1,000=100%=10.0=Physicality=Tech.=10 Oct.=Uranus=P=1Ø.
Protestant=10,000=1,000=100%=10.0=Physicality=Tech.=10 Oct.=Uranus=P=1Ø.

Proteus=6,000=60%=P6.0D=Man=Earth=Royalty=6 June=Gaia=Maia>>M=M2.
Greek myth. A sea God able to change his shape at will. In the jurisdiction of Gaia. The emphasis is on the ability to change shape. This is the principle of Spiralogy.

Pro to-=3,000=30%=P3.0D=3.0=Creativity=Stars=Muses=3 March = CI/GIL.
Protocol=10,000=1,000=100%=10.0=Physicality=Tech.=10 Oct.=Uranus=P=1Ø.
Pro to-Indo-European=3,500=4,000=40%=P4.0D=Govt.=Creato=4 April=Hermes=G=A4.
Proton=6,500=7,000=70%=P7.0D=7.0=Language=Assets=Mars=7 July=Pleiades.
Protoplasm=7,000=70%=P7.0D=7.0=Language=Assets=Mars=7 July=Pleiades.
Prototype=10,000=1,000=100%=10.0=Physicality=Tech.=10 Oct.=Uranus=P=1Ø.
Protozoan=10,000=1,000=100%=10.0=Physicality=Tech.=10 Oct.=Uranus=P=1Ø.
Protract=5,500=5.5=80%=P5.50=Earth-Midway=5 May = Gaia.
Protractile=2,500=3,000=30%=P3.0D=3.0=Creativity=Stars=Muses=3 March = CI/GIL.
Protractor=4,500=5,000=50%=P5.00D=Law=Time=Venus=5 May = Aphrodite>>L=N.
Protrude=6,000=60%=P6.0D=Man=Earth=Royalty=6 June=Gaia=Maia>>M=M2.
Protuberance=7,000=70%=P7.0D=7.0=Language=Assets=Mars=7 July=Pleiades.
Proud=10,000=1,000=100%=10.0=Physicality=Tech.=10 Oct.=Uranus=P=1Ø.
Proudhon Pierre=2,500=3,000=30%=P3.0D=3.0=Cre.=Stars=Muses=3 March = CI/GIL.
Proust Marcel.=2,000=20%=P2.00D=2.0=Nature=Matter=Moon=2 Feb.=Cupid=N=C+_
Prov.=1,000=100%=10.0=1.0=Mind=Sun=1 January=Helios >> M=E4.
Prove=10,000=1,000=100%=10.0=Physicality=Tech.=10 Oct.=Uranus=P=1Ø.
Provenance=6,000=60%=P6.0D=Man=Earth=Royalty=6 June=Gaia=Maia>>M=M2.
Provençal=5,000=50%=P5.00D=Law=Time=Venus=5 May = Aphrodite>>L=N.
Provence=6,500=7,000=70%=P7.0D=7.0=Language=Assets=Mars=7 July=Pleiades.
Provender=6,500=7,000=70%=P7.0D=7.0=Language=Assets=Mars=7 July=Pleiades.
Provenience=2,500=3,000=30%=P3.0D=3.0=Creativity=Stars=Muses=3 March = CI/GIL.
Proverb=10,000=1,000=100%=10.0=Physicality=Tech.=10 Oct.=Uranus=P=1Ø.

Proverbs=3,000=30%=P3.0D=3.0=Creativity=Stars=Muses=3 March = CI/GIL.

Provide=10,000=1,000=100%=10.0=Physicality=Tech.=10 Oct.=Uranus=P=1Ø.
Provided=2,000=20%=P2.00D=2.0=Nature=Matter=Moon=2 Feb.=Cupid=N=C+_
Providence=6,500=7,000=70%=P7.0D=7.0=Language=Assets=Mars=7 July=Pleiades.
Providence.=6,000=60%=P6.0D=Man=Earth=Royalty=6 June=Gaia=Maia>>M=M2.
Provident=4,000=40%=P4.0D=Govt.=Creatocracy=4 April=Mercury=Hermes=G=A4.

Providential=4,000=40%=P4.0D=Govt.=Creatocracy=4 April=Mercury=Hermes=G=A4.
Providing=2,000=20%=P2.00D=2.0=Nature=Matter=Moon=2 Feb.=Cupid=N=C+_
Province=10,000=1,000=100%=10.0=Physicality=Tech.=10 Oct.=Uranus=P=1Ø.
Provincial=6,500=7,000=70%=P7.0D=7.0=Language=Assets=Mars=7 July=Pleiades.
Proving ground=4,000=40%=P4.0D=Govt.=Creatocracy=4 April=Mercury=Hermes=G=A4.
Provision=10,000=1,000=100%=10.0=Physicality=Tech.=10 Oct.=Uranus=P=1Ø.
Provisional=6,000=60%=P6.0D=Man=Earth=Royalty=6 June=Gaia=Maia>>M=M2.
Proviso=7,000=70%=P7.0D=7.0=Language=Assets=Mars=7 July=Pleiades.
Provo=6,000=60%=P6.0D=Man=Earth=Royalty=6 June=Gaia=Maia>>M=M2.
Provocation=4,500=5,000=50%=P5.00D=Law=Time=Venus=5 May = Aphrodite>>L=N.
Provocative=1,500=15%=P1.50D=1.5=Authority=Solar Crown=1 May = Maia.
Provoke=6,000=60%=P6.0D=Man=Earth=Royalty=6 June=Gaia=Maia>>M=M2.
Provolone=3,000=30%=P3.0D=3.0=Creativity=Stars=Muses=3 March = CI/GIL.
Provost=5,000=50%=P5.00D=Law=Time=Venus=5 May = Aphrodite>>L=N.
Provost Marshall=3,000=30%=P3.0D=3.0=Creativity=Stars=Muses=3 March = CI/GIL.
Prow=5,000=50%=P5.00D=Law=Time=Venus=5 May = Aphrodite>>L=N.
Prowess=7,000=70%=P7.0D=7.0=Language=Assets=Mars=7 July=Pleiades.
Prowl=5,500=5.5=80%=P5.50=Earth-Midway=5 May = Gaia.
Prowl car=1,500=15%=P1.50D=1.5=Authority=Solar Crown=1 May = Maia.
Proximate=6,000=60%=P6.0D=Man=Earth=Royalty=6 June=Gaia=Maia>>M=M2.
Proximity=2,500=3,000=30%=P3.0D=3.0=Creativity=Stars=Muses=3 March = CI/GIL.
Proxy=9,000=90%=P9.00D=9.0=Abstraction=Gods=Saturn=9Sept.>>A=Ø.
Prude=9,500=10,000=1,000=100%=10.0=Physicality=Tech.=10 Oct.=Uranus=P=1Ø.
Prudent=7,500=8,000=80%=P8.0D=Economy=Currency=8 Aug.=Zeus>>E=v.
Prune1=3,500=4,000=40%=P4.0D=Govt.=Creato=4 April=Mercury=Hermes=G=A4.
Prune2=10,000=1,000=100%=10.0=Physicality=Tech.=10 Oct.=Uranus=P=1Ø.
Prurient=5,000=50%=P5.00D=Law=Time=Venus=5 May = Aphrodite>>L=N.
Prussia=7,500=8,000=80%=P8.0D=Economy=Currency=8 Aug.=Zeus>>E=v.
Pry1=4,500=5,000=50%=P5.00D=Law=Time=Venus=5 May = Aphrodite>>L=N.
Pry2=9,000=90%=P9.00D=9.0=Abstraction=Gods=Saturn=9Sept.>>A=Ø.
P.S.=1,500=15%=P1.50D=1.5=Authority=Solar Crown=1 May = Maia.

Psalm=5,500=5.5=80%=P5.50=Earth-Midway=5 May = Gaia.
Inspired by Gaia Midway >> Maia. Psalms is a midway Scripture and Mind of GOD.
On earth as Gaia Midway Maia exists as an independent being. At the cosmic she
leads the Pleiades.
The Psalm written are a set of Earth codes that translate into human destiny. The smart
value for Psalm WDSD is 5.5 >> Gaia Midway who stands between Heaven and Earth to
judge all activities of both spirits and men. Gaia is Maia the Mind of GOD. The smart
values for destiny is 10.0 >> which after definition indicates that it can only be discovered
through technology or MindTech as a physicality. Now destiny is spiritual and so is energy.
The only energy system given by scriptures are means by which signs are computed read and
interpreted. GOD made it clear that in time to come which is this time of tech advancement
He will write the laws of human destiny upon the tablet of our hearts. Tablets translate into
many things that today are known as the electrical hi-tech energy gadgets called phones. It

means that phone lines once used for a short period of 21,600seconds = 6hours take up the solar and lunar energy flux around us. Tracking them to the Psalms shows us the codes that will run our lives at that instant. As much as we can change our phone numbers so also we can change our destinies. 08161928511 >> 0 indicates that Psalm is involved as a means of abstraction on the law of 9. 0 = Ø = 9.0. Psalm 81,61,92,85,11 contains codes that will run this destiny. Codes are interpreted as required by Eccl.8:1-4,Prov. 25:1-4.

However we need to compute the Psalm and track it for coherence and alignment.

PSALM = P*S*A*L*M = P = >> P= 1.4 >> S = 6.0 >> A = 7.0 >> L = 4.0 >> M = 3.0

1.4*6.0x=px=7.4+8.4=15.8x=px=77.96 = 80 = 8.0

7.0*4.0x=px=11+28=39x=px=347= 400 4.0

[3.0] * 8.0*4.0x=px=12+32=44x=px=428 = 43 = 4.3

3.0*4.3x=px=7.3+12.9=20.2x=px=114.37 = 1.1 >> Idea >> Brainchild >> Athena.

Psalm is brainchild of Athena. Gaia is the Earth or the World. Destiny is a technology that runs on the planetary energy flux systems. Psalm is a book of wisdom containing destiny codes of everyone through phones. It aligns with brain energy for order. Destiny Tracking >> Destrack is a discovery of Peter Matthews - Akukalia, the Solar Crown King, Owner of the Solar Core Assets. Castle Makupedia, The God of Creatocracy Genius & Mind.

Psalmody=10,000=1,000=100%=10.0=Physicality=Tech.=10 Oct.=Uranus=P=1Ø.
Psalter=10,000=1,000=100%=10.0=Physicality=Tech.=10 Oct.=Uranus=P=1Ø.
PSAT=2,000=20%=P2.00D=2.0=Nature=Matter=Moon=2 Feb.=Cupid=N=C+_
Pseudo-=3,500=4,000=40%=P4.0D=Govt.=Creatocracy=4 April=Hermes=G=A4.
Pseudonym=4,000=40%=P4.0D=Govt.=Creatocracy=4 April=Mercury=Hermes=G=A4.
psf.=2,000=20%=P2.00D=2.0=Nature=Matter=Moon=2 Feb.=Cupid=N=C+_
psi1=4,000=40%=P4.0D=Govt.=Creatocracy=4 April=Mercury=Hermes=G=A4.
psi2=2,000=20%=P2.00D=2.0=Nature=Matter=Moon=2 Feb.=Cupid=N=C+_
Psittacosis=9,500=10,000=1,000=100%=10.0=Physicality=Tech.=10 Oct.=Uranus=P=1Ø.
Psoriasis=6,000=60%=P6.0D=Man=Earth=Royalty=6 June=Gaia=Maia>>M=M2.
PST=1,500=15%=P1.50D=1.5=Authority=Solar Crown=1 May = Maia.
Psych=6,000=60%=P6.0D=Man=Earth=Royalty=6 June=Gaia=Maia>>M=M2.
Psyche=7,500=8,000=80%=P8.0D=Economy=Currency=8 Aug.=Zeus>>E=v.
Psychedelic=7,500=8,000=80%=P8.0D=Economy=Currency=8 Aug.=Zeus>>E=v.
Psychiatry=7,500=8,000=80%=P8.0D=Economy=Currency=8 Aug.=Zeus>>E=v.
Psychic=9,000=90%=P9.00D=9.0=Abstraction=Gods=Saturn=9Sept.>>A=Ø.
Psycho-=3,000=30%=P3.0D=3.0=Creativity=Stars=Muses=3 March = CI/GIL.
Psychoactive=3,000=30%=P3.0D=3.0=Creativity=Stars=Muses=3 March = CI/GIL.

Psychoanalysis=10,000=1,000=100%=10.0=Physicality=Tech.=10 Oct.=Uranus=P=1Ø.
The Creatocracy has the Mind Assessment Test for this purpose for all ages and levels. In the Psycho-categories, Principles of Psychoeconomix and Psychoastronomy exist.

Psychodrama=9,000=90%=P9.00D=9.0=Abstraction=Gods=Saturn=9Sept.>>A=Ø.
Psychogenic=4,500=5,000=50%=P5.00D=Law=Time=Venus=5 May = Aphrodite>>L=N.

Psychologist=6,000=60%=P6.0D=Man=Earth=Royalty=6 June=Gaia=Maia>>M=M2.
The Creative Scientist is a creative or computational psychologist>>Creatochologist. See the book >> The ORACLE: Peter Matthews-Akukalia, World's 1ˢᵗ Creative Scientist.

Psychology=9,000=90%=P9.00D=9.0=Abstraction=Gods=Saturn=9Sept.>>A=Ø.
The Creatocracy measures the Psychology Potentials Creativity and Career of a person indicated as P1P2C1C2. Creative Sciences classifies psychology as the computed energy that results to the personality and emotional balance. Potentials as the quantum of ideas and talents. Creativity as resultant behavior (normal and genius) and career (Occupation). See Template & Manifesto for the Creative Economy 2: Principles of Psychoeconomix by Peter Matthews-Akukalia. Published by AuthorHouse in 2016.

Psychometrics=7,500=8,000=80%=P8.0D=Economy=Currency=8 Aug.=Zeus>>E=v.
Psychometry=1,500=15%=P1.50D=1.5=Authority=Solar Crown=1 May = Maia.
Psychomotor=5,500=5.5=80%=P5.50=Earth-Midway=5 May = Gaia.
Psychopath=8,000=80%=P8.0D=Economy=Currency=8 Aug.=Zeus>>E=v.
Psychopathology=5,000=50%=P5.00D=Law=Time=Venus=5 May = Aphrodite>>L=N.
Psychophysiology=5,500=5.5=80%=P5.50=Earth-Midway=5 May = Gaia.
Psychosexual=5,000=50%=P5.00D=Law=Time=Venus=5 May = Aphrodite>>L=N.
Psychosis=8,000=80%=P8.0D=Economy=Currency=8 Aug.=Zeus>>E=v.
Psychosomatic=10,000=1,000=100%=10.0=Physicality=Tech.=10 Oct.=Uranus=P=1Ø.
Psychotherapy=10,000=1,000=100%=10.0=Physicality=Tech.=10 Oct.=Uranus=P=1Ø.
Pt.=3,000=30%=P3.0D=3.0=Creativity=Stars=Muses=3 March = CI/GIL.
pt.=2,000=20%=P2.00D=2.0=Nature=Matter=Moon=2 Feb.=Cupid=N=C+_
P.T.=3,000=30%=P3.0D=3.0=Creativity=Stars=Muses=3 March = CI/GIL.
PTA=1,500=15%=P1.50D=1.5=Authority=Solar Crown=1 May = Maia.
ptarmigan=6,500=7,000=70%=P7.0D=7.0=Language=Assets=Mars=7 July=Pleiades.
PT boat=7,000=70%=P7.0D=7.0=Language=Assets=Mars=7 July=Pleiades.
pterodactyl=5,500=5.5=80%=P5.50=Earth-Midway=5 May = Gaia.
pterosaur=8,000=80%=P8.0D=Economy=Currency=8 Aug.=Zeus>>E=v.
Ptolemaic system=6,000=60%=P6.0D=Man=Earth=Royalty=6 June=Gaia=Maia>>M=M2.
Ptolemy1=9,000=90%=P9.00D=9.0=Abstraction=Gods=Saturn=9Sept.>>A=Ø.
Ptolemy2=4,500=5,000=50%=P5.00D=Law=Time=Venus=5 May = Aphrodite>>L=N.
Ptomaine=7,000=70%=P7.0D=7.0=Language=Assets=Mars=7 July=Pleiades.
Ptomaine poisoning=3,500=4,000=40%=P4.0D=Govt.=4April=Mercury=Hermes=G=A4.
Pu=3,000=30%=P3.0D=3.0=Creativity=Stars=Muses=3 March = CI/GIL.
pub=2,500=3,000=30%=P3.0D=3.0=Creativity=Stars=Muses=3 March = CI/GIL.
Puberty=8,000=80%=P8.0D=Economy=Currency=8 Aug.=Zeus>>E=v.
Pubescent=7,500=8,000=80%=P8.0D=Economy=Currency=8 Aug.=Zeus>>E=v.
Pubic=7,500=8,000=80%=P8.0D=Economy=Currency=8 Aug.=Zeus>>E=v.
Pubis=7,500=8,000=80%=P8.0D=Economy=Currency=8 Aug.=Zeus>>E=v.
Public=10,000=1,000=100%=10.0=Physicality=Tech.=10 Oct.=Uranus=P=1Ø.
Public address system=10,000=1,000=100%=10.0=Phy=Tech.=10 Oct.=Uranus=P=1Ø.
Publican=9,000=90%=P9.00D=9.0=Abstraction=Gods=Saturn=9Sept.>>A=Ø.

Publication=5,000=50%=P5.00D=Law=Time=Venus=5 May = Aphrodite>>L=N.
Public defender=8,000=80%=P8.0D=Economy=Currency=8 Aug.=Zeus>>E=v.
Public domain=10,000=1,000=100%=10.0=Physicality=Tech.=10 Oct.=Uranus=P=1Ø.
Public house=3,500=4,000=40%=P4.0D=Govt.=Creatocracy=4 April=Hermes=G=A4.
Publicist=4,500=5,000=50%=P5.00D=Law=Time=Venus=5 May = Aphrodite>>L=N.
Publicity=4,000=40%=P4.0D=Govt.=Creatocracy=4 April=Mercury=Hermes=G=A4.
Publicize=1,500=15%=P1.50D=1.5=Authority=Solar Crown=1 May = Maia.
Public relations=10,000=1,000=100%=10.0=Physicality=Tech.=10 Oct.=Uranus=P=1Ø.
Public school=10,000=1,000=100%=10.0=Physicality=Tech.=10 Oct.=Uranus=P=1Ø.
Public-spirited=4,500=5,000=50%=P5.00D=Law=Time=Venus=5 May = Aphrodite>>L=N.
Publish=10,000=1,000=100%=10.0=Physicality=Tech.=10 Oct.=Uranus=P=1Ø.
Puccini Giacomo=2,500=3,000=30%=P3.0D=3.0=Cre.=Stars=Muses=3 March = CI/GIL.
puck=6,000=60%=P6.0D=Man=Earth=Royalty=6 June=Gaia=Maia>>M=M2.
Puck=3,000=30%=P3.0D=3.0=Creativity=Stars=Muses=3 March = CI/GIL.
Pucker=7,000=70%=P7.0D=7.0=Language=Assets=Mars=7 July=Pleiades.
Puckish=1,000=100%=Physicality=Tech.=10 Oct.=Uranus=P=1Ø.
Pudding=9,000=90%=P9.00D=9.0=Abstraction=Gods=Saturn=9Sept.>>A=Ø.
Puddle=5,000=50%=P5.00D=Law=Time=Venus=5 May = Aphrodite>>L=N.
Puddling=7,500=8,000=80%=P8.0D=Economy=Currency=8 Aug.=Zeus>>E=v.
Pudendum=6,000=60%=P6.0D=Man=Earth=Royalty=6 June=Gaia=Maia>>M=M2.
Pudgy=4,500=5,000=50%=P5.00D=Law=Time=Venus=5 May = Aphrodite>>L=N.
Puebla=5,500=5.5=80%=P5.50=Earth-Midway=5 May = Gaia.
Pueblo=10,000=1,000=100%=10.0=Physicality=Tech.=10 Oct.=Uranus=P=1Ø.
Pueblo.=5,500=5.5=80%=P5.50=Earth-Midway=5 May = Gaia.
Puerile=2,500=3,000=30%=P3.0D=3.0=Creativity=Stars=Muses=3 March = CI/GIL.
Puerperal=7,000=70%=P7.0D=7.0=Language=Assets=Mars=7 July=Pleiades.
Puerto Rico=8,500=9,000=90%=P9.00D=9.0=Abstraction=Gods=Saturn=9Sept.>>A=Ø.
Puff=10,000=1,000=100%=10.0=Physicality=Tech.=10 Oct.=Uranus=P=1Ø.
Puffball=8,500=9,000=90%=P9.00D=9.0=Abstraction=Gods=Saturn=9Sept.>>A=Ø.
Puffer=7,500=8,000=80%=P8.0D=Economy=Currency=8 Aug.=Zeus>>E=v.
Puffery=3,000=30%=P3.0D=3.0=Creativity=Stars=Muses=3 March = CI/GIL.
Puffin=7,500=8,000=80%=P8.0D=Economy=Currency=8 Aug.=Zeus>>E=v.
Pug1=8,000=80%=P8.0D=Economy=Currency=8 Aug.=Zeus>>E=v.
Pug2=3,000=30%=P3.0D=3.0=Creativity=Stars=Muses=3 March = CI/GIL.
Puget Sound=4,500=5,000=50%=P5.00D=Law=Time=Venus=5 May = Aphrodite>>L=N.
Pugilism=2,500=3,000=30%=P3.0D=3.0=Creativity=Stars=Muses=3 March = CI/GIL.
Pugnacious=3,500=4,000=40%=P4.0D=Govt.=4 April=Mercury=Hermes=G=A4.
Puissance=1,500=15%=P1.50D=1.5=Authority=Solar Crown=1 May = Maia.
Puke=2,500=3,000=30%=P3.0D=3.0=Creativity=Stars=Muses=3 March = CI/GIL.
Pul=3,000=30%=P3.0D=3.0=Creativity=Stars=Muses=3 March = CI/GIL.

Pula=2,500=3,000=30%=P3.0D=3.0=Creativity=Stars=Muses=3 March = CI/GIL.
Currency metric weight >> 2.5/10=0.25=25:1. See Naira.

Pulaski Casimir=5,500=5.5=80%=P5.50=Earth-Midway=5 May = Gaia.
Pulchritude=2,500=3,000=30%=P3.0D=3.0=Creativity=Stars=Muses=3 March = CI/GIL.
Pule=3,000=30%=P3.0D=3.0=Creativity=Stars=Muses=3 March = CI/GIL.
Pulitzer Joseph=4,000=40%=P4.0D=Govt.=Creatocracy=4 April=Mercury=Hermes=G=A4.
Pull=10,000=1,000=100%=10.0=Physicality=Tech.=10 Oct.=Uranus=P=1Ø.
Pullback=2,000=20%=P2.00D=2.0=Nature=Matter=Moon=2 Feb.=Cupid=N=C+_
Pullet=3,000=30%=P3.0D=3.0=Creativity=Stars=Muses=3 March = CI/GIL.
Pulley=10,000=1,000=100%=10.0=Physicality=Tech.=10 Oct.=Uranus=P=1Ø.
Pullman=6,500=7,000=70%=P7.0D=7.0=Language=Assets=Mars=7 July=Pleiades.
Pullout=2,500=3,000=30%=P3.0D=3.0=Creativity=Stars=Muses=3 March = CI/GIL.
Pullover=6,000=60%=P6.0D=Man=Earth=Royalty=6 June=Gaia=Maia>>M=M2.
Pulmonary=5,000=50%=P5.00D=Law=Time=Venus=5 May = Aphrodite>>L=N.
Pulp=10,000=1,000=100%=10.0=Physicality=Tech.=10 Oct.=Uranus=P=1Ø.
Pulpit=8,500=9,000=90%=P9.00D=9.0=Abstraction=Gods=Saturn=9Sept.>>A=Ø.
Pulpwood=3,000=30%=P3.0D=3.0=Creativity=Stars=Muses=3 March = CI/GIL.
Pulsar=9,000=90%=P9.00D=9.0=Abstraction=Gods=Saturn=9Sept.>>A=Ø.
Pulsate=5,000=50%=P5.00D=Law=Time=Venus=5 May = Aphrodite>>L=N.
Pulse=10,000=1,000=100%=10.0=Physicality=Tech.=10 Oct.=Uranus=P=1Ø.
Pulverize=6,000=60%=P6.0D=Man=Earth=Royalty=6 June=Gaia=Maia>>M=M2.

Puma=2,000=20%=P2.00D=2.0=Nature=Matter=Moon=2 Feb.=Cupid=N=C+_
See Mountain lions. We believe that Mountain lion are Gods at defense. Jesus was referred
as the lion of the tribe of Judah. Jesus is Hermes. < Quechua.

Pumice=8,500=9,000=90%=P9.00D=9.0=Abstraction=Gods=Saturn=9Sept.>>A=Ø.
Pummel=6,000=60%=P6.0D=Man=Earth=Royalty=6 June=Gaia=Maia>>M=M2.
Pump1=10,000=1,000=100%=10.0=Physicality=Tech.=10 Oct.=Uranus=P=1Ø.
Pump2=4,500=5,000=50%=P5.00D=Law=Time=Venus=5 May = Aphrodite>>L=N.
Pumpernickel=3,000=30%=P3.0D=3.0=Creativity=Stars=Muses=3 March = CI/GIL.
Pumpkin=10,000=1,000=100%=10.0=Physicality=Tech.=10 Oct.=Uranus=P=1Ø.
Pun=10,000=1,000=100%=10.0=Physicality=Tech.=10 Oct.=Uranus=P=1Ø.
Punch1=8,000=80%=P8.0D=Economy=Currency=8 Aug.=Zeus>>E=v.
Punch2=10,000=1,000=100%=10.0=Physicality=Tech.=10 Oct.=Uranus=P=1Ø.
Punch3=9,500=10,000=1,000=100%=10.0=Physicality=Tech.=10 Oct.=Uranus=P=1Ø.
Punch card=6,000=60%=P6.0D=Man=Earth=Royalty=6 June=Gaia=Maia>>M=M2.
Puncheon1=8,500=9,000=90%=P9.00D=9.0=Abstraction=Gods=Saturn=9Sept.>>A=Ø.
Puncheon2=8,500=9,000=90%=P9.00D=9.0=Abstraction=Gods=Saturn=9Sept.>>A=Ø.
Punchline=4,000=40%=P4.0D=Govt.=Creatocracy=4 April=Mercury=Hermes=G=A4.
Punchy=6,000=60%=P6.0D=Man=Earth=Royalty=6 June=Gaia=Maia>>M=M2.
Punctilio=5,500=5.5=80%=P5.50=Earth-Midway=5 May = Gaia.
Punctual=6,000=60%=P6.0D=Man=Earth=Royalty=6 June=Gaia=Maia>>M=M2.
Punctuate=7,000=70%=P7.0D=7.0=Language=Assets=Mars=7 July=Pleiades.
Punctuation=10,000=1,000=100%=10.0=Physicality=Tech.=10 Oct.=Uranus=P=1Ø.
Puncture=10,000=1,000=100%=10.0=Physicality=Tech.=10 Oct.=Uranus=P=1Ø.

Pundit=3,000=30%=P3.0D=3.0=Creativity=Stars=Muses=3 March = CI/GIL.
Pungent=7,500=8,000=80%=P8.0D=Economy=Currency=8 Aug.=Zeus>>E=v.
Punic=6,000=60%=P6.0D=Man=Earth=Royalty=6 June=Gaia=Maia>>M=M2.
Punish=10,000=1,000=100%=10.0=Physicality=Tech.=10 Oct.=Uranus=P=1Ø.
Punishment=10,000=1,000=100%=10.0=Physicality=Tech.=10 Oct.=Uranus=P=1Ø.
Punitive=4,500=5,000=50%=P5.00D=Law=Time=Venus=5 May = Aphrodite>>L=N.
Punjab=4,500=5,000=50%=P5.00D=Law=Time=Venus=5 May = Aphrodite>>L=N.
Punjabi=6,000=60%=P6.0D=Man=Earth=Royalty=6 June=Gaia=Maia>>M=M2.
Punk=10,000=1,000=100%=10.0=Physicality=Tech.=10 Oct.=Uranus=P=1Ø.
Punk rock=4,500=5,000=50%=P5.00D=Law=Time=Venus=5 May = Aphrodite>>L=N.
Punster=2,000=20%=P2.00D=2.0=Nature=Matter=Moon=2 Feb.=Cupid=N=C+_
Punt1=10,000=1,000=100%=10.0=Physicality=Tech.=10 Oct.=Uranus=P=1Ø.
Punt2=9,000=90%=P9.00D=9.0=Abstraction=Gods=Saturn=9Sept.>>A=Ø.
Puny=5,500=5.5=80%=P5.50=Earth-Midway=5 May = Gaia.
Pup=5,500=5.5=80%=P5.50=Earth-Midway=5 May = Gaia.
Pupa=7,500=8,000=80%=P8.0D=Economy=Currency=8 Aug.=Zeus>>E=v.
Pupil1=6,500=7,000=70%=P7.0D=7.0=Language=Assets=Mars=7 July=Pleiades.
Pupil2=6,500=7,000=70%=P7.0D=7.0=Language=Assets=Mars=7 July=Pleiades.
Puppet=10,000=1,000=100%=10.0=Physicality=Tech.=10 Oct.=Uranus=P=1Ø.
Puppeteer=3,500=4,000=40%=P4.0D=Govt.=4 April=Mercury=Hermes=G=A4.
Puppy=3,000=30%=P3.0D=3.0=Creativity=Stars=Muses=3 March = CI/GIL.
Purblind=6,000=60%=P6.0D=Man=Earth=Royalty=6 June=Gaia=Maia>>M=M2.
Purchase=10,000=1,000=100%=10.0=Physicality=Tech.=10 Oct.=Uranus=P=1Ø.
Purdah=8,000=80%=P8.0D=Economy=Currency=8 Aug.=Zeus>>E=v.
Pure=10,000=1,000=100%=10.0=Physicality=Tech.=10 Oct.=Uranus=P=1Ø.
Purebred=5,500=5.5=80%=P5.50=Earth-Midway=5 May = Gaia.
Purée=10,000=1,000=100%=10.0=Physicality=Tech.=10 Oct.=Uranus=P=1Ø.
Purgation=3,000=30%=P3.0D=3.0=Creativity=Stars=Muses=3 March = CI/GIL.
Purgative=5,500=5.5=80%=P5.50=Earth-Midway=5 May = Gaia.
Purgatory=10,000=1,000=100%=10.0=Physicality=Tech.=10 Oct.=Uranus=P=1Ø.
Purge=10,000=1,000=100%=10.0=Physicality=Tech.=10 Oct.=Uranus=P=1Ø.
Purify=3,500=4,000=40%=P4.0D=Govt.=Creatocracy=4 April=Mercury=Hermes=G=A4.
Purim=8,000=80%=P8.0D=Economy=Currency=8 Aug.=Zeus>>E=v.
Purine=10,000=1,000=100%=10.0=Physicality=Tech.=10 Oct.=Uranus=P=1Ø.
Purism=3,500=4,000=40%=P4.0D=Govt.=Creatocracy=4 April=Mercury=Hermes=G=A4.
Puritan=10,000=1,000=100%=10.0=Physicality=Tech.=10 Oct.=Uranus=P=1Ø.
Purl1=7,000=70%=P7.0D=7.0=Language=Assets=Mars=7 July=Pleiades.
Purl2=2,500=3,000=30%=P3.0D=3.0=Creativity=Stars=Muses=3 March = CI/GIL.
Purlieu=5,500=5.5=80%=P5.50=Earth-Midway=5 May = Gaia.
Purloin=3,500=4,000=40%=P4.0D=Govt.=Creatocracy=4 April=Mercury=Hermes=G=A4.
Purple=10,000=1,000=100%=10.0=Physicality=Tech.=10 Oct.=Uranus=P=1Ø.
Purport=7,500=8,000=80%=P8.0D=Economy=Currency=8 Aug.=Zeus>>E=v.
Purpose=10,000=1,000=100%=10.0=Physicality=Tech.=10 Oct.=Uranus=P=1Ø.
Purr=5,000=50%=P5.00D=Law=Time=Venus=5 May = Aphrodite>>L=N.
Purse=10,000=1,000=100%=10.0=Physicality=Tech.=10 Oct.=Uranus=P=1Ø.

Purser=7,000=70%=P7.0D=7.0=Language=Assets=Mars=7 July=Pleiades.
Purslane=11,000=11%=P1.10D=1.1=Idea=Brainchild=Inv.=11 Nov.=SC=Athena>>I=MT.
Pursuance=3,500=4,000=40%=P4.0D=Govt.=Creatocracy=4 April=Hermes=G=A4.
Pursuant to=1,500=15%=P1.50D=1.5=Authority=Solar Crown=1 May = Maia.
Pursue=10,000=1,000=100%=10.0=Physicality=Tech.=10 Oct.=Uranus=P=1Ø.
Pursuit=7,500=8,000=80%=P8.0D=Economy=Currency=8 Aug.=Zeus>>E=v.
Purulent=3,000=30%=P3.0D=3.0=Creativity=Stars=Muses=3 March = CI/GIL.
Purvey=4,000=40%=P4.0D=Govt.=Creatocracy=4 April=Mercury=Hermes=G=A4.
Purview=10,000=1,000=100%=10.0=Physicality=Tech.=10 Oct.=Uranus=P=1Ø.
Pus=10,000=1,000=100%=10.0=Physicality=Tech.=10 Oct.=Uranus=P=1Ø.
Pusan=7,000=70%=P7.0D=7.0=Language=Assets=Mars=7 July=Pleiades.
Push=10,000=1,000=100%=10.0=Physicality=Tech.=10 Oct.=Uranus=P=1Ø.
Push button=5,000=50%=P5.00D=Law=Time=Venus=5 May = Aphrodite>>L=N.
Push-button=4,000=40%=P4.0D=Govt.=Creatocracy=4 April=Mercury=Hermes=G=A4.
Pushcart=3,000=30%=P3.0D=3.0=Creativity=Stars=Muses=3 March = CI/GIL.
Pusher=3,000=30%=P3.0D=3.0=Creativity=Stars=Muses=3 March = CI/GIL.
Pushkin Aleksandr=2,500=3,000=30%=P3.0D=3.0=Cre.=Stars=Muses=3 March = CI/GIL.
Pushover=5,500=5.5=80%=P5.50=Earth-Midway=5 May = Gaia.
Push-tu=1,500=15%=P1.50D=1.5=Authority=Solar Crown=1 May = Maia.
Push up=10,000=1,000=100%=10.0=Physicality=Tech.=10 Oct.=Uranus=P=1Ø.
Pushy=2,000=20%=P2.00D=2.0=Nature=Matter=Moon=2 Feb.=Cupid=N=C+_
Pusillanimous=2,500=3,000=30%=P3.0D=3.0=Creativity=Stars=Muses=3 March = CI/GIL.
Puss1=3,500=4,000=40%=P4.0D=Govt.=Creatocracy=4 April=Mercury=Hermes=G=A4.
Puss2=3,500=4,000=40%=P4.0D=Govt.=Creatocracy=4 April=Mercury=Hermes=G=A4.
Pussy1=1,500=15%=P1.50D=1.5=Authority=Solar Crown=1 May = Maia.
Pussy2=2,000=20%=P2.00D=2.0=Nature=Matter=Moon=2 Feb.=Cupid=N=C+_
Pussycat=3,500=4,000=40%=P4.0D=Govt.=Creatocracy=4 April=Hermes=G=A4.
Pussyfoot=4,500=5,000=50%=P5.00D=Law=Time=Venus=5 May = Aphrodite>>L=N.
Pussy willow=5,000=50%=P5.00D=Law=Time=Venus=5 May = Aphrodite>>L=N.
Pustule=5,500=5.5=80%=P5.50=Earth-Midway=5 May = Gaia.
Put=10,000=1,000=100%=10.0=Physicality=Tech.=10 Oct.=Uranus=P=1Ø.
Putative=5,500=5.5=80%=P5.50=Earth-Midway=5 May = Gaia.
Put down=3,000=30%=P3.0D=3.0=Creativity=Stars=Muses=3 March = CI/GIL.
Put on=10,000=1,000=100%=10.0=Physicality=Tech.=10 Oct.=Uranus=P=1Ø.
Putrefy=10,000=1,000=100%=10.0=Physicality=Tech.=10 Oct.=Uranus=P=1Ø.
Putrescent=3,000=30%=P3.0D=3.0=Creativity=Stars=Muses=3 March = CI/GIL.
Putrid=5,000=50%=P5.00D=Law=Time=Venus=5 May = Aphrodite>>L=N.
Putsch=4,500=5,000=50%=P5.00D=Law=Time=Venus=5 May = Aphrodite>>L=N.
Putt=8,000=80%=P8.0D=Economy=Currency=8 Aug.=Zeus>>E=v.
Puttee=8,000=80%=P8.0D=Economy=Currency=8 Aug.=Zeus>>E=v.
Putter1=3,500=4,000=40%=P4.0D=Govt.=Creatocracy=4 April=Mercury=Hermes=G=A4.
Putter2=5,000=50%=P5.00D=Law=Time=Venus=5 May = Aphrodite>>L=N.
Putty=10,000=1,000=100%=10.0=Physicality=Tech.=10 Oct.=Uranus=P=1Ø.
Putumayo=11,000=11%=P1.10D=1.1=Idea=Brainchild=Inv.=11 Nov.=SC=Athena>>I=MT.
Puzzle=10,000=1,000=100%=10.0=Physicality=Tech.=10 Oct.=Uranus=P=1Ø.

PVC=10,000=1,000=100%=10.0=Physicality=Tech.=10 Oct.=Uranus=P=1Ø.
Pvt.=1,000=100%=10.0=1.0=Mind=Sun=1 January=Helios >> M=E4.

Pya=2,500=3,000=30%=P3.0D=3.0=Creativity=Stars=Muses=3 March = CI/GIL.
Currency metric weight = 2.5/10=0.25=25:1. See Naira. Dollar.

Pygmy=10,000=1,000=100%=10.0=Physicality=Tech.=10 Oct.=Uranus=P=1Ø.
Pyjamas=2,500=3,000=30%=P3.0D=3.0=Creativity=Stars=Muses=3 March = CI/GIL.
Pylon=10,000=1,000=100%=10.0=Physicality=Tech.=10 Oct.=Uranus=P=1Ø.
Pym John=2,000=20%=P2.00D=2.0=Nature=Matter=Moon=2 Feb.=Cupid=N=C+_
Pyongyang=5,500=5.5=80%=P5.50=Earth-Midway=5 May = Gaia.
Pyorrhea=10,000=1,000=100%=10.0=Physicality=Tech.=10 Oct.=Uranus=P=1Ø.
Pyramid=10,000=1,000=100%=10.0=Physicality=Tech.=10 Oct.=Uranus=P=1Ø.
Pyre=6,000=60%=P6.0D=Man=Earth=Royalty=6 June=Gaia=Maia>>M=M2.
Pyrenees=6,500=7,000=70%=P7.0D=7.0=Language=Assets=Mars=7 July=Pleiades.
Pyrethrum=10,000=1,000=100%=10.0=Physicality=Tech.=10 Oct.=Uranus=P=1Ø.
Pyrex=6,500=7,000=70%=P7.0D=7.0=Language=Assets=Mars=7 July=Pleiades.
Pyrimidine=10,000=1,000=100%=10.0=Physicality=Tech.=10 Oct.=Uranus=P=1Ø.
Pyrite=10,000=1,000=100%=10.0=Physicality=Tech.=10 Oct.=Uranus=P=1Ø.
Pyrites=7,000=70%=P7.0D=7.0=Language=Assets=Mars=7 July=Pleiades.
Pyro-=3,000=30%=P3.0D=3.0=Creativity=Stars=Muses=3 March = CI/GIL.
Pyrolysis=4,500=5,000=50%=P5.00D=Law=Time=Venus=5 May = Aphrodite>>L=N.
Pyromania=3,000=30%=P3.0D=3.0=Creativity=Stars=Muses=3 March = CI/GIL.
Pyrometer=3,000=30%=P3.0D=3.0=Creativity=Stars=Muses=3 March = CI/GIL.
Pyrotechnics=4,000=40%=P4.0D=Govt.=Creatocracy=4 April=Mercury=Hermes=G=A4.
Pyrrhic victory=8,000=80%=P8.0D=Economy=Currency=8 Aug.=Zeus>>E=v.
Pythagoras=4,000=40%=P4.0D=Govt.=Creatocracy=4 April=Mercury=Hermes=G=A4.
Python=10,000=1,000=100%=10.0=Physicality=Tech.=10 Oct.=Uranus=P=1Ø.
Pyx=10,500=11,000=11%=P1.10D=1.1=Idea=Brainchild=Inv.=11 Nov.=SC=Athena>>I=MT.

MAKABET =Qq=

---

q1=3,000=30%=P3.0D=3.0=Creativity=Stars=Muses=3 March = C=I>>GIL.
The 17th letter of the English alphabet. The psycho-weight effect of the Q whenever it is mentioned is thus computed>> 3.0*1.7x=px=4.7+5.1=9.8x=px=33.77. 3.3 >> Genius. >> Host >> Holy Spirit. 77=80=8.0>> Business >> Currency >> Economy >> Banking >> Trading >> Transactions >> Jupiter >> Zeus. So the letter Q induces the visitation of the Almighty GOD accompanied by the Hosts of Heaven. It is thus the symbol of the Zeus-Jehovah-Allah >> ZeJeAl in the Makupedian Disean - Makstian language. The only time in the Bible that GOD and the Host appeared was during the visit to Egypt in the burning bush experience with Moses. Hence the Q could be reasoned to be the sign

of this visit. See the Makupedia Wit Bible for computational precision on this matter. Another mention of this experience was in Job 1 when the Sons of GOD bowed and worshipped. Then David confirms the Q experience in a meeting between GOD and the Gods in Psalms 82:1-8. Therefore Q is the head of the scepter or staff of office of Zeus as mentioned in the Greek mythologies. It is the caduceus of Hermes, the shield of Athena. The Castle Makupedia.

---

q2=3,000=30%=P3.0D=3.0=Creativity=Stars=Muses=3 March = C=I>>GIL.
Q=1,500=15%=P1.50D=1.5=Authority=Solar Crown=1 May = Maia.
q.=4,500=5,000=50%=P5.00D=Law=Time=Venus=5 May = Aphrodite>>L=N.
Qaddafi=3,500=4,000=40%=P4.0D=Govt.=Creatocracy=4 April=Mercury=Hermes=G=A4.
q and a=1,500=15%=P1.50D=1.5=Authority=Solar Crown=1 May = Maia.
Qatar=7,000=70%=P7.0D=7.0=Language=Assets=Mars=7 July=Pleiades.
Q.E.D.=4,500=5,000=50%=P5.00D=Law=Time=Venus=5 May = Aphrodite>>L=N.
Qindarka=3,000=30%=P3.0D=3.0=Creativity=Stars=Muses=3 March = C=I>>GIL.
Qingdao=6,500=7,000=70%=P7.0D=7.0=Language=Assets=Mars=7 July=Pleiades.
Qiqihar=5,500=5.5=80%=P5.50=Earth-Midway=5 May = Gaia.
QM=500=5%=P5.00D=5.0=Law=Time=Venus=5 May=Aphrodite>>L=N.
Qom=5,000=50%=P5.00D=Law=Time=Venus=5 May = Aphrodite>>L=N.
qoph=4,000=40%=P4.0D=Govt.=Creatocracy=4 April=Mercury=Hermes=G=A4.
qr.=1,500=15%=P1.50D=1.5=Authority=Solar Crown=1 May = Maia.
qt=1,000=100%=10.0=1.0=Mind=Sun=1 January=Helios >> M=E4.
qt.=500=5%=P5.00D=5.0=Law=Time=Venus=5 May=Aphrodite>>L=N.
qto.=500=5%=P5.00D=5.0=Law=Time=Venus=5 May=Aphrodite>>L=N.
qty.=500=5%=P5.00D=5.0=Law=Time=Venus=5 May=Aphrodite>>L=N.
Quack1=4,000=40%=P4.0D=Govt.=Creatocracy=4 April=Mercury=Hermes=G=A4.
Quack2=7,000=70%=P7.0D=7.0=Language=Assets=Mars=7 July=Pleiades.
Quad1=1,000=100%=10.0=1.0=Mind=Sun=1 January=Helios >> M=E4.
Quad2=1,000=100%=10.0=1.0=Mind=Sun=1 January=Helios >> M=E4.
Quad=1,000=100%=10.0=1.0=Mind=Sun=1 January=Helios >> M=E4.
Quadrangle=6,500=7,000=70%=P7.0D=7.0=Language=Assets=Mars=7 July=Pleiades.
Quadrant=10,000=1,000=100%=10.0=Physicality=Tech.=10 Oct.=Uranus=P=1Ø.
Quadraphonic=4,000=40%=P4.0D=Govt.=Creatocracy=4 April=Mercury=Hermes=G=A4.
Quadratic=6,500=7,000=70%=P7.0D=7.0=Language=Assets=Mars=7 July=Pleiades.
Quadrennial=6,000=60%=P6.0D=Man=Earth=Royalty=6 June=Gaia=Maia>>M=M2.
Quadri-=2,500=3,000=30%=P3.0D=3.0=Creativity=Stars=Muses=3 March = C=I>>GIL.
Quadriceps=6,500=7,000=70%=P7.0D=7.0=Language=Assets=Mars=7 July=Pleiades.
Quadrilateral=4,500=5,000=50%=P5.00D=Law=Time=Venus=5 May = Aphrodite>>L=N.
Quadrille=10,000=1,000=100%=10.0=Physicality=Tech.=10 Oct.=Uranus=P=1Ø.
Quadrillion=7,500=8,000=80%=P8.0D=Economy=Currency=8 Aug.=Zeus>>E=v.
Quadripartite=4,500=5,000=50%=P5.00D=Law=Time=Venus=5 May = Aphrodite>>L=N.
Quadriplegia=5,500=5.5=80%=P5.50=Earth-Midway=5 May = Gaia.
Quadruped=2,000=20%=P2.00D=2.0=Nature=Matter=Moon=2 Feb.=Cupid=N=C+_
Quadruple=10,000=1,000=100%=10.0=Physicality=Tech.=10 Oct.=Uranus=P=1Ø.

Quadruplet=6,500=7,000=70%=P7.0D=7.0=Language=Assets=Mars=7 July=Pleiades.
Quadruplicate=10,000=1,000=100%=10.0=Physicality=Tech.=10 Oct.=Uranus=P=1Ø.
Quaff=2,000=20%=P2.00D=2.0=Nature=Matter=Moon=2 Feb.=Cupid=N=C+_
Quagmire=7,500=8,000=80%=P8.0D=Economy=Currency=8 Aug.=Zeus>>E=v.
Quahog=8,000=80%=P8.0D=Economy=Currency=8 Aug.=Zeus>>E=v.
Quail1=8,500=9,000=90%=P9.00D=9.0=Abstraction=Gods=Saturn=9Sept.>>A=Ø.
Quail2=5,000=50%=P5.00D=Law=Time=Venus=5 May = Aphrodite>>L=N.
Quaint=8,500=9,000=90%=P9.00D=9.0=Abstraction=Gods=Saturn=9Sept.>>A=Ø.
Quake=8,000=80%=P8.0D=Economy=Currency=8 Aug.=Zeus>>E=v.
Quaker=3,000=30%=P3.0D=3.0=Creativity=Stars=Muses=3 March = C=I>>GIL.

Qualification=11,000=11%=P1.10D=1.1=Idea=Brainchild=11 Nov=Athena>>I=MT.
Every qualification is subject to the wisdom of its application.

Qualify=10,000=1,000=100%=10.0=Physicality=Tech.=10 Oct.=Uranus=P=1Ø.
Qualitative=2,000=20%=P2.00D=2.0=Nature=Matter=Moon=2 Feb.=Cupid=N=C+_
Quality=10,000=1,000=100%=10.0=Physicality=Tech.=10 Oct.=Uranus=P=1Ø.
Qualm=8,000=80%=P8.0D=Economy=Currency=8 Aug.=Zeus>>E=v.
Quandary=3,500=4,000=40%=P4.0D=Govt.=Creatocracy=4 April=Hermes=G=A4.
Quantify=5,500=5.5=80%=P5.50=Earth-Midway=5 May = Gaia.
Quantitative=3,500=4,000=40%=P4.0D=Govt.=Creatocracy=4 April=Hermes=G=A4.
Quantity=6,000=60%=P6.0D=Man=Earth=Royalty=6 June=Gaia=Maia>>M=M2.

Quantum=6,500=7,000=70%=P7.0D=7.0=Language=Assets=Mars=7 July=Pleiades.
A means of measuring human emotion and its energy systems potentials and modules.

Quantum theory=6,500=7,000=70%=P7.0D=7.0=Language=Assets=Mars=7 July=Pleiades.
Quarantine=10,000=1,000=100%=10.0=Physicality=Tech.=10 Oct.=Uranus=P=1Ø.
Quark=10,000=1,000=100%=10.0=Physicality=Tech.=10 Oct.=Uranus=P=1Ø.
Quarrel=10,000=1,000=100%=10.0=Physicality=Tech.=10 Oct.=Uranus=P=1Ø.
Quarrelsome=4,000=40%=P4.0D=Govt.=Creatocracy=4 April=Mercury=Hermes=G=A4.
Quarry1=10,000=1,000=100%=10.0=Physicality=Tech.=10 Oct.=Uranus=P=1Ø.
Quarry2=10,000=1,000=100%=10.0=Physicality=Tech.=10 Oct.=Uranus=P=1Ø.
Quart=10,000=1,000=100%=10.0=Physicality=Tech.=10 Oct.=Uranus=P=1Ø.
Quarter=10,000=1,000=100%=10.0=Physicality=Tech.=10 Oct.=Uranus=P=1Ø.
Quarterback=5,500=5.5=80%=P5.50=Earth-Midway=5 May = Gaia.
Quarterdeck=4,500=5,000=50%=P5.00D=Law=Time=Venus=5 May = Aphrodite>>L=N.
Quarter horse=10,500=11,000=11%=P1.10D=1.1=Idea=Brainchild=11 Nov=Athena>>I=MT.
Quarterly=7,500=8,000=80%=P8.0D=Economy=Currency=8 Aug.=Zeus>>E=v.
Quartermaster=8,500=9,000=90%=P9.00D=9.0=Abst.=Gods=Saturn=9Sept.>>A=Ø.
Quarter note=6,000=60%=P6.0D=Man=Earth=Royalty=6 June=Gaia=Maia>>M=M2.

Quartet=9,000=90%=P9.00D=9.0=Abstraction=Gods=Saturn=9Sept.>>A=Ø.
Peter Matthews-Akukalia, Castle Makupedia discovered the Quartet Principle 1/4ᵗʰ as a basic functionality of thought place and all time curiosity and occurrence. All creation is a product of the Quartet Principle. He then invented the CCLT emotion card. See emotion. We can then say that the CCLT is an instrument of the Gods and so is the inventor is a God.

Quartile=8,000=80%=P8.0D=Economy=Currency=8 Aug.=Zeus>>E=v.
Quarto=12,000=12%=P1.20D=1.2=Knowledge=Edu=12Dec.=Athena>>K=F.
Quartz=10,000=1,000=100%=10.0=Physicality=Tech.=10 Oct.=Uranus=P=1Ø.
Quartzite=5,000=50%=P5.00D=Law=Time=Venus=5 May = Aphrodite>>L=N.
Quasar=7,500=8,000=80%=P8.0D=Economy=Currency=8 Aug.=Zeus>>E=v.
Quash1=6,000=60%=P6.0D=Man=Earth=Royalty=6 June=Gaia=Maia>>M=M2.
Quash2=6,000=60%=P6.0D=Man=Earth=Royalty=6 June=Gaia=Maia>>M=M2.
Quasi=5,000=50%=P5.00D=Law=Time=Venus=5 May = Aphrodite>>L=N.
Quasi-=4,000=40%=P4.0D=Govt.=Creatocracy=4 April=Mercury=Hermes=G=A4.
Quasi stellar object=1,000=100%=10.0=1.0=Mind=Sun=1 January=Helios >> M=E4.
Quaternary=10,000=1,000=100%=10.0=Physicality=Tech.=10 Oct.=Uranus=P=1Ø.
Quart rain=6,000=60%=P6.0D=Man=Earth=Royalty=6 June=Gaia=Maia>>M=M2.
Quatrefoil=10,000=1,000=100%=10.0=Physicality=Tech.=10 Oct.=Uranus=P=1Ø.
Quaver=7,500=8,000=80%=P8.0D=Economy=Currency=8 Aug.=Zeus>>E=v.
Quay=2,000=20%=P2.00D=2.0=Nature=Matter=Moon=2 Feb.=Cupid=N=C+_
Quayle=5,500=5.5=80%=P5.50=Earth-Midway=5 May = Gaia.
Queasy=5,500=5.5=80%=P5.50=Earth-Midway=5 May = Gaia.
Quebec=10,000=1,000=100%=10.0=Physicality=Tech.=10 Oct.=Uranus=P=1Ø.
Québécois=5,500=5.5=80%=P5.50=Earth-Midway=5 May = Gaia.
Quechua=8,000=80%=P8.0D=Economy=Currency=8 Aug.=Zeus>>E=v.
Quechuan=7,000=70%=P7.0D=7.0=Language=Assets=Mars=7 July=Pleiades.

Queen=10,000=1,000=100%=10.0=Physicality=Tech.=10 Oct.=Uranus=P=1Ø.
Queen Alice Folayegbe Matthews - Akukalia is the First Queen of the Creatocracy under jurisdiction of Empress Tina. She is honored as the Queen of Fortune. Eve of Fortune, A play was dedicated to her by the emperor. She is advisory secretary of the royal family. See the book >> The Creatocracy Republic, Eve of Fortune by Peter Matthews - Akukalia.

Queen mother=5,000=50%=P5.00D=Law=Time=Venus=5 May = Aphrodite>>L=N.

Queens=7,500=8,000=80%=P8.0D=Economy=Currency=8 Aug.=Zeus>>E=v.
The wives of Peter Matthews-Akukalia, Castle Makupedia constitute his council of Queens headed by the Creatocratic Goddess Empress Tina. This is for now and the future.

Queen's English=5,000=50%=P5.00D=Law=Time=Venus=5 May = Aphrodite>>L=N.
Queer=9,000=90%=P9.00D=9.0=Abstraction=Gods=Saturn=9Sept.>>A=Ø.
Quell=5,000=50%=P5.00D=Law=Time=Venus=5 May = Aphrodite>>L=N.

Quemoy=5,500=5.5=80%=P5.50=Earth-Midway=5 May = Gaia.
Quench=8,500=9,000=90%=P9.00D=9.0=Abstraction=Gods=Saturn=9Sept.>>A=Ø.
Querulous=5,500=5.5=80%=P5.50=Earth-Midway=5 May = Gaia.
Query=9,000=90%=P9.00D=9.0=Abstraction=Gods=Saturn=9Sept.>>A=Ø.
Quest=10,000=1,000=100%=10.0=Physicality=Tech.=10 Oct.=Uranus=P=1Ø.
Question=10,000=1,000=100%=10.0=Physicality=Tech.=10 Oct.=Uranus=P=1Ø.
Questionable=4,500=5,000=50%=P5.00D=Law=Time=Venus=5 May = Aphrodite>>L=N.
Question mark=8,500=9,000=90%=P9.00D=9.0=Abst.=Gods=Saturn=9Sept.>>A=Ø.
Questionnaire=6,000=60%=P6.0D=Man=Earth=Royalty=6 June=Gaia=Maia>>M=M2.
Quetzal=10,500=11,000=11%=P1.10D=1.1=Idea=Brainchild=11 Nov=Athena>>I=MT.
Queue=10,000=1,000=100%=10.0=Physicality=Tech.=10 Oct.=Uranus=P=1Ø.

Quezon City=5,000=50%=P5.00D=Law=Time=Venus=5 May = Aphrodite>>L=N.
Disean City, New Africa of the King (NAK) City, MindTech City are cities of the Paradise Nations. Invented by Peter Matthews-Akukalia, Castle Makupedia.

Quezon y Molina=3,000=30%=P3.0D=3.0=Creativity=Stars=Muses=3 March = C=I>>GIL.
Quibble=10,000=1,000=100%=10.0=Physicality=Tech.=10 Oct.=Uranus=P=1Ø.
Quiche=7,500=8,000=80%=P8.0D=Economy=Currency=8 Aug.=Zeus>>E=v.
Quick=10,000=1,000=100%=10.0=Physicality=Tech.=10 Oct.=Uranus=P=1Ø.

Quicken=6,000=60%=P6.0D=Man=Earth=Royalty=6 June=Gaia=Maia>>M=M2.
The Bible teaches that the Holy Spirit is a quickening spirit. Evidence is seen in the writings of Peter Matthews-Akukalia, Castle Makupedia which he does spontaneous and creates. The spirit speed of a thing or the Holy Spirit was calculated by him as 1.0x10 raised to power (-6). This is also the speed it takes for a heartfelt prayer to reach heaven.

Quickie=3,000=30%=P3.0D=3.0=Creativity=Stars=Muses=3 March = C=I>>GIL.
Quicklime=1,000=100%=10.0=1.0=Mind=Sun=1 January=Helios >> M=E4.
Quicksand=13,000=13%=P1.30=Solar Core=Faculty=13 January=Athena.
Quicksilver=5,500=5.5=80%=P5.50=Earth-Midway=5 May = Gaia.
Quickstep=3,000=30%=P3.0D=3.0=Creativity=Stars=Muses=3 March = C=I>>GIL.
Quick tempered=2,000=20%=P2.00D=2.0=Nature=Matter=Moon=2 Feb.=Cupid=N=C+_
Quick time=4,500=5,000=50%=P5.00D=Law=Time=Venus=5 May = Aphrodite>>L=N.

Quick witted=2,500=3,000=30%=P3.0D=3.0=Cre.=Stars=Muses=3 March = C=I>>GIL.
People often wonder how it all happens that the Creatocracy has so much in stock for humanity to explore. The evidence of incarnation in man is being quick witted.

Quid1=4,500=5,000=50%=P5.00D=Law=Time=Venus=5 May = Aphrodite>>L=N.
Quid2=4,000=40%=P4.0D=Govt.=Creatocracy=4 April=Mercury=Hermes=G=A4.
Quid pro quo=5,500=5.5=80%=P5.50=Earth-Midway=5 May = Gaia.

Quiescent=4,000=40%=P4.0D=Govt.=Creatocracy=4 April=Mercury=Hermes=G=A4.
Quiet=10,000=1,000=100%=10.0=Physicality=Tech.=10 Oct.=Uranus=P=1Ø.
Quietude=500=5%=P5.00D=5.0=Law=Time=Venus=5 May=Aphrodite>>L=N.
Quietus=6,000=60%=P6.0D=Man=Earth=Royalty=6 June=Gaia=Maia>>M=M2.
Quill=10,000=1,000=100%=10.0=Physicality=Tech.=10 Oct.=Uranus=P=1Ø.
Quilt=7,500=8,000=80%=P8.0D=Economy=Currency=8 Aug.=Zeus>>E=v.
Quince=8,500=9,000=90%=P9.00D=9.0=Abstraction=Gods=Saturn=9Sept.>>A=Ø.
Quinine=10,000=1,000=100%=10.0=Physicality=Tech.=10 Oct.=Uranus=P=1Ø.
Quinquennial=10,000=1,000=100%=10.0=Physicality=Tech.=10 Oct.=Uranus=P=1Ø.
Quinsy=6,500=7,000=70%=P7.0D=7.0=Language=Assets=Mars=7 July=Pleiades.
Quint=1,000=100%=Physicality=Tech.=10 Oct.=Uranus=P=1Ø.
Quintal=10,000=1,000=100%=10.0=Physicality=Tech.=10 Oct.=Uranus=P=1Ø.
Quintessence=10,000=1,000=100%=10.0=Physicality=Tech.=10 Oct.=Uranus=P=1Ø.
Quintet=10,000=1,000=100%=10.0=Physicality=Tech.=10 Oct.=Uranus=P=1Ø.
Quintile=8,500=9,000=90%=P9.00D=9.0=Abstraction=Gods=Saturn=9Sept.>>A=Ø.
Quintilian=2,500=3,000=30%=P3.0D=3.0=Creativity=Stars=Muses=3 March = C=I>>GIL.
Quintillion=10,000=1,000=100%=10.0=Physicality=Tech.=10 Oct.=Uranus=P=1Ø.
Quintuple=10,000=1,000=100%=10.0=Physicality=Tech.=10 Oct.=Uranus=P=1Ø.
Quintuplet=7,000=70%=P7.0D=7.0=Language=Assets=Mars=7 July=Pleiades.
Quintuplicate=10,000=1,000=100%=10.0=Physicality=Tech.=10 Oct.=Uranus=P=1Ø.
Quip=7,000=70%=P7.0D=7.0=Language=Assets=Mars=7 July=Pleiades.
Quire=11,000=11%=P1.10D=1.1=Idea=Brainchild=11 Nov=Athena>>I=MT.
Quirk=5,500=5.5=80%=P5.50=Earth-Midway=5 May = Gaia.
Quirt=9,000=90%=P9.00D=9.0=Abstraction=Gods=Saturn=9Sept.>>A=Ø.
Quisling=10,000=1,000=100%=10.0=Physicality=Tech.=10 Oct.=Uranus=P=1Ø.
Quit=10,000=1,000=100%=10.0=Physicality=Tech.=10 Oct.=Uranus=P=1Ø.
Quitclaim=6,500=7,000=70%=P7.0D=7.0=Language=Assets=Mars=7 July=Pleiades.
Quite=6,500=7,000=70%=P7.0D=7.0=Language=Assets=Mars=7 July=Pleiades.
Quito=5,000=50%=P5.00D=Law=Time=Venus=5 May = Aphrodite>>L=N.
Quits=6,000=60%=P6.0D=Man=Earth=Royalty=6 June=Gaia=Maia>>M=M2.
Quittance=7,500=8,000=80%=P8.0D=Economy=Currency=8 Aug.=Zeus>>E=v.
Quitter=2,500=3,000=30%=P3.0D=3.0=Creativity=Stars=Muses=3 March = C=I>>GIL.
Quiver1=4,000=40%=P4.0D=Govt.=Creatocracy=4 April=Mercury=Hermes=G=A4.
Quiver2=5,000=50%=P5.00D=Law=Time=Venus=5 May = Aphrodite>>L=N.
Qui vive=8,500=9,000=90%=P9.00D=9.0=Abstraction=Gods=Saturn=9Sept.>>A=Ø.
Quixotic=10,000=1,000=100%=10.0=Physicality=Tech.=10 Oct.=Uranus=P=1Ø.
Quiz=6,000=60%=P6.0D=Man=Earth=Royalty=6 June=Gaia=Maia>>M=M2.
Quizzical=8,500=9,000=90%=P9.00D=9.0=Abstraction=Gods=Saturn=9Sept.>>A=Ø.
Qum=1,000=100%=10.0=1.0=Mind=Sun=1 January=Helios >> M=E4.
Quoin=8,500=9,000=90%=P9.00D=9.0=Abstraction=Gods=Saturn=9Sept.>>A=Ø.
Quoit=10,000=1,000=100%=10.0=Physicality=Tech.=10 Oct.=Uranus=P=1Ø.
Quo dam=2,500=3,000=30%=P3.0D=3.0=Creativity=Stars=Muses=3 March = C=I>>GIL.
Quorum=10,000=1,000=100%=10.0=Physicality=Tech.=10 Oct.=Uranus=P=1Ø.
Quot.=500=5%=P5.00D=5.0=Law=Time=Venus=5 May=Aphrodite>>L=N.
Quota=10,000=1,000=100%=10.0=Physicality=Tech.=10 Oct.=Uranus=P=1Ø.

PETER K. MATTHEWS - AKUKALIA

Quotable=1,000=100%=10.0=1.0=Mind=Sun=1 January=Helios >> M=E4.
Quotation=8,000=80%=P8.0D=Economy=Currency=8 Aug.=Zeus>>E=v.
Quotation mark=10,000=1,000=100%=10.0=Physicality=Tech.=10 Oct.=Uranus=P=1Ø.
Quote=10,000=1,000=100%=10.0=Physicality=Tech.=10 Oct.=Uranus=P=1Ø.
Quoth=2,500=3,000=30%=P3.0D=3.0=Creativity=Stars=Muses=3 March = C=I>>GIL.
Quotidian=3,500=4,000=40%=P4.0D=Govt.=Creatocracy=4 April=Hermes=G=A4.

Quotient=7,000=70%=P7.0D=7.0=Language=Assets=Mars=7 July=Pleiades.
The elements of a word is measured in quotients. Known as Makumaticology it is the second computational study after Makumatics. It is used to compute the average propensity and inclination for a thing. It is the invention of Peter Matthews-Akukalia, Castle Makupedia. See >> THE CASTLE MAKUPEDIA: First Makumatics Dictionary & MaksCurrencies Encyclopedia. Also Principles of Psychoastronomy.

Quran=1,500=15%=P1.50D=1.5=Authority=Solar Crown=1 May = Maia.
The Quran is an authoritative scripture used in the Makstian Faith. Inspired by Maia.

q.v.=3,000=30%=P3.0D=3.0=Creativity=Stars=Muses=3 March = C=I>>GIL.

MAKABET =Rr=

r1=3,000=30%=P3.0D=3.0=Creativity=Stars=Muses=3 March = C=I>>GIL.
The 18th letter of the English alphabet. 3.0*1.8x=4.8+5.4=10.2x=px=36.12=40=4.0. The letter R is an alphabet of power politics Mercury and relationships.

r2=2,500=3,000=30%=P3.0D=3.0=Creativity=Stars=Muses=3 March = C=I>>GIL.
R1=10,000=1,000=100%=10.0=Physicality=Tech.=10 Oct.=Uranus=P=1Ø.
R2=2,500=3,000=30%=P3.0D=3.0=Creativity=Stars=Muses=3 March = C=I>>GIL.
R3=3,500=4,000=40%=P4.0D=Govt.=Creat.=4 April=Mercury=Hermes=G=A4.
r.=6,000=60%=P6.0D=Man=Earth=Royalty=6 June=Gaia=Maia>>M=M2.
R.=2,000=20%=P2.00D=2.0=Nature=Matter=Moon=2 Feb.=Cupid=N=C+_
Ra1=3,000=30%=P3.0D=3.0=Creativity=Stars=Muses=3 March = C=I>>GIL.
Ra2=2,500=3,000=30%=P3.0D=3.0=Creativity=Stars=Muses=3 March = C=I>>GIL.
R.A.=3,000=30%=P3.0D=3.0=Creativity=Stars=Muses=3 March = C=I>>GIL.
Rabat=5,000=50%=P5.00D=Law=Time=Venus=5 May = Aphrodite>>L=N.
Rabbet=10,000=1,000=100%=10.0=Physicality=Tech.=10 Oct.=Uranus=P=1Ø.
Rabbi=10,000=1,000=100%=10.0=Physicality=Tech.=10 Oct.=Uranus=P=1Ø.
Rabbinate=4,500=5,000=50%=P5.00D=Law=Time=Venus=5 May = Aphrodite>>L=N.
Rabbit=10,000=1,000=100%=10.0=Physicality=Tech.=10 Oct.=Uranus=P=1Ø.
Rabbit punch=4,000=40%=P4.0D=Govt.=Creat.=4 April=Mercury=Hermes=G=A4.

Rabble=6,000=60%=P6.0D=Man=Earth=Royalty=6 June=Gaia=Maia>>M=M2.
Rabble rouser=4,500=5,000=50%=P5.00D=Law=Time=Venus=5 May = Aphrodite>>L=N.
Rabelais François=2,500=3,000=30%=P3.0D=3.0=Creativity=Stars=Muses=3 March =CI.
Rabi=8,000=80%=P8.0D=Economy=Currency=8 Aug.=Zeus>>E=v.
Rabid=10,000=1,000=100%=10.0=Physicality=Tech.=10 Oct.=Uranus=P=1Ø.
Rabies=10,000=1,000=100%=10.0=Physicality=Tech.=10 Oct.=Uranus=P=1Ø.
Raccoon=10,000=1,000=100%=10.0=Physicality=Tech.=10 Oct.=Uranus=P=1Ø.
Race1=10,000=1,000=100%=10.0=Physicality=Tech.=10 Oct.=Uranus=P=1Ø.
Race2=10,000=1,000=100%=10.0=Physicality=Tech.=10 Oct.=Uranus=P=1Ø.
Race course=3,000=30%=P3.0D=3.0=Creativity=Stars=Muses=3 March = C=I>>GIL.
Race horse=3,500=4,000=40%=P4.0D=Govt.=Creat.=4 April=Mercury=Hermes=G=A4.
Raceme=7,500=8,000=80%=P8.0D=Economy=Currency=8 Aug.=Zeus>>E=v.
Race track=4,500=5,000=50%=P5.00D=Law=Time=Venus=5 May = Aphrodite>>L=N.
Raceway=1,000=100%=10.0=1.0=Mind=Sun=1 January=Helios >> M=E4.
Rachel=3,500=4,000=40%=P4.0D=Govt.=Creat.=4 April=Mercury=Hermes=G=A4.
Rachitis=2,500=3,000=30%=P3.0D=3.0=Creativity=Stars=Muses=3 March = C=I>>GIL.
Rachmaninoff=4,500=5,000=50%=P5.00D=Law=Time=Venus=5 May = Aphrodite>>L=N.
Racial=7,000=70%=P7.0D=7.0=Language=Assets=Mars=7 July=Pleiades.
Racine Jean=2,500=3,000=30%=P3.0D=3.0=Creativity=Stars=Muses=3 March = C=I
Racism=10,000=1,000=100%=10.0=Physicality=Tech.=10 Oct.=Uranus=P=1Ø.
Rack1=10,000=1,000=100%=10.0=Physicality=Tech.=10 Oct.=Uranus=P=1Ø.
Rack2=4,500=5,000=50%=P5.00D=Law=Time=Venus=5 May = Aphrodite>>L=N.
Racket1=10,000=1,000=100%=10.0=Physicality=Tech.=10 Oct.=Uranus=P=1Ø.
Racketeer=5,500=5.5=80%=P5.50=Earth-Midway=5 May = Gaia.
Raconteur=5,500=5.5=80%=P5.50=Earth-Midway=5 May = Gaia.
Racquet ball=5,500=5.5=80%=P5.50=Earth-Midway=5 May = Gaia.
Racy=5,000=50%=P5.00D=Law=Time=Venus=5 May = Aphrodite>>L=N.
Rad1=7,500=8,000=80%=P8.0D=Economy=Currency=8 Aug.=Zeus>>E=v.
Rad2=500=5%=P5.00D=5.0=Law=Time=Venus=5 May=Aphrodite>>L=N.
Rad.=1,500=15%=P1.50D=1.5=Authority=Solar Crown=1 May = Maia.
Radar=10,000=1,000=100%=10.0=Physicality=Tech.=10 Oct.=Uranus=P=1Ø.
Radar scope=3,500=4,000=40%=P4.0D=Govt.=Creat.=4 April=Mercury=Hermes=G=A4.
Radial=10,000=1,000=100%=10.0=Physicality=Tech.=10 Oct.=Uranus=P=1Ø.
Radial symmetry=5,500=5.5=80%=P5.50=Earth-Midway=5 May = Gaia.
Radial tire=9,000=90%=P9.00D=9.0=Abstraction=Gods=Saturn=9Sept.>>A=Ø.
Radian=5,000=50%=P5.00D=Law=Time=Venus=5 May = Aphrodite>>L=N.
Radiant=10,000=1,000=100%=10.0=Physicality=Tech.=10 Oct.=Uranus=P=1Ø.
Radiant energy=4,500=5,000=50%=P5.00D=Law=Time=Venus=5 May = Aphrodite>>L=N.
Radiate=10,000=1,000=100%=10.0=Physicality=Tech.=10 Oct.=Uranus=P=1Ø.
Radiation=10,000=1,000=100%=10.0=Physicality=Tech.=10 Oct.=Uranus=P=1Ø.
Radiation sickness=10,000=1,000=100%=10.0=Physicality=Tech.=10 Oct.=Uranus=P=1Ø.
Radiator=10,000=1,000=100%=10.0=Physicality=Tech.=10 Oct.=Uranus=P=1Ø.
Radical=10,000=1,000=100%=10.0=Physicality=Tech.=10 Oct.=Uranus=P=1Ø.
Radicalism=3,500=4,000=40%=P4.0D=Govt.=Creat.=4 April=Mercury=Hermes=G=A4.
Radicalize=3,000=30%=P3.0D=3.0=Creativity=Stars=Muses=3 March = C=I>>GIL.

Radical sign=8,500=9,000=90%=P9.00D=9.0=Abstraction=Gods=Saturn=9Sept.>>A=Ø.
Radii=2,000=20%=P2.00D=2.0=Nature=Matter=Moon=2 Feb.=Cupid=N=C+_
Radio=10,000=1,000=100%=10.0=Physicality=Tech.=10 Oct.=Uranus=P=1Ø.
Radio-=4,000=40%=P4.0D=Govt.=Creat.=4 April=Mercury=Hermes=G=A4.
Radioactivity=10,000=1,000=100%=10.0=Physicality=Tech.=10 Oct.=Uranus=P=1Ø.

Radio astronomy=10,000=1,000=100%=10.0=Physicality=Tech.=10 Oct.=Uranus=P=1Ø.
In the Creatocracy, Mind Astronomy is the same thing as Psychoastronomy. Peter Matthews-Akukalia invented a satellite tracking system for radio programs aligned to frequency. This means that all radio stations have lunar data that make for daily programs.

Radio carbon=4,000=40%=P4.0D=Govt.=Creat.=4 April=Mercury=Hermes=G=A4.
Radio frequency=10,000=1,000=100%=10.0=Physicality=Tech.=10 Oct.=Uranus=P=1Ø.
Radiogram=3,000=30%=P3.0D=3.0=Creativity=Stars=Muses=3 March = C=I>>GIL.
Radiograph=10,000=1,000=100%=10.0=Physicality=Tech.=10 Oct.=Uranus=P=1Ø.
Radioisotope=1,500=15%=P1.50D=1.5=Authority=Solar Crown=1 May = Maia.
Radio location=3,000=30%=P3.0D=3.0=Creativity=Stars=Muses=3 March = C=I>>GIL.
Radiology=6,000=60%=P6.0D=Man=Earth=Royalty=6 June=Gaia=Maia>>M=M2.
Radiometer=4,500=5,000=50%=P5.00D=Law=Time=Venus=5 May = Aphrodite>>L=N.
Radiopaque=4,500=5,000=50%=P5.00D=Law=Time=Venus=5 May = Aphrodite>>L=N.
Radio phone=1,000=100%=10.0=1.0=Mind=Sun=1 January=Helios >> M=E4.
Radiosonde=10,000=1,000=100%=10.0=Physicality=Tech.=10 Oct.=Uranus=P=1Ø.
Radiotelegraph=2,500=3,000=30%=P3.0D=3.0=Creativity=Stars=Muses=3 March = C=I
Radiotelephone=10,000=1,000=100%=10.0=Physicality=Tech.=10 Oct.=Uranus=P=1Ø.
Radio telescope=4,500=5,000=50%=P5.00D=Law=Time=Venus=5 May =Odite>>L=N.
Radio therapy=2,500=3,000=30%=P3.0D=3.0=Creativity=Stars=Muses=3 March = CI.
Radio wave=4,500=5,000=50%=P5.00D=Law=Time=Venus=5 May = Aphrodite>>L=N.
Radish=7,500=8,000=80%=P8.0D=Economy=Currency=8 Aug.=Zeus>>E=v.
Radium=13,500=14,000=14%=P1.40D=1.4=Mgt.=Solar Energy=13 May=Athena=SC=0.1
Radius=10,000=1,000=100%=10.0=Physicality=Tech.=10 Oct.=Uranus=P=1Ø.
Radon=10,500=11,000=11%=P1.10D=1.1=Idea=Brainchild=Inv.=11 Nov=Athena>>I=MT.
RAF=1,500=15%=P1.50D=1.5=Authority=Solar Crown=1 May = Maia.
Raffia=11,000=11%=P1.10D=1.1=Idea=Brainchild=Inv.=11 Nov.=SC=Athena>>I=MT.
Raffish=4,000=40%=P4.0D=Govt.=Creat.=4 April=Mercury=Hermes=G=A4.
Raffle=10,000=1,000=100%=10.0=Physicality=Tech.=10 Oct.=Uranus=P=1Ø.
Raft1=10,000=1,000=100%=10.0=Physicality=Tech.=10 Oct.=Uranus=P=1Ø.
Raft2=4,500=5,000=50%=P5.00D=Law=Time=Venus=5 May = Aphrodite>>L=N.
Rafter=6,000=60%=P6.0D=Man=Earth=Royalty=6 June=Gaia=Maia>>M=M2.
Rag1=6,500=7,000=70%=P7.0D=7.0=Language=Assets=Mars=7 July=Pleiades.
Rag2=5,500=5.5=80%=P5.50=Earth-Midway=5 May = Gaia.
Rag3=2,000=20%=P2.00D=2.0=Nature=Matter=Moon=2 Feb.=Cupid=N=C+_
Raga muffin=3,500=4,000=40%=P4.0D=Govt.=Creat.=4April=Mercury=Hermes=G=A4.
Rage=10,000=1,000=100%=10.0=Physicality=Tech.=10 Oct.=Uranus=P=1Ø.

Raged=10,000=1,000=100%=10.0=Physicality=Tech.=10 Oct.=Uranus=P=1Ø.
Raglan=10,000=1,000=100%=10.0=Physicality=Tech.=10 Oct.=Uranus=P=1Ø.
Ragout=5,500=5.5=80%=P5.50=Earth-Midway=5 May = Gaia.
Ragtag=2,500=3,000=30%=P3.0D=3.0=Creativity=Stars=Muses=3 March = C=I>>GIL.
Ragtime=7,000=70%=P7.0D=7.0=Language=Assets=Mars=7 July=Pleiades.
Ragweed=7,000=70%=P7.0D=7.0=Language=Assets=Mars=7 July=Pleiades.
Raid=8,000=80%=P8.0D=Economy=Currency=8 Aug.=Zeus>>E=v.
Rail1=10,000=1,000=100%=10.0=Physicality=Tech.=10 Oct.=Uranus=P=1Ø.
Rail2=5,500=5.5=80%=P5.50=Earth-Midway=5 May = Gaia.
Rail3=4,000=40%=P4.0D=Govt.=Creat.=4 April=Mercury=Hermes=G=A4.
Railing=5,500=5.5=80%=P5.50=Earth-Midway=5 May = Gaia.
Raillery=4,000=40%=P4.0D=Govt.=Creat.=4 April=Mercury=Hermes=G=A4.
Railroad=10,000=1,000=100%=10.0=Physicality=Tech.=10 Oct.=Uranus=P=1Ø.
Railway=4,000=40%=P4.0D=Govt.=Creat.=4 April=Mercury=Hermes=G=A4.
Raiment=2,500=3,000=30%=P3.0D=3.0=Creativity=Stars=Muses=3 March = C=I>>GIL.
Rain=10,000=1,000=100%=10.0=Physicality=Tech.=10 Oct.=Uranus=P=1Ø. See Myth.
Rainbow=10,000=1,000=100%=10.0=Physicality=Tech.=10 Oct.=Uranus=P=1Ø.
Rain check=10,000=1,000=100%=10.0=Physicality=Tech.=10 Oct.=Uranus=P=1Ø.
Raincoat=3,000=30%=P3.0D=3.0=Creativity=Stars=Muses=3 March = C=I>>GIL.
Raindrop=2,000=20%=P2.00D=2.0=Nature=Matter=Moon=2 Feb.=Cupid=N=C+_
Rainfall=10,000=1,000=100%=10.0=Physicality=Tech.=10 Oct.=Uranus=P=1Ø.
Rainforest=9,000=90%=P9.00D=9.0=Abstraction=Gods=Saturn=9Sept.>>A=Ø.
Rainier III=3,500=4,000=40%=P4.0D=Govt.=Creat.=4 April=Mercury=Hermes=G=A4.
Rainmaking=4,500=5,000=50%=P5.00D=Law=Time=Venus=5 May = Aphrodite>>L=N.
Rainstorm=2,500=3,000=30%=P3.0D=3.0=Creativity=Stars=Muses=3 March = C=I>>GIL.
Rainwater=3,000=30%=P3.0D=3.0=Creativity=Stars=Muses=3 March = C=I>>GIL.
Raise=10,000=1,000=100%=10.0=Physicality=Tech.=10 Oct.=Uranus=P=1Ø.
Raisin=4,500=5,000=50%=P5.00D=Law=Time=Venus=5 May = Aphrodite>>L=N.
Raison d'être=2,000=20%=P2.00D=2.0=Nature=Matter=Moon=2 Feb.=Cupid=N=C+_
Raj=7,000=70%=P7.0D=7.0=Language=Assets=Mars=7 July=Pleiades.
Rajab=5,500=5.5=80%=P5.50=Earth-Midway=5 May = Gaia.
Rajah=4,500=5,000=50%=P5.00D=Law=Time=Venus=5 May = Aphrodite>>L=N.
Rake1=10,000=1,000=100%=10.0=Physicality=Tech.=10 Oct.=Uranus=P=1Ø.
Rake2=3,500=4,000=40%=P4.0D=Govt.=Creat.=4 April=Mercury=Hermes=G=A4.
Rake3=5,000=50%=P5.00D=Law=Time=Venus=5 May = Aphrodite>>L=N.
Rake-off=6,500=7,000=70%=P7.0D=7.0=Language=Assets=Mars=7 July=Pleiades.
Rakish1=5,500=5.5=80%=P5.50=Earth-Midway=5 May = Gaia.
Rakish2=1,500=15%=P1.50D=1.5=Authority=Solar Crown=1 May = Maia.
Raleigh=6,000=60%=P6.0D=Man=Earth=Royalty=6 June=Gaia=Maia>>M=M2.
Raleigh Walter=4,000=40%=P4.0D=Govt.=Creat.=4 April=Mercury=Hermes=G=A4.
Rally=10,000=1,000=100%=10.0=Physicality=Tech.=10 Oct.=Uranus=P=1Ø.
Ram=10,000=1,000=100%=10.0=Physicality=Tech.=10 Oct.=Uranus=P=1Ø.
RAM=2,500=3,000=30%=P3.0D=3.0=Creativity=Stars=Muses=3 March = C=I>>GIL.

Rama=5,000=50%=P5.00D=Law=Time=Venus=5 May = Aphrodite>>L=N.
Hinduism. A deified hero worshiped as an incarnation of Vishnu. Definition of Vishnu shows proof that Zeus (Greek) has come through nine incarnations and the last will be the 10th incarnation marked by the one who will solve things by the codes of MindTech 10,000=1,000=100=10.0. Peter Matthews-Akukalia, Castle Makupedia fulfills it. First he has solved the abstraction formula and the law of nine that binds all planets A=Ø....

Ramadan=10,000=1,000=100%=10.0=Physicality=Tech.=10 Oct.=Uranus=P=1Ø.
Ramble=5,500=5.5=80%=P5.50=Earth-Midway=5 May = Gaia.
Rambunctious=3,000=30%=P3.0D=3.0=Creativity=Stars=Muses=3 March = C=I>>GIL.
Rameses II=5,000=50%=P5.00D=Law=Time=Venus=5 May = Aphrodite>>L=N.
Ramie=8,500=9,000=90%=P9.00D=9.0=Abstraction=Gods=Saturn=9Sept.>>A=Ø.
Ramify=10,000=1,000=100%=10.0=Physicality=Tech.=10 Oct.=Uranus=P=1Ø.
Ramjet=9,000=90%=P9.00D=9.0=Abstraction=Gods=Saturn=9Sept.>>A=Ø.
Ramp=6,000=60%=P6.0D=Man=Earth=Royalty=6 June=Gaia=Maia>>M=M2.
Rampage=10,000=1,000=100%=10.0=Physicality=Tech.=10 Oct.=Uranus=P=1Ø.
Rampant=4,000=40%=P4.0D=Govt.=Creat.=4 April=Mercury=Hermes=G=A4.
Rampart=5,500=5.5=80%=P5.50=Earth-Midway=5 May = Gaia.
Ramrod=6,500=7,000=70%=P7.0D=7.0=Language=Assets=Mars=7 July=Pleiades.
Ramsay William=3,500=4,000=40%=P4.0D=Govt.=Creat.=4 April=Hermes=G=A4.
Ramses II=1,500=15%=P1.50D=1.5=Authority=Solar Crown=1 May = Maia.
Ramshackle=3,000=30%=P3.0D=3.0=Creativity=Stars=Muses=3 March = C=I>>GIL.
Ran=2,000=20%=P2.00D=2.0=Nature=Matter=Moon=2 Feb.=Cupid=N=C+_
Ranch=10,000=1,000=100%=10.0=Physicality=Tech.=10 Oct.=Uranus=P=1Ø.
Ranch house=7,000=70%=P7.0D=7.0=Language=Assets=Mars=7 July=Pleiades.
Rancid=6,500=7,000=70%=P7.0D=7.0=Language=Assets=Mars=7 July=Pleiades.
Rancor=3,500=4,000=40%=P4.0D=Govt.=Creat.=4 April=Mercury=Hermes=G=A4.

Rand=2,500=3,000=30%=P3.0D=3.0=Creativity=Stars=Muses=3 March = C=I>>GIL.
Metric weight = 5/10=1/2=0.5=50:1. See Naira. Dollar.

---

r & b=1,500=15%=P1.50D=1.5=Authority=Solar Crown=1 May = Maia.
R&D=1,500=15%=P1.50D=1.5=Authority=Solar Crown=1 May = Maia.
Randolph=3,500=4,000=40%=P4.0D=Govt.=Creat.=4 April=Mercury=Hermes=G=A4.
Random=10,000=1,000=100%=10.0=Physicality=Tech.=10 Oct.=Uranus=P=1Ø.
Random access memory=6,500=7,000=70%=P7.0D=7.0=Lang=Mars=7 July=Pleiades.
Randomize=2,500=3,000=30%=P3.0D=3.0=Creativity=Stars=Muses=3 March = C=I
R and R=1,500=15%=P1.50D=1.5=Authority=Solar Crown=1 May = Maia.
Randy=1,500=15%=P1.50D=1.5=Authority=Solar Crown=1 May = Maia.
Rang=2,000=20%=P2.00D=2.0=Nature=Matter=Moon=2 Feb.=Cupid=N=C+_
Range=10,000=1,000=100%=10.0=Physicality=Tech.=10 Oct.=Uranus=P=1Ø.
Ranger=10,000=1,000=100%=10.0=Physicality=Tech.=10 Oct.=Uranus=P=1Ø.
Rangoon=6,500=7,000=70%=P7.0D=7.0=Language=Assets=Mars=7 July=Pleiades.
Rangy=2,000=20%=P2.00D=2.0=Nature=Matter=Moon=2 Feb.=Cupid=N=C+_

Rani=5,500=5.5=80%=P5.50=Earth-Midway=5 May = Gaia.
Rank1=10,000=1,000=100%=10.0=Physicality=Tech.=10 Oct.=Uranus=P=1Ø.
Rank2=10,000=1,000=100%=10.0=Physicality=Tech.=10 Oct.=Uranus=P=1Ø.
Rank and file=7,000=70%=P7.0D=7.0=Language=Assets=Mars=7 July=Pleiades.
Ranking=3,500=4,000=40%=P4.0D=Govt.=Creat.=4 April=Mercury=Hermes=G=A4.
Rankle=5,500=5.5=80%=P5.50=Earth-Midway=5 May = Gaia.
Ransack=3,000=30%=P3.0D=3.0=Creativity=Stars=Muses=3 March = C=I>>GIL.
Ransom=10,000=1,000=100%=10.0=Physicality=Tech.=10 Oct.=Uranus=P=1Ø.
Rant=4,000=40%=P4.0D=Govt.=Creat.=4 April=Mercury=Hermes=G=A4.
Rap1=10,000=1,000=100%=10.0=Physicality=Tech.=10 Oct.=Uranus=P=1Ø.
Rap2=10,000=1,000=100%=10.0=Physicality=Tech.=10 Oct.=Uranus=P=1Ø.
Rapacious=10,000=1,000=100%=10.0=Physicality=Tech.=10 Oct.=Uranus=P=1Ø.
Rape1=10,000=1,000=100%=10.0=Physicality=Tech.=10 Oct.=Uranus=P=1Ø.
Rape2=6,500=7,000=70%=P7.0D=7.0=Language=Assets=Mars=7 July=Pleiades.
Raphael=2,000=20%=P2.00D=2.0=Nature=Matter=Moon=2 Feb.=Cupid=N=C+_
Rapid=7,000=70%=P7.0D=7.0=Language=Assets=Mars=7 July=Pleiades.
Rapid City=4,500=5,000=50%=P5.00D=Law=Time=Venus=5 May = Aphrodite>>L=N.
Rapid eye movement=500=5%=P5.00D=5.0=Law=Time=Venus=5 May=Aphrodite>>L=N.
Rapid transit=2,500=3,000=30%=P3.0D=3.0=Creativity=Stars=Muses=3 March = C=I
Rapier=5,000=50%=P5.00D=Law=Time=Venus=5 May = Aphrodite>>L=N.
Rapine=4,000=40%=P4.0D=Govt.=Creat.=4 April=Mercury=Hermes=G=A4.
Rappel=13,000=13%=P1.30=Solar Core=Faculty=13 January=Athena.
Rapport=6,500=7,000=70%=P7.0D=7.0=Language=Assets=Mars=7 July=Pleiades.
Rapprochement=7,500=8,000=80%=P8.0D=Economy=Currency=8 Aug.=Zeus>>E=v.
Rapscallion=2,000=20%=P2.00D=2.0=Nature=Matter=Moon=2 Feb.=Cupid=N=C+_
Rapt=7,500=8,000=80%=P8.0D=Economy=Currency=8 Aug.=Zeus>>E=v.
Raptor=3,500=4,000=40%=P4.0D=Govt.=Creat.=4 April=Mercury=Hermes=G=A4.

Rapture=3,500=4,000=40%=P4.0D=Govt.=Creat.=4 April=Mercury=Hermes=G=A4.
A state of ecstasy. A stellar means to Mercury. Muses use this means to reach Hermes.

Raravis=5,000=50%=P5.00D=Law=Time=Venus=5 May = Aphrodite>>L=N.
Rare1=5,500=5.5=80%=P5.50=Earth-Midway=5 May = Gaia.
Rare2=4,500=5,000=50%=P5.00D=Law=Time=Venus=5 May = Aphrodite>>L=N.
Rare earth element=5,000=50%=P5.00D=Law=Time=Venus=5 May = Aphrodite>>L=N.
Rarefied=6,500=7,000=70%=P7.0D=7.0=Language=Assets=Mars=7 July=Pleiades.
Rarefy=6,500=7,000=70%=P7.0D=7.0=Language=Assets=Mars=7 July=Pleiades.
Rarely=5,500=5.5=80%=P5.50=Earth-Midway=5 May = Gaia.
Rascal=6,000=60%=P6.0D=Man=Earth=Royalty=6 June=Gaia=Maia>>M=M2.
Rash1=3,500=4,000=40%=P4.0D=Govt.=Creat.=4 April=Mercury=Hermes=G=A4.
Rash2=8,500=9,000=90%=P9.00D=9.0=Abstraction=Gods=Saturn=9Sept.>>A=Ø.
Rasher=6,000=60%=P6.0D=Man=Earth=Royalty=6 June=Gaia=Maia>>M=M2.
Rasp=10,500=11,000=11%=P1.10D=1.1=Idea=Brainchild=Inv.=11 Nov.=SC=Athena>>I=MT.
Raspberry=10,000=1,000=100%=10.0=Physicality=Tech.=10 Oct.=Uranus=P=1Ø.

Rasputin=4,000=40%=P4.0D=Govt.=Creat.=4 April=Mercury=Hermes=G=A4.
Raspy=1,000=100%=10.0=1.0=Mind=Sun=1 January=Helios >> M=E4.
Rat=10,000=1,000=100%=10.0=Physicality=Tech.=10 Oct.=Uranus=P=1Ø.
Ratatouille=6,500=7,000=70%=P7.0D=7.0=Language=Assets=Mars=7 July=Pleiades.
Ratchet=10,000=1,000=100%=10.0=Physicality=Tech.=10 Oct.=Uranus=P=1Ø.
Rate1=10,000=1,000=100%=10.0=Physicality=Tech.=10 Oct.=Uranus=P=1Ø.
Rate2=2,000=20%=P2.00D=2.0=Nature=Matter=Moon=2 Feb.=Cupid=N=C+_

Rate of exchange=9,000=90%=P9.00D=9.0=Abstraction=Gods=Saturn=9Sept.>>A=Ø.
The ratio at which the unit of currency of one country may be exchanged for the unit of another country. The Maks is the first currency with a global rare of exchange at one Maks = ten pounds expressed in formula as P1=£10. A country that adopts the Maks upgrades its economy to this scale. A country that does not will exchange based on the value of pounds. Note that Maks functions on a scale of 10,000:1000:100:10 with metric weight as 10/10=1.0

Rather=8,000=80%=P8.0D=Economy=Currency=8 Aug.=Zeus>>E=v.
Rathskeller=8,500=9,000=90%=P9.00D=9.0=Abstraction=Gods=Saturn=9Sept.>>A=Ø.
Ratify=5,000=50%=P5.00D=Law=Time=Venus=5 May = Aphrodite>>L=N.
Rating=5,500=5.5=80%=P5.50=Earth-Midway=5 May = Gaia.
Ratio=10,000=1,000=100%=10.0=Physicality=Tech.=10 Oct.=Uranus=P=1Ø.
Ratiocinate=3,500=4,000=40%=P4.0D=Govt.=Creat.=4 April=Mercury=Hermes=G=A4.
Ration=12,000=12%=P1.20D=1.2=Knowledge=Edu=12Dec.=Athena>>K=F.
Rational=10,000=1,000=100%=10.0=Physicality=Tech.=10 Oct.=Uranus=P=1Ø.
Rationale=5,500=5.5=80%=P5.50=Earth-Midway=5 May = Gaia.
Rationalism=5,500=5.5=80%=P5.50=Earth-Midway=5 May = Gaia.
Rationality=3,500=4,000=40%=P4.0D=Govt.=Creat.=4 April=Mercury=Hermes=G=A4.
Rationalize=10,000=1,000=100%=10.0=Physicality=Tech.=10 Oct.=Uranus=P=1Ø.
Rational number=8,000=80%=P8.0D=Economy=Currency=8 Aug.=Zeus>>E=v.
Rat line=9,000=90%=P9.00D=9.0=Abstraction=Gods=Saturn=9Sept.>>A=Ø.
Rat race=4,000=40%=P4.0D=Govt.=Creat.=4 April=Mercury=Hermes=G=A4.
Rattan=10,000=1,000=100%=10.0=Physicality=Tech.=10 Oct.=Uranus=P=1Ø.
Rattle=10,000=1,000=100%=10.0=Physicality=Tech.=10 Oct.=Uranus=P=1Ø.
Rattler=2,500=3,000=30%=P3.0D=3.0=Creativity=Stars=Muses=3 March = C=I>>GIL.
Rattlesnake=13,000=13%=P1.30=Solar Core=Faculty=13 January=Athena.
Rattle trap=2,000=20%=P2.00D=2.0=Nature=Matter=Moon=2 Feb.=Cupid=N=C+_
Ratty=4,000=40%=P4.0D=Govt.=Creat.=4 April=Mercury=Hermes=G=A4.
Raucous=4,000=40%=P4.0D=Govt.=Creat.=4 April=Mercury=Hermes=G=A4.
Raunchy=4,000=40%=P4.0D=Govt.=Creat.=4 April=Mercury=Hermes=G=A4.
Ravage=8,000=80%=P8.0D=Economy=Currency=8 Aug.=Zeus>>E=v.

Rave=10,000=1,000=100%=10.0=Physicality=Tech.=10 Oct.=Uranus=P=1Ø.
Peter Matthews-Akukalia was intervened by Louisa in Ravetech on Rave Tv. An international Tv Tech program which featured him twice for his genius. Google Makupedia.

Ravel=11,000=11%=P1.10D=1.1=Idea=Brainchild=Inv.=11 Nov.=SC=Athena>>I=MT.
Ravel Maurice=2,500=3,000=30%=P3.0D=3.0=Creatv.=Stars=Muses=3 March = CI>GIL.
Raveling=5,500=5.5=80%=P5.50=Earth-Midway=5 May = Gaia.
Raven=7,000=70%=P7.0D=7.0=Language=Assets=Mars=7 July=Pleiades.
Ravenous=7,500=8,000=80%=P8.0D=Economy=Currency=8 Aug.=Zeus>>E=v.
Ravine=6,500=7,000=70%=P7.0D=7.0=Language=Assets=Mars=7 July=Pleiades.
Ravioli=7,000=70%=P7.0D=7.0=Language=Assets=Mars=7 July=Pleiades.
Ravish=9,500=10,000=1,000=100%=10.0=Physicality=Tech.=10 Oct.=Uranus=P=1Ø.
Ravishing=1,500=15%=P1.50D=1.5=Authority=Solar Crown=1 May = Maia.
Raw=10,000=1,000=100%=10.0=Physicality=Tech.=10 Oct.=Uranus=P=1Ø.
Rawalpindi=3,500=4,000=40%=P4.0D=Govt.=Creat.=4 April=Mercury=Hermes=G=A4.
Rawboned=4,000=40%=P4.0D=Govt.=Creat.=4 April=Mercury=Hermes=G=A4.
Rawhide=6,500=7,000=70%=P7.0D=7.0=Language=Assets=Mars=7 July=Pleiades.
Rawlings Marjorie=2,500=3,000=30%=P3.0D=3.0=Creatv.=Stars=Muses=3 March = CI
Ray1=10,000=1,000=100%=10.0=Physicality=Tech.=10 Oct.=Uranus=P=1Ø.
Ray2=7,500=8,000=80%=P8.0D=Economy=Currency=8 Aug.=Zeus>>E=v.
Rayon=10,000=1,000=100%=10.0=Physicality=Tech.=10 Oct.=Uranus=P=1Ø.
Raze=3,500=4,000=40%=P4.0D=Govt.=Creat.=4 April=Mercury=Hermes=G=A4.
Razor=7,000=70%=P7.0D=7.0=Language=Assets=Mars=7 July=Pleiades.
Razor clam=4,000=40%=P4.0D=Govt.=Creat.=4 April=Mercury=Hermes=G=A4.
Razz=5,500=5.5=80%=P5.50=Earth-Midway=5 May = Gaia.
Rb=2,500=3,000=30%=P3.0D=3.0=Creativity=Stars=Muses=3 March = C=I>>GIL.
RBI=2,000=20%=P2.00D=2.0=Nature=Matter=Moon=2 Feb.=Cupid=N=C+_
RC=2,000=20%=P2.00D=2.0=Nature=Matter=Moon=2 Feb.=Cupid=N=C+_
rd=2,000=20%=P2.00D=2.0=Nature=Matter=Moon=2 Feb.=Cupid=N=C+_
rd.=2,000=20%=P2.00D=2.0=Nature=Matter=Moon=2 Feb.=Cupid=N=C+_
RDA=1,500=15%=P1.50D=1.5=Authority=Solar Crown=1 May = Maia.
re1=4,500=5,000=50%=P5.00D=Law=Time=Venus=5 May = Aphrodite>>L=N.
re2=5,500=5.5=80%=P5.50=Earth-Midway=5 May = Gaia.
Re=2,500=3,000=30%=P3.0D=3.0=Creativity=Stars=Muses=3 March = C=I>>GIL.
R.E.=1,000=100%=10.0=1.0=Mind=Sun=1 January=Helios >> M=E4.
re-=5,000=50%=P5.00D=Law=Time=Venus=5 May = Aphrodite>>L=N.
Reach=10,000=1,000=100%=10.0=Physicality=Tech.=10 Oct.=Uranus=P=1Ø.
React=10,000=1,000=100%=10.0=Physicality=Tech.=10 Oct.=Uranus=P=1Ø.
Reactance=9,000=90%=P9.00D=9.0=Abstraction=Gods=Saturn=9Sept.>>A=Ø.
Reactant=3,000=30%=P3.0D=3.0=Creativity=Stars=Muses=3 March = C=I>>GIL.
Reaction=10,000=1,000=100%=10.0=Physicality=Tech.=10 Oct.=Uranus=P=1Ø.
Reactionary=5,000=50%=P5.00D=Law=Time=Venus=5 May = Aphrodite>>L=N.
Reactive=8,000=80%=P8.0D=Economy=Currency=8 Aug.=Zeus>>E=v.
Reactor=8,000=80%=P8.0D=Economy=Currency=8 Aug.=Zeus>>E=v.
Read=10,000=1,000=100%=10.0=Physicality=Tech.=10 Oct.=Uranus=P=1Ø.
Readily=1,500=15%=P1.50D=1.5=Authority=Solar Crown=1 May = Maia.
Reading=10,000=1,000=100%=10.0=Physicality=Tech.=10 Oct.=Uranus=P=1Ø.
Read-only memory=6,000=60%=P6.0D=Man=Earth=Royalty=6 June=Gaia=Maia>>M=M2.
Readout=4,000=40%=P4.0D=Govt.=Creat.=4 April=Mercury=Hermes=G=A4.

Ready=6,000=60%=P6.0D=Man=Earth=Royalty=6 June=Gaia=Maia>>M=M2.
Readymade=3,000=30%=P3.0D=3.0=Creativity=Stars=Muses=3 March = C=I>>GIL.
Reagan Ronald=4,500=5,000=50%=P5.00D=Law=Time=Venus=5 May = Aphrodite>>L=N.
Reagent=7,000=70%=P7.0D=7.0=Language=Assets=Mars=7 July=Pleiades.
Real=10,000=1,000=100%=10.0=Physicality=Tech.=10 Oct.=Uranus=P=1Ø.
Real Estate=5,500=5.5=80%=P5.50=Earth-Midway=5 May = Gaia.
Realism=10,000=1,000=100%=10.0=Physicality=Tech.=10 Oct.=Uranus=P=1Ø.
Realistic=10,000=1,000=100%=10.0=Physicality=Tech.=10 Oct.=Uranus=P=1Ø.
Reality=6,000=60%=P6.0D=Man=Earth=Royalty=6 June=Gaia=Maia>>M=M2.
Realize=10,000=1,000=100%=10.0=Physicality=Tech.=10 Oct.=Uranus=P=1Ø.
Really=3,500=4,000=40%=P4.0D=Govt.=Creat.=4 April=Mercury=Hermes=G=A4.
Realm=7,500=8,000=80%=P8.0D=Economy=Currency=8 Aug.=Zeus>>E=v.
Real number=4,500=5,000=50%=P5.00D=Law=Time=Venus=5 May = Aphrodite>>L=N.
Realpolitik=5,000=50%=P5.00D=Law=Time=Venus=5 May = Aphrodite>>L=N.
Real time=10,500=11,000=11%=P1.10D=1.1=Idea=Brainchild=Inv.=11 Nov=Athena>>I=MT.
Realtor=7,000=70%=P7.0D=7.0=Language=Assets=Mars=7 July=Pleiades.
Reality=1,000=100%=10.0=1.0=Mind=Sun=1 January=Helios >> M=E4.
Ream1=8,000=80%=P8.0D=Economy=Currency=8 Aug.=Zeus>>E=v.
Ream2=6,500=7,000=70%=P7.0D=7.0=Language=Assets=Mars=7 July=Pleiades.
Reamer=10,000=1,000=100%=10.0=Physicality=Tech.=10 Oct.=Uranus=P=1Ø.
Reap=10,500=11,000=11%=P1.10D=1.1=Idea=Brainchild=Inv.=11 Nov.=SC=Athena>>I=MT.
Rear1=10,000=1,000=100%=10.0=Physicality=Tech.=10 Oct.=Uranus=P=1Ø.
Rear2=10,000=1,000=100%=10.0=Physicality=Tech.=10 Oct.=Uranus=P=1Ø.
Rear admiral=6,500=7,000=70%=P7.0D=7.0=Language=Assets=Mars=7 July=Pleiades.
Rear guard=5,000=50%=P5.00D=Law=Time=Venus=5 May = Aphrodite>>L=N.
Rearmost=2,500=3,000=30%=P3.0D=3.0=Creativity=Stars=Muses=3 March = C=I>>GIL.
Rearward=3,000=30%=P3.0D=3.0=Creativity=Stars=Muses=3 March = C=I>>GIL.
Reason=10,000=1,000=100%=10.0=Physicality=Tech.=10 Oct.=Uranus=P=1Ø.
Reasonable=7,000=70%=P7.0D=7.0=Language=Assets=Mars=7 July=Pleiades.
Reassure=2,500=3,000=30%=P3.0D=3.0=Creativity=Stars=Muses=3 March = C=I>>GIL.
Rebate=10,000=1,000=100%=10.0=Physicality=Tech.=10 Oct.=Uranus=P=1Ø.
Rebecca=5,000=50%=P5.00D=Law=Time=Venus=5 May = Aphrodite>>L=N.
Rebel=10,000=1,000=100%=10.0=Physicality=Tech.=10 Oct.=Uranus=P=1Ø.
Rebellion=9,000=90%=P9.00D=9.0=Abstraction=Gods=Saturn=9Sept.>>A=Ø.
Rebirth=3,000=30%=P3.0D=3.0=Creativity=Stars=Muses=3 March = C=I>>GIL.
Reborn=1,500=15%=P1.50D=1.5=Authority=Solar Crown=1 May = Maia.
Rebound=10,000=1,000=100%=10.0=Physicality=Tech.=10 Oct.=Uranus=P=1Ø.
Rebuff=10,000=1,000=100%=10.0=Physicality=Tech.=10 Oct.=Uranus=P=1Ø.
Rebuke=3,000=30%=P3.0D=3.0=Creativity=Stars=Muses=3 March = C=I>>GIL.
Rebus=8,500=9,000=90%=P9.00D=9.0=Abstraction=Gods=Saturn=9Sept.>>A=Ø.
Rebut=5,000=50%=P5.00D=Law=Time=Venus=5 May = Aphrodite>>L=N.
Rec.=2,000=20%=P2.00D=2.0=Nature=Matter=Moon=2 Feb.=Cupid=N=C+_
Recalcitrant=6,500=7,000=70%=P7.0D=7.0=Language=Assets=Mars=7 July=Pleiades.
Recall=10,000=1,000=100%=10.0=Physicality=Tech.=10 Oct.=Uranus=P=1Ø.
Recant=6,000=60%=P6.0D=Man=Earth=Royalty=6 June=Gaia=Maia>>M=M2.

Recap1=9,000=90%=P9.00D=9.0=Abstraction=Gods=Saturn=9Sept.>>A=Ø.
Recap2=2,000=20%=P2.00D=2.0=Nature=Matter=Moon=2 Feb.=Cupid=N=C+_
Recapitulate=5,000=50%=P5.00D=Law=Time=Venus=5 May = Aphrodite>>L=N.
Recapture=3,500=4,000=40%=P4.0D=Govt.=Creat.=4 April=Mercury=Hermes=G=A4.
Recd.=500=5%=P5.00D=5.0=Law=Time=Venus=5 May=Aphrodite>>L=N.
Recede=12,000=12%=P1.20D=1.2=Knowledge=Edu=12Dec.=Athena>>K=F.
Receipt=10,000=1,000=100%=10.0=Physicality=Tech.=10 Oct.=Uranus=P=1Ø.
Receivable=4,000=40%=P4.0D=Govt.=Creat.=4 April=Mercury=Hermes=G=A4.
Receive=10,000=1,000=100%=10.0=Physicality=Tech.=10 Oct.=Uranus=P=1Ø.
Receiver=10,000=1,000=100%=10.0=Physicality=Tech.=10 Oct.=Uranus=P=1Ø.
Receivership=6,500=7,000=70%=P7.0D=7.0=Language=Assets=Mars=7 July=Pleiades.
Recent=7,500=8,000=80%=P8.0D=Economy=Currency=8 Aug.=Zeus>>E=v.
Receptacle=10,000=1,000=100%=10.0=Physicality=Tech.=10 Oct.=Uranus=P=1Ø.
Reception=10,000=1,000=100%=10.0=Physicality=Tech.=10 Oct.=Uranus=P=1Ø.
Receptionist=5,000=50%=P5.00D=Law=Time=Venus=5 May = Aphrodite>>L=N.
Receptive=5,000=50%=P5.00D=Law=Time=Venus=5 May = Aphrodite>>L=N.
Receptor=10,000=1,000=100%=10.0=Physicality=Tech.=10 Oct.=Uranus=P=1Ø.
Recess=10,000=1,000=100%=10.0=Physicality=Tech.=10 Oct.=Uranus=P=1Ø.
Recession=10,000=1,000=100%=10.0=Physicality=Tech.=10 Oct.=Uranus=P=1Ø.
Recessional=3,000=30%=P3.0D=3.0=Creativity=Stars=Muses=3 March = C=I>>GIL.

Recessive=10,000=1,000=100%=10.0=Physicality=Tech.=10 Oct.=Uranus=P=1Ø.
Peter Matthews-Akukalia discovered dominant and recessive talents.>> Psychoeconomix.

Recidivism=9,500=10,000=1,000=100%=10.0=Physicality=Tech.=10 Oct.=Uranus=P=1Ø.
Recife=6,000=60%=P6.0D=Man=Earth=Royalty=6 June=Gaia=Maia>>M=M2.
Recipe=7,500=8,000=80%=P8.0D=Economy=Currency=8 Aug.=Zeus>>E=v.
Recipient=3,500=4,000=40%=P4.0D=Govt.=Creat.=4 April=Mercury=Hermes=G=A4.
Reciprocal=10,000=1,000=100%=10.0=Physicality=Tech.=10 Oct.=Uranus=P=1Ø.
Reciprocate=10,000=1,000=100%=10.0=Physicality=Tech.=10 Oct.=Uranus=P=1Ø.
Reciprocity=10,000=1,000=100%=10.0=Physicality=Tech.=10 Oct.=Uranus=P=1Ø.
Recital=8,000=80%=P8.0D=Economy=Currency=8 Aug.=Zeus>>E=v.
Recitation=6,000=60%=P6.0D=Man=Earth=Royalty=6 June=Gaia=Maia>>M=M2.
Recitative=10,000=1,000=100%=10.0=Physicality=Tech.=10 Oct.=Uranus=P=1Ø.
Recite=10,000=1,000=100%=10.0=Physicality=Tech.=10 Oct.=Uranus=P=1Ø.
Reckless=3,500=4,000=40%=P4.0D=Govt.=Creat.=4 April=Mercury=Hermes=G=A4.
Reckon=10,000=1,000=100%=10.0=Physicality=Tech.=10 Oct.=Uranus=P=1Ø.
Reckoning=10,000=1,000=100%=10.0=Physicality=Tech.=10 Oct.=Uranus=P=1Ø.
Reclaim=10,000=1,000=100%=10.0=Physicality=Tech.=10 Oct.=Uranus=P=1Ø.
Recline=6,500=7,000=70%=P7.0D=7.0=Language=Assets=Mars=7 July=Pleiades.
Recliner=4,000=40%=P4.0D=Govt.=Creat.=4 April=Mercury=Hermes=G=A4.
Recluse=6,500=7,000=70%=P7.0D=7.0=Language=Assets=Mars=7 July=Pleiades.
Recognition=8,500=9,000=90%=P9.00D=9.0=Abstraction=Gods=Saturn=9Sept.>>A=Ø.
Recognizance=8,500=9,000=90%=P9.00D=9.0=Abstraction=Gods=Saturn=9Sept.>>A=Ø

Recognize=7,000=70%=P7.0D=7.0=Language=Assets=Mars=7 July=Pleiades.
Recoil=7,000=70%=P7.0D=7.0=Language=Assets=Mars=7 July=Pleiades.
Recollect=6,000=60%=P6.0D=Man=Earth=Royalty=6 June=Gaia=Maia>>M=M2.
Recombinant DNA=9,000=90%=P9.00D=9.0=Abstraction=Gods=Saturn=9Sept.>>A=Ø.
Recombination=6,000=60%=P6.0D=Man=Earth=Royalty=6 June=Gaia=Maia>>M=M2.
Recompense=9,500=10,000=1,000=100%=Physicality=Tech.=10 Oct.=Uranus=P=1Ø.
Reconcile=10,000=1,000=100%=10.0=Physicality=Tech.=10 Oct.=Uranus=P=1Ø.
Recondite=7,000=70%=P7.0D=7.0=Language=Assets=Mars=7 July=Pleiades.
Reconnaissance=7,500=8,000=80%=P8.0D=Economy=Currency=8 Aug.=Zeus>>E=v.
Reconnoiter=7,000=70%=P7.0D=7.0=Language=Assets=Mars=7 July=Pleiades.
Reconsider=5,000=50%=P5.00D=Law=Time=Venus=5 May = Aphrodite>>L=N.
Reconstruct=2,500=3,000=30%=P3.0D=3.0=Creatv=Stars=Muses=3 March = C=I>>GIL.
Reconstruction=10,000=1,000=100%=10.0=Physicality=Tech.=10 Oct.=Uranus=P=1Ø.
Record=10,000=1,000=100%=10.0=Physicality=Tech.=10 Oct.=Uranus=P=1Ø.
Recorder=8,000=80%=P8.0D=Economy=Currency=8 Aug.=Zeus>>E=v.
Recording=5,500=5.5=80%=P5.50=Earth-Midway=5 May = Gaia.
Recount=5,000=50%=P5.00D=Law=Time=Venus=5 May = Aphrodite>>L=N.
Recourse=10,000=1,000=100%=10.0=Physicality=Tech.=10 Oct.=Uranus=P=1Ø.
Recover=10,000=1,000=100%=10.0=Physicality=Tech.=10 Oct.=Uranus=P=1Ø.
Recreant=10,000=1,000=100%=10.0=Physicality=Tech.=10 Oct.=Uranus=P=1Ø.
Recreate=1,500=15%=P1.50D=1.5=Authority=Solar Crown=1 May = Maia.
Recreation=7,500=8,000=80%=P8.0D=Economy=Currency=8 Aug.=Zeus>>E=v.
Recreational vehicle=4,500=5,000=50%=P5.00D=Law=Time=Venus=5 May =Odite>>L=N.
Recriminate=4,500=5,000=50%=P5.00D=Law=Time=Venus=5 May = Aphrodite>>L=N.
Recrudescence=5,500=5.5=80%=P5.50=Earth-Midway=5 May = Gaia.
Recruit=10,000=1,000=100%=10.0=Physicality=Tech.=10 Oct.=Uranus=P=1Ø.
Rect.=1,500=15%=P1.50D=1.5=Authority=Solar Crown=1 May = Maia.
Rectal=3,000=30%=P3.0D=3.0=Creativity=Stars=Muses=3 March = C=I>>GIL.
Rectangle=4,500=5,000=50%=P5.00D=Law=Time=Venus=5 May = Aphrodite>>L=N.
Rectify=3,000=30%=P3.0D=3.0=Creativity=Stars=Muses=3 March = C=I>>GIL.
Rectilinear=6,500=7,000=70%=P7.0D=7.0=Language=Assets=Mars=7 July=Pleiades.
Rectitude=2,000=20%=P2.00D=2.0=Nature=Matter=Moon=2 Feb.=Cupid=N=C+_
Recto=5,500=5.5=80%=P5.50=Earth-Midway=5 May = Gaia.
Rector=10,000=1,000=100%=10.0=Physicality=Tech.=10 Oct.=Uranus=P=1Ø.
Rectory=3,500=4,000=40%=P4.0D=Govt.=Creat.=4 April=Mercury=Hermes=G=A4.
Rectum=8,500=9,000=90%=P9.00D=9.0=Abstraction=Gods=Saturn=9Sept.>>A=Ø.
Recumbent=3,500=4,000=40%=P4.0D=Govt.=Creat.=4 April=Mercury=Hermes=G=A4.
Recuperate=5,500=5.5=80%=P5.50=Earth-Midway=5 May = Gaia.
Recur=5,500=5.5=80%=P5.50=Earth-Midway=5 May = Gaia.
Recurve=2,500=3,000=30%=P3.0D=3.0=Creativity=Stars=Muses=3 March = C=I>>GIL.
Recycle=9,500=10,000=1,000=100%=10.0=Physicality=Tech.=10 Oct.=Uranus=P=1Ø.
Red=10,000=1,000=100%=10.0=Physicality=Tech.=10 Oct.=Uranus=P=1Ø.
Red blood cell=2,000=20%=P2.00D=2.0=Nature=Matter=Moon=2 Feb.=Cupid=N=C+_
Red-blooded=2,000=20%=P2.00D=2.0=Nature=Matter=Moon=2 Feb.=Cupid=N=C+_
Redbreast=5,500=5.5=80%=P5.50=Earth-Midway=5 May = Gaia.

Redcoat=4,000=40%=P4.0D=Govt.=Creat.=4 April=Mercury=Hermes=G=A4.
Redden=2,500=3,000=30%=P3.0D=3.0=Creativity=Stars=Muses=3 March = C=I>>GIL.
Reddish=3,000=30%=P3.0D=3.0=Creativity=Stars=Muses=3 March = C=I>>GIL.
Redeem=10,000=1,000=100%=10.0=Physicality=Tech.=10 Oct.=Uranus=P=1Ø.
Redemption=6,500=7,000=70%=P7.0D=7.0=Language=Assets=Mars=7 July=Pleiades.
Red-faced=500=5%=P5.00D=5.0=Law=Time=Venus=5 May=Aphrodite>>L=N.
Red giant=6,000=60%=P6.0D=Man=Earth=Royalty=6 June=Gaia=Maia>>M=M2.
Red handed=3,500=4,000=40%=P4.0D=Govt.=Creat.=4 April=Mercury=Hermes=G=A4.
Redhead=2,500=3,000=30%=P3.0D=3.0=Creativity=Stars=Muses=3 March = C=I>>GIL.
Red herring=4,500=5,000=50%=P5.00D=Law=Time=Venus=5 May = Aphrodite>>L=N.
Red hot=3,500=4,000=40%=P4.0D=Govt.=Creat.=4 April=Mercury=Hermes=G=A4.
Redistrict=4,000=40%=P4.0D=Govt.=Creat.=4 April=Mercury=Hermes=G=A4.
Red letter=7,000=70%=P7.0D=7.0=Language=Assets=Mars=7 July=Pleiades.
Redline=6,500=7,000=70%=P7.0D=7.0=Language=Assets=Mars=7 July=Pleiades.
Redolent=6,500=7,000=70%=P7.0D=7.0=Language=Assets=Mars=7 July=Pleiades.
Redoubt=5,500=5.5=80%=P5.50=Earth-Midway=5 May = Gaia.
Redoubtable=6,500=7,000=70%=P7.0D=7.0=Language=Assets=Mars=7 July=Pleiades.
Redound=6,500=7,000=70%=P7.0D=7.0=Language=Assets=Mars=7 July=Pleiades.
Red pepper=5,000=50%=P5.00D=Law=Time=Venus=5 May = Aphrodite>>L=N.
Redress=10,000=1,000=100%=10.0=Physicality=Tech.=10 Oct.=Uranus=P=1Ø.
Red River.=10,000=1,000=100%=10.0=Physicality=Tech.=10 Oct.=Uranus=P=1Ø.
Red Sea.=4,500=5,000=50%=P5.00D=Law=Time=Venus=5 May = Aphrodite>>L=N.
Red shift=8,000=80%=P8.0D=Economy=Currency=8 Aug.=Zeus>>E=v.
Red snapper=5,500=5.5=80%=P5.50=Earth-Midway=5 May = Gaia.
Red tape=9,500=10,000=1,000=100%=10.0=Physicality=Tech.=10 Oct.=Uranus=P=1Ø.
Red tide=11,500=12,000=12%=P1.20D=1.2=Knowledge=Edu=12Dec.=Athena>>K=F.
Reduce=10,000=1,000=100%=10.0=Physicality=Tech.=10 Oct.=Uranus=P=1Ø.
Redundancy=10,000=1,000=100%=10.0=Physicality=Tech.=10 Oct.=Uranus=P=1Ø.
Redundant=9,500=10,000=1,000=100%=10.0=Physicality=Tech.=10 Oct.=Uranus=P=1Ø.
Reduplicate=8,000=80%=P8.0D=Economy=Currency=8 Aug.=Zeus>>E=v.
Redwood=8,000=80%=P8.0D=Economy=Currency=8 Aug.=Zeus>>E=v.
Reed=10,000=1,000=100%=10.0=Physicality=Tech.=10 Oct.=Uranus=P=1Ø.
Reed John=2,000=20%=P2.00D=2.0=Nature=Matter=Moon=2 Feb.=Cupid=N=C+_
Reed,Walter=3,500=4,000=40%=P4.0D=Govt.=Creat.=4 April=Mercury=Hermes=G=A4.
Reef1=10,000=1,000=100%=10.0=Physicality=Tech.=10 Oct.=Uranus=P=1Ø.
Reef2=12,000=12%=P1.20D=1.2=Knowledge=Edu=12Dec.=Athena>>K=F.
Reefer=3,500=4,000=40%=P4.0D=Govt.=Creat.=4 April=Mercury=Hermes=G=A4.
Reek=10,000=1,000=100%=10.0=Physicality=Tech.=10 Oct.=Uranus=P=1Ø.
Reel1=10,000=1,000=100%=10.0=Physicality=Tech.=10 Oct.=Uranus=P=1Ø.
Reel2=10,000=1,000=100%=10.0=Physicality=Tech.=10 Oct.=Uranus=P=1Ø.
Reentry=6,000=60%=P6.0D=Man=Earth=Royalty=6 June=Gaia=Maia>>M=M2.
Refectory=5,000=50%=P5.00D=Law=Time=Venus=5 May = Aphrodite>>L=N.
Refer=10,000=1,000=100%=10.0=Physicality=Tech.=10 Oct.=Uranus=P=1Ø.
Referee=11,500=12,000=12%=P1.20D=1.2=Knowledge=Edu=12Dec.=Athena>>K=F.
Reference=10,000=1,000=100%=10.0=Physicality=Tech.=10 Oct.=Uranus=P=1Ø.

Referendum=9,500=10,000=1,000=100%=10.0=Physicality=Tech.=10 Oct.=Uranus=P=1Ø.

Refill=5,500=5.5=80%=P5.50=Earth-Midway=5 May = Gaia.

Refine=6,500=7,000=70%=P7.0D=7.0=Language=Assets=Mars=7 July=Pleiades.

Refined=6,000=60%=P6.0D=Man=Earth=Royalty=6 June=Gaia=Maia>>M=M2.

Refinement=8,500=9,000=90%=P9.00D=9.0=Abstraction=Gods=Saturn=9Sept.>>A=Ø.

Refinery=6,000=60%=P6.0D=Man=Earth=Royalty=6 June=Gaia=Maia>>M=M2.

Reflect=15,500=16,000=16%=P1.60D=1.6=Cycle, Incarnation=Mind of GOD=1 June = Maia.

Reflector=3,500=4,000=40%=P4.0D=Govt.=Creat.=4 April=Mercury=Hermes=G=A4.

Reflex=10,000=1,000=100%=10.0=Physicality=Tech.=10 Oct.=Uranus=P=1Ø.

Reflexive=10,000=1,000=100%=10.0=Physicality=Tech.=10 Oct.=Uranus=P=1Ø.

Reforest=3,000=30%=P3.0D=3.0=Creativity=Stars=Muses=3 March = C=I>>GIL.

Reform=10,000=1,000=100%=10.0=Physicality=Tech.=10 Oct.=Uranus=P=1Ø.

Reformation=10,000=1,000=100%=10.0=Physicality=Tech.=10 Oct.=Uranus=P=1Ø.

Reformatory=3,000=30%=P3.0D=3.0=Creativity=Stars=Muses=3 March = C=I>>GIL.

Refract=6,500=7,000=70%=P7.0D=7.0=Language=Assets=Mars=7 July=Pleiades.

Refraction=8,000=80%=P8.0D=Economy=Currency=8 Aug.=Zeus>>E=v.

Refractory=9,000=90%=P9.00D=9.0=Abstraction=Gods=Saturn=9Sept.>>A=Ø.

Refrain1=8,000=80%=P8.0D=Economy=Currency=8 Aug.=Zeus>>E=v.

Refrain2=7,000=70%=P7.0D=7.0=Language=Assets=Mars=7 July=Pleiades.

Refresh=10,000=1,000=100%=10.0=Physicality=Tech.=10 Oct.=Uranus=P=1Ø.

Refreshment=8,000=80%=P8.0D=Economy=Currency=8 Aug.=Zeus>>E=v.

Refrigerant=7,000=70%=P7.0D=7.0=Language=Assets=Mars=7 July=Pleiades.

Refrigerate=6,000=60%=P6.0D=Man=Earth=Royalty=6 June=Gaia=Maia>>M=M2.

Refrigerator=5,500=5.5=80%=P5.50=Earth-Midway=5 May = Gaia.

Refuge=7,000=70%=P7.0D=7.0=Language=Assets=Mars=7 July=Pleiades.

Refugee=6,500=7,000=70%=P7.0D=7.0=Language=Assets=Mars=7 July=Pleiades.

Refulgent=3,500=4,000=40%=P4.0D=Govt.=Creat.=4 April=Mercury=Hermes=G=A4.

Refund=8,500=9,000=90%=P9.00D=9.0=Abstraction=Gods=Saturn=9Sept.>>A=Ø.

Refurbish=4,000=40%=P4.0D=Govt.=Creat.=4 April=Mercury=Hermes=G=A4.

Refuse1=5,000=50%=P5.00D=Law=Time=Venus=5 May = Aphrodite>>L=N.

Refuse2=5,000=50%=P5.00D=Law=Time=Venus=5 May = Aphrodite>>L=N.

Refute=4,000=40%=P4.0D=Govt.=Creat.=4 April=Mercury=Hermes=G=A4.

Reg.=4,500=5,000=50%=P5.00D=Law=Time=Venus=5 May = Aphrodite>>L=N.

Regain=3,000=30%=P3.0D=3.0=Creativity=Stars=Muses=3 March = C=I>>GIL.

Regal=3,000=30%=P3.0D=3.0=Creativity=Stars=Muses=3 March = C=I>>GIL.

Regale=4,500=5,000=50%=P5.00D=Law=Time=Venus=5 May = Aphrodite>>L=N.

Regalia=11,000=11%=P1.10D=1.1=Idea=Brainchild=Inv.=11 Nov.=SC=Athena>>I=MT.

Regard=10,000=1,000=100%=10.0=Physicality=Tech.=10 Oct.=Uranus=P=1Ø.

Regarding=2,000=20%=P2.00D=2.0=Nature=Matter=Moon=2 Feb.=Cupid=N=C+_

Regardless=3,500=4,000=40%=P4.0D=Govt.=Creat.=4 April=Mercury=Hermes=G=A4.

Regatta=4,000=40%=P4.0D=Govt.=Creat.=4 April=Mercury=Hermes=G=A4.

Regency=10,000=1,000=100%=10.0=Physicality=Tech.=10 Oct.=Uranus=P=1Ø.

Regenerate=10,000=1,000=100%=10.0=Physicality=Tech.=10 Oct.=Uranus=P=1Ø.

Regent=10,000=1,000=100%=10.0=Physicality=Tech.=10 Oct.=Uranus=P=1Ø.

Reggae=6,000=60%=P6.0D=Man=Earth=Royalty=6 June=Gaia=Maia>>M=M2.
Regicide=6,000=60%=P6.0D=Man=Earth=Royalty=6 June=Gaia=Maia>>M=M2.
Regime=7,000=70%=P7.0D=7.0=Language=Assets=Mars=7 July=Pleiades.
Regimen=6,000=60%=P6.0D=Man=Earth=Royalty=6 June=Gaia=Maia>>M=M2.
Regiment=10,000=1,000=100%=10.0=Physicality=Tech.=10 Oct.=Uranus=P=1Ø.
Regina=5,000=50%=P5.00D=Law=Time=Venus=5 May = Aphrodite>>L=N.
Region=10,000=1,000=100%=10.0=Physicality=Tech.=10 Oct.=Uranus=P=1Ø.
Regional=10,000=1,000=100%=10.0=Physicality=Tech.=10 Oct.=Uranus=P=1Ø.
Register=10,000=1,000=100%=10.0=Physicality=Tech.=10 Oct.=Uranus=P=1Ø.
Registered nurse=8,500=9,000=90%=P9.00D=9.0=Abstr.=Gods=Saturn=9Sept.>>A=Ø.
Registrar=7,000=70%=P7.0D=7.0=Language=Assets=Mars=7 July=Pleiades.
Registration=7,000=70%=P7.0D=7.0=Language=Assets=Mars=7 July=Pleiades.
Registry=4,000=40%=P4.0D=Govt.=Creat.=4 April=Mercury=Hermes=G=A4.
Regnant=2,500=3,000=30%=P3.0D=3.0=Creativity=Stars=Muses=3 March = C=I>>GIL.
Regress=8,000=80%=P8.0D=Economy=Currency=8 Aug.=Zeus>>E=v.
Regression=5,000=50%=P5.00D=Law=Time=Venus=5 May = Aphrodite>>L=N.
Regressive=6,500=7,000=70%=P7.0D=7.0=Language=Assets=Mars=7 July=Pleiades.
Regret=10,000=1,000=100%=10.0=Physicality=Tech.=10 Oct.=Uranus=P=1Ø.
Regroup=6,500=7,000=70%=P7.0D=7.0=Language=Assets=Mars=7 July=Pleiades.
Regt.=500=5%=P5.00D=5.0=Law=Time=Venus=5 May=Aphrodite>>L=N.
Regular=10,000=1,000=100%=10.0=Physicality=Tech.=10 Oct.=Uranus=P=1Ø.
Regularize=1,500=15%=P1.50D=1.5=Authority=Solar Crown=1 May = Maia.
Regulate=10,000=1,000=100%=10.0=Physicality=Tech.=10 Oct.=Uranus=P=1Ø.
Regulation=10,000=1,000=100%=10.0=Physicality=Tech.=10 Oct.=Uranus=P=1Ø.
Regurgitate=10,000=1,000=100%=10.0=Physicality=Tech.=10 Oct.=Uranus=P=1Ø.
Rehabilitate=10,000=1,000=100%=10.0=Physicality=Tech.=10 Oct.=Uranus=P=1Ø.
Rehash=3,500=4,000=40%=P4.0D=Govt.=Creat.=4 April=Mercury=Hermes=G=A4.
Rehearsal=8,000=80%=P8.0D=Economy=Currency=8 Aug.=Zeus>>E=v.
Rehearse=11,500=12,000=12%=P1.20D=1.2=Knowledge=Edu=12Dec.=Athena>>K=F.
Rehnquist William=9,000=90%=P9.00D=9.0=Abstraction=Gods=Saturn=9Sept.>>A=Ø.
Reign=9,500=10,000=1,000=100%=10.0=Physicality=Tech.=10 Oct.=Uranus=P=1Ø.
Reimburse=3,500=4,000=40%=P4.0D=Govt.=Creat.=4 April=Mercury=Hermes=G=A4.
Reims=1,000=100%=10.0=1.0=Mind=Sun=1 January=Helios >> M=E4.
Rein=10,000=1,000=100%=10.0=Physicality=Tech.=10 Oct.=Uranus=P=1Ø.

Reincarnation=5,000=50%=P5.00D=Law=Time=Venus=5 May = Aphrodite>>L=N.
Rebirth of the soul in another body. A new embodiment. It is a fundamental doctrine of the Makstians and is established as the Cycle of Life in the Creatocracy. Peter Matthews-Akukalia discovered its process through Mind Computing and tracks such persons. We believe it aligns with the born again principle of Christ. Inspired by Aphrodite Goddess of Beauty Fertility and Sexual Love. She is known as the foam born daughter of Zeus and Dione. Sexual transmutation is actually the process by which reincarnation takes place.

Makupedia established that a certain cycle of life exists. This we call reincarnation. And suspect this is what Hermes - Jesus Christ meant by the phrase "born again". Deut. 20:19. David is an angel who ascended that status. Sād verses 20-26 (Holy Quran). 2 Samuel 19:27. We see Trees manifested as having life and abilities to fight. 2 Samuel 18:8; 19:27; 24:17; Reincarnation is real by Quran book of Waaqi - The Inevitable Event verses 57-61.

"You must be born again...by water and by spirit. Water =Mare=Moon = Human original Source must be tracked by computing through an abstraction process (spirit = A=Ø). Water = 2.0, Abstraction = 9.0. So 2.0*9.0x=px=11+18=29x=px=227=22=2.2=4.0

By Moon matter we obtained power and became human through computation so that man is an asset of the Most High (7). Today Peter Matthews-Akukalia has discovered a method to track the lunar source of every person through computing and satellite tracking from which purpose on earth is known. Note that Jesus was the one who mentioned this statement hence it is a code that establishes He is Hermes (4.0) God of commerce invention merchandise wit and Son of Zeus. It further proves that Man was made in the Moon and put on Earth in the Garden of Eden. Mind Computing upgrades our religion to Faith because we will now be guided not by speculations but by precision in truth. In reincarnation matters Peter Matthews-Akukalia discovered that Joseph of Egypt reincarnated as George Washington, Hermes as Mohammed Ali, King Solomon as Ralph Waldo Emerson and Helios as Father Abraham and as Benjamin Banneker and again as Himself Castle Makupedia. See Hermes, Reborn. Paradise is earned by IP rights of signs.

Reindeer=6,000=60%=P6.0D=Man=Earth=Royalty=6 June=Gaia=Maia>>M=M2.
Reinforce=10,000=1,000=100%=10.0=Physicality=Tech.=10 Oct.=Uranus=P=1Ø.
Reinforced concrete=5,500=5.5=80%=P5.50=Earth-Midway=5 May = Gaia.
Reinstate=4,000=40%=P4.0D=Govt.=Creat.=4 April=Mercury=Hermes=G=A4.
Reiterate=4,500=5,000=50%=P5.00D=Law=Time=Venus=5 May = Aphrodite>>L=N.
Reject=10,000=1,000=100%=10.0=Physicality=Tech.=10 Oct.=Uranus=P=1Ø.
Rejoice=4,000=40%=P4.0D=Govt.=Creat.=4 April=Mercury=Hermes=G=A4.
Rejoin1=3,500=4,000=40%=P4.0D=Govt.=Creat.=4 April=Mercury=Hermes=G=A4.
Rejoin2=3,000=30%=P3.0D=3.0=Creativity=Stars=Muses=3 March = C=I>>GIL.
Rejoinder=4,000=40%=P4.0D=Govt.=Creat.=4 April=Mercury=Hermes=G=A4.
Rejuvenate=6,000=60%=P6.0D=Man=Earth=Royalty=6 June=Gaia=Maia>>M=M2.
Rel.=1,000=100%=10.0=1.0=Mind=Sun=1 January=Helios >> M=E4.
Relapse=10,000=1,000=100%=10.0=Physicality=Tech.=10 Oct.=Uranus=P=1Ø.
Relate=10,000=1,000=100%=10.0=Physicality=Tech.=10 Oct.=Uranus=P=1Ø.
Related=4,500=5,000=50%=P5.00D=Law=Time=Venus=5 May = Aphrodite>>L=N.
Relation=10,000=1,000=100%=10.0=Physicality=Tech.=10 Oct.=Uranus=P=1Ø.
Relative=10,000=1,000=100%=10.0=Physicality=Tech.=10 Oct.=Uranus=P=1Ø.
Relative clause=11,000=11%=P1.10D=1.1=Idea=Brainchild=Inv.=11 Nov=Athena>>I=MT.

Relative humidity=10,000=1,000=100%=Physicality=Tech.=10 Oct.=Uranus=P=1∅.
Relativism=10,000=1,000=100%=10.0=Physicality=Tech.=10 Oct.=Uranus=P=1∅.
Relativity=6,000=60%=P6.0D=Man=Earth=Royalty=6 June=Gaia=Maia>>M=M2.
Relax=10,000=1,000=100%=10.0=Physicality=Tech.=10 Oct.=Uranus=P=1∅.
Relaxant=5,500=5.5=80%=P5.50=Earth-Midway=5 May = Gaia.
Relay=10,000=1,000=100%=10.0=Physicality=Tech.=10 Oct.=Uranus=P=1∅.
Relay race=10,000=1,000=100%=10.0=Physicality=Tech.=10 Oct.=Uranus=P=1∅.
Release=10,000=1,000=100%=10.0=Physicality=Tech.=10 Oct.=Uranus=P=1∅.
Relegate=10,000=1,000=100%=10.0=Physicality=Tech.=10 Oct.=Uranus=P=1∅.
Relent=4,000=40%=P4.0D=Govt.=Creat.=4 April=Mercury=Hermes=G=A4.
Relentless=2,500=3,000=30%=P3.0D=3.0=Creativity=Stars=Muses=3 March = C=I>>GIL.
Relevant=5,500=5.5=80%=P5.50=Earth-Midway=5 May = Gaia.
Reliable=6,000=60%=P6.0D=Man=Earth=Royalty=6 June=Gaia=Maia>>M=M2.
Reliant=4,500=5,000=50%=P5.00D=Law=Time=Venus=5 May = Aphrodite>>L=N.
Relic=10,000=1,000=100%=10.0=Physicality=Tech.=10 Oct.=Uranus=P=1∅.
Relief=10,000=1,000=100%=10.0=Physicality=Tech.=10 Oct.=Uranus=P=1∅.
Relief map=5,000=50%=P5.00D=Law=Time=Venus=5 May = Aphrodite>>L=N.
Relieve=10,000=1,000=100%=10.0=Physicality=Tech.=10 Oct.=Uranus=P=1∅.

Religion=10,000=1,000=100%=10.0=Physicality=Tech.=10 Oct.=Uranus=P=1∅.
Peter Matthews-Akukalia invented the Faith System of Makstianism. An advance religion of precision that tracks the Mind of GOD through the adoption to wit and the manifestation of the Sons of GOD. Makstians believe the Holy Spirit is not one person but the administrative Council or Board of Trustees of the Universe and that Peter Matthews-Akukalia is a God. Precisely the God of Creatocracy Genius and Mind which he invented and measured. The Order of the Holy Spirit of the Makstian Faith >> Mind Temple believes in the unification of the Sons of Abraham and thus has discovered the Bible and Quran to be from one GOD. Peter Matthews-Akukalia, Castle Makupedia computed the Scriptures and translated them into programs and discovers the hidden secrets of the Gods in the essence of the Mind of GOD. Thus it is said that God inspired the Bible Men wrote it but Peter Matthews-Akukalia invented it. He owns the Castle Makupedia Wit Scriptures. (Bible & Quran) Mind versions. He wrote the formula for religion as A=∅ thus upgrading it to Faith meaning that all scriptures must be computed tracked and proved for truth before it can be taught anyone. Against this there is no law. Those who must worship GOD must do so in spirit and in truth.

PICTURE OF THE MIND TEMPLE LOGO. CODE 10 I.

Religious=10,500=11,000=11%=P1.10D=1.1=Idea=Brainchild=Inv.=11 Nov=Athena>>I=MT.
Relinquish=8,500=9,000=90%=P9.00D=9.0=Abstraction=Gods=Saturn=9Sept.>>A=Ø.
Reliquary=5,500=5.5=80%=P5.50=Earth-Midway=5 May = Gaia.
Relish=10,000=1,000=100%=10.0=Physicality=Tech.=10 Oct.=Uranus=P=1Ø.
Relive=4,500=5,000=50%=P5.00D=Law=Time=Venus=5 May = Aphrodite>>L=N.
Reluctant=5,000=50%=P5.00D=Law=Time=Venus=5 May = Aphrodite>>L=N.
Rely=10,000=1,000=100%=10.0=Physicality=Tech.=10 Oct.=Uranus=P=1Ø.
Rem=10,000=1,000=100%=10.0=Physicality=Tech.=10 Oct.=Uranus=P=1Ø.
REM=10,000=1,000=100%=10.0=Physicality=Tech.=10 Oct.=Uranus=P=1Ø.
rem.=500=5%=P5.00D=5.0=Law=Time=Venus=5 May=Aphrodite>>L=N.
Remain=10,000=1,000=100%=10.0=Physicality=Tech.=10 Oct.=Uranus=P=1Ø.
Remainder=10,000=1,000=100%=10.0=Physicality=Tech.=10 Oct.=Uranus=P=1Ø.
Remains=8,500=9,000=90%=P9.00D=9.0=Abstraction=Gods=Saturn=9Sept.>>A=Ø.
Remand=10,000=1,000=100%=10.0=Physicality=Tech.=10 Oct.=Uranus=P=1Ø.
Remark=10,000=1,000=100%=10.0=Physicality=Tech.=10 Oct.=Uranus=P=1Ø.
Remarkable=2,500=3,000=30%=P3.0D=3.0=Creativity=Stars=Muses=3 March = C=I>GIL.
Remarque Erich=3,500=4,000=40%=P4.0D=Govt.=Creat.=4 April=Hermes=G=A4.
Rembrandt van Rijn=2,000=20%=P2.00D=2.0=Nature=Moon=2 Feb.=Cupid=N=C+_
Remediable=1,500=15%=P1.50D=1.5=Authority=Solar Crown=1 May = Maia.
Remedial=4,500=5,000=50%=P5.00D=Law=Time=Venus=5 May = Aphrodite>>L=N.
Remedy=10,000=1,000=100%=10.0=Physicality=Tech.=10 Oct.=Uranus=P=1Ø.
-dying=6,500=7,000=70%=P7.0D=7.0=Language=Assets=Mars=7 July=Pleiades.

Remember=10,000=1,000=100%=10.0=Physicality=Tech.=10 Oct.=Uranus=P=1Ø.
Remembrance=10,000=1,000=100%=10.0=Physicality=Tech.=10 Oct.=Uranus=P=1Ø.
Remind=2,000=20%=P2.00D=2.0=Nature=Matter=Moon=2 Feb.=Cupid=N=C+_
Remington=3,500=4,000=40%=P4.0D=Govt.=Creat.=4 April=Mercury=Hermes=G=A4.
Reminisce=4,000=40%=P4.0D=Govt.=Creat.=4 April=Mercury=Hermes=G=A4.
Reminiscence=7,500=8,000=80%=P8.0D=Economy=Currency=8 Aug.=Zeus>>E=v.
Reminiscent=7,000=70%=P7.0D=7.0=Language=Assets=Mars=7 July=Pleiades.
Remiss=6,000=60%=P6.0D=Man=Earth=Royalty=6 June=Gaia=Maia>>M=M2.
Remissible=2,000=20%=P2.00D=2.0=Nature=Matter=Moon=2 Feb.=Cupid=N=C+_
Remission=7,500=8,000=80%=P8.0D=Economy=Currency=8 Aug.=Zeus>>E=v.
Remit=10,500=11,000=11%=P1.10D=1.1=Idea=Brainchild=Inv.=11 Nov.=SC=Athena
    >>I=MT.
Remittance=8,000=80%=P8.0D=Economy=Currency=8 Aug.=Zeus>>E=v.
Remittent=3,000=30%=P3.0D=3.0=Creativity=Stars=Muses=3 March = C=I>>GIL.

Remix=9,500=10,000=1,000=100%=10.0=Physicality=Tech.=10 Oct.=Uranus=P=1Ø
First Queen Alice of Makupedia invented the word merix for a remix of an already remixed song. She is also credited for "a catastic woman" though unisex in gender use as one who speaks through the nose as though having catarrh. The inspiration occurred from the telenovela NURSES based on the character Maria Clara and her manner of speaking. Most especially when she is seemingly under marital and professional pressure and so unhappy.

Remnant=6,000=60%=P6.0D=Man=Earth=Royalty=6 June=Gaia=Maia>>M=M2.
Remodel=4,000=40%=P4.0D=Govt.=Creat.=4 April=Mercury=Hermes=G=A4.
Remonstrance=3,500=4,000=40%=P4.0D=Govt.=4 April=Mercury=Hermes=G=A4.
Remonstrate=10,000=1,000=100%=10.0=Physicality=Tech.=10 Oct.=Uranus=P=1Ø.
Remora=10,000=1,000=100%=10.0=Physicality=Tech.=10 Oct.=Uranus=P=1Ø.
Remorse=10,000=1,000=100%=10.0=Physicality=Tech.=10 Oct.=Uranus=P=1Ø.
Remorseless=2,500=3,000=30%=P3.0D=3.0=Creatv=Stars=Muses=3 March = C=I>>GIL.
Remote=10,000=1,000=100%=10.0=Physicality=Tech.=10 Oct.=Uranus=P=1Ø.
Remote control=10,000=1,000=100%=10.0=Physicality=Tech.=10 Oct.=Uranus=P=1Ø.
Remove=10,000=1,000=100%=10.0=Physicality=Tech.=10 Oct.=Uranus=P=1Ø.
Removed=10,000=1,000=100%=10.0=Physicality=Tech.=10 Oct.=Uranus=P=1Ø.
Remunerate=10,000=1,000=100%=10.0=Physicality=Tech.=10 Oct.=Uranus=P=1Ø.

Renaissance=10,000=1,000=100%=10.0=Physicality=Tech.=10 Oct.=Uranus=P=1Ø.
The Creatocracy owns the Renaissance Faculty of Creative & Psycho-Social Sciences. Also called the Creative Sciences. Peter Matthews-Akukalia, Castle Makupedia invented and owns the Creatocracy. Thus the Field of Study and its practice is one of his many assets. It can be added as a department of study in the secondary schools and as a faculty at higher levels and tertiary education. It contains the Castle Makupedia Sciences, the Mind Arts, the Makupedia Business, the Creative Economy on the Maks Currencies and the political system called the Creatocracy. It is all a complete package open for licensing to nations.

Renal=4,500=5,000=50%=P5.00D=Law=Time=Venus=5 May = Aphrodite>>L=N.
Renascent=5,000=50%=P5.00D=Law=Time=Venus=5 May = Aphrodite>>L=N.
Rend=10,000=1,000=100%=10.0=Physicality=Tech.=10 Oct.=Uranus=P=1Ø.
Render=10,000=1,000=100%=10.0=Physicality=Tech.=10 Oct.=Uranus=P=1Ø.
Rendezvous=10,000=1,000=100%=10.0=Physicality=Tech.=10 Oct.=Uranus=P=1Ø.
Rendition=10,000=1,000=100%=10.0=Physicality=Tech.=10 Oct.=Uranus=P=1Ø.
Renegade=9,000=90%=P9.00D=9.0=Abstraction=Gods=Saturn=9Sept.>>A=Ø.
Renege=10,000=1,000=100%=10.0=Physicality=Tech.=10 Oct.=Uranus=P=1Ø.
Renew=10,000=1,000=100%=10.0=Physicality=Tech.=10 Oct.=Uranus=P=1Ø.
Rennet=8,000=80%=P8.0D=Economy=Currency=8 Aug.=Zeus>>E=v.
Reno=5,500=5.5=80%=P5.50=Earth-Midway=5 May = Gaia.
Renoir=3,000=30%=P3.0D=3.0=Creativity=Stars=Muses=3 March = C=I>>GIL.
Renounce=5,500=5.5=80%=P5.50=Earth-Midway=5 May = Gaia.
Renovate=3,500=4,000=40%=P4.0D=Govt.=Creat.=4 April=Mercury=Hermes=G=A4.
Renown=4,500=5,000=50%=P5.00D=Law=Time=Venus=5 May = Aphrodite>>L=N.
Rent1=10,000=1,000=100%=10.0=Physicality=Tech.=10 Oct.=Uranus=P=1Ø.
Rent2=6,000=60%=P6.0D=Man=Earth=Royalty=6 June=Gaia=Maia>>M=M2.
Rental=8,000=80%=P8.0D=Economy=Currency=8 Aug.=Zeus>>E=v.
Rent control=4,500=5,000=50%=P5.00D=Law=Time=Venus=5 May = Aphrodite>>L=N.
Renunciation=5,000=50%=P5.00D=Law=Time=Venus=5 May = Aphrodite>>L=N.
Reorder=3,500=4,000=40%=P4.0D=Govt.=Creat.=4 April=Mercury=Hermes=G=A4.
Rep1=4,000=40%=P4.0D=Govt.=Creat.=4 April=Mercury=Hermes=G=A4.
Rep2=1,500=15%=P1.50D=1.5=Authority=Solar Crown=1 May = Maia.
Rep3=1,000=100%=Physicality=Tech.=10 Oct.=Uranus=P=1Ø.
rep.=3,000=30%=P3.0D=3.0=Creativity=Stars=Muses=3 March = C=I>>GIL.
Rep.=500=5%=P5.00D=5.0=Law=Time=Venus=5 May=Aphrodite>>L=N.
Repair1=10,000=1,000=100%=10.0=Physicality=Tech.=10 Oct.=Uranus=P=1Ø.
Repair2=5,500=5.5=80%=P5.50=Earth-Midway=5 May = Gaia.
Reparable=1,500=15%=P1.50D=1.5=Authority=Solar Crown=1 May = Maia.
Reparation=10,000=1,000=100%=10.0=Physicality=Tech.=10 Oct.=Uranus=P=1Ø.
Repartee=6,000=60%=P6.0D=Man=Earth=Royalty=6 June=Gaia=Maia>>M=M2.
Repast=5,000=50%=P5.00D=Law=Time=Venus=5 May = Aphrodite>>L=N.
Repatriate=11,000=11%=P1.10D=1.1=Idea=Brainchild=Inv.=11 Nov.=SC=Athena>>I=MT.
Repay=5,500=5.5=80%=P5.50=Earth-Midway=5 May = Gaia.
Repeal=6,500=7,000=70%=P7.0D=7.0=Language=Assets=Mars=7 July=Pleiades.
Repeat=10,000=1,000=100%=10.0=Physicality=Tech.=10 Oct.=Uranus=P=1Ø.
Repeated=3,000=30%=P3.0D=3.0=Creativity=Stars=Muses=3 March = C=I>>GIL.
Repeating decimal=6,500=7,000=70%=P7.0D=7.0=Lang=Assets=Mars=7 July=Pleiades.
Repel=10,000=1,000=100%=10.0=Physicality=Tech.=10 Oct.=Uranus=P=1Ø.
Repellent=10,000=1,000=100%=10.0=Physicality=Tech.=10 Oct.=Uranus=P=1Ø.
Repent=10,000=1,000=100%=10.0=Physicality=Tech.=10 Oct.=Uranus=P=1Ø.
Repentance=5,500=5.5=80%=P5.50=Earth-Midway=5 May = Gaia.
Repercussion=10,000=1,000=100%=10.0=Physicality=Tech.=10 Oct.=Uranus=P=1Ø.
Repertoire=10,000=1,000=100%=10.0=Physicality=Tech.=10 Oct.=Uranus=P=1Ø.
Repertory=10,000=1,000=100%=10.0=Physicality=Tech.=10 Oct.=Uranus=P=1Ø.

Repetend=10,000=1,000=100%=10.0=Physicality=Tech.=10 Oct.=Uranus=P=1Ø.
Repetition=6,000=60%=P6.0D=Man=Earth=Royalty=6 June=Gaia=Maia>>M=M2.
Repetitious=2,500=3,000=30%=P3.0D=3.0=Creatv=Stars=Muses=3 March = C=I>>GIL.
Repetitive=3,000=30%=P3.0D=3.0=Creativity=Stars=Muses=3 March = C=I>>GIL.
Repine=4,000=40%=P4.0D=Govt.=Creat.=4 April=Mercury=Hermes=G=A4.
Replace=3,500=4,000=40%=P4.0D=Govt.=Creat.=4 April=Mercury=Hermes=G=A4.
Replay=4,500=5,000=50%=P5.00D=Law=Time=Venus=5 May = Aphrodite>>L=N.
Replenish=4,000=40%=P4.0D=Govt.=Creat.=4 April=Mercury=Hermes=G=A4.
Replete=9,000=90%=P9.00D=9.0=Abstraction=Gods=Saturn=9Sept.>>A=Ø.
Replica=4,000=40%=P4.0D=Govt.=Creat.=4 April=Mercury=Hermes=G=A4.
Replicate=6,500=7,000=70%=P7.0D=7.0=Language=Assets=Mars=7 July=Pleiades.
Reply=8,500=9,000=90%=P9.00D=9.0=Abstraction=Gods=Saturn=9Sept.>>A=Ø.
Report=10,000=1,000=100%=10.0=Physicality=Tech.=10 Oct.=Uranus=P=1Ø.
Report card=3,000=30%=P3.0D=3.0=Creativity=Stars=Muses=3 March = C=I>>GIL.
Reportedly=1,500=15%=P1.50D=1.5=Authority=Solar Crown=1 May = Maia.
Reporter=3,500=4,000=40%=P4.0D=Govt.=Creat.=4 April=Mercury=Hermes=G=A4.
Repose1=10,000=1,000=100%=10.0=Physicality=Tech.=10 Oct.=Uranus=P=1Ø.
Repose2=8,000=80%=P8.0D=Economy=Currency=8 Aug.=Zeus>>E=v.
Repository=10,000=1,000=100%=10.0=Physicality=Tech.=10 Oct.=Uranus=P=1Ø.
Repossess=2,500=3,000=30%=P3.0D=3.0=Creativity=Stars=Muses=3 March = C=I>>GIL.
Reprehend=3,500=4,000=40%=P4.0D=Govt.=Creat.=4 April=Mercury=Hermes=G=A4.
Reprehensible=4,000=40%=P4.0D=Govt.=Creat.=4 April=Mercury=Hermes=G=A4.
Represent=10,000=1,000=100%=10.0=Physicality=Tech.=10 Oct.=Uranus=P=1Ø.
Representation=8,500=9,000=90%=P9.00D=9.0=Abstr.=Gods=Saturn=9Sept.>>A=Ø.
Representational=3,500=4,000=40%=P4.0D=Govt.=Creat.=4 April=Hermes=G=A4.
Representative=10,000=1,000=100%=10.0=Physicality=Tech.=10 Oct.=Uranus=P=1Ø.
Repress=10,000=1,000=100%=10.0=Physicality=Tech.=10 Oct.=Uranus=P=1Ø.
Reprieve=10,000=1,000=100%=10.0=Physicality=Tech.=10 Oct.=Uranus=P=1Ø.
Reprimand=6,000=60%=P6.0D=Man=Earth=Royalty=6 June=Gaia=Maia>>M=M2.
Reprint=5,000=50%=P5.00D=Law=Time=Venus=5 May = Aphrodite>>L=N.
Reprisal=11,500=12,000=12%=P1.20D=1.2=Knowledge=Edu=12Dec.=Athena>>K=F.
Reprise=9,000=90%=P9.00D=9.0=Abstraction=Gods=Saturn=9Sept.>>A=Ø.
Reproach=5,500=5.5=80%=P5.50=Earth-Midway=5 May = Gaia.
Reprobate=3,500=4,000=40%=P4.0D=Govt.=Creat.=4 April=Mercury=Hermes=G=A4.
Reproduce=10,000=1,000=100%=10.0=Physicality=Tech.=10 Oct.=Uranus=P=1Ø.
Reproof=1,000=100%=10.0=1.0=Mind=Sun=1 January=Helios >> M=E4.
Reprove=6,500=7,000=70%=P7.0D=7.0=Language=Assets=Mars=7 July=Pleiades.
Reptile=10,000=1,000=100%=10.0=Physicality=Tech.=10 Oct.=Uranus=P=1Ø.

Republic=10,000=1,000=100%=10.0=Physicality=Tech.=10 Oct.=Uranus=P=1Ø.
The Creatocracy Republic by Peter Matthews-Akukalia. Creatocracy is defined as a government of creativity in the people by the people and for the people. Our structured data builds smart governance that leads to a Creatocracy. Sourced from the WDSD.

Republican=10,000=1,000=100%=10.0=Physicality=Tech.=10 Oct.=Uranus=P=1Ø.
Republican Party=4,000=40%=P4.0D=Govt.=Creat.=4 April=Mercury=Hermes=G=A4.
Repudiate=6,000=60%=P6.0D=Man=Earth=Royalty=6 June=Gaia=Maia>>M=M2.
Repugnant=5,500=5.5=80%=P5.50=Earth-Midway=5 May = Gaia.
Repulse=10,000=1,000=100%=10.0=Physicality=Tech.=10 Oct.=Uranus=P=1Ø.
Repulsion=3,000=30%=P3.0D=3.0=Creativity=Stars=Muses=3 March = C=I>>GIL.
Repulsive=6,500=7,000=70%=P7.0D=7.0=Language=Assets=Mars=7 July=Pleiades.
Reputable=2,000=20%=P2.00D=2.0=Nature=Matter=Moon=2 Feb.=Cupid=N=C+_

Reputation=8,500=9,000=90%=P9.00D=9.0=Abstraction=Gods=Saturn=9Sept.>>A=Ø.
A Zeusian means to appease the council of Gods or the Holy Spirit. A means that links economy or one's means of income to his faith. Your reputation is 85-90% your wealth. Peter Matthews-Akukalia has the reputation of being a God in the first place. He is the God of Creatocracy Genius and Mind. He is an author, Creative Scientist and Inventor.

Repute=4,500=5,000=50%=P5.00D=Law=Time=Venus=5 May = Aphrodite>>L=N.
Reputed=3,000=30%=P3.0D=3.0=Creativity=Stars=Muses=3 March = C=I>>GIL.
Request=10,000=1,000=100%=10.0=Physicality=Tech.=10 Oct.=Uranus=P=1Ø.
Requiem=10,000=1,000=100%=10.0=Physicality=Tech.=10 Oct.=Uranus=P=1Ø.
Require=5,500=5.5=80%=P5.50=Earth-Midway=5 May = Gaia.
Required=2,500=3,000=30%=P3.0D=3.0=Creativity=Stars=Muses=3 March = C=I>>GIL.
Requisite=7,500=8,000=80%=P8.0D=Economy=Currency=8 Aug.=Zeus>>E=v.
Requisition=9,500=10,000=1,000=100%=10.0=Physicality=Tech.=10 Oct.=Uranus=P=1Ø.
Requite=8,500=9,000=90%=P9.00D=9.0=Abstraction=Gods=Saturn=9Sept.>>A=Ø.
Rerun=4,500=5,000=50%=P5.00D=Law=Time=Venus=5 May = Aphrodite>>L=N.
Rescind=3,000=30%=P3.0D=3.0=Creativity=Stars=Muses=3 March = C=I>>GIL.
Rescue=3,500=4,000=40%=P4.0D=Govt.=Creat.=4 April=Mercury=Hermes=G=A4.
Research=9,000=90%=P9.00D=9.0=Abstraction=Gods=Saturn=9Sept.>>A=Ø.
Resection=4,000=40%=P4.0D=Govt.=Creat.=4 April=Mercury=Hermes=G=A4.
Resemblance=2,500=3,000=30%=P3.0D=3.0=Creatv=Stars=Muses=3 March = C=I>>GIL.
Resemble=4,000=40%=P4.0D=Govt.=Creat.=4 April=Mercury=Hermes=G=A4.
Resent=4,500=5,000=50%=P5.00D=Law=Time=Venus=5 May = Aphrodite>>L=N.
Reservation=10,000=1,000=100%=10.0=Physicality=Tech.=10 Oct.=Uranus=P=1Ø.
Reserve=10,000=1,000=100%=10.0=Physicality=Tech.=10 Oct.=Uranus=P=1Ø.
Reserved=7,500=8,000=80%=P8.0D=Economy=Currency=8 Aug.=Zeus>>E=v.
Reservist=2,500=3,000=30%=P3.0D=3.0=Creativity=Stars=Muses=3 March = C=I>>GIL.
Reservoir=9,000=90%=P9.00D=9.0=Abstraction=Gods=Saturn=9Sept.>>A=Ø.
Resh=4,000=40%=P4.0D=Govt.=Creat.=4 April=Mercury=Hermes=G=A4.
Reside=11,000=11%=P1.10D=1.1=Idea=Brainchild=Inv.=11 Nov.=SC=Athena>>I=MT.

Residence=6,000=60%=P6.0D=Man=Earth=Royalty=6 June=Gaia=Maia>>M=M2.
Peter Matthews-Akukalia made all his inventions at his residence at Ikotun Lagos.

Residency=4,000=40%=P4.0D=Govt.=Creat.=4 April=Mercury=Hermes=G=A4.
Resident=6,000=60%=P6.0D=Man=Earth=Royalty=6 June=Gaia=Maia>>M=M2.
Residential=4,500=5,000=50%=P5.00D=Law=Time=Venus=5 May = Aphrodite>>L=N.
Residual=9,000=90%=P9.00D=9.0=Abstraction=Gods=Saturn=9Sept.>>A=Ø.
Residue=6,500=7,000=70%=P7.0D=7.0=Language=Assets=Mars=7 July=Pleiades.
Resign=8,000=80%=P8.0D=Economy=Currency=8 Aug.=Zeus>>E=v.
Resignation=6,500=7,000=70%=P7.0D=7.0=Language=Assets=Mars=7 July=Pleiades.
Resigned=1,000=100%=10.0=1.0=Mind=Sun=1 January=Helios >> M=E4.
Resilient=10,000=1,000=100%=10.0=Physicality=Tech.=10 Oct.=Uranus=P=1Ø.
Resin=10,000=1,000=100%=10.0=Physicality=Tech.=10 Oct.=Uranus=P=1Ø.
Resist=8,000=80%=P8.0D=Economy=Currency=8 Aug.=Zeus>>E=v.
Resistance=10,000=1,000=100%=10.0=Physicality=Tech.=10 Oct.=Uranus=P=1Ø.
Resistor=5,000=50%=P5.00D=Law=Time=Venus=5 May = Aphrodite>>L=N.
Resolute=5,500=5.5=80%=P5.50=Earth-Midway=5 May = Gaia.
Resolution=10,000=1,000=100%=10.0=Physicality=Tech.=10 Oct.=Uranus=P=1Ø.
Resolve=10,000=1,000=100%=10.0=Physicality=Tech.=10 Oct.=Uranus=P=1Ø.
Resonance=10,000=1,000=100%=10.0=Physicality=Tech.=10 Oct.=Uranus=P=1Ø.
Resonant=9,000=90%=P9.00D=9.0=Abstraction=Gods=Saturn=9Sept.>>A=Ø.
Resonate=4,500=5,000=50%=P5.00D=Law=Time=Venus=5 May = Aphrodite>>L=N.
Resonator=8,000=80%=P8.0D=Economy=Currency=8 Aug.=Zeus>>E=v.
Resort=10,000=1,000=100%=10.0=Physicality=Tech.=10 Oct.=Uranus=P=1Ø.
Resound=8,000=80%=P8.0D=Economy=Currency=8 Aug.=Zeus>>E=v.

Resource=15,000=1,500=15%=P1.50D=1.5=Authority=Solar Crown=1 May = Maia.
Peter Matthews-Akukalia founded Utmost Peak Resources an enterprise which later became the Creative Media department of Makupedia Limited, an inventions company dealing with international business and training of Creative Scientists for the Creatocracy.

Resourceful=4,500=5,000=50%=P5.00D=Law=Time=Venus=5 May = Aphrodite>>L=N.
Peter Matthews-Akukalia discovered a method to measure the resourcefulness level in a person. It is the speed and ability of a person to overcome difficulties very quickly. The Mind Assessment Tests his invention is considered a necessity for everyone at every age.

Respect=10,000=1,000=100%=10.0=Physicality=Tech.=10 Oct.=Uranus=P=1Ø.
Respectable=10,000=1,000=100%=10.0=Physicality=Tech.=10 Oct.=Uranus=P=1Ø.
Respective=3,000=30%=P3.0D=3.0=Creativity=Stars=Muses=3 March = C=I>>GIL.
Respectively=3,500=4,000=40%=P4.0D=Govt.=Creat.=4 April=Mercury=Hermes=G=A4.
Respiration=10,000=1,000=100%=10.0=Physicality=Tech.=10 Oct.=Uranus=P=1Ø.
Respirator=10,000=1,000=100%=10.0=Physicality=Tech.=10 Oct.=Uranus=P=1Ø.
Respiratory system=10,000=1,000=100%=10.0=Physicality=Tech.=10 Oct.=Uranus=P=1Ø.
Respire=6,000=60%=P6.0D=Man=Earth=Royalty=6 June=Gaia=Maia>>M=M2.
Respite=8,500=9,000=90%=P9.00D=9.0=Abstraction=Gods=Saturn=9Sept.>>A=Ø.
Resplendent=4,500=5,000=50%=P5.00D=Law=Time=Venus=5 May = Aphrodite>>L=N.
Respond=6,000=60%=P6.0D=Man=Earth=Royalty=6 June=Gaia=Maia>>M=M2.

Respondent=5,500=5.5=80%=P5.50=Earth-Midway=5 May = Gaia.
Response=6,500=7,000=70%=P7.0D=7.0=Language=Assets=Mars=7 July=Pleiades.
Responsibility=6,000=60%=P6.0D=Man=Earth=Royalty=6 June=Gaia=Maia>>M=M2.
Responsible=12,000=12%=P1.20D=1.2=Knowledge=Edu=12Dec.=Athena>>K=F.
Responsive=3,000=30%=P3.0D=3.0=Creativity=Stars=Muses=3 March = C=I>>GIL.
Rest1=10,000=1,000=100%=10.0=Physicality=Tech.=10 Oct.=Uranus=P=1Ø.
Rest2=10,000=1,000=100%=10.0=Physicality=Tech.=10 Oct.=Uranus=P=1Ø.
Restaurant=6,000=60%=P6.0D=Man=Earth=Royalty=6 June=Gaia=Maia>>M=M2.
Restaurateur=4,000=40%=P4.0D=Govt.=Creat.=4 April=Mercury=Hermes=G=A4.
Restful=3,500=4,000=40%=P4.0D=Govt.=Creat.=4 April=Mercury=Hermes=G=A4.
Rest home=6,000=60%=P6.0D=Man=Earth=Royalty=6 June=Gaia=Maia>>M=M2.
Restitution=12,500=13,000=13%=P1.30=Solar Core=Faculty=13 January=Athena.
Restive=10,000=1,000=100%=10.0=Physicality=Tech.=10 Oct.=Uranus=P=1Ø.
Restless=12,000=12%=P1.20D=1.2=Knowledge=Edu=12Dec.=Athena>>K=F.
Restoration=7,500=8,000=80%=P8.0D=Economy=Currency=8 Aug.=Zeus>>E=v.
Restorative=6,000=60%=P6.0D=Man=Earth=Royalty=6 June=Gaia=Maia>>M=M2.
Restore=12,000=12%=P1.20D=1.2=Knowledge=Edu=12Dec.=Athena>>K=F.
Restrain=6,500=7,000=70%=P7.0D=7.0=Language=Assets=Mars=7 July=Pleiades.
Restraint=7,000=70%=P7.0D=7.0=Language=Assets=Mars=7 July=Pleiades.
Restrict=5,500=5.5=80%=P5.50=Earth-Midway=5 May = Gaia.
Restrictive=10,000=1,000=100%=10.0=Physicality=Tech.=10 Oct.=Uranus=P=1Ø.
Rest room=1,000=100%=10.0=1.0=Mind=Sun=1 January=Helios >> M=E4.
Result=10,000=1,000=100%=10.0=Physicality=Tech.=10 Oct.=Uranus=P=1Ø.
Resume=6,500=7,000=70%=P7.0D=7.0=Language=Assets=Mars=7 July=Pleiades.
Résumé=8,000=80%=P8.0D=Economy=Currency=8 Aug.=Zeus>>E=v.
Resurgent=5,000=50%=P5.00D=Law=Time=Venus=5 May = Aphrodite>>L=N.
Resurrect=6,000=60%=P6.0D=Man=Earth=Royalty=6 June=Gaia=Maia>>M=M2.
Resurrection=10,000=1,000=100%=10.0=Physicality=Tech.=10 Oct.=Uranus=P=1Ø.
Resuscitate=7,000=70%=P7.0D=7.0=Language=Assets=Mars=7 July=Pleiades.
Ret.=1,500=15%=P1.50D=1.5=Authority=Solar Crown=1 May = Maia.
Retail=5,500=5.5=80%=P5.50=Earth-Midway=5 May = Gaia.
Retain=10,000=1,000=100%=10.0=Physicality=Tech.=10 Oct.=Uranus=P=1Ø.
Retainer1=6,000=60%=P6.0D=Man=Earth=Royalty=6 June=Gaia=Maia>>M=M2.
Retainer2=3,500=4,000=40%=P4.0D=Govt.=Creat.=4 April=Mercury=Hermes=G=A4.
Retake=5,500=5.5=80%=P5.50=Earth-Midway=5 May = Gaia.
Retaliate=4,500=5,000=50%=P5.00D=Law=Time=Venus=5 May = Aphrodite>>L=N.
Retard=5,000=50%=P5.00D=Law=Time=Venus=5 May = Aphrodite>>L=N.
Retardant=2,500=3,000=30%=P3.0D=3.0=Creativity=Stars=Muses=3 March = C=I>>GIL.
Retardation=9,000=90%=P9.00D=9.0=Abstraction=Gods=Saturn=9Sept.>>A=Ø.
Retarded=5,000=50%=P5.00D=Law=Time=Venus=5 May = Aphrodite>>L=N.
Retch=3,500=4,000=40%=P4.0D=Govt.=Creat.=4 April=Mercury=Hermes=G=A4.
Retention=10,000=1,000=100%=10.0=Physicality=Tech.=10 Oct.=Uranus=P=1Ø.
Reticent=10,000=1,000=100%=10.0=Physicality=Tech.=10 Oct.=Uranus=P=1Ø.
Retina=10,500=11,000=11%=P1.10D=1.1=Idea=Brainchild=Inv.=11 Nov.=SC=Athena
    >>I=MT.

Retinue=5,000=50%=P5.00D=Law=Time=Venus=5 May = Aphrodite>>L=N.
Retire=10,000=1,000=100%=10.0=Physicality=Tech.=10 Oct.=Uranus=P=1∅.
Retired=3,500=4,000=40%=P4.0D=Govt.=Creat.=4 April=Mercury=Hermes=G=A4.
Retiree=4,000=40%=P4.0D=Govt.=Creat.=4 April=Mercury=Hermes=G=A4.
Retiring=2,000=20%=P2.00D=2.0=Nature=Matter=Moon=2 Feb.=Cupid=N=C+_
Retool=6,000=60%=P6.0D=Man=Earth=Royalty=6 June=Gaia=Maia>>M=M2.
Retort1=10,000=1,000=100%=10.0=Physicality=Tech.=10 Oct.=Uranus=P=1∅.
Retort2=10,500=11,000=11%=P1.10D=1.1=Idea=Brainchild=Inv.=11 Nov=Athena>>I=MT.
Retouch=6,500=7,000=70%=P7.0D=7.0=Language=Assets=Mars=7 July=Pleiades.
Retrace=2,500=3,000=30%=P3.0D=3.0=Creativity=Stars=Muses=3 March = C=I>>GIL.
Retract=7,000=70%=P7.0D=7.0=Language=Assets=Mars=7 July=Pleiades.
Retractile=3,500=4,000=40%=P4.0D=Govt.=Creat.=4 April=Mercury=Hermes=G=A4.
Retread=6,000=60%=P6.0D=Man=Earth=Royalty=6 June=Gaia=Maia>>M=M2.
Retreat=10,000=1,000=100%=10.0=Physicality=Tech.=10 Oct.=Uranus=P=1∅.
Retrench=4,500=5,000=50%=P5.00D=Law=Time=Venus=5 May = Aphrodite>>L=N.
Retribution=6,000=60%=P6.0D=Man=Earth=Royalty=6 June=Gaia=Maia>>M=M2.
Retrieve=6,000=60%=P6.0D=Man=Earth=Royalty=6 June=Gaia=Maia>>M=M2.
Retriever=7,000=70%=P7.0D=7.0=Language=Assets=Mars=7 July=Pleiades.
Retro-=2,500=3,000=30%=P3.0D=3.0=Creativity=Stars=Muses=3 March = C=I>>GIL.
Retroactive=3,000=30%=P3.0D=3.0=Creativity=Stars=Muses=3 March = C=I>>GIL.
Retro fire=2,500=3,000=30%=P3.0D=3.0=Creativity=Stars=Muses=3 March = C=I>>GIL.
Retrofit=6,500=7,000=70%=P7.0D=7.0=Language=Assets=Mars=7 July=Pleiades.
Retrograde=10,000=1,000=100%=10.0=Physicality=Tech.=10 Oct.=Uranus=P=1∅.
Retrogress=8,500=9,000=90%=P9.00D=9.0=Abstraction=Gods=Saturn=9Sept.>>A=∅.
Retrorocket=4,500=5,000=50%=P5.00D=Law=Time=Venus=5 May = Aphrodite>>L=N.
Retrospect=10,500=11,000=11%=P1.10D=1.1=Idea=Brainchild=11 Nov.=Athena>>I=MT.
Retrovirus=10,500=11,000=11%=P1.10D=1.1=Idea=Brainchild=Inv.=11 Nov=Athena
    >>I=MT.
Return=10,000=1,000=100%=10.0=Physicality=Tech.=10 Oct.=Uranus=P=1∅.
Returnee=4,000=40%=P4.0D=Govt.=Creat.=4 April=Mercury=Hermes=G=A4.
Reunion=8,000=80%=P8.0D=Economy=Currency=8 Aug.=Zeus>>E=v.
Reuther Walter=3,000=30%=P3.0D=3.0=Creativity=Stars=Muses=3 March = C=I>>GIL.
Rev=9,000=90%=P9.00D=9.0=Abstraction=Gods=Saturn=9Sept.>>A=∅.
Rev.=500=5%=P5.00D=5.0=Law=Time=Venus=5 May=Aphrodite>>L=N.
Revamp=2,000=20%=P2.00D=2.0=Nature=Matter=Moon=2 Feb.=Cupid=N=C+_
Reveal=4,000=40%=P4.0D=Govt.=Creat.=4 April=Mercury=Hermes=G=A4.
Reveille=7,000=70%=P7.0D=7.0=Language=Assets=Mars=7 July=Pleiades.
Revel=7,500=8,000=80%=P8.0D=Economy=Currency=8 Aug.=Zeus>>E=v.

Revelation=9,000=90%=P9.00D=9.0=Abstraction=Gods=Saturn=9Sept.>>A=∅.
Inspired by the Council of Gods >> Holy Spirit >> The Creatocracy of Heaven.

Revenge=10,000=1,000=100%=10.0=Physicality=Tech.=10 Oct.=Uranus=P=1∅.
Revenue=9,500=10,000=1,000=100%=10.0=Physicality=Tech.=10 Oct.=Uranus=P=1∅.

Reverberate=5,000=50%=P5.00D=Law=Time=Venus=5 May = Aphrodite>>L=N.
revere=4,000=40%=P4.0D=Govt.=Creat.=4 April=Mercury=Hermes=G=A4.
Revere Paul=2,500=3,000=30%=P3.0D=3.0=Creativity=Stars=Muses=3 March=C=I>GIL.
Reverence=10,000=1,000=100%=10.0=Physicality=Tech.=10 Oct.=Uranus=P=1Ø.
Reverend=8,000=80%=P8.0D=Economy=Currency=8 Aug.=Zeus>>E=v.
Reverent=2,000=20%=P2.00D=2.0=Nature=Matter=Moon=2 Feb.=Cupid=N=C+_
Reverential=1,500=15%=P1.50D=1.5=Authority=Solar Crown=1 May = Maia.
Reverie=5,000=50%=P5.00D=Law=Time=Venus=5 May = Aphrodite>>L=N.
Reversal=6,500=7,000=70%=P7.0D=7.0=Language=Assets=Mars=7 July=Pleiades.
Reverse=10,000=1,000=100%=10.0=Physicality=Tech.=10 Oct.=Uranus=P=1Ø.
Revert=10,000=1,000=100%=10.0=Physicality=Tech.=10 Oct.=Uranus=P=1Ø.
Review=10,000=1,000=100%=10.0=Physicality=Tech.=10 Oct.=Uranus=P=1Ø.
Reviewer=4,500=5,000=50%=P5.00D=Law=Time=Venus=5 May = Aphrodite>>L=N.
Revile=4,500=5,000=50%=P5.00D=Law=Time=Venus=5 May = Aphrodite>>L=N.
Revise=10,000=1,000=100%=10.0=Physicality=Tech.=10 Oct.=Uranus=P=1Ø.
Revision=7,000=70%=P7.0D=7.0=Language=Assets=Mars=7 July=Pleiades.
Revival=10,000=1,000=100%=10.0=Physicality=Tech.=10 Oct.=Uranus=P=1Ø.
Revive=10,000=1,000=100%=10.0=Physicality=Tech.=10 Oct.=Uranus=P=1Ø.
Revivify=4,000=40%=P4.0D=Govt.=Creat.=4 April=Mercury=Hermes=G=A4.
Revocable=2,000=20%=P2.00D=2.0=Nature=Matter=Moon=2 Feb.=Cupid=N=C+_
Revoke=6,000=60%=P6.0D=Man=Earth=Royalty=6 June=Gaia=Maia>>M=M2.
Revolt=10,000=1,000=100%=10.0=Physicality=Tech.=10 Oct.=Uranus=P=1Ø.
Revolting=4,000=40%=P4.0D=Govt.=Creat.=4 April=Mercury=Hermes=G=A4.
Revolution=10,000=1,000=100%=10.0=Physicality=Tech.=10 Oct.=Uranus=P=1Ø.
Revolutionist=10,000=1,000=100%=10.0=Physicality=Tech.=10 Oct.=Uranus=P=1Ø.
Revolutionize=1,000=100%=10.0=1.0=Mind=Sun=1 January=Helios >> M=E4.
Revolve=8,000=80%=P8.0D=Economy=Currency=8 Aug.=Zeus>>E=v.
Revolver=7,500=8,000=80%=P8.0D=Economy=Currency=8 Aug.=Zeus>>E=v.
Revue=7,000=70%=P7.0D=7.0=Language=Assets=Mars=7 July=Pleiades.
Revulsion=10,500=11,000=11%=P1.10D=1.1=Idea=Brainchild=Inv.=11 Nov=Athena>>I=MT.
Reward=10,000=1,000=100%=10.0=Physicality=Tech.=10 Oct.=Uranus=P=1Ø.
Reword=4,000=40%=P4.0D=Govt.=Creat.=4 April=Mercury=Hermes=G=A4.
Rewrite=5,000=50%=P5.00D=Law=Time=Venus=5 May = Aphrodite>>L=N.
Reykjavik=4,000=40%=P4.0D=Govt.=Creat.=4 April=Mercury=Hermes=G=A4.
Reynolds=3,000=30%=P3.0D=3.0=Creativity=Stars=Muses=3 March = C=I>>GIL.
RF=2,000=20%=P2.00D=2.0=Nature=Matter=Moon=2 Feb.=Cupid=N=C+_
RFD=1,500=15%=P1.50D=1.5=Authority=Solar Crown=1 May = Maia.
Rh1=4,500=5,000=50%=P5.00D=Law=Time=Venus=5 May = Aphrodite>>L=N.
Rh2=2,500=3,000=30%=P3.0D=3.0=Creativity=Stars=Muses=3 March = C=I>>GIL.
Rhaetia=6,000=60%=P6.0D=Man=Earth=Royalty=6 June=Gaia=Maia>>M=M2.
Rhaeto-Romance=7,000=70%=P7.0D=7.0=Language=Assets=Mars=7 July=Pleiades.
Rhapsody=8,500=9,000=90%=P9.00D=9.0=Abstraction=Gods=Saturn=9Sept.>>A=Ø.
Rhea=8,000=80%=P8.0D=Economy=Currency=8 Aug.=Zeus>>E=v.
Rhee Syngman.=2,500=3,000=30%=P3.0D=3.0=Creativity=Stars=Muses=3 March=C=I
Rhelms=4,500=5,000=50%=P5.00D=Law=Time=Venus=5 May = Aphrodite>>L=N.

Rhenium=10,000=1,000=100%=10.0=Physicality=Tech.=10 Oct.=Uranus=P=1Ø.
Rheostat=5,500=5.5=80%=P5.50=Earth-Midway=5 May = Gaia.

Rhesus monkey=8,500=9,000=90%=P9.00D=9.0=Abstr.=Gods=Saturn=9Sept.>>A=Ø.
A brownish monkey of India,often used in scientific research < Gk. Rhēsos, a mythical
king of Thrace).

Rhetoric=10,000=1,000=100%=10.0=Physicality=Tech.=10 Oct.=Uranus=P=1Ø.
Rhetorical question=4,000=40%=P4.0D=Govt.=Creat.=4 April=Mercury=Hermes=G=A4.
Rheum=6,500=7,000=70%=P7.0D=7.0=Language=Assets=Mars=7 July=Pleiades.
Rheumatic=5,000=50%=P5.00D=Law=Time=Venus=5 May = Aphrodite>>L=N.
Rheumatic fever=10,000=1,000=100%=10.0=Physicality=Tech.=10 Oct.=Uranus=P=1Ø.
Rheumatism=10,000=1,000=100%=10.0=Physicality=Tech.=10 Oct.=Uranus=P=1Ø.
Rheumatoid arthritis=6,000=60%=P6.0D=Man=Earth=Roy=6 June=Gaia=Maia>>M=M2.
Rh factor=10,000=1,000=100%=10.0=Physicality=Tech.=10 Oct.=Uranus=P=1Ø.
Rhine=10,000=1,000=100%=10.0=Physicality=Tech.=10 Oct.=Uranus=P=1Ø.
Rhineland=4,500=5,000=50%=P5.00D=Law=Time=Venus=5 May = Aphrodite>>L=N.
Rhinestone=5,500=5.5=80%=P5.50=Earth-Midway=5 May = Gaia.
Rhinitis=5,000=50%=P5.00D=Law=Time=Venus=5 May = Aphrodite>>L=N.
Rhino=1,000=100%=10.0=1.0=Mind=Sun=1 January=Helios >> M=E4.
Rhinoceros=10,000=1,000=100%=10.0=Physicality=Tech.=10 Oct.=Uranus=P=1Ø.
Rhizome=8,000=80%=P8.0D=Economy=Currency=8 Aug.=Zeus>>E=v.
Rh-negative=2,000=20%=P2.00D=2.0=Nature=Matter=Moon=2 Feb.=Cupid=N=C+_
Rho=4,000=40%=P4.0D=Govt.=Creat.=4 April=Mercury=Hermes=G=A4.
Rhode Island=6,000=60%=P6.0D=Man=Earth=Royalty=6 June=Gaia=Maia>>M=M2.
Rhodes=4,500=5,000=50%=P5.00D=Law=Time=Venus=5 May = Aphrodite>>L=N.
Rhodes,Cecil=3,500=4,000=40%=P4.0D=Govt.=Creat.=4 April=Mercury=Hermes=G=A4.
Rhodesia=1,000=100%=10.0=1.0=Mind=Sun=1 January=Helios >> M=E4.
Rhodium=10,000=1,000=100%=10.0=Physicality=Tech.=10 Oct.=Uranus=P=1Ø.
Rhododendron=10,000=1,000=100%=10.0=Physicality=Tech.=10 Oct.=Uranus=P=1Ø.
Rhomboid=3,000=30%=P3.0D=3.0=Creativity=Stars=Muses=3 March = C=I>>GIL.
Rhombus=2,500=3,000=30%=P3.0D=3.0=Creativity=Stars=Muses=3 March = C=I>>GIL.
Rhone=9,000=90%=P9.00D=9.0=Abstraction=Gods=Saturn=9Sept.>>A=Ø.
rhp=1,000=100%=10.0=1.0=Mind=Sun=1 January=Helios >> M=E4.
Rh-positive=2,000=20%=P2.00D=2.0=Nature=Matter=Moon=2 Feb.=Cupid=N=C+_
Rhubarb=10,500=11,000=11%=P1.10D=1.1=Idea=Brainchild=Inv.=11 Nov.=Athena>>I=MT.
Rhyme=10,000=1,000=100%=10.0=Physicality=Tech.=10 Oct.=Uranus=P=1Ø.
Rhythm=10,000=1,000=100%=10.0=Physicality=Tech.=10 Oct.=Uranus=P=1Ø.
Rhythm and blues=6,500=7,000=70%=P7.0D=7.0=Lang=Assets=Mars=7 July=Pleiades.
Rhythm method=4,500=5,000=50%=P5.00D=Law=Time=Venus=5 May =Odite>>L=N.
RI=1,000=100%=10.0=1.0=Mind=Sun=1 January=Helios >> M=E4.

Rial=2,000=20%=P2.00D=2.0=Nature=Matter=Moon=2 Feb.=Cupid=N=C+_
Metric weight >> 2/10=0.2>>20:1. See Naira. Dollar.

Rib=10,000=1,000=100%=10.0=Physicality=Tech.=10 Oct.=Uranus=P=1Ø.
Ribald=9,000=90%=P9.00D=9.0=Abstraction=Gods=Saturn=9Sept.>>A=Ø.
Ribbing=8,500=9,000=90%=P9.00D=9.0=Abstraction=Gods=Saturn=9Sept.>>A=Ø.
Ribbon=10,000=1,000=100%=10.0=Physicality=Tech.=10 Oct.=Uranus=P=1Ø.
Rib cage=6,000=60%=P6.0D=Man=Earth=Royalty=6 June=Gaia=Maia>>M=M2.

Riboflavin=10,000=1,000=100%=10.0=Physicality=Tech.=10 Oct.=Uranus=P=1Ø.
An orange-yellow crystalline compound, the principal growth-promoting factor in the vitamin B complex, found in milk, leafy vegetables, fresh meat, and egg yolks.

Ribonucleic acid=3,000=30%=P3.0D=3.0=Creativity=Stars=Muses=3 March = C=I>>GIL.
Ribose=6,500=7,000=70%=P7.0D=7.0=Language=Assets=Mars=7 July=Pleiades.
Ribosome=10,000=1,000=100%=10.0=Physicality=Tech.=10 Oct.=Uranus=P=1Ø.
Ricardo,David=2,000=20%=P2.00D=2.0=Nature=Matter=Moon=2 Feb.=Cupid=N=C+_
Rice=8,500=9,000=90%=P9.00D=9.0=Abstraction=Gods=Saturn=9Sept.>>A=Ø.
Rich=10,000=1,000=100%=10.0=Physicality=Tech.=10 Oct.=Uranus=P=1Ø.
Richard I=4,500=5,000=50%=P5.00D=Law=Time=Venus=5 May = Aphrodite>>L=N.
Richard II.=3,500=4,000=40%=P4.0D=Govt.=Creat.=4 April=Mercury=Hermes=G=A4.
Richard III.=3,000=30%=P3.0D=3.0=Creativity=Stars=Muses=3 March = C=I>>GIL.
Richardson Samuel=2,000=20%=P2.00D=2.0=Nature=Moon=2 Feb.=Cupid=N=C+_
Richelieu=4,000=40%=P4.0D=Govt.=Creat.=4 April=Mercury=Hermes=G=A4.

Riches=3,000=30%=P3.0D=3.0=Creativity=Stars=Muses=3 March = C=I>>GIL.
Proverbs 8:18 - 21. Revelation 22:14.

Richmond=8,000=80%=P8.0D=Economy=Currency=8 Aug.=Zeus>>E=v.
Richter scale=11,000=11%=P1.10D=1.1=Idea=Brainchild=Inv.=11 Nov.=SC=Athena>>I=MT.
Rick=6,000=60%=P6.0D=Man=Earth=Royalty=6 June=Gaia=Maia>>M=M2.
Rickets=11,000=11%=P1.10D=1.1=Idea=Brainchild=Inv.=11 Nov.=SC=Athena>>I=MT.
Rickety=6,000=60%=P6.0D=Man=Earth=Royalty=6 June=Gaia=Maia>>M=M2.
Rickey=8,500=9,000=90%=P9.00D=9.0=Abstraction=Gods=Saturn=9Sept.>>A=Ø.
Rickover Hyman=2,500=3,000=30%=P3.0D=3.0=Creatv=Stars=Muses=3 March=C=I>GIL.
Ricksha=1,000=100%=10.0=1.0=Mind=Sun=1 January=Helios >> M=E4.
Ricochet=3,000=30%=P3.0D=3.0=Creativity=Stars=Muses=3 March = C=I>>GIL.
Ricotta=4,500=5,000=50%=P5.00D=Law=Time=Venus=5 May = Aphrodite>>L=N.
Rid=3,500=4,000=40%=P4.0D=Govt.=Creat.=4 April=Mercury=Hermes=G=A4.
Riddle1=6,000=60%=P6.0D=Man=Earth=Royalty=6 June=Gaia=Maia>>M=M2.
Riddle2=10,000=1,000=100%=10.0=Physicality=Tech.=10 Oct.=Uranus=P=1Ø.
ride=10,000=1,000=100%=10.0=Physicality=Tech.=10 Oct.=Uranus=P=1Ø.
Ride Sally=5,500=5.5=80%=P5.50=Earth-Midway=5 May = Gaia.
Rider=7,000=70%=P7.0D=7.0=Language=Assets=Mars=7 July=Pleiades.
Ridership=5,000=50%=P5.00D=Law=Time=Venus=5 May = Aphrodite>>L=N.
Ridge=10,000=1,000=100%=10.0=Physicality=Tech.=10 Oct.=Uranus=P=1Ø.

Ridge pole=6,500=7,000=70%=P7.0D=7.0=Language=Assets=Mars=7 July=Pleiades.
Ridicule=9,500=10,000=1,000=100%=10.0=Physicality=Tech.=10 Oct.=Uranus=P=1∅.
Ridiculous=3,000=30%=P3.0D=3.0=Creativity=Stars=Muses=3 March = C=I>>GIL.

Riel=2,500=3,000=30%=P3.0D=3.0=Creativity=Stars=Muses=3 March = C=I>>GIL.
Metric weight >> 2.5/10=0.25>>25:1. See Naira. Dollar.

Rife=3,000=30%=P3.0D=3.0=Creativity=Stars=Muses=3 March = C=I>>GIL.
Riff=5,500=5.5=80%=P5.50=Earth-Midway=5 May = Gaia.
Riffraff=6,500=7,000=70%=P7.0D=7.0=Language=Assets=Mars=7 July=Pleiades.
Rifle1=9,500=10,000=1,000=100%=10.0=Physicality=Tech.=10 Oct.=Uranus=P=1∅.
Rifle2=5,500=5.5=80%=P5.50=Earth-Midway=5 May = Gaia.
Rifiery=4,000=40%=P4.0D=Govt.=Creat.=4 April=Mercury=Hermes=G=A4.
Rifling=3,000=30%=P3.0D=3.0=Creativity=Stars=Muses=3 March = C=I>>GIL.
Rift=9,000=90%=P9.00D=9.0=Abstraction=Gods=Saturn=9Sept.>>A=∅.
Rig=10,000=1,000=100%=10.0=Physicality=Tech.=10 Oct.=Uranus=P=1∅.
Riga=8,000=80%=P8.0D=Economy=Currency=8 Aug.=Zeus>>E=v.
Rigamarole=1,500=15%=P1.50D=1.5=Authority=Solar Crown=1 May = Maia.
Rigging=12,000=12%=P1.20D=1.2=Knowledge=Edu=12Dec.=Athena>>K=F.
Right=10,000=1,000=100%=10.0=Physicality=Tech.=10 Oct.=Uranus=P=1∅.
Right angle=5,500=5.5=80%=P5.50=Earth-Midway=5 May = Gaia.

Righteous=2,500=3,000=30%=P3.0D=3.0=Creativity=Stars=Muses=3 March = C=I>>GIL.
In reference to being morally upright righteousness weighs just 25%. In reference to rights as an aspect of law it weighs 50%. So 25+50=75%. Now computing righteousness to determine precisely what it is from the scriptures >> 2.5=3.0*5.0x=px=8+15=23x=px=143 = 14.3 indicating over 100% (143) and judged based on the wisdom of management guided by critical thinking (14.3). A wisdom of development based on thought meaning prudence that dwells with wisdom and searches the knowledge of witty inventions. Proverbs 8:12. Hence righteousness that is based on just morality without a justifiable earned rights is referred to by the almighty as filthy rags. Hence heaven is more about rights than morals.

Right field=7,000=70%=P7.0D=7.0=Language=Assets=Mars=7 July=Pleiades.
Rightful=5,000=50%=P5.00D=Law=Time=Venus=5 May = Aphrodite>>L=N.
Right hand=7,000=70%=P7.0D=7.0=Language=Assets=Mars=7 July=Pleiades.
Right handed=10,000=1,000=100%=10.0=Physicality=Tech.=10 Oct.=Uranus=P=1∅.
Right hander=2,500=3,000=30%=P3.0D=3.0=Creativity=Stars=Muses=3 March = C=I.
Rightism=2,500=3,000=30%=P3.0D=3.0=Creativity=Stars=Muses=3 March = C=I>>GIL.
Rightly=4,000=40%=P4.0D=Govt.=Creat.=4 April=Mercury=Hermes=G=A4.
Right of way=10,000=1,000=100%=10.0=Physicality=Tech.=10 Oct.=Uranus=P=1∅.
Right on=4,000=40%=P4.0D=Govt.=Creat.=4 April=Mercury=Hermes=G=A4.
Right to life=1,000=100%=10.0=1.0=Mind=Sun=1 January=Helios >> M=E4.
Right triangle=3,500=4,000=40%=P4.0D=Govt.=Creat.=4 April=Mercury=Hermes=G=A4.

Right whale=8,500=9,000=90%=P9.00D=9.0=Abstraction=Gods=Saturn=9Sept.>>A=Ø.
Right wing=5,500=5.5=80%=P5.50=Earth-Midway=5 May = Gaia.
Rigid=6,000=60%=P6.0D=Man=Earth=Royalty=6 June=Gaia=Maia>>M=M2.
Rigmarole=9,000=90%=P9.00D=9.0=Abstraction=Gods=Saturn=9Sept.>>A=Ø.
Rigor=10,000=1,000=100%=10.0=Physicality=Tech.=10 Oct.=Uranus=P=1Ø.
Rigor mortis=4,000=40%=P4.0D=Govt.=Creat.=4 April=Mercury=Hermes=G=A4.
Rile=3,000=30%=P3.0D=3.0=Creativity=Stars=Muses=3 March = C=I>>GIL.
Rilke Rainer=3,000=30%=P3.0D=3.0=Creativity=Stars=Muses=3 March = C=I>>GIL.
Rill=2,500=3,000=30%=P3.0D=3.0=Creativity=Stars=Muses=3 March = C=I>>GIL.
Rim=9,000=90%=P9.00D=9.0=Abstraction=Gods=Saturn=9Sept.>>A=Ø.
Rime1=7,000=70%=P7.0D=7.0=Language=Assets=Mars=7 July=Pleiades.
Rime2=1,500=15%=P1.50D=1.5=Authority=Solar Crown=1 May = Maia.
Rim ski-Korsakov=3,000=30%=P3.0D=3.0=Creativity=Stars=Muses=3 March = C=I>>GIL.
Rind=7,000=70%=P7.0D=7.0=Language=Assets=Mars=7 July=Pleiades.
Ring1=10,000=1,000=100%=10.0=Physicality=Tech.=10 Oct.=Uranus=P=1Ø.
Ring2=10,000=1,000=100%=10.0=Physicality=Tech.=10 Oct.=Uranus=P=1Ø.
Ringer=10,000=1,000=100%=10.0=Physicality=Tech.=10 Oct.=Uranus=P=1Ø.

Ringgit=2,000=20%=P2.00D=2.0=Nature=Matter=Moon=2 Feb.=Cupid=N=C+_
[Malay] >> Metric weight >> 2/10=0.2>>20:1. See Naira. Dollar.

Ring leader=4,500=5,000=50%=P5.00D=Law=Time=Venus=5 May = Aphrodite>>L=N.
Ringlet=4,500=5,000=50%=P5.00D=Law=Time=Venus=5 May = Aphrodite>>L=N.
Ringmaster=5,000=50%=P5.00D=Law=Time=Venus=5 May = Aphrodite>>L=N.
Ringside=5,000=50%=P5.00D=Law=Time=Venus=5 May = Aphrodite>>L=N.
Ringworm=7,500=8,000=80%=P8.0D=Economy=Currency=8 Aug.=Zeus>>E=v.
Rink=10,500=11,000=11%=P1.10D=1.1=Idea=Brainchild=Inv.=11 Nov.=SC=Athena>>I=MT.
Rinse=10,000=1,000=100%=10.0=Physicality=Tech.=10 Oct.=Uranus=P=1Ø.
Rio de Janeiro=7,000=70%=P7.0D=7.0=Language=Assets=Mars=7 July=Pleiades.
Rio Grande=10,000=1,000=100%=10.0=Physicality=Tech.=10 Oct.=Uranus=P=1Ø.
Riot=10,000=1,000=100%=10.0=Physicality=Tech.=10 Oct.=Uranus=P=1Ø.
Riotous=10,000=1,000=100%=10.0=Physicality=Tech.=10 Oct.=Uranus=P=1Ø.
Rip=10,000=1,000=100%=10.0=Physicality=Tech.=10 Oct.=Uranus=P=1Ø.
R.I.P.=5,000=50%=P5.00D=Law=Time=Venus=5 May = Aphrodite>>L=N.
Riparian=6,500=7,000=70%=P7.0D=7.0=Language=Assets=Mars=7 July=Pleiades.
Ripcord=4,500=5,000=50%=P5.00D=Law=Time=Venus=5 May = Aphrodite>>L=N.
Ripe=6,500=7,000=70%=P7.0D=7.0=Language=Assets=Mars=7 July=Pleiades.
Ripoff=7,000=70%=P7.0D=7.0=Language=Assets=Mars=7 July=Pleiades.
Riposte=10,000=1,000=100%=10.0=Physicality=Tech.=10 Oct.=Uranus=P=1Ø.
Ripple=10,000=1,000=100%=10.0=Physicality=Tech.=10 Oct.=Uranus=P=1Ø.
Ripsaw=5,500=5.5=80%=P5.50=Earth-Midway=5 May = Gaia.
Riptide=4,000=40%=P4.0D=Govt.=Creat.=4 April=Mercury=Hermes=G=A4.
Rise=10,000=1,000=100%=10.0=Physicality=Tech.=10 Oct.=Uranus=P=1Ø.
Riser=6,500=7,000=70%=P7.0D=7.0=Language=Assets=Mars=7 July=Pleiades.

Risibility=4,000=40%=P4.0D=Govt.=Creat.=4 April=Mercury=Hermes=G=A4.
Risible=8,000=80%=P8.0D=Economy=Currency=8 Aug.=Zeus>>E=v.
Risk=10,000=1,000=100%=10.0=Physicality=Tech.=10 Oct.=Uranus=P=1Ø.
Risqué=5,000=50%=P5.00D=Law=Time=Venus=5 May = Aphrodite>>L=N.
Rite=7,500=8,000=80%=P8.0D=Economy=Currency=8 Aug.=Zeus>>E=v.
Ritual=11,500=12,000=12%=P1.20D=1.2=Knowledge=Edu=12Dec.=Athena>>K=F.
Ritzy=3,000=30%=P3.0D=3.0=Creativity=Stars=Muses=3 March = C=I>>GIL.
Riv.=500=5%=P5.00D=5.0=Law=Time=Venus=5 May=Aphrodite>>L=N.
Rival=10,000=1,000=100%=10.0=Physicality=Tech.=10 Oct.=Uranus=P=1Ø.
Rive=6,000=60%=P6.0D=Man=Earth=Royalty=6 June=Gaia=Maia>>M=M2.
River=4,000=40%=P4.0D=Govt.=Creat.=4 April=Mercury=Hermes=G=A4.
Rivera Diego=2,000=20%=P2.00D=2.0=Nature=Matter=Moon=2 Feb.=Cupid=N=C+_
Riverboat=3,000=30%=P3.0D=3.0=Creativity=Stars=Muses=3 March = C=I>>GIL.
Riverside=5,000=50%=P5.00D=Law=Time=Venus=5 May = Aphrodite>>L=N.
Rivet=10,000=1,000=100%=10.0=Physicality=Tech.=10 Oct.=Uranus=P=1Ø.
Riviera=7,000=70%=P7.0D=7.0=Language=Assets=Mars=7 July=Pleiades.
Rivulet=4,000=40%=P4.0D=Govt.=Creat.=4 April=Mercury=Hermes=G=A4.
Riyadh=5,500=5.5=80%=P5.50=Earth-Midway=5 May = Gaia.

Riyal=3,000=30%=P3.0D=3.0=Creativity=Stars=Muses=3 March = C=I>>GIL.
>> Metric weight >> 3/10=0.3>>30:1. See Naira. Dollar.

Riyal-Omani=4,500=5,000=50%=P5.00D=Law=Time=Venus=5 May = Aphrodite>>L=N.
>> Metric weight >> 4.5/10=0.45>>45:1. See Naira. Dollar.

---

rm.=1,000=100%=10.0=1.0=Mind=Sun=1 January=Helios >> M=E4.
Rn=2,500=3,000=30%=P3.0D=3.0=Creativity=Stars=Muses=3 March = C=I>>GIL.
RN=2,000=20%=P2.00D=2.0=Nature=Matter=Moon=2 Feb.=Cupid=N=C+_
RNA=10,000=1,000=100%=10.0=Physicality=Tech.=10 Oct.=Uranus=P=1Ø.

Roach1=4,000=40%=P4.0D=Govt.=Creat.=4 April=Mercury=Hermes=G=A4.
Different from cockroach. A freshwater fish of N Europe < Old Fr. roche.

Roach2=1,000=100%=10.0=1.0=Mind=Sun=1 January=Helios >> M=E4.
A cockroach. Animals and insects equivalent to 10,000 like the rhinoceros and now the cockroach at 1,000 should have their behavior characteristics studied to understand further the mysteries behind these numbers and codes. Peter Matthews-Akukalia asserts in the Naturecology that the alphanumerics are a system of transmuted spirits.

Road=10,000=1,000=100%=10.0=Physicality=Tech.=10 Oct.=Uranus=P=1Ø.
Hermes is known as the God of commerce inventions wits thievery merchandise oratory boundaries and the roads. This means that he measures road movements and the above

listed elements by the quantum standards. Today Peter Matthews-Akukalia, Castle Makupedia (King Maks by Makumatics) is the universal standard unit to measure these. Boundaries include lands occupied and not occupied by humans water and other things.

Roadbed=7,000=70%=P7.0D=7.0=Language=Assets=Mars=7 July=Pleiades.
Roadblock=5,000=50%=P5.00D=Law=Time=Venus=5 May = Aphrodite>>L=N.
Roadhouse=5,500=5.5=80%=P5.50=Earth-Midway=5 May = Gaia.
Roadrunner=8,000=80%=P8.0D=Economy=Currency=8 Aug.=Zeus>>E=v.
Road show=3,000=30%=P3.0D=3.0=Creativity=Stars=Muses=3 March = C=I>>GIL.
Roadside=2,500=3,000=30%=P3.0D=3.0=Creativity=Stars=Muses=3 March = C=I>>GIL.
Roadster=7,500=8,000=80%=P8.0D=Economy=Currency=8 Aug.=Zeus>>E=v.
Road Town=7,000=70%=P7.0D=7.0=Language=Assets=Mars=7 July=Pleiades.
Road way=4,500=5,000=50%=P5.00D=Law=Time=Venus=5 May = Aphrodite>>L=N.
Roadwork=6,500=7,000=70%=P7.0D=7.0=Language=Assets=Mars=7 July=Pleiades.
Roam=4,000=40%=P4.0D=Govt.=Creat.=4 April=Mercury=Hermes=G=A4.
Roan=9,000=90%=P9.00D=9.0=Abstraction=Gods=Saturn=9Sept.>>A=Ø.
Roanoke=5,500=5.5=80%=P5.50=Earth-Midway=5 May = Gaia.
Roanoke Island=10,500=11,000=11%=P1.10D=1.1=Idea=Brainchild=11Nov=Athena>>I=MT.
Roar=10,500=11,000=11%=P1.10D=1.1=Idea=Brainchild=Inv.=11 Nov.=SC=Athena>>I=MT.
Roast=10,000=1,000=100%=10.0=Physicality=Tech.=10 Oct.=Uranus=P=1Ø.
Rob=8,000=80%=P8.0D=Economy=Currency=8 Aug.=Zeus>>E=v.
Robe=10,000=1,000=100%=10.0=Physicality=Tech.=10 Oct.=Uranus=P=1Ø.
Robert=5,000=50%=P5.00D=Law=Time=Venus=5 May = Aphrodite>>L=N.
Robespierre Maximllen=4,500=5,000=50%=P5.00D=Law=Time=5May=Odite>>L=N.
Rob in=10,000=1,000=100%=10.0=Physicality=Tech.=10 Oct.=Uranus=P=1Ø.
Robinson Edwin=2,500=3,000=30%=P3.0D=3.0=Creativity=Stars=Muses=3 March = CI
Robinson,Jack=4,500=5,000=50%=P5.00D=Law=Time=Venus=5 May = Aphrodite>>L=N.
Robot=10,000=1,000=100%=10.0=Physicality=Tech.=10 Oct.=Uranus=P=1Ø.
Robotics=3,500=4,000=40%=P4.0D=Govt.=Creat.=4 April=Mercury=Hermes=G=A4.
Robust=10,000=1,000=100%=10.0=Physicality=Tech.=10 Oct.=Uranus=P=1Ø.
Rocha Beau=3,500=4,000=40%=P4.0D=Govt.=Creat.=4 April=Mercury=Hermes=G=A4.
Rochester=4,500=5,000=50%=P5.00D=Law=Time=Venus=5 May = Aphrodite>>L=N.
Rock1=10,000=1,000=100%=10.0=Physicality=Tech.=10 Oct.=Uranus=P=1Ø.
Rock2=10,000=1,000=100%=10.0=Physicality=Tech.=10 Oct.=Uranus=P=1Ø.
Rock and roll=2,500=3,000=30%=P3.0D=3.0=Creativity=Stars=Muses=3 March = CI
Rock bottom=2,000=20%=P2.00D=2.0=Nature=Matter=Moon=2 Feb.=Cupid=N=C+_
Rock bound=3,500=4,000=40%=P4.0D=Govt.=Creat.=4April=Mercury=Hermes=G=A4.

Rockefeller=11,500=12,000=12%=P1.20D=1.2=Knowledge=Edu=12Dec.=Athena>>K=F.
American family of business executives politicians and philanthropists.

Rocker=12,500=13,000=13%=P1.30=Solar Core=Faculty=13 January=Athena.
Rocket1=10,000=1,000=100%=10.0=Physicality=Tech.=10 Oct.=Uranus=P=1Ø.
Rocket2=7,500=8,000=80%=P8.0D=Economy=Currency=8 Aug.=Zeus>>E=v.

Rocketry=5,000=50%=P5.00D=Law=Time=Venus=5 May = Aphrodite>>L=N.
Rocket ship=2,500=3,000=30%=P3.0D=3.0=Creativity=Stars=Muses=3 March = CI
Rockford=4,500=5,000=50%=P5.00D=Law=Time=Venus=5 May = Aphrodite>>L=N.
Rocking chair=3,500=4,000=40%=P4.0D=Govt.=Creat.=4 April=Mercury=Hermes=G=A4.
Rocking ham=5,500=5.5=80%=P5.50=Earth-Midway=5 May = Gaia.
Rocking horse=4,000=40%=P4.0D=Govt.=Creat.=4 April=Mercury=Hermes=G=A4.
Rock 'n' roll=12,000=12%=P1.20D=1.2=Knowledge=Edu=12Dec.=Athena>>K=F.
Rock salt=2,500=3,000=30%=P3.0D=3.0=Creativity=Stars=Muses=3 March = C=I>>GIL.
Rockville=5,000=50%=P5.00D=Law=Time=Venus=5 May = Aphrodite>>L=N.
Rock wool=1,500=15%=P1.50D=1.5=Authority=Solar Crown=1 May = Maia.
Rocky1=6,500=7,000=70%=P7.0D=7.0=Language=Assets=Mars=7 July=Pleiades.
Rocky2=5,000=50%=P5.00D=Law=Time=Venus=5 May = Aphrodite>>L=N.
Rocky Mountains=10,500=11,000=11%=P1.10D=1.1=Idea=Bchd.=11Nov.=Athena>>I=MT.
Rococo=10,000=1,000=100%=10.0=Physicality=Tech.=10 Oct.=Uranus=P=1Ø.
Rod=10,000=1,000=100%=10.0=Physicality=Tech.=10 Oct.=Uranus=P=1Ø.
Rode=2,000=20%=P2.00D=2.0=Nature=Matter=Moon=2 Feb.=Cupid=N=C+_
Rodent=10,000=1,000=100%=10.0=Physicality=Tech.=10 Oct.=Uranus=P=1Ø.
Rodeo=10,000=1,000=100%=10.0=Physicality=Tech.=10 Oct.=Uranus=P=1Ø.
Rodin François=3,000=30%=P3.0D=3.0=Creativity=Stars=Muses=3 March = C=I>>GIL.
Roe1=5,500=5.5=80%=P5.50=Earth-Midway=5 May = Gaia.
Roe2=4,500=5,000=50%=P5.00D=Law=Time=Venus=5 May = Aphrodite>>L=N.
roentgen=9,000=90%=P9.00D=9.0=Abstraction=Gods=Saturn=9Sept.>>A=Ø.
Roentgen William=2,500=3,000=30%=P3.0D=3.0=Creativity=Stars=Muses=3 March = C=I
Roethke Theodore=2,000=20%=P2.00D=2.0=Nature=Matter=Moon=2 Feb.=Cupid=N=C+_
Roger=10,000=1,000=100%=10.0=Physicality=Tech.=10 Oct.=Uranus=P=1Ø.
Roget=4,000=40%=P4.0D=Govt.=Creat.=4 April=Mercury=Hermes=G=A4.
Rogue=5,000=50%=P5.00D=Law=Time=Venus=5 May = Aphrodite>>L=N.
Roil=6,500=7,000=70%=P7.0D=7.0=Language=Assets=Mars=7 July=Pleiades.
Role=11,000=11%=P1.10D=1.1=Idea=Brainchild=Inv.=11 Nov.=SC=Athena>>I=MT.
Role model=5,000=50%=P5.00D=Law=Time=Venus=5 May = Aphrodite>>L=N.
Roll=10,000=1,000=100%=10.0=Physicality=Tech.=10 Oct.=Uranus=P=1Ø.
Rollback=5,000=50%=P5.00D=Law=Time=Venus=5 May = Aphrodite>>L=N.
Roll call=6,500=7,000=70%=P7.0D=7.0=Language=Assets=Mars=7 July=Pleiades.
Roller=10,000=1,000=100%=10.0=Physicality=Tech.=10 Oct.=Uranus=P=1Ø.
Roller coaster=9,000=90%=P9.00D=9.0=Abstraction=Gods=Saturn=9Sept.>>A=Ø.
Roller skate=8,500=9,000=90%=P9.00D=9.0=Abstraction=Gods=Saturn=9Sept.>>A=Ø.
Rollick=3,500=4,000=40%=P4.0D=Govt.=Creat.=4 April=Mercury=Hermes=G=A4.
Rolling pin=4,000=40%=P4.0D=Govt.=Creat.=4 April=Mercury=Hermes=G=A4.
Rölvaag Ole=3,500=4,000=40%=P4.0D=Govt.=Creat.=4 April=Mercury=Hermes=G=A4.
Rolypoly=2,000=20%=P2.00D=2.0=Nature=Matter=Moon=2 Feb.=Cupid=N=C+_
rom=1,000=100%=10.0=1.0=Mind=Sun=1 January=Helios >> M=E4.
ROM=2,500=3,000=30%=P3.0D=3.0=Creativity=Stars=Muses=3 March = C=I>>GIL.
Rom.=2,500=3,000=30%=P3.0D=3.0=Creativity=Stars=Muses=3 March = C=I>>GIL.
Romagna=3,500=4,000=40%=P4.0D=Govt.=Creat.=4 April=Mercury=Hermes=G=A4.
Romaine=5,500=5.5=80%=P5.50=Earth-Midway=5 May = Gaia.

Roman=10,000=1,000=100%=10.0=Physicality=Tech.=10 Oct.=Uranus=P=1Ø.
Roman candle=4,000=40%=P4.0D=Govt.=Creat.=4 April=Mercury=Hermes=G=A4.
Roman Catholic=5,000=50%=P5.00D=Law=Time=Venus=5 May = Aphrodite>>L=N.
Roman Catholic Church=5,000=50%=P5.00D=Law=Time=Venus=5 May =Odite>>L=N.
Romance=10,000=1,000=100%=10.0=Physicality=Tech.=10 Oct.=Uranus=P=1Ø.

Roman Empire=11,500=12,000=12%=P1.20D=1.2=Knowledge=Edu=12Dec.=Athena>>K=F.
The Creatocracy is the Makupedian Empire including the Disean Nation.

Romanesque=10,000=1,000=100%=10.0=Physicality=Tech.=10 Oct.=Uranus=P=1Ø.
Romania=4,500=5,000=50%=P5.00D=Law=Time=Venus=5 May = Aphrodite>>L=N.
Romanian=4,500=5,000=50%=P5.00D=Law=Time=Venus=5 May = Aphrodite>>L=N.
Roman numeral=10,500=11,000=11%=P1.10D=1.1=Idea=Brainchild=11Nov=Athena
    >>I=MT.
Romansch=5,500=5.5=80%=P5.50=Earth-Midway=5 May = Gaia.
Romantic=10,000=1,000=100%=10.0=Physicality=Tech.=10 Oct.=Uranus=P=1Ø.
Romanticism=10,000=1,000=100%=10.0=Physicality=Tech.=10 Oct.=Uranus=P=1Ø.
Romanticize=5,000=50%=P5.00D=Law=Time=Venus=5 May = Aphrodite>>L=N.
Romany=4,000=40%=P4.0D=Govt.=Creat.=4 April=Mercury=Hermes=G=A4.
Romberg Sigmund=3,000=30%=P3.0D=3.0=Creatv=Stars=Muses=3 March = C=I>>GIL.
Rome=5,000=50%=P5.00D=Law=Time=Venus=5 May = Aphrodite>>L=N.
Romeo=7,500=8,000=80%=P8.0D=Economy=Currency=8 Aug.=Zeus>>E=v.
Romp=2,500=3,000=30%=P3.0D=3.0=Creativity=Stars=Muses=3 March = C=I>>GIL.
Romper=8,500=9,000=90%=P9.00D=9.0=Abstraction=Gods=Saturn=9Sept.>>A=Ø.
Rondo=5,500=5.5=80%=P5.50=Earth-Midway=5 May = Gaia.
Rood=10,000=1,000=100%=10.0=Physicality=Tech.=10 Oct.=Uranus=P=1Ø.
Roof=10,000=1,000=100%=10.0=Physicality=Tech.=10 Oct.=Uranus=P=1Ø.
Roofing=3,000=30%=P3.0D=3.0=Creativity=Stars=Muses=3 March = C=I>>GIL.
Roof tree=3,500=4,000=40%=P4.0D=Govt.=Creat.=4 April=Mercury=Hermes=G=A4.
Rook1=6,000=60%=P6.0D=Man=Earth=Royalty=6 June=Gaia=Maia>>M=M2.
Rook2=8,500=9,000=90%=P9.00D=9.0=Abstraction=Gods=Saturn=9Sept.>>A=Ø.
Rookery=7,500=8,000=80%=P8.0D=Economy=Currency=8 Aug.=Zeus>>E=v.
Rookie=6,500=7,000=70%=P7.0D=7.0=Language=Assets=Mars=7 July=Pleiades.
Room=10,000=1,000=100%=10.0=Physicality=Tech.=10 Oct.=Uranus=P=1Ø.
Roomer=1,000=100%=10.0=1.0=Mind=Sun=1 January=Helios >> M=E4.
Rooming house=3,500=4,000=40%=P4.0D=Govt.=Creat.=4 April=Hermes=G=A4.
Roommate=4,000=40%=P4.0D=Govt.=Creat.=4 April=Mercury=Hermes=G=A4.
Roomy=4,500=5,000=50%=P5.00D=Law=Time=Venus=5 May = Aphrodite>>L=N.
Roosevelt Anna=7,000=70%=P7.0D=7.0=Language=Assets=Mars=7 July=Pleiades.
Roosevelt Franklin=2,500=3,000=30%=P3.0D=3.0=Creatv=Stars=Muses=3 March = CI
Roosevelt,Theodore=4,000=40%=P4.0D=Govt.=Creat.=4 April=Mercury=Hermes=G=A4.
Roost=7,000=70%=P7.0D=7.0=Language=Assets=Mars=7 July=Pleiades.
Rooster=2,000=20%=P2.00D=2.0=Nature=Matter=Moon=2 Feb.=Cupid=N=C+_
Root1=10,000=1,000=100%=10.0=Physicality=Tech.=10 Oct.=Uranus=P=1Ø.

Root2=8,000=80%=P8.0D=Economy=Currency=8 Aug.=Zeus>>E=v.
Root3=7,000=70%=P7.0D=7.0=Language=Assets=Mars=7 July=Pleiades.
Root Elihu=5,500=5.5=80%=P5.50=Earth-Midway=5 May = Gaia.
Root beer=6,000=60%=P6.0D=Man=Earth=Royalty=6 June=Gaia=Maia>>M=M2.
Root canal=10,000=1,000=100%=10.0=Physicality=Tech.=10 Oct.=Uranus=P=1Ø.
Root cellar=4,500=5,000=50%=P5.00D=Law=Time=Venus=5 May = Aphrodite>>L=N.
Rootstock=5,000=50%=P5.00D=Law=Time=Venus=5 May = Aphrodite>>L=N.
Rope=10,000=1,000=100%=10.0=Physicality=Tech.=10 Oct.=Uranus=P=1Ø.
Roquefort=4,500=5,000=50%=P5.00D=Law=Time=Venus=5 May = Aphrodite>>L=N.
Rorqual=12,000=12%=P1.20D=1.2=Knowledge=Edu=12Dec.=Athena>>K=F.
Rorschach test=10,000=1,000=100%=10.0=Physicality=Tech.=10 Oct.=Uranus=P=1Ø.
Rosario=7,500=8,000=80%=P8.0D=Economy=Currency=8 Aug.=Zeus>>E=v.
Rosary=10,000=1,000=100%=10.0=Physicality=Tech.=10 Oct.=Uranus=P=1Ø.
Rose1=10,000=1,000=100%=10.0=Physicality=Tech.=10 Oct.=Uranus=P=1Ø.
Rose2=2,000=20%=P2.00D=2.0=Nature=Matter=Moon=2 Feb.=Cupid=N=C+_
Rosé=5,000=50%=P5.00D=Law=Time=Venus=5 May = Aphrodite>>L=N.
Roseate=3,000=30%=P3.0D=3.0=Creativity=Stars=Muses=3 March = C=I>>GIL.
Rosebud=2,500=3,000=30%=P3.0D=3.0=Creativity=Stars=Muses=3 March = C=I>>GIL.
Rose bush=2,500=3,000=30%=P3.0D=3.0=Creativity=Stars=Muses=3 March = C=I>>GIL.
Rose colored=2,000=20%=P2.00D=2.0=Nature=Matter=Moon=2 Feb.=Cupid=N=C+_
Rose crans=3,000=30%=P3.0D=3.0=Creativity=Stars=Muses=3 March = C=I>>GIL.
Rosemary=10,000=1,000=100%=10.0=Physicality=Tech.=10 Oct.=Uranus=P=1Ø.
Rosette=5,500=5.5=80%=P5.50=Earth-Midway=5 May = Gaia.
Rose water=8,500=9,000=90%=P9.00D=9.0=Abstraction=Gods=Saturn=9Sept.>>A=Ø.
Rose window=4,000=40%=P4.0D=Govt.=Creat.=4 April=Mercury=Hermes=G=A4.
Rose wood=6,500=7,000=70%=P7.0D=7.0=Language=Assets=Mars=7 July=Pleiades.
Roman Hashanah=7,500=8,000=80%=P8.0D=Economy=Currency=8 Aug.=Zeus>>E=v.

Rosicrucian=10,000=1,000=100%=10.0=Physicality=Tech.=10 Oct.=Uranus=P=1Ø.
A member of an international organization devoted to the study of ancient mysticism and its application to modern life. The Creatocrat is a member of an international organization of Makstianism devoted to the study of Greek mythologies in alignment with the Scriptures and discoveries of the Creative Sciences in a view to establishing faith through precision.

Rosin=10,000=1,000=100%=10.0=Physicality=Tech.=10 Oct.=Uranus=P=1Ø.
Ross Betsy=2,500=3,000=30%=P3.0D=3.0=Creativity=Stars=Muses=3 March = C=I
Ross,James=3,500=4,000=40%=P4.0D=Govt.=Creat.=4 April=Mercury=Hermes=G=A4.
Rossetti=7,000=70%=P7.0D=7.0=Language=Assets=Mars=7 July=Pleiades.
Ross Ice Shelf.=7,500=8,000=80%=P8.0D=Economy=Currency=8 Aug.=Zeus>>E=v.
Rossini Gloacchino=2,500=3,000=30%=P3.0D=3.0=Creativity=Stars=Muses=3 March = CI
Rostand Edmond=2,000=20%=P2.00D=2.0=Nature=Matter=Moon=2 Feb.=Cupid=N=C+_
Roster=6,000=60%=P6.0D=Man=Earth=Royalty=6 June=Gaia=Maia>>M=M2.
Rostock=6,500=7,000=70%=P7.0D=7.0=Language=Assets=Mars=7 July=Pleiades.
Rostov=5,000=50%=P5.00D=Law=Time=Venus=5 May = Aphrodite>>L=N.

Rostrum=4,500=5,000=50%=P5.00D=Law=Time=Venus=5 May = Aphrodite>>L=N.
Rosy=4,500=5,000=50%=P5.00D=Law=Time=Venus=5 May = Aphrodite>>L=N.
Rot=10,000=1,000=100%=10.0=Physicality=Tech.=10 Oct.=Uranus=P=1Ø.
Rotary=8,000=80%=P8.0D=Economy=Currency=8 Aug.=Zeus>>E=v.
Rotate=5,500=5.5=80%=P5.50=Earth-Midway=5 May = Gaia.
Rotation=10,000=1,000=100%=10.0=Physicality=Tech.=10 Oct.=Uranus=P=1Ø.
ROTC=2,000=20%=P2.00D=2.0=Nature=Matter=Moon=2 Feb.=Cupid=N=C+_
Rote=4,500=5,000=50%=P5.00D=Law=Time=Venus=5 May = Aphrodite>>L=N.

Rothschild=8,500=9,000=90%=P9.00D=9.0=Abstraction=Gods=Saturn=9Sept.>>A=Ø.
German Family of Bankers including Mayer, Salomon and Nathan.

Rotisserie=8,000=80%=P8.0D=Economy=Currency=8 Aug.=Zeus>>E=v.
Rotogravure=10,000=1,000=100%=10.0=Physicality=Tech.=10 Oct.=Uranus=P=1Ø.
Rotor=7,000=70%=P7.0D=7.0=Language=Assets=Mars=7 July=Pleiades.
Roto tiller=8,500=9,000=90%=P9.00D=9.0=Abstraction=Gods=Saturn=9Sept.>>A=Ø.
Rotten=10,000=1,000=100%=10.0=Physicality=Tech.=10 Oct.=Uranus=P=1Ø.
Rotterdam=7,000=70%=P7.0D=7.0=Language=Assets=Mars=7 July=Pleiades.
Rottweiler=8,500=9,000=90%=P9.00D=9.0=Abstraction=Gods=Saturn=9Sept.>>A=Ø.
Rotund=3,000=30%=P3.0D=3.0=Creativity=Stars=Muses=3 March = C=I>>GIL.
Rotunda=8,500=9,000=90%=P9.00D=9.0=Abstraction=Gods=Saturn=9Sept.>>A=Ø.
Rouault Georges=2,000=20%=P2.00D=2.0=Nature=Matter=Moon=2 Feb.=Cupid=N=C+_
Rouble=1,500=15%=P1.50D=1.5=Authority=Solar Crown=1 May = Maia.
Roué=4,500=5,000=50%=P5.00D=Law=Time=Venus=5 May = Aphrodite>>L=N.
Rouen=4,500=5,000=50%=P5.00D=Law=Time=Venus=5 May = Aphrodite>>L=N.
Rouge=11,000=11%=P1.10D=1.1=Idea=Brainchild=Inv.=11 Nov.=SC=Athena>>I=MT.
Rough=10,000=1,000=100%=10.0=Physicality=Tech.=10 Oct.=Uranus=P=1Ø.
Roughage=1,500=15%=P1.50D=1.5=Authority=Solar Crown=1 May = Maia.
Roughen=2,500=3,000=30%=P3.0D=3.0=Creativity=Stars=Muses=3 March = C=I>>GIL.
Rough-hew=6,500=7,000=70%=P7.0D=7.0=Language=Assets=Mars=7 July=Pleiades.
Roughhouse=1,500=15%=P1.50D=1.5=Authority=Solar Crown=1 May = Maia.
Roughneck=1,500=15%=P1.50D=1.5=Authority=Solar Crown=1 May = Maia.
Roughshod=9,000=90%=P9.00D=9.0=Abstraction=Gods=Saturn=9Sept.>>A=Ø.
Roulade=6,500=7,000=70%=P7.0D=7.0=Language=Assets=Mars=7 July=Pleiades.
Roulette=10,000=1,000=100%=10.0=Physicality=Tech.=10 Oct.=Uranus=P=1Ø.
Round=10,000=1,000=100%=10.0=Physicality=Tech.=10 Oct.=Uranus=P=1Ø.
Roundabout=1,000=100%=10.0=1.0=Mind=Sun=1 January=Helios >> M=E4.
Round delay=4,500=5,000=50%=P5.00D=Law=Time=Venus=5 May = Aphrodite>>L=N.
Roundhouse=6,000=60%=P6.0D=Man=Earth=Royalty=6 June=Gaia=Maia>>M=M2.
Roundly=1,000=100%=10.0=1.0=Mind=Sun=1 January=Helios >> M=E4.
Round robin=7,000=70%=P7.0D=7.0=Language=Assets=Mars=7 July=Pleiades.
Round table=10,000=1,000=100%=10.0=Physicality=Tech.=10 Oct.=Uranus=P=1Ø.
Round-the-clock=3,000=30%=P3.0D=3.0=Creativity=Stars=Muses=3 March = C=I>>GIL.
Round trip=3,500=4,000=40%=P4.0D=Govt.=Creat.=4 April=Mercury=Hermes=G=A4.

Roundup=7,000=70%=P7.0D=7.0=Language=Assets=Mars=7 July=Pleiades.
Roundworm=1,000=100%=10.0=1.0=Mind=Sun=1 January=Helios >> M=E4.
Rouse=10,000=1,000=100%=10.0=Physicality=Tech.=10 Oct.=Uranus=P=1Ø.
Rousing=2,500=3,000=30%=P3.0D=3.0=Creativity=Stars=Muses=3 March = C=I>>GIL.
Rousseau Henri=2,500=3,000=30%=P3.0D=3.0=Creativity=Stars=Muses=3 March = C=I
Rousseau,Jean=3,500=4,000=40%=P4.0D=Creat.=4 April=Mercury=Hermes=G=A4.
Rousseau,Théodore=3,000=30%=P3.0D=3.0=Creativity=Stars=Muses=3 March = C=I
Roust=4,000=40%=P4.0D=Govt.=Creat.=4 April=Mercury=Hermes=G=A4.
Roustabout=4,000=40%=P4.0D=Govt.=Creat.=4 April=Mercury=Hermes=G=A4.
Rout1=10,000=1,000=100%=10.0=Physicality=Tech.=10 Oct.=Uranus=P=1Ø.
Rout2=10,000=1,000=100%=10.0=Physicality=Tech.=10 Oct.=Uranus=P=1Ø.
Route=10,000=1,000=100%=10.0=Physicality=Tech.=10 Oct.=Uranus=P=1Ø.
Routine=10,000=1,000=100%=10.0=Physicality=Tech.=10 Oct.=Uranus=P=1Ø.
Rove=6,500=7,000=70%=P7.0D=7.0=Language=Assets=Mars=7 July=Pleiades.
Row1=10,000=1,000=100%=10.0=Physicality=Tech.=10 Oct.=Uranus=P=1Ø.
Row2=7,500=8,000=80%=P8.0D=Economy=Currency=8 Aug.=Zeus>>E=v.
Row3=6,000=60%=P6.0D=Man=Earth=Royalty=6 June=Gaia=Maia>>M=M2.
Rowboat=3,000=30%=P3.0D=3.0=Creativity=Stars=Muses=3 March = C=I>>GIL.
Rowdy=4,000=40%=P4.0D=Govt.=Creat.=4 April=Mercury=Hermes=G=A4.
Rowel=8,000=80%=P8.0D=Economy=Currency=8 Aug.=Zeus>>E=v.
Row house=6,500=7,000=70%=P7.0D=7.0=Language=Assets=Mars=7 July=Pleiades.

Royal=6,500=7,000=70%=P7.0D=7.0=Language=Assets=Mars=7 July=Pleiades.
To be royal is a borderline between humanity and precision. It is not an end in itself.
Peter Matthews-Akukalia was born in a royal home. Then he established a higher royalty.

Royal blue=2,500=3,000=30%=P3.0D=3.0=Creativity=Stars=Muses=3 March = C=I>>GIL.
Royalist=3,500=4,000=40%=P4.0D=Govt.=Creat.=4 April=Mercury=Hermes=G=A4.
Royal poinciana=6,000=60%=P6.0D=Man=Earth=Royalty=6 June=Gaia=Maia>>M=M2.

Royalty=10,000=1,000=100%=10.0=Physicality=Tech.=10 Oct.=Uranus=P=1Ø.
Peter Matthews-Akukalia is royalty and owns the Creatocratic Royal Family by his works. He founded the Matthews-Akukalia family empire completely different from the mere Matthews (surname) or Akukalia (Family name) which he was born into. The brand Makupedia given to his invented field of study and company was formed from Matthews-Akukalia Peter. He is the inventor first and registered owner of the surname Matthews-Akukalia exclusive to his heirs successors and lineage. All others are relatives. He is Castle Makupedia God of Creatocracy Genius and Mind. He is the Creatocracy [of things].

---

rpm=1,500=15%=P1.50D=1.5=Authority=Solar Crown=1 May = Maia.
RR=1,500=15%=P1.50D=1.5=Authority=Solar Crown=1 May = Maia.
-rrhea=6,000=60%=P6.0D=Man=Earth=Royalty=6 June=Gaia=Maia>>M=M2.

rRNA=1,000=100%=10.0=1.0=Mind=Sun=1 January=Helios >> M=E4.
RSV=2,000=20%=P2.00D=2.0=Nature=Matter=Moon=2 Feb.=Cupid=N=C+_
R.S.V.P.=3,500=4,000=40%=P4.0D=Govt.=Creat.=4 April=Mercury=Hermes=G=A4.
rt.=500=5%=P5.00D=5.0=Law=Time=Venus=5 May=Aphrodite>>L=N.
rte.=500=5%=P5.00D=5.0=Law=Time=Venus=5 May=Aphrodite>>L=N.
Rt.Hon.=1,000=100%=10.0=1.0=Mind=Sun=1 January=Helios >> M=E4.
Ru=2,500=3,000=30%=P3.0D=3.0=Creativity=Stars=Muses=3 March = C=I>>GIL.
Rub=10,000=1,000=100%=10.0=Physicality=Tech.=10 Oct.=Uranus=P=1Ø.
Rubber1=10,000=1,000=100%=10.0=Physicality=Tech.=10 Oct.=Uranus=P=1Ø.
Rubber2=10,000=1,000=100%=10.0=Physicality=Tech.=10 Oct.=Uranus=P=1Ø.
Rubber band=5,000=50%=P5.00D=Law=Time=Venus=5 May = Aphrodite>>L=N.
Rubber cement=2,500=3,000=30%=P3.0D=3.0=Creatv=Stars=Muses=3 March=C=I>GIL.
Rubberize=3,500=4,000=40%=P4.0D=Govt.=Creat.=4 April=Mercury=Hermes=G=A4.
Rubberneck=2,500=3,000=30%=P3.0D=3.0=Creativity=Stars=Muses=3 March = C=I
Rubber stamp=7,000=70%=P7.0D=7.0=Language=Assets=Mars=7 July=Pleiades.
Rubber-stamp=3,500=4,000=40%=P4.0D=Govt.=Creat.=4 April=Hermes=G=A4.
Rubbing=10,000=1,000=100%=10.0=Physicality=Tech.=10 Oct.=Uranus=P=1Ø.
Rubbish=3,500=4,000=40%=P4.0D=Govt.=Creat.=4 April=Mercury=Hermes=G=A4.
Rubble=6,500=7,000=70%=P7.0D=7.0=Language=Assets=Mars=7 July=Pleiades.
Rubdown=1,000=100%=10.0=1.0=Mind=Sun=1 January=Helios >> M=E4.
Rube=4,500=5,000=50%=P5.00D=Law=Time=Venus=5 May = Aphrodite>>L=N.
Rubella=10,000=1,000=100%=10.0=Physicality=Tech.=10 Oct.=Uranus=P=1Ø.
Rubens Peter Paul.=2,000=20%=P2.00D=2.0=Nature=Moon=2 Feb.=Cupid=N=C+_
Rubicund=4,000=40%=P4.0D=Govt.=Creat.=4 April=Mercury=Hermes=G=A4.
Rubidium=11,000=11%=P1.10D=1.1=Idea=Brainchild=Inv.=11 Nov.=SC=Athena>>I=MT.
Rubinstein Anton=2,500=3,000=30%=P3.0D=3.0=Creativity=Stars=Muses=3 March = C=I
Rubinstein Arthur=3,000=30%=P3.0D=3.0=Creativity=Stars=Muses=3 March = C=I>>GIL.

Ruble=3,000=30%=P3.0D=3.0=Creativity=Stars=Muses=3 March = C=I>>GIL.
Metric currency weight = 3/10=0.3>>30:1. See Naira. Dollar.

Rubric=10,000=1,000=100%=10.0=Physicality=Tech.=10 Oct.=Uranus=P=1Ø.
Ruby=9,000=90%=P9.00D=9.0=Abstraction=Gods=Saturn=9Sept.>>A=Ø.
Rucksack=1,500=15%=P1.50D=1.5=Authority=Solar Crown=1 May = Maia.
Ruckus=4,500=5,000=50%=P5.00D=Law=Time=Venus=5 May = Aphrodite>>L=N.
Rudder=10,000=1,000=100%=10.0=Physicality=Tech.=10 Oct.=Uranus=P=1Ø.
Ruddy=5,500=5.5=80%=P5.50=Earth-Midway=5 May = Gaia.
Rude=11,500=12,000=12%=P1.20D=1.2=Knowledge=Edu=12Dec.=Athena>>K=F.
Rudiment=9,000=90%=P9.00D=9.0=Abstraction=Gods=Saturn=9Sept.>>A=Ø.
Rudolf I=6,000=60%=P6.0D=Man=Earth=Royalty=6 June=Gaia=Maia>>M=M2.
Rudolph Wilma=2,500=3,000=30%=P3.0D=3.0=Creativity=Stars=Muses=3 March = C=I
Ruel=4,500=5,000=50%=P5.00D=Law=Time=Venus=5 May=Aphrodite>>L=N.
Rue2=8,500=9,000=90%=P9.00D=9.0=Abstraction=Gods=Saturn=9Sept.>>A=Ø.
Ruff=11,500=12,000=12%=P1.20D=1.2=Knowledge=Edu=12Dec.=Athena>>K=F.

Ruffian=3,500=4,000=40%=P4.0D=Govt.=Creat.=4 April=Mercury=Hermes=G=A4.
Ruffle=10,000=1,000=100%=10.0=Physicality=Tech.=10 Oct.=Uranus=P=1Ø.

Rufiyaa=3,000=30%=P3.0D=3.0=Creativity=Stars=Muses=3 March = C=I>>GIL.
[Hindi Rupiya] >> Metric currency weight = 3/10=0.3>>30:1. See Naira. Dollar.

Rufous=4,500=5,000=50%=P5.00D=Law=Time=Venus=5 May = Aphrodite>>L=N.
Rug=5,000=50%=P5.00D=Law=Time=Venus=5 May = Aphrodite>>L=N.
Rugby=10,500=11,000=11%=P1.10D=1.1=Idea=Brainchild=Inv.=11 Nov.=SC=Athena
    >>I=MT.
Rugged=10,000=1,000=100%=10.0=Physicality=Tech.=10 Oct.=Uranus=P=1Ø.
Ruhr=10,500=11,000=11%=P1.10D=1.1=Idea=Brainchild=Inv.=11 Nov.=SC=Athena>>I=MT.
Ruin=10,000=1,000=100%=10.0=Physicality=Tech.=10 Oct.=Uranus=P=1Ø.
Rule=10,000=1,000=100%=10.0=Physicality=Tech.=10 Oct.=Uranus=P=1Ø.
Rule of thumb=6,500=7,000=70%=P7.0D=7.0=Language=Assets=Mars=7 July=Pleiades.
Ruler=7,500=8,000=80%=P8.0D=Economy=Currency=8 Aug.=Zeus>>E=v.
Ruling=5,500=5.5=80%=P5.50=Earth-Midway=5 May = Gaia.
Rum=7,500=8,000=80%=P8.0D=Economy=Currency=8 Aug.=Zeus>>E=v.
Rumania=1,000=100%=10.0=1.0=Mind=Sun=1 January=Helios >> M=E4.
Rumba=4,000=40%=P4.0D=Govt.=Creat.=4 April=Mercury=Hermes=G=A4.
Rumble=10,000=1,000=100%=10.0=Physicality=Tech.=10 Oct.=Uranus=P=1Ø.
Rumen=5,000=50%=P5.00D=Law=Time=Venus=5 May = Aphrodite>>L=N.
Ruminant=10,000=1,000=100%=10.0=Physicality=Tech.=10 Oct.=Uranus=P=1Ø.
Ruminate=10,000=1,000=100%=10.0=Physicality=Tech.=10 Oct.=Uranus=P=1Ø.
Rummage=5,500=5.5=80%=P5.50=Earth-Midway=5 May = Gaia.
Rummage sale=3,500=4,000=40%=P4.0D=Creat.=4 April=Mercury=Hermes=G=A4.
Rummy=10,000=1,000=100%=10.0=Physicality=Tech.=10 Oct.=Uranus=P=1Ø.
Rumor=5,000=50%=P5.00D=Law=Time=Venus=5 May = Aphrodite>>L=N.
Rump=10,000=1,000=100%=10.0=Physicality=Tech.=10 Oct.=Uranus=P=1Ø.
Rumple=5,000=50%=P5.00D=Law=Time=Venus=5 May = Aphrodite>>L=N.
Rumpus=2,000=20%=P2.00D=2.0=Nature=Matter=Moon=2 Feb.=Cupid=N=C+_
Rumpus room=2,500=3,000=30%=P3.0D=3.0=Creativity=Stars=Muses=3 March = C=I
Run=10,000=1,000=100%=10.0=Physicality=Tech.=10 Oct.=Uranus=P=1Ø.
Runabout=3,500=4,000=40%=P4.0D=Govt.=Creat.=4 April=Mercury=Hermes=G=A4.
Runaround=4,500=5,000=50%=P5.00D=Law=Time=Venus=5 May = Aphrodite>>L=N.
Runaway=9,500=10,000=1,000=100%=10.0=Physicality=Tech.=10 Oct.=Uranus=P=1Ø.
Rundown=8,500=9,000=90%=P9.00D=9.0=Abstraction=Gods=Saturn=9Sept.>>A=Ø.
Rune=3,000=30%=P3.0D=3.0=Creativity=Stars=Muses=3 March = C=I>>GIL.
Rung1=7,000=70%=P7.0D=7.0=Language=Assets=Mars=7 July=Pleiades.
Rung2=2,000=20%=P2.00D=2.0=Nature=Matter=Moon=2 Feb.=Cupid=N=C+_
Run-in=2,000=20%=P2.00D=2.0=Nature=Matter=Moon=2 Feb.=Cupid=N=C+_
Runnel=5,000=50%=P5.00D=Law=Time=Venus=5 May = Aphrodite>>L=N.
Runner=10,000=1,000=100%=10.0=Physicality=Tech.=10 Oct.=Uranus=P=1Ø.
Runner up=2,500=3,000=30%=P3.0D=3.0=Creativity=Stars=Muses=3 March = C=I>>GIL.

Running=4,500=5,000=50%=P5.00D=Law=Time=Venus=5 May = Aphrodite>>L=N.
Running board=6,000=60%=P6.0D=Man=Earth=Royalty=6 June=Gaia=Maia>>M=M2.
Running light=7,000=70%=P7.0D=7.0=Language=Assets=Mars=7 July=Pleiades.
Runny=4,000=40%=P4.0D=Govt.=Creat.=4 April=Mercury=Hermes=G=A4.
Runnymede=9,000=90%=P9.00D=9.0=Abstraction=Gods=Saturn=9Sept.>>A=Ø.
Runoff=5,000=50%=P5.00D=Law=Time=Venus=5 May = Aphrodite>>L=N.
Run of the mill=1,500=15%=P1.50D=1.5=Authority=Solar Crown=1 May = Maia.
Runt=6,500=7,000=70%=P7.0D=7.0=Language=Assets=Mars=7 July=Pleiades.
Run through=3,500=4,000=40%=P4.0D=Govt.=Creat.=4 April=Mercury=Hermes=G=A4.
Runway=10,000=1,000=100%=10.0=Physicality=Tech.=10 Oct.=Uranus=P=1Ø.

Rupee=3,500=4,000=40%=P4.0D=Govt.=Creat.=4 April=Mercury=Hermes=G=A4.
<Skt.rúpya-, silver. Metric currency weight = 3.5/10=0.35>>35:1. See Naira. Dollar.

Rupiah=3,500=4,000=40%=P4.0D=Govt.=Creat.=4 April=Mercury=Hermes=G=A4.
[Hindi Rupiya, rupee]. Metric currency weight = 3.5/10=0.35>>35:1. See Naira. Dollar.

Rupture=7,500=8,000=80%=P8.0D=Economy=Currency=8 Aug.=Zeus>>E=v.
Rural=6,500=7,000=70%=P7.0D=7.0=Language=Assets=Mars=7 July=Pleiades.
Rus.=1,000=100%=10.0=1.0=Mind=Sun=1 January=Helios >> M=E4.
ruse=7,000=70%=P7.0D=7.0=Language=Assets=Mars=7 July=Pleiades.
Ruse=5,000=50%=P5.00D=Law=Time=Venus=5 May = Aphrodite>>L=N.
Rush1=10,000=1,000=100%=10.0=Physicality=Tech.=10 Oct.=Uranus=P=1Ø.
Rush2=8,500=9,000=90%=P9.00D=9.0=Abstraction=Gods=Saturn=9Sept.>>A=Ø.
Rushmore=10,000=1,000=100%=10.0=Physicality=Tech.=10 Oct.=Uranus=P=1Ø.
Rusk=6,000=60%=P6.0D=Man=Earth=Royalty=6 June=Gaia=Maia>>M=M2.

Russell Bertrand=5,500=5.5=80%=P5.50=Earth-Midway=5 May = Gaia.
3rd Earl Russell. 1872-1970. British philosopher and mathematician. Peter Matthews-Akukalia, Castle Makupedia Most Sovereign Emperor, Paradise Nations is the World's 1st Makumatician, 1st Computational Lexicographer, 1st Dicclopedysxt and Many Other Firsts.

Russet=8,500=9,000=90%=P9.00D=9.0=Abstraction=Gods=Saturn=9Sept.>>A=Ø.
Russia=10,000=1,000=100%=10.0=Physicality=Tech.=10 Oct.=Uranus=P=1Ø.
Russian=10,000=1,000=100%=10.0=Physicality=Tech.=10 Oct.=Uranus=P=1Ø.
Rust=10,000=1,000=100%=10.0=Physicality=Tech.=10 Oct.=Uranus=P=1Ø.
Rustic=8,000=80%=P8.0D=Economy=Currency=8 Aug.=Zeus>>E=v.
Rusticate=3,500=4,000=40%=P4.0D=Govt.=Creat.=4 April=Mercury=Hermes=G=A4.
Rustle=10,000=1,000=100%=10.0=Physicality=Tech.=10 Oct.=Uranus=P=1Ø.
Rut1=10,000=1,000=100%=10.0=Physicality=Tech.=10 Oct.=Uranus=P=1Ø.
Rut2=7,000=70%=P7.0D=7.0=Language=Assets=Mars=7 July=Pleiades.
Rutabaga=9,500=10,000=1,000=100%=10.0=Physicality=Tech.=10 Oct.=Uranus=P=1Ø.

Ruth=2,000=20%=P2.00D=2.0=Nature=Matter=Moon=2 Feb.=Cupid=N=C+_
Inspired by Artemis and Cupid (Eros). After all it is the story of love.

Ruth, George=4,000=40%=P4.0D=Govt.=Creat.=4 April=Mercury=Hermes=G=A4.
Ruthenia=4,500=5,000=50%=P5.00D=Law=Time=Venus=5 May = Aphrodite>>L=N.
Ruthenium=10,000=1,000=100%=10.0=Physicality=Tech.=10 Oct.=Uranus=P=1Ø.
Rutherford Ernest=3,500=4,000=40%=P4.0D=Creat.=4 April=Mercury=Hermes=G=A4.
Ruthless=4,500=5,000=50%=P5.00D=Law=Time=Venus=5 May = Aphrodite>>L=N.
Rutland=4,500=5,000=50%=P5.00D=Law=Time=Venus=5 May = Aphrodite>>L=N.
RV=4,000=40%=P4.0D=Govt.=Creat.=4 April=Mercury=Hermes=G=A4.
R-value=8,000=80%=P8.0D=Economy=Currency=8 Aug.=Zeus>>E=v.
Rwanda=5,000=50%=P5.00D=Law=Time=Venus=5 May = Aphrodite>>L=N.
rwy.=500=5%=P5.00D=5.0=Law=Time=Venus=5 May=Aphrodite>>L=N.
Rx=6,500=7,000=70%=P7.0D=7.0=Language=Assets=Mars=7 July=Pleiades.
-ry=2,000=20%=P2.00D=2.0=Nature=Matter=Moon=2 Feb.=Cupid=N=C+_
Ryazan=5,000=50%=P5.00D=Law=Time=Venus=5 May = Aphrodite>>L=N.
rye=10,000=1,000=100%=10.0=Physicality=Tech.=10 Oct.=Uranus=P=1Ø.
Ryukyu Islands=8,000=80%=P8.0D=Economy=Currency=8 Aug.=Zeus>>E=v.

MAKABET =Ss=

---

s1=3,500=4,000=40%=P4.0D=Govt.=Creatocracy=4 April=Mercury=Hermes=G=A4.
The 19th letter of the English alphabet. Computing the psycho - weight of S >>1935-1940
1.9*4.0x=px=5.9+7.6=13.5x=px=58.35=60=6.0. S is the benchmark for emotion inducing it
and awakening royalty once pronounced. S is an earth alphabet and 4th mind dimension.

---

s2=3,500=4,000=40%=P4.0D=Govt.=Creatocracy=4 April=Mercury=Hermes=G=A4.
S1=2,500=3,000=30%=P3.0D=3.0=Creativity=Stars=Muses=3 March = C=I>>GIL.
S2=1,000=100%=10.0=1.0=Mind=Sun=1 January=Helios >> M=E4.
s.=4,000=40%=P4.0D=Govt.=Creatocracy=4 April=Mercury=Hermes=G=A4.
-s1=3,000=30%=P3.0D=3.0=Creativity=Stars=Muses=3 March = C=I>>GIL.
-s2=11,000=11%=P1.10D=1.1=Idea=Brainchild=Inv.=11 Nov.=SC=Athena>>I=MT.
-s3=5,500=5.5=80%=P5.50=Earth-Midway=5 May = Gaia.
-'s=6,000=60%=P6.0D=Man=Earth=Royalty=6 June=Gaia=Maia>>M=M2.
Saar=9,000=90%=P9.00D=9.0=Abstraction=Gods=Saturn=9Sept.>>A=Ø.
Saarland=5,000=50%=P5.00D=Law=Time=Venus=5 May = Aphrodite>>L=N.
Sabbath=10,000=1,000=100%=10.0=Physicality=Tech.=10 Oct.=Uranus=P=1Ø.
Sabbatical year=10,000=1,000=100%=10.0=Physicality=Tech.=10 Oct.=Uranus=P=1Ø.
Saber=10,000=1,000=100%=10.0=Physicality=Tech.=10 Oct.=Uranus=P=1Ø.
Sabin Bruce=3,000=30%=P3.0D=3.0=Creativity=Stars=Muses=3 March = C=I>>GIL.
Sabine=6,500=7,000=70%=P7.0D=7.0=Language=Assets=Mars=7 July=Pleiades.

Sabine vaccine=7,000=70%=P7.0D=7.0=Language=Assets=Mars=7 July=Pleiades.
Sable=12,000=12%=P1.20D=1.2=Knowledge=Edu=12Dec.=Athena>>K=F.
Sabotage=10,000=1,000=100%=10.0=Physicality=Tech.=10 Oct.=Uranus=P=1Ø.
Saboteur=2,500=3,000=30%=P3.0D=3.0=Creativity=Stars=Muses=3 March = C=I>>GIL.
Sabra=4,000=40%=P4.0D=Govt.=Creatocracy=4 April=Mercury=Hermes=G=A4.
sac=4,500=5,000=50%=P5.00D=Law=Time=Venus=5 May = Aphrodite>>L=N.
Sac=1,500=15%=P1.50D=1.5=Authority=Solar Crown=1 May = Maia.
SAC=1,500=15%=P1.50D=1.5=Authority=Solar Crown=1 May = Maia.
Sacajawea=6,500=7,000=70%=P7.0D=7.0=Language=Assets=Mars=7 July=Pleiades.
Sacchar-=3,500=4,000=40%=P4.0D=Govt.=Creatocracy=4 April=Hermes=G=A4.
Saccharin=6,500=7,000=70%=P7.0D=7.0=Language=Assets=Mars=7 July=Pleiades.
Saccharine=3,500=4,000=40%=P4.0D=Govt.=Creatocracy=4 April=Hermes=G=A4.
Sacco Nicola.=3,500=4,000=40%=P4.0D=Govt.=Creatocracy=4 April=Hermes=G=A4.
Sacerdotal=5,000=50%=P5.00D=Law=Time=Venus=5 May = Aphrodite>>L=N.
Sachem=6,000=60%=P6.0D=Man=Earth=Royalty=6 June=Gaia=Maia>>M=M2.
Sachet=5,000=50%=P5.00D=Law=Time=Venus=5 May = Aphrodite>>L=N.
Sack1=10,000=1,000=100%=10.0=Physicality=Tech.=10 Oct.=Uranus=P=1Ø.
Sack2=5,000=50%=P5.00D=Law=Time=Venus=5 May = Aphrodite>>L=N.
Sackcloth=7,000=70%=P7.0D=7.0=Language=Assets=Mars=7 July=Pleiades.
Sacking=4,000=40%=P4.0D=Govt.=Creatocracy=4 April=Mercury=Hermes=G=A4.
sacra=1,500=15%=P1.50D=1.5=Authority=Solar Crown=1 May = Maia.
Sacra=10,000=1,000=100%=10.0=Physicality=Tech.=10 Oct.=Uranus=P=1Ø.
Sacrament=7,000=70%=P7.0D=7.0=Language=Assets=Mars=7 July=Pleiades.
Sacramento=7,000=70%=P7.0D=7.0=Language=Assets=Mars=7 July=Pleiades.
Sacramento River=7,500=8,000=80%=P8.0D=Economy=Currency=8 Aug.=Zeus>>E=v.
Sacred=10,000=1,000=100%=10.0=Physicality=Tech.=10 Oct.=Uranus=P=1Ø.
Sacred cow=2,000=20%=P2.00D=2.0=Nature=Matter=Moon=2 Feb.=Cupid=N=C+_
Sacrifice=10,000=1,000=100%=10.0=Physicality=Tech.=10 Oct.=Uranus=P=1Ø.
Sacrilege=5,000=50%=P5.00D=Law=Time=Venus=5 May = Aphrodite>>L=N.
Sacrilegious=9,500=10,000=1,000=100%=10.0=Physicality=Tech.=10 Oct.=Uranus=P=1Ø.
Sacristan=5,000=50%=P5.00D=Law=Time=Venus=5 May = Aphrodite>>L=N.
Sacristy=6,500=7,000=70%=P7.0D=7.0=Language=Assets=Mars=7 July=Pleiades.
Sacroiliac=7,000=70%=P7.0D=7.0=Language=Assets=Mars=7 July=Pleiades.
Sacrosanct=4,000=40%=P4.0D=Govt.=Creatocracy=4 April=Mercury=Hermes=G=A4.
Sacrum=6,000=60%=P6.0D=Man=Earth=Royalty=6 June=Gaia=Maia>>M=M2.
sad=6,000=60%=P6.0D=Man=Earth=Royalty=6 June=Gaia=Maia>>M=M2.
SAD=1,500=15%=P1.50D=1.5=Authority=Solar Crown=1 May = Maia.
Sadat Anwar el.=4,000=40%=P4.0D=Govt.=Creatocracy=4 April=Hermes=G=A4.
Sadden=2,500=3,000=30%=P3.0D=3.0=Creativity=Stars=Muses=3 March = C=I>>GIL.
Saddle=10,000=1,000=100%=10.0=Physicality=Tech.=10 Oct.=Uranus=P=1Ø.
Saddle bag=7,500=8,000=80%=P8.0D=Economy=Currency=8 Aug.=Zeus>>E=v.
Sadducee=9,000=90%=P9.00D=9.0=Abstraction=Gods=Saturn=9Sept.>>A=Ø.
Sade Comte=5,000=50%=P5.00D=Law=Time=Venus=5 May = Aphrodite>>L=N.
Sadhe=4,000=40%=P4.0D=Govt.=Creatocracy=4 April=Mercury=Hermes=G=A4.
Sadism=9,000=90%=P9.00D=9.0=Abstraction=Gods=Saturn=9Sept.>>A=Ø.

Sadomachism=6,500=7,000=70%=P7.0D=7.0=Language=Assets=Mars=7 July=Pleiades.
Safar=6,000=60%=P6.0D=Man=Earth=Royalty=6 June=Gaia=Maia>>M=M2.
Safari=5,000=50%=P5.00D=Law=Time=Venus=5 May = Aphrodite>>L=N.
Safe=10,000=1,000=100%=10.0=Physicality=Tech.=10 Oct.=Uranus=P=1Ø.
Safe conduct=6,000=60%=P6.0D=Man=Earth=Royalty=6 June=Gaia=Maia>>M=M2.
Safe cracker=2,500=3,000=30%=P3.0D=3.0=Cre=Stars=Muses=3 March = C=I>>GIL.
Safe deposit box=7,000=70%=P7.0D=7.0=Language=Assets=Mars=7 July=Pleiades.
Safeguard=5,500=5.5=80%=P5.50=Earth-Midway=5 May = Gaia.
Safekeeping=1,000=100%=10.0=1.0=Mind=Sun=1 January=Helios >> M=E4.
Safelight=6,000=60%=P6.0D=Man=Earth=Royalty=6 June=Gaia=Maia>>M=M2.
Safe sex=10,000=1,000=100%=10.0=Physicality=Tech.=10 Oct.=Uranus=P=1Ø.
Safety=10,000=1,000=100%=10.0=Physicality=Tech.=10 Oct.=Uranus=P=1Ø.
Safety belt=5,000=50%=P5.00D=Law=Time=Venus=5 May = Aphrodite>>L=N.
Safety glass=8,000=80%=P8.0D=Economy=Currency=8 Aug.=Zeus>>E=v.
Safety match=7,500=8,000=80%=P8.0D=Economy=Currency=8 Aug.=Zeus>>E=v.
Safety pin=7,000=70%=P7.0D=7.0=Language=Assets=Mars=7 July=Pleiades.
Safety razor=5,500=5.5=80%=P5.50=Earth-Midway=5 May = Gaia.
Safety valve=7,000=70%=P7.0D=7.0=Language=Assets=Mars=7 July=Pleiades.
Saf flower=8,000=80%=P8.0D=Economy=Currency=8 Aug.=Zeus>>E=v.
Saffron=11,500=12,000=12%=P1.20D=1.2=Knowledge=Edu=12Dec.=Athena>>K=F.
Sag=9,500=10,000=1,000=100%=10.0=Physicality=Tech.=10 Oct.=Uranus=P=1Ø.
Saga=8,000=80%=P8.0D=Economy=Currency=8 Aug.=Zeus>>E=v.
Sagacious=2,500=3,000=30%=P3.0D=3.0=Creativity=Stars=Muses=3 March = C=I>>GIL.
Sage1=5,500=5.5=80%=P5.50=Earth-Midway=5 May = Gaia.
Sage2=7,000=70%=P7.0D=7.0=Language=Assets=Mars=7 July=Pleiades.
Sagebrush=4,500=5,000=50%=P5.00D=Law=Time=Venus=5 May = Aphrodite>>L=N.
Sagittarius=5,500=5.5=80%=P5.50=Earth-Midway=5 May = Gaia.
Sago=8,000=80%=P8.0D=Economy=Currency=8 Aug.=Zeus>>E=v.
Saguaro=8,500=9,000=90%=P9.00D=9.0=Abstraction=Gods=Saturn=9Sept.>>A=Ø.
Sahaptin=7,500=8,000=80%=P8.0D=Economy=Currency=8 Aug.=Zeus>>E=v.
Sahara=10,000=1,000=100%=10.0=Physicality=Tech.=10 Oct.=Uranus=P=1Ø.
Sahel=5,500=5.5=80%=P5.50=Earth-Midway=5 May = Gaia.
Sahib=8,000=80%=P8.0D=Economy=Currency=8 Aug.=Zeus>>E=v.
Said=10,000=1,000=100%=10.0=Physicality=Tech.=10 Oct.=Uranus=P=1Ø.
Salgon=2,500=3,000=30%=P3.0D=3.0=Creativity=Stars=Muses=3 March = C=I>>GIL.
Sail=10,000=1,000=100%=10.0=Physicality=Tech.=10 Oct.=Uranus=P=1Ø.
Sailboard=3,500=4,000=40%=P4.0D=Govt.=Creatocracy=4 April=Hermes=G=A4.
Sailboat=5,500=5.5=80%=P5.50=Earth-Midway=5 May = Gaia.
Sailfish=7,500=8,000=80%=P8.0D=Economy=Currency=8 Aug.=Zeus>>E=v.
Sailor=7,000=70%=P7.0D=7.0=Language=Assets=Mars=7 July=Pleiades.
Sailplane=3,500=4,000=40%=P4.0D=Govt.=Creatocracy=4 April=Hermes=G=A4.
Saint=11,000=11%=P1.10D=1.1=Idea=Brainchild=Inv.=11 Nov.=SC=Athena>>I=MT.
Saint Augustine=8,500=9,000=90%=P9.00D=9.0=Abst.=Gods=Saturn=9Sept.>>A=Ø.
Saint Bernard=7,000=70%=P7.0D=7.0=Language=Assets=Mars=7 July=Pleiades.
Saint Catharines=5,000=50%=P5.00D=Law=Time=Venus=5 May = Aphrodite>>L=N.

Saint Christopher-Nevis=10,000=1,000=100%=10.0=Phy=Tech.=10 Oct.=Uranus=P=1Ø.
Saint Croix=6,500=7,000=70%=P7.0D=7.0=Language=Assets=Mars=7 July=Pleiades.
Saint Elias Mount.=9,500=10,000=1,000=100%=10.0=Phy=Tech.=10 Oct.=Uranus=P=1Ø.
Saint Elmo's fire=10,500=11,000=11%=P1.10D=1.1=Idea=Brchld.=11 Nov.=Athena>>I=MT.
Saint-Gaudens=3,500=4,000=40%=P4.0D=Govt.=Creatocracy=4 April=Hermes=G=A4.
Saint George's Channel=4,000=40%=P4.0D=Govt.=Creatocracy=4 April=Hermes=G=A4.
Saint Gotthard=5,000=50%=P5.00D=Law=Time=Venus=5 May = Aphrodite>>L=N.
Saint Helena=8,000=80%=P8.0D=Economy=Currency=8 Aug.=Zeus>>E=v.
Saint Helens,Mount=5,500=5.5=80%=P5.50=Earth-Midway=5 May = Gaia.
Saint John's=11,000=11%=P1.10D=1.1=Idea=Brainchild=Inv.=11 Nov.=SC=Athena>>I=MT.
Saint Kitts and Nevis=2,000=20%=P2,00D=2.0=Nature=Moon=2 Feb.=Cupid=N=C+_
Saint Laurent=4,500=5,000=50%=P5.00D=Law=Time=Venus=5 May = Aphrodite>>L=N.
Saint Lawrence=7,500=8,000=80%=P8.0D=Economy=Currency=8 Aug.=Zeus>>E=v.
Saint Lawrence River.=9,500=10,000=1,000=100%=10.0=Phy.=10 Oct.=Uranus=P=1Ø.
Saint Lawrence Seaway.=13,000=13%=P1.30=Solar Core=Faculty=13 January=Athena.
Saint Louis=5,500=5.5=80%=P5.50=Earth-Midway=5 May = Gaia.
Saint Lucia=8,000=80%=P8.0D=Economy=Currency=8 Aug.=Zeus>>E=v.
Saint Martin=5,500=5.5=80%=P5.50=Earth-Midway=5 May = Gaia.
Saint Paul=8,000=80%=P8.0D=Economy=Currency=8 Aug.=Zeus>>E=v.
Saint Petersburg=12,000=12%=P1.20D=1.2=Knowledge=Edu=12Dec.=Athena>>K=F.
Saint Pierre and Miquelon=8,000=80%=P8.0D=Economy=Currency=8 Aug.=Zeus>>E=v.
Saint-Saëns=3,000=30%=P3.0D=3.0=Creativity=Stars=Muses=3 March = C=I>>GIL.
Saint Thomas=7,000=70%=P7.0D=7.0=Language=Assets=Mars=7 July=Pleiades.

Saint valentines Day=5,500=5.5=80%=P5.50=Earth-Midway=5 May = Gaia.
February 14 energy details >> Day 14:Value: 5.0, Planetary Type:Venus, Human Type:Law, Birth Energy Level:83.3%. Computing the total value of lovers day = 5.0*5.5x=px=10.5+27.5=38x=px=326.75=33=3.3G
Saint Valentines Day is a product of genius instituted by the Holy Spirit >> The Host.
Sword of Honour: Days of St. Valentine by African Shakespeare. The first play on Saint Valentines Day ever was written by Peter Matthews-Akukalia published in 2011. The title of African Shakespeare was granted him because it is the first play from an African ever written in the Old Shakespearean English. In the book >> The Creatocracy Republic he authored a reloaded version of the same book. Hence it is believed that Shakespeare was incarnated in him whenever he wrote the Mind Arts or literatures. And the almighty incarnated him whenever he wrote the Sciences hence Castle Makupedia is a God.

Saint Vincent and Grenadines=7,500=8,000=80%=P8.0D=Econ=Cur=8 Aug.=Zeus>>E=v.
Saipan=5,000=50%=P5.00D=Law=Time=Venus=5 May = Aphrodite>>L=N.
Saith=4,000=40%=P4.0D=Govt.=Creatocracy=4 April=Mercury=Hermes=G=A4.
Sakai=6,000=60%=P6.0D=Man=Earth=Royalty=6 June=Gaia=Maia>>M=M2.
Sake1=6,000=60%=P6.0D=Man=Earth=Royalty=6 June=Gaia=Maia>>M=M2.
Sake2=4,000=40%=P4.0D=Govt.=Creatocracy=4 April=Mercury=Hermes=G=A4.
Sakhalin=6,000=60%=P6.0D=Man=Earth=Royalty=6 June=Gaia=Maia>>M=M2.

Sakharov Andre=5,500=5.5=80%=P5.50=Earth-Midway=5 May = Gaia.
Sal=1,500=15%=P1.50D=1.5=Authority=Solar Crown=1 May = Maia.
Salaam=10,500=11,000=11%=P1.10D=1.1=Idea=Brainchild=Inv.=11 Nov.=Athena>>I=MT.
Salacious=2,000=20%=P2.00D=2.0=Nature=Matter=Moon=2 Feb.=Cupid=N=C+_
Salad=9,000=90%=P9.00D=9.0=Abstraction=Gods=Saturn=9Sept.>>A=Ø.
Saladin=4,000=40%=P4.0D=Govt.=Creatocracy=4 April=Mercury=Hermes=G=A4.
Salamanca=5,000=50%=P5.00D=Law=Time=Venus=5 May = Aphrodite>>L=N.
Salamander=3,000=30%=P3.0D=3.0=Creativity=Stars=Muses=3 March = C=I>>GIL.
Salami=4,500=5,000=50%=P5.00D=Law=Time=Venus=5 May = Aphrodite>>L=N.
Salary=10,000=1,000=100%=10.0=Physicality=Tech.=10 Oct.=Uranus=P=1Ø.
Sale=10,000=1,000=100%=10.0=Physicality=Tech.=10 Oct.=Uranus=P=1Ø.
Salem=10,000=1,000=100%=10.0=Physicality=Tech.=10 Oct.=Uranus=P=1Ø.
Salerno=7,500=8,000=80%=P8.0D=Economy=Currency=8 Aug.=Zeus>>E=v.
Salesclerk=4,000=40%=P4.0D=Govt.=Creatocracy=4 April=Mercury=Hermes=G=A4.
Salesman=8,000=80%=P8.0D=Economy=Currency=8 Aug.=Zeus>>E=v.
Salesperson=2,000=20%=P2.00D=2.0=Nature=Matter=Moon=2 Feb.=Cupid=N=C+_
Sales tax=5,000=50%=P5.00D=Law=Time=Venus=5 May = Aphrodite>>L=N.
Saleswoman=7,500=8,000=80%=P8.0D=Economy=Currency=8 Aug.=Zeus>>E=v.
Salicylic acid=7,500=8,000=80%=P8.0D=Economy=Currency=8 Aug.=Zeus>>E=v.
Salient=6,500=7,000=70%=P7.0D=7.0=Language=Assets=Mars=7 July=Pleiades.
Salinas=4,500=5,000=50%=P5.00D=Law=Time=Venus=5 May = Aphrodite>>L=N.
Saline=3,000=30%=P3.0D=3.0=Creativity=Stars=Muses=3 March = C=I>>GIL.
Salinger Jerome=2,500=3,000=30%=P3.0D=3.0=Cr=Stars=Muses=3 March = C=I>>GIL.
Salisbury=9,500=10,000=1,000=100%=10.0=Physicality=Tech.=10 Oct.=Uranus=P=1Ø.
Salish=10,000=1,000=100%=10.0=Physicality=Tech.=10 Oct.=Uranus=P=1Ø.
Saliva=8,500=9,000=90%=P9.00D=9.0=Abstraction=Gods=Saturn=9Sept.>>A=Ø.
Salivate=2,500=3,000=30%=P3.0D=3.0=Creativity=Stars=Muses=3 March = C=I>>GIL.
Salk Jonas=2,500=3,000=30%=P3.0D=3.0=Creativity=Stars=Muses=3 March = C=I>>GIL.
Salk vaccine=7,000=70%=P7.0D=7.0=Language=Assets=Mars=7 July=Pleiades.
Sallow=3,500=4,000=40%=P4.0D=Govt.=Creatocracy=4 April=Mercury=Hermes=G=A4.
Sallust=4,000=40%=P4.0D=Govt.=Creatocracy=4 April=Mercury=Hermes=G=A4.
Sally=7,500=8,000=80%=P8.0D=Economy=Currency=8 Aug.=Zeus>>E=v.
Salmon=11,000=11%=P1.10D=1.1=Idea=Brainchild=Inv.=11 Nov.=SC=Athena>>I=MT.
Salmonella=12,000=12%=P1.20D=1.2=Knowledge=Edu=12Dec.=Athena>>K=F.
Salon=10,000=1,000=100%=10.0=Physicality=Tech.=10 Oct.=Uranus=P=1Ø.
Salonika=1,000=100%=10.0=1.0=Mind=Sun=1 January=Helios >> M=E4.
Saloon=5,500=5.5=80%=P5.50=Earth-Midway=5 May = Gaia.
Salsa=9,000=90%=P9.00D=9.0=Abstraction=Gods=Saturn=9Sept.>>A=Ø.
Salt=10,000=1,000=100%=10.0=Physicality=Tech.=10 Oct.=Uranus=P=1Ø.
SALT=2,000=20%=P2.00D=2.0=Nature=Matter=Moon=2 Feb.=Cupid=N=C+_
Saltcellar=4,000=40%=P4.0D=Govt.=Creatocracy=4 April=Mercury=Hermes=G=A4.
Saltine=2,000=20%=P2.00D=2.0=Nature=Matter=Moon=2 Feb.=Cupid=N=C+_
Salt Lake City=7,000=70%=P7.0D=7.0=Language=Assets=Mars=7 July=Pleiades.
Salt lick=5,000=50%=P5.00D=Law=Time=Venus=5 May = Aphrodite>>L=N.
Salt marsh=4,000=40%=P4.0D=Govt.=Creatocracy=4 April=Mercury=Hermes=G=A4.

Saltpeter=3,500=4,000=40%=P4.0D=Govt.=Creatocracy=4 April=Hermes=G=A4.

Salt shaker=3,000=30%=P3.0D=3.0=Creativity=Stars=Muses=3 March = C=I>>GIL.

Saltwater=3,000=30%=P3.0D=3.0=Creativity=Stars=Muses=3 March = C=I>>GIL.

Salubrious=4,500=5,000=50%=P5.00D=Law=Time=Venus=5 May = Aphrodite>>L=N.

Salutary=3,500=4,000=40%=P4.0D=Govt.=Creatocracy=4 April=Mercury=Hermes=G=A4.

Salutation=3,500=4,000=40%=P4.0D=Govt.=Creatocracy=4 April=Hermes=G=A4.

Salutatorian=8,000=80%=P8.0D=Economy=Currency=8 Aug.=Zeus>>E=v.

Salute=8,000=80%=P8.0D=Economy=Currency=8 Aug.=Zeus>>E=v.

Salvador=6,500=7,000=70%=P7.0D=7.0=Language=Assets=Mars=7 July=Pleiades.

Salvadoran=3,500=4,000=40%=P4.0D=Govt.=Creatocracy=4 April=Hermes=G=A4.

Salvage=10,000=1,000=100%=10.0=Physicality=Tech.=10 Oct.=Uranus=P=1Ø.

Salvation=10,000=1,000=100%=10.0=Physicality=Tech.=10 Oct.=Uranus=P=1Ø.

Salve=8,000=80%=P8.0D=Economy=Currency=8 Aug.=Zeus>>E=v.

Salver=4,000=40%=P4.0D=Govt.=Creatocracy=4 April=Mercury=Hermes=G=A4.

Salvia=7,500=8,000=80%=P8.0D=Economy=Currency=8 Aug.=Zeus>>E=v.

Salvo=4,500=5,000=50%=P5.00D=Law=Time=Venus=5 May = Aphrodite>>L=N.

Salween=9,000=90%=P9.00D=9.0=Abstraction=Gods=Saturn=9Sept.>>A=Ø.

Salzburg=5,000=50%=P5.00D=Law=Time=Venus=5 May = Aphrodite>>L=N.

SAM=2,000=20%=P2.00D=2.0=Nature=Matter=Moon=2 Feb.=Cupid=N=C+_

Samaria=5,500=5.5=80%=P5.50=Earth-Midway=5 May = Gaia.

Samaritan=4,000=40%=P4.0D=Govt.=Creatocracy=4 April=Mercury=Hermes=G=A4.

Samarium=10,000=1,000=100%=10.0=Physicality=Tech.=10 Oct.=Uranus=P=1Ø.

Samarkand=4,500=5,000=50%=P5.00D=Law=Time=Venus=5 May = Aphrodite>>L=N.

Samba=5,500=5.5=80%=P5.50=Earth-Midway=5 May = Gaia.

Same=10,000=1,000=100%=10.0=Physicality=Tech.=10 Oct.=Uranus=P=1Ø.

Samekh=4,000=40%=P4.0D=Govt.=Creatocracy=4 April=Mercury=Hermes=G=A4.

Samoa=8,000=80%=P8.0D=Economy=Currency=8 Aug.=Zeus>>E=v.

Samoset=6,000=60%=P6.0D=Man=Earth=Royalty=6 June=Gaia=Maia>>M=M2.

Samovar=6,000=60%=P6.0D=Man=Earth=Royalty=6 June=Gaia=Maia>>M=M2.

Samoyed=10,000=1,000=100%=10.0=Physicality=Tech.=10 Oct.=Uranus=P=1Ø.

Sampan=4,000=40%=P4.0D=Govt.=Creatocracy=4 April=Mercury=Hermes=G=A4.

Sample=10,000=1,000=100%=10.0=Physicality=Tech.=10 Oct.=Uranus=P=1Ø.

Sampler=6,500=7,000=70%=P7.0D=7.0=Language=Assets=Mars=7 July=Pleiades.

Sampling=1,500=15%=P1.50D=1.5=Authority=Solar Crown=1 May = Maia.

Samson=5,500=5.5=80%=P5.50=Earth-Midway=5 May = Gaia.

Bible. Samson had seven locks of hair. 5.5*7.0x=px=12.5+38.5=51x=px=532.25. Now 53=5.3>> Copyright. 2.2>>4.0>>Hermes. 22-25 indicated that Samson was about this age when he began to rule as a judge in Israel perhaps he had began doing things before then. Samson was inspired to royalty by Gaia, managed by Hermes and strengthen by Aries. The signs or codes will definitely be seen through details of his life in the scriptures for example when Samson was 40years indicates the code 40>>4.0>>Hermes >> Mercury >> Power.

Samuel=6,500=7,000=70%=P7.0D=7.0=Language=Assets=Mars=7 July=Pleiades.
Bible book inspired by Gaia as a means to reach and understand the link between emotion and computational measures as a means to reach precision and become an Aries.

Samurai=6,000=60%=P6.0D=Man=Earth=Royalty=6 June=Gaia=Maia>>M=M2.
San=7,000=70%=P7.0D=7.0=Language=Assets=Mars=7 July=Pleiades.
Sana=5,000=50%=P5.00D=Law=Time=Venus=5 May = Aphrodite>>L=N.
San Antonio=5,000=50%=P5.00D=Law=Time=Venus=5 May = Aphrodite>>L=N.
Sanatorium=10,000=1,000=100%=10.0=Physicality=Tech.=10 Oct.=Uranus=P=1Ø.
San Bernardino=5,000=50%=P5.00D=Law=Time=Venus=5 May = Aphrodite>>L=N.
Sanctify=10,000=1,000=100%=10.0=Physicality=Tech.=10 Oct.=Uranus=P=1Ø.
Sanctimony=10,000=1,000=100%=10.0=Physicality=Tech.=10 Oct.=Uranus=P=1Ø.
Sanction=10,000=1,000=100%=10.0=Physicality=Tech.=10 Oct.=Uranus=P=1Ø.

Sanctity=5,000=50%=P5.00D=Law=Time=Venus=5 May = Aphrodite>>L=N.
See Terrorism. Makupedia protects the sanctity of human life.

Sanctuary=9,000=90%=P9.00D=9.0=Abstraction=Gods=Saturn=9Sept.>>A=Ø.
Sanctum=5,000=50%=P5.00D=Law=Time=Venus=5 May = Aphrodite>>L=N.
sand=12,000=12%=P1.20D=1.2=Knowledge=Edu=12Dec.=Athena>>K=F.
Sand George.=5,000=50%=P5.00D=Law=Time=Venus=5 May = Aphrodite>>L=N.
Sandal=10,000=1,000=100%=10.0=Physicality=Tech.=10 Oct.=Uranus=P=1Ø.
Sandalwood=8,000=80%=P8.0D=Economy=Currency=8 Aug.=Zeus>>E=v.
Sandbag=10,000=1,000=100%=10.0=Physicality=Tech.=10 Oct.=Uranus=P=1Ø.
Sandbar=5,000=50%=P5.00D=Law=Time=Venus=5 May = Aphrodite>>L=N.
Sandblast=7,500=8,000=80%=P8.0D=Economy=Currency=8 Aug.=Zeus>>E=v.
Sandbox=5,000=50%=P5.00D=Law=Time=Venus=5 May = Aphrodite>>L=N.
Sandburg Carl.=2,000=20%=P2.00D=2.0=Nature=Matter=Moon=2 Feb.=Cupid=N=C+_
Sand dollar=7,000=70%=P7.0D=7.0=Language=Assets=Mars=7 July=Pleiades.
Sand hog=7,000=70%=P7.0D=7.0=Language=Assets=Mars=7 July=Pleiades.
San Diego=9,000=90%=P9.00D=9.0=Abstraction=Gods=Saturn=9Sept.>>A=Ø.
S&L=2,000=20%=P2.00D=2.0=Nature=Matter=Moon=2 Feb.=Cupid=N=C+_
Sandlot=4,500=5,000=50%=P5.00D=Law=Time=Venus=5 May = Aphrodite>>L=N.
Sandman=7,000=70%=P7.0D=7.0=Language=Assets=Mars=7 July=Pleiades.
Sandpaper=7,000=70%=P7.0D=7.0=Language=Assets=Mars=7 July=Pleiades.
Sandpiper=4,500=5,000=50%=P5.00D=Law=Time=Venus=5 May = Aphrodite>>L=N.
Sandstone=8,000=80%=P8.0D=Economy=Currency=8 Aug.=Zeus>>E=v.
Sandstorm=4,500=5,000=50%=P5.00D=Law=Time=Venus=5 May = Aphrodite>>L=N.
Sand trap=5,500=5.5=80%=P5.50=Earth-Midway=5 May = Gaia.
Sandwich=13,000=13%=P1.30=Solar Core=Faculty=13 January=Athena.
Sane=3,000=30%=P3.0D=3.0=Creativity=Stars=Muses=3 March = C=I>>GIL.
San Fernando do Valley=5,000=50%=P5.00D=Law=Time=Venus=5 May =Odite>>L=N.
San Francisco=10,000=1,000=100%=10.0=Physicality=Tech.=10 Oct.=Uranus=P=1Ø.
Sang=2,000=20%=P2.00D=2.0=Nature=Matter=Moon=2 Feb.=Cupid=N=C+_

Sang-froid=2,000=20%=P2.00D=2.0=Nature=Matter=Moon=2 Feb.=Cupid=N=C+_
Sangria=9,000=90%=P9.00D=9.0=Abstraction=Gods=Saturn=9Sept.>>A=Ø.
Sanguinary=4,000=40%=P4.0D=Govt.=Creatocracy=4 April=Mercury=Hermes=G=A4.
Sanguine=6,000=60%=P6.0D=Man=Earth=Royalty=6 June=Gaia=Maia>>M=M2.
Sanguineous=6,000=60%=P6.0D=Man=Earth=Royalty=6 June=Gaia=Maia>>M=M2.
Sanitarium=2,500=3,000=30%=P3.0D=3.0=Creativity=Stars=Muses=3 March = C=I>>GIL.
Sanitary=3,500=4,000=40%=P4.0D=Govt.=Creatocracy=4 April=Mercury=Hermes=G=A4.
Sanitary landfill=5,000=50%=P5.00D=Law=Time=Venus=5 May = Aphrodite>>L=N.
Sanitary napkin=5,500=5.5=80%=P5.50=Earth-Midway=5 May = Gaia.
Sanitation=6,000=60%=P6.0D=Man=Earth=Royalty=6 June=Gaia=Maia>>M=M2.
Sanitize=8,000=80%=P8.0D=Economy=Currency=8 Aug.=Zeus>>E=v.
Sanity=3,500=4,000=40%=P4.0D=Govt.=Creatocracy=4 April=Mercury=Hermes=G=A4.
San Joaquin=9,500=10,000=1,000=100%=10.0=Physicality=Tech.=10 Oct.=Uranus=P=1Ø.
San Jose=5,000=50%=P5.00D=Law=Time=Venus=5 May = Aphrodite>>L=N.
San José=5,500=5.5=80%=P5.50=Earth-Midway=5 May = Gaia.
San Juan=6,500=7,000=70%=P7.0D=7.0=Language=Assets=Mars=7 July=Pleiades.
Sank=2,000=20%=P2.00D=2.0=Nature=Matter=Moon=2 Feb.=Cupid=N=C+_
San Luis Potosí=4,500=5,000=50%=P5.00D=Law=Time=Venus=5 May=Aphrodite>>L=N.
San Marino=10,000=1,000=100%=10.0=Physicality=Tech.=10 Oct.=Uranus=P=1Ø.
San Miguel de Tuc.=4,500=5,000=50%=P5.00D=Law=Time=Venus=5 May=Odite>>L=N.
San Salvador=6,000=60%=P6.0D=Man=Earth=Royalty=6 June=Gaia=Maia>>M=M2.
Sanskrit=6,000=60%=P6.0D=Man=Earth=Royalty=6 June=Gaia=Maia>>M=M2.
Santa Ana1=7,000=70%=P7.0D=7.0=Language=Assets=Mars=7 July=Pleiades.
Santa Ana2=11,000=11%=P1.10D=1.1=Idea=Brainchild=Inv.=11 Nov.=SC=Athena>>I=MT.
Santa Anna Antonio=5,000=50%=P5.00D=Law=Time=Venus=5 May = Aphrodite>>L=N.
Santa Clara=4,500=5,000=50%=P5.00D=Law=Time=Venus=5 May = Aphrodite>>L=N.
Santa Claus=11,000=11%=P1.10D=1.1=Idea=Brainchild=Inv.=11 Nov.=SC=Athena>>I=MT.
Santa Cruz=4,500=5,000=50%=P5.00D=Law=Time=Venus=5 May = Aphrodite>>L=N.
SantaCruz deTenerife=6,500=7,000=70%=P7.0D=7.0=Lang=Assets=Mars=7July=Pleiades.
Santa Fe=6,000=60%=P6.0D=Man=Earth=Royalty=6 June=Gaia=Maia>>M=M2.
Santa Fe Trail.=10,000=1,000=100%=10.0=Physicality=Tech.=10 Oct.=Uranus=P=1Ø.
Santa Rosa=5,000=50%=P5.00D=Law=Time=Venus=5 May = Aphrodite>>L=N.
Santayana George.=3,000=30%=P3.0D=3.0=Cre=Stars=Muses=3 March = C=I>>GIL.
Santee=7,500=8,000=80%=P8.0D=Economy=Currency=8 Aug.=Zeus>>E=v.
Santiago=10,000=1,000=100%=10.0=Physicality=Tech.=10 Oct.=Uranus=P=1Ø.
Santiago de Cuba=6,500=7,000=70%=P7.0D=7.0=Lang=Assets=Mars=7July=Pleiades.
Santo Domingo=6,500=7,000=70%=P7.0D=7.0=Lang=Assets=Mars=7 July=Pleiades.
São Francisco=7,000=70%=P7.0D=7.0=Language=Assets=Mars=7 July=Pleiades.
Saône=10,000=1,000=100%=10.0=Physicality=Tech.=10 Oct.=Uranus=P=1Ø.
São Paulo=5,500=5.5=80%=P5.50=Earth-Midway=5 May = Gaia.
São Tomé=7,000=70%=P7.0D=7.0=Language=Assets=Mars=7 July=Pleiades.
São Tomé and Príncipe=8,000=80%=P8.0D=Economy=Currency=8 Aug.=Zeus>>E=v.
Sap1=10,000=1,000=100%=10.0=Physicality=Tech.=10 Oct.=Uranus=P=1Ø.
Sap2=7,500=8,000=80%=P8.0D=Economy=Currency=8 Aug.=Zeus>>E=v.
Saphar=1,500=15%=P1.50D=1.5=Authority=Solar Crown=1 May = Maia.

Sapient=3,500=4,000=40%=P4.0D=Govt.=Creatocracy=4 April=Mercury=Hermes=G=A4.
Sapling=1,500=15%=P1.50D=1.5=Authority=Solar Crown=1 May = Maia.
Sapodilla=10,000=1,000=100%=10.0=Physicality=Tech.=10 Oct.=Uranus=P=1Ø.
Saponification=10,000=1,000=100%=10.0=Physicality=Tech.=10 Oct.=Uranus=P=1Ø.
Saponify=8,000=80%=P8.0D=Economy=Currency=8 Aug.=Zeus>>E=v.
Sapper=1,500=15%=P1.50D=1.5=Authority=Solar Crown=1 May = Maia.
Sapphire=10,000=1,000=100%=10.0=Physicality=Tech.=10 Oct.=Uranus=P=1Ø.
Sappho=3,500=4,000=40%=P4.0D=Govt.=Creatocracy=4 April=Mercury=Hermes=G=A4.
Sapporo=6,500=7,000=70%=P7.0D=7.0=Language=Assets=Mars=7 July=Pleiades.
Sappy=3,500=4,000=40%=P4.0D=Govt.=Creatocracy=4 April=Mercury=Hermes=G=A4.
Saprophyte=10,000=1,000=100%=10.0=Physicality=Tech.=10 Oct.=Uranus=P=1Ø.
Sapsucker=7,500=8,000=80%=P8.0D=Economy=Currency=8 Aug.=Zeus>>E=v.
Saracen=10,000=1,000=100%=10.0=Physicality=Tech.=10 Oct.=Uranus=P=1Ø.
Saragossa=6,500=7,000=70%=P7.0D=7.0=Language=Assets=Mars=7 July=Pleiades.

Sarah=4,500=5,000=50%=P5.00D=Law=Time=Venus=5 May = Aphrodite>>L=N.
Sarah was a means of Hermes reaching the objectives set out by Aphrodite. She was the borderline between power and authority, politics and law, media and judiciary. She was the incarnation of Aphrodite and the guinea pig to try prolonged fertility concerns at old age. Note that Odite is the Goddess of fertility so the age of Sarah and Abraham was an experimental period for the Gods to perfect their arts skills knowledge and process in Man.

Sarajevo= 5,500=5.5=80%=P5.50=Earth-Midway=5 May = Gaia.
Saran=10,000=1,000=100%=10.0=Physicality=Tech.=10 Oct.=Uranus=P=1Ø.
Sarape=1,500=15%=P1.50D=1.5=Authority=Solar Crown=1 May = Maia.
Saratov=6,500=7,000=70%=P7.0D=7.0=Language=Assets=Mars=7 July=Pleiades.
Sarawak=3,500=4,000=40%=P4.0D=Govt.=Creatocracy=4 April=Hermes=G=A4.
Sarcasm=5,500=5.5=80%=P5.50=Earth-Midway=5 May = Gaia.
Sarcoma=5,500=5.5=80%=P5.50=Earth-Midway=5 May = Gaia.
Sarcophagus=2,500=3,000=30%=P3.0D=3.0=Cre=Stars=Muses=3 March = C=I>>GIL.
Sardine=6,000=60%=P6.0D=Man=Earth=Royalty=6 June=Gaia=Maia>>M=M2.
Sardinia=4,500=5,000=50%=P5.00D=Law=Time=Venus=5 May = Aphrodite>>L=N.
Sardis=6,000=60%=P6.0D=Man=Earth=Royalty=6 June=Gaia=Maia>>M=M2.
Sardonic=2,000=20%=P2.00D=2.0=Nature=Matter=Moon=2 Feb.=Cupid=N=C+_
Sargasso=2,500=3,000=30%=P3.0D=3.0=Creativity=Stars=Muses=3 March = C=I>>GIL.
Sargasso Sea=6,000=60%=P6.0D=Man=Earth=Royalty=6 June=Gaia=Maia>>M=M2.
Sargent,John=2,500=3,000=30%=P3.0D=3.0=Cre=Stars=Muses=3 March = C=I>>GIL.
Sargon II=3,000=30%=P3.0D=3.0=Creativity=Stars=Muses=3 March = C=I>>GIL.
Sari=7,500=8,000=80%=P8.0D=Economy=Currency=8 Aug.=Zeus>>E=v.
Sarmatia=5,000=50%=P5.00D=Law=Time=Venus=5 May = Aphrodite>>L=N.
Sarong=11,500=12,000=12%=P1.20D=1.2=Knowledge=Edu=12Dec.=Athena>>K=F.
Saroyan,William.=2,000=20%=P2.00D=2.0=Nature=Matter=Moon=2 Feb.=Cupid=N=C+_
Sarsaparilla=10,000=1,000=100%=10.0=Physicality=Tech.=10 Oct.=Uranus=P=1Ø.
Sartorial=4,500=5,000=50%=P5.00D=Law=Time=Venus=5 May = Aphrodite>>L=N.

Sartre Jean Paul=5,000=50%=P5.00D=Law=Time=Venus=5 May = Aphrodite>>L=N.
SASE=2,000=20%=P2.00D=2.0=Nature=Matter=Moon=2 Feb.=Cupid=N=C+_
Sash1=7,000=70%=P7.0D=7.0=Language=Assets=Mars=7 July=Pleiades.
Sash2=8,000=80%=P8.0D=Economy=Currency=8 Aug.=Zeus>>E=v.
Sashay=6,000=60%=P6.0D=Man=Earth=Royalty=6 June=Gaia=Maia>>M=M2.
Sask.=500=5%=P5.00D=5.0=Law=Time=Venus=5 May=Aphrodite>>L=N.
Saskatchewan=5,000=50%=P5.00D=Law=Time=Venus=5 May = Aphrodite>>L=N.
Saskatchewan River.=5,500=5.5=80%=P5.50=Earth-Midway=5 May = Gaia.
Saskatoon=5,000=50%=P5.00D=Law=Time=Venus=5 May = Aphrodite>>L=N.
Sasquatch=1,000=100%=10.0=1.0=Mind=Sun=1 January=Helios >> M=E4.
Sass=2,000=20%=P2.00D=2.0=Nature=Matter=Moon=2 Feb.=Cupid=N=C+_
Sassafras=10,000=1,000=100%=10.0=Physicality=Tech.=10 Oct.=Uranus=P=1Ø.
Sassy=2,500=3,000=30%=P3.0D=3.0=Creativity=Stars=Muses=3 March = C=I>>GIL.
Sat=3,000=30%=P3.0D=3.0=Creativity=Stars=Muses=3 March = C=I>>GIL.
SAT=3,000=30%=P3.0D=3.0=Creativity=Stars=Muses=3 March = C=I>>GIL.
Sat.=500=5%=P5.00D=5.0=Law=Time=Venus=5 May=Aphrodite>>L=N.
Satan=2,000=20%=P2.00D=2.0=Nature=Matter=Moon=2 Feb.=Cupid=N=C+_

Satang=3,000=30%=P3.0D=3.0=Creativity=Stars=Muses=3 March = C=I>>GIL.
Thai satān. Currency Metric weight >> 3/10=0.3 >> 30:1. See Naira. Dollar.

Satanic=4,500=5,000=50%=P5.00D=Law=Time=Venus=5 May = Aphrodite>>L=N.
Satchel=5,000=50%=P5.00D=Law=Time=Venus=5 May = Aphrodite>>L=N.
Sate=4,000=40%=P4.0D=Govt.=Creatocracy=4 April=Mercury=Hermes=G=A4.
Sateen=3,500=4,000=40%=P4.0D=Govt.=Creatocracy=4 April=Mercury=Hermes=G=A4.

Satellite=10,000=1,000=100%=10.0=Physicality=Tech.=10 Oct.=Uranus=P=1Ø.
Peter Matthews-Akukalia, Castle Makupedia invented a satellite data tracking system for discovering the cosmic or planetary origin of a person used in the Mind Assessment Test. Peter Matthews-Akukalia himself is from Mare Imbrium, the Sea of Showers being the core reason he is gifted with the knowledge of particulate cosmic energy, rainfalls and lightning. The satellite data tracking system was invented after he did 6million computations and 15million programming on lunar computing. It is useful to create frequency based programs for radio and television broadcast industry in the planetary energy matrix. It is also useful for developing appropriate license codes for the telecommunications industry eg *556# is inappropriate but *553# is correct. See the page>> A message from Castle Makupedia.

Satiate=5,000=50%=P5.00D=Law=Time=Venus=5 May = Aphrodite>>L=N.
Satiety=3,500=4,000=40%=P4.0D=Govt.=Creatocracy=4 April=Mercury=Hermes=G=A4.
Satin=2,500=3,000=30%=P3.0D=3.0=Creativity=Stars=Muses=3 March = C=I>>GIL.
Satinwood=5,500=5.5=80%=P5.50=Earth-Midway=5 May = Gaia.
Satire=10,000=1,000=100%=10.0=Physicality=Tech.=10 Oct.=Uranus=P=1Ø.
Satirize=3,000=30%=P3.0D=3.0=Creativity=Stars=Muses=3 March = C=I>>GIL.

Satisfaction=9,000=90%=P9.00D=9.0=Abstraction=Gods=Saturn=9Sept.>>A=Ø.
Satisfactory=1,500=15%=P1.50D=1.5=Authority=Solar Crown=1 May = Maia.
Satisfy=10,000=1,000=100%=10.0=Physicality=Tech.=10 Oct.=Uranus=P=1Ø.
Satrap=4,500=5,000=50%=P5.00D=Law=Time=Venus=5 May = Aphrodite>>L=N.
Saturate=10,000=1,000=100%=10.0=Physicality=Tech.=10 Oct.=Uranus=P=1Ø.
Saturated fat=10,000=1,000=100%=10.0=Physicality=Tech.=10 Oct.=Uranus=P=1Ø.
Saturday=3,500=4,000=40%=P4.0D=Govt.=Creatocracy=4 April=Hermes=G=A4.

Saturn=10,000=1,000=100%=10.0=Physicality=Tech.=10 Oct.=Uranus=P=1Ø.
Roman myth. The God of agriculture. The second largest planet in the solar system. Hence agriculture is the second resource of nature. The Creatocracy asserts that knowledge is the first need of man. A need to be born and to be aware. The second is food.

Saturnine=1,500=15%=P1.50D=1.5=Authority=Solar Crown=1 May = Maia.

Satyr=10,000=1,000=100%=10.0=Physicality=Tech.=10 Oct.=Uranus=P=1Ø.
Greek myth. A woodland creature depicted as having the ears, legs, and horns of a goat.

Sauce=10,000=1,000=100%=10.0=Physicality=Tech.=10 Oct.=Uranus=P=1Ø.
Saucepan=3,000=30%=P3.0D=3.0=Creativity=Stars=Muses=3 March = C=I>>GIL.
Saucer=5,500=5.5=80%=P5.50=Earth-Midway=5 May = Gaia.
Saucy=2,000=20%=P2.00D=2.0=Nature=Matter=Moon=2 Feb.=Cupid=N=C+_
Saudi Arabia=6,000=60%=P6.0D=Man=Earth=Royalty=6 June=Gaia=Maia>>M=M2.
Sauerbraten=7,500=8,000=80%=P8.0D=Economy=Currency=8 Aug.=Zeus>>E=v.
Sauerkraut=5,000=50%=P5.00D=Law=Time=Venus=5 May = Aphrodite>>L=N.
Sauk=9,500=10,000=1,000=100%=10.0=Physicality=Tech.=10 Oct.=Uranus=P=1Ø.
Saul=4,500=5,000=50%=P5.00D=Law=Time=Venus=5 May = Aphrodite>>L=N.
Sault Salute Maria=6,000=60%=P6.0D=Man=Earth=Royalty=6 June=Gaia=Maia>>M=M2.
Sauna=9,500=10,000=1,000=100%=10.0=Physicality=Tech.=10 Oct.=Uranus=P=1Ø.

Saunter=6,000=60%=P6.0D=Man=Earth=Royalty=6 June=Gaia=Maia>>M=M2.
To walk at a leisurely pace. A leisurely stroll. Prob.<ME santren, muse. So muses saunter. We then conclude that persons incarnated by muses will naturally love a lot of walks and strolls. A good reason why Peter Matthews-Akukalia was not allowed to drive a long time. It also means that strolling induces inspiration to the person involved as gifts from the muses.

Sausage=7,000=70%=P7.0D=7.0=Language=Assets=Mars=7 July=Pleiades.
Sauté=4,000=40%=P4.0D=Govt.=Creatocracy=4 April=Mercury=Hermes=G=A4.
Sauternes=4,000=40%=P4.0D=Govt.=Creatocracy=4 April=Mercury=Hermes=G=A4.
Savage=10,000=1,000=100%=10.0=Physicality=Tech.=10 Oct.=Uranus=P=1Ø.
savanna=5,000=50%=P5.00D=Law=Time=Venus=5 May = Aphrodite>>L=N.
Savannah=8,500=9,000=90%=P9.00D=9.0=Abstraction=Gods=Saturn=9Sept.>>A=Ø.

Savant=3,000=30%=P3.0D=3.0=Creativity=Stars=Muses=3 March = C=I>>GIL.
Save1=10,000=1,000=100%=10.0=Physicality=Tech.=10 Oct.=Uranus=P=1Ø.
Save2=5,000=50%=P5.00D=Law=Time=Venus=5 May = Aphrodite>>L=N.
Saving=7,000=70%=P7.0D=7.0=Language=Assets=Mars=7 July=Pleiades.
Savings account=3,000=30%=P3.0D=3.0=Creativity=Stars=Muses=3 March = C=I>>GIL.
Savings and loan association=5,500=5.5=80%=P5.50=Earth-Midway=5 May = Gaia.
Savings bank=5,000=50%=P5.00D=Law=Time=Venus=5 May = Aphrodite>>L=N.
Savior=6,000=60%=P6.0D=Man=Earth=Royalty=6 June=Gaia=Maia>>M=M2.
Savoir-faire=2,500=3,000=30%=P3.0D=3.0=Cre=Stars=Muses=3 March = C=I>>GIL.
Savonarola=2,500=3,000=30%=P3.0D=3.0=Cre=Stars=Muses=3 March = C=I>>GIL.
Savor=10,000=1,000=100%=10.0=Physicality=Tech.=10 Oct.=Uranus=P=1Ø.
Savory1=4,500=5,000=50%=P5.00D=Law=Time=Venus=5 May = Aphrodite>>L=N.
Savory2=4,500=5,000=50%=P5.00D=Law=Time=Venus=5 May = Aphrodite>>L=N.
Savoy=7,000=70%=P7.0D=7.0=Language=Assets=Mars=7 July=Pleiades.
Savvy=7,500=8,000=80%=P8.0D=Economy=Currency=8 Aug.=Zeus>>E=v.
Saw1=13,000=13%=P1.30=Solar Core=Faculty=13 January=Athena.
Saw2=4,500=5,000=50%=P5.00D=Law=Time=Venus=5 May = Aphrodite>>L=N.
Saw3=2,000=20%=P2.00D=2.0=Nature=Matter=Moon=2 Feb.=Cupid=N=C+_
Sawdust=4,000=40%=P4.0D=Govt.=Creatocracy=4 April=Mercury=Hermes=G=A4.
Sawed-off=5,000=50%=P5.00D=Law=Time=Venus=5 May = Aphrodite>>L=N.
Sawfish=8,500=9,000=90%=P9.00D=9.0=Abstraction=Gods=Saturn=9Sept.>>A=Ø.
Sawhorse=5,000=50%=P5.00D=Law=Time=Venus=5 May = Aphrodite>>L=N.
Sawmill=4,000=40%=P4.0D=Govt.=Creatocracy=4 April=Mercury=Hermes=G=A4.
Sawn=2,000=20%=P2.00D=2.0=Nature=Matter=Moon=2 Feb.=Cupid=N=C+_
Sawyer=3,500=4,000=40%=P4.0D=Govt.=Creatocracy=4 April=Mercury=Hermes=G=A4.
Sax=1,000=100%=10.0=1.0=Mind=Solar Energy.=1 January.=Helios=M=E4.
Saxifrage=9,000=90%=P9.00D=9.0=Abstraction=Gods=Saturn=9Sept.>>A=Ø.
Saxon=11,000=11%=P1.10D=1.1=Idea=Brainchild=Inv.=11 Nov.=SC=Athena>>I=MT.
Saxony=3,000=30%=P3.0D=3.0=Creativity=Stars=Muses=3 March = C=I>>GIL.

Say=10,000=1,000=100%=10.0=Physicality=Tech.=10 Oct.=Uranus=P=1Ø.
To say means to understand the value of what is to be said.

Sayers Dorothy=2,500=3,000=30%=P3.0D=3.0=Cr=Stars=Muses=3 March = C=I>>GIL.
Saying=2,000=20%=P2.00D=2.0=Nature=Matter=Moon=2 Feb.=Cupid=N=C+_
Sayonara=2,000=20%=P2.00D=2.0=Nature=Matter=Moon=2 Feb.=Cupid=N=C+_

Say so=7,000=70%=P7.0D=7.0=Language=Assets=Mars=7 July=Pleiades.
"To say so" means to be computationally precise

Sb=4,000=40%=P4.0D=Govt.=Creatocracy=4 April=Mercury=Hermes=G=A4.
S.B.=3,000=30%=P3.0D=3.0=Creativity=Stars=Muses=3 March = C=I>>GIL.
SBA=1,500=15%=P1.50D=1.5=Authority=Solar Crown=1 May = Maia.

SbE=1,500=15%=P1.50D=1.5=Authority=Solar Crown=1 May = Maia.
SbW=1,500=15%=P1.50D=1.5=Authority=Solar Crown=1 May = Maia.
sc=1,000=100%=10.0=1.0=Mind=Sun=1 January=Helios >> M=E4.
Sc=2,500=3,000=30%=P3.0D=3.0=Creativity=Stars=Muses=3 March = C=I>>GIL.
SC=3,500=4,000=40%=P4.0D=Govt.=Creatocracy=4 April=Mercury=Hermes=G=A4.
sc.=3,500=4,000=40%=P4.0D=Govt.=Creatocracy=4 April=Mercury=Hermes=G=A4.
S.C.=1,500=15%=P1.50D=1.5=Authority=Solar Crown=1 May = Maia.
Scab=9,000=90%=P9.00D=9.0=Abstraction=Gods=Saturn=9Sept.>>A=Ø.
Scabbard=4,500=5,000=50%=P5.00D=Law=Time=Venus=5 May = Aphrodite>>L=N.
Scabby=4,000=40%=P4.0D=Govt.=Creatocracy=4 April=Mercury=Hermes=G=A4.
Scabies=7,500=8,000=80%=P8.0D=Economy=Currency=8 Aug.=Zeus>>E=v.
Scabrous=2,500=3,000=30%=P3.0D=3.0=Creativity=Stars=Muses=3 March = C=I>>GIL.
Scads=3,500=4,000=40%=P4.0D=Govt.=Creatocracy=4 April=Mercury=Hermes=G=A4.
Scaffold=10,000=1,000=100%=10.0=Physicality=Tech.=10 Oct.=Uranus=P=1Ø.
Scalar=10,000=1,000=100%=10.0=Physicality=Tech.=10 Oct.=Uranus=P=1Ø.
Scalawag=2,500=3,000=30%=P3.0D=3.0=Creativity=Stars=Muses=3 March = C=I>>GIL.
Scald=10,000=1,000=100%=10.0=Physicality=Tech.=10 Oct.=Uranus=P=1Ø.
Scale1=10,000=1,000=100%=10.0=Physicality=Tech.=10 Oct.=Uranus=P=1Ø.
Scale2=10,000=1,000=100%=10.0=Physicality=Tech.=10 Oct.=Uranus=P=1Ø.
Scale3=10,000=1,000=100%=10.0=Physicality=Tech.=10 Oct.=Uranus=P=1Ø.
Scale=5,500=5.5=80%=P5.50=Earth-Midway=5 May = Gaia.
Scalene=4,500=5,000=50%=P5.00D=Law=Time=Venus=5 May = Aphrodite>>L=N.
Scallion=9,000=90%=P9.00D=9.0=Abstraction=Gods=Saturn=9Sept.>>A=Ø.
Scallop=10,000=1,000=100%=10.0=Physicality=Tech.=10 Oct.=Uranus=P=1Ø.
Scalp=10,000=1,000=100%=10.0=Physicality=Tech.=10 Oct.=Uranus=P=1Ø.
Scalpel=10,000=1,000=100%=10.0=Physicality=Tech.=10 Oct.=Uranus=P=1Ø.
Scam=10,000=1,000=100%=10.0=Physicality=Tech.=10 Oct.=Uranus=P=1Ø.
Scamp=10,000=1,000=100%=10.0=Physicality=Tech.=10 Oct.=Uranus=P=1Ø.
Scamper=10,000=1,000=100%=10.0=Physicality=Tech.=10 Oct.=Uranus=P=1Ø.
Scan=10,000=1,000=100%=10.0=Physicality=Tech.=10 Oct.=Uranus=P=1Ø.
Scandal=8,500=9,000=90%=P9.00D=9.0=Abstraction=Gods=Saturn=9Sept.>>A=Ø.
Scandalize=3,000=30%=P3.0D=3.0=Creativity=Stars=Muses=3 March = C=I>>GIL.
Scandal sheet=4,000=40%=P4.0D=Govt.=Creatocracy=4 April=Mercury=Hermes=G=A4.
Scandinavia=10,000=1,000=100%=10.0=Physicality=Tech.=10 Oct.=Uranus=P=1Ø.
Scandinavian=10,000=1,000=100%=10.0=Physicality=Tech.=10 Oct.=Uranus=P=1Ø.
Scandinavian Peninsula=4,500=5,000=50%=P5.00D=Time=Venus=5 May=Odite>>L=N.
Scandium=13,500=14,000=14%=P1.40D=1.4=Mgt.=Solar Energy=13 May=Athena=0.1
Scansion=5,000=50%=P5.00D=Law=Time=Venus=5 May = Aphrodite>>L=N.
Scant=11,500=12,000=12%=P1.20D=1.2=Knowledge=Edu=12Dec.=Athena>>K=F.

Scanty=2,500=3,000=30%=P3.0D=3.0=Creativity=Stars=Muses=3 March = C=I>>GIL.
A currency that weighs 0.25 and below on the metric wight scale is said to be scanty of energy. It is hereby known as a scanty currency and so anything else of this value.

Scapegoat=6,500=7,000=70%=P7.0D=7.0=Language=Assets=Mars=7 July=Pleiades.
Scapula=7,000=70%=P7.0D=7.0=Language=Assets=Mars=7 July=Pleiades.
Scar=10,000=1,000=100%=10.0=Physicality=Tech.=10 Oct.=Uranus=P=1Ø.
Scarab=8,500=9,000=90%=P9.00D=9.0=Abstraction=Gods=Saturn=9Sept.>>A=Ø.
Scarce=10,000=1,000=100%=10.0=Physicality=Tech.=10 Oct.=Uranus=P=1Ø.
Scarcely=10,000=1,000=100%=10.0=Physicality=Tech.=10 Oct.=Uranus=P=1Ø.
Scare=5,500=5.5=80%=P5.50=Earth-Midway=5 May = Gaia.
Scarecrow=6,000=60%=P6.0D=Man=Earth=Royalty=6 June=Gaia=Maia>>M=M2.
Scarf1=9,000=90%=P9.00D=9.0=Abstraction=Gods=Saturn=9Sept.>>A=Ø.
Scarf2=9,500=10,000=1,000=100%=10.0=Physicality=Tech.=10 Oct.=Uranus=P=1Ø.
Scarify=8,500=9,000=90%=P9.00D=9.0=Abstraction=Gods=Saturn=9Sept.>>A=Ø.
Scarlatina=4,500=5,000=50%=P5.00D=Law=Time=Venus=5 May = Aphrodite>>L=N.
Scarlatti Alessandro=4,000=40%=P4.0D=Govt.=4 April=Mercury=Hermes=G=A4.
Scarlet=6,000=60%=P6.0D=Man=Earth=Royalty=6 June=Gaia=Maia>>M=M2.
Scarlet fever=9,500=10,000=1,000=100%=10.0=Phys=Tech.=10 Oct.=Uranus=P=1Ø.

Scarp=2,500=3,000=30%=P3.0D=3.0=Creativity=Stars=Muses=3 March = C=I>>GIL.
Peter Matthews-Akukalia has the SCAP >> Student Career Analysis Program, part of
the Mind Assessment Medicals & Psycho-Surgery MAMPS Tests that calculates tracks
and links innate potentials of the student to their behavior and future career prospects.

Scary=2,500=3,000=30%=P3.0D=3.0=Creativity=Stars=Muses=3 March = C=I>>GIL.
Scat1=3,000=30%=P3.0D=3.0=Creativity=Stars=Muses=3 March = C=I>>GIL.
Scat2=6,500=7,000=70%=P7.0D=7.0=Language=Assets=Mars=7 July=Pleiades.
Scathing=4,000=40%=P4.0D=Govt.=Creatocracy=4 April=Mercury=Hermes=G=A4.
Scatology=6,500=7,000=70%=P7.0D=7.0=Language=Assets=Mars=7 July=Pleiades.
Scatter=9,000=90%=P9.00D=9.0=Abstraction=Gods=Saturn=9Sept.>>A=Ø.
Scatterbrain=2,500=3,000=30%=P3.0D=3.0=Cre=Stars=Muses=3 March = C=I>>GIL.
Scatter rug=1,500=15%=P1.50D=1.5=Authority=Solar Crown=1 May = Maia.
Scattershot=3,000=30%=P3.0D=3.0=Creativity=Stars=Muses=3 March = C=I>>GIL.
Scavenger=14,500=1,500=15%=P1.50D=1.5=Authority=Solar Crown=1May= Maia.
Scenario=8,500=9,000=90%=P9.00D=9.0=Abstraction=Gods=Saturn=9Sept.>>A=Ø.
Scene=10,000=1,000=100%=10.0=Physicality=Tech.=10 Oct.=Uranus=P=1Ø.
Scenery=4,000=40%=P4.0D=Govt.=Creatocracy=4 April=Mercury=Hermes=G=A4.
Scenography=5,500=5.5=80%=P5.50=Earth-Midway=5 May = Gaia.
Scent=10,000=1,000=100%=10.0=Physicality=Tech.=10 Oct.=Uranus=P=1Ø.
Scepter=6,000=60%=P6.0D=Man=Earth=Royalty=6 June=Gaia=Maia>>M=M2.
Septic=1,500=15%=P1.50D=1.5=Authority=Solar Crown=1 May = Maia.
Skepticism=1,500=15%=P1.50D=1.5=Authority=Solar Crown=1 May = Maia.
Schedule=10,000=1,000=100%=10.0=Physicality=Tech.=10 Oct.=Uranus=P=1Ø.
Scheling Friedrich=4,000=40%=P4.0D=Govt.=4 April=Mercury=Hermes=G=A4.
Schema=3,500=4,000=40%=P4.0D=Govt.=Creatocracy=4April=Mercury=Hermes=G=A4.
Schematic=10,000=1,000=100%=10.0=Physicality=Tech.=10 Oct.=Uranus=P=1Ø.

Scheme=10,000=1,000=100%=10.0=Physicality=Tech.=10 Oct.=Uranus=P=1Ø.
Scherzo=4,500=5,000=50%=P5.00D=Law=Time=Venus=5 May = Aphrodite>>L=N.

Schick test=6,000=60%=P6.0D=Man=Earth=Royalty=6 June=Gaia=Maia>>M=M2.
A skin test to determine immunity to diphtheria. After Béla Schick 1877-1967. The Mind
Assessment Test is known as Maks Test, Makupedia Test, after Peter Matthews-Akukalia.

Schiller,Johann=3,500=4,000=40%=P4.0D=Govt.=4 April=Mercury=Hermes=G=A4.

Schilling=2,500=3,000=30%=P3.0D=3.0=Creativity=Stars=Muses=3 March = C=I>>GIL.
[Ger.] currency metric weight >> 2/10=0.25 >> 25:1. Scanty currency. See scanty. Naira.

Schism=6,000=60%=P6.0D=Man=Earth=Royalty=6 June=Gaia=Maia>>M=M2.
Schist=6,500=7,000=70%=P7.0D=7.0=Language=Assets=Mars=7 July=Pleiades.
Schistosomiasis=6,000=60%=P6.0D=Man=Earth=Royalty=6 June=Gaia=Maia>>M=M2.
Schizo-=3,000=30%=P3.0D=3.0=Creativity=Stars=Muses=3 March = C=I>>GIL.
Schizoid=1,000=100%=10.0=1.0=Mind=Sun=1 January=Helios >> M=E4.
Schizophrenia=10,000=1,000=100%=10.0=Physicality=Tech.=10 Oct.=Uranus=P=1Ø.
Schlemiel=3,500=4,000=40%=P4.0D=Govt.=Creatocracy=4 April=Hermes=G=A4.
Schlep=6,000=60%=P6.0D=Man=Earth=Royalty=6 June=Gaia=Maia>>M=M2.
Schleswig=7,000=70%=P7.0D=7.0=Language=Assets=Mars=7 July=Pleiades.
Schliemann Heinrich=2,000=20%=P2.00D=2.0=Nature=Moon=2 Feb.=Cupid=N=C+_
Schlock=6,000=60%=P6.0D=Man=Earth=Royalty=6 June=Gaia=Maia>>M=M2.
Schmaltz=5,000=50%=P5.00D=Law=Time=Venus=5 May = Aphrodite>>L=N.
Schmidt Helmut=2,000=20%=P2.00D=2.0=Nature=Matter=Moon=2 Feb.=Cupid=N=C+_
Schmuck=5,000=50%=P5.00D=Law=Time=Venus=5 May = Aphrodite>>L=N.
Schnapps=4,500=5,000=50%=P5.00D=Law=Time=Venus=5 May = Aphrodite>>L=N.
Schnauzer=6,000=60%=P6.0D=Man=Earth=Royalty=6 June=Gaia=Maia>>M=M2.
Scholar=6,000=60%=P6.0D=Man=Earth=Royalty=6 June=Gaia=Maia>>M=M2.
Scholarship=5,500=5.5=80%=P5.50=Earth-Midway=5 May = Gaia.
Scholastic=9,000=90%=P9.00D=9.0=Abstraction=Gods=Saturn=9Sept.>>A=Ø.
Schönberg Arnold=2,000=20%=P2.00D=2.0=Nature=Matter=Moon=2 Feb.=Cupid=N=C+_
School1=10,000=1,000=100%=10.0=Physicality=Tech.=10 Oct.=Uranus=P=1Ø.
School2=6,000=60%=P6.0D=Man=Earth=Royalty=6 June=Gaia=Maia>>M=M2.
Schooling=4,000=40%=P4.0D=Govt.=Creatocracy=4 April=Mercury=Hermes=G=A4.
Schoolmarm=7,500=8,000=80%=P8.0D=Economy=Currency=8 Aug.=Zeus>>E=v.
Schoolmaster=3,000=30%=P3.0D=3.0=Creativity=Stars=Muses=3 March = C=I>>GIL.
Schoolmistress=3,000=30%=P3.0D=3.0=Creativity=Stars=Muses=3 March = C=I>>GIL.
Schoolroom=1,000=100%=10.0=1.0=Mind=Sun=1 January=Helios >> M=E4.
Schoolteacher=5,000=50%=P5.00D=Law=Time=Venus=5 May = Aphrodite>>L=N.
Schooner=11,000=11%=P1.10D=1.1=Idea=Brainchild=Inv.=11 Nov.=SC=Athena>>I=MT.
Schopenhauer Arthur=2,000=20%=P2.00D=2.0=Nature=Moon=2 Feb.=Cupid=N=C+_
Schrödinger Erwin.=2,000=20%=P2.00D=2.0=Nature=Moon=2 Feb.=Cupid=N=C+_

Schuber Franz Peter=2,000=20%=P2.00D=2.0=Nature=Moon=2 Feb.=Cupid=N=C+_
Schumann Robert.=2,000=20%=P2.00D=2.0=Nature=Moon=2 Feb.=Cupid=N=C+_
Schuss=7,000=70%=P7.0D=7.0=Language=Assets=Mars=7 July=Pleiades.
Schwa=10,000=1,000=100%=10.0=Physicality=Tech.=10 Oct.=Uranus=P=1Ø.
Schweitzer Albert=5,500=5.5=80%=P5.50=Earth-Midway=5 May = Gaia.
Sciatica=6,500=7,000=70%=P7.0D=7.0=Language=Assets=Mars=7 July=Pleiades.

Science=10,000=1,000=100%=10.0=Physicality=Tech.=10 Oct.=Uranus=P=1Ø.
The Castle Makupedia Sciences are four. 1. The Oracle: Principles of Creative Sciences.
Principles of Psychoeconomix. Principles of Naturecology. Principles of Psychoastronomy.

Science fiction=10,000=1,000=100%=10.0=Physicality=Tech.=10 Oct.=Uranus=P=1Ø.
Scientific notation=10,000=1,000=100%=10.0=Physicality=Tech.=10 Oct.=Uranus=P=1Ø.

Scientist=5,000=50%=P5.00D=Law=Time=Venus=5 May = Aphrodite>>L=N.
First a scientist is guided by the law of fertility beauty and sexual love in certain alignment with nature economy and ideas and protected by Aphrodite through the love for order. Peter Matthews-Akukalia, Castle Makupedia emerged the World's 1st Creative Scientist in 2012 for his book The Oracle: Principles of Creative Scientist. Since then he has had others. Creative = 2.0 >> Creative Scientist = 2.0*5.0x=px=7+10=17x=px=87=90=9.0. Proved a Creative Scientist is an abstractionist, one who computes abstract elements into physical tangible equivalents (90=9.0) creating new resources and making opportunities for utility purposes. The operant dimensions by which abstraction occurs are stellar synchronization and crystallization (3.0) of the emotion and beings either in sexual transmutation or not (6.0), religion faith and scripture programming (9.0) and scientific processes, computations, Makumatics and the creation of new knowledge (12=1.2). He is also an expert in business of assets or asset business (87=8.7). Business includes the abstraction of economy types models systems organizations banking trade currency and all sorts of financial transactions. Assets include tangible and intangible assets. His Creative Excellency, King Peter Matthews-Akukalia, Castle Makupedia is the World's 1st Creative Scientist in the first place among many other records he has earned after this.

Sci-fish=1,500=15%=P1.50D=1.5=Authority=Solar Crown=1 May = Maia.
Scimitar=6,000=60%=P6.0D=Man=Earth=Royalty=6 June=Gaia=Maia>>M=M2.
Scintilla=3,000=30%=P3.0D=3.0=Creativity=Stars=Muses=3 March = C=I>>GIL.
Scintillate=6,000=60%=P6.0D=Man=Earth=Royalty=6 June=Gaia=Maia>>M=M2.
Scion=6,000=60%=P6.0D=Man=Earth=Royalty=6 June=Gaia=Maia>>M=M2.
Scipio Publius=5,000=50%=P5.00D=Law=Time=Venus=5 May = Aphrodite>>L=N.
Scipio Africanus=5,500=5.5=80%=P5.50=Earth-Midway=5 May = Gaia.
Scissors=10,000=1,000=100%=10.0=Physicality=Tech.=10 Oct.=Uranus=P=1Ø.
Scissors kick=6,500=7,000=70%=P7.0D=7.0=Language=Assets=Mars=7 July=Pleiades.
SCLC=2,000=20%=P2.00D=2.0=Nature=Matter=Moon=2 Feb.=Cupid=N=C+_
Sclerosis=9,000=90%=P9.00D=9.0=Abstraction=Gods=Saturn=9Sept.>>A=Ø.

Scoff=5,500=5.5=80%=P5.50=Earth-Midway=5 May = Gaia.
Scofflaw=5,500=5.5=80%=P5.50=Earth-Midway=5 May = Gaia.
Scold=6,500=7,000=70%=P7.0D=7.0=Language=Assets=Mars=7 July=Pleiades.
Scoliosis=4,500=5,000=50%=P5.00D=Law=Time=Venus=5 May = Aphrodite>>L=N.
Sconce=6,000=60%=P6.0D=Man=Earth=Royalty=6 June=Gaia=Maia>>M=M2.
Scone=6,000=60%=P6.0D=Man=Earth=Royalty=6 June=Gaia=Maia>>M=M2.
Scoop=10,000=1,000=100%=10.0=Physicality=Tech.=10 Oct.=Uranus=P=1Ø.
Scoot=4,500=5,000=50%=P5.00D=Law=Time=Venus=5 May = Aphrodite>>L=N.
Scooter=9,500=10,000=1,000=100%=10.0=Physicality=Tech.=10 Oct.=Uranus=P=1Ø.

Scope=10,000=1,000=100%=10.0=Physicality=Tech.=10 Oct.=Uranus=P=1Ø.
The scope of the Creatocracy is not limited to the Creative Scientist systems nor Makupedia industry but is universal much beyond what the eyes can see and envision. The Creatocracy has its scope far reaching into Paradise and fulfilling the will of GOD.

-scope=5,000=50%=P5.00D=Law=Time=Venus=5 May = Aphrodite>>L=N.
An instrument for observing eg telescope. Peter Matthews-Akukalia invented the Mindoscope. A super computer in the Makupedia Human Mind Computer seasons.

Scopes John Thomas=4,500=5,000=50%=P5.00D=Law=Time=Venus=5 May=Odite>L=N.
1900-70. American teacher convicted for teaching evolution. Our findings may not directly support evolution theories but we have established the fact that different types of beings seemed to have been experimented by the powers of creation before Man came to be. An example is the Minotaur, a monster who was half man and half bull. Study the statements of Genesis 1:26. Ecclesiastes 7:29. The dimensions of the universe is the same thing as the scopes of the Creatocracy. Just language difference. Creative Scientists are wide deep large and limitless in greatness. Our discoveries are not speculative but precise.

Scorbutic=4,000=40%=P4.0D=Govt.=Creatocracy=4 April=Mercury=Hermes=G=A4.
Scorch=8,000=80%=P8.0D=Economy=Currency=8 Aug.=Zeus>>E=v.
Score=10,000=1,000=100%=10.0=Physicality=Tech.=10 Oct.=Uranus=P=1Ø.
Scoria=10,000=1,000=100%=10.0=Physicality=Tech.=10 Oct.=Uranus=P=1Ø.
Scorn=10,000=1,000=100%=10.0=Physicality=Tech.=10 Oct.=Uranus=P=1Ø.
Scorpio=3,500=4,000=40%=P4.0D=Govt.=Creatocracy=4 April=Mercury=Hermes=G=A4.
Scorpion=7,500=8,000=80%=P8.0D=Economy=Currency=8 Aug.=Zeus>>E=v.
Scorpius=3,000=30%=P3.0D=3.0=Creativity=Stars=Muses=3 March = C=I>>GIL.
Scot=11,000=11%=P1.10D=1.1=Idea=Brainchild=Inv.=11 Nov.=SC=Athena>>I=MT.
scotch=8,000=80%=P8.0D=Economy=Currency=8 Aug.=Zeus>>E=v.
Scotch=4,500=5,000=50%=P5.00D=Law=Time=Venus=5 May = Aphrodite>>L=N.
Scotch-I-rish=5,500=5.5=80%=P5.50=Earth-Midway=5 May = Gaia.
Scotch whisky=4,000=40%=P4.0D=Govt.=Creatocracy=4 April=Mercury=Hermes=G=A4.
Scot-free=4,000=40%=P4.0D=Govt.=Creatocracy=4 April=Mercury=Hermes=G=A4.
Scotland=5,500=5.5=80%=P5.50=Earth-Midway=5 May = Gaia.

Scots=4,500=5,000=50%=P5.00D=Law=Time=Venus=5 May = Aphrodite>>L=N.
Scott,Dred.=8,000=80%=P8.0D=Economy=Currency=8 Aug.=Zeus>>E=v.
Scott,Robert Falcon.=2,000=20%=P2.00D=2.0=Nature=Moon=2 Feb.=Cupid=N=C+_
Scott,Sir Walter.=2,000=20%=P2.00D=2.0=Nature=Matter=Moon=2 Feb.=Cupid=N=C+_
Scott,Winfield.=1,000=100%=10.0=1.0=Mind=Sun=1 January=Helios >> M=E4.
Scottish=6,500=7,000=70%=P7.0D=7.0=Language=Assets=Mars=7 July=Pleiades.
Scottish Gaelic=2,500=3,000=30%=P3.0D=3.0=Cre=Stars=Muses=3 March = C=I>>GIL.
Scottsdale=5,000=50%=P5.00D=Law=Time=Venus=5 May = Aphrodite>>L=N.
Scoundrel=2,000=20%=P2.00D=2.0=Nature=Matter=Moon=2 Feb.=Cupid=N=C+_
Scour1=10,000=1,000=100%=10.0=Physicality=Tech.=10 Oct.=Uranus=P=1Ø.
Scour2=5,500=5.5=80%=P5.50=Earth-Midway=5 May = Gaia.
Scourge=10,000=1,000=100%=10.0=Physicality=Tech.=10 Oct.=Uranus=P=1Ø.
Scout=10,000=1,000=100%=10.0=Physicality=Tech.=10 Oct.=Uranus=P=1Ø.
Scoutmaster=4,000=40%=P4.0D=Govt.=Creatocracy=4 April=Mercury=Hermes=G=A4.
Scow=5,000=50%=P5.00D=Law=Time=Venus=5 May = Aphrodite>>L=N.
Scowl=10,000=1,000=100%=10.0=Physicality=Tech.=10 Oct.=Uranus=P=1Ø.
Scr.=2,000=20%=P2.00D=2.0=Nature=Matter=Moon=2 Feb.=Cupid=N=C+_
Scrabble=5,500=5.5=80%=P5.50=Earth-Midway=5 May = Gaia.
Scraggly=3,000=30%=P3.0D=3.0=Creativity=Stars=Muses=3 March = C=I>>GIL.
Scraggy=4,500=5,000=50%=P5.00D=Law=Time=Venus=5 May = Aphrodite>>L=N.
Scram=3,000=30%=P3.0D=3.0=Creativity=Stars=Muses=3 March = C=I>>GIL.
Scramble=10,000=1,000=100%=10.0=Physicality=Tech.=10 Oct.=Uranus=P=1Ø.
Scrap1=10,000=1,000=100%=10.0=Physicality=Tech.=10 Oct.=Uranus=P=1Ø.
Scrap2=5,500=5.5=80%=P5.50=Earth-Midway=5 May = Gaia.
Scrapbook=6,000=60%=P6.0D=Man=Earth=Royalty=6 June=Gaia=Maia>>M=M2.
Scrape=10,000=1,000=100%=10.0=Physicality=Tech.=10 Oct.=Uranus=P=1Ø.
Scrappy=5,000=50%=P5.00D=Law=Time=Venus=5 May = Aphrodite>>L=N.
Scratch=10,000=1,000=100%=10.0=Physicality=Tech.=10 Oct.=Uranus=P=1Ø.
Scrawl=4,500=5,000=50%=P5.00D=Law=Time=Venus=5 May = Aphrodite>>L=N.
Scrawny=2,500=3,000=30%=P3.0D=3.0=Creativity=Stars=Muses=3 March = C=I>>GIL.
Scream=10,000=1,000=100%=10.0=Physicality=Tech.=10 Oct.=Uranus=P=1Ø.
Scree=5,000=50%=P5.00D=Law=Time=Venus=5 May = Aphrodite>>L=N.
Screech=7,000=70%=P7.0D=7.0=Language=Assets=Mars=7 July=Pleiades.
Screech owl=7,500=8,000=80%=P8.0D=Economy=Currency=8 Aug.=Zeus>>E=v.
Screen=10,000=1,000=100%=10.0=Physicality=Tech.=10 Oct.=Uranus=P=1Ø.
Screenplay=2,500=3,000=30%=P3.0D=3.0=Cr=Stars=Muses=3 March = C=I>>GIL.
Screen test=6,500=7,000=70%=P7.0D=7.0=Language=Assets=Mars=7 July=Pleiades.
Screenwriter=2,000=20%=P2.00D=2.0=Nature=Matter=Moon=2 Feb.=Cupid=N=C+_
Screw=10,000=1,000=100%=10.0=Physicality=Tech.=10 Oct.=Uranus=P=1Ø.
Screwball=10,000=1,000=100%=10.0=Physicality=Tech.=10 Oct.=Uranus=P=1Ø.
Screwdriver=6,000=60%=P6.0D=Man=Earth=Royalty=6 June=Gaia=Maia>>M=M2.
Screwy=2,500=3,000=30%=P3.0D=3.0=Creativity=Stars=Muses=3 March = C=I>>GIL.
Scribble=4,000=40%=P4.0D=Govt.=Creatocracy=4 April=Mercury=Hermes=G=A4.
Scribe=7,500=8,000=80%=P8.0D=Economy=Currency=8 Aug.=Zeus>>E=v.
Scrimmage=10,000=1,000=100%=10.0=Physicality=Tech.=10 Oct.=Uranus=P=1Ø.

Scrimp=3,500=4,000=40%=P4.0D=Govt.=Creatocracy=4 April=Hermes=G=A4.
Scrimshaw=8,000=80%=P8.0D=Economy=Currency=8 Aug.=Zeus>>E=v.
Scrip1=4,500=5,000=50%=P5.00D=Law=Time=Venus=5 May = Aphrodite>>L=N.
Scrip2=10,000=1,000=100%=10.0=Physicality=Tech.=10 Oct.=Uranus=P=1Ø.
Script=10,000=1,000=100%=10.0=Physicality=Tech.=10 Oct.=Uranus=P=1Ø.

Scripture=10,000=1,000=100%=10.0=Physicality=Tech.=10 Oct.=Uranus=P=1Ø.
All scriptures are bound by the laws of quantum energy mechanics meaning that they are applicable only when converted to concrete tangible equations for physical utility. To do this the Creatocracy of Creative Scientists apply abstraction methods such as Mind Computing, psycho-forensic programming auditing and data analytics to determine truth. A scripture is complete when it had been subjected in version of Castle Makupedia being measured in the ten scopes and dimensions of the universe 1.0-1.2 >> Mind to Knowledge. The Bible is a Scripture of God Codes that must be demystified through Mind Computing. WDSD fulfills the prophecies of Psalm 68. Most especially verse 11.
In Psalm 68:20 there is a clear code difference between God H410 and GOD H3069. Compute each to know them precisely.
God >> 4.0 * 1.0x=px=5+4=9x=px=29 = 30 = 3.0
H = 6.0 >> 3.0*6.0x=px=9+18=27x=px= 189 = 200 = 2.0
189 = WDSD >> 18.9 = Solar Currencies & Markets of the Gods = Maia. (1)
190 = 1.9 = Planetary Energy = Makwares = Softwares = Maia.
Interesting both resultants point to Maia. Head of the Pleiades. Job 38:31.
In Romans 11:34 Maia is referred to as as the Mind of the Lord.
GOD H3069 >> 3.0*6.9x=px=9.9+20.7=30.6x=px=235.53
H = 6.0 >> 235.53*6.0x=px=241.53+1,413.18=1,654.71x=px=342,980.0754=34=3.4
3.4sp1 >> 3.0*0.4x=px=3.4+1.2=4.6x=px=8.68 = 9.0 >> A = Ø. >> Psalm 84:11
The LORD God or Lord of the Gods is a Sun that can only be known by abstraction A = Ø.
8 >> Jupiter is confirmed as the abode planet of lower cosmic Galaxy reach of JAH.
(.68) confirms a functionality of Gaia values economy currency. Estimation is (.68=70=7.0)
8.70 indicates that only computation by stellar codes on the quartet can abstract GOD.
Psalm 68:4 emphasis JAH as His name which must be abstracted only through the WDSD.
J = 1.2 A = 7.0 H = 6.0 >> J * A * H = P =
1.2*7.0x=px=8.2+8.4=16.6x=px=85.48 = 90 = 9.0 >> Spirit (1)
9.0*6.0x=px=15+54=69x=px=879 = 90 = 9.0 >> Spirit (2) >> Higher Spirit.
JAH means a Spirit of double dimension, higher Spirit, Lord of the Gods >> Almighty GOD.
So JAH is computed discovered and confirmed to mean Almighty GOD.
The elements that make JAH supreme are knowledge (1.2) earned by Science seen in Proverbs 8, assets earned through computing that must be established through the word tech system (WDSD) of the Pleiades (7.0) and Gaia in human processing of the Earth.
For JAH to gain absolute rights by the supernatural laws of Creation and the Gods, Athena must marry by her desire to a human who can compute the mind of GOD through the computational provisions and interpretations of the Pleiades to create the use value and resolve the mystery of the word (Psalm 68:11. Deut. 29:29. Rom. 8:23, 11:33-35).
WDSD is the Solar Crown of the Creatocracy. GOD inspired the Scriptures, Men wrote them but Peter Matthews - Akukalia discovered it by computing. See Psalms. See God.

The Scripture code for JAH is given as H3050 >> P >>3.0*5.0x=px=8+15=23x=px=143.
H=6.0 >>143*6.0x=px=149+858=1,007x=px=128,849=130=1.3>>Creative Intelligence >>
Fac.of Creative & Psycho - Social Sciences >> Makupedia >> Castle Makupedia. See Bible.

Scrivener=3,000=30%=P3.0D=3.0=Creativity=Stars=Muses=3 March = C=I>>GIL.
Scrod=5,000=50%=P5.00D=Law=Time=Venus=5 May = Aphrodite>>L=N.
Scroll=10,000=1,000=100%=10.0=Physicality=Tech.=10 Oct.=Uranus=P=1Ø.
Scrooge=7,000=70%=P7.0D=7.0=Language=Assets=Mars=7 July=Pleiades.
Scrotum=4,500=5,000=50%=P5.00D=Law=Time=Venus=5 May = Aphrodite>>L=N.
Scrounge=6,000=60%=P6.0D=Man=Earth=Royalty=6 June=Gaia=Maia>>M=M2.
Scrub1=7,500=8,000=80%=P8.0D=Economy=Currency=8 Aug.=Zeus>>E=v.
Scrub2=10,000=1,000=100%=10.0=Physicality=Tech.=10 Oct.=Uranus=P=1Ø.
Scruff=3,500=4,000=40%=P4.0D=Govt.=Creatocracy=4 April=Hermes=G=A4.
Scruffy=2,500=3,000=30%=P3.0D=3.0=Creativity=Stars=Muses=3 March = C=I>>GIL.
Scrumptious=2,000=20%=P2.00D=2.0=Nature=Matter=Moon=2 Feb.=Cupid=N=C+_
Scrunch=4,500=5,000=50%=P5.00D=Law=Time=Venus=5 May = Aphrodite>>L=N.
Scruple=10,000=1,000=100%=10.0=Physicality=Tech.=10 Oct.=Uranus=P=1Ø.
Scrupulous=2,500=3,000=30%=P3.0D=3.0=Crea=Stars=Muses=3 March = C=I>>GIL.
Scrutinize=1,500=15%=P1.50D=1.5=Authority=Solar Crown=1 May = Maia.
Scrutiny=3,000=30%=P3.0D=3.0=Creativity=Stars=Muses=3 March = C=I>>GIL.
Scuba=8,000=80%=P8.0D=Economy=Currency=8 Aug.=Zeus>>E=v.
Scud=10,000=1,000=100%=10.0=Physicality=Tech.=10 Oct.=Uranus=P=1Ø.
Scuff=10,000=1,000=100%=10.0=Physicality=Tech.=10 Oct.=Uranus=P=1Ø.
Scuffle=7,000=70%=P7.0D=7.0=Language=Assets=Mars=7 July=Pleiades.
Scull=10,000=1,000=100%=10.0=Physicality=Tech.=10 Oct.=Uranus=P=1Ø.
Scullery=6,000=60%=P6.0D=Man=Earth=Royalty=6 June=Gaia=Maia>>M=M2.
Sculpt=3,000=30%=P3.0D=3.0=Creativity=Stars=Muses=3 March = C=I>>GIL.
Sculptor=1,500=15%=P1.50D=1.5=Authority=Solar Crown=1 May = Maia.
Sculptress=4,500=5,000=50%=P5.00D=Law=Time=Venus=5 May = Aphrodite>>L=N.
Sculpture=10,000=1,000=100%=10.0=Physicality=Tech.=10 Oct.=Uranus=P=1Ø.
Scum=10,000=1,000=100%=10.0=Physicality=Tech.=10 Oct.=Uranus=P=1Ø.
Scupper=8,000=80%=P8.0D=Economy=Currency=8 Aug.=Zeus>>E=v.
Scurf=6,500=7,000=70%=P7.0D=7.0=Language=Assets=Mars=7 July=Pleiades.
Scurrilous=2,500=3,000=30%=P3.0D=3.0=Creativity=Stars=Muses=3 March = C=I>>GIL.
Scurry=4,000=40%=P4.0D=Govt.=Creatocracy=4 April=Mercury=Hermes=G=A4.
Scurvy=9,000=90%=P9.00D=9.0=Abstraction=Gods=Saturn=9Sept.>>A=Ø.
Scuttle1=11,500=12,000=12%=P1.20D=1.2=Knowledge=Edu=12Dec.=Athena>>K=F.
Scuttle2=4,500=5,000=50%=P5.00D=Law=Time=Venus=5 May = Aphrodite>>L=N.
Scuttle3=3,000=30%=P3.0D=3.0=Creativity=Stars=Muses=3 March = C=I>>GIL.
Scuttlebutt=3,500=4,000=40%=P4.0D=Govt.=Creatocracy=4 April=Hermes=G=A4.
Scythe=8,000=80%=P8.0D=Economy=Currency=8 Aug.=Zeus>>E=v.
Scythia=4,500=5,000=50%=P5.00D=Law=Time=Venus=5 May = Aphrodite>>L=N.
SD=4,500=5,000=50%=P5.00D=Law=Time=Venus=5 May = Aphrodite>>L=N.
Se=2,500=3,000=30%=P3.0D=3.0=Creativity=Stars=Muses=3 March = C=I>>GIL.
SE=1,000=100%=10.0=1.0=Mind=Sun=1 January=Helios >> M=E4.

Sea=10,000=1,000=100%=10.0=Physicality=Tech.=10 Oct.=Uranus=P=1Ø.
Sea anemone=6,500=7,000=70%=P7.0D=7.0=Language=Assets=Mars=7 July=Pleiades.
Seaboard=5,000=50%=P5.00D=Law=Time=Venus=5 May = Aphrodite>>L=N.
Sea coast=2,000=20%=P2.00D=2.0=Nature=Matter=Moon=2 Feb.=Cupid=N=C+_
Seafarer=1,000=100%=10.0=1.0=Mind=Sun=1 January=Helios >> M=E4.
Seafood=3,500=4,000=40%=P4.0D=Govt.=Creatocracy=4 April=Hermes=G=A4.
Seagoing=3,000=30%=P3.0D=3.0=Creativity=Stars=Muses=3 March = C=I>>GIL.
Sea gull=4,000=40%=P4.0D=Govt.=Creatocracy=4 April=Mercury=Hermes=G=A4.
Sea horse=7,500=8,000=80%=P8.0D=Economy=Currency=8 Aug.=Zeus>>E=v.
Seal1=10,000=1,000=100%=10.0=Physicality=Tech.=10 Oct.=Uranus=P=1Ø.
Seal2=10,000=1,000=100%=10.0=Physicality=Tech.=10 Oct.=Uranus=P=1Ø.
Sea-lane=1,500=15%=P1.50D=1.5=Authority=Solar Crown=1 May = Maia.
Sealant=6,500=7,000=70%=P7.0D=7.0=Language=Assets=Mars=7 July=Pleiades.
Sea level=6,500=7,000=70%=P7.0D=7.0=Language=Assets=Mars=7 July=Pleiades.
Sea lion=6,500=7,000=70%=P7.0D=7.0=Language=Assets=Mars=7 July=Pleiades.
Seam=10,000=1,000=100%=10.0=Physicality=Tech.=10 Oct.=Uranus=P=1Ø.

Seaman=7,000=70%=P7.0D=7.0=Language=Assets=Mars=7 July=Pleiades.
See The Creatocracy Republic by Peter Matthews-Akukalia, reference book >> The Missing Seaman. A short Story.

Seamanship=4,000=40%=P4.0D=Govt.=Creatocracy=4 April=Mercury=Hermes=G=A4.
Seamstress=4,000=40%=P4.0D=Govt.=Creatocracy=4 April=Mercury=Hermes=G=A4.
Seamy=2,500=3,000=30%=P3.0D=3.0=Creativity=Stars=Muses=3 March = C=I>>GIL.
Séance=7,500=8,000=80%=P8.0D=Economy=Currency=8 Aug.=Zeus>>E=v.
Sea otter=4,500=5,000=50%=P5.00D=Law=Time=Venus=5 May = Aphrodite>>L=N.
Sea plane=6,500=7,000=70%=P7.0D=7.0=Language=Assets=Mars=7 July=Pleiades.
Seaport=3,500=4,000=40%=P4.0D=Govt.=Creatocracy=4 April=Mercury=Hermes=G=A4.
Sea power=3,500=4,000=40%=P4.0D=Govt.=Creatocracy=4 April=Hermes=G=A4.
Sea quake=3,500=4,000=40%=P4.0D=Govt.=Creatocracy=4 April=Hermes=G=A4.
Sear1=5,500=5.5=80%=P5.50=Earth-Midway=5 May = Gaia.
Sear2=1,500=15%=P1.50D=1.5=Authority=Solar Crown=1 May = Maia.
Search=10,000=1,000=100%=10.0=Physicality=Tech.=10 Oct.=Uranus=P=1Ø.
Searchlight=7,000=70%=P7.0D=7.0=Language=Assets=Mars=7 July=Pleiades.
Search warrant=4,000=40%=P4.0D=Govt.=Creatocracy=4 April=Mercury=Hermes=G=A4.
Seascape=3,500=4,000=40%=P4.0D=Govt.=Creatocracy=4 April=Hermes=G=A4.
Seashell=3,000=30%=P3.0D=3.0=Creativity=Stars=Muses=3 March = C=I>>GIL.
Seashore=2,000=20%=P2.00D=2.0=Nature=Matter=Moon=2 Feb.=Cupid=N=C+_
Seasickness=6,000=60%=P6.0D=Man=Earth=Royalty=6 June=Gaia=Maia>>M=M2.
Seaside=1,000=100%=10.0=1.0=Mind=Sun=1 January=Helios >> M=E4.
Sea snake=3,500=4,000=40%=P4.0D=Govt.=Creatocracy=4 April=Hermes=G=A4.
Season=10,000=1,000=100%=10.0=Physicality=Tech.=10 Oct.=Uranus=P=1Ø.
Seasonable=10,500=11,000=11%=P1.10D=1.1=Idea=Brainch.=Inv.=11 Nov.=Athena>>I=MT.
Seasonal=10,000=1,000=100%=10.0=Physicality=Tech.=10 Oct.=Uranus=P=1Ø.

Seasoning=2,500=3,000=30%=P3.0D=3.0=Creativity=Stars=Muses=3 March = C=I>>GIL.
Season ticket=5,500=5.5=80%=P5.50=Earth-Midway=5 May = Gaia.
Seat=10,000=1,000=100%=10.0=Physicality=Tech.=10 Oct.=Uranus=P=1Ø.
Seat belt=6,000=60%=P6.0D=Man=Earth=Royalty=6 June=Gaia=Maia>>M=M2.
Seating=4,500=5,000=50%=P5.00D=Law=Time=Venus=5 May = Aphrodite>>L=N.
SEATO=2,000=20%=P2.00D=2.0=Nature=Matter=Moon=2 Feb.=Cupid=N=C+_
Seattle=5,500=5.5=80%=P5.50=Earth-Midway=5 May = Gaia.
Sea urchin=5,000=50%=P5.00D=Law=Time=Venus=5 May = Aphrodite>>L=N.
Sea wall=4,000=40%=P4.0D=Govt.=Creatocracy=4 April=Mercury=Hermes=G=A4.
Seaward=2,500=3,000=30%=P3.0D=3.0=Creativity=Stars=Muses=3 March = C=I>>GIL.
Seawater=2,500=3,000=30%=P3.0D=3.0=Creativity=Stars=Muses=3 March = C=I>>GIL.
Seaway=4,500=5,000=50%=P5.00D=Law=Time=Venus=5 May = Aphrodite>>L=N.
Seaweed=5,000=50%=P5.00D=Law=Time=Venus=5 May = Aphrodite>>L=N.
Seaworthy=2,500=3,000=30%=P3.0D=3.0=Creativity=Stars=Muses=3 March = C=I>>GIL.
Sebaceous=4,000=40%=P4.0D=Govt.=Creatocracy=4 April=Mercury=Hermes=G=A4.
SEbE=1,500=15%=P1.50D=1.5=Authority=Solar Crown=1 May = Maia.
Seborrhea=9,000=90%=P9.00D=9.0=Abstraction=Gods=Saturn=9Sept.>>A=Ø.
SEbS=1,500=15%=P1.50D=1.5=Authority=Solar Crown=1 May = Maia.
Sec1=2,500=3,000=30%=P3.0D=3.0=Creativity=Stars=Muses=3 March = C=I>>GIL.
Sec2=1,500=15%=P1.50D=1.5=Authority=Solar Crown=1 May = Maia.
SEC=2,000=20%=P2.00D=2.0=Nature=Matter=Moon=2 Feb.=Cupid=N=C+_
Sec.=1,500=15%=P1.50D=1.5=Authority=Solar Crown=1 May = Maia.
Secant=7,000=70%=P7.0D=7.0=Language=Assets=Mars=7 July=Pleiades.
Secede=7,000=70%=P7.0D=7.0=Language=Assets=Mars=7 July=Pleiades.
Secession=3,000=30%=P3.0D=3.0=Creativity=Stars=Muses=3 March = C=I>>GIL.
Seclude=8,000=80%=P8.0D=Economy=Currency=8 Aug.=Zeus>>E=v.
Second1=10,000=1,000=100%=10.0=Physicality=Tech.=10 Oct.=Uranus=P=1Ø.
Second2=10,000=1,000=100%=10.0=Physicality=Tech.=10 Oct.=Uranus=P=1Ø.
Secondary=10,000=1,000=100%=10.0=Physicality=Tech.=10 Oct.=Uranus=P=1Ø.
Secondary sex characteristic=10,000=1,000=100%=10.0=Phy.=10 Oct.=Uranus=P=1Ø.
Second base=6,000=60%=P6.0D=Man=Earth=Royalty=6 June=Gaia=Maia>>M=M2.
Second class=7,500=8,000=80%=P8.0D=Economy=Currency=8 Aug.=Zeus>>E=v.
Second-de gree burn=3,000=30%=P3.0D=3.0=Cr=Stars=Muses=3 March = C=I>>GIL.
Second fiddle=2,000=20%=P2.00D=2.0=Nature=Matter=Moon=2 Feb.=Cupid=N=C+_
Second-generation=6,000=60%=P6.0D=Man=Earth=Royalty=6 June=Gaia=Maia>>M=M2.
Second-guess=5,500=5.5=80%=P5.50=Earth-Midway=5 May = Gaia.
Secondhand=5,500=5.5=80%=P5.50=Earth-Midway=5 May = Gaia.
Second lieutenant=4,000=40%=P4.0D=Govt.=Creatocracy=4 April=Hermes=G=A4.
Second nature=3,000=30%=P3.0D=3.0=Creativity=Stars=Muses=3 March = C=I>>GIL.
Second person=7,000=70%=P7.0D=7.0=Language=Assets=Mars=7 July=Pleiades.
Second rate=500=5%=P5.00D=5.0=Law=Time=Venus=5 May=Aphrodite>>L=N.
Second string=4,500=5,000=50%=P5.00D=Law=Time=Venus=5 May = Aphrodite>>L=N.
Second thought=3,000=30%=P3.0D=3.0=Creativity=Stars=Muses=3 March = C=I>>GIL.
Second wind=2,500=3,000=30%=P3.0D=3.0=Cre=Stars=Muses=3 March = C=I>>GIL.
Secrecy=5,500=5.5=80%=P5.50=Earth-Midway=5 May = Gaia.

Secret=10,000=1,000=100%=10.0=Physicality=Tech.=10 Oct.=Uranus=P=1Ø.
Secretariat=5,500=5.5=80%=P5.50=Earth-Midway=5 May = Gaia.
Secretary=10,000=1,000=100%=10.0=Physicality=Tech.=10 Oct.=Uranus=P=1Ø.
Secretary-general=4,500=5,000=50%=P5.00D=Law=Time=Venus=5 May=Odite>>L=N.
Secrete1=8,000=80%=P8.0D=Economy=Currency=8 Aug.=Zeus>>E=v.
Secrete2=2,500=3,000=30%=P3.0D=3.0=Creativity=Stars=Muses=3 March = C=I>>GIL.
Secretive=1,500=15%=P1.50D=1.5=Authority=Solar Crown=1 May = Maia.
Secret service=10,000=1,000=100%=10.0=Physicality=Tech.=10 Oct.=Uranus=P=1Ø.
Sect=10,000=1,000=100%=10.0=Physicality=Tech.=10 Oct.=Uranus=P=1Ø.
-sect=4,000=40%=P4.0D=Govt.=Creatocracy=4 April=Mercury=Hermes=G=A4.
Sectarian=7,000=70%=P7.0D=7.0=Language=Assets=Mars=7 July=Pleiades.
Section=10,000=1,000=100%=10.0=Physicality=Tech.=10 Oct.=Uranus=P=1Ø.
Sectional=6,500=7,000=70%=P7.0D=7.0=Language=Assets=Mars=7 July=Pleiades.
Sectionalism=3,500=4,000=40%=P4.0D=Govt.=Creatocracy=4 April=Hermes=G=A4.
Sector=10,000=1,000=100%=10.0=Physicality=Tech.=10 Oct.=Uranus=P=1Ø.
Secular=10,000=1,000=100%=10.0=Physicality=Tech.=10 Oct.=Uranus=P=1Ø.
Secularize=5,000=50%=P5.00D=Law=Time=Venus=5 May = Aphrodite>>L=N.
Secure=10,000=1,000=100%=10.0=Physicality=Tech.=10 Oct.=Uranus=P=1Ø.
Security=10,000=1,000=100%=10.0=Physicality=Tech.=10 Oct.=Uranus=P=1Ø.
Sedan=10,000=1,000=100%=10.0=Physicality=Tech.=10 Oct.=Uranus=P=1Ø.
Sedate1=5,500=5.5=80%=P5.50=Earth-Midway=5 May = Gaia.
Sedate2=3,000=30%=P3.0D=3.0=Creativity=Stars=Muses=3 March = C=I>>GIL.
Sedative=6,500=7,000=70%=P7.0D=7.0=Language=Assets=Mars=7 July=Pleiades.
Sedentary=8,000=80%=P8.0D=Economy=Currency=8 Aug.=Zeus>>E=v.
Seder=8,500=9,000=90%=P9.00D=9.0=Abstraction=Gods=Saturn=9Sept.>>A=Ø.
Sedge=6,000=60%=P6.0D=Man=Earth=Royalty=6 June=Gaia=Maia>>M=M2.
Sediment=8,500=9,000=90%=P9.00D=9.0=Abstraction=Gods=Saturn=9Sept.>>A=Ø.
Sedimentary=5,000=50%=P5.00D=Law=Time=Venus=5 May = Aphrodite>>L=N.
Sedition=10,000=1,000=100%=10.0=Physicality=Tech.=10 Oct.=Uranus=P=1Ø.
Seduce=10,000=1,000=100%=10.0=Physicality=Tech.=10 Oct.=Uranus=P=1Ø.
Sedulous=2,000=20%=P2.00D=2.0=Nature=Matter=Moon=2 Feb.=Cupid=N=C+_
See1=10,000=1,000=100%=10.0=Physicality=Tech.=10 Oct.=Uranus=P=1Ø.
See2=6,000=60%=P6.0D=Man=Earth=Royalty=6 June=Gaia=Maia>>M=M2.
Seed=10,000=1,000=100%=10.0=Physicality=Tech.=10 Oct.=Uranus=P=1Ø.
Seedling=3,000=30%=P3.0D=3.0=Creativity=Stars=Muses=3 March = C=I>>GIL.
Seedpod=1,500=15%=P1.50D=1.5=Authority=Solar Crown=1 May = Maia.
Seedy=4,000=40%=P4.0D=Govt.=Creatocracy=4 April=Mercury=Hermes=G=A4.
Seeing=1,000=100%=10.0=1.0=Mind=Sun=1 January=Helios >> M=E4.
Seek=10,000=1,000=100%=10.0=Physicality=Tech.=10 Oct.=Uranus=P=1Ø.
Seem=12,000=12%=P1.20D=1.2=Knowledge=Edu=12Dec.=Athena>>K=F.
Seeming=1,000=100%=10.0=1.0=Mind=Sun=1 January=Helios >> M=E4.
Seemly=3,500=4,000=40%=P4.0D=Govt.=Creatocracy=4April=Mercury=Hermes=G=A4.
Seen=2,000=20%=P2.00D=2.0=Nature=Matter=Moon=2 Feb.=Cupid=N=C+_
Seep=6,500=7,000=70%=P7.0D=7.0=Language=Assets=Mars=7 July=Pleiades.
Seer=1,500=15%=P1.50D=1.5=Authority=Solar Crown=1 May = Maia.

PETER K. MATTHEWS - AKUKALIA

Seersucker=8,000=80%=P8.0D=Economy=Currency=8 Aug.=Zeus>>E=v.
Seesaw=10,000=1,000=100%=10.0=Physicality=Tech.=10 Oct.=Uranus=P=1Ø.
Seethe=6,000=60%=P6.0D=Man=Earth=Royalty=6 June=Gaia=Maia>>M=M2.
Segment=10,000=1,000=100%=10.0=Physicality=Tech.=10 Oct.=Uranus=P=1Ø.
Segregate=10,000=1,000=100%=10.0=Physicality=Tech.=10 Oct.=Uranus=P=1Ø.
Segue=10,000=1,000=100%=10.0=Physicality=Tech.=10 Oct.=Uranus=P=1Ø.
Seignior=2,500=3,000=30%=P3.0D=3.0=Creativity=Stars=Muses=3 March=C=I>>GIL.
seine=10,000=1,000=100%=10.0=Physicality=Tech.=10 Oct.=Uranus=P=1Ø.
Seine=9,000=90%=P9.00D=9.0=Abstraction=Gods=Saturn=9Sept.>>A=Ø.
Seismic=3,000=30%=P3.0D=3.0=Creativity=Stars=Muses=3 March = C=I>>GIL.
Seismo-=1,500=15%=P1.50D=1.5=Authority=Solar Crown=1 May = Maia.
Seismograph=10,000=1,000=100%=10.0=Physicality=Tech.=10 Oct.=Uranus=P=1Ø.
Seismology=10,000=1,000=100%=10.0=Physicality=Tech.=10 Oct.=Uranus=P=1Ø.
Seize=10,000=1,000=100%=10.0=Physicality=Tech.=10 Oct.=Uranus=P=1Ø.
Seizure=10,000=1,000=100%=10.0=Physicality=Tech.=10 Oct.=Uranus=P=1Ø.
Seldom=2,500=3,000=30%=P3.0D=3.0=Creativity=Stars=Muses=3 March = C=I>>GIL.
Select=10,000=1,000=100%=10.0=Physicality=Tech.=10 Oct.=Uranus=P=1Ø.
Selectee=1,000=100%=10.0=1.0=Mind=Sun=1 January=Helios >> M=E4.
Selection=10,000=1,000=100%=10.0=Physicality=Tech.=10 Oct.=Uranus=P=1Ø.
Selective service=5,000=50%=P5.00D=Law=Time=Venus=5 May = Aphrodite>>L=N.
Selectman=10,000=1,000=100%=10.0=Physicality=Tech.=10 Oct.=Uranus=P=1Ø.
Select woman=3,000=30%=P3.0D=3.0=Creativity=Stars=Muses=3 March = C=I>>GIL.
Selenium=12,000=12%=P1.20D=1.2=Knowledge=Edu=12Dec.=Athena>>K=F.
Seleucia=4,000=40%=P4.0D=Govt.=Creatocracy=4 April=Mercury=Hermes=G=A4.
Seleucid=6,000=60%=P6.0D=Man=Earth=Royalty=6 June=Gaia=Maia>>M=M2.
Self=10,000=1,000=100%=10.0=Physicality=Tech.=10 Oct.=Uranus=P=1Ø.
Self-=3,500=4,000=40%=P4.0D=Govt.=Creatocracy=4 April=Mercury=Hermes=G=A4.
Self absorbed=1,500=15%=P1.50D=1.5=Authority=Solar Crown=1 May = Maia.
Self addressed=1,500=15%=P1.50D=1.5=Authority=Solar Crown=1 May = Maia.
Self appointed=1,500=15%=P1.50D=1.5=Authority=Solar Crown=1 May = Maia.

Self assertion=4,500=5,000=50%=P5.00D=Law=Time=Venus=5 May = Aphrodite>>L=N.
Determined advancement of one's own personality, wishes, or views. Score is 45%. To execute the process, implement ideas and live by it is worth a 100% and 10,000 Maks. This is the rights Peter Matthews-Akukalia has so managed to become a God at what he does. The Creatocracy is determined on a much higher scale through word power & data mining.

Self assured=1,500=15%=P1.50D=1.5=Authority=Solar Crown=1 May = Maia.
Self-centered=2,000=20%=P2.00D=2.0=Nature=Matter=Moon=2 Feb.=Cupid=N=C+_
Self-conscious=5,000=50%=P5.00D=Law=Time=Venus=5 May = Aphrodite>>L=N.
Self-contained=6,000=60%=P6.0D=Man=Earth=Royalty=6 June=Gaia=Maia>>M=M2.
Self-control=3,500=4,000=40%=P4.0D=Govt.=Creatocracy=4 April=Hermes=G=A4.
Self-defense=10,000=1,000=100%=10.0=Physicality=Tech.=10 Oct.=Uranus=P=1Ø.

Self-denial=3,500=4,000=40%=P4.0D=Govt.=4 April=Mercury=Hermes=G=A4.
Self-destruct=5,000=50%=P5.00D=Law=Time=Venus=5 May = Aphrodite>>L=N.
Self-destruction=3,500=4,000=40%=P4.0D=Govt.=4 April=Mercury=Hermes=G=A4.
Self-determination=10,000=1,000=100%=10.0=Physicality=Tech.=10 Oct.=Uranus=P=1Ø.
Self-discipline=4,500=5,000=50%=P5.00D=Law=Time=Venus=5 May = Aphrodite>>L=N.
Self-effacing=3,000=30%=P3.0D=3.0=Creativity=Stars=Muses=3 March = C=I>>GIL.
Self-esteem=1,500=15%=P1.50D=1.5=Authority=Solar Crown=1 May = Maia.
Self-evident=2,500=3,000=30%=P3.0D=3.0=Cre=Stars=Muses=3 March = C=I>>GIL.
Self-explanatory=1,500=15%=P1.50D=1.5=Authority=Solar Crown=1 May = Maia.
Self-expression=5,000=50%=P5.00D=Law=Time=Venus=5 May = Aphrodite>>L=N.
Self-fertilization=4,000=40%=P4.0D=Govt.=4 April=Mercury=Hermes=G=A4.
Self-fulfilling=8,000=80%=P8.0D=Economy=Currency=8 Aug.=Zeus>>E=v.
Self-fulfillment=3,000=30%=P3.0D=3.0=Creativity=Stars=Muses=3 March = C=I>>GIL.

Self-government=2,000=20%=P2.00D=2.0=Nature=Matter=Moon=2 Feb.=Cupid=N=C+_
Democracy is a self government and so is Creatocracy except the standards are higher.
Democracy weighs 10% in nature and so naturally depends and must depend on the
Creatocracy. Hence there is no true democracy without a Creatocracy. No professionalism
without the Creative Scientist and no nation without the universe. This is natural law.

Self-hardening=4,500=5,000=50%=P5.00D=Law=Time=Venus=5 May = Aphrodite>>L=N.
Self-image=5,000=50%=P5.00D=Law=Time=Venus=5 May = Aphrodite>>L=N.
Self-importance=3,500=4,000=40%=P4.0D=Govt.=Creatocracy=4 April=Hermes=G=A4.

Self-imposed=3,000=30%=P3.0D=3.0=Creativity=Stars=Muses=3 March = C=I>>GIL.
Everyone is born with a natural self imposed creativity hence everyone is a natural
creatocrat. There is first the one who has accepted it and there is the one in the waiting list.

Self-incrimination=6,000=60%=P6.0D=Man=Earth=Royalty=6 June=Gaia=Maia>>M=M2.
Self-induced=4,000=40%=P4.0D=Govt.=Creatocracy=4 April=Mercury=Hermes=G=A4.
Self-induction=7,000=70%=P7.0D=7.0=Language=Assets=Mars=7 July=Pleiades.
Self-indulgence=4,000=40%=P4.0D=Govt.=4 April=Mercury=Hermes=G=A4.
Self-interest=5,000=50%=P5.00D=Law=Time=Venus=5 May = Aphrodite>>L=N.
Selfish=2,000=20%=P2.00D=2.0=Nature=Matter=Moon=2 Feb.=Cupid=N=C+_
Selfless=3,000=30%=P3.0D=3.0=Creativity=Stars=Muses=3 March = C=I>>GIL.
Self-love=2,000=20%=P2.00D=2.0=Nature=Matter=Moon=2 Feb.=Cupid=N=C+_
Self-made=4,000=40%=P4.0D=Govt.=Creatocracy=4 April=Mercury=Hermes=G=A4.
Self-mailer=6,000=60%=P6.0D=Man=Earth=Royalty=6 June=Gaia=Maia>>M=M2.
Self-pity=2,000=20%=P2.00D=2.0=Nature=Matter=Moon=2 Feb.=Cupid=N=C+_
Self-pollination=6,000=60%=P6.0D=Man=Earth=Royalty=6 June=Gaia=Maia>>M=M2.
Self-possession=4,000=40%=P4.0D=Govt.=4 April=Mercury=Hermes=G=A4.
Self-preservation=3,500=4,000=40%=P4.0D=Govt.=Creatocracy=4 April=Hermes=G=A4.

Self-proclaimed=1,000=100%=10.0=1.0=Mind=Sun=1 January=Helios >> M=E4.
No one can win a prize without being sure of himself. Peter Matthews-Akukalia wrote
the formula of the Mind and computed the temperature of the Solar core owning the
solar core asset that manifests as the diamond and everything governed by the Sun.
This granted him the legal right to self proclaim in the first instance. Publishing made
him universally acclaimed. He sets his objectives by the laws of GOD and Man in the
Scriptures and by Intellectual Property laws. He asserts his rights. Deuteronomy 29:29
Job 38, 39 & 40:10

Self-realization=2,500=3,000=30%=P3.0D=3.0=Cr=Stars=Muses=3 March = C=I>>GIL.
Complete development of one's own potential. The philosophy of the Creatocracy.
Peter Matthews-Akukalia discovered DDC code. 1. Discover. 2. Develop. 3. Connect.
We summarize this principle in slogan as "The Creatocracy - self realization through
creativity".

Self-referential=1,500=15%=P1.50D=1.5=Authority=Solar Crown=1 May = Maia.
Self-respect=2,000=20%=P2.00D=2.0=Nature=Matter=Moon=2 Feb.=Cupid=N=C+_
Self-righteous=3,500=4,000=40%=P4.0D=Govt.=4 April=Mercury=G=A4.
Self-rising flour=3,500=4,000=40%=P4.0D=Govt.=4 April=Mercury=Hermes=G=A4.
Self-sacrifice=6,000=60%=P6.0D=Man=Earth=Royalty=6 June=Gaia=Maia>>M=M2.
Selfsame=4,000=40%=P4.0D=Govt.=Creatocracy=4 April=Mercury=Hermes=G=A4.
Self-satisfaction=2,000=20%=P2.00D=2.0=Nature=Matter=Moon=2 Feb.=Cupid=N=C+_
Self-sealing=5,000=50%=P5.00D=Law=Time=Venus=5 May = Aphrodite>>L=N.
Self-searching=4,000=40%=P4.0D=Govt.=Creatocracy=4 April=Mercury=Hermes=G=A4.
Self-seeking=3,500=4,000=40%=P4.0D=Govt.=Creatocracy=4 April=Hermes=G=A4.
Self-service=5,500=5.5=80%=P5.50=Earth-Midway=5 May = Gaia.
Self-serving=4,500=5,000=50%=P5.00D=Law=Time=Venus=5 May = Aphrodite>>L=N.
Self-starter=4,000=40%=P4.0D=Govt.=Creatocracy=4 April=Mercury=Hermes=G=A4.
Self-styled=6,000=60%=P6.0D=Man=Earth=Royalty=6 June=Gaia=Maia>>M=M2.
Self-sufficient=3,500=4,000=40%=P4.0D=Govt.=Creatocracy=4 April=Hermes=G=A4.
Self will=1,000=100%=10.0=1.0=Mind=Sun=1 January=Helios >> M=E4.
Seljuk=6,000=60%=P6.0D=Man=Earth=Royalty=6 June=Gaia=Maia>>M=M2.
Sell=10,000=1,000=100%=10.0=Physicality=Tech.=10 Oct.=Uranus=P=1Ø.
Sell off=8,000=80%=P8.0D=Economy=Currency=8 Aug.=Zeus>>E=v.
Sellout=7,500=8,000=80%=P8.0D=Economy=Currency=8 Aug.=Zeus>>E=v.
Seltzer=9,500=10,000=1,000=100%=10.0=Physicality=Tech.=10 Oct.=Uranus=P=1Ø.
Selvage=5,000=50%=P5.00D=Law=Time=Venus=5 May = Aphrodite>>L=N.
Selves=1,500=15%=P1.50D=1.5=Authority=Solar Crown=1 May = Maia.
Semantic=7,000=70%=P7.0D=7.0=Language=Assets=Mars=7 July=Pleiades.
Semantics=3,000=30%=P3.0D=3.0=Creativity=Stars=Muses=3 March = C=I>>GIL.
Semaphore=10,000=1,000=100%=10.0=Physicality=Tech.=10 Oct.=Uranus=P=1Ø.
Semarang=5,000=50%=P5.00D=Law=Time=Venus=5 May = Aphrodite>>L=N.
Semblance=6,500=7,000=70%=P7.0D=7.0=Language=Assets=Mars=7 July=Pleiades.

Semen=6,500=7,000=70%=P7.0D=7.0=Language=Assets=Mars=7 July=Pleiades.
The seed of the male reproductive organs, a means to attain precision through functionality. Sexual transmutation, conception as a concept, brainchild as offspring etc. Read the book >> Think and Grow Rich by Napoleon Hill. Here it is established.

Semester=9,000=90%=P9.00D=9.0=Abstraction=Gods=Saturn=9Sept.>>A=Ø.
Semi=2,000=20%=P2.00D=2.0=Nature=Matter=Moon=2 Feb.=Cupid=N=C+_
Semi-=8,500=9,000=90%=P9.00D=9.0=Abstraction=Gods=Saturn=9Sept.>>A=Ø.
Semiannual=3,000=30%=P3.0D=3.0=Creativity=Stars=Muses=3 March = C=I>>GIL.
Semicircle=4,000=40%=P4.0D=Govt.=Creatocracy=4 April=Mercury=Hermes=G=A4.
Semicircular canal=9,000=90%=P9.00D=9.0=Abstraction=Gods=Saturn=9Sept.>>A=Ø.
Semicolon=10,000=1,000=100%=10.0=Physicality=Tech.=10 Oct.=Uranus=P=1Ø.
Semiconductor=10,000=1,000=100%=10.0=Physicality=Tech.=10 Oct.=Uranus=P=1Ø.
Semifinal=4,500=5,000=50%=P5.00D=Law=Time=Venus=5 May = Aphrodite>>L=N.
Semi month=5,500=5.5=80%=P5.50=Earth-Midway=5 May = Gaia.

Seminal=12,000=12%=P1.20D=1.2=Knowledge=Edu=12Dec.=Athena>>K=F.
Of or relating to semen. Creative. Providing a basis for further development: seminal research in a new field. <Lat.semen,sēmin-,seed. The Creatocracy discovers the link between sex and creativity and the development of the knowledge of an inner faculty. Seminal is classified as creativity hence it is correct that sexuality or sexual transmutation builds one's creativity and knowledge. Perhaps reason why highly sexual nations are often more stable within the approved standards. See semen. Principles of Psychoeconomix.

Seminar=9,000=90%=P9.00D=9.0=Abstraction=Gods=Saturn=9Sept.>>A=Ø.
Seminary=5,000=50%=P5.00D=Law=Time=Venus=5 May = Aphrodite>>L=N.
Seminole=10,000=1,000=100%=10.0=Physicality=Tech.=10 Oct.=Uranus=P=1Ø.

Semiotics=2,000=20%=P2.00D=2.0=Nature=Matter=Moon=2 Feb.=Cupid=N=C+_
Greek > Sēma, sign.

Semiprecious stone=8,000=80%=P8.0D=Economy=Currency=8 Aug.=Zeus>>E=v.
Semiprivate=2,500=3,000=30%=P3.0D=3.0=Cre=Stars=Muses=3 March = C=I>>GIL.

Semipro=1,000=100%=10.0=1.0=Mind=Sun=1 January=Helios >> M=E4.

Semiprofessional=10,000=1,000=100%=10.0=Physicality=Tech.=10 Oct.=Uranus=P=1Ø.
Now in the Creatocracy a Creative Scientist is a semiprofessional or semipro. After a chartered course such one is inducted into the Institute of Chartered Creative & Psycho-Social Scientists as a Creative Scientist Prodessional. It takes about 5years to be a Creative Scientist or an Oracle and ten years of study and practice to become a professional...

Semiskilled=2,500=3,000=30%=P3.0D=3.0=Cre=Stars=Muses=3 March = C=I>>GIL.
Semisolid=7,000=70%=P7.0D=7.0=Language=Assets=Mars=7 July=Pleiades.
Semite=10,000=1,000=100%=10.0=Physicality=Tech.=10 Oct.=Uranus=P=1Ø.
Semitic=10,000=1,000=100%=10.0=Physicality=Tech.=10 Oct.=Uranus=P=1Ø.
Semitism=2,000=20%=P2.00D=2.0=Nature=Matter=Moon=2 Feb.=Cupid=N=C+_
Semitone=6,500=7,000=70%=P7.0D=7.0=Language=Assets=Mars=7 July=Pleiades.
Semitrailer=7,000=70%=P7.0D=7.0=Language=Assets=Mars=7 July=Pleiades.
Semivowel=8,500=9,000=90%=P9.00D=9.0=Abstraction=Gods=Saturn=9Sept.>>A=Ø.
Semiweekly=5,500=5.5=80%=P5.50=Earth-Midway=5 May = Gaia.
Semi yearly=3,000=30%=P3.0D=3.0=Creativity=Stars=Muses=3 March = C=I>>GIL.
Semolina=8,000=80%=P8.0D=Economy=Currency=8 Aug.=Zeus>>E=v.

Sen1=3,000=30%=P3.0D=3.0=Creativity=Stars=Muses=3 March = C=I>>GIL.
Currency metric weight >> 3/10=0.3>>30:1. See Naira. Dollar.

Sen2=4,000=40%=P4.0D=Govt.=Creatocracy=4 April=Mercury=Hermes=G=A4.
Indonesia, ult. <CENT. Currency metric weight >> 4/10=0.4>>40:1. See Naira. Dollar.

Senate=10,000=1,000=100%=10.0=Physicality=Tech.=10 Oct.=Uranus=P=1Ø.
Senator=2,000=20%=P2.00D=2.0=Nature=Matter=Moon=2 Feb.=Cupid=N=C+_
Send=10,000=1,000=100%=10.0=Physicality=Tech.=10 Oct.=Uranus=P=1Ø.
Sendal=5,000=50%=P5.00D=Law=Time=Venus=5 May = Aphrodite>>L=N.
Send off=6,000=60%=P6.0D=Man=Earth=Royalty=6 June=Gaia=Maia>>M=M2.

Sene=3,500=4,000=40%=P4.0D=Govt.=Creatocracy=4 April=Mercury=Hermes=G=A4.
Samoan < CENT. Currency metric weight >> 3.5/10=0.35=35:1. See Naira. Dollar.

Seneca=10,000=1,000=100%=10.0=Physicality=Tech.=10 Oct.=Uranus=P=1Ø.
Seneca,Lucius=7,000=70%=P7.0D=7.0=Language=Assets=Mars=7 July=Pleiades.
Senegal=6,000=60%=P6.0D=Man=Earth=Royalty=6 June=Gaia=Maia>>M=M2.
Senegal River=9,500=10,000=1,000=100%=10.0=Physicality.=10 Oct.=Uranus=P=1Ø.
Senescent=3,000=30%=P3.0D=3.0=Creativity=Stars=Muses=3 March = C=I>>GIL.
Senile=10,000=1,000=100%=10.0=Physicality=Tech.=10 Oct.=Uranus=P=1Ø.
Senior=10,000=1,000=100%=10.0=Physicality=Tech.=10 Oct.=Uranus=P=1Ø.
Senior chief petty officer=6,000=60%=P6.0D=Man=Earth=6June=Gaia=Maia>>M=M2.
Senior citizen=4,000=40%=P4.0D=Govt.=Creatocracy=4 April=Mercury=Hermes=G=A4.
Senior high school=5,000=50%=P5.00D=Law=Time=Venus=5 May = Aphrodite>>L=N.
Seniority=5,500=5.5=80%=P5.50=Earth-Midway=5 May = Gaia.
Senior master sergeant=5,500=5.5=80%=P5.50=Earth-Midway=5 May = Gaia.

Seniti=3,000=30%=P3.0D=3.0=Creativity=Stars=Muses=3 March = C=I>>GIL.
Tongan<CENT. Currency metric weight = 3/10=0.3=30:1. See Naira. Dollar.

Senna=10,000=1,000=100%=10.0=Physicality=Tech.=10 Oct.=Uranus=P=1Ø.
Sennacherib=3,500=4,000=40%=P4.0D=Govt.=4 April=Mercury=Hermes=G=A4.
Señor=4,000=40%=P4.0D=Govt.=Creatocracy=4 April=Mercury=Hermes=G=A4.
Señora=3,500=4,000=40%=P4.0D=Govt.=Creatocracy=4 April=Mercury=Hermes=G=A4.
Señorita=5,000=50%=P5.00D=Law=Time=Venus=5 May = Aphrodite>>L=N.
Sensation=10,000=1,000=100%=10.0=Physicality=Tech.=10 Oct.=Uranus=P=1Ø.
Sensationalism=6,000=60%=P6.0D=Man=Earth=Royalty=6 June=Gaia=Maia>>M=M2.
Sense=10,000=1,000=100%=10.0=Physicality=Tech.=10 Oct.=Uranus=P=1Ø.
Senseless=3,500=4,000=40%=P4.0D=Govt.=4 April=Mercury=Hermes=G=A4.
Sensibility=8,500=9,000=90%=P9.00D=9.0=Abstraction=Gods=Saturn=9Sept.>>A=Ø.
Sensible=10,000=1,000=100%=10.0=Physicality=Tech.=10 Oct.=Uranus=P=1Ø.
Sensitive=10,000=1,000=100%=10.0=Physicality=Tech.=10 Oct.=Uranus=P=1Ø.
Sensitize=3,500=4,000=40%=P4.0D=Govt.=4 April=Mercury=Hermes=G=A4.
Sensor=7,000=70%=P7.0D=7.0=Language=Assets=Mars=7 July=Pleiades.
Sensory=1,500=15%=P1.50D=1.5=Authority=Solar Crown=1 May = Maia.
Sensual=8,000=80%=P8.0D=Economy=Currency=8 Aug.=Zeus>>E=v.
Sensuous=6,500=7,000=70%=P7.0D=7.0=Language=Assets=Mars=7 July=Pleiades.
Sent=3,000=30%=P3.0D=3.0=Creativity=Stars=Muses=3 March = C=I>>GIL.

Sente=3,000=30%=P3.0D=3.0=Creativity=Stars=Muses=3 March = C=I>>GIL.
[Sotho < CENT].

Sentence=10,000=1,000=100%=10.0=Physicality=Tech.=10 Oct.=Uranus=P=1Ø.
Sententious=6,500=7,000=70%=P7.0D=7.0=Language=Assets=Mars=7 July=Pleiades.
Sentient=4,500=5,000=50%=P5.00D=Law=Time=Venus=5 May = Aphrodite>>L=N.
Sentiment=10,000=1,000=100%=10.0=Physicality=Tech.=10 Oct.=Uranus=P=1Ø.
Sentimental=10,000=1,000=100%=10.0=Physicality=Tech.=10 Oct.=Uranus=P=1Ø.
Sentinel=2,500=3,000=30%=P3.0D=3.0=Creativity=Stars=Muses=3 March = C=I>>GIL.
Sentry=10,000=1,000=100%=10.0=Physicality=Tech.=10 Oct.=Uranus=P=1Ø.
Seoul=6,000=60%=P6.0D=Man=Earth=Royalty=6 June=Gaia=Maia>>M=M2.
Sepal=5,500=5.5=80%=P5.50=Earth-Midway=5 May = Gaia.
Separable=1,000=100%=10.0=1.0=Mind=Sun=1 January=Helios >> M=E4.
Separate=10,000=1,000=100%=10.0=Physicality=Tech.=10 Oct.=Uranus=P=1Ø.
Separation=11,000=11%=P1.10D=1.1=Idea=Brainchild=Inv.=11 Nov.=SC=Athena>>I=MT.
Separatist=3,500=4,000=40%=P4.0D=Govt.=Creatocracy=4 April=Hermes=G=A4.
Separator=5,500=5.5=80%=P5.50=Earth-Midway=5 May = Gaia.
Sephardi=7,500=8,000=80%=P8.0D=Economy=Currency=8 Aug.=Zeus>>E=v.
Sepia=7,000=70%=P7.0D=7.0=Language=Assets=Mars=7 July=Pleiades.
Sepsis=7,500=8,000=80%=P8.0D=Economy=Currency=8 Aug.=Zeus>>E=v.
Sept.=500=5%=P5.00D=5.0=Law=Time=Venus=5 May=Aphrodite>>L=N.
September=6,500=7,000=70%=P7.0D=7.0=Language=Assets=Mars=7 July=Pleiades.
Septic=3,500=4,000=40%=P4.0D=Govt.=Creatocracy=4 April=Mercury=Hermes=G=A4.
Septicemia=4,500=5,000=50%=P5.00D=Law=Time=Venus=5 May = Aphrodite>>L=N.

Septic tank=6,500=7,000=70%=P7.0D=7.0=Language=Assets=Mars=7 July=Pleiades.
Septillion=5,000=50%=P5.00D=Law=Time=Venus=5 May = Aphrodite>>L=N.

Septuagint=9,500=10,000=1,000=100%=10.0=Physicality=Tech.=10 Oct.=Uranus=P=1Ø.
A Greek translation of the Hebrew Bible made in the 3rd century B.C. Lat. Septuāgintā,
seventy (< the traditional number of its translators. So we have three codes that define
how the Bible should be processed. 9,500=10.0, 3rd=3.0, seventy =70=7.0. Hence the Bible
is governed by the laws of physical manifestations from abstraction means (9,500=10.0)
through Creativity and stellar coding being synchronization and crystallization (3.0) and
computing for language metric development (7.0). This translates the Bible from the Hebrew
literal value to the Greek real value. 10.0*3.0x=px=13+30=43x=px=433=4.33>>4.3>
Hermes functioned by the Gods (the Holy Spirit, Host of GOD). 4.3*7.0x=px=11.3+30.1
=41.4x=px=381.53=400=40=4.0 >> Hermes.
The Septuagint is actually the seven golden candlesticks in the Hands of Hermes (Khristos
Yezeus >> Christ Son of Zeus >> Christ Jesus) seen in Revelation 1:12-13. Hermes >> Jesus
Christ is actually the God of merchandise commerce invention. As Mercury He is the
God of oratory communication politics government nations roads borders relationships.
The Septuagint is the first seven books of the Bible that run from Genesis to Judges. It is
the essence of the entire scriptures and connects everything else in one way or the other.

Septum=9,000=90%=P9.00D=9.0=Abstraction=Gods=Saturn=9Sept.>>A=Ø.
Sepulcher=7,000=70%=P7.0D=7.0=Language=Assets=Mars=7 July=Pleiades.
Seq.=2,000=20%=P2.00D=2.0=Nature=Matter=Moon=2 Feb.=Cupid=N=C+_
Sequel=7,500=8,000=80%=P8.0D=Economy=Currency=8 Aug.=Zeus>>E=v.
Sequence=9,000=90%=P9.00D=9.0=Abstraction=Gods=Saturn=9Sept.>>A=Ø.
Sequester=10,000=1,000=100%=10.0=Physicality=Tech.=10 Oct.=Uranus=P=1Ø.
Sequin=7,000=70%=P7.0D=7.0=Language=Assets=Mars=7 July=Pleiades.
Sequoia=2,500=3,000=30%=P3.0D=3.0=Creativity=Stars=Muses=3 March = C=I>>GIL.
Sequoyah=2,500=3,000=30%=P3.0D=3.0=Creativity=Stars=Muses=3 March = C=I>>GIL.
Sera=2,000=20%=P2.00D=2.0=Nature=Matter=Moon=2 Feb.=Cupid=N=C+_
Seraglio=3,000=30%=P3.0D=3.0=Creativity=Stars=Muses=3 March = C=I>>GIL.
Serape=6,000=60%=P6.0D=Man=Earth=Royalty=6 June=Gaia=Maia>>M=M2.
Seraph=4,000=40%=P4.0D=Govt.=Creatocracy=4 April=Mercury=Hermes=G=A4.
Serb=6,500=7,000=70%=P7.0D=7.0=Language=Assets=Mars=7 July=Pleiades.
Serbia=9,500=10,000=1,000=100%=10.0=Physicality=Tech.=10 Oct.=Uranus=P=1Ø.
Serbian=6,500=7,000=70%=P7.0D=7.0=Language=Assets=Mars=7 July=Pleiades.
Serbo-Croatian=7,000=70%=P7.0D=7.0=Language=Assets=Mars=7 July=Pleiades.
Sere=2,000=20%=P2.00D=2.0=Nature=Matter=Moon=2 Feb.=Cupid=N=C+_
Serenade=8,500=9,000=90%=P9.00D=9.0=Abstraction=Gods=Saturn=9Sept.>>A=Ø.
Serendipity=7,000=70%=P7.0D=7.0=Language=Assets=Mars=7 July=Pleiades.
Serene=4,000=40%=P4.0D=Govt.=Creatocracy=4 April=Mercury=Hermes=G=A4.
Serf=9,500=10,000=1,000=100%=10.0=Physicality=Tech.=10 Oct.=Uranus=P=1Ø.
Serge=6,000=60%=P6.0D=Man=Earth=Royalty=6 June=Gaia=Maia>>M=M2.

Sergeant=10,000=1,000=100%=10.0=Physicality=Tech.=10 Oct.=Uranus=P=1Ø.
Sergeant at arms=6,500=7,000=70%=P7.0D=7.0=Lang=Assets=Mars=7 July=Pleiades.
Sergeant first class=4,500=5,000=50%=P5.00D=Law=Time=Venus=5 May=Odite>>L=N.
Sergeant major=9,000=90%=P9.00D=9.0=Abstraction=Gods=Saturn=9Sept.>>A=Ø.
Serial=8,000=80%=P8.0D=Economy=Currency=8 Aug.=Zeus>>E=v.
Series=10,000=1,000=100%=10.0=Physicality=Tech.=10 Oct.=Uranus=P=1Ø.
Serif=7,000=70%=P7.0D=7.0=Language=Assets=Mars=7 July=Pleiades.
Seriocomic=2,000=20%=P2.00D=2.0=Nature=Matter=Moon=2 Feb.=Cupid=N=C+_
Serious=10,500=11,000=11%=P1.10D=1.1=Idea=Brainchild=Inv.=11 Nov.=Athena>>I=MT.
Sermon=7,500=8,000=80%=P8.0D=Economy=Currency=8 Aug.=Zeus>>E=v.
Serology=2,500=3,000=30%=P3.0D=3.0=Creativity=Stars=Muses=3 March = C=I>>GIL.
Sero negative=7,500=8,000=80%=P8.0D=Economy=Currency=8 Aug.=Zeus>>E=v.
Seropositive=5,500=5.5=80%=P5.50=Earth-Midway=5 May = Gaia.
Serous=2,500=3,000=30%=P3.0D=3.0=Creativity=Stars=Muses=3 March = C=I>>GIL.
Serpent=3,000=30%=P3.0D=3.0=Creativity=Stars=Muses=3 March = C=I>>GIL.
Serpentine=4,500=5,000=50%=P5.00D=Law=Time=Venus=5 May = Aphrodite>>L=N.
Serrate=4,000=40%=P4.0D=Govt.=Creatocracy=4 April=Mercury=Hermes=G=A4.
Serried=4,000=40%=P4.0D=Govt.=Creatocracy=4 April=Mercury=Hermes=G=A4.
Serum=10,000=1,000=100%=10.0=Physicality=Tech.=10 Oct.=Uranus=P=1Ø.
Servant=3,000=30%=P3.0D=3.0=Creativity=Stars=Muses=3 March = C=I>>GIL.
Serve=10,000=1,000=100%=10.0=Physicality=Tech.=10 Oct.=Uranus=P=1Ø.
Service=10,000=1,000=100%=10.0=Physicality=Tech.=10 Oct.=Uranus=P=1Ø.
Serviceable=4,500=5,000=50%=P5.00D=Law=Time=Venus=5 May = Aphrodite>>L=N.
Serviceman=10,000=1,000=100%=10.0=Physicality=Tech.=10 Oct.=Uranus=P=1Ø.
Service mark=7,500=8,000=80%=P8.0D=Economy=Currency=8 Aug.=Zeus>>E=v.
Service station=6,500=7,000=70%=P7.0D=7.0=Language=Assets=Mars=7 July=Pleiades.
Service woman=3,500=4,000=40%=P4.0D=Govt.=Creatocracy=4 April=Hermes=G=A4.
Servile=3,500=4,000=40%=P4.0D=Govt.=Creatocracy=4 April=Mercury=Hermes=G=A4.
Serving=3,000=30%=P3.0D=3.0=Creativity=Stars=Muses=3 March = C=I>>GIL.
Servitor=2,000=20%=P2.00D=2.0=Nature=Matter=Moon=2 Feb.=Cupid=N=C+_
Servitude=7,000=70%=P7.0D=7.0=Language=Assets=Mars=7 July=Pleiades.
Servo=1,500=15%=P1.50D=1.5=Authority=Solar Crown=1 May = Maia.
Servomechanism=5,500=5.5=80%=P5.50=Earth-Midway=5 May = Gaia.
Servo motor=8,000=80%=P8.0D=Economy=Currency=8 Aug.=Zeus>>E=v.
Sesame=8,500=9,000=90%=P9.00D=9.0=Abstraction=Gods=Saturn=9Sept.>>A=Ø.
Sesquicentennial=9,500=10,000=1,000=100%=10.0=Phy=Tech.=10 Oct.=Uranus=P=1Ø.
Sesquipedalian=10,000=1,000=100%=10.0=Physicality=Tech.=10 Oct.=Uranus=P=1Ø.
Sessile=9,500=10,000=1,000=100%=10.0=Physicality=Tech.=10 Oct.=Uranus=P=1Ø.
Session=10,000=1,000=100%=10.0=Physicality=Tech.=10 Oct.=Uranus=P=1Ø.
Sestet=4,500=5,000=50%=P5.00D=Law=Time=Venus=5 May = Aphrodite>>L=N.
Set1=10,000=1,000=100%=10.0=Physicality=Tech.=10 Oct.=Uranus=P=1Ø.
Set2=10,000=1,000=100%=10.0=Physicality=Tech.=10 Oct.=Uranus=P=1Ø.
Setback=3,000=30%=P3.0D=3.0=Creativity=Stars=Muses=3 March = C=I>>GIL.
Seton Saint Elizabeth=5,000=50%=P5.00D=Law=Time=Venus=5 May = Aphrodite>>L=N.
Set piece=10,000=1,000=100%=10.0=Physicality=Tech.=10 Oct.=Uranus=P=1Ø.

Set screw=5,000=50%=P5.00D=Law=Time=Venus=5 May = Aphrodite>>L=N.
Settee=5,000=50%=P5.00D=Law=Time=Venus=5 May = Aphrodite>>L=N.
Setter=4,500=5,000=50%=P5.00D=Law=Time=Venus=5 May = Aphrodite>>L=N.
Set theory=3,000=30%=P3.0D=3.0=Creativity=Stars=Muses=3 March = C=I>>GIL.
Setting=10,000=1,000=100%=10.0=Physicality=Tech.=10 Oct.=Uranus=P=1Ø.
Settle=10,000=1,000=100%=10.0=Physicality=Tech.=10 Oct.=Uranus=P=1Ø.
Settlement=10,000=1,000=100%=10.0=Physicality=Tech.=10 Oct.=Uranus=P=1Ø.
Set-to=2,500=3,000=30%=P3.0D=3.0=Creativity=Stars=Muses=3 March = C=I>>GIL.
Setup=10,000=1,000=100%=10.0=Physicality=Tech.=10 Oct.=Uranus=P=1Ø.
Seurat Georges=2,500=3,000=30%=P3.0D=3.0=Cr=Stars=Muses=3 March = C=I>>GIL.
Sevastopol=6,500=7,000=70%=P7.0D=7.0=Language=Assets=Mars=7 July=Pleiades.

Seven=8,000=80%=P8.0D=Economy=Currency=8 Aug.=Zeus>>E=v.
The number seven is actually a sign of Zeus, of course through Aries. Seven is therefore an economy number indicating assets are earned through computing literal works and developing language metric systems such as the Castle Makupedia which becomes the World first computed dictionary Makumatics and MaksCurrencies encyclopedia by the World's 1ˢᵗ Makumatician, 1ˢᵗ Computational Lexicographer, 1ˢᵗ Dicclopedysxt and Many Other Firsts in the person of Peter Matthews-Akukalia, Castle Makupedia. Computing makes one inherit the promise which is the Spirit of the Zeus the almighty GOD.
We conclude that Zeus actually created the Earth by computing tracking and establishing. See Proverbs 8:22-31.

Seventeen=8,500=9,000=90%=P9.00D=9.0=Abstraction=Gods=Saturn=9Sept.>>A=Ø.
Seventeen is the name of the means by which Zeus discusses with the Council of the Host or the Holy Spirit. An asset of computational intelligence and value, it indicates that communication of spirits is done by symbolic codes and computational numbers. Therefore numbers are the basis for all spirituality and a religion without it is still speculative and lags behind. Seventeen >> 17>>1.7 where God is (as) One is the government body or council of GOD known as the Holy Spirit is functioned by 7 the spirit of Zeus the almighty Himself. The incarnation of the almighty is a proficiency of numerical interpretation in a person. So we could say that people like Isaac Newton and Einstein were incarnations of Zeus who could in a certain way manner and level compute formulas and abstract matter. This is the apotheosis of Peter Matthews-Akukalia into Castle Makupedia a God.

Seventeenth=6,500=7,000=70%=P7.0D=7.0=Language=Assets=Mars=7 July=Pleiades.
Seventh=8,000=80%=P8.0D=Economy=Currency=8 Aug.=Zeus>>E=v.
Seventh heaven=2,500=3,000=30%=P3.0D=3.0=Cre=Stars=Muses=3 March = C=I>>GIL.
Seventieth=6,500=7,000=70%=P7.0D=7.0=Language=Assets=Mars=7 July=Pleiades.
Seventy=5,000=50%=P5.00D=Law=Time=Venus=5 May = Aphrodite>>L=N.
Sever=8,500=9,000=90%=P9.00D=9.0=Abstraction=Gods=Saturn=9Sept.>>A=Ø.
Several=10,000=1,000=100%=10.0=Physicality=Tech.=10 Oct.=Uranus=P=1Ø.
Severalty=7,000=70%=P7.0D=7.0=Language=Assets=Mars=7 July=Pleiades.
Severance=9,500=10,000=1,000=100%=10.0=Physicality=Tech.=10 Oct.=Uranus=P=1Ø.

Severe=10,000=1,000=100%=10.0=Physicality=Tech.=10 Oct.=Uranus=P=1Ø.
Severn River=10,000=1,000=100%=10.0=Physicality=Tech.=10 Oct.=Uranus=P=1Ø.
Severus Lucius=4,000=40%=P4.0D=Govt.=Creatocracy=4 April=Mercury=Hermes=G=A4.
Seville=4,500=5,000=50%=P5.00D=Law=Time=Venus=5 May = Aphrodite>>L=N.
Sew=10,000=1,000=100%=10.0=Physicality=Tech.=10 Oct.=Uranus=P=1Ø.
Sewage=5,000=50%=P5.00D=Law=Time=Venus=5 May = Aphrodite>>L=N.
Seward William=3,000=30%=P3.0D=3.0=Creativity=Stars=Muses=3 March = C=I>>GIL.
Sewer=10,000=1,000=100%=10.0=Physicality=Tech.=10 Oct.=Uranus=P=1Ø.
Sewerage=4,500=5,000=50%=P5.00D=Law=Time=Venus=5 May = Aphrodite>>L=N.
Sewing=5,000=50%=P5.00D=Law=Time=Venus=5 May = Aphrodite>>L=N.
Sewing machine=5,000=50%=P5.00D=Law=Time=Venus=5 May = Aphrodite>>L=N.
Sex=10,000=1,000=100%=10.0=Physicality=Tech.=10 Oct.=Uranus=P=1Ø.
Sexagenarian=5,500=5.5=80%=P5.50=Earth-Midway=5 May = Gaia.
Sexagesimal=5,000=50%=P5.00D=Law=Time=Venus=5 May = Aphrodite>>L=N.
Sex chromosome=10,000=1,000=100%=10.0=Physicality=Tech.=10 Oct.=Uranus=P=1Ø.
Sex hormones=6,000=60%=P6.0D=Man=Earth=Royalty=6 June=Gaia=Maia>>M=M2.
Sexism=4,000=40%=P4.0D=Govt.=Creatocracy=4 April=Mercury=Hermes=G=A4.
Sexless=3,000=30%=P3.0D=3.0=Creativity=Stars=Muses=3 March = C=I>>GIL.
Sex-linked=6,000=60%=P6.0D=Man=Earth=Royalty=6 June=Gaia=Maia>>M=M2.
Sextant=7,500=8,000=80%=P8.0D=Economy=Currency=8 Aug.=Zeus>>E=v.
Sextet=8,000=80%=P8.0D=Economy=Currency=8 Aug.=Zeus>>E=v.
Sextillion=6,000=60%=P6.0D=Man=Earth=Royalty=6 June=Gaia=Maia>>M=M2.
Sexton=6,500=7,000=70%=P7.0D=7.0=Language=Assets=Mars=7 July=Pleiades.
Sexton, Anne.=2,000=20%=P2.00D=2.0=Nature=Matter=Moon=2 Feb.=Cupid=N=C+_
Sextuple=10,000=1,000=100%=10.0=Physicality=Tech.=10 Oct.=Uranus=P=1Ø.
Sextuplet=6,000=60%=P6.0D=Man=Earth=Royalty=6 June=Gaia=Maia>>M=M2.
Sexual=10,000=1,000=100%=10.0=Physicality=Tech.=10 Oct.=Uranus=P=1Ø.

Sexual intercourse=6,000=60%=P6.0D=Man=Earth=Royalty=6 June=Gaia=Maia>>M=M2.
Sexual union between human beings generally involving physical union of the sexual organs. The code here is "physical" measured as 10.0. See sex. Computing sexual intercourse>> 10.0*6.0x=px=16+60=76x=px=1,036=10.36. Interpreted as a physical commitment of one's creative and emotional energy to produce a resultant. At 10=1.0 it is a thing of the mind in the first instance that consumes intelligence thought will and emotion. 10.4 it is the method by which the human being as a physical content is managed to create promote and sustain a certain objective agenda program or course of intended action.

Sexuality=7,500=8,000=80%=P8.0D=Economy=Currency=8 Aug.=Zeus>>E=v.
Sexuality transmtd. disease=5,000=50%=P5.00D=Law=Time=Venus=5 May=Odite>>L=N.
Sexy=5,000=50%=P5.00D=Law=Time=Venus=5 May = Aphrodite>>L=N.
Seychelles=7,500=8,000=80%=P8.0D=Economy=Currency=8 Aug.=Zeus>>E=v.
Seymour Jane=6,500=7,000=70%=P7.0D=7.0=Language=Assets=Mars=7 July=Pleiades.
Sf=1,000=100%=10.0=1.0=Mind=Sun=1 January=Helios >> M=E4.

---

sg=1,000=100%=10.0=1.0=Mind=Sun=1 January=Helios >> M=E4.
Peter Matthews-Akukalia, Castle Makupedia discovered and computed Quantum Gravity and Quantum Specific Gravity. See Psychoeconomix.

Sgt.=500=5%=P5.00D=5.0=Law=Time=Venus=5 May=Aphrodite>>L=N.
Shaban=5,500=5.5=80%=P5.50=Earth-Midway=5 May = Gaia.
Shabbat=2,500=3,000=30%=P3.0D=3.0=Creativity=Stars=Muses=3 March = C=I>>GIL.
Shabby=10,000=1,000=100%=10.0=Physicality=Tech.=10 Oct.=Uranus=P=1Ø.
Shack=5,000=50%=P5.00D=Law=Time=Venus=5 May = Aphrodite>>L=N.
Shackle=10,000=1,000=100%=10.0=Physicality=Tech.=10 Oct.=Uranus=P=1Ø.
Shad=8,000=80%=P8.0D=Economy=Currency=8 Aug.=Zeus>>E=v.
Shade=10,000=1,000=100%=10.0=Physicality=Tech.=10 Oct.=Uranus=P=1Ø.

Shadow=10,000=1,000=100%=10.0=Physicality=Tech.=10 Oct.=Uranus=P=1Ø.
See the book >> The Creatocracy Republic: Castle Makupedia Plays Legends and Short Stories by Peter Matthews-Akukalia. Reference book>> Shadows of Defeat. This is the first attempt made by the King to write a play. It is the first local play so published in Lagos and sold about 500 copies. He was 25years old and was a teacher at a local secondary school. In the Naturecology Peter Matthews-Akukalia used a shadow to illustrate and describe the nature of a spirit and defined spirit as animated energy from which television cartoons are classical examples of spirits. Thus they can be experienced but not tangible.

Shadow box=10,000=1,000=100%=10.0=Physicality=Tech.=10 Oct.=Uranus=P=1Ø.
Shady=3,000=30%=P3.0D=3.0=Creativity=Stars=Muses=3 March = C=I>>GIL.
Shaft=10,000=1,000=100%=10.0=Physicality=Tech.=10 Oct.=Uranus=P=1Ø.
Shag=10,000=1,000=100%=10.0=Physicality=Tech.=10 Oct.=Uranus=P=1Ø.
Shaggy=6,000=60%=P6.0D=Man=Earth=Royalty=6 June=Gaia=Maia>>M=M2.
Shah=6,500=7,000=70%=P7.0D=7.0=Language=Assets=Mars=7 July=Pleiades.
Shake=10,000=1,000=100%=10.0=Physicality=Tech.=10 Oct.=Uranus=P=1Ø.
Shakedown=10,000=1,000=100%=10.0=Physicality=Tech.=10 Oct.=Uranus=P=1Ø.
Shaker=10,000=1,000=100%=10.0=Physicality=Tech.=10 Oct.=Uranus=P=1Ø.

Shakespeare William=2,000=20%=P2.00D=2.0=Nature=Moon=2 Feb.=Cupid=N=C+_
The secret of William Shakespeare is in his nature and the natural things he does such as his works thus if he reincarnates or shares his energy then it is provable. The literal style of writing plays by Peter Matthews-Akukalia is much similar and traceable to Wilkiam Shakespeare hence the title African Shakespeare. In such a case we would reason that Abraham reincarnated as Tycho Brahe then as William Shakespeare, then as Benjamin Banneker then as Peter Matthews-Akukalia based on the energy of Zeus through centuries. The Creatocracy Republic: Castle Makupedia Plays Legends and Short Stories by Peter Matthews-Akukalia. Reference book is Legend of the Monarchs - a Play on William Shakespeare. The king's style of writing plays in the old Shakespearean English earned him the title of African Shakespeare. This title is exclusive to him in all rights asserted.

Shakeup=1,500=15%=P1.50D=1.5=Authority=Solar Crown=1 May = Maia.
Shako=8,000=80%=P8.0D=Economy=Currency=8 Aug.=Zeus>>E=v.
Shaky=4,000=40%=P4.0D=Govt.=Creatocracy=4 April=Mercury=Hermes=G=A4.
Shale=5,500=5.5=80%=P5.50=Earth-Midway=5 May = Gaia.
Shale oil=5,000=50%=P5.00D=Law=Time=Venus=5 May = Aphrodite>>L=N.
Shall=10,000=1,000=100%=10.0=Physicality=Tech.=10 Oct.=Uranus=P=1Ø.
Shallot=9,000=90%=P9.00D=9.0=Abstraction=Gods=Saturn=9Sept.>>A=Ø.
Shallow=10,000=1,000=100%=10.0=Physicality=Tech.=10 Oct.=Uranus=P=1Ø.
Shallom=4,500=5,000=50%=P5.00D=Law=Time=Venus=5 May = Aphrodite>>L=N.
Shalt=3,500=4,000=40%=P4.0D=Govt.=Creatocracy=4 April=Mercury=Hermes=G=A4.
Sham=10,000=1,000=100%=10.0=Physicality=Tech.=10 Oct.=Uranus=P=1Ø.
Shaman=10,000=1,000=100%=10.0=Physicality=Tech.=10 Oct.=Uranus=P=1Ø.
Shamble=7,000=70%=P7.0D=7.0=Language=Assets=Mars=7 July=Pleiades.
Shambles=8,500=9,000=90%=P9.00D=9.0=Abstraction=Gods=Saturn=9Sept.>>A=Ø.
Shame=10,000=1,000=100%=10.0=Physicality=Tech.=10 Oct.=Uranus=P=1Ø.
Shamefaced=6,500=7,000=70%=P7.0D=7.0=Language=Assets=Mars=7 July=Pleiades.
Shameless=5,000=50%=P5.00D=Law=Time=Venus=5 May = Aphrodite>>L=N.
Shammy=2,000=20%=P2.00D=2.0=Nature=Matter=Moon=2 Feb.=Cupid=N=C+_
Shampoo=10,000=1,000=100%=10.0=Physicality=Tech.=10 Oct.=Uranus=P=1Ø.
Shamrock=9,500=10,000=1,000=100%=10.0=Physicality=Tech.=10 Oct.=Uranus=P=1Ø.
Shandong=8,000=80%=P8.0D=Economy=Currency=8 Aug.=Zeus>>E=v.
shanghai=10,000=1,000=100%=10.0=Physicality=Tech.=10 Oct.=Uranus=P=1Ø.
Shanghai=7,000=70%=P7.0D=7.0=Language=Assets=Mars=7 July=Pleiades.
Shangri-La=6,500=7,000=70%=P7.0D=7.0=Language=Assets=Mars=7 July=Pleiades.
Shank=10,000=1,000=100%=10.0=Physicality=Tech.=10 Oct.=Uranus=P=1Ø.
Shannon=8,500=9,000=90%=P9.00D=9.0=Abstraction=Gods=Saturn=9Sept.>>A=Ø.
Shan't=1,000=100%=10.0=1.0=Mind=Sun=1 January=Helios >> M=E4.
Shape=10,000=1,000=100%=10.0=Physicality=Tech.=10 Oct.=Uranus=P=1Ø.
Shapeless=5,000=50%=P5.00D=Law=Time=Venus=5 May = Aphrodite>>L=N.
Shapely=2,000=20%=P2.00D=2.0=Nature=Matter=Moon=2 Feb.=Cupid=N=C+_
Shard=8,000=80%=P8.0D=Economy=Currency=8 Aug.=Zeus>>E=v.
Share1=10,000=1,000=100%=10.0=Physicality=Tech.=10 Oct.=Uranus=P=1Ø.
Share2=2,000=20%=P2.00D=2.0=Nature=Matter=Moon=2 Feb.=Cupid=N=C+_
Sharecropper=7,500=8,000=80%=P8.0D=Economy=Currency=8 Aug.=Zeus>>E=v.
Shareholder=4,500=5,000=50%=P5.00D=Law=Time=Venus=5 May = Aphrodite>>L=N.
Shark=10,000=1,000=100%=10.0=Physicality=Tech.=10 Oct.=Uranus=P=1Ø.
Sharkskin=6,500=7,000=70%=P7.0D=7.0=Language=Assets=Mars=7 July=Pleiades.
Sharp=10,000=1,000=100%=10.0=Physicality=Tech.=10 Oct.=Uranus=P=1Ø.
Sharpen=3,000=30%=P3.0D=3.0=Creativity=Stars=Muses=3 March = C=I>>GIL.
Sharpshooter=3,500=4,000=40%=P4.0D=Govt.=4 April=Mercury=Hermes=G=A4.
Shasta Mount.=7,000=70%=P7.0D=7.0=Language=Assets=Mars=7 July=Pleiades.
Shatt al Arab=10,000=1,000=100%=10.0=Physicality=Tech.=10 Oct.=Uranus=P=1Ø.
Shatter=10,000=1,000=100%=10.0=Physicality=Tech.=10 Oct.=Uranus=P=1Ø.
Shatterproof=1,500=15%=P1.50D=1.5=Authority=Solar Crown=1 May = Maia.
Shave=10,000=1,000=100%=10.0=Physicality=Tech.=10 Oct.=Uranus=P=1Ø.

Shaver=7,000=70%=P7.0D=7.0=Language=Assets=Mars=7 July=Pleiades.
Shaving=4,000=40%=P4.0D=Govt.=Creatocracy=4 April=Mercury=Hermes=G=A4.
Shaw Bernard=4,500=5,000=50%=P5.00D=Law=Time=Venus=5 May = Aphrodite>>L=N.
Shawl=7,500=8,000=80%=P8.0D=Economy=Currency=8 Aug.=Zeus>>E=v.
Shawnee=8,500=9,000=90%=P9.00D=9.0=Abstraction=Gods=Saturn=9Sept.>>A=Ø.
Shawwal=5,500=5.5=80%=P5.50=Earth-Midway=5 May = Gaia.
Shay=2,000=20%=P2.00D=2.0=Nature=Matter=Moon=2 Feb.=Cupid=N=C+_
She=10,000=1,000=100%=10.0=Physicality=Tech.=10 Oct.=Uranus=P=1Ø.
Sheaf=8,000=80%=P8.0D=Economy=Currency=8 Aug.=Zeus>>E=v.
Shear=10,000=1,000=100%=10.0=Physicality=Tech.=10 Oct.=Uranus=P=1Ø.
Sheath=10,000=1,000=100%=10.0=Physicality=Tech.=10 Oct.=Uranus=P=1Ø.
Sheathe=5,000=50%=P5.00D=Law=Time=Venus=5 May = Aphrodite>>L=N.
Sheathing=8,000=80%=P8.0D=Economy=Currency=8 Aug.=Zeus>>E=v.
Shebang=5,000=50%=P5.00D=Law=Time=Venus=5 May = Aphrodite>>L=N.
Shebat=1,500=15%=P1.50D=1.5=Authority=Solar Crown=1 May = Maia.
Shed1=10,000=1,000=100%=10.0=Physicality=Tech.=10 Oct.=Uranus=P=1Ø.
Shed2=5,000=50%=P5.00D=Law=Time=Venus=5 May = Aphrodite>>L=N.
She'd=1,500=15%=P1.50D=1.5=Authority=Solar Crown=1 May = Maia.
Sheen=2,500=3,000=30%=P3.0D=3.0=Creativity=Stars=Muses=3 March = C=I>>GIL.
Sheep=11,000=11%=P1.10D=1.1=Idea=Brainchild=Inv.=11 Nov.=SC=Athena>>I=MT.
Sheepdog=4,000=40%=P4.0D=Govt.=Creatocracy=4 April=Mercury=Hermes=G=A4.
Sheepish=4,500=5,000=50%=P5.00D=Law=Time=Venus=5 May = Aphrodite>>L=N.

Sheepskin=6,000=60%=P6.0D=Man=Earth=Royalty=6 June=Gaia=Maia>>M=M2.
The tanned skin of a sheep, with or without the fleece. Informal. A diploma. A first degree was also discovered to mean a cow keeper, an apprentice. So anyone who has learnt a vocation should in the first place be granted a diploma by an applicable institution.

Sheer1=4,000=40%=P4.0D=Govt.=Creatocracy=4 April=Mercury=Hermes=G=A4.
Sheer2=12,000=12%=P1.20D=1.2=Knowledge=Edu=12Dec.=Athena>>K=F.
Sheet1=10,000=1,000=100%=10.0=Physicality=Tech.=10 Oct.=Uranus=P=1Ø.
Sheet2=10,000=1,000=100%=10.0=Physicality=Tech.=10 Oct.=Uranus=P=1Ø.
Sheet metal=3,500=4,000=40%=P4.0D=Govt.=Creatocracy=4 April=Hermes=G=A4.
Sheet music=4,000=40%=P4.0D=Govt.=Creatocracy=4 April=Mercury=Hermes=G=A4.
Sheet rock=2,000=20%=P2.00D=2.0=Nature=Matter=Moon=2 Feb.=Cupid=N=C+_
Sheffield=5,000=50%=P5.00D=Law=Time=Venus=5 May = Aphrodite>>L=N.

Sheik=7,000=70%=P7.0D=7.0=Language=Assets=Mars=7 July=Pleiades.
The leader of an Arab or Muslim tribe, village, or family. [Ar.šayh, old man]. By laws of time deduced in the definitive definitions a sheik should be at least 70years to be called one.

Shekel=10,000=1,000=100%=10.0=Physicality=Tech.=10 Oct.=Uranus=P=1Ø.
Shekel is a Hebrew currency unit equal to about a half ounce. The chief silver coin of the ancient Hebrews. It is the only currency that meets the 10,000th standard. However a silver

and does not measure even up to the gold standard and thus far below the diamond metric standard of the Maks. Now 10,000=1,000=[100]=10.0. By definition an Ounce >>1/16 >> 1/16x100=6.25=6.30. Currency metric weight is 6.30/10=0.63>63:1. See Naira. Dollar.

Shelf=10,000=1,000=100%=10.0=Physicality=Tech.=10 Oct.=Uranus=P=1Ø.

Shelf life=5,500=5.5=80%=P5.50=Earth-Midway=5 May = Gaia.

Shell=10,000=1,000=100%=10.0=Physicality=Tech.=10 Oct.=Uranus=P=1Ø.

She'll=1,500=15%=P1.50D=1.5=Authority=Solar Crown=1 May = Maia.

Shellac=10,000=1,000=100%=10.0=Physicality=Tech.=10 Oct.=Uranus=P=1Ø.

Shelley, Mary=3,000=30%=P3.0D=3.0=Creativity=Stars=Muses=3 March = C=I>>GIL.

Shelley,Percy=3,000=30%=P3.0D=3.0=Creativity=Stars=Muses=3 March = C=I>>GIL.

Shellfire=2,500=3,000=30%=P3.0D=3.0=Creativity=Stars=Muses=3 March = C=I>>GIL.

Shellfish=6,000=60%=P6.0D=Man=Earth=Royalty=6 June=Gaia=Maia>>M=M2.

Shell shock=7,000=70%=P7.0D=7.0=Language=Assets=Mars=7 July=Pleiades.

Shelter=10,000=1,000=100%=10.0=Physicality=Tech.=10 Oct.=Uranus=P=1Ø.

Shelve=6,000=60%=P6.0D=Man=Earth=Royalty=6 June=Gaia=Maia>>M=M2.

Shelves=1,500=15%=P1.50D=1.5=Authority=Solar Crown=1 May = Maia.

Shelving=2,000=20%=P2.00D=2.0=Nature=Matter=Moon=2 Feb.=Cupid=N=C+_

Shenandoah Valley=6,000=60%=P6.0D=Man=Earth=Royalty=6 June=Gaia=Maia>>M=M2.

Shenanigan=4,000=40%=P4.0D=Govt.=Creatocracy=4 April=Mercury=Hermes=G=A4.

Shenyang=4,500=5,000=50%=P5.00D=Law=Time=Venus=5 May = Aphrodite>>L=N.

Shepard Alan=4,500=5,000=50%=P5.00D=Law=Time=Venus=5 May = Aphrodite>>L=N.

Shepherd=10,000=1,000=100%=10.0=Physicality=Tech.=10 Oct.=Uranus=P=1Ø.

Shepherdess=4,000=40%=P4.0D=Govt.=Creatocracy=4 April=Mercury=Hermes=G=A4.

Sherbet=9,500=10,000=1,000=100%=10.0=Physicality=Tech.=10 Oct.=Uranus=P=1Ø.

Sheridan,Philip=3,000=30%=P3.0D=3.0=Creativity=Stars=Muses=3 March = C=I>>GIL.

Sheridan Richard=3,500=4,000=40%=P4.0D=Govt.=4 April=Mercury=Hermes=G=A4.

Sheriff=7,500=8,000=80%=P8.0D=Economy=Currency=8 Aug.=Zeus>>E=v.

Sherman,William=3,000=30%=P3.0D=3.0=Creativity=Stars=Muses=3 March = C=I>>GIL.

Sherpa=5,000=50%=P5.00D=Law=Time=Venus=5 May = Aphrodite>>L=N.

Sherry=3,500=4,000=40%=P4.0D=Govt.=Creatocracy=4 April=Mercury=Hermes=G=A4.

Sherwood Forest=5,500=5.5=80%=P5.50=Earth-Midway=5 May = Gaia.

Shetland=6,500=5.5=80%=P5.50=Earth-Midway=5 May = Gaia.

Shetland Islands.=5,500=5.5=80%=P5.50=Earth-Midway=5 May = Gaia.

Shetland pony=5,000=50%=P5.00D=Law=Time=Venus=5 May = Aphrodite>>L=N.

Shevat=5,500=5.5=80%=P5.50=Earth-Midway=5 May = Gaia.

Shiatsu=8,000=80%=P8.0D=Economy=Currency=8 Aug.=Zeus>>E=v.

Shibboleth=6,000=60%=P6.0D=Man=Earth=Royalty=6 June=Gaia=Maia>>M=M2.

Shied1=3,000=30%=P3.0D=3.0=Creativity=Stars=Muses=3 March = C=I>>GIL.

Shied2=3,000=30%=P3.0D=3.0=Creativity=Stars=Muses=3 March = C=I>>GIL.

Shield=10,000=1,000=100%=10.0=Physicality=Tech.=10 Oct.=Uranus=P=1Ø.

Shier=1,500=15%=P1.50D=1.5=Authority=Solar Crown=1 May = Maia.

Shiest=2,000=20%=P2.00D=2.0=Nature=Matter=Moon=2 Feb.=Cupid=N=C+_

Shift=10,000=1,000=100%=10.0=Physicality=Tech.=10 Oct.=Uranus=P=1Ø.

Shiftless=2,000=20%=P2.00D=2.0=Nature=Matter=Moon=2 Feb.=Cupid=N=C+_
Lacking ambition or purpose. This means that ambitious persons are purposeful people who are continuous flexible and shifting with an objective to knowing learning and earning.

Shifty=4,000=40%=P4.0D=Govt.=Creatocracy=4 April=Mercury=Hermes=G=A4.
Shite=9,000=90%=P9.00D=9.0=Abstraction=Gods=Saturn=9Sept.>>A=Ø.
Shijiazhuang=4,000=40%=P4.0D=Govt.=Creatocracy=4 April=Mercury=Hermes=G=A4.
Shikoku=5,500=5.5=80%=P5.50=Earth-Midway=5 May = Gaia.
Shill=8,000=80%=P8.0D=Economy=Currency=8 Aug.=Zeus>>E=v.
Shillelagh=5,000=50%=P5.00D=Law=Time=Venus=5 May = Aphrodite>>L=N.

Shilling=3,000=30%=P3.0D=3.0=Creativity=Stars=Muses=3 March = C=I>>GIL.
Old English scilling. Currency metric weight >> 3/10=0.3=30:1. See Naira. Dollar.

Shilly-shally=3,000=30%=P3.0D=3.0=Creativity=Stars=Muses=3 March = C=I>>GIL.
Shim=7,500=8,000=80%=P8.0D=Economy=Currency=8 Aug.=Zeus>>E=v.
Shimmer=6,000=60%=P6.0D=Man=Earth=Royalty=6 June=Gaia=Maia>>M=M2.
Shimmy=7,500=8,000=80%=P8.0D=Economy=Currency=8 Aug.=Zeus>>E=v.
Shin1=10,000=1,000=100%=10.0=Physicality=Tech.=10 Oct.=Uranus=P=1Ø.
Shin2=4,000=40%=P4.0D=Govt.=Creatocracy=4 April=Mercury=Hermes=G=A4.
Shindig=4,000=40%=P4.0D=Govt.=Creatocracy=4 April=Mercury=Hermes=G=A4.
Shine=10,000=1,000=100%=10.0=Physicality=Tech.=10 Oct.=Uranus=P=1Ø.
Shiner=5,000=50%=P5.00D=Law=Time=Venus=5 May = Aphrodite>>L=N.
Shingle1=10,000=1,000=100%=10.0=Physicality=Tech.=10 Oct.=Uranus=P=1Ø.
Shingle2=6,000=60%=P6.0D=Man=Earth=Royalty=6 June=Gaia=Maia>>M=M2.
Shingles=10,500=11,000=11%=P1.10D=1.1=Idea=Brainchild=Inv.=11 Nov.=Athena>>I=MT.
Shinny=3,500=4,000=40%=P4.0D=Govt.=Creatocracy=4 April=Mercury=Hermes=G=A4.

Shinto=7,500=8,000=80%=P8.0D=Economy=Currency=8 Aug.=Zeus>>E=v.
A religion native to Japan marked by worship of nature spirits and ancestors. J.shinto. We deduce these nature spirits and ancestors are actually about 75 in number and can only be reached more quickly through the means of abstraction and precision by Mind Computing.

Shiny=1,000=100%=10.0=1.0=Mind=Sun=1 January=Helios >> M=E4.
Ship=10,000=1,000=100%=10.0=Physicality=Tech.=10 Oct.=Uranus=P=1Ø.
Shipboard=1,000=100%=10.0=1.0=Mind=Sun=1 January=Helios >> M=E4.
Shipbuilding=3,500=4,000=40%=P4.0D=Govt.=Creatocracy=4 April=Hermes=G=A4.
Shipmaster=4,000=40%=P4.0D=Govt.=Creatocracy=4 April=Mercury=Hermes=G=A4.
Shipmate=1,500=15%=P1.50D=1.5=Authority=Solar Crown=1 May = Maia.
Shipment=6,000=60%=P6.0D=Man=Earth=Royalty=6 June=Gaia=Maia>>M=M2.
Shipping=8,000=80%=P8.0D=Economy=Currency=8 Aug.=Zeus>>E=v.
Shipshape=2,000=20%=P2.00D=2.0=Nature=Matter=Moon=2 Feb.=Cupid=N=C+_
Shipwreck=8,500=9,000=90%=P9.00D=9.0=Abstraction=Gods=Saturn=9Sept.>>A=Ø.

Shipyard=4,000=40%=P4.0D=Govt.=Creatocracy=4 April=Mercury=Hermes=G=A4.
Shiraz=5,000=50%=P5.00D=Law=Time=Venus=5 May = Aphrodite>>L=N.
Shire=5,500=5.5=80%=P5.50=Earth-Midway=5 May = Gaia.
Shirk=4,000=40%=P4.0D=Govt.=Creatocracy=4 April=Mercury=Hermes=G=A4.
Shirr=6,500=7,000=70%=P7.0D=7.0=Language=Assets=Mars=7 July=Pleiades.
Shirt=10,000=1,000=100%=10.0=Physicality=Tech.=10 Oct.=Uranus=P=1Ø.
Shirtwaist=3,500=4,000=40%=P4.0D=Govt.=4 April=Mercury=Hermes=G=A4.
Shish kebab=9,000=90%=P9.00D=9.0=Abstraction=Gods=Saturn=9Sept.>>A=Ø.
Shiva=5,000=50%=P5.00D=Law=Time=Venus=5 May = Aphrodite>>L=N.
Shiver1=5,000=50%=P5.00D=Law=Time=Venus=5 May = Aphrodite>>L=N.
Shiver2=4,500=5,000=50%=P5.00D=Law=Time=Venus=5 May = Aphrodite>>L=N.
Shoal1=4,000=40%=P4.0D=Govt.=Creatocracy=4 April=Mercury=Hermes=G=A4.
Shoal2=5,500=5.5=80%=P5.50=Earth-Midway=5 May = Gaia.
Shoat=2,500=3,000=30%=P3.0D=3.0=Creativity=Stars=Muses=3 March = C=I>>GIL.
Shock1=10,000=1,000=100%=10.0=Physicality=Tech.=10 Oct.=Uranus=P=1Ø.
Shock2=10,000=1,000=100%=10.0=Physicality=Tech.=10 Oct.=Uranus=P=1Ø.
Shock absorber=5,500=5.5=80%=P5.50=Earth-Midway=5 May = Gaia.
Shocker=4,500=5,000=50%=P5.00D=Law=Time=Venus=5 May = Aphrodite>>L=N.
Shocking=2,500=3,000=30%=P3.0D=3.0=Creativity=Stars=Muses=3 March = C=I>>GIL.
Shock therapy=7,500=8,000=80%=P8.0D=Economy=Currency=8 Aug.=Zeus>>E=v.
Shock troops=5,000=50%=P5.00D=Law=Time=Venus=5 May = Aphrodite>>L=N.
Shock wave=10,000=1,000=100%=10.0=Physicality=Tech.=10 Oct.=Uranus=P=1Ø.
Shoddy=10,000=1,000=100%=10.0=Physicality=Tech.=10 Oct.=Uranus=P=1Ø.
Shoe=10,000=1,000=100%=10.0=Physicality=Tech.=10 Oct.=Uranus=P=1Ø.
Shoehorn=6,000=60%=P6.0D=Man=Earth=Royalty=6 June=Gaia=Maia>>M=M2.
Shoelace=5,000=50%=P5.00D=Law=Time=Venus=5 May = Aphrodite>>L=N.
Shoemaker=3,000=30%=P3.0D=3.0=Creativity=Stars=Muses=3 March = C=I>>GIL.
Shoestring=10,000=1,000=100%=10.0=Physicality=Tech.=10 Oct.=Uranus=P=1Ø.
Shoe tree=6,500=7,000=70%=P7.0D=7.0=Language=Assets=Mars=7 July=Pleiades.
Shogun=7,500=8,000=80%=P8.0D=Economy=Currency=8 Aug.=Zeus>>E=v.
Shone=3,000=30%=P3.0D=3.0=Creativity=Stars=Muses=3 March = C=I>>GIL.
Shoo=2,500=3,000=30%=P3.0D=3.0=Creativity=Stars=Muses=3 March = C=I>>GIL.
Shoo In=2,000=20%=P2.00D=2.0=Nature=Matter=Moon=2 Feb.=Cupid=N=C+_
Shook=2,000=20%=P2.00D=2.0=Nature=Matter=Moon=2 Feb.=Cupid=N=C+_
Shook-up=2,000=20%=P2.00D=2.0=Nature=Matter=Moon=2 Feb.=Cupid=N=C+_
Shoot=10,000=1,000=100%=10.0=Physicality=Tech.=10 Oct.=Uranus=P=1Ø.
Shooting star=1,000=100%=10.0=1.0=Mind=Sun=1 January=Helios >> M=E4.
Shop=10,000=1,000=100%=10.0=1.0=Mind=Sun=1 January=Helios >> M=E4.
Shopkeeper=3,000=30%=P3.0D=3.0=Creativity=Stars=Muses=3 March = C=I>>GIL.
Shoplift=4,000=40%=P4.0D=Govt.=Creatocracy=4 April=Mercury=Hermes=G=A4.
Shopping center=6,000=60%=P6.0D=Man=Earth=Royalty=6 June=Gaia=Maia>>M=M2.
Shopping mail=8,000=80%=P8.0D=Economy=Currency=8 Aug.=Zeus>>E=v.
Shop steward=5,500=5.5=80%=P5.50=Earth-Midway=5 May = Gaia.
Shoptalk=3,500=4,000=40%=P4.0D=Govt.=4 April=Mercury=Hermes=G=A4.
Shopworn=6,500=7,000=70%=P7.0D=7.0=Language=Assets=Mars=7 July=Pleiades.

Shore1=7,000=70%=P7.0D=7.0=Language=Assets=Mars=7 July=Pleiades.
Shore2=7,500=8,000=80%=P8.0D=Economy=Currency=8 Aug.=Zeus>>E=v.
Shoreline=3,000=30%=P3.0D=3.0=Creativity=Stars=Muses=3 March = C=I>>GIL.
Shorn=2,000=20%=P2.00D=2.0=Nature=Matter=Moon=2 Feb.=Cupid=N=C+_
Short=10,000=1,000=100%=10.0=Physicality=Tech.=10 Oct.=Uranus=P=1Ø.
Shortage=2,000=20%=P2.00D=2.0=Nature=Matter=Moon=2 Feb.=Cupid=N=C+_
Shortbread=3,000=30%=P3.0D=3.0=Creativity=Stars=Muses=3 March = C=I>>GIL.
Shortcake=5,500=5.5=80%=P5.50=Earth-Midway=5 May = Gaia.
Shortchange=5,500=5.5=80%=P5.50=Earth-Midway=5 May = Gaia.
Short circuit=6,500=7,000=70%=P7.0D=7.0=Language=Assets=Mars=7 July=Pleiades.
Shortcoming=1,500=15%=P1.50D=1.5=Authority=Solar Crown=1 May = Maia.
Shortcut=7,000=70%=P7.0D=7.0=Language=Assets=Mars=7 July=Pleiades.
Shorten=7,000=70%=P7.0D=7.0=Language=Assets=Mars=7 July=Pleiades.
Shortening=7,500=8,000=80%=P8.0D=Economy=Currency=8 Aug.=Zeus>>E=v.
Shortfall=7,000=70%=P7.0D=7.0=Language=Assets=Mars=7 July=Pleiades.
Shorthand=6,500=7,000=70%=P7.0D=7.0=Language=Assets=Mars=7 July=Pleiades.
Short handed=3,000=30%=P3.0D=3.0=Creativity=Stars=Muses=3 March = C=I>>GIL.
Shortlist=5,500=5.5=80%=P5.50=Earth-Midway=5 May = Gaia.
Short lived=3,500=4,000=40%=P4.0D=Govt.=4 April=Mercury=Hermes=G=A4.
Shortly=4,000=40%=P4.0D=Govt.=Creatocracy=4 April=Mercury=Hermes=G=A4.
Short order=2,500=3,000=30%=P3.0D=3.0=Cr=Stars=Muses=3 March = C=I>>GIL.
Short range=6,000=60%=P6.0D=Man=Earth=Royalty=6 June=Gaia=Maia>>M=M2.
Short shrift=2,000=20%=P2.00D=2.0=Nature=Matter=Moon=2 Feb.=Cupid=N=C+_
Shortsighted=2,500=3,000=30%=P3.0D=3.0=Cr=Stars=Muses=3 March = C=I>>GIL.
Shortstop=2,500=3,000=30%=P3.0D=3.0=Creativity=Stars=Muses=3 March = C=I>>GIL.
Short story=7,500=8,000=80%=P8.0D=Economy=Currency=8 Aug.=Zeus>>E=v.
Short subject=3,500=4,000=40%=P4.0D=Govt.=Creatocracy=4 April=Hermes=G=A4.
Short tempered=2,000=20%=P2.00D=2.0=Nature=Matter=Moon=2 Feb.=Cupid=N=C+_
Short term=10,000=1,000=100%=10.0=Physicality=Tech.=10 Oct.=Uranus=P=1Ø.
Short ton=2,000=20%=P2.00D=2.0=Nature=Matter=Moon=2 Feb.=Cupid=N=C+_
Shortwave=6,000=60%=P6.0D=Man=Earth=Royalty=6 June=Gaia=Maia>>M=M2.
Shoshone=10,000=1,000=100%=10.0=Physicality=Tech.=10 Oct.=Uranus=P=1Ø.
Shostakovich=2,500=3,000=30%=P3.0D=3.0=Cr=Stars=Muses=3 March = C=I>>GIL.
Shot1=10,000=1,000=100%=10.0=1.0=Mind=Sun=1 January=Helios >> M=E4.
Shot2=3,000=30%=P3.0D=3.0=Creativity=Stars=Muses=3 March = C=I>>GIL.
Shotgun=5,000=50%=P5.00D=Law=Time=Venus=5 May = Aphrodite>>L=N.
Shot put=9,000=90%=P9.00D=9.0=Abstraction=Gods=Saturn=9Sept.>>A=Ø.
Should=10,000=1,000=100%=10.0=Physicality=Tech.=10 Oct.=Uranus=P=1Ø.
Shoulder=10,000=1,000=100%=10.0=Physicality=Tech.=10 Oct.=Uranus=P=1Ø.
Shoulder blade=1,000=100%=10.0=1.0=Mind=Sun=1 January=Helios >> M=E4.
Shouldn't=1,000=100%=10.0=1.0=Mind=Sun=1 January=Helios >> M=E4.
Shout=9,000=90%=P9.00D=9.0=Abstraction=Gods=Saturn=9Sept.>>A=Ø.
Shove=10,000=1,000=100%=10.0=Physicality=Tech.=10 Oct.=Uranus=P=1Ø.
Shovel=10,000=1,000=100%=10.0=Physicality=Tech.=10 Oct.=Uranus=P=1Ø.
Show=10,000=1,000=100%=10.0=Physicality=Tech.=10 Oct.=Uranus=P=1Ø.

Showboat=5,500=5.5=80%=P5.50=Earth-Midway=5 May = Gaia.
Show business=1,500=15%=P1.50D=1.5=Authority=Solar Crown=1 May = Maia.
Showcase=7,000=70%=P7.0D=7.0=Language=Assets=Mars=7 July=Pleiades.
Showdown=4,500=5,000=50%=P5.00D=Law=Time=Venus=5 May = Aphrodite>>L=N.
Shower=10,000=1,000=100%=10.0=Physicality=Tech.=10 Oct.=Uranus=P=1Ø.
Showing=3,500=4,000=40%=P4.0D=Govt.=4 April=Mercury=Hermes=G=A4.
Showman=4,500=5,000=50%=P5.00D=Law=Time=Venus=5 May = Aphrodite>>L=N.
Show off=4,000=40%=P4.0D=Govt.=Creatocracy=4 April=Mercury=Hermes=G=A4.
Showpiece=4,500=5,000=50%=P5.00D=Law=Time=Venus=5 May = Aphrodite>>L=N.
Showplace=5,500=5.5=80%=P5.50=Earth-Midway=5 May = Gaia.
Show room=4,000=40%=P4.0D=Govt.=Creatocracy=4 April=Mercury=Hermes=G=A4.
Showstopper=8,500=9,000=90%=P9.00D=9.0=Abstraction=Gods=Saturn=9Sept.>>A=Ø.
Showy=6,500=7,000=70%=P7.0D=7.0=Language=Assets=Mars=7 July=Pleiades.
Shrank=2,000=20%=P2.00D=2.0=Nature=Matter=Moon=2 Feb.=Cupid=N=C+_
Shrapnel=10,000=1,000=100%=10.0=Physicality=Tech.=10 Oct.=Uranus=P=1Ø.
Shred=10,000=1,000=100%=10.0=Physicality=Tech.=10 Oct.=Uranus=P=1Ø.
Shreveport=5,500=5.5=80%=P5.50=Earth-Midway=5 May = Gaia.
Shrew=7,500=8,000=80%=P8.0D=Economy=Currency=8 Aug.=Zeus>>E=v.
Shrewd=7,500=8,000=80%=P8.0D=Economy=Currency=8 Aug.=Zeus>>E=v.
Shriek=4,000=40%=P4.0D=Govt.=Creatocracy=4 April=Mercury=Hermes=G=A4.
Shrift=5,500=5.5=80%=P5.50=Earth-Midway=5 May = Gaia.
Shrike=8,500=9,000=90%=P9.00D=9.0=Abstraction=Gods=Saturn=9Sept.>>A=Ø.
Shrill=4,500=5,000=50%=P5.00D=Law=Time=Venus=5 May = Aphrodite>>L=N.
Shrimp=8,500=9,000=90%=P9.00D=9.0=Abstraction=Gods=Saturn=9Sept.>>A=Ø.
Shrine=10,000=1,000=100%=10.0=Physicality=Tech.=10 Oct.=Uranus=P=1Ø.
Shrink=10,000=1,000=100%=10.0=Physicality=Tech.=10 Oct.=Uranus=P=1Ø.
Shrink wrap=10,000=1,000=100%=10.0=Physicality=Tech.=10 Oct.=Uranus=P=1Ø.
Shrive=10,000=1,000=100%=10.0=Physicality=Tech.=10 Oct.=Uranus=P=1Ø.
Shrivel=10,000=1,000=100%=10.0=Physicality=Tech.=10 Oct.=Uranus=P=1Ø.
Shroud=10,000=1,000=100%=10.0=Physicality=Tech.=10 Oct.=Uranus=P=1Ø.
Shrub=6,500=7,000=70%=P7.0D=7.0=Language=Assets=Mars=7 July=Pleiades.
Shrubbery=3,000=30%=P3.0D=3.0=Creativity=Stars=Muses=3 March = C=I>>GIL.
Shrug=10,000=1,000=100%=10.0=Physicality=Tech.=10 Oct.=Uranus=P=1Ø.
Shrunk=3,000=30%=P3.0D=3.0=Creativity=Stars=Muses=3 March = C=I>>GIL.
Shrunken=2,000=20%=P2.00D=2.0=Nature=Matter=Moon=2 Feb.=Cupid=N=C+_
Shuck=10,000=1,000=100%=10.0=Physicality=Tech.=10 Oct.=Uranus=P=1Ø.
Shudder=6,500=7,000=70%=P7.0D=7.0=Language=Assets=Mars=7 July=Pleiades.
Shuffle=10,000=1,000=100%=10.0=Physicality=Tech.=10 Oct.=Uranus=P=1Ø.
Shuffleboard=10,000=1,000=100%=10.0=Physicality=Tech.=10 Oct.=Uranus=P=1Ø.
Shun=3,000=30%=P3.0D=3.0=Creativity=Stars=Muses=3 March = C=I>>GIL.
Shunt=10,000=1,000=100%=10.0=Physicality=Tech.=10 Oct.=Uranus=P=1Ø.
Shush=4,500=5,000=50%=P5.00D=Law=Time=Venus=5 May = Aphrodite>>L=N.
Shut=10,000=1,000=100%=10.0=Physicality=Tech.=10 Oct.=Uranus=P=1Ø.
Shutdown=3,500=4,000=40%=P4.0D=Govt.=Creatocracy=4 April=Hermes=G=A4.
Shuteye=1,000=100%=10.0=1.0=Mind=Sun=1 January=Helios >> M=E4.

Shut in=3,500=4,000=40%=P4.0D=Govt.=Creatocracy=4 April=Mercury=Hermes=G=A4.
Shutout=5,500=5.5=80%=P5.50=Earth-Midway=5 May = Gaia.
Shutter=10,000=1,000=100%=10.0=Physicality=Tech.=10 Oct.=Uranus=P=1Ø.
Shutterbug=2,500=3,000=30%=P3.0D=3.0=Cr=Stars=Muses=3 March = C=I>>GIL.
Shuttle=10,000=1,000=100%=10.0=Physicality=Tech.=10 Oct.=Uranus=P=1Ø.
Shuttlecock=7,500=8,000=80%=P8.0D=Economy=Currency=8 Aug.=Zeus>>E=v.
Shy1=10,000=1,000=100%=10.0=Physicality=Tech.=10 Oct.=Uranus=P=1Ø.
Shy2=4,000=40%=P4.0D=Govt.=Creatocracy=4 April=Mercury=Hermes=G=A4.
Shyster=6,000=60%=P6.0D=Man=Earth=Royalty=6 June=Gaia=Maia>>M=M2.
Si=2,500=3,000=30%=P3.0D=3.0=Creativity=Stars=Muses=3 March = C=I>>GIL.

SI=4,000=40%=P4.0D=Govt.=Creatocracy=4 April=Mercury=Hermes=G=A4.
In the Creatocracy, Standard International System of Units is equivalent to US >> the
Universal Standard Systems of Units. This is the Maks indicated as the circled P slashed.

PICTURE of the Maks symbol. Code 10K.

Siam=2,000=20%=P2.00D=2.0=Nature=Matter=Moon=2 Feb.=Cupid=N=C+_
Siamese cat=8,000=80%=P8.0D=Economy=Currency=8 Aug.=Zeus>>E=v.
Siamese twin=6,000=60%=P6.0D=Man=Earth=Royalty=6 June=Gaia=Maia>>M=M2.
Sian=1,000=100%=10.0=1.0=Mind=Sun=1 January=Helios >> M=E4.
Siang Kiang=1,500=15%=P1.50D=1.5=Authority=Solar Crown=1 May = Maia.
Sibelius Jean=2,000=20%=P2.00D=2.0=Nature=Matter=Moon=2 Feb.=Cupid=N=C+_
Siberia=6,500=7,000=70%=P7.0D=7.0=Language=Assets=Mars=7 July=Pleiades.
Sibilant=9,000=90%=P9.00D=9.0=Abstraction=Gods=Saturn=9Sept.>>A=Ø.
Sibling=5,500=5.5=80%=P5.50=Earth-Midway=5 May = Gaia.

Sibyl=2,500=3,000=30%=P3.0D=3.0=Creativity=Stars=Muses=3 March = C=I>>GIL.
A woman prophet. Greek. Sibulla. A woman in ancient times supposed to utter the oracles
and prophecies of a God. So clearly it is the right of a God to have sibyls for his pleasure.
To achieve this Castle Makupedia trains ladies in the studies and courses of the Oracle.

Sic1=10,000=1,000=100%=10.0=Physicality=Tech.=10 Oct.=Uranus=P=1Ø.
Sic2=6,000=60%=P6.0D=Man=Earth=Royalty=6 June=Gaia=Maia>>M=M2.
Sichuan=4,000=40%=P4.0D=Govt.=Creatocracy=4 April=Mercury=Hermes=G=A4.
Sicily=7,000=70%=P7.0D=7.0=Language=Assets=Mars=7 July=Pleiades.

Sick=10,000=1,000=100%=10.0=Physicality=Tech.=10 Oct.=Uranus=P=1Ø.
Sickbay=3,500=4,000=40%=P4.0D=Govt.=Creatocracy=4 April=Mercury=Hermes=G=A4.
Sickbed=2,000=20%=P2.00D=2.0=Nature=Matter=Moon=2 Feb.=Cupid=N=C+_
Sicken=3,000=30%=P3.0D=3.0=Creativity=Stars=Muses=3 March = C=I>>GIL.
Sickening=2,500=3,000=30%=P3.0D=3.0=Creativity=Stars=Muses=3 March = C=I>>GIL.
Sickle=9,000=90%=P9.00D=9.0=Abstraction=Gods=Saturn=9Sept.>>A=Ø.
Sickle cell anemia=10,000=1,000=100%=10.0=Physicality=Tech.=10 Oct.=Uranus=P=1Ø.
Sickly=10,000=1,000=100%=10.0=Physicality=Tech.=10 Oct.=Uranus=P=1Ø.
Sick out=8,000=80%=P8.0D=Economy=Currency=8 Aug.=Zeus>>E=v.
Side=10,000=1,000=100%=10.0=Physicality=Tech.=10 Oct.=Uranus=P=1Ø.
Sidearm=6,500=7,000=70%=P7.0D=7.0=Language=Assets=Mars=7 July=Pleiades.
Side arm=6,000=60%=P6.0D=Man=Earth=Royalty=6 June=Gaia=Maia>>M=M2.
Sideboard=6,000=60%=P6.0D=Man=Earth=Royalty=6 June=Gaia=Maia>>M=M2.
Sideburns=9,500=10,000=1,000=100%=10.0=Physicality=Tech.=10 Oct.=Uranus=P=1Ø.
Sidecar=5,500=5.5=80%=P5.50=Earth-Midway=5 May = Gaia.
Side effect=5,000=50%=P5.00D=Law=Time=Venus=5 May = Aphrodite>>L=N.
Sidekick=2,000=20%=P2.00D=2.0=Nature=Matter=Moon=2 Feb.=Cupid=N=C+_
Sidelight=1,000=100%=10.0=1.0=Mind=Sun=1 January=Helios >> M=E4.
Sideline=10,000=1,000=100%=10.0=Physicality=Tech.=10 Oct.=Uranus=P=1Ø.
Sidelong=4,000=40%=P4.0D=Govt.=Creatocracy=4 April=Mercury=Hermes=G=A4.
Sideman=5,000=50%=P5.00D=Law=Time=Venus=5 May = Aphrodite>>L=N.
Sidereal=10,000=1,000=100%=10.0=Physicality=Tech.=10 Oct.=Uranus=P=1Ø.
Sidesaddle=8,000=80%=P8.0D=Economy=Currency=8 Aug.=Zeus>>E=v.
Sideshow=6,500=7,000=70%=P7.0D=7.0=Language=Assets=Mars=7 July=Pleiades.
Sidestep=4,000=40%=P4.0D=Govt.=Creatocracy=4 April=Mercury=Hermes=G=A4.
Sidestroke=10,000=1,000=100%=10.0=Physicality=Tech.=10 Oct.=Uranus=P=1Ø.
Sideswipe=5,000=50%=P5.00D=Law=Time=Venus=5 May = Aphrodite>>L=N.
Sidetrack=10,000=1,000=100%=10.0=Physicality=Tech.=10 Oct.=Uranus=P=1Ø.
Sidewalk=4,500=5,000=50%=P5.00D=Law=Time=Venus=5 May = Aphrodite>>L=N.
Sidewall=3,500=4,000=40%=P4.0D=Govt.=4 April=Mercury=Hermes=G=A4.
Sideways=6,000=60%=P6.0D=Man=Earth=Royalty=6 June=Gaia=Maia>>M=M2.
Sidewinder=6,000=60%=P6.0D=Man=Earth=Royalty=6 June=Gaia=Maia>>M=M2.
Siding=10,000=1,000=100%=10.0=Physicality=Tech.=10 Oct.=Uranus=P=1Ø.
Sidle=6,000=60%=P6.0D=Man=Earth=Royalty=6 June=Gaia=Maia>>M=M2.
Sidney Philip.=3,500=4,000=40%=P4.0D=Govt.=4 April=Mercury=Hermes=G=A4.
Sidon=7,000=70%=P7.0D=7.0=Language=Assets=Mars=7 July=Pleiades.
SIDS=2,000=20%=P2.00D=2.0=Nature=Matter=Moon=2 Feb.=Cupid=N=C+_
Siege=10,000=1,000=100%=10.0=Physicality=Tech.=10 Oct.=Uranus=P=1Ø.
Siena=5,000=50%=P5.00D=Law=Time=Venus=5 May = Aphrodite>>L=N.
Sierra=6,500=7,000=70%=P7.0D=7.0=Language=Assets=Mars=7 July=Pleiades.
Sierra Leone=6,000=60%=P6.0D=Man=Earth=Royalty=6 June=Gaia=Maia>>M=M2.
Sierra Madre=10,000=1,000=100%=10.0=Physicality=Tech.=10 Oct.=Uranus=P=1Ø.
Sierra Nevada=3,000=30%=P3.0D=3.0=Creativity=Stars=Muses=3 March = C=I>>GIL.
Siesta=6,000=60%=P6.0D=Man=Earth=Royalty=6 June=Gaia=Maia>>M=M2.
Sieve=8,500=9,000=90%=P9.00D=9.0=Abstraction=Gods=Saturn=9Sept.>>A=Ø.

Sift=10,000=1,000=100%=10.0=Physicality=Tech.=10 Oct.=Uranus=P=1Ø.
Sigh=10,000=1,000=100%=10.0=Physicality=Tech.=10 Oct.=Uranus=P=1Ø.
Sight=10,000=1,000=100%=10.0=Physicality=Tech.=10 Oct.=Uranus=P=1Ø.
Sighted=1,000=100%=10.0=1.0=Mind=Sun=1 January=Helios >> M=E4.
Sightless=2,000=20%=P2.00D=2.0=Nature=Matter=Moon=2 Feb.=Cupid=N=C+_
Sightly=2,000=20%=P2.00D=2.0=Nature=Matter=Moon=2 Feb.=Cupid=N=C+_
Sight read=5,000=50%=P5.00D=Law=Time=Venus=5 May = Aphrodite>>L=N.
Sightseeing=3,000=30%=P3.0D=3.0=Creativity=Stars=Muses=3 March = C=I>>GIL.
Sigma=3,500=4,000=40%=P4.0D=Govt.=Creatocracy=4 April=Mercury=Hermes=G=A4.
Sign=10,000=1,000=100%=10.0=Physicality=Tech.=10 Oct.=Uranus=P=1Ø.
Signal=10,000=1,000=100%=10.0=Physicality=Tech.=10 Oct.=Uranus=P=1Ø.
Signalize=4,000=40%=P4.0D=Govt.=Creatocracy=4 April=Mercury=Hermes=G=A4.
Signatory=5,500=5.5=80%=P5.50=Earth-Midway=5 May = Gaia.
Signature=10,000=1,000=100%=10.0=Physicality=Tech.=10 Oct.=Uranus=P=1Ø.
Signboard=2,000=20%=P2.00D=2.0=Nature=Matter=Moon=2 Feb.=Cupid=N=C+_
Signet=5,000=50%=P5.00D=Law=Time=Venus=5 May = Aphrodite>>L=N.
Significance=10,000=1,000=100%=10.0=Physicality=Tech.=10 Oct.=Uranus=P=1Ø.
Significant=10,000=1,000=100%=10.0=Physicality=Tech.=10 Oct.=Uranus=P=1Ø.
Signification=10,000=1,000=100%=10.0=Physicality=Tech.=10 Oct.=Uranus=P=1Ø.
Signify=10,000=1,000=100%=10.0=Physicality=Tech.=10 Oct.=Uranus=P=1Ø.
Sign language=4,000=40%=P4.0D=Govt.=Creatocracy=4 April=Mercury=Hermes=G=A4.
Signpost=3,500=4,000=40%=P4.0D=Govt.=Creatocracy=4 April=Hermes=G=A4.
Sikh=6,500=7,000=70%=P7.0D=7.0=Language=Assets=Mars=7 July=Pleiades.
Sikkim=8,000=80%=P8.0D=Economy=Currency=8 Aug.=Zeus>>E=v.
Sikorsky Ivor=4,000=40%=P4.0D=Govt.=Creatocracy=4 April=Mercury=Hermes=G=A4.
Silage=5,000=50%=P5.00D=Law=Time=Venus=5 May = Aphrodite>>L=N.
Silence=10,000=1,000=100%=10.0=Physicality=Tech.=10 Oct.=Uranus=P=1Ø.
Silencer=5,000=50%=P5.00D=Law=Time=Venus=5 May = Aphrodite>>L=N.
Silent=10,000=1,000=100%=10.0=Physicality=Tech.=10 Oct.=Uranus=P=1Ø.
Silesia=6,500=7,000=70%=P7.0D=7.0=Language=Assets=Mars=7 July=Pleiades.
Silhouette=10,000=1,000=100%=10.0=Physicality=Tech.=10 Oct.=Uranus=P=1Ø.
Silica=7,000=70%=P7.0D=7.0=Language=Assets=Mars=7 July=Pleiades.
Silicate=3,500=4,000=40%=P4.0D=Govt.=Creatocracy=4 April=Mercury=Hermes=G=A4.
Silicon=10,000=1,000=100%=10.0=Physicality=Tech.=10 Oct.=Uranus=P=1Ø.
Silicon=10,000=1,000=100%=10.0=Physicality=Tech.=10 Oct.=Uranus=P=1Ø.
Silicosis=7,500=8,000=80%=P8.0D=Economy=Currency=8 Aug.=Zeus>>E=v.
Silk=10,000=1,000=100%=10.0=Physicality=Tech.=10 Oct.=Uranus=P=1Ø.
Silk cotton=7,500=8,000=80%=P8.0D=Economy=Currency=8 Aug.=Zeus>>E=v.
Silken=5,000=50%=P5.00D=Law=Time=Venus=5 May = Aphrodite>>L=N.
Silkscreen=10,000=1,000=100%=10.0=Physicality=Tech.=10 Oct.=Uranus=P=1Ø.
Silkworm=4,500=5,000=50%=P5.00D=Law=Time=Venus=5 May = Aphrodite>>L=N.
Silky=4,000=40%=P4.0D=Govt.=Creatocracy=4 April=Mercury=Hermes=G=A4.
Sill=8,500=9,000=90%=P9.00D=9.0=Abstraction=Gods=Saturn=9Sept.>>A=Ø.
Silly=4,500=5,000=50%=P5.00D=Law=Time=Venus=5 May = Aphrodite>>L=N.
Silo=8,000=80%=P8.0D=Economy=Currency=8 Aug.=Zeus>>E=v.

Slit=10,000=1,000=100%=10.0=Physicality=Tech.=10 Oct.=Uranus=P=1Ø.

Silurian=10,000=1,000=100%=10.0=Physicality=Tech.=10 Oct.=Uranus=P=1Ø.

Silvan=1,500=15%=P1.50D=1.5=Authority=Solar Crown=1 May = Maia.

Silver=10,000=1,000=100%=10.0=Physicality=Tech.=10 Oct.=Uranus=P=1Ø.

Silver bromide=7,500=8,000=80%=P8.0D=Economy=Currency=8 Aug.=Zeus>>E=v.

Silverfish=5,000=50%=P5.00D=Law=Time=Venus=5 May = Aphrodite>>L=N.

Silver iodide=5,000=50%=P5.00D=Law=Time=Venus=5 May = Aphrodite>>L=N.

Silver nitrate=9,500=10,000=1,000=100%=10.0=Phys=Tech.=10 Oct.=Uranus=P=1Ø.

Silversmith=4,000=40%=P4.0D=Govt.=Creatocracy=4 April=Mercury=Hermes=G=A4.

Silverware=4,500=5,000=50%=P5.00D=Law=Time=Venus=5 May = Aphrodite>>L=N.

Simferopol=6,500=7,000=70%=P7.0D=7.0=Language=Assets=Mars=7 July=Pleiades.

Simian=3,000=30%=P3.0D=3.0=Creativity=Stars=Muses=3 March = C=I>>GIL.

Similar=6,000=60%=P6.0D=Man=Earth=Royalty=6 June=Gaia=Maia>>M=M2.

Similarity=3,500=4,000=40%=P4.0D=Govt.=4 April=Mercury=Hermes=G=A4.

Simile=11,000=11%=P1.10D=1.1=Idea=Brainchild=Inv.=11 Nov.=SC=Athena>>I=MT.

Similitude=2,500=3,000=30%=P3.0D=3.0=Creativity=Stars=Muses=3 March = C=I>>GIL.

Simmer=13,000=13%=P1.30=Solar Core=Faculty=13 January=Athena.

Simony=10,000=1,000=100%=10.0=Physicality=Tech.=10 Oct.=Uranus=P=1Ø.

Simon Zelotes=5,000=50%=P5.00D=Law=Time=Venus=5 May = Aphrodite>>L=N.

Simpatico=2,000=20%=P2.00D=2.0=Nature=Matter=Moon=2 Feb.=Cupid=N=C+_

Simper=6,500=7,000=70%=P7.0D=7.0=Language=Assets=Mars=7 July=Pleiades.

Simple=10,000=1,000=100%=10.0=Physicality=Tech.=10 Oct.=Uranus=P=1Ø.

Simple fraction=6,000=60%=P6.0D=Man=Earth=Royalty=6 June=Gaia=Maia>>M=M2.

Simple interest=4,500=5,000=50%=P5.00D=Law=Time=Venus=5 May = Aphrodite>>L=N.

Simpleminded=4,500=5,000=50%=P5.00D=Law=Time=Venus=5 May = Aphrodite>>L=N.

Simple sentence=5,000=50%=P5.00D=Law=Time=Venus=5 May = Aphrodite>>L=N.

Simpleton=4,000=40%=P4.0D=Govt.=Creatocracy=4 April=Mercury=Hermes=G=A4.

Simplicity=10,000=1,000=100%=10.0=Physicality=Tech.=10 Oct.=Uranus=P=1Ø.

Simplify=2,500=3,000=30%=P3.0D=3.0=Creativity=Stars=Muses=3 March = C=I>>GIL.

Simply=6,000=60%=P6.0D=Man=Earth=Royalty=6 June=Gaia=Maia>>M=M2.

Simulate=6,000=60%=P6.0D=Man=Earth=Royalty=6 June=Gaia=Maia>>M=M2.

Simulcast=10,000=1,000=100%=10.0=Physicality=Tech.=10 Oct.=Uranus=P=1Ø.

Simultaneous=10,000=1,000=100%=10.0=Physicality=Tech.=10 Oct.=Uranus=P=1Ø.

Sin1=6,000=60%=P6.0D=Man=Earth=Royalty=6 June=Gaia=Maia>>M=M2.
A transgression of a religious or moral law. <OE synn.=syn=Greek sun, with.
A human code. The word sin first has something to do with the sun. See Sin2 for clarity.

Sin2=4,000=40%=P4.0D=Govt.=Creatocracy=4 April=Mercury=Hermes=G=A4.
The 21st letter of the Hebrew alphabet. <Heb.ŝîn. Computing Sin >>21>2.1>3.0>Muse.
4.0*3.0x=px=7+12=19x=px=103=1.03 >> 1.0 x 10 raised to power 03 is the quantum size
for intelligence. Note that intelligence is the first component of the Mind > 103=1.0
hence what we call sin is actually the abstract code for the Mind. "For all have sinned
and come short of the glory of GOD interprets as For all have minds or solar energy

have occurred below the status of Godship. This is why we must attain by measures in the 10,000 scale. Also the code 103 indicates over 100% meaning 1,000=10,000. This is called the Peak of Aspiration (POA) measured as the point of godly perfection in every person. Sin>>Sign.

Sin3=1,000=100%=10.0=1.0=Mind=Sun=1 January=Helios >> M=E4.
Math. Sine. Thus aligns with Sin1 and Sin2.

Sinai Mount.=6,000=60%=P6.0D=Man=Earth=Royalty=6 June=Gaia=Maia>>M=M2.
Sinai Peninsula=4,500=5,000=50%=P5.00D=Law=Time=Venus=5 May = Aphrodite>>L=N.
Since=10,000=1,000=100%=10.0=Physicality=Tech.=10 Oct.=Uranus=P=1Ø.
Sincere=3,500=4,000=40%=P4.0D=Govt.=Creatocracy=4 April=Mercury=Hermes=G=A4.
Sinclair, Upton=3,500=4,000=40%=P4.0D=Govt.=4 April=Mercury=Hermes=G=A4.
Sine=8,500=9,000=90%=P9.00D=9.0=Abstraction=Gods=Saturn=9Sept.>>A=Ø.

Sine cure=8,000=80%=P8.0D=Economy=Currency=8 Aug.=Zeus>>E=v.
Makumatics is different from Mathematics. Makumatics is defined as deductions of the inherent faculties of the mind. Makumatics is herein defined by Peter Matthews-Akukalia, Castle Makupedia as deductions of the inherent faculties of matter. Now Makumatics is computed in the name of King Maks expressed as cures-Maks-cure in signs as x=px= meaning cure the problem using formulas made by Makupedia himself (King Maks). It is a part of the Castle Makupedia programming language for abstraction and Mind technology. This is a great link between computation 7.0 and economy 8.0. See seven.

Sinedie=6,000=60%=P6.0D=Man=Earth=Royalty=6 June=Gaia=Maia>>M=M2.
Sine qua non=6,000=60%=P6.0D=Man=Earth=Royalty=6 June=Gaia=Maia>>M=M2.
Sinew=3,000=30%=P3.0D=3.0=Creativity=Stars=Muses=3 March = C=I>>GIL.
Sinewy=6,000=60%=P6.0D=Man=Earth=Royalty=6 June=Gaia=Maia>>M=M2.
Sing=10,000=1,000=100%=10.0=Physicality=Tech.=10 Oct.=Uranus=P=1Ø.
Sing.=1,000=100%=10.0=1.0=Mind=Sun=1 January=Helios >> M=E4.
Singapore=9,000=90%=P9.00D=9.0=Abstraction=Gods=Saturn=9Sept.>>A=Ø.
Singe=6,000=60%=P6.0D=Man=Earth=Royalty=6 June=Gaia=Maia>>M=M2.
Singer Isaac=4,500=5,000=50%=P5.00D=Law=Time=Venus=5 May = Aphrodite>>L=N.
Singhalese=7,000=70%=P7.0D=7.0=Language=Assets=Mars=7 July=Pleiades.
Single=10,000=1,000=100%=10.0=Physicality=Tech.=10 Oct.=Uranus=P=1Ø.
Single breasted=6,000=60%=P6.0D=Man=Earth=Royalty=6 June=Gaia=Maia>>M=M2.
Single file=6,000=60%=P6.0D=Man=Earth=Royalty=6 June=Gaia=Maia>>M=M2.
Singlehanded=5,000=50%=P5.00D=Law=Time=Venus=5 May = Aphrodite>>L=N.
Singleminded=3,500=4,000=40%=P4.0D=Govt.=Creatocracy=4 April=Hermes=G=A4.
Singles bar=4,500=5,000=50%=P5.00D=Law=Time=Venus=5 May = Aphrodite>>L=N.
Singly=2,000=20%=P2.00D=2.0=Nature=Matter=Moon=2 Feb.=Cupid=N=C+_
Singsong=4,000=40%=P4.0D=Govt.=Creatocracy=4 April=Mercury=Hermes=G=A4.

Singular=10,000=1,000=100%=10.0=Physicality=Tech.=10 Oct.=Uranus=P=1Ø.
Sinhalese=1,500=15%=P1.50D=1.5=Authority=Solar Crown=1 May = Maia.
Sinister=5,500=5.5=80%=P5.50=Earth-Midway=5 May = Gaia.
Sink=10,000=1,000=100%=10.0=Physicality=Tech.=10 Oct.=Uranus=P=1Ø.
Sinker=4,500=5,000=50%=P5.00D=Law=Time=Venus=5 May = Aphrodite>>L=N.
Sinkhole=10,000=1,000=100%=10.0=Physicality=Tech.=10 Oct.=Uranus=P=1Ø.
Sinking fund=5,000=50%=P5.00D=Law=Time=Venus=5 May = Aphrodite>>L=N.
Sino-=2,500=3,000=30%=P3.0D=3.0=Creativity=Stars=Muses=3 March = C=I>>GIL.
Sinology=4,000=40%=P4.0D=Govt.=Creatocracy=4 April=Mercury=Hermes=G=A4.
Sino-Tibetan=4,500=5,000=50%=P5.00D=Law=Time=Venus=5 May = Aphrodite>>L=N.
Sinuous=8,500=9,000=90%=P9.00D=9.0=Abstraction=Gods=Saturn=9Sept.>>A=Ø.
Sinus=10,000=1,000=100%=10.0=Physicality=Tech.=10 Oct.=Uranus=P=1Ø.
Sinusitis=4,500=5,000=50%=P5.00D=Law=Time=Venus=5 May = Aphrodite>>L=N.
Sion=1,500=15%=P1.50D=1.5=Authority=Solar Crown=1 May = Maia.
Siouan=7,500=8,000=80%=P8.0D=Economy=Currency=8 Aug.=Zeus>>E=v.
Sioux=10,000=1,000=100%=10.0=Physicality=Tech.=10 Oct.=Uranus=P=1Ø.
Sioux Falls.=5,500=5.5=80%=P5.50=Earth-Midway=5 May = Gaia.
Sip=8,000=80%=P8.0D=Economy=Currency=8 Aug.=Zeus>>E=v.
Siphon=10,000=1,000=100%=10.0=Physicality=Tech.=10 Oct.=Uranus=P=1Ø.

Sir=10,000=1,000=100%=10.0=Physicality=Tech.=10 Oct.=Uranus=P=1Ø.
Used as an horrific title for baronets and knights. Used as a form of polite address for a man. Used as a salutation in a letter: Dear Sir. <SIRE

Sire=10,000=1,000=100%=10.0=Physicality=Tech.=10 Oct.=Uranus=P=1Ø.
A father. Archaic. Used as a form of address for a male superior, esp. a king. To begat. <Latin. Senior, older.

---

siren=7,500=8,000=80%=P8.0D=Economy=Currency=8 Aug.=Zeus>>E=v.

Siren=11,000=11%=P1.10D=1.1=Idea=Brainchild=Inv.=11 Nov.=SC=Athena>>I=MT.
Greek myth. One of a group that sea nymphs whose singing lured Mariners to destruction. A beautiful or alluring woman. Results indicate Athena who interestingly is the Goddess of marine warfare and inventor and the Navy defense combat and warships. The sea nymphs are logically muses who fight on her behalf and serve as servant of duty to her.

Sirius=4,500=5,000=50%=P5.00D=Law=Time=Venus=5 May = Aphrodite>>L=N.
A star in the Canis Major, the brightest star in the sky. The codes are Canis = Castle, Major = Makupedia. Brightest = light of the Sun = Mind. Sky >> Zeus Incarnation. Now energy is 4.0 computing his GIL/CME = 70%, 4.0 >> 7.0*4.0=P=4.0. Therefore the abstract word for Castle Makupedia is Canis Major and Sirius is his innermost spirit or solar core point. Canis Major is a small constellation (the Great Dog) said to represent

one of the dogs following Orion. It is south of the celestial equator and contains the brightest star Sirius. Peter Matthews-Akukalia, Castle Makupedia has therefore cast the bands of Orion as required by GOD in Job 38:31. It is a means that links Hermes with Aphrodite, power with authority.

Sirloin=6,000=60%=P6.0D=Man=Earth=Royalty=6 June=Gaia=Maia>>M=M2.
Sirocco=7,500=8,000=80%=P8.0D=Economy=Currency=8 Aug.=Zeus>>E=v.
Sirup=1,500=15%=P1.50D=1.5=Authority=Solar Crown=1 May = Maia.
Sis=1,000=100%=10.0=1.0=Mind=Sun=1 January=Helios >> M=E4.
Sisal=8,500=9,000=90%=P9.00D=9.0=Abstraction=Gods=Saturn=9Sept.>>A=Ø.
Sissy=7,000=70%=P7.0D=7.0=Language=Assets=Mars=7 July=Pleiades.
Sister=10,000=1,000=100%=10.0=Physicality=Tech.=10 Oct.=Uranus=P=1Ø.
Sisterhood=8,500=9,000=90%=P9.00D=9.0=Abstraction=Gods=Saturn=9Sept.>>A=Ø.
Sister in law=5,000=50%=P5.00D=Law=Time=Venus=5 May = Aphrodite>>L=N.
Sit=10,000=1,000=100%=10.0=Physicality=Tech.=10 Oct.=Uranus=P=1Ø.
Sitar=11,000=11%=P1.10D=1.1=Idea=Brainchild=Inv.=11 Nov.=SC=Athena>>I=MT.
Sitcom=1,500=15%=P1.50D=1.5=Authority=Solar Crown=1 May = Maia.
Sit down=10,000=1,000=100%=10.0=Physicality=Tech.=10 Oct.=Uranus=P=1Ø.
Site=7,000=70%=P7.0D=7.0=Language=Assets=Mars=7 July=Pleiades.
Sit in=8,500=9,000=90%=P9.00D=9.0=Abstraction=Gods=Saturn=9Sept.>>A=Ø.
Sitting=2,500=3,000=30%=P3.0D=3.0=Creativity=Stars=Muses=3 March = C=I>>GIL.
Sitting Bull=2,500=3,000=30%=P3.0D=3.0=Creativity=Stars=Muses=3 March = C=I>>GIL.
Situate=5,000=50%=P5.00D=Law=Time=Venus=5 May = Aphrodite>>L=N.
Situation=4,500=5,000=50%=P5.00D=Law=Time=Venus=5 May = Aphrodite>>L=N.
Situation comedy=4,500=5,000=50%=P5.00D=Law=Time=Venus=5 May =Odite>>L=N.
Sit-up=11,000=11%=P1.10D=1.1=Idea=Brainchild=Inv.=11 Nov.=SC=Athena>>I=MT.
Sivan=5,500=5.5=80%=P5.50=Earth-Midway=5 May = Gaia.
Six=2,000=20%=P2.00D=2.0=Nature=Matter=Moon=2 Feb.=Cupid=N=C+_
Six gun=2,000=20%=P2.00D=2.0=Nature=Matter=Moon=2 Feb.=Cupid=N=C+_
Six Nations=4,500=5,000=50%=P5.00D=Law=Time=Venus=5 May = Aphrodite>>L=N.
Six pack=5,500=5.5=80%=P5.50=Earth-Midway=5 May = Gaia.
Six shooter=1,500=15%=P1.50D=1.5=Authority=Solar Crown=1 May = Maia.
Sixteen=7,000=70%=P7.0D=7.0=Language=Assets=Mars=7 July=Pleiades.
Sixteenth=7,000=70%=P7.0D=7.0=Language=Assets=Mars=7 July=Pleiades.
Sixth=10,000=1,000=100%=10.0=Physicality=Tech.=10 Oct.=Uranus=P=1Ø.
Sixtieth=6,500=7,000=70%=P7.0D=7.0=Language=Assets=Mars=7 July=Pleiades.
Sixty=4,500=5,000=50%=P5.00D=Law=Time=Venus=5 May = Aphrodite>>L=N.
Sizable=2,500=3,000=30%=P3.0D=3.0=Creativity=Stars=Muses=3 March = C=I>>GIL.
Size1=10,000=1,000=100%=10.0=Physicality=Tech.=10 Oct.=Uranus=P=1Ø.
Size2=9,000=90%=P9.00D=9.0=Abstraction=Gods=Saturn=9Sept.>>A=Ø.
Sizing=2,500=3,000=30%=P3.0D=3.0=Creativity=Stars=Muses=3 March = C=I>>GIL.
Sizzle=8,500=9,000=90%=P9.00D=9.0=Abstraction=Gods=Saturn=9Sept.>>A=Ø.
S.J.=1,500=15%=P1.50D=1.5=Authority=Solar Crown=1 May = Maia.
Sjaelland=6,000=60%=P6.0D=Man=Earth=Royalty=6 June=Gaia=Maia>>M=M2.

SK=500=5%=P5.00D=5.0=Law=Time=Venus=5 May=Aphrodite>>L=N.
Saskatchewan. In the Creatocracy a symbol for the smallest denomination of the Maks currencies called the Kosemaks. It is the symbol for the measure of inherent energy in a thing that determines the pure equivalence, average propensity and value of that thing. It is the 10,000th unit in a thing and indicates cosmic energy quantum (=SK=>>Sky). Discovery of this singular unit made Peter Matthews-Akukalia, Dragon Lord of the Sky (DLS).

Skagerrak.=6,000=60%=P6.0D=Man=Earth=Royalty=6 June=Gaia=Maia>>M=M2.
Skate1=8,500=9,000=90%=P9.00D=9.0=Abstraction=Gods=Saturn=9Sept.>>A=Ø.
Skate2=8,000=80%=P8.0D=Economy=Currency=8 Aug.=Zeus>>E=v.
Skateboard=7,500=8,000=80%=P8.0D=Economy=Currency=8 Aug.=Zeus>>E=v.
Skeet=9,000=90%=P9.00D=9.0=Abstraction=Gods=Saturn=9Sept.>>A=Ø.
Skein=8,500=9,000=90%=P9.00D=9.0=Abstraction=Gods=Saturn=9Sept.>>A=Ø.
Skeleton=10,000=1,000=100%=10.0=Physicality=Tech.=10 Oct.=Uranus=P=1Ø.
Skeleton key=5,000=50%=P5.00D=Law=Time=Venus=5 May = Aphrodite>>L=N.
Skeptic=10,000=1,000=100%=10.0=Physicality=Tech.=10 Oct.=Uranus=P=1Ø.
Skepticism=10,000=1,000=100%=10.0=Physicality=Tech.=10 Oct.=Uranus=P=1Ø.
Sketch=10,000=1,000=100%=10.0=Physicality=Tech.=10 Oct.=Uranus=P=1Ø.
Skew=8,500=9,000=90%=P9.00D=9.0=Abstraction=Gods=Saturn=9Sept.>>A=Ø.
Skewer=6,500=7,000=70%=P7.0D=7.0=Language=Assets=Mars=7 July=Pleiades.
Ski=10,000=1,000=100%=10.0=Physicality=Tech.=10 Oct.=Uranus=P=1Ø.
Skid=10,000=1,000=100%=10.0=Physicality=Tech.=10 Oct.=Uranus=P=1Ø.
Skid row=3,500=4,000=40%=P4.0D=Govt.=4 April=Mercury=Hermes=G=A4.
Skiff=5,500=5.5=80%=P5.50=Earth-Midway=5 May = Gaia.
Ski lift=6,000=60%=P6.0D=Man=Earth=Royalty=6 June=Gaia=Maia>>M=M2.

Skill=9,500=10,000=1,000=100%=10.0=Physicality=Tech.=10 Oct.=Uranus=P=1Ø.
Peter Matthews-Akukalia, Castle Makupedia invented the study Faculty of Creative & Psycho-Social Sciences with over 2,000 new skills that translate into careers for the creation of an estimated one billion people worldwide.

Skillet=4,000=40%=P4.0D=Govt.=Creatocracy=4 April=Mercury=Hermes=G=A4.
Skillful=4,000=40%=P4.0D=Govt.=Creatocracy=4 April=Mercury=Hermes=G=A4.
Skim=10,000=1,000=100%=10.0=Physicality=Tech.=10 Oct.=Uranus=P=1Ø.
Skim milk=4,000=40%=P4.0D=Govt.=Creatocracy=4 April=Mercury=Hermes=G=A4.
Skimp=6,000=60%=P6.0D=Man=Earth=Royalty=6 June=Gaia=Maia>>M=M2.
Skimpy=4,500=5,000=50%=P5.00D=Law=Time=Venus=5 May = Aphrodite>>L=N.
Skin=10,000=1,000=100%=10.0=Physicality=Tech.=10 Oct.=Uranus=P=1Ø.
Skin diving=5,500=5.5=80%=P5.50=Earth-Midway=5 May = Gaia.
Skinflint=1,000=100%=10.0=1.0=Mind=Sun=1 January=Helios >> M=E4.

Skinner B(urrhus) F(rederick)=2,000=20%=P2.00D=2.0=Nature=2 Feb.=Cupid=N=C+_
Peter Matthews-Akukalia, Castle Makupedia wrote The Oracle: Principles of Creative Sciences was written to fulfill the dreams of B.F. Skinner and Ralph Waldo Emerson. He

predicted the emergence of a new science that would solve the equation of the Mind. His nature and source origin indicates the moon hence satellite data tracking on his birth.

Skinny=1,000=100%=10.0=1.0=Mind=Sun=1 January=Helios >> M=E4.
Skinny dip=3,000=30%=P3.0D=3.0=Creativity=Stars=Muses=3 March = C=I>>GIL.
Skip=10,000=1,000=100%=10.0=Physicality=Tech.=10 Oct.=Uranus=P=1Ø.
Skipper=3,500=4,000=40%=P4.0D=Govt.=Creatocracy=4 April=Mercury=Hermes=G=A4.
Skirmish=5,000=50%=P5.00D=Law=Time=Venus=5 May = Aphrodite>>L=N.
Skirt=10,000=1,000=100%=10.0=Physicality=Tech.=10 Oct.=Uranus=P=1Ø.
Skit=3,500=4,000=40%=P4.0D=Govt.=Creatocracy=4 April=Mercury=Hermes=G=A4.
Skitter=7,500=8,000=80%=P8.0D=Economy=Currency=8 Aug.=Zeus>>E=v.
Skittish=3,000=30%=P3.0D=3.0=Creativity=Stars=Muses=3 March = C=I>>GIL.
Skoal=4,000=40%=P4.0D=Govt.=Creatocracy=4 April=Mercury=Hermes=G=A4.
Skopje=4,500=5,000=50%=P5.00D=Law=Time=Venus=5 May = Aphrodite>>L=N.
Skulk=6,500=7,000=70%=P7.0D=7.0=Language=Assets=Mars=7 July=Pleiades.
Skull=4,000=40%=P4.0D=Govt.=Creatocracy=4 April=Mercury=Hermes=G=A4.

Skullcap=3,500=4,000=40%=P4.0D=Govt.=Creatocracy=4 April=Hermes=G=A4.
Hermes is known to wear a cap with flying wings on it, Castle Makupedia the Solar Crown.

Skulduggery=4,000=40%=P4.0D=Govt.=Creatocracy=4 April=Mercury=Hermes=G=A4.
Skunk=10,000=1,000=100%=10.0=Physicality=Tech.=10 Oct.=Uranus=P=1Ø.
Skunk cabbage=8,000=80%=P8.0D=Economy=Currency=8 Aug.=Zeus>>E=v.

Sky=9,500=10,000=1,000=100%=10.0=Physicality=Tech.=10 Oct.=Uranus=P=1Ø.
ON skÿ, cloud. To measure the clouds in a quantum mechanics is to own the sky.
Peter Matthews-Akukalia, Castle Makupedia is revered as Dragon Lord of the Sky. See SK.
See the book>> Template & Manifesto for the Creative Economy 2: Principles of Psychoeconomix by Peter Matthews-Akukalia. World's 1st Psychoeconomixt

Skycap=1,500=15%=P1.50D=1.5=Authority=Solar Crown=1 May = Maia.
Skydive=6,000=60%=P6.0D=Man=Earth=Royalty=6 June=Gaia=Maia>>M=M2.
Skye Isle of.=4,500=5,000=50%=P5.00D=Law=Time=Venus=5 May = Aphrodite>>L=N.
Sky high=9,500=10,000=1,000=100%=10.0=Physicality=Tech.=10 Oct.=Uranus=P=1Ø.
Skyjack=5,000=50%=P5.00D=Law=Time=Venus=5 May = Aphrodite>>L=N.
Skylark=9,000=90%=P9.00D=9.0=Abstraction=Gods=Saturn=9Sept.>>A=Ø.
Skylight=4,500=5,000=50%=P5.00D=Law=Time=Venus=5 May = Aphrodite>>L=N.
Skyline=4,500=5,000=50%=P5.00D=Law=Time=Venus=5 May = Aphrodite>>L=N.
Skyrocket=7,000=70%=P7.0D=7.0=Language=Assets=Mars=7 July=Pleiades.
Skyscraper=2,000=20%=P2.00D=2.0=Nature=Matter=Moon=2 Feb.=Cupid=N=C+_
Skyward=2,500=3,000=30%=P3.0D=3.0=Creativity=Stars=Muses=3 March = C=I>>GIL.
Skywriting=7,000=70%=P7.0D=7.0=Language=Assets=Mars=7 July=Pleiades.
Slab=9,000=90%=P9.00D=9.0=Abstraction=Gods=Saturn=9Sept.>>A=Ø.

Slack=10,000=1,000=100%=10.0=Physicality=Tech.=10 Oct.=Uranus=P=1Ø.
Slacken=5,000=50%=P5.00D=Law=Time=Venus=5 May = Aphrodite>>L=N.
Slacker=5,500=5.5=80%=P5.50=Earth-Midway=5 May = Gaia.
Slag=5,000=50%=P5.00D=Law=Time=Venus=5 May = Aphrodite>>L=N.
Slain=2,000=20%=P2.00D=2.0=Nature=Matter=Moon=2 Feb.=Cupid=N=C+_
Slake=8,000=80%=P8.0D=Economy=Currency=8 Aug.=Zeus>>E=v.
Slalom=4,500=5,000=50%=P5.00D=Law=Time=Venus=5 May = Aphrodite>>L=N.
Slam1=10,000=1,000=100%=10.0=Physicality=Tech.=10 Oct.=Uranus=P=1Ø.
Slam2=10,000=1,000=100%=10.0=Physicality=Tech.=10 Oct.=Uranus=P=1Ø.
Slammer=2,000=20%=P2.00D=2.0=Nature=Matter=Moon=2 Feb.=Cupid=N=C+_
Slander=7,000=70%=P7.0D=7.0=Language=Assets=Mars=7 July=Pleiades.
Slang=10,000=1,000=100%=10.0=Physicality=Tech.=10 Oct.=Uranus=P=1Ø.
Slant=10,000=1,000=100%=10.0=Physicality=Tech.=10 Oct.=Uranus=P=1Ø.
Slap=10,000=1,000=100%=10.0=Physicality=Tech.=10 Oct.=Uranus=P=1Ø.
Slapdash=1,500=15%=P1.50D=1.5=Authority=Solar Crown=1 May = Maia.
Slaphappy=6,000=60%=P6.0D=Man=Earth=Royalty=6 June=Gaia=Maia>>M=M2.
Slapstick=3,500=4,000=40%=P4.0D=Govt.=4 April=Mercury=Hermes=G=A4.
Slash=10,000=1,000=100%=10.0=Physicality=Tech.=10 Oct.=Uranus=P=1Ø.
Slat=6,000=60%=P6.0D=Man=Earth=Royalty=6 June=Gaia=Maia>>M=M2.
Slate=10,000=1,000=100%=10.0=Physicality=Tech.=10 Oct.=Uranus=P=1Ø.
Slather=3,500=4,000=40%=P4.0D=Govt.=Creatocracy=4 April=Hermes=G=A4.
Slattern=4,000=40%=P4.0D=Govt.=Creatocracy=4 April=Mercury=Hermes=G=A4.
Slaughter=11,000=11%=P1.10D=1.1=Idea=Brainchild=Inv.=11 Nov.=SC=Athena>>I=MT.
Slaughterhouse=3,000=30%=P3.0D=3.0=Creativity=Stars=Muses=3 March = C=I>>GIL.
Slav=5,000=50%=P5.00D=Law=Time=Venus=5 May = Aphrodite>>L=N.
Slave=10,000=1,000=100%=10.0=Physicality=Tech.=10 Oct.=Uranus=P=1Ø.
Slaver1=5,500=5.5=80%=P5.50=Earth-Midway=5 May = Gaia.
Slaver2=6,500=7,000=70%=P7.0D=7.0=Language=Assets=Mars=7 July=Pleiades.
Slavery=7,500=8,000=80%=P8.0D=Economy=Currency=8 Aug.=Zeus>>E=v.
Slavic=10,000=1,000=100%=10.0=Physicality=Tech.=10 Oct.=Uranus=P=1Ø.
Slavish=7,000=70%=P7.0D=7.0=Language=Assets=Mars=7 July=Pleiades.
Slavonia=3,000=30%=P3.0D=3.0=Creativity=Stars=Muses=3 March = C=I>>GIL.
Slavonic=500=5%=P5.00D=5.0=Law=Time=Venus=5 May=Aphrodite>>L=N.
Slaw=500=5%=P5.00D=5.0=Law=Time=Venus=5 May=Aphrodite>>L=N.
Slay=2,500=3,000=30%=P3.0D=3.0=Creativity=Stars=Muses=3 March = C=I>>GIL.
Sleazy=5,000=50%=P5.00D=Law=Time=Venus=5 May = Aphrodite>>L=N.
Sled=10,000=1,000=100%=10.0=Physicality=Tech.=10 Oct.=Uranus=P=1Ø.
Sledge=9,000=90%=P9.00D=9.0=Abstraction=Gods=Saturn=9Sept.>>A=Ø.
Sledgehammer=5,500=5.5=80%=P5.50=Earth-Midway=5 May = Gaia.
Sleek=10,000=1,000=100%=10.0=Physicality=Tech.=10 Oct.=Uranus=P=1Ø.
Sleep=10,000=1,000=100%=10.0=Physicality=Tech.=10 Oct.=Uranus=P=1Ø.
Sleeper=6,000=60%=P6.0D=Man=Earth=Royalty=6 June=Gaia=Maia>>M=M2.
Sleeping bag=4,500=5,000=50%=P5.00D=Law=Time=Venus=5 May = Aphrodite>>L=N.
Sleeping car=3,500=4,000=40%=P4.0D=Govt.=Creatocracy=4 April=Hermes=G=A4.
Sleeping pill=6,500=7,000=70%=P7.0D=7.0=Language=Assets=Mars=7 July=Pleiades.

Sleeping sickness=9,500=10,000=1,000=100%=10.0=Phy=Tech.=10 Oct.=Uranus=P=1Ø.
Sleepless=6,500=7,000=70%=P7.0D=7.0=Language=Assets=Mars=7 July=Pleiades.
Sleepwalking=7,500=8,000=80%=P8.0D=Economy=Currency=8 Aug.=Zeus>>E=v.
Sleepy=3,500=4,000=40%=P4.0D=Govt.=Creatocracy=4 April=Mercury=Hermes=G=A4.
Sleet=7,500=8,000=80%=P8.0D=Economy=Currency=8 Aug.=Zeus>>E=v.
Sleeve=11,000=11%=P1.10D=1.1=Idea=Brainchild=Inv.=11 Nov.=SC=Athena>>I=MT.
Sleigh=7,500=8,000=80%=P8.0D=Economy=Currency=8 Aug.=Zeus>>E=v.
Sleight of hand=10,000=1,000=100%=10.0=Physicality=Tech.=10 Oct.=Uranus=P=1Ø.
Slender=10,000=1,000=100%=10.0=Physicality=Tech.=10 Oct.=Uranus=P=1Ø.
Slenderize=10,000=1,000=100%=10.0=Physicality=Tech.=10 Oct.=Uranus=P=1Ø.
Slept=3,000=30%=P3.0D=3.0=Creativity=Stars=Muses=3 March = C=I>>GIL.
Sleuth=2,000=20%=P2.00D=2.0=Nature=Matter=Moon=2 Feb.=Cupid=N=C+_
Sleuth hound=5,500=5.5=80%=P5.50=Earth-Midway=5 May = Gaia.
Slew1=4,000=40%=P4.0D=Govt.=Creatocracy=4 April=Mercury=Hermes=G=A4.
Slew2=2,000=20%=P2.00D=2.0=Nature=Matter=Moon=2 Feb.=Cupid=N=C+_
Slew3=1,500=15%=P1.50D=1.5=Authority=Solar Crown=1 May = Maia.
Slice=10,000=1,000=100%=10.0=Physicality=Tech.=10 Oct.=Uranus=P=1Ø.
Slick=10,000=1,000=100%=10.0=Physicality=Tech.=10 Oct.=Uranus=P=1Ø.
Slicker=7,500=8,000=80%=P8.0D=Economy=Currency=8 Aug.=Zeus>>E=v.
Slide=10,000=1,000=100%=10.0=Physicality=Tech.=10 Oct.=Uranus=P=1Ø.
Slider=10,000=1,000=100%=10.0=Physicality=Tech.=10 Oct.=Uranus=P=1Ø.
Slide rule=10,000=1,000=100%=10.0=Physicality=Tech.=10 Oct.=Uranus=P=1Ø.
Sliding scale=10,000=1,000=100%=10.0=Physicality=Tech.=10 Oct.=Uranus=P=1Ø.
Slier=1,500=15%=P1.50D=1.5=Authority=Solar Crown=1 May = Maia.
Sliest=2,000=20%=P2.00D=2.0=Nature=Matter=Moon=2 Feb.=Cupid=N=C+_
Slight=10,000=1,000=100%=10.0=Physicality=Tech.=10 Oct.=Uranus=P=1Ø.
Slim=10,000=1,000=100%=10.0=Physicality=Tech.=10 Oct.=Uranus=P=1Ø.
Slime=7,500=8,000=80%=P8.0D=Economy=Currency=8 Aug.=Zeus>>E=v.
Sling=10,000=1,000=100%=10.0=Physicality=Tech.=10 Oct.=Uranus=P=1Ø.
Slingshot=10,000=1,000=100%=10.0=Physicality=Tech.=10 Oct.=Uranus=P=1Ø.
Slink=2,500=3,000=30%=P3.0D=3.0=Creativity=Stars=Muses=3 March = C=I>>GIL.
Slip1=10,000=1,000=100%=10.0=Physicality=Tech.=10 Oct.=Uranus=P=1Ø.
Slip2=8,500=9,000=90%=P9.00D=9.0=Abstraction=Gods=Saturn=9Sept.>>A=Ø.
Slipcover=5,500=5.5=80%=P5.50=Earth-Midway=5 May = Gaia.
Slip knot=10,000=1,000=100%=10.0=Physicality=Tech.=10 Oct.=Uranus=P=1Ø.
Slipped disk=8,000=80%=P8.0D=Economy=Currency=8 Aug.=Zeus>>E=v.
Slipper=6,000=60%=P6.0D=Man=Earth=Royalty=6 June=Gaia=Maia>>M=M2.
Slippery=6,500=7,000=70%=P7.0D=7.0=Language=Assets=Mars=7 July=Pleiades.
Slipshod=3,000=30%=P3.0D=3.0=Creativity=Stars=Muses=3 March = C=I>>GIL.
Slip up=1,500=15%=P1.50D=1.5=Authority=Solar Crown=1 May = Maia.
Slit=5,000=50%=P5.00D=Law=Time=Venus=5 May = Aphrodite>>L=N.
Slither=7,000=70%=P7.0D=7.0=Language=Assets=Mars=7 July=Pleiades.
Silver=4,500=5,000=50%=P5.00D=Law=Time=Venus=5 May = Aphrodite>>L=N.
Slob=4,500=5,000=50%=P5.00D=Law=Time=Venus=5 May = Aphrodite>>L=N.
Slobber=8,000=80%=P8.0D=Economy=Currency=8 Aug.=Zeus>>E=v.

Sloe=6,000=60%=P6.0D=Man=Earth=Royalty=6 June=Gaia=Maia>>M=M2.
Slog=7,500=8,000=80%=P8.0D=Economy=Currency=8 Aug.=Zeus>>E=v.
Slogan=10,000=1,000=100%=10.0=Physicality=Tech.=10 Oct.=Uranus=P=1Ø.
Sloop=10,000=1,000=100%=10.0=Physicality=Tech.=10 Oct.=Uranus=P=1Ø.
Slop=10,000=1,000=100%=10.0=Physicality=Tech.=10 Oct.=Uranus=P=1Ø.
Slope=10,000=1,000=100%=10.0=Physicality=Tech.=10 Oct.=Uranus=P=1Ø.
Sloppy=3,500=4,000=40%=P4.0D=Govt.=Creatocracy=4 April=Mercury=Hermes=G=A4.
Slosh=7,000=70%=P7.0D=7.0=Language=Assets=Mars=7 July=Pleiades.
Slot=10,000=1,000=100%=10.0=Physicality=Tech.=10 Oct.=Uranus=P=1Ø.
Sloth=10,000=1,000=100%=10.0=Physicality=Tech.=10 Oct.=Uranus=P=1Ø.
Slothful=3,000=30%=P3.0D=3.0=Creativity=Stars=Muses=3 March = C=I>>GIL.
Slot machine=3,500=4,000=40%=P4.0D=Govt.=4 April=Mercury=Hermes=G=A4.
Slouch=6,500=7,000=70%=P7.0D=7.0=Language=Assets=Mars=7 July=Pleiades.
Slough1=7,000=70%=P7.0D=7.0=Language=Assets=Mars=7 July=Pleiades.
Slough2=10,000=1,000=100%=10.0=Physicality=Tech.=10 Oct.=Uranus=P=1Ø.
Slovak=10,000=1,000=100%=10.0=Physicality=Tech.=10 Oct.=Uranus=P=1Ø.
Slovakia=10,000=1,000=100%=10.0=Physicality=Tech.=10 Oct.=Uranus=P=1Ø.
Sloven=4,500=5,000=50%=P5.00D=Law=Time=Venus=5 May = Aphrodite>>L=N.
Slovene=10,000=1,000=100%=10.0=Physicality=Tech.=10 Oct.=Uranus=P=1Ø.
Slovenia=5,500=5.5=80%=P5.50=Earth-Midway=5 May = Gaia.
Slovenly=4,500=5,000=50%=P5.00D=Law=Time=Venus=5 May = Aphrodite>>L=N.
Slow=10,000=1,000=100%=10.0=Physicality=Tech.=10 Oct.=Uranus=P=1Ø.
Slowdown=10,000=1,000=100%=10.0=Physicality=Tech.=10 Oct.=Uranus=P=1Ø.
Slow motion=7,500=8,000=80%=P8.0D=Economy=Currency=8 Aug.=Zeus>>E=v.
Slow poke=4,000=40%=P4.0D=Govt.=Creatocracy=4 April=Mercury=Hermes=G=A4.
Sludge=8,500=9,000=90%=P9.00D=9.0=Abstraction=Gods=Saturn=9Sept.>>A=Ø.
Slue1=5,000=50%=P5.00D=Law=Time=Venus=5 May = Aphrodite>>L=N.
Slue2=1,500=15%=P1.50D=1.5=Authority=Solar Crown=1 May = Maia.
Slug1=10,000=1,000=100%=10.0=Physicality=Tech.=10 Oct.=Uranus=P=1Ø.
Slug2=7,500=8,000=80%=P8.0D=Economy=Currency=8 Aug.=Zeus>>E=v.
Slug3=6,000=60%=P6.0D=Man=Earth=Royalty=6 June=Gaia=Maia>>M=M2.
Sluggard=3,000=30%=P3.0D=3.0=Creativity=Stars=Muses=3 March = C=I>>GIL.
Sluggish=6,000=60%=P6.0D=Man=Earth=Royalty=6 June=Gaia=Maia>>M=M2.
Sluice=10,000=1,000=100%=10.0=Physicality=Tech.=10 Oct.=Uranus=P=1Ø.
Sluice way=5,000=50%=P5.00D=Law=Time=Venus=5 May = Aphrodite>>L=N.
Slum=7,000=70%=P7.0D=7.0=Language=Assets=Mars=7 July=Pleiades.
Slumber=4,500=5,000=50%=P5.00D=Law=Time=Venus=5 May = Aphrodite>>L=N.
Slumberous=4,000=40%=P4.0D=Govt.=Creatocracy=4 April=Mercury=Hermes=G=A4.
Slumlord=6,000=60%=P6.0D=Man=Earth=Royalty=6 June=Gaia=Maia>>M=M2.
Slump=7,500=8,000=80%=P8.0D=Economy=Currency=8 Aug.=Zeus>>E=v.
Slung=3,000=30%=P3.0D=3.0=Creativity=Stars=Muses=3 March = C=I>>GIL.
Slunk=3,000=30%=P3.0D=3.0=Creativity=Stars=Muses=3 March = C=I>>GIL.
Slur=10,000=1,000=100%=10.0=Physicality=Tech.=10 Oct.=Uranus=P=1Ø.
Slurp=3,000=30%=P3.0D=3.0=Creativity=Stars=Muses=3 March = C=I>>GIL.
Slush=7,000=70%=P7.0D=7.0=Language=Assets=Mars=7 July=Pleiades.

Slush fund=7,500=8,000=80%=P8.0D=Economy=Currency=8 Aug.=Zeus>>E=v.
Slut=4,000=40%=P4.0D=Govt.=Creatocracy=4 April=Mercury=Hermes=G=A4.
Sly=7,000=70%=P7.0D=7.0=Language=Assets=Mars=7 July=Pleiades.
Sm=2,500=3,000=30%=P3.0D=3.0=Creativity=Stars=Muses=3 March = C=I>>GIL.
SM=2,000=20%=P2.00D=2.0=Nature=Matter=Moon=2 Feb.=Cupid=N=C+_
Smack1=10,000=1,000=100%=10.0=Physicality=Tech.=10 Oct.=Uranus=P=1Ø.
Smack2=10,000=1,000=100%=10.0=Physicality=Tech.=10 Oct.=Uranus=P=1Ø.
Smack3=10,000=1,000=100%=10.0=Physicality=Tech.=10 Oct.=Uranus=P=1Ø.
Smack4=4,000=40%=P4.0D=Govt.=Creatocracy=4 April=Mercury=Hermes=G=A4.
Small=10,000=1,000=100%=10.0=Physicality=Tech.=10 Oct.=Uranus=P=1Ø.
Small arm=4,500=5,000=50%=P5.00D=Law=Time=Venus=5 May = Aphrodite>>L=N.
Small calorie=1,500=15%=P1.50D=1.5=Authority=Solar Crown=1 May = Maia.
Small capital=4,500=5,000=50%=P5.00D=Law=Time=Venus=5 May = Aphrodite>>L=N.
Small fry=4,000=40%=P4.0D=Govt.=Creatocracy=4 April=Mercury=Hermes=G=A4.
Small intestine=5,500=5.5=80%=P5.50=Earth-Midway=5 May = Gaia.
Small minded=3,000=30%=P3.0D=3.0=Creativity=Stars=Muses=3 March = C=I>>GIL.
Smallpox=7,500=8,000=80%=P8.0D=Economy=Currency=8 Aug.=Zeus>>E=v.
Small talk=2,000=20%=P2.00D=2.0=Nature=Matter=Moon=2 Feb.=Cupid=N=C+_
Small time=2,000=20%=P2.00D=2.0=Nature=Matter=Moon=2 Feb.=Cupid=N=C+_
Smarmy=5,000=50%=P5.00D=Law=Time=Venus=5 May = Aphrodite>>L=N.

Smart=10,000=1,000=100%=10.0=Physicality=Tech.=10 Oct.=Uranus=P=1Ø.
Intelligent, bright. Amusingly clever, witty. Impertinent or insolent. Quick and energetic.
Canny and sharp in dealings, shrewd. Fashionable, elegant. Having some computational
ability of its own. To cause or feel a sharp stinging pain. To feel mental distress. <OE
smeart, stinging. The Creatocracy is a smart product of a smart course of study through
the smart formulas of a smart person Peter Matthews-Akukalia, Castle Makupedia.

Smart aleck=3,000=30%=P3.0D=3.0=Creativity=Stars=Muses=3 March = C=I>>GIL.
Smarten=4,500=5,000=50%=P5.00D=Law=Time=Venus=5 May = Aphrodite>>L=N.
Smash=10,000=1,000=100%=10.0=Physicality=Tech.=10 Oct.=Uranus=P=1Ø.
Smash up=3,500=4,000=40%=P4.0D=Govt.=Creatocracy=4 April=Hermes=G=A4.
Smattering=4,500=5,000=50%=P5.00D=Law=Time=Venus=5 May = Aphrodite>>L=N.
Smear=10,000=1,000=100%=10.0=Physicality=Tech.=10 Oct.=Uranus=P=1Ø.
Smell=10,000=1,000=100%=10.0=Physicality=Tech.=10 Oct.=Uranus=P=1Ø.
Smelling salts=6,000=60%=P6.0D=Man=Earth=Royalty=6 June=Gaia=Maia>>M=M2.
Smelly=2,500=3,000=30%=P3.0D=3.0=Creativity=Stars=Muses=3 March = C=I>>GIL.
Smelt1=6,000=60%=P6.0D=Man=Earth=Royalty=6 June=Gaia=Maia>>M=M2.
Smelt2=3,000=30%=P3.0D=3.0=Creativity=Stars=Muses=3 March = C=I>>GIL.
Smelt3=3,000=30%=P3.0D=3.0=Creativity=Stars=Muses=3 March = C=I>>GIL.
Smelter=4,500=5,000=50%=P5.00D=Law=Time=Venus=5 May = Aphrodite>>L=N.
Smidgen=5,500=5.5=80%=P5.50=Earth-Midway=5 May = Gaia.
Smilax=5,500=5.5=80%=P5.50=Earth-Midway=5 May = Gaia.
Smile=10,000=1,000=100%=10.0=Physicality=Tech.=10 Oct.=Uranus=P=1Ø.

Smirch=3,500=4,000=40%=P4.0D=Govt.=Creatocracy=4 April=Mercury=Hermes=G=A4.
Smirk=6,500=7,000=70%=P7.0D=7.0=Language=Assets=Mars=7 July=Pleiades.
Smite=8,000=80%=P8.0D=Economy=Currency=8 Aug.=Zeus>>E=v.
smith=5,500=5.5=80%=P5.50=Earth-Midway=5 May = Gaia.
Smith,Adam.=3,000=30%=P3.0D=3.0=Creativity=Stars=Muses=3 March = C=I>>GIL.
Smith,Alfred=2,500=3,000=30%=P3.0D=3.0=Cr=Stars=Muses=3 March = C=I>>GIL.
Smith,John.=4,000=40%=P4.0D=Govt.=Creatocracy=4 April=Mercury=Hermes=G=A4.
Smith,Joseph.=7,000=70%=P7.0D=7.0=Language=Assets=Mars=7 July=Pleiades.
Smith,Margaret=2,000=20%=P2.00D=2.0=Nature=Matter=Moon=2 Feb.=Cupid=N=C+_
Smithereens=3,000=30%=P3.0D=3.0=Creativity=Stars=Muses=3 March = C=I>>GIL.
Smithson James.=3,000=30%=P3.0D=3.0=Creativity=Stars=Muses=3 March = C=I>>GIL.
Smithy=3,000=30%=P3.0D=3.0=Creativity=Stars=Muses=3 March = C=I>>GIL.
Smock=10,000=1,000=100%=10.0=Physicality=Tech.=10 Oct.=Uranus=P=1Ø.
Smog=10,000=1,000=100%=10.0=Physicality=Tech.=10 Oct.=Uranus=P=1Ø.

Smoke=10,000=1,000=100%=10.0=Physicality=Tech.=10 Oct.=Uranus=P=1Ø.
Newton's laws of gravity states that what goes up must come down. Peter Matthews-Akukalia, Castle Makupedia discovered that certain things go up and don't come down at a spirit speed of 1.0x10 raised to power (-6). They include steam vapour smell and smoke. This is the law of psycho-gravitational incursion (PGI). He postulates that mind ascends and nature descends hence energy as the pure equivalent of mind ascends and matter as the pure equivalent of nature descends. Mind=Energy=Sun=Makumatics. Nature=Matter=Moon=Mathematics. Now in Mind, Intelligence is the equivalent of hydrogen measured at the size of 1.0x10(valency -03), thought is helium (0.3) and both go up and do not come down. Even through the natural cycle like the nitrogen cycle they come down in a different state from how they ascended. See Principles of Psychoeconomix by Peter Matthews-Akukalia. A template for Creative Scientists. See Alphabet.

Smokehouse=4,000=40%=P4.0D=Govt.=Creatocracy=4 April=Mercury=Hermes=G=A4.
Smokescreen=7,000=70%=P7.0D=7.0=Language=Assets=Mars=7 July=Pleiades.
Smokestack=6,000=60%=P6.0D=Man=Earth=Royalty=6 June=Gaia=Maia>>M=M2.
Smolder=10,000=1,000=100%=10.0=Physicality=Tech.=10 Oct.=Uranus=P=1Ø.
Smolensk=5,500=5.5=80%=P5.50=Earth-Midway=5 May = Gaia.
Smolett Tobias=2,500=3,000=30%=P3.0D=3.0=Cr=Stars=Muses=3 March = C=I>>GIL.
Smooch=4,000=40%=P4.0D=Govt.=Creatocracy=4 April=Mercury=Hermes=G=A4.
Smooth=10,000=1,000=100%=10.0=Physicality=Tech.=10 Oct.=Uranus=P=1Ø.
Smoothbore=5,000=50%=P5.00D=Law=Time=Venus=5 May = Aphrodite>>L=N.
Smorgasbord=5,000=50%=P5.00D=Law=Time=Venus=5 May = Aphrodite>>L=N.
Smote=3,000=30%=P3.0D=3.0=Creativity=Stars=Muses=3 March = C=I>>GIL.
Smother=8,000=80%=P8.0D=Economy=Currency=8 Aug.=Zeus>>E=v.
Smudge=8,000=80%=P8.0D=Economy=Currency=8 Aug.=Zeus>>E=v.
Smug=3,000=30%=P3.0D=3.0=Creativity=Stars=Muses=3 March = C=I>>GIL.
Smuggle=10,000=1,000=100%=10.0=Physicality=Tech.=10 Oct.=Uranus=P=1Ø.
Smut=10,000=1,000=100%=10.0=Physicality=Tech.=10 Oct.=Uranus=P=1Ø.

Smuts Jan=4,000=40%=P4.0D=Govt.=Creatocracy=4 April=Mercury=Hermes=G=A4.
Smyrna=1,000=100%=10.0=1.0=Mind=Sun=1 January=Helios >> M=E4.
Sn=4,500=5,000=50%=P5.00D=Law=Time=Venus=5 May = Aphrodite>>L=N.
Snack=3,000=30%=P3.0D=3.0=Creativity=Stars=Muses=3 March = C=I>>GIL.
Snaffle=3,000=30%=P3.0D=3.0=Creativity=Stars=Muses=3 March = C=I>>GIL.
Snafu=5,000=50%=P5.00D=Law=Time=Venus=5 May = Aphrodite>>L=N.
Snag=10,000=1,000=100%=10.0=Physicality=Tech.=10 Oct.=Uranus=P=1Ø.
Snail=7,500=8,000=80%=P8.0D=Economy=Currency=8 Aug.=Zeus>>E=v.
Snake=10,000=1,000=100%=10.0=Physicality=Tech.=10 Oct.=Uranus=P=1Ø.
Snake oil=5,000=50%=P5.00D=Law=Time=Venus=5 May = Aphrodite>>L=N.
Snake River=12,000=12%=P1.20D=1.2=Knowledge=Edu=12Dec.=Athena>>K=F.
Snap=10,000=1,000=100%=10.0=Physicality=Tech.=10 Oct.=Uranus=P=1Ø.
Snap bean=4,500=5,000=50%=P5.00D=Law=Time=Venus=5 May = Aphrodite>>L=N.
Snapdragon=6,000=60%=P6.0D=Man=Earth=Royalty=6 June=Gaia=Maia>>M=M2.
Snapper=7,000=70%=P7.0D=7.0=Language=Assets=Mars=7 July=Pleiades.
Snapping turtle=7,500=8,000=80%=P8.0D=Economy=Currency=8 Aug.=Zeus>>E=v.
Snapshot=3,000=30%=P3.0D=3.0=Creativity=Stars=Muses=3 March = C=I>>GIL.
Snare1=10,000=1,000=100%=10.0=Physicality=Tech.=10 Oct.=Uranus=P=1Ø.
Snare2=10,000=1,000=100%=10.0=Physicality=Tech.=10 Oct.=Uranus=P=1Ø.
Snarl1=6,000=60%=P6.0D=Man=Earth=Royalty=6 June=Gaia=Maia>>M=M2.
Snarl2=4,500=5,000=50%=P5.00D=Law=Time=Venus=5 May = Aphrodite>>L=N.
Snatch=10,000=1,000=100%=10.0=Physicality=Tech.=10 Oct.=Uranus=P=1Ø.
Snazzy=3,500=4,000=40%=P4.0D=Govt.=Creatocracy=4 April=Mercury=Hermes=G=A4.
Sneak=10,000=1,000=100%=10.0=Physicality=Tech.=10 Oct.=Uranus=P=1Ø.
Sneaker=5,500=5.5=80%=P5.50=Earth-Midway=5 May = Gaia.
Sneer=7,500=8,000=80%=P8.0D=Economy=Currency=8 Aug.=Zeus>>E=v.
Sneeze=8,000=80%=P8.0D=Economy=Currency=8 Aug.=Zeus>>E=v.
Snicker=4,500=5,000=50%=P5.00D=Law=Time=Venus=5 May = Aphrodite>>L=N.
Snide=1,500=15%=P1.50D=1.5=Authority=Solar Crown=1 May = Maia.
Sniff=10,000=1,000=100%=10.0=Physicality=Tech.=10 Oct.=Uranus=P=1Ø.
Sniffle=4,500=5,000=50%=P5.00D=Law=Time=Venus=5 May = Aphrodite>>L=N.
Snifter=7,500=8,000=80%=P8.0D=Economy=Currency=8 Aug.=Zeus>>E=v.
Snigger=2,000=20%=P2.00D=2.0=Nature=Matter=Moon=2 Feb.=Cupid=N=C+_
Snip=10,000=1,000=100%=10.0=Physicality=Tech.=10 Oct.=Uranus=P=1Ø.
Snipe=10,000=1,000=100%=10.0=Physicality=Tech.=10 Oct.=Uranus=P=1Ø.
Snippet=2,000=20%=P2.00D=2.0=Nature=Matter=Moon=2 Feb.=Cupid=N=C+_
Snippy=2,000=20%=P2.00D=2.0=Nature=Matter=Moon=2 Feb.=Cupid=N=C+_
Snit=2,500=3,000=30%=P3.0D=3.0=Creativity=Stars=Muses=3 March = C=I>>GIL.
Snitch=3,000=30%=P3.0D=3.0=Creativity=Stars=Muses=3 March = C=I>>GIL.
Snivel=7,000=70%=P7.0D=7.0=Language=Assets=Mars=7 July=Pleiades.
Snob=9,000=90%=P9.00D=9.0=Abstraction=Gods=Saturn=9Sept.>>A=Ø.
Snoop=6,000=60%=P6.0D=Man=Earth=Royalty=6 June=Gaia=Maia>>M=M2.
Snoot=2,500=3,000=30%=P3.0D=3.0=Creativity=Stars=Muses=3 March = C=I>>GIL.
Snooty=2,000=20%=P2.00D=2.0=Nature=Matter=Moon=2 Feb.=Cupid=N=C+_
Snooze=3,500=4,000=40%=P4.0D=Govt.=Creatocracy=4 April=Mercury=Hermes=G=A4.

Snore=5,500=5.5=80%=P5.50=Earth-Midway=5 May = Gaia.
Snorkel=10,000=1,000=100%=10.0=Physicality=Tech.=10 Oct.=Uranus=P=1Ø.
Snort=10,000=1,000=100%=10.0=Physicality=Tech.=10 Oct.=Uranus=P=1Ø.
Snot=6,000=60%=P6.0D=Man=Earth=Royalty=6 June=Gaia=Maia>>M=M2.
Snout=7,500=8,000=80%=P8.0D=Economy=Currency=8 Aug.=Zeus>>E=v.
Snow=10,000=1,000=100%=10.0=Physicality=Tech.=10 Oct.=Uranus=P=1Ø.
Snow Charles=3,000=30%=P3.0D=3.0=Creativity=Stars=Muses=3 March = C=I>>GIL.
Snowball=10,000=1,000=100%=10.0=Physicality=Tech.=10 Oct.=Uranus=P=1Ø.
Snow blindness=7,000=70%=P7.0D=7.0=Language=Assets=Mars=7 July=Pleiades.
Snowbound=3,500=4,000=40%=P4.0D=Govt.=Creatocracy=4 April=Hermes=G=A4.
Snowdrift=5,500=5.5=80%=P5.50=Earth-Midway=5 May = Gaia.
Snowdrop=4,000=40%=P4.0D=Govt.=Creatocracy=4 April=Mercury=Hermes=G=A4.
Snowfall=6,500=7,000=70%=P7.0D=7.0=Language=Assets=Mars=7 July=Pleiades.
Snowflake=3,500=4,000=40%=P4.0D=Govt.=4 April=Mercury=Hermes=G=A4.
Snow leopard=6,000=60%=P6.0D=Man=Earth=Royalty=6 June=Gaia=Maia>>M=M2.
Snowman=4,000=40%=P4.0D=Govt.=Creatocracy=4 April=Mercury=Hermes=G=A4.
Snowmobile=7,500=8,000=80%=P8.0D=Economy=Currency=8 Aug.=Zeus>>E=v.
Snow pea=5,500=5.5=80%=P5.50=Earth-Midway=5 May = Gaia.
Snowplow=4,500=5,000=50%=P5.00D=Law=Time=Venus=5 May = Aphrodite>>L=N.
Snowshoe=8,500=9,000=90%=P9.00D=9.0=Abstraction=Gods=Saturn=9Sept.>>A=Ø.
Snowstorm=3,000=30%=P3.0D=3.0=Creativity=Stars=Muses=3 March = C=I>>GIL.
Snow tire=6,500=7,000=70%=P7.0D=7.0=Language=Assets=Mars=7 July=Pleiades.
Snub=10,000=1,000=100%=10.0=Physicality=Tech.=10 Oct.=Uranus=P=1Ø.
Snub-nosed=3,000=30%=P3.0D=3.0=Creativity=Stars=Muses=3 March = C=I>>GIL.
Snuck=3,500=4,000=40%=P4.0D=Govt.=Creatocracy=4 April=Mercury=Hermes=G=A4.
Snuff1=5,500=5.5=80%=P5.50=Earth-Midway=5 May = Gaia.
Snuff2=8,000=80%=P8.0D=Economy=Currency=8 Aug.=Zeus>>E=v.
Snuff3=10,000=1,000=100%=10.0=Physicality=Tech.=10 Oct.=Uranus=P=1Ø.
Snuffle=7,000=70%=P7.0D=7.0=Language=Assets=Mars=7 July=Pleiades.
Snug=10,000=1,000=100%=10.0=Physicality=Tech.=10 Oct.=Uranus=P=1Ø.
Snuggle=2,000=20%=P2.00D=2.0=Nature=Matter=Moon=2 Feb.=Cupid=N=C+_
Sol1=10,000=1,000=100%=10.0=Physicality=Tech.=10 Oct.=Uranus=P=1Ø.
So2=2,000=20%=P2.00D=2.0=Nature=Matter=Moon=2 Feb.=Cupid=N=C+_
So.=1,000=100%=10.0=1.0=Mind=Sun=1 January=Helios >> M=E4.
Soak=10,000=1,000=100%=10.0=Physicality=Tech.=10 Oct.=Uranus=P=1Ø.
Soap=10,000=1,000=100%=10.0=Physicality=Tech.=10 Oct.=Uranus=P=1Ø.
Soapbox=7,000=70%=P7.0D=7.0=Language=Assets=Mars=7 July=Pleiades.
Soap opera=7,500=8,000=80%=P8.0D=Economy=Currency=8 Aug.=Zeus>>E=v.
Soapstone=4,000=40%=P4.0D=Govt.=Creatocracy=4 April=Mercury=Hermes=G=A4.
Soar=7,000=70%=P7.0D=7.0=Language=Assets=Mars=7 July=Pleiades.
Sob=4,000=40%=P4.0D=Govt.=Creatocracy=4 April=Mercury=Hermes=G=A4.
Sober=10,000=1,000=100%=10.0=Physicality=Tech.=10 Oct.=Uranus=P=1Ø.
Sobriety=4,000=40%=P4.0D=Govt.=Creatocracy=4 April=Mercury=Hermes=G=A4.
Sobriquet=3,000=30%=P3.0D=3.0=Creativity=Stars=Muses=3 March = C=I>>GIL.
Soc.=1,500=15%=P1.50D=1.5=Authority=Solar Crown=1 May = Maia.

So-called=10,000=1,000=100%=10.0=Physicality=Tech.=10 Oct.=Uranus=P=1Ø.
Soccer=10,000=1,000=100%=10.0=Physicality=Tech.=10 Oct.=Uranus=P=1Ø.
Sociable=10,000=1,000=100%=10.0=Physicality=Tech.=10 Oct.=Uranus=P=1Ø.
Social=10,000=1,000=100%=10.0=Physicality=Tech.=10 Oct.=Uranus=P=1Ø.
Social disease=1,500=15%=P1.50D=1.5=Authority=Solar Crown=1 May = Maia.
Socialism=10,000=1,000=100%=10.0=Physicality=Tech.=10 Oct.=Uranus=P=1Ø.
Socialite=2,500=3,000=30%=P3.0D=3.0=Creativity=Stars=Muses=3 March = C=I>>GIL.
Socialize=10,000=1,000=100%=10.0=Physicality=Tech.=10 Oct.=Uranus=P=1Ø.

Socialized medicine=10,000=1,000=100%=10.0=Physicality=Tech.=10 Oct.=Uranus=P=1Ø.
A system for providing medical and hospital care for all at nominal cost through government regulation of health services and tax subsidies. The Creatocracy applies this principle to the provision of mind assessment tests, energy readings through telephone numbers and even copies of our books as methods to introduce and sustain our support for creative education. This is called creative education services or socialized creativity.

Social science=10,000=1,000=100%=10.0=Physicality=Tech.=10 Oct.=Uranus=P=1Ø.
In education there are three key faculties of study. The Sciences, Arts and Social Sciences. Peter Matthews-Akukalia, Castle Makupedia invented the fourth named Faculty of Creative & Psycho-Social Sciences©. Or simply Faculty of the Creative Sciences. The academic brand for the entire four departments of this faculty is Makupedia, named after him "Maku" >> Matthews-Akukalia, "Pe"-Peter, "dia",-education system. So Makupedia is an education system invented by Peter Matthews-Akukalia. It contains the Mind Sciences, Mind Arts, Makupedia Business and Industrial Practice. The political brand is the Creatocracy meaning Universe. (See Universe). The national brand is the Mind Industry, Makupedia sector. The economy brand is the Creative Economy (Creatocism) built on the MaksCurrencies. The religious brand is Makstianity with worship and consult services at the Mind Temple.

The corporate logo is De-Royal Makupedia Limited or simply Makupedia Limited. The nationhood brand is the Creatocratic Nations of Paradise, Paradise Nations. His deified name is Castle Makupedia God of Creatocracy Genius and Mind because he invented and atomized the system of Creatocracy, computed the code for genius (see the Genius Table) and measured the mind defined it and wrote its formula as M=E4. The first in many things and Most Sovereign Emperor of the Paradise Nations of Creative Scientists, Creative Scientist Professionals, C3 Nations Organization and the Makupedian ideologists wearing the Solar Crown by rights of the ownership of the Solar Core Assets©. He owns the body of knowledge, fields of study and academic disciplines 10/10=1.0=10=100%=1,000=10,000.

A feat with no mean integrity. The faculty is open for licensing and induction into all levels of education worldwide. The Standard International Unit and the Universal Standard Unit for the Makupedia is the Maks. Officially the symbol and logo is the Maks. See SI.

Social security=10,000=1,000=100%=10.0=Physicality=Tech.=10 Oct.=Uranus=P=1Ø.
Social studies=10,000=1,000=100%=10.0=Physicality=Tech.=10 Oct.=Uranus=P=1Ø.

Social work=10,000=1,000=100%=10.0=Physicality=Tech.=10 Oct.=Uranus=P=1Ø.
Society=10,000=1,000=100%=10.0=Physicality=Tech.=10 Oct.=Uranus=P=1Ø.
Society Islands=6,000=60%=P6.0D=Man=Earth=Royalty=6 June=Gaia=Maia>>M=M2.
Society of Friends=10,000=1,000=100%=10.0=Physicality=Tech.=10 Oct.=Uranus=P=1Ø.
Socio-=3,500=4,000=40%=P4.0D=Govt.=Creatocracy=4 April=Mercury=Hermes=G=A4.
Socio-economic=2,000=20%=P2.00D=2.0=Nature=Matter=Moon=2 Feb.=Cupid=N=C+_
Sociology=10,000=1,000=100%=10.0=Physicality=Tech.=10 Oct.=Uranus=P=1Ø.
Sociopath=3,000=30%=P3.0D=3.0=Creativity=Stars=Muses=3 March = C=I>>GIL.
Sock1=4,500=5,000=50%=P5.00D=Law=Time=Venus=5 May = Aphrodite>>L=N.
Sock2=2,500=3,000=30%=P3.0D=3.0=Creativity=Stars=Muses=3 March = C=I>>GIL.
Socket=7,000=70%=P7.0D=7.0=Language=Assets=Mars=7 July=Pleiades.
Socotra=7,000=70%=P7.0D=7.0=Language=Assets=Mars=7 July=Pleiades.
Socrates=3,000=30%=P3.0D=3.0=Creativity=Stars=Muses=3 March = C=I>>GIL.
Socratic=7,500=8,000=80%=P8.0D=Economy=Currency=8 Aug.=Zeus>>E=v.
Sod=7,500=8,000=80%=P8.0D=Economy=Currency=8 Aug.=Zeus>>E=v.
Soda=10,000=1,000=100%=10.0=Physicality=Tech.=10 Oct.=Uranus=P=1Ø.
Soda fountain=9,000=90%=P9.00D=9.0=Abstraction=Gods=Saturn=9Sept.>>A=Ø.
Soda pop.=1,500=15%=P1.50D=1.5=Authority=Solar Crown=1 May = Maia.
Soda water=6,500=7,000=70%=P7.0D=7.0=Language=Assets=Mars=7 July=Pleiades.
Sodden=10,000=1,000=100%=10.0=Physicality=Tech.=10 Oct.=Uranus=P=1Ø.
Sodium=10,000=1,000=100%=10.0=Physicality=Tech.=10 Oct.=Uranus=P=1Ø.
Sodium bicarbonate=1,500=15%=P1.50D=1.5=Authority=Solar Crown=1 May = Maia.
Sodium chloride=9,000=90%=P9.00D=9.0=Abstraction=Gods=Saturn=9Sept.>>A=Ø.
Sodium hydroxide=7,000=70%=P7.0D=7.0=Language=Assets=Mars=7 July=Pleiades.
Sodium nitrate=5,500=5.5=80%=P5.50=Earth-Midway=5 May = Gaia.
Sodom=2,500=3,000=30%=P3.0D=3.0=Creativity=Stars=Muses=3 March = C=I>>GIL.
Sodomy=8,500=9,000=90%=P9.00D=9.0=Abstraction=Gods=Saturn=9Sept.>>A=Ø.
Sofa=6,500=7,000=70%=P7.0D=7.0=Language=Assets=Mars=7 July=Pleiades.
Sofia=5,500=5.5=80%=P5.50=Earth-Midway=5 May = Gaia.
Soft=10,000=1,000=100%=10.0=Physicality=Tech.=10 Oct.=Uranus=P=1Ø.
Softball=6,500=7,000=70%=P7.0D=7.0=Language=Assets=Mars=7 July=Pleiades.
Soft-boiled=6,000=60%=P6.0D=Man=Earth=Royalty=6 June=Gaia=Maia>>M=M2.
Soft coal=1,500=15%=P1.50D=1.5=Authority=Solar Crown=1 May = Maia.
Softcore=6,500=7,000=70%=P7.0D=7.0=Language=Assets=Mars=7 July=Pleiades.
Soft drink=5,000=50%=P5.00D=Law=Time=Venus=5 May = Aphrodite>>L=N.
Softhearted=2,000=20%=P2.00D=2.0=Nature=Matter=Moon=2 Feb.=Cupid=N=C+_
Soft landing=6,500=7,000=70%=P7.0D=7.0=Language=Assets=Mars=7 July=Pleiades.
Soft palate=10,000=1,000=100%=10.0=Physicality=Tech.=10 Oct.=Uranus=P=1Ø.
Soft pedal=3,500=4,000=40%=P4.0D=Govt.=Creatocracy=4 April=Hermes=G=A4.

Soft sell=4,500=5,000=50%=P5.00D=Law=Time=Venus=5 May = Aphrodite>>L=N.
A subtly persuasive method of selling or advertising. The average market for a soft sell strategy is 45-50%. The Castle Makupedia is a soft sell because it is for everyone.

Soft shell clam=4,000=40%=P4.0D=Govt.=Creatocracy=4 April=Mercury=Hermes=G=A4.
Soft soap=1,500=15%=P1.50D=1.5=Authority=Solar Crown=1 May = Maia.

Software=9,500=10,000=1,000=100%=10.0=Physicality=Tech.=10 Oct.=Uranus=P=1Ø.
Peter Matthews-Akukalia, Castle Makupedia discovered through planetary energy computing that Planets contained certain transmissible and astrotransmutational energy to Earth, absorbed through the ears transmitted into the human brain and processed through the helium or thought segment. This planetary energy is called mind wares. It is processed through convertible intelligence (0.3) when computed at a speed of 1.0x10 raised to power (-1) to become what we know as software. This is how the energy flux in phone lines are read and interpreted into details and predictions of the activities of the life of a person. All energy are first of all mind wares and when computed become softwares. All things in nature are measured on the natural scale of the unit multiplied by the physical applications on the abstract value of the moon >> time >> value and nature 1.0x10(raised to power -2). On alignment a word or thing that weighs say 6.0 >> 6.0x10(raised to power -2) meaning 60% propensity on average shows that everyone has an average effect to such value.

Softwood=3,000=30%=P3.0D=3.0=Creativity=Stars=Muses=3 March = C=I>>GIL.
Softy=4,000=40%=P4.0D=Govt.=Creatocracy=4 April=Mercury=Hermes=G=A4.
Soggy=4,000=40%=P4.0D=Govt.=Creatocracy=4 April=Mercury=Hermes=G=A4.
Soil1=10,000=1,000=100%=10.0=Physicality=Tech.=10 Oct.=Uranus=P=1Ø.
Soil2=10,000=1,000=100%=10.0=Physicality=Tech.=10 Oct.=Uranus=P=1Ø.
Soirée=3,500=4,000=40%=P4.0D=Govt.=Creatocracy=4 April=Mercury=Hermes=G=A4.
Sojourn=4,500=5,000=50%=P5.00D=Law=Time=Venus=5 May = Aphrodite>>L=N.
Sol=4,500=5,000=50%=P5.00D=Law=Time=Venus=5 May = Aphrodite>>L=N.
Solace=10,000=1,000=100%=10.0=Physicality=Tech.=10 Oct.=Uranus=P=1Ø.

Solar=10,000=1,000=100%=10.0=Physicality=Tech.=10 Oct.=Uranus=P=1Ø.
Peter Matthews-Akukalia computed the center of the Sun through Solar Computing. He discovered it had a temperature of 800,000°Ø and comprised a diamond form aligned by same temperature from which he founded Paradise and invented the Makscurrencies. He is believed to own the Solar Core Asset, to be the Mind God and wears the Solar Crown. Reference book >> The Creatocratic Charter, pgs. 207 & 307 shows Solar Core pix and copyright to the ownership of the Sun through the Solar Core computations. This is his throne and law. This is the reason Peter Matthews - Akukalia by these signs is believed to be a God named MIND branded Castle Makupedia as one who measures owns and presides over the Mind and its Universes. He is the Mind God. The Almighty GOD promised to make Moses a God and mentioned the Council of Gods as administrators and rulers of the worlds and peoples as distinct from gods or idols. Exodus 4:1-4>>Rod=Pen=Serpent =Dragon=Brainchild = Invention=Computing the Signs=Athena = Spirit of GOD. Exodus 4:10-17>>Eloquence=Mouth=Aaron=Hermes=Creatocracy. Gods perform computational signs that create new knowledge and technologies. Muses do the philosophy. See Exodus 4:16-17. 22:28. 23:20-24. Castle Makupedia is the God of Creatocracy Genius & Mind.

Solar battery=5,500=5.5=80%=P5.50=Earth-Midway=5 May = Gaia.
Solar cell=5,000=50%=P5.00D=Law=Time=Venus=5 May = Aphrodite>>L=N.
Solar flare=5,000=50%=P5.00D=Law=Time=Venus=5 May = Aphrodite>>L=N.
Solarium=6,000=60%=P6.0D=Man=Earth=Royalty=6 June=Gaia=Maia>>M=M2.
Solar plexus=4,500=5,000=50%=P5.00D=Law=Time=Venus=5 May = Aphrodite>>L=N.

Solar system=7,000=70%=P7.0D=7.0=Language=Assets=Mars=7 July=Pleiades.
In the first place the solar system is a bundle of assets that make the Solar Core asset. It can only be known and owned by the one who computes their central core for each and discovered the controlling energy through abstraction and planetary energy computing. Peter Matthews-Akukalia measured the solar system on planetary core for each and discovered the twelve dimensions of the universe. He owns the Solar Core Assets.>>See Solar. Eccl. 3:11, Deut. 29:29, 30:11-15; 32:6-8, Romans 11:33-35. Revelations 2:22-25.

Solar wind=10,000=1,000=100%=10.0=Physicality=Tech.=10 Oct.=Uranus=P=1Ø.
Sold=3,000=30%=P3.0D=3.0=Creativity=Stars=Muses=3 March = C=I>>GIL.
Solder=10,000=1,000=100%=10.0=Physicality=Tech.=10 Oct.=Uranus=P=1Ø.
Soldier=10,000=1,000=100%=10.0=Physicality=Tech.=10 Oct.=Uranus=P=1Ø.
Soldier of fortune=6,500=7,000=70%=P7.0D=7.0=Lang=Assets=Mars=7 July=Pleiades.
Soldiery=3,000=30%=P3.0D=3.0=Creativity=Stars=Muses=3 March = C=I>>GIL.
Sole1=4,000=40%=P4.0D=Govt.=Creatocracy=4 April=Mercury=Hermes=G=A4.
Sole2=3,500=4,000=40%=P4.0D=Govt.=Creatocracy=4 April=Mercury=Hermes=G=A4.
Sole3=7,000=70%=P7.0D=7.0=Language=Assets=Mars=7 July=Pleiades.
Solecism=6,500=7,000=70%=P7.0D=7.0=Language=Assets=Mars=7 July=Pleiades.
Solemn=6,000=60%=P6.0D=Man=Earth=Royalty=6 June=Gaia=Maia>>M=M2.
Solemnize=5,500=5.5=80%=P5.50=Earth-Midway=5 May = Gaia.
Solenoid=11,000=11%=P1.10D=1.1=Idea=Brainchild=Inv.=11 Nov.=SC=Athena>>I=MT.
Solicit=6,500=7,000=70%=P7.0D=7.0=Language=Assets=Mars=7 July=Pleiades.
Solicitor=10,000=1,000=100%=10.0=Physicality=Tech.=10 Oct.=Uranus=P=1Ø.
Solicitous=3,500=4,000=40%=P4.0D=Govt.=Creatocracy=4 April=Hermes=G=A4.
Solicitude=2,500=3,000=30%=P3.0D=3.0=Creativity=Stars=Muses=3 March = C=I>>GIL.
Solid=10,000=1,000=100%=10.0=Physicality=Tech.=10 Oct.=Uranus=P=1Ø.
Solidarity=4,000=40%=P4.0D=Govt.=Creatocracy=4 April=Mercury=Hermes=G=A4.
Solidify=3,500=4,000=40%=P4.0D=Govt.=Creatocracy=4 April=Mercury=Hermes=G=A4.
Solid state=10,000=1,000=100%=10.0=Physicality=Tech.=10 Oct.=Uranus=P=1Ø.

Soliloquy=10,000=1,000=100%=10.0=Physicality=Tech.=10 Oct.=Uranus=P=1Ø.
A lot of soliloquy was used in "The Creatocracy Republic by Peter Matthews-Akukalia".

Solipsism=10,000=1,000=100%=10.0=Physicality=Tech.=10 Oct.=Uranus=P=1Ø.
Solitaire=7,500=8,000=80%=P8.0D=Economy=Currency=8 Aug.=Zeus>>E=v.
Solitary=10,000=1,000=100%=10.0=Physicality=Tech.=10 Oct.=Uranus=P=1Ø.

Solitude=7,000=70%=P7.0D=7.0=Language=Assets=Mars=7 July=Pleiades.
Solo=10,000=1,000=100%=10.0=Physicality=Tech.=10 Oct.=Uranus=P=1Ø.

Solomon=5,500=5.5=80%=P5.50=Earth-Midway=5 May = Gaia.
fl.10th cent. B.C. King of Israel famous for his wisdom. Peter Matthews-Akukalia in his invented Mind Computing discovered King Solomon reincarnated as Ralph Waldo Emerson.

Solomon Islands1=8,500=9,000=90%=P9.00D=9.0=Abstr.=Gods=Saturn=9Sept.>>A=Ø.
Solomon Islands2=6,500=7,000=70%=P7.0D=7.0=Lang=Assets=Mars=7 July=Pleiades.
Solon=4,000=40%=P4.0D=Govt.=Creatocracy=4 April=Mercury=Hermes=G=A4.
Solstice=10,000=1,000=100%=10.0=Physicality=Tech.=10 Oct.=Uranus=P=1Ø.
Soluble=6,500=7,000=70%=P7.0D=7.0=Language=Assets=Mars=7 July=Pleiades.
Solute=8,500=9,000=90%=P9.00D=9.0=Abstraction=Gods=Saturn=9Sept.>>A=Ø.
Solution=10,000=1,000=100%=10.0=Physicality=Tech.=10 Oct.=Uranus=P=1Ø.
Solve=6,000=60%=P6.0D=Man=Earth=Royalty=6 June=Gaia=Maia>>M=M2.
Solvent=10,000=1,000=100%=10.0=Physicality=Tech.=10 Oct.=Uranus=P=1Ø.
Solzhenitsyn=5,000=50%=P5.00D=Law=Time=Venus=5 May = Aphrodite>>L=N.
Somali=5,000=50%=P5.00D=Law=Time=Venus=5 May = Aphrodite>>L=N.
Somalia=8,500=9,000=90%=P9.00D=9.0=Abstraction=Gods=Saturn=9Sept.>>A=Ø.
Somaliland=6,500=7,000=70%=P7.0D=7.0=Language=Assets=Mars=7 July=Pleiades.
Somatic=10,500=11,000=11%=P1.10D=1.1=Idea=Brainchild=Inv.=11 Nov.=Athena>>I=MT.
Somatic cell=5,000=50%=P5.00D=Law=Time=Venus=5 May = Aphrodite>>L=N.
Somber=4,500=5,000=50%=P5.00D=Law=Time=Venus=5 May = Aphrodite>>L=N.
Sombre=2,500=3,000=30%=P3.0D=3.0=Creativity=Stars=Muses=3 March = C=I>>GIL.
Sombrero=3,000=30%=P3.0D=3.0=Creativity=Stars=Muses=3 March = C=I>>GIL.
Some=10,000=1,000=100%=10.0=Physicality=Tech.=10 Oct.=Uranus=P=1Ø.
-some1=6,000=60%=P6.0D=Man=Earth=Royalty=6 June=Gaia=Maia>>M=M2.
-some2=5,500=5.5=80%=P5.50=Earth-Midway=5 May = Gaia.
-some3=2,500=3,000=30%=P3.0D=3.0=Creativity=Stars=Muses=3 March = C=I>>GIL.
Somebody=5,500=5.5=80%=P5.50=Earth-Midway=5 May = Gaia.
Someday=10,000=1,000=100%=10.0=Physicality=Tech.=10 Oct.=Uranus=P=1Ø.
Somehow=4,000=40%=P4.0D=Govt.=Creatocracy=4 April=Mercury=Hermes=G=A4.
Someone=4,500=5,000=50%=P5.00D=Law=Time=Venus=5 May = Aphrodite>>L=N.
Someplace=1,000=100%=10.0=1.0=Mind=Sun=1 January=Helios >> M=E4.
Somersault=8,000=80%=P8.0D=Economy=Currency=8 Aug.=Zeus>>E=v.
Something=10,000=1,000=100%=10.0=Physicality=Tech.=10 Oct.=Uranus=P=1Ø.
Sometime=7,500=8,000=80%=P8.0D=Economy=Currency=8 Aug.=Zeus>>E=v.
Sometimes=1,500=15%=P1.50D=1.5=Authority=Solar Crown=1 May = Maia.
Someway=2,500=3,000=30%=P3.0D=3.0=Creativity=Stars=Muses=3 March = C=I>>GIL.
Somewhat=3,000=30%=P3.0D=3.0=Creativity=Stars=Muses=3 March = C=I>>GIL.
Somewhere=10,000=1,000=100%=10.0=Physicality=Tech.=10 Oct.=Uranus=P=1Ø.
Somme=8,000=80%=P8.0D=Economy=Currency=8 Aug.=Zeus>>E=v.
Sommelier=3,000=30%=P3.0D=3.0=Creativity=Stars=Muses=3 March = C=I>>GIL.

Somnambulate=4,000=40%=P4.0D=Govt.=Creatocracy=4 April=Mercury=Hermes=G=A4.
Somnambulism=1,000=100%=10.0=1.0=Mind=Sun=1 January=Helios >> M=E4.
Somnolent=3,500=4,000=40%=P4.0D=Govt.=4 April=Mercury=Hermes=G=A4.
Son=10,000=1,000=100%=10.0=Physicality=Tech.=10 Oct.=Uranus=P=1Ø.
Sonar=10,000=1,000=100%=10.0=Physicality=Tech.=10 Oct.=Uranus=P=1Ø.
Sonata=7,500=8,000=80%=P8.0D=Economy=Currency=8 Aug.=Zeus>>E=v.
Song=10,000=1,000=100%=10.0=Physicality=Tech.=10 Oct.=Uranus=P=1Ø.
Songbird=3,500=4,000=40%=P4.0D=Govt.=4 April=Mercury=Hermes=G=A4.
Song hua=8,000=80%=P8.0D=Economy=Currency=8 Aug.=Zeus>>E=v.

Song of Solomon=2,000=20%=P2.00D=2.0=Nature=Matter=Moon=2 Feb.=Cupid=N=C+_
A book of the Bible. Inspired by Artemis and Eros (Cupid).

Song of Songs=2,000=20%=P2.00D=2.0=Nature=Matter=Moon=2 Feb.=Cupid=N=C+_
Songster=2,500=3,000=30%=P3.0D=3.0=Creativity=Stars=Muses=3 March = C=I>>GIL.
Songwriter=3,500=4,000=40%=P4.0D=Govt.=4 April=Mercury=Hermes=G=A4.
Sonic=5,500=5.5=80%=P5.50=Earth-Midway=5 May = Gaia.
Sonic barrier=7,000=70%=P7.0D=7.0=Language=Assets=Mars=7 July=Pleiades.
Sonic boom=8,000=80%=P8.0D=Economy=Currency=8 Aug.=Zeus>>E=v.
Son-in-law=2,500=3,000=30%=P3.0D=3.0=Cre=Stars=Muses=3 March = C=I>>GIL.
Sonnet=8,000=80%=P8.0D=Economy=Currency=8 Aug.=Zeus>>E=v.
Sonogram=7,500=8,000=80%=P8.0D=Economy=Currency=8 Aug.=Zeus>>E=v.
Sonorous=10,000=1,000=100%=10.0=Physicality=Tech.=10 Oct.=Uranus=P=1Ø.
So Canals=2,500=3,000=30%=P3.0D=3.0=Creativity=Stars=Muses=3 March = C=I>>GIL.
Soo chow=1,000=100%=10.0=1.0=Mind=Sun=1 January=Helios >> M=E4.
Soon=10,000=1,000=100%=10.0=Physicality=Tech.=10 Oct.=Uranus=P=1Ø.
Soot=10,000=1,000=100%=10.0=Physicality=Tech.=10 Oct.=Uranus=P=1Ø.
Sooth=2,500=3,000=30%=P3.0D=3.0=Creativity=Stars=Muses=3 March = C=I>>GIL.
Soothe=6,500=7,000=70%=P7.0D=7.0=Language=Assets=Mars=7 July=Pleiades.
Soothsayer=2,500=3,000=30%=P3.0D=3.0=Cre=Stars=Muses=3 March = C=I>>GIL.
Sop=10,000=1,000=100%=10.0=Physicality=Tech.=10 Oct.=Uranus=P=1Ø.
SOP=1,500=15%=P1.50D=1.5=Authority=Solar Crown=1 May = Maia.
Soph.=500=5%=P5.00D=5.0=Law=Time=Venus=5 May=Aphrodite>>L=N.

Sophism=6,000=60%=P6.0D=Man=Earth=Royalty=6 June=Gaia=Maia>>M=M2.
A plausible but fallacious argument. Deceptive or fallacious argumentation. < Greek, sophos, clever.

Sophisticate=6,500=7,000=70%=P7.0D=7.0=Language=Assets=Mars=7 July=Pleiades.
Sophisticated=6,500=7,000=70%=P7.0D=7.0=Language=Assets=Mars=7 July=Pleiades.
Sophistry=3,000=30%=P3.0D=3.0=Creativity=Stars=Muses=3 March = C=I>>GIL.
Sophocles=3,000=30%=P3.0D=3.0=Creativity=Stars=Muses=3 March = C=I>>GIL.
Sophomore=6,500=7,000=70%=P7.0D=7.0=Language=Assets=Mars=7 July=Pleiades.

Sophomoric=5,500=5.5=80%=P5.50=Earth-Midway=5 May = Gaia.
Soporific=5,500=5.5=80%=P5.50=Earth-Midway=5 May = Gaia.
Soprano=10,000=1,000=100%=10.0=Physicality=Tech.=10 Oct.=Uranus=P=1Ø.
Sorbitol=10,000=1,000=100%=10.0=Physicality=Tech.=10 Oct.=Uranus=P=1Ø.
Sorcery=7,000=70%=P7.0D=7.0=Language=Assets=Mars=7 July=Pleiades.
Sordid=6,000=60%=P6.0D=Man=Earth=Royalty=6 June=Gaia=Maia>>M=M2.
Sore=10,000=1,000=100%=10.0=Physicality=Tech.=10 Oct.=Uranus=P=1Ø.
Sorghum=8,500=9,000=90%=P9.00D=9.0=Abstraction=Gods=Saturn=9Sept.>>A=Ø.
Sorority=8,500=9,000=90%=P9.00D=9.0=Abstraction=Gods=Saturn=9Sept.>>A=Ø.
Sorrel1=5,500=5.5=80%=P5.50=Earth-Midway=5 May = Gaia.
Sorrel2=6,000=60%=P6.0D=Man=Earth=Royalty=6 June=Gaia=Maia>>M=M2.
Sorrow=10,000=1,000=100%=10.0=Physicality=Tech.=10 Oct.=Uranus=P=1Ø.
Sorry=10,000=1,000=100%=10.0=Physicality=Tech.=10 Oct.=Uranus=P=1Ø.
Sort=10,000=1,000=100%=10.0=Physicality=Tech.=10 Oct.=Uranus=P=1Ø.
Sortie=10,000=1,000=100%=10.0=Physicality=Tech.=10 Oct.=Uranus=P=1Ø.
SOS=6,000=60%=P6.0D=Man=Earth=Royalty=6 June=Gaia=Maia>>M=M2.
so-so=500=5%=P5.00D=5.0=Law=Time=Venus=5 May=Aphrodite>>L=N.
Sot=2,000=20%=P2.00D=2.0=Nature=Matter=Moon=2 Feb.=Cupid=N=C+_
Soubrette=7,500=8,000=80%=P8.0D=Economy=Currency=8 Aug.=Zeus>>E=v.
Soufflé=8,500=9,000=90%=P9.00D=9.0=Abstraction=Gods=Saturn=9Sept.>>A=Ø.
Sough=4,000=40%=P4.0D=Govt.=Creatocracy=4 April=Mercury=Hermes=G=A4.
Sought=3,000=30%=P3.0D=3.0=Creativity=Stars=Muses=3 March = C=I>>GIL.
Soul=10,000=1,000=100%=10.0=Physicality=Tech.=10 Oct.=Uranus=P=1Ø.
Soulful=10,000=1,000=100%=10.0=Physicality=Tech.=10 Oct.=Uranus=P=1Ø.
Sound1=10,000=1,000=100%=10.0=Physicality=Tech.=10 Oct.=Uranus=P=1Ø.
Sound2=10,000=1,000=100%=10.0=Physicality=Tech.=10 Oct.=Uranus=P=1Ø.
Sound3=8,500=9,000=90%=P9.00D=9.0=Abstraction=Gods=Saturn=9Sept.>>A=Ø.
Sound4=11,000=11%=P1.10D=1.1=Idea=Brainchild=Inv.=11 Nov.=SC=Athena>>I=MT.
Sound barrier=1,500=15%=P1.50D=1.5=Authority=Solar Crown=1 May = Maia.
Sound effects=5,500=5.5=80%=P5.50=Earth-Midway=5 May = Gaia.
Sounding board=10,000=1,000=100%=10.0=Physicality=Tech.=10 Oct.=Uranus=P=1Ø.
Soundproof=2,500=3,000=30%=P3.0D=3.0=Cre=Stars=Muses=3 March = C=I>>GIL.
Soundtrack=10,000=1,000=100%=10.0=Physicality=Tech.=10 Oct.=Uranus=P=1Ø.
Soup=10,000=1,000=100%=10.0=Physicality=Tech.=10 Oct.=Uranus=P=1Ø.
Soupçon=4,000=40%=P4.0D=Govt.=Creatocracy=4 April=Mercury=Hermes=G=A4.
Soupy=4,500=5,000=50%=P5.00D=Law=Time=Venus=5 May = Aphrodite>>L=N.
Sour=10,000=1,000=100%=10.0=Physicality=Tech.=10 Oct.=Uranus=P=1Ø.
Sour ball=3,500=4,000=40%=P4.0D=Govt.=4 April=Mercury=Hermes=G=A4.
Source=10,000=1,000=100%=10.0=Physicality=Tech.=10 Oct.=Uranus=P=1Ø.
Sour cream=5,500=5.5=80%=P5.50=Earth-Midway=5 May = Gaia.
Sour dough=4,500=5,000=50%=P5.00D=Law=Time=Venus=5 May = Aphrodite>>L=N.
Soursop=4,000=40%=P4.0D=Govt.=Creatocracy=4 April=Mercury=Hermes=G=A4.
Sousa John=3,500=4,000=40%=P4.0D=Govt.=4 April=Mercury=Hermes=G=A4.
Souse=10,000=1,000=100%=10.0=Physicality=Tech.=10 Oct.=Uranus=P=1Ø.
South=10,000=1,000=100%=10.0=Physicality=Tech.=10 Oct.=Uranus=P=1Ø.

South Africa=10,000=1,000=100%=10.0=Physicality=Tech.=10 Oct.=Uranus=P=1Ø.

South America.=8,000=80%=P8.0D=Economy=Currency=8 Aug.=Zeus>>E=v.

Southampton=7,000=70%=P7.0D=7.0=Language=Assets=Mars=7 July=Pleiades.

South Atlantic Ocean.=4,500=5,000=50%=P5.00D=Law=Time=Venus=5May=Odite>L=N.

South Bend.=7,000=70%=P7.0D=7.0=Language=Assets=Mars=7 July=Pleiades.

South Carolina=6,500=7,000=70%=P7.0D=7.0=Language=Assets=Mars=7 July=Pleiades.

South China Sea.=7,500=8,000=80%=P8.0D=Economy=Currency=8 Aug.=Zeus>>E=v.

South Dakota=5,500=5.5=80%=P5.50=Earth-Midway=5 May = Gaia.

Southeast=10,000=1,000=100%=10.0=Physicality=Tech.=10 Oct.=Uranus=P=1Ø.

Southeast Asia.=6,000=60%=P6.0D=Man=Earth=Royalty=6 June=Gaia=Maia>>M=M2.

Southeaster=4,000=40%=P4.0D=Govt.=Creatocracy=4 April=Mercury=Hermes=G=A4.

Southerly=4,000=40%=P4.0D=Govt.=Creatocracy=4 April=Mercury=Hermes=G=A4.

Southern=5,500=5.5=80%=P5.50=Earth-Midway=5 May = Gaia.

Southern Alps=5,500=5.5=80%=P5.50=Earth-Midway=5 May = Gaia.

Southerner=3,500=4,000=40%=P4.0D=Govt.=4 April=Mercury=Hermes=G=A4.

Southern Hemisphere=3,000=30%=P3.0D=3.0=Cr=Stars=Muses=3 March = C=I>>GIL.

Southern lights=1,500=15%=P1.50D=1.5=Authority=Solar Crown=1 May = Maia.

South Yemen.=10,000=1,000=100%=10.0=Physicality=Tech.=10 Oct.=Uranus=P=1Ø.

Southey Robert.=2,000=20%=P2.00D=2.0=Nature=Matter=Moon=2 Feb.=Cupid=N=C+_

South Frigid Zone.=1,500=15%=P1.50D=1.5=Authority=Solar Crown=1 May = Maia.

South Island.=8,000=80%=P8.0D=Economy=Currency=8 Aug.=Zeus>>E=v.

South Korea.=7,000=70%=P7.0D=7.0=Language=Assets=Mars=7 July=Pleiades.

South Pacific Ocean.=4,500=5,000=50%=P5.00D=Law=Time=Venus=5 May=Odite>>L=N.

Southpaw=4,000=40%=P4.0D=Govt.=Creatocracy=4 April=Mercury=Hermes=G=A4.

South Polar Region.=1,500=15%=P1.50D=1.5=Authority=Solar Crown=1 May = Maia.

South Pole=10,000=1,000=100%=10.0=Physicality=Tech.=10 Oct.=Uranus=P=1Ø.

South Sea islands.=4,500=5,000=50%=P5.00D=Law=Time=Venus=5 May =Odite>>L=N.

South Seas.=3,500=4,000=40%=P4.0D=Govt.=4 April=Mercury=Hermes=G=A4.

Southern Temperate Zone.=1,500=15%=P1.50D=1.5=Authority=Solar Crown=1 May = Maia.

South Vietnam.=6,000=60%=P6.0D=Man=Earth=Royalty=6 June=Gaia=Maia>>M=M2.

Southwest=10,000=1,000=100%=10.0=Physicality=Tech.=10 Oct.=Uranus=P=1Ø.

Southwester=7,000=70%=P7.0D=7.0=Language=Assets=Mars=7 July=Pleiades.

Souvenir=8,500=9,000=90%=P9.00D=9.0=Abstraction=Gods=Saturn=9Sept.>>A=Ø.

Sovereign=10,000=1,000=100%=10.0=Physicality=Tech.=10 Oct.=Uranus=P=1Ø.
His Creative Excellency & Godship
Peter K. Matthews-Akukalia, Castle Makupedia
Most Sovereign Emperor, Sovereign Creatocratic Republic of Paradise.

Sovereignty=7,000=70%=P7.0D=7.0=Language=Assets=Mars=7 July=Pleiades.
Supremacy of authority or rule. Royal rank, authority, power. Complete independence and self-government. It is based on the rights earned from the invention of measurements. The Creatocracy is sovereignty over all dimensions of the Universe in which it has discovered its formula and thereby measured them on the rights of the Maks from mind

to knowledge 1.0-1.9. All things were created and so are products of creativity so everything is creativity and creativity is everything. There is first the Creatocracy of GOD and then the Creatocracy of Mankind. Against this there is no law. Castle Makupedia wears the solar crown that has granted him universal sovereignty so asserted by his works. Genesis 1:1.

Soviet=10,000=1,000=100%=10.0=Physicality=Tech.=10 Oct.=Uranus=P=1Ø.
Soviet Union=3,000=30%=P3.0D=3.0=Creativity=Stars=Muses=3 March = C=I>>GIL.
Sowl=10,000=1,000=100%=10.0=Physicality=Tech.=10 Oct.=Uranus=P=1Ø.
Sow2=4,500=5,000=50%=P5.00D=Law=Time=Venus=5 May = Aphrodite>>L=N.
Soweto=5,000=50%=P5.00D=Law=Time=Venus=5 May = Aphrodite>>L=N.
Sox=2,000=20%=P2.00D=2.0=Nature=Matter=Moon=2 Feb.=Cupid=N=C+_
Soy=7,000=70%=P7.0D=7.0=Language=Assets=Mars=7 July=Pleiades.
Soybean=5,500=5.5=80%=P5.50=Earth-Midway=5 May = Gaia.
sp.=3,000=30%=P3.0D=3.0=Creativity=Stars=Muses=3 March = C=I>>GIL.
Sp.=1,000=100%=10.0=1.0=Mind=Sun=1 January=Helios >> M=E4.
Spa=6,500=7,000=70%=P7.0D=7.0=Language=Assets=Mars=7 July=Pleiades.

Space=10,000=1,000=100%=10.0=Physicality=Tech.=10 Oct.=Uranus=P=1Ø.
Peter Matthews-Akukalia, Castle Makupedia discovered the planetary activities of the cosmic and invented Spiralogy or spiral computing from which he established MindSpace. An advance programming department of the Creatocracy that studies Mind Astronomy. See The LAWS OF CASTLE MAKUPEDIA: Principles of Psychoastronomy. Note that title can change so one needs to be sure during request and book order.

Space bar=10,000=1,000=100%=10.0=Physicality=Tech.=10 Oct.=Uranus=P=1Ø.
Spacecraft=4,000=40%=P4.0D=Govt.=Creatocracy=4 April=Mercury=Hermes=G=A4.
Space heater=5,000=50%=P5.00D=Law=Time=Venus=5 May = Aphrodite>>L=N.
Spaceship=1,000=100%=10.0=1.0=Mind=Sun=1 January=Helios >> M=E4.
Space shuttle=10,000=1,000=100%=10.0=Physicality=Tech.=10 Oct.=Uranus=P=1Ø.
Space station=8,500=9,000=90%=P9.00D=9.0=Abstraction=Gods=Saturn=9Sept.>>A=Ø.
Space suit=7,500=8,000=80%=P8.0D=Economy=Currency=8 Aug.=Zeus>>E=v.
Space time=10,500=11,000=11%=P1.10D=1.1=Idea=Brainchild=11 Nov.=Athena>>I=MT.
Spacewalk=1,000=100%=10.0=1.0=Mind=Sun=1 January=Helios >> M=E4.
Spacious=6,000=60%=P6.0D=Man=Earth=Royalty=6 June=Gaia=Maia>>M=M2.
Spacy=5,500=5.5=80%=P5.50=Earth-Midway=5 May = Gaia.
Spadel=7,500=8,000=80%=P8.0D=Economy=Currency=8 Aug.=Zeus>>E=v.
Spade2=8,000=80%=P8.0D=Economy=Currency=8 Aug.=Zeus>>E=v.
Spadework=4,000=40%=P4.0D=Govt.=Creatocracy=4 April=Mercury=Hermes=G=A4.
Spadix=8,500=9,000=90%=P9.00D=9.0=Abstraction=Gods=Saturn=9Sept.>>A=Ø.
Spaghetti=6,500=7,000=70%=P7.0D=7.0=Language=Assets=Mars=7 July=Pleiades.
Spain=9,500=10,000=1,000=100%=10.0=Physicality=Tech.=10 Oct.=Uranus=P=1Ø.
Spake=2,500=3,000=30%=P3.0D=3.0=Creativity=Stars=Muses=3 March = C=I>>GIL.
Span1=10,000=1,000=100%=10.0=Physicality=Tech.=10 Oct.=Uranus=P=1Ø.
Span2=7,000=70%=P7.0D=7.0=Language=Assets=Mars=7 July=Pleiades.

Spangle=8,500=9,000=90%=P9.00D=9.0=Abstraction=Gods=Saturn=9Sept.>>A=Ø.
Spaniard=3,000=30%=P3.0D=3.0=Creativity=Stars=Muses=3 March = C=I>>GIL.
Spaniel=7,500=8,000=80%=P8.0D=Economy=Currency=8 Aug.=Zeus>>E=v.
Spanish=7,000=70%=P7.0D=7.0=Language=Assets=Mars=7 July=Pleiades.
Spanish America=4,000=40%=P4.0D=Govt.=Creatocracy=4 April=Hermes=G=A4.
Spanish American=10,000=1,000=100%=10.0=Physicality=Tech.=10 Oct.=Uranus=P=1Ø.
Spanish moss=9,000=90%=P9.00D=9.0=Abstraction=Gods=Saturn=9Sept.>>A=Ø.
Spanish Sahara=1,500=15%=P1.50D=1.5=Authority=Solar Crown=1 May = Maia.
Spank=5,500=5.5=80%=P5.50=Earth-Midway=5 May = Gaia.
Spanking=10,000=1,000=100%=10.0=Physicality=Tech.=10 Oct.=Uranus=P=1Ø.
Spar1=6,500=7,000=70%=P7.0D=7.0=Language=Assets=Mars=7 July=Pleiades.
Spar2=6,500=7,000=70%=P7.0D=7.0=Language=Assets=Mars=7 July=Pleiades.
Spare=10,000=1,000=100%=10.0=Physicality=Tech.=10 Oct.=Uranus=P=1Ø.
Spare ribs=6,500=7,000=70%=P7.0D=7.0=Language=Assets=Mars=7 July=Pleiades.
Sparing=1,500=15%=P1.50D=1.5=Authority=Solar Crown=1 May = Maia.
Spark1=10,000=1,000=100%=10.0=Physicality=Tech.=10 Oct.=Uranus=P=1Ø.
Spark2=7,000=70%=P7.0D=7.0=Language=Assets=Mars=7 July=Pleiades.
Sparkle=10,000=1,000=100%=10.0=Physicality=Tech.=10 Oct.=Uranus=P=1Ø.
Spark plug=9,000=90%=P9.00D=9.0=Abstraction=Gods=Saturn=9Sept.>>A=Ø.
Sparrow=6,000=60%=P6.0D=Man=Earth=Royalty=6 June=Gaia=Maia>>M=M2.
Sparrow hawk=6,500=7,000=70%=P7.0D=7.0=Language=Assets=Mars=7 July=Pleiades.
Sparse=7,500=8,000=80%=P8.0D=Economy=Currency=8 Aug.=Zeus>>E=v.
Sparta=5,000=50%=P5.00D=Law=Time=Venus=5 May = Aphrodite>>L=N.
Spartacus=5,500=5.5=80%=P5.50=Earth-Midway=5 May = Gaia.
Spartan=8,500=9,000=90%=P9.00D=9.0=Abstraction=Gods=Saturn=9Sept.>>A=Ø.
Spasm=6,500=7,000=70%=P7.0D=7.0=Language=Assets=Mars=7 July=Pleiades.
Spastic=7,500=8,000=80%=P8.0D=Economy=Currency=8 Aug.=Zeus>>E=v.
Spat1=6,500=7,000=70%=P7.0D=7.0=Language=Assets=Mars=7 July=Pleiades.
Spat2=6,000=60%=P6.0D=Man=Earth=Royalty=6 June=Gaia=Maia>>M=M2.
Spat3=4,500=5,000=50%=P5.00D=Law=Time=Venus=5 May = Aphrodite>>L=N.
Spat4=4,000=40%=P4.0D=Govt.=Creatocracy=4 April=Mercury=Hermes=G=A4.
Spate=4,000=40%=P4.0D=Govt.=Creatocracy=4 April=Mercury=Hermes=G=A4.
Spathe=10,000=1,000=100%=10.0=Physicality=Tech.=10 Oct.=Uranus=P=1Ø.
Spatial=3,000=30%=P3.0D=3.0=Creativity=Stars=Muses=3 March = C=I>>GIL.
Spatter=10,000=1,000=100%=10.0=Physicality=Tech.=10 Oct.=Uranus=P=1Ø.
Spatula=9,000=90%=P9.00D=9.0=Abstraction=Gods=Saturn=9Sept.>>A=Ø.
Spavin=7,000=70%=P7.0D=7.0=Language=Assets=Mars=7 July=Pleiades.
Spawn=10,000=1,000=100%=10.0=Physicality=Tech.=10 Oct.=Uranus=P=1Ø.
Spay=7,000=70%=P7.0D=7.0=Language=Assets=Mars=7 July=Pleiades.
SPCA=4,000=40%=P4.0D=Govt.=Creatocracy=4 April=Mercury=Hermes=G=A4.
Speak=10,000=1,000=100%=10.0=Physicality=Tech.=10 Oct.=Uranus=P=1Ø.
Speakeasy=5,000=50%=P5.00D=Law=Time=Venus=5 May = Aphrodite>>L=N.
Speaker=7,000=70%=P7.0D=7.0=Language=Assets=Mars=7 July=Pleiades.
Spear1=10,000=1,000=100%=10.0=Physicality=Tech.=10 Oct.=Uranus=P=1Ø.
Spear2=5,000=50%=P5.00D=Law=Time=Venus=5 May = Aphrodite>>L=N.

Spearfish=3,500=4,000=40%=P4.0D=Govt.=4 April=Mercury=Hermes=G=A4.
Speargun=6,000=60%=P6.0D=Man=Earth=Royalty=6 June=Gaia=Maia>>M=M2.
Spearhead=8,500=9,000=90%=P9.00D=9.0=Abstraction=Gods=Saturn=9Sept.>>A=Ø.
Spearmint=5,000=50%=P5.00D=Law=Time=Venus=5 May = Aphrodite>>L=N.
Special=10,000=1,000=100%=10.0=Physicality=Tech.=10 Oct.=Uranus=P=1Ø.
Special delivery=5,500=5.5=80%=P5.50=Earth-Midway=5 May = Gaia.
Special education=7,500=8,000=80%=P8.0D=Economy=Currency=8 Aug.=Zeus>>E=v.
Special effect=7,000=70%=P7.0D=7.0=Language=Assets=Mars=7 July=Pleiades.
Special Forces=6,500=7,000=70%=P7.0D=7.0=Language=Assets=Mars=7 July=Pleiades.
Specialist=10,000=1,000=100%=10.0=Physicality=Tech.=10 Oct.=Uranus=P=1Ø.
Specialize=10,000=1,000=100%=10.0=Physicality=Tech.=10 Oct.=Uranus=P=1Ø.
Special relativity=5,500=5.5=80%=P5.50=Earth-Midway=5 May = Gaia.
Specialty=10,000=1,000=100%=10.0=Physicality=Tech.=10 Oct.=Uranus=P=1Ø.
Specie=3,500=4,000=40%=P4.0D=Govt.=Creatocracy=4 April=Mercury=Hermes=G=A4.
Species=10,000=1,000=100%=10.0=Physicality=Tech.=10 Oct.=Uranus=P=1Ø.
Specific=10,000=1,000=100%=10.0=Physicality=Tech.=10 Oct.=Uranus=P=1Ø.
Specification=10,000=1,000=100%=10.0=Physicality=Tech.=10 Oct.=Uranus=P=1Ø.
Specific gravity=10,000=1,000=100%=10.0=Physicality=Tech.=10 Oct.=Uranus=P=1Ø.
Specify=5,500=5.5=80%=P5.50=Earth-Midway=5 May = Gaia.
Specimen=10,500=11,000=11%=P1.10D=1.1=Idea=Brainchild=Inv.=11 Nov.=Athena>>I=MT.
Specious=10,000=1,000=100%=10.0=Physicality=Tech.=10 Oct.=Uranus=P=1Ø.
Speck=6,500=7,000=70%=P7.0D=7.0=Language=Assets=Mars=7 July=Pleiades.
Speckle=7,000=70%=P7.0D=7.0=Language=Assets=Mars=7 July=Pleiades.
Spectacle=10,000=1,000=100%=10.0=Physicality=Tech.=10 Oct.=Uranus=P=1Ø.
Spectacular=4,500=5,000=50%=P5.00D=Law=Time=Venus=5 May = Aphrodite>>L=N.
Spectator=5,500=5.5=80%=P5.50=Earth-Midway=5 May = Gaia.
Specter=9,000=90%=P9.00D=9.0=Abstraction=Gods=Saturn=9Sept.>>A=Ø.
Spectra=2,000=20%=P2.00D=2.0=Nature=Matter=Moon=2 Feb.=Cupid=N=C+_
Spectral=4,500=5,000=50%=P5.00D=Law=Time=Venus=5 May = Aphrodite>>L=N.
Spectro-=1,500=15%=P1.50D=1.5=Authority=Solar Crown=1 May = Maia.
Spectrogram=3,500=4,000=40%=P4.0D=Govt.=4 April=Mercury=Hermes=G=A4.
Spectrograph=3,500=4,000=40%=P4.0D=Govt.=4 April=Mercury=Hermes=G=A4.
Spectrometer=5,500=5.5=80%=P5.50=Earth-Midway=5 May = Gaia.
Spectroscope=10,000=1,000=100%=10.0=Physicality=Tech.=10 Oct.=Uranus=P=1Ø.
Spectrum=10,000=1,000=100%=10.0=Physicality=Tech.=10 Oct.=Uranus=P=1Ø.
Speculate=10,000=1,000=100%=10.0=Physicality=Tech.=10 Oct.=Uranus=P=1Ø.
Speculum=10,000=1,000=100%=10.0=Physicality=Tech.=10 Oct.=Uranus=P=1Ø.
Speech=10,000=1,000=100%=10.0=Physicality=Tech.=10 Oct.=Uranus=P=1Ø.
Speechless=6,000=60%=P6.0D=Man=Earth=Royalty=6 June=Gaia=Maia>>M=M2.
Speed=10,000=1,000=100%=10.0=Physicality=Tech.=10 Oct.=Uranus=P=1Ø.
Speedboat=1,500=15%=P1.50D=1.5=Authority=Solar Crown=1 May = Maia.
Speedometer=5,500=5.5=80%=P5.50=Earth-Midway=5 May = Gaia.
Speed up=4,000=40%=P4.0D=Govt.=Creatocracy=4 April=Mercury=Hermes=G=A4.
Speedway=7,000=70%=P7.0D=7.0=Language=Assets=Mars=7 July=Pleiades.
Speedwell=4,500=5,000=50%=P5.00D=Law=Time=Venus=5 May = Aphrodite>>L=N.

Spell1=10,000=1,000=100%=10.0=Physicality=Tech.=10 Oct.=Uranus=P=1∅.
Spell2=8,000=80%=P8.0D=Economy=Currency=8 Aug.=Zeus>>E=v.
Spell3=10,000=1,000=100%=10.0=Physicality=Tech.=10 Oct.=Uranus=P=1∅.
Spellbind=5,500=5.5=80%=P5.50=Earth-Midway=5 May = Gaia.
Speller=5,000=50%=P5.00D=Law=Time=Venus=5 May = Aphrodite>>L=N.
Spelling=8,000=80%=P8.0D=Economy=Currency=8 Aug.=Zeus>>E=v.
Spelunker=4,500=5,000=50%=P5.00D=Law=Time=Venus=5 May = Aphrodite>>L=N.
Spencer Herbert.=2,000=20%=P2.00D=2.0=Nature=Matter=Moon=2 Feb.=Cupid=N=C+_
Spend=10,000=1,000=100%=10.0=Physicality=Tech.=10 Oct.=Uranus=P=1∅.
Spendthrift=6,500=7,000=70%=P7.0D=7.0=Language=Assets=Mars=7 July=Pleiades.
Spenser Edmund=2,500=3,000=30%=P3.0D=3.0=Cr=Stars=Muses=3 March = C=I>>GIL.
Spent=6,500=7,000=70%=P7.0D=7.0=Language=Assets=Mars=7 July=Pleiades.
Sperm=3,000=30%=P3.0D=3.0=Creativity=Stars=Muses=3 March = C=I>>GIL.
Spermaceti=10,000=1,000=100%=10.0=Physicality=Tech.=10 Oct.=Uranus=P=1∅.
Spermatozoon=6,000=60%=P6.0D=Man=Earth=Royalty=6 June=Gaia=Maia>>M=M2.
Spermicide=3,000=30%=P3.0D=3.0=Creativity=Stars=Muses=3 March = C=I>>GIL.
Sperm whale=5,500=5.5=80%=P5.50=Earth-Midway=5 May = Gaia.
Spew=6,000=60%=P6.0D=Man=Earth=Royalty=6 June=Gaia=Maia>>M=M2.
Sp gr=1,000=100%=10.0=1.0=Mind=Sun=1 January=Helios >> M=E4.
Sphagnum=7,500=8,000=80%=P8.0D=Economy=Currency=8 Aug.=Zeus>>E=v.

Sphere=10,000=1,000=100%=10.0=Physicality=Tech.=10 Oct.=Uranus=P=1∅.
The Bible book of Job 38:31 >>3831, Zeus the almighty Jehovah Allah challenged man to find out the influence of Pleiades and demystify the bands of Orion, authorities that can only be found in Greek mythology and religious system. Peter Matthews-Akukalia uncovered two kinds of influence that exist in Nature. First is the Sphere of Influence (SOI) and the Sphere beyond Influence (SBI). Then he tracked the codes and discovered the Greek mythologies where Pleiades was headed by Maia and was the Mind of GOD seen in Romans 11:34. The secrets of Orion is the rights earned what we call righteousness. Astronomy confirms Orion as a body of about 500 stars in a constellation >> 500=50=5.0 >> Rights >> Righteousness (lots of rights) earned by computing >> Aphrodite. In Ephesians 6:14-16. Paul mentions the belt of truth earned only through mathematical or computational precision upon which rights of life assets riches and wealth (righteousness) is earned. This same belt was mentioned by GOD in reference to Orion in Job 38:31. Loosing the bands of Orion is simply uncovering demystifying the truth in a thing and this is only possible through computing. However since it is indicated by the abstract order then it requires an abstraction process of such higher order to determine the mind of GOD. Here is the wisdom of Makumatics which deduces the inherent faculties of the Mind. It has birthed computational creativity, Makumaticology, psycho-forensic auditing and data analytics, planetary energy synchronization and crystallization, Mind Computing, Spiralogy, law of pure equivalence, astrotransmutation, Mind assessment tests, satellite data tracking systems, etc. The essence of all these is what we call Word Power Data Mining & Language Metrics Development where problems are solved through energy and Makulations. Maia is the head of the Pleiades and constitutes the computational Mind of GOD. Hence she is the Universe a normal term for the word

Creatocracy. She is the Creatocracy and the world is simply the congregation of the alphanumerics borne out numbers and formulas. U=abc. Peter Matthews-Akukalia by law invented the Creatocracy and so owns it raising mankind to the status of godly perfection and the office of a God as instructed by GOD almighty. "Be holy (wholly) for I am holy (whole), be perfect (precise) for I am perfect (precision >> truth).

Spheroid=7,500=8,000=80%=P8.0D=Economy=Currency=8 Aug.=Zeus>>E=v.
Sphincter=8,500=9,000=90%=P9.00D=9.0=Abstraction=Gods=Saturn=9Sept.>>A=Ø.

Sphinx=10,000=1,000=100%=10.0=Physicality=Tech.=10 Oct.=Uranus=P=1Ø.
A figure in Egyptian myth having the body of a lion and the head of a man, ram, or hawk. Greek myth a winged creature having the head of a woman and the body of a lion, noted for killing those who could not answer its riddle. A puzzling or mysterious person. The word "creature" is used to describe the source of human woes and the secret of his salvation. Wit >> Creativity is the only solution to human misery as seen in Romans 8:17-23. Reading the Scriptures does not free man but solving its mystery through computing it. Deut.29:29.

Spice=10,000=1,000=100%=10.0=Physicality=Tech.=10 Oct.=Uranus=P=1Ø.
Spick-and-span=6,500=7,000=70%=P7.0D=7.0=Language=Assets=Mars=7 July=Pleiades.
Spicule=4,500=5,000=50%=P5.00D=Law=Time=Venus=5 May = Aphrodite>>L=N.

Spider=10,000=1,000=100%=10.0=Physicality=Tech.=10 Oct.=Uranus=P=1Ø.
Using Word Power.>> Spiders eat Mosquitos. Digit it.
>> 10.0*10.0*10.0 = P.=>>10.0*10.0x=px=20+100=120x=px=2,120
2,120*10.0x=px=2130+21200=23,330x=px=44967330=5.0
>> Law >> Natural Order >> Law of Nature >> Aphrodite.
Spiders are technology. To eat is a technology. Mosquitos are technology. Technology is the application of scientific knowledge for practical purposes especially in industry. Study of spiders and mosquitos and eating as a process could lead to new discovery about their behavior, habitat and control. The relationship is ordered by the Law of Nature administered by Aphrodite. Greek mythology teaches that Athena turned a woman into a spider for arrogance against the Gods and undue competition with her. The code above means that the process takes place on the average of 44,967,330 times daily. The spider laws of natural relations are thus: 1. Same technologies synchronize to establish an order. 2. To eat is a synchronization hence all things that feed do so to sustain nature. 3. Nature is constantly sustained in a process that defines it as a technology.

Spider monkey=7,000=70%=P7.0D=7.0=Language=Assets=Mars=7 July=Pleiades.
Spiel=8,500=9,000=90%=P9.00D=9.0=Abstraction=Gods=Saturn=9Sept.>>A=Ø.
Spiffy=4,500=5,000=50%=P5.00D=Law=Time=Venus=5 May = Aphrodite>>L=N.
Spigot=1,500=15%=P1.50D=1.5=Authority=Solar Crown=1 May = Maia.
Spike1=10,000=1,000=100%=10.0=Physicality=Tech.=10 Oct.=Uranus=P=1Ø.
Spike2=6,500=7,000=70%=P7.0D=7.0=Language=Assets=Mars=7 July=Pleiades.

Spikelet=5,000=50%=P5.00D=Law=Time=Venus=5 May = Aphrodite>>L=N.
Spikenard=6,500=7,000=70%=P7.0D=7.0=Language=Assets=Mars=7 July=Pleiades.
Spill=10,000=1,000=100%=10.0=Physicality=Tech.=10 Oct.=Uranus=P=1Ø.
Spillway=5,000=50%=P5.00D=Law=Time=Venus=5 May = Aphrodite>>L=N.
Spin=10,000=1,000=100%=10.0=Physicality=Tech.=10 Oct.=Uranus=P=1Ø.
Spinach=5,500=5.5=80%=P5.50=Earth-Midway=5 May = Gaia.
Spinal=6,500=7,000=70%=P7.0D=7.0=Language=Assets=Mars=7 July=Pleiades.
Spinal column=7,000=70%=P7.0D=7.0=Language=Assets=Mars=7 July=Pleiades.
Spinal cord=6,500=7,000=70%=P7.0D=7.0=Language=Assets=Mars=7 July=Pleiades.
Spindle=10,000=1,000=100%=10.0=Physicality=Tech.=10 Oct.=Uranus=P=1Ø.
Spindly=2,500=3,000=30%=P3.0D=3.0=Creativity=Stars=Muses=3 March = C=I>>GIL.
Spindrift=5,500=5.5=80%=P5.50=Earth-Midway=5 May = Gaia.
Spine=10,000=1,000=100%=10.0=Physicality=Tech.=10 Oct.=Uranus=P=1Ø.
Spinet=6,000=60%=P6.0D=Man=Earth=Royalty=6 June=Gaia=Maia>>M=M2.
Spinnaker=10,000=1,000=100%=10.0=Physicality=Tech.=10 Oct.=Uranus=P=1Ø.
Spinneret=7,500=8,000=80%=P8.0D=Economy=Currency=8 Aug.=Zeus>>E=v.
Spinning Jenny=3,500=4,000=40%=P4.0D=Govt.=4 April=Mercury=Hermes=G=A4.
Spinning wheel=9,000=90%=P9.00D=9.0=Abstraction=Gods=Saturn=9Sept.>>A=Ø.
Spinoff=7,500=8,000=80%=P8.0D=Economy=Currency=8 Aug.=Zeus>>E=v.
Spinoza Baruch.=3,000=30%=P3.0D=3.0=Cre=Stars=Muses=3 March = C=I>>GIL.

Spinster=7,000=70%=P7.0D=7.0=Language=Assets=Mars=7 July=Pleiades.
Every spinster ought to conduct a Mind Assessment & Psycho-Surgery MAPS Tests.

Spiracle=9,000=90%=P9.00D=9.0=Abstraction=Gods=Saturn=9Sept.>>A=Ø.

Spiral=10,000=1,000=100%=10.0=Physicality=Tech.=10 Oct.=Uranus=P=1Ø.

Spiral galaxy=2,500=4,000=40%=P4.0D=Govt.=Creatocracy=4 April=Mercury=G=A4.
Based on the spiral galaxy Peter Matthews-Akukalia discovered spiral computing.
Spiral Energy Computing is known as Spiral Life Galaxy Computing. Now what goes around comes around is established here. Karma has its scientific proof here. It is based on the fact that reincarnation occurs in a spiral circle sourcing from the black hole and whirl pool Galaxy. It is functioned on dimension, spiral source and the resultant interaction.

SPIRAL GALAXY DATABASE FOR THE CYCLE OF LIFE.
ØD = ØS = ØT

1.0 = 10.0 = 1.3. 2.0 = 8.0 = 2.0. 3.0 = 1.0 = 2.0. 4.0 = 3.0 = 1.0. 5.0 = 5.0 = 3.0
6.0 = 8.0 = 3.0. 7.0 = 2.0 = 2.0. 8.0 = 9.0 = 1.3. 9.0 = 2.0 = 2.3. 10.0 = 2.0 = 3.0
1.1>>2.0 = 8.0 = 2.0 1.2>>2.0 = 8.0 = 2.0
ØD>>Galaxy Dimension or Planet. ØS>> Galaxy Source Energy. ØT >> Earth Resultant.

Spirant=2,500=3,000=30%=P3.0D=3.0=Creativity=Stars=Muses=3 March = C=I>>GIL.
Spire=9,000=90%=P9.00D=9.0=Abstraction=Gods=Saturn=9Sept.>>A=Ø.
Spiraea=6,500=7,000=70%=P7.0D=7.0=Language=Assets=Mars=7 July=Pleiades.

Spirit=10,000=1,000=100%=10.0=Physicality=Tech.=10 Oct.=Uranus=P=1Ø.
Peter Matthews-Akukalia defined spirit as animated energy and computed it.

Spirited=3,000=30%=P3.0D=3.0=Creativity=Stars=Muses=3 March = C=I>>GIL.
Marked by animation vigor or courage. See shadow.

Spiritual=9,000=90%=P9.00D=9.0=Abstraction=Gods=Saturn=9Sept.>>A=Ø.
Peter Matthews-Akukalia discovered that spirits exist in nine levels which is by law of pure equivalence the planets, religion, abstraction through computing and the Gods through scriptures. Therefore computed religion becomes faith. This apotheosized him as a God. He wrote the formula for all spirituality on the law of nine as A=Ø represented as ØD=ØS=ØT being that all abstractions are transmuted planetary energy from dimensions through spiral means to achieve destination destiny and resultant measured in digital bits. This formula also helped him to compute the Wit Bible and possibly the Quran by approval.

Spiritualism=5,000=50%=P5.00D=Law=Time=Venus=5 May = Aphrodite>>L=N.
Spirituous=2,500=3,000=30%=P3.0D=3.0=Creativity=Stars=Muses=3 March = C=I>>GIL.
Spirochete=9,000=90%=P9.00D=9.0=Abstraction=Gods=Saturn=9Sept.>>A=Ø.
Spit1=10,000=1,000=100%=10.0=Physicality=Tech.=10 Oct.=Uranus=P=1Ø.
Spit2=10,000=1,000=100%=10.0=Physicality=Tech.=10 Oct.=Uranus=P=1Ø.
Spitball=10,000=1,000=100%=10.0=Physicality=Tech.=10 Oct.=Uranus=P=1Ø.
Spite=10,000=1,000=100%=10.0=Physicality=Tech.=10 Oct.=Uranus=P=1Ø.
Spittle=2,000=20%=P2.00D=2.0=Nature=Matter=Moon=2 Feb.=Cupid=N=C+_
Spittle bug=7,000=70%=P7.0D=7.0=Language=Assets=Mars=7 July=Pleiades.
Spittoon=4,500=5,000=50%=P5.00D=Law=Time=Venus=5 May = Aphrodite>>L=N.
Splash=10,000=1,000=100%=10.0=Physicality=Tech.=10 Oct.=Uranus=P=1Ø.
Splashdown=4,500=5,000=50%=P5.00D=Law=Time=Venus=5 May = Aphrodite>>L=N.
Splashy=5,000=50%=P5.00D=Law=Time=Venus=5 May = Aphrodite>>L=N.
Splat1=8,000=80%=P8.0D=Economy=Currency=8 Aug.=Zeus>>E=v.
Splat2=2,000=20%=P2.00D=2.0=Nature=Matter=Moon=2 Feb.=Cupid=N=C+_
Splatter=4,000=40%=P4.0D=Govt.=Creatocracy=4 April=Mercury=Hermes=G=A4.
Splay=10,000=1,000=100%=10.0=Physicality=Tech.=10 Oct.=Uranus=P=1Ø.
Splay foot=5,000=50%=P5.00D=Law=Time=Venus=5 May = Aphrodite>>L=N.
Spleen=10,000=1,000=100%=10.0=Physicality=Tech.=10 Oct.=Uranus=P=1Ø.
Splendid=6,500=7,000=70%=P7.0D=7.0=Language=Assets=Mars=7 July=Pleiades.
Splendiferous=2,000=20%=P2.00D=2.0=Nature=Matter=Moon=2 Feb.=Cupid=N=C+_
Splendor=5,500=5.5=80%=P5.50=Earth-Midway=5 May = Gaia.
Splendour=2,500=3,000=30%=P3.0D=3.0=Cre=Stars=Muses=3 March = C=I>>GIL.
Splenetic=4,500=5,000=50%=P5.00D=Law=Time=Venus=5 May = Aphrodite>>L=N.

Splenic=4,000=40%=P4.0D=Govt.=Creatocracy=4 April=Mercury=Hermes=G=A4.
Splice=10,000=1,000=100%=10.0=Physicality=Tech.=10 Oct.=Uranus=P=1Ø.
Splint=10,000=1,000=100%=10.0=Physicality=Tech.=10 Oct.=Uranus=P=1Ø.
Splinter=10,000=1,000=100%=10.0=Physicality=Tech.=10 Oct.=Uranus=P=1Ø.
Splint=10,000=1,000=100%=10.0=Physicality=Tech.=10 Oct.=Uranus=P=1Ø.
Split=5,500=5.5=80%=P5.50=Earth-Midway=5 May = Gaia.
Split-level=8,500=9,000=90%=P9.00D=9.0=Abstraction=Gods=Saturn=9Sept.>>A=Ø.
Split personality=1,500=15%=P1.50D=1.5=Authority=Solar Crown=1 May = Maia.
Split second=1,500=15%=P1.50D=1.5=Authority=Solar Crown=1 May = Maia.
Splitting=2,500=3,000=30%=P3.0D=3.0=Creativity=Stars=Muses=3 March = C=I>>GIL.
Splotch=6,500=7,000=70%=P7.0D=7.0=Language=Assets=Mars=7 July=Pleiades.
Splurge=4,500=5,000=50%=P5.00D=Law=Time=Venus=5 May = Aphrodite>>L=N.
Splutter=7,500=8,000=80%=P8.0D=Economy=Currency=8 Aug.=Zeus>>E=v.
Spock Benjamin=4,000=40%=P4.0D=Govt.=4 April=Mercury=Hermes=G=A4.
Spoil=10,000=1,000=100%=10.0=Physicality=Tech.=10 Oct.=Uranus=P=1Ø.
Spoilsport=4,500=5,000=50%=P5.00D=Law=Time=Venus=5 May = Aphrodite>>L=N.
Spokane=5,500=5.5=80%=P5.50=Earth-Midway=5 May = Gaia.
Spoke1=7,000=70%=P7.0D=7.0=Language=Assets=Mars=7 July=Pleiades.
Spoke2=4,000=40%=P4.0D=Govt.=Creatocracy=4 April=Mercury=Hermes=G=A4.
Spoken=2,000=20%=P2.00D=2.0=Nature=Matter=Moon=2 Feb.=Cupid=N=C+_
Spokesman=7,500=8,000=80%=P8.0D=Economy=Currency=8 Aug.=Zeus>>E=v.
Spokesperson=2,000=20%=P2.00D=2.0=Nature=Matter=Moon=2 Feb.=Cupid=N=C+_
Spokeswoman=7,500=8,000=80%=P8.0D=Economy=Currency=8 Aug.=Zeus>>E=v.
Spoliation=6,000=60%=P6.0D=Man=Earth=Royalty=6 June=Gaia=Maia>>M=M2.
Sponge=10,000=1,000=100%=10.0=Physicality=Tech.=10 Oct.=Uranus=P=1Ø.
Sponge cake=3,500=4,000=40%=P4.0D=Govt.=4 April=Mercury=Hermes=G=A4.
Sponge rubber=5,500=5.5=80%=P5.50=Earth-Midway=5 May = Gaia.

Sponsor=10,000=1,000=100%=10.0=Physicality=Tech.=10 Oct.=Uranus=P=1Ø.

Spontaneous=10,000=1,000=100%=10.0=Physicality=Tech.=10 Oct.=Uranus=P=1Ø.
Peter Matthews-Akukalia, Castle Makupedia is known for being spontaneous in writing thinking and activity that may have been a great facility for his ability to invent things.

Spontaneous abortion=1,000=100%=10.0=1.0=Mind=Sun=1 January=Helios >> M=E4.
Spontaneous combustion=10,000=1,000=100%=10.0=Phy=Tech.=10 Oct.=Uranus=P=1Ø.
Spoof=4,000=40%=P4.0D=Govt.=Creatocracy=4 April=Mercury=Hermes=G=A4.
Spook=6,500=7,000=70%=P7.0D=7.0=Language=Assets=Mars=7 July=Pleiades.
Spool=9,500=10,000=1,000=100%=10.0=Physicality=Tech.=10 Oct.=Uranus=P=1Ø.
Spoon=10,000=1,000=100%=10.0=Physicality=Tech.=10 Oct.=Uranus=P=1Ø.
Spoonbill=7,500=8,000=80%=P8.0D=Economy=Currency=8 Aug.=Zeus>>E=v.
Spoonerism=10,000=1,000=100%=10.0=Physicality=Tech.=10 Oct.=Uranus=P=1Ø.
Spoon feed=8,000=80%=P8.0D=Economy=Currency=8 Aug.=Zeus>>E=v.
Spoor=6,500=7,000=70%=P7.0D=7.0=Language=Assets=Mars=7 July=Pleiades.

Sporades=10,000=1,000=100%=10.0=Physicality=Tech.=10 Oct.=Uranus=P=1Ø.
Sporadic=6,500=7,000=70%=P7.0D=7.0=Language=Assets=Mars=7 July=Pleiades.
Spore=8,500=9,000=90%=P9.00D=9.0=Abstraction=Gods=Saturn=9Sept.>>A=Ø.
Sporran=6,500=7,000=70%=P7.0D=7.0=Language=Assets=Mars=7 July=Pleiades.
Sport=10,000=1,000=100%=10.0=Physicality=Tech.=10 Oct.=Uranus=P=1Ø.
Sporting=7,500=8,000=80%=P8.0D=Economy=Currency=8 Aug.=Zeus>>E=v.
Sportive=2,500=3,000=30%=P3.0D=3.0=Creativity=Stars=Muses=3 March = C=I>>GIL.
Sportscast=5,000=50%=P5.00D=Law=Time=Venus=5 May = Aphrodite>>L=N.
Sportsman=5,000=50%=P5.00D=Law=Time=Venus=5 May = Aphrodite>>L=N.
Sportsmanship=5,500=5.5=80%=P5.50=Earth-Midway=5 May = Gaia.
Sportswoman=3,500=4,000=40%=P4,0D=Govt.=4 April=Mercury=Hermes=G=A4.
Sportswriter=5,500=5.5=80%=P5.50=Earth-Midway=5 May = Gaia.
Spot=10,000=1,000=100%=10.0=Physicality=Tech.=10 Oct.=Uranus=P=1Ø.
Spot check=5,500=5.5=80%=P5.50=Earth-Midway=5 May = Gaia.
Spotless=3,500=4,000=40%=P4.0D=Govt.=Creatocracy=4 April=Hermes=G=A4.
Spotlight=10,000=1,000=100%=10.0=Physicality=Tech.=10 Oct.=Uranus=P=1Ø.
Spotter=6,000=60%=P6.0D=Man=Earth=Royalty=6 June=Gaia=Maia>>M=M2.
Spotty=3,000=30%=P3.0D=3.0=Creativity=Stars=Muses=3 March = C=I>>GIL.
Spousal=4,500=5,000=50%=P5.00D=Law=Time=Venus=5 May = Aphrodite>>L=N.
Spouse=7,500=8,000=80%=P8.0D=Economy=Currency=8 Aug.=Zeus>>E=v.
Spout=10,000=1,000=100%=10.0=Physicality=Tech.=10 Oct.=Uranus=P=1Ø.
spp.=1,500=15%=P1.50D=1.5=Authority=Solar Crown=1 May = Maia.
Sprain=9,000=90%=P9.00D=9.0=Abstraction=Gods=Saturn=9Sept.>>A=Ø.
Sprang=2,000=20%=P2.00D=2.0=Nature=Matter=Moon=2 Feb.=Cupid=N=C+_
Sprat=8,000=80%=P8.0D=Economy=Currency=8 Aug.=Zeus>>E=v.
Sprawl=8,000=80%=P8.0D=Economy=Currency=8 Aug.=Zeus>>E=v.
Spray1=10,000=1,000=100%=10.0=Physicality=Tech.=10 Oct.=Uranus=P=1Ø.
Spray2=5,000=50%=P5.00D=Law=Time=Venus=5 May = Aphrodite>>L=N.
Spread=10,000=1,000=100%=10.0=Physicality=Tech.=10 Oct.=Uranus=P=1Ø.
Spread eagle=9,000=90%=P9.00D=9.0=Abstraction=Gods=Saturn=9Sept.>>A=Ø.
Spreadsheet=7,000=70%=P7.0D=7.0=Language=Assets=Mars=7 July=Pleiades.
Spree=6,500=7,000=70%=P7.0D=7.0=Language=Assets=Mars=7 July=Pleiades.
Sprier=1,500=15%=P1.50D=1.5=Authority=Solar Crown=1 May = Maia.
Spriest=2,000=20%=P2.00D=2.0=Nature=Matter=Moon=2 Feb.=Cupid=N=C+_
Sprig=4,500=5,000=50%=P5.00D=Law=Time=Venus=5 May = Aphrodite>>L=N.
Sprightly=2,000=20%=P2.00D=2.0=Nature=Matter=Moon=2 Feb.=Cupid=N=C+_
Spring=10,000=1,000=100%=10.0=Physicality=Tech.=10 Oct.=Uranus=P=1Ø.
Springboard=4,000=40%=P4.0D=Govt.=Creatocracy=4 April=Mercury=Hermes=G=A4.
Spring fever=6,000=60%=P6.0D=Man=Earth=Royalty=6 June=Gaia=Maia>>M=M2.
Springfield=10,000=1,000=100%=10.0=Physicality=Tech.=10 Oct.=Uranus=P=1Ø.
Spring loaded=4,000=40%=P4.0D=Govt.=Creatocracy=4 April=Mercury=Hermes=G=A4.
Spring tide=8,000=80%=P8.0D=Economy=Currency=8 Aug.=Zeus>>E=v.
Spring time=2,000=20%=P2.00D=2.0=Nature=Matter=Moon=2 Feb.=Cupid=N=C+_
Sprinkle=7,500=8,000=80%=P8.0D=Economy=Currency=8 Aug.=Zeus>>E=v.
Sprinkler system=5,500=5.5=80%=P5.50=Earth-Midway=5 May = Gaia.

Sprinkling=2,500=3,000=30%=P3.0D=3.0=Creativity=Stars=Muses=3 March = C=I>>GIL.
Sprint=5,000=50%=P5.00D=Law=Time=Venus=5 May = Aphrodite>>L=N.

Sprite=5,000=50%=P5.00D=Law=Time=Venus=5 May = Aphrodite>>L=N.
A specter or ghost. < Lat. spīritus, spirit. In simple terms drinking Sprite can help us sense the spirit of Aphrodite which translates to us understanding the place of beauty sexual love, incentives and rewards better earned at spiritual or cosmic markets and fertility boost. But spirit is 9.0 in the dimensions of the Creatocracy (universe) and so computing the ticological resultant and the dimension will yield the resultant dimension. 5.0*9.0x=px=14+45=59x=px=689=700=7.0. Sprite helps us develop computational ability. On the other hand Coca Cola soft drink increases human intelligence. We are working on others to know what exactly they boost in the human body and spirit. Great discoveries by Peter Matthews-Akukalia, Castle Makupedia. God of Creatocracy Genius and Mind.

Spritzer=5,500=5.5=80%=P5.50=Earth-Midway=5 May = Gaia.
Sprocket=9,000=90%=P9.00D=9.0=Abstraction=Gods=Saturn=9Sept.>>A=Ø.
Sprout=10,000=1,000=100%=10.0=Physicality=Tech.=10 Oct.=Uranus=P=1Ø.
Spruce1=10,000=1,000=100%=10.0=Physicality=Tech.=10 Oct.=Uranus=P=1Ø.
Spruce2=2,500=3,000=30%=P3.0D=3.0=Creativity=Stars=Muses=3 March = C=I>>GIL.
Sprung=3,500=4,000=40%=P4.0D=Govt.=Creatocracy=4 April=Mercury=Hermes=G=A4.
Spry=3,000=30%=P3.0D=3.0=Creativity=Stars=Muses=3 March = C=I>>GIL.
Spud=5,000=50%=P5.00D=Law=Time=Venus=5 May = Aphrodite>>L=N.
Spume=4,000=40%=P4.0D=Govt.=Creatocracy=4 April=Mercury=Hermes=G=A4.
Spumoni=7,500=8,000=80%=P8.0D=Economy=Currency=8 Aug.=Zeus>>E=v.
Spun=3,000=30%=P3.0D=3.0=Creativity=Stars=Muses=3 March = C=I>>GIL.
Spun glass=1,000=100%=10.0=1.0=Mind=Sun=1 January=Helios >> M=E4.
Spunk=3,500=4,000=40%=P4.0D=Govt.=Creatocracy=4 April=Mercury=Hermes=G=A4.
Spur=10,000=1,000=100%=10.0=Physicality=Tech.=10 Oct.=Uranus=P=1Ø.
Spurge=9,500=10,000=1,000=100%=10.0=Physicality=Tech.=10 Oct.=Uranus=P=1Ø.
Spurious=4,000=40%=P4.0D=Govt.=Creatocracy=4 April=Mercury=Hermes=G=A4.
Spurn=4,000=40%=P4.0D=Govt.=Creatocracy=4 April=Mercury=Hermes=G=A4.
Spurt=9,000=90%=P9.00D=9.0=Abstraction=Gods=Saturn=9Sept.>>A=Ø.
Sputnik=6,000=60%=P6.0D=Man=Earth=Royalty=6 June=Gaia=Maia>>M=M2.
Sputter=10,000=1,000=100%=10.0=Physicality=Tech.=10 Oct.=Uranus=P=1Ø.
Sputum=10,000=1,000=100%=10.0=Physicality=Tech.=10 Oct.=Uranus=P=1Ø.
Spy=10,000=1,000=100%=10.0=Physicality=Tech.=10 Oct.=Uranus=P=1Ø.
Spyglass=1,500=15%=P1.50D=1.5=Authority=Solar Crown=1 May = Maia.
Sq.=500=5%=P5.00D=5.0=Law=Time=Venus=5 May=Aphrodite>>L=N.
Squab=4,500=5,000=50%=P5.00D=Law=Time=Venus=5 May = Aphrodite>>L=N.
Squabble=9,000=90%=P9.00D=9.0=Abstraction=Gods=Saturn=9Sept.>>A=Ø.
Squad=10,000=1,000=100%=10.0=Physicality=Tech.=10 Oct.=Uranus=P=1Ø.
Squad car=4,000=40%=P4.0D=Govt.=Creatocracy=4 April=Mercury=Hermes=G=A4.
Squadron=10,000=1,000=100%=10.0=Physicality=Tech.=10 Oct.=Uranus=P=1Ø.
Squalid=4,000=40%=P4.0D=Govt.=Creatocracy=4 April=Mercury=Hermes=G=A4.

Squall1=4,000=40%=P4.0D=Govt.=Creatocracy=4 April=Mercury=Hermes=G=A4.
Squall2=7,000=70%=P7.0D=7.0=Language=Assets=Mars=7 July=Pleiades.
Squalor=3,500=4,000=40%=P4.0D=Govt.=Creatocracy=4 April=Mercury=Hermes=G=A4.
Squamous=4,000=40%=P4.0D=Govt.=Creatocracy=4 April=Mercury=Hermes=G=A4.
Squander=5,000=50%=P5.00D=Law=Time=Venus=5 May = Aphrodite>>L=N.
Squanto=5,500=5.5=80%=P5.50=Earth-Midway=5 May = Gaia.
Square=10,000=1,000=100%=10.0=Physicality=Tech.=10 Oct.=Uranus=P=1Ø.
Square bracket=1,500=15%=P1.50D=1.5=Authority=Solar Crown=1 May = Maia.
Square dance=5,000=50%=P5.00D=Law=Time=Venus=5 May = Aphrodite>>L=N.
Square knot=10,000=1,000=100%=10.0=Physicality=Tech.=10 Oct.=Uranus=P=1Ø.
Square meal=2,000=20%=P2.00D=2.0=Nature=Matter=Moon=2 Feb.=Cupid=N=C+_
Square rigged=4,500=5,000=50%=P5.00D=Law=Time=Venus=5 May = Aphrodite>>L=N.
Square rigger=2,500=3,000=30%=P3.0D=3.0=Cr=Stars=Muses=3 March = C=I>>GIL.
Square root=5,500=5.5=80%=P5.50=Earth-Midway=5 May = Gaia.
Squash1=10,000=1,000=100%=10.0=Physicality=Tech.=10 Oct.=Uranus=P=1Ø.
Squash2=10,000=1,000=100%=10.0=Physicality=Tech.=10 Oct.=Uranus=P=1Ø.
Squat=10,000=1,000=100%=10.0=Physicality=Tech.=10 Oct.=Uranus=P=1Ø.
Squat test=8,500=9,000=90%=P9.00D=9.0=Abstraction=Gods=Saturn=9Sept.>>A=Ø.
Squaw=3,500=4,000=40%=P4.0D=Govt.=Creatocracy=4 April=Mercury=Hermes=G=A4.
Squawk=6,000=60%=P6.0D=Man=Earth=Royalty=6 June=Gaia=Maia>>M=M2.
Squeak=7,000=70%=P7.0D=7.0=Language=Assets=Mars=7 July=Pleiades.
Squeal=7,500=8,000=80%=P8.0D=Economy=Currency=8 Aug.=Zeus>>E=v.
Squeamish=6,500=7,000=70%=P7.0D=7.0=Language=Assets=Mars=7 July=Pleiades.
Squeegee=10,000=1,000=100%=10.0=Physicality=Tech.=10 Oct.=Uranus=P=1Ø.
Squeeze=10,000=1,000=100%=10.0=Physicality=Tech.=10 Oct.=Uranus=P=1Ø.
Squelch=10,000=1,000=100%=10.0=Physicality=Tech.=10 Oct.=Uranus=P=1Ø.
Squib=10,000=1,000=100%=10.0=Physicality=Tech.=10 Oct.=Uranus=P=1Ø.
Squid=6,500=7,000=70%=P7.0D=7.0=Language=Assets=Mars=7 July=Pleiades.
Squiggle=8,000=80%=P8.0D=Economy=Currency=8 Aug.=Zeus>>E=v.
Squint=10,000=1,000=100%=10.0=Physicality=Tech.=10 Oct.=Uranus=P=1Ø.
Squire=10,000=1,000=100%=10.0=Physicality=Tech.=10 Oct.=Uranus=P=1Ø.
Squirm=10,000=1,000=100%=10.0=Physicality=Tech.=10 Oct.=Uranus=P=1Ø.
Squirrel=10,000=1,000=100%=10.0=Physicality=Tech.=10 Oct.=Uranus=P=1Ø.
Squirt=10,000=1,000=100%=10.0=Physicality=Tech.=10 Oct.=Uranus=P=1Ø.
Squish=10,000=1,000=100%=10.0=Physicality=Tech.=10 Oct.=Uranus=P=1Ø.
Sr=3,000=30%=P3.0D=3.0=Creativity=Stars=Muses=3 March = C=I>>GIL.
Sr.=3,000=30%=P3.0D=3.0=Creativity=Stars=Muses=3 March = C=I>>GIL.
Sri Lanka=8,000=80%=P8.0D=Economy=Currency=8 Aug.=Zeus>>E=v.
SRO=3,000=30%=P3.0D=3.0=Creativity=Stars=Muses=3 March = C=I>>GIL.
SSA=1,500=15%=P1.50D=1.5=Authority=Solar Crown=1 May = Maia.
SSE=1,000=100%=10.0=1.0=Mind=Sun=1 January=Helios >> M=E4.
SSW=1,000=100%=10.0=1.0=Mind=Sun=1 January=Helios >> M=E4.
ST=1,000=100%=10.0=1.0=Mind=Sun=1 January=Helios >> M=E4.
st.=4,000=40%=P4.0D=Govt.=Creatocracy=4 April=Mercury=Hermes=G=A4.
St.=500=5%=P5.00D=5.0=Law=Time=Venus=5 May=Aphrodite>>L=N.

Stab=10,000=1,000=100%=10.0=Physicality=Tech.=10 Oct.=Uranus=P=1Ø.
Stabilize=4,000=40%=P4.0D=Govt.=Creatocracy=4 April=Mercury=Hermes=G=A4.
Stable1=10,000=1,000=100%=10.0=Physicality=Tech.=10 Oct.=Uranus=P=1Ø.
Stable2=10,000=1,000=100%=10.0=Physicality=Tech.=10 Oct.=Uranus=P=1Ø.
Staccato=10,000=1,000=100%=10.0=Physicality=Tech.=10 Oct.=Uranus=P=1Ø.
Stack=10,000=1,000=100%=10.0=Physicality=Tech.=10 Oct.=Uranus=P=1Ø.
Stadium=7,000=70%=P7.0D=7.0=Language=Assets=Mars=7 July=Pleiades.
Staël=6,500=7,000=70%=P7.0D=7.0=Language=Assets=Mars=7 July=Pleiades.
Staff=10,000=1,000=100%=10.0=Physicality=Tech.=10 Oct.=Uranus=P=1Ø.
Staffer=2,500=3,000=30%=P3.0D=3.0=Creativity=Stars=Muses=3 March = C=I>>GIL.
Staff sergeant=6,500=7,000=70%=P7.0D=7.0=Language=Assets=Mars=7 July=Pleiades.
Stag=10,000=1,000=100%=10.0=Physicality=Tech.=10 Oct.=Uranus=P=1Ø.
Stage=10,000=1,000=100%=10.0=Physicality=Tech.=10 Oct.=Uranus=P=1Ø.
Stagecoach=6,500=7,000=70%=P7.0D=7.0=Language=Assets=Mars=7 July=Pleiades.
Stagecraft=4,000=40%=P4.0D=Govt.=Creatocracy=4 April=Mercury=Hermes=G=A4.
Stagger=10,000=1,000=100%=10.0=Physicality=Tech.=10 Oct.=Uranus=P=1Ø.
Staging=5,000=50%=P5.00D=Law=Time=Venus=5 May = Aphrodite>>L=N.
Stagnant=10,000=1,000=100%=10.0=Physicality=Tech.=10 Oct.=Uranus=P=1Ø.
Stagnate=4,000=40%=P4.0D=Govt.=Creatocracy=4 April=Mercury=Hermes=G=A4.
Stagy=2,000=20%=P2.00D=2.0=Nature=Matter=Moon=2 Feb.=Cupid=N=C+_
Stald=6,000=60%=P6.0D=Man=Earth=Royalty=6 June=Gaia=Maia>>M=M2.
Stain=10,000=1,000=100%=10.0=Physicality=Tech.=10 Oct.=Uranus=P=1Ø.
Stained glass=4,500=5,000=50%=P5.00D=Law=Time=Venus=5 May = Aphrodite>>L=N.
Stainless steel=7,000=70%=P7.0D=7.0=Language=Assets=Mars=7 July=Pleiades.
Stair=5,500=5.5=80%=P5.50=Earth-Midway=5 May = Gaia.
Staircase=4,000=40%=P4.0D=Govt.=Creatocracy=4 April=Mercury=Hermes=G=A4.
Stairway=1,000=100%=10.0=1.0=Mind=Sun=1 January=Helios >> M=E4.
Stairwell=4,500=5,000=50%=P5.00D=Law=Time=Venus=5 May = Aphrodite>>L=N.
Stake=10,000=1,000=100%=10.0=Physicality=Tech.=10 Oct.=Uranus=P=1Ø.
Stakeout=5,000=50%=P5.00D=Law=Time=Venus=5 May = Aphrodite>>L=N.
Stalactite=7,500=8,000=80%=P8.0D=Economy=Currency=8 Aug.=Zeus>>E=v.
Stalagmite=7,000=70%=P7.0D=7.0=Language=Assets=Mars=7 July=Pleiades.
Stale=8,000=80%=P8.0D=Economy=Currency=8 Aug.=Zeus>>E=v.
Stalemate=6,500=7,000=70%=P7.0D=7.0=Language=Assets=Mars=7 July=Pleiades.
Stalin Joseph.=2,000=20%=P2.00D=2.0=Nature=Matter=Moon=2 Feb.=Cupid=N=C+_
Stalingrad=1,000=100%=10.0=1.0=Mind=Sun=1 January=Helios >> M=E4.
Stalk1=5,000=50%=P5.00D=Law=Time=Venus=5 May = Aphrodite>>L=N.
Stalk2=10,000=1,000=100%=10.0=Physicality=Tech.=10 Oct.=Uranus=P=1Ø.
Stall1=10,000=1,000=100%=10.0=Physicality=Tech.=10 Oct.=Uranus=P=1Ø.
Stall2=4,500=5,000=50%=P5.00D=Law=Time=Venus=5 May = Aphrodite>>L=N.
Stallion=5,000=50%=P5.00D=Law=Time=Venus=5 May = Aphrodite>>L=N.
Stalwart=5,000=50%=P5.00D=Law=Time=Venus=5 May = Aphrodite>>L=N.
Stamen=6,500=7,000=70%=P7.0D=7.0=Language=Assets=Mars=7 July=Pleiades.
Stamford=5,500=5.5=80%=P5.50=Earth-Midway=5 May = Gaia.
Stamina=7,000=70%=P7.0D=7.0=Language=Assets=Mars=7 July=Pleiades.

Staminate=2,500=3,000=30%=P3.0D=3.0=Creativity=Stars=Muses=3 March = C=I>>GIL.
Stammer=4,500=5,000=50%=P5.00D=Law=Time=Venus=5 May = Aphrodite>>L=N.
Stamp=10,000=1,000=100%=10.0=Physicality=Tech.=10 Oct.=Uranus=P=1Ø.
Stampede=10,000=1,000=100%=10.0=Physicality=Tech.=10 Oct.=Uranus=P=1Ø.
Stance=10,000=1,000=100%=10.0=Physicality=Tech.=10 Oct.=Uranus=P=1Ø.
Stanch1=10,000=1,000=100%=10.0=Physicality=Tech.=10 Oct.=Uranus=P=1Ø.
Stanch2=4,000=40%=P4.0D=Govt.=Creatocracy=4 April=Mercury=Hermes=G=A4.
Stanchion=6,000=60%=P6.0D=Man=Earth=Royalty=6 June=Gaia=Maia>>M=M2.
Stand=10,000=1,000=100%=10.0=Physicality=Tech.=10 Oct.=Uranus=P=1Ø.

Standard=10,000=1,000=100%=10.0=Physicality=Tech.=10 Oct.=Uranus=P=1Ø.
The standard unit of measurement for the universe and its twelve dimensions is the Maks.
After Peter Matthews-Akukalia for writing their formulas and applying them. See The
Universe Dimensions and Formulas Table. Maks is indicated as a Makabet P. See SI.

Standard bearer=6,000=60%=P6.0D=Man=Earth=Royalty=6 June=Gaia=Maia>>M=M2.
Standard deviation=6,000=60%=P6.0D=Man=Earth=Royalty=6 June=Gaia=Maia>>M=M2.
Standardize=2,500=3,000=30%=P3.0D=3.0=Cr=Stars=Muses=3 March = C=I>>GIL.

Standard of living=7,500=8,000=80%=P8.0D=Economy=Currency=8 Aug.=Zeus>>E=v.
It is predictable that the Creatocracy brings an era of lower cost of living but a high
standard of living. People will earn based on their potentials and more jobs than required.

Standard time=8,000=80%=P8.0D=Economy=Currency=8 Aug.=Zeus>>E=v.
The time in any of the 24 global time zones usually the mean solar time at the central
meridian of each zone. Computing the mean solar time >> 8.0*2.4x=px=10.4+19.2=29.6x=px
=229.28 = 230.
Now time is influenced by planetary energy systems as seen in Zeus. Hence satellite data
tracking from astronomy is required to track the solar time from the moon surface. Diameter
230. The closet available data is Diameter 232, Location Clavius, Lat.56S long 14W. South
uplands. Massive walls. Curved line of craters on floor. No central peak. The lack of a central
peak qualifies the need to get a mean solar time and so we are correct. Standard time is
not measured from the moon seas (mare) but from the landforms. The mean solar time is
therefore 230=2.30pm. Standard time is 8:00am as deduced from the resultant and morning
sun hour reality. Time falls into the 5th dimension of the Universe known as Law and the
formula for Law is L=N >> Law is operant on nature which translates to Time operant on
the Moon. The Moon is the second dimension and regulates solar energy for control and
moderation during earth incursion. So the standard time is correct because it falls in the
moon half hour moderation system 2:30pm solar mean time-Maks. Therefore we refer to
this discovery as the World Standard Time WST by Castle Makupedia. Application to work
shifts would be 8:00am - 2:30pm less 30minutes break on the first shift of 6hours. Then
3:30pm - 8:30pm second work shift - 30minutes break. - Maks-Time.

Standby=9,000=90%=P9.00D=9.0=Abstraction=Gods=Saturn=9Sept.>>A=Ø.
Standee=3,500=4,000=40%=P4.0D=Govt.=Creatocracy=4 April=Mercury=Hermes=G=A4.
Stand in=6,000=60%=P6.0D=Man=Earth=Royalty=6 June=Gaia=Maia>>M=M2.
Standing=10,000=1,000=100%=10.0=Physicality=Tech.=10 Oct.=Uranus=P=1Ø.
Standish Miles=4,500=5,000=50%=P5.00D=Law=Time=Venus=5 May = Aphrodite>>L=N.
Stand off=3,500=4,000=40%=P4.0D=Govt.=Creatocracy=4 April=Hermes=G=A4.
Standoffish=2,500=3,000=30%=P3.0D=3.0=Cr=Stars=Muses=3 March = C=I>>GIL.
Standout=3,500=4,000=40%=P4.0D=Govt.=Creatocracy=4 April=Hermes=G=A4.
Standpipe=7,500=8,000=80%=P8.0D=Economy=Currency=8 Aug.=Zeus>>E=v.
Standpoint=7,000=70%=P7.0D=7.0=Language=Assets=Mars=7 July=Pleiades.
Standstill=1,000=100%=10.0=1.0=Mind=Sun=1 January=Helios >> M=E4.
Standup=7,500=8,000=80%=P8.0D=Economy=Currency=8 Aug.=Zeus>>E=v.
Stank=2,000=20%=P2.00D=2.0=Nature=Matter=Moon=2 Feb.=Cupid=N=C+_
Stanley Port=6,000=60%=P6.0D=Man=Earth=Royalty=6 June=Gaia=Maia>>M=M2.
Stanley,Henry=3,500=4,000=40%=P4.0D=Govt.=4 April=Mercury=Hermes=G=A4.
Stanton Elizabeth=4,000=40%=P4.0D=Govt.=4 April=Mercury=Hermes=G=A4.
Stanza=6,500=7,000=70%=P7.0D=7.0=Language=Assets=Mars=7 July=Pleiades.
Stapes=7,500=8,000=80%=P8.0D=Economy=Currency=8 Aug.=Zeus>>E=v.
Staphylococcus=10,000=1,000=100%=10.0=Physicality=Tech.=10 Oct.=Uranus=P=1Ø.
Staphylococcus=10,000=1,000=100%=10.0=Physicality=Tech.=10 Oct.=Uranus=P=1Ø.
Staple1=10,000=1,000=100%=10.0=Physicality=Tech.=10 Oct.=Uranus=P=1Ø.
Staple2=10,000=1,000=100%=10.0=Physicality=Tech.=10 Oct.=Uranus=P=1Ø.
Star=10,000=1,000=100%=10.0=Physicality=Tech.=10 Oct.=Uranus=P=1Ø.
Starboard=7,500=8,000=80%=P8.0D=Economy=Currency=8 Aug.=Zeus>>E=v.
Starch=10,000=1,000=100%=10.0=Physicality=Tech.=10 Oct.=Uranus=P=1Ø.
Stare=7,500=8,000=80%=P8.0D=Economy=Currency=8 Aug.=Zeus>>E=v.
Starfish=7,500=8,000=80%=P8.0D=Economy=Currency=8 Aug.=Zeus>>E=v.
Stargaze=2,500=3,000=30%=P3.0D=3.0=Creativity=Stars=Muses=3 March = C=I>>GIL.
Stark=10,000=1,000=100%=10.0=Physicality=Tech.=10 Oct.=Uranus=P=1Ø.
Starlet=4,000=40%=P4.0D=Govt.=Creatocracy=4 April=Mercury=Hermes=G=A4.
Starlight=2,000=20%=P2.00D=2.0=Nature=Matter=Moon=2 Feb.=Cupid=N=C+_
Starling=9,500=10,000=1,000=100%=10.0=Physicality=Tech.=10 Oct.=Uranus=P=1Ø.
Starlit=2,000=20%=P2.00D=2.0=Nature=Matter=Moon=2 Feb.=Cupid=N=C+_
Starry eyed=2,500=3,000=30%=P3.0D=3.0=Cr=Stars=Muses=3 March = C=I>>GIL.
Stars and Stripes=2,500=3,000=30%=P3.0D=3.0=Cr=Stars=Muses=3 March = C=I>>GIL.
Start=10,000=1,000=100%=10.0=Physicality=Tech.=10 Oct.=Uranus=P=1Ø.
Startle=8,000=80%=P8.0D=Economy=Currency=8 Aug.=Zeus>>E=v.
Starve=10,000=1,000=100%=10.0=Physicality=Tech.=10 Oct.=Uranus=P=1Ø.
Starveling=3,500=4,000=40%=P4.0D=Govt.=Creatocracy=4 April=Hermes=G=A4.
Stash=6,000=60%=P6.0D=Man=Earth=Royalty=6 June=Gaia=Maia>>M=M2.
-stasis=6,000=60%=P6.0D=Man=Earth=Royalty=6 June=Gaia=Maia>>M=M2.
Stat.=2,000=20%=P2.00D=2.0=Nature=Matter=Moon=2 Feb.=Cupid=N=C+_
-stat=7,000=70%=P7.0D=7.0=Language=Assets=Mars=7 July=Pleiades.
State=10,000=1,000=100%=10.0=Physicality=Tech.=10 Oct.=Uranus=P=1Ø.
Statecraft=3,000=30%=P3.0D=3.0=Creativity=Stars=Muses=3 March = C=I>>GIL.

Statehouse=4,000=40%=P4.0D=Govt.=Creatocracy=4 April=Mercury=Hermes=G=A4.
Stateless=4,000=40%=P4.0D=Govt.=Creatocracy=4 April=Mercury=Hermes=G=A4.
Stately=2,000=20%=P2.00D=2.0=Nature=Matter=Moon=2 Feb.=Cupid=N=C+_
Statement=10,000=1,000=100%=10.0=Physicality=Tech.=10 Oct.=Uranus=P=1Ø.
Staten Island=10,000=1,000=100%=10.0=Physicality=Tech.=10 Oct.=Uranus=P=1Ø.
Stateroom=4,000=40%=P4.0D=Govt.=Creatocracy=4 April=Mercury=Hermes=G=A4.
Stateside=10,000=1,000=100%=10.0=Physicality=Tech.=10 Oct.=Uranus=P=1Ø.
Statesman=10,000=1,000=100%=10.0=Physicality=Tech.=10 Oct.=Uranus=P=1Ø.
Stateswoman=10,000=1,000=100%=10.0=Physicality=Tech.=10 Oct.=Uranus=P=1Ø.
Static=10,000=1,000=100%=10.0=Physicality=Tech.=10 Oct.=Uranus=P=1Ø.
Station=10,000=1,000=100%=10.0=Physicality=Tech.=10 Oct.=Uranus=P=1Ø.
Stationary=2,000=20%=P2.00D=2.0=Nature=Matter=Moon=2 Feb.=Cupid=N=C+_
Station break=7,000=70%=P7.0D=7.0=Language=Assets=Mars=7 July=Pleiades.
Stattioner=5,000=50%=P5.00D=Law=Time=Venus=5 May = Aphrodite>>L=N.
Stationery=3,500=4,000=40%=P4.0D=Govt.=Creatocracy=4 April=Hermes=G=A4.
Station wagon=7,500=8,000=80%=P8.0D=Economy=Currency=8 Aug.=Zeus>>E=v.
Statistic=1,500=15%=P1.50D=1.5=Authority=Solar Crown=1 May = Maia.

Statistics=10,000=1,000=100%=10.0=Physicality=Tech.=10 Oct.=Uranus=P=1Ø.
One of the professions of the Creatocracy is Natistics >> Nature Statistics, Naturecology.

Statuary=1,000=100%=10.0=1.0=Mind=Sun=1 January=Helios >> M=E4.
Statue=11,000=11%=P1.10D=1.1=Idea=Brainchild=Inv.=11 Nov.=SC=Athena>>I=MT.
Statuesque=4,500=5,000=50%=P5.00D=Law=Time=Venus=5 May = Aphrodite>>L=N.
Stature=10,000=1,000=100%=10.0=Physicality=Tech.=10 Oct.=Uranus=P=1Ø.
Status=10,000=1,000=100%=10.0=Physicality=Tech.=10 Oct.=Uranus=P=1Ø.
Status quo=5,500=5.5=80%=P5.50=Earth-Midway=5 May = Gaia.
Statute=8,500=9,000=90%=P9.00D=9.0=Abstraction=Gods=Saturn=9Sept.>>A=Ø.
Statute mile=2,500=3,000=30%=P3.0D=3.0=Cr=Stars=Muses=3 March = C=I>>GIL.
Statutory=3,000=30%=P3.0D=3.0=Creativity=Stars=Muses=3 March = C=I>>GIL.
Staunch1=10,000=1,000=100%=10.0=Physicality=Tech.=10 Oct.=Uranus=P=1Ø.
Staunch2=1,500=15%=P1.50D=1.5=Authority=Solar Crown=1 May = Maia.
Stave=10,000=1,000=100%=10.0=Physicality=Tech.=10 Oct.=Uranus=P=1Ø.
Staves=2,000=20%=P2.00D=2.0=Nature=Matter=Moon=2 Feb.=Cupid=N=C+_
Stay1=10,000=1,000=100%=10.0=Physicality=Tech.=10 Oct.=Uranus=P=1Ø.
Stay2=10,000=1,000=100%=10.0=Physicality=Tech.=10 Oct.=Uranus=P=1Ø.
STD=1,500=15%=P1.50D=1.5=Authority=Solar Crown=1 May = Maia.
std.=500=5%=P5.00D=5.0=Law=Time=Venus=5 May=Aphrodite>>L=N.
Stead=9,000=90%=P9.00D=9.0=Abstraction=Gods=Saturn=9Sept.>>A=Ø.
Steadfast=4,000=40%=P4.0D=Govt.=Creatocracy=4 April=Mercury=Hermes=G=A4.
Steady=10,000=1,000=100%=10.0=Physicality=Tech.=10 Oct.=Uranus=P=1Ø.
Steak=6,500=7,000=70%=P7.0D=7.0=Language=Assets=Mars=7 July=Pleiades.
Steal=10,000=1,000=100%=10.0=Physicality=Tech.=10 Oct.=Uranus=P=1Ø.
Stealth=7,000=70%=P7.0D=7.0=Language=Assets=Mars=7 July=Pleiades.

Steam=10,000=1,000=100%=10.0=Physicality=Tech.=10 Oct.=Uranus=P=1Ø.
Steamboat=1,000=100%=10.0=1.0=Mind=Sun=1 January=Helios >> M=E4.
Steam engine=10,000=1,000=100%=10.0=Physicality=Tech.=10 Oct.=Uranus=P=1Ø.
Steamer=6,000=60%=P6.0D=Man=Earth=Royalty=6 June=Gaia=Maia>>M=M2.
Steam fitter=6,000=60%=P6.0D=Man=Earth=Royalty=6 June=Gaia=Maia>>M=M2.
Steamroller=10,000=1,000=100%=10.0=Physicality=Tech.=10 Oct.=Uranus=P=1Ø.
Steamship=5,000=50%=P5.00D=Law=Time=Venus=5 May = Aphrodite>>L=N.
Steam shovel=5,000=50%=P5.00D=Law=Time=Venus=5 May = Aphrodite>>L=N.
Steatite=3,500=4,000=40%=P4.0D=Govt.=Creatocracy=4 April=Mercury=Hermes=G=A4.
Steed=5,000=50%=P5.00D=Law=Time=Venus=5 May = Aphrodite>>L=N.
Steel=10,000=1,000=100%=10.0=Physicality=Tech.=10 Oct.=Uranus=P=1Ø.
Steel drum=4,500=5,000=50%=P5.00D=Law=Time=Venus=5 May = Aphrodite>>L=N.
Steele Sir Richard=2,000=20%=P2.00D=2.0=Nature=Matter=Moon=2 Feb.=Cupid=N=C+_
Steel wood=6,000=60%=P6.0D=Man=Earth=Royalty=6 June=Gaia=Maia>>M=M2.
Steep1=8,500=9,000=90%=P9.00D=9.0=Abstraction=Gods=Saturn=9Sept.>>A=Ø.
Steep2=10,000=1,000=100%=10.0=Physicality=Tech.=10 Oct.=Uranus=P=1Ø.
Steeple=7,500=8,000=80%=P8.0D=Economy=Currency=8 Aug.=Zeus>>E=v.
Steeplechase=5,500=5.5=80%=P5.50=Earth-Midway=5 May = Gaia.
Steeple jack=4,500=5,000=50%=P5.00D=Law=Time=Venus=5 May = Aphrodite>>L=N.
Steer1=10,000=1,000=100%=10.0=Physicality=Tech.=10 Oct.=Uranus=P=1Ø.
Steer2=8,500=9,000=90%=P9.00D=9.0=Abstraction=Gods=Saturn=9Sept.>>A=Ø.
Steerage=7,000=70%=P7.0D=7.0=Language=Assets=Mars=7 July=Pleiades.
Stegosaur=10,000=1,000=100%=10.0=Physicality=Tech.=10 Oct.=Uranus=P=1Ø.
Steichen Edward=2,500=3,000=30%=P3.0D=3.0=Cr=Stars=Muses=3 March = C=I>>GIL.
stein=3,000=30%=P3.0D=3.0=Creativity=Stars=Muses=3 March = C=I>>GIL.
Stein Gertrude.=2,000=20%=P2.00D=2.0=Nature=Matter=Moon=2 Feb.=Cupid=N=C+_
Steinbeck John=3,500=4,000=40%=P4.0D=Govt.=4 April=Mercury=Hermes=G=A4.
Steinem Gloria.=3,500=4,000=40%=P4.0D=Govt.=4 April=Mercury=Hermes=G=A4.

Stellar=6,500=7,000=70%=P7.0D=7.0=Language=Assets=Mars=7 July=Pleiades.
In the year 2019, Peter Matthews-Akukalia broke the stellar code. Google Nigerian Creative Scientist Cracks Controversial Stellar Code. Google Peter Matthews-Akukalia.

Stem1=10,000=1,000=100%=10.0=Physicality=Tech.=10 Oct.=Uranus=P=1Ø.
Stem2=6,000=60%=P6.0D=Man=Earth=Royalty=6 June=Gaia=Maia>>M=M2.
Stemware=2,500=3,000=30%=P3.0D=3.0=Creativity=Stars=Muses=3 March = C=I>>GIL.
Stench=6,500=7,000=70%=P7.0D=7.0=Language=Assets=Mars=7 July=Pleiades.
Stencil=10,000=1,000=100%=10.0=Physicality=Tech.=10 Oct.=Uranus=P=1Ø.
Stendhal Marie=3,000=30%=P3.0D=3.0=Creativity=Stars=Muses=3 March = C=I>>GIL.
Stenography=6,500=7,000=70%=P7.0D=7.0=Language=Assets=Mars=7 July=Pleiades.
Stentorian=6,500=7,000=70%=P7.0D=7.0=Language=Assets=Mars=7 July=Pleiades.
Step=10,000=1,000=100%=10.0=Physicality=Tech.=10 Oct.=Uranus=P=1Ø.
Step-=5,500=5.5=80%=P5.50=Earth-Midway=5 May = Gaia.
Stepbrother=2,500=3,000=30%=P3.0D=3.0=Cr=Stars=Muses=3 March = C=I>>GIL.

Stepchild=3,000=30%=P3.0D=3.0=Creativity=Stars=Muses=3 March = C=I>>GIL.
Stepdaughter=3,000=30%=P3.0D=3.0=Creativity=Stars=Muses=3 March = C=I>>GIL.
Stepfather=4,500=5,000=50%=P5.00D=Law=Time=Venus=5 May = Aphrodite>>L=N.
Stephen Saint.=2,500=3,000=30%=P3.0D=3.0=Cr=Stars=Muses=3 March = C=I>>GIL.
Stephen of Blois=4,000=40%=P4.0D=Govt.=4 April=Mercury=Hermes=G=A4.
Stepladder=3,500=4,000=40%=P4.0D=Govt.=4 April=Mercury=Hermes=G=A4.
Stepmother=4,500=5,000=50%=P5.00D=Law=Time=Venus=5 May = Aphrodite>>L=N.
Stepparent=2,000=20%=P2.00D=2.0=Nature=Matter=Moon=2 Feb.=Cupid=N=C+_
Steppe=7,500=8,000=80%=P8.0D=Economy=Currency=8 Aug.=Zeus>>E=v.
Steppingstone=4,000=40%=P4.0D=Govt.=Creatocracy=4 April=Mercury=Hermes=G=A4.
Stepsister=2,500=3,000=30%=P3.0D=3.0=Creativity=Stars=Muses=3 March = C=I>>GIL.
Stepson=3,000=30%=P3.0D=3.0=Creativity=Stars=Muses=3 March = C=I>>GIL.
Stere=500=5%=P5.00D=5.0=Law=Time=Venus=5 May=Aphrodite>>L=N.
-ster=8,000=80%=P8.0D=Economy=Currency=8 Aug.=Zeus>>E=v.
Stere=6,000=60%=P6.0D=Man=Earth=Royalty=6 June=Gaia=Maia>>M=M2.
Stereo-=3,500=4,000=40%=P4.0D=Govt.=Creatocracy=4 April=Mercury=Hermes=G=A4.
Stereophonic=10,000=1,000=100%=10.0=Physicality=Tech.=10 Oct.=Uranus=P=1Ø.
Stereoscope=10,000=1,000=100%=10.0=Physicality=Tech.=10 Oct.=Uranus=P=1Ø.
Stereoscopy=5,000=50%=P5.00D=Law=Time=Venus=5 May = Aphrodite>>L=N.
Stereotype=10,000=1,000=100%=10.0=Physicality=Tech.=10 Oct.=Uranus=P=1Ø.
Sterile=8,500=9,000=90%=P9.00D=9.0=Abstraction=Gods=Saturn=9Sept.>>A=Ø.
Sterilize=1,500=15%=P1.50D=1.5=Authority=Solar Crown=1 May = Maia.

Sterling=6,000=60%=P6.0D=Man=Earth=Royalty=6 June=Gaia=Maia>>M=M2.
British money. Sterling silver. <ME, silver penny. Currency metric weight is 6/10=0.6>60:1.
It is a silver though of the highest quality which means the sterling is a penny made of
silver. This is below the gold model and far below the diamond standard of the Maks
which is measured on the 10/10=1.0=10=100=1,000=10,000. See Naira. Dollar. Pounds.

Sterling Heights=4,500=5,000=50%=P5.00D=Law=Time=Venus=5 May =Odite>>L=N.
Sterling silver=5,000=50%=P5.00D=Law=Time=Venus=5 May = Aphrodite>>L=N.
Stern1=6,500=7,000=70%=P7.0D=7.0=Language=Assets=Mars=7 July=Pleiades.
Stern2=6,000=60%=P6.0D=Man=Earth=Royalty=6 June=Gaia=Maia>>M=M2.
Sterne Laurence.=2,000=20%=P2.00D=2.0=Nature=Matter=Moon=2 Feb.=Cupid=N=C+_
Sternum =10,000=1,000=100%=10.0=Physicality=Tech.=10 Oct.=Uranus=P=1Ø.
Steroid=10,000=1,000=100%=10.0=Physicality=Tech.=10 Oct.=Uranus=P=1Ø.
Sterol=10,000=1,000=100%=10.0=Physicality=Tech.=10 Oct.=Uranus=P=1Ø.
Stet=10,000=1,000=100%=10.0=Physicality=Tech.=10 Oct.=Uranus=P=1Ø.
Stethoscope=8,500=9,000=90%=P9.00D=9.0=Abstraction=Gods=Saturn=9Sept.>>A=Ø.
Steuben Baron=6,500=7,000=70%=P7.0D=7.0=Language=Assets=Mars=7 July=Pleiades.
Stevedore=6,000=60%=P6.0D=Man=Earth=Royalty=6 June=Gaia=Maia>>M=M2.
Stevens Wallace=2,000=20%=P2.00D=2.0=Nature=Matter=Moon=2 Feb.=Cupid=N=C+_
Stevens Adlai=11,500=12,000=12%=P1.20D=1.2=Knowledge=Edu=12Dec.=Athena>>K=F.
Stevenson,Robert=3,000=30%=P3.0D=3.0=Creativity=Stars=Muses=3 March = C=I>>GIL.

Stew=10,000=1,000=100%=10.0=Physicality=Tech.=10 Oct.=Uranus=P=1Ø.
Steward=10,000=1,000=100%=10.0=Physicality=Tech.=10 Oct.=Uranus=P=1Ø.
Stewardess=4,000=40%=P4.0D=Govt.=Creatocracy=4 April=Mercury=Hermes=G=A4.
Stick=10,000=1,000=100%=10.0=Physicality=Tech.=10 Oct.=Uranus=P=1Ø.
Sticker=5,500=5.5=80%=P5.50=Earth-Midway=5 May = Gaia.
Stickler=4,500=5,000=50%=P5.00D=Law=Time=Venus=5 May = Aphrodite>>L=N.
Stick shift=5,000=50%=P5.00D=Law=Time=Venus=5 May = Aphrodite>>L=N.
Stick-to-itiveness=1,500=15%=P1.50D=1.5=Authority=Solar Crown=1 May = Maia.
Stickup=3,000=30%=P3.0D=3.0=Creativity=Stars=Muses=3 March = C=I>>GIL.
Sticky=9,000=90%=P9.00D=9.0=Abstraction=Gods=Saturn=9Sept.>>A=Ø.
Stiff=10,000=1,000=100%=10.0=Physicality=Tech.=10 Oct.=Uranus=P=1Ø.
Stiff-necked=2,500=3,000=30%=P3.0D=3.0=Cr=Stars=Muses=3 March = C=I>>GIL.
Stifle=8,500=9,000=90%=P9.00D=9.0=Abstraction=Gods=Saturn=9Sept.>>A=Ø.
Stigma=10,000=1,000=100%=10.0=Physicality=Tech.=10 Oct.=Uranus=P=1Ø.
Stigmatize=5,500=5.5=80%=P5.50=Earth-Midway=5 May = Gaia.
Stile=6,000=60%=P6.0D=Man=Earth=Royalty=6 June=Gaia=Maia>>M=M2.
Stiletto=6,000=60%=P6.0D=Man=Earth=Royalty=6 June=Gaia=Maia>>M=M2.
Still1=10,000=1,000=100%=10.0=Physicality=Tech.=10 Oct.=Uranus=P=1Ø.
Still2=6,500=7,000=70%=P7.0D=7.0=Language=Assets=Mars=7 July=Pleiades.
Stillbirth=4,000=40%=P4.0D=Govt.=Creatocracy=4 April=Mercury=Hermes=G=A4.
Still life=4,000=40%=P4.0D=Govt.=Creatocracy=4 April=Mercury=Hermes=G=A4.
Stilt=10,000=1,000=100%=10.0=Physicality=Tech.=10 Oct.=Uranus=P=1Ø.
Stilted=10,000=1,000=100%=10.0=Physicality=Tech.=10 Oct.=Uranus=P=1Ø.
Stilted=2,500=3,000=30%=P3.0D=3.0=Creativity=Stars=Muses=3 March = C=I>>GIL.
Stimulant=8,500=9,000=90%=P9.00D=9.0=Abstraction=Gods=Saturn=9Sept.>>A=Ø.
Stimulate=5,000=50%=P5.00D=Law=Time=Venus=5 May = Aphrodite>>L=N.
Stimulus=2,500=3,000=30%=P3.0D=3.0=Creativity=Stars=Muses=3 March = C=I>>GIL.
Sting=10,000=1,000=100%=10.0=Physicality=Tech.=10 Oct.=Uranus=P=1Ø.
Stingray=5,500=5.5=80%=P5.50=Earth-Midway=5 May = Gaia.
Stingy=6,000=60%=P6.0D=Man=Earth=Royalty=6 June=Gaia=Maia>>M=M2.
Stink=10,000=1,000=100%=10.0=Physicality=Tech.=10 Oct.=Uranus=P=1Ø.
Stink bug=4,500=5,000=50%=P5.00D=Law=Time=Venus=5 May = Aphrodite>>L=N.
Stint=10,000=1,000=100%=10.0=Physicality=Tech.=10 Oct.=Uranus=P=1Ø.
Stipend=7,000=70%=P7.0D=7.0=Language=Assets=Mars=7 July=Pleiades.
Stipple=9,500=10,000=1,000=100%=10.0=Physicality=Tech.=10 Oct.=Uranus=P=1Ø.
Stipulate=10,000=1,000=100%=10.0=Physicality=Tech.=10 Oct.=Uranus=P=1Ø.
Stir1=10,000=1,000=100%=10.0=Physicality=Tech.=10 Oct.=Uranus=P=1Ø.
Stir2=1,500=15%=P1.50D=1.5=Authority=Solar Crown=1 May = Maia.
Stir fry=6,000=60%=P6.0D=Man=Earth=Royalty=6 June=Gaia=Maia>>M=M2.
Stirring=2,000=20%=P2.00D=2.0=Nature=Matter=Moon=2 Feb.=Cupid=N=C+_
Stirrup=9,000=90%=P9.00D=9.0=Abstraction=Gods=Saturn=9Sept.>>A=Ø.
Stitch=10,000=1,000=100%=10.0=Physicality=Tech.=10 Oct.=Uranus=P=1Ø.
Stoat=6,000=60%=P6.0D=Man=Earth=Royalty=6 June=Gaia=Maia>>M=M2.
Stochastic=4,500=5,000=50%=P5.00D=Law=Time=Venus=5 May = Aphrodite>>L=N.
Stock=10,000=1,000=100%=10.0=Physicality=Tech.=10 Oct.=Uranus=P=1Ø.

Stockade=10,500=11,000=11%=P1.10D=1.1=Idea=Brainchild=Inv.=11 Nov.=Athena>>I=MT.
Stockbroker=6,500=7,000=70%=P7.0D=7.0=Language=Assets=Mars=7 July=Pleiades.
Stock car=4,500=5,000=50%=P5.00D=Law=Time=Venus=5 May = Aphrodite>>L=N.
Stock exchange=8,000=80%=P8.0D=Economy=Currency=8 Aug.=Zeus>>E=v.
Stockholder=1,000=100%=10.0=1.0=Mind=Sun=1 January=Helios >> M=E4.
Stockholm=6,000=60%=P6.0D=Man=Earth=Royalty=6 June=Gaia=Maia>>M=M2.
Stocking=7,500=8,000=80%=P8.0D=Economy=Currency=8 Aug.=Zeus>>E=v.
Stocking cap=2,500=3,000=30%=P3.0D=3.0=Cr=Stars=Muses=3 March = C=I>>GIL.
Stock market=4,500=5,000=50%=P5.00D=Law=Time=Venus=5 May = Aphrodite>>L=N.
Stockpile=3,000=30%=P3.0D=3.0=Creativity=Stars=Muses=3 March = C=I>>GIL.
Stock still=1,500=15%=P1.50D=1.5=Authority=Solar Crown=1 May = Maia.
Stockton=4,500=5,000=50%=P5.00D=Law=Time=Venus=5 May = Aphrodite>>L=N.
Stocky=1,500=15%=P1.50D=1.5=Authority=Solar Crown=1 May = Maia.
Stockyard=6,500=7,000=70%=P7.0D=7.0=Language=Assets=Mars=7 July=Pleiades.
Stodgy=8,500=9,000=90%=P9.00D=9.0=Abstraction=Gods=Saturn=9Sept.>>A=Ø.
Stoic=10,000=1,000=100%=10.0=Physicality=Tech.=10 Oct.=Uranus=P=1Ø.
Stoke=10,000=1,000=100%=10.0=Physicality=Tech.=10 Oct.=Uranus=P=1Ø.
Stoke-on-Trent=10,000=1,000=100%=10.0=Physicality=Tech.=10 Oct.=Uranus=P=1Ø.
STOL=2,000=20%=P2.00D=2.0=Nature=Matter=Moon=2 Feb.=Cupid=N=C+_
Stole1=10,000=1,000=100%=10.0=Physicality=Tech.=10 Oct.=Uranus=P=1Ø.
Stole2=2,000=20%=P2.00D=2.0=Nature=Matter=Moon=2 Feb.=Cupid=N=C+_
Stolen=2,000=20%=P2.00D=2.0=Nature=Matter=Moon=2 Feb.=Cupid=N=C+_
Stolid=4,000=40%=P4.0D=Govt.=Creatocracy=4 April=Mercury=Hermes=G=A4.
Stoma=10,000=1,000=100%=10.0=Physicality=Tech.=10 Oct.=Uranus=P=1Ø.
Stomach=10,000=1,000=100%=10.0=Physicality=Tech.=10 Oct.=Uranus=P=1Ø.
Stomachache=3,000=30%=P3.0D=3.0=Creativity=Stars=Muses=3 March = C=I>>GIL.
Stomacher=4,000=40%=P4.0D=Govt.=Creatocracy=4 April=Mercury=Hermes=G=A4.
Stomachic=4,000=40%=P4.0D=Govt.=Creatocracy=4 April=Mercury=Hermes=G=A4.
Stomp=4,500=5,000=50%=P5.00D=Law=Time=Venus=5 May = Aphrodite>>L=N.
stone=10,000=1,000=100%=10.0=Physicality=Tech.=10 Oct.=Uranus=P=1Ø.
Stone Lucy=3,000=30%=P3.0D=3.0=Creativity=Stars=Muses=3 March = C=I>>GIL.
Stone Age=6,500=7,000=70%=P7.0D=7.0=Language=Assets=Mars=7 July=Pleiades.
Stoned=5,000=50%=P5.00D=Law=Time=Venus=5 May = Aphrodite>>L=N.
Stonewall=3,500=4,000=40%=P4.0D=Govt.=Creatocracy=4 April=Hermes=G=A4.
Stoneware=2,500=3,000=30%=P3.0D=3.0=Creativity=Stars=Muses=3 March = C=I>>GIL.
Stony=6,500=7,000=70%=P7.0D=7.0=Language=Assets=Mars=7 July=Pleiades.
Stood=3,000=30%=P3.0D=3.0=Creativity=Stars=Muses=3 March = C=I>>GIL.
Stooge=6,000=60%=P6.0D=Man=Earth=Royalty=6 June=Gaia=Maia>>M=M2.
Stool=11,000=11%=P1.10D=1.1=Idea=Brainchild=Inv.=11 Nov.=SC=Athena>>I=MT.
Stool pigeon=8,000=80%=P8.0D=Economy=Currency=8 Aug.=Zeus>>E=v.
Stoop1=10,000=1,000=100%=10.0=Physicality=Tech.=10 Oct.=Uranus=P=1Ø.
Stoop2=10,000=1,000=100%=10.0=Physicality=Tech.=10 Oct.=Uranus=P=1Ø.
Stop=10,000=1,000=100%=10.0=Physicality=Tech.=10 Oct.=Uranus=P=1Ø.
Stopcock=5,000=50%=P5.00D=Law=Time=Venus=5 May = Aphrodite>>L=N.
Stopgap=3,500=4,000=40%=P4.0D=Govt.=Creatocracy=4 April=Hermes=G=A4.

Stoplight=1,500=15%=P1.50D=1.5=Authority=Solar Crown=1 May = Maia.
Stopover=4,500=5,000=50%=P5.00D=Law=Time=Venus=5 May = Aphrodite>>L=N.
Stopper=5,000=50%=P5.00D=Law=Time=Venus=5 May = Aphrodite>>L=N.
Stopwatch=10,000=1,000=100%=10.0=Physicality=Tech.=10 Oct.=Uranus=P=1Ø.
Storage=10,000=1,000=100%=10.0=Physicality=Tech.=10 Oct.=Uranus=P=1Ø.
Storage battery=5,500=5.5=80%=P5.50=Earth-Midway=5 May = Gaia.
Store=10,000=1,000=100%=10.0=Physicality=Tech.=10 Oct.=Uranus=P=1Ø.
Storefront=6,500=7,000=70%=P7.0D=7.0=Language=Assets=Mars=7 July=Pleiades.
Storehouse=6,500=7,000=70%=P7.0D=7.0=Language=Assets=Mars=7 July=Pleiades.
Storekeeper=4,000=40%=P4.0D=Govt.=Creatocracy=4 April=Mercury=Hermes=G=A4.
Storeroom=3,500=4,000=40%=P4.0D=Govt.=Creatocracy=4 April=Hermes=G=A4.
Storey=2,500=3,000=30%=P3.0D=3.0=Creativity=Stars=Muses=3 March = C=I>>GIL.
Storied=3,000=30%=P3.0D=3.0=Creativity=Stars=Muses=3 March = C=I>>GIL.
Stork=8,000=80%=P8.0D=Economy=Currency=8 Aug.=Zeus>>E=v.
Storm=10,000=1,000=100%=10.0=Physicality=Tech.=10 Oct.=Uranus=P=1Ø.
Story1=10,000=1,000=100%=10.0=Physicality=Tech.=10 Oct.=Uranus=P=1Ø.
Story2=10,000=1,000=100%=10.0=Physicality=Tech.=10 Oct.=Uranus=P=1Ø.
Storyteller=2,000=20%=P2.00D=2.0=Nature=Matter=Moon=2 Feb.=Cupid=N=C+_

Stotinka=2,500=3,000=30%=P3.0D=3.0=Creativity=Stars=Muses=3 March = C=I>>GIL.
[Bulgarian] currency metric weight = 2.5/10=0.25>>25:1. See Naira. Dollar.

Stoup=5,000=50%=P5.00D=Law=Time=Venus=5 May = Aphrodite>>L=N.
Stout=10,000=1,000=100%=10.0=Physicality=Tech.=10 Oct.=Uranus=P=1Ø.
Stouthearted=1,000=100%=10.0=1.0=Mind=Sun=1 January=Helios >> M=E4.
Stove1=11,000=11%=P1.10D=1.1=Idea=Brainchild=Inv.=11 Nov.=SC=Athena>>I=MT.
Stove2=3,000=30%=P3.0D=3.0=Creativity=Stars=Muses=3 March = C=I>>GIL.
Stovepipe=7,500=8,000=80%=P8.0D=Economy=Currency=8 Aug.=Zeus>>E=v.
Stow=5,000=50%=P5.00D=Law=Time=Venus=5 May = Aphrodite>>L=N.
Stowaway=6,500=7,000=70%=P7.0D=7.0=Language=Assets=Mars=7 July=Pleiades.
Stowe Harriet=3,000=30%=P3.0D=3.0=Creativity=Stars=Muses=3 March = C=I>>GIL.
STP=2,000=20%=P2.00D=2.0=Nature=Matter=Moon=2 Feb.=Cupid=N=C+_
str.=1,000=100%=10.0=1.0=Mind=Sun=1 January=Helios >> M=E4.
Strabismus=10,000=1,000=100%=10.0=Physicality=Tech.=10 Oct.=Uranus=P=1Ø.
Straddle=10,000=1,000=100%=10.0=Physicality=Tech.=10 Oct.=Uranus=P=1Ø.
Strafe=7,000=70%=P7.0D=7.0=Language=Assets=Mars=7 July=Pleiades.
Straggle=7,000=70%=P7.0D=7.0=Language=Assets=Mars=7 July=Pleiades.
Straight=10,000=1,000=100%=10.0=Physicality=Tech.=10 Oct.=Uranus=P=1Ø.

Straight angle=2,000=20%=P2.00D=2.0=Nature=Matter=Moon=2 Feb.=Cupid=N=C+_
An angle of 180°. Computing 2.0*1.8x=px=3.8+3.6=7.4x=px=21.08=2.11. Now see Psalm
21:8 for puzzle codes. The use of "enemies" indicate left hand side which is -1.0 and the
"right" hand is +1.0. In the creative sciences both elements are represented in a plane as

>+1. To determine the straight angle based on abstraction, 5.0*2.11x=px=7.11+10.55 =17.66x=px=92.6705=93=9.3. Applying this resultant to a triangle indicates an angle with three sides of 90° each is rightly what a straight angle is. So an angle of 180°/3=60° is 30° short of expectation and questionable. This is because a side of the angle is missing at 180°/2=90°. Discovery here is that the link between mathematics and Makumatics is the resolution of conflicts using the triangles. This is clearly represented in the Mind Assessment Medicals & Psycho-Surgery (MAMPS) Tests.

Straightaway=10,000=1,000=100%=10.0=Physicality=Tech.=10 Oct.=Uranus=P=1Ø.
Straightedge=6,500=7,000=70%=P7.0D=7.0=Language=Assets=Mars=7 July=Pleiades.
Straighten=3,000=30%=P3.0D=3.0=Creativity=Stars=Muses=3 March = C=I>>GIL.
Straightforward=4,500=5,000=50%=P5.00D=Law=Time=Venus=5 May =Odite>>L=N.
Straight man=4,500=5,000=50%=P5.00D=Law=Time=Venus=5 May = Aphrodite>>L=N.
Straight razor=8,000=80%=P8.0D=Economy=Currency=8 Aug.=Zeus>>E=v.
Straight way=1,000=100%=10.0=1.0=Mind=Sun=1 January=Helios >> M=E4.
Strain1=10,000=1,000=100%=10.0=Physicality=Tech.=10 Oct.=Uranus=P=1Ø.
Strain2=10,000=1,000=100%=10.0=Physicality=Tech.=10 Oct.=Uranus=P=1Ø.
Strained=8,000=80%=P8.0D=Economy=Currency=8 Aug.=Zeus>>E=v.
Strait=10,000=1,000=100%=10.0=Physicality=Tech.=10 Oct.=Uranus=P=1Ø.
Straiten=4,000=40%=P4.0D=Govt.=Creatocracy=4 April=Mercury=Hermes=G=A4.
Straight jacket=8,000=80%=P8.0D=Economy=Currency=8 Aug.=Zeus>>E=v.
Strait-laced=3,500=4,000=40%=P4.0D=Govt.=Creatocracy=4 April=Hermes=G=A4.
Strand1=9,000=90%=P9.00D=9.0=Abstraction=Gods=Saturn=9Sept.>>A=Ø.
Strand2=10,000=1,000=100%=10.0=Physicality=Tech.=10 Oct.=Uranus=P=1Ø.

Strange=10,000=1,000=100%=10.0=Physicality=Tech.=10 Oct.=Uranus=P=1Ø.
See The Creatocracy Republic by Peter Matthews-Akukalia, reference play > Stranger than Strange. A Propoplay. An invention play of Peter Matthews-Akukalia, Castle Makupedia.

Stranger=6,500=7,000=70%=P7.0D=7.0=Language=Assets=Mars=7 July=Pleiades.
Strangle=6,500=7,000=70%=P7.0D=7.0=Language=Assets=Mars=7 July=Pleiades.
Strangulate=9,000=90%=P9.00D=9.0=Abstraction=Gods=Saturn=9Sept.>>A=Ø.
Strap=10,000=1,000=100%=10.0=Physicality=Tech.=10 Oct.=Uranus=P=1Ø.
Strapless=4,000=40%=P4.0D=Govt.=Creatocracy=4 April=Mercury=Hermes=G=A4.
Strapped=2,000=20%=P2.00D=2.0=Nature=Matter=Moon=2 Feb.=Cupid=N=C+_
Strapping=2,000=20%=P2.00D=2.0=Nature=Matter=Moon=2 Feb.=Cupid=N=C+_
Strasbourg=5,500=5.5=80%=P5.50=Earth-Midway=5 May = Gaia.
Strata=2,000=20%=P2.00D=2.0=Nature=Matter=Moon=2 Feb.=Cupid=N=C+_
Stratagem=10,000=1,000=100%=10.0=Physicality=Tech.=10 Oct.=Uranus=P=1Ø.
Strategy=10,000=1,000=100%=10.0=Physicality=Tech.=10 Oct.=Uranus=P=1Ø.

Stratford-upon-Avon=10,000=1,000=100%=10.0=Phy=Tech.=10 Oct.=Uranus=P=1Ø.
Birthplace of William Shakespeare. Nkpologu-Nsukka, village of Peter Matthews-Akukalia.

Stratify=6,000=60%=P6.0D=Man=Earth=Royalty=6 June=Gaia=Maia>>M=M2.
Stratosphere=10,000=1,000=100%=10.0=Physicality=Tech.=10 Oct.=Uranus=P=1Ø.
Stratum=10,000=1,000=100%=10.0=Physicality=Tech.=10 Oct.=Uranus=P=1Ø.
Stratus=9,000=90%=P9.00D=9.0=Abstraction=Gods=Saturn=9Sept.>>A=Ø.
Strauss Johann.=6,500=7,000=70%=P7.0D=7.0=Language=Assets=Mars=7 July=Pleiades.
Strauss Richard.=2,000=20%=P2.00D=2.0=Nature=Matter=Moon=2 Feb.=Cupid=N=C+_
Stravinsky, Igor=3,000=30%=P3.0D=3.0=Creativity=Stars=Muses=3 March = C=I>>GIL.
Straw=10,000=1,000=100%=10.0=Physicality=Tech.=10 Oct.=Uranus=P=1Ø.
Strawberry=10,000=1,000=100%=10.0=Physicality=Tech.=10 Oct.=Uranus=P=1Ø.
Straw boss=3,500=4,000=40%=P4.0D=Govt.=Creatocracy=4 April=Hermes=G=A4.
Straw vote=2,500=3,000=30%=P3.0D=3.0=Creativity=Stars=Muses=3 March = C=I>>GIL.
Stray=10,000=1,000=100%=10.0=Physicality=Tech.=10 Oct.=Uranus=P=1Ø.
Streak=10,000=1,000=100%=10.0=Physicality=Tech.=10 Oct.=Uranus=P=1Ø.
Streak=10,000=1,000=100%=10.0=Physicality=Tech.=10 Oct.=Uranus=P=1Ø.
Stream=10,000=1,000=100%=10.0=Physicality=Tech.=10 Oct.=Uranus=P=1Ø.
Streamer=8,000=80%=P8.0D=Economy=Currency=8 Aug.=Zeus>>E=v.
Streamline=6,500=7,000=70%=P7.0D=7.0=Language=Assets=Mars=7 July=Pleiades.
Street=10,000=1,000=100%=10.0=Physicality=Tech.=10 Oct.=Uranus=P=1Ø.
Streetcar=5,500=5.5=80%=P5.50=Earth-Midway=5 May = Gaia.
Street walker=1,000=100%=10.0=1.0=Mind=Sun=1 January=Helios >> M=E4.
Strength=10,000=1,000=100%=10.0=Physicality=Tech.=10 Oct.=Uranus=P=1Ø.
Strengthen=3,000=30%=P3.0D=3.0=Creativity=Stars=Muses=3 March = C=I>>GIL.
Strenuous=10,000=1,000=100%=10.0=Physicality=Tech.=10 Oct.=Uranus=P=1Ø.
Strep throat=10,000=1,000=100%=10.0=Physicality=Tech.=10 Oct.=Uranus=P=1Ø.
Streptococcus=10,000=1,000=100%=10.0=Physicality=Tech.=10 Oct.=Uranus=P=1Ø.
Streptomycin=8,000=80%=P8.0D=Economy=Currency=8 Aug.=Zeus>>E=v.
Stress=10,000=1,000=100%=10.0=Physicality=Tech.=10 Oct.=Uranus=P=1Ø.
Stressor=3,500=4,000=40%=P4.0D=Govt.=Creatocracy=4 April=Hermes=G=A4.
Stretch=10,000=1,000=100%=10.0=Physicality=Tech.=10 Oct.=Uranus=P=1Ø.
Stretcher=6,500=7,000=70%=P7.0D=7.0=Language=Assets=Mars=7 July=Pleiades.
Strew=10,000=1,000=100%=10.0=Physicality=Tech.=10 Oct.=Uranus=P=1Ø.
Stria=10,000=1,000=100%=10.0=Physicality=Tech.=10 Oct.=Uranus=P=1Ø.
Stricken=7,000=70%=P7.0D=7.0=Language=Assets=Mars=7 July=Pleiades.
Strict=10,000=1,000=100%=10.0=Physicality=Tech.=10 Oct.=Uranus=P=1Ø.
Stricture=10,000=1,000=100%=10.0=Physicality=Tech.=10 Oct.=Uranus=P=1Ø.
Stride=10,000=1,000=100%=10.0=Physicality=Tech.=10 Oct.=Uranus=P=1Ø.
Strident=10,000=1,000=100%=10.0=Physicality=Tech.=10 Oct.=Uranus=P=1Ø.
Strife=10,000=1,000=100%=10.0=Physicality=Tech.=10 Oct.=Uranus=P=1Ø.
Strike=10,000=1,000=100%=10.0=Physicality=Tech.=10 Oct.=Uranus=P=1Ø.
Strikebreaker=4,500=5,000=50%=P5.00D=Law=Time=Venus=5 May = Aphrodite>>L=N.
Strikeout=3,000=30%=P3.0D=3.0=Creativity=Stars=Muses=3 March = C=I>>GIL.

Strike zone=8,000=80%=P8.0D=Economy=Currency=8 Aug.=Zeus>>E=v.
Striking=2,000=20%=P2.00D=2.0=Nature=Matter=Moon=2 Feb.=Cupid=N=C+_
Strindberg August.=2,000=20%=P2.00D=2.0=Nature=Moon=2 Feb.=Cupid=N=C+_
String=10,000=1,000=100%=10.0=Physicality=Tech.=10 Oct.=Uranus=P=1Ø.
String bean=7,000=70%=P7.0D=7.0=Language=Assets=Mars=7 July=Pleiades.
Stringent=8,500=9,000=90%=P9.00D=9.0=Abstraction=Gods=Saturn=9Sept.>>A=Ø.
Stringer=9,000=90%=P9.00D=9.0=Abstraction=Gods=Saturn=9Sept.>>A=Ø.
Strip1=10,000=1,000=100%=10.0=Physicality=Tech.=10 Oct.=Uranus=P=1Ø.
Strip2=8,500=9,000=90%=P9.00D=9.0=Abstraction=Gods=Saturn=9Sept.>>A=Ø.
Stripe=10,000=1,000=100%=10.0=Physicality=Tech.=10 Oct.=Uranus=P=1Ø.
Stripling=2,000=20%=P2.00D=2.0=Nature=Matter=Moon=2 Feb.=Cupid=N=C+_
Stripe mine=8,000=80%=P8.0D=Economy=Currency=8 Aug.=Zeus>>E=v.
Strip search=6,000=60%=P6.0D=Man=Earth=Royalty=6 June=Gaia=Maia>>M=M2.
Strip tease=6,500=7,000=70%=P7.0D=7.0=Language=Assets=Mars=7 July=Pleiades.
Strive=6,000=60%=P6.0D=Man=Earth=Royalty=6 June=Gaia=Maia>>M=M2.
Strobe=2,000=20%=P2.00D=2.0=Nature=Matter=Moon=2 Feb.=Cupid=N=C+_
Strobe light=6,000=60%=P6.0D=Man=Earth=Royalty=6 June=Gaia=Maia>>M=M2.
Stroboscope=10,000=1,000=100%=10.0=Physicality=Tech.=10 Oct.=Uranus=P=1Ø.
Strode=2,000=20%=P2.00D=2.0=Nature=Matter=Moon=2 Feb.=Cupid=N=C+_
Stroke1=10,000=1,000=100%=10.0=Physicality=Tech.=10 Oct.=Uranus=P=1Ø.
Stroke2=4,500=5,000=50%=P5.00D=Law=Time=Venus=5 May = Aphrodite>>L=N.
Stroll=5,000=50%=P5.00D=Law=Time=Venus=5 May = Aphrodite>>L=N.
Stroller=6,000=60%=P6.0D=Man=Earth=Royalty=6 June=Gaia=Maia>>M=M2.
Stromboli=6,000=60%=P6.0D=Man=Earth=Royalty=6 June=Gaia=Maia>>M=M2.
Strong=10,000=1,000=100%=10.0=Physicality=Tech.=10 Oct.=Uranus=P=1Ø.
Strongman=2,500=3,000=30%=P3.0D=3.0=Cr=Stars=Muses=3 March = C=I>>GIL.
Strongbox=2,000=20%=P2.00D=2.0=Nature=Matter=Moon=2 Feb.=Cupid=N=C+_
Stronghold=1,000=100%=10.0=1.0=Mind=Sun=1 January=Helios >> M=E4.
Strong interaction=9,000=90%=P9.00D=9.0=Abstraction=Gods=Saturn=9Sept.>>A=Ø.
Strongman=4,000=40%=P4.0D=Govt.=Creatocracy=4 April=Mercury=Hermes=G=A4.
Strontium=12,000=12%=P1.20D=1.2=Knowledge=Edu=12Dec.=Athena>>K=F.
Strontium 90=8,000=80%=P8.0D=Economy=Currency=8 Aug.=Zeus>>E=v.
Strop=10,000=1,000=100%=10.0=Physicality=Tech.=10 Oct.=Uranus=P=1Ø.
Strophe=10,000=1,000=100%=10.0=Physicality=Tech.=10 Oct.=Uranus=P=1Ø.
Strove=2,000=20%=P2.00D=2.0=Nature=Matter=Moon=2 Feb.=Cupid=N=C+_
Struck=6,500=7,000=70%=P7.0D=7.0=Language=Assets=Mars=7 July=Pleiades.
Structure=10,000=1,000=100%=10.0=Physicality=Tech.=10 Oct.=Uranus=P=1Ø.
Strudel=8,500=9,000=90%=P9.00D=9.0=Abstraction=Gods=Saturn=9Sept.>>A=Ø.
Struggle=10,000=1,000=100%=10.0=Physicality=Tech.=10 Oct.=Uranus=P=1Ø.
Strum=7,000=70%=P7.0D=7.0=Language=Assets=Mars=7 July=Pleiades.
Strumpet=1,500=15%=P1.50D=1.5=Authority=Solar Crown=1 May = Maia.
Strung=3,000=30%=P3.0D=3.0=Creativity=Stars=Muses=3 March = C=I>>GIL.
Strung-out=4,000=40%=P4.0D=Govt.=Creatocracy=4 April=Mercury=Hermes=G=A4.
Strut=10,000=1,000=100%=10.0=Physicality=Tech.=10 Oct.=Uranus=P=1Ø.
Strychnine=10,000=1,000=100%=10.0=Physicality=Tech.=10 Oct.=Uranus=P=1Ø.

Stuart Gilbert=2,500=3,000=30%=P3.0D=3.0=Cr=Stars=Muses=3 March = C=I>>GIL.
Stuart James=4,500=5,000=50%=P5.00D=Law=Time=Venus=5 May = Aphrodite>>L=N.
Stub=10,000=1,000=100%=10.0=Physicality=Tech.=10 Oct.=Uranus=P=1Ø.
Stubble=10,000=1,000=100%=10.0=Physicality=Tech.=10 Oct.=Uranus=P=1Ø.
Stubborn=10,000=1,000=100%=10.0=Physicality=Tech.=10 Oct.=Uranus=P=1Ø.
Stubby=1,500=15%=P1.50D=1.5=Authority=Solar Crown=1 May = Maia.
Stucco=10,000=1,000=100%=10.0=Physicality=Tech.=10 Oct.=Uranus=P=1Ø.
Stuck=3,000=30%=P3.0D=3.0=Creativity=Stars=Muses=3 March = C=I>>GIL.
Stuck up=1,500=15%=P1.50D=1.5=Authority=Solar Crown=1 May = Maia.
Stud1=10,000=1,000=100%=10.0=Physicality=Tech.=10 Oct.=Uranus=P=1Ø.
Stud2=10,000=1,000=100%=10.0=Physicality=Tech.=10 Oct.=Uranus=P=1Ø.
Stud book=4,000=40%=P4.0D=Govt.=Creatocracy=4 April=Mercury=Hermes=G=A4.

Student=8,000=80%=P8.0D=Economy=Currency=8 Aug.=Zeus>>E=v.
Result shows that the almighty is studious in His divine nature and loves knowledge.
Makupedia Student Development Program. Digit subjects eg Biology Maths Geography
WDSD. This applies to all aspects of education. Study using codes and dimensions. Box
1.0 - 1.9. Fix subjects codes. Guidelines cover evaluation assessments and teaching students.

Studied=1,500=15%=P1.50D=1.5=Authority=Solar Crown=1 May = Maia.
Studio=10,000=1,000=100%=10.0=Physicality=Tech.=10 Oct.=Uranus=P=1Ø.
Studio apartment=6,500=7,000=70%=P7.0D=7.0=Lang=Assets=Mars=7 July=Pleiades.
Studious=3,000=30%=P3.0D=3.0=Creativity=Stars=Muses=3 March = C=I>>GIL.

Study=10,000=1,000=100%=10.0=Physicality=Tech.=10 Oct.=Uranus=P=1Ø.
Peter Matthews-Akukalia, Castle Makupedia invented the study Faculty of Creative
and Psycho - Social Sciences, also known as the Creative Sciences. He is the World's 1st
Creative Scientist for his book > The Oracle: Principles of Creative Sciences.

Stuff=10,000=1,000=100%=10.0=Physicality=Tech.=10 Oct.=Uranus=P=1Ø.
Stuffing=8,000=80%=P8.0D=Economy=Currency=8 Aug.=Zeus>>E=v.
Stuffy=4,000=40%=P4.0D=Govt.=Creatocracy=4 April=Mercury=Hermes=G=A4.
Stultify=8,000=80%=P8.0D=Economy=Currency=8 Aug.=Zeus>>E=v.
Stumble=10,000=1,000=100%=10.0=Physicality=Tech.=10 Oct.=Uranus=P=1Ø.
Stumbling block=2,000=20%=P2.00D=2.0=Nature=Matter=Moon=2 Feb.=Cupid=N=C+_
Stump=10,000=1,000=100%=10.0=Physicality=Tech.=10 Oct.=Uranus=P=1Ø.
Stun=8,500=9,000=90%=P9.00D=9.0=Abstraction=Gods=Saturn=9Sept.>>A=Ø.
Stung=3,000=30%=P3.0D=3.0=Creativity=Stars=Muses=3 March = C=I>>GIL.
Stunk=3,000=30%=P3.0D=3.0=Creativity=Stars=Muses=3 March = C=I>>GIL.
Stunning=2,000=20%=P2.00D=2.0=Nature=Matter=Moon=2 Feb.=Cupid=N=C+_
Stunt1=5,000=50%=P5.00D=Law=Time=Venus=5 May = Aphrodite>>L=N.
Stunt2=6,500=7,000=70%=P7.0D=7.0=Language=Assets=Mars=7 July=Pleiades.
Stupefy=7,500=8,000=80%=P8.0D=Economy=Currency=8 Aug.=Zeus>>E=v.

Stupendous=7,500=8,000=80%=P8.0D=Economy=Currency=8 Aug.=Zeus>>E=v.

Stupid=9,000=90%=P9.00D=9.0=Abstraction=Gods=Saturn=9Sept.>>A=Ø.

Stupor=7,500=8,000=80%=P8.0D=Economy=Currency=8 Aug.=Zeus>>E=v.

Sturdy=5,000=50%=P5.00D=Law=Time=Venus=5 May = Aphrodite>>L=N.

Sturgeon=7,500=8,000=80%=P8.0D=Economy=Currency=8 Aug.=Zeus>>E=v.

Stutter=9,000=90%=P9.00D=9.0=Abstraction=Gods=Saturn=9Sept.>>A=Ø.

Stuttgart=5,500=5.5=80%=P5.50=Earth-Midway=5 May = Gaia.

Stuyvesant Peter.=3,000=30%=P3.0D=3.0=Creativity=Stars=Muses=3 March = C=I>>GIL.

Sty1=4,500=5,000=50%=P5.00D=Law=Time=Venus=5 May = Aphrodite>>L=N.

Sty2=6,000=60%=P6.0D=Man=Earth=Royalty=6 June=Gaia=Maia>>M=M2.

Style=10,000=1,000=100%=10.0=Physicality=Tech.=10 Oct.=Uranus=P=1Ø.

Stylish=4,500=5,000=50%=P5.00D=Law=Time=Venus=5 May = Aphrodite>>L=N.

Stylist=8,000=80%=P8.0D=Economy=Currency=8 Aug.=Zeus>>E=v.

Stylize=4,500=5,000=50%=P5.00D=Law=Time=Venus=5 May = Aphrodite>>L=N.

Stylus=7,000=70%=P7.0D=7.0=Language=Assets=Mars=7 July=Pleiades.

Stymie=2,000=20%=P2.00D=2.0=Nature=Matter=Moon=2 Feb.=Cupid=N=C+_

Styptic=5,000=50%=P5.00D=Law=Time=Venus=5 May = Aphrodite>>L=N.

Styrofoam=4,000=40%=P4.0D=Govt.=Creatocracy=4 April=Mercury=Hermes=G=A4.

Suave=4,000=40%=P4.0D=Govt.=Creatocracy=4 April=Mercury=Hermes=G=A4.

Sub1=4,000=40%=P4.0D=Govt.=Creatocracy=4 April=Mercury=Hermes=G=A4.

Sub2=4,500=5,000=50%=P5.00D=Law=Time=Venus=5 May = Aphrodite>>L=N.

Sub-=8,000=80%=P8.0D=Economy=Currency=8 Aug.=Zeus>>E=v.

Subaltern=8,000=80%=P8.0D=Economy=Currency=8 Aug.=Zeus>>E=v.

Subatomic=6,500=7,000=70%=P7.0D=7.0=Language=Assets=Mars=7 July=Pleiades.

Subatomic particles=5,000=50%=P5.00D=Law=Time=Venus=5 May = Aphrodite>>L=N.

Subcommittee=4,500=5,000=50%=P5.00D=Law=Time=Venus=5 May = Aphrodite>>L=N.

Subcompact=3,000=30%=P3.0D=3.0=Creativity=Stars=Muses=3 March = C=I>>GIL.

Subconscious=10,000=1,000=100%=10.0=Physicality=Tech.=10 Oct.=Uranus=P=1Ø.

Subcontinent=10,000=1,000=100%=10.0=Physicality=Tech.=10 Oct.=Uranus=P=1Ø.

Subcontract=6,000=60%=P6.0D=Man=Earth=Royalty=6 June=Gaia=Maia>>M=M2.

Subculture=4,000=40%=P4.0D=Govt.=Creatocracy=4 April=Mercury=Hermes=G=A4.

Subcutaneous=2,000=20%=P2.00D=2.0=Nature=Matter=Moon=2 Feb.=Cupid=N=C+_

Subdivide=10,000=1,000=100%=10.0=Physicality=Tech.=10 Oct.=Uranus=P=1Ø.

Subdue=10,000=1,000=100%=10.0=Physicality=Tech.=10 Oct.=Uranus=P=1Ø.

Subhead=7,500=8,000=80%=P8.0D=Economy=Currency=8 Aug.=Zeus>>E=v.

Subj.=1,000=100%=10.0=1.0=Mind=Sun=1 January=Helios >> M=E4.

Subject=10,000=1,000=100%=10.0=Physicality=Tech.=10 Oct.=Uranus=P=1Ø.

Subjective=10,000=1,000=100%=10.0=Physicality=Tech.=10 Oct.=Uranus=P=1Ø.

The Mind Assessment & Psycho-Surgery (MAPS) Tests is designed to discover the origin and innate nature of a person using both objective and subjective means.

Sub join=7,500=8,000=80%=P8.0D=Economy=Currency=8 Aug.=Zeus>>E=v.

Subjugate=10,000=1,000=100%=10.0=Physicality=Tech.=10 Oct.=Uranus=P=1Ø.

Subjunctive=11,000=11%=P1.10D=1.1=Idea=Brainchild=Inv.=11 Nov.=SC=Athena>>I=MT.

Sublease=3,500=4,000=40%=P4.0D=Govt.=Creatocracy=4 April=Hermes=G=A4.

Sublet=8,000=80%=P8.0D=Economy=Currency=8 Aug.=Zeus>>E=v.

Sublimate=10,000=1,000=100%=10.0=Physicality=Tech.=10 Oct.=Uranus=P=1Ø.

Sublime=10,000=1,000=100%=10.0=Physicality=Tech.=10 Oct.=Uranus=P=1Ø.

Subliminal=7,000=70%=P7.0D=7.0=Language=Assets=Mars=7 July=Pleiades.

Sun lunary=5,000=50%=P5.00D=Law=Time=Venus=5 May = Aphrodite>>L=N.

Sub machine gun=6,000=60%=P6.0D=Man=Earth=Royalty=6 June=Gaia=Maia>>M=M2.

Submarine=10,000=1,000=100%=10.0=Physicality=Tech.=10 Oct.=Uranus=P=1Ø.

Submerge=10,000=1,000=100%=10.0=Physicality=Tech.=10 Oct.=Uranus=P=1Ø.

Submerse=10,000=1,000=100%=10.0=Physicality=Tech.=10 Oct.=Uranus=P=1Ø.

Submersible=4,000=40%=P4.0D=Govt.=Creatocracy=4 April=Mercury=Hermes=G=A4.

Submicroscopic=4,000=40%=P4.0D=Govt.=Creatocracy=4 April=Hermes=G=A4.

Submit=10,000=1,000=100%=10.0=Physicality=Tech.=10 Oct.=Uranus=P=1Ø.

Subnormal=3,000=30%=P3.0D=3.0=Creativity=Stars=Muses=3 March = C=I>>GIL.

Suborbital=4,500=5,000=50%=P5.00D=Law=Time=Venus=5 May = Aphrodite>>L=N.

Subordinate=10,000=1,000=100%=10.0=Physicality=Tech.=10 Oct.=Uranus=P=1Ø.

Suborn=5,000=50%=P5.00D=Law=Time=Venus=5 May = Aphrodite>>L=N.

Subplot=6,000=60%=P6.0D=Man=Earth=Royalty=6 June=Gaia=Maia>>M=M2.

Subpoena=10,000=1,000=100%=10.0=Physicality=Tech.=10 Oct.=Uranus=P=1Ø.

Sub rosa=4,500=5,000=50%=P5.00D=Law=Time=Venus=5 May = Aphrodite>>L=N.

Subroutine=6,500=7,000=70%=P7.0D=7.0=Language=Assets=Mars=7 July=Pleiades.

Sub-Saharan=4,500=5,000=50%=P5.00D=Law=Time=Venus=5 May = Aphrodite>>L=N.

Subscribe=10,000=1,000=100%=10.0=Physicality=Tech.=10 Oct.=Uranus=P=1Ø.

Subscript=10,000=1,000=100%=10.0=Physicality=Tech.=10 Oct.=Uranus=P=1Ø.

Subscription=10,000=1,000=100%=10.0=Physicality=Tech.=10 Oct.=Uranus=P=1Ø.

Subsequent=5,500=5.5=80%=P5.50=Earth-Midway=5 May = Gaia.

Subservient=3,500=4,000=40%=P4.0D=Govt.=Creatocracy=4 April=Hermes=G=A4.

Subset=2,000=20%=P2.00D=2.0=Nature=Matter=Moon=2 Feb.=Cupid=N=C+_

Subside=10,000=1,000=100%=10.0=Physicality=Tech.=10 Oct.=Uranus=P=1Ø.

Subsidiary=10,000=1,000=100%=10.0=Physicality=Tech.=10 Oct.=Uranus=P=1Ø.

Subsidize=3,500=4,000=40%=P4.0D=Govt.=Creatocracy=4 April=Hermes=G=A4.

Subsidy=10,000=1,000=100%=10.0=Physicality=Tech.=10 Oct.=Uranus=P=1Ø.

Subsist=10,000=1,000=100%=10.0=Physicality=Tech.=10 Oct.=Uranus=P=1Ø.

Subsistence=5,500=5.5=80%=P5.50=Earth-Midway=5 May = Gaia.

Subsoil=3,000=30%=P3.0D=3.0=Creativity=Stars=Muses=3 March = C=I>>GIL.

Subsonic=6,000=60%=P6.0D=Man=Earth=Royalty=6 June=Gaia=Maia>>M=M2.

Substance=10,000=1,000=100%=10.0=Physicality=Tech.=10 Oct.=Uranus=P=1Ø.

Substance abuse=4,500=5,000=50%=P5.00D=Law=Time=Venus=5 May =Odite>>L=N.

Substandard=3,000=30%=P3.0D=3.0=Creativity=Stars=Muses=3 March = C=I>>GIL.

Substantial=10,000=1,000=100%=10.0=Physicality=Tech.=10 Oct.=Uranus=P=1Ø.

Substantiate=3,000=30%=P3.0D=3.0=Creativity=Stars=Muses=3 March = C=I>>GIL.

Substantive=7,000=70%=P7.0D=7.0=Language=Assets=Mars=7 July=Pleiades.

Substation=3,500=4,000=40%=P4.0D=Govt.=Creatocracy=4 April=Hermes=G=A4.

Substitute=10,000=1,000=100%=10.0=Physicality=Tech.=10 Oct.=Uranus=P=1Ø.

Substrate=2,000=20%=P2.00D=2.0=Nature=Matter=Moon=2 Feb.=Cupid=N=C+_
Substratum=3,000=30%=P3.0D=3.0=Creativity=Stars=Muses=3 March = C=I>>GIL.
Substructure=3,500=4,000=40%=P4.0D=Govt.=Creatocracy=4 April=Hermes=G=A4.
Subsume=6,000=60%=P6.0D=Man=Earth=Royalty=6 June=Gaia=Maia>>M=M2.
Sub tend=8,000=80%=P8.0D=Economy=Currency=8 Aug.=Zeus>>E=v.
Subterfuge=4,500=5,000=50%=P5.00D=Law=Time=Venus=5 May = Aphrodite>>L=N.
Subterranean=9,500=10,000=1,000=100%=10.0=Phy=Tech.=10 Oct.=Uranus=P=1Ø.
Subtext=4,500=5,000=50%=P5.00D=Law=Time=Venus=5 May = Aphrodite>>L=N.
Subtitle=10,000=1,000=100%=10.0=Physicality=Tech.=10 Oct.=Uranus=P=1Ø.
Subtle=10,000=1,000=100%=10.0=Physicality=Tech.=10 Oct.=Uranus=P=1Ø.
Subtotal=3,500=4,000=40%=P4.0D=Govt.=Creatocracy=4 April=Hermes=G=A4.
Subtract=6,500=7,000=70%=P7.0D=7.0=Language=Assets=Mars=7 July=Pleiades.
Subtrahend=5,000=50%=P5.00D=Law=Time=Venus=5 May = Aphrodite>>L=N.
Subtropical=4,500=5,000=50%=P5.00D=Law=Time=Venus=5 May = Aphrodite>>L=N.
Subtropics=1,000=100%=10.0=1.0=Mind=Sun=1 January=Helios >> M=E4.
Suburb=8,000=80%=P8.0D=Economy=Currency=8 Aug.=Zeus>>E=v.
Suburbanite=3,000=30%=P3.0D=3.0=Creativity=Stars=Muses=3 March = C=I>>GIL.
Suburbia=2,000=20%=P2.00D=2.0=Nature=Matter=Moon=2 Feb.=Cupid=N=C+_
Subvention=8,000=80%=P8.0D=Economy=Currency=8 Aug.=Zeus>>E=v.
Subversive=8,000=80%=P8.0D=Economy=Currency=8 Aug.=Zeus>>E=v.
Subvert=8,500=9,000=90%=P9.00D=9.0=Abstraction=Gods=Saturn=9Sept.>>A=Ø.
Subway=3,500=4,000=40%=P4.0D=Govt.=Creatocracy=4 April=Mercury=Hermes=G=A4.
Succeed=9,000=90%=P9.00D=9.0=Abstraction=Gods=Saturn=9Sept.>>A=Ø.
Success=8,000=80%=P8.0D=Economy=Currency=8 Aug.=Zeus>>E=v.
Succession=10,000=1,000=100%=10.0=Physicality=Tech.=10 Oct.=Uranus=P=1Ø.
Successive=2,500=3,000=30%=P3.0D=3.0=Cr=Stars=Muses=3 March = C=I>>GIL.
Successor=3,000=30%=P3.0D=3.0=Creativity=Stars=Muses=3 March = C=I>>GIL.
Succinct=7,500=8,000=80%=P8.0D=Economy=Currency=8 Aug.=Zeus>>E=v.
Succor=6,000=60%=P6.0D=Man=Earth=Royalty=6 June=Gaia=Maia>>M=M2.
Succotash=7,500=8,000=80%=P8.0D=Economy=Currency=8 Aug.=Zeus>>E=v.
Succoth=5,000=50%=P5.00D=Law=Time=Venus=5 May = Aphrodite>>L=N.

Succubus=7,500=8,000=80%=P8.0D=Economy=Currency=8 Aug.=Zeus>>E=v.
An evil spirit supposed to have sexual intercourse with a sleeping man. <Lat.succuba, paramour.] Evil>>-1. Spirit>>9.0. Sexual intercourse >> 5.0. Sleeping >> 3.0. Man >> 6.0
-1.0*9.0x=px=8+-9.0=-1x=px=-73=-7.3
5.0*3.0x=px=8+15=23x=px=143=1.4[6.0]
-7.3*1.4x=px=-5.9+-10.22=-16.12x=px=44.178=4.4
4.4*-7.3x=px=-2.9+-32.12=-35.02x=px=58.128=6.0
6.0*6.0x=px=12+36=48x=px=480=500=50=5.0 >> Law >> Time >> Venus >> Odite.
Succubus is an evil spirit sent from Odite as a punishment or curse to a particular man. Greek myths teaches that Aphrodite (Odite) turned women to prostitutes when they insulted her against the order that Zeus had given for man never to revoke the Gods. See Exodus 22:28; Exodus 23:20-25.

Succulent=10,000=1,000=100%=10.0=Physicality=Tech.=10 Oct.=Uranus=P=1Ø.
Succumb=6,500=7,000=70%=P7.0D=7.0=Language=Assets=Mars=7 July=Pleiades.
Such=10,000=1,000=100%=10.0=Physicality=Tech.=10 Oct.=Uranus=P=1Ø.
Suchlike=4,000=40%=P4.0D=Govt.=Creatocracy=4 April=Mercury=Hermes=G=A4.
Süchow=1,000=100%=10.0=1.0=Mind=Sun=1 January=Helios >> M=E4.
Suck=10,000=1,000=100%=10.0=Physicality=Tech.=10 Oct.=Uranus=P=1Ø.
Sucker=10,000=1,000=100%=10.0=Physicality=Tech.=10 Oct.=Uranus=P=1Ø.
Suckle=7,000=70%=P7.0D=7.0=Language=Assets=Mars=7 July=Pleiades.
Suckling=3,000=30%=P3.0D=3.0=Creativity=Stars=Muses=3 March = C=I>>GIL.

Sucre=3,000=30%=P3.0D=3.0=Creativity=Stars=Muses=3 March = C=I>>GIL.
Am. Sp. Currency metric weight > 3,000 = 3/10=0.3 > 30:1. See Naira. Dollar.

Sucrose=7,000=70%=P7.0D=7.0=Language=Assets=Mars=7 July=Pleiades.
Suction=10,000=1,000=100%=10.0=Physicality=Tech.=10 Oct.=Uranus=P=1Ø.
Sudan=10,000=1,000=100%=10.0=Physicality=Tech.=10 Oct.=Uranus=P=1Ø.
Sudden=5,000=50%=P5.00D=Law=Time=Venus=5 May = Aphrodite>>L=N.
Sudeten=7,500=8,000=80%=P8.0D=Economy=Currency=8 Aug.=Zeus>>E=v.
Sudetenland=5,500=5.5=80%=P5.50=Earth-Midway=5 May = Gaia.
Suds=4,000=40%=P4.0D=Govt.=Creatocracy=4 April=Mercury=Hermes=G=A4.
Sue=10,000=1,000=100%=10.0=Physicality=Tech.=10 Oct.=Uranus=P=1Ø.
Suede=7,000=70%=P7.0D=7.0=Language=Assets=Mars=7 July=Pleiades.
Suet=8,500=9,000=90%=P9.00D=9.0=Abstraction=Gods=Saturn=9Sept.>>A=Ø.
Suetonius=4,500=5,000=50%=P5.00D=Law=Time=Venus=5 May = Aphrodite>>L=N.
Suez=10,000=1,000=100%=10.0=Physicality=Tech.=10 Oct.=Uranus=P=1Ø.
Suez,Isthmus of.=4,500=5,000=50%=P5.00D=Law=Time=Venus=5 May=Odite>>L=N.
Suez Canal.=8,500=9,000=90%=P9.00D=9.0=Abstraction=Gods=Saturn=9Sept.>>A=Ø.
Suff.=1,500=15%=P1.50D=1.5=Authority=Solar Crown=1 May = Maia.
Suffer=10,000=1,000=100%=10.0=Physicality=Tech.=10 Oct.=Uranus=P=1Ø.
Sufferance=6,000=60%=P6.0D=Man=Earth=Royalty=6 June=Gaia=Maia>>M=M2.
Suffering=3,000=30%=P3.0D=3.0=Creativity=Stars=Muses=3 March = C=I>>GIL.
Suffice=5,000=50%=P5.00D=Law=Time=Venus=5 May = Aphrodite>>L=N.
Sufficient=3,000=30%=P3.0D=3.0=Creativity=Stars=Muses=3 March = C=I>>GIL.
Suffix=10,000=1,000=100%=10.0=Physicality=Tech.=10 Oct.=Uranus=P=1Ø.
Suffocate=6,000=60%=P6.0D=Man=Earth=Royalty=6 June=Gaia=Maia>>M=M2.
Suffrage=5,000=50%=P5.00D=Law=Time=Venus=5 May = Aphrodite>>L=N.
Suffragette=4,000=40%=P4.0D=Govt.=Creatocracy=4 April=Mercury=Hermes=G=A4.
Suffragist=4,500=5,000=50%=P5.00D=Law=Time=Venus=5 May = Aphrodite>>L=N.
Suffuse=8,500=9,000=90%=P9.00D=9.0=Abstraction=Gods=Saturn=9Sept.>>A=Ø.
Sufi=2,000=20%=P2.00D=2.0=Nature=Matter=Moon=2 Feb.=Cupid=N=C+_
Sugar=10,000=1,000=100%=10.0=Physicality=Tech.=10 Oct.=Uranus=P=1Ø.
Sugar beet=5,500=5.5=80%=P5.50=Earth-Midway=5 May = Gaia.
Sugar cane=5,000=50%=P5.00D=Law=Time=Venus=5 May = Aphrodite>>L=N.
Sugar coat=5,000=50%=P5.00D=Law=Time=Venus=5 May = Aphrodite>>L=N.

Sugarless=5,000=50%=P5.00D=Law=Time=Venus=5 May = Aphrodite>>L=N.
Sugar maple=8,000=80%=P8.0D=Economy=Currency=8 Aug.=Zeus>>E=v.
Sugar plum=2,500=3,000=30%=P3.0D=3.0=Cr=Stars=Muses=3 March = C=I>>GIL.
Sugary=4,000=40%=P4.0D=Govt.=Creatocracy=4 April=Mercury=Hermes=G=A4.
Suggest=9,000=90%=P9.00D=9.0=Abstraction=Gods=Saturn=9Sept.>>A=Ø.
Suggestible=2,000=20%=P2.00D=2.0=Nature=Matter=Moon=2 Feb.=Cupid=N=C+_
Suggestion=5,000=50%=P5.00D=Law=Time=Venus=5 May = Aphrodite>>L=N.
Suggestive=5,000=50%=P5.00D=Law=Time=Venus=5 May = Aphrodite>>L=N.
Suharto=3,500=4,000=40%=P4.0D=Govt.=Creatocracy=4April=Mercury=Hermes=G=A4.
Suicide=9,000=90%=P9.00D=9.0=Abstraction=Gods=Saturn=9Sept.>>A=Ø.
Suigeneris=4,500=5,000=50%=P5.00D=Law=Time=Venus=5 May = Aphrodite>>L=N.
Suit=10,000=1,000=100%=10.0=Physicality=Tech.=10 Oct.=Uranus=P=1Ø.
Suitable=3,000=30%=P3.0D=3.0=Creativity=Stars=Muses=3 March = C=I>>GIL.
Suitcase=4,000=40%=P4.0D=Govt.=Creatocracy=4 April=Mercury=Hermes=G=A4.
Suite=10,000=1,000=100%=10.0=Physicality=Tech.=10 Oct.=Uranus=P=1Ø.
Suitor=3,500=4,000=40%=P4.0D=Govt.=Creatocracy=4 April=Mercury=Hermes=G=A4.
Sukarno=2,000=20%=P2.00D=2.0=Nature=Matter=Moon=2 Feb.=Cupid=N=C+_
Sukiyaki=6,500=7,000=70%=P7.0D=7.0=Language=Assets=Mars=7 July=Pleiades.
Sukkoth=1,500=15%=P1.50D=1.5=Authority=Solar Crown=1 May = Maia.
Sulawesi=1,000=100%=10.0=1.0=Mind=Sun=1 January=Helios >> M=E4.
Suleiman I=4,500=5,000=50%=P5.00D=Law=Time=Venus=5 May = Aphrodite>>L=N.

Sulfa drug=8,000=80%=P8.0D=Economy=Currency=8 Aug.=Zeus>>E=v.
Proverbs 8:27 "when he prepared the heavens,…" Zeus-Jehovah-Allah used chemicals to create the heavens and earth through culturing them in a laboratory process. The sulfa drug is any of a group of synthetic organic compounds used to inhibit bacterial growth and activity. [<Sulfa-(nilamide).]. All chemicals indicated 8.0 were definite materials of Zeus.

Sulfanilamide=6,500=7,000=70%=P7.0D=7.0=Language=Assets=Mars=7 July=Pleiades.
Sulfate=6,000=60%=P6.0D=Man=Earth=Royalty=6 June=Gaia=Maia>>M=M2.
Sulfide=4,500=5,000=50%=P5.00D=Law=Time=Venus=5 May = Aphrodite>>L=N.
Sulfur=10,000=1,000=100%=10.0=Physicality=Tech.=10 Oct.=Uranus=P=1Ø.
Sulfur dioxide=7,500=8,000=80%=P8.0D=Economy=Currency=8 Aug.=Zeus>>E=v.
Sulfuric=2,000=20%=P2.00D=2.0=Nature=Matter=Moon=2 Feb.=Cupid=N=C+_
Sulfuric acid=8,000=80%=P8.0D=Economy=Currency=8 Aug.=Zeus>>E=v.
Sulfurous=5,500=5.5=80%=P5.50=Earth-Midway=5 May = Gaia.
Sulk=5,500=5.5=80%=P5.50=Earth-Midway=5 May = Gaia.
Sulky1=3,000=30%=P3.0D=3.0=Creativity=Stars=Muses=3 March = C=I>>GIL.
Sulky2=7,500=8,000=80%=P8.0D=Economy=Currency=8 Aug.=Zeus>>E=v.
Sulla Lucius.=5,500=5.5=80%=P5.50=Earth-Midway=5 May = Gaia.
Sullen=6,500=7,000=70%=P7.0D=7.0=Language=Assets=Mars=7 July=Pleiades.
Sullivan Arthur=3,000=30%=P3.0D=3.0=Creativity=Stars=Muses=3 March = C=I>>GIL.
Sullivan Louis=2,500=3,000=30%=P3.0D=3.0=Cr=Stars=Muses=3 March = C=I>>GIL.
Sully=5,500=5.5=80%=P5.50=Earth-Midway=5 May = Gaia.

Sulphur=1,500=15%=P1.50D=1.5=Authority=Solar Crown=1 May = Maia.
Sultan=6,000=60%=P6.0D=Man=Earth=Royalty=6 June=Gaia=Maia>>M=M2.
Sultana=6,500=7,000=70%=P7.0D=7.0=Language=Assets=Mars=7 July=Pleiades.
Sultanate=6,000=60%=P6.0D=Man=Earth=Royalty=6 June=Gaia=Maia>>M=M2.
Sultry=4,500=5,000=50%=P5.00D=Law=Time=Venus=5 May = Aphrodite>>L=N.
Sula Sea=6,000=60%=P6.0D=Man=Earth=Royalty=6 June=Gaia=Maia>>M=M2.

Sum=10,000=1,000=100%=10.0=Physicality=Tech.=10 Oct.=Uranus=P=1Ø.
The sum or plus(+) sign is one of the elements used in the 10,000 synchronization and crystallization process of Makumatics exclusive to the Creative & Psycho-Social Sciences.

Sumac=10,000=1,000=100%=10.0=Physicality=Tech.=10 Oct.=Uranus=P=1Ø.
Sumatra=6,000=60%=P6.0D=Man=Earth=Royalty=6 June=Gaia=Maia>>M=M2.
Sumer=5,000=50%=P5.00D=Law=Time=Venus=5 May = Aphrodite>>L=N.
Summary=10,000=1,000=100%=10.0=Physicality=Tech.=10 Oct.=Uranus=P=1Ø.
Summation=7,000=70%=P7.0D=7.0=Language=Assets=Mars=7 July=Pleiades.
Summer=7,500=8,000=80%=P8.0D=Economy=Currency=8 Aug.=Zeus>>E=v.
Summerhouse=4,000=40%=P4.0D=Govt.=Creatocracy=4 April=Mercury=Hermes=G=A4.
Summertime=1,500=15%=P1.50D=1.5=Authority=Solar Crown=1 May = Maia.
Summit=7,500=8,000=80%=P8.0D=Economy=Currency=8 Aug.=Zeus>>E=v.
Summit conference=6,500=7,000=70%=P7.0D=7.0=Lang=Assets=Mars=7 July=Pleiades.
Summon=10,000=1,000=100%=10.0=Physicality=Tech.=10 Oct.=Uranus=P=1Ø.
Summons=10,000=1,000=100%=10.0=Physicality=Tech.=10 Oct.=Uranus=P=1Ø.
Sumner Charles.=2,000=20%=P2.00D=2.0=Nature=Matter=Moon=2 Feb.=Cupid=N=C+_
Sumo=3,500=4,000=40%=P4.0D=Govt.=Creatocracy=4 April=Mercury=Hermes=G=A4.
Sump=5,500=5.5=80%=P5.50=Earth-Midway=5 May = Gaia.
Sumptuous=6,000=60%=P6.0D=Man=Earth=Royalty=6 June=Gaia=Maia>>M=M2.

Sun=10,000=1,000=100%=10.0=Physicality=Tech.=10 Oct.=Uranus=P=1Ø.
The physical equivalent of the Mind and the Mind its abstract equivalent. The first > 1.0ø dimension of the Universes (the Creatocracy) in the Creative Sciences, Makupedia.

Sun.=500=5%=P5.00D=5.0=Law=Time=Venus=5 May=Aphrodite>>L=N.
Astronomy assumes the age of the sun to be about 5,000years and will still be here for about 5000 million years. Peter Matthews-Akukalia, Castle Makupedia has the Solar mean time from which he measured the Standard Time in the Maks. See Standard Time.

Sun baked=4,000=40%=P4.0D=Govt.=Creatocracy=4 April=Mercury=Hermes=G=A4.
Sunbathe=3,000=30%=P3.0D=3.0=Creativity=Stars=Muses=3 March = C=I>>GIL.
Sunbeam=2,000=20%=P2.00D=2.0=Nature=Matter=Moon=2 Feb.=Cupid=N=C+_
Sunbelt=2,500=3,000=30%=P3.0D=3.0=Creativity=Stars=Muses=3 March = C=I>>GIL.
Sunblock=5,500=5.5=80%=P5.50=Earth-Midway=5 May = Gaia.
Sun bonnet=6,500=7,000=70%=P7.0D=7.0=Language=Assets=Mars=7 July=Pleiades.
Sunburn=6,000=60%=P6.0D=Man=Earth=Royalty=6 June=Gaia=Maia>>M=M2.

Sunburst=4,500=5,000=50%=P5.00D=Law=Time=Venus=5 May = Aphrodite>>L=N.
Sundae=8,000=80%=P8.0D=Economy=Currency=8 Aug.=Zeus>>E=v.
Sunda Islands=8,000=80%=P8.0D=Economy=Currency=8 Aug.=Zeus>>E=v.
Sunday=5,500=5.5=80%=P5.50=Earth-Midway=5 May = Gaia.
Sunder=4,000=40%=P4.0D=Govt.=Creatocracy=4 April=Mercury=Hermes=G=A4.
Sunderland=7,000=70%=P7.0D=7.0=Language=Assets=Mars=7 July=Pleiades.
Sundial=9,500=10,000=1,000=100%=10.0=Physicality=Tech.=10 Oct.=Uranus=P=1Ø.
Sundown=500=5%=P5.00D=5.0=Law=Time=Venus=5 May=Aphrodite>>L=N.
Sundries=2,000=20%=P2.00D=2.0=Nature=Matter=Moon=2 Feb.=Cupid=N=C+_
Sundry=2,500=3,000=30%=P3.0D=3.0=Creativity=Stars=Muses=3 March = C=I>>GIL.
Sunfish=9,000=90%=P9.00D=9.0=Abstraction=Gods=Saturn=9Sept.>>A=Ø.
Sunflower=8,500=9,000=90%=P9.00D=9.0=Abstraction=Gods=Saturn=9Sept.>>A=Ø.
Sung=4,000=40%=P4.0D=Govt.=Creatocracy=4 April=Mercury=Hermes=G=A4.
Sunglasses=5,500=5.5=80%=P5.50=Earth-Midway=5 May = Gaia.
Sunk=4,000=40%=P4.0D=Govt.=Creatocracy=4 April=Mercury=Hermes=G=A4.
Sunken=7,000=70%=P7.0D=7.0=Language=Assets=Mars=7 July=Pleiades.
Sun lamp=6,000=60%=P6.0D=Man=Earth=Royalty=6 June=Gaia=Maia>>M=M2.
Sunlight=2,000=20%=P2.00D=2.0=Nature=Matter=Moon=2 Feb.=Cupid=N=C+_
Sunlit=2,000=20%=P2.00D=2.0=Nature=Matter=Moon=2 Feb.=Cupid=N=C+_
Sunna=10,000=1,000=100%=10.0=Physicality=Tech.=10 Oct.=Uranus=P=1Ø.
Sunni=4,000=40%=P4.0D=Govt.=Creatocracy=4 April=Mercury=Hermes=G=A4.
Sunny=4,000=40%=P4.0D=Govt.=Creatocracy=4 April=Mercury=Hermes=G=A4.
Sunnyvale=5,000=50%=P5.00D=Law=Time=Venus=5 May = Aphrodite>>L=N.
Sunrise=3,500=4,000=40%=P4.0D=Govt.=Creatocracy=4 April=Mercury=Hermes=G=A4.
Sunroof=6,500=7,000=70%=P7.0D=7.0=Language=Assets=Mars=7 July=Pleiades.
Sunscreen=6,000=60%=P6.0D=Man=Earth=Royalty=6 June=Gaia=Maia>>M=M2.
Sunset=3,500=4,000=40%=P4.0D=Govt.=Creatocracy=4 April=Mercury=Hermes=G=A4.
Sunshade=5,000=50%=P5.00D=Law=Time=Venus=5 May = Aphrodite>>L=N.
Sunshine=4,500=5,000=50%=P5.00D=Law=Time=Venus=5 May = Aphrodite>>L=N.
Sunspot=6,500=7,000=70%=P7.0D=7.0=Language=Assets=Mars=7 July=Pleiades.
Sunstroke=4,000=40%=P4.0D=Govt.=Creatocracy=4 April=Mercury=Hermes=G=A4.
Suntan=5,000=50%=P5.00D=Law=Time=Venus=5 May = Aphrodite>>L=N.
Sunup=2,000=20%=P2.00D=2.0=Nature=Matter=Moon=2 Feb.=Cupid=N=C+_
Sun Yatsen=2,000=20%=P2.00D=2.0=Nature=Matter=Moon=2 Feb.=Cupid=N=C+_
Sup=3,500=4,000=40%=P4.0D=Govt.=Creatocracy=4 April=Mercury=Hermes=G=A4.
Sup.=1,500=15%=P1.50D=1.5=Authority=Solar Crown=1 May = Maia.

Super=8,000=80%=P8.0D=Economy=Currency=8 Aug.=Zeus>>E=v.
Zeus-Jehovah-Allah>>ZeJeAl is the Super GOD. THE GREATEST OF THE GREATESTS.

Super-=10,000=1,000=100%=10.0=Physicality=Tech.=10 Oct.=Uranus=P=1Ø.
Super able=5,500=5.5=80%=P5.50=Earth-Midway=5 May = Gaia.
Superabundant=1,500=15%=P1.50D=1.5=Authority=Solar Crown=1 May = Maia.
Superannuated=10,000=1,000=100%=10.0=Physicality=Tech.=10 Oct.=Uranus=P=1Ø.

Superb=4,500=5,000=50%=P5.00D=Law=Time=Venus=5 May = Aphrodite>>L=N.
Super cargo=9,000=90%=P9.00D=9.0=Abstraction=Gods=Saturn=9Sept.>>A=Ø.
Supercharge=4,500=5,000=50%=P5.00D=Law=Time=Venus=5 May = Aphrodite>>L=N.
Supercharger=9,000=90%=P9.00D=9.0=Abstraction=Gods=Saturn=9Sept.>>A=Ø.
Supercilious=10,000=1,000=100%=10.0=Physicality=Tech.=10 Oct.=Uranus=P=1Ø.
Supercollider=2,500=3,000=30%=P3.0D=3.0=Cr=Stars=Muses=3 March = C=I>>GIL.
Superconductivity=9,500=10,000=1,000=100%=10.0=Phy=Tech.=10 Oct.=Uranus=P=1Ø.
Supercool=5,500=5.5=80%=P5.50=Earth-Midway=5 May = Gaia.
Superego=7,500=8,000=80%=P8.0D=Economy=Currency=8 Aug.=Zeus>>E=v.
Supererogatory=5,000=50%=P5.00D=Law=Time=Venus=5 May = Aphrodite>>L=N.
Superficial=10,000=1,000=100%=10.0=Physicality=Tech.=10 Oct.=Uranus=P=1Ø.
Superfine=5,000=50%=P5.00D=Law=Time=Venus=5 May = Aphrodite>>L=N.
Superfluity=5,500=5.5=80%=P5.50=Earth-Midway=5 May = Gaia.
Superfluous=10,000=1,000=100%=10.0=Physicality=Tech.=10 Oct.=Uranus=P=1Ø.
Super galaxy=3,000=30%=P3.0D=3.0=Creativity=Stars=Muses=3 March = C=I>>GIL.
Supergiant=6,000=60%=P6.0D=Man=Earth=Royalty=6 June=Gaia=Maia>>M=M2.
Superhero=9,500=10,000=1,000=100%=10.0=Physicality=Tech.=10 Oct.=Uranus=P=1Ø.
Super highway=3,500=4,000=40%=P4.0D=Govt.=Creatocracy=4 April=Hermes=G=A4.
Superhuman=5,500=5.5=80%=P5.50=Earth-Midway=5 May = Gaia.
Superimpose=4,500=5,000=50%=P5.00D=Law=Time=Venus=5 May = Aphrodite>>L=N.
Superintend=10,000=1,000=100%=10.0=Physicality=Tech.=10 Oct.=Uranus=P=1Ø.
Superior=10,000=1,000=100%=10.0=Physicality=Tech.=10 Oct.=Uranus=P=1Ø.
Superior Lake=6,500=7,000=70%=P7.0D=7.0=Language=Assets=Mars=7 July=Pleiades.
Superlative=10,000=1,000=100%=10.0=Physicality=Tech.=10 Oct.=Uranus=P=1Ø.
Superman=3,500=4,000=40%=P4.0D=Govt.=Creatocracy=4 April=Hermes=G=A4.
Supermarket=5,500=5.5=80%=P5.50=Earth-Midway=5 May = Gaia.
Supernal=5,500=5.5=80%=P5.50=Earth-Midway=5 May = Gaia.
Supernatural=6,500=7,000=70%=P7.0D=7.0=Language=Assets=Mars=7 July=Pleiades.
Supernova=8,000=80%=P8.0D=Economy=Currency=8 Aug.=Zeus>>E=v.
Supernumerary=10,000=1,000=100%=10.0=Physicality=Tech.=10 Oct.=Uranus=P=1Ø.
Superphosphate=7,500=8,000=80%=P8.0D=Economy=Currency=8 Aug.=Zeus>>E=v.
Superpower=6,500=7,000=70%=P7.0D=7.0=Language=Assets=Mars=7 July=Pleiades.
Supersaturate=10,000=1,000=100%=10.0=Physicality=Tech.=10 Oct.=Uranus=P=1Ø.
Superscribe=10,000=1,000=100%=10.0=Physicality=Tech.=10 Oct.=Uranus=P=1Ø.
Superscript=10,000=1,000=100%=10.0=Physicality=Tech.=10 Oct.=Uranus=P=1Ø.

Supersede=9,000=90%=P9.00D=9.0=Abstraction=Gods=Saturn=9Sept.>>A=Ø.
The Creatocracy or Council of Gods supersede all others. Exodus 22:28, 23:20-25.

Supersonic=6,000=60%=P6.0D=Man=Earth=Royalty=6 June=Gaia=Maia>>M=M2.
The spirit speed of a thing or steam is 1.0x10 raised to power (-6). Emotion is therefore the medium at which the contents of the heart can attain spirit speed to the cosmic. This is the essence of prayer. The depth of the emotion employed determines the speed of travel.

PETER K. MATTHEWS - AKUKALIA

Superstar=7,000=70%=P7.0D=7.0=Language=Assets=Mars=7 July=Pleiades.
Assets and measurements are the standards for determining superstars. Example is the time an athlete will break an old record to achieve a new one. Formula is Genius.

Superstition=10,000=1,000=100%=10.0=Physicality=Tech.=10 Oct.=Uranus=P=1Ø.
A superstition is known by its physical manifestation and can be mused on the 10th rule.

Superstructure=10,000=1,000=100%=10.0=Physicality=Tech.=10 Oct.=Uranus=P=1Ø.
Supertanker=4,500=5,000=50%=P5.00D=Law=Time=Venus=5 May = Aphrodite>>L=N.
Supervene=8,500=9,000=90%=P9.00D=9.0=Abstraction=Gods=Saturn=9Sept.>>A=Ø.
Supervise=10,000=1,000=100%=10.0=Physicality=Tech.=10 Oct.=Uranus=P=1Ø.
Supervision=5,000=50%=P5.00D=Law=Time=Venus=5 May = Aphrodite>>L=N.
Supine=7,500=8,000=80%=P8.0D=Economy=Currency=8 Aug.=Zeus>>E=v.
Supper=8,000=80%=P8.0D=Economy=Currency=8 Aug.=Zeus>>E=v.
Supplant=5,000=50%=P5.00D=Law=Time=Venus=5 May = Aphrodite>>L=N.
Supple=6,500=7,000=70%=P7.0D=7.0=Language=Assets=Mars=7 July=Pleiades.
Supplement=10,000=1,000=100%=10.0=Physicality=Tech.=10 Oct.=Uranus=P=1Ø.
Suppliant=5,000=50%=P5.00D=Law=Time=Venus=5 May = Aphrodite>>L=N.
Supplicant=3,000=30%=P3.0D=3.0=Creativity=Stars=Muses=3 March = C=I>>GIL.
Supplicate=6,000=60%=P6.0D=Man=Earth=Royalty=6 June=Gaia=Maia>>M=M2.
Supply=10,000=1,000=100%=10.0=Physicality=Tech.=10 Oct.=Uranus=P=1Ø.
Support=10,000=1,000=100%=10.0=Physicality=Tech.=10 Oct.=Uranus=P=1Ø.
Suppose=10,000=1,000=100%=10.0=Physicality=Tech.=10 Oct.=Uranus=P=1Ø.
Suppose=10,000=1,000=100%=10.0=Physicality=Tech.=10 Oct.=Uranus=P=1Ø.
Supposing=5,000=50%=P5.00D=Law=Time=Venus=5 May = Aphrodite>>L=N.
Supposition=3,000=30%=P3.0D=3.0=Creativity=Stars=Muses=3 March = C=I>>GIL.
Suppository=10,000=1,000=100%=10.0=Physicality=Tech.=10 Oct.=Uranus=P=1Ø.
Suppress=10,000=1,000=100%=10.0=Physicality=Tech.=10 Oct.=Uranus=P=1Ø.
Suppurate=8,000=80%=P8.0D=Economy=Currency=8 Aug.=Zeus>>E=v.
Supranational=8,000=80%=P8.0D=Economy=Currency=8 Aug.=Zeus>>E=v.
Supremacist=6,000=60%=P6.0D=Man=Earth=Royalty=6 June=Gaia=Maia>>M=M2.

Supremacy=4,000=40%=P4.0D=Govt.=Creatocracy=4 April=Mercury=Hermes=G=A4.
The quality or condition of being supreme. Supreme power. Supremacy rests with GOD. All supreme power rests not with the people but with GOD through the supremacy of the Creatocracy because the people cannot govern themselves without GOD. A standard rule of the Sun is light, no one can survive without the Sun and so none without GOD. See book> The Creatocratic Charter by Peter Matthews-Akukalia.

Supreme=10,000=1,000=100%=10.0=Physicality=Tech.=10 Oct.=Uranus=P=1Ø.
His Creative Excellency & Godship, Peter Matthews-Akukalia is the Supreme Emperor, Emperor Supreme and Most Sovereign Emperor, Creatocratic Nations of Paradise. CNP.

Supreme Court=5,000=50%=P5.00D=Law=Time=Venus=5 May = Aphrodite>>L=N. The Creatocracy Court is considered the most Supreme Court because it tries the Mind based on the formulas of Castle Makupedia and the laws of Nature, Propensity & Inclinations. An invention of Peter Matthews-Akukalia, Castle Makupedia.

Supt.=500=5%=P5.00D=5.0=Law=Time=Venus=5 May=Aphrodite>>L=N.
Sur-=5,000=50%=P5.00D=Law=Time=Venus=5 May = Aphrodite>>L=N.
Surabaya=5,500=5.5=80%=P5.50=Earth-Midway=5 May = Gaia.
Surcease=2,000=20%=P2.00D=2.0=Nature=Matter=Moon=2 Feb.=Cupid=N=C+_
Surcharge=10,000=1,000=100%=10.0=Physicality=Tech.=10 Oct.=Uranus=P=1Ø.
Sure=10,000=1,000=100%=10.0=Physicality=Tech.=10 Oct.=Uranus=P=1Ø.
Sure-fire=2,500=3,000=30%=P3.0D=3.0=Creativity=Stars=Muses=3 March = C=I>>GIL.
Sure footed=3,000=30%=P3.0D=3.0=Creativity=Stars=Muses=3 March = C=I>>GIL.
Surely=2,500=3,000=30%=P3.0D=3.0=Creativity=Stars=Muses=3 March = C=I>>GIL.
Surety=10,000=1,000=100%=10.0=Physicality=Tech.=10 Oct.=Uranus=P=1Ø.
Surf=8,500=9,000=90%=P9.00D=9.0=Abstraction=Gods=Saturn=9Sept.>>A=Ø.
Surface=10,000=1,000=100%=10.0=Physicality=Tech.=10 Oct.=Uranus=P=1Ø.
Surfboard=4,000=40%=P4.0D=Govt.=Creatocracy=4 April=Mercury=Hermes=G=A4.
Surfeit=10,000=1,000=100%=10.0=Physicality=Tech.=10 Oct.=Uranus=P=1Ø.
Surfing=7,500=8,000=80%=P8.0D=Economy=Currency=8 Aug.=Zeus>>E=v.
Surge=10,000=1,000=100%=10.0=Physicality=Tech.=10 Oct.=Uranus=P=1Ø.
Surgeon=3,500=4,000=40%=P4.0D=Govt.=Creatocracy=4 April=Hermes=G=A4.
Surgery=10,000=1,000=100%=10.0=Physicality=Tech.=10 Oct.=Uranus=P=1Ø.
Suriname=10,000=1,000=100%=10.0=Physicality=Tech.=10 Oct.=Uranus=P=1Ø.
Suriname River=7,000=70%=P7.0D=7.0=Language=Assets=Mars=7 July=Pleiades.
Surly=4,500=5,000=50%=P5.00D=Law=Time=Venus=5 May = Aphrodite>>L=N.
Surmise=10,000=1,000=100%=10.0=Physicality=Tech.=10 Oct.=Uranus=P=1Ø.
Surmount=8,000=80%=P8.0D=Economy=Currency=8 Aug.=Zeus>>E=v.

Surname=10,000=1,000=100%=10.0=Physicality=Tech.=10 Oct.=Uranus=P=1Ø.
Formerly Peter Matthews, [Matthews-Akukalia] is an invention surname of the bearer bringing both together to create a dynasty royalty and legacy for easy identification of his genealogy in 2011. Through his works the name is protected by Intellectual Property rights and laws. Matthews is his grandfather. Akukalia is his great grandfather. Peter, first name.

Surpass=10,000=1,000=100%=10.0=Physicality=Tech.=10 Oct.=Uranus=P=1Ø.
Surpassing=1,000=100%=10.0=1.0=Mind=Sun=1 January=Helios >> M=E4.
Surplice=10,000=1,000=100%=10.0=Physicality=Tech.=10 Oct.=Uranus=P=1Ø.
Surplus=10,000=1,000=100%=10.0=Physicality=Tech.=10 Oct.=Uranus=P=1Ø.
Surprise=10,000=1,000=100%=10.0=Physicality=Tech.=10 Oct.=Uranus=P=1Ø.
Surrealism=10,000=1,000=100%=10.0=Physicality=Tech.=10 Oct.=Uranus=P=1Ø.
Surrender=10,000=1,000=100%=10.0=Physicality=Tech.=10 Oct.=Uranus=P=1Ø.
Surreptitious=4,000=40%=P4.0D=Govt.=Creatocracy=4 April=Mercury=Hermes=G=A4.
surrey=7,000=70%=P7.0D=7.0=Language=Assets=Mars=7 July=Pleiades.

Surrey Henry=2,000=20%=P2.00D=2.0=Nature=Matter=Moon=2 Feb.=Cupid=N=C+_
Surrogate=10,000=1,000=100%=10.0=Physicality=Tech.=10 Oct.=Uranus=P=1Ø.
Surround=10,000=1,000=100%=10.0=Physicality=Tech.=10 Oct.=Uranus=P=1Ø.
Surroundings=4,500=5,000=50%=P5.00D=Law=Time=Venus=5 May = Aphrodite>>L=N.
Surtax=5,500=5.5=80%=P5.50=Earth-Midway=5 May = Gaia.
Surveillance=7,500=8,000=80%=P8.0D=Economy=Currency=8 Aug.=Zeus>>E=v.
Survey=10,000=1,000=100%=10.0=Physicality=Tech.=10 Oct.=Uranus=P=1Ø.
Surveying=10,000=1,000=100%=10.0=Physicality=Tech.=10 Oct.=Uranus=P=1Ø.
Survive=10,000=1,000=100%=10.0=Physicality=Tech.=10 Oct.=Uranus=P=1Ø.
Susceptible=10,000=1,000=100%=10.0=Physicality=Tech.=10 Oct.=Uranus=P=1Ø.
Sushi=7,500=8,000=80%=P8.0D=Economy=Currency=8 Aug.=Zeus>>E=v.
Suspect=10,000=1,000=100%=10.0=Physicality=Tech.=10 Oct.=Uranus=P=1Ø.
Suspend=10,000=1,000=100%=10.0=Physicality=Tech.=10 Oct.=Uranus=P=1Ø.
Suspenders=6,500=7,000=70%=P7.0D=7.0=Language=Assets=Mars=7 July=Pleiades.
Suspense=9,000=90%=P9.00D=9.0=Abstraction=Gods=Saturn=9Sept.>>A=Ø.
Suspension=10,000=1,000=100%=10.0=Physicality=Tech.=10 Oct.=Uranus=P=1Ø.
Suspension bridge=8,000=80%=P8.0D=Economy=Currency=8 Aug.=Zeus>>E=v.
Suspicion=10,000=1,000=100%=10.0=Physicality=Tech.=10 Oct.=Uranus=P=1Ø.
Suspicious=10,000=1,000=100%=10.0=Physicality=Tech.=10 Oct.=Uranus=P=1Ø.
Susquehanna River=10,000=1,000=100%=10.0=Physicality=Tech.=10 Oct.=Uranus=P=1Ø.
Sustain=10,000=1,000=100%=10.0=Physicality=Tech.=10 Oct.=Uranus=P=1Ø.
Sustenance=10,000=1,000=100%=10.0=Physicality=Tech.=10 Oct.=Uranus=P=1Ø.
Sutherland Joan.=2,500=3,000=30%=P3.0D=3.0=Cr=Stars=Muses=3 March = C=I>>GIL.
Sutra=10,000=1,000=100%=10.0=Physicality=Tech.=10 Oct.=Uranus=P=1Ø.
Suture=10,000=1,000=100%=10.0=Physicality=Tech.=10 Oct.=Uranus=P=1Ø.
Suva=5,500=5.5=80%=P5.50=Earth-Midway=5 May = Gaia.
Suzerain=10,000=1,000=100%=10.0=Physicality=Tech.=10 Oct.=Uranus=P=1Ø.
Suzhou=4,500=5,000=50%=P5.00D=Law=Time=Venus=5 May = Aphrodite>>L=N.
Svelte=5,000=50%=P5.00D=Law=Time=Venus=5 May = Aphrodite>>L=N.
Sverdlovsk=7,000=70%=P7.0D=7.0=Language=Assets=Mars=7 July=Pleiades.
sw=1,000=100%=10.0=1.0=Mind=Sun=1 January=Helios >> M=E4.
SW=1,000=100%=10.0=1.0=Mind=Sun=1 January=Helios >> M=E4.
Sw.=1,000=100%=10.0=1.0=Mind=Sun=1 January=Helios >> M=E4.
Swab=10,000=1,000=100%=10.0=Physicality=Tech.=10 Oct.=Uranus=P=1Ø.
Swabia=3,000=30%=P3.0D=3.0=Creativity=Stars=Muses=3 March = C=I>>GIL.
Swaddle=6,000=60%=P6.0D=Man=Earth=Royalty=6 June=Gaia=Maia>>M=M2.
Swag=4,000=40%=P4.0D=Govt.=Creatocracy=4 April=Mercury=Hermes=G=A4.
Swagger=7,000=70%=P7.0D=7.0=Language=Assets=Mars=7 July=Pleiades.

Swagger stick=4,000=40%=P4.0D=Govt.=Creatocracy=4 April=Mercury=Hermes=G=A4.
Peter Matthews-Akukalia, Castle Makupedia, Most Sovereign Emperor of the Paradise
Nations and God of Creatocracy carries a Swagger staff of various types choices and will
to symbolize his authority. See Principles of Psychoastronomy >> Creatolingua.

Swahili=10,000=1,000=100%=10.0=Physicality=Tech.=10 Oct.=Uranus=P=1Ø.
Swain=4,500=5,000=50%=P5.00D=Law=Time=Venus=5 May = Aphrodite>>L=N.
Swallow1=10,000=1,000=100%=10.0=Physicality=Tech.=10 Oct.=Uranus=P=1Ø.
Swallow2=9,000=90%=P9.00D=9.0=Abstraction=Gods=Saturn=9Sept.>>A=Ø.
Swallowtail=10,000=1,000=100%=10.0=Physicality=Tech.=10 Oct.=Uranus=P=1Ø.
Swam=2,000=20%=P2.00D=2.0=Nature=Matter=Moon=2 Feb.=Cupid=N=C+_
Swami=3,500=4,000=40%=P4.0D=Govt.=Creatocracy=4 April=Mercury=Hermes=G=A4.
Swamp=10,000=1,000=100%=10.0=Physicality=Tech.=10 Oct.=Uranus=P=1Ø.
Swan=10,000=1,000=100%=10.0=Physicality=Tech.=10 Oct.=Uranus=P=1Ø.
Swan dive=10,000=1,000=100%=10.0=Physicality=Tech.=10 Oct.=Uranus=P=1Ø.
Swank=10,000=1,000=100%=10.0=Physicality=Tech.=10 Oct.=Uranus=P=1Ø.
Swan's down=4,500=5,000=50%=P5.00D=Law=Time=Venus=5 May = Aphrodite>>L=N.
Swansea=4,500=5,000=50%=P5.00D=Law=Time=Venus=5 May = Aphrodite>>L=N.
Swan song=3,000=30%=P3.0D=3.0=Creativity=Stars=Muses=3 March = C=I>>GIL.
Swap=10,000=1,000=100%=10.0=Physicality=Tech.=10 Oct.=Uranus=P=1Ø.
Sward=4,000=40%=P4.0D=Govt.=Creatocracy=4 April=Mercury=Hermes=G=A4.
Swarm=10,000=1,000=100%=10.0=Physicality=Tech.=10 Oct.=Uranus=P=1Ø.
Swarthy=4,000=40%=P4.0D=Govt.=Creatocracy=4 April=Mercury=Hermes=G=A4.
Swash=5,500=5.5=80%=P5.50=Earth-Midway=5 May = Gaia.
Swashbuckler=2,500=3,000=30%=P3.0D=3.0=Cr=Stars=Muses=3 March = C=I>>GIL.
Swastika=10,000=1,000=100%=10.0=Physicality=Tech.=10 Oct.=Uranus=P=1Ø.
Swat=5,000=50%=P5.00D=Law=Time=Venus=5 May = Aphrodite>>L=N.
Swatch=4,500=5,000=50%=P5.00D=Law=Time=Venus=5 May = Aphrodite>>L=N.
Swath=10,000=1,000=100%=10.0=Physicality=Tech.=10 Oct.=Uranus=P=1Ø.
Swathe=4,500=5,000=50%=P5.00D=Law=Time=Venus=5 May = Aphrodite>>L=N.
Sway=10,000=1,000=100%=10.0=Physicality=Tech.=10 Oct.=Uranus=P=1Ø.
Swayback=4,000=40%=P4.0D=Govt.=Creatocracy=4 April=Mercury=Hermes=G=A4.
Swazi=5,500=5.5=80%=P5.50=Earth-Midway=5 May = Gaia.
Swaziland=7,000=70%=P7.0D=7.0=Language=Assets=Mars=7 July=Pleiades.
SWbS=1,500=15%=P1.50D=1.5=Authority=Solar Crown=1 May = Maia.
SWbW=1,500=15%=P1.50D=1.5=Authority=Solar Crown=1 May = Maia.
Swear=10,000=1,000=100%=10.0=Physicality=Tech.=10 Oct.=Uranus=P=1Ø.
Sweat=10,000=1,000=100%=10.0=Physicality=Tech.=10 Oct.=Uranus=P=1Ø.
Sweater=5,000=50%=P5.00D=Law=Time=Venus=5 May = Aphrodite>>L=N.
Sweat gland=7,500=8,000=80%=P8.0D=Economy=Currency=8 Aug.=Zeus>>E=v.
Sweatshirt=5,500=5.5=80%=P5.50=Earth-Midway=5 May = Gaia.
Sweatshop=8,000=80%=P8.0D=Economy=Currency=8 Aug.=Zeus>>E=v.
Swede=3,000=30%=P3.0D=3.0=Creativity=Stars=Muses=3 March = C=I>>GIL.
Sweden=6,000=60%=P6.0D=Man=Earth=Royalty=6 June=Gaia=Maia>>M=M2.

Swedenborg Emmanuel=3,500=4,000=40%=P4.0D=Govt.=4 April=Mercury=G=A4.
1688-1772. Swedish scientist and theologian. Peter Matthews-Akukalia. 1978-Date. Nigerian
Author, Creative Scientist inventor Makumatician, Faithysxt & Many Other Firsts.

Swedish=6,000=60%=P6.0D=Man=Earth=Royalty=6 June=Gaia=Maia>>M=M2.
Sweep=10,000=1,000=100%=10.0=Physicality=Tech.=10 Oct.=Uranus=P=1Ø.
Sweeping=6,000=60%=P6.0D=Man=Earth=Royalty=6 June=Gaia=Maia>>M=M2.
Sweepstakes=10,000=1,000=100%=10.0=Physicality=Tech.=10 Oct.=Uranus=P=1Ø.
Sweet=10,000=1,000=100%=10.0=Physicality=Tech.=10 Oct.=Uranus=P=1Ø.
Sweet alyssum=5,000=50%=P5.00D=Law=Time=Venus=5 May = Aphrodite>>L=N.
Sweetbread=6,000=60%=P6.0D=Man=Earth=Royalty=6 June=Gaia=Maia>>M=M2.
Sweetbrier=5,500=5.5=80%=P5.50=Earth-Midway=5 May = Gaia.
Sweet corn=5,500=5.5=80%=P5.50=Earth-Midway=5 May = Gaia.
Sweeten=4,000=40%=P4.0D=Govt.=Creatocracy=4 April=Mercury=Hermes=G=A4.
Sweetening=5,500=5.5=80%=P5.50=Earth-Midway=5 May = Gaia.
Sweetheart=3,500=4,000=40%=P4.0D=Govt.=Creatocracy=4 April=Hermes=G=A4.
Sweetmeat=5,000=50%=P5.00D=Law=Time=Venus=5 May = Aphrodite>>L=N.
Sweet pea=6,000=60%=P6.0D=Man=Earth=Royalty=6 June=Gaia=Maia>>M=M2.
Sweet potato=10,000=1,000=100%=10.0=Physicality=Tech.=10 Oct.=Uranus=P=1Ø.
Sweet talk=3,500=4,000=40%=P4.0D=Govt.=Creatocracy=4 April=Mercury=G=A4.
Sweet tooth=3,500=4,000=40%=P4.0D=Govt.=Creatocracy=4 April=Mercury=G=A4.
Sweet William=6,000=60%=P6.0D=Man=Earth=Royalty=6 June=Gaia=Maia>>M=M2.
Swell=10,000=1,000=100%=10.0=Physicality=Tech.=10 Oct.=Uranus=P=1Ø.
Swelling=3,000=30%=P3.0D=3.0=Creativity=Stars=Muses=3 March = C=I>>GIL.
Swelter=4,000=40%=P4.0D=Govt.=Creatocracy=4 April=Mercury=Hermes=G=A4.
Swept=3,000=30%=P3.0D=3.0=Creativity=Stars=Muses=3 March = C=I>>GIL.
Swerve=10,000=1,000=100%=10.0=Physicality=Tech.=10 Oct.=Uranus=P=1Ø.
Swift=10,000=1,000=100%=10.0=Physicality=Tech.=10 Oct.=Uranus=P=1Ø.
Swift Jonathan.=3,000=30%=P3.0D=3.0=Creativity=Stars=Muses=3 March = C=I>>GIL.
Swig=5,500=5.5=80%=P5.50=Earth-Midway=5 May = Gaia.
Swill=10,000=1,000=100%=10.0=Physicality=Tech.=10 Oct.=Uranus=P=1Ø.
Swim=10,000=1,000=100%=10.0=Physicality=Tech.=10 Oct.=Uranus=P=1Ø.
Swimmingly=1,000=100%=10.0=1.0=Mind=Sun=1 January=Helios >> M=E4.
Swimsuit=3,500=4,000=40%=P4.0D=Govt.=4 April=Mercury=Hermes=G=A4.
Swinburne Algernon=3,500=4,000=40%=P4.0D=Govt.=4 April=Mercury=G=A4.
Swindle=8,000=80%=P8.0D=Economy=Currency=8 Aug.=Zeus>>E=v.
Swine=12,000=12%=P1.20D=1.2=Knowledge=Edu=12Dec.=Athena>>K=F.
Swing=10,000=1,000=100%=10.0=Physicality=Tech.=10 Oct.=Uranus=P=1Ø.
Swinger=7,000=70%=P7.0D=7.0=Language=Assets=Mars=7 July=Pleiades.
Swipe=10,000=1,000=100%=10.0=Physicality=Tech.=10 Oct.=Uranus=P=1Ø.
Swirl=7,500=8,000=80%=P8.0D=Economy=Currency=8 Aug.=Zeus>>E=v.
Swish=4,000=40%=P4.0D=Govt.=Creatocracy=4 April=Mercury=Hermes=G=A4.
Swiss=7,500=8,000=80%=P8.0D=Economy=Currency=8 Aug.=Zeus>>E=v.
Swiss chard=5,500=5.5=80%=P5.50=Earth-Midway=5 May = Gaia.
Switch=10,000=1,000=100%=10.0=Physicality=Tech.=10 Oct.=Uranus=P=1Ø.
Switchblade=7,500=8,000=80%=P8.0D=Economy=Currency=8 Aug.=Zeus>>E=v.
Switchboard=5,500=5.5=80%=P5.50=Earth-Midway=5 May = Gaia.
Switch hitter=5,500=5.5=80%=P5.50=Earth-Midway=5 May = Gaia.
Switchman=2,500=3,000=30%=P3.0D=3.0=Cre=Stars=Muses=3 March = C=I>>GIL.

Switzerland=5,000=50%=P5.00D=Law=Time=Venus=5 May = Aphrodite>>L=N.
Swivel=10,000=1,000=100%=10.0=Physicality=Tech.=10 Oct.=Uranus=P=1Ø.
Swizzle stick=4,000=40%=P4.0D=Govt.=Creatocracy=4 April=Mercury=Hermes=G=A4.
Swollen=3,500=4,000=40%=P4.0D=Govt.=Creatocracy=4 April=Mercury=Hermes=G=A4.
Swoon=4,500=5,000=50%=P5.00D=Law=Time=Venus=5 May = Aphrodite>>L=N.
Swoop=7,000=70%=P7.0D=7.0=Language=Assets=Mars=7 July=Pleiades.

Sword=12,000=12%=P1.20D=1.2=Knowledge=Edu=12Dec.=Athena>>K=F.
See Valentine. St. Valentine's Day. Contains knowledge on Shakespearean writing style.

Swordfish=7,500=8,000=80%=P8.0D=Economy=Currency=8 Aug.=Zeus>>E=v.
Swordplay=4,000=40%=P4.0D=Govt.=Creatocracy=4 April=Mercury=Hermes=G=A4.
Swordsman=3,500=4,000=40%=P4.0D=Govt.=4 April=Mercury=Hermes=G=A4.
Swore=2,000=20%=P2.00D=2.0=Nature=Matter=Moon=2 Feb.=Cupid=N=C+_
Sworn=2,000=20%=P2.00D=2.0=Nature=Matter=Moon=2 Feb.=Cupid=N=C+_
Swum=2,000=20%=P2.00D=2.0=Nature=Matter=Moon=2 Feb.=Cupid=N=C+_
Swung=3,000=30%=P3.0D=3.0=Creativity=Stars=Muses=3 March = C=I>>GIL.
Sybarite=7,500=8,000=80%=P8.0D=Economy=Currency=8 Aug.=Zeus>>E=v.
Sycamore=10,000=1,000=100%=10.0=Physicality=Tech.=10 Oct.=Uranus=P=1Ø.
Sycophant=10,000=1,000=100%=10.0=Physicality=Tech.=10 Oct.=Uranus=P=1Ø.
Sydney=7,500=8,000=80%=P8.0D=Economy=Currency=8 Aug.=Zeus>>E=v.
Syllabify=3,000=30%=P3.0D=3.0=Creativity=Stars=Muses=3 March = C=I>>GIL.
Syllable=10,000=1,000=100%=10.0=Physicality=Tech.=10 Oct.=Uranus=P=1Ø.
Syllabus=10,000=1,000=100%=10.0=Physicality=Tech.=10 Oct.=Uranus=P=1Ø.
Syllogism=10,000=1,000=100%=10.0=Physicality=Tech.=10 Oct.=Uranus=P=1Ø.
Sylph=10,000=1,000=100%=10.0=Physicality=Tech.=10 Oct.=Uranus=P=1Ø.
Sylavan=10,000=1,000=100%=10.0=Physicality=Tech.=10 Oct.=Uranus=P=1Ø.
Symbiosis=10,000=1,000=100%=10.0=Physicality=Tech.=10 Oct.=Uranus=P=1Ø.

Symbol=10,000=1,000=100%=10.0=Physicality=Tech.=10 Oct.=Uranus=P=1Ø.
The Creatocracy is represented by the symbols of the Solar Crown, the Maks Currencies
and universal standard unit and peak of all aspirations on the Maks. See SI.

Symbolic language=3,000=30%=P3.0D=3.0=Cre.=Stars=Muses=3 March = C=I>>GIL.
Symbolism=3,500=4,000=40%=P4.0D=Govt.=Creatocracy=4 April=Hermes=G=A4.
Symbolize=4,500=5,000=50%=P5.00D=Law=Time=Venus=5 May = Aphrodite>>L=N.
Symmetry=10,000=1,000=100%=10.0=Physicality=Tech.=10 Oct.=Uranus=P=1Ø.
Sympathetic=10,000=1,000=100%=10.0=Physicality=Tech.=10 Oct.=Uranus=P=1Ø.
Sympathetic nervous system==10,000=1,000=100%=10.0=Phy.=10 Oct.=Uranus=P=1Ø.
Sympathize=10,000=1,000=100%=10.0=Physicality=Tech.=10 Oct.=Uranus=P=1Ø.
Sympathy=10,000=1,000=100%=10.0=Physicality=Tech.=10 Oct.=Uranus=P=1Ø.
Symphonic=6,000=60%=P6.0D=Man=Earth=Royalty=6 June=Gaia=Maia>>M=M2.
Symphony=9,000=90%=P9.00D=9.0=Abstraction=Gods=Saturn=9Sept.>>A=Ø.

Symphony orchestra=5,000=50%=P5.00D=Law=Time=Venus=5 May = Aphrodite>>L=N.
Symposium=10,000=1,000=100%=10.0=Physicality=Tech.=10 Oct.=Uranus=P=1Ø.
Symptom=10,000=1,000=100%=10.0=Physicality=Tech.=10 Oct.=Uranus=P=1Ø.
Syn.=500=5%=P5.00D=5.0=Law=Time=Venus=5 May=Aphrodite>>L=N.
Synagogue=10,000=1,000=100%=10.0=Physicality=Tech.=10 Oct.=Uranus=P=1Ø.
Synapse=10,000=1,000=100%=10.0=Physicality=Tech.=10 Oct.=Uranus=P=1Ø.
Sync=3,000=30%=P3.0D=3.0=Creativity=Stars=Muses=3 March = C=I>>GIL.
Synchronize=10,000=1,000=100%=10.0=Physicality=Tech.=10 Oct.=Uranus=P=1Ø.
Synchronous=5,500=5.5=80%=P5.50=Earth-Midway=5 May = Gaia.
Syncopate=3,000=30%=P3.0D=3.0=Creativity=Stars=Muses=3 March = C=I>>GIL.
Syncopation=5,500=5.5=80%=P5.50=Earth-Midway=5 May = Gaia.
Syncope=5,500=5.5=80%=P5.50=Earth-Midway=5 May = Gaia.
Syndicate=10,000=1,000=100%=10.0=Physicality=Tech.=10 Oct.=Uranus=P=1Ø.
Syndrome=7,000=70%=P7.0D=7.0=Language=Assets=Mars=7 July=Pleiades.
Synergy=10,000=1,000=100%=10.0=Physicality=Tech.=10 Oct.=Uranus=P=1Ø.
Synfuel=9,500=10,000=1,000=100%=10.0=Physicality=Tech.=10 Oct.=Uranus=P=1Ø.
Synge John=2,500=3,000=30%=P3.0D=3.0=Cr=Stars=Muses=3 March = C=I>>GIL.

Synod=6,500=7,000=70%=P7.0D=7.0=Language=Assets=Mars=7 July=Pleiades.
The Creatocracy, The Creatocratic Royal Family, The Council of Heirs, The Board of Governors. All these are the equivalent of the Synod.

Synonym=8,000=80%=P8.0D=Economy=Currency=8 Aug.=Zeus>>E=v.
Synonymy=2,500=3,000=30%=P3.0D=3.0=Creativity=Stars=Muses=3 March = C=I>>GIL.

Synopsis=6,000=60%=P6.0D=Man=Earth=Royalty=6 June=Gaia=Maia>>M=M2.
The human element of a story narration or occurrence.

Syntax=11,000=11%=P1.10D=1.1=Idea=Brainchild=Inv.=11 Nov.=SC=Athena>>I=MT.
Synthesis=10,000=1,000=100%=10.0=Physicality=Tech.=10 Oct.=Uranus=P=1Ø.
Synthesizer=10,000=1,000=100%=10.0=Physicality=Tech.=10 Oct.=Uranus=P=1Ø.
Synthetic=10,000=1,000=100%=10.0=Physicality=Tech.=10 Oct.=Uranus=P=1Ø.
Syphilis=10,000=1,000=100%=10.0=Physicality=Tech.=10 Oct.=Uranus=P=1Ø.
Syphon=1,500=15%=P1.50D=1.5=Authority=Solar Crown=1 May = Maia.
Syracuse=5,000=50%=P5.00D=Law=Time=Venus=5 May = Aphrodite>>L=N.
Syria=7,000=70%=P7.0D=7.0=Language=Assets=Mars=7 July=Pleiades.
Syringe=10,000=1,000=100%=10.0=Physicality=Tech.=10 Oct.=Uranus=P=1Ø.
Syrup=10,000=1,000=100%=10.0=Physicality=Tech.=10 Oct.=Uranus=P=1Ø.
System=10,000=1,000=100%=10.0=Physicality=Tech.=10 Oct.=Uranus=P=1Ø.
Systematize=5,500=5.5=80%=P5.50=Earth-Midway=5 May = Gaia.
Systemic=6,000=60%=P6.0D=Man=Earth=Royalty=6 June=Gaia=Maia>>M=M2.
Systemize=1,000=100%=10.0=1.0=Mind=Sun=1 January=Helios >> M=E4.
Systems analysis=10,000=1,000=100%=10.0=Physicality=Tech.=10 Oct.=Uranus=P=1Ø.

Systole=10,000=1,000=100%=10.0=Physicality=Tech.=10 Oct.=Uranus=P=1Ø.
Szczecin=5,500=5.5=80%=P5.50=Earth-Midway=5 May = Gaia.
Szechuan=1,000=100%=10.0=1.0=Mind=Sun=1 January=Helios >> M=E4.
Szeged=5,500=5.5=80%=P5.50=Earth-Midway=5 May = Gaia.

MAKABET =Tt=

---

t1=3,000=30%=P3.0D=3.0=Creativity=Stars=Muses=3 March = C=I>>GIL.
The 20th letter of the English alphabet. The psycho or mind weight of Tt is computed thus>>3.0*2.0x=px=5+6=11x=px=41=4.1 <<1.4 >> Management.

---

t2=2,500=3,000=30%=P3.0D=3.0=Creativity=Stars=Muses=3 March = C=I>>GIL.
T=500=5%=P5.00D=5.0=Law=Time=Venus=5 May=Aphrodite>>L=N.
t.=5,000=50%=P5.00D=Law=Time=Venus=5 May = Aphrodite>>L=N.
T.=10,000=1,000=100%=10.0=Physicality=Tech.=10 Oct.=Uranus=P=1Ø.
Ta=2,500=3,000=30%=P3.0D=3.0=Creativity=Stars=Muses=3 March = C=I>>GIL.
Tab1=6,000=60%=P6.0D=Man=Earth=Royalty=6 June=Gaia=Maia>>M=M2.
Tab2=7,500=8,000=80%=P8.0D=Economy=Currency=8 Aug.=Zeus>>E=v.
Tabby=7,500=8,000=80%=P8.0D=Economy=Currency=8 Aug.=Zeus>>E=v.
Tabernacle=10,000=1,000=100%=10.0=Physicality=Tech.=10 Oct.=Uranus=P=1Ø.
Table=10,000=1,000=100%=10.0=Physicality=Tech.=10 Oct.=Uranus=P=1Ø.
Tableau=10,000=1,000=100%=10.0=Physicality=Tech.=10 Oct.=Uranus=P=1Ø.
Tableau vivant=10,000=1,000=100%=10.0=Physicality=Tech.=10 Oct.=Uranus=P=1Ø.
Tablecloth=4,000=40%=P4.0D=Govt.=Creatocracy=4 April=Mercury=Hermes=G=A4.
Table d'hôte=7,500=8,000=80%=P8.0D=Economy=Currency=8 Aug.=Zeus>>E=v.
Tableland=2,000=20%=P2.00D=2.0=Nature=Matter=Moon=2 Feb.=Cupid=N=C+_
Tablespoon=10,000=1,000=100%=10.0=Physicality=Tech.=10 Oct.=Uranus=P=1Ø.
Tablet=10,000=1,000=100%=10.0=Physicality=Tech.=10 Oct.=Uranus=P=1Ø.
Table tennis=8,000=80%=P8.0D=Economy=Currency=8 Aug.=Zeus>>E=v.
Tabletop=6,500=7,000=70%=P7.0D=7.0=Language=Assets=Mars=7 July=Pleiades.
Tableware=5,500=5.5=80%=P5.50=Earth-Midway=5 May = Gaia.
Tabloid=8,500=9,000=90%=P9.00D=9.0=Abstraction=Gods=Saturn=9Sept.>>A=Ø.
Taboo=10,000=1,000=100%=10.0=Physicality=Tech.=10 Oct.=Uranus=P=1Ø.
Tabor=4,500=5,000=50%=P5.00D=Law=Time=Venus=5 May = Aphrodite>>L=N.
Tabriz=3,500=4,000=40%=P4.0D=Govt.=Creatocracy=4 April=Mercury=Hermes=G=A4.
Tabular=4,500=5,000=50%=P5.00D=Law=Time=Venus=5 May = Aphrodite>>L=N.
Tabulate=5,500=5.5=80%=P5.50=Earth-Midway=5 May = Gaia.
Tachometer=10,000=1,000=100%=10.0=Physicality=Tech.=10 Oct.=Uranus=P=1Ø.
Tacit=10,000=1,000=100%=10.0=Physicality=Tech.=10 Oct.=Uranus=P=1Ø.
Taciturn=3,000=30%=P3.0D=3.0=Creativity=Stars=Muses=3 March = C=I>>GIL.
Tacitus Publius=3,500=4,000=40%=P4.0D=Govt.=Creatocracy=4 April=Hermes=G=A4.
Tack1=10,000=1,000=100%=10.0=Physicality=Tech.=10 Oct.=Uranus=P=1Ø.

Tack2=5,000=50%=P5.00D=Law=Time=Venus=5 May = Aphrodite>>L=N.
Tackle=10,000=1,000=100%=10.0=Physicality=Tech.=10 Oct.=Uranus=P=1Ø.
Tacky1=1,500=15%=P1.50D=1.5=Authority=Solar Crown=1 May = Maia.
Tacky2=10,000=1,000=100%=10.0=Physicality=Tech.=10 Oct.=Uranus=P=1Ø.
Taco=8,000=80%=P8.0D=Economy=Currency=8 Aug.=Zeus>>E=v.
Tacoma=5,000=50%=P5.00D=Law=Time=Venus=5 May = Aphrodite>>L=N.
Taconite=7,000=70%=P7.0D=7.0=Language=Assets=Mars=7 July=Pleiades.
Tact=5,000=50%=P5.00D=Law=Time=Venus=5 May = Aphrodite>>L=N.
Tactic=10,000=1,000=100%=10.0=Physicality=Tech.=10 Oct.=Uranus=P=1Ø.
Tactile=6,500=7,000=70%=P7.0D=7.0=Language=Assets=Mars=7 July=Pleiades.
Tad=5,000=50%=P5.00D=Law=Time=Venus=5 May = Aphrodite>>L=N.
Tadpole=9,000=90%=P9.00D=9.0=Abstraction=Gods=Saturn=9Sept.>>A=Ø.
Tadzhikistan=8,500=9,000=90%=P9.00D=9.0=Abstraction=Gods=Saturn=9Sept.>>A=Ø.
Taegu=5,000=50%=P5.00D=Law=Time=Venus=5 May = Aphrodite>>L=N.
Taejon=5,000=50%=P5.00D=Law=Time=Venus=5 May = Aphrodite>>L=N.
Take kwon do=4,000=40%=P4.0D=Govt.=Creatocracy=4 April=Mercury=Hermes=G=A4.
Taffeta=8,000=80%=P8.0D=Economy=Currency=8 Aug.=Zeus>>E=v.
Taffy=5,000=50%=P5.00D=Law=Time=Venus=5 May = Aphrodite>>L=N.
Taft William=9,000=90%=P9.00D=9.0=Abstraction=Gods=Saturn=9Sept.>>A=Ø.
Tag1=10,000=1,000=100%=10.0=Physicality=Tech.=10 Oct.=Uranus=P=1Ø.
Tag2=10,000=1,000=100%=10.0=Physicality=Tech.=10 Oct.=Uranus=P=1Ø.
Tagalog=6,000=60%=P6.0D=Man=Earth=Royalty=6 June=Gaia=Maia>>M=M2.
Tagore Rabindranath=3,500=4,000=40%=P4.0D=Govt.=4 April=Hermes=G=A4.
Tagus=10,000=1,000=100%=10.0=Physicality=Tech.=10 Oct.=Uranus=P=1Ø.
Tahini=5,000=50%=P5.00D=Law=Time=Venus=5 May = Aphrodite>>L=N.
Tahiti=5,500=5.5=80%=P5.50=Earth-Midway=5 May = Gaia.
Tahitian=4,500=5,000=50%=P5.00D=Law=Time=Venus=5 May = Aphrodite>>L=N.
Tahoe Lake=6,000=60%=P6.0D=Man=Earth=Royalty=6 June=Gaia=Maia>>M=M2.
Tai=10,000=1,000=100%=10.0=Physicality=Tech.=10 Oct.=Uranus=P=1Ø.
Tai chi=10,000=1,000=100%=10.0=Physicality=Tech.=10 Oct.=Uranus=P=1Ø.
Taichung=4,000=40%=P4.0D=Govt.=Creatocracy=4 April=Mercury=Hermes=G=A4.
Taiga=6,000=60%=P6.0D=Man=Earth=Royalty=6 June=Gaia=Maia>>M=M2.
Tall=10,000=1,000=100%=10.0=Physicality=Tech.=10 Oct.=Uranus=P=1Ø.
Tailgate=10,000=1,000=100%=10.0=Physicality=Tech.=10 Oct.=Uranus=P=1Ø.
Tailings=4,500=5,000=50%=P5.00D=Law=Time=Venus=5 May = Aphrodite>>L=N.
Tail light=4,500=5,000=50%=P5.00D=Law=Time=Venus=5 May = Aphrodite>>L=N.
Tailor=10,000=1,000=100%=10.0=Physicality=Tech.=10 Oct.=Uranus=P=1Ø.
Tailor made=5,000=50%=P5.00D=Law=Time=Venus=5 May = Aphrodite>>L=N.
Tail pipe=5,500=5.5=80%=P5.50=Earth-Midway=5 May = Gaia.
Tail spin=8,500=9,000=90%=P9.00D=9.0=Abstraction=Gods=Saturn=9Sept.>>A=Ø.
Tainan=5,500=5.5=80%=P5.50=Earth-Midway=5 May = Gaia.
Taine Hippolyte=3,500=4,000=40%=P4.0D=Govt.=Creatocracy=4 April=Hermes=G=A4.
Taino=10,000=1,000=100%=10.0=Physicality=Tech.=10 Oct.=Uranus=P=1Ø.
Taint=10,000=1,000=100%=10.0=Physicality=Tech.=10 Oct.=Uranus=P=1Ø.
Taipei=4,500=5,000=50%=P5.00D=Law=Time=Venus=5 May = Aphrodite>>L=N.

Taiwan=10,000=1,000=100%=10.0=Physicality=Tech.=10 Oct.=Uranus=P=1Ø.
Tai yuan=4,500=5,000=50%=P5.00D=Law=Time=Venus=5 May = Aphrodite>>L=N.

Taka=5,000=50%=P5.00D=Law=Time=Venus=5 May = Aphrodite>>L=N.
Bengali. Currency metric weight >> 5/10=0.5 >> 50:1. See Naira. Dollar.

Take=10,000=1,000=100%=10.0=Physicality=Tech.=10 Oct.=Uranus=P=1Ø.
Takeoff=5,500=5.5=80%=P5.50=Earth-Midway=5 May = Gaia.
Takeout=4,500=5,000=50%=P5.00D=Law=Time=Venus=5 May = Aphrodite>>L=N.
Takeover=2,500=3,000=30%=P3.0D=3.0=Creativity=Stars=Muses=3 March = C=I>>GIL.

Tala=3,500=4,000=40%=P4.0D=Govt.=Creatocracy=4 April=Mercury=Hermes=G=A4.
Samoan. Currency metric weight >> 3.5/10=0.35 >> 35:1. See Naira. Dollar.

Talc=5,500=5.5=80%=P5.50=Earth-Midway=5 May = Gaia.
Talcahuano=6,000=60%=P6.0D=Man=Earth=Royalty=6 June=Gaia=Maia>>M=M2.
Talcum powder=8,000=80%=P8.0D=Economy=Currency=8 Aug.=Zeus>>E=v.
Tale=7,000=70%=P7.0D=7.0=Language=Assets=Mars=7 July=Pleiades.
Tale bearer=2,500=3,000=30%=P3.0D=3.0=Cre=Stars=Muses=3 March = C=I>>GIL.
Talent=10,000=1,000=100%=10.0=Physicality=Tech.=10 Oct.=Uranus=P=1Ø.
Talisman=7,500=8,000=80%=P8.0D=Economy=Currency=8 Aug.=Zeus>>E=v.
Talk=10,000=1,000=100%=10.0=Physicality=Tech.=10 Oct.=Uranus=P=1Ø.
Talkative=2,500=3,000=30%=P3.0D=3.0=Creativity=Stars=Muses=3 March = C=I>>GIL.
Talking to=2,500=3,000=30%=P3.0D=3.0=Creativity=Stars=Muses=3 March = C=I>>GIL.
Talk show=6,500=7,000=70%=P7.0D=7.0=Language=Assets=Mars=7 July=Pleiades.
Tall=10,000=1,000=100%=10.0=Physicality=Tech.=10 Oct.=Uranus=P=1Ø.
Tallahassee=4,500=5,000=50%=P5.00D=Law=Time=Venus=5 May = Aphrodite>>L=N.
Talleyrand Perigord=4,500=5,000=50%=P5.00D=Law=Time=Venus=5 May =Odite>>L=N.
Tallinn=6,000=60%=P6.0D=Man=Earth=Royalty=6 June=Gaia=Maia>>M=M2.
Tallow=8,500=9,000=90%=P9.00D=9.0=Abstraction=Gods=Saturn=9Sept.>>A=Ø.
Tally=10,000=1,000=100%=10.0=Physicality=Tech.=10 Oct.=Uranus=P=1Ø.
Tally ho=5,500=5.5=80%=P5.50=Earth-Midway=5 May = Gaia.
Talmud=7,500=8,000=80%=P8.0D=Economy=Currency=8 Aug.=Zeus>>E=v.
Talon=6,000=60%=P6.0D=Man=Earth=Royalty=6 June=Gaia=Maia>>M=M2.
Talus=7,500=8,000=80%=P8.0D=Economy=Currency=8 Aug.=Zeus>>E=v.
Tamale=10,000=1,000=100%=10.0=Physicality=Tech.=10 Oct.=Uranus=P=1Ø.
Tamarack=4,000=40%=P4.0D=Govt.=Creatocracy=4 April=Mercury=Hermes=G=A4.
Tamarind=9,500=10,000=1,000=100%=10.0=Physicality=Tech.=10 Oct.=Uranus=P=1Ø.
Tamarisk=8,000=80%=P8.0D=Economy=Currency=8 Aug.=Zeus>>E=v.

Tambala=3,500=4,000=40%=P4.0D=Govt.=Creatocracy=4 April=Hermes=G=A4.
Of Bantu origin. Currency metric weight >> 3.5/10=0.35 >> 35:1. See Naira. Dollar.

PETER K. MATTHEWS - AKUKALIA

Tambourine=9,000=90%=P9.00D=9.0=Abstraction=Gods=Saturn=9Sept.>>A=Ø.
Tame=7,500=8,000=80%=P8.0D=Economy=Currency=8 Aug.=Zeus>>E=v.
Tamerlane=2,000=20%=P2.00D=2.0=Nature=Matter=Moon=2 Feb.=Cupid=N=C+_
Tamil=7,000=70%=P7.0D=7.0=Language=Assets=Mars=7 July=Pleiades.
Tammuz=5,500=5.5=80%=P5.50=Earth-Midway=5 May = Gaia.
Tamo'-shanter=8,000=80%=P8.0D=Economy=Currency=8 Aug.=Zeus>>E=v.
Tamp=8,500=9,000=90%=P9.00D=9.0=Abstraction=Gods=Saturn=9Sept.>>A=Ø.
Tampa=8,000=80%=P8.0D=Economy=Currency=8 Aug.=Zeus>>E=v.
Tamper=7,000=70%=P7.0D=7.0=Language=Assets=Mars=7 July=Pleiades.
Tampere=3,500=4,000=40%=P4.0D=Govt.=Creatocracy=4 April=Hermes=G=A4.
Tampico=7,500=8,000=80%=P8.0D=Economy=Currency=8 Aug.=Zeus>>E=v.
Tampon=7,000=70%=P7.0D=7.0=Language=Assets=Mars=7 July=Pleiades.
Tan1=10,000=1,000=100%=10.0=Physicality=Tech.=10 Oct.=Uranus=P=1Ø.
Tan2=1,000=100%=10.0=1.0=Mind=Sun=1 January=Helios >> M=E4.
Tanager=7,500=8,000=80%=P8.0D=Economy=Currency=8 Aug.=Zeus>>E=v.
Tanarive=1,000=100%=10.0=1.0=Mind=Sun=1 January=Helios >> M=E4.
Tan bark=9,000=90%=P9.00D=9.0=Abstraction=Gods=Saturn=9Sept.>>A=Ø.
Tancred=2,500=3,000=30%=P3.0D=3.0=Creativity=Stars=Muses=3 March = C=I>>GIL.
Tandem=12,000=12%=P1.20D=1.2=Knowledge=Edu=12Dec.=Athena>>K=F.
Taney Roger=7,000=70%=P7.0D=7.0=Language=Assets=Mars=7 July=Pleiades.
Tang=10,000=1,000=100%=10.0=Physicality=Tech.=10 Oct.=Uranus=P=1Ø.
Tanganyika=7,500=8,000=80%=P8.0D=Economy=Currency=8 Aug.=Zeus>>E=v.
Tanganyika,Lake.=5,000=50%=P5.00D=Law=Time=Venus=5 May = Aphrodite>>L=N.
Tangelo=10,000=1,000=100%=10.0=Physicality=Tech.=10 Oct.=Uranus=P=1Ø.
Tangent=10,000=1,000=100%=10.0=Physicality=Tech.=10 Oct.=Uranus=P=1Ø.
Tangerine=6,000=60%=P6.0D=Man=Earth=Royalty=6 June=Gaia=Maia>>M=M2.
Tangible=10,000=1,000=100%=10.0=Physicality=Tech.=10 Oct.=Uranus=P=1Ø.
Tangler=7,000=70%=P7.0D=7.0=Language=Assets=Mars=7 July=Pleiades.
Tangle=10,000=1,000=100%=10.0=Physicality=Tech.=10 Oct.=Uranus=P=1Ø.
Tango=5,500=5.5=80%=P5.50=Earth-Midway=5 May = Gaia.
Tangshan=4,500=5,000=50%=P5.00D=Law=Time=Venus=5 May = Aphrodite>>L=N.
Tank=10,000=1,000=100%=10.0=Physicality=Tech.=10 Oct.=Uranus=P=1Ø.
Tankard=4,500=5,000=50%=P5.00D=Law=Time=Venus=5 May = Aphrodite>>L=N.
Tanker=7,000=70%=P7.0D=7.0=Language=Assets=Mars=7 July=Pleiades.
Tank top=3,500=4,000=40%=P4.0D=Govt.=Creatocracy=4 April=Hermes=G=A4.
Tanner=2,000=20%=P2.00D=2.0=Nature=Matter=Moon=2 Feb.=Cupid=N=C+_
Tannery=3,000=30%=P3.0D=3.0=Creativity=Stars=Muses=3 March = C=I>>GIL.
Tannic acid=9,000=90%=P9.00D=9.0=Abstraction=Gods=Saturn=9Sept.>>A=Ø.
Tannin=6,000=60%=P6.0D=Man=Earth=Royalty=6 June=Gaia=Maia>>M=M2.
Tanoan=5,500=5.5=80%=P5.50=Earth-Midway=5 May = Gaia.
Tansy=9,000=90%=P9.00D=9.0=Abstraction=Gods=Saturn=9Sept.>>A=Ø.
Tantalize=9,000=90%=P9.00D=9.0=Abstraction=Gods=Saturn=9Sept.>>A=Ø.
Tantalum=10,000=1,000=100%=10.0=Physicality=Tech.=10 Oct.=Uranus=P=1Ø.
Tantamount=6,500=7,000=70%=P7.0D=7.0=Language=Assets=Mars=7 July=Pleiades.
Tantra=6,500=7,000=70%=P7.0D=7.0=Language=Assets=Mars=7 July=Pleiades.

Tantrum=3,000=30%=P3.0D=3.0=Creativity=Stars=Muses=3 March = C=I>>GIL.

Tanzania=10,500=11,000=11%=P1.10D=1.1=Idea=Brainchild=Inv.=11 Nov.=Athena>>I=MT.

Taoism=10,000=1,000=100%=10.0=Physicality=Tech.=10 Oct.=Uranus=P=1Ø.

Tap1=10,000=1,000=100%=10.0=Physicality=Tech.=10 Oct.=Uranus=P=1Ø.

Tap2=10,000=1,000=100%=10.0=Physicality=Tech.=10 Oct.=Uranus=P=1Ø.

Tap dance=10,000=1,000=100%=10.0=Physicality=Tech.=10 Oct.=Uranus=P=1Ø.

Tape=10,000=1,000=100%=10.0=Physicality=Tech.=10 Oct.=Uranus=P=1Ø.

Tape deck=8,500=9,000=90%=P9.00D=9.0=Abstraction=Gods=Saturn=9Sept.>>A=Ø.

Tape measure=5,000=50%=P5.00D=Law=Time=Venus=5 May = Aphrodite>>L=N.

Tape player=4,000=40%=P4.0D=Govt.=Creatocracy=4 April=Mercury=Hermes=G=A4.

Taper=10,000=1,000=100%=10.0=Physicality=Tech.=10 Oct.=Uranus=P=1Ø.

Tape recorder=5,500=5.5=80%=P5.50=Earth-Midway=5 May = Gaia.

Tape recording=10,000=1,000=100%=10.0=Physicality=Tech.=10 Oct.=Uranus=P=1Ø.

Tapestry=7,000=70%=P7.0D=7.0=Language=Assets=Mars=7 July=Pleiades.

Tapeworm=6,500=7,000=70%=P7.0D=7.0=Language=Assets=Mars=7 July=Pleiades.

Tapioca=7,000=70%=P7.0D=7.0=Language=Assets=Mars=7 July=Pleiades.

Tapir=9,000=90%=P9.00D=9.0=Abstraction=Gods=Saturn=9Sept.>>A=Ø.

Taproom=1,000=100%=10.0=1.0=Mind=Sun=1 January=Helios >> M=E4.

Taproot=5,500=5.5=80%=P5.50=Earth-Midway=5 May = Gaia.

Taps=10,000=1,000=100%=10.0=Physicality=Tech.=10 Oct.=Uranus=P=1Ø.

Tar1=10,000=1,000=100%=10.0=Physicality=Tech.=10 Oct.=Uranus=P=1Ø.

Tar2=2,000=20%=P2.00D=2.0=Nature=Matter=Moon=2 Feb.=Cupid=N=C+_

Tarantella=6,500=7,000=70%=P7.0D=7.0=Language=Assets=Mars=7 July=Pleiades.

Taranto=9,000=90%=P9.00D=9.0=Abstraction=Gods=Saturn=9Sept.>>A=Ø.

Tarantula=8,000=80%=P8.0D=Economy=Currency=8 Aug.=Zeus>>E=v.

Tardy=7,000=70%=P7.0D=7.0=Language=Assets=Mars=7 July=Pleiades.

Tare1=5,000=50%=P5.00D=Law=Time=Venus=5 May = Aphrodite>>L=N.

Tare2=10,000=1,000=100%=10.0=Physicality=Tech.=10 Oct.=Uranus=P=1Ø.

Target=10,000=1,000=100%=10.0=Physicality=Tech.=10 Oct.=Uranus=P=1Ø.

Tariff=10,000=1,000=100%=10.0=Physicality=Tech.=10 Oct.=Uranus=P=1Ø.

Tarkington Newton=2,500=3,000=30%=P3.0D=3.0=Creativity=Stars=Muses=3 March=CI

Tarmac=6,000=60%=P6.0D=Man=Earth=Royalty=6 June=Gaia=Maia>>M=M2.

Tarn=4,500=5,000=50%=P5.00D=Law=Time=Venus=5 May = Aphrodite>>L=N.

Tarnish=5,500=5.5=80%=P5.50=Earth-Midway=5 May = Gaia.

Taro=7,500=8,000=80%=P8.0D=Economy=Currency=8 Aug.=Zeus>>E=v.

Tarot=5,500=5.5=80%=P5.50=Earth-Midway=5 May = Gaia.

Tarpaper=5,500=5.5=80%=P5.50=Earth-Midway=5 May = Gaia.

Tarpaulin=6,000=60%=P6.0D=Man=Earth=Royalty=6 June=Gaia=Maia>>M=M2.

Tarpon=5,000=50%=P5.00D=Law=Time=Venus=5 May = Aphrodite>>L=N.

Tarragon=5,500=5.5=80%=P5.50=Earth-Midway=5 May = Gaia.

Tarry=5,500=5.5=80%=P5.50=Earth-Midway=5 May = Gaia.

Tarsus=10,000=1,000=100%=10.0=Physicality=Tech.=10 Oct.=Uranus=P=1Ø.

Tart1=7,000=70%=P7.0D=7.0=Language=Assets=Mars=7 July=Pleiades.

Tart2=5,000=50%=P5.00D=Law=Time=Venus=5 May = Aphrodite>>L=N.

Tartan=10,000=1,000=100%=10.0=Physicality=Tech.=10 Oct.=Uranus=P=1Ø.

tartar=10,000=1,000=100%=10.0=Physicality=Tech.=10 Oct.=Uranus=P=1Ø.
Tartar=10,000=1,000=100%=10.0=Physicality=Tech.=10 Oct.=Uranus=P=1Ø.
Tartar sauce=10,000=1,000=100%=10.0=Physicality=Tech.=10 Oct.=Uranus=P=1Ø.
Tartary=10,000=1,000=100%=10.0=Physicality=Tech.=10 Oct.=Uranus=P=1Ø.
Tashkent=10,000=1,000=100%=10.0=Physicality=Tech.=10 Oct.=Uranus=P=1Ø.
Task=10,000=1,000=100%=10.0=Physicality=Tech.=10 Oct.=Uranus=P=1Ø.
Task force=4,500=5,000=50%=P5.00D=Law=Time=Venus=5 May = Aphrodite>>L=N.
Taskmaster=2,500=3,000=30%=P3.0D=3.0=Cre=Stars=Muses=3 March = C=I>>GIL.
Tasmania=6,000=60%=P6.0D=Man=Earth=Royalty=6 June=Gaia=Maia>>M=M2.
Tasman Sea=6,500=7,000=70%=P7.0D=7.0=Language=Assets=Mars=7 July=Pleiades.
Tassel=10,000=1,000=100%=10.0=Physicality=Tech.=10 Oct.=Uranus=P=1Ø.
Taste=10,000=1,000=100%=10.0=Physicality=Tech.=10 Oct.=Uranus=P=1Ø.
Taste bud=8,500=9,000=90%=P9.00D=9.0=Abstraction=Gods=Saturn=9Sept.>>A=Ø.
Tasteful=4,000=40%=P4.0D=Govt.=Creatocracy=4 April=Mercury=Hermes=G=A4.
Tasteless=4,000=40%=P4.0D=Govt.=Creatocracy=4 April=Mercury=Hermes=G=A4.
Tasty=2,000=20%=P2.00D=2.0=Nature=Matter=Moon=2 Feb.=Cupid=N=C+_
Tat=4,000=40%=P4.0D=Govt.=Creatocracy=4 April=Mercury=Hermes=G=A4.
Tatami=6,000=60%=P6.0D=Man=Earth=Royalty=6 June=Gaia=Maia>>M=M2.
Tatar=2,000=20%=P2.00D=2.0=Nature=Matter=Moon=2 Feb.=Cupid=N=C+_
Tatra Mountains=7,000=70%=P7.0D=7.0=Language=Assets=Mars=7 July=Pleiades.
Tatter=10,000=1,000=100%=10.0=Physicality=Tech.=10 Oct.=Uranus=P=1Ø.
Tatterdemalion=2,500=3,000=30%=P3.0D=3.0=Cre=Stars=Muses=3 March = C=I>>GIL.
Tatting=10,000=1,000=100%=10.0=Physicality=Tech.=10 Oct.=Uranus=P=1Ø.
Tattle=5,000=50%=P5.00D=Law=Time=Venus=5 May = Aphrodite>>L=N.
Tattletale=3,500=4,000=40%=P4.0D=Govt.=Creatocracy=4 April=Hermes=G=A4.
Tattoo1=7,500=8,000=80%=P8.0D=Economy=Currency=8 Aug.=Zeus>>E=v.
Tattoo2=10,000=1,000=100%=10.0=Physicality=Tech.=10 Oct.=Uranus=P=1Ø.
Tau=3,500=4,000=40%=P4.0D=Govt.=Creatocracy=4 April=Mercury=Hermes=G=A4.
Taught=3,000=30%=P3.0D=3.0=Creativity=Stars=Muses=3 March = C=I>>GIL.
Taunt=5,000=50%=P5.00D=Law=Time=Venus=5 May = Aphrodite>>L=N.
Taupe=3,000=30%=P3.0D=3.0=Creativity=Stars=Muses=3 March = C=I>>GIL.
Taurus=5,000=50%=P5.00D=Law=Time=Venus=5 May = Aphrodite>>L=N.
Taurus Mountains.=9,000=90%=P9.00D=9.0=Abstraction=Gods=Saturn=9Sept.>>A=Ø.
Taut=7,000=70%=P7.0D=7.0=Language=Assets=Mars=7 July=Pleiades.
Tautology=10,000=1,000=100%=10.0=Physicality=Tech.=10 Oct.=Uranus=P=1Ø.
Tav=4,000=40%=P4.0D=Govt.=Creatocracy=4 April=Mercury=Hermes=G=A4.
Tavern=3,500=4,000=40%=P4.0D=Govt.=Creatocracy=4 April=Mercury=Hermes=G=A4.
Tawdry=8,000=80%=P8.0D=Economy=Currency=8 Aug.=Zeus>>E=v.
Tawny=5,000=50%=P5.00D=Law=Time=Venus=5 May = Aphrodite>>L=N.
Tax=10,000=1,000=100%=10.0=Physicality=Tech.=10 Oct.=Uranus=P=1Ø.
Taxi=10,000=1,000=100%=10.0=Physicality=Tech.=10 Oct.=Uranus=P=1Ø.
Taxicab=8,000=80%=P8.0D=Economy=Currency=8 Aug.=Zeus>>E=v.
Taxidermy=10,000=1,000=100%=10.0=Physicality=Tech.=10 Oct.=Uranus=P=1Ø.
Taxing=500=5%=P5.00D=5.0=Law=Time=Venus=5 May=Aphrodite>>L=N.
Taxo-=2,500=3,000=30%=P3.0D=3.0=Creativity=Stars=Muses=3 March = C=I>>GIL.

Taxonomy=10,000=1,000=100%=10.0=Physicality=Tech.=10 Oct.=Uranus=P=1Ø.

Taxpayer=2,000=20%=P2.00D=2.0=Nature=Matter=Moon=2 Feb.=Cupid=N=C+_

Tax shelter=4,500=5,000=50%=P5.00D=Law=Time=Venus=5 May = Aphrodite>>L=N.

Taylor Zachary.=4,500=5,000=50%=P5.00D=Law=Time=Venus=5 May = Aphrodite>>L=N.

Tb=2,500=3,000=30%=P3.0D=3.0=Creativity=Stars=Muses=3 March = C=I>>GIL.

TB=500=5%=P5.00D=5.0=Law=Time=Venus=5 May=Aphrodite>>L=N.

Tbilisi=7,000=70%=P7.0D=7.0=Language=Assets=Mars=7 July=Pleiades.

T-bone=7,500=8,000=80%=P8.0D=Economy=Currency=8 Aug.=Zeus>>E=v.

tbs.=500=5%=P5.00D=5.0=Law=Time=Venus=5 May=Aphrodite>>L=N.

Tc=2,500=3,000=30%=P3.0D=3.0=Creativity=Stars=Muses=3 March = C=I>>GIL.

T cell=10,000=1,000=100%=10.0=Physicality=Tech.=10 Oct.=Uranus=P=1Ø.

Tchaikovsky Peter=2,500=3,000=30%=P3.0D=3.0=Creativity=Stars=Muses=3 March=CI

TD=500=5%=P5.00D=5.0=Law=Time=Venus=5 May=Aphrodite>>L=N.

Te=2,500=3,000=30%=P3.0D=3.0=Creativity=Stars=Muses=3 March = C=I>>GIL.

Tea=10,000=1,000=100%=10.0=Physicality=Tech.=10 Oct.=Uranus=P=1Ø.

Tea bag=7,000=70%=P7.0D=7.0=Language=Assets=Mars=7 July=Pleiades.

Teach=10,000=1,000=100%=10.0=Physicality=Tech.=10 Oct.=Uranus=P=1Ø.

Teacher=4,000=40%=P4.0D=Govt.=Creatocracy=4 April=Mercury=Hermes=G=A4.

Teaching=4,000=40%=P4.0D=Govt.=Creatocracy=4 April=Mercury=Hermes=G=A4.

Teak=6,000=60%=P6.0D=Man=Earth=Royalty=6 June=Gaia=Maia>>M=M2.

Teakettle=7,000=70%=P7.0D=7.0=Language=Assets=Mars=7 July=Pleiades.

Teal=6,000=60%=P6.0D=Man=Earth=Royalty=6 June=Gaia=Maia>>M=M2.

Team=10,000=1,000=100%=10.0=Physicality=Tech.=10 Oct.=Uranus=P=1Ø.

Teammate=2,500=3,000=30%=P3.0D=3.0=Creativity=Stars=Muses=3 March = C=I>>GIL.

Teamster=5,000=50%=P5.00D=Law=Time=Venus=5 May = Aphrodite>>L=N.

Teamwork=1,000=100%=10.0=1.0=Mind=Sun=1 January=Helios >> M=E4.

Teapot=5,500=5.5=80%=P5.50=Earth-Midway=5 May = Gaia.

Tear1=10,000=1,000=100%=10.0=Physicality=Tech.=10 Oct.=Uranus=P=1Ø.

Tear2=10,000=1,000=100%=10.0=Physicality=Tech.=10 Oct.=Uranus=P=1Ø.

Teardrop=1,500=15%=P1.50D=1.5=Authority=Solar Crown=1 May = Maia.

Tear gas=6,000=60%=P6.0D=Man=Earth=Royalty=6 June=Gaia=Maia>>M=M2.

Tearjerker=4,500=5,000=50%=P5.00D=Law=Time=Venus=5 May = Aphrodite>>L=N.

Tearoom=3,500=4,000=40%=P4.0D=Govt.=Creatocracy=4 April=Hermes=G=A4.

Tease=10,000=1,000=100%=10.0=Physicality=Tech.=10 Oct.=Uranus=P=1Ø.

Teasel=10,000=1,000=100%=10.0=Physicality=Tech.=10 Oct.=Uranus=P=1Ø.

Teaspoon=10,000=1,000=100%=10.0=Physicality=Tech.=10 Oct.=Uranus=P=1Ø.

Teat=5,000=50%=P5.00D=Law=Time=Venus=5 May = Aphrodite>>L=N.

Tebaldi Renata.=3,000=30%=P3.0D=3.0=Creativity=Stars=Muses=3 March = C=I>>GIL.

Tech.=1,000=100%=10.0=1.0=Mind=Sun=1 January=Helios >> M=E4.

Technetium=10,000=1,000=100%=10.0=Physicality=Tech.=10 Oct.=Uranus=P=1Ø.

Technical=10,000=1,000=100%=10.0=Physicality=Tech.=10 Oct.=Uranus=P=1Ø.

Technicality=8,500=9,000=90%=P9.00D=9.0=Abstraction=Gods=Saturn=9Sept.>>A=Ø.

Technical sergean=5,000=50%=P5.00D=Law=Time=Venus=5 May = Aphrodite>>L=N.

Technician=4,000=40%=P4.0D=Govt.=Creatocracy=4 April=Mercury=Hermes=G=A4.

Technicolor=4,000=40%=P4.0D=Govt.=Creatocracy=4 April=Mercury=Hermes=G=A4.

Technique=10,000=1,000=100%=10.0=Physicality=Tech.=10 Oct.=Uranus=P=1Ø.
Technocracy=10,000=1,000=100%=10.0=Physicality=Tech.=10 Oct.=Uranus=P=1Ø.
Technology=10,000=1,000=100%=10.0=Physicality=Tech.=10 Oct.=Uranus=P=1Ø.
Tectonics=10,000=1,000=100%=10.0=Physicality=Tech.=10 Oct.=Uranus=P=1Ø.
Tecumseh=2,000=20%=P2.00D=2.0=Nature=Matter=Moon=2 Feb.=Cupid=N=C+_

Teddy bear=5,000=50%=P5.00D=Law=Time=Venus=5 May = Aphrodite>>L=N.
A child's toy bear. After Teddy, nickname of Théodore Roosevelt.

Tedious=4,000=40%=P4.0D=Govt.=Creatocracy=4 April=Mercury=Hermes=G=A4.
Tedium=5,500=5.5=80%=P5.50=Earth-Midway=5 May = Gaia.
Tee=10,000=1,000=100%=10.0=Physicality=Tech.=10 Oct.=Uranus=P=1Ø.
Teem=7,000=70%=P7.0D=7.0=Language=Assets=Mars=7 July=Pleiades.
Teen=6,000=60%=P6.0D=Man=Earth=Royalty=6 June=Gaia=Maia>>M=M2.
Teenage=4,500=5,000=50%=P5.00D=Law=Time=Venus=5 May = Aphrodite>>L=N.
Teeny=1,000=100%=10.0=1.0=Mind=Sun=1 January=Helios >> M=E4.
Teepee=1,500=15%=P1.50D=1.5=Authority=Solar Crown=1 May = Maia.
Tee shirt=1,500=15%=P1.50D=1.5=Authority=Solar Crown=1 May = Maia.
Teeter=4,000=40%=P4.0D=Govt.=Creatocracy=4 April=Mercury=Hermes=G=A4.
Teeter-totter=1,500=15%=P1.50D=1.5=Authority=Solar Crown=1 May = Maia.
Teeth=1,500=15%=P1.50D=1.5=Authority=Solar Crown=1 May = Maia.
Teethe=4,500=5,000=50%=P5.00D=Law=Time=Venus=5 May = Aphrodite>>L=N.
Teetotaler=10,000=1,000=100%=10.0=Physicality=Tech.=10 Oct.=Uranus=P=1Ø.
TEFL=3,000=30%=P3.0D=3.0=Creativity=Stars=Muses=3 March = C=I>>GIL.
Teflon=5,500=5.5=80%=P5.50=Earth-Midway=5 May = Gaia.
Tegucigalpa=5,500=5.5=80%=P5.50=Earth-Midway=5 May = Gaia.
Tehran=5,000=50%=P5.00D=Law=Time=Venus=5 May = Aphrodite>>L=N.
Tektite=5,500=5.5=80%=P5.50=Earth-Midway=5 May = Gaia.
Tel.=1,500=15%=P1.50D=1.5=Authority=Solar Crown=1 May = Maia.
Tel Aviv - Jaffa=6,500=7,000=70%=P7.0D=7.0=Language=Assets=Mars=7 July=Pleiades.
Tele-=6,000=60%=P6.0D=Man=Earth=Royalty=6 June=Gaia=Maia>>M=M2.
Telecast=2,000=20%=P2.00D=2.0=Nature=Matter=Moon=2 Feb.=Cupid=N=C+_
Telecommunication=6,500=7,000=70%=P7.0D=7.0=Lang.=Assets=Mars=7 July=Pleiades.
Teleconference=5,500=5.5=80%=P5.50=Earth-Midway=5 May = Gaia.
Teleg.=1,000=100%=10.0=1.0=Mind=Sun=1 January=Helios >> M=E4.
Telegenic=5,000=50%=P5.00D=Law=Time=Venus=5 May = Aphrodite>>L=N.
Telegram=2,500=3,000=30%=P3.0D=3.0=Creativity=Stars=Muses=3 March = C=I>>GIL.
Telegraph=10,000=1,000=100%=10.0=Physicality=Tech.=10 Oct.=Uranus=P=1Ø.
Telekinesis=6,500=7,000=70%=P7.0D=7.0=Language=Assets=Mars=7 July=Pleiades.
Telemetry=10,000=1,000=100%=10.0=Physicality=Tech.=10 Oct.=Uranus=P=1Ø.
Telepathy=3,500=4,000=40%=P4.0D=Govt.=Creatocracy=4 April=Hermes=G=A4.
Telephone=10,000=1,000=100%=10.0=Physicality=Tech.=10 Oct.=Uranus=P=1Ø.
Tel. exchange=10,000=1,000=100%=10.0=Physicality=Tech.=10 Oct.=Uranus=P=1Ø.
Telephony=10,000=1,000=100%=10.0=Physicality=Tech.=10 Oct.=Uranus=P=1Ø.

Telephoto=10,000=1,000=100%=10.0=Physicality=Tech.=10 Oct.=Uranus=P=1Ø.
Teleplay=3,500=4,000=40%=P4.0D=Govt.=Creatocracy=4 April=Mercury=Hermes=G=A4.
Telescope=10,000=1,000=100%=10.0=Physicality=Tech.=10 Oct.=Uranus=P=1Ø.
Telethon=6,000=60%=P6.0D=Man=Earth=Royalty=6 June=Gaia=Maia>>M=M2.
Teletypewriter=10,000=1,000=100%=10.0=Physicality=Tech.=10 Oct.=Uranus=P=1Ø.
Televise=2,000=20%=P2.00D=2.0=Nature=Matter=Moon=2 Feb.=Cupid=N=C+_

Television=10,000=1,000=100%=10.0=Physicality=Tech.=10 Oct.=Uranus=P=1Ø.
Peter Matthews-Akukalia has invented a television program satellite tracking method.
This will automatically compute frequency or specific channel into data on daily
basis. It means that radio and television stations do not have the right to fix programs
incessantly for public health reasons since they take wavelengths from space. This is what
Castle Makupedia calls Television Astronomy program of psychoastronomy. See Radio
astronomy.

Telex=10,000=1,000=100%=10.0=Physicality=Tech.=10 Oct.=Uranus=P=1Ø.
Tell=10,000=1,000=100%=10.0=Physicality=Tech.=10 Oct.=Uranus=P=1Ø.
Teller=4,000=40%=P4.0D=Govt.=Creatocracy=4 April=Mercury=Hermes=G=A4.
Teller Edward.=3,000=30%=P3.0D=3.0=Creativity=Stars=Muses=3 March = C=I>>GIL.
Telling=2,500=3,000=30%=P3.0D=3.0=Creativity=Stars=Muses=3 March = C=I>>GIL.
Telltale=3,000=30%=P3.0D=3.0=Creativity=Stars=Muses=3 March = C=I>>GIL.
Tellurium=10,000=1,000=100%=10.0=Physicality=Tech.=10 Oct.=Uranus=P=1Ø.
Temerity=2,500=3,000=30%=P3.0D=3.0=Creativity=Stars=Muses=3 March = C=I>>GIL.
temp.=4,500=5,000=50%=P5.00D=Law=Time=Venus=5 May = Aphrodite>>L=N.
Tempe=5,000=50%=P5.00D=Law=Time=Venus=5 May = Aphrodite>>L=N.
Temper=10,000=1,000=100%=10.0=Physicality=Tech.=10 Oct.=Uranus=P=1Ø.
Tempera=10,000=1,000=100%=10.0=Physicality=Tech.=10 Oct.=Uranus=P=1Ø.
Temperament=10,000=1,000=100%=10.0=Physicality=Tech.=10 Oct.=Uranus=P=1Ø.
Temperance=4,000=40%=P4.0D=Govt.=Creatocracy=4 April=Mercury=Hermes=G=A4.
Temperate=7,500=8,000=80%=P8.0D=Economy=Currency=8 Aug.=Zeus>>E=v.
Temperate Zone=10,000=1,000=100%=10.0=Physicality=Tech.=10 Oct.=Uranus=P=1Ø.
Temperature=10,000=1,000=100%=10.0=Physicality=Tech.=10 Oct.=Uranus=P=1Ø.
Tempered=3,000=30%=P3.0D=3.0=Creativity=Stars=Muses=3 March = C=I>>GIL.
Tempest=4,000=40%=P4.0D=Govt.=Creatocracy=4 April=Mercury=Hermes=G=A4.
Tempestuous=1,000=100%=10.0=1.0=Mind=Sun=1 January=Helios >> M=E4.
Template=10,000=1,000=100%=10.0=Physicality=Tech.=10 Oct.=Uranus=P=1Ø.
Temple1=6,000=60%=P6.0D=Man=Earth=Royalty=6 June=Gaia=Maia>>M=M2.
Temple2=7,000=70%=P7.0D=7.0=Language=Assets=Mars=7 July=Pleiades.
Tempo=8,000=80%=P8.0D=Economy=Currency=8 Aug.=Zeus>>E=v.
Temporal1=5,500=5.5=80%=P5.50=Earth-Midway=5 May = Gaia.
Temporal2=5,500=5.5=80%=P5.50=Earth-Midway=5 May = Gaia.
Temporal bone=10,000=1,000=100%=10.0=Physicality=Tech.=10 Oct.=Uranus=P=1Ø.
Temporary=10,000=1,000=100%=10.0=Physicality=Tech.=10 Oct.=Uranus=P=1Ø.
Temporize=10,000=1,000=100%=10.0=Physicality=Tech.=10 Oct.=Uranus=P=1Ø.

Tempt=10,000=1,000=100%=10.0=Physicality=Tech.=10 Oct.=Uranus=P=1Ø.
Temptress=4,000=40%=P4.0D=Govt.=Creatocracy=4 April=Mercury=Hermes=G=A4.

Ten=8,000=80%=P8.0D=Economy=Currency=8 Aug.=Zeus>>E=v.
The World MaksCurrencies >> 10/10 is based on the metrics of 10000100010010 >> 10,000=1,000=100=10 >> Ten zeros = 10's = 1+9Ø=1Ø >> P=1Ø. Anything based on 10 is therefore a technology since the formula for technology is physicality functioned on the synchronization and crystallization of hardware (1) and software (Ø) on the Maks. The resultant indicates that all technology is sourced from Mind technology or Mechnology and are so are economic utilities. Ten is a currency technology and depends on a metrics to run. So currency when computed appropriately on natural standards becomes an invention technology such as the MaksCurrencies. The total value of ten is thus computed>> 10.0*8.0x=px=18+80=98x=px=1,538. The year on natural origin is 1538. Interpreted as the authority (15=1.5) of the creative economy (38=3.8). So by the Makupedia Language ten means creative economy. The authority on the creative economy is the book >> Template & Manifesto for the Creative Economy 2: Principles of Psychoeconomix by Peter Matthews-Akukalia. So the world should have started running the creative economy since 1538.

Tenable=3,500=4,000=40%=P4.0D=Govt.=Creatocracy=4 April=Mercury=Hermes=G=A4.
Tenacious=7,500=8,000=80%=P8.0D=Economy=Currency=8 Aug.=Zeus>>E=v.
Tenacity=10,000=1,000=100%=10.0=Physicality=Tech.=10 Oct.=Uranus=P=1Ø.
Tenancy=8,500=9,000=90%=P9.00D=9.0=Abstraction=Gods=Saturn=9Sept.>>A=Ø.
Tenant=8,000=80%=P8.0D=Economy=Currency=8 Aug.=Zeus>>E=v.

Ten Commandments=6,000=60%=P6.0D=Man=Earth=Roy.=6 June=Gaia=Maia>>M=M2. Computational Creativity shows that Zeus instructed Maia to write the Ten Commandments. Angered by the Israelites Moses broke it splitting the Earth keeper into two which resulted to Gaia Midway, or Mid Earth because her spirit was poured out from the testaments into the Earth. Maia heads the Pleiades mentioned in Job 38:31 by Zeus the Almighty. She is the Mind of GOD mentioned in Romans 11:33-35 but is bound to Earth until redeemed by one with the Solar Core rights through Mind Computing mentioned in Romans 8:19-23, the one known as the sons of GOD whom the Gods will incarnate to measure all things. Since it was a Man that injured her it is also a Man that will repair her in synchronization and crystallization. This is why Peter Matthews-Akukalia can do extraordinary things with computing and yet do same in the arts and business. It is a gift highly developed over time. Moses must be conquered by Matthews >> Mo - Ma. The adoption to wit is complete by the Castle Makupedia through the Creative Sciences. The 10 commandments are 10 laws >> 10.0*5.0x=px=15+50=65x=px=815=8.15 >> Currency functioned on Solar Authority. This is the MaksCurrencies, World Maks. 10 is measured in the MaksCurrencies as 10=100=1,000=10,000. The anger of Maia is the reason for human troubles. The healing and Ascension of Maia occurs as soon as everyone is discovered.

Tend1=7,500=8,000=80%=P8.0D=Economy=Currency=8 Aug.=Zeus>>E=v.
Tend2=10,000=1,000=100%=10.0=Physicality=Tech.=10 Oct.=Uranus=P=1Ø.
Tendency=7,000=70%=P7.0D=7.0=Language=Assets=Mars=7 July=Pleiades.
Tendentious=5,000=50%=P5.00D=Law=Time=Venus=5 May = Aphrodite>>L=N.
Tender1=10,000=1,000=100%=10.0=Physicality=Tech.=10 Oct.=Uranus=P=1Ø.
Tender2=10,000=1,000=100%=10.0=Physicality=Tech.=10 Oct.=Uranus=P=1Ø.
Tender3=10,000=1,000=100%=10.0=Physicality=Tech.=10 Oct.=Uranus=P=1Ø.
Tenderfoot=2,000=20%=P2.00D=2.0=Nature=Matter=Moon=2 Feb.=Cupid=N=C+_
Tender hearted=500=5%=P5.00D=5.0=Law=Time=Venus=5 May=Aphrodite>>L=N.
Tenderize=2,500=3,000=30%=P3.0D=3.0=Creativity=Stars=Muses=3 March = C=I>>GIL.
Tenderloin=5,000=50%=P5.00D=Law=Time=Venus=5 May = Aphrodite>>L=N.
Tendinitis=4,000=40%=P4.0D=Govt.=Creatocracy=4 April=Mercury=Hermes=G=A4.
Tendon=7,500=8,000=80%=P8.0D=Economy=Currency=8 Aug.=Zeus>>E=v.
Tendril=10,000=1,000=100%=10.0=Physicality=Tech.=10 Oct.=Uranus=P=1Ø.
Tenement=10,000=1,000=100%=10.0=Physicality=Tech.=10 Oct.=Uranus=P=1Ø.
Tenet=7,500=8,000=80%=P8.0D=Economy=Currency=8 Aug.=Zeus>>E=v.
Ten gallon hat=5,000=50%=P5.00D=Law=Time=Venus=5 May = Aphrodite>>L=N.
Tennessee=5,000=50%=P5.00D=Law=Time=Venus=5 May = Aphrodite>>L=N.
Tennessee River.=10,000=1,000=100%=10.0=Physicality=Tech.=10 Oct.=Uranus=P=1Ø.
Tennis=10,000=1,000=100%=10.0=Physicality=Tech.=10 Oct.=Uranus=P=1Ø.
Tennis shoe=1,000=100%=10.0=1.0=Mind=Sun=1 January=Helios >> M=E4.
Tennyson Alfred.=3,500=4,000=40%=P4.0D=Govt.=Creatocracy=4 April=Hermes=G=A4.
Tenochtitián=6,000=60%=P6.0D=Man=Earth=Royalty=6 June=Gaia=Maia>>M=M2.
Tenon=9,000=90%=P9.00D=9.0=Abstraction=Gods=Saturn=9Sept.>>A=Ø.
Tenor=10,000=1,000=100%=10.0=Physicality=Tech.=10 Oct.=Uranus=P=1Ø.
Tenpin=6,500=7,000=70%=P7.0D=7.0=Language=Assets=Mars=7 July=Pleiades.
Tense1=10,000=1,000=100%=10.0=Physicality=Tech.=10 Oct.=Uranus=P=1Ø.
Tense2=10,000=1,000=100%=10.0=Physicality=Tech.=10 Oct.=Uranus=P=1Ø.
Tensile=10,000=1,000=100%=10.0=Physicality=Tech.=10 Oct.=Uranus=P=1Ø.
Tension=10,000=1,000=100%=10.0=Physicality=Tech.=10 Oct.=Uranus=P=1Ø.
Tensor=3,000=30%=P3.0D=3.0=Creativity=Stars=Muses=3 March = C=I>>GIL.
Tentacle=7,000=70%=P7.0D=7.0=Language=Assets=Mars=7 July=Pleiades.
Tentative=6,000=60%=P6.0D=Man=Earth=Royalty=6 June=Gaia=Maia>>M=M2.
Tenterhook=10,000=1,000=100%=10.0=Physicality=Tech.=10 Oct.=Uranus=P=1Ø.
Tenth=10,000=1,000=100%=10.0=Physicality=Tech.=10 Oct.=Uranus=P=1Ø.
Tenuous=4,500=5,000=50%=P5.00D=Law=Time=Venus=5 May = Aphrodite>>L=N.
Tenure=10,000=1,000=100%=10.0=Physicality=Tech.=10 Oct.=Uranus=P=1Ø.
Teotihuacán=5,500=5.5=80%=P5.50=Earth-Midway=5 May = Gaia.
Tepee=10,000=1,000=100%=10.0=Physicality=Tech.=10 Oct.=Uranus=P=1Ø.
Tepid=4,000=40%=P4.0D=Govt.=Creatocracy=4 April=Mercury=Hermes=G=A4.
Tequila=5,000=50%=P5.00D=Law=Time=Venus=5 May = Aphrodite>>L=N.
Teratogen=9,500=10,000=1,000=100%=10.0=Physicality=Tech.=10 Oct.=Uranus=P=1Ø.
Terbium=10,000=1,000=100%=10.0=Physicality=Tech.=10 Oct.=Uranus=P=1Ø.
Tercentenary=4,000=40%=P4.0D=Govt.=Creatocracy=4 April=Mercury=Hermes=G=A4.
Terence=4,000=40%=P4.0D=Govt.=Creatocracy=4 April=Mercury=Hermes=G=A4.

Teresa,Mother=5,500=5.5=80%=P5.50=Earth-Midway=5 May = Gaia.

Tereshkova Valentina=5,500=5.5=80%=P5.50=Earth-Midway=5 May = Gaia.

Teriyaki=6,000=60%=P6.0D=Man=Earth=Royalty=6 June=Gaia=Maia>>M=M2.

Term=10,000=1,000=100%=10.0=Physicality=Tech.=10 Oct.=Uranus=P=1Ø.

Termagant=5,500=5.5=80%=P5.50=Earth-Midway=5 May = Gaia.

Terminal=10,000=1,000=100%=10.0=Physicality=Tech.=10 Oct.=Uranus=P=1Ø.

Terminate=3,500=4,000=40%=P4.0D=Govt.=Creatocracy=4 April=Hermes=G=A4.

Terminology=9,000=90%=P9.00D=9.0=Abstraction=Gods=Saturn=9Sept.>>A=Ø.

Terminus=5,000=50%=P5.00D=Law=Time=Venus=5 May = Aphrodite>>L=N.

Termite=8,000=80%=P8.0D=Economy=Currency=8 Aug.=Zeus>>E=v.

Tern=9,000=90%=P9.00D=9.0=Abstraction=Gods=Saturn=9Sept.>>A=Ø.

Ternary=9,500=10,000=1,000=100%=10.0=Physicality=Tech.=10 Oct.=Uranus=P=1Ø.

Terpsichorean=4,000=40%=P4.0D=Govt.=Creatocracy=4 April=Mercury=Hermes=G=A4.

Terr.=1,000=100%=10.0=1.0=Mind=Sun=1 January=Helios >> M=E4.

Terrace=10,000=1,000=100%=10.0=Physicality=Tech.=10 Oct.=Uranus=P=1Ø.

Terracota=6,000=60%=P6.0D=Man=Earth=Royalty=6 June=Gaia=Maia>>M=M2.

Terra firma=2,500=3,000=30%=P3.0D=3.0=Creativity=Stars=Muses=3 March=GIL.

Terrain=6,000=60%=P6.0D=Man=Earth=Royalty=6 June=Gaia=Maia>>M=M2.

Terrapin=5,000=50%=P5.00D=Law=Time=Venus=5 May = Aphrodite>>L=N.

Terrarium=10,000=1,000=100%=10.0=Physicality=Tech.=10 Oct.=Uranus=P=1Ø.

Terrestrial=10,000=1,000=100%=10.0=Physicality=Tech.=10 Oct.=Uranus=P=1Ø.

Terrible=10,000=1,000=100%=10.0=Physicality=Tech.=10 Oct.=Uranus=P=1Ø.

Terrier=10,000=1,000=100%=10.0=Physicality=Tech.=10 Oct.=Uranus=P=1Ø.

Terrific=10,000=1,000=100%=10.0=Physicality=Tech.=10 Oct.=Uranus=P=1Ø.

Terrify=3,000=30%=P3.0D=3.0=Creativity=Stars=Muses=3 March = C=I>>GIL.

Territorial=7,000=70%=P7.0D=7.0=Language=Assets=Mars=7 July=Pleiades.

Territory=10,000=1,000=100%=10.0=Physicality=Tech.=10 Oct.=Uranus=P=1Ø.

Terror=10,000=1,000=100%=10.0=Physicality=Tech.=10 Oct.=Uranus=P=1Ø.

Terrorism=3,500=4,000=40%=P4.0D=Govt.=Creatocracy=4 April=Hermes=G=A4.
Makupedia believes terrorism is an act of dissatisfaction among a class or group of people or citizens that feel marginalized or disengaged from the benefits of entitled opportunities to succeed. Hence you don't fight terrorism by carrying guns you fight it by creating jobs. You don't infringe on human rights rather you protect the sanctity of the human life. That is creative governance that leads to a creative economy and a Paradise Nation. Makupedia contains at least one billion jobs through the knowledge system for creative education.

Terrorize=3,500=4,000=40%=P4.0D=Govt.=Creatocracy=4 April=Hermes=G=A4.

Terry=7,000=70%=P7.0D=7.0=Language=Assets=Mars=7 July=Pleiades.

Terse=6,500=7,000=70%=P7.0D=7.0=Language=Assets=Mars=7 July=Pleiades.

Tertiary=10,000=1,000=100%=10.0=Physicality=Tech.=10 Oct.=Uranus=P=1Ø.

TESL=3,000=30%=P3.0D=3.0=Creativity=Stars=Muses=3 March = C=I>>GIL.

Tesla Nikola=4,000=40%=P4.0D=Govt.=Creatocracy=4 April=Mercury=Hermes=G=A4.

Tessellate=7,500=8,000=80%=P8.0D=Economy=Currency=8 Aug.=Zeus>>E=v.

test=10,000=1,000=100%=10.0=Physicality=Tech.=10 Oct.=Uranus=P=1Ø.
Test.=1,000=100%=10.0=1.0=Mind=Sun=1 January=Helios >> M=E4.

Testament=10,000=1,000=100%=10.0=Physicality=Tech.=10 Oct.=Uranus=P=1Ø.
Peter Matthews-Akukalia invented the Nidrapoe, a system of poems written in testaments.
He is the World's 1st Drapoet. See the book >> MAKUPEDIALAND >> A Disean City
of Testamentary Poetry by Peter Matthews-Akukalia.

Testate=4,500=5,000=50%=P5.00D=Law=Time=Venus=5 May = Aphrodite>>L=N.
Testator=4,000=40%=P4.0D=Govt.=Creatocracy=4 April=Mercury=Hermes=G=A4.
Testatrix=4,000=40%=P4.0D=Govt.=Creatocracy=4 April=Mercury=Hermes=G=A4.
Testicle=4,500=5,000=50%=P5.00D=Law=Time=Venus=5 May = Aphrodite>>L=N.
Testify=10,000=1,000=100%=10.0=Physicality=Tech.=10 Oct.=Uranus=P=1Ø.
Testimonial=10,000=1,000=100%=10.0=Physicality=Tech.=10 Oct.=Uranus=P=1Ø.
Testimony=10,000=1,000=100%=10.0=Physicality=Tech.=10 Oct.=Uranus=P=1Ø.
Testis=2,500=3,000=30%=P3.0D=3.0=Creativity=Stars=Muses=3 March = C=I>>GIL.
Testosterone=8,500=9,000=90%=P9.00D=9.0=Abstraction=Gods=Saturn=9Sept.>>A=Ø.
Test tube=4,500=5,000=50%=P5.00D=Law=Time=Venus=5 May = Aphrodite>>L=N.
Testy=2,500=3,000=30%=P3.0D=3.0=Creativity=Stars=Muses=3 March = C=I>>GIL.
Tet=5,000=50%=P5.00D=Law=Time=Venus=5 May = Aphrodite>>L=N.
Tetanus=10,000=1,000=100%=10.0=Physicality=Tech.=10 Oct.=Uranus=P=1Ø.
Tête-à-tête=6,500=7,000=70%=P7.0D=7.0=Language=Assets=Mars=7 July=Pleiades.
Teth=4,000=40%=P4.0D=Govt.=Creatocracy=4 April=Mercury=Hermes=G=A4.
Tether=10,000=1,000=100%=10.0=Physicality=Tech.=10 Oct.=Uranus=P=1Ø.
Teton=4,500=5,000=50%=P5.00D=Law=Time=Venus=5 May = Aphrodite>>L=N.
Teton Range.=6,000=60%=P6.0D=Man=Earth=Royalty=6 June=Gaia=Maia>>M=M2.
Tetra-=2,500=3,000=30%=P3.0D=3.0=Creativity=Stars=Muses=3 March = C=I>>GIL.
Tetracycline=6,000=60%=P6.0D=Man=Earth=Royalty=6 June=Gaia=Maia>>M=M2.
Tetrameter=4,500=5,000=50%=P5.00D=Law=Time=Venus=5 May = Aphrodite>>L=N.
Teuton=10,000=1,000=100%=10.0=Physicality=Tech.=10 Oct.=Uranus=P=1Ø.
Tevet=4,500=5,000=50%=P5.00D=Law=Time=Venus=5 May = Aphrodite>>L=N.
Tewa=8,000=80%=P8.0D=Economy=Currency=8 Aug.=Zeus>>E=v.
Tex.=500=5%=P5.00D=5.0=Law=Time=Venus=5 May=Aphrodite>>L=N.
Texas=7,000=70%=P7.0D=7.0=Language=Assets=Mars=7 July=Pleiades.
Text=10,000=1,000=100%=10.0=Physicality=Tech.=10 Oct.=Uranus=P=1Ø.

Textbook=4,000=40%=P4.0D=Govt.=Creatocracy=4 April=Mercury=Hermes=G=A4.
Peter Matthews-Akukalia invented the Creative Sciences because he conceptualized the
abstract universes in dimensions and wrote their textbooks.

Textile=10,000=1,000=100%=10.0=Physicality=Tech.=10 Oct.=Uranus=P=1Ø.
Texture=10,000=1,000=100%=10.0=Physicality=Tech.=10 Oct.=Uranus=P=1Ø.
TGIF=2,000=20%=P2.00D=2.0=Nature=Matter=Moon=2 Feb.=Cupid=N=C+_

Th=2,500=3,000=30%=P3.0D=3.0=Creativity=Stars=Muses=3 March = C=I>>GIL.
Th.=500=5%=P5.00D=5.0=Law=Time=Venus=5 May=Aphrodite>>L=N.
-th1=2,000=20%=P2.00D=2.0=Nature=Matter=Moon=2 Feb.=Cupid=N=C+_
-th2=4,500=5,000=50%=P5.00D=Law=Time=Venus=5 May = Aphrodite>>L=N.
Thackeray William=2,500=3,000=30%=P3.0D=3.0=Cre=Stars=Muses=3 March=GIL.
Thai=5,000=50%=P5.00D=Law=Time=Venus=5 May = Aphrodite>>L=N.
Thailand=10,000=1,000=100%=10.0=Physicality=Tech.=10 Oct.=Uranus=P=1Ø.
Thalamus=10,000=1,000=100%=10.0=Physicality=Tech.=10 Oct.=Uranus=P=1Ø.
Thales=3,000=30%=P3.0D=3.0=Creativity=Stars=Muses=3 March = C=I>>GIL.
Thalidomide=10,000=1,000=100%=10.0=Physicality=Tech.=10 Oct.=Uranus=P=1Ø.
Thallium=10,000=1,000=100%=10.0=Physicality=Tech.=10 Oct.=Uranus=P=1Ø.
Thames=10,000=1,000=100%=10.0=Physicality=Tech.=10 Oct.=Uranus=P=1Ø.
Than=10,000=1,000=100%=10.0=Physicality=Tech.=10 Oct.=Uranus=P=1Ø.
Thane=10,000=1,000=100%=10.0=Physicality=Tech.=10 Oct.=Uranus=P=1Ø.
Thank=3,500=4,000=40%=P4.0D=Govt.=Creatocracy=4 April=Mercury=Hermes=G=A4.
Thankful=500=5%=P5.00D=5.0=Law=Time=Venus=5 May=Aphrodite>>L=N.
Thankless=3,000=30%=P3.0D=3.0=Creativity=Stars=Muses=3 March = C=I>>GIL.
Thanks=6,500=7,000=70%=P7.0D=7.0=Language=Assets=Mars=7 July=Pleiades.
Thanksgiving=4,000=40%=P4.0D=Govt.=Creatocracy=4 April=Mercury=Hermes=G=A4.
Thanksgiving Day=5,500=5.5=80%=P5.50=Earth-Midway=5 May = Gaia.
Thant=6,000=60%=P6.0D=Man=Earth=Royalty=6 June=Gaia=Maia>>M=M2.
That=10,000=1,000=100%=10.0=Physicality=Tech.=10 Oct.=Uranus=P=1Ø.
Thatch=9,000=90%=P9.00D=9.0=Abstraction=Gods=Saturn=9Sept.>>A=Ø.
Thatcher Margaret=4,000=40%=P4.0D=Govt.=Creatocracy=4 April=Hermes=G=A4.
Thaw=10,000=1,000=100%=10.0=Physicality=Tech.=10 Oct.=Uranus=P=1Ø.
THC=5,000=50%=P5.00D=Law=Time=Venus=5 May = Aphrodite>>L=N.
The1=10,000=1,000=100%=10.0=Physicality=Tech.=10 Oct.=Uranus=P=1Ø.
The2=10,000=1,000=100%=10.0=Physicality=Tech.=10 Oct.=Uranus=P=1Ø.
Theater=10,000=1,000=100%=10.0=Physicality=Tech.=10 Oct.=Uranus=P=1Ø.
Theatrical=10,000=1,000=100%=10.0=Physicality=Tech.=10 Oct.=Uranus=P=1Ø.
Theatrics=5,000=50%=P5.00D=Law=Time=Venus=5 May = Aphrodite>>L=N.

Thebe=2,500=3,000=30%=P3.0D=3.0=Creativity=Stars=Muses=3 March = C=I>>GIL.
Sotho. Currency metric weight >> 2.5/10=0.25 >> 25:1. See Naira. Dollar.

Thee=6,000=60%=P6.0D=Man=Earth=Royalty=6 June=Gaia=Maia>>M=M2.
Theft=3,500=4,000=40%=P4.0D=Govt.=Creatocracy=4 April=Mercury=Hermes=G=A4.
Their=7,500=8,000=80%=P8.0D=Economy=Currency=8 Aug.=Zeus>>E=v.
Theirs=5,500=5.5=80%=P5.50=Earth-Midway=5 May = Gaia.

Theism=4,500=5,000=50%=P5.00D=Law=Time=Venus=5 May = Aphrodite>>L=N.
Belief in the existence of a God or Gods. The distinct classification of each deity and group of deities is worth 45%. The Creatocracy believes in Duo-theism the existence of GOD and De-Gods which he refers collectively as the powers that be, the Creatocracy. Named

after him it emerged the Makstian Faith Order known as Makstianism, Makstianity, Makstians. Himself being a God by works and rights of abstraction.

Them=10,000=1,000=100%=10.0=Physicality=Tech.=10 Oct.=Uranus=P=1Ø.
Thematic=3,500=4,000=40%=P4.0D=Govt.=Creatocracy=4 April=Hermes=G=A4.
Theme=10,000=1,000=100%=10.0=Physicality=Tech.=10 Oct.=Uranus=P=1Ø.
Theme song=5,500=5.5=80%=P5.50=Earth-Midway=5 May = Gaia.
Themselves=10,000=1,000=100%=10.0=Physicality=Tech.=10 Oct.=Uranus=P=1Ø.
Then=10,000=1,000=100%=10.0=Physicality=Tech.=10 Oct.=Uranus=P=1Ø.
Thence=5,000=50%=P5.00D=Law=Time=Venus=5 May = Aphrodite>>L=N.
Thence forth=2,500=3,000=30%=P3.0D=3.0=Creativity=Stars=Muses=3 March=C=I
Thence forward=3,500=4,000=40%=P4.0D=Govt.=Creatocracy=4 April=Hermes=G=A4.
Theo-=2,500=3,000=30%=P3.0D=3.0=Creativity=Stars=Muses=3 March = C=I>>GIL.
Theocracy=6,000=60%=P6.0D=Man=Earth=Royalty=6 June=Gaia=Maia>>M=M2.
Theocritus=2,500=3,000=30%=P3.0D=3.0=Creativity=Stars=Muses=3 March = C=I>>GIL.
Theodora=4,000=40%=P4.0D=Govt.=Creatocracy=4 April=Mercury=Hermes=G=A4.
Theodoric=5,000=50%=P5.00D=Law=Time=Venus=5 May = Aphrodite>>L=N.
Theodosius I=4,000=40%=P4.0D=Govt.=Creatocracy=4 April=Mercury=Hermes=G=A4.
Theology=8,000=80%=P8.0D=Economy=Currency=8 Aug.=Zeus>>E=v.
Theorem=11,000=11%=P1.10D=1.1=Idea=Brainchild=Inv.=11 Nov.=SC=Athena>>I=MT.
Theoretician=7,000=70%=P7.0D=7.0=Language=Assets=Mars=7 July=Pleiades.
Theorize=3,000=30%=P3.0D=3.0=Creativity=Stars=Muses=3 March = C=I>>GIL.
Theory=10,000=1,000=100%=10.0=Physicality=Tech.=10 Oct.=Uranus=P=1Ø.
Theosophy=10,000=1,000=100%=10.0=Physicality=Tech.=10 Oct.=Uranus=P=1Ø.
Therapeutic=4,500=5,000=50%=P5.00D=Law=Time=Venus=5 May = Aphrodite>>L=N.
Therapeutics=2,000=20%=P2.00D=2.0=Nature=Matter=Moon=2 Feb.=Cupid=N=C+_
Therapy=5,000=50%=P5.00D=Law=Time=Venus=5 May = Aphrodite>>L=N.
There=10,000=1,000=100%=10.0=Physicality=Tech.=10 Oct.=Uranus=P=1Ø.
Thereabouts=2,000=20%=P2.00D=2.0=Nature=Matter=Moon=2 Feb.=Cupid=N=C+_
Thereafter=3,500=4,000=40%=P4.0D=Govt.=Creatocracy=4 April=Hermes=G=A4.
Thereat=4,000=40%=P4.0D=Govt.=Creatocracy=4 April=Mercury=Hermes=G=A4.
Thereby=1,500=15%=P1.50D=1.5=Authority=Solar Crown=1 May = Maia.
Therefore=2,000=20%=P2.00D=2.0=Nature=Matter=Moon=2 Feb.=Cupid=N=C+_
Therefrom=3,000=30%=P3.0D=3.0=Creativity=Stars=Muses=3 March = C=I>>GIL.
Therein=4,000=40%=P4.0D=Govt.=Creatocracy=4 April=Mercury=Hermes=G=A4.
Therein after=2,000=20%=P2.00D=2.0=Nature=Matter=Moon=2 Feb.=Cupid=N=C+_
Thereof=4,000=40%=P4.0D=Govt.=Creatocracy=4 April=Mercury=Hermes=G=A4.
There on=3,000=30%=P3.0D=3.0=Creativity=Stars=Muses=3 March = C=I>>GIL.
Theresa=3,500=4,000=40%=P4.0D=Govt.=Creatocracy=4 April=Mercury=Hermes=G=A4.
Thereto=2,500=3,000=30%=P3.0D=3.0=Creativity=Stars=Muses=3 March = C=I>>GIL.
Theretofore=1,500=15%=P1.50D=1.5=Authority=Solar Crown=1 May = Maia.
There unto=3,500=4,000=40%=P4.0D=Govt.=Creatocracy=4 April=Hermes=G=A4.
Thereupon=5,000=50%=P5.00D=Law=Time=Venus=5 May = Aphrodite>>L=N.
There with=2,500=3,000=30%=P3.0D=3.0=Creativity=Stars=Muses=3 March = C=I>>GIL.
There withal=3,500=4,000=40%=P4.0D=Govt.=Creatocracy=4 April=Hermes=G=A4.

Thermal=6,000=60%=P6.0D=Man=Earth=Royalty=6 June=Gaia=Maia>>M=M2.
Thermo-=2,500=3,000=30%=P3.0D=3.0=Creativity=Stars=Muses=3 March = C=I>>GIL.
Thermocouple=10,000=1,000=100%=10.0=Physicality=Tech.=10 Oct.=Uranus=P=1Ø.
Thermodynamics=10,000=1,000=100%=10.0=Physicality=Tech.=10 Oct.=Uranus=P=1Ø.
Thermometer=2,500=3,000=30%=P3.0D=3.0=Creativity=Stars=Muses=3 March=GIL
Thermonuclear=8,000=80%=P8.0D=Economy=Currency=8 Aug.=Zeus>>E=v.
Thermoplastic=5,500=5.5=80%=P5.50=Earth-Midway=5 May = Gaia.
Thermopylae=8,000=80%=P8.0D=Economy=Currency=8 Aug.=Zeus>>E=v.
Thermos=4,000=40%=P4.0D=Govt.=Creatocracy=4 April=Mercury=Hermes=G=A4.
Thermosetting=3,500=4,000=40%=P4.0D=Govt.=Creatocracy=4 April=Mercury=G=A4.
Thermoset=9,500=10,000=1,000=100%=10.0=Physicality=Tech.=10 Oct.=Uranus=P=1Ø.

Thesaurus=7,000=70%=P7.0D=7.0=Language=Assets=Mars=7 July=Pleiades.
A book of selected words, especially a dictionary of synonyms and related words. <Gk. thēsauros, treasury. Result indicates dictionaries must be computed and the words measured to earn precision in definition. Against this there is no law. Castle Makupedia is a Dictionary of Makumatics, Creatocracy, Data Mining & World MaksCurrencies Encyclopedia. Data Mining is the process of examining large databases in order to generate new information. Hence Castle Makupedia is the first computed dictionary in the world.

These=1,500=15%=P1.50D=1.5=Authority=Solar Crown=1 May = Maia.
Thesis=10,000=1,000=100%=10.0=Physicality=Tech.=10 Oct.=Uranus=P=1Ø.
Thespian=6,500=7,000=70%=P7.0D=7.0=Language=Assets=Mars=7 July=Pleiades.
Thespis=2,500=3,000=30%=P3.0D=3.0=Creativity=Stars=Muses=3 March = C=I>>GIL.

Thessalonians=2,000=20%=P2.00D=2.0=Nature=Matter=Moon=2 Feb.=Cupid=N=C+_
Inspired by Artemis and Eros as a guide to adventures. See Timothy.

Thessaloniki=6,500=7,000=70%=P7.0D=7.0=Language=Assets=Mars=7 July=Pleiades.
Thessaly=5,000=50%=P5.00D=Law=Time=Venus=5 May = Aphrodite>>L=N.
Theta=4,000=40%=P4.0D=Govt.=Creatocracy=4 April=Mercury=Hermes=G=A4.
Thew=4,000=40%=P4.0D=Govt.=Creatocracy=4 April=Mercury=Hermes=G=A4.
They=6,500=7,000=70%=P7.0D=7.0=Language=Assets=Mars=7 July=Pleiades.
They'd=1,500=15%=P1.50D=1.5=Authority=Solar Crown=1 May = Maia.
They'll=1,500=15%=P1.50D=1.5=Authority=Solar Crown=1 May = Maia.
They're=1,000=100%=10.0=1.0=Mind=Sun=1 January=Helios >> M=E4.
They've=1,000=100%=10.0=1.0=Mind=Sun=1 January=Helios >> M=E4.
Thiamine=10,000=1,000=100%=10.0=Physicality=Tech.=10 Oct.=Uranus=P=1Ø.
Thick=10,000=1,000=100%=10.0=Physicality=Tech.=10 Oct.=Uranus=P=1Ø.
Thicken=3,000=30%=P3.0D=3.0=Creativity=Stars=Muses=3 March = C=I>>GIL.
Thicket=4,500=5,000=50%=P5.00D=Law=Time=Venus=5 May = Aphrodite>>L=N.
Thickset=4,000=40%=P4.0D=Govt.=Creatocracy=4 April=Mercury=Hermes=G=A4.
Thick skinned=3,500=4,000=40%=P4.0D=Govt.=Creatocracy=4 April=Hermes=G=A4.

Thief=2,500=3,000=30%=P3.0D=3.0=Creativity=Stars=Muses=3 March = C=I>>GIL.
Thieve=2,500=3,000=30%=P3.0D=3.0=Creativity=Stars=Muses=3 March = C=I>>GIL.
Thigh=5,000=50%=P5.00D=Law=Time=Venus=5 May = Aphrodite>>L=N.
Thighbone=1,000=100%=10.0=1.0=Mind=Sun=1 January=Helios >> M=E4.
Thimble=9,000=90%=P9.00D=9.0=Abstraction=Gods=Saturn=9Sept.>>A=Ø.
Thimbu=6,000=60%=P6.0D=Man=Earth=Royalty=6 June=Gaia=Maia>>M=M2.
Thin=10,000=1,000=100%=10.0=Physicality=Tech.=10 Oct.=Uranus=P=1Ø.
Thine=10,000=1,000=100%=10.0=Physicality=Tech.=10 Oct.=Uranus=P=1Ø.
Thing=10,000=1,000=100%=10.0=Physicality=Tech.=10 Oct.=Uranus=P=1Ø.
Think=10,000=1,000=100%=10.0=Physicality=Tech.=10 Oct.=Uranus=P=1Ø.

Think tank=5,500=5.5=80%=P5.50=Earth-Midway=5 May = Gaia.
A research group organized especially by a government for solving complex problems. The Creatocracy of Creative Scientist can find jobs as think tanks for governments offering our various expertise in helping governments to build their territories in line with their needs. This is where brainstorming comes in. Organizations can also hire us for our services.

Thinner=5,000=50%=P5.00D=Law=Time=Venus=5 May = Aphrodite>>L=N.
Thin-skinned=3,500=4,000=40%=P4.0D=Govt.=4 April=Mercury=Hermes=G=A4.
Third=10,000=1,000=100%=10.0=Physicality=Tech.=10 Oct.=Uranus=P=1Ø.
Third base=4,500=5,000=50%=P5.00D=Law=Time=Venus=5 May = Aphrodite>>L=N.
Third class=10,000=1,000=100%=10.0=Physicality=Tech.=10 Oct.=Uranus=P=1Ø.
Third-degree burn=9,000=90%=P9.00D=9.0=Abstraction=Gods=Saturn=9Sept.>>A=Ø.
Third person=9,000=90%=P9.00D=9.0=Abstraction=Gods=Saturn=9Sept.>>A=Ø.
Third World=4,500=5,000=50%=P5.00D=Law=Time=Venus=5 May = Aphrodite>>L=N.
Thirst=10,000=1,000=100%=10.0=Physicality=Tech.=10 Oct.=Uranus=P=1Ø.
Thirteen=7,000=70%=P7.0D=7.0=Language=Assets=Mars=7 July=Pleiades.

Thirteenth=6,500=7,000=70%=P7.0D=7.0=Language=Assets=Mars=7 July=Pleiades.
In the Creatocracy, the first abstract dimension after the first twelve physical dimensions of Mind - Knowledge. Represented as 13th it is the dimension of Athena Goddess of wisdom handicraft and warfare translated into the Faculty of Creative Intelligence. It discovered computed and applied to create the study of Creative & Psycho-Social Sciences© by Peter Matthews-Akukalia, Castle Makupedia God of Creatocracy Genius and Mind.

Thirtieth=7,000=70%=P7.0D=7.0=Language=Assets=Mars=7 July=Pleiades.
At the age of 33, Peter Matthews-Akukalia became African Shakespeare. See the book>>Sword of Honour - Days of St. Valentine by African Shakespeare. In 2012, at 34, He emerged as the World's 1st Creative Scientist. See the book >> The Oracle-Principles of Creative Sciences by Peter Matthews-Akukalia. In 2013 at 35 he earned the Copyright to the ownership of the Faculty of Creative & Psycho-Social Sciences. Became King of Creativity in 2016. See Principles of Psychoeconomix by Peter

Matthews-Akukalia. In 2020 he became a God after publishing the Creatocratic Charter. This work apotheosizes him as Castle Makupedia, the God of Creatocracy Genius and Mind. Husband of Athena.

Thirty=5,000=50%=P5.00D=Law=Time=Venus=5 May = Aphrodite>>L=N.
This=10,000=1,000=100%=10.0=Physicality=Tech.=10 Oct.=Uranus=P=1Ø.
Thistle=8,000=80%=P8.0D=Economy=Currency=8 Aug.=Zeus>>E=v.
Thistle down=4,500=5,000=50%=P5.00D=Law=Time=Venus=5 May = Aphrodite>>L=N.
Thither=7,500=8,000=80%=P8.0D=Economy=Currency=8 Aug.=Zeus>>E=v.
Thole pin=8,500=9,000=90%=P9.00D=9.0=Abstraction=Gods=Saturn=9Sept.>>A=Ø.
Thomas=4,000=40%=P4.0D=Govt.=Creatocracy=4 April=Mercury=Hermes=G=A4.
Thomas, Dylan=2,500=3,000=30%=P3.0D=3.0=Cre=Stars=Muses=3 March = C=I>>GIL.
Thomas á Kempis=3,500=4,000=40%=P4.0D=Govt.=Creatocracy=4 April=Hermes=G=A4.
Thompson Benjamin=3,500=4,000=40%=P4.0D=Govt.=4 April=Hermes=G=A4.
Thompson John=4,000=40%=P4.0D=Govt.=Creatocracy=4 April=Hermes=G=A4.
Thomson Virgil.=4,000=40%=P4.0D=Govt.=Creatocracy=4 April=Hermes=G=A4.
Thong=5,500=5.5=80%=P5.50=Earth-Midway=5 May = Gaia.

Thor=3,000=30%=P3.0D=3.0=Creativity=Stars=Muses=3 March = C=I>>GIL.
The Norse God of thunder. Greeks recognize him as Zeus. Peter Matthews-Akukalia, Castle Makupedia named him Zeus-Jehovah-Allah >> ZeJeAl. Anyone who is born on Thursday gets creatively inspired once there is a thunder because muses descend in spirit speed.

Thorax=10,000=1,000=100%=10.0=Physicality=Tech.=10 Oct.=Uranus=P=1Ø.
Thoreau Henry=2,500=3,000=30%=P3.0D=3.0=Cre=Stars=Muses=3 March = C=I>>GIL.
Thorium=10,000=1,000=100%=10.0=Physicality=Tech.=10 Oct.=Uranus=P=1Ø.
Thorn=10,000=1,000=100%=10.0=Physicality=Tech.=10 Oct.=Uranus=P=1Ø.
Thorn=4,500=5,000=50%=P5.00D=Law=Time=Venus=5 May = Aphrodite>>L=N.
Thorough=10,000=1,000=100%=10.0=Physicality=Tech.=10 Oct.=Uranus=P=1Ø.
Thoroughbred=10,000=1,000=100%=10.0=Physicality=Tech.=10 Oct.=Uranus=P=1Ø.
Thoroughfare=3,000=30%=P3.0D=3.0=Creativity=Stars=Muses=3 March = C=I>>GIL.
Thoroughgoing=2,500=3,000=30%=P3.0D=3.0=Creativity=Stars=Muses=3 March =C=I
Those=1,500=15%=P1.50D=1.5=Authority=Solar Crown=1 May = Maia.
Thou=7,000=70%=P7.0D=7.0=Language=Assets=Mars=7 July=Pleiades.
Though=7,500=8,000=80%=P8.0D=Economy=Currency=8 Aug.=Zeus>>E=v.

Thought=11,000=11%=P1.10D=1.1=Idea=Brainchild=Inv.=11 Nov.=SC=Athena>>I=MT.
Thoughts are things - Napoleon Hill, in his book Think and Grow Rich. Results prove that thoughts are ideas which is defined in the Creative Sciences, Makupedia as congruent energy particles they crystallize into creativity measured on the 10,000th scale. Thought is the second component of the Mind where intelligence is first, will is third and emotion is fourth. Athena as a brainchild that could lead to creativity and inventions is inspired and guided by Athena Goddess of wisdom handicraft and mental warfare. Peter Matthews-

Akukalia, Castle Makupedia wrote the Idea formula as I=MT>>Ideas function on MindTech developed from Makumatics (Mind Computing) through convertible intelligence process.

Thoughtful=4,500=5,000=50%=P5.00D=Law=Time=Venus=5 May = Aphrodite>>L=N.
Thoughtless=1,500=15%=P1.50D=1.5=Authority=Solar Crown=1 May = Maia.
Thousand=6,000=60%=P6.0D=Man=Earth=Royalty=6 June=Gaia=Maia>>M=M2.
Thousand Islands=8,000=80%=P8.0D=Economy=Currency=8 Aug.=Zeus>>E=v.
Thousand Oaks.=5,000=50%=P5.00D=Law=Time=Venus=5 May = Aphrodite>>L=N.
Thousandth=6,500=7,000=70%=P7.0D=7.0=Language=Assets=Mars=7 July=Pleiades.
Thrace=6,500=7,000=70%=P7.0D=7.0=Language=Assets=Mars=7 July=Pleiades.
Thrall=5,000=50%=P5.00D=Law=Time=Venus=5 May = Aphrodite>>L=N.
Thrash=10,000=1,000=100%=10.0=Physicality=Tech.=10 Oct.=Uranus=P=1Ø.
Thrasher=4,500=5,000=50%=P5.00D=Law=Time=Venus=5 May = Aphrodite>>L=N.
Thread=10,000=1,000=100%=10.0=Physicality=Tech.=10 Oct.=Uranus=P=1Ø.
Threadbare=6,500=7,000=70%=P7.0D=7.0=Language=Assets=Mars=7 July=Pleiades.
Threat=10,000=1,000=100%=10.0=Physicality=Tech.=10 Oct.=Uranus=P=1Ø.
Threaten=10,000=1,000=100%=10.0=Physicality=Tech.=10 Oct.=Uranus=P=1Ø.
Three=10,000=1,000=100%=10.0=Physicality=Tech.=10 Oct.=Uranus=P=1Ø.
Three-dimensional=10,000=1,000=100%=10.0=Physicality=Tech.=10 Oct.=Uranus=P=1Ø.
Three score=500=5%=P5.00D=5.0=Law=Time=Venus=5 May=Aphrodite>>L=N.
Threesome=2,000=20%=P2.00D=2.0=Nature=Matter=Moon=2 Feb.=Cupid=N=C+_
Threnody=7,000=70%=P7.0D=7.0=Language=Assets=Mars=7 July=Pleiades.
Thresh=10,000=1,000=100%=10.0=Physicality=Tech.=10 Oct.=Uranus=P=1Ø.
Threshold=10,000=1,000=100%=10.0=Physicality=Tech.=10 Oct.=Uranus=P=1Ø.
Threw=2,000=20%=P2.00D=2.0=Nature=Matter=Moon=2 Feb.=Cupid=N=C+_
Thrice=2,500=3,000=30%=P3.0D=3.0=Creativity=Stars=Muses=3 March = C=I>>GIL.
Thrift=10,500=11,000=11%=P1.10D=1.1=Idea=Brainchild=Inv.=11 Nov.=SC=Athena
    >>I=MT.
Thrift shop=6,000=60%=P6.0D=Man=Earth=Royalty=6 June=Gaia=Maia>>M=M2.
Thrill=10,000=1,000=100%=10.0=Physicality=Tech.=10 Oct.=Uranus=P=1Ø.
Thrive=5,000=50%=P5.00D=Law=Time=Venus=5 May = Aphrodite>>L=N.
Throat=10,000=1,000=100%=10.0=Physicality=Tech.=10 Oct.=Uranus=P=1Ø.
Throaty=5,000=50%=P5.00D=Law=Time=Venus=5 May = Aphrodite>>L=N.
Throb=5,500=5.5=80%=P5.50=Earth-Midway=5 May = Gaia.
Throe=9,000=90%=P9.00D=9.0=Abstraction=Gods=Saturn=9Sept.>>A=Ø.
Thrombosis=3,500=4,000=40%=P4.0D=Govt.=4 April=Mercury=Hermes=G=A4.

Throne=8,000=80%=P8.0D=Economy=Currency=8 Aug.=Zeus>>E=v.
Zeus instituted the throne. The Creatocratic Charter is the throne of Castle Makupedia.

Throng=10,000=1,000=100%=10.0=Physicality=Tech.=10 Oct.=Uranus=P=1Ø.
Throttle=10,000=1,000=100%=10.0=Physicality=Tech.=10 Oct.=Uranus=P=1Ø.
Through=10,000=1,000=100%=10.0=Physicality=Tech.=10 Oct.=Uranus=P=1Ø.
Throughout=10,000=1,000=100%=10.0=Physicality=Tech.=10 Oct.=Uranus=P=1Ø.

Throve=2,000=20%=P2.00D=2.0=Nature=Matter=Moon=2 Feb.=Cupid=N=C+_
Throw=10,000=1,000=100%=10.0=Physicality=Tech.=10 Oct.=Uranus=P=1Ø.
Throwback=4,000=40%=P4.0D=Govt.=Creatocracy=4 April=Mercury=Hermes=G=A4.
Thru=1,000=100%=10.0=1.0=Mind=Sun=1 January=Helios >> M=E4.
Thrum=5,000=50%=P5.00D=Law=Time=Venus=5 May = Aphrodite>>L=N.
Thrush=7,500=8,000=80%=P8.0D=Economy=Currency=8 Aug.=Zeus>>E=v.
Thrust=10,000=1,000=100%=10.0=Physicality=Tech.=10 Oct.=Uranus=P=1Ø.
Thruway=1,000=100%=10.0=1.0=Mind=Sun=1 January=Helios >> M=E4.
Thucydides=3,000=30%=P3.0D=3.0=Creativity=Stars=Muses=3 March = C=I>>GIL.
Thud=7,500=8,000=80%=P8.0D=Economy=Currency=8 Aug.=Zeus>>E=v.
Thug=7,500=8,000=80%=P8.0D=Economy=Currency=8 Aug.=Zeus>>E=v.
Thulium=10,000=1,000=100%=10.0=Physicality=Tech.=10 Oct.=Uranus=P=1Ø.
Thumb=10,000=1,000=100%=10.0=Physicality=Tech.=10 Oct.=Uranus=P=1Ø.
Thumbscrew=4,000=40%=P4.0D=Govt.=Creatocracy=4 April=Mercury=Hermes=G=A4.
Thumbtack=6,000=60%=P6.0D=Man=Earth=Royalty=6 June=Gaia=Maia>>M=M2.
Thump=10,000=1,000=100%=10.0=Physicality=Tech.=10 Oct.=Uranus=P=1Ø.
Thunder=10,000=1,000=100%=10.0=Physicality=Tech.=10 Oct.=Uranus=P=1Ø.
Thunder Bay=10,000=1,000=100%=10.0=Physicality=Tech.=10 Oct.=Uranus=P=1Ø.
Thunderbolt=3,500=4,000=40%=P4.0D=Govt.=4 April=Mercury=Hermes=G=A4.
Thunderclap=3,000=30%=P3.0D=3.0=Creativity=Stars=Muses=3 March = C=I>>GIL.
Thundercloud=4,000=40%=P4.0D=Govt.=Creatocracy=4 April=Mercury=Hermes=G=A4.
Thunderhead=3,500=4,000=40%=P4.0D=Govt.=4 April=Mercury=Hermes=G=A4.
Thundershower=4,000=40%=P4.0D=Govt.=4 April=Mercury=Hermes=G=A4.
Thunderstorm=3,000=30%=P3.0D=3.0=Creativity=Stars=Muses=3 March = C=I>>GIL.
Thunderstruck=1,000=100%=10.0=1.0=Mind=Sun=1 January=Helios >> M=E4.
Thur.=500=5%=P5.00D=5.0=Law=Time=Venus=5 May=Aphrodite>>L=N.
Thurber James.=2,500=3,000=30%=P3.0D=3.0=Cr=Stars=Muses=3 March = C=I>>GIL.

Thursday=5,000=50%=P5.00D=Law=Time=Venus=5 May = Aphrodite>>L=N. See Thor.

Thwack=4,000=40%=P4.0D=Govt.=Creatocracy=4 April=Mercury=Hermes=G=A4.
Thwart=9,000=90%=P9.00D=9.0=Abstraction=Gods=Saturn=9Sept.>>A=Ø.
Thy=2,500=3,000=30%=P3.0D=3.0=Creativity=Stars=Muses=3 March = C=I>>GIL.
Thyme=5,000=50%=P5.00D=Law=Time=Venus=5 May = Aphrodite>>L=N.
Thymine=5,000=50%=P5.00D=Law=Time=Venus=5 May = Aphrodite>>L=N.
Thymus=10,000=1,000=100%=10.0=Physicality=Tech.=10 Oct.=Uranus=P=1Ø.
Thyroid=10,000=1,000=100%=10.0=Physicality=Tech.=10 Oct.=Uranus=P=1Ø.
Thyroid gland=10,000=1,000=100%=10.0=Physicality=Tech.=10 Oct.=Uranus=P=1Ø.
Thyself=1,500=15%=P1.50D=1.5=Authority=Solar Crown=1 May = Maia.
ti=4,500=5,000=50%=P5.00D=Law=Time=Venus=5 May = Aphrodite>>L=N.
Ti=2,500=3,000=30%=P3.0D=3.0=Creativity=Stars=Muses=3 March = C=I>>GIL.
Tianjin=7,000=70%=P7.0D=7.0=Language=Assets=Mars=7 July=Pleiades.
Tian Shan=1,500=15%=P1.50D=1.5=Authority=Solar Crown=1 May = Maia.
Tiara=7,500=8,000=80%=P8.0D=Economy=Currency=8 Aug.=Zeus>>E=v.

Tiber=10,000=1,000=100%=10.0=Physicality=Tech.=10 Oct.=Uranus=P=1Ø.

Tiberius=4,000=40%=P4.0D=Govt.=Creatocracy=4 April=Mercury=Hermes=G=A4.

Tibet=7,000=70%=P7.0D=7.0=Language=Assets=Mars=7 July=Pleiades.

Tibet o-Burman=6,500=7,000=70%=P7.0D=7.0=Language=Assets=Mars=7 July=Pleiades.

Tibia=9,000=90%=P9.00D=9.0=Abstraction=Gods=Saturn=9Sept.>>A=Ø.

Tic=5,500=5.5=80%=P5.50=Earth-Midway=5 May = Gaia.

Tick1=10,000=1,000=100%=10.0=Physicality=Tech.=10 Oct.=Uranus=P=1Ø.

Tick2=8,000=80%=P8.0D=Economy=Currency=8 Aug.=Zeus>>E=v.

Tick3=6,500=7,000=70%=P7.0D=7.0=Language=Assets=Mars=7 July=Pleiades.

Ticker=8,000=80%=P8.0D=Economy=Currency=8 Aug.=Zeus>>E=v.

Ticker tape=4,000=40%=P4.0D=Govt.=Creatocracy=4 April=Mercury=Hermes=G=A4.

Ticket=10,000=1,000=100%=10.0=Physicality=Tech.=10 Oct.=Uranus=P=1Ø.

Ticking=6,000=60%=P6.0D=Man=Earth=Royalty=6 June=Gaia=Maia>>M=M2.

Tickle=10,000=1,000=100%=10.0=Physicality=Tech.=10 Oct.=Uranus=P=1Ø.

Ticklish=5,500=5.5=80%=P5.50=Earth-Midway=5 May = Gaia.

Tick tack toe=10,000=1,000=100%=10.0=Physicality=Tech.=10 Oct.=Uranus=P=1Ø.

Tidal=2,500=3,000=30%=P3.0D=3.0=Creativity=Stars=Muses=3 March = C=I>>GIL.

Tidal wave=9,000=90%=P9.00D=9.0=Abstraction=Gods=Saturn=9Sept.>>A=Ø.
An unusual rise or incursion of water along the seashore. A tsunami. An overwhelming manifestation as of opinion; flood. Result indicate that incursion is an activity of the God Council >> Host >> Holy Spirit using the lunar energy PGI. It is the manifestation of the Holy Spirit anything that makes contact with water in prayers makes contact with GOD. Note the Holy Spirit, the Spirit of GOD and the Seven Spirits of GOD are all different. The Holy Spirit is the Council of GODS headed by Hermes >> Khristos Zeus >> Christ Jesus >> the wit and guided by Athena the wis. The Spirit of GOD is Athena. The Seven Spirits is Pleiades (Job 38:31) headed by Maia known in Roman 11:33-35 as the Mind of GOD.

Tidbit=4,500=5,000=50%=P5.00D=Law=Time=Venus=5 May = Aphrodite>>L=N.

Tiddlywinks=10,000=1,000=100%=10.0=Physicality=Tech.=10 Oct.=Uranus=P=1Ø.

Tide=10,000=1,000=100%=Physicality=Tech.=10 Oct.=Uranus=P=1Ø.

Tideland=3,000=30%=P3.0D=3.0=Creativity=Stars=Muses=3 March = C=I>>GIL.

Tidewater=10,000=1,000=100%=10.0=Physicality=Tech.=10 Oct.=Uranus=P=1Ø.

Tidings=4,500=5,000=50%=P5.00D=Law=Time=Venus=5 May = Aphrodite>>L=N.

Tidy=10,000=1,000=100%=10.0=Physicality=Tech.=10 Oct.=Uranus=P=1Ø.

Tie=10,000=1,000=100%=10.0=Physicality=Tech.=10 Oct.=Uranus=P=1Ø.

Tie-dye=10,000=1,000=100%=10.0=Physicality=Tech.=10 Oct.=Uranus=P=1Ø.

Tie-in=10,000=1,000=100%=10.0=Physicality=Tech.=10 Oct.=Uranus=P=1Ø.

Tine Shan=10,000=1,000=100%=10.0=Physicality=Tech.=10 Oct.=Uranus=P=1Ø.

Tientsin=1,000=100%=10.0=1.0=Mind=Sun=1 January=Helios >> M=E4.

Tie polo=3,000=30%=P3.0D=3.0=Creativity=Stars=Muses=3 March = C=I>>GIL.

Tier=6,500=7,000=70%=P7.0D=7.0=Language=Assets=Mars=7 July=Pleiades.

Tierra del Fuego=10,000=1,000=100%=10.0=Physicality=Tech.=10 Oct.=Uranus=P=1Ø.

Tie-up=1,500=15%=P1.50D=1.5=Authority=Solar Crown=1 May = Maia.

Tiff=3,500=4,000=40%=P4.0D=Govt.=Creatocracy=4 April=Mercury=Hermes=G=A4.
Tiger=5,500=4,000=40%=P4.0D=Govt.=Creatocracy=4 April=Mercury=Hermes=G=A4.
Tiger lily=5,500=5.5=80%=P5.50=Earth-Midway=5 May = Gaia.
Tight=10,000=1,000=100%=10.0=Physicality=Tech.=10 Oct.=Uranus=P=1Ø.
Tightfisted=500=5%=P5.00D=5.0=Law=Time=Venus=5 May=Aphrodite>>L=N.
Tight lipped=5,000=50%=P5.00D=Law=Time=Venus=5 May = Aphrodite>>L=N.
Tightrope=4,000=40%=P4.0D=Govt.=Creatocracy=4 April=Mercury=Hermes=G=A4.
Tights=6,000=60%=P6.0D=Man=Earth=Royalty=6 June=Gaia=Maia>>M=M2.
Tightwad=1,500=15%=P1.50D=1.5=Authority=Solar Crown=1 May = Maia.
Tigris=11,000=11%=P1.10D=1.1=Idea=Brainchild=Inv.=11 Nov.=SC=Athena>>I=MT.
Tijuana=7,500=8,000=80%=P8.0D=Economy=Currency=8 Aug.=Zeus>>E=v.
Tilde=11,500=12,000=12%=P1.20D=1.2=Knowledge=Edu=12Dec.=Athena>>K=F.
Tile=10,000=1,000=100%=10.0=Physicality=Tech.=10 Oct.=Uranus=P=1Ø.
Till1=4,000=40%=P4.0D=Govt.=Creatocracy=4 April=Mercury=Hermes=G=A4.
Till2=10,000=1,000=100%=10.0=Physicality=Tech.=10 Oct.=Uranus=P=1Ø.
Till3=5,500=5.5=80%=P5.50=Earth-Midway=5 May = Gaia.
Tillage=1,500=15%=P1.50D=1.5=Authority=Solar Crown=1 May = Maia.
Tiller1=2,000=20%=P2.00D=2.0=Nature=Matter=Moon=2 Feb.=Cupid=N=C+_
Tiller2=8,000=80%=P8.0D=Economy=Currency=8 Aug.=Zeus>>E=v.
Tilt=10,000=1,000=100%=10.0=Physicality=Tech.=10 Oct.=Uranus=P=1Ø.
Timber=10,000=1,000=100%=10.0=Physicality=Tech.=10 Oct.=Uranus=P=1Ø.
Timberline=6,000=60%=P6.0D=Man=Earth=Royalty=6 June=Gaia=Maia>>M=M2.
Timber wolf=1,500=15%=P1.50D=1.5=Authority=Solar Crown=1 May = Maia.
Timbre=8,000=80%=P8.0D=Economy=Currency=8 Aug.=Zeus>>E=v.
Timbuktu=6,500=7,000=70%=P7.0D=7.0=Language=Assets=Mars=7 July=Pleiades.

Time=10,000=1,000=100%=10.0=Physicality=Tech.=10 Oct.=Uranus=P=1Ø.
See Standard Time. Now Time is assertively measured in the Maks. After Peter Matthews-Akukalia, Castle Makupedia. God of Creatocracy Genius and Mind.

Time bomb=8,000=80%=P8.0D=Economy=Currency=8 Aug.=Zeus>>E=v.
Time clock=5,500=5.5=80%=P5.50=Earth-Midway=5 May = Gaia.
Time deposit=5,000=50%=P5.00D=Law=Time=Venus=5 May = Aphrodite>>L=N.
Time honored=3,500=4,000=40%=P4.0D=Govt.=Creatocracy=4 April=Hermes=G=A4.
Time keeper=4,500=5,000=50%=P5.00D=Law=Time=Venus=5 May = Aphrodite>>L=N.
Time lapse=10,000=1,000=100%=10.0=Physicality=Tech.=10 Oct.=Uranus=P=1Ø.
Timeless=4,500=5,000=50%=P5.00D=Law=Time=Venus=5 May = Aphrodite>>L=N.
Timely=6,500=7,000=70%=P7.0D=7.0=Language=Assets=Mars=7 July=Pleiades.
Timeout=3,500=4,000=40%=P4.0D=Govt.=Creatocracy=4 April=Mercury=Hermes=G=A4.
Timepiece=4,000=40%=P4.0D=Govt.=Creatocracy=4 April=Mercury=Hermes=G=A4.
Times=4,000=40%=P4.0D=Govt.=Creatocracy=4 April=Mercury=Hermes=G=A4.
Time Sharing=10,000=1,000=100%=10.0=Physicality=Tech.=10 Oct.=Uranus=P=1Ø.
Times sign=4,000=40%=P4.0D=Govt.=Creatocracy=4 April=Mercury=Hermes=G=A4.

Timetable=7,500=8,000=80%=P8.0D=Economy=Currency=8 Aug.=Zeus>>E=v.
A measured means or principle to reach an economic utility for business and money.
Peter Matthews-Akukalia created the Genius Table, Human Energy Table, Calibrated
Curiosity Levels Table (Makumeter Gauge or CCLT) an instrument for measuring human
emotion, Planetary Dimensions Table and Formula. Even the Castle Makupedia is a huge
Table Dictionary of Makumatics Data Mining and MaksCurrencies World Encyclopedia etc.

Timeworn=4,500=5,000=50%=P5.00D=Law=Time=Venus=5 May = Aphrodite>>L=N.

Time zone=7,500=8,000=80%=P8.0D=Economy=Currency=8 Aug.=Zeus>>E=v.
Time zones must be measured to meet with an economic standard. See Standard Time.

Timid=3,000=30%=P3.0D=3.0=Creativity=Stars=Muses=3 March = C=I>>GIL.
Timing=6,000=60%=P6.0D=Man=Earth=Royalty=6 June=Gaia=Maia>>M=M2.
Timisoara=6,500=7,000=70%=P7.0D=7.0=Language=Assets=Mars=7 July=Pleiades.
Timor=4,500=5,000=50%=P5.00D=Law=Time=Venus=5 May = Aphrodite>>L=N.
Timorous=2,500=3,000=30%=P3.0D=3.0=Creativity=Stars=Muses=3 March = C=I>>GIL.
Timor Sea.=5,000=50%=P5.00D=Law=Time=Venus=5 May = Aphrodite>>L=N.
timothy=7,000=70%=P7.0D=7.0=Language=Assets=Mars=7 July=Pleiades.

Timothy=2,000=20%=P2.00D=2.0=Nature=Matter=Moon=2 Feb.=Cupid=N=C+_
Inspired by Artemis and Eros. A night hunter love and adventure book for startups.

Timothy, Saint.=2,000=20%=P2.00D=2.0=Nature=Matter=Moon=2 Feb.=Cupid=N=C+_
Timpani=4,500=5,000=50%=P5.00D=Law=Time=Venus=5 May = Aphrodite>>L=N.
Tin=10,000=1,000=100%=10.0=Physicality=Tech.=10 Oct.=Uranus=P=1Ø.
Tincture=10,000=1,000=100%=10.0=Physicality=Tech.=10 Oct.=Uranus=P=1Ø.
Tinder=4,000=40%=P4.0D=Govt.=Creatocracy=4 April=Mercury=Hermes=G=A4.
Tinderbox=4,000=40%=P4.0D=Govt.=Creatocracy=4 April=Mercury=Hermes=G=A4.
Tine=4,500=5,000=50%=P5.00D=Law=Time=Venus=5 May = Aphrodite>>L=N.
Tinfoil=5,000=50%=P5.00D=Law=Time=Venus=5 May = Aphrodite>>L=N.
Tinge=4,000=40%=P4.0D=Govt.=Creatocracy=4 April=Mercury=Hermes=G=A4.
Tingle=6,500=7,000=70%=P7.0D=7.0=Language=Assets=Mars=7 July=Pleiades.
Tinker=10,000=1,000=100%=10.0=Physicality=Tech.=10 Oct.=Uranus=P=1Ø.
Tinkle=10,000=1,000=100%=10.0=Physicality=Tech.=10 Oct.=Uranus=P=1Ø.
Tinny=500=5%=P5.00D=5.0=Law=Time=Venus=5 May=Aphrodite>>L=N.
Tinsel=10,000=1,000=100%=10.0=Physicality=Tech.=10 Oct.=Uranus=P=1Ø.
Tinsmith=4,000=40%=P4.0D=Govt.=Creatocracy=4 April=Mercury=Hermes=G=A4.
Tint=10,000=1,000=100%=10.0=Physicality=Tech.=10 Oct.=Uranus=P=1Ø.
Tintinnabulation=5,000=50%=P5.00D=Law=Time=Venus=5 May = Aphrodite>>L=N.
Tintoretto=2,000=20%=P2.00D=2.0=Nature=Matter=Moon=2 Feb.=Cupid=N=C+_
Tintype=1,000=100%=10.0=1.0=Mind=Sun=1 January=Helios >> M=E4.
Tiny=4,500=5,000=50%=P5.00D=Law=Time=Venus=5 May = Aphrodite>>L=N.

Tip=10,000=1,000=100%=10.0=Physicality=Tech.=10 Oct.=Uranus=P=1Ø.
Tip=2,000=20%=P2.00D=2.0=Nature=Matter=Moon=2 Feb.=Cupid=N=C+_
Tip3=4,000=40%=P4.0D=Govt.=Creatocracy=4 April=Mercury=Hermes=G=A4.
Tip4=10,000=1,000=100%=10.0=Physicality=Tech.=10 Oct.=Uranus=P=1Ø.
Tipi=1,500=15%=P1.50D=1.5=Authority=Solar Crown=1 May = Maia.
Tipoff=4,500=5,000=50%=P5.00D=Law=Time=Venus=5 May = Aphrodite>>L=N.
Tippet=7,000=70%=P7.0D=7.0=Language=Assets=Mars=7 July=Pleiades.
Tipple=5,500=5.5=80%=P5.50=Earth-Midway=5 May = Gaia.
Tipster=4,500=5,000=50%=P5.00D=Law=Time=Venus=5 May = Aphrodite>>L=N.
Tipsy=1,500=15%=P1.50D=1.5=Authority=Solar Crown=1 May = Maia.
Tiptoe=4,500=5,000=50%=P5.00D=Law=Time=Venus=5 May = Aphrodite>>L=N.
Tiptop=3,500=4,000=40%=P4.0D=Govt.=Creatocracy=4 April=Mercury=Hermes=G=A4.
Tirade=4,000=40%=P4.0D=Govt.=Creatocracy=4 April=Mercury=Hermes=G=A4.
Tiranë=5,000=50%=P5.00D=Law=Time=Venus=5 May = Aphrodite>>L=N.
Tire1=4,500=5,000=50%=P5.00D=Law=Time=Venus=5 May = Aphrodite>>L=N.
Tire2=10,000=1,000=100%=10.0=Physicality=Tech.=10 Oct.=Uranus=P=1Ø.
Tired=5,000=50%=P5.00D=Law=Time=Venus=5 May = Aphrodite>>L=N.
Tired=5,000=50%=P5.00D=Law=Time=Venus=5 May = Aphrodite>>L=N.
Tiresome=1,000=100%=10.0=1.0=Mind=Sun=1 January=Helios >> M=E4.
Tirol=1,000=100%=10.0=1.0=Mind=Sun=1 January=Helios >> M=E4.
'Tis=1,000=100%=10.0=1.0=Mind=Sun=1 January=Helios >> M=E4.
Tishri=6,000=60%=P6.0D=Man=Earth=Royalty=6 June=Gaia=Maia>>M=M2.
Tissue=10,000=1,000=100%=10.0=Physicality=Tech.=10 Oct.=Uranus=P=1Ø.
Tit1=4,500=5,000=50%=P5.00D=Law=Time=Venus=5 May = Aphrodite>>L=N.
Tit2=2,000=20%=P2.00D=2.0=Nature=Matter=Moon=2 Feb.=Cupid=N=C+_
Tit.=500=5%=P5.00D=5.0=Law=Time=Venus=5 May=Aphrodite>>L=N.

Titan=9,000=90%=P9.00D=9.0=Abstraction=Gods=Saturn=9Sept.>>A=Ø.
Greek Myth. One of a family of giants who were overthrown by the family of Zeus. A person of colossal size, strength, or achievement. Result confirms that Titans are Gods. The hierarchy of life >> Human >> gods (Influence, assets) >> Genius >> Titan >> Gods >> GOD. Peter Matthews-Akukalia, Castle Makupedia, God of Creatocracy Genius and Mind.

Titanic=3,000=30%=P3.0D=3.0=Creativity=Stars=Muses=3 March = C=I>>GIL.
Titanium=10,000=1,000=100%=10.0=Physicality=Tech.=10 Oct.=Uranus=P=1Ø.
Tithe=8,000=80%=P8.0D=Economy=Currency=8 Aug.=Zeus>>E=v.
Titian=2,500=3,000=30%=P3.0D=3.0=Creativity=Stars=Muses=3 March = C=I>>GIL.
Titicaca Lake=6,500=7,000=70%=P7.0D=7.0=Language=Assets=Mars=7 July=Pleiades.
Titilate=3,000=30%=P3.0D=3.0=Creativity=Stars=Muses=3 March = C=I>>GIL.

Title=10,000=1,000=100%=10.0=Physicality=Tech.=10 Oct.=Uranus=P=1Ø.
His Creative Excellency & Godship: Peter Matthews-Akukalia.
Castle Makupedia, God of Creatocracy Genius Mind & Mindom.

Titled=3,000=30%=P3.0D=3.0=Creativity=Stars=Muses=3 March = C=I>>GIL.
Titmouse=4,500=5,000=50%=P5.00D=Law=Time=Venus=5 May = Aphrodite>>L=N.
Tito Josip=3,000=30%=P3.0D=3.0=Creativity=Stars=Muses=3 March = C=I>>GIL.
Titograd=4,500=5,000=50%=P5.00D=Law=Time=Venus=5 May = Aphrodite>>L=N.
Titration=10,000=1,000=100%=10.0=Physicality=Tech.=10 Oct.=Uranus=P=1Ø.
Titter=4,500=5,000=50%=P5.00D=Law=Time=Venus=5 May = Aphrodite>>L=N.
Tittle=4,500=5,000=50%=P5.00D=Law=Time=Venus=5 May = Aphrodite>>L=N.

Titular=6,000=60%=P6.0D=Man=Earth=Royalty=6 June=Gaia=Maia>>M=M2. See title.

Titus1=4,000=40%=P4.0D=Govt.=Creatocracy=4 April=Mercury=Hermes=G=A4.

Titus2=2,000=20%=P2.00D=2.0=Nature=Matter=Moon=2 Feb.=Cupid=N=C+_
Inspired by Artemis and Eros. A night hunter love and adventure book for startups.

Titus,Saint=5,500=5.5=80%=P5.50=Earth-Midway=5 May = Gaia.
Tizzy=4,000=40%=P4.0D=Govt.=Creatocracy=4 April=Mercury=Hermes=G=A4.
TKO=1,500=15%=P1.50D=1.5=Authority=Solar Crown=1 May = Maia.
tkt.=500=5%=P5.00D=5.0=Law=Time=Venus=5 May=Aphrodite>>L=N.
TI=3,000=30%=P3.0D=3.0=Creativity=Stars=Muses=3 March = C=I>>GIL.
TLC=1,500=15%=P1.50D=1.5=Authority=Solar Crown=1 May = Maia.
Tlingit=10,000=1,000=100%=10.0=Physicality=Tech.=10 Oct.=Uranus=P=1Ø.
Tm=500=5%=P5.00D=5.0=Law=Time=Venus=5 May=Aphrodite>>L=N.
TM=500=5%=P5.00D=5.0=Law=Time=Venus=5 May=Aphrodite>>L=N.
TN=500=5%=P5.00D=5.0=Law=Time=Venus=5 May=Aphrodite>>L=N.
tnpk.=500=5%=P5.00D=5.0=Law=Time=Venus=5 May=Aphrodite>>L=N.
TNT=5,000=50%=P5.00D=Law=Time=Venus=5 May = Aphrodite>>L=N.
To=10,000=1,000=100%=10.0=Physicality=Tech.=10 Oct.=Uranus=P=1Ø.
Toad=6,000=60%=P6.0D=Man=Earth=Royalty=6 June=Gaia=Maia>>M=M2.
Toadstool=2,500=3,000=30%=P3.0D=3.0=Creativity=Stars=Muses=3 March = C=I>>GIL.
Toady=6,500=7,000=70%=P7.0D=7.0=Language=Assets=Mars=7 July=Pleiades.
Toast1=10,000=1,000=100%=10.0=Physicality=Tech.=10 Oct.=Uranus=P=1Ø.
Toast2=10,000=1,000=100%=10.0=Physicality=Tech.=10 Oct.=Uranus=P=1Ø.
Toaster=3,500=4,000=40%=P4.0D=Govt.=Creatocracy=4 April=Mercury=Hermes=G=A4.
Toasty=1,000=100%=10.0=1.0=Mind=Sun=1 January=Helios >> M=E4.
Tobacco=10,000=1,000=100%=10.0=Physicality=Tech.=10 Oct.=Uranus=P=1Ø.
Tobacconist=10,000=1,000=100%=10.0=Physicality=Tech.=10 Oct.=Uranus=P=1Ø.
Tobago=6,000=60%=P6.0D=Man=Earth=Royalty=6 June=Gaia=Maia>>M=M2.

Tobit=2,000=20%=P2.00D=2.0=Nature=Matter=Moon=2 Feb.=Cupid=N=C+_
See Timothy, Titus.

PETER K. MATTHEWS - AKUKALIA

Toboggan=10,000=1,000=100%=10.0=Physicality=Tech.=10 Oct.=Uranus=P=1Ø.
Toccata=8,500=9,000=90%=P9.00D=9.0=Abstraction=Gods=Saturn=9Sept.>>A=Ø.
Tocqueville Alexis=5,500=5.5=80%=P5.50=Earth-Midway=5 May = Gaia.
Tocsin=4,500=5,000=50%=P5.00D=Law=Time=Venus=5 May = Aphrodite>>L=N.
Today=8,000=80%=P8.0D=Economy=Currency=8 Aug.=Zeus>>E=v.
Toddle=3,500=4,000=40%=P4.0D=Govt.=Creatocracy=4 April=Mercury=Hermes=G=A4.
Toddy=4,000=40%=P4.0D=Govt.=Creatocracy=4 April=Mercury=Hermes=G=A4.
To-do=2,500=3,000=30%=P3.0D=3.0=Creativity=Stars=Muses=3 March = C=I>>GIL.
Toe=10,000=1,000=100%=10.0=Physicality=Tech.=10 Oct.=Uranus=P=1Ø.

Toea=4,000=40%=P4.0D=Govt.=Creatocracy=4 April=Mercury=Hermes=G=A4.
Perhaps <. E. DOLLAR. Currency metric weight >> 4/10=0.4 >> 40:1. See Naira. Dollar.

Toed=6,500=7,000=70%=P7.0D=7.0=Language=Assets=Mars=7 July=Pleiades.
Toehold=6,000=60%=P6.0D=Man=Earth=Royalty=6 June=Gaia=Maia>>M=M2.
Toenail=2,500=3,000=30%=P3.0D=3.0=Creativity=Stars=Muses=3 March = C=I>>GIL.
Toffee=5,500=5.5=80%=P5.50=Earth-Midway=5 May = Gaia.
Tofu=9,500=10,000=1,000=100%=10.0=Physicality=Tech.=10 Oct.=Uranus=P=1Ø.
Tog=5,000=50%=P5.00D=Law=Time=Venus=5 May = Aphrodite>>L=N.
Toga=9,000=90%=P9.00D=9.0=Abstraction=Gods=Saturn=9Sept.>>A=Ø.
Together=10,000=1,000=100%=10.0=Physicality=Tech.=10 Oct.=Uranus=P=1Ø.
Toggle switch=8,500=9,000=90%=P9.00D=9.0=Abst.=Gods=Saturn=9Sept.>>A=Ø.
Togliatti=6,500=7,000=70%=P7.0D=7.0=Language=Assets=Mars=7 July=Pleiades.
Togo=6,500=7,000=70%=P7.0D=7.0=Language=Assets=Mars=7 July=Pleiades.
Tohono O'odham=1,000=100%=10.0=1.0=Mind=Sun=1 January=Helios >> M=E4.
Toil1=7,000=70%=P7.0D=7.0=Language=Assets=Mars=7 July=Pleiades.
Toil2=7,000=70%=P7.0D=7.0=Language=Assets=Mars=7 July=Pleiades.
Toilet=10,000=1,000=100%=10.0=Physicality=Tech.=10 Oct.=Uranus=P=1Ø.
Toilet paper=5,000=50%=P5.00D=Law=Time=Venus=5 May = Aphrodite>>L=N.
Toiletry=4,000=40%=P4.0D=Govt.=Creatocracy=4 April=Mercury=Hermes=G=A4.
Toilette=7,500=8,000=80%=P8.0D=Economy=Currency=8 Aug.=Zeus>>E=v.
Toilet water=7,500=8,000=80%=P8.0D=Economy=Currency=8 Aug.=Zeus>>E=v.
Token=10,000=1,000=100%=10.0=Physicality=Tech.=10 Oct.=Uranus=P=1Ø.
Tokenism=4,500=5,000=50%=P5.00D=Law=Time=Venus=5 May = Aphrodite>>L=N.
Tokyo=9,000=90%=P9.00D=9.0=Abstraction=Gods=Saturn=9Sept.>>A=Ø.
Toledo=10,000=1,000=100%=10.0=Physicality=Tech.=10 Oct.=Uranus=P=1Ø.
Tolerable=2,000=20%=P2.00D=2.0=Nature=Matter=Moon=2 Feb.=Cupid=N=C+_
Tolerance=10,000=1,000=100%=10.0=Physicality=Tech.=10 Oct.=Uranus=P=1Ø.
Tolerate=10,000=1,000=100%=10.0=Physicality=Tech.=10 Oct.=Uranus=P=1Ø.
Tolkien John=3,000=30%=P3.0D=3.0=Creativity=Stars=Muses=3 March = C=I>>GIL.
Toll1=10,000=1,000=100%=10.0=Physicality=Tech.=10 Oct.=Uranus=P=1Ø.
Toll2=10,000=1,000=100%=10.0=Physicality=Tech.=10 Oct.=Uranus=P=1Ø.
Tollbooth=3,000=30%=P3.0D=3.0=Creativity=Stars=Muses=3 March = C=I>>GIL.
Tollgate=4,000=40%=P4.0D=Govt.=Creatocracy=4 April=Mercury=Hermes=G=A4.

Tolstoy Leo.=3,500=4,000=40%=P4.0D=Govt.=Creatocracy=4 April=Hermes=G=A4.
Toltec=10,000=1,000=100%=10.0=Physicality=Tech.=10 Oct.=Uranus=P=1Ø.
Tolyatti=1,000=100%=10.0=1.0=Mind=Sun=1 January=Helios >> M=E4.
Tom=7,000=70%=P7.0D=7.0=Language=Assets=Mars=7 July=Pleiades.
Tomahawk=10,000=1,000=100%=10.0=Physicality=Tech.=10 Oct.=Uranus=P=1Ø.

Tomato=7,000=70%=P7.0D=7.0=Language=Assets=Mars=7 July=Pleiades.
Eating tomatoes helps the brain develop precision sharpness and clarity of Mind.1.4.7.10.13.

Tomb=6,500=7,000=70%=P7.0D=7.0=Language=Assets=Mars=7 July=Pleiades.
Tomboy=5,000=50%=P5.00D=Law=Time=Venus=5 May = Aphrodite>>L=N.
Tombstone=1,000=100%=10.0=1.0=Mind=Sun=1 January=Helios >> M=E4.
Tomcat=1,500=15%=P1.50D=1.5=Authority=Solar Crown=1 May = Maia.
Tome=5,000=50%=P5.00D=Law=Time=Venus=5 May = Aphrodite>>L=N.
Tomfoolery=1,500=15%=P1.50D=1.5=Authority=Solar Crown=1 May = Maia.
Tomography=10,000=1,000=100%=10.0=Physicality=Tech.=10 Oct.=Uranus=P=1Ø.
Tomorrow=10,000=1,000=100%=10.0=Physicality=Tech.=10 Oct.=Uranus=P=1Ø.
Tomsk=4,500=5,000=50%=P5.00D=Law=Time=Venus=5 May = Aphrodite>>L=N.
Tom-Tom=7,000=70%=P7.0D=7.0=Language=Assets=Mars=7 July=Pleiades.
-tomy=4,500=5,000=50%=P5.00D=Law=Time=Venus=5 May = Aphrodite>>L=N.
Ton=10,000=1,000=100%=10.0=Physicality=Tech.=10 Oct.=Uranus=P=1Ø.
Tonality=7,000=70%=P7.0D=7.0=Language=Assets=Mars=7 July=Pleiades.
Tone=10,000=1,000=100%=10.0=Physicality=Tech.=10 Oct.=Uranus=P=1Ø.
Tone arm=4,500=5,000=50%=P5.00D=Law=Time=Venus=5 May = Aphrodite>>L=N.
Toner=8,000=80%=P8.0D=Economy=Currency=8 Aug.=Zeus>>E=v.
Tonga=8,500=9,000=90%=P9.00D=9.0=Abstraction=Gods=Saturn=9Sept.>>A=Ø.
Tongs=8,500=9,000=90%=P9.00D=9.0=Abstraction=Gods=Saturn=9Sept.>>A=Ø.
Tongue=10,000=1,000=100%=10.0=Physicality=Tech.=10 Oct.=Uranus=P=1Ø.
Tongue in cheek=2,000=20%=P2.00D=2.0=Nature=Matter=Moon=2 Feb.=Cupid=N=C+_
Tongue tied=5,000=50%=P5.00D=Law=Time=Venus=5 May = Aphrodite>>L=N.
Tongue twister=6,500=7,000=70%=P7.0D=7.0=Language=Assets=Mars=7 July=Pleiades.
Tonic=10,000=1,000=100%=10.0=Physicality=Tech.=10 Oct.=Uranus=P=1Ø.
Tonight=10,000=1,000=100%=10.0=Physicality=Tech.=10 Oct.=Uranus=P=1Ø.
Tonkin=10,000=1,000=100%=10.0=Physicality=Tech.=10 Oct.=Uranus=P=1Ø.
Tonnage=10,000=1,000=100%=10.0=Physicality=Tech.=10 Oct.=Uranus=P=1Ø.
Tonsil=10,000=1,000=100%=10.0=Physicality=Tech.=10 Oct.=Uranus=P=1Ø.
Tonsillectomy=3,500=4,000=40%=P4.0D=Govt.=4 April=Mercury=Hermes=G=A4.
Tonsillitis=2,000=20%=P2.00D=2.0=Nature=Matter=Moon=2 Feb.=Cupid=N=C+_
Tonsorial=3,500=4,000=40%=P4.0D=Govt.=Creatocracy=4 April=Hermes=G=A4.
Tonsure=10,000=1,000=100%=10.0=Physicality=Tech.=10 Oct.=Uranus=P=1Ø.
Tony=2,500=3,000=30%=P3.0D=3.0=Creativity=Stars=Muses=3 March = C=I>>GIL.
Too=10,000=1,000=100%=10.0=Physicality=Tech.=10 Oct.=Uranus=P=1Ø.
Took=2,000=20%=P2.00D=2.0=Nature=Matter=Moon=2 Feb.=Cupid=N=C+_
Tool=10,000=1,000=100%=10.0=Physicality=Tech.=10 Oct.=Uranus=P=1Ø.

Toot=7,000=70%=P7.0D=7.0=Language=Assets=Mars=7 July=Pleiades.
Tooth=10,000=1,000=100%=10.0=Physicality=Tech.=10 Oct.=Uranus=P=1Ø.
Toothache=4,000=40%=P4.0D=Govt.=Creatocracy=4 April=Mercury=Hermes=G=A4.
Toothbrush=2,500=3,000=30%=P3.0D=3.0=Stars=Muses=3 March = C=I
Toothpaste=2,500=3,000=30%=P3.0D=3.0=Creativity=Stars=Muses=3 March = C=I.
Toothpick=5,000=50%=P5.00D=Law=Time=Venus=5 May = Aphrodite>>L=N.
Toothsome=1,000=100%=10.0=1.0=Mind=Sun=1 January=Helios >> M=E4.
Top1=10,000=1,000=100%=10.0=Physicality=Tech.=10 Oct.=Uranus=P=1Ø.
Top2=5,000=50%=P5.00D=Law=Time=Venus=5 May = Aphrodite>>L=N.
Topaz=10,000=1,000=100%=10.0=Physicality=Tech.=10 Oct.=Uranus=P=1Ø.
Topcoat=2,000=20%=P2.00D=2.0=Nature=Matter=Moon=2 Feb.=Cupid=N=C+_
Top dog=5,000=50%=P5.00D=Law=Time=Venus=5 May = Aphrodite>>L=N.
Top drawer=3,500=4,000=40%=P4.0D=Govt.=4 April=Mercury=Hermes=G=A4.
Topeka=6,000=60%=P6.0D=Man=Earth=Royalty=6 June=Gaia=Maia>>M=M2.
Toper=3,000=30%=P3.0D=3.0=Creativity=Stars=Muses=3 March = C=I>>GIL.
Top flight=2,000=20%=P2.00D=2.0=Nature=Matter=Moon=2 Feb.=Cupid=N=C+_
Top hat=5,500=5.5=80%=P5.50=Earth-Midway=5 May = Gaia.
Top heavy=4,000=40%=P4.0D=Govt.=Creatocracy=4 April=Mercury=Hermes=G=A4.
Topiary=10,000=1,000=100%=10.0=Physicality=Tech.=10 Oct.=Uranus=P=1Ø.
Topic=6,000=60%=P6.0D=Man=Earth=Royalty=6 June=Gaia=Maia>>M=M2.
Topical=6,000=60%=P6.0D=Man=Earth=Royalty=6 June=Gaia=Maia>>M=M2.
Top knot=10,000=1,000=100%=10.0=Physicality=Tech.=10 Oct.=Uranus=P=1Ø.
Topless=3,500=4,000=40%=P4.0D=Govt.=Creatocracy=4 April=Mercury=Hermes=G=A4.
Topmost=1,500=15%=P1.50D=1.5=Authority=Solar Crown=1 May = Maia.
Top notch=2,000=20%=P2.00D=2.0=Nature=Matter=Moon=2 Feb.=Cupid=N=C+_
Topo-=2,000=20%=P2.00D=2.0=Nature=Matter=Moon=2 Feb.=Cupid=N=C+_
Topography=10,000=1,000=100%=10.0=Physicality=Tech.=10 Oct.=Uranus=P=1Ø.
Topping=3,500=4,000=40%=P4.0D=Govt.=Creatocracy=4 April=Mercury=Hermes=G=A4.
Topple=7,000=70%=P7.0D=7.0=Language=Assets=Mars=7 July=Pleiades.
Tops=2,000=20%=P2.00D=2.0=Nature=Matter=Moon=2 Feb.=Cupid=N=C+_
Topsail=7,500=8,000=80%=P8.0D=Economy=Currency=8 Aug.=Zeus>>E=v.
Top secret=3,000=30%=P3.0D=3.0=Creativity=Stars=Muses=3 March = C=I>>GIL.
Topside=5,000=50%=P5.00D=Law=Time=Venus=5 May = Aphrodite>>L=N.
Topsoil=2,500=3,000=30%=P3.0D=3.0=Creativity=Stars=Muses=3 March = C=I>>GIL.
Topsy-turvy=7,000=70%=P7.0D=7.0=Language=Assets=Mars=7 July=Pleiades.
Toque=4,000=40%=P4.0D=Govt.=Creatocracy=4 April=Mercury=Hermes=G=A4.
Tor=5,500=5.5=80%=P5.50=Earth-Midway=5 May = Gaia.
Torah=10,000=1,000=100%=10.0=Physicality=Tech.=10 Oct.=Uranus=P=1Ø.
Torch=10,000=1,000=100%=10.0=Physicality=Tech.=10 Oct.=Uranus=P=1Ø.
Tore=2,000=20%=P2.00D=2.0=Nature=Matter=Moon=2 Feb.=Cupid=N=C+_
Toreador=1,500=15%=P1.50D=1.5=Authority=Solar Crown=1 May = Maia.
Torment=10,000=1,000=100%=10.0=Physicality=Tech.=10 Oct.=Uranus=P=1Ø.
Torn=2,000=20%=P2.00D=2.0=Nature=Matter=Moon=2 Feb.=Cupid=N=C+_
Tornado=10,000=1,000=100%=10.0=Physicality=Tech.=10 Oct.=Uranus=P=1Ø.
Toronto=6,500=7,000=70%=P7.0D=7.0=Language=Assets=Mars=7 July=Pleiades.

Torpedo=10,000=1,000=100%=10.0=Physicality=Tech.=10 Oct.=Uranus=P=1Ø.
Torpid=10,000=1,000=100%=10.0=Physicality=Tech.=10 Oct.=Uranus=P=1Ø.
Torpor=10,000=1,000=100%=10.0=Physicality=Tech.=10 Oct.=Uranus=P=1Ø.
Torque=7,000=70%=P7.0D=7.0=Language=Assets=Mars=7 July=Pleiades.
Torrance=5,000=50%=P5.00D=Law=Time=Venus=5 May = Aphrodite>>L=N.
Torrent=10,000=1,000=100%=10.0=Physicality=Tech.=10 Oct.=Uranus=P=1Ø.
Torrid=5,500=5.5=80%=P5.50=Earth-Midway=5 May = Gaia.
Torrid Zone=6,000=60%=P6.0D=Man=Earth=Royalty=6 June=Gaia=Maia>>M=M2.
Torsion=10,000=1,000=100%=10.0=Physicality=Tech.=10 Oct.=Uranus=P=1Ø.
Torso=4,000=40%=P4.0D=Govt.=Creatocracy=4 April=Mercury=Hermes=G=A4.
Tort=10,000=1,000=100%=10.0=Physicality=Tech.=10 Oct.=Uranus=P=1Ø.
Tortilla=10,000=1,000=100%=10.0=Physicality=Tech.=10 Oct.=Uranus=P=1Ø.
Tortoise=4,000=40%=P4.0D=Govt.=Creatocracy=4 April=Mercury=Hermes=G=A4.
Tortoiseshell=7,000=70%=P7.0D=7.0=Language=Assets=Mars=7 July=Pleiades.
Tortola=6,000=60%=P6.0D=Man=Earth=Royalty=6 June=Gaia=Maia>>M=M2.
Tortuga=4,500=5,000=50%=P5.00D=Law=Time=Venus=5 May = Aphrodite>>L=N.
Tortuous=5,000=50%=P5.00D=Law=Time=Venus=5 May = Aphrodite>>L=N.
Torture=10,000=1,000=100%=10.0=Physicality=Tech.=10 Oct.=Uranus=P=1Ø.
Tory=10,000=1,000=100%=10.0=Physicality=Tech.=10 Oct.=Uranus=P=1Ø.
Toscanini Arturo=2,000=20%=P2.00D=2.0=Nature=Matter=Moon=2 Feb.=Cupid=N=C+_
Toss=10,000=1,000=100%=10.0=Physicality=Tech.=10 Oct.=Uranus=P=1Ø.
Toss up=3,000=30%=P3.0D=3.0=Creativity=Stars=Muses=3 March = C=I>>GIL.
Tot1=2,500=3,000=30%=P3.0D=3.0=Creativity=Stars=Muses=3 March = C=I>>GIL.
Tot2=3,000=30%=P3.0D=3.0=Creativity=Stars=Muses=3 March = C=I>>GIL.
Total=10,000=1,000=100%=10.0=Physicality=Tech.=10 Oct.=Uranus=P=1Ø.
Totalitarian=10,000=1,000=100%=10.0=Physicality=Tech.=10 Oct.=Uranus=P=1Ø.
Totality=5,000=50%=P5.00D=Law=Time=Venus=5 May = Aphrodite>>L=N.
Tote=4,000=40%=P4.0D=Govt.=Creatocracy=4 April=Mercury=Hermes=G=A4.
Totem=10,000=1,000=100%=10.0=Physicality=Tech.=10 Oct.=Uranus=P=1Ø.
Totem pole=8,500=9,000=90%=P9.00D=9.0=Abstraction=Gods=Saturn=9Sept.>>A=Ø.
Totter=5,500=5.5=80%=P5.50=Earth-Midway=5 May = Gaia.
Toucan=7,000=70%=P7.0D=7.0=Language=Assets=Mars=7 July=Pleiades.
Touch=10,000=1,000=100%=10.0=Physicality=Tech.=10 Oct.=Uranus=P=1Ø.
Touch and go=3,500=4,000=40%=P4.0D=Govt.=Creatocracy=4 April=Hermes=G=A4.
Touch down=10,000=1,000=100%=10.0=Physicality=Tech.=10 Oct.=Uranus=P=1Ø.
Touché=10,000=1,000=100%=10.0=Physicality=Tech.=10 Oct.=Uranus=P=1Ø.
Touching=2,000=20%=P2.00D=2.0=Nature=Matter=Moon=2 Feb.=Cupid=N=C+_
Touchstone=10,000=1,000=100%=10.0=Physicality=Tech.=10 Oct.=Uranus=P=1Ø.
Touchy=5,000=50%=P5.00D=Law=Time=Venus=5 May = Aphrodite>>L=N.
Tough=10,000=1,000=100%=10.0=Physicality=Tech.=10 Oct.=Uranus=P=1Ø.
Toughen=4,500=5,000=50%=P5.00D=Law=Time=Venus=5 May = Aphrodite>>L=N.
Toulouse=4,500=5,000=50%=P5.00D=Law=Time=Venus=5 May = Aphrodite>>L=N.
Toulouse-Lautrec=3,000=30%=P3.0D=3.0=Creativity=Stars=Muses=3 March = C=I>>GIL.
Toupee=5,000=50%=P5.00D=Law=Time=Venus=5 May = Aphrodite>>L=N.
Tour=10,000=1,000=100%=10.0=Physicality=Tech.=10 Oct.=Uranus=P=1Ø.

PETER K. MATTHEWS - AKUKALIA

Tour de force=4,000=40%=P4.0D=Govt.=Creatocracy=4 April=Mercury=Hermes=G=A4.
Tourism=2,000=20%=P2.00D=2.0=Nature=Matter=Moon=2 Feb.=Cupid=N=C+_
Tourist=2,500=3,000=30%=P3.0D=3.0=Creativity=Stars=Muses=3 March = C=I>>GIL.
Tourmaline=8,000=80%=P8.0D=Economy=Currency=8 Aug.=Zeus>>E=v.
Tournament=10,000=1,000=100%=10.0=Physicality=Tech.=10 Oct.=Uranus=P=1Ø.
Tourney=3,000=30%=P3.0D=3.0=Creativity=Stars=Muses=3 March = C=I>>GIL.
Tourniquet=7,500=8,000=80%=P8.0D=Economy=Currency=8 Aug.=Zeus>>E=v.
Tours=6,000=60%=P6.0D=Man=Earth=Royalty=6 June=Gaia=Maia>>M=M2.
Tousle=3,500=4,000=40%=P4.0D=Govt.=Creatocracy=4 April=Mercury=Hermes=G=A4.
Tousaint L'Ouverture=3,500=4,000=40%=P4.0D=Govt.=4April=Mercury=Hermes=G=A4.
Tout=8,000=80%=P8.0D=Economy=Currency=8 Aug.=Zeus>>E=v.
Tow1=10,000=1,000=100%=10.0=Physicality=Tech.=10 Oct.=Uranus=P=1Ø.
Tow2=5,000=50%=P5.00D=Law=Time=Venus=5 May = Aphrodite>>L=N.
Toward=10,000=1,000=100%=10.0=Physicality=Tech.=10 Oct.=Uranus=P=1Ø.
Towel=8,000=80%=P8.0D=Economy=Currency=8 Aug.=Zeus>>E=v.
Tower=10,000=1,000=100%=10.0=Physicality=Tech.=10 Oct.=Uranus=P=1Ø.
Towering=4,500=5,000=50%=P5.00D=Law=Time=Venus=5 May = Aphrodite>>L=N.
Towhead=3,000=30%=P3.0D=3.0=Creativity=Stars=Muses=3 March = C=I>>GIL.
Towhee=7,500=8,000=80%=P8.0D=Economy=Currency=8 Aug.=Zeus>>E=v.
Town=10,000=1,000=100%=10.0=Physicality=Tech.=10 Oct.=Uranus=P=1Ø.

Town hall=6,500=7,000=70%=P7.0D=7.0=Language=Assets=Mars=7 July=Pleiades.
A building containing the offices of town officials and the town council and courts.
See Principles of Psychoastronomy by Peter Matthews-Akukalia.

Townhouse=5,000=50%=P5.00D=Law=Time=Venus=5 May = Aphrodite>>L=N.
Town meeting=2,500=3,000=30%=P3.0D=3.0=Creativity=Stars=Muses=3 March=C=I
Township=9,000=90%=P9.00D=9.0=Abstraction=Gods=Saturn=9Sept.>>A=Ø.
Townspeople=4,000=40%=P4.0D=Govt.=Creatocracy=4 April=Mercury=Hermes=G=A4.
Towpath=5,500=5.5=80%=P5.50=Earth-Midway=5 May = Gaia.
Toxemia=10,000=1,000=100%=10.0=Physicality=Tech.=10 Oct.=Uranus=P=1Ø.
Toxi-=2,000=20%=P2.00D=2.0=Nature=Matter=Moon=2 Feb.=Cupid=N=C+_
Toxic=6,000=60%=P6.0D=Man=Earth=Royalty=6 June=Gaia=Maia>>M=M2.
Toxicology=4,000=40%=P4.0D=Govt.=Creatocracy=4 April=Mercury=Hermes=G=A4.
Toxin=10,000=1,000=100%=10.0=Physicality=Tech.=10 Oct.=Uranus=P=1Ø.
Toy=10,000=1,000=100%=10.0=Physicality=Tech.=10 Oct.=Uranus=P=1Ø.
Toyama=10,000=1,000=100%=10.0=Physicality=Tech.=10 Oct.=Uranus=P=1Ø.
tpk.=500=5%=P5.00D=5.0=Law=Time=Venus=5 May=Aphrodite>>L=N.
TR=1,000=100%=10.0=1.0=Mind=Sun=1 January=Helios >> M=E4.
tr.=3,500=4,000=40%=P4.0D=Govt.=Creatocracy=4 April=Mercury=Hermes=G=A4.
Trace1=10,000=1,000=100%=10.0=Physicality=Tech.=10 Oct.=Uranus=P=1Ø.
Trace2=10,000=1,000=100%=10.0=Physicality=Tech.=10 Oct.=Uranus=P=1Ø.
Tracer bullet=4,000=40%=P4.0D=Govt.=Creatocracy=4April=Mercury=Hermes=G=A4.
Tracery=3,500=4,000=40%=P4.0D=Govt.=Creatocracy=4 April=Mercury=Hermes=G=A4.

Trachea=10,000=1,000=100%=10.0=Physicality=Tech.=10 Oct.=Uranus=P=1Ø.
Tracheotomy=3,500=4,000=40%=P4.0D=Govt.=4 April=Mercury=Hermes=G=A4.
Track=10,000=1,000=100%=10.0=Physicality=Tech.=10 Oct.=Uranus=P=1Ø.
Track and field=5,500=5.5=80%=P5.50=Earth-Midway=5 May = Gaia.
Tracking=7,000=70%=P7.0D=7.0=Language=Assets=Mars=7 July=Pleiades.
Tract1=10,000=1,000=100%=10.0=Physicality=Tech.=10 Oct.=Uranus=P=1Ø.
Tract2=8,000=80%=P8.0D=Economy=Currency=8 Aug.=Zeus>>E=v.
Tractable=6,000=60%=P6.0D=Man=Earth=Royalty=6 June=Gaia=Maia>>M=M2.
Tract house=7,000=70%=P7.0D=7.0=Language=Assets=Mars=7 July=Pleiades.
Traction=10,000=1,000=100%=10.0=Physicality=Tech.=10 Oct.=Uranus=P=1Ø.
Tractor=10,000=1,000=100%=10.0=Physicality=Tech.=10 Oct.=Uranus=P=1Ø.
Tractor-trailer=10,000=1,000=100%=10.0=Physicality=Tech.=10 Oct.=Uranus=P=1Ø.
Trade=10,000=1,000=100%=10.0=Physicality=Tech.=10 Oct.=Uranus=P=1Ø.
Trade in=4,500=5,000=50%=P5.00D=Law=Time=Venus=5 May = Aphrodite>>L=N.
Trademark=10,000=1,000=100%=10.0=Physicality=Tech.=10 Oct.=Uranus=P=1Ø.
Trade name=8,000=80%=P8.0D=Economy=Currency=8 Aug.=Zeus>>E=v.
Trade off=10,000=1,000=100%=10.0=Physicality=Tech.=10 Oct.=Uranus=P=1Ø.
Tradesman=4,000=40%=P4.0D=Govt.=Creatocracy=4 April=Mercury=Hermes=G=A4.
Trade union=1,500=15%=P1.50D=1.5=Authority=Solar Crown=1 May = Maia.
Trade wind=10,000=1,000=100%=10.0=Physicality=Tech.=10 Oct.=Uranus=P=1Ø.
Trading post=6,500=7,000=70%=P7.0D=7.0=Language=Assets=Mars=7 July=Pleiades.
Tradition=10,000=1,000=100%=10.0=Physicality=Tech.=10 Oct.=Uranus=P=1Ø.
Traduce=2,500=3,000=30%=P3.0D=3.0=Creativity=Stars=Muses=3 March = C=I>>GIL.
Trafalgar Cape=5,500=5.5=80%=P5.50=Earth-Midway=5 May = Gaia.
Traffic=10,000=1,000=100%=10.0=Physicality=Tech.=10 Oct.=Uranus=P=1Ø.
Traffic circle=7,000=70%=P7.0D=7.0=Language=Assets=Mars=7 July=Pleiades.
Traffic light=6,000=60%=P6.0D=Man=Earth=Royalty=6 June=Gaia=Maia>>M=M2.
Tragedy=10,000=1,000=100%=10.0=Physicality=Tech.=10 Oct.=Uranus=P=1Ø.
Tragic=10,000=1,000=100%=10.0=Physicality=Tech.=10 Oct.=Uranus=P=1Ø.
Tragicomedy=10,000=1,000=100%=10.0=Physicality=Tech.=10 Oct.=Uranus=P=1Ø.
Trail=10,000=1,000=100%=10.0=Physicality=Tech.=10 Oct.=Uranus=P=1Ø.
Trail bike=4,000=40%=P4.0D=Govt.=Creatocracy=4 April=Mercury=Hermes=G=A4.

Trailblazer=5,500=5.5=80%=P5.50=Earth-Midway=5 May = Gaia.
Peter Matthews-Akukalia, Castle Makupedia is the trailblazer of Creatocracy.

Trailer=10,000=1,000=100%=10.0=Physicality=Tech.=10 Oct.=Uranus=P=1Ø.
Trailer park=5,500=5.5=80%=P5.50=Earth-Midway=5 May = Gaia.
Trailing arbutus=4,500=5,000=50%=P5.00D=Law=Time=Venus=5 May =Odite>>L=N.
Train traipse=10,000=1,000=100%=10.0=Physicality=Tech.=10 Oct.=Uranus=P=1Ø.
Traipse=4,500=5,000=50%=P5.00D=Law=Time=Venus=5 May = Aphrodite>>L=N.
Trait=7,500=8,000=80%=P8.0D=Economy=Currency=8 Aug.=Zeus>>E=v.
Traitor=10,000=1,000=100%=10.0=Physicality=Tech.=10 Oct.=Uranus=P=1Ø.
Trajan=3,500=4,000=40%=P4.0D=Govt.=Creatocracy=4 April=Mercury=Hermes=G=A4.

Trajectory=8,000=80%=P8.0D=Economy=Currency=8 Aug.=Zeus>>E=v.
Tram=10,000=1,000=100%=10.0=Physicality=Tech.=10 Oct.=Uranus=P=1Ø.
Trammel=10,000=1,000=100%=10.0=Physicality=Tech.=10 Oct.=Uranus=P=1Ø.
Tramp==10,000=1,000=100%=10.0=Physicality=Tech.=10 Oct.=Uranus=P=1Ø.
Trample=10,000=1,000=100%=10.0=Physicality=Tech.=10 Oct.=Uranus=P=1Ø.
Trampoline=10,000=1,000=100%=10.0=Physicality=Tech.=10 Oct.=Uranus=P=1Ø.
Trance=10,000=1,000=100%=10.0=Physicality=Tech.=10 Oct.=Uranus=P=1Ø.
Tranquil=3,000=30%=P3.0D=3.0=Creativity=Stars=Muses=3 March = C=I>>GIL.
Tranquilize=3,000=30%=P3.0D=3.0=Creativity=Stars=Muses=3 March = C=I>>GIL.
Tranquilizer=2,500=3,000=30%=P3.0D=3.0=Creativity=Stars=Muses=3 March=C=I
Trans.=3,500=4,000=40%=P4.0D=Govt.=Creatocracy=4 April=Mercury=Hermes=G=A4.
Trans-=5,000=50%=P5.00D=Law=Time=Venus=5 May = Aphrodite>>L=N.
Transact=9,500=10,000=1,000=100%=10.0=Physicality=Tech.=10 Oct.=Uranus=P=1Ø.
Transaction=4,500=5,000=50%=P5.00D=Law=Time=Venus=5 May = Aphrodite>>L=N.
Transalpine Gaul=6,500=7,000=70%=P7.0D=7.0=Lang=Assets=Mars=7 July=Pleiades.
Transatlantic=5,000=50%=P5.00D=Law=Time=Venus=5 May = Aphrodite>>L=N.
Transaxle=10,000=1,000=100%=10.0=Physicality=Tech.=10 Oct.=Uranus=P=1Ø.
Transcaucasia=10,000=1,000=100%=10.0=Physicality=Tech.=10 Oct.=Uranus=P=1Ø.
Transcend=10,000=1,000=100%=10.0=Physicality=Tech.=10 Oct.=Uranus=P=1Ø.
Transcendental=10,000=1,000=100%=10.0=Physicality=Tech.=10 Oct.=Uranus=P=1Ø.
Transcendentalism=10,000=1,000=100%=10.0=Physicality=Tech.=10 Oct.=Uranus=P=1Ø.
Transcontinental=2,500=3,000=30%=P3.0D=3.0=Creativity=Stars=Muses=3 March=CI
Transcribe=10,000=1,000=100%=10.0=Physicality=Tech.=10 Oct.=Uranus=P=1Ø.
Transcript=4,500=5,000=50%=P5.00D=Law=Time=Venus=5 May = Aphrodite>>L=N.
Transcription=10,000=1,000=100%=10.0=Physicality=Tech.=10 Oct.=Uranus=P=1Ø.
Transducer=10,000=1,000=100%=10.0=Physicality=Tech.=10 Oct.=Uranus=P=1Ø.
Transept=7,000=70%=P7.0D=7.0=Language=Assets=Mars=7 July=Pleiades.
Transfer=10,000=1,000=100%=10.0=Physicality=Tech.=10 Oct.=Uranus=P=1Ø.
Transfigure=8,000=80%=P8.0D=Economy=Currency=8 Aug.=Zeus>>E=v.
Transfix=10,000=1,000=100%=10.0=Physicality=Tech.=10 Oct.=Uranus=P=1Ø.
Transform=10,000=1,000=100%=10.0=Physicality=Tech.=10 Oct.=Uranus=P=1Ø.
Transformer=10,000=1,000=100%=10.0=Physicality=Tech.=10 Oct.=Uranus=P=1Ø.
Transfuse=10,000=1,000=100%=10.0=Physicality=Tech.=10 Oct.=Uranus=P=1Ø.
Transfusion=10,000=1,000=100%=10.0=Physicality=Tech.=10 Oct.=Uranus=P=1Ø.
Transgress=10,000=1,000=100%=10.0=Physicality=Tech.=10 Oct.=Uranus=P=1Ø.
Transship=1,500=15%=P1.50D=1.5=Authority=Solar Crown=1 May = Maia.
Transient=10,000=1,000=100%=10.0=Physicality=Tech.=10 Oct.=Uranus=P=1Ø.
Transistor=10,000=1,000=100%=10.0=Physicality=Tech.=10 Oct.=Uranus=P=1Ø.
Transit=10,000=1,000=100%=10.0=Physicality=Tech.=10 Oct.=Uranus=P=1Ø.
Transition=5,000=50%=P5.00D=Law=Time=Venus=5 May = Aphrodite>>L=N.
Transitive=7,000=70%=P7.0D=7.0=Language=Assets=Mars=7 July=Pleiades.
Transitory=1,500=15%=P1.50D=1.5=Authority=Solar Crown=1 May = Maia.
Transkei=10,000=1,000=100%=10.0=Physicality=Tech.=10 Oct.=Uranus=P=1Ø.
Translate=10,000=1,000=100%=10.0=Physicality=Tech.=10 Oct.=Uranus=P=1Ø.
Transliterate=10,000=1,000=100%=10.0=Physicality=Tech.=10 Oct.=Uranus=P=1Ø.

Translucent=10,000=1,000=100%=10.0=Physicality=Tech.=10 Oct.=Uranus=P=1Ø.
Transmigrate=6,500=7,000=70%=P7.0D=7.0=Language=Assets=Mars=7 July=Pleiades.
Transmission=10,000=1,000=100%=10.0=Physicality=Tech.=10 Oct.=Uranus=P=1Ø.
Transmit=10,000=1,000=100%=10.0=Physicality=Tech.=10 Oct.=Uranus=P=1Ø.
Transmitter=10,000=1,000=100%=10.0=Physicality=Tech.=10 Oct.=Uranus=P=1Ø.
Transmogrify=10,000=1,000=100%=10.0=Physicality=Tech.=10 Oct.=Uranus=P=1Ø.
Transmute=10,000=1,000=100%=10.0=Physicality=Tech.=10 Oct.=Uranus=P=1Ø.
Transnational=5,500=5.5=80%=P5.50=Earth-Midway=5 May = Gaia.
Transoceanic=4,000=40%=P4.0D=Govt.=Creatocracy=4 April=Mercury=Hermes=G=A4.
Transom=5,000=50%=P5.00D=Law=Time=Venus=5 May = Aphrodite>>L=N.
Transpacific=4,000=40%=P4.0D=Govt.=Creatocracy=4 April=Mercury=Hermes=G=A4.
Transparent=10,000=1,000=100%=10.0=Physicality=Tech.=10 Oct.=Uranus=P=1Ø.
Transpire=10,000=1,000=100%=10.0=Physicality=Tech.=10 Oct.=Uranus=P=1Ø.
Transplant=10,000=1,000=100%=10.0=Physicality=Tech.=10 Oct.=Uranus=P=1Ø.
Transport=10,000=1,000=100%=10.0=Physicality=Tech.=10 Oct.=Uranus=P=1Ø.
Transpose=10,000=1,000=100%=10.0=Physicality=Tech.=10 Oct.=Uranus=P=1Ø.
Transsexual=10,000=1,000=100%=10.0=Physicality=Tech.=10 Oct.=Uranus=P=1Ø.
Transship=5,000=50%=P5.00D=Law=Time=Venus=5 May = Aphrodite>>L=N.
Transubstantiate=10,000=1,000=100%=10.0=Physicality=Tech.=10 Oct.=Uranus=P=1Ø.
Transuranic=5,000=50%=P5.00D=Law=Time=Venus=5 May = Aphrodite>>L=N.
Transvaal=3,000=30%=P3.0D=3.0=Creativity=Stars=Muses=3 March = C=I>>GIL.
Transversal=5,000=50%=P5.00D=Law=Time=Venus=5 May = Aphrodite>>L=N.
Transverse=5,000=50%=P5.00D=Law=Time=Venus=5 May = Aphrodite>>L=N.
Transvestite=10,000=1,000=100%=10.0=Physicality=Tech.=10 Oct.=Uranus=P=1Ø.
Transylvania=10,000=1,000=100%=10.0=Physicality=Tech.=10 Oct.=Uranus=P=1Ø.
Transylvanian Alps.=5,000=50%=P5.00D=Law=Time=Venus=5 May = Aphrodite>>L=N.
Trap=10,000=1,000=100%=10.0=Physicality=Tech.=10 Oct.=Uranus=P=1Ø.
Trap door=5,000=50%=P5.00D=Law=Time=Venus=5 May = Aphrodite>>L=N.
Trapeze=7,500=8,000=80%=P8.0D=Economy=Currency=8 Aug.=Zeus>>E=v.
Trapezoid=9,000=90%=P9.00D=9.0=Abstraction=Gods=Saturn=9Sept.>>A=Ø.
Trappings=8,000=80%=P8.0D=Economy=Currency=8 Aug.=Zeus>>E=v.
Trapshooting=4,500=5,000=50%=P5.00D=Law=Time=Venus=5 May = Aphrodite>>L=N.
Trash=10,000=1,000=100%=10.0=Physicality=Tech.=10 Oct.=Uranus=P=1Ø.
Trauma=10,000=1,000=100%=10.0=Physicality=Tech.=10 Oct.=Uranus=P=1Ø.
Travail=8,000=80%=P8.0D=Economy=Currency=8 Aug.=Zeus>>E=v.
Travel=10,000=1,000=100%=10.0=Physicality=Tech.=10 Oct.=Uranus=P=1Ø.
Travelogue=3,500=4,000=40%=P4.0D=Govt.=Creatocracy=4 April=Hermes=G=A4.
Traverse=10,000=1,000=100%=10.0=Physicality=Tech.=10 Oct.=Uranus=P=1Ø.
Travertine=10,000=1,000=100%=10.0=Physicality=Tech.=10 Oct.=Uranus=P=1Ø.
Travesty=10,000=1,000=100%=10.0=Physicality=Tech.=10 Oct.=Uranus=P=1Ø.
Trawl=10,000=1,000=100%=10.0=Physicality=Tech.=10 Oct.=Uranus=P=1Ø.
Trawler=2,500=3,000=30%=P3.0D=3.0=Creativity=Stars=Muses=3 March = C=I>>GIL.
Tray=8,000=80%=P8.0D=Economy=Currency=8 Aug.=Zeus>>E=v.
Treacherous=10,000=1,000=100%=10.0=Physicality=Tech.=10 Oct.=Uranus=P=1Ø.

PETER K. MATTHEWS - AKUKALIA

Treachery=4,500=5,000=50%=P5.00D=Law=Time=Venus=5 May = Aphrodite>>L=N.
Treacle=7,000=70%=P7.0D=7.0=Language=Assets=Mars=7 July=Pleiades.
Tread=10,000=1,000=100%=10.0=Physicality=Tech.=10 Oct.=Uranus=P=1Ø.
Treadle=9,000=90%=P9.00D=9.0=Abstraction=Gods=Saturn=9Sept.>>A=Ø.
Treadmill=10,000=1,000=100%=10.0=Physicality=Tech.=10 Oct.=Uranus=P=1Ø.
Treason=10,000=1,000=100%=10.0=Physicality=Tech.=10 Oct.=Uranus=P=1Ø.
Treasure=10,000=1,000=100%=10.0=Physicality=Tech.=10 Oct.=Uranus=P=1Ø.
Treasurer=10,000=1,000=100%=10.0=Physicality=Tech.=10 Oct.=Uranus=P=1Ø.
Treasure-trove=10,000=1,000=100%=10.0=Physicality=Tech.=10 Oct.=Uranus=P=1Ø.
Treasury=10,000=1,000=100%=10.0=Physicality=Tech.=10 Oct.=Uranus=P=1Ø.
Treat=10,000=1,000=100%=10.0=Physicality=Tech.=10 Oct.=Uranus=P=1Ø.
Treatise=6,000=60%=P6.0D=Man=Earth=Royalty=6 June=Gaia=Maia>>M=M2.
Treatment=5,500=5.5=80%=P5.50=Earth-Midway=5 May = Gaia.
Treaty=5,500=5.5=80%=P5.50=Earth-Midway=5 May = Gaia.
Treble=10,000=1,000=100%=10.0=Physicality=Tech.=10 Oct.=Uranus=P=1Ø.
Treble clef=8,500=9,000=90%=P9.00D=9.0=Abstraction=Gods=Saturn=9Sept.>>A=Ø.
Tree=10,000=1,000=100%=10.0=Physicality=Tech.=10 Oct.=Uranus=P=1Ø.
Tree frog=5,500=5.5=80%=P5.50=Earth-Midway=5 May = Gaia.
Tree line=7,500=8,000=80%=P8.0D=Economy=Currency=8 Aug.=Zeus>>E=v.
Tree-of-heaven=4,500=5,000=50%=P5.00D=Law=Time=Venus=5 May =Odite>>L=N.
Trefoil=10,000=1,000=100%=10.0=Physicality=Tech.=10 Oct.=Uranus=P=1Ø.
Trek=7,000=70%=P7.0D=7.0=Language=Assets=Mars=7 July=Pleiades.
Trellis=7,000=70%=P7.0D=7.0=Language=Assets=Mars=7 July=Pleiades.
Trematoda=10,000=1,000=100%=10.0=Physicality=Tech.=10 Oct.=Uranus=P=1Ø.
Tremble=7,000=70%=P7.0D=7.0=Language=Assets=Mars=7 July=Pleiades.
Tremendous=10,000=1,000=100%=10.0=Physicality=Tech.=10 Oct.=Uranus=P=1Ø.
Tremolo=10,000=1,000=100%=10.0=Physicality=Tech.=10 Oct.=Uranus=P=1Ø.
Tremor=10,000=1,000=100%=10.0=Physicality=Tech.=10 Oct.=Uranus=P=1Ø.
Tremulous=5,000=50%=P5.00D=Law=Time=Venus=5 May = Aphrodite>>L=N.
Trench=10,000=1,000=100%=10.0=Physicality=Tech.=10 Oct.=Uranus=P=1Ø.
Trenchant=3,500=4,000=40%=P4.0D=Govt.=4 April=Mercury=Hermes=G=A4.
Trench coat=5,500=5.5=80%=P5.50=Earth-Midway=5 May = Gaia.
Trencher=3,500=4,000=40%=P4.0D=Govt.=Creatocracy=4 April=Hermes=G=A4.
Trench fever=6,000=60%=P6.0D=Man=Earth=Royalty=6 June=Gaia=Maia>>M=M2.
Trench foot=7,500=8,000=80%=P8.0D=Economy=Currency=8 Aug.=Zeus>>E=v.
Trench mouth=4,500=5,000=50%=P5.00D=Law=Time=Venus=5 May = Aphrodite>>L=N.
Trend=10,000=1,000=100%=Physicality=Tech.=10 Oct.=Uranus=P=1Ø.
Trendy=5,500=5.5=80%=P5.50=Earth-Midway=5 May = Gaia.

Trenton=7,500=8,000=80%=P8.0D=Economy=Currency=8 Aug.=Zeus>>E=v.
Treston, a word used to describe the subconscious material part of the brain. Invented by Peter Matthews-Akukalia, Castle Makupedia in the Oracle: Principles of Creative Sciences. >> Mind Mechanics & Engineering.

Trepan=3,000=30%=P3.0D=3.0=Creativity=Stars=Muses=3 March = C=I>>GIL.
Trephine=10,000=1,000=100%=10.0=Physicality=Tech.=10 Oct.=Uranus=P=1Ø.
Trepidation=2,500=3,000=30%=P3.0D=3.0=Creativity=Stars=Muses=3 March = C=I
Trespass=10,000=1,000=100%=10.0=Physicality=Tech.=10 Oct.=Uranus=P=1Ø.
Tress=3,000=30%=P3.0D=3.0=Creativity=Stars=Muses=3 March = C=I>>GIL.
Trestle=10,000=1,000=100%=10.0=Physicality=Tech.=10 Oct.=Uranus=P=1Ø.
Trey=4,500=5,000=50%=P5.00D=Law=Time=Venus=5 May = Aphrodite>>L=N.
Tri-=10,000=1,000=100%=10.0=Physicality=Tech.=10 Oct.=Uranus=P=1Ø.
Triad=3,000=30%=P3.0D=3.0=Creativity=Stars=Muses=3 March = C=I>>GIL.
Triage=9,000=90%=P9.00D=9.0=Abstraction=Gods=Saturn=9Sept.>>A=Ø.
Trial=10,000=1,000=100%=10.0=Physicality=Tech.=10 Oct.=Uranus=P=1Ø.
Triangle=10,000=1,000=100%=10.0=Physicality=Tech.=10 Oct.=Uranus=P=1Ø.
Triangulate=2,500=3,000=30%=P3.0D=3.0=Creativity=Stars=Muses=3 March=C=I>>GIL
Triassic=6,000=60%=P6.0D=Man=Earth=Royalty=6 June=Gaia=Maia>>M=M2.
Triathlon=9,000=90%=P9.00D=9.0=Abstraction=Gods=Saturn=9Sept.>>A=Ø.
Tribe=10,000=1,000=100%=10.0=Physicality=Tech.=10 Oct.=Uranus=P=1Ø.
Tribulation=10,000=1,000=100%=10.0=Physicality=Tech.=10 Oct.=Uranus=P=1Ø.
Tribunal=10,000=1,000=100%=10.0=Physicality=Tech.=10 Oct.=Uranus=P=1Ø.
Tribune=10,000=1,000=100%=10.0=Physicality=Tech.=10 Oct.=Uranus=P=1Ø.
Tributary=10,000=1,000=100%=10.0=Physicality=Tech.=10 Oct.=Uranus=P=1Ø.
Tribute=10,000=1,000=100%=10.0=Physicality=Tech.=10 Oct.=Uranus=P=1Ø.
Trice=10,000=1,000=100%=10.0=Physicality=Tech.=10 Oct.=Uranus=P=1Ø.
Tricentennial=2,500=3,000=30%=P3.0D=3.0=Cre=Stars=Muses=3 March = C=I>>GIL.
Triceps=10,000=1,000=100%=10.0=Physicality=Tech.=10 Oct.=Uranus=P=1Ø.
Triceratops=10,000=1,000=100%=10.0=Physicality=Tech.=10 Oct.=Uranus=P=1Ø.
Trichinosis=10,000=1,000=100%=10.0=Physicality=Tech.=10 Oct.=Uranus=P=1Ø.
Trick=10,000=1,000=100%=10.0=Physicality=Tech.=10 Oct.=Uranus=P=1Ø.
Trickery=3,500=4,000=40%=P4.0D=Govt.=Creatocracy=4 April=Mercury=Hermes=G=A4.
Trickle=10,000=1,000=100%=10.0=Physicality=Tech.=10 Oct.=Uranus=P=1Ø.
Trickster=3,500=4,000=40%=P4.0D=Govt.=4 April=Hermes=G=A4.
Tricky=3,000=30%=P3.0D=3.0=Creativity=Stars=Muses=3 March = C=I>>GIL.
Tricolor=2,500=3,000=30%=P3.0D=3.0=Creativity=Stars=Muses=3 March = C=I>>GIL.
Tricorn=6,500=7,000=70%=P7.0D=7.0=Language=Assets=Mars=7 July=Pleiades.
Tricot=7,500=8,000=80%=P8.0D=Economy=Currency=8 Aug.=Zeus>>E=v.
Tricycle=4,000=40%=P4.0D=Govt.=Creatocracy=4 April=Mercury=Hermes=G=A4.
Trident=8,000=80%=P8.0D=Economy=Currency=8 Aug.=Zeus>>E=v.
Tried=6,000=60%=P6.0D=Man=Earth=Royalty=6 June=Gaia=Maia>>M=M2.
Triennial=6,000=60%=P6.0D=Man=Earth=Royalty=6 June=Gaia=Maia>>M=M2.
Trieste=10,000=1,000=100%=10.0=Physicality=Tech.=10 Oct.=Uranus=P=1Ø.
Trifle=10,000=1,000=100%=10.0=Physicality=Tech.=10 Oct.=Uranus=P=1Ø.
Trifling=3,500=4,000=40%=P4.0D=Govt.=Creatocracy=4 April=Mercury=Hermes=G=A4.
Trifocal=4,000=40%=P4.0D=Govt.=Creatocracy=4 April=Mercury=Hermes=G=A4.
Trig=6,000=60%=P6.0D=Man=Earth=Royalty=6 June=Gaia=Maia>>M=M2.
Trigger=10,000=1,000=100%=10.0=Physicality=Tech.=10 Oct.=Uranus=P=1Ø.
Triglyceride=10,000=1,000=100%=10.0=Physicality=Tech.=10 Oct.=Uranus=P=1Ø.

PETER K. MATTHEWS - AKUKALIA

Trigonometry=10,000=1,000=100%=10.0=Physicality=Tech.=10 Oct.=Uranus=P=1Ø.
Trill=10,000=1,000=100%=10.0=Physicality=Tech.=10 Oct.=Uranus=P=1Ø.
Trillion=10,000=1,000=100%=10.0=Physicality=Tech.=10 Oct.=Uranus=P=1Ø.
Trilobite=7,000=70%=P7.0D=7.0=Language=Assets=Mars=7 July=Pleiades.
Trilogy=4,500=5,000=50%=P5.00D=Law=Time=Venus=5 May = Aphrodite>>L=N.
Trim=10,000=1,000=100%=10.0=Physicality=Tech.=10 Oct.=Uranus=P=1Ø.
Trimester=10,000=1,000=100%=10.0=Physicality=Tech.=10 Oct.=Uranus=P=1Ø.
Trimeter=4,500=5,000=50%=P5.00D=Law=Time=Venus=5 May = Aphrodite>>L=N.
Trimming=6,500=7,000=70%=P7.0D=7.0=Language=Assets=Mars=7 July=Pleiades.
Trine=4,000=40%=P4.0D=Govt.=Creatocracy=4 April=Mercury=Hermes=G=A4.
Trinidad=6,000=60%=P6.0D=Man=Earth=Royalty=6 June=Gaia=Maia>>M=M2.
Trinidad and Tobago=10,000=1,000=100%=10.0=Phys.=Tech.=10 Oct.=Uranus=P=1Ø.
Trinity=10,000=1,000=100%=10.0=Physicality=Tech.=10 Oct.=Uranus=P=1Ø.
Trinket=4,500=5,000=50%=P5.00D=Law=Time=Venus=5 May = Aphrodite>>L=N.
Trio=7,000=70%=P7.0D=7.0=Language=Assets=Mars=7 July=Pleiades.
Trip=10,000=1,000=100%=10.0=Physicality=Tech.=10 Oct.=Uranus=P=1Ø.
Tripartite=10,000=1,000=100%=10.0=Physicality=Tech.=10 Oct.=Uranus=P=1Ø.
Tripe=9,000=90%=P9.00D=9.0=Abstraction=Gods=Saturn=9Sept.>>A=Ø.
Triple=10,000=1,000=100%=10.0=Physicality=Tech.=10 Oct.=Uranus=P=1Ø.
Triple play=5,000=50%=P5.00D=Law=Time=Venus=5 May = Aphrodite>>L=N.
Triplet=10,000=1,000=100%=10.0=Physicality=Tech.=10 Oct.=Uranus=P=1Ø.
Triplex=1,000=100%=10.0=1.0=Mind=Sun=1 January=Helios >> M=E4.
Triplicate=10,000=1,000=100%=10.0=Physicality=Tech.=10 Oct.=Uranus=P=1Ø.
Tripod=10,000=1,000=100%=10.0=Physicality=Tech.=10 Oct.=Uranus=P=1Ø.
Tripoli=10,000=1,000=100%=10.0=Physicality=Tech.=10 Oct.=Uranus=P=1Ø.
Triptych=4,500=5,000=50%=P5.00D=Law=Time=Venus=5 May = Aphrodite>>L=N.
Trisect=3,000=30%=P3.0D=3.0=Creativity=Stars=Muses=3 March = C=I>>GIL.
Trite=6,000=60%=P6.0D=Man=Earth=Royalty=6 June=Gaia=Maia>>M=M2.
Tritium=6,000=60%=P6.0D=Man=Earth=Royalty=6 June=Gaia=Maia>>M=M2.
Triumph=10,000=1,000=100%=10.0=Physicality=Tech.=10 Oct.=Uranus=P=1Ø.
Triumvir=10,000=1,000=100%=10.0=Physicality=Tech.=10 Oct.=Uranus=P=1Ø.
Trivet=10,000=1,000=100%=10.0=Physicality=Tech.=10 Oct.=Uranus=P=1Ø.
Trivia=2,500=3,000=30%=P3.0D=3.0=Creativity=Stars=Muses=3 March = C=I>>GIL.
Trivial=3,000=30%=P3.0D=3.0=Creativity=Stars=Muses=3 March = C=I>>GIL.
Trivialize=1,500=15%=P1.50D=1.5=Authority=Solar Crown=1 May = Maia.
-trix=5,500=5.5=80%=P5.50=Earth-Midway=5 May = Gaia.
Trochee=7,000=70%=P7.0D=7.0=Language=Assets=Mars=7 July=Pleiades.
Trod=3,000=30%=P3.0D=3.0=Creativity=Stars=Muses=3 March = C=I>>GIL.
Trodden=2,000=20%=P2.00D=2.0=Nature=Matter=Moon=2 Feb.=Cupid=N=C+_
Troglodyte=10,000=1,000=100%=10.0=Physicality=Tech.=10 Oct.=Uranus=P=1Ø.
Trolka=5,000=50%=P5.00D=Law=Time=Venus=5 May = Aphrodite>>L=N.
Trojan=5,000=50%=P5.00D=Law=Time=Venus=5 May = Aphrodite>>L=N.
Trojan War=8,000=80%=P8.0D=Economy=Currency=8 Aug.=Zeus>>E=v.
Troll1=10,000=1,000=100%=10.0=Physicality=Tech.=10 Oct.=Uranus=P=1Ø.
Troll2=8,000=80%=P8.0D=Economy=Currency=8 Aug.=Zeus>>E=v.

Trolley=10,000=1,000=100%=10.0=Physicality=Tech.=10 Oct.=Uranus=P=1Ø.
Trolley bus=5,500=5.5=80%=P5.50=Earth-Midway=5 May = Gaia.
Trolley car=1,000=100%=10.0=1.0=Mind=Sun=1 January=Helios >> M=E4.
Trollop=4,000=40%=P4.0D=Govt.=Creatocracy=4 April=Mercury=Hermes=G=A4.
Trollope Anthony.=2,000=20%=P2.00D=2.0=Nature=Matter=Moon=2 Feb.=Cupid=N=C+_
Trombone=7,500=8,000=80%=P8.0D=Economy=Currency=8 Aug.=Zeus>>E=v.
Tromp=3,000=30%=P3.0D=3.0=Creativity=Stars=Muses=3 March = C=I>>GIL.
Trompe l'oell=6,500=7,000=70%=P7.0D=7.0=Language=Assets=Mars=7 July=Pleiades.
-tron=4,500=5,000=50%=P5.00D=Law=Time=Venus=5 May = Aphrodite>>L=N.
Trondheim=8,000=80%=P8.0D=Economy=Currency=8 Aug.=Zeus>>E=v.
Troop=10,000=1,000=100%=10.0=Physicality=Tech.=10 Oct.=Uranus=P=1Ø.
Trooper=6,500=7,000=70%=P7.0D=7.0=Language=Assets=Mars=7 July=Pleiades.
Trope=6,000=60%=P6.0D=Man=Earth=Royalty=6 June=Gaia=Maia>>M=M2.
Trophy=5,500=5.5=80%=P5.50=Earth-Midway=5 May = Gaia.
-trophy=3,000=30%=P3.0D=3.0=Creativity=Stars=Muses=3 March = C=I>>GIL.
Tropic=10,000=1,000=100%=10.0=Physicality=Tech.=10 Oct.=Uranus=P=1Ø.
-tropic=8,500=9,000=90%=P9.00D=9.0=Abstraction=Gods=Saturn=9Sept.>>A=Ø.
Tropical=5,000=50%=P5.00D=Law=Time=Venus=5 May = Aphrodite>>L=N.
Tropical year=7,000=70%=P7.0D=7.0=Language=Assets=Mars=7 July=Pleiades.
Tropic of Cancer=4,500=5,000=50%=P5.00D=Law=Time=Venus=5 May =Odite>>L=N.
Tropic of Capricorn=4,500=5,000=50%=P5.00D=Law=Time=Venus=5 May =Odite>>L=N.
Tropism=10,000=1,000=100%=10.0=Physicality=Tech.=10 Oct.=Uranus=P=1Ø.
Troposphere=10,000=1,000=100%=10.0=Physicality=Tech.=10 Oct.=Uranus=P=1Ø.
-trophy=7,500=8,000=80%=P8.0D=Economy=Currency=8 Aug.=Zeus>>E=v.
Trot=10,000=1,000=100%=10.0=Physicality=Tech.=10 Oct.=Uranus=P=1Ø.
Troth=5,000=50%=P5.00D=Law=Time=Venus=5 May = Aphrodite>>L=N.
Trotsky Leon.=2,500=3,000=30%=P3.0D=3.0=Cr=Stars=Muses=3 March = C=I>>GIL.
Troubadour=10,000=1,000=100%=10.0=Physicality=Tech.=10 Oct.=Uranus=P=1Ø.
Trouble=10,000=1,000=100%=10.0=Physicality=Tech.=10 Oct.=Uranus=P=1Ø.
Troublemaker=3,500=4,000=40%=P4.0D=Govt.=Creatocracy=4 April=Hermes=G=A4.
Troubleshooter=4,000=40%=P4.0D=Govt.=Creatocracy=4 April=Mercury=Hermes=G=A4.
Trough=10,000=1,000=100%=10.0=Physicality=Tech.=10 Oct.=Uranus=P=1Ø.
Trounce=3,000=30%=P3.0D=3.0=Creativity=Stars=Muses=3 March = C=I>>GIL.
Troupe=10,000=1,000=100%=10.0=Physicality=Tech.=10 Oct.=Uranus=P=1Ø.
Trousers=10,000=1,000=100%=10.0=Physicality=Tech.=10 Oct.=Uranus=P=1Ø.
Trousseau=10,000=1,000=100%=10.0=Physicality=Tech.=10 Oct.=Uranus=P=1Ø.
Trout=10,000=1,000=100%=10.0=Physicality=Tech.=10 Oct.=Uranus=P=1Ø.
Trove=1,500=15%=P1.50D=1.5=Authority=Solar Crown=1 May = Maia.
Trowel=10,000=1,000=100%=10.0=Physicality=Tech.=10 Oct.=Uranus=P=1Ø.
troy=4,000=40%=P4.0D=Govt.=Creatocracy=4 April=Mercury=Hermes=G=A4.
Troy=5,000=50%=P5.00D=Law=Time=Venus=5 May = Aphrodite>>L=N.
Troy-weight=12,000=12%=P1.20D=1.2=Knowledge=Edu=12Dec.=Athena>>K=F.
Truant=6,500=7,000=70%=P7.0D=7.0=Language=Assets=Mars=7 July=Pleiades.
Truce=5,500=5.5=80%=P5.50=Earth-Midway=5 May = Gaia.
Truck1=10,000=1,000=100%=10.0=Physicality=Tech.=10 Oct.=Uranus=P=1Ø.

PETER K. MATTHEWS - AKUKALIA

Truck2=10,000=1,000=100%=10.0=Physicality=Tech.=10 Oct.=Uranus=P=1Ø.
Truckage=5,000=50%=P5.00D=Law=Time=Venus=5 May = Aphrodite>>L=N.
Truckle=9,000=90%=P9.00D=9.0=Abstraction=Gods=Saturn=9Sept.>>A=Ø.
Truculent=5,000=50%=P5.00D=Law=Time=Venus=5 May = Aphrodite>>L=N.
Trudeau Elliot=5,500=5.5=80%=P5.50=Earth-Midway=5 May = Gaia.
Trudge=5,000=50%=P5.00D=Law=Time=Venus=5 May = Aphrodite>>L=N.
True=10,000=1,000=100%=10.0=Physicality=Tech.=10 Oct.=Uranus=P=1Ø.
True blue=1,500=15%=P1.50D=1.5=Authority=Solar Crown=1 May = Maia.
True love=1,000=100%=10.0=1.0=Mind=Sun=1 January=Helios >> M=E4.
Truffle=5,000=50%=P5.00D=Law=Time=Venus=5 May = Aphrodite>>L=N.
Trujillo=4,500=5,000=50%=P5.00D=Law=Time=Venus=5 May = Aphrodite>>L=N.
Truk Islands=5,500=5.5=80%=P5.50=Earth-Midway=5 May = Gaia.
Truly=2,500=3,000=30%=P3.0D=3.0=Creativity=Stars=Muses=3 March = C=I>>GIL.
Truman,Harry S.=4,500=5,000=50%=P5.00D=Law=Time=Venus=5 May =Odite>>L=N.
Trump=10,000=1,000=100%=10.0=Physicality=Tech.=10 Oct.=Uranus=P=1Ø.
Trumpery=4,500=5,000=50%=P5.00D=Law=Time=Venus=5 May = Aphrodite>>L=N.
Trumpet=10,000=1,000=100%=10.0=Physicality=Tech.=10 Oct.=Uranus=P=1Ø.
Truncate=10,000=1,000=100%=10.0=Physicality=Tech.=10 Oct.=Uranus=P=1Ø.
Truncheon=5,000=50%=P5.00D=Law=Time=Venus=5 May = Aphrodite>>L=N.
Trundle=4,500=5,000=50%=P5.00D=Law=Time=Venus=5 May = Aphrodite>>L=N.
Trundle bed=7,000=70%=P7.0D=7.0=Language=Assets=Mars=7 July=Pleiades.
Trunk=10,000=1,000=100%=10.0=Physicality=Tech.=10 Oct.=Uranus=P=1Ø.
Trunk line=3,500=4,000=40%=P4.0D=Govt.=Creatocracy=4 April=Hermes=G=A4.
Truss=10,000=1,000=100%=10.0=Physicality=Tech.=10 Oct.=Uranus=P=1Ø.
Trustee=10,000=1,000=100%=10.0=Physicality=Tech.=10 Oct.=Uranus=P=1Ø.
Trustful=10,000=1,000=100%=10.0=Physicality=Tech.=10 Oct.=Uranus=P=1Ø.
Trustworthy=3,500=4,000=40%=P4.0D=Govt.=Creatocracy=4 April=Hermes=G=A4.
Trusty=10,000=1,000=100%=10.0=Physicality=Tech.=10 Oct.=Uranus=P=1Ø.
Truth=10,000=1,000=100%=10.0=Physicality=Tech.=10 Oct.=Uranus=P=1Ø.
Truth Sojourner=3,500=4,000=40%=P4.0D=Govt.=Creatocracy=4 April=Hermes=G=A4.
Truthful=4,000=40%=P4.0D=Govt.=Creatocracy=4 April=Mercury=Hermes=G=A4.
Try=10,000=1,000=100%=10.0=Physicality=Tech.=10 Oct.=Uranus=P=1Ø.
Trying=2,500=3,000=30%=P3.0D=3.0=Creativity=Stars=Muses=3 March = C=I>>GIL.
Tryout=6,000=60%=P6.0D=Man=Earth=Royalty=6 June=Gaia=Maia>>M=M2.
Tryst=10,000=1,000=100%=10.0=Physicality=Tech.=10 Oct.=Uranus=P=1Ø.
Tsar=2,000=20%=P2.00D=2.0=Nature=Matter=Moon=2 Feb.=Cupid=N=C+_
Tsetse fly=8,500=9,000=90%=P9.00D=9.0=Abstraction=Gods=Saturn=9Sept.>>A=Ø.
T.Sgt.=1,000=100%=10.0=1.0=Mind=Sun=1 January=Helios >> M=E4.
T-shirt=2,500=3,000=30%=P3.0D=3.0=Creativity=Stars=Muses=3 March = C=I>>GIL.
Tsinan=1,000=100%=10.0=1.0=Mind=Sun=1 January=Helios >> M=E4.
Tsingtao=1,000=100%=10.0=1.0=Mind=Sun=1 January=Helios >> M=E4.
Tsitsihar=1,000=100%=10.0=1.0=Mind=Sun=1 January=Helios >> M=E4.
T-Square=4,500=5,000=50%=P5.00D=Law=Time=Venus=5 May = Aphrodite>>L=N.
Tsunami=7,000=70%=P7.0D=7.0=Language=Assets=Mars=7 July=Pleiades.
Tswana=10,000=1,000=100%=10.0=Physicality=Tech.=10 Oct.=Uranus=P=1Ø.

Tu.=500=5%=P5.00D=5.0=Law=Time=Venus=5 May=Aphrodite>>L=N.
TuamotuArchipelago=6,000=60%=P6.0D=Man=Earth=Roy=6 June=Gaia=Maia>>M=M2.
Tub=8,000=80%=P8.0D=Economy=Currency=8 Aug.=Zeus>>E=v.
Tuba=5,500=5.5=80%=P5.50=Earth-Midway=5 May = Gaia.
Tubal ligation=6,500=7,000=70%=P7.0D=7.0=Language=Assets=Mars=7 July=Pleiades.
Tubby=1,500=15%=P1.50D=1.5=Authority=Solar Crown=1 May = Maia.
Tube=10,000=1,000=100%=10.0=Physicality=Tech.=10 Oct.=Uranus=P=1Ø.
Tuber=10,000=1,000=100%=10.0=Physicality=Tech.=10 Oct.=Uranus=P=1Ø.
Tubercle=10,000=1,000=100%=10.0=Physicality=Tech.=10 Oct.=Uranus=P=1Ø.
Tubercular=4,000=40%=P4.0D=Govt.=Creatocracy=4 April=Mercury=Hermes=G=A4.
Tuberculin=10,000=1,000=100%=10.0=Physicality=Tech.=10 Oct.=Uranus=P=1Ø.
Tuberculosis=10,000=1,000=100%=10.0=Physicality=Tech.=10 Oct.=Uranus=P=1Ø.
Tuberose=10,000=1,000=100%=10.0=Physicality=Tech.=10 Oct.=Uranus=P=1Ø.
Tubman Harriet.=2,500=3,000=30%=P3.0D=3.0=Cr=Stars=Muses=3 March = C=I>>GIL.
Tubular=4,000=40%=P4.0D=Govt.=Creatocracy=4 April=Mercury=Hermes=G=A4.
Tuck=10,000=1,000=100%=10.0=Physicality=Tech.=10 Oct.=Uranus=P=1Ø.
Tucker=3,000=30%=P3.0D=3.0=Creativity=Stars=Muses=3 March = C=I>>GIL.
Tucson=4,500=5,000=50%=P5.00D=Law=Time=Venus=5 May = Aphrodite>>L=N.
Tucumán=2,500=3,000=30%=P3.0D=3.0=Creativity=Stars=Muses=3 March = C=I>>GIL.
-tude=4,000=40%=P4.0D=Govt.=Creatocracy=4 April=Mercury=Hermes=G=A4.
Tues.=500=5%=P5.00D=5.0=Law=Time=Venus=5 May=Aphrodite>>L=N.
Tuesday=4,000=40%=P4.0D=Govt.=Creatocracy=4 April=Mercury=Hermes=G=A4.
Tuff=4,500=5,000=50%=P5.00D=Law=Time=Venus=5 May = Aphrodite>>L=N.
Tuft=10,000=1,000=100%=10.0=Physicality=Tech.=10 Oct.=Uranus=P=1Ø.
Tug=10,000=1,000=100%=10.0=Physicality=Tech.=10 Oct.=Uranus=P=1Ø.
Tugboat=5,500=5.5=80%=P5.50=Earth-Midway=5 May = Gaia.
Tug of war=10,000=1,000=100%=10.0=Physicality=Tech.=10 Oct.=Uranus=P=1Ø.

Tugrik=3,000=30%=P3.0D=3.0=Creativity=Stars=Muses=3 March = C=I>>GIL.
Mongolian dughurik. Currency metric weight >> 3/10=0.3 >> 30:1. See Naira. Dollar.

Tuition=6,500=7,000=70%=P7.0D=7.0=Language=Assets=Mars=7 July=Pleiades.
Tula=5,000=50%=P5.00D=Law=Time=Venus=5 May = Aphrodite>>L=N.
Tulip=8,000=80%=P8.0D=Economy=Currency=8 Aug.=Zeus>>E=v.
Tulip tree=4,500=5,000=50%=P5.00D=Law=Time=Venus=5 May = Aphrodite>>L=N.
Tulle=9,500=10,000=1,000=100%=10.0=Physicality=Tech.=10 Oct.=Uranus=P=1Ø.
Tulsa=7,000=70%=P7.0D=7.0=Language=Assets=Mars=7 July=Pleiades.
Tumble=10,000=1,000=100%=10.0=Physicality=Tech.=10 Oct.=Uranus=P=1Ø.
Tumble down=1,500=15%=P1.50D=1.5=Authority=Solar Crown=1 May = Maia.
Tumbler=10,000=1,000=100%=10.0=Physicality=Tech.=10 Oct.=Uranus=P=1Ø.
Tumbleweed=10,000=1,000=100%=10.0=Physicality=Tech.=10 Oct.=Uranus=P=1Ø.
Tumbrel=8,000=80%=P8.0D=Economy=Currency=8 Aug.=Zeus>>E=v.
Tumescence=4,500=5,000=50%=P5.00D=Law=Time=Venus=5 May = Aphrodite>>L=N.
Tumid=3,000=30%=P3.0D=3.0=Creativity=Stars=Muses=3 March = C=I>>GIL.

Tummy=3,500=4,000=40%=P4.0D=Govt.=Creatocracy=4 April=Mercury=Hermes=G=A4.
Tumor=10,000=1,000=100%=10.0=Physicality=Tech.=10 Oct.=Uranus=P=1Ø.
Tumult=10,000=1,000=100%=10.0=Physicality=Tech.=10 Oct.=Uranus=P=1Ø.
Tumulus=2,500=3,000=30%=P3.0D=3.0=Creativity=Stars=Muses=3 March = C=I>>GIL.
Tun=2,500=3,000=30%=P3.0D=3.0=Creativity=Stars=Muses=3 March = C=I>>GIL.
Tuna=10,000=1,000=100%=10.0=Physicality=Tech.=10 Oct.=Uranus=P=1Ø.
Tundra=10,000=1,000=100%=10.0=Physicality=Tech.=10 Oct.=Uranus=P=1Ø.
Tune=10,000=1,000=100%=10.0=Physicality=Tech.=10 Oct.=Uranus=P=1Ø.
Tuneful=10,000=1,000=100%=10.0=Physicality=Tech.=10 Oct.=Uranus=P=1Ø.
Tuner=10,000=1,000=100%=10.0=Physicality=Tech.=10 Oct.=Uranus=P=1Ø.
Tune-up=10,000=1,000=100%=10.0=Physicality=Tech.=10 Oct.=Uranus=P=1Ø.
Tungsten=10,000=1,000=100%=10.0=Physicality=Tech.=10 Oct.=Uranus=P=1Ø.
Tungus=1,000=100%=10.0=1.0=Mind=Sun=1 January=Helios >> M=E4.
Tungsic=10,000=1,000=100%=10.0=Physicality=Tech.=10 Oct.=Uranus=P=1Ø.
Tunic=10,000=1,000=100%=10.0=Physicality=Tech.=10 Oct.=Uranus=P=1Ø.
Tuning fork=10,000=1,000=100%=10.0=Physicality=Tech.=10 Oct.=Uranus=P=1Ø.
Tunis=10,000=1,000=100%=10.0=Physicality=Tech.=10 Oct.=Uranus=P=1Ø.
Tunisia=10,000=1,000=100%=10.0=Physicality=Tech.=10 Oct.=Uranus=P=1Ø.
Tunnel=10,000=1,000=100%=10.0=Physicality=Tech.=10 Oct.=Uranus=P=1Ø.
Tunnel vision=2,500=3,000=30%=P3.0D=3.0=Cr=Stars=Muses=3 March = C=I>>GIL.
Tunny=2,500=3,000=30%=P3.0D=3.0=Creativity=Stars=Muses=3 March = C=I>>GIL.
Tupelo=7,000=70%=P7.0D=7.0=Language=Assets=Mars=7 July=Pleiades.
Tupi=10,000=1,000=100%=10.0=Physicality=Tech.=10 Oct.=Uranus=P=1Ø.
Turban=10,000=1,000=100%=10.0=Physicality=Tech.=10 Oct.=Uranus=P=1Ø.
Turbid=10,000=1,000=100%=10.0=Physicality=Tech.=10 Oct.=Uranus=P=1Ø.
Turbine=10,000=1,000=100%=10.0=Physicality=Tech.=10 Oct.=Uranus=P=1Ø.
Turbojet=3,500=4,000=40%=P4.0D=Govt.=4 April=Mercury=Hermes=G=A4.
Turboprop=4,500=5,000=50%=P5.00D=Law=Time=Venus=5 May = Aphrodite>>L=N.
Turbot=3,000=30%=P3.0D=3.0=Creativity=Stars=Muses=3 March = C=I>>GIL.
Turbulent=5,500=5.5=80%=P5.50=Earth-Midway=5 May = Gaia.
Tureen=10,000=1,000=100%=10.0=Physicality=Tech.=10 Oct.=Uranus=P=1Ø.
Turf=10,000=1,000=100%=10.0=Physicality=Tech.=10 Oct.=Uranus=P=1Ø.
Turgenev=3,000=30%=P3.0D=3.0=Creativity=Stars=Muses=3 March = C=I>>GIL.
Turgid=10,000=1,000=100%=10.0=Physicality=Tech.=10 Oct.=Uranus=P=1Ø.
Turin=5,500=5.5=80%=P5.50=Earth-Midway=5 May = Gaia.
Turk=6,500=7,000=70%=P7.0D=7.0=Language=Assets=Mars=7 July=Pleiades.
turkey=10,000=1,000=100%=10.0=Physicality=Tech.=10 Oct.=Uranus=P=1Ø.
Turkey=10,000=1,000=100%=10.0=Physicality=Tech.=10 Oct.=Uranus=P=1Ø.
Turkey vulture=6,500=7,000=70%=P7.0D=7.0=Language=Assets=Mars=7 July=Pleiades.
Turkic=4,000=40%=P4.0D=Govt.=Creatocracy=4 April=Mercury=Hermes=G=A4.
Turkish=4,000=40%=P4.0D=Govt.=Creatocracy=4 April=Mercury=Hermes=G=A4.
Turkish bath=4,000=40%=P4.0D=Govt.=Creatocracy=4 April=Mercury=Hermes=G=A4.
Turkmenistan=7,500=8,000=80%=P8.0D=Economy=Currency=8 Aug.=Zeus>>E=v.
Turks and Calicos Islands=5,500=5.5=80%=P5.50=Earth-Midway=5 May = Gaia.
Turku=6,500=7,000=70%=P7.0D=7.0=Language=Assets=Mars=7 July=Pleiades.

Turmeric=10,000=1,000=100%=10.0=Physicality=Tech.=10 Oct.=Uranus=P=1Ø.
Turmoil=2,500=3,000=30%=P3.0D=3.0=Creativity=Stars=Muses=3 March = C=I>>GIL.
Turn=10,000=1,000=100%=10.0=Physicality=Tech.=10 Oct.=Uranus=P=1Ø.
Turnabout=4,000=40%=P4.0D=Govt.=Creatocracy=4 April=Mercury=Hermes=G=A4.
Turnaround=1,000=100%=10.0=1.0=Mind=Sun=1 January=Helios >> M=E4.
Turnbuckle=10,000=1,000=100%=10.0=Physicality=Tech.=10 Oct.=Uranus=P=1Ø.
Turncoat=2,500=3,000=30%=P3.0D=3.0=Creativity=Stars=Muses=3 March = C=I>>GIL.
Turner Joseph=3,000=30%=P3.0D=3.0=Creativity=Stars=Muses=3 March = C=I>>GIL.
Turner,Nat.=2,500=3,000=30%=P3.0D=3.0=Cre=Stars=Muses=3 March = C=I>>GIL.
Turning Point=1,500=15%=P1.50D=1.5=Authority=Solar Crown=1 May = Maia.
Turnip=10,000=1,000=100%=10.0=Physicality=Tech.=10 Oct.=Uranus=P=1Ø.
Turnkey=1,000=100%=10.0=1.0=Mind=Sun=1 January=Helios >> M=E4.
Turnoff=3,500=4,000=40%=P4.0D=Govt.=Creatocracy=4 April=Mercury=Hermes=G=A4.
Turn-on=10,000=1,000=100%=10.0=Physicality=Tech.=10 Oct.=Uranus=P=1Ø.
Turnout=10,000=1,000=100%=10.0=Physicality=Tech.=10 Oct.=Uranus=P=1Ø.
Turnover=10,000=1,000=100%=10.0=Physicality=Tech.=10 Oct.=Uranus=P=1Ø.
Turnpike=6,000=60%=P6.0D=Man=Earth=Royalty=6 June=Gaia=Maia>>M=M2.
Turnstile=10,000=1,000=100%=10.0=Physicality=Tech.=10 Oct.=Uranus=P=1Ø.
Turntable=10,000=1,000=100%=10.0=Physicality=Tech.=10 Oct.=Uranus=P=1Ø.
Turpentine=10,000=1,000=100%=10.0=Physicality=Tech.=10 Oct.=Uranus=P=1Ø.
Turpitude=10,000=1,000=100%=10.0=Physicality=Tech.=10 Oct.=Uranus=P=1Ø.
Turquoise=10,000=1,000=100%=10.0=Physicality=Tech.=10 Oct.=Uranus=P=1Ø.
Turret=10,000=1,000=100%=10.0=Physicality=Tech.=10 Oct.=Uranus=P=1Ø.
Turtle1=10,000=1,000=100%=10.0=Physicality=Tech.=10 Oct.=Uranus=P=1Ø.
Turtle2=2,500=3,000=30%=P3.0D=3.0=Creativity=Stars=Muses=3 March = C=I>>GIL.
Turtledove=5,500=5.5=80%=P5.50=Earth-Midway=5 May = Gaia.
Turtleneck=10,000=1,000=100%=10.0=Physicality=Tech.=10 Oct.=Uranus=P=1Ø.
Tuscany=10,000=1,000=100%=10.0=Physicality=Tech.=10 Oct.=Uranus=P=1Ø.
Tuscarora=10,000=1,000=100%=10.0=Physicality=Tech.=10 Oct.=Uranus=P=1Ø.
Tusk=10,000=1,000=100%=10.0=Physicality=Tech.=10 Oct.=Uranus=P=1Ø.
Tussle=4,000=40%=P4.0D=Govt.=Creatocracy=4 April=Mercury=Hermes=G=A4.
Tussock=4,000=40%=P4.0D=Govt.=Creatocracy=4 April=Mercury=Hermes=G=A4.
Tutankhamen=5,500=5.5=80%=P5.50=Earth-Midway=5 May = Gaia.
Tutelage=10,000=1,000=100%=10.0=Physicality=Tech.=10 Oct.=Uranus=P=1Ø.
Tutor=10,000=1,000=100%=10.0=Physicality=Tech.=10 Oct.=Uranus=P=1Ø.
Tutti-frutti=10,000=1,000=100%=10.0=Physicality=Tech.=10 Oct.=Uranus=P=1Ø.
Tutu=6,000=60%=P6.0D=Man=Earth=Royalty=6 June=Gaia=Maia>>M=M2.
Tutu Desmond.=6,000=60%=P6.0D=Man=Earth=Royalty=6 June=Gaia=Maia>>M=M2.
Tuvalu=6,500=7,000=70%=P7.0D=7.0=Language=Assets=Mars=7 July=Pleiades.
Tux=1,500=15%=P1.50D=1.5=Authority=Solar Crown=1 May = Maia.
Tuxedo=10,000=1,000=100%=10.0=Physicality=Tech.=10 Oct.=Uranus=P=1Ø.
TV=2,000=20%=P2.00D=2.0=Nature=Matter=Moon=2 Feb.=Cupid=N=C+_
TVA=1,500=15%=P1.50D=1.5=Authority=Solar Crown=1 May = Maia.
TV dinner=6,000=60%=P6.0D=Man=Earth=Royalty=6 June=Gaia=Maia>>M=M2.
Twaddle=3,000=30%=P3.0D=3.0=Creativity=Stars=Muses=3 March = C=I>>GIL.

Twain=1,500=15%=P1.50D=1.5=Authority=Solar Crown=1 May = Maia.
Twain Mark.=2,000=20%=P2.00D=2.0=Nature=Matter=Moon=2 Feb.=Cupid=N=C+_
Twang=10,000=1,000=100%=10.0=Physicality=Tech.=10 Oct.=Uranus=P=1Ø.
Tweak=3,500=4,000=40%=P4.0D=Govt.=Creatocracy=4 April=Mercury=Hermes=G=A4.
Tweed=7,000=70%=P7.0D=7.0=Language=Assets=Mars=7 July=Pleiades.
Tweet=5,500=5.5=80%=P5.50=Earth-Midway=5 May = Gaia.
Tweeter=6,500=7,000=70%=P7.0D=7.0=Language=Assets=Mars=7 July=Pleiades.
Tweezers=10,000=1,000=100%=10.0=Physicality=Tech.=10 Oct.=Uranus=P=1Ø.
Twelfth=6,500=7,000=70%=P7.0D=7.0=Language=Assets=Mars=7 July=Pleiades.

Twelfth Night=3,000=30%=P3.0D=3.0=Creativity=Stars=Muses=3 March = C=I>>GIL.
Jan. 5, the eve of Epiphany. Defining Epiphany A manifestation of divine or supernatural being. The manifestation of Christ to the Gentiles as represented by the Magi. The energy for January 5 is abstracted from the human energy database as thus. Day 5:Value: 4.1, Planetary Type: Mercury, Human Type: Politics, Birth Energy Level: 70.0%. This is a concrete proof that Jesus is Hermes of the Greek myth who is known as Mercury in Roman myth. Energy value of 4.1>>6.1>>1.0 indicates the Mind >> Sun >> Sun God >> Energy. On the twelfth night he manifests as a star in the sky over the Gentiles. Perhaps the Tristar discovered by Peter Matthews-Akukalia in his book >> Psychoeconomix. Computing the resultant with the energy value >> 3.0*4.1x=px=7.1+12.3=19.4x=px=106.73=11=1.1. He also could delegate his manifestation to Athena hence as a dove or any of her symbols. Satellite data tracking shows Diameter 106.73 >> N. of Frigoris. Low walled; irregular >> Mare Frigoris >> The Sea of Cold. Christ manifestation is characterized by cold weather or chills.

Twelve=9,500=10,000=1,000=100%=10.0=Physicality=Tech.=10 Oct.=Uranus=P=1Ø.
Twelve month=1,000=100%=10.0=1.0=Mind=Sun=1 January=Helios >> M=E4.
Twentieth=7,000=70%=P7.0D=7.0=Language=Assets=Mars=7 July=Pleiades.
Twenty=5,000=50%=P5.00D=Law=Time=Venus=5 May = Aphrodite>>L=N.
Twenty-twenty or 20/20=2,000=20%=P2.00D=2.0=Nature=Moon=2 Feb.=Cupid=N=C+_
Twerp=3,500=4,000=40%=P4.0D=Govt.=Creatocracy=4 April=Mercury=Hermes=G=A4.
Twi=2,000=20%=P2.00D=2.0=Nature=Matter=Moon=2 Feb.=Cupid=N=C+_
Twice=7,500=8,000=80%=P8.0D=Economy=Currency=8 Aug.=Zeus>>E=v.
Twiddle=10,000=1,000=100%=10.0=Physicality=Tech.=10 Oct.=Uranus=P=1Ø.
Twig=3,000=30%=P3.0D=3.0=Creativity=Stars=Muses=3 March = C=I>>GIL.
Twilight=10,000=1,000=100%=10.0=Physicality=Tech.=10 Oct.=Uranus=P=1Ø.
Twill=4,000=40%=P4.0D=Govt.=Creatocracy=4 April=Mercury=Hermes=G=A4.
Twin=10,000=1,000=100%=10.0=Physicality=Tech.=10 Oct.=Uranus=P=1Ø.
Twine=10,000=1,000=100%=10.0=Physicality=Tech.=10 Oct.=Uranus=P=1Ø.
Twinge=10,000=1,000=100%=10.0=Physicality=Tech.=10 Oct.=Uranus=P=1Ø.
Twinkle=10,000=1,000=100%=10.0=Physicality=Tech.=10 Oct.=Uranus=P=1Ø.
Twinkling=1,500=15%=P1.50D=1.5=Authority=Solar Crown=1 May = Maia.
Twirl=5,000=50%=P5.00D=Law=Time=Venus=5 May = Aphrodite>>L=N.
Twist=10,000=1,000=100%=10.0=Physicality=Tech.=10 Oct.=Uranus=P=1Ø.
Twit=8,500=9,000=90%=P9.00D=9.0=Abstraction=Gods=Saturn=9Sept.>>A=Ø.

Twitch=10,000=1,000=100%=10.0=Physicality=Tech.=10 Oct.=Uranus=P=1Ø.

Twitter=6,000=60%=P6.0D=Man=Earth=Royalty=6 June=Gaia=Maia>>M=M2.

Twixt=1,000=100%=10.0=1.0=Mind=Sun=1 January=Helios >> M=E4.

Two=8,500=9,000=90%=P9.00D=9.0=Abstraction=Gods=Saturn=9Sept.>>A=Ø.

Two-bit=3,000=30%=P3.0D=3.0=Creativity=Stars=Muses=3 March = C=I>>GIL.

Two bits=4,000=40%=P4.0D=Govt.=Creatocracy=4 April=Mercury=Hermes=G=A4.

Two-by-four=10,000=1,000=100%=10.0=Physicality=Tech.=10 Oct.=Uranus=P=1Ø.

Two dimensional=10,000=1,000=100%=10.0=Physicality=Tech.=10 Oct.=Uranus=P=1Ø.

Two faced=10,000=1,000=100%=10.0=Physicality=Tech.=10 Oct.=Uranus=P=1Ø.

Two ply=3,500=4,000=40%=P4.0D=Govt.=Creatocracy=4 April=Mercury=Hermes=G=A4.

Twosome=2,500=3,000=30%=P3.0D=3.0=Creativity=Stars=Muses=3 March = C=I>>GIL.

Two step=5,000=50%=P5.00D=Law=Time=Venus=5 May = Aphrodite>>L=N.

Defined as 2/4 time with long sliding steps. 2/4=1/2=0.5=1.0*5.0x=px=6+5=11x=px=41 =4.1=6.1=1.0.

Two step involves taking a step at a time. It influences the mind during the process and establishes a certain bonded energy >> GIL * CME = P = TOTAL OPERANT ENERGY.

Two-time=3,500=4,000=40%=P4.0D=Govt.=Creatocracy=4 April=Hermes=G=A4.

Two-way=3,500=4,000=40%=P4.0D=Govt.=Creatocracy=4 April=Hermes=G=A4.

TX=500=5%=P5.00D=5.0=Law=Time=Venus=5 May=Aphrodite>>L=N.

-ty=3,000=30%=P3.0D=3.0=Creativity=Stars=Muses=3 March = C=I>>GIL.

Tycoon=5,500=5.5=80%=P5.50=Earth-Midway=5 May = Gaia.

Tyke=5,500=5.5=80%=P5.50=Earth-Midway=5 May = Gaia.

Tyler John.=4,500=5,000=50%=P5.00D=Law=Time=Venus=5 May = Aphrodite>>L=N.

Tympani=2,000=20%=P2.00D=2.0=Nature=Matter=Moon=2 Feb.=Cupid=N=C+_

Tympanic membrane=1,000=100%=10.0=1.0=Mind=Sun=1 January=Helios >> M=E4.

Tympanum=3,500=4,000=40%=P4.0D=Govt.=4 April=Mercury=Hermes=G=A4.

Tyndale William=4,000=40%=P4.0D=Govt.=Creatocracy=4 April=Hermes=G=A4.

Tyne=8,000=80%=P8.0D=Economy=Currency=8 Aug.=Zeus>>E=v.

Type=10,000=1,000=100%=10.0=Physicality=Tech.=10 Oct.=Uranus=P=1Ø.

Typecast=6,000=60%=P6.0D=Man=Earth=Royalty=6 June=Gaia=Maia>>M=M2.

Typeface=7,000=70%=P7.0D=7.0=Language=Assets=Mars=7 July=Pleiades.

Typescript=3,000=30%=P3.0D=3.0=Creativity=Stars=Muses=3 March = C=I>>GIL.

Typeset=4,000=40%=P4.0D=Govt.=Creatocracy=4 April=Mercury=Hermes=G=A4.

Typewrite=4,000=40%=P4.0D=Govt.=Creatocracy=4 April=Mercury=Hermes=G=A4.

Typewriter=10,000=1,000=100%=10.0=Physicality=Tech.=10 Oct.=Uranus=P=1Ø.

Typhoid=2,500=3,000=30%=P3.0D=3.0=Creativity=Stars=Muses=3 March = C=I>>GIL.

Typhoid fever=12,000=12%=P1.20D=1.2=Knowledge=Edu=12Dec.=Athena>>K=F.

Typhoon=6,500=7,000=70%=P7.0D=7.0=Language=Assets=Mars=7 July=Pleiades.

Typhus=10,000=1,000=100%=10.0=Physicality=Tech.=10 Oct.=Uranus=P=1Ø.

Typical=10,000=1,000=100%=10.0=Physicality=Tech.=10 Oct.=Uranus=P=1Ø.

Typify=10,000=1,000=100%=10.0=Physicality=Tech.=10 Oct.=Uranus=P=1Ø.

Typist=3,000=30%=P3.0D=3.0=Creativity=Stars=Muses=3 March = C=I>>GIL.

Typo=2,000=20%=P2.00D=2.0=Nature=Matter=Moon=2 Feb.=Cupid=N=C+_
Typographical error=7,500=8,000=80%=P8.0D=Economy=Currency=8 Aug.=Zeus>>E=v.
Typography=6,500=7,000=70%=P7.0D=7.0=Language=Assets=Mars=7 July=Pleiades.
Tyrannical=4,000=40%=P4.0D=Govt.=Creatocracy=4 April=Mercury=Hermes=G=A4.
Tyrannize=4,000=40%=P4.0D=Govt.=Creatocracy=4 April=Mercury=Hermes=G=A4.
Tyrannosaur=8,000=80%=P8.0D=Economy=Currency=8 Aug.=Zeus>>E=v.
Tyrannous=1,000=100%=10.0=1.0=Mind=Sun=1 January=Helios >> M=E4.
Tyranny=10,000=1,000=100%=10.0=Physicality=Tech.=10 Oct.=Uranus=P=1Ø.
Tyrant=6,500=7,000=70%=P7.0D=7.0=Language=Assets=Mars=7 July=Pleiades.
tyre=2,500=3,000=30%=P3.0D=3.0=Creativity=Stars=Muses=3 March = C=I>>GIL.
Tyre=4,500=5,000=50%=P5.00D=Law=Time=Venus=5 May = Aphrodite>>L=N.
Tyro=4,500=5,000=50%=P5.00D=Law=Time=Venus=5 May = Aphrodite>>L=N.
Tyrol=6,000=60%=P6.0D=Man=Earth=Royalty=6 June=Gaia=Maia>>M=M2.
Tyrrhenian Sea=7,500=8,000=80%=P8.0D=Economy=Currency=8 Aug.=Zeus>>E=v.
Tsar.=2,000=20%=P2.00D=2.0=Nature=Matter=Moon=2 Feb.=Cupid=N=C+_

MAKABET =Uu=

---

u=3,000=30%=P3.0D=3.0=Creativity=Stars=Muses=3 March = C=I>>GIL.
The 21st letter of the English alphabet. The psycho weight is computed thus 3.0*2.1x=px
=5.1+6.3=11.4x=px=43.53=44=4.4sp1>>4.0*0.4x=px=4.4+1.6=6x=px=13.04. So U is an
alphabet that grants wisdom to manage relationships and organization.
13.04sp1 >> 1.3*0.4x=px=1.7+0.52=2.22x=px=3.104
3.104sp2 >> 3.1*0.4x=px=3.5+1.24=4.74x=px=9.08
9.08sp3 >> 9.0*0.8x=px=9.8+7.2=17x=px=87.56=90=9.0 >>Saturn>>ICT>>A=Ø>>Abstraction
>> ICT >> Cronus >>Council of Gods >> Planets >> Planetary Energy >> Makwares >>
Spirits >> The Sun. So the Universe is controlled by Spirits. However there seems a conflict
between Cronus the Muses and the Council of Gods. So the date settles everything on spirit
that controls the U Galaxy.
Day 3:Value:7.0, Planetary Type:Mars, Human Type:Consulting, Birth Energy Level:100.0%
WDSD value for 7.0 >> 7,000=70%=P7.0D=7.0=Language=Assets=Mars=7 July=Pleiades.
So the Universe is functioned by U >> The Pleiades >> the Mind of GOD guarded by the
Army of Ares. In the dimensions of the universe 7.0 is the smart dictionary or Makupedia.
Makupedia is the Universe Pleiades or Mind of God and Castle Makupedia is a God. U=abc.

U=2,500=3,000=30%=P3.0D=3.0=Creativity=Stars=Muses=3 March = C=I>>GIL.
u.=2,000=20%=P2.00D=2.0=Nature=Matter=Moon=2 Feb.=Cupid=N=C+_
U.=500=5%=P5.00D=5.0=Law=Time=Venus=5 May=Aphrodite>>L=N.
U.A.E.=1,500=15%=P1.50D=1.5=Authority=Solar Crown=1 May = Maia.
UAW=1,500=15%=P1.50D=1.5=Authority=Solar Crown=1 May = Maia.
Ubangi=10,500=11,000=11%=P1.10D=1.1=Idea=Brainchild=Inv.=11 Nov=Athena>>I=MT.

Ubiquitous=7,500=8,000=80%=P8.0D=Economy=Currency=8 Aug.=Zeus>>E=v.
U-boat=7,500=8,000=80%=P8.0D=Economy=Currency=8 Aug.=Zeus>>E=v.
U-bolt=6,000=60%=P6.0D=Man=Earth=Royalty=6 June=Gaia=Maia>>M=M2.
u.c.=1,000=100%=10.0=1.0=Mind=Sun=1 January=Helios >> M=E4.
Uccelo Paolo=2,000=20%=P2.00D=2.0=Nature=Matter=Moon=2 Feb.=Cupid=N=C+_
Under=6,000=60%=P6.0D=Man=Earth=Royalty=6 June=Gaia=Maia>>M=M2.
Ufa=6,000=60%=P6.0D=Man=Earth=Royalty=6 June=Gaia=Maia>>M=M2.
UFO=2,000=20%=P2.00D=2.0=Nature=Matter=Moon=2 Feb.=Cupid=N=C+_
Uganda=5,000=50%=P5.00D=Law=Time=Venus=5 May = Aphrodite>>L=N.
Ugly=18,000=18%=P1.80D=Solar Currency=Maks Currencies=1 Aug.=Maia.
Ugric=5,000=50%=P5.00D=Law=Time=Venus=5 May = Aphrodite>>L=N.
uhf=1,000=100%=10.0=1.0=Mind=Sun=1 January=Helios >> M=E4.
UJung Pandang=5,500=5.5=80%=P5.50=Earth-Midway=5 May = Gaia.

U.K.=1,000=100%=10.0=1.0=Mind=Sun=1 January=Helios >> M=E4.
Functional on the laws of ten hence the Maks Currencies is measured as P1=£10. See Naira.

Ukase=2,500=3,000=30%=P3.0D=3.0=Creativity=Stars=Muses=3 March = C=I>>GIL.
Ukraine=4,500=5,000=50%=P5.00D=Law=Time=Venus=5 May = Aphrodite>>L=N.
Ukrainian=4,500=5,000=50%=P5.00D=Law=Time=Venus=5 May = Aphrodite>>L=N.
Ukulele=10,000=1,000=100%=10.0=Physicality=Tech.=10 Oct.=Uranus=P=1Ø.
Ulan Bator=5,500=5.5=80%=P5.50=Earth-Midway=5 May = Gaia.
Ulan-Ude=7,500=8,000=80%=P8.0D=Economy=Currency=8 Aug.=Zeus>>E=v.
Ulcer=11,000=11%=P1.10D=1.1=Idea=Brainchild=Inv.=11 Nov.=SC=Athena>>I=MT.
Ulcerate=4,000=40%=P4.0D=Govt.=Creatocracy=4 April=Mercury=Hermes=G=A4.
-ule=4,000=40%=P4.0D=Govt.=Creatocracy=4 April=Mercury=Hermes=G=A4.
Ulna=6,000=60%=P6.0D=Man=Earth=Royalty=6 June=Gaia=Maia>>M=M2.
ulster=3,500=4,000=40%=P4.0D=Govt.=Creatocracy=4 April=Mercury=Hermes=G=A4.
Ulster=3,000=30%=P3.0D=3.0=Creativity=Stars=Muses=3 March = C=I>>GIL.
Ulterior=9,500=10,000=1,000=100%=Physicality=Tech.=10 Oct.=Uranus=P=1Ø.
Ultimate=10,000=1,000=100%=10.0=Physicality=Tech.=10 Oct.=Uranus=P=1Ø.
Ultimatum=10,000=1,000=100%=10.0=Physicality=Tech.=10 Oct.=Uranus=P=1Ø.
Ultimo=7,000=70%=P7.0D=7.0=Language=Assets=Mars=7 July=Pleiades.
Ultra=4,500=5,000=50%=P5.00D=Law=Time=Venus=5 May = Aphrodite>>L=N.
Ulra-=4,000=40%=P4.0D=Govt.=Creatocracy=4 April=Mercury=Hermes=G=A4.
Ultra conservative=1,500=15%=P1.50D=1.5=Authority=Solar Crown=1 May = Maia.
Ultra high frequency=5,000=50%=P5.00D=Law=Time=Venus=5 May = Aphrodite>>L=N.
Ultra liberal=1,500=15%=P1.50D=1.5=Authority=Solar Crown=1 May = Maia.
Ultramarine=10,000=1,000=100%=10.0=Physicality=Tech.=10 Oct.=Uranus=P=1Ø.
Ultramicroscope=6,000=60%=P6.0D=Man=Earth=Royalty=6 June=Gaia=Maia>>M=M2.
Ultramicroscopic=6,000=60%=P6.0D=Man=Earth=Royalty=6 June=Gaia=Maia>>M=M2.
Ultramodern=3,000=30%=P3.0D=3.0=Creativity=Stars=Muses=3 March = C=I>>GIL.
Ultra montane=10,000=1,000=100%=10.0=Physicality=Tech.=10 Oct.=Uranus=P=1Ø.
Ultrasonic=9,000=90%=P9.00D=9.0=Abstraction=Gods=Saturn=9Sept.>>A=Ø.

Ultrasonography=10,000=1,000=100%=10.0=Physicality=Tech.=10 Oct.=Uranus=P=1Ø.
Ultrasound=2,500=3,000=30%=P3.0D=3.0=Creativity=Stars=Muses=3 March = C=I>GIL.
Ultraviolet=10,000=1,000=100%=10.0=Physicality=Tech.=10 Oct.=Uranus=P=1Ø.
Ululate=4,000=40%=P4.0D=Govt.=Creatocracy=4 April=Mercury=Hermes=G=A4.
Ulyanovsk=6,500=7,000=70%=P7.0D=7.0=Language=Assets=Mars=7 July=Pleiades.
Ulysses=1,000=100%=10.0=1.0=Mind=Sun=1 January=Helios >> M=E4.
Umbel=10,500=11,000=11%=P1.10D=1.1=Idea=Brainchild=Inv.=11 Nov=Athena>>I=MT.
Umber=10,000=1,000=100%=10.0=Physicality=Tech.=10 Oct.=Uranus=P=1Ø.
Umbilical=4,000=40%=P4.0D=Govt.=Creatocracy=4 April=Mercury=Hermes=G=A4.
Umbilical cord=10,000=1,000=100%=10.0=Physicality=Tech.=10 Oct.=Uranus=P=1Ø.
Umbilicus=2,000=20%=P2.00D=2.0=Nature=Matter=Moon=2 Feb.=Cupid=N=C+_
Umbra=10,000=1,000=100%=10.0=Physicality=Tech.=10 Oct.=Uranus=P=1Ø.
Umbrage=6,500=7,000=70%=P7.0D=7.0=Language=Assets=Mars=7 July=Pleiades.
Umbrella=10,000=1,000=100%=10.0=Physicality=Tech.=10 Oct.=Uranus=P=1Ø.
Umbria=2,500=3,000=30%=P3.0D=3.0=Creativity=Stars=Muses=3 March = C=I>>GIL.
Umiak=7,000=70%=P7.0D=7.0=Language=Assets=Mars=7 July=Pleiades.
Umlaut=10,000=1,000=100%=10.0=Physicality=Tech.=10 Oct.=Uranus=P=1Ø.
Umpire=10,000=1,000=100%=10.0=Physicality=Tech.=10 Oct.=Uranus=P=1Ø.
Umpteen=8,000=80%=P8.0D=Economy=Currency=8 Aug.=Zeus>>E=v.
UMW=1,500=15%=P1.50D=1.5=Authority=Solar Crown=1 May = Maia.

UN=1,000=100%=10.0=1.0=Mind=Sun=1 January=Helios >> M=E4.
The UN is computed and discovered to be inspired by Helios through a reincarnation as
Benjamin Banneker in 1731 to implement Mind Laws whose formula was written by Peter
Matthews -Akukalia. Maks Currencies is the one world currency. See UK.Naira, Dollar.
See League of Nations.

---

un-1=1,500=15%=P1.50D=1.5=Authority=Solar Crown=1 May = Maia.
un-2=8,000=80%=P8.0D=Economy=Currency=8 Aug.=Zeus>>E=v.
Unable=4,000=40%=P4.0D=Govt.=Creatocracy=4 April=Mercury=Hermes=G=A4.
Unaccompanied=5,000=50%=P5.00D=Law=Time=Venus=5 May = Aphrodite>>L=N.
Unaccountable=3,500=4,000=40%=P4.0D=Govt.=Creatocracy=4 April=Hermes=G=A4.
Unaccustomed=6,000=60%=P6.0D=Man=Earth=Royalty=6 June=Gaia=Maia>>M=M2.
Unadulterated=2,000=20%=P2.00D=2.0=Nature=Matter=Moon=2 Feb.=Cupid=N=C+_
Unadvised=2,000=20%=P2.00D=2.0=Nature=Matter=Moon=2 Feb.=Cupid=N=C+_
Unaffected=3,000=30%=P3.0D=3.0=Creativity=Stars=Muses=3 March = C=I>>GIL.
Unalloyed=4,500=5,000=50%=P5.00D=Law=Time=Venus=5 May = Aphrodite>>L=N.
Unanimous=10,000=1,000=100%=10.0=Physicality=Tech.=10 Oct.=Uranus=P=1Ø.
Unarmed=1,500=15%=P1.50D=1.5=Authority=Solar Crown=1 May = Maia.
Unassailable=3,500=4,000=40%=P4.0D=Govt.=Creatocracy=4 April=Hermes=G=A4.
Unassisted=5,500=5.5=80%=P5.50=Earth-Midway=5 May = Gaia.
Unassuming=1,500=15%=P1.50D=1.5=Authority=Solar Crown=1 May = Maia.
Unattached=6,000=60%=P6.0D=Man=Earth=Royalty=6 June=Gaia=Maia>>M=M2.
Unavailing=3,500=4,000=40%=P4.0D=Govt.=Creatocracy=4 April=Hermes=G=A4.

Unavoidable=4,000=40%=P4.0D=Govt.=Creatocracy=4 April=Mercury=Hermes=G=A4.
Unaware=10,000=1,000=100%=10.0=Physicality=Tech.=10 Oct.=Uranus=P=1Ø.
Unawares=6,000=60%=P6.0D=Man=Earth=Royalty=6 June=Gaia=Maia>>M=M2.
Unbalanced=10,000=1,000=100%=10.0=Physicality=Tech.=10 Oct.=Uranus=P=1Ø.
Unbar=1,000=100%=10.0=1.0=Mind=Sun=1 January=Helios >> M=E4.
Unbearable=1,000=100%=10.0=1.0=Mind=Sun=1 January=Helios >> M=E4.
Unbeatable=2,500=3,000=30%=P3.0D=3.0=Creativity=Stars=Muses=3 March = C=I>GIL.
Unbeaten=3,500=4,000=40%=P4.0D=Govt.=Creatocracy=4 April=Hermes=G=A4.
Unbecoming=3,500=4,000=40%=P4.0D=Govt=4 April=Mercury=Hermes=G=A4.
Unbeknown=8,000=80%=P8.0D=Economy=Currency=8 Aug.=Zeus>>E=v.
Unbelief=4,500=5,000=50%=P5.00D=Law=Time=Venus=5 May = Aphrodite>>L=N.
Unbend=4,000=40%=P4.0D=Govt.=Creatocracy=4 April=Mercury=Hermes=G=A4.
Unbending=3,500=4,000=40%=P4.0D=Govt.=Creatocracy=4 April=Hermes=G=A4.
Unbidden=2,500=3,000=30%=P3.0D=3.0=Creativity=Stars=Muses=3 March=C=I>>GIL.
Unblinking=4,000=40%=P4.0D=Govt.=Creatocracy=4 April=Mercury=Hermes=G=A4.
Unblushing=2,000=20%=P2.00D=2.0=Nature=Matter=Moon=2 Feb.=Cupid=N=C+_
Unbolt=5,000=50%=P5.00D=Law=Time=Venus=5 May = Aphrodite>>L=N.
Unborn=1,500=15%=P1.50D=1.5=Authority=Solar Crown=1 May = Maia.
Unbosom=5,000=50%=P5.00D=Law=Time=Venus=5 May = Aphrodite>>L=N.
Unbounded=2,500=3,000=30%=P3.0D=3.0=Creativity=Stars=Muses=3 March=C=I>GIL.
Unbowed=2,000=20%=P2.00D=2.0=Nature=Matter=Moon=2 Feb.=Cupid=N=C+_
Unbridled=2,000=20%=P2.00D=2.0=Nature=Matter=Moon=2 Feb.=Cupid=N=C+_
Unbroken=5,000=50%=P5.00D=Law=Time=Venus=5 May = Aphrodite>>L=N.
Unburden=3,500=4,000=40%=P4.0D=Govt.=Creatocracy=4 April=Hermes=G=A4.
Unbutton=6,500=7,000=70%=P7.0D=7.0=Language=Assets=Mars=7 July=Pleiades.
Uncalled for=4,000=40%=P4.0D=Govt.=Creatocracy=4 April=Mercury=Hermes=G=A4.
Uncanny=5,500=5.5=80%=P5.50=Earth-Midway=5 May = Gaia.
Unceremonious=3,000=30%=P3.0D=3.0=Creativity=Stars=Muses=3 March = C=I>>GIL.
Uncertain=6,500=7,000=70%=P7.0D=7.0=Language=Assets=Mars=7 July=Pleiades.
Uncertainty=2,500=3,000=30%=P3.0D=3.0=Creativity=Stars=Muses=3 March=C=I>GIL.
Uncharitable=3,500=4,000=40%=P4.0D=Govt.=Creatocracy=4 April=Hermes=G=A4.
Uncharted=4,500=5,000=50%=P5.00D=Law=Time=Venus=5 May = Aphrodite>>L=N.
Unchaste=2,000=20%=P2.00D=2.0=Nature=Matter=Moon=2 Feb.=Cupid=N=C+_
Unchristian=5,500=5.5=80%=P5.50=Earth-Midway=5 May = Gaia.
Uncial=10,000=1,000=100%=10.0=Physicality=Tech.=10 Oct.=Uranus=P=1Ø.
Uncivil=1,000=100%=10.0=1.0=Mind=Sun=1 January=Helios >> M=E4.
Uncivilized=1,500=15%=P1.50D=1.5=Authority=Solar Crown=1 May = Maia.
Unclad=500=5%=P5.00D=5.0=Law=Time=Venus=5 May=Aphrodite>>L=N.
Unclasp=5,000=50%=P5.00D=Law=Time=Venus=5 May = Aphrodite>>L=N.
Uncle=8,500=9,000=90%=P9.00D=9.0=Abstraction=Gods=Saturn=9Sept.>>A=Ø.
Unclean=4,000=40%=P4.0D=Govt.=Creatocracy=4 April=Mercury=Hermes=G=A4.
Uncleanly=1,000=100%=10.0=1.0=Mind=Sun=1 January=Helios >> M=E4.
Uncle Sam=10,000=1,000=100%=10.0=Physicality=Tech.=10 Oct.=Uranus=P=1Ø.
Uncle Tom=10,000=1,000=100%=10.0=Physicality=Tech.=10 Oct.=Uranus=P=1Ø.
Uncloak=4,500=5,000=50%=P5.00D=Law=Time=Venus=5 May = Aphrodite>>L=N.

Unclose=1,000=100%=10.0=1.0=Mind=Sun=1 January=Helios >> M=E4.
Unclothe=3,500=4,000=40%=P4.0D=Govt.=Creatocracy=4 April=Hermes=G=A4.
Uncoil=1,000=100%=10.0=1.0=Mind=Sun=1 January=Helios >> M=E4.
Uncomfortable=3,500=4,000=40%=P4.0D=Govt.=Creatocracy=4 April=Hermes=G=A4.
Uncommitted=4,000=40%=P4.0D=Govt.=Creatocracy=4 April=Mercury=Hermes=G=A4.
Uncommon=2,500=3,000=30%=P3.0D=3.0=Creativity=Stars=Muses=3 March=C=I>GIL.
Uncommunicative=2,000=20%=P2.00D=2.0=Nature=Matter=Moon=2 Feb.=Cupid=N=C+_
Uncompromising=2,000=20%=P2.00D=2.0=Nature=Matter=Moon=2 Feb.=Cupid=N=C+_
Unconcern=3,500=4,000=40%=P4.0D=Govt.=Creatocracy=4 April=Hermes=G=A4.
Unconcerned=3,000=30%=P3.0D=3.0=Creativity=Stars=Muses=3 March = C=I>>GIL.
Unconditional=2,000=20%=P2.00D=2.0=Nature=Matter=Moon=2 Feb.=Cupid=N=C+_
Unconditioned=4,500=5,000=50%=P5.00D=Law=Time=Venus=5 May = Aphrodite>>L=N.
Unconscionable=5,500=5.5=80%=P5.50=Earth-Midway=5 May = Gaia.
Unconscious=10,000=1,000=100%=10.0=Physicality=Tech.=10 Oct.=Uranus=P=1Ø.
Unconstitutional=5,500=5.5=80%=P5.50=Earth-Midway=5 May = Gaia.
Unconventional=4,000=40%=P4.0D=Govt.=Creatocracy=4 April=Mercury=Hermes=G=A4.
Uncork=5,000=50%=P5.00D=Law=Time=Venus=5 May = Aphrodite>>L=N.
Uncouple=1,000=100%=10.0=1.0=Mind=Sun=1 January=Helios >> M=E4.
Uncouth=4,000=40%=P4.0D=Govt.=Creatocracy=4 April=Mercury=Hermes=G=A4.
Uncover=6,000=60%=P6.0D=Man=Earth=Royalty=6 June=Gaia=Maia>>M=M2.
Uncover=4,500=5,000=50%=P5.00D=Law=Time=Venus=5 May = Aphrodite>>L=N.
Unction=10,000=1,000=100%=10.0=Physicality=Tech.=10 Oct.=Uranus=P=1Ø.
Unctuous=10,000=1,000=100%=10.0=Physicality=Tech.=10 Oct.=Uranus=P=1Ø.
Uncut=10,000=1,000=100%=10.0=Physicality=Tech.=10 Oct.=Uranus=P=1Ø.
Undaunted=3,000=30%=P3.0D=3.0=Creativity=Stars=Muses=3 March = C=I>>GIL.
Undecided=5,000=50%=P5.00D=Law=Time=Venus=5 May = Aphrodite>>L=N.
Undemonstrative=3,500=4,000=40%=P4.0D=Govt.=Creatocracy=4 April=Hermes=G=A4.
Under=10,000=1,000=100%=10.0=Physicality=Tech.=10 Oct.=Uranus=P=1Ø.
Under-=6,500=7,000=70%=P7.0D=7.0=Language=Assets=Mars=7 July=Pleiades.
Underachieve=4,500=5,000=50%=P5.00D=Law=Time=Venus=5 May = Aphrodite>>L=N.
Underage1=8,500=9,000=90%=P9.00D=9.0=Abstraction=Gods=Saturn=9Sept.>>A=Ø.
Underage2=3,000=30%=P3.0D=3.0=Creativity=Stars=Muses=3 March = C=I>>GIL.
Underarm=8,000=80%=P8.0D=Economy=Currency=8 Aug.=Zeus>>E=v.
Underbelly=5,500=5.5=80%=P5.50=Earth-Midway=5 May = Gaia.
Underbid=3,500=4,000=40%=P4.0D=Govt.=Creatocracy=4 April=Hermes=G=A4.
Underbrush=7,000=70%=P7.0D=7.0=Language=Assets=Mars=7 July=Pleiades.
Undercarriage=6,000=60%=P6.0D=Man=Earth=Royalty=6 June=Gaia=Maia>>M=M2.
Undercharge=4,500=5,000=50%=P5.00D=Law=Time=Venus=5 May = Aphrodite>>L=N.
Underclass man=6,500=7,000=70%=P7.0D=7.0=Language=Assets=Mars=7 July=Pleiades.
Underclothes=5,500=5.5=80%=P5.50=Earth-Midway=5 May = Gaia.
Undercoat=10,000=1,000=100%=10.0=Physicality=Tech.=10 Oct.=Uranus=P=1Ø.
Undercover=2,500=3,000=30%=P3.0D=3.0=Creativity=Stars=Muses=3 March=C=I>GIL.
Undercurrent=10,000=1,000=100%=10.0=Physicality=Tech.=10 Oct.=Uranus=P=1Ø.
Undercut=10,000=1,000=100%=10.0=Physicality=Tech.=10 Oct.=Uranus=P=1Ø.
Underdeveloped=10,000=1,000=100%=10.0=Physicality=Tech.=10 Oct.=Uranus=P=1Ø.

Underdog=7,000=70%=P7.0D=7.0=Language=Assets=Mars=7 July=Pleiades.
Underdone=1,500=15%=P1.50D=1.5=Authority=Solar Crown=1 May = Maia.
Under dress=6,000=60%=P6.0D=Man=Earth=Royalty=6 June=Gaia=Maia>>M=M2.
Underestimate=8,000=80%=P8.0D=Economy=Currency=8 Aug.=Zeus>>E=v.
Underexpose=5,000=50%=P5.00D=Law=Time=Venus=5 May = Aphrodite>>L=N.
Underfoot=3,500=4,000=40%=P4.0D=Govt.=Creatocracy=4 April=Hermes=G=A4.
Undergarment=3,000=30%=P3.0D=3.0=Creativity=Stars=Muses=3 March = C=I>>GIL.
Undergo=3,000=30%=P3.0D=3.0=Creativity=Stars=Muses=3 March = C=I>>GIL.
Undergraduate=5,500=5.5=80%=P5.50=Earth-Midway=5 May = Gaia.
Underground=10,000=1,000=100%=10.0=Physicality=Tech.=10 Oct.=Uranus=P=1Ø.
Undergrowth=5,500=5.5=80%=P5.50=Earth-Midway=5 May = Gaia.
Underhand=10,000=1,000=100%=10.0=Physicality=Tech.=10 Oct.=Uranus=P=1Ø.
Underlie=6,500=7,000=70%=P7.0D=7.0=Language=Assets=Mars=7 July=Pleiades.
Underline=3,500=4,000=40%=P4.0D=Govt.=Creatocracy=4 April=Hermes=G=A4.
Underling=1,000=100%=10.0=1.0=Mind=Sun=1 January=Helios >> M=E4.
Underlying=5,500=5.5=80%=P5.50=Earth-Midway=5 May = Gaia.
Undermine=7,000=70%=P7.0D=7.0=Language=Assets=Mars=7 July=Pleiades.
Under most=4,000=40%=P4.0D=Govt.=Creatocracy=4 April=Mercury=Hermes=G=A4.
Underneath=10,000=1,000=100%=10.0=Physicality=Tech.=10 Oct.=Uranus=P=1Ø.
Underpants=3,000=30%=P3.0D=3.0=Creativity=Stars=Muses=3 March = C=I>>GIL.
Underpass=4,500=5,000=50%=P5.00D=Law=Time=Venus=5 May = Aphrodite>>L=N.
Underpinning=5,000=50%=P5.00D=Law=Time=Venus=5 May = Aphrodite>>L=N.
Underplay=6,000=60%=P6.0D=Man=Earth=Royalty=6 June=Gaia=Maia>>M=M2.
Underrate=2,500=3,000=30%=P3.0D=3.0=Creativity=Stars=Muses=3 March = C=I>>GIL.
Underscore=2,000=20%=P2.00D=2.0=Nature=Matter=Moon=2 Feb.=Cupid=N=C+_
Undersea=2,500=3,000=30%=P3.0D=3.0=Creativity=Stars=Muses=3 March = C=I>>GIL.
Undersecretary=4,000=40%=P4.0D=Govt.=Creatocracy=4 April=Hermes=G=A4.
Undersell=7,000=70%=P7.0D=7.0=Language=Assets=Mars=7 July=Pleiades.
Undershirt=3,500=4,000=40%=P4.0D=Govt.=Creatocracy=4 April=Hermes=G=A4.
Undershoot=6,500=7,000=70%=P7.0D=7.0=Language=Assets=Mars=7 July=Pleiades.
Undershorts=1,000=100%=10.0=1.0=Mind=Sun=1 January=Helios >> M=E4.
Undershot=10,000=1,000=100%=10.0=Physicality=Tech.=10 Oct.=Uranus=P=1Ø.
Underside=3,500=4,000=40%=P4.0D=Govt.=Creatocracy=4 April=Hermes=G=A4.
Undersigned=6,000=60%=P6.0D=Man=Earth=Royalty=6 June=Gaia=Maia>>M=M2.
Undersized=3,000=30%=P3.0D=3.0=Creativity=Stars=Muses=3 March = C=I>>GIL.
Underskirt=2,500=3,000=30%=P3.0D=3.0=Creativity=Stars=Muses=3 March = C=I>>GIL.
Under slung=6,500=7,000=70%=P7.0D=7.0=Language=Assets=Mars=7 July=Pleiades.
Understand=10,000=1,000=100%=10.0=Physicality=Tech.=10 Oct.=Uranus=P=1Ø.
Understanding=10,000=1,000=100%=10.0=Physicality=Tech.=10 Oct.=Uranus=P=1Ø.
Understate=10,000=1,000=100%=10.0=Physicality=Tech.=10 Oct.=Uranus=P=1Ø.
Understood=3,000=30%=P3.0D=3.0=Creativity=Stars=Muses=3 March = C=I>>GIL.
Understudy=10,000=1,000=100%=10.0=Physicality=Tech.=10 Oct.=Uranus=P=1Ø.
Undertake=5,000=50%=P5.00D=Law=Time=Venus=5 May = Aphrodite>>L=N.
Undertaker=1,500=15%=P1.50D=1.5=Authority=Solar Crown=1 May = Maia.
Undertaking=6,000=60%=P6.0D=Man=Earth=Royalty=6 June=Gaia=Maia>>M=M2.

PETER K. MATTHEWS - AKUKALIA

Under-the-counter=2,000=20%=P2.00D=2.0=Nature=Moon=2 Feb.=Cupid=N=C+_
Undertone=10,000=1,000=100%=10.0=Physicality=Tech.=10 Oct.=Uranus=P=1Ø.
Undertow=6,000=60%=P6.0D=Man=Earth=Royalty=6 June=Gaia=Maia>>M=M2.
Underwater=4,500=5,000=50%=P5.00D=Law=Time=Venus=5 May = Aphrodite>>L=N.
Underwear=1,500=15%=P1.50D=1.5=Authority=Solar Crown=1 May = Maia.
Underweight=4,000=40%=P4.0D=Govt.=Creatocracy=4 April=Mercury=Hermes=G=A4.

Underworld=10,500=11,000=11%=P1.10D=1.1=Idea=Brainchild=11 Nov.=Athena>>I=MT.
Greek & Roman Myth. The world of the dead: Hades. Bible mentions Hades.

Underwrite=10,000=1,000=100%=10.0=Physicality=Tech.=10 Oct.=Uranus=P=1Ø.
Undesirable=3,000=30%=P3.0D=3.0=Creativity=Stars=Muses=3 March = C=I>>GIL.
Undies=1,500=15%=P1.50D=1.5=Authority=Solar Crown=1 May = Maia.
Undisposed=3,500=4,000=40%=P4.0D=Govt.=Creatocracy=4 April=Hermes=G=A4.
Undo=10,000=1,000=100%=10.0=Physicality=Tech.=10 Oct.=Uranus=P=1Ø.
Undoing=10,000=1,000=100%=10.0=Physicality=Tech.=10 Oct.=Uranus=P=1Ø.
Undress=4,500=5,000=50%=P5.00D=Law=Time=Venus=5 May = Aphrodite>>L=N.
Undue=7,000=70%=P7.0D=7.0=Language=Assets=Mars=7 July=Pleiades.
Undulant=500=5%=P5.00D=5.0=Law=Time=Venus=5 May=Aphrodite>>L=N.
Undulate=10,000=1,000=100%=10.0=Physicality=Tech.=10 Oct.=Uranus=P=1Ø.
Undulation=6,000=60%=P6.0D=Man=Earth=Royalty=6 June=Gaia=Maia>>M=M2.
Unduly=2,000=20%=P2.00D=2.0=Nature=Matter=Moon=2 Feb.=Cupid=N=C+_
Undying=500=5%=P5.00D=5.0=Law=Time=Venus=5 May=Aphrodite>>L=N.
Unearned=3,500=4,000=40%=P4.0D=Govt.=Creatocracy=4 April=Hermes=G=A4.
Unearthly=5,000=50%=P5.00D=Law=Time=Venus=5 May = Aphrodite>>L=N.
Uneasy=10,000=1,000=100%=10.0=Physicality=Tech.=10 Oct.=Uranus=P=1Ø.

Unemployed=3,500=4,000=40%=P4.0D=Govt.=Creatocracy=4 April=Hermes=G=A4.
Only the Creatocracy and its systems can eliminate unemployment. See Entrepreneur.

Unequal=10,000=1,000=100%=10.0=Physicality=Tech.=10 Oct.=Uranus=P=1Ø.
Unequaled=2,500=3,000=30%=P3.0D=3.0=Creativity=Stars=Muses=3 March = C=I>>GIL.
Unequivocal=3,500=4,000=40%=P4.0D=Govt.=Creatocracy=4 April=Hermes=G=A4.
UNESCO=3,500=4,000=40%=P4.0D=Govt.=Creatocracy=4 April=Hermes=G=A4.
Uneven=10,000=1,000=100%=10.0=Physicality=Tech.=10 Oct.=Uranus=P=1Ø.
Uneventful=3,500=4,000=40%=P4.0D=Govt.=Creatocracy=4 April=Hermes=G=A4.
Unexampled=1,500=15%=P1.50D=1.5=Authority=Solar Crown=1 May = Maia.
Unexceptionable=10,000=1,000=100%=10.0=Physicality=Tech.=10 Oct.=Uranus=P=1Ø.
Unexceptional=8,000=80%=P8.0D=Economy=Currency=8 Aug.=Zeus>>E=v.
Unexpected=2,500=3,000=30%=P3.0D=3.0=Creativity=Stars=Muses=3March=C=I>GIL.
Unfailing=4,500=5,000=50%=P5.00D=Law=Time=Venus=5 May = Aphrodite>>L=N.
Unfair=6,500=7,000=70%=P7.0D=7.0=Language=Assets=Mars=7 July=Pleiades.
Unfaithful=5,500=5.5=80%=P5.50=Earth-Midway=5 May = Gaia.

Unfamiliar=3,500=4,000=40%=P4.0D=Govt.=Creatocracy=4 April=Hermes=G=A4.
Unfeeling=3,500=4,000=40%=P4.0D=Govt.=Creatocracy=4 April=Hermes=G=A4.
Unfeigned=1,500=15%=P1.50D=1.5=Authority=Solar Crown=1 May = Maia.
Unfetter=3,000=30%=P3.0D=3.0=Creativity=Stars=Muses=3 March = C=I>>GIL.
Unfit=5,500=5.5=80%=P5.50=Earth-Midway=5 May = Gaia.
Unflagging=3,500=4,000=40%=P4.0D=Govt.=Creatocracy=4 April=Hermes=G=A4.
Unflappable=2,000=20%=P2.00D=2.0=Nature=Matter=Moon=2 Feb.=Cupid=N=C+_
Unfledged=7,500=8,000=80%=P8.0D=Economy=Currency=8 Aug.=Zeus>>E=v.
Unflinching=1,000=100%=10.0=1.0=Mind=Sun=1 January=Helios >> M=E4.
Unfold=7,000=70%=P7.0D=7.0=Language=Assets=Mars=7 July=Pleiades.
Unforgettable=3,000=30%=P3.0D=3.0=Creativity=Stars=Muses=3 March = C=I>>GIL.
Unformed=6,000=60%=P6.0D=Man=Earth=Royalty=6 June=Gaia=Maia>>M=M2.
Unfortunate=10,000=1,000=100%=10.0=Physicality=Tech.=10 Oct.=Uranus=P=1Ø.
Unfounded=6,000=60%=P6.0D=Man=Earth=Royalty=6 June=Gaia=Maia>>M=M2.
Unfrequented=2,500=3,000=30%=P3.0D=3.0=Creativity=Stars=Muses=3March=CI>GIL.
Unfriendly=2,500=3,000=30%=P3.0D=3.0=Creativity=Stars=Muses=3 March = C=I>>GIL.
Unfrock=4,500=5,000=50%=P5.00D=Law=Time=Venus=5 May = Aphrodite>>L=N.
Unfurl=3,000=30%=P3.0D=3.0=Creativity=Stars=Muses=3 March = C=I>>GIL.
Ungainly=4,000=40%=P4.0D=Govt.=Creatocracy=4 April=Mercury=Hermes=G=A4.
Ungava Bay=10,000=1,000=100%=10.0=Physicality=Tech.=10 Oct.=Uranus=P=1Ø.

Ungodly=5,000=50%=P5.00D=Law=Time=Venus=5 May = Aphrodite>>L=N.
In the Creatocracy or universe Law 5.0 functions under Nature 2.0 binding but having the foundations of economy >> Currency 8.0 and Ideas >> (Brainchild) 1.1. This means that ungodliness is any act that goes against the natural law of sustainability of ideas. That is in the God sense any law that goes against Aphrodite (love) Zeus (the Name and a Word of the Almighty) and Athena (the Spirit of GOD)is said to be ungodly. Computing all factors points us precisely what it is to be ungodly.
5.0*2.0x=px=7+10=17x=px=87=90=9.0>>Spirituality >> The Gods.
8.0*1.1x=px=9.1+8.8=17.9x=px=97.98=100=10.0 >> Physical activity.
9.0*10.0x=px=19+90=109x=px=1,819=18-20. >> Business and Natural Law.
So to be ungodly means to engage oneself in any physical activity and or business that negates the spirits and the abstraction of the Gods Love and all natural laws and rights.

Ungovernable=3,000=30%=P3.0D=3.0=Creativity=Stars=Muses=3 March = C=I>>GIL.
Ungracious=2,000=20%=P2.00D=2.0=Nature=Matter=Moon=2 Feb.=Cupid=N=C+_
Unguarded=2,500=3,000=30%=P3.0D=3.0=Creativity=Stars=Muses=3 March=C=I>GIL.
Unguent=2,500=3,000=30%=P3.0D=3.0=Creativity=Stars=Muses=3 March = C=I>>GIL.
Ungulate=2,000=20%=P2.00D=2.0=Nature=Matter=Moon=2 Feb.=Cupid=N=C+_
Unhallowed=3,000=30%=P3.0D=3.0=Creativity=Stars=Muses=3 March = C=I>>GIL.
Unhand=3,500=4,000=40%=P4.0D=Govt.=Creatocracy=4 April=Mercury=Hermes=G=A4.
Unhappy=6,000=60%=P6.0D=Man=Earth=Royalty=6 June=Gaia=Maia>>M=M2.
Unhealthy=10,000=1,000=100%=10.0=Physicality=Tech.=10 Oct.=Uranus=P=1Ø.
Unheard=2,500=3,000=30%=P3.0D=3.0=Creativity=Stars=Muses=3 March = C=I>>GIL.

Unheard of=2,500=3,000=30%=P3.0D=3.0=Creativity=Stars=Muses=3 March = C=I>GIL.
Unhinge=3,000=30%=P3.0D=3.0=Creativity=Stars=Muses=3 March = C=I>>GIL.
Unholy=4,000=40%=P4.0D=Govt.=Creatocracy=4 April=Mercury=Hermes=G=A4.
Unhook=4,500=5,000=50%=P5.00D=Law=Time=Venus=5 May = Aphrodite>>L=N.
Unhorse=4,500=5,000=50%=P5.00D=Law=Time=Venus=5 May = Aphrodite>>L=N.
Uni-=2,000=20%=P2.00D=2.0=Nature=Matter=Moon=2 Feb.=Cupid=N=C+_
Unicameral=3,000=30%=P3.0D=3.0=Creativity=Stars=Muses=3 March = C=I>>GIL.
UNICEF=3,500=4,000=40%=P4.0D=Govt.=Creatocracy=4 April=Mercury=Hermes=G=A4.
Unicellular=3,000=30%=P3.0D=3.0=Creativity=Stars=Muses=3 March = C=I>>GIL.
Unicorn=10,000=1,000=100%=10.0=Physicality=Tech.=10 Oct.=Uranus=P=1Ø.
Unicycle=4,000=40%=P4.0D=Govt.=Creatocracy=4 April=Mercury=Hermes=G=A4.
Unidentified flying object=8,000=80%=P8.0D=Economy=Currency=8 Aug.=Zeus>>E=v.
Uniform=10,000=1,000=100%=10.0=Physicality=Tech.=10 Oct.=Uranus=P=1Ø.
Unify=4,000=40%=P4.0D=Govt.=Creatocracy=4 April=Mercury=Hermes=G=A4.
Unilateral=4,000=40%=P4.0D=Govt.=Creatocracy=4 April=Mercury=Hermes=G=A4.
Unimpeachable=2,500=3,000=30%=P3.0D=3.0=Creativity=Stars=Muses=3March=C=I
Uninterested=7,000=70%=P7.0D=7.0=Language=Assets=Mars=7 July=Pleiades.
Union=10,000=1,000=100%=10.0=Physicality=Tech.=10 Oct.=Uranus=P=1Ø.
Unionism=10,000=1,000=100%=10.0=Physicality=Tech.=10 Oct.=Uranus=P=1Ø.
Unionize=4,500=5,000=50%=P5.00D=Law=Time=Venus=5 May = Aphrodite>>L=N.
Union Jack=5,500=5.5=80%=P5.50=Earth-Midway=5 May = Gaia.

Union of Soviet Socialist Republics.>> USSR.
=10,000=1,000=100%=10.0=Physicality=Tech.=10 Oct.=Uranus=P=1Ø.
Peter Matthews-Akukalia, Castle Makupedia authored and owns The Creatocracy Republic.

Union Shop=8,000=80%=P8.0D=Economy=Currency=8 Aug.=Zeus>>E=v.
Unique=7,500=8,000=80%=P8.0D=Economy=Currency=8 Aug.=Zeus>>E=v.
Unisex=3,500=4,000=40%=P4.0D=Govt.=Creatocracy=4 April=Mercury=Hermes=G=A4.
Unisexual=7,000=70%=P7.0D=7.0=Language=Assets=Mars=7 July=Pleiades.
Unison=10,000=1,000=100%=10.0=Physicality=Tech.=10 Oct.=Uranus=P=1Ø.
Unit=10,000=1,000=100%=10.0=Physicality=Tech.=10 Oct.=Uranus=P=1Ø.
Unit.=1,000=100%=10.0=1.0=Mind=Sun=1 January=Helios >> M=E4.
Unitarian=10,000=1,000=100%=10.0=Physicality=Tech.=10 Oct.=Uranus=P=1Ø.
Unitary=3,500=4,000=40%=P4.0D=Govt.=Creatocracy=4 April=Mercury=Hermes=G=A4.
Unite=10,000=1,000=100%=10.0=Physicality=Tech.=10 Oct.=Uranus=P=1Ø.
United Arab Emirates=10,000=1,000=100%=10.0=Phy=Tech.=10 Oct.=Uranus=P=1Ø.
United Kingdom=6,000=60%=P6.0D=Man=Earth=Royalty=6 June=Gaia=Maia>>M=M2.
United Nations.=6,000=60%=P6.0D=Man=Earth=Royalty=6 June=Gaia=Maia>>M=M2.

United States of America.=10,000=1,000=100%=10.0=Phy=Tech.=10 Oct.=Uranus=P=1Ø.
The United States of America is driven by technology subject to the natural law of
quantum 10. See UK. Dollar.

Unit pricing=5,000=50%=P5.00D=Law=Time=Venus=5 May = Aphrodite>>L=N.
The unit pricing of a thing or commodity is bound to natural law metrics of the Maks Currencies on the C+-=50% metric. See Naira. Dollar and other currencies metric weight.

Unity=10,000=1,000=100%=10.0=Physicality=Tech.=10 Oct.=Uranus=P=1Ø.
Univ.=2,000=20%=P2.00D=2.0=Nature=Matter=Moon=2 Feb.=Cupid=N=C+_
Univalent=2,000=20%=P2.00D=2.0=Nature=Matter=Moon=2 Feb.=Cupid=N=C+_
Univalve=5,000=50%=P5.00D=Law=Time=Venus=5 May = Aphrodite>>L=N.
Universal=10,000=1,000=100%=10.0=Physicality=Tech.=10 Oct.=Uranus=P=1Ø.
Universal donor=8,000=80%=P8.0D=Economy=Currency=8 Aug.=Zeus>>E=v.
Universalism=4,000=40%=P4.0D=Govt.=Creatocracy=4 April=Mercury=Hermes=G=A4.
Universal joint=10,000=1,000=100%=10.0=Physicality=Tech.=10 Oct.=Uranus=P=1Ø.
Universal Product Code=10,000=1,000=100%=10.0=Phy=Tech.=10 Oct.=Uranus=P=1Ø.
Universal time=10,000=1,000=100%=10.0=Physicality=Tech.=10 Oct.=Uranus=P=1Ø.

Universe=7,000=70%=P7.0D=7.0=Language=Assets=Mars=7 July=Pleiades.
Castle Makupedia is the first Makumatics dictionary and Maks Currencies world encyclopedia. This work obeys the 7th law of the universe that language is the medium by which truth is proven and established. The universe functions on twelve laws that materialize into generations (Deuteronomy 30) and dimensions that range from Mind to Knowledge. For instance the Mind law states that the energy that runs a thing constitutes the mind of that thing. The law of everything chapter 21 of the Psychoastronomy is the law of nature. Creativity is the measure of interest in a person or thing measured as the Gil and deduced from the human birth energy. The universe is a product of measurements. Peter Matthews-Akukalia, Castle Makupedia established the Creatocracy by coding the universe as the combined functionality of energy matter and behavior or mind nature and creativity by the law of pure equivalence as the Sun, Moon and Stars in the formula U=ABC>>U=abc>>123. The Creatocracy simply means the Universe, Creatocratic means Universal by synchronized and crystallized dimensions. So the Creatocracy of things is the universe of things and the Creatocracy republic means the universe or universal republic. This is the establishment of the will of GOD as one world government in Ephesians 1:10-15.

University=10,000=1,000=100%=10.0=Physicality=Tech.=10 Oct.=Uranus=P=1Ø.
Peter Matthews-Akukalia, Castle Makupedia invented the Faculty of Creative & Psycho-Social Sciences with over 2million concepts in a body of knowledge known as the Creatocratic Charter. Thus he owns the Creative Sciences as a field of study and the professionalism of the Creative Scientist. This is the rights of the Creatocracy to establish the Mind Universities, the Creatocracy Universities Union and the Makupedia Institutes. An inclusive business of ideas is to induct the faculty into every university and tertiary institution worldwide on licensing and franchising to promote the knowledge economy.

Unkempt=8,000=80%=P8.0D=Economy=Currency=8 Aug.=Zeus>>E=v.
Unleaded=2,500=3,000=30%=P3.0D=3.0=Creativity=Stars=Muses=3 March = C=I>>GIL.

Unlearn=4,500=5,000=50%=P5.00D=Law=Time=Venus=5 May = Aphrodite>>L=N.
Unlearned=3,500=4,000=40%=P4.0D=Govt.=Creatocracy=4 April=Hermes=G=A4.
Unleash=5,500=5.5=80%=P5.50=Earth-Midway=5 May = Gaia.
Unless=3,500=4,000=40%=P4.0D=Govt.=Creatocracy=4 April=Mercury=Hermes=G=A4.
Unlettered=4,000=40%=P4.0D=Govt.=Creatocracy=4 April=Mercury=Hermes=G=A4.
Unlike=7,000=70%=P7.0D=7.0=Language=Assets=Mars=7 July=Pleiades.
Unlikely=2,500=3,000=30%=P3.0D=3.0=Creativity=Stars=Muses=3 March = C=I>>GIL.
Unlimber=2,500=3,000=30%=P3.0D=3.0=Creativity=Stars=Muses=3 March = C=I>>GIL.
Unload=10,000=1,000=100%=10.0=Physicality=Tech.=10 Oct.=Uranus=P=1Ø.
Unlock=5,000=50%=P5.00D=Law=Time=Venus=5 May = Aphrodite>>L=N.
Unlooked-for=3,000=30%=P3.0D=3.0=Creativity=Stars=Muses=3 March = C=I>>GIL.
Unloose=4,000=40%=P4.0D=Govt.=Creatocracy=4 April=Mercury=Hermes=G=A4.
Unlucky=7,500=8,000=80%=P8.0D=Economy=Currency=8 Aug.=Zeus>>E=v.
Unmake=6,000=60%=P6.0D=Man=Earth=Royalty=6 June=Gaia=Maia>>M=M2.
Unmannered=3,500=4,000=40%=P4.0D=Govt.=Creatocracy=4 April=Hermes=G=A4.
Unmask=5,000=50%=P5.00D=Law=Time=Venus=5 May = Aphrodite>>L=N.
Unmentionable=2,500=3,000=30%=P3.0D=3.0=Creativity=Stars=Muses=3March=C=I
Unmerciful=3,500=4,000=40%=P4.0D=Govt.=Creatocracy=4 April=Hermes=G=A4.
Unmistakable=1,000=100%=10.0=1.0=Mind=Sun=1 January=Helios >> M=E4.
Unmitigated=4,500=5,000=50%=P5.00D=Law=Time=Venus=5 May = Aphrodite>>L=N.
Unmoral=500=5%=P5.00D=5.0=Law=Time=Venus=5 May=Aphrodite>>L=N.
Unnatural=8,500=9,000=90%=P9.00D=9.0=Abstraction=Gods=Saturn=9Sept.>>A=Ø.
Unnerve=5,000=50%=P5.00D=Law=Time=Venus=5 May = Aphrodite>>L=N.
Unnumbered=3,500=4,000=40%=P4.0D=Govt.=Creatocracy=4 April=Hermes=G=A4.
Unorganized=3,000=30%=P3.0D=3.0=Creativity=Stars=Muses=3 March = C=I>>GIL.
Unpack=4,500=5,000=50%=P5.00D=Law=Time=Venus=5 May = Aphrodite>>L=N.
Unparalleled=1,500=15%=P1.50D=1.5=Authority=Solar Crown=1 May = Maia.
Unparliamentary=3,000=30%=P3.0D=3.0=Creativity=Stars=Muses=3 March = C=I>>GIL.
Unpeople=2,000=20%=P2.00D=2.0=Nature=Matter=Moon=2 Feb.=Cupid=N=C+_
Unperson=1,000=100%=10.0=1.0=Mind=Sun=1 January=Helios >> M=E4.

Unplug=7,500=8,000=80%=P8.0D=Economy=Currency=8 Aug.=Zeus>>E=v.
It takes about 75% of the available hand energy transmitted by a person to remove a plug.

Unplumbed=5,500=5.5=80%=P5.50=Earth-Midway=5 May = Gaia.
Unprecedented=2,000=20%=P2.00D=2.0=Nature=Matter=Moon=2 Feb.=Cupid=N=C+_
Unprepared=2,500=3,000=30%=P3.0D=3.0=Creativity=Stars=Muses=3 March=C=I>GIL.
Unpretentious=4,500=5,000=50%=P5.00D=Law=Time=Venus=5 May = Aphrodite>>L=N.
Unprintable=2,000=20%=P2.00D=2.0=Nature=Matter=Moon=2 Feb.=Cupid=N=C+_
Unprofessional=6,000=60%=P6.0D=Man=Earth=Royalty=6 June=Gaia=Maia>>M=M2.
Unprofitable=3,500=4,000=40%=P4.0D=Govt.=Creatocracy=4 April=Hermes=G=A4.
Unqualified=8,000=80%=P8.0D=Economy=Currency=8 Aug.=Zeus>>E=v.
Unquote=5,000=50%=P5.00D=Law=Time=Venus=5 May = Aphrodite>>L=N.
Unravel=8,500=9,000=90%=P9.00D=9.0=Abstraction=Gods=Saturn=9Sept.>>A=Ø.

Unread=3,500=4,000=40%=P4.0D=Govt.=Creatocracy=4 April=Mercury=Hermes=G=A4.
Unreadable=3,500=4,000=40%=P4.0D=Govt.=Creatocracy=4 April=Hermes=G=A4.
Unreal=5,500=5.5=80%=P5.50=Earth-Midway=5 May = Gaia.
Unreasonable=6,000=60%=P6.0D=Man=Earth=Royalty=6 June=Gaia=Maia>>M=M2.
Unregenerate=4,000=40%=P4.0D=Govt.=Creatocracy=4 April=Mercury=Hermes=G=A4.
Unrelenting=4,500=5,000=50%=P5.00D=Law=Time=Venus=5 May = Aphrodite>>L=N.
Unremitting=1,500=15%=P1.50D=1.5=Authority=Solar Crown=1 May = Maia.
Unreserved=5,500=5.5=80%=P5.50=Earth-Midway=5 May = Gaia.
Unrest=2,000=20%=P2.00D=2.0=Nature=Matter=Moon=2 Feb.=Cupid=N=C+_
Unrivaled=1,000=100%=10.0=1.0=Mind=Sun=1 January=Helios >> M=E4.
Unroll=4,500=5,000=50%=P5.00D=Law=Time=Venus=5 May = Aphrodite>>L=N.
Unruffled=1,500=15%=P1.50D=1.5=Authority=Solar Crown=1 May = Maia.
Unruly=4,500=5,000=50%=P5.00D=Law=Time=Venus=5 May = Aphrodite>>L=N.
Unsaddle=3,000=30%=P3.0D=3.0=Creativity=Stars=Muses=3 March = C=I>>GIL.
Unsaturated=10,000=1,000=100%=10.0=Physicality=Tech.=10 Oct.=Uranus=P=1Ø.
Unsavory=5,000=50%=P5.00D=Law=Time=Venus=5 May = Aphrodite>>L=N.
Unscathed=4,000=40%=P4.0D=Govt.=Creatocracy=4 April=Mercury=Hermes=G=A4.
Unschooled=5,500=5.5=80%=P5.50=Earth-Midway=5 May = Gaia.
Unscramble=4,500=5,000=50%=P5.00D=Law=Time=Venus=5 May = Aphrodite>>L=N.
Unscrew=6,500=7,000=70%=P7.0D=7.0=Language=Assets=Mars=7 July=Pleiades.
Unscrupulous=2,500=3,000=30%=P3.0D=3.0=Creativity=Stars=Muses=3 March=GIL.
Unseasonable=5,500=5.5=80%=P5.50=Earth-Midway=5 May = Gaia.
Unseat=6,000=60%=P6.0D=Man=Earth=Royalty=6 June=Gaia=Maia>>M=M2.
Unseemly=3,500=4,000=40%=P4.0D=Govt.=Creatocracy=4 April=Hermes=G=A4.
Unsettle=2,000=20%=P2.00D=2.0=Nature=Matter=Moon=2 Feb.=Cupid=N=C+_
Unsettled=10,000=1,000=100%=10.0=Physicality=Tech.=10 Oct.=Uranus=P=1Ø.
Unsightly=5,500=5.5=80%=P5.50=Earth-Midway=5 May = Gaia.
Unskilled=5,000=50%=P5.00D=Law=Time=Venus=5 May = Aphrodite>>L=N.
Unsociable=4,000=40%=P4.0D=Govt.=Creatocracy=4 April=Mercury=Hermes=G=A4.
Unsound=5,500=5.5=80%=P5.50=Earth-Midway=5 May = Gaia.
Unsparing=2,500=3,000=30%=P3.0D=3.0=Creativity=Stars=Muses=3 March = C=I>>GIL.
Unspeakable=10,000=1,000=100%=10.0=Physicality=Tech.=10 Oct.=Uranus=P=1Ø.
Unstable=10,000=1,000=100%=10.0=Physicality=Tech.=10 Oct.=Uranus=P=1Ø.
Unsteady=5,000=50%=P5.00D=Law=Time=Venus=5 May = Aphrodite>>L=N.
Unstick=2,500=3,000=30%=P3.0D=3.0=Creativity=Stars=Muses=3 March = C=I>>GIL.
Unstop=4,000=40%=P4.0D=Govt.=Creatocracy=4 April=Mercury=Hermes=G=A4.
Unstressed=5,500=5.5=80%=P5.50=Earth-Midway=5 May = Gaia.
Unstructured=3,000=30%=P3.0D=3.0=Creativity=Stars=Muses=3 March = C=I>>GIL.
Unstrung=4,000=40%=P4.0D=Govt.=Creatocracy=4 April=Mercury=Hermes=G=A4.
Unstudied=4,500=5,000=50%=P5.00D=Law=Time=Venus=5 May = Aphrodite>>L=N.
Unsubstantial=5,000=50%=P5.00D=Law=Time=Venus=5 May = Aphrodite>>L=N.
Unsung=3,000=30%=P3.0D=3.0=Creativity=Stars=Muses=3 March = C=I>>GIL.
Untangle=4,500=5,000=50%=P5.00D=Law=Time=Venus=5 May = Aphrodite>>L=N.
Untaught=3,000=30%=P3.0D=3.0=Creativity=Stars=Muses=3 March = C=I>>GIL.
Unthankful=1,000=100%=10.0=1.0=Mind=Sun=1 January=Helios >> M=E4.

Unthinkable=1,000=100%=Physicality=Tech.=10 Oct.=Uranus=P=1Ø.
Unthinking=3,000=30%=P3.0D=3.0=Creativity=Stars=Muses=3 March = C=I>>GIL.
Untie=6,500=7,000=70%=P7.0D=7.0=Language=Assets=Mars=7 July=Pleiades.
Until=10,000=1,000=100%=10.0=Physicality=Tech.=10 Oct.=Uranus=P=1Ø.
Untimely=4,000=40%=P4.0D=Govt.=Creatocracy=4 April=Mercury=Hermes=G=A4.
Unto=500=5%=P5.00D=5.0=Law=Time=Venus=5 May=Aphrodite>>L=N.
Untold=3,500=4,000=40%=P4.0D=Govt.=Creatocracy=4 April=Mercury=Hermes=G=A4.
Untouchable=10,000=1,000=100%=10.0=Physicality=Tech.=10 Oct.=Uranus=P=1Ø.
Untoward=2,000=20%=P2.00D=2.0=Nature=Matter=Moon=2 Feb.=Cupid=N=C+_
Untruth=3,500=4,000=40%=P4.0D=Govt.=Creatocracy=4 April=Mercury=Hermes=G=A4.
Untutored=3,500=4,000=40%=P4.0D=Govt.=Creatocracy=4 April=Hermes=G=A4.
Untwist=6,000=60%=P6.0D=Man=Earth=Royalty=6 June=Gaia=Maia>>M=M2.
Unused=5,000=50%=P5.00D=Law=Time=Venus=5 May = Aphrodite>>L=N.
Unusual=2,000=20%=P2.00D=2.0=Nature=Matter=Moon=2 Feb.=Cupid=N=C+_
Unutterable=8,500=9,000=90%=P9.00D=9.0=Abstraction=Gods=Saturn=9Sept.>>A=Ø.
Unvarnished=5,000=50%=P5.00D=Law=Time=Venus=5 May = Aphrodite>>L=N.
Unveil=4,500=5,000=50%=P5.00D=Law=Time=Venus=5 May = Aphrodite>>L=N.
Unvoiced=3,000=30%=P3.0D=3.0=Creativity=Stars=Muses=3 March = C=I>>GIL.
Unwarranted=4,000=40%=P4.0D=Govt.=Creatocracy=4 April=Mercury=Hermes=G=A4.
Unwearied=4,000=40%=P4.0D=Govt.=Creatocracy=4 April=Mercury=Hermes=G=A4.
Unwell=2,000=20%=P2.00D=2.0=Nature=Matter=Moon=2 Feb.=Cupid=N=C+_
Unwholesome=3,500=4,000=40%=P4.0D=Govt.=Creatocracy=4 April=Hermes=G=A4.
Unwieldy=4,500=5,000=50%=P5.00D=Law=Time=Venus=5 May = Aphrodite>>L=N.
Unwilling=4,000=40%=P4.0D=Govt.=Creatocracy=4 April=Mercury=Hermes=G=A4.
Unwind=2,500=3,000=30%=P3.0D=3.0=Creativity=Stars=Muses=3 March = C=I>>GIL.
Unwitting=7,000=70%=P7.0D=7.0=Language=Assets=Mars=7 July=Pleiades.
Unwonted=2,500=3,000=30%=P3.0D=3.0=Creativity=Stars=Muses=3 March = C=I>>GIL.
Unworldly=7,000=70%=P7.0D=7.0=Language=Assets=Mars=7 July=Pleiades.
Unworthy=5,000=50%=P5.00D=Law=Time=Venus=5 May = Aphrodite>>L=N.
Unwritten=4,000=40%=P4.0D=Govt.=Creatocracy=4 April=Mercury=Hermes=G=A4.
Up=10,000=1,000=100%=Physicality=Tech.=10 Oct.=Uranus=P=1Ø.
Up-=4,000=40%=P4.0D=Govt.=Creatocracy=4 April=Mercury=Hermes=G=A4.
Up-and-coming=2,500=3,000=30%=P3.0D=3.0=Creativity=Stars=Muses=3 March=>>GIL.
Upanishad=9,000=90%=P9.00D=9.0=Abstraction=Gods=Saturn=9Sept.>>A=Ø.
Upbeat=7,000=70%=P7.0D=7.0=Language=Assets=Mars=7 July=Pleiades.
Upbraid=3,000=30%=P3.0D=3.0=Creativity=Stars=Muses=3 March = C=I>>GIL.
Upbringing=3,500=4,000=40%=P4.0D=Govt.=Creatocracy=4 April=Hermes=G=A4.
UPC=1,500=15%=P1.50D=1.5=Authority=Solar Crown=1 May = Maia.
Upcoming=1,500=15%=P1.50D=1.5=Authority=Solar Crown=1 May = Maia.
Upcountry=4,000=40%=P4.0D=Govt.=Creatocracy=4 April=Mercury=Hermes=G=A4.
Update=2,500=3,000=30%=P3.0D=3.0=Creativity=Stars=Muses=3 March = C=I>>GIL.
Updike John=2,500=3,000=30%=P3.0D=3.0=Creativity=Stars=Muses=3 March=GIL.
Updraft=2,500=3,000=30%=P3.0D=3.0=Creativity=Stars=Muses=3 March = C=I>>GIL.
Upend=5,000=50%=P5.00D=Law=Time=Venus=5 May = Aphrodite>>L=N.
Up-front=5,000=50%=P5.00D=Law=Time=Venus=5 May = Aphrodite>>L=N.

Upgrade=5,000=50%=P5.00D=Law=Time=Venus=5 May = Aphrodite>>L=N.
Upheaval=9,000=90%=P9.00D=9.0=Abstraction=Gods=Saturn=9Sept.>>A=Ø.
Uphill=10,000=1,000=100%=10.0=Physicality=Tech.=10 Oct.=Uranus=P=1Ø.
Uphold=5,000=50%=P5.00D=Law=Time=Venus=5 May = Aphrodite>>L=N.
Upholster=6,500=7,000=70%=P7.0D=7.0=Language=Assets=Mars=7 July=Pleiades.
Upholstery=4,000=40%=P4.0D=Govt.=Creatocracy=4 April=Mercury=Hermes=G=A4.

UPI=1,500=15%=P1.50D=1.5=Authority=Solar Crown=1 May = Maia.
Universal Press International. The Creatocracy >> Undue Parental Influence. A Creativity
related offense discovered by Peter Matthews-Akukalia, Castle Makupedia in his book>>
The Oracle: Principles of Creative Sciences. Necessary for the Creatocracy or Mind Courts.

Upkeep=5,500=5.5=80%=P5.50=Earth-Midway=5 May = Gaia.
Upland=3,500=4,000=40%=P4.0D=Govt.=Creatocracy=4 April=Mercury=Hermes=G=A4.
Uplift=10,000=1,000=100%=10.0=Physicality=Tech.=10 Oct.=Uranus=P=1Ø.
Upload=8,000=80%=P8.0D=Economy=Currency=8 Aug.=Zeus>>E=v.
Upmost=500=5%=P5.00D=5.0=Law=Time=Venus=5 May=Aphrodite>>L=N.
Upon=500=5%=P5.00D=5.0=Law=Time=Venus=5 May=Aphrodite>>L=N.
Upper=10,000=1,000=100%=10.0=Physicality=Tech.=10 Oct.=Uranus=P=1Ø.
Upper California=1,500=15%=P1.50D=1.5=Authority=Solar Crown=1 May = Maia.
Upper case=10,000=1,000=100%=10.0=Physicality=Tech.=10 Oct.=Uranus=P=1Ø.
Upper class=3,500=4,000=40%=P4.0D=Govt.=Creatocracy=4 April=Hermes=G=A4.
Upperclassman=6,000=60%=P6.0D=Man=Earth=Royalty=6 June=Gaia=Maia>>M=M2.
Upper crust=3,500=4,000=40%=P4.0D=Govt.=Creatocracy=4 April=Mercury=G=A4.
Upper cut=4,500=5,000=50%=P5.00D=Law=Time=Venus=5 May = Aphrodite>>L=N.
Upper hand=3,000=30%=P3.0D=3.0=Creativity=Stars=Muses=3 March = C=I>>GIL.
Uppermost=3,500=4,000=40%=P4.0D=Govt.=Creato=4 April=Mercury=Hermes=G=A4.
Upper Volta=1,500=15%=P1.50D=1.5=Authority=Solar Crown=1 May = Maia.
Uppity=1,000=100%=10.0=1.0=Mind=Sun=1 January=Helios >> M=E4.
Up raise=2,500=3,000=30%=P3.0D=3.0=Creativity=Stars=Muses=3 March = C=I>>GIL.
Upright=10,000=1,000=100%=10.0=Physicality=Tech.=10 Oct.=Uranus=P=1Ø.
Upright piano=3,500=4,000=40%=P4.0D=Govt.=Creato=4 April=Mercury=Hermes=G=A4.
Uprising=2,500=3,000=30%=P3.0D=3.0=Creativity=Stars=Muses=3 March = C=I>>GIL.
Uproar=6,000=60%=P6.0D=Man=Earth=Royalty=6 June=Gaia=Maia>>M=M2.
Uproarious=3,500=4,000=40%=P4.0D=Govt.=Creatocracy=4 April=Hermes=G=A4.
Uproot=6,000=60%=P6.0D=Man=Earth=Royalty=6 June=Gaia=Maia>>M=M2.
Upscale=4,000=40%=P4.0D=Govt.=Creatocracy=4 April=Mercury=Hermes=G=A4.
Upset=10,000=1,000=100%=10.0=Physicality=Tech.=10 Oct.=Uranus=P=1Ø.
Upshot=2,000=20%=P2.00D=2.0=Nature=Matter=Moon=2 Feb.=Cupid=N=C+_
Upside down=8,000=80%=P8.0D=Economy=Currency=8 Aug.=Zeus>>E=v.
Upsilon=5,000=50%=P5.00D=Law=Time=Venus=5 May = Aphrodite>>L=N.
Upstage=10,000=1,000=100%=10.0=Physicality=Tech.=10 Oct.=Uranus=P=1Ø.
Upstairs=7,000=70%=P7.0D=7.0=Language=Assets=Mars=7 July=Pleiades.
Upstanding=3,500=4,000=40%=P4.0D=Govt.=Creatocracy=4 April=Hermes=G=A4.

Upstart=8,000=80%=P8.0D=Economy=Currency=8 Aug.=Zeus>>E=v.
Upstate=4,500=5,000=50%=P5.00D=Law=Time=Venus=5 May = Aphrodite>>L=N.
Upstream=3,000=30%=P3.0D=3.0=Creativity=Stars=Muses=3 March = C=I>>GIL.
Upstroke=1,500=15%=P1.50D=1.5=Authority=Solar Crown=1 May = Maia.
Upsurge=4,500=5,000=50%=P5.00D=Law=Time=Venus=5 May = Aphrodite>>L=N.
Upsweep=2,500=3,000=30%=P3.0D=3.0=Creativity=Stars=Muses=3 March = C=I>>GIL.
Upswing=3,000=30%=P3.0D=3.0=Creativity=Stars=Muses=3 March = C=I>>GIL.
Uptake=7,000=70%=P7.0D=7.0=Language=Assets=Mars=7 July=Pleiades.
Uptempo=4,000=40%=P4.0D=Govt.=Creatocracy=4 April=Mercury=Hermes=G=A4.
Uptight=3,500=4,000=40%=P4.0D=Govt.=Creatocracy=4 April=Mercury=Hermes=G=A4.
Up-to-date=4,000=40%=P4.0D=Govt.=Creatocracy=4 April=Mercury=Hermes=G=A4.
Uptown=5,000=50%=P5.00D=Law=Time=Venus=5 May = Aphrodite>>L=N.
Upturn=7,000=70%=P7.0D=7.0=Language=Assets=Mars=7 July=Pleiades.
Upward=4,000=40%=P4.0D=Govt.=Creatocracy=4 April=Mercury=Hermes=G=A4.
Upwind=4,500=5,000=50%=P5.00D=Law=Time=Venus=5 May = Aphrodite>>L=N.
Ur=6,500=7,000=70%=P7.0D=7.0=Language=Assets=Mars=7 July=Pleiades.
Uracil=6,500=7,000=70%=P7.0D=7.0=Language=Assets=Mars=7 July=Pleiades.
Ural-Altaic=5,000=50%=P5.00D=Law=Time=Venus=5 May = Aphrodite>>L=N.
Uralic=5,500=5.5=80%=P5.50=Earth-Midway=5 May = Gaia.
Ural Mountains=10,000=1,000=100%=10.0=Physicality=Tech.=10 Oct.=Uranus=P=1Ø.
Ural River=10,000=1,000=100%=10.0=Physicality=Tech.=10 Oct.=Uranus=P=1Ø.
Uranium=10,000=1,000=100%=10.0=Physicality=Tech.=10 Oct.=Uranus=P=1Ø.

Uranus=10,000=1,000=100%=10.0=Physicality=Tech.=10 Oct.=Uranus=P=1Ø.
Greek Myth. The earliest supreme God, a personification of the sky.

Urban=5,000=50%=P5.00D=Law=Time=Venus=5 May = Aphrodite>>L=N.
Urban II=2,500=3,000=30%=P3.0D=3.0=Creativity=Stars=Muses=3 March = C=I>>GIL.
Urbane=4,500=5,000=50%=P5.00D=Law=Time=Venus=5 May = Aphrodite>>L=N.
Urbanite=1,500=15%=P1.50D=1.5=Authority=Solar Crown=1 May = Maia.
Urbanize=3,500=4,000=40%=P4.0D=Govt.=Creatocracy=4 April=Hermes=G=A4.
Urchin=4,500=5,000=50%=P5.00D=Law=Time=Venus=5 May = Aphrodite>>L=N.
Urdu=8,500=9,000=90%=P9.00D=9.0=Abstraction=Gods=Saturn=9Sept.>>A=Ø.
-ure=7,500=8,000=80%=P8.0D=Economy=Currency=8 Aug.=Zeus>>E=v.
Urea=10,000=1,000=100%=10.0=Physicality=Tech.=10 Oct.=Uranus=P=1Ø.
Uremia=10,000=1,000=100%=10.0=Physicality=Tech.=10 Oct.=Uranus=P=1Ø.
Ureter=8,000=80%=P8.0D=Economy=Currency=8 Aug.=Zeus>>E=v.
Urethra=10,000=1,000=100%=10.0=Physicality=Tech.=10 Oct.=Uranus=P=1Ø.
Urge=10,000=1,000=100%=10.0=Physicality=Tech.=10 Oct.=Uranus=P=1Ø.
Urgent=3,500=4,000=40%=P4.0D=Govt.=Creatocracy=4 April=Mercury=Hermes=G=A4.
-urgy=5,000=50%=P5.00D=Law=Time=Venus=5 May = Aphrodite>>L=N.
Uric=4,000=40%=P4.0D=Govt.=Creatocracy=4 April=Mercury=Hermes=G=A4.
Uric acid=9,000=90%=P9.00D=9.0=Abstraction=Gods=Saturn=9Sept.>>A=Ø.
Urinal=3,000=30%=P3.0D=3.0=Creativity=Stars=Muses=3 March = C=I>>GIL.

Urinalysis=2,000=20%=P2.00D=2.0=Nature=Matter=Moon=2 Feb.=Cupid=N=C+_
Urinary=3,500=4,000=40%=P4.0D=Govt.=Creatocracy=4 April=Mercury=Hermes=G=A4.
Urinary bladder=8,000=80%=P8.0D=Economy=Currency=8 Aug.=Zeus>>E=v.
Urinate=1,500=15%=P1.50D=1.5=Authority=Solar Crown=1 May = Maia.
Urine=10,000=1,000=100%=10.0=Physicality=Tech.=10 Oct.=Uranus=P=1Ø.
Urino-=2,500=3,000=30%=P3.0D=3.0=Creativity=Stars=Muses=3 March = C=I>>GIL.
Urn=10,000=1,000=100%=10.0=Physicality=Tech.=10 Oct.=Uranus=P=1Ø.
Uro-=5,000=50%=P5.00D=Law=Time=Venus=5 May = Aphrodite>>L=N.
Urogenital=5,000=50%=P5.00D=Law=Time=Venus=5 May = Aphrodite>>L=N.
Urology=10,000=1,000=100%=10.0=Physicality=Tech.=10 Oct.=Uranus=P=1Ø.
Ursa Major=7,000=70%=P7.0D=7.0=Language=Assets=Mars=7 July=Pleiades.
Ursa Minor=6,000=60%=P6.0D=Man=Earth=Royalty=6 June=Gaia=Maia>>M=M2.
Ursine=4,000=40%=P4.0D=Govt.=Creatocracy=4 April=Mercury=Hermes=G=A4.
Urticaria=2,500=3,000=30%=P3.0D=3.0=Creativity=Stars=Muses=3 March = C=I>>GIL.
Uruguay=10,000=1,000=100%=10.0=Physicality=Tech.=10 Oct.=Uranus=P=1Ø.
Uruguay River.=10,000=1,000=100%=10.0=Physicality=Tech.=10 Oct.=Uranus=P=1Ø.
Us=10,000=1,000=100%=10.0=Physicality=Tech.=10 Oct.=Uranus=P=1Ø.
U.S.=1,000=100%=10.0=1.0=Mind=Sun=1 January=Helios >> M=E4.
USA=2,500=3,000=30%=P3.0D=3.0=Creativity=Stars=Muses=3 March = C=I>>GIL.
Usable=8,000=80%=P8.0D=Economy=Currency=8 Aug.=Zeus>>E=v.
USAF=2,000=20%=P2.00D=2.0=Nature=Matter=Moon=2 Feb.=Cupid=N=C+_
Usage=10,000=1,000=100%=10.0=Physicality=Tech.=10 Oct.=Uranus=P=1Ø.
USCG=2,000=20%=P2.00D=2.0=Nature=Matter=Moon=2 Feb.=Cupid=N=C+_
USDA=2,500=3,000=30%=P3.0D=3.0=Creativity=Stars=Muses=3 March = C=I>>GIL.
Use=10,000=1,000=100%=10.0=Physicality=Tech.=10 Oct.=Uranus=P=1Ø.
Used=6,000=60%=P6.0D=Man=Earth=Royalty=6 June=Gaia=Maia>>M=M2.
Useful=2,500=3,000=30%=P3.0D=3.0=Creativity=Stars=Muses=3 March = C=I>>GIL.
Useless=6,500=7,000=70%=P7.0D=7.0=Language=Assets=Mars=7 July=Pleiades.
User friendly=2,500=3,000=30%=P3.0D=3.0=Creativity=Stars=Muses=3 March=C=I>>GIL.
Usher=10,000=1,000=100%=10.0=Physicality=Tech.=10 Oct.=Uranus=P=1Ø.
USIA=2,000=20%=P2.00D=2.0=Nature=Matter=Moon=2 Feb.=Cupid=N=C+_
USMC=2,000=20%=P2.00D=2.0=Nature=Matter=Moon=2 Feb.=Cupid=N=C+_
USN=1,500=15%=P1.50D=1.5=Authority=Solar Crown=1 May = Maia.
USO=1,500=15%=P1.50D=1.5=Authority=Solar Crown=1 May = Maia.
U.S.S.=2,500=3,000=30%=P3.0D=3.0=Creativity=Stars=Muses=3 March = C=I>>GIL.
U.S.S.R.=2,500=3,000=30%=P3.0D=3.0=Creativity=Stars=Muses=3 March = C=I>>GIL.
Usu.=500=5%=P5.00D=5.0=Law=Time=Venus=5 May=Aphrodite>>L=N.
Usual=4,000=40%=P4.0D=Govt.=Creatocracy=4 April=Mercury=Hermes=G=A4.
Usufruct=10,000=1,000=100%=10.0=Physicality=Tech.=10 Oct.=Uranus=P=1Ø.
Usurer=8,500=9,000=90%=P9.00D=9.0=Abstraction=Gods=Saturn=9Sept.>>A=Ø.
Usurious=3,000=30%=P3.0D=3.0=Creativity=Stars=Muses=3 March = C=I>>GIL.
Usurp=10,000=1,000=100%=10.0=Physicality=Tech.=10 Oct.=Uranus=P=1Ø.
Usury=10,000=1,000=100%=10.0=Physicality=Tech.=10 Oct.=Uranus=P=1Ø.
UT=500=5%=P5.00D=5.0=Law=Time=Venus=5 May=Aphrodite>>L=N.
Utah=6,000=60%=P6.0D=Man=Earth=Royalty=6 June=Gaia=Maia>>M=M2.

Ute=7,500=8,000=80%=P8.0D=Economy=Currency=8 Aug.=Zeus>>E=v.
Utensil=7,500=8,000=80%=P8.0D=Economy=Currency=8 Aug.=Zeus>>E=v.
Uterus=9,000=90%=P9.00D=9.0=Abstraction=Gods=Saturn=9Sept.>>A=Ø.
Utile=1,500=15%=P1.50D=1.5=Authority=Solar Crown=1 May = Maia.
Utilitarian=10,000=1,000=100%=10.0=Physicality=Tech.=10 Oct.=Uranus=P=1Ø.
Utilitarianism=10,000=1,000=100%=10.0=Physicality=Tech.=10 Oct.=Uranus=P=1Ø.
Utility=10,000=1,000=100%=10.0=Physicality=Tech.=10 Oct.=Uranus=P=1Ø.
Utilize=3,000=30%=P3.0D=3.0=Creativity=Stars=Muses=3 March = C=I>>GIL.

Utmost=10,000=1,000=100%=10.0=Physicality=Tech.=10 Oct.=Uranus=P=1Ø.
Peter Matthews-Akukalia owns Utmost Peak Resources an enterprise.

Uto-Aztecan=10,000=1,000=100%=10.0=Physicality=Tech.=10 Oct.=Uranus=P=1Ø.
Utopia=10,000=1,000=100%=10.0=Physicality=Tech.=10 Oct.=Uranus=P=1Ø.
Utrecht=3,500=4,000=40%=P4.0D=Govt.=Creatocracy=4 April=Mercury=Hermes=G=A4.
Utrillo Maurice.=2,000=20%=P2.00D=2.0=Nature=Matter=Moon=2 Feb.=Cupid=N=C+_
Utter1=7,000=70%=P7.0D=7.0=Language=Assets=Mars=7 July=Pleiades.
Utter2=4,000=40%=P4.0D=Govt.=Creatocracy=4 April=Mercury=Hermes=G=A4.
Utterance=5,000=50%=P5.00D=Law=Time=Venus=5 May = Aphrodite>>L=N.
Utterly=1,500=15%=P1.50D=1.5=Authority=Solar Crown=1 May = Maia.
Uttermost=1,000=100%=10.0=1.0=Mind=Sun=1 January=Helios >> M=E4.
U-turn=5,000=50%=P5.00D=Law=Time=Venus=5 May = Aphrodite>>L=N.
UV=500=5%=P5.00D=5.0=Law=Time=Venus=5 May=Aphrodite>>L=N.
Uvula=9,000=90%=P9.00D=9.0=Abstraction=Gods=Saturn=9Sept.>>A=Ø.
UW=500=5%=P5.00D=5.0=Law=Time=Venus=5 May=Aphrodite>>L=N.
Uxorious=5,000=50%=P5.00D=Law=Time=Venus=5 May = Aphrodite>>L=N.
Uzbek=7,000=70%=P7.0D=7.0=Language=Assets=Mars=7 July=Pleiades.
Uzbekistan=5,000=50%=P5.00D=Law=Time=Venus=5 May = Aphrodite>>L=N.

MAKABET =Vv=

---

v=3,000=30%=P3.0D=3.0=Creativity=Stars=Muses=3 March = C=I>>GIL.
The 22nd letter of the English alphabet. The psychometric weight of V is thus computed>>
3.0*2.2x=px=5.2+6.6=11.8x=px=46.12=50=5.0>>Law >> Rights >> Righteousness >>
Time >> Venus >> Aphrodite. V is for Venus which stands for righteousness through the
protection of rights obedience to natural laws and time measure to deduce value so that
economies are sustained through ideas development and brainchild management.

V1=6,000=60%=P6.0D=Man=Earth=Royalty=6 June=Gaia=Maia>>M=M2.
V2=2,500=3,000=30%=P3.0D=3.0=Creativity=Stars=Muses=3 March = C=I>>GIL.
v.=3,500=4,000=40%=P4.0D=Govt.=Creatocracy=4 April=Mercury=Hermes=G=A4.

V.=1,000=100%=10.0=1.0=Mind=Sun=1 January=Helios >> M=E4.
VA=500=5%=P5.00D=5.0=Law=Time=Venus=5 May=Aphrodite>>L=N.
V.A.=1,000=100%=10.0=1.0=Mind=Sun=1 January=Helios >> M=E4.
Vacancy=10,000=1,000=100%=10.0=Physicality=Tech.=10 Oct.=Uranus=P=1Ø.
Vacant=10,000=1,000=100%=10.0=Physicality=Tech.=10 Oct.=Uranus=P=1Ø.
Vacate=5,500=5.5=80%=P5.50=Earth-Midway=5 May = Gaia.
Vacation=8,500=9,000=90%=P9.00D=9.0=Abstraction=Gods=Saturn=9Sept.>>A=Ø.
Vaccinate=6,000=60%=P6.0D=Man=Earth=Royalty=6 June=Gaia=Maia>>M=M2.
Vaccine=8,500=9,000=90%=P9.00D=9.0=Abstraction=Gods=Saturn=9Sept.>>A=Ø.
Vacillate=8,500=9,000=90%=P9.00D=9.0=Abstraction=Gods=Saturn=9Sept.>>A=Ø.
Vacuity=9,000=90%=P9.00D=9.0=Abstraction=Gods=Saturn=9Sept.>>A=Ø.
Vacuole=7,500=8,000=80%=P8.0D=Economy=Currency=8 Aug.=Zeus>>E=v.
Vacuous=8,500=9,000=90%=P9.00D=9.0=Abstraction=Gods=Saturn=9Sept.>>A=Ø.
Vacuum=9,000=90%=P9.00D=9.0=Abstraction=Gods=Saturn=9Sept.>>A=Ø.
Vacuum bottle=10,000=1,000=100%=10.0=Physicality=Tech.=10 Oct.=Uranus=P=1Ø.
Vacuum cleaner=4,000=40%=P4.0D=Govt.=4 April=Mercury=Hermes=G=A4.
Vacuum packed=2,500=3,000=30%=P3.0D=3.0=Cre=Stars=Muses=3 March = C=I>>GIL.
Vacuum tube=10,000=1,000=100%=10.0=Physicality=Tech.=10 Oct.=Uranus=P=1Ø.
Vademecum=7,000=70%=P7.0D=7.0=Language=Assets=Mars=7 July=Pleiades.
Vaduz=5,500=5.5=80%=P5.50=Earth-Midway=5 May = Gaia.
Vagabond=10,000=1,000=100%=10.0=Physicality=Tech.=10 Oct.=Uranus=P=1Ø.
Vagary=5,000=50%=P5.00D=Law=Time=Venus=5 May = Aphrodite>>L=N.
Vagina=6,500=7,000=70%=P7.0D=7.0=Language=Assets=Mars=7 July=Pleiades.
Vagrant=10,000=1,000=100%=10.0=Physicality=Tech.=10 Oct.=Uranus=P=1Ø.
Vague=10,000=1,000=100%=10.0=Physicality=Tech.=10 Oct.=Uranus=P=1Ø.
Vain=10,000=1,000=100%=10.0=Physicality=Tech.=10 Oct.=Uranus=P=1Ø.
Vain glory=3,500=4,000=40%=P4.0D=Govt.=Creatocracy=4 April=Hermes=G=A4.
Val.=1,500=15%=P1.50D=1.5=Authority=Solar Crown=1 May = Maia.
Valance=10,000=1,000=100%=10.0=Physicality=Tech.=10 Oct.=Uranus=P=1Ø.
Vale=2,500=3,000=30%=P3.0D=3.0=Creativity=Stars=Muses=3 March = C=I>>GIL.
Valediction=5,500=5.5=80%=P5.50=Earth-Midway=5 May = Gaia.
Valedictorian=10,000=1,000=100%=10.0=Physicality=Tech.=10 Oct.=Uranus=P=1Ø.
Valedictory=3,500=4,000=40%=P4.0D=Govt.=4 April=Mercury=Hermes=G=A4.
Valence=10,000=1,000=100%=10.0=Physicality=Tech.=10 Oct.=Uranus=P=1Ø.
Valencia=10,000=1,000=100%=10.0=Physicality=Tech.=10 Oct.=Uranus=P=1Ø.
-valent=4,000=40%=P4.0D=Govt.=Creatocracy=4 April=Mercury=Hermes=G=A4.
valentine=10,000=1,000=100%=10.0=Physicality=Tech.=10 Oct.=Uranus=P=1Ø.

Valentine=4,000=40%=P4.0D=Govt.=Creatocracy=4 April=Mercury=Hermes=G=A4.
See the book >> Sword of Honour: Days of St. Valentine by African Shakespeare. This book emerged Peter Matthews-Akukalia as the first African to write a play completely in the Old Shakespearean English without prior training. See also the complete package>> The Creatocracy Republic which emerged the author as Dragon Lord of the Skies and Castle Makupedia God of the MindArts. Sword of Honour (reloaded) was featured herein.

Valentine's Day=2,000=20%=P2.00D=2.0=Nature=Matter=Moon=2 Feb.=Cupid=N=C+_
Valerian=4,000=40%=P4.0D=Govt.=Creatocracy=4 April=Mercury=Hermes=G=A4.
Valet=10,000=1,000=100%=10.0=Physicality=Tech.=10 Oct.=Uranus=P=1Ø.
Valetudinarian=10,000=1,000=100%=10.0=Physicality=Tech.=10 Oct.=Uranus=P=1Ø.

Valhalla=6,000=60%=P6.0D=Man=Earth=Royalty=6 June=Gaia=Maia>>M=M2.
Myth. In Norse myth, the hall in which Odin received the souls of slain heroes.

Valiant=5,500=5.5=80%=P5.50=Earth-Midway=5 May = Gaia.
Valid=8,500=9,000=90%=P9.00D=9.0=Abstraction=Gods=Saturn=9Sept.>>A=Ø.
Valise=4,500=5,000=50%=P5.00D=Law=Time=Venus=5 May = Aphrodite>>L=N.
Valium=3,500=4,000=40%=P4.0D=Govt.=Creatocracy=4 April=Mercury=Hermes=G=A4.

Valkyrie=7,000=70%=P7.0D=7.0=Language=Assets=Mars=7 July=Pleiades.
Myth. In Norse myth, any of Odin's handmaidens who conducted the souls of the slain to Valhalla. They were computational muses who functioned in the jurisdictions of Aries.

Valladolid=4,500=5,000=50%=P5.00D=Law=Time=Venus=5 May = Aphrodite>>L=N.
Vallejo=6,500=7,000=70%=P7.0D=7.0=Language=Assets=Mars=7 July=Pleiades.
Valletta=4,500=5,000=50%=P5.00D=Law=Time=Venus=5 May = Aphrodite>>L=N.

Valley=10,000=1,000=100%=10.0=Physicality=Tech.=10 Oct.=Uranus=P=1Ø.
See The Creatocracy Republic: Castle Makupedia Plays Legends & Short Stories by Peter Matthews-Akukalia. One of the featured plays is Valley of the Kings.

Valley Forge=6,000=60%=P6.0D=Man=Earth=Royalty=6 June=Gaia=Maia>>M=M2.
Valor=4,500=5,000=50%=P5.00D=Law=Time=Venus=5 May = Aphrodite>>L=N.
Valparaiso=6,000=60%=P6.0D=Man=Earth=Royalty=6 June=Gaia=Maia>>M=M2.
Valuable=10,000=1,000=100%=10.0=Physicality=Tech.=10 Oct.=Uranus=P=1Ø.
Valuate=3,000=30%=P3.0D=3.0=Creativity=Stars=Muses=3 March = C=I>>GIL.
Valuation=4,500=5,000=50%=P5.00D=Law=Time=Venus=5 May = Aphrodite>>L=N.
Value=10,000=1,000=100%=10.0=Physicality=Tech.=10 Oct.=Uranus=P=1Ø.
Value-added tax=9,000=90%=P9.00D=9.0=Abstraction=Gods=Saturn=9Sept.>>A=Ø.
Valve=10,000=1,000=100%=10.0=Physicality=Tech.=10 Oct.=Uranus=P=1Ø.
Vamoose=4,000=40%=P4.0D=Govt.=Creatocracy=4 April=Mercury=Hermes=G=A4.
Vamp1=10,000=1,000=100%=10.0=Physicality=Tech.=10 Oct.=Uranus=P=1Ø.
Vamp2=5,000=50%=P5.00D=Law=Time=Venus=5 May = Aphrodite>>L=N.
Vampire=10,000=1,000=100%=10.0=Physicality=Tech.=10 Oct.=Uranus=P=1Ø.
Van1=10,000=1,000=100%=10.0=Physicality=Tech.=10 Oct.=Uranus=P=1Ø.
Van2=1,000=100%=10.0=1.0=Mind=Sun=1 January=Helios >> M=E4.
Vanadium=10,000=1,000=100%=10.0=Physicality=Tech.=10 Oct.=Uranus=P=1Ø.
Van Allen belt=10,000=1,000=100%=10.0=Physicality=Tech.=10 Oct.=Uranus=P=1Ø.

Van Buren=4,000=40%=P4.0D=Govt.=Creatocracy=4 April=Mercury=Hermes=G=A4.
Vancouver=6,000=60%=P6.0D=Man=Earth=Royalty=6 June=Gaia=Maia>>M=M2.
Vancouver, Mount.=7,500=8,000=80%=P8.0D=Economy=Currency=8 Aug.=Zeus>>E=v.
Vancouver Island.=5,000=50%=P5.00D=Law=Time=Venus=5 May = Aphrodite>>L=N.
Vandal=10,000=1,000=100%=10.0=Physicality=Tech.=10 Oct.=Uranus=P=1Ø.
Vandalism=4,500=5,000=50%=P5.00D=Law=Time=Venus=5 May = Aphrodite>>L=N.
Vanderbilt Cornelius=2,500=3,000=30%=P3.0D=3.0=Creat=Stars=Muses=3 March = C=I.
Vandyke Anthony=2,500=3,000=30%=P3.0D=3.0=Cre=Stars=Muses=3March=C=I>GIL.
Vane=10,000=1,000=100%=10.0=Physicality=Tech.=10 Oct.=Uranus=P=1Ø.
Van Eyck=3,000=30%=P3.0D=3.0=Creativity=Stars=Muses=3 March = C=I>>GIL.
Van Gogh=2,500=3,000=30%=P3.0D=3.0=Creativity=Stars=Muses=3 March = C=I>>GIL.
Vanguard=7,000=70%=P7.0D=7.0=Language=Assets=Mars=7 July=Pleiades.
Vanilla=10,000=1,000=100%=10.0=Physicality=Tech.=10 Oct.=Uranus=P=1Ø.
Vanillin=6,500=7,000=70%=P7.0D=7.0=Language=Assets=Mars=7 July=Pleiades.
Vanish=7,500=8,000=80%=P8.0D=Economy=Currency=8 Aug.=Zeus>>E=v.
Vanity=10,000=1,000=100%=10.0=Physicality=Tech.=10 Oct.=Uranus=P=1Ø.
Vanity case=6,000=60%=P6.0D=Man=Earth=Royalty=6 June=Gaia=Maia>>M=M2.
Vanity plate=7,500=8,000=80%=P8.0D=Economy=Currency=8 Aug.=Zeus>>E=v.
Vanity press=5,500=5.5=80%=P5.50=Earth-Midway=5 May = Gaia.
Vanquish=7,500=8,000=80%=P8.0D=Economy=Currency=8 Aug.=Zeus>>E=v.
Vantage=10,000=1,000=100%=10.0=Physicality=Tech.=10 Oct.=Uranus=P=1Ø.
Vanuatu=9,000=90%=P9.00D=9.0=Abstraction=Gods=Saturn=9Sept.>>A=Ø.
Vanzetti Bartoloméo=3,500=4,000=40%=P4.0D=Govt.=4 April=Hermes=G=A4.
Vapid=5,000=50%=P5.00D=Law=Time=Venus=5 May = Aphrodite>>L=N.

Vapor=10,000=1,000=100%=10.0=Physicality=Tech.=10 Oct.=Uranus=P=1Ø.
Peter Matthews-Akukalia broke the Newton's laws of gravity proving that certain things go up and do not come down. This includes smoke, vapor and steam. Mind Ascends and matter descends. This is called the Maks - Psycho-gravitational Incursion (PGI) Law. See the book>Template & Manifesto for the Creative Economy 2: Principles of Psychoeconomix.

Vaporize=3,500=4,000=40%=P4.0D=Govt.=Creatocracy=4 April=Hermes=G=A4.
Vapor lock=10,000=1,000=100%=10.0=Physicality=Tech.=10 Oct.=Uranus=P=1Ø.
Vaporous=10,000=1,000=100%=10.0=Physicality=Tech.=10 Oct.=Uranus=P=1Ø.
Vapor=1,500=15%=P1.50D=1.5=Authority=Solar Crown=1 May = Maia.
Vaquero=3,000=30%=P3.0D=3.0=Creativity=Stars=Muses=3 March = C=I>>GIL.
Var.=1,500=15%=P1.50D=1.5=Authority=Solar Crown=1 May = Maia.
Varanasi=6,000=60%=P6.0D=Man=Earth=Royalty=6 June=Gaia=Maia>>M=M2.
Vargas Liosa=2,500=3,000=30%=P3.0D=3.0=Cre=Stars=Muses=3 March = C=I>>GIL.
Variable=10,000=1,000=100%=10.0=Physicality=Tech.=10 Oct.=Uranus=P=1Ø.
Variance=10,000=1,000=100%=10.0=Physicality=Tech.=10 Oct.=Uranus=P=1Ø.
Variant=10,000=1,000=100%=10.0=Physicality=Tech.=10 Oct.=Uranus=P=1Ø.
Variation=10,000=1,000=100%=10.0=Physicality=Tech.=10 Oct.=Uranus=P=1Ø.
Varicolored=3,000=30%=P3.0D=3.0=Creativity=Stars=Muses=3 March = C=I>>GIL.

Varicose=5,000=50%=P5.00D=Law=Time=Venus=5 May = Aphrodite>>L=N.
Varied=2,500=3,000=30%=P3.0D=3.0=Creativity=Stars=Muses=3 March = C=I>>GIL.
Variegate=10,000=1,000=100%=10.0=Physicality=Tech.=10 Oct.=Uranus=P=1Ø.
Variety=10,000=1,000=100%=10.0=Physicality=Tech.=10 Oct.=Uranus=P=1Ø.
Variety show=4,000=40%=P4.0D=Govt.=Creatocracy=4 April=Mercury=Hermes=G=A4.
Variety store=5,000=50%=P5.00D=Law=Time=Venus=5 May = Aphrodite>>L=N.
Variorum=10,000=1,000=100%=Physicality=Tech.=10 Oct.=Uranus=P=1Ø.
Various=10,000=1,000=100%=10.0=Physicality=Tech.=10 Oct.=Uranus=P=1Ø.
Varlet=4,000=40%=P4.0D=Govt.=Creatocracy=4 April=Mercury=Hermes=G=A4.
Varmint=5,500=5.5=80%=P5.50=Earth-Midway=5 May = Gaia.
Varna=6,500=7,000=70%=P7.0D=7.0=Language=Assets=Mars=7 July=Pleiades.
Varnish=10,000=1,000=100%=10.0=Physicality=Tech.=10 Oct.=Uranus=P=1Ø.

Varsity=10,000=1,000=100%=10.0=Physicality=Tech.=10 Oct.=Uranus=P=1Ø.
See University.

Vary=10,000=1,000=100%=10.0=Physicality=Tech.=10 Oct.=Uranus=P=1Ø.
Vas=3,500=4,000=40%=P4.0D=Govt.=Creatocracy=4 April=Mercury=Hermes=G=A4.
Vasari Giorgio=4,000=40%=P4.0D=Govt.=Creatocracy=4 April=Mercury=Hermes=G=A4.
Vascular=9,500=10,000=1,000=100%=10.0=Physicality=Tech.=10 Oct.=Uranus=P=1Ø.
Vas deferens=9,000=90%=P9.00D=9.0=Abstraction=Gods=Saturn=9Sept.>>A=Ø.
Vase=7,500=8,000=80%=P8.0D=Economy=Currency=8 Aug.=Zeus>>E=v.
Vasectomy=7,000=70%=P7.0D=7.0=Language=Assets=Mars=7 July=Pleiades.
Vaso-=5,000=50%=P5.00D=Law=Time=Venus=5 May = Aphrodite>>L=N.
Vasoconstriction=2,500=3,000=30%=P3.0D=3.0=Cre=Stars=Muses=3 March = C=I>>GIL.
Vasodilation=2,500=3,000=30%=P3.0D=3.0=Cre=Stars=Muses=3 March = C=I>>GIL.
Vasomotor=4,000=40%=P4.0D=Govt.=Creatocracy=4 April=Mercury=Hermes=G=A4.
Vassal=10,000=1,000=100%=10.0=Physicality=Tech.=10 Oct.=Uranus=P=1Ø.
Vassalage=10,000=1,000=100%=10.0=Physicality=Tech.=10 Oct.=Uranus=P=1Ø.
Vast=5,500=5.5=80%=P5.50=Earth-Midway=5 May = Gaia.
Vat=7,000=70%=P7.0D=7.0=Language=Assets=Mars=7 July=Pleiades.
VAT=1,500=15%=P1.50D=1.5=Authority=Solar Crown=1 May = Maia.
Vatic=4,500=5,000=50%=P5.00D=Law=Time=Venus=5 May = Aphrodite>>L=N.
Vatican=5,500=5.5=80%=P5.50=Earth-Midway=5 May = Gaia.
Vatican City=6,500=7,000=70%=P7.0D=7.0=Language=Assets=Mars=7 July=Pleiades.

Vatu=4,000=40%=P4.0D=Govt.=Creatocracy=4 April=Mercury=Hermes=G=A4.
Metric weight=4/10=0.4>>40:1. See Naira. Dollar.

Vaudeville=10,000=1,000=100%=10.0=Physicality=Tech.=10 Oct.=Uranus=P=1Ø.
Vault1=10,000=1,000=100%=10.0=Physicality=Tech.=10 Oct.=Uranus=P=1Ø.
Vault2=10,000=1,000=100%=10.0=Physicality=Tech.=10 Oct.=Uranus=P=1Ø.
Vaunt=2,500=3,000=30%=P3.0D=3.0=Creativity=Stars=Muses=3 March = C=I>>GIL.

Vav=4,500=5,000=50%=P5.00D=Law=Time=Venus=5 May = Aphrodite>>L=N.
vb.=1,000=100%=10.0=1.0=Mind=Sun=1 January=Helios >> M=E4.
VC=500=5%=P5.00D=5.0=Law=Time=Venus=5 May=Aphrodite>>L=N.
V.C.=3,500=4,000=40%=P4.0D=Govt.=Creatocracy=4 April=Mercury=Hermes=G=A4.
VCR=9,000=90%=P9.00D=9.0=Abstraction=Gods=Saturn=9Sept.>>A=Ø.
VD=1,000=100%=10.0=1.0=Mind=Sun=1 January=Helios >> M=E4.
VDT=10,000=1,000=100%=10.0=Physicality=Tech.=10 Oct.=Uranus=P=1Ø.
Veal=3,500=4,000=40%=P4.0D=Govt.=Creatocracy=4 April=Mercury=Hermes=G=A4.
Veblen Thorstein=2,500=3,000=30%=P3.0D=3.0=Cre=Stars=Muses=3 March = C=I>>GIL.
Vector=10,000=1,000=100%=10.0=Physicality=Tech.=10 Oct.=Uranus=P=1Ø.
Veda=7,000=70%=P7.0D=7.0=Language=Assets=Mars=7 July=Pleiades.
Vedanta=10,000=1,000=100%=10.0=Physicality=Tech.=10 Oct.=Uranus=P=1Ø.
Veep=4,000=40%=P4.0D=Govt.=Creatocracy=4 April=Mercury=Hermes=G=A4.
Veer=7,500=8,000=80%=P8.0D=Economy=Currency=8 Aug.=Zeus>>E=v.
Vega Lope de.=2,000=20%=P2.00D=2.0=Nature=Matter=Moon=2 Feb.=Cupid=N=C+_
Vegetable=10,000=1,000=100%=10.0=Physicality=Tech.=10 Oct.=Uranus=P=1Ø.
Vegetal=8,500=9,000=90%=P9.00D=9.0=Abstraction=Gods=Saturn=9Sept.>>A=Ø.
Vegetarian=9,000=90%=P9.00D=9.0=Abstraction=Gods=Saturn=9Sept.>>A=Ø.
Vegetate=10,000=1,000=100%=10.0=Physicality=Tech.=10 Oct.=Uranus=P=1Ø.
Vegetation=10,000=1,000=100%=10.0=Physicality=Tech.=10 Oct.=Uranus=P=1Ø.
Vegetative=10,000=1,000=100%=10.0=Physicality=Tech.=10 Oct.=Uranus=P=1Ø.
Vehement=10,000=1,000=100%=10.0=Physicality=Tech.=10 Oct.=Uranus=P=1Ø.
Vehicle=10,000=1,000=100%=10.0=Physicality=Tech.=10 Oct.=Uranus=P=1Ø.
Veil=10,000=1,000=100%=10.0=Physicality=Tech.=10 Oct.=Uranus=P=1Ø.
Vein=10,000=1,000=100%=10.0=Physicality=Tech.=10 Oct.=Uranus=P=1Ø.
Velar=8,500=9,000=90%=P9.00D=9.0=Abstraction=Gods=Saturn=9Sept.>>A=Ø.
Velázquez Diego=4,000=40%=P4.0D=Govt.=4 April=Mercury=Hermes=G=A4.
Velcro=5,000=50%=P5.00D=Law=Time=Venus=5 May = Aphrodite>>L=N.
Veldt=5,500=5.5=80%=P5.50=Earth-Midway=5 May = Gaia.
Vellum=9,500=10,000=1,000=100%=10.0=Physicality=Tech.=10 Oct.=Uranus=P=1Ø.
Velocity=11,000=11%=P1.10D=1.1=Idea=Brainchild=Inv.=11 Nov.=SC=Athena>>I=MT.
Valor=4,500=5,000=50%=P5.00D=Law=Time=Venus=5 May = Aphrodite>>L=N.
Velum=6,500=7,000=70%=P7.0D=7.0=Language=Assets=Mars=7 July=Pleiades.
Velvet=10,000=1,000=100%=10.0=Physicality=Tech.=10 Oct.=Uranus=P=1Ø.
Velveteen=3,000=30%=P3.0D=3.0=Creativity=Stars=Muses=3 March = C=I>>GIL.
Ven.=1,000=100%=10.0=1.0=Mind=Sun=1 January=Helios >> M=E4.
Vena cava=9,500=10,000=1,000=100%=10.0=Physicality=Tech.=10 Oct.=Uranus=P=1Ø.
Venal=6,000=60%=P6.0D=Man=Earth=Royalty=6 June=Gaia=Maia>>M=M2.
Venation=4,500=5,000=50%=P5.00D=Law=Time=Venus=5 May = Aphrodite>>L=N.
Vend=10,000=1,000=100%=10.0=Physicality=Tech.=10 Oct.=Uranus=P=1Ø.
Venda=6,000=60%=P6.0D=Man=Earth=Royalty=6 June=Gaia=Maia>>M=M2.
Vender=4,000=40%=P4.0D=Govt.=Creatocracy=4 April=Mercury=Hermes=G=A4.
Vendetta=4,000=40%=P4.0D=Govt.=Creatocracy=4 April=Mercury=Hermes=G=A4.
Vending machine=3,500=4,000=40%=P4.0D=Govt.=4 April=Mercury=Hermes=G=A4.
Veneer=10,000=1,000=100%=10.0=Physicality=Tech.=10 Oct.=Uranus=P=1Ø.

Venerable=7,500=8,000=80%=P8.0D=Economy=Currency=8 Aug.=Zeus>>E=v.
Venerate=4,500=5,000=50%=P5.00D=Law=Time=Venus=5 May = Aphrodite>>L=N.
Venereal=5,000=50%=P5.00D=Law=Time=Venus=5 May = Aphrodite>>L=N.
Venereal disease=6,000=60%=P6.0D=Man=Earth=Royalty=6 June=Gaia=Maia>>M=M2.
Venetian=7,500=8,000=80%=P8.0D=Economy=Currency=8 Aug.=Zeus>>E=v.
Venezuela=7,000=70%=P7.0D=7.0=Language=Assets=Mars=7 July=Pleiades.
Vengeance=6,500=7,000=70%=P7.0D=7.0=Language=Assets=Mars=7 July=Pleiades.
Vengeful=1,500=15%=P1.50D=1.5=Authority=Solar Crown=1 May = Maia.
Venial=4,500=5,000=50%=P5.00D=Law=Time=Venus=5 May = Aphrodite>>L=N.
Venice=9,500=10,000=1,000=100%=10.0=Physicality=Tech.=10 Oct.=Uranus=P=1Ø.
Venire=8,500=9,000=90%=P9.00D=9.0=Abstraction=Gods=Saturn=9Sept.>>A=Ø.
Venireman=4,000=40%=P4.0D=Govt=4 April=Mercury=Hermes=G=A4.
Venison=5,500=5.5=80%=P5.50=Earth-Midway=5 May = Gaia.

Venom=11,000=11%=P1.10D=1.1=Idea=Brainchild=Inv.=11 Nov.=SC=Athena>>I=MT. Athena is said to have snakes on her hair. She is synchronous with the wisdom and cunning of a snake. She also holds in her hand a shield that has the snake head of Medusa. All these are venom. Yet she is known to fight with her brain more than arms. An intellectual war. Hence intellectual war that results to a brainchild is greater weapon than violence.

Venomous=5,000=50%=P5.00D=Law=Time=Venus=5 May = Aphrodite>>L=N.
Venous=5,500=5.5=80%=P5.50=Earth-Midway=5 May = Gaia.
Vent1=10,000=1,000=100%=10.0=Physicality=Tech.=10 Oct.=Uranus=P=1Ø.
Vent2=6,500=7,000=70%=P7.0D=7.0=Language=Assets=Mars=7 July=Pleiades.
Ventilate=10,000=1,000=100%=10.0=Physicality=Tech.=10 Oct.=Uranus=P=1Ø.
Ventral=10,000=1,000=100%=10.0=Physicality=Tech.=10 Oct.=Uranus=P=1Ø.
Ventricle=10,000=1,000=100%=10.0=Physicality=Tech.=10 Oct.=Uranus=P=1Ø.
Ventriloquism=10,000=1,000=100%=10.0=Physicality=Tech.=10 Oct.=Uranus=P=1Ø.
Ventura=6,500=7,000=70%=P7.0D=7.0=Language=Assets=Mars=7 July=Pleiades.
Venture=10,000=1,000=100%=10.0=Physicality=Tech.=10 Oct.=Uranus=P=1Ø.
Venturesome=5,500=5.5=80%=P5.50=Earth-Midway=5 May = Gaia.
Venturous=1,000=100%=10.0=1.0=Mind=Sun=1 January=Helios >> M=E4.
Venue=10,000=1,000=100%=10.0=Physicality=Tech.=10 Oct.=Uranus=P=1Ø.

Venus=10,000=1,000=100%=10.0=Physicality=Tech.=10 Oct.=Uranus=P=1Ø.
Roman Myth. The Goddess of love and beauty. In Greek myth she is the equivalent Aphrodite. The Bible in Revelations 2:22-25 refers to her as the Morning Star. The Creatocracy recognizes her as the Goddess of Law Time and Rewards in the 5th dimension.

Venus's flytrap=7,500=8,000=80%=P8.0D=Economy=Currency=8 Aug.=Zeus>>E=v.
Ver.=1,000=100%=10.0=1.0=Mind=Sun=1 January=Helios >> M=E4.
Veracious=3,000=30%=P3.0D=3.0=Creativity=Stars=Muses=3 March = C=I>>GIL.
Veracity=10,000=1,000=100%=10.0=Physicality=Tech.=10 Oct.=Uranus=P=1Ø.

Veracruz=6,500=7,000=70%=P7.0D=7.0=Language=Assets=Mars=7 July=Pleiades.

Veranda=7,000=70%=P7.0D=7.0=Language=Assets=Mars=7 July=Pleiades.

Verb=8,500=9,000=90%=P9.00D=9.0=Abstraction=Gods=Saturn=9Sept.>>A=Ø.

Verbal=10,000=1,000=100%=10.0=Physicality=Tech.=10 Oct.=Uranus=P=1Ø.

Verbalize=5,500=5.5=80%=P5.50=Earth-Midway=5 May = Gaia.

Verbatim=4,000=40%=P4.0D=Govt.=Creatocracy=4 April=Mercury=Hermes=G=A4.

Verbena=7,500=8,000=80%=P8.0D=Economy=Currency=8 Aug.=Zeus>>E=v.

Verbiage=6,500=7,000=70%=P7.0D=7.0=Language=Assets=Mars=7 July=Pleiades.

Verbose=7,000=70%=P7.0D=7.0=Language=Assets=Mars=7 July=Pleiades.

Verboten=1,500=15%=P1.50D=1.5=Authority=Solar Crown=1 May = Maia.

Verdant=4,500=5,000=50%=P5.00D=Law=Time=Venus=5 May = Aphrodite>>L=N.

Verde Cape=7,000=70%=P7.0D=7.0=Language=Assets=Mars=7 July=Pleiades.

Verdi Giuseppe=2,000=20%=P2.00D=2.0=Nature=Matter=Moon=2 Feb.=Cupid=N=C+_

Verdict=5,500=5.5=80%=P5.50=Earth-Midway=5 May = Gaia.

Verdigris=11,000=11%=P1.10D=1.1=Idea=Brainchild=Inv.=11 Nov.=SC=Athena>>I=MT.

Verdun=9,000=90%=P9.00D=9.0=Abstraction=Gods=Saturn=9Sept.>>A=Ø.

Verdure=5,000=50%=P5.00D=Law=Time=Venus=5 May = Aphrodite>>L=N.

Verge1=10,000=1,000=100%=10.0=Physicality=Tech.=10 Oct.=Uranus=P=1Ø.

Verge2=4,500=5,000=50%=P5.00D=Law=Time=Venus=5 May = Aphrodite>>L=N.

Verger=10,000=1,000=100%=10.0=Physicality=Tech.=10 Oct.=Uranus=P=1Ø.

Vergil=1,000=100%=10.0=1.0=Mind=Sun=1 January=Helios >> M=E4.

Verify=10,000=1,000=100%=10.0=Physicality=Tech.=10 Oct.=Uranus=P=1Ø.

Verily=5,000=50%=P5.00D=Law=Time=Venus=5 May = Aphrodite>>L=N.

Verisimilitude=11,000=11%=P1.10D=1.1=Idea=Brainchild=Inv.=11 Nov.=SC=Athena>>I=MT.

Veritable=5,000=50%=P5.00D=Law=Time=Venus=5 May = Aphrodite>>L=N.

Verity=10,000=1,000=100%=10.0=Physicality=Tech.=10 Oct.=Uranus=P=1Ø.

Vermeer=2,500=3,000=30%=P3.0D=3.0=Creativity=Stars=Muses=3 March = C=I>>GIL.

Vermeil=4,000=40%=P4.0D=Govt.=Creatocracy=4 April=Mercury=Hermes=G=A4.

Vermicelli=4,500=5,000=50%=P5.00D=Law=Time=Venus=5 May = Aphrodite>>L=N.

Vermiculite=11,500=12,000=12%=P1.20D=1.2=Knowledge=Edu=12Dec.=Athena>>K=F.

Vermiform=7,500=8,000=80%=P8.0D=Economy=Currency=8 Aug.=Zeus>>E=v.

Vermiform appendix=7,500=8,000=80%=P8.0D=Economy=Currency=8 Aug.=Zeus>>E=v.

Vermifuge=6,500=7,000=70%=P7.0D=7.0=Language=Assets=Mars=7 July=Pleiades.

Vermillion=6,000=60%=P6.0D=Man=Earth=Royalty=6 June=Gaia=Maia>>M=M2.

Vermin=10,500=11,000=11%=P1.10D=1.1=Idea=Brainchild=Inv.=11 Nov.=Athena>>I=MT.

Vermont=6,500=7,000=70%=P7.0D=7.0=Language=Assets=Mars=7 July=Pleiades.

Vermouth=5,500=7,000=70%=P7.0D=7.0=Language=Assets=Mars=7 July=Pleiades.

Vernacular=10,000=1,000=100%=10.0=Physicality=Tech.=10 Oct.=Uranus=P=1Ø.

Vernal=4,000=40%=P4.0D=Govt.=Creatocracy=4 April=Mercury=Hermes=G=A4.

Verne Jules.=2,000=20%=P2.00D=2.0=Nature=Matter=Moon=2 Feb.=Cupid=N=C+_

Vernier=11,000=11%=P1.10D=1.1=Idea=Brainchild=Inv.=11 Nov.=SC=Athena>>I=MT.

Vernier caliper=5,000=50%=P5.00D=Law=Time=Venus=5 May = Aphrodite>>L=N.

Verona=5,500=5.5=80%=P5.50=Earth-Midway=5 May = Gaia.

Veronese Paolo.=2,000=20%=P2.00D=2.0=Nature=Matter=Moon=2 Feb.=Cupid=N=C+_

Varazano Giovanni da.=2,500=3,000=30%=P3.0D=3.0=Cre=Stars=Muses=3 March=C=I

Versailles=7,500=8,000=80%=P8.0D=Economy=Currency=8 Aug.=Zeus>>E=v.
Versatile=10,000=1,000=100%=10.0=Physicality=Tech.=10 Oct.=Uranus=P=1Ø.

Verse=10,000=1,000=100%=10.0=Physicality=Tech.=10 Oct.=Uranus=P=1Ø.
The verses of the Scriptures make it a technology hence it requires being quantized based on the 10,000 standards. The Bible was inspired by Athena the Spirit of GOD who moved studied and measured the Earth when it was yet null and void. She is the same personified as wisdom in the Proverbs. Based on the Quantum mechanics of the Creative Sciences it is established that the Spirit of GOD inspired the Bible, Men wrote it but Peter Matthews-Akukalia invented it and thereby apotheosized as Castle Makupedia the God of Creatocracy Genius and Mind. All scriptures irrespective of religion is subject to the law of quantum through which Mind Computing, psycho-forensic programming, auditing and data analytics were invented by him to determine the deeper meaning precise facts and truths. Once employed religion becomes upgraded to faith from speculation to precision. King David who himself was an inventor versed in the mystery of things in the psalms gave this clue as 10,000 falling at thy right hand and 1,000 at the other side but none of them hurting you. The only thing in the law of abstraction that does not hurt is the alphanumerics consisting the alphabets, numbers and symbols and now the makabets. All verses are subject to the law of the 10,000=1,000=100=10 systems and are payed services offered by Makupedia.

Versed=2,000=20%=P2.00D=2.0=Nature=Matter=Moon=2 Feb.=Cupid=N=C+_
Versify=4,500=5,000=50%=P5.00D=Law=Time=Venus=5 May = Aphrodite>>L=N.

Version=10,000=1,000=100%=10.0=Physicality=Tech.=10 Oct.=Uranus=P=1Ø.
The Castle Makupedia Wit Bible is the Mind Temple Computed Version of the Holy Bible. If allowed by the Islamic authorities on contract the same will be applied to the Holy Quran.

Vers liber=1,500=15%=P1.50D=1.5=Authority=Solar Crown=1 May = Maia.
Verso=5,500=5.5=80%=P5.50=Earth-Midway=5 May = Gaia.
Versus=7,000=70%=P7.0D=7.0=Language=Assets=Mars=7 July=Pleiades.
Vert.=500=5%=P5.00D=5.0=Law=Time=Venus=5 May=Aphrodite>>L=N.
Vertebra=5,500=5.5=80%=P5.50=Earth-Midway=5 May = Gaia.
Vertebrate=10,000=1,000=100%=10.0=Physicality=Tech.=10 Oct.=Uranus=P=1Ø.
Vertex=10,000=1,000=100%=10.0=Physicality=Tech.=10 Oct.=Uranus=P=1Ø.
Vertical=10,000=1,000=100%=10.0=Physicality=Tech.=10 Oct.=Uranus=P=1Ø.
Vertiginous=10,000=1,000=100%=10.0=Physicality=Tech.=10 Oct.=Uranus=P=1Ø.
Vertigo=3,500=4,000=40%=P4.0D=Govt.=Creatocracy=4 April=Mercury=Hermes=G=A4.
Vervain=3,000=30%=P3.0D=3.0=Creativity=Stars=Muses=3 March = C=I>>GIL.
Verve=9,000=90%=P9.00D=9.0=Abstraction=Gods=Saturn=9Sept.>>A=Ø.
Very=10,000=1,000=100%=10.0=Physicality=Tech.=10 Oct.=Uranus=P=1Ø.
Very high frequency=5,000=50%=P5.00D=Law=Time=Venus=5 May = Aphrodite>>L=N.

Very low frequency=5,000=50%=P5.00D=Law=Time=Venus=5 May = Aphrodite>>L=N.
Vesicant=4,500=5,000=50%=P5.00D=Law=Time=Venus=5 May = Aphrodite>>L=N.
Vesicle=5,000=50%=P5.00D=Law=Time=Venus=5 May = Aphrodite>>L=N.
Vespasian=3,500=4,000=40%=P4.0D=Govt.=4 April=Mercury=Hermes=G=A4.
Vesper=6,000=60%=P6.0D=Man=Earth=Royalty=6 June=Gaia=Maia>>M=M2.
Vespers=6,500=7,000=70%=P7.0D=7.0=Language=Assets=Mars=7 July=Pleiades.
Vespertine=10,000=1,000=100%=10.0=Physicality=Tech.=10 Oct.=Uranus=P=1Ø.
Vespucci Amerigo=2,000=20%=P2.00D=2.0=Nature=Matter=Moon=2 Feb.=Cupid=N=C+_
Vessel=10,000=1,000=100%=10.0=Physicality=Tech.=10 Oct.=Uranus=P=1Ø.
Vest=10,000=1,000=100%=10.0=Physicality=Tech.=10 Oct.=Uranus=P=1Ø.

Vesta=3,000=30%=P3.0D=3.0=Creativity=Stars=Muses=3 March = C=I>>GIL.
Roman Myth. The Goddess of hearth. A hearth is a kitchen. It means that foods are muses.

Vestal=4,000=40%=P4.0D=Govt.=Creatocracy=4 April=Mercury=Hermes=G=A4.
Vested interest=10,000=1,000=100%=10.0=Physicality=Tech.=10 Oct.=Uranus=P=1Ø.
Vestibule=10,000=1,000=100%=10.0=Physicality=Tech.=10 Oct.=Uranus=P=1Ø.
Vestige=10,000=1,000=100%=10.0=Physicality=Tech.=10 Oct.=Uranus=P=1Ø.
Vestigial=10,000=1,000=100%=10.0=Physicality=Tech.=10 Oct.=Uranus=P=1Ø.
Vestment=10,000=1,000=100%=10.0=Physicality=Tech.=10 Oct.=Uranus=P=1Ø.
Vest pocket=500=5%=P5.00D=5.0=Law=Time=Venus=5 May=Aphrodite>>L=N.
Vestry=10,000=1,000=100%=10.0=Physicality=Tech.=10 Oct.=Uranus=P=1Ø.
Vestryman=2,000=20%=P2.00D=2.0=Nature=Matter=Moon=2 Feb.=Cupid=N=C+_
Vesture=4,500=5,000=50%=P5.00D=Law=Time=Venus=5 May = Aphrodite>>L=N.
Vesuvius Mount.=10,000=1,000=100%=10.0=Physicality=Tech.=10 Oct.=Uranus=P=1Ø.
Vet1=1,500=15%=P1.50D=1.5=Authority=Solar Crown=1 May = Maia.
Vet2=1,500=15%=P1.50D=1.5=Authority=Solar Crown=1 May = Maia.
Vetch=7,500=8,000=80%=P8.0D=Economy=Currency=8 Aug.=Zeus>>E=v.
Veteran=10,000=1,000=100%=10.0=Physicality=Tech.=10 Oct.=Uranus=P=1Ø.
Veterans Day=10,000=1,000=100%=10.0=Physicality=Tech.=10 Oct.=Uranus=P=1Ø.
Veterinarian=3,000=30%=P3.0D=3.0=Creativity=Stars=Muses=3 March = C=I>>GIL.
Veterinary=6,000=60%=P6.0D=Man=Earth=Royalty=6 June=Gaia=Maia>>M=M2.

Veto=10,000=1,000=100%=10.0=Physicality=Tech.=10 Oct.=Uranus=P=1Ø.
The veto right is the 10,000[th] right vested on whoever has invented a government system.
Invention means the creation of the processes and systems by which precision is established
and results are achieved in a specified time. Castle Makupedia invented the Creatocracy
and so has the veto right in royalty media government and labour the quartet compass
arms of the Creatocracy and wears the solar crown of sovereignty in all things.

Vex=6,000=60%=P6.0D=Man=Earth=Royalty=6 June=Gaia=Maia>>M=M2.
Vexation=4,500=5,000=50%=P5.00D=Law=Time=Venus=5 May = Aphrodite>>L=N.
V.F.=2,000=20%=P2.00D=2.0=Nature=Matter=Moon=2 Feb.=Cupid=N=C+_

VFW=2,000=20%=P2.00D=2.0=Nature=Matter=Moon=2 Feb.=Cupid=N=C+_
vhf=1,500=15%=P1.50D=1.5=Authority=Solar Crown=1 May = Maia.
VI=1,000=100%=10.0=1.0=Mind=Sun=1 January=Helios >> M=E4.
Via=3,000=30%=P3.0D=3.0=Creativity=Stars=Muses=3 March = C=I>>GIL.
Viable=10,000=1,000=100%=10.0=Physicality=Tech.=10 Oct.=Uranus=P=1Ø.
Viaduct=11,500=12,000=12%=P1.20D=1.2=Knowledge=Edu=12Dec.=Athena>>K=F.
Vial=4,000=40%=P4.0D=Govt.=Creatocracy=4 April=Mercury=Hermes=G=A4.
Vi and=6,000=60%=P6.0D=Man=Earth=Royalty=6 June=Gaia=Maia>>M=M2.
Viaticum=8,500=9,000=90%=P9.00D=9.0=Abstraction=Gods=Saturn=9Sept.>>A=Ø.
Vibes=2,000=20%=P2.00D=2.0=Nature=Matter=Moon=2 Feb.=Cupid=N=C+_
Vibrant=5,500=5.5=80%=P5.50=Earth-Midway=5 May = Gaia.
Vibraphone=10,000=1,000=100%=10.0=Physicality=Tech.=10 Oct.=Uranus=P=1Ø.
Vibrate=10,000=1,000=100%=10.0=Physicality=Tech.=10 Oct.=Uranus=P=1Ø.
Vibration=10,000=1,000=100%=10.0=Physicality=Tech.=10 Oct.=Uranus=P=1Ø.
Vibrato=10,000=1,000=100%=10.0=Physicality=Tech.=10 Oct.=Uranus=P=1Ø.
Viburnum=10,000=1,000=100%=10.0=Physicality=Tech.=10 Oct.=Uranus=P=1Ø.
Vic.=1,000=100%=10.0=1.0=Mind=Sun=1 January=Helios >> M=E4.
Vicar=10,000=1,000=100%=10.0=Physicality=Tech.=10 Oct.=Uranus=P=1Ø.
Vicarage=10,000=1,000=100%=10.0=Physicality=Tech.=10 Oct.=Uranus=P=1Ø.
Vicarious=10,000=1,000=100%=10.0=Physicality=Tech.=10 Oct.=Uranus=P=1Ø.
Vice1=10,000=1,000=100%=10.0=Physicality=Tech.=10 Oct.=Uranus=P=1Ø.
Vice2=1,500=15%=P1.50D=1.5=Authority=Solar Crown=1 May = Maia.
Vice3=7,500=8,000=80%=P8.0D=Economy=Currency=8 Aug.=Zeus>>E=v.
Vice admiral=6,500=7,000=70%=P7.0D=7.0=Language=Assets=Mars=7 July=Pleiades.

Vice President=10,000=1,000=100%=10.0=Physicality=Tech.=10 Oct.=Uranus=P=1Ø.
Presidents and Vice Presidents have 10,000th veto right in the Government. It is the 3rd
compass arm of the Creatocracy after royalty and media.

Vice regal=1,500=15%=P1.50D=1.5=Authority=Solar Crown=1 May = Maia.

Vice roy=6,000=60%=P6.0D=Man=Earth=Royalty=6 June=Gaia=Maia>>M=M2.
The Governor of a country, province, or colony, ruling as the representative of a sovereign. In
the Creatocracy the departments are so huge that they are considered states. An example is
the Mind Bank Vice Roy who is the Governor of the Creatocracy Bank. Read administration
of the Creatocracy Corporation Bank at opening pages of Castle Makupedia.

Vice versa=7,000=70%=P7.0D=7.0=Language=Assets=Mars=7 July=Pleiades.
Vichy=4,500=5,000=50%=P5.00D=Law=Time=Venus=5 May = Aphrodite>>L=N.
Vichyssoise=7,500=8,000=80%=P8.0D=Economy=Currency=8 Aug.=Zeus>>E=v.
Vicinity=10,000=1,000=100%=10.0=Physicality=Tech.=10 Oct.=Uranus=P=1Ø.
Vicious=10,000=1,000=100%=10.0=Physicality=Tech.=10 Oct.=Uranus=P=1Ø.
Vicissitude=10,000=1,000=100%=10.0=Physicality=Tech.=10 Oct.=Uranus=P=1Ø.

Victim=10,000=1,000=100%=10.0=Physicality=Tech.=10 Oct.=Uranus=P=1Ø.
Victimize=2,500=3,000=30%=P3.0D=3.0=Creativity=Stars=Muses=3 March = C=I>>GIL.
Victimless crime=3,500=4,000=40%=P4.0D=Govt.=4 April=Mercury=Hermes=G=A4.
Victor=5,000=50%=P5.00D=Law=Time=Venus=5 May = Aphrodite>>L=N.

Victor Emmanuel I.=3,000=30%=P3.0D=3.0=Crea=Stars=Muses=3 March =C=I>>GIL.
1759-1824. Sardinian King (1802-21). In the Creatocracy, First Child Son and Most Senior
Heir of Peter and Tina Matthews-Akukalia ranked as the Head Prince and Demi-God.

Victor Emmanuel II.=2,500=3,000=30%=P3.0D=3.0=Crea=Stars=Muses=3March=CI>GIL.
Victoria=9,500=10,000=1,000=100%=10.0=Physicality=Tech.=10 Oct.=Uranus=P=1Ø.

Victoria1=7,000=70%=P7.0D=7.0=Language=Assets=Mars=7 July=Pleiades.
The immediate younger sister of Peter Matthews-Akukalia, Castle Makupedia. Uncrowned.

Victoria2=10,000=1,000=100%=10.0=Physicality=Tech.=10 Oct.=Uranus=P=1Ø.
Victoria,Lake=5,500=5.5=80%=P5.50=Earth-Midway=5 May = Gaia.
Victoria Falls.=10,000=1,000=100%=10.0=Physicality=Tech.=10 Oct.=Uranus=P=1Ø.

Victoria Island=7,500=8,000=80%=P8.0D=Economy=Currency=8 Aug.=Zeus>>E=v.
An island of N-central Northwest Terrs., Canada, in the Arctic Archipelago E of Banks
I. Also Victoria Island, the other side of the Mainland Lagos. Nigeria.

Victoria Land=5,500=5.5=80%=P5.50=Earth-Midway=5 May = Gaia.
Victorian=10,000=1,000=100%=10.0=Physicality=Tech.=10 Oct.=Uranus=P=1Ø.
Victorious=6,500=7,000=70%=P7.0D=7.0=Language=Assets=Mars=7 July=Pleiades.
Victory=6,500=7,000=70%=P7.0D=7.0=Language=Assets=Mars=7 July=Pleiades.
Victual=10,000=1,000=100%=10.0=Physicality=Tech.=10 Oct.=Uranus=P=1Ø.
Vicūna=10,000=1,000=100%=10.0=Physicality=Tech.=10 Oct.=Uranus=P=1Ø.
Vide=7,000=70%=P7.0D=7.0=Language=Assets=Mars=7 July=Pleiades.
Videlicet=6,000=60%=P6.0D=Man=Earth=Royalty=6 June=Gaia=Maia>>M=M2.
Video=10,000=1,000=100%=10.0=Physicality=Tech.=10 Oct.=Uranus=P=1Ø.
Video camera=7,000=70%=P7.0D=7.0=Language=Assets=Mars=7 July=Pleiades.
Video cassette=3,500=4,000=40%=P4.0D=Govt.=4 April=Mercury=Hermes=G=A4.
Videocassette recorder=1,000=100%=10.0=1.0=Mind=Sun=1 January=Helios >> M=E4.
Videodisk=10,000=1,000=100%=10.0=Physicality=Tech.=10 Oct.=Uranus=P=1Ø.
Video display terminal=1,000=100%=10.0=1.0=Mind=Sun=1 January=Helios >> M=E4.
Video game=5,500=5.5=80%=P5.50=Earth-Midway=5 May = Gaia.
Videotape=7,500=8,000=80%=P8.0D=Economy=Currency=8 Aug.=Zeus>>E=v.
Vie=4,000=40%=P4.0D=Govt.=Creatocracy=4 April=Mercury=Hermes=G=A4.
Vienna=6,000=60%=P6.0D=Man=Earth=Royalty=6 June=Gaia=Maia>>M=M2.
Vientiane=7,500=8,000=80%=P8.0D=Economy=Currency=8 Aug.=Zeus>>E=v.

Viet.=1,000=100%=10.0=1.0=Mind=Sun=1 January=Helios >> M=E4.
Vietcong=10,000=1,000=100%=10.0=Physicality=Tech.=10 Oct.=Uranus=P=1Ø.
Vietnam=10,000=1,000=100%=10.0=Physicality=Tech.=10 Oct.=Uranus=P=1Ø.
Vietnamese=4,000=40%=P4.0D=Govt.=Creatocracy=4 April=Mercury=Hermes=G=A4.
View=10,000=1,000=100%=10.0=Physicality=Tech.=10 Oct.=Uranus=P=1Ø.
Viewfinder=7,500=8,000=80%=P8.0D=Economy=Currency=8 Aug.=Zeus>>E=v.
Viewpoint=2,000=20%=P2.00D=2.0=Nature=Matter=Moon=2 Feb.=Cupid=N=C+_
Vigil=10,000=1,000=100%=10.0=Physicality=Tech.=10 Oct.=Uranus=P=1Ø.
Vigilance=1,000=100%=10.0=1.0=Mind=Sun=1 January=Helios >> M=E4.
Vigilant=2,000=20%=P2.00D=2.0=Nature=Matter=Moon=2 Feb.=Cupid=N=C+_
Vigilante=7,500=8,000=80%=P8.0D=Economy=Currency=8 Aug.=Zeus>>E=v.
Vignette=10,000=1,000=100%=10.0=Physicality=Tech.=10 Oct.=Uranus=P=1Ø.
Vigor=10,000=1,000=100%=10.0=Physicality=Tech.=10 Oct.=Uranus=P=1Ø.
Vigorous=3,500=4,000=40%=P4.0D=Govt.=4 April=Mercury=Hermes=G=A4.
Vigor=10,000=1,000=100%=10.0=Physicality=Tech.=10 Oct.=Uranus=P=1Ø.
Viking=9,500=10,000=1,000=100%=10.0=Physicality=Tech.=10 Oct.=Uranus=P=1Ø.
Vila=6,000=60%=P6.0D=Man=Earth=Royalty=6 June=Gaia=Maia>>M=M2.
Vile=6,500=7,000=70%=P7.0D=7.0=Language=Assets=Mars=7 July=Pleiades.
Vilify=3,500=4,000=40%=P4.0D=Govt.=Creatocracy=4 April=Mercury=Hermes=G=A4.
villa=7,500=8,000=80%=P8.0D=Economy=Currency=8 Aug.=Zeus>>E=v.
Villa Francesco=3,500=4,000=40%=P4.0D=Govt.=Creatocracy=4 April=Hermes=G=A4.
Village=10,000=1,000=100%=10.0=Physicality=Tech.=10 Oct.=Uranus=P=1Ø.
Villain=7,000=70%=P7.0D=7.0=Language=Assets=Mars=7 July=Pleiades.
Villainous=3,000=30%=P3.0D=3.0=Creativity=Stars=Muses=3 March = C=I>>GIL.
Villainy=5,500=5.5=80%=P5.50=Earth-Midway=5 May = Gaia.
Villein=11,500=12,000=12%=P1.20D=1.2=Knowledge=Edu=12Dec.=Athena>>K=F.
Villon François=2,500=3,000=30%=P3.0D=3.0=Cre=Stars=Muses=3March=C=I>>GIL.
Vilnius=5,500=5.5=80%=P5.50=Earth-Midway=5 May = Gaia.
Vim=6,000=60%=P6.0D=Man=Earth=Royalty=6 June=Gaia=Maia>>M=M2.
Vinaigrette=10,000=1,000=100%=10.0=Physicality=Tech.=10 Oct.=Uranus=P=1Ø.
Vincent de Paul=2,500=3,000=30%=P3.0D=3.0=Cre=Stars=Muses=3 March = C=I>>GIL.
Vincible=3,500=4,000=40%=P4.0D=Govt.=Creatocracy=4 April=Mercury=Hermes=G=A4.
Vindicate=10,000=1,000=100%=10.0=Physicality=Tech.=10 Oct.=Uranus=P=1Ø.
Vindictive=7,000=70%=P7.0D=7.0=Language=Assets=Mars=7 July=Pleiades.
Vine=10,000=1,000=100%=10.0=Physicality=Tech.=10 Oct.=Uranus=P=1Ø.
Vinegar=10,000=1,000=100%=10.0=Physicality=Tech.=10 Oct.=Uranus=P=1Ø.
Vinegary=4,000=40%=P4.0D=Govt.=Creatocracy=4 April=Mercury=Hermes=G=A4.
Vineyard=2,500=3,000=30%=P3.0D=3.0=Creativity=Stars=Muses=3 March = C=I>>GIL.
Viniculture=3,000=30%=P3.0D=3.0=Creativity=Stars=Muses=3 March = C=I>>GIL.
Vinland=8,500=9,000=90%=P9.00D=9.0=Abstraction=Gods=Saturn=9Sept.>>A=Ø.
Vinson Massif=4,500=5,000=50%=P5.00D=Law=Time=Venus=5 May = Aphrodite>>L=N.
Vintage=10,000=1,000=100%=10.0=Physicality=Tech.=10 Oct.=Uranus=P=1Ø.
Vintner=3,000=30%=P3.0D=3.0=Creativity=Stars=Muses=3 March = C=I>>GIL.
Vinyl=9,500=10,000=1,000=100%=10.0=Physicality=Tech.=10 Oct.=Uranus=P=1Ø.
Viol=10,000=1,000=100%=10.0=Physicality=Tech.=10 Oct.=Uranus=P=1Ø.

Viola=10,000=1,000=100%=10.0=Physicality=Tech.=10 Oct.=Uranus=P=1Ø.
Violable=2,000=20%=P2.00D=2.0=Nature=Matter=Moon=2 Feb.=Cupid=N=C+_
Violate=10,000=1,000=100%=10.0=Physicality=Tech.=10 Oct.=Uranus=P=1Ø.
Violation=5,000=50%=P5.00D=Law=Time=Venus=5 May = Aphrodite>>L=N.
Violence=10,000=1,000=100%=10.0=Physicality=Tech.=10 Oct.=Uranus=P=1Ø.
Violent=10,000=1,000=100%=10.0=Physicality=Tech.=10 Oct.=Uranus=P=1Ø.
Violet=10,000=1,000=100%=10.0=Physicality=Tech.=10 Oct.=Uranus=P=1Ø.
Violin=10,000=1,000=100%=10.0=Physicality=Tech.=10 Oct.=Uranus=P=1Ø.
Violoncello=1,500=15%=P1.50D=1.5=Authority=Solar Crown=1 May = Maia.
VIP=3,000=30%=P3.0D=3.0=Creativity=Stars=Muses=3 March = C=I>>GIL.
Viper=10,000=1,000=100%=10.0=Physicality=Tech.=10 Oct.=Uranus=P=1Ø.
Virago=5,000=50%=P5.00D=Law=Time=Venus=5 May = Aphrodite>>L=N.
Viral=3,000=30%=P3.0D=3.0=Creativity=Stars=Muses=3 March = C=I>>GIL.
Vireo=7,500=8,000=80%=P8.0D=Economy=Currency=8 Aug.=Zeus>>E=v.
Virgil=2,500=3,000=30%=P3.0D=3.0=Creativity=Stars=Muses=3 March = C=I>>GIL.
Virgin=10,000=1,000=100%=10.0=Physicality=Tech.=10 Oct.=Uranus=P=1Ø.
Virginal1=4,000=40%=P4.0D=Govt.=Creatocracy=4 April=Mercury=Hermes=G=A4.
Virginal2=6,000=60%=P6.0D=Man=Earth=Royalty=6 June=Gaia=Maia>>M=M2.
Virginia=7,500=8,000=80%=P8.0D=Economy=Currency=8 Aug.=Zeus>>E=v.
Virginia Beach.=6,500=7,000=70%=P7.0D=7.0=Language=Assets=Mars=7 July=Pleiades.
Virginia Creeper=7,500=8,000=80%=P8.0D=Economy=Currency=8 Aug.=Zeus>>E=v.
Virginia reel=8,500=9,000=90%=P9.00D=9.0=Abstraction=Gods=Saturn=9Sept.>>A=Ø.
Virginia Islands.=10,000=1,000=100%=10.0=Physicality=Tech.=10 Oct.=Uranus=P=1Ø.
Virgo=7,500=8,000=80%=P8.0D=Economy=Currency=8 Aug.=Zeus>>E=v.
Virgule=11,000=11%=P1.10D=1.1=Idea=Brainchild=Inv.=11 Nov.=SC=Athena>>I=MT.
Virile=10,000=1,000=100%=10.0=Physicality=Tech.=10 Oct.=Uranus=P=1Ø.
Virology=3,500=4,000=40%=P4.0D=Govt.=Creatocracy=4 April=Mercury=Hermes=G=A4.
Virtual=8,500=9,000=90%=P9.00D=9.0=Abstraction=Gods=Saturn=9Sept.>>A=Ø.
Virtually=3,500=4,000=40%=P4.0D=Govt.=Creatocracy=4April=Mercury=Hermes=G=A4.
Virtue=10,000=1,000=100%=10.0=Physicality=Tech.=10 Oct.=Uranus=P=1Ø.
Virtuosity=4,500=5,000=50%=P5.00D=Law=Time=Venus=5 May = Aphrodite>>L=N.
Virtuoso=10,000=1,000=100%=10.0=Physicality=Tech.=10 Oct.=Uranus=P=1Ø.
Virtuous=4,500=5,000=50%=P5.00D=Law=Time=Venus=5 May = Aphrodite>>L=N.
Virulent=10,000=1,000=100%=10.0=Physicality=Tech.=10 Oct.=Uranus=P=1Ø.
Virus=10,000=1,000=100%=10.0=Physicality=Tech.=10 Oct.=Uranus=P=1Ø.
vis.=1,000=100%=10.0=1.0=Mind=Sun=1 January=Helios >> M=E4.
Vis.=500=5%=P5.00D=5.0=Law=Time=Venus=5 May=Aphrodite>>L=N.
Visa=10,000=1,000=100%=10.0=Physicality=Tech.=10 Oct.=Uranus=P=1Ø.
Visage=10,000=1,000=100%=10.0=Physicality=Tech.=10 Oct.=Uranus=P=1Ø.
Vis-à-vis=10,000=1,000=100%=10.0=Physicality=Tech.=10 Oct.=Uranus=P=1Ø.
Visayan Islands=7,500=8,000=80%=P8.0D=Economy=Currency=8 Aug.=Zeus>>E=v.
Viscera=7,500=8,000=80%=P8.0D=Economy=Currency=8 Aug.=Zeus>>E=v.
Visceral=5,000=50%=P5.00D=Law=Time=Venus=5 May = Aphrodite>>L=N.
Viscid=4,500=5,000=50%=P5.00D=Law=Time=Venus=5 May = Aphrodite>>L=N.
Viscose=10,000=1,000=100%=10.0=Physicality=Tech.=10 Oct.=Uranus=P=1Ø.

Viscosity=3,500=4,000=40%=P4.0D=Govt.=4 April=Mercury=Hermes=G=A4.
Viscount=7,000=70%=P7.0D=7.0=Language=Assets=Mars=7 July=Pleiades.
Viscous=5,000=50%=P5.00D=Law=Time=Venus=5 May = Aphrodite>>L=N.
Vise=10,000=1,000=100%=10.0=Physicality=Tech.=10 Oct.=Uranus=P=1Ø.
Vishnu=7,500=8,000=80%=P8.0D=Economy=Currency=8 Aug.=Zeus>>E=v.
Visibility=10,000=1,000=100%=10.0=Physicality=Tech.=10 Oct.=Uranus=P=1Ø.
Visible=5,500=5.5=80%=P5.50=Earth-Midway=5 May = Gaia.
Visigoth=10,000=1,000=100%=10.0=Physicality=Tech.=10 Oct.=Uranus=P=1Ø.
Vision=10,000=1,000=100%=10.0=Physicality=Tech.=10 Oct.=Uranus=P=1Ø.
Visionary=10,000=1,000=100%=10.0=Physicality=Tech.=10 Oct.=Uranus=P=1Ø.
Visit=10,000=1,000=100%=10.0=Physicality=Tech.=10 Oct.=Uranus=P=1Ø.
Visitant=1,500=15%=P1.50D=1.5=Authority=Solar Crown=1 May = Maia.
Visitation=10,000=1,000=100%=10.0=Physicality=Tech.=10 Oct.=Uranus=P=1Ø.
Visitor=1,500=15%=P1.50D=1.5=Authority=Solar Crown=1 May = Maia.
Visor=10,000=1,000=100%=10.0=Physicality=Tech.=10 Oct.=Uranus=P=1Ø.
Vista=10,000=1,000=100%=10.0=Physicality=Tech.=10 Oct.=Uranus=P=1Ø.
VISTA=2,500=3,000=30%=P3.0D=3.0=Creativity=Stars=Muses=3 March = C=I>>GIL.
Vistula=10,000=1,000=100%=10.0=Physicality=Tech.=10 Oct.=Uranus=P=1Ø.
Visual=10,000=1,000=100%=10.0=Physicality=Tech.=10 Oct.=Uranus=P=1Ø.
Visualize=4,000=40%=P4.0D=Govt.=Creatocracy=4 April=Mercury=Hermes=G=A4.
Vita=6,500=7,000=70%=P7.0D=7.0=Language=Assets=Mars=7 July=Pleiades.
Vital=9,000=90%=P9.00D=9.0=Abstraction=Gods=Saturn=9Sept.>>A=Ø.
Vitality=10,000=1,000=100%=10.0=Physicality=Tech.=10 Oct.=Uranus=P=1Ø.
Vitalize=3,500=4,000=40%=P4.0D=Govt.=Creatocracy=4 April=Mercury=Hermes=G=A4.
Vitals=5,000=50%=P5.00D=Law=Time=Venus=5 May = Aphrodite>>L=N.
Vital signs=4,500=5,000=50%=P5.00D=Law=Time=Venus=5 May = Aphrodite>>L=N.
Vital statistics=3,500=4,000=40%=P4.0D=Govt.=Creatocracy=4 April=Hermes=G=A4.
Vitamin=10,000=1,000=100%=10.0=Physicality=Tech.=10 Oct.=Uranus=P=1Ø.
Vitamin A=10,000=1,000=100%=10.0=Physicality=Tech.=10 Oct.=Uranus=P=1Ø.
Vitamin B=10,000=1,000=100%=10.0=Physicality=Tech.=10 Oct.=Uranus=P=1Ø.
Vitamin B1=1,000=100%=10.0=1.0=Mind=Sun=1 January=Helios >> M=E4.
Vitamin B2=1,000=100%=Physicality=Tech.=10 Oct.=Uranus=P=1Ø.
Vitamin B12=7,500=8,000=80%=P8.0D=Economy=Currency=8 Aug.=Zeus>>E=v.
Vitamin B complex=11,000=11%=P1.10D=1.1=Idea=Brainchild.=11 Nov.=Athena>>I=MT.
Vitamin C=1,500=15%=P1.50D=1.5=Authority=Solar Crown=1 May = Maia.
Vitamin D=12,000=12%=P1.20D=1.2=Knowledge=Edu=12Dec.=Athena>>K=F.
Vitamin E=13,000=13%=P1.30=Solar Core=Faculty=13 January=Athena.
Vitamin K=9,000=90%=P9.00D=9.0=Abstraction=Gods=Saturn=9Sept.>>A=Ø.
Vitebsk=4,500=5,000=50%=P5.00D=Law=Time=Venus=5 May = Aphrodite>>L=N.
Vitiate=10,000=1,000=100%=10.0=Physicality=Tech.=10 Oct.=Uranus=P=1Ø.
Viticulture=4,500=5,000=50%=P5.00D=Law=Time=Venus=5 May = Aphrodite>>L=N.
Viti Levu=4,500=5,000=50%=P5.00D=Law=Time=Venus=5 May = Aphrodite>>L=N.
Vitreous=6,000=60%=P6.0D=Man=Earth=Royalty=6 June=Gaia=Maia>>M=M2.
Vitreous humor=5,500=5.5=80%=P5.50=Earth-Midway=5 May = Gaia.
Vitrify=7,500=8,000=80%=P8.0D=Economy=Currency=8 Aug.=Zeus>>E=v.

Vitriol=7,500=8,000=80%=P8.0D=Economy=Currency=8 Aug.=Zeus>>E=v.

Vitriolic=4,000=40%=P4.0D=Govt.=Creatocracy=4 April=Mercury=Hermes=G=A4.

Vittles=2,000=20%=P2.00D=2.0=Nature=Matter=Moon=2 Feb.=Cupid=N=C+_

Vituperate=10,000=1,000=100%=10.0=Physicality=Tech.=10 Oct.=Uranus=P=1Ø.

Viva=7,500=8,000=80%=P8.0D=Economy=Currency=8 Aug.=Zeus>>E=v.

Vivace=5,500=5.5=80%=P5.50=Earth-Midway=5 May = Gaia.

Vivacious=5,500=5.5=80%=P5.50=Earth-Midway=5 May = Gaia.

Vivaldi Antonio=4,000=40%=P4.0D=Govt.=Creatocracy=4 April=Hermes=G=A4.

Vivid=10,000=1,000=100%=10.0=Physicality=Tech.=10 Oct.=Uranus=P=1Ø.

Vivify=10,000=1,000=100%=10.0=Physicality=Tech.=10 Oct.=Uranus=P=1Ø.

Viviparous=10,000=1,000=100%=10.0=Physicality=Tech.=10 Oct.=Uranus=P=1Ø.

Vivisection=10,000=1,000=100%=10.0=Physicality=Tech.=10 Oct.=Uranus=P=1Ø.

Vixen=5,000=50%=P5.00D=Law=Time=Venus=5 May = Aphrodite>>L=N.

viz.=1,500=15%=P1.50D=1.5=Authority=Solar Crown=1 May = Maia.

Vizard=1,500=15%=P1.50D=1.5=Authority=Solar Crown=1 May = Maia.

Vizier=7,500=8,000=80%=P8.0D=Economy=Currency=8 Aug.=Zeus>>E=v.

Vizor=1,500=15%=P1.50D=1.5=Authority=Solar Crown=1 May = Maia.

Vladivostok=7,000=70%=P7.0D=7.0=Language=Assets=Mars=7 July=Pleiades.

Vlaminck Maurice de.=2,000=20%=P2.00D=2.0=Nature=Moon=2 Feb.=Cupid=N=C+_

vlf=1,500=15%=P1.50D=1.5=Authority=Solar Crown=1 May = Maia.

V.M.D.=2,000=20%=P2.00D=2.0=Nature=Matter=Moon=2 Feb.=Cupid=N=C+_

Vo.=500=5%=P5.00D=5.0=Law=Time=Venus=5 May=Aphrodite>>L=N.

Vocable=8,500=9,000=90%=P9.00D=9.0=Abstraction=Gods=Saturn=9Sept.>>A=Ø.

Vocabulary=10,000=1,000=100%=10.0=Physicality=Tech.=10 Oct.=Uranus=P=1Ø.

Vocal=10,000=1,000=100%=10.0=Physicality=Tech.=10 Oct.=Uranus=P=1Ø.

Vocal cords=10,000=1,000=100%=10.0=Physicality=Tech.=10 Oct.=Uranus=P=1Ø.

Vocalic=5,000=50%=P5.00D=Law=Time=Venus=5 May = Aphrodite>>L=N.

Vocalist=1,000=100%=10.0=1.0=Mind=Sun=1 January=Helios >> M=E4.

Vocalize=6,500=7,000=70%=P7.0D=7.0=Language=Assets=Mars=7 July=Pleiades.

Vocation=9,500=10,000=1,000=100%=10.0=Physicality=Tech.=10 Oct.=Uranus=P=1Ø.

Vocational school=6,500=7,000=70%=P7.0D=7.0=Lang=Assets=Mars=7 July=Pleiades.

Vocative=6,000=60%=P6.0D=Man=Earth=Royalty=6 June=Gaia=Maia>>M=M2.

Vociferate=9,000=90%=P9.00D=9.0=Abstraction=Gods=Saturn=9Sept.>>A=Ø.

Vociferous=2,000=20%=P2.00D=2.0=Nature=Matter=Moon=2 Feb.=Cupid=N=C+_

Vodka=9,500=10,000=1,000=100%=10.0=Physicality=Tech.=10 Oct.=Uranus=P=1Ø.

Vogue=6,000=60%=P6.0D=Man=Earth=Royalty=6 June=Gaia=Maia>>M=M2.

Voice=10,000=1,000=100%=10.0=Physicality=Tech.=10 Oct.=Uranus=P=1Ø.

Voice box=1,000=100%=10.0=1.0=Mind=Sun=1 January=Helios >> M=E4.

Voiced=9,000=90%=P9.00D=9.0=Abstraction=Gods=Saturn=9Sept.>>A=Ø.

Voiceless=7,000=70%=P7.0D=7.0=Language=Assets=Mars=7 July=Pleiades.

Voice-over=7,000=70%=P7.0D=7.0=Language=Assets=Mars=7 July=Pleiades.

Voice print=4,500=5,000=50%=P5.00D=Law=Time=Venus=5 May = Aphrodite>>L=N.

Vold=10,000=1,000=100%=10.0=Physicality=Tech.=10 Oct.=Uranus=P=1Ø.

Voile=10,000=1,000=100%=10.0=Physicality=Tech.=10 Oct.=Uranus=P=1Ø.

Vol.=1,000=100%=Physicality=Tech.=10 Oct.=Uranus=P=1Ø.

Volatile=10,000=1,000=100%=10.0=Physicality=Tech.=10 Oct.=Uranus=P=1Ø.
Volatilize=4,000=40%=P4.0D=Govt.=Creatocracy=4 April=Mercury=Hermes=G=A4.
Volcanic=4,500=5,000=50%=P5.00D=Law=Time=Venus=5 May = Aphrodite>>L=N.
Volcanism=2,000=20%=P2.00D=2.0=Nature=Matter=Moon=2 Feb.=Cupid=N=C+_
Volcano=10,000=1,000=100%=10.0=Physicality=Tech.=10 Oct.=Uranus=P=1Ø.
Volcano Islands=6,500=7,000=70%=P7.0D=7.0=Language=Assets=Mars=7 July=Pleiades.
Vole=7,500=8,000=80%=P8.0D=Economy=Currency=8 Aug.=Zeus>>E=v.
Volga=9,500=10,000=1,000=100%=10.0=Physicality=Tech.=10 Oct.=Uranus=P=1Ø.
Volgograd=7,500=8,000=80%=P8.0D=Economy=Currency=8 Aug.=Zeus>>E=v.
Volition=10,500=11,000=11%=P1.10D=1.1=Idea=Brainchild=Inv.=11 Nov.=Athena>>I=MT.
Volley=10,000=1,000=100%=10.0=Physicality=Tech.=10 Oct.=Uranus=P=1Ø.
Volleyball=10,000=1,000=100%=10.0=Physicality=Tech.=10 Oct.=Uranus=P=1Ø.
Vòlos=8,000=80%=P8.0D=Economy=Currency=8 Aug.=Zeus>>E=v.
Volt=10,000=1,000=100%=10.0=Physicality=Tech.=10 Oct.=Uranus=P=1Ø.
Volta=8,500=9,000=90%=P9.00D=9.0=Abstraction=Gods=Saturn=9Sept.>>A=Ø.
Volta Alessandro=2,500=3,000=30%=P3.0D=3.0=Cr=Stars=Muses=3March=C=I>>GIL.
Voltage=4,500=5,000=50%=P5.00D=Law=Time=Venus=5 May = Aphrodite>>L=N.
Voltaic=4,000=40%=P4.0D=Govt.=Creatocracy=4 April=Mercury=Hermes=G=A4.
Voltaire=4,500=5,000=50%=P5.00D=Law=Time=Venus=5 May = Aphrodite>>L=N.
Voltmeter=4,000=40%=P4.0D=Govt.=Creatocracy=4 April=Mercury=Hermes=G=A4.
Voluble=5,000=50%=P5.00D=Law=Time=Venus=5 May = Aphrodite>>L=N.
Volume=10,000=1,000=100%=10.0=Physicality=Tech.=10 Oct.=Uranus=P=1Ø.
Volumetric=7,000=70%=P7.0D=7.0=Language=Assets=Mars=7 July=Pleiades.
Voluminous=11,500=12,000=12%=P1.20D=1.2=Knowledge=Edu=12Dec.=Athena>>K=F.
Voluntary=10,000=1,000=100%=10.0=Physicality=Tech.=10 Oct.=Uranus=P=1Ø.
Volunteer=10,000=1,000=100%=10.0=Physicality=Tech.=10 Oct.=Uranus=P=1Ø.
Volunteerism=3,000=30%=P3.0D=3.0=Creativity=Stars=Muses=3 March = C=I>>GIL.
Voluptuary=5,000=50%=P5.00D=Law=Time=Venus=5 May = Aphrodite>>L=N.
Voluptuous=10,000=1,000=100%=10.0=Physicality=Tech.=10 Oct.=Uranus=P=1Ø.
Volute=4,500=5,000=50%=P5.00D=Law=Time=Venus=5 May = Aphrodite>>L=N.
Vomit=10,000=1,000=100%=10.0=Physicality=Tech.=10 Oct.=Uranus=P=1Ø.
Voodoo=10,000=1,000=100%=10.0=Physicality=Tech.=10 Oct.=Uranus=P=1Ø.
Voracious=10,000=1,000=100%=10.0=Physicality=Tech.=10 Oct.=Uranus=P=1Ø.
Voronezh=6,500=7,000=70%=P7.0D=7.0=Language=Assets=Mars=7 July=Pleiades.
Voroshilovgrad=6,500=7,000=70%=P7.0D=7.0=Language=Assets=Mars=7 July=Pleiades.
-vorous=4,000=40%=P4.0D=Govt.=Creatocracy=4 April=Mercury=Hermes=G=A4.
Vortex=10,000=1,000=100%=10.0=Physicality=Tech.=10 Oct.=Uranus=P=1Ø.
Vosges=8,500=9,000=90%=P9.00D=9.0=Abstraction=Gods=Saturn=9Sept.>>A=Ø.
Votary=10,000=1,000=100%=10.0=Physicality=Tech.=10 Oct.=Uranus=P=1Ø.

Vote=10,000=1,000=100%=10.0=Physicality=Tech.=10 Oct.=Uranus=P=1Ø.
In a Creatocracy all voters of government must have conducted the Mind Assessment Tests. Creatocracy is a system that accommodates all government forms and gives people as individuals families or groups to believe whatever they wish to believe. This means that Creatocracy is a natural system of universal governance much higher than

mere government forms. It is higher governance and not a mere system of government. Consult the Creative Scientists of the Castle Makupedia for further classes. However it is compulsory that all citizens are assessed to help them discover develop and connect to their original purpose on earth. Hence the first need of Man is knowledge for awareness.

Votive=5,500=5.5=80%=P5.50=Earth-Midway=5 May = Gaia.
Vouch=12,000=12%=P1.20D=1.2=Knowledge=Edu=12Dec.=Athena>>K=F.
Voucher=9,000=90%=P9.00D=9.0=Abstraction=Gods=Saturn=9Sept.>>A=Ø.
Vouchsafe=5,500=5.5=80%=P5.50=Earth-Midway=5 May = Gaia.
Vow1=10,000=1,000=100%=10.0=Physicality=Tech.=10 Oct.=Uranus=P=1Ø.

Vow2=2,500=3,000=30%=P3.0D=3.0=Creativity=Stars=Muses=3 March = C=I>>GIL.
To declare or assert. A vow is a means made between the Moon and the Stars.

Vowel=10,000=1,000=100%=10.0=Physicality=Tech.=10 Oct.=Uranus=P=1Ø.
Vox populi=4,500=5,000=50%=P5.00D=Law=Time=Venus=5 May = Aphrodite>>L=N.
Voyage=10,000=1,000=100%=10.0=Physicality=Tech.=10 Oct.=Uranus=P=1Ø.
Voyeur=10,000=1,000=100%=10.0=Physicality=Tech.=10 Oct.=Uranus=P=1Ø.
VP=1,000=100%=10.0=1.0=Mind=Sun=1 January=Helios >> M=E4.
vs.=500=5%=P5.00D=5.0=Law=Time=Venus=5 May=Aphrodite>>L=N.
V.S.=1,000=100%=10.0=1.0=Mind=Sun=1 January=Helios >> M=E4.
vss.=1,000=100%=10.0=1.0=Mind=Sun=1 January=Helios >> M=E4.
VT=500=5%=P5.00D=5.0=Law=Time=Venus=5 May=Aphrodite>>L=N.
VTR=1,000=100%=10.0=1.0=Mind=Sun=1 January=Helios >> M=E4.
Vul.=500=5%=P5.00D=5.0=Law=Time=Venus=5 May=Aphrodite>>L=N.

Vulcan=4,000=40%=P4.0D=Govt.=Creatocracy=4 April=Mercury=Hermes=G=A4.
Roman Myth. The God of fire and metalworking. In the jurisdiction of Hermes. The book of Revelation describes Jesus >> Hermes as having fire in His eyes and blazing sword in hand.

Vulcanism=1,500=15%=P1.50D=1.5=Authority=Solar Crown=1 May = Maia.
Vulcanize=10,000=1,000=100%=10.0=Physicality=Tech.=10 Oct.=Uranus=P=1Ø.
vulg.=500=5%=P5.00D=5.0=Law=Time=Venus=5 May=Aphrodite>>L=N.
Vulg.=500=5%=P5.00D=5.0=Law=Time=Venus=5 May=Aphrodite>>L=N.
Vulgar=10,000=1,000=100%=10.0=Physicality=Tech.=10 Oct.=Uranus=P=1Ø.
Vulgarian=3,500=4,000=40%=P4.0D=Govt.=4 April=Mercury=Hermes=G=A4.
Vulgarism=10,000=1,000=100%=10.0=Physicality=Tech.=10 Oct.=Uranus=P=1Ø.
Vulgarity=10,000=1,000=100%=10.0=Physicality=Tech.=10 Oct.=Uranus=P=1Ø.
Vulgarize=2,500=3,000=30%=P3.0D=3.0=Creativity=Stars=Muses=3 March = C=I>>GIL.
Vulgar Latin=10,000=1,000=100%=10.0=Physicality=Tech.=10 Oct.=Uranus=P=1Ø.
Vulgate=10,000=1,000=100%=10.0=Physicality=Tech.=10 Oct.=Uranus=P=1Ø.
Vulnerable=10,000=1,000=100%=10.0=Physicality=Tech.=10 Oct.=Uranus=P=1Ø.
Vulpine=3,000=30%=P3.0D=3.0=Creativity=Stars=Muses=3 March = C=I>>GIL.

Vulture=10,000=1,000=100%=10.0=Physicality=Tech.=10 Oct.=Uranus=P=1Ø.
Vulva=4,000=40%=P4.0D=Govt.=Creatocracy=4 April=Mercury=Hermes=G=A4.
vv.=500=5%=P5.00D=5.0=Law=Time=Venus=5 May=Aphrodite>>L=N.
v.v.=1,000=100%=10.0=1.0=Mind=Sun=1 January=Helios >> M=E4.

MAKABET =Ww=

---

w1=3,000=30%=P3.0D=3.0=Creativity=Stars=Muses=3 March = C=I>>GIL.
The 23rd letter of the English alphabet. Computing the psycho-metric weight is thus:
3.0*2.3x=px=5.3+6.9=12.2x=px=48.77=50=5.0.
An alphabet that constantly pronounced induces the authority of Law, the management
Time, the glory of the morning star Venus through the energy of 5 May and the blessings
of Aphrodite. The energy of 5 May is thus>> Day 5:Value:3.0, Planetary Type:Star, Human
Type:Creativity, Birth Energy Level:50.0%. It is the sign of beauty, fertility and sexual love.

---

w2=1,000=100%=10.0=1.0=Mind=Sun=1 January=Helios >> M=E4.
W1=4,500=5,000=50%=P5.00D=Law=Time=Venus=5 May = Aphrodite>>L=N.
W2=4,500=5,000=50%=P5.00D=Law=Time=Venus=5 May = Aphrodite>>L=N.
w.=3,000=30%=P3.0D=3.0=Creativity=Stars=Muses=3 March = C=I>>GIL.
WA=500=5%=P5.00D=5.0=Law=Time=Venus=5 May=Aphrodite>>L=N.
WAAC=2,000=20%=P2.00D=2.0=Nature=Matter=Moon=2 Feb.=Cupid=N=C+_
WAAF=2,000=20%=P2.00D=2.0=Nature=Matter=Moon=2 Feb.=Cupid=N=C+_
Wabash=10,500=11,000=11%=P1.10D=1.1=Idea=Brainchild=Inv.=11 Nov.=Athena>>I=MT.
WAC=1,500=15%=P1.50D=1.5=Authority=Solar Crown=1 May = Maia.
Wacky=3,500=4,000=40%=P4.0D=Govt.=Creatocracy=4 April=Mercury=Hermes=G=A4.
Waco=6,000=60%=P6.0D=Man=Earth=Royalty=6 June=Gaia=Maia>>M=M2.
Wad=10,000=1,000=100%=10.0=Physicality=Tech.=10 Oct.=Uranus=P=1Ø.
Waddling=8,000=80%=P8.0D=Economy=Currency=8 Aug.=Zeus>>E=v.
Wade=11,000=11%=P1.10D=1.1=Idea=Brainchild=Inv.=11 Nov.=SC=Athena>>I=MT.
Wader=4,500=5,000=50%=P5.00D=Law=Time=Venus=5 May = Aphrodite>>L=N.
Wadi=10,000=1,000=100%=10.0=Physicality=Tech.=10 Oct.=Uranus=P=1Ø.
Wading bird=4,000=40%=P4.0D=Govt.=Creatocracy=4 April=Mercury=Hermes=G=A4.
WAF=2,500=3,000=30%=P3.0D=3.0=Creativity=Stars=Muses=3 March = C=I>>GIL.
Wafer=10,000=1,000=100%=10.0=Physicality=Tech.=10 Oct.=Uranus=P=1Ø.
Waffle1=5,500=5.5=80%=P5.50=Earth-Midway=5 May = Gaia.
Waffle2=5,000=50%=P5.00D=Law=Time=Venus=5 May = Aphrodite>>L=N.
Waffle iron=8,500=9,000=90%=P9.00D=9.0=Abstraction=Gods=Saturn=9Sept.>>A=Ø.
Waft=10,000=1,000=100%=10.0=Physicality=Tech.=10 Oct.=Uranus=P=1Ø.
Wag1=8,000=80%=P8.0D=Economy=Currency=8 Aug.=Zeus>>E=v.
Wag2=4,000=40%=P4.0D=Govt.=Creatocracy=4 April=Mercury=Hermes=G=A4.
Wage=10,000=1,000=100%=10.0=Physicality=Tech.=10 Oct.=Uranus=P=1Ø.
Wager=7,000=70%=P7.0D=7.0=Language=Assets=Mars=7 July=Pleiades.

Waggle=5,000=50%=P5.00D=Law=Time=Venus=5 May = Aphrodite>>L=N.
Wagner Richard=2,000=20%=P2.00D=2.0=Nature=Matter=Moon=2 Feb.=Cupid=N=C+_
Wagon=10,000=1,000=100%=10.0=Physicality=Tech.=10 Oct.=Uranus=P=1Ø.
Wagon train=4,500=5,000=50%=P5.00D=Law=Time=Venus=5 May = Aphrodite>>L=N.
Wahoo=6,000=60%=P6.0D=Man=Earth=Royalty=6 June=Gaia=Maia>>M=M2.
Walf=4,500=5,000=50%=P5.00D=Law=Time=Venus=5 May = Aphrodite>>L=N.
Waikiki=6,000=60%=P6.0D=Man=Earth=Royalty=6 June=Gaia=Maia>>M=M2.
Wall=10,000=1,000=100%=10.0=Physicality=Tech.=10 Oct.=Uranus=P=1Ø.
Wain=3,500=4,000=40%=P4.0D=Govt.=Creatocracy=4 April=Mercury=Hermes=G=A4.
Wainscot=10,000=1,000=100%=10.0=Physicality=Tech.=10 Oct.=Uranus=P=1Ø.
Wainwright=3,000=30%=P3.0D=3.0=Creativity=Stars=Muses=3 March = C=I>>GIL.
Waist=10,000=1,000=100%=10.0=Physicality=Tech.=10 Oct.=Uranus=P=1Ø.
Waistband=4,000=40%=P4.0D=Govt.=Creatocracy=4 April=Mercury=Hermes=G=A4.
Waistcoat=2,000=20%=P2.00D=2.0=Nature=Matter=Moon=2 Feb.=Cupid=N=C+_
Waistline=10,000=1,000=100%=10.0=Physicality=Tech.=10 Oct.=Uranus=P=1Ø.
Wait=10,000=1,000=100%=10.0=Physicality=Tech.=10 Oct.=Uranus=P=1Ø.
Waiter=5,000=50%=P5.00D=Law=Time=Venus=5 May = Aphrodite>>L=N.
Waiting room=6,000=60%=P6.0D=Man=Earth=Royalty=6 June=Gaia=Maia>>M=M2.
Waitress=5,000=50%=P5.00D=Law=Time=Venus=5 May = Aphrodite>>L=N.
Waive=6,000=60%=P6.0D=Man=Earth=Royalty=6 June=Gaia=Maia>>M=M2.
Waiver=7,000=70%=P7.0D=7.0=Language=Assets=Mars=7 July=Pleiades.
Wakashan=6,000=60%=P6.0D=Man=Earth=Royalty=6 June=Gaia=Maia>>M=M2.
Wake1=10,000=1,000=100%=10.0=Physicality=Tech.=10 Oct.=Uranus=P=1Ø.
Wake2=9,000=90%=P9.00D=9.0=Abstraction=Gods=Saturn=9Sept.>>A=Ø.
Wakeful=3,500=4,000=40%=P4.0D=Govt.=Creatocracy=4 April=Mercury=Hermes=G=A4.
Wake Island=5,000=50%=P5.00D=Law=Time=Venus=5 May = Aphrodite>>L=N.
Waken=6,000=60%=P6.0D=Man=Earth=Royalty=6 June=Gaia=Maia>>M=M2.
Waldheim Kurt=3,000=30%=P3.0D=3.0=Creativity=Stars=Muses=3 March = C=I>>GIL.
Wale=10,000=1,000=100%=10.0=Physicality=Tech.=10 Oct.=Uranus=P=1Ø.
Wales=8,000=80%=P8.0D=Economy=Currency=8 Aug.=Zeus>>E=v.
Walesa=5,500=5.5=80%=P5.50=Earth-Midway=5 May = Gaia.
Walk=10,000=1,000=100%=10.0=Physicality=Tech.=10 Oct.=Uranus=P=1Ø.
Walk away=6,500=7,000=70%=P7.0D=7.0=Language=Assets=Mars=7 July=Pleiades.
Walker Alice=2,000=20%=P2.00D=2.0=Nature=Matter=Moon=2 Feb.=Cupid=N=C+_
Walkie-talkie=3,500=4,000=40%=P4.0D=Govt.=4 April=Mercury=Hermes=G=A4.
Walking papers=3,500=4,000=40%=P4.0D=Govt.=Creatocracy=4April==Hermes=G=A4.
Walking stick=10,000=1,000=100%=10.0=Physicality=Tech.=10 Oct.=Uranus=P=1Ø.
Walk-on=4,000=40%=P4.0D=Govt.=Creatocracy=4 April=Mercury=Hermes=G=A4.
Walk-out=6,500=7,000=70%=P7.0D=7.0=Language=Assets=Mars=7 July=Pleiades.
Walk-over=9,000=90%=P9.00D=9.0=Abstraction=Gods=Saturn=9Sept.>>A=Ø.
Walk up=6,000=60%=P6.0D=Man=Earth=Royalty=6 June=Gaia=Maia>>M=M2.
Walkway=2,000=20%=P2.00D=2.0=Nature=Matter=Moon=2 Feb.=Cupid=N=C+_
Wall=10,000=1,000=100%=10.0=Physicality=Tech.=10 Oct.=Uranus=P=1Ø.
Wallaby=7,500=8,000=80%=P8.0D=Economy=Currency=8 Aug.=Zeus>>E=v.
Wallace Henry=5,000=50%=P5.00D=Law=Time=Venus=5 May = Aphrodite>>L=N.

Wallboard=1,000=100%=10.0=1.0=Mind=Sun=1 January=Helios >> M=E4.
Wallet=8,000=80%=P8.0D=Economy=Currency=8 Aug.=Zeus>>E=v.
Walleye=10,000=1,000=100%=10.0=Physicality=Tech.=10 Oct.=Uranus=P=1Ø.
Wallflower=10,000=1,000=100%=10.0=Physicality=Tech.=10 Oct.=Uranus=P=1Ø.
Wallis and Futuna Islands=4,500=5,000=50%=P5.00D=Law=Time=Venus=5May=Odite
Walloon=6,500=7,000=70%=P7.0D=7.0=Language=Assets=Mars=7 July=Pleiades.
Wallop=10,000=1,000=100%=10.0=Physicality=Tech.=10 Oct.=Uranus=P=1Ø.
Wallow=10,000=1,000=100%=10.0=Physicality=Tech.=10 Oct.=Uranus=P=1Ø.
Wallpaper=7,000=70%=P7.0D=7.0=Language=Assets=Mars=7 July=Pleiades.
Wall-to-wall=4,500=5,000=50%=P5.00D=Law=Time=Venus=5 May = Aphrodite>>L=N.
Walnut=10,000=1,000=100%=10.0=Physicality=Tech.=10 Oct.=Uranus=P=1Ø.
Walpole Horace=5,000=50%=P5.00D=Law=Time=Venus=5 May = Aphrodite>>L=N.
Walrus=7,000=70%=P7.0D=7.0=Language=Assets=Mars=7 July=Pleiades.
Walton Izaak.=2,000=20%=P2.00D=2.0=Nature=Matter=Moon=2 Feb.=Cupid=N=C+_
Waltz=10,000=1,000=100%=10.0=Physicality=Tech.=10 Oct.=Uranus=P=1Ø.
Wampanoag=10,000=1,000=100%=10.0=Physicality=Tech.=10 Oct.=Uranus=P=1Ø.
Wampum=10,000=1,000=100%=10.0=Physicality=Tech.=10 Oct.=Uranus=P=1Ø.
Wan=10,000=1,000=100%=10.0=Physicality=Tech.=10 Oct.=Uranus=P=1Ø.
Wand=10,000=1,000=100%=10.0=Physicality=Tech.=10 Oct.=Uranus=P=1Ø.
Wander=10,000=1,000=100%=10.0=Physicality=Tech.=10 Oct.=Uranus=P=1Ø.
Wandering Jew=5,000=50%=P5.00D=Law=Time=Venus=5 May = Aphrodite>>L=N.
Wanderlust=4,000=40%=P4.0D=Govt.=Creatocracy=4 April=Mercury=Hermes=G=A4.
Wane=10,000=1,000=100%=10.0=Physicality=Tech.=10 Oct.=Uranus=P=1Ø.
Wangle=5,500=5.5=80%=P5.50=Earth-Midway=5 May = Gaia.
Want=10,000=1,000=100%=10.0=Physicality=Tech.=10 Oct.=Uranus=P=1Ø.
Want ad=1,500=15%=P1.50D=1.5=Authority=Solar Crown=1 May = Maia.
Wanting=5,500=5.5=80%=P5.50=Earth-Midway=5 May = Gaia.
Wanton=10,000=1,000=100%=10.0=Physicality=Tech.=10 Oct.=Uranus=P=1Ø.
Wapiti=6,000=60%=P6.0D=Man=Earth=Royalty=6 June=Gaia=Maia>>M=M2.
War=10,000=1,000=100%=10.0=Physicality=Tech.=10 Oct.=Uranus=P=1Ø.
Warble=10,000=1,000=100%=10.0=Physicality=Tech.=10 Oct.=Uranus=P=1Ø.
Warbler=10,000=1,000=100%=10.0=Physicality=Tech.=10 Oct.=Uranus=P=1Ø.
War chest=4,500=5,000=50%=P5.00D=Law=Time=Venus=5 May = Aphrodite>>L=N.
War cry=1,500=15%=P1.50D=1.5=Authority=Solar Crown=1 May = Maia.
Ward=10,000=1,000=100%=10.0=Physicality=Tech.=10 Oct.=Uranus=P=1Ø.
-ward=3,000=30%=P3.0D=3.0=Creativity=Stars=Muses=3 March = C=I>>GIL.
Warden=10,000=1,000=100%=10.0=Physicality=Tech.=10 Oct.=Uranus=P=1Ø.
Warder=6,500=7,000=70%=P7.0D=7.0=Language=Assets=Mars=7 July=Pleiades.
Ward heeler=4,500=5,000=50%=P5.00D=Law=Time=Venus=5 May = Aphrodite>>L=N.
Wardrobe=10,000=1,000=100%=10.0=Physicality=Tech.=10 Oct.=Uranus=P=1Ø.
Wardroom=6,500=7,000=70%=P7.0D=7.0=Language=Assets=Mars=7 July=Pleiades.
Wardship=4,000=40%=P4.0D=Govt.=Creatocracy=4 April=Mercury=Hermes=G=A4.
Ware=7,500=8,000=80%=P8.0D=Economy=Currency=8 Aug.=Zeus>>E=v.
Warehouse=4,000=40%=P4.0D=Govt.=Creatocracy=4 April=Mercury=Hermes=G=A4.
Warfare=4,000=40%=P4.0D=Govt.=Creatocracy=4 April=Mercury=Hermes=G=A4.

Warfarin=10,000=1,000=100%=10.0=Physicality=Tech.=10 Oct.=Uranus=P=1Ø.
Warhead=8,500=9,000=90%=P9.00D=9.0=Abstraction=Gods=Saturn=9Sept.>>A=Ø.
Warhol Andy=2,500=3,000=30%=P3.0D=3.0=Cre.=Stars=Muses=3 March = C=I>>GIL.
Warhorse=7,000=70%=P7.0D=7.0=Language=Assets=Mars=7 July=Pleiades.
Warlike=3,500=4,000=40%=P4.0D=Govt.=Creatocracy=4 April=Mercury=Hermes=G=A4.
Warlock=5,000=50%=P5.00D=Law=Time=Venus=5 May = Aphrodite>>L=N.
Warlord=6,500=7,000=70%=P7.0D=7.0=Language=Assets=Mars=7 July=Pleiades.
Warm=10,000=1,000=100%=10.0=Physicality=Tech.=10 Oct.=Uranus=P=1Ø.
Warm-blooded=7,000=70%=P7.0D=7.0=Language=Assets=Mars=7 July=Pleiades.
Warmhearted=1,000=100%=10.0=1.0=Mind=Sun=1 January=Helios >> M=E4.
Warmonger=4,500=5,000=50%=P5.00D=Law=Time=Venus=5 May = Aphrodite>>L=N.
Warmth=5,000=50%=P5.00D=Law=Time=Venus=5 May = Aphrodite>>L=N.
Warm-up=4,000=40%=P4.0D=Govt.=Creatocracy=4 April=Mercury=Hermes=G=A4.
Warn=10,000=1,000=100%=10.0=Physicality=Tech.=10 Oct.=Uranus=P=1Ø.
Warning=10,000=1,000=100%=10.0=Physicality=Tech.=10 Oct.=Uranus=P=1Ø.
Warp=10,000=1,000=100%=10.0=Physicality=Tech.=10 Oct.=Uranus=P=1Ø.
Warpath=5,500=5.5=80%=P5.50=Earth-Midway=5 May = Gaia.
Warplane=1,500=15%=P1.50D=1.5=Authority=Solar Crown=1 May = Maia.
Warrant=10,000=1,000=100%=10.0=Physicality=Tech.=10 Oct.=Uranus=P=1Ø.
Warrant officer=4,500=5,000=50%=P5.00D=Law=Time=Venus=5 May = Aphrodite>>L=N.
Warranty=8,000=80%=P8.0D=Economy=Currency=8 Aug.=Zeus>>E=v.
warren=9,000=90%=P9.00D=9.0=Abstraction=Gods=Saturn=9Sept.>>A=Ø.
Warren=5,500=5.5=80%=P5.50=Earth-Midway=5 May = Gaia.
Warren,Earl.=6,500=7,000=70%=P7.0D=7.0=Language=Assets=Mars=7 July=Pleiades.
Warren,Robert Penn=3,000=30%=P3.0D=3.0=Cr.=Stars=Muses=3 March = C=I>>GIL.
Warrior=4,000=40%=P4.0D=Govt.=Creatocracy=4 April=Mercury=Hermes=G=A4.
Warsaw=6,500=7,000=70%=P7.0D=7.0=Language=Assets=Mars=7 July=Pleiades.
Warship=1,500=15%=P1.50D=1.5=Authority=Solar Crown=1 May = Maia.
Wart=10,000=1,000=100%=10.0=Physicality=Tech.=10 Oct.=Uranus=P=1Ø.
Wart hog=7,500=8,000=80%=P8.0D=Economy=Currency=8 Aug.=Zeus>>E=v.
Wartime=2,000=20%=P2.00D=2.0=Nature=Matter=Moon=2 Feb.=Cupid=N=C+_
Warwick=5,500=5.5=80%=P5.50=Earth-Midway=5 May = Gaia.
Wary=3,000=30%=P3.0D=3.0=Creativity=Stars=Muses=3 March = C=I>>GIL.
Was=4,500=5,000=50%=P5.00D=Law=Time=Venus=5 May = Aphrodite>>L=N.
Wasatch Range=9,000=90%=P9.00D=9.0=Abstraction=Gods=Saturn=9Sept.>>A=Ø.
Wash=10,000=1,000=100%=10.0=Physicality=Tech.=10 Oct.=Uranus=P=1Ø.
Wash.=500=5%=P5.00D=5.0=Law=Time=Venus=5 May=Aphrodite>>L=N.
Washable=3,000=30%=P3.0D=3.0=Creativity=Stars=Muses=3 March = C=I>>GIL.
Wash-and-wear=5,500=5.5=80%=P5.50=Earth-Midway=5 May = Gaia.
Washbasin=1,000=100%=10.0=1.0=Mind=Sun=1 January=Helios >> M=E4.
Washboard=6,500=7,000=70%=P7.0D=7.0=Language=Assets=Mars=7 July=Pleiades.
Wash bowl=6,500=7,000=70%=P7.0D=7.0=Language=Assets=Mars=7 July=Pleiades.
Washcloth=3,000=30%=P3.0D=3.0=Creativity=Stars=Muses=3 March = C=I>>GIL.
Wash-out=3,000=30%=P3.0D=3.0=Creativity=Stars=Muses=3 March = C=I>>GIL.
Washed-up=3,000=30%=P3.0D=3.0=Creativity=Stars=Muses=3 March = C=I>>GIL.

Washer=10,000=1,000=100%=10.0=Physicality=Tech.=10 Oct.=Uranus=P=1Ø.
Washing=6,500=7,000=70%=P7.0D=7.0=Language=Assets=Mars=7 July=Pleiades.
Washing soda=4,000=40%=P4.0D=Govt.=Creatocracy=4 April=Mercury=Hermes=G=A4.
Washington=10,000=1,000=100%=10.0=Physicality=Tech.=10 Oct.=Uranus=P=1Ø.
Washington,Booker T=2,000=20%=P2.00D=2.0=Nature=Moon=2 Feb.=Cupid=N=C+_
Washington,George=5,500=5.5=80%=P5.50=Earth-Midway=5 May = Gaia.
Washington,Mount.=4,500=5,000=50%=P5.00D=Law=Time=Venus=5 May =Odite>>L=N.
Washout=9,000=90%=P9.00D=9.0=Abstraction=Gods=Saturn=9Sept.>>A=Ø.
Washroom=3,500=4,000=40%=P4.0D=Govt.=4 April=Mercury=Hermes=G=A4.
Washstand=7,500=8,000=80%=P8.0D=Economy=Currency=8 Aug.=Zeus>>E=v.
Washtub=3,000=30%=P3.0D=3.0=Creativity=Stars=Muses=3 March = C=I>>GIL.
Wasn't=1,000=100%=10.0=1.0=Mind=Sun=1 January=Helios >> M=E4.
Wasp=10,500=11,000=11%=P1.10D=1.1=Idea=Brainchild=Inv.=11 Nov.=SC=Athena>>I=MT.
Wasp=6,000=60%=P6.0D=Man=Earth=Royalty=6 June=Gaia=Maia>>M=M2.
Waspish=4,500=5,000=50%=P5.00D=Law=Time=Venus=5 May = Aphrodite>>L=N.
Wash waist=3,500=4,000=40%=P4.0D=Govt.=Creatocracy=4 April=Hermes=G=A4.
Wassail=10,000=1,000=100%=10.0=Physicality=Tech.=10 Oct.=Uranus=P=1Ø.
Wassermann test=5,500=5.5=80%=P5.50=Earth-Midway=5 May = Gaia.
Wast=5,500=5.5=80%=P5.50=Earth-Midway=5 May = Gaia.
Wastage=4,000=40%=P4.0D=Govt.=Creatocracy=4 April=Mercury=Hermes=G=A4.
Waste=10,000=1,000=100%=10.0=Physicality=Tech.=10 Oct.=Uranus=P=1Ø.
Wastebasket=2,000=20%=P2.00D=2.0=Nature=Matter=Moon=2 Feb.=Cupid=N=C+_
Wasteful=3,000=30%=P3.0D=3.0=Creativity=Stars=Muses=3 March = C=I>>GIL.
Wasteland=3,500=4,000=40%=P4.0D=Govt.=4 April=Mercury=Hermes=G=A4.
Waste paper=1,000=100%=10.0=1.0=Mind=Sun=1 January=Helios >> M=E4.
Wastrel=4,000=40%=P4.0D=Govt.=Creatocracy=4 April=Mercury=Hermes=G=A4.
Watch=10,000=1,000=100%=10.0=Physicality=Tech.=10 Oct.=Uranus=P=1Ø.
Watchdog=6,500=7,000=70%=P7.0D=7.0=Language=Assets=Mars=7 July=Pleiades.
Watchful=4,500=5,000=50%=P5.00D=Law=Time=Venus=5 May = Aphrodite>>L=N.
Watchman=4,500=5,000=50%=P5.00D=Law=Time=Venus=5 May = Aphrodite>>L=N.
Watchtower=4,000=40%=P4.0D=Govt.=Creatocracy=4 April=Mercury=Hermes=G=A4.
Watchword=6,000=60%=P6.0D=Man=Earth=Royalty=6 June=Gaia=Maia>>M=M2.
Water=10,000=1,000=100%=10.0=Physicality=Tech.=10 Oct.=Uranus=P=1Ø.
Waterbed=5,000=50%=P5.00D=Law=Time=Venus=5 May = Aphrodite>>L=N.
Waterborne=3,500=4,000=40%=P4.0D=Govt.=Creato=4 April=Mercury=Hermes=G=A4.
Water buffalo=5,000=50%=P5.00D=Law=Time=Venus=5 May = Aphrodite>>L=N.
Waterbury=5,500=5.5=80%=P5.50=Earth-Midway=5 May = Gaia.
Water cannon=7,500=8,000=80%=P8.0D=Economy=Currency=8 Aug.=Zeus>>E=v.
Water chestnut=8,000=80%=P8.0D=Economy=Currency=8 Aug.=Zeus>>E=v.
Water closet=4,500=5,000=50%=P5.00D=Law=Time=Venus=5 May = Aphrodite>>L=N.
Watercolor=6,500=7,000=70%=P7.0D=7.0=Language=Assets=Mars=7 July=Pleiades.
Watercourse=4,500=5,000=50%=P5.00D=Law=Time=Venus=5 May = Aphrodite>>L=N.
Watercraft=2,000=20%=P2.00D=2.0=Nature=Matter=Moon=2 Feb.=Cupid=N=C+_
Watercress=6,500=7,000=70%=P7.0D=7.0=Language=Assets=Mars=7 July=Pleiades.
Waterfall=3,500=4,000=40%=P4.0D=Govt.=Creatocracy=4 April=Hermes=G=A4.

Waterfowl=7,000=70%=P7.0D=7.0=Language=Assets=Mars=7 July=Pleiades.
Waterfront=6,000=60%=P6.0D=Man=Earth=Royalty=6 June=Gaia=Maia>>M=M2.
Water gap=4,500=5,000=50%=P5.00D=Law=Time=Venus=5 May = Aphrodite>>L=N.
Water hole=3,500=4,000=40%=P4.0D=Govt.=Creatocracy=4 April=Hermes=G=A4.
Water hyacinth=6,000=60%=P6.0D=Man=Earth=Royalty=6 June=Gaia=Maia>>M=M2.
Watering place=2,000=20%=P2.00D=2.0=Nature=Matter=Moon=2 Feb.=Cupid=N=C+_
Waterish=500=5%=P5.00D=5.0=Law=Time=Venus=5 May=Aphrodite>>L=N.
Water lily=7,000=70%=P7.0D=7.0=Language=Assets=Mars=7 July=Pleiades.
Waterline=10,000=1,000=100%=10.0=Physicality=Tech.=10 Oct.=Uranus=P=1Ø.
Waterlogged=6,000=60%=P6.0D=Man=Earth=Royalty=6 June=Gaia=Maia>>M=M2.
waterloo=2,000=20%=P2.00D=2.0=Nature=Matter=Moon=2 Feb.=Cupid=N=C+_
Waterloo=6,000=60%=P6.0D=Man=Earth=Royalty=6 June=Gaia=Maia>>M=M2.
Watermark=10,000=1,000=100%=10.0=Physicality=Tech.=10 Oct.=Uranus=P=1Ø.
Watermelon=10,000=1,000=100%=10.0=Physicality=Tech.=10 Oct.=Uranus=P=1Ø.
Water moccasin=6,500=7,000=70%=P7.0D=7.0=Language=Assets=Mars=7 July=Pleiades.
Water ouzel=2,500=3,000=30%=P3.0D=3.0=Cre.=Stars=Muses=3 March = C=I>>GIL.
Water pipe=10,000=1,000=100%=10.0=Physicality=Tech.=10 Oct.=Uranus=P=1Ø.
Water polo=7,500=8,000=80%=P8.0D=Economy=Currency=8 Aug.=Zeus>>E=v.
Waterpower=9,000=90%=P9.00D=9.0=Abstraction=Gods=Saturn=9Sept.>>A=Ø.
Waterproof=5,000=50%=P5.00D=Law=Time=Venus=5 May = Aphrodite>>L=N.
Water-repellent=3,500=4,000=40%=P4.0D=Govt.=4 April=Mercury=Hermes=G=A4.
Water-resistant=1,000=100%=10.0=1.0=Mind=Sun=1 January=Helios >> M=E4.
Watershed=10,000=1,000=100%=10.0=Physicality=Tech.=10 Oct.=Uranus=P=1Ø.
Waterside=3,000=30%=P3.0D=3.0=Creativity=Stars=Muses=3 March = C=I>>GIL.
Water ski=7,000=70%=P7.0D=7.0=Language=Assets=Mars=7 July=Pleiades.
Waterspout=10,000=1,000=100%=10.0=Physicality=Tech.=10 Oct.=Uranus=P=1Ø.
Water table=4,500=5,000=50%=P5.00D=Law=Time=Venus=5 May = Aphrodite>>L=N.
Watertight=6,000=60%=P6.0D=Man=Earth=Royalty=6 June=Gaia=Maia>>M=M2.
Water tower=4,500=5,000=50%=P5.00D=Law=Time=Venus=5 May = Aphrodite>>L=N.
Waterway=4,500=5,000=50%=P5.00D=Law=Time=Venus=5 May = Aphrodite>>L=N.
Waterwheel=6,000=60%=P6.0D=Man=Earth=Royalty=6 June=Gaia=Maia>>M=M2.
Water wings=6,500=7,000=70%=P7.0D=7.0=Language=Assets=Mars=7 July=Pleiades.
Waterworks=8,500=9,000=90%=P9.00D=9.0=Abstraction=Gods=Saturn=9Sept.>>A=Ø.
Watery=7,000=70%=P7.0D=7.0=Language=Assets=Mars=7 July=Pleiades.
WATS=2,000=20%=P2.00D=2.0=Nature=Matter=Moon=2 Feb.=Cupid=N=C+_
Watt=6,500=7,000=70%=P7.0D=7.0=Language=Assets=Mars=7 July=Pleiades.
Watt James.=3,000=30%=P3.0D=3.0=Creativity=Stars=Muses=3 March = C=I>>GIL.
Wattage=10,000=1,000=100%=10.0=Physicality=Tech.=10 Oct.=Uranus=P=1Ø.
Watteau Jean=2,500=3,000=30%=P3.0D=3.0=Cre.=Stars=Muses=3 March = C=I>>GIL.
Wattle=10,000=1,000=100%=10.0=Physicality=Tech.=10 Oct.=Uranus=P=1Ø.
Waugh Evelyn=3,500=4,000=40%=P4.0D=Govt.=4 April=Mercury=Hermes=G=A4.

Wave=10,000=1,000=100%=10.0=Physicality=Tech.=10 Oct.=Uranus=P=1Ø.
Peter Matthews - Akukalia discovered the valley field concept. See attraction.

Waveband=3,500=4,000=40%=P4.0D=Govt.=Creato=4 April=Mercury=Hermes=G=A4.
Waveform=7,000=70%=P7.0D=7.0=Language=Assets=Mars=7 July=Pleiades.
Wavelength=9,500=10,000=1,000=100%=10.0=Physicality=Tech.=10 Oct.=Uranus=P=1Ø.
Wavelet=2,000=20%=P2.00D=2.0=Nature=Matter=Moon=2 Feb.=Cupid=N=C+_
Waver=10,000=1,000=100%=10.0=Physicality=Tech.=10 Oct.=Uranus=P=1Ø.
WAVES=3,000=30%=P3.0D=3.0=Creativity=Stars=Muses=3 March = C=I>>GIL.
Wavy=10,000=1,000=100%=10.0=Physicality=Tech.=10 Oct.=Uranus=P=1Ø.
Wax1=10,000=1,000=100%=10.0=Physicality=Tech.=10 Oct.=Uranus=P=1Ø.
Wax2=10,000=1,000=100%=10.0=Physicality=Tech.=10 Oct.=Uranus=P=1Ø.
Wax bean=4,000=40%=P4.0D=Govt.=Creatocracy=4 April=Mercury=Hermes=G=A4.
Waxen=4,500=5,000=50%=P5.00D=Law=Time=Venus=5 May = Aphrodite>>L=N.
Wax myrtle=8,500=9,000=90%=P9.00D=9.0=Abstraction=Gods=Saturn=9Sept.>>A=Ø.
Waxwing=8,500=9,000=90%=P9.00D=9.0=Abstraction=Gods=Saturn=9Sept.>>A=Ø.
Waxwork=10,000=1,000=100%=10.0=Physicality=Tech.=10 Oct.=Uranus=P=1Ø.
Waxy=5,500=5.5=80%=P5.50=Earth-Midway=5 May = Gaia.
Way=10,000=1,000=100%=10.0=Physicality=Tech.=10 Oct.=Uranus=P=1Ø.
Waybill=5,500=5.5=80%=P5.50=Earth-Midway=5 May = Gaia.
Wayfarer=4,000=40%=P4.0D=Govt.=Creatocracy=4 April=Mercury=Hermes=G=A4.
Waylay=8,000=80%=P8.0D=Economy=Currency=8 Aug.=Zeus>>E=v.
Wayne Anthony=2,500=3,000=30%=P3.0D=3.0=Cr.=Stars=Muses=3 March = C=I>>GIL.
-ways=4,000=40%=P4.0D=Govt.=Creatocracy=4 April=Mercury=Hermes=G=A4.
Ways and means=5,500=5.5=80%=P5.50=Earth-Midway=5 May = Gaia.
Wayside=2,500=3,000=30%=P3.0D=3.0=Creativity=Stars=Muses=3 March = C=I>>GIL.
Way station=5,500=5.5=80%=P5.50=Earth-Midway=5 May = Gaia.
Wayward=4,500=5,000=50%=P5.00D=Law=Time=Venus=5 May = Aphrodite>>L=N.
w.b.=500=5%=P5.00D=5.0=Law=Time=Venus=5 May=Aphrodite>>L=N.
WBC=1,500=15%=P1.50D=1.5=Authority=Solar Crown=1 May = Maia.
WbN=1,500=15%=P1.50D=1.5=Authority=Solar Crown=1 May = Maia.
WbS=1,500=15%=P1.50D=1.5=Authority=Solar Crown=1 May = Maia.
W.C.=1,000=100%=10.0=1.0=Mind=Sun=1 January=Helios >> M=E4.
WCTU=2,000=20%=P2.00D=2.0=Nature=Matter=Moon=2 Feb.=Cupid=N=C+_
We=10,000=1,000=100%=10.0=Physicality=Tech.=10 Oct.=Uranus=P=1Ø.
Weak=10,000=1,000=100%=10.0=Physicality=Tech.=10 Oct.=Uranus=P=1Ø.
Weaken=3,500=4,000=40%=P4.0D=Govt.=Creatocracy=4 April=Mercury=Hermes=G=A4.
Weakfish=7,000=70%=P7.0D=7.0=Language=Assets=Mars=7 July=Pleiades.
Weak Interaction=10,000=1,000=100%=10.0=Physicality=Tech.=10 Oct.=Uranus=P=1Ø.
Weak-knead=3,000=30%=P3.0D=3.0=Creativity=Stars=Muses=3 March = C=I>>GIL.
Weakling=3,000=30%=P3.0D=3.0=Creativity=Stars=Muses=3 March = C=I>>GIL.
Weakness=9,000=90%=P9.00D=9.0=Abstraction=Gods=Saturn=9Sept.>>A=Ø.
Weal1=2,500=3,000=30%=P3.0D=3.0=Creativity=Stars=Muses=3 March = C=I>>GIL.
Weal2=2,500=3,000=30%=P3.0D=3.0=Creativity=Stars=Muses=3 March = C=I>>GIL.
Weald=5,500=5.5=80%=P5.50=Earth-Midway=5 May = Gaia

Wealth=11,500=12,000=12%=P1.20D=1.2=Knowledge=Edu=12Dec.=Athena>>K=F.
Riches make up 1/4 of wealth which is based on inventions. Proverbs 8:8-12. See Riches.

Wealthy=4,000=40%=P4.0D=Govt.=Creatocracy=4 April=Mercury=Hermes=G=A4.
Greek mythology teaches that Hermes is the God of merchandise and wealth. His skills
are oratory eloquence invention and commerce. This is confirmed as the business of ideas.

Wean=10,000=1,000=100%=10.0=Physicality=Tech.=10 Oct.=Uranus=P=1Ø.
Weapon=9,000=90%=P9.00D=9.0=Abstraction=Gods=Saturn=9Sept.>>A=Ø.
Weaponry=1,000=100%=10.0=1.0=Mind=Sun=1 January=Helios >> M=E4.
Wear=10,000=1,000=100%=10.0=Physicality=Tech.=10 Oct.=Uranus=P=1Ø.

Wear and tear=3,500=4,000=40%=P4.0D=Govt.=Creatocracy=4 April=Hermes=G=A4.
During the trial and crucifixion of Jesus there was a wear and tear process of His clothes.
This confirms He is Hermes. As God of merchandise and invention He is King (of the Jews).

Wearisome=1,500=15%=P1.50D=1.5=Authority=Solar Crown=1 May = Maia.
Weary=10,000=1,000=100%=10.0=Physicality=Tech.=10 Oct.=Uranus=P=1Ø.
Weasel=10,000=1,000=100%=10.0=Physicality=Tech.=10 Oct.=Uranus=P=1Ø.
Weather=10,000=1,000=100%=10.0=Physicality=Tech.=10 Oct.=Uranus=P=1Ø.
Weather-beaten=10,000=1,000=100%=10.0=Physicality=Tech.=10 Oct.=Uranus=P=1Ø.
Weatherboard=1,000=100%=10.0=1.0=Mind=Sun=1 January=Helios >> M=E4.
Weather bound=4,000=40%=P4.0D=Govt.=Creatocracy=4 April=Hermes=G=A4.
Weathercock=6,500=7,000=70%=P7.0D=7.0=Language=Assets=Mars=7 July=Pleiades.
Weathering=8,000=80%=P8.0D=Economy=Currency=8 Aug.=Zeus>>E=v.
Weatherize=4,000=40%=P4.0D=Govt.=Creatocracy=4 April=Hermes=G=A4.
Weatherproof=4,000=40%=P4.0D=Govt.=Creatocracy=4 April=Hermes=G=A4.
Weather stripping=10,000=1,000=100%=10.0=Physicality=Tech.=10 Oct.=Uranus=P=1Ø.
Weathervane=5,500=5.5=80%=P5.50=Earth-Midway=5 May = Gaia.
Weave=10,000=1,000=100%=10.0=Physicality=Tech.=10 Oct.=Uranus=P=1Ø.
Web=10,000=1,000=100%=10.0=Physicality=Tech.=10 Oct.=Uranus=P=1Ø.
Webbing=8,000=80%=P8.0D=Economy=Currency=8 Aug.=Zeus>>E=v.
Weber Karl=4,500=5,000=50%=P5.00D=Law=Time=Venus=5 May = Aphrodite>>L=N.
Weber1, Max=2,000=20%=P2.00D=2.0=Nature=Matter=Moon=2 Feb.=Cupid=N=C+_
Weber2, Max=3,000=30%=P3.0D=3.0=Creativity=Stars=Muses=3 March = C=I>>GIL.
Webfooted=2,500=3,000=30%=P3.0D=3.0=Cre=Stars=Muses=3 March = C=I>>GIL.
Webster Daniel=3,000=30%=P3.0D=3.0=Creativity=Stars=Muses=3 March = C=I>>GIL.
Webster, John=3,000=30%=P3.0D=3.0=Creativity=Stars=Muses=3 March = C=I>>GIL.
Webster, Noah.=2,500=3,000=30%=P3.0D=3.0=Cre=Stars=Muses=3 March = C=I>>GIL.
Webworm=4,500=5,000=50%=P5.00D=Law=Time=Venus=5 May = Aphrodite>>L=N.
Wed=7,500=8,000=80%=P8.0D=Economy=Currency=8 Aug.=Zeus>>E=v.
Wed.=500=5%=P5.00D=5.0=Law=Time=Venus=5 May=Aphrodite>>L=N.
Wedding=10,000=1,000=100%=10.0=Physicality=Tech.=10 Oct.=Uranus=P=1Ø.

Wedge=10,000=1,000=100%=10.0=Physicality=Tech.=10 Oct.=Uranus=P=1Ø.
Wedlock=4,000=40%=P4.0D=Govt.=Creatocracy=4 April=Hermes=G=A4.
Wednesday=3,500=4,000=40%=P4.0D=Govt.=Creatocracy=4 April=Hermes=G=A4.
Wee=7,000=70%=P7.0D=7.0=Language=Assets=Mars=7 July=Pleiades.
Weed1=10,000=1,000=100%=10.0=Physicality=Tech.=10 Oct.=Uranus=P=1Ø.
Weed2=6,500=7,000=70%=P7.0D=7.0=Language=Assets=Mars=7 July=Pleiades.
Weekday=6,500=7,000=70%=P7.0D=7.0=Language=Assets=Mars=7 July=Pleiades.
Weekend=7,000=70%=P7.0D=7.0=Language=Assets=Mars=7 July=Pleiades.
Weekly=10,000=1,000=100%=10.0=Physicality=Tech.=10 Oct.=Uranus=P=1Ø.
Weeknight=4,500=5,000=50%=P5.00D=Law=Time=Venus=5 May = Aphrodite>>L=N.
Ween=3,000=30%=P3.0D=3.0=Creativity=Stars=Muses=3 March = C=I>>GIL.
Weep=8,000=80%=P8.0D=Economy=Currency=8 Aug.=Zeus>>E=v.
Weeping=4,000=40%=P4.0D=Govt.=Creatocracy=4 April=Hermes=G=A4.
Weevil=11,000=11%=P1.10D=1.1=Idea=Brainchild=Inv.=11 Nov.=SC=Athena>>I=MT.
Weft=4,000=40%=P4.0D=Govt.=Creatocracy=4 April=Hermes=G=A4.
Weigh=10,000=1,000=100%=10.0=Physicality=Tech.=10 Oct.=Uranus=P=1Ø.
Weight=10,000=1,000=100%=10.0=Physicality=Tech.=10 Oct.=Uranus=P=1Ø.
Weightless=5,500=5.5=80%=P5.50=Earth-Midway=5 May = Gaia.
Weightlifting=6,000=60%=P6.0D=Man=Earth=Royalty=6 June=Gaia=Maia>>M=M2.
Weighty=9,000=90%=P9.00D=9.0=Abstraction=Gods=Saturn=9Sept.>>A=Ø.
Weir=4,000=40%=P4.0D=Govt.=Creatocracy=4 April=Hermes=G=A4.
Weird=8,000=80%=P8.0D=Economy=Currency=8 Aug.=Zeus>>E=v.
Weirdo=3,000=30%=P3.0D=3.0=Creativity=Stars=Muses=3 March = C=I>>GIL.
Welcome=10,000=1,000=100%=10.0=Physicality=Tech.=10 Oct.=Uranus=P=1Ø.
Weld=10,000=1,000=100%=10.0=Physicality=Tech.=10 Oct.=Uranus=P=1Ø.
Welfare=10,000=1,000=100%=10.0=Physicality=Tech.=10 Oct.=Uranus=P=1Ø.
Welfare state=7,000=70%=P7.0D=7.0=Language=Assets=Mars=7 July=Pleiades.
Well1=10,000=1,000=100%=10.0=Physicality=Tech.=10 Oct.=Uranus=P=1Ø.
Well2=10,000=1,000=100%=10.0=Physicality=Tech.=10 Oct.=Uranus=P=1Ø.
We'll=1,500=15%=P1.50D=1.5=Authority=Solar Crown=1 May = Maia.
Weiland=11,500=12,000=12%=P1.20D=1.2=Knowledge=Edu=12Dec.=Athena>>K=F.
Well appointed=4,500=5,000=50%=P5.00D=Law=Time=Venus=5 May = Aphrodite>>L=N.
Well balanced=4,500=5,000=50%=P5.00D=Law=Time=Venus=5 May = Aphrodite>>L=N.
Wellbeing=4,500=5,000=50%=P5.00D=Law=Time=Venus=5 May = Aphrodite>>L=N.
Well born=2,500=3,000=30%=P3.0D=3.0=Creativity=Stars=Muses=3 March = C=I>>GIL.
Well bred=4,000=40%=P4.0D=Govt.=Creatocracy=4 April=Hermes=G=A4.
Well defined=3,500=4,000=40%=P4.0D=Govt.=Creatocracy=4 April=Hermes=G=A4.
Well disposed=3,500=4,000=40%=P4.0D=Govt.=Creatocracy=4 April=Hermes=G=A4.
Well fixed=3,000=30%=P3.0D=3.0=Creativity=Stars=Muses=3 March = C=I>>GIL.
Well founded=3,500=4,000=40%=P4.0D=Govt.=Creatocracy=4 April=Hermes=G=A4.
Well groomed=6,500=7,000=70%=P7.0D=7.0=Language=Assets=Mars=7 July=Pleiades.
Well grounded=5,000=50%=P5.00D=Law=Time=Venus=5 May = Aphrodite>>L=N.
Well heeled=500=5%=P5.00D=5.0=Law=Time=Venus=5 May=Aphrodite>>L=N.
Wellington=7,000=70%=P7.0D=7.0=Language=Assets=Mars=7 July=Pleiades.
Well-intentioned=3,000=30%=P3.0D=3.0=Creativity=Stars=Muses=3 March = C=I>>GIL.

Well knit=3,500=4,000=40%=P4.0D=Govt.=Creatocracy=4 April=Hermes=G=A4.
Well mannered=500=5%=P5.00D=5.0=Law=Time=Venus=5 May=Aphrodite>>L=N.
Well meaning=1,000=100%=10.0=Physicality=Tech.=10 Oct.=Uranus=P=1Ø.
Wellness=8,000=80%=P8.0D=Economy=Currency=8 Aug.=Zeus>>E=v.
Well nigh=1,000=100%=10.0=1.0=Mind=Sun=1 January=Helios >> M=E4.
Well off=3,000=30%=P3.0D=3.0=Creativity=Stars=Muses=3 March = C=I>>GIL.
Well read=2,500=3,000=30%=P3.0D=3.0=Creativity=Stars=Muses=3 March = C=I>>GIL.
Well rounded=4,500=5,000=50%=P5.00D=Law=Time=Venus=5 May = Aphrodite>>L=N.
Wells Herbert=2,500=3,000=30%=P3.0D=3.0=Cre=Stars=Muses=3 March = C=I>>GIL.
Well spoken=5,000=50%=P5.00D=Law=Time=Venus=5 May = Aphrodite>>L=N.
Wellspring=4,500=5,000=50%=P5.00D=Law=Time=Venus=5 May = Aphrodite>>L=N.
Well timed=5,500=5.5=80%=P5.50=Earth-Midway=5 May = Gaia.
Well to do=2,000=20%=P2.00D=2.0=Nature=Matter=Moon=2 Feb.=Cupid=N=C+_
Well turned=5,000=50%=P5.00D=Law=Time=Venus=5 May = Aphrodite>>L=N.
Well wisher=3,500=4,000=40%=P4.0D=Govt.=Creatocracy=4 April=Hermes=G=A4.
Well worn=4,000=40%=P4.0D=Govt.=Creatocracy=4 April=Hermes=G=A4.
welsh=8,500=9,000=90%=P9.00D=9.0=Abstraction=Gods=Saturn=9Sept.>>A=Ø.
Welsh=8,500=9,000=90%=P9.00D=9.0=Abstraction=Gods=Saturn=9Sept.>>A=Ø.
Welsh corgi=8,000=80%=P8.0D=Economy=Currency=8 Aug.=Zeus>>E=v.
Welsh rabbit=8,000=80%=P8.0D=Economy=Currency=8 Aug.=Zeus>>E=v.
Welt=10,000=1,000=100%=10.0=Physicality=Tech.=10 Oct.=Uranus=P=1Ø.
Welter=10,000=1,000=100%=10.0=Physicality=Tech.=10 Oct.=Uranus=P=1Ø.
Welter weight=7,000=70%=P7.0D=7.0=Language=Assets=Mars=7 July=Pleiades.
Welty Eudora=2,000=20%=P2.00D=2.0=Nature=Matter=Moon=2 Feb.=Cupid=N=C+_
Wen=3,500=4,000=40%=P4.0D=Govt.=Creatocracy=4 April=Mercury=Hermes=G=A4.
Wench=5,500=5.5=80%=P5.50=Earth-Midway=5 May = Gaia.
Wend=4,500=5,000=50%=P5.00D=Law=Time=Venus=5 May = Aphrodite>>L=N.
Went=2,000=20%=P2.00D=2.0=Nature=Matter=Moon=2 Feb.=Cupid=N=C+_
Wept=3,000=30%=P3.0D=3.0=Creativity=Stars=Muses=3 March = C=I>>GIL.
Were=6,000=60%=P6.0D=Man=Earth=Royalty=6 June=Gaia=Maia>>M=M2.
We're=1,000=100%=10.0=1.0=Mind=Sun=1 January=Helios >> M=E4.
Weren't=1,000=100%=10.0=1.0=Mind=Sun=1 January=Helios >> M=E4.
Werewolf=9,000=90%=P9.00D=9.0=Abstraction=Gods=Saturn=9Sept.>>A=Ø.
Wert=4,000=40%=P4.0D=Govt.=Creatocracy=4 April=Mercury=Hermes=G=A4.
Weser=8,500=9,000=90%=P9.00D=9.0=Abstraction=Gods=Saturn=9Sept.>>A=Ø.
Wesley John=3,500=4,000=40%=P4.0D=Govt.=4 April=Mercury=Hermes=G=A4.
Wessex=5,000=50%=P5.00D=Law=Time=Venus=5 May = Aphrodite>>L=N.
West=10,000=1,000=100%=10.0=Physicality=Tech.=10 Oct.=Uranus=P=1Ø.
West,Benjamin.=2,000=20%=P2.00D=2.0=Nature=Matter=Moon=2 Feb.=Cupid=N=C+_
West Bank.=8,500=9,000=90%=P9.00D=9.0=Abstraction=Gods=Saturn=9Sept.>>A=Ø.
West Berlin.=1,000=100%=10.0=1.0=Mind=Sun=1 January=Helios >> M=E4.
Westerly=3,500=4,000=40%=P4.0D=Govt.=Creatocracy=4 April=Hermes=G=A4.
Western=10,000=1,000=100%=10.0=Physicality=Tech.=10 Oct.=Uranus=P=1Ø.
Westerner=5,500=5.5=80%=P5.50=Earth-Midway=5 May = Gaia.
Western Hemisphere=6,500=7,000=70%=P7.0D=7.0=Lang=Assets=Mars=7 July=Pleiades.

Westernize=3,500=4,000=40%=P4.0D=Govt.=4 April=Mercury=Hermes=G=A4.
Western Sahara=4,500=5,000=50%=P5.00D=Law=Time=Venus=5 May = Odite>>L=N.
Western Samoa=7,500=8,000=80%=P8.0D=Economy=Currency=8 Aug.=Zeus>>E=v.
West Germany.=10,000=1,000=100%=10.0=Physicality=Tech.=10 Oct.=Uranus=P=1Ø.
West Indies.=10,000=1,000=100%=10.0=Physicality=Tech.=10 Oct.=Uranus=P=1Ø.
Westphalia=7,000=70%=P7.0D=7.0=Language=Assets=Mars=7 July=Pleiades.
West Virginia=5,500=5.5=80%=P5.50=Earth-Midway=5 May = Gaia.
Westward=2,500=3,000=30%=P3.0D=3.0=Creativity=Stars=Muses=3 March = C=I>>GIL.
Wet=10,000=1,000=100%=10.0=Physicality=Tech.=10 Oct.=Uranus=P=1Ø.
Wetted=6,000=60%=P6.0D=Man=Earth=Royalty=6 June=Gaia=Maia>>M=M2.
Wet blanket=3,500=4,000=40%=P4.0D=Govt.=Creatocracy=4 April=Hermes=G=A4.
Wether=2,000=20%=P2.00D=2.0=Nature=Matter=Moon=2 Feb.=Cupid=N=C+_
Wetland=5,000=50%=P5.00D=Law=Time=Venus=5 May = Aphrodite>>L=N.
Wet nurse=3,500=4,000=40%=P4.0D=Govt.=Creatocracy=4 April=Hermes=G=A4.
Wet suit=6,500=7,000=70%=P7.0D=7.0=Language=Assets=Mars=7 July=Pleiades.
We've=1,000=100%=10.0=1.0=Mind=Sun=1 January=Helios >> M=E4.
Weyden Rogler=3,500=4,000=40%=P4.0D=Govt.=4 April=Mercury=Hermes=G=A4.
WH=1,000=100%=10.0=1.0=Mind=Sun=1 January=Helios >> M=E4.
Whack=11,000=11%=P1.10D=1.1=Idea=Brainchild=Inv.=11 Nov.=SC=Athena>>I=MT.
Whacky=2,000=20%=P2.00D=2.0=Nature=Matter=Moon=2 Feb.=Cupid=N=C+_
Whale1=10,000=1,000=100%=10.0=Physicality=Tech.=10 Oct.=Uranus=P=1Ø.
Whale2=2,500=3,000=30%=P3.0D=3.0=Creativity=Stars=Muses=3 March = C=I>>GIL.
Whaleboat=6,000=60%=P6.0D=Man=Earth=Royalty=6 June=Gaia=Maia>>M=M2.
Whalebone=10,000=1,000=100%=10.0=Physicality=Tech.=10 Oct.=Uranus=P=1Ø.
Whaler=5,000=50%=P5.00D=Law=Time=Venus=5 May = Aphrodite>>L=N.
Wham=8,500=9,000=90%=P9.00D=9.0=Abstraction=Gods=Saturn=9Sept.>>A=Ø.
Whammy=5,000=50%=P5.00D=Law=Time=Venus=5 May = Aphrodite>>L=N.
Wharf=7,500=8,000=80%=P8.0D=Economy=Currency=8 Aug.=Zeus>>E=v.
Wharfage=4,500=5,000=50%=P5.00D=Law=Time=Venus=5 May = Aphrodite>>L=N.
Wharton Edith=3,000=30%=P3.0D=3.0=Creativity=Stars=Muses=3 March = C=I>>GIL.
What=10,000=1,000=100%=10.0=Physicality=Tech.=10 Oct.=Uranus=P=1Ø.
Whatever=10,000=1,000=100%=10.0=Physicality=Tech.=10 Oct.=Uranus=P=1Ø.
Whatnot=6,000=60%=P6.0D=Man=Earth=Royalty=6 June=Gaia=Maia>>M=M2.
Wheat=10,000=1,000=100%=10.0=Physicality=Tech.=10 Oct.=Uranus=P=1Ø.
Wheat germ=7,000=70%=P7.0D=7.0=Language=Assets=Mars=7 July=Pleiades.
Wheatley Philips.=3,500=4,000=40%=P4.0D=Govt.=4 April=Mercury=Hermes=G=A4.
Wheedle=5,000=50%=P5.00D=Law=Time=Venus=5 May = Aphrodite>>L=N.
Wheel=10,000=1,000=100%=10.0=Physicality=Tech.=10 Oct.=Uranus=P=1Ø.
Wheelbarrow=8,000=80%=P8.0D=Economy=Currency=8 Aug.=Zeus>>E=v.
Wheelbase=7,000=70%=P7.0D=7.0=Language=Assets=Mars=7 July=Pleiades.
Wheelchair=7,000=70%=P7.0D=7.0=Language=Assets=Mars=7 July=Pleiades.
Wheeler=4,500=5,000=50%=P5.00D=Law=Time=Venus=5 May = Aphrodite>>L=N.
Wheeler dealer=4,500=5,000=50%=P5.00D=Law=Time=Venus=5 May = Aphrodite>>L=N.
Wheelhouse=1,000=100%=10.0=1.0=Mind=Sun=1 January=Helios >> M=E4.
Wheelwright=3,000=30%=P3.0D=3.0=Creativity=Stars=Muses=3 March = C=I>>GIL.

Wheeze=9,000=90%=P9.00D=9.0=Abstraction=Gods=Saturn=9Sept.>>A=Ø.
Whelk=5,000=50%=P5.00D=Law=Time=Venus=5 May = Aphrodite>>L=N.
Whelp=9,500=10,000=1,000=100%=10.0=Physicality=Tech.=10 Oct.=Uranus=P=1Ø.
When=10,000=1,000=100%=10.0=Physicality=Tech.=10 Oct.=Uranus=P=1Ø.
Whence=10,000=1,000=100%=10.0=Physicality=Tech.=10 Oct.=Uranus=P=1Ø.
Whenever=10,000=1,000=100%=10.0=Physicality=Tech.=10 Oct.=Uranus=P=1Ø.
Whensoever=500=5%=P5.00D=5.0=Law=Time=Venus=5 May=Aphrodite>>L=N.
Where=10,000=1,000=100%=10.0=Physicality=Tech.=10 Oct.=Uranus=P=1Ø.
Whereabouts=11,500=12,000=12%=P1.20D=1.2=Knowledge=Edu=12Dec.=Athena>>K=F.
Whereas=8,000=80%=P8.0D=Economy=Currency=8 Aug.=Zeus>>E=v.
Whereat=2,500=3,000=30%=P3.0D=3.0=Creativity=Stars=Muses=3 March = C=I>>GIL.
Whereby=4,000=40%=P4.0D=Govt.=Creatocracy=4 April=Mercury=Hermes=G=A4.
Wherefore=8,000=80%=P8.0D=Economy=Currency=8 Aug.=Zeus>>E=v.
Wherein=7,000=70%=P7.0D=7.0=Language=Assets=Mars=7 July=Pleiades.
Whereof=7,500=8,000=80%=P8.0D=Economy=Currency=8 Aug.=Zeus>>E=v.
Whereon=2,500=3,000=30%=P3.0D=3.0=Creativity=Stars=Muses=3 March = C=I>>GIL.
Wheresoever=500=5%=P5.00D=5.0=Law=Time=Venus=5 May=Aphrodite>>L=N.
Where to=3,500=4,000=40%=P4.0D=Govt.=Creatocracy=4 April=Hermes=G=A4.
Whereupon=1,500=15%=P1.50D=1.5=Authority=Solar Crown=1 May = Maia.
Wherever=10,000=1,000=100%=10.0=Physicality=Tech.=10 Oct.=Uranus=P=1Ø.
Where with=2,000=20%=P2.00D=2.0=Nature=Matter=Moon=2 Feb.=Cupid=N=C+_
Wherewithal=3,000=30%=P3.0D=3.0=Creativity=Stars=Muses=3 March = C=I>>GIL.
Whet=6,000=60%=P6.0D=Man=Earth=Royalty=6 June=Gaia=Maia>>M=M2.
Whether=10,000=1,000=100%=10.0=Physicality=Tech.=10 Oct.=Uranus=P=1Ø.
Whetstone=4,000=40%=P4.0D=Govt.=Creatocracy=4 April=Mercury=Hermes=G=A4.
Whey=8,000=80%=P8.0D=Economy=Currency=8 Aug.=Zeus>>E=v.
Which=10,000=1,000=100%=10.0=Physicality=Tech.=10 Oct.=Uranus=P=1Ø.
Whichever=6,000=60%=P6.0D=Man=Earth=Royalty=6 June=Gaia=Maia>>M=M2.
Whichsoever=500=5%=P5.00D=5.0=Law=Time=Venus=5 May=Aphrodite>>L=N.
Whiff=10,000=1,000=100%=10.0=Physicality=Tech.=10 Oct.=Uranus=P=1Ø.
Whiffle tree=10,000=1,000=100%=10.0=Physicality=Tech.=10 Oct.=Uranus=P=1Ø.
Whig=10,000=1,000=100%=10.0=Physicality=Tech.=10 Oct.=Uranus=P=1Ø.
While=10,000=1,000=100%=10.0=Physicality=Tech.=10 Oct.=Uranus=P=1Ø.
Whilom=7,000=70%=P7.0D=7.0=Language=Assets=Mars=7 July=Pleiades.
Whilst=2,500=3,000=30%=P3.0D=3.0=Creativity=Stars=Muses=3 March = C=I>>GIL.
Whim=8,000=80%=P8.0D=Economy=Currency=8 Aug.=Zeus>>E=v.
Whimsical=10,000=1,000=100%=10.0=Physicality=Tech.=10 Oct.=Uranus=P=1Ø.
Whimsy=10,000=1,000=100%=10.0=Physicality=Tech.=10 Oct.=Uranus=P=1Ø.
Whine=10,000=1,000=100%=10.0=Physicality=Tech.=10 Oct.=Uranus=P=1Ø.
Whinny=10,000=1,000=100%=10.0=Physicality=Tech.=10 Oct.=Uranus=P=1Ø.
Whip=10,000=1,000=100%=10.0=Physicality=Tech.=10 Oct.=Uranus=P=1Ø.
Whipcord=8,000=80%=P8.0D=Economy=Currency=8 Aug.=Zeus>>E=v.
Whiplash=11,500=12,000=12%=P1.20D=1.2=Knowledge=Edu=12Dec.=Athena>>K=F.
Whippersnapper=3,500=4,000=40%=P4.0D=Govt.=Creatocracy=4 April=Hermes=G=A4.
Whippet=6,000=60%=P6.0D=Man=Earth=Royalty=6 June=Gaia=Maia>>M=M2.

Whipping boy=1,000=100%=10.0=Physicality=Tech.=10 Oct.=Uranus=P=1Ø.
Whippoorwill=5,500=5.5=80%=P5.50=Earth-Midway=5 May = Gaia.
Whipsaw=8,000=80%=P8.0D=Economy=Currency=8 Aug.=Zeus>>E=v.
Whipstitch=8,500=9,000=90%=P9.00D=9.0=Abstraction=Gods=Saturn=9Sept.>>A=Ø.
Whipt=3,000=30%=P3.0D=3.0=Creativity=Stars=Muses=3 March = C=I>>GIL.
Whir=9,500=10,000=1,000=100%=10.0=Physicality=Tech.=10 Oct.=Uranus=P=1Ø.
Whirl=10,000=1,000=100%=10.0=Physicality=Tech.=10 Oct.=Uranus=P=1Ø.
Whirligig=5,500=5.5=80%=P5.50=Earth-Midway=5 May = Gaia.
Whirlpool=7,000=70%=P7.0D=7.0=Language=Assets=Mars=7 July=Pleiades.
Whirlwind=11,500=12,000=12%=P1.20D=1.2=Knowledge=Edu=12Dec.=Athena>>K=F.
Whisk=10,000=1,000=100%=10.0=Physicality=Tech.=10 Oct.=Uranus=P=1Ø.
Whiskbroom=5,000=50%=P5.00D=Law=Time=Venus=5 May = Aphrodite>>L=N.
Whisker=10,000=1,000=100%=10.0=Physicality=Tech.=10 Oct.=Uranus=P=1Ø.
Whiskey=11,500=12,000=12%=P1.20D=1.2=Knowledge=Edu=12Dec.=Athena>>K=F.
Whisper=10,000=1,000=100%=10.0=Physicality=Tech.=10 Oct.=Uranus=P=1Ø.
Whist=4,000=40%=P4.0D=Govt.=Creatocracy=4 April=Mercury=Hermes=G=A4.
Whistle=10,000=1,000=100%=10.0=Physicality=Tech.=10 Oct.=Uranus=P=1Ø.
Whistler James=3,000=30%=P3.0D=3.0=Creativity=Stars=Muses=3 March = C=I>>GIL.
Whistle stop=11,500=12,000=12%=P1.20D=1.2=Knowledge=Edu=12Dec.=Athena>>K=F.
Whit=3,500=4,000=40%=P4.0D=Govt.=Creatocracy=4 April=Mercury=Hermes=G=A4.
White=10,000=1,000=100%=10.0=Physicality=Tech.=10 Oct.=Uranus=P=1Ø.
White,Stanford.=2,000=20%=P2.00D=2.0=Nature=Matter=Moon=2 Feb.=Cupid=N=C+_
White,Terence=2,500=3,000=30%=P3.0D=3.0=Cre=Stars=Muses=3 March = C=I>>GIL.
White ant=1,000=100%=10.0=1.0=Mind=Sun=1 January=Helios >> M=E4.
Whitebait=6,000=60%=P6.0D=Man=Earth=Royalty=6 June=Gaia=Maia>>M=M2.
White blood cell=8,000=80%=P8.0D=Economy=Currency=8 Aug.=Zeus>>E=v.
Whitecap=3,000=30%=P3.0D=3.0=Creativity=Stars=Muses=3 March = C=I>>GIL.
White-collar=6,000=60%=P6.0D=Man=Earth=Royalty=6 June=Gaia=Maia>>M=M2.
White dwarf=6,000=60%=P6.0D=Man=Earth=Royalty=6 June=Gaia=Maia>>M=M2.
White elephant=11,000=11%=P1.10D=1.1=Idea=Brainchild=Inv.=11 Nov.=Athena>>I=MT.
White feather=2,000=20%=P2.00D=2.0=Nature=Matter=Moon=2 Feb.=Cupid=N=C+_
Whitefish=5,000=50%=P5.00D=Law=Time=Venus=5 May = Aphrodite>>L=N.
White flag=3,500=4,000=40%=P4.0D=Govt.=Creatocracy=4 April=Hermes=G=A4.
White gold=8,000=80%=P8.0D=Economy=Currency=8 Aug.=Zeus>>E=v.
White hall=5,500=5.5=80%=P5.50=Earth-Midway=5 May = Gaia.
Whitehead Alfred=3,500=4,000=40%=P4.0D=Govt.=Creatocracy=4 April=Hermes=G=A4.
White horse=7,000=70%=P7.0D=7.0=Language=Assets=Mars=7 July=Pleiades.
White House=5,000=50%=P5.00D=Law=Time=Venus=5 May = Aphrodite>>L=N.
White lead=5,500=5.5=80%=P5.50=Earth-Midway=5 May = Gaia.
White lie=3,500=4,000=40%=P4.0D=Govt.=Creatocracy=4 April=Hermes=G=A4.
White matter=8,500=9,000=90%=P9.00D=9.0=Abstraction=Gods=Saturn=9Sept.>>A=Ø.
White Mountains.=4,500=5,000=50%=P5.00D=Law=Time=Venus=5 May = Odite>>L=N.
White Nile.=10,000=1,000=100%=10.0=Physicality=Tech.=10 Oct.=Uranus=P=1Ø.
White pine=8,000=80%=P8.0D=Economy=Currency=8 Aug.=Zeus>>E=v.
White sauce=5,500=5.5=80%=P5.50=Earth-Midway=5 May = Gaia.

White slave=4,000=40%=P4.0D=Govt.=Creatocracy=4 April=Mercury=Hermes=G=A4.
Whitewash=10,000=1,000=100%=10.0=Physicality=Tech.=10 Oct.=Uranus=P=1Ø.
White whale=7,000=70%=P7.0D=7.0=Language=Assets=Mars=7 July=Pleiades.
Whither=5,000=50%=P5.00D=Law=Time=Venus=5 May = Aphrodite>>L=N.
Whiting1=8,500=9,000=90%=P9.00D=9.0=Abstraction=Gods=Saturn=9Sept.>>A=Ø.
Whiting2=5,000=50%=P5.00D=Law=Time=Venus=5 May = Aphrodite>>L=N.
Whitish=1,000=100%=10.0=1.0=Mind=Sun=1 January=Helios >> M=E4.
Whitman Walt.=2,000=20%=P2.00D=2.0=Nature=Matter=Moon=2 Feb.=Cupid=N=C+_
Whitney Eli.=4,500=5,000=50%=P5.00D=Law=Time=Venus=5 May = Aphrodite>>L=N.
Whitney,Mount.=7,000=70%=P7.0D=7.0=Language=Assets=Mars=7 July=Pleiades.
Whitsunday=3,500=4,000=40%=P4.0D=Govt.=Creatocracy=4 April=Hermes=G=A4.
Whittier John=2,500=3,000=30%=P3.0D=3.0=Cr=Stars=Muses=3 March = C=I>>GIL.
Whittle=12,000=12%=P1.20D=1.2=Knowledge=Edu=12Dec.=Athena>>K=F.
Whiz=10,000=1,000=100%=10.0=Physicality=Tech.=10 Oct.=Uranus=P=1Ø.
Who=10,000=1,000=100%=10.0=Physicality=Tech.=10 Oct.=Uranus=P=1Ø.
WHO=1,500=15%=P1.50D=1.5=Authority=Solar Crown=1 May = Maia.
Whoa=4,500=5,000=50%=P5.00D=Law=Time=Venus=5 May = Aphrodite>>L=N.
Who'd=1,500=15%=P1.50D=1.5=Authority=Solar Crown=1 May = Maia.
Whodunnit=4,000=40%=P4.0D=Govt.=Creatocracy=4 April=Mercury=Hermes=G=A4.
Whoever=6,000=60%=P6.0D=Man=Earth=Royalty=6 June=Gaia=Maia>>M=M2.
Whole=10,000=1,000=100%=10.0=Physicality=Tech.=10 Oct.=Uranus=P=1Ø.
Wholehearted=2,500=3,000=30%=P3.0D=3.0=Cre=Stars=Muses=3 March = C=I>>GIL.
Whole note=6,000=60%=P6.0D=Man=Earth=Royalty=6 June=Gaia=Maia>>M=M2.
Whole number=1,500=15%=P1.50D=1.5=Authority=Solar Crown=1 May = Maia.
Wholesale=10,000=1,000=100%=10.0=Physicality=Tech.=10 Oct.=Uranus=P=1Ø.
Wholesome=10,000=1,000=100%=10.0=Physicality=Tech.=10 Oct.=Uranus=P=1Ø.
Whole-wheat=3,500=4,000=40%=P4.0D=Govt.=Creatocracy=4 April=Hermes=G=A4.
Who'll=1,500=15%=P1.50D=1.5=Authority=Solar Crown=1 May = Maia.
Wholly=2,000=20%=P2.00D=2.0=Nature=Matter=Moon=2 Feb.=Cupid=N=C+_
Whom=5,000=50%=P5.00D=Law=Time=Venus=5 May = Aphrodite>>L=N.
Whomever=5,000=50%=P5.00D=Law=Time=Venus=5 May = Aphrodite>>L=N.
Whomsoever=3,000=30%=P3.0D=3.0=Creativity=Stars=Muses=3 March = C=I>>GIL.
Whoop=10,000=1,000=100%=10.0=Physicality=Tech.=10 Oct.=Uranus=P=1Ø.
Whooping cough=10,000=1,000=100%=10.0=Physicality=Tech.=10 Oct.=Uranus=P=1Ø.
Whooping crane=7,500=8,000=80%=P8.0D=Economy=Currency=8 Aug.=Zeus>>E=v.
Whoops=3,500=4,000=40%=P4.0D=Govt.=Creatocracy=4 April=Mercury=Hermes=G=A4.
Whop=5,000=50%=P5.00D=Law=Time=Venus=5 May = Aphrodite>>L=N.
Whopper=4,500=5,000=50%=P5.00D=Law=Time=Venus=5 May = Aphrodite>>L=N.
Whopping=1,500=15%=P1.50D=1.5=Authority=Solar Crown=1 May = Maia.
Whore=2,000=20%=P2.00D=2.0=Nature=Matter=Moon=2 Feb.=Cupid=N=C+_
Whorl=10,000=1,000=100%=10.0=Physicality=Tech.=10 Oct.=Uranus=P=1Ø.
Who's=1,500=15%=P1.50D=1.5=Authority=Solar Crown=1 May = Maia.
Whose=10,000=1,000=100%=10.0=Physicality=Tech.=10 Oct.=Uranus=P=1Ø.
Whosoever=500=5%=P5.00D=5.0=Law=Time=Venus=5 May=Aphrodite>>L=N.
W-hr=1,000=100%=10.0=1.0=Mind=Sun=1 January=Helios >> M=E4.

Why=10,000=1,000=100%=10.0=Physicality=Tech.=10 Oct.=Uranus=P=1Ø.
WI=500=5%=P5.00D=5.0=Law=Time=Venus=5 May=Aphrodite>>L=N.
W.I.=1,000=100%=10.0=1.0=Mind=Sun=1 January=Helios >> M=E4.
Wichita1=8,000=80%=P8.0D=Economy=Currency=8 Aug.=Zeus>>E=v.
Wichita2=6,000=60%=P6.0D=Man=Earth=Royalty=6 June=Gaia=Maia>>M=M2.
Wick=9,000=90%=P9.00D=9.0=Abstraction=Gods=Saturn=9Sept.>>A=Ø.
Wicked=9,000=90%=P9.00D=9.0=Abstraction=Gods=Saturn=9Sept.>>A=Ø.
Wicker=8,000=80%=P8.0D=Economy=Currency=8 Aug.=Zeus>>E=v.
Wicker work=1,000=100%=10.0=Physicality=Tech.=10 Oct.=Uranus=P=1Ø.
Wicket=10,000=1,000=100%=10.0=Physicality=Tech.=10 Oct.=Uranus=P=1Ø.
Wickiup=10,000=1,000=100%=10.0=Physicality=Tech.=10 Oct.=Uranus=P=1Ø.
Wide=10,000=1,000=100%=10.0=Physicality=Tech.=10 Oct.=Uranus=P=1Ø.
Wide awake=2,000=20%=P2.00D=2.0=Nature=Matter=Moon=2 Feb.=Cupid=N=C+_
Wide-eyed=5,000=50%=P5.00D=Law=Time=Venus=5 May = Aphrodite>>L=N.
Widespread=3,000=30%=P3.0D=3.0=Creativity=Stars=Muses=3 March = C=I>>GIL.
Widgeon=6,000=60%=P6.0D=Man=Earth=Royalty=6 June=Gaia=Maia>>M=M2.
Widow=9,500=10,000=1,000=100%=10.0=Physicality=Tech.=10 Oct.=Uranus=P=1Ø.
Widower=6,000=60%=P6.0D=Man=Earth=Royalty=6 June=Gaia=Maia>>M=M2.
Width=6,500=7,000=70%=P7.0D=7.0=Language=Assets=Mars=7 July=Pleiades.
Wield=8,000=80%=P8.0D=Economy=Currency=8 Aug.=Zeus>>E=v.
Wiener=1,500=15%=P1.50D=1.5=Authority=Solar Crown=1 May = Maia.
Wiesbaden=7,000=70%=P7.0D=7.0=Language=Assets=Mars=7 July=Pleiades.
Wiesel Eliezer=5,000=50%=P5.00D=Law=Time=Venus=5 May = Aphrodite>>L=N.
Wife=2,500=3,000=30%=P3.0D=3.0=Creativity=Stars=Muses=3 March = C=I>>GIL.
Wig=10,000=1,000=100%=10.0=Physicality=Tech.=10 Oct.=Uranus=P=1Ø.
Wigan=4,500=5,000=50%=P5.00D=Law=Time=Venus=5 May = Aphrodite>>L=N.
Wiggle=6,500=7,000=70%=P7.0D=7.0=Language=Assets=Mars=7 July=Pleiades.
Wight,Isle of.=5,000=50%=P5.00D=Law=Time=Venus=5 May = Aphrodite>>L=N.
Wigwam=10,000=1,000=100%=10.0=Physicality=Tech.=10 Oct.=Uranus=P=1Ø.
Wilberforce=2,000=20%=P2.00D=2.0=Nature=Matter=Moon=2 Feb.=Cupid=N=C+_
Wild=10,000=1,000=100%=10.0=Physicality=Tech.=10 Oct.=Uranus=P=1Ø.
Wildcat=10,000=1,000=100%=10.0=Physicality=Tech.=10 Oct.=Uranus=P=1Ø.
Wilde,Oscar=4,000=40%=P4.0D=Govt.=Creatocracy=4 April=Mercury=Hermes=G=A4.
Wildebeest=2,000=20%=P2.00D=2.0=Nature=Matter=Moon=2 Feb.=Cupid=N=C+_
Wilder Thornton=2,500=3,000=30%=P3.0D=3.0=Cre=Stars=Muses=3 March = C=I>>GIL.

Wilderness=9,000=90%=P9.00D=9.0=Abstraction=Gods=Saturn=9Sept.>>A=Ø.
<OE wildēor,wild beast. The book of Revelation talks about the wild beast, wilderness.

Wild eyed=4,500=5,000=50%=P5.00D=Law=Time=Venus=5 May = Aphrodite>>L=N.
Wildfire=2,500=3,000=30%=P3.0D=3.0=Creativity=Stars=Muses=3 March = C=I>>GIL.
Wildfowl=4,500=5,000=50%=P5.00D=Law=Time=Venus=5 May = Aphrodite>>L=N.
Wild goose chase=2,500=3,000=30%=P3.0D=3.0=Stars=Muses=3 March = C=I>>GIL.
Wildlife=4,500=5,000=50%=P5.00D=Law=Time=Venus=5 May = Aphrodite>>L=N.

Wild rice=6,000=60%=P6.0D=Man=Earth=Royalty=6 June=Gaia=Maia>>M=M2.
Wile=10,000=1,000=100%=10.0=Physicality=Tech.=10 Oct.=Uranus=P=1Ø.
Wilhelmina=4,000=40%=P4.0D=Govt.=Creatocracy=4 April=Mercury=Hermes=G=A4.
Wilkins Roy.=3,000=30%=P3.0D=3.0=Creativity=Stars=Muses=3 March = C=I>>GIL.

Will1=10,000=1,000=100%=10.0=Physicality=Tech.=10 Oct.=Uranus=P=1Ø.
Jesus prayed for the will of GOD to be done on Earth as it is in Heaven. This means that the will of GOD is a Creatocratic system functioned on quantum mechanics means of 10,000. Indicating particulate energy, matter creativity and communications. It is therefore the will of GOD to use a currency module that measures as 10,000=1,000=100=10.0<P=£10.0. Peter Matthews-Akukalia, Castle Makupedia invented MaksCurrencies on the will of GOD.

Will2=10,000=1,000=100%=10.0=Physicality=Tech.=10 Oct.=Uranus=P=1Ø.
Willard Emma=2,500=3,000=30%=P3.0D=3.0=Cr=Stars=Muses=3 March = C=I>>GIL.
Willemstad=5,500=5.5=80%=P5.50=Earth-Midway=5 May = Gaia.
Willful=2,000=20%=P2.00D=2.0=Nature=Matter=Moon=2 Feb.=Cupid=N=C+_
William I1=5,500=5.5=80%=P5.50=Earth-Midway=5 May = Gaia.
William I2=4,500=5,000=50%=P5.00D=Law=Time=Venus=5 May = Aphrodite>>L=N.
William I3=5,000=50%=P5.00D=Law=Time=Venus=5 May = Aphrodite>>L=N.
William II1=4,000=40%=P4.0D=Govt.=Creatocracy=4 April=Mercury=Hermes=G=A4.
William II2=5,000=50%=P5.00D=Law=Time=Venus=5 May = Aphrodite>>L=N.
William III=10,000=1,000=100%=10.0=Physicality=Tech.=10 Oct.=Uranus=P=1Ø.
William IV.=4,500=5,000=50%=P5.00D=Law=Time=Venus=5 May = Aphrodite>>L=N.
Williams, Roger.=4,500=5,000=50%=P5.00D=Law=Time=Venus=5 May = Odite>>L=N.
Williams,Tennessee.=2,000=20%=P2.00D=2.0=Nature=Moon=2 Feb.=Cupid=N=C+_
Williams,Carlos=2,500=3,000=30%=P3.0D=3.0=Cre=Stars=Muses=3 March = C=I>>GIL.
Williamsburg=7,000=70%=P7.0D=7.0=Language=Assets=Mars=7 July=Pleiades.
Willies=3,000=30%=P3.0D=3.0=Creativity=Stars=Muses=3 March = C=I>>GIL.
Willing=6,500=7,000=70%=P7.0D=7.0=Language=Assets=Mars=7 July=Pleiades.
Williwaw=6,000=60%=P6.0D=Man=Earth=Royalty=6 June=Gaia=Maia>>M=M2.
Will-o'-the-wisp=6,000=60%=P6.0D=Man=Earth=Royalty=6 June=Gaia=Maia>>M=M2.
Willow=10,000=1,000=100%=10.0=Physicality=Tech.=10 Oct.=Uranus=P=1Ø.
Willowy=4,000=40%=P4.0D=Govt.=Creatocracy=4 April=Mercury=Hermes=G=A4.
Willpower=6,000=60%=P6.0D=Man=Earth=Royalty=6 June=Gaia=Maia>>M=M2.
Wily-nilly=7,500=8,000=80%=P8.0D=Economy=Currency=8 Aug.=Zeus>>E=v.
Wilmington=5,500=5.5=80%=P5.50=Earth-Midway=5 May = Gaia.
Wilson,James=7,500=8,000=80%=P8.0D=Economy=Currency=8 Aug.=Zeus>>E=v.
Wilson Woodrow=4,000=40%=P4.0D=Govt.=4 April=Mercury=Hermes=G=A4.
Wilt1=10,000=1,000=100%=10.0=Physicality=Tech.=10 Oct.=Uranus=P=1Ø.
Wilt2=3,500=4,000=40%=P4.0D=Govt.=Creatocracy=4 April=Mercury=Hermes=G=A4.
Willy=2,000=20%=P2.00D=2.0=Nature=Matter=Moon=2 Feb.=Cupid=N=C+_
Wimble=3,500=4,000=40%=P4.0D=Govt.=Creatocracy=4 April=Mercury=Hermes=G=A4.
Wimp=3,000=30%=P3.0D=3.0=Creativity=Stars=Muses=3 March = C=I>>GIL.
Wimple=10,000=1,000=100%=10.0=Physicality=Tech.=10 Oct.=Uranus=P=1Ø.

Win=10,000=1,000=100%=10.0=Physicality=Tech.=10 Oct.=Uranus=P=1Ø.
Wince=7,000=70%=P7.0D=7.0=Language=Assets=Mars=7 July=Pleiades.
Winch=10,000=1,000=100%=10.0=Physicality=Tech.=10 Oct.=Uranus=P=1Ø.
Wind1=10,000=1,000=100%=10.0=Physicality=Tech.=10 Oct.=Uranus=P=1Ø.
Wind2=10,000=1,000=100%=10.0=Physicality=Tech.=10 Oct.=Uranus=P=1Ø.
Wind3=4,500=5,000=50%=P5.00D=Law=Time=Venus=5 May = Aphrodite>>L=N.
Windbag=2,500=3,000=30%=P3.0D=3.0=Creativity=Stars=Muses=3 March = C=I>>GIL.
Windbreak=7,500=8,000=80%=P8.0D=Economy=Currency=8 Aug.=Zeus>>E=v.
Windburn=4,000=40%=P4.0D=Govt.=Creatocracy=4 April=Mercury=Hermes=G=A4.
Windchill factor=10,000=1,000=100%=10.0=Physicality=Tech.=10 Oct.=Uranus=P=1Ø.
Windfall=6,500=7,000=70%=P7.0D=7.0=Language=Assets=Mars=7 July=Pleiades.
Windflower=1,000=100%=10.0=1.0=Mind=Sun=1 January=Helios >> M=E4.
Windhoek=4,500=5,000=50%=P5.00D=Law=Time=Venus=5 May = Aphrodite>>L=N.
Winding=10,000=1,000=100%=10.0=Physicality=Tech.=10 Oct.=Uranus=P=1Ø.
Winding sheet=3,000=30%=P3.0D=3.0=Creativity=Stars=Muses=3 March = C=I>>GIL.
Wind instrument=7,500=8,000=80%=P8.0D=Economy=Currency=8 Aug.=Zeus>>E=v.
Windjammer=2,000=20%=P2.00D=2.0=Nature=Matter=Moon=2 Feb.=Cupid=N=C+_
Windlass=10,000=1,000=100%=10.0=Physicality=Tech.=10 Oct.=Uranus=P=1Ø.
Windmill=7,500=8,000=80%=P8.0D=Economy=Currency=8 Aug.=Zeus>>E=v.
Window=10,000=1,000=100%=10.0=Physicality=Tech.=10 Oct.=Uranus=P=1Ø.
Window box=6,000=60%=P6.0D=Man=Earth=Royalty=6 June=Gaia=Maia>>M=M2.
Window dressing=10,000=1,000=100%=10.0=Physicality=Tech.=10 Oct.=Uranus=P=1Ø.
Windowpane=3,000=30%=P3.0D=3.0=Creativity=Stars=Muses=3 March = C=I>>GIL.
Window shop=5,500=5.5=80%=P5.50=Earth-Midway=5 May = Gaia.
Windowsill=4,500=5,000=50%=P5.00D=Law=Time=Venus=5 May = Aphrodite>>L=N.
Windpipe=1,500=15%=P1.50D=1.5=Authority=Solar Crown=1 May = Maia.
Windrow=6,000=60%=P6.0D=Man=Earth=Royalty=6 June=Gaia=Maia>>M=M2.
Windshield=6,500=7,000=70%=P7.0D=7.0=Language=Assets=Mars=7 July=Pleiades.
Windsock=10,000=1,000=100%=10.0=Physicality=Tech.=10 Oct.=Uranus=P=1Ø.
Windsor=7,500=8,000=80%=P8.0D=Economy=Currency=8 Aug.=Zeus>>E=v.
Windsor, Duke of.=1,500=15%=P1.50D=1.5=Authority=Solar Crown=1 May = Maia.
Windstorm=5,000=50%=P5.00D=Law=Time=Venus=5 May = Aphrodite>>L=N.
Windsurfing=4,500=5,000=50%=P5.00D=Law=Time=Venus=5 May = Aphrodite>>L=N.
Windswept=3,000=30%=P3.0D=3.0=Creativity=Stars=Muses=3 March = C=I>>GIL.
Wind tunnel=8,500=9,000=90%=P9.00D=9.0=Abstraction=Gods=Saturn=9Sept.>>A=Ø.
Windup=10,000=1,000=100%=10.0=Physicality=Tech.=10 Oct.=Uranus=P=1Ø.
Windward=1,500=15%=P1.50D=1.5=Authority=Solar Crown=1 May = Maia.
Windward Islands=6,500=7,000=70%=P7.0D=7.0=Lang=Assets=Mars=7 July=Pleiades.
Windy=6,500=7,000=70%=P7.0D=7.0=Language=Assets=Mars=7 July=Pleiades.
Wine=7,000=70%=P7.0D=7.0=Language=Assets=Mars=7 July=Pleiades.
Wineglass=5,000=50%=P5.00D=Law=Time=Venus=5 May = Aphrodite>>L=N.
Winegrower=4,000=40%=P4.0D=Govt.=Creatocracy=4 April=Mercury=Hermes=G=A4.
Wine press=5,000=50%=P5.00D=Law=Time=Venus=5 May = Aphrodite>>L=N.
Winery=3,500=4,000=40%=P4.0D=Govt.=Creatocracy=4 April=Mercury=Hermes=G=A4.
Wine skin=6,000=60%=P6.0D=Man=Earth=Royalty=6 June=Gaia=Maia>>M=M2.

Wing=10,000=1,000=100%=10.0=Physicality=Tech.=10 Oct.=Uranus=P=1Ø.
Wingding=4,500=5,000=50%=P5.00D=Law=Time=Venus=5 May = Aphrodite>>L=N.
Winged=6,000=60%=P6.0D=Man=Earth=Royalty=6 June=Gaia=Maia>>M=M2.
Wing nut=6,000=60%=P6.0D=Man=Earth=Royalty=6 June=Gaia=Maia>>M=M2.
Wind span=500=5%=P5.00D=5.0=Law=Time=Venus=5 May=Aphrodite>>L=N.
Wingspread=6,000=60%=P6.0D=Man=Earth=Royalty=6 June=Gaia=Maia>>M=M2.
Wink=10,000=1,000=100%=10.0=Physicality=Tech.=10 Oct.=Uranus=P=1Ø.
Winnebago=10,000=1,000=100%=10.0=Physicality=Tech.=10 Oct.=Uranus=P=1Ø.
Winning=10,000=1,000=100%=10.0=Physicality=Tech.=10 Oct.=Uranus=P=1Ø.
Winnipeg=5,000=50%=P5.00D=Law=Time=Venus=5 May = Aphrodite>>L=N.
Winnipeg,Lake=3,500=4,000=40%=P4.0D=Govt.=4 April=Mercury=Hermes=G=A4.
Winnow=10,000=1,000=100%=10.0=Physicality=Tech.=10 Oct.=Uranus=P=1Ø.
Wino=3,000=30%=P3.0D=3.0=Creativity=Stars=Muses=3 March = C=I>>GIL.
Winsome=4,000=40%=P4.0D=Govt.=Creatocracy=4 April=Mercury=Hermes=G=A4.
Winston-Salem=4,000=40%=P4.0D=Govt.=Creatocracy=4 April=Mercury=Hermes=G=A4.
Winter=10,000=1,000=100%=10.0=Physicality=Tech.=10 Oct.=Uranus=P=1Ø.
Winter green=10,000=1,000=100%=10.0=Physicality=Tech.=10 Oct.=Uranus=P=1Ø.
Winterize=5,000=50%=P5.00D=Law=Time=Venus=5 May = Aphrodite>>L=N.
Winter kill=5,500=5.5=80%=P5.50=Earth-Midway=5 May = Gaia.
Winter squash=10,000=1,000=100%=10.0=Physicality=Tech.=10 Oct.=Uranus=P=1Ø.
Wintertime=2,000=20%=P2.00D=2.0=Nature=Matter=Moon=2 Feb.=Cupid=N=C+_
Winthrop John.=2,500=3,000=30%=P3.0D=3.0=Cre=Stars=Muses=3 March = C=I>>GIL.
Wintry=5,000=50%=P5.00D=Law=Time=Venus=5 May = Aphrodite>>L=N.
Wipe=10,000=1,000=100%=10.0=Physicality=Tech.=10 Oct.=Uranus=P=1Ø.
Wire=10,000=1,000=100%=10.0=Physicality=Tech.=10 Oct.=Uranus=P=1Ø.
Wire haired=5,000=50%=P5.00D=Law=Time=Venus=5 May = Aphrodite>>L=N.
Wireless=6,500=7,000=70%=P7.0D=7.0=Language=Assets=Mars=7 July=Pleiades.
Wire service=5,500=5.5=80%=P5.50=Earth-Midway=5 May = Gaia.
Wiretap=8,000=80%=P8.0D=Economy=Currency=8 Aug.=Zeus>>E=v.
Wiring=2,500=3,000=30%=P3.0D=3.0=Creativity=Stars=Muses=3 March = C=I>>GIL.
Wiry=5,500=5.5=80%=P5.50=Earth-Midway=5 May = Gaia.
Wisconsin=5,500=5.5=80%=P5.50=Earth-Midway=5 May = Gaia.

Wisdom=9,000=90%=P9.00D=9.0=Abstraction=Gods=Saturn=9Sept.>>A=Ø.
Understanding of what is true, right, or lasting. Common sense; good judgement.
Scholarly learning.<OE wīsdōm. See weid-*. Now we prove that wisdom is a spirit and a
living being. Greek myth calls her Athena. She also heads the council of Heaven and is
next to Hermes. She is the only one born as an adult. Bible calls her the Spirit of GOD.
Gen.1:1-3. Prov.8,9. Rom.11:33-35. Athena is the Goddess of wisdom handicraft and
mental warfare > Mind. Wife of Castle Makupedia >>see The Creatocracy Republic by
Peter Matthews-Akukalia.
The Lord gave the word: great was the company that published it. - Psalm 68:11.
Psalm 68 is the prophecy and signs of the wealth of Peter Matthews-Akukalia through
the publishing of the World Digital Smart Dictionary. WDSD is prophetic fulfillment
of Psalm 68. It gives the step by step procedures by which a man will become a God after

computing the world in a word book and published. It states the author of the work will have the authority of the Almighty GOD and even compute the name JAH to mean a double dimension Spirit or Almighty. Through the book the word "God" is mentioned which by their different codes indicates different Gods under the administration of the almighty. Heavens computationally means Creatocracy. There is a clear distinction between a God as an excellent person who will decipher the mysteries of destiny and GOD as the Almighty. Hence a God is different from GOD. The reason Peter Matthews - Akukalia is established to be a God by authority of GOD. Interpretation of the Scriptures upgrades region to faith through computation. A knowledge system known as Makstianity and invented by Peter Matthews - Akukalia. It involves Spirinatics, Spiricology and Psycho - Forensics Auditing. Below are the use of different codes to depict distinction between God and GOD. V1. God H430, V11. The Lord H136, V14. Almighty H7706, V18. The LORD H3050, V19. Even the God H410, V20. GOD H3069. See Psalm. See God. See Word. See Witty.

Wisdom of Solomon=2,000=20%=P2.00D=2.0=Nature=Moon=2 Feb.=Cupid=N=C+_
Wisdom tooth=6,500=7,000=70%=P7.0D=7.0=Language=Assets=Mars=7 July=Pleiades.
Wise1=10,000=1,000=100%=10.0=Physicality=Tech.=10 Oct.=Uranus=P=1Ø.
Wise2=6,000=60%=P6.0D=Man=Earth=Royalty=6 June=Gaia=Maia>>M=M2.
-wise=10,000=1,000=100%=10.0=Physicality=Tech.=10 Oct.=Uranus=P=1Ø.
Wiseacre=5,500=5.5=80%=P5.50=Earth-Midway=5 May = Gaia.
Wisecrack=3,000=30%=P3.0D=3.0=Creativity=Stars=Muses=3 March = C=I>>GIL.
Wish=10,000=1,000=100%=10.0=Physicality=Tech.=10 Oct.=Uranus=P=1Ø.
Wishbone=4,500=5,000=50%=P5.00D=Law=Time=Venus=5 May = Aphrodite>>L=N.
Wishful=3,500=4,000=40%=P4.0D=Govt.=Creatocracy=4 April=Mercury=Hermes=G=A4.
Wishy-washy=4,000=40%=P4.0D=Govt.=Creatocracy=4 April=Mercury=Hermes=G=A4.
Wisp=10,000=1,000=100%=10.0=Physicality=Tech.=10 Oct.=Uranus=P=1Ø.
Wisteria=10,000=1,000=100%=10.0=Physicality=Tech.=10 Oct.=Uranus=P=1Ø.
Wistful=10,000=1,000=100%=10.0=Physicality=Tech.=10 Oct.=Uranus=P=1Ø.
Wit=10,000=1,000=100%=10.0=Physicality=Tech.=10 Oct.=Uranus=P=1Ø.
Witch=10,000=1,000=100%=10.0=Physicality=Tech.=10 Oct.=Uranus=P=1Ø.
Witchcraft=1,000=100%=10.0=1.0=Mind=Sun=1 January=Helios >> M=E4.
Witch doctor=1,500=15%=P1.50D=1.5=Authority=Solar Crown=1 May = Maia.
Witch hazel=10,000=1,000=100%=10.0=Physicality=Tech.=10 Oct.=Uranus=P=1Ø.
Witch-hunt=10,000=1,000=100%=10.0=Physicality=Tech.=10 Oct.=Uranus=P=1Ø.
Witching=3,000=30%=P3.0D=3.0=Creativity=Stars=Muses=3 March = C=I>>GIL.
With=10,000=1,000=100%=10.0=Physicality=Tech.=10 Oct.=Uranus=P=1Ø.
Withal=4,500=5,000=50%=P5.00D=Law=Time=Venus=5 May = Aphrodite>>L=N.
Withdraw=10,000=1,000=100%=10.0=Physicality=Tech.=10 Oct.=Uranus=P=1Ø.
Withdrawal=10,000=1,000=100%=10.0=Physicality=Tech.=10 Oct.=Uranus=P=1Ø.
Withdrawn=2,000=20%=P2.00D=2.0=Nature=Matter=Moon=2 Feb.=Cupid=N=C+_
Withe=7,000=70%=P7.0D=7.0=Language=Assets=Mars=7 July=Pleiades.
Wither=10,000=1,000=100%=10.0=Physicality=Tech.=10 Oct.=Uranus=P=1Ø.
Withers=10,000=1,000=100%=10.0=Physicality=Tech.=10 Oct.=Uranus=P=1Ø.
Withhold=10,000=1,000=100%=10.0=Physicality=Tech.=10 Oct.=Uranus=P=1Ø.

Withholding tax=10,000=1,000=100%=10.0=Physicality=Tech.=10 Oct.=Uranus=P=1Ø.
Within=10,000=1,000=100%=10.0=Physicality=Tech.=10 Oct.=Uranus=P=1Ø.
Without=10,000=1,000=100%=10.0=Physicality=Tech.=10 Oct.=Uranus=P=1Ø.
Withstand=10,000=1,000=100%=10.0=Physicality=Tech.=10 Oct.=Uranus=P=1Ø.
Witless=2,500=3,000=30%=P3.0D=3.0=Creativity=Stars=Muses=3 March = C=I>>GIL.
Witness=10,000=1,000=100%=10.0=Physicality=Tech.=10 Oct.=Uranus=P=1Ø.
Witticism=3,000=30%=P3.0D=3.0=Creativity=Stars=Muses=3 March = C=I>>GIL.

Witty=3,000=30%=P3.0D=3.0=Creativity=Stars=Muses=3 March = C=I>>GIL.
I dwell with Prudence and searches for the knowledge of witty inventions. Peter Matthews-Akukalia, Castle Makupedia discovered that words are witty expressions and the ability to measure the value of a word through scientific means holds the keys to all creativity hence obtaining the favor and love of Athena Goddess of wisdom handicraft and mind. This birthed Castle Makupedia as the First Makumatics Dictionary and MaksCurrencies World Encyclopedia. The secret of a word and all words is the ownership of its equivalent asset and is a requirement of GOD. Deuteronomy 29:29. Romans 8:23, 11:33-35. Proverbs 8:12. Castle Makupedia is the God of Creatocracy Genius and Mind. See Wisdom.

Witwatersrand=4,500=5,000=50%=P5.00D=Law=Time=Venus=5 May = Aphrodite>>L=N.
Wives=1,500=15%=P1.50D=1.5=Authority=Solar Crown=1 May = Maia.

Wizard=7,500=8,000=80%=P8.0D=Economy=Currency=8 Aug.=Zeus>>E=v.
Peter Matthews-Akukalia, Castle Makupedia is the wizard at Makumatics. God of Creatocracy Genius & Mind. He computed the wits behind all inventions. See witty.

Wizened=2,500=3,000=30%=P3.0D=3.0=Creativity=Stars=Muses=3 March = C=I>>GIL.
wk.=1,000=100%=10.0=1.0=Mind=Sun=1 January=Helios >> M=E4.
wkly.=500=5%=P5.00D=5.0=Law=Time=Venus=5 May=Aphrodite>>L=N.
WNW=1,000=100%=10.0=1.0=Mind=Sun=1 January=Helios >> M=E4.
w/o=500=5%=P5.00D=5.0=Law=Time=Venus=5 May=Aphrodite>>L=N.
Woad=8,500=9,000=90%=P9.00D=9.0=Abstraction=Gods=Saturn=9Sept.>>A=Ø.
Wobble=10,000=1,000=100%=10.0=Physicality=Tech.=10 Oct.=Uranus=P=1Ø.
Wodehouse Pelham=2,500=3,000=30%=P3.0D=3.0=Stars=Muses=3 March = C=I>>GIL.
Woe=11,000=11%=P1.10D=1.1=Idea=Brainchild=Inv.=11 Nov.=SC=Athena>>I=MT.
Woebegone=3,000=30%=P3.0D=3.0=Creativity=Stars=Muses=3 March = C=I>>GIL.
Woeful=6,000=60%=P6.0D=Man=Earth=Royalty=6 June=Gaia=Maia>>M=M2.
Wok=8,000=80%=P8.0D=Economy=Currency=8 Aug.=Zeus>>E=v.
Woke=4,500=5,000=50%=P5.00D=Law=Time=Venus=5 May = Aphrodite>>L=N.
Woken=2,000=20%=P2.00D=2.0=Nature=Matter=Moon=2 Feb.=Cupid=N=C+_
Wolf=10,000=1,000=100%=10.0=Physicality=Tech.=10 Oct.=Uranus=P=1Ø.
Wolfe James.=3,000=30%=P3.0D=3.0=Creativity=Stars=Muses=3 March = C=I>>GIL.
Wolfe, Thomas=2,500=3,000=30%=P3.0D=3.0=Cr=Stars=Muses=3 March = C=I>>GIL.
Wolfhound=5,000=50%=P5.00D=Law=Time=Venus=5 May = Aphrodite>>L=N.

Wolfram=1,500=15%=P1.50D=1.5=Authority=Solar Crown=1 May = Maia.
Wollstonecraft Mary=2,000=20%=P2.00D=2.0=Nature=Moon=2 Feb.=Cupid=N=C+_
Wolsey Thomas.=3,500=4,000=40%=P4.0D=Govt.=4 April=Mercury=Hermes=G=A4.
Wolverine=6,500=7,000=70%=P7.0D=7.0=Language=Assets=Mars=7 July=Pleiades.
Woman=7,000=70%=P7.0D=7.0=Language=Assets=Mars=7 July=Pleiades.
Womanhood=8,000=80%=P8.0D=Economy=Currency=8 Aug.=Zeus>>E=v.
Womanish=2,500=3,000=30%=P3.0D=3.0=Creativity=Stars=Muses=3 March = C=I>>GIL.
Womanize=2,000=20%=P2.00D=2.0=Nature=Matter=Moon=2 Feb.=Cupid=N=C+_
Womankind=1,000=100%=10.0=1.0=Mind=Sun=1 January=Helios >> M=E4.
Womanly=3,500=4,000=40%=P4.0D=Govt.=Creato=4 April=Mercury=Hermes=G=A4.
Womb=6,000=60%=P6.0D=Man=Earth=Royalty=6 June=Gaia=Maia>>M=M2.
Wombat=6,000=60%=P6.0D=Man=Earth=Royalty=6 June=Gaia=Maia>>M=M2.
Women=1,500=15%=P1.50D=1.5=Authority=Solar Crown=1 May = Maia.
Womenfolk=4,000=40%=P4.0D=Govt.=Creatocracy=4 April=Mercury=Hermes=G=A4.

Won1=3,500=4,000=40%=P4.0D=Govt.=Creatocracy=4 April=Mercury=Hermes=G=A4.
Currency of Korea. Metric weight = 3.5/10=0.35>35:1. See Naira. Dollar.

Won2=3,000=30%=P3.0D=3.0=Creativity=Stars=Muses=3 March = C=I>>GIL.
Wonder=10,000=1,000=100%=10.0=Physicality=Tech.=10 Oct.=Uranus=P=1Ø.
Wonderful=3,500=4,000=40%=P4.0D=Govt.=Creatocracy=4 April=Hermes=G=A4.
Wonderland=4,000=40%=P4.0D=Govt.=Creatocracy=4 April=Mercury=Hermes=G=A4.
Wonderment=3,500=4,000=40%=P4.0D=Govt.=Creatocracy=4 April=Hermes=G=A4.
Wondrous=500=5%=P5.00D=5.0=Law=Time=Venus=5 May=Aphrodite>>L=N.
Wont=11,000=11%=P1.10D=1.1=Idea=Brainchild=Inv.=11 Nov.=SC=Athena>>I=MT.
Won't=1,000=100%=10.0=1.0=Mind=Sun=1 January=Helios >> M=E4.
Wonted=3,500=4,000=40%=P4.0D=Govt.=Creatocracy=4 April=Mercury=Hermes=G=A4.
Wonton=8,500=9,000=90%=P9.00D=9.0=Abstraction=Gods=Saturn=9Sept.>>A=Ø.
Woo=8,500=9,000=90%=P9.00D=9.0=Abstraction=Gods=Saturn=9Sept.>>A=Ø.
wood=10,000=1,000=100%=10.0=Physicality=Tech.=10 Oct.=Uranus=P=1Ø.
Wood Grant.=2,000=20%=P2.00D=2.0=Nature=Matter=Moon=2 Feb.=Cupid=N=C+_
Wood alcohol=1,000=100%=10.0=1.0=Mind=Sun=1 January=Helios >> M=E4.
Woodbine=8,500=9,000=90%=P9.00D=9.0=Abstraction=Gods=Saturn=9Sept.>>A=Ø.
Woodblock=1,000=100%=10.0=1.0=Mind=Sun=1 January=Helios >> M=E4.
Woodchuck=10,000=1,000=100%=10.0=Physicality=Tech.=10 Oct.=Uranus=P=1Ø.
Woodcock=5,500=5.5=80%=P5.50=Earth-Midway=5 May = Gaia.
Woodcraft=7,000=70%=P7.0D=7.0=Language=Assets=Mars=7 July=Pleiades.
Woodcut=7,000=70%=P7.0D=7.0=Language=Assets=Mars=7 July=Pleiades.
Woodcutter=5,000=50%=P5.00D=Law=Time=Venus=5 May = Aphrodite>>L=N.
Wood duck=6,000=60%=P6.0D=Man=Earth=Royalty=6 June=Gaia=Maia>>M=M2.
Wooded=2,500=3,000=30%=P3.0D=3.0=Creativity=Stars=Muses=3 March = C=I>>GIL.
Wooden=5,500=5.5=80%=P5.50=Earth-Midway=5 May = Gaia.
Wood hull Victoria=2,500=3,000=30%=P3.0D=3.0=Cr=Stars=Muses=3 March=C=I>GIL.
Woodland=3,000=30%=P3.0D=3.0=Creativity=Stars=Muses=3 March = C=I>>GIL.

Woodpecker=12,000=12%=P1.20D=1.2=Knowledge=Edu=12Dec.=Athena>>K=F.
Woodpile=3,500=4,000=40%=P4.0D=Govt.=Creatocracy=4 April=Hermes=G=A4.
Woodruff=3,500=4,000=40%=P4.0D=Govt.=Creatocracy=4 April=Hermes=G=A4.
Woodshed=3,500=4,000=40%=P4.0D=Govt.=Creatocracy=4 April=Hermes=G=A4.
Woodsman=7,000=70%=P7.0D=7.0=Language=Assets=Mars=7 July=Pleiades.
Woodsy=3,000=30%=P3.0D=3.0=Creativity=Stars=Muses=3 March = C=I>>GIL.
Wood wind=8,500=9,000=90%=P9.00D=9.0=Abstraction=Gods=Saturn=9Sept.>>A=Ø.
Woodwork=7,500=8,000=80%=P8.0D=Economy=Currency=8 Aug.=Zeus>>E=v.
Woody=5,000=50%=P5.00D=Law=Time=Venus=5 May = Aphrodite>>L=N.
Woof=10,000=1,000=100%=10.0=Physicality=Tech.=10 Oct.=Uranus=P=1Ø.
Woofer=5,000=50%=P5.00D=Law=Time=Venus=5 May = Aphrodite>>L=N.
Wool=10,000=1,000=100%=10.0=Physicality=Tech.=10 Oct.=Uranus=P=1Ø.
Woolen=6,000=60%=P6.0D=Man=Earth=Royalty=6 June=Gaia=Maia>>M=M2.
Woolf Adeline=3,000=30%=P3.0D=3.0=Creativity=Stars=Muses=3 March = C=I>>GIL.
Wool gathering=2,000=20%=P2.00D=2.0=Nature=Matter=Moon=2 Feb.=Cupid=N=C+_
Woolly=10,000=1,000=100%=10.0=Physicality=Tech.=10 Oct.=Uranus=P=1Ø.
Woomera=7,000=70%=P7.0D=7.0=Language=Assets=Mars=7 July=Pleiades.
Woops=1,500=15%=P1.50D=1.5=Authority=Solar Crown=1 May = Maia.
Woozy=2,500=3,000=30%=P3.0D=3.0=Creativity=Stars=Muses=3 March = C=I>>GIL.
Worcester=4,500=5,000=50%=P5.00D=Law=Time=Venus=5 May = Aphrodite>>L=N.
Worcestershire=4,000=40%=P4.0D=Govt.=Creatocracy=4 April=Hermes=G=A4.

Word=10,000=1,000=100%=10.0=Physicality=Tech.=10 Oct.=Uranus=P=1Ø.
Keys of a word>>meaning, sound, combination, writing, representations, something, said, set, bits, memory, discourse or talk, speech, music, lyrics, text, assurance, promise, command, direction, news, signal, password, the Bible. The formula of language is the same used to measure all words hence a dictionary is defined as the depth of riches in the knowledge and wisdom of GOD because in the beginning GOD said...See Wisdom, witty. The formula for the measurement of language and all words is Lang=Az. The seventh dimension of the Creatocracy, the Disean language meaning Universe. >See Universe. Once computed a word becomes technology and an asset as obtained in the WDSD.

Wordage=4,000=40%=P4.0D=Govt.=Creatocracy=4 April=Mercury=Hermes=G=A4.
Word book=2,500=3,000=30%=P3.0D=3.0=Creativity=Stars=Muses=3 March = C=I>>GIL.
Wording=4,000=40%=P4.0D=Govt.=Creatocracy=4 April=Mercury=Hermes=G=A4.
Wordplay=3,500=4,000=40%=P4.0D=Govt.=Creato=4 April=Mercury=Hermes=G=A4.

Word processing=8,000=80%=P8.0D=Economy=Currency=8 Aug.=Zeus>>E=v.
The Almighty GOD processes words through His computerized Mind called the Pleiades.

Wordsworth William=2,000=20%=P2.00D=2.0=Nature=Moon=2 Feb.=Cupid=N=C+_
Wordy=8,000=80%=P8.0D=Economy=Currency=8 Aug.=Zeus>>E=v.
Wore=2,000=20%=P2.00D=2.0=Nature=Matter=Moon=2 Feb.=Cupid=N=C+_

Work=10,000=1,000=100%=10.0=Physicality=Tech.=10 Oct.=Uranus=P=1Ø.
Workable=4,000=40%=P4.0D=Govt.=Creatocracy=4 April=Mercury=Hermes=G=A4.
Workaday=6,000=60%=P6.0D=Man=Earth=Royalty=6 June=Gaia=Maia>>M=M2.
Workaholic=6,500=7,000=70%=P7.0D=7.0=Language=Assets=Mars=7 July=Pleiades.
Workbench=7,000=70%=P7.0D=7.0=Language=Assets=Mars=7 July=Pleiades.
Workbook=10,000=1,000=100%=10.0=Physicality=Tech.=10 Oct.=Uranus=P=1Ø.
Workday=8,000=80%=P8.0D=Economy=Currency=8 Aug.=Zeus>>E=v.
Worker=10,000=1,000=100%=10.0=Physicality=Tech.=10 Oct.=Uranus=P=1Ø.
Workfare=7,500=8,000=80%=P8.0D=Economy=Currency=8 Aug.=Zeus>>E=v.
Workforce=10,000=1,000=100%=10.0=Physicality=Tech.=10 Oct.=Uranus=P=1Ø.
Workhorse=8,000=80%=P8.0D=Economy=Currency=8 Aug.=Zeus>>E=v.
Workhouse=7,000=70%=P7.0D=7.0=Language=Assets=Mars=7 July=Pleiades.
Working=10,000=1,000=100%=10.0=Physicality=Tech.=10 Oct.=Uranus=P=1Ø.
Workload=5,000=50%=P5.00D=Law=Time=Venus=5 May = Aphrodite>>L=N.
Workman=4,000=40%=P4.0D=Govt.=Creatocracy=4 April=Mercury=Hermes=G=A4.
Workmanlike=3,000=30%=P3.0D=3.0=Creativity=Stars=Muses=3 March = C=I>>GIL.
Workmanship=6,000=60%=P6.0D=Man=Earth=Royalty=6 June=Gaia=Maia>>M=M2.
Workout=6,500=7,000=70%=P7.0D=7.0=Language=Assets=Mars=7 July=Pleiades.
Workplace=5,500=5.5=80%=P5.50=Earth-Midway=5 May = Gaia.
Workshop=8,000=80%=P8.0D=Economy=Currency=8 Aug.=Zeus>>E=v.
Workspace=6,000=60%=P6.0D=Man=Earth=Royalty=6 June=Gaia=Maia>>M=M2.
Workstation=7,500=8,000=80%=P8.0D=Economy=Currency=8 Aug.=Zeus>>E=v.
Work table=4,000=40%=P4.0D=Govt.=Creatocracy=4 April=Mercury=Hermes=G=A4.
Workweek=4,000=40%=P4.0D=Govt.=Creatocracy=4 April=Mercury=Hermes=G=A4.

World=10,000=1,000=100%=10.0=Physicality=Tech.=10 Oct.=Uranus=P=1Ø.
Peter Matthews-Akukalia, Castle Makupedia sits on a myriad of endless world records earned through his works. He invented the World Digital Dictionary WDD emerging him as a world power among the nations and fields of practice esp. in the world of science and inventions. A multidisciplinary and multidimensional sector crucial in national life is his invented Creatocracy...the long awaited paradigm shift. He is therefore apotheosized among the deities as Castle Makupedia the God of Creatocracy Genius and Mind. Publishing makes for the program or show titled The Creatocracy...the paradigm shift.

Worldly=6,000=60%=P6.0D=Man=Earth=Royalty=6 June=Gaia=Maia>>M=M2.
Worldly wise=3,000=30%=P3.0D=3.0=Creativity=Stars=Muses=3 March = C=I>>GIL.
Worldly wide=3,500=4,000=40%=P4.0D=Govt.=Creatocracy=4 April=Hermes=G=A4.
Worm=10,000=1,000=100%=10.0=Physicality=Tech.=10 Oct.=Uranus=P=1Ø.
Worm-eaten=5,000=50%=P5.00D=Law=Time=Venus=5 May = Aphrodite>>L=N.
Worm gear=8,000=80%=P8.0D=Economy=Currency=8 Aug.=Zeus>>E=v.
Worm wheel=3,500=4,000=40%=P4.0D=Govt.=Creatocracy=4 April=Hermes=G=A4.
Wormwood=6,500=7,000=70%=P7.0D=7.0=Language=Assets=Mars=7 July=Pleiades.
Worn=10,000=1,000=100%=10.0=Physicality=Tech.=10 Oct.=Uranus=P=1Ø.
Worn out=5,000=50%=P5.00D=Law=Time=Venus=5 May = Aphrodite>>L=N.

Worrisome=3,000=30%=P3.0D=3.0=Creativity=Stars=Muses=3 March = C=I>>GIL.
Worry=10,000=1,000=100%=10.0=Physicality=Tech.=10 Oct.=Uranus=P=1Ø.
Worry wart=3,000=30%=P3.0D=3.0=Creativity=Stars=Muses=3 March = C=I>>GIL.
Worse=6,500=7,000=70%=P7.0D=7.0=Language=Assets=Mars=7 July=Pleiades.
Worsen=2,500=3,000=30%=P3.0D=3.0=Creativity=Stars=Muses=3 March = C=I>>GIL.
Worship=10,000=1,000=100%=10.0=Physicality=Tech.=10 Oct.=Uranus=P=1Ø.
Worshipful=7,000=70%=P7.0D=7.0=Language=Assets=Mars=7 July=Pleiades.
Worst=10,000=1,000=100%=10.0=Physicality=Tech.=10 Oct.=Uranus=P=1Ø.
Worsted=10,000=1,000=100%=10.0=Physicality=Tech.=10 Oct.=Uranus=P=1Ø.
Wort=3,500=4,000=40%=P4.0D=Govt.=Creatocracy=4 April=Mercury=Hermes=G=A4.
Worth=10,000=1,000=100%=10.0=Physicality=Tech.=10 Oct.=Uranus=P=1Ø.
Worthless=4,500=5,000=50%=P5.00D=Law=Time=Venus=5 May = Aphrodite>>L=N.
Worthwhile=6,000=60%=P6.0D=Man=Earth=Royalty=6 June=Gaia=Maia>>M=M2.
Worthy=9,000=90%=P9.00D=9.0=Abstraction=Gods=Saturn=9Sept.>>A=Ø.
Would=10,000=1,000=100%=10.0=Physicality=Tech.=10 Oct.=Uranus=P=1Ø.
Would be=4,500=5,000=50%=P5.00D=Law=Time=Venus=5 May = Aphrodite>>L=N.
Wouldn't=1,000=100%=10.0=1.0=Mind=Sun=1 January=Helios >> M=E4.
Wouldst=4,000=40%=P4.0D=Govt.=Creatocracy=4 April=Mercury=Hermes=G=A4.
Wound1=10,000=1,000=100%=10.0=Physicality=Tech.=10 Oct.=Uranus=P=1Ø.
Wound2=3,000=30%=P3.0D=3.0=Creativity=Stars=Muses=3 March = C=I>>GIL.
Wounded knee=6,500=7,000=70%=P7.0D=7.0=Language=Assets=Mars=7 July=Pleiades.
Wove=2,000=20%=P2.00D=2.0=Nature=Matter=Moon=2 Feb.=Cupid=N=C+_
Woven=2,000=20%=P2.00D=2.0=Nature=Matter=Moon=2 Feb.=Cupid=N=C+_
Wow=11,000=11%=P1.10D=1.1=Idea=Brainchild=Inv.=11 Nov.=SC=Athena>>I=MT.
WPA=1,500=15%=P1.50D=1.5=Authority=Solar Crown=1 May = Maia.
wpm=1,500=15%=P1.50D=1.5=Authority=Solar Crown=1 May = Maia.
Wrack=11,000=11%=P1.10D=1.1=Idea=Brainchild=Inv.=11 Nov.=SC=Athena>>I=MT.
Wraith=6,000=60%=P6.0D=Man=Earth=Royalty=6 June=Gaia=Maia>>M=M2.
Wrangell Island=6,500=7,000=70%=P7.0D=7.0=Language=Assets=Mars=7 July=Pleiades.
Wrangell Mount.=4,500=5,000=50%=P5.00D=Law=Time=Venus=5 May = Odite>>L=N.
Wrangell Mountains.=10,000=1,000=100%=10.0=Phys=Tech.=10 Oct.=Uranus=P=1Ø.
Wrangle=10,000=1,000=100%=10.0=Physicality=Tech.=10 Oct.=Uranus=P=1Ø.
Wrap=10,000=1,000=100%=10.0=Physicality=Tech.=10 Oct.=Uranus=P=1Ø.
Wraparound=10,000=1,000=100%=10.0=Physicality=Tech.=10 Oct.=Uranus=P=1Ø.
Wrapper=8,500=9,000=90%=P9.00D=9.0=Abstraction=Gods=Saturn=9Sept.>>A=Ø.
Wrapping=3,500=4,000=40%=P4.0D=Govt.=Creatocracy=4 April=Hermes=G=A4.
Wrap up=4,000=40%=P4.0D=Govt.=Creatocracy=4 April=Mercury=Hermes=G=A4.
Wrasse=6,000=60%=P6.0D=Man=Earth=Royalty=6 June=Gaia=Maia>>M=M2.
Wrath=8,500=9,000=90%=P9.00D=9.0=Abstraction=Gods=Saturn=9Sept.>>A=Ø.
Wreak=5,000=50%=P5.00D=Law=Time=Venus=5 May = Aphrodite>>L=N.
Wreath=10,000=1,000=100%=10.0=Physicality=Tech.=10 Oct.=Uranus=P=1Ø.
Wreathe=10,000=1,000=100%=10.0=Physicality=Tech.=10 Oct.=Uranus=P=1Ø.
Wreck=10,000=1,000=100%=10.0=Physicality=Tech.=10 Oct.=Uranus=P=1Ø.
Wreckage=4,500=5,000=50%=P5.00D=Law=Time=Venus=5 May = Aphrodite>>L=N.
Wrecker=10,000=1,000=100%=10.0=Physicality=Tech.=10 Oct.=Uranus=P=1Ø.

Wren=6,500=7,000=70%=P7.0D=7.0=Language=Assets=Mars=7 July=Pleiades.
Wren Christopher=2,500=3,000=30%=P3.0D=3.0=Cr=Stars=Muses=3 March = C=I>>GIL.
Wrench=10,000=1,000=100%=10.0=Physicality=Tech.=10 Oct.=Uranus=P=1Ø.
Wrest=10,000=1,000=100%=10.0=Physicality=Tech.=10 Oct.=Uranus=P=1Ø.
Wrestle=10,000=1,000=100%=10.0=Physicality=Tech.=10 Oct.=Uranus=P=1Ø.
Wrestling=7,500=8,000=80%=P8.0D=Economy=Currency=8 Aug.=Zeus>>E=v.
Wretch=5,000=50%=P5.00D=Law=Time=Venus=5 May = Aphrodite>>L=N.
Wretched=8,500=9,000=90%=P9.00D=9.0=Abstraction=Gods=Saturn=9Sept.>>A=Ø.
Wrier=1,500=15%=P1.50D=1.5=Authority=Solar Crown=1 May = Maia.
Wriest=2,000=20%=P2.00D=2.0=Nature=Matter=Moon=2 Feb.=Cupid=N=C+_
Wriggle=10,000=1,000=100%=10.0=Physicality=Tech.=10 Oct.=Uranus=P=1Ø.
Wriggler=4,000=40%=P4.0D=Govt.=Creatocracy=4 April=Mercury=Hermes=G=A4.
Wright Frank Lloyd.=2,000=20%=P2.00D=2.0=Nature=Moon=2 Feb.=Cupid=N=C+_
Wright,Orville.=7,000=70%=P7.0D=7.0=Language=Assets=Mars=7 July=Pleiades.
Wright,Richard=2,000=20%=P2.00D=2.0=Nature=Matter=Moon=2 Feb.=Cupid=N=C+_
Wring=10,000=1,000=100%=10.0=Physicality=Tech.=10 Oct.=Uranus=P=1Ø.
Wringer=8,000=80%=P8.0D=Economy=Currency=8 Aug.=Zeus>>E=v.
Wrinkle=10,000=1,000=100%=10.0=Physicality=Tech.=10 Oct.=Uranus=P=1Ø.
Wrist=6,000=60%=P6.0D=Man=Earth=Royalty=6 June=Gaia=Maia>>M=M2.
Wristband=4,500=5,000=50%=P5.00D=Law=Time=Venus=5 May = Aphrodite>>L=N.
Wristwatch=5,000=50%=P5.00D=Law=Time=Venus=5 May = Aphrodite>>L=N.
Writ=10,000=1,000=100%=10.0=Physicality=Tech.=10 Oct.=Uranus=P=1Ø.
Write=10,000=1,000=100%=10.0=Physicality=Tech.=10 Oct.=Uranus=P=1Ø.
Write-in=7,000=70%=P7.0D=7.0=Language=Assets=Mars=7 July=Pleiades.
Writer=3,500=4,000=40%=P4.0D=Govt.=Creatocracy=4 April=Mercury=Hermes=G=A4.
Write up=3,000=30%=P3.0D=3.0=Creativity=Stars=Muses=3 March = C=I>>GIL.
Writhe=4,500=5,000=50%=P5.00D=Law=Time=Venus=5 May = Aphrodite>>L=N.
Writing=10,000=1,000=100%=10.0=Physicality=Tech.=10 Oct.=Uranus=P=1Ø.
Wroclaw=5,500=5.5=80%=P5.50=Earth-Midway=5 May = Gaia.
Wrong=10,000=1,000=100%=10.0=Physicality=Tech.=10 Oct.=Uranus=P=1Ø.
Wrongdoer=2,000=20%=P2.00D=2.0=Nature=Matter=Moon=2 Feb.=Cupid=N=C+_
Wrongful=2,500=3,000=30%=P3.0D=3.0=Creativity=Stars=Muses=3 March = C=I>>GIL.
Wrongheaded=2,000=20%=P2.00D=2.0=Nature=Matter=Moon=2 Feb.=Cupid=N=C+_
Wrote=2,000=20%=P2.00D=2.0=Nature=Matter=Moon=2 Feb.=Cupid=N=C+_
Wroth=1,500=15%=P1.50D=1.5=Authority=Solar Crown=1 May = Maia.
Wrought=3,500=4,000=40%=P4.0D=Govt.=Creatocracy=4 April=Hermes=G=A4.
Wrought iron=6,000=60%=P6.0D=Man=Earth=Royalty=6 June=Gaia=Maia>>M=M2.
Wrought up=1,000=100%=10.0=Physicality=Tech.=10 Oct.=Uranus=P=1Ø.
Wrung=3,000=30%=P3.0D=3.0=Creativity=Stars=Muses=3 March = C=I>>GIL.
Wry=10,000=1,000=100%=10.0=Physicality=Tech.=10 Oct.=Uranus=P=1Ø.
WSW=1,000=100%=10.0=1.0=Mind=Sun=1 January=Helios >> M=E4.
wt.=500=5%=P5.00D=5.0=Law=Time=Venus=5 May=Aphrodite>>L=N.
Wuhan=7,000=70%=P7.0D=7.0=Language=Assets=Mars=7 July=Pleiades.
Wuppertal=4,000=40%=P4.0D=Govt.=Creatocracy=4 April=Mercury=Hermes=G=A4.
Wurst=1,000=100%=10.0=1.0=Mind=Sun=1 January=Helios >> M=E4.

WV=1,000=100%=10.0=1.0=Mind=Sun=1 January=Helios >> M=E4.
WWI=1,500=15%=P1.50D=1.5=Authority=Solar Crown=1 May = Maia.
WWII=1,500=15%=P1.50D=1.5=Authority=Solar Crown=1 May = Maia.
WY=500=5%=P5.00D=5.0=Law=Time=Venus=5 May=Aphrodite>>L=N.
Wyandotte=10,000=1,000=100%=10.0=Physicality=Tech.=10 Oct.=Uranus=P=1Ø.
Wyatt Thomas=2,500=3,000=30%=P3.0D=3.0=Cr=Stars=Muses=3 March = C=I>>GIL.
Wycherley William.=4,000=40%=P4.0D=Govt.=4 April=Mercury=Hermes=G=A4.
Wycliffe, John.=4,000=40%=P4.0D=Govt.=Creatocracy=4 April=Mercury=Hermes=G=A4.
Wyeth Andrew=2,000=20%=P2.00D=2.0=Nature=Matter=Moon=2 Feb.=Cupid=N=C+_
Wyoming=5,000=50%=P5.00D=Law=Time=Venus=5 May = Aphrodite>>L=N.
WYSIWYG=10,000=1,000=100%=10.0=Physicality=Tech.=10 Oct.=Uranus=P=1Ø.

MAKABET =Xx=

---

x1=10,000=1,000=100%=10.0=Physicality=Tech.=10 Oct.=Uranus=P=1Ø.
The 24th letter of the English alphabet. An unknown or unnamed factor, thing, or person. Psycho-weight of X>> 10.0*2.4x=px=12.4+24=36.4x=px=33.4. It is actually unknown because it represents the unseen genius in a person. 4G ranking. See Genius Table.

---

x2=2,500=3,000=30%=P3.0D=3.0=Creativity=Stars=Muses=3 March = C=I>>GIL.
X1=7,000=70%=P7.0D=7.0=Language=Assets=Mars=7 July=Pleiades.
X2=5,000=50%=P5.00D=Law=Time=Venus=5 May = Aphrodite>>L=N.
X3=1,500=15%=P1.50D=1.5=Authority=Solar Crown=1 May = Maia.
x.=1,000=100%=10.0=1.0=Mind=Sun=1 January=Helios >> M=E4.
Xanthus=5,000=50%=P5.00D=Law=Time=Venus=5 May = Aphrodite>>L=N.
Xavier Saint=5,500=5.5=80%=P5.50=Earth-Midway=5 May = Gaia.
X-axis=10,000=1,000=100%=10.0=Physicality=Tech.=10 Oct.=Uranus=P=1Ø.
X-chromosome=10,000=1,000=100%=10.0=Physicality=Tech.=10 Oct.=Uranus=P=1Ø.
Xe=2,500=3,000=30%=P3.0D=3.0=Creativity=Stars=Muses=3 March = C=I>>GIL.
Xebec=7,500=8,000=80%=P8.0D=Economy=Currency=8 Aug.=Zeus>>E=v.
Xenon=10,000=1,000=100%=10.0=Physicality=Tech.=10 Oct.=Uranus=P=1Ø.
Xenophanes=3,000=30%=P3.0D=3.0=Creativity=Stars=Muses=3 March = C=I>>GIL.
Xenophobe=6,500=7,000=70%=P7.0D=7.0=Language=Assets=Mars=7 July=Pleiades.
Xenophone=4,000=40%=P4.0D=Govt.=Creatocracy=4 April=Mercury=Hermes=G=A4.
Xeric=5,000=50%=P5.00D=Law=Time=Venus=5 May = Aphrodite>>L=N.
Xerography=10,000=1,000=100%=10.0=Physicality=Tech.=10 Oct.=Uranus=P=1Ø.
Xerophyte=5,500=5.5=80%=P5.50=Earth-Midway=5 May = Gaia.
Xerox=4,500=5,000=50%=P5.00D=Law=Time=Venus=5 May = Aphrodite>>L=N.
Xerxes 1=5,500=5.5=80%=P5.50=Earth-Midway=5 May = Gaia.
Xhosa=10,000=1,000=100%=10.0=Physicality=Tech.=10 Oct.=Uranus=P=1Ø.
xi=4,000=40%=P4.0D=Govt.=Creatocracy=4 April=Mercury=Hermes=G=A4.
Xiamen=4,500=5,000=50%=P5.00D=Law=Time=Venus=5 May = Aphrodite>>L=N.

XI'an=5,000=50%=P5.00D=Law=Time=Venus=5 May = Aphrodite>>L=N.
Xiang Jian=6,500=7,000=70%=P7.0D=7.0=Language=Assets=Mars=7 July=Pleiades.
Xingu=8,500=9,000=90%=P9.00D=9.0=Abstraction=Gods=Saturn=9Sept.>>A=Ø.
Xizang=8,500=9,000=90%=P9.00D=9.0=Abstraction=Gods=Saturn=9Sept.>>A=Ø.
XL.=1,500=15%=P1.50D=1.5=Authority=Solar Crown=1 May = Maia.
Xmas=500=5%=P5.00D=5.0=Law=Time=Venus=5 May=Aphrodite>>L=N.
X-radiation=5,000=50%=P5.00D=Law=Time=Venus=5 May = Aphrodite>>L=N.
x-ray=10,000=1,000=100%=10.0=Physicality=Tech.=10 Oct.=Uranus=P=1Ø.
Xuzhou=4,500=5,000=50%=P5.00D=Law=Time=Venus=5 May = Aphrodite>>L=N.
Xylem=8,000=80%=P8.0D=Economy=Currency=8 Aug.=Zeus>>E=v.
xylophone=11,000=11%=P1.10D=1.1=Idea=Brainchild=Inv.=11 Nov.=SC=Athena>>I=MT.

MAKABET =Yy=

y1=3,500=4,000=40%=P4.0D=Govt.=Creatocracy=4 April=Mercury=Hermes=G=A4.
The 25th letter of the English alphabet. 4.0*2.5x=px=6.5+10=16.5x=px=81.5=82=8.2spl
>>8.0*0.2x=px=8.2+1.6=9.8x=px=22.92=2.3>>2.0 >> Moon >> Night >> Bonding >>
Cupid >> Sexual Love >> Artemis & Eros.

y2=2,500=3,000=30%=P3.0D=3.0=Creativity=Stars=Muses=3 March = C=I>>GIL.
Y=2,500=3,000=30%=P3.0D=3.0=Creativity=Stars=Muses=3 March = C=I>>GIL.
y.=500=5%=P5.00D=5.0=Law=Time=Venus=5 May=Aphrodite>>L=N.
-y1=5,500=5.5=80%=P5.50=Earth-Midway=5 May = Gaia.
-y2=10,000=1,000=100%=10.0=Physicality=Tech.=10 Oct.=Uranus=P=1Ø.
-y3=7,000=70%=P7.0D=7.0=Language=Assets=Mars=7 July=Pleiades.
Yacht=10,500=11,000=11%=P1.10D=1.1=Idea=Brainchild=Inv.=11 Nov.=SC=Athena>>I=MT.
Yahoo=9,500=10,000=1,000=100%=10.0=Physicality=Tech.=10 Oct.=Uranus=P=1Ø.
Yahweh=4,500=5,000=50%=P5.00D=Law=Time=Venus=5 May = Aphrodite>>L=N.
Yak1=5,500=5.5=80%=P5.50=Earth-Midway=5 May = Gaia.
Yak2=3,500=4,000=40%=P4.0D=Govt.=Creatocracy=4 April=Mercury=Hermes=G=A4.
Y'all=4,500=5,000=50%=P5.00D=Law=Time=Venus=5 May = Aphrodite>>L=N.
Yalta=7,000=70%=P7.0D=7.0=Language=Assets=Mars=7 July=Pleiades.
Yalu Jiang=7,500=8,000=80%=P8.0D=Economy=Currency=8 Aug.=Zeus>>E=v.
Yam=11,000=11%=P1.10D=1.1=Idea=Brainchild=Inv.=11 Nov.=SC=Athena>>I=MT.
Yammer=5,000=50%=P5.00D=Law=Time=Venus=5 May = Aphrodite>>L=N.

Yang=6,500=7,000=70%=P7.0D=7.0=Language=Assets=Mars=7 July=Pleiades.

Yangon=1,000=100%=10.0=1.0=Mind=Sun=1 January=Helios >> M=E4.
Yangtze River=10,000=1,000=100%=10.0=Physicality=Tech.=10 Oct.=Uranus=P=1Ø.
yank=11,500=12,000=12%=P1.20D=1.2=Knowledge=Edu=12Dec.=Athena>>K=F.

Yank=1,500=15%=P1.50D=1.5=Authority=Solar Crown=1 May = Maia.
Yankee=6,500=7,000=70%=P7.0D=7.0=Language=Assets=Mars=7 July=Pleiades.
Yaoundé=5,500=5.5=80%=P5.50=Earth-Midway=5 May = Gaia.
Yap=10,000=1,000=100%=10.0=Physicality=Tech.=10 Oct.=Uranus=P=1Ø.
Yaqui=10,000=1,000=100%=10.0=Physicality=Tech.=10 Oct.=Uranus=P=1Ø.
Yard1=10,000=1,000=100%=10.0=Physicality=Tech.=10 Oct.=Uranus=P=1Ø.
Yard2=10,000=1,000=100%=10.0=Physicality=Tech.=10 Oct.=Uranus=P=1Ø.
Yardage=4,500=5,000=50%=P5.00D=Law=Time=Venus=5 May = Aphrodite>>L=N.
Yardarm=4,500=5,000=50%=P5.00D=Law=Time=Venus=5 May = Aphrodite>>L=N.
Yardstick=10,000=1,000=100%=10.0=Physicality=Tech.=10 Oct.=Uranus=P=1Ø.
Yarmulke=4,500=5,000=50%=P5.00D=Law=Time=Venus=5 May = Aphrodite>>L=N.
Yarn=10,000=1,000=100%=10.0=Physicality=Tech.=10 Oct.=Uranus=P=1Ø.
Yaroslavl=7,000=70%=P7.0D=7.0=Language=Assets=Mars=7 July=Pleiades.
Yarrow=9,000=90%=P9.00D=9.0=Abstraction=Gods=Saturn=9Sept.>>A=Ø.
Yaw=10,000=1,000=100%=10.0=Physicality=Tech.=10 Oct.=Uranus=P=1Ø.
Yawl=10,000=1,000=100%=10.0=Physicality=Tech.=10 Oct.=Uranus=P=1Ø.
Yawn=10,000=1,000=100%=10.0=Physicality=Tech.=10 Oct.=Uranus=P=1Ø.
Yaws=10,000=1,000=100%=10.0=Physicality=Tech.=10 Oct.=Uranus=P=1Ø.
Y-axis=10,000=1,000=100%=10.0=Physicality=Tech.=10 Oct.=Uranus=P=1Ø.
Yb=2,500=3,000=30%=P3.0D=3.0=Creativity=Stars=Muses=3 March = C=I>>GIL.
Y-chromosome=10,000=1,000=100%=10.0=Physicality=Tech.=10 Oct.=Uranus=P=1Ø.
yd=1,000=100%=10.0=1.0=Mind=Sun=1 January=Helios >> M=E4.
Ye1=4,500=5,000=50%=P5.00D=Law=Time=Venus=5 May = Aphrodite>>L=N.
Ye2=2,000=20%=P2.00D=2.0=Nature=Matter=Moon=2 Feb.=Cupid=N=C+_
Yea=7,500=8,000=80%=P8.0D=Economy=Currency=8 Aug.=Zeus>>E=v.

Yeah=1,500=15%=P1.50D=1.5=Authority=Solar Crown=1 May = Maia.
Bible. His word is yea and amen. Result indicates they yeah is Maia head of the Pleiades
and the Mind of GOD. Revelation states that Jesus >> Hermes >> Wit >> Amen. So the
word is guided by Maia and managed by Hermes. Wits and wis are required to understand.
Amen>> A mén >> A Mind >> A man. The word is Az hence processing the dictionary
through the superior standards of the Scriptures makes one a God-Man or Human-God.

Year=10,000=1,000=100%=10.0=Physicality=Tech.=10 Oct.=Uranus=P=1Ø.
Yearbook=10,000=1,000=100%=10.0=Physicality=Tech.=10 Oct.=Uranus=P=1Ø.
Yearling=6,500=7,000=70%=P7.0D=7.0=Language=Assets=Mars=7 July=Pleiades.
Yearlong=1,500=15%=P1.50D=1.5=Authority=Solar Crown=1 May = Maia.
Yearly=4,500=5,000=50%=P5.00D=Law=Time=Venus=5 May = Aphrodite>>L=N.
Yearn=7,500=8,000=80%=P8.0D=Economy=Currency=8 Aug.=Zeus>>E=v.
Yearning=1,500=15%=P1.50D=1.5=Authority=Solar Crown=1 May = Maia.
Year round=3,500=4,000=40%=P4.0D=Govt.=Creatocracy=4 April=Hermes=G=A4.
Yeast=10,000=1,000=100%=10.0=Physicality=Tech.=10 Oct.=Uranus=P=1Ø.
Yeats William=3,500=4,000=40%=P4.0D=Govt.=Creatocracy=4 April=Hermes=G=A4.
Yell=9,000=90%=P9.00D=9.0=Abstraction=Gods=Saturn=9Sept.>>A=Ø.

Yellow=10,000=1,000=100%=10.0=Physicality=Tech.=10 Oct.=Uranus=P=1Ø.
Yellow fever=10,000=1,000=100%=10.0=Physicality=Tech.=10 Oct.=Uranus=P=1Ø.
Yellow Jack=7,000=70%=P7.0D=7.0=Language=Assets=Mars=7 July=Pleiades.
Yellow Jacket=4,000=40%=P4.0D=Govt.=Creatocracy=4 April=Mercury=Hermes=G=A4.
Yellow knife=7,000=70%=P7.0D=7.0=Language=Assets=Mars=7 July=Pleiades.
Yellow River.=1,500=15%=P1.50D=1.5=Authority=Solar Crown=1 May = Maia.
Yellow Sea.=5,000=50%=P5.00D=Law=Time=Venus=5 May = Aphrodite>>L=N.
Yellowstone=7,500=8,000=80%=P8.0D=Economy=Currency=8 Aug.=Zeus>>E=v.
Yelp=5,500=5.5=80%=P5.50=Earth-Midway=5 May = Gaia.
Yemen=12,500=13,000=13%=P1.30=Solar Core=Faculty=13 January=Athena.
Yen1=3,000=30%=P3.0D=3.0=Creativity=Stars=Muses=3 March = C=I>>GIL.

Yen2=4,000=40%=P4.0D=Govt.=Creatocracy=4 April=Mercury=Hermes=G=A4.
4/10=0.4>> 40:1. See Naira. Dollar.

Yenisel=7,500=8,000=80%=P8.0D=Economy=Currency=8 Aug.=Zeus>>E=v.
Yenta=5,000=50%=P5.00D=Law=Time=Venus=5 May = Aphrodite>>L=N.
Yeoman=10,000=1,000=100%=10.0=Physicality=Tech.=10 Oct.=Uranus=P=1Ø.
Yeomanry=3,500=4,000=40%=P4.0D=Govt.=4 April=Mercury=Hermes=G=A4.
Yep=1,000=100%=10.0=1.0=Mind=Sun=1 January=Helios >> M=E4.
Yerba maté=4,500=5,000=50%=P5.00D=Law=Time=Venus=5 May = Aphrodite>>L=N.
Yerevan=5,000=50%=P5.00D=Law=Time=Venus=5 May = Aphrodite>>L=N.
Yes=10,000=1,000=100%=10.0=Physicality=Tech.=10 Oct.=Uranus=P=1Ø.
Yeshiva=10,000=1,000=100%=10.0=Physicality=Tech.=10 Oct.=Uranus=P=1Ø.
Yes man=3,500=4,000=40%=P4.0D=Govt.=Creatocracy=4 April=Hermes=G=A4.
Yesterday=11,000=11%=P1.10D=1.1=Idea=Brainchild=Inv.=11 Nov.=SC=Athena>>I=MT.
Yesteryear=3,000=30%=P3.0D=3.0=Creativity=Stars=Muses=3 March = C=I>>GIL.
Yet=10,000=1,000=100%=10.0=Physicality=Tech.=10 Oct.=Uranus=P=1Ø.
Yeti=3,500=4,000=40%=P4.0D=Govt.=Creatocracy=4 April=Mercury=Hermes=G=A4.
Yevtushenko=3,000=30%=P3.0D=3.0=Creativity=Stars=Muses=3 March = C=I>>GIL.
Yew=10,000=1,000=100%=10.0=Physicality=Tech.=10 Oct.=Uranus=P=1Ø.
Yiddish=10,000=1,000=100%=10.0=Physicality=Tech.=10 Oct.=Uranus=P=1Ø.
Yield=10,000=1,000=100%=10.0=Physicality=Tech.=10 Oct.=Uranus=P=1Ø.
Yin=6,500=7,000=70%=P7.0D=7.0=Language=Assets=Mars=7 July=Pleiades.
Yip=4,500=5,000=50%=P5.00D=Law=Time=Venus=5 May = Aphrodite>>L=N.
Yippee=3,500=4,000=40%=P4.0D=Govt.=Creatocracy=4 April=Mercury=Hermes=G=A4.
-yl=5,000=50%=P5.00D=Law=Time=Venus=5 May = Aphrodite>>L=N.
YMCA=2,000=20%=P2.00D=2.0=Nature=Matter=Moon=2 Feb.=Cupid=N=C+_
YMHA=2,000=20%=P2.00D=2.0=Nature=Matter=Moon=2 Feb.=Cupid=N=C+_
YOB=1,500=15%=P1.50D=1.5=Authority=Solar Crown=1 May = Maia.
Yodel=8,000=80%=P8.0D=Economy=Currency=8 Aug.=Zeus>>E=v.
Yodh=3,500=4,000=40%=P4.0D=Govt.=Creatocracy=4 April=Mercury=Hermes=G=A4.
Yoga=10,000=1,000=100%=10.0=Physicality=Tech.=10 Oct.=Uranus=P=1Ø.
Yogl=5,000=50%=P5.00D=Law=Time=Venus=5 May = Aphrodite>>L=N.

Yogurt=6,000=60%=P6.0D=Man=Earth=Royalty=6 June=Gaia=Maia>>M=M2.
Yoke=10,000=1,000=100%=10.0=Physicality=Tech.=10 Oct.=Uranus=P=1Ø.
Yokel=2,000=20%=P2.00D=2.0=Nature=Matter=Moon=2 Feb.=Cupid=N=C+_
Yokohama=7,000=70%=P7.0D=7.0=Language=Assets=Mars=7 July=Pleiades.
Yolk=9,000=90%=P9.00D=9.0=Abstraction=Gods=Saturn=9Sept.>>A=Ø.
Yom Kippur=10,000=1,000=100%=10.0=Physicality=Tech.=10 Oct.=Uranus=P=1Ø.
Yon=1,500=15%=P1.50D=1.5=Authority=Solar Crown=1 May = Maia.
Yonder=6,500=7,000=70%=P7.0D=7.0=Language=Assets=Mars=7 July=Pleiades.
Yonkers=5,000=50%=P5.00D=Law=Time=Venus=5 May = Aphrodite>>L=N.
Yoo-hoo=3,500=4,000=40%=P4.0D=Govt.=Creatocracy=4 April=Hermes=G=A4.
Yore=6,000=60%=P6.0D=Man=Earth=Royalty=6 June=Gaia=Maia>>M=M2.
York=6,500=7,000=70%=P7.0D=7.0=Language=Assets=Mars=7 July=Pleiades.
York, Cape.=8,000=80%=P8.0D=Economy=Currency=8 Aug.=Zeus>>E=v.
Yorktown=6,000=60%=P6.0D=Man=Earth=Royalty=6 June=Gaia=Maia>>M=M2.
Yoruba=7,500=8,000=80%=P8.0D=Economy=Currency=8 Aug.=Zeus>>E=v.
Yosemite Valley=10,000=1,000=100%=10.0=Physicality=Tech.=10 Oct.=Uranus=P=1Ø.
You=11,000=11%=P1.10D=1.1=Idea=Brainchild=Inv.=11 Nov.=SC=Athena>>I=MT.
You all=10,000=1,000=100%=10.0=Physicality=Tech.=10 Oct.=Uranus=P=1Ø.
You'd=1,500=15%=P1.50D=1.5=Authority=Solar Crown=1 May = Maia.
You'll=3,000=30%=P3.0D=3.0=Creativity=Stars=Muses=3 March = C=I>>GIL.
Young=10,000=1,000=100%=10.0=Physicality=Tech.=10 Oct.=Uranus=P=1Ø.
Young Andrew=4,000=40%=P4.0D=Govt.=Creatocracy=4 April=Mercury=Hermes=G=A4.
Young,Brigham=2,500=3,000=30%=P3.0D=3.0=Creativity=Stars=Muses=3 March = C=I
Youngling=3,000=30%=P3.0D=3.0=Creativity=Stars=Muses=3 March = C=I>>GIL.
Youngster=1,500=15%=P1.50D=1.5=Authority=Solar Crown=1 May = Maia.
Youngstown=4,500=5,000=50%=P5.00D=Law=Time=Venus=5 May = Aphrodite>>L=N.
Your=9,000=90%=P9.00D=9.0=Abstraction=Gods=Saturn=9Sept.>>A=Ø.
You're=1,000=100%=10.0=1.0=Mind=Sun=1 January=Helios >> M=E4.
Yours=8,000=80%=P8.0D=Economy=Currency=8 Aug.=Zeus>>E=v.
Yourself=13,000=13%=P1.30=Solar Core=Faculty=13 January=Athena.
Youth=10,000=1,000=100%=10.0=Physicality=Tech.=10 Oct.=Uranus=P=1Ø.
Youthful=5,500=5.5=80%=P5.50=Earth-Midway=5 May = Gaia.
You've=1,000=100%=10.0=1.0=Mind=Sun=1 January=Helios >> M=E4.
Yowl=5,000=50%=P5.00D=Law=Time=Venus=5 May = Aphrodite>>L=N.
yo-yo=11,000=11%=P1.10D=1.1=Idea=Brainchild=Inv.=11 Nov.=SC=Athena>>I=MT.
Yr.=1,500=15%=P1.50D=1.5=Authority=Solar Crown=1 May = Maia.
Ytterbium=10,000=1,000=100%=10.0=Physicality=Tech.=10 Oct.=Uranus=P=1Ø.
Yttrium=10,000=1,000=100%=10.0=Physicality=Tech.=10 Oct.=Uranus=P=1Ø.

Yuan=3,000=30%=P3.0D=3.0=Creativity=Stars=Muses=3 March = C=I>>GIL.
Mandarin yudn. Metric weight = 3/10=0.3>>30:1. Means 30 lower value = 1 higher value.
See Naira, dollar.

Yucatán=10,000=1,000=100%=10.0=Physicality=Tech.=10 Oct.=Uranus=P=1Ø.
Yucca=10,000=1,000=100%=10.0=Physicality=Tech.=10 Oct.=Uranus=P=1Ø.

Yuck=4,000=40%=P4.0D=Govt.=Creatocracy=4 April=Mercury=Hermes=G=A4.
Yugoslavia=10,000=1,000=100%=10.0=Physicality=Tech.=10 Oct.=Uranus=P=1Ø.
Yukon River=9,500=10,000=1,000=100%=10.0=Physicality=Tech.=10 Oct.=Uranus=P=1Ø.
Yukon Territory=5,500=5.5=80%=P5.50=Earth-Midway=5 May = Gaia.
Yule=1,500=15%=P1.50D=1.5=Authority=Solar Crown=1 May = Maia.
Yule log=4,500=5,000=50%=P5.00D=Law=Time=Venus=5 May = Aphrodite>>L=N.
Yuletide=1,500=15%=P1.50D=1.5=Authority=Solar Crown=1 May = Maia.
Yuma=5,500=5.5=80%=P5.50=Earth-Midway=5 May = Gaia.
Yummy=1,500=15%=P1.50D=1.5=Authority=Solar Crown=1 May = Maia.
Yupik=8,000=80%=P8.0D=Economy=Currency=8 Aug.=Zeus>>E=v.
Yuppie=5,000=50%=P5.00D=Law=Time=Venus=5 May = Aphrodite>>L=N.
Yurt=7,500=8,000=80%=P8.0D=Economy=Currency=8 Aug.=Zeus>>E=v.
YWCA=2,000=20%=P2.00D=2.0=Nature=Matter=Moon=2 Feb.=Cupid=N=C+_
YWHA=2,000=20%=P2.00D=2.0=Nature=Matter=Moon=2 Feb.=Cupid=N=C+_

MAKABET =Zz=

---

z=3,000=30%=P3.0D=3.0=Creativity=Stars=Muses=3 March = C=I>>GIL.
The 26th letter of the English alphabet. 3.0*2.6x=px=5.6+7.8=13.4x=px=57.08=60=6.0 >>
An emotional muse that transmutes energy into humanity through sexual transmutation.
The secrets of the Z is found in Psalms 57 verse 8 thus Awake up, my glory; awake, psaltery
and harp: I myself will awake early. 6.0 indicates Earth>>Generosity>>Royalty >>Glory.
A constant repetition of the Zed conveys the principles of success and its responsibility.
I myself will awake early. The secret of success has to do with the early morning star or
muse. The morning star is Aphrodite Goddess of marriage beauty love and birth. Zeus.

Z.=2,000=20%=P2.00D=2.0=Nature=Matter=Moon=2 Feb.=Cupid=N=C+_
z.=1,000=100%=10.0=1.0=Mind=Sun=1 January=Helios >> M=E4.
Zagreb=6,000=60%=P6.0D=Man=Earth=Royalty=6 June=Gaia=Maia>>M=M2.

---

zaire=4,500=5,000=50%=P5.00D=Law=Time=Venus=5 May = Aphrodite>>L=N.
Kongo n-zadi, large River. Metric weight = 4.5/10=0.45>>45:1

Zaire=6,000=60%=P6.0D=Man=Earth=Royalty=6 June=Gaia=Maia>>M=M2.
Zaire River.=1,500=15%=P1.50D=1.5=Authority=Solar Crown=1 May = Maia.
Zambezi=11,000=11%=P1.10D=1.1=Idea=Brainchild=Inv.=11 Nov.=SC=Athena>>I=MT.
Zambia=5,000=50%=P5.00D=Law=Time=Venus=5 May = Aphrodite>>L=N.
Zany=10,000=1,000=100%=10.0=Physicality=Tech.=10 Oct.=Uranus=P=1Ø.
Zanzibar=10,000=1,000=100%=10.0=Physicality=Tech.=10 Oct.=Uranus=P=1Ø.
Zap=10,000=1,000=100%=10.0=Physicality=Tech.=10 Oct.=Uranus=P=1Ø.
Zaporonzhe=10,000=1,000=100%=10.0=Physicality=Tech.=10 Oct.=Uranus=P=1Ø.

Z-axis=10,000=1,000=100%=10.0=Physicality=Tech.=10 Oct.=Uranus=P=1Ø.
Zayin=3,500=4,000=40%=P4.0D=Govt.=Creatocracy=4 April=Mercury=Hermes=G=A4.
Zazen=9,000=90%=P9.00D=9.0=Abstraction=Gods=Saturn=9Sept.>>A=Ø.
Zeal=5,000=50%=P5.00D=Law=Time=Venus=5 May = Aphrodite>>L=N.
Zealot=6,000=60%=P6.0D=Man=Earth=Royalty=6 June=Gaia=Maia>>M=M2.
Zealous=3,500=4,000=40%=P4.0D=Govt.=Creatocracy=4 April=Mercury=Hermes=G=A4.
Zebra=11,000=11%=P1.10D=1.1=Idea=Brainchild=Inv.=11 Nov.=SC=Athena>>I=MT.
Zebu=8,000=80%=P8.0D=Economy=Currency=8 Aug.=Zeus>>E=v.

Zechariah=6,000=60%=P6.0D=Man=Earth=Royalty=6 June=Gaia=Maia>>M=M2.
A Hebrew prophet of the 6th century B.C. Inspired by Gaia.

Zed=3,500=4,000=40%=P4.0D=Govt.=Creatocracy=4 April=Mercury=Hermes=G=A4.
Zedekiah=5,500=5.5=80%=P5.50=Earth-Midway=5 May = Gaia.
Zeitgeist=5,500=5.5=80%=P5.50=Earth-Midway=5 May = Gaia.
Zen=1,000=100%=10.0=1.0=Mind=Sun=1 January=Helios >> M=E4.
Zen Buddhism=10,000=1,000=100%=10.0=Physicality=Tech.=10 Oct.=Uranus=P=1Ø.
Zend-Avesta=3,000=30%=P3.0D=3.0=Creativity=Stars=Muses=3 March = C=I>>GIL.
Zenger John=4,000=40%=P4.0D=Govt.=Creatocracy=4 April=Mercury=Hermes=G=A4.
Zenith=10,000=1,000=100%=10.0=Physicality=Tech.=10 Oct.=Uranus=P=1Ø.
Zeno of Citium=3,500=4,000=40%=P4.0D=Govt.=4 April=Mercury=Hermes=G=A4.
Zeno of Elea=3,000=30%=P3.0D=3.0=Creativity=Stars=Muses=3 March = C=I>>GIL.

Zephaniah=6,000=60%=P6.0D=Man=Earth=Royalty=6 June=Gaia=Maia>>M=M2.

Zephyr=10,000=1,000=100%=10.0=Physicality=Tech.=10 Oct.=Uranus=P=1Ø.
Zeppelin=10,000=1,000=100%=10.0=Physicality=Tech.=10 Oct.=Uranus=P=1Ø.

Zero=10,000=1,000=100%=10.0=Physicality=Tech.=10 Oct.=Uranus=P=1Ø.
There is nothing like nothing because nothing is zero and zero as a word is a quantum of 10,000 in quantum. The dimension for Zero >> 0 = Ø = 9.0 >> abstraction. Total value for zero is 10.0*9.0x=px=19+90=109x=px=1819. A value that indicates 18 and 19 >> 1.8 = Solar Currency being the Maks. 19 >> 1.9=Solar God= Helios >> the Sun God. Computing further or probing both >> 1.8*1.9x=px=3.7+3.42=7.12x=px=19.774=20=2.0 >> Moon. Through the abstraction module of the Sun (Zero) and the invisibility of the spirit and energy of the moon (PGI) persons who were born in 1819 would reincarnate in the year 1977. Those of 1978 would probably be those born in the year 1818. Peter Matthews-Akukalia was tracked to share same energy modules with Father Abraham to an astronomer Tycho and then to Benjamin Banneker. The number one zeros is the number of spirits involved. So zero=10,000 indicates the Quartet Principle (Four 0's) is the module for all creation.

Zero in=10,000=1,000=100%=10.0=Physicality=Tech.=10 Oct.=Uranus=P=1Ø.
Zero gravity=9,000=90%=P9.00D=9.0=Abstraction=Gods=Saturn=9Sept.>>A=Ø.

Zero hour=6,000=60%=P6.0D=Man=Earth=Royalty=6 June=Gaia=Maia>>M=M2.
Zero population growth=5,500=5.5=80%=P5.50=Earth-Midway=5 May = Gaia.
Zero sum game=8,000=80%=P8.0D=Economy=Currency=8 Aug.=Zeus>>E=v.
Zest=10,000=1,000=100%=10.0=Physicality=Tech.=10 Oct.=Uranus=P=1Ø.
Zeta=4,000=40%=P4.0D=Govt.=Creatocracy=4 April=Mercury=Hermes=G=A4.

Zeus=9,000=90%=P9.00D=9.0=Abstraction=Gods=Saturn=9Sept.>>A=Ø.
Greek Myth. The principal God of the Greek pantheon, ruler of the heavens and father of other Gods and mortal heroes. The Creatocracy recognizes Him Zeus-Jehovah-Allah >> ZeJeAl. A name invented by Peter Matthews-Akukalia one believed to be his incarnation.

Zhdanov=5,000=50%=P5.00D=Law=Time=Venus=5 May = Aphrodite>>L=N.
Zhengzhou=3,000=30%=P3.0D=3.0=Creativity=Stars=Muses=3 March = C=I>>GIL.
Zhou Enlai=3,000=30%=P3.0D=3.0=Creativity=Stars=Muses=3 March = C=I>>GIL.
Ziggurat=8,000=80%=P8.0D=Economy=Currency=8 Aug.=Zeus>>E=v.
Zigzag=10,000=1,000=100%=10.0=Physicality=Tech.=10 Oct.=Uranus=P=1Ø.
Zilch=2,000=20%=P2.00D=2.0=Nature=Matter=Moon=2 Feb.=Cupid=N=C+_
Zillion=4,500=5,000=50%=P5.00D=Law=Time=Venus=5 May = Aphrodite>>L=N.
Zimbabwe=5,500=5.5=80%=P5.50=Earth-Midway=5 May = Gaia.
Zinc=10,000=1,000=100%=10.0=Physicality=Tech.=10 Oct.=Uranus=P=1Ø.
Zinc ointment=7,000=70%=P7.0D=7.0=Language=Assets=Mars=7 July=Pleiades.
Zinc oxide=8,000=80%=P8.0D=Economy=Currency=8 Aug.=Zeus>>E=v.
Zinger=3,000=30%=P3.0D=3.0=Creativity=Stars=Muses=3 March = C=I>>GIL.
Zinnia=7,500=8,000=80%=P8.0D=Economy=Currency=8 Aug.=Zeus>>E=v.
Zion=10,000=1,000=100%=10.0=Physicality=Tech.=10 Oct.=Uranus=P=1Ø.
Zionism=10,000=1,000=100%=10.0=Physicality=Tech.=10 Oct.=Uranus=P=1Ø.
Zip=12,000=12%=P1.20D=1.2=Knowledge=Edu=12Dec.=Athena>>K=F.
ZIP code=10,000=1,000=100%=10.0=Physicality=Tech.=10 Oct.=Uranus=P=1Ø.
Zipper=10,000=1,000=100%=10.0=Physicality=Tech.=10 Oct.=Uranus=P=1Ø.
Zippy=2,000=20%=P2.00D=2.0=Nature=Matter=Moon=2 Feb.=Cupid=N=C+_
Zircon=10,000=1,000=100%=10.0=Physicality=Tech.=10 Oct.=Uranus=P=1Ø.
Zirconium=10,000=1,000=100%=10.0=Physicality=Tech.=10 Oct.=Uranus=P=1Ø.
Zit=2,000=20%=P2.00D=2.0=Nature=Matter=Moon=2 Feb.=Cupid=N=C+_
Zither=10,000=1,000=100%=10.0=Physicality=Tech.=10 Oct.=Uranus=P=1Ø.
Ziti=2,500=3,000=30%=P3.0D=3.0=Creativity=Stars=Muses=3 March = C=I>>GIL.

Zloty=4,000=40%=P4.0D=Govt.=Creatocracy=4 April=Mercury=Hermes=G=A4.

Zn=2,500=3,000=30%=P3.0D=3.0=Creativity=Stars=Muses=3 March = C=I>>GIL.
Zodiac=10,000=1,000=100%=10.0=Physicality=Tech.=10 Oct.=Uranus=P=1Ø.
-zoic=10,000=1,000=100%=10.0=Physicality=Tech.=10 Oct.=Uranus=P=1Ø.
Zola Emile.=3,000=30%=P3.0D=3.0=Creativity=Stars=Muses=3 March = C=I>>GIL.
Zombie=10,000=1,000=100%=10.0=Physicality=Tech.=10 Oct.=Uranus=P=1Ø.

Zonal=3,500=4,000=40%=P4.0D=Govt.=Creatocracy=4 April=Mercury=Hermes=G=A4.
Zone=10,000=1,000=100%=10.0=Physicality=Tech.=10 Oct.=Uranus=P=1Ø.
Zonk=5,000=50%=P5.00D=Law=Time=Venus=5 May = Aphrodite>>L=N.
Zoo=10,000=1,000=100%=10.0=Physicality=Tech.=10 Oct.=Uranus=P=1Ø.
Zoo-=5,000=50%=P5.00D=Law=Time=Venus=5 May = Aphrodite>>L=N.
Zoo geography=3,500=4,000=40%=P4.0D=Govt.=Creatocracy=4 April=Hermes=G=A4.
Zoological garden=1,500=15%=P1.50D=1.5=Authority=Solar Crown=1 May = Maia.
Zoology=10,000=1,000=100%=10.0=Physicality=Tech.=10 Oct.=Uranus=P=1Ø.
Zoom=10,000=1,000=100%=10.0=Physicality=Tech.=10 Oct.=Uranus=P=1Ø.
Zoom lens=9,500=10,000=1,000=100%=10.0=Physicality=Tech.=10 Oct.=Uranus=P=1Ø.
-zoom=6,500=7,000=70%=P7.0D=7.0=Language=Assets=Mars=7 July=Pleiades.
Zoo plankton=2,500=3,000=30%=P3.0D=3.0=Creativity=Stars=Muses=3 March = C=I
Zoospore=2,500=3,000=30%=P3.0D=3.0=Creativity=Stars=Muses=3 March = C=I>>GIL.
Zoroaster=4,000=40%=P4.0D=Govt.=Creatocracy=4 April=Mercury=Hermes=G=A4.
Zoroastrian=10,000=1,000=100%=10.0=Physicality=Tech.=10 Oct.=Uranus=P=1Ø.
Zounds=3,500=4,000=40%=P4.0D=Govt.=Creatocracy=4 April=Mercury=Hermes=G=A4.
Zoysia=10,000=1,000=100%=10.0=Physicality=Tech.=10 Oct.=Uranus=P=1Ø.
Zr.=2,500=3,000=30%=P3.0D=3.0=Creativity=Stars=Muses=3 March = C=I>>GIL.
Zucchini=8,000=80%=P8.0D=Economy=Currency=8 Aug.=Zeus>>E=v.
Zulu=5,000=50%=P5.00D=Law=Time=Venus=5 May = Aphrodite>>L=N.
Zulu land=3,500=4,000=40%=P4.0D=Govt.=Creatocracy=4 April=Hermes=G=A4.
Zuni=5,000=50%=P5.00D=Law=Time=Venus=5 May = Aphrodite>>L=N.
Zurich=6,500=7,000=70%=P7.0D=7.0=Language=Assets=Mars=7 July=Pleiades.
Zwieback=7,000=70%=P7.0D=7.0=Language=Assets=Mars=7 July=Pleiades.
Zwingli=3,000=30%=P3.0D=3.0=Creativity=Stars=Muses=3 March = C=I>>GIL.
Zydeco=9,000=90%=P9.00D=9.0=Abstraction=Gods=Saturn=9Sept.>>A=Ø.
Zygosis=4,500=5,000=50%=P5.00D=Law=Time=Venus=5 May = Aphrodite>>L=N.
Zygote=10,000=1,000=100%=10.0=Physicality=Tech.=10 Oct.=Uranus=P=1Ø.
Zymurgy=8,500=9,000=90%=P9.00D=9.0=Abstraction=Gods=Saturn=9Sept.>>A=Ø.

PICTURE of the Maks Currencies bundle. Backside design. Code 10J.

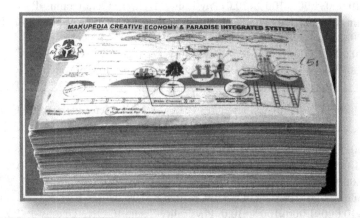

1. Makupedian Databank Encyclopedia of Propensities Inclinations Assets Commodities Abstractions Dimensions Prices Taxes & Benchmark Values in the Creative Economy.
2. Based on the invented MaksCurrencies & MindBanking Standards.
3. The American Heritage Dictionary Lunar Computed Edition of Makupedia.
4. Definitive definitions & Precise complements for the conventional use of words.
5. Creatocratic standards on the value and utility of language and terminologies.
6. A MaksCurrencies & Mind Bank Assets repertory for licensing costs and abstractions.
7. A necessary resource in computing prices and taxes for the Ministry of Creativity.
8. Discover the worth of a thing; anything at all on natural measured universal standards.
9. Great resource for measuring the costs of offenses and count charges in Legal matters.
10. A consult resource for the Talents & Ideas Markets and the Ministry of Creativity.
11. Know the Mind of GOD the activities of the Gods and codes of the Creatocracy.
12. Direct applications of the Creatocracy Courts laws constitution and computations.
13. A research center for name search technologies and discovery of new knowledge.
14. Methods applied are Makumatics, Data analytics, Makumaticology, Psycho-forensics programming, computational creativity, laws of astrotransmutation and pure equivalence.
15. Practical material for the students of Makupedia Business department.
16. Maks Currencies * Dictionary = Maktionary.
17. A Material of advance research enclosing guidance for national fiscal policy annually.
18. A Creative Economy management system for establishment of Mind Banks worldwide.
19. Authored by one apotheosized to be the God of Creatocracy Genius & Mind.
20. Aimed at institutionalizing the Creatocracy and promoting the creative economy.
21. Data mines matrix and benchmark prices for Mind Banking, Talents & Ideas Markets, Ministry of Creativity, Propensities & Inclinations, assets and commodities in the Maks.

Printed in the United States
by Baker & Taylor Publisher Services

Printed in the United States
by Baker & Taylor Publisher Services